Business Statistics

of the United States

Fifth Edition, 1999

Business Statistics
of the United States

Fifth Edition, 1999

Editors
Courtenay M. Slater
Cornelia J. Strawser

Associate Editor
James B. Rice

BERNAN PRESS
Lanham, MD

© 1999 Bernan Press, an imprint of Bernan Associates, a division of the Kraus Organization Limited.

All rights reserved. No part of this work covered by the copyrights hereon may be reproduced or used in any form or by any means, whether graphic, electronic, or mechanical—including photocopying, recording, taping, or information storage and retrieval systems—without written permission from the publisher.

ISBN: 0-89059-213-6

ISSN: 1086-8488

Printed by Automated Graphic Systems, Inc., White Plains, MD, on acid-free paper that meets the American National Standards Institute Z39-48 standard.

2000 1999   4 3 2 1

Bernan Press
4611-F Assembly Drive
Lanham, MD 20706
email: info@bernan.com

Contents

Preface

Business Statistics of the United States is a basic desk reference for everyone requiring recent or historical information about the U.S. economy. It contains some 2,000 economic time series, predominantly from federal government sources, presenting a rich selection of the data most needed for analysis of economic trends and patterns. Of equal importance with the data themselves are the extensive background notes that enable the user to understand the data, use them appropriately, and, if desired, seek additional information from the source agencies.

THE 1999 EDITION

As always, each table in the 1999 edition of Business Statistics has been updated through the latest year available and all historical revisions to the data have been incorporated. All the standard features that have made earlier editions a must-have for every business reference shelf have been maintained. These include:

- Approximately 2,000 data series covering virtually every aspect of the U.S. economy, including GDP, employment, production, prices, productivity, international trade, money supply, and interest rates;

- Statistical profiles of each major industry group, from mining through retail trade;

- Tables presenting 29 years of annual data and 4 years of monthly or 9 years of quarterly data;

- Additional historical data for selected key series;

- An introductory section describing major economic trends over the nearly 30 years covered by the book;

- A review of major new developments in federal statistical programs;

- Annual time series covering personal income and employment for each state and region;

- Detailed background notes providing definitions, data revision schedules, and sources of additional information.

USING THIS BOOK

TIME PERIOD COVERAGE. The 1999 edition of Business Statistics contains annual data for 1970 through 1998; quarterly data for 1990 through 1998; and monthly data for 1995 through 1998. To make the volume even more timely, key 1999 data are found in Table 2 (monthly data through July 1999) and Table 3 (quarterly data through the second quarter) of the lead section, "The 1990s: Prosperous Prelude to the Twenty-first Century" beginning on page 1. Part III contains selected quarterly and monthly data for earlier time periods. In general, these quarterly data begin with 1962, and the monthly data, with 1971.

Annual data for certain series particularly important to an understanding of the U.S. economy also are included even though monthly or quarterly data are not available. This is the case for the data in the chapter on income distribution and poverty. These data are annual time series through 1998. Other examples are the inclusion of available data from the Census Bureau's Annual Capital Expenditure Survey (page 87) and Annual Survey of Services (page 284).

SUBJECT MATTER COVERAGE. Part I covers the U.S. economy as a whole. It contains 12 chapters:

> National Product and Income and Cyclical
>   Indicators
> Income Distribution and Poverty
> Consumer Income and Spending
> Industrial Production and Capacity Utilization
> Saving and Investment; Business Sales and
>   Inventories
> Prices
> Employment Costs, Productivity, and Profits
> Employment, Hours, and Earnings
> Energy
> Money and Financial Markets
> U.S. Foreign Trade and Finance
> International Comparisons

Part II presents data by major industry group, following the structure of the Standard Industrial Classification (SIC). Basic data are repeated from Part I and are supplemented by additional industry detail. The user thus has the convenience of a profile of the industry in a single location. The industry groups covered are:

> Mining, Oil, and Gas
> Construction and Housing
> Manufacturing
> Durable Goods Manufacturing
>   (nine 2-digit industries)
> Nondurable Goods Manufacturing
>   (ten 2-digit industries)
> Transportation, Communications, and Utilities
> Retail and Wholesale Trade
> Finance, Insurance, Real Estate, and Private
> Services
> Government

Part III, as noted, contains additional historical data for

selected series. Part IV contains annual data (1969 through 1998) for each state and region. The state data cover personal income and its major components, as well as employment and population.

SPECIAL FEATURES. Each chapter in Parts I and II begins with a chart and brief text highlighting some of the trends reflected in the data.

Two introductory features provide perspective on the tables that make up the heart of the book. The first describes overall trends in the U.S. economy during the period covered by the book, with particular emphasis on the most recent few years. This analysis is carried through the first half of 1999. The second special feature describes important recent developments in federal statistical programs. It discusses the recent comprehensive revision of the National Income and Product Accounts; the measurement of prices and productivity; different approaches to the measurement of saving; the differences between the two basic measures of employment—total civilian employment and nonfarm payroll employment; and the impact of alternative definitions on the measurement of income and poverty.

THE NOTES. The background notes beginning on page 405 contain definitions, descriptions of recent data revisions, information about data availability and release schedules, and references to sources of additional technical information. They are arranged in the order in which the data appear in the book, with references to the data pages and the subject to which they pertain shown at the beginning of each group of notes.

THE HISTORY OF BUSINESS STATISTICS

The history of *Business Statistics* begins with the publication, many years ago, by the U.S. Commerce Department's Bureau of Economic Analysis (BEA) of the first edition of a volume of the same name and general purpose. After 27 periodic editions, the last of which appeared in 1992, the BEA found it necessary, for budgetary and other reasons, to discontinue not only that publication but also maintenance of the database from which the publication was derived.

The individual statistical series in Business Statistics are publicly available. However, the task of gathering them from a number of sources within the government, plus a few private sources, and assembling them into one coherent database is highly impractical for most data users. Even when current data are more-or-less readily available, obtaining the full historical time series often is time-consuming and difficult. Believing that a Business Statistics compilation was too valuable to be lost to the public, Bernan Press published the first edition of the present publication in 1995. The first edition received a warm welcome among users of economic data, and the volume's popularity has been sustained through three subsequent editions. As noted above, this 1999

edition contains new features and additional data series that should enhance the book's usefulness.

The great majority of the statistical data in this book are from federal government sources and are in the public domain. A few series are from private sources and further use may be subject to copyright restrictions. Sources for all the data are given in the notes.

The data in this volume meet the publication standards of the federal statistical agencies from which they were obtained. Every effort has been made to select data that are accurate, meaningful, and useful. All statistical data are subject to error arising from sampling variability, reporting errors, incomplete coverage, imputation, and other causes. The responsibility of the editor and publisher of this volume is limited to reasonable care in the reproduction and presentation of data obtained from established sources.

The 1999 edition has been edited by Courtenay M. Slater and Cornelia J. Strawser. Dr. Slater is Manager of Economic Publications for Bernan and former Chief Economist for the U.S. Department of Commerce. Dr. Strawser is Senior Economic Consultant to Bernan; she was formerly Senior Economist at the U.S. House of Representatives Budget Committee and has also served at the Senate Budget Committee, the Congressional Budget Office, and the Federal Reserve Board. The editors participated jointly in overseeing preparation of the data and the background notes; Dr. Slater prepared the introductory section on economic trends, and Dr. Strawser prepared the introductory section on developments in federal statistics. The editors assume full responsibility for any interpretations or misinterpretations found in the introductory sections.

ACKNOWLEDGEMENTS

The editors are profoundly grateful to all those at Bernan who assisted in the preparation of this edition of *Business Statistics of the United States*. This volume would not have been possible without the careful and reliable work of the analysts who maintain the database, prepare the data tables, and review and fact-check all the material. Over the past year this team included: Kendall Golladay, James Rice, Elizabeth Rogers, and Steven Thomas.

Copy editing, layout, and graphics preparation were done by Bernan's production department, under the direction of Sean Long. Benjamin Shupe prepared the graphics, and he, Joyce Goodwine, and Dan Parham capably handled all production aspects of the volume.

Finally, special thanks are due to the many federal agency personnel who, as always, responded generously to our frequent need for assistance in obtaining data and background information.

The 1990s: Prosperous Prelude to the Twenty-first Century

by Courtenay Slater

In mid-1999, continued economic growth, sustained high employment, and low inflation were bringing many benefits to the U.S. economy. Real incomes were gaining and new employment opportunities were emerging for those who traditionally have had the greatest difficulty finding jobs. Increased tax receipts were producing a growing federal budget surplus. Economic forecasts were for continued moderate expansion of the U.S. economy in the months ahead. Amidst the general prosperity, however, the farm sector and some mining and manufacturing industries faced severe difficulties stemming from low prices in world markets.

As of mid-1999, there was every prospect that the U.S. economy would enter the 21st century in a strong and vibrant condition, with output growing, incomes and employment rising, inflation remaining subdued, and the federal budget registering a large and growing surplus. Throughout 1998 and into 1999 the U.S. economy continued to maintain a satisfying combination of sturdy economic growth, high employment, and low inflation. The combined value of the unemployment rate and the inflation rate, often referred to as the "misery index," remained near its lowest level of the past three decades (Figure 1). Real average hourly earnings recovered much, though not all, of the ground lost to inflation since the mid-1970s. Lower unemployment rates for all major demographic groups indicated widespread success in finding jobs. Buoyed by high tax receipts stemming from prosperity and capital gains, the federal budget moved solidly into surplus, and, under current tax and spending plans, the surplus was projected to increase through fiscal year 2009.[1] Policy debate about uses of the surplus intensified as the surplus increased in early 1999.

But not all the news was good. Many farmers, as well as some mining and manufacturing industries, were hard hit by low world prices and stiff foreign competition. Overall, however, sustained prosperity was bringing substantial benefits to the U.S. populace.

The term "virtuous cycle" has come into widespread use to describe the recent workings of the U.S. economy. The phrase implies no moral judgements, but rather describes the relationships believed to underlie the extended period of non-inflationary growth. According to this theory, improving productivity bolsters corporate earnings expectations and thus encourages capital investment. Investment, in turn, brings further productivity gains that, in their turn, help maintain price stability. Price stability, in its turn, fosters an environment in which growth of output and employment can continue.

As 1998 began, there was general concern about the possible impact on the U.S. economy of the "Asian crisis." Severe financial or economic problems had emerged in Japan and in several of the more newly industrialized Asian countries, and subsequently seemed to be spreading to Brazil and elsewhere. Although the ramifications of these world financial problems dampened U.S. exports and squeezed some corporate profits, the U.S. economy weathered the international crisis with no interruption of domestic growth. By mid-1999, encouraging signs of stabilization and recovery had emerged in many of the world's troubled economies.

The "good news" U.S. economy of the 1990s has contrasted dramatically with the deep recessions, high unemployment, and troublesome inflation that characterized much of the 1970s and early 1980s. The three decades covered by this book have been marked by technological advances, shifts in job requirements and work force composition, and dramatic changes in the global economic and political environment. These changes were at times disruptive and evoked periodic expressions of concern about the strength, stability, and international competitiveness of the U.S. economy. Yet from these years of change and turbulence has emerged a prosperous, dynamic, and competitive economy that is widely viewed as a model for nations either making the transition from managed to free market economies or seeking to join the ranks of wealthy industrialized nations.

This review briefly examines major trends from 1970 to 1990 and then takes a closer look at the 1990s, including developments in recent months and projections for 1999 and 2000. The comprehensive statistical tables that form the main body of this book permit users to assemble additional information about the U.S. economy and make their own assessments of the U.S. economic situation.

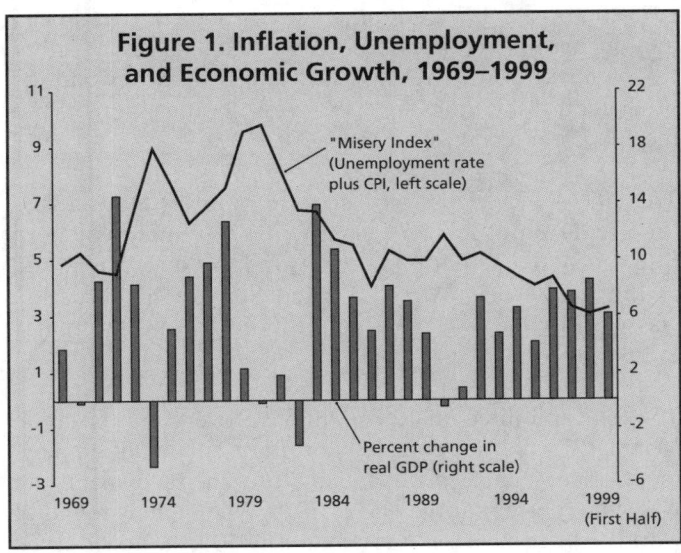

Figure 1. Inflation, Unemployment, and Economic Growth, 1969–1999

"Misery Index" (Unemployment rate plus CPI, left scale)

Percent change in real GDP (right scale)

Source: Bureau of Labor Statistics, Bureau of Economic Analysis

THE 1970s: A TURBULENT DECADE

In 1969, the U.S. economy, which had performed so well in the early 1960s, was experiencing the strains of financing the war in Vietnam without offsetting cutbacks in civilian production. Consumer prices rose over 6 percent from December 1968 to December 1969, and the unemployment rate averaged 3.5 percent (the lowest in 16 years), a combination that clearly indicated an overextended economy. An income tax surcharge and a leveling-off of defense spending moved the federal budget into surplus, but this fiscal restraint came too late to slow the economic overheating without a recession.

The recession of 1969–1970, although it lasted 11 months, appears relatively mild in retrospect (Table 1). Few observers suspected that it marked the beginning of a decade of abrupt and unsettling economic change; a decade to be marked by the deepest recession since the 1930s.

STRUCTURAL SHIFTS DURING THE 1970s. Although marred by a deep recession, the 1970s were not a period of economic stagnation. Quite the opposite. As measured by real gross domestic product (GDP), the economy grew by more than one-third during the decade, and employment rose by an average of about 2 million jobs per year. Almost 90 percent of these new jobs were in service-producing industries (Figure 2). Over one-half the new jobs were filled by women. These were related developments. Service industry growth offered attractive job opportunities for women, and the rapid rise in women's labor force participation, from 43 percent of the female population age 20 and over in 1970 to 51 percent in 1980, was in part a response to these new opportunities.

As more and more of the post-World War II "baby boomers" reached working age, the 1970s also saw a dramatic increase in the number of 16 to 19 year olds entering the labor force. The labor force of 1979 included 9.6 million teenagers, or 38 percent more than in 1969. In no subsequent year has the number of teenagers participating in the labor force been this great.

Table 1. Recessions, 1969–1999

Onset [1]	Trough [1]	Duration (months)	Change in real output (percent) [2]	Peak unemployment rate [3]
December 1969	November 1970	11	-0.7	6.1
November 1973	March 1975	16	-3.7	9.0
January 1980	July 1980	6	-2.5	7.8
July 1981	November 1982	16	-3.0	10.8
July 1990	March 1991	8	-2.0	7.8

Sources: National Bureau of Economic Research, Bureau of Economic Analysis, Bureau of Labor Statistics.
1. Onset and trough are the business cycle peaks and troughs as identified by the National Bureau of Economic Reserch (NBER).
2. Total percent change in real GDP from quarterly peak to quarterly trough. These quarters do not necessarily include the monthly peaks and troughs as identified by the NBER.
3. Monthly unemployment peak, seasonally adjusted. The peak may occur after the trough month identified by the NBER.

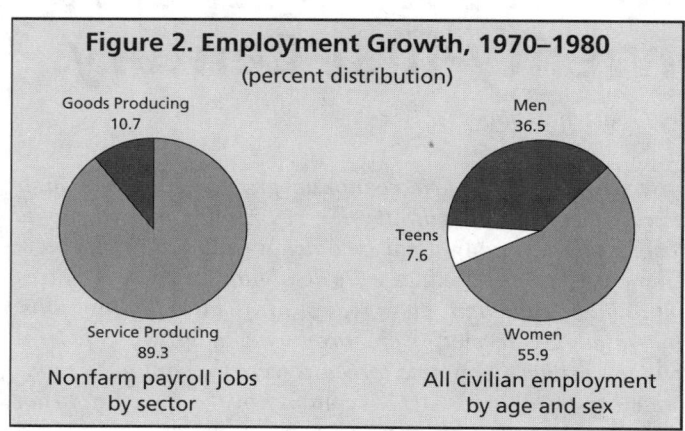

Figure 2. Employment Growth, 1970–1980
(percent distribution)

Goods Producing 10.7
Service Producing 89.3
Nonfarm payroll jobs by sector

Men 36.5
Teens 7.6
Women 55.9
All civilian employment by age and sex

Source: Bureau of Labor Statistics

The unusually high proportion of young and inexperienced workers entering the labor force contributed to the combination of low productivity gains, high unemployment, and troublesome inflation that characterized much of the 1970s. But abrupt changes in world oil prices and supply were among the immediate precipitants of the worst recession since the 1930s.

THE 1973 RECESSION. By the middle of 1973, the economy had come back from the 1969–1970 recession. Strains on productive capacity and accompanying price increases were again a problem. The unemployment rate had dropped below 5 percent, industrial capacity utilization had reached an unusually high 88 percent, and consumer prices had risen nearly 6 percent from July 1972 to July 1973, with most of the increase concentrated in food and energy prices. This overheating economy was then hit by large increases in world oil prices stemming from an oil embargo imposed by the Organization of Petroleum Exporting Countries (OPEC). The price impacts were immediate; consumer prices for fuel oil, for example, rose 42 percent in the four months from September 1973 to January 1974. Oil price increases quickly translated into higher overall producer costs and consumer prices. Coupled with restrictive monetary and fiscal policy and the production dislocations induced by oil shortages, this led to the deepest recession since the 1930s.

The 1973–1975 recession lasted 16 months. During that time real output fell 3.7 percent, and the unemployment rate reached a peak of 9 percent—a level unprecedented in the post-World War II United States. The recession was world-wide, with production falling in all the major industrial countries.

The four and three-quarter years of recovery that began in March 1975 did not completely restore either full employment or reasonable price stability. The unemployment rate was still 6 percent at the end of 1979. When a new round of world oil price increases was initiated in 1979, the added strain helped bring on a new recession at the beginning of 1980.

THE 1980s: EXPANSION, INFLATION, AND DEFICITS

1980–1982: TWO RECESSIONS IN TWO YEARS. The 1980 recession was sharp but brief. However, the subsequent recovery lasted just a year. High inflation continued, monetary policy was tightened while projected federal deficits rose, and the 1981–1982 recession that followed lasted 16 months and brought the unemployment rate to an extraordinarily high 10.8 percent. In examining long-term trends, 1980–1982 can be viewed as a single recessionary period. Real output was no higher in 1982 than in 1979, and the unemployment rate remained above 9 percent until late in 1983.

The period from late 1982 to mid-1990 was one of uninterrupted economic growth, but also one of accumulating structural imbalances. Output grew throughout the period, 20 million nonfarm jobs were added, and the unemployment rate came down from its 10.8-percent recession peak

Table 2. Recent Economic Indicators: Monthly Data

(Seasonally adjusted, except as noted)

	1998						1999						
	Jul	Aug	Sep	Oct	Nov	Dec	Jan	Feb	Mar	Apr	May	Jun	Jul
Labor measures													
Civilian labor force (thousands) ..	137 407	137 481	138 081	138 116	138 193	138 547	139 347	139 271	138 816	139 091	139 019	139 408	139 254
Civilian employment (thousands)	131 176	131 264	131 818	131 858	132 113	132 526	133 396	133 144	133 033	133 069	133 224	133 432	133 307
Unemployment rate (percent)	4.5	4.5	4.5	4.5	4.4	4.3	4.3	4.4	4.2	4.3	4.2	4.3	4.3
Nonagricultural payroll employment (thousands)	125 808	126 170	126 361	126 567	126 841	127 186	127 378	127 730	127 813	128 134	128 162	128 443	128 781
Production and nonsupervisory workers (private nonfarm):													
Average weekly hours	34.6	34.6	34.5	34.6	34.6	34.6	34.6	34.6	34.5	34.4	34.4	34.5	34.5
Average hourly earnings (dollars)	12.80	12.85	12.88	12.91	12.94	12.98	13.04	13.06	13.11	13.14	13.18	13.23	13.29
Real average hourly earnings (1982 dollars)	7.76	7.78	7.80	7.80	7.80	7.81	7.83	7.84	7.86	7.83	7.85	7.88	.....
Production and sales measures													
Industrial production (1992=100)	130.5	132.4	131.9	132.4	132.2	132.4	132.3	132.5	133.3	133.7	134.0	134.2	135.1
Capacity utilization (percent of capacity)	81.1	82.0	81.3	81.3	80.8	80.7	80.4	80.2	80.5	80.4	80.4	80.3	80.7
Manufacturers' new orders ($ billions)	334.8	337.8	340.4	334.7	335.9	344.0	349.3	343.0	349.7	344.9	348.3	350.7	.....
Inventory to sales ratio, manufacturing and trade	1.39	1.40	1.39	1.39	1.39	1.37	1.38	1.37	1.36	1.35	1.35	1.34	.....
Retail sales ($ billions)	228.2	228.4	229.3	232.4	234.5	236.8	239.6	243.6	243.4	244.7	247.2	246.8	248.7
Domestic new car and light truck sales (millions of units, annual rate)	11.8	12.7	13.5	14.2	13.2	14.8	13.4	14.5	14.0	13.8	14.7	14.6	14.4
New private housing units started (thousands, annual rate)	1 719	1 615	1 576	1 698	1 654	1 750	1 820	1 752	1 746	1 577	1 668	1 571	1 661
New one-family homes sold (thousands, annual rate)	883	836	861	903	985	958	908	909	885	952	912	978	980
Price measures													
Consumer price index, all urban consumers (1982-1984=100):													
All items	163.3	163.5	163.6	163.9	164.2	164.4	164.6	164.7	165.0	166.2	166.2	166.2	166.7
All items less food and energy	173.8	174.2	174.5	174.8	175.0	175.6	175.7	175.8	176.0	176.7	176.9	177.0	177.3
Producer price index: Finished goods (1982=100) ...	130.7	130.3	130.6	131.0	130.7	131.3	131.7	131.1	131.5	132.2	132.4	132.3	132.6
Foreign trade price indexes (1995=100, not seasonally adjusted):													
Import price index	91.8	91.4	91.6	91.8	91.3	90.4	90.8	90.7	90.9	91.9	92.5	92.3	93.1
Export price index	95.8	95.3	94.8	94.7	94.9	94.8	94.8	94.6	94.2	94.4	94.5	94.5	94.3
Interest rates *(percent, not seasonally adjusted)*													
3-month treasury bill	4.96	4.94	4.74	4.08	4.44	4.42	4.34	4.45	4.48	4.28	4.51	4.59	4.60
US treasury bonds, 30 year	5.68	5.54	5.20	5.01	5.25	5.06	5.16	5.37	5.58	5.55	5.81	6.04	5.98
Fixed rate first mortgages	6.95	6.92	6.72	6.71	6.87	6.72	6.79	6.81	7.04	6.92	7.15	7.55	7.63
International trade *(millions of dollars)*													
Exports of goods and services ...	75 824	76 227	77 234	79 617	79 126	78 161	77 903	77 139	77 054	78 224	77 955	78 370	.....
Imports of goods and services ...	90 513	92 086	92 409	93 975	93 789	92 402	94 172	95 682	96 001	96 815	99 124	102 992	.....
Trade surplus (+) or deficit (-)	-14 689	-15 860	-15 174	-14 358	-14 664	-14 241	-16 270	-18 544	-18 948	-18 591	-21 169	-24 622	.....

Sources: Bureau of Labor Statistics, Federal Reserve Board of Governors, Bureau of the Census, Bureau of Economic Analysis. Some data are preliminary.

Table 3. Recent Economic Indicators: Quarterly Data

(Seasonally adjusted)

	1998:I	1998:II	1998:III	1998:IV	1999:I	1999:II
National Income and Product Account data:						
Percent change (annual rate)						
Real quantity measures:						
Gross domestic product	5.5	1.8	3.7	6.0	4.3	1.8
Personal consumption expenditures	6.1	6.1	4.1	5.0	6.7	4.6
Nonresidential fixed investment	22.2	12.8	-0.7	14.6	8.5	11.2
Residential fixed investment	15.6	15.0	9.9	10.0	15.4	7.7
Price indexes:						
Gross domestic product	0.9	0.9	1.0	0.8	1.6	1.5
Gross domestic purchases	-0.2	0.4	0.7	0.9	1.2	2.1
Billions of current dollars (annual rate):						
Gross domestic product	8 384.2	8 440.6	8 537.9	8 681.2	8 808.7	8 881.9
Personal consumption expenditures	5 676.5	5 773.7	5 846.7	5 934.8	6 050.6	6 155.9
Nonresidential fixed investment	921.3	941.9	931.6	957.9	972.6	995.1
Residential fixed investment	349.8	363.8	375.8	388.9	405.3	415.8
Change in business inventories	95.5	39.2	57.0	45.7	39.5	12.4
Net exports of goods and services	-123.7	-159.3	-165.5	-156.2	-196.9	-240.0
Exports	973.3	949.6	936.2	976.8	962.7	972.6
Imports	1 097.1	1 108.9	1 101.7	1 133.0	1 159.6	1 212.7
Federal government						
Receipts	1 809.1	1 838.3	1 858.8	1 870.4	1 914.7	1 946.9
Current expenditures	1 750.3	1 763.9	1 766.7	1 804.6	1 792.0	1 806.1
Current surplus or deficit (-)	58.8	74.4	92.0	65.8	122.7	140.8
Corporate profits with inventory valuation and capital consumption adjustments	829.2	820.6	827.0	821.7	868.8	859.6
Personal income	7 003.9	7 081.9	7 160.8	7 257.9	7 349.3	7 442.3
Disposable personal income	5 937.1	5 988.9	6 052.4	6 133.1	6 205.2	6 279.6
Personal saving (percent of disposable personal income)	1.2	0.4	0.2	0.0	-0.7	-1.3
Per capita disposable personal income:						
Current dollars	22 046	22 192	22 373	22 604	22 811	23 031
Chained 1992 dollars	19 632	19 719	19 829	19 980	20 101	20 172
Productivity and cost measures:						
Output per hour (1992=100):						
Nonfarm business	106.5	106.6	107.3	108.4	109.4	109.6
Manufacturing	122.1	123.2	124.6	126.2	128.2	129.7
Employment cost index (July 1989=100):						
Total compensation, private industry	136.1	137.3	138.7	139.7	140.2	141.8
Wages and salaries, private industry	133.6	134.9	136.5	137.5	138.1	139.8

Sources: Bureau of Economic Analysis, Bureau of Labor Statistics.

to 5.2 percent in June 1990. The rate of price increase remained fairly high, however, with the underlying inflation rate (the Consumer Price Index for all items except food and energy) dropping below 4 percent only briefly in 1986.

The 1982–1990 economic expansion was fueled by growth of consumer spending that exceeded the growth of disposable personal income. As a result, the personal saving rate, which had ranged between 6.7 and 9.5 percent from 1970 to 1985, dropped to a range of 5.0 to 5.5 percent from 1987 through 1990.

Tax reductions and defense spending increases helped stimulate economic growth during this period, but they also produced a federal budget deficit that remained near or above 4 percent of GDP from mid-1982 through 1986. Although economic growth helped lower the deficit to 2.0 percent of GDP by 1989, it climbed again to 2.7 percent in 1990 as the economy weakened. These large and persistent deficits made the federal government a drain on the national saving pool rather than a contributor to it. Federal dissaving, combined with the decline in the personal saving rate, caused total gross saving by households, businesses, and government to fall from 21 percent of GDP in 1981 to 16 percent in 1990.

The foreign trade deficit also burgeoned during the mid-1980s, and the United States became heavily dependent on an inflow of foreign funds to help finance government borrowing and business investment needs. Real interest rates were high; business investment grew slowly, especially from 1985 on; and productivity gains were disappointing.

THE 1990s: ACHIEVING A NEW PROSPERITY

By 1989, the economy had reached a high level of resource utilization, but not one that was sustained. Concerned about renewed inflation, the Federal Reserve had tightened monetary policy, raising the discount rate several times between mid-1987 and early 1989. The Iraqi invasion of Kuwait in August 1990 brought with it world oil price increases that, although not on the scale of the oil shocks of the 1970s, helped push the economy into recession. The brief 1990–91 recession lasted eight months, with recovery beginning in March 1991.

The recovery was weak at first, with the unemployment rate continuing to rise until June 1992. In late 1993 the economy began to grow more briskly, initiating the sustained period of steady growth and moderate inflation which continued into 1999. Real GDP grew at an average rate of 3.4 percent per year from the fourth quarter of 1993 through the second quarter of 1999, and the GDP price index rose an average of only 1.8 percent per year during these five and one-half years. Continuing economic growth reduced the unemployment rate to an average of 4.3 percent during the first half of 1999, the lowest since 1969, while price increases remained moderate (Tables 2 and 3).

Various aspects of economic performance during the 1990s; a summary of economic projections for 1999 and 2000 as published by the Federal Reserve, the Administration, and the Congressional Budget Office; and a brief review of some factors that may influence future economic developments are discussed in the sections that follow.

EMPLOYMENT. The vigorous employment growth that characterized the 1970s and 1980s has continued in the 1990s, with an average of 2 million new nonfarm payroll jobs added each year from 1989 through mid-1999 (Table 4). Virtually all the employment growth since 1989 has occurred in private service-producing industries and in state and local government (Figure 3). Federal government employment fell more than 10 percent from 1989 to mid-1999. Hit hard by recession, private goods-producing

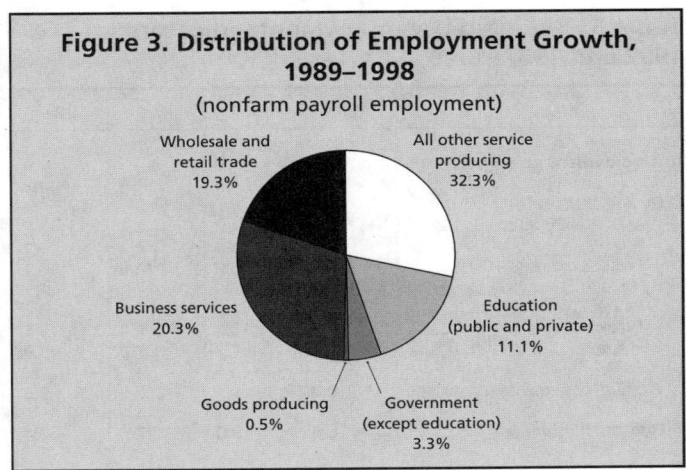

Figure 3. Distribution of Employment Growth, 1989–1998 (nonfarm payroll employment)

Source: Bureau of Labor Statistics

employment fell 8 percent from 1989 to 1992 but, helped by gains in construction employment, regained its 1989 level for the first time in 1998. However, manufacturing employment, which was still 3 percent below its 1989 peak in 1998, began a new decline in mid-1998, falling more than 2 percent from June 1998 to June 1999.

Almost two-thirds of total nonfarm payroll employment growth from 1989 to 1998 occurred in four industry groups: business services, wholesale and retail trade, health services, and education. Business services alone accounted for 20 percent of non-farm payroll employment growth, wholesale and retail trade for 19 percent, health services for 13 percent, and education (public and private) for 11 percent. The broad business services category includes many types of services, ranging from building cleaning and maintenance to construction equipment rental. Among the most rapidly growing business services have been com-

Table 4: Labor Force and Employment Measures, 1989–1999

(Seasonally adjusted)

	1989	1990	1991	1992	1993	1994	1995	1996	1997	1998	1999 [1]
Civilian population, age 16 and over:											
Population (thousands)	186 393	189 164	190 925	192 805	194 838	196 814	198 584	200 591	203 133	205 220	207 432
Labor force (thousands)	123 869	125 840	126 346	128 105	129 200	131 056	132 304	133 943	136 297	137 673	139 173
Employment (thousands)	117 342	118 793	117 718	118 492	120 259	123 060	124 900	126 708	129 558	131 463	133 242
Unemployment (thousands)	6 528	7 047	8 628	9 613	8 940	7 996	7 404	7 236	6 739	6 210	5 931
Unemployment rate (percent of labor force)	5.3	5.6	6.8	7.5	6.9	6.1	5.6	5.4	4.9	4.5	4.3
Employment to population ratio (percent)	63.0	62.8	61.7	61.5	61.7	62.5	62.9	63.2	63.8	64.1	64.3
Labor force participation rate (percent of population)	66.5	66.5	66.2	66.4	66.3	66.6	66.6	66.8	67.1	67.1	67.1
Nonfarm payroll employees (thousands):											
Total	107 884	109 403	108 249	108 601	110 713	114 163	117 191	119 608	122 690	125 826	128 243
Goods producing	25 254	24 905	23 745	23 231	23 352	23 908	24 265	24 493	24 962	25 347	25 222
Service producing	82 630	84 497	84 504	85 370	87 361	90 256	92 925	95 115	97 727	100 480	103 021
By sector											
Private sector	90 105	91 098	89 847	89 956	91 872	95 036	97 885	100 189	103 133	106 007	108 148
Federal government	2 988	3 085	2 966	2 969	2 915	2 870	2 822	2 757	2 699	2 686	2 672
State and local government	14 791	15 219	15 436	15 675	15 926	16 258	16 484	16 662	16 858	17 133	17 423

Sources: Bureau of Economic Analysis, Bureau of Labor Statistics.
1. Second quarter average, seasonally adjusted.

Table 5. Selected Unemployment Indicators, 1992 and 1997–1999

	1992	1997	1998	1999 [1]
Unemployment rates (percent):				
All civilian workers	7.5	4.9	4.5	4.3
By age and sex				
Men age 20 and over	7.1	4.2	3.7	3.5
Women age 20 and over	6.3	4.4	4.1	3.9
Both sexes, age 16-19	20.1	16.0	14.6	13.4
By race and ethnicity				
White	6.6	4.2	3.9	3.8
Black	14.2	10.0	8.9	7.5
Hispanic	11.6	7.7	7.2	6.8
Women who maintain families	10.0	8.1	7.2	6.6
Construction workers	16.8	9.0	7.5	7.4
Median weeks unemployed, all civilian workers	8.7	8.0	6.7	6.3

Source: Bureau of Labor Statistics.
1. Second quarter average.

puter and data processing services (860,000 jobs added) and help supply services (1.7 million jobs added). The latter consists largely of temporary help supplied to businesses throughout the industrial spectrum; counts of workers by industry to which the help is supplied are not read-

ily available. It may well be that part of the decline in manufacturing employment represents the substitution of workers on the payrolls of help supply services for workers on manufacturing payrolls.

Tight labor markets have drawn additional workers into the labor force. A record 64.3 percent of the population age 16 and over held jobs in the first half of 1999. Unemployment rates were the lowest in many years for all major groups in the labor force, and the reductions have been particularly dramatic among groups with traditionally high unemployment rates, indicating the expanding job opportunities for individuals who have greatest difficulty finding jobs. The unemployment rate for Blacks rose to 14.2 percent in 1992 and still was 10 percent in 1997; by the second quarter of 1999 it had fallen to 7.5 percent (Table 5). Similar trends can be seen in the unemployment rates for Hispanics, for women who maintain families, and for construction workers.

The sustained ability of the U.S. economy to create new jobs and the willingness of the U.S. population to respond to employment opportunities are remarkable success stories. Entry and reentry into the labor force, shifts by workers from declining to growing industries, and the absorp-

Table 6: Price and Cost Measures, 1989–1999

(Annual percent change, fourth quarter to fourth quarter or December to December.)

	1989	1990	1991	1992	1993	1994	1995	1996	1997	1998	1999 [1]
Fourth quarter to fourth quarter:											
Price indexes:											
Gross domestic product	3.9	4.6	3.4	2.6	2.6	2.5	2.1	1.8	1.7	0.9	1.6
Gross domestic purchases	4.0	5.2	2.7	3.0	2.3	2.5	2.0	1.8	1.3	0.4	1.7
Employment cost index, private industry											
Total compensation	4.8	4.6	4.4	3.5	3.6	3.1	2.6	3.1	3.4	3.5	3.0
Wages and salaries	4.1	4.0	3.7	2.6	3.1	2.8	2.8	3.4	3.9	3.9	3.4
Productivity (output per worker hour)											
Nonfarm business	0.2	-0.6	2.2	3.5	-0.4	0.1	1.2	2.0	1.6	2.6	2.4
Manufacturing	-0.3	3.3	3.3	4.5	1.5	3.6	4.0	4.3	5.3	3.8	5.6
December to December:											
Consumer price indexes, all urban consumers											
All items	4.6	6.1	3.1	2.9	2.7	2.7	2.5	3.3	1.7	1.6	2.2
All items less food and energy	4.4	5.2	4.4	3.3	3.2	2.6	3.0	2.6	2.2	2.4	1.6
Food	5.6	5.3	1.9	1.5	2.9	2.9	2.1	4.3	1.5	2.3	1.7
Housing	3.9	4.5	3.4	2.6	2.7	2.2	3.0	2.9	2.4	2.3	2.0
Apparel	1.0	5.1	3.4	1.4	0.9	-1.6	0.1	-0.2	1.0	-0.7	-1.4
Transportation	4.0	10.4	-1.5	3.0	2.4	3.8	1.5	4.4	-1.4	-1.7	3.4
Medical care	8.5	9.6	7.9	6.6	5.4	4.9	3.9	3.0	2.8	3.4	3.6
Energy	5.1	18.1	-7.4	2.0	-1.4	2.2	-1.3	8.6	-3.4	-8.8	9.9
Producer price indexes											
Finished goods	4.9	5.7	-0.1	1.6	0.2	1.7	2.3	2.8	-1.2	0.0	1.5
Finished goods less food & energy	4.2	3.5	3.1	2.0	0.4	1.6	2.6	0.6	0.0	2.5	-0.4
Finished energy goods	9.5	30.7	-9.6	-0.3	-4.1	3.5	1.1	11.7	-6.4	-11.7	13.5
Finished consumer foods	5.2	2.6	-1.5	1.6	2.4	1.1	1.9	3.4	-0.8	0.1	1.2
Intermediate materials, supplies, and components	2.3	4.3	-2.6	1.0	1.0	4.4	3.3	0.7	-0.8	-3.3	2.5
Crude materials	7.1	6.0	-11.6	3.3	0.1	-0.5	5.5	14.7	-11.3	-16.7	15.1
Crude foodstuffs and feedstuffs	2.8	-4.2	-5.8	3.0	7.2	-9.4	12.9	-1.0	-4.0	-11.0	2.0
Crude nonfood materials	10.4	13.6	-14.6	3.4	-4.8	6.4	0.5	27.1	-15.8	-20.9	26.5
Foreign trade price indexes											
Exports	0.6	2.1	-0.6	0.7	1.1	3.7	3.4	-1.2	-1.1	-3.5	-0.6
Imports	2.6	7.4	-4.2	0.2	-1.0	5.3	2.6	1.5	-5.2	-6.4	4.2

Sources: Bureau of Economic Analysis, Bureau of Labor Statistics.
1. Compound annual rate of change 4th quarter 1998 to 2nd quarter 1999 or December 1998 to June 1999, seasonally adjusted. Some data are preliminary.

tion of immigrant labor into the work force all have demonstrated the responsiveness and flexibility of the U.S. economy. By mid-1999, however, with labor force participation already at record levels, concern was increasing over whether the strong demand for additional workers could be met without the lure of higher wages, possibly leading in turn to inflationary price increases.

PRICES AND COSTS. During the 1990s, the United States has moved from a situation of persistent, troubling inflation to one of near price stability. The yearly increase in the price index for gross domestic purchases—the index which measures prices paid by U.S. residents, including prices paid for imported goods—fell from 5.2 percent in 1990 to only 1.3 percent in 1997 (Table 6). Helped by falling prices for many imports—including a large drop in oil prices—the 1998 increase in the gross domestic purchases price index was even smaller, only 0.4 percent. During the first half of 1999 import prices recovered some of their 1998 decline, rising at an annual rate of 4.2 percent. Even incorporating this import price rise, however, the price index for gross domestic purchases rose at a still-modest annual rate of 1.7 percent.

Similarly, the Consumer Price Index (CPI), which rose 6.1 percent in 1990, rose only 1.6 percent in 1998 and at a 2.2 percent rate during the first half of 1999. The Producer Price Index (PPI) for finished goods, which rose 5.7 percent during 1990, actually declined during 1997, remained unchanged in 1998, and, had it not been for rising prices for food and energy, would have fallen again in the first half of 1999.

As in earlier decades, energy prices have been a highly volatile component of the price indexes throughout the 1990s. Measured either at the producer or the consumer level, energy prices fell in 1997 and 1998 and rose again in the first half of 1999. Even so, in mid-1999, both consumer and producer prices for energy remained below their levels at the beginning of 1997.

Consumer prices for transportation are heavily influenced by energy prices and have followed a similar pattern of ups and downs during the 1990s, but with less pronounced swings. Prices for crude foodstuffs and feedstuffs fell in 1997 and 1998 and rose only a little during the first half of 1999. While these declines have helped hold down consumer food prices, low prices have caused severe problems for many farmers.

Apparel prices have shown small yearly ups and downs, but on balance their mid-1999 level was about equal to prices at the end of 1991.

Prices for medical care have shown increases of less than 4 percent per year from 1995 through mid-1999, a far cry from the 8 to 9.5 percent rates of the 1989–1991 period, and closer to the general inflation rate than in the earlier period.

In summary, despite strong economic growth and tight labor markets, inflation remained subdued in 1998 and early 1999, with rates of change for major groups in the consumer price index ranging from price declines for apparel to less than 4 percent per year increases for medical care.

Fundamental factors in determining price levels are labor costs and labor productivity. The employment cost index, a comprehensive measure of labor costs, has held to moderate rates of increase during the past six years, and productivity gains since 1995 have been the most encouraging in many years. In the second quarter of 1999, however, the employment cost index for wages and salaries in private industry rose at an annual rate of 5 percent, compared to only a 1.8 percent rate in the first quarter, giving rise to concerns that tight labor markets had begun to generate more rapid labor cost increases. However, the still low rate of increase when the two quarters are averaged together suggests that, unless additional data indicate otherwise, the second quarter rise may have been merely a temporary spurt.

PRODUCTIVITY AND REAL WAGES. Output gains are achieved through some combination of increases in hours worked and labor productivity gains; that is, increases in the amount produced per worker hour. Productivity gains permit society to enjoy more goods and services for any given amount of time worked. Productivity gains also help hold down price increases; if increases in money wages are matched by increases in output, labor costs do not rise and prices need not be increased to cover these costs.

From the mid-1970s to the mid-1990s, productivity gains were puzzlingly small by earlier historical standards. However, the picture improved beginning late in 1995. For the nonfarm business sector, labor productivity grew an average of slightly over 2 percent per year from mid-1995 to mid-1999. These gains have been important both in helping to hold down price increases and in providing real wage gains. After nearly two decades of stagnation or decline, real (inflation-adjusted) average hourly earnings

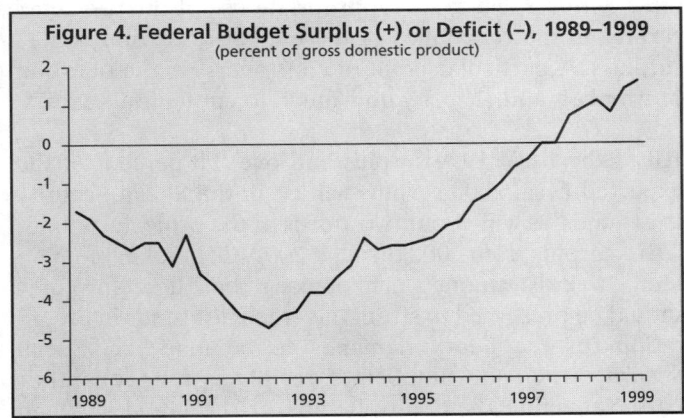

Figure 4. Federal Budget Surplus (+) or Deficit (–), 1989–1999
(percent of gross domestic product)

Source: Bureau of Economic Analysis

began rising during 1997, and the gains continued in 1998 and the first half of 1999. By mid-1999, average hourly earnings were at their highest level since 1979, although still shy of their 1973 peak.

FEDERAL BUDGET TRENDS. After many years of deficits, the federal budget (measured on a National Income and Product Account basis) moved into balance in the second half of 1997, following some 28 years of persistent deficits. In 1998, there was a surplus of $73 billion, or 0.9 percent of GDP, and in the first half of 1999, the surplus increased to $132 billion (1.5 percent of GDP) (Figure 4).

This rapid emergence of a surplus is explained by the increased tax receipts and lower costs of assistance programs associated with strong economic growth. The surplus came as a happy surprise to many observers. Spending limitations agreed to by Congress and the Administration in 1997 had been designed to produce a balanced budget by the year 2002.

The most recent analysis by the Congressional Budget Office (CBO) shows the surplus rising to $413 billion (3.1 percent of GDP) by fiscal 2009[2]. These projections assume continuation of tax and spending as provided in current law (including adherence to tight ceilings on discretionary spending), a steady growth of real GDP of between 2.3 and 2.5 percent per year from 2001 through 2009, and a rate of consumer price increase of 2.5 percent per year over the same period. Were the CBO projections to be realized, federal debt held by the public would fall from $3,720 billion at the end of 1998 to $865 billion at the end of 2009, and, with GDP growing, would plummet from 44.3 percent of GDP at the end of 1998 to only 6.4 percent at the end of 2009.

The prospect of large and growing federal surpluses has generated intense discussion of the possible uses of these funds. A broad consensus seems to have emerged regarding the portion of the surplus accruing to the Social Security trust funds. There appears to be much less agreement with respect to the appropriate use of the projected surplus in the remainder of the budget (the "on-budget" surplus). A particular point of controversy is the question of whether, and, if so, by how much to cut federal taxes.

All of the fiscal 1999 surplus and over 90 percent of the expected fiscal 2000 surplus will be in the Social Security trust funds, as will about two-thirds of the projected cumulative surplus from 2000 through 2009. General agreement seems to exist among policy-makers that these surpluses should be preserved to strengthen the trust funds in preparation for the heavy demands to be made on Social Security when the number of recipients burgeons after 2010, reflecting the "baby boom" of the late 1940s and 1950s. Preserving these surpluses, which could reach a cumulative total of almost $2 trillion over the 10 years from 2000 through 2009, will provide for major reduction in the federal debt. This debt reduction will contribute to the overall supply of saving in the economy and provide fiscal restraint that many see as appropriate in a fully-employed economy.

Excluding Social Security, the budget surpluses are projected to be quite small in fiscal 2000 and 2001 but to increase thereafter, and to total almost $1 trillion over the ten years 2000 to 2009. As of mid-1999 there was no consensus in Washington concerning the best division of this anticipated "on-budget" surplus among tax cuts, expenditure increases, and debt reduction. In August, the Congress approved a package of tax cuts with an estimated 10 year cumulative cost of $792 billion. The President, arguing that so large a tax cut would be irresponsible and would force reductions in important government programs, indicated his firm intention to veto this legislation, but also indicated his willingness to support a much smaller tax cut, one with a cumulative cost of no more than $300 billion. Meanwhile, increases in appropriations exceeding the spending "caps" set by law were being justified by Congress as "emergency spending," and many foresaw that these caps would be exceeded in FY2000.

Whether the projected budget surpluses actually will be realized also is dependent on the accuracy of the assumptions underlying the projections. Comparing projections made in 1997—showing a budget barely in balance by 2002—with the current projection of a $246 billion surplus in that year is a reminder of how rapidly the budget outlook can change. In its January 1999 report, the CBO published rules of thumb for estimating the impact of lower economic growth, higher inflation, or higher interest rates on future budget surpluses.[3] As an example, higher interest rates, which necessitate increased federal spending, could greatly reduce future surpluses. Applying the CBO rule of thumb, interest rates one percentage point higher than those assumed in the latest CBO projections, if sustained over the projection period, would—other things equal—reduce the cumulative on-budget surplus to a figure less than the $792 billion tax cut approved by Congress. In other words, if CBO has underestimated future interest rates by one percentage point, a tax cut of this magnitude could well produce a renewed "on-budget" deficit. Similarly, slower growth of real GDP would work to reduce future budget surpluses, while a higher rate of inflation could lead to larger surpluses, as inflation tends to increase tax receipts more than current spending.

Economic growth has strengthened state and local budgets as well as the federal budget. According to a Federal Reserve analysis, fiscal 1999 was the seventh consecutive year of improving fiscal positions at the state level; of the 46 states whose fiscal years end on June 30, all appear to

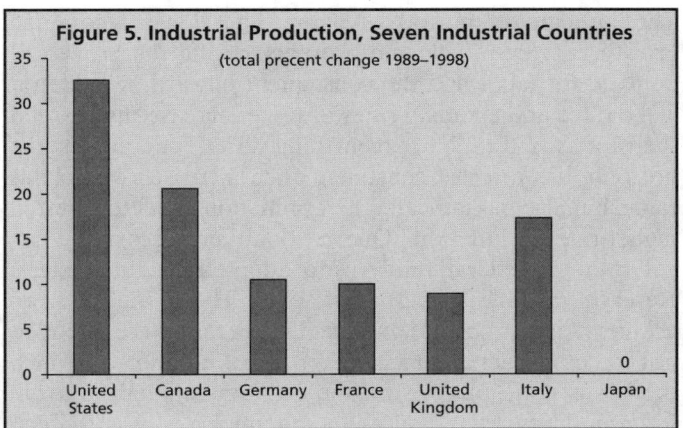

Figure 5. Industrial Production, Seven Industrial Countries
(total precent change 1989–1998)

Source: U.S. Department of Commerce, International Trade Administration

have achieved fiscal 1999 surpluses in their general funds.[4]

THE UNITED STATES IN THE WORLD ECONOMY. Economic growth in the 1990s has been stronger in the United States than in other major industrial countries (Figure 5). Recession spread to all the major countries in the early 1990s, and recovery in most was slower and less certain than in the United States. The strength of the U.S. economy contributed to a strong dollar and large inflows of foreign funds. U.S. purchases of imported goods and the nation's ability to tolerate a large foreign trade deficit helped sustain weaker economies abroad. At the same time, a strong dollar and the availability of imported goods have helped hold down the U.S. inflation rate.

Exports have become increasingly important to the U.S. economy over the past three decades, constituting 11 percent of GDP in mid-1999, compared to only 5 percent in 1968. Strong growth of U.S. exports has demonstrated international competitiveness. Imports also have grown, however, and the trade deficit has remained large. This deficit stems entirely from trade in goods. U.S. trade in services—which includes travel, transportation, royalties and license fees, and other services—now provides the United States with an important positive factor in its international payments balance. The surplus on trade in services offset $83 billion, or 33 percent, of the deficit on trade in goods in 1997.

Asian nations, including not only Japan but also rapidly industrializing nations such as South Korea, Thailand, and Singapore, have become increasingly important trading partners for the United States during the 1990s. In 1996, 33 percent of U.S. goods exports went to Asia, up from 31 percent in 1991. But in mid-1997 several Asian nations, including South Korea, Thailand, and Indonesia, encountered financial crises and abrupt reversals of their previously impressive economic growth. Around the same time, the Japanese economy moved into renewed recession. Growth of U.S. exports to Asia slowed and competition in

world markets intensified as several Asian nations devalued their currencies and cut prices of their exports.

The Asian crisis aroused concern that it might become a global crisis, with serious economic consequences in the United States and elsewhere. The devaluation of several Asian currencies and reductions in worldwide demand led to sharply lower world prices for many commodities. The U.S. import price index fell 5.2 percent during 1997 and a further 6.4 percent during 1998 with much larger declines in prices for oil and for many agricultural commodities.

The Asian crisis persisted into 1998 and created a situation of uncertainty in U.S. financial markets, with investors seeking to reduce their exposure to credit risks. Common stock prices took an abrupt dip in late summer. The Federal Reserve responded to the financial stresses with a series of reductions—totaling three-quarters of a percentage point—in its target interest rate for federal funds. Confidence in U.S. markets was restored, and, despite new concerns that were aroused when Brazil was forced to devalue its currency at the beginning of 1999, U.S. economic growth continued at a healthy pace throughout 1998 and into 1999.

By mid-1999, global economic prospects had brightened considerably. Signs of recovery were increasingly visible in Asian countries, the Brazilian economy seemed to be on the way back, the fallout from Brazil on other Latin American economies was less than had been feared, and

Table 7: Economic Projections for 1999 and 2000

	Actual	Projected	
	1998	1999	2000
Real GDP, percent change			
Fourth quarter to fourth quarter			
Federal Reserve	4.3	3.5 to 3.75	2.5 to 3.0
Administration	4.3	3.2	2.1
Congressional Budget Office	4.3	3.6	2.1
Unemployment rate			
Fourth quarter			
Federal Reserve	4.4	4.0 to 4.25	4.25 to 4.5
Administration	4.4	4.3	4.7
Annual average			
Congressional Budget Office	4.5	4.2	4.3
Consumer price index, percent change			
Fourth quarter to fourth quarter			
Federal Reserve	1.5	2.25 to 2.5	2.0 to 2.5
Administration	1.5	2.4	2.4
Congressional Budget Office	1.5	2.5	2.4

Sources:
Federal Reserve: Central tendency of estimates of Federal Reserve Governors and Reserve Bank Presidents as presented in Board of Governors of the Federal Reserve System, "Monetary Policy Report to the Congress," July 22, 1999.
Administration: Office of Management and Budget, "Mid-Session Review, Budget of the United States Government, Fiscal Year 2000," June 28,1999.
Congressional Budget Office: "The Economic and Budget Outlook: An Update," July 1, 1999.

the Canadian economy was expanding at a brisk pace. In Europe, a new common currency, the Euro, was introduced at the beginning of 1999 in the 11 countries participating the European Monetary Union.[5] Economic growth in West Europe was sluggish in 1998, but it was expected that renewed export demand from Asia would provide a boost as 1999 progressed.

U.S. PROSPECTS FOR THE FUTURE. The general expectation, as of mid-1999, was for the U.S. economy to continue on a path of healthy economic growth. Table 7 summarizes economic projections prepared by the Federal Reserve, the Administration, and the Congressional Budget Office. Although the projections differ somewhat, all three anticipate moderate GDP growth and an unemployment rate that rises slightly in 2000 but remains near 4.5 percent. Consumer prices are projected to rise somewhat more in 1999 and 2000 than in 1998 but still to remain in a relatively comfortable range of a 2 to 2.5 percent annual increase.

The projected real GDP gain of between 2 and 3 percent during the year 2000 would be slower than the 3.4 percent average achieved from late 1993 through mid-1999. There are several reasons to anticipate this moderation of economic growth. The stock market gains that have helped finance consumer spending during the past few years are unlikely to continue at such a rapid pace. The high levels of consumer purchases of motor vehicles and other durables during recent years suggests that consumers may now be "stocked up" and that purchases of durables will grow more slowly. Slightly higher interest rates are expected to slow the pace of residential construction. Industrial plant capacity utilization rates declined during 1998 and remained low during the first half of 1999, suggesting limited need for new industrial construction, and the very rapid pace of investment in producers' durable equipment during recent years suggests that this category of business investment also may grow more slowly in 2000.

The factors mentioned above argue for a more slowly growing economy, but not a weak economy. Real business fixed investment has increased an average of 10 percent per year over the past five years, the most rapid sustained expansion in more than 30 years. Continued investment at a somewhat slower pace would still represent strong performance. Although consumer purchasing recently has exceeded growth of disposable personal income, gains in wealth created by the buoyant stock market have helped finance these purchases. Consumer finances remain in good shape, with measures of financial stress improving. In the first half of 1999, personal bankruptcies declined, as did delinquency rates on household loans and credit card debt.[6] The federal government, with its rising budget surplus, is making a growing contribution to the pool of national saving, so that, despite the low personal saving rate, total gross saving by households, business, and governments is higher relative to GDP than was the case in the early 1990s.

The anticipated period of somewhat slower economic growth may be a welcome prospect, easing the growth of demand for labor and the consequent upward pressure on wage rates and avoiding rates of price increase that exceed the predicted 2 to 2.5 percent range. The Federal Reserve not only has forecast consumer price increases within this range but also has indicated determination to act to forestall higher rates of inflation.[7] Quarter point increases in the target rate for federal funds were adopted by the Federal Reserve in June and August 1999. These moves were acknowledged to be preemptive. That is, they were intended not to counteract a current outbreak of inflation, of which there was none, but to slow the economy enough to avoid future inflationary pressures. In announcing its August decision, the Federal Reserve indicated that it expected the actions taken to be adequate and did not anticipate further interest rate increases during the remainder of 1999.[8]

As the history of past decades has demonstrated, unanticipated world events can produce unanticipated economic dislocations. This vulerability has increased with the more rapid transmission of the effects of political and economic change throughout the global economy. However, economic forecasts must be based on what presently can be observed and reasonably foreseen. With the strong, balanced economic foundation that has been established during the 1990s, the United States seems ready both to extend its impressive record of economic growth and to weather the challenges that may lie ahead.

1. "The Economic and Budget Outlook: An Update," Congressional Budget Office, July 1, 1999.

2. Ibid. The estimated surplus is for the unified budget and for the fiscal year. It is not precisely comparable to the National Income and Product Account figures referenced earlier.

3. "How the Economy Affects the Budget," Appendix C of "The Economic and Budget Outlook: Fiscal Years 2000–2009," Congressional Budget Office, January 1999.

4. "Monetary Policy Report to the Congress," Board of Governors of the Federal Reserve System, July 1999.

5. The 11 countries are Austria, Belgium, France, Finland, Germany, Ireland, Italy, Luxembourg, Netherlands, Portugal, and Spain.

6. Board of Governors of the Federal Reserve System, Op. Cit.

7. Alan Greenspan, Chairman of the Federal Reserve Board of Governors stated in testimony to the Committee on Banking and Financial Services, U.S. House of Representatives, July 22, 1999, "If new data suggest it is likely that the pace of cost and price increases will be picking up, the Federal Reserve will have to act promptly and forcefully so as to preclude imbalances from arising that would only require a more disruptive adjustment later..."

8. The Federal Open Market Committee stated "Today's increase in the federal funds rate, together with the policy action in June and the firming of conditions more generally in U.S. financial markets over recent months, should markedly diminish the risk of rising inflation going forward. As a consequence, the directive the Federal Open Market Committee adopted is symmetrical with regard to the outlook for policy over the near term."

Current Issues in Economic Measurement

by Cornelia J. Strawser

INTRODUCTION

As the contents of this book suggest, the United States has a large, comprehensive, and complex system of statistics measuring the course of its economy. But the economy itself is large, complex, and rapidly changing. Data users often find areas in which the statistics appear not to have kept up with the economy.

U.S. statistical agencies themselves continually study ways in which their data can be improved, and improvements are routinely introduced into important statistical systems such as the National Income and Product Accounts (NIPAs), which encompass Gross Domestic Product (GDP), national and personal income (and related aggregate statistics), and the Consumer Price Index (CPI), which provides data about inflation and key inputs for the measurement of real output and productivity.

Below we outline some of the changes that are being made in the 1999 comprehensive revision of the NIPAs, and then discuss recent developments concerning four current issues: measuring prices, with implications for GDP and productivity; measuring personal income, saving, and taxes; measuring the level of employment; and measuring poverty.

COMPREHENSIVE NIPA REVISION

At intervals of five years, more or less, the Bureau of Economic Analysis (BEA) undertakes a comprehensive, or benchmark, revision of the NIPAs. Release of data incorporating the results of the latest such revision is beginning in late October 1999. (Data in this edition of *Business Statistics* are those available as of September 1999 and do not include any of the benchmark revisions.) In addition to the usual annual revisions that reflect revised and more comprehensive source data, the benchmark revision incorporates definitional and classification changes, and new and improved methodologies. The revised estimates that are being released in 1999 begin with 1959; comparable estimates back to 1929 will be released early in 2000. Measures of real (constant-dollar) output reflect a shift in the reference year from 1992 to 1996.[1]

Innovations in this revision that affect the measurement of real output and productivity include:

- Recognition of business and government purchases of computer software as fixed investment. In the accounts as previously published, software was included as business investment if it was packaged with hardware, but was otherwise considered to be intermediate to the production of other goods and services in the current year, and therefore not included in the comprehensive measure of output. This revision extends back to 1959 and increases output

and productivity growth, adding about 1.5 percent to GDP in 1996.

- Introduction of revised CPI deflators for many components of personal consumption expenditures (PCE) for the years 1967–95, which tend to raise real output growth during that period. The new CPI indexes were already being used from 1995 to date; this will be explained more fully below.

- Introduction of an improved measure of the growth of real output of banks, which should increase output and productivity (see below).

Other definitional and classificational changes have little or no effect on real output growth but change allocation of income and saving among sectors:

- Government employee pension plans are being treated the same way as private pension plans. Prior to the revisions, federal civilian and military retirement and state and local government retirement plans were treated similarly to the Social Security plan, and any surpluses they accumulate counted as part of the government surplus or deficit. In the revision, surpluses in those employee retirement accounts (but not in Social Security) are counted as personal saving. See Section 3.

- Some transactions are reclassified as capital transfers.

- Miscellaneous redefinitions and reclassifications are made.

MEASUREMENT OF PRICES, GDP, AND PRODUCTIVITY

Comprehensive revisions of the CPI introduced in January 1998 have been followed by additional methodological changes in 1999. A new "research series" of the CPI has been developed that carries back to December 1977 the effects of these changes, as well as those of other major methodological changes made during that time. It provides a historical series that is consistent in methodology with the current index, and is shown in this volume along with the official CPI-U (Consumer Price Index for all Urban Consumers); the official CPI-W (Consumer Price Index for Urban Wage Earners and Clerical Workers); and the CPI-U-X1, a historical series incorporating the current rental equivalence method for owner-occupied housing for the years before 1983.

Components of the new "CPI-U-RS" have already been used to calculate the changes in real output and productivity shown in this volume from 1995 forward, and the comprehensive revisions in the NIPAs and the productivity data derived from them will incorporate the revised CPI deflators for the years before 1995.

CONSUMER PRICE INDEX

In this year's edition of *Business Statistics* the Consumer Price Index is presented following the new structure that was introduced in January 1998. At that time, a new market basket was introduced, derived from Consumer Expenditure Survey data covering the years 1993–95; item categories were updated; and new samples and sampling procedures were introduced.[2]

Improvements in the Consumer Price Index are not restricted to major revisions such as that in January 1998, which are undertaken at intervals of approximately 10 years. In January 1999, an important change in the formula used for calculating the basic components of the index was introduced. A geometric mean formula is now used for calculating most of the basic components. "In contrast to the fixed quantity weights of the current CPI arithmetic mean formula, the geometric mean estimator employs a set of fixed expenditure proportions as weights to be used in averaging the prices of individual items within a CPI basic index. Fixing the relative expenditure proportions, rather than the relative quantities, implies that consumers can alter the quantities of goods and services they buy— albeit within the narrow range of a CPI category—when the relative prices of those goods and services change."[3]

The new geometric mean formula is being used for categories making up approximately 61 percent of the total consumer spending represented by the CPI-U. The traditional arithmetic mean formula, holding quantities rather than expenditure constant, will continue to be used for several important categories where the ability of consumers to change their mix of purchases is severely limited: rent of housing, including the imputed rent on owner-occupied housing; selected utilities and government charges; and selected medical care services. BLS expects that the use of the new formula will reduce the annual rate of increase in the CPI by approximately 0.2 of a percentage point per year.[4]

Three other changes were introduced in January 1999:

- A new "hedonic" model to adjust television prices for changes in quality. Hedonic models were developed in response to the problem of separating price change from the value of quality change when a product is substantially altered in both characteristics and price at the time of a model changeover. A hedonic model is one that estimates the consumer valuation of various individual features of a product based on concurrent variations in the prices of products of different specifications. Hedonic models were already in use for estimating apparel and computer price changes in the CPI.

- A change in the treatment of utility rebates.

- A change in the treatment of mandated anti-pollution devices. In March 1971, a decision by an interagency committee led BLS to treat anti-pollution devices as quality improvements, meaning that the cost increase caused by the device would not be treated as a consumer price increase. This decision was inconsistent with the treatment of benefits and costs to the general population—"public goods" and "public bads"—in the rest of the CPI. For example, increased electricity prices resulting from the installation of smokestack scrubbers have been treated as price increases. From now on, changes in the price of motor vehicles and gasoline that result from meeting air quality standards will be counted as price increases to the consumer, though they will still be considered as quality changes in the Producer Price Index, where the focus is on firms and their output rather than consumer utility.

As these examples demonstrate, the Bureau of Labor Statistics (BLS) does not make important changes in the calculation of the CPI only at the time of major market-basket revisions. Other changes in the last decade have been quality adjustment of personal computer prices, introduced in 1998; elimination of automobile finance charges as being out of the scope of the index, also in 1998; revisions of various formulas to eliminate bias, in 1995; treating shifts between brand-name and generic drugs as price changes, also in 1995; and quality adjustment for apparel prices, in 1991. In each case, the changes are introduced as soon as feasible, once the need for the change and its practicality have been established by professional research inside and outside of the BLS.

NEW "RESEARCH SERIES" CPI

The official Consumer Price Indexes (CPI-U and CPI-W) are not retroactively revised when changes are made of the kind discussed above. That would cause great difficulties in statistical series that are widely used in legislation and contracts. However, people who use the CPI as an indicator of inflation over time in economic modeling and other time series applications understandably prefer to have a historical series consistent with the current best thinking about price measurement.

Up until recently, the best historical series available was the BLS' "CPI-U-X1," which carries back to 1967 the treatment of owner-occupied housing that has been used in the CPI-U since 1982. That index (shown on p. 95 of this volume) is also used in the constant-dollar income calculations and some of the alternative poverty series in this book's chapter on "Income Distribution and Poverty."

In a recent issue of the *Monthly Labor Review*, the BLS presented a new "research series" index.[5] This index, known as CPI-U-RS, carries major changes in current methods (or estimates of their likely effects, where retrospective use of the new methods is not feasible) back to December 1977. The CPI-U-RS includes the rental equivalence method for owner-occupied housing; quality adjust-

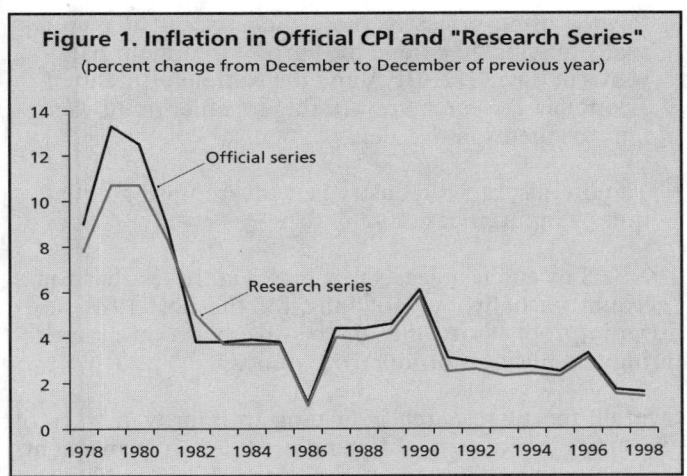

Figure 1. Inflation in Official CPI and "Research Series"
(percent change from December to December of previous year)

Source: U.S. Department of Labor, Bureau of Labor Statistics, *Monthly Labor Review,* June 1999, p. 35.

ments for used cars and housing, which were introduced in 1987 and 1988; and all the changes made in the 1990s that were outlined previously in this section.

Most of the changes tended to reduce measured inflation over the 21-year period, and overall, inflation in the research index averaged 0.45 percent per year less than in the official CPI-U. However, some of the changes tended to raise the official index. Before the newer methods, housing rental measures were biased downward because of "aging bias," as BLS priced the same unit year after year while its quality gradually deteriorated. Also, apparel quality improvements were overstated. Treating pollution control costs as quality increases also introduced a downward bias in the official index. These three downward biases are removed in the CPI-U-RS.

The yearly inflation rates yielded by the official CPI-U and the new CPI-U-RS are shown in Figure 1. The new series does not change the basic story that inflation accelerated to high rates in the late 1970s and early 1980s, was rapidly reduced by the 1981–82 recession, and has remained much lower since then. The largest year-to-year differences are in the period before introduction of rental equivalence.

The user should be cautious about applying the difference between the "CPI-U" and the "CPI-U-RS" to other areas where inflation measurement is important. The potential effect of this difference on measurement of Gross Domestic Product and productivity is limited, and will be discussed in the next subsection. The biggest single source of difference between the two CPIs is the rental equivalence method, which has always been used in estimation of GDP and the associated price indexes and deflators.

The CPI is an important factor in the federal budget, but it should be remembered that it is the CPI-W, not the CPI-U, which is used to escalate federal Social Security and other retirement payments. (The CPI-U is used in portions of the tax code, however.) The CPI-W incorporated rental

equivalence two years later than the CPI-U. During those two years the old method actually showed less increase in housing prices than the new one, with the result that over the affected period as a whole, the official CPI-W rises somewhat less than the official CPI-U.

Poverty thresholds are escalated with the CPI-U; are they therefore too high? Some points relative to this question are discussed in the final section of this chapter. It is also questionable whether some of the new CPI methods, which are appropriate for measuring prices for the population in general, are particularly appropriate for measuring the change in the price of a subsistence level of living. People who are already buying the cheapest commodity in any category have few possibilities of substituting when its price goes up. And better measurement of personal computer prices hardly seems relevant to the poverty budget.

PRODUCTIVITY MEASUREMENT

Improvements in a nation's living standards require either an increase in the nation's effort—labor and capital inputs—or an increase in the productivity of its inputs, or both. Labor inputs dominate the production process, and "labor productivity"—output per hour worked—is central to the nation's ability to raise living standards. Table 1 below shows the annual rate of increase in business output per hour over recent decades. Each of the years shown through 1989 is a business cycle peak, so the figures for 1959 through 1989 are trend estimates, not affected by the typical cycle of productivity over the course of a business cycle.

These data indicate a sharp slowdown in productivity growth since 1973, and some pickup beginning in 1995. There has been much debate on the causes of the slowdown; on whether the recent acceleration will endure; and on the role of measurement error in our perceptions of these developments.

The figures in Table 1 are based on the BLS productivity and cost indexes, shown in more detail on p. 106 of this volume. In these measures, output is derived from GDP statistics, while labor input is calculated using BLS data on employment and hours. Private business output is total real GDP minus the government, nonprofit, and household sectors; these excluded sectors are measured by their labor input in the GDP, hence it would be meaningless to

Table 1. Annual Rates of Increase in Output per Hour, Private Business

(percent)

1959–1969	3.2
1969–1973	3.2
1973–1979	1.2
1979–1989	1.2
1989–1995	0.9
1995:II–1999:II	2.3

Source: Bureau of Labor Statistics.

include them in a productivity index. BLS also removes the imputed rental of owner-occupied and nonprofit buildings, because no corresponding labor input measures can be developed.

Thus, output per hour in private business depends on how output is measured in the GDP accounts. Personal consumption expenditures (PCE) is a large proportion of GDP, and real PCE is heavily dependent on CPI components to deflate current values. BLS calculates that the CPI affects 57 percent of business sector output. CPIs using the geometric mean formula (see above) have already been incorporated in the deflation of PCE beginning with 1995; in the comprehensive revision of the National Income and Product Accounts (NIPAs) being introduced in late October 1999, real PCE estimates beginning with 1978 are recalculated using CPI-U-RS components. This will in turn be reflected in subsequent revisions of productivity using the revised NIPAs. In the meantime, the Federal Reserve estimates that about .25 percentage point of the improvement in productivity growth since 1995 is because of changes in price measurement.[6] As can be seen in Table 1, there has been a considerable acceleration of productivity growth since 1995 even after allowing for this.

Another productivity issue has been the divergence between total business and manufacturing productivity trends. The manufacturing data are generated separately from the business totals using a different set of output data, and do not show the slowdown evident in the business data. While some of this divergence may arise from inconsistency between the two data sets, it still suggests that there may be some significant downward biases in the measurement of nonmanufacturing industries. BLS has undertaken extensive research in this area, the results of which were published in February 1999.[7]

As it turns out, BLS does find likely problems in several nonmanufacturing industries, most of which do not derive from problems in the CPI.

• Banking is a major problem area. Most banking output has been represented in the NIPAs by labor input measures, a procedure that biases the productivity growth measure toward zero. BEA is introducing a new treatment of banking using transactions volume data (developed by BLS) in the October 1999 comprehensive revision.

• Construction values in the NIPAs are converted to constant dollars using input cost, not output, deflators—another method that biases productivity growth toward zero. BLS, BEA, and the Census Bureau are working together to improve measurement in this area.

• The health industries are difficult to measure, starting with the difficulty of defining the unit of output. The Producer Price Indexes and Consumer Price Indexes have both recently updated their approach to measuring prices in these industry, but it is not really possible to extend the current treatment backwards in time. BLS, BEA and the National Bureau of Economic Research are working together on further improvements in this field.

• The life insurance industry is measured using deflation by input prices.

The BLS research suggests that biases in these areas could "account partially, but not fully, for the post-1973 slowdown in productivity and for the divergence of manufacturing and business productivity trends."[8]

Overall, recent research is leading to improved ways of measuring productivity. Extending these improvements back into the 1970s, 1980s, and early 1990s is likely to lessen the apparent slowdown in productivity growth at that time, but probably not erase it entirely.

Many of these same improvements also imply more improvement in general standards of living over the last two decades than had been shown by previous measures. It is less clear that measures of the extent of poverty—discussed above and in the last section of this chapter—would be affected by these improved ways of measuring prices and output.

INCOME, SAVING, AND TAXES

Is it true that Americans aren't saving any money and are going hopelessly into debt? Is it true that Americans are paying unprecedentedly high taxes?

Statistics can be found in this book, or derived from figures found in this book, that would seem to give an answer of "Yes" to both questions. The personal saving[9] rate—personal saving as a percent of disposable personal income—has been around zero recently, as is shown on p. 52. In some periods it has even fallen into negative territory, suggesting spending down past savings and/or borrowing more than is saved or repaid. And it is frequently pointed out that federal taxes have reached a peacetime high relative to Gross Domestic Product (GDP).

However, both of these percentages have a problem of incompatibility between numerator and denominator. The National Income and Product Accounts (NIPAs), the source of GDP and personal income figures, are not designed to provide a comprehensive aggregate measure of the resources available to individuals. According to the Bureau of Economic Analysis (BEA) which compiles these figures, "The NIPAs focus on the production of goods and services in the U.S. economy and on the income arising from that production. Changes in the value of existing assets play a role in that production, but these changes fall outside the scope of the NIPAs."[10]

Recently, "changes in the value of existing assets," i.e. rapid increases in prices of common stocks, have provided huge increases to the taxable and spendable income of

U.S. shareholders. These capital gains provide real increases in spending power to their recipients, even though they do not correspond to anything defined as output in the GDP. The taxes paid on realized capital gains rise without a corresponding rise in GDP. To the extent that consumers spend from their capital gains, personal consumption expenditures (PCE) rises even though personal income does not. Since personal saving is simply the residual left when personal outlays are subtracted from disposable personal income, it can decline or even go negative without additional borrowing or drawing on past savings, if those outlays are financed from capital gains (which could be on other types of assets such as homes as well as on stocks).

How the statistics user should deal with this situation depends on the nature of the inquiry.

- For anyone making or evaluating a forecast of the economy, a low personal saving rate raises a caution flag. The forecaster needs to estimate how consumers have been financing their current rate of spending—whether by debt, spending down assets, or capital gains—and make a judgment about how long that source of financing will be available in the forecast period.

- Others may be concerned about the longer-term issue of whether individuals are accumulating adequate savings to finance emergencies and retirement.

- Finally, macroeconomic growth analysts may be concerned as to whether there is enough saving and investment in the economy as a whole.

ADJUSTMENTS TO NIPA SAVING

An extensive discussion and analysis of personal saving measurement by William G. Gale and John Sabelhaus recently has been published.[11] They suggest a number of adjustments to the NIPA personal saving estimate that would make it more consistent with economic theory and consumer behavior: treating consumer durables as investment rather than consumption, treating government pension plans as if they were private pensions, adjusting interest payments for inflation, and allowing for future taxation of pension benefits. The last three of these do not increase total saving in the economy but only reallocate it from the government and corporate to the personal sector. The personal saving rate so measured—still excluding capital gains, to be consistent with the NIPA concept—declines less than the official figure.

Gale and Sabelhaus also calculate personal saving according to their definition from a different data source, the Federal Reserve Flow of Funds Accounts (FOF). In these accounts, saving is measured as the increase in assets minus the increase in liabilities. "FOF" measures, adjusted for comparability with NIPA measures, show levels and changes in personal saving that are similar to the NIPA estimates in recent years.

However, Gale and Sabelhaus find that including capital gains "fundamentally changes recent trends. If all capital gains are included, the current adjusted household saving rate is the highest in at least the last forty years, despite a personal saving rate of zero."[12]

NATIONAL SAVING AND INVESTMENT

For those concerned with the adequacy of saving to finance investment, it is the level of *national* saving that measures the amount of plant, equipment, and housing investment that can be financed domestically. (In addition, investment can be financed by an inflow of net foreign investment, which corresponds to a deficit on current account in the international transactions accounts.) In its February 1999 "Note", BEA points out that "…as personal saving has fallen, saving by business (mainly in the form of retained earnings and consumption of fixed capital) and by government (in the form of the NIPA surplus and consumption of fixed capital) have risen….Gross saving combined with net foreign investment, which reflects the acquisition of U.S. assets by foreign residents, has been adequate to finance high levels of investment in recent years."[13] (It should perhaps be explained that "consumption of fixed capital" means depreciation allowances, which BEA adjusts for consistency with NIPA concepts and subtracts from gross output to calculate income. These allowances represent saving that is available to finance the replacement of the used-up capital. Gross saving, like GDP and its investment components, is calculated before deducting the consumption of fixed capital.) As Figure 1 indicates, gross saving has increased from about 14.5 percent of GNP[14] in 1992-1993 to over 17 percent recently, as corporate and other private saving has increased and government (federal, state, and local) has moved from deficit to surplus.

CONSUMER FINANCIAL STRAIN

The points made by Gale and Sabelhaus make it clear that the personal saving rate is not a good gauge of the extent

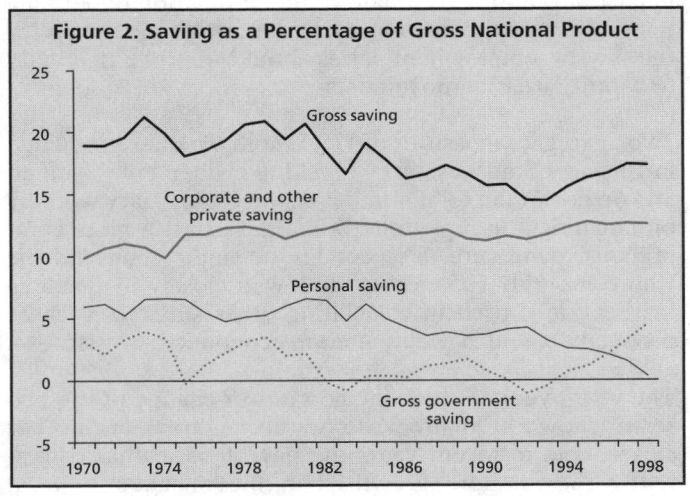

Figure 2. Saving as a Percentage of Gross National Product

Source: U.S. Department of Commerce, Bureau of Economic Analysis

of financial strain on consumers. Some have proposed using household net worth as part of this evaluation. For example, in the Federal Reserve "Monetary Policy Report to Congress," July 22, 1999, the Federal Reserve charted the wealth-to-income ratio along with the personal saving rate. However, the accumulation of wealth may be concentrated in higher-income households while debt burdens may be most onerous in middle and lower income households. For that reason, it is desirable to look directly at debt burdens. The Federal Reserve used to make available a ratio of debt service payments to income, which was published in last year's Business Statistics, but this has been discontinued because of statistical difficulties. A revised version may be available later. In the meantime, some direct measures of the extent of debt distress are available; measures of credit card delinquency at banks and mortgage delinquency rates may be found on p. 149 of this volume.

PERSONAL SAVING IN THE NIPA REVISION

In the October 1999 revision of the NIPAs, one of the changes recommended by Gale and Sabelhaus and others is being made: government employee pension plans (but not Social Security) are treated in the same way as private pension plans. This means that any accumulation of surpluses in federal, state, and local employee retirement plan accounts will be treated as personal saving. In the previous treatment, these surpluses were counted as part of government, and accounted for a significant portion of the government surpluses shown in Figure 2. The new treatment will reduce government saving (or increase government deficits) and increase personal saving, with no net effect on national saving.[15]

MEASURING EMPLOYMENT

In recent years, total nonfarm payroll employment has consistently grown faster than total civilian employment. There are definitional differences between the two measures, but even after these are adjusted for, some unexplained difference remains, possibly accounted for, at least in part, by an underestimate of the population underlying the civilian employment number. A new sample design for the payroll employment series should improve its ability to capture cyclical movements.

Two aggregate measures of U.S. employment are provided in Business Statistics: on p. 111, total civilian employment; and on p. 117, the total number of wage and salary workers on nonagricultural payrolls. While the first is a more comprehensive measure, the second is the employment statistic whose monthly changes are followed closely in financial markets; it is used in calculating other statistics such as productivity and is widely used in economic analysis.

The year-over-year percentage rates of change of the two series, shown in Figure 3, do not always track each other closely, and in recent years the payroll series has consistently shown more growth than the measure of total employment. This section will discuss the definitional and

technical differences between these two measures of this central aspect of the economy's well-being.[16]

Total employment is estimated monthly from the Current Population Survey (CPS), a large sample survey of about 50,000 households which is the source of unemployment, labor force, household income, and related data. The advantages of this survey include the ability to relate labor market outcomes to demographic characteristics such as race, sex, age, family structure, occupation, education, and training. The notes to p. 112 give a detailed explanation. To summarize the characteristics relevant to comparison, total civilian employment:

- Covers not only wage and salary jobs but other forms of employment, specifically self-employment, unpaid family work, and private household work (domestic service);

- Includes all agricultural employment;

- Covers persons 16 years and older;

- Includes persons with jobs who are on strike or unpaid leave;

- Covers only U.S. households that are part of the civilian noninstitutional population;

- Is subject to discontinuity when new information about the overall population, such as data from a new Census, are introduced into the procedure that converts sample data into estimates for the total economy;

- Counts each employed person only once, even if he or she has two or more jobs.

Payroll employment is derived from the Current Employment Statistics (CES) survey, a monthly survey of nearly 400,000 businesses, a sample which covers about 46

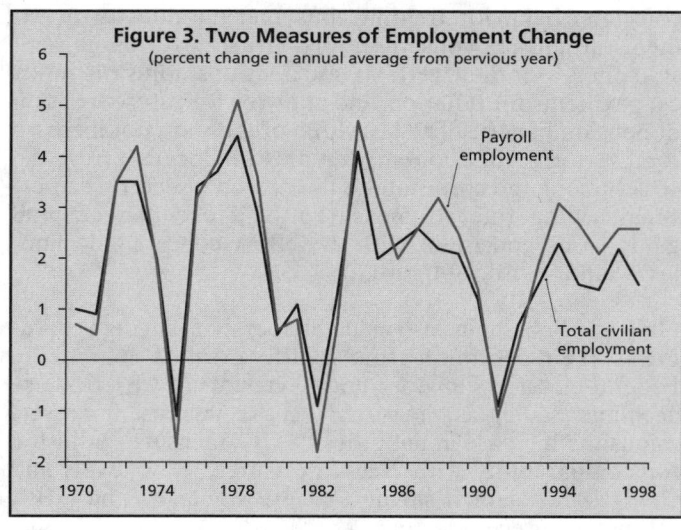

Figure 3. Two Measures of Employment Change
(percent change in annual average from pervious year)

Payroll employment

Total civilian employment

Sources: U.S. Department of Labor, Bureau of Labor Statistics

percent of total payroll employment. This survey also supplies information on the workweeks and hourly and weekly earnings of production or nonsupervisory workers. Its advantages, in addition to the smaller amount of random "noise" consequent on its very large sample, include greater geographic detail, and more detailed and reliable industry classifications. The notes to p. 117 give a detailed explanation. In comparison to the CPS, the CES:

- Covers only wage and salary jobs;

- Has no age limit;

- Includes persons on paid leave, but not those with a job but on strike or unpaid leave;

- Covers all nonagricultural industries plus "agricultural services", a category which includes landscape and veterinary services outside of the traditional rural farm sector;

- Can include persons not part of a U.S. civilian noninstitutional household, e.g. residents of Canada or Mexico who commute to U.S. jobs, inmates of institutions if they hold payroll jobs, and uniformed military personnel who hold civilian jobs;

- Is annually benchmarked to a count of total jobs (based on unemployment insurance system records) using a smooth interpolation that avoids abrupt discontinuities;

- Is currently adjusted for bias revealed by the benchmarking process. Bias occurs because it takes time for new establishments to get into the sample, while establishments that go out of business leave the monthly sample immediately;

- Is a count of jobs, not of individuals; thus, a person with two payroll jobs is counted twice, and one with three payroll jobs, three times.

- Finally, but probably more relevant for month-to-month than for longer-term comparisons, the reference period for the CPS is the week that includes the 12th day of the month, while for the CES survey it is the pay period that includes the 12th.

Despite these differences, the two series in Figure 3 clearly are describing the same business cycle behavior in the U.S. economy: contractions of employment in 1975, 1982, and 1991, presaged by growth slowdowns in the preceding year or years; and low growth, rather than decline, in the lesser recessions of 1970 and 1980. Both series also show substantial growth in other years. The payroll employment series is a little more volatile, with higher high-growth years and deeper declines in the major recessions.

Data permit the BLS staff to compare the two series and eliminate many of the conceptual and definitional differences between them. For example, it can be anticipated

that the types of employment in the CPS that are excluded from the CES might help to explain the lower volatility of the total employment series. But BLS staff finds that these adjustments do not completely eliminate the gap between the two series, nor the apparent cyclical component of that gap.

A new sample design for the CES will be implemented over the next four years, with more up-to-date incorporation of new businesses, which may increase the cyclical accuracy of the CES survey and reduce the need for estimated bias adjustments.

Similarly, the results of the 2000 Census will provide a benchmark for the CPS that will reveal whether adequate allowance for immigration has been made in the population control figures. To give an idea of the size of such adjustments in the past, the introduction of 1990 census-based population controls, adjusted for the estimated undercount, raised employment in 1990 and subsequent years by 880,000, or 0.75 percent of the prior year's employment level. An even larger adjustment—over 2 million—was made in January 1982 when data from the 1980 census were introduced.

One question raised by this discrepancy is whether labor markets are actually even tighter than is measured by the CPS. If employment is rising faster than the CPS reports, wouldn't the unemployment rate be lower? However, it is likely that if CPS employment is rising too slowly, the same is true of CPS labor force: labor force is not calculated independently of reported employment, but rather defined as the sum of employment and unemployment. Thus, bias in CPS employment does not necessarily imply bias in the unemployment rate.

Another question is which series is a better indicator of trend growth of potential employment, which along with productivity growth determines the potential rate of growth of GDP.

Whatever the ultimate answers are to these questions, the payroll employment survey remains a sensitive indication of the cyclical state of the economy, with relatively modest amounts of random statistical "noise," thanks to its huge sample.

INCOME AND POVERTY: NEW EXPERIMENTAL POVERTY MEASURES

The 1998 edition of *Business Statistics* introduced a new chapter of data tables presenting both official and alternative income and poverty data from the Current Population Survey. Updated Census Bureau data through 1998 are presented in this edition. The Census Bureau has also issued a new report, *Experimental Poverty Measures, 1990 to 1997.*[17]

This section presents and discusses experimental measures of poverty from this new report and compares them with the Census Bureau's official and alternative measures.

In 1997, all the major measures of median household and family income increased, in inflation-adjusted terms, and all measures of the incidence of poverty declined.[18]

While there is general agreement that the incidence of poverty declined in 1997, and has been declining since 1993, there is much controversy about the extent of poverty, as measured by the poverty rate. "Poverty" does not have an agreed-on definition. Any specific poverty threshold is bound to be a matter of judgment, and further judg-

Most of the measures of business activity presented in this book are gauges of aggregate economic performance, not the economic status of individuals or families. For example, gross domestic product (GDP) is the aggregate value, in current or constant dollars, of production within the boundaries of the United States; personal disposable income is the aggregate value of after-tax income received by all persons in the United States. The Bureau of Economic Analysis does calculate "real per capita disposable income" (see p. 34, but this is done simply by dividing aggregate real disposable income by the number of persons in the population. It cannot be inferred from real per capita disposable income that any particular individual or group in the population enjoyed that level of income or its rate of increase.

A separate set of statistics, developed by the Census Bureau over the years, provides data on how income is distributed among individuals and families, and produces measures of economic deprivation. Business Statistics now includes historical Census Bureau data on the median incomes of households and families and the changing distribution of income and on poverty and near-poverty (see p. 45). Several of these measures are shown using not only the official definitions of income and poverty, but also alternative definitions.

The Census Bureau measures are derived from a large sample survey of the U.S. population, the Current Population Survey (CPS)–the same survey that yields the monthly unemployment rate, labor force participation, and many other important labor force statistics. In March of each year, the CPS includes additional questions about the previous year's income and related matters. The answers to these questions provide the basis for tabulating distributions of household and family income; identifying the median income (the income of the family or household at the exact middle of the distribution); and comparing the income of each family or unrelated individual with a poverty threshold for that size family so as to identify the number and percentage in poverty.

ment is involved in deciding how that poverty threshold should be changed over time. In addition, the definition of a threshold requires consistency with the income or resources measure with which it is compared.

Figure 4 presents four poverty rates, all based on the same

data source—Current Population Survey data collected in March 1998 and previous years—but using different definitions of resources and poverty.

- The highest rate, shown from 1990 through 1997, is based on the resource and threshold concepts recommended by the National Academy of Sciences, National Research Council (NAS). It was 15.4 percent in 1997.

- The next highest measure, extending all the way back to 1959, is the official measure, based on cash income and the threshold concept first defined in 1964. In 1997 it was 13.3 percent.

- The two lowest measures, shown from 1979 to date, are calculated using different income concepts but the same thresholds as the official measure. "Alternative 14," which takes account of all taxes and transfer payments, was 10.0 percent in 1997; "Alternative 15," which in addition includes a value for the imputed return on equity in owner-occupied homes, was 9.2 percent.

These four series do not encompass the entire range of available poverty measures, but they provide a framework for discussion of several of the most important issues in poverty measurement.

Except for the experimental NAS calculations, all of the rates shown start off with the poverty level basically defined by Mollie Orshansky in 1964. The value of an "economy food plan," the least costly of four nutritionally adequate plans, was multiplied by a factor which was set at 3 for most family sizes. This factor was derived from the ratio of total after-tax income to food spending, as reported in an Agriculture Department 1955 survey. Subsequent annual updates of the thresholds have been *for price change only;* the official measure uses the Consumer Price Index for all urban consumers (CPI-U) for this purpose.

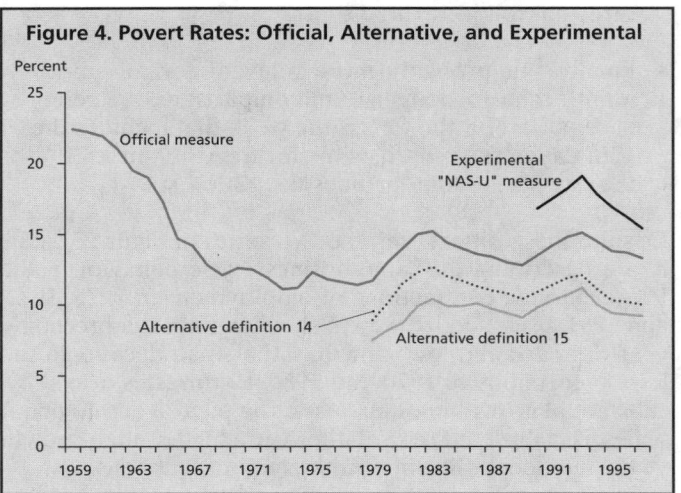

Figure 4. Povert Rates: Official, Alternative, and Experimental

Source: U.S. Bureau of Census. Experimental measure uses definitions recommended by the National Academy of Sciences, National Research Council. Others use official thresholds. In alternative definition 14, income includes all taxes and transfers; in alternative definition 15, income includes all taxes and transfers and adjustments for homeownership.

The alternative definitions 14 and 15 selected for Figure 4 accept this poverty threshold but define income differently. Income and payroll taxes are subtracted from cash income; capital gains, the value of employer-provided health insurance, and the Earned Income Tax Credit are added; and the values or estimated values of noncash transfer payments—food stamps, school lunches, rent subsidies, and the "fungible value" of Medicare and Medicaid—are included in income in both of the alternative poverty rates shown. In the lower one, the annual value to the householder of owner-occupied housing is also included in income. Some of these adjustments to income—notably, the employer-provided health insurance and owner-occupied housing adjustments—also should require adjustments to the poverty threshold, but that has not been done in these alternative rates.

EXPERIMENTAL RATE

The new experimental rate follows—to the extent feasible—the recommendations of the NAS panel. These recommendations differ from the present official method in many ways, some of which, when taken in isolation, tend to reduce measured poverty and some of which tend to increase it.

First of all, the NAS recommended a completely different method to determine the poverty threshold. The recommended threshold for 1997 is based on about 80 percent of median expenditures by two-parent, two-child families for food, clothing, shelter, and utilities (FCSU), derived from the Consumer Expenditure Surveys for 1995, 1996, and 1997; this FCSU estimate is increased by a multiplier of 1.2 to account for other common needs (e.g., household supplies and personal care items), and adjusted by scaling factors to meet the needs of other family sizes and compositions.

This recommendation led to a poverty threshold of $15,998 for the four-person family in 1997, which was 1.7 percent lower than the corresponding official threshold of $16,276. The experimental poverty rate is higher than the official rate, not because the income threshold is set higher, but because of the adjustments made to incomes to better measure family resources relative to the threshold concept.

Tending to reduce the overall incidence of measured poverty (taken by themselves and compared with the official measure) were the following recommendations:

- Using more precise adjustments for family size, taking better account of economies of scale.

- Making a geographic adjustment for housing costs. This raises poverty in the Northeast and the West, which is more than offset by reducing it in the South and Midwest.

- Adjusting family resources for tax payments and tax credits. The effects of the federal Earned Income Tax

Credit more than offset the income reductions caused by subtracting income and payroll taxes. (Property and sales taxes are part of the threshold value, and hence should not be deducted from resources.)

- Including as family resources in-kind transfers—food stamps, school lunches, housing subsidies, and heating assistance.

The following recommendations tended to increase overall poverty rates:

- Subtracting estimates of child-care expenses from income. This tended to increase poverty rates for working families.

- Deducting medical out-of-pocket expenses. This tended to increase poverty rates for the elderly.

The experimental measure shown here is for illustration only. The report presents several other experimental measures based on differing methods or assumptions. It emphasizes that further research is required before the NAS recommendations can be fully implemented.

COMPARING POVERTY RATES

Although these rates differ in level, they are similar with respect to the effect of general business conditions on the poverty rate. However it is measured, poverty peaked in 1993 as the effects of the 1990–91 recession lingered in the labor market, and has declined each year since. The Census alternatives, like the official measure, peak in 1983 just after the end of the 1981–82 recession and then decline to a low point in 1989, the last full year before the recession began in 1990, and then begin to climb to a 1993 peak.

One difference that is evident is the effect of including all taxes, including the Earned Income Credit, which for lower-income working families can more than offset the effect of income and payroll taxes. Substantial expansions of this credit were enacted in 1990 and again in 1993. This is an important factor in the more rapid decline since 1993 in the "NAS" poverty measure and in the Census Definition 14 measure, compared with the official measure which does not include the effects of taxes.

The NAS poverty rate is based on out-of-pocket shelter costs, and therefore underestimates the resources of homeowners with substantial equity. The new Census report makes a strong case that for homeowners, the thresholds should include estimated rental equivalent shelter costs (instead of the out-of-pocket costs included in FCSU) and resources should include some value for the net return to home equity. They calculate that such an adjustment would reduce the official poverty rate in 1997 from 13.3 percent to 11.0 percent, suggesting that it would also lead to a poverty rate lower than the experimental "NAS-U" rate. "Definition 15" uses this definition for income but does not adjust the threshold.

THE COMPOSITION OF POVERTY

An important consequence of the NAS recommendations is a change in the current composition of measured poverty. Table 2 compares poverty rates for 1997 calculated using the NAS-U recommendation for a number of population subgroups with the official rates.

Almost all NAS-U rates are higher. The exceptions are for nonmetropolitan areas, lower due to the geographic adjustment for housing costs, and female-householder families, where noncash benefits offset other factors that tend to raise rates. (Welfare reform may well change this comparison in subsequent years, as many mothers who used to stay at home are required to go to work.) But the rates which had been lowest under the official measure go up the most in the alternative, so that the dispersion of poverty rates among these subgroups is reduced somewhat.

There are striking increases in reported poverty rates for the elderly, reflecting their out-of-pocket medical care costs. The overall rate for the elderly goes from being just over half of the official rate for children to 86 percent of that rate in NAS-U. The rate for persons living in a family with an elderly householder or spouse goes from 5.3 percent, less than half of the official overall rate, to a NAS-U level of 14.5 percent, very close to the NAS-U overall rate. Inclusion of the treatment of owner-occupied housing suggested by the Census report might reduce elderly poverty rates below the levels shown in the NAS-U calculations, however.

POVERTY AND OTHER MEASUREMENT ERRORS

In earlier sections, new research on measurement error in the CPI has been discussed. The question obviously arises, if the CPI is over-estimated, doesn't that mean that poverty thresholds have been progressively overstated, and that poverty has been reduced more over the last two or more decades than the official measure shows?

If one accepts the NAS concept for determining the poverty threshold, however, errors in the CPI would become immaterial. Changes in poverty thresholds would be determined by changes in actual median spending on FCSU, not by changes in the CPI. This could be seen as an improvement in that some of the new methodology being used in the CPI—allowing for substitution and improving the quality adjustment for computers—is of dubious relevance to the determination of a poverty level of resources.

Interestingly, the Census study reports that median FCSU over the period 1961–96 increased 439.8 percent, compared with a change in the official CPI-U of 424.8 percent—a difference of only 0.1 percent per year at a compound annual rate. In other words, the NAS proposal not only leads to a lower threshold currently than the official method, but also would increase at about the same rate (over the entire period) as the official threshold with its overstatement in the CPI. This is not to say that a NAS-

Table 2. Official and Experimental Poverty Rates, 1997

(Percent)

Category	Official	NAS/U
All persons	13.3	15.4
By age:		
Children	19.9	20.3
Nonelderly adults	10.9	12.8
Elderly	10.5	17.4
Unrelated individuals	21.0	23.9
Family members:		
Householder or spouse	5.3	14.5
Other relative	6.1	10.3
By race or Hispanic origin:		
White	11.0	13.4
Black	26.5	26.8
Other	16.1	18.8
Hispanic origin	27.1	31.6
Number of workers:		
No workers	36.3	38.4
One or more workers	9.5	11.6
Persons in family of type:		
Married couple	6.4	9.4
Male householder	16.1	17.5
Female householder	31.5	31.4
Geographic regions:		
Northeast	12.6	16.2
Midwest	10.4	11.6
South	14.6	15.3
West	14.6	18.6
Metropolitan areas:		
Central city	18.8	21.2
Not central city	9.0	11.9
Nonmetropolitan area	15.9	15.4

Source: U.S. Census Bureau, *Experimental Poverty Measures, 1990 to 1997.*

method poverty rate, with or without a further adjustment for homeownership, would behave the same way as the official rate, because there are so many differences in the family resource concept involved. Without further analysis and research, it will be difficult to establish how the behavior of an improved poverty measure over the years since 1961 would differ from that of the official rate.

---

1. BEA, "Technical Note," July 2, 1999; "A Preview of the 1999 Comprehensive Revision of the National Income and Product Accounts: Definitional and Classificational Changes," *Survey of Current Business,* August 1999.

2. See "Overview of the 1998 Revision of the Consumer Price Index" in Bernan Press, *Handbook of U.S. Labor Statistics,* Second Edition, 1998.

3. Dalton, Greenlees, and Stewart, "Incorporating a geometric mean formula into the CPI," *Monthly Labor Review,* October 1998, p. 4.

4. Ibid.

5. "Consumer Price Index research series using current methods, 1978-98," *Monthly Labor Review,* June 1999.

6. Board of Governors of the Federal Reserve System, "Monetary Policy Report to the Congress, July 1999," p. 14.

7. Gullickson and Harper, "Possible measurement bias in aggregate productivity growth," *Monthly Labor Review,* February 1999.

8. Ibid., p. 59.

9. Economists distinguish between "saving" and "savings." Saving refers to the portion of national output (GNP) in a given period that is not used up in current consumption; it is a flow, measured for a particular time period. In total national production, saving and investment must be equal (apart from measurement error). Savings is a stock, referring to sums of money accumulated in bank accounts or other financial assets.

10. "Note on the Personal Saving Rate," *Survey of Current Business*, February 1999, pp. 8-9.

11. Gale and Sabelhaus, "Perspectives on the Household Saving Rate," *Brookings Papers on Economic Activity*, 1:1999.

12. Ibid., p. 210.

13. "Note on the Personal Saving Rate."

14. Gross National Product measures the value of production by labor and property supplied by U.S. residents, rather than production in the United States which is measured by GDP. GNP is a better measure of the flow from which saving is accumulated by U.S. residents and businesses.

15. BEA, "Technical Note," July 2, 1999.

16. The discussion that follows is based on "Conceptual differences between employment estimates from the Current Population Survey (household survey) and the Current Employment Statistics survey (establishment survey)," *Monthly Labor Review*, February 1999, p. 4.

17. U.S. Census Bureau, *Current Population Reports: Consumer Income*, P60-205, June 1999.

18. Indeed, according to the Census Bureau, both real income and the poverty rate returned—for the first time since the recession of the early 1990s—to levels not different, in terms of statistical significance, from their 1989 levels. However, this conclusion was based on a special retabulation of 1989 data using population controls from the 1990 Census of Population, which reduced 1989's median income and increased its poverty rate, compared with the previous estimates for that year that were based on 1980 population controls. This retabulation has not been incorporated in the Bureau's official historical series, and would affect the comparability of adjacent years if it was; therefore, the original 1989 data are presented in this article and in the data tables. In all of the data presented here, the estimates use 1980 census population controls for the years 1979 through 1991, and 1990 census population controls for subsequent years.

Part I: The U.S. Economy

National Product and Income and Cyclical Indicators

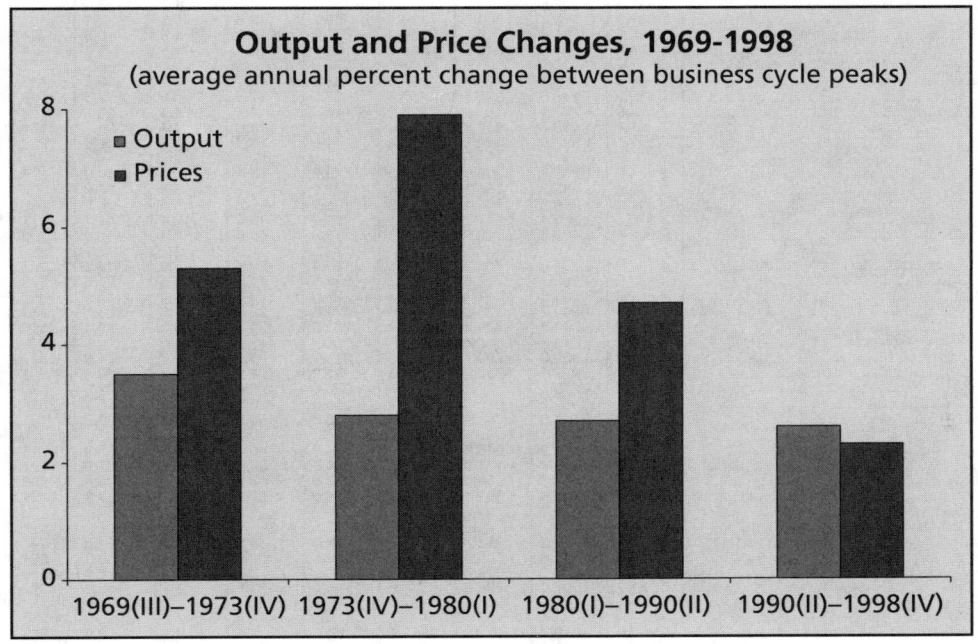

Output and Price Changes, 1969-1998
(average annual percent change between business cycle peaks)

- Output
- Prices

1969(III)–1973(IV) 1973(IV)–1980(I) 1980(I)–1990(II) 1990(II)–1998(IV)

- Both prices (gross domestic product price index) and to a lesser degree output (real gross domestic product) have increased more slowly from 1990 to 1998 than in previous business cycles. From mid-1990 to the end of 1998, output grew at an annual rate of 2.6 percent per year, while the annual rate of price increase was 2.3 percent. The annual rate of increase for prices in the 1990-1998 period is substantially less than in the previous 3 business cycles, when the annual rate of price increases ranged from 4.6 to 7.6 percent.

- In 1998 imports of goods and services, in constant 1992 dollars, exceeded exports by $238 billion, compared with $136 billion in 1997. This was largely a result of a sharp 10.6 percent increase in the real volume of imports. Because import prices were declining, the cost of imports, measured in the current dollars of each year, rose only about one-half as much (4.9 percent) as the real volume.

- Real government consumption expenditures increased by $12 billion in 1998 (in constant 1992 dollars), to $1,297 billion from $1,285 billion. Federal government consumption expenditures declined by nearly $5 billion, while state and local government consumption expenditures increased by nearly $17 billion to $843.8 billion.

Gross Domestic Product

(Billions of dollars, quarterly data are at seasonally adjusted annual rates)

Year and quarter	Gross domestic product	Personal consumption expenditures	Gross private domestic investment Total	Fixed investment Nonresidential	Fixed investment Residential	Change in business inventories Nonfarm	Change in business inventories Farm	Net exports	Exports	Imports	Government Total	Government Federal	Government State and local
1970	1 035.6	648.1	150.2	106.7	41.4	3.0	-0.8	1.2	57.0	55.8	236.1	115.9	120.2
1971	1 125.4	702.5	176.0	111.7	55.8	6.8	1.7	-3.0	59.3	62.3	249.9	117.1	132.8
1972	1 237.3	770.7	205.6	126.1	69.7	9.6	0.3	-8.0	66.2	74.2	268.9	125.1	143.8
1973	1 382.6	851.6	242.9	150.0	75.3	15.9	1.5	0.6	91.8	91.2	287.6	128.2	159.4
1974	1 496.9	931.2	245.6	165.6	66.0	16.9	-2.8	-3.1	124.3	127.5	323.2	139.9	183.3
1975	1 630.6	1 029.1	225.4	169.0	62.7	-9.7	3.4	13.6	136.3	122.7	362.6	154.5	208.1
1976	1 819.0	1 148.8	286.6	187.2	82.5	17.8	-0.8	-2.3	148.9	151.1	385.9	162.7	223.1
1977	2 026.9	1 277.1	356.6	223.2	110.3	18.5	4.5	-23.7	158.8	182.4	416.9	178.4	238.5
1978	2 291.4	1 428.8	430.8	272.0	131.6	25.8	1.4	-26.1	186.1	212.3	457.9	194.4	263.4
1979	2 557.5	1 593.5	480.9	323.0	141.0	13.3	3.6	-24.0	228.7	252.7	507.1	215.0	292.0
1980	2 784.2	1 760.4	465.9	350.3	123.2	-1.5	-6.1	-14.9	278.9	293.8	572.8	248.4	324.4
1981	3 115.9	1 941.3	556.2	405.4	122.6	19.4	8.8	-15.0	302.8	317.8	633.4	284.1	349.2
1982	3 242.1	2 076.8	501.1	409.9	105.7	-20.2	5.8	-20.5	282.6	303.2	684.8	313.2	371.6
1983	3 514.5	2 283.4	547.1	399.4	152.5	10.4	-15.4	-51.7	277.0	328.6	735.7	344.5	391.2
1984	3 902.4	2 492.3	715.6	468.3	179.8	61.8	5.7	-102.0	303.1	405.1	796.6	372.6	424.0
1985	4 180.7	2 704.8	715.1	502.0	186.9	20.4	5.8	-114.2	303.0	417.2	875.0	410.1	464.9
1986	4 422.2	2 892.7	722.5	494.8	218.1	11.1	-1.5	-131.5	320.7	452.2	938.5	435.2	503.3
1987	4 692.3	3 094.5	747.2	495.4	227.6	30.7	-6.4	-142.1	365.7	507.9	992.8	455.7	537.2
1988	5 049.6	3 349.7	773.9	530.6	232.5	22.8	-11.9	-106.1	447.2	553.2	1 032.0	457.3	574.7
1989	5 438.7	3 594.8	829.2	566.2	231.3	31.7	0.0	-80.4	509.3	589.7	1 095.1	477.2	617.9
1990	5 743.8	3 839.3	799.7	575.9	215.7	5.4	2.6	-71.3	557.3	628.6	1 176.1	503.6	672.6
1991	5 916.7	3 975.1	736.2	547.3	191.2	-1.2	-1.1	-20.5	601.8	622.3	1 225.9	522.6	703.4
1992	6 244.4	4 219.8	790.4	557.9	225.6	2.0	5.0	-29.5	639.4	669.0	1 263.8	528.0	735.8
1993	6 558.1	4 459.2	876.2	604.1	251.6	26.7	-6.2	-60.7	658.6	719.3	1 283.4	518.3	765.0
1994	6 947.0	4 717.0	1 007.9	660.6	286.0	50.5	10.8	-90.9	721.2	812.1	1 313.0	510.2	802.8
1995	7 269.6	4 953.9	1 043.2	727.7	284.8	40.1	-9.3	-83.9	819.4	903.3	1 356.4	509.1	847.3
1996	7 661.6	5 215.7	1 131.9	787.9	311.8	24.5	7.6	-91.2	873.8	965.0	1 405.2	518.4	886.8
1997	8 110.9	5 493.7	1 256.0	860.7	327.9	63.1	4.3	-93.4	965.4	1 058.8	1 454.6	520.2	934.4
1998	8 511.0	5 807.9	1 367.1	938.2	369.6	52.7	6.7	-151.2	959.0	1 110.2	1 487.1	520.6	966.5
1990:													
1st quarter	5 660.6	3 759.2	822.7	581.2	232.7	8.9	-0.1	-74.3	541.6	615.9	1 153.0	496.4	656.6
2nd quarter	5 750.8	3 811.8	835.0	571.6	222.4	36.9	4.1	-60.3	554.8	615.1	1 164.3	500.1	664.2
3rd quarter	5 782.2	3 879.2	804.7	580.3	210.9	5.4	8.1	-78.5	555.5	634.1	1 176.9	501.2	675.7
4th quarter	5 781.7	3 907.0	736.3	570.6	196.9	-29.6	-1.7	-72.0	577.3	649.2	1 210.4	516.7	693.7
1991:													
1st quarter	5 821.9	3 910.7	723.5	555.4	184.3	-14.8	-1.5	-32.9	577.4	610.3	1 220.6	525.6	695.0
2nd quarter	5 892.5	3 961.0	716.4	550.2	185.9	-23.3	3.5	-12.3	602.7	615.0	1 227.4	528.2	699.2
3rd quarter	5 950.2	4 001.6	744.1	544.3	194.3	13.5	-8.1	-22.0	602.6	624.5	1 226.5	520.9	705.5
4th quarter	6 002.1	4 027.1	760.7	539.2	200.3	19.6	1.6	-14.8	624.4	639.3	1 229.2	515.5	713.6
1992:													
1st quarter	6 121.8	4 127.6	755.2	544.1	211.3	-7.5	7.3	-8.9	632.4	641.3	1 247.9	521.8	726.1
2nd quarter	6 201.2	4 183.0	790.7	556.8	223.7	1.1	9.1	-29.0	635.9	664.9	1 256.4	523.2	733.2
3rd quarter	6 271.7	4 238.9	799.7	561.0	227.1	6.8	4.8	-37.6	640.2	677.8	1 270.7	532.0	738.7
4th quarter	6 383.1	4 329.6	816.1	569.6	240.1	7.8	-1.3	-42.7	649.1	691.8	1 280.0	535.0	745.1
1993:													
1st quarter	6 444.5	4 365.4	854.3	580.5	243.0	37.1	-6.3	-46.6	647.1	693.7	1 271.5	521.3	750.1
2nd quarter	6 509.1	4 428.1	857.4	598.8	244.1	19.8	-5.3	-57.5	661.2	718.7	1 281.2	517.8	763.4
3rd quarter	6 574.6	4 488.6	872.8	606.4	252.4	25.2	-11.2	-72.1	646.8	718.9	1 285.3	515.7	769.6
4th quarter	6 704.2	4 554.9	920.3	630.6	266.8	24.8	-2.0	-66.6	679.4	746.0	1 295.5	518.5	777.0
1994:													
1st quarter	6 794.3	4 616.6	963.4	634.6	276.4	38.9	13.4	-76.6	678.5	755.1	1 291.0	506.9	784.1
2nd quarter	6 911.4	4 680.5	1 017.9	652.9	288.7	60.9	15.3	-87.9	710.1	797.9	1 300.8	505.3	795.5
3rd quarter	6 986.5	4 750.6	1 007.1	667.4	289.5	40.1	10.1	-103.4	732.6	836.0	1 332.3	520.4	811.9
4th quarter	7 095.7	4 820.2	1 043.1	687.5	289.5	62.0	4.2	-95.6	763.7	859.2	1 328.0	508.3	819.6
1995:													
1st quarter	7 170.8	4 862.5	1 058.9	713.6	286.4	66.7	-7.7	-94.7	787.8	882.5	1 344.1	512.3	831.8
2nd quarter	7 210.9	4 931.5	1 029.6	728.1	276.2	39.4	-14.1	-108.0	803.4	911.4	1 357.8	511.7	846.2
3rd quarter	7 304.8	4 986.4	1 030.6	729.5	284.0	32.6	-15.5	-74.5	835.1	909.6	1 362.3	511.2	851.1
4th quarter	7 391.9	5 035.3	1 053.6	739.5	292.6	21.6	-0.1	-58.4	851.5	909.9	1 361.4	501.2	860.2
1996:													
1st quarter	7 495.3	5 108.2	1 075.3	759.0	300.1	11.2	5.0	-75.7	856.6	932.3	1 387.5	517.1	870.4
2nd quarter	7 629.2	5 199.0	1 118.3	774.8	315.0	15.9	12.7	-94.0	863.0	957.0	1 406.0	523.1	882.9
3rd quarter	7 703.4	5 242.5	1 167.9	801.1	317.0	40.1	9.7	-115.5	861.4	976.9	1 408.6	519.0	889.6
4th quarter	7 818.4	5 313.2	1 166.0	816.8	315.3	30.7	3.1	-79.6	914.2	993.8	1 418.8	514.6	904.2
1997:													
1st quarter	7 955.0	5 402.4	1 206.4	827.1	319.5	60.8	-1.1	-93.3	930.2	1 023.5	1 439.4	517.0	922.4
2nd quarter	8 063.4	5 438.8	1 259.9	850.5	325.9	77.2	6.2	-86.8	961.1	1 047.9	1 451.5	522.9	928.6
3rd quarter	8 170.8	5 540.3	1 265.7	882.3	328.8	47.3	7.3	-94.7	981.7	1 076.4	1 459.5	521.0	938.5
4th quarter	8 254.5	5 593.2	1 292.0	882.8	337.4	66.9	4.9	-98.8	988.6	1 087.4	1 468.1	520.1	947.9
1998:													
1st quarter	8 384.2	5 676.5	1 366.6	921.3	349.8	90.5	5.0	-123.7	973.3	1 097.1	1 464.9	511.6	953.3
2nd quarter	8 440.6	5 773.7	1 345.0	941.9	363.8	31.5	7.7	-159.3	949.6	1 108.9	1 481.2	520.7	960.4
3rd quarter	8 537.9	5 846.7	1 364.4	931.6	375.8	49.3	7.7	-165.5	936.2	1 101.7	1 492.3	519.4	972.9
4th quarter	8 681.2	5 934.8	1 392.4	957.9	388.9	39.3	6.3	-156.2	976.8	1 133.0	1 510.2	530.7	979.5

Real Gross Domestic Product

(Billions of chained [1992] dollars, quarterly data are at seasonally adjusted annual rates)

Year and quarter	Gross domestic product	Personal consumption expenditures	Gross private domestic investment					Exports and imports of goods and services			Government consumption expenditures and gross investment		
			Total	Fixed investment		Change in business inventories		Net exports	Exports	Imports	Total	Federal	State and local
				Nonresidential	Residential	Nonfarm	Farm						
1970	3 397.6	2 197.8	426.1	282.8	149.1	8.3	-2.4	-65.0	158.1	223.1	866.8	427.2	440.0
1971	3 510.0	2 279.5	474.9	282.4	190.0	18.0	4.0	-75.8	159.2	235.0	851.0	397.0	454.4
1972	3 702.3	2 415.9	531.8	307.7	223.8	25.4	0.3	-89.0	172.0	261.0	854.1	390.2	464.5
1973	3 916.3	2 532.6	595.5	352.5	222.3	38.5	1.4	-63.0	209.6	272.6	848.4	371.1	478.5
1974	3 891.2	2 514.7	546.5	354.4	176.4	31.9	-4.7	-35.6	229.8	265.3	862.9	368.8	495.6
1975	3 873.9	2 570.0	446.6	317.3	153.5	-18.5	6.1	-7.2	228.2	235.4	876.3	367.9	510.0
1976	4 082.9	2 714.3	537.4	332.6	189.7	32.1	-1.3	-39.9	241.6	281.5	876.8	364.3	514.3
1977	4 273.6	2 829.8	622.1	371.8	229.8	31.7	6.8	-64.2	247.4	311.7	884.7	370.1	516.4
1978	4 503.0	2 951.6	693.4	422.6	245.0	41.4	2.6	-65.6	273.1	338.6	910.6	377.7	534.7
1979	4 630.6	3 020.2	709.8	463.3	236.0	19.3	3.8	-45.3	299.0	344.3	924.9	383.3	543.5
1980	4 615.0	3 009.7	628.3	461.1	186.1	-1.5	-7.1	10.1	331.4	321.3	941.4	399.3	543.6
1981	4 720.7	3 046.4	686.0	485.7	171.2	22.8	9.6	5.6	335.3	329.7	947.7	415.9	532.8
1982	4 620.3	3 081.5	587.2	464.3	140.1	-22.9	7.3	-14.1	311.4	325.5	960.1	429.4	531.4
1983	4 803.7	3 240.6	642.1	456.4	197.6	12.1	-16.9	-63.3	303.3	366.6	987.3	452.7	534.9
1984	5 140.1	3 407.6	833.4	535.4	226.4	69.1	6.4	-127.3	328.4	455.7	1 018.4	463.7	555.0
1985	5 323.5	3 566.5	823.8	568.4	229.5	23.3	6.9	-147.9	337.3	485.2	1 080.1	495.6	584.7
1986	5 487.7	3 708.7	811.8	548.5	257.0	12.4	-1.6	-163.9	362.2	526.1	1 135.0	518.4	616.9
1987	5 649.5	3 822.3	821.5	542.4	257.6	34.2	-8.8	-156.2	402.0	558.2	1 165.9	534.4	631.8
1988	5 865.2	3 972.7	828.2	566.0	252.5	24.7	-12.6	-114.4	465.8	580.2	1 180.9	524.6	656.6
1989	6 062.0	4 064.6	863.5	588.8	243.2	33.5	0.0	-82.7	520.2	603.0	1 213.9	531.5	682.6
1990	6 136.3	4 132.2	815.0	585.2	220.6	7.8	2.5	-61.9	564.4	626.3	1 250.4	541.9	708.6
1991	6 079.4	4 105.8	738.1	547.7	193.4	-1.2	-1.7	-22.3	599.9	622.2	1 258.0	539.4	718.7
1992	6 244.4	4 219.8	790.4	557.9	225.6	2.0	5.0	-29.5	639.4	669.0	1 263.8	528.0	735.8
1993	6 389.6	4 343.6	863.6	600.2	242.6	29.5	-7.3	-70.2	658.2	728.4	1 252.1	505.7	746.4
1994	6 610.7	4 486.0	975.7	648.4	267.0	49.0	11.7	-104.6	712.4	817.0	1 252.3	486.6	765.7
1995	6 761.7	4 605.6	996.1	710.6	256.8	37.7	-11.0	-96.5	792.6	889.0	1 254.5	470.6	783.9
1996	6 994.8	4 752.4	1 084.1	776.6	275.9	23.2	7.1	-111.2	860.0	971.2	1 268.2	465.6	802.7
1997	7 269.8	4 913.5	1 206.4	859.4	282.8	58.8	4.3	-136.1	970.0	1 106.1	1 285.0	458.0	827.1
1998	7 551.9	5 153.3	1 330.1	960.7	312.0	50.1	7.6	-238.2	984.7	1 222.9	1 296.9	453.3	843.8
1990:													
1st quarter	6 152.6	4 128.9	842.6	595.3	239.4	10.9	-0.1	-67.1	555.2	622.3	1 246.5	542.9	703.8
2nd quarter	6 171.6	4 134.7	853.4	583.4	227.8	39.2	4.2	-66.7	566.8	633.5	1 248.2	543.0	705.4
3rd quarter	6 142.1	4 148.5	817.9	588.1	214.9	6.7	7.9	-71.2	561.8	633.0	1 246.8	538.2	708.7
4th quarter	6 079.0	4 116.4	746.1	573.9	200.3	-25.9	-2.0	-42.5	573.9	616.4	1 259.9	543.5	716.5
1991:													
1st quarter	6 047.5	4 084.5	725.1	555.1	187.4	-15.0	-2.1	-24.3	572.3	596.6	1 262.6	547.3	715.5
2nd quarter	6 074.7	4 110.0	718.5	550.9	188.3	-23.4	2.7	-17.1	600.3	617.4	1 263.8	547.1	716.8
3rd quarter	6 090.1	4 119.5	745.8	545.3	195.6	13.6	-9.0	-29.8	603.6	633.4	1 255.1	536.3	718.8
4th quarter	6 105.3	4 109.1	763.2	539.5	202.4	19.9	1.4	-17.9	623.5	641.4	1 250.7	526.9	723.8
1992:													
1st quarter	6 175.7	4 173.8	758.2	544.4	213.9	-7.7	7.1	-14.8	633.0	647.8	1 258.5	525.1	733.5
2nd quarter	6 214.2	4 196.4	792.8	557.5	224.9	1.6	9.4	-32.5	635.8	668.3	1 257.5	523.3	734.2
3rd quarter	6 260.7	4 226.7	798.5	560.6	226.7	6.9	5.0	-30.8	639.7	670.5	1 266.5	529.6	736.9
4th quarter	6 327.1	4 282.3	812.2	569.1	236.7	7.4	-1.7	-40.0	649.1	689.1	1 272.5	534.0	738.5
1993:													
1st quarter	6 327.9	4 286.8	845.5	577.8	237.0	40.0	-7.6	-54.7	647.2	701.9	1 250.1	512.1	738.0
2nd quarter	6 359.9	4 322.8	846.1	595.1	236.1	23.4	-6.6	-62.6	660.1	722.7	1 253.1	507.8	745.3
3rd quarter	6 393.5	4 366.6	858.6	602.3	242.2	27.8	-12.3	-83.1	646.3	729.4	1 250.5	501.5	749.1
4th quarter	6 476.9	4 398.0	904.0	625.6	255.1	26.9	-2.6	-80.5	679.1	759.7	1 254.7	501.3	753.4
1994:													
1st quarter	6 524.5	4 439.4	939.9	626.2	261.3	39.6	13.8	-97.6	676.0	773.6	1 241.9	487.2	754.7
2nd quarter	6 600.3	4 472.2	987.8	641.2	271.5	59.6	16.6	-103.9	704.1	808.0	1 243.3	481.2	762.2
3rd quarter	6 629.5	4 498.2	972.2	653.2	269.4	38.2	11.6	-111.1	722.1	833.2	1 268.1	496.4	771.7
4th quarter	6 688.6	4 534.1	1 003.0	672.9	265.9	58.7	4.8	-105.9	747.3	853.2	1 255.8	481.7	774.1
1995:													
1st quarter	6 717.5	4 555.3	1 013.5	698.4	259.9	62.5	-9.5	-109.5	763.9	873.4	1 256.2	478.6	777.6
2nd quarter	6 724.2	4 593.6	982.0	710.2	249.5	36.7	-16.4	-114.7	774.0	888.7	1 259.9	476.2	783.7
3rd quarter	6 779.5	4 623.4	983.4	711.7	255.6	30.6	-17.1	-86.8	806.3	893.1	1 257.6	473.1	784.5
4th quarter	6 825.8	4 650.0	1 005.4	722.3	262.1	20.8	-0.8	-74.8	826.1	900.9	1 244.5	454.6	790.0
1996:													
1st quarter	6 882.0	4 692.1	1 029.3	744.8	268.0	10.4	4.3	-95.5	833.6	929.1	1 254.5	463.5	791.0
2nd quarter	6 983.9	4 746.6	1 072.8	764.4	280.2	15.2	11.6	-113.5	845.5	958.9	1 276.2	472.6	803.6
3rd quarter	7 020.0	4 768.3	1 118.1	790.1	279.0	38.6	9.2	-140.1	849.9	990.0	1 271.1	467.0	804.2
4th quarter	7 093.1	4 802.6	1 116.1	807.0	276.3	28.7	3.3	-95.9	911.1	1 007.0	1 271.2	459.5	811.8
1997:													
1st quarter	7 166.7	4 853.4	1 156.6	820.9	278.4	56.2	-0.5	-121.5	929.4	1 050.9	1 277.7	456.3	821.5
2nd quarter	7 236.5	4 872.7	1 211.3	848.2	282.5	72.1	6.8	-131.6	963.6	1 095.2	1 284.4	460.4	824.2
3rd quarter	7 311.2	4 947.0	1 215.8	882.2	282.3	44.0	7.3	-142.4	988.1	1 130.5	1 288.9	458.9	830.1
4th quarter	7 364.6	4 981.0	1 241.9	886.2	287.9	62.7	3.7	-149.0	998.8	1 147.8	1 289.2	456.5	832.9
1998:													
1st quarter	7 464.7	5 055.1	1 321.8	931.9	298.5	85.9	5.3	-198.5	991.9	1 190.4	1 283.0	446.1	837.1
2nd quarter	7 498.6	5 130.2	1 306.5	960.4	309.1	29.9	8.7	-245.2	972.1	1 217.3	1 294.8	454.1	840.9
3rd quarter	7 566.5	5 181.8	1 331.6	958.7	316.5	47.0	9.1	-259.0	965.3	1 224.3	1 299.6	452.5	847.3
4th quarter	7 677.7	5 246.0	1 360.6	991.9	324.1	37.5	7.2	-250.0	1 009.6	1 259.6	1 310.3	460.6	850.0

Price Indexes for Gross Domestic Product and Domestic Purchases

(Index numbers, 1992=100)

Year and quarter	Gross domestic product	Personal consumption expenditures	Private fixed investment			Exports and imports of goods and services		Government consumption expenditures and gross investment			Gross domestic purchases
			Total	Nonresidential	Residential	Export	Imports	Total	Federal	State and local	
1970	30.5	29.5	34.3	37.8	27.7	36.0	25.0	27.2	27.1	27.3	29.7
1971	32.1	30.8	36.1	39.6	29.4	37.3	26.5	29.3	29.4	29.2	31.3
1972	33.4	31.9	37.6	41.0	31.1	38.5	28.4	31.5	32.0	31.0	32.7
1973	35.3	33.6	39.7	42.6	33.9	43.8	33.4	33.9	34.5	33.3	34.6
1974	38.5	37.0	43.7	46.8	37.4	54.1	48.0	37.5	37.9	37.0	38.2
1975	42.1	40.0	49.2	53.3	40.9	59.7	52.1	41.4	42.0	40.8	41.7
1976	44.6	42.3	52.1	56.3	43.5	61.6	53.7	44.0	44.6	43.4	44.2
1977	47.4	45.1	56.2	60.1	48.0	64.2	58.5	47.1	48.2	46.2	47.2
1978	50.9	48.4	61.1	64.4	53.7	68.2	62.7	50.3	51.5	49.3	50.7
1979	55.2	52.8	66.7	69.7	59.8	76.5	73.4	54.8	56.1	53.7	55.2
1980	60.3	58.5	73.0	76.0	66.2	84.2	91.5	60.9	62.2	59.7	61.1
1981	66.0	63.7	79.9	83.5	71.6	90.3	96.4	66.8	68.3	65.6	66.7
1982	70.2	67.4	84.5	88.3	75.5	90.8	93.1	71.3	72.9	69.9	70.6
1983	73.2	70.5	84.4	87.5	77.2	91.3	89.6	74.5	76.1	73.2	73.3
1984	75.9	73.1	85.0	87.5	79.4	92.3	88.9	78.2	80.4	76.4	75.9
1985	78.5	75.8	86.2	88.3	81.5	89.8	86.0	81.0	82.7	79.5	78.3
1986	80.6	78.0	88.6	90.2	84.9	88.5	86.0	82.7	84.0	81.6	80.4
1987	83.1	81.0	90.4	91.3	88.3	91.0	91.0	85.2	85.3	85.0	83.1
1988	86.1	84.3	93.3	93.7	92.1	96.0	95.4	87.4	87.2	87.5	86.1
1989	89.7	88.4	95.9	96.2	95.1	97.9	97.8	90.2	89.8	90.5	89.8
1990	93.6	92.9	98.2	98.4	97.8	98.7	100.4	94.1	92.9	94.9	93.8
1991	97.3	96.8	99.6	99.9	98.9	100.3	100.0	97.5	96.9	97.9	97.3
1992	100.0	100.0	100.0	100.0	100.0	100.0	100.0	100.0	100.0	100.0	100.0
1993	102.6	102.7	101.5	100.7	103.7	100.1	98.8	102.5	102.5	102.5	102.5
1994	105.1	105.2	103.4	101.9	107.1	101.2	99.4	104.9	104.8	104.9	104.9
1995	107.5	107.6	104.8	102.4	110.9	103.4	101.6	108.1	108.2	108.1	107.3
1996	109.5	109.8	104.7	101.5	113.0	101.6	99.4	110.8	111.4	110.5	109.2
1997	111.6	111.8	104.5	100.2	116.0	99.5	95.7	113.2	113.6	113.0	110.9
1998	112.7	112.7	103.2	97.7	118.4	97.4	90.7	114.7	114.8	114.6	111.5
1990:											
1st quarter	92.0	91.1	97.5	97.6	97.2	97.5	98.8	92.5	91.4	93.3	92.2
2nd quarter	93.2	92.2	97.9	98.0	97.6	97.9	97.1	93.3	92.1	94.2	93.1
3rd quarter	94.2	93.5	98.5	98.7	98.1	98.9	100.0	94.4	93.1	95.3	94.3
4th quarter	95.1	94.9	99.1	99.4	98.3	100.6	105.6	96.1	95.0	96.8	95.7
1991:											
1st quarter	96.3	95.7	99.6	100.1	98.4	100.9	102.2	96.6	95.9	97.2	96.4
2nd quarter	97.0	96.4	99.6	100.0	98.7	100.5	99.7	97.2	96.6	97.6	97.0
3rd quarter	97.7	97.1	99.7	99.8	99.3	99.8	98.6	97.7	97.1	98.2	97.6
4th quarter	98.3	98.0	99.6	99.9	99.0	100.1	99.6	98.3	97.9	98.6	98.3
1992:											
1st quarter	99.1	98.9	99.6	99.9	98.8	99.9	99.0	99.2	99.4	99.0	99.0
2nd quarter	99.8	99.7	99.8	99.9	99.5	100.1	99.6	99.9	100.0	99.9	99.8
3rd quarter	100.2	100.3	100.1	100.1	100.2	100.1	101.0	100.3	100.4	100.3	100.3
4th quarter	100.9	101.1	100.5	100.1	101.5	100.0	100.4	100.6	100.2	100.9	100.9
1993:											
1st quarter	101.9	101.8	101.1	100.5	102.5	100.0	98.8	101.7	101.8	101.7	101.7
2nd quarter	102.4	102.5	101.5	100.7	103.4	100.2	99.5	102.2	101.9	102.4	102.3
3rd quarter	102.8	102.8	101.7	100.7	104.3	100.0	98.6	102.8	102.8	102.7	102.6
4th quarter	103.5	103.6	101.9	100.8	104.6	100.0	98.2	103.3	103.5	103.1	103.3
1994:											
1st quarter	104.2	104.0	102.6	101.4	105.8	100.4	97.6	104.0	104.0	103.9	103.8
2nd quarter	104.7	104.7	103.2	101.9	106.4	101.0	98.9	104.6	105.0	104.4	104.5
3rd quarter	105.4	105.6	103.7	102.2	107.5	101.4	100.3	105.1	104.8	105.2	105.2
4th quarter	106.1	106.3	104.0	102.1	108.8	102.1	100.7	105.8	105.5	105.9	105.9
1995:											
1st quarter	106.7	106.8	104.5	102.2	110.2	103.1	101.1	107.0	107.0	107.0	106.5
2nd quarter	107.3	107.4	105.0	102.7	110.7	104.0	102.8	107.8	107.4	108.0	107.1
3rd quarter	107.8	107.9	104.9	102.5	111.1	103.5	101.8	108.3	108.1	108.5	107.5
4th quarter	108.3	108.3	104.9	102.3	111.6	102.9	100.8	109.4	110.2	108.9	108.0
1996:											
1st quarter	108.9	108.9	104.7	101.9	112.0	102.6	100.3	110.5	111.4	110.1	108.6
2nd quarter	109.3	109.6	104.6	101.5	112.4	102.2	99.9	110.2	110.8	109.9	108.9
3rd quarter	109.8	110.0	104.8	101.4	113.6	101.4	98.6	110.9	111.3	110.6	109.3
4th quarter	110.2	110.6	104.7	101.1	114.1	100.3	98.6	111.6	112.0	111.4	109.9
1997:											
1st quarter	111.0	111.3	104.5	100.7	114.8	100.0	97.5	112.7	113.3	112.3	110.5
2nd quarter	111.5	111.6	104.4	100.3	115.4	99.8	95.7	113.0	113.6	112.7	110.8
3rd quarter	111.8	112.0	104.5	100.0	116.5	99.4	95.2	113.2	113.5	113.1	111.1
4th quarter	112.1	112.3	104.4	99.6	117.2	99.0	94.6	113.9	113.9	113.8	111.3
1998:											
1st quarter	112.3	112.3	103.8	98.9	117.2	98.1	92.1	114.2	114.7	113.9	111.3
2nd quarter	112.6	112.6	103.3	98.1	117.7	97.7	91.0	114.4	114.7	114.2	111.4
3rd quarter	112.9	112.8	102.9	97.2	118.8	97.0	89.9	114.8	114.8	114.8	111.6
4th quarter	113.1	113.1	102.8	96.6	120.0	96.8	89.8	115.3	115.2	115.3	111.8

Implicit Price Deflators for Gross Domestic Product

(Index numbers, 1992=100)

Year and quarter	Gross domestic product	Personal consumption expenditures	Private fixed investment			Exports and imports of goods and services		Government consumption expenditures and gross investment		
			Total	Nonresidential	Residential	Export	Imports	Total	Federal	State and local
1970	30.5	29.5	34.3	37.7	27.7	36.0	25.0	27.2	27.1	27.3
1971	32.1	30.8	36.0	39.6	29.4	37.3	26.5	29.4	29.5	29.2
1972	33.4	31.9	37.6	41.0	31.1	38.5	28.4	31.5	32.1	31.0
1973	35.3	33.6	39.7	42.6	33.9	43.8	33.4	33.9	34.6	33.3
1974	38.5	37.0	43.7	46.7	37.4	54.1	48.0	37.5	37.9	37.0
1975	42.1	40.0	49.2	53.3	40.9	59.7	52.1	41.4	42.0	40.8
1976	44.6	42.3	52.1	56.3	43.5	61.6	53.7	44.0	44.7	43.4
1977	47.4	45.1	56.2	60.0	48.0	64.2	58.5	47.1	48.2	46.2
1978	50.9	48.4	61.1	64.4	53.7	68.2	62.7	50.3	51.5	49.3
1979	55.2	52.8	66.7	69.7	59.8	76.5	73.4	54.8	56.1	53.7
1980	60.3	58.5	73.0	76.0	66.2	84.2	91.5	60.9	62.2	59.7
1981	66.0	63.7	79.9	83.5	71.6	90.3	96.4	66.8	68.3	65.6
1982	70.2	67.4	84.5	88.3	75.5	90.8	93.1	71.3	72.9	69.9
1983	73.2	70.5	84.4	87.5	77.2	91.3	89.6	74.5	76.1	73.2
1984	75.9	73.1	85.0	87.5	79.4	92.3	88.9	78.2	80.4	76.4
1985	78.5	75.8	86.2	88.3	81.5	89.8	86.0	81.0	82.7	79.5
1986	80.6	78.0	88.6	90.2	84.9	88.5	86.0	82.7	84.0	81.6
1987	83.1	81.0	90.4	91.3	88.3	91.0	91.0	85.2	85.3	85.0
1988	86.1	84.3	93.3	93.7	92.1	96.0	95.4	87.4	87.2	87.5
1989	89.7	88.4	95.9	96.2	95.1	97.9	97.8	90.2	89.8	90.5
1990	93.6	92.9	98.2	98.4	97.8	98.7	100.4	94.1	92.9	94.9
1991	97.3	96.8	99.6	99.9	98.9	100.3	100.0	97.5	96.9	97.9
1992	100.0	100.0	100.0	100.0	100.0	100.0	100.0	100.0	100.0	100.0
1993	102.6	102.7	101.5	100.7	103.7	100.1	98.8	102.5	102.5	102.5
1994	105.1	105.2	103.4	101.9	107.1	101.2	99.4	104.9	104.9	104.9
1995	107.5	107.6	104.8	102.4	110.9	103.4	101.6	108.1	108.2	108.1
1996	109.5	109.8	104.7	101.5	113.0	101.6	99.4	110.8	111.3	110.5
1997	111.6	111.8	104.5	100.2	116.0	99.5	95.7	113.2	113.6	113.0
1998	112.7	112.7	103.2	97.7	118.4	97.4	90.8	114.7	114.8	114.5
1990:										
1st quarter	92.0	91.1	97.5	97.6	97.2	97.6	99.0	92.5	91.4	93.3
2nd quarter	93.2	92.2	97.9	98.0	97.6	97.9	97.1	93.3	92.1	94.2
3rd quarter	94.1	93.5	98.5	98.7	98.1	98.9	100.2	94.4	93.1	95.3
4th quarter	95.1	94.9	99.1	99.4	98.3	100.6	105.3	96.1	95.1	96.8
1991:										
1st quarter	96.3	95.8	99.6	100.1	98.4	100.9	102.3	96.7	96.0	97.1
2nd quarter	97.0	96.4	99.6	99.9	98.7	100.4	99.6	97.1	96.5	97.6
3rd quarter	97.7	97.1	99.7	99.8	99.3	99.8	98.6	97.7	97.1	98.2
4th quarter	98.3	98.0	99.7	99.9	98.9	100.2	99.7	98.3	97.8	98.6
1992:										
1st quarter	99.1	98.9	99.6	100.0	98.8	99.9	99.0	99.2	99.4	99.0
2nd quarter	99.8	99.7	99.8	99.9	99.5	100.0	99.5	99.9	100.0	99.9
3rd quarter	100.2	100.3	100.1	100.1	100.2	100.1	101.1	100.3	100.5	100.3
4th quarter	100.9	101.1	100.5	100.1	101.4	100.0	100.4	100.6	100.2	100.9
1993:										
1st quarter	101.8	101.8	101.1	100.5	102.5	100.0	98.8	101.7	101.8	101.7
2nd quarter	102.4	102.4	101.4	100.6	103.4	100.2	99.5	102.2	102.0	102.4
3rd quarter	102.8	102.8	101.7	100.7	104.2	100.1	98.6	102.8	102.9	102.7
4th quarter	103.5	103.6	101.9	100.8	104.6	100.0	98.2	103.3	103.4	103.1
1994:										
1st quarter	104.1	104.0	102.6	101.4	105.8	100.4	97.6	104.0	104.0	103.9
2nd quarter	104.7	104.7	103.1	101.8	106.4	100.8	98.8	104.6	105.0	104.4
3rd quarter	105.4	105.6	103.7	102.2	107.5	101.5	100.3	105.1	104.8	105.2
4th quarter	106.1	106.3	104.1	102.2	108.8	102.2	100.7	105.8	105.5	105.9
1995:										
1st quarter	106.8	106.7	104.5	102.2	110.2	103.1	101.0	107.0	107.0	107.0
2nd quarter	107.2	107.4	104.9	102.5	110.7	103.8	102.6	107.8	107.4	108.0
3rd quarter	107.8	107.9	104.9	102.5	111.1	103.6	101.8	108.3	108.1	108.5
4th quarter	108.3	108.3	105.0	102.4	111.6	103.1	101.0	109.4	110.2	108.9
1996:										
1st quarter	108.9	108.9	104.7	101.9	111.9	102.8	100.4	110.6	111.6	110.0
2nd quarter	109.2	109.5	104.4	101.4	112.4	102.1	99.8	110.2	110.7	109.9
3rd quarter	109.7	109.9	104.8	101.4	113.6	101.4	98.7	110.8	111.2	110.6
4th quarter	110.2	110.6	104.8	101.2	114.1	100.4	98.7	111.6	112.0	111.4
1997:										
1st quarter	111.0	111.3	104.6	100.8	114.8	100.1	97.4	112.7	113.3	112.3
2nd quarter	111.4	111.6	104.4	100.3	115.3	99.7	95.7	113.0	113.6	112.7
3rd quarter	111.8	112.0	104.5	100.0	116.5	99.4	95.2	113.2	113.5	113.1
4th quarter	112.1	112.3	104.3	99.6	117.2	99.0	94.7	113.9	113.9	113.8
1998:										
1st quarter	112.3	112.3	103.8	98.9	117.2	98.1	92.2	114.2	114.7	113.9
2nd quarter	112.6	112.5	103.3	98.1	117.7	97.7	91.1	114.4	114.7	114.2
3rd quarter	112.8	112.8	102.9	97.2	118.8	97.0	90.0	114.8	114.8	114.8
4th quarter	113.1	113.1	102.7	96.6	120.0	96.8	90.0	115.3	115.2	115.2

Final Sales

Year and quarter	Final sales of domestic product			Final sales to domestic purchasers		
	Billions of dollars [1]	Billions of chained (1992) dollars [1]	Price Index, 1992=100	Billions of dollars [1]	Billions of chained (1992) dollars [1]	Price index, 1992=100
1970	1 033.4	3 406.5	30.3	1 032.2	3 488.3	29.6
1971	1 116.9	3 499.8	31.9	1 119.9	3 592.6	31.2
1972	1 227.4	3 689.5	33.3	1 235.4	3 793.8	32.6
1973	1 365.2	3 883.9	35.2	1 364.6	3 956.8	34.5
1974	1 482.8	3 873.4	38.3	1 485.9	3 910.8	38.0
1975	1 636.9	3 906.4	41.9	1 623.4	3 908.5	41.5
1976	1 802.0	4 061.7	44.4	1 804.3	4 103.3	44.0
1977	2 003.8	4 240.8	47.3	2 027.5	4 312.8	47.0
1978	2 264.2	4 464.4	50.7	2 290.3	4 536.2	50.5
1979	2 540.6	4 614.4	55.1	2 564.6	4 658.2	55.1
1980	2 791.9	4 641.9	60.2	2 806.7	4 607.8	60.9
1981	3 087.8	4 691.6	65.8	3 102.7	4 664.0	66.5
1982	3 256.6	4 651.2	70.0	3 277.1	4 649.7	70.5
1983	3 519.4	4 821.2	73.0	3 571.1	4 881.6	73.2
1984	3 835.0	5 061.6	75.8	3 937.0	5 197.7	75.8
1985	4 154.5	5 296.9	78.4	4 268.7	5 456.3	78.2
1986	4 412.6	5 480.9	80.5	4 544.1	5 657.2	80.3
1987	4 668.1	5 626.0	83.0	4 810.2	5 793.4	83.0
1988	5 038.7	5 855.1	86.1	5 144.8	5 976.1	86.1
1989	5 407.0	6 028.7	89.7	5 487.4	6 114.5	89.7
1990	5 735.8	6 126.7	93.6	5 807.1	6 190.2	93.8
1991	5 919.0	6 082.6	97.3	5 939.5	6 104.9	97.3
1992	6 237.4	6 237.4	100.0	6 267.0	6 267.0	100.0
1993	6 537.6	6 368.9	102.7	6 598.3	6 438.3	102.5
1994	6 885.7	6 551.2	105.1	6 976.6	6 653.2	104.9
1995	7 238.9	6 731.7	107.5	7 322.8	6 824.9	107.3
1996	7 629.5	6 961.6	109.6	7 720.7	7 068.0	109.2
1997	8 043.5	7 203.7	111.7	8 136.9	7 330.2	111.0
1998	8 451.6	7 491.3	112.8	8 602.8	7 705.2	111.7
1990:						
1st quarter	5 651.8	6 144.6	92.0	5 726.1	6 213.5	92.2
2nd quarter	5 709.8	6 127.5	93.2	5 770.1	6 196.0	93.1
3rd quarter	5 768.7	6 126.6	94.2	5 847.2	6 199.9	94.3
4th quarter	5 812.9	6 108.1	95.1	5 884.9	6 151.4	95.7
1991:						
1st quarter	5 838.2	6 065.4	96.3	5 871.1	6 089.6	96.4
2nd quarter	5 912.2	6 095.9	97.0	5 924.6	6 112.9	96.9
3rd quarter	5 944.7	6 085.4	97.7	5 966.7	6 115.3	97.6
4th quarter	5 980.9	6 083.8	98.3	5 995.7	6 101.6	98.3
1992:						
1st quarter	6 122.1	6 175.8	99.1	6 131.0	6 190.5	99.0
2nd quarter	6 191.0	6 203.8	99.8	6 220.0	6 236.3	99.8
3rd quarter	6 260.1	6 249.5	100.2	6 297.7	6 280.5	100.3
4th quarter	6 376.6	6 320.7	100.9	6 419.3	6 360.7	100.9
1993:						
1st quarter	6 413.8	6 297.3	101.9	6 460.4	6 351.7	101.7
2nd quarter	6 494.7	6 344.9	102.4	6 552.2	6 407.0	102.3
3rd quarter	6 560.6	6 379.3	102.8	6 632.7	6 461.4	102.7
4th quarter	6 681.3	6 453.8	103.5	6 747.9	6 533.1	103.3
1994:						
1st quarter	6 741.9	6 473.0	104.2	6 818.5	6 568.7	103.8
2nd quarter	6 835.1	6 526.7	104.8	6 923.0	6 628.0	104.5
3rd quarter	6 936.3	6 580.4	105.4	7 039.8	6 688.4	105.3
4th quarter	7 029.6	6 624.8	106.1	7 125.1	6 727.5	105.9
1995:						
1st quarter	7 111.8	6 661.8	106.8	7 206.5	6 767.5	106.5
2nd quarter	7 185.6	6 700.0	107.3	7 293.6	6 810.4	107.1
3rd quarter	7 287.7	6 761.7	107.8	7 362.2	6 845.7	107.6
4th quarter	7 370.4	6 803.3	108.3	7 428.8	6 875.9	108.0
1996:						
1st quarter	7 479.1	6 863.6	108.9	7 554.8	6 955.7	108.6
2nd quarter	7 600.6	6 954.7	109.3	7 694.6	7 063.5	109.0
3rd quarter	7 653.6	6 970.3	109.8	7 769.1	7 102.7	109.4
4th quarter	7 784.6	7 057.9	110.3	7 864.2	7 149.9	110.0
1997:						
1st quarter	7 895.2	7 108.1	111.0	7 988.5	7 222.6	110.6
2nd quarter	7 979.9	7 155.5	111.5	8 066.7	7 278.3	110.8
3rd quarter	8 116.2	7 256.3	111.9	8 210.9	7 388.0	111.2
4th quarter	8 182.6	7 294.8	112.2	8 281.4	7 432.1	111.4
1998:						
1st quarter	8 288.7	7 372.5	112.5	8 412.5	7 552.2	111.4
2nd quarter	8 401.3	7 456.4	112.7	8 560.6	7 676.4	111.5
3rd quarter	8 480.9	7 507.6	113.0	8 646.4	7 739.8	111.7
4th quarter	8 635.5	7 628.9	113.2	8 791.7	7 852.5	112.0

1. Quarterly data are at seasonally adjusted annual rates.

Gross Domestic Product, Gross and Net National Product, and National Income

(Billions of dollars, quarterly data are at seasonally adjusted annual rates)

Year and quarter	Gross domestic product	Plus: Receipts of factor income from rest of world	Less: Payments of factor income to rest of world	Equals: Gross national product	Less: Consumption of fixed capital	Equals: Net national product	Less			Plus: Subsidies less current surplus of government enterprises	Equals: National income
							Indirect business taxes and nontaxes	Business transfer payments	Statistical discrepancy		
1970	1 035.6	13.0	6.6	1 042.0	107.0	935.0	94.3	3.2	1.9	4.9	840.6
1971	1 125.4	14.1	6.4	1 133.1	116.5	1 016.6	103.6	3.4	6.1	5.1	908.6
1972	1 237.3	16.4	7.7	1 246.0	127.6	1 118.3	111.4	3.9	4.3	6.4	1 005.3
1973	1 382.6	23.8	11.1	1 395.4	140.0	1 255.4	121.0	4.5	3.4	5.9	1 132.3
1974	1 496.9	30.3	14.6	1 512.6	162.5	1 350.0	129.3	5.0	5.5	4.5	1 214.9
1975	1 630.6	28.2	14.9	1 643.9	188.7	1 455.2	140.0	5.2	12.1	8.1	1 305.9
1976	1 819.0	32.9	15.7	1 836.1	206.0	1 630.0	151.6	6.5	19.9	7.4	1 459.4
1977	2 026.9	37.9	17.2	2 047.5	228.6	1 818.9	165.5	7.3	18.2	10.1	1 638.0
1978	2 291.4	47.4	25.3	2 313.5	258.3	2 055.2	177.8	8.2	18.1	11.1	1 862.3
1979	2 557.5	70.4	37.5	2 590.4	296.7	2 293.6	188.7	9.9	28.2	11.7	2 078.5
1980	2 784.2	81.8	46.5	2 819.5	339.4	2 480.1	212.0	11.2	27.6	15.2	2 244.5
1981	3 115.9	95.6	60.9	3 150.6	388.5	2 762.1	249.3	13.4	14.9	16.9	2 501.4
1982	3 242.1	96.9	65.8	3 273.2	424.3	2 848.9	256.4	15.2	-2.5	21.1	2 600.8
1983	3 514.5	97.6	65.6	3 546.5	445.3	3 101.3	280.1	16.2	37.1	25.6	2 793.3
1984	3 902.4	118.7	87.6	3 933.5	461.5	3 472.0	309.5	18.6	5.0	25.5	3 164.4
1985	4 180.7	108.1	87.7	4 201.0	486.6	3 714.5	329.6	20.9	2.4	21.9	3 383.4
1986	4 422.2	106.5	93.6	4 435.1	517.9	3 917.2	344.7	23.9	23.3	25.1	3 550.3
1987	4 692.3	116.0	107.1	4 701.3	545.8	4 155.5	364.8	24.2	-15.4	31.0	3 813.0
1988	5 049.6	144.7	131.7	5 062.6	582.2	4 480.5	385.5	25.4	-47.3	28.5	4 145.3
1989	5 438.7	169.0	154.8	5 452.8	625.4	4 827.4	414.7	26.3	13.2	24.2	4 397.3
1990	5 743.8	177.5	156.4	5 764.9	651.5	5 113.4	442.6	26.5	17.4	25.3	4 652.1
1991	5 916.7	156.2	140.5	5 932.4	679.9	5 252.5	478.1	26.3	10.1	23.6	4 761.6
1992	6 244.4	137.9	126.8	6 255.5	713.5	5 542.0	505.6	28.4	44.8	27.1	4 990.4
1993	6 558.1	150.8	132.1	6 576.8	727.9	5 848.9	532.5	28.2	52.6	31.1	5 266.8
1994	6 947.0	176.5	168.3	6 955.2	777.5	6 177.7	568.5	30.5	14.6	26.6	5 590.7
1995	7 269.6	225.2	207.6	7 287.1	800.8	6 486.3	581.2	32.9	-26.5	25.1	5 923.7
1996	7 661.6	235.5	223.1	7 674.0	832.0	6 842.0	606.4	33.8	-32.2	22.0	6 256.0
1997	8 110.9	265.5	273.5	8 102.9	871.8	7 231.1	627.2	35.1	-55.8	21.9	6 646.5
1998	8 511.0	269.2	289.6	8 490.5	908.0	7 582.5	655.3	36.1	-76.5	27.1	6 994.7
1990:											
1st quarter	5 660.6	173.6	152.5	5 681.6	639.1	5 042.5	432.1	26.1	44.4	23.8	4 563.7
2nd quarter	5 750.8	173.3	156.4	5 767.6	646.0	5 121.6	436.1	26.8	18.7	24.5	4 664.5
3rd quarter	5 782.2	173.1	158.7	5 796.6	655.7	5 140.9	447.3	26.9	17.6	25.7	4 674.8
4th quarter	5 781.7	190.0	157.9	5 813.8	665.3	5 148.5	455.0	26.4	-11.0	27.3	4 705.4
1991:											
1st quarter	5 821.9	174.0	147.1	5 848.8	671.9	5 176.9	464.7	26.0	-5.2	24.4	4 715.8
2nd quarter	5 892.5	156.0	143.8	5 904.7	676.4	5 228.3	472.9	26.3	6.9	22.7	4 744.9
3rd quarter	5 950.2	148.1	138.7	5 959.6	680.9	5 278.7	483.7	26.0	18.5	23.5	4 774.1
4th quarter	6 002.1	146.6	132.2	6 016.5	690.4	5 326.1	491.2	26.8	20.1	23.6	4 811.7
1992:											
1st quarter	6 121.8	140.7	124.2	6 138.3	687.2	5 451.1	495.7	27.6	24.5	24.6	4 927.9
2nd quarter	6 201.2	143.3	132.3	6 212.2	692.4	5 519.7	497.9	28.5	37.4	25.4	4 981.5
3rd quarter	6 271.7	133.8	124.3	6 281.1	770.1	5 510.9	507.1	28.6	52.7	26.9	4 949.5
4th quarter	6 383.1	133.9	126.4	6 390.5	704.3	5 686.2	521.7	28.8	64.6	31.5	5 102.6
1993:											
1st quarter	6 444.5	145.6	122.1	6 468.1	721.8	5 746.2	520.6	27.8	71.0	33.0	5 159.8
2nd quarter	6 509.1	148.9	132.7	6 525.3	720.7	5 804.6	525.9	27.7	46.9	32.8	5 236.9
3rd quarter	6 574.6	153.2	130.9	6 596.9	735.3	5 861.5	534.4	28.2	47.5	30.2	5 281.7
4th quarter	6 704.2	155.6	142.7	6 717.1	733.6	5 983.5	549.4	29.0	45.0	28.5	5 388.7
1994:											
1st quarter	6 794.3	161.1	144.2	6 811.2	823.3	5 987.9	556.9	29.7	6.3	28.1	5 423.2
2nd quarter	6 911.4	168.3	159.3	6 920.3	753.1	6 167.3	564.4	30.1	42.4	25.9	5 556.3
3rd quarter	6 986.5	181.9	176.1	6 992.3	762.2	6 230.1	573.2	30.7	15.2	25.1	5 636.1
4th quarter	7 095.7	194.6	193.5	7 096.8	771.4	6 325.4	579.4	31.5	-5.4	27.4	5 747.3
1995:											
1st quarter	7 170.8	216.9	198.4	7 189.3	783.1	6 406.2	579.1	32.5	3.1	24.6	5 816.1
2nd quarter	7 210.9	227.4	205.0	7 233.3	794.4	6 438.9	580.6	32.6	-22.7	24.9	5 873.5
3rd quarter	7 304.8	224.6	216.2	7 313.2	803.5	6 509.7	579.6	33.3	-43.0	25.5	5 965.3
4th quarter	7 391.9	231.6	210.9	7 412.6	822.2	6 590.5	585.6	33.4	-43.2	25.2	6 039.8
1996:											
1st quarter	7 495.3	229.7	210.0	7 515.0	818.6	6 696.4	593.9	33.2	-26.3	24.0	6 119.6
2nd quarter	7 629.2	229.3	215.2	7 643.3	826.4	6 816.9	599.7	33.7	-20.6	22.8	6 226.8
3rd quarter	7 703.4	234.7	229.5	7 708.6	836.5	6 872.1	603.8	33.9	-49.3	20.0	6 303.6
4th quarter	7 818.4	248.2	237.6	7 829.0	846.4	6 982.6	628.3	34.2	-32.6	21.2	6 373.9
1997:											
1st quarter	7 955.0	253.1	255.6	7 952.4	856.1	7 096.3	617.2	34.5	-43.1	21.3	6 509.0
2nd quarter	8 063.4	268.3	269.4	8 062.3	866.5	7 195.8	625.0	35.0	-47.7	21.0	6 604.5
3rd quarter	8 170.8	274.3	283.0	8 162.0	877.0	7 285.1	632.0	35.4	-65.1	22.0	6 704.8
4th quarter	8 254.5	266.3	285.9	8 234.9	887.6	7 347.3	634.5	35.6	-67.3	23.4	6 767.9
1998:											
1st quarter	8 384.2	270.3	285.1	8 369.4	894.5	7 474.9	641.9	35.6	-54.1	23.5	6 875.0
2nd quarter	8 440.6	270.6	289.3	8 421.8	902.3	7 519.6	647.7	36.0	-85.7	23.9	6 945.5
3rd quarter	8 537.9	265.0	292.1	8 510.9	912.3	7 598.5	656.5	36.3	-102.0	24.6	7 032.3
4th quarter	8 681.2	270.7	291.9	8 660.0	923.0	7 737.1	675.1	36.4	-64.2	36.3	7 126.0

National Income by Type of Income

(Billions of dollars, quarterly data are at seasonally adjusted annual rates)

Year and quarter	National income	Compensation of employees Total	Wage and salary accruals	Supplements to wages and salaries	Proprietors' income with IVA[1] and CCAdj[2] Total	Farm	Nonfarm	Rental income of persons with CCAdj[2]	Corporate profits Total with IVA[1] and CCAdj[2]	Profits before tax	Profits after tax Total	Dividends	Undistributed profits	Net interest
1970	840.6	618.1	551.5	66.6	80.2	14.8	65.4	23.6	78.7	78.4	44.0	23.7	20.3	40.0
1971	908.6	660.1	584.5	75.6	86.5	15.4	71.1	24.6	92.0	90.1	52.4	23.7	28.6	45.4
1972	1 005.3	726.8	638.7	88.1	98.3	19.5	78.8	24.3	106.7	104.5	62.6	25.8	36.9	49.3
1973	1 132.3	813.1	708.6	104.4	116.8	32.6	84.2	25.8	120.1	130.9	81.6	28.1	53.5	56.5
1974	1 214.9	892.4	772.2	120.3	115.7	25.8	89.8	25.7	109.2	142.8	91.0	30.4	60.6	71.8
1975	1 305.9	951.3	814.7	136.6	121.8	24.1	97.7	24.7	128.2	140.4	89.5	30.1	59.4	80.0
1976	1 459.4	1 061.5	899.6	162.0	133.6	18.6	115.0	24.3	154.9	173.8	109.6	35.9	73.7	85.1
1977	1 638.0	1 182.9	994.0	188.9	147.4	17.5	129.9	22.8	184.3	203.5	130.4	40.8	89.6	100.7
1978	1 862.3	1 338.5	1 121.1	217.4	169.5	22.2	147.4	24.8	209.0	238.1	154.6	46.0	108.6	120.5
1979	2 078.5	1 503.3	1 255.7	247.5	185.0	25.3	159.7	26.9	213.1	261.8	173.8	52.5	121.3	150.3
1980	2 244.5	1 653.9	1 377.6	276.3	176.6	12.2	164.4	33.9	188.3	241.4	156.6	59.3	97.3	191.9
1981	2 501.4	1 827.8	1 517.6	310.2	187.6	21.9	165.7	44.5	207.0	229.8	148.6	69.5	79.1	234.5
1982	2 600.8	1 927.6	1 593.9	333.7	179.6	14.5	165.1	46.5	182.3	176.7	113.6	66.7	46.9	264.9
1983	2 793.3	2 044.2	1 684.8	359.4	191.9	4.1	187.8	46.1	235.2	212.8	135.5	74.4	61.2	275.9
1984	3 164.4	2 257.0	1 855.3	401.7	248.7	23.2	225.5	50.1	290.1	244.2	150.1	79.3	70.9	318.5
1985	3 383.4	2 425.7	1 995.7	430.0	268.6	23.6	245.0	48.1	304.0	229.9	133.4	83.9	49.6	337.2
1986	3 550.3	2 572.4	2 116.5	455.9	279.5	24.2	255.3	41.5	293.8	222.6	116.1	91.4	24.7	363.1
1987	3 813.0	2 757.7	2 272.7	485.0	305.1	31.5	273.6	44.8	333.2	293.6	166.5	96.0	70.5	372.2
1988	4 145.3	2 973.9	2 453.6	520.3	335.3	27.5	307.8	55.1	382.1	354.3	217.3	111.1	106.3	398.9
1989	4 397.3	3 151.6	2 598.1	553.5	357.4	36.3	321.1	51.7	380.0	348.1	206.8	134.4	72.4	456.6
1990	4 652.1	3 352.8	2 757.5	595.2	374.0	35.4	338.6	61.0	397.1	371.7	231.2	143.9	87.3	467.3
1991	4 761.6	3 457.9	2 827.6	630.4	376.5	29.3	347.2	67.9	411.3	374.2	240.8	147.2	93.6	448.0
1992	4 990.4	3 644.9	2 970.6	674.3	423.8	37.1	386.7	79.4	427.0	406.4	263.4	147.9	115.5	414.3
1993	5 266.8	3 814.9	3 094.0	720.8	450.8	32.4	418.4	105.7	492.8	465.4	300.2	157.6	142.6	402.5
1994	5 590.7	4 012.0	3 254.0	758.0	471.6	36.9	434.7	124.4	570.5	535.1	348.5	182.4	166.1	412.3
1995	5 923.7	4 208.9	3 441.9	767.0	488.1	22.4	465.6	133.7	672.4	635.6	424.6	205.3	219.3	420.6
1996	6 256.0	4 409.0	3 640.4	768.6	527.7	38.9	488.8	150.2	750.4	680.2	454.1	261.9	192.3	418.6
1997	6 646.5	4 687.2	3 893.6	793.7	551.2	35.5	515.8	158.2	817.9	734.4	488.3	275.1	213.2	432.0
1998	6 994.7	4 981.0	4 153.9	827.1	577.2	28.7	548.5	162.6	824.6	717.8	477.7	279.2	198.5	449.3
1990:														
1st quarter	4 563.7	3 285.5	2 704.0	581.5	367.7	35.5	332.2	55.1	396.4	354.7	221.7	144.8	76.9	458.9
2nd quarter	4 664.5	3 344.7	2 753.0	591.7	375.4	38.3	337.1	57.6	421.8	373.4	232.2	145.5	86.7	465.0
3rd quarter	4 674.8	3 384.9	2 784.5	600.5	378.6	34.9	343.7	64.4	379.2	381.9	233.9	143.8	90.1	467.7
4th quarter	4 705.4	3 395.9	2 788.8	607.1	374.4	33.1	341.3	66.7	390.9	376.7	237.1	141.5	95.6	477.5
1991:														
1st quarter	4 715.8	3 405.7	2 789.5	616.2	362.4	26.5	336.0	66.3	420.9	370.7	240.7	145.8	94.9	460.4
2nd quarter	4 744.9	3 440.7	2 814.7	626.0	378.7	33.4	345.4	66.0	408.8	368.7	236.4	147.6	88.8	450.6
3rd quarter	4 774.1	3 474.2	2 838.8	635.4	378.9	27.3	351.7	67.1	407.2	374.6	238.6	148.7	89.9	446.6
4th quarter	4 811.7	3 511.0	2 867.1	643.8	385.7	30.0	355.8	72.3	408.4	382.8	247.6	146.5	101.0	434.3
1992:														
1st quarter	4 927.9	3 577.1	2 916.5	660.7	410.2	35.9	374.4	77.2	444.2	411.1	267.2	142.6	124.6	419.2
2nd quarter	4 981.5	3 626.5	2 956.2	670.3	420.8	37.1	383.8	79.5	437.2	426.2	275.2	144.0	131.3	417.5
3rd quarter	4 949.5	3 669.2	2 988.2	681.0	426.6	39.0	387.6	69.5	376.1	368.0	240.4	148.7	91.7	408.1
4th quarter	5 102.6	3 707.0	3 021.7	685.3	437.4	36.5	401.0	91.2	454.6	420.3	270.6	156.4	114.2	412.4
1993:														
1st quarter	5 159.8	3 749.3	3 045.5	703.8	440.3	29.7	410.6	99.7	459.2	431.7	282.5	150.7	131.8	411.2
2nd quarter	5 236.9	3 796.3	3 079.3	717.0	452.2	36.3	416.0	105.6	478.2	461.5	296.1	154.5	141.6	404.6
3rd quarter	5 281.7	3 837.6	3 111.0	726.6	446.2	25.6	420.6	106.1	492.8	459.6	298.4	159.8	138.6	398.9
4th quarter	5 388.7	3 876.2	3 140.4	735.8	464.4	38.0	426.5	111.5	541.2	508.9	324.0	165.4	158.6	395.4
1994:														
1st quarter	5 423.2	3 937.4	3 190.7	746.7	463.9	46.4	417.5	112.7	512.0	475.1	312.1	170.2	141.9	397.2
2nd quarter	5 556.3	3 988.0	3 232.3	755.6	474.7	38.8	435.9	126.0	552.4	525.3	342.5	178.1	164.4	405.6
3rd quarter	5 636.1	4 028.7	3 267.2	761.5	471.6	33.2	438.4	130.1	590.1	556.2	361.6	186.0	175.6	415.6
4th quarter	5 747.3	4 093.9	3 325.9	768.1	476.1	29.1	447.0	128.9	617.7	583.9	377.7	195.3	182.4	430.7
1995:														
1st quarter	5 816.1	4 150.3	3 381.6	768.8	478.6	22.8	455.7	131.1	629.3	610.5	407.6	197.1	210.5	426.9
2nd quarter	5 873.3	4 183.6	3 416.8	766.7	482.4	20.4	462.0	133.3	653.9	629.4	421.9	199.0	222.8	420.2
3rd quarter	5 965.3	4 230.0	3 462.7	767.2	489.8	19.1	470.7	131.9	698.6	650.8	431.6	204.4	227.2	415.2
4th quarter	6 039.8	4 271.6	3 506.5	765.1	501.5	27.4	474.1	138.7	707.8	651.8	437.5	220.7	216.8	420.2
1996:														
1st quarter	6 119.6	4 303.5	3 542.0	761.5	516.1	34.8	481.3	145.0	735.9	669.9	446.0	247.6	198.4	419.2
2nd quarter	6 226.8	4 382.4	3 615.2	767.2	528.0	41.0	487.0	148.4	748.3	683.4	454.8	257.1	197.6	419.7
3rd quarter	6 303.6	4 444.4	3 673.6	770.9	533.5	43.2	490.3	152.1	755.4	681.9	454.2	269.1	185.1	418.1
4th quarter	6 373.9	4 505.9	3 730.9	775.0	533.1	36.7	496.4	155.3	762.0	685.7	461.5	273.6	187.9	417.5
1997:														
1st quarter	6 509.0	4 586.3	3 802.2	784.1	540.5	36.4	504.1	157.5	794.3	712.4	473.6	274.1	199.5	430.4
2nd quarter	6 604.5	4 649.2	3 859.2	790.0	549.9	37.8	512.1	158.0	815.5	729.8	487.8	274.7	213.2	431.8
3rd quarter	6 704.8	4 715.5	3 919.3	796.2	556.5	36.3	520.2	158.6	840.9	758.9	504.7	275.1	229.5	433.3
4th quarter	6 767.9	4 798.0	3 993.6	804.4	558.0	31.4	526.6	158.8	820.8	736.4	487.1	276.4	210.6	432.4
1998:														
1st quarter	6 875.0	4 882.8	4 065.9	816.8	564.2	27.4	536.8	158.3	829.2	719.1	479.2	277.3	201.8	440.5
2nd quarter	6 945.5	4 945.2	4 121.6	823.5	571.7	27.7	544.0	161.0	820.6	723.5	481.8	278.1	203.7	447.1
3rd quarter	7 032.3	5 011.6	4 181.1	830.5	576.1	25.2	550.9	163.6	827.0	720.5	477.3	279.0	198.3	454.0
4th quarter	7 126.0	5 084.3	4 246.8	837.5	596.9	34.7	562.2	167.5	821.7	708.1	472.5	282.3	190.2	455.6

1. Inventory valuation adjustment.
2. Capital consumption adjustment.

Domestic Product and Income of Nonfinacial Corporate Business

(Billions of dollars, quarterly data are at seasonally adjusted annual rates)

Year and quarter	Gross domestic product	Less: Consumption of fixed capital	Equals: Net domestic product	Less: Indirect business taxes plus business transfer payments less subsides	Equals: Domestic income	Components of domestic income									
						Compensation of employees	Corporate profits with inventory valuation and capital consumption adjustments						Inventory valuation adjustment	Capital consumption adjustment	Net interest
							Total	Profits							
								Profits before tax	Profits tax liability	Profits after tax					
										Total	Dividends	Undistributed profits			
1970	561.4	48.5	512.8	58.8	454.0	378.7	58.3	58.1	27.2	31.0	18.5	12.5	-6.6	6.7	17.1
1971	606.4	53.0	553.4	64.5	488.9	402.0	68.8	67.1	29.9	37.1	18.5	18.7	-4.6	6.3	18.1
1972	673.3	57.6	615.8	69.2	546.6	447.1	80.4	78.6	33.8	44.8	20.1	24.7	-6.6	8.4	19.2
1973	754.5	62.6	691.8	76.3	615.5	505.9	87.1	98.6	40.2	58.4	21.1	37.3	-20.0	8.6	22.5
1974	814.6	73.3	741.3	81.4	659.9	556.8	74.8	109.2	42.2	67.0	21.7	45.2	-39.5	5.1	28.3
1975	881.2	87.5	793.7	87.4	706.3	580.3	97.3	109.9	41.5	68.4	24.8	43.6	-11.0	-1.6	28.7
1976	995.3	96.9	898.4	95.1	803.3	657.4	118.4	137.3	53.0	84.4	28.0	56.3	-14.9	-4.0	27.5
1977	1 125.4	108.8	1 016.7	104.1	912.6	742.6	139.4	158.6	59.9	98.7	31.5	67.2	-16.6	-2.6	30.6
1978	1 284.1	124.4	1 159.7	116.4	1 043.2	852.9	154.0	183.5	67.1	116.4	36.4	80.0	-25.0	-4.5	36.3
1979	1 429.7	143.9	1 285.8	125.4	1 160.4	968.1	147.2	195.5	69.6	125.9	38.1	87.9	-41.6	-6.8	45.1
1980	1 553.8	165.4	1 388.4	141.6	1 246.8	1 058.5	130.1	181.6	67.0	114.6	45.3	69.2	-43.0	-8.4	58.2
1981	1 767.3	193.2	1 574.1	170.4	1 403.7	1 171.5	160.3	181.4	63.9	117.5	53.3	64.2	-25.7	4.6	71.9
1982	1 823.4	209.7	1 613.7	172.1	1 441.6	1 217.0	142.1	133.7	46.3	87.4	53.3	34.2	-9.9	18.3	82.5
1983	1 950.3	222.7	1 727.6	189.0	1 538.6	1 280.5	181.5	157.4	59.4	97.9	64.2	33.8	-9.1	33.2	76.6
1984	2 187.5	228.7	1 958.8	210.2	1 748.6	1 421.7	239.0	191.0	73.7	117.3	67.8	49.5	-5.6	53.7	87.8
1985	2 319.3	238.9	2 080.4	224.4	1 856.0	1 521.9	243.5	167.6	69.9	97.6	72.3	25.4	0.5	75.4	90.6
1986	2 416.3	253.2	2 163.1	235.8	1 927.3	1 603.2	226.0	151.5	75.6	75.9	73.9	2.1	11.4	63.1	98.1
1987	2 589.6	263.6	2 326.1	246.7	2 079.3	1 715.5	258.6	214.9	93.5	121.4	75.9	45.5	-20.7	64.4	105.3
1988	2 805.2	279.7	2 525.5	263.5	2 262.0	1 846.7	294.3	260.6	101.7	158.8	79.4	79.4	-29.3	63.1	121.0
1989	2 950.9	297.4	2 653.5	280.8	2 372.7	1 950.0	276.7	237.0	98.8	138.3	103.5	34.8	-17.5	57.2	145.9
1990	3 084.0	308.4	2 775.6	296.8	2 478.8	2 056.0	275.3	237.3	95.7	141.6	118.4	23.3	-13.5	51.5	147.5
1991	3 132.1	320.2	2 811.9	318.0	2 493.9	2 090.6	269.7	218.1	85.4	132.8	124.6	8.2	4.0	47.6	133.7
1992	3 262.6	330.5	2 932.2	337.0	2 595.1	2 195.3	295.6	257.8	91.1	166.7	133.6	33.1	-7.5	45.3	104.2
1993	3 430.4	340.3	3 090.1	358.5	2 731.6	2 290.7	346.4	308.6	105.0	203.6	147.7	55.9	-8.5	46.3	94.5
1994	3 709.7	360.7	3 349.0	389.0	2 960.1	2 426.7	437.1	392.3	128.8	263.5	158.6	104.9	-16.1	60.8	96.3
1995	3 920.4	375.6	3 544.8	397.3	3 147.5	2 556.0	487.4	441.5	136.7	304.7	179.3	125.4	-22.6	68.5	104.2
1996	4 134.4	393.4	3 741.0	411.6	3 329.4	2 679.7	548.5	473.1	151.5	321.5	217.1	104.4	-1.2	76.7	101.2
1997	4 414.5	415.4	3 999.1	436.8	3 562.3	2 871.2	594.2	505.4	169.8	335.6	229.3	106.3	6.9	81.9	96.9
1998	4 657.4	435.3	4 222.1	461.3	3 760.8	3 066.6	598.7	487.9	160.4	327.4	249.6	77.9	14.5	96.3	95.6
1990:															
1st quarter	3 042.8	303.2	2 739.6	290.5	2 449.1	2 022.0	280.7	227.9	90.5	137.3	119.5	17.8	-1.3	54.2	146.5
2nd quarter	3 103.0	306.1	2 796.9	292.6	2 504.3	2 055.8	299.6	239.0	96.4	142.7	116.5	26.2	7.7	52.9	148.9
3rd quarter	3 092.7	310.2	2 782.6	299.7	2 482.9	2 074.7	260.6	250.1	101.1	148.9	118.1	30.8	-40.0	50.6	147.6
4th quarter	3 097.4	314.2	2 783.3	304.3	2 478.9	2 071.4	260.4	232.3	94.7	137.7	119.5	18.2	-20.3	48.3	147.1
1991:															
1st quarter	3 107.7	318.3	2 789.3	309.2	2 480.2	2 060.0	277.5	213.3	83.1	130.3	120.7	9.5	17.6	46.5	142.7
2nd quarter	3 119.1	319.3	2 799.9	314.2	2 485.7	2 078.8	269.3	215.0	84.0	131.0	125.4	5.6	6.8	47.5	137.6
3rd quarter	3 142.0	320.8	2 821.2	321.2	2 500.0	2 101.2	267.6	220.6	86.8	133.8	124.9	8.9	-0.8	47.9	131.1
4th quarter	3 159.5	322.3	2 837.2	327.3	2 509.9	2 122.2	264.3	223.7	87.5	136.2	127.5	8.7	-7.6	48.3	123.3
1992:															
1st quarter	3 202.2	323.3	2 878.9	330.4	2 548.4	2 152.8	285.5	236.3	82.4	153.9	124.0	29.9	0.3	48.9	110.2
2nd quarter	3 236.1	325.1	2 911.0	331.8	2 579.2	2 183.2	290.0	262.6	93.6	169.0	129.7	39.3	-21.9	49.3	106.0
3rd quarter	3 270.5	343.8	2 926.7	337.8	2 588.9	2 209.3	278.9	254.4	89.9	164.5	134.3	30.2	-8.6	33.0	100.8
4th quarter	3 341.7	329.7	3 012.0	348.0	2 664.0	2 236.1	328.2	277.9	98.4	179.5	146.3	33.2	0.2	50.1	99.7
1993:															
1st quarter	3 351.8	335.8	3 015.9	348.2	2 667.7	2 253.5	316.0	275.6	92.5	183.1	143.5	39.6	-12.5	52.9	98.2
2nd quarter	3 400.3	337.3	3 063.0	353.8	2 709.2	2 279.9	334.4	306.9	104.7	202.2	144.2	58.0	-17.1	44.5	95.0
3rd quarter	3 444.3	344.5	3 099.8	359.7	2 740.1	2 301.5	345.5	303.1	102.9	200.2	147.6	52.5	0.2	42.2	93.1
4th quarter	3 525.2	343.4	3 181.9	372.3	2 809.6	2 327.8	389.9	349.0	120.0	228.9	155.6	73.4	-4.8	45.7	91.9
1994:															
1st quarter	3 624.5	375.1	3 249.3	380.4	2 868.9	2 372.5	405.4	359.1	119.5	239.6	150.4	89.2	-4.3	50.6	91.1
2nd quarter	3 668.9	351.6	3 317.3	386.1	2 931.1	2 409.8	427.0	380.7	124.6	256.1	158.7	97.4	-15.1	61.4	94.3
3rd quarter	3 729.1	355.9	3 373.2	392.3	2 980.9	2 439.2	444.1	400.7	130.1	270.6	158.5	112.1	-21.2	64.6	97.6
4th quarter	3 816.4	360.0	3 456.4	397.1	3 059.2	2 485.2	472.0	428.9	141.1	287.8	166.8	121.0	-23.6	66.7	102.1
1995:															
1st quarter	3 844.1	365.6	3 478.5	396.1	3 082.4	2 519.5	460.0	431.5	134.6	296.9	169.0	127.9	-37.9	66.3	103.0
2nd quarter	3 879.3	372.6	3 506.7	397.0	3 109.7	2 539.5	466.2	432.1	132.8	299.2	171.2	128.0	-33.9	68.1	104.0
3rd quarter	3 956.5	378.1	3 578.3	396.0	3 182.3	2 569.6	508.3	451.4	139.3	312.0	184.5	127.6	-13.4	70.3	104.5
4th quarter	4 001.7	385.9	3 615.8	400.2	3 215.6	2 595.3	515.0	450.9	140.3	310.7	192.7	118.0	-5.3	69.5	105.3
1996:															
1st quarter	4 033.0	385.8	3 647.2	405.3	3 241.9	2 607.1	533.0	460.8	146.8	314.0	208.4	105.5	-2.9	75.1	101.9
2nd quarter	4 106.4	390.6	3 715.8	409.1	3 306.7	2 661.8	543.4	473.3	151.3	321.9	210.4	111.5	-6.2	76.3	101.6
3rd quarter	4 168.9	395.9	3 773.1	412.7	3 360.4	2 704.3	554.9	476.5	152.5	324.0	222.2	101.8	1.2	77.2	101.2
4th quarter	4 229.3	401.3	3 828.0	419.5	3 408.5	2 745.7	562.8	481.8	155.5	326.3	227.3	99.0	3.0	78.0	100.0
1997:															
1st quarter	4 307.1	406.5	3 900.6	425.6	3 475.0	2 799.1	575.4	488.3	164.4	323.9	227.0	96.8	8.1	79.1	100.6
2nd quarter	4 375.7	412.2	3 963.5	434.5	3 529.0	2 843.4	586.7	495.6	166.4	329.2	224.6	104.6	10.3	80.7	99.0
3rd quarter	4 461.9	418.4	4 043.4	442.1	3 601.4	2 889.8	615.2	528.0	178.1	349.9	226.1	123.8	4.8	82.5	96.3
4th quarter	4 513.2	424.4	4 088.8	445.0	3 643.8	2 952.6	599.3	509.8	170.1	339.6	239.6	100.1	4.3	85.3	91.9
1998:															
1st quarter	4 574.2	428.5	4 145.7	450.5	3 695.2	3 002.3	599.3	484.2	159.7	324.5	237.3	87.2	25.3	89.8	93.6
2nd quarter	4 618.8	433.1	4 185.7	454.2	3 731.4	3 043.1	593.2	491.8	162.1	329.6	254.3	75.3	7.8	93.7	95.2
3rd quarter	4 688.9	437.4	4 251.4	461.1	3 790.3	3 086.3	607.5	497.3	163.8	333.5	247.3	86.2	11.7	98.5	96.5
4th quarter	4 747.8	442.3	4 305.5	479.2	3 826.4	3 134.6	594.8	478.2	156.1	322.1	259.3	62.8	13.4	103.2	96.9

Per Capita Product and Income and U.S. Population

(Dollars, except as noted; quarterly data are at seasonally adjusted annual rates)

| Year and quarter | Current dollars | | | | | | | Chained (1992) dollars | | | | | | Population (Mid-period, thousands) |
| | Gross domestic product | Personal income | Disposable personal income | Personal consumption expenditures | | | | Gross domestic product | Disposable personal income | Personal consumption expenditures | | | | |
				Total	Durable goods	Nondurable goods	Services			Total	Durable goods	Nondurable	Services	
1970	5 050	4 082	3 550	3 160	414	1 326	1 419	16 566	12 039	10 717	912	4 189	5 634	205 089
1971	5 419	4 334	3 811	3 383	467	1 375	1 541	16 900	12 366	10 975	990	4 211	5 768	207 692
1972	5 894	4 710	4 082	3 671	526	1 467	1 678	17 637	12 794	11 508	1 105	4 349	6 014	209 924
1973	6 524	5 226	4 562	4 018	583	1 619	1 816	18 479	13 566	11 950	1 207	4 449	6 225	211 939
1974	6 998	5 685	4 941	4 353	572	1 797	1 984	18 192	13 344	11 756	1 114	4 322	6 317	213 898
1975	7 550	6 107	5 383	4 765	618	1 948	2 199	17 936	13 444	11 899	1 103	4 344	6 474	215 981
1976	8 341	6 692	5 856	5 268	728	2 101	2 438	18 721	13 837	12 446	1 231	4 516	6 681	218 086
1977	9 201	7 336	6 383	5 797	822	2 256	2 719	19 400	14 142	12 846	1 332	4 587	6 892	220 289
1978	10 292	8 201	7 123	6 418	905	2 470	3 043	20 226	14 715	13 258	1 387	4 697	7 139	222 629
1979	11 361	9 133	7 888	7 079	950	2 772	3 357	20 571	14 951	13 417	1 365	4 752	7 285	225 106
1980	12 226	10 069	8 697	7 730	938	3 054	3 739	20 265	14 867	13 216	1 241	4 677	7 336	227 726
1981	13 547	11 167	9 601	8 440	1 002	3 296	4 142	20 524	15 064	13 245	1 243	4 671	7 374	230 008
1982	13 961	11 731	10 132	8 943	1 030	3 388	4 525	19 896	15 034	13 270	1 229	4 654	7 442	232 218
1983	14 998	12 352	10 776	9 744	1 194	3 543	5 007	20 499	15 293	13 829	1 397	4 747	7 720	234 332
1984	16 508	13 585	11 912	10 543	1 375	3 738	5 430	21 744	16 286	14 415	1 586	4 872	7 966	236 394
1985	17 529	14 427	12 592	11 341	1 514	3 889	5 938	22 320	16 604	14 954	1 725	4 941	8 290	238 506
1986	18 374	15 122	13 211	12 019	1 656	3 977	6 385	22 801	16 939	15 409	1 863	5 052	8 482	240 682
1987	19 323	15 968	13 851	12 743	1 716	4 175	6 851	23 264	17 109	15 740	1 873	5 103	8 758	242 842
1988	20 605	17 052	14 881	13 669	1 840	4 411	7 417	23 934	17 650	16 211	1 973	5 200	9 028	245 061
1989	21 984	18 176	15 771	14 531	1 911	4 704	7 915	24 504	17 833	16 430	2 006	5 269	9 145	247 387
1990	22 979	19 188	16 689	15 360	1 906	4 982	8 472	24 549	17 962	16 532	1 974	5 265	9 287	249 956
1991	23 416	19 652	17 179	15 732	1 802	5 056	8 874	24 060	17 744	16 249	1 828	5 156	9 265	252 680
1992	24 447	20 576	18 029	16 520	1 913	5 175	9 433	24 447	18 029	16 520	1 913	5 175	9 433	255 432
1993	25 403	21 231	18 558	17 273	2 054	5 309	9 910	24 750	18 077	16 825	2 029	5 233	9 563	258 161
1994	26 647	22 086	19 251	18 093	2 223	5 479	10 391	25 357	18 308	17 207	2 153	5 331	9 725	260 705
1995	27 621	23 071	20 050	18 822	2 322	5 599	10 902	25 691	18 640	17 499	2 238	5 386	9 877	263 194
1996	28 849	24 193	20 840	19 639	2 422	5 795	11 421	26 338	18 989	17 894	2 358	5 463	10 079	265 579
1997	30 278	25 325	21 633	20 508	2 512	5 975	12 021	27 138	19 349	18 342	2 496	5 548	10 309	267 880
1998	31 492	26 368	22 304	21 490	2 681	6 151	12 658	27 943	19 790	19 068	2 727	5 713	10 655	270 258
1990:														
1st quarter	22 740	18 859	16 396	15 102	1 982	4 904	8 216	24 716	18 009	16 587	2 053	5 299	9 222	248 928
2nd quarter	23 043	19 142	16 624	15 274	1 914	4 929	8 431	24 729	18 033	16 568	1 985	5 277	9 301	249 564
3rd quarter	23 101	19 346	16 826	15 498	1 891	5 019	8 589	24 539	17 994	16 574	1 959	5 273	9 338	250 299
4th quarter	23 032	19 404	16 905	15 564	1 840	5 076	8 648	24 216	17 811	16 398	1 897	5 212	9 287	251 031
1991:														
1st quarter	23 135	19 415	16 942	15 540	1 784	5 040	8 716	24 031	17 695	16 231	1 822	5 168	9 240	251 650
2nd quarter	23 355	19 614	17 154	15 700	1 794	5 072	8 833	24 078	17 800	16 290	1 825	5 185	9 281	252 295
3rd quarter	23 515	19 702	17 238	15 815	1 826	5 072	8 917	24 069	17 746	16 280	1 847	5 166	9 268	253 033
4th quarter	23 654	19 874	17 381	15 871	1 802	5 041	9 028	24 061	17 736	16 194	1 819	5 106	9 269	253 743
1992:														
1st quarter	24 070	20 228	17 725	16 229	1 864	5 124	9 241	24 281	17 923	16 410	1 872	5 168	9 370	254 338
2nd quarter	24 315	20 456	17 947	16 402	1 887	5 130	9 384	24 366	18 004	16 454	1 887	5 144	9 423	255 032
3rd quarter	24 516	20 544	18 001	16 570	1 925	5 185	9 460	24 474	17 949	16 522	1 923	5 164	9 435	255 815
4th quarter	24 881	21 070	18 440	16 877	1 973	5 260	9 643	24 663	18 238	16 692	1 968	5 223	9 502	256 543
1993:														
1st quarter	25 061	20 735	18 159	16 976	1 969	5 267	9 740	24 608	17 832	16 671	1 960	5 201	9 509	257 151
2nd quarter	25 250	21 204	18 545	17 177	2 033	5 300	9 844	24 671	18 104	16 769	2 014	5 228	9 527	257 785
3rd quarter	25 432	21 297	18 607	17 363	2 078	5 315	9 970	24 732	18 101	16 891	2 050	5 248	9 593	258 516
4th quarter	25 866	21 684	18 920	17 574	2 134	5 355	10 084	24 989	18 268	16 968	2 092	5 254	9 624	259 191
1994:														
1st quarter	26 158	21 496	18 752	17 774	2 168	5 407	10 199	25 120	18 032	17 092	2 120	5 307	9 667	259 738
2nd quarter	26 546	22 021	19 138	17 978	2 199	5 439	10 341	25 352	18 286	17 178	2 135	5 322	9 723	260 351
3rd quarter	26 764	22 234	19 400	18 199	2 235	5 514	10 450	25 396	18 369	17 232	2 152	5 337	9 745	261 040
4th quarter	27 115	22 589	19 711	18 419	2 290	5 555	10 574	25 559	18 541	17 326	2 203	5 359	9 767	261 692
1995:														
1st quarter	27 345	22 802	19 876	18 542	2 282	5 566	10 695	25 616	18 621	17 371	2 193	5 378	9 802	262 235
2nd quarter	27 434	22 942	19 915	18 762	2 306	5 595	10 861	25 582	18 551	17 476	2 220	5 387	9 872	262 847
3rd quarter	27 719	23 123	20 091	18 922	2 341	5 604	10 977	25 726	18 628	17 544	2 259	5 383	9 905	263 527
4th quarter	27 982	23 413	20 316	19 061	2 358	5 631	11 072	25 839	18 761	17 602	2 280	5 397	9 929	264 169
1996:														
1st quarter	28 318	23 743	20 533	19 299	2 389	5 693	11 217	26 001	18 860	17 727	2 308	5 416	10 007	264 680
2nd quarter	28 761	24 090	20 722	19 600	2 440	5 798	11 361	26 329	18 919	17 894	2 373	5 468	10 060	265 258
3rd quarter	28 972	24 359	20 976	19 717	2 417	5 806	11 495	26 402	19 079	17 934	2 356	5 471	10 110	265 887
4th quarter	29 338	24 578	21 127	19 938	2 443	5 885	11 610	26 617	19 096	18 021	2 392	5 498	10 138	266 491
1997:														
1st quarter	29 795	24 970	21 391	20 235	2 505	5 954	11 775	26 843	19 217	18 178	2 458	5 536	10 196	266 987
2nd quarter	30 138	25 206	21 558	20 329	2 467	5 936	11 926	27 048	19 315	18 213	2 444	5 521	10 255	267 545
3rd quarter	30 468	25 435	21 709	20 660	2 540	6 008	12 111	27 263	19 385	18 447	2 534	5 578	10 349	268 171
4th quarter	30 707	25 686	21 871	20 807	2 538	6 001	12 268	27 397	19 478	18 529	2 547	5 559	10 434	268 815
1998:														
1st quarter	31 132	26 007	22 046	21 078	2 618	6 064	12 396	27 718	19 632	18 770	2 637	5 649	10 506	269 309
2nd quarter	31 277	26 242	22 192	21 394	2 668	6 134	12 593	27 786	19 719	19 010	2 703	5 710	10 623	269 867
3rd quarter	31 561	26 470	22 373	21 612	2 657	6 173	12 782	27 970	19 829	19 155	2 712	5 726	10 738	270 523
4th quarter	31 995	26 749	22 604	21 873	2 781	6 233	12 859	28 297	19 980	19 334	2 856	5 768	10 751	271 331

Composite Indexes of Economic Activity and Selected Index Components

Year and month	Cyclical composite indexes, 1992=100				Selected components of leading index			Selected components of lagging index	
	Leading	Coincident	Lagging	Ratio, coincident to lagging	Vendor performance (slower deliveries diffusion index, percent)	Interest rate spread, 10 year Treasury bonds less federal funds [1]	Index of consumer expecta- tions [1,2]	Change in manufac- turing labor cost per unit of output [3]	Consumer installment credit outstanding (percent of personal income)
1970	84.7	61.3	101.3	60.5	50.3	0.17	73.7	0.4	15.5
1971	87.3	62.1	98.7	62.9	48.0	1.50	77.1	-2.2	15.5
1972	90.7	65.5	97.3	67.3	62.7	1.78	87.3	0.4	15.8
1973	91.4	69.2	100.5	68.9	88.0	-1.89	67.6	3.0	16.3
1974	87.6	69.4	104.1	66.7	65.8	-2.95	56.0	9.2	16.2
1975	86.6	67.1	100.8	66.6	30.2	2.16	65.5	-1.0	15.1
1976	90.7	70.3	97.4	72.2	54.4	2.57	82.7	3.0	14.7
1977	92.4	73.8	97.8	75.5	55.7	1.88	81.3	5.6	15.0
1978	92.7	77.9	100.0	77.9	60.5	0.48	69.3	0.3	15.6
1979	91.3	80.6	103.5	77.8	57.9	-1.75	52.8	10.9	16.0
1980	89.5	80.2	104.6	76.7	40.6	-1.90	56.8	11.8	15.2
1981	90.0	81.3	103.5	78.5	46.3	-2.47	65.0	8.3	14.0
1982	89.7	79.5	102.3	77.8	43.5	0.74	62.7	3.3	13.8
1983	94.6	80.9	98.5	82.1	56.8	2.02	84.7	-4.6	14.0
1984	96.3	86.2	102.0	84.6	57.3	2.21	92.7	3.6	14.8
1985	97.2	88.8	104.6	84.9	48.0	2.52	86.5	-2.6	16.2
1986	98.5	90.8	105.1	86.4	50.6	0.88	85.8	-3.8	17.2
1987	100.0	93.6	104.7	89.4	57.4	1.73	81.3	-0.9	17.0
1988	100.3	97.0	105.3	92.1	57.7	1.28	85.2	-0.2	16.8
1989	99.6	99.3	107.0	92.8	47.6	-0.72	85.3	1.1	16.9
1990	99.2	100.3	106.8	93.9	47.9	0.45	70.2	2.9	16.4
1991	99.1	98.8	104.2	94.8	47.3	2.17	70.3	-2.0	15.8
1992	100.0	100.0	100.0	100.0	50.2	3.49	70.3	0.4	14.8
1993	100.4	102.3	99.5	102.8	51.6	2.85	72.8	3.4	14.7
1994	101.3	105.9	100.4	105.6	60.1	2.88	83.8	-2.2	15.6
1995	100.8	109.3	104.0	105.1	52.8	0.74	83.2	-2.0	17.0
1996	102.1	112.5	105.1	107.1	50.5	1.14	85.7	-1.3	17.9
1997	103.9	116.7	105.6	110.6	53.9	0.89	97.7	-1.7	17.9
1998	105.5	120.9	107.2	112.8	51.1	-0.09	98.3	-0.6	17.8
1995:									
January	101.3	108.5	102.3	106.1	62.7	2.25	88.4	-4.0	16.3
February	101.0	108.6	102.8	105.6	60.7	1.55	85.9	-2.8	16.4
March	100.7	108.7	103.1	105.4	56.9	1.22	79.8	-3.4	16.6
April	100.5	108.7	103.6	104.9	56.3	1.01	83.8	-2.6	16.7
May	100.4	108.7	103.9	104.6	53.3	0.62	80.1	-2.6	16.9
June	100.5	109.1	104.4	104.5	51.8	0.17	84.1	-1.8	17.0
July	100.7	109.0	104.5	104.3	51.3	0.43	87.4	0.6	17.1
August	101.0	109.5	104.5	104.8	49.1	0.75	86.1	-1.8	17.2
September	101.0	109.8	104.7	104.9	50.0	0.40	78.8	-2.0	17.4
October	100.9	110.0	104.8	105.0	48.4	0.28	80.8	-2.4	17.4
November	100.9	110.4	104.8	105.3	45.3	0.13	79.7	-1.6	17.6
December	101.1	110.6	104.9	105.4	47.5	0.11	83.7	-1.8	17.6
1996:									
January	100.6	110.3	105.0	105.0	47.8	0.09	78.7	-5.0	17.7
February	101.4	111.1	104.9	105.9	49.5	0.59	77.8	-3.5	17.7
March	101.5	111.3	104.8	106.2	49.7	0.96	86.2	-3.7	17.7
April	101.8	111.7	104.9	106.5	49.4	1.29	83.0	-3.1	17.8
May	102.1	112.2	104.9	107.0	49.9	1.50	79.2	-4.1	17.9
June	102.3	112.6	104.9	107.3	52.7	1.64	84.0	-3.5	17.9
July	102.3	112.8	105.2	107.2	50.8	1.47	86.5	-2.5	18.0
August	102.4	113.2	105.2	107.6	51.9	1.42	87.3	-2.5	18.0
September	102.5	113.4	105.3	107.7	50.0	1.53	90.1	-1.3	18.0
October	102.5	113.6	105.2	108.0	50.9	1.29	89.9	-1.9	18.0
November	102.7	114.0	105.2	108.4	51.1	0.89	93.9	-1.5	18.0
December	102.6	114.2	105.3	108.5	52.1	1.01	91.8	-0.8	17.9
1997:									
January	102.9	114.6	105.3	108.8	49.6	1.33	91.3	-0.4	18.0
February	103.4	115.2	105.2	109.5	52.0	1.23	94.9	-1.3	17.9
March	103.4	115.5	105.3	109.7	53.2	1.30	93.6	-0.8	17.9
April	103.4	115.9	105.4	110.0	53.4	1.38	92.5	-1.3	17.9
May	103.6	116.1	105.6	109.9	54.8	1.21	96.6	-0.6	17.9
June	103.7	116.5	105.6	110.3	54.7	0.93	98.9	-1.7	17.9
July	104.1	117.0	105.3	111.1	54.7	0.70	102.6	-2.1	17.9
August	104.2	117.2	105.6	111.0	55.2	0.76	100.3	-1.1	17.9
September	104.4	117.6	105.6	111.4	55.0	0.67	100.7	-1.7	17.8
October	104.6	118.0	105.8	111.5	55.0	0.53	102.8	1.3	17.8
November	104.7	118.4	106.1	111.6	55.0	0.36	102.3	0.4	17.8
December	104.6	118.8	105.9	112.2	54.3	0.31	96.1	1.9	17.8
1998:									
January	104.8	119.2	106.2	112.2	52.9	-0.02	102.2	2.8	17.7
February	105.2	119.6	106.5	112.3	52.5	0.06	104.2	3.2	17.7
March	105.4	120.0	106.8	112.4	53.1	0.16	101.9	3.0	17.7
April	105.4	120.2	106.7	112.7	52.4	0.19	104.3	0.4	17.7
May	105.4	120.6	106.8	112.9	51.3	0.16	101.7	1.3	17.7
June	105.2	120.7	107.3	112.5	51.1	-0.06	99.3	0.4	17.8
July	105.6	120.8	107.4	112.5	50.3	-0.08	100.0	-0.4	17.8
August	105.6	121.4	107.7	112.7	50.2	-0.21	98.3	-2.3	17.8
September	105.6	121.6	107.9	112.7	51.0	-0.70	93.9	-0.6	17.8
October	105.7	121.9	108.0	112.9	50.1	-0.54	87.5	-0.9	17.9
November	106.2	122.4	107.8	113.5	50.0	0.00	94.3	-1.5	17.8
December	106.4	122.7	107.5	114.1	48.7	-0.03	91.9	-2.9	17.9

1. Not seasonally adjusted.
2. Copyright, University of Michigan, first quarter 1996=100.
3. Monthly data are six month percent change at annual rate; annual data are for the six month period ending in September.

Income Distribution and Proverty

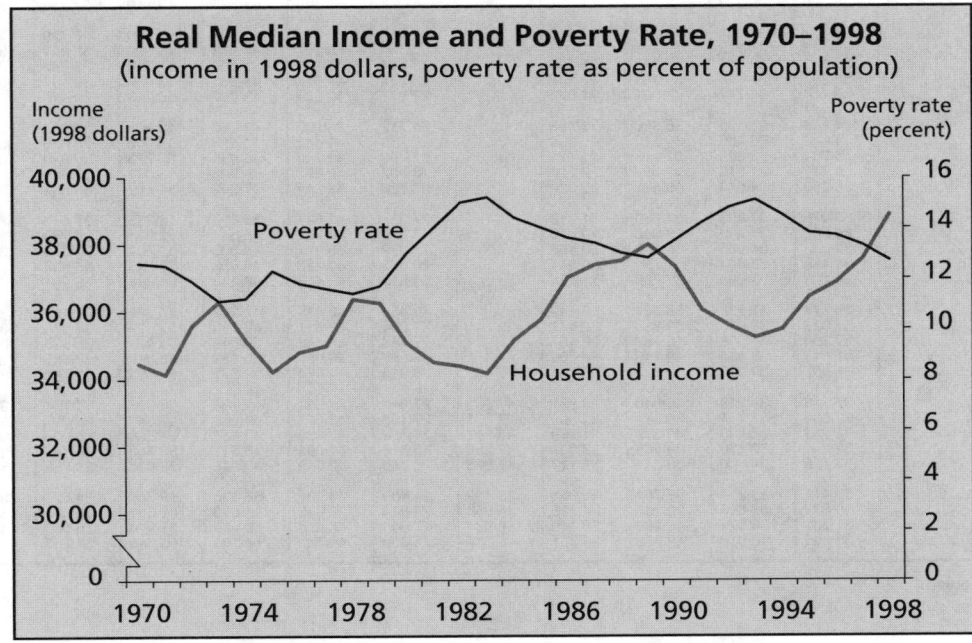

Real Median Income and Poverty Rate, 1970–1998
(income in 1998 dollars, poverty rate as percent of population)

- Real median household income in 1998 increased to an all-time high of $38,885. Median earnings of year-round full-time male workers increased to $35,345, the highest since 1989. Year-round, full-time female worker earnings rose to a record high of $25,862.

- The poverty rate in 1998 was at 12.7 percent, the lowest level since 1979. The rate for people in households with a female head declined to 33.1 percent, the lowest level in at least 39 years.

- Income inequality as measured by the Gini coefficient declined slightly in 1998, based on the official definition of income, but it remained near its 31-year high reached in 1997. Adjusted for taxes and transfer payments, inequality was lower than in the official definition but still increasing in 1998.

Median Income and Earnings

(1998 dollars)

Year	Median household income						Median family income						Median earnings of year-round, full-time workers	
	All races	White		Black	Asian and Pacific Islander	Hispanic	All families	Married couples			Male house-holder [1]	Female house-holder [1]	Male workers	Female workers
		Total	Not Hispanic					Total	Wife in workforce	Wife not in workforce				
1967	32 075	33 449	.....	19 421	.....	.....	35 622	37 903	44 706	34 176	30 597	19 282	32 250	18 635
1968	33 478	34 857	.....	20 554	.....	.....	37 321	39 535	46 202	35 518	31 653	19 357	33 136	19 271
1969	34 706	36 220	.....	21 893	.....	.....	39 025	41 375	48 110	36 733	34 503	19 949	34 978	20 590
1970	34 471	35 903	.....	21 853	.....	.....	38 942	41 504	48 450	36 720	35 568	20 101	35 387	21 008
1971	34 143	35 713	.....	21 095	.....	.....	38 897	41 563	48 609	36 851	32 986	19 341	35 546	21 152
1972	35 599	37 347	37 879	21 799	.....	28 184	40 809	43 698	51 018	38 753	37 831	19 611	37 453	21 671
1973	36 302	38 046	38 381	22 395	.....	28 124	41 617	44 991	52 619	39 431	37 096	20 019	38 629	21 878
1974	35 166	36 777	37 091	21 872	.....	27 971	40 521	43 727	50 945	38 413	36 614	20 377	37 257	21 891
1975	34 224	35 790	36 060	21 486	.....	25 712	39 790	43 120	49 993	36 985	37 690	19 850	37 003	21 764
1976	34 812	36 466	36 684	21 684	.....	26 258	41 046	44 463	51 400	38 228	35 289	19 788	36 922	22 225
1977	35 004	36 809	37 539	21 721	.....	27 460	41 289	45 434	52 273	38 849	37 444	20 027	37 723	22 227
1978	36 377	37 816	38 528	22 726	.....	28 502	42 597	46 703	53 389	39 014	38 555	20 615	37 985	22 578
1979	36 259	38 016	38 552	22 320	.....	28 728	43 144	47 202	54 761	39 001	37 023	21 763	37 477	22 360
1980	35 076	37 005	37 660	21 319	.....	27 037	41 637	45 832	53 235	37 575	34 697	20 614	36 862	22 176
1981	34 507	36 459	36 985	20 459	.....	27 679	40 502	45 345	52 911	36 770	35 981	19 828	36 652	21 711
1982	34 392	36 005	36 609	20 406	.....	25 879	39 954	44 363	51 734	36 315	35 937	19 580	35 937	22 189
1983	34 179	35 844	.....	20 341	.....	26 031	40 226	44 655	52 545	35 824	35 750	19 293	35 809	22 772
1984	35 165	37 098	37 868	21 134	.....	26 657	41 469	46 456	54 388	36 996	36 593	20 086	36 425	23 187
1985	35 778	37 732	38 581	22 449	.....	26 457	42 015	47 112	55 188	37 199	34 269	20 693	36 652	23 668
1986	37 027	38 928	39 813	22 427	.....	27 294	43 811	48 788	57 029	38 375	37 124	20 296	37 561	24 140
1987	37 394	39 398	40 482	22 487	.....	27 744	44 438	50 046	58 472	38 225	36 170	21 068	37 229	24 265
1988	37 512	39 656	40 749	22 606	44 459	28 052	44 354	50 139	58 847	37 505	36 964	21 145	36 728	24 258
1989	37 997	39 969	40 829	23 770	47 457	28 816	44 974	50 671	59 503	37 788	36 605	21 613	35 927	24 672
1990	37 343	38 949	39 840	23 291	47 952	27 848	44 090	49 754	58 337	37 744	36 224	21 116	34 518	24 720
1991	36 054	37 781	38 683	22 508	43 621	27 156	43 011	49 062	57 647	35 993	33 930	19 976	35 210	24 597
1992	35 593	37 420	38 676	21 789	43 917	26 253	42 490	48 668	57 828	35 056	32 038	19 780	35 083	24 834
1993	35 241	37 180	38 548	22 034	43 256	25 816	41 691	48 511	57 760	34 087	29 856	19 676	34 300	24 531
1994	35 486	37 426	38 634	23 127	44 525	25 760	42 655	49 449	58 633	34 289	30 522	20 057	33 935	24 423
1995	36 446	38 254	39 764	23 951	43 439	24 450	43 436	50 335	59 706	34 627	32 470	21 061	33 687	24 062
1996	36 872	38 606	40 295	24 395	44 958	25 874	43 945	51 640	60 651	35 060	32 829	20 685	33 394	24 632
1997	37 581	39 579	41 209	25 440	45 954	27 043	45 262	52 395	61 614	36 588	33 473	21 350	34 199	25 362
1998	38 885	40 912	42 439	25 351	46 637	28 330	46 737	54 180	63 368	35 665	35 681	22 163	35 345	25 862

1. No spouse present.

Shares of Aggregate Household Income by Race and Hispanic Origin

Year, race and Hispanic origin	Number of households (thousands)	Share of aggregate income (percent)						Mean household income (1998 dollars)						Gini coefficient
		Lowest fifth	Second fifth	Third fifth	Fourth fifth	Highest fifth	Top five percent	Lowest fifth	Second fifth	Third fifth	Fourth fifth	Highest fifth	Top five percent	
All races:														
1967	60 813	4.0	10.8	17.3	24.2	43.8	17.5	7 301	19 906	31 783	44 468	80 584	128 447	0.399
1968	62 214	4.2	11.1	17.5	24.4	42.8	16.6	7 921	20 935	33 201	46 319	81 120	125 592	0.388
1969	62 874	4.1	10.9	17.5	24.5	43.0	16.6	8 096	21 579	34 482	48 296	84 892	130 673	0.391
1970	64 374	4.1	10.8	17.4	24.5	43.3	16.6	8 008	21 293	34 289	48 336	85 581	131 359	0.394
1971	66 676	4.1	10.6	17.3	24.5	43.5	16.7	8 040	20 910	33 905	48 200	85 407	130 994	0.396
1972	68 251	4.1	10.5	17.1	24.5	43.9	17.0	8 502	21 653	35 335	50 725	91 067	141 146	0.401
1973	69 859	4.2	10.5	17.1	24.6	43.6	16.6	8 868	21 984	35 922	51 642	91 587	139 576	0.397
1974	71 163	4.4	10.6	17.1	24.7	43.1	15.9	9 142	21 900	35 194	50 819	88 752	130 868	0.395
1975	72 867	4.4	10.5	17.1	24.8	43.2	15.9	8 800	20 894	34 186	49 645	86 457	127 442	0.397
1976	74 142	4.4	10.4	17.1	24.8	43.3	16.0	8 995	21 349	35 020	50 824	88 690	131 182	0.398
1977	76 030	4.4	10.3	17.0	24.8	43.6	16.1	9 060	21 383	35 259	51 629	90 504	133 577	0.402
1978	77 330	4.3	10.3	16.9	24.8	43.7	16.2	9 193	22 004	36 246	53 078	93 673	139 154	0.402
1979	80 776	4.2	10.3	16.9	24.7	44.0	16.4	9 062	22 073	36 334	53 290	94 694	141 407	0.404
1980	82 368	4.3	10.3	16.9	24.9	43.7	15.8	8 879	21 428	35 268	51 928	91 211	131 939	0.403
1981	83 527	4.2	10.2	16.8	25.0	43.8	15.6	8 749	20 966	34 628	51 581	90 350	128 618	0.406
1982	83 918	4.1	10.1	16.6	24.7	44.5	16.2	8 530	20 866	34 433	51 195	92 351	134 603	0.412
1983	85 290	4.1	10.0	16.5	24.7	44.7	16.4	8 574	20 941	34 539	51 825	93 779	137 377	0.414
1984	86 789	4.1	9.9	16.4	24.7	44.9	16.5	8 795	21 389	35 372	53 252	96 714	142 180	0.415
1985	88 458	4.0	9.7	16.3	24.6	45.3	17.0	8 782	21 708	35 955	54 072	99 741	149 890	0.419
1986	89 479	3.9	9.7	16.2	24.5	45.7	17.5	8 840	22 250	37 149	55 952	104 611	159 794	0.425
1987	91 124	3.8	9.6	16.1	24.3	46.2	18.2	8 849	22 361	37 385	56 509	107 467	169 313	0.426
1988	92 830	3.8	9.6	16.0	24.3	46.3	18.3	8 962	22 482	37 603	56 842	108 518	171 150	0.427
1989	93 347	3.8	9.5	15.8	24.0	46.8	18.9	9 229	22 874	38 022	57 514	112 429	181 646	0.431
1990	94 312	3.9	9.6	15.9	24.0	46.6	18.6	8 973	22 486	37 141	55 997	108 671	173 047	0.428
1991	95 669	3.8	9.6	15.9	24.2	46.5	18.1	8 692	21 720	36 079	55 000	105 471	164 594	0.428
1992	96 426	3.8	9.4	15.8	24.2	46.9	18.6	8 467	21 123	35 587	54 629	105 851	168 005	0.434
1993	97 107	3.6	9.0	15.1	23.5	48.9	21.0	8 361	21 044	35 276	54 821	114 216	196 033	0.454
1994	98 990	3.6	8.9	15.0	23.4	49.1	21.2	8 537	21 144	35 619	55 428	116 525	201 324	0.456
1995	99 627	3.7	9.1	15.2	23.3	48.7	21.0	8 931	21 816	36 478	56 076	117 021	201 962	0.450
1996	101 018	3.7	9.0	15.1	23.3	49.0	21.4	8 930	21 917	36 866	57 057	120 005	209 043	0.455
1997	102 528	3.6	8.9	15.0	23.2	49.4	21.7	9 010	22 442	37 756	58 479	124 676	218 792	0.459
1998	103 874	3.6	9.0	15.0	23.2	49.2	21.4	9 223	23 288	38 967	60 266	127 529	222 283	0.456
White:														
1967	54 188	4.1	11.2	17.4	24.0	43.3	17.3	7 863	21 383	33 152	45 775	82 465	131 680	0.391
1968	55 394	4.4	11.4	17.6	24.3	42.3	16.5	8 552	22 427	34 602	47 620	83 104	129 263	0.381
1969	56 248	4.3	11.3	17.6	24.3	42.5	16.4	8 762	23 159	36 059	49 785	87 139	134 640	0.383
1970	57 575	4.2	11.1	17.5	24.3	42.9	16.5	8 643	22 717	35 714	49 725	87 633	134 887	0.387
1971	59 463	4.3	11.0	17.4	24.4	43.0	16.5	8 664	22 355	35 414	49 619	87 536	134 481	0.389
1972	60 618	4.3	10.8	17.2	24.3	43.4	16.8	9 193	23 275	37 053	52 303	93 541	145 041	0.393
1973	61 965	4.4	10.8	17.3	24.5	43.1	16.4	9 573	23 587	37 642	53 341	93 981	143 457	0.389
1974	62 984	4.6	11.0	17.2	24.6	42.6	15.7	9 893	23 439	36 783	52 414	90 928	133 826	0.387
1975	64 392	4.6	10.8	17.2	24.7	42.7	15.7	9 525	22 315	35 753	51 191	88 615	130 551	0.390
1976	65 353	4.6	10.7	17.3	24.7	42.8	15.9	9 728	22 828	36 700	52 454	91 052	134 887	0.391
1977	66 934	4.5	10.6	17.2	24.7	43.0	15.8	9 808	22 962	37 049	53 372	92 778	136 719	0.394
1978	68 028	4.5	10.6	17.1	24.6	43.2	16.1	10 012	23 494	37 961	54 705	95 977	142 655	0.394
1979	70 766	4.4	10.6	17.0	24.6	43.4	16.2	9 934	23 681	38 120	55 008	97 212	145 158	0.396
1980	71 872	4.5	10.6	17.1	24.7	43.1	15.5	9 798	23 074	37 070	53 697	93 502	134 912	0.394
1981	72 845	4.5	10.5	17.0	24.8	43.2	15.3	9 691	22 574	36 493	53 392	92 782	131 712	0.397
1982	73 182	4.4	10.4	16.8	24.6	43.9	15.9	9 429	22 474	36 163	53 062	94 809	137 452	0.403
1983	74 170	4.4	10.4	16.6	24.6	44.1	16.1	9 585	22 604	36 330	53 661	96 250	140 614	0.404
1984	75 328	4.3	10.3	16.6	24.6	44.2	16.2	9 745	23 071	37 241	55 127	99 235	145 641	0.405
1985	76 576	4.2	10.2	16.5	24.4	44.7	16.8	9 697	23 334	37 779	55 976	102 517	153 831	0.411
1986	77 284	4.1	10.1	16.4	24.3	45.1	17.2	9 878	23 986	39 111	57 966	107 394	163 999	0.415
1987	78 519	4.1	10.0	16.3	24.2	45.5	17.9	9 961	24 223	39 482	58 580	110 263	173 868	0.415
1988	79 734	4.1	10.0	16.2	24.1	45.6	18.0	10 069	24 365	39 659	58 838	111 470	176 010	0.416
1989	80 163	4.1	9.8	16.0	23.8	46.3	18.7	10 331	24 614	39 932	59 506	115 684	187 251	0.422
1990	80 968	4.2	10.0	16.0	23.9	46.0	18.3	10 081	24 166	38 878	57 940	111 614	178 027	0.419
1991	81 675	4.1	9.9	16.0	24.1	45.8	17.9	9 799	23 400	37 945	57 043	108 358	168 930	0.418
1992	81 795	4.1	9.7	15.9	24.1	46.2	18.4	9 557	22 897	37 583	56 811	109 006	173 077	0.423
1993	82 387	3.9	9.3	15.3	23.3	48.2	20.7	9 405	22 759	37 322	56 962	117 749	202 451	0.444
1994	83 737	3.8	9.2	15.1	23.2	48.6	21.1	9 498	22 714	37 482	57 535	120 483	209 307	0.448
1995	84 511	4.0	9.3	15.3	23.3	48.1	20.7	9 881	23 330	38 265	58 145	120 283	206 824	0.442
1996	85 059	3.9	9.2	15.2	23.2	48.4	21.1	9 890	23 456	38 751	59 110	123 288	214 277	0.446
1997	86 106	3.8	9.1	15.0	23.0	49.1	21.7	9 919	23 929	39 629	60 734	129 378	228 647	0.453
1998	87 212	3.8	9.2	15.1	23.1	48.8	21.5	10 262	24 921	41 031	62 469	132 350	232 849	0.450

Note: An updating of survey methodology affected the reported income of higher income households and the Gini coefficient beginning in 1993. The increases in both would have been less sharp without this change. See Notes for explanation of the Gini coefficient.

Shares of Aggregate Household Income by Race and Hispanic Origin—*Continued*

Year, race and Hispanic origin	Number of households (thousands)	Share of aggregate income (percent)						Mean household income (1998 dollars)						Gini coefficient
		Lowest fifth	Second fifth	Third fifth	Fourth fifth	Highest fifth	Top five percent	Lowest fifth	Second fifth	Third fifth	Fourth fifth	Highest fifth	Top five percent	
Black:														
1967	5 728	3.8	9.3	15.9	24.3	46.7	18.2	4 567	11 248	19 282	29 470	56 614	88 128	0.432
1968	5 870	4.0	9.8	16.3	25.1	44.9	15.9	4 981	12 236	20 373	31 450	56 146	79 736	0.412
1969	6 053	3.9	9.7	16.5	25.1	44.7	15.9	5 084	12 626	21 442	32 592	57 886	82 547	0.411
1970	6 180	3.7	9.3	16.3	25.2	45.5	16.4	4 949	12 468	21 687	33 610	60 720	87 578	0.422
1971	6 578	4.0	9.4	16.1	25.1	45.4	16.4	5 215	12 219	21 099	32 812	59 406	85 668	0.419
1972	6 809	3.9	9.2	15.8	24.9	46.2	16.9	5 408	12 621	21 737	34 307	63 629	92 796	0.427
1973	7 040	4.1	9.4	16.0	25.1	45.5	16.6	5 684	13 064	22 202	34 862	63 242	92 319	0.419
1974	7 263	4.2	9.4	16.2	25.2	45.0	15.7	5 694	12 823	21 975	34 258	61 262	85 124	0.414
1975	7 489	4.2	9.1	16.0	25.5	45.3	15.9	5 569	12 150	21 451	34 195	60 748	85 062	0.419
1976	7 776	4.3	9.2	15.8	25.5	45.2	15.7	5 903	12 716	21 909	35 402	62 686	87 161	0.421
1977	7 977	4.2	9.2	15.5	24.9	46.3	16.7	5 803	12 756	21 572	34 648	64 388	92 714	0.425
1978	8 066	4.0	8.7	15.6	25.3	46.4	16.3	5 735	12 695	22 719	36 778	67 318	94 914	0.431
1979	8 586	3.9	8.8	15.5	25.4	46.3	16.1	5 511	12 668	22 261	36 437	66 356	92 417	0.433
1980	8 847	3.7	8.7	15.4	25.3	46.9	16.6	5 165	12 018	21 271	34 991	64 923	91 912	0.439
1981	8 961	3.8	8.6	15.3	25.4	46.9	16.1	5 076	11 549	20 553	34 161	63 098	86 450	0.440
1982	8 916	3.6	8.6	15.3	25.5	47.0	16.9	4 830	11 528	20 598	34 266	63 033	90 886	0.442
1983	9 243	3.6	8.3	15.2	25.2	47.8	16.9	4 829	11 333	20 612	34 232	64 951	91 753	0.448
1984	9 480	3.6	8.4	15.0	24.7	48.3	17.4	5 078	11 865	21 118	34 873	68 022	98 095	0.450
1985	9 797	3.5	8.3	15.2	25.0	48.0	17.5	5 149	12 222	22 225	36 564	70 308	102 752	0.450
1986	9 922	3.2	8.0	15.0	25.1	48.8	18.2	4 738	12 063	22 542	37 722	73 411	109 713	0.464
1987	10 192	3.3	7.9	14.8	24.4	49.7	19.3	4 927	11 928	22 454	37 015	75 494	116 878	0.468
1988	10 561	3.3	7.7	14.6	24.7	49.7	18.7	5 109	11 991	22 577	38 240	77 021	116 000	0.468
1989	10 486	3.2	8.0	15.0	24.9	48.9	18.2	4 986	12 614	23 711	39 279	77 129	114 727	0.461
1990	10 671	3.1	7.9	15.0	25.1	49.0	18.5	4 791	12 170	23 259	38 776	75 757	114 613	0.464
1991	11 083	3.1	7.8	15.0	25.2	48.9	18.3	4 627	11 756	22 522	37 720	73 258	109 972	0.464
1992	11 269	3.1	7.8	14.7	24.8	49.7	19.1	4 555	11 503	21 735	36 622	73 442	113 197	0.470
1993	11 281	3.0	7.7	14.3	23.7	51.3	21.1	4 655	11 747	21 975	36 401	78 807	129 297	0.484
1994	11 655	3.0	7.9	14.3	24.3	50.5	20.1	4 891	12 632	23 084	39 091	81 236	129 160	0.477
1995	11 577	3.2	8.2	14.8	24.2	49.6	20.2	5 149	13 341	24 111	39 263	80 709	131 082	0.468
1996	12 109	3.1	8.0	14.5	23.7	50.7	21.7	5 245	13 503	24 364	39 964	85 533	146 456	0.479
1997	12 474	3.2	8.5	15.1	24.5	48.7	19.1	5 344	14 202	25 323	41 050	81 476	127 863	0.458
1998	12 579	3.1	8.2	14.8	24.4	49.5	19.1	5 194	14 036	25 262	41 670	84 533	130 383	0.466
Hispanic:														
1972	2 655	5.3	11.2	17.2	24.0	42.3	16.2	8 440	17 945	27 637	38 573	67 917	103 795	0.373
1973	2 722	5.1	11.1	17.1	24.7	42.0	15.0	8 440	18 389	28 207	40 791	69 247	99 074	0.371
1974	2 897	5.2	10.9	17.2	24.7	42.0	15.1	8 351	17 666	27 829	40 065	68 130	97 904	0.376
1975	2 948	4.8	10.7	16.9	24.9	42.9	15.8	7 265	16 268	25 729	37 986	65 458	96 475	0.388
1976	3 081	4.7	10.5	16.9	25.1	42.8	15.2	7 357	16 218	26 157	39 002	66 451	94 556	0.387
1977	3 304	4.9	10.8	16.9	24.7	42.8	15.4	7 931	17 435	27 354	39 956	69 386	100 054	0.383
1978	3 291	4.7	10.7	16.9	24.9	42.8	15.4	7 906	18 046	28 420	41 989	72 007	103 651	0.385
1979	3 684	4.6	10.5	16.6	24.6	43.7	15.9	7 958	18 315	28 897	42 750	75 956	110 274	0.396
1980	3 906	4.4	10.2	16.4	24.9	44.1	16.0	7 231	16 851	27 130	41 065	72 924	105 374	0.405
1981	3 980	4.5	10.3	16.7	24.8	43.6	15.3	7 515	17 165	27 829	41 309	72 476	101 791	0.398
1982	4 085	4.2	9.6	16.2	24.7	45.3	16.7	6 725	15 401	25 814	39 422	72 385	106 516	0.417
1983	4 666	4.2	9.7	16.3	24.9	44.9	16.0	6 638	15 343	25 875	39 343	71 139	101 121	0.413
1984	4 883	3.9	9.5	16.2	25.0	45.3	16.6	6 522	15 818	26 886	41 385	75 162	110 084	0.420
1985	5 213	4.1	9.5	16.1	24.8	45.6	16.5	6 829	15 638	26 569	40 958	75 315	108 856	0.418
1986	5 418	4.0	9.5	15.9	24.8	45.8	16.5	6 810	16 370	27 352	42 819	79 021	113 755	0.424
1987	5 642	3.7	9.1	15.5	24.1	47.6	19.2	6 609	16 257	27 478	42 786	84 730	136 673	0.441
1988	5 910	3.7	9.3	15.6	24.2	47.2	19.0	6 572	16 716	27 980	43 265	84 573	135 888	0.437
1989	5 933	3.8	9.5	15.7	24.4	46.6	18.1	6 937	17 562	28 977	44 906	85 699	133 568	0.430
1990	6 220	4.0	9.5	15.9	24.3	46.3	17.9	7 038	16 515	27 785	42 305	80 810	124 982	0.425
1991	6 379	4.0	9.4	15.8	24.3	46.5	17.7	6 885	16 302	27 255	41 954	80 399	122 591	0.427
1992	7 153	4.0	9.4	15.7	24.1	46.9	18.1	6 611	15 753	26 240	40 381	78 460	120 939	0.430
1993	7 362	3.9	9.1	15.1	23.1	48.7	20.4	6 684	15 556	25 835	39 526	83 289	139 604	0.447
1994	7 735	3.7	8.7	14.8	23.3	49.6	21.0	6 398	15 111	25 717	40 382	86 111	145 976	0.459
1995	7 939	3.8	8.9	14.8	23.3	49.3	20.8	6 291	14 872	24 634	38 796	82 265	138 953	0.455
1996	8 225	3.8	9.0	14.7	23.1	49.5	21.5	6 725	15 805	25 881	40 770	87 453	151 617	0.457
1997	8 590	3.6	8.9	14.9	23.1	49.5	21.5	6 612	16 291	27 074	42 032	90 221	156 682	0.458
1998	9 060	3.6	8.9	14.8	22.9	49.7	21.9	6 891	17 124	28 346	43 841	95 200	167 944	0.460

Note: An updating of survey methodology affected the reported income of higher income households and the Gini coefficient beginning in 1993. The increases in both would have been less sharp without this change. See Notes for explanation of the Gini coefficient.

Average Poverty Thresholds by Family Size

(Dollars)

Year	Unrelated individuals			Families of 2 persons			Families, all ages								CPI-U, all items (1982–1984 = 100)
	All ages	Under age 65	Age 65 and older	All ages	Householder under age 65	Householder age 65 and older	3 persons	4 persons	5 persons	6 persons	7 persons or more (before 1980)	7 persons	8 persons	9 persons or more	
1959	1 467	1 503	1 397	1 894	1 952	1 761	2 324	2 973	3 506	3 944	4 849	.....	.....	.....	29.2
1960	1 490	1 526	1 418	1 924	1 982	1 788	2 359	3 022	3 560	4 002	4 921	.....	.....	.....	29.6
1961	1 506	1 545	1 433	1 942	2 005	1 808	2 383	3 054	3 597	4 041	4 967	.....	.....	.....	29.9
1962	1 519	1 562	1 451	1 962	2 027	1 828	2 412	3 089	3 639	4 088	5 032	.....	.....	.....	30.3
1963	1 539	1 581	1 470	1 988	2 052	1 850	2 442	3 128	3 685	4 135	5 092	.....	.....	.....	30.6
1964	1 558	1 601	1 488	2 015	2 079	1 875	2 473	3 169	3 732	4 193	5 156	.....	.....	.....	31.0
1965	1 582	1 626	1 512	2 048	2 114	1 906	2 514	3 223	3 797	4 264	5 248	.....	.....	.....	31.5
1966	1 628	1 674	1 556	2 107	2 175	1 961	2 588	3 317	3 908	4 388	5 395	.....	.....	.....	32.5
1967	1 675	1 722	1 600	2 168	2 238	2 017	2 661	3 410	4 019	4 516	5 550	.....	.....	.....	33.4
1968	1 748	1 797	1 667	2 262	2 333	2 102	2 774	3 553	4 188	4 706	5 789	.....	.....	.....	34.8
1969	1 840	1 893	1 757	2 383	2 458	2 215	2 924	3 743	4 415	4 958	6 101	.....	.....	.....	36.7
1970	1 954	2 010	1 861	2 525	2 604	2 348	3 099	3 968	4 680	5 260	6 468	.....	.....	.....	38.8
1971	2 040	2 098	1 940	2 633	2 716	2 448	3 229	4 137	4 880	5 489	6 751	.....	.....	.....	40.5
1972	2 109	2 168	2 005	2 724	2 808	2 530	3 339	4 275	5 044	5 673	6 983	.....	.....	.....	41.8
1973	2 247	2 307	2 130	2 895	2 984	2 688	3 548	4 540	5 358	6 028	7 435	.....	.....	.....	44.4
1974	2 495	2 562	2 364	3 211	3 312	2 982	3 936	5 038	5 950	6 699	8 253	.....	.....	.....	49.3
1975	2 724	2 797	2 581	3 506	3 617	3 257	4 293	5 500	6 499	7 316	9 022	.....	.....	.....	53.8
1976	2 884	2 959	2 730	3 711	3 826	3 445	4 540	5 815	6 876	7 760	9 588	.....	.....	.....	56.9
1977	3 075	3 152	2 906	3 951	4 072	3 666	4 833	6 191	7 320	8 261	10 216	.....	.....	.....	60.6
1978	3 311	3 392	3 127	4 249	4 383	3 944	5 201	6 662	7 880	8 891	11 002	.....	.....	.....	65.2
1979	3 689	3 778	3 479	4 725	4 878	4 390	5 784	7 412	8 775	9 914	12 280	.....	.....	.....	72.6
1980	4 190	4 290	3 949	5 363	5 537	4 983	6 565	8 414	9 966	11 269	13 955	12 761	14 199	16 896	82.4
1981	4 620	4 729	4 359	5 917	6 111	5 498	7 250	9 287	11 007	12 449	.....	14 110	15 655	18 572	90.9
1982	4 901	5 019	4 626	6 281	6 487	5 836	7 693	9 862	11 684	13 207	.....	15 036	16 719	19 698	96.5
1983	5 061	5 180	4 775	6 483	6 697	6 023	7 938	10 178	12 049	13 630	.....	15 500	17 170	20 310	99.6
1984	5 278	5 400	4 979	6 762	6 983	6 282	8 277	10 609	12 566	14 207	.....	16 096	17 961	21 247	103.9
1985	5 469	5 593	5 156	6 998	7 231	6 503	8 573	10 989	13 007	14 696	.....	16 656	18 512	22 083	107.6
1986	5 572	5 701	5 255	7 138	7 372	6 630	8 737	11 203	13 259	14 986	.....	17 049	18 791	22 497	109.6
1987	5 778	5 909	5 447	7 397	7 641	6 872	9 056	11 611	13 737	15 509	.....	17 649	19 515	23 105	113.6
1988	6 022	6 155	5 674	7 704	7 958	7 157	9 435	12 092	14 304	16 146	.....	18 232	20 253	24 129	118.3
1989	6 310	6 451	5 947	8 076	8 343	7 501	9 885	12 674	14 990	16 921	.....	19 162	21 328	25 480	124.0
1990	6 652	6 800	6 268	8 509	8 794	7 905	10 419	13 359	15 792	17 839	.....	20 241	22 582	26 848	130.7
1991	6 932	7 086	6 532	8 865	9 165	8 241	10 860	13 924	16 456	18 587	.....	21 058	23 582	27 942	136.2
1992	7 143	7 299	6 729	9 137	9 443	8 487	11 186	14 335	16 952	19 137	.....	21 594	24 053	28 745	140.3
1993	7 363	7 518	6 930	9 414	9 728	8 740	11 522	14 763	17 449	19 718	.....	22 383	24 838	29 529	144.5
1994	7 547	7 710	7 108	9 661	9 976	8 967	11 821	15 141	17 900	20 235	.....	22 923	25 427	30 300	148.2
1995	7 763	7 929	7 309	9 933	10 259	9 219	12 158	15 569	18 408	20 804	.....	23 552	26 237	31 280	152.4
1996	7 995	8 163	7 525	10 233	10 564	9 491	12 516	16 036	18 952	21 389	.....	24 268	27 091	31 971	156.9
1997	8 183	8 350	7 698	10 473	10 805	9 712	12 802	16 400	19 380	21 886	.....	24 802	27 593	32 566	160.5
1998	8 316	8 480	7 818	10 634	10 972	9 862	13 003	16 660	19 680	22 228		25 257	28 166	33 339	163.0

Poverty Status of Persons by Family Relationship, Race, and Hispanic Origin

(Thousands)

Year, race, and Hispanic origin	All persons Total	Below poverty level Number	Below poverty level Percent	Married couple families [1] Total	Below poverty level Number	Below poverty level Percent	Female householder, no spouse present Total	Below poverty level Number	Below poverty level Percent	Unrelated individuals Total	Below poverty level Number	Below poverty level Percent
All races:												
1959	176 557	39 490	22.4	39 335	.....	.....	.....	7 014	49.4	10 699	4 928	46.1
1960	179 503	39 851	22.2	39 624	.....	.....	.....	7 247	48.9	10 888	4 926	45.2
1961	181 277	39 628	21.9	40 405	.....	.....	.....	7 252	48.1	11 146	5 119	45.9
1962	184 276	38 625	21.0	40 923	.....	.....	.....	7 781	50.3	11 013	5 002	45.4
1963	187 258	36 436	19.5	41 311	.....	.....	.....	7 646	47.7	11 182	4 938	44.2
1964	189 710	36 055	19.0	41 648	.....	.....	.....	7 297	44.4	12 057	5 143	42.7
1965	191 413	33 185	17.3	42 107	.....	.....	16 371	7 524	46.0	12 132	4 827	39.8
1966	193 388	28 510	14.7	42 553	.....	.....	17 240	6 861	39.8	12 271	4 701	38.3
1967	195 672	27 769	14.2	43 292	.....	.....	17 788	6 898	38.8	13 114	4 998	38.1
1968	197 628	25 389	12.8	43 842	.....	.....	18 048	6 990	38.7	13 803	4 694	34.0
1969	199 517	24 147	12.1	44 436	.....	.....	17 995	6 879	38.2	14 626	4 972	34.0
1970	202 183	25 420	12.6	44 739	.....	.....	19 673	7 503	38.1	15 491	5 090	32.9
1971	204 554	25 559	12.5	45 752	.....	.....	20 153	7 797	38.7	16 311	5 154	31.6
1972	206 004	24 460	11.9	46 314	.....	.....	21 264	8 114	38.2	16 811	4 883	29.0
1973	207 621	22 973	11.1	46 812	2 482	5.3	21 823	8 178	37.5	18 260	4 674	25.6
1974	209 362	23 370	11.2	47 069	2 474	5.3	23 165	8 462	36.5	18 926	4 553	24.1
1975	210 864	25 877	12.3	47 318	2 904	6.1	23 580	8 846	37.5	20 234	5 088	25.1
1976	212 303	24 975	11.8	47 497	2 606	5.5	24 204	9 029	37.3	21 459	5 344	24.9
1977	213 867	24 720	11.6	47 385	2 524	5.3	25 404	9 205	36.2	23 110	5 216	22.6
1978	215 656	24 497	11.4	47 692	2 474	5.2	26 032	9 269	35.6	24 585	5 435	22.1
1979	222 903	26 072	11.7	49 112	2 640	5.4	26 927	9 400	34.9	26 170	5 743	21.9
1980	225 027	29 272	13.0	49 294	3 032	6.2	27 565	10 120	36.7	27 133	6 227	22.9
1981	227 157	31 822	14.0	49 630	3 394	6.8	28 587	11 051	38.7	27 714	6 490	23.4
1982	229 412	34 398	15.0	49 908	3 789	7.6	28 834	11 701	40.6	27 908	6 458	23.1
1983	231 700	35 303	15.2	50 081	3 815	7.6	30 049	12 072	40.2	29 158	6 740	23.1
1984	233 816	33 700	14.4	50 350	3 488	6.9	30 844	11 831	38.4	30 268	6 609	21.8
1985	236 594	33 064	14.0	50 933	3 438	6.7	30 878	11 600	37.6	31 351	6 725	21.5
1986	238 554	32 370	13.6	51 537	3 123	6.1	31 152	11 944	38.3	31 679	6 846	21.6
1987	240 982	32 221	13.4	51 675	3 011	5.8	31 893	12 148	38.1	32 992	6 857	20.8
1988	243 530	31 745	13.0	52 100	2 897	5.6	32 164	11 972	37.2	34 340	7 070	20.6
1989	245 992	31 528	12.8	52 137	2 931	5.6	32 525	11 668	35.9	35 185	6 760	19.2
1990	248 644	33 585	13.5	52 147	2 981	5.7	33 795	12 578	37.2	36 056	7 446	20.7
1991	251 179	35 708	14.2	52 457	3 158	6.0	34 790	13 824	39.7	36 839	7 773	21.1
1992	256 549	38 014	14.8	53 090	3 385	6.4	36 446	14 205	39.0	36 842	8 075	21.9
1993	259 278	39 265	15.1	53 181	3 481	6.5	37 861	14 636	38.7	38 038	8 388	22.1
1994	261 616	38 059	14.5	53 865	3 272	6.1	37 253	14 380	38.6	38 538	8 287	21.5
1995	263 733	36 425	13.8	53 570	2 982	5.6	38 908	14 205	36.5	39 484	8 247	20.9
1996	266 218	36 529	13.7	53 604	3 010	5.6	38 584	13 796	35.8	40 727	8 452	20.8
1997	268 480	35 574	13.3	54 321	2 821	5.2	38 412	13 494	35.1	41 672	8 687	20.8
1998	271 059	34 476	12.7	54 778	2 879	5.3	39 000	12 907	33.1	42 539	8 478	19.9
White:												
1959	156 956	28 484	18.1	36 217	.....	.....	.....	4 232	40.2	9 154	4 041	44.1
1960	158 863	28 309	17.8	36 400	.....	.....	.....	4 296	39.0	9 405	4 047	43.0
1961	160 306	27 890	17.4	37 185	.....	.....	.....	4 062	37.6	9 589	4 143	43.2
1962	162 842	26 672	16.4	37 657	.....	.....	.....	4 089	37.9	9 494	4 059	42.7
1963	165 309	25 238	15.3	37 799	.....	.....	.....	4 051	35.6	9 725	4 089	42.0
1964	167 313	24 957	14.9	38 171	.....	.....	.....	3 911	33.4	10 415	4 241	40.7
1965	168 732	22 496	13.3	38 632	.....	.....	11 573	4 092	35.4	10 477	3 988	38.1
1966	170 247	19 290	11.3	39 007	.....	.....	12 261	3 646	29.7	10 686	3 860	36.1
1967	172 038	18 983	11.0	39 821	.....	.....	12 131	3 453	28.5	11 318	4 132	36.5
1968	173 732	17 395	10.0	40 355	.....	.....	12 190	3 551	29.1	11 955	3 849	32.2
1969	175 349	16 659	9.5	40 802	.....	.....	12 285	3 577	29.1	12 570	4 036	32.1
1970	177 376	17 484	9.9	41 092	.....	.....	13 226	3 761	28.4	13 500	4 161	30.8
1971	179 398	17 780	9.9	42 039	.....	.....	13 502	4 099	30.4	14 214	4 214	29.6
1972	180 125	16 203	9.0	42 585	.....	.....	13 739	3 770	27.4	14 495	3 935	27.1
1973	181 185	15 142	8.4	43 805	2 306	5.3	14 303	4 003	28.0	15 761	3 730	23.7
1974	182 376	15 736	8.6	43 049	1 977	4.6	15 433	4 278	27.7	16 295	3 555	21.8
1975	183 164	17 770	9.7	43 311	2 363	5.5	15 577	4 577	29.4	17 503	3 972	22.7
1976	184 165	16 713	9.1	43 397	2 071	4.8	15 941	4 463	28.0	18 594	4 213	22.7
1977	185 254	16 416	8.9	43 423	2 028	4.7	16 721	4 474	26.8	19 869	4 051	20.4
1978	186 450	16 259	8.7	43 636	2 033	4.7	16 877	4 371	25.9	21 257	4 209	19.8
1979	191 742	17 214	9.0	44 751	2 099	4.7	17 349	4 375	25.2	22 587	4 452	19.7
1980	192 912	19 699	10.2	44 860	2 437	5.4	17 642	4 940	28.0	23 370	4 760	20.4
1981	194 504	21 553	11.1	45 007	2 712	6.0	18 795	5 600	29.8	23 913	5 061	21.2
1982	195 919	23 517	12.0	45 252	3 104	6.9	18 374	5 686	30.9	24 300	5 041	20.7
1983	197 496	23 984	12.1	45 470	3 125	6.9	19 256	6 017	31.2	25 206	5 189	20.6
1984	198 941	22 955	11.5	45 643	2 858	6.3	19 727	5 866	29.7	26 094	5 181	19.9
1985	200 918	22 860	11.4	45 924	2 815	6.1	20 105	5 990	29.8	27 067	5 299	19.6
1986	202 282	22 183	11.0	46 410	2 591	5.6	20 163	6 171	30.6	27 143	5 198	19.2
1987	203 605	21 195	10.4	46 510	2 382	5.1	20 244	5 989	29.6	28 290	5 174	18.3
1988	205 235	20 715	10.1	46 877	2 294	4.9	20 396	5 950	29.2	29 315	5 314	18.1
1989	206 853	20 785	10.0	46 981	2 329	5.0	20 362	5 723	28.1	29 993	5 063	16.9
1990	208 611	22 326	10.7	47 014	2 386	5.1	20 845	6 210	29.8	30 833	5 739	18.6
1991	210 121	23 747	11.3	47 124	2 573	5.5	21 604	6 806	31.5	31 201	5 872	18.8
1992	213 060	25 259	11.9	47 383	2 677	5.7	22 453	6 907	30.8	31 170	6 147	19.7
1993	214 899	26 226	12.2	47 452	2 757	5.8	23 224	7 199	31.0	32 112	6 443	20.1
1994	216 460	25 379	11.7	47 905	2 629	5.5	22 713	7 228	31.8	32 569	6 292	19.3
1995	218 028	24 423	11.2	47 877	2 443	5.1	23 732	7 047	29.7	33 399	6 336	19.0
1996	219 656	24 650	11.2	47 650	2 416	5.1	23 744	7 073	29.8	34 274	6 463	18.9
1997	221 200	24 396	11.0	48 070	2 312	4.8	23 773	7 296	30.7	34 858	6 593	18.9
1998	222 837	23 454	10.5	48 461	2 400	5.0	24 211	6 674	27.6	35 563	6 386	18.0

1. These numbers and rates refer to families rather than persons; data on persons were not available.

Poverty Status of Persons by Family Relationship, Race, and Hispanic Origin—*Continued*

(Thousands)

Year, race, and Hispanic origin	All persons			Married couple families [1]			Female householder, no spouse present			Unrelated individuals		
	Total	Below poverty level		Total	Below poverty level		Total	Below poverty level		Total	Below poverty level	
		Number	Percent		Number	Percent		Number	Percent		Number	Percent
Black:												
1959	18 013	9 927	55.1	.....	.....	.....	.....	2 416	70.6	1 430	815	57.0
1966	21 206	8 867	41.8	.....	.....	.....	.....	3 160	65.3	.....	777	54.4
1967	21 590	8 486	39.3	3 118	.....	.....	.....	3 362	61.6	.....	809	49.3
1968	21 944	7 616	34.7	3 141	.....	.....	.....	3 312	58.9	.....	777	46.3
1969	22 011	7 095	32.2	3 323	.....	.....	5 537	3 225	58.2	1 819	850	46.7
1970	22 515	7 548	33.5	3 301	.....	.....	6 225	3 656	58.7	1 791	865	48.3
1971	22 784	7 396	32.5	3 289	.....	.....	6 398	3 587	56.1	1 884	866	46.0
1972	23 144	7 710	33.3	3 233	.....	.....	7 125	4 139	58.1	2 028	870	42.9
1973	23 512	7 388	31.4	3 360	.....	.....	7 188	4 064	56.5	2 183	828	37.9
1974	23 699	7 182	30.3	3 357	435	13.0	7 483	4 116	55.0	2 359	927	39.3
1975	24 089	7 545	31.3	3 352	479	14.3	7 679	4 168	54.3	2 402	1 011	42.1
1976	24 399	7 595	31.1	3 406	450	13.2	7 926	4 415	55.7	2 559	1 019	39.8
1977	24 710	7 726	31.3	3 260	429	13.1	8 315	4 595	55.3	2 860	1 059	37.0
1978	24 956	7 625	30.6	3 244	366	11.3	8 689	4 712	54.2	2 929	1 132	38.6
1979	25 944	8 050	31.0	3 433	453	13.2	9 065	4 816	53.1	3 127	1 168	37.3
1980	26 408	8 579	32.5	3 392	474	14.0	9 338	4 984	53.4	3 208	1 314	41.0
1981	26 834	9 173	34.2	3 535	543	15.4	9 214	5 222	56.7	3 277	1 296	39.6
1982	27 216	9 697	35.6	3 486	543	15.6	9 699	5 698	58.8	3 051	1 229	40.3
1983	27 678	9 882	35.7	3 454	535	15.5	10 059	5 736	57.0	3 287	1 338	40.7
1984	28 087	9 490	33.8	3 469	479	13.8	10 384	5 666	54.6	3 501	1 255	35.8
1985	28 485	8 926	31.3	3 680	447	12.2	10 041	5 342	53.2	3 641	1 264	34.7
1986	28 871	8 983	31.1	3 742	403	10.8	10 175	5 473	53.8	3 714	1 431	38.5
1987	29 362	9 520	32.4	3 681	439	11.9	10 701	5 789	54.1	3 977	1 471	37.0
1988	29 849	9 356	31.3	3 722	421	11.3	10 794	5 601	51.9	4 095	1 509	36.8
1989	30 332	9 302	30.7	3 750	443	11.8	11 190	5 530	49.4	4 180	1 471	35.2
1990	30 806	9 837	31.9	3 569	448	12.6	11 866	6 005	50.6	4 244	1 491	35.1
1991	31 312	10 242	32.7	3 631	399	11.0	11 959	6 557	54.8	4 505	1 590	35.3
1992	32 411	10 827	33.4	3 777	490	13.0	12 591	6 799	54.0	4 410	1 569	35.6
1993	32 910	10 877	33.1	3 715	458	12.3	13 132	6 955	53.0	4 608	1 541	33.4
1994	33 353	10 196	30.6	3 842	336	8.7	12 926	6 489	50.2	4 649	1 617	34.8
1995	33 740	9 872	29.3	3 713	314	8.5	13 604	6 553	48.2	4 756	1 551	32.6
1996	34 110	9 694	28.4	3 851	352	9.1	13 193	6 123	46.4	4 989	1 606	32.2
1997	34 458	9 116	26.5	3 921	312	8.0	13 218	5 654	42.8	5 316	1 645	31.0
1998	34 877	9 091	26.1	3 979	290	7.3	13 156	5 629	42.8	5 390	1 752	32.5
Hispanic:												
1973	10 795	2 366	21.9	1 876	239	12.7	1 534	881	57.4	526	157	29.9
1974	11 201	2 575	23.0	1 926	278	14.4	1 723	915	53.1	617	201	32.6
1975	11 117	2 991	26.9	1 896	335	17.7	1 842	1 053	57.2	645	236	36.6
1976	11 269	2 783	24.7	1 978	312	15.8	1 766	1 000	56.6	716	266	37.2
1977	12 046	2 700	22.4	2 104	280	13.3	1 901	1 077	56.7	797	237	29.8
1978	12 079	2 607	21.6	2 089	248	11.9	1 817	1 024	56.4	886	264	29.8
1979	13 371	2 921	21.8	2 282	298	13.1	2 058	1 053	51.2	991	286	28.8
1980	13 600	3 491	25.7	2 365	363	15.3	2 421	1 319	54.5	970	312	32.2
1981	14 021	3 713	26.5	2 414	366	15.1	2 622	1 465	55.9	1 005	313	31.1
1982	14 385	4 301	29.9	2 448	465	19.0	2 664	1 601	60.1	1 018	358	35.1
1983	16 544	4 633	28.0	2 752	437	17.7	3 032	1 670	55.1	1 364	457	33.5
1984	16 916	4 806	28.4	2 824	469	16.6	3 139	1 764	56.2	1 481	545	36.8
1985	18 075	5 236	29.0	2 962	505	17.0	3 561	1 983	55.7	1 602	532	33.2
1986	18 758	5 117	27.3	3 118	518	16.6	3 631	1 921	52.9	1 685	553	32.8
1987	19 395	5 422	28.0	3 196	556	17.4	3 678	2 045	55.6	1 933	598	31.0
1988	20 064	5 357	26.7	3 398	547	16.1	3 734	2 052	55.0	1 864	597	32.0
1989	20 746	5 430	26.2	3 395	549	16.2	3 763	1 902	50.6	2 045	634	31.0
1990	21 405	6 006	28.1	3 454	605	17.5	3 993	2 115	53.0	2 254	774	34.3
1991	22 068	6 339	28.7	3 532	674	19.1	4 326	2 282	52.7	2 145	667	31.1
1992	25 646	7 592	29.6	3 940	743	18.8	4 806	2 474	51.5	2 577	881	34.2
1993	26 559	8 126	30.6	4 038	770	19.1	5 333	2 837	53.2	2 717	972	35.8
1994	27 442	8 416	30.7	4 236	827	19.5	5 328	2 920	54.8	2 798	926	33.1
1995	28 344	8 574	30.3	4 247	803	18.9	5 785	3 053	52.8	2 947	1 092	37.0
1996	29 614	8 697	29.4	4 520	815	18.0	5 641	3 020	53.5	2 985	1 066	35.7
1997	30 637	8 308	27.1	4 804	836	17.4	5 718	2 911	50.9	2 976	1 017	34.2
1998	31 515	8 070	25.6	4 945	775	15.7	6 074	2 837	46.7	3 218	1 097	34.1

1. These numbers and rates refer to families rather than persons; data on persons were not available.

Poverty Status of Persons by Sex and Age

Year	Poverty status of persons by sex				Poverty status of persons by age					
	Males below poverty level		Females below poverty level		Children under 18 below poverty level		Persons 18 to 64 years old below poverty level		Persons 65 years and older below poverty level	
	Number (thousands)	Poverty rate	Number (thousands)	Poverty rate	Number (thousands)	Poverty rate	Number (thousands)	Poverty rate	Number (thousands)	Poverty rate
1966	12 225	13.0	16 265	16.3	12 389	17.6	11 007	10.5	5 114	28.5
1967	11 813	12.5	15 951	15.8	11 656	16.6	10 725	10.0	5 388	29.5
1968	10 793	11.3	14 578	14.3	10 954	15.6	9 803	9.0	4 632	25.0
1969	10 292	10.6	13 978	13.6	9 691	14.0	9 669	8.7	4 787	25.3
1970	10 879	11.1	14 632	14.0	10 440	15.1	10 187	9.0	4 793	24.6
1971	10 708	10.8	14 841	14.1	10 551	15.3	10 735	9.3	4 273	21.6
1972	10 190	10.2	14 258	13.4	10 284	15.1	10 438	8.8	3 738	18.6
1973	9 642	9.6	13 316	12.5	9 642	14.4	9 977	8.3	3 354	16.3
1974	10 313	10.2	13 881	12.9	10 156	15.4	10 132	8.3	3 085	14.6
1975	10 908	10.7	14 970	13.8	11 104	17.1	11 456	9.2	3 317	15.3
1976	10 373	10.1	14 603	13.4	10 273	16.0	11 389	9.0	3 313	15.0
1977	10 340	10.0	14 381	13.0	10 288	16.2	11 316	8.8	3 177	14.1
1978	10 017	9.6	14 480	13.0	9 931	15.9	11 332	8.7	3 233	14.0
1979	10 535	10.0	14 810	13.2	10 377	16.4	12 014	8.9	3 682	15.2
1980	12 207	11.2	17 065	14.7	11 543	18.3	13 858	10.1	3 871	15.7
1981	13 360	12.1	18 462	15.8	12 505	20.0	15 464	11.1	3 853	15.3
1982	14 842	13.4	19 556	16.5	13 647	21.9	17 000	12.0	3 751	14.6
1983	15 182	13.5	20 084	16.8	13 911	22.3	17 767	12.4	3 625	13.8
1984	14 537	12.8	19 163	15.9	13 420	21.5	16 952	11.7	3 330	12.4
1985	14 140	12.3	18 923	15.6	13 010	20.7	16 598	11.3	3 456	12.6
1986	13 721	11.8	18 649	15.2	12 876	20.5	16 017	10.8	3 477	12.4
1987	14 029	12.0	18 518	15.0	12 843	20.3	15 815	10.6	3 563	12.5
1988	13 599	11.5	18 146	14.5	12 455	19.5	15 809	10.5	3 481	12.0
1989	13 366	11.2	18 162	14.4	12 590	19.6	15 575	10.2	3 363	11.4
1990	14 211	11.7	19 373	15.2	13 431	20.6	16 496	10.7	3 658	12.2
1991	15 082	12.3	20 626	16.0	14 341	21.8	17 585	11.4	3 781	12.4
1992	16 222	12.9	21 792	16.6	15 294	22.3	18 793	11.9	3 928	12.9
1993	16 900	13.3	22 365	16.9	15 727	22.7	19 781	12.4	3 755	12.2
1994	16 316	12.8	21 744	16.3	15 289	21.8	19 107	11.9	3 663	11.7
1995	15 683	12.2	20 742	15.4	14 665	20.8	18 442	11.4	3 318	10.5
1996	15 611	12.0	20 918	15.4	14 463	20.5	18 638	11.4	3 428	10.8
1997	15 187	11.6	20 387	14.9	14 113	19.9	18 084	10.9	3 376	10.5
1998	14 714	11.1	19 764	14.3	13 467	18.9	17 624	10.5	3 386	10.5

Poverty Status of Persons Inside and Outside Metropolitan Areas, and Persons In and Near Poverty

| Year | Inside metropolitan areas | | | | | | Outside metropolitan areas | | Total in and near poverty (income below 1.25 times the poverty level) | | Near-poor (income between 1 and 1.25 times poverty level) | |
| | Number (thousands) | Poverty rate | Central city | | Outside central city | | Number (thousands) | Poverty rate | Number (thousands) | Percent | Number (thousands) | Percent |
			Number (thousands)	Poverty rate	Number (thousands)	Poverty rate						
1959	17 019	15.3	10 437	18.3	6 582	12.2	21 747	33.2	54 942	31.1	15 452	8.7
1960	.....	.....	.....	.....	.....	.....	.....	.....	54 560	30.4	14 709	8.2
1961	.....	.....	.....	.....	.....	.....	.....	.....	54 280	30.0	14 652	8.1
1962	.....	.....	.....	.....	.....	.....	.....	.....	53 119	28.8	14 494	7.9
1963	.....	.....	.....	.....	.....	.....	.....	.....	50 778	27.1	14 342	7.7
1964	.....	.....	.....	.....	.....	.....	.....	.....	49 819	26.3	13 764	7.3
1965	.....	.....	.....	.....	.....	.....	.....	.....	46 163	24.1	12 978	6.8
1966	.....	.....	.....	.....	.....	.....	.....	.....	41 267	21.3	12 757	6.6
1967	13 832	10.9	8 649	15.0	5 183	7.5	13 936	20.2	39 206	20.0	11 437	5.8
1968	12 871	10.0	7 754	13.4	5 117	7.3	12 518	18.0	35 905	18.2	10 516	5.3
1969	13 084	9.5	7 993	12.7	5 091	6.8	11 063	17.9	34 665	17.4	10 518	5.3
1970	13 317	10.2	8 118	14.2	5 199	7.1	12 103	16.9	35 624	17.6	10 204	5.0
1971	14 561	10.4	8 912	14.2	5 649	7.2	10 999	17.2	36 501	17.8	10 942	5.3
1972	14 508	10.3	9 179	14.7	5 329	6.8	9 952	15.3	34 653	16.8	10 193	4.9
1973	13 759	9.7	8 594	14.0	5 165	6.4	9 214	14.0	32 828	15.8	9 855	4.7
1974	13 851	9.7	8 373	13.7	5 477	6.7	9 519	14.2	33 666	16.1	10 296	4.9
1975	15 348	10.8	9 090	15.0	6 259	7.6	10 529	15.4	37 182	17.6	11 305	5.4
1976	15 229	10.7	9 482	15.8	5 747	6.9	9 746	14.0	35 509	16.7	10 534	5.0
1977	14 859	10.4	9 203	15.4	5 657	6.8	9 861	13.9	35 659	16.7	10 939	5.1
1978	15 090	10.4	9 285	15.4	5 805	6.8	9 407	13.5	34 155	15.8	9 658	4.5
1979	16 135	10.7	9 720	15.7	6 415	7.2	9 937	13.8	36 616	16.4	10 544	4.7
1980	18 021	11.9	10 644	17.2	7 377	8.2	11 251	15.4	40 658	18.1	11 386	5.1
1981	19 347	12.6	11 231	18.0	8 116	8.9	12 475	17.0	43 748	19.3	11 926	5.3
1982	21 247	13.7	12 696	19.9	8 551	9.3	13 152	17.8	46 520	20.3	12 122	5.3
1983	21 750	13.8	12 872	19.8	8 878	9.6	13 516	18.3	47 150	20.3	11 847	5.1
1984	.....	.....	.....	.....	.....	.....	.....	.....	45 288	19.4	11 588	5.0
1985	23 275	12.7	14 177	19.0	9 097	8.4	9 789	18.3	44 166	18.7	11 102	4.7
1986	22 657	12.3	13 295	18.0	9 362	8.4	9 712	18.1	43 486	18.2	11 116	4.7
1987	23 054	12.3	13 697	18.3	9 357	8.3	9 167	17.0	43 032	17.9	10 811	4.5
1988	23 059	12.2	13 615	18.1	9 444	8.3	8 686	16.0	42 551	17.5	10 806	4.4
1989	22 917	12.0	13 592	18.1	9 326	8.0	8 611	15.7	42 653	17.3	11 125	4.5
1990	24 510	12.7	14 254	19.0	10 255	8.7	9 075	16.3	44 837	18.0	11 252	4.5
1991	26 827	13.7	15 314	20.2	11 513	9.6	8 881	16.1	47 527	18.9	11 819	4.7
1992	28 380	14.2	16 346	20.9	12 034	9.9	9 634	16.9	50 592	19.7	12 578	4.9
1993	29 615	14.6	16 805	21.5	12 810	10.3	9 650	17.2	51 801	20.0	12 536	4.8
1994	29 610	14.2	16 098	20.9	13 511	10.3	8 449	16.0	50 401	19.3	12 342	4.7
1995	28 342	13.4	16 269	20.6	12 072	9.1	8 083	15.6	48 761	18.5	12 336	4.7
1996	28 211	13.2	15 645	19.6	12 566	9.4	8 318	15.9	49 310	18.5	12 781	4.8
1997	27 273	12.6	15 018	18.8	12 255	9.0	8 301	15.9	47 853	17.8	12 279	4.6
1998	26 997	12.3	14 921	18.5	12 076	8.7	7 479	14.4	46 036	17.0	11 560	4.3

Poor Persons 16 Years and Over by Work Experience

| Year | Number | Worked | | Worked year-round, full-time | | Worked less than year-round or full-time | | Did not work | |
		Number	Percent of total poor	Number	Percent of total poor	Number	Percent of total poor	Number	Percent of total poor
1978	16 914	6 599	39.0	1 309	7.7	5 290	31.3	10 315	61.0
1979	16 803	6 601	39.3	1 394	8.3	5 207	31.0	10 202	60.7
1980	18 892	7 674	40.6	1 644	8.7	6 030	31.9	11 218	59.4
1981	20 571	8 524	41.4	1 881	9.1	6 643	32.3	12 047	58.6
1982	22 100	9 013	40.8	1 999	9.0	7 014	31.7	13 087	59.2
1983	22 741	9 329	41.0	2 064	9.1	7 265	31.9	13 412	59.0
1984	21 541	8 999	41.8	2 076	9.6	6 923	32.1	12 542	58.2
1985	21 243	9 008	42.4	1 972	9.3	7 036	33.1	12 235	57.6
1986	20 688	8 743	42.3	2 007	9.7	6 736	32.6	11 945	57.7
1987	20 546	8 258	40.2	1 821	8.9	6 437	31.3	12 288	59.8
1988	20 323	8 363	41.2	1 929	9.5	6 434	31.7	11 960	58.8
1989	19 952	8 376	42.0	1 908	9.6	6 468	32.4	11 576	58.0
1990	21 242	8 716	41.0	2 076	9.8	6 640	31.3	12 526	59.0
1991	22 530	9 208	40.9	2 103	9.3	7 105	31.5	13 322	59.1
1992	23 951	9 739	40.6	2 211	9.2	7 528	31.4	14 212	59.3
1993	24 832	10 144	40.8	2 408	9.7	7 736	31.2	14 688	59.1
1994	24 108	9 829	40.8	2 520	10.5	7 309	30.3	14 279	59.2
1995	23 077	9 484	41.1	2 418	10.5	7 066	30.6	13 593	58.9
1996	23 472	9 586	40.8	2 263	9.6	7 323	31.2	13 886	59.2
1997	22 754	9 444	41.5	2 345	10.3	7 099	31.2	13 310	58.5
1998	22 255	9 133	41.0	2 804	12.6	6 329	28.4	13 122	59.0

Median Income and Poverty Rate, Based on Alternative Definitions of Income

Year	Definition 1: Money income excluding capital gains (current official measure)				Definition 4: Money income before taxes and transfers, plus health insurance supplements			
	Median income (1998 dollars)	Poverty rate (percent)		Gini coefficient	Median income (1998 dollars)	Poverty rate (percent)		Gini coefficient
		Official threshold	CPI-U-X1 threshold			Official threshold	CPI-U-X1 threshold	
1979	36 259	11.7	10.6	0.403	35 739	18.8	17.8	0.460
1980	35 076	13.0	11.5	0.401	33 899	20.1	19.0	0.462
1981	34 507	14.0	12.2	0.404	33 125	21.1	19.8	0.466
1982	34 391	15.0	13.2	0.409	32 670	22.0	20.6	0.475
1983	34 397	15.2	13.7	0.412	33 081	21.8	20.6	0.478
1984	35 165	14.4	12.8	0.413	34 060	20.8	19.5	0.477
1985	35 778	14.0	12.5	0.418	34 615	20.4	19.1	0.486
1986	37 028	13.6	12.2	0.423	36 007	19.9	18.7	0.505
1987	37 394	13.4	12.0	0.424	36 156	19.7	18.7	0.488
1988	37 512	13.0	11.7	0.425	36 477	19.7	18.6	0.489
1989	37 998	12.8	11.4	0.429	36 971	19.4	18.3	0.492
1990	37 343	13.5	12.1	0.426	35 803	19.9	18.8	0.487
1991	36 054	14.2	12.7	0.425	34 457	21.1	20.0	0.490
1992	35 593	14.8	13.4	0.430	33 923	22.1	20.9	0.497
1993	35 240	15.1	13.7	0.448	33 647	22.6	21.4	0.514
1994	35 486	14.5	13.2	0.450	34 286	22.0	20.8	0.515
1995	36 446	13.8	12.3	0.444	35 101	21.1	19.9	0.509
1996	36 872	13.7	12.2	0.447	35 712	20.8	19.5	0.511
1997	37 581	13.3	11.8	0.448	36 536	20.3	19.1	0.513
1998	38 885	12.7	11.3	0.446	37 673	19.3	18.1	0.509

Year	Definition 14: Income after all taxes and transfers				Definition 15: Income after all taxes and transfers, plus net imputed return on equity in own home			
	Median income (1998 dollars)	Poverty rate (percent)		Gini coefficient	Median income (1998 dollars)	Poverty rate (percent)		Gini coefficient
		Official threshold	CPI-U-X1 threshold			Official threshold	CPI-U-X1 threshold	
1979	33 243	8.9	7.9	0.359	35 440	7.5	6.7	0.352
1980	32 119	10.1	8.6	0.354	35 410	8.2	7.0	0.347
1981	31 359	11.5	9.8	0.358	36 689	8.7	7.3	0.350
1982	31 608	12.3	10.6	0.366	35 875	9.9	8.5	0.359
1983	32 092	12.7	11.0	0.374	35 683	10.4	9.0	0.368
1984	32 635	12.0	10.4	0.378	36 557	9.9	8.6	0.372
1985	33 176	11.7	10.1	0.385	36 615	9.9	8.6	0.381
1986	34 547	11.3	9.8	0.409	37 175	10.1	8.6	0.404
1987	34 929	11.0	9.5	0.382	38 050	9.7	8.3	0.380
1988	34 855	10.8	9.5	0.385	37 989	9.4	8.2	0.384
1989	35 378	10.4	8.9	0.389	38 227	9.1	7.7	0.387
1990	34 689	10.9	9.5	0.382	37 034	9.8	8.5	0.381
1991	34 022	11.4	9.9	0.380	36 547	10.3	8.9	0.379
1992	34 125	11.9	10.5	0.385	36 191	10.7	9.5	0.381
1993	34 287	12.1	10.7	0.398	36 199	11.2	9.8	0.395
1994	34 704	11.1	9.8	0.400	36 830	10.0	8.8	0.395
1995	35 622	10.3	9.0	0.394	37 711	9.4	8.1	0.388
1996	35 861	10.2	8.9	0.398	37 773	9.3	8.1	0.392
1997	36 419	10.0	8.8	0.403	38 209	9.2	8.0	0.397
1998	37 673	9.5	8.2	0.405	39 308	8.8	7.6	0.399

See Notes for explanation of alternative definitions and thresholds, and of the Gini coefficient.

Median Income and Poverty Rate by State

State	Median household income (1998 dollars)							Poverty rate						
	1992	1993	1994	1995	1996	1997	Standard error[1], 1997	1992	1993	1994	1995	1996	1997	Standard error[1], 1997
United States	35 593	35 240	35 486	36 446	36 872	37 581	174	14.8	15.1	14.5	13.8	13.7	13.3	0.21
Alabama	29 984	28 293	29 912	27 798	31 480	32 436	1 632	17.3	17.4	16.4	20.1	14.0	15.7	1.81
Alaska	48 566	48 428	49 897	51 290	54 831	48 742	1 278	10.2	9.1	10.2	7.1	8.2	8.8	1.40
Arizona	34 108	34 416	34 418	33 009	32 867	33 250	1 317	15.8	15.4	15.9	16.1	20.5	17.2	1.76
Arkansas	27 746	25 989	28 118	27 609	28 177	26 570	1 172	17.5	20.0	15.3	14.9	17.2	19.7	1.92
California	40 550	38 436	38 859	39 583	40 321	40 312	877	16.4	18.2	17.9	16.7	16.9	16.6	0.75
Colorado	37 740	38 904	41 611	43 538	42 542	43 906	1 974	10.8	9.9	9.0	8.8	10.6	8.2	1.36
Connecticut	47 449	44 575	45 201	43 042	43 756	44 670	2 020	9.8	8.5	10.8	9.7	11.7	8.6	1.57
Delaware	41 451	40 681	39 455	37 357	40 837	43 703	2 094	7.8	10.2	8.3	10.3	8.6	9.6	1.63
District of Columbia	35 141	30 799	33 124	32 886	33 208	32 356	999	20.3	26.4	21.2	22.2	24.1	21.8	2.34
Florida	31 774	32 205	32 219	31 814	31 832	32 961	592	15.6	17.8	14.9	16.2	14.2	14.3	0.93
Georgia	33 456	35 717	34 610	36 470	33 760	37 234	930	17.7	13.5	14.0	12.1	14.8	14.5	1.54
Hawaii	48 926	48 124	46 475	45 832	43 396	41 572	1 420	11.2	8.0	8.7	10.3	12.1	13.9	1.92
Idaho	32 187	34 981	34 685	34 949	36 058	33 924	1 360	15.2	13.1	12.0	14.5	11.9	14.7	1.67
Illinois	36 656	37 063	38 585	40 719	41 092	41 926	794	15.6	13.6	12.4	12.4	12.1	11.2	0.92
Indiana	33 146	33 249	30 640	35 707	36 513	39 495	1 201	11.8	12.2	13.7	9.6	7.5	8.8	1.40
Iowa	33 393	32 333	36 382	37 990	34 500	34 309	1 302	11.5	10.3	10.7	12.2	9.6	9.6	1.50
Kansas	35 256	33 581	31 151	32 452	33 852	37 039	1 639	11.1	13.1	14.9	10.8	11.2	9.7	1.51
Kentucky	27 284	27 497	29 251	31 883	33 673	33 973	1 686	19.7	20.4	18.5	14.7	17.0	15.9	1.81
Louisiana	29 555	29 680	28 240	29 892	31 438	33 778	1 575	24.5	26.4	25.7	19.7	20.5	16.3	1.78
Maine	34 409	30 951	33 343	36 213	36 045	33 282	1 321	13.5	15.4	9.4	11.2	11.2	10.1	1.69
Maryland	43 222	45 052	43 112	43 895	45 703	47 412	1 499	11.8	9.7	10.7	10.1	10.3	8.4	1.48
Massachusetts	42 242	41 809	44 544	41 257	41 029	42 678	1 405	10.3	10.7	11.0	10.1	11.2	12.2	1.23
Michigan	37 488	36 844	38 807	38 960	40 750	39 345	1 125	13.6	15.4	14.1	12.2	11.2	10.3	0.95
Minnesota	35 994	37 995	37 004	40 571	42 585	43 227	1 534	13.0	11.6	11.7	9.2	9.8	9.6	1.45
Mississippi	23 899	25 032	27 936	28 383	27 714	28 943	1 408	24.6	24.7	19.9	23.5	20.6	16.7	1.84
Missouri	31 788	32 354	33 205	37 247	35 597	37 122	2 092	15.7	16.1	15.6	9.4	9.5	11.8	1.67
Montana	30 817	29 859	30 390	29 687	29 799	29 667	1 162	13.8	14.9	11.5	15.3	17.0	15.6	1.75
Nebraska	34 909	34 977	34 969	35 219	35 336	35 232	1 552	10.6	10.3	8.8	9.6	10.2	9.8	1.53
Nevada	37 071	40 400	39 453	38 594	40 038	39 459	1 601	14.7	9.8	11.1	11.1	8.1	11.0	1.61
New Hampshire	45 817	42 825	38 765	41 896	40 939	41 637	1 630	8.7	9.9	7.7	5.3	6.4	9.1	1.65
New Jersey	45 310	45 685	46 502	46 980	49 313	48 769	1 446	10.3	10.9	9.2	7.8	9.2	9.3	0.95
New Mexico	30 044	30 184	29 592	27 798	26 062	30 555	1 174	21.6	17.4	21.1	25.3	25.5	21.2	1.95
New York	36 075	35 755	35 084	35 325	36 786	36 356	644	15.7	16.4	17.0	16.5	16.7	16.5	0.84
North Carolina	32 264	32 510	33 121	34 204	36 985	36 398	931	15.8	14.4	14.2	12.6	12.2	11.4	1.16
North Dakota	31 320	31 717	31 102	31 112	32 693	32 154	1 383	12.1	11.2	10.4	12.0	11.0	13.6	1.75
Ohio	36 485	35 290	35 036	37 371	35 395	36 697	908	12.5	13.0	14.1	11.5	12.7	11.0	0.96
Oklahoma	29 375	29 622	29 686	28 141	28 504	31 839	1 041	18.6	19.9	16.7	17.1	16.6	13.7	1.64
Oregon	37 093	37 380	34 598	38 904	36 872	37 827	1 816	11.4	11.8	11.8	11.2	11.8	11.6	1.67
Pennsylvania	34 716	34 963	35 268	36 925	36 256	38 101	979	11.9	13.2	12.5	12.2	11.6	11.2	0.91
Rhode Island	35 356	37 799	35 117	37 818	38 424	35 339	2 269	12.4	11.2	10.3	10.6	11.0	12.7	1.92
South Carolina	32 040	29 389	32 826	31 093	36 012	34 796	1 634	19.0	18.7	13.8	19.9	13.0	13.1	1.77
South Dakota	30 508	31 288	32 703	31 635	30 673	30 157	1 163	15.1	14.2	14.5	14.5	11.8	16.5	1.85
Tennessee	28 252	28 315	31 499	31 033	31 987	31 113	1 379	17.0	19.6	14.6	15.5	15.9	14.3	1.75
Texas	32 476	32 405	33 827	34 268	34 358	35 621	894	18.3	17.4	19.1	17.4	16.6	16.7	0.94
Utah	39 792	40 367	39 282	39 017	38 478	43 441	1 813	9.4	10.7	8.0	8.4	7.7	8.9	1.31
Vermont	38 055	35 042	39 377	36 177	33 616	35 599	1 753	10.5	10.0	7.6	10.3	12.6	9.3	1.64
Virginia	44 379	41 097	41 407	38 741	40 736	43 626	1 927	9.5	9.7	10.7	10.2	12.3	12.7	1.59
Washington	39 385	40 220	36 882	38 041	38 102	45 256	1 742	11.2	12.1	11.7	12.5	11.9	9.2	1.49
West Virginia	23 551	25 292	25 918	26 610	26 228	27 916	1 335	22.3	22.2	18.6	16.7	18.5	16.4	1.79
Wisconsin	38 698	35 833	38 922	43 804	41 556	40 212	1 168	10.9	12.6	9.0	8.5	8.8	8.2	1.37
Wyoming	35 096	33 211	36 449	33 722	32 156	33 944	1 463	10.3	13.3	9.3	12.2	11.9	13.5	1.73

1. See Notes for an explanation of standard errors.

Consumer Income and Spending

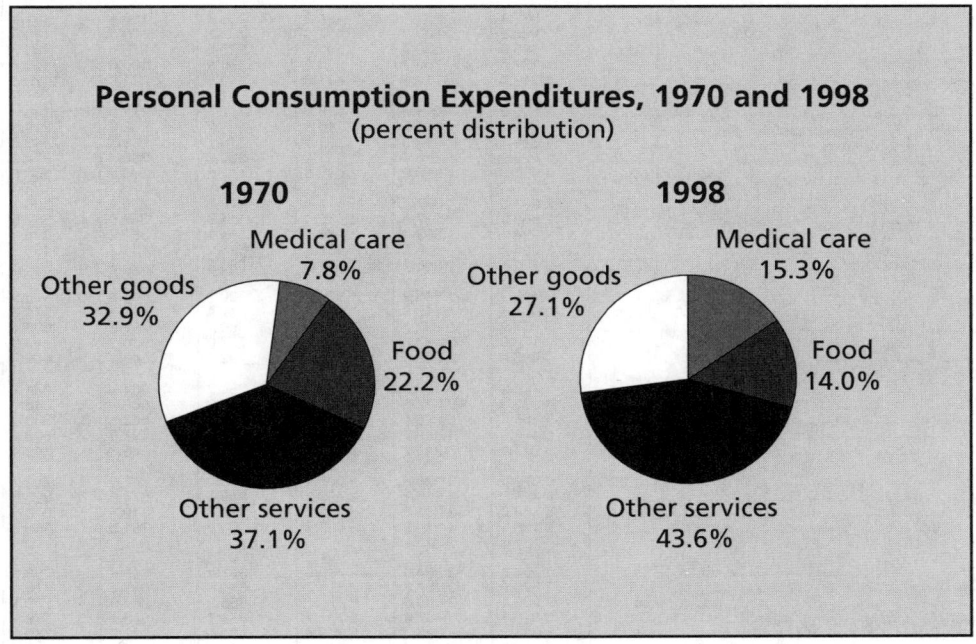

Personal Consumption Expenditures, 1970 and 1998
(percent distribution)

1970

Medical care
7.8%

Other goods
32.9%

Food
22.2%

Other services
37.1%

1998

Medical care
15.3%

Other goods
27.1%

Food
14.0%

Other services
43.6%

- The percentage of personal income devoted to medical care doubled from 1970 to 1998. The share of other services also grew, while the shares of food and other goods fell.

- Total wage and salary payments rose at a 7.5 percent annual rate from 1970 to 1998; the service industries were the leading sector with a 10.2 percent rate, while manufacturing trailed with a growth rate of 5.7 percent.

- Personal saving was negative in late 1998, the first time since the Great Depression. For a discussion of the statistical and economic significance of recent low and negative measured saving rates, see "Current Issues in Economic Measurement" at the front of this book.

- Adjusted for inflation, disposable personal income rose at a 2.8 percent annual rate from 1970 to 1998, while personal consumption expenditures rose at a 3.1 percent rate. With population rising at a rate of 1.0 percent, the increase in real per capita income was 1.8 percent per year.

Personal Income by Source

(Billions of dollars, monthly data are at seasonally adjusted annual rates.)

Year and month	Total	Wage and salary disbursements						Government	Other labor income
		Total	Private industries						
			Total	Commodity-producing industries		Distributive industries	Service industries		
				Total	Manufactur-ing				
1970	837.1	551.5	434.3	203.7	158.4	131.2	99.4	117.1	32.5
1971	900.2	583.9	457.4	209.1	160.5	140.4	107.9	126.5	36.7
1972	988.8	638.7	501.2	228.2	175.6	153.3	119.7	137.4	43.0
1973	1 107.5	708.7	560.0	255.9	196.6	170.3	133.9	148.7	49.2
1974	1 215.9	772.6	611.8	276.5	211.8	186.8	148.6	160.9	56.5
1975	1 319.0	814.6	638.6	277.1	211.6	198.1	163.4	176.0	65.9
1976	1 459.4	899.5	710.8	309.7	238.0	219.5	181.6	188.6	79.7
1977	1 616.1	993.9	791.6	346.1	266.7	242.7	202.8	202.3	94.7
1978	1 825.9	1 120.8	901.2	392.6	300.1	274.9	233.7	219.6	110.1
1979	2 055.8	1 255.9	1 018.8	442.5	335.3	308.5	267.8	237.1	124.3
1980	2 293.0	1 377.7	1 116.4	472.5	356.4	336.7	307.2	261.3	139.8
1981	2 568.5	1 517.6	1 232.0	514.9	388.0	368.5	348.6	285.6	153.0
1982	2 724.1	1 593.9	1 286.7	515.1	386.2	385.9	385.7	307.3	165.4
1983	2 894.4	1 685.3	1 360.3	528.2	401.2	405.7	426.5	325.0	177.2
1984	3 211.4	1 855.1	1 507.5	586.6	445.9	445.3	475.6	347.6	188.9
1985	3 440.9	1 995.9	1 622.2	620.7	468.9	476.5	525.0	373.8	203.1
1986	3 639.6	2 116.6	1 720.0	637.4	481.3	501.6	581.0	396.6	216.0
1987	3 877.8	2 272.7	1 849.5	660.4	497.2	535.4	653.7	423.1	235.4
1988	4 178.9	2 453.6	2 003.2	707.0	530.1	575.3	720.9	450.4	251.7
1989	4 496.4	2 598.1	2 118.7	732.4	548.1	606.8	779.5	479.4	273.1
1990	4 796.2	2 757.5	2 240.3	754.2	561.2	634.1	852.1	517.2	300.6
1991	4 965.6	2 827.6	2 281.6	746.3	562.5	646.6	888.7	546.1	322.7
1992	5 255.7	2 986.4	2 418.6	765.7	583.5	680.3	972.6	567.8	351.3
1993	5 481.0	3 089.6	2 505.3	781.2	592.9	699.4	1 024.7	584.3	385.1
1994	5 757.9	3 240.7	2 638.5	824.4	620.8	741.4	1 072.7	602.2	405.0
1995	6 072.1	3 428.6	2 805.8	864.0	647.9	782.9	1 158.9	622.7	401.6
1996	6 425.2	3 631.1	2 990.2	909.0	674.6	823.3	1 257.9	640.9	387.0
1997	6 784.0	3 889.8	3 225.7	975.0	719.5	879.8	1 370.8	664.2	392.9
1998	7 126.1	4 149.9	3 460.5	1 026.9	751.5	939.6	1 494.0	689.3	406.9
1995:									
January	5 963.5	3 354.5	2 739.8	851.4	641.4	768.2	1 120.2	614.7	408.0
February	5 979.9	3 369.3	2 751.7	854.8	643.0	770.0	1 126.8	617.6	407.2
March	5 995.1	3 380.8	2 761.4	855.3	642.9	772.1	1 134.0	619.4	406.2
April	6 015.1	3 397.4	2 777.7	858.1	644.1	778.5	1 141.1	619.7	404.7
May	6 025.3	3 396.4	2 775.4	855.9	642.9	775.5	1 144.0	621.0	403.6
June	6 050.5	3 416.7	2 793.6	860.3	645.1	780.7	1 152.6	623.1	402.4
July	6 067.0	3 434.8	2 810.8	864.7	648.5	784.5	1 161.6	624.0	401.6
August	6 091.0	3 447.5	2 822.9	867.6	650.0	788.1	1 167.2	624.6	400.3
September	6 122.5	3 465.7	2 840.7	872.2	652.6	791.9	1 176.7	625.0	398.9
October	6 155.8	3 482.3	2 856.1	875.0	654.2	792.9	1 188.2	626.2	397.6
November	6 184.9	3 493.9	2 866.2	876.8	655.5	795.7	1 193.6	627.7	395.7
December	6 214.4	3 503.3	2 873.7	875.3	654.2	797.2	1 201.2	629.6	393.5
1996:									
January	6 231.7	3 498.1	2 864.7	870.6	647.7	792.2	1 202.0	633.3	389.4
February	6 294.9	3 543.4	2 909.0	887.1	660.3	806.6	1 215.3	634.4	387.6
March	6 326.3	3 556.6	2 921.1	883.9	655.8	811.2	1 225.9	635.6	386.7
April	6 354.8	3 576.8	2 939.4	897.9	668.3	808.4	1 233.1	637.5	387.8
May	6 384.7	3 601.3	2 961.9	903.5	671.8	815.3	1 243.2	639.4	387.6
June	6 430.6	3 639.4	2 998.8	911.2	676.7	827.6	1 260.0	640.6	387.3
July	6 447.1	3 639.0	2 997.2	913.9	678.4	822.2	1 261.2	641.7	386.6
August	6 477.0	3 664.8	3 022.3	920.0	682.6	830.0	1 272.3	642.5	386.3
September	6 506.0	3 688.9	3 045.0	924.2	685.3	837.1	1 283.7	643.9	386.1
October	6 517.0	3 694.6	3 049.3	925.4	684.8	836.7	1 287.2	645.3	385.8
November	6 547.3	3 719.6	3 072.3	931.1	688.5	842.4	1 298.9	647.3	385.9
December	6 585.0	3 750.6	3 101.5	939.3	694.7	849.7	1 312.4	649.1	386.4
1997:									
January	6 627.3	3 767.0	3 111.9	943.9	697.7	851.2	1 316.8	655.0	389.0
February	6 668.1	3 802.2	3 144.7	951.8	701.5	857.9	1 335.0	657.5	389.7
March	6 704.9	3 826.2	3 167.7	959.2	707.9	865.3	1 343.2	658.5	390.3
April	6 720.3	3 837.1	3 177.0	961.4	709.6	866.8	1 348.8	660.1	390.7
May	6 744.1	3 856.9	3 195.4	966.2	712.1	871.0	1 358.1	661.6	391.5
June	6 766.4	3 872.3	3 209.2	968.5	714.2	872.7	1 367.9	663.1	392.5
July	6 785.8	3 886.9	3 222.0	972.2	716.7	877.0	1 372.8	664.9	392.0
August	6 826.7	3 922.7	3 255.9	980.9	723.7	889.1	1 386.0	666.8	393.5
September	6 850.1	3 937.1	3 268.8	985.3	726.6	892.7	1 390.7	668.3	395.3
October	6 875.5	3 964.0	3 294.0	995.2	735.1	898.7	1 400.2	670.0	394.4
November	6 910.9	3 998.0	3 326.3	1 004.0	741.8	908.7	1 413.7	671.6	396.9
December	6 928.3	4 007.7	3 335.0	1 012.1	746.8	906.3	1 416.7	672.7	399.7
1998:									
January	6 970.5	4 040.0	3 362.9	1 016.7	748.7	915.3	1 430.8	677.2	401.7
February	7 007.3	4 066.4	3 386.5	1 020.2	750.8	920.8	1 445.5	680.0	402.8
March	7 033.9	4 079.3	3 397.0	1 020.1	751.8	920.5	1 457.3	681.4	403.8
April	7 055.6	4 097.9	3 414.3	1 022.8	750.8	926.4	1 465.0	683.6	404.7
May	6 784.0	3 889.8	3 225.7	975.0	719.5	879.8	1 370.8	664.2	392.9
June	7 104.4	4 131.0	3 442.8	1 021.3	748.3	934.4	1 487.1	688.1	406.6
July	7 133.7	4 153.6	3 463.4	1 020.9	743.8	941.5	1 501.0	690.2	407.5
August	7 164.1	4 183.4	3 490.6	1 030.6	752.4	946.3	1 513.8	692.8	408.3
September	7 184.6	4 194.3	3 499.2	1 032.7	756.4	949.6	1 516.9	695.1	409.2
October	7 217.2	4 220.9	3 523.5	1 034.3	754.5	956.3	1 533.0	697.4	410.1
November	7 279.8	4 243.9	3 544.4	1 036.5	753.5	961.9	1 546.1	699.4	411.0
December	7 276.8	4 263.5	3 562.7	1 041.6	754.2	966.2	1 554.8	700.9	411.9

Personal Income by Source—*Continued*

(Billions of dollars, monthly data are at seasonally adjusted annual rates)

| Year and month | Proprietors income [1] | | | Rental income of persons [2] | Personal dividend income | Personal interest income | Transfer payments to persons | | | | Less: Personal contributions for social insurance |
	Total	Farm	Nonfarm				Total	Social Security and Medicare	Unemploy-ment insurance benefits	Other transfers	
1970	80.2	14.8	65.4	23.6	23.5	69.2	84.6	38.5	4.0	42.1	27.9
1971	86.5	15.4	71.1	24.6	23.5	75.7	100.1	44.5	5.8	49.8	30.7
1972	98.3	19.5	78.8	24.3	25.5	81.8	111.8	49.6	5.7	56.5	34.4
1973	116.8	32.6	84.2	25.8	27.6	94.1	127.9	60.4	4.4	63.1	42.6
1974	115.7	25.8	89.8	25.7	29.6	112.4	151.3	70.1	6.8	74.4	47.9
1975	121.8	24.1	97.7	24.7	29.2	123.0	190.2	81.4	17.6	91.2	50.4
1976	133.6	18.6	115.0	24.3	35.0	134.6	208.3	92.9	15.8	99.6	55.5
1977	147.4	17.5	129.9	22.8	39.5	155.7	223.3	104.9	12.7	105.7	61.2
1978	169.5	22.2	147.4	24.8	44.3	184.5	241.6	116.2	9.7	115.7	69.8
1979	185.0	25.3	159.7	26.9	50.5	223.6	270.7	131.8	9.8	129.1	81.0
1980	176.6	12.2	164.4	33.9	57.5	274.2	321.5	154.2	16.1	151.2	88.6
1981	187.6	21.9	165.7	44.5	67.2	337.2	365.9	182.0	15.9	168.0	104.5
1982	179.6	14.5	165.1	46.5	63.8	379.2	408.1	204.5	25.2	178.4	112.3
1983	191.9	4.1	187.8	46.1	71.0	403.2	439.4	221.7	26.3	191.4	119.7
1984	248.7	23.2	225.5	50.1	75.4	472.3	453.6	235.7	15.9	202.0	132.7
1985	268.6	23.6	245.0	48.1	79.4	508.4	486.5	253.4	15.7	217.4	149.0
1986	279.5	24.2	255.3	41.5	86.3	543.3	518.6	269.2	16.3	233.1	162.1
1987	305.1	31.5	273.6	44.8	90.2	560.0	543.3	282.9	14.5	245.9	173.7
1988	335.3	27.5	307.8	55.1	104.2	595.5	577.6	300.4	13.3	263.9	194.2
1989	357.4	36.3	321.1	51.7	126.3	674.5	626.0	325.1	14.4	286.5	210.8
1990	374.0	35.5	338.6	61.0	134.9	704.4	687.8	352.0	18.1	317.7	223.9
1991	376.5	29.3	347.2	67.9	137.7	699.3	769.9	382.3	26.8	360.8	235.8
1992	423.8	37.1	386.7	79.4	137.9	667.2	858.2	414.0	38.9	405.3	248.4
1993	450.8	32.4	418.4	105.7	147.1	651.0	912.0	444.4	34.0	433.6	260.3
1994	471.6	36.9	434.7	124.4	171.0	668.1	954.7	473.0	23.6	458.1	277.5
1995	488.1	22.4	465.7	133.8	192.8	704.9	1 015.6	507.8	21.4	485.8	293.6
1996	527.7	38.9	488.8	150.2	248.2	719.4	1 068.0	538.0	21.9	508.0	306.3
1997	551.2	35.5	515.8	158.2	260.3	747.3	1 110.4	565.9	19.9	524.6	326.2
1998	577.2	28.7	548.5	162.6	263.1	764.8	1 149.0	586.5	19.5	542.9	347.4
1995:											
January	48.6	24.3	454.0	130.1	184.8	705.6	990.0	494.7	21.2	475.5	287.7
February	45.4	22.7	455.7	131.1	184.8	702.4	995.7	498.6	20.9	477.0	288.9
March	43.0	21.5	457.6	132.1	185.3	698.9	1 002.7	502.0	20.8	480.3	289.9
April	42.0	21.0	457.4	133.1	185.5	701.5	1 005.9	503.4	20.3	481.4	291.4
May	40.6	20.3	462.5	133.4	186.3	701.5	1 012.8	506.5	21.6	484.0	291.5
June	39.6	19.8	466.3	133.3	188.3	701.6	1 015.0	507.6	21.2	485.2	292.9
July	36.2	18.1	467.1	130.9	188.4	700.9	1 019.6	509.0	22.2	487.2	294.3
August	37.6	18.8	472.1	131.5	190.7	702.3	1 022.9	510.5	21.6	489.2	295.2
September	41.0	20.5	472.8	133.2	196.3	704.8	1 026.6	513.8	21.6	489.4	296.4
October	49.6	24.8	473.1	133.6	200.0	711.2	1 030.6	513.6	22.5	492.8	297.4
November	54.8	27.4	474.6	140.3	206.6	713.5	1 031.1	514.3	22.3	492.7	298.2
December	60.0	30.0	474.6	142.4	217.0	714.8	1 037.6	520.2	21.1	493.7	298.8
1996:											
January	509.7	32.5	477.2	143.6	226.0	713.1	1 049.4	525.2	23.8	499.1	297.6
February	516.7	34.9	481.8	145.0	235.2	713.4	1 054.1	529.2	22.7	500.6	300.5
March	521.9	37.1	484.8	146.3	241.9	714.0	1 060.2	534.2	22.3	502.4	301.3
April	525.6	39.5	486.1	147.3	241.4	714.6	1 064.1	533.9	23.4	506.2	302.7
May	528.8	41.2	487.6	148.4	242.5	715.7	1 064.6	535.2	21.2	507.3	304.3
June	529.7	42.3	487.4	149.6	246.4	717.3	1 067.7	537.1	21.6	508.6	306.8
July	535.2	44.8	490.4	151.0	251.1	720.7	1 070.4	538.8	21.9	509.9	306.8
August	532.7	43.5	489.2	152.2	255.8	721.5	1 072.2	540.6	20.4	511.4	308.5
September	532.7	41.3	491.4	153.3	259.2	722.3	1 073.5	540.8	21.7	511.8	310.1
October	533.5	38.9	494.6	154.4	259.3	723.9	1 076.0	542.3	21.3	513.4	310.5
November	532.1	35.9	496.2	155.4	259.6	726.5	1 080.3	546.2	21.1	514.5	312.2
December	533.5	35.2	498.3	156.2	259.8	730.1	1 082.9	548.2	22.3	515.0	314.4
1997:											
January	537.2	36.2	501.0	157.0	259.6	735.3	1 099.4	559.5	22.1	523.9	317.3
February	540.9	36.3	504.6	157.5	259.6	740.4	1 097.5	555.6	22.0	526.5	319.8
March	543.2	36.6	506.6	157.9	259.8	744.6	1 104.3	561.5	22.0	528.4	321.5
April	546.8	37.8	509.0	157.8	259.8	745.4	1 105.1	562.4	22.0	530.3	322.3
May	549.7	38.0	511.7	158.0	259.9	745.7	1 106.2	564.8	21.9	529.8	323.8
June	553.3	37.8	515.5	158.2	260.1	745.9	1 109.1	566.3	21.9	531.9	324.9
July	554.3	37.3	517.0	158.4	260.1	749.2	1 110.9	567.3	21.7	533.1	326.1
August	555.6	36.4	519.2	158.6	260.3	750.6	1 114.1	570.4	21.4	534.1	328.6
September	559.6	35.1	524.5	158.7	260.7	751.7	1 116.8	570.0	22.0	537.0	329.7
October	558.9	33.5	525.4	158.7	261.0	752.5	1 117.5	572.0	21.0	538.0	331.7
November	557.7	31.5	526.2	158.8	261.3	753.0	1 119.3	573.0	21.0	539.0	334.1
December	557.5	29.1	528.4	158.9	261.4	753.3	1 124.7	578.0	22.0	541.0	334.9
1998:											
January	559.8	28.2	531.6	158.3	261.5	754.7	1 133.8	579.3	19.6	534.9	339.3
February	563.9	27.3	536.6	158.4	261.6	757.0	1 138.4	581.2	19.5	537.7	341.2
March	568.8	26.6	542.2	158.3	261.8	759.3	1 144.7	584.4	19.7	540.6	342.2
April	569.8	26.5	543.3	159.8	262.0	761.1	1 143.8	583.7	19.5	540.5	343.5
May	551.2	35.5	515.8	158.2	260.3	747.3	1 110.4	565.9	19.9	524.6	326.2
June	574.8	28.2	546.6	162.6	262.3	765.0	1 148.3	586.2	19.6	542.5	346.2
July	577.2	26.8	550.5	163.0	262.4	767.3	1 150.4	588.0	19.5	542.9	347.7
August	574.7	25.2	549.5	163.5	262.8	769.4	1 151.8	588.5	19.4	544.0	349.9
September	576.4	23.5	552.9	164.4	263.7	770.7	1 156.6	590.4	19.6	546.6	350.8
October	582.9	25.7	557.3	164.8	264.7	770.5	1 155.8	588.8	19.4	547.6	352.5
November	614.8	53.0	561.7	171.6	265.7	769.8	1 157.3	589.6	19.5	458.1	354.2
December	592.9	25.4	567.5	166.3	266.7	769.4	1 161.7	593.2	19.6	548.9	355.6

1. Includes inventory valuation and capital consumption adjustments.
2. Includes capital consumption adjustment.

Disposition of Personal Income

(Billions of dollars, except as noted; monthly data are at seasonally adjusted annual rates)

Year and month	Total personal income	Less: Personal tax and nontax payments	Equals: Disposable personal income	Less: Personal outlays Total	Personal consumption expenditures	Interest paid by persons	Personal transfer payments to the rest of the world	Equals: Personal saving Billions of dollars	Percent of disposable personal income	Disposable personal income Total, chained (1992) dollars	Per capita (dollars) Current dollars	Per capita (dollars) Chained 1992 dollars	Population (thousands)
1970	837.1	109.0	728.1	666.1	648.1	16.8	1.2	62.0	8.5	2 469.0	3 550	12 039	205 089
1971	900.2	108.7	791.5	721.6	702.5	17.8	1.3	69.9	8.8	2 568.3	3 811	12 366	207 692
1972	988.8	132.0	856.8	791.6	770.7	19.6	1.3	65.2	7.6	2 685.7	4 082	12 794	209 924
1973	1 107.6	140.6	967.0	875.4	851.6	22.4	1.4	91.5	9.5	2 875.2	4 562	13 566	211 939
1974	1 215.9	159.1	1 056.8	956.6	931.2	24.2	1.2	100.2	9.5	2 854.2	4 941	13 344	213 898
1975	1 319.0	156.4	1 162.6	1 054.8	1 029.1	24.5	1.2	107.8	9.3	2 903.6	5 383	13 444	215 981
1976	1 459.4	182.3	1 277.1	1 176.7	1 148.8	26.7	1.2	100.4	7.9	3 017.6	5 856	13 837	218 086
1977	1 616.1	210.0	1 406.1	1 308.9	1 277.1	30.7	1.2	97.2	6.9	3 115.4	6 383	14 142	220 289
1978	1 825.9	240.1	1 585.8	1 467.6	1 428.8	37.5	1.3	118.2	7.5	3 276.0	7 123	14 715	222 629
1979	2 055.9	280.2	1 775.7	1 639.5	1 593.5	44.5	1.4	136.2	7.7	3 365.5	7 888	14 951	225 106
1980	2 292.9	312.4	1 980.5	1 811.5	1 760.4	49.4	1.6	169.1	8.5	3 385.7	8 697	14 867	227 726
1981	2 568.5	360.2	2 208.3	2 001.1	1 941.3	54.6	5.2	207.2	9.4	3 464.9	9 601	15 064	230 008
1982	2 724.1	371.4	2 352.7	2 141.8	2 076.8	58.8	6.2	210.9	9.0	3 491.1	10 131	15 034	232 218
1983	2 894.4	369.3	2 525.1	2 355.5	2 283.4	65.5	6.5	169.7	6.7	3 583.7	10 775	15 293	234 333
1984	3 211.4	395.5	2 815.9	2 574.4	2 492.3	74.7	7.4	241.5	8.6	3 850.0	11 911	16 286	236 394
1985	3 440.9	437.7	3 003.2	2 795.8	2 704.8	83.2	7.8	207.4	6.9	3 960.3	12 591	16 604	238 506
1986	3 639.6	459.9	3 179.7	2 991.1	2 892.7	90.4	8.1	188.6	6.0	4 076.9	13 211	16 939	240 682
1987	3 877.8	514.2	3 363.6	3 194.7	3 094.5	91.5	8.7	168.9	5.0	4 154.7	13 851	17 108	242 843
1988	4 178.9	532.0	3 646.9	3 451.7	3 349.7	92.9	9.1	195.2	5.4	4 325.3	14 881	17 650	245 061
1989	4 496.4	594.9	3 901.6	3 706.7	3 594.8	102.4	9.6	194.9	5.0	4 411.6	15 771	17 833	247 388
1990	4 796.2	624.8	4 171.4	3 958.1	3 839.3	108.9	9.9	213.3	5.1	4 489.6	16 688	17 962	249 956
1991	4 965.6	624.8	4 340.9	4 097.4	3 975.1	111.9	10.4	243.5	5.6	4 483.5	17 179	17 744	252 680
1992	5 255.7	650.6	4 605.1	4 341.0	4 219.8	111.7	9.6	264.1	5.7	4 605.1	18 028	18 029	255 432
1993	5 481.0	690.0	4 791.1	4 580.7	4 459.3	108.2	13.3	210.3	4.4	4 666.7	18 558	18 077	258 161
1994	5 757.9	739.1	5 018.9	4 842.1	4 717.0	110.9	14.2	176.8	3.5	4 772.9	19 250	18 307	260 705
1995	6 072.1	795.0	5 277.1	5 097.2	4 953.9	127.6	15.7	179.8	3.4	4 906.1	20 050	18 640	263 195
1996	6 425.2	890.5	5 534.7	5 376.2	5 215.7	143.6	16.9	158.5	2.9	5 043.0	20 840	18 989	265 579
1997	6 784.0	989.0	5 795.1	5 674.1	5 493.7	161.5	18.9	121.0	2.1	5 183.1	21 633	19 349	267 880
1998	7 126.1	1 098.3	6 027.9	6 000.2	5 807.9	172.4	19.9	27.7	0.5	5 348.5	22 304	19 790	270 258
1995:													
January	5 963.5	763.5	5 200.0	4 997.9	4 863.7	119.0	15.2	202.2	3.9	4 878.0	19 843	18 614	262 057
February	5 979.9	768.1	5 211.7	4 982.5	4 847.9	119.4	15.2	229.2	4.4	4 882.9	19 875	18 621	262 223
March	5 995.1	769.9	5 225.2	5 011.9	4 875.8	120.9	15.2	213.3	4.1	4 888.1	19 911	18 627	262 427
April	6 015.1	823.9	5 191.2	5 019.2	4 882.2	122.2	14.8	172.0	3.3	4 845.5	19 766	18 449	262 639
May	6 025.3	778.3	5 247.1	5 075.8	4 936.7	124.3	14.8	171.3	3.3	4 885.6	19 963	18 588	262 842
June	6 050.5	784.8	5 265.7	5 116.9	4 975.5	126.6	14.8	148.7	2.8	4 897.1	20 017	18 616	263 060
July	6 067.0	792.4	5 274.7	5 102.3	4 959.0	127.8	15.6	172.3	3.3	4 899.1	20 034	18 607	263 289
August	6 091.0	799.0	5 291.9	5 148.7	5 003.5	129.6	15.6	143.3	2.7	4 902.9	20 081	18 605	263 525
September	6 122.5	805.6	5 316.9	5 145.3	4 996.7	133.0	15.6	171.6	3.2	4 925.3	20 157	18 673	263 767
October	6 155.8	811.7	5 344.2	5 150.3	4 998.7	134.4	17.2	193.8	3.6	4 939.0	20 244	18 709	263 984
November	6 184.9	818.6	5 366.3	5 189.8	5 036.0	136.6	17.2	176.5	3.3	4 957.6	20 314	18 766	264 172
December	6 214.4	824.5	5 389.8	5 226.2	5 071.1	137.9	17.2	163.6	3.0	4 971.7	20 389	18 807	264 351
1996:													
January	6 231.7	837.5	5 394.2	5 226.0	5 073.3	136.9	15.8	168.2	3.1	4 964.4	20 394	18 769	264 505
February	6 294.9	852.2	5 442.7	5 267.6	5 114.8	137.0	15.8	175.0	3.2	5 001.6	20 564	18 898	264 667
March	6 326.3	859.2	5 467.0	5 289.7	5 136.4	137.5	15.8	177.3	3.2	5 000.9	20 640	18 914	264 870
April	6 354.8	916.7	5 438.1	5 345.4	5 189.9	138.8	16.6	92.7	1.7	4 969.8	20 516	18 749	265 066
May	6 384.7	876.2	5 508.5	5 367.8	5 210.4	140.8	16.6	140.7	2.6	5 028.0	20 767	18 955	265 253
June	6 430.6	887.0	5 543.6	5 355.6	5 196.6	142.4	16.6	188.0	3.4	5 057.4	20 883	19 052	265 456
July	6 447.1	891.6	5 555.5	5 391.8	5 231.0	144.2	16.6	163.7	2.9	5 057.9	20 912	19 038	265 669
August	6 477.0	899.1	5 578.0	5 404.7	5 242.0	146.2	16.6	173.2	3.1	5 075.4	20 979	19 089	265 886
September	6 506.0	907.6	5 598.4	5 418.9	5 254.4	147.9	16.6	179.5	3.2	5 085.2	21 038	19 110	266 106
October	6 517.0	912.0	5 605.0	5 458.8	5 292.0	148.3	18.5	146.1	2.6	5 076.3	21 047	19 062	266 308
November	6 547.3	918.8	5 628.5	5 478.3	5 309.4	150.4	18.5	150.2	2.7	5 088.2	21 121	19 093	266 492
December	6 585.0	928.1	5 656.9	5 510.3	5 338.4	153.3	18.5	146.6	2.6	5 102.4	21 213	19 134	266 672
1997:													
January	6 627.3	947.1	5 680.2	5 560.3	5 388.1	154.3	18.0	119.8	2.1	5 113.7	21 288	19 165	266 826
February	6 668.1	956.2	5 711.8	5 576.9	5 403.6	155.3	18.0	134.9	2.4	5 130.7	21 395	19 218	266 975
March	6 704.9	963.4	5 741.5	5 590.1	5 415.7	156.4	18.0	151.5	2.6	5 147.8	21 491	19 269	267 161
April	6 720.3	967.9	5 752.4	5 597.7	5 421.9	157.6	18.2	154.7	2.7	5 152.8	21 516	19 273	267 354
May	6 744.1	976.0	5 768.1	5 604.1	5 427.0	158.8	18.2	164.0	2.8	5 171.7	21 560	19 331	267 541
June	6 766.4	983.3	5 783.1	5 646.2	5 467.5	160.5	18.2	136.9	2.4	5 178.0	21 600	19 340	267 741
July	6 785.8	990.0	5 795.7	5 709.8	5 529.1	161.2	19.5	85.9	1.5	5 181.3	21 630	19 337	267 952
August	6 826.7	1 000.3	5 826.4	5 720.6	5 537.7	163.3	19.5	105.8	1.8	5 203.2	21 726	19 403	268 171
September	6 850.1	1 006.7	5 843.4	5 739.6	5 554.0	166.0	19.5	103.8	1.8	5 210.7	21 772	19 415	268 391
October	6 875.5	1 015.5	5 860.0	5 752.7	5 565.8	167.2	19.8	107.2	1.8	5 221.4	21 814	19 437	268 633
November	6 910.9	1 026.9	5 884.0	5 783.4	5 596.4	167.2	19.8	100.6	1.7	5 239.7	21 888	19 491	268 823
December	6 928.3	1 034.1	5 894.2	5 807.4	5 617.4	170.2	19.8	86.8	1.5	5 246.5	21 912	19 504	268 989
1998:													
January	6 970.5	1 058.7	5 911.8	5 837.3	5 649.3	168.8	19.2	74.5	1.3	5 264.9	21 965	19 562	269 143
February	7 007.3	1 069.4	5 937.9	5 870.0	5 682.7	168.1	19.2	67.9	1.1	5 287.0	22 049	19 632	269 302
March	7 033.9	1 072.4	5 961.5	5 884.7	5 697.5	168.0	19.2	76.8	1.3	5 309.5	22 122	19 703	269 482
April	7 055.6	1 076.7	5 978.8	5 915.1	5 727.3	168.0	19.9	63.7	1.1	5 318.1	22 171	19 721	269 669
May	7 085.9	1 094.9	5 990.9	5 970.4	5 782.1	168.4	19.9	20.5	0.5	5 324.2	22 223	19 729	269 862
June	7 104.4	1 100.5	6 004.0	6 005.2	5 815.0	170.4	19.9	-1.2	0.2	5 331.9	22 241	19 743	270 067
July	7 133.7	1 102.0	6 031.7	6 009.5	5 817.7	171.9	20.0	22.2	0.4	5 347.1	22 316	19 783	270 289
August	7 164.1	1 110.8	6 053.3	6 036.4	5 843.1	173.3	20.0	16.9	0.3	5 363.0	22 376	19 825	270 522
September	7 184.6	1 112.4	6 072.2	6 073.7	5 879.2	174.5	20.0	-1.4	0.0	5 382.3	22 427	19 879	270 757
October	7 217.2	1 119.1	6 098.1	6 109.3	5 912.0	176.7	20.6	-11.2	-0.2	5 393.8	22 504	19 905	270 973
November	7 279.8	1 125.4	6 154.5	6 117.9	5 919.2	178.1	20.6	36.6	0.6	5 441.3	22 682	20 054	271 336
December	7 276.8	1 130.1	6 146.7	6 173.7	5 973.1	180.1	20.6	-27.1	-0.4	5 428.6	22 624	19 981	271 684

Disposition of Personal Income—*Continued*

(Billions of dollars, except as noted; monthly data are at seasonally adjusted annual rates)

Year and month	Personal consumption expenditure											
	Current dollars				Chained (1992) dollars				Implicit price deflators for personal consumption expenditure (1992=100)			
	Total	Durable goods	Nondura-ble goods	Services	Total	Durable goods	Nondura-ble goods	Services	Total	Durable goods	Nondura-ble goods	Services
1970	648.1	85.0	272.0	291.1	2 197.8	187.0	859.1	1 155.4	29.5	45.4	31.7	25.2
1971	702.5	96.9	285.5	320.1	2 279.5	205.7	874.5	1 197.9	30.8	47.1	32.6	26.7
1972	770.7	110.4	308.0	352.3	2 415.9	231.9	912.9	1 262.5	31.9	47.6	33.7	27.9
1973	851.6	123.5	343.1	384.9	2 532.6	255.8	942.9	1 319.4	33.6	48.3	36.4	29.2
1974	931.2	122.3	384.5	424.4	2 514.7	238.2	924.5	1 351.2	37.0	51.3	41.6	31.4
1975	1 029.1	133.5	420.6	475.0	2 570.0	238.1	938.3	1 398.3	40.0	56.0	44.8	34.0
1976	1 148.8	158.8	458.2	531.8	2 714.3	268.5	984.8	1 457.1	42.3	59.2	46.5	36.5
1977	1 277.1	181.1	496.9	599.0	2 829.8	293.4	1 010.4	1 518.2	45.1	61.7	49.2	39.5
1978	1 428.8	201.4	549.9	677.4	2 951.6	308.8	1 045.7	1 589.3	48.4	65.2	52.6	42.6
1979	1 593.5	213.9	624.0	755.6	3 020.1	307.3	1 069.7	1 639.8	52.8	69.6	58.3	46.1
1980	1 760.4	213.5	695.5	851.4	3 009.7	282.6	1 065.1	1 670.7	58.5	75.6	65.3	51.0
1981	1 941.3	230.5	758.2	952.6	3 046.4	285.8	1 074.3	1 696.1	63.7	80.6	70.6	56.2
1982	2 076.8	239.3	786.8	1 050.7	3 081.5	285.5	1 080.6	1 728.2	67.4	83.8	72.8	60.8
1983	2 283.4	279.9	830.3	1 173.3	3 240.6	327.4	1 112.4	1 809.0	70.5	85.5	74.6	64.9
1984	2 492.3	325.1	883.6	1 283.7	3 407.6	374.9	1 151.8	1 883.0	73.1	86.7	76.7	68.2
1985	2 704.8	361.1	927.6	1 416.1	3 566.5	411.4	1 178.4	1 977.3	75.8	87.8	78.7	71.6
1986	2 892.7	398.7	957.2	1 536.8	3 708.7	448.4	1 215.9	2 041.4	78.0	88.9	78.7	75.3
1987	3 094.5	416.7	1 014.0	1 663.8	3 822.3	455.0	1 239.3	2 126.9	81.0	91.6	81.8	78.2
1988	3 349.7	451.0	1 081.1	1 817.6	3 972.7	483.5	1 274.4	2 212.4	84.3	93.3	84.8	82.2
1989	3 594.8	472.8	1 163.8	1 958.1	4 064.6	496.2	1 303.5	2 262.3	88.4	95.3	89.3	86.6
1990	3 839.3	476.5	1 245.3	2 117.5	4 132.1	493.3	1 316.1	2 321.4	92.9	96.6	94.6	91.2
1991	3 975.1	455.2	1 277.6	2 242.3	4 105.8	462.0	1 302.9	2 341.0	96.8	98.5	98.1	95.8
1992	4 219.8	488.5	1 321.8	2 409.4	4 219.8	488.5	1 321.8	2 409.4	100.0	100.0	100.0	100.0
1993	4 459.3	530.2	1 370.7	2 558.4	4 343.6	523.8	1 351.0	2 468.9	102.7	101.2	101.5	103.6
1994	4 717.0	579.5	1 428.4	2 709.1	4 486.0	561.2	1 389.9	2 535.5	105.2	103.3	102.8	106.9
1995	4 953.9	611.0	1 473.7	2 869.2	4 605.6	589.1	1 417.6	2 599.6	107.6	103.7	104.0	110.4
1996	5 215.7	643.3	1 539.2	3 033.2	4 752.4	626.1	1 450.9	2 676.7	109.8	102.8	106.1	113.3
1997	5 493.7	673.0	1 600.6	3 220.1	4 913.5	668.6	1 486.3	2 761.5	111.8	100.7	107.7	116.6
1998	5 807.9	724.7	1 662.4	3 420.8	5 153.3	737.1	1 544.1	2 879.5	112.7	98.3	107.7	118.8
1995:												
January	4 863.7	604.7	1 471.5	2 787.4	4 562.4	581.8	1 422.2	2 559.9	106.6	103.9	103.5	108.9
February	4 847.9	587.8	1 451.3	2 808.8	4 542.1	565.1	1 402.3	2 574.8	106.7	104.0	103.5	109.1
March	4 875.8	602.6	1 455.9	2 817.3	4 561.3	578.6	1 406.5	2 576.7	106.9	104.2	103.5	109.3
April	4 882.2	588.3	1 463.5	2 830.5	4 557.0	564.6	1 410.2	2 582.3	107.1	104.2	103.8	109.6
May	4 936.7	608.7	1 473.3	2 854.7	4 596.6	586.3	1 417.6	2 593.4	107.4	103.8	103.9	110.1
June	4 975.5	621.2	1 475.5	2 878.8	4 627.2	599.6	1 419.8	2 608.6	107.5	103.6	103.9	110.4
July	4 959.0	608.7	1 471.2	2 879.1	4 605.9	587.5	1 413.7	2 605.0	107.7	103.6	104.1	110.5
August	5 003.5	626.2	1 475.8	2 901.5	4 635.6	603.9	1 417.8	2 614.8	107.9	103.7	104.1	111.0
September	4 996.7	616.0	1 483.3	2 897.5	4 628.7	594.6	1 423.9	2 611.1	108.0	103.6	104.2	111.0
October	4 998.7	613.6	1 476.9	2 908.2	4 619.7	592.9	1 414.8	2 612.5	108.2	103.5	104.4	111.3
November	5 036.0	620.6	1 487.5	2 927.9	4 652.5	601.1	1 427.1	2 625.1	108.2	103.3	104.2	111.5
December	5 071.1	634.1	1 498.1	2 938.9	4 677.7	613.1	1 435.0	2 631.1	108.4	103.4	104.4	111.7
1996:												
January	5 073.3	622.2	1 497.6	2 953.5	4 669.0	601.0	1 428.5	2 640.0	108.7	103.5	104.8	111.9
February	5 114.8	642.4	1 508.3	2 964.1	4 700.3	620.8	1 436.4	2 644.7	108.8	103.5	105.0	112.1
March	5 136.4	632.4	1 514.6	2 989.4	4 706.9	611.1	1 435.7	2 660.8	109.1	103.5	105.5	112.4
April	5 189.9	649.3	1 538.3	3 002.3	4 743.0	629.4	1 450.9	2 664.6	109.4	103.2	106.0	112.7
May	5 210.4	653.3	1 540.3	3 016.8	4 755.8	635.8	1 451.1	2 671.1	109.6	102.8	106.2	112.9
June	5 196.6	639.4	1 535.2	3 021.9	4 740.8	623.3	1 449.3	2 669.6	109.6	102.6	105.9	113.2
July	5 231.0	638.9	1 540.4	3 051.8	4 762.4	622.7	1 451.7	2 688.6	109.8	102.6	106.1	113.5
August	5 242.0	647.6	1 540.2	3 054.1	4 769.7	631.6	1 454.3	2 685.3	109.9	102.5	105.9	113.7
September	5 254.4	641.1	1 550.2	3 063.1	4 772.8	625.2	1 458.1	2 690.4	110.1	102.6	106.3	113.9
October	5 292.0	652.8	1 563.8	3 075.4	4 792.8	637.4	1 465.2	2 692.2	110.4	102.4	106.7	114.2
November	5 309.4	651.0	1 567.4	3 090.9	4 799.7	637.2	1 464.3	2 699.9	110.6	102.2	107.0	114.5
December	5 338.4	649.4	1 573.6	3 115.4	4 815.1	637.9	1 465.6	2 713.0	110.9	101.8	107.4	114.8
1997:												
January	5 388.1	670.8	1 585.8	3 131.5	4 850.7	659.3	1 474.9	2 719.6	111.1	101.8	107.5	115.1
February	5 403.6	668.4	1 589.5	3 145.7	4 853.8	654.9	1 476.8	2 724.8	111.3	102.1	107.6	115.5
March	5 415.7	667.4	1 593.8	3 154.5	4 855.6	654.6	1 482.1	2 721.8	111.5	102.0	107.5	115.9
April	5 421.9	656.3	1 585.4	3 180.2	4 856.7	648.3	1 472.0	2 737.8	111.6	101.2	107.7	116.2
May	5 427.0	656.7	1 586.9	3 183.5	4 865.9	650.8	1 476.5	2 740.3	111.5	100.9	107.5	116.2
June	5 467.5	666.8	1 592.3	3 208.4	4 895.4	662.2	1 482.9	2 752.8	111.7	100.7	107.4	116.6
July	5 529.1	682.9	1 608.6	3 237.7	4 942.9	679.4	1 497.2	2 770.3	111.9	100.5	107.4	116.9
August	5 537.7	683.5	1 610.8	3 243.5	4 945.4	682.6	1 495.4	2 771.7	112.0	100.1	107.7	117.0
September	5 554.0	677.1	1 614.4	3 262.5	4 952.6	676.9	1 494.6	2 784.1	112.1	100.0	108.0	117.2
October	5 565.8	671.7	1 614.6	3 279.5	4 959.3	673.0	1 494.4	2 794.0	112.2	99.8	108.0	117.4
November	5 596.4	684.8	1 614.8	3 296.7	4 983.6	687.9	1 495.7	2 803.3	112.3	99.6	108.0	117.6
December	5 617.4	690.1	1 610.2	3 317.1	5 000.1	693.3	1 492.6	2 817.3	112.4	99.5	107.9	117.7
1998:												
January	5 649.3	709.6	1 623.8	3 315.9	5 031.1	713.8	1 508.6	2 814.9	112.3	99.4	107.6	117.8
February	5 682.7	708.2	1 636.7	3 337.8	5 059.7	713.1	1 523.7	2 829.0	112.3	99.3	107.4	118.0
March	5 697.5	697.6	1 638.8	3 361.0	5 074.3	703.8	1 531.4	2 843.8	112.3	99.1	107.0	118.2
April	5 727.3	698.5	1 646.9	3 381.8	5 094.4	704.2	1 536.9	2 857.4	112.4	99.2	107.2	118.4
May	5 776.1	722.1	1 661.3	3 392.8	5 127.9	731.7	1 543.8	2 860.0	112.6	98.7	107.6	118.6
June	5 809.7	733.9	1 664.8	3 411.0	5 157.1	746.3	1 548.7	2 871.3	112.6	98.3	107.5	118.6
July	5 817.7	707.4	1 669.9	3 440.4	5 157.4	719.3	1 551.2	2 891.5	112.8	98.4	107.7	119.0
August	5 843.1	715.4	1 669.4	3 458.2	5 176.8	729.8	1 546.6	2 905.4	112.9	98.0	107.9	119.0
September	5 879.2	733.8	1 670.8	3 474.7	5 211.2	751.8	1 549.3	2 917.5	112.8	97.6	107.8	119.1
October	5 912.0	748.5	1 683.2	3 480.4	5 229.3	767.1	1 557.9	2 914.3	113.1	97.6	108.0	119.4
November	5 919.2	742.0	1 691.2	3 486.0	5 233.3	761.8	1 567.0	2 914.2	113.1	97.4	107.9	119.4
December	5 973.1	773.2	1 699.6	3 500.3	5 275.3	796.1	1 570.4	2 923.0	113.2	97.1	108.2	119.8

Personal Consumption Expenditures by Major Type of Product

(Billions of dollars, quarterly data are seasonally adjusted annual rates)

Year and quarter	Total	Durable goods				Nondurable goods					
		Total	Motor vehicles and parts	Furniture and house-hold equip-ment	Other	Total	Food	Clothing and shoes	Gasoline and oil	Fuel oil and coal	Other
1970	648.1	85.0	35.5	35.7	13.7	272.0	143.8	47.8	21.9	4.4	54.1
1971	702.5	96.9	44.5	37.8	14.6	285.5	149.7	51.7	23.2	4.6	56.4
1972	770.7	110.4	51.1	42.4	16.9	308.0	161.4	56.4	24.4	5.1	60.8
1973	851.6	123.5	56.1	47.9	19.5	343.1	179.6	62.5	28.1	6.3	66.6
1974	931.2	122.3	49.5	51.5	21.3	384.5	201.8	66.0	36.1	7.8	72.7
1975	1 029.1	133.5	54.8	54.5	24.2	420.6	223.1	70.8	39.7	8.4	78.5
1976	1 148.8	158.9	71.3	60.2	27.4	458.2	242.4	76.6	43.0	10.1	86.0
1977	1 277.1	181.1	83.5	67.1	30.5	496.9	262.4	84.1	46.9	11.1	92.4
1978	1 428.8	201.4	93.1	74.0	34.3	549.9	289.2	94.3	50.1	11.5	104.7
1979	1 593.5	213.9	93.5	82.3	38.2	624.0	324.2	101.2	66.2	14.4	118.0
1980	1 760.4	213.5	87.0	86.0	40.5	695.5	355.4	107.3	86.7	15.4	130.6
1981	1 941.3	230.5	95.8	91.3	43.4	758.2	382.8	117.2	97.9	15.8	144.5
1982	2 076.8	239.3	102.9	92.5	43.9	786.8	402.6	120.5	94.1	14.5	155.2
1983	2 283.4	279.8	126.9	105.3	47.7	830.3	422.9	130.9	93.1	13.6	169.8
1984	2 492.3	325.1	152.5	117.2	55.4	883.6	446.3	142.5	94.6	13.9	186.3
1985	2 704.8	361.1	175.7	126.3	59.0	927.6	466.5	152.1	97.2	13.6	198.2
1986	2 892.7	398.7	192.4	140.3	66.0	957.2	490.8	163.1	80.1	11.3	211.9
1987	3 094.5	416.7	193.1	150.4	73.2	1 014.0	513.9	174.4	85.4	11.2	229.1
1988	3 349.7	451.0	207.5	162.8	80.7	1 081.1	551.2	185.9	87.1	11.4	245.3
1989	3 594.8	472.8	214.4	173.3	85.2	1 163.8	588.4	199.9	96.6	11.4	267.5
1990	3 839.3	476.5	210.3	176.0	90.1	1 245.3	630.5	205.9	109.2	12.0	287.6
1991	3 975.1	455.2	187.6	178.5	89.1	1 277.6	650.0	211.3	103.9	11.3	301.2
1992	4 219.8	488.5	206.9	189.4	92.3	1 321.8	660.0	225.5	106.6	10.9	318.8
1993	4 459.2	530.2	226.2	204.9	99.1	1 370.7	686.8	236.5	107.6	10.7	329.0
1994	4 717.0	579.5	246.6	226.2	106.7	1 428.4	714.5	247.8	109.4	10.5	346.2
1995	4 953.9	611.0	255.4	241.2	114.4	1 473.6	731.8	254.1	115.6	10.9	361.3
1996	5 215.7	643.3	264.8	256.0	122.5	1 539.2	755.0	265.7	124.5	12.2	381.8
1997	5 493.7	673.0	269.5	271.4	132.1	1 600.6	780.9	278.0	126.5	11.2	403.9
1998	5 807.9	724.7	290.5	292.2	141.9	1 662.4	815.3	293.8	112.1	9.6	431.6
1990:											
1st quarter	3 759.2	493.3	223.4	178.9	90.9	1 220.7	617.6	205.8	102.8	11.5	283.0
2nd quarter	3 811.8	477.6	211.5	176.4	89.7	1 230.2	627.5	205.6	100.4	11.3	285.3
3rd quarter	3 879.2	473.2	208.5	175.0	89.7	1 256.2	637.1	206.8	109.6	12.7	290.0
4th quarter	3 907.0	461.9	198.0	173.7	90.2	1 274.1	639.7	205.5	124.1	12.6	292.2
1991:											
1st quarter	3 910.7	449.0	183.6	175.2	90.2	1 268.3	644.0	207.2	108.4	11.9	296.8
2nd quarter	3 961.0	452.7	183.3	179.7	89.7	1 279.7	652.9	212.7	103.6	10.8	299.6
3rd quarter	4 001.6	462.0	192.5	180.6	88.8	1 283.4	653.2	214.1	102.1	11.3	302.7
4th quarter	4 027.1	457.3	191.1	178.3	87.9	1 279.0	649.8	211.1	101.4	11.0	305.8
1992:											
1st quarter	4 127.6	474.1	199.1	184.8	90.2	1 303.1	657.3	219.6	102.3	10.4	313.5
2nd quarter	4 183.0	481.3	204.0	186.5	90.8	1 308.4	652.3	222.3	105.8	11.8	316.2
3rd quarter	4 238.9	492.5	208.3	190.6	93.6	1 326.3	657.9	228.1	109.4	10.6	320.2
4th quarter	4 329.6	506.2	216.1	195.5	94.6	1 349.5	672.3	232.1	108.9	10.8	325.4
1993:											
1st quarter	4 365.4	506.4	212.4	198.0	95.9	1 354.4	676.4	231.3	109.7	10.8	326.3
2nd quarter	4 428.1	524.2	224.3	202.1	97.8	1 366.3	684.1	235.4	107.6	10.5	328.8
3rd quarter	4 488.6	537.2	228.5	207.6	101.1	1 373.9	690.2	238.0	105.5	10.9	329.3
4th quarter	4 554.9	553.1	239.6	212.0	101.5	1 388.0	696.6	241.6	107.7	10.7	331.4
1994:											
1st quarter	4 616.6	563.2	244.1	216.2	102.9	1 404.4	703.9	244.1	106.2	11.7	338.4
2nd quarter	4 680.5	572.4	243.3	223.5	105.7	1 416.0	711.8	245.0	105.1	10.1	344.0
3rd quarter	4 750.6	583.3	245.4	229.7	108.2	1 439.5	718.5	249.0	111.8	10.6	349.6
4th quarter	4 820.2	599.3	253.7	235.4	110.2	1 453.7	723.7	253.2	114.3	9.8	352.7
1995:											
1st quarter	4 862.5	598.4	250.3	236.2	111.9	1 459.6	726.1	251.4	116.1	10.1	355.9
2nd quarter	4 931.5	606.0	254.4	237.9	113.7	1 470.7	730.4	252.9	116.8	11.1	359.5
3rd quarter	4 986.4	616.9	257.9	243.2	115.8	1 476.8	733.0	255.3	115.2	11.0	362.2
4th quarter	5 035.3	622.8	259.1	247.4	116.3	1 487.5	737.6	256.8	114.3	11.3	367.5
1996:											
1st quarter	5 108.2	632.3	264.9	248.9	118.5	1 506.8	743.3	260.1	118.8	12.6	371.9
2nd quarter	5 199.0	647.3	267.7	257.1	122.6	1 537.9	751.8	267.3	127.5	12.0	379.5
3rd quarter	5 242.5	642.5	262.8	257.2	122.6	1 543.6	757.5	266.5	123.4	11.8	384.5
4th quarter	5 313.2	651.1	264.0	260.8	126.3	1 568.3	767.4	268.8	128.3	12.3	391.5
1997:											
1st quarter	5 402.4	668.9	271.3	266.6	131.0	1 589.7	775.4	274.8	130.7	11.6	397.2
2nd quarter	5 438.8	659.9	260.7	269.2	130.0	1 588.2	775.8	275.6	123.7	11.5	401.5
3rd quarter	5 540.3	681.2	274.5	273.8	132.8	1 611.3	785.3	280.9	125.7	11.2	408.1
4th quarter	5 593.2	682.2	271.6	276.0	134.6	1 613.2	787.1	280.7	125.9	10.7	408.8
1998:											
1st quarter	5 676.5	705.1	277.0	288.5	139.6	1 633.1	796.9	291.0	116.2	9.5	419.4
2nd quarter	5 773.7	720.1	288.8	288.9	142.3	1 655.2	810.2	295.3	111.6	9.8	428.3
3rd quarter	5 846.7	718.9	282.6	294.1	142.2	1 670.0	818.7	293.7	111.7	9.8	436.2
4th quarter	5 934.8	754.5	313.6	297.3	143.6	1 691.3	835.6	295.1	109.0	9.0	442.7

Personal Consumption Expenditures by Major Type of Product—*Continued*

(Billions of dollars, quarterly data are seasonally adjusted annual rates)

Year and quarter	Services Total	Housing	Household operation Total	Electricity and gas	Other household operation	Transpor- tation	Medical care	Other
1970	291.1	94.0	37.8	15.2	22.6	23.7	50.4	85.3
1971	320.1	102.7	41.0	16.6	24.4	27.1	56.9	92.5
1972	352.3	112.1	45.3	18.4	26.9	29.8	63.8	101.3
1973	384.9	122.7	49.8	20.0	29.8	31.2	71.6	109.6
1974	424.4	134.1	55.5	23.5	32.0	33.3	80.6	120.8
1975	475.0	147.0	63.7	28.5	35.2	35.7	93.5	135.0
1976	531.8	161.5	72.4	32.5	40.0	41.3	106.7	149.8
1977	599.0	179.5	81.9	37.6	44.3	49.2	123.0	165.4
1978	677.4	201.7	91.2	42.1	49.1	53.5	140.0	191.0
1979	755.6	226.6	100.0	46.8	53.2	59.1	158.0	212.0
1980	851.4	255.2	113.0	56.3	56.7	64.7	181.2	237.3
1981	952.6	287.9	126.0	63.4	62.5	68.7	213.0	257.0
1982	1 050.7	313.2	141.4	72.6	68.8	70.9	239.4	285.7
1983	1 173.3	339.0	155.9	80.7	75.2	79.4	267.8	331.3
1984	1 283.6	370.6	168.0	84.7	83.3	90.0	294.1	361.0
1985	1 416.1	407.1	180.3	88.8	91.4	100.0	321.8	407.0
1986	1 536.8	442.2	186.9	87.2	99.7	107.3	346.1	454.2
1987	1 663.8	476.6	194.9	88.9	106.0	118.2	381.1	493.0
1988	1 817.6	512.9	206.6	94.1	112.5	130.5	428.7	538.9
1989	1 958.1	547.4	219.8	98.8	121.0	137.8	477.1	576.1
1990	2 117.5	586.3	226.3	98.7	127.6	143.7	537.7	623.5
1991	2 242.3	616.5	237.6	104.9	132.7	145.3	586.5	656.4
1992	2 409.4	646.8	248.2	106.6	141.7	158.1	646.6	709.7
1993	2 558.4	672.8	268.8	115.8	153.0	170.2	695.6	751.0
1994	2 709.1	712.7	283.7	116.6	167.0	186.2	731.6	794.8
1995	2 869.2	750.4	296.9	119.2	177.7	203.1	776.2	842.6
1996	3 033.2	787.4	314.5	125.5	189.0	222.3	806.8	902.3
1997	3 220.1	829.8	327.3	126.2	201.1	240.3	843.4	979.3
1998	3 420.8	877.9	338.6	122.1	216.5	252.7	888.2	1 063.5
1990:								
1st quarter	2 045.3	571.1	219.1	93.5	125.6	141.5	514.2	599.3
2nd quarter	2 104.1	581.5	227.0	99.5	127.5	143.2	530.6	621.8
3rd quarter	2 149.8	593.5	229.6	101.0	128.5	144.2	547.2	635.3
4th quarter	2 171.0	599.2	229.6	100.9	128.8	145.8	558.8	637.5
1991:								
1st quarter	2 193.5	605.8	230.7	101.6	129.2	143.0	568.2	645.7
2nd quarter	2 228.6	612.9	239.9	108.1	131.8	143.9	578.6	653.3
3rd quarter	2 256.3	619.7	240.5	106.1	134.4	145.9	591.3	658.8
4th quarter	2 290.7	627.5	239.3	104.0	135.3	148.5	607.7	667.8
1992:								
1st quarter	2 350.4	636.6	241.5	102.1	139.4	154.9	624.2	693.2
2nd quarter	2 393.3	643.4	248.8	106.2	142.7	156.9	640.6	703.6
3rd quarter	2 420.1	649.9	243.6	106.6	137.0	156.0	655.0	715.7
4th quarter	2 473.9	657.4	259.0	111.4	147.7	164.5	666.8	726.3
1993:								
1st quarter	2 504.6	662.2	260.3	112.4	147.9	166.8	680.8	734.4
2nd quarter	2 537.6	668.8	264.0	112.6	151.4	168.6	690.8	745.3
3rd quarter	2 577.4	675.8	274.1	119.2	154.9	170.7	701.6	755.2
4th quarter	2 613.8	684.4	276.7	118.8	157.9	174.5	709.2	768.9
1994:								
1st quarter	2 649.0	698.1	274.8	118.2	156.6	179.6	717.8	778.7
2nd quarter	2 692.2	707.8	287.1	120.0	167.1	184.5	726.5	786.4
3rd quarter	2 727.8	717.7	286.2	115.6	170.7	188.3	735.9	799.7
4th quarter	2 767.2	727.2	286.6	112.8	173.7	192.6	746.4	814.5
1995:								
1st quarter	2 804.5	736.9	288.0	113.5	174.5	195.7	762.3	821.6
2nd quarter	2 854.7	745.9	295.2	118.9	176.3	200.5	771.4	841.7
3rd quarter	2 892.7	754.5	303.0	123.8	179.2	206.2	780.8	848.2
4th quarter	2 925.0	764.5	301.5	120.7	180.8	209.9	790.2	858.9
1996:								
1st quarter	2 969.0	773.2	308.6	124.5	184.1	213.5	792.6	881.2
2nd quarter	3 013.7	782.1	315.4	126.7	188.8	219.9	803.7	892.5
3rd quarter	3 056.3	792.1	313.9	124.7	189.3	224.5	809.7	916.0
4th quarter	3 093.9	802.2	320.0	126.1	193.9	231.1	821.3	919.3
1997:								
1st quarter	3 143.9	812.8	318.3	123.2	195.2	234.4	829.3	949.1
2nd quarter	3 190.7	824.0	323.6	125.4	198.1	238.4	837.7	967.1
3rd quarter	3 247.9	835.4	330.4	127.0	203.4	242.2	848.7	991.3
4th quarter	3 297.8	847.0	337.0	129.2	207.8	246.3	857.9	1 009.5
1998:								
1st quarter	3 338.2	859.1	327.6	116.8	210.9	249.5	871.5	1 030.5
2nd quarter	3 398.4	871.9	339.2	124.1	215.1	253.2	884.2	1 049.8
3rd quarter	3 457.7	883.8	348.4	129.8	218.5	253.4	893.0	1 079.1
4th quarter	3 488.9	896.7	339.0	117.6	221.5	254.8	904.0	1 094.4

Real Personal Consumption Expenditures by Major Type of Product

(Billions of chained [1992] dollars, quarterly data are seasonally adjusted annual rates)

Year and quarter	Total	Durable goods				Nondurable goods					
		Total	Motor vehicles and parts	Furniture and house-hold equip-ment	Other	Total	Food	Clothing and shoes	Gasoline and oil	Fuel oil and coal	Other
1970	2 197.8	187.0	91.2	58.6	38.3	859.1	477.2	94.8	77.3	23.8	191.3
1971	2 279.5	205.7	108.7	60.9	38.9	874.5	481.6	99.4	81.1	23.0	192.6
1972	2 415.9	231.9	124.3	67.5	43.9	912.9	496.8	106.1	84.4	25.3	202.6
1973	2 532.6	255.8	135.7	74.9	49.3	942.9	498.4	113.5	88.8	27.5	216.4
1974	2 514.7	238.2	112.5	75.6	50.8	924.5	490.6	111.9	84.4	21.7	216.5
1975	2 570.0	238.1	113.2	73.9	52.8	938.3	502.6	115.7	86.9	21.3	209.7
1976	2 714.3	268.5	136.8	78.8	56.9	984.8	529.4	121.2	90.4	23.9	217.7
1977	2 829.8	293.4	151.5	85.5	61.0	1 010.4	541.2	127.8	93.2	23.1	221.2
1978	2 951.6	308.8	158.0	90.5	65.0	1 045.7	545.7	139.9	95.3	23.0	236.5
1979	3 020.2	307.3	147.4	95.4	67.4	1 069.7	555.1	145.8	94.0	21.3	249.2
1980	3 009.7	282.6	127.5	93.5	62.3	1 065.1	558.7	148.1	88.6	16.5	252.5
1981	3 046.4	285.8	130.5	93.5	63.0	1 074.3	557.9	156.1	89.9	13.8	256.8
1982	3 081.5	285.5	133.9	91.3	61.9	1 080.6	565.1	157.1	91.0	12.8	254.6
1983	3 240.6	327.4	160.5	103.5	65.3	1 112.4	579.7	167.3	93.0	12.9	259.3
1984	3 407.6	374.9	187.7	115.5	74.6	1 151.8	589.9	179.9	95.9	12.8	273.4
1985	3 566.5	411.4	211.2	125.3	78.1	1 178.3	602.2	186.5	97.8	13.0	279.1
1986	3 708.7	448.4	224.8	140.6	85.7	1 215.9	614.0	199.9	102.5	13.4	285.5
1987	3 822.3	454.9	216.2	149.9	90.9	1 239.3	620.8	205.4	105.3	13.0	294.5
1988	3 972.7	483.5	229.4	160.8	95.2	1 274.4	641.6	210.0	106.5	13.2	302.6
1989	4 064.6	496.2	230.3	170.9	96.4	1 303.5	650.1	220.7	108.1	12.6	311.5
1990	4 132.2	493.3	224.3	173.5	96.6	1 316.1	662.9	217.9	107.3	11.2	316.7
1991	4 105.8	462.0	193.2	177.0	91.8	1 302.9	659.6	215.9	103.4	10.8	313.2
1992	4 219.8	488.5	206.9	189.4	92.3	1 321.8	660.0	225.5	106.6	10.9	318.8
1993	4 343.6	523.8	218.9	207.8	97.2	1 351.0	675.3	234.2	108.7	10.7	322.1
1994	4 486.0	561.2	230.0	229.4	102.3	1 389.9	687.9	247.1	109.8	10.7	334.3
1995	4 605.6	589.1	230.6	251.2	109.0	1 417.6	689.5	260.1	114.3	11.2	343.1
1996	4 752.4	626.1	235.0	277.5	117.1	1 450.9	692.6	276.1	116.0	11.2	356.7
1997	4 913.5	668.6	239.3	307.7	127.7	1 486.5	699.3	288.4	117.9	10.3	373.0
1998	5 153.3	737.1	259.6	347.3	138.5	1 544.1	718.0	310.3	119.9	9.6	390.3
1990:											
1st quarter	4 128.9	511.2	237.6	176.0	98.9	1 319.2	659.0	221.5	109.3	10.7	318.5
2nd quarter	4 134.7	495.4	226.4	173.9	96.1	1 316.9	664.2	217.3	107.5	11.8	315.8
3rd quarter	4 148.5	490.4	223.1	172.5	95.8	1 319.8	665.5	217.6	107.4	12.3	316.7
4th quarter	4 116.4	476.3	210.0	171.5	95.5	1 308.4	662.9	215.1	104.9	9.9	315.6
1991:											
1st quarter	4 084.5	458.6	191.4	173.0	94.4	1 300.6	658.7	214.0	103.3	10.4	314.3
2nd quarter	4 110.0	460.5	189.6	177.7	93.2	1 308.0	661.5	218.9	104.0	10.8	312.8
3rd quarter	4 119.5	467.3	197.2	179.2	90.9	1 307.1	661.6	217.5	103.8	11.4	312.7
4th quarter	4 109.1	461.5	194.6	178.0	88.9	1 295.7	656.5	213.1	102.5	10.6	312.8
1992:											
1st quarter	4 173.8	476.1	201.7	183.7	90.7	1 314.4	661.0	220.4	104.8	10.5	317.7
2nd quarter	4 196.4	481.1	204.5	186.0	90.6	1 312.0	653.9	223.2	106.1	11.9	316.9
3rd quarter	4 226.7	491.9	207.4	191.3	93.3	1 321.1	656.4	227.7	108.2	10.5	318.4
4th quarter	4 282.3	505.0	213.9	196.4	94.6	1 339.8	668.6	230.9	107.3	10.7	322.3
1993:											
1st quarter	4 286.8	504.0	209.1	200.4	94.6	1 337.5	670.1	228.8	107.2	10.8	320.6
2nd quarter	4 322.8	519.3	218.4	205.0	95.9	1 347.8	674.1	233.4	108.6	10.3	321.4
3rd quarter	4 366.6	529.9	219.8	210.9	99.3	1 356.8	677.9	235.9	109.8	10.9	322.3
4th quarter	4 398.0	542.1	228.4	214.8	99.0	1 361.8	679.2	238.6	109.0	10.9	324.0
1994:											
1st quarter	4 439.4	550.7	231.6	219.1	100.0	1 378.4	684.3	243.1	109.2	11.9	329.9
2nd quarter	4 472.2	555.8	228.4	226.1	101.6	1 385.5	689.8	242.7	109.6	10.2	333.0
3rd quarter	4 498.2	561.7	227.3	232.2	102.9	1 393.2	687.9	248.1	109.9	10.7	336.7
4th quarter	4 534.1	576.6	232.6	240.3	104.5	1 402.5	689.5	254.7	110.7	10.2	337.8
1995:											
1st quarter	4 555.3	575.2	227.4	242.6	106.5	1 410.4	689.5	256.4	113.5	10.4	340.9
2nd quarter	4 593.6	583.5	229.5	246.6	108.7	1 415.9	689.6	258.4	114.2	11.4	342.8
3rd quarter	4 623.4	595.3	232.6	254.1	110.3	1 418.5	688.9	262.1	114.3	11.3	342.7
4th quarter	4 650.0	602.4	232.8	261.4	110.5	1 425.6	690.0	263.5	115.3	11.7	346.0
1996:											
1st quarter	4 692.1	611.0	235.9	265.0	112.3	1 433.5	691.1	268.0	114.7	11.9	348.9
2nd quarter	4 746.6	629.5	237.9	277.7	117.0	1 450.4	693.4	276.4	116.2	11.1	355.0
3rd quarter	4 768.3	626.5	232.8	280.0	117.6	1 454.7	691.4	279.8	116.0	11.3	358.2
4th quarter	4 802.6	637.5	233.3	287.2	121.5	1 465.1	694.3	280.3	117.0	10.6	364.8
1997:											
1st quarter	4 853.4	656.3	239.1	296.2	125.8	1 477.9	699.4	286.0	116.7	9.8	368.3
2nd quarter	4 872.7	653.8	230.8	303.7	125.9	1 477.1	697.3	283.3	118.3	10.4	369.9
3rd quarter	4 947.0	679.6	244.4	312.7	128.5	1 495.7	700.6	291.9	118.4	10.7	377.0
4th quarter	4 981.0	684.8	242.7	318.1	130.8	1 494.3	699.9	292.3	118.1	10.1	376.8
1998:											
1st quarter	5 055.1	710.3	247.8	335.8	135.1	1 521.2	706.8	307.4	118.5	9.2	383.5
2nd quarter	5 130.2	729.4	258.9	339.3	138.6	1 540.9	716.3	311.4	118.4	9.7	389.2
3rd quarter	5 181.8	733.7	252.6	352.0	139.1	1 549.1	718.9	309.8	121.1	9.9	393.4
4th quarter	5 246.0	775.0	279.3	362.1	141.0	1 565.1	730.1	312.5	121.5	9.5	395.2

Real Personal Consumption Expenditures by Major Type of Product— *Continued*

(Billions of chained [1992] dollars, quarterly data are seasonally adjusted annual rates)

Year and quarter	Services								Residual
	Total	Housing	Household operation			Transpor-tation	Medical care	Other	
			Total	Electricity and gas	Other household operation				
1970	1 155.5	329.3	130.2	65.4	64.7	89.1	250.8	344.0	2.0
1971	1 197.9	343.5	132.2	67.2	65.2	92.4	268.3	350.8	6.0
1972	1 262.5	361.5	139.0	70.8	68.4	98.1	286.4	367.0	12.8
1973	1 319.4	379.5	146.0	72.8	72.9	100.6	307.6	376.2	18.7
1974	1 351.2	399.1	147.5	73.7	73.6	101.1	320.2	374.3	8.7
1975	1 398.3	410.6	154.6	77.8	76.7	103.0	337.3	384.5	4.1
1976	1 457.1	422.9	161.4	80.5	80.6	107.3	353.5	403.8	10.7
1977	1 518.2	433.3	170.3	84.4	85.5	114.8	371.2	420.2	16.0
1978	1 589.3	454.5	178.6	87.7	90.5	118.0	385.7	443.2	18.2
1979	1 639.8	472.7	183.3	88.3	94.4	121.8	401.1	452.0	14.4
1980	1 670.7	486.7	187.4	90.7	96.0	115.6	415.5	457.8	-0.3
1981	1 696.1	497.8	185.9	89.4	95.9	111.7	436.4	459.8	-6.0
1982	1 728.2	500.9	187.0	90.3	96.0	109.9	442.2	484.5	-10.0
1983	1 809.0	511.8	193.0	93.0	99.3	117.0	459.7	524.9	-6.6
1984	1 883.0	531.8	197.7	93.6	103.6	128.6	472.4	549.9	-2.0
1985	1 977.3	551.1	205.6	96.1	109.1	140.6	490.7	587.0	-1.3
1986	2 041.4	565.5	209.8	95.1	114.7	145.7	510.3	608.5	2.5
1987	2 126.9	583.4	219.4	98.4	120.9	151.0	537.3	635.0	0.3
1988	2 212.4	600.9	229.2	103.4	125.7	159.0	561.3	661.6	1.5
1989	2 262.3	614.6	237.6	105.6	132.0	160.8	575.8	672.8	2.4
1990	2 321.3	627.2	240.1	103.7	136.4	159.9	602.8	691.2	0.6
1991	2 341.0	635.2	243.4	107.0	136.4	152.3	621.6	688.4	0.0
1992	2 409.4	646.8	248.2	106.6	141.7	158.1	646.6	709.7	-0.1
1993	2 468.9	654.7	261.5	112.3	149.2	163.1	655.3	734.5	-0.4
1994	2 535.5	674.3	270.5	112.5	158.0	175.2	662.1	754.0	-1.6
1995	2 599.6	688.6	280.6	114.7	165.8	186.4	675.0	769.8	-3.7
1996	2 676.7	700.9	291.4	118.0	173.3	200.5	686.6	798.6	-7.7
1997	2 761.5	717.4	301.3	116.0	185.1	212.2	701.7	830.5	-13.0
1998	2 879.5	735.0	316.8	116.2	200.5	220.4	723.2	886.0	-21.5
1990:									
1st quarter	2 295.7	623.4	233.7	98.6	135.2	161.7	591.9	684.9	1.7
2nd quarter	2 321.1	626.3	241.3	104.8	136.4	160.9	600.7	691.7	0.9
3rd quarter	2 337.3	628.5	243.7	106.2	137.4	159.7	608.0	697.4	0.4
4th quarter	2 331.2	630.6	241.9	105.3	136.6	157.3	610.6	690.8	-0.2
1991:									
1st quarter	2 325.3	631.6	238.2	103.5	134.7	152.6	614.3	688.7	-0.4
2nd quarter	2 341.5	634.1	246.9	110.9	136.0	152.1	617.9	690.4	0.1
3rd quarter	2 345.0	636.4	246.1	108.5	137.6	151.8	623.3	687.3	0.3
4th quarter	2 352.0	638.6	242.5	105.1	137.4	152.6	630.8	687.4	0.2
1992:									
1st quarter	2 383.2	642.6	243.6	103.2	140.5	155.4	638.2	703.4	0.0
2nd quarter	2 403.2	645.2	249.9	106.8	143.0	156.7	645.9	705.3	0.1
3rd quarter	2 413.6	648.5	243.3	106.6	136.7	160.5	650.3	710.9	0.0
4th quarter	2 437.6	650.6	256.1	109.7	146.5	159.6	652.2	719.1	-0.1
1993:									
1st quarter	2 445.3	650.6	256.6	111.0	145.7	160.3	653.7	724.1	-0.2
2nd quarter	2 455.9	652.4	257.7	109.2	148.5	161.9	654.3	729.7	-0.3
3rd quarter	2 480.0	655.8	265.2	114.7	150.5	163.8	656.4	739.0	-0.4
4th quarter	2 494.4	660.0	266.3	114.1	152.2	166.6	656.7	745.2	-0.7
1994:									
1st quarter	2 510.9	666.8	263.1	113.8	149.3	170.3	658.1	753.0	-1.0
2nd quarter	2 531.4	672.2	274.1	115.8	158.4	173.6	661.1	750.9	-1.2
3rd quarter	2 543.8	677.0	272.3	111.4	160.9	176.7	663.2	755.1	-1.8
4th quarter	2 555.9	681.1	272.4	108.9	163.4	180.1	666.0	756.9	-2.6
1995:									
1st quarter	2 570.4	684.9	272.8	109.4	163.3	182.8	669.1	761.4	-2.8
2nd quarter	2 594.8	687.0	279.6	114.8	164.8	184.2	673.0	771.7	-3.1
3rd quarter	2 610.3	689.7	286.0	119.1	166.9	187.6	677.2	770.7	-4.1
4th quarter	2 622.9	692.7	283.8	115.6	168.1	191.0	680.9	775.3	-4.8
1996:									
1st quarter	2 648.5	695.7	289.0	118.8	170.2	195.5	679.5	790.1	-5.5
2nd quarter	2 668.4	698.6	292.7	119.6	173.0	199.1	685.6	793.8	-7.8
3rd quarter	2 688.1	702.6	289.6	116.5	173.0	202.1	687.7	807.3	-8.0
4th quarter	2 701.7	706.7	294.4	117.2	177.1	205.3	693.5	803.1	-9.3
1997:									
1st quarter	2 722.1	711.2	291.1	112.4	178.6	208.6	694.8	817.5	-11.0
2nd quarter	2 743.6	715.1	297.8	116.0	181.6	210.7	698.6	823.0	-11.9
3rd quarter	2 775.4	719.5	305.0	117.2	187.7	213.7	704.2	834.8	-14.3
4th quarter	2 804.8	723.9	311.1	118.4	192.5	215.9	709.4	846.6	-14.5
1998:									
1st quarter	2 829.3	728.7	306.3	110.5	195.6	217.9	714.9	862.9	-19.5
2nd quarter	2 866.8	732.7	316.5	117.4	198.9	221.4	721.6	876.7	-20.3
3rd quarter	2 904.8	737.1	326.3	123.8	202.4	220.5	725.3	898.2	-22.3
4th quarter	2 917.2	741.5	318.2	112.9	205.0	221.8	730.8	906.3	-23.5

Industrial Production and Capacity Utilization

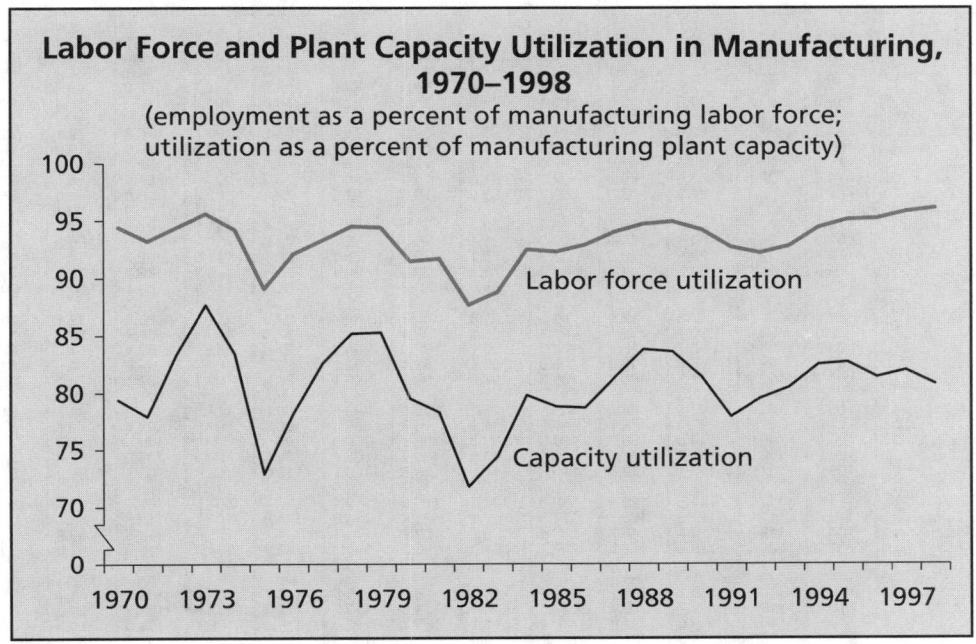

Labor Force and Plant Capacity Utilization in Manufacturing, 1970–1998

(employment as a percent of manufacturing labor force; utilization as a percent of manufacturing plant capacity)

Labor force utilization

Capacity utilization

- Despite a 4.2 percent rise in output, manufacturing plant capacity utilization declined in 1998; at 80.8 percent, the plant utilization rate was down from a high point three years earlier and substantially below its peaks in 1973 and 1979.

- In contrast to declining plant capacity utilization, manufacturing labor force utilization (measured as 100 minus the unemployment rate for workers last employed in manufacturing) rose to 96.1 percent in 1998, the highest since 1968 and 1969, when it was 96.7 percent.

- The 35 percent rise in manufacturing production from 1992 to 1998 was concentrated primarily in durable goods industries, where production rose 58 percent during the six years; production of nondurable goods was up 12 percent overall even though production of apparel and leather products declined.

- Among major market categories, production of business equipment has shown by far the strongest gains since 1992, with 1998 production of computers and office equipment more than six times its 1992 level.

Industrial Production and Capacity Utilization Summary

(Seasonally adjusted)

Year and month	Industrial production indexes (1992=100)											Capacity utilization (output as a percent of capacity)					
	Total indus-trial produc-tion	Major market groups					Major industry groups					Total industry	Manufacturing			Mining	Utilities
		Products				Mater-ials	Manufacturing			Mining	Utilities		Total	Primary process-ing	Ad-vanced process-ing		
		Total	Con-sumer goods	Busi-ness equip-ment	Constr-uction supplies		Total	Primary process-ing	Ad-vanced process-ing								
1970	58.7	57.2	60.8	45.3	70.8	60.5	54.8	67.2	48.9	101.8	66.5	81.1	79.4	79.9	78.9	88.8	96.2
1971	59.5	58.0	64.3	43.1	73.0	61.4	55.6	68.7	49.4	99.3	69.6	79.4	77.9	78.7	77.1	87.3	94.6
1972	65.3	63.4	69.5	49.1	82.9	67.7	61.5	77.3	54.3	101.4	74.1	84.4	83.4	85.5	82.2	90.3	95.2
1973	70.6	68.0	72.6	57.5	88.7	74.2	66.9	84.6	59.0	102.3	77.0	88.4	87.7	90.5	86.2	92.3	93.5
1974	69.6	67.2	70.3	60.0	83.1	72.6	65.9	82.0	58.6	101.8	76.1	84.3	83.4	85.1	82.5	92.3	87.3
1975	63.5	62.8	67.7	53.6	71.4	63.8	59.4	71.4	53.8	99.5	76.8	74.6	72.9	72.1	73.3	89.7	84.4
1976	69.3	67.6	74.3	55.5	79.8	71.3	65.4	80.3	58.6	100.3	79.9	79.3	78.2	79.2	77.6	89.8	85.2
1977	74.9	73.2	79.5	62.0	87.0	76.9	71.2	86.7	64.0	103.4	82.0	83.5	82.6	83.8	81.9	90.9	85.0
1978	79.3	77.8	82.6	69.3	92.1	81.0	75.8	90.7	68.9	106.5	84.4	85.8	85.2	85.9	84.8	90.9	85.4
1979	82.0	80.2	81.5	77.3	93.1	83.9	78.5	92.5	72.0	108.3	86.8	86.0	85.3	86.0	84.9	91.4	86.6
1980	79.7	78.9	79.6	76.7	84.9	80.3	75.5	84.4	71.4	111.5	87.3	81.5	79.5	77.2	80.8	93.4	85.9
1981	81.0	80.4	80.1	78.0	82.3	81.4	76.7	85.2	72.8	115.6	85.0	80.8	78.3	77.2	78.8	93.9	82.5
1982	76.7	77.7	78.8	70.6	75.7	75.1	72.1	75.7	70.5	111.2	82.3	74.5	71.8	68.6	73.5	86.3	79.3
1983	79.5	80.2	83.2	68.3	84.2	78.3	76.3	82.1	73.6	106.6	83.7	75.7	74.4	74.5	74.4	80.4	79.7
1984	86.6	86.9	86.7	79.2	90.4	85.9	83.8	88.4	81.7	113.9	86.7	80.8	79.8	80.0	79.7	86.0	81.9
1985	88.0	89.2	87.6	82.5	93.5	86.3	85.7	88.4	84.5	111.0	88.8	79.8	78.8	79.1	78.6	84.3	83.5
1986	89.0	90.9	90.7	82.0	98.4	86.3	88.1	90.0	87.2	102.6	86.4	78.7	78.7	79.9	78.1	77.6	80.6
1987	93.2	95.1	93.7	85.1	104.7	90.9	92.8	95.3	91.6	102.1	89.4	81.3	81.3	84.5	79.9	80.3	82.5
1988	97.4	99.0	96.7	93.5	106.3	95.1	97.1	99.0	96.2	104.7	93.9	84.0	83.8	86.8	82.3	85.2	84.9
1989	99.1	100.6	97.7	98.8	105.5	97.0	99.0	99.9	98.6	103.2	97.1	84.1	83.6	86.1	82.5	86.9	86.3
1990	98.9	100.1	97.3	98.2	102.9	97.2	98.5	99.3	98.2	104.8	98.3	82.3	81.4	83.9	80.3	89.8	85.7
1991	97.0	97.6	97.0	95.7	96.2	95.9	96.2	95.7	96.4	102.6	100.4	79.3	77.9	79.6	77.2	88.4	86.3
1992	100.0	100.0	100.0	100.0	100.0	100.0	100.0	100.0	100.0	100.0	100.0	80.3	79.5	82.3	78.3	86.4	84.5
1993	103.5	103.2	103.1	105.6	103.4	103.9	103.7	103.6	103.8	99.9	103.9	81.3	80.5	84.0	79.0	86.0	87.2
1994	109.1	107.2	107.1	112.8	110.6	111.9	109.9	109.7	110.0	102.4	105.3	83.2	82.5	87.1	80.6	87.5	87.4
1995	114.4	110.7	109.5	122.5	112.6	120.4	115.9	112.1	117.7	102.0	109.0	83.4	82.7	86.5	81.0	86.8	89.2
1996	119.5	114.4	111.3	133.5	117.9	127.8	121.4	114.5	124.8	103.7	112.6	82.4	81.4	85.1	79.8	88.5	90.5
1997	126.8	119.6	114.1	148.7	122.4	138.2	129.7	119.1	134.7	105.8	112.8	82.9	82.0	85.3	80.7	89.1	89.7
1998	131.3	123.5	115.2	163.5	127.2	144.0	135.1	120.7	142.1	104.0	113.9	81.8	80.8	83.6	79.9	86.7	90.9
1995:																	
January	113.4	110.2	109.1	120.1	114.5	118.6	115.0	113.6	115.6	103.0	104.9	84.7	84.4	89.0	82.3	87.5	86.5
February	113.4	110.1	109.0	120.4	113.5	118.6	114.8	113.2	115.6	102.5	106.2	84.3	83.8	88.4	81.8	87.0	87.5
March	113.6	110.1	109.0	121.1	112.5	119.1	115.1	112.9	116.1	102.1	106.5	84.1	83.6	88.0	81.7	86.8	87.5
April	113.4	109.9	108.9	121.2	112.2	119.0	115.0	112.2	116.3	100.6	106.6	83.5	83.1	87.2	81.3	85.5	87.5
May	113.8	110.0	109.1	120.7	110.6	119.9	115.1	111.9	116.7	102.4	108.6	83.4	82.8	86.7	81.0	87.0	89.0
June	114.3	110.5	109.8	121.9	111.0	120.1	115.7	111.7	117.6	102.3	108.5	83.4	82.7	86.3	81.1	86.9	88.8
July	113.9	110.2	109.2	121.3	111.8	119.6	115.1	110.7	117.2	101.9	109.9	82.7	81.9	85.3	80.4	86.7	89.8
August	115.1	111.2	110.3	123.6	111.1	121.3	116.2	111.4	118.5	102.1	114.7	83.3	82.3	85.6	80.8	86.9	93.6
September	115.4	111.4	110.1	124.8	112.7	121.7	117.0	112.1	119.3	102.1	109.9	83.1	82.4	85.9	80.9	87.0	89.6
October	115.5	111.2	109.7	124.3	113.0	122.3	117.1	111.9	119.6	101.1	109.3	82.8	82.1	85.5	80.6	86.3	89.0
November	115.7	111.4	110.2	124.9	112.9	122.6	117.2	111.8	119.8	102.3	111.2	82.6	81.7	85.1	80.2	87.3	90.3
December	115.8	111.7	110.9	126.3	115.6	122.3	117.3	111.9	119.9	101.3	112.1	82.3	81.3	84.9	79.7	86.6	90.9
1996:																	
January	115.5	111.0	109.0	127.3	112.4	122.8	116.9	111.4	119.6	100.9	113.1	81.7	80.7	84.3	79.1	86.3	91.6
February	117.0	112.7	110.6	130.6	113.7	123.8	118.4	111.7	121.7	102.3	114.2	82.4	81.3	84.3	80.0	87.5	92.4
March	116.8	112.5	110.0	128.8	115.8	123.7	118.1	112.8	120.6	103.2	114.5	81.8	80.6	84.8	78.8	88.3	92.5
April	118.2	113.2	110.6	131.6	114.8	126.1	119.7	112.8	123.1	104.2	113.5	82.4	81.3	84.6	79.9	89.1	91.5
May	119.2	113.8	110.9	132.1	117.1	127.8	120.9	113.9	124.3	104.3	114.0	82.7	81.7	85.1	80.2	89.2	91.8
June	120.0	114.7	111.6	133.6	119.4	128.5	121.8	115.0	125.1	104.7	113.3	82.9	81.9	85.6	80.2	89.5	91.1
July	120.3	115.1	111.9	135.0	119.1	128.6	122.4	114.9	126.1	105.0	109.7	82.7	81.9	85.3	80.4	89.7	88.1
August	120.9	115.2	111.8	134.8	120.0	130.1	123.0	115.7	126.5	105.0	111.8	82.8	81.8	85.6	80.2	89.6	89.6
September	121.1	115.7	112.2	135.7	120.8	129.5	123.3	116.0	126.8	104.0	111.1	82.5	81.6	85.6	79.9	88.6	88.9
October	121.2	115.4	111.8	135.7	119.6	130.4	123.3	116.3	126.7	104.4	111.7	82.2	81.2	85.5	79.4	88.9	89.2
November	121.9	116.3	112.5	137.5	122.0	130.8	124.2	116.5	127.9	103.3	112.6	82.3	81.4	85.4	79.7	87.8	89.8
December	122.3	116.7	112.8	139.0	119.9	131.3	124.7	116.6	128.7	103.1	112.1	82.2	81.3	85.2	79.7	87.6	89.2
1997:																	
January	123.0	117.0	112.8	140.3	120.0	132.6	125.3	116.6	129.5	104.3	113.4	82.3	81.3	84.9	79.8	88.4	90.2
February	123.9	117.7	112.9	142.6	122.3	133.8	126.4	117.7	130.7	105.5	111.0	82.6	81.7	85.5	80.1	89.4	88.3
March	124.4	118.3	113.6	143.5	122.8	134.0	127.0	117.9	131.5	106.3	109.6	82.5	81.7	85.4	80.2	89.9	87.1
April	125.1	118.5	113.3	144.6	122.7	135.6	127.7	118.7	132.1	105.4	112.7	82.7	81.7	85.7	80.2	88.9	89.6
May	125.5	118.9	113.6	145.8	122.6	136.0	128.1	118.7	132.8	106.6	111.4	82.6	81.6	85.4	80.1	89.9	88.5
June	126.1	119.2	113.8	147.5	122.3	137.2	129.0	118.8	133.9	105.9	111.4	82.6	81.7	85.2	80.4	89.1	88.5
July	127.0	119.5	113.7	148.9	122.5	139.2	129.8	119.4	134.9	106.1	113.7	82.9	81.9	85.3	80.6	89.2	90.4
August	127.8	120.6	114.6	152.0	122.6	139.4	130.8	119.4	136.5	105.5	113.1	83.1	82.2	85.1	81.1	88.6	89.9
September	128.5	120.7	114.4	152.7	121.4	141.0	131.4	120.0	137.0	106.6	114.4	83.2	82.2	85.2	81.1	89.4	90.9
October	129.3	121.5	114.9	154.4	122.3	141.9	132.2	120.3	138.1	106.2	116.1	83.4	82.4	85.2	81.3	89.0	92.3
November	129.9	122.2	115.9	155.4	123.6	142.4	133.3	121.1	139.3	104.9	113.6	83.4	82.6	85.4	81.6	87.9	90.3
December	130.3	122.3	115.4	156.5	124.2	143.4	133.7	121.5	139.7	106.4	113.1	83.4	82.5	85.4	81.4	89.0	89.9
1998:																	
January	130.3	122.6	116.0	156.3	125.5	142.6	133.8	121.6	139.8	107.6	109.8	83.0	82.2	85.2	81.0	90.0	87.2
February	130.2	122.5	115.2	157.0	125.7	142.5	133.7	121.1	140.0	107.5	109.0	82.6	81.8	84.7	80.7	89.9	86.6
March	130.7	123.2	115.8	160.1	124.7	142.7	134.1	121.0	140.6	105.8	114.0	82.6	81.6	84.4	80.6	88.4	90.5
April	131.3	124.0	116.4	162.2	125.4	143.1	134.9	121.5	141.6	105.7	112.8	82.6	81.7	84.6	80.7	88.2	89.5
May	131.9	124.5	116.8	163.1	126.6	143.6	135.4	121.4	142.3	105.4	115.2	82.6	81.6	84.3	80.7	87.9	91.3
June	130.6	123.6	115.1	163.6	126.1	141.8	133.7	120.2	140.4	104.7	118.7	81.5	80.2	83.3	79.2	87.3	94.0
July	130.5	123.3	114.0	163.5	128.5	141.9	133.6	120.7	139.9	104.6	118.3	81.1	79.8	83.4	78.5	87.2	93.7
August	132.4	124.9	116.1	166.6	128.0	144.4	135.7	120.6	143.3	103.7	120.2	82.0	80.7	83.1	79.9	86.3	95.1
September	131.9	124.1	114.8	167.4	126.9	144.4	135.2	119.3	143.2	102.4	120.3	81.3	80.1	82.1	79.5	85.2	95.0
October	132.4	124.9	115.2	169.0	128.4	144.5	136.1	120.1	144.2	102.0	116.5	81.3	80.3	82.4	79.6	84.7	92.0
November	132.2	124.5	114.8	168.1	129.6	144.6	136.4	120.3	144.6	101.1	110.6	80.8	80.1	82.4	79.4	83.8	87.3
December	132.4	124.4	114.9	167.9	131.0	145.2	136.7	121.3	144.4	99.0	111.8	80.7	80.0	82.9	79.0	82.0	88.2

Industrial Production Indexes by Market Groups

(Seasonally adjusted, 1992=100)

Year and month	Total industrial production	Products										
		Total	Final products									
			Total	Total consumer goods	Durable consumer goods						Other consumer durables	
					Total	Automotive products					Total	Total appliances and electronics
						Total	Total autos and trucks	Autos	Trucks	Auto parts and allied products		
1970	58.7	57.2	56.7	60.8	52.6	49.7	49.3	.....	14.2	51.3	54.6	34.0
1971	59.5	58.0	57.2	64.3	59.6	63.3	67.7	.....	20.0	55.1	57.7	35.8
1972	65.3	63.4	62.0	69.5	66.7	68.4	72.3	130.9	25.8	61.2	66.1	40.8
1973	70.6	68.0	66.7	72.6	71.8	75.2	82.8	140.8	33.6	62.8	70.0	45.7
1974	69.6	67.2	66.4	70.3	64.4	65.0	66.1	102.0	31.5	61.7	64.7	42.2
1975	63.5	62.8	62.6	67.7	58.7	61.8	60.7	94.7	28.5	61.6	56.9	34.4
1976	69.3	67.6	67.0	74.3	68.8	76.3	82.8	126.5	40.1	65.4	63.8	38.5
1977	74.9	73.2	72.4	79.5	77.9	87.2	95.4	136.2	50.1	73.6	71.8	44.4
1978	79.3	77.8	77.2	82.6	80.7	89.6	97.8	133.6	55.7	75.8	74.9	47.1
1979	82.0	80.2	79.7	81.5	76.7	81.4	87.5	123.1	45.8	70.4	73.6	47.3
1980	79.7	78.9	79.3	79.6	66.9	62.3	61.5	97.1	24.6	59.3	69.7	45.9
1981	81.0	80.4	81.2	80.1	67.2	61.6	61.2	93.7	26.8	58.3	70.7	46.2
1982	76.7	77.7	78.3	78.8	62.5	59.1	57.2	78.3	34.0	57.4	64.4	40.6
1983	79.5	80.2	80.0	83.2	73.8	74.3	79.9	111.0	45.9	64.7	73.1	54.0
1984	86.6	86.9	87.0	86.7	84.1	89.4	96.0	127.1	60.8	77.8	80.1	61.7
1985	88.0	89.2	89.3	87.6	84.7	95.4	103.9	134.9	68.2	81.6	77.3	58.1
1986	89.0	90.9	90.3	90.7	88.7	97.5	104.1	132.7	70.8	85.8	82.6	66.8
1987	93.2	95.1	93.3	93.7	93.9	100.7	104.0	123.9	80.1	94.1	89.1	73.0
1988	97.4	99.0	97.9	96.7	99.8	107.1	111.1	131.1	87.0	99.3	94.5	84.2
1989	99.1	100.6	99.9	97.7	101.3	108.9	114.0	131.5	92.5	99.2	95.9	86.3
1990	98.9	100.1	99.5	97.3	98.0	100.9	103.3	115.2	88.4	96.1	96.0	87.7
1991	97.0	97.6	97.7	97.0	93.0	90.3	89.6	94.5	83.4	91.6	95.2	92.5
1992	100.0	100.0	100.0	100.0	100.0	100.0	100.0	100.0	100.0	100.0	100.0	100.0
1993	103.5	103.2	103.4	103.1	109.4	111.3	114.8	110.3	120.3	105.6	107.9	113.1
1994	109.1	107.2	107.5	107.1	119.5	122.7	131.0	125.1	138.2	109.5	117.2	134.8
1995	114.4	110.7	111.5	109.5	121.5	121.6	128.0	120.3	137.2	111.5	121.4	146.5
1996	119.5	114.4	115.5	111.3	124.5	123.3	128.9	115.6	143.5	114.3	125.5	159.8
1997	126.8	119.6	121.1	114.1	129.6	129.1	135.7	114.9	157.1	118.5	130.1	176.1
1998	131.3	123.5	125.4	115.2	135.7	132.9	137.8	109.2	166.2	125.0	137.8	206.2
1995:												
January	113.4	110.2	110.8	109.1	124.0	126.2	135.5	133.1	135.4	111.6	122.4	145.9
February	113.4	110.1	110.7	109.0	123.5	125.3	134.6	130.6	136.5	110.6	122.2	144.8
March	113.6	110.1	110.8	109.0	121.8	123.2	132.3	128.2	134.5	108.8	120.7	144.0
April	113.4	109.9	110.7	108.9	122.0	123.8	131.1	123.9	137.2	112.1	120.7	143.0
May	113.8	110.0	110.8	109.1	119.7	119.7	126.0	115.8	135.7	109.5	119.7	144.0
June	114.3	110.5	111.5	109.8	119.4	120.2	126.6	114.4	138.8	109.8	118.8	141.0
July	113.9	110.2	111.0	109.2	117.8	115.3	117.6	113.5	122.5	111.5	119.7	142.7
August	115.1	111.2	112.3	110.3	120.9	120.8	127.0	113.1	141.8	110.7	121.1	146.2
September	115.4	111.4	112.4	110.1	122.6	122.1	127.8	116.8	140.3	113.0	123.0	150.8
October	115.5	111.2	112.0	109.7	121.6	120.1	125.1	116.4	136.0	111.9	122.8	151.7
November	115.7	111.4	112.3	110.2	121.9	120.4	124.9	115.4	137.1	113.1	123.0	152.9
December	115.8	111.7	112.5	109.9	123.0	122.7	127.2	117.0	140.6	115.4	123.2	151.4
1996:												
January	115.5	111.0	112.2	109.0	119.1	117.6	120.9	110.1	135.3	112.2	120.3	144.6
February	117.0	112.7	114.2	110.6	122.4	122.5	127.7	115.5	143.9	114.1	122.3	151.7
March	116.8	112.5	113.4	110.0	117.5	110.5	106.3	87.7	128.2	117.0	123.0	152.7
April	118.2	113.2	114.6	110.6	124.2	124.8	132.8	122.3	148.3	112.0	123.8	156.0
May	119.2	113.8	115.0	110.9	125.7	124.8	131.5	123.4	144.9	114.0	126.4	159.3
June	120.0	114.7	115.7	111.6	129.0	127.3	133.7	128.1	144.9	117.1	130.4	168.3
July	120.3	115.1	116.3	111.9	128.5	130.5	141.5	131.5	156.9	113.3	126.9	162.7
August	120.9	115.2	116.2	111.8	127.2	126.5	134.9	126.9	148.2	113.1	127.8	162.4
September	121.1	115.7	116.8	112.2	125.9	124.7	130.7	123.2	143.0	115.1	126.9	163.5
October	121.2	115.4	116.4	111.8	123.4	120.6	124.1	107.2	144.2	114.8	125.5	163.0
November	121.9	116.3	117.3	112.5	125.0	123.9	129.3	116.5	145.8	115.2	125.8	165.0
December	122.3	116.7	117.8	112.8	126.6	125.8	133.3	111.8	157.3	113.9	127.1	168.7
1997:												
January	123.0	117.0	118.0	112.8	126.5	127.7	135.0	114.0	158.1	116.0	125.5	161.1
February	123.9	117.7	118.8	112.9	128.0	128.6	135.4	115.9	156.7	117.7	127.6	168.3
March	124.4	118.3	119.6	113.6	129.1	128.5	135.4	116.1	156.1	117.4	129.7	171.5
April	125.1	118.5	119.6	113.3	126.4	122.4	125.4	110.7	141.3	117.3	129.6	172.0
May	125.5	118.9	120.1	113.6	127.5	124.4	128.2	111.7	145.5	117.9	129.9	173.1
June	126.1	119.2	120.6	113.8	129.6	127.1	132.3	112.6	152.3	118.6	131.6	175.6
July	127.0	119.5	120.9	113.7	127.2	120.5	120.5	112.5	130.1	119.2	132.5	180.8
August	127.8	120.6	122.4	114.6	131.3	132.1	139.7	120.3	159.2	120.1	130.6	178.1
September	128.5	120.7	122.4	114.4	130.9	132.9	142.2	119.0	164.8	118.5	129.2	177.8
October	129.3	121.5	123.1	114.9	131.0	132.0	141.1	114.4	166.6	118.0	130.1	181.3
November	129.9	122.2	124.1	115.9	135.1	138.4	149.1	119.4	177.3	122.1	132.4	186.5
December	130.3	122.3	124.0	115.4	133.3	134.5	144.1	113.1	173.5	119.8	132.3	187.4
1998:												
January	130.3	122.6	124.5	116.0	135.1	133.0	141.0	115.1	166.1	120.5	136.7	195.5
February	130.2	122.5	124.2	115.2	134.5	131.5	138.6	104.8	170.5	120.3	136.9	197.9
March	130.7	123.2	125.3	115.8	135.9	132.7	138.9	106.5	169.8	122.7	138.5	203.8
April	131.3	124.0	126.2	116.4	136.9	134.6	141.3	107.4	173.8	123.7	138.8	203.4
May	131.9	124.5	126.6	116.8	138.3	136.8	143.5	108.4	177.1	126.0	139.4	202.7
June	130.6	123.6	125.5	115.1	130.7	121.7	118.2	93.8	142.2	125.4	137.8	199.9
July	130.5	123.3	124.7	114.0	124.6	107.3	92.8	75.8	110.0	125.6	138.7	207.8
August	132.4	124.9	126.8	116.1	140.1	141.7	151.4	124.4	178.9	127.6	138.5	209.4
September	131.9	124.1	126.0	114.8	137.4	136.4	143.4	128.3	161.1	126.0	138.0	209.9
October	132.4	124.9	126.7	115.2	140.5	141.1	150.6	119.9	181.0	127.4	139.7	215.2
November	132.2	124.5	126.1	114.8	138.9	139.6	149.1	113.7	183.2	125.9	137.9	222.5
December	132.4	124.4	125.9	114.9	139.8	139.8	147.7	115.5	179.1	128.2	139.5	226.0

Industrial Production Indexes by Market Groups—*Continued*

(Seasonally adjusted, 1992=100)

Year and month	Durable consumer goods				Final products—*Continued* Nondurable consumer goods								
	Appliances and air conditioners	Home electronics	Carpeting and furniture	Miscellaneous home goods	Total	Nonenergy products					Energy products		
						Total	Foods and tobacco	Clothing	Chemical products	Paper products	Total	Fuels	Utilities
1970	63.3	.....	64.2	70.5	64.2	62.8	62.3	95.9	45.9	58.9	72.1	81.8	62.7
1971	65.5	.....	69.1	74.3	66.0	64.4	64.2	95.5	48.5	60.1	75.5	85.1	66.0
1972	74.6	.....	83.3	83.3	70.3	68.6	67.8	103.9	53.0	60.6	79.8	89.3	69.9
1973	84.4	.....	88.5	84.1	72.4	70.6	69.8	104.4	57.0	60.8	83.2	93.6	72.7
1974	79.6	.....	80.4	78.7	72.4	70.7	70.2	99.3	59.7	62.1	82.3	90.4	72.8
1975	64.2	.....	70.2	73.7	71.0	68.7	70.2	92.0	57.9	59.2	85.2	91.6	76.1
1976	72.2	.....	79.3	82.5	76.2	74.3	74.3	103.8	63.2	63.4	86.8	97.2	76.0
1977	80.2	.....	89.7	91.2	79.8	78.2	77.0	108.8	65.9	71.4	88.0	102.6	77.0
1978	82.2	.....	95.8	92.7	82.9	81.6	80.0	111.4	70.1	76.1	89.8	102.6	79.7
1979	84.2	.....	96.4	88.3	82.9	81.7	80.8	106.7	71.6	77.2	88.9	99.1	81.0
1980	79.3	.....	88.9	83.4	83.8	83.4	82.4	107.5	75.0	77.9	85.8	91.1	82.7
1981	79.7		87.8	86.3	84.3	84.1	83.9	107.1	73.3	80.4	85.1	90.0	82.3
1982	69.7	21.6	78.8	81.2	84.2	84.1	84.7	105.8	71.0	82.1	85.2	89.1	83.3
1983	82.0	33.9	87.8	82.6	86.2	86.4	86.6	107.9	73.4	85.9	85.3	87.8	84.3
1984	91.5	39.9	94.2	88.6	87.5	87.5	88.2	106.4	73.5	90.1	87.7	91.6	86.0
1985	85.4	38.1	92.9	85.9	88.5	88.5	90.6	100.8	74.5	92.1	88.5	91.2	87.3
1986	90.4	48.6	98.3	86.8	91.3	91.5	92.8	102.1	80.3	94.7	90.7	95.4	88.8
1987	95.7	55.2	103.5	94.2	93.6	93.8	95.3	104.2	83.0	96.4	92.7	95.6	91.3
1988	100.2	70.7	103.4	97.5	95.9	95.7	96.9	102.2	87.6	98.3	97.0	97.9	96.5
1989	101.7	73.3	103.5	99.0	96.7	96.4	97.4	100.1	89.7	100.2	98.3	98.2	98.2
1990	98.2	78.9	100.8	99.4	97.1	97.1	98.3	96.6	92.4	100.6	97.7	98.5	97.2
1991	91.9	93.1	94.5	97.3	98.1	97.8	98.5	97.6	95.1	99.6	100.4	99.0	100.9
1992	100.0	100.0	100.0	100.0	100.0	100.0	100.0	100.0	100.0	100.0	100.0	100.0	100.0
1993	109.6	116.7	104.9	106.4	101.4	100.9	99.3	102.4	102.8	102.4	105.2	102.5	106.3
1994	123.7	147.0	108.8	111.1	104.0	103.8	103.5	105.0	105.2	101.7	105.1	101.9	106.3
1995	116.6	183.8	109.3	113.0	106.5	106.3	105.9	104.5	109.9	103.7	107.7	104.3	109.0
1996	118.7	213.6	111.1	113.5	108.0	107.3	106.3	102.6	114.4	103.8	112.3	106.8	114.6
1997	116.9	261.1	112.8	114.2	110.2	109.9	108.2	101.1	119.5	108.0	111.6	109.3	112.3
1998	125.4	331.7	117.1	114.8	110.1	109.9	109.0	97.8	120.5	105.8	112.2	110.5	112.3
1995:													
January	123.4	173.2	112.0	113.8	105.4	105.8	105.6	106.0	108.6	102.0	103.1	104.2	102.4
February	119.2	176.4	113.8	113.1	105.3	105.3	104.7	105.3	108.1	103.4	105.4	104.6	105.5
March	114.6	180.8	109.4	112.8	105.8	105.9	105.3	107.1	108.4	103.1	105.5	105.5	105.2
April	116.2	176.4	112.0	111.9	105.5	105.7	105.4	105.3	107.6	104.3	104.7	104.0	104.8
May	115.7	179.6	107.2	111.7	106.3	106.2	106.2	105.5	108.2	103.9	107.3	103.1	108.9
June	106.7	184.8	106.5	111.9	107.3	107.3	107.8	104.9	109.8	104.0	107.3	103.7	108.7
July	113.1	179.0	108.5	111.9	107.0	106.9	107.5	102.9	109.0	104.5	108.1	104.0	109.7
August	114.2	186.3	107.8	113.2	107.6	106.7	106.4	104.3	110.5	104.1	113.2	103.7	117.3
September	119.0	190.2	109.6	113.8	106.9	106.4	105.5	103.6	111.0	104.4	110.4	106.1	112.0
October	118.5	193.1	108.4	113.6	106.7	106.8	105.9	104.0	112.5	103.5	106.2	103.4	107.3
November	118.9	195.7	106.9	114.1	107.2	106.8	105.7	103.2	112.6	104.3	110.0	104.0	112.5
December	119.9	190.3	109.6	113.9	106.6	106.0	105.2	101.3	112.2	102.8	111.1	105.0	113.6
1996:													
January	112.0	185.7	108.9	111.8	106.4	105.5	104.9	99.2	112.4	101.6	112.9	105.2	116.2
February	114.7	199.2	107.8	112.8	107.6	106.6	105.8	102.7	112.5	103.0	114.4	107.3	117.5
March	118.4	195.9	110.5	112.4	108.1	107.1	107.1	102.4	112.4	102.8	114.8	107.0	118.2
April	117.5	205.8	108.8	113.1	107.2	106.2	105.8	102.7	111.2	102.8	113.5	106.4	116.6
May	118.4	212.3	112.2	114.8	107.2	106.4	105.5	103.0	112.2	103.4	112.9	106.6	115.6
June	126.8	221.6	116.3	116.3	107.3	106.4	106.1	103.0	111.4	102.9	113.1	106.5	116.0
July	119.8	219.3	108.5	116.2	107.7	107.4	106.4	102.9	114.7	103.5	109.4	106.2	110.5
August	120.0	218.0	113.2	115.4	108.0	107.5	105.8	103.9	115.0	104.5	111.3	107.2	113.0
September	120.4	220.1	112.6	113.6	108.8	108.6	107.3	103.2	116.6	104.7	111.3	105.7	112.1
October	116.4	226.1	111.9	111.6	108.9	108.5	106.7	103.0	117.6	105.1	111.3	108.2	112.3
November	116.7	230.9	112.3	111.0	109.3	108.9	107.3	102.8	117.9	105.5	112.3	108.2	113.9
December	123.5	228.0	110.2	113.0	109.3	109.0	107.3	102.1	118.3	105.9	111.4	107.1	113.1
1997:													
January	114.9	223.2	109.7	113.5	109.3	109.0	108.4	101.4	118.1	103.1	111.4	106.0	113.6
February	115.9	240.9	110.1	114.0	109.1	109.1	108.0	101.0	117.6	105.8	109.3	107.0	109.9
March	121.1	239.6	113.1	115.2	109.7	110.0	110.1	101.5	115.9	107.0	107.5	108.5	106.5
April	117.6	247.5	112.9	114.8	109.9	109.6	107.7	102.0	119.7	106.9	111.9	109.2	112.8
May	116.3	252.7	112.3	115.3	110.1	109.7	107.5	101.4	120.0	108.0	112.3	111.3	112.2
June	118.1	256.0	114.5	116.3	109.8	109.7	107.1	101.1	120.4	109.1	110.2	111.1	109.2
July	118.2	271.3	113.4	116.6	110.3	110.1	108.5	101.2	118.4	109.3	111.7	108.4	112.9
August	113.0	274.8	113.1	114.2	110.4	110.1	107.9	101.2	120.2	109.0	112.7	110.6	113.3
September	112.1	276.0	112.3	112.2	110.3	110.1	108.2	101.0	119.3	109.1	112.0	110.5	112.2
October	114.8	280.4	113.0	112.2	110.8	110.2	107.8	101.1	121.3	108.2	115.6	111.5	117.1
November	121.0	281.9	116.8	112.4	111.2	111.1	109.2	100.0	120.9	110.8	112.0	107.4	113.9
December	119.1	288.7	112.6	114.1	110.9	110.7	108.4	100.6	121.8	109.5	112.5	110.2	113.2
1998:													
January	125.3	298.8	119.2	115.6	111.3	111.6	110.4	100.7	121.3	109.2	109.1	111.0	107.6
February	126.4	303.6	115.8	116.8	110.5	111.0	110.1	99.3	121.2	107.7	106.5	110.4	104.0
March	123.6	327.2	114.3	118.3	110.8	110.5	109.1	100.4	121.3	106.3	113.2	111.2	113.7
April	124.4	324.2	115.9	118.2	111.4	111.4	110.2	99.9	123.2	106.2	111.5	111.6	111.0
May	127.7	314.7	119.1	117.9	111.5	111.3	110.8	98.8	122.5	105.7	112.5	110.9	112.9
June	121.9	319.7	117.0	117.1	111.2	110.1	108.5	98.8	122.8	105.3	118.2	111.4	121.2
July	127.9	328.9	117.3	115.9	111.2	110.1	108.5	98.4	122.2	106.3	118.4	112.9	120.7
August	128.6	332.0	116.7	115.3	110.3	108.9	107.5	97.7	119.0	106.6	120.1	112.1	123.7
September	123.3	348.5	116.3	114.5	109.3	108.2	106.9	97.1	118.0	105.9	116.8	108.3	120.7
October	129.1	349.9	120.3	113.6	109.1	108.3	108.0	95.4	117.2	105.2	115.0	108.4	117.8
November	132.3	365.0	117.5	109.5	109.0	109.3	109.6	94.5	119.3	104.1	106.5	109.1	104.5
December	133.7	372.5	116.8	111.4	108.9	109.1	109.6	94.6	118.7	103.6	107.1	109.6	105.2

Industrial Production Indexes by Market Groups—*Continued*

(Seasonally adjusted, 1992=100)

Year and month	Final products—*Continued* Equipment	Business equipment Total	Information processing and related Total	Computer and office equipment	Industrial equipment	Transit Total	Autos and trucks	Other business equipment	Defense and space	Oil and gas well drilling	Manufactured homes	Intermediate products Total	Construction supplies	Business supplies
1970	52.5	45.3	15.3	2.7	100.9	57.3	39.4	63.0	64.8	85.2	96.5	59.2	70.8	51.7
1971	49.2	43.1	14.2	2.3	94.4	55.3	46.7	64.7	58.2	81.8	118.6	61.0	73.0	53.2
1972	53.8	49.1	16.6	2.8	104.7	60.4	50.1	79.7	56.6	93.9	146.6	68.1	82.9	58.5
1973	60.1	57.5	19.6	3.5	120.0	72.8	59.7	93.9	55.3	101.9	144.0	72.5	88.7	61.9
1974	62.0	60.0	21.8	4.1	126.0	70.3	54.2	92.9	54.5	126.4	101.7	69.9	83.1	61.4
1975	56.8	53.6	20.5	3.7	109.5	64.2	50.5	77.4	53.5	143.4	81.5	63.1	71.4	57.8
1976	58.8	55.5	22.3	4.5	108.8	61.8	61.5	86.9	54.3	144.1	107.1	69.5	79.8	62.9
1977	64.3	62.0	26.0	6.0	118.2	65.8	71.4	94.9	54.4	175.0	118.7	75.7	87.0	68.4
1978	71.0	69.3	31.8	8.9	125.3	76.7	74.9	97.4	55.9	196.4	126.0	79.9	92.1	72.0
1979	77.6	77.3	38.6	12.2	130.8	88.1	70.9	106.0	57.7	190.7	121.2	82.0	93.1	74.9
1980	79.1	76.7	43.3	16.4	126.5	81.3	53.6	95.7	63.2	236.8	99.6	77.7	84.9	73.2
1981	82.8	78.0	48.1	21.7	126.5	74.6	55.5	94.9	64.5	315.6	101.8	77.6	82.3	74.7
1982	77.7	70.6	51.2	25.2	103.7	62.0	49.3	84.1	72.6	296.0	89.3	75.8	75.7	75.8
1983	76.4	68.3	56.0	33.4	87.3	58.4	64.2	85.3	80.4	257.6	110.5	81.0	84.2	79.1
1984	87.6	79.2	67.9	48.6	98.1	67.0	80.9	95.2	89.5	296.1	104.7	86.9	90.4	84.9
1985	91.8	82.5	74.9	58.8	97.4	73.0	91.6	90.5	103.8	259.9	102.5	89.1	93.5	86.4
1986	90.0	82.0	73.8	58.9	95.6	74.6	92.2	91.8	113.0	143.3	102.5	92.7	98.4	89.3
1987	92.9	85.1	78.9	67.3	95.4	75.4	92.5	98.4	117.5	130.7	106.4	100.7	104.7	98.4
1988	99.9	93.5	86.3	77.9	105.2	84.9	94.1	105.5	117.1	150.0	103.1	102.5	106.3	100.3
1989	103.7	98.8	90.7	88.4	109.6	94.4	96.0	109.5	117.4	139.9	96.3	102.9	105.5	101.3
1990	103.2	98.2	90.5	84.1	107.3	95.2	93.7	108.7	115.9	151.1	94.0	101.9	102.9	101.4
1991	98.8	95.7	91.1	79.9	100.9	96.4	91.6	98.2	106.7	128.6	84.5	97.5	96.2	98.3
1992	100.0	100.0	100.0	100.0	100.0	100.0	100.0	100.0	100.0	100.0	100.0	100.0	100.0	100.0
1993	104.0	105.6	107.8	119.7	106.5	98.5	109.1	107.8	93.8	122.6	115.3	102.5	103.4	102.0
1994	108.3	112.8	117.5	144.6	116.5	97.4	123.3	113.4	87.0	127.0	127.0	106.3	110.6	103.7
1995	114.9	122.5	134.2	208.5	126.9	95.3	122.8	119.2	83.0	126.4	135.8	108.1	112.6	105.5
1996	122.7	133.5	157.8	296.2	131.2	99.3	117.8	122.0	79.0	138.0	144.7	110.9	117.9	106.8
1997	133.9	148.7	181.6	415.8	136.1	116.7	124.0	136.0	76.2	149.3	141.4	115.2	122.4	111.0
1998	144.2	163.5	209.9	646.0	140.0	133.7	124.6	138.9	75.7	134.7	149.2	118.0	127.2	112.6
1995:														
January	113.7	120.1	126.3	176.8	124.1	101.2	132.4	120.2	86.1	125.3	141.3	108.4	114.5	104.7
February	113.5	120.4	127.2	186.4	124.4	100.9	130.9	119.3	84.6	126.4	131.5	108.2	113.5	105.0
March	114.0	121.1	129.2	190.1	124.4	100.7	129.3	119.4	84.6	124.1	130.5	107.9	112.5	105.2
April	113.8	121.2	130.6	196.4	124.4	99.5	126.7	117.7	84.1	120.6	130.2	107.5	112.2	104.7
May	113.8	120.7	130.4	200.7	125.3	95.8	120.8	117.4	84.3	128.9	131.7	107.4	110.6	105.5
June	114.5	121.9	132.6	202.6	126.1	95.6	120.5	119.7	84.2	125.5	132.4	107.5	111.0	105.4
July	114.0	121.3	133.6	211.0	125.6	92.4	115.2	118.5	83.8	126.2	133.2	107.8	111.8	105.5
August	115.7	123.6	136.8	214.3	128.5	93.4	119.2	118.8	83.1	127.0	136.0	107.9	111.1	106.0
September	116.5	124.8	138.3	218.7	128.5	95.4	121.7	121.0	82.1	128.8	138.0	108.4	112.7	105.9
October	115.9	124.3	140.7	228.8	129.7	88.5	118.8	119.0	81.1	127.7	139.1	108.6	113.0	106.0
November	116.1	124.9	142.3	233.9	130.7	87.4	116.9	119.4	79.6	126.8	142.3	108.5	112.9	105.9
December	116.9	126.3	142.5	241.7	130.9	92.3	120.9	119.9	78.2	129.6	147.9	109.3	115.6	105.6
1996:														
January	117.6	127.3	145.8	245.7	129.4	94.5	112.6	118.5	77.4	134.0	141.8	107.4	112.4	104.4
February	120.4	130.6	150.9	259.7	131.5	97.6	118.3	119.5	78.5	136.5	139.6	108.4	113.7	105.3
March	119.2	128.8	152.3	267.1	131.3	87.9	98.1	119.4	79.4	134.1	146.0	109.5	115.8	105.8
April	121.4	131.6	153.4	270.8	131.2	98.6	122.5	119.7	78.9	139.5	146.2	110.4	117.1	106.5
May	121.9	132.1	155.1	282.3	130.8	98.4	122.2	120.7	79.0	141.8	146.7	111.6	119.4	107.0
June	122.9	133.6	158.7	294.8	130.3	100.7	125.2	119.0	78.5	139.9	149.1	111.6	119.4	107.0
July	124.1	135.0	159.2	307.6	131.3	102.8	127.5	122.9	79.6	139.8	144.3	111.3	119.1	106.7
August	123.9	134.8	159.8	311.2	130.5	102.0	122.2	123.7	79.6	138.6	147.7	112.0	120.0	107.2
September	124.6	135.7	162.0	316.1	131.4	102.0	119.3	122.5	80.0	138.2	147.1	112.5	120.8	107.6
October	124.5	135.7	163.9	325.5	131.6	98.5	109.6	124.0	79.3	138.2	146.6	112.1	119.6	107.7
November	125.6	137.5	165.2	332.9	132.2	103.3	117.8	124.0	78.8	137.3	143.2	113.4	122.0	108.3
December	126.6	139.0	166.9	341.1	132.2	104.6	118.6	130.0	78.5	137.8	136.7	113.2	119.9	109.3
1997:														
January	127.3	140.3	168.0	345.9	133.3	106.5	121.1	131.3	77.0	138.4	140.5	113.7	120.0	110.0
February	129.1	142.6	171.9	359.9	133.6	109.6	122.9	132.2	77.1	142.7	142.0	114.4	122.3	109.7
March	130.1	143.5	172.7	368.2	133.8	111.4	122.7	133.8	76.8	152.4	141.8	114.4	122.8	109.4
April	130.8	144.6	175.2	377.7	135.3	110.3	116.4	134.7	76.3	149.2	144.1	115.2	122.7	110.8
May	131.6	145.8	177.3	386.5	135.1	112.5	118.9	135.1	76.2	149.8	142.7	115.1	122.6	110.6
June	132.9	147.5	180.8	405.4	134.6	114.9	121.1	136.6	76.0	150.3	141.7	114.7	122.3	110.2
July	133.7	148.9	184.0	425.9	136.6	113.5	119.0	136.8	74.9	151.9	142.3	115.1	122.5	110.7
August	136.3	152.0	185.0	434.8	138.1	122.2	128.3	138.2	76.2	152.9	140.8	115.1	122.6	110.7
September	136.7	152.7	188.3	449.5	136.5	123.5	128.9	136.5	76.2	152.4	139.7	115.4	121.4	111.8
October	137.9	154.4	190.3	465.0	138.6	123.7	127.7	139.7	75.8	150.6	139.8	116.5	122.3	113.0
November	138.6	155.4	191.8	474.3	138.0	127.0	133.4	138.8	75.7	151.6	141.5	116.3	123.6	112.0
December	139.4	156.5	194.5	496.8	139.8	125.6	127.4	138.7	75.8	149.6	142.3	117.0	124.2	112.6
1998:														
January	139.5	156.3	195.3	520.3	138.4	126.0	126.2	137.7	76.2	153.9	147.1	117.0	125.5	112.0
February	140.3	157.0	199.2	547.4	136.6	126.8	120.9	136.9	76.3	157.4	149.6	117.1	125.7	112.1
March	142.4	160.1	202.3	584.9	139.4	130.3	121.6	139.8	75.9	155.7	148.0	116.9	124.7	112.2
April	143.6	162.2	206.0	601.5	139.4	133.6	123.4	140.8	75.9	147.6	149.0	117.3	125.4	112.5
May	144.2	163.1	209.2	620.6	138.1	135.5	125.1	139.6	76.0	147.1	149.0	118.2	126.6	113.3
June	144.1	163.6	210.3	638.6	142.9	128.2	108.6	141.7	75.8	136.7	146.1	118.0	126.1	113.2
July	143.9	163.5	211.8	654.6	144.2	121.9	91.7	146.6	76.1	131.9	151.1	119.1	128.5	113.6
August	146.0	166.6	213.1	671.6	142.3	141.6	136.9	132.6	76.5	127.7	145.7	119.1	128.0	113.8
September	146.2	167.4	217.3	693.6	139.5	140.1	135.6	140.9	75.5	123.4	147.8	118.3	126.9	113.3
October	147.5	169.0	219.0	716.7	141.6	141.6	136.1	141.1	76.4	117.4	150.9	119.0	128.4	113.5
November	146.5	168.1	219.7	745.2	139.9	140.5	136.4	138.5	75.7	115.2	154.6	119.3	129.6	113.2
December	145.6	167.9	220.8	759.9	141.3	139.6	136.0	131.7	74.6	103.2	156.6	119.8	131.0	113.3

Industrial Production Indexes by Market Groups—*Continued*

(Seasonally adjusted, 1992=100)

Year and month	Total	Materials													
		Durable					Nondurable					Energy		
		Total	Consumer parts	Equipment parts	Other		Total	Textile	Paper	Chemical	Other	Total	Primary	Converted fuel
					Total	Basic metals								
1970	60.5	48.3	71.0	23.8	68.3	97.2	59.4	80.3	58.2	51.4	64.5	93.6	101.0	87.5
1971	61.4	48.4	78.6	23.9	65.7	91.0	62.0	84.1	60.8	54.5	65.4	94.3	100.2	89.8
1972	67.7	54.8	87.4	27.4	74.4	101.3	68.3	88.6	64.9	63.4	69.2	98.0	101.9	95.5
1973	74.2	62.6	100.0	32.4	83.6	113.7	73.2	91.4	68.0	72.0	72.0	98.7	100.6	98.6
1974	72.6	60.8	89.5	33.0	82.0	110.5	73.6	84.9	67.4	74.1	72.6	96.0	98.1	95.7
1975	63.8	50.6	72.7	28.0	68.5	88.7	65.5	80.3	58.1	62.5	68.8	93.9	96.1	93.4
1976	71.3	58.4	92.2	31.4	76.6	98.4	74.2	91.0	66.4	72.5	74.5	96.2	95.5	99.2
1977	76.9	64.6	104.7	36.1	81.7	100.4	78.9	94.5	67.1	80.8	77.1	97.9	96.7	102.8
1978	81.0	70.2	107.9	41.4	88.1	108.9	81.6	93.2	69.3	85.0	79.8	98.9	98.5	102.3
1979	83.9	73.3	103.0	47.1	90.8	111.8	84.4	96.4	72.5	89.0	80.2	101.4	100.2	106.4
1980	80.3	67.7	82.3	49.6	81.4	94.3	80.7	93.7	72.6	81.5	79.6	102.2	102.1	104.8
1981	81.4	70.4	81.2	53.2	84.4	100.5	82.3	91.7	74.3	84.0	81.3	100.2	101.6	98.7
1982	75.1	62.6	71.0	51.5	70.1	73.3	74.6	82.0	72.2	71.1	78.9	96.7	100.1	90.0
1983	78.3	68.2	81.7	54.7	76.2	79.7	81.0	92.8	78.8	78.5	81.6	94.7	97.1	90.7
1984	85.9	79.5	94.0	67.0	85.2	89.6	84.5	92.5	83.1	83.1	84.6	99.5	102.2	94.5
1985	86.3	80.9	95.1	68.9	86.1	88.8	83.2	86.8	81.3	82.8	84.2	99.1	101.2	95.6
1986	86.3	82.3	92.3	73.3	85.9	83.7	85.7	91.8	85.8	83.4	87.0	95.2	99.7	87.3
1987	90.4	87.5	95.0	78.6	92.2	90.7	90.9	99.5	90.2	88.8	91.1	96.3	99.2	90.9
1988	95.1	93.6	100.4	85.3	97.9	99.6	94.8	98.6	93.7	95.2	93.1	98.5	100.5	94.9
1989	97.0	95.7	99.6	89.6	99.3	100.6	97.2	98.4	94.6	98.8	96.2	99.5	100.1	98.3
1990	97.2	95.3	93.2	92.3	98.8	100.9	98.1	94.4	96.3	100.3	97.3	100.6	101.7	98.5
1991	95.9	93.2	89.5	93.3	94.7	96.2	96.9	93.5	97.1	97.3	97.4	100.8	102.0	98.6
1992	100.0	100.0	100.0	100.0	100.0	100.0	100.0	100.0	100.0	100.0	100.0	100.0	100.0	100.0
1993	103.9	106.8	111.8	106.5	104.8	103.8	101.9	104.3	103.6	99.9	102.9	99.5	98.1	102.0
1994	111.9	118.9	127.5	121.7	113.1	110.1	106.9	111.1	108.2	105.2	106.7	101.2	99.9	103.6
1995	120.4	133.8	133.2	155.3	118.1	113.9	108.5	110.6	109.8	107.7	107.5	102.4	100.9	105.1
1996	127.8	147.7	138.3	190.6	122.0	116.4	108.2	108.2	109.0	108.2	107.2	103.5	101.8	106.9
1997	138.2	165.0	143.1	238.5	127.2	121.9	113.4	111.2	115.9	114.4	110.0	103.7	101.4	108.0
1998	144.0	176.4	144.0	277.4	129.0	121.2	113.5	108.7	116.0	114.5	111.5	103.6	101.2	108.1
1995:														
January	118.6	129.0	134.4	139.7	118.6	115.4	111.3	117.8	111.4	109.9	110.6	102.0	101.1	103.7
February	118.6	129.5	132.9	142.9	118.0	114.2	110.2	115.6	110.9	109.4	108.2	101.9	100.5	104.5
March	119.1	130.5	131.2	146.4	118.2	113.7	110.1	115.6	111.5	109.2	107.6	102.0	100.7	104.5
April	119.0	130.6	129.4	149.1	117.4	113.4	109.9	114.3	110.8	108.7	108.9	101.5	99.5	105.2
May	119.9	131.9	131.8	151.4	117.5	113.3	109.9	113.8	112.3	108.7	107.9	102.5	101.1	105.2
June	120.1	132.9	132.3	154.1	117.5	112.7	108.8	110.1	110.5	108.1	107.6	102.5	101.4	104.5
July	119.6	132.6	131.1	156.0	116.1	111.9	107.2	102.8	110.7	107.2	105.4	102.8	100.7	106.8
August	121.3	134.9	131.9	160.0	117.9	112.4	107.8	110.0	109.3	106.7	107.4	104.3	101.0	110.6
September	121.7	137.2	135.8	163.3	118.9	115.0	107.1	107.7	107.3	107.0	106.7	101.8	100.5	104.3
October	122.3	138.1	136.5	165.3	119.1	113.8	107.5	107.9	110.8	106.1	106.4	101.9	101.5	102.6
November	122.6	139.1	135.8	167.4	120.0	116.6	106.1	106.0	105.8	106.4	105.7	102.8	101.9	104.4
December	122.3	138.6	135.8	168.3	118.5	113.9	106.1	105.5	105.9	105.3	108.0	102.3	100.5	105.5
1996:														
January	122.8	140.0	139.2	169.0	119.4	112.8	105.3	102.9	106.1	105.2	105.5	102.4	100.4	106.2
February	123.8	141.3	137.5	173.5	120.0	113.9	105.7	105.1	105.4	105.5	106.2	103.5	101.9	106.5
March	123.7	140.6	125.4	177.8	120.8	115.7	106.0	107.0	105.9	105.5	106.5	104.0	102.5	106.7
April	126.1	144.8	139.6	182.3	120.6	114.8	107.2	107.8	108.8	106.0	107.4	104.1	103.3	105.6
May	127.8	147.6	142.0	187.8	121.8	115.8	107.8	109.1	108.2	107.1	108.1	104.5	102.9	107.4
June	128.5	148.8	141.5	191.9	122.0	116.1	108.1	108.6	108.0	107.9	107.9	104.2	102.4	107.6
July	128.6	149.1	141.1	193.8	121.6	114.9	108.8	109.8	109.8	108.3	108.1	103.4	102.3	105.3
August	130.1	151.5	143.3	197.2	123.3	117.2	109.1	110.4	110.2	109.2	106.7	104.1	102.5	107.0
September	129.5	150.6	137.3	199.3	122.9	118.1	109.6	109.6	109.3	110.1	108.7	103.2	101.3	106.6
October	130.4	151.8	137.4	202.1	123.7	119.4	110.0	110.1	110.9	111.7	105.5	103.7	101.7	107.7
November	130.8	152.8	138.8	204.8	123.6	118.7	110.3	110.1	112.3	110.6	108.0	102.9	99.9	108.8
December	131.3	153.6	136.6	208.1	124.3	119.7	110.9	107.8	113.3	111.8	108.1	102.6	100.2	107.3
1997:														
January	132.6	155.3	140.1	211.7	124.1	118.4	111.0	109.1	112.0	112.3	108.2	104.2	101.7	108.9
February	133.8	157.1	140.4	216.2	124.9	119.1	112.3	110.4	115.8	112.5	109.3	103.9	102.1	107.3
March	134.0	157.7	139.1	220.5	124.3	118.2	112.4	109.1	115.8	113.0	109.6	103.4	101.5	107.0
April	135.6	160.4	140.8	224.9	126.4	120.9	113.1	112.0	114.8	114.2	109.8	103.7	101.4	108.1
May	136.0	161.5	138.7	230.7	126.2	121.2	112.3	108.8	115.6	113.1	109.2	103.7	102.1	106.8
June	137.2	164.0	140.9	237.0	126.8	122.5	112.4	110.2	113.9	113.1	110.5	103.4	101.1	107.7
July	139.2	167.0	145.5	243.1	127.5	122.6	113.6	114.0	115.6	114.1	110.2	104.0	101.7	108.3
August	139.4	168.2	143.9	248.1	127.8	122.8	113.0	110.3	116.7	113.6	109.4	103.1	101.0	107.3
September	141.0	169.8	144.6	252.2	128.6	123.5	114.4	112.4	117.5	115.9	109.6	104.8	101.9	110.4
October	141.9	171.9	146.1	256.6	129.6	124.0	114.4	112.8	117.7	116.1	108.4	104.2	101.6	109.2
November	142.4	173.2	147.0	259.2	130.5	125.8	115.5	112.4	116.8	116.9	113.0	102.2	99.7	107.1
December	143.4	174.1	150.0	261.1	130.0	123.5	116.1	113.5	117.9	117.6	112.3	103.8	101.1	109.1
1998:														
January	142.6	173.6	143.1	263.4	130.7	126.1	114.8	109.9	117.2	117.2	110.0	103.0	101.6	105.8
February	142.5	173.5	144.2	264.5	129.7	125.9	114.9	111.1	117.0	116.5	111.4	102.8	101.4	105.6
March	142.7	173.7	143.7	265.8	129.7	123.7	114.2	110.6	116.3	115.6	111.0	103.7	101.0	109.0
April	143.1	174.5	144.4	266.9	130.3	123.5	114.4	110.5	116.3	116.2	110.9	103.8	101.3	108.6
May	143.6	175.4	147.9	268.6	129.6	123.0	114.1	111.0	115.5	115.6	111.2	104.3	101.0	110.8
June	141.8	171.7	131.9	271.0	128.3	120.1	113.9	110.2	117.3	114.8	110.6	104.8	101.8	110.7
July	141.9	171.8	129.7	274.1	128.1	120.2	114.1	110.1	117.3	114.6	111.7	104.8	102.9	108.6
August	144.4	177.4	149.6	278.0	128.3	121.9	113.1	107.7	116.4	113.6	111.6	104.4	101.2	110.7
September	144.4	177.7	147.7	282.7	127.7	118.2	112.0	107.6	115.0	111.8	111.5	105.2	102.3	110.9
October	144.5	178.8	146.2	287.0	128.4	118.3	111.7	108.8	115.8	111.1	110.4	103.7	102.6	106.1
November	144.6	179.9	145.6	289.9	129.3	117.3	112.2	103.0	112.7	113.7	113.2	101.5	99.8	104.9
December	145.2	180.4	144.8	292.6	129.3	116.3	112.5	102.5	114.7	113.0	114.4	102.6	100.3	107.2

Industrial Production Indexes by Market Groups—*Continued*

(Seasonally adjusted, 1992=100)

Year and month	Total excluding				Consumer goods excluding		Business equipment excluding		Materials, excluding energy
	Autos and trucks	Motor vehicles and parts	Computer and office equipment	Computers and semiconductors	Autos and trucks	Energy	Autos and trucks	Computer and office equipment	
1970	59.3	59.3	62.6	65.7	61.9	59.5	45.8	63.4	51.3
1971	59.7	59.5	63.7	66.8	64.2	63.1	43.3	61.1	52.2
1972	65.5	65.3	69.7	72.9	69.4	68.3	49.4	68.9	58.5
1973	70.6	70.3	75.3	78.5	71.9	71.3	57.7	80.4	65.5
1974	70.0	69.8	73.9	77.1	70.8	69.0	60.8	82.8	64.3
1975	63.8	63.9	67.4	70.4	68.3	65.9	54.1	73.8	54.8
1976	69.2	69.0	73.4	76.5	73.7	72.9	55.5	75.0	62.7
1977	74.6	74.2	79.1	82.6	78.5	78.5	61.4	81.4	68.6
1978	79.1	78.6	83.3	86.8	81.6	81.7	69.0	88.6	73.4
1979	82.0	81.8	85.6	88.9	81.1	80.6	77.8	96.8	76.4
1980	80.2	80.4	82.8	85.7	80.5	78.8	78.4	93.0	71.4
1981	81.5	81.8	83.7	86.4	81.0	79.4	79.7	91.9	73.8
1982	77.1	77.6	78.9	81.0	79.9	78.0	72.2	80.7	66.0
1983	79.6	79.9	81.3	83.3	83.2	82.9	68.6	74.9	71.8
1984	86.5	86.6	88.0	89.7	86.1	86.6	79.0	84.1	80.9
1985	87.8	87.7	89.1	90.8	86.6	87.5	81.8	85.8	81.6
1986	88.8	88.8	90.0	91.6	89.9	90.7	81.2	85.2	83.3
1987	93.0	93.1	94.0	95.4	93.0	93.8	84.5	87.3	88.5
1988	97.2	97.3	97.9	99.2	95.8	96.7	93.5	95.3	94.0
1989	98.9	99.1	99.5	100.5	96.7	97.6	99.2	99.8	96.2
1990	98.9	99.1	99.3	100.1	97.0	97.3	98.6	99.6	96.1
1991	97.2	97.4	97.2	97.7	97.5	96.7	96.2	97.4	94.3
1992	100.0	100.0	100.0	100.0	100.0	100.0	100.0	100.0	100.0
1993	103.2	103.0	103.2	102.9	102.4	102.8	105.3	104.4	105.3
1994	108.5	108.0	108.5	107.3	105.8	107.4	111.8	110.3	115.3
1995	114.1	113.5	113.2	110.1	108.5	109.7	122.6	116.6	126.0
1996	119.4	118.9	117.5	112.6	110.3	111.2	135.3	123.5	135.2
1997	126.6	126.1	123.8	116.7	112.9	114.4	151.5	134.4	149.0
1998	131.3	130.8	127.1	118.5	113.9	115.5	167.9	142.4	156.7
1995:									
January	112.9	112.2	112.5	110.3	107.7	109.9	118.9	115.9	123.7
February	112.8	112.3	112.3	109.9	107.6	109.4	119.4	115.6	123.7
March	113.1	112.6	112.5	110.0	107.7	109.4	120.3	116.1	124.3
April	113.0	112.5	112.2	109.5	107.6	109.4	120.7	115.8	124.3
May	113.5	113.0	112.6	109.8	108.1	109.3	120.7	114.9	125.2
June	114.0	113.4	113.0	110.1	108.8	110.1	122.1	116.1	125.5
July	113.8	113.2	112.6	109.5	108.8	109.4	122.0	115.0	124.8
August	114.9	114.4	113.8	110.6	109.4	109.9	124.1	117.3	126.5
September	115.2	114.5	114.1	110.6	109.1	110.0	125.2	118.3	127.8
October	115.3	114.6	114.0	110.4	108.8	110.1	124.9	117.3	128.5
November	115.6	115.0	114.2	110.5	109.3	110.2	125.9	117.7	128.7
December	115.6	114.9	114.2	110.4	109.0	109.8	126.9	118.7	128.4
1996:									
January	115.5	114.8	113.9	110.1	108.3	108.5	128.9	119.5	129.0
February	116.9	116.3	115.3	111.3	109.6	110.1	132.0	122.2	130.1
March	117.2	117.1	115.0	110.8	110.3	109.5	132.2	120.0	129.7
April	117.9	117.3	116.4	111.9	109.4	110.3	132.6	122.7	132.9
May	119.0	118.3	117.3	112.5	109.8	110.7	133.3	122.6	135.0
June	119.7	119.2	118.0	113.0	110.4	111.5	134.5	123.5	135.9
July	119.9	119.3	118.1	113.0	110.2	112.2	135.8	124.5	136.3
August	120.7	120.1	118.7	113.5	110.6	111.9	136.3	124.1	138.0
September	120.9	120.5	118.8	113.5	111.2	112.5	137.6	124.9	137.6
October	121.3	120.9	118.8	113.4	111.1	111.9	138.7	124.5	138.6
November	121.9	121.4	119.5	113.9	111.6	112.5	139.8	126.0	139.4
December	122.2	121.9	119.9	114.1	111.6	113.0	141.4	127.3	140.2
1997:									
January	122.9	122.3	120.5	114.6	111.5	112.9	142.5	128.4	141.3
February	123.8	123.3	121.3	115.2	111.7	113.3	144.8	130.1	143.0
March	124.2	123.8	121.7	115.4	112.4	114.3	145.9	130.7	143.5
April	125.3	124.8	122.4	115.9	112.6	113.4	147.9	131.6	145.6
May	125.6	125.2	122.7	115.9	112.7	113.7	148.9	132.5	146.1
June	126.1	125.6	123.2	116.2	112.7	114.2	150.6	133.5	147.8
July	127.3	126.7	124.0	116.7	113.3	113.9	152.4	134.3	150.2
August	127.7	127.1	124.7	117.2	113.2	114.8	154.8	137.0	150.8
September	128.3	127.7	125.3	117.7	112.9	114.7	155.4	137.2	152.4
October	129.2	128.6	126.0	118.3	113.4	114.8	157.5	138.5	153.7
November	129.6	129.0	126.6	118.7	114.2	116.4	157.9	139.2	155.1
December	130.2	129.5	126.9	119.0	113.8	115.7	159.9	139.7	155.8
1998:									
January	130.2	129.7	126.7	118.7	114.7	116.8	159.7	138.8	155.0
February	130.2	129.7	126.4	118.4	113.9	116.2	161.1	138.7	155.0
March	130.7	130.3	126.7	118.8	114.5	116.1	164.6	140.8	154.9
April	131.3	130.9	127.3	119.3	115.1	117.0	166.7	142.4	155.5
May	131.8	131.3	127.7	119.6	115.3	117.3	167.4	142.6	156.0
June	131.2	131.2	126.4	118.2	114.8	114.7	170.0	142.7	153.4
July	131.6	131.7	126.2	117.8	114.9	113.5	171.8	142.2	153.6
August	132.1	131.3	128.0	119.5	114.3	115.7	169.9	144.8	156.9
September	131.7	131.0	127.4	118.7	113.2	114.6	171.0	145.1	156.7
October	132.1	131.5	127.8	118.9	113.4	115.3	172.7	146.2	157.3
November	131.9	131.4	127.4	118.4	113.0	115.8	171.6	144.6	158.2
December	132.1	131.7	127.5	118.4	113.2	115.8	171.5	144.1	158.6

Industrial Production Indexes by Industry Groups

(Seasonally adjusted, 1992=100)

Year and month	Total	Manufacturing										
		Total	Primary processing	Advanced processing	Durable goods manufacturing							
					Total	Lumber and products	Furniture and fixtures	Stone, clay, and glass products	Primary metals			
									Total	Iron and steel		Nonferrous
										Total	Raw steel	
1970	58.7	54.8	67.2	48.9	52.7	68.6	56.2	74.8	111.2	139.0	139.2	75.9
1971	59.5	55.6	68.7	49.4	52.4	70.4	58.6	78.5	104.9	126.3	127.1	76.6
1972	65.3	61.5	77.3	54.3	58.5	80.6	70.7	86.9	118.3	141.5	143.9	87.0
1973	70.6	66.9	84.6	59.0	65.3	80.9	75.4	93.9	134.1	161.0	164.3	98.1
1974	69.6	65.9	82.0	58.6	64.0	73.4	70.1	92.4	129.7	155.7	163.1	94.8
1975	63.5	59.4	71.4	53.8	56.1	68.3	60.0	81.8	103.4	125.1	128.6	74.3
1976	69.3	65.4	80.3	58.6	61.8	77.8	67.0	91.5	115.7	137.9	140.9	85.7
1977	74.9	71.2	86.7	64.0	68.1	86.1	74.8	98.3	119.0	138.0	139.3	93.0
1978	79.3	75.8	90.7	68.9	73.6	87.5	80.4	106.0	128.0	147.5	154.9	101.1
1979	82.0	78.5	92.5	72.0	77.4	86.3	80.5	106.8	130.0	148.4	154.4	104.6
1980	79.7	75.5	84.4	71.4	73.4	80.4	79.1	96.5	108.0	119.0	126.9	92.4
1981	81.0	76.7	85.2	72.8	74.6	78.1	78.4	94.3	113.9	126.6	138.5	96.1
1982	76.7	72.1	75.7	70.5	68.2	70.3	74.6	84.2	80.5	80.5	82.6	80.7
1983	79.5	76.3	82.1	73.6	72.2	83.3	80.2	91.2	88.2	90.0	94.1	85.9
1984	86.6	83.8	88.4	81.7	82.7	89.9	88.6	98.6	98.7	98.9	102.6	98.6
1985	88.0	85.7	88.4	84.5	85.6	92.0	88.9	98.0	98.4	98.8	97.7	98.2
1986	89.0	88.1	90.0	87.2	87.4	99.6	93.3	101.7	91.2	86.8	89.7	97.6
1987	93.2	92.8	95.3	91.6	92.0	104.9	100.9	104.8	97.8	95.4	98.8	101.2
1988	97.4	97.1	99.0	96.2	98.1	105.1	101.1	107.5	106.2	107.6	111.2	104.6
1989	99.1	99.0	99.9	98.6	100.5	104.3	102.4	107.4	104.9	106.2	107.2	103.2
1990	98.9	98.5	99.3	98.2	99.0	101.6	100.9	105.0	104.0	106.4	108.3	100.9
1991	97.0	96.2	95.7	96.4	95.5	94.5	94.8	97.2	96.7	96.0	96.2	97.7
1992	100.0	100.0	100.0	100.0	100.0	100.0	100.0	100.0	100.0	100.0	100.0	100.0
1993	103.5	103.7	103.6	103.8	105.4	100.8	104.9	102.1	105.7	107.1	104.4	104.0
1994	109.1	109.9	109.7	110.0	114.2	105.9	108.1	107.8	113.4	113.7	106.6	113.0
1995	114.4	115.9	112.1	117.7	124.0	107.9	111.4	110.9	116.8	117.7	113.3	115.8
1996	119.5	121.4	114.5	124.8	134.1	110.4	113.2	118.3	119.8	119.2	112.2	120.6
1997	126.8	129.7	119.1	134.7	147.1	114.2	117.7	122.3	125.3	124.2	115.9	126.7
1998	131.3	135.1	120.7	142.1	157.5	117.0	121.4	126.2	123.8	121.1	115.7	127.0
1995:												
January	113.4	115.0	113.6	115.6	121.7	110.3	112.2	110.4	119.7	120.9	113.3	118.2
February	113.4	114.8	113.2	115.6	121.8	108.4	114.1	110.4	118.2	119.6	114.9	116.4
March	113.6	115.1	112.9	116.1	122.2	106.8	112.4	111.0	117.6	119.3	114.7	115.6
April	113.4	115.0	112.2	116.3	122.2	106.9	111.1	108.9	116.6	116.7	113.4	116.3
May	113.8	115.1	111.9	116.7	122.4	105.0	109.9	110.2	116.2	117.0	112.0	115.2
June	114.3	115.7	111.7	117.6	123.2	105.9	111.2	110.1	115.9	116.5	111.7	115.2
July	113.9	115.1	110.7	117.2	122.7	107.2	111.0	109.2	113.9	112.1	112.0	116.2
August	115.1	116.2	111.4	118.5	124.7	107.7	111.1	110.1	114.7	116.2	113.2	112.7
September	115.4	117.0	112.1	119.3	126.3	109.5	112.1	110.4	118.1	121.0	116.9	114.5
October	115.5	117.1	111.9	119.6	126.4	109.2	110.7	112.3	115.7	114.3	111.2	117.3
November	115.7	117.2	111.8	119.8	126.9	107.1	110.8	114.1	118.8	121.5	114.4	115.5
December	115.8	117.3	111.9	119.9	127.5	110.8	110.0	114.1	116.6	117.2	113.9	115.9
1996:												
January	115.5	116.9	111.4	119.6	127.5	106.9	111.1	114.7	116.1	117.7	112.3	114.2
February	117.0	118.4	111.7	121.7	129.8	107.3	110.9	114.2	116.8	115.6	111.0	118.2
March	116.8	118.1	112.8	120.6	128.6	110.3	109.6	115.2	118.7	118.1	112.7	119.4
April	118.2	119.7	112.8	123.1	132.0	110.7	110.9	114.5	118.2	117.0	111.5	119.7
May	119.2	120.9	113.9	124.3	133.8	110.7	114.1	117.3	119.2	118.0	112.4	120.6
June	120.0	121.8	115.0	125.1	135.2	112.5	112.6	119.3	119.9	119.7	114.8	120.2
July	120.3	122.4	114.9	126.1	135.8	109.9	112.2	121.4	118.5	118.5	114.0	118.5
August	120.9	123.0	115.7	126.5	136.7	111.8	115.5	119.5	121.5	121.4	113.5	121.6
September	121.1	123.3	116.0	126.8	136.6	111.7	114.6	121.0	121.8	119.1	112.5	125.2
October	121.2	123.3	116.3	126.7	136.7	110.6	116.0	121.2	123.1	123.7	112.1	122.3
November	121.9	124.2	116.5	127.9	138.1	112.3	115.8	121.2	121.9	121.5	109.1	122.5
December	122.3	124.7	116.6	128.7	138.7	110.0	115.3	119.8	122.2	120.5	112.7	124.3
1997:												
January	123.0	125.3	116.6	129.5	139.8	111.3	115.2	122.3	120.7	120.8	111.6	120.6
February	123.9	126.4	117.7	130.7	141.7	113.6	116.4	121.8	122.3	120.6	112.1	124.4
March	124.4	127.0	117.9	131.5	142.3	114.4	116.4	121.1	121.1	117.8	114.3	125.2
April	125.1	127.7	118.7	132.1	143.6	114.5	118.2	121.9	124.2	124.8	114.8	123.4
May	125.5	128.1	118.7	132.8	144.5	115.2	117.1	121.1	124.8	123.9	115.1	126.0
June	126.1	129.0	118.8	133.9	146.3	115.6	117.7	121.6	126.2	124.5	115.0	128.2
July	127.0	129.8	119.4	134.9	147.7	115.1	118.7	122.4	126.2	124.5	116.5	128.3
August	127.8	130.8	119.4	136.5	149.6	114.0	116.6	121.7	126.2	123.4	116.1	129.6
September	128.5	131.4	120.0	137.0	150.3	113.2	117.5	122.4	127.0	126.6	118.7	127.5
October	129.3	132.2	120.3	138.1	151.8	113.5	118.6	123.0	128.2	128.2	118.5	128.2
November	129.9	133.3	121.1	139.3	153.3	114.8	119.7	123.7	129.3	128.0	120.2	130.9
December	130.3	133.7	121.5	139.7	154.0	115.0	120.4	125.0	127.8	127.6	119.6	128.1
1998:												
January	130.3	133.8	121.6	139.8	153.9	115.2	119.4	124.6	129.2	128.9	122.5	129.7
February	130.2	133.7	121.1	140.0	154.0	116.2	118.6	124.0	128.1	128.2	123.3	128.0
March	130.7	134.1	121.0	140.6	155.2	115.3	121.5	124.5	127.1	127.7	120.0	126.4
April	131.3	134.9	121.5	141.6	156.2	116.1	121.0	124.0	127.5	126.7	122.4	128.4
May	131.9	135.4	121.4	142.3	157.2	116.4	120.6	124.5	126.5	125.5	121.9	127.6
June	130.6	133.7	120.2	140.4	154.8	116.7	122.0	123.5	122.1	119.8	116.0	124.9
July	130.5	133.6	120.7	139.9	154.4	117.5	120.8	125.4	122.6	120.2	118.3	125.4
August	132.4	135.7	120.6	143.3	159.8	118.5	120.1	127.0	124.4	122.5	120.3	126.7
September	131.9	135.2	119.3	143.2	159.6	117.0	121.6	126.6	120.1	113.4	112.6	128.1
October	132.4	136.1	120.1	144.2	161.2	118.0	124.5	128.3	120.6	114.4	109.7	128.0
November	132.2	136.4	120.3	144.6	161.0	118.3	123.6	130.5	118.7	109.7	100.2	129.3
December	132.4	136.7	121.3	144.4	161.5	121.4	122.9	131.7	118.6	114.6	102.0	123.4

Industrial Production Indexes by Industry Groups—*Continued*

(Seasonally adjusted, 1992=100)

Year and month	Fabricated metal products	Industrial machinery and equipment		Electrical machinery		Transportation equipment				Instruments	Miscellaneous
							Motor vehicles and parts		Aerospace and miscellaneous		
		Total	Computer and office equipment	Total	Semiconductors	Total	Total	Autos and light trucks			
1970	77.7	41.1	2.3	26.2	.....	54.1	52.0	.....	62.3	36.2	72.1
1971	77.3	38.2	2.0	26.3	.....	58.5	65.2	.....	55.9	37.9	72.4
1972	84.8	44.3	2.4	30.1	.....	62.4	71.1	.....	57.7	42.5	84.6
1973	94.3	51.8	2.9	34.3	.....	71.1	82.8	.....	63.8	48.5	85.7
1974	90.5	55.2	3.5	33.9	.....	64.6	71.4	.....	62.0	51.4	81.9
1975	78.4	47.8	3.2	29.2	.....	58.2	61.0	.....	59.3	48.9	76.0
1976	86.9	50.2	3.9	32.8	.....	66.3	80.0	.....	56.6	53.7	82.5
1977	94.7	56.6	5.1	38.1	.....	71.9	92.4	84.2	55.6	60.1	92.6
1978	98.2	63.3	7.5	42.2	.....	77.5	96.8	87.5	62.2	66.2	92.7
1979	101.6	70.2	10.3	46.9	.....	78.7	89.0	80.1	71.1	71.7	92.1
1980	94.4	70.5	13.9	48.6	.....	70.3	65.8	58.1	74.3	73.6	86.9
1981	93.0	74.7	18.4	51.0	.....	66.9	62.8	59.3	70.5	75.4	89.6
1982	84.9	65.8	21.3	51.7	.....	63.0	56.9	54.4	68.3	76.3	85.5
1983	87.2	65.2	29.5	55.9	.....	70.5	72.1	74.7	69.3	77.7	83.2
1984	95.2	78.9	42.0	66.7	.....	80.5	87.3	90.7	75.1	86.0	87.6
1985	96.5	81.2	50.3	68.4	.....	88.8	95.0	99.1	83.7	89.3	82.2
1986	95.6	81.8	53.7	71.0	42.9	94.1	94.2	99.2	94.2	88.8	83.5
1987	101.9	86.0	62.2	75.6	50.6	96.1	94.9	98.7	97.5	93.8	93.5
1988	106.1	97.1	74.6	82.5	57.3	101.1	100.2	103.1	102.1	97.2	99.8
1989	104.8	103.0	83.0	85.8	64.2	105.1	101.2	106.5	109.4	98.2	100.3
1990	101.2	100.1	81.4	87.7	71.7	102.3	95.3	99.3	109.8	98.4	100.0
1991	96.2	95.4	82.3	89.6	80.8	96.5	88.5	91.0	105.0	99.8	98.4
1992	100.0	100.0	100.0	100.0	100.0	100.0	100.0	100.0	100.0	100.0	100.0
1993	104.4	109.9	120.5	109.6	115.5	103.6	113.2	111.5	93.9	100.8	105.7
1994	112.2	124.9	149.3	131.4	155.9	107.4	130.4	125.2	85.0	99.8	110.0
1995	116.4	143.9	211.3	166.3	248.1	106.4	132.7	121.7	80.7	103.6	113.0
1996	120.2	159.8	298.8	206.0	365.7	107.9	132.6	122.5	83.8	107.7	116.5
1997	124.7	179.4	423.7	253.4	540.7	117.1	139.9	127.8	94.7	110.3	119.1
1998	127.3	203.7	649.1	291.9	700.6	123.0	141.1	128.5	104.9	113.0	117.7
1995:											
January	116.0	138.3	181.3	150.5	202.8	110.4	138.1	129.8	83.4	101.8	112.2
February	117.0	138.5	190.6	153.0	211.9	109.2	135.6	128.6	83.4	101.3	112.4
March	116.8	139.1	194.0	156.9	220.8	108.5	134.2	126.4	83.4	102.1	112.1
April	115.0	140.3	200.0	158.8	228.7	107.5	132.2	124.8	83.4	102.9	112.3
May	116.2	141.3	204.0	161.2	234.3	106.3	130.9	119.4	82.2	102.3	112.1
June	116.5	142.0	205.5	164.0	240.9	106.4	131.2	119.7	82.1	103.8	113.1
July	115.2	142.7	213.3	165.5	247.4	104.1	127.3	112.3	81.5	103.4	111.7
August	116.7	145.8	216.4	170.5	257.3	105.4	130.5	119.9	80.9	105.0	113.0
September	117.0	147.0	220.9	174.5	269.8	107.0	133.9	121.1	80.9	105.2	114.0
October	116.4	149.5	230.8	178.8	281.3	104.2	132.9	118.9	76.3	105.0	113.9
November	117.0	150.4	235.7	180.7	289.2	102.9	131.4	118.7	75.1	105.9	114.7
December	117.2	152.1	243.2	181.5	292.9	104.5	133.6	120.8	76.3	104.5	114.7
1996:											
January	117.7	151.2	247.0	182.3	296.1	104.8	130.6	114.7	79.7	105.6	113.8
February	118.9	154.3	261.0	188.7	306.9	106.7	132.8	121.1	81.3	107.8	115.6
March	118.9	155.5	268.4	192.4	319.9	96.3	111.1	99.5	81.6	108.0	116.1
April	118.7	155.8	272.2	197.7	336.3	109.1	137.2	126.3	81.7	107.5	115.4
May	119.6	158.1	283.9	203.4	355.0	109.7	138.1	125.6	82.0	107.5	116.3
June	120.3	160.0	296.7	208.8	368.3	109.6	137.7	128.1	82.3	108.2	117.2
July	120.8	161.6	309.9	209.8	375.5	111.8	140.4	135.0	83.9	107.2	116.6
August	121.4	162.7	313.8	212.8	386.8	111.1	138.2	129.0	84.8	107.5	117.1
September	121.4	162.5	319.4	215.3	395.6	108.9	132.1	125.0	86.2	107.8	117.5
October	121.6	163.4	329.5	217.6	406.2	106.8	127.1	117.1	86.8	108.0	116.9
November	121.7	165.2	337.7	220.3	415.0	110.1	133.1	122.9	87.5	108.2	116.8
December	121.4	167.6	346.7	223.3	427.1	110.0	132.2	125.3	88.3	108.6	118.9
1997:											
January	121.7	169.0	352.3	226.0	439.4	112.5	137.0	127.1	88.6	107.7	119.1
February	123.1	171.5	367.2	231.6	456.0	113.2	136.7	127.7	90.2	109.1	119.7
March	123.6	172.8	376.2	235.2	472.9	113.5	136.1	127.7	91.3	108.6	119.1
April	124.8	175.5	386.1	240.5	487.3	112.3	132.4	118.8	92.4	108.7	118.7
May	124.1	176.3	395.1	245.6	507.6	112.6	132.4	121.3	93.1	109.8	119.0
June	123.7	177.9	414.3	251.6	533.4	115.4	137.3	124.7	93.9	110.3	119.0
July	125.2	181.1	435.1	259.5	559.0	114.4	135.0	115.4	94.0	110.4	119.6
August	124.5	183.7	444.5	262.6	581.8	120.0	143.6	132.0	96.9	111.4	119.2
September	124.7	182.7	458.1	266.4	596.0	121.7	145.5	133.7	98.3	111.2	118.3
October	126.1	186.4	472.0	269.8	609.9	121.7	144.9	131.9	98.9	112.5	119.0
November	126.8	187.3	481.3	274.9	618.4	123.8	149.0	139.2	99.0	111.8	118.6
December	128.2	189.0	502.2	276.5	626.3	124.1	148.6	134.1	100.0	112.0	119.9
1998:											
January	127.6	191.8	526.3	277.7	630.7	121.3	141.9	132.0	100.9	111.5	119.7
February	126.6	192.3	552.6	278.5	633.8	121.5	140.4	128.2	102.6	112.5	119.9
March	127.2	198.4	589.6	278.2	630.0	122.3	140.0	128.8	104.5	112.8	120.0
April	127.8	200.6	605.4	280.8	635.3	123.3	140.8	130.9	105.7	113.0	120.1
May	128.7	202.5	623.9	282.0	643.1	125.2	144.1	132.7	106.3	113.8	119.1
June	128.0	205.8	641.4	285.5	660.3	114.2	121.1	110.1	106.3	112.4	118.5
July	127.8	209.0	657.0	289.4	676.7	108.2	107.6	86.9	107.1	112.6	118.5
August	126.3	207.0	673.6	290.8	697.5	130.3	154.2	142.0	106.9	113.0	117.7
September	126.2	207.7	695.5	297.7	725.6	127.6	149.9	136.5	105.8	114.2	117.0
October	126.9	211.2	718.5	302.4	756.3	128.4	150.2	140.4	106.9	114.6	115.9
November	127.7	211.1	746.9	304.8	779.3	127.1	148.8	138.1	105.7	114.1	114.1
December	128.7	212.7	761.6	307.3	794.8	125.6	146.6	137.3	104.8	113.9	115.4

Industrial Production Indexes by Industry Groups—*Continued*

(Seasonally adjusted, 1992=100)

Year and month	Nondurable goods manufacturing										
	Total	Foods	Tobacco products	Textile mill products	Apparel products	Paper and products	Printing and publishing	Chemicals and products	Petroleum and products	Rubber and plastics products	Leather and products
1970	58.0	60.6	94.3	71.8	81.8	56.7	54.4	48.8	80.8	33.0	235.0
1971	60.3	62.5	93.1	75.8	82.9	59.1	54.8	51.9	83.5	35.9	225.7
1972	65.7	65.8	96.6	83.1	87.9	64.3	58.5	58.4	87.4	43.7	234.2
1973	69.0	67.1	101.7	86.5	88.5	68.8	60.1	63.9	92.2	49.0	217.9
1974	68.5	68.0	99.4	78.7	84.5	68.2	59.1	66.2	89.0	47.9	207.2
1975	64.2	67.5	101.7	75.0	77.4	59.4	55.4	60.3	88.0	41.6	206.6
1976	70.7	71.4	106.8	83.3	91.1	67.4	60.5	67.5	93.6	48.1	205.1
1977	75.7	74.6	102.8	88.3	98.0	70.1	66.3	72.4	101.5	56.0	200.6
1978	78.9	77.2	107.4	88.6	100.4	73.4	70.1	76.4	104.9	59.3	201.6
1979	79.9	77.9	106.9	91.5	95.3	76.0	72.0	79.2	103.9	58.7	184.4
1980	78.3	79.7	108.5	89.0	95.4	75.2	72.4	75.9	95.9	53.3	181.6
1981	79.5	81.4	109.9	86.3	97.3	76.6	74.3	77.3	91.2	57.5	176.0
1982	77.7	82.4	106.2	80.1	96.3	74.3	77.5	71.0	86.6	56.8	163.1
1983	81.9	84.6	101.6	89.9	100.3	81.0	81.4	76.0	86.9	64.0	158.3
1984	85.3	86.4	101.7	90.4	102.2	85.0	87.0	79.3	89.9	72.1	141.9
1985	86.0	88.9	101.8	86.5	98.6	83.8	90.2	79.4	89.5	73.8	126.1
1986	89.1	91.2	100.3	90.5	101.8	88.3	93.4	82.4	95.7	78.2	115.0
1987	93.8	93.5	104.7	96.3	105.5	90.9	102.5	87.0	97.0	86.0	112.4
1988	96.0	94.9	106.5	95.0	103.6	93.8	103.4	92.2	98.8	88.2	112.0
1989	97.3	95.9	105.4	96.5	100.3	95.4	103.5	95.1	99.3	91.2	111.9
1990	97.9	97.0	105.4	93.2	97.2	96.0	103.1	97.3	100.3	92.2	107.8
1991	97.0	98.4	98.9	92.7	97.8	96.8	99.1	96.4	99.1	90.7	98.4
1992	100.0	100.0	100.0	100.0	100.0	100.0	100.0	100.0	100.0	100.0	100.0
1993	101.8	102.0	84.1	105.3	102.4	104.0	100.7	101.5	102.9	106.9	101.0
1994	105.2	103.7	104.4	110.6	106.3	108.4	100.7	104.7	102.7	116.5	93.6
1995	107.1	105.8	111.8	110.2	107.1	109.6	101.4	107.3	104.5	119.7	86.9
1996	107.9	105.4	113.5	108.9	104.7	108.8	101.6	110.0	106.8	123.3	87.3
1997	111.3	108.0	110.9	112.2	102.8	114.4	105.2	114.9	109.8	128.2	81.9
1998	111.9	109.6	106.0	112.2	99.2	115.0	105.1	115.5	112.0	132.6	75.3
1995:											
January	107.7	105.7	108.7	114.9	109.1	111.9	101.0	107.9	104.4	120.6	89.7
February	107.3	104.8	107.8	113.3	108.8	111.1	101.7	107.3	104.2	120.8	88.9
March	107.3	105.0	111.1	113.6	109.5	110.9	101.2	107.4	105.2	119.9	88.5
April	107.2	105.3	113.0	113.6	107.3	110.8	101.4	106.6	103.7	120.6	86.8
May	107.2	106.3	111.4	110.8	108.3	110.8	101.4	107.0	103.4	118.7	86.9
June	107.5	107.0	118.7	109.5	106.6	109.4	101.3	107.5	104.6	118.5	86.4
July	106.9	106.3	120.6	105.0	106.0	109.6	101.4	106.7	105.4	117.4	84.5
August	107.0	106.6	110.7	110.1	106.5	108.6	101.7	106.8	104.7	119.1	86.4
September	106.9	106.1	106.7	108.5	106.5	108.2	101.8	107.3	105.7	120.0	87.3
October	107.2	106.1	108.8	108.7	106.1	109.8	101.0	108.2	103.4	120.4	85.7
November	106.8	105.5	111.1	106.9	105.6	106.4	101.7	108.0	104.0	120.4	85.9
December	106.3	104.6	113.3	107.0	104.3	107.6	100.6	107.3	105.3	119.7	85.4
1996:											
January	105.6	104.6	108.9	103.6	101.7	106.3	99.0	107.5	105.6	120.0	85.2
February	106.3	105.1	113.0	106.1	105.0	104.7	100.4	107.7	106.5	120.5	87.1
March	106.9	105.7	117.3	109.3	104.1	106.3	100.4	107.6	106.2	121.3	87.3
April	106.7	105.1	113.8	107.8	105.1	108.2	100.5	107.4	105.8	120.7	87.8
May	107.3	104.7	112.3	109.1	105.4	108.3	101.6	108.4	106.3	122.8	87.3
June	107.7	104.9	115.3	111.8	105.3	109.3	101.2	108.5	106.6	124.1	88.7
July	108.2	105.3	115.0	110.0	105.1	109.9	101.6	110.4	105.6	124.0	88.2
August	108.5	104.5	114.2	110.8	106.2	109.1	102.2	111.0	107.7	125.2	88.1
September	109.2	105.6	118.7	109.8	105.7	109.5	102.6	111.9	107.3	125.8	87.9
October	109.1	106.1	110.3	109.8	104.8	109.3	102.8	112.9	108.7	124.4	86.9
November	109.5	106.5	112.7	110.1	104.4	111.4	103.1	112.8	108.0	124.6	86.4
December	110.0	106.9	110.0	108.9	103.7	112.6	103.4	113.8	107.6	126.0	87.0
1997:											
January	110.0	107.1	117.7	109.9	103.1	111.7	102.7	114.0	107.6	124.8	86.3
February	110.4	107.4	112.8	110.0	102.7	113.6	103.9	113.8	108.6	126.6	84.2
March	111.0	108.7	120.5	111.2	103.7	114.0	104.1	113.0	108.3	127.2	85.1
April	111.1	107.6	109.2	112.4	103.4	113.4	105.0	115.4	110.0	126.4	84.4
May	111.0	107.7	107.0	110.5	103.2	113.9	105.3	114.8	111.8	127.2	83.3
June	110.9	107.6	105.3	112.3	103.2	113.4	104.8	114.8	111.4	127.5	82.3
July	111.2	108.7	108.1	114.0	103.0	114.4	105.1	114.1	109.0	127.9	82.3
August	111.3	107.9	108.2	112.8	102.5	115.5	105.2	114.6	110.1	129.7	78.9
September	111.8	107.6	112.1	112.8	102.5	116.0	105.8	115.5	110.1	129.6	78.9
October	112.0	107.5	112.0	113.1	102.7	115.0	106.4	116.3	111.1	129.2	80.0
November	112.6	109.1	112.1	114.1	101.8	116.1	107.1	116.2	109.1	130.9	78.7
December	112.7	109.0	106.4	113.1	102.3	116.2	107.0	117.3	110.6	130.9	78.8
1998:											
January	113.1	110.5	110.1	115.0	102.5	115.7	106.4	117.0	111.2	131.0	77.3
February	112.8	109.9	112.7	113.2	101.1	115.9	106.4	116.7	110.5	131.1	78.3
March	112.4	109.7	105.3	112.6	101.6	115.0	105.4	116.6	113.0	131.4	77.9
April	113.0	110.3	109.8	113.3	101.0	115.2	105.5	117.7	112.8	133.2	76.3
May	113.0	110.7	111.5	114.5	100.4	115.0	105.6	116.9	111.5	133.1	75.8
June	112.0	109.2	104.7	112.0	100.5	114.9	105.5	116.2	111.6	132.4	74.5
July	112.1	109.0	106.0	113.2	100.1	115.9	105.4	115.7	113.4	132.7	75.3
August	111.3	107.9	107.0	111.8	99.2	115.3	104.9	114.3	114.1	132.2	74.0
September	110.6	107.7	104.2	111.2	98.3	113.9	104.6	113.3	110.7	132.6	73.5
October	110.9	109.1	101.9	112.4	97.3	115.4	104.2	113.1	110.4	133.4	72.8
November	111.6	111.3	99.8	108.8	95.5	112.3	105.4	114.7	112.8	135.0	74.3
December	111.7	111.1	100.0	109.4	95.4	115.3	105.1	114.0	112.5	136.0	73.0

Industrial Production Indexes by Industry Groups—*Continued*

(Seasonally adjusted, 1992=100)

Year and month	Mining					Utilities			Special aggregates		
									Manufacturing excluding:		
	Total	Metal mining	Coal mining	Oil and gas extraction	Stone and earth minerals	Total	Electric	Gas	Motor vehicles and parts	Computer and office equipment	Computers and semiconductors
1970	101.8	77.1	62.3	116.5	89.5	66.5	51.0	130.5	.....	.....	.....
1971	99.3	68.6	57.3	115.2	89.9	69.6	53.9	134.4	.....	.....	.....
1972	101.4	66.3	61.3	117.2	93.9	74.1	58.4	136.5	.....	.....	.....
1973	102.3	70.0	60.7	116.6	102.5	77.0	62.3	134.4	.....	.....	.....
1974	101.8	68.0	61.6	115.8	102.1	76.1	61.9	131.2	.....	.....	.....
1975	99.5	63.5	66.2	113.1	91.9	76.8	64.0	125.2	.....	.....	.....
1976	100.3	69.2	68.9	111.2	97.2	79.9	67.1	127.1	.....	.....	.....
1977	103.4	61.1	70.6	116.8	99.4	82.0	70.7	120.7	.....	.....	.....
1978	106.5	69.5	67.6	121.1	104.7	84.4	73.3	122.6	.....	.....	.....
1979	108.3	72.2	78.6	119.5	107.1	86.8	75.2	126.6	.....	.....	.....
1980	111.5	65.2	83.4	124.4	97.9	87.3	76.4	124.8	.....	.....	.....
1981	115.6	73.5	82.9	129.7	94.1	85.0	78.0	109.3	.....	.....	.....
1982	111.2	54.8	84.5	125.6	78.7	82.3	76.7	102.4	.....	.....	.....
1983	106.6	52.8	79.0	120.2	84.0	83.7	79.2	100.4	.....	.....	.....
1984	113.9	57.2	90.2	126.9	94.7	86.7	82.4	102.6	.....	.....	.....
1985	111.0	56.6	89.1	123.0	97.9	88.8	84.6	104.3	.....	.....	.....
1986	102.6	59.3	89.7	111.0	96.6	86.4	86.2	87.0	87.8	89.2	91.1
1987	102.1	61.9	92.5	108.9	100.9	89.4	89.4	89.0	92.7	93.7	95.4
1988	104.7	74.3	95.4	110.4	103.2	93.9	93.6	94.5	97.0	97.7	99.3
1989	103.2	85.6	98.9	106.1	101.8	97.1	96.8	98.1	98.9	99.4	100.7
1990	104.8	93.1	103.7	106.4	103.3	98.3	99.2	94.4	98.7	98.9	99.9
1991	102.6	93.3	100.1	104.7	96.7	100.4	101.2	97.3	96.7	96.5	97.0
1992	100.0	100.0	100.0	100.0	100.0	100.0	100.0	100.0	100.0	100.0	100.0
1993	99.9	98.8	93.7	101.1	102.3	103.9	103.8	104.3	103.1	103.4	103.0
1994	102.4	100.5	102.5	101.7	108.6	105.3	105.5	104.6	108.7	109.2	107.9
1995	102.0	101.5	101.9	100.5	112.9	109.0	109.5	107.2	114.9	114.4	110.9
1996	103.7	104.0	105.0	101.8	114.9	112.6	112.7	112.3	120.7	119.0	113.3
1997	105.8	110.0	107.8	103.1	120.3	112.8	113.2	111.2	129.1	126.3	118.0
1998	104.0	110.0	109.7	99.6	124.7	113.9	117.2	101.9	134.7	130.2	120.1
1995:											
January	103.0	100.9	104.0	101.1	117.2	104.9	105.7	102.0	113.7	113.9	111.4
February	102.5	101.6	102.7	101.1	113.0	106.2	106.6	105.0	113.6	113.6	110.9
March	102.1	99.8	105.3	100.1	113.6	106.5	107.3	103.4	114.0	113.8	110.9
April	100.6	100.7	94.9	100.4	111.5	106.6	107.2	104.3	114.0	113.6	110.5
May	102.4	100.5	101.7	101.6	110.9	108.6	108.6	108.3	114.2	113.7	110.5
June	102.3	101.0	103.4	100.8	111.5	108.5	109.0	106.6	114.8	114.3	110.8
July	101.9	102.4	98.9	100.6	115.3	109.9	109.8	110.1	114.4	113.6	110.1
August	102.1	102.0	103.8	100.4	111.8	114.7	116.2	109.0	115.3	114.6	110.9
September	102.1	101.1	104.1	100.0	114.8	109.9	110.3	108.4	116.0	115.4	111.4
October	101.1	102.9	102.6	99.2	110.9	109.3	111.0	102.9	116.2	115.4	111.2
November	102.3	104.0	103.5	100.6	110.8	111.2	111.0	112.0	116.4	115.4	111.1
December	101.3	101.5	98.0	100.1	113.9	112.1	111.4	114.6	116.3	115.4	111.0
1996:											
January	100.9	98.9	97.0	100.7	109.1	113.1	112.9	114.1	116.1	115.0	110.6
February	102.3	97.7	103.0	101.2	111.9	114.2	114.0	115.3	117.6	116.4	111.7
March	103.2	103.4	103.8	101.5	113.3	114.5	114.1	116.1	118.5	116.0	111.0
April	104.2	101.5	105.6	102.7	113.9	113.5	112.9	115.6	118.7	117.6	112.4
May	104.3	103.2	107.6	102.2	114.7	114.0	114.5	112.0	119.9	118.6	113.1
June	104.7	103.6	103.5	103.2	117.7	113.3	113.7	111.5	120.9	119.4	113.6
July	105.0	105.4	109.7	102.4	116.9	109.7	110.5	106.8	121.3	119.9	114.0
August	105.0	105.2	110.4	102.4	116.0	111.8	112.3	109.5	122.1	120.4	114.3
September	104.0	106.5	102.7	102.5	114.0	111.1	111.1	111.1	122.7	120.7	114.5
October	104.4	106.8	107.4	101.9	117.1	111.7	111.8	111.2	123.1	120.6	114.2
November	103.3	106.6	104.2	100.7	118.9	112.6	112.6	113.0	123.7	121.4	114.9
December	103.1	109.0	105.6	100.4	115.9	112.1	112.3	111.3	124.3	121.9	115.2
1997:											
January	104.3	109.7	108.2	101.5	115.0	113.4	113.7	112.1	124.6	122.4	115.6
February	105.5	108.1	108.9	102.6	121.0	111.0	111.4	109.7	125.9	123.4	116.3
March	106.3	109.1	105.6	104.0	122.4	109.6	111.0	104.0	126.5	123.9	116.6
April	105.4	108.0	105.9	103.3	117.8	112.7	113.0	111.8	127.5	124.6	117.0
May	106.6	108.6	113.4	103.4	119.3	111.4	110.3	116.2	127.9	124.9	117.0
June	105.9	110.1	106.5	103.1	123.0	111.4	110.8	114.1	128.5	125.6	117.4
July	106.1	109.0	108.1	103.7	118.9	113.7	114.0	112.6	129.5	126.3	117.8
August	105.5	109.2	104.3	103.3	121.3	113.1	113.4	111.9	130.1	127.2	118.5
September	106.6	111.7	108.9	103.8	121.0	114.4	115.2	110.5	130.6	127.7	118.8
October	106.2	113.2	107.7	103.5	119.8	116.1	117.4	110.2	131.5	128.4	119.4
November	104.9	115.9	100.3	102.6	122.0	113.6	114.1	111.0	132.4	129.4	120.2
December	106.4	107.5	116.1	102.2	121.9	113.1	113.8	109.9	132.8	129.7	120.4
1998:											
January	107.6	110.9	112.4	103.6	127.5	109.8	111.4	102.2	133.4	129.6	120.3
February	107.5	123.2	104.3	104.6	123.1	109.0	111.2	99.3	133.4	129.4	120.1
March	105.8	109.3	103.4	104.0	120.0	114.0	115.7	106.3	133.8	129.5	120.2
April	105.7	106.9	107.2	102.9	123.3	112.8	115.2	102.0	134.6	130.2	120.9
May	105.4	108.5	106.0	102.4	124.4	115.2	118.9	98.3	134.9	130.6	121.1
June	104.7	108.0	110.4	100.4	125.6	118.7	121.0	108.4	134.5	128.8	119.2
July	104.6	105.7	112.8	100.0	125.4	118.3	119.8	111.7	135.1	128.6	118.9
August	103.7	109.0	109.7	99.2	124.3	120.2	121.2	115.7	134.6	130.6	120.6
September	102.4	106.4	115.8	96.8	120.3	120.3	122.6	109.7	134.4	130.0	119.9
October	102.0	113.6	110.8	96.8	118.8	116.5	120.3	98.7	135.3	130.8	120.4
November	101.1	110.7	108.6	94.2	132.1	110.6	114.6	92.0	135.7	130.9	120.4
December	99.0	108.3	114.5	91.0	125.6	111.8	115.2	96.0	136.2	131.1	120.5

Capacity Utilization

(Output as a percent of capacity, seasonally adjusted)

Year and month	Total industry	Manufacturing			Durable goods				Primary metals					
		Total	Primary process-ing	Advanced process-ing	Total	Lumber and products	Furniture and fixtures	Stone, clay, and glass products	Total	Iron and steel		Nonferrous		
										Total	Raw steel	Total	Primary copper	Primary aluminum
1970	81.1	79.4	79.9	78.9	77.2	80.5	81.0	73.9	80.8	84.9	83.4	74.3	88.4	97.4
1971	79.4	77.9	78.7	77.1	74.7	80.0	80.7	75.6	74.8	76.6	76.0	71.7	74.9	88.1
1972	84.4	83.4	85.5	82.2	81.4	88.2	93.0	81.7	83.7	86.2	85.6	79.2	85.1	87.4
1973	88.4	87.7	90.5	86.2	88.0	85.5	93.9	86.0	94.5	98.0	97.1	88.1	85.0	94.0
1974	84.3	83.4	85.1	82.5	83.1	75.8	82.9	81.9	90.7	94.7	96.0	83.7	73.0	100.2
1975	74.6	72.9	72.1	73.3	70.6	69.5	68.9	70.3	71.7	75.9	75.2	64.1	61.9	78.4
1976	79.3	78.2	79.2	77.6	75.7	78.2	75.7	77.2	79.0	82.4	80.7	72.9	67.9	83.1
1977	83.5	82.6	83.8	81.9	80.8	85.7	82.1	81.8	80.1	80.7	78.6	79.4	63.2	87.4
1978	85.8	85.2	85.9	84.8	84.4	86.1	84.5	86.5	86.6	86.5	87.6	86.9	67.9	92.3
1979	86.0	85.3	86.0	84.9	85.6	83.8	81.0	85.5	88.4	88.6	88.3	88.0	71.8	95.7
1980	81.5	79.5	77.2	80.8	78.4	77.7	77.2	76.3	73.5	71.6	73.4	76.9	56.7	95.0
1981	80.8	78.3	77.2	78.8	76.8	74.9	74.7	75.0	77.6	76.4	80.5	79.1	72.0	90.3
1982	74.5	71.8	68.6	73.5	68.0	66.6	70.2	67.5	54.5	48.9	48.3	65.6	54.0	65.9
1983	75.7	74.4	74.5	74.4	70.1	78.8	74.9	73.1	61.7	56.9	57.4	69.6	56.8	67.4
1984	80.8	79.8	80.0	79.7	77.6	84.0	81.4	78.3	71.9	66.5	66.4	81.0	66.9	83.6
1985	79.8	78.8	79.1	78.6	76.8	84.0	79.5	76.3	73.2	68.9	65.8	80.3	71.9	74.9
1986	78.7	78.7	79.9	78.1	75.7	89.0	81.5	78.3	70.1	64.1	63.9	80.3	74.4	71.9
1987	81.3	81.3	84.5	79.9	77.9	92.1	86.0	79.8	79.2	76.2	77.7	84.1	77.2	84.1
1988	84.0	83.8	86.8	82.3	81.7	91.1	84.0	81.6	87.4	87.4	88.9	87.5	78.4	97.4
1989	84.1	83.6	86.1	82.5	82.0	88.7	83.1	81.1	85.2	84.7	84.1	85.9	76.3	98.6
1990	82.3	81.4	83.9	80.3	79.0	85.1	80.1	78.6	83.4	83.6	84.5	83.1	77.8	98.3
1991	79.3	77.9	79.6	77.2	74.7	78.5	74.7	72.2	77.6	75.7	75.8	80.1	81.3	99.6
1992	80.3	79.5	82.3	78.3	76.7	82.7	78.2	74.0	80.7	80.5	80.8	81.2	85.7	97.0
1993	81.3	80.5	84.0	79.0	78.8	82.6	80.3	75.5	85.7	87.6	87.7	83.4	93.6	88.8
1994	83.2	82.5	87.1	80.6	81.7	84.9	80.9	80.0	90.6	91.8	90.8	89.1	87.7	79.1
1995	83.4	82.7	86.5	81.0	82.0	83.9	81.6	79.8	90.5	92.7	94.1	87.9	95.4	80.7
1996	82.4	81.4	85.1	79.8	80.7	82.9	79.3	80.5	90.0	90.7	90.5	89.4	82.4	85.1
1997	82.9	82.0	85.3	80.7	81.2	82.3	78.1	80.4	90.8	90.3	89.5	91.6	90.5	85.8
1998	81.8	80.8	83.6	79.9	80.4	81.7	78.1	81.7	86.8	84.3	83.9	90.2	86.8	88.4
1995:														
January	84.7	84.4	89.0	82.3	84.1	86.9	83.1	81.7	93.8	96.0	95.4	91.2	93.8	78.8
February	84.3	83.8	88.4	81.8	83.5	85.2	84.3	81.3	92.4	94.8	96.5	89.6	94.1	78.6
March	84.1	83.6	88.0	81.7	83.1	83.7	82.9	81.3	91.7	94.4	96.1	88.6	97.4	78.6
April	83.5	83.1	87.2	81.3	82.4	83.6	81.8	79.3	90.7	92.3	94.7	88.9	96.8	79.3
May	83.4	82.8	86.7	81.0	81.9	81.9	80.7	79.8	90.2	92.4	93.3	87.8	102.4	80.1
June	83.4	82.7	86.3	81.1	81.8	82.4	81.5	79.4	89.8	91.9	92.8	87.5	94.3	80.6
July	82.7	81.9	85.3	80.4	80.8	83.2	81.2	78.3	88.1	88.2	92.8	88.0	96.4	81.1
August	83.3	82.3	85.6	80.8	81.5	83.4	81.1	78.6	88.5	91.4	93.5	85.2	97.0	81.2
September	83.1	82.4	85.9	80.9	81.9	84.6	81.6	78.4	91.0	95.0	96.3	86.4	92.6	82.0
October	82.8	82.1	85.5	80.6	81.3	84.2	80.5	79.3	88.9	89.7	91.4	88.2	95.2	81.6
November	82.6	81.7	85.1	80.2	81.1	82.3	80.4	80.1	91.2	95.1	93.8	86.7	94.8	82.7
December	82.3	81.3	84.9	79.7	80.8	84.9	79.6	79.7	89.3	91.6	93.1	86.8	89.9	83.7
1996:														
January	81.7	80.7	84.3	79.1	80.1	81.7	80.1	79.7	88.7	91.8	91.5	85.3	88.8	84.4
February	82.4	81.3	84.3	80.0	81.0	81.8	79.5	79.1	89.0	89.7	90.3	88.3	86.5	84.9
March	81.8	80.6	84.8	78.8	79.5	83.8	78.2	79.5	90.2	91.3	91.5	89.0	83.8	84.9
April	82.4	81.3	84.6	79.9	81.0	83.8	78.7	78.7	89.5	90.0	90.3	89.1	84.0	85.3
May	82.7	81.7	85.1	80.2	81.4	83.5	80.6	80.3	90.0	90.3	90.8	89.7	82.2	85.1
June	82.9	81.9	85.6	80.2	81.6	84.6	79.1	81.4	90.3	91.2	92.6	89.3	80.7	85.0
July	82.7	81.9	85.3	80.4	81.4	82.4	78.4	82.6	88.9	89.9	91.7	87.8	81.6	84.8
August	82.8	81.8	85.6	80.2	81.4	83.5	80.3	80.9	90.9	91.7	91.1	90.0	77.3	85.5
September	82.5	81.6	85.6	79.9	80.7	83.2	79.3	81.6	90.9	89.6	90.1	92.4	79.4	85.4
October	82.2	81.2	85.5	79.4	80.2	82.1	79.8	81.5	91.5	92.6	89.6	90.1	82.8	85.4
November	82.3	81.4	85.4	79.7	80.4	83.1	79.3	81.2	90.3	90.6	87.0	90.1	79.1	85.5
December	82.2	81.3	85.2	79.7	80.1	81.2	78.5	79.9	90.2	89.4	89.7	91.3	82.8	85.2
1997:														
January	82.3	81.3	84.9	79.8	80.2	81.8	78.1	81.4	88.8	89.4	88.5	88.3	86.3	85.3
February	82.6	81.7	85.5	80.1	80.7	83.2	78.6	80.8	89.8	89.0	88.4	90.9	85.7	85.7
March	82.5	81.7	85.4	80.2	80.5	83.5	78.3	80.2	88.7	86.6	89.7	91.3	89.2	85.8
April	82.7	81.7	85.7	80.2	80.7	83.3	79.2	80.6	90.6	91.4	89.7	89.7	87.4	85.5
May	82.6	81.6	85.4	80.1	80.6	83.5	78.1	79.9	90.8	90.5	89.4	91.3	81.5	85.3
June	82.6	81.7	85.2	80.4	81.0	83.5	78.3	80.0	91.6	90.7	88.9	92.7	88.1	85.8
July	82.9	81.9	85.3	80.6	81.3	82.9	78.6	80.4	91.3	90.4	89.6	92.6	93.2	85.8
August	83.1	82.2	85.1	81.1	81.8	81.8	76.9	79.7	91.1	89.4	88.8	93.3	92.5	85.8
September	83.2	82.2	85.2	81.1	81.7	80.9	77.2	80.0	91.4	91.4	90.4	91.6	95.8	85.6
October	83.4	82.4	85.2	81.3	82.0	80.9	77.6	80.2	92.0	92.3	89.7	91.9	96.6	86.3
November	83.4	82.6	85.4	81.6	82.2	81.5	78.0	80.5	92.6	91.9	90.6	93.6	94.8	86.3
December	83.4	82.5	85.4	81.4	82.0	81.4	78.2	81.2	91.3	91.3	89.7	91.5	95.3	86.4
1998:														
January	83.0	82.2	85.2	81.0	81.4	81.3	77.3	80.9	92.1	91.9	91.4	92.4	89.7	86.4
February	82.6	81.8	84.7	80.7	81.0	81.9	76.7	80.4	91.0	91.0	91.5	91.2	91.0	86.5
March	82.6	81.6	84.4	80.6	81.1	81.0	78.5	80.7	90.0	90.2	88.5	89.9	87.9	87.3
April	82.6	81.7	84.6	80.7	81.1	81.4	78.1	80.4	90.0	89.1	89.8	91.2	88.9	88.2
May	82.6	81.6	84.3	80.7	81.1	81.4	77.7	80.7	89.1	87.9	88.9	90.6	83.1	88.5
June	81.5	80.2	83.3	79.2	79.3	81.5	78.5	80.0	85.8	83.5	84.1	88.6	84.2	88.9
July	81.1	79.8	83.4	78.5	78.6	81.8	77.6	81.2	85.9	83.5	85.3	88.9	85.7	89.6
August	82.0	80.7	83.1	79.9	80.9	82.3	77.1	82.2	86.9	84.7	86.3	89.7	89.3	89.7
September	81.3	80.1	82.1	79.5	80.3	81.1	78.0	81.9	83.7	78.1	80.4	90.6	83.9	90.1
October	81.3	80.3	82.4	79.6	80.6	81.6	79.7	83.1	83.7	78.4	77.8	90.4	87.6	88.3
November	80.8	80.1	82.4	79.4	80.0	81.6	79.1	84.4	82.2	74.9	70.7	91.3	88.9	88.9
December	80.7	80.0	82.9	79.0	79.8	83.6	78.5	85.1	81.9	77.9	71.6	87.0	81.6	88.4

Capacity Utilization—*Continued*

(Output as a percent of capacity, seasonally adjusted)

Year and month	Fabricated metal products	Industrial machinery and equipment		Electrical machinery	Transportation equipment			Aerospace and miscellaneous	Instruments	Miscellaneous
		Total	Computer and office equipment		Total	Motor vehicles and parts				
						Total	Autos and light trucks			
1970	75.0	81.3	90.9	76.6	70.5	66.6	.....	76.7	77.4	77.9
1971	73.7	73.0	70.9	73.5	74.2	79.5	.....	68.7	76.3	74.3
1972	79.9	82.5	79.2	81.1	76.8	82.5	.....	70.6	81.4	82.7
1973	86.8	93.0	86.3	88.0	84.7	91.6	.....	77.3	87.6	79.9
1974	80.9	94.6	91.7	81.9	75.0	76.4	.....	73.9	86.5	73.5
1975	68.6	78.4	74.0	67.0	65.8	63.1	.....	69.6	77.1	66.9
1976	74.6	78.8	75.6	72.8	72.7	80.2	.....	65.3	80.5	71.8
1977	79.9	83.9	78.1	80.1	76.4	90.3	89.8	63.2	86.1	79.5
1978	81.0	88.2	87.3	83.9	80.7	91.0	88.3	70.2	89.5	78.2
1979	82.0	91.6	89.3	87.7	80.2	82.0	78.3	78.4	90.6	76.1
1980	74.9	85.9	88.2	84.0	70.9	61.3	57.8	79.1	87.2	70.6
1981	73.2	84.8	85.7	81.2	66.1	59.3	60.3	72.2	84.8	72.4
1982	66.9	70.5	74.3	76.7	60.9	52.8	53.5	67.8	81.7	69.1
1983	68.4	66.2	78.7	77.8	66.7	66.2	71.9	67.2	79.7	67.3
1984	74.3	75.7	86.1	85.8	74.1	79.0	81.6	70.0	84.6	70.7
1985	74.9	72.8	80.0	80.5	77.9	83.1	81.5	73.8	83.6	65.9
1986	73.6	70.3	72.5	77.8	78.6	78.7	76.7	78.5	79.1	66.6
1987	78.1	72.1	74.6	78.7	77.5	76.8	74.7	78.1	80.2	74.0
1988	81.1	79.6	79.5	82.3	80.6	81.2	79.2	80.0	80.8	78.2
1989	80.0	83.4	81.2	81.3	81.8	79.5	79.8	84.4	79.8	77.4
1990	77.3	79.4	73.7	78.9	77.7	71.6	71.0	84.0	78.5	75.6
1991	73.4	74.2	68.8	76.3	71.8	64.1	64.6	80.8	78.7	73.2
1992	76.9	75.4	75.1	80.0	73.8	70.7	71.2	77.2	77.4	73.3
1993	79.7	78.7	76.7	81.4	75.7	77.6	78.6	73.5	77.0	76.2
1994	83.1	83.1	77.7	86.2	76.9	85.5	86.7	67.2	75.4	78.1
1995	82.8	86.5	85.3	88.1	73.4	80.9	80.4	64.1	76.6	79.0
1996	81.0	85.4	84.8	83.6	72.1	76.3	79.7	66.5	78.6	80.0
1997	79.2	85.2	82.9	81.4	76.6	78.0	83.3	74.8	80.0	80.2
1998	76.9	85.5	83.6	77.5	78.8	76.2	82.0	82.4	80.5	78.0
1995:										
January	84.5	87.5	84.7	90.2	77.7	87.4	87.4	66.2	76.2	79.1
February	84.9	86.8	86.8	89.8	76.5	85.2	86.3	66.1	75.6	79.1
March	84.3	86.4	86.1	90.1	75.8	83.7	84.5	66.2	76.1	78.8
April	82.7	86.3	86.4	89.2	74.9	81.9	83.1	66.2	76.5	78.8
May	83.2	86.1	85.9	88.4	73.7	80.5	79.3	65.3	75.9	78.5
June	83.0	85.7	84.3	87.9	73.5	80.2	79.2	65.2	76.8	79.1
July	81.7	85.4	85.3	86.9	71.7	77.2	74.0	64.7	76.4	78.1
August	82.4	86.5	84.3	87.6	72.3	78.7	78.7	64.3	77.4	78.8
September	82.2	86.4	83.8	87.7	73.2	80.2	79.2	64.3	77.3	79.4
October	81.4	87.1	85.3	87.9	71.0	79.0	77.6	60.7	77.0	79.2
November	81.5	86.8	84.9	86.9	69.8	77.7	77.2	59.7	77.5	79.7
December	81.3	87.0	85.4	85.2	70.7	78.5	78.3	60.7	76.3	79.6
1996:										
January	81.3	85.6	84.2	83.6	70.7	76.3	74.3	63.4	77.0	78.8
February	81.8	86.5	86.1	84.7	71.9	77.4	78.4	64.6	78.6	79.9
March	81.3	86.2	85.8	84.4	64.7	64.6	64.5	64.9	78.8	80.1
April	80.9	85.5	84.2	84.8	73.2	79.5	81.9	64.9	78.4	79.6
May	81.1	85.8	85.0	85.2	73.4	79.8	81.5	65.1	78.5	80.0
June	81.3	85.9	86.0	85.4	73.2	79.4	83.2	65.3	79.0	80.5
July	81.2	85.9	87.0	84.1	74.6	80.7	87.7	66.6	78.3	79.9
August	81.2	85.6	85.3	83.6	74.0	79.3	84.0	67.2	78.5	80.2
September	80.9	84.7	84.0	82.9	72.4	75.6	81.5	68.3	78.7	80.3
October	80.7	84.3	83.9	82.0	70.8	72.5	76.4	68.7	78.9	79.8
November	80.4	84.3	83.3	81.3	72.9	75.7	80.3	69.3	79.1	79.6
December	79.9	84.7	82.8	80.6	72.7	75.0	82.0	69.8	79.4	80.9
1997:										
January	79.6	84.5	81.6	80.0	74.3	77.5	83.2	70.0	78.7	80.9
February	80.1	85.0	82.5	80.6	74.6	77.2	83.6	71.2	79.6	81.2
March	80.0	84.8	82.1	80.4	74.7	76.7	83.6	72.1	79.1	80.6
April	80.4	85.3	81.8	80.8	73.8	74.4	77.7	73.0	79.1	80.3
May	79.5	84.9	81.3	81.0	73.9	74.2	79.3	73.6	79.8	80.3
June	78.8	84.8	82.7	81.5	75.6	76.8	81.5	74.2	80.0	80.3
July	79.3	85.6	84.3	82.7	74.8	75.3	75.3	74.2	80.1	80.5
August	78.4	86.0	83.7	82.4	78.4	79.9	86.0	76.5	80.6	80.1
September	78.1	84.8	83.7	82.2	79.3	80.7	87.0	77.6	80.4	79.4
October	78.6	85.7	83.7	81.9	79.2	80.1	85.7	78.1	81.2	79.8
November	78.6	85.3	82.9	82.0	80.4	82.2	90.3	78.1	80.6	79.3
December	79.0	85.3	84.0	81.1	80.5	81.7	86.8	78.9	80.7	80.1
1998:										
January	78.3	85.7	85.0	80.2	78.5	77.8	85.3	79.6	80.2	79.8
February	77.5	84.9	85.7	79.3	78.5	76.8	82.7	80.8	80.7	79.9
March	77.6	86.6	87.9	78.1	78.9	76.4	82.8	82.2	80.8	79.8
April	77.7	86.6	86.7	77.7	79.4	76.7	83.9	83.0	80.8	79.7
May	78.0	86.3	85.8	76.9	80.5	78.3	84.9	83.4	81.1	78.9
June	77.3	86.6	84.7	76.8	73.3	65.7	70.3	83.2	80.0	78.4
July	77.0	87.0	83.4	76.8	69.3	58.3	55.3	83.8	80.0	78.3
August	75.8	85.2	82.1	76.2	83.3	83.4	90.2	83.5	80.1	77.6
September	75.6	84.5	81.4	77.0	81.5	80.9	86.5	82.6	80.8	77.0
October	75.7	84.9	80.7	77.2	81.8	80.9	88.8	83.3	80.9	76.2
November	75.9	83.9	80.7	76.8	80.8	80.0	87.1	82.3	80.4	74.9
December	76.4	83.6	79.2	76.5	79.8	78.7	86.5	81.5	80.1	75.7

Capacity Utilization—*Continued*

(Output as a percent of capacity, seasonally adjusted)

Year and month	Total	Foods	Textile mill products	Apparel products	Paper and products — Total	Paper and products — Pulp and paper	Printing and publishing	Chemicals — Total	Chemicals — Plastics materials	Chemicals — Synthetic fibers	Petroleum products
1970	82.8	83.6	83.5	78.9	86.5	92.2	86.9	77.7	82.3	81.9	93.9
1971	82.6	83.6	84.7	78.6	87.4	93.3	85.3	77.5	81.3	87.6	91.8
1972	86.4	85.5	88.6	82.0	91.9	95.8	88.3	82.3	98.5	87.6	92.8
1973	87.3	85.0	89.7	81.4	95.4	96.1	87.7	85.5	98.5	91.5	94.2
1974	83.9	83.6	80.5	76.5	91.9	93.5	83.9	84.4	93.8	89.9	87.1
1975	76.3	80.4	76.1	69.3	78.1	79.4	77.0	73.3	64.8	76.3	83.7
1976	81.8	82.4	83.6	80.3	87.0	89.8	82.6	78.4	74.5	77.7	85.2
1977	85.3	83.5	87.2	84.8	90.1	90.8	89.4	80.8	80.6	81.1	87.6
1978	86.4	83.6	86.0	85.9	92.5	92.4	91.7	82.7	85.3	86.5	87.6
1979	84.9	82.0	87.7	80.5	92.6	94.6	89.5	83.7	86.7	91.4	84.1
1980	81.0	81.6	84.8	79.4	88.4	92.2	85.8	78.4	75.2	65.3	74.7
1981	80.4	81.2	81.6	80.6	87.2	91.3	83.9	78.1	76.9	81.2	70.7
1982	77.5	80.2	75.5	79.7	83.1	86.2	83.8	70.7	71.2	68.6	70.1
1983	80.8	80.9	85.3	82.6	89.5	91.7	85.2	75.2	82.3	84.9	73.4
1984	82.9	81.5	85.8	84.1	92.1	93.4	87.7	77.4	86.3	85.4	77.8
1985	81.5	82.2	81.5	80.4	88.2	90.4	86.4	75.6	85.7	78.4	78.4
1986	82.8	82.9	85.4	82.3	90.3	94.0	85.6	77.6	89.4	86.3	83.7
1987	85.9	84.1	90.5	85.2	90.8	95.7	91.0	81.3	98.7	92.1	83.5
1988	86.4	84.4	88.0	83.6	92.2	95.6	89.5	84.0	95.5	91.7	85.3
1989	85.7	84.3	87.9	80.9	91.1	93.9	87.7	83.7	90.3	94.8	87.0
1990	84.4	83.9	83.5	78.3	88.9	93.9	85.2	83.0	87.1	86.7	.87.6
1991	81.9	83.4	81.7	78.7	86.7	91.7	80.8	80.1	81.4	85.6	* 86.6
1992	82.8	83.0	87.3	80.1	87.5	92.1	81.4	80.2	89.0	86.0	88.6
1993	82.4	83.2	89.6	81.3	88.9	93.2	81.7	78.7	86.7	87.7	92.1
1994	83.6	83.3	91.2	83.4	90.8	94.9	81.2	78.9	95.9	85.8	91.1
1995	83.5	83.3	88.5	82.5	90.1	94.2	81.2	79.0	91.7	86.1	91.9
1996	82.2	81.3	85.8	79.5	86.7	90.9	81.0	78.2	89.1	85.3	93.8
1997	83.1	82.0	85.3	77.1	89.2	94.3	83.8	79.5	91.7	87.3	95.3
1998	81.7	81.6	83.2	74.2	87.1	92.6	82.5	77.8	91.1	85.3	96.1
1995:											
January	84.8	84.2	93.0	85.0	93.0	96.9	81.2	80.4	102.4	86.9	91.6
February	84.3	83.2	91.6	84.5	92.2	96.3	81.7	79.8	97.2	89.3	91.5
March	84.2	83.3	91.7	85.0	91.9	96.6	81.3	79.7	94.8	90.3	92.4
April	84.0	83.4	91.6	83.1	91.7	96.0	81.4	78.9	94.3	85.4	91.1
May	83.9	84.0	89.2	83.7	91.6	96.9	81.4	79.1	92.1	88.5	90.9
June	83.9	84.4	88.0	82.2	90.2	95.5	81.2	79.3	90.8	87.0	92.0
July	83.3	83.7	84.3	81.6	90.2	94.8	81.2	78.5	88.9	82.7	92.8
August	83.2	83.7	88.2	81.8	89.1	93.5	81.4	78.3	85.7	84.6	92.2
September	83.0	83.2	86.8	81.7	88.5	91.9	81.5	78.5	89.0	85.0	93.1
October	83.0	83.1	86.9	81.1	89.6	93.2	80.8	78.9	88.6	84.3	91.2
November	82.5	82.4	85.3	80.6	86.5	89.4	81.3	78.5	88.9	85.8	91.7
December	82.0	81.5	85.3	79.4	87.2	88.9	80.4	77.8	87.3	83.5	92.9
1996:											
January	81.3	81.4	82.4	77.4	85.9	89.0	79.0	77.7	88.1	81.3	93.1
February	81.7	81.7	84.2	79.9	84.4	88.1	80.1	77.6	88.5	81.2	93.9
March	82.0	82.0	86.7	79.1	85.5	88.8	80.2	77.3	88.5	81.1	93.5
April	81.7	81.4	85.3	79.9	86.8	90.8	80.2	76.9	88.3	80.8	93.1
May	81.9	81.0	86.2	80.1	86.6	90.4	81.1	77.4	89.6	83.5	93.5
June	82.1	81.0	88.1	80.0	87.2	90.4	80.7	77.2	89.9	84.7	93.6
July	82.4	81.1	86.6	79.8	87.5	91.7	81.1	78.4	88.8	86.9	92.7
August	82.4	80.4	87.0	80.6	86.7	91.7	81.5	78.6	89.6	86.6	94.4
September	82.8	81.1	86.0	80.2	86.8	91.1	81.8	79.0	89.9	86.5	94.0
October	82.6	81.4	85.9	79.5	86.5	92.1	81.9	79.5	89.6	91.9	95.1
November	82.8	81.6	85.9	79.2	88.1	92.7	82.2	79.2	88.5	88.8	94.5
December	82.9	81.8	84.8	78.6	88.9	93.8	82.4	79.7	89.7	90.1	94.1
1997:											
January	82.8	81.7	85.4	78.0	87.9	92.7	81.8	79.7	89.7	92.5	93.9
February	83.0	81.9	85.1	77.6	89.3	94.5	82.8	79.4	90.5	87.0	94.7
March	83.3	82.8	85.7	78.2	89.5	94.7	82.9	78.7	91.3	86.8	94.3
April	83.3	81.9	86.3	77.9	88.8	93.3	83.7	80.3	90.9	93.4	95.7
May	83.1	81.9	84.5	77.6	89.0	93.7	83.8	79.6	90.9	83.8	97.2
June	82.8	81.7	85.5	77.5	88.5	93.1	83.5	79.5	91.3	83.4	96.7
July	82.9	82.5	86.5	77.2	89.1	93.8	83.7	78.8	92.9	88.5	94.5
August	82.9	81.8	85.2	76.7	89.7	95.2	83.8	79.0	91.8	86.0	95.4
September	83.1	81.5	84.9	76.6	90.0	95.6	84.3	79.5	92.9	87.9	95.3
October	83.1	81.4	84.8	76.6	89.0	95.4	84.7	79.8	91.7	86.1	96.0
November	83.4	82.5	85.2	75.8	89.6	94.7	85.3	79.5	93.1	83.6	94.2
December	83.4	82.3	84.1	76.1	89.4	94.7	85.2	80.1	93.6	88.1	95.4
1998:											
January	83.5	83.3	85.3	76.2	88.8	94.7	84.6	79.7	93.4	87.9	95.8
February	83.1	82.7	84.0	75.2	88.8	94.0	84.4	79.3	91.0	90.2	95.2
March	82.6	82.4	83.5	75.6	87.9	93.1	83.3	79.1	89.5	89.5	97.2
April	82.9	82.5	84.0	75.2	87.8	93.5	83.1	79.7	91.7	90.0	96.9
May	82.7	82.7	84.8	74.9	87.4	92.6	83.0	79.0	90.5	86.4	95.7
June	81.8	81.3	83.0	75.0	87.1	93.1	82.7	78.3	89.7	86.3	95.7
July	81.7	81.0	83.9	74.8	87.7	93.5	82.4	77.9	91.6	85.5	97.2
August	80.9	80.0	82.8	74.2	87.0	92.6	81.7	76.7	92.9	85.0	97.7
September	80.2	79.6	82.3	73.5	85.7	91.4	81.3	75.9	87.1	85.5	94.7
October	80.3	80.5	83.2	72.9	86.7	92.4	80.8	75.7	89.1	81.7	94.4
November	80.7	81.8	80.5	71.6	84.2	89.3	81.4	76.6	94.1	79.6	96.3
December	80.6	81.6	80.9	71.6	86.2	90.8	81.0	76.1	93.1	76.2	96.0

Capacity Utilization—*Continued*

(Output as a percent of capacity, seasonally adjusted)

Year and month	Nondurable goods manufacturing —Continued		Mining						Utilities		
	Rubber and plastics products	Leather and products	Total	Metal mining	Coal mining	Oil and gas extraction		Stone and earth minerals	Total	Electric	Gas
						Total	Oil and gas well drilling				
1970	81.2	81.8	88.8	93.6	95.8	87.7	69.7	87.2	96.2	98.9	91.9
1971	82.6	79.9	87.3	83.2	86.0	88.5	68.6	85.9	94.6	96.5	92.3
1972	91.6	84.2	90.3	80.7	89.2	92.3	79.1	87.8	95.2	97.0	92.5
1973	93.3	79.6	92.3	84.6	85.7	94.8	85.2	92.8	93.5	95.4	90.7
1974	84.9	77.4	92.3	82.1	84.2	96.1	98.9	89.6	87.3	87.3	88.6
1975	70.1	79.7	89.7	76.4	87.5	93.8	99.2	79.1	84.4	84.8	84.8
1976	78.5	81.7	89.8	81.0	88.9	92.1	91.5	83.0	85.2	85.1	86.6
1977	88.3	83.3	90.9	69.4	88.2	94.2	101.7	85.4	85.0	86.0	83.2
1978	89.2	86.8	90.9	78.5	80.3	94.7	100.0	89.2	85.4	85.3	85.5
1979	84.2	82.2	91.4	81.4	88.8	92.8	88.2	90.6	86.6	85.3	89.5
1980	73.9	84.1	93.4	72.8	90.3	95.8	95.7	82.7	85.9	84.7	89.3
1981	77.9	83.9	93.9	79.1	86.7	96.1	98.0	79.8	82.5	84.3	79.1
1982	74.4	80.7	86.3	57.5	86.1	88.2	70.3	67.4	79.3	81.3	74.9
1983	79.2	82.8	80.4	57.9	79.1	81.7	52.6	72.6	79.7	82.3	74.4
1984	84.3	78.6	86.0	63.3	88.6	86.7	63.4	81.8	81.9	84.0	77.1
1985	82.1	74.1	84.3	62.7	85.7	84.9	58.5	84.4	83.5	84.7	79.8
1986	82.9	71.9	77.6	65.9	84.7	76.4	34.3	82.7	80.6	84.9	67.6
1987	89.0	74.7	80.3	70.9	85.7	79.3	38.4	85.7	82.5	86.1	69.9
1988	87.8	78.7	85.2	80.5	86.8	85.0	56.0	86.9	84.9	87.8	73.7
1989	87.4	82.5	86.9	85.4	88.3	87.0	63.7	85.2	86.3	89.4	75.7
1990	84.6	82.7	89.8	85.7	90.7	90.3	75.6	86.3	85.7	89.6	72.9
1991	80.3	78.8	88.4	82.9	85.7	90.4	69.4	81.1	86.3	89.1	75.1
1992	84.7	83.0	86.4	87.1	84.7	87.0	55.2	83.9	84.5	86.8	77.2
1993	86.2	86.1	86.0	84.4	79.1	88.1	67.7	82.8	87.2	88.8	80.4
1994	89.6	81.4	87.5	86.2	84.5	88.6	70.7	85.4	87.4	89.2	80.4
1995	88.0	74.6	86.8	87.6	82.6	87.8	71.2	86.7	89.2	91.1	82.0
1996	86.6	72.3	88.5	88.3	84.2	89.8	78.8	85.8	90.5	91.8	84.8
1997	85.6	68.1	89.1	91.5	84.9	90.1	85.3	86.1	89.7	91.5	82.2
1998	84.6	63.9	86.7	89.8	84.9	86.7	76.0	85.5	90.9	94.6	75.2
1995:											
January	90.5	78.4	87.5	87.4	84.4	87.9	70.1	91.0	86.5	88.9	78.2
February	90.3	77.5	87.0	88.0	83.3	87.9	70.7	87.6	87.5	89.4	80.5
March	89.3	76.8	86.8	86.4	85.4	87.0	69.6	87.8	87.5	89.8	79.2
April	89.5	75.2	85.5	87.2	76.9	87.3	67.7	86.0	87.5	89.6	79.9
May	87.7	75.0	87.0	86.9	82.4	88.5	72.5	85.3	89.0	90.6	82.9
June	87.3	74.3	86.9	87.4	83.8	87.9	70.6	85.6	88.8	90.7	81.6
July	86.1	72.5	86.7	88.4	80.2	87.8	71.1	88.4	89.8	91.3	84.2
August	87.1	73.9	86.9	88.0	84.1	87.7	71.7	85.6	93.6	96.3	83.3
September	87.4	74.3	87.0	87.1	84.3	87.5	72.8	87.8	89.6	91.3	82.9
October	87.4	72.7	86.3	88.5	83.1	87.0	72.3	84.6	89.0	91.7	78.6
November	87.1	72.6	87.3	89.4	83.8	88.4	71.9	84.4	90.3	91.5	85.5
December	86.3	72.0	86.6	87.0	79.4	88.1	73.6	86.7	90.9	91.7	87.5
1996:											
January	86.3	71.6	86.3	84.6	78.5	88.7	76.2	82.8	91.6	92.7	87.0
February	86.2	73.0	87.5	83.5	83.2	89.3	77.7	84.7	92.4	93.4	87.8
March	86.5	73.0	88.3	88.3	83.6	89.6	76.4	85.5	92.5	93.4	88.2
April	85.7	73.2	89.1	86.5	84.9	90.7	79.5	85.7	91.5	92.3	87.7
May	86.9	72.6	89.2	87.7	86.4	90.2	80.9	86.1	91.8	93.4	84.8
June	87.4	73.5	89.5	88.0	83.0	91.1	79.9	88.1	91.1	92.7	84.2
July	87.0	72.9	89.7	89.4	87.9	90.4	79.9	87.2	88.1	89.9	80.5
August	87.4	72.6	89.6	89.2	88.3	90.4	79.3	86.2	89.6	91.3	82.4
September	87.5	72.2	88.6	90.2	82.0	90.4	79.2	84.5	88.9	90.2	83.4
October	86.2	71.2	88.9	90.4	85.6	89.8	79.2	86.5	89.2	90.6	83.4
November	85.9	70.6	87.8	90.1	82.9	88.6	78.8	87.5	89.8	91.1	84.6
December	86.6	70.9	87.6	92.0	84.0	88.2	79.1	84.9	89.2	90.7	83.1
1997:											
January	85.3	70.3	88.4	92.5	85.9	89.2	79.5	84.0	90.2	91.8	83.6
February	86.2	68.9	89.4	90.9	86.3	90.0	81.9	88.0	88.3	89.9	81.7
March	86.3	69.8	89.9	91.5	83.6	91.1	87.4	88.8	87.1	89.6	77.3
April	85.3	69.5	88.9	90.4	83.7	90.4	85.5	85.1	89.6	91.3	83.0
May	85.5	68.8	89.9	90.7	89.5	90.5	85.8	85.8	88.5	89.1	86.1
June	85.4	68.3	89.1	91.7	83.9	90.1	85.9	88.2	88.5	89.6	84.5
July	85.3	68.5	89.2	90.5	85.1	90.5	86.8	85.0	90.4	92.2	83.2
August	86.1	66.0	88.6	90.5	82.0	90.1	87.3	86.4	89.9	91.8	82.6
September	85.7	66.2	89.4	92.3	85.4	90.5	86.9	85.9	90.9	93.2	81.4
October	85.1	67.4	89.0	93.3	84.4	90.2	85.8	84.8	92.3	95.0	81.0
November	85.9	66.5	87.9	95.2	78.5	89.4	86.3	86.0	90.3	92.4	81.5
December	85.5	66.9	89.0	88.1	90.7	89.1	85.0	85.7	89.9	92.2	80.6
1998:											
January	85.3	65.7	90.0	90.7	87.7	90.3	87.4	89.3	87.2	90.2	74.8
February	85.0	66.5	89.9	100.7	81.2	91.2	89.2	86.0	86.6	90.0	72.6
March	84.9	66.2	88.4	89.3	80.5	90.6	88.1	83.6	90.5	93.6	77.6
April	85.7	64.8	88.2	87.3	83.3	89.6	83.4	85.6	89.5	93.1	74.4
May	85.3	64.4	87.9	88.6	82.2	89.2	82.9	86.0	91.3	96.0	71.6
June	84.6	63.3	87.3	88.1	85.5	87.5	77.0	86.6	94.0	97.7	78.9
July	84.4	63.9	87.2	86.3	87.3	87.1	74.2	86.2	93.7	96.7	81.2
August	83.7	62.8	86.3	88.9	84.7	86.4	71.7	85.1	95.1	97.8	84.0
September	83.7	62.4	85.2	86.8	89.3	84.2	69.1	82.1	95.0	98.8	79.6
October	83.8	61.8	84.7	92.6	85.3	84.1	66.8	80.8	92.0	96.9	71.5
November	84.5	63.0	83.8	90.2	83.6	81.8	64.3	89.5	87.3	92.2	66.5
December	84.8	62.0	82.0	88.3	87.9	78.9	57.5	84.8	88.2	92.6	69.4

Saving and Investment; Business Sales and Inventories

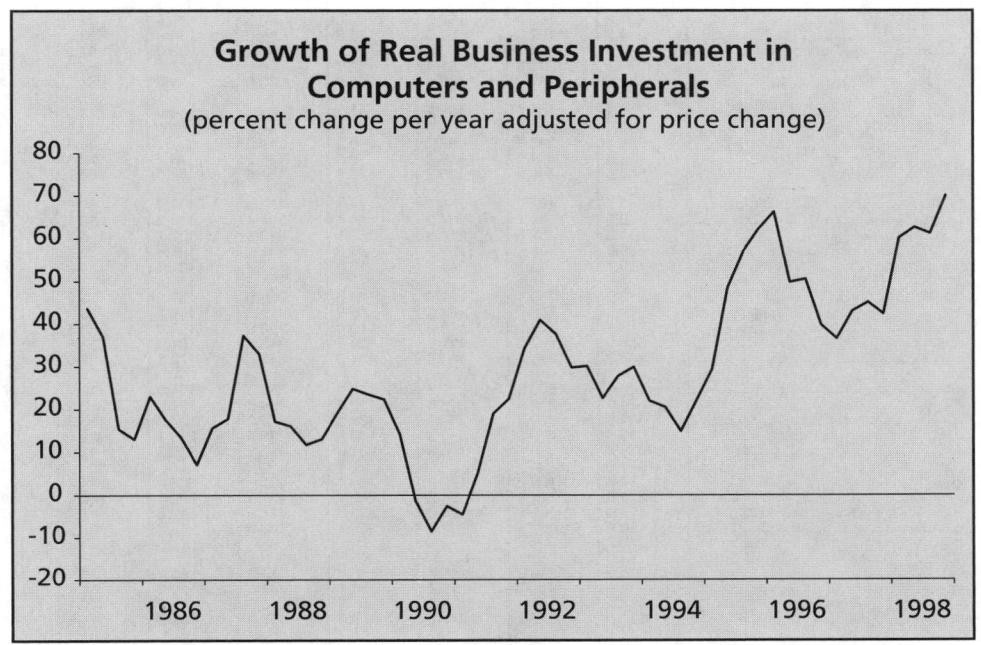

Growth of Real Business Investment in Computers and Peripherals
(percent change per year adjusted for price change)

- Except for a brief recession-related pause in 1990, real business investment in computers and peripherals has increased strongly throughout the 1980s and 1990s, with especially dramatic gains from 1994 through 1998.

- Other major components of business fixed investment also increased, if less dramatically. Total real business fixed investment grew 10.3 percent per year from 1994 to 1998, with an especially strong 11.8 percent gain in 1998.

- Real residential investment grew rather slowly from 1994 to 1997, but moved ahead 10.4 percent in 1998, with the strongest rise occurring in single family housing.

- The emergence of a federal budget surplus contributed to a rise in economy-wide gross saving (personal, business and government) to more than 17 percent of gross domestic product in 1997 and 1998. These were the highest percentages since 1988, but still well below the averages of the 1970s and early 1980s.

Gross Saving and Investment

(Billions of dollars, quarterly data are at seasonally adjusted annual rates)

Year and quarter	Total	Gross saving Private[1] Total	Personal	Undistributed corporate profits[2]	Consumption of fixed capital Corporate	Noncorporate	Government Total	Consumption of fixed capital Federal	State and local	Current surplus or deficit Federal	State and local
1970	197.3	163.8	62.0	20.7	50.3	30.9	32.6	16.2	9.6	-14.1	20.8
1971	214.3	189.7	69.9	30.5	55.0	33.9	23.9	16.9	10.7	-25.3	21.7
1972	243.9	201.7	65.2	39.0	59.8	38.0	41.5	18.2	11.7	-20.5	32.2
1973	296.4	241.3	91.5	42.7	65.2	41.9	55.1	19.9	13.0	-11.1	33.4
1974	301.2	251.7	100.2	27.0	76.5	48.0	51.5	22.0	16.0	-16.9	30.5
1975	297.3	301.2	107.8	47.2	91.4	54.9	-3.9	24.0	18.4	-73.9	27.6
1976	340.0	316.5	100.4	54.8	101.4	59.9	23.5	25.4	19.4	-57.2	35.9
1977	394.7	348.6	97.2	70.5	114.0	67.0	46.1	27.0	20.7	-46.3	44.7
1978	476.9	404.5	118.2	79.5	130.6	76.2	72.4	28.9	22.5	-31.7	52.6
1979	540.6	448.8	136.2	72.6	151.6	88.3	90.7	31.5	25.4	-18.4	52.3
1980	547.2	489.2	169.1	44.1	175.0	101.0	56.8	34.1	29.2	-61.0	54.4
1981	650.8	581.7	207.2	56.4	205.1	113.0	68.1	37.1	33.3	-57.8	55.4
1982	604.3	609.6	210.9	52.5	223.5	122.7	-5.3	41.9	36.2	-134.7	51.3
1983	589.0	618.4	169.7	83.6	238.4	126.8	-29.4	42.6	37.5	-174.4	64.9
1984	750.7	736.7	241.5	116.8	246.9	131.5	14.0	44.1	39.0	-156.0	86.9
1985	745.6	730.5	207.4	123.6	260.0	139.4	15.2	46.1	41.0	-162.9	91.0
1986	719.8	708.9	188.6	95.9	278.3	146.1	10.8	49.6	43.9	-177.5	94.9
1987	779.6	726.0	168.9	110.0	292.9	154.2	53.6	51.7	47.1	-128.9	83.8
1988	876.0	807.2	195.2	134.0	313.5	164.5	68.8	54.3	49.9	-121.3	85.9
1989	906.3	814.3	194.8	104.3	335.8	179.3	92.0	57.0	53.3	-113.4	95.1
1990	903.1	860.3	213.3	112.7	350.3	184.0	42.7	60.7	56.6	-154.7	80.1
1991	934.0	930.6	243.5	130.8	364.5	191.9	3.3	63.9	59.6	-196.0	75.8
1992	904.3	970.7	264.1	137.1	376.4	209.0	-66.5	65.9	62.3	-280.9	86.3
1993	949.5	979.3	210.3	170.1	388.4	206.1	-29.8	67.9	65.5	-250.7	87.4
1994	1 079.2	1 030.2	176.8	201.4	412.3	226.3	49.0	69.5	69.4	-186.7	96.8
1995	1 187.4	1 106.2	179.8	256.1	431.1	225.9	81.2	70.7	73.2	-174.4	111.7
1996	1 274.5	1 114.5	158.5	262.4	452.0	232.3	160.0	70.6	77.1	-110.3	122.6
1997	1 406.3	1 141.6	121.0	296.7	477.3	242.8	264.7	70.6	81.1	-21.1	134.1
1998	1 468.0	1 090.4	27.7	305.4	500.6	252.7	377.6	69.7	85.0	72.8	150.2
1990:											
1st quarter	894.9	849.0	205.8	118.6	343.9	180.7	45.9	59.3	55.2	-154.1	85.5
2nd quarter	939.2	884.7	219.4	135.1	347.6	182.6	54.5	59.7	56.1	-144.1	82.8
3rd quarter	893.5	837.4	212.2	87.5	352.5	185.3	56.1	60.8	57.2	-142.6	80.7
4th quarter	884.6	870.1	215.8	109.7	357.3	187.3	14.5	62.8	57.9	-177.7	71.5
1991:											
1st quarter	982.0	926.7	230.9	145.1	362.1	188.6	55.3	62.6	58.6	-134.6	68.8
2nd quarter	926.9	926.7	244.7	128.8	363.4	189.7	0.2	63.9	59.4	-196.7	73.7
3rd quarter	904.3	916.9	237.8	122.5	365.2	191.4	-12.6	64.3	60.0	-214.0	77.1
4th quarter	922.6	952.3	260.6	126.6	367.1	197.9	-29.7	64.8	60.6	-238.8	83.8
1992:											
1st quarter	920.3	976.6	258.1	157.6	368.6	192.3	-56.3	65.2	61.1	-267.4	84.8
2nd quarter	914.0	979.3	272.2	142.3	370.7	194.0	-65.3	65.8	62.0	-279.6	86.6
3rd quarter	899.9	986.7	245.4	99.8	389.9	251.6	-86.9	66.0	62.7	-297.5	82.0
4th quarter	883.0	940.3	280.6	148.4	376.3	198.0	-57.3	66.5	63.5	-279.0	91.7
1993:											
1st quarter	932.0	1 001.1	181.2	159.2	383.0	207.5	-69.1	67.0	64.3	-278.2	77.8
2nd quarter	942.1	977.3	231.0	158.3	385.0	203.0	-35.2	67.5	65.2	-249.2	81.3
3rd quarter	943.8	973.3	200.5	171.8	393.0	208.1	-29.4	68.4	65.8	-250.6	86.9
4th quarter	980.1	965.6	228.7	191.0	392.6	205.5	14.5	68.8	66.6	-224.6	103.7
1994:											
1st quarter	1 062.4	1 048.6	132.3	178.7	425.3	259.9	13.8	69.1	69.0	-209.0	84.7
2nd quarter	1 065.5	995.7	179.3	201.2	402.8	212.1	69.7	69.6	68.5	-163.2	94.8
3rd quarter	1 071.0	1 021.2	188.1	209.5	408.2	215.1	49.7	69.3	69.6	-187.6	98.4
4th quarter	1 118.0	1 055.3	207.5	216.2	413.1	218.1	62.7	69.8	70.4	-186.8	109.3
1995:											
1st quarter	1 161.5	1 098.7	214.9	229.3	419.6	221.5	62.8	70.3	71.7	-189.6	110.4
2nd quarter	1 153.8	1 075.8	164.0	247.3	427.9	223.2	78.0	70.7	72.6	-177.9	112.6
3rd quarter	1 190.4	1 110.0	162.4	275.0	434.2	225.0	80.4	70.7	73.6	-176.9	113.0
4th quarter	1 244.0	1 140.5	178.0	272.7	442.7	233.7	103.5	71.0	74.7	-153.0	110.7
1996:											
1st quarter	1 233.0	1 119.4	173.5	264.4	443.2	229.0	113.6	70.7	75.7	-150.1	117.3
2nd quarter	1 255.3	1 091.6	140.5	262.6	448.6	230.6	163.7	70.7	76.5	-112.6	129.1
3rd quarter	1 298.8	1 128.6	172.2	258.7	454.9	233.6	170.2	70.5	77.5	-100.1	122.3
4th quarter	1 311.0	1 118.4	147.6	264.2	461.2	236.1	192.5	70.7	78.5	-78.3	121.7
1997:											
1st quarter	1 353.9	1 126.3	135.4	281.4	467.2	238.6	227.5	70.8	79.5	-51.2	128.4
2nd quarter	1 416.3	1 169.5	151.9	299.0	473.7	241.3	246.9	70.9	80.6	-34.8	130.1
3rd quarter	1 427.0	1 139.0	98.5	311.5	480.8	244.4	288.0	70.3	81.4	-0.3	136.6
4th quarter	1 428.0	1 131.6	98.2	295.0	487.7	247.0	296.4	70.2	82.7	2.2	141.4
1998:											
1st quarter	1 482.5	1 130.1	73.0	312.0	492.5	248.6	352.4	69.9	83.5	58.8	140.2
2nd quarter	1 448.5	1 079.0	25.6	300.9	497.8	250.7	369.4	69.5	84.3	74.4	141.3
3rd quarter	1 474.5	1 078.7	12.6	304.8	503.1	254.2	395.7	69.6	85.4	92.0	148.7
4th quarter	1 466.6	1 073.7	-0.6	303.9	508.9	257.5	392.9	70.0	86.6	65.8	170.5

1. Includes wage and salary accruals less disbursements, not shown separately.
2. Includes inventory valuation and capital consumption adjustments.

Gross Saving and Investment—*Continued*

(Billions of dollars, quarterly data are at seasonally adjusted annual rates)

Year and quarter	Gross investment				Statistical discrepancy [1]	Gross savings as a percent of GNP
	Total	Private domestic	Government	Net foreign		
1970	199.1	150.2	44.0	4.9	1.9	18.9
1971	220.4	176.0	43.1	1.3	6.1	18.9
1972	248.1	205.6	45.4	-2.9	4.3	19.6
1973	299.9	242.9	48.3	8.7	3.4	21.2
1974	306.7	245.6	56.0	5.1	5.5	19.9
1975	309.5	225.4	62.7	21.4	12.1	18.1
1976	359.9	286.6	64.4	8.9	19.9	18.5
1977	413.0	356.6	65.4	-9.0	18.2	19.3
1978	494.9	430.8	74.6	-10.4	18.1	20.6
1979	568.7	480.9	85.3	2.6	28.2	20.9
1980	574.8	465.9	96.4	12.5	27.6	19.4
1981	665.7	556.2	102.1	7.4	14.9	20.7
1982	601.8	501.1	106.9	-6.1	-2.5	18.5
1983	626.2	547.1	116.5	-37.3	37.1	16.6
1984	755.7	715.6	131.7	-91.5	5.0	19.1
1985	748.0	715.1	149.9	-116.9	2.4	17.7
1986	743.1	722.5	163.5	-142.9	23.3	16.2
1987	764.2	747.2	173.5	-156.4	-15.4	16.6
1988	828.7	773.9	172.9	-118.1	-47.3	17.3
1989	919.5	829.2	182.7	-92.4	13.2	16.6
1990	920.5	799.7	199.4	-78.6	17.4	15.7
1991	944.0	736.2	200.5	7.3	10.1	15.7
1992	949.1	790.4	209.1	-50.5	44.8	14.5
1993	1 002.1	876.2	204.5	-78.6	52.6	14.4
1994	1 093.8	1 007.9	205.9	-120.0	14.6	15.5
1995	1 160.9	1 043.2	218.3	-100.6	-26.5	16.3
1996	1 242.3	1 131.9	229.7	-119.2	-32.2	16.6
1997	1 350.5	1 256.0	235.4	-140.9	-55.8	17.4
1998	1 391.5	1 367.1	237.0	-212.6	-76.5	17.3
1990:						
1st quarter	939.3	822.7	196.0	-79.4	44.4	15.8
2nd quarter	957.9	835.0	196.7	-73.8	18.7	16.3
3rd quarter	911.1	804.7	199.7	-93.3	17.6	15.4
4th quarter	873.6	736.3	205.4	-68.1	-11.0	15.2
1991:						
1st quarter	976.8	723.5	198.1	55.3	-5.2	16.8
2nd quarter	933.8	716.4	201.5	16.0	6.9	15.7
3rd quarter	922.7	744.1	201.3	-22.6	18.5	15.2
4th quarter	942.7	760.7	201.4	-19.4	20.1	15.3
1992:						
1st quarter	944.8	755.2	209.5	-19.9	24.5	15.0
2nd quarter	951.3	790.7	209.3	-48.7	37.4	14.7
3rd quarter	952.5	799.7	208.9	-56.0	52.7	14.3
4th quarter	947.7	816.1	208.8	-77.2	64.6	13.8
1993:						
1st quarter	1 003.0	854.3	202.9	-54.2	71.0	14.4
2nd quarter	989.0	857.4	206.5	-74.9	46.9	14.4
3rd quarter	991.3	872.8	203.4	-84.9	47.5	14.3
4th quarter	1 025.1	920.3	205.2	-100.4	45.0	14.6
1994:						
1st quarter	1 068.7	963.4	197.0	-91.6	6.3	15.6
2nd quarter	1 107.8	1 017.9	202.4	-112.5	42.4	15.4
3rd quarter	1 086.2	1 007.1	213.2	-134.2	15.2	15.3
4th quarter	1 112.6	1 043.1	211.2	-141.8	-5.4	15.8
1995:						
1st quarter	1 164.6	1 058.9	216.3	-110.7	3.1	16.2
2nd quarter	1 131.1	1 029.6	219.6	-118.0	-22.7	16.0
3rd quarter	1 147.3	1 030.6	216.8	-100.1	-43.0	16.3
4th quarter	1 200.8	1 053.6	220.7	-73.5	-43.2	16.8
1996:						
1st quarter	1 206.7	1 075.3	229.2	-97.8	-26.3	16.4
2nd quarter	1 234.7	1 118.3	231.3	-114.9	-20.6	16.4
3rd quarter	1 249.5	1 167.9	227.9	-146.2	-49.3	16.8
4th quarter	1 278.3	1 166.0	230.3	-118.0	-32.6	16.7
1997:						
1st quarter	1 310.8	1 206.4	235.3	-130.9	-43.1	17.0
2nd quarter	1 368.6	1 259.9	232.6	-123.9	-47.7	17.6
3rd quarter	1 361.9	1 265.7	237.3	-141.0	-65.1	17.5
4th quarter	1 360.7	1 292.0	236.5	-167.8	-67.3	17.3
1998:						
1st quarter	1 428.4	1 366.6	237.4	-175.6	-54.1	17.7
2nd quarter	1 362.7	1 345.0	232.5	-214.8	-85.7	17.2
3rd quarter	1 372.5	1 364.4	239.7	-231.6	-102.0	17.3
4th quarter	1 402.4	1 392.4	238.3	-228.3	-64.2	16.9

1. Gross investment less gross saving.

Private Fixed Investment by Type

(Gross private domestic fixed investment—Billions of dollars, quarterly data are at seasonally adjusted annual rates)

Year and quarter	Total	Nonresidential Total	Structures Total	Nonresidential buildings including farm	Utilities	Mining exploration, shafts, and wells	Other Structures	Producers durable equipment Total	Information processing and related equipment Total	Computers and peripheral equipment[1]	Other
1970	148.1	106.7	40.3	25.4	11.1	2.8	1.0	66.4	14.3	2.7	11.6
1971	167.5	111.7	42.7	27.1	11.9	2.7	1.0	69.1	14.9	2.8	12.1
1972	195.7	126.1	47.2	30.1	13.1	3.1	0.9	78.9	16.5	3.5	13.1
1973	225.4	150.0	55.0	35.5	15.0	3.5	1.0	95.1	19.8	3.5	16.3
1974	231.5	165.6	61.2	38.3	16.5	5.2	1.2	104.3	22.9	3.9	19.0
1975	231.7	169.0	61.4	35.6	17.1	7.4	1.3	107.6	23.5	3.6	19.9
1976	269.6	187.2	65.9	35.9	20.0	8.6	1.4	121.2	27.2	4.4	22.8
1977	333.5	223.2	74.6	39.9	21.5	11.5	1.8	148.7	33.1	5.7	27.5
1978	403.6	272.0	91.4	49.7	24.1	15.4	2.2	180.6	41.8	7.6	34.2
1979	464.0	323.0	114.9	65.7	27.5	19.0	2.6	208.1	49.9	10.2	39.8
1980	473.5	350.3	133.9	73.7	30.2	27.4	2.6	216.4	58.9	12.5	46.4
1981	528.1	405.4	164.6	86.3	33.0	42.5	2.8	240.9	69.5	17.1	52.3
1982	515.6	409.9	175.0	94.5	32.5	44.8	3.2	234.9	72.7	18.9	53.9
1983	552.0	399.4	152.7	90.5	28.7	30.0	3.5	246.7	82.0	23.9	58.1
1984	648.1	468.3	176.0	110.0	30.0	31.3	4.7	292.3	98.6	31.6	67.0
1985	688.9	502.0	193.3	128.0	30.6	27.9	6.8	308.7	104.2	33.7	70.5
1986	712.9	494.8	175.8	123.3	31.2	15.7	5.7	319.0	108.8	33.4	75.4
1987	722.9	495.4	172.1	126.0	26.5	13.1	6.5	323.3	109.8	35.8	74.0
1988	763.1	530.6	181.3	133.3	27.1	15.7	5.2	349.3	118.2	38.1	80.1
1989	797.5	566.2	192.3	142.7	29.4	14.4	6.0	373.9	127.1	43.3	83.8
1990	791.6	575.9	200.8	148.9	27.5	17.5	6.9	375.1	124.2	38.9	85.2
1991	738.5	547.3	181.7	126.1	31.6	17.1	6.9	365.6	122.6	38.1	84.5
1992	783.4	557.9	169.2	113.2	34.5	13.3	8.2	388.7	134.2	43.9	90.2
1993	855.7	604.1	176.4	119.2	32.8	16.6	7.8	427.7	141.6	48.6	93.0
1994	946.6	660.6	184.5	128.7	32.0	16.7	7.1	476.1	152.1	51.8	100.3
1995	1 012.5	727.7	201.3	143.8	33.9	16.3	7.3	526.4	173.0	64.9	108.1
1996	1 099.8	787.9	216.9	160.9	31.7	18.1	6.2	571.0	189.4	74.4	114.9
1997	1 188.6	860.7	240.2	177.3	33.5	22.7	6.7	620.5	206.6	81.1	125.5
1998	1 307.8	938.2	246.9	184.1	34.7	21.3	6.8	691.3	233.3	95.1	138.3
1990:											
1st quarter	813.9	581.2	201.9	150.8	27.0	16.8	7.3	379.3	127.8	41.3	86.5
2nd quarter	794.0	571.6	202.4	151.2	27.0	17.6	6.7	369.2	123.9	38.9	85.0
3rd quarter	791.2	580.3	203.5	151.4	27.5	17.6	7.0	376.7	121.5	36.8	84.7
4th quarter	767.5	570.6	195.4	142.1	28.4	18.1	6.8	375.1	123.4	38.6	84.7
1991:											
1st quarter	739.7	555.4	192.3	136.4	30.0	19.4	6.6	363.1	119.3	36.7	82.7
2nd quarter	736.2	550.2	187.6	130.9	31.3	18.9	6.6	362.6	121.6	37.2	84.5
3rd quarter	738.6	544.3	176.1	121.4	32.3	15.2	7.1	368.2	123.5	37.8	85.6
4th quarter	739.5	539.2	170.8	115.7	33.0	15.0	7.2	368.4	125.9	40.7	85.2
1992:											
1st quarter	755.4	544.1	171.6	117.2	34.3	12.8	7.3	372.5	129.2	41.9	87.3
2nd quarter	780.5	556.8	170.4	114.0	34.8	13.3	8.4	386.3	133.0	44.4	88.6
3rd quarter	788.1	561.0	167.6	110.6	34.7	13.3	9.0	393.4	137.7	44.6	93.1
4th quarter	809.7	569.6	167.1	111.0	34.2	13.8	8.1	402.5	136.8	44.9	91.9
1993:											
1st quarter	823.5	580.5	171.7	113.6	33.8	16.0	8.3	408.9	137.2	47.1	90.1
2nd quarter	842.9	598.8	175.2	117.6	32.7	16.8	8.1	423.6	138.1	47.1	91.0
3rd quarter	858.8	606.4	177.8	121.5	32.2	16.8	7.3	428.6	145.0	49.8	95.2
4th quarter	897.5	630.6	180.7	124.2	32.5	16.6	7.5	449.9	146.0	50.5	95.5
1994:											
1st quarter	911.0	634.6	175.4	120.7	32.1	15.7	6.8	459.3	147.6	49.9	97.7
2nd quarter	941.7	652.9	185.2	130.9	31.6	15.8	6.9	467.7	149.4	50.6	98.8
3rd quarter	956.9	667.4	186.8	130.0	32.0	17.0	7.7	480.6	152.8	51.5	101.2
4th quarter	977.0	687.5	190.7	133.2	32.4	18.1	7.0	496.8	158.5	55.1	103.4
1995:											
1st quarter	1 000.0	713.6	197.9	139.7	33.6	17.3	7.4	515.6	162.6	56.1	106.4
2nd quarter	1 004.3	728.1	201.8	144.2	34.5	15.6	7.6	526.3	173.6	64.1	109.6
3rd quarter	1 013.5	729.5	203.0	144.7	34.4	16.2	7.7	526.5	174.8	66.6	108.2
4th quarter	1 032.1	739.5	202.2	146.6	33.2	16.0	6.5	537.2	181.1	72.8	108.3
1996:											
1st quarter	1 059.1	759.0	206.5	151.1	31.9	16.7	6.7	552.6	185.0	73.4	111.5
2nd quarter	1 089.7	774.8	211.3	157.0	31.2	16.9	6.3	563.5	185.2	72.0	113.2
3rd quarter	1 118.1	801.1	218.0	162.4	31.0	18.6	5.9	583.1	192.7	75.5	117.2
4th quarter	1 132.2	816.8	232.1	173.2	32.9	20.3	5.7	584.8	194.6	76.8	117.8
1997:											
1st quarter	1 146.7	827.1	236.2	177.5	32.5	20.6	5.6	591.0	197.1	76.8	120.3
2nd quarter	1 176.4	850.5	234.3	172.9	33.4	22.2	5.8	616.2	202.6	79.9	122.7
3rd quarter	1 211.1	882.3	243.8	180.0	34.1	23.8	6.1	638.5	213.0	84.0	129.0
4th quarter	1 220.1	882.8	246.4	178.9	34.1	24.3	9.2	636.4	213.6	83.7	129.9
1998:											
1st quarter	1 271.1	921.3	245.0	180.6	34.2	23.5	6.6	676.3	226.5	91.8	134.7
2nd quarter	1 305.8	941.9	245.4	181.8	34.7	22.4	6.5	696.6	231.6	94.8	136.8
3rd quarter	1 307.5	931.6	246.2	183.7	35.0	20.7	6.8	685.4	235.2	95.6	139.5
4th quarter	1 346.7	957.9	250.9	190.1	35.1	18.7	7.1	706.9	239.9	98.0	142.0

1. New computers and peripheral equipment only.

Private Fixed Investment by Type—*Continued*

(Gross private domestic fixed investment—Billions of dollars, quarterly data are at seasonally adjusted annual rates)

| Year and quarter | Nonresidential—*Continued* | | | | Residential | | | | |
| | Producers durable equipment—*Continued* | | | Total | Structures | | | | Producers' durable equipment |
	Industrial equipment	Transportation and related equipment	Other		Total	Single family	Multifamily	Other structures	
1970	20.2	16.2	15.6	41.4	40.2	17.5	9.5	13.2	1.1
1971	19.4	18.4	16.4	55.8	54.5	25.8	12.9	15.8	1.3
1972	21.3	21.8	19.2	69.7	68.1	32.8	17.2	18.0	1.5
1973	25.9	26.6	22.8	75.3	73.6	35.2	19.4	19.0	1.7
1974	30.5	26.3	24.6	66.0	64.1	29.7	13.7	20.7	1.9
1975	31.1	25.2	27.9	62.7	60.8	29.6	6.7	24.5	1.9
1976	33.9	30.0	30.1	82.5	80.4	43.9	6.9	29.6	2.1
1977	39.2	39.3	37.1	110.3	107.9	62.2	10.0	35.7	2.4
1978	47.4	47.3	44.2	131.6	128.9	72.8	12.8	43.3	2.7
1979	55.8	53.6	48.7	141.0	137.9	72.3	17.0	48.6	3.2
1980	60.4	48.4	48.7	123.2	119.9	53.0	16.7	50.2	3.4
1981	65.2	50.6	55.7	122.6	119.0	52.0	17.5	49.5	3.6
1982	62.2	46.8	53.1	105.7	102.0	41.5	15.5	45.0	3.7
1983	58.2	53.7	52.7	152.5	148.3	72.2	22.4	53.7	4.2
1984	67.4	64.8	61.4	179.8	175.1	85.6	28.2	61.3	4.7
1985	71.7	69.7	63.0	186.9	181.9	86.1	28.5	67.2	5.1
1986	74.6	71.8	63.8	218.1	212.6	102.2	31.0	79.4	5.5
1987	75.9	70.4	67.2	227.6	221.8	114.5	25.5	81.9	5.8
1988	82.9	76.0	72.3	232.5	226.4	116.6	22.3	87.5	6.1
1989	91.5	71.2	84.1	231.3	225.1	116.9	22.3	85.9	6.2
1990	89.8	75.5	85.6	215.7	209.7	108.7	19.3	81.7	6.1
1991	86.4	79.5	77.1	191.2	185.4	95.4	15.1	74.8	5.8
1992	89.3	86.2	79.0	225.6	219.5	116.5	13.1	89.9	6.0
1993	97.9	99.9	88.3	251.6	245.2	133.3	10.8	101.1	6.4
1994	109.3	118.6	96.2	286.0	279.1	153.8	14.1	111.2	6.9
1995	123.8	126.2	103.4	284.8	277.5	145.0	17.9	114.6	7.3
1996	131.7	137.2	112.7	311.8	304.3	159.1	20.3	124.8	7.6
1997	138.6	152.0	123.3	327.9	319.9	164.4	22.6	132.8	8.0
1998	147.0	175.1	135.9	369.6	361.1	187.3	24.4	149.4	8.5
1990:									
1st quarter	91.7	74.0	85.8	232.7	226.4	120.2	20.0	86.2	6.2
2nd quarter	88.9	71.4	84.9	222.4	216.3	113.5	19.5	83.3	6.1
3rd quarter	90.3	78.5	86.4	210.9	204.9	104.7	19.2	81.0	6.0
4th quarter	88.1	78.3	85.4	196.9	191.0	96.5	18.3	76.2	6.0
1991:									
1st quarter	87.8	78.1	77.8	184.3	178.5	87.7	17.3	73.4	5.8
2nd quarter	86.4	77.3	77.2	185.9	180.0	89.8	15.3	75.0	5.9
3rd quarter	86.3	81.9	76.5	194.3	188.4	100.4	14.0	74.0	5.9
4th quarter	85.2	80.6	76.8	200.3	194.5	103.9	14.0	76.7	5.7
1992:									
1st quarter	86.2	79.5	77.6	211.3	205.4	108.8	13.1	83.4	6.0
2nd quarter	87.7	87.8	77.7	223.7	217.7	115.7	15.1	86.9	6.0
3rd quarter	90.5	85.5	79.7	227.1	221.1	117.9	12.5	90.7	6.1
4th quarter	92.8	91.9	81.1	240.1	233.9	123.6	11.6	98.6	6.2
1993:									
1st quarter	94.0	92.9	84.7	243.0	236.7	127.5	10.6	98.7	6.3
2nd quarter	95.4	102.9	87.3	244.1	237.7	128.5	10.3	98.9	6.4
3rd quarter	98.1	96.4	89.0	252.4	245.9	133.7	11.2	101.0	6.6
4th quarter	104.1	107.5	92.2	266.8	260.3	143.4	11.0	105.8	6.6
1994:									
1st quarter	105.4	113.1	93.3	276.4	269.7	150.4	11.7	107.6	6.6
2nd quarter	107.0	115.5	95.8	288.7	281.9	156.9	13.3	111.6	6.9
3rd quarter	110.8	119.9	97.3	289.5	282.5	155.0	15.1	112.4	7.0
4th quarter	114.0	126.1	98.3	289.5	282.3	153.0	16.2	113.1	7.2
1995:									
1st quarter	119.3	131.0	102.7	286.4	279.2	149.2	17.2	112.7	7.2
2nd quarter	124.8	125.5	102.3	276.2	269.0	140.1	17.1	111.8	7.2
3rd quarter	125.8	122.5	103.5	284.0	276.6	142.4	18.4	115.9	7.3
4th quarter	125.3	125.8	105.1	292.6	285.3	148.3	18.9	118.0	7.4
1996:									
1st quarter	129.6	130.0	107.9	300.1	292.7	153.3	20.0	119.4	7.4
2nd quarter	133.1	134.3	111.0	315.0	307.4	160.1	21.7	125.6	7.6
3rd quarter	131.7	143.4	115.3	317.0	309.4	162.5	19.4	127.5	7.6
4th quarter	132.3	141.2	116.6	315.3	307.6	160.6	20.2	126.8	7.8
1997:									
1st quarter	132.7	141.5	119.7	319.5	311.6	161.6	22.0	128.0	7.9
2nd quarter	138.9	151.9	122.8	325.9	317.9	163.5	22.7	131.8	8.0
3rd quarter	140.7	158.8	126.0	328.8	320.8	164.0	22.0	134.7	8.0
4th quarter	142.1	155.9	124.8	337.4	329.4	168.7	23.8	136.8	8.0
1998:									
1st quarter	145.4	172.4	132.0	349.8	341.5	175.8	25.1	140.6	8.3
2nd quarter	146.8	181.2	137.0	363.8	355.4	183.8	23.5	148.1	8.5
3rd quarter	147.4	164.0	138.8	375.8	367.3	190.9	23.9	152.6	8.5
4th quarter	148.3	182.8	135.9	388.9	380.3	198.7	25.3	156.3	8.6

Real Private Fixed Investment by Type

(Gross private domestic fixed investment—Billions of chained [1992] dollars, quarterly data are at seasonally adjusted annual rates)

Year and quarter	Total	Nonresidential									
		Total	Structures					Producers durable equipment			
			Total	Nonresidential buildings including farm	Utilities	Mining exploration, shafts, and wells	Other Structures	Total	Information processing and related equipment		
									Total	Computers and peripheral equipment [1]	Other
1970	432.1	282.8	141.7	91.1	35.7	9.8	3.6	149.5	.....	.....	.....
1971	464.9	282.4	139.4	89.4	36.1	9.1	3.2	150.7	.....	.....	.....
1972	520.3	307.7	143.7	91.8	37.6	9.7	2.8	169.8	.....	.....	.....
1973	567.5	352.5	155.4	100.3	40.0	10.4	2.9	201.2	.....	.....	.....
1974	530.2	354.4	152.2	97.6	37.6	12.4	2.9	205.4	.....	.....	.....
1975	471.0	317.3	136.2	82.5	34.4	14.4	2.8	183.9	.....	.....	.....
1976	517.6	332.6	139.6	80.6	38.0	15.6	2.8	195.2	.....	.....	.....
1977	593.7	371.8	146.4	83.6	38.2	18.1	3.5	225.6	.....	.....	.....
1978	660.8	422.6	162.3	95.3	40.0	20.0	4.0	259.6	.....	.....	.....
1979	695.6	463.3	182.7	113.5	41.3	21.3	4.5	280.7	.....	.....	.....
1980	648.4	461.1	195.0	114.4	41.3	30.0	3.9	268.2	.....	.....	.....
1981	660.6	485.7	210.4	122.8	42.0	34.9	3.8	278.2	.....	.....	.....
1982	610.4	464.3	207.2	126.6	39.5	32.2	4.0	260.3	54.5	4.7	67.0
1983	654.2	456.4	185.7	117.6	34.2	26.7	4.3	272.4	63.4	7.1	70.4
1984	762.4	535.4	212.2	137.6	35.4	30.3	5.8	324.6	79.8	11.6	79.0
1985	799.3	568.4	227.8	155.2	35.6	27.0	8.3	342.4	88.0	14.5	81.9
1986	805.0	548.5	203.3	144.5	36.5	15.8	6.6	345.9	94.1	16.7	84.6
1987	799.4	542.4	195.9	142.4	30.7	15.5	7.3	346.9	97.5	21.0	80.2
1988	818.3	566.0	196.8	145.3	30.0	15.8	5.7	369.2	106.6	24.0	85.7
1989	832.0	588.8	201.2	150.2	30.9	13.9	6.4	387.6	116.2	29.4	88.1
1990	805.8	585.2	203.3	152.0	28.1	16.1	7.2	381.9	116.2	29.4	88.2
1991	741.3	547.7	181.6	126.9	32.0	15.7	6.9	366.2	117.8	32.4	85.9
1992	783.4	557.9	169.2	113.2	34.5	13.3	8.2	388.7	134.2	43.9	90.2
1993	842.8	600.2	170.8	115.3	31.8	16.0	7.7	429.6	147.9	56.1	92.3
1994	915.5	648.4	172.5	119.9	29.9	15.8	6.9	476.8	165.1	67.2	99.4
1995	966.0	710.6	180.7	128.8	30.6	14.4	6.7	531.7	201.5	100.8	108.1
1996	1 050.6	776.6	189.7	141.0	27.8	15.3	5.5	589.8	245.4	151.3	115.4
1997	1 138.0	859.4	203.2	150.5	28.7	17.9	5.8	660.9	298.0	214.8	126.6
1998	1 267.8	960.7	203.0	150.9	29.5	16.7	5.7	770.2	388.1	351.8	141.2
1990:											
1st quarter	834.7	595.3	206.5	155.4	27.7	15.8	7.6	388.8	119.2	30.6	89.8
2nd quarter	811.2	583.4	205.5	154.7	27.6	16.3	6.9	377.8	116.1	29.3	88.2
3rd quarter	803.1	588.1	205.2	153.8	28.1	16.1	7.2	383.0	113.8	27.9	87.6
4th quarter	774.4	573.9	196.0	143.8	28.9	16.3	6.9	377.9	115.7	29.9	87.1
1991:											
1st quarter	742.6	555.1	192.2	137.6	30.4	17.3	6.7	362.9	112.5	29.2	84.3
2nd quarter	739.4	550.9	187.2	131.7	31.7	17.0	6.6	363.8	116.2	30.8	86.2
3rd quarter	741.0	545.3	175.5	121.7	32.6	14.0	7.1	369.8	119.7	33.2	87.1
4th quarter	742.0	539.5	171.4	116.4	33.3	14.4	7.2	368.1	122.5	36.6	86.2
1992:											
1st quarter	758.3	544.4	172.7	118.1	34.6	12.7	7.3	371.7	126.7	39.2	87.7
2nd quarter	782.4	557.5	171.0	114.4	34.8	13.3	8.4	386.4	132.4	43.4	88.9
3rd quarter	787.3	560.6	167.4	110.4	34.6	13.4	9.0	393.1	138.6	45.7	92.8
4th quarter	805.8	569.1	165.6	109.8	33.9	13.7	8.1	403.5	138.9	47.5	91.5
1993:											
1st quarter	814.8	577.8	168.0	111.3	33.4	15.2	8.2	409.8	140.5	51.0	89.6
2nd quarter	831.1	595.1	170.3	114.4	31.7	16.2	8.0	424.9	143.2	53.2	90.3
3rd quarter	844.5	602.3	171.7	117.1	31.0	16.4	7.2	430.7	152.5	58.4	94.6
4th quarter	880.8	625.6	173.1	118.5	31.0	16.2	7.4	452.9	155.5	61.7	94.8
1994:											
1st quarter	887.8	626.2	166.3	114.3	30.3	15.1	6.7	460.6	158.1	62.2	96.8
2nd quarter	913.2	641.2	174.5	123.1	29.6	15.1	6.7	467.3	160.8	64.1	97.8
3rd quarter	922.7	653.2	174.0	120.6	29.8	16.2	7.4	480.0	166.1	67.1	100.2
4th quarter	938.5	672.9	175.0	121.8	29.8	16.7	6.7	499.1	175.6	75.3	102.8
1995:											
1st quarter	957.1	698.4	179.5	126.1	30.7	15.7	6.9	520.4	183.7	80.4	106.1
2nd quarter	957.8	710.2	181.7	129.5	31.3	13.9	7.0	529.9	199.2	95.2	109.2
3rd quarter	965.8	711.7	181.5	129.3	30.9	14.2	7.1	531.8	205.2	105.3	108.2
4th quarter	983.1	722.3	179.8	130.4	29.6	13.9	5.9	544.8	217.7	122.1	108.7
1996:											
1st quarter	1 011.4	744.8	182.6	133.9	28.3	14.4	6.0	565.0	229.5	133.6	111.9
2nd quarter	1 043.5	764.4	185.9	138.3	27.5	14.4	5.6	581.6	238.0	142.6	113.7
3rd quarter	1 067.1	790.1	189.9	141.6	27.1	15.6	5.3	604.0	253.1	158.5	117.9
4th quarter	1 080.4	807.0	200.6	150.2	28.4	16.7	5.1	608.8	260.9	170.7	118.2
1997:											
1st quarter	1 096.0	820.9	202.5	152.8	28.1	16.6	4.9	621.0	271.8	182.5	121.1
2nd quarter	1 127.0	848.2	199.3	147.8	28.6	17.6	5.1	653.8	288.1	203.9	123.7
3rd quarter	1 159.3	882.2	205.2	152.0	29.1	18.6	5.2	682.6	311.5	229.9	130.0
4th quarter	1 169.5	886.2	205.7	149.5	29.2	18.9	7.8	686.4	320.7	242.9	131.5
1998:											
1st quarter	1 224.9	931.9	203.1	150.1	29.2	17.9	5.6	738.8	353.4	292.2	136.7
2nd quarter	1 264.1	960.4	201.9	149.8	29.5	17.0	5.5	771.3	376.8	331.5	139.7
3rd quarter	1 270.9	958.7	202.0	150.1	29.7	16.4	5.8	769.3	399.6	370.5	142.8
4th quarter	1 311.0	991.9	205.0	153.8	29.7	15.3	6.0	801.5	422.5	413.0	145.6

1. New computers and peripheral equipment only.

Real Private Fixed Investment by Type—*Continued*

(Gross private domestic fixed investment—Billions of chained [1992] dollars, quarterly data are at seasonally adjusted annual rates)

Year and quarter	Nonresidential—*Continued* Producers durable equipment—*Continued* Industrial equipment	Transportation and related equipment	Other	Residential Total	Structures Total	Single family	Multifamily	Other structures	Producers' durable equipment
1970	.....	.....	.....	149.1	147.4	62.6	36.7	47.8	2.1
1971	.....	.....	.....	190.0	188.4	86.9	46.7	54.3	2.4
1972	.....	.....	.....	223.8	221.8	103.3	58.5	59.5	2.9
1973	.....	.....	.....	222.3	219.8	101.1	60.1	58.2	3.2
1974	.....	.....	.....	176.4	173.2	77.6	38.7	56.7	3.3
1975	.....	.....	.....	153.5	150.4	70.8	17.3	61.4	3.1
1976	.....	.....	.....	189.7	186.7	98.6	16.7	69.6	3.2
1977	.....	.....	.....	229.8	226.8	126.2	21.9	76.3	3.5
1978	.....	.....	.....	245.0	241.7	130.9	25.0	83.4	3.8
1979	.....	.....	.....	236.0	232.2	116.0	30.5	84.2	4.2
1980	.....	.....	.....	186.1	182.0	76.3	27.3	78.6	4.2
1981	.....	.....	.....	171.2	167.0	69.5	26.3	71.6	4.2
1982	85.5	63.7	70.2	140.1	135.9	53.2	21.4	61.8	4.0
1983	78.5	71.7	68.0	197.6	193.2	92.0	29.3	71.7	4.5
1984	89.9	85.1	77.9	226.4	221.5	106.2	35.8	79.2	5.0
1985	94.1	88.4	78.3	229.5	224.2	104.8	34.9	84.3	5.4
1986	93.5	85.6	76.8	257.0	251.3	119.3	35.9	95.8	5.8
1987	91.1	82.1	79.0	257.6	251.6	128.3	28.3	94.8	6.1
1988	95.3	87.1	82.4	252.5	246.3	126.1	23.4	96.8	6.3
1989	101.5	78.9	92.3	243.2	237.0	121.9	23.3	91.8	6.3
1990	95.0	81.2	90.4	220.6	214.5	110.4	19.7	84.4	6.1
1991	88.3	81.7	78.8	193.4	187.6	96.4	15.4	75.7	5.9
1992	89.3	86.2	79.0	225.6	219.5	116.5	13.1	89.9	6.0
1993	96.5	98.3	86.8	242.6	236.2	127.1	10.6	98.6	6.4
1994	105.5	113.2	92.9	267.0	260.3	140.1	13.6	106.5	6.7
1995	115.4	119.4	97.9	256.8	249.8	126.8	16.9	106.6	7.0
1996	120.5	127.6	104.2	275.9	268.6	136.6	18.7	113.8	7.3
1997	125.9	140.3	113.0	282.8	275.1	137.2	20.2	118.5	7.7
1998	132.7	162.0	123.3	312.0	303.9	153.0	21.3	130.2	8.2
1990:									
1st quarter	98.6	80.3	91.6	239.4	233.1	122.8	20.6	89.7	6.3
2nd quarter	94.8	77.4	90.3	227.8	221.6	115.4	20.0	86.3	6.2
3rd quarter	95.1	84.3	91.0	214.9	208.8	105.8	19.5	83.6	6.1
4th quarter	91.4	82.8	88.8	200.3	194.4	97.6	18.6	78.1	6.0
1991:									
1st quarter	89.7	81.2	80.1	187.4	181.5	88.8	17.7	75.0	5.9
2nd quarter	88.7	79.9	79.2	188.3	182.3	90.8	15.6	76.0	6.0
3rd quarter	88.4	83.9	78.0	195.6	189.8	100.9	14.2	74.7	5.9
4th quarter	86.4	81.6	77.7	202.4	196.6	105.1	14.2	77.3	5.8
1992:									
1st quarter	86.8	79.9	78.2	213.9	207.9	110.4	13.3	84.3	6.0
2nd quarter	88.1	87.9	78.1	224.9	218.9	116.4	15.2	87.3	6.0
3rd quarter	89.8	85.4	79.3	226.7	220.7	117.7	12.5	90.6	6.0
4th quarter	92.6	91.5	80.5	236.7	230.5	121.6	11.5	97.4	6.2
1993:									
1st quarter	93.4	91.9	83.9	237.0	230.7	123.5	10.4	96.9	6.3
2nd quarter	94.2	101.5	85.8	236.1	229.8	123.6	10.1	96.1	6.3
3rd quarter	96.5	94.8	87.3	242.2	235.7	126.8	11.0	97.9	6.5
4th quarter	102.0	105.2	90.1	255.1	248.6	134.3	10.7	103.5	6.5
1994:									
1st quarter	102.8	108.8	90.9	261.3	254.8	139.4	11.4	103.8	6.5
2nd quarter	103.8	110.0	92.6	271.5	264.8	144.5	13.0	107.2	6.7
3rd quarter	106.7	113.5	93.7	269.4	262.7	140.5	14.7	107.6	6.7
4th quarter	108.9	120.5	94.5	265.9	259.0	136.1	15.5	107.6	6.9
1995:									
1st quarter	113.2	125.3	98.5	259.9	252.9	131.2	16.3	105.7	7.0
2nd quarter	116.4	119.1	97.1	249.5	242.6	122.7	16.2	104.2	6.9
3rd quarter	116.6	115.3	97.8	255.6	248.5	124.2	17.4	107.6	7.1
4th quarter	115.6	118.0	98.4	262.1	255.0	128.9	17.8	108.8	7.1
1996:									
1st quarter	119.1	121.9	100.4	268.0	261.0	133.0	18.7	109.8	7.1
2nd quarter	122.0	125.0	103.1	280.2	272.9	138.5	20.1	114.8	7.3
3rd quarter	120.4	132.7	106.4	279.0	271.7	138.6	17.7	115.9	7.3
4th quarter	120.6	130.8	106.9	276.3	268.9	136.3	18.3	114.8	7.4
1997:									
1st quarter	120.8	131.1	109.8	278.4	270.9	136.3	19.8	115.3	7.5
2nd quarter	126.4	140.5	112.4	282.5	274.9	137.2	20.3	118.0	7.6
3rd quarter	127.7	145.9	115.6	282.3	274.5	136.1	19.5	119.7	7.8
4th quarter	128.6	143.8	114.1	287.9	280.1	139.0	21.0	120.9	7.8
1998:									
1st quarter	131.5	159.6	120.2	298.5	290.5	145.2	22.1	123.8	8.0
2nd quarter	132.5	167.9	124.6	309.1	300.9	151.3	20.7	129.6	8.2
3rd quarter	133.1	151.7	125.8	316.5	308.3	155.6	20.8	132.6	8.2
4th quarter	133.5	168.7	122.5	324.1	315.7	159.7	21.7	135.0	8.3

Inventories to Sales Ratios

(Seasonally adjusted; ratio of inventories at end of quarter to monthly rate of sales during the quarter; annual data are for fourth quater)

Year and quarter	Total inventories to final sales of domestic business		Nonfarm inventories to:			
			Final sales of domestic business		Final sales of goods and structures	
	Current dollars	Chained (1992) dollars	Current dollars	Chained (1992) dollars	Current dollars	Chained (1992) dollars
1970	3.31	2.84	2.74	2.38	4.12	4.05
1971	3.27	2.81	2.66	2.35	4.03	4.00
1972	3.25	2.71	2.59	2.28	3.87	3.84
1973	3.52	2.76	2.75	2.36	4.08	3.98
1974	3.76	2.93	3.13	2.54	4.77	4.44
1975	3.46	2.77	2.87	2.37	4.37	4.13
1976	3.40	2.76	2.89	2.38	4.45	4.15
1977	3.40	2.75	2.90	2.37	4.48	4.11
1978	3.46	2.71	2.89	2.35	4.39	4.03
1979	3.62	2.72	3.01	2.36	4.60	4.05
1980	3.59	2.69	3.04	2.35	4.73	4.09
1981	3.53	2.80	3.06	2.43	4.83	4.26
1982	3.29	0.00	2.83	0.00	4.63	0.00
1983	3.08	0.00	2.67	0.00	4.38	0.00
1984	3.11	2.66	2.72	2.34	4.46	4.11
1985	2.94	2.63	2.58	2.31	4.35	4.10
1986	2.73	2.57	2.43	2.26	4.14	4.00
1987	2.78	2.58	2.49	2.29	4.30	4.10
1988	2.74	2.49	2.46	2.25	4.25	4.02
1989	2.71	2.52	2.44	2.28	4.27	4.09
1990	2.68	2.54	2.41	2.30	4.30	4.16
1991	2.56	2.55	2.33	2.31	4.25	4.24
1992	2.44	2.45	2.20	2.21	4.04	4.04
1993	2.40	2.45	2.19	2.23	4.02	4.05
1994	2.45	2.50	2.24	2.27	4.13	4.11
1995	2.45	2.48	2.26	2.28	4.20	4.11
1996	2.38	2.44	2.19	2.23	4.08	4.01
1997	2.35	2.48	2.16	2.26	4.04	4.05
1998	2.26	2.46	2.09	2.25	3.89	3.97
1990:						
1st quarter	2.67	2.49	2.40	2.26	4.16	4.02
2nd quarter	2.67	2.53	2.40	2.29	4.23	4.12
3rd quarter	2.71	2.54	2.44	2.30	4.32	4.16
4th quarter	2.68	2.54	2.41	2.30	4.30	4.16
1991:						
1st quarter	2.66	2.55	2.38	2.31	4.26	4.20
2nd quarter	2.58	2.55	2.33	2.28	4.19	4.17
3rd quarter	2.56	2.53	2.32	2.29	4.20	4.20
4th quarter	2.56	2.55	2.33	2.31	4.25	4.24
1992:						
1st quarter	2.52	2.50	2.27	2.26	4.14	4.14
2nd quarter	2.50	2.49	2.26	2.25	4.14	4.13
3rd quarter	2.49	2.48	2.24	2.24	4.12	4.11
4th quarter	2.44	2.45	2.20	2.21	4.04	4.04
1993:						
1st quarter	2.48	2.48	2.23	2.25	4.11	4.12
2nd quarter	2.45	2.47	2.22	2.24	4.08	4.09
3rd quarter	2.43	2.47	2.21	2.24	4.09	4.11
4th quarter	2.40	2.45	2.19	2.23	4.02	4.05
1994:						
1st quarter	2.42	2.47	2.19	2.24	4.04	4.08
2nd quarter	2.42	2.49	2.21	2.25	4.08	4.10
3rd quarter	2.42	2.49	2.22	2.25	4.09	4.10
4th quarter	2.45	2.50	2.24	2.27	4.13	4.11
1995:						
1st quarter	2.50	2.52	2.29	2.29	4.22	4.14
2nd quarter	2.50	2.51	2.30	2.29	4.27	4.17
3rd quarter	2.46	2.49	2.28	2.28	4.23	4.14
4th quarter	2.45	2.48	2.26	2.28	4.20	4.11
1996:						
1st quarter	2.43	2.46	2.24	2.26	4.14	4.07
2nd quarter	2.41	2.45	2.21	2.24	4.09	4.02
3rd quarter	2.42	2.46	2.21	2.25	4.11	4.04
4th quarter	2.38	2.44	2.19	2.23	4.08	4.01
1997:						
1st quarter	2.37	2.45	2.17	2.24	4.03	4.01
2nd quarter	2.37	2.47	2.17	2.26	4.05	4.05
3rd quarter	2.35	2.46	2.16	2.25	4.02	4.01
4th quarter	2.35	2.48	2.16	2.26	4.04	4.05
1998:						
1st quarter	2.34	2.49	2.15	2.28	4.01	4.04
2nd quarter	2.31	2.48	2.13	2.26	3.99	4.03
3rd quarter	2.30	2.49	2.12	2.27	3.99	4.05
4th quarter	2.26	2.46	2.09	2.25	3.89	3.97

Manufacturing and Trade Sales

(Millions of dollars)

Year and month	Total		Seasonally adjusted								
			Manufacturing			Retail trade			Merchant wholesalers		
	Not seasonally adjusted	Seasonally adjusted	Total	Durable goods industries	Nondurable goods industries	Total	Durable goods stores	Nondurable goods stores	Total	Durable goods establishments	Nondurable goods establishments
1970	1 298 651	1 298 651	633 663	337 876	295 787	374 989	114 586	260 403	289 999	133 778	156 221
1971	1 402 745	1 402 745	670 877	359 089	311 788	413 969	135 113	278 856	317 899	147 761	170 138
1972	1 572 976	1 572 976	756 321	407 844	348 477	458 267	155 937	302 330	358 388	168 879	189 509
1973	1 844 121	1 844 121	875 173	475 621	399 552	511 570	176 817	334 753	457 378	208 554	248 824
1974	2 134 949	2 134 949	1 017 477	530 074	487 403	541 686	172 497	369 189	575 786	255 863	319 923
1975	2 186 375	2 186 375	1 039 065	523 178	515 887	587 704	185 479	402 225	559 606	235 723	323 883
1976	2 449 803	2 449 803	1 185 563	607 475	578 088	655 859	219 908	435 951	608 381	263 605	344 776
1977	2 754 158	2 754 158	1 358 416	710 017	648 399	722 109	249 078	473 031	673 633	304 721	368 912
1978	3 123 838	3 123 838	1 522 858	812 776	710 082	804 019	280 899	523 120	796 961	372 176	424 785
1979	3 572 409	3 572 409	1 727 234	911 124	816 110	896 561	306 561	590 000	948 614	436 254	512 360
1980	3 926 797	3 926 797	1 852 689	929 027	923 662	956 921	298 618	658 303	1 117 187	486 509	630 678
1981	4 269 863	4 269 863	2 017 544	1 004 725	1 012 819	1 038 163	324 211	713 952	1 214 156	525 607	688 549
1982	4 171 496	4 171 496	1 960 214	950 541	1 009 673	1 068 747	335 587	733 160	1 142 535	480 318	662 217
1983	4 431 432	4 431 432	2 070 564	1 025 770	1 044 794	1 170 163	390 849	779 314	1 190 705	523 080	667 625
1984	4 921 490	4 921 490	2 288 184	1 175 276	1 112 908	1 286 914	454 481	832 433	1 346 392	622 361	724 031
1985	5 070 990	5 070 990	2 334 456	1 215 352	1 119 104	1 375 027	498 125	876 902	1 361 507	651 864	709 643
1986	5 165 031	5 165 031	2 335 881	1 238 859	1 097 022	1 449 636	540 688	908 948	1 379 514	681 691	697 823
1987	5 492 818	5 492 818	2 475 906	1 297 532	1 178 374	1 541 299	575 863	965 436	1 475 613	730 592	745 021
1988	5 965 883	5 965 883	2 695 432	1 421 501	1 273 931	1 656 202	629 154	1 027 048	1 614 249	801 751	812 498
1989	6 324 469	6 324 469	2 840 375	1 477 900	1 362 475	1 758 971	657 154	1 101 817	1 725 123	851 550	873 573
1990	6 550 911	6 550 911	2 912 228	1 485 313	1 426 915	1 844 611	668 835	1 175 776	1 794 072	880 767	913 305
1991	6 513 777	6 513 777	2 878 167	1 451 998	1 426 169	1 855 937	649 974	1 205 963	1 779 673	860 138	919 535
1992	6 806 114	6 806 114	3 004 727	1 541 866	1 462 861	1 951 589	703 604	1 247 985	1 849 798	908 917	940 881
1993	7 145 329	7 145 329	3 127 625	1 630 635	1 496 990	2 083 029	782 264	1 300 765	1 934 675	990 282	944 393
1994	7 664 899	7 664 899	3 348 019	1 789 576	1 558 443	2 250 033	887 443	1 362 590	2 066 847	1 091 483	975 364
1995	8 211 129	8 211 129	3 594 663	1 927 029	1 667 634	2 361 793	948 652	1 413 141	2 254 673	1 196 306	1 058 367
1996	8 605 620	8 605 620	3 715 460	2 004 159	1 711 301	2 506 141	1 020 861	1 485 280	2 384 019	1 246 078	1 137 941
1997	9 025 137	9 025 137	3 929 419	2 159 699	1 770 720	2 615 669	1 066 087	1 549 582	2 480 049	1 312 427	1 167 622
1998	9 333 267	9 333 267	4 052 248	2 275 987	1 776 261	2 746 011	1 138 286	1 607 725	2 535 008	1 359 989	1 175 019
1995:											
January	609 303	675 603	296 963	159 920	137 043	194 807	77 593	117 214	183 833	97 858	85 975
February	628 812	674 152	297 287	159 099	138 188	191 635	76 049	115 586	185 230	98 562	86 668
March	701 922	675 703	298 648	160 614	138 034	193 235	77 115	116 120	183 820	97 934	85 886
April	658 872	674 244	294 788	157 020	137 768	193 768	77 095	116 673	185 688	97 961	87 727
May	696 732	680 514	297 738	158 975	138 763	195 870	78 347	117 523	186 906	99 694	87 212
June	720 384	686 071	299 770	159 772	139 998	197 529	79 393	118 136	188 772	99 797	88 975
July	641 023	678 227	294 172	155 735	138 437	197 195	79 395	117 800	186 860	98 180	88 680
August	710 327	691 674	302 528	162 070	140 458	199 045	80 847	118 198	190 101	100 869	89 232
September	706 910	691 581	302 571	162 669	139 902	198 960	80 118	118 842	190 050	100 752	89 298
October	708 363	691 500	301 954	162 533	139 421	198 786	80 494	118 292	190 760	100 759	90 001
November	700 631	696 908	303 049	163 364	139 685	200 973	81 718	119 255	192 886	102 406	90 480
December	727 850	701 292	303 823	164 018	139 805	202 317	82 066	120 251	195 152	103 951	91 201
1996:											
January	634 566	695 315	300 389	161 326	139 063	201 610	81 782	119 828	193 316	101 900	91 416
February	668 392	700 056	302 541	163 002	139 539	204 570	83 626	120 944	192 945	101 577	91 368
March	717 033	702 053	301 083	160 941	140 142	205 955	84 530	121 425	195 015	102 661	92 354
April	707 274	710 568	307 672	164 906	142 766	207 142	84 088	123 054	195 754	102 215	93 539
May	737 372	718 200	312 489	169 351	143 138	208 566	85 279	123 287	197 145	103 610	93 535
June	733 606	712 856	308 248	167 004	141 244	207 568	84 511	123 057	197 040	103 062	93 978
July	690 958	718 160	310 576	167 129	143 447	208 074	84 952	123 122	199 510	102 810	96 700
August	736 765	720 935	312 153	168 808	143 345	208 414	84 771	123 643	200 368	103 508	96 860
September	734 245	723 371	313 159	170 292	142 867	210 571	85 977	124 594	199 641	104 135	95 506
October	754 630	728 359	313 737	168 855	144 882	212 329	86 609	125 720	202 293	105 277	97 016
November	730 765	732 704	317 744	171 970	145 774	212 216	85 945	126 271	202 744	106 278	96 466
December	760 014	727 266	313 779	169 204	144 575	213 061	85 969	127 092	200 426	104 701	95 725
1997:											
January	674 348	738 654	319 150	172 304	146 846	215 250	87 435	127 815	204 254	106 325	97 929
February	696 983	746 169	321 274	174 534	146 740	217 338	89 191	128 147	207 557	108 738	98 819
March	760 684	743 427	320 700	175 504	145 196	217 731	88 772	128 959	204 996	106 755	98 241
April	741 676	746 575	325 639	178 523	147 116	215 044	87 594	127 450	205 892	108 890	97 002
May	757 845	742 014	322 260	175 749	146 511	213 890	85 935	127 955	205 864	108 659	97 205
June	775 896	749 031	326 118	180 038	146 080	216 311	87 557	128 754	206 602	109 755	96 847
July	730 004	756 950	331 331	183 484	147 847	218 992	89 260	129 732	206 627	110 726	95 901
August	759 941	754 571	328 250	180 554	147 696	220 627	90 423	130 204	205 694	108 986	96 708
September	784 233	762 818	333 422	184 966	148 456	220 430	89 863	130 567	208 966	111 483	97 483
October	788 634	761 118	332 321	183 225	149 096	219 841	89 367	130 474	208 956	111 410	97 546
November	747 289	759 407	331 404	182 791	148 613	220 740	90 312	130 428	207 263	110 560	96 703
December	807 604	766 195	336 424	186 007	150 417	221 660	91 578	130 082	208 111	110 907	97 204
1998:											
January	692 927	764 610	331 937	182 303	149 634	223 038	92 538	130 500	209 635	112 602	97 033
February	720 192	769 153	335 883	187 298	148 585	224 158	92 576	131 582	209 112	112 224	96 888
March	797 710	774 054	338 991	189 998	148 993	224 508	92 689	131 819	210 555	113 400	97 155
April	771 370	773 653	335 553	186 843	148 710	226 659	93 990	132 669	211 441	114 414	97 027
May	777 715	772 689	333 622	185 789	147 833	228 631	94 915	133 716	210 436	112 993	97 443
June	813 712	775 765	335 110	186 536	148 574	229 520	95 671	133 849	211 135	114 077	97 058
July	748 807	775 499	335 380	186 907	148 473	228 189	93 620	134 569	211 930	114 485	97 445
August	777 164	773 999	336 445	188 789	147 656	228 410	93 774	134 636	209 144	113 303	95 841
September	803 255	781 728	340 481	192 842	147 639	229 283	94 545	134 738	211 964	112 979	98 985
October	807 722	783 878	340 133	193 818	146 315	232 379	96 724	135 655	211 366	112 441	98 925
November	779 603	788 294	341 423	194 823	146 600	234 504	97 782	136 722	212 367	112 597	99 770
December	843 090	796 583	344 247	195 531	148 716	236 786	99 500	137 286	215 550	114 522	101 028

Manufacturing and Trade Inventories

(Book value, end of period—millions of dollars)

Year and month	Total		Seasonally adjusted								
			Manufacturing			Retail trade			Merchant wholesalers		
	Not seasonally adjusted	Seasonally adjusted	Total	Durable goods industries	Nondurable goods industries	Total	Durable goods stores	Nondurable goods stores	Total	Durable goods establishments	Nondurable goods establishments
1970	.....	.....	.....	.....	.....	.....	.....	.....	.....	.....	.....
1971	.....	.....	.....	.....	.....	.....	.....	.....	.....	.....	.....
1972	.....	.....	.....	.....	.....	.....	.....	.....	.....	.....	.....
1973	.....	.....	.....	.....	.....	.....	.....	.....	.....	.....	.....
1974	.....	.....	.....	.....	.....	.....	.....	.....	.....	.....	.....
1975	.....	.....	.....	.....	.....	.....	.....	.....	.....	.....	.....
1976	.....	.....	.....	.....	.....	.....	.....	.....	.....	.....	.....
1977	.....	.....	.....	.....	.....	.....	.....	.....	.....	.....	.....
1978	.....	.....	.....	.....	.....	.....	.....	.....	.....	.....	.....
1979	.....	.....	.....	.....	.....	.....	.....	.....	.....	.....	.....
1980	.....	.....	.....	.....	.....	121 078	55 799	65 279	122 631	79 372	43 259
1981	.....	.....	.....	.....	.....	132 719	61 050	71 669	129 654	85 856	43 798
1982	566 523	573 908	311 852	200 444	111 408	134 628	61 316	73 312	127 428	85 222	42 206
1983	582 494	590 287	312 379	199 854	112 525	147 833	68 856	78 977	130 075	85 180	44 895
1984	640 467	649 780	339 516	221 330	118 186	167 812	79 074	88 738	142 452	95 474	46 978
1985	654 899	664 039	334 749	218 193	116 556	181 881	88 315	93 566	147 409	97 371	50 038
1986	653 299	662 738	322 654	211 997	110 657	186 510	89 983	96 527	153 574	102 349	51 225
1987	700 139	709 848	338 109	220 799	117 310	207 836	105 481	102 355	163 903	108 112	55 791
1988	757 952	767 222	369 374	242 468	126 906	219 047	112 453	106 594	178 801	117 045	61 756
1989	805 579	815 455	391 212	257 513	133 699	237 234	121 347	115 887	187 009	122 237	64 772
1990	830 883	840 663	405 073	263 209	141 864	239 815	121 194	118 621	195 775	880 767	69 362
1991	824 764	834 715	390 950	250 019	140 931	243 389	119 189	124 200	200 376	127 342	73 034
1992	832 779	842 939	382 510	238 105	144 405	252 185	123 152	129 033	208 244	131 458	76 786
1993	859 459	870 316	384 039	239 334	144 705	269 303	135 088	134 215	216 974	137 042	79 932
1994	922 285	934 342	404 877	253 624	151 253	294 052	153 019	141 033	235 413	150 928	84 485
1995	981 682	994 826	430 985	268 353	162 632	310 276	165 108	145 168	253 565	163 474	90 091
1996	999 202	1 013 201	436 729	273 815	162 914	320 601	170 849	149 752	255 871	166 185	89 686
1997	1 045 768	1 060 326	456 133	286 372	169 761	330 308	176 483	153 825	273 885	177 746	96 139
1998	1 079 784	1 095 042	466 798	295 344	171 454	340 760	181 070	159 690	287 484	187 734	99 750
1995:											
January	939 639	944 734	409 071	255 847	153 224	297 969	156 120	141 849	237 694	152 238	85 456
February	952 264	951 323	412 092	257 193	154 899	299 510	157 041	142 469	239 721	154 136	85 585
March	960 314	960 069	415 625	259 004	156 621	302 054	159 361	142 693	242 390	155 829	86 561
April	972 610	967 875	418 586	260 531	158 055	304 161	161 286	142 875	245 128	157 028	88 100
May	974 323	974 040	421 634	262 135	159 499	306 316	162 454	143 862	246 090	158 159	87 931
June	967 045	978 289	423 425	262 709	160 716	306 980	162 480	144 500	247 884	159 202	88 682
July	972 209	981 775	425 920	264 569	161 351	305 494	161 414	144 080	250 361	160 083	90 278
August	975 225	985 663	426 131	264 748	161 383	308 770	163 319	145 451	250 762	160 203	90 559
September	983 889	989 019	428 522	266 034	162 488	308 619	163 401	145 218	251 878	160 913	90 965
October	1 015 537	994 079	429 878	267 719	162 159	311 056	164 906	146 150	253 145	162 259	90 886
November	1 023 380	996 455	429 716	267 826	161 890	313 453	167 026	146 427	253 286	163 172	90 114
December	981 682	994 826	430 985	268 353	162 632	310 276	165 108	145 168	253 565	163 474	90 091
1996:											
January	995 284	1 000 084	433 597	270 707	162 890	311 493	166 040	145 453	254 994	164 493	90 501
February	1 002 403	1 000 460	434 023	271 111	162 912	311 995	166 154	145 841	254 442	164 108	90 334
March	997 875	997 640	434 157	271 251	162 906	309 364	164 151	145 213	254 119	163 720	90 399
April	1 006 800	1 001 557	433 815	271 153	162 662	309 629	164 078	145 551	258 113	164 970	93 143
May	1 002 386	1 002 800	432 518	270 995	161 523	312 253	166 266	145 987	258 029	164 437	93 592
June	989 431	1 001 929	432 102	270 682	161 420	312 786	166 941	145 845	257 041	164 170	92 871
July	996 161	1 006 741	432 854	271 759	161 095	316 480	168 952	147 528	257 407	165 050	92 357
August	997 797	1 008 658	433 794	272 684	161 110	318 148	170 368	147 780	256 716	165 433	91 283
September	1 004 001	1 008 618	434 864	273 092	161 772	318 718	170 945	147 773	255 036	165 939	89 097
October	1 035 549	1 013 399	436 428	274 146	162 282	321 153	172 408	148 745	255 818	165 657	90 161
November	1 040 707	1 013 472	437 606	274 896	162 710	319 714	170 384	149 330	256 152	166 442	89 710
December	999 202	1 013 201	436 729	273 815	162 914	320 601	170 849	149 752	255 871	166 185	89 686
1997:											
January	1 011 841	1 017 484	438 641	275 517	163 124	320 527	170 836	149 691	258 316	167 292	91 024
February	1 023 374	1 021 878	440 915	277 080	163 835	322 714	172 415	150 299	258 249	167 400	90 849
March	1 022 931	1 022 294	441 676	277 399	164 277	320 987	171 684	149 303	259 631	168 848	90 783
April	1 033 544	1 027 400	444 714	279 880	164 834	322 666	172 184	150 482	260 020	169 656	90 364
May	1 032 051	1 032 186	446 888	281 143	165 745	324 143	173 365	150 778	261 155	170 836	90 319
June	1 026 785	1 038 996	447 947	282 013	165 934	325 290	174 349	150 941	265 759	174 939	90 820
July	1 030 761	1 041 204	449 657	283 723	165 934	326 937	175 410	151 527	264 610	173 180	91 430
August	1 032 344	1 043 207	451 737	284 982	166 755	325 596	174 640	150 956	265 874	173 326	92 548
September	1 044 661	1 049 494	452 224	284 660	167 564	328 245	175 725	152 520	269 025	175 648	93 377
October	1 076 358	1 053 865	455 553	286 654	168 899	328 645	176 383	152 262	269 667	175 116	94 551
November	1 085 607	1 057 865	457 766	287 949	168 817	328 371	175 665	152 706	271 728	175 953	95 775
December	1 045 768	1 060 326	456 133	286 372	169 761	330 308	176 483	153 825	273 885	177 746	96 139
1998:											
January	1 056 951	1 063 043	458 197	288 086	170 111	331 323	175 817	155 506	273 523	178 685	94 838
February	1 071 112	1 069 619	461 178	290 153	171 025	331 938	176 200	155 738	276 503	180 803	95 700
March	1 075 688	1 074 243	461 948	290 887	171 061	334 282	177 346	156 936	278 013	182 230	95 783
April	1 084 113	1 077 101	464 668	293 393	171 275	335 270	177 584	157 686	277 163	182 385	94 778
May	1 077 206	1 077 294	465 729	294 375	171 354	332 728	175 598	157 130	278 837	182 755	96 082
June	1 066 165	1 078 803	466 701	295 143	171 558	333 042	174 303	158 739	279 060	182 433	96 627
July	1 069 390	1 079 285	467 636	295 669	171 967	332 881	174 098	158 783	278 768	182 189	96 579
August	1 072 921	1 083 792	468 445	296 871	171 528	333 432	174 523	158 909	281 915	184 028	97 887
September	1 083 782	1 089 349	468 552	296 757	171 795	335 965	176 303	159 662	284 832	185 366	99 466
October	1 114 477	1 091 438	471 031	298 561	172 470	335 911	177 448	158 463	284 496	186 129	98 367
November	1 123 945	1 095 493	471 000	297 981	173 019	338 348	179 586	158 762	286 145	186 525	99 620
December	1 079 784	1 095 042	466 798	295 344	171 454	340 760	181 070	159 690	287 484	187 734	99 750

Manufacturing and Trade Inventory to Sales Ratios

(Seasonally adjusted; annual figures are averages of seasonally adjusted monthly ratios)

Year and month	Total	Manufacturing			Retail trade			Merchant wholesalers		
		Total	Durable goods industries	Nondurable goods industries	Total	Durable goods stores	Nondurable goods stores	Total	Durable goods establishments	Nondurable goods establishments
1970	.....	.....	.....	.....	.....	.....	.....	.....	.....	.....
1971	.....	.....	.....	.....	.....	.....	.....	.....	.....	.....
1972	.....	.....	.....	.....	.....	.....	.....	.....	.....	.....
1973	.....	.....	.....	.....	.....	.....	.....	.....	.....	.....
1974	.....	.....	.....	.....	.....	.....	.....	.....	.....	.....
1975	.....	.....	.....	.....	.....	.....	.....	.....	.....	.....
1976	.....	.....	.....	.....	.....	.....	.....	.....	.....	.....
1977	.....	.....	.....	.....	.....	.....	.....	.....	.....	.....
1978	.....	.....	.....	.....	.....	.....	.....	.....	.....	.....
1979	.....	.....	.....	.....	.....	.....	.....	.....	.....	.....
1980	.....	.....	.....	.....	.....	.....	.....	.....	.....	.....
1981					1.48	2.18	1.16	1.25	1.88	0.76
1982	1.67	1.95	2.60	1.34	1.49	2.17	1.18	1.36	2.15	0.77
1983	1.56	1.78	2.30	1.27	1.44	1.98	1.17	1.28	1.89	0.78
1984	1.53	1.73	2.16	1.27	1.49	1.96	1.23	1.23	1.74	0.78
1985	1.55	1.73	2.18	1.25	1.52	2.02	1.25	1.28	1.77	0.82
1986	1.55	1.68	2.08	1.22	1.56	2.07	1.26	1.32	1.77	0.87
1987	1.50	1.59	1.99	1.16	1.55	2.08	1.24	1.29	1.72	0.86
1988	1.49	1.57	1.95	1.15	1.54	2.05	1.23	1.30	1.71	0.89
1989	1.52	1.63	2.06	1.16	1.58	2.18	1.22	1.28	1.70	0.86
1990	1.52	1.65	2.12	1.16	1.56	2.17	1.20	1.29	1.70	0.88
1991	1.53	1.65	2.12	1.18	1.54	2.18	1.20	1.33	1.76	0.92
1992	1.48	1.54	1.90	1.17	1.52	2.06	1.22	1.32	1.70	0.96
1993	1.44	1.47	1.76	1.17	1.51	1.98	1.23	1.32	1.62	1.00
1994	1.41	1.41	1.65	1.13	1.50	1.95	1.21	1.31	1.58	1.00
1995	1.43	1.41	1.64	1.15	1.55	2.05	1.22	1.32	1.59	1.00
1996	1.41	1.40	1.63	1.14	1.51	1.98	1.19	1.29	1.60	0.97
1997	1.38	1.37	1.57	1.13	1.49	1.96	1.17	1.28	1.58	0.95
1998	1.39	1.38	1.56	1.16	1.46	1.86	1.18	1.33	1.62	0.99
1995:										
January	1.40	1.38	1.60	1.12	1.53	2.01	1.21	1.29	1.56	0.99
February	1.41	1.39	1.62	1.12	1.56	2.06	1.23	1.29	1.56	0.99
March	1.42	1.39	1.61	1.13	1.56	2.07	1.23	1.32	1.59	1.01
April	1.44	1.42	1.66	1.15	1.57	2.09	1.22	1.32	1.60	1.00
May	1.43	1.42	1.65	1.15	1.56	2.07	1.22	1.32	1.59	1.01
June	1.43	1.41	1.64	1.15	1.55	2.05	1.22	1.31	1.60	1.00
July	1.45	1.45	1.70	1.17	1.55	2.03	1.22	1.34	1.63	1.02
August	1.43	1.41	1.63	1.15	1.55	2.02	1.23	1.32	1.59	1.01
September	1.43	1.42	1.64	1.16	1.55	2.04	1.22	1.33	1.60	1.02
October	1.44	1.42	1.65	1.16	1.56	2.05	1.24	1.33	1.61	1.01
November	1.43	1.42	1.64	1.16	1.56	2.04	1.23	1.31	1.59	1.00
December	1.42	1.42	1.64	1.16	1.53	2.01	1.21	1.30	1.57	0.99
1996:										
January	1.44	1.44	1.68	1.17	1.55	2.03	1.21	1.32	1.61	0.99
February	1.43	1.43	1.66	1.17	1.53	1.99	1.21	1.32	1.62	0.99
March	1.42	1.44	1.69	1.16	1.50	1.94	1.20	1.30	1.59	0.98
April	1.41	1.41	1.64	1.14	1.49	1.95	1.18	1.32	1.61	1.00
May	1.40	1.38	1.60	1.13	1.50	1.95	1.18	1.31	1.59	1.00
June	1.41	1.40	1.62	1.14	1.51	1.98	1.19	1.30	1.59	0.99
July	1.40	1.39	1.63	1.12	1.52	1.99	1.20	1.29	1.61	0.96
August	1.40	1.39	1.62	1.12	1.53	2.01	1.20	1.28	1.60	0.94
September	1.39	1.39	1.60	1.13	1.51	1.99	1.19	1.28	1.59	0.93
October	1.39	1.39	1.62	1.12	1.51	1.99	1.18	1.26	1.57	0.93
November	1.38	1.38	1.60	1.12	1.51	1.98	1.18	1.26	1.57	0.93
December	1.39	1.39	1.62	1.13	1.50	1.99	1.18	1.28	1.59	0.94
1997:										
January	1.38	1.37	1.60	1.11	1.49	1.95	1.17	1.26	1.57	0.93
February	1.37	1.37	1.59	1.12	1.48	1.93	1.17	1.24	1.54	0.92
March	1.38	1.38	1.58	1.13	1.47	1.93	1.16	1.27	1.58	0.92
April	1.38	1.37	1.57	1.12	1.50	1.97	1.18	1.26	1.56	0.93
May	1.39	1.39	1.60	1.13	1.52	2.02	1.18	1.27	1.57	0.93
June	1.39	1.37	1.57	1.14	1.50	1.99	1.17	1.29	1.59	0.94
July	1.38	1.36	1.55	1.12	1.49	1.97	1.17	1.28	1.56	0.95
August	1.38	1.38	1.58	1.13	1.48	1.93	1.16	1.29	1.59	0.96
September	1.38	1.36	1.54	1.13	1.49	1.96	1.17	1.29	1.58	0.96
October	1.38	1.37	1.56	1.13	1.49	1.97	1.17	1.29	1.57	0.97
November	1.39	1.38	1.58	1.14	1.49	1.95	1.17	1.31	1.59	0.99
December	1.38	1.36	1.54	1.13	1.49	1.93	1.18	1.32	1.60	0.99
1998:										
January	1.39	1.38	1.58	1.14	1.49	1.90	1.19	1.30	1.59	0.98
February	1.39	1.37	1.55	1.15	1.48	1.90	1.18	1.32	1.61	0.99
March	1.39	1.36	1.53	1.15	1.49	1.91	1.19	1.32	1.61	0.99
April	1.39	1.38	1.57	1.15	1.48	1.89	1.19	1.31	1.59	0.98
May	1.39	1.40	1.58	1.16	1.46	1.85	1.18	1.33	1.62	0.99
June	1.39	1.39	1.58	1.15	1.45	1.82	1.19	1.32	1.60	1.00
July	1.39	1.39	1.58	1.16	1.46	1.86	1.18	1.32	1.59	0.99
August	1.40	1.39	1.57	1.16	1.46	1.86	1.18	1.35	1.62	1.02
September	1.39	1.38	1.54	1.16	1.47	1.86	1.18	1.34	1.64	1.00
October	1.39	1.38	1.54	1.18	1.45	1.83	1.17	1.35	1.66	0.99
November	1.39	1.38	1.53	1.18	1.44	1.84	1.16	1.35	1.66	1.00
December	1.37	1.36	1.51	1.15	1.44	1.82	1.16	1.33	1.64	0.99

Real Manufacturing and Trade Sales and Inventories

(Billions of chained [1992] dollars, except as noted; seasonally adjusted)

Year and month	Sales				Inventories (Book value, end of period)				Inventory-sales ratios (Based on chained [1992] dollars)			
	Total	Manufacturing	Retail trade	Merchant wholesalers	Total	Manufacturing	Retail trade	Merchant wholesalers	Total	Manufacturing	Retail trade	Merchant wholesalers
1970	316.0	158.6	90.5	67.6	442.1	256.0	102.4	79.6	1.40	1.62	1.13	1.18
1971	330.6	162.9	96.7	71.4	458.3	253.1	116.1	85.8	1.39	1.55	1.20	1.20
1972	359.8	178.1	104.9	77.4	478.8	259.8	124.9	90.9	1.33	1.46	1.19	1.17
1973	389.8	192.4	110.3	87.4	509.4	277.7	134.8	93.4	1.31	1.44	1.22	1.07
1974	387.5	187.9	105.2	93.9	536.1	296.8	132.9	102.3	1.38	1.58	1.26	1.09
1975	359.1	169.0	105.9	84.5	516.8	289.7	126.4	96.6	1.44	1.71	1.19	1.14
1976	385.2	184.5	112.8	88.2	547.2	303.4	136.0	103.7	1.42	1.65	1.21	1.18
1977	412.1	199.4	118.2	94.6	573.7	311.8	143.7	114.5	1.39	1.56	1.22	1.21
1978	437.7	208.9	124.0	104.6	609.5	325.8	153.1	127.2	1.39	1.56	1.24	1.22
1979	448.1	211.6	126.1	110.0	629.3	338.5	153.1	133.8	1.40	1.60	1.21	1.22
1980	434.3	199.7	121.5	112.3	631.9	338.9	148.9	140.1	1.46	1.70	1.23	1.25
1981	437.0	201.1	122.0	113.0	647.8	343.5	157.2	143.5	1.48	1.71	1.29	1.27
1982	419.1	191.6	120.8	106.5	628.1	329.5	153.3	142.1	1.50	1.72	1.27	1.34
1983	439.7	200.5	129.8	109.5	639.5	329.5	166.2	141.9	1.46	1.64	1.28	1.30
1984	476.6	216.5	139.1	121.0	703.1	358.4	186.4	156.2	1.48	1.66	1.34	1.29
1985	490.4	220.4	145.2	124.9	718.7	353.9	201.3	162.5	1.47	1.61	1.39	1.30
1986	509.3	224.3	153.2	131.9	724.6	349.7	204.4	169.7	1.42	1.56	1.33	1.29
1987	528.0	234.1	157.6	136.4	755.9	354.8	223.9	177.0	1.43	1.52	1.42	1.30
1988	551.6	244.6	164.1	143.0	780.8	364.3	231.3	185.2	1.42	1.49	1.41	1.30
1989	561.3	246.6	167.7	147.0	817.6	383.5	245.0	189.2	1.46	1.56	1.46	1.29
1990	563.0	245.9	168.7	148.4	830.1	390.1	243.5	196.3	1.47	1.59	1.44	1.32
1991	554.2	241.8	164.5	147.9	829.2	384.0	243.3	201.9	1.50	1.59	1.48	1.37
1992	573.7	250.3	169.8	153.6	831.7	374.8	247.2	209.8	1.45	1.50	1.46	1.37
1993	594.7	256.8	177.5	160.4	859.1	380.9	263.0	215.1	1.45	1.48	1.48	1.34
1994	628.0	271.3	187.5	169.1	901.0	392.0	279.9	229.1	1.44	1.45	1.49	1.36
1995	652.8	281.0	193.4	178.9	933.2	403.2	290.3	239.7	1.43	1.44	1.50	1.34
1996	675.4	288.7	202.2	185.1	954.1	415.2	296.1	242.8	1.41	1.44	1.46	1.31
1997	714.3	307.1	210.7	197.1	999.4	435.2	302.9	261.3	1.37	1.39	1.42	1.28
1998	756.2	323.5	224.4	209.0	1 039.3	455.1	305.7	278.8	1.35	1.39	1.36	1.29
1995:												
January	650.8	282.2	192.3	177.1	907.6	394.3	282.8	230.5	1.40	1.40	1.47	1.30
February	647.5	281.3	189.3	177.7	909.8	394.5	283.7	231.6	1.41	1.40	1.50	1.30
March	647.2	281.8	190.2	175.8	914.4	395.9	284.9	233.5	1.41	1.41	1.50	1.33
April	642.4	276.4	190.6	176.0	918.1	397.1	286.4	234.6	1.43	1.44	1.50	1.33
May	647.0	278.5	192.8	176.2	919.6	398.1	287.0	234.5	1.42	1.43	1.49	1.33
June	652.5	280.7	193.9	178.5	923.5	398.9	288.9	235.7	1.42	1.42	1.49	1.32
July	645.9	275.3	193.5	177.7	926.3	400.7	288.2	237.4	1.43	1.46	1.49	1.34
August	657.5	283.1	194.8	180.0	927.4	399.9	290.0	237.6	1.41	1.41	1.49	1.32
September	656.7	283.0	194.8	179.4	930.3	401.9	289.6	238.8	1.42	1.42	1.49	1.33
October	657.4	282.4	194.4	181.0	934.2	402.9	291.7	239.6	1.42	1.43	1.50	1.32
November	662.5	283.7	196.7	182.6	934.4	402.0	292.8	239.6	1.41	1.42	1.49	1.31
December	665.7	284.2	197.8	184.1	933.2	403.2	290.3	239.7	1.40	1.42	1.47	1.30
1996:												
January	658.3	280.5	196.8	181.5	936.5	406.4	289.5	240.5	1.42	1.45	1.47	1.33
February	664.3	283.4	199.8	181.6	936.7	406.4	290.2	240.1	1.41	1.43	1.45	1.32
March	664.0	281.8	200.4	182.5	934.8	407.3	287.3	240.1	1.41	1.45	1.43	1.32
April	670.2	287.4	201.1	182.3	939.0	407.8	288.7	242.5	1.40	1.42	1.44	1.33
May	675.3	290.9	202.9	182.2	938.0	406.8	289.4	241.8	1.39	1.40	1.43	1.33
June	671.6	287.4	202.1	182.8	938.6	407.2	290.4	240.9	1.40	1.42	1.44	1.32
July	677.5	290.0	202.2	186.0	943.8	408.7	293.9	241.2	1.39	1.41	1.45	1.30
August	677.9	291.0	202.4	185.2	945.1	409.7	294.2	241.1	1.39	1.41	1.45	1.30
September	680.8	291.1	203.8	186.5	947.1	411.4	295.3	240.3	1.39	1.41	1.45	1.29
October	686.1	291.9	205.3	189.5	950.8	413.7	295.7	241.4	1.39	1.42	1.44	1.27
November	691.1	296.1	204.7	190.9	953.7	415.6	295.9	242.3	1.38	1.40	1.44	1.27
December	687.0	292.6	205.1	189.9	954.1	415.2	296.1	242.8	1.39	1.42	1.44	1.28
1997:												
January	696.6	297.7	207.2	192.3	958.1	416.9	296.2	245.0	1.38	1.40	1.43	1.27
February	705.3	300.2	209.4	196.3	962.5	419.2	298.0	245.4	1.37	1.40	1.42	1.25
March	703.6	300.0	209.3	195.0	963.8	420.2	296.0	247.7	1.37	1.40	1.41	1.27
April	707.7	304.8	207.6	195.9	969.5	423.3	299.5	246.7	1.37	1.39	1.44	1.26
May	704.6	301.9	207.6	195.8	972.6	425.6	299.0	248.0	1.38	1.41	1.44	1.27
June	713.0	306.1	209.5	198.0	977.4	426.9	297.5	253.1	1.37	1.39	1.42	1.28
July	722.9	311.6	212.1	199.8	979.4	428.8	298.9	251.8	1.36	1.38	1.41	1.26
August	715.8	308.0	213.1	195.3	980.6	430.3	296.8	253.6	1.37	1.40	1.39	1.30
September	724.1	312.5	212.3	199.9	986.3	430.8	298.7	256.8	1.36	1.38	1.41	1.29
October	722.8	312.5	212.2	198.7	991.2	433.9	300.3	257.0	1.37	1.39	1.42	1.29
November	722.7	311.9	213.3	198.1	995.5	435.4	301.5	258.6	1.38	1.40	1.41	1.31
December	731.8	317.7	214.5	200.2	999.4	435.2	302.9	261.3	1.37	1.37	1.41	1.31
1998:												
January	734.9	315.5	217.3	202.7	1 002.3	437.8	303.7	260.9	1.36	1.39	1.40	1.29
February	743.7	320.4	219.7	204.2	1 010.8	441.3	304.5	265.0	1.36	1.38	1.39	1.30
March	752.2	324.2	220.7	207.9	1 017.5	442.8	307.3	267.5	1.35	1.37	1.39	1.29
April	749.4	320.4	222.1	207.5	1 021.6	445.8	309.8	266.1	1.36	1.39	1.40	1.28
May	750.1	318.7	224.7	207.4	1 022.1	447.3	306.7	268.2	1.36	1.40	1.37	1.29
June	754.3	320.5	225.3	209.1	1 021.5	448.7	304.3	268.7	1.35	1.40	1.35	1.29
July	753.4	321.0	223.7	209.3	1 021.0	452.0	300.5	268.7	1.36	1.41	1.34	1.28
August	755.6	323.4	223.9	209.0	1 027.3	453.2	302.2	272.1	1.36	1.40	1.35	1.30
September	762.7	327.0	225.3	211.2	1 032.0	453.5	303.0	275.7	1.35	1.39	1.35	1.31
October	765.3	327.5	228.1	210.2	1 035.7	456.6	303.8	275.6	1.35	1.39	1.33	1.31
November	771.6	329.5	230.0	212.7	1 041.6	458.2	306.3	277.3	1.35	1.39	1.33	1.30
December	781.4	333.5	232.2	216.3	1 039.3	455.1	305.7	278.8	1.33	1.37	1.32	1.29

1. Annual figures for sales and inventory-sales ratios are averages of seasonally adjusted monthly data; annual figures for inventories are as of end of December.

Capital Expenditures for All Companies and Businesses

Capital expenditures	All companies and businesses		Companies with one or more employees		Nonemployer businesses	
	1996	1997	1996	1997	1996	1997
Total	807 070	870 221	707 110	770 799	99 960	99 422
Structures	243 427	272 669	204 345	235 537	39 082	37 132
New	223 588	253 822	191 867	224 478	31 721	29 344
Used	19 839	18 849	12 478	11 060	7 361	7 789
Equipment	563 641	597 550	502 762	535 261	60 878	62 289
New	526 016	561 103	481 785	515 049	44 231	46 054
Used	37 625	36 447	20 977	20 212	16 648	16 235
Not distributed as structures or equipment	2	.....	2	.....	.....	.....
Capital Lease and Capitalized Interest Expenses [1]						
Capital leases	15 675	16 066	13 023	14 549	2 652	1 517
Capitalized interest	.....	.....	6 827	7 241	.....	.....

1. Included in data shown above.

Capital Expenditures for Companies with One or More Employees by Major Industry Sector: 1996 and 1997

Industry	SIC	1996					1997				
		Total	Structures		Equipment		Total	Structures		Equipment	
			New	Used	New	Used		New	Used	New	Used
Total expenditures	.....	707 110	191 867	12 478	481 785	20 977	770 799	224 478	11 060	515 049	20 212
Mining	10-14	30 155	18 696	717	9 370	1 372	37 412	24 831	677	10 491	1 414
Construction	15-17	13 806	826	299	10 166	2 515	15 531	1 426	131	11 477	2 497
Manufacturing	20-39	191 762	35 636	1 807	147 944	6 375	192 271	37 310	1 056	149 547	4 357
Durable goods industries	24, 25, 32-39	109 898	18 698	842	86 759	3 599	108 331	18 894	616	86 137	2 684
Nondurable goods industries	20-23, 26-31	81 864	16 938	966	61 185	2 776	83 940	18 417	440	63 411	1 672
Transportation	40-42, 44-47	36 698	7 035	703	25 048	3 913	45 045	9 000	374	32 165	3 506
Communications	48	57 133	12 568	264	43 917	385	68 403	14 572	377	52 776	677
Utilities	49	36 744	15 687	583	19 901	573	38 719	16 907	626	20 472	713
Electric and gas services	491, 493	25 531	9 901	118	15 265	248	26 503	10 280	329	15 752	142
Gas, water, and other utilities	492, 494-497	11 212	5 786	465	4 636	325	12 216	6 628	297	4 721	571
Wholesale trade	50, 51	26 026	5 329	452	19 197	1 049	28 847	6 346	431	21 218	851
Retail trade	52-59	55 831	23 883	1 009	29 426	1 512	55 868	24 182	1 070	28 903	1 714
Finance	60-62, 67	87 144	8 724	1 085	76 895	439	91 328	11 414	1 335	77 959	620
Insurance and real estate	63-65	23 410	13 313	1 453	8 350	294	29 270	18 846	1 310	8 791	323
Services	07-09, 70-89	145 896	49 470	4 071	89 831	2 522	165 113	58 874	3 664	99 099	3 476
Rental and business services	07-09, 70, 72, 73, 75, 76, 78, 79	78 064	15 345	1 504	59 332	1 882	86 749	18 675	813	65 042	2 220
Health services	80	34 176	16 362	1 047	16 386	381	37 015	17 396	1 532	17 356	730
Membership organizations, educational, and miscellaneous services	81-84, 86, 87, 89	33 657	17 763	1 519	14 113	259	41 349	22 803	1 320	16 701	525
Structures and equipment expenditures serving multiple industry categories	.....	2 503	701	34	1 741	27	2 992	769	9	2 150	65

1. Included in data shown above.

Prices

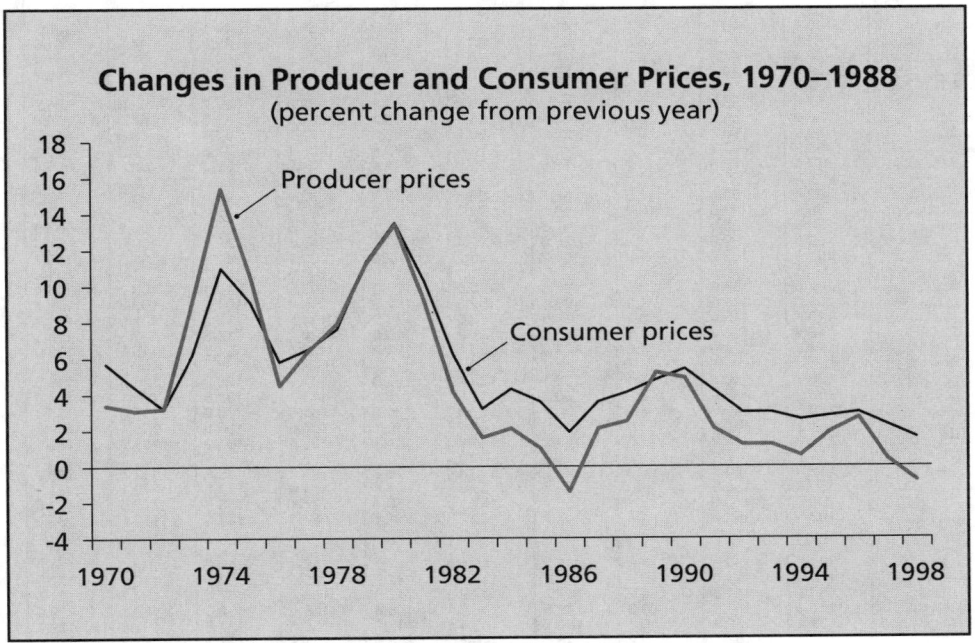

Changes in Producer and Consumer Prices, 1970–1988
(percent change from previous year)

- The recent U.S. record of essential price stability was extended in 1998, when consumer prices rose only 1.6 percent, marking the seventh consecutive year in which consumer prices rose 3 percent or less.

- Producer prices for finished goods declined 0.8 percent in 1998, the result of a large drop in energy prices coupled with a small 0.6 percent rise in prices of finished goods other than energy.

- Prices received by farmers fell for the second consecutive year in 1998, bringing the prices received index 9.8 percent below its 1996 peak. Thus, even though prices paid by farmers rose little over the two years, the ratio of prices received to prices paid fell to 87 percent of its 1990-1992 base.

Consumer Price Indexes

(All urban consumers—1982–1984=100; seasonally adjusted)

Year and month	All items Not seasonally adjusted	All items Seasonally adjusted Index	All items Seasonally adjusted Percent change	Total	Total food	Food at home Total	Cereals and bakery products	Meats, poultry, fish, and eggs	Dairy and related products	Fruits and vege-tables	Non-alcoholic beverages	Other food at home	Food away from home	Alcoholic beverages
1970	38.8	38.8	5.7	40.1	39.2	39.9	37.1	44.6	44.7	37.8	27.1	32.9	37.5	.....
1971	40.5	40.5	4.4	41.4	40.4	40.9	38.8	44.1	46.1	39.7	28.1	34.3	39.4	.....
1972	41.8	41.8	3.2	43.1	42.1	42.7	39.0	48.0	46.8	41.6	28.0	34.6	41.0	.....
1973	44.4	44.4	6.2	48.8	48.2	49.7	43.5	60.9	51.2	47.4	30.1	36.7	44.2	.....
1974	49.3	49.3	11.0	55.5	55.1	57.1	56.5	62.2	60.7	55.2	35.9	47.8	49.8	.....
1975	53.8	53.8	9.1	60.2	59.8	61.8	62.9	67.0	62.6	56.9	41.3	55.4	54.5	.....
1976	56.9	56.9	5.8	62.1	61.6	63.1	61.5	68.0	67.7	58.4	49.4	56.4	58.2	.....
1977	60.6	60.6	6.5	65.8	65.5	66.8	62.5	67.4	69.5	63.8	74.4	68.4	62.6	.....
1978	65.2	65.2	7.6	72.2	72.0	73.8	68.1	77.6	74.2	70.9	78.7	73.6	68.3	74.8
1979	72.6	72.6	11.3	79.9	79.9	81.8	74.9	89.0	82.8	76.6	82.6	79.0	75.9	80.6
1980	82.4	82.4	13.5	86.7	86.8	88.4	83.9	92.0	90.9	82.1	91.4	88.4	83.4	87.3
1981	90.9	90.9	10.3	93.5	93.6	94.8	92.3	96.0	97.4	92.0	95.3	94.9	90.9	93.1
1982	96.5	96.5	6.2	97.3	97.4	98.1	96.5	99.6	98.8	97.0	97.9	97.3	95.8	97.0
1983	99.6	99.6	3.2	99.5	99.4	99.1	99.6	99.2	100.0	97.3	99.8	99.5	100.0	100.6
1984	103.9	103.9	4.3	103.2	103.2	102.8	103.9	101.3	101.3	105.7	102.3	103.1	104.2	102.4
1985	107.6	107.6	3.6	105.6	105.6	104.3	107.9	100.1	103.2	108.4	104.3	105.7	108.3	105.2
1986	109.6	109.6	1.9	109.1	109.0	107.3	110.9	104.5	103.3	109.4	110.4	109.4	112.5	109.3
1987	113.6	113.6	3.6	113.5	113.5	111.9	114.8	110.5	105.9	119.1	107.5	110.5	117.0	111.5
1988	118.3	118.3	4.1	118.2	118.2	116.6	122.1	114.3	108.4	128.1	107.5	113.1	121.8	114.2
1989	124.0	124.0	4.8	124.9	125.1	124.2	132.4	121.3	115.6	138.0	111.3	119.1	127.4	117.9
1990	130.7	130.7	5.4	132.1	132.4	132.3	140.0	130.0	126.5	149.0	113.5	123.4	133.4	123.0
1991	136.2	136.2	4.2	136.8	136.3	135.8	145.8	132.6	125.1	155.8	114.1	127.3	137.9	137.8
1992	140.3	140.3	3.0	138.7	137.9	136.8	151.5	130.9	128.5	155.4	114.3	128.8	140.7	141.6
1993	144.5	144.5	3.0	141.6	140.9	140.1	156.6	135.5	129.4	159.0	114.6	130.5	143.2	142.2
1994	148.2	148.2	2.6	144.9	144.3	144.1	163.0	137.2	131.7	165.0	123.2	135.6	145.7	142.5
1995	152.4	152.4	2.8	148.9	148.4	148.8	167.5	138.8	132.8	177.7	131.7	140.8	149.0	143.1
1996	156.9	156.9	3.0	153.7	153.3	154.3	174.0	144.8	142.1	183.9	128.6	142.9	152.7	146.8
1997	160.5	160.5	2.3	157.7	157.3	158.1	177.6	148.5	145.5	187.5	133.4	147.3	157.0	149.5
1998	163.0	163.0	1.6	161.1	160.7	161.1	181.1	147.3	150.8	198.2	133.0	150.8	161.1	150.6
1995:														
January	150.3	150.6	-7.6	147.2	146.9	147.0	164.7	136.6	132.7	174.8	133.0	140.0	147.4	142.3
February	150.9	151.0	0.3	147.7	147.5	147.7	165.5	137.5	132.1	177.0	132.6	140.0	147.6	142.1
March	151.4	151.3	0.2	147.5	147.2	147.0	165.7	137.8	132.2	171.4	132.3	140.3	148.1	142.6
April	151.9	151.8	0.3	148.5	148.3	148.6	166.6	137.8	132.1	179.9	132.4	140.5	148.3	142.9
May	152.2	152.2	0.3	148.7	148.4	148.7	166.6	137.9	132.8	179.7	131.5	140.5	148.6	143.2
June	152.5	152.5	0.2	148.8	148.5	148.6	167.1	137.7	132.2	179.9	131.6	140.5	148.8	142.9
July	152.5	152.7	0.1	149.0	148.7	148.8	167.7	138.1	132.9	178.8	131.5	140.8	149.1	142.7
August	152.9	153.0	0.2	149.2	148.9	148.9	168.2	138.8	132.8	177.1	131.8	141.2	149.4	143.6
September	153.2	153.2	0.1	149.6	149.3	149.5	168.5	139.4	132.3	179.9	131.7	141.1	149.6	143.3
October	153.7	153.7	0.3	150.1	149.8	150.0	169.1	140.6	133.2	179.3	130.9	141.1	150.0	143.7
November	153.6	153.8	0.1	150.1	149.8	149.9	169.8	141.1	133.7	177.0	130.9	141.2	150.2	144.1
December	153.5	154.1	0.2	150.4	150.1	150.3	170.1	141.5	135.0	176.9	130.5	141.4	150.4	143.7
1996:														
January	154.4	154.7	0.4	150.8	150.5	150.8	171.6	142.0	136.3	176.5	129.8	141.5	150.6	144.4
February	154.9	155.1	0.3	151.3	150.9	151.3	171.8	142.2	137.2	178.5	129.0	141.3	150.9	145.1
March	155.7	155.6	0.3	151.7	151.4	151.9	172.4	142.1	136.7	181.3	129.1	142.0	151.2	145.8
April	156.3	156.2	0.4	152.4	152.1	152.8	173.1	142.0	137.0	185.8	129.3	142.3	151.6	145.9
May	156.6	156.6	0.3	152.5	152.1	152.6	173.6	142.0	137.6	182.7	129.1	142.6	152.0	146.3
June	156.7	156.8	0.1	153.4	153.1	154.0	173.7	144.0	139.8	185.5	128.5	142.8	152.3	146.6
July	157.0	157.2	0.3	154.0	153.7	154.6	174.2	144.7	142.0	185.5	128.2	143.0	152.8	147.0
August	157.3	157.3	0.1	154.4	154.2	155.2	174.4	145.6	144.6	184.7	128.9	143.1	153.1	147.3
September	157.8	157.8	0.3	155.1	154.9	156.1	174.8	147.0	146.7	184.8	127.8	143.6	153.5	147.8
October	158.3	158.3	0.3	155.9	155.7	157.0	175.2	147.6	149.3	186.6	127.6	143.8	154.2	148.1
November	158.6	158.7	0.3	156.5	156.3	157.6	176.1	148.2	149.3	187.9	127.6	144.2	154.7	148.1
December	158.6	159.1	0.3	156.7	156.5	157.7	176.3	149.3	148.6	186.4	127.9	144.4	155.0	148.6
1997:														
January	159.1	159.4	0.2	156.3	156.1	156.9	176.6	148.7	147.8	182.5	128.2	144.5	155.3	148.8
February	159.6	159.8	0.3	156.9	156.7	157.7	176.4	148.7	146.2	188.6	127.7	144.8	155.6	149.0
March	160.0	159.9	0.1	156.8	156.5	157.2	177.1	147.5	146.1	187.2	128.9	145.0	156.0	149.0
April	160.2	160.1	0.1	156.9	156.6	157.1	176.7	148.1	145.7	184.2	131.1	146.3	156.2	149.1
May	160.1	160.1	0.0	157.2	156.8	157.6	177.0	148.6	145.4	184.9	133.2	146.9	156.3	149.5
June	160.3	160.3	0.1	157.4	157.1	157.8	177.7	148.7	144.1	185.5	134.9	147.7	156.6	149.4
July	160.5	160.6	0.2	157.8	157.5	158.1	177.7	149.0	143.3	185.8	137.0	148.6	157.1	149.5
August	160.8	160.9	0.2	158.3	158.0	158.8	177.9	148.9	143.4	189.9	137.0	148.6	157.4	149.9
September	161.2	161.3	0.2	158.6	158.3	158.9	178.2	148.9	143.5	189.9	136.7	148.9	157.8	149.8
October	161.6	161.5	0.1	158.8	158.5	159.1	178.6	148.5	145.7	190.0	136.6	148.9	158.2	149.9
November	161.5	161.7	0.1	159.1	158.9	159.4	178.7	148.6	147.0	190.9	135.1	148.5	158.6	149.7
December	161.3	161.8	0.1	159.3	159.0	159.3	179.0	147.7	147.8	191.2	134.2	148.6	159.0	149.9
1998:														
January	161.6	162.0	0.1	159.9	159.6	160.1	179.1	147.4	148.3	198.4	134.0	148.6	159.2	150.2
February	161.9	162.1	0.1	159.8	159.5	159.9	179.5	147.3	147.7	195.9	134.0	148.9	159.6	149.8
March	162.2	162.1	0.0	159.8	159.5	159.7	180.0	146.9	148.4	194.0	133.5	149.3	159.9	149.7
April	162.5	162.5	0.2	159.9	159.6	159.7	180.1	146.7	148.5	194.8	133.1	149.2	160.2	150.0
May	162.8	162.9	0.2	160.7	160.4	160.7	180.6	146.9	148.1	202.8	132.7	149.4	160.6	150.1
June	163.0	163.0	0.1	160.7	160.4	160.6	181.1	146.8	148.1	199.8	132.9	150.3	160.7	150.5
July	163.2	163.3	0.2	161.1	160.9	161.1	181.2	147.3	148.2	200.9	133.0	151.0	161.1	150.6
August	163.4	163.5	0.1	161.6	161.3	161.6	182.0	147.8	150.5	199.8	132.3	152.0	161.5	150.7
September	163.6	163.6	0.1	161.6	161.4	161.3	182.0	146.9	152.9	196.5	132.2	152.5	162.1	151.0
October	164.0	163.9	0.2	162.4	162.2	162.5	182.4	147.4	155.0	201.7	132.6	152.7	162.3	151.2
November	164.0	164.2	0.2	162.7	162.4	162.7	182.7	147.1	155.9	200.4	133.1	153.8	162.6	151.7
December	163.9	164.4	0.1	162.8	162.5	162.7	182.9	146.7	157.6	200.4	132.8	153.2	163.0	152.0

Consumer Price Indexes—*Continued*

(All urban consumers—1982–1984=100, except as noted; seasonally adjusted)

Year and month	Total	Shelter						Fuels and utilities				Household furnishings and operations	
		Total	Rent of shelter [1]	Rent of primary residence	Lodging away from home [2]	Owners' equivalent rent of primary residence [1]	Tenants' and household insurance [2]	Total	Fuels		Water and sewer and trash collection services [2]	Total	House-hold operations [2]
									Fuel oil and other fuels	Gas (piped) and electricity			
1970	36.4	35.5	.....	46.5	.....	.....	.....	29.1	17.0	25.4	.....	46.8	.....
1971	38.0	37.0	.....	48.7	.....	.....	.....	31.1	18.2	27.1	.....	48.6	.....
1972	39.4	38.7	.....	50.4	.....	.....	.....	32.5	18.3	28.5	.....	49.7	.....
1973	41.2	40.5	.....	52.5	.....	.....	.....	34.3	21.1	29.9	.....	51.1	.....
1974	45.8	44.4	.....	55.2	.....	.....	.....	40.7	33.2	34.5	.....	56.8	.....
1975	50.7	48.8	.....	58.0	.....	.....	.....	45.4	36.4	40.1	.....	63.4	.....
1976	53.8	51.5	.....	61.1	.....	.....	.....	49.4	38.8	44.7	.....	67.3	.....
1977	57.4	54.9	.....	64.8	.....	.....	.....	54.7	43.9	50.5	.....	70.4	.....
1978	62.4	60.5	.....	69.3	.....	.....	.....	58.5	46.2	55.0	.....	74.7	.....
1979	70.1	68.9	.....	74.3	.....	.....	.....	64.8	62.4	61.0	.....	79.9	.....
1980	81.1	81.0	.....	80.9	.....	.....	.....	75.4	86.1	71.4	.....	86.3	.....
1981	90.4	90.5	.....	87.9	.....	.....	.....	86.4	104.6	81.9	.....	93.0	.....
1982	96.9	96.9	.....	94.6	.....	.....	.....	94.9	103.4	93.2	.....	98.0	.....
1983	99.5	99.1	102.7	100.1	.....	102.5	.....	100.2	97.2	101.5	.....	100.2	.....
1984	103.6	104.0	107.7	105.3	.....	107.3	.....	104.8	99.4	105.4	.....	101.9	.....
1985	107.7	109.8	113.9	111.8	.....	113.2	.....	106.5	95.9	107.1	.....	103.8	.....
1986	110.9	115.8	120.2	118.3	.....	119.4	.....	104.1	77.6	105.7	.....	105.2	.....
1987	114.2	121.3	125.9	123.1	.....	124.8	.....	103.0	77.9	103.8	.....	107.1	.....
1988	118.5	127.1	132.0	127.8	.....	131.1	.....	104.4	78.1	104.6	.....	109.4	.....
1989	123.0	132.8	138.0	132.8	.....	137.4	.....	107.8	81.7	107.5	.....	111.2	.....
1990	128.5	140.0	145.5	138.4	.....	144.8	.....	111.6	99.3	109.3	.....	113.3	.....
1991	133.6	146.3	152.1	143.3	.....	150.4	.....	115.3	94.6	112.6	.....	116.0	.....
1992	137.5	151.2	157.3	146.9	.....	155.5	.....	117.8	90.7	114.8	.....	118.0	.....
1993	141.2	155.7	162.0	150.3	.....	160.5	.....	121.3	90.3	118.5	.....	119.3	.....
1994	144.8	160.5	167.0	154.0	.....	165.8	.....	122.8	88.8	119.2	.....	121.0	.....
1995	148.5	165.7	172.4	157.8	.....	171.3	.....	123.7	88.1	119.2	.....	123.0	.....
1996	152.8	171.0	178.0	162.0	.....	176.8	.....	127.5	99.2	122.1	.....	124.7	.....
1997	156.8	176.3	183.4	166.7	.....	181.9	.....	130.8	99.8	125.1	.....	125.4	.....
1998	160.4	182.1	189.6	172.1	109.0	187.8	99.8	128.5	90.0	121.2	101.6	126.6	101.5
1995:													
January	146.5	162.8	169.5	156.1	.....	168.6	.....	123.5	87.6	118.5	.....	121.9	.....
February	146.8	163.2	170.1	156.3	.....	169.0	.....	123.3	87.1	118.8	.....	122.3	.....
March	147.2	163.8	170.6	156.7	.....	169.5	.....	123.3	87.3	118.7	.....	122.4	.....
April	147.5	164.3	171.2	157.0	.....	170.0	.....	123.4	87.4	118.5	.....	122.4	.....
May	147.8	164.8	171.8	157.3	.....	170.6	.....	123.0	88.1	117.8	.....	122.5	.....
June	148.1	165.3	172.2	157.6	.....	171.1	.....	123.4	88.8	118.1	.....	122.4	.....
July	148.5	165.7	172.7	158.0	.....	171.5	.....	123.5	89.3	118.0	.....	122.9	.....
August	148.9	166.0	173.0	158.2	.....	172.0	.....	124.2	89.3	119.3	.....	123.3	.....
September	149.1	166.6	173.6	158.5	.....	172.5	.....	123.4	88.8	117.6	.....	123.6	.....
October	149.7	167.2	174.2	158.8	.....	173.2	.....	124.1	87.8	118.8	.....	123.8	.....
November	149.9	167.6	174.6	159.2	.....	173.7	.....	124.0	87.4	118.5	.....	123.7	.....
December	150.2	167.9	175.2	159.6	.....	174.2	.....	124.4	88.4	118.7	.....	124.0	.....
1996:													
January	150.8	168.5	175.7	160.0	.....	174.6	.....	125.3	95.7	119.2	.....	124.3	.....
February	151.1	168.8	176.0	160.3	.....	174.9	.....	125.8	94.9	120.3	.....	124.1	.....
March	151.5	169.3	176.4	160.6	.....	175.4	.....	126.2	97.2	119.8	.....	124.4	.....
April	151.9	169.7	176.9	160.9	.....	175.8	.....	126.7	100.9	120.9	.....	124.5	.....
May	152.2	170.1	177.3	161.3	.....	176.2	.....	127.3	99.4	121.2	.....	124.2	.....
June	152.3	170.4	177.6	161.8	.....	176.5	.....	126.8	95.6	120.4	.....	124.4	.....
July	152.9	171.2	178.4	162.3	.....	177.0	.....	127.4	94.7	121.6	.....	124.6	.....
August	153.3	171.5	178.7	162.5	.....	177.4	.....	128.0	95.2	122.4	.....	124.7	.....
September	153.6	171.8	179.0	162.9	.....	177.7	.....	128.3	98.1	122.2	.....	124.9	.....
October	153.9	172.2	179.4	163.2	.....	178.2	.....	128.9	104.0	122.1	.....	124.9	.....
November	154.3	172.7	179.9	163.6	.....	178.6	.....	129.2	105.6	122.3	.....	124.9	.....
December	154.6	172.9	180.3	164.0	.....	179.0	.....	129.9	108.8	123.1	.....	125.2	.....
1997:													
January	155.2	173.5	180.8	164.4	.....	179.4	.....	131.2	109.3	125.3	.....	125.0	.....
February	155.6	174.0	181.3	164.7	.....	179.9	.....	131.7	106.3	126.4	.....	125.1	.....
March	155.7	174.3	181.7	165.1	.....	180.2	.....	131.0	103.2	125.2	.....	125.1	.....
April	155.9	174.8	182.2	165.6	.....	180.7	.....	130.2	100.9	123.8	.....	125.3	.....
May	156.1	175.3	182.7	166.0	.....	181.2	.....	129.6	100.1	122.6	.....	125.6	.....
June	156.5	175.7	183.1	166.5	.....	181.6	.....	130.4	99.1	123.8	.....	125.6	.....
July	156.8	176.2	183.6	166.8	.....	182.2	.....	130.5	97.3	123.9	.....	125.5	.....
August	156.9	176.7	184.1	167.3	.....	182.7	.....	130.0	96.6	123.0	.....	125.1	.....
September	157.3	177.0	184.5	167.7	.....	183.0	.....	130.7	96.1	124.2	.....	125.2	.....
October	157.7	177.5	185.0	168.1	.....	183.3	.....	131.0	96.4	124.4	.....	125.3	.....
November	158.2	178.0	185.5	168.6	.....	183.9	.....	131.8	96.3	125.8	.....	125.4	.....
December	158.3	178.7	186.3	169.1	100.0	184.6	100.0	130.5	95.9	123.2	100.0	125.3	100.0
1998:													
January	158.5	179.1	186.7	169.5	100.0	185.0	100.3	129.4	94.4	121.9	100.1	125.8	100.1
February	158.7	179.6	187.2	169.8	100.4	185.5	100.2	128.4	92.2	120.8	100.6	126.1	100.3
March	159.0	180.0	187.5	170.3	100.2	186.0	100.3	128.7	92.3	121.0	100.9	126.1	100.3
April	159.6	180.6	188.2	170.8	101.1	186.6	100.4	129.0	91.7	121.4	101.1	126.7	100.7
May	159.9	181.2	188.9	171.3	102.1	187.1	99.6	128.8	91.5	121.1	101.3	126.4	101.0
June	160.1	181.6	189.3	171.8	101.8	187.6	99.1	128.4	90.5	120.6	101.5	126.5	101.7
July	160.4	181.9	189.6	172.2	101.0	188.1	99.3	128.3	90.3	120.5	101.6	127.0	101.9
August	160.7	182.5	190.2	172.8	101.7	188.6	99.2	127.9	89.6	119.9	101.8	126.8	102.0
September	161.0	183.2	191.1	173.3	103.8	189.1	99.2	127.1	88.2	119.1	102.0	126.4	102.2
October	161.3	183.7	191.6	173.8	103.8	189.6	99.7	126.8	87.4	118.7	102.2	126.7	102.4
November	161.8	184.3	192.1	174.4	104.8	190.0	99.9	127.2	86.6	119.2	102.4	126.9	102.8
December	162.0	184.6	192.5	174.9	103.8	190.6	99.9	127.0	84.9	119.1	102.7	127.0	103.0

1. December 1982=100.
2. December 1997=100.

Consumer Price Indexes—*Continued*

(All urban consumers—1982–1984=100, except as noted; seasonally adjusted)

Year and month	Apparel					Transportation								
						Total	Private transportation							
	Total	Men's and boys' apparel	Women's and girls' apparel	Infants' and toddlers' apparel	Footwear		Total	New and used motor vehicles			Motor fuel		Motor vehicle parts and equipment	Motor vehicle maintenance and repair
								Total [1]	New vehicles	Used cars and trucks	Total	Gasoline (all types)		
1970	59.2	62.2	71.8	39.2	56.8	37.5	37.5	.....	53.1	31.2	27.9	27.9	.....	36.6
1971	61.1	63.9	74.4	40.0	58.6	39.5	39.4	.....	55.3	33.0	28.1	28.1	.....	39.3
1972	62.3	64.7	76.2	41.1	60.3	39.9	39.7	.....	54.8	33.1	28.4	28.4	.....	41.1
1973	64.6	67.1	78.8	42.5	62.8	41.2	41.0	.....	54.8	35.2	31.2	31.2	.....	43.2
1974	69.4	72.4	83.5	54.2	66.6	45.8	46.2	.....	58.0	36.7	42.2	42.2	.....	47.6
1975	72.5	75.5	85.5	64.5	69.6	50.1	50.6	.....	63.0	43.8	45.1	45.1	.....	53.7
1976	75.2	78.1	87.9	68.0	72.3	55.1	55.6	.....	67.0	50.3	47.0	47.0	.....	57.6
1977	78.6	81.7	90.6	74.6	75.7	59.0	59.7	.....	70.5	54.7	49.7	49.7	.....	61.9
1978	81.4	83.5	92.4	77.4	79.0	61.7	62.5	.....	75.9	55.8	51.8	51.8	77.6	67.0
1979	84.9	85.4	94.0	79.0	85.3	70.5	71.7	.....	81.9	60.2	70.1	70.2	85.1	73.7
1980	90.9	89.4	96.0	85.5	91.8	83.1	84.2	.....	88.5	62.3	97.4	97.5	95.3	81.5
1981	95.3	94.2	97.5	92.9	96.7	93.2	93.8	.....	93.9	76.9	108.5	108.5	101.0	89.2
1982	97.8	97.6	98.5	96.3	99.1	97.0	97.1	.....	97.5	88.8	102.8	102.8	103.6	96.0
1983	100.2	100.3	100.2	101.1	99.8	99.3	99.3	.....	99.9	98.7	99.4	99.4	100.7	100.3
1984	102.1	102.1	101.3	102.6	101.1	103.7	103.6	.....	102.6	112.5	97.9	97.8	95.6	103.8
1985	105.0	105.0	104.9	107.2	102.3	106.4	106.2	.....	106.1	113.7	98.7	98.6	95.9	106.8
1986	105.9	106.2	104.0	111.8	101.9	102.3	101.2	.....	110.6	108.8	77.1	77.0	95.4	110.3
1987	110.6	109.1	110.4	112.1	105.1	105.4	104.2	.....	114.4	113.1	80.2	80.1	96.1	114.8
1988	115.4	113.4	114.9	116.4	109.9	108.7	107.6	.....	116.5	118.0	80.9	80.8	97.9	119.7
1989	118.6	117.0	116.4	119.1	114.4	114.1	112.9	.....	119.2	120.4	88.5	88.5	100.2	124.9
1990	124.1	120.4	122.6	125.8	117.4	120.5	118.8	.....	121.4	117.6	101.2	101.0	100.9	130.1
1991	128.7	124.2	127.6	128.9	120.9	123.8	121.9	.....	126.0	118.1	99.4	99.2	102.2	136.0
1992	131.9	126.5	130.4	129.3	125.0	126.5	124.6	.....	129.2	123.2	99.0	99.0	103.1	141.3
1993	133.7	127.5	132.6	127.1	125.9	130.4	127.5	91.8	132.7	133.9	98.0	97.7	101.6	145.9
1994	133.4	126.4	130.9	128.1	126.0	134.3	131.4	95.5	137.6	141.7	98.5	98.2	101.4	150.2
1995	132.0	126.2	126.9	127.2	125.4	139.1	136.3	99.4	141.0	156.5	100.0	99.8	102.1	154.0
1996	131.7	127.7	124.7	129.7	126.6	143.0	140.0	101.0	143.7	157.0	106.3	105.9	102.2	158.4
1997	132.9	130.1	126.1	129.0	127.6	144.3	141.0	100.5	144.3	151.1	106.2	105.8	101.9	162.7
1998	133.0	131.8	126.0	126.1	128.0	141.6	137.9	100.1	143.4	150.6	92.2	91.6	101.1	167.1
1995:														
January	132.2	126.4	127.4	129.0	125.4	137.5	135.3	98.6	139.8	152.4	100.9	100.9	101.4	152.1
February	131.9	126.6	126.7	126.8	125.4	138.0	135.6	98.8	139.9	153.3	101.1	100.9	101.7	152.4
March	132.2	126.1	127.3	127.1	125.5	138.5	135.9	99.0	140.0	154.8	100.5	100.3	101.9	152.7
April	132.0	125.9	126.8	127.1	125.6	139.3	136.6	99.6	140.6	156.7	100.8	100.6	102.0	153.2
May	131.6	126.4	126.7	123.6	125.0	139.9	137.2	99.9	140.9	157.7	102.5	102.3	102.2	153.8
June	131.3	126.2	125.8	121.6	124.5	140.6	137.5	100.1	141.1	158.3	103.0	103.1	102.3	153.8
July	131.4	125.8	126.4	123.0	124.7	140.0	136.9	100.0	141.0	157.5	101.3	101.2	102.3	154.2
August	132.4	126.0	127.6	128.0	125.1	139.5	136.7	99.9	141.1	157.0	99.8	99.6	102.4	154.6
September	132.3	126.4	126.3	131.2	126.9	139.2	136.5	100.0	141.4	156.5	98.4	98.3	102.3	154.9
October	132.4	126.5	127.5	131.0	125.9	139.5	136.6	100.3	141.7	157.2	97.9	97.6	102.4	155.2
November	132.0	126.1	126.8	129.7	125.7	139.2	136.3	100.6	142.0	157.8	95.9	95.6	102.3	155.6
December	132.2	126.4	126.9	128.7	125.1	139.1	136.8	100.7	142.1	158.2	97.6	97.3	102.2	155.7
1996:														
January	132.7	127.0	127.6	131.5	124.8	140.0	137.7	100.7	142.3	157.9	100.6	100.4	102.3	156.2
February	132.0	127.5	125.4	134.4	126.4	140.8	138.1	100.9	142.7	157.5	101.1	100.9	102.2	156.5
March	132.6	127.9	125.7	133.3	127.9	141.7	138.9	100.9	142.8	157.3	104.6	104.4	102.3	156.9
April	132.0	127.9	124.9	133.7	126.6	143.3	140.6	101.0	142.9	157.4	110.0	109.7	102.3	157.2
May	131.9	127.8	124.7	130.4	126.8	144.0	141.3	101.2	143.2	157.6	111.7	111.2	102.2	157.6
June	131.5	127.9	124.0	129.1	127.1	143.5	140.7	101.4	143.6	157.2	108.1	107.8	102.5	157.9
July	131.3	127.5	123.7	125.7	127.1	143.4	140.5	101.5	143.9	156.9	106.8	106.5	102.0	158.3
August	130.4	127.7	122.4	125.1	126.2	143.1	140.3	101.6	144.1	156.6	105.1	104.7	102.0	158.7
September	131.2	127.0	123.5	131.4	126.8	143.7	140.6	101.9	144.6	157.0	104.9	104.4	102.2	159.8
October	131.5	127.3	124.3	128.5	126.2	144.0	140.8	101.9	144.6	157.0	105.3	104.5	102.2	160.2
November	131.6	128.8	124.1	126.7	126.6	144.4	141.2	101.8	144.6	156.5	107.0	106.5	102.1	160.3
December	131.9	128.4	125.4	126.9	126.8	145.2	141.9	101.8	144.7	155.6	109.6	109.0	102.1	160.6
1997:														
January	132.2	129.3	125.4	127.9	126.5	145.1	142.1	101.6	144.6	154.7	110.5	110.0	102.2	161.1
February	132.8	128.5	126.8	127.2	127.0	145.2	142.5	101.5	144.6	154.4	111.3	110.7	102.3	161.1
March	132.3	128.0	125.9	129.7	126.9	145.4	142.2	101.5	144.6	154.4	109.9	109.3	102.1	161.5
April	133.2	130.2	126.3	133.7	127.8	145.1	141.7	101.5	144.6	154.3	107.5	107.0	102.0	162.0
May	133.3	130.2	126.7	133.8	127.7	144.0	140.7	101.4	144.4	153.9	104.0	103.4	101.9	162.3
June	133.1	129.8	126.7	132.9	126.3	143.6	140.4	101.0	144.3	151.8	103.1	102.5	101.9	162.8
July	133.2	130.5	126.3	131.3	127.3	143.7	140.2	100.8	144.4	149.9	102.1	101.5	102.4	163.1
August	132.4	130.4	125.0	127.3	127.7	144.1	141.2	100.5	144.2	148.5	106.4	106.1	101.8	163.4
September	132.9	131.1	126.0	126.7	127.5	144.7	141.7	100.4	144.1	148.2	108.2	108.0	101.7	163.3
October	133.0	131.1	125.7	126.2	128.7	144.5	141.1	100.4	144.1	147.9	105.8	105.6	101.5	163.6
November	132.9	130.6	126.1	126.0	128.0	143.5	140.4	100.2	143.8	147.6	103.6	103.2	101.4	163.8
December	133.2	131.9	125.8	125.8	129.0	143.1	140.0	100.0	143.4	147.9	102.4	101.9	101.3	164.7
1998:														
January	132.7	132.1	124.7	124.8	129.0	142.8	139.5	100.1	143.6	148.1	99.4	99.0	101.1	164.9
February	132.8	132.0	125.4	123.1	127.4	142.5	139.0	100.2	143.6	148.4	96.9	96.4	101.1	165.4
March	132.5	132.3	125.6	124.4	126.5	141.9	138.2	100.0	143.6	147.3	94.0	93.5	101.1	165.7
April	132.7	132.1	125.6	126.6	126.5	141.8	138.1	100.2	143.7	148.2	93.2	92.7	100.7	165.8
May	132.9	131.7	126.2	126.9	127.0	141.7	138.2	100.2	143.1	150.0	93.3	92.8	100.9	166.1
June	133.1	131.8	126.7	124.7	128.2	141.4	138.0	100.1	142.7	150.9	92.5	91.9	101.2	166.7
July	132.7	132.0	125.7	122.0	128.5	141.8	138.2	100.5	143.4	151.3	92.2	91.6	101.2	167.0
August	134.0	132.2	128.2	124.4	129.1	141.6	137.9	100.8	144.0	151.1	90.6	89.9	101.2	167.5
September	133.2	130.9	127.3	124.9	128.6	141.1	137.5	100.7	143.6	151.9	89.1	88.5	101.2	168.1
October	133.2	132.1	125.8	130.2	128.4	141.3	137.8	100.7	143.3	153.0	89.8	89.3	101.4	168.7
November	133.1	131.6	125.3	131.3	129.0	141.1	137.7	101.0	143.3	154.0	88.6	88.2	101.2	169.3
December	132.3	131.0	124.6	129.6	128.2	140.6	137.1	100.9	143.4	153.1	86.4	85.9	101.1	169.6

1. December 1997=100.

Consumer Price Indexes—Continued

(All urban consumers—1982–1984=100, except as noted; seasonally adjusted)

Year and month	Transportation—Continued		Medical care					Recreation		Education and communication			
					Medical care services						Education		
	Public transportation	Transportation services	Medical care	Medical Care Commodities	Total	Professional services	Hospital and related services	Total [1]	Video and audio [1]	Total [1]	Total [1]	Educational books and supplies	Tuition, other school fees, and childcare
1970	35.2	40.2	34.0	46.5	32.3	37.0	.....	.....	.....	.....	.....	38.8	.....
1971	37.8	43.4	36.1	47.3	34.7	39.4	.....	.....	.....	.....	.....	41.4	.....
1972	39.3	44.4	37.3	47.4	35.9	40.8	.....	.....	.....	.....	.....	44.2	.....
1973	39.7	44.7	38.8	47.5	37.5	42.2	.....	.....	.....	.....	.....	45.6	.....
1974	40.6	46.3	42.4	49.2	41.4	45.8	.....	.....	.....	.....	.....	47.2	.....
1975	43.5	49.8	47.5	53.3	46.6	50.8	.....	.....	.....	.....	.....	50.3	.....
1976	47.8	56.9	52.0	56.5	51.3	55.5	.....	.....	.....	.....	.....	53.7	.....
1977	50.0	61.5	57.0	60.2	56.4	60.0	.....	.....	.....	.....	.....	56.9	.....
1978	51.5	64.4	61.8	64.4	61.2	64.5	55.1	.....	.....	.....	.....	61.6	59.8
1979	54.9	69.5	67.5	69.0	67.2	70.1	61.0	.....	.....	.....	.....	65.7	64.7
1980	69.0	79.2	74.9	75.4	74.8	77.9	69.2	.....	.....	.....	.....	71.4	71.2
1981	85.6	88.6	82.9	83.7	82.8	85.9	79.1	.....	.....	.....	.....	80.3	79.9
1982	94.9	96.1	92.5	92.3	92.6	93.2	90.3	.....	.....	.....	.....	91.0	90.5
1983	99.5	99.1	100.6	100.2	100.7	99.8	100.5	.....	.....	.....	.....	100.3	99.7
1984	105.7	104.8	106.8	107.5	106.7	107.0	109.2	.....	.....	.....	.....	108.7	109.8
1985	110.5	110.0	113.5	115.2	113.2	113.5	116.1	.....	.....	.....	.....	118.2	119.7
1986	117.0	116.3	122.0	122.8	121.9	120.8	123.1	.....	.....	.....	.....	128.1	129.6
1987	121.1	121.9	130.1	131.0	130.0	128.8	131.6	.....	.....	.....	.....	138.1	140.0
1988	123.3	128.0	138.6	139.9	138.3	137.5	143.9	.....	.....	.....	.....	148.1	151.0
1989	129.5	135.6	149.3	150.8	148.9	146.4	160.5	.....	.....	.....	.....	158.0	162.7
1990	142.6	144.2	162.8	163.4	162.7	156.1	178.0	.....	.....	.....	.....	171.3	175.7
1991	148.9	151.2	177.0	176.8	177.1	165.7	196.1	.....	.....	.....	.....	180.3	191.4
1992	151.4	155.7	190.1	188.1	190.5	175.8	214.0	.....	.....	.....	.....	190.3	208.5
1993	167.0	162.9	201.4	195.0	202.9	184.7	231.9	90.7	96.5	85.5	78.4	197.6	225.3
1994	172.0	168.6	211.0	200.7	213.4	192.5	245.6	92.7	95.4	88.8	83.3	205.5	239.8
1995	175.9	175.9	220.5	204.5	224.2	201.0	257.8	94.5	95.1	92.2	88.0	214.4	253.8
1996	181.9	180.5	228.2	210.4	232.4	208.3	269.5	97.4	96.6	95.3	92.7	226.9	267.1
1997	186.7	185.0	234.6	215.3	239.1	215.4	278.4	99.6	99.4	98.4	97.3	238.4	280.4
1998	190.3	187.9	242.1	221.8	246.8	222.2	287.5	101.1	101.1	100.3	102.1	250.8	294.2
1995:													
January	168.4	172.1	216.8	203.3	219.7	197.4	252.6	93.5	95.0	91.3	86.2	210.2	247.2
February	169.9	172.8	217.6	203.2	220.7	198.2	253.5	93.7	95.0	91.5	86.8	211.0	249.1
March	174.5	174.6	218.3	203.3	221.5	198.7	254.3	93.8	94.9	91.6	87.2	211.7	250.2
April	176.7	175.9	218.9	203.3	222.2	199.2	255.3	94.2	95.3	91.8	87.5	212.4	251.0
May	176.7	176.0	219.5	203.3	223.0	199.9	256.1	94.4	95.8	92.0	87.8	212.9	252.0
June	182.5	177.2	220.1	203.6	223.7	200.6	256.8	94.1	95.0	92.3	88.1	213.8	253.0
July	181.8	176.9	220.9	204.1	224.5	201.4	257.7	94.2	94.9	92.5	88.5	214.3	254.2
August	177.1	176.5	221.8	204.7	225.5	202.0	259.4	94.5	94.9	92.9	89.2	214.1	256.2
September	176.1	176.6	222.6	205.1	226.4	202.6	260.6	94.9	95.0	93.1	89.4	216.2	256.7
October	178.7	177.6	223.2	205.9	227.0	203.2	261.4	95.0	94.9	93.3	89.8	217.5	257.7
November	177.5	177.5	224.0	206.8	227.7	203.8	262.3	95.5	95.0	93.5	90.2	218.9	258.9
December	170.7	175.9	224.6	207.1	228.4	204.6	263.2	95.6	95.1	93.9	90.6	220.0	260.0
1996:													
January	171.6	176.2	225.4	207.9	229.2	205.2	264.4	96.0	94.9	94.1	91.0	222.0	261.0
February	177.4	178.0	225.9	208.3	229.7	205.8	265.2	96.7	95.3	94.4	91.4	223.1	262.3
March	178.9	178.0	226.4	208.6	230.3	206.1	266.1	96.8	95.5	94.8	91.9	224.2	263.5
April	179.3	178.8	227.0	209.2	230.9	206.7	267.0	96.9	95.8	94.6	92.3	225.1	264.8
May	180.2	179.4	227.6	209.5	231.5	207.3	268.1	97.0	96.0	95.2	92.6	225.4	265.7
June	182.2	180.3	228.2	210.2	232.1	207.7	269.6	97.2	96.4	95.6	93.0	225.8	266.8
July	182.7	180.8	228.9	210.6	232.9	208.5	270.4	97.3	97.3	95.8	93.3	226.3	267.9
August	181.4	181.0	229.3	211.1	233.3	209.2	271.1	97.4	97.2	96.1	93.8	228.7	269.1
September	184.6	182.3	229.9	211.6	233.9	209.8	272.0	97.7	97.4	96.3	93.9	229.3	269.4
October	187.2	183.0	230.5	212.7	234.3	210.5	272.5	98.0	97.8	96.6	94.3	230.3	270.6
November	187.3	183.2	231.1	212.5	235.2	211.4	273.2	98.3	97.9	96.8	94.7	231.0	271.7
December	189.9	183.8	231.5	212.5	235.6	211.7	274.1	98.4	98.2	97.1	95.1	232.1	272.8
1997:													
January	185.8	182.9	232.1	213.0	236.2	212.4	274.9	98.7	98.4	97.4	95.5	232.6	274.0
February	182.4	182.8	232.4	213.7	236.5	212.9	275.4	99.0	98.6	97.7	95.9	233.6	275.2
March	188.1	184.5	233.2	214.4	237.3	213.8	276.2	99.2	98.7	97.9	96.3	234.4	276.2
April	189.8	185.2	233.7	214.8	237.8	214.3	277.0	99.2	97.9	98.1	96.6	235.3	277.1
May	188.1	184.9	234.3	215.3	238.4	214.8	277.8	99.3	98.8	98.4	97.1	236.6	278.6
June	186.6	185.0	234.7	215.5	238.9	215.3	278.4	99.6	99.5	98.7	97.5	238.5	279.6
July	189.4	186.0	235.0	215.6	239.2	215.7	278.1	99.6	99.8	99.0	97.9	239.4	280.8
August	183.4	184.8	235.4	215.5	239.7	216.3	278.9	99.8	99.9	98.9	98.4	241.1	282.2
September	186.0	185.5	235.9	215.7	240.3	216.6	279.8	99.9	100.1	99.2	98.8	241.0	283.3
October	190.9	186.8	236.3	216.0	240.7	217.1	280.4	99.9	100.2	99.5	99.2	242.1	284.6
November	185.9	185.6	237.0	216.5	241.5	217.6	281.4	100.0	100.6	99.8	99.6	242.6	285.7
December	184.3	185.6	237.9	217.3	242.4	218.2	282.8	100.0	100.5	100.0	100.0	243.7	286.9
1998:													
January	187.1	186.7	238.3	217.8	242.8	218.7	282.7	100.2	100.9	100.0	100.4	243.2	288.1
February	191.2	187.7	239.0	218.2	243.6	219.3	284.0	100.4	100.8	99.9	100.8	245.1	289.2
March	193.7	188.4	239.7	218.3	244.4	220.0	284.7	100.7	100.9	100.2	101.2	246.5	290.4
April	193.4	188.3	240.5	219.7	245.1	220.7	285.6	100.8	100.9	100.4	101.7	248.3	291.7
May	190.4	187.8	241.4	221.1	245.8	221.3	286.1	100.8	101.1	100.7	102.2	249.6	293.3
June	188.2	187.4	242.1	221.5	246.6	222.3	286.8	101.0	101.1	100.8	102.5	249.9	294.0
July	192.0	188.2	242.7	221.8	247.3	222.6	288.2	100.9	101.0	100.9	102.8	250.9	295.0
August	192.2	188.3	243.7	223.1	248.1	223.3	289.4	101.1	101.1	100.4	103.1	250.3	296.0
September	190.2	187.8	244.4	224.4	248.7	223.9	289.6	101.2	101.6	100.5	103.5	253.3	296.7
October	189.9	187.9	244.9	224.6	249.2	224.5	290.4	101.0	101.4	100.6	103.8	256.6	297.6
November	187.4	187.8	245.4	225.3	249.7	224.9	291.0	101.1	101.1	100.9	104.3	257.2	298.8
December	188.4	188.1	246.1	226.1	250.3	225.4	291.7	101.2	101.3	100.7	104.7	258.2	300.0

1. December 1997=100.

Consumer Price Indexes—*Continued*

(All urban consumers—1982–1984=100, except as noted; seasonally adjusted)

Year and month	Education and communication—*Continued*					Other goods and services				
	Communication					Total	Tobacco and smoking products	Personal care		
	Information and information processing									
	Total [1]	Total [1]	Telephone services [1]	Information and information processing other than telephone services				Total	Personal care products	Personal care services
				Total [2]	Personal computers and peripheral equipment [1]					
1970	.....	.....	.....	.....	.....	40.9	43.1	43.5	42.7	44.2
1971	.....	.....	.....	.....	.....	42.9	44.9	44.9	44.0	45.7
1972	.....	.....	.....	.....	.....	44.7	47.4	46.0	45.2	46.8
1973	.....	.....	.....	.....	.....	46.4	48.7	48.1	46.4	49.7
1974	.....	.....	.....	.....	.....	49.8	51.1	52.8	51.5	53.9
1975	.....	.....	.....	.....	.....	53.9	54.7	57.9	58.0	57.7
1976	.....	.....	.....	.....	.....	57.0	57.0	61.7	61.3	61.9
1977	.....	.....	.....	.....	.....	60.4	59.8	65.7	64.7	66.4
1978	.....	.....	.....	.....	.....	64.3	63.0	69.9	68.2	71.3
1979	.....	.....	.....	.....	.....	68.9	66.8	75.2	72.9	77.2
1980	.....	.....	.....	.....	.....	75.2	72.0	81.9	79.6	83.7
1981	.....	.....	.....	.....	.....	82.6	77.8	89.1	87.8	90.2
1982	.....	.....	.....	.....	.....	91.1	86.5	95.4	95.1	95.7
1983	.....	.....	.....	.....	.....	101.1	103.4	100.3	100.7	100.0
1984	.....	.....	.....	.....	.....	107.9	110.1	104.3	104.2	104.4
1985	.....	.....	.....	.....	.....	114.5	116.7	108.3	107.6	108.9
1986	.....	.....	.....	.....	.....	121.4	124.7	111.9	111.3	112.5
1987	.....	.....	.....	.....	.....	128.5	133.6	115.1	113.9	116.2
1988	.....	.....	.....	.....	.....	137.0	145.8	119.4	118.1	120.7
1989	.....	.....	.....	96.3	.....	147.7	164.4	125.0	123.2	126.8
1990	.....	.....	.....	93.5	.....	159.0	181.5	130.4	128.2	132.8
1991	.....	.....	.....	88.6	.....	171.6	202.7	134.9	132.8	137.0
1992	.....	.....	.....	83.7	.....	183.3	219.8	138.3	136.5	140.0
1993	96.7	97.7	.....	78.8	.....	192.9	228.4	141.5	139.0	144.0
1994	97.6	98.6	.....	72.0	.....	198.5	220.0	144.6	141.5	147.9
1995	98.8	98.7	.....	63.8	.....	206.9	225.7	147.1	143.1	151.5
1996	99.6	99.5	.....	57.2	.....	215.4	232.8	150.1	144.3	156.6
1997	100.3	100.4	.....	50.1	.....	224.8	243.7	152.7	144.2	162.4
1998	98.7	98.5	100.7	39.9	78.2	237.7	274.8	156.7	148.3	166.0
1995:										
January	99.5	99.4	.....	66.5	.....	203.3	221.9	145.7	142.2	149.4
February	98.8	98.7	.....	66.1	.....	204.6	222.5	146.2	142.6	150.1
March	98.6	98.3	.....	64.2	.....	205.0	222.7	146.0	142.2	150.2
April	98.6	98.4	.....	64.0	.....	205.4	222.9	146.3	142.2	150.7
May	98.6	98.3	.....	64.7	.....	206.2	224.1	146.6	142.9	150.6
June	98.9	98.7	.....	64.6	.....	207.2	226.7	146.7	142.8	151.0
July	98.8	98.7	.....	63.7	.....	207.7	226.3	146.9	142.7	151.4
August	98.8	98.6	.....	63.7	.....	208.8	227.6	147.3	143.2	151.7
September	98.9	98.7	.....	63.5	.....	209.7	228.3	147.5	143.0	152.4
October	98.9	98.7	.....	62.5	.....	210.3	227.9	148.5	144.4	153.0
November	98.7	98.6	.....	61.4	.....	211.2	228.8	148.9	144.8	153.5
December	99.0	98.9	.....	61.0	.....	211.7	228.8	148.9	144.1	154.3
1996:										
January	99.0	98.9	.....	60.7	.....	212.4	229.1	149.1	143.7	155.0
February	99.1	99.0	.....	61.0	.....	213.2	229.8	149.3	144.1	155.2
March	99.5	99.4	.....	60.4	.....	213.9	231.2	149.4	144.0	155.3
April	98.1	97.9	.....	58.9	.....	214.4	230.2	149.7	144.2	155.7
May	99.3	99.2	.....	58.0	.....	215.4	231.9	150.3	145.3	155.8
June	99.8	99.7	.....	58.2	.....	216.0	233.5	149.6	143.9	155.9
July	99.7	99.7	.....	55.8	.....	216.6	233.5	150.0	144.4	156.3
August	99.9	99.8	.....	55.0	.....	217.3	233.8	150.5	145.0	156.5
September	100.0	100.0	.....	55.3	.....	217.8	234.2	150.8	145.1	157.2
October	100.2	100.2	.....	55.2	.....	218.3	234.9	150.9	144.6	157.9
November	100.2	100.2	.....	54.4	.....	219.2	235.7	151.2	144.7	158.6
December	100.3	100.3	.....	53.9	.....	219.4	235.0	150.5	142.8	159.2
1997:										
January	100.5	100.5	.....	53.5	.....	220.5	236.2	151.6	143.6	160.7
February	100.5	100.6	.....	53.2	.....	221.3	237.5	151.5	143.3	160.7
March	100.6	100.7	.....	52.4	.....	222.4	238.7	151.8	143.6	161.2
April	100.6	100.6	.....	51.4	.....	223.8	242.6	152.7	144.5	162.0
May	100.6	100.6	.....	50.8	.....	224.5	242.7	152.6	144.1	162.3
June	100.7	100.8	.....	49.9	.....	225.1	242.2	152.8	144.2	162.6
July	100.6	100.7	.....	49.1	.....	225.6	242.2	152.6	143.7	162.5
August	99.8	99.8	.....	48.2	.....	226.8	244.1	152.5	143.5	162.7
September	99.8	99.8	.....	48.5	.....	227.6	246.7	152.7	143.7	162.8
October	100.0	100.0	.....	48.9	.....	228.9	249.4	153.3	144.5	163.4
November	100.1	100.1	.....	47.6	.....	229.8	249.9	154.3	146.1	163.5
December	100.0	100.0	100.0	47.4	100.0	230.8	251.8	154.0	145.3	163.9
1998:										
January	99.6	99.6	99.9	46.2	96.9	231.8	253.5	154.6	146.1	164.3
February	99.2	99.1	100.0	44.3	91.3	233.7	261.4	155.0	146.7	164.3
March	99.3	99.3	100.4	43.4	88.7	233.1	254.8	155.5	147.3	164.7
April	99.3	99.2	100.5	42.8	86.6	235.1	262.6	155.9	147.3	165.2
May	99.4	99.3	101.1	41.5	82.7	237.0	268.8	156.6	149.3	165.4
June	99.4	99.3	101.4	40.6	80.0	237.2	268.2	156.8	149.2	165.3
July	99.1	99.0	101.5	39.1	75.2	238.4	273.5	157.0	149.1	166.1
August	97.9	97.7	100.4	37.6	71.1	238.8	274.8	157.1	148.5	166.6
September	97.9	97.7	100.7	36.7	68.5	241.0	283.8	157.5	149.1	167.1
October	97.8	97.6	100.7	36.1	67.5	241.7	283.7	158.1	149.4	167.5
November	97.8	97.6	101.1	35.3	65.6	240.9	280.2	158.0	148.8	167.6
December	97.1	96.9	100.3	34.8	64.2	251.0	331.9	158.3	148.7	168.3

1. December 1997=100.
2. December 1988=100.

Consumer Price Indexes—Continued

(All urban consumers, except as noted—1982–1984=100, except as noted; seasonally adjusted)

Year and month	Commodities Total	Commodities less food and beverages Total	Commodities less food and beverages Durables	Non-durables	Services	Energy	All items less: Food	All items less: Energy	All items less: Food and energy	CPI-U-X1 [1]	CPI-U-RS [2]	Consumer Price Index, Urban wage earners and clerical workers (CPI-W)
1970	41.7	43.1	44.1	40.8	35.0	25.5	39.0	40.3	40.8	41.3	.....	39.0
1971	43.2	44.7	46.0	42.1	37.0	26.5	40.8	42.0	42.7	43.1	.....	40.7
1972	44.5	45.8	46.9	43.5	38.4	27.2	42.0	43.4	44.0	44.4	.....	42.1
1973	47.8	47.3	48.1	47.5	40.1	29.4	43.7	46.1	45.6	47.2	.....	44.7
1974	53.5	52.4	51.5	54.0	43.8	38.1	48.0	50.6	49.4	51.9	.....	49.6
1975	58.2	57.3	57.4	58.3	48.0	42.1	52.5	55.1	53.9	56.2	.....	54.1
1976	60.7	60.2	60.9	60.5	52.0	45.1	56.0	58.2	57.4	59.4	.....	57.2
1977	64.2	63.6	64.4	64.0	56.0	49.4	59.6	61.9	61.0	63.2	.....	60.9
1978	68.8	67.3	68.6	68.6	60.8	52.5	63.9	66.7	65.5	67.5	104.4	65.6
1979	76.6	75.2	75.4	77.2	67.5	65.7	71.2	73.4	71.9	74.0	114.2	73.1
1980	86.0	85.7	83.0	87.6	77.9	86.0	81.5	81.9	80.8	82.3	126.9	82.9
1981	93.2	93.1	89.6	95.2	88.1	97.7	90.4	90.1	89.2	90.1	138.8	91.4
1982	97.0	96.9	95.1	97.8	96.0	99.2	96.3	96.1	95.8	95.6	147.1	96.9
1983	99.8	100.0	99.8	99.7	99.4	99.9	99.7	99.6	99.6	99.6	153.2	99.8
1984	103.2	103.1	105.1	102.5	104.6	100.9	104.0	104.3	104.6	103.9	159.4	103.3
1985	105.4	105.2	106.8	104.8	109.9	101.6	108.0	108.4	109.1	107.6	164.8	106.9
1986	104.4	101.4	106.6	103.5	115.4	88.2	109.8	112.6	113.5	109.6	167.8	108.6
1987	107.7	104.0	108.2	107.5	120.2	88.6	113.6	117.2	118.2	113.6	173.6	112.5
1988	111.5	107.3	110.4	111.8	125.7	89.3	118.3	122.3	123.4	118.3	179.9	117.0
1989	116.7	111.6	112.2	118.2	131.9	94.3	123.7	128.1	129.0	124.0	187.7	122.6
1990	122.8	117.0	113.4	126.0	139.2	102.1	130.3	134.7	135.5	130.7	197.1	129.0
1991	126.6	120.4	116.0	130.3	146.3	102.5	136.1	140.9	142.1	136.2	204.4	134.3
1992	129.1	123.2	118.6	132.8	152.0	103.0	140.8	145.4	147.3	140.3	209.7	138.2
1993	131.5	125.3	121.3	135.1	157.9	104.2	145.1	150.0	152.2	144.5	215.1	142.1
1994	133.8	126.9	124.8	136.8	163.1	104.6	149.0	154.1	156.5	148.2	219.8	145.6
1995	136.4	128.9	128.0	139.3	168.7	105.2	153.1	158.7	161.2	152.4	225.7	149.8
1996	139.9	131.5	129.4	143.5	174.1	110.1	157.5	163.1	165.6	156.9	231.8	154.1
1997	141.8	132.2	128.7	146.4	179.4	111.5	161.1	167.1	169.5	160.5	236.9	157.6
1998	141.9	130.5	127.6	146.9	184.2	102.9	163.4	170.9	173.4	163.0	240.1	159.7
1995:												
January	135.4	128.2	127.0	138.3	166.1	105.3	151.2	156.7	159.2	150.3	222.8	148.0
February	135.7	128.3	127.4	138.5	166.6	105.5	151.5	157.1	159.6	150.9	223.5	148.4
March	135.6	128.4	127.6	138.5	167.2	105.2	151.9	157.5	160.1	151.4	224.2	148.7
April	136.2	128.6	127.8	138.9	167.7	105.2	152.4	158.1	160.6	151.9	224.9	149.2
May	136.5	129.0	128.0	139.2	168.1	105.7	152.7	158.4	160.9	152.2	225.4	149.5
June	136.6	129.2	127.9	139.6	168.6	106.2	153.1	158.7	161.3	152.5	225.9	149.8
July	136.6	129.0	128.0	139.6	168.9	105.4	153.3	159.0	161.6	152.5	226.0	149.9
August	136.8	129.2	128.2	139.7	169.4	105.3	153.6	159.4	162.0	152.9	226.4	150.2
September	136.9	129.1	128.4	139.8	169.7	103.8	153.8	159.8	162.4	153.2	226.8	150.5
October	137.1	129.3	128.5	139.9	170.4	104.0	154.2	160.3	162.9	153.7	227.4	150.9
November	137.0	129.0	128.6	139.9	170.7	103.0	154.4	160.5	163.2	153.6	227.3	150.9
December	137.4	129.4	128.7	140.2	170.9	103.9	154.6	160.7	163.4	153.5	227.2	151.3
1996:												
January	138.1	130.3	129.0	141.2	171.5	106.0	155.3	161.2	163.8	154.4	228.2	151.9
February	138.3	130.3	129.1	141.3	172.1	106.6	155.7	161.6	164.2	154.9	229.1	152.3
March	139.0	131.2	129.3	142.4	172.5	108.2	156.3	162.0	164.7	155.7	230.2	152.9
April	139.7	132.0	129.2	143.1	173.0	111.4	156.9	162.4	164.9	156.3	231.0	153.5
May	139.9	132.2	129.2	143.5	173.5	112.2	157.3	162.6	165.3	156.6	231.6	153.9
June	139.9	131.6	129.2	143.6	173.8	110.0	157.3	163.1	165.6	156.7	231.7	154.0
July	139.9	131.4	129.3	143.8	174.5	109.9	157.7	163.5	166.0	157.0	232.1	154.3
August	139.9	131.1	129.4	143.6	174.9	109.4	157.8	163.8	166.2	157.3	232.3	154.5
September	140.4	131.5	129.8	144.0	175.4	109.5	158.2	164.3	166.7	157.8	233.1	155.0
October	140.9	131.8	129.6	144.6	175.8	110.0	158.6	164.8	167.1	158.3	233.8	155.4
November	141.3	132.1	129.5	145.3	176.3	110.9	159.0	165.2	167.4	158.6	234.2	155.9
December	141.7	132.6	129.7	145.7	176.7	112.7	159.4	165.4	167.7	158.6	234.3	156.2
1997:												
January	141.7	132.8	129.4	146.0	177.2	114.1	159.9	165.6	167.9	159.1	235.0	156.5
February	142.1	133.1	129.5	146.2	177.7	114.8	160.2	166.0	168.3	159.6	235.6	156.9
March	141.8	132.8	129.6	146.1	178.2	113.4	160.4	166.3	168.7	160.0	236.1	157.0
April	141.8	132.7	129.3	145.8	178.5	111.5	160.6	166.7	169.2	160.2	236.4	157.1
May	141.6	132.2	129.3	145.7	178.8	109.3	160.6	166.9	169.5	160.1	236.3	157.1
June	141.5	131.8	129.0	145.8	179.3	109.4	160.8	167.2	169.7	160.3	236.7	157.3
July	141.4	131.6	128.5	146.1	179.8	108.8	161.0	167.5	170.0	160.5	236.8	157.5
August	141.9	131.9	128.2	146.6	179.9	110.4	161.2	167.6	170.0	160.8	237.2	157.8
September	142.2	132.4	128.2	147.1	180.4	111.8	161.7	167.9	170.4	161.2	238.0	158.2
October	142.2	132.1	128.1	146.9	181.0	110.8	161.9	168.3	170.8	161.6	238.4	158.4
November	142.1	131.8	127.9	147.0	181.4	110.3	162.1	168.6	171.0	161.5	238.3	158.5
December	142.0	131.6	127.8	146.9	181.7	108.6	162.2	168.9	171.4	161.3	237.9	158.6
1998:												
January	142.0	131.2	127.9	146.6	182.0	106.6	162.2	169.3	171.7	161.6	238.3	158.7
February	141.8	131.0	127.8	146.4	182.4	104.8	162.4	169.6	172.2	161.9	238.6	158.7
March	141.4	130.4	127.7	146.1	182.9	103.6	162.5	169.8	172.4	162.2	239.0	158.7
April	141.6	130.7	127.8	145.9	183.4	103.4	162.9	170.3	172.9	162.5	239.5	159.1
May	141.9	130.8	127.5	146.8	183.8	103.3	163.2	170.7	173.3	162.8	239.9	159.4
June	141.8	130.6	127.4	147.0	184.1	102.7	163.3	170.9	173.5	163.0	240.0	159.5
July	142.0	130.7	127.7	147.1	184.5	102.5	163.5	171.2	173.8	163.2	240.3	159.8
August	142.2	130.7	127.7	147.3	184.8	101.5	163.7	171.6	174.2	163.4	240.6	160.0
September	142.0	130.4	127.4	147.1	185.2	100.3	163.9	171.9	174.5	163.6	240.9	160.1
October	142.3	130.5	127.2	147.6	185.5	100.4	164.1	172.2	174.8	164.0	241.4	160.4
November	142.2	130.2	127.4	147.5	186.0	100.1	164.3	172.5	175.0	164.0	241.4	160.7
December	142.5	130.5	127.2	147.8	186.3	99.0	164.6	173.0	175.6	163.9	241.2	161.0

1. See Notes for definition.
2. December 1977=100; see Notes for more information.

Producer Price Indexes

(Seasonally adjusted, 1982=100)

Year and month	Finished goods		Finished consumer goods				Finished consumer goods, except foods			Capital equipment		
	Total	Percent change from previous period	Total	Finished consumer foods			Total	Nondurable goods less foods	Durable goods	Total	Manu-facturing industries	Nonmanu-facturing industries
				Total	Crude	Processed						
1970	39.3	3.4	39.1	43.8	46.0	43.9	37.4	32.5	47.2	40.1	38.1	41.3
1971	40.5	3.1	40.2	44.5	45.8	44.7	38.7	33.5	48.9	41.7	39.6	43.0
1972	41.8	3.2	41.5	46.9	48.0	47.2	39.4	34.1	50.0	42.8	40.5	44.2
1973	45.6	9.1	46.0	56.5	63.6	55.8	41.2	36.1	50.9	44.2	42.2	45.3
1974	52.6	15.4	53.1	64.4	71.6	63.9	48.2	44.0	55.5	50.5	48.8	51.2
1975	58.2	10.6	58.2	69.8	71.7	70.3	53.2	48.9	61.0	58.2	56.5	58.9
1976	60.8	4.5	60.4	69.6	76.7	69.0	56.5	52.4	63.7	62.1	60.3	62.9
1977	64.7	6.4	64.3	73.3	79.5	72.7	60.6	56.8	67.4	66.1	64.5	66.8
1978	69.8	7.9	69.4	79.9	85.8	79.4	64.9	60.0	73.6	71.3	70.1	71.8
1979	77.6	11.2	77.5	87.3	92.3	86.8	73.5	69.3	80.8	77.5	77.1	77.7
1980	88.0	13.4	88.6	92.4	93.9	92.3	87.1	85.1	91.0	85.8	86.0	85.7
1981	96.1	9.2	96.6	97.8	104.4	97.2	96.1	95.8	96.4	94.6	94.9	94.4
1982	100.0	4.1	100.0	100.0	100.0	100.0	100.0	100.0	100.0	100.0	100.0	100.0
1983	101.6	1.6	101.3	101.0	102.4	100.9	101.2	100.5	102.8	102.8	102.3	103.0
1984	103.7	2.1	103.3	105.4	111.4	104.9	102.2	101.1	104.5	105.2	104.9	105.4
1985	104.7	1.0	103.8	104.6	102.9	104.8	103.3	101.7	106.5	107.5	107.4	107.6
1986	103.2	-1.4	101.4	107.3	105.6	107.4	98.5	93.3	108.9	109.7	109.7	109.7
1987	105.4	2.1	103.6	109.5	107.1	109.6	100.7	94.9	111.5	111.7	111.8	111.6
1988	108.0	2.5	106.2	112.6	109.8	112.7	103.1	97.3	113.8	114.3	115.5	113.9
1989	113.6	5.2	112.1	118.7	119.6	118.6	108.9	103.8	117.6	118.8	120.3	118.2
1990	119.2	4.9	118.2	124.4	123.0	124.4	115.3	111.5	120.4	122.9	124.5	122.2
1991	121.7	2.1	120.5	124.1	119.3	124.4	118.7	115.0	123.9	126.7	127.8	126.3
1992	123.2	1.2	121.7	123.3	107.6	124.4	120.8	117.3	125.7	129.1	129.3	129.0
1993	124.7	1.2	123.0	125.7	114.4	126.5	121.7	117.6	128.0	131.4	131.2	131.4
1994	125.5	0.6	123.3	126.8	111.3	127.9	121.6	116.2	130.9	134.1	133.2	134.3
1995	127.9	1.9	125.6	129.0	118.8	129.8	124.0	118.8	132.7	136.7	135.8	137.0
1996	131.3	2.7	129.5	133.6	129.2	133.8	127.6	123.3	134.2	138.3	137.2	138.6
1997	131.8	0.4	130.2	134.5	126.6	135.1	128.2	124.3	133.7	138.2	137.7	138.4
1998	130.7	-0.8	128.9	134.3	127.2	134.8	126.4	122.2	132.9	137.6	137.9	137.4
1995:												
January	126.9	0.2	124.7	128.3	121.8	128.8	122.9	117.6	132.0	135.5	134.5	135.8
February	127.2	0.2	124.9	128.6	118.2	129.3	123.2	117.9	132.1	135.7	134.8	136.0
March	127.3	0.1	125.1	128.5	118.5	129.2	123.4	118.3	132.0	135.9	135.0	136.1
April	127.7	0.3	125.4	128.9	131.3	128.7	123.7	118.7	132.3	136.3	135.3	136.5
May	127.9	0.2	125.6	128.1	125.5	128.3	124.3	119.5	132.4	136.5	135.5	136.8
June	127.8	-0.1	125.5	127.6	111.9	128.7	124.4	119.6	132.2	136.6	135.7	136.8
July	128.0	0.2	125.6	128.6	110.7	129.9	124.1	119.1	132.6	136.9	136.0	137.1
August	127.9	-0.1	125.4	128.2	106.1	129.8	124.1	118.9	132.7	137.0	136.1	137.2
September	128.1	0.2	125.8	129.7	120.3	130.3	123.9	118.9	132.3	136.9	136.2	137.1
October	128.4	0.2	126.0	129.7	113.2	130.9	124.2	118.9	133.2	137.6	136.9	137.7
November	128.6	0.2	126.1	130.9	124.8	131.3	124.0	118.3	133.9	138.0	137.2	138.2
December	129.4	0.6	127.1	131.0	122.5	131.6	125.2	120.0	134.1	138.0	136.8	138.3
1996:												
January	129.8	0.3	127.6	131.3	127.4	131.6	125.9	121.0	133.6	138.0	137.1	138.2
February	129.7	-0.1	127.5	131.1	123.9	131.6	125.8	121.0	133.7	138.0	137.1	138.3
March	130.5	0.6	128.5	132.2	146.2	131.1	126.8	122.2	133.9	138.1	137.1	138.3
April	130.9	0.3	129.0	131.8	132.9	131.6	127.7	123.5	133.8	138.2	137.0	138.5
May	131.0	0.1	129.2	131.7	120.2	132.6	127.9	123.6	134.4	138.3	137.1	138.6
June	131.3	0.2	129.5	133.7	129.6	134.0	127.5	123.0	134.6	138.3	137.2	138.7
July	131.3	0.0	129.5	133.8	123.7	134.5	127.4	123.0	134.4	138.4	137.2	138.7
August	131.5	0.2	129.8	134.2	118.3	135.4	127.7	123.2	134.6	138.6	137.3	139.0
September	131.7	0.2	130.0	134.8	122.8	135.6	127.9	123.4	134.6	138.5	137.3	138.9
October	132.3	0.5	130.8	136.0	134.3	136.1	128.4	124.4	134.2	138.4	137.2	138.7
November	132.5	0.2	131.0	135.9	135.3	135.9	128.8	124.8	134.3	138.4	137.3	138.7
December	133.0	0.4	131.7	135.6	133.4	135.7	129.8	126.3	134.4	138.5	137.4	138.8
1997:												
January	133.0	0.0	131.6	134.9	132.4	135.1	130.0	126.6	134.4	138.6	137.7	138.9
February	132.7	-0.2	131.2	134.5	135.0	134.4	129.7	126.1	134.4	138.5	137.7	138.7
March	132.5	-0.2	131.1	135.7	141.2	135.2	128.9	125.0	134.5	138.5	137.8	138.7
April	131.9	-0.5	130.2	135.1	122.6	136.0	128.0	123.7	134.4	138.4	137.8	138.6
May	131.6	-0.2	129.9	135.4	127.1	136.0	127.3	123.0	133.9	138.2	137.6	138.4
June	131.3	-0.2	129.5	134.1	116.8	135.4	127.4	123.2	133.7	138.3	137.6	138.4
July	131.0	-0.2	129.2	133.8	115.7	135.1	127.1	123.1	133.0	138.1	137.6	138.2
August	131.3	0.2	129.6	133.6	114.3	135.0	127.7	123.9	133.2	138.1	137.7	138.2
September	131.7	0.3	130.1	133.8	119.0	134.8	128.4	124.7	133.5	138.3	137.8	138.4
October	131.8	0.1	130.3	134.6	132.0	134.8	128.3	124.4	133.7	138.0	137.6	138.0
November	131.5	-0.2	130.0	134.2	129.3	134.6	128.0	124.2	133.2	137.9	137.6	137.9
December	131.4	-0.1	129.8	134.3	133.0	134.4	127.7	123.9	132.9	137.7	137.6	137.7
1998:												
January	130.6	-0.6	128.8	133.9	129.1	134.2	126.5	122.3	132.8	137.6	137.8	137.5
February	130.5	-0.1	128.7	134.3	131.6	134.5	126.2	121.8	132.8	137.6	137.8	137.5
March	130.5	0.0	128.7	134.0	131.4	134.1	126.2	121.9	132.7	137.7	137.9	137.6
April	130.7	0.2	128.9	134.6	134.0	134.6	126.4	122.1	132.8	137.6	137.7	137.5
May	130.6	-0.1	128.9	133.9	124.2	134.6	126.6	122.5	132.5	137.5	137.9	137.2
June	130.4	-0.2	128.7	133.8	118.6	135.0	126.3	122.3	132.1	137.3	138.0	137.0
July	130.7	0.2	129.1	134.5	128.0	135.0	126.5	122.4	132.7	137.4	137.9	137.2
August	130.3	-0.3	128.6	134.1	119.3	135.2	126.1	121.9	132.4	137.2	137.8	136.9
September	130.6	0.2	128.8	134.4	122.7	135.3	126.2	121.8	133.1	137.6	138.0	137.4
October	131.0	0.3	129.3	135.0	133.5	135.0	126.7	122.3	133.4	137.7	138.0	137.5
November	130.7	-0.2	128.9	134.5	126.6	135.1	126.3	121.7	133.5	137.8	138.1	137.6
December	131.3	0.5	129.7	134.5	129.3	134.8	127.5	123.5	133.3	137.7	138.1	137.5

Producer Price Indexes—Continued

(1982=100, seasonally adjusted)

Year and month	Total	Materials and components for manufacturing					Materials and components for construction	Processed fuels and lubricants			Containers, nonreturnable	Supplies	
		Total	Materials for food manufacturing	Materials for nondurable manufacturing	Materials for durable manufacturing	Components for manufacturing		Total	Manufacturing industries	Nonmanufacturing industries		Total	Manufacturing industries
1970	35.4	38.0	44.3	36.5	37.0	40.6	38.3	17.7	21.5	15.2	39.0	39.7	41.4
1971	36.8	38.9	45.7	37.0	38.1	41.9	40.8	19.5	23.6	16.6	40.8	40.8	42.5
1972	38.2	40.4	47.0	38.5	39.9	42.9	43.0	20.1	24.5	16.9	42.7	42.5	43.3
1973	42.4	44.1	57.2	42.6	43.1	44.3	46.5	22.2	26.4	19.4	45.2	51.7	45.6
1974	52.5	56.0	82.0	54.6	55.4	51.1	55.0	33.6	35.5	32.7	53.3	56.8	53.3
1975	58.0	61.7	82.1	61.4	60.8	57.8	60.1	39.4	41.9	38.0	60.0	61.8	59.4
1976	60.9	64.0	70.6	64.8	64.8	60.8	64.1	42.3	44.8	41.1	63.1	65.8	62.6
1977	64.9	67.4	71.9	66.8	70.2	64.5	69.3	47.7	51.0	46.2	65.9	69.3	66.6
1978	69.5	72.0	81.0	69.2	76.2	69.2	76.5	49.9	53.7	48.1	71.0	72.9	71.2
1979	78.4	80.9	89.9	78.3	87.3	75.8	84.2	61.6	64.3	60.4	79.4	80.2	78.1
1980	90.3	91.7	103.7	91.2	97.1	84.6	91.3	85.0	85.5	84.7	89.1	89.9	87.2
1981	98.6	98.7	102.1	100.5	100.7	94.7	97.9	100.6	100.2	101.0	96.7	96.9	95.2
1982	100.0	100.0	100.0	100.0	100.0	100.0	100.0	100.0	100.0	100.0	100.0	100.0	100.0
1983	100.6	101.2	101.3	98.5	103.0	102.4	102.8	95.4	96.2	94.9	100.4	101.8	101.5
1984	103.1	104.1	106.3	102.1	104.9	105.0	105.6	95.7	97.1	94.6	105.9	104.1	105.0
1985	102.7	103.3	101.5	100.5	103.3	106.4	107.3	92.8	93.8	92.0	109.0	104.4	107.3
1986	99.1	102.2	98.4	98.1	101.2	107.5	108.1	72.7	75.1	71.2	110.3	105.6	108.3
1987	101.5	105.3	100.8	102.2	106.2	108.8	109.8	73.3	75.9	71.7	114.5	107.7	110.0
1988	107.1	113.2	106.0	112.9	118.7	112.3	116.1	71.2	73.3	69.9	120.1	113.7	114.8
1989	112.0	118.1	112.7	118.5	123.6	116.4	121.3	76.4	78.3	75.3	125.4	118.1	119.8
1990	114.5	118.7	117.9	118.0	120.7	119.0	122.9	85.9	87.3	85.0	127.7	119.4	122.1
1991	114.4	118.1	115.3	116.7	117.2	121.0	124.5	85.3	88.4	83.4	128.1	121.4	124.4
1992	114.7	117.9	113.9	115.4	117.2	122.0	126.5	84.5	87.5	82.6	127.7	122.7	125.9
1993	116.2	118.9	115.6	115.5	119.1	123.0	132.0	84.7	88.1	82.6	126.4	125.0	128.5
1994	118.5	122.1	118.5	119.2	125.2	124.3	136.6	83.1	86.1	81.1	129.7	127.0	130.7
1995	124.9	130.4	119.5	135.1	135.6	126.5	142.1	84.2	87.1	82.3	148.8	132.1	137.0
1996	125.7	128.6	125.3	130.5	131.3	126.9	143.6	90.0	92.4	88.4	141.1	135.9	138.7
1997	125.6	128.3	123.2	129.6	132.8	126.4	146.5	89.3	92.0	87.6	136.0	135.9	139.4
1998	123.0	126.1	123.2	126.7	128.0	125.9	146.8	81.1	85.8	78.1	140.8	134.8	140.6
1995:													
January	122.8	128.1	118.6	129.6	134.6	125.7	140.6	83.8	86.9	81.8	139.8	129.4	134.6
February	123.7	129.3	119.0	132.0	136.0	126.0	141.0	84.3	87.6	82.2	144.5	129.9	135.2
March	124.3	129.8	119.1	133.2	136.5	126.1	141.7	84.6	87.7	82.6	145.9	130.5	135.8
April	125.0	130.7	117.5	135.7	136.8	126.3	142.1	85.1	87.7	83.4	146.8	131.2	136.4
May	125.2	130.9	116.4	136.9	136.3	126.3	142.1	85.5	88.3	83.6	149.0	131.4	136.8
June	125.5	131.0	117.2	137.3	135.9	126.4	142.0	85.5	88.8	83.4	151.4	131.9	137.3
July	125.6	131.4	119.3	137.5	136.4	126.5	142.6	84.5	87.5	82.5	152.0	132.4	137.7
August	125.7	131.4	119.1	137.4	136.4	126.6	142.9	84.0	87.1	82.1	152.1	132.7	137.8
September	125.5	131.3	120.0	137.0	136.0	126.7	143.1	82.8	85.1	81.3	151.8	133.2	138.1
October	125.4	130.9	122.0	136.1	134.8	126.9	142.8	83.2	86.2	81.3	151.3	133.6	138.2
November	125.2	130.5	122.8	134.9	133.9	127.1	142.4	82.7	85.5	80.8	151.1	134.4	138.3
December	125.4	130.1	123.1	134.0	133.3	127.1	142.2	84.5	86.9	82.9	150.3	134.8	138.3
1996:													
January	125.5	129.5	121.5	133.2	132.2	127.3	142.0	86.8	89.1	85.2	148.1	135.2	138.3
February	125.0	129.0	121.6	132.3	131.0	127.4	142.1	85.9	89.0	83.9	146.0	135.2	138.3
March	125.2	128.6	120.8	131.4	131.0	127.2	142.3	88.0	90.6	86.4	144.6	135.3	138.3
April	125.7	128.3	122.2	130.4	131.1	126.9	142.4	91.0	93.1	89.7	143.0	135.6	138.3
May	126.2	128.8	126.6	130.2	132.4	126.8	143.4	91.5	94.5	89.6	141.6	136.1	138.6
June	125.8	128.8	128.2	130.1	132.6	126.6	143.9	89.3	92.2	87.5	140.1	136.1	138.7
July	125.5	128.3	128.2	129.6	130.7	126.7	143.6	89.2	91.4	87.8	139.7	136.4	138.9
August	125.7	128.3	128.2	129.7	130.6	126.8	144.0	89.7	92.0	88.2	138.5	136.5	139.0
September	126.1	128.6	128.5	130.1	131.2	126.8	144.7	90.6	92.5	89.4	138.6	136.9	139.1
October	126.0	128.3	128.7	129.6	130.5	126.6	144.3	91.9	94.0	90.5	137.9	136.0	138.9
November	125.8	128.0	124.6	129.5	130.9	126.6	145.0	91.6	94.0	90.0	137.5	135.5	138.9
December	126.3	128.2	123.9	129.7	131.5	126.7	144.9	93.9	96.3	92.4	137.8	135.6	138.9
1997:													
January	126.5	128.4	123.9	130.0	131.9	126.8	145.1	94.8	97.4	93.0	137.7	135.4	138.7
February	126.4	128.4	123.6	129.7	132.5	126.8	145.8	94.1	96.1	92.8	136.8	135.4	138.8
March	126.0	128.5	124.6	129.3	133.3	126.7	146.3	91.1	93.0	89.9	136.0	135.7	138.7
April	125.6	128.4	124.7	129.0	133.3	126.6	146.7	88.7	91.0	87.2	135.1	136.0	138.9
May	125.4	128.4	123.9	129.1	133.4	126.5	147.1	87.4	89.9	85.8	134.6	136.2	139.0
June	125.4	128.3	122.8	129.2	133.7	126.4	146.9	88.0	90.4	86.4	134.3	136.0	139.1
July	125.2	128.3	122.0	129.4	133.3	126.4	147.1	87.1	89.5	85.6	134.2	135.9	139.4
August	125.4	128.3	121.6	129.9	133.2	126.2	147.0	87.9	90.4	86.3	133.5	135.8	139.5
September	125.5	128.3	122.3	129.9	133.0	126.2	146.8	88.2	91.3	86.2	135.4	136.2	139.6
October	125.4	128.0	121.9	129.8	132.3	126.0	146.5	88.7	92.1	86.5	136.4	135.8	140.0
November	125.6	128.2	123.9	129.9	132.2	126.0	146.7	88.5	91.9	86.4	138.0	136.1	140.3
December	125.3	128.0	123.2	130.0	131.4	126.0	146.5	87.2	90.7	85.0	139.8	136.1	140.3
1998:													
January	124.4	127.5	120.6	129.8	130.5	126.0	146.4	84.6	88.3	82.2	141.3	135.4	140.3
February	124.1	127.3	122.1	129.0	130.3	126.0	146.5	83.5	87.4	80.9	141.8	135.2	140.4
March	123.7	126.9	121.5	128.6	129.7	126.0	146.7	81.8	86.0	79.1	141.6	135.4	140.4
April	123.7	126.9	122.6	128.2	129.9	126.0	146.9	82.0	86.6	79.1	141.0	135.0	140.7
May	123.6	126.8	124.0	128.0	129.1	126.0	146.8	82.1	86.7	79.3	141.8	134.8	140.6
June	123.2	126.4	123.2	127.6	128.1	126.0	146.6	81.3	86.1	78.3	141.5	134.7	140.6
July	123.2	126.1	122.8	127.1	127.8	125.8	147.0	81.3	86.3	78.2	141.4	135.1	140.7
August	122.8	125.9	123.6	126.4	127.8	125.8	147.3	80.0	85.0	77.0	140.9	134.8	140.6
September	122.4	125.4	124.3	125.1	127.2	125.8	147.3	79.6	84.7	76.5	140.7	134.3	140.7
October	122.2	125.0	124.8	124.3	126.0	125.8	146.8	80.5	85.4	77.4	139.4	134.2	140.7
November	121.9	124.6	125.0	123.8	125.2	125.8	146.7	79.5	84.6	76.4	139.2	134.4	140.7
December	121.1	124.1	123.8	123.2	124.3	125.8	146.7	76.8	82.8	73.2	138.5	134.4	140.7

Producer Price Indexes—*Continued*

(1982=100, seasonally adjusted)

| Year and month | Intermediate materials, supplies, and components—*Continued* Supplies—*Continued* Nonmanufacturing industries | | | Crude materials for further processing | | Nonfood materials | | | | | | |
	Total	Feeds	Other supplies	Total	Foodstuffs and feedstuffs	Total	Nonfood materials except fuel Total	Manu-facturing	Construc-tion	Crude fuel Total	Manu-facturing industries	Nonmanu-facturing industries
1970	38.9	49.9	37.6	35.2	45.2	23.8	29.1	28.3	42.1	13.8	11.3	16.6
1971	39.9	50.4	38.9	36.0	46.1	24.7	29.4	28.4	44.1	15.7	12.6	19.3
1972	42.0	56.1	39.8	39.9	51.5	27.0	32.3	31.5	45.0	16.8	13.5	20.6
1973	54.7	97.3	42.7	54.5	72.6	34.3	42.9	42.7	46.2	18.6	14.8	22.9
1974	58.4	90.2	50.5	61.4	76.4	44.1	54.5	55.0	50.0	24.8	19.1	31.8
1975	62.9	84.0	58.9	61.6	77.4	43.7	50.0	49.7	55.9	30.6	24.4	38.0
1976	67.3	95.1	62.0	63.4	76.8	48.2	54.9	54.7	59.6	34.5	29.0	40.5
1977	70.7	99.3	65.2	65.5	77.5	51.7	56.3	56.0	63.1	42.0	37.2	47.4
1978	73.8	95.5	69.7	73.4	87.3	57.5	61.9	61.5	68.7	48.2	43.1	53.8
1979	81.2	106.9	76.3	85.9	100.0	69.6	75.5	75.6	76.6	57.3	53.1	62.0
1980	91.1	110.6	87.5	95.3	104.6	84.6	91.8	92.3	87.9	69.4	66.7	72.5
1981	97.8	111.3	95.4	103.0	103.9	101.8	109.8	110.9	96.8	84.8	83.6	86.2
1982	100.0	100.0	100.0	100.0	100.0	100.0	100.0	100.0	100.0	100.0	100.0	100.0
1983	102.0	109.1	101.0	101.3	101.8	100.7	98.8	98.6	100.1	105.1	105.8	104.4
1984	103.7	104.2	103.7	103.5	104.7	102.2	101.0	100.8	103.1	105.1	105.6	104.6
1985	103.0	86.6	105.3	95.8	94.8	96.9	94.3	93.1	105.7	102.7	102.7	102.5
1986	104.2	90.5	106.2	87.7	93.2	81.6	76.0	72.6	106.5	92.2	91.1	93.6
1987	106.6	94.6	108.3	93.7	96.2	87.9	88.5	84.7	114.8	84.1	82.1	86.3
1988	113.2	115.0	112.7	96.0	106.1	85.5	85.9	81.5	126.5	82.1	80.1	84.5
1989	117.2	114.4	117.5	103.1	111.2	93.4	95.8	91.0	136.9	85.3	83.9	87.0
1990	118.0	102.8	120.2	108.9	113.1	101.5	107.3	102.5	145.2	84.8	82.9	87.0
1991	119.9	101.3	122.5	101.2	105.5	94.6	97.5	92.2	147.5	82.9	82.3	84.1
1992	121.1	103.0	123.7	100.4	105.1	93.5	94.2	87.9	162.1	84.0	83.1	85.2
1993	123.2	105.4	125.8	102.4	108.4	94.7	94.1	85.6	193.6	87.1	85.9	88.6
1994	125.1	105.8	127.9	101.8	106.5	94.8	97.0	88.3	199.1	82.4	81.7	83.6
1995	129.5	103.4	133.2	102.7	105.8	96.8	105.8	97.3	201.7	72.1	72.5	72.9
1996	134.4	133.1	134.6	113.8	121.5	104.5	105.7	97.6	195.7	92.6	90.7	94.3
1997	134.1	129.1	134.8	111.1	112.2	106.4	103.5	95.0	201.4	101.3	98.4	103.3
1998	132.2	100.2	136.2	96.8	103.9	88.4	84.5	76.7	196.0	86.7	84.8	88.5
1995:												
January	126.7	97.5	130.8	102.1	103.6	97.2	103.6	95.2	199.1	77.1	76.8	78.1
February	127.0	95.9	131.4	102.9	105.3	97.4	106.5	98.2	201.1	72.3	72.6	73.1
March	127.7	97.2	132.0	102.0	103.1	97.4	107.3	98.9	202.0	71.0	71.5	71.8
April	128.4	98.7	132.5	103.3	102.0	100.1	110.9	102.7	202.7	71.9	72.3	72.7
May	128.5	97.0	133.0	102.2	98.6	100.5	111.1	102.8	204.0	72.6	72.9	73.4
June	129.1	98.4	133.4	102.8	101.2	99.9	109.3	100.8	205.0	74.1	74.3	75.0
July	129.5	99.5	133.8	101.6	103.3	96.7	105.1	96.6	202.3	72.9	73.3	73.6
August	130.0	102.6	133.9	100.0	103.4	94.0	104.7	96.2	201.8	66.5	67.6	67.0
September	130.6	105.0	134.2	102.3	108.0	94.8	105.3	96.9	201.6	67.4	68.4	68.0
October	131.2	110.1	134.2	102.2	110.0	93.3	101.8	93.2	201.0	69.7	70.4	70.3
November	132.3	117.0	134.5	104.5	115.3	93.6	100.8	92.2	199.3	72.5	72.8	73.3
December	133.0	122.1	134.5	106.8	116.3	96.6	102.4	94.0	198.9	77.6	77.3	78.6
1996:												
January	133.6	126.9	134.6	109.7	117.0	100.8	103.9	95.5	198.3	86.1	85.0	87.5
February	133.6	126.3	134.6	111.6	116.8	104.1	102.5	94.2	196.3	97.1	94.8	99.0
March	133.8	128.2	134.5	109.8	116.1	101.7	104.0	95.8	194.3	88.2	86.8	89.7
April	134.2	132.3	134.5	114.3	120.0	106.3	107.7	100.0	188.9	93.9	91.8	95.6
May	134.9	137.1	134.6	115.0	125.8	103.6	105.8	97.9	191.9	90.1	88.5	91.6
June	134.8	136.9	134.5	112.5	127.3	98.6	102.7	94.6	192.4	82.3	81.5	83.5
July	135.1	138.5	134.6	114.6	128.4	101.3	102.7	94.6	194.0	89.2	87.6	90.8
August	135.2	139.0	134.7	115.1	127.1	102.9	104.7	96.5	195.6	90.2	88.6	91.7
September	135.7	141.9	134.8	112.5	123.8	101.0	107.4	99.1	197.3	80.5	80.0	81.6
October	134.5	133.1	134.7	111.5	119.7	102.1	109.9	101.6	198.8	79.1	78.7	80.2
November	133.8	128.4	134.5	115.5	118.9	109.0	108.1	99.7	200.0	100.4	97.6	102.4
December	133.8	128.3	134.6	122.5	115.5	122.7	109.3	101.0	200.0	134.1	127.6	137.5
1997:												
January	133.7	127.2	134.7	127.4	114.8	131.0	112.9	104.6	200.1	149.8	141.6	153.9
February	133.7	127.7	134.5	116.8	113.0	115.0	107.8	99.4	199.7	116.6	112.0	119.3
March	134.2	132.6	134.5	107.5	114.2	99.1	103.6	95.1	200.3	82.1	81.4	83.3
April	134.5	134.3	134.5	108.0	117.6	97.7	102.9	94.5	199.7	79.6	79.2	80.7
May	134.8	136.7	134.5	109.8	116.0	101.6	105.0	96.5	201.5	86.3	85.1	87.7
June	134.5	133.6	134.6	106.6	110.2	100.4	100.7	92.0	202.1	90.4	88.7	92.0
July	134.1	128.7	134.8	106.2	109.8	100.0	101.5	92.9	203.1	88.0	86.5	89.5
August	134.0	127.6	134.8	106.5	109.0	101.0	102.5	93.8	203.1	88.9	87.3	90.5
September	134.5	131.4	135.0	108.1	109.4	103.3	101.3	92.7	202.7	97.1	94.5	99.0
October	133.6	122.3	135.2	112.8	110.1	110.6	103.1	94.6	201.6	112.9	108.7	115.5
November	134.0	123.8	135.4	115.4	111.6	113.7	102.2	93.6	201.6	122.7	117.4	125.7
December	133.9	123.1	135.4	108.7	110.8	103.4	99.1	90.5	201.3	100.9	97.9	103.0
1998:												
January	133.1	115.4	135.4	102.6	107.5	95.5	93.1	84.8	200.5	91.1	89.8	92.8
February	132.8	111.1	135.6	100.7	106.8	92.9	92.8	84.6	200.3	85.5	83.4	87.3
March	133.0	106.9	136.2	99.3	106.5	90.8	87.2	79.2	200.2	88.5	86.8	90.2
April	132.5	101.6	136.3	100.6	106.8	92.7	87.9	79.9	200.2	91.8	89.8	93.6
May	132.2	99.5	136.2	100.0	105.2	92.7	88.0	80.0	198.4	91.8	89.9	93.6
June	132.1	99.0	136.2	97.3	105.6	88.1	84.8	77.0	196.6	85.7	83.4	87.4
July	132.5	101.4	136.4	97.4	102.0	90.7	85.3	77.6	193.6	90.7	88.6	92.5
August	132.2	98.0	136.3	93.3	100.9	84.8	80.1	72.6	194.1	84.4	83.4	86.0
September	131.6	92.9	136.3	91.6	100.0	82.6	83.1	75.4	192.7	75.3	74.3	76.7
October	131.4	90.4	136.3	93.9	103.2	84.1	80.8	73.2	192.5	81.9	80.0	83.6
November	131.6	92.9	136.3	93.8	102.6	84.3	77.9	70.5	192.1	86.4	83.8	88.2
December	131.6	93.2	136.3	90.4	98.2	81.8	72.7	65.6	190.8	87.7	84.2	89.6

Producer Price Indexes—Continued

(1982=100, seasonally adjusted)

Year and month	Finished energy goods	Finished goods excluding: Foods	Finished goods excluding: Energy	Finished goods excluding: Foods and energy	Finished consumer goods excluding: Energy	Finished consumer goods excluding: Foods and energy	Intermediate materials: Foods and feeds	Intermediate materials: Energy goods	Intermediate materials less: Foods and feeds	Intermediate materials less: Energy	Intermediate materials less: Foods and energy	Crude materials: Energy materials	Crude materials: Less energy	Crude materials: Nonfood materials less energy
1970	.....	38.2	.....	.....	.....	.....	45.6	.....	34.8	.....	.....	.....	.....	.....
1971	.....	39.6	.....	.....	.....	.....	46.7	.....	36.2	.....	.....	.....	.....	.....
1972	.....	40.4	.....	.....	.....	.....	49.5	.....	37.7	.....	.....	.....	.....	.....
1973	.....	42.0	.....	48.1	.....	50.4	70.3	.....	40.6	.....	44.3	.....	.....	70.8
1974	26.2	48.8	.....	53.6	58.7	55.5	83.6	33.1	50.5	56.2	54.0	27.8	78.4	83.3
1975	30.7	54.7	62.4	59.7	63.9	60.6	81.6	38.7	56.6	61.7	60.2	33.3	75.9	69.3
1976	34.3	58.1	64.8	63.1	65.7	63.7	77.4	41.5	60.0	64.7	63.8	35.3	77.6	80.2
1977	39.7	62.2	68.6	66.9	69.4	67.3	79.6	46.8	64.1	68.5	67.6	40.4	78.1	79.8
1978	42.3	66.7	74.0	71.9	74.9	72.2	84.8	49.1	68.6	73.4	72.5	45.2	87.5	87.8
1979	57.1	74.6	80.7	78.3	81.7	78.8	94.5	61.1	77.4	81.7	80.7	54.9	101.5	106.2
1980	85.2	86.7	88.4	87.1	89.3	87.8	105.5	84.9	89.4	91.4	90.3	73.1	106.5	113.1
1981	101.5	95.6	95.4	94.6	95.7	94.6	104.6	100.5	98.2	98.2	97.7	97.7	105.7	111.7
1982	100.0	100.0	100.0	100.0	100.0	100.0	100.0	100.0	100.0	100.0	100.0	100.0	100.0	100.0
1983	95.2	101.8	102.5	103.0	102.4	103.1	103.6	95.3	100.5	101.7	101.6	98.7	102.6	105.3
1984	91.2	103.2	105.5	105.5	105.6	105.7	105.7	95.5	103.0	104.6	104.7	98.0	106.3	111.7
1985	87.6	104.6	107.2	108.1	107.0	108.4	97.3	92.6	103.0	104.7	105.2	93.3	97.0	104.9
1986	63.0	101.9	109.7	110.6	109.7	111.1	96.2	72.6	99.3	104.5	104.9	71.8	95.4	103.1
1987	61.8	104.0	112.3	113.3	112.5	114.2	99.2	73.0	101.7	107.3	107.8	75.0	100.9	115.7
1988	59.8	106.5	115.8	117.0	116.3	118.5	109.5	70.9	106.9	114.6	115.2	67.7	112.6	133.0
1989	65.7	111.8	121.2	122.1	122.1	124.0	113.8	76.1	111.9	119.5	120.2	75.9	117.7	137.9
1990	75.0	117.4	126.0	126.6	127.2	128.8	113.3	85.5	114.5	120.4	120.9	85.9	118.6	136.3
1991	78.1	120.9	129.1	131.1	130.0	133.7	111.1	85.1	114.6	120.8	121.4	80.4	110.9	128.2
1992	77.8	123.1	131.1	134.2	131.8	137.3	110.7	84.3	114.9	121.3	122.0	78.8	110.7	128.4
1993	78.0	124.4	132.9	135.8	133.5	138.5	112.7	84.6	116.4	123.2	123.8	76.7	116.3	140.2
1994	77.0	125.1	134.2	137.1	134.2	139.0	114.8	83.0	118.7	126.3	127.1	72.1	119.3	156.2
1995	78.1	127.5	136.9	140.0	136.9	141.9	114.8	84.1	125.5	134.0	135.2	69.4	123.5	173.6
1996	83.2	130.5	139.6	142.0	140.1	144.3	128.1	89.8	125.6	133.6	134.0	85.0	130.0	155.8
1997	83.4	130.9	140.2	142.4	141.0	145.1	125.4	89.0	125.7	133.7	134.2	87.3	123.5	156.5
1998	75.1	129.5	141.1	143.7	142.5	147.7	116.2	80.8	123.4	132.4	133.5	68.6	113.6	142.1
1995:														
January	78.3	126.4	135.6	138.4	135.6	140.3	112.3	83.7	123.3	131.4	132.6	69.8	122.0	174.1
February	78.5	126.7	135.9	138.7	135.9	140.6	112.1	84.2	124.3	132.4	133.7	69.6	123.7	175.7
March	78.5	126.9	136.1	139.0	136.1	140.9	112.6	84.5	124.9	133.0	134.3	69.1	122.6	177.3
April	78.8	127.2	136.4	139.3	136.4	141.3	111.9	85.0	125.6	133.8	135.2	72.0	122.2	179.0
May	79.4	127.7	136.5	139.7	136.4	141.8	110.6	85.3	126.0	134.0	135.5	72.4	119.8	179.1
June	79.3	127.8	136.4	139.8	136.3	141.9	111.7	85.4	126.2	134.3	135.7	71.5	121.7	179.5
July	78.2	127.7	136.9	140.1	136.9	142.2	113.4	84.4	126.3	134.7	136.1	68.2	122.7	177.2
August	77.9	127.7	136.9	140.2	136.8	142.3	114.3	83.9	126.2	134.9	136.2	65.6	122.1	174.8
September	77.2	127.5	137.3	140.3	137.5	142.5	115.6	82.7	126.0	134.9	136.2	67.4	124.6	171.8
October	77.0	128.0	137.8	140.9	137.9	143.1	118.6	83.1	125.8	134.8	135.8	66.9	124.8	167.3
November	75.8	127.9	138.4	141.3	138.5	143.5	121.2	82.6	125.4	134.6	135.5	68.3	127.8	164.1
December	78.4	128.8	138.6	141.5	138.8	143.7	123.0	84.3	125.5	134.4	135.2	72.5	128.0	162.4
1996:														
January	80.1	129.2	138.6	141.4	138.8	143.6	123.5	86.6	125.6	134.1	134.8	78.1	128.4	162.0
February	79.7	129.2	138.7	141.6	138.9	143.8	123.4	85.8	125.1	133.7	134.4	82.7	128.1	161.5
March	82.0	129.9	139.0	141.6	139.3	143.8	123.5	87.9	125.3	133.4	134.1	80.6	126.7	158.0
April	84.1	130.5	138.9	141.6	139.1	143.8	125.7	90.8	125.7	133.3	133.8	87.3	129.0	156.1
May	83.6	130.7	139.2	142.0	139.5	144.4	130.3	91.3	126.0	133.8	134.0	83.3	133.4	157.4
June	82.6	130.5	139.8	142.2	140.4	144.6	131.3	89.2	125.5	133.8	134.0	77.6	133.8	154.7
July	82.4	130.4	139.9	142.2	140.4	144.6	131.8	89.1	125.2	133.5	133.6	81.8	134.0	152.6
August	82.9	130.7	140.1	142.3	140.6	144.6	131.9	89.5	125.3	133.6	133.7	83.8	133.3	153.2
September	83.3	130.8	140.2	142.3	140.8	144.6	133.1	90.4	125.8	133.9	134.0	81.0	131.1	154.1
October	84.5	131.1	140.6	142.3	141.3	144.7	130.4	91.6	125.7	133.5	133.7	82.7	128.0	153.4
November	85.4	131.4	140.5	142.2	141.3	144.6	126.1	91.3	125.8	133.3	133.7	91.9	127.3	153.0
December	87.6	132.1	140.5	142.4	141.3	144.9	125.6	93.6	126.3	133.4	133.9	109.6	125.0	153.4
1997:														
January	88.0	132.3	140.4	142.5	141.0	144.9	125.3	94.6	126.6	133.5	134.0	119.4	125.4	156.6
February	87.3	132.1	140.2	142.4	140.8	144.8	125.2	93.9	126.5	133.6	134.1	98.0	124.5	158.1
March	85.1	131.5	140.7	142.5	141.5	145.1	127.4	90.9	126.0	133.7	134.1	77.1	125.4	158.5
April	82.7	130.8	140.5	142.6	141.3	145.2	128.0	88.5	125.5	133.7	134.1	76.4	126.9	155.0
May	81.5	130.3	140.5	142.4	141.3	145.0	128.3	87.1	125.3	133.8	134.2	80.8	126.4	157.1
June	81.6	130.4	140.1	142.4	140.8	145.0	126.5	87.7	125.4	133.7	134.2	79.2	122.2	157.0
July	81.4	130.1	139.9	142.2	140.5	144.7	124.4	86.8	125.3	133.7	134.3	79.1	121.5	155.9
August	82.6	130.6	139.9	142.3	140.5	144.9	123.8	87.6	125.5	133.7	134.3	79.7	121.5	157.8
September	83.3	131.1	140.2	142.7	140.9	145.5	125.5	87.9	125.5	133.8	134.3	83.2	121.5	156.5
October	82.9	130.9	140.4	142.6	141.3	145.6	122.3	88.4	125.6	133.5	134.3	92.8	121.8	156.1
November	82.3	130.6	140.2	142.5	141.1	145.4	124.2	88.2	125.7	133.8	134.4	97.1	122.7	155.5
December	81.8	130.4	140.2	142.4	141.1	145.3	123.4	86.9	125.4	133.7	134.4	84.3	121.6	153.3
1998:														
January	78.8	129.5	140.0	142.4	140.9	145.4	119.2	84.3	124.7	133.3	134.2	74.9	118.5	150.7
February	77.7	129.3	140.3	142.5	141.2	145.7	118.8	83.2	124.4	133.2	134.1	71.7	117.9	150.4
March	76.0	129.4	140.7	143.2	141.8	146.8	117.2	81.5	124.1	133.0	134.1	69.6	117.1	148.3
April	75.7	129.4	141.0	143.4	142.3	147.2	116.2	81.7	124.1	133.0	134.1	72.7	116.9	146.5
May	76.0	129.6	140.8	143.5	142.1	147.4	116.5	81.9	124.0	132.8	133.9	72.7	115.7	146.7
June	75.4	129.3	140.7	143.4	142.1	147.3	115.8	81.0	123.6	132.6	133.7	66.9	115.9	146.1
July	75.3	129.5	141.2	143.7	142.6	147.8	116.3	81.0	123.6	132.5	133.6	70.9	112.6	143.9
August	73.9	129.1	141.0	143.7	142.5	147.9	115.8	79.8	123.2	132.4	133.5	64.5	110.8	139.9
September	73.6	129.4	141.4	144.1	142.9	148.4	114.7	79.4	122.9	132.0	133.1	62.2	109.7	138.2
October	74.2	129.7	141.7	144.3	143.3	148.7	114.2	80.2	122.7	131.6	132.7	65.6	110.9	134.0
November	73.2	129.5	141.7	144.4	143.2	148.7	115.1	79.3	122.3	131.4	132.4	66.9	109.7	131.1
December	71.9	130.2	142.8	145.9	144.8	151.4	114.4	76.5	121.5	131.1	132.2	64.2	105.9	128.9

Producer Price Indexes—*Continued*, and Purchasing Power of the Dollar

(1982=100, except as noted; not seasonally adjusted)

Year and month	Finished goods Total	Finished consumer goods Total	Finished consumer goods Foods	Goods except foods Total	Goods except foods Durable	Goods except foods Non-durable	Capital equipment	Inter-mediate materials, supplies, and com-ponents	Crude materials for further processing	Producer prices for finished goods (1982-1994= $1.00)[1]	Consumer prices (1982-1984= $1.00)
1970	39.3	39.1	43.8	37.4	47.2	32.5	40.1	35.4	35.2	2.589	2.577
1971	40.5	40.2	44.5	38.7	48.9	33.5	41.7	36.8	36.0	2.513	2.469
1972	41.8	41.5	46.9	39.4	50.0	34.1	42.8	38.2	39.9	2.435	2.392
1973	45.6	46.0	56.5	41.2	50.9	36.1	44.2	42.4	54.5	2.232	2.252
1974	52.6	53.1	64.4	48.2	55.5	44.0	50.5	52.5	61.4	1.935	2.028
1975	58.2	58.2	69.8	53.2	61.0	48.9	58.2	58.0	61.6	1.749	1.859
1976	60.8	60.4	69.6	56.5	63.7	52.4	62.1	60.9	63.4	1.674	1.757
1977	64.7	64.3	73.3	60.6	67.4	56.8	66.1	64.9	65.5	1.573	1.650
1978	69.8	69.4	79.9	64.9	73.6	60.0	71.3	69.5	73.4	1.458	1.534
1979	77.6	77.5	87.3	73.5	80.8	69.3	77.5	78.4	85.9	1.311	1.377
1980	88.0	88.6	92.4	87.1	91.0	85.1	85.8	90.3	95.3	1.156	1.214
1981	96.1	96.6	97.8	96.1	96.4	95.8	94.6	98.6	103.0	1.059	1.100
1982	100.0	100.0	100.0	100.0	100.0	100.0	100.0	100.0	100.0	1.018	1.036
1983	101.6	101.3	101.0	101.2	102.8	100.5	102.8	100.6	101.3	1.002	1.004
1984	103.7	103.3	105.4	102.2	104.5	101.1	105.2	103.1	103.5	0.981	0.962
1985	104.7	103.8	104.6	103.3	106.5	101.7	107.5	102.7	95.8	0.972	0.929
1986	103.2	101.4	107.3	98.5	108.9	93.3	109.7	99.1	87.7	0.986	0.912
1987	105.4	103.6	109.5	100.7	111.5	94.9	111.7	101.5	93.7	0.966	0.880
1988	108.0	106.2	112.6	103.1	113.8	97.3	114.3	107.1	96.0	0.942	0.845
1989	113.6	112.1	118.7	108.9	117.6	103.8	118.8	112.0	103.1	0.896	0.806
1990	119.2	118.2	124.4	115.3	120.4	111.5	122.9	114.5	108.9	0.854	0.765
1991	121.7	120.5	124.1	118.7	123.9	115.0	126.7	114.4	101.2	0.836	0.734
1992	123.2	121.7	123.3	120.8	125.7	117.3	129.1	114.7	100.4	0.826	0.713
1993	124.7	123.0	125.7	121.7	128.0	117.6	131.4	116.2	102.4	0.816	0.692
1994	125.5	123.3	126.8	121.6	130.9	116.2	134.1	118.5	101.8	0.811	0.675
1995	127.9	125.6	129.0	124.0	132.7	118.8	136.7	124.9	102.7	0.796	0.656
1996	131.3	129.5	133.6	127.6	134.2	123.3	138.3	125.7	113.8	0.775	0.637
1997	131.8	130.2	134.5	128.2	133.7	124.3	138.2	125.6	111.1	0.772	0.623
1998	130.7	128.9	134.3	126.4	132.9	122.2	137.6	123.0	96.8	0.779	0.613
1995:											
January	126.6	124.2	127.9	122.4	132.6	116.7	135.9	122.5	101.5	0.804	0.665
February	126.9	124.5	128.4	122.6	132.7	116.9	136.1	123.4	102.6	0.802	0.663
March	127.1	124.7	128.7	122.9	132.4	117.3	136.2	124.0	102.3	0.801	0.661
April	127.6	125.2	128.7	123.6	132.4	118.4	136.4	124.7	103.6	0.798	0.658
May	128.1	125.9	128.0	124.7	132.3	120.1	136.5	125.3	102.8	0.794	0.657
June	128.2	126.0	127.4	125.1	132.0	120.8	136.4	125.8	103.4	0.794	0.656
July	128.2	126.0	128.5	124.7	132.1	120.1	136.6	126.0	102.1	0.794	0.656
August	128.1	125.9	128.8	124.4	131.9	119.8	136.6	126.0	100.5	0.794	0.654
September	127.9	125.9	130.1	123.9	130.0	119.9	135.7	125.9	102.5	0.796	0.653
October	128.7	126.3	129.9	124.5	134.1	119.0	138.0	125.4	101.7	0.791	0.651
November	128.7	126.2	131.1	123.9	134.7	117.8	138.3	125.1	103.8	0.791	0.651
December	129.1	126.7	131.0	124.6	134.7	118.9	138.1	125.1	106.0	0.788	0.651
1996:											
January	129.4	127.1	130.7	125.4	134.2	120.1	138.3	125.2	108.8	0.786	0.648
February	129.4	127.0	130.7	125.3	134.3	119.9	138.4	124.7	111.1	0.786	0.646
March	130.1	128.0	132.0	126.1	134.3	121.2	138.3	124.9	110.0	0.782	0.642
April	130.6	128.7	131.2	127.4	134.0	123.1	138.3	125.4	114.4	0.779	0.640
May	131.1	129.3	131.5	128.2	134.2	124.1	138.2	126.2	115.9	0.776	0.639
June	131.7	130.0	133.6	128.3	134.4	124.2	138.2	126.2	113.3	0.773	0.638
July	131.5	129.9	133.9	128.0	133.8	124.0	138.1	125.9	115.6	0.774	0.637
August	131.9	130.4	135.3	128.1	133.7	124.2	138.2	126.1	116.0	0.772	0.636
September	131.8	130.4	135.6	128.0	132.4	124.6	137.3	126.7	112.9	0.772	0.634
October	132.7	131.2	136.6	128.8	135.2	124.5	138.9	126.0	111.3	0.767	0.632
November	132.6	131.1	136.1	128.8	135.2	124.5	138.7	125.7	114.8	0.767	0.631
December	132.7	131.2	135.5	129.2	135.0	125.2	138.7	126.0	121.6	0.767	0.631
1997:											
January	132.6	131.0	134.1	129.5	134.9	125.7	139.0	126.3	126.3	0.767	0.629
February	132.2	130.6	133.8	129.0	135.0	124.9	138.9	126.1	116.1	0.770	0.627
March	132.1	130.4	135.2	128.2	135.0	123.8	138.8	125.6	107.6	0.770	0.625
April	131.6	129.8	134.3	127.7	134.5	123.2	138.6	125.3	107.9	0.773	0.624
May	131.6	130.0	135.2	127.6	133.6	123.5	138.1	125.4	110.4	0.773	0.625
June	131.6	130.0	134.0	128.1	133.4	124.4	138.1	125.8	107.1	0.773	0.624
July	131.3	129.7	134.0	127.6	132.4	124.1	137.8	125.5	107.1	0.775	0.623
August	131.7	130.3	134.9	128.1	132.3	124.8	137.7	125.8	107.5	0.773	0.622
September	131.8	130.5	134.7	128.6	131.4	125.8	137.2	126.0	108.5	0.772	0.620
October	132.3	130.7	135.1	128.7	134.7	124.6	138.5	125.5	112.7	0.769	0.619
November	131.7	130.1	134.6	128.0	134.1	123.9	138.3	125.5	114.7	0.773	0.619
December	131.1	129.4	134.4	127.2	133.4	123.0	137.9	125.0	107.8	0.776	0.620
1998:											
January	130.3	128.3	133.1	126.1	133.4	121.5	137.9	124.2	101.7	0.781	0.619
February	130.2	128.2	133.6	125.6	133.4	120.8	137.9	123.8	100.1	0.782	0.618
March	130.1	128.1	133.4	125.6	133.2	120.9	137.9	123.3	99.4	0.782	0.617
April	130.4	128.5	133.8	126.0	133.0	121.5	137.7	123.3	100.3	0.780	0.615
May	130.6	128.9	133.6	126.7	132.3	122.8	137.3	123.5	100.5	0.779	0.614
June	130.7	129.1	133.8	127.0	131.8	123.4	137.2	123.5	97.6	0.779	0.613
July	131.0	129.4	134.7	127.0	132.0	123.3	137.1	123.5	98.1	0.777	0.613
August	130.7	129.2	135.2	126.4	131.5	122.7	136.8	123.2	94.3	0.779	0.612
September	130.6	129.1	135.4	126.3	131.0	122.8	136.7	122.9	92.1	0.779	0.611
October	131.4	129.8	135.5	127.1	134.4	122.5	138.1	122.3	94.0	0.774	0.610
November	130.9	129.0	134.9	126.4	134.4	121.4	138.2	121.8	93.6	0.777	0.610
December	131.1	129.4	134.5	127.1	133.8	122.7	137.9	120.9	89.8	0.776	0.610

1. Calculations by the editors.

Prices Received and Paid by Farmers

(All urban consumers—1990–1992=100, not seasonally adjusted)

| Year and month | All farm products | Prices received by farmers | | | | | | | | | | | | | Food commodities | Prices paid by farmers [1] | | Ratio of prices received to prices paid |
| | | Crops | | | | | | | | | Livestock and products | | | | | All commodities and services | Production items | |
		Total	Food grains	Feed grains and hay	Cotton	Tobacco	Oil-bearing crops	Fruit and nuts	Commercial vegetables	Potatoes and dry beans	Total	Meat animals	Dairy products	Poultry and eggs				
1975	73	88	128	112	68	56	93	46	66	78	62	56	67	83	69	47	55	158
1976	75	87	105	105	99	63	97	45	67	75	64	57	74	83	71	50	59	150
1977	73	83	83	87	100	66	119	54	70	71	64	56	74	81	71	53	61	138
1978	83	89	102	88	91	72	110	72	74	73	78	75	81	87	83	58	67	144
1979	94	98	121	100	96	75	121	77	79	65	90	90	92	90	95	66	76	144
1980	98	107	136	115	114	80	118	73	80	93	89	84	100	91	96	75	85	131
1981	100	111	138	122	111	94	122	76	99	126	89	82	105	94	97	82	92	121
1982	94	98	119	103	92	99	103	78	92	88	90	86	104	89	95	86	94	109
1983	98	108	120	125	104	96	118	71	96	89	91	83	104	95	95	86	92	113
1984	101	111	117	127	108	98	125	85	97	111	91	83	103	109	98	89	94	114
1985	91	98	108	105	93	92	96	84	95	87	86	78	97	97	89	86	91	106
1986	87	87	89	84	91	82	89	83	92	81	88	80	96	105	87	85	86	103
1987	89	86	83	72	98	83	90	93	105	89	91	90	96	87	91	87	87	102
1988	99	104	113	102	95	86	126	96	104	88	93	91	93	98	99	91	90	108
1989	104	109	127	109	98	96	118	99	103	131	100	94	104	111	104	96	95	108
1990	104	103	100	105	107	97	105	97	102	133	105	105	105	105	104	99	99	105
1991	100	101	94	101	108	102	99	112	100	99	99	101	94	99	99	100	100	99
1992	98	101	113	98	88	101	100	99	111	88	97	96	100	97	99	101	101	97
1993	101	102	105	99	89	101	108	93	116	107	100	100	98	102	102	104	103	97
1994	100	105	119	106	109	101	110	90	109	110	95	90	99	106	98	106	106	94
1995	102	112	134	112	127	103	104	99	120	107	92	85	98	107	99	109	108	93
1996	112	126	157	146	122	105	128	118	109	114	99	87	114	120	108	115	115	98
1997	107	116	128	117	112	104	131	108	122	90	98	92	102	113	105	118	118	90
1998	101	106	103	100	107	104	107	110	119	99	97	79	119	117	100	117	116	87
1995:																		
January	98	103	120	97	130	108	98	73	120	92	93	89	96	101	95	107	108	90
February	97	102	116	99	132	113	96	73	115	89	94	92	96	100	95	107	108	89
March	99	107	113	102	136	99	98	76	147	96	93	89	96	100	97	109	108	91
April	99	112	113	104	128	88	99	81	172	100	89	84	94	100	97	109	108	91
May	100	116	119	108	126	.....	99	100	155	105	88	82	94	97	98	109	108	92
June	100	113	128	110	131	.....	102	104	122	121	90	85	93	101	98	110	108	92
July	102	115	137	114	132	101	105	114	98	144	90	85	92	105	100	110	108	94
August	103	115	141	115	119	101	104	127	101	116	92	85	95	112	101	110	109	94
September	105	115	148	116	123	105	104	122	117	98	93	85	98	115	102	111	109	95
October	105	114	154	122	122	104	107	122	98	106	92	83	103	113	101	111	110	95
November	106	117	157	125	124	106	113	106	98	108	94	82	107	119	101	111	110	95
December	108	119	161	131	125	106	119	94	101	108	96	84	106	117	103	112	112	96
1996:																		
January	108	121	158	133	126	109	120	94	93	111	94	82	108	117	102	113	112	96
February	106	123	159	140	125	118	125	98	108	116	93	82	106	113	101	113	113	94
March	109	128	161	146	127	100	125	103	140	125	94	83	106	112	104	114	114	96
April	108	128	168	159	130	92	132	103	118	132	93	81	106	112	102	114	114	95
May	112	131	184	170	127	.....	137	117	100	138	97	84	109	116	105	115	115	97
June	118	140	175	165	127	.....	133	133	115	139	100	85	113	122	113	115	115	102
July	119	136	159	169	121	92	136	131	97	139	102	89	118	122	113	115	116	103
August	117	133	153	166	119	100	138	130	114	106	104	91	122	123	113	115	116	102
September	116	125	147	147	118	109	124	141	100	94	105	92	126	123	112	115	116	100
October	112	119	140	125	118	110	118	139	107	91	103	91	126	121	110	115	115	97
November	110	117	139	116	115	111	119	124	119	90	102	90	116	126	109	115	114	96
December	110	115	137	116	115	111	124	101	123	84	103	90	109	130	108	115	115	96
1997:																		
January	107	115	137	118	112	111	127	93	113	84	98	90	103	119	105	117	117	91
February	105	113	134	118	112	110	131	90	107	85	98	90	103	116	102	117	117	90
March	108	118	136	123	114	111	142	97	122	86	99	92	104	113	106	118	118	92
April	106	116	140	127	112	.....	146	88	115	85	99	94	101	111	104	118	118	90
May	108	118	139	124	113	.....	149	106	111	94	100	97	97	112	106	119	119	91
June	107	119	120	118	111	.....	145	127	118	85	97	94	93	111	106	119	118	90
July	107	115	111	112	111	91	134	127	114	99	99	95	93	118	106	118	118	91
August	108	117	122	114	111	92	128	126	125	107	99	94	97	117	108	118	118	92
September	107	114	126	113	115	101	113	131	119	87	99	92	100	116	106	119	119	90
October	107	115	124	112	115	103	112	120	147	85	97	89	108	108	106	119	118	90
November	107	115	123	112	112	106	120	106	142	90	98	88	113	112	106	119	119	90
December	105	111	119	112	105	110	120	89	136	94	98	87	113	107	103	119	118	88
1998:																		
January	103	109	116	113	101	110	119	80	120	97	95	84	113	106	100	119	119	87
February	101	109	117	113	103	110	117	86	112	104	94	82	113	104	98	119	118	85
March	102	111	118	113	105	104	114	93	120	109	95	82	111	108	100	118	117	86
April	104	114	114	109	105	97	112	102	147	108	95	84	107	109	103	118	117	88
May	103	112	109	108	105	.....	112	111	126	110	96	87	102	108	102	117	117	88
June	102	107	96	105	115	.....	111	121	105	106	98	86	108	116	101	117	116	87
July	102	107	89	101	112	94	111	129	119	105	96	80	109	123	101	116	115	88
August	101	103	85	91	109	93	98	133	111	96	99	78	119	131	102	116	115	88
September	99	100	88	86	111	103	93	128	111	88	98	73	129	128	100	115	113	87
October	99	100	100	85	110	107	93	123	132	82	98	75	136	126	100	116	114	85
November	99	101	105	86	107	109	101	115	113	89	97	72	136	124	100	116	115	86
December	98	100	101	89	100	110	102	93	112	91	97	66	139	119	98	116	114	85

1. Includes commodities, services, taxes, and wage rates.

Employment Costs, Productivity, and Profits

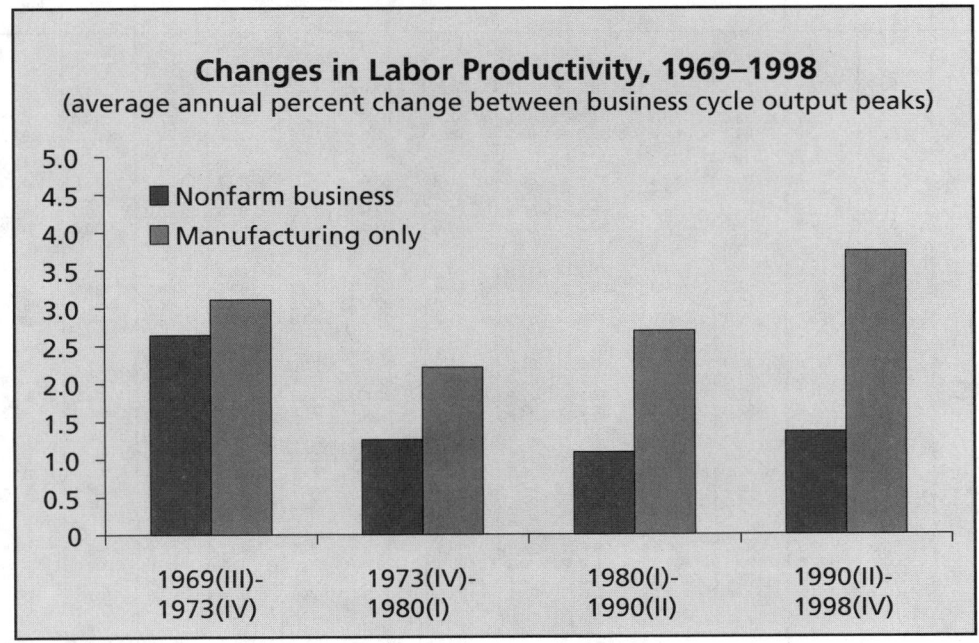

Changes in Labor Productivity, 1969–1998
(average annual percent change between business cycle output peaks)

- For all nonfarm business, annual average gains in labor productivity during the 1990s have slightly exceeded the limited gains achieved from 1973 to 1990, but have not equaled the strong 1969-1973 performance. In manufacturing, however, 1990s labor productivity gains have been even more rapid than from 1969 to 1973.

- Productivity gains in 1998 were especially strong: 2.2 percent for all nonfarm business and 4.0 percent for manufacturing.

- Employment cost increases remained moderate in 1998, with the index for total compensation for all civilian workers rising 3.3 percent from the fourth quarter of 1997 to the fourth quarter of 1998.

- Although down 3 percent from the 1997 record, after-tax corporate profits in manufacturing in 1998 still were quite strong, maintaining the string of high-profit years that began in 1994.

Employment Cost Indexes—Total Compensation

(Seasonally adjusted, except as noted; June 1989, not seasonally adjusted=100)

Year and quarter	All civilian workers [1]	State and local government workers	All private industry workers	Private industry workers excluding sales occupations [2]	By occupational group			By industry division									
					White-collar occupations	Blue-collar occupations	Service occupations	Goods-producing industries			Service-producing industries						
								Total	Construction	Manufacturing	Total	Transportation and utilities	Wholesale trade	Retail trade	Finance, insurance, and real estate [2]	Services	Nonmanufacturing industry
1984:																	
1st quarter	80.7	76.4	81.4	81.7	79.7	83.5	82.5	82.9	84.3	82.0	80.3	84.6	79.1	82.2	.....	77.6	80.9
2nd quarter	81.7	77.5	82.4	82.5	80.8	84.2	83.1	83.6	84.5	83.0	81.6	85.4	80.3	83.2	.....	78.5	81.8
3rd quarter	82.4	78.7	83.0	83.3	81.3	84.9	84.4	84.5	84.7	83.9	81.7	86.0	81.0	83.7	.....	79.2	82.3
4th quarter	83.5	80.0	84.1	84.3	82.6	85.9	85.9	85.6	85.2	85.1	82.8	87.0	82.7	84.9	.....	81.0	83.5
1985:																	
1st quarter	84.5	81.2	85.0	85.2	83.6	86.6	85.9	86.6	86.2	86.1	83.7	87.5	83.0	85.6	83.1	81.2	84.2
2nd quarter	85.4	82.2	85.9	85.8	84.6	87.3	86.7	87.2	86.9	86.8	84.8	88.3	84.4	86.5	83.0	82.4	85.1
3rd quarter	86.4	83.5	86.9	86.9	85.6	88.2	88.1	87.9	87.5	87.5	86.0	89.6	85.2	88.0	84.6	83.6	86.3
4th quarter	87.1	84.6	87.5	87.3	86.6	88.6	88.5	88.4	88.4	88.0	86.7	90.2	85.9	89.0	85.9	84.1	87.1
1986:																	
1st quarter	87.9	85.6	88.3	88.3	87.3	89.3	89.0	89.2	88.6	88.7	87.5	91.1	86.5	89.3	86.7	85.1	87.8
2nd quarter	88.5	86.8	89.0	88.9	88.2	89.8	89.8	90.1	89.7	89.7	88.2	91.3	87.0	89.7	87.4	86.1	88.5
3rd quarter	89.1	87.8	89.6	89.6	88.7	90.5	90.5	90.6	90.5	90.2	88.7	91.8	87.8	90.4	87.9	86.6	89.1
4th quarter	89.9	88.9	90.2	90.2	89.6	91.1	91.2	91.2	90.9	90.9	89.5	92.2	88.8	91.0	88.6	87.8	89.9
1987:																	
1st quarter	90.6	89.8	90.9	91.0	90.5	91.2	91.9	91.5	91.6	90.9	90.5	92.9	89.8	91.5	90.9	88.9	90.9
2nd quarter	91.4	90.9	91.6	91.7	91.1	92.1	92.6	92.1	92.5	91.7	91.2	93.8	90.8	92.3	90.0	89.8	91.5
3rd quarter	92.2	91.5	92.5	92.7	92.1	92.9	92.9	93.0	93.3	92.6	92.0	94.3	91.6	92.8	90.2	91.1	92.3
4th quarter	93.1	92.8	93.3	93.4	92.9	93.9	93.4	94.0	94.2	93.7	92.8	95.0	92.3	93.2	90.4	92.3	93.1
1988:																	
1st quarter	94.4	94.2	94.5	94.9	93.8	95.3	94.5	95.5	95.3	95.1	93.8	95.8	93.2	94.7	91.5	93.5	94.1
2nd quarter	95.5	95.3	95.7	95.9	95.0	96.3	95.7	96.5	96.2	96.1	95.0	96.6	94.4	96.1	92.8	94.8	95.4
3rd quarter	96.5	96.5	96.6	96.9	96.1	97.1	97.1	97.2	97.1	96.9	96.1	97.4	95.5	97.1	92.9	96.2	96.4
4th quarter	97.7	98.1	97.8	97.7	97.5	98.1	98.2	98.1	98.2	97.8	97.6	97.8	96.3	98.6	96.2	97.6	97.7
1989:																	
1st quarter	98.8	99.3	98.9	99.0	98.8	98.7	99.1	98.9	99.1	98.7	98.9	98.7	98.7	99.3	98.3	98.9	98.8
2nd quarter	100.0	100.8	100.0	100.0	99.9	99.9	100.1	100.0	99.8	99.9	100.0	99.8	99.8	99.8	100.0	100.3	99.9
3rd quarter	101.4	102.7	101.2	101.2	101.3	101.1	101.1	101.2	101.1	101.2	101.2	100.6	102.5	100.9	100.4	101.6	101.2
4th quarter	102.7	104.2	102.4	102.1	102.6	102.1	102.5	102.3	102.6	102.4	102.5	101.5	104.7	101.8	101.4	103.0	102.5
1990:																	
1st quarter	104.0	105.7	103.8	103.9	104.0	103.4	103.8	103.8	103.2	103.8	103.8	103.0	105.0	103.2	102.6	104.9	103.8
2nd quarter	105.4	107.3	105.1	105.1	105.4	104.6	105.0	105.1	104.1	105.1	105.1	103.1	105.2	104.6	104.4	106.7	105.0
3rd quarter	106.6	108.8	106.2	106.3	106.6	105.6	105.7	106.2	105.0	106.4	106.2	104.1	105.8	105.3	105.4	107.9	106.1
4th quarter	107.7	110.3	107.2	107.1	107.6	106.6	107.4	107.2	105.8	107.5	107.2	105.4	106.6	106.3	105.5	109.4	107.1
1991:																	
1st quarter	108.9	111.7	108.4	108.6	108.9	107.8	108.2	108.4	107.5	108.4	108.4	105.9	107.9	107.5	108.3	110.7	108.4
2nd quarter	110.2	112.7	109.7	109.8	110.2	108.9	110.0	109.7	108.4	109.9	109.7	107.6	109.3	108.7	109.5	111.7	109.7
3rd quarter	111.2	113.3	110.9	111.1	111.4	110.2	111.5	110.8	109.1	111.2	110.9	108.9	110.7	109.9	109.7	113.0	110.8
4th quarter	112.2	114.2	111.9	112.0	112.4	111.2	112.5	112.0	110.1	112.4	111.8	110.0	111.3	110.7	110.0	114.1	111.7
1992:																	
1st quarter	113.3	115.2	113.0	113.3	113.3	112.4	113.5	113.3	110.7	113.8	112.7	111.0	112.6	111.0	111.7	115.2	112.6
2nd quarter	114.1	116.4	113.7	114.1	114.1	113.3	114.3	114.1	111.6	114.7	113.5	111.8	113.2	111.9	110.8	116.6	113.5
3rd quarter	115.0	117.2	114.7	115.1	115.0	114.3	115.4	115.2	112.9	115.7	114.3	112.8	113.2	112.7	111.1	117.7	114.3
4th quarter	116.1	118.5	115.7	115.9	116.1	115.2	115.9	116.2	114.0	116.8	115.3	113.8	114.5	113.6	111.3	119.0	115.4
1993:																	
1st quarter	117.2	119.3	116.9	117.5	117.3	116.5	117.2	117.8	115.1	118.5	116.3	114.6	115.4	114.8	112.6	120.0	116.2
2nd quarter	118.2	120.1	117.9	118.5	118.2	117.6	118.1	118.8	115.8	119.6	117.2	116.0	116.1	115.4	113.1	121.0	117.1
3rd quarter	119.2	120.8	118.9	119.5	119.3	118.4	118.9	119.7	116.5	120.6	118.3	116.7	116.6	116.0	115.7	122.2	118.3
4th quarter	120.1	121.7	119.9	120.2	120.4	119.5	119.5	120.6	116.8	121.6	119.4	117.8	118.0	116.9	116.4	123.2	119.2
1994:																	
1st quarter	121.2	122.7	120.9	121.4	121.4	120.3	120.5	121.8	118.8	122.4	120.3	119.0	118.0	117.7	117.7	124.3	120.2
2nd quarter	122.3	123.6	121.9	122.3	122.4	121.1	121.0	123.0	120.0	123.4	121.2	119.8	119.4	119.0	117.7	125.0	121.2
3rd quarter	123.3	124.6	123.0	123.4	123.4	122.2	121.7	123.9	121.1	124.5	122.2	121.3	120.6	120.1	118.5	125.8	122.1
4th quarter	124.0	125.3	123.7	123.9	124.3	122.8	122.8	124.6	121.1	125.3	123.0	122.4	121.7	120.4	118.9	126.7	122.8
1995:																	
1st quarter	124.9	126.4	124.5	125.0	125.2	123.5	123.3	125.5	121.3	126.1	124.0	123.8	123.2	121.0	120.2	127.4	123.6
2nd quarter	125.8	127.4	125.4	125.7	126.2	124.3	124.0	126.2	121.8	126.8	125.0	124.8	124.5	121.7	121.8	128.3	124.6
3rd quarter	126.5	128.3	126.1	126.5	126.9	125.0	124.5	126.8	122.7	127.3	125.8	125.9	126.1	122.3	122.7	128.8	125.3
4th quarter	127.4	129.1	127.0	127.1	127.8	125.8	125.0	127.8	123.7	128.4	126.5	126.8	127.3	123.0	123.1	129.5	126.1
1996:																	
1st quarter	128.2	129.9	127.9	128.3	128.9	126.6	125.6	128.5	124.6	129.1	127.6	127.6	127.5	124.6	124.5	130.6	127.1
2nd quarter	129.3	130.8	128.9	129.2	130.0	127.5	126.4	129.6	125.1	130.3	128.6	128.5	129.1	124.7	126.3	131.8	128.2
3rd quarter	130.1	131.5	129.7	130.2	131.0	128.0	127.1	130.4	125.5	131.2	129.4	129.3	129.9	125.9	126.7	132.6	128.9
4th quarter	131.0	132.5	130.7	130.8	132.0	129.2	128.5	131.2	126.7	132.1	130.4	130.6	130.1	127.7	126.0	133.5	130.0
1997:																	
1st quarter	131.9	133.2	131.6	131.9	133.0	129.6	129.5	131.7	127.5	132.5	131.5	131.0	132.8	128.6	128.6	134.6	131.0
2nd quarter	132.9	133.9	132.7	133.0	134.1	130.7	130.7	132.9	128.5	133.6	132.6	131.8	133.6	129.6	129.4	135.8	132.1
3rd quarter	133.9	134.6	133.7	134.1	135.1	131.6	132.7	133.8	129.3	134.5	133.7	132.9	134.6	130.8	130.5	136.9	133.1
4th quarter	135.2	135.5	135.2	135.2	137.0	132.5	133.7	134.3	130.0	135.3	135.6	134.4	135.4	132.0	134.5	138.6	134.9
1998:																	
1st quarter	136.2	136.5	136.1	136.4	138.0	133.2	134.9	135.2	130.9	136.3	136.6	135.6	137.6	133.2	136.7	139.3	136.0
2nd quarter	137.4	137.5	137.3	137.5	139.4	134.2	135.8	136.3	132.5	137.1	137.8	137.2	138.4	134.3	138.4	140.4	137.2
3rd quarter	138.7	138.5	138.7	138.8	141.0	135.1	136.9	137.2	133.0	138.1	139.5	138.5	140.8	135.6	141.0	141.7	138.7
4th quarter	139.7	139.5	139.7	139.4	142.3	136.1	137.6	137.9	134.6	138.9	140.6	139.5	143.1	135.9	142.5	142.8	139.9

1. Includes private industry and state and local government workers. Federal government workers are not included.
2. Not seasonally adjusted.

Employment Cost Indexes—Wages and Salaries

(Seasonally adjusted, except as noted; June 1989, not seasonally adjusted=100)

Year and quarter	All civilian workers [1]	State and local government workers	Private industry workers															
			All private industry workers	Private industry workers excluding sales occupations [2]	By occupational group			By industry division									
					White-collar occupations	Blue-collar occupations	Service occupations	Goods-producing industries			Service-producing industries						
								Total	Construction	Manufacturing	Total	Transportation and utilities	Wholesale trade	Retail trade	Finance, insurance, and real estate [2]	Services	Non-manufacturing industry
1984:																	
1st quarter	81.8	77.8	82.5	82.7	80.5	84.8	84.5	84.0	86.3	83.4	81.3	87.6	79.3	83.0	80.0	78.5	82.0
2nd quarter	82.6	78.7	83.3	83.4	81.4	85.4	84.9	84.6	86.5	84.1	82.2	88.2	80.1	83.6	80.5	79.4	82.8
3rd quarter	83.2	79.8	83.9	84.2	81.9	86.0	86.2	85.4	86.7	85.0	82.6	88.5	81.0	84.2	79.4	80.2	83.2
4th quarter	84.3	81.0	84.9	85.3	83.1	86.9	87.8	86.3	87.0	86.1	83.7	89.4	82.8	85.5	79.8	82.2	84.3
1985:																	
1st quarter	85.3	82.1	85.9	86.0	84.3	87.7	87.5	87.4	88.0	87.2	84.6	89.9	83.1	86.0	84.0	82.1	85.2
2nd quarter	86.3	83.1	86.9	86.9	85.2	88.6	88.5	88.2	88.5	88.1	85.7	90.8	84.7	86.9	83.8	83.4	86.1
3rd quarter	87.3	84.4	87.9	88.1	86.3	89.7	89.8	89.0	88.9	88.8	87.0	92.1	85.7	88.5	85.5	84.6	87.4
4th quarter	88.0	85.5	88.5	88.4	87.2	89.9	89.9	89.4	89.7	89.2	87.8	92.7	86.3	89.6	87.1	85.1	88.1
1986:																	
1st quarter	88.9	86.6	89.4	89.3	88.0	90.7	90.5	90.3	90.0	90.3	88.5	93.3	87.1	90.1	87.2	86.2	88.7
2nd quarter	89.6	87.7	90.0	90.0	89.0	91.2	91.0	91.2	90.9	91.1	89.2	93.6	87.8	90.5	88.2	87.2	89.4
3rd quarter	90.2	89.0	90.5	90.6	89.5	91.9	91.6	91.7	91.5	91.6	89.7	94.0	88.5	91.1	88.7	87.3	90.0
4th quarter	91.0	90.1	91.2	91.2	90.2	92.4	92.3	92.2	91.9	92.1	90.4	94.4	89.5	91.5	89.5	88.5	90.7
1987:																	
1st quarter	91.9	91.0	92.0	92.1	91.4	92.8	93.1	92.8	92.6	92.7	91.5	94.7	90.7	92.2	91.9	89.8	91.7
2nd quarter	92.5	92.1	92.6	92.7	91.8	93.5	93.8	93.3	93.1	93.3	92.1	95.5	91.8	93.0	90.6	90.9	92.3
3rd quarter	93.3	92.6	93.5	93.8	92.9	94.3	94.1	94.3	94.0	94.2	92.9	96.0	92.4	93.6	90.8	92.2	93.2
4th quarter	94.1	93.9	94.2	94.5	93.5	95.1	94.5	95.1	94.9	95.2	93.5	96.4	93.1	93.9	90.6	93.2	93.8
1988:																	
1st quarter	95.0	95.0	95.0	95.4	94.4	95.9	95.4	96.0	95.8	96.0	94.3	97.1	93.5	95.1	91.5	94.1	94.5
2nd quarter	96.1	96.0	96.1	96.3	95.5	96.8	96.5	96.9	96.9	96.8	95.5	97.8	94.8	96.3	92.9	95.2	95.8
3rd quarter	97.0	97.0	96.9	97.3	96.6	97.4	97.7	97.4	97.6	97.3	96.5	98.5	96.1	97.5	92.9	96.6	96.8
4th quarter	98.1	98.5	98.0	98.0	97.9	98.1	98.6	98.1	98.4	98.1	97.9	98.8	96.6	98.7	96.3	97.9	97.9
1989:																	
1st quarter	99.2	99.5	99.1	99.1	99.0	99.0	99.4	99.0	99.3	99.0	99.2	99.5	99.2	99.4	98.3	99.0	99.1
2nd quarter	100.2	100.8	100.0	100.0	99.9	100.0	100.1	100.0	99.9	100.0	100.0	99.9	99.7	99.7	100.0	100.3	100.0
3rd quarter	101.4	102.4	101.1	101.1	101.3	101.0	100.9	100.9	101.0	100.9	101.2	100.6	102.8	100.9	100.6	101.3	101.3
4th quarter	102.5	103.7	102.2	101.9	102.5	101.7	102.2	101.9	101.8	101.9	102.3	101.4	105.3	101.8	101.3	102.5	102.3
1990:																	
1st quarter	103.6	105.1	103.2	103.2	103.6	102.8	103.1	103.1	102.2	103.3	103.3	102.6	104.9	103.0	101.8	104.1	103.2
2nd quarter	104.8	106.5	104.4	104.4	104.8	103.9	104.3	104.2	102.8	104.5	104.6	103.1	105.0	104.1	103.5	106.0	104.5
3rd quarter	105.8	107.9	105.4	105.4	105.9	104.7	104.8	105.1	103.3	105.4	105.6	104.0	105.3	104.8	104.9	106.9	105.3
4th quarter	106.8	109.3	106.2	106.2	106.7	105.4	106.4	105.8	103.9	106.2	106.4	104.8	106.3	105.5	104.8	108.4	106.2
1991:																	
1st quarter	107.9	110.6	107.3	107.4	107.9	106.6	106.9	107.0	105.3	107.4	107.5	105.4	107.6	106.6	107.0	109.4	107.3
2nd quarter	109.0	111.6	108.4	108.4	109.0	107.4	108.4	108.0	105.8	108.4	108.7	106.5	109.0	107.7	108.1	110.2	108.4
3rd quarter	109.8	112.2	109.2	109.4	110.0	108.2	109.7	108.8	106.1	109.3	109.6	107.6	110.3	108.7	108.0	111.3	109.2
4th quarter	110.6	113.1	110.1	110.2	110.8	108.9	110.6	109.7	106.9	110.3	110.3	108.9	110.3	109.4	108.4	112.2	109.9
1992:																	
1st quarter	111.5	113.8	111.0	111.1	111.7	109.8	111.2	110.7	107.4	111.5	111.1	109.7	111.7	109.7	109.5	113.1	110.7
2nd quarter	112.2	114.9	111.6	111.8	112.2	110.6	111.7	111.4	107.8	112.2	111.7	110.5	112.2	110.3	108.2	114.2	111.3
3rd quarter	112.7	115.3	112.1	112.5	112.8	111.3	112.4	112.2	108.5	112.9	112.2	111.2	111.9	111.1	108.2	115.0	111.8
4th quarter	113.7	116.5	113.0	113.2	113.8	111.9	112.8	112.9	109.0	113.7	113.1	111.9	113.5	111.9	108.3	116.2	112.7
1993:																	
1st quarter	114.5	117.2	113.9	114.2	114.7	112.7	113.5	113.8	109.7	114.7	113.9	112.8	114.2	112.9	109.3	116.9	113.4
2nd quarter	115.2	118.1	114.6	115.0	115.4	113.4	114.2	114.6	110.3	115.5	114.7	114.0	114.8	113.6	109.3	117.8	114.2
3rd quarter	116.2	118.8	115.6	115.9	116.6	114.4	114.8	115.4	111.1	116.3	115.8	114.7	115.2	114.3	112.3	118.8	115.3
4th quarter	117.1	119.5	116.5	116.6	117.6	115.0	115.2	116.2	111.3	117.3	116.7	115.5	116.4	115.1	112.9	119.7	116.2
1994:																	
1st quarter	117.7	120.4	117.1	117.5	118.3	115.8	116.3	117.0	112.4	118.0	117.3	116.3	116.5	115.4	113.7	120.7	116.8
2nd quarter	118.7	121.3	118.1	118.3	119.2	116.7	116.9	118.0	113.5	119.0	118.2	117.2	118.0	116.8	113.2	121.4	117.7
3rd quarter	119.6	122.3	119.0	119.4	120.1	117.8	117.5	119.0	114.4	120.0	119.1	118.9	119.0	117.7	113.8	122.1	118.6
4th quarter	120.4	123.2	119.7	120.0	121.0	118.2	118.7	119.6	114.9	120.8	119.8	119.7	119.9	118.1	114.2	123.1	119.2
1995:																	
1st quarter	121.3	124.3	120.6	121.0	121.7	119.2	119.4	120.5	115.0	121.9	120.7	121.1	121.1	118.9	115.0	123.8	120.0
2nd quarter	122.2	125.3	121.5	121.8	122.6	120.3	120.1	121.4	115.5	122.9	121.6	122.1	122.4	119.4	117.0	124.5	120.9
3rd quarter	123.1	126.1	122.4	122.6	123.5	121.1	120.8	122.1	116.5	123.5	122.5	122.9	124.0	120.2	118.0	125.2	121.8
4th quarter	123.9	127.0	123.2	123.4	124.5	121.7	121.3	122.9	117.6	124.3	123.3	123.7	125.5	120.9	118.4	126.1	122.6
1996:																	
1st quarter	125.1	127.8	124.4	124.7	125.8	122.8	122.2	123.9	118.5	125.4	124.7	124.5	126.3	122.9	119.8	127.5	123.9
2nd quarter	126.2	128.8	125.6	125.7	127.0	123.9	123.2	125.1	119.4	126.5	125.8	125.1	127.7	123.0	121.9	128.8	125.1
3rd quarter	127.0	129.7	126.4	126.8	127.9	124.5	124.1	126.1	120.1	127.7	126.6	125.9	128.5	124.1	122.2	129.6	125.8
4th quarter	128.0	130.6	127.4	127.5	128.9	125.4	125.6	126.8	121.0	128.4	127.6	127.0	129.7	126.1	122.2	130.6	127.0
1997:																	
1st quarter	129.1	131.4	128.5	128.6	130.2	126.2	126.6	127.6	122.3	129.1	129.0	128.1	131.6	127.2	124.5	131.7	128.2
2nd quarter	130.2	132.2	129.7	129.9	131.3	127.5	127.8	128.9	123.4	130.3	130.1	129.0	132.0	128.4	125.3	133.1	129.3
3rd quarter	131.3	133.2	130.9	131.2	132.6	128.4	129.8	129.9	124.4	131.3	131.4	130.1	133.0	129.6	126.4	134.6	130.5
4th quarter	132.7	134.1	132.4	132.4	134.4	129.3	131.0	130.6	125.1	132.2	133.2	131.3	133.7	130.9	130.6	136.3	132.3
1998:																	
1st quarter	133.9	135.1	133.6	133.7	135.6	130.4	132.1	132.0	126.3	133.7	134.4	132.0	136.3	132.0	134.8	137.2	133.4
2nd quarter	135.1	136.1	134.9	134.8	137.0	131.4	133.2	133.3	127.9	134.6	135.6	133.0	136.9	133.2	134.8	138.4	134.7
3rd quarter	136.6	137.1	136.5	136.3	138.9	132.6	134.3	134.4	128.2	136.0	137.5	134.3	139.3	134.9	138.1	139.9	136.3
4th quarter	137.6	138.2	137.5	136.9	140.1	133.3	135.1	135.2	129.5	136.8	138.5	135.1	141.4	135.1	139.8	140.9	137.6

1. Includes private industry and state and local government workers. Federal government workers are not included.
2. Not seasonally adjusted.

Productivity and Related Data

(Seasonally adjusted, 1992=100)

Year and quarter	Business sector								Nonfarm business sector							
	Output per hour of all persons	Output	Hours of all persons	Compensation per hour	Real compensation per hour	Unit labor costs	Unit nonlabor payments	Implicit price deflator	Output per hour of all persons	Output	Hours of all persons	Compensation per hour	Real compensation per hour	Unit labor costs	Unit nonlabor payments	Implicit price deflator
1970	70.6	52.0	73.6	23.6	85.4	33.5	30.6	32.4	72.7	52.1	71.8	23.8	86.1	32.8	30.3	31.9
1971	73.6	54.0	73.3	25.1	87.1	34.2	33.4	33.9	75.7	54.1	71.5	25.4	87.9	33.5	33.0	33.3
1972	76.0	57.6	75.7	26.7	89.6	35.1	34.8	35.0	78.3	57.8	73.9	27.0	90.6	34.5	34.0	34.3
1973	78.4	61.6	78.5	29.0	91.6	37.0	36.6	36.8	80.7	62.0	76.9	29.2	92.3	36.2	34.3	35.5
1974	77.1	60.6	78.6	31.8	90.6	41.3	38.6	40.3	79.4	61.1	76.9	32.1	91.3	40.4	36.7	39.1
1975	79.8	60.0	75.2	35.1	91.5	44.0	44.5	44.2	81.6	60.0	73.6	35.3	92.2	43.3	43.0	43.2
1976	82.5	64.0	77.5	38.2	94.1	46.2	47.1	46.5	84.5	64.3	76.1	38.4	94.7	45.4	46.0	45.6
1977	84.0	67.6	80.6	41.2	95.3	49.0	50.0	49.4	85.8	67.9	79.1	41.5	96.0	48.3	49.0	48.6
1978	84.9	71.7	84.5	44.9	96.5	52.8	53.3	53.0	87.0	72.3	83.1	45.2	97.3	52.0	51.8	51.9
1979	84.5	73.9	87.4	49.2	95.0	58.2	56.5	57.6	86.3	74.3	86.1	49.5	95.7	57.4	54.7	56.4
1980	84.2	73.0	86.6	54.5	92.8	64.7	59.6	62.8	86.0	73.4	85.4	54.8	93.4	63.8	58.6	61.9
1981	85.8	74.8	87.2	59.6	92.1	69.6	67.1	68.7	87.0	74.8	86.0	60.2	92.8	69.2	65.6	67.9
1982	85.3	72.5	85.0	64.1	93.2	75.1	68.3	72.7	86.3	72.4	83.9	64.6	93.9	74.8	67.4	72.2
1983	88.0	76.1	86.4	66.8	94.0	75.8	74.6	75.4	89.9	76.8	85.4	67.3	94.8	74.9	74.7	74.7
1984	90.2	82.5	91.5	69.7	94.1	77.2	78.5	77.7	91.4	82.8	90.6	70.2	94.8	76.8	77.4	77.0
1985	91.7	85.7	93.5	73.1	95.3	79.7	80.5	80.0	92.3	85.8	92.9	73.4	95.7	79.5	79.9	79.6
1986	94.1	88.5	94.1	76.8	98.4	81.7	81.7	81.7	94.7	88.7	93.6	77.2	98.8	81.5	81.3	81.4
1987	94.0	91.1	96.9	79.8	98.6	84.9	81.9	83.8	94.5	91.3	96.6	80.1	98.9	84.7	81.4	83.6
1988	94.7	94.6	99.9	83.6	99.1	88.3	84.1	86.8	95.3	95.1	99.8	83.7	99.3	87.8	83.8	86.4
1989	95.5	97.8	102.4	85.9	97.2	90.0	91.3	90.4	95.8	98.1	102.4	86.0	97.3	89.7	90.7	90.0
1990	96.1	98.6	102.6	90.8	97.4	94.4	93.5	94.1	96.3	98.8	102.6	90.7	97.3	94.2	93.1	93.8
1991	96.7	96.9	100.2	95.1	98.0	98.3	96.6	97.7	97.0	97.1	100.1	95.1	98.0	98.1	96.8	97.6
1992	100.0	100.0	100.0	100.0	100.0	100.0	100.0	100.0	100.0	100.0	100.0	100.0	100.0	100.0	100.0	100.0
1993	100.1	102.7	102.6	102.5	99.5	102.4	102.7	102.5	100.1	103.0	102.9	102.2	99.3	102.2	103.1	102.5
1994	100.7	107.0	106.2	104.4	98.8	103.7	106.8	104.8	100.6	107.0	106.3	104.2	98.7	103.6	107.3	104.9
1995	101.0	109.9	108.8	106.8	98.4	105.8	108.8	106.9	101.2	110.2	108.9	106.7	98.2	105.4	109.9	107.0
1996	103.7	114.5	110.4	110.7	99.0	106.8	111.8	108.6	103.7	114.8	110.7	110.4	98.7	106.5	112.1	108.5
1997	105.2	119.8	113.8	114.7	100.3	109.0	112.9	110.4	104.9	119.9	114.3	114.3	99.9	108.9	113.6	110.6
1998	107.7	125.3	116.3	119.7	103.0	111.1	110.9	111.0	107.2	125.5	117.0	119.1	102.5	111.1	112.0	111.4
1990:																
1st quarter	96.1	99.3	103.4	88.6	97.0	92.2	93.2	92.5	96.3	99.6	103.4	88.5	96.9	91.9	92.7	92.2
2nd quarter	96.6	99.5	103.0	90.4	98.0	93.6	94.0	93.7	96.7	99.7	103.0	90.2	97.8	93.3	93.5	93.4
3rd quarter	96.5	98.6	102.2	91.7	97.7	95.1	93.7	94.6	96.5	98.8	102.4	91.5	97.6	94.8	93.3	94.3
4th quarter	95.4	97.1	101.8	92.5	96.9	96.9	93.2	95.6	95.6	97.2	101.8	92.4	96.8	96.7	93.0	95.4
1991:																
1st quarter	95.8	96.3	100.6	93.2	97.0	97.4	95.6	96.7	96.0	96.5	100.5	93.2	97.0	97.1	95.9	96.7
2nd quarter	96.7	96.9	100.2	94.7	98.0	97.9	96.5	97.4	96.9	97.0	100.1	94.7	98.0	97.8	96.4	97.3
3rd quarter	97.0	97.2	100.2	95.7	98.2	98.6	97.1	98.1	97.3	97.4	100.1	95.7	98.2	98.4	97.4	98.0
4th quarter	97.5	97.4	99.9	96.8	98.5	99.3	97.3	98.6	97.6	97.5	99.9	96.8	98.5	99.1	97.4	98.5
1992:																
1st quarter	99.6	98.8	99.3	98.9	100.0	99.3	99.2	99.3	99.6	98.8	99.3	98.8	99.9	99.3	99.2	99.2
2nd quarter	99.7	99.6	99.9	99.3	99.6	99.6	100.0	99.7	99.8	99.6	99.8	99.4	99.7	99.6	100.0	99.8
3rd quarter	99.6	99.8	100.2	100.6	100.2	100.9	98.6	100.1	99.6	99.8	100.2	100.6	100.2	101.0	98.4	100.1
4th quarter	101.1	101.7	100.7	101.2	99.9	100.1	102.2	100.9	101.1	101.8	100.7	101.2	99.9	100.1	102.3	100.9
1993:																
1st quarter	99.9	101.4	101.5	101.6	99.6	101.7	101.8	101.7	99.9	101.6	101.7	101.5	99.5	101.6	102.3	101.8
2nd quarter	99.8	102.1	102.3	102.5	99.7	102.7	101.5	102.3	99.7	102.3	102.6	102.2	99.4	102.5	101.8	102.3
3rd quarter	99.9	102.8	102.9	102.9	99.6	103.0	102.2	102.7	100.0	103.2	103.2	102.5	99.3	102.5	102.9	102.6
4th quarter	100.8	104.6	103.7	103.1	99.1	102.3	105.3	103.4	100.7	104.8	104.1	102.8	98.8	102.1	105.5	103.3
1994:																
1st quarter	100.8	105.2	104.4	104.1	99.6	103.3	104.9	103.9	100.7	105.2	104.5	103.9	99.3	103.2	105.0	103.8
2nd quarter	100.8	106.9	106.0	104.1	98.9	103.2	106.5	104.4	100.8	106.9	106.1	103.9	98.7	103.1	107.0	104.5
3rd quarter	100.4	107.3	106.8	104.3	98.2	103.8	107.4	105.1	100.3	107.3	106.9	104.1	98.0	103.7	108.2	105.3
4th quarter	100.7	108.5	107.7	105.1	98.3	104.3	108.3	105.8	100.8	108.6	107.8	105.0	98.2	104.2	109.2	106.0
1995:																
1st quarter	100.5	109.0	108.5	105.6	98.2	105.1	108.3	106.3	100.6	109.2	108.6	105.5	98.0	104.8	109.4	106.4
2nd quarter	100.7	109.1	108.3	106.4	98.1	105.7	108.5	106.7	100.9	109.4	108.4	106.2	97.9	105.3	109.7	106.9
3rd quarter	101.0	110.3	109.1	107.2	98.3	106.1	108.9	107.1	101.3	110.7	109.2	107.0	98.2	105.6	110.0	107.2
4th quarter	101.8	111.2	109.2	108.2	98.6	106.2	109.6	107.4	102.0	111.6	109.4	108.0	98.4	105.8	110.3	107.4
1996:																
1st quarter	103.0	112.5	109.2	108.9	98.5	105.7	111.9	107.9	103.1	112.8	109.4	108.7	98.3	105.4	112.3	107.9
2nd quarter	103.8	114.2	110.0	110.4	98.9	106.3	112.1	108.4	103.8	114.5	110.3	110.1	98.7	106.0	112.3	108.2
3rd quarter	103.8	114.9	110.7	111.4	99.3	107.3	111.5	108.8	103.8	115.2	111.0	111.0	99.0	107.0	111.6	108.6
4th quarter	104.2	116.4	111.7	112.3	99.2	107.8	111.8	109.2	104.0	116.6	112.1	111.9	98.9	107.5	112.2	109.2
1997:																
1st quarter	104.4	117.8	112.9	113.2	99.5	108.5	112.4	109.9	104.1	117.9	113.3	112.9	99.2	108.5	112.9	110.0
2nd quarter	104.8	119.1	113.6	113.9	99.8	108.7	113.2	110.3	104.5	119.2	114.1	113.6	99.5	108.7	113.7	110.4
3rd quarter	105.8	120.6	114.0	115.0	100.3	108.8	113.8	110.6	105.4	120.6	114.5	114.6	99.9	108.8	114.6	110.8
4th quarter	106.0	121.7	114.8	116.5	101.1	109.9	112.4	110.8	105.6	121.8	115.3	116.0	100.7	109.8	113.3	111.1
1998:																
1st quarter	107.1	123.7	115.6	117.9	102.1	110.2	112.2	110.9	106.6	123.9	116.3	117.4	101.6	110.1	113.2	111.2
2nd quarter	107.1	124.3	116.1	119.1	102.7	111.2	110.5	111.0	106.6	124.4	116.7	118.5	102.1	111.1	111.6	111.3
3rd quarter	107.8	125.5	116.4	120.2	103.2	111.5	110.4	111.1	107.3	125.6	117.1	119.7	102.7	111.5	111.4	111.5
4th quarter	109.0	127.7	117.2	121.5	103.9	111.5	110.7	111.2	108.5	127.9	117.9	120.9	103.3	111.4	111.7	111.5

Productivity and Related Data—*Continued*

(Seasonally adjusted, 1992=100)

Year and quarter	Nonfinancial corporations										Manufacturing					
	Output per hour of all persons	Output	Employee hours	Compensation per hour	Real compensation per hour	Unit costs			Implicit price deflator	Unit nonlabor payments	Output per hour of all persons	Output	Hours of all persons	Compensation per hour	Real compensation per hour	Unit labor costs
						Total	Labor costs	Nonlabor costs								
1970	69.1	47.0	68.0	25.4	91.7	36.1	36.7	34.3	36.6	36.4	54.4	56.8	104.4	23.8	86.2	43.8
1971	72.0	48.9	67.9	27.0	93.4	37.1	37.5	36.0	38.0	39.2	58.2	58.5	100.5	25.3	87.6	43.5
1972	73.9	52.7	71.4	28.5	95.8	37.9	38.6	35.9	39.2	40.2	60.7	63.7	105.1	26.6	89.3	43.9
1973	74.5	55.8	74.9	30.8	97.2	40.3	41.3	37.5	41.5	41.7	61.9	68.3	110.4	28.7	90.6	46.3
1974	72.7	54.8	75.3	33.7	95.9	45.5	46.3	43.3	45.6	44.1	61.6	66.5	107.9	31.8	90.6	51.7
1975	75.6	53.9	71.3	37.1	96.6	49.0	49.0	48.9	50.1	52.3	64.7	62.9	97.2	35.7	93.1	55.2
1976	78.2	58.3	74.6	40.2	99.0	50.7	51.4	48.8	52.4	54.3	67.4	68.6	101.9	38.7	95.3	57.4
1977	80.1	62.6	78.1	43.3	100.3	53.1	54.0	50.4	55.1	57.3	70.1	74.3	106.1	42.0	97.3	60.0
1978	80.8	66.7	82.6	47.0	101.2	57.1	58.2	53.8	59.0	60.5	70.7	78.2	110.6	45.4	97.7	64.2
1979	79.4	68.2	85.8	51.4	99.3	63.4	64.7	59.8	64.3	63.4	70.2	79.1	112.7	49.9	96.4	71.0
1980	80.4	68.3	85.1	56.7	96.5	70.2	70.5	69.2	69.7	67.9	70.4	75.7	107.5	55.8	95.0	79.3
1981	82.9	71.5	86.2	61.9	95.5	75.8	74.7	79.0	75.8	78.1	71.1	76.0	107.0	61.3	94.7	86.3
1982	84.2	70.5	83.7	66.3	96.3	80.4	78.7	85.4	79.3	80.6	74.7	73.1	97.9	67.3	97.8	90.1
1983	86.9	73.7	84.9	68.7	96.8	80.9	79.1	85.8	81.1	85.1	77.1	76.3	98.9	69.1	97.4	89.6
1984	89.6	81.0	90.3	71.7	96.8	81.1	80.0	84.3	82.8	88.6	79.8	84.0	105.3	71.5	96.5	89.6
1985	91.1	84.2	92.5	75.0	97.8	83.1	82.3	85.2	84.4	88.7	82.8	86.6	104.6	75.3	98.2	91.0
1986	93.7	86.9	92.7	78.8	100.8	84.9	84.0	87.5	85.2	87.7	86.5	89.1	103.0	78.7	100.7	91.0
1987	95.2	91.1	95.8	81.6	100.8	86.2	85.7	87.5	87.1	89.9	88.8	92.1	103.8	80.9	99.9	91.2
1988	96.9	95.9	99.1	84.9	100.7	88.2	87.7	89.7	89.6	93.6	90.5	96.5	106.6	84.2	99.9	93.0
1989	95.5	97.5	102.0	87.1	98.5	92.5	91.1	96.3	92.8	96.2	90.7	97.1	107.1	86.9	98.3	95.8
1990	96.1	98.4	102.4	91.5	98.2	96.2	95.2	99.1	96.1	97.9	93.0	97.5	104.8	91.0	97.7	97.9
1991	97.6	97.1	99.6	95.7	98.5	99.3	98.0	103.0	98.8	100.5	95.1	95.5	100.4	95.8	98.7	100.7
1992	100.0	100.0	100.0	100.0	100.0	100.0	100.0	100.0	100.0	100.0	100.0	100.0	100.0	100.0	100.0	100.0
1993	101.1	103.4	102.3	102.0	99.1	100.5	100.9	99.4	101.7	103.2	102.2	103.6	101.4	102.9	99.9	100.7
1994	103.5	109.9	106.2	104.1	98.5	100.3	100.6	99.7	103.4	109.4	105.3	109.1	103.6	105.8	100.2	100.5
1995	104.8	114.8	109.6	106.2	97.8	100.8	101.4	99.0	104.7	111.4	109.4	113.8	104.0	108.3	99.7	99.0
1996	107.6	120.0	111.5	109.5	97.9	100.7	101.7	97.9	105.6	113.6	113.8	118.0	103.7	110.7	99.0	97.2
1997	110.3	127.3	115.4	113.3	99.0	101.1	102.7	96.6	106.3	113.6	119.2	125.7	105.5	115.1	100.6	96.6
1998	113.6	134.5	118.4	118.0	101.6	101.7	103.8	95.6	106.1	110.8	124.0	130.9	105.6	120.0	103.3	96.8
1990:																
1st quarter	95.4	98.3	103.0	89.4	97.9	94.7	93.7	97.6	94.9	97.3	92.1	97.4	105.7	89.0	97.5	96.6
2nd quarter	96.6	99.3	102.8	91.1	98.7	95.1	94.3	97.5	95.8	98.8	92.4	97.7	105.8	90.6	98.3	98.1
3rd quarter	96.1	98.2	102.3	92.4	98.5	97.2	96.2	99.9	96.5	97.1	93.7	98.1	104.7	91.7	97.7	97.8
4th quarter	96.5	97.7	101.2	93.2	97.7	97.9	96.6	101.6	97.2	98.4	93.8	96.6	103.0	92.8	97.2	98.9
1991:																
1st quarter	97.1	97.0	99.9	93.9	97.7	98.4	96.8	102.9	98.2	101.2	93.5	94.2	100.8	94.0	97.8	100.6
2nd quarter	97.5	96.8	99.3	95.4	98.6	99.2	97.8	103.2	98.8	100.7	94.2	94.5	100.3	95.3	98.5	101.1
3rd quarter	97.7	97.1	99.5	96.2	98.8	99.7	98.5	103.1	99.1	100.4	96.0	96.4	100.5	96.5	99.1	100.6
4th quarter	98.2	97.6	99.4	97.3	99.0	100.0	99.1	102.6	99.2	99.6	96.9	97.0	100.2	97.5	99.3	100.7
1992:																
1st quarter	99.4	98.6	99.2	98.9	100.0	99.7	99.5	100.4	99.5	99.7	98.4	97.9	99.5	98.6	99.7	100.2
2nd quarter	99.3	99.3	100.0	99.4	99.8	100.0	100.2	99.6	99.9	99.4	99.6	99.7	100.1	99.7	100.0	100.1
3rd quarter	100.1	100.1	100.1	100.6	100.1	100.7	100.5	101.3	100.1	99.3	100.7	100.7	99.9	100.6	100.2	99.9
4th quarter	101.3	102.0	100.7	101.2	99.9	99.6	99.9	98.8	100.4	101.6	101.3	101.7	100.4	101.0	99.7	99.8
1993:																
1st quarter	100.2	101.5	101.3	101.4	99.4	100.8	101.2	99.9	101.3	101.4	102.1	102.9	100.8	101.5	99.5	99.5
2nd quarter	100.9	102.8	101.9	101.9	99.2	100.6	101.1	99.1	101.4	102.2	102.1	103.3	101.2	102.5	99.7	100.4
3rd quarter	101.2	103.8	102.6	102.2	99.0	100.6	101.0	99.5	101.7	103.1	101.8	103.3	101.5	103.4	100.1	101.6
4th quarter	102.1	105.7	103.5	102.4	98.4	100.0	100.3	99.0	102.2	106.2	102.8	104.9	102.0	104.3	100.2	101.4
1994:																
1st quarter	103.8	108.1	104.1	103.8	99.2	100.4	100.0	101.5	102.8	108.5	104.0	106.3	102.2	105.3	100.6	101.2
2nd quarter	103.1	109.1	105.8	103.7	98.6	100.1	100.6	98.8	103.1	108.1	105.2	108.4	103.0	105.3	100.1	100.1
3rd quarter	103.0	110.2	106.9	103.9	97.8	100.5	100.9	99.5	103.7	109.7	105.5	109.7	104.0	105.9	99.7	100.4
4th quarter	103.7	112.3	108.3	104.6	97.9	100.3	100.8	99.1	104.1	111.0	106.5	111.9	105.1	106.7	99.9	100.2
1995:																
1st quarter	103.4	112.9	109.1	105.2	97.8	101.1	101.7	99.3	104.4	110.0	108.0	113.4	105.0	107.3	99.7	99.3
2nd quarter	104.0	113.7	109.4	105.8	97.5	101.2	101.7	99.6	104.6	110.4	109.0	113.4	104.0	108.0	99.6	99.0
3rd quarter	105.3	115.7	109.9	106.5	97.7	100.4	101.1	98.4	104.8	112.3	109.8	113.9	103.7	108.8	99.8	99.1
4th quarter	106.1	116.9	110.2	107.3	97.8	100.5	101.1	98.8	104.9	112.7	110.8	114.6	103.4	109.3	99.6	98.6
1996:																
1st quarter	106.4	117.3	110.2	107.8	97.5	100.6	101.2	98.7	105.4	113.9	112.0	114.8	102.6	109.2	98.8	97.5
2nd quarter	107.3	119.3	111.2	109.1	97.7	100.7	101.7	97.9	105.5	113.5	113.2	117.5	103.8	110.3	98.9	97.5
3rd quarter	108.0	120.9	112.0	110.0	98.1	100.8	101.9	97.5	105.7	113.5	114.6	119.3	104.1	111.2	99.1	97.0
4th quarter	108.6	122.5	112.9	110.8	98.0	100.9	102.1	97.4	105.8	113.5	115.5	120.4	104.2	111.9	98.9	96.9
1997:																
1st quarter	108.9	124.3	114.1	111.8	98.2	101.2	102.6	97.3	106.2	113.7	116.7	122.5	105.0	113.1	99.4	96.9
2nd quarter	109.5	126.2	115.2	112.4	98.5	101.2	102.6	97.1	106.3	113.8	118.0	124.5	105.5	114.1	99.9	96.7
3rd quarter	111.0	128.7	115.9	113.6	99.0	100.7	102.3	96.4	106.3	114.5	120.4	126.8	105.3	115.5	100.7	95.9
4th quarter	111.4	130.2	116.9	115.1	99.8	101.3	103.3	95.7	106.3	112.3	121.6	129.1	106.2	117.7	102.1	96.8
1998:																
1st quarter	112.1	132.1	117.8	116.1	100.5	101.4	103.5	95.4	106.2	111.5	122.1	129.9	106.4	118.8	102.8	97.3
2nd quarter	112.9	133.4	118.1	117.3	101.1	101.7	103.9	95.5	106.1	110.7	123.2	130.7	106.1	119.5	103.0	97.0
3rd quarter	114.2	135.4	118.6	118.6	101.8	101.6	103.8	95.2	106.1	110.9	124.6	130.8	105.0	120.4	103.3	96.6
4th quarter	115.1	137.2	119.3	119.7	102.3	102.0	104.1	96.2	106.0	110.1	126.2	132.4	104.9	121.4	103.8	96.2

Corporate Profits

(Net profits after taxes—Millions of dollars)

Year and quarter	Total	Manufacturing											Petroleum and coal products	Rubber and plastics products
		Nondurable goods												
								Chemicals						
		Total	Food and tobacco	Textiles	Apparel (including leather)	Paper	Printing	Total	Industrial chemicals and synthetics	Drugs	Other chemicals			
1970	28 572	.....	2 549	413	.....	719	.....	3 434	.....	.....	.....	5 893	.....
1971	31 038	.....	2 754	558	.....	501	.....	3 780	.....	.....	.....	5 829	.....
1972	36 467	.....	3 021	659	.....	941	.....	4 499	.....	.....	.....	5 151	.....
1973	48 259	.....	3 723	831	.....	1 427	.....	5 670	.....	.....	.....	7 759	.....
1974	58 747	.....	4 601	780	.....	2 287	.....	7 175	.....	.....	.....	14 483	.....
1975	49 135	.....	5 154	409	.....	1 801	.....	6 703	.....	.....	.....	9 307	.....
1976	64 519	.....	5 826	809	.....	2 270	.....	7 610	.....	.....	.....	11 725	.....
1977	70 366	.....	5 575	828	.....	2 367	.....	8 060	.....	.....	.....	12 179	.....
1978	81 148	.....	6 213	1 170	.....	2 598	.....	9 117	.....	.....	.....	12 805	.....
1979	98 698	.....	7 340	1 340	.....	3 723	.....	10 896	.....	.....	.....	21 936	.....
1980	92 579	.....	8 222	977	.....	2 789	.....	11 578	.....	.....	.....	25 133	.....
1981	101 302	.....	9 109	1 157	.....	3 110	.....	12 973	.....	.....	.....	23 733	.....
1982	71 028	.....	8 383	851	.....	1 460	.....	10 324	.....	.....	.....	19 666	.....
1983	85 834	.....	9 436	1 599	.....	2 327	.....	11 644	.....	.....	.....	19 297	.....
1984	107 648	.....	9 760	1 635	.....	3 015	.....	13 883	.....	.....	.....	17 154	.....
1985	87 648	.....	12 798	1 200	.....	2 880	.....	9 542	.....	.....	.....	12 739	.....
1986	83 121	.....	13 292	1 706	.....	3 280	.....	12 900	.....	.....	.....	8 823	.....
1987	115 498	.....	4 966	1 882	.....	5 505	.....	16 572	.....	.....	.....	10 867	.....
1988	153 764	86 813	20 591	1 493	1 853	8 021	7 407	23 448	10 129	7 367	.....	21 087	2 911
1989	135 141	79 611	16 482	670	2 071	6 981	7 799	23 994	9 017	7 741	.....	19 366	2 246
1990	110 128	69 441	15 997	345	1 260	4 846	5 110	22 710	7 448	9 309	.....	17 811	1 365
1991	66 407	59 255	19 576	691	1 896	2 134	3 921	19 527	4 406	10 185	.....	10 786	724
1992	22 085	46 043	17 502	1 991	3 473	1 176	4 792	12 446	-2 962	9 487	5 921	3 142	1 522
1993	83 156	55 713	15 811	1 449	2 430	-255	5 492	15 198	3 873	10 196	1 128	12 970	2 621
1994	174 874	87 816	21 913	1 754	1 963	5 168	8 350	29 608	8 069	13 340	8 197	14 880	4 176
1995	198 151	103 889	24 806	893	1 956	11 784	9 978	36 007	10 516	15 468	10 024	13 929	4 540
1996	224 869	118 785	26 432	1 844	1 925	6 249	11 181	39 843	8 063	16 431	15 349	26 640	4 675
1997	244 505	123 119	26 615	1 883	3 247	3 606	10 889	41 981	9 391	17 732	14 858	29 447	5 452
1998	236 631	108 943	27 057	2 083	2 533	4 746	15 891	42 736	7 916	22 747	12 074	8 364	5 531
1990:													
1st quarter	27 718	16 010	3 480	41	256	1 445	1 010	5 294	1 582	2 082	.....	4 062	424
2nd quarter	34 762	19 148	5 146	217	265	1 583	1 220	6 192	2 587	1 993	.....	3 939	587
3rd quarter	29 195	19 894	5 095	111	546	1 202	1 526	6 070	1 779	2 434	.....	5 017	326
4th quarter	18 453	14 389	2 276	-24	193	616	1 354	5 154	1 500	2 800	.....	4 793	28
1991:													
1st quarter	18 011	16 619	4 957	-55	318	852	684	5 084	1 735	2 243	.....	4 833	-53
2nd quarter	22 793	15 231	5 163	148	335	812	696	5 253	1 196	2 158	.....	2 512	311
3rd quarter	17 298	16 257	5 469	177	802	846	1 515	5 240	601	3 097	.....	1 573	634
4th quarter	8 305	11 148	3 987	421	441	-376	1 026	3 950	874	2 687	.....	1 868	-168
1992:													
1st quarter	-44 377	-4 160	3 113	254	748	-509	124	-3 213	-5 832	1 472	1 147	-3 934	-743
2nd quarter	29 596	18 503	5 924	502	441	864	1 670	6 023	1 824	2 688	1 511	2 181	898
3rd quarter	27 449	18 588	4 584	568	1 711	720	1 775	6 088	1 500	2 825	1 763	2 331	811
4th quarter	9 417	13 112	3 881	667	573	101	1 223	3 548	-454	2 502	1 500	2 564	556
1993:													
1st quarter	10 998	12 683	2 910	227	642	714	962	4 226	1 474	3 014	-261	2 593	408
2nd quarter	24 961	15 690	4 813	597	574	803	1 622	3 031	1 911	2 611	-1 491	3 243	1 008
3rd quarter	24 729	13 251	4 459	321	883	-1 757	1 147	4 582	-39	3 273	1 347	2 961	658
4th quarter	22 468	14 089	3 629	304	331	-15	1 761	3 359	527	1 298	1 533	4 173	547
1994:													
1st quarter	35 085	18 939	5 505	336	176	661	1 914	7 418	2 015	3 891	1 511	2 265	663
2nd quarter	46 557	19 977	4 635	526	679	1 000	2 277	6 936	2 019	2 790	2 127	2 609	1 314
3rd quarter	46 452	24 165	5 799	661	731	1 275	2 248	8 027	2 471	3 111	2 445	4 255	1 168
4th quarter	46 780	24 735	5 974	231	377	2 232	1 911	7 227	1 564	3 548	2 114	5 751	1 031
1995:													
1st quarter	51 960	25 968	5 851	339	403	2 452	3 473	8 934	3 388	3 299	2 247	3 331	1 185
2nd quarter	57 023	28 007	6 675	388	196	3 192	2 079	10 303	3 855	3 909	2 539	3 755	1 419
3rd quarter	50 291	29 622	6 655	194	893	3 474	1 940	10 348	2 515	5 003	2 831	5 029	1 092
4th quarter	38 877	20 292	5 625	-28	464	2 666	2 486	6 422	758	3 257	2 407	1 814	844
1996:													
1st quarter	50 749	28 163	6 368	213	195	2 125	2 886	9 913	3 380	3 437	3 096	5 148	1 315
2nd quarter	58 871	27 996	6 176	596	254	1 555	1 942	7 755	-344	4 163	3 937	8 079	1 639
3rd quarter	62 063	34 473	6 810	657	815	1 721	2 936	13 678	3 305	4 453	5 920	6 456	1 401
4th quarter	53 186	28 153	7 078	378	661	848	3 417	8 497	1 722	4 378	2 396	6 957	320
1997:													
1st quarter	60 589	33 558	6 053	418	870	1 102	2 980	12 998	3 405	5 221	4 371	7 871	1 266
2nd quarter	66 877	30 532	7 231	650	912	1 033	2 840	8 572	3 853	1 208	3 512	7 353	1 941
3rd quarter	62 498	33 017	8 067	506	1 164	1 568	2 611	11 054	2 174	4 351	4 530	6 639	1 408
4th quarter	54 541	26 012	5 264	309	301	-97	2 458	9 357	-41	6 952	2 445	7 584	837
1998:													
1st quarter	74 680	29 867	6 747	587	765	1 325	3 180	11 697	2 884	5 222	3 592	3 968	1 598
2nd quarter	55 877	30 065	6 233	530	733	1 590	4 152	11 832	2 751	5 303	3 778	3 109	1 885
3rd quarter	61 393	33 182	9 221	663	1 010	1 408	4 405	10 532	1 322	5 665	3 546	4 878	1 064
4th quarter	44 681	15 829	4 856	303	25	423	4 154	8 675	959	6 557	1 158	-3 591	984

1. The tobacco industry is included beginning with the data for 1985.

Corporate Profits—*Continued*

(Net profits after taxes—Millions of dollars)

Year and quarter	Total	Stone, clay, and glass products	Primary metals Total	Iron and steel	Nonferrous metals	Fabricated metal products	Machinery (except electrical)	Electrical and electronic equipment	Transportation equipment Total	Motor vehicles and equipment	Aircraft, missiles, parts	Instruments
1970	.....	627	.....	692	1 297	1 066	2 689	2 349	.....	1 424	.....	.....
1971	.....	853	.....	748	621	1 070	2 489	2 563	.....	3 097	.....	.....
1972	.....	1 060	.....	1 022	687	1 569	3 481	2 999	.....	3 639	.....	.....
1973	.....	1 266	.....	1 695	1 343	2 207	4 936	3 883	.....	4 122	.....	.....
1974	.....	1 204	.....	3 149	2 035	2 837	5 648	2 940	.....	1 957	.....	.....
1975	.....	968	.....	2 280	663	2 523	6 311	2 564	.....	1 737	.....	.....
1976	.....	1 447	.....	2 085	913	3 196	7 889	4 073	.....	5 099	.....	.....
1977	.....	1 686	.....	864	873	3 458	9 131	5 383	.....	6 133	.....	.....
1978	.....	2 353	.....	2 124	1 362	3 815	10 746	6 500	.....	6 211	.....	.....
1979	.....	2 373	.....	2 185	2 691	4 431	11 530	7 386	.....	4 382	.....	.....
1980	.....	1 833	.....	2 334	2 768	3 967	11 459	7 114	.....	-3 424	.....	.....
1981	.....	1 627	.....	3 507	2 124	4 235	12 580	7 872	.....	-209	.....	.....
1982	.....	408	.....	-3 705	-333	2 320	8 038	6 449	.....	734	.....	.....
1983	.....	1 002	.....	-3 746	-288	2 693	7 680	6 367	.....	7 168	.....	.....
1984	.....	1 870	.....	-379	-84	4 646	11 963	8 616	.....	10 575	.....	.....
1985	.....	1 627	.....	-1 349	-1 000	3 388	9 676	6 886	.....	9 087	.....	.....
1986	.....	2 120	.....	-3 372	760	3 232	6 551	7 619	.....	8 363	.....	.....
1987	.....	2 907	.....	1 353	1 065	4 428	10 205	9 585	.....	10 642	.....	.....
1988	66 948	2 443	5 177	984	4 195	5 334	13 758	11 137	17 468	12 454	4 880	7 728
1989	55 532	1 950	5 223	1 491	3 733	5 506	9 666	9 643	13 108	8 799	3 860	6 069
1990	40 686	1 049	3 084	544	2 541	4 577	11 127	6 390	4 576	-566	4 491	6 697
1991	7 152	-1 568	-523	-1 482	958	3 341	-2 763	4 686	-4 827	-7 602	2 477	6 680
1992	-23 960	-427	-2 440	-1 245	-1 195	4 036	-9 261	8 356	-32 394	-30 720	-1 839	4 250
1993	27 442	1 052	-775	-235	-538	2 773	-6 774	12 552	7 756	2 738	4 603	5 758
1994	87 061	1 837	4 786	2 488	2 297	5 499	15 624	18 308	22 764	16 484	5 594	11 504
1995	94 261	2 825	8 150	2 716	5 436	5 493	16 168	26 354	21 364	15 404	4 301	9 349
1996	106 086	3 593	5 396	1 677	3 718	9 249	22 932	26 201	23 845	14 986	7 125	8 319
1997	121 385	3 066	6 563	2 765	3 798	10 130	24 044	34 220	27 734	19 132	7 222	7 729
1998	127 688	4 171	5 376	1 825	3 550	10 168	22 688	28 524	43 300	34 196	7 701	6 093
1990:												
1st quarter	11 708	-10	1 107	314	794	1 335	2 324	2 040	2 766	1 357	1 293	1 483
2nd quarter	15 613	994	1 374	455	919	1 490	2 890	2 030	3 393	2 122	1 161	2 242
3rd quarter	9 301	547	981	307	674	1 272	2 570	2 012	-349	-1 937	1 587	1 268
4th quarter	4 064	-482	-378	-532	154	480	3 343	308	-1 234	-2 108	450	1 704
1991:												
1st quarter	1 392	-559	270	-268	537	499	-1 250	1 870	-1 011	-1 975	951	1 486
2nd quarter	7 562	144	342	-62	404	1 485	76	2 242	211	-1 292	1 364	2 211
3rd quarter	1 041	239	256	7	249	1 083	-325	-1 324	-1 595	-1 679	-39	1 844
4th quarter	-2 843	-1 392	-1 391	-1 159	-232	274	-1 264	1 898	-2 432	-2 656	201	1 139
1992:												
1st quarter	-40 217	-1 112	-2 918	-1 131	-1 787	918	-3 919	631	-33 975	-28 471	-5 493	-539
2nd quarter	11 092	506	676	251	425	1 621	1 150	2 932	1 124	-79	1 076	1 974
3rd quarter	8 860	508	862	384	478	1 498	-460	2 720	37	-1 227	1 192	2 243
4th quarter	-3 695	-329	-1 060	-749	-311	-1	-6 032	2 073	420	-943	1 386	572
1993:												
1st quarter	-1 684	-766	-1 358	-787	-570	701	-1 085	2 065	-2 276	-3 560	1 180	1
2nd quarter	9 271	1 445	939	680	259	1 596	-7 068	4 045	4 242	2 633	1 380	2 568
3rd quarter	11 476	709	197	40	157	1 310	369	3 369	1 966	689	1 147	2 046
4th quarter	8 379	-336	-553	-168	-384	-834	1 010	3 073	3 824	2 976	896	1 143
1994:												
1st quarter	16 147	-484	713	421	291	1 507	2 112	3 939	4 540	3 182	1 265	2 419
2nd quarter	26 581	1 020	1 179	660	518	1 892	5 308	5 024	7 110	5 408	1 488	3 185
3rd quarter	22 288	873	1 307	712	596	1 706	3 458	5 217	4 569	3 023	1 369	2 983
4th quarter	22 045	428	1 587	695	892	394	4 746	4 128	6 545	4 871	1 472	2 917
1995:												
1st quarter	25 991	235	2 412	842	1 571	1 808	4 702	5 547	6 582	5 012	1 230	3 459
2nd quarter	29 015	683	2 055	618	1 437	2 109	6 317	6 679	6 212	4 830	918	3 361
3rd quarter	20 669	1 299	2 047	728	1 320	1 342	1 992	6 792	4 046	2 002	1 587	2 022
4th quarter	18 586	608	1 636	528	1 108	234	3 157	7 336	4 524	3 560	566	507
1996:												
1st quarter	22 587	377	1 334	232	1 103	2 134	3 840	6 155	5 596	3 327	1 512	1 910
2nd quarter	30 875	1 206	1 776	675	1 101	2 413	6 434	6 447	8 177	5 584	2 099	2 537
3rd quarter	27 590	1 433	1 443	626	817	3 146	5 839	6 030	5 471	3 293	1 801	2 277
4th quarter	25 034	577	843	144	697	1 556	6 819	7 569	4 601	2 782	1 713	1 595
1997:												
1st quarter	27 031	-818	1 703	595	1 108	2 367	5 475	8 303	6 885	4 807	1 792	1 471
2nd quarter	36 344	1 277	2 130	920	1 210	2 898	7 213	9 464	8 778	6 094	2 175	2 125
3rd quarter	29 481	1 693	1 640	637	1 003	2 909	4 567	8 363	5 820	3 257	2 240	2 364
4th quarter	28 529	914	1 090	613	477	1 956	6 789	8 090	6 251	4 974	1 015	1 769
1998:												
1st quarter	44 813	515	1 796	652	1 145	2 805	6 160	6 404	23 804	21 837	1 615	1 840
2nd quarter	25 812	1 758	1 485	696	789	3 291	3 623	3 907	8 111	5 462	2 106	1 317
3rd quarter	28 211	2 009	1 446	440	1 005	2 665	5 972	8 275	4 582	1 966	2 125	1 312
4th quarter	28 852	-111	649	37	611	1 407	6 933	9 938	6 803	4 931	1 855	1 624

Corporate Profits—*Continued,* and Dividends Paid, All Manufacturing

(Net profits after taxes—Millions of dollars)

Year and quarter	Durable goods manufacturing- Continued				Mining	Wholesale trade			Retail trade				Dividends paid, all manufacturing
		Other durable goods											
	Total	Lumber and wood products	Furniture and fixtures	Miscellaneous manufacturing		Total	Durable goods	Nondurable goods	Total	General merchandise stores	Food stores	All others	
1970	.....	.....	.....	.....	.....	.....	.....	.....	.....	.....	.....	.....	15 070
1971	.....	.....	.....	.....	.....	.....	.....	.....	.....	.....	.....	.....	15 252
1972	.....	.....	.....	.....	.....	.....	.....	.....	.....	.....	.....	.....	16 110
1973	.....	.....	.....	.....	.....	.....	.....	.....	.....	.....	.....	.....	17 734
1974	.....	.....	.....	.....	.....	.....	.....	.....	.....	.....	.....	.....	19 467
1975	.....	.....	.....	.....	.....	.....	.....	.....	.....	.....	.....	.....	19 968
1976	.....	.....	.....	.....	.....	.....	.....	.....	.....	.....	.....	.....	22 763
1977	.....	.....	.....	.....	.....	.....	.....	.....	.....	.....	.....	.....	26 585
1978	.....	.....	.....	.....	.....	.....	.....	.....	.....	.....	.....	.....	28 932
1979	.....	.....	.....	.....	.....	.....	.....	.....	.....	.....	.....	.....	32 491
1980	.....	.....	.....	.....	.....	.....	.....	.....	.....	.....	.....	.....	36 495
1981	.....	.....	.....	.....	.....	.....	.....	.....	.....	.....	.....	.....	40 317
1982	.....	.....	.....	.....	.....	.....	.....	.....	.....	.....	.....	.....	41 259
1983	.....	.....	.....	.....	.....	.....	.....	.....	.....	.....	.....	.....	41 624
1984	.....	.....	.....	.....	.....	.....	.....	.....	.....	.....	.....	.....	45 102
1985	.....	.....	.....	.....	.....	.....	.....	.....	.....	.....	.....	.....	45 517
1986	.....	.....	.....	.....	.....	.....	.....	.....	.....	.....	.....	.....	46 044
1987	.....	.....	.....	.....	.....	.....	.....	.....	.....	.....	.....	.....	49 512
1988	3 901	.....	.....	.....	584	7 583	3 532	4 051	10 961	5 685	1 491	3 785	57 064
1989	4 370	.....	.....	.....	1 613	7 275	2 731	4 543	8 380	3 560	540	4 281	65 243
1990	3 186	.....	.....	.....	2 469	4 415	519	3 896	7 192	3 285	1 013	2 897	62 201
1991	2 125	.....	.....	.....	759	3 916	333	3 584	6 798	2 747	1 601	2 450	60 231
1992	3 921	1 753	955	1 213	-240	5 121	1 355	3 766	6 170	2 288	1 007	2 872	63 061
1993	5 095	2 357	1 339	1 401	1 476	6 717	2 069	4 649	11 357	6 281	1 672	3 402	66 756
1994	6 738	3 274	1 593	1 870	820	5 698	1 433	4 266	18 144	7 468	2 981	7 693	69 977
1995	4 560	2 095	1 061	1 404	863	11 245	4 779	6 464	14 855	6 654	3 228	4 974	80 866
1996	6 552	2 619	2 284	1 648	5 828	13 371	5 538	7 833	18 197	6 902	3 627	7 668	95 517
1997	7 898	3 731	2 744	1 422	5 288	16 810	7 187	9 624	21 231	7 923	3 796	9 512	108 029
1998	7 370	2 616	3 134	1 622	-3 611	13 880	7 472	6 409	26 606	9 636	4 397	12 573	119 959
1990:													
1st quarter	661	.....	.....	.....	666	1 293	208	1 085	150	135	-383	399	15 149
2nd quarter	1 200	.....	.....	.....	362	1 109	150	959	1 417	224	546	648	16 339
3rd quarter	1 001	.....	.....	.....	658	1 269	61	1 208	1 518	567	244	707	14 759
4th quarter	324	.....	.....	.....	783	744	100	644	4 107	2 359	606	1 143	15 954
1991:													
1st quarter	87	.....	.....	.....	443	671	-264	935	731	388	331	12	14 722
2nd quarter	850	.....	.....	.....	340	1 015	-58	1 073	1 887	658	654	575	14 982
3rd quarter	861	.....	.....	.....	241	1 335	204	1 132	1 394	468	455	472	14 647
4th quarter	327	.....	.....	.....	-265	895	451	444	2 786	1 233	161	1 391	15 880
1992:													
1st quarter	698	380	138	181	-684	621	-170	792	-735	-1 220	264	221	14 765
2nd quarter	1 109	465	260	384	142	1 470	232	1 238	2 411	1 433	435	542	15 533
3rd quarter	1 453	562	423	468	170	1 447	423	1 024	1 551	719	292	539	15 519
4th quarter	661	346	134	180	132	1 583	870	712	2 943	1 356	16	1 570	17 244
1993:													
1st quarter	1 035	541	342	153	241	674	-167	841	1 511	1 020	-149	639	16 137
2nd quarter	1 501	746	348	407	779	2 474	908	1 566	3 661	1 927	670	1 064	16 982
3rd quarter	1 508	640	322	546	362	1 268	503	766	2 609	1 234	518	857	16 246
4th quarter	1 051	430	327	295	94	2 301	825	1 476	3 576	2 100	633	842	17 391
1994:													
1st quarter	1 401	716	217	468	-538	2 149	794	1 355	2 704	816	624	1 264	16 269
2nd quarter	1 863	991	475	396	694	2 535	1 312	1 223	4 143	1 563	851	1 729	17 187
3rd quarter	2 173	1 020	570	584	556	-890	-1 841	951	3 805	1 398	783	1 623	17 533
4th quarter	1 301	547	331	422	108	1 904	1 168	737	7 492	3 691	723	3 077	18 988
1995:													
1st quarter	1 247	621	289	337	244	2 594	956	1 637	3 201	1 353	767	1 081	18 292
2nd quarter	1 599	733	594	272	646	2 606	874	1 731	3 621	1 422	894	1 306	20 646
3rd quarter	1 129	362	505	262	-438	2 930	1 437	1 493	3 593	1 284	706	1 603	20 980
4th quarter	585	379	-327	533	411	3 115	1 512	1 603	4 440	2 595	861	984	20 948
1996:													
1st quarter	1 239	368	413	459	794	3 388	1 473	1 915	2 943	941	888	1 114	20 048
2nd quarter	1 888	926	544	416	1 435	3 277	1 242	2 035	3 916	1 466	925	1 525	27 067
3rd quarter	1 949	957	616	376	2 074	3 464	1 968	1 496	4 858	1 665	875	2 318	23 387
4th quarter	1 476	368	711	397	1 525	3 242	855	2 387	6 480	2 830	939	2 711	25 015
1997:													
1st quarter	1 644	883	455	307	2 082	3 822	1 483	2 339	3 651	1 224	893	1 533	21 815
2nd quarter	2 459	1 219	797	442	1 432	4 568	1 710	2 858	3 826	1 111	766	1 950	25 734
3rd quarter	2 125	945	784	395	1 697	4 982	2 168	2 814	4 974	1 443	878	2 653	25 586
4th quarter	1 670	684	708	278	77	3 438	1 826	1 613	8 780	4 145	1 259	3 376	34 894
1998:													
1st quarter	1 489	600	676	213	625	3 128	1 067	2 061	5 550	1 636	958	2 956	31 131
2nd quarter	2 321	1 014	904	403	468	3 813	1 586	2 227	6 324	2 173	1 177	2 974	28 145
3rd quarter	1 951	593	787	572	5	4 166	3 198	969	5 349	1 343	1 044	2 962	27 123
4th quarter	1 609	409	767	434	-4 709	2 773	1 621	1 152	9 383	4 484	1 218	3 681	33 560

Employment, Hours, and Earnings

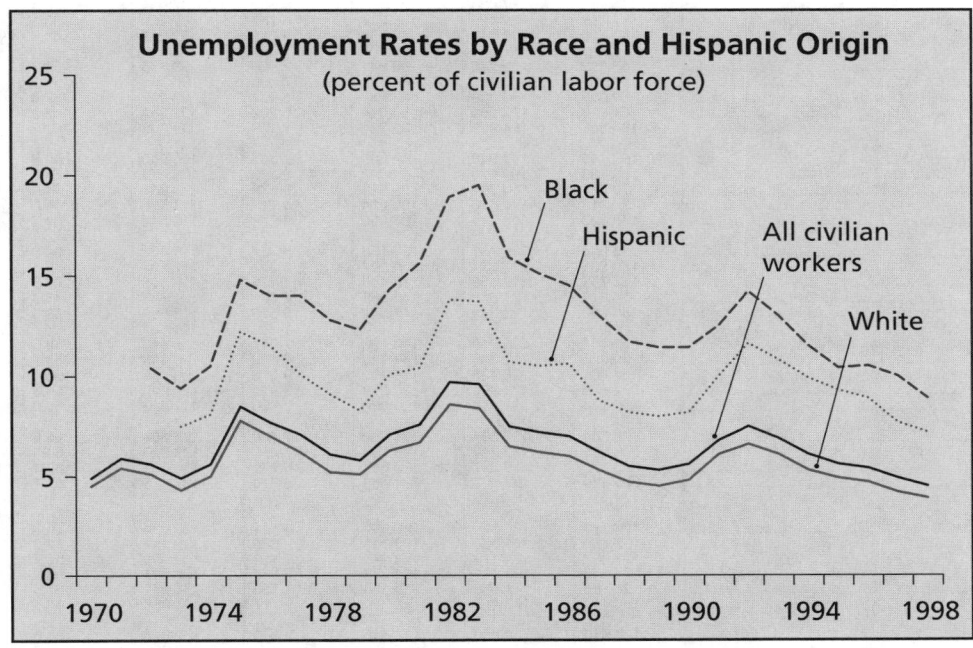

- The 1998 unemployment rate of 4.5 percent was the lowest recorded in 30 years. The rates for Blacks and Hispanics remained higher, but each fell to its lowest point since these data first became available in the mid-1970s.

- 1998 saw 64.1 percent of the civilian noninstitutional population holding jobs, an all-time record.

- Nonagricultural payroll employment grew by 3.1 million to 125.8 million in 1998. Of the 3.1 million net new jobs created, 2.7 million were in the service-producing industries. The industry group with the most rapid job growth was business services, which includes both computer and temporary help supply services.

- Adjusted for inflation, average hourly earnings of production or nonsupervisory workers declined during and after the 1990–1991 recession. Beginning in 1996, however, hourly wages started an upward trend that continued through 1998. The 2.65 percent increase recorded in 1998 represented the largest single year increase since 1972. From 1995 to 1998, real wages increased an average 1.6 percent per year, roughly consistent with an upturn in nonfarm productivity growth to a 1.9 percent rate.

Civilian Population and Labor Force [1]

(Thousands of persons, 16 years of age and over)

Year and month	Population	Not seasonally adjusted			Labor force (seasonally adjusted)				
		Labor force			Total		Persons 20 years and over		Both sexes, 16 to 19 years
		Total	Employed	Unemployed	Thousands of persons	Participation rate [2]	Men	Women	
1970	137 085	82 771	78 678	4 093	82 771	60.4	47 220	28 301	7 249
1971	140 216	84 382	79 367	5 016	84 382	60.2	48 009	28 904	7 470
1972	144 126	87 034	82 153	4 882	87 034	60.4	49 079	29 901	8 054
1973	147 096	89 429	85 064	4 365	89 429	60.8	49 932	30 991	8 507
1974	150 120	91 949	86 794	5 156	91 949	61.3	50 879	32 201	8 871
1975	153 153	93 775	85 846	7 929	93 775	61.2	51 494	33 410	8 870
1976	156 150	96 158	88 752	7 406	96 158	61.6	52 288	34 814	9 056
1977	159 033	99 009	92 017	6 991	99 009	62.3	53 348	36 310	9 351
1978	161 911	102 251	96 048	6 202	102 251	63.2	54 471	38 128	9 652
1979	164 863	104 962	98 824	6 137	104 962	63.7	55 615	39 708	9 638
1980	167 745	106 940	99 303	7 637	106 940	63.8	56 455	41 106	9 378
1981	170 130	108 670	100 397	8 273	108 670	63.9	57 197	42 485	8 988
1982	172 271	110 204	99 526	10 678	110 204	64.0	57 980	43 699	8 526
1983	174 215	111 550	100 834	10 717	111 550	64.0	58 744	44 636	8 171
1984	176 383	113 544	105 005	8 539	113 544	64.4	59 701	45 900	7 943
1985	178 206	115 461	107 150	8 312	115 461	64.8	60 277	47 283	7 901
1986	180 587	117 834	109 597	8 237	117 834	65.3	61 320	48 589	7 926
1987	182 753	119 865	112 440	7 425	119 865	65.6	62 095	49 783	7 988
1988	184 613	121 669	114 968	6 701	121 669	65.9	62 768	50 870	8 031
1989	186 393	123 869	117 342	6 528	123 869	66.5	63 704	52 212	7 954
1990	189 164	125 840	118 793	7 047	125 840	66.5	64 916	53 131	7 792
1991	190 925	126 346	117 718	8 628	126 346	66.2	65 374	53 708	7 265
1992	192 805	128 105	118 492	9 613	128 105	66.4	66 213	54 796	7 096
1993	194 838	129 200	120 259	8 940	129 200	66.3	66 642	55 388	7 170
1994	196 814	131 056	123 060	7 996	131 056	66.6	66 921	56 655	7 481
1995	198 584	132 304	124 900	7 404	132 304	66.6	67 324	57 215	7 765
1996	200 591	133 943	126 708	7 236	133 943	66.8	68 044	58 094	7 806
1997	203 133	136 297	129 558	6 739	136 297	67.1	69 166	59 198	7 932
1998	205 220	137 673	131 463	6 210	137 673	67.1	69 715	59 702	8 256
1995:									
January	197 753	130 698	122 597	8 101	132 034	66.8	67 516	56 871	7 647
February	197 886	131 028	123 343	7 685	132 111	66.8	67 469	56 975	7 667
March	198 007	131 423	123 943	7 480	132 099	66.7	67 464	56 897	7 738
April	198 148	131 657	124 278	7 378	132 591	66.9	67 464	57 357	7 770
May	198 286	131 739	124 554	7 185	131 881	66.5	67 192	57 005	7 684
June	198 453	133 447	125 720	7 727	131 956	66.5	67 229	56 881	7 846
July	198 615	134 440	126 548	7 892	132 336	66.6	67 181	57 371	7 784
August	198 801	133 383	125 926	7 457	132 329	66.6	67 155	57 271	7 903
September	199 005	132 341	125 173	7 167	132 608	66.6	67 442	57 344	7 822
October	199 192	132 863	125 979	6 884	132 698	66.6	67 330	57 589	7 779
November	199 355	132 622	125 599	7 024	132 611	66.5	67 247	57 601	7 763
December	199 508	132 008	125 136	6 872	132 510	66.4	67 324	57 414	7 772
1996:									
January	199 634	131 396	123 126	8 270	132 665	66.5	67 434	57 503	7 728
February	199 773	131 995	124 137	7 858	133 022	66.6	67 713	57 588	7 721
March	199 921	132 692	124 992	7 700	133 188	66.6	67 820	57 695	7 673
April	200 101	132 513	125 388	7 124	133 407	66.7	67 775	57 856	7 776
May	200 278	133 558	126 391	7 166	133 718	66.8	67 980	57 885	7 853
June	200 459	135 083	127 706	7 377	133 711	66.7	68 090	57 894	7 727
July	200 641	136 272	128 579	7 693	134 247	66.9	68 211	58 197	7 839
August	200 847	135 011	128 143	6 868	134 021	66.7	68 089	58 228	7 704
September	201 061	134 230	127 529	6 700	134 464	66.9	68 213	58 324	7 927
October	201 273	135 015	128 439	6 577	134 847	67.0	68 359	58 496	7 992
November	201 463	134 973	128 157	6 816	134 944	67.0	68 399	58 679	7 866
December	201 636	134 583	127 903	6 680	135 063	67.0	68 378	58 791	7 894
1997:									
January	202 285	134 317	126 384	7 933	135 598	67.0	68 884	58 788	7 926
February	202 389	134 535	126 887	7 647	135 563	67.0	68 837	58 723	8 003
March	202 513	135 524	128 125	7 399	135 950	67.1	69 008	58 995	7 947
April	202 674	135 181	128 629	6 551	136 052	67.1	69 072	59 002	7 978
May	202 832	135 963	129 565	6 398	136 103	67.1	69 004	59 144	7 955
June	203 000	137 557	130 463	7 094	136 254	67.1	69 187	59 220	7 847
July	203 166	138 331	131 350	6 981	136 378	67.1	69 160	59 276	7 942
August	203 364	137 460	130 865	6 594	136 540	67.1	69 280	59 385	7 875
September	203 570	136 375	129 972	6 403	136 565	67.1	69 266	59 451	7 848
October	203 767	136 665	130 671	5 995	136 500	67.0	69 236	59 364	7 900
November	203 941	136 912	130 999	5 914	136 835	67.1	69 440	59 349	8 046
December	204 098	136 742	130 785	5 957	137 086	67.2	69 489	59 638	7 959
1998:									
January	204 238	135 951	128 882	7 069	137 288	67.2	69 547	59 583	8 158
February	204 400	136 286	129 482	6 804	137 384	67.2	69 559	59 625	8 200
March	204 547	136 967	130 150	6 816	137 340	67.1	69 446	59 666	8 228
April	204 731	136 379	130 735	5 643	137 232	67.0	69 616	59 539	8 077
May	204 899	137 240	131 476	5 764	137 369	67.0	69 608	59 583	8 178
June	205 085	138 798	132 265	6 534	137 498	67.0	69 590	59 613	8 295
July	205 270	139 336	132 769	6 567	137 407	66.9	69 738	59 465	8 204
August	205 479	138 379	132 206	6 173	137 481	66.9	69 518	59 708	8 255
September	205 699	137 903	131 864	6 039	138 081	67.1	69 869	59 804	8 408
October	205 919	138 255	132 424	5 831	138 116	67.1	69 913	59 826	8 377
November	206 104	138 288	132 577	5 711	138 193	67.1	70 023	59 896	8 274
December	206 270	138 297	132 732	5 565	138 547	67.2	70 069	60 078	8 400

1. Changes in survey design, population coverage, methodology in 1994, 1986, 1982, 1978, and 1972 affect year-to-year comparisions. See Notes for more information.
2. Civilian labor force as a percent of the civilian noninstitutional population. 16 years and over.

Civilian Employment and Unemployment [1]

(Thousands of persons, 16 years and over, seasonally adjusted)

Year and month	Employment						Unemployment						
	Total		By age and sex			By industry				Persons 20 years and over		Both sexes, 16 to 19 years	Average weeks unem-ployed	Median weeks unem-ployed
	Thousands of persons	Ratio: employ-ment to popu-lation [2]	Persons 20 years and over		Both sexes, 16 to 19 years	Agricul-tural	Nonagri-cultural	Total	Long-term [3]	Men	Women			
			Men	Women										
1970	78 678	57.4	45 581	26 952	6 144	3 463	75 215	4 093	663	1 638	1 349	1 107	8.6	4.9
1971	79 367	56.6	45 912	27 246	6 208	3 394	75 972	5 016	1 187	2 097	1 658	1 263	11.3	6.3
1972	82 153	57.0	47 130	28 276	6 746	3 484	78 669	4 882	1 167	1 948	1 625	1 310	12.0	6.2
1973	85 064	57.8	48 310	29 484	7 271	3 470	81 594	4 365	826	1 624	1 507	1 237	10.0	5.2
1974	86 794	57.8	48 922	30 424	7 448	3 515	83 279	5 156	955	1 957	1 777	1 423	9.8	5.2
1975	85 846	56.1	48 018	30 726	7 104	3 408	82 438	7 929	2 505	3 476	2 684	1 768	14.2	8.4
1976	88 752	56.8	49 190	32 226	7 336	3 331	85 421	7 406	2 366	3 098	2 588	1 719	15.8	8.2
1977	92 017	57.9	50 555	33 775	7 688	3 283	88 734	6 991	1 942	2 794	2 535	1 662	14.0	7.0
1978	96 048	59.3	52 143	35 836	8 070	3 387	92 661	6 202	1 414	2 328	2 292	1 583	12.0	6.0
1979	98 824	59.9	53 308	37 434	8 083	3 347	95 477	6 137	1 241	2 308	2 276	1 554	11.0	5.0
1980	99 303	59.2	53 101	38 492	7 710	3 364	95 938	7 637	1 871	3 353	2 615	1 668	11.9	6.5
1981	100 397	59.0	53 582	39 590	7 225	3 368	97 030	8 273	2 285	3 615	2 895	1 762	13.7	6.9
1982	99 526	57.8	52 891	40 086	6 549	3 401	96 125	10 678	3 485	5 089	3 613	1 976	15.6	8.7
1983	100 834	57.9	53 487	41 004	6 342	3 383	97 450	10 717	4 210	5 257	3 632	1 829	20.0	10.1
1984	105 005	59.5	55 769	42 793	6 444	3 321	101 685	8 539	2 737	3 932	3 107	1 500	18.2	7.9
1985	107 150	60.1	56 562	44 154	6 434	3 179	103 971	8 312	2 305	3 715	3 129	1 469	15.6	6.8
1986	109 597	60.7	57 569	45 556	6 472	3 163	106 434	8 237	2 232	3 751	3 032	1 454	15.0	6.9
1987	112 440	61.5	58 726	47 074	6 640	3 208	109 232	7 425	1 983	3 369	2 709	1 347	14.5	6.5
1988	114 968	62.3	59 781	48 383	6 805	3 169	111 800	6 701	1 610	2 987	2 487	1 226	13.5	5.9
1989	117 342	63.0	60 837	49 745	6 759	3 199	114 142	6 528	1 375	2 867	2 467	1 194	11.9	4.8
1990	118 793	62.8	61 678	50 535	6 581	3 223	115 570	7 047	1 525	3 239	2 596	1 212	12.0	5.3
1991	117 718	61.7	61 178	50 634	5 906	3 269	114 449	8 628	2 357	4 195	3 074	1 359	13.7	6.8
1992	118 492	61.5	61 496	51 328	5 669	3 247	115 245	9 613	3 408	4 717	3 469	1 427	17.7	8.7
1993	120 259	61.7	62 355	52 099	5 805	3 115	117 144	8 940	3 094	4 287	3 288	1 365	18.0	8.3
1994	123 060	62.5	63 294	53 606	6 161	3 409	119 651	7 996	2 860	3 627	3 049	1 320	18.8	9.2
1995	124 900	62.9	64 085	54 396	6 419	3 440	121 460	7 404	2 363	3 239	2 819	1 346	16.6	8.3
1996	126 708	63.2	64 897	55 311	6 500	3 443	123 264	7 236	2 316	3 146	2 783	1 306	16.7	8.3
1997	129 558	63.8	66 284	56 613	6 661	3 399	126 159	6 739	2 062	2 882	2 585	1 271	15.8	8.0
1998	131 463	64.1	67 135	57 278	7 051	3 378	128 085	6 210	1 637	2 580	2 424	1 205	14.5	6.7
1995:														
January	124 696	63.1	64 194	54 116	6 386	3 520	121 176	7 338	2 394	3 322	2 755	1 261	17.1	8.0
February	124 922	63.1	64 375	54 219	6 328	3 609	121 313	7 189	2 343	3 094	2 756	1 339	17.0	8.1
March	124 957	63.1	64 327	54 140	6 490	3 634	121 323	7 142	2 268	3 137	2 757	1 248	17.3	8.3
April	124 955	63.1	64 174	54 369	6 412	3 575	121 380	7 636	2 460	3 290	2 988	1 358	17.6	8.3
May	124 445	62.8	63 825	54 280	6 340	3 350	121 095	7 436	2 575	3 367	2 725	1 344	17.0	9.1
June	124 525	62.7	63 992	54 026	6 507	3 466	121 059	7 431	2 299	3 237	2 855	1 339	16.0	7.8
July	124 800	62.8	63 961	54 463	6 376	3 378	121 422	7 536	2 313	3 220	2 908	1 408	16.5	8.5
August	124 833	62.8	63 868	54 427	6 538	3 374	121 459	7 496	2 393	3 287	2 844	1 365	16.2	8.3
September	125 111	62.9	64 172	54 497	6 442	3 282	121 829	7 497	2 309	3 270	2 847	1 380	16.2	7.8
October	125 358	62.9	64 249	54 683	6 426	3 430	121 928	7 340	2 278	3 081	2 906	1 353	16.0	8.2
November	125 184	62.8	63 931	54 849	6 404	3 339	121 845	7 427	2 343	3 316	2 752	1 359	16.4	8.0
December	125 081	62.7	64 047	54 659	6 375	3 350	121 731	7 429	2 336	3 277	2 755	1 397	16.3	8.2
1996:														
January	125 201	62.7	64 213	54 633	6 355	3 489	121 712	7 464	2 364	3 221	2 870	1 373	16.1	8.3
February	125 687	62.9	64 417	54 856	6 414	3 541	122 146	7 335	2 304	3 296	2 732	1 307	16.4	7.9
March	125 890	63.0	64 530	55 000	6 360	3 491	122 399	7 298	2 422	3 290	2 695	1 313	17.3	8.4
April	126 017	63.0	64 489	55 078	6 450	3 414	122 603	7 390	2 422	3 286	2 778	1 326	17.5	8.6
May	126 264	63.0	64 662	55 054	6 548	3 479	122 785	7 454	2 406	3 318	2 831	1 305	17.0	8.7
June	126 608	63.2	64 935	55 191	6 482	3 427	123 181	7 103	2 379	3 155	2 703	1 245	17.7	8.2
July	126 908	63.3	65 058	55 330	6 520	3 437	123 471	7 339	2 309	3 153	2 867	1 319	16.8	8.3
August	127 130	63.3	65 207	55 512	6 411	3 400	123 730	6 891	2 275	2 882	2 716	1 293	17.3	8.4
September	127 470	63.4	65 152	55 634	6 684	3 437	124 033	6 994	2 226	3 061	2 690	1 243	16.8	8.4
October	127 813	63.5	65 406	55 723	6 684	3 448	124 365	7 034	2 284	2 953	2 773	1 308	16.4	8.4
November	127 717	63.4	65 309	55 868	6 540	3 355	124 362	7 227	2 176	3 090	2 811	1 326	15.9	7.6
December	127 819	63.4	65 430	55 811	6 578	3 426	124 393	7 244	2 141	2 948	2 980	1 316	15.6	7.7
1997:														
January	128 472	63.5	65 778	56 112	6 582	3 462	125 010	7 126	2 150	3 106	2 676	1 344	15.9	7.8
February	128 409	63.4	65 804	55 993	6 612	3 346	125 063	7 154	2 137	3 033	2 730	1 391	15.8	8.2
March	128 954	63.7	66 017	56 294	6 643	3 418	125 536	6 996	2 075	2 991	2 701	1 304	15.5	8.0
April	129 210	63.8	66 122	56 376	6 712	3 496	125 714	6 842	2 138	2 950	2 626	1 266	15.5	8.3
May	129 425	63.8	66 242	56 478	6 705	3 437	125 988	6 678	2 130	2 762	2 666	1 250	15.3	8.0
June	129 430	63.8	66 285	56 605	6 540	3 409	126 021	6 824	2 090	2 902	2 615	1 307	15.6	7.9
July	129 745	63.9	66 400	56 729	6 616	3 428	126 317	6 633	2 140	2 760	2 547	1 326	16.5	8.2
August	129 910	63.9	66 484	56 815	6 611	3 354	126 556	6 630	2 018	2 796	2 570	1 264	16.0	7.8
September	129 911	63.8	66 478	56 861	6 572	3 382	126 529	6 654	2 063	2 788	2 590	1 276	15.8	8.1
October	130 055	63.8	66 427	56 929	6 699	3 289	126 766	6 445	1 972	2 809	2 435	1 201	16.2	7.8
November	130 546	64.0	66 735	56 969	6 842	3 377	127 169	6 289	1 844	2 705	2 380	1 204	15.4	7.6
December	130 638	64.0	66 636	57 165	6 837	3 383	127 255	6 448	1 926	2 853	2 473	1 122	16.0	7.4
1998:														
January	130 943	64.1	66 892	57 051	7 000	3 337	127 606	6 345	1 811	2 655	2 532	1 158	15.5	7.3
February	131 021	64.1	66 927	57 097	6 997	3 345	127 676	6 363	1 804	2 632	2 528	1 203	15.4	7.1
March	130 908	64.0	66 769	57 136	7 003	3 173	127 735	6 432	1 728	2 677	2 530	1 225	14.6	6.9
April	131 280	64.1	67 173	57 117	6 990	3 381	127 899	5 952	1 461	2 443	2 422	1 087	14.5	6.6
May	131 330	64.1	67 084	57 235	7 011	3 351	127 979	6 039	1 509	2 524	2 348	1 167	14.7	6.1
June	131 253	64.0	66 994	57 190	7 069	3 363	127 890	6 245	1 641	2 596	2 423	1 226	14.1	6.7
July	131 176	63.9	67 056	57 078	7 042	3 423	127 753	6 231	1 606	2 682	2 387	1 162	14.3	6.7
August	131 264	63.9	66 940	57 295	7 029	3 492	127 772	6 217	1 644	2 578	2 413	1 226	13.7	6.8
September	131 818	64.1	67 262	57 426	7 130	3 470	128 348	6 263	1 636	2 607	2 378	1 278	14.3	6.6
October	131 858	64.0	67 362	57 437	7 059	3 558	128 300	6 258	1 598	2 551	2 389	1 318	14.1	5.9
November	132 113	64.1	67 503	57 503	7 037	3 348	128 765	6 080	1 611	2 450	2 393	1 237	14.4	6.7
December	132 526	64.2	67 553	57 745	7 228	3 222	129 304	6 021	1 578	2 516	2 333	1 172	14.1	6.7

1. Changes in survey design, population coverage, methodology in 1994, 1986, 1982, 1978, and 1972 affect year-to-year comparisions. See Notes for more information.
2. Civilian employment as a percent of the civilian noninstitutional population.
3. Fifteen weeks and over.

Unemployment Rates [1]

(Percent of the civilian labor force in group, seasonally adjusted)

Year and month	All civilian workers	By sex and age — 20 years and over — Men	By sex and age — 20 years and over — Women	Both sexes, 16 to 19 years	By race — White	By race — Black	Persons of Hispanic origin	Married men, spouse present	Married women, spouse present	Women who maintain families	Private nonagricultural wage and salary workers — Total	Private nonagricultural wage and salary workers — Construction
1970	4.9	3.5	4.8	15.3	4.5	.....	.....	2.6	4.9	5.4	5.2	9.7
1971	5.9	4.4	5.7	16.9	5.4	.....	.....	3.2	5.7	7.3	6.2	10.4
1972	5.6	4.0	5.4	16.2	5.1	10.4	.....	2.8	5.4	7.2	5.7	10.3
1973	4.9	3.3	4.9	14.5	4.3	9.4	7.5	2.3	4.7	7.1	4.9	8.9
1974	5.6	3.8	5.5	16.0	5.0	10.5	8.1	2.7	5.3	7.0	5.7	10.7
1975	8.5	6.8	8.0	19.9	7.8	14.8	12.2	5.1	7.9	10.0	9.1	18.0
1976	7.7	5.9	7.4	19.0	7.0	14.0	11.5	4.2	7.1	10.1	7.9	15.5
1977	7.1	5.2	7.0	17.8	6.2	14.0	10.1	3.6	6.5	9.4	7.1	12.7
1978	6.1	4.3	6.0	16.4	5.2	12.8	9.1	2.8	5.5	8.5	5.9	10.6
1979	5.8	4.2	5.7	16.1	5.1	12.3	8.3	2.8	5.1	8.3	5.8	10.3
1980	7.1	5.9	6.4	17.8	6.3	14.3	10.1	4.2	5.8	9.2	7.4	14.1
1981	7.6	6.3	6.8	19.6	6.7	15.6	10.4	4.3	6.0	10.4	7.7	15.6
1982	9.7	8.8	8.3	23.2	8.6	18.9	13.8	6.5	7.4	11.7	10.1	20.0
1983	9.6	8.9	8.1	22.4	8.4	19.5	13.7	6.5	7.0	12.2	9.9	18.4
1984	7.5	6.6	6.8	18.9	6.5	15.9	10.7	4.6	5.7	10.4	7.4	14.3
1985	7.2	6.2	6.6	18.6	6.2	15.1	10.5	4.3	5.6	10.4	7.2	13.1
1986	7.0	6.1	6.2	18.3	6.0	14.5	10.6	4.4	5.2	9.8	7.0	13.1
1987	6.2	5.4	5.4	16.9	5.3	13.0	8.8	3.9	4.3	9.2	6.2	11.6
1988	5.5	4.8	4.9	15.3	4.7	11.7	8.2	3.3	3.9	8.1	5.5	10.6
1989	5.3	4.5	4.7	15.0	4.5	11.4	8.0	3.0	3.7	8.1	5.3	10.0
1990	5.6	5.0	4.9	15.5	4.8	11.4	8.2	3.4	3.8	8.3	5.8	11.1
1991	6.8	6.4	5.7	18.7	6.1	12.5	10.0	4.4	4.5	9.3	7.1	15.5
1992	7.5	7.1	6.3	20.1	6.6	14.2	11.6	5.1	5.0	10.0	7.8	16.8
1993	6.9	6.4	5.9	19.0	6.1	13.0	10.8	4.4	4.6	9.7	7.1	14.4
1994	6.1	5.4	5.4	17.6	5.3	11.5	9.9	3.7	4.1	8.9	6.3	11.8
1995	5.6	4.8	4.9	17.3	4.9	10.4	9.3	3.3	3.9	8.0	5.8	11.5
1996	5.4	4.6	4.8	16.7	4.7	10.5	8.9	3.0	3.6	8.2	5.5	10.1
1997	4.9	4.2	4.4	16.0	4.2	10.0	7.7	2.7	3.1	8.1	5.0	9.0
1998	4.5	3.7	4.1	14.6	3.9	8.9	7.2	2.4	2.9	7.2	4.6	7.5
1995:												
January	5.6	4.9	4.8	16.5	4.8	10.3	10.2	3.3	3.7	8.6	5.6	11.4
February	5.4	4.6	4.8	17.5	4.7	10.1	9.0	3.2	3.7	8.3	5.6	10.6
March	5.4	4.6	4.8	16.1	4.7	9.7	8.9	3.2	3.9	7.6	5.6	11.0
April	5.8	4.9	5.2	17.5	5.0	10.7	8.9	3.4	4.1	9.4	5.9	11.8
May	5.6	5.0	4.8	17.5	5.0	10.0	9.8	3.4	3.8	8.1	6.0	12.4
June	5.6	4.8	5.0	17.1	4.9	10.7	9.1	3.4	3.8	8.5	5.7	11.3
July	5.7	4.8	5.1	18.1	4.9	10.9	8.8	3.4	4.0	8.2	5.9	11.3
August	5.7	4.9	5.0	17.3	4.9	11.1	9.6	3.3	4.2	7.0	5.9	12.1
September	5.7	4.8	5.0	17.6	4.9	11.1	9.1	3.4	4.0	8.1	5.9	12.5
October	5.5	4.6	5.0	17.4	4.9	10.0	9.5	3.1	3.9	7.9	5.8	11.6
November	5.6	4.9	4.8	17.5	5.0	9.7	9.5	3.3	3.7	7.6	5.7	11.6
December	5.6	4.9	4.8	18.0	4.9	10.3	9.3	3.1	3.7	6.9	5.8	11.3
1996:												
January	5.6	4.8	5.0	17.8	4.9	10.6	9.4	3.2	3.9	7.9	5.8	10.7
February	5.5	4.9	4.7	16.9	4.8	10.0	9.6	3.1	3.7	7.4	5.6	11.1
March	5.5	4.9	4.7	17.1	4.8	10.6	9.6	3.1	3.5	7.4	5.7	10.1
April	5.5	4.8	4.8	17.1	4.8	10.6	9.6	3.0	3.8	7.6	5.7	10.6
May	5.6	4.9	4.9	16.6	4.9	10.2	9.5	3.0	3.7	8.6	5.8	10.4
June	5.3	4.6	4.7	16.1	4.6	10.3	8.8	3.0	3.5	7.8	5.4	9.8
July	5.5	4.6	4.9	16.8	4.7	10.6	8.8	3.0	3.5	9.1	5.6	10.0
August	5.1	4.2	4.7	16.8	4.4	10.6	8.8	2.9	3.4	8.5	5.3	8.9
September	5.2	4.5	4.6	15.7	4.5	10.6	8.3	3.0	3.4	8.4	5.3	9.1
October	5.2	4.3	4.7	16.4	4.5	10.8	8.1	3.0	3.6	8.5	5.3	9.6
November	5.4	4.5	4.8	16.9	4.6	10.6	8.6	3.1	3.6	8.6	5.5	10.1
December	5.4	4.3	5.1	16.7	4.6	10.6	7.3	2.9	3.8	8.6	5.4	9.5
1997:												
January	5.3	4.5	4.6	17.0	4.5	10.8	8.2	2.8	3.3	8.7	5.4	9.9
February	5.3	4.4	4.6	17.4	4.5	10.8	8.2	2.8	3.3	8.8	5.3	9.3
March	5.1	4.3	4.6	16.4	4.4	10.5	8.3	2.7	3.2	8.7	5.2	9.4
April	5.0	4.3	4.5	15.9	4.3	10.0	8.2	2.7	3.2	7.8	5.1	9.1
May	4.9	4.0	4.5	15.7	4.1	10.3	7.7	2.7	3.2	7.7	5.0	8.5
June	5.0	4.2	4.4	16.7	4.2	10.6	7.6	2.7	3.1	8.2	5.0	8.7
July	4.9	4.0	4.3	16.7	4.2	9.5	7.8	2.7	3.1	7.8	4.9	8.8
August	4.9	4.0	4.3	16.1	4.2	9.5	7.2	2.6	3.0	8.1	5.0	9.0
September	4.9	4.0	4.4	16.3	4.2	9.5	7.5	2.6	3.2	7.8	5.0	8.3
October	4.7	4.1	4.1	15.2	4.1	9.5	7.9	2.6	2.9	7.8	4.8	8.7
November	4.6	3.9	4.0	15.0	3.9	9.5	7.1	2.4	2.8	7.9	4.6	7.5
December	4.7	4.1	4.1	14.1	3.9	10.1	7.2	2.6	2.9	7.8	4.8	9.3
1998:												
January	4.6	3.8	4.2	14.2	4.0	9.4	7.0	2.5	3.0	7.6	4.7	8.1
February	4.6	3.8	4.2	14.7	3.9	9.4	6.9	2.5	3.0	7.5	4.7	8.0
March	4.7	3.9	4.2	14.9	4.0	9.2	7.0	2.5	3.2	7.5	4.7	8.4
April	4.3	3.5	4.1	13.5	3.7	9.0	6.7	2.3	2.8	7.5	4.4	6.6
May	4.4	3.6	3.9	14.3	3.8	8.9	6.9	2.4	2.8	7.5	4.5	8.0
June	4.5	3.7	4.1	14.8	4.0	8.5	7.5	2.2	2.9	7.1	4.6	7.9
July	4.5	3.8	4.0	14.2	3.8	9.6	7.2	2.3	2.8	6.9	4.6	6.8
August	4.5	3.7	4.0	14.9	3.9	8.9	7.4	2.3	3.1	6.8	4.7	7.4
September	4.5	3.7	4.0	15.2	3.9	9.0	7.4	2.3	2.7	7.6	4.8	8.6
October	4.5	3.6	4.0	15.7	3.9	8.6	7.3	2.3	2.8	6.9	4.6	6.7
November	4.4	3.5	4.0	15.0	3.8	8.6	7.3	2.2	2.9	6.9	4.5	7.0
December	4.3	3.6	3.9	14.0	3.8	7.9	7.6	2.3	2.8	6.3	4.4	6.4

1. Changes in survey design, population coverage, methodology in 1994, 1986, 1982, 1978, and 1972 affect year-to-year comparisions. See Notes for more information.

Unemployment Rates [1]—Continued

(Percent of the civilian labor force in group, seasonally adjusted, except as noted)

Year and month	By industry of last job—Continued									By occupation					
	Private nonagricultural wage and salary workers—Continued							Govern-ment workers	Agricul-tural wage and salary workers	Manager-ial and profes-sional specialty	Tech-nical, sales, and adminis-trative support	Preci-sion produc-tion, craft, and repair	Oper-ators, fabri-cators, and laborers	Farming, forestry, fishing	Service occupa-tions [2]
	Manufacturing			Transpor-tation and utilities	Whole-sale and retail trade	Finance, insur-ance, real estate	Services								
	Total	Durable goods	Nondur-able goods												
1970	5.6	5.7	5.4	3.2	5.3	2.8	4.7	2.2	7.5	.....	.....	.....	.....	.....	.....
1971	6.8	7.0	6.5	3.8	6.4	3.3	5.6	2.9	7.9	.....	.....	.....	.....	.....	.....
1972	5.6	5.5	5.7	3.5	6.4	3.4	5.3	2.9	7.7	.....	.....	.....	.....	.....	.....
1973	4.4	3.9	4.9	3.0	5.6	2.7	4.8	2.7	7.0	.....	.....	.....	.....	.....	.....
1974	5.8	5.4	6.2	3.2	6.4	3.1	5.2	3.0	7.5	.....	.....	.....	.....	.....	.....
1975	10.9	11.3	10.4	5.6	8.7	4.9	7.1	4.1	10.4	.....	.....	.....	.....	.....	.....
1976	7.9	7.7	8.1	5.0	8.6	4.4	7.2	4.4	11.8	.....	.....	.....	.....	.....	.....
1977	6.7	6.2	7.4	4.7	8.0	3.9	6.6	4.2	11.2	.....	.....	.....	.....	.....	.....
1978	5.5	5.0	6.3	3.7	6.9	3.1	5.7	3.9	8.9	.....	.....	.....	.....	.....	.....
1979	5.6	5.0	6.4	3.7	6.5	3.0	5.5	3.7	9.3	.....	.....	.....	.....	.....	.....
1980	8.5	8.9	7.9	4.9	7.4	3.4	5.9	4.1	11.0	.....	.....	.....	.....	.....	.....
1981	8.3	8.2	8.4	5.2	8.1	3.5	6.6	4.7	12.1	.....	.....	.....	.....	.....	.....
1982	12.3	13.3	10.8	6.9	10.0	4.7	7.6	4.9	14.7	3.3	6.1	10.6	16.7	8.5	10.8
1983	11.2	12.1	10.0	7.4	10.0	4.5	7.9	5.3	16.0	3.3	6.3	10.6	15.5	10.0	10.9
1984	7.5	7.2	7.8	5.5	8.0	3.7	6.6	4.5	13.5	2.6	5.0	7.4	11.5	8.4	9.1
1985	7.7	7.6	7.8	5.2	7.7	3.5	6.2	3.9	13.2	2.4	4.8	7.2	11.3	8.3	8.8
1986	7.1	6.9	7.4	5.1	7.6	3.5	6.1	3.6	12.5	2.4	4.7	7.2	10.9	7.8	8.6
1987	6.0	5.8	6.3	4.5	6.9	3.1	5.4	3.5	10.5	2.3	4.3	6.1	9.4	7.1	7.7
1988	5.3	5.0	5.7	3.9	6.2	3.0	4.9	2.8	10.6	1.9	4.0	5.4	8.3	7.0	6.9
1989	5.1	4.8	5.5	3.9	6.0	3.1	4.8	2.7	9.6	2.0	3.9	5.2	8.0	6.4	6.5
1990	5.8	5.8	5.8	3.9	6.4	3.0	5.0	2.7	9.8	2.1	4.3	5.9	8.7	6.4	6.6
1991	7.3	7.5	6.9	5.3	7.6	4.0	5.8	3.3	11.8	2.8	5.2	8.0	10.6	7.9	7.6
1992	7.8	8.0	7.6	5.5	8.4	4.6	6.6	3.6	12.5	3.1	5.9	8.9	11.1	8.3	8.2
1993	7.2	7.1	7.4	5.1	7.8	4.1	6.1	3.3	11.7	3.0	5.4	7.9	10.0	8.4	7.7
1994	5.6	5.2	6.0	4.8	7.4	3.6	5.9	3.4	11.3	2.6	5.0	6.3	9.0	8.4	8.0
1995	4.9	4.4	5.7	4.5	6.5	3.3	5.4	2.9	11.1	2.4	4.5	6.0	8.2	7.9	7.5
1996	4.8	4.5	5.2	4.1	6.4	2.7	5.4	2.9	10.2	2.3	4.5	5.5	7.9	7.6	7.2
1997	4.2	3.5	5.1	3.5	6.2	3.0	4.6	2.6	9.1	2.0	4.1	4.8	7.5	7.1	6.7
1998	3.9	3.4	4.7	3.4	5.5	2.5	4.5	2.3	8.3	1.8	3.9	4.2	6.7	6.5	6.4
1995:															
January	4.8	4.2	5.5	4.7	6.5	2.8	5.2	3.1	11.0	2.3	4.5	5.8	8.2	7.6	7.7
February	4.5	4.0	5.2	4.6	6.4	3.6	5.2	2.9	9.8	2.3	4.4	5.6	7.8	7.4	7.6
March	4.6	4.2	5.1	4.5	6.3	3.4	5.3	2.9	10.1	2.5	4.4	5.5	7.5	7.9	7.2
April	4.8	4.3	5.5	4.6	6.8	3.5	5.6	3.1	11.1	2.5	4.8	6.1	8.1	8.4	7.4
May	5.3	5.0	5.8	4.3	6.6	3.6	5.5	2.8	12.3	2.2	4.6	6.3	8.6	8.6	7.4
June	5.0	4.2	6.1	4.4	6.2	3.4	5.4	3.1	11.8	2.5	4.4	6.0	8.4	8.0	7.5
July	5.2	4.8	5.7	4.5	6.6	3.4	5.7	2.7	11.0	2.5	4.4	6.4	8.2	8.2	8.0
August	4.9	4.2	5.9	4.2	6.5	3.5	5.6	3.0	10.0	2.5	4.4	6.5	8.4	7.6	7.6
September	5.0	4.4	5.9	4.4	7.1	2.9	5.2	2.7	11.3	2.4	4.5	6.1	8.5	7.3	7.6
October	4.9	4.4	5.6	4.2	6.4	3.3	5.6	2.9	11.9	2.4	4.5	5.9	8.0	8.5	7.7
November	5.1	4.6	5.8	4.3	6.3	2.9	5.5	3.0	11.2	2.5	4.2	6.1	8.3	7.8	7.8
December	5.0	4.4	5.8	4.9	6.6	2.9	5.5	2.8	11.6	2.4	4.4	5.7	8.4	7.3	7.0
1996:															
January	5.0	4.4	5.8	3.8	6.6	2.7	5.7	2.8	10.8	2.4	4.5	5.3	8.4	7.9	8.1
February	4.8	5.0	4.4	3.9	6.3	2.4	5.6	2.9	10.7	2.3	4.5	6.1	8.1	7.6	7.4
March	5.3	5.0	5.7	4.1	6.8	2.5	5.5	2.8	10.2	2.4	4.4	5.8	8.2	7.7	7.5
April	4.8	4.7	4.9	4.4	6.7	2.4	5.7	3.0	10.8	2.3	4.5	5.7	8.2	8.1	7.6
May	5.1	4.8	5.4	4.3	6.6	2.6	5.7	3.3	10.7	2.3	4.7	5.5	8.5	9.2	7.2
June	4.9	4.6	5.5	4.4	6.3	2.7	5.0	2.8	9.5	2.5	4.1	5.4	8.0	7.4	7.3
July	4.6	4.2	5.2	4.3	6.4	2.8	5.6	3.0	9.5	2.4	4.6	5.4	7.7	6.9	7.5
August	4.7	3.8	5.9	3.9	6.3	2.5	5.2	2.7	8.7	2.1	4.4	5.2	7.8	6.6	6.9
September	4.3	4.1	4.6	3.9	6.1	3.0	5.2	2.9	10.7	2.3	4.5	5.4	7.3	7.0	6.8
October	4.7	4.5	5.1	4.5	6.2	2.9	5.0	2.9	9.8	2.2	4.5	5.4	7.8	6.8	6.9
November	4.8	4.6	5.3	3.8	6.3	2.9	5.2	2.9	10.9	2.3	4.6	5.6	7.7	7.8	7.0
December	4.8	4.6	5.0	4.0	6.2	3.1	5.1	3.1	9.4	2.3	4.6	5.2	7.6	7.3	6.3
1997:															
January	4.5	4.3	5.0	3.9	6.3	3.3	5.0	2.9	8.6	2.1	4.3	5.1	8.0	7.2	7.5
February	4.5	4.1	5.1	4.2	6.4	3.1	4.9	2.9	9.0	2.1	4.3	5.0	8.1	7.4	7.5
March	4.4	3.7	5.4	4.0	6.4	3.1	4.8	2.8	8.9	2.1	4.3	4.9	8.0	7.2	7.1
April	4.4	3.6	5.6	3.0	6.4	3.4	4.7	2.5	9.5	2.0	4.3	4.9	7.6	7.0	6.7
May	4.3	3.6	5.2	3.7	6.2	3.3	4.6	2.4	7.5	2.1	3.9	4.7	7.3	6.7	6.9
June	4.2	3.6	5.0	2.9	6.4	2.6	4.7	2.9	10.7	2.0	4.2	4.9	7.4	7.9	7.1
July	4.2	3.3	5.4	3.4	6.1	3.3	4.4	2.6	8.3	2.0	4.1	4.8	7.3	6.2	6.4
August	4.1	3.4	5.1	3.6	6.1	3.0	4.5	2.6	9.9	1.9	4.2	4.6	7.4	7.7	6.3
September	4.1	3.2	5.3	3.7	6.1	3.0	4.7	2.5	8.9	2.0	4.0	4.7	7.6	6.2	6.6
October	3.8	3.2	4.7	3.2	6.1	2.9	4.3	2.4	9.9	1.8	3.9	5.3	7.0	7.7	6.3
November	3.7	3.2	4.4	3.1	6.1	2.3	4.4	2.3	8.7	1.7	4.0	4.3	7.1	6.7	6.1
December	3.8	3.1	4.8	3.3	5.8	2.7	4.6	2.1	9.4	1.9	4.0	4.7	6.8	6.9	5.7
1998:															
January	3.8	3.3	4.6	3.8	5.8	2.6	4.4	2.4	10.3	1.9	4.1	4.6	6.1	6.7	6.5
February	3.8	3.0	4.9	3.3	5.7	2.5	4.6	2.3	8.5	2.0	4.0	4.3	6.6	6.4	6.4
March	3.9	3.6	4.3	3.3	5.5	2.5	4.7	2.8	9.2	1.8	4.0	4.4	6.8	6.9	6.9
April	3.9	3.4	4.5	3.2	5.4	2.3	4.3	2.0	8.0	1.9	3.7	3.8	6.4	6.1	6.1
May	3.6	3.0	4.6	3.1	5.3	2.1	4.7	2.4	8.0	1.7	3.9	4.4	6.6	6.5	5.7
June	3.6	3.0	4.6	3.5	5.6	2.2	4.6	2.2	8.4	1.7	3.9	4.3	6.9	6.4	6.5
July	4.3	4.1	4.6	3.4	5.6	2.1	4.6	2.4	8.2	1.7	3.8	4.3	6.9	6.6	6.6
August	3.9	3.5	4.5	3.5	5.6	2.7	4.7	2.2	7.4	1.9	3.7	4.5	6.6	5.9	6.7
September	4.0	3.7	4.6	3.5	5.7	2.4	4.5	2.2	7.9	1.8	3.9	4.3	7.0	7.0	6.5
October	3.9	3.2	5.1	3.5	5.6	2.5	4.7	2.2	6.7	1.9	3.9	4.0	6.8	5.4	6.6
November	3.8	3.2	4.8	3.2	5.2	2.8	4.6	2.1	7.6	1.8	3.7	3.8	6.7	6.3	6.4
December	4.0	3.4	4.9	3.2	5.5	2.8	4.1	2.0	8.3	1.8	3.7	3.2	6.7	7.5	5.6

1. Changes in survey design, population coverage, methodology in 1994, 1986, 1982, 1978, and 1972 affect year-to-year comparisions. See Notes for more information.
2. Not seasonally adjusted.

Insured Unemployment

(Weekly averages—Thousands of persons)

Year and month	State programs (seasonally adjusted)			Federal programs (not seasonally adjusted)					
				Initial claims		Persons claiming benefits			
	Initial claims	Insured unemploy-ment	Insured unemploy-ment rate [1]	Federal employees	Newly discharged veterans	Federal employees	Newly discharged veterans	Railroad retirement	Extended benefits
1970	296	1 805	3.4	.....	.....	.....	.....	.....	.....
1971	295	2 150	4.1	.....	.....	.....	.....	.....	.....
1972	261	1 848	3.5	.....	.....	.....	.....	.....	.....
1973	247	1 632	2.7	.....	.....	.....	.....	.....	.....
1974	363	2 262	3.5	.....	.....	.....	.....	.....	.....
1975	478	3 986	6.0	.....	.....	.....	.....	.....	.....
1976	386	2 991	4.6	.....	.....	.....	.....	.....	.....
1977	375	2 655	3.9	.....	.....	.....	.....	.....	.....
1978	346	2 359	3.3	.....	.....	.....	.....	.....	.....
1979	388	2 434	2.9	.....	.....	.....	.....	.....	.....
1980	488	3 350	3.9	.....	.....	.....	.....	.....	.....
1981	460	3 047	3.5	.....	.....	.....	.....	.....	.....
1982	583	4 059	4.6	.....	.....	.....	.....	.....	.....
1983	438	3 395	3.9	.....	.....	.....	.....	.....	.....
1984	377	2 475	2.8	.....	.....	.....	.....	.....	.....
1985	397	2 617	2.9	.....	.....	.....	.....	.....	.....
1986	378	2 643	2.8	2.13	2.52	20.24	17.11	.....	.....
1987	328	2 300	2.4	2.19	2.57	21.29	17.71	.....	8.64
1988	310	2 081	2.0	2.32	2.74	22.91	18.13	13.28	1.21
1989	330	2 158	2.1	2.14	2.31	22.17	15.09	10.37	0.60
1990	388	2 522	2.4	2.45	2.54	23.89	18.43	10.56	2.23
1991	447	3 342	3.2	2.55	2.93	30.50	22.12	10.73	32.05
1992	408	3 245	3.1	2.75	4.95	32.10	60.25	8.77	4.63
1993	341	2 751	2.6	2.55	3.94	32.06	54.90	7.40	8.02
1994	340	2 670	2.5	2.54	3.02	32.21	37.65	6.21	31.23
1995	357	2 572	2.3	4.57	2.51	31.68	29.78	5.48	14.31
1996	356	2 595	2.3	7.33	2.13	29.84	24.30	5.40	5.51
1997	323	2 323	2.0	2.01	1.75	23.58	19.66	4.00	5.07
1998	320	2 220	1.9	1.64	1.41	19.60	15.68	3.17	6.31
1995:									
January	329	2 494	2.3	3.29	2.96	37.59	36.36	7.50	12.71
February	333	2 508	2.3	2.38	2.65	37.07	36.01	8.75	13.15
March	336	2 508	2.3	1.88	2.45	34.27	33.52	8.00	15.92
April	351	2 501	2.3	1.89	2.23	29.44	30.15	6.00	16.62
May	374	2 570	2.4	1.86	2.33	25.77	28.03	4.25	20.63
June	373	2 619	2.4	2.43	2.44	24.42	27.00	3.25	18.73
July	372	2 651	2.4	2.93	2.95	27.05	27.68	3.80	15.09
August	352	2 613	2.4	2.15	2.77	29.48	29.26	4.00	11.79
September	361	2 640	2.4	2.65	2.46	27.75	28.40	4.00	10.99
October	371	2 689	2.4	3.59	2.37	33.28	28.05	4.50	12.10
November	379	2 688	2.4	17.29	2.20	35.20	27.22	5.50	11.23
December	365	2 623	2.4	12.38	2.38	40.83	28.18	6.80	12.72
1996:									
January	368	2 629	2.3	66.18	2.50	49.79	28.61	9.50	10.99
February	370	2 676	2.4	4.39	2.22	36.15	28.53	9.50	9.39
March	383	2 648	2.4	1.82	2.15	32.26	26.84	8.00	3.04
April	360	2 601	2.3	2.28	2.02	27.94	25.09	6.00	3.25
May	347	2 572	2.3	1.80	1.97	24.84	23.86	4.50	5.11
June	350	2 552	2.3	2.39	2.08	24.26	22.66	4.00	11.75
July	334	2 515	2.2	2.96	2.23	26.63	22.61	4.00	13.88
August	326	2 504	2.2	1.98	2.30	27.40	22.74	4.20	8.27
September	341	2 470	2.2	2.03	2.23	25.76	22.68	4.00	0.23
October	338	2 477	2.2	2.95	2.15	27.40	22.99	3.75	0.11
November	338	2 453	2.2	2.32	1.84	28.07	22.49	3.80	0.09
December	354	2 508	2.2	2.07	1.91	29.50	23.14	4.00	0.06
1997:									
January	336	2 477	2.1	2.59	2.05	29.47	23.79	6.50	0.06
February	314	2 402	2.1	1.83	1.87	27.40	23.72	7.50	0.18
March	313	2 309	2.0	1.42	1.79	24.16	22.12	6.60	2.45
April	329	2 284	2.0	1.62	1.66	21.19	20.57	5.00	2.69
May	328	2 276	2.0	1.61	1.57	18.52	19.02	3.40	1.96
June	335	2 298	2.0	2.06	1.68	18.59	18.16	2.75	1.38
July	321	2 305	2.0	2.69	1.87	21.31	18.04	2.50	0.38
August	324	2 282	2.0	1.75	2.10	23.00	19.01	2.80	0.11
September	313	2 233	1.9	1.82	1.71	22.10	18.38	2.50	8.43
October	310	2 232	1.9	2.85	1.79	24.40	18.21	2.50	15.10
November	319	2 244	1.9	2.15	1.43	26.14	17.52	2.80	18.19
December	315	2 261	2.0	2.00	1.56	27.37	17.59	3.25	9.94
1998:									
January	318	2 267	1.9	2.27	1.71	27.40	18.36	4.60	0.44
February	309	2 197	1.8	1.43	1.48	24.53	17.73	5.00	0.24
March	308	2 170	1.8	1.28	1.50	21.98	16.87	4.25	7.29
April	311	2 136	1.8	1.34	1.35	19.09	15.82	3.25	14.59
May	316	2 112	1.8	1.29	1.26	15.99	14.94	2.00	19.90
June	353	2 235	1.9	1.64	1.38	15.42	14.41	2.00	14.57
July	325	2 372	2.0	2.16	1.50	17.10	14.78	2.00	0.27
August	305	2 230	1.9	1.31	1.42	18.31	15.21	2.00	0.05
September	301	2 166	1.8	1.46	1.39	16.90	14.89	2.00	0.03
October	313	2 195	1.8	1.98	1.33	18.28	14.83	2.40	.....
November	320	2 238	1.9	1.73	1.21	19.09	14.74	3.50	6.21
December	323	2 262	1.9	1.70	1.33	20.75	15.40	5.50	13.40

1. Insured unemployed as a percent of employment covered by state programs.

Nonagricultural Employment

(Wage and salary workers on nonagricultural payrolls—Thousands)

Year and month	Not seasonally adjusted		Seasonally adjusted		Diffusion index, 6-month span, private industry [1]	Goods-producing industries (seasonally adjusted)						
						Total	Mining [2]	Construc-tion [2]	Manufacturing			
	Total	Private Sector	Total	Private Sector					Total	Production workers	Durable goods	
											Total	Production workers
1970	70 880	58 325	70 880	58 325	.....	23 578	623	3 588	19 367	14 044	11 176	8 088
1971	71 211	58 331	71 211	58 331	.....	22 935	609	3 704	18 623	13 544	10 604	7 697
1972	73 675	60 341	73 675	60 341	.....	23 668	628	3 889	19 151	14 045	11 022	8 025
1973	76 790	63 058	76 790	63 058	.....	24 893	642	4 097	20 154	14 834	11 863	8 699
1974	78 265	64 095	78 265	64 095	.....	24 794	697	4 020	20 077	14 638	11 897	8 634
1975	76 945	62 259	76 945	62 259	.....	22 600	752	3 525	18 323	13 043	10 662	7 532
1976	79 382	64 511	79 382	64 511	79.7	23 352	779	3 576	18 997	13 638	11 051	7 888
1977	82 471	67 344	82 471	67 344	76.2	24 346	813	3 851	19 682	14 135	11 570	8 280
1978	86 697	71 026	86 697	71 026	57.9	25 585	851	4 229	20 505	14 734	12 245	8 777
1979	89 823	73 876	89 823	73 876		26 461	958	4 463	21 040	15 068	12 730	9 082
1980	90 406	74 166	90 406	74 166	37.5	25 658	1 027	4 346	20 285	14 214	12 159	8 416
1981	91 152	75 121	91 152	75 121	58.0	25 497	1 139	4 188	20 170	14 020	12 082	8 270
1982	89 544	73 707	89 544	73 707	36.8	23 812	1 128	3 904	18 780	12 742	11 014	7 290
1983	90 152	74 282	90 152	74 282	78.2	23 330	952	3 946	18 432	12 528	10 707	7 095
1984	94 408	78 384	94 408	78 384	72.6	24 718	966	4 380	19 372	13 280	11 476	7 715
1985	97 387	80 992	97 387	80 992	57.6	24 842	927	4 668	19 248	13 084	11 458	7 618
1986	99 344	82 651	99 344	82 651	57.6	24 533	777	4 810	18 947	12 864	11 195	7 399
1987	101 958	84 948	101 958	84 948	69.5	24 674	717	4 958	18 999	12 952	11 154	7 409
1988	105 209	87 823	105 209	87 823	66.3	25 125	713	5 098	19 314	13 193	11 363	7 582
1989	107 884	90 105	107 884	90 105	53.7	25 254	692	5 171	19 391	13 230	11 394	7 594
1990	109 403	91 098	109 403	91 098	43.4	24 905	709	5 120	19 076	12 947	11 109	7 363
1991	108 249	89 847	108 249	89 847	43.8	23 745	689	4 650	18 406	12 434	10 569	6 967
1992	108 601	89 956	108 601	89 956	57.4	23 231	635	4 492	18 104	12 287	10 277	6 822
1993	110 713	91 872	110 713	91 872	66.0	23 352	610	4 668	18 075	12 341	10 221	6 849
1994	114 163	95 036	114 163	95 036	69.7	23 908	601	4 986	18 321	12 632	10 448	7 104
1995	117 191	97 885	117 191	97 885	60.0	24 265	581	5 160	18 524	12 826	10 683	7 317
1996	119 608	100 189	119 608	100 189	64.6	24 493	580	5 418	18 495	12 776	10 789	7 386
1997	122 690	103 133	122 690	103 133	64.9	24 962	596	5 691	18 675	12 907	11 010	7 553
1998	125 826	106 007	125 826	106 007	61.1	25 347	590	5 985	18 772	12 930	11 170	7 643
1995:												
January	114 435	95 243	116 259	97 007	66.7	24 274	592	5 129	18 553	12 856	10 636	7 284
February	115 093	95 524	116 521	97 254	59.7	24 275	588	5 133	18 554	12 861	10 658	7 308
March	115 849	96 175	116 687	97 409	58.6	24 272	587	5 130	18 555	12 862	10 673	7 321
April	116 674	97 009	116 864	97 574	56.5	24 292	586	5 136	18 570	12 872	10 690	7 332
May	117 409	97 743	116 841	97 566	59.0	24 239	582	5 113	18 544	12 851	10 683	7 323
June	118 138	98 761	117 050	97 754	60.0	24 247	581	5 141	18 525	12 836	10 672	7 313
July	116 926	98 673	117 137	97 848	57.7	24 240	580	5 153	18 507	12 802	10 676	7 304
August	117 180	99 062	117 449	98 154	61.0	24 270	577	5 178	18 515	12 817	10 689	7 321
September	118 083	98 987	117 648	98 353	60.5	24 306	576	5 215	18 515	12 815	10 699	7 328
October	118 665	99 052	117 784	98 461	59.3	24 301	575	5 236	18 490	12 789	10 692	7 316
November	118 917	99 172	117 942	98 614	61.7	24 288	573	5 241	18 474	12 769	10 693	7 309
December	118 918	99 221	118 087	98 753	63.2	24 300	573	5 228	18 499	12 798	10 737	7 358
1996:												
January	116 210	96 957	118 080	98 760	62.6	24 250	573	5 212	18 465	12 765	10 724	7 343
February	117 146	97 486	118 534	99 175	65.2	24 365	577	5 299	18 489	12 777	10 743	7 353
March	117 952	98 158	118 795	99 398	64.5	24 369	578	5 337	18 454	12 737	10 714	7 322
April	118 779	99 017	118 958	99 570	65.2	24 399	579	5 353	18 467	12 752	10 755	7 357
May	119 922	100 092	119 288	99 870	64.7	24 445	581	5 381	18 483	12 761	10 775	7 374
June	120 589	101 111	119 535	100 131	64.6	24 486	581	5 417	18 488	12 770	10 791	7 388
July	119 558	101 204	119 742	100 338	67.0	24 508	580	5 437	18 491	12 770	10 793	7 390
August	119 829	101 586	120 020	100 600	65.4	24 558	581	5 468	18 509	12 787	10 816	7 408
September	120 569	101 347	120 172	100 739	65.9	24 578	579	5 488	18 511	12 786	10 822	7 411
October	121 287	101 565	120 413	100 984	66.7	24 617	581	5 517	18 519	12 792	10 828	7 416
November	121 740	101 830	120 698	101 268	66.9	24 652	583	5 545	18 524	12 795	10 841	7 423
December	121 716	101 911	120 893	101 449	66.7	24 678	584	5 558	18 536	12 805	10 858	7 436
1997:												
January	119 166	99 784	121 131	101 670	67.4	24 697	587	5 558	18 552	12 817	10 875	7 452
February	120 017	100 262	121 427	101 968	68.3	24 764	592	5 601	18 571	12 828	10 895	7 465
March	120 903	101 040	121 782	102 313	65.6	24 851	592	5 658	18 601	12 847	10 917	7 483
April	121 879	102 018	122 065	102 575	67.0	24 849	593	5 647	18 609	12 855	10 933	7 492
May	122 970	103 058	122 292	102 798	65.6	24 886	596	5 669	18 621	12 873	10 949	7 510
June	123 615	104 004	122 524	102 987	64.9	24 915	596	5 670	18 649	12 887	10 978	7 529
July	122 662	104 141	122 822	103 238	66.3	24 956	598	5 687	18 671	12 905	11 013	7 553
August	122 714	104 312	122 894	103 309	68.4	25 018	599	5 712	18 707	12 931	11 060	7 596
September	123 703	104 329	123 302	103 720	69.7	25 051	601	5 734	18 716	12 939	11 065	7 600
October	124 575	104 658	123 626	104 008	71.3	25 109	601	5 745	18 763	12 972	11 106	7 627
November	124 969	104 900	123 949	104 311	71.3	25 181	601	5 767	18 813	13 006	11 154	7 659
December	125 103	105 088	124 263	104 613	71.9	25 253	602	5 813	18 838	13 023	11 179	7 677
1998:												
January	122 554	102 974	124 580	104 920	70.6	25 355	606	5 879	18 870	13 047	11 219	7 705
February	123 335	103 358	124 773	105 095	66.9	25 366	606	5 885	18 875	13 051	11 229	7 714
March	124 050	103 965	124 961	105 267	65.9	25 367	605	5 879	18 883	13 040	11 237	7 709
April	125 082	104 992	125 220	105 494	62.4	25 418	600	5 943	18 875	13 031	11 238	7 708
May	126 139	105 969	125 478	105 715	62.6	25 379	595	5 932	18 852	12 999	11 225	7 686
June	126 804	106 956	125 689	105 913	61.1	25 381	593	5 962	18 826	12 970	11 210	7 668
July	125 762	107 010	125 808	106 009	58.0	25 240	588	5 990	18 662	12 801	11 066	7 521
August	125 966	107 290	126 170	106 301	59.8	25 344	585	6 005	18 754	12 891	11 177	7 634
September	126 769	107 086	126 361	106 470	60.0	25 333	583	6 009	18 741	12 893	11 159	7 628
October	127 523	107 311	126 567	106 654	60.8	25 306	578	6 042	18 686	12 849	11 128	7 605
November	127 902	107 489	126 841	106 893	60.8	25 298	574	6 085	18 639	12 808	11 092	7 577
December	128 028	107 686	127 186	107 213	58.0	25 354	570	6 173	18 611	12 795	11 074	7 568

1. Percent of private industries with employment increasing over a 6-month span plus one-half of private industries with no change, based on seasonally adjusted data and centered within the span. June index used for the annual data.
2. Additional industry detail availible in individual industry profile sections.

Nonagricultural Employment—*Continued*

(Wage and salary workers on nonagricultural payrolls—Thousands, seasonally adjusted)

Year and month	Lumber and wood products	Furniture and fixtures	Stone, clay, and glass products	Primary metal industries[1]	Fabricated metal products	Industrial machinery and equipment[1]	Electronic and electrical equipment	Transportation equipment[1]	Instruments and related products	Miscellaneous manufacturing
1970	658	440	610	1 260	1 559	2 003	1 584	1 833	804	426
1971	681	444	611	1 171	1 479	1 834	1 477	1 743	753	412
1972	740	483	645	1 173	1 541	1 909	1 535	1 777	786	433
1973	774	507	680	1 259	1 645	2 111	1 667	1 915	851	454
1974	727	489	673	1 289	1 632	2 230	1 666	1 853	885	452
1975	627	417	598	1 139	1 453	2 076	1 442	1 700	804	407
1976	693	444	613	1 155	1 505	2 085	1 503	1 785	840	429
1977	736	464	636	1 182	1 577	2 195	1 591	1 857	895	438
1978	770	494	664	1 215	1 667	2 347	1 699	1 987	952	452
1979	782	498	674	1 254	1 713	2 508	1 793	2 059	1 006	445
1980	704	466	629	1 142	1 609	2 517	1 771	1 881	1 022	418
1981	680	464	606	1 122	1 586	2 521	1 774	1 879	1 041	408
1982	610	432	548	922	1 424	2 264	1 701	1 718	1 013	382
1983	671	448	541	832	1 368	2 053	1 704	1 730	990	370
1984	718	486	562	857	1 462	2 218	1 869	1 883	1 040	382
1985	711	493	557	808	1 464	2 195	1 859	1 960	1 045	367
1986	724	498	554	751	1 422	2 074	1 790	2 003	1 018	361
1987	754	515	554	746	1 399	2 028	1 750	2 028	1 011	370
1988	767	527	567	770	1 428	2 089	1 764	2 036	1 031	383
1989	756	524	568	772	1 445	2 125	1 744	2 052	1 026	381
1990	733	506	556	756	1 419	2 095	1 673	1 989	1 006	375
1991	675	475	522	723	1 355	2 000	1 591	1 890	974	366
1992	680	478	513	695	1 329	1 929	1 528	1 830	929	368
1993	709	487	517	683	1 339	1 931	1 526	1 756	896	378
1994	754	505	532	698	1 388	1 990	1 571	1 761	861	389
1995	769	510	540	712	1 437	2 067	1 625	1 790	843	390
1996	778	504	544	711	1 449	2 115	1 661	1 785	855	388
1997	796	512	552	711	1 479	2 168	1 689	1 845	866	392
1998	813	530	563	712	1 501	2 203	1 704	1 884	868	393
1995:										
January	771	514	539	712	1 427	2 028	1 608	1 800	845	392
February	773	515	540	712	1 434	2 038	1 609	1 802	844	391
March	771	516	542	712	1 438	2 044	1 613	1 805	841	391
April	768	514	543	714	1 442	2 055	1 617	1 806	841	390
May	766	511	540	714	1 441	2 056	1 621	1 803	842	389
June	765	508	540	712	1 436	2 063	1 622	1 795	842	389
July	765	505	539	709	1 437	2 071	1 624	1 794	844	388
August	767	507	539	711	1 437	2 077	1 626	1 792	844	389
September	769	507	539	711	1 436	2 080	1 633	1 790	845	389
October	771	507	538	711	1 438	2 091	1 638	1 765	844	389
November	773	507	538	712	1 439	2 098	1 641	1 750	844	391
December	774	508	537	712	1 439	2 103	1 646	1 782	846	390
1996:										
January	765	506	535	714	1 439	2 105	1 648	1 774	849	389
February	772	504	539	713	1 439	2 106	1 651	1 779	851	389
March	771	503	540	711	1 439	2 112	1 651	1 745	853	389
April	775	501	540	710	1 438	2 111	1 655	1 784	854	387
May	776	503	542	711	1 442	2 113	1 658	1 786	857	387
June	780	503	543	712	1 446	2 115	1 661	1 787	856	388
July	781	504	543	706	1 452	2 115	1 664	1 786	855	387
August	783	505	545	713	1 454	2 116	1 665	1 791	857	387
September	783	506	546	713	1 456	2 116	1 667	1 791	857	387
October	784	505	548	708	1 458	2 119	1 668	1 792	858	388
November	787	506	549	707	1 460	2 120	1 669	1 797	858	388
December	784	507	550	707	1 461	2 125	1 670	1 804	861	389
1997:										
January	785	507	551	707	1 461	2 133	1 670	1 812	859	390
February	788	508	551	708	1 463	2 139	1 672	1 816	860	390
March	791	508	552	708	1 466	2 145	1 674	1 824	859	390
April	793	509	551	709	1 470	2 151	1 675	1 822	862	391
May	796	510	551	707	1 473	2 156	1 676	1 826	862	392
June	796	512	550	707	1 476	2 162	1 683	1 836	864	392
July	797	514	553	707	1 476	2 169	1 691	1 846	867	393
August	799	512	553	712	1 484	2 178	1 696	1 866	868	392
September	799	513	553	713	1 487	2 182	1 700	1 857	869	392
October	800	516	555	714	1 492	2 193	1 707	1 864	872	393
November	803	518	554	716	1 497	2 201	1 713	1 886	874	392
December	805	520	555	717	1 501	2 207	1 718	1 886	876	394
1998:										
January	806	523	563	720	1 505	2 214	1 725	1 891	877	395
February	808	525	561	719	1 507	2 217	1 725	1 898	873	396
March	809	527	559	719	1 508	2 219	1 725	1 898	877	396
April	811	530	561	718	1 509	2 215	1 722	1 901	875	396
May	811	531	561	716	1 507	2 215	1 718	1 897	874	395
June	811	531	562	716	1 503	2 215	1 715	1 891	872	394
July	812	532	563	705	1 491	2 208	1 705	1 788	869	393
August	813	532	564	713	1 502	2 203	1 698	1 894	866	392
September	815	532	565	712	1 500	2 197	1 692	1 891	863	392
October	817	532	566	705	1 498	2 188	1 683	1 892	859	388
November	820	532	568	700	1 494	2 177	1 673	1 887	855	386
December	823	534	570	699	1 493	2 167	1 669	1 882	851	386

1. Additional data availible in individual industry profile sections.

Nonagricultural Employment—*Continued*

(Wage and salary workers on nonagricultural payrolls—Thousands, seasonally adjusted)

| Year and month | Manufacturing—*Conitued* | | | | | | | | | | | |
| | Nondurable—*Continued* | | | | | | | | | | | |
	Total	Production workers	Food and products	Tobacco products	Textile mill products	Apparel and other textile products	Paper and products	Printing and publishing	Chemicals and products	Petroleum and coal products	Rubber and miscellaneous plastics products	Leather and products
1970	8 190	5 956	1 786	83	975	1 364	701	1 104	1 049	191	617	320
1971	8 019	5 847	1 766	77	955	1 343	677	1 081	1 011	194	617	299
1972	8 129	6 022	1 745	75	986	1 383	679	1 094	1 009	195	667	296
1973	8 291	6 138	1 715	78	1 010	1 438	694	1 111	1 038	193	731	284
1974	8 181	6 004	1 707	77	965	1 363	696	1 111	1 061	197	733	271
1975	7 661	5 510	1 658	76	868	1 243	633	1 083	1 015	194	643	248
1976	7 946	5 750	1 689	77	919	1 318	666	1 099	1 043	199	675	263
1977	8 112	5 855	1 711	71	910	1 316	682	1 141	1 074	202	750	255
1978	8 259	5 956	1 724	71	899	1 332	689	1 192	1 096	208	793	257
1979	8 310	5 986	1 733	70	885	1 304	697	1 235	1 109	210	821	246
1980	8 127	5 798	1 708	69	848	1 264	685	1 252	1 107	198	764	233
1981	8 089	5 751	1 671	70	823	1 244	681	1 266	1 109	214	772	238
1982	7 766	5 451	1 636	69	749	1 161	655	1 272	1 075	201	729	219
1983	7 725	5 433	1 614	68	741	1 163	654	1 298	1 043	196	743	205
1984	7 896	5 565	1 611	64	746	1 185	674	1 375	1 049	189	813	189
1985	7 790	5 466	1 601	64	702	1 120	671	1 426	1 044	179	818	165
1986	7 752	5 465	1 607	59	703	1 100	667	1 456	1 021	169	823	149
1987	7 845	5 543	1 617	55	725	1 097	674	1 503	1 025	164	842	143
1988	7 951	5 611	1 626	54	728	1 085	689	1 543	1 057	160	866	143
1989	7 997	5 636	1 644	50	720	1 076	696	1 556	1 074	156	888	138
1990	7 968	5 584	1 661	49	691	1 036	697	1 569	1 086	157	888	133
1991	7 837	5 467	1 667	49	670	1 006	688	1 536	1 076	160	862	124
1992	7 827	5 466	1 663	48	674	1 007	690	1 507	1 084	158	878	120
1993	7 854	5 492	1 680	44	675	989	692	1 517	1 081	152	909	117
1994	7 873	5 528	1 678	43	676	974	692	1 537	1 057	149	953	113
1995	7 841	5 508	1 692	42	663	936	693	1 546	1 038	145	980	106
1996	7 706	5 390	1 692	41	627	868	684	1 540	1 034	142	983	96
1997	7 665	5 354	1 685	41	616	824	683	1 552	1 036	141	996	91
1998	7 602	5 287	1 686	41	598	763	675	1 565	1 043	140	1 009	83
1995:												
January	7 917	5 572	1 690	43	681	972	695	1 547	1 045	148	985	111
February	7 896	5 553	1 681	42	681	963	695	1 549	1 043	148	985	109
March	7 882	5 541	1 680	41	679	960	694	1 548	1 040	148	983	109
April	7 880	5 540	1 683	42	680	955	695	1 547	1 039	147	984	108
May	7 861	5 528	1 684	42	672	948	695	1 545	1 038	147	983	107
June	7 853	5 523	1 695	42	667	940	694	1 547	1 037	146	980	105
July	7 831	5 498	1 694	42	659	934	694	1 546	1 037	145	975	105
August	7 826	5 496	1 696	43	658	929	695	1 544	1 036	144	976	105
September	7 816	5 487	1 701	43	653	921	693	1 544	1 036	143	977	105
October	7 798	5 473	1 702	42	648	910	691	1 543	1 037	143	978	104
November	7 781	5 460	1 702	41	645	901	688	1 544	1 037	142	979	102
December	7 762	5 440	1 701	42	640	895	688	1 544	1 033	142	977	100
1996:												
January	7 741	5 422	1 701	41	632	885	687	1 542	1 035	143	976	99
February	7 746	5 424	1 703	42	635	889	685	1 540	1 035	143	975	99
March	7 740	5 415	1 707	41	632	880	684	1 543	1 037	143	975	98
April	7 712	5 395	1 697	42	627	877	681	1 538	1 035	142	976	97
May	7 708	5 387	1 696	41	627	873	682	1 538	1 034	142	978	97
June	7 697	5 382	1 687	42	626	868	682	1 538	1 033	142	982	97
July	7 698	5 380	1 687	41	626	868	681	1 539	1 033	142	985	96
August	7 693	5 379	1 686	40	624	861	682	1 540	1 035	142	988	95
September	7 689	5 375	1 686	42	621	859	683	1 541	1 033	142	988	94
October	7 691	5 376	1 687	42	623	856	683	1 543	1 033	141	989	94
November	7 683	5 372	1 686	42	620	852	684	1 541	1 033	142	991	92
December	7 678	5 369	1 686	42	620	847	685	1 541	1 033	141	989	94
1997:												
January	7 677	5 365	1 689	42	621	844	684	1 541	1 034	141	988	93
February	7 676	5 363	1 687	42	619	844	684	1 543	1 033	141	990	93
March	7 684	5 364	1 693	42	621	837	685	1 545	1 035	141	992	93
April	7 676	5 363	1 688	41	618	834	684	1 550	1 035	141	993	92
May	7 672	5 363	1 685	41	616	830	684	1 553	1 036	141	994	92
June	7 671	5 358	1 685	41	616	827	683	1 556	1 036	141	995	91
July	7 658	5 352	1 683	42	617	821	682	1 555	1 033	141	994	90
August	7 647	5 335	1 675	41	614	818	682	1 555	1 034	141	997	90
September	7 651	5 339	1 682	41	613	812	681	1 556	1 037	141	999	89
October	7 657	5 345	1 684	41	613	811	682	1 557	1 038	141	1 001	89
November	7 659	5 347	1 686	42	612	807	682	1 559	1 040	141	1 002	88
December	7 659	5 346	1 686	41	612	803	681	1 561	1 041	142	1 004	88
1998:												
January	7 651	5 342	1 685	40	609	798	682	1 563	1 040	140	1 007	87
February	7 646	5 337	1 684	41	608	792	681	1 564	1 041	140	1 008	87
March	7 646	5 331	1 685	42	606	788	679	1 564	1 043	141	1 010	86
April	7 637	5 323	1 686	42	606	781	679	1 565	1 042	141	1 010	85
May	7 627	5 313	1 687	41	604	773	678	1 566	1 044	141	1 009	84
June	7 616	5 302	1 686	40	601	768	676	1 568	1 044	141	1 009	83
July	7 596	5 280	1 684	40	597	764	674	1 567	1 044	140	1 004	82
August	7 577	5 257	1 675	40	594	755	673	1 566	1 044	140	1 009	81
September	7 582	5 265	1 687	40	593	751	672	1 565	1 043	140	1 010	81
October	7 558	5 244	1 685	40	590	738	669	1 565	1 042	140	1 009	80
November	7 547	5 231	1 690	40	586	729	666	1 564	1 043	140	1 010	79
December	7 537	5 227	1 693	40	582	724	666	1 560	1 042	140	1 012	78

Nonagricultural Employment—*Continued*

(Wage and salary workers on nonagricultural payrolls—Thousands, seasonally adjusted)

Year and month	Total	Transportation and public utilities [1]	Wholesale trade	Service-producing industries — Retail trade [1] — Total	General merchandise stores	Food stores	Automotive dealers and service stations	Eating and drinking places	Finance, insurance, and real estate — Total	Finance — Total	Finance — Depository institutions	Insurance	Real estate
1970	47 302	4 515	4 006	11 034	.....	1 731	1 617	2 575	3 645	.....	.....	.....	.....
1971	48 278	4 476	4 014	11 338	.....	1 752	1 642	2 700	3 772	.....	.....	.....	.....
1972	50 007	4 541	4 127	11 822	2 149	1 805	1 723	2 860	3 908	1 778	.....	1 373	756
1973	51 897	4 656	4 291	12 315	2 229	1 856	1 778	3 054	4 046	1 866	.....	1 401	778
1974	53 471	4 725	4 447	12 539	2 210	1 948	1 666	3 231	4 148	1 936	.....	1 434	778
1975	54 345	4 542	4 430	12 630	2 113	2 007	1 677	3 380	4 165	1 964	.....	1 442	760
1976	56 030	4 582	4 562	13 193	2 155	2 039	1 744	3 656	4 271	2 026	.....	1 468	776
1977	58 125	4 713	4 723	13 792	2 204	2 106	1 801	3 949	4 467	2 113	.....	1 528	826
1978	61 113	4 923	4 985	14 556	2 308	2 199	1 861	4 277	4 724	2 233	.....	1 591	900
1979	63 363	5 136	5 221	14 972	2 287	2 297	1 812	4 513	4 975	2 369	.....	1 643	963
1980	64 748	5 146	5 292	15 018	2 245	2 384	1 689	4 626	5 160	2 483	.....	1 688	989
1981	65 655	5 165	5 375	15 171	2 230	2 448	1 653	4 749	5 298	2 593	.....	1 713	992
1982	65 732	5 081	5 295	15 158	2 184	2 477	1 632	4 829	5 340	2 647	.....	1 723	970
1983	66 821	4 952	5 283	15 587	2 165	2 556	1 674	5 038	5 466	2 741	.....	1 728	997
1984	69 690	5 156	5 568	16 512	2 267	2 636	1 798	5 381	5 684	2 852	.....	1 765	1 067
1985	72 544	5 233	5 727	17 315	2 323	2 774	1 889	5 699	5 948	2 974	.....	1 840	1 135
1986	74 811	5 247	5 761	17 880	2 365	2 896	1 941	5 902	6 273	3 145	.....	1 944	1 184
1987	77 284	5 362	5 848	18 422	2 411	2 958	2 001	6 086	6 533	3 264	.....	2 027	1 242
1988	80 084	5 512	6 030	19 023	2 472	3 074	2 071	6 258	6 630	3 274	2 255	2 075	1 280
1989	82 630	5 614	6 187	19 475	2 544	3 164	2 092	6 402	6 668	3 283	2 273	2 090	1 296
1990	84 497	5 777	6 173	19 601	2 540	3 215	2 063	6 509	6 709	3 268	2 251	2 126	1 315
1991	84 504	5 755	6 081	19 284	2 453	3 204	1 984	6 476	6 646	3 187	2 164	2 161	1 299
1992	85 370	5 718	5 997	19 356	2 451	3 180	1 966	6 609	6 602	3 160	2 096	2 152	1 290
1993	87 361	5 811	5 981	19 773	2 488	3 224	2 014	6 821	6 757	3 238	2 089	2 197	1 322
1994	90 256	5 984	6 162	20 507	2 583	3 291	2 116	7 078	6 896	3 299	2 066	2 236	1 361
1995	92 925	6 132	6 378	21 187	2 681	3 366	2 190	7 354	6 806	3 231	2 025	2 225	1 351
1996	95 115	6 253	6 482	21 597	2 702	3 436	2 267	7 517	6 911	3 303	2 019	2 226	1 382
1997	97 727	6 408	6 648	21 966	2 701	3 478	2 311	7 646	7 109	3 424	2 027	2 264	1 421
1998	100 480	6 600	6 831	22 296	2 730	3 482	2 341	7 760	7 407	3 593	2 042	2 344	1 471
1995:													
January	91 985	6 092	6 311	21 008	2 680	3 330	2 166	7 259	6 822	3 244	2 040	2 227	1 351
February	92 246	6 108	6 339	21 065	2 678	3 338	2 173	7 278	6 815	3 236	2 035	2 230	1 349
March	92 415	6 114	6 356	21 047	2 643	3 342	2 179	7 291	6 811	3 233	2 034	2 234	1 344
April	92 572	6 123	6 363	21 126	2 678	3 355	2 181	7 310	6 800	3 224	2 031	2 233	1 343
May	92 602	6 110	6 368	21 123	2 677	3 357	2 182	7 312	6 793	3 222	2 026	2 227	1 344
June	92 803	6 112	6 381	21 192	2 688	3 367	2 184	7 354	6 790	3 218	2 022	2 225	1 347
July	92 897	6 109	6 391	21 213	2 688	3 368	2 186	7 374	6 793	3 222	2 022	2 221	1 350
August	93 179	6 137	6 395	21 254	2 686	3 380	2 193	7 392	6 801	3 225	2 020	2 222	1 354
September	93 342	6 139	6 401	21 293	2 691	3 382	2 199	7 413	6 805	3 228	2 019	2 222	1 355
October	93 483	6 182	6 403	21 276	2 699	3 379	2 205	7 401	6 812	3 233	2 018	2 221	1 358
November	93 654	6 201	6 410	21 310	2 682	3 392	2 211	7 421	6 818	3 239	2 018	2 218	1 361
December	93 787	6 185	6 418	21 335	2 674	3 403	2 219	7 435	6 827	3 247	2 019	2 215	1 365
1996:													
January	93 830	6 199	6 421	21 339	2 677	3 404	2 226	7 438	6 831	3 257	2 020	2 216	1 358
February	94 169	6 202	6 426	21 394	2 686	3 407	2 234	7 453	6 851	3 267	2 021	2 215	1 369
March	94 426	6 207	6 434	21 447	2 691	3 411	2 242	7 476	6 859	3 271	2 018	2 216	1 372
April	94 559	6 229	6 442	21 460	2 681	3 413	2 250	7 485	6 870	3 280	2 017	2 217	1 373
May	94 843	6 242	6 457	21 540	2 711	3 425	2 259	7 498	6 890	3 291	2 017	2 222	1 377
June	95 049	6 264	6 472	21 574	2 710	3 430	2 269	7 505	6 905	3 300	2 018	2 225	1 380
July	95 234	6 285	6 479	21 621	2 709	3 439	2 277	7 522	6 919	3 307	2 017	2 228	1 384
August	95 462	6 285	6 499	21 655	2 704	3 445	2 282	7 534	6 935	3 319	2 017	2 228	1 388
September	95 594	6 280	6 517	21 681	2 704	3 451	2 286	7 532	6 949	3 324	2 018	2 234	1 391
October	95 796	6 281	6 539	21 770	2 716	3 458	2 289	7 573	6 962	3 335	2 020	2 233	1 394
November	96 046	6 298	6 550	21 801	2 711	3 465	2 294	7 581	6 973	3 339	2 018	2 236	1 398
December	96 215	6 282	6 559	21 852	2 715	3 467	2 296	7 593	6 989	3 349	2 018	2 238	1 402
1997:													
January	96 434	6 333	6 563	21 839	2 687	3 472	2 299	7 608	7 004	3 359	2 019	2 241	1 404
February	96 663	6 356	6 585	21 842	2 677	3 474	2 303	7 619	7 015	3 364	2 019	2 244	1 407
March	96 931	6 377	6 605	21 895	2 701	3 479	2 306	7 626	7 033	3 376	2 021	2 246	1 411
April	97 216	6 398	6 614	21 920	2 702	3 479	2 307	7 633	7 058	3 391	2 023	2 250	1 417
May	97 406	6 407	6 626	21 917	2 694	3 477	2 307	7 636	7 074	3 402	2 024	2 253	1 419
June	97 609	6 419	6 633	21 945	2 698	3 476	2 306	7 650	7 086	3 411	2 025	2 258	1 417
July	97 866	6 425	6 656	21 933	2 697	3 481	2 308	7 624	7 113	3 424	2 028	2 264	1 425
August	97 876	6 283	6 669	21 986	2 704	3 481	2 314	7 647	7 134	3 439	2 029	2 269	1 426
September	98 251	6 454	6 678	22 012	2 698	3 477	2 317	7 664	7 155	3 453	2 028	2 273	1 429
October	98 517	6 480	6 699	22 047	2 704	3 482	2 318	7 666	7 181	3 468	2 032	2 281	1 432
November	98 768	6 483	6 712	22 109	2 715	3 481	2 321	7 690	7 207	3 485	2 036	2 288	1 434
December	99 010	6 474	6 732	22 139	2 732	3 475	2 321	7 691	7 233	3 502	2 041	2 299	1 432
1998:													
January	99 225	6 505	6 755	22 142	2 712	3 482	2 322	7 703	7 258	3 513	2 037	2 304	1 441
February	99 407	6 528	6 767	22 149	2 711	3 479	2 321	7 720	7 282	3 527	2 039	2 309	1 446
March	99 594	6 545	6 780	22 155	2 709	3 477	2 323	7 719	7 317	3 547	2 041	2 317	1 453
April	99 802	6 559	6 798	22 177	2 716	3 474	2 327	7 718	7 348	3 559	2 042	2 326	1 463
May	100 099	6 577	6 814	22 237	2 725	3 478	2 333	7 736	7 374	3 574	2 043	2 336	1 464
June	100 308	6 589	6 826	22 257	2 725	3 474	2 338	7 740	7 400	3 589	2 043	2 343	1 468
July	100 568	6 606	6 836	22 321	2 728	3 484	2 343	7 767	7 430	3 606	2 043	2 349	1 475
August	100 826	6 625	6 846	22 353	2 733	3 483	2 345	7 779	7 445	3 616	2 043	2 355	1 474
September	101 028	6 637	6 871	22 382	2 745	3 486	2 349	7 782	7 467	3 623	2 040	2 362	1 482
October	101 261	6 657	6 876	22 392	2 744	3 485	2 356	7 787	7 494	3 642	2 044	2 367	1 485
November	101 543	6 671	6 891	22 443	2 750	3 488	2 361	7 808	7 520	3 651	2 044	2 375	1 494
December	101 832	6 684	6 901	22 525	2 758	3 487	2 370	7 857	7 542	3 663	2 047	2 379	1 500

1. Additional industry detail availible in individual industry profile sections.

Nonagricultural Employment—*Continued*

(Wage and salary workers on nonagricultural payrolls—Thousands, seasonally adjusted)

Year and month	Total	Hotels and other lodging places	Personal services	Business services			Computer and data processing	Auto repair services, and parking	Amusement and recreation	Health services			Hospitals
				Total	Personnel supply					Total	Offices and clinics of medical doctors	Nursing and personal care facilities	
					Total	Help supply							
1970	11 548	.....	898	1 397	.....	.....	.....	.....	.....	3 053	.....	.....	1 863
1971	11 797	.....	848	1 402	.....	.....	.....	.....	.....	3 239	.....	.....	1 935
1972	12 276	813	828	1 491	214	.....	107	399	.....	3 412	467	591	1 980
1973	12 857	854	823	1 610	247	.....	120	422	.....	3 641	519	659	2 051
1974	13 441	878	807	1 686	257	.....	135	430	.....	3 887	567	708	2 160
1975	13 892	898	782	1 697	242	.....	143	439	.....	4 134	608	759	2 274
1976	14 551	929	790	1 806	293	.....	159	466	.....	4 350	644	809	2 363
1977	15 302	956	806	1 958	357	.....	187	498	.....	4 584	681	860	2 465
1978	16 252	988	827	2 181	438	.....	224	549	.....	4 792	720	911	2 538
1979	17 112	1 060	821	2 410	508	.....	271	575	.....	4 993	761	951	2 608
1980	17 890	1 076	818	2 564	543	.....	304	571	.....	5 278	802	997	2 750
1981	18 615	1 119	828	2 700	585	.....	337	574	.....	5 562	845	1 029	2 904
1982	19 021	1 133	844	2 722	541	417	365	589	.....	5 811	887	1 067	3 014
1983	19 664	1 172	869	2 948	619	488	416	619	.....	5 986	934	1 106	3 037
1984	20 746	1 263	918	3 353	797	643	474	682	.....	6 118	977	1 147	3 004
1985	21 927	1 331	957	3 679	891	732	542	730	.....	6 293	1 028	1 198	2 997
1986	22 957	1 378	991	3 957	990	837	588	762	.....	6 528	1 081	1 245	3 037
1987	24 110	1 464	1 027	4 278	1 177	989	629	794	.....	6 794	1 139	1 283	3 142
1988	25 504	1 540	1 056	4 638	1 350	1 126	673	834	977	7 105	1 200	1 311	3 294
1989	26 907	1 596	1 086	4 941	1 455	1 216	736	884	1 033	7 463	1 268	1 356	3 439
1990	27 934	1 631	1 104	5 139	1 535	1 288	772	914	1 076	7 814	1 338	1 415	3 549
1991	28 336	1 589	1 112	5 086	1 485	1 268	797	882	1 122	8 183	1 405	1 493	3 655
1992	29 052	1 576	1 116	5 315	1 629	1 411	836	881	1 188	8 490	1 463	1 533	3 750
1993	30 197	1 596	1 137	5 735	1 906	1 669	893	925	1 258	8 756	1 506	1 585	3 779
1994	31 579	1 631	1 140	6 281	2 272	2 017	959	968	1 334	8 992	1 545	1 649	3 763
1995	33 117	1 668	1 163	6 812	2 476	2 189	1 090	1 020	1 417	9 230	1 609	1 691	3 772
1996	34 454	1 715	1 180	7 293	2 654	2 352	1 228	1 080	1 476	9 478	1 678	1 730	3 812
1997	36 040	1 746	1 186	7 988	2 985	2 656	1 409	1 120	1 552	9 703	1 739	1 756	3 860
1998	37 526	1 776	1 195	8 584	3 230	2 872	1 599	1 144	1 601	9 846	1 803	1 762	3 926
1995:													
January	32 500	1 652	1 154	6 629	2 440	2 167	1 020	1 000	1 360	9 117	1 575	1 671	3 762
February	32 652	1 657	1 157	6 654	2 453	2 175	1 034	1 002	1 380	9 139	1 583	1 676	3 760
March	32 809	1 661	1 162	6 691	2 451	2 173	1 046	1 006	1 418	9 163	1 589	1 678	3 764
April	32 870	1 657	1 161	6 703	2 447	2 164	1 058	1 008	1 425	9 178	1 594	1 681	3 770
May	32 933	1 662	1 163	6 733	2 437	2 155	1 074	1 011	1 412	9 190	1 599	1 682	3 767
June	33 032	1 668	1 164	6 761	2 431	2 149	1 085	1 017	1 417	9 213	1 605	1 687	3 769
July	33 102	1 673	1 167	6 780	2 435	2 150	1 097	1 021	1 418	9 235	1 610	1 691	3 770
August	33 297	1 677	1 165	6 863	2 474	2 185	1 110	1 026	1 427	9 262	1 616	1 697	3 773
September	33 409	1 679	1 164	6 930	2 530	2 228	1 123	1 026	1 434	9 281	1 624	1 702	3 775
October	33 487	1 679	1 163	6 956	2 520	2 228	1 134	1 035	1 435	9 301	1 630	1 704	3 779
November	33 587	1 675	1 164	7 004	2 544	2 246	1 145	1 040	1 427	9 327	1 638	1 710	3 784
December	33 688	1 678	1 168	7 028	2 543	2 243	1 160	1 047	1 422	9 351	1 646	1 712	3 788
1996:													
January	33 720	1 679	1 170	7 011	2 491	2 203	1 165	1 052	1 436	9 357	1 646	1 713	3 792
February	33 937	1 690	1 174	7 100	2 555	2 258	1 176	1 059	1 449	9 387	1 655	1 717	3 798
March	34 082	1 700	1 176	7 141	2 572	2 272	1 186	1 067	1 459	9 413	1 661	1 722	3 803
April	34 170	1 705	1 178	7 182	2 596	2 297	1 196	1 069	1 471	9 430	1 668	1 724	3 804
May	34 296	1 711	1 180	7 217	2 623	2 321	1 205	1 073	1 469	9 454	1 672	1 728	3 808
June	34 430	1 732	1 182	7 261	2 653	2 353	1 213	1 077	1 474	9 471	1 678	1 732	3 808
July	34 526	1 719	1 181	7 310	2 672	2 372	1 229	1 084	1 479	9 490	1 683	1 734	3 810
August	34 668	1 719	1 182	7 393	2 707	2 407	1 243	1 090	1 488	9 505	1 689	1 734	3 810
September	34 734	1 722	1 182	7 419	2 727	2 425	1 257	1 092	1 482	9 527	1 692	1 737	3 819
October	34 815	1 724	1 185	7 413	2 697	2 394	1 273	1 098	1 498	9 547	1 695	1 739	3 823
November	34 994	1 730	1 186	7 516	2 765	2 454	1 289	1 099	1 502	9 569	1 700	1 741	3 829
December	35 089	1 736	1 185	7 561	2 775	2 467	1 304	1 103	1 505	9 585	1 704	1 744	3 833
1997:													
January	35 234	1 737	1 184	7 626	2 811	2 505	1 322	1 105	1 520	9 613	1 711	1 745	3 836
February	35 406	1 742	1 186	7 719	2 852	2 538	1 339	1 111	1 529	9 628	1 719	1 746	3 842
March	35 552	1 743	1 184	7 797	2 892	2 574	1 358	1 115	1 537	9 645	1 720	1 747	3 848
April	35 736	1 747	1 182	7 873	2 931	2 607	1 374	1 118	1 541	9 669	1 726	1 753	3 849
May	35 888	1 743	1 185	7 933	2 958	2 630	1 390	1 121	1 556	9 692	1 736	1 757	3 853
June	35 989	1 739	1 184	7 985	2 985	2 652	1 407	1 116	1 563	9 691	1 736	1 756	3 856
July	36 155	1 738	1 184	8 041	3 020	2 686	1 418	1 120	1 565	9 715	1 742	1 758	3 861
August	36 219	1 737	1 185	8 055	3 004	2 673	1 431	1 120	1 556	9 727	1 742	1 760	3 865
September	36 370	1 746	1 188	8 127	3 045	2 711	1 447	1 124	1 557	9 738	1 747	1 760	3 870
October	36 492	1 758	1 190	8 158	3 067	2 727	1 460	1 126	1 558	9 756	1 755	1 762	3 876
November	36 619	1 758	1 194	8 230	3 107	2 767	1 470	1 128	1 557	9 771	1 761	1 764	3 882
December	36 782	1 759	1 187	8 302	3 153	2 804	1 491	1 132	1 567	9 790	1 772	1 767	3 888
1998:													
January	36 905	1 766	1 184	8 362	3 185	2 829	1 505	1 134	1 565	9 796	1 773	1 763	3 896
February	37 003	1 764	1 190	8 398	3 198	2 844	1 520	1 130	1 571	9 801	1 777	1 766	3 898
March	37 103	1 766	1 193	8 428	3 200	2 846	1 537	1 131	1 573	9 807	1 782	1 766	3 902
April	37 194	1 771	1 195	8 457	3 195	2 843	1 555	1 130	1 580	9 817	1 787	1 765	3 912
May	37 334	1 774	1 197	8 513	3 212	2 858	1 573	1 137	1 584	9 830	1 793	1 766	3 918
June	37 460	1 777	1 196	8 573	3 248	2 886	1 593	1 142	1 587	9 842	1 798	1 765	3 925
July	37 576	1 782	1 197	8 601	3 234	2 873	1 613	1 146	1 599	9 847	1 803	1 762	3 931
August	37 688	1 784	1 197	8 649	3 249	2 887	1 626	1 150	1 608	9 859	1 811	1 760	3 937
September	37 780	1 785	1 195	8 654	3 230	2 874	1 639	1 153	1 622	9 873	1 818	1 761	3 943
October	37 929	1 784	1 194	8 729	3 254	2 891	1 658	1 155	1 626	9 883	1 825	1 759	3 948
November	38 070	1 782	1 198	8 779	3 267	2 903	1 675	1 160	1 641	9 892	1 831	1 757	3 950
December	38 207	1 783	1 202	8 829	3 292	2 922	1 691	1 163	1 647	9 899	1 833	1 756	3 952

1. Additional industry detail availible in individual industry profile sections.

Nonagricultural Employment—*Continued*

(Wage and salary workers on nonagricultural payrolls—Thousands, seasonally adjusted)

| Year and month | Services (private) [1]—*Continued* | | | | | Government | | | | | |
| | Legal services | Educational services | Social services | Membership organizations | Engineering and management services | Total | Federal | State | | Local | |
								Total	Education	Total	Education
1970	.....	940	.....	.....	.....	12 554	2 731	2 664	1 104	7 158	4 004
1971	.....	948	.....	.....	.....	12 881	2 696	2 747	1 149	7 437	4 188
1972	271	958	553	1 403	.....	13 334	2 684	2 859	1 188	7 790	4 363
1973	296	975	552	1 410	.....	13 732	2 663	2 923	1 205	8 146	4 537
1974	326	990	625	1 438	.....	14 170	2 724	3 039	1 267	8 407	4 692
1975	341	1 001	690	1 452	.....	14 686	2 748	3 179	1 323	8 758	4 834
1976	364	1 013	763	1 487	.....	14 871	2 733	3 273	1 371	8 865	4 899
1977	394	1 031	855	1 495	.....	15 127	2 727	3 377	1 385	9 023	4 974
1978	427	1 062	991	1 502	.....	15 672	2 753	3 474	1 367	9 446	5 075
1979	460	1 090	1 081	1 516	.....	15 947	2 773	3 541	1 378	9 633	5 107
1980	498	1 138	1 134	1 539	.....	16 241	2 866	3 610	1 398	9 765	5 210
1981	532	1 179	1 149	1 527	.....	16 031	2 772	3 640	1 420	9 619	5 216
1982	565	1 199	1 149	1 526	.....	15 837	2 739	3 640	1 433	9 458	5 169
1983	602	1 225	1 188	1 510	.....	15 869	2 774	3 662	1 450	9 434	5 139
1984	645	1 270	1 222	1 504	.....	16 024	2 807	3 734	1 488	9 482	5 196
1985	692	1 359	1 325	1 517	.....	16 394	2 875	3 832	1 540	9 687	5 344
1986	747	1 421	1 406	1 536	.....	16 693	2 899	3 893	1 561	9 901	5 484
1987	801	1 449	1 454	1 614	.....	17 010	2 943	3 967	1 586	10 100	5 598
1988	845	1 567	1 552	1 740	2 230	17 386	2 971	4 076	1 621	10 339	5 722
1989	880	1 647	1 644	1 836	2 389	17 779	2 988	4 182	1 668	10 609	5 875
1990	908	1 661	1 734	1 946	2 478	18 304	3 085	4 305	1 730	10 914	6 042
1991	912	1 710	1 845	1 982	2 433	18 402	2 966	4 355	1 768	11 081	6 136
1992	914	1 678	1 959	1 973	2 471	18 645	2 969	4 408	1 799	11 267	6 220
1993	924	1 711	2 070	2 035	2 521	18 841	2 915	4 488	1 834	11 438	6 353
1994	924	1 850	2 200	2 082	2 579	19 128	2 870	4 576	1 882	11 682	6 479
1995	921	1 965	2 336	2 146	2 731	19 305	2 822	4 635	1 919	11 849	6 606
1996	928	2 030	2 413	2 201	2 844	19 419	2 757	4 606	1 911	12 056	6 748
1997	944	2 104	2 518	2 277	2 988	19 557	2 699	4 582	1 904	12 276	6 918
1998	973	2 177	2 644	2 361	3 185	19 819	2 686	4 612	1 916	12 521	7 082
1995:											
January	923	1 923	2 296	2 123	2 666	19 252	2 840	4 645	1 919	11 767	6 543
February	923	1 943	2 308	2 127	2 685	19 267	2 836	4 649	1 924	11 782	6 555
March	923	1 949	2 320	2 133	2 697	19 278	2 832	4 653	1 926	11 793	6 564
April	922	1 952	2 327	2 134	2 707	19 290	2 828	4 647	1 922	11 815	6 582
May	921	1 963	2 332	2 139	2 715	19 275	2 831	4 640	1 922	11 804	6 579
June	919	1 966	2 336	2 144	2 731	19 296	2 833	4 638	1 921	11 825	6 585
July	920	1 967	2 321	2 148	2 741	19 289	2 828	4 626	1 922	11 835	6 592
August	921	1 984	2 347	2 158	2 751	19 295	2 827	4 628	1 916	11 840	6 596
September	921	1 977	2 357	2 155	2 757	19 295	2 816	4 621	1 912	11 858	6 613
October	921	1 983	2 358	2 153	2 766	19 323	2 804	4 626	1 917	11 893	6 623
November	920	1 984	2 361	2 165	2 775	19 328	2 794	4 623	1 916	11 911	6 636
December	920	1 993	2 371	2 171	2 781	19 334	2 789	4 621	1 913	11 924	6 651
1996:											
January	922	1 986	2 372	2 172	2 786	19 320	2 780	4 613	1 907	11 927	6 645
February	924	2 002	2 384	2 179	2 801	19 359	2 782	4 626	1 918	11 951	6 660
March	924	2 009	2 391	2 181	2 816	19 397	2 780	4 626	1 921	11 991	6 687
April	923	2 014	2 399	2 185	2 809	19 388	2 774	4 620	1 918	11 994	6 701
May	926	2 017	2 406	2 195	2 833	19 418	2 770	4 621	1 919	12 027	6 712
June	927	2 030	2 411	2 199	2 844	19 404	2 762	4 615	1 916	12 027	6 728
July	928	2 045	2 417	2 199	2 846	19 404	2 756	4 603	1 915	12 045	6 743
August	930	2 047	2 422	2 212	2 856	19 420	2 739	4 600	1 912	12 081	6 764
September	928	2 038	2 428	2 216	2 871	19 433	2 740	4 598	1 910	12 095	6 778
October	931	2 051	2 438	2 221	2 878	19 429	2 732	4 586	1 901	12 111	6 792
November	933	2 060	2 446	2 227	2 890	19 430	2 727	4 584	1 899	12 119	6 803
December	933	2 063	2 449	2 231	2 901	19 444	2 725	4 580	1 897	12 139	6 815
1997:											
January	936	2 069	2 460	2 235	2 906	19 461	2 730	4 575	1 894	12 156	6 829
February	937	2 074	2 471	2 239	2 926	19 459	2 714	4 576	1 895	12 169	6 843
March	939	2 078	2 482	2 245	2 935	19 469	2 711	4 572	1 892	12 186	6 856
April	942	2 089	2 495	2 256	2 953	19 490	2 707	4 576	1 896	12 207	6 867
May	942	2 092	2 502	2 265	2 964	19 494	2 704	4 577	1 900	12 213	6 871
June	943	2 100	2 512	2 272	2 976	19 537	2 699	4 577	1 904	12 261	6 903
July	945	2 111	2 535	2 283	2 994	19 584	2 694	4 600	1 922	12 290	6 919
August	946	2 117	2 536	2 290	3 009	19 585	2 689	4 581	1 904	12 315	6 937
September	948	2 123	2 545	2 296	3 022	19 582	2 682	4 583	1 908	12 317	6 953
October	950	2 127	2 554	2 305	3 042	19 618	2 684	4 585	1 906	12 349	6 963
November	952	2 132	2 560	2 309	3 053	19 638	2 686	4 588	1 908	12 364	6 972
December	955	2 134	2 569	2 325	3 071	19 650	2 685	4 581	1 905	12 384	6 982
1998:											
January	957	2 142	2 579	2 336	3 087	19 660	2 680	4 577	1 900	12 403	6 996
February	959	2 147	2 589	2 345	3 099	19 678	2 677	4 574	1 898	12 427	7 014
March	962	2 154	2 600	2 354	3 114	19 694	2 674	4 583	1 904	12 437	7 021
April	964	2 158	2 611	2 356	3 130	19 726	2 675	4 591	1 908	12 460	7 034
May	968	2 164	2 624	2 357	3 158	19 763	2 675	4 597	1 908	12 491	7 052
June	971	2 171	2 638	2 360	3 178	19 776	2 677	4 598	1 911	12 501	7 060
July	974	2 177	2 650	2 362	3 201	19 799	2 675	4 612	1 915	12 512	7 078
August	977	2 176	2 660	2 365	3 214	19 869	2 688	4 633	1 931	12 548	7 109
September	980	2 189	2 672	2 369	3 231	19 881	2 689	4 647	1 939	12 555	7 103
October	985	2 206	2 682	2 374	3 248	19 913	2 711	4 633	1 923	12 569	7 108
November	986	2 214	2 695	2 375	3 273	19 948	2 723	4 637	1 923	12 588	7 132
December	988	2 223	2 708	2 380	3 292	19 973	2 701	4 652	1 932	12 620	7 148

1. Additional industry detail availible in individual industry profile sections.

Average Weekly Hours

(Production or nonsupervisory workers on private nonagricultural payrolls—Seasonally adjusted, except as noted)

Year and month	All industries					Total manufacturing		Durable goods manufacturing					
	Not seasonally adjusted	Seasonally adjusted	Goods producing industries [1]	Mining	Construction	Average weekly hours	Overtime hours	Total		Lumber and products	Furniture and fixtures	Stone, clay, and glass products	Primary metal industries
								Average weekly hours	Overtime hours				
1970	37.1	37.1	39.4	42.7	37.3	39.8	3.0	40.3	3.0	39.6	39.2	41.2	40.4
1971	36.9	36.9	39.4	42.4	37.2	39.9	2.9	40.3	2.9	39.8	39.8	41.6	40.1
1972	37.0	37.0	39.9	42.6	36.5	40.5	3.5	41.2	3.6	40.4	40.2	42.0	41.4
1973	36.9	36.9	40.0	42.4	36.8	40.7	3.8	41.4	4.1	40.0	40.0	41.9	42.3
1974	36.5	36.5	39.5	41.9	36.6	40.0	3.3	40.6	3.4	39.2	39.1	41.3	41.6
1975	36.1	36.1	39.0	41.9	36.4	39.5	2.6	39.9	2.6	38.8	38.0	40.4	40.0
1976	36.1	36.1	39.6	42.4	36.8	40.1	3.1	40.6	3.2	39.9	38.8	41.1	40.8
1977	36.0	36.0	39.8	43.4	36.5	40.3	3.5	41.0	3.7	39.9	39.0	41.3	41.3
1978	35.8	35.8	39.9	43.4	36.8	40.4	3.6	41.1	3.8	39.8	39.3	41.6	41.8
1979	35.7	35.7	39.7	43.0	37.0	40.2	3.3	40.8	3.5	39.5	38.7	41.5	41.4
1980	35.3	35.3	39.3	43.3	37.0	39.7	2.8	40.1	2.8	38.6	38.1	40.8	40.1
1981	35.2	35.2	39.5	43.7	36.9	39.8	2.8	40.2	2.8	38.7	38.4	40.6	40.5
1982	34.8	34.8	38.7	42.7	36.7	38.9	2.3	39.3	2.2	38.1	37.2	40.1	38.6
1983	35.0	35.0	39.7	42.5	37.1	40.1	3.0	40.7	3.0	40.1	39.4	41.5	40.5
1984	35.2	35.2	40.2	43.3	37.8	40.7	3.4	41.4	3.6	39.9	39.7	42.0	41.7
1985	34.9	34.9	40.0	43.4	37.7	40.5	3.3	41.2	3.5	39.9	39.4	41.9	41.5
1986	34.8	34.8	40.1	42.2	37.4	40.7	3.4	41.3	3.5	40.4	39.8	42.2	41.9
1987	34.8	34.8	40.3	42.4	37.8	41.0	3.7	41.5	3.8	40.6	40.0	42.3	43.1
1988	34.7	34.7	40.4	42.3	37.9	41.1	3.9	41.8	4.1	40.1	39.4	42.3	43.5
1989	34.6	34.6	40.3	43.0	37.9	41.0	3.8	41.6	3.9	40.1	39.5	42.3	43.0
1990	34.5	34.5	40.3	44.1	38.2	40.8	3.6	41.3	3.7	40.2	39.1	42.0	42.7
1991	34.3	34.3	40.3	44.4	38.1	40.7	3.6	41.1	3.5	40.0	38.9	41.7	42.2
1992	34.4	34.4	40.5	43.9	38.0	41.0	3.8	41.5	3.7	40.6	39.7	42.2	43.0
1993	34.5	34.5	40.9	44.3	38.5	41.4	4.1	42.1	4.3	40.8	40.1	42.7	43.7
1994	34.7	34.7	41.4	44.8	38.9	42.0	4.7	42.9	5.0	41.2	40.4	43.4	44.7
1995	34.5	34.5	41.0	44.7	38.9	41.6	4.4	42.4	4.7	40.6	39.6	43.0	44.0
1996	34.4	34.4	41.1	45.3	39.0	41.6	4.5	42.4	4.8	40.8	39.4	43.3	44.2
1997	34.6	34.6	41.3	45.4	39.0	42.0	4.8	42.8	5.1	41.0	40.2	43.2	44.9
1998	34.6	34.6	41.0	43.9	38.8	41.7	4.6	42.3	4.8	41.1	40.6	43.5	44.2
1995:													
January	34.4	34.6	41.5	45.1	39.1	42.1	4.8	43.0	5.2	41.0	40.7	43.6	44.9
February	34.2	34.5	41.0	44.6	37.8	41.9	4.7	42.7	5.1	40.9	40.3	42.7	44.6
March	34.2	34.5	41.2	44.5	38.9	41.8	4.6	42.7	5.0	40.8	39.7	43.2	44.5
April	34.3	34.5	41.0	44.8	38.8	41.6	4.4	42.4	4.7	40.6	39.2	43.0	44.3
May	34.2	34.3	40.7	44.4	38.0	41.5	4.3	42.2	4.6	40.4	39.3	42.6	43.8
June	34.6	34.5	41.0	44.7	38.9	41.5	4.3	42.3	4.6	40.5	39.5	43.0	43.9
July	34.8	34.4	40.9	44.7	38.9	41.4	4.3	42.2	4.6	40.4	39.3	43.0	43.3
August	34.8	34.4	41.0	44.4	38.8	41.5	4.4	42.3	4.7	40.6	39.7	43.1	43.7
September	34.6	34.4	40.9	44.6	38.7	41.5	4.4	42.3	4.7	40.6	39.4	43.2	43.7
October	34.7	34.4	41.0	44.9	39.1	41.5	4.4	42.4	4.7	40.8	39.6	43.1	43.8
November	34.4	34.4	41.0	44.7	38.8	41.5	4.4	42.4	4.7	40.8	39.7	43.0	43.9
December	34.4	34.3	40.7	44.6	38.6	41.2	4.3	41.9	4.6	40.2	39.4	42.8	43.7
1996:													
January	33.4	33.9	39.5	44.1	37.9	39.9	4.1	40.9	4.4	38.9	35.9	42.0	43.3
February	34.1	34.4	41.0	45.2	39.0	41.5	4.3	42.2	4.6	40.7	39.2	43.3	43.9
March	34.2	34.5	40.9	45.7	38.8	41.4	4.3	42.0	4.5	40.7	39.4	43.4	43.8
April	34.1	34.4	41.0	45.0	38.9	41.5	4.4	42.3	4.7	40.7	39.4	43.4	43.8
May	34.3	34.4	41.0	45.1	38.5	41.7	4.5	42.5	4.8	41.0	39.6	43.2	44.2
June	34.9	34.5	41.2	45.7	39.0	41.8	4.6	42.6	4.9	41.2	39.6	43.6	44.3
July	34.6	34.4	41.1	44.9	38.7	41.7	4.5	42.5	4.8	41.1	39.8	43.3	44.3
August	34.8	34.5	41.2	45.2	39.0	41.8	4.6	42.6	4.9	41.1	39.7	43.4	44.4
September	34.9	34.6	41.3	45.6	39.0	41.9	4.6	42.7	4.9	41.2	39.8	43.4	44.5
October	34.5	34.5	41.1	45.2	38.9	41.7	4.5	42.5	4.8	41.0	39.8	43.3	44.4
November	34.5	34.5	41.2	45.3	39.0	41.7	4.5	42.5	4.8	41.0	39.9	43.2	44.0
December	34.9	34.6	41.3	45.6	39.0	41.9	4.6	42.7	4.9	41.1	40.3	43.2	44.5
1997:													
January	33.9	34.4	40.9	44.7	38.1	41.8	4.7	42.5	5.0	40.6	39.6	42.3	44.4
February	34.5	34.6	41.3	46.0	38.8	41.9	4.7	42.7	5.0	40.9	39.5	43.1	44.7
March	34.6	34.7	41.4	46.5	39.1	42.1	4.9	42.9	5.2	41.1	40.3	43.2	44.8
April	34.4	34.6	41.5	45.2	39.0	42.2	4.9	43.1	5.3	41.2	40.2	43.1	45.0
May	34.5	34.6	41.5	45.7	39.4	42.0	4.9	42.8	5.2	41.1	40.2	43.3	44.8
June	34.9	34.5	41.3	45.6	39.1	41.9	4.7	42.7	5.0	41.1	40.0	43.1	44.7
July	34.8	34.5	41.3	45.3	39.0	41.9	4.8	42.8	5.1	41.2	40.1	43.2	44.8
August	35.0	34.7	41.3	45.5	38.9	42.0	4.8	42.8	5.1	41.0	40.2	43.1	45.0
September	34.8	34.6	41.4	45.2	39.3	42.0	4.8	42.7	5.1	41.1	40.5	43.3	45.0
October	34.7	34.6	41.4	45.0	39.0	42.0	4.9	42.8	5.2	41.1	40.3	43.3	45.3
November	34.8	34.7	41.2	45.1	38.4	42.1	4.9	42.8	5.2	41.1	40.6	43.0	45.1
December	34.8	34.6	41.4	44.9	38.9	42.1	4.9	42.9	5.2	41.0	40.8	43.7	45.2
1998:													
January	34.2	34.8	41.5	45.7	39.1	42.2	4.9	42.9	5.2	41.1	40.9	43.7	45.3
February	34.6	34.7	41.4	44.2	39.3	42.0	4.8	42.7	5.1	41.3	41.0	43.7	44.8
March	34.5	34.6	41.1	44.1	38.7	41.8	4.8	42.5	5.0	41.1	40.7	43.3	44.5
April	34.2	34.6	41.0	44.3	38.9	41.6	4.6	42.2	4.8	41.2	40.7	43.4	44.1
May	34.6	34.7	41.1	44.3	38.9	41.8	4.6	42.4	4.8	41.1	40.8	43.6	44.3
June	34.7	34.6	41.1	43.7	38.8	41.8	4.6	42.3	4.8	41.1	40.9	43.4	44.4
July	34.8	34.6	41.2	44.3	39.2	41.7	4.6	42.3	4.8	41.2	40.7	43.6	44.0
August	35.2	34.6	41.1	43.7	39.2	41.7	4.5	42.3	4.7	41.2	40.6	43.6	44.1
September	34.3	34.5	40.9	43.3	38.6	41.6	4.5	42.2	4.7	40.7	40.2	43.4	43.9
October	34.6	34.6	41.1	43.7	39.2	41.7	4.5	42.3	4.7	41.1	40.5	43.6	43.7
November	34.7	34.6	41.0	43.3	39.1	41.7	4.5	42.3	4.6	41.2	40.3	43.6	43.8
December	34.7	34.6	41.1	43.3	39.4	41.7	4.5	42.2	4.6	41.5	40.2	43.8	43.7

1. Includes mining, construction, and manufacturing. Additional industry detail availible in individual industry profile sections.

Average Weekly Hours—*Continued*

(Production or nonsupervisory workers on private nonagricultural payrolls—Seasonally adjusted, except as noted)

Year and month	Durable goods manufacturing—*Continued*						Nondurable good manufacturing					
	Fabricated metal products	Industrial machinery and equipment [1]	Electronic and electrical equipment	Transportation equipment [1]	Instruments and related products	Miscellaneous manufacturing	Total		Food and products	Tobacco products	Textile mill products	Apparel and other textile products
							Average weekly hours	Overtime hours				
1970	40.7	41.1	.....	40.3	.....	38.7	39.1	3.0	40.5	37.8	39.9	35.3
1971	40.4	40.6	.....	40.7	.....	38.9	39.3	3.0	40.3	37.8	40.6	35.6
1972	41.2	42.1	.....	41.7	.....	39.5	39.7	3.3	40.5	37.6	41.3	36.0
1973	41.6	42.8	.....	42.1	.....	39.0	39.6	3.4	40.4	38.6	40.9	35.9
1974	40.8	42.1	.....	40.5	.....	38.7	39.1	3.0	40.4	38.3	39.5	35.2
1975	40.1	40.8	.....	40.4	.....	38.5	38.8	2.7	40.3	38.2	39.3	35.2
1976	40.8	41.2	.....	41.7	.....	38.8	39.4	3.0	40.5	37.5	40.1	35.8
1977	41.0	41.5	.....	42.5	.....	38.8	39.4	3.2	40.0	37.8	40.4	35.6
1978	41.0	42.0	.....	42.2	.....	38.8	39.4	3.2	39.7	38.1	40.4	35.6
1979	40.7	41.7	.....	41.1	.....	38.8	39.3	3.1	39.9	38.0	40.4	35.3
1980	40.4	41.0	.....	40.6	.....	38.7	39.0	2.8	39.7	38.1	40.1	35.4
1981	40.3	40.9	.....	40.9	.....	38.8	39.2	2.8	39.7	38.8	39.6	35.7
1982	39.2	39.7	.....	40.5	.....	38.4	38.4	2.5	39.4	37.8	37.5	34.7
1983	40.6	40.5	.....	42.1	.....	39.1	39.4	3.0	39.5	37.4	40.4	36.2
1984	41.4	41.9	.....	42.7	.....	39.4	39.7	3.1	39.8	38.9	39.9	36.4
1985	41.3	41.5	.....	42.6	.....	39.4	39.6	3.1	40.0	37.2	39.7	36.4
1986	41.3	41.6	.....	42.3	.....	39.6	39.9	3.3	40.0	37.4	41.1	36.7
1987	41.6	42.2	.....	42.0	.....	39.4	40.2	3.6	40.2	39.0	41.8	37.0
1988	41.9	42.7	41.0	42.7	41.4	39.2	40.2	3.6	40.3	39.8	41.0	37.0
1989	41.6	42.4	40.8	42.4	41.1	39.4	40.2	3.6	40.7	38.6	40.9	36.9
1990	41.3	41.9	40.8	42.0	41.1	39.5	40.0	3.6	40.8	39.2	39.9	36.4
1991	41.2	41.7	40.7	41.9	41.0	39.7	40.2	3.7	40.6	39.1	40.6	37.0
1992	41.6	42.2	41.2	41.8	41.1	39.9	40.4	3.8	40.6	38.6	41.1	37.2
1993	42.1	43.0	41.8	43.0	41.1	39.8	40.6	4.0	40.7	37.4	41.4	37.2
1994	42.9	43.7	42.2	44.3	41.7	40.0	40.9	4.3	41.3	39.3	41.6	37.5
1995	42.4	43.4	41.6	43.8	41.4	39.9	40.5	4.0	41.1	39.6	40.8	37.0
1996	42.4	43.1	41.5	44.0	41.7	39.7	40.5	4.1	41.0	40.0	40.6	37.0
1997	42.6	43.6	42.0	44.5	42.0	40.4	40.9	4.4	41.3	38.9	41.4	37.3
1998	42.3	42.8	41.4	43.4	41.3	39.9	40.9	4.3	41.7	38.3	41.0	37.3
1995:												
January	43.2	43.9	41.9	44.5	41.6	40.1	41.0	4.3	41.5	39.8	41.7	37.6
February	42.9	43.8	41.6	44.4	41.4	40.1	40.9	4.2	41.3	39.2	41.5	37.5
March	42.8	43.7	41.7	44.4	41.5	40.0	40.7	4.1	41.2	38.7	41.2	37.3
April	42.1	43.4	41.6	43.9	41.4	40.0	40.6	4.0	41.0	40.1	41.0	37.0
May	42.1	43.4	41.5	43.4	41.3	39.8	40.5	3.9	41.1	40.2	40.6	37.0
June	42.2	43.2	41.5	43.7	41.4	40.0	40.5	3.9	41.2	40.7	40.4	36.9
July	42.1	43.1	41.5	43.7	41.4	39.8	40.4	3.9	41.3	40.6	40.5	36.9
August	42.3	43.4	41.6	43.6	41.5	40.0	40.5	4.0	41.3	40.2	40.8	36.8
September	42.4	43.3	41.8	43.6	41.4	39.9	40.5	4.0	41.2	38.4	40.6	36.9
October	42.4	43.2	42.1	43.6	41.5	39.8	40.4	4.0	40.9	39.1	40.5	36.7
November	42.3	43.4	41.7	43.9	41.4	39.7	40.4	3.9	40.8	39.7	40.5	36.8
December	42.1	43.0	41.1	42.8	41.3	39.4	40.2	3.8	40.5	38.3	40.3	36.8
1996:												
January	41.0	41.9	40.1	42.4	40.2	37.8	38.6	3.8	39.6	36.5	36.1	33.7
February	42.1	43.1	41.7	43.2	41.7	39.5	40.4	4.0	41.1	39.4	40.4	36.9
March	42.1	43.1	41.6	42.1	41.7	39.7	40.5	4.0	41.1	40.1	40.7	36.9
April	42.2	43.1	41.2	44.1	41.6	39.6	40.4	4.1	41.1	40.0	40.3	36.8
May	42.5	43.2	41.5	44.2	41.7	39.8	40.6	4.1	41.0	39.9	40.8	37.3
June	42.6	43.2	41.6	44.4	42.0	39.8	40.7	4.1	41.1	40.0	41.0	37.5
July	42.6	43.1	41.4	44.4	41.6	39.7	40.6	4.1	40.9	39.9	41.0	37.3
August	42.6	43.1	41.7	44.5	41.7	39.8	40.7	4.1	40.9	39.9	41.1	37.5
September	42.5	43.2	41.7	44.6	41.9	40.0	40.7	4.2	41.1	40.6	41.0	37.4
October	42.4	43.1	41.5	44.0	41.8	39.8	40.7	4.1	41.2	39.8	41.0	37.4
November	42.4	43.1	41.6	44.1	41.9	40.0	40.7	4.2	41.2	40.2	41.2	37.4
December	42.5	43.4	41.8	44.3	42.1	40.4	40.9	4.3	41.2	40.9	41.5	37.4
1997:												
January	42.4	43.3	41.4	44.8	41.7	40.1	40.7	4.2	41.0	39.8	41.1	37.2
February	42.6	43.5	42.0	44.5	41.9	40.3	40.8	4.3	41.3	40.7	40.8	37.1
March	42.7	43.6	42.3	44.7	42.0	40.2	40.9	4.4	41.3	39.8	41.3	37.4
April	42.8	44.0	42.4	44.8	42.0	40.5	40.9	4.3	41.3	39.0	41.6	37.4
May	42.6	43.7	42.1	44.4	42.0	40.3	40.8	4.4	41.3	38.6	41.4	37.2
June	42.5	43.3	42.1	44.5	41.9	40.2	40.7	4.2	41.0	38.2	41.3	37.3
July	42.5	43.5	42.1	44.3	41.8	40.4	40.7	4.3	41.2	36.5	41.4	37.1
August	42.5	43.5	41.9	44.5	42.1	40.2	40.8	4.3	41.3	37.8	41.4	37.1
September	42.5	43.6	41.8	43.9	42.0	40.4	40.8	4.3	41.2	38.1	41.5	37.3
October	42.6	43.5	41.9	44.2	42.0	40.4	40.9	4.4	41.4	39.0	41.4	37.3
November	42.7	43.7	41.9	44.0	42.2	40.6	41.0	4.5	41.5	39.2	41.5	37.3
December	42.8	43.7	42.0	44.2	42.0	40.7	41.0	4.5	41.6	39.2	41.6	37.5
1998:												
January	42.9	43.6	42.0	44.0	41.9	40.5	41.1	4.4	41.7	38.5	41.7	37.6
February	42.6	43.4	41.8	43.6	41.9	40.4	41.0	4.4	41.5	38.9	41.5	37.3
March	42.4	43.3	41.5	43.5	41.5	40.4	40.8	4.4	41.5	37.7	41.3	37.1
April	42.1	42.9	41.3	42.9	41.5	40.0	40.8	4.2	41.5	38.2	41.2	37.5
May	42.5	43.0	41.4	43.3	41.4	40.1	40.9	4.4	41.7	39.1	41.2	37.4
June	42.4	43.1	41.4	42.9	41.4	40.1	40.9	4.3	41.7	38.8	41.2	37.3
July	42.4	42.9	41.4	43.0	41.4	40.0	41.0	4.4	41.8	40.1	41.0	37.4
August	42.3	42.9	41.5	43.0	41.3	40.0	40.9	4.3	41.7	39.2	41.0	37.4
September	42.2	42.6	41.4	43.8	41.1	39.5	40.8	4.3	41.7	37.7	40.4	37.2
October	42.3	42.6	41.5	43.9	41.2	39.7	40.9	4.3	41.6	38.5	41.1	37.3
November	42.2	42.4	41.4	44.1	41.1	39.4	40.8	4.3	41.7	38.5	40.8	37.3
December	42.2	42.1	41.1	44.1	41.1	39.6	40.9	4.3	42.0	36.6	40.8	37.3

1. Additional industry detail available in individual industry profile sections.

Average Weekly Hours—Continued

(Production or nonsupervisory workers on private nonagricultural payrolls—Seasonally adjusted, except as noted)

Year and month	Nondurable goods manufacturing—Continued						Service-producing industries					
	Paper and products	Printing and publishing	Chemicals and products	Petroleum and coal products [1]	Rubber and miscellaneous plastics products	Leather and products	Total	Transportation and public utilities	Wholesale trade	Retail trade	Finance, insurance, real estate [1]	Services
1970	41.9	37.7	41.6	42.8	40.3	37.2	35.8	40.5	39.9	33.8	36.7	34.4
1971	42.1	37.5	41.6	42.8	40.4	37.7	35.5	40.1	39.4	33.7	36.6	33.9
1972	42.8	37.7	41.7	42.7	41.2	38.3	35.4	40.4	39.4	33.4	36.6	33.9
1973	42.9	37.7	41.8	42.4	41.2	37.8	35.2	40.5	39.2	33.1	36.6	33.8
1974	42.2	37.5	41.5	42.1	40.6	36.9	34.9	40.2	38.8	32.7	36.5	33.6
1975	41.6	36.9	41.0	41.2	39.9	37.1	34.7	39.7	38.6	32.4	36.5	33.5
1976	42.5	37.5	41.6	42.1	40.7	37.4	34.4	39.8	38.7	32.1	36.4	33.3
1977	42.9	37.7	41.7	42.7	41.1	36.9	34.2	39.9	38.8	31.6	36.4	33.0
1978	42.9	37.6	41.9	43.6	40.9	37.1	33.9	40.0	38.8	31.0	36.4	32.8
1979	42.6	37.5	41.9	43.8	40.6	36.5	33.7	39.9	38.8	30.6	36.2	32.7
1980	42.2	37.1	41.5	41.8	40.0	36.7	33.5	39.6	38.4	30.2	36.2	32.6
1981	42.5	37.3	41.6	43.2	40.3	36.7	33.5	39.4	38.5	30.1	36.3	32.6
1982	41.8	37.1	40.9	43.9	39.6	35.6	33.3	39.0	38.3	29.9	36.2	32.6
1983	42.6	37.6	41.6	43.9	41.2	36.8	33.3	39.0	38.5	29.8	36.2	32.7
1984	43.1	37.9	41.9	43.7	41.7	36.8	33.3	39.4	38.5	29.8	36.5	32.6
1985	43.1	37.8	41.9	43.0	41.1	37.2	33.1	39.5	38.4	29.4	36.4	32.5
1986	43.2	38.0	41.9	43.8	41.4	36.9	32.9	39.2	38.3	29.2	36.4	32.5
1987	43.4	38.0	42.3	44.0	41.6	38.2	32.9	39.2	38.1	29.2	36.3	32.5
1988	43.3	38.0	42.2	44.4	41.7	37.5	32.8	38.2	38.1	29.1	35.9	32.6
1989	43.3	37.9	42.4	44.3	41.4	37.9	32.7	38.3	38.0	28.9	35.8	32.6
1990	43.3	37.9	42.6	44.6	41.1	37.4	32.7	38.4	38.1	28.8	35.8	32.5
1991	43.3	37.7	42.9	44.1	41.1	37.5	32.5	38.1	38.1	28.6	35.7	32.4
1992	43.6	38.1	43.1	43.8	41.7	38.0	32.7	38.3	38.2	28.8	35.8	32.5
1993	43.6	38.3	43.1	44.2	41.8	38.6	32.7	39.3	38.2	28.8	35.8	32.5
1994	43.9	38.6	43.2	44.4	42.2	38.5	32.8	39.7	38.4	28.9	35.8	32.5
1995	43.1	38.2	43.2	43.7	41.5	38.0	32.7	39.4	38.3	28.8	35.9	32.4
1996	43.3	38.2	43.2	43.6	41.5	38.1	32.7	39.6	38.3	28.8	35.9	32.4
1997	43.7	38.5	43.2	43.1	41.8	38.4	32.9	39.7	38.4	28.9	36.1	32.6
1998	43.4	38.3	43.2	43.6	41.7	37.6	32.9	39.5	38.4	29.0	36.4	32.6
1995:												
January	43.9	38.4	43.4	43.8	42.1	38.1	32.7	39.5	38.4	28.8	36.3	32.4
February	43.6	38.4	43.3	44.4	42.1	38.5	32.6	39.5	38.3	28.7	35.8	32.4
March	43.4	38.4	43.3	43.3	41.9	38.3	32.6	39.4	38.3	28.7	35.5	32.4
April	43.3	38.4	43.4	43.9	41.7	38.3	32.7	39.4	38.3	28.8	36.3	32.4
May	43.0	38.3	43.2	43.2	41.5	38.4	32.6	39.3	38.2	28.8	35.4	32.3
June	43.0	38.2	43.3	43.7	41.4	38.1	32.7	39.4	38.2	28.8	35.6	32.5
July	43.0	38.2	43.2	44.1	41.0	37.3	32.6	39.4	38.2	28.7	36.3	32.4
August	43.0	38.1	43.1	43.2	41.3	38.2	32.6	39.3	38.3	28.8	35.6	32.4
September	43.0	38.1	43.2	43.8	41.5	37.9	32.7	39.2	38.3	28.8	35.7	32.4
October	42.9	38.1	43.2	44.3	41.5	37.8	32.6	39.2	38.2	28.7	36.4	32.3
November	43.0	38.3	43.0	43.8	41.5	37.6	32.6	39.3	38.2	28.8	35.7	32.4
December	42.9	37.9	43.1	43.2	41.3	37.6	32.6	39.4	38.2	28.7	35.7	32.4
1996:												
January	41.5	37.0	42.5	43.1	40.2	35.0	32.4	39.1	38.0	28.5	35.5	32.2
February	43.1	38.1	43.2	42.8	41.4	37.6	32.6	39.6	38.2	28.8	35.7	32.3
March	43.1	38.2	43.1	42.9	41.4	37.9	32.7	39.8	38.3	28.9	35.7	32.4
April	43.2	38.2	43.0	43.3	41.5	37.9	32.6	39.4	38.2	28.7	35.6	32.3
May	43.3	38.3	43.2	42.6	41.6	38.4	32.7	39.5	38.3	28.8	35.6	32.4
June	43.4	38.3	43.4	44.7	41.6	38.6	32.7	39.6	38.4	28.8	36.5	32.5
July	43.3	38.3	43.3	44.3	41.5	38.5	32.6	39.5	38.1	28.7	35.6	32.3
August	43.5	38.3	43.2	43.9	41.7	38.8	32.7	39.7	38.3	28.8	35.8	32.4
September	43.5	38.3	43.1	44.2	41.8	38.7	32.8	39.7	38.4	28.9	36.5	32.5
October	43.4	38.2	43.1	43.6	41.5	38.6	32.7	39.8	38.3	28.8	35.7	32.4
November	43.6	38.3	43.3	43.9	41.4	38.9	32.7	39.8	38.3	28.8	35.8	32.4
December	43.7	38.4	43.5	43.9	41.7	38.7	32.8	39.8	38.4	28.9	36.7	32.5
1997:												
January	43.7	38.3	43.1	44.9	41.6	38.3	32.7	39.5	38.3	28.9	35.7	32.4
February	43.8	38.5	43.3	43.4	41.7	38.5	32.8	39.5	38.4	28.9	36.7	32.6
March	43.8	38.7	43.2	43.0	41.8	38.7	32.9	39.9	38.4	29.0	36.5	32.6
April	43.7	38.5	43.2	42.4	42.1	38.6	32.8	39.6	38.4	28.9	35.9	32.5
May	43.7	38.5	43.3	42.4	41.7	38.4	32.8	39.6	38.5	28.9	35.9	32.6
June	43.4	38.4	43.1	42.9	41.7	38.3	32.7	39.4	38.4	28.8	36.7	32.5
July	43.5	38.4	43.1	42.8	41.7	38.6	32.8	39.3	38.4	28.9	35.9	32.5
August	43.5	38.4	43.2	43.0	41.8	38.2	32.9	40.1	38.4	29.0	36.1	32.7
September	43.6	38.7	43.2	43.3	41.7	38.5	32.9	40.0	38.4	28.9	35.8	32.6
October	43.7	38.7	43.3	43.3	41.9	38.4	32.8	39.8	38.4	28.9	35.9	32.6
November	43.9	38.7	43.4	43.3	42.0	37.9	32.9	39.9	38.5	29.0	36.7	32.7
December	43.8	38.6	43.2	42.2	42.1	38.2	32.8	39.9	38.4	28.9	35.9	32.6
1998:												
January	43.7	38.5	43.5	44.5	42.1	38.3	33.0	39.9	38.5	29.0	36.1	32.7
February	43.6	38.6	43.4	42.2	41.9	38.5	32.9	39.9	38.4	29.0	37.1	32.6
March	43.4	38.4	43.4	43.1	41.6	37.8	32.9	39.7	38.3	29.0	36.8	32.6
April	43.1	38.3	43.2	42.8	41.7	37.5	32.9	39.6	38.3	29.0	36.1	32.6
May	43.5	38.4	43.1	42.9	41.8	37.5	33.0	39.7	38.4	29.1	36.1	32.7
June	43.5	38.3	43.2	43.2	41.9	37.6	32.9	39.5	38.3	29.0	36.0	32.6
July	43.6	38.4	43.1	44.8	41.9	37.3	33.0	39.5	38.4	29.1	36.1	32.7
August	43.3	38.5	43.2	44.0	41.7	37.9	32.9	39.4	38.4	29.0	36.9	32.7
September	43.6	38.2	43.2	43.2	41.7	37.4	32.8	39.3	38.3	29.0	35.9	32.5
October	43.5	38.2	43.2	44.0	41.8	37.4	32.9	39.3	38.3	29.1	36.1	32.7
November	43.5	38.1	42.9	43.9	41.6	37.4	32.9	39.2	38.4	29.0	36.9	32.7
December	43.4	38.1	42.7	44.7	41.7	37.5	32.9	39.1	38.4	29.0	36.2	32.7

1. Not seasonally adjusted.

Indexes of Aggregate Weekly Hours

(Production or nonsupervisory workers on private nonagricultural payrolls—1982=100, seasonally adjusted)

Year and month	Total private	Goods-producing industries									
		Total	Mining	Construction	Manufacturing						
					Total	Durable goods					
						Total	Lumber and wood products	Furniture and fixtures	Stone, clay, and glass products	Primary metal industries [1]	Fabricated metal products
1970	86.3	107.8	57.6	101.3	112.8	113.0	117.9	111.6	120.9	152.9	120.3
1971	85.8	105.0	54.9	103.6	108.8	107.4	123.8	114.0	122.2	140.5	113.2
1972	89.2	110.5	57.8	107.9	114.8	115.4	136.1	126.6	131.1	146.3	121.9
1973	93.2	116.9	58.8	113.7	121.7	125.8	140.6	132.0	138.4	161.8	131.8
1974	93.2	113.7	63.4	109.5	118.1	122.4	128.2	123.4	134.5	162.4	127.4
1975	88.8	99.9	68.3	92.7	103.8	104.9	107.8	100.7	115.6	134.3	108.4
1976	92.3	105.4	71.5	94.0	110.3	111.9	123.5	111.0	120.8	140.0	115.3
1977	96.0	110.3	76.5	100.2	115.0	118.4	132.0	117.2	125.9	144.2	121.9
1978	100.7	116.5	79.0	112.2	120.1	125.9	138.3	125.6	132.1	151.3	129.3
1979	104.0	119.9	88.2	119.9	122.1	129.1	138.6	123.5	132.8	154.8	131.4
1980	102.8	112.9	94.1	115.1	113.8	117.8	119.9	112.4	119.8	133.4	119.8
1981	104.1	111.6	104.8	109.3	112.5	116.1	115.1	112.7	114.1	132.5	117.1
1982	100.0	100.0	100.0	100.0	100.0	100.0	100.0	100.0	100.0	100.0	100.0
1983	101.5	100.5	81.5	102.2	101.4	100.7	117.7	110.3	103.2	95.2	100.3
1984	107.7	109.0	84.9	116.8	109.0	111.5	126.3	121.6	109.5	102.9	111.0
1985	110.5	108.7	81.4	125.3	106.9	109.5	124.9	121.9	108.1	96.1	111.2
1986	112.3	107.3	65.7	128.2	105.7	106.8	129.2	124.2	108.7	89.8	107.8
1987	115.6	109.0	61.8	132.7	107.0	107.4	134.9	129.5	109.7	91.8	107.1
1988	119.3	111.4	61.7	136.9	109.3	110.5	135.6	130.1	113.3	97.2	110.5
1989	122.1	111.7	60.5	138.9	109.3	110.1	132.6	129.6	113.5	96.0	110.6
1990	123.0	109.5	63.9	138.0	106.4	106.1	128.2	122.8	109.7	93.0	107.1
1991	120.4	103.4	62.0	122.8	102.1	99.3	116.9	113.9	101.4	87.2	101.4
1992	121.2	102.1	56.2	118.4	101.7	98.2	119.9	117.6	101.2	85.6	100.7
1993	124.6	104.2	54.3	125.4	103.1	100.0	126.1	121.3	102.9	86.2	103.3
1994	130.0	109.2	54.6	136.3	107.0	105.5	135.9	127.0	107.9	90.9	110.5
1995	133.4	110.3	54.1	140.8	107.5	107.5	135.8	125.6	108.8	92.1	113.6
1996	136.7	111.5	55.6	148.7	107.2	109.2	138.0	123.4	110.8	92.6	114.5
1997	141.5	114.6	58.3	156.2	109.4	112.9	142.1	128.6	112.4	94.5	118.1
1998	145.1	115.3	56.1	163.7	108.8	112.8	145.2	134.7	115.7	93.4	118.8
1995:											
January	132.7	111.7	55.3	141.5	109.1	109.2	137.7	130.2	109.9	93.8	115.2
February	132.6	110.7	54.3	137.5	108.7	108.9	137.8	129.2	107.9	93.5	115.1
March	132.9	111.0	54.2	140.5	108.5	109.0	137.2	127.3	109.4	93.3	115.1
April	133.0	110.6	54.4	140.0	108.0	108.4	135.7	125.4	109.2	93.0	113.5
May	132.5	109.5	53.8	136.5	107.4	107.8	134.6	124.8	107.6	92.0	113.3
June	133.3	110.2	54.1	140.5	107.4	107.9	134.5	124.8	108.9	92.2	113.1
July	133.2	109.9	54.1	140.8	106.9	107.5	134.4	122.9	108.4	90.3	112.7
August	133.7	110.2	53.6	141.2	107.4	108.1	135.0	125.1	108.9	91.4	113.3
September	134.1	110.3	53.7	141.8	107.3	108.3	135.7	124.2	109.2	91.4	113.4
October	134.0	110.5	54.1	144.0	107.1	108.2	136.6	124.8	108.9	91.6	113.6
November	134.3	110.2	53.4	142.7	106.9	108.1	136.8	124.8	108.7	92.0	113.5
December	134.2	109.4	53.4	141.4	106.3	107.7	135.0	124.2	107.9	91.6	113.0
1996:											
January	132.6	106.3	52.8	139.6	102.7	104.7	129.0	112.6	105.4	91.3	110.0
February	135.1	110.7	54.9	145.9	106.8	108.3	136.2	122.6	109.4	92.4	112.9
March	135.6	110.3	55.7	145.9	106.3	107.4	136.0	122.9	109.9	92.0	112.9
April	135.5	110.8	55.1	146.4	106.8	108.6	136.9	122.3	110.2	91.5	113.0
May	136.2	111.1	55.3	145.7	107.3	109.3	138.3	123.6	110.2	92.8	114.2
June	137.0	111.9	56.3	148.7	107.7	109.9	139.6	123.6	111.2	93.2	115.0
July	136.6	111.6	55.2	148.1	107.4	109.7	139.5	124.5	110.7	92.2	115.6
August	137.4	112.2	55.8	150.1	107.8	110.1	139.9	124.5	111.5	93.6	115.6
September	138.0	112.4	56.2	150.5	107.9	110.3	140.1	125.1	111.8	93.8	115.6
October	137.9	112.3	55.8	151.2	107.6	109.9	140.0	125.1	111.8	92.9	115.4
November	138.3	112.6	56.2	152.3	107.7	110.0	140.5	125.4	111.5	92.1	115.6
December	139.0	113.1	56.7	152.7	108.3	110.8	140.4	127.0	112.0	93.1	115.9
1997:											
January	138.7	112.2	56.1	149.5	107.9	110.6	138.7	125.1	109.7	92.9	115.7
February	139.7	113.4	58.4	153.0	108.4	111.3	140.1	125.1	111.8	93.5	116.5
March	140.6	114.4	59.0	156.5	109.0	112.1	141.5	127.6	112.3	93.7	117.1
April	140.7	114.3	57.6	154.8	109.3	112.6	142.3	127.3	111.8	94.3	117.7
May	141.2	114.6	58.7	157.3	109.0	112.3	142.3	128.0	112.6	93.9	117.4
June	140.9	114.2	58.5	156.0	108.8	112.3	142.3	127.6	111.5	93.7	117.5
July	141.4	114.4	58.5	156.1	109.1	112.7	142.7	128.6	112.8	94.1	117.6
August	141.9	114.7	58.8	156.4	109.4	113.4	142.4	128.6	112.3	95.2	118.3
September	142.4	115.1	58.7	158.5	109.5	113.3	143.0	130.2	112.8	95.0	118.4
October	142.7	115.3	58.4	157.6	110.0	113.9	143.2	130.2	113.3	96.0	119.1
November	143.3	115.4	58.4	156.0	110.4	114.4	143.6	131.8	112.6	95.9	119.8
December	143.5	116.2	58.4	159.2	110.7	115.0	143.7	132.7	114.7	96.3	120.4
1998:											
January	144.3	117.0	60.0	162.7	110.9	115.3	144.3	134.0	116.2	96.8	121.1
February	144.3	116.7	58.4	162.9	110.5	114.9	145.2	135.0	116.0	95.8	120.6
March	144.1	115.8	57.7	160.6	110.0	114.3	144.5	134.3	114.1	95.3	119.9
April	144.3	115.7	57.5	162.2	109.4	113.5	145.1	135.3	114.9	94.3	119.1
May	145.0	115.8	57.2	162.3	109.6	113.7	144.7	135.6	115.2	94.2	120.0
June	144.8	115.5	56.2	162.7	109.2	113.3	144.7	135.6	114.9	94.4	119.1
July	145.2	114.8	56.5	165.1	107.8	110.9	145.5	135.3	115.7	91.7	118.4
August	145.5	115.4	55.3	165.4	108.5	112.6	145.5	135.3	116.0	93.3	118.6
September	145.1	114.7	54.6	162.7	108.3	112.4	144.0	134.0	115.7	92.7	118.4
October	146.0	115.2	54.6	166.4	108.1	112.3	145.6	134.6	116.5	91.4	118.4
November	146.1	115.0	53.7	167.5	107.7	111.8	146.6	134.3	116.8	90.8	117.9
December	146.6	115.5	53.4	171.3	107.5	111.5	148.1	134.6	118.1	90.4	117.7

1. Additional industry detail availible in individual industry profile sections.

Indexes of Aggregate Weekly Hours—*Continued*

(Production or nonsupervisory workers on private nonagricultural payrolls—1982=100, seasonally adjusted)

Year and month	Manufacturing—Continued										
	Durable goods—*Continued*					Nondurable goods					
	Industrial machinery and equipment	Electronic and electrical equipment	Transportation equipment [1]	Instruments and related products	Miscellaneous manufacturing	Total	Food and products	Tobacco products	Textile mill products	Apparel and other textile products	Paper and products
1970	101.2	.....	114.1	.....	119.8	112.4	110.2	129.2	141.8	123.9	110.2
1971	89.5	.....	112.6	.....	116.2	110.8	109.3	118.7	141.3	122.9	106.4
1972	97.8	.....	118.4	.....	126.2	114.1	108.7	115.9	148.9	127.8	110.3
1973	111.8	.....	129.1	.....	130.9	116.0	106.3	124.0	150.7	131.7	112.7
1974	116.1	.....	117.9	.....	128.8	112.1	106.0	120.9	138.5	121.3	111.2
1975	101.6	.....	106.8	.....	112.5	102.1	101.8	118.1	122.9	110.2	96.8
1976	102.6	.....	117.9	.....	120.1	108.1	104.4	118.2	133.3	119.3	104.7
1977	109.8	.....	125.6	.....	122.2	110.2	104.6	106.8	132.9	117.9	107.6
1978	119.4	.....	133.6	.....	125.9	112.0	105.1	106.1	131.6	119.5	109.0
1979	126.9	.....	134.1	.....	123.8	112.3	107.0	104.4	129.3	115.6	110.5
1980	122.1	.....	114.6	.....	113.9	108.1	105.1	101.2	122.7	112.2	106.9
1981	120.2	.....	114.2	.....	110.5	107.6	102.8	105.1	117.3	111.0	106.8
1982	100.0	.....	100.0	.....	100.0	100.0	100.0	100.0	100.0	100.0	100.0
1983	90.1	.....	105.7	.....	98.1	102.4	99.1	96.3	107.4	104.5	102.1
1984	103.8	.....	118.9	.....	102.9	105.5	100.3	93.5	107.0	107.2	106.8
1985	101.0	.....	122.7	.....	97.8	103.4	100.6	88.4	100.1	100.7	106.8
1986	94.7	.....	123.3	.....	97.5	104.2	101.7	81.6	103.8	99.7	106.9
1987	93.8	.....	124.3	.....	99.9	106.6	103.7	80.1	109.4	100.1	108.5
1988	98.8	113.1	125.8	89.9	103.5	107.7	105.0	80.1	107.7	99.0	108.9
1989	100.3	111.5	125.3	89.6	103.0	108.2	107.8	70.6	105.6	98.3	109.9
1990	97.5	106.5	119.1	87.6	101.1	106.8	109.7	70.6	98.4	92.9	110.4
1991	91.8	100.7	113.3	84.0	98.1	105.9	110.2	70.2	97.0	91.3	109.3
1992	89.6	99.1	110.9	80.2	99.4	106.6	110.9	68.2	98.6	92.2	110.5
1993	92.7	100.9	111.4	77.0	101.6	107.4	112.6	60.7	98.9	90.4	110.9
1994	99.3	105.7	118.5	75.2	104.2	109.2	114.6	64.1	99.4	89.7	112.3
1995	103.5	107.8	121.6	73.7	103.3	107.6	115.5	62.8	94.9	84.2	110.5
1996	105.0	108.5	123.1	75.4	102.1	104.3	115.9	63.3	89.2	77.2	109.5
1997	109.6	111.1	129.2	76.7	104.4	104.6	116.6	61.4	89.8	73.7	111.0
1998	109.8	109.5	126.4	76.4	103.0	103.3	117.6	59.8	86.4	67.2	108.9
1995:											
January	102.5	108.1	123.6	73.8	104.9	109.1	116.4	65.0	99.8	89.7	113.0
February	102.8	107.4	123.8	73.5	104.5	108.4	115.1	62.1	99.3	88.5	112.0
March	103.1	107.8	124.2	73.5	104.3	107.8	114.7	61.3	98.3	87.6	111.5
April	103.1	107.5	123.0	73.5	104.3	107.5	114.4	63.5	98.0	86.3	111.5
May	103.2	107.3	121.4	73.3	103.0	106.9	114.8	63.7	95.8	85.7	110.7
June	103.0	107.1	121.8	73.8	103.5	106.8	116.6	64.5	94.5	84.4	110.5
July	103.1	107.1	121.8	73.8	101.9	106.2	116.1	64.3	93.6	83.5	110.5
August	104.0	107.7	121.8	74.2	103.2	106.3	116.3	65.7	94.1	83.0	110.3
September	104.0	108.3	121.7	74.0	103.3	106.1	116.6	60.9	92.9	82.4	110.1
October	104.4	109.4	119.2	74.3	102.6	105.6	115.9	62.0	92.0	81.0	109.4
November	105.2	108.5	118.3	74.2	103.1	105.3	115.7	61.0	91.7	80.3	109.2
December	104.7	107.1	119.3	74.0	102.3	104.5	114.7	60.7	90.4	79.5	109.0
1996:											
January	101.9	104.5	117.9	72.0	97.8	100.1	112.3	57.9	79.6	71.9	105.4
February	104.8	108.8	120.3	74.9	102.2	104.8	116.7	62.5	90.0	79.0	109.1
March	104.8	108.5	114.3	75.1	102.4	104.7	116.8	63.5	90.3	78.3	108.8
April	104.8	107.7	123.4	75.1	101.8	104.3	116.3	63.4	88.7	77.8	108.7
May	105.0	108.6	123.8	75.6	102.3	104.5	116.0	63.2	89.7	78.4	108.9
June	105.1	108.9	124.8	76.0	102.3	104.8	115.8	63.4	90.1	78.4	109.2
July	105.0	108.6	124.5	74.9	101.6	104.4	115.2	63.2	89.9	77.8	108.9
August	105.0	109.2	125.3	75.6	101.9	104.6	115.1	61.3	90.3	77.6	109.9
September	105.2	109.3	125.5	76.0	102.4	104.6	115.7	64.3	89.6	77.2	110.3
October	105.1	108.7	124.0	76.1	101.9	104.5	116.2	63.1	89.9	76.8	110.2
November	105.3	108.9	124.2	76.3	102.8	104.6	116.2	65.7	89.9	76.4	110.8
December	106.4	109.3	125.6	76.9	104.2	104.8	116.4	66.9	90.5	76.1	111.2
1997:											
January	106.7	108.3	127.7	75.8	103.8	104.3	116.0	63.1	89.8	75.4	111.0
February	107.6	110.1	127.0	76.1	104.3	104.5	116.5	64.5	89.0	75.1	111.5
March	108.4	111.0	128.0	76.3	103.7	104.8	116.7	63.1	90.3	75.2	111.5
April	109.9	111.2	128.0	76.3	104.4	104.9	116.8	59.9	90.6	74.9	111.2
May	109.4	110.5	127.5	76.3	104.3	104.6	116.3	61.2	89.8	74.2	111.2
June	108.8	110.9	128.4	76.5	104.0	104.1	115.6	60.5	89.6	74.1	110.2
July	109.4	111.4	128.8	76.3	104.6	104.1	116.1	57.9	90.1	73.1	110.3
August	110.0	111.4	131.4	76.9	104.0	104.0	115.7	58.0	89.4	72.6	110.1
September	110.6	111.4	129.0	76.9	104.2	104.2	116.1	60.4	89.5	72.5	110.3
October	110.8	112.1	130.3	76.9	104.9	104.6	116.6	61.8	89.4	72.4	110.8
November	111.8	112.5	130.9	77.6	105.1	104.8	117.1	62.1	89.5	71.9	111.3
December	112.1	113.3	131.4	77.4	105.7	104.8	117.4	62.1	89.9	71.8	111.0
1998:											
January	112.3	113.5	130.8	77.8	105.6	105.0	117.6	61.0	89.6	71.4	111.2
February	112.0	112.9	130.0	77.6	105.3	104.5	117.2	61.7	89.1	70.2	110.5
March	111.8	111.7	129.4	77.2	105.7	104.0	117.1	61.6	88.2	69.4	110.0
April	110.7	110.7	127.4	77.2	105.0	103.8	117.2	62.5	88.0	69.2	109.1
May	110.9	110.7	127.7	77.0	104.2	103.9	117.9	62.0	87.8	68.3	109.6
June	111.3	110.3	125.7	76.8	103.8	103.7	117.8	59.6	87.3	67.7	109.2
July	110.1	109.4	114.5	76.6	103.5	103.4	117.9	61.6	86.0	67.4	109.0
August	110.0	109.1	125.1	76.3	103.2	102.8	116.5	60.2	85.7	66.5	108.1
September	109.1	108.6	127.2	75.7	101.5	102.7	117.7	57.9	84.3	65.8	108.6
October	108.6	108.1	127.8	75.7	100.5	102.4	117.4	59.1	85.2	64.7	108.0
November	107.6	106.9	127.6	75.2	99.8	102.0	118.1	59.1	83.9	63.6	107.5
December	106.3	105.9	127.3	75.0	100.3	102.1	119.3	56.2	83.4	63.4	107.1

1. Additional industry detail availible in individual industry profile sections.

Indexes of Aggregate Weekly Hours—*Continued*

(Production or nonsupervisory workers on private nonagricultural payrolls—1982=100, seasonally adjusted)

Year and month	Nondurable goods manufacturing—*Continued*					Service-producing industries					
	Printing and publishing	Chemicals and products	Petroleum and coal products	Rubber and miscellaneous plastics products	Leather and products	Total	Transportation and public utilities	Wholesale trade	Retail trade	Finance, insurance, real estate	Services
1970	98.9	102.5	96.2	86.3	156.4	76.7	96.9	81.7	83.4	73.0	65.3
1971	95.3	99.8	100.9	87.5	148.7	77.2	95.1	80.4	85.3	74.3	65.6
1972	96.5	100.9	101.5	97.8	150.7	79.6	97.3	82.5	88.2	76.5	68.0
1973	97.4	104.2	99.9	107.9	142.3	82.5	99.9	85.6	90.9	78.9	71.3
1974	95.5	105.7	100.9	105.8	131.8	84.0	100.4	87.6	91.0	79.8	73.9
1975	88.9	97.1	96.3	89.0	121.3	83.9	94.6	86.4	90.6	79.9	76.0
1976	90.3	102.0	102.3	96.1	130.6	86.4	95.5	89.1	93.9	81.5	78.8
1977	94.1	105.0	106.6	109.2	123.9	89.5	97.9	92.5	96.5	85.4	82.0
1978	97.5	107.4	112.2	115.3	125.5	93.6	101.3	97.7	100.0	90.3	86.3
1979	101.0	108.3	114.0	118.2	117.1	96.9	104.9	102.0	101.5	94.4	90.2
1980	100.1	106.0	99.1	106.7	110.7	98.3	104.1	101.9	100.1	97.8	94.3
1981	100.6	106.8	110.0	109.0	113.6	100.8	103.3	103.3	100.6	105.5	98.2
1982	100.0	100.0	100.0	100.0	100.0	100.0	100.0	100.0	100.0	100.0	100.0
1983	103.3	98.3	98.4	107.2	96.8	102.0	97.3	99.9	102.7	101.6	103.6
1984	110.9	99.8	92.5	119.6	89.3	107.1	102.8	105.3	108.2	106.4	108.2
1985	114.9	98.9	88.7	117.6	78.1	111.3	104.6	108.4	111.7	110.9	114.0
1986	119.6	97.3	88.1	119.6	69.5	114.6	104.0	108.5	114.3	116.7	119.2
1987	123.2	99.3	89.4	123.1	70.3	118.5	106.5	109.4	117.9	120.1	124.9
1988	126.7	102.9	88.1	127.3	67.9	122.8	108.2	113.3	121.0	119.2	132.2
1989	126.2	104.5	85.7	129.6	66.4	126.8	111.1	116.1	122.9	119.5	139.3
1990	127.5	104.3	87.2	127.9	62.8	129.1	114.5	115.7	123.0	120.2	144.2
1991	123.3	101.6	86.7	123.2	57.7	128.0	113.4	113.7	119.5	118.3	145.3
1992	122.3	100.0	86.0	127.8	56.6	129.7	113.6	112.8	120.6	118.1	149.3
1993	123.9	100.9	83.1	133.2	55.6	133.7	118.2	112.8	123.4	121.2	155.4
1994	125.9	102.0	81.4	141.9	53.0	139.3	122.4	116.9	128.6	124.0	162.9
1995	125.0	102.5	77.9	143.4	48.3	143.8	123.9	121.1	132.2	122.9	170.5
1996	124.0	101.5	76.3	143.2	43.3	148.0	127.5	122.9	134.6	125.0	177.4
1997	126.0	101.2	76.1	146.4	40.6	153.6	130.5	126.1	137.7	129.6	186.6
1998	124.9	103.4	76.7	147.9	36.0	158.4	132.1	128.8	140.0	136.6	194.3
1995:											
January	125.8	102.3	80.3	146.4	50.9	142.1	123.5	120.1	131.0	123.1	167.3
February	126.0	102.1	81.6	146.4	50.9	142.4	123.7	120.5	130.9	122.6	168.2
March	125.8	101.9	79.9	145.6	50.0	142.7	123.4	120.8	130.8	122.2	169.0
April	125.8	102.3	80.4	144.9	49.4	143.1	123.4	121.0	131.7	122.4	169.3
May	125.4	102.0	78.7	144.0	49.6	142.9	123.0	120.7	131.7	122.0	169.1
June	125.0	102.4	78.1	142.9	48.6	143.7	123.4	121.0	132.1	122.5	170.6
July	125.0	102.7	78.6	140.8	47.0	143.6	123.4	121.3	131.8	122.8	170.4
August	124.6	102.7	76.7	142.0	48.1	144.3	123.7	121.6	132.5	122.7	171.4
September	124.4	102.9	76.0	142.5	47.7	144.7	123.6	121.7	132.7	123.5	172.2
October	124.1	103.1	77.3	142.9	47.0	144.5	124.4	121.4	132.2	123.3	172.1
November	124.9	102.4	74.7	143.4	46.2	145.1	125.1	121.4	132.8	123.1	173.0
December	123.5	102.5	74.2	142.0	45.1	145.3	125.4	121.6	132.4	123.2	173.6
1996:											
January	120.4	101.1	75.6	138.0	41.4	144.4	124.6	120.9	131.5	122.8	172.4
February	124.0	102.6	75.6	141.6	44.5	146.0	126.5	121.7	133.4	123.5	174.3
March	124.5	102.1	75.7	141.6	44.2	147.0	127.2	122.2	134.3	124.0	175.6
April	124.0	101.6	75.4	142.1	43.7	146.5	126.3	121.9	133.4	124.0	175.5
May	124.2	101.7	74.6	142.6	43.7	147.4	126.8	122.5	134.3	124.3	176.7
June	124.2	102.1	78.4	143.4	43.9	148.2	127.7	123.1	134.6	125.3	177.9
July	124.2	101.6	77.1	143.6	43.2	147.8	127.7	122.2	134.4	124.9	177.3
August	124.3	101.3	76.8	144.9	43.5	148.7	128.3	123.2	135.0	125.5	178.6
September	124.2	100.9	76.6	145.2	43.4	149.4	128.3	123.9	135.6	126.8	179.4
October	124.0	100.6	75.4	144.2	42.7	149.5	128.7	124.0	135.8	126.1	179.4
November	124.3	101.0	75.9	144.4	42.4	149.9	128.9	124.3	135.9	126.6	180.1
December	124.5	101.3	76.1	144.9	43.4	150.6	128.9	124.6	136.7	127.2	181.2
1997:											
January	124.2	100.2	78.2	144.3	42.4	150.6	128.6	124.4	136.7	126.7	181.3
February	125.0	100.7	77.4	145.1	42.0	151.5	129.1	125.1	136.7	127.4	183.3
March	125.8	100.6	76.4	145.6	42.2	152.4	131.0	125.6	137.7	127.6	184.1
April	125.7	100.6	75.7	146.8	41.5	152.5	130.4	125.6	137.3	128.4	184.5
May	126.6	101.0	75.9	145.6	41.3	153.1	130.5	126.0	137.3	128.8	185.9
June	126.3	100.4	75.2	145.1	40.6	152.9	130.0	125.8	137.0	129.0	185.9
July	126.1	100.6	75.2	145.8	40.3	153.5	129.6	126.2	137.4	129.5	186.9
August	125.8	101.0	75.9	146.3	39.9	154.1	127.8	126.3	138.1	130.3	188.3
September	126.5	101.5	75.9	146.4	39.6	154.6	131.9	126.4	137.8	130.3	188.5
October	126.8	102.1	75.9	147.3	39.5	154.9	131.4	126.7	138.1	130.9	189.0
November	127.0	102.7	76.4	148.0	39.0	155.8	131.7	127.3	138.9	131.8	190.2
December	126.7	102.6	74.9	148.5	38.7	155.7	131.5	127.3	138.5	131.7	190.4
1998:											
January	126.3	103.6	76.4	148.9	38.8	156.6	131.8	127.9	138.9	133.4	191.6
February	126.5	103.7	74.5	148.4	39.0	156.6	131.8	127.7	139.0	134.3	191.5
March	125.7	103.9	75.7	147.7	37.7	156.8	131.5	127.6	139.1	134.7	192.0
April	125.2	103.6	75.2	148.3	36.9	157.1	131.3	127.9	139.1	135.3	192.4
May	125.6	103.6	76.1	148.2	36.9	158.1	132.2	128.5	140.1	135.8	193.7
June	125.2	103.8	76.6	148.6	36.4	157.9	131.7	128.4	139.6	136.0	193.7
July	125.4	103.4	77.7	147.6	35.5	158.9	132.3	129.0	140.5	136.9	195.0
August	125.4	103.4	76.6	147.7	35.5	159.0	132.6	129.2	140.1	137.2	195.4
September	124.5	103.4	76.3	147.9	34.5	158.8	132.5	129.3	140.2	137.5	194.7
October	124.3	103.3	76.3	148.1	34.5	159.8	132.9	129.3	140.8	138.1	196.6
November	123.5	102.5	77.3	147.5	33.9	160.1	132.9	130.0	140.6	138.6	197.2
December	123.0	102.2	79.4	148.1	33.4	160.5	133.0	130.2	140.9	138.9	197.8

Average Hourly Earnings

(Average earnings per hour of production or nonsupervisory workers on private nonagricultural payrolls—Dollars, seasonally adjusted)

| Year and month | Total private | | Goods-producing industries | | | | | Service-producing industries | | | | | |
| | Current dollars | 1982 dollars | Total | Mining[1] | Construction[1] | Manufacturing | | Total | Transportation and public utilities[1] | Wholesale trade | Retail trade[1] | Finance, insurance, and real estate[1] | Services[1] |
						Total	Excluding overtime						
1970	3.23	8.03	3.67	3.85	5.24	3.35	3.23	2.95	3.85	3.43	2.44	3.07	2.81
1971	3.45	8.21	3.94	4.06	5.69	3.57	3.45	3.15	4.21	3.64	2.60	3.22	3.04
1972	3.70	8.53	4.22	4.44	6.06	3.82	3.66	3.38	4.65	3.85	2.75	3.36	3.27
1973	3.94	8.55	4.50	4.75	6.41	4.09	3.91	3.59	5.02	4.07	2.91	3.53	3.47
1974	4.24	8.28	4.84	5.23	6.81	4.42	4.25	3.87	5.41	4.38	3.14	3.77	3.75
1975	4.53	8.12	5.27	5.95	7.31	4.83	4.67	4.14	5.88	4.72	3.36	4.06	4.02
1976	4.86	8.24	5.65	6.46	7.71	5.22	5.02	4.43	6.45	5.02	3.57	4.27	4.31
1977	5.25	8.36	6.10	6.94	8.10	5.68	5.44	4.77	6.99	5.39	3.85	4.54	4.65
1978	5.69	8.40	6.64	7.67	8.66	6.17	5.91	5.17	7.57	5.88	4.20	4.89	4.99
1979	6.16	8.17	7.21	8.49	9.27	6.70	6.43	5.58	8.16	6.39	4.53	5.27	5.36
1980	6.66	7.78	7.83	9.17	9.94	7.27	7.02	6.06	8.87	6.95	4.88	5.79	5.85
1981	7.25	7.69	8.57	10.04	10.82	7.99	7.72	6.59	9.70	7.55	5.25	6.31	6.41
1982	7.68	7.68	9.16	10.77	11.63	8.49	8.25	7.02	10.32	8.08	5.48	6.78	6.92
1983	8.02	7.79	9.48	11.28	11.94	8.83	8.52	7.37	10.79	8.54	5.74	7.29	7.31
1984	8.32	7.80	9.83	11.63	12.13	9.19	8.82	7.62	11.12	8.88	5.85	7.63	7.59
1985	8.57	7.77	10.19	11.98	12.32	9.54	9.16	7.86	11.40	9.15	5.94	7.94	7.90
1986	8.76	7.81	10.39	12.46	12.48	9.73	9.34	8.08	11.70	9.34	6.03	8.36	8.18
1987	8.98	7.73	10.58	12.54	12.71	9.91	9.48	8.32	12.03	9.59	6.12	8.73	8.49
1988	9.28	7.69	10.88	12.80	13.08	10.19	9.73	8.64	12.24	9.98	6.31	9.06	8.88
1989	9.66	7.64	11.22	13.26	13.54	10.48	10.02	9.04	12.57	10.39	6.53	9.53	9.38
1990	10.01	7.52	11.56	13.68	13.77	10.83	10.37	9.42	12.92	10.79	6.75	9.97	9.83
1991	10.32	7.45	11.86	14.19	14.00	11.18	10.71	9.77	13.20	11.15	6.94	10.39	10.23
1992	10.57	7.41	12.09	14.54	14.15	11.46	10.95	10.04	13.43	11.39	7.12	10.82	10.54
1993	10.83	7.39	12.37	14.60	14.38	11.74	11.18	10.30	13.55	11.74	7.29	11.35	10.78
1994	11.12	7.40	12.71	14.88	14.73	12.07	11.43	10.56	13.78	12.06	7.49	11.83	11.04
1995	11.43	7.39	13.04	15.30	15.09	12.37	11.74	10.88	14.13	12.43	7.69	12.32	11.39
1996	11.82	7.43	13.47	15.62	15.47	12.77	12.12	11.26	14.45	12.87	7.99	12.80	11.79
1997	12.28	7.55	13.92	16.15	16.04	13.17	12.45	11.73	14.92	13.45	8.33	13.34	12.28
1998	12.78	7.75	14.34	16.90	16.59	13.49	12.79	12.27	15.31	14.06	8.73	14.06	12.85
1995:													
January	11.27	7.38	12.85	15.05	14.78	12.21	11.56	10.71	13.96	12.27	7.58	12.08	11.22
February	11.30	7.38	12.91	15.09	14.96	12.26	11.61	10.74	13.95	12.29	7.61	12.13	11.25
March	11.33	7.38	12.93	15.16	14.98	12.26	11.63	10.77	14.00	12.32	7.61	12.18	11.27
April	11.35	7.37	12.96	15.22	15.01	12.29	11.68	10.79	14.03	12.35	7.63	12.20	11.31
May	11.37	7.37	12.97	15.21	15.05	12.30	11.69	10.82	14.04	12.37	7.65	12.25	11.35
June	11.41	7.38	13.03	15.29	15.11	12.34	11.73	10.85	14.11	12.42	7.68	12.29	11.36
July	11.45	7.40	13.09	15.44	15.12	12.41	11.80	10.88	14.16	12.43	7.71	12.33	11.39
August	11.47	7.40	13.10	15.41	15.13	12.42	11.79	10.91	14.17	12.47	7.73	12.39	11.42
September	11.50	7.41	13.11	15.41	15.16	12.43	11.82	10.95	14.24	12.52	7.76	12.44	11.46
October	11.53	7.41	13.16	15.44	15.18	12.47	11.84	10.97	14.32	12.53	7.75	12.45	11.48
November	11.56	7.42	13.18	15.44	15.24	12.49	11.87	11.00	14.32	12.55	7.77	12.49	11.52
December	11.58	7.42	13.17	15.47	15.10	12.52	11.90	11.05	14.30	12.61	7.80	12.55	11.57
1996:													
January	11.63	7.42	13.31	15.45	15.35	12.62	12.01	11.07	14.26	12.62	7.84	12.59	11.60
February	11.64	7.40	13.26	15.46	15.25	12.58	11.95	11.09	14.32	12.66	7.85	12.63	11.62
March	11.66	7.39	13.23	15.46	15.27	12.53	11.91	11.14	14.35	12.75	7.88	12.70	11.66
April	11.72	7.40	13.38	15.48	15.31	12.72	12.07	11.16	14.38	12.74	7.90	12.73	11.69
May	11.75	7.40	13.40	15.55	15.37	12.73	12.07	11.19	14.42	12.78	7.93	12.75	11.71
June	11.81	7.43	13.46	15.61	15.43	12.78	12.11	11.25	14.49	12.88	8.00	12.80	11.76
July	11.83	7.43	13.50	15.66	15.48	12.81	12.16	11.26	14.44	12.87	7.99	12.82	11.80
August	11.87	7.45	13.54	15.70	15.53	12.84	12.18	11.30	14.48	12.91	8.02	12.84	11.84
September	11.91	7.44	13.57	15.70	15.58	12.87	12.20	11.34	14.55	12.99	8.03	12.88	11.89
October	11.93	7.44	13.58	15.66	15.59	12.87	12.21	11.38	14.48	12.99	8.09	12.91	11.94
November	11.99	7.45	13.63	15.77	15.62	12.92	12.25	11.43	14.57	13.07	8.12	12.99	11.99
December	12.02	7.46	13.67	15.89	15.62	12.98	12.29	11.47	14.61	13.13	8.16	12.97	12.03
1997:													
January	12.06	7.47	13.74	16.05	15.82	13.01	12.32	11.49	14.68	13.14	8.17	13.00	12.06
February	12.09	7.47	13.76	15.98	15.87	13.02	12.32	11.53	14.66	13.22	8.20	13.03	12.10
March	12.14	7.49	13.79	15.99	15.83	13.06	12.35	11.58	14.76	13.27	8.24	13.09	12.14
April	12.16	7.50	13.81	16.02	15.89	13.07	12.35	11.60	14.79	13.31	8.25	13.10	12.16
May	12.21	7.53	13.85	16.12	15.94	13.10	12.38	11.65	14.83	13.36	8.28	13.22	12.20
June	12.24	7.54	13.88	16.16	15.99	13.12	12.42	11.69	14.89	13.39	8.30	13.29	12.24
July	12.27	7.55	13.89	16.16	16.00	13.14	12.43	11.73	14.97	13.45	8.33	13.34	12.27
August	12.33	7.57	13.95	16.13	16.07	13.20	12.49	11.79	15.01	13.55	8.36	13.50	12.33
September	12.37	7.58	13.98	16.19	16.12	13.21	12.50	11.83	15.00	13.56	8.40	13.53	12.37
October	12.43	7.60	14.07	16.27	16.19	13.31	12.57	11.88	15.05	13.63	8.45	13.59	12.42
November	12.47	7.62	14.10	16.38	16.23	13.34	12.62	11.94	15.09	13.73	8.49	13.63	12.48
December	12.51	7.64	14.15	16.38	16.32	13.38	12.64	11.96	15.12	13.73	8.50	13.63	12.51
1998:													
January	12.54	7.66	14.17	16.45	16.34	13.38	12.65	11.99	15.17	13.76	8.54	13.69	12.53
February	12.60	7.69	14.22	16.75	16.39	13.41	12.69	12.06	15.21	13.84	8.57	13.81	12.61
March	12.64	7.72	14.25	16.84	16.43	13.45	12.72	12.10	15.23	13.89	8.62	13.85	12.66
April	12.69	7.73	14.27	16.72	16.48	13.45	12.75	12.17	15.27	13.91	8.68	13.95	12.74
May	12.73	7.74	14.29	16.72	16.50	13.48	12.77	12.22	15.27	14.02	8.70	14.00	12.79
June	12.76	7.75	14.31	16.71	16.54	13.48	12.77	12.26	15.27	14.05	8.71	14.05	12.85
July	12.80	7.76	14.33	16.87	16.63	13.46	12.75	12.30	15.31	14.09	8.76	14.08	12.89
August	12.85	7.78	14.39	17.00	16.67	13.53	12.82	12.35	15.33	14.17	8.80	14.14	12.94
September	12.88	7.80	14.41	17.06	16.60	13.58	12.86	12.38	15.37	14.18	8.84	14.16	12.98
October	12.91	7.80	14.44	17.15	16.72	13.57	12.87	12.41	15.38	14.23	8.83	14.23	13.02
November	12.94	7.80	14.47	17.27	16.76	13.58	12.88	12.45	15.41	14.27	8.85	14.32	13.05
December	12.98	7.81	14.51	17.18	16.80	13.60	12.90	12.49	15.47	14.30	8.89	14.40	13.08

1. Additional industry detail availible in individual industry profile sections.

Average Hourly Earnings—Continued

(Average earnings per hour of production or nonsupervisory workers on private nonagricultural payrolls—Dollars, not seasonally adjusted)

Year and month	Total private	Goods producing industries								
		Total	Mining	Construction	Manufacturing					
					Total	Durable goods				
						Total	Lumber and wood products	Furniture and fixtures	Stone, clay, and glass products	Primary metal industries [1]
1970	3.23	3.67	3.85	5.24	3.35	3.55	2.97	2.77	3.40	3.93
1971	3.45	3.94	4.06	5.69	3.57	3.79	3.18	2.90	3.67	4.23
1972	3.70	4.22	4.44	6.06	3.82	4.07	3.34	3.08	3.94	4.66
1973	3.94	4.50	4.75	6.41	4.09	4.35	3.62	3.29	4.22	5.04
1974	4.24	4.84	5.23	6.81	4.42	4.70	3.90	3.53	4.54	5.60
1975	4.53	5.27	5.95	7.31	4.83	5.15	4.28	3.78	4.92	6.18
1976	4.86	5.65	6.46	7.71	5.22	5.57	4.74	3.99	5.33	6.77
1977	5.25	6.10	6.94	8.10	5.68	6.06	5.11	4.34	5.81	7.40
1978	5.69	6.64	7.67	8.66	6.17	6.58	5.62	4.68	6.32	8.20
1979	6.16	7.21	8.49	9.27	6.70	7.12	6.08	5.06	6.85	8.98
1980	6.66	7.83	9.17	9.94	7.27	7.75	6.57	5.49	7.50	9.77
1981	7.25	8.57	10.04	10.82	7.99	8.53	7.02	5.91	8.27	10.81
1982	7.68	9.16	10.77	11.63	8.49	9.03	7.46	6.31	8.87	11.33
1983	8.02	9.48	11.28	11.94	8.83	9.38	7.82	6.62	9.27	11.35
1984	8.32	9.83	11.63	12.13	9.19	9.73	8.05	6.84	9.57	11.47
1985	8.57	10.19	11.98	12.32	9.54	10.09	8.25	7.17	9.84	11.67
1986	8.76	10.39	12.46	12.48	9.73	10.28	8.37	7.46	10.04	11.86
1987	8.98	10.58	12.54	12.71	9.91	10.43	8.43	7.67	10.25	11.94
1988	9.28	10.88	12.80	13.08	10.19	10.71	8.59	7.95	10.56	12.16
1989	9.66	11.22	13.26	13.54	10.48	11.01	8.84	8.25	10.82	12.43
1990	10.01	11.56	13.68	13.77	10.83	11.35	9.08	8.52	11.12	12.92
1991	10.32	11.86	14.19	14.00	11.18	11.75	9.24	8.76	11.36	13.33
1992	10.57	12.09	14.54	14.15	11.46	12.02	9.44	9.01	11.60	13.66
1993	10.83	12.37	14.60	14.38	11.74	12.33	9.61	9.27	11.85	13.99
1994	11.12	12.71	14.88	14.73	12.07	12.68	9.84	9.55	12.13	14.34
1995	11.43	13.04	15.30	15.09	12.37	12.94	10.12	9.82	12.41	14.62
1996	11.82	13.47	15.62	15.47	12.77	13.33	10.44	10.15	12.82	14.97
1997	12.28	13.92	16.15	16.04	13.17	13.73	10.76	10.55	13.18	15.22
1998	12.78	14.34	16.90	16.59	13.49	13.98	11.10	10.90	13.60	15.49
1995:										
January	11.35	12.81	15.23	14.71	12.25	12.84	9.95	9.68	12.20	14.57
February	11.35	12.83	15.24	14.87	12.26	12.86	9.94	9.67	12.24	14.46
March	11.34	12.87	15.22	14.88	12.27	12.86	9.94	9.68	12.26	14.45
April	11.38	12.94	15.30	14.93	12.30	12.84	9.97	9.76	12.44	14.76
May	11.35	12.97	15.19	15.01	12.30	12.87	10.01	9.71	12.32	14.53
June	11.33	13.02	15.23	15.04	12.32	12.89	10.11	9.78	12.37	14.61
July	11.39	13.14	15.34	15.15	12.40	12.94	10.21	9.83	12.46	14.69
August	11.36	13.10	15.29	15.20	12.35	12.93	10.20	9.89	12.47	14.63
September	11.54	13.22	15.35	15.35	12.47	13.06	10.28	9.95	12.55	14.70
October	11.59	13.20	15.33	15.35	12.43	12.98	10.27	9.92	12.54	14.64
November	11.58	13.19	15.35	15.26	12.49	13.03	10.22	9.95	12.57	14.73
December	11.60	13.22	15.54	15.15	12.60	13.13	10.29	10.00	12.54	14.69
1996:										
January	11.70	13.27	15.63	15.26	12.66	13.17	10.28	10.01	12.60	14.84
February	11.68	13.19	15.61	15.16	12.57	13.12	10.23	9.95	12.56	14.70
March	11.68	13.17	15.50	15.16	12.54	13.05	10.29	10.00	12.60	14.73
April	11.74	13.36	15.55	15.22	12.73	13.28	10.33	10.06	12.77	14.99
May	11.72	13.38	15.45	15.30	12.70	13.27	10.35	10.08	12.74	14.82
June	11.75	13.45	15.59	15.35	12.75	13.32	10.45	10.11	12.82	14.91
July	11.73	13.54	15.55	15.52	12.79	13.35	10.47	10.13	12.94	15.08
August	11.76	13.55	15.52	15.58	12.79	13.38	10.54	10.19	12.92	15.02
September	11.96	13.66	15.74	15.77	12.89	13.51	10.57	10.27	12.99	15.18
October	11.96	13.62	15.56	15.77	12.83	13.41	10.56	10.27	12.91	15.09
November	12.01	13.63	15.69	15.64	12.92	13.48	10.57	10.28	12.96	15.18
December	12.07	13.73	15.97	15.68	13.07	13.64	10.62	10.42	12.93	15.15
1997:										
January	12.12	13.68	16.20	15.76	13.03	13.61	10.58	10.38	12.99	15.12
February	12.15	13.67	16.09	15.72	13.01	13.57	10.61	10.34	13.04	15.09
March	12.18	13.73	16.01	15.71	13.07	13.63	10.61	10.43	13.02	15.16
April	12.18	13.78	16.08	15.78	13.08	13.63	10.65	10.42	13.06	15.15
May	12.18	13.83	16.00	15.86	13.08	13.63	10.71	10.47	13.12	15.09
June	12.18	13.86	16.13	15.91	13.09	13.64	10.77	10.51	13.13	15.16
July	12.17	13.94	16.05	16.04	13.10	13.61	10.82	10.53	13.20	15.28
August	12.23	13.97	15.96	16.13	13.14	13.69	10.80	10.60	13.21	15.16
September	12.41	14.08	16.24	16.31	13.23	13.79	10.86	10.70	13.27	15.27
October	12.45	14.12	16.19	16.34	13.28	13.88	10.87	10.67	13.32	15.33
November	12.54	14.13	16.38	16.30	13.36	13.95	10.90	10.70	13.36	15.38
December	12.53	14.21	16.49	16.39	13.47	14.06	10.92	10.79	13.39	15.43
1998:										
January	12.61	14.11	16.60	16.28	13.40	13.95	10.89	10.75	13.38	15.48
February	12.66	14.12	16.85	16.23	13.41	13.95	10.90	10.78	13.45	15.46
March	12.68	14.18	16.85	16.31	13.47	14.01	10.94	10.81	13.46	15.53
April	12.70	14.24	16.79	16.36	13.46	13.95	10.98	10.86	13.63	15.66
May	12.71	14.29	16.67	16.44	13.48	13.97	11.05	10.80	13.58	15.55
June	12.68	14.28	16.68	16.47	13.44	13.93	11.09	10.82	13.58	15.54
July	12.68	14.35	16.76	16.66	13.38	13.77	11.17	10.91	13.59	15.56
August	12.76	14.41	16.88	16.77	13.45	13.92	11.18	10.96	13.63	15.45
September	12.90	14.49	17.11	16.79	13.60	14.07	11.17	10.99	13.82	15.61
October	12.93	14.51	17.07	16.89	13.55	14.02	11.22	10.99	13.68	15.32
November	13.00	14.50	17.29	16.82	13.60	14.07	11.24	10.99	13.65	15.35
December	13.00	14.56	17.29	16.87	13.69	14.16	11.33	11.10	13.70	15.36

1. Additional industry detail availible in individual industry profile sections.

Average Hourly Earnings—*Continued*

(Average earnings per hour of production or nonsupervisory workers on private nonagricultural payrolls—Dollars, not seasonally adjusted)

Year and month	Manufacturing—*Continued*										
	Durable goods—*Continued*						Nondurable goods				
	Fabricated metal products	Industrial machinery and equipment[1]	Electronic and electric equipment	Transportation equipment[1]	Instrument and products	Miscellaneous manufacturing	Total	Food and products	Tobacco products	Textile mill products	Apparel and other textile products
1970	3.53	3.77	.....	4.06	.....	2.83	3.08	3.16	2.91	2.45	2.39
1971	3.77	4.02	.....	4.45	.....	2.97	3.27	3.38	3.16	2.57	2.49
1972	4.05	4.32	.....	4.81	.....	3.11	3.48	3.60	3.47	2.75	2.60
1973	4.29	4.60	.....	5.15	.....	3.29	3.70	3.85	3.76	2.95	2.76
1974	4.61	4.94	.....	5.54	.....	3.53	4.01	4.19	4.12	3.20	2.97
1975	5.05	5.37	.....	6.07	.....	3.81	4.37	4.61	4.55	3.42	3.17
1976	5.50	5.79	.....	6.62	.....	4.04	4.71	4.98	4.98	3.69	3.40
1977	5.91	6.26	.....	7.29	.....	4.36	5.11	5.37	5.54	3.99	3.62
1978	6.35	6.78	.....	7.91	.....	4.69	5.54	5.80	6.13	4.30	3.94
1979	6.85	7.32	.....	8.53	.....	5.03	6.01	6.27	6.67	4.66	4.23
1980	7.45	8.00	.....	9.35	.....	5.46	6.56	6.85	7.74	5.07	4.56
1981	8.20	8.81	.....	10.39	.....	5.97	7.19	7.44	8.88	5.52	4.97
1982	8.77	9.26	.....	11.11	.....	6.42	7.75	7.92	9.79	5.83	5.20
1983	9.12	9.56	.....	11.67	.....	6.81	8.09	8.19	10.38	6.18	5.38
1984	9.40	9.97	.....	12.20	.....	7.05	8.39	8.39	11.22	6.46	5.55
1985	9.71	10.30	.....	12.71	.....	7.30	8.72	8.57	11.96	6.70	5.73
1986	9.89	10.58	.....	12.81	.....	7.55	8.95	8.75	12.88	6.93	5.84
1987	10.01	10.73	.....	12.94	.....	7.76	9.19	8.93	14.07	7.17	5.94
1988	10.29	11.08	9.79	13.29	10.60	8.00	9.45	9.12	14.67	7.38	6.12
1989	10.57	11.40	10.05	13.67	10.83	8.29	9.75	9.38	15.31	7.67	6.35
1990	10.83	11.77	10.30	14.08	11.29	8.61	10.12	9.62	16.23	8.02	6.57
1991	11.19	12.15	10.70	14.75	11.64	8.85	10.44	9.90	16.77	8.30	6.77
1992	11.42	12.41	11.00	15.20	11.89	9.15	10.73	10.20	16.92	8.60	6.95
1993	11.69	12.73	11.24	15.80	12.23	9.39	10.98	10.45	16.89	8.88	7.09
1994	11.93	13.00	11.50	16.51	12.47	9.67	11.24	10.66	19.07	9.13	7.34
1995	12.13	13.24	11.69	16.74	12.71	10.05	11.58	10.93	19.41	9.41	7.64
1996	12.50	13.59	12.18	17.19	13.13	10.38	11.97	11.20	19.35	9.69	7.96
1997	12.78	14.07	12.70	17.55	13.52	10.60	12.34	11.48	19.24	10.03	8.25
1998	13.06	14.47	13.09	17.53	13.81	10.89	12.76	11.80	18.55	10.39	8.52
1995:											
January	12.04	13.16	11.58	16.68	12.53	10.01	11.43	10.85	18.60	9.34	7.55
February	12.03	13.17	11.53	16.78	12.62	9.98	11.41	10.82	19.53	9.31	7.49
March	12.05	13.17	11.54	16.75	12.62	9.94	11.44	10.87	20.30	9.29	7.53
April	12.03	13.07	11.52	16.56	12.67	9.98	11.56	10.92	19.98	9.35	7.62
May	12.08	13.17	11.56	16.65	12.65	10.02	11.50	10.90	20.97	9.34	7.57
June	12.05	13.17	11.63	16.71	12.68	9.98	11.53	10.92	21.85	9.37	7.62
July	12.11	13.23	11.74	16.72	12.76	10.06	11.65	10.92	21.71	9.39	7.64
August	12.11	13.25	11.76	16.66	12.70	9.98	11.56	10.89	18.49	9.45	7.68
September	12.22	13.34	11.81	16.95	12.81	10.11	11.65	10.97	17.57	9.50	7.72
October	12.19	13.33	11.79	16.74	12.76	10.13	11.67	10.92	18.09	9.49	7.73
November	12.26	13.39	11.83	16.79	12.83	10.15	11.73	11.05	19.48	9.53	7.77
December	12.42	13.47	11.93	16.88	12.89	10.27	11.84	11.17	17.71	9.57	7.83
1996:											
January	12.38	13.44	11.95	16.88	13.00	10.30	11.91	11.08	18.38	9.56	7.87
February	12.32	13.40	11.88	16.95	12.94	10.25	11.79	11.03	18.13	9.55	7.82
March	12.32	13.36	11.91	16.64	12.96	10.24	11.83	11.10	19.34	9.55	7.86
April	12.46	13.44	12.01	17.22	13.03	10.33	11.93	11.19	20.40	9.65	7.95
May	12.45	13.45	12.09	17.19	13.03	10.34	11.88	11.18	21.06	9.62	7.94
June	12.51	13.52	12.19	17.22	13.08	10.33	11.92	11.22	21.40	9.68	7.99
July	12.50	13.55	12.25	17.28	13.17	10.37	12.00	11.25	20.98	9.69	7.95
August	12.52	13.64	12.28	17.27	13.15	10.37	11.95	11.16	20.24	9.72	7.94
September	12.65	13.77	12.35	17.43	13.29	10.47	12.01	11.19	18.39	9.78	7.99
October	12.53	13.71	12.33	17.23	13.24	10.47	12.00	11.16	17.75	9.73	8.02
November	12.59	13.81	12.35	17.32	13.30	10.52	12.11	11.38	18.65	9.78	8.01
December	12.76	13.98	12.54	17.55	13.36	10.59	12.23	11.45	18.68	9.93	8.14
1997:											
January	12.72	13.92	12.46	17.43	13.35	10.58	12.20	11.41	18.58	9.94	8.12
February	12.71	13.90	12.41	17.36	13.35	10.55	12.19	11.32	18.59	9.90	8.18
March	12.74	13.95	12.49	17.48	13.42	10.55	12.25	11.40	19.46	9.93	8.23
April	12.75	13.96	12.55	17.44	13.43	10.52	12.26	11.45	20.34	9.95	8.21
May	12.74	13.94	12.55	17.43	13.48	10.51	12.26	11.47	20.75	9.95	8.22
June	12.72	13.97	12.59	17.41	13.52	10.50	12.27	11.44	21.12	9.98	8.25
July	12.65	14.03	12.68	17.19	13.51	10.51	12.37	11.52	20.93	10.02	8.19
August	12.75	14.04	12.74	17.42	13.50	10.58	12.34	11.51	19.79	10.02	8.23
September	12.80	14.20	12.84	17.55	13.65	10.66	12.41	11.51	18.26	10.10	8.33
October	12.85	14.24	12.90	17.86	13.62	10.65	12.40	11.45	18.00	10.11	8.33
November	12.92	14.31	12.98	17.91	13.69	10.73	12.49	11.59	17.80	10.16	8.33
December	13.02	14.42	13.11	18.05	13.71	10.82	12.58	11.71	18.63	10.25	8.42
1998:											
January	12.98	14.35	12.98	17.72	13.67	10.81	12.57	11.66	18.36	10.26	8.42
February	12.97	14.38	12.95	17.74	13.71	10.80	12.58	11.63	18.12	10.26	8.38
March	12.99	14.38	13.04	17.88	13.76	10.80	12.64	11.69	18.42	10.29	8.43
April	12.88	14.34	13.06	17.67	13.78	10.77	12.72	11.74	18.84	10.39	8.48
May	13.03	14.38	13.02	17.61	13.78	10.80	12.72	11.78	20.24	10.37	8.47
June	13.01	14.42	13.06	17.41	13.75	10.83	12.70	11.76	20.78	10.36	8.50
July	12.88	14.43	13.13	16.86	13.78	10.85	12.81	11.80	20.59	10.36	8.48
August	13.04	14.46	13.10	17.29	13.79	10.85	12.75	11.76	18.96	10.37	8.54
September	13.16	14.55	13.23	17.49	13.88	10.98	12.93	11.95	17.92	10.48	8.63
October	13.17	14.57	13.13	17.46	13.86	11.02	12.84	11.82	16.95	10.45	8.65
November	13.21	14.64	13.17	17.52	13.91	11.03	12.90	11.95	17.31	10.51	8.64
December	13.34	14.73	13.26	17.56	14.00	11.12	12.99	12.02	17.05	10.56	8.71

1. Additional industry detail availible in individual industry profile sections.

Average Hourly Earnings—*Continued*

(Average earnings per hour of production or nonsupervisory workers on private nonagricultural payrolls—Dollars, not seasonally adjusted)

Year and month	Manfacturing—*Continued* Nondurable—*Continued*						Service-producing industries					
	Paper and products	Printing and publishing	Chemicals and products	Petroleum and coal products	Rubber and miscellaneous plastics products	Leather and products	Total	Transportation and public utilities [1]	Wholesale trade	Retail trade [1]	Finance, insurance, and real estate [1]	Services [1]
1970	3.44	3.92	3.69	4.28	3.21	2.49	2.95	3.85	3.43	2.44	3.07	2.81
1971	3.67	4.20	3.97	4.57	3.41	2.59	3.15	4.21	3.64	2.60	3.22	3.04
1972	3.95	4.51	4.26	4.96	3.63	2.68	3.38	4.65	3.85	2.75	3.36	3.27
1973	4.20	4.75	4.51	5.28	3.84	2.79	3.59	5.02	4.07	2.91	3.53	3.47
1974	4.53	5.03	4.88	5.68	4.09	2.99	3.87	5.41	4.38	3.14	3.77	3.75
1975	5.01	5.38	5.39	6.48	4.42	3.21	4.14	5.88	4.72	3.36	4.06	4.02
1976	5.47	5.71	5.91	7.21	4.71	3.40	4.43	6.45	5.02	3.57	4.27	4.31
1977	5.96	6.12	6.43	7.83	5.21	3.61	4.77	6.99	5.39	3.85	4.54	4.65
1978	6.52	6.51	7.02	8.63	5.57	3.89	5.17	7.57	5.88	4.20	4.89	4.99
1979	7.13	6.94	7.60	9.36	6.02	4.22	5.58	8.16	6.39	4.53	5.27	5.36
1980	7.84	7.53	8.30	10.10	6.58	4.58	6.06	8.87	6.95	4.88	5.79	5.85
1981	8.60	8.19	9.12	11.38	7.22	4.99	6.59	9.70	7.55	5.25	6.31	6.41
1982	9.32	8.74	9.96	12.46	7.70	5.33	7.02	10.32	8.08	5.48	6.78	6.92
1983	9.93	9.11	10.58	13.28	8.06	5.54	7.37	10.79	8.54	5.74	7.29	7.31
1984	10.41	9.41	11.07	13.44	8.35	5.71	7.62	11.12	8.88	5.85	7.63	7.59
1985	10.83	9.71	11.56	14.06	8.60	5.83	7.86	11.40	9.15	5.94	7.94	7.90
1986	11.18	9.99	11.98	14.19	8.79	5.92	8.08	11.70	9.34	6.03	8.36	8.18
1987	11.43	10.28	12.37	14.58	8.98	6.08	8.32	12.03	9.59	6.12	8.73	8.49
1988	11.69	10.53	12.71	14.97	9.19	6.28	8.64	12.24	9.98	6.31	9.06	8.88
1989	11.96	10.88	13.09	15.41	9.46	6.59	9.04	12.57	10.39	6.53	9.53	9.38
1990	12.31	11.24	13.54	16.24	9.76	6.91	9.42	12.92	10.79	6.75	9.97	9.83
1991	12.72	11.48	14.04	17.04	10.07	7.18	9.77	13.20	11.15	6.94	10.39	10.23
1992	13.07	11.74	14.51	17.90	10.36	7.42	10.04	13.43	11.39	7.12	10.82	10.54
1993	13.42	11.93	14.82	18.53	10.57	7.63	10.30	13.55	11.74	7.29	11.35	10.78
1994	13.77	12.14	15.13	19.07	10.70	7.97	10.56	13.78	12.06	7.49	11.83	11.04
1995	14.23	12.33	15.62	19.36	10.91	8.17	10.88	14.13	12.43	7.69	12.32	11.39
1996	14.67	12.65	16.17	19.32	11.24	8.57	11.26	14.45	12.87	7.99	12.80	11.79
1997	15.05	13.06	16.57	20.20	11.57	8.97	11.73	14.92	13.45	8.33	13.34	12.28
1998	15.51	13.45	17.12	20.92	11.87	9.32	12.27	15.31	14.06	8.73	14.06	12.85
1995:												
January	14.00	12.25	15.37	19.18	10.81	8.10	10.84	14.01	12.33	7.63	12.17	11.36
February	14.01	12.25	15.39	19.55	10.75	8.11	10.84	13.97	12.31	7.63	12.20	11.35
March	14.02	12.27	15.39	19.37	10.79	8.10	10.82	13.98	12.27	7.63	12.21	11.32
April	14.26	12.22	15.69	19.55	10.76	8.28	10.86	14.04	12.47	7.65	12.32	11.38
May	14.15	12.23	15.49	19.17	10.85	8.15	10.79	13.96	12.35	7.64	12.24	11.31
June	14.13	12.25	15.49	19.16	10.90	8.10	10.74	14.02	12.34	7.65	12.19	11.22
July	14.41	12.33	15.68	19.25	11.01	8.01	10.80	14.16	12.46	7.66	12.32	11.26
August	14.20	12.36	15.56	19.14	10.93	8.14	10.76	14.14	12.41	7.65	12.27	11.22
September	14.33	12.50	15.71	19.41	10.99	8.24	10.95	14.25	12.52	7.77	12.39	11.45
October	14.31	12.44	15.79	19.68	11.01	8.23	11.03	14.35	12.56	7.77	12.52	11.54
November	14.38	12.41	15.88	19.46	11.01	8.23	11.02	14.34	12.55	7.78	12.48	11.57
December	14.51	12.50	16.03	19.44	11.15	8.33	11.06	14.32	12.63	7.80	12.56	11.66
1996:												
January	14.58	12.49	16.08	19.41	11.13	8.51	11.18	14.32	12.66	7.89	12.61	11.73
February	14.43	12.49	15.96	19.54	11.14	8.41	11.18	14.34	12.68	7.87	12.69	11.72
March	14.44	12.53	16.00	19.21	11.15	8.46	11.18	14.33	12.69	7.90	12.73	11.72
April	14.61	12.53	16.15	19.32	11.20	8.40	11.20	14.40	12.78	7.92	12.75	11.71
May	14.58	12.54	16.04	18.98	11.20	8.43	11.16	14.35	12.75	7.92	12.74	11.67
June	14.63	12.54	16.11	18.88	11.16	8.48	11.18	14.41	12.88	7.98	12.76	11.66
July	14.78	12.63	16.16	19.01	11.25	8.44	11.13	14.45	12.83	7.93	12.69	11.61
August	14.69	12.70	16.22	18.98	11.23	8.63	11.15	14.50	12.85	7.95	12.72	11.63
September	14.73	12.82	16.26	19.34	11.30	8.71	11.37	14.59	13.04	8.06	12.91	11.90
October	14.73	12.81	16.29	19.34	11.28	8.73	11.38	14.51	12.95	8.11	12.88	11.94
November	14.85	12.82	16.38	19.61	11.33	8.74	11.45	14.59	13.07	8.13	12.99	12.04
December	14.93	12.90	16.45	20.25	11.51	8.85	11.51	14.63	13.21	8.15	13.04	12.16
1997:												
January	14.82	12.86	16.37	20.11	11.48	8.86	11.61	14.75	13.19	8.24	13.02	12.19
February	14.76	12.89	16.49	20.39	11.45	8.94	11.65	14.69	13.27	8.24	13.17	12.24
March	14.92	13.01	16.42	20.48	11.50	8.89	11.67	14.74	13.29	8.26	13.22	12.24
April	14.98	12.98	16.42	19.94	11.53	8.89	11.64	14.80	13.35	8.27	13.12	12.19
May	14.97	12.93	16.48	19.96	11.50	8.92	11.62	14.76	13.34	8.27	13.21	12.16
June	14.97	12.90	16.53	19.92	11.52	8.94	11.62	14.81	13.38	8.27	13.26	12.14
July	15.16	13.01	16.58	20.02	11.57	8.77	11.58	14.98	13.39	8.26	13.21	12.06
August	15.11	13.07	16.57	19.99	11.57	8.89	11.64	15.03	13.50	8.29	13.38	12.12
September	15.17	13.22	16.62	20.27	11.64	9.11	11.83	15.04	13.55	8.44	13.48	12.36
October	15.18	13.20	16.64	20.32	11.64	9.15	11.88	15.07	13.59	8.46	13.56	12.41
November	15.22	13.25	16.84	20.42	11.64	9.13	12.00	15.17	13.79	8.50	13.73	12.57
December	15.28	13.31	16.91	20.58	11.76	9.21	11.97	15.15	13.76	8.50	13.64	12.61
1998:												
January	15.19	13.28	16.88	20.66	11.74	9.31	12.11	15.24	13.81	8.61	13.71	12.66
February	15.21	13.34	16.92	20.95	11.77	9.28	12.18	15.25	13.89	8.60	13.95	12.75
March	15.28	13.38	16.96	21.20	11.78	9.30	12.19	15.21	13.90	8.64	13.98	12.77
April	15.45	13.34	17.15	21.02	11.83	9.27	12.20	15.24	13.95	8.69	13.98	12.77
May	15.51	13.33	17.11	20.81	11.85	9.31	12.19	15.18	14.00	8.69	13.99	12.76
June	15.46	13.34	17.04	20.74	11.81	9.33	12.14	15.19	13.94	8.68	13.94	12.71
July	15.64	13.44	17.19	20.83	11.91	9.14	12.14	15.27	14.04	8.69	13.94	12.68
August	15.54	13.47	17.14	20.80	11.84	9.28	12.22	15.30	14.18	8.72	14.12	12.75
September	15.84	13.65	17.30	20.83	11.98	9.35	12.38	15.41	14.16	8.88	14.10	12.97
October	15.60	13.61	17.21	21.06	11.88	9.45	12.41	15.39	14.19	8.84	14.20	13.01
November	15.64	13.57	17.27	20.96	11.97	9.44	12.52	15.48	14.34	8.86	14.43	13.15
December	15.78	13.68	17.31	21.22	12.08	9.43	12.50	15.50	14.32	8.88	14.40	13.18

1. Additional industry detail availible in individual industry profile sections.

Average Weekly Earnings

(Average earnings per week of production or nonsupervisory workers on private nonagricultural payrolls—Dollars)

Year and month	Total private — Seasonally adjusted	Total private — Not seasonally adjusted	Goods-producing [1]	Mining [2]	Construc-tion [2]	Manufacturing Total	Durable goods Total	Lumber and wood products	Furniture and fixtures	Stone, clay, and glass products	Primary metal industries [2]
1970	119.83	119.83	144.60	164.40	195.45	133.33	143.07	117.61	108.58	140.08	158.77
1971	127.31	127.31	155.24	172.14	211.67	142.44	152.74	126.56	115.42	152.67	169.62
1972	136.90	136.90	168.38	189.14	221.19	154.71	167.68	134.94	123.82	165.48	192.92
1973	145.39	145.39	180.00	201.40	235.89	166.46	180.09	144.80	131.60	176.82	213.19
1974	154.76	154.76	191.18	219.14	249.25	176.80	190.82	152.88	138.02	187.50	232.96
1975	163.53	163.53	205.53	249.31	266.08	190.79	205.49	166.06	143.64	198.77	247.20
1976	175.45	175.45	223.74	273.90	283.73	209.32	226.14	189.13	154.81	219.06	276.22
1977	189.00	189.00	242.78	301.20	295.65	228.90	248.46	203.89	169.26	239.95	305.62
1978	203.70	203.70	264.94	332.88	318.69	249.27	270.44	223.68	183.92	262.91	342.76
1979	219.91	219.91	286.24	365.07	342.99	269.34	290.50	240.16	195.82	284.28	371.77
1980	235.10	235.10	307.72	397.06	367.78	288.62	310.78	253.60	209.17	306.00	391.78
1981	255.20	255.20	338.52	438.75	399.26	318.00	342.91	271.67	226.94	335.76	437.81
1982	267.26	267.26	354.49	459.88	426.82	330.26	354.88	284.23	234.73	355.69	437.34
1983	280.70	280.70	376.36	479.40	442.97	354.08	381.77	313.58	260.83	384.71	459.68
1984	292.86	292.86	395.17	503.58	458.51	374.03	402.82	321.20	271.55	401.94	478.30
1985	299.09	299.09	407.60	519.93	464.46	386.37	415.71	329.18	282.50	412.30	484.31
1986	304.85	304.85	416.64	525.81	466.75	396.01	424.56	338.15	296.91	423.69	496.93
1987	312.50	312.50	426.37	531.70	480.44	406.31	432.85	342.26	306.80	433.58	514.61
1988	322.02	322.02	439.55	541.44	495.73	418.81	447.68	344.46	313.23	446.69	528.96
1989	334.24	334.24	452.17	570.18	513.17	429.68	458.02	354.48	325.88	457.69	534.49
1990	345.35	345.35	465.87	603.29	526.01	441.86	468.76	365.02	333.13	467.04	551.68
1991	353.98	353.98	477.96	630.04	533.40	455.03	482.93	369.60	340.76	473.71	562.53
1992	363.61	363.61	489.65	638.31	537.70	469.86	498.83	383.26	357.70	489.52	587.38
1993	373.64	373.64	505.93	646.78	553.63	486.04	519.09	392.09	371.73	506.00	611.36
1994	385.86	385.86	526.19	666.62	573.00	506.94	543.97	405.41	385.82	526.44	641.00
1995	394.34	394.34	534.64	683.91	587.00	514.59	548.66	410.87	388.87	533.63	643.28
1996	406.61	406.61	553.62	707.59	603.33	531.23	565.19	425.95	399.91	555.11	661.67
1997	424.89	424.89	574.90	733.21	625.56	553.14	587.64	441.16	424.11	569.38	683.38
1998	442.19	442.19	587.94	741.91	643.69	562.53	591.35	456.21	442.54	591.60	684.66
1995:											
January	389.94	390.44	527.77	683.83	556.04	514.50	550.84	404.97	393.01	516.06	655.65
February	389.85	388.17	523.46	678.18	550.19	511.24	547.84	397.60	383.90	512.86	646.36
March	390.89	387.83	527.67	668.16	568.42	511.66	547.83	401.58	381.39	522.28	643.03
April	391.58	390.33	516.31	677.79	562.86	496.92	526.44	400.79	367.95	526.21	639.11
May	389.99	388.17	529.18	672.92	577.89	509.22	543.11	406.41	375.78	530.99	637.87
June	393.65	392.02	536.42	685.35	595.58	512.51	546.54	412.49	386.31	539.33	642.84
July	393.88	396.37	534.80	682.63	606.00	505.92	535.72	408.40	381.40	538.27	628.73
August	394.57	395.33	539.72	683.46	604.96	512.53	546.94	419.22	396.59	544.94	634.94
September	395.60	399.28	549.95	696.89	612.47	523.74	558.97	422.51	399.99	552.20	643.86
October	396.63	402.17	546.48	697.52	615.54	518.33	552.95	423.12	397.79	549.25	639.77
November	397.66	398.35	543.43	687.68	590.56	523.33	557.68	415.95	399.99	543.02	652.54
December	397.19	399.04	544.66	697.75	577.22	529.20	561.96	415.72	407.00	534.20	652.24
1996:											
January	394.26	390.78	521.51	686.16	560.04	503.87	538.65	396.81	359.36	515.34	644.06
February	400.42	398.29	536.83	704.01	579.11	519.14	552.35	407.15	384.07	532.54	648.27
March	402.27	399.46	536.02	697.50	577.60	517.90	548.10	415.72	390.00	538.02	645.17
April	403.17	400.33	543.75	698.20	587.49	524.48	557.76	420.43	389.32	551.66	653.56
May	404.20	402.00	548.58	696.80	595.17	528.32	562.65	426.42	394.13	555.46	653.56
June	407.45	410.08	556.83	717.14	607.86	534.23	568.76	434.72	399.35	565.36	660.51
July	406.95	405.86	552.43	696.64	617.70	525.67	556.70	426.13	398.11	562.89	657.49
August	409.52	409.25	560.97	701.50	621.64	534.62	568.65	436.36	408.62	568.48	662.38
September	412.09	417.40	570.99	724.04	627.65	545.25	582.28	439.71	414.91	575.46	680.06
October	411.59	412.62	565.23	714.20	629.22	537.58	572.61	437.18	413.26	568.04	670.00
November	413.66	414.35	564.28	712.33	606.83	543.93	578.29	433.37	416.34	563.76	675.51
December	415.89	421.24	573.91	734.62	605.25	559.40	594.70	437.54	433.47	558.58	686.30
1997:											
January	414.86	410.87	552.67	716.04	573.66	540.75	574.34	418.97	407.93	531.29	672.84
February	418.31	419.18	557.74	733.70	589.50	541.22	576.73	426.52	402.23	547.68	673.01
March	421.26	421.43	565.68	731.66	603.26	548.94	584.73	431.83	416.16	553.35	679.17
April	420.74	418.99	567.74	725.21	612.26	546.74	582.00	438.78	411.59	560.27	677.21
May	422.47	420.21	572.56	734.40	629.64	548.05	583.36	442.32	416.71	573.34	674.52
June	422.28	425.08	573.80	738.75	630.04	549.78	583.79	446.96	419.35	572.47	679.17
July	423.32	423.52	571.54	723.86	643.20	539.72	570.26	441.46	415.94	571.56	670.79
August	427.85	428.05	579.76	727.78	641.97	551.88	584.56	446.04	429.30	578.60	677.65
September	428.00	431.87	589.95	738.92	654.03	560.95	594.35	450.69	440.84	586.53	691.73
October	430.08	432.02	588.80	733.41	650.33	560.42	596.84	451.11	435.34	584.75	691.38
November	432.71	436.39	584.98	746.93	617.77	569.14	604.04	451.26	440.84	575.82	699.79
December	432.85	436.04	596.82	747.00	631.02	579.21	617.23	449.90	454.26	585.14	711.32
1998:											
January	436.39	431.26	577.10	748.66	610.50	561.46	594.27	437.78	437.53	565.97	702.79
February	437.22	438.04	577.51	739.72	616.74	559.20	592.88	441.45	436.59	572.97	691.06
March	437.34	437.46	579.96	731.29	619.78	561.70	595.43	445.26	436.72	573.40	691.09
April	439.07	434.34	572.45	727.01	623.32	549.17	576.14	447.98	431.14	584.73	679.64
May	441.73	439.77	588.75	738.48	646.09	563.46	593.73	456.37	433.08	597.52	691.98
June	441.50	440.00	588.34	733.92	645.62	561.79	590.63	461.34	441.46	596.16	689.98
July	442.88	441.26	586.92	735.76	669.73	549.92	571.46	460.20	439.67	595.24	670.64
August	444.61	449.15	596.57	742.72	674.15	560.87	587.42	465.09	449.36	602.45	676.71
September	444.36	442.47	586.85	734.02	629.63	564.40	588.13	452.39	437.40	606.70	683.72
October	446.69	447.38	600.71	751.08	675.60	567.75	595.85	465.63	449.49	603.29	667.95
November	447.72	451.10	597.40	757.30	649.25	573.92	602.20	466.46	449.49	597.87	678.47
December	449.11	451.10	607.15	755.57	659.62	583.19	613.13	472.46	460.65	600.06	685.06

1. Includes mining, construction, and manufacturing.
2. Additional industry detail availible in individual industry profile sections.

Average Weekly Earnings—*Continued*

(Average earnings per week of production or nonsupervisory workers on private nonagricultural payrolls—Dollars, not seasonally adjusted)

Year and month	Durable goods—*Continued*						Nondurable goods by industry				
	Fabricated metal products	Industrial machinery and equipment [1]	Electronic and electric equipment	Transportation equipment [1]	Instrument and products	Miscellaneous manufacturing	Total	Food and products	Tobacco products	Textile mill products	Apparel and other textile products
1970	143.67	154.95	154.95	163.62	163.62	109.52	120.43	127.98	110.00	97.76	84.37
1971	152.31	163.21	163.21	181.12	181.12	115.53	128.51	136.21	119.45	104.34	88.64
1972	166.86	181.87	181.87	200.58	200.58	122.85	138.16	145.80	130.47	113.58	93.60
1973	178.46	196.88	196.88	216.82	216.82	128.31	146.52	155.54	145.14	120.66	99.08
1974	188.09	207.97	207.97	224.37	224.37	136.61	156.79	169.28	157.80	126.40	104.54
1975	202.51	219.10	219.10	245.23	245.23	146.69	169.56	185.78	173.81	134.41	111.58
1976	224.40	238.55	238.55	276.05	276.05	156.75	185.57	201.69	186.75	147.97	121.72
1977	242.31	259.79	259.79	309.83	309.83	169.17	201.33	214.80	209.41	161.20	128.87
1978	260.35	284.76	284.76	333.80	333.80	181.97	218.28	230.26	233.55	173.72	140.26
1979	278.80	305.24	305.24	350.58	350.58	195.16	236.19	250.17	253.46	188.26	149.32
1980	300.98	328.00	328.00	379.61	379.61	211.30	255.84	271.95	294.89	203.31	161.42
1981	330.46	360.33	360.33	424.95	424.95	231.64	281.85	295.37	344.54	218.59	177.43
1982	343.78	367.62	367.62	449.96	449.96	246.53	297.60	312.05	370.06	218.63	180.44
1983	370.27	387.18	387.18	491.31	491.31	266.27	318.75	323.51	388.21	249.67	194.76
1984	389.16	417.74	417.74	520.94	520.94	277.77	333.08	333.92	436.46	257.75	202.02
1985	401.02	427.45	427.45	541.45	541.45	287.62	345.31	342.80	444.91	265.99	208.57
1986	408.46	440.13	440.13	541.86	541.86	298.98	357.11	350.00	481.71	284.82	214.33
1987	416.42	452.81	452.81	543.48	543.48	305.74	369.44	358.99	548.73	299.71	219.78
1988	431.15	473.12	401.39	567.48	438.84	313.60	379.89	367.54	583.87	302.58	226.44
1989	439.71	483.36	410.04	579.61	445.11	326.63	391.95	381.77	590.97	313.70	234.32
1990	447.28	493.16	420.24	591.36	464.02	340.10	404.80	392.50	636.22	320.00	239.15
1991	461.03	506.66	435.49	618.03	477.24	351.35	419.69	401.94	655.71	336.98	250.49
1992	475.07	523.70	453.20	635.36	488.68	365.09	433.49	414.12	653.11	353.46	258.54
1993	492.15	547.39	469.83	679.40	502.65	373.72	445.79	425.32	631.69	367.63	263.75
1994	511.80	568.10	485.30	731.39	520.00	386.80	459.72	440.26	749.45	379.81	275.25
1995	514.31	574.62	486.30	733.21	526.19	401.00	468.99	449.22	768.64	383.93	282.68
1996	530.00	585.73	505.47	756.36	547.52	412.09	484.79	459.20	774.00	393.41	294.52
1997	544.43	613.45	533.40	780.98	567.84	428.24	504.71	474.12	748.44	415.24	307.73
1998	552.44	619.32	541.93	760.80	570.35	434.51	521.88	492.06	710.47	425.99	317.80
1995:											
January	518.92	581.67	488.68	738.92	525.01	399.40	465.20	445.94	727.26	387.61	280.86
February	513.68	579.48	478.50	746.71	523.73	398.20	462.11	439.29	751.91	382.64	280.13
March	512.13	578.16	480.06	747.05	526.25	397.60	463.32	441.32	773.43	382.75	280.87
April	484.81	546.33	463.10	698.83	513.14	388.22	457.78	434.62	767.23	373.07	271.27
May	508.57	571.58	477.43	729.27	521.18	397.79	463.45	444.72	838.80	378.27	280.09
June	509.72	570.26	482.65	733.57	523.68	399.20	466.97	449.90	908.96	382.30	283.46
July	498.93	560.95	476.64	705.58	520.61	391.33	467.17	449.90	853.20	373.72	278.86
August	511.04	569.75	488.04	724.71	523.24	398.20	468.18	454.11	747.00	387.45	284.16
September	524.24	578.96	498.38	752.58	530.33	407.43	477.65	461.84	702.80	390.45	287.18
October	519.29	575.86	497.54	731.54	528.26	408.24	473.80	452.09	730.84	385.29	285.24
November	525.95	585.14	500.41	743.80	536.29	410.06	478.58	457.47	790.89	389.78	288.27
December	536.54	594.03	504.64	741.03	543.96	411.83	483.07	460.20	692.46	389.50	292.06
1996:											
January	506.34	568.51	482.78	714.02	525.20	386.25	457.34	435.44	658.00	344.16	262.07
February	517.44	580.22	494.21	733.94	540.89	402.83	472.78	445.61	701.63	383.91	287.78
March	516.21	578.49	494.27	703.87	543.02	407.55	476.75	449.55	762.00	388.69	290.82
April	520.83	573.89	490.01	757.68	538.14	405.97	477.20	449.84	801.72	386.97	289.38
May	526.64	578.35	496.90	764.96	540.75	408.43	479.95	455.03	840.29	390.57	296.16
June	535.43	585.42	507.10	766.29	549.36	410.10	486.34	458.90	877.40	400.75	302.82
July	520.00	574.52	497.35	737.86	539.97	402.36	482.40	459.00	809.83	389.54	292.56
August	533.35	582.43	510.85	765.06	547.04	412.73	488.76	463.14	809.60	401.44	299.34
September	543.95	596.24	518.70	786.09	558.18	422.99	496.01	472.22	772.38	404.89	300.42
October	535.03	588.16	514.16	761.57	552.11	420.89	490.80	464.26	731.30	399.90	301.55
November	541.37	597.97	519.94	770.74	561.26	427.11	498.93	475.68	768.38	407.83	301.18
December	556.34	620.71	537.97	800.28	574.48	435.25	508.77	480.90	782.69	417.06	308.51
1997:											
January	535.51	602.74	513.35	777.38	556.70	418.97	494.10	464.39	728.34	407.54	299.63
February	537.63	606.04	518.74	769.05	560.70	423.06	492.48	460.72	726.87	399.96	301.02
March	541.45	611.01	527.08	786.60	566.32	425.17	498.58	463.98	760.89	410.11	308.63
April	540.60	608.66	525.85	779.57	560.03	422.90	496.53	462.58	781.06	411.93	304.59
May	* 541.45	606.39	524.59	779.12	562.12	420.40	497.76	470.27	803.03	409.94	305.78
June	541.87	606.30	528.78	774.75	566.49	421.05	499.39	466.75	827.90	416.17	311.03
July	526.24	600.48	522.42	728.86	556.61	415.15	499.75	473.47	738.83	406.81	299.75
August	541.88	605.12	531.26	771.71	568.35	426.37	504.71	481.12	748.06	416.83	307.80
September	550.40	620.54	540.56	777.47	574.67	434.93	513.77	486.87	719.44	424.20	312.38
October	551.27	616.59	540.51	794.77	570.68	434.52	509.64	478.61	712.80	418.55	313.21
November	559.44	629.64	554.25	797.00	583.19	443.15	518.34	487.94	703.10	425.70	313.21
December	572.88	646.02	566.35	823.08	588.16	447.95	525.84	496.50	747.06	431.53	320.80
1998:											
January	552.95	627.10	542.56	776.14	572.77	432.40	514.11	482.72	694.01	426.82	314.07
February	548.63	625.53	538.72	771.69	577.19	435.24	510.75	475.67	677.69	421.69	310.90
March	548.18	625.53	538.55	781.36	573.79	437.40	514.45	478.12	683.38	423.95	313.60
April	526.79	600.85	527.62	731.54	560.85	425.42	508.80	474.30	697.08	417.68	309.52
May	553.78	619.78	536.42	769.56	569.11	430.92	518.98	488.87	789.36	426.21	316.78
June	554.23	622.94	540.68	746.89	569.25	433.20	519.43	488.04	829.12	429.94	321.30
July	535.81	610.39	533.08	691.26	560.85	425.32	520.09	490.88	809.19	418.54	312.91
August	550.29	616.00	543.65	740.01	568.15	434.00	522.75	493.92	745.13	427.24	321.10
September	547.46	608.19	542.43	757.32	563.53	431.51	530.13	507.88	670.21	424.44	316.72
October	561.04	617.77	544.90	771.73	569.65	443.00	527.72	496.44	662.75	429.50	325.24
November	565.39	625.13	554.46	781.39	577.27	441.20	532.77	506.68	673.36	431.96	325.73
December	578.96	636.34	560.90	802.49	588.00	447.02	540.38	514.46	639.38	437.18	330.11

1. Additional industry detail availible in individual industry profile sections.

Average Weekly Earnings—*Continued*

(Average earnings per week of production or nonsupervisory workers on private nonagricultural payrolls—Dollars, not seasonally adjusted)

| Year and month | Manufacturing—*Continued* | | | | | | Service-producing industries | | | | | |
| | Nondurable goods—*Continued* | | | | | | | | | | | |
	Paper and products	Printing and publishing	Chemicals and products	Petroleum and coal products	Rubber and miscellaneous plastics products	Leather and products	Total	Transportation and public utilities [1]	Wholesale trade	Retail trade [1]	Finance, insurance, and real estate [1]	Services [1]
1970	144.14	147.78	153.50	183.18	129.36	92.63	105.37	155.93	136.86	82.47	112.67	96.66
1971	154.51	157.50	165.15	195.60	137.76	97.64	111.84	168.82	143.42	87.62	117.85	103.06
1972	169.06	170.03	177.64	211.79	149.56	102.64	119.65	187.86	151.69	91.85	122.98	110.85
1973	180.18	179.08	188.52	223.87	158.21	105.46	126.37	203.31	159.54	96.32	129.20	117.29
1974	191.17	188.63	202.52	239.13	166.05	110.33	135.06	217.48	169.94	102.68	137.61	126.00
1975	208.42	198.52	220.99	266.98	176.36	119.09	143.66	233.44	182.19	108.86	148.19	134.67
1976	232.48	214.13	245.86	303.54	191.70	127.16	152.39	256.71	194.27	114.60	155.43	143.52
1977	255.68	230.72	268.13	334.34	214.13	133.21	163.13	278.90	209.13	121.66	165.26	153.45
1978	279.71	244.78	294.14	376.27	227.81	144.32	175.26	302.80	228.14	130.20	178.00	163.67
1979	303.74	260.25	318.44	409.97	244.41	154.03	188.05	325.58	247.93	138.62	190.77	175.27
1980	330.85	279.36	344.45	422.18	263.20	168.09	203.01	351.25	266.88	147.38	209.60	190.71
1981	365.50	305.49	379.39	491.62	290.97	183.13	220.77	382.18	290.68	158.03	229.05	208.97
1982	389.58	324.25	407.36	546.99	304.92	189.75	233.77	402.48	309.46	163.85	245.44	225.59
1983	423.02	342.54	440.13	582.99	332.07	203.87	245.42	420.81	328.79	171.05	263.90	239.04
1984	448.67	356.64	463.83	587.33	348.20	210.13	253.75	438.13	341.88	174.33	278.50	247.43
1985	466.77	367.04	484.36	604.58	353.46	216.88	260.17	450.30	351.36	174.64	289.02	256.75
1986	482.98	379.62	501.96	621.52	363.91	218.45	265.83	458.64	357.72	176.08	304.30	265.85
1987	496.06	390.64	523.25	641.52	373.57	232.26	273.73	471.58	365.38	178.70	316.90	275.93
1988	506.18	400.14	536.36	664.67	383.22	235.50	283.39	467.57	380.24	183.62	325.25	289.49
1989	517.87	412.35	555.02	682.66	391.64	249.76	295.61	481.43	394.82	188.72	341.17	305.79
1990	533.02	426.00	576.80	724.30	401.14	258.43	308.03	496.13	411.10	194.40	356.93	319.48
1991	550.78	432.80	602.32	751.46	413.88	269.25	317.53	502.92	424.82	198.48	370.92	331.45
1992	569.85	447.29	625.38	784.02	432.01	281.96	328.31	514.37	435.10	205.06	387.36	342.55
1993	585.11	456.92	638.74	819.03	441.83	294.52	336.81	532.52	448.47	209.95	406.33	350.35
1994	604.50	468.60	653.62	846.71	451.54	306.85	346.37	547.07	463.10	216.46	423.51	358.80
1995	613.31	471.01	674.78	846.03	452.77	310.46	355.78	556.72	476.07	221.47	442.29	369.04
1996	635.21	483.23	698.54	842.35	466.46	326.52	368.20	572.22	492.92	230.11	459.52	382.00
1997	657.69	502.81	715.82	870.62	483.63	344.45	385.92	592.32	516.48	240.74	481.57	400.33
1998	673.13	515.14	739.58	912.11	494.98	350.43	403.68	604.75	539.90	253.17	511.78	418.91
1995:												
January	616.00	466.73	665.52	840.08	456.18	306.18	352.30	549.19	471.01	215.17	441.77	368.06
February	606.63	467.95	664.85	868.02	451.50	307.37	351.22	547.62	469.01	214.40	436.76	366.61
March	604.26	471.17	666.39	838.72	451.02	308.61	350.57	546.62	467.49	215.93	433.46	364.50
April	603.20	461.92	679.38	858.25	434.70	307.19	356.21	554.58	477.60	221.09	447.22	369.85
May	605.62	464.74	667.62	828.14	451.36	313.78	349.60	545.84	470.54	219.27	433.30	363.05
June	606.18	464.28	670.72	837.29	454.53	313.47	352.27	553.79	472.62	222.62	433.96	364.65
July	616.75	467.31	671.10	848.93	443.70	293.17	358.56	566.40	479.71	227.50	447.22	369.33
August	606.34	472.15	665.97	826.85	449.22	314.20	355.08	561.36	475.30	225.68	436.81	366.89
September	621.92	482.50	678.67	850.16	459.38	318.06	356.97	562.88	479.52	224.55	442.32	369.84
October	616.76	476.45	682.13	871.82	456.92	314.39	361.78	566.83	483.56	223.78	455.73	376.20
November	624.09	480.27	689.19	852.35	460.22	312.74	358.15	563.56	479.41	222.51	445.54	373.71
December	634.09	481.25	703.72	839.81	470.53	317.37	360.56	562.78	483.73	226.20	448.39	376.62
1996:												
January	607.99	458.38	681.79	836.57	448.54	294.45	356.64	551.32	476.02	216.98	447.66	373.01
February	617.60	473.37	687.88	836.31	460.08	312.01	362.23	563.56	481.84	221.93	453.03	377.38
March	618.03	478.65	689.60	824.11	460.50	319.79	363.35	564.60	483.49	225.15	454.46	377.38
April	626.77	474.89	691.22	836.56	460.32	315.00	362.88	563.04	486.92	224.93	453.90	377.06
May	626.94	476.52	689.72	808.55	465.92	322.03	362.70	563.96	487.05	227.30	453.54	375.77
June	634.94	475.27	699.17	843.94	465.37	331.57	371.18	577.84	499.74	234.61	465.74	382.45
July	638.50	479.94	691.65	842.14	459.00	318.19	366.18	573.67	488.82	233.14	451.76	377.33
August	637.55	490.22	695.84	833.22	467.17	335.71	367.95	581.45	493.44	234.53	455.38	380.30
September	648.12	497.42	704.06	854.83	477.85	341.43	375.21	587.98	503.34	234.55	471.22	387.94
October	642.23	493.19	702.10	843.22	469.25	341.34	370.99	576.05	495.99	232.76	459.82	386.86
November	654.89	496.13	715.81	860.88	471.33	343.48	373.27	580.68	500.58	232.52	465.04	390.10
December	664.39	503.10	730.38	888.98	490.33	347.81	379.83	583.74	511.23	238.80	478.57	397.63
1997:												
January	649.12	486.11	705.55	902.94	475.27	334.02	373.84	573.78	499.90	229.90	464.81	390.08
February	637.63	491.11	710.72	884.93	475.18	337.93	383.29	580.26	510.90	236.49	483.34	400.25
March	649.02	503.49	709.34	880.64	480.70	342.27	383.94	583.70	511.67	237.06	482.53	399.02
April	650.13	497.13	706.06	845.46	480.80	338.71	379.46	581.64	511.31	236.52	471.01	394.96
May	649.70	492.63	710.29	846.30	479.55	340.74	379.97	580.07	513.59	238.18	474.24	393.98
June	649.70	490.20	712.44	854.57	480.38	346.87	384.62	590.92	517.81	243.14	486.64	398.19
July	656.43	495.68	707.97	856.86	474.37	331.51	383.30	591.71	512.84	244.50	474.24	395.57
August	655.77	504.50	712.51	859.57	482.47	341.38	387.61	608.72	519.75	246.21	483.02	398.75
September	669.00	518.22	722.97	877.69	488.88	356.20	388.02	606.11	520.32	244.76	482.58	401.70
October	664.88	513.48	720.51	879.86	487.72	353.19	389.66	599.79	521.86	243.65	486.80	404.57
November	675.77	520.73	735.91	884.19	494.70	351.51	396.00	612.87	533.67	244.80	503.89	412.30
December	683.02	521.75	744.04	868.48	505.68	357.35	393.81	602.97	528.38	248.20	489.68	411.09
1998:												
January	663.80	504.64	732.59	919.37	491.91	350.99	393.58	598.93	526.16	241.94	494.93	410.18
February	654.03	509.59	732.64	884.09	489.63	351.71	401.94	608.48	534.77	246.82	517.55	418.20
March	658.57	515.13	736.06	913.72	488.87	350.61	401.05	599.27	533.76	247.97	514.46	416.30
April	656.63	504.25	735.74	899.66	485.03	338.36	397.72	595.88	531.50	249.40	504.68	413.75
May	671.58	507.87	734.02	892.75	496.52	348.19	399.83	599.61	537.60	252.01	505.04	414.70
June	672.51	506.92	734.42	895.97	496.02	355.47	400.62	601.52	535.30	254.32	501.84	415.62
July	674.08	512.06	734.01	933.18	489.50	337.27	403.05	606.22	537.73	258.96	503.23	417.17
August	669.77	519.94	737.02	915.20	491.36	356.35	409.37	610.47	548.77	260.73	521.03	423.30
September	698.54	526.89	750.82	899.86	495.97	348.76	404.83	605.61	539.50	258.41	506.19	418.93
October	680.16	522.62	743.47	926.64	496.58	355.32	407.05	604.83	543.48	255.48	512.62	424.13
November	686.60	525.16	746.06	920.14	503.94	358.72	413.16	614.56	554.96	256.05	532.47	431.32
December	699.05	530.78	752.99	948.53	515.82	359.28	411.25	606.05	549.89	259.30	521.28	429.67

1. Additional industry detail availible in individual industry profile sections.

Energy

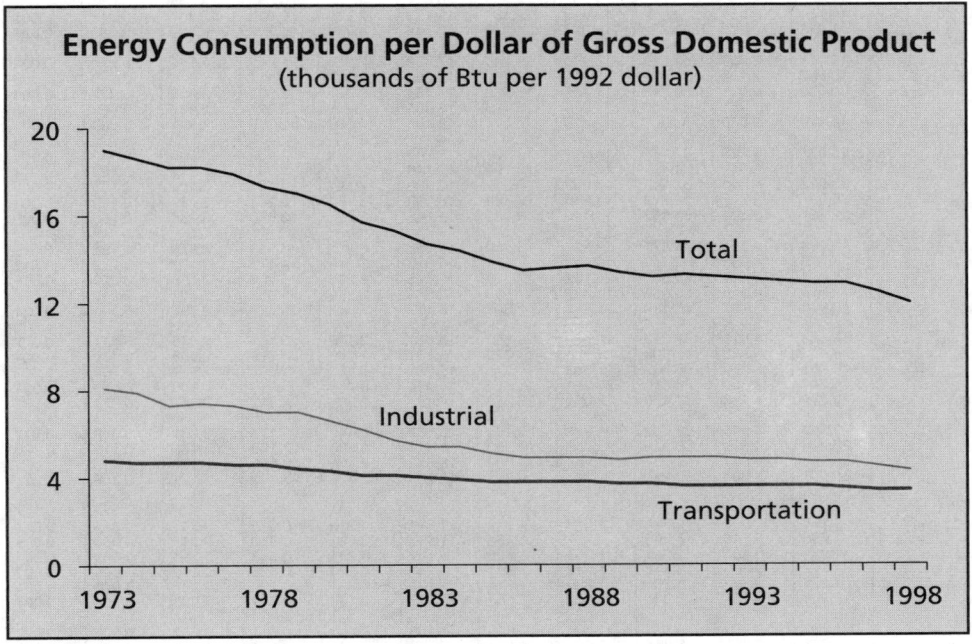

Energy Consumption per Dollar of Gross Domestic Product
(thousands of Btu per 1992 dollar)

- The decline in energy consumption per dollar of GDP slowed during the late 1980s and early 1990s, when energy prices were relatively stable, but accelerated again in 1997 and 1998, even though energy prices were declining.

- Industrial energy use has shown the greatest decline relative to GDP. In absolute amount (measured in Btu's), industrial energy use in 1998 was about equal to 1979, even though industrial production rose 60 percent over this period.

- While use of petroleum and natural gas declined rapidly relative to GDP in the late 1980s, the ratio of other energy use to GDP was little changed. In contrast, the ratios for both categories of energy use fell at similar rates from 1996 to 1998.

Energy Supply and Consumption

(Quadrillion Btu)

Year and month	Imports	Exports	Production, by source									Consumption, by end-use sector			
			Total	Coal	Natural gas	Crude oil	Natural gas plant liquids	Nuclear electric power	Hydro-electric power	Geo-thermal energy	Other	Total	Residen-tial and commer-cial	Industrial	Transpor-tation
1970	8.385	2.662	.....	14.607	21.666	20.401	2.512	0.239	2.634	0.011	.....	67.858	22.120	29.649	16.092
1971	9.585	2.176	.....	13.186	22.280	20.033	2.544	0.413	2.824	0.012	.....	69.314	22.981	29.614	16.722
1972	11.460	2.138	.....	14.092	22.208	20.041	2.598	0.583	2.864	0.031	.....	72.758	24.074	30.975	17.712
1973	14.731	2.051	62.060	13.993	22.187	19.493	2.569	0.910	2.861	0.043	0.003	74.282	24.143	31.528	18.605
1974	14.413	2.223	60.835	14.074	21.210	18.575	2.471	1.272	3.177	0.053	0.003	72.543	23.725	30.694	18.117
1975	14.111	2.359	59.860	14.990	19.640	17.729	2.374	1.900	3.155	0.070	0.002	70.546	23.899	28.402	18.244
1976	16.837	2.188	59.892	15.654	19.480	17.262	2.327	2.111	2.976	0.078	0.003	74.362	25.018	30.236	19.101
1977	20.090	2.071	60.219	15.755	19.565	17.454	2.327	2.702	2.333	0.077	0.005	76.288	25.384	31.077	19.819
1978	19.254	1.931	61.103	14.910	19.485	18.434	2.245	3.024	2.937	0.064	0.003	78.089	26.084	31.392	20.611
1979	19.616	2.870	63.801	17.539	20.076	18.104	2.286	2.776	2.931	0.084	0.005	78.898	25.808	32.616	20.472
1980	15.971	3.723	64.761	18.597	19.908	18.249	2.254	2.739	2.900	0.110	0.005	75.955	25.655	30.606	19.695
1981	13.975	4.329	64.421	18.376	19.699	18.146	2.307	3.008	2.758	0.123	0.004	73.990	25.241	29.240	19.507
1982	12.092	4.633	63.962	18.639	18.319	18.309	2.191	3.131	3.266	0.105	0.003	70.848	25.629	26.145	19.069
1983	12.027	3.717	61.279	17.246	16.593	18.392	2.184	3.203	3.527	0.129	0.004	70.524	25.627	25.759	19.135
1984	12.767	3.804	65.962	19.719	18.008	18.848	2.274	3.553	3.386	0.165	0.009	74.144	26.474	27.867	19.801
1985	12.103	4.231	64.871	19.325	16.980	18.992	2.241	4.149	2.970	0.198	0.015	73.981	26.704	27.214	20.067
1986	14.438	4.055	64.350	19.510	16.541	18.376	2.149	4.471	3.071	0.219	0.012	74.297	26.852	26.630	20.812
1987	15.764	3.853	64.952	20.142	17.136	17.675	2.215	4.906	2.635	0.229	0.016	76.894	27.623	27.826	21.447
1988	17.564	4.415	66.105	20.737	17.599	17.279	2.260	5.661	2.334	0.217	0.017	80.218	28.924	28.985	22.305
1989	18.950	4.767	66.160	21.345	17.847	16.117	2.158	5.677	2.798	0.197	0.021	81.358	29.424	29.365	22.561
1990	18.988	4.911	67.872	22.456	18.362	15.571	2.175	6.161	2.945	0.181	0.022	81.284	28.799	29.944	22.533
1991	18.582	5.222	67.508	21.594	18.229	15.701	2.306	6.579	2.908	0.170	0.021	81.142	29.441	29.580	22.121
1992	19.661	5.019	66.863	21.593	18.375	15.223	2.363	6.607	2.510	0.169	0.022	82.162	29.106	30.589	22.461
1993	21.547	4.356	65.171	20.221	18.584	14.494	2.408	6.519	2.765	0.158	0.021	83.881	30.239	30.762	22.884
1994	22.740	4.133	67.459	22.068	19.348	14.103	2.391	6.837	2.547	0.145	0.021	85.635	30.441	31.622	23.571
1995	22.519	4.595	67.762	21.978	19.101	13.887	2.442	7.177	3.061	0.099	0.017	87.243	31.272	31.897	24.068
1996	23.996	4.718	68.919	22.646	19.300	13.723	2.530	7.168	3.422	0.110	0.020	90.063	32.644	32.796	24.616
1997	25.565	4.644	69.034	23.164	19.394	13.658	2.495	6.678	3.510	0.115	0.021	90.644	32.790	32.923	24.930
1998	26.907	4.384	69.230	23.764	19.353	13.235	2.420	7.157	3.171	0.108	0.021	90.955	32.850	32.705	25.380
1995:															
January	1.766	0.360	5.874	1.893	1.642	1.201	0.210	0.675	0.243	0.009	0.001	7.979	3.334	2.743	1.902
February	1.656	0.346	5.363	1.797	1.464	1.103	0.189	0.553	0.249	0.006	0.001	7.374	3.022	2.580	1.773
March	1.954	0.380	5.861	1.994	1.625	1.187	0.209	0.553	0.286	0.007	0.001	7.465	2.770	2.673	2.024
April	1.779	0.380	5.418	1.716	1.571	1.149	0.204	0.526	0.245	0.006	0.002	6.815	2.298	2.597	1.922
May	1.875	0.390	5.665	1.785	1.614	1.192	0.211	0.580	0.277	0.005	0.001	6.871	2.180	2.665	2.027
June	1.962	0.394	5.605	1.805	1.554	1.145	0.198	0.601	0.296	0.006	0.001	6.912	2.244	2.576	2.090
July	1.897	0.356	5.614	1.704	1.605	1.159	0.206	0.661	0.270	0.006	0.002	7.216	2.559	2.598	2.055
August	1.951	0.362	5.754	1.888	1.594	1.159	0.204	0.657	0.239	0.011	0.002	7.479	2.661	2.734	2.079
September	1.996	0.366	5.558	1.895	1.548	1.116	0.200	0.594	0.196	0.008	0.002	6.780	2.201	2.578	2.001
October	1.851	0.396	5.681	1.927	1.577	1.155	0.207	0.579	0.223	0.013	0.002	6.882	2.166	2.682	2.035
November	1.883	0.389	5.644	1.846	1.623	1.146	0.205	0.562	0.250	0.012	0.002	7.282	2.595	2.701	1.987
December	1.883	0.453	5.720	1.730	1.683	1.174	0.199	0.638	0.284	0.011	0.001	8.138	3.280	2.794	2.063
1996:															
January	2.010	0.389	5.766	1.784	1.634	1.168	0.201	0.669	0.301	0.007	0.002	8.480	3.671	2.813	1.995
February	1.714	0.376	5.548	1.799	1.544	1.106	0.184	0.594	0.311	0.008	0.001	7.865	3.307	2.661	1.898
March	1.947	0.359	5.909	1.946	1.635	1.182	0.212	0.589	0.336	0.007	0.002	7.908	3.049	2.812	2.049
April	1.934	0.378	5.701	1.897	1.612	1.121	0.209	0.535	0.318	0.008	0.001	7.119	2.493	2.610	2.018
May	2.131	0.378	5.836	1.906	1.641	1.150	0.212	0.591	0.331	0.005	0.001	7.142	2.322	2.691	2.130
June	2.034	0.387	5.668	1.804	1.597	1.124	0.208	0.611	0.315	0.008	0.002	7.084	2.346	2.729	2.008
July	2.094	0.396	5.834	1.900	1.634	1.140	0.214	0.648	0.286	0.012	0.002	7.347	2.542	2.617	2.185
August	2.129	0.381	5.944	2.024	1.633	1.144	0.218	0.653	0.259	0.012	0.002	7.453	2.523	2.717	2.208
September	1.912	0.428	5.589	1.868	1.572	1.128	0.212	0.580	0.216	0.010	0.002	6.796	2.197	2.655	1.942
October	2.093	0.425	5.779	2.017	1.600	1.165	0.224	0.538	0.221	0.011	0.002	7.236	2.218	2.847	2.171
November	1.935	0.412	5.569	1.850	1.578	1.127	0.217	0.554	0.229	0.011	0.002	7.476	2.685	2.772	2.019
December	2.029	0.399	5.777	1.850	1.618	1.170	0.220	0.607	0.300	0.010	0.002	8.135	3.275	2.824	2.036
1997:															
January	2.102	0.402	5.960	1.973	1.669	1.151	0.208	0.626	0.323	0.009	0.002	8.545	3.697	2.871	1.978
February	1.855	0.344	5.503	1.880	1.512	1.058	0.197	0.538	0.310	0.006	0.002	7.554	3.091	2.615	1.850
March	2.100	0.378	5.923	1.973	1.679	1.160	0.219	0.536	0.346	0.009	0.002	7.694	2.890	2.748	2.059
April	2.082	0.366	5.612	1.879	1.600	1.121	0.206	0.477	0.317	0.010	0.002	7.205	2.451	2.703	2.053
May	2.266	0.371	5.904	2.014	1.661	1.164	0.212	0.500	0.341	0.010	0.002	7.147	2.282	2.735	2.132
June	2.189	0.367	5.652	1.847	1.573	1.121	0.206	0.553	0.341	0.008	0.002	7.133	2.342	2.695	2.095
July	2.138	0.382	5.829	1.896	1.634	1.152	0.212	0.609	0.313	0.011	0.002	7.676	2.713	2.730	2.227
August	2.230	0.444	5.819	1.907	1.631	1.141	0.214	0.649	0.265	0.011	0.002	7.517	2.591	2.739	2.182
September	2.169	0.388	5.700	1.970	1.593	1.129	0.208	0.559	0.229	0.010	0.002	7.054	2.343	2.664	2.045
October	2.287	0.419	5.785	2.019	1.638	1.163	0.211	0.499	0.242	0.010	0.002	7.298	2.367	2.793	2.137
November	2.098	0.366	5.472	1.779	1.587	1.124	0.195	0.544	0.231	0.010	0.002	7.470	2.694	2.743	2.035
December	2.047	0.418	5.877	2.026	1.616	1.174	0.207	0.589	0.252	0.011	0.002	8.346	3.329	2.886	2.131
1998:															
January	2.192	0.418	6.061	2.085	1.676	1.176	0.211	0.615	0.286	0.010	0.002	8.322	3.496	2.823	2.002
February	1.942	0.327	5.463	1.854	1.510	1.052	0.196	0.542	0.299	0.008	0.001	7.415	2.973	2.585	1.857
March	2.151	0.370	5.967	2.046	1.655	1.152	0.217	0.571	0.315	0.010	0.002	7.903	3.029	2.779	2.097
April	2.273	0.380	5.684	1.958	1.593	1.128	0.211	0.505	0.280	0.007	0.002	7.222	2.428	2.687	2.109
May	2.329	0.410	5.805	1.929	1.642	1.141	0.214	0.547	0.323	0.006	0.002	7.215	2.349	2.737	2.128
June	2.252	0.382	5.767	1.966	1.597	1.091	0.198	0.592	0.315	0.007	0.001	7.375	2.556	2.658	2.156
July	2.470	0.377	5.793	1.935	1.616	1.114	0.185	0.653	0.278	0.009	0.002	7.854	2.849	2.733	2.266
August	2.359	0.338	5.798	1.948	1.638	1.115	0.201	0.641	0.242	0.010	0.002	7.783	2.789	2.733	2.254
September	2.183	0.354	5.652	2.038	1.589	1.007	0.194	0.608	0.205	0.010	0.002	7.206	2.479	2.624	2.099
October	2.308	0.361	5.813	2.067	1.632	1.104	0.204	0.610	0.183	0.011	0.002	7.255	2.318	2.757	2.180
November	2.222	0.315	5.580	1.924	1.574	1.068	0.200	0.609	0.194	0.010	0.002	7.222	2.466	2.707	2.050
December	2.226	0.353	5.847	2.015	1.630	1.087	0.189	0.664	0.251	0.009	0.002	8.183	3.119	2.883	2.182

Energy Consumption per Dollar of Real Gross Domestic Product

(Seasonally adjusted annual rate)

Year and quarter	Consumption (quadrillion Btu)			Gross domestic product (billions of chained [1992] dollars)	Energy consumption per dollar of GDP (thousand Btu per chained [1992] dollar)		
	Total	Petroleum and natural gas	Other energy		Total	Petroleum and natural gas	Other energy
1970	67.858	.....	.....	3 397.6	19.97	.....	.....
1971	69.314	.....	.....	3 510.0	19.75	.....	.....
1972	72.758	.....	.....	3 702.3	19.65	.....	.....
1973	74.282	57.352	16.930	3 916.3	18.97	14.64	4.32
1974	72.543	55.187	17.356	3 891.2	18.64	14.18	4.46
1975	70.546	52.678	17.867	3 873.9	18.21	13.60	4.61
1976	74.362	55.520	18.842	4 082.9	18.21	13.60	4.61
1977	76.288	57.053	19.236	4 273.6	17.85	13.35	4.50
1978	78.089	57.966	20.123	4 503.0	17.34	12.87	4.47
1979	78.898	57.789	21.108	4 630.6	17.04	12.48	4.56
1980	75.955	54.596	21.359	4 615.0	16.46	11.83	4.63
1981	73.990	51.859	22.131	4 720.7	15.67	10.99	4.69
1982	70.848	48.736	22.111	4 620.3	15.33	10.55	4.79
1983	70.524	47.411	23.114	4 803.7	14.68	9.87	4.81
1984	74.144	49.558	24.586	5 140.1	14.42	9.64	4.78
1985	73.981	48.756	25.225	5 323.5	13.90	9.16	4.74
1986	74.297	48.904	25.393	5 487.7	13.54	8.91	4.63
1987	76.894	50.609	26.285	5 649.5	13.61	8.96	4.65
1988	80.218	52.774	27.443	5 865.2	13.68	9.00	4.68
1989	81.358	53.595	27.763	6 062.0	13.42	8.84	4.58
1990	81.284	52.849	28.434	6 136.3	13.25	8.61	4.63
1991	81.142	52.452	28.687	6 079.4	13.35	8.63	4.72
1992	82.162	53.657	28.504	6 244.4	13.16	8.59	4.56
1993	83.881	54.668	29.213	6 389.6	13.13	8.56	4.57
1994	85.635	56.022	29.612	6 610.7	12.95	8.47	4.47
1995	87.243	56.827	30.416	6 761.7	12.90	8.40	4.49
1996	90.063	58.424	31.640	6 994.8	12.87	8.35	4.52
1997	90.644	58.925	31.719	7 269.8	12.46	8.11	4.36
1998	90.955	58.967	31.989	7 551.9	12.04	7.81	4.23
1990:							
1st quarter	80.421	52.241	28.180	6 152.6	13.07	8.49	4.58
2nd quarter	82.415	54.069	28.346	6 171.6	13.35	8.76	4.59
3rd quarter	81.870	53.459	28.411	6 142.1	13.33	8.70	4.63
4th quarter	80.166	51.627	28.538	6 079.0	13.19	8.49	4.69
1991:							
1st quarter	80.611	52.249	28.362	6 047.5	13.33	8.64	4.69
2nd quarter	81.122	51.976	29.146	6 074.7	13.35	8.56	4.80
3rd quarter	81.453	52.712	28.741	6 090.1	13.37	8.66	4.72
4th quarter	81.268	52.860	28.409	6 105.3	13.31	8.66	4.65
1992:							
1st quarter	81.808	53.676	28.132	6 175.7	13.25	8.69	4.56
2nd quarter	82.583	54.051	28.532	6 214.2	13.29	8.70	4.59
3rd quarter	81.131	52.840	28.291	6 260.7	12.96	8.44	4.52
4th quarter	83.055	54.066	28.989	6 327.1	13.13	8.55	4.58
1993:							
1st quarter	84.575	55.300	29.275	6 327.9	13.37	8.74	4.63
2nd quarter	83.235	53.653	29.581	6 359.9	13.09	8.44	4.65
3rd quarter	83.581	54.487	29.094	6 393.5	13.07	8.52	4.55
4th quarter	84.066	55.231	28.835	6 476.9	12.98	8.53	4.45
1994:							
1st quarter	87.845	57.900	29.944	6 524.5	13.46	8.87	4.59
2nd quarter	85.756	55.837	29.918	6 600.3	12.99	8.46	4.53
3rd quarter	84.829	55.655	29.174	6 629.5	12.80	8.40	4.40
4th quarter	84.159	54.924	29.235	6 688.6	12.58	8.21	4.37
1995:							
1st quarter	86.395	56.537	29.859	6 717.5	12.86	8.42	4.44
2nd quarter	87.141	57.101	30.040	6 724.2	12.96	8.49	4.47
3rd quarter	87.649	56.813	30.836	6 779.5	12.93	8.38	4.55
4th quarter	87.570	56.854	30.716	6 825.8	12.83	8.33	4.50
1996:							
1st quarter	90.910	59.282	31.628	6 882.0	13.21	8.61	4.60
2nd quarter	90.558	58.591	31.967	6 983.9	12.97	8.39	4.58
3rd quarter	88.650	57.442	31.208	7 020.0	12.63	8.18	4.45
4th quarter	90.063	58.392	31.671	7 093.1	12.70	8.23	4.47
1997:							
1st quarter	90.826	58.618	32.208	7 166.7	12.62	8.18	4.44
2nd quarter	90.931	59.407	31.524	7 236.5	12.58	8.21	4.37
3rd quarter	90.345	59.038	31.307	7 311.2	12.39	8.08	4.31
4th quarter	90.462	58.617	31.845	7 364.6	12.28	7.96	4.32
1998:							
1st quarter	89.678	57.925	31.753	7 464.7	12.01	7.76	4.25
2nd quarter	92.438	59.831	32.607	7 498.6	12.33	7.98	4.35
3rd quarter	92.883	60.474	32.409	7 566.5	12.27	7.99	4.28
4th quarter	88.825	57.635	31.190	7 677.7	11.57	7.51	4.06

Money and Financial Markets

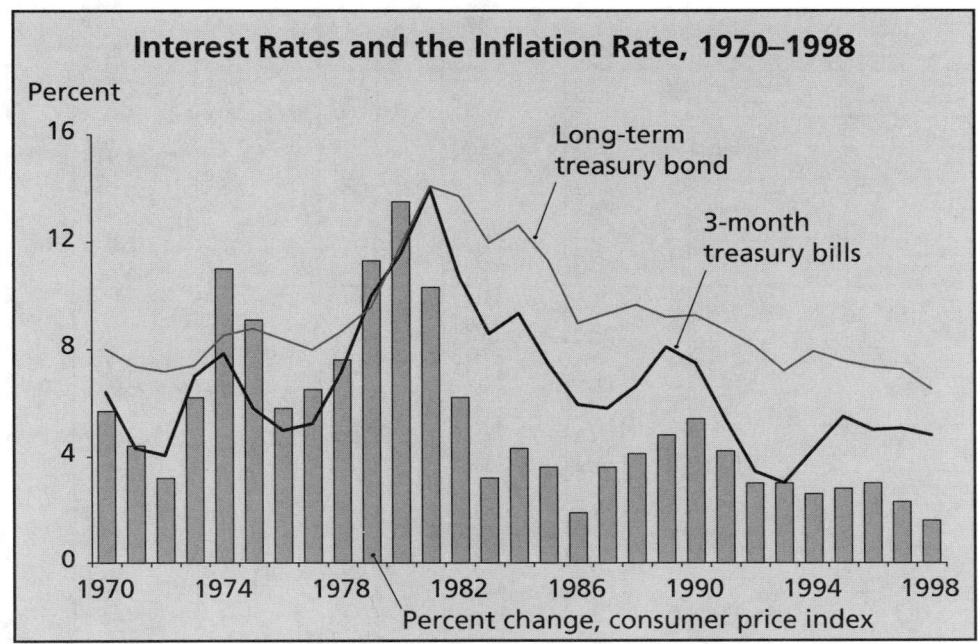

Interest Rates and the Inflation Rate, 1970–1998

Long-term treasury bond

3-month treasury bills

Percent change, consumer price index

- Short- and long-term interest rates roughly tracked the rate of price inflation from 1970 to 1980, though they did not match the inflationary spike of 1974–75. During the 1980s, short-term rates fell faster than long-term, and inflation fell faster than either. As a result, rates of return were positive after adjustment for inflation; these positive real rates have continued into the 1990s.

- Currency was 22.7 percent of M1 in 1970; by 1998, it had risen to 42.0 percent. Demand deposits were 76.8 percent of M1 in 1970 but by 1998 had fallen to 34.5 percent. Other checkable deposits, which include credit union share draft balances and demand deposits at thrift institutions, grew rapidly, from less than a tenth of one percent in 1970 to 22.8 percent of M1 by 1998.

- Credit market debt outstanding grew over 14 times from 1970 to 1998. The largest growth took place in the domestic financial sectors, increasing by a factor of 50. In this category, the federal government related debt (credit agencies such as FNMA and mortgage pools) was 75 times higher than it had been in 1970, while private debt was only 38 times higher.

- Credit market debt owed by the domestic private nonfinancial sectors stood about 11 times higher in 1998 than in 1970. Household debt increased the most in this category, growing about 13 times.

Money Stock, Liquid Assets, and Debt [1]

(Billions of dollars; annual data are for December)

Year and month	Money stock measures (monthly data are averages of daily figures)						Debt (monthly average, seasonally adjusted)	
	Seasonally adjusted			Not seasonally adjusted			Federal	Non-federal
	M1	M2	M3	M1	M2	M3		
1970	214.4	626.5	677.1	220.1	627.8	678.2	298.9	1 118.0
1971	228.3	710.3	776.0	234.5	711.2	776.6	321.0	1 229.6
1972	249.2	802.3	885.9	256.1	803.1	886.2	338.0	1 368.9
1973	262.9	855.5	985.0	270.2	856.5	985.2	345.6	1 546.5
1974	274.2	902.4	1 070.2	281.8	903.8	1 071.1	356.4	1 708.6
1975	287.1	1 016.6	1 171.9	295.3	1 018.3	1 173.8	440.5	1 812.1
1976	306.2	1 152.6	1 312.3	314.5	1 154.1	1 314.2	510.6	1 987.0
1977	330.9	1 271.1	1 472.7	340.0	1 273.8	1 477.0	565.2	2 249.4
1978	357.3	1 366.9	1 646.5	367.9	1 371.8	1 653.5	621.0	2 582.3
1979	381.8	1 474.7	1 810.1	393.2	1 480.2	1 816.4	653.3	2 938.9
1980	408.1	1 600.4	1 996.3	419.5	1 606.2	2 002.2	729.6	3 204.7
1981	436.2	1 756.1	2 254.9	447.0	1 761.8	2 260.1	814.3	3 531.5
1982	474.3	1 911.2	2 460.9	485.8	1 919.8	2 470.0	967.7	3 814.2
1983	520.8	2 127.8	2 699.2	533.3	2 139.1	2 710.9	1 162.3	4 189.2
1984	551.2	2 311.7	2 992.8	564.6	2 324.2	3 007.2	1 354.2	4 794.4
1985	619.4	2 497.4	3 209.8	633.4	2 510.1	3 224.0	1 575.0	5 493.5
1986	724.3	2 734.0	3 501.2	740.0	2 747.3	3 516.1	1 793.2	6 139.9
1987	749.7	2 832.8	3 692.0	765.5	2 845.4	3 705.0	1 943.5	6 730.1
1988	786.3	2 995.8	3 935.2	803.3	3 008.9	3 948.1	2 096.9	7 366.7
1989	792.6	3 159.9	4 091.0	811.0	3 173.7	4 104.1	2 244.9	7 911.9
1990	824.6	3 279.1	4 155.6	843.2	3 292.7	4 167.2	2 487.8	8 335.4
1991	896.7	3 379.8	4 208.6	916.0	3 394.4	4 222.1	2 759.9	8 536.2
1992	1 024.4	3 434.0	4 220.0	1 046.0	3 451.5	4 236.3	3 064.2	8 753.5
1993	1 129.3	3 487.4	4 279.7	1 153.7	3 508.6	4 299.3	3 323.6	9 081.9
1994	1 149.7	3 502.0	4 353.9	1 174.4	3 523.8	4 372.8	3 492.4	9 508.5
1995	1 126.7	3 649.1	4 618.5	1 152.4	3 671.7	4 638.0	3 638.9	10 058.8
1996	1 081.3	3 823.9	4 955.6	1 104.9	3 843.7	4 972.5	3 780.6	10 612.3
1997	1 074.9	4 046.6	5 403.7	1 097.4	4 064.8	5 419.9	3 798.4	11 296.5
1998	1 093.4	4 402.0	5 996.9	1 115.3	4 418.8	6 013.0	3 747.4	12 278.7
1995:								
January	1 150.6	3 507.5	4 377.8	1 159.3	3 511.4	4 380.8	3 504.1	9 545.2
February	1 146.7	3 506.2	4 380.5	1 135.1	3 490.8	4 370.0	3 527.9	9 589.4
March	1 146.5	3 506.4	4 395.4	1 139.1	3 507.6	4 398.3	3 540.0	9 636.6
April	1 149.5	3 516.4	4 418.9	1 160.1	3 538.2	4 435.9	3 543.6	9 688.5
May	1 144.6	3 538.6	4 455.8	1 133.8	3 522.6	4 441.2	3 564.3	9 744.2
June	1 144.2	3 566.5	4 494.2	1 140.8	3 562.4	4 490.4	3 590.5	9 793.2
July	1 146.5	3 586.3	4 524.0	1 145.6	3 587.3	4 520.1	3 608.1	9 827.2
August	1 146.1	3 606.2	4 555.1	1 139.2	3 603.1	4 551.1	3 614.0	9 862.8
September	1 142.3	3 619.1	4 575.8	1 138.4	3 611.7	4 565.1	3 617.2	9 913.3
October	1 136.4	3 628.7	4 593.2	1 132.7	3 619.1	4 586.7	3 627.3	9 964.9
November	1 133.5	3 637.7	4 607.5	1 138.4	3 640.1	4 613.2	3 636.4	10 013.2
December	1 126.7	3 649.1	4 618.5	1 152.4	3 671.7	4 638.0	3 638.9	10 058.8
1996:								
January	1 122.6	3 666.3	4 648.6	1 129.8	3 669.7	4 651.9	3 638.6	10 104.4
February	1 117.5	3 680.1	4 676.3	1 105.3	3 665.2	4 668.4	3 654.9	10 151.5
March	1 122.6	3 705.5	4 708.6	1 117.5	3 712.7	4 720.1	3 679.8	10 193.2
April	1 124.5	3 717.6	4 726.6	1 131.3	3 739.6	4 744.6	3 693.2	10 236.6
May	1 116.3	3 726.8	4 759.5	1 105.5	3 708.2	4 742.9	3 702.4	10 278.9
June	1 115.5	3 742.5	4 785.0	1 114.6	3 739.4	4 781.3	3 711.8	10 328.0
July	1 112.3	3 755.5	4 808.5	1 110.4	3 754.0	4 800.6	3 731.7	10 380.2
August	1 102.2	3 764.6	4 825.9	1 097.4	3 763.4	4 822.2	3 745.2	10 421.8
September	1 095.6	3 774.9	4 853.6	1 091.5	3 766.4	4 840.7	3 747.7	10 468.8
October	1 082.6	3 786.1	4 890.1	1 077.9	3 773.8	4 880.4	3 759.0	10 518.6
November	1 080.5	3 803.4	4 915.5	1 086.6	3 806.3	4 921.4	3 771.9	10 569.2
December	1 081.3	3 823.9	4 955.6	1 104.9	3 843.7	4 972.5	3 780.6	10 612.3
1997:								
January	1 080.5	3 838.8	4 981.1	1 086.6	3 841.0	4 983.8	3 777.3	10 653.9
February	1 076.2	3 848.2	5 012.9	1 065.5	3 836.4	5 009.8	3 780.6	10 704.0
March	1 072.4	3 862.7	5 044.2	1 067.8	3 875.1	5 064.8	3 793.1	10 749.3
April	1 067.5	3 882.4	5 086.5	1 073.4	3 908.3	5 109.0	3 801.3	10 811.3
May	1 063.4	3 892.8	5 108.3	1 053.8	3 873.8	5 092.4	3 792.3	10 869.0
June	1 066.0	3 911.6	5 135.5	1 064.1	3 905.3	5 128.0	3 783.5	10 908.3
July	1 067.6	3 929.1	5 185.8	1 065.6	3 925.1	5 171.6	3 788.3	10 962.8
August	1 072.1	3 961.1	5 232.5	1 069.2	3 960.4	5 226.5	3 792.5	11 024.3
September	1 064.8	3 981.7	5 269.2	1 059.6	3 970.7	5 251.5	3 795.0	11 089.4
October	1 062.1	4 000.2	5 306.1	1 057.6	3 986.7	5 294.3	3 795.1	11 161.1
November	1 067.5	4 023.1	5 352.8	1 074.1	4 025.7	5 358.4	3 793.7	11 232.2
December	1 074.9	4 046.6	5 403.7	1 097.4	4 064.8	5 419.9	3 798.4	11 296.5
1998:								
January	1 073.8	4 071.4	5 448.5	1 079.9	4 073.7	5 452.7	3 796.8	11 361.6
February	1 076.0	4 100.9	5 483.6	1 066.0	4 092.1	5 485.3	3 792.9	11 442.3
March	1 080.6	4 126.2	5 541.9	1 075.7	4 143.6	5 571.3	3 797.2	11 523.1
April	1 082.1	4 155.2	5 586.9	1 087.4	4 186.2	5 616.6	3 791.5	11 605.9
May	1 078.2	4 174.8	5 628.7	1 070.5	4 155.9	5 615.3	3 778.8	11 688.2
June	1 077.8	4 198.6	5 671.3	1 074.7	4 188.7	5 659.0	3 775.8	11 764.1
July	1 075.4	4 216.1	5 691.4	1 073.6	4 209.0	5 669.1	3 772.9	11 846.3
August	1 072.2	4 241.7	5 747.5	1 068.6	4 238.7	5 735.9	3 770.3	11 925.9
September	1 074.7	4 285.5	5 811.0	1 069.9	4 273.4	5 788.2	3 760.0	12 006.5
October	1 080.4	4 326.9	5 873.1	1 076.2	4 311.7	5 858.1	3 750.3	12 100.1
November	1 089.0	4 365.2	5 938.1	1 094.3	4 365.7	5 942.9	3 748.8	12 196.4
December	1 093.4	4 402.0	5 996.9	1 115.3	4 418.8	6 013.0	3 747.4	12 278.7

1. See Notes for definitions of M1, M2, M3, and debt.

Selected Components of the Money Stock

(Billions of dollars; monthly data are averages of daily figures, annual data are for December)

Year and month	Currency	Demand deposits	Other checkable deposits	Overnight RPs	Eurodollars	Money market funds Retail	Money market funds Institutional	Savings deposits	Small time deposits	Large time deposits
						Seasonally adjusted				
1970	48.6	164.7	0.1	3.0	2.4	.....	.....	260.9	151.2	45.1
1971	52.0	175.1	0.2	5.2	2.9	.....	.....	292.2	189.8	57.6
1972	56.2	191.6	0.2	6.6	3.8	.....	.....	321.4	231.7	73.3
1973	60.8	200.3	0.3	12.8	5.8	0.1	.....	326.7	265.8	111.0
1974	67.0	205.1	0.4	14.5	8.5	1.7	0.2	338.6	287.9	144.7
1975	72.8	211.3	0.9	15.0	10.2	2.8	0.5	388.8	337.8	129.7
1976	79.5	221.5	2.7	25.5	15.4	2.5	0.6	453.2	390.7	118.1
1977	87.4	236.4	4.2	33.5	21.9	2.6	1.0	492.2	445.5	145.2
1978	96.0	249.5	8.5	45.2	35.3	6.7	3.5	481.9	520.9	195.6
1979	104.8	256.6	16.8	49.2	52.8	34.9	10.4	423.8	634.2	223.1
1980	115.3	261.2	28.1	58.2	61.5	63.5	16.0	400.2	728.5	260.2
1981	122.5	231.4	78.7	67.8	88.9	152.9	38.2	343.9	823.1	303.9
1982	132.5	234.1	104.1	71.8	104.3	185.9	48.8	400.1	850.9	324.9
1983	146.2	238.5	132.1	97.3	116.6	138.1	40.9	684.9	784.0	316.5
1984	156.1	243.4	147.4	107.3	108.9	167.0	61.8	704.7	888.8	403.2
1985	167.9	266.9	179.8	121.2	104.2	177.1	64.6	815.2	885.7	422.4
1986	180.7	302.8	235.6	145.8	115.7	210.4	85.5	940.9	858.4	420.2
1987	196.9	287.6	259.5	178.0	121.5	224.7	92.7	937.4	921.0	467.0
1988	212.2	287.0	280.9	196.5	131.7	246.1	92.8	926.3	1 037.1	518.3
1989	222.6	278.7	285.1	169.1	109.4	322.3	111.1	893.7	1 151.4	541.5
1990	247.0	276.9	293.7	151.5	103.3	358.0	139.6	923.2	1 173.4	482.1
1991	267.5	289.7	332.5	131.1	92.3	373.1	187.7	1 044.4	1 065.7	417.6
1992	292.5	340.0	384.4	141.6	79.5	354.7	210.5	1 186.7	868.2	354.5
1993	322.0	385.4	414.6	172.6	72.7	357.0	212.5	1 219.1	782.1	334.5
1994	354.2	383.6	404.1	196.4	86.1	385.8	204.7	1 150.0	816.5	364.5
1995	372.3	389.4	356.7	198.7	93.7	455.5	255.9	1 135.1	931.7	421.1
1996	394.1	403.0	276.2	211.3	113.9	522.8	313.3	1 272.3	947.5	493.2
1997	424.5	396.5	246.2	251.7	149.3	602.3	379.9	1 400.2	969.3	576.1
1998	459.2	377.5	248.8	297.8	150.7	751.7	516.2	1 605.0	951.9	630.1
1995:										
January	357.3	384.5	401.1	201.2	89.2	389.2	210.7	1 135.3	832.4	369.2
February	358.4	383.5	397.0	204.2	88.6	389.1	207.2	1 118.1	852.4	374.2
March	362.1	381.6	394.6	203.9	90.8	386.8	215.5	1 097.9	875.1	378.8
April	365.4	380.7	394.8	204.6	93.1	389.7	221.8	1 085.3	891.9	383.0
May	368.1	381.3	386.4	208.3	93.8	399.9	228.7	1 088.6	905.4	386.4
June	367.8	384.5	382.4	205.6	95.0	412.7	237.1	1 097.0	912.5	390.0
July	368.0	386.8	381.8	202.1	97.5	424.3	242.9	1 097.3	918.1	395.2
August	369.0	388.5	378.6	207.2	98.0	434.9	244.8	1 103.6	921.6	398.8
September	369.7	388.6	374.4	206.7	98.5	440.6	248.4	1 112.0	924.2	403.2
October	370.8	390.4	366.2	205.4	96.7	445.5	250.7	1 120.6	926.2	411.7
November	371.4	390.3	363.3	202.3	94.8	450.6	253.8	1 123.7	929.8	419.0
December	372.3	389.4	356.7	198.7	93.7	455.5	255.9	1 135.1	931.7	421.1
1996:										
January	373.2	394.8	346.5	200.4	96.0	460.6	260.7	1 150.6	932.5	425.1
February	372.5	396.9	339.9	201.4	97.8	467.2	268.6	1 161.9	933.5	428.3
March	374.6	402.7	336.9	200.1	97.8	476.9	273.9	1 173.8	932.2	431.3
April	376.2	405.8	334.0	201.6	99.5	479.7	274.8	1 181.6	931.7	433.1
May	377.7	407.6	322.4	215.7	99.3	485.8	276.8	1 193.8	930.9	441.0
June	380.2	410.1	316.1	213.3	101.2	492.6	281.3	1 204.4	930.1	446.6
July	383.0	410.8	309.0	212.2	99.7	497.9	287.6	1 212.9	932.3	453.4
August	385.6	406.0	301.1	210.6	98.1	500.2	293.2	1 225.3	936.9	459.4
September	387.7	405.4	293.4	212.9	100.6	502.6	298.7	1 236.0	940.6	466.5
October	389.8	400.0	284.0	215.8	106.7	508.5	301.2	1 251.2	943.9	480.3
November	391.8	402.6	277.9	212.7	108.2	513.6	306.9	1 263.0	946.4	484.2
December	394.1	403.0	276.2	211.3	113.9	522.8	313.3	1 272.3	947.5	493.2
1997:										
January	396.4	402.5	273.6	212.8	116.5	527.7	313.6	1 281.9	948.8	499.4
February	398.7	401.4	268.1	216.9	119.8	533.1	322.4	1 288.7	950.1	505.6
March	401.5	400.9	261.9	215.2	124.0	540.3	329.6	1 298.9	951.1	512.6
April	403.4	397.1	258.9	219.1	127.6	549.8	331.9	1 311.7	953.4	525.6
May	406.4	396.1	252.7	219.3	133.3	551.5	335.7	1 320.0	958.1	527.3
June	408.6	398.0	251.0	219.1	130.1	556.4	341.7	1 327.5	961.7	533.1
July	410.9	399.1	248.4	226.6	132.3	562.9	349.4	1 334.1	964.5	548.4
August	413.0	401.3	248.6	228.8	135.9	575.9	355.7	1 347.0	966.1	551.2
September	415.5	392.3	248.4	226.0	137.9	584.9	362.9	1 364.8	967.2	560.7
October	417.9	389.6	246.3	238.5	135.5	589.9	368.0	1 380.0	968.3	563.8
November	421.2	393.2	245.3	249.2	139.9	598.4	370.6	1 388.6	968.6	570.1
December	424.5	396.5	246.2	251.7	149.3	602.3	379.9	1 400.2	969.3	576.1
1998:										
January	427.0	392.8	246.3	258.8	150.0	612.9	385.9	1 413.9	970.8	582.4
February	430.0	392.3	246.1	253.5	145.4	626.3	391.3	1 428.4	970.0	592.4
March	432.1	391.0	249.8	267.4	141.8	637.3	399.8	1 439.4	968.9	606.7
April	434.2	389.2	250.9	268.0	141.9	646.3	414.4	1 459.2	967.6	607.5
May	436.4	387.8	246.2	269.1	145.4	658.4	426.9	1 472.3	966.0	612.6
June	439.2	384.7	245.9	268.0	146.3	669.7	437.7	1 485.9	965.2	620.7
July	442.3	379.3	245.3	270.7	149.2	672.5	441.9	1 505.8	962.4	613.6
August	444.8	374.8	244.0	277.6	153.5	687.2	454.5	1 522.5	959.8	620.2
September	449.6	374.4	242.4	282.0	154.4	708.4	467.8	1 543.8	958.6	621.3
October	453.3	374.7	244.2	282.6	155.5	725.5	486.7	1 563.1	957.9	621.5
November	456.5	377.0	247.6	289.2	154.5	737.9	503.8	1 582.6	955.7	625.4
December	459.2	377.5	248.8	297.8	150.7	751.7	516.2	1 605.0	951.9	630.1

Aggregate Reserves of Depository Institutions and Monetary Base [1]

(Millions of dollars, adjusted for seasonality and changes in reserve requirements)

Year and month	Reserves				Monetary base
	Total	Non-borrowed	Non-borrowed plus extended credit	Required	
1970	14 558	14 225	14 225	14 309	65 013
1971	15 230	15 104	15 104	15 049	69 108
1972	16 645	15 595	15 595	16 361	75 167
1973	17 021	15 723	15 723	16 717	81 073
1974	17 550	16 823	16 970	17 292	87 535
1975	17 822	17 692	17 704	17 556	93 887
1976	18 388	18 335	18 335	18 115	101 515
1977	18 990	18 420	18 420	18 800	110 324
1978	19 753	18 885	18 885	19 521	120 445
1979	20 720	19 248	19 248	20 279	131 143
1980	22 015	20 325	20 328	21 501	142 004
1981	22 443	21 807	21 956	22 124	149 021
1982	23 600	22 966	23 152	23 100	160 127
1983	25 367	24 593	24 595	24 806	175 467
1984	26 912	23 726	26 330	26 078	187 236
1985	31 558	30 239	30 739	30 495	203 552
1986	38 826	37 999	38 302	37 653	223 426
1987	38 896	38 119	38 602	37 877	239 850
1988	40 435	38 719	39 963	39 374	256 888
1989	40 469	40 204	40 224	39 528	267 701
1990	41 747	41 422	41 445	40 083	293 240
1991	45 493	45 301	45 301	44 504	317 512
1992	54 388	54 265	54 265	53 235	350 865
1993	60 530	60 448	60 448	59 460	386 451
1994	59 419	59 210	59 210	58 260	418 072
1995	56 454	56 197	56 197	55 164	434 098
1996	50 162	50 008	50 008	48 746	451 373
1997	46 861	46 537	46 537	45 176	478 877
1998	44 902	44 785	44 785	43 319	512 321
1995:					
January	59 403	59 267	59 271	58 064	420 944
February	58 662	58 603	58 603	57 701	421 660
March	58 229	58 160	58 160	57 415	424 768
April	57 994	57 883	57 883	57 241	428 042
May	57 665	57 515	57 515	56 791	430 731
June	57 393	57 121	57 121	56 411	430 333
July	57 840	57 469	57 469	56 736	430 798
August	57 578	57 296	57 296	56 573	431 439
September	57 334	57 057	57 057	56 366	431 797
October	56 734	56 489	56 489	55 649	432 563
November	56 311	56 106	56 106	55 357	432 960
December	56 454	56 197	56 197	55 164	434 098
1996:					
January	55 881	55 843	55 843	54 417	434 625
February	54 636	54 601	54 601	53 779	432 706
March	55 309	55 287	55 287	54 169	435 905
April	55 179	55 089	55 089	54 056	437 192
May	54 040	53 912	53 912	53 134	437 876
June	54 136	53 750	53 750	53 027	440 191
July	53 387	53 019	53 019	52 369	442 703
August	52 182	51 848	51 848	51 223	444 768
September	51 306	50 939	50 939	50 259	446 073
October	50 036	49 749	49 749	49 030	446 708
November	49 779	49 565	49 565	48 727	448 465
December	50 162	50 008	50 008	48 746	451 373
1997:					
January	49 676	49 631	49 631	48 453	453 122
February	48 719	48 677	48 677	47 688	454 528
March	47 852	47 695	47 695	46 686	456 534
April	47 341	47 081	47 081	46 332	458 256
May	46 635	46 392	46 392	45 372	460 100
June	46 900	46 533	46 533	45 586	462 511
July	46 737	46 328	46 328	45 520	464 900
August	46 907	46 309	46 309	45 652	466 928
September	46 224	45 787	45 787	44 923	469 180
October	45 959	45 689	45 689	44 544	471 568
November	46 424	46 271	46 271	44 755	475 364
December	46 861	46 537	46 537	45 176	478 877
1998:					
January	46 680	46 470	46 470	44 887	481 483
February	45 744	45 686	45 686	44 211	483 250
March	45 854	45 813	45 813	44 503	485 295
April	46 119	46 047	46 047	44 731	487 571
May	45 516	45 363	45 363	44 243	489 571
June	45 410	45 159	45 159	43 794	492 314
July	44 895	44 637	44 637	43 524	494 736
August	44 983	44 712	44 712	43 453	497 869
September	44 540	44 290	44 290	42 846	502 038
October	44 405	44 231	44 231	42 831	505 843
November	44 497	44 414	44 414	42 873	509 144
December	44 902	44 785	44 785	43 319	512 321

1. Monthly data are averages of daily figures. Annual data are for December.

Assets and Liabilities of Commercial Banks [1]

(All commercial banks in the United States—Billions of dollars, seasonally adjusted)

Year and month	Assets — Bank credit								
		Securities in bank credit			Loans and leases in bank credit				
							Real estate		
	Total	Total	U.S. government securities	Other securities	Total	Commercial and industrial	Total	Revolving home equity	Other
1970	.....	.....	.....	.....	.....	.....	.....	.....	.....
1971	.....	.....	.....	.....	.....	.....	.....	.....	.....
1972	.....	.....	.....	.....	.....	.....	.....	.....	.....
1973	660.4	180.5	90.5	90.1	479.9	167.3	123.3	.....	123.3
1974	725.4	185.6	88.7	96.9	539.8	198.7	136.7	.....	136.7
1975	758.8	221.8	119.8	102.1	537.0	188.9	141.9	.....	141.9
1976	818.5	245.3	140.1	105.2	573.2	191.5	156.0	.....	156.0
1977	905.7	253.4	140.4	112.9	652.4	211.3	183.8	.....	183.8
1978	1 021.6	259.4	141.7	117.8	762.2	246.2	220.9	.....	220.9
1979	1 133.3	266.6	148.1	118.5	866.7	285.6	252.6	.....	252.6
1980	1 226.4	300.8	174.3	126.4	925.7	317.1	272.9	.....	272.9
1981	1 319.0	313.8	182.4	131.4	1 005.2	356.0	294.5	.....	294.5
1982	1 424.0	339.1	204.5	134.6	1 085.0	397.5	309.1	.....	309.1
1983	1 573.7	402.9	261.7	141.2	1 170.8	419.7	337.5	.....	337.5
1984	1 743.5	406.8	263.1	143.7	1 336.7	480.1	383.4	.....	383.4
1985	1 925.2	453.8	272.7	181.0	1 471.4	505.7	432.3	.....	432.3
1986	2 106.5	506.5	310.4	196.2	1 599.9	541.9	500.8	.....	500.8
1987	2 252.0	534.0	338.6	195.4	1 718.0	570.5	590.7	31.0	559.7
1988	2 429.9	562.6	367.6	195.0	1 867.3	611.4	674.7	42.0	632.8
1989	2 604.1	585.2	400.8	184.3	2 019.0	643.0	770.6	52.8	717.9
1990	2 750.8	634.3	456.4	177.9	2 116.5	645.8	857.9	65.4	792.4
1991	2 856.9	746.0	566.5	179.5	2 110.9	624.3	883.7	73.3	810.3
1992	2 955.5	841.5	664.8	176.7	2 114.1	600.6	906.0	77.4	828.6
1993	3 115.0	915.0	730.3	184.7	2 200.0	591.3	947.7	77.0	870.6
1994	3 321.6	939.8	721.7	218.1	2 381.8	651.4	1 011.0	79.3	931.7
1995	3 604.8	984.7	701.8	282.9	2 620.1	723.1	1 090.0	83.2	1 006.8
1996	3 761.5	978.7	699.2	279.5	2 782.7	787.1	1 141.8	89.4	1 052.4
1997	4 103.1	1 085.9	748.1	337.8	3 017.2	854.5	1 247.2	103.3	1 143.8
1998	4 545.6	1 225.8	791.7	434.1	3 319.8	951.7	1 337.8	102.4	1 235.4
1995:									
January	3 343.3	940.5	722.4	218.2	2 402.8	659.8	1 020.0	79.7	940.3
February	3 362.2	935.3	718.3	216.9	2 426.9	671.4	1 028.3	79.9	948.4
March	3 391.9	944.5	710.2	234.3	2 447.4	677.4	1 034.1	80.0	954.0
April	3 467.4	995.2	704.0	291.3	2 472.2	686.7	1 041.5	80.6	960.9
May	3 484.3	984.4	703.3	281.1	2 499.9	695.1	1 047.3	81.3	966.0
June	3 506.9	980.7	703.3	277.4	2 526.2	700.5	1 058.2	82.0	976.2
July	3 532.5	982.8	700.3	282.5	2 549.7	705.7	1 068.1	82.4	985.6
August	3 553.5	990.4	707.5	282.9	2 563.2	710.1	1 073.1	82.6	990.5
September	3 575.6	994.8	705.7	289.0	2 580.8	712.9	1 077.8	82.6	995.3
October	3 581.0	991.8	707.1	284.7	2 589.2	714.5	1 083.5	82.7	1 000.8
November	3 594.0	987.3	707.0	280.3	2 606.8	720.9	1 088.1	83.0	1 005.1
December	3 604.8	984.7	701.8	282.9	2 620.1	723.1	1 090.0	83.2	1 006.8
1996:									
January	3 625.1	984.2	695.7	288.5	2 640.9	728.7	1 095.5	83.7	1 011.8
February	3 644.4	994.5	707.0	287.5	2 649.9	732.2	1 099.4	83.9	1 015.5
March	3 639.4	984.4	699.1	285.3	2 655.0	734.2	1 103.2	84.0	1 019.2
April	3 657.5	985.4	695.7	289.6	2 672.1	739.3	1 104.0	84.1	1 019.9
May	3 661.8	992.8	700.4	292.4	2 669.1	744.7	1 105.9	84.0	1 022.0
June	3 673.1	987.5	699.6	287.9	2 685.6	748.2	1 110.1	83.8	1 026.3
July	3 687.4	986.6	702.9	283.7	2 700.8	753.4	1 111.6	84.5	1 027.1
August	3 684.7	979.0	701.4	277.7	2 705.6	757.1	1 117.3	85.5	1 031.9
September	3 698.5	972.8	700.9	271.9	2 725.7	767.4	1 120.7	86.4	1 034.3
October	3 717.2	972.3	701.1	271.2	2 744.9	774.6	1 124.8	87.5	1 037.3
November	3 741.6	977.9	702.3	275.6	2 763.8	780.0	1 133.2	88.4	1 044.8
December	3 761.5	978.7	699.2	279.5	2 782.7	787.1	1 141.8	89.4	1 052.4
1997:									
January	3 799.2	999.1	699.9	299.2	2 800.1	790.7	1 147.4	89.9	1 057.5
February	3 836.6	1 017.9	699.0	318.9	2 818.7	798.2	1 150.3	90.6	1 059.7
March	3 851.8	1 015.0	705.1	309.9	2 836.8	802.7	1 162.3	92.2	1 070.2
April	3 891.0	1 030.7	715.0	315.7	2 860.3	809.9	1 175.9	94.2	1 081.7
May	3 905.0	1 019.3	715.5	303.9	2 885.6	817.0	1 185.5	95.6	1 089.9
June	3 933.5	1 020.0	722.6	297.3	2 913.5	821.7	1 198.3	97.7	1 100.6
July	3 975.1	1 043.2	726.7	316.5	2 932.0	824.0	1 205.5	98.9	1 106.6
August	3 989.7	1 042.2	722.0	320.1	2 947.5	833.0	1 210.9	99.8	1 111.1
September	4 005.4	1 041.7	728.6	313.1	2 963.7	839.3	1 221.1	100.9	1 120.2
October	4 039.1	1 052.1	735.3	316.8	2 987.0	844.5	1 231.7	101.7	1 129.9
November	4 079.1	1 077.9	744.5	333.4	3 001.1	848.4	1 240.9	102.5	1 138.4
December	4 103.1	1 085.9	748.1	337.8	3 017.2	854.5	1 247.2	103.3	1 143.8
1998:									
January	4 157.9	1 111.3	760.7	350.5	3 046.7	866.9	1 248.3	104.0	1 144.3
February	4 186.3	1 113.0	765.4	347.6	3 073.3	873.9	1 262.5	104.0	1 158.5
March	4 216.1	1 125.2	777.2	347.9	3 090.9	877.9	1 275.1	104.0	1 171.1
April	4 218.9	1 112.7	764.3	348.4	3 106.2	876.6	1 280.7	104.1	1 176.6
May	4 240.8	1 125.1	768.8	356.3	3 115.7	887.6	1 277.3	103.8	1 173.5
June	4 265.5	1 125.8	759.2	366.6	3 139.7	900.9	1 277.8	103.6	1 174.2
July	4 285.2	1 134.0	763.6	370.3	3 151.2	906.3	1 282.3	103.5	1 178.8
August	4 344.4	1 159.4	776.0	383.4	3 185.0	914.2	1 291.9	103.3	1 188.6
September	4 392.5	1 177.6	771.6	406.1	3 214.9	920.9	1 294.1	103.6	1 190.5
October	4 487.9	1 218.7	776.7	441.9	3 269.2	942.9	1 301.1	102.4	1 198.7
November	4 527.1	1 221.9	790.0	431.9	3 305.1	954.0	1 323.5	102.6	1 220.9
December	4 545.6	1 225.8	791.7	434.1	3 319.8	951.7	1 337.8	102.4	1 235.4

1. Monthly data are prorated averages of Wednesday figures. Annual data are for December.

Assets and Liabilities of Commercial Banks [1]—*Continued*

(All commercial banks in the United states—Billions of dollars, seasonally adjusted)

Year and month	Assets—*Continued*						
	Bank credit—*Continued*			Interbank loans	Cash assets	Other assets	Total assets
	Loans and leases in bank credit—*Continued*						
	Consumer	Security	Other				
1970	.....	.....	.....	.....	.....	.....	.....
1971	. .....	. .....	.....	.....	.....	.....	.....
1972	.....	.....	.....	.....	.....	.....	.....
1973	100.9	10.9	77.5	35.3	90.2	36.4	816.5
1974	104.8	10.4	89.2	39.4	98.9	48.5	905.7
1975	107.4	12.4	86.4	37.5	101.0	51.0	942.0
1976	119.0	17.3	89.5	45.8	110.7	46.7	1 014.8
1977	141.4	20.3	95.5	53.0	119.7	49.1	1 120.1
1978	168.3	19.0	107.9	56.5	138.1	59.8	1 267.6
1979	188.8	17.1	122.6	74.8	162.4	78.9	1 440.0
1980	182.1	16.8	136.8	100.6	177.9	99.8	1 594.3
1981	185.0	19.6	150.1	109.5	168.3	134.8	1 720.4
1982	190.9	22.9	164.4	116.9	187.0	146.8	1 862.3
1983	215.7	25.5	172.4	109.3	188.2	150.7	2 008.9
1984	256.6	32.7	183.8	126.9	192.3	157.8	2 204.3
1985	296.6	40.8	196.0	149.8	206.6	161.7	2 424.3
1986	316.1	36.7	204.4	164.1	226.4	175.9	2 650.6
1987	330.2	34.9	191.7	162.8	214.3	177.0	2 766.5
1988	354.9	39.8	186.6	160.8	222.1	189.8	2 940.4
1989	375.4	40.4	189.5	182.7	226.7	195.0	3 142.8
1990	380.9	44.5	187.5	195.0	212.5	209.0	3 302.5
1991	363.9	53.8	185.3	168.3	212.5	211.9	3 385.8
1992	356.2	63.9	187.3	163.3	212.0	213.0	3 481.6
1993	387.7	88.1	185.2	154.4	218.4	218.3	3 647.3
1994	448.2	77.7	193.6	175.6	209.0	227.5	3 877.3
1995	491.3	84.6	231.1	201.2	223.5	246.9	4 219.8
1996	512.5	76.8	264.5	204.5	231.9	266.1	4 407.6
1997	502.5	97.0	316.0	210.3	262.5	298.8	4 818.0
1998	497.8	150.4	382.0	217.7	252.7	341.5	5 299.6
1995:							
January	452.5	74.8	195.7	179.7	215.9	234.3	3 916.4
February	455.8	73.6	197.8	180.1	213.7	236.5	3 935.7
March	460.7	74.3	201.0	181.9	211.5	240.3	3 969.0
April	466.3	77.1	200.6	180.1	208.5	230.8	4 029.9
May	469.3	83.5	204.7	184.4	210.6	231.0	4 053.2
June	473.8	85.6	208.1	188.4	212.7	230.5	4 081.6
July	477.5	84.9	213.6	195.2	216.6	232.0	4 119.5
August	481.6	83.3	215.1	191.3	212.5	231.4	4 131.9
September	484.6	86.6	218.8	194.2	217.3	236.7	4 166.9
October	485.5	84.3	221.4	198.5	222.5	239.9	4 185.2
November	488.1	85.8	223.8	195.1	215.3	241.3	4 189.2
December	491.3	84.6	231.1	201.2	223.5	246.9	4 219.8
1996:							
January	493.1	86.0	237.7	207.6	229.0	247.7	4 252.6
February	493.8	85.9	238.6	194.8	219.3	247.3	4 249.1
March	496.3	81.7	239.5	201.4	216.6	246.2	4 246.7
April	499.9	84.0	244.8	205.8	221.2	247.0	4 274.5
May	498.1	76.1	244.3	207.8	220.6	248.8	4 282.4
June	502.4	77.7	247.2	206.4	220.2	253.4	4 296.5
July	506.5	77.0	252.2	200.5	223.3	258.6	4 312.7
August	507.2	71.9	252.1	200.9	224.5	262.7	4 315.7
September	510.1	73.6	253.8	205.9	226.5	263.8	4 337.5
October	511.3	74.6	259.6	203.6	226.2	256.0	4 346.4
November	511.9	76.5	262.3	209.8	230.4	263.8	4 389.2
December	512.5	76.8	264.5	204.5	231.9	266.1	4 407.6
1997:							
January	514.2	79.8	268.0	202.5	228.5	265.0	4 439.1
February	513.8	82.6	273.9	207.8	230.6	270.6	4 489.6
March	510.2	83.9	277.6	213.9	234.1	278.0	4 521.8
April	508.2	88.2	278.1	209.5	241.0	278.5	4 563.6
May	510.6	87.7	285.0	216.5	240.2	284.5	4 589.8
June	513.4	91.1	289.1	189.5	244.4	286.1	4 596.9
July	513.9	92.6	296.0	182.6	244.3	286.5	4 631.9
August	513.4	92.9	297.4	189.3	255.9	287.6	4 665.8
September	509.3	94.8	299.1	193.7	252.1	287.1	4 681.7
October	504.0	102.5	304.3	194.8	261.5	293.5	4 732.3
November	504.0	98.0	309.8	197.8	272.7	300.7	4 793.6
December	502.5	97.0	316.0	210.3	262.5	298.8	4 818.0
1998:							
January	498.9	116.6	316.0	204.8	258.8	303.0	4 867.9
February	496.4	119.5	321.0	203.4	263.4	307.3	4 903.8
March	495.3	114.7	327.9	215.0	272.1	303.1	4 949.4
April	498.7	116.5	333.7	213.0	266.8	308.7	4 950.2
May	497.5	120.1	333.3	203.9	249.1	313.9	4 950.5
June	495.7	127.8	337.5	218.8	249.9	310.0	4 986.7
July	489.3	130.6	342.8	212.7	246.4	314.7	5 001.7
August	488.5	136.2	354.2	206.1	249.5	320.2	5 063.0
September	491.3	141.7	366.8	217.0	252.3	327.5	5 131.8
October	493.1	156.5	375.6	219.2	246.1	329.0	5 224.3
November	496.1	150.0	381.5	217.9	251.2	339.7	5 277.9
December	497.8	150.4	382.0	217.7	252.7	341.5	5 299.6

1. Monthly data are prorated averages of Wedensday figures. Annual data are for December.

Assets and Liabilities of Commercial Banks [1]—*Continued*

(All commercial banks in the United states—Billions of dollars, seasonally adjusted)

Year and month	Liabilities											Residual (assets less liabilities)
	Deposits					Borrowings			Net due foreign offices	Other liabilities	Total liabilities	
	Total	Trans-action	Nontransaction			Total	From banks in the U.S.	From nonbanks in the U.S.				
			Total	Large time	Other							
1970	.....	.....	.....	.....	.....	.....	.....	.....	.....	.....	.....	.....
1971	.....	.....	.....	.....	.....	.....	.....	.....	.....	.....	.....	.....
1972	.....	.....	.....	.....	.....	.....	.....	.....	.....	.....	.....	.....
1973	650.5	280.2	370.3	114.7	255.6	71.0	44.1	26.9	3.8	26.8	752.1	64.4
1974	717.4	288.5	428.9	137.9	291.0	76.6	47.8	28.8	3.9	35.6	833.6	72.1
1975	757.9	295.8	462.0	143.3	318.8	72.5	45.3	27.3	2.1	32.6	865.0	76.9
1976	813.7	316.6	497.1	142.9	354.2	96.5	56.8	39.8	1.7	27.7	939.7	75.2
1977	897.3	344.9	552.3	161.2	391.1	113.7	62.8	50.9	2.0	31.5	1 044.5	75.7
1978	994.3	371.4	622.9	191.4	431.5	141.6	74.2	67.5	6.9	46.3	1 189.1	78.5
1979	1 067.0	391.0	676.0	213.2	462.8	176.1	96.9	79.2	15.5	77.4	1 336.0	104.0
1980	1 178.9	406.9	772.1	254.3	517.8	212.2	117.7	94.4	13.9	94.1	1 499.1	95.1
1981	1 245.1	343.7	901.4	302.1	599.3	255.9	142.1	113.8	-0.9	98.3	1 598.4	122.0
1982	1 362.8	347.6	1 015.2	333.6	681.6	281.7	153.6	128.1	-10.9	108.8	1 742.5	119.9
1983	1 475.9	356.2	1 119.7	326.2	793.6	281.6	148.5	133.1	-7.8	117.1	1 866.8	142.2
1984	1 605.5	464.7	1 140.8	345.7	795.0	314.8	164.7	150.1	-6.5	122.2	2 036.0	168.3
1985	1 751.6	516.1	1 235.5	363.8	871.7	371.0	191.5	179.4	-1.1	117.7	2 239.2	185.2
1986	1 911.8	598.3	1 313.5	377.9	935.6	408.6	212.4	196.2	3.7	122.6	2 446.7	203.9
1987	1 972.9	586.0	1 386.9	411.7	975.2	425.8	221.4	204.4	23.9	131.5	2 554.1	212.4
1988	2 112.1	607.9	1 504.2	440.4	1 063.8	488.9	251.0	237.9	11.9	136.9	2 749.8	190.5
1989	2 237.1	608.6	1 628.4	473.5	1 155.0	550.6	281.9	268.7	13.4	140.9	2 941.9	200.8
1990	2 338.4	610.5	1 727.9	448.6	1 279.2	574.2	295.5	278.7	38.1	138.8	3 089.5	213.0
1991	2 465.8	649.2	1 816.7	444.9	1 371.8	496.1	221.8	274.3	42.6	133.5	3 138.0	247.8
1992	2 499.7	744.9	1 754.8	379.1	1 375.7	498.3	212.6	285.7	70.9	130.2	3 199.1	282.5
1993	2 533.2	815.9	1 717.3	347.1	1 370.2	535.4	213.6	321.8	129.2	133.2	3 331.0	316.3
1994	2 537.4	799.2	1 738.2	356.8	1 381.4	622.1	256.2	365.8	226.0	177.0	3 562.4	314.8
1995	2 668.6	774.4	1 894.2	415.9	1 478.3	696.9	287.4	409.5	259.5	238.8	3 863.8	356.0
1996	2 864.5	713.4	2 151.1	534.5	1 616.6	727.9	300.4	427.5	238.1	222.1	4 052.7	354.9
1997	3 119.0	686.8	2 432.2	652.7	1 779.4	854.4	308.2	546.2	203.2	255.1	4 431.7	386.3
1998	3 338.3	671.6	2 666.7	717.4	1 949.3	1 021.4	322.6	698.8	214.1	306.2	4 880.1	419.5
1995:												
January	2 547.8	801.6	1 746.1	362.2	1 383.9	632.9	264.9	368.0	244.8	171.8	3 597.3	319.1
February	2 554.7	801.1	1 753.6	371.6	1 382.0	645.4	267.9	377.5	244.5	176.5	3 621.1	314.5
March	2 554.3	793.4	1 760.9	379.8	1 381.1	651.0	266.6	384.4	244.9	199.6	3 649.9	319.1
April	2 558.4	786.9	1 771.5	385.1	1 386.5	668.0	273.4	394.5	240.6	231.7	3 698.7	331.1
May	2 576.0	785.2	1 790.8	390.2	1 400.6	676.5	279.2	397.3	240.1	227.7	3 720.4	332.8
June	2 598.3	784.7	1 813.6	394.4	1 419.2	683.0	281.3	401.7	244.6	223.4	3 749.3	332.3
July	2 621.8	793.3	1 828.5	398.1	1 430.5	701.4	288.5	412.9	239.1	223.8	3 786.1	333.4
August	2 630.4	787.7	1 842.7	404.7	1 438.0	696.8	284.3	412.5	248.0	225.8	3 801.1	330.8
September	2 641.4	785.8	1 855.6	409.8	1 445.8	695.2	286.4	408.7	252.4	236.0	3 825.0	341.9
October	2 656.0	785.3	1 870.7	417.4	1 453.3	692.1	286.3	405.8	257.5	233.8	3 839.4	345.8
November	2 651.8	771.2	1 880.7	418.8	1 461.9	685.0	285.5	399.6	262.1	237.2	3 836.2	353.0
December	2 668.6	774.4	1 894.2	415.9	1 478.3	696.9	287.4	409.5	259.5	238.8	3 863.8	356.0
1996:												
January	2 697.8	777.4	1 920.4	417.8	1 502.5	688.7	286.0	402.6	270.5	237.1	3 894.0	358.6
February	2 698.2	767.5	1 930.7	422.3	1 508.4	692.5	283.7	408.9	271.3	237.0	3 899.1	350.0
March	2 705.7	763.8	1 941.9	424.6	1 517.3	695.1	286.5	408.6	263.6	228.8	3 893.3	353.4
April	2 711.1	760.6	1 950.6	429.4	1 521.2	706.9	290.8	416.0	260.6	231.0	3 909.5	365.0
May	2 721.8	755.6	1 966.2	438.9	1 527.3	711.6	290.7	420.9	255.6	225.7	3 914.7	367.7
June	2 730.6	750.1	1 980.5	442.5	1 537.9	716.2	291.5	424.7	255.0	230.7	3 932.5	363.9
July	2 747.4	743.9	2 003.6	449.4	1 554.1	719.4	291.6	427.8	257.8	231.7	3 956.3	356.4
August	2 763.1	740.3	2 022.8	455.3	1 567.5	722.4	293.4	429.0	247.0	226.1	3 958.6	357.1
September	2 776.0	726.5	2 049.5	470.0	1 579.5	723.3	294.4	428.9	250.5	221.8	3 971.5	366.0
October	2 819.5	722.1	2 097.4	515.3	1 582.0	719.1	290.7	428.4	256.4	204.6	3 999.6	346.8
November	2 838.7	718.0	2 120.7	522.3	1 598.4	736.7	297.2	439.5	246.7	214.2	4 036.3	352.9
December	2 864.5	713.4	2 151.1	534.5	1 616.6	727.9	300.4	427.5	238.1	222.1	4 052.7	354.9
1997:												
January	2 877.1	706.5	2 170.7	544.3	1 626.4	734.2	298.4	435.8	237.9	237.0	4 086.2	352.9
February	2 900.6	700.5	2 200.1	560.4	1 639.7	750.6	299.4	451.2	231.9	254.2	4 137.3	352.3
March	2 920.9	693.9	2 227.0	569.2	1 657.7	764.5	308.1	456.4	224.6	245.6	4 155.5	366.4
April	2 944.2	693.8	2 250.3	585.9	1 664.4	792.6	317.8	474.8	220.9	244.8	4 202.4	361.1
May	2 944.0	689.5	2 254.5	584.8	1 669.7	792.3	314.4	477.9	235.4	245.8	4 217.5	372.3
June	2 975.0	690.4	2 284.7	597.5	1 687.1	772.7	288.3	484.4	228.9	247.7	4 224.3	372.6
July	3 016.3	690.7	2 325.7	613.0	1 712.6	775.1	283.7	491.5	224.2	260.2	4 275.8	356.0
August	3 042.7	700.7	2 342.0	621.8	1 720.1	789.2	294.8	494.4	214.6	261.6	4 308.2	357.6
September	3 052.7	684.1	2 368.6	630.2	1 738.4	804.0	298.1	506.0	211.4	244.4	4 312.6	369.1
October	3 070.8	686.9	2 383.9	638.1	1 745.8	830.9	296.4	534.6	195.9	249.8	4 347.4	384.9
November	3 106.8	693.3	2 413.5	651.0	1 762.5	846.0	301.8	544.2	192.6	258.2	4 403.6	389.9
December	3 119.0	686.8	2 432.2	652.7	1 779.4	854.4	308.2	546.2	203.2	255.1	4 431.7	386.3
1998:												
January	3 127.6	677.8	2 449.8	654.6	1 795.2	860.0	293.4	566.6	232.4	263.6	4 483.6	384.4
February	3 167.3	684.1	2 483.2	668.3	1 814.8	865.3	295.2	570.1	216.5	267.2	4 516.3	387.5
March	3 197.5	689.8	2 507.6	687.0	1 820.6	889.9	306.4	583.5	205.4	263.1	4 555.8	393.6
April	3 202.7	688.5	2 514.2	688.3	1 825.9	906.8	305.7	601.1	185.6	263.4	4 558.5	391.7
May	3 204.2	683.5	2 520.7	690.7	1 830.0	898.2	283.5	614.7	175.5	266.2	4 544.2	406.3
June	3 224.5	679.7	2 544.8	702.1	1 842.7	905.9	293.0	612.9	180.4	271.3	4 582.0	404.7
July	3 213.3	668.0	2 545.3	687.0	1 858.3	912.5	294.0	618.4	195.8	281.1	4 602.6	399.0
August	3 242.4	669.2	2 573.2	698.1	1 875.0	915.8	296.0	619.8	207.6	295.3	4 661.0	402.0
September	3 264.8	675.3	2 589.5	702.7	1 886.8	944.1	305.0	639.1	206.4	302.8	4 718.1	413.7
October	3 287.6	673.0	2 614.6	714.8	1 899.8	983.4	315.5	667.9	221.0	316.5	4 808.4	415.8
November	3 322.7	670.2	2 652.5	726.1	1 926.4	1 016.4	324.1	692.4	214.5	303.2	4 856.9	421.0
December	3 338.3	671.6	2 666.7	717.4	1 949.3	1 021.4	322.6	698.8	214.1	306.2	4 880.1	419.5

1. Monthly data are prorated averages of Wedensday figures. Annual data are for December.

Credit Market Debt Outstanding and Delinquency Rates

(Billions of dollars, end of period, not seasonally adjusted)

Year and quarter	Total	Credit market debt outstanding — Owed by:							
		Domestic financial sectors			Domestic nonfinancial sectors				
						Federal government			
		Total	Federal government-related	Private	Total	Total	Treasury securities	Budget agency securities and mortgages	Households
1970	1 602.1	127.8	43.6	84.1	1 422.3	299.5	289.9	9.6	445.4
1971	1 752.9	138.9	49.6	89.3	1 557.5	324.4	315.9	8.5	487.1
1972	1 937.4	162.8	58.0	104.8	1 713.5	339.4	330.1	9.3	544.5
1973	2 175.2	209.8	77.9	131.9	1 898.0	346.3	336.7	9.6	614.1
1974	2 411.9	258.3	98.6	159.7	2 072.3	358.2	348.8	9.4	663.5
1975	2 620.7	260.4	108.9	151.6	2 264.7	443.9	434.9	9.0	715.3
1976	2 908.3	283.9	123.1	160.8	2 508.3	513.1	503.7	9.3	802.3
1977	3 296.8	337.8	145.5	192.3	2 829.6	569.4	561.0	8.4	934.6
1978	3 784.6	412.5	182.6	229.9	3 214.5	621.9	614.9	7.0	1 094.1
1979	4 284.4	504.9	231.8	273.1	3 606.5	657.7	652.1	5.6	1 258.5
1980	4 733.2	578.1	276.6	301.5	3 957.9	735.0	730.0	5.0	1 374.2
1981	5 269.4	682.4	324.0	358.3	4 366.4	820.5	815.9	4.6	1 480.8
1982	5 776.8	778.1	388.9	389.2	4 788.3	981.8	978.1	3.7	1 547.7
1983	6 475.4	882.8	456.7	426.1	5 364.9	1 167.0	1 163.4	3.6	1 706.2
1984	7 439.2	1 052.4	531.2	521.2	6 151.2	1 364.2	1 360.8	3.4	1 918.4
1985	8 627.7	1 258.3	632.7	625.6	7 132.7	1 589.9	1 586.6	3.3	2 235.9
1986	9 804.9	1 593.6	810.3	783.3	7 973.1	1 805.9	1 802.2	3.6	2 489.0
1987	10 816.4	1 896.5	978.6	917.9	8 675.0	1 949.8	1 944.6	5.2	2 743.3
1988	11 855.8	2 145.8	1 098.4	1 047.4	9 457.6	2 104.9	2 082.3	22.6	3 011.3
1989	12 822.5	2 399.3	1 247.9	1 151.4	10 161.0	2 251.2	2 227.0	24.2	3 280.8
1990	13 745.1	2 615.8	1 418.4	1 197.4	10 843.4	2 498.1	2 465.8	32.4	3 554.3
1991	14 395.3	2 786.7	1 564.2	1 222.5	11 307.6	2 776.4	2 757.8	18.6	3 725.4
1992	15 194.7	3 046.3	1 720.0	1 326.3	11 832.7	3 080.4	3 061.6	18.8	3 893.4
1993	16 165.9	3 346.1	1 885.2	1 460.8	12 434.1	3 336.5	3 309.9	26.6	4 110.3
1994	17 209.1	3 822.2	2 172.7	1 649.5	13 016.1	3 492.3	3 465.6	26.8	4 429.1
1995	18 439.3	4 281.3	2 376.8	1 904.5	13 716.1	3 636.8	3 608.5	28.2	4 783.0
1996	19 766.6	4 838.6	2 608.3	2 230.4	14 409.2	3 781.8	3 755.1	26.6	5 100.2
1997	21 157.4	5 457.5	2 821.0	2 636.5	15 130.2	3 804.9	3 778.3	26.5	5 429.5
1998	23 184.9	6 526.1	3 292.0	3 234.1	16 067.3	3 752.2	3 723.7	28.5	5 902.3
1990:									
1st quarter	13 055.9	2 439.1	1 288.2	1 150.9	10 354.5	2 310.0	2 278.4	31.6	3 347.3
2nd quarter	13 274.9	2 487.5	1 330.1	1 157.4	10 514.1	2 347.4	2 314.4	32.9	3 427.1
3rd quarter	13 488.7	2 529.8	1 367.9	1 161.9	10 679.0	2 410.4	2 377.8	32.6	3 496.5
4th quarter	13 745.1	2 615.8	1 418.4	1 197.4	10 843.4	2 498.1	2 465.8	32.4	3 554.3
1991:									
1st quarter	13 849.0	2 645.8	1 452.1	1 193.7	10 903.4	2 548.8	2 522.4	26.4	3 563.6
2nd quarter	14 005.4	2 680.0	1 482.8	1 197.3	11 039.2	2 591.9	2 567.1	24.8	3 626.9
3rd quarter	14 176.0	2 715.6	1 522.9	1 192.7	11 169.6	2 687.2	2 669.6	17.6	3 662.9
4th quarter	14 395.3	2 786.7	1 564.2	1 222.5	11 307.6	2 776.4	2 757.8	18.6	3 725.4
1992:									
1st quarter	14 560.4	2 843.6	1 590.3	1 253.3	11 425.6	2 859.8	2 844.0	15.8	3 738.5
2nd quarter	14 762.9	2 913.2	1 641.6	1 271.5	11 543.0	2 923.3	2 907.5	15.9	3 769.9
3rd quarter	14 986.3	2 988.7	1 683.5	1 305.1	11 683.9	2 998.9	2 980.7	18.1	3 828.3
4th quarter	15 194.7	3 046.3	1 720.0	1 326.3	11 832.7	3 080.4	3 061.6	18.8	3 893.4
1993:									
1st quarter	15 328.1	3 088.9	1 755.8	1 333.1	11 911.9	3 140.2	3 120.6	19.6	3 883.4
2nd quarter	15 568.1	3 137.7	1 774.5	1 363.2	12 086.0	3 201.2	3 180.6	20.6	3 946.5
3rd quarter	15 854.4	3 247.6	1 845.7	1 401.9	12 232.9	3 247.3	3 222.6	24.7	4 024.9
4th quarter	16 165.9	3 346.1	1 885.2	1 460.8	12 434.1	3 336.5	3 309.9	26.6	4 110.3
1994:									
1st quarter	16 402.3	3 474.9	1 963.0	1 511.9	12 565.1	3 387.7	3 361.4	26.3	4 142.7
2nd quarter	16 616.9	3 576.8	2 032.7	1 544.1	12 684.4	3 395.4	3 368.0	27.4	4 226.3
3rd quarter	16 871.5	3 682.1	2 093.3	1 588.9	12 829.5	3 432.3	3 404.1	28.2	4 320.8
4th quarter	17 209.1	3 822.2	2 172.7	1 649.5	13 016.1	3 492.3	3 465.6	26.8	4 429.1
1995:									
1st quarter	17 469.2	3 893.9	2 196.2	1 697.8	13 189.5	3 557.9	3 531.5	26.4	4 467.3
2nd quarter	17 794.4	4 007.2	2 247.1	1 760.1	13 389.9	3 583.5	3 556.7	26.8	4 566.8
3rd quarter	18 086.1	4 130.5	2 300.1	1 830.4	13 535.0	3 603.4	3 576.5	27.0	4 679.0
4th quarter	18 439.3	4 281.3	2 376.8	1 904.5	13 716.1	3 636.8	3 608.5	28.2	4 783.0
1996:									
1st quarter	18 718.7	4 367.6	2 414.0	1 953.6	13 898.3	3 717.2	3 689.6	27.7	4 829.0
2nd quarter	19 062.6	4 555.4	2 489.4	2 066.0	14 043.5	3 693.8	3 665.6	28.2	4 902.1
3rd quarter	19 382.6	4 672.8	2 545.1	2 127.8	14 215.7	3 733.1	3 705.7	27.4	5 006.2
4th quarter	19 766.6	4 838.6	2 608.3	2 230.4	14 409.2	3 781.8	3 755.1	26.6	5 100.2
1997:									
1st quarter	20 013.1	4 920.7	2 634.7	2 286.0	14 568.2	3 829.8	3 803.5	26.3	5 133.5
2nd quarter	20 313.0	5 091.8	2 706.2	2 385.6	14 682.0	3 760.6	3 734.3	26.3	5 223.2
3rd quarter	20 653.6	5 214.2	2 746.5	2 467.7	14 881.7	3 771.2	3 745.1	26.1	5 333.0
4th quarter	21 157.4	5 457.5	2 821.0	2 636.5	15 130.2	3 804.9	3 778.3	26.5	5 429.5
1998:									
1st quarter	21 628.0	5 685.7	2 877.9	2 807.9	15 358.2	3 830.8	3 804.8	25.9	5 487.5
2nd quarter	22 091.0	5 937.4	2 981.2	2 956.2	15 547.0	3 749.0	3 723.4	25.6	5 608.2
3rd quarter	22 561.1	6 206.2	3 121.6	3 084.6	15 754.7	3 720.2	3 694.7	25.5	5 738.5
4th quarter	23 184.9	6 526.1	3 292.0	3 234.1	16 067.3	3 752.2	3 723.7	28.5	5 902.3

Credit Market Debt Outstanding and Delinquency Rates—Continued

(Billions of dollars, except as noted, end of period, not seasonally adjusted)

Year and quarter	Credit market debt outstanding, owed by:					Foreign credit market debt held in United States	Household debt delinquency rates (percent of loans serviced)	
	Domestic nonfinancial sectors—continued							
	Nonfinancial business				State and local governments		Credit card accounts held at banks	Mortgage (90 days)
	Total	Corporate	Nonfarm noncorporate	Farm				
1970	527.2	367.4	112.2	47.6	150.3	52.1	.....	.....
1971	579.2	395.6	132.1	51.6	166.8	56.6	.....	.....
1972	649.0	433.0	159.2	56.8	180.7	61.1	.....	.....
1973	742.8	497.0	180.4	65.4	194.8	67.4	.....	.....
1974	842.4	554.6	214.4	73.3	208.2	81.2	.....	.....
1975	886.2	575.2	228.9	82.1	219.4	95.6	.....	.....
1976	955.2	614.3	248.7	92.2	237.8	116.0	.....	.....
1977	1 069.5	687.6	275.9	105.9	256.2	129.4	.....	.....
1978	1 203.0	761.6	319.1	122.2	295.6	157.6	.....	.....
1979	1 368.2	845.4	377.0	145.7	322.2	172.9	.....	0.51
1980	1 504.3	911.7	431.2	161.5	344.4	197.2	.....	0.62
1981	1 693.0	1 028.6	486.6	177.8	372.1	220.7	.....	0.64
1982	1 845.0	1 117.9	542.6	184.5	413.8	210.4	.....	0.84
1983	2 030.6	1 228.8	613.4	188.4	461.1	227.7	.....	0.86
1984	2 355.0	1 434.8	732.2	188.0	513.6	235.5	.....	0.92
1985	2 629.0	1 612.4	843.1	173.4	677.9	236.7	.....	0.96
1986	2 926.1	1 832.9	937.2	156.0	752.1	238.3	.....	0.99
1987	3 141.0	2 004.5	992.1	144.4	841.0	244.8	.....	0.89
1988	3 446.5	2 214.3	1 098.5	133.7	895.0	252.4	.....	0.83
1989	3 683.8	2 397.0	1 152.5	134.4	945.2	262.2	.....	0.75
1990	3 798.7	2 515.3	1 147.9	135.4	992.3	285.9	.....	0.73
1991	3 728.2	2 463.2	1 130.1	134.8	1 077.7	301.1	5.32	0.81
1992	3 757.1	2 506.5	1 115.3	135.3	1 101.8	315.8	4.68	0.76
1993	3 819.4	2 563.0	1 118.5	137.9	1 167.9	385.8	3.90	0.75
1994	3 972.9	2 708.9	1 121.8	142.2	1 121.7	370.8	3.27	0.72
1995	4 226.1	2 928.6	1 152.4	145.1	1 070.2	441.9	3.93	0.69
1996	4 463.8	3 077.7	1 236.1	149.9	1 063.4	518.9	4.60	0.59
1997	4 776.4	3 306.7	1 313.6	156.1	1 119.5	569.6	4.79	0.61
1998	5 213.0	3 638.2	1 411.9	162.9	1 199.8	591.6	4.75	0.60
1990:								
1st quarter	3 735.9	2 445.2	1 156.9	133.9	961.2	262.3	.....	0.70
2nd quarter	3 766.9	2 475.8	1 156.5	134.6	972.8	273.3	.....	0.70
3rd quarter	3 787.4	2 500.7	1 151.2	135.6	984.7	279.8	.....	0.71
4th quarter	3 798.7	2 515.3	1 147.9	135.4	992.3	285.9	.....	0.73
1991:								
1st quarter	3 785.3	2 508.9	1 144.6	131.8	1 005.8	299.8	5.29	0.78
2nd quarter	3 798.5	2 521.5	1 142.3	134.7	1 021.9	286.1	5.46	0.78
3rd quarter	3 768.3	2 494.6	1 137.3	136.4	1 051.2	290.8	5.39	0.81
4th quarter	3 728.2	2 463.2	1 130.1	134.8	1 077.7	301.1	5.32	0.81
1992:								
1st quarter	3 746.0	2 484.5	1 128.5	133.0	1 081.4	291.2	5.28	0.81
2nd quarter	3 756.0	2 497.1	1 122.9	136.0	1 093.8	306.7	5.06	0.83
3rd quarter	3 748.0	2 494.2	1 118.0	135.8	1 108.8	313.7	4.99	0.82
4th quarter	3 757.1	2 506.5	1 115.3	135.3	1 101.8	315.8	4.68	0.76
1993:								
1st quarter	3 767.5	2 520.1	1 115.3	132.1	1 120.8	327.4	4.60	0.79
2nd quarter	3 789.3	2 538.4	1 114.4	136.5	1 149.0	344.4	4.44	0.78
3rd quarter	3 795.3	2 541.6	1 114.8	138.9	1 165.5	373.9	4.09	0.77
4th quarter	3 819.4	2 563.0	1 118.5	137.9	1 167.9	385.8	3.90	0.75
1994:								
1st quarter	3 869.8	2 616.2	1 117.0	136.6	1 164.9	362.3	3.59	0.77
2nd quarter	3 910.8	2 652.3	1 116.5	142.0	1 151.9	355.7	3.30	0.80
3rd quarter	3 937.2	2 675.6	1 117.6	143.9	1 139.3	359.9	3.24	0.74
4th quarter	3 972.9	2 708.9	1 121.8	142.2	1 121.7	370.8	3.27	0.72
1995:								
1st quarter	4 056.4	2 788.1	1 128.7	139.6	1 107.9	385.8	3.46	0.72
2nd quarter	4 138.3	2 860.2	1 133.4	144.7	1 101.3	397.2	3.70	0.76
3rd quarter	4 174.6	2 888.2	1 139.2	147.3	1 077.9	420.6	3.83	0.79
4th quarter	4 226.1	2 928.6	1 152.4	145.1	1 070.2	441.9	3.93	0.69
1996:								
1st quarter	4 285.5	2 967.8	1 174.7	143.0	1 066.6	452.8	4.03	0.70
2nd quarter	4 378.4	3 033.1	1 196.8	148.5	1 069.2	463.8	4.25	0.63
3rd quarter	4 424.4	3 060.0	1 214.7	149.7	1 051.9	494.1	4.47	0.60
4th quarter	4 463.8	3 077.7	1 236.1	149.9	1 063.4	518.9	4.60	0.59
1997:								
1st quarter	4 535.9	3 138.6	1 249.1	148.2	1 069.0	524.3	4.66	0.57
2nd quarter	4 612.1	3 188.9	1 269.7	153.5	1 086.1	539.2	4.68	0.58
3rd quarter	4 682.0	3 235.5	1 291.3	155.2	1 095.5	557.7	4.68	0.57
4th quarter	4 776.4	3 306.7	1 313.6	156.1	1 119.5	569.6	4.79	0.61
1998:								
1st quarter	4 895.6	3 402.6	1 337.9	155.1	1 144.3	584.1	4.69	0.61
2nd quarter	5 019.0	3 496.7	1 361.8	160.6	1 170.9	606.6	4.70	0.61
3rd quarter	5 117.3	3 569.4	1 385.5	162.5	1 178.8	600.2	4.71	0.61
4th quarter	5 213.0	3 638.2	1 411.9	162.9	1 199.8	591.6	4.75	0.60

Consumer Installment Credit

(Outstanding at end of period, billions of dollars)

Year and month	Seasonally adjusted			Not seasonally adjusted						
	Total	By major credit type		Total	By major holder					
		Revolving	Non-revolving		Commercial banks	Finance companies	Credit unions	Savings institutions	Non-financial businesses	Asset pools [1]
1970	131.5	4.9	126.6	133.7	65.6	27.6	13.0	4.4	23.0	.....
1971	146.9	8.3	138.7	149.2	74.3	29.2	14.8	4.7	26.2	.....
1972	166.2	9.4	156.8	168.8	87.0	31.9	17.0	5.1	27.8	.....
1973	190.1	11.3	178.7	193.0	99.6	35.4	19.6	8.5	29.8	.....
1974	198.9	13.2	185.7	201.9	103.0	36.1	21.9	9.1	31.8	.....
1975	204.0	14.5	189.5	207.0	106.1	32.6	25.7	10.1	32.6	.....
1976	225.8	16.6	209.2	229.0	118.0	33.7	31.2	10.8	35.2	.....
1977	259.3	36.7	222.6	264.4	140.3	37.3	37.6	11.8	37.4	.....
1978	304.7	45.2	259.5	310.4	166.5	44.4	45.2	13.1	41.2	.....
1979	346.9	53.4	293.5	353.1	185.7	55.4	47.4	20.0	44.6	.....
1980	349.4	55.1	294.3	355.4	180.2	62.2	44.1	22.7	46.2	.....
1981	366.7	61.1	305.6	373.1	184.2	70.1	46.7	24.0	48.1	.....
1982	383.6	66.5	317.1	390.3	190.9	75.3	48.8	26.6	48.7	.....
1983	432.6	79.1	353.5	440.3	213.7	83.3	56.1	31.5	55.7	.....
1984	511.7	100.4	411.4	521.0	258.8	89.9	67.9	44.2	60.2	.....
1985	593.2	124.7	468.5	603.8	297.2	111.7	74.0	57.6	63.3	.....
1986	646.8	141.2	505.6	658.2	320.2	134.0	77.1	62.9	64.0	.....
1987	676.4	160.9	515.5	688.6	334.1	140.0	81.0	65.3	68.1	.....
1988	718.8	184.6	534.2	732.0	360.8	144.7	88.3	66.8	71.4	.....
1989	778.8	211.2	567.6	793.3	383.3	138.9	91.7	62.5	69.6	47.3
1990	789.3	238.6	550.7	805.1	382.0	133.4	91.6	49.6	71.9	76.7
1991	777.4	263.7	513.7	794.5	370.2	121.6	90.3	42.2	67.3	103.0
1992	780.3	278.2	502.1	798.3	362.9	118.1	89.4	37.4	70.3	120.3
1993	839.2	310.0	529.2	859.0	395.7	116.1	101.6	37.9	77.2	130.5
1994	960.7	365.6	595.1	983.9	458.8	134.4	119.6	38.5	86.6	146.1
1995	1 096.0	443.2	652.8	1 122.8	502.0	152.1	131.9	40.1	85.1	211.6
1996	1 182.4	499.5	682.9	1 211.6	526.8	152.4	144.1	44.7	77.7	265.8
1997	1 234.1	531.3	702.8	1 264.1	512.6	160.0	152.4	47.2	78.9	313.1
1998	1 300.5	560.7	739.8	1 331.7	508.9	168.5	155.4	51.6	74.9	372.4
1995:										
January	972.8	372.0	600.8	980.7	457.0	137.1	119.6	38.2	82.8	146.1
February	980.4	378.1	602.3	976.1	455.7	134.3	119.7	37.8	80.2	148.2
March	995.0	385.5	609.5	986.2	459.7	135.4	120.6	37.5	79.7	153.3
April	1 004.8	389.7	615.1	996.7	466.4	137.4	121.4	37.8	79.1	154.6
May	1 018.2	398.1	620.1	1 009.3	469.6	139.2	122.8	38.2	80.0	159.6
June	1 029.9	406.1	623.8	1 023.8	471.6	141.3	125.7	38.5	80.5	166.2
July	1 037.8	409.2	628.5	1 031.4	475.3	141.7	126.8	38.9	80.0	168.7
August	1 049.2	417.6	631.6	1 049.0	484.4	145.1	128.7	39.3	78.6	173.0
September	1 065.6	429.1	636.6	1 068.4	485.9	145.7	129.2	39.7	78.3	189.6
October	1 071.2	433.4	637.8	1 074.5	485.6	148.2	130.3	40.1	78.8	191.6
November	1 088.4	436.4	652.0	1 093.7	490.0	148.3	130.9	40.5	77.9	206.0
December	1 096.0	443.2	652.8	1 122.8	502.0	152.1	131.9	40.1	85.1	211.6
1996:										
January	1 103.1	447.1	656.0	1 111.6	493.2	152.1	131.5	40.2	80.7	213.9
February	1 114.4	453.6	660.8	1 109.0	490.4	153.9	131.2	40.4	78.1	215.0
March	1 123.7	459.6	664.1	1 113.2	490.4	152.5	131.5	40.7	76.7	221.4
April	1 132.5	465.9	666.7	1 123.2	498.1	154.3	132.8	41.1	73.7	223.0
May	1 141.9	471.6	670.3	1 131.9	498.3	156.1	134.6	41.6	74.1	227.2
June	1 151.1	475.3	675.7	1 144.5	503.3	153.9	136.1	42.1	72.0	237.2
July	1 161.6	480.8	680.7	1 154.8	507.4	155.8	137.9	43.0	69.9	240.8
August	1 168.1	483.7	684.5	1 168.3	513.4	154.7	140.0	44.0	71.0	245.3
September	1 170.4	485.7	684.8	1 173.5	513.4	154.6	140.9	44.9	68.5	251.2
October	1 172.6	488.8	683.8	1 176.8	517.9	151.4	143.0	44.9	68.0	251.7
November	1 181.0	495.4	685.6	1 186.6	520.0	151.0	143.3	44.8	69.8	257.8
December	1 182.4	499.5	682.9	1 211.6	526.8	152.4	144.1	44.7	77.7	265.8
1997:										
January	1 191.0	504.9	686.1	1 199.6	521.4	153.5	144.2	45.1	73.6	261.8
February	1 196.5	508.5	688.0	1 190.5	512.9	153.3	143.4	45.5	70.6	264.8
March	1 198.0	508.8	689.2	1 186.4	504.3	153.8	143.9	45.9	70.0	268.5
April	1 205.6	511.5	694.0	1 195.6	510.3	152.7	145.6	46.1	69.3	271.6
May	1 210.2	515.0	695.2	1 199.3	511.6	154.9	146.7	46.3	67.7	272.1
June	1 211.7	516.7	695.0	1 205.0	510.7	156.7	147.6	46.5	68.0	275.6
July	1 216.3	522.0	694.3	1 209.6	514.5	156.4	148.8	47.2	67.6	275.2
August	1 220.2	524.1	696.1	1 220.7	516.2	157.2	149.3	47.8	68.6	281.6
September	1 223.6	527.0	696.6	1 226.7	507.5	158.4	150.0	48.5	68.7	293.5
October	1 227.9	528.6	699.3	1 232.5	506.3	156.9	150.6	48.0	68.5	302.2
November	1 228.6	530.6	698.0	1 234.5	506.5	156.4	150.6	47.6	70.5	302.9
December	1 234.1	531.3	702.8	1 264.1	512.6	160.0	152.4	47.2	78.9	313.1
1998:										
January	1 235.4	532.3	703.0	1 244.0	499.3	159.5	151.5	47.1	75.4	311.1
February	1 240.1	534.8	705.4	1 234.2	492.5	155.7	150.8	47.1	72.8	315.3
March	1 248.5	539.5	709.0	1 236.0	492.1	156.5	150.7	47.1	72.7	316.8
April	1 251.3	541.4	709.9	1 241.1	500.1	154.3	151.1	47.5	65.1	323.1
May	1 254.4	541.2	713.2	1 243.1	497.3	153.6	152.2	47.9	65.2	326.9
June	1 263.8	545.2	718.5	1 256.8	491.4	154.3	152.4	48.3	65.3	345.1
July	1 268.9	544.4	724.5	1 262.4	491.4	156.1	153.5	49.0	65.5	346.9
August	1 275.5	548.6	726.8	1 276.4	498.2	159.6	153.6	49.6	66.0	349.4
September	1 283.3	551.9	731.4	1 286.6	497.9	159.1	154.3	50.3	65.5	359.4
October	1 292.8	557.2	735.6	1 297.6	502.1	165.6	155.0	51.0	66.0	358.0
November	1 298.3	556.9	741.4	1 304.5	498.8	166.6	155.2	51.6	66.6	365.6
December	1 300.5	560.7	739.8	1 331.7	508.9	168.5	155.4	51.6	74.9	372.4

1. Outstanding balances of pools upon which securities have been issued; these balances are no longer carried on the balance sheets of the loan originators.

Selected Interest Rates and Bond Yields

(Percent per annum)

Year and month	Short-term rates							
	Federal funds	Federal Reserve discount rate [1]	Eurodollar deposits, one-month	U.S. Treasury bills, 3-month	U.S. Treasury bills, 6-month	Bankers acceptances, 3-month	CDs (secondary market), 3-month	Bank prime rate
1970	7.18	5.95	.....	6.44	6.53	7.27	7.56	7.91
1971	4.66	4.88	6.39	4.34	4.51	4.84	5.01	5.72
1972	4.43	4.50	5.01	4.07	4.47	4.47	4.67	5.25
1973	8.73	6.44	9.28	7.03	7.18	8.08	8.42	8.02
1974	10.50	7.83	10.74	7.88	7.93	9.94	10.24	10.80
1975	5.82	6.25	6.34	5.83	6.12	6.31	6.44	7.86
1976	5.05	5.50	5.26	5.00	5.27	5.08	5.27	6.84
1977	5.54	5.46	5.74	5.26	5.52	5.54	5.64	6.82
1978	7.93	7.46	8.36	7.22	7.58	8.06	8.22	9.06
1979	11.19	10.28	11.67	10.04	10.02	10.99	11.23	12.67
1980	13.36	11.77	13.81	11.62	11.37	12.72	13.07	15.27
1981	16.38	13.42	16.72	14.08	13.78	15.32	15.91	18.87
1982	12.26	11.02	12.78	10.73	11.08	11.89	12.27	14.86
1983	9.09	8.50	9.37	8.62	8.75	8.90	9.07	10.79
1984	10.23	8.80	10.43	9.39	9.77	10.14	10.37	12.04
1985	8.10	7.69	8.12	7.49	7.64	7.92	8.05	9.93
1986	6.81	6.33	6.79	5.97	6.03	6.39	6.52	8.33
1987	6.66	5.66	6.88	5.83	6.05	6.74	6.86	8.20
1988	7.57	6.20	7.69	6.67	6.92	7.56	7.73	9.32
1989	9.22	6.92	9.16	8.12	8.04	8.87	9.09	10.87
1990	8.10	6.98	8.16	7.51	7.47	7.93	8.15	10.01
1991	5.69	5.45	5.82	5.41	5.49	5.71	5.84	8.46
1992	3.52	3.25	3.63	3.46	3.57	3.62	3.68	6.25
1993	3.02	3.00	3.07	3.02	3.14	3.13	3.17	6.00
1994	4.20	3.60	4.34	4.27	4.66	4.62	4.63	7.14
1995	5.83	5.21	5.86	5.51	5.59	5.81	5.92	8.83
1996	5.30	5.02	5.32	5.02	5.09	5.31	5.39	8.27
1997	5.46	5.00	5.52	5.07	5.18	5.54	5.62	8.44
1998	5.35	4.92	5.45	4.81	4.85	5.39	5.47	8.35
1995:								
January	5.53	4.75	5.82	5.81	6.31	6.12	6.24	8.50
February	5.92	5.25	5.99	5.80	6.10	6.05	6.16	9.00
March	5.98	5.25	6.01	5.73	5.91	6.04	6.15	9.00
April	6.05	5.25	6.02	5.67	5.80	6.00	6.11	9.00
May	6.01	5.25	5.98	5.70	5.73	5.91	6.07	9.00
June	6.00	5.25	5.95	5.50	5.46	5.80	5.90	9.00
July	5.85	5.25	5.81	5.47	5.41	5.66	5.77	8.80
August	5.74	5.25	5.78	5.41	5.40	5.68	5.77	8.75
September	5.80	5.25	5.73	5.26	5.28	5.66	5.73	8.75
October	5.76	5.25	5.74	5.30	5.34	5.71	5.79	8.75
November	5.80	5.25	5.72	5.35	5.29	5.64	5.74	8.75
December	5.60	5.25	5.74	5.16	5.15	5.52	5.14	8.65
1996:								
January	5.56	5.24	5.45	5.02	4.97	5.31	5.39	8.50
February	5.22	5.00	5.20	4.87	4.79	5.07	5.15	8.25
March	5.31	5.00	5.26	4.96	4.96	5.21	5.29	8.25
April	5.22	5.00	5.32	4.99	5.08	5.28	5.36	8.25
May	5.24	5.00	5.30	5.02	5.12	5.29	5.36	8.25
June	5.27	5.00	5.33	5.11	5.26	5.38	5.46	8.25
July	5.40	5.00	5.31	5.17	5.32	5.45	5.53	8.25
August	5.22	5.00	5.28	5.09	5.17	5.32	5.40	8.25
September	5.30	5.00	5.40	5.20	5.29	5.40	5.50	8.30
October	5.24	5.00	5.30	5.00	5.12	5.30	5.40	8.30
November	5.31	5.00	5.26	5.03	5.07	5.29	5.38	8.25
December	5.29	5.00	5.48	4.87	5.02	5.35	5.44	8.25
1997:								
January	5.25	5.00	5.33	5.05	5.11	5.34	5.43	8.25
February	5.19	5.00	5.27	5.00	5.05	5.29	5.37	8.25
March	5.39	5.00	5.40	5.14	5.24	5.44	5.53	8.30
April	5.51	5.00	5.56	5.17	5.35	5.62	5.71	8.50
May	5.50	5.00	5.56	5.13	5.35	5.62	5.70	8.50
June	5.56	5.00	5.56	4.92	5.14	5.59	5.66	8.50
July	5.52	5.00	5.54	5.07	5.12	5.53	5.60	8.50
August	5.54	5.00	5.50	5.13	5.17	5.53	5.60	8.50
September	5.54	5.00	5.58	4.97	5.11	5.54	5.60	8.50
October	5.50	5.00	5.52	4.95	5.09	5.57	5.65	8.50
November	5.52	5.00	5.56	5.15	5.17	5.66	5.74	8.50
December	5.50	5.00	5.82	5.16	5.24	5.75	5.80	8.50
1998:								
January	5.56	5.00	5.51	5.09	5.07	5.48	5.54	8.50
February	5.51	5.00	5.48	5.11	5.07	5.46	5.54	8.50
March	5.49	5.00	5.56	5.03	5.04	5.50	5.58	8.50
April	5.45	5.00	5.54	5.00	5.08	5.48	5.58	8.50
May	5.49	5.00	5.52	5.03	5.15	5.48	5.59	8.50
June	5.56	5.00	5.53	4.99	5.12	5.50	5.60	8.50
July	5.54	5.00	5.51	4.96	5.03	5.50	5.59	8.50
August	5.55	5.00	5.51	4.94	4.97	5.49	5.58	8.50
September	5.51	5.00	5.43	4.74	4.75	5.38	5.41	8.49
October	5.07	4.86	5.21	4.08	4.15	5.12	5.21	8.12
November	4.83	4.63	5.13	4.44	4.43	5.15	5.24	7.89
December	4.68	4.50	5.42	4.42	4.43	5.08	5.14	7.75

1. Discount window borrowing, Federal Reserve Bank of New York.

Selected Interest Rates and Bond Yields—*Continued*

(Percent per annum)

Year and month	U.S. Treasury securities				Bond yields			Fixed-rate first mortgages
	One-year	Ten-year	Thirty-year	Long-term composite [1]	Domestic corporate (Moody's)		State and local bonds (Bond Buyer)	
					Aaa	Baa		
1970	6.90	7.35	.....	6.58	8.04	9.11	.....	.....
1971	4.88	6.16	.....	5.74	7.39	8.56	.....	.....
1972	4.96	6.21	.....	5.63	7.21	8.16	.....	7.38
1973	7.31	6.84	.....	6.30	7.44	8.24	.....	8.04
1974	8.18	7.56	.....	6.98	8.57	9.50	.....	9.19
1975	6.76	7.99	.....	6.98	8.83	10.61	.....	9.04
1976	5.87	7.61	.....	6.78	8.43	9.75	.....	8.87
1977	6.09	7.42	.....	7.06	8.02	8.97	.....	8.84
1978	8.34	8.41	8.49	7.89	8.73	9.49	.....	9.64
1979	10.67	9.44	9.29	8.74	9.63	10.69	.....	11.19
1980	12.05	11.46	11.30	10.81	11.94	13.67	.....	13.77
1981	14.78	13.91	13.44	12.89	14.17	16.04	11.33	16.63
1982	12.28	13.00	12.76	12.23	13.79	16.11	11.66	16.08
1983	9.57	11.11	11.18	10.84	12.04	13.55	9.51	13.23
1984	10.89	12.44	12.39	11.99	12.71	14.19	10.10	13.87
1985	8.43	10.62	10.79	10.75	11.37	12.72	9.10	12.42
1986	6.46	7.68	7.80	8.14	9.02	10.39	7.32	10.18
1987	6.76	8.38	8.58	8.63	9.38	10.58	7.64	10.20
1988	7.65	8.85	8.96	8.98	9.71	10.83	7.68	10.34
1989	8.54	8.50	8.45	8.59	9.26	10.18	7.23	10.32
1990	7.88	8.55	8.61	8.73	9.32	10.36	7.27	10.13
1991	5.86	7.86	8.14	8.16	8.77	9.80	6.92	9.25
1992	3.89	7.01	7.67	7.52	8.14	8.98	6.44	8.40
1993	3.43	5.87	6.60	6.46	7.22	7.93	5.60	7.33
1994	5.31	7.08	7.37	7.41	7.96	8.62	6.18	8.36
1995	5.94	6.57	6.88	6.93	7.59	8.20	5.95	7.95
1996	5.52	6.44	6.71	6.80	7.37	8.05	5.75	7.80
1997	5.63	6.35	6.61	6.67	7.27	7.87	5.52	7.60
1998	5.05	5.26	5.58	5.69	6.53	7.22	5.09	6.94
1995:								
January	7.05	7.78	7.85	7.93	8.46	9.08	6.53	9.15
February	6.70	7.47	7.61	7.69	8.26	8.85	6.22	8.83
March	6.43	7.20	7.45	7.52	8.12	8.70	6.10	8.46
April	6.27	7.06	7.36	7.41	8.03	8.60	6.02	8.32
May	6.00	6.63	6.95	6.99	7.65	8.20	5.95	7.96
June	5.64	6.17	6.57	6.59	7.30	7.90	5.84	7.57
July	5.59	6.28	6.72	6.71	7.41	8.04	5.92	7.61
August	5.75	6.49	6.86	6.90	7.57	8.19	6.06	7.86
September	5.62	6.20	6.55	6.63	7.32	7.93	5.91	7.64
October	5.59	6.04	6.37	6.43	7.12	7.75	5.80	7.48
November	5.43	5.93	6.26	6.31	7.02	7.68	5.64	7.38
December	5.31	5.71	6.06	6.11	6.82	7.49	5.45	7.20
1996:								
January	5.09	5.65	6.05	6.07	6.80	7.47	5.43	7.03
February	4.94	5.81	6.24	6.28	6.99	7.63	5.43	7.08
March	5.34	6.27	6.60	6.72	7.35	8.03	5.79	7.62
April	5.54	6.51	6.79	6.94	7.50	8.19	5.94	7.93
May	5.64	6.74	6.93	7.08	7.62	8.20	5.87	8.07
June	5.81	6.91	7.06	7.20	7.71	8.40	6.02	8.32
July	5.85	6.87	7.03	7.13	7.65	8.35	5.92	8.25
August	5.67	6.64	6.84	6.94	7.46	8.18	5.76	8.00
September	5.80	6.80	7.00	7.10	7.70	8.40	5.90	8.23
October	5.60	6.50	6.80	6.90	7.40	8.10	5.70	7.92
November	5.42	6.20	6.48	6.55	7.10	7.79	5.59	7.62
December	5.47	6.30	6.55	6.63	7.20	7.89	5.64	7.60
1997:								
January	5.61	6.58	6.83	6.89	7.42	8.09	5.72	7.82
February	5.53	6.42	6.69	6.76	7.31	7.94	5.63	7.65
March	5.80	6.69	6.93	7.03	7.55	8.18	5.76	7.90
April	5.99	6.89	7.09	7.18	7.73	8.34	5.88	8.14
May	5.87	6.71	6.94	7.00	7.58	8.20	5.70	7.94
June	5.69	6.49	6.77	6.82	7.41	8.02	5.53	7.69
July	5.54	6.22	6.51	6.55	7.14	7.75	5.35	7.50
August	5.56	6.30	6.58	6.64	7.22	7.82	5.41	7.48
September	5.52	6.21	6.50	6.54	7.15	7.70	5.39	7.43
October	5.46	6.03	6.33	6.37	7.00	7.57	5.38	7.29
November	5.46	5.88	6.11	6.18	6.87	7.42	5.33	7.21
December	5.53	5.81	5.99	6.06	6.76	7.32	5.19	7.10
1998:								
January	5.24	5.54	5.81	5.87	6.61	7.19	5.06	6.99
February	5.31	5.57	5.89	5.94	6.67	7.25	5.10	7.04
March	5.39	5.65	5.95	6.00	6.72	7.32	5.21	7.13
April	5.38	5.64	5.92	5.98	6.69	7.33	5.23	7.14
May	5.44	5.65	5.93	5.99	6.69	7.30	5.20	7.14
June	5.41	5.50	5.70	5.78	6.53	7.13	5.12	7.00
July	5.36	5.46	5.68	5.76	6.55	7.15	5.14	6.95
August	5.21	5.34	5.54	5.64	6.52	7.14	5.10	6.92
September	4.71	4.81	5.20	5.34	6.40	7.09	4.99	6.72
October	4.12	4.53	5.01	5.24	6.37	7.18	4.93	6.71
November	4.53	4.83	5.25	5.43	6.41	7.34	5.03	6.87
December	4.52	4.65	5.06	5.29	6.22	7.23	4.98	6.72

1. Maturities of more than ten years.

Common Stock Prices and Yields

| Year and month | Dow Jones industrials (30 stocks) | Standard and Poor's composite (500 stocks) [1] | New York Stock Exchange (December 31, 1965=50, except as noted) | | | | | Stock dividend-price ratio, Standard and Poor's composite (percent) |
			Composite	Industrial	Transportation	Utility (Dec. 31, 1965=100)	Finance	
1970	753.20	83.22	45.72	48.03	32.14	74.48	60.00	3.83
1971	884.76	98.29	54.22	57.92	44.35	79.04	70.38	3.14
1972	950.71	109.20	60.29	65.73	50.17	76.96	78.35	2.84
1973	923.88	107.43	57.42	63.08	37.74	75.38	70.12	3.06
1974	759.37	82.85	43.84	48.08	31.89	59.58	49.67	4.47
1975	802.49	86.16	45.73	50.52	31.10	63.00	47.14	4.31
1976	974.92	102.01	54.46	60.44	39.57	73.94	52.94	3.77
1977	894.62	98.20	53.69	57.86	41.08	81.84	55.25	4.62
1978	820.23	96.02	53.70	58.23	43.50	78.44	56.65	5.28
1979	844.40	103.01	58.32	64.75	47.34	76.40	61.42	5.47
1980	891.41	118.78	68.10	78.70	60.61	74.70	64.25	5.26
1981	932.92	128.04	74.02	85.44	72.61	77.82	73.52	5.20
1982	884.36	119.71	68.93	78.18	60.41	79.48	71.99	5.81
1983	1 190.34	160.41	92.63	107.45	89.36	94.00	95.34	4.40
1984	1 178.48	160.46	92.46	108.01	85.63	92.88	89.28	4.64
1985	1 328.23	186.84	108.09	123.78	104.10	113.48	114.21	4.25
1986	1 792.76	236.34	136.00	155.85	119.87	142.72	147.20	3.48
1987	2 275.99	286.83	161.70	195.31	140.39	148.59	146.48	3.08
1988	2 060.82	265.79	149.91	180.95	134.12	143.53	127.26	3.64
1989	2 508.91	322.84	180.02	216.23	175.28	174.87	151.88	3.45
1990	2 678.94	334.59	183.46	225.78	158.62	181.20	133.26	3.61
1991	2 929.33	376.17	206.33	258.14	173.99	185.32	150.82	3.24
1992	3 284.29	415.74	229.01	284.62	201.09	198.91	179.26	2.99
1993	3 522.06	451.41	249.58	299.99	242.49	228.90	216.42	2.78
1994	3 793.77	460.42	254.12	315.25	247.29	209.06	209.73	2.82
1995	4 493.76	541.72	291.15	367.34	269.41	220.30	238.45	2.56
1996	5 742.89	670.50	358.17	453.98	327.33	249.77	303.89	2.19
1997	7 441.15	873.43	456.54	574.52	414.60	283.82	424.48	1.77
1998	8 625.52	1 085.50	550.26	681.57	468.69	378.12	516.35	1.49
1995:								
January	3 872.46	465.25	253.56	319.93	230.25	201.16	201.05	2.87
February	3 953.72	481.92	261.86	328.98	237.29	207.73	211.76	2.81
March	4 062.78	493.15	266.81	337.96	244.45	204.16	213.29	2.76
April	4 230.66	507.91	274.37	347.69	254.36	208.93	219.38	2.68
May	4 391.57	523.81	281.81	357.01	254.69	211.58	228.55	2.60
June	4 510.76	539.35	289.52	366.75	256.80	216.27	236.26	2.55
July	4 684.76	557.37	298.18	379.13	279.15	219.18	240.50	2.50
August	4 639.27	559.11	300.05	379.79	285.63	221.99	245.27	2.49
September	4 746.76	578.77	310.41	390.42	295.54	229.64	260.72	2.42
October	4 760.46	582.92	311.78	389.63	291.16	236.43	265.12	2.41
November	4 935.81	595.53	317.58	398.66	300.06	238.98	266.12	2.37
December	5 136.10	614.57	327.90	412.11	303.53	247.59	273.36	2.30
1996:								
January	5 179.37	614.42	329.22	412.71	300.03	254.07	273.73	2.31
February	5 518.73	649.54	346.46	435.92	315.29	257.80	290.97	2.22
March	5 612.24	647.07	346.73	439.56	324.76	245.77	290.45	2.22
April	5 579.86	647.17	347.50	441.99	326.42	244.87	287.92	2.24
May	5 616.71	661.23	354.84	452.63	334.66	249.73	290.43	2.21
June	5 671.51	668.50	358.32	458.30	331.57	247.20	294.42	2.21
July	5 496.26	644.07	345.52	438.58	316.66	245.31	287.89	2.28
August	5 685.50	662.68	354.59	449.41	321.61	244.74	302.95	2.22
September	5 804.01	674.88	360.96	459.69	323.12	242.25	308.16	2.20
October	5 996.21	701.46	373.54	473.98	332.93	249.61	324.42	2.11
November	6 318.36	735.67	388.75	490.60	348.32	258.85	345.30	2.01
December	6 435.87	743.25	391.61	494.38	352.28	257.09	350.01	2.01
1997:								
January	6 707.03	766.22	403.58	509.84	359.40	263.91	361.45	1.95
February	6 917.48	798.39	418.57	524.30	364.15	271.36	388.75	1.89
March	6 901.12	792.16	416.72	523.08	372.87	264.78	387.21	1.91
April	6 657.50	763.93	401.00	506.69	366.67	253.18	364.25	1.98
May	7 242.36	833.09	433.36	549.65	395.50	268.18	392.32	1.85
June	7 599.60	876.29	457.07	578.57	410.94	280.48	419.12	1.77
July	7 990.65	925.29	480.94	610.42	433.75	288.51	441.59	1.66
August	7 948.43	927.74	481.53	609.54	439.71	287.63	446.93	1.65
September	7 866.59	937.02	489.74	617.94	451.63	291.87	459.86	1.65
October	7 875.82	951.16	499.25	625.22	466.04	302.83	476.70	1.61
November	7 677.36	938.92	492.08	615.57	453.49	307.52	465.29	1.65
December	7 909.82	962.37	504.66	623.57	461.04	325.60	490.30	1.62
1998:								
January	7 808.35	963.36	504.13	624.61	458.49	332.50	479.81	1.62
February	8 323.61	1 023.74	532.15	660.91	485.73	341.91	508.97	1.55
March	8 709.47	1 076.83	560.70	693.13	508.06	367.48	539.47	1.48
April	9 037.44	1 112.20	578.05	711.89	523.73	378.92	563.07	1.43
May	9 080.07	1 108.42	574.46	712.39	505.02	372.62	551.28	1.45
June	8 872.96	1 108.39	569.76	704.14	492.98	376.51	548.57	1.45
July	9 097.14	1 156.58	586.39	718.54	503.89	388.78	579.67	1.39
August	8 478.52	1 074.62	539.16	665.66	441.36	372.48	511.22	1.48
September	7 909.79	1 020.64	506.56	629.51	408.75	372.33	454.28	1.59
October	8 164.47	1 032.47	511.49	636.62	396.61	390.17	448.12	1.59
November	9 005.75	1 144.43	564.26	704.46	442.95	412.59	501.45	1.43
December	9 018.68	1 190.05	576.05	717.00	456.70	431.14	510.31	1.37

1.1941-1943=10.

U.S. Foreign Trade and Finance

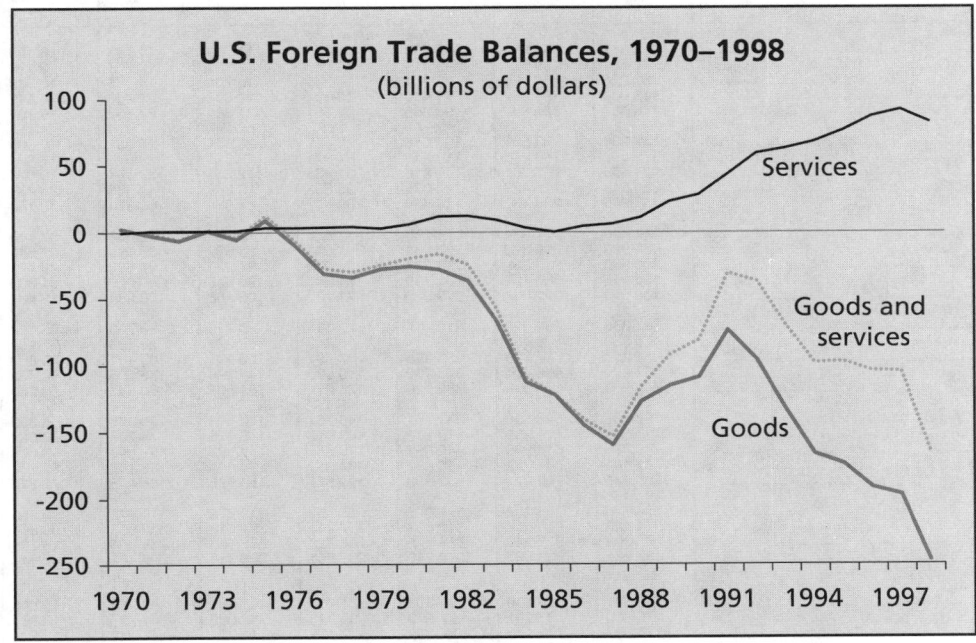

- The U.S. foreign trade deficit on goods and services reached a record $164 billion in 1998.

- The current-account deficit, which includes income payments and unilateral transfers and which measures the net amount of financial inflows from abroad, expanded to $221 billion, also a record.

- In 1998, the trade surplus in services declined for the first time since 1985, due to slower growth in exports of services and an 8.4 percent increase in imports. Even so, at $83 billion, the services surplus offset 33 percent of the deficit on trade in goods.

- Total goods exports declined 1.4 percent in 1998, while imports increased 4.7 percent. Exports of goods to major Asian trading partners declined sharply while those to Europe and the Americas continued to grow.

- As a percentage of GDP, exports of goods and services have doubled from 1970 to 1998, from 5.5 percent to 11 percent. Over this same period, imports have gained even more, from 5.3 percent to 12.9 percent.

U.S. International Transactions

(Millions of dollars, seasonally adjusted)

Year and quarter	Current account									
	Exports of goods and services and income reciepts									
						Income receipts				
							Income receipts on U.S. assets abroad			
	Total	Exports of goods and services	Exports of goods	Exports of services	Total	Total	Direct investment receipts	Other private receipts	U.S. government receipts	Compensation of employees
1970	68 387	56 640	42 469	14 171	11 748	11 748	8 169	2 671	907	.....
1971	72 384	59 677	43 319	16 358	12 707	12 707	9 160	2 641	906	.....
1972	81 986	67 222	49 381	17 841	14 765	14 765	10 949	2 949	866	.....
1973	113 050	91 242	71 410	19 832	21 808	21 808	16 542	4 330	936	.....
1974	148 484	120 897	98 306	22 591	27 587	27 587	19 157	7 356	1 074	.....
1975	157 936	132 585	107 088	25 497	25 351	25 351	16 595	7 644	1 112	.....
1976	172 090	142 716	114 745	27 971	29 375	29 375	18 999	9 043	1 332	.....
1977	184 655	152 301	120 816	31 485	32 354	32 354	19 673	11 057	1 625	.....
1978	220 516	178 428	142 075	36 353	42 088	42 088	25 458	14 788	1 843	.....:
1979	287 965	224 131	184 439	39 692	63 834	63 834	38 183	23 356	2 295	.....
1980	344 440	271 834	224 250	47 584	72 606	72 606	37 146	32 898	2 562	.....
1981	380 928	294 398	237 044	57 354	86 529	86 529	32 549	50 300	3 680	.....
1982	366 926	275 236	211 157	64 079	91 690	91 690	29 412	58 160	4 118	.....
1983	356 156	266 106	201 799	64 307	90 050	90 050	31 800	53 418	4 832	.....
1984	400 052	291 094	219 926	71 168	108 958	108 958	35 464	68 267	5 227	.....
1985	387 806	289 070	215 915	73 155	98 736	98 736	35 604	57 633	5 499	.....
1986	406 060	308 786	223 344	85 442	97 274	96 366	37 148	52 806	6 413	908
1987	456 227	347 799	250 208	97 591	108 428	107 434	46 532	55 592	5 311	994
1988	567 260	430 260	320 230	110 030	137 000	136 005	58 732	70 571	6 703	995
1989	649 902	488 336	362 120	126 216	161 566	160 549	62 260	92 638	5 651	1 017
1990	708 135	536 058	389 307	146 751	172 078	170 906	66 309	94 072	10 525	1 172
1991	729 513	579 956	416 913	163 043	149 558	148 268	59 062	81 186	8 019	1 290
1992	748 431	615 909	440 352	175 557	132 523	131 098	58 005	65 977	7 115	1 425
1993	776 404	641 783	456 832	184 951	134 621	133 187	67 708	60 353	5 126	1 434
1994	868 041	702 073	502 398	199 675	165 968	164 425	77 874	82 423	4 128	1 543
1995	1 005 715	793 482	575 845	217 637	212 233	210 472	95 991	109 768	4 713	1 761
1996	1 074 425	849 806	612 057	237 749	224 619	222 863	103 314	114 958	4 591	1 756
1997	1 197 206	938 543	679 715	258 828	258 663	256 861	115 795	137 507	3 559	1 802
1998	1 192 231	933 907	670 246	263 661	258 324	256 467	102 846	150 001	3 620	1 857
1990:										
1st quarter	171 897	130 046	95 301	34 745	41 851	41 569	16 618	23 001	1 950	282
2nd quarter	175 380	133 291	97 573	35 718	42 089	41 797	16 764	23 073	1 960	292
3rd quarter	175 393	133 471	96 339	37 132	41 922	41 630	15 973	23 660	1 997	292
4th quarter	185 468	139 252	100 094	39 158	46 216	45 910	16 953	24 338	4 619	306
1991:										
1st quarter	181 160	138 932	101 345	37 587	42 228	41 910	16 622	22 679	2 609	318
2nd quarter	182 260	144 970	104 529	40 441	37 290	36 971	14 634	20 486	1 851	319
3rd quarter	180 925	145 288	103 732	41 556	35 637	35 312	13 547	19 821	1 944	325
4th quarter	185 176	150 769	107 307	43 462	34 407	34 079	14 262	18 200	1 617	328
1992:										
1st quarter	185 931	152 050	108 344	43 706	33 881	33 543	14 824	17 083	1 636	338
2nd quarter	187 219	152 726	109 025	43 701	34 493	34 147	15 664	16 678	1 805	346
3rd quarter	186 166	153 791	109 593	44 198	32 375	32 012	14 383	15 771	1 858	363
4th quarter	189 114	157 341	113 390	43 951	31 773	31 395	13 134	16 445	1 816	378
1993:										
1st quarter	190 577	157 562	111 862	45 700	33 015	32 675	16 314	15 040	1 321	340
2nd quarter	193 492	160 382	114 185	46 197	33 110	32 760	16 854	14 575	1 331	350
3rd quarter	191 999	157 907	111 429	46 478	34 092	33 727	17 273	15 124	1 330	365
4th quarter	200 335	165 931	119 356	46 575	34 404	34 025	17 267	15 614	1 144	379
1994:										
1st quarter	203 174	166 542	118 382	48 160	36 632	36 266	17 919	17 301	1 046	366
2nd quarter	212 111	172 841	123 025	49 816	39 270	38 895	18 302	19 605	988	375
3rd quarter	221 275	178 136	127 629	50 507	43 139	42 746	20 343	21 437	966	393
4th quarter	231 483	184 557	133 362	51 195	46 926	46 517	21 308	24 080	1 129	409
1995:										
1st quarter	242 057	190 821	139 016	51 805	51 236	50 797	22 747	26 855	1 195	439
2nd quarter	248 496	194 870	142 103	52 767	53 626	53 186	24 592	27 225	1 369	440
3rd quarter	254 785	201 944	145 909	56 035	52 841	52 399	23 690	27 677	1 032	442
4th quarter	260 373	205 844	148 817	57 027	54 529	54 089	24 962	28 011	1 116	440
1996:										
1st quarter	262 090	207 366	150 438	56 928	54 724	54 285	25 082	27 935	1 268	439
2nd quarter	265 687	211 454	152 612	58 842	54 233	53 795	24 746	27 942	1 107	438
3rd quarter	266 217	210 095	151 991	58 104	56 122	55 682	25 395	29 008	1 279	440
4th quarter	280 425	220 887	157 016	63 871	59 538	59 099	28 087	30 073	939	439
1997:										
1st quarter	287 363	225 760	162 979	62 781	61 603	61 152	28 443	31 847	862	451
2nd quarter	300 113	234 683	169 895	64 788	65 430	64 980	30 098	33 916	966	450
3rd quarter	305 865	239 285	173 447	65 838	66 580	66 129	30 312	34 936	881	451
4th quarter	303 869	238 819	173 394	65 425	65 050	64 600	26 942	36 808	850	450
1998:										
1st quarter	302 289	235 831	170 665	65 166	66 458	65 994	27 338	37 826	830	464
2nd quarter	298 463	231 889	165 198	66 691	66 574	66 111	26 744	38 412	955	463
3rd quarter	291 493	229 284	164 259	65 025	62 209	61 744	23 124	37 744	876	465
4th quarter	299 985	236 904	170 124	66 780	63 081	62 617	25 639	36 019	959	464

U.S. International Transactions—*Continued*

(Millions of dollars, seasonally adjusted)

Year and quarter	Current account—*Continued*									
	Imports of goods and services and income payments [1]									
						Income payments				
							Income payments on U.S. assets abroad			Compensation of employees
	Total	Imports of goods and services	Imports of goods	Imports of services	Total	Total	Direct investment payments	Other private payments	U.S. government payments	
1970	-59 901	-54 386	-39 866	-14 520	-5 515	-5 515	-875	-3 617	-1 024	.....
1971	-66 414	-60 979	-45 579	-15 400	-5 435	-5 435	-1 164	-2 428	-1 844	.....
1972	-79 237	-72 665	-55 797	-16 868	-6 572	-6 572	-1 284	-2 604	-2 684	.....
1973	-98 997	-89 342	-70 499	-18 843	-9 655	-9 655	-1 610	-4 209	-3 836	.....
1974	-137 274	-125 190	-103 811	-21 379	-12 084	-12 084	-1 331	-6 491	-4 262	.....
1975	-132 745	-120 181	-98 185	-21 996	-12 564	-12 564	-2 234	-5 788	-4 542	.....
1976	-162 109	-148 798	-124 228	-24 570	-13 311	-13 311	-3 110	-5 681	-4 520	.....
1977	-193 764	-179 547	-151 907	-27 640	-14 217	-14 217	-2 834	-5 841	-5 542	.....
1978	-229 870	-208 191	-176 002	-32 189	-21 680	-21 680	-4 211	-8 795	-8 674	.....
1979	-281 657	-248 696	-212 007	-36 689	-32 961	-32 961	-6 357	-15 481	-11 122	.....
1980	-333 774	-291 241	-249 750	-41 491	-42 532	-42 532	-8 635	-21 214	-12 684	.....
1981	-364 196	-310 570	-265 067	-45 503	-53 626	-53 626	-6 898	-29 415	-17 313	.....
1982	-355 964	-299 391	-247 642	-51 749	-56 572	-56 572	-2 103	-35 187	-19 282	.....
1983	-377 577	-323 874	-268 901	-54 973	-53 703	-53 703	-4 209	-30 501	-18 993	.....
1984	-474 144	-400 166	-332 418	-67 748	-73 977	-73 977	-8 664	-44 158	-21 155	.....
1985	-484 106	-410 950	-338 088	-72 862	-73 156	-73 156	-7 282	-42 745	-23 129	.....
1986	-530 478	-448 572	-368 425	-80 147	-81 907	-79 229	-7 192	-47 412	-24 625	-2 678
1987	-594 825	-500 552	-409 765	-90 787	-94 273	-91 935	-8 058	-57 659	-26 218	-2 338
1988	-664 167	-545 715	-447 189	-98 526	-118 452	-116 605	-12 576	-72 314	-31 715	-1 847
1989	-721 686	-579 844	-477 365	-102 479	-141 842	-139 556	-7 424	-93 768	-38 364	-2 286
1990	-759 646	-615 996	-498 308	-117 659	-143 649	-140 185	-3 907	-95 508	-40 770	-3 464
1991	-735 048	-609 440	-490 981	-118 459	-125 608	-121 582	1 742	-82 452	-40 872	-4 026
1992	-763 187	-652 934	-536 458	-116 476	-110 253	-105 501	-3 341	-63 079	-39 081	-4 752
1993	-823 167	-711 722	-589 441	-122 281	-111 445	-106 313	-9 133	-57 804	-39 376	-5 132
1994	-950 529	-800 468	-668 590	-131 878	-150 061	-144 109	-23 467	-76 450	-44 192	-5 952
1995	-1 083 844	-891 021	-749 574	-141 447	-192 823	-186 560	-32 186	-97 004	-57 370	-6 263
1996	-1 161 533	-954 124	-803 327	-150 797	-207 409	-201 109	-35 568	-97 901	-67 640	-6 300
1997	-1 298 705	-1 043 273	-876 366	-166 907	-255 432	-248 676	-46 575	-114 051	-88 050	-6 756
1998	-1 368 718	-1 098 189	-917 178	-181 011	-270 529	-263 423	-43 441	-128 863	-91 119	-7 106
1990:										
1st quarter	-186 573	-150 620	-122 447	-28 173	-35 953	-35 135	-1 231	-23 882	-10 022	-818
2nd quarter	-186 647	-150 933	-122 169	-28 764	-35 714	-34 875	-1 208	-23 546	-10 121	-839
3rd quarter	-192 037	-155 312	-125 389	-29 923	-36 725	-35 858	-1 596	-24 039	-10 223	-867
4th quarter	-194 385	-159 127	-128 332	-30 795	-35 258	-34 317	128	-24 041	-10 404	-941
1991:										
1st quarter	-184 081	-149 942	-120 141	-29 801	-34 139	-33 240	759	-23 549	-10 450	-899
2nd quarter	-182 409	-150 365	-120 705	-29 660	-32 044	-31 063	91	-20 934	-10 220	-981
3rd quarter	-183 969	-152 679	-123 479	-29 200	-31 290	-30 267	-207	-19 794	-10 266	-1 023
4th quarter	-184 594	-156 455	-126 656	-29 799	-28 139	-27 013	1 098	-18 175	-9 936	-1 126
1992:										
1st quarter	-183 456	-155 587	-126 284	-29 303	-27 869	-26 692	432	-17 333	-9 791	-1 177
2nd quarter	-190 988	-162 325	-133 277	-29 048	-28 663	-27 477	-1 503	-16 152	-9 822	-1 186
3rd quarter	-192 461	-165 165	-136 887	-28 278	-27 296	-26 122	-1 346	-14 996	-9 780	-1 174
4th quarter	-196 284	-169 858	-140 010	-29 848	-26 426	-25 210	-924	-14 598	-9 688	-1 216
1993:										
1st quarter	-196 453	-170 725	-141 069	-29 656	-25 728	-24 518	-333	-14 483	-9 702	-1 210
2nd quarter	-205 324	-177 868	-147 571	-30 297	-27 456	-26 185	-2 672	-13 826	-9 687	-1 271
3rd quarter	-205 492	-178 459	-147 926	-30 533	-27 033	-25 750	-1 910	-13 878	-9 962	-1 283
4th quarter	-215 901	-184 671	-152 875	-31 796	-31 230	-29 861	-4 219	-15 617	-10 025	-1 369
1994:										
1st quarter	-219 188	-187 420	-155 009	-32 411	-31 768	-30 325	-4 107	-16 032	-10 186	-1 443
2nd quarter	-231 932	-196 519	-163 852	-32 667	-35 413	-33 919	-5 228	-18 112	-10 579	-1 494
3rd quarter	-244 852	-205 325	-171 977	-33 348	-39 527	-38 031	-6 666	-20 225	-11 140	-1 496
4th quarter	-254 558	-211 206	-177 752	-33 454	-43 352	-41 834	-7 466	-22 081	-12 287	-1 518
1995:										
1st quarter	-263 716	-217 626	-183 093	-34 533	-46 090	-44 539	-7 325	-23 914	-13 300	-1 551
2nd quarter	-273 314	-225 775	-190 539	-35 236	-47 539	-45 978	-7 481	-24 391	-14 106	-1 561
3rd quarter	-274 013	-223 742	-188 077	-35 665	-50 271	-48 710	-9 445	-24 413	-14 852	-1 561
4th quarter	-272 802	-223 880	-187 865	-36 015	-48 922	-47 333	-7 935	-24 286	-15 112	-1 589
1996:										
1st quarter	-277 914	-229 711	-193 038	-36 673	-48 203	-46 693	-7 946	-23 596	-15 151	-1 510
2nd quarter	-287 958	-237 934	-200 763	-37 171	-50 024	-48 464	-8 667	-23 974	-15 823	-1 560
3rd quarter	-295 037	-241 563	-203 196	-38 367	-53 474	-51 904	-9 486	-24 767	-17 651	-1 570
4th quarter	-300 625	-244 917	-206 330	-38 587	-55 708	-54 048	-9 469	-25 564	-19 015	-1 660
1997:										
1st quarter	-312 914	-252 372	-212 187	-40 185	-60 542	-58 908	-11 855	-26 744	-20 309	-1 634
2nd quarter	-322 090	-258 872	-217 773	-41 099	-63 218	-61 543	-11 426	-28 083	-22 034	-1 675
3rd quarter	-331 384	-265 008	-222 362	-42 646	-66 376	-64 673	-13 001	-28 818	-22 854	-1 703
4th quarter	-332 317	-267 020	-224 044	-42 976	-65 297	-63 552	-10 293	-30 406	-22 853	-1 745
1998:										
1st quarter	-335 380	-269 169	-225 541	-43 628	-66 211	-64 476	-10 501	-31 292	-22 683	-1 735
2nd quarter	-340 977	-273 850	-228 698	-45 152	-67 127	-65 376	-10 567	-31 849	-22 960	-1 751
3rd quarter	-344 182	-275 008	-229 228	-45 780	-69 174	-67 381	-11 290	-33 314	-22 777	-1 793
4th quarter	-348 180	-280 166	-233 711	-46 455	-68 014	-66 188	-11 081	-32 408	-22 699	-1 826

1. A minus sign indicates imports of goods and services, or payments of income.

U.S. International Transactions—*Continued*

(Millions of dollars, seasonally adjusted)

Year and quarter	Current account—*Continued* Unilateral current transfers, net[1]				Capital account transactions, net	Financial account U.S.-owned assets abroad, net[1]					
		U.S. government		Private remittances and other transfers			U.S. official reserve assets, net				
	Total	Grants	Pensions and other transfers			Total	Total	Gold	Special drawing rights	Reserve position in the IMF	Foreign currencies
1970	-6 156	-4 449	-611	-1 096	.....	-8 470	3 348	787	16	389	2 156
1971	-7 402	-5 589	-696	-1 117	.....	-11 758	3 066	866	468	1 350	382
1972	-8 544	-6 665	-770	-1 109	.....	-13 787	706	547	7	153	-1
1973	-6 913	-4 748	-915	-1 250	.....	-22 874	158	.....	9	-33	182
1974	-9 249	-7 293	-939	-1 017	.....	-34 745	-1 467	.....	-172	-1 265	-30
1975	-7 075	-5 101	-1 068	-906	.....	-39 703	-849	.....	-66	-466	-317
1976	-5 686	-3 519	-1 250	-917	.....	-51 269	-2 558	.....	-78	-2 212	-268
1977	-5 226	-2 990	-1 378	-859	.....	-34 785	-375	-118	-121	-294	158
1978	-5 788	-3 412	-1 532	-844	.....	-61 130	732	-65	1 249	4 231	-4 683
1979	-6 593	-4 015	-1 658	-920	.....	-64 915	6	-65	3	-189	257
1980	-8 349	-5 486	-1 818	-1 044	.....	-85 815	-7 003	.....	1 136	-1 667	-6 472
1981	-11 702	-5 145	-2 041	-4 516	.....	-113 054	-4 082	.....	-730	-2 491	-861
1982	-17 139	-6 087	-2 251	-8 801	199	-127 825	-4 965	.....	-1 371	-2 552	-1 041
1983	-17 778	-6 469	-2 207	-9 103	209	-66 423	-1 196	.....	-66	-4 434	3 304
1984	-20 661	-8 696	-2 159	-9 805	235	-40 515	-3 131	.....	-979	-995	-1 156
1985	-22 762	-11 268	-2 138	-9 357	315	-44 946	-3 858	.....	-897	908	-3 869
1986	-24 818	-11 883	-2 372	-10 564	301	-111 933	312	.....	-246	1 501	-942
1987	-24 047	-10 309	-2 409	-11 330	365	-79 540	9 149	.....	-509	2 070	7 588
1988	-26 139	-10 537	-2 709	-12 893	493	-106 860	-3 912	.....	127	1 025	-5 064
1989	-27 116	-10 860	-2 775	-13 481	336	-175 662	-25 293	.....	-535	471	-25 229
1990	-27 821	-10 359	-3 224	-14 238	-6 579	-81 570	-2 158	.....	-192	731	-2 697
1991	9 819	29 193	-3 775	-15 599	-4 479	-64 732	5 763	.....	-177	-367	6 307
1992	-35 873	-16 320	-4 043	-15 510	612	-74 877	3 901	.....	2 316	-2 692	4 277
1993	-38 522	-17 036	-4 104	-17 383	-88	-201 014	-1 379	.....	-537	-44	-797
1994	-39 192	-14 978	-4 556	-19 658	-469	-176 586	5 346	.....	-441	494	5 293
1995	-35 437	-11 190	-3 451	-20 796	372	-330 675	-9 742	.....	-808	-2 466	-6 468
1996	-42 187	-15 337	-4 466	-22 384	672	-380 762	6 668	.....	370	-1 280	7 578
1997	-41 966	-12 386	-4 239	-25 341	292	-465 296	-1 010	.....	-350	-3 575	2 915
1998	-44 075	-13 057	-4 350	-26 668	617	-292 818	-6 784	.....	-149	-5 118	-1 517
1990:											
1st quarter	-6 793	-2 556	-803	-3 434	-19	37 747	-3 177	.....	-247	234	-3 164
2nd quarter	-7 923	-3 613	-811	-3 499	157	-37 288	371	.....	-216	493	94
3rd quarter	-7 635	-3 088	-812	-3 735	165	-43 801	1 739	.....	363	8	1 368
4th quarter	-5 472	-1 102	-798	-3 572	-6 882	-38 228	-1 091	.....	-93	-4	-995
1991:											
1st quarter	14 756	19 444	-869	-3 819	-941	-10 651	-353	.....	31	-341	-43
2nd quarter	3 536	8 285	-877	-3 872	73	663	1 014	.....	-190	72	1 132
3rd quarter	-3 039	1 730	-880	-3 889	-3 786	-15 988	3 877	.....	6	-114	3 986
4th quarter	-5 438	-267	-1 150	-4 021	175	-38 757	1 225	.....	-23	17	1 232
1992:											
1st quarter	-7 767	-3 040	-907	-3 820	152	-11 538	-1 057	.....	-172	111	-996
2nd quarter	-8 631	-3 532	-1 197	-3 902	111	-16 351	1 464	.....	-168	1	1 631
3rd quarter	-8 046	-3 161	-1 021	-3 864	173	-13 690	1 952	.....	-173	-118	2 243
4th quarter	-11 430	-6 586	-919	-3 925	176	-33 298	1 542	.....	2 829	-2 685	1 398
1993:											
1st quarter	-8 138	-3 007	-904	-4 227	-459	-21 606	-983	.....	-140	-228	-615
2nd quarter	-8 791	-3 468	-1 068	-4 255	147	-45 958	822	.....	-166	313	675
3rd quarter	-9 557	-4 097	-1 071	-4 389	83	-53 090	-545	.....	-118	-48	-378
4th quarter	-12 036	-6 463	-1 061	-4 512	141	-80 360	-673	.....	-113	-80	-480
1994:											
1st quarter	-8 193	-2 488	-964	-4 741	152	-39 860	-59	.....	-101	-3	45
2nd quarter	-8 717	-2 946	-974	-4 797	-704	-43 198	3 537	.....	-108	251	3 394
3rd quarter	-9 843	-3 323	-1 555	-4 965	-70	-31 121	-165	.....	-111	273	-327
4th quarter	-12 438	-6 221	-1 063	-5 154	153	-62 409	2 033	.....	-121	-27	2 181
1995:											
1st quarter	-8 868	-2 964	-762	-5 142	146	-63 976	-5 318	.....	-867	-526	-3 925
2nd quarter	-8 397	-2 491	-980	-4 926	272	-113 618	-2 722	.....	-156	-786	-1 780
3rd quarter	-8 836	-2 698	-973	-5 165	-299	-41 527	-1 893	.....	362	-991	-1 264
4th quarter	-9 336	-3 037	-736	-5 563	253	-111 552	191	.....	-147	-163	501
1996:											
1st quarter	-10 920	-4 447	-1 157	-5 316	152	-71 680	17	.....	-199	-849	1 065
2nd quarter	-9 185	-2 503	-1 103	-5 579	168	-61 367	-523	.....	-133	-220	-170
3rd quarter	-9 507	-2 777	-1 111	-5 619	172	-84 509	7 489	.....	848	-183	6 824
4th quarter	-12 574	-5 610	-1 095	-5 869	180	-163 203	-315	.....	-146	-28	-141
1997:											
1st quarter	-9 347	-2 306	-1 026	-6 015	135	-144 665	4 480	.....	72	1 055	3 353
2nd quarter	-9 494	-2 290	-1 070	-6 134	56	-91 124	-236	.....	-133	54	-157
3rd quarter	-10 096	-2 423	-1 074	-6 599	19	-112 578	-730	.....	-139	-463	-128
4th quarter	-13 030	-5 367	-1 069	-6 594	82	-116 929	-4 524	.....	-150	-4 221	-153
1998:											
1st quarter	-9 927	-2 340	-1 079	-6 508	143	-59 599	-444	.....	-182	-85	-177
2nd quarter	-9 886	-2 168	-1 095	-6 623	160	-120 517	-1 945	.....	72	-1 031	-986
3rd quarter	-10 787	-2 807	-1 106	-6 874	148	-62 097	-2 026	.....	188	-2 078	-136
4th quarter	-13 474	-5 742	-1 071	-6 661	166	-50 607	-2 369	.....	-227	-1 924	-218

1. A minus sign indicates net unilateral transfers to foreigners, capital or financial outflows, or increases in U.S. official reserve assets.

U.S. International Transactions—*Continued*

(Millions of dollars, seasonally adjusted)

Year and quarter	Financial account—*Continued*								
	U.S. assets abroad, net [1]—*Continued*								
	U.S. government assets other than official reserve assets, net				U.S. private assets, net				
								U.S. claims	
	Total	U.S. credits and other long-term assets	Repayments on U.S. credits and other long-term assets	U.S. foreign currency holdings and short-term assets, net	Total	Direct investment	Foreign securities	On unaffiliated foreigners reported by U.S. nonbanking concerns	Reported by U.S. banks, not included elsewhere
1970	-1 589	-3 293	1 721	-16	-10 229	-7 590	-1 076	-596	-967
1971	-1 884	-4 181	2 115	182	-12 940	-7 618	-1 113	-1 229	-2 980
1972	-1 568	-3 819	2 086	165	-12 925	-7 747	-618	-1 054	-3 506
1973	-2 644	-4 638	2 596	-602	-20 388	-11 353	-671	-2 383	-5 980
1974	366	-5 001	4 826	541	-33 643	-9 052	-1 854	-3 221	-19 516
1975	-3 474	-5 941	2 475	-9	-35 380	-14 244	-6 247	-1 357	-13 532
1976	-4 214	-6 943	2 596	133	-44 498	-11 949	-8 885	-2 296	-21 368
1977	-3 693	-6 445	2 719	33	-30 717	-11 890	-5 460	-1 940	-11 427
1978	-4 660	-7 470	2 941	-131	-57 202	-16 056	-3 626	-3 853	-33 667
1979	-3 746	-7 697	3 926	25	-61 176	-25 222	-4 726	-5 014	-26 213
1980	-5 162	-9 860	4 456	242	-73 651	-19 222	-3 568	-4 023	-46 838
1981	-5 097	-9 674	4 413	164	-103 875	-9 624	-5 699	-4 377	-84 175
1982	-6 131	-10 063	4 292	-360	-116 729	-4 499	-7 983	6 823	-111 070
1983	-5 006	-9 967	5 012	-51	-60 222	-12 578	-6 762	-10 954	-29 928
1984	-5 489	-9 599	4 490	-379	-31 896	-16 546	-4 756	533	-11 127
1985	-2 821	-7 657	4 719	117	-38 268	-19 121	-7 481	-10 342	-1 323
1986	-2 022	-9 084	6 089	973	-110 224	-24 205	-4 271	-21 773	-59 975
1987	1 006	-6 506	7 625	-113	-89 694	-35 278	-5 251	-7 046	-42 119
1988	2 967	-7 680	10 370	277	-105 915	-22 815	-7 980	-21 193	-53 927
1989	1 233	-5 608	6 725	115	-151 602	-43 726	-22 070	-27 646	-58 160
1990	2 317	-8 410	10 856	-130	-81 729	-37 519	-28 765	-27 824	12 379
1991	2 924	-12 879	16 776	-974	-73 419	-38 233	-45 673	11 097	-610
1992	-1 667	-7 408	5 807	-66	-77 111	-48 733	-49 166	-387	21 175
1993	-351	-6 311	6 270	-310	-199 284	-84 412	-146 253	766	30 615
1994	-390	-5 383	5 088	-95	-181 542	-80 697	-60 309	-36 336	-4 200
1995	-984	-4 859	4 125	-250	-319 949	-99 481	-100 074	-45 286	-75 108
1996	-989	-5 025	3 930	106	-386 441	-92 694	-115 859	-86 333	-91 555
1997	68	-5 417	5 438	47	-464 354	-109 955	-89 174	-120 403	-144 822
1998	-429	-4 676	4 102	145	-285 605	-132 829	-102 817	-25 041	-24 918
1990:									
1st quarter	-756	-1 871	1 189	-74	41 680	-10 472	-8 580	3 019	57 713
2nd quarter	-796	-2 019	1 209	14	-36 863	-4 735	-11 037	-5 069	-16 022
3rd quarter	-338	-1 349	1 039	-28	-45 202	-17 983	-1 037	-15 514	-10 668
4th quarter	4 205	-3 171	7 419	-43	-41 341	-4 326	-8 111	-10 260	-18 644
1991:									
1st quarter	549	-2 018	2 630	-63	-10 847	-14 399	-9 960	-40	13 552
2nd quarter	-423	-1 061	840	-202	72	-1 312	-12 021	7 902	5 503
3rd quarter	3 256	-8 724	12 417	-437	-23 122	-9 444	-12 550	3 341	-4 469
4th quarter	-459	-1 077	890	-272	-39 524	-13 080	-11 142	-106	-15 196
1992:									
1st quarter	-259	-1 517	1 326	-68	-10 222	-20 805	-8 668	7 562	11 689
2nd quarter	-302	-1 247	1 084	-139	-17 513	-10 384	-8 196	-6 620	7 687
3rd quarter	-392	-1 980	1 359	229	-15 250	-5 277	-13 059	-3 737	6 823
4th quarter	-715	-2 664	2 038	-89	-34 125	-12 266	-19 243	2 408	-5 024
1993:									
1st quarter	487	-945	1 763	-331	-21 110	-15 097	-28 208	-6 130	28 325
2nd quarter	-304	-773	891	-422	-46 476	-23 379	-29 833	-725	7 461
3rd quarter	-194	-1 668	2 036	-562	-52 352	-13 270	-51 940	5 896	6 962
4th quarter	-340	-2 925	1 580	1 005	-79 347	-32 667	-36 272	1 725	-12 133
1994:									
1st quarter	399	-757	1 120	36	-40 200	-28 674	-19 540	-2 215	10 229
2nd quarter	477	-1 006	1 648	-165	-47 212	-15 058	-9 229	-20 966	-1 959
3rd quarter	-323	-1 372	1 383	-334	-30 633	-17 452	-12 405	-960	184
4th quarter	-943	-2 248	937	368	-63 499	-19 515	-19 135	-12 195	-12 654
1995:									
1st quarter	-553	-1 622	1 072	-3	-58 105	-19 495	-7 631	-2 631	-28 348
2nd quarter	-225	-862	649	-12	-110 671	-15 258	-23 313	-24 580	-47 520
3rd quarter	252	-1 028	1 522	-242	-39 886	-21 960	-36 144	13 729	4 489
4th quarter	-458	-1 347	882	7	-111 285	-42 766	-32 986	-31 804	-3 729
1996:									
1st quarter	-210	-1 076	1 013	-147	-71 487	-23 926	-34 620	-15 210	2 269
2nd quarter	-568	-1 512	683	261	-60 276	-15 279	-23 640	-22 000	643
3rd quarter	105	-1 192	1 214	83	-92 103	-23 341	-25 895	-9 090	-33 777
4th quarter	-316	-1 245	1 020	-91	-162 572	-30 145	-31 704	-40 033	-60 690
1997:									
1st quarter	-76	-1 170	1 119	-25	-149 069	-30 726	-16 787	-37 880	-63 676
2nd quarter	-298	-1 616	1 329	-11	-90 590	-25 907	-23 949	-9 825	-30 909
3rd quarter	377	-1 426	1 832	-29	-112 225	-22 381	-39 462	-24 791	-25 591
4th quarter	65	-1 205	1 158	112	-112 470	-30 941	-8 976	-47 907	-24 646
1998:									
1st quarter	-81	-1 192	1 133	-22	-59 074	-37 300	-14 116	-6 596	-1 062
2nd quarter	-483	-1 156	699	-26	-118 089	-43 172	-32 886	-14 327	-27 704
3rd quarter	185	-1 285	1 332	138	-60 256	-21 586	14 994	-20 320	-33 344
4th quarter	-50	-1 043	938	55	-48 188	-30 773	-70 809	16 202	37 192

1. A minus sign indicates financial outflows.

U.S. International Transactions—*Continued*

(Millions of dollars, seasonally adjusted)

Year and quarter	Total	Foreign-owned assets in the United States, net [1]											
		Foreign official assets in the United States, net							Other foreign assets in the United States, net				
		Total	U.S. government securities			Other U.S. govern-ment liabilities	U.S. liabilities reported by U.S. banks, not included elsewhere	Other foreign official assets	Total	Direct investment	U.S. Treasury securities	U.S. securities other than Treasury securities	U.S. currency
			Total	U.S. Treasury securities	Other								
1970	6 359	6 908	9 439	9 411	28	-456	-2 075	.....	-550	1 464	81	2 189	.....
1971	22 970	26 879	26 570	26 578	-8	-510	819	.....	-3 909	367	-24	2 289	.....
1972	21 461	10 475	8 470	8 213	257	182	1 638	.....	10 986	949	-39	4 507	.....
1973	18 388	6 026	641	59	582	936	4 126	185	12 362	2 800	-216	4 041	.....
1974	35 341	10 546	4 172	3 270	902	301	5 818	254	24 796	4 760	697	378	1 100
1975	17 170	7 027	5 563	4 658	905	1 517	-2 158	2 104	10 143	2 603	2 590	2 503	1 500
1976	38 018	17 693	9 892	9 319	573	4 627	969	2 205	20 326	4 347	2 783	1 284	1 500
1977	53 219	36 816	32 538	30 230	2 308	1 400	773	2 105	16 403	3 728	534	2 437	1 900
1978	67 036	33 678	24 221	23 555	666	2 476	5 551	1 430	33 358	7 897	2 178	2 254	3 000
1979	40 852	-13 665	-21 972	-22 435	463	-40	7 213	1 135	54 516	11 877	4 060	1 351	3 000
1980	62 612	15 497	11 895	9 708	2 187	615	-159	3 145	47 115	16 918	2 645	5 457	4 500
1981	86 232	4 960	6 322	5 019	1 303	-338	-3 670	2 646	81 272	25 195	2 927	6 905	3 200
1982	96 578	3 593	5 085	5 779	-694	605	-1 747	-350	92 986	12 624	7 027	6 085	4 000
1983	88 783	5 845	6 496	6 972	-476	602	545	-1 798	82 938	10 461	8 689	8 164	5 400
1984	117 973	3 140	4 703	4 690	13	739	555	-2 857	114 833	24 689	23 001	12 568	4 100
1985	146 452	-1 119	-1 139	-838	-301	844	645	-1 469	147 570	20 079	20 433	50 962	5 200
1986	230 345	35 648	33 150	34 364	-1 214	2 195	1 187	-884	194 696	35 756	3 809	70 969	4 100
1987	249 016	45 387	44 802	43 238	1 564	-2 326	3 918	-1 007	203 629	58 852	-7 643	42 120	5 400
1988	246 948	39 758	43 050	41 741	1 309	-467	-319	-2 506	207 190	58 161	20 239	26 353	5 800
1989	225 307	8 503	1 532	149	1 383	160	4 976	1 835	216 804	68 653	29 618	38 767	5 900
1990	142 028	33 910	30 243	29 576	667	1 868	3 385	-1 586	108 118	48 951	-2 534	1 592	18 800
1991	111 332	17 389	16 147	14 846	1 301	1 367	-1 484	1 359	93 944	23 695	18 826	35 144	15 400
1992	171 815	40 477	22 403	18 454	3 949	2 191	16 571	-688	131 338	20 975	37 131	30 043	13 400
1993	283 230	71 753	53 014	48 952	4 062	1 313	14 841	2 585	211 477	52 552	24 381	80 092	18 900
1994	307 306	39 583	36 827	30 750	6 077	1 564	3 665	-2 473	267 723	47 438	34 274	56 971	23 400
1995	467 552	109 880	72 712	68 977	3 735	-105	34 008	3 265	357 672	59 644	99 548	96 367	12 300
1996	574 847	127 390	120 679	115 671	5 008	-316	5 704	1 323	447 457	88 977	154 996	130 240	17 362
1997	751 661	18 119	-2 161	-6 690	4 529	-1 798	22 286	-208	733 542	109 264	146 433	196 258	24 782
1998	502 637	-21 684	-3 625	-9 957	6 332	-3 113	-11 469	-3 477	524 321	193 375	46 155	218 026	16 622
1990:													
1st quarter	-22 713	-6 421	-6 698	-6 177	-521	-195	598	-126	-16 292	15 885	-1 891	1 311	3 600
2nd quarter	41 329	6 207	4 081	3 735	346	1 160	1 240	-274	35 122	13 887	1 857	2 114	4 400
3rd quarter	63 347	13 977	12 469	12 335	134	-408	2 141	-265	49 410	8 429	544	-2 874	5 500
4th quarter	60 065	20 186	20 391	19 683	708	1 310	-594	-921	39 879	10 751	-3 044	1 041	5 300
1991:													
1st quarter	8 446	5 569	126	155	-29	769	3 908	766	2 877	4 175	4 739	5 023	4 800
2nd quarter	12 790	-4 914	-3 764	-3 545	-219	253	-1 517	115	17 703	13 490	13 461	14 872	2 200
3rd quarter	33 374	3 854	6 095	5 621	474	771	-3 107	95	29 520	-1 216	-1 196	10 310	4 200
4th quarter	56 724	12 879	13 690	12 615	1 075	-426	-768	383	43 845	7 247	1 822	4 939	4 200
1992:													
1st quarter	31 326	20 988	15 380	14 916	464	-73	5 568	113	10 338	2 333	686	4 569	1 300
2nd quarter	50 587	20 879	12 950	11 251	1 699	518	7 486	-75	29 708	6 199	10 231	10 467	1 100
3rd quarter	35 775	-7 524	593	-319	912	607	-7 724	-1 000	43 299	3 204	4 908	2 531	6 100
4th quarter	54 125	6 133	-6 520	-7 394	874	1 138	11 241	274	47 992	9 238	21 306	12 476	4 900
1993:													
1st quarter	25 399	10 937	1 745	1 080	665	-469	8 257	1 404	14 462	8 360	13 363	9 694	3 000
2nd quarter	59 335	17 466	6 750	5 668	1 082	132	9 485	1 099	41 869	11 683	-292	15 205	5 900
3rd quarter	85 990	19 073	20 443	19 098	1 345	932	-2 486	184	66 917	11 984	3 258	17 782	6 400
4th quarter	112 507	24 277	24 076	23 106	970	718	-415	-102	88 230	20 526	8 052	37 411	3 600
1994:													
1st quarter	90 581	10 568	1 074	897	177	659	9 588	-753	80 013	6 184	9 912	21 070	5 500
2nd quarter	57 157	9 455	8 282	5 922	2 360	-5	2 143	-965	47 702	6 082	-7 098	12 352	6 300
3rd quarter	82 270	19 358	18 697	16 475	2 222	284	1 177	-800	62 912	14 045	5 661	13 389	4 700
4th quarter	77 298	202	8 774	7 456	1 318	626	-9 243	45	77 096	21 127	25 799	10 160	6 900
1995:													
1st quarter	103 645	21 956	11 258	10 132	1 126	-562	10 995	265	81 689	10 319	30 011	15 734	6 400
2nd quarter	129 345	37 072	26 560	25 234	1 326	54	7 510	2 948	92 273	12 328	30 439	20 606	1 900
3rd quarter	124 768	39 302	21 116	20 598	518	-504	18 918	-228	85 466	17 255	37 295	32 128	1 900
4th quarter	109 794	11 550	13 778	13 013	765	907	-3 415	280	98 244	19 742	1 803	27 899	2 100
1996:													
1st quarter	92 184	51 950	55 839	55 685	154	-375	-3 303	-211	40 234	29 146	18 031	29 391	-2 391
2nd quarter	111 759	13 616	-1 934	-3 378	1 444	48	14 217	1 285	98 143	16 829	26 967	31 179	4 542
3rd quarter	149 096	23 284	26 135	24 908	1 227	411	-1 677	-1 585	125 812	15 884	38 727	35 118	7 382
4th quarter	221 807	38 540	40 639	38 456	2 183	-400	-3 533	1 834	183 267	27 117	71 271	34 552	7 829
1997:													
1st quarter	185 303	27 524	23 105	22 351	754	-394	8 123	-3 310	157 779	26 856	33 050	45 015	3 484
2nd quarter	152 767	-6 177	-11 411	-12 373	962	-444	4 643	1 035	158 944	24 304	37 928	53 890	4 822
3rd quarter	188 126	23 260	10 316	7 604	2 712	-776	12 817	903	164 866	24 128	40 133	62 673	6 576
4th quarter	225 466	-26 488	-24 171	-24 272	101	-184	-3 297	1 164	251 954	33 977	35 322	34 680	9 900
1998:													
1st quarter	96 817	11 004	13 946	11 336	2 610	-1 028	-958	-956	85 813	27 016	-2 557	76 810	746
2nd quarter	162 466	-10 551	-20 064	-20 318	254	-807	9 488	832	173 017	20 946	25 759	71 785	2 349
3rd quarter	93 547	-46 489	-30 905	-32 811	1 906	-224	-12 866	-2 494	140 036	24 906	-1 438	20 103	7 277
4th quarter	149 805	24 352	33 398	31 836	1 562	-1 054	-7 133	-859	125 453	120 505	24 391	49 328	6 250

1. A minus sign indicates financial outflows or decrease in foreign official assets in the United States.

U.S. International Transactions— *Continued*

(Millions of dollars, seasonally adjusted)

Year and quarter	Financial account—Continued		Statistical discrepancy [2]		Balance on:						
	Other foreign assets in the U.S., net [1] —Continued				Goods	Services	Goods and services	Income	Goods, services, and income	Unilateral current transfers	Current account
	U.S. liabilities		Total	Seasonal adjustment discrepancy							
	To unaffiliated foreigners reported by U.S. nonbanking concerns	Reported by U.S. banks not included elsewhere									
1970	2 014	-6 298	-219	.....	2 603	-349	2 254	6 233	8 487	-6 156	2 331
1971	369	-6 911	-9 779	.....	-2 260	957	-1 303	7 272	5 969	-7 402	-1 433
1972	815	4 754	-1 879	.....	-6 416	973	-5 443	8 192	2 749	-8 544	-5 795
1973	1 035	4 702	-2 654	.....	911	989	1 900	12 153	14 053	-6 913	7 140
1974	1 844	16 017	-2 558	.....	-5 505	1 213	-4 292	15 503	11 211	-9 249	1 962
1975	319	628	4 417	.....	8 903	3 501	12 404	12 787	25 191	-7 075	18 116
1976	-578	10 990	8 955	.....	-9 483	3 401	-6 082	16 063	9 981	-5 686	4 295
1977	1 086	6 719	-4 099	.....	-31 091	3 845	-27 246	18 137	-9 109	-5 226	-14 335
1978	1 889	16 141	9 236	.....	-33 927	4 164	-29 763	20 408	-9 355	-5 788	-15 143
1979	1 621	32 607	24 349	.....	-27 568	3 003	-24 565	30 873	6 308	-6 593	-285
1980	6 852	10 743	20 886	.....	-25 500	6 093	-19 407	30 073	10 666	-8 349	2 317
1981	917	42 128	21 792	.....	-28 023	11 852	-16 172	32 903	16 731	-11 702	5 030
1982	-2 383	65 633	37 224	.....	-36 485	12 329	-24 156	35 118	10 962	-17 139	-6 177
1983	-118	50 342	16 630	.....	-67 102	9 335	-57 767	36 347	-21 420	-17 778	-39 198
1984	16 626	33 849	17 059	.....	-112 492	3 419	-109 073	34 981	-74 092	-20 661	-94 753
1985	9 851	41 045	17 242	.....	-122 173	294	-121 880	25 580	-96 300	-22 762	-119 062
1986	3 325	76 737	30 524	.....	-145 081	5 295	-139 786	15 368	-124 418	-24 818	-149 236
1987	18 363	86 537	-7 196	.....	-159 557	6 804	-152 753	14 155	-138 598	-24 047	-162 645
1988	32 893	63 744	-17 535	.....	-126 959	11 504	-115 455	18 548	-96 907	-26 139	-123 046
1989	22 086	51 780	48 920	.....	-115 245	23 736	-91 509	19 724	-71 785	-27 116	-98 900
1990	45 133	-3 824	25 454	.....	-109 030	29 091	-79 939	28 429	-51 510	-27 821	-79 332
1991	-3 115	3 994	-46 405	.....	-74 068	44 584	-29 484	23 950	-5 534	9 819	4 284
1992	13 573	16 216	-46 921	.....	-96 106	59 081	-37 025	22 269	-14 756	-35 873	-50 629
1993	10 489	25 063	3 157	.....	-132 609	62 669	-69 940	23 176	-46 764	-38 522	-85 286
1994	1 302	104 338	-8 571	.....	-166 192	67 797	-98 395	15 907	-82 488	-39 192	-121 680
1995	59 637	30 176	-23 683	.....	-173 729	76 190	-97 539	19 410	-78 129	-35 437	-113 566
1996	39 404	16 478	-65 462	.....	-191 270	86 952	-104 318	17 210	-87 108	-42 187	-129 295
1997	107 779	149 026	-143 192	.....	-196 651	91 921	-104 730	3 231	-101 499	-41 966	-143 465
1998	9 412	40 731	10 126	.....	-246 932	82 650	-164 282	-12 205	-176 487	-44 075	-220 562
1990:											
1st quarter	12 904	-48 101	6 454	4 101	-27 146	6 572	-20 574	5 898	-14 676	-6 793	-21 469
2nd quarter	6 713	6 151	14 992	142	-24 596	6 954	-17 642	6 375	-11 267	-7 923	-19 190
3rd quarter	16 838	20 973	4 568	-5 581	-29 050	7 209	-21 841	5 197	-16 644	-7 635	-24 279
4th quarter	8 678	17 153	-566	1 332	-28 238	8 363	-19 875	10 958	-8 917	-5 472	-14 389
1991:											
1st quarter	-586	-15 274	-8 689	4 665	-18 796	7 786	-11 010	8 089	-2 921	14 756	11 835
2nd quarter	-2 549	-23 771	-16 913	103	-16 176	10 781	-5 395	5 246	-149	3 536	3 387
3rd quarter	4 761	12 661	-7 517	-6 032	-19 747	12 356	-7 391	4 347	-3 044	-3 039	-6 083
4th quarter	-4 741	30 378	-13 286	1 265	-19 349	13 663	-5 686	6 268	582	-5 438	-4 856
1992:											
1st quarter	5 689	-4 239	-14 648	4 424	-17 940	14 403	-3 537	6 012	2 475	-7 767	-5 292
2nd quarter	3 954	-2 243	-21 947	451	-24 252	14 653	-9 599	5 830	-3 769	-8 631	-12 400
3rd quarter	4 854	21 702	-7 917	-6 232	-27 294	15 920	-11 374	5 079	-6 295	-8 046	-14 341
4th quarter	-924	996	-2 403	1 363	-26 620	14 103	-12 517	5 347	-7 170	-11 430	-18 600
1993:											
1st quarter	-215	-19 740	10 680	5 523	-29 207	16 044	-13 163	7 287	-5 876	-8 138	-14 014
2nd quarter	6 531	2 842	7 099	58	-33 386	15 900	-17 486	5 654	-11 832	-8 791	-20 623
3rd quarter	288	27 205	-9 933	-6 250	-36 497	15 945	-20 552	7 059	-13 493	-9 557	-23 050
4th quarter	3 885	14 756	-4 686	671	-33 519	14 779	-18 740	3 174	-15 566	-12 036	-27 602
1994:											
1st quarter	5 856	31 491	-26 666	3 922	-36 627	15 749	-20 878	4 864	-16 014	-8 193	-24 207
2nd quarter	4 269	25 797	15 283	-207	-40 827	17 149	-23 678	3 857	-19 821	-8 717	-28 538
3rd quarter	-1 620	26 737	-17 659	-6 807	-44 348	17 159	-27 189	3 612	-23 577	-9 843	-33 420
4th quarter	-7 203	20 313	20 471	3 092	-44 390	17 741	-26 649	3 574	-23 075	-12 438	-35 513
1995:											
1st quarter	17 764	1 461	-9 288	4 743	-44 077	17 272	-26 805	5 146	-21 659	-8 868	-30 527
2nd quarter	11 864	15 136	17 216	357	-48 436	17 531	-30 905	6 087	-24 818	-8 397	-33 215
3rd quarter	13 493	-16 605	-54 878	-7 545	-42 168	20 370	-21 798	2 570	-19 228	-8 836	-28 064
4th quarter	16 516	30 184	23 270	2 448	-39 048	21 012	-18 036	5 607	-12 429	-9 336	-21 765
1996:											
1st quarter	-557	-33 386	6 088	4 984	-42 600	20 255	-22 345	6 521	-15 824	-10 920	-26 744
2nd quarter	16 367	2 259	-19 104	-604	-48 151	21 671	-26 480	4 209	-22 271	-9 185	-31 456
3rd quarter	25 629	3 072	-26 432	-9 200	-51 205	19 737	-31 468	2 648	-28 820	-9 507	-38 327
4th quarter	-2 035	44 533	-26 010	4 824	-49 314	25 284	-24 030	3 830	-20 200	-12 574	-32 774
1997:											
1st quarter	28 840	20 534	-5 875	4 724	-49 208	22 596	-26 612	1 061	-25 551	-9 347	-34 898
2nd quarter	5 274	32 726	-30 228	-682	-47 878	23 689	-24 189	2 212	-21 977	-9 494	-31 471
3rd quarter	26 275	5 081	-39 952	-10 546	-48 915	23 192	-25 723	204	-25 519	-10 096	-35 615
4th quarter	47 390	90 685	-67 141	6 500	-50 650	22 449	-28 201	-247	-28 448	-13 030	-41 478
1998:											
1st quarter	32 707	-48 909	5 657	5 915	-54 876	21 538	-33 338	247	-33 091	-9 927	-43 018
2nd quarter	18 040	34 138	10 291	528	-63 500	21 539	-41 961	-553	-42 514	-9 886	-52 400
3rd quarter	11 875	77 313	31 878	-10 582	-64 969	19 245	-45 724	-6 965	-52 689	-10 787	-63 476
4th quarter	-53 210	-21 811	-37 695	4 144	-63 587	20 325	-43 262	-4 933	-48 195	-13 474	-61 669

1. A minus sign indicates financial outflows or decreases in foreign official assets in the United States.
2. Sum of credits and debits with the sign reversed.

U.S. Exports and Imports of Goods and Services

(Balance of payments basis, millions of dollars, seasonally adjusted)

Year and month	Goods and services			Goods			Services		
	Exports	Imports	Balance	Exports	Imports	Balance	Exports	Imports	Balance
1970	56 640	54 386	2 254	42 469	39 866	2 603	14 171	14 520	-349
1971	59 677	60 979	-1 302	43 319	45 579	-2 260	16 358	15 400	958
1972	67 222	72 665	-5 443	49 381	55 797	-6 416	17 841	16 868	973
1973	91 242	89 342	1 900	71 410	70 499	911	19 832	18 843	989
1974	120 897	125 190	-4 293	98 306	103 811	-5 505	22 591	21 379	1 212
1975	132 585	120 181	12 404	107 088	98 185	8 903	25 497	21 996	3 501
1976	142 716	148 798	-6 082	114 745	124 228	-9 483	27 971	24 570	3 401
1977	152 301	179 547	-27 246	120 816	151 907	-31 091	31 485	27 640	3 845
1978	178 428	208 191	-29 763	142 075	176 002	-33 927	36 353	32 189	4 164
1979	224 131	248 696	-24 565	184 439	212 007	-27 568	39 692	36 689	3 003
1980	271 834	291 241	-19 407	224 250	249 750	-25 500	47 584	41 491	6 093
1981	294 398	310 570	-16 172	237 044	265 067	-28 023	57 354	45 503	11 851
1982	275 236	299 391	-24 156	211 157	247 642	-36 485	64 079	51 749	12 330
1983	266 106	323 874	-57 767	201 799	268 901	-67 102	64 307	54 973	9 334
1984	291 094	400 166	-109 073	219 926	332 418	-112 492	71 168	67 748	3 420
1985	289 070	410 950	-121 880	215 915	338 088	-122 173	73 155	72 862	293
1986	309 694	450 260	-140 566	223 344	368 425	-145 081	86 350	81 835	4 515
1987	348 801	502 114	-153 313	250 208	409 765	-159 557	98 593	92 349	6 244
1988	431 298	547 154	-115 856	320 230	447 189	-126 959	111 068	99 965	11 103
1989	489 353	581 550	-92 197	362 120	477 365	-115 245	127 233	104 185	23 048
1990	537 229	618 358	-81 129	389 307	498 337	-109 030	147 922	120 021	27 901
1991	581 246	612 177	-30 931	416 913	490 981	-74 068	164 333	121 196	43 137
1992	615 909	652 934	-37 025	440 352	536 458	-96 106	175 557	116 476	59 081
1993	641 783	711 722	-69 940	456 832	589 441	-132 609	184 951	122 281	62 669
1994	702 073	800 468	-98 395	502 398	668 590	-166 192	199 675	131 878	67 797
1995	793 482	891 021	-97 539	575 845	749 574	-173 729	217 637	141 447	76 190
1996	849 806	954 124	-104 318	612 057	803 327	-191 270	237 749	150 797	86 952
1997	938 543	1 043 273	-104 731	679 715	876 366	-196 652	258 828	166 907	91 921
1998	933 907	1 098 189	-164 282	670 246	917 178	-246 932	263 661	181 011	82 650
1995:									
January	63 134	72 185	-9 051	45 619	60 745	-15 126	17 515	11 440	6 075
February	62 843	71 491	-8 648	45 914	60 076	-14 162	16 929	11 415	5 514
March	64 844	73 950	-9 106	47 483	62 272	-14 789	17 361	11 678	5 683
April	64 812	75 114	-10 302	47 032	63 448	-16 416	17 780	11 666	6 114
May	65 526	75 205	-9 679	47 646	63 474	-15 828	17 880	11 731	6 149
June	64 532	75 456	-10 924	47 425	63 617	-16 192	17 107	11 839	5 268
July	65 817	74 549	-8 731	47 377	62 700	-15 322	18 440	11 849	6 591
August	67 121	74 200	-7 079	48 555	62 289	-13 734	18 566	11 911	6 655
September	69 005	74 993	-5 988	49 976	63 088	-13 112	19 029	11 905	7 124
October	68 033	74 382	-6 349	49 332	62 462	-13 130	18 701	11 920	6 781
November	68 485	74 498	-6 014	49 455	62 459	-13 005	19 030	12 039	6 991
December	69 326	75 000	-5 674	50 030	62 944	-12 914	19 296	12 056	7 240
1996:									
January	68 281	76 164	-7 883	49 579	64 102	-14 523	18 702	12 062	6 640
February	69 485	76 264	-6 780	50 835	63 911	-13 077	18 650	12 353	6 297
March	69 599	77 283	-7 684	50 023	65 025	-15 002	19 576	12 258	7 318
April	69 667	78 427	-8 760	50 502	66 076	-15 574	19 165	12 351	6 814
May	70 867	80 270	-9 402	50 884	67 718	-16 833	19 983	12 552	7 431
June	70 920	79 237	-8 316	51 226	66 969	-15 742	19 694	12 268	7 426
July	68 969	79 651	-10 681	49 883	66 687	-16 803	19 086	12 964	6 122
August	70 672	80 898	-10 226	51 159	68 111	-16 952	19 513	12 787	6 726
September	70 454	81 015	-10 561	50 949	68 399	-17 450	19 505	12 616	6 889
October	73 735	80 638	-6 903	52 407	67 747	-15 340	21 328	12 891	8 437
November	74 384	81 493	-7 109	52 841	68 660	-15 819	21 543	12 833	8 710
December	72 768	82 786	-10 018	51 768	69 923	-18 155	21 000	12 863	8 137
1997:									
January	73 707	83 400	-9 693	52 796	70 071	-17 275	20 911	13 329	7 582
February	75 169	84 151	-8 982	54 409	70 729	-16 320	20 760	13 422	7 338
March	76 884	84 821	-7 937	55 774	71 387	-15 613	21 110	13 434	7 676
April	77 949	85 897	-7 948	56 575	72 391	-15 816	21 374	13 506	7 868
May	77 737	86 444	-8 707	56 028	72 726	-16 698	21 709	13 718	7 991
June	78 997	86 531	-7 534	57 292	72 656	-15 364	21 705	13 875	7 830
July	80 110	87 717	-7 607	58 379	73 635	-15 256	21 731	14 082	7 649
August	79 571	88 457	-8 886	57 496	74 308	-16 812	22 075	14 149	7 926
September	79 604	88 834	-9 230	57 572	74 419	-16 847	22 032	14 415	7 617
October	80 232	88 782	-8 550	58 044	74 532	-16 488	22 188	14 250	7 938
November	79 001	88 437	-9 436	57 319	74 114	-16 795	21 682	14 323	7 359
December	79 586	89 801	-10 215	58 031	75 398	-17 367	21 555	14 403	7 152
1998:									
January	79 397	89 247	-9 850	57 748	74 889	-17 141	21 649	14 358	7 291
February	77 999	88 705	-10 706	56 512	74 018	-17 506	21 487	14 687	6 800
March	78 436	91 217	-12 782	56 406	76 634	-20 229	22 030	14 583	7 447
April	78 040	91 257	-13 217	55 330	76 190	-20 860	22 710	15 067	7 643
May	77 126	92 027	-14 901	54 853	77 089	-22 236	22 273	14 938	7 335
June	76 723	90 566	-13 843	55 015	75 419	-20 404	21 708	15 147	6 561
July	75 824	90 513	-14 689	54 164	75 230	-21 066	21 660	15 283	6 377
August	76 227	92 086	-15 860	54 624	76 914	-22 291	21 603	15 172	6 431
September	77 234	92 409	-15 174	55 472	77 084	-21 611	21 762	15 325	6 437
October	79 617	93 975	-14 358	57 193	78 183	-20 990	22 424	15 792	6 632
November	79 126	93 789	-14 664	56 926	78 464	-21 539	22 200	15 325	6 875
December	78 161	92 402	-14 241	56 005	77 064	-21 059	22 156	15 338	6 818

U.S. Exports of Goods by Selected Countries and Regions

(Census basis, except as noted; millions of dollars, not seasonally adjusted)

Year and month	Total exports of goods			North America			Central and South America [1]						
	Total: Balance of payments basis	Net adjustments	Total: Census basis	Total	Canada	Mexico	Total [2]	Argentina	Brazil	Chile	Colombia	Dominican Republic	Venezuela
1970	42 469	.....	.....	11 300	9 596	1 704	.....	.....	841	.....	.....	.....	759
1971	43 319	.....	.....	12 523	10 903	1 620	.....	.....	966	.....	.....	.....	787
1972	49 381	.....	.....	15 052	13 070	1 982	.....	.....	1 243	.....	.....	.....	924
1973	71 410	.....	.....	19 083	16 146	2 937	.....	.....	1 916	.....	.....	.....	1 033
1974	98 306	.....	.....	26 136	21 281	4 855	.....	.....	3 088	.....	.....	.....	1 768
1975	107 088	.....	.....	28 089	22 948	5 141	.....	.....	3 056	.....	.....	.....	2 243
1976	114 745	.....	.....	30 667	25 677	4 990	.....	.....	2 809	.....	.....	.....	2 628
1977	120 816	.....	.....	32 544	27 738	4 806	.....	.....	2 490	.....	.....	.....	3 171
1978	142 075	.....	.....	37 220	30 540	6 680	.....	.....	2 981	.....	.....	.....	3 728
1979	184 439	.....	.....	47 446	37 599	9 847	.....	.....	3 442	.....	.....	.....	3 934
1980	224 250	.....	.....	55 476	40 331	15 145	.....	2 625	4 344	.....	1 736	.....	4 573
1981	237 044	.....	.....	62 391	44 602	17 789	.....	2 192	3 798	.....	1 771	.....	5 445
1982	211 157	.....	.....	49 704	37 887	11 817	.....	1 294	3 423	.....	1 903	.....	5 206
1983	201 799	91	201 708	52 427	43 345	9 082	.....	965	2 557	.....	1 514	.....	2 811
1984	219 926	1 183	218 743	63 769	51 777	11 992	.....	900	2 640	.....	1 450	.....	3 377
1985	215 915	3 294	212 621	66 922	53 287	13 635	.....	721	3 140	.....	1 468	.....	3 399
1986	223 344	-3 127	226 471	67 904	55 512	12 392	.....	944	3 885	.....	1 319	.....	3 141
1987	250 208	-3 696	253 904	74 396	59 814	14 582	.....	1 090	4 040	.....	1 412	.....	3 586
1988	320 230	-3 105	323 335	92 250	71 622	20 628	.....	1 054	4 267	.....	1 754	.....	4 612
1989	362 120	-1 716	363 836	103 791	78 809	24 982	.....	1 039	4 804	.....	1 924	.....	3 025
1990	389 307	-3 617	392 924	112 241	83 866	28 375	.....	1 179	5 062	.....	2 029	.....	3 107
1991	416 913	-4 851	421 764	118 427	85 150	33 277	.....	2 045	6 148	1 839	1 952	1 743	4 656
1992	440 352	-7 809	448 161	131 186	90 594	40 592	35 204	3 223	5 751	2 466	3 286	2 100	5 444
1993	456 832	-8 258	465 090	142 025	100 444	41 581	36 842	3 776	6 058	2 599	3 235	2 350	4 590
1994	502 398	-10 228	512 626	165 283	114 439	50 844	41 708	4 462	8 102	2 774	4 064	2 799	4 039
1995	575 845	-8 897	584 742	173 518	127 226	46 292	49 992	4 189	11 439	3 615	4 624	3 015	4 640
1996	612 057	-13 018	625 075	191 002	134 210	56 792	52 599	4 517	12 718	4 140	4 714	3 191	4 750
1997	679 715	-9 468	689 182	223 155	151 767	71 388	63 021	5 810	15 915	4 368	5 197	3 924	6 602
1998	670 246	-11 892	682 138	235 376	156 603	78 773	63 395	5 886	15 142	3 979	4 816	3 944	6 516
1995:													
January	42 998	-635	43 633	14 103	10 101	4 001	3 731	400	853	251	329	204	333
February	44 319	-680	44 999	13 834	10 162	3 672	3 694	301	895	243	367	218	339
March	51 809	-770	52 579	15 639	11 719	3 921	4 477	372	1 102	283	442	266	372
April	47 160	-649	47 808	13 984	10 601	3 383	4 232	350	1 082	247	401	284	365
May	49 100	-755	49 855	15 201	11 420	3 781	4 350	325	981	397	391	289	387
June	48 550	-843	49 393	14 642	10 938	3 704	4 137	316	968	291	373	260	456
July	43 672	-718	44 390	11 901	8 435	3 466	3 945	282	818	295	386	231	438
August	48 221	-751	48 972	15 021	10 834	4 187	4 203	327	915	353	357	261	444
September	49 061	-662	49 723	14 840	10 778	4 062	4 232	395	854	316	403	246	422
October	51 024	-804	51 828	15 742	11 429	4 313	4 254	376	912	314	407	267	405
November	49 906	-805	50 710	15 046	11 078	3 968	4 331	342	1 015	317	383	267	356
December	50 052	-801	50 853	13 567	9 732	3 835	4 406	403	1 046	308	388	223	325
1996:													
January	47 072	-695	47 767	14 578	10 301	4 276	3 773	311	829	287	380	209	332
February	50 322	-791	51 112	15 476	11 212	4 265	3 965	327	858	390	402	247	335
March	54 048	-904	54 952	16 059	11 600	4 459	4 100	346	941	280	373	259	412
April	51 029	-843	51 872	15 858	11 500	4 359	4 015	334	879	309	403	256	376
May	52 230	-1 130	53 359	16 196	11 456	4 740	4 396	383	990	308	407	294	466
June	50 939	-882	51 821	15 881	11 320	4 560	4 404	439	1 116	296	395	237	393
July	46 158	-1 440	47 598	14 214	9 647	4 567	4 463	387	1 033	403	377	271	378
August	50 223	-1 352	51 575	15 765	10 935	4 830	4 614	389	1 239	323	385	297	453
September	49 289	-1 309	50 598	16 623	11 673	4 950	4 447	395	1 203	317	387	262	371
October	55 042	-1 065	56 107	17 747	12 120	5 627	4 905	404	1 238	379	447	306	436
November	53 737	-1 279	55 016	17 261	12 145	5 116	4 773	421	1 244	356	386	305	440
December	51 980	-1 316	53 295	15 344	10 302	5 041	4 745	380	1 147	492	372	247	359
1997:													
January	50 025	-566	50 591	16 651	11 733	4 917	4 327	407	1 013	300	382	259	433
February	52 467	-685	53 153	17 431	12 102	5 330	4 360	378	1 049	309	364	311	384
March	60 203	-999	61 201	18 425	13 001	5 425	5 179	448	1 323	442	418	320	483
April	57 477	-703	58 180	19 010	13 289	5 721	5 065	424	1 208	363	470	345	513
May	57 736	-1 003	58 738	18 397	12 977	5 420	5 332	498	1 341	349	476	343	569
June	57 207	-842	58 049	18 419	12 506	5 913	5 278	477	1 335	331	445	329	581
July	53 868	-1 041	54 909	17 097	11 113	5 984	5 232	430	1 315	354	434	334	603
August	55 615	-1 047	56 662	18 527	12 256	6 271	5 444	545	1 372	339	455	346	623
September	56 731	-739	57 470	19 733	13 407	6 326	5 394	509	1 440	368	403	323	609
October	61 351	-1 050	62 402	21 258	14 093	7 165	6 103	527	1 568	387	508	380	684
November	57 494	-670	58 164	19 485	12 867	6 618	5 769	610	1 485	369	420	323	621
December	59 151	-513	59 664	18 721	12 422	6 299	5 540	558	1 466	478	423	310	500
1998:													
January	54 535	-637	55 172	18 352	12 118	6 234	4 944	468	1 123	330	401	262	608
February	54 426	-808	55 234	19 345	12 924	6 421	5 001	425	1 078	311	416	318	609
March	61 410	-887	62 297	21 484	14 573	6 911	5 722	517	1 294	294	496	370	665
April	56 014	-660	56 675	20 317	13 921	6 396	5 336	474	1 217	326	439	321	573
May	55 918	-754	56 672	19 951	13 543	6 408	5 548	496	1 311	515	407	331	624
June	56 090	-905	56 994	19 828	13 379	6 449	5 368	607	1 283	321	471	327	573
July	50 604	-973	51 578	16 659	10 517	6 142	5 409	539	1 205	311	367	375	571
August	52 101	-1 320	53 420	18 305	12 124	6 181	5 262	499	1 296	278	360	355	446
September	54 681	-946	55 627	20 151	13 255	6 896	4 759	462	1 198	352	323	284	426
October	60 105	-1 208	61 313	21 279	14 010	7 269	5 643	524	1 471	303	408	380	528
November	56 787	-1 608	58 395	20 555	13 576	6 979	5 196	434	1 330	250	356	322	488
December	57 576	-1 186	58 762	19 149	12 664	6 486	5 208	443	1 336	389	371	300	405

1. Includes Caribbean.
2. Includes countries not shown separately. See Notes for list of included countries.

U.S. Exports of Goods by Selected Countries and Regions—*Continued*

(Census basis, millions of dollars, not seasonally adjusted)

Year and month	Total¹	Western Europe — European Union									
		Total¹	Belgium	France	Germany	Ireland	Italy	Netherlands	Spain	Sweden	United Kingdom
1970	.....	.....	.....	1 483	2 741	.....	1 353	.....	.....	.....	2 536
1971	.....	.....	.....	1 373	2 831	.....	1 314	.....	.....	.....	2 369
1972	.....	.....	.....	1 609	2 808	.....	1 434	.....	.....	.....	2 658
1973	.....	.....	.....	2 263	3 756	.....	2 119	.....	.....	.....	3 564
1974	28 639	28 268	.....	2 942	4 985	.....	2 752	3 979	.....	.....	4 574
1975	29 939	22 862	.....	3 031	5 194	.....	2 867	4 183	.....	.....	4 527
1976	32 401	25 406	.....	3 446	5 731	.....	3 071	4 645	.....	.....	4 801
1977	33 752	26 476	.....	3 503	5 989	.....	2 790	4 796	.....	.....	5 951
1978	39 936	32 051	.....	4 166	6 957	.....	3 361	5 683	.....	.....	7 116
1979	54 331	42 582	.....	5 587	8 478	.....	4 362	6 907	.....	.....	10 635
1980	67 512	53 679	.....	7 485	10 960	.....	5 511	8 669	3 340	1 767	12 694
1981	65 377	52 363	.....	7 341	10 277	.....	5 360	8 595	3 563	1 842	12 439
1982	60 054	47 932	.....	7 110	9 291	.....	4 616	8 604	3 590	1 689	10 645
1983	55 980	44 311	.....	5 961	8 737	.....	3 908	7 767	2 915	1 581	10 621
1984	58 019	46 976	.....	6 037	9 084	.....	4 375	7 554	2 561	1 542	12 210
1985	56 763	48 994	.....	6 096	9 050	.....	4 625	7 269	2 524	1 925	11 273
1986	61 642	53 154	.....	7 216	10 561	.....	4 838	7 848	2 615	1 871	11 418
1987	69 718	60 575	.....	7 943	11 748	.....	5 530	8 217	3 148	1 894	14 114
1988	87 858	75 755	.....	9 970	14 348	.....	6 775	10 117	4 215	2 700	18 364
1989	100 165	86 331	.....	11 579	16 862	.....	7 215	11 364	4 796	3 138	20 837
1990	112 975	98 027	.....	13 652	18 693	.....	7 987	13 016	5 213	3 405	23 484
1991	118 682	103 123	10 572	15 346	21 302	2 681	8 570	13 511	5 474	3 287	22 046
1992	117 100	102 958	9 775	14 593	21 249	2 862	8 721	13 752	5 537	2 845	22 800
1993	113 681	96 973	8 878	13 267	18 932	2 728	6 464	12 839	4 168	2 354	26 438
1994	118 177	102 818	10 939	13 619	19 229	3 419	7 183	13 582	4 622	2 518	26 900
1995	134 863	123 671	12 466	14 245	22 394	4 109	8 862	16 558	5 526	3 080	28 857
1996	141 543	127 710	12 532	14 455	23 495	3 669	8 797	16 662	6 500	3 431	30 962
1997	155 384	140 773	13 420	15 965	24 458	4 642	8 995	19 827	5 539	3 314	36 425
1998	162 571	149 035	13 918	17 729	26 657	5 647	8 991	18 978	5 454	3 822	39 058
1995:											
January	9 648	8 986	886	1 166	1 709	326	640	1 174	456	209	1 949
February	10 266	9 505	977	1 256	1 740	310	707	1 209	391	208	2 065
March	12 571	11 295	1 140	1 288	1 906	403	780	1 506	589	247	2 750
April	11 767	11 017	1 139	1 236	1 944	337	727	1 481	483	269	2 802
May	11 755	10 528	1 066	1 267	1 825	295	717	1 597	499	247	2 410
June	11 023	9 658	966	1 159	1 756	272	862	1 212	415	237	2 239
July	9 910	9 168	929	1 044	1 699	307	580	1 198	363	226	2 172
August	10 729	9 937	1 039	1 075	1 760	347	690	1 400	382	262	2 307
September	11 114	10 324	1 063	1 112	1 912	310	727	1 217	526	268	2 557
October	12 029	10 996	1 115	1 215	2 070	357	873	1 491	451	308	2 451
November	11 745	10 911	1 100	1 159	1 914	442	741	1 580	423	267	2 510
December	12 306	11 348	1 045	1 268	2 160	404	819	1 494	548	332	2 647
1996:											
January	10 993	10 208	978	1 204	1 903	334	745	1 249	589	257	2 342
February	11 727	10 729	1 087	1 221	1 932	317	900	1 374	535	276	2 481
March	12 869	11 285	1 048	1 313	2 169	327	807	1 593	502	307	2 613
April	12 590	11 367	1 004	1 252	1 964	342	871	1 231	428	268	3 346
May	12 771	11 483	1 085	1 154	2 044	332	756	1 340	499	277	3 150
June	11 971	10 613	1 000	1 157	1 927	247	734	1 377	432	251	2 708
July	9 805	8 775	890	953	1 662	225	602	1 025	363	221	2 155
August	11 169	10 042	1 087	1 106	1 853	253	613	1 322	362	254	2 620
September	11 125	9 868	1 051	1 112	1 907	303	614	1 238	373	268	2 360
October	12 620	11 412	1 102	1 346	2 043	336	733	1 826	465	313	2 467
November	12 031	11 013	1 067	1 316	2 086	299	694	1 554	466	379	2 410
December	11 873	10 916	1 134	1 322	2 007	355	730	1 533	484	360	2 310
1997:											
January	11 261	10 424	1 099	1 233	1 838	345	684	1 445	498	262	2 466
February	12 928	11 834	1 064	1 213	2 034	325	750	1 659	525	249	3 331
March	15 014	13 210	1 218	1 433	2 300	336	811	1 682	526	315	3 838
April	13 753	12 150	1 070	1 377	2 370	375	842	1 610	457	297	3 124
May	13 513	11 919	1 137	1 314	2 010	427	753	1 760	463	286	3 113
June	13 220	11 533	1 125	1 331	1 964	391	752	1 494	449	250	3 204
July	* 11 567	10 450	1 010	1 232	1 813	349	690	1 433	374	234	2 749
August	11 824	10 820	1 128	1 233	1 990	385	646	1 513	335	252	2 599
September	12 519	11 605	1 087	1 284	2 007	345	687	1 867	385	272	2 934
October	13 525	12 521	1 176	1 466	2 137	425	811	1 932	544	302	2 906
November	12 627	11 746	1 192	1 391	2 008	466	769	1 669	482	287	2 841
December	13 634	12 563	1 115	1 460	1 989	473	800	1 764	501	309	3 320
1998:											
January	13 042	12 054	1 208	1 501	1 980	519	813	1 707	537	253	2 951
February	13 481	12 616	1 240	1 478	2 139	462	758	1 679	461	289	3 313
March	15 305	14 164	1 392	1 722	2 329	478	822	1 749	503	340	3 964
April	13 041	11 957	1 179	1 544	2 193	500	732	1 452	475	291	2 981
May	13 740	12 682	1 123	1 521	2 148	484	690	1 468	423	330	3 749
June	13 496	12 431	1 197	1 368	2 291	497	751	1 580	436	279	3 256
July	12 042	11 030	1 084	1 243	2 047	382	693	1 417	366	238	2 752
August	12 915	11 805	1 165	1 267	2 033	419	604	1 557	350	268	3 361
September	13 481	12 457	1 106	1 379	2 264	421	743	1 378	400	404	3 594
October	14 566	12 964	1 132	1 542	2 559	500	830	1 583	495	430	3 230
November	13 707	12 234	1 029	1 438	2 217	468	765	1 738	518	419	3 003
December	13 755	12 641	1 062	1 725	2 458	517	791	1 671	490	282	2 906

1. Includes countries not shown separately. See Notes for list of included countries.

U.S. Exports of Goods by Selected Countries and Regions—*Continued*

(Census basis, millions of dollars, not seasonally adjusted)

Year and month	Western Europe—*Continued* — European Free Trade Association			Eastern Europe and former Soviet Republics					Near and Middle Eastern countries		
	Total¹	Norway	Switzerland	Total¹	Hungary	Poland	Former Soviet Republics — Total¹	Russia	Israel	Saudi Arabia	Turkey
1970	.....	.....	.....	.....	.....	.....	119	.....	.....	.....	.....
1971	.....	.....	.....	.....	.....	.....	161	.....	.....	.....	.....
1972	.....	.....	.....	.....	.....	.....	542	.....	.....	.....	.....
1973	.....	.....	.....	.....	.....	.....	1 194	.....	.....	.....	.....
1974	.....	.....	.....	1 432	.....	.....	609	.....	.....	835	.....
1975	.....	.....	.....	2 788	.....	.....	1 835	.....	.....	1 502	.....
1976	.....	.....	.....	3 502	.....	.....	2 310	.....	.....	2 774	.....
1977	.....	.....	.....	2 544	.....	.....	1 628	.....	.....	3 575	.....
1978	.....	.....	.....	3 679	.....	.....	2 252	.....	.....	4 370	.....
1979	.....	.....	.....	5 683	.....	.....	3 607	.....	.....	4 875	.....
1980	.....	843	3 781	3 860	80	714	1 513	.....	.....	5 769	.....
1981	.....	892	3 022	4 338	78	681	2 431	.....	.....	7 327	.....
1982	.....	950	2 707	3 610	68	295	2 587	.....	.....	9 026	.....
1983	.....	813	2 960	2 891	110	324	2 003	.....	.....	7 903	.....
1984	.....	859	2 562	4 188	88	318	3 284	.....	.....	5 564	.....
1985	.....	666	2 288	3 215	94	238	2 423	.....	.....	4 474	.....
1986	.....	937	2 976	1 989	98	151	1 248	.....	.....	3 449	.....
1987	.....	842	3 151	2 200	95	239	1 480	.....	.....	3 373	.....
1988	.....	929	4 196	3 650	76	304	2 769	.....	.....	3 776	.....
1989	.....	1 037	4 911	5 307	122	413	4 284	.....	.....	3 574	.....
1990	.....	1 281	4 943	4 263	156	406	3 088	.....	.....	4 035	.....
1991	12 507	1 489	5 557	4 787	256	459	3 578	.....	3 911	6 557	2 468
1992	10 837	1 279	4 540	4 069	295	641	2 764	2 112	4 077	7 167	2 735
1993	12 704	1 212	6 806	6 104	435	912	3 984	2 970	4 429	6 661	3 429
1994	11 975	1 267	5 624	5 301	309	625	3 562	2 578	4 996	6 013	2 752
1995	7 706	1 293	6 227	5 701	295	776	3 807	2 823	5 621	6 155	2 768
1996	10 198	1 559	8 373	7 267	331	968	5 078	3 346	6 012	7 311	2 847
1997	10 220	1 721	8 307	7 889	486	1 170	5 191	3 365	5 995	8 438	3 540
1998	9 201	1 709	7 247	12 367	483	882	4 930	3 553	6 983	10 520	3 506
1995:											
January	453	90	354	368	27	45	225	178	415	733	167
February	432	85	338	369	26	38	245	195	421	398	268
March	1 003	115	874	434	25	52	285	217	634	411	210
April	515	109	391	436	24	54	292	220	406	402	185
May	889	107	765	536	22	134	319	249	608	629	244
June	1 044	94	933	490	22	54	346	266	432	619	268
July	457	97	342	421	23	55	291	230	428	406	226
August	499	97	385	454	19	58	319	233	445	368	246
September	523	106	399	516	26	67	354	258	425	526	209
October	731	157	554	508	24	62	350	250	435	543	244
November	566	111	437	597	27	73	411	271	434	589	208
December	596	125	455	573	29	84	371	257	538	531	294
1996:											
January	513	106	393	491	25	69	323	243	443	428	219
February	650	126	509	757	31	63	596	355	531	501	266
March	1 258	137	1 044	620	28	78	448	330	540	732	257
April	903	118	769	590	29	73	401	277	475	565	257
May	997	113	867	544	25	94	363	273	524	561	227
June	1 072	146	908	498	25	65	328	238	554	449	202
July	795	125	653	504	23	98	316	232	448	787	192
August	817	125	670	743	24	69	575	323	486	734	251
September	911	100	792	532	27	81	360	248	424	609	271
October	946	156	774	666	26	80	488	282	488	658	195
November	720	191	510	748	42	120	491	272	574	710	236
December	617	118	484	573	27	78	389	272	524	578	274
1997:											
January	516	113	387	524	33	63	377	234	464	439	241
February	726	141	571	509	39	68	331	222	458	510	261
March	1 356	208	1 128	774	47	77	480	262	564	795	381
April	1 296	199	1 079	738	43	127	468	325	514	560	257
May	1 108	175	916	715	39	163	398	259	498	640	421
June	1 287	114	1 156	717	48	184	407	245	532	529	335
July	745	138	589	536	35	67	377	264	462	563	284
August	669	140	513	640	27	88	447	255	503	513	288
September	618	111	495	646	39	82	453	309	407	749	239
October	650	122	514	742	40	93	519	294	479	550	287
November	538	112	412	765	47	83	547	445	455	587	263
December	710	149	548	584	50	77	388	251	661	2 003	284
1998:											
January	664	139	448	878	35	80	341	247	570	944	254
February	559	122	422	908	43	78	362	257	698	831	235
March	622	151	455	1 599	40	89	678	557	574	960	415
April	741	164	561	1 129	47	71	423	297	516	767	242
May	735	141	577	1 256	36	73	495	363	511	674	261
June	623	122	488	1 465	40	69	634	460	680	823	382
July	640	103	520	1 216	42	76	507	345	519	628	315
August	792	147	630	970	41	60	403	288	564	656	266
September	787	167	606	591	34	59	212	109	546	897	171
October	1 123	142	965	878	41	75	337	246	557	779	419
November	1 101	165	922	796	41	88	290	209	583	1 651	316
December	813	146	654	683	42	64	250	176	666	909	232

1. Includes countries not shown separately. See Notes for list of included countries.

U.S. Exports of Goods by Selected Countries and Regions—*Continued*

(Census basis, millions of dollars, not seasonally adjusted)

Year and month	Selected Asian and Oceanic countries											
	Australia	China	Hong Kong	India	Indonesia	Japan	South Korea	Malaysia	Phil-ippines	Singapore	Thailand	Taiwan
1970	.....	.....	.....	.....	.....	4 652	.....	.....	.....	.....	.....	.....
1971	.....	.....	.....	.....	.....	4 055	.....	.....	.....	.....	.....	.....
1972	.....	.....	.....	.....	.....	4 963	.....	.....	.....	.....	.....	.....
1973	.....	.....	.....	.....	.....	8 313	.....	.....	.....	.....	.....	.....
1974	2 157	807	882	.....	.....	10 679	.....	.....	.....	988	.....	1 427
1975	1 816	304	808	.....	.....	9 563	.....	.....	.....	994	.....	1 660
1976	2 185	135	1 115	.....	.....	10 145	.....	.....	.....	965	.....	1 635
1977	2 356	171	1 292	.....	.....	10 529	.....	.....	.....	1 172	.....	1 798
1978	2 910	824	1 625	.....	.....	12 885	.....	.....	.....	1 462	.....	2 340
1979	3 617	1 724	2 083	.....	.....	17 581	.....	.....	.....	2 331	.....	3 271
1980	4 093	3 755	2 686	.....	1 545	20 790	.....	.....	.....	3 033	.....	4 337
1981	5 242	3 603	2 635	.....	1 302	21 823	.....	.....	.....	3 003	.....	4 305
1982	4 535	2 912	2 453	.....	2 025	20 966	.....	.....	.....	3 214	.....	4 367
1983	3 954	2 173	2 564	.....	1 466	21 894	.....	.....	.....	3 759	.....	4 667
1984	4 793	3 004	3 062	.....	1 216	23 575	.....	.....	.....	3 675	.....	5 003
1985	5 441	3 856	2 786	.....	795	22 631	5 956	.....	.....	3 476	.....	4 700
1986	5 551	3 106	3 030	.....	946	26 882	6 355	.....	.....	3 380	.....	5 524
1987	5 495	3 497	3 983	.....	767	28 249	8 099	.....	.....	4 053	.....	7 413
1988	6 973	5 021	5 687	.....	1 059	37 725	11 232	.....	.....	5 768	.....	12 129
1989	8 331	5 755	6 246	.....	1 247	44 494	13 478	.....	.....	7 345	.....	11 335
1990	8 535	4 807	6 841	.....	1 897	48 585	14 399	.....	.....	8 019	.....	11 482
1991	8 404	6 278	8 137	1 999	1 891	48 125	15 505	3 900	2 265	8 804	3 753	13 182
1992	8 876	7 418	9 077	1 917	2 779	47 813	14 639	4 363	2 759	9 626	3 989	15 250
1993	8 277	8 763	9 874	2 778	2 770	47 892	14 782	6 064	3 529	11 678	3 766	16 168
1994	9 781	9 282	11 441	2 294	2 809	53 488	18 025	6 969	3 886	13 020	4 865	17 109
1995	10 789	11 754	14 232	3 296	3 360	64 343	25 380	8 816	5 295	15 333	6 665	19 290
1996	12 008	11 993	13 966	3 328	3 977	67 607	26 621	8 546	6 142	16 720	7 198	18 460
1997	12 063	12 862	15 117	3 608	4 522	65 549	25 046	10 780	7 417	17 696	7 349	20 366
1998	11 918	14 241	12 925	3 564	2 299	57 831	16 486	8 957	6 737	15 694	5 239	18 165
1995:												
January	829	745	1 030	200	252	4 492	1 645	603	366	950	461	1 453
February	847	1 086	1 027	208	262	4 987	1 956	581	327	1 187	538	1 529
March	972	1 070	1 235	260	285	5 581	2 481	687	415	1 305	516	1 793
April	832	896	1 133	249	241	5 287	2 046	628	514	1 110	477	1 530
May	915	831	1 397	273	242	5 035	2 056	687	397	1 113	454	1 726
June	989	947	1 231	293	241	5 542	2 238	754	455	1 299	515	1 864
July	857	986	1 237	353	311	5 474	2 111	806	405	1 267	516	1 475
August	852	881	1 156	318	262	5 435	2 202	834	514	1 417	498	1 716
September	964	960	1 181	345	311	5 685	2 065	805	438	1 306	640	1 654
October	958	1 097	1 223	285	339	5 510	2 126	780	514	1 541	678	1 389
November	869	1 125	1 202	267	323	5 442	2 055	796	490	1 317	831	1 459
December	904	1 130	1 181	247	290	5 873	2 399	857	460	1 521	540	1 702
1996:												
January	1 013	929	996	250	336	5 222	1 925	832	469	1 276	527	1 571
February	966	1 147	970	252	307	5 875	2 067	665	455	1 439	710	1 341
March	1 076	1 093	1 192	298	350	6 412	2 567	765	496	1 713	565	1 606
April	952	841	1 126	242	386	5 440	2 144	687	617	1 340	678	1 613
May	1 099	882	1 267	257	290	5 903	2 195	693	518	1 349	535	1 719
June	946	772	1 228	229	327	5 644	2 260	649	467	1 540	664	1 432
July	950	998	997	259	281	5 432	2 053	677	460	1 437	505	1 440
August	1 062	778	1 215	250	281	5 741	2 419	605	503	1 335	524	1 400
September	957	753	1 129	273	240	5 359	2 025	580	475	1 250	480	1 422
October	1 025	928	1 392	387	311	5 810	2 221	868	569	1 309	670	1 484
November	1 019	1 586	1 197	390	339	5 372	2 269	792	575	1 393	467	1 612
December	943	1 286	1 257	240	531	5 398	2 476	733	539	1 341	873	1 821
1997:												
January	873	938	1 054	250	310	5 073	1 986	725	557	1 497	583	1 444
February	882	913	1 092	285	361	5 435	1 986	706	563	1 207	602	1 429
March	1 094	1 022	1 351	395	360	6 184	2 482	821	679	1 673	639	1 770
April	880	965	1 306	309	329	5 389	2 460	968	672	1 350	674	1 541
May	1 008	1 057	1 307	327	493	5 655	2 403	1 142	618	1 536	566	1 565
June	1 258	920	1 339	283	409	5 775	2 239	947	675	1 437	558	1 735
July	1 029	1 097	1 244	261	358	5 409	2 342	941	607	1 559	539	1 790
August	1 053	938	1 344	367	327	5 519	1 916	832	620	1 674	589	1 750
September	1 044	1 040	1 231	296	323	5 038	1 707	861	578	1 527	751	1 608
October	1 009	1 439	1 289	280	361	5 424	2 069	1 200	649	1 432	677	1 856
November	965	1 301	1 250	287	422	5 433	1 822	800	607	1 391	648	1 685
December	968	1 233	1 310	269	470	5 216	1 634	837	593	1 416	523	2 193
1998:												
January	927	1 271	1 025	241	283	5 161	1 089	903	583	1 203	561	1 655
February	1 093	1 019	1 036	208	163	4 636	1 127	654	579	1 359	410	1 597
March	1 133	1 034	1 147	322	159	5 228	1 289	972	573	1 378	464	1 636
April	963	985	1 072	277	161	4 869	1 395	992	574	1 177	420	1 509
May	975	911	1 240	273	133	4 753	1 238	813	543	1 248	383	1 445
June	939	1 283	1 115	311	168	4 756	1 190	640	566	1 412	363	1 326
July	990	1 101	934	275	181	4 968	1 211	729	565	1 346	356	1 288
August	1 060	870	991	325	155	4 770	1 219	595	540	1 306	328	1 335
September	901	1 215	1 198	371	153	4 572	1 299	609	530	1 337	345	1 320
October	1 082	1 855	1 051	267	178	4 965	1 504	787	598	1 207	380	1 660
November	948	1 317	1 009	221	148	4 499	1 542	615	523	1 177	370	1 711
December	907	1 380	1 108	473	418	4 656	2 383	649	564	1 545	859	1 683

U.S. Exports of Goods by Selected Countries and Regions—*Continued*

(Census basis, millions of dollars, not seasonally adjusted)

Year and month	Selected African countries				Special country groupings [1]					
	Angola	Egypt	Nigeria	South Africa	ASEAN [2]	MERCOSUR [3]	Central American Common Market	Newly industrialized Pacific Rim countries	OPEC [4]	Pacific Rim Countries
1970	.....	.....	.....	563	.....	.....	.....	.....	.....	.....
1971	.....	.....	.....	622	.....	.....	.....	.....	.....	.....
1972	.....	.....	.....	603	.....	.....	.....	.....	.....	.....
1973	.....	.....	.....	746	.....	.....	.....	.....	6 723	.....
1974	.....	.....	286	1 160	.....	.....	.....	.....		.....
1975	.....	.....	536	1 302	.....	.....	.....	.....	10 767	.....
1976	.....	.....	770	1 348	.....	.....	.....	.....	12 566	.....
1977	.....	.....	958	1 054	.....	.....	.....	.....	14 019	.....
1978	.....	.....	985	1 080	.....	.....	.....	.....	16 655	.....
1979	.....	.....	632	1 413	.....	.....	.....	.....	15 051	.....
1980	.....	1 874	1 150	2 464	.....	.....	.....	.....	17 759	.....
1981	.....	2 159	1 523	2 912	.....	.....	.....	.....	21 533	.....
1982	.....	2 875	1 295	2 368	.....	.....	.....	.....	22 863	.....
1983	.....	2 813	864	2 129	.....	.....	.....	.....	16 905	.....
1984	.....	2 704	577	2 265	.....	.....	.....	.....	14 387	.....
1985	.....	2 323	676	1 205	.....	.....	.....	16 918	12 480	.....
1986	.....	1 982	409	1 158	.....	.....	.....	18 289	10 844	.....
1987	.....	2 210	295	1 281	.....	.....	.....	23 548	11 058	.....
1988	.....	2 332	357	1 688	.....	.....	.....	34 816	13 994	.....
1989	.....	2 612	490	1 659	.....	.....	.....	38 404	13 196	.....
1990	.....	2 249	552	1 732	.....	.....	.....	40 741	13 679	.....
1991	186	2 720	831	2 113	20 775	8 783	3 287	45 628	19 054	117 767
1992	158	3 088	1 001	2 434	23 969	9 620	4 300	48 592	21 960	124 451
1993	174	2 768	895	2 188	28 281	10 609	4 777	52 502	19 500	131 595
1994	197	2 855	509	2 174	31 925	13 663	5 351	59 595	17 868	147 779
1995	260	2 985	603	2 751	39 659	17 016	6 023	74 234	19 533	180 552
1996	268	3 153	818	3 112	42 958	18 616	6 362	75 768	22 275	188 243
1997	281	3 835	813	2 997	47 943	23 186	7 463	78 225	25 526	193 740
1998	355	3 059	817	3 628	39 048	22 405	8 402	63 269	25 154	167 367
1995:										
January	18	226	46	177	2 640	1 367	442	5 078	1 872	12 493
February	14	224	47	217	2 900	1 316	421	5 700	1 364	13 916
March	9	265	48	224	3 212	1 597	553	6 813	1 633	15 991
April	15	237	37	238	2 973	1 546	537	5 818	1 427	14 425
May	16	229	47	212	2 898	1 428	516	6 292	1 797	14 533
June	30	201	55	239	3 376	1 408	501	6 633	1 766	15 819
July	16	234	78	210	3 311	1 223	517	6 090	1 550	15 083
August	28	254	59	254	3 534	1 364	528	6 491	1 470	15 434
September	24	245	48	280	3 507	1 371	461	6 205	1 615	15 528
October	23	309	57	265	3 863	1 405	536	6 278	1 726	15 623
November	24	217	45	221	3 769	1 456	527	6 033	1 742	15 235
December	43	345	36	214	3 678	1 539	485	6 803	1 571	16 471
1996:										
January	20	212	68	268	3 453	1 245	487	5 768	1 512	14 719
February	47	294	56	253	3 622	1 283	471	5 816	1 572	15 415
March	19	239	68	275	4 050	1 409	527	7 078	1 944	17 587
April	14	223	60	243	3 795	1 318	497	6 223	1 708	15 388
May	20	201	57	236	3 394	1 498	506	6 530	1 777	16 086
June	17	216	47	286	3 657	1 676	530	6 460	1 886	15 419
July	13	293	75	250	3 370	1 576	534	5 928	2 124	14 882
August	26	320	74	294	3 258	1 734	527	6 368	1 936	15 524
September	17	269	79	285	3 029	1 708	555	5 826	1 801	14 343
October	32	231	67	257	3 733	1 757	591	6 406	2 027	16 084
November	22	287	122	222	3 571	1 779	594	6 471	1 950	16 320
December	23	370	46	245	4 028	1 631	542	6 896	2 038	16 477
1997:										
January	13	288	49	228	3 675	1 544	553	5 980	1 534	14 615
February	28	218	46	227	3 444	1 538	577	5 714	1 623	14 705
March	33	380	71	254	4 181	1 910	618	7 277	2 082	17 595
April	30	199	56	254	3 999	1 754	613	6 657	1 950	16 024
May	21	355	74	262	4 393	1 954	625	6 810	2 286	16 984
June	24	265	58	243	4 035	1 931	642	6 749	1 927	16 996
July	22	479	62	223	4 060	1 865	605	6 935	2 188	16 610
August	22	560	136	277	4 057	2 039	638	6 684	2 074	16 179
September	21	300	72	284	4 051	2 077	598	6 074	2 288	15 132
October	25	254	57	269	4 326	2 233	663	6 647	2 047	17 011
November	21	235	56	219	3 876	2 209	709	6 148	2 101	15 862
December	21	303	78	258	3 848	2 134	621	6 553	3 425	16 028
1998:										
January	43	317	65	236	3 538	1 691	633	4 972	2 376	14 291
February	31	195	65	223	3 169	1 586	652	5 119	1 975	13 415
March	22	225	92	275	3 551	1 961	773	5 449	2 476	14 744
April	34	232	48	265	3 329	1 825	742	5 152	1 878	13 831
May	18	163	52	264	3 164	1 895	708	5 170	1 829	13 469
June	20	210	71	444	3 156	1 994	679	5 042	2 107	13 531
July	39	214	63	272	3 182	1 852	677	4 779	1 801	13 449
August	17	319	71	279	2 927	1 915	711	4 851	1 628	13 030
September	38	236	61	254	2 978	1 788	664	5 154	1 829	13 299
October	33	270	104	269	3 154	2 126	744	5 422	2 152	15 219
November	28	362	56	398	2 837	1 884	739	5 439	2 912	13 625
December	32	316	69	450	4 061	1 889	679	6 720	2 191	15 463

1. See Notes for list of countries included in each group.
2. Association of Southeast Asian Nations.
3. Argentina, Brazil, Paraguay, and Uruguay.
4. Organization of Petroleum Exporting Countries.

U.S. Imports of Goods by Selected Countries and Regions

(Census basis, except as noted; millions of dollars, not seasonally adjusted)

Year and month	Total imports of goods			North America			Central and South America [1]						
	Total: Balance of payments basis	Net adjustments	Total: Census basis	Total	Canada	Mexico	Total [2]	Argentina	Brazil	Chile	Colombia	Dominican Republic	Venezuela
1970	39 866	.....	.....	12 311	11 092	1 219	.....	.....	670	.....	.....	.....	1 082
1971	45 579	.....	.....	13 954	12 692	1 262	.....	.....	762	.....	.....	.....	1 216
1972	55 797	.....	.....	16 559	14 927	1 632	.....	.....	942	.....	.....	.....	1 298
1973	70 499	.....	.....	20 021	17 715	2 306	.....	.....	1 189	.....	.....	.....	1 787
1974	103 811	.....	.....	25 314	21 924	3 390	.....	.....	1 700	.....	.....	.....	4 671
1975	98 185	.....	.....	24 806	21 747	3 059	.....	.....	1 464	.....	.....	.....	3 624
1976	124 228	.....	.....	29 835	26 237	3 598	.....	.....	1 737	.....	.....	.....	3 574
1977	151 907	.....	.....	34 293	29 599	4 694	.....	.....	2 241	.....	.....	.....	4 084
1978	176 002	.....	.....	39 619	33 525	6 094	.....	.....	2 826	.....	.....	.....	3 545
1979	212 007	.....	.....	46 846	38 046	8 800	.....	.....	3 118	.....	.....	.....	5 166
1980	249 750	.....	.....	53 975	41 455	12 520	.....	741	3 715	.....	1 248	.....	5 297
1981	265 067	.....	.....	60 179	46 414	13 765	.....	1 125	4 475	.....	822	.....	5 566
1982	247 642	.....	.....	62 043	46 477	15 566	.....	1 128	4 285	.....	801	.....	4 768
1983	268 901	7 178	261 723	68 906	52 130	16 776	.....	853	4 946	.....	970	.....	4 938
1984	332 418	1 908	330 510	84 498	66 478	18 020	.....	954	7 621	.....	1 146	.....	6 543
1985	338 088	1 705	336 383	88 138	69 006	19 132	.....	1 069	7 526	.....	1 331	.....	6 537
1986	368 425	2 753	365 672	85 555	68 253	17 302	.....	856	6 813	.....	1 874	.....	5 097
1987	409 765	3 482	406 283	91 356	71 085	20 271	.....	1 080	7 865	.....	2 232	.....	5 579
1988	447 189	5 263	441 926	104 658	81 398	23 260	.....	1 436	9 294	.....	2 161	.....	5 157
1989	477 365	3 718	473 647	115 115	87 953	27 162	.....	1 391	8 410	.....	2 555	.....	6 771
1990	498 337	2 357	495 980	121 544	91 372	30 172	.....	1 511	7 976	.....	3 168	.....	9 446
1991	490 981	2 529	488 452	122 194	91 064	31 130	.....	1 287	6 717	1 302	2 736	2 008	8 179
1992	536 458	3 795	532 663	133 841	98 630	35 211	33 531	1 256	7 609	1 388	2 837	2 373	8 181
1993	589 441	8 783	580 658	151 133	111 216	39 917	34 456	1 206	7 479	1 462	3 032	2 672	8 140
1994	668 590	5 334	663 256	177 900	128 406	49 494	38 461	1 725	8 683	1 821	3 171	3 091	8 371
1995	749 574	6 031	743 543	207 033	145 349	61 684	42 255	1 761	8 830	1 931	3 751	3 399	9 721
1996	803 327	8 037	795 289	230 190	155 893	74 297	49 547	2 279	8 773	2 262	4 424	3 575	13 173
1997	876 366	6 662	869 704	254 138	168 201	85 938	53 697	2 228	9 626	2 293	4 737	4 327	13 477
1998	917 178	5 282	911 896	267 885	173 256	94 629	50 266	2 231	10 102	2 453	4 656	4 441	9 181
1995:													
January	57 536	243	57 293	16 286	11 579	4 707	3 261	121	805	160	266	159	772
February	55 447	230	55 217	16 281	11 494	4 787	3 168	119	633	176	264	247	727
March	64 454	870	63 583	18 161	12 688	5 473	3 784	145	745	216	334	321	864
April	60 672	880	59 792	16 813	12 100	4 713	3 216	158	647	195	282	257	719
May	64 351	1 153	63 198	17 869	12 602	5 267	3 720	175	702	146	333	306	901
June	64 997	907	64 090	17 702	12 499	5 204	3 647	162	732	170	321	317	859
July	62 064	210	61 854	14 469	9 748	4 722	3 539	132	715	158	279	298	854
August	64 684	232	64 452	17 572	12 285	5 287	3 691	172	812	133	374	322	768
September	63 648	231	63 417	17 892	12 542	5 350	3 471	150	692	116	294	298	859
October	67 810	420	67 390	18 943	13 264	5 680	3 578	162	775	142	340	318	729
November	63 885	308	63 577	18 402	12 762	5 639	3 638	131	775	152	319	309	849
December	59 883	204	59 679	16 644	11 787	4 857	3 543	134	797	166	344	248	821
1996:													
January	62 184	275	61 910	17 819	12 211	5 607	3 734	195	741	211	301	178	956
February	60 968	388	60 580	17 978	12 396	5 582	3 444	122	633	207	302	275	802
March	64 577	1 213	63 364	18 462	12 761	5 701	3 817	158	686	210	403	277	914
April	66 277	1 613	64 664	19 041	13 047	5 994	4 104	184	716	253	374	290	1 058
May	68 104	1 247	66 857	20 169	13 749	6 420	4 325	206	723	195	350	309	1 223
June	65 070	874	64 196	19 645	13 479	6 166	3 925	207	737	181	335	307	990
July	68 107	425	67 682	17 636	11 595	6 041	4 341	176	729	172	386	354	1 160
August	68 795	770	68 025	19 635	13 163	6 472	4 148	205	859	162	344	328	1 030
September	68 616	307	68 309	19 985	13 488	6 497	4 353	250	732	143	379	306	1 262
October	74 433	315	74 118	20 617	13 501	7 116	4 595	233	706	136	437	356	1 314
November	68 304	289	68 016	20 376	13 773	6 603	4 087	152	747	162	384	284	1 108
December	67 805	235	67 570	18 828	12 729	6 099	4 674	192	764	229	429	313	1 357
1997:													
January	67 604	252	67 352	19 954	13 767	6 187	4 317	161	870	259	297	211	1 263
February	65 602	430	65 171	20 092	13 558	6 534	4 235	223	707	222	387	324	960
March	72 145	1 458	70 687	21 106	14 148	6 958	4 414	180	750	221	417	343	1 097
April	72 271	1 021	71 250	21 324	14 227	7 097	4 296	180	815	220	377	377	990
May	72 408	897	71 511	21 526	14 414	7 112	4 682	188	886	186	415	379	1 190
June	72 548	892	71 656	21 004	13 895	7 108	4 459	180	804	157	358	378	1 109
July	75 125	228	74 896	19 478	12 455	7 023	4 744	166	946	173	409	405	1 064
August	73 251	245	73 006	20 916	13 637	7 279	4 502	185	837	188	413	387	1 078
September	77 097	266	76 831	22 261	14 554	7 707	4 677	201	762	171	393	396	1 259
October	81 685	255	81 430	23 503	15 045	8 458	4 711	211	786	161	428	407	1 207
November	72 372	242	72 130	21 783	14 265	7 518	4 098	167	722	140	406	325	1 135
December	75 173	423	74 750	21 192	14 236	6 957	4 562	189	739	197	440	395	1 125
1998:													
January	70 804	580	70 224	20 234	13 229	7 006	4 049	207	799	205	447	204	918
February	68 622	228	68 394	20 926	13 967	6 960	3 968	168	702	219	361	357	793
March	78 606	511	78 096	23 718	15 392	8 326	4 218	184	780	245	371	397	769
April	76 068	325	75 744	22 794	14 981	7 813	4 165	225	839	236	372	388	783
May	74 289	291	73 998	22 712	14 769	7 943	4 205	186	873	186	375	387	806
June	77 276	358	76 918	22 353	14 371	7 983	4 350	186	936	181	372	411	758
July	76 698	361	76 337	19 612	12 266	7 346	4 336	178	913	180	368	432	757
August	76 713	699	76 014	21 714	13 753	7 961	4 190	176	901	177	375	387	726
September	78 983	549	78 434	23 493	15 158	8 335	4 149	168	869	199	384	359	710
October	84 303	592	83 712	24 694	15 714	8 980	4 394	190	855	183	428	399	817
November	78 541	522	78 020	23 390	15 190	8 200	4 042	166	788	217	386	365	736
December	76 274	267	76 007	22 245	14 467	7 779	4 200	198	848	224	417	354	610

1. Includes Caribbean.
2. Includes countries not shown separately. See Notes for list of included countries.

U.S. Imports of Goods by Selected Countries and Regions—*Continued*

(Census basis, millions of dollars, not seasonally adjusted)

Year and month	Total[1]	Western Europe — European Union									
		Total[1]	Belgium	France	Germany	Ireland	Italy	Nether-lands	Spain	Sweden	United Kingdom
1970	.....	.....	.....	942	3 127	.....	1 316	.....	.....	.....	2 194
1971	.....	.....	.....	1 088	3 651	.....	1 406	.....	.....	.....	2 499
1972	.....	.....	.....	1 369	4 250	.....	1 757	.....	.....	.....	2 987
1973	.....	.....	.....	1 732	5 345	.....	2 002	.....	.....	.....	3 657
1974	23 522	19 035	.....	2 257	6 324	.....	2 585	1 433	.....	.....	4 061
1975	20 735	16 610	.....	2 137	5 382	.....	2 397	1 083	.....	.....	3 784
1976	22 784	17 848	.....	2 509	5 592	.....	2 530	1 080	.....	.....	4 254
1977	27 417	22 087	.....	3 032	7 238	.....	3 037	1 477	.....	.....	5 141
1978	36 485	29 009	.....	4 051	9 962	.....	4 102	1 603	.....	.....	6 514
1979	41 684	33 295	.....	4 768	10 955	.....	4 918	1 852	.....	.....	8 028
1980	46 416	35 958	.....	5 247	11 681	.....	4 313	1 910	1 230	1 631	9 755
1981	51 855	41 624	.....	5 851	11 379	.....	5 189	2 366	1 537	1 714	12 835
1982	52 346	42 509	.....	5 545	11 975	.....	5 301	2 494	1 508	1 992	13 095
1983	53 884	43 892	.....	6 025	12 695	.....	5 455	2 970	1 536	2 429	12 470
1984	71 153	57 360	.....	8 113	16 996	.....	7 935	4 069	2 391	3 244	14 492
1985	79 756	67 822	.....	9 482	20 239	.....	9 674	4 081	2 515	4 124	14 937
1986	89 825	75 736	.....	10 129	25 124	.....	10 607	4 066	2 702	4 419	15 396
1987	95 496	81 188	.....	10 730	27 069	.....	11 040	3 964	2 839	4 758	17 341
1988	100 443	84 939	.....	12 509	26 362	.....	11 576	4 559	3 204	4 985	17 976
1989	101 764	85 153	.....	13 013	24 832	.....	11 933	4 810	3 317	4 892	18 319
1990	108 901	91 868	.....	13 124	28 109	.....	12 723	4 972	3 311	4 937	20 288
1991	102 262	86 481	3 929	13 333	26 137	1 948	11 764	4 811	2 848	4 524	18 413
1992	110 727	93 993	4 476	14 797	28 820	2 262	12 314	5 300	3 002	4 716	20 093
1993	115 557	97 941	5 149	15 279	28 562	2 519	13 216	5 443	2 992	4 534	21 730
1994	130 730	110 875	6 354	16 699	31 744	2 894	14 802	6 007	3 555	5 041	25 058
1995	145 320	131 871	6 054	17 209	36 844	4 079	16 348	6 405	3 880	6 256	26 930
1996	157 601	142 947	6 776	18 646	38 945	4 804	18 325	6 583	4 280	7 153	28 979
1997	172 957	157 528	7 912	20 636	43 122	5 867	19 408	7 293	4 606	7 299	32 659
1998	191 971	176 380	8 440	24 016	49 842	8 401	20 959	7 599	4 780	7 848	34 838
1995:											
January	10 814	9 875	503	1 367	2 689	263	1 300	484	290	514	1 875
February	10 632	9 657	538	1 225	2 576	265	1 198	436	288	496	2 053
March	12 638	11 467	545	1 609	3 006	277	1 375	501	350	629	2 538
April	12 204	11 093	468	1 507	3 246	309	1 300	532	320	531	2 225
May	12 678	11 391	555	1 526	3 116	360	1 320	542	325	593	2 394
June	12 699	11 473	445	1 384	3 306	392	1 472	558	360	532	2 332
July	13 064	11 855	592	1 496	3 633	347	1 576	565	338	493	2 110
August	11 450	10 388	346	1 471	2 992	272	1 420	492	341	312	2 075
September	11 135	10 068	461	1 264	2 665	398	1 056	492	269	494	2 313
October	13 221	12 033	552	1 708	2 937	430	1 529	716	363	549	2 566
November	12 505	11 404	578	1 419	3 161	398	1 439	543	343	551	2 294
December	12 282	11 166	473	1 235	3 520	368	1 362	544	292	562	2 156
1996:											
January	11 960	10 862	494	1 294	2 914	455	1 526	457	315	567	2 182
February	11 899	10 773	532	1 354	2 857	345	1 420	501	333	581	2 217
March	13 306	12 018	577	1 679	3 312	366	1 537	568	353	623	2 328
April	13 276	11 958	566	1 491	3 225	394	1 466	544	371	636	2 470
May	13 595	12 346	575	1 607	3 423	412	1 476	578	360	643	2 583
June	12 674	11 474	548	1 560	2 970	389	1 536	533	328	593	2 364
July	14 267	12 974	682	1 621	3 613	381	1 785	560	403	629	2 475
August	12 637	11 503	422	1 533	3 268	378	1 680	542	335	338	2 329
September	12 236	11 061	570	1 531	2 958	430	1 204	554	302	565	2 246
October	14 404	13 067	692	1 815	3 448	399	1 598	636	419	682	2 624
November	13 353	12 077	556	1 509	3 404	450	1 537	558	378	639	2 366
December	13 994	12 835	562	1 653	3 555	407	1 560	553	381	658	2 795
1997:											
January	12 549	11 400	543	1 430	3 082	393	1 373	534	369	497	2 544
February	12 655	11 544	589	1 471	3 234	396	1 450	461	334	574	2 405
March	14 749	13 363	676	1 686	3 772	486	1 681	585	367	714	2 674
April	14 483	13 302	742	1 636	3 820	450	1 547	561	391	671	2 731
May	14 650	13 226	677	1 622	3 735	415	1 582	607	405	610	2 799
June	14 162	12 904	622	1 770	3 486	469	1 664	640	404	631	2 469
July	15 973	14 555	802	2 057	3 771	569	1 948	692	412	656	2 866
August	13 347	12 241	484	1 655	3 354	434	1 661	583	419	392	2 557
September	13 856	12 589	723	1 783	3 199	565	1 305	674	309	590	2 730
October	16 202	14 804	738	2 008	3 883	545	1 808	718	384	696	3 208
November	14 372	13 046	648	1 629	3 667	599	1 634	553	399	588	2 603
December	15 959	14 553	668	1 891	4 119	547	1 755	685	414	681	3 073
1998:											
January	13 759	12 589	626	1 661	3 291	624	1 558	565	381	507	2 659
February	13 798	12 678	695	1 675	3 510	503	1 579	536	349	572	2 550
March	16 984	15 620	780	2 061	4 692	667	1 888	605	404	663	3 003
April	16 228	14 829	663	1 976	4 315	742	1 674	646	419	642	2 991
May	15 405	14 054	675	1 957	4 047	606	1 637	580	427	615	2 816
June	16 432	15 143	728	2 193	4 022	736	1 833	668	447	641	3 012
July	17 321	15 850	844	2 234	4 291	801	2 034	673	430	740	2 921
August	14 926	13 889	472	1 816	4 030	719	1 834	620	381	472	2 780
September	15 407	14 170	766	1 978	3 759	874	1 376	619	301	692	2 982
October	17 933	16 444	773	2 348	4 643	807	1 894	790	374	778	3 124
November	16 718	15 321	734	2 109	4 323	727	1 831	639	425	716	2 990
December	17 061	15 793	685	2 007	4 918	595	1 821	659	444	810	3 011

1. Includes countries not shown separately. See Notes for list of included countries.

U.S. Imports of Goods by Selected Countries and Regions—*Continued*

(Census basis, millions of dollars, not seasonally adjusted)

Year and month	Western Europe—*Continued* European Free Trade Association			Eastern Europe and former Soviet Republics					Near and Middle Eastern countries		
	Total 1	Norway	Switzer-land	Total 1	Hungary	Poland	Former Soviet Republics Total 1	Russia	Israel	Saudi Arabia	Turkey
1970	.....	.....	.....	.....	.....	.....	72	.....	.....	.....	.....
1971	.....	.....	.....	.....	.....	.....	57	.....	.....	.....	.....
1972	.....	.....	.....	.....	.....	.....	95	.....	.....	.....	.....
1973	.....	.....	.....	.....	.....	.....	220	.....	.....	.....	.....
1974	.....	.....	.....	890	.....	.....	350	.....	.....	.....	.....
1975	.....	.....	.....	731	.....	.....	254	.....	.....	.....	.....
1976	.....	.....	.....	856	.....	.....	220	.....	.....	.....	.....
1977	.....	.....	.....	914	.....	.....	453	.....	.....	.....	.....
1978	.....	.....	.....	1 503	.....	.....	539	.....	.....	.....	.....
1979	.....	.....	.....	1 865	.....	.....	874	.....	.....	.....	.....
1980	.....	2 633	2 796	1 433	107	417	453	.....	.....	.....	.....
1981	.....	2 478	2 448	1 555	129	365	348	.....	.....	.....	.....
1982	.....	1 973	2 340	1 067	133	212	228	.....	.....	.....	.....
1983	.....	1 358	2 494	1 359	158	189	347	.....	.....	.....	.....
1984	.....	1 904	3 117	2 154	221	220	554	.....	.....	.....	.....
1985	.....	1 164	3 476	1 936	218	220	409	.....	.....	1 907	.....
1986	.....	1 079	5 253	2 001	225	233	558	.....	.....	3 612	.....
1987	.....	1 404	4 249	1 923	279	296	425	.....	.....	4 433	.....
1988	.....	1 446	4 611	2 163	293	377	586	.....	.....	5 620	.....
1989	.....	1 991	4 714	2 064	328	387	710	.....	.....	7 181	.....
1990	.....	1 830	5 587	2 275	348	408	1 065	.....	.....	9 974	.....
1991	14 302	1 624	5 576	1 800	367	357	813	.....	3 484	10 900	1 006
1992	15 021	1 969	5 645	1 551	347	375	658	481	3 816	10 371	1 110
1993	15 816	1 958	5 973	3 526	401	454	2 094	1 743	4 420	7 708	1 198
1994	17 665	2 353	6 373	5 832	470	651	3 848	3 245	5 229	7 688	1 575
1995	11 039	3 087	7 594	7 020	547	664	4 896	4 030	5 709	8 377	1 798
1996	12 112	3 993	7 792	6 987	676	628	4 690	3 577	6 434	10 467	1 778
1997	12 504	3 752	8 405	8 483	1 079	696	5 350	4 319	7 326	9 365	2 121
1998	12 072	2 872	8 690	17 991	1 567	784	7 089	5 747	8 640	6 241	2 543
1995:											
January	720	208	494	626	45	57	449	385	519	647	172
February	775	190	557	550	41	58	391	313	434	656	147
March	923	274	620	784	50	57	579	497	513	745	191
April	912	241	626	683	45	52	515	430	388	717	157
May	1 070	287	748	571	45	60	390	317	482	766	167
June	1 031	326	673	704	45	52	539	478	469	638	146
July	964	228	706	526	49	55	339	253	544	685	181
August	888	310	558	590	42	48	423	345	455	624	134
September	891	249	611	509	43	50	341	272	493	745	128
October	1 032	235	761	454	51	59	282	219	450	634	102
November	893	244	621	552	48	59	358	294	531	760	145
December	942	295	619	471	45	57	290	227	431	761	127
1996:											
January	885	260	592	416	44	54	244	184	538	747	154
February	908	242	646	466	44	47	297	237	507	571	151
March	1 078	322	721	468	48	48	301	232	486	750	152
April	1 091	400	663	581	49	50	414	340	434	910	163
May	1 051	353	668	564	52	60	389	288	534	911	140
June	1 023	370	633	538	47	48	366	254	494	635	120
July	1 079	398	654	519	54	53	323	232	661	916	148
August	927	344	553	663	59	53	467	357	498	932	140
September	994	337	638	588	59	51	392	299	565	1 068	126
October	1 095	377	687	714	67	61	509	394	613	939	161
November	1 046	323	697	685	77	51	438	331	567	823	166
December	936	268	641	784	78	52	551	430	538	1 265	156
1997:											
January	893	284	580	660	62	54	423	286	642	765	181
February	881	251	606	537	62	45	339	260	543	641	177
March	1 120	381	715	656	71	54	437	377	565	779	198
April	928	242	658	657	84	49	412	318	526	782	191
May	1 145	413	705	713	104	62	445	368	613	889	200
June	1 033	299	710	660	93	55	403	325	528	699	162
July	1 179	354	795	728	102	65	440	353	723	736	166
August	878	257	597	795	94	62	490	390	556	823	173
September	1 040	303	709	827	99	64	549	446	731	869	162
October	1 132	310	784	758	102	68	457	376	615	838	194
November	1 108	324	746	614	91	52	369	310	640	777	155
December	1 168	334	799	876	115	66	587	510	642	768	163
1998:											
January	880	240	614	1 311	91	73	498	419	732	713	215
February	868	193	638	1 243	88	59	487	405	652	481	182
March	1 039	255	743	1 386	112	87	533	441	761	609	227
April	1 098	223	836	1 572	113	63	645	542	662	584	228
May	1 069	267	758	1 449	122	57	582	474	689	551	208
June	978	241	698	1 810	125	62	745	616	710	461	227
July	1 165	317	809	1 552	134	67	605	459	880	534	201
August	772	188	554	1 490	122	60	591	445	644	510	184
September	967	227	694	1 705	177	68	674	548	729	451	190
October	1 126	235	846	1 513	157	66	582	464	709	489	273
November	1 067	237	778	1 513	146	69	598	501	792	406	259
December	1 044	249	725	1 448	180	54	550	435	681	453	149

1. Includes countries not shown separately. See Notes for list of included countries.

U.S. Imports of Goods by Selected Countries and Regions—*Continued*

(Census basis, millions of dollars, not seasonally adjusted)

Year and month	Selected Asian and Oceanic countries											
	Australia	China	Hong Kong	India	Indonesia	Japan	South Korea	Malaysia	Philippines	Singapore	Thailand	Taiwan
1970	.....	.....	.....	.....	.....	5 875	.....	.....	.....	.....	.....	.....
1971	.....	.....	.....	.....	.....	7 259	.....	.....	.....	.....	.....	.....
1972	.....	.....	.....	.....	.....	9 064	.....	.....	.....	.....	.....	.....
1973	.....	.....	.....	.....	.....	9 676	.....	.....	.....	.....	.....	.....
1974	.....	.....	.....	.....	.....	12 338	.....	.....	.....	.....	.....	.....
1975	.....	.....	.....	.....	.....	11 268	.....	.....	.....	.....	.....	.....
1976	.....	.....	.....	.....	.....	15 504	.....	.....	.....	.....	.....	.....
1977	.....	.....	.....	.....	.....	18 550	.....	.....	.....	.....	.....	.....
1978	.....	.....	.....	.....	.....	24 458	.....	.....	.....	.....	.....	.....
1979	.....	.....	.....	.....	.....	26 248	.....	.....	.....	.....	.....	.....
1980	.....	.....	.....	.....	5 183	30 701	.....	.....	.....	.....	.....	.....
1981	.....	.....	.....	.....	6 022	37 612	.....	.....	.....	.....	.....	.....
1982	.....	.....	.....	.....	4 224	37 744	.....	.....	.....	.....	.....	.....
1983	.....	.....	.....	.....	5 285	41 183	.....	.....	.....	.....	.....	.....
1984	.....	.....	.....	.....	5 461	57 135	.....	.....	.....	.....	.....	.....
1985	2 837	3 862	8 396	.....	4 569	68 783	10 031	.....	.....	4 260	.....	16 396
1986	2 632	4 771	8 891	.....	3 312	81 911	12 729	.....	.....	4 725	.....	19 791
1987	3 007	6 294	9 854	.....	3 394	84 575	16 987	.....	.....	6 201	.....	24 622
1988	3 541	8 511	10 238	.....	3 150	89 519	20 105	.....	.....	7 973	.....	24 714
1989	3 898	11 989	9 739	.....	3 529	93 586	19 742	.....	.....	8 950	.....	24 326
1990	4 442	15 224	9 488	.....	3 341	89 655	18 493	.....	.....	9 839	.....	22 667
1991	3 988	18 969	9 279	3 193	3 241	91 511	17 019	6 102	3 471	9 957	6 122	23 023
1992	3 688	25 728	9 793	3 780	4 529	97 414	16 682	8 294	4 355	11 313	7 529	24 596
1993	3 297	31 540	9 554	4 554	5 435	107 246	17 118	10 563	4 894	12 798	8 542	25 102
1994	3 202	38 787	9 696	5 310	6 547	119 156	19 629	13 982	5 719	15 358	10 306	26 706
1995	3 323	45 543	10 291	5 726	7 435	123 479	24 184	17 455	7 007	18 560	11 348	28 972
1996	3 869	51 513	9 865	6 170	8 250	115 187	22 655	17 829	8 161	20 343	11 336	29 907
1997	4 602	62 558	10 288	7 322	9 188	121 663	23 173	18 027	10 445	20 075	12 602	32 629
1998	5 387	71 169	10 538	8 237	9 341	121 845	23 942	19 000	11 947	18 356	13 436	33 125
1995:												
January	272	3 451	903	467	577	9 234	1 870	1 278	507	1 392	908	2 387
February	298	3 002	661	458	532	9 733	1 499	1 107	489	1 064	770	1 898
March	259	2 910	656	524	592	11 732	1 819	1 200	554	1 438	934	2 351
April	261	3 148	670	433	494	11 180	1 747	1 268	468	1 355	846	2 186
May	299	3 655	811	452	612	10 510	1 983	1 404	536	1 376	859	2 448
June	265	3 961	881	458	677	10 885	2 003	1 429	590	1 609	944	2 363
July	294	4 312	950	518	736	10 549	2 132	1 524	608	1 592	1 006	2 492
August	283	4 805	1 013	551	691	10 459	2 310	1 625	666	1 688	1 087	2 667
September	271	4 584	1 024	527	657	10 050	2 181	1 723	675	1 793	1 029	2 554
October	261	4 714	1 077	543	672	10 235	2 395	1 750	705	1 819	1 099	2 745
November	305	3 868	901	437	594	9 552	2 260	1 583	628	1 728	976	2 503
December	256	3 134	746	360	601	9 360	1 986	1 562	582	1 708	892	2 378
1996:												
January	255	3 658	912	489	617	8 955	2 268	1 504	663	1 665	937	2 453
February	289	3 540	720	471	629	9 575	1 996	1 301	636	1 417	829	2 252
March	283	2 864	640	495	567	10 241	1 940	1 423	657	1 980	915	2 165
April	277	3 248	669	514	630	9 913	1 919	1 426	569	1 699	890	2 304
May	303	3 954	806	474	593	9 082	1 937	1 443	615	1 713	817	2 476
June	302	4 111	763	446	679	8 964	1 660	1 348	655	1 611	900	2 467
July	315	4 817	953	564	751	9 781	1 816	1 500	726	1 695	1 004	2 648
August	353	5 496	889	584	736	9 453	1 770	1 596	733	1 699	1 008	2 567
September	325	5 481	902	590	715	9 205	1 725	1 638	767	1 801	1 000	2 731
October	365	5 813	1 017	638	898	10 741	1 912	1 685	783	1 759	1 110	2 818
November	407	4 585	835	479	715	9 620	1 826	1 496	655	1 601	997	2 493
December	396	3 947	758	426	722	9 657	1 887	1 469	704	1 704	931	2 533
1997:												
January	345	4 668	904	556	765	9 433	1 793	1 362	737	1 567	952	2 531
February	244	4 262	623	540	633	9 721	1 506	1 199	732	1 332	868	2 301
March	343	3 629	605	624	608	10 948	1 801	1 420	866	1 669	973	2 428
April	351	4 445	683	577	679	10 344	1 916	1 415	739	1 699	976	2 577
May	408	4 795	711	536	777	9 167	1 908	1 398	831	1 713	955	2 617
June	367	5 214	848	583	755	9 895	1 985	1 509	807	1 717	1 022	2 735
July	444	5 777	995	651	860	10 528	2 216	1 557	939	1 711	1 150	2 819
August	423	6 074	972	639	807	10 063	1 943	1 670	951	1 812	1 149	2 873
September	425	6 561	1 113	741	930	10 141	2 094	1 702	1 020	1 875	1 180	2 968
October	463	6 607	1 079	795	882	11 203	2 113	1 737	967	1 773	1 172	3 068
November	387	5 426	906	516	760	9 790	1 880	1 515	932	1 528	1 056	2 756
December	403	5 101	848	566	734	10 432	2 019	1 543	925	1 679	1 150	2 958
1998:												
January	354	5 453	960	652	799	9 426	1 954	1 417	914	1 490	1 033	2 755
February	437	4 560	649	641	666	9 910	1 726	1 319	945	1 341	977	2 327
March	475	4 798	708	760	680	10 986	1 950	1 524	1 065	1 715	1 131	2 699
April	473	5 263	750	684	733	10 327	1 924	1 511	924	1 540	987	2 653
May	482	5 539	789	632	707	9 655	1 895	1 462	889	1 530	1 001	2 580
June	483	6 020	948	689	765	9 971	2 101	1 489	1 022	1 616	1 136	2 780
July	445	6 556	1 016	748	867	10 210	2 023	1 576	1 041	1 514	1 187	2 841
August	442	6 780	1 059	784	846	9 890	1 998	1 754	1 143	1 516	1 221	2 900
September	434	7 125	1 058	774	880	9 736	2 062	1 747	1 105	1 589	1 233	2 947
October	489	7 378	978	757	902	10 924	2 097	1 887	1 048	1 537	1 265	2 949
November	402	6 374	840	569	778	10 334	2 102	1 720	955	1 433	1 165	2 869
December	472	5 322	784	547	718	10 476	2 110	1 596	898	1 537	1 100	2 826

U.S. Imports of Goods by Selected Countries and Regions—*Continued*

(Census basis, millions of dollars, not seasonally adjusted)

Year and month	Selected African countries				Special country groupings [1]					
	Angola	Egypt	Nigeria	South Africa	ASEAN [2]	MERCOSUR [3]	Central American Common Market	Newly industrialized Pacific Rim countries	OPEC [4]	Pacific Rim Countries
1970	.....	.....	.....	290	.....	.....	.....	.....	.....	.....
1971	.....	.....	.....	287	.....	.....	.....	.....	.....	.....
1972	.....	.....	.....	325	.....	.....	.....	.....	.....	.....
1973	.....	.....	.....	377	.....	.....	.....	.....	.....	.....
1974	.....	.....	.....	609	.....	.....	.....	.....	.....	.....
1975	.....	.....	.....	841	.....	.....	.....	.....	.....	.....
1976	.....	.....	.....	925	.....	.....	.....	.....	.....	.....
1977	.....	.....	.....	1 261	.....	.....	.....	.....	.....	.....
1978	.....	.....	.....	2 259	.....	.....	.....	.....	.....	.....
1979	.....	.....	.....	2 616	.....	.....	.....	.....	.....	.....
1980	.....	459	.....	3 321	.....	.....	.....	.....	.....	.....
1981	.....	397	.....	2 445	.....	.....	.....	.....	.....	.....
1982	.....	547	.....	1 967	.....	.....	.....	.....	.....	.....
1983	.....	303	.....	2 027	.....	.....	.....	.....	.....	.....
1984	.....	169	.....	2 488	.....	.....	.....	.....	.....	.....
1985	.....	79	3 002	2 071	.....	.....	.....	.....	22 800	.....
1986	.....	112	2 530	2 365	.....	.....	.....	.....	19 750	.....
1987	.....	465	3 573	1 346	.....	.....	.....	.....	23 953	.....
1988	.....	220	3 279	1 513	.....	.....	.....	.....	22 962	.....
1989	.....	226	5 226	1 529	.....	.....	.....	.....	30 601	.....
1990	.....	398	5 977	1 701	.....	.....	.....	.....	38 017	.....
1991	1 775	206	5 168	1 728	28 918	8 004	2 972	59 277	32 644	188 407
1992	2 303	434	5 103	1 727	36 050	8 865	3 727	62 384	33 200	208 424
1993	2 092	613	5 301	1 845	42 262	8 685	4 266	64 572	31 739	229 552
1994	2 061	549	4 430	2 031	51 957	10 408	4 804	71 388	31 685	261 153
1995	2 232	606	4 931	2 208	61 844	10 591	5 862	82 008	35 197	288 685
1996	2 902	680	5 978	2 323	65 968	11 052	6 774	82 770	44 285	290 033
1997	2 779	658	6 349	2 510	70 392	12 124	8 421	86 164	44 025	315 368
1998	2 241	660	4 194	3 049	72 291	12 622	9 252	85 961	33 925	327 743
1995:										
January	113	59	396	182	4 665	926	404	6 552	2 700	22 095
February	183	51	336	143	3 966	752	476	5 122	2 697	20 458
March	193	49	467	165	4 721	890	551	6 264	3 025	23 689
April	201	53	307	163	4 433	805	431	5 957	2 617	22 957
May	250	63	492	201	4 790	877	493	6 618	3 187	23 861
June	163	41	431	216	5 250	894	499	6 855	3 062	24 882
July	231	43	412	186	5 470	847	489	7 165	3 123	25 412
August	147	62	417	191	5 762	984	541	7 679	2 965	26 432
September	207	42	454	198	5 880	842	505	7 552	3 024	25 712
October	206	40	444	166	6 050	937	489	8 036	2 874	26 586
November	173	48	336	206	5 511	906	506	7 392	2 939	24 112
December	167	58	439	190	5 346	931	480	6 816	2 984	22 490
1996:										
January	197	62	549	146	5 392	936	454	7 298	3 280	23 163
February	165	56	405	156	4 815	755	537	6 385	2 809	22 534
March	128	62	367	191	5 544	844	547	6 725	2 964	22 930
April	224	81	484	239	5 216	900	538	6 591	3 555	22 842
May	278	46	552	215	5 184	929	565	6 933	3 896	23 162
June	214	47	523	165	5 196	944	550	6 501	3 401	22 763
July	204	79	667	223	5 679	905	617	7 113	4 090	25 243
August	270	42	499	204	5 777	1 064	580	6 925	3 835	25 516
September	293	32	648	184	5 925	982	586	7 159	4 235	25 498
October	353	58	523	194	6 241	939	619	7 505	4 263	27 996
November	289	65	414	226	5 468	899	565	6 756	3 643	24 420
December	287	51	349	180	5 532	956	618	6 882	4 313	23 967
1997:										
January	247	52	621	184	5 388	1 048	551	6 795	3 877	24 326
February	349	44	388	140	4 769	946	646	5 762	3 175	22 744
March	271	41	523	175	5 538	950	724	6 503	3 409	24 513
April	268	69	639	210	5 510	1 024	658	6 874	3 590	25 093
May	168	41	667	215	5 679	1 108	721	6 950	3 935	24 561
June	236	43	529	202	5 815	1 007	725	7 284	3 644	26 105
July	227	67	494	239	6 223	1 142	789	7 741	3 690	28 105
August	134	50	619	198	6 393	1 047	677	7 599	3 746	27 825
September	215	52	514	257	6 713	983	745	8 050	3 998	29 074
October	277	70	571	231	6 536	1 017	751	8 031	4 038	30 115
November	250	51	405	228	5 794	905	647	7 071	3 520	26 053
December	138	78	381	231	6 035	950	789	7 504	3 402	26 854
1998:										
January	242	58	414	229	5 657	1 037	629	7 158	3 252	25 769
February	183	55	301	239	5 256	892	763	6 044	2 587	24 074
March	182	63	449	247	6 120	983	846	7 070	2 908	26 811
April	204	50	463	287	5 702	1 083	704	6 867	3 038	26 318
May	201	53	474	231	5 594	1 079	734	6 794	2 944	25 736
June	180	55	388	282	6 059	1 140	818	7 444	2 740	27 493
July	201	56	339	263	6 211	1 110	810	7 393	2 915	28 410
August	180	76	343	274	6 491	1 114	799	7 473	2 943	28 623
September	187	57	253	258	6 589	1 068	775	7 655	2 737	28 972
October	127	53	295	222	6 647	1 078	801	7 561	2 988	30 452
November	216	38	279	259	6 087	973	728	7 244	2 574	28 060
December	139	48	195	261	5 879	1 065	846	7 258	2 300	27 025

1. See Notes for list of countries included in each group.
2. Association of Southeast Asian Nations.
3. Argentina, Brazil, Paraguay, and Uruguay.
4. Organization of Petroleum Exporting Countries.

U.S. Exports of Goods by Principal End-Use Category

(Census basis, except as noted; billions of dollars, seasonally adjusted)

Year and month	Total exports of goods			Foods, feeds, and beverages	Industrial supplies and materials		Capital goods, except automotive	Automotive vehicles, engines, and parts	Consumer goods (nonfood) except automotive	Other goods
	Total: Balance of payments basis	Net adjustments	Total: Census basis		Total	Petroleum and products				
1970	42.47	.....	.....	.....	.....	.....	.....	.....	.....	.....
1971	43.32	.....	.....	.....	.....	.....	.....	.....	.....	.....
1972	49.38	.....	.....	.....	.....	.....	.....	.....	.....	.....
1973	71.41	.....	.....	.....	.....	.....	.....	.....	.....	.....
1974	98.31	.....	.....	.....	.....	.....	.....	.....	.....	.....
1975	107.09	.....	.....	.....	.....	.....	.....	.....	.....	.....
1976	114.75	.....	.....	.....	.....	.....	.....	.....	.....	.....
1977	120.82	.....	.....	.....	.....	.....	.....	.....	.....	.....
1978	142.08	.....	.....	25.57	39.05	.....	46.81	14.56	11.20	.....
1979	184.44	.....	.....	30.26	57.30	.....	58.71	16.56	13.58	.....
1980	224.25	.....	.....	36.01	70.59	.....	74.65	15.98	17.31	.....
1981	237.04	.....	.....	38.57	67.79	.....	82.47	18.23	17.26	.....
1982	211.16	.....	.....	31.96	62.13	.....	75.03	15.94	15.75	.....
1983	201.80	0.09	201.71	31.83	57.43	.....	70.02	17.02	14.50	.....
1984	219.93	1.18	218.74	31.93	62.59	.....	75.41	20.99	14.64	.....
1985	215.92	3.29	212.62	24.42	59.17	.....	76.89	22.99	14.01	.....
1986	223.34	-3.13	226.47	22.84	61.89	.....	79.47	22.16	15.86	.....
1987	250.21	-3.70	253.90	24.74	67.84	.....	90.66	25.74	19.76	.....
1988	320.23	-3.11	323.34	32.86	86.73	.....	115.42	30.21	26.00	.....
1989	362.12	-1.72	363.84	37.06	99.33	.....	138.71	34.94	36.57	.....
1990	389.31	-3.62	392.92	34.95	104.92	7.65	152.12	36.50	42.78	20.73
1991	416.91	-4.85	421.76	35.74	109.57	7.59	165.96	40.01	46.86	23.66
1992	440.35	-7.81	448.16	40.27	109.14	7.62	175.92	47.03	51.42	24.39
1993	456.83	-8.26	465.09	40.63	111.81	7.50	181.70	52.40	54.66	23.89
1994	502.40	-10.23	512.63	41.96	121.40	6.97	205.02	57.78	59.98	26.50
1995	575.85	-8.90	584.74	50.47	146.25	8.10	233.05	61.83	64.43	28.72
1996	612.06	-13.02	625.08	55.53	147.65	9.63	252.98	65.02	70.06	33.84
1997	679.72	-9.47	689.18	51.51	158.23	10.42	294.55	74.03	77.37	33.51
1998	670.25	-11.89	682.14	46.40	148.27	8.08	299.61	73.16	79.26	35.44
1995:										
January	45.62	-0.64	46.26	3.87	11.54	0.63	17.72	5.52	5.15	2.46
February	45.91	-0.68	46.60	4.00	11.71	0.64	18.31	5.22	5.24	2.12
March	47.48	-0.78	48.26	4.10	12.50	0.67	18.61	5.25	5.34	2.47
April	47.03	-0.65	47.68	4.17	12.38	0.69	18.66	4.98	5.30	2.21
May	47.65	-0.76	48.41	4.04	12.37	0.70	19.01	5.18	5.36	2.44
June	47.43	-0.85	48.27	3.95	12.57	0.64	19.21	4.84	5.39	2.33
July	47.38	-0.72	48.10	4.14	12.02	0.66	19.66	4.81	5.26	2.20
August	48.56	-0.75	49.31	4.37	12.11	0.61	19.90	5.11	5.53	2.28
September	49.98	-0.66	50.64	4.68	12.60	0.60	20.13	5.41	5.48	2.35
October	49.33	-0.80	50.13	4.30	12.47	0.74	20.23	5.19	5.45	2.49
November	49.46	-0.81	50.26	4.37	11.83	0.66	20.73	5.01	5.42	2.91
December	50.03	-0.80	50.83	4.49	12.14	0.88	20.88	5.32	5.53	2.48
1996:										
January	49.58	-0.70	50.28	4.65	12.00	0.89	20.46	5.43	5.59	2.16
February	50.84	-0.79	51.63	4.52	12.19	0.79	21.28	5.38	5.79	2.47
March	50.02	-0.88	50.90	4.80	12.47	0.73	20.58	4.79	5.68	2.57
April	50.50	-0.85	51.35	4.71	12.68	0.65	20.78	5.03	5.72	2.44
May	50.88	-1.13	52.01	4.82	12.35	0.68	20.78	5.40	5.72	2.95
June	51.23	-0.89	52.11	4.81	12.23	0.62	20.71	5.46	5.82	3.08
July	49.88	-1.45	51.33	4.74	11.65	0.72	20.53	5.55	5.68	3.17
August	51.16	-1.36	52.52	4.56	12.31	0.78	21.11	5.60	5.86	3.08
September	50.95	-1.32	52.26	4.39	12.30	0.88	20.63	5.90	5.97	3.08
October	52.41	-1.07	53.47	4.48	12.63	1.09	22.20	5.37	6.05	2.75
November	52.84	-1.28	54.12	4.66	12.30	0.85	22.39	5.67	6.06	3.04
December	51.77	-1.32	53.09	4.38	12.54	0.95	21.54	5.45	6.11	3.06
1997:										
January	52.80	-0.56	53.35	4.34	12.22	0.89	22.33	5.85	6.15	2.47
February	54.41	-0.69	55.09	4.36	12.83	0.84	23.14	5.90	6.35	2.51
March	55.77	-1.00	56.77	4.22	13.50	0.81	23.98	5.85	6.37	2.86
April	56.58	-0.70	57.27	4.33	13.46	0.86	24.50	6.07	6.35	2.57
May	56.03	-1.00	57.03	4.22	13.25	0.77	24.35	5.90	6.45	2.85
June	57.29	-0.84	58.13	4.20	13.77	0.86	24.46	6.37	6.59	2.74
July	58.38	-0.69	59.07	3.96	13.13	0.92	25.85	6.58	6.49	3.06
August	57.50	-1.05	58.55	4.21	13.36	0.91	25.16	6.32	6.52	2.98
September	57.57	-0.75	58.32	4.29	13.15	0.87	25.18	6.21	6.44	3.05
October	58.04	-1.04	59.09	4.55	13.20	0.91	25.33	6.45	6.66	2.90
November	57.32	-0.66	57.98	4.53	13.12	0.82	24.74	6.48	6.55	2.58
December	58.03	-0.50	58.53	4.31	13.23	0.97	25.53	6.06	6.46	2.95
1998:										
January	57.75	-0.64	58.39	4.14	13.25	0.86	25.34	6.43	6.65	2.57
February	56.51	-0.81	57.32	4.22	12.69	0.75	24.87	6.36	6.48	2.70
March	56.41	-0.89	57.29	3.99	12.69	0.71	24.62	6.48	6.46	3.05
April	55.33	-0.66	55.99	3.81	12.44	0.74	24.09	6.33	6.55	2.76
May	54.85	-0.75	55.61	3.79	12.46	0.70	24.00	6.00	6.52	2.85
June	55.02	-0.91	55.92	3.87	12.03	0.66	24.66	5.81	6.72	2.83
July	54.16	-0.97	55.14	3.72	11.87	0.64	24.94	5.07	6.71	2.83
August	54.62	-1.32	55.94	3.67	12.13	0.66	24.33	5.87	6.69	3.26
September	55.47	-0.95	56.42	3.32	12.02	0.63	25.48	6.12	6.69	2.80
October	57.19	-1.21	58.40	4.02	12.37	0.59	26.12	6.16	6.62	3.12
November	56.93	-1.61	58.53	3.87	12.48	0.54	25.70	6.34	6.65	3.50
December	56.01	-1.19	57.19	3.99	11.83	0.61	25.47	6.19	6.53	3.18

U.S. Imports of Goods by Principal End-Use Category

(Census basis, except as noted; billions of dollars, seasonally adjusted)

Year and month	Total imports of goods			Foods, feeds, and beverages	Industrial supplies and materials		Capital goods, except automotive	Automotive vehicles, engines, and parts	Consumer goods (nonfood) except automotive	Other goods
	Total: Balance of payments basis	Net adjustments	Total: Census basis		Total	Petroleum and products				
1970	39.87	.....	.....	.....	.....	.....	.....	.....	.....	.....
1971	45.58	.....	.....	.....	.....	.....	.....	.....	.....	.....
1972	55.80	.....	.....	.....	.....	.....	.....	.....	.....	.....
1973	70.50	.....	.....	.....	.....	.....	.....	.....	.....	.....
1974	103.81	.....	.....	.....	.....	.....	.....	.....	.....	.....
1975	98.19	.....	.....	.....	.....	.....	.....	.....	.....	.....
1976	124.23	.....	.....	.....	.....	.....	.....	.....	.....	.....
1977	151.91	.....	.....	.....	.....	.....	.....	.....	.....	.....
1978	176.00	.....	.....	15.84	79.26	.....	19.29	25.11	29.40	.....
1979	212.01	.....	.....	18.01	102.67	.....	24.49	26.51	31.22	.....
1980	249.75	.....	.....	18.55	124.96	.....	30.72	28.13	34.22	.....
1981	265.07	.....	.....	18.53	131.10	.....	36.86	30.80	38.30	.....
1982	247.64	.....	.....	17.47	107.82	.....	38.22	34.26	39.66	.....
1983	268.90	7.18	261.72	18.56	105.63	.....	42.61	42.04	46.59	.....
1984	332.42	1.91	330.51	21.92	122.72	.....	60.15	56.77	61.19	.....
1985	338.09	1.71	336.38	21.89	112.48	.....	60.81	65.21	66.43	.....
1986	368.43	2.75	365.67	24.40	101.37	.....	71.86	78.25	79.43	.....
1987	409.77	3.48	406.28	24.81	110.67	.....	84.77	85.17	88.82	.....
1988	447.19	5.26	441.93	24.93	118.06	.....	101.79	87.95	96.42	.....
1989	477.37	3.72	473.65	25.08	132.40	.....	112.45	87.38	102.26	.....
1990	498.34	2.36	495.98	26.65	143.41	62.16	116.04	87.69	105.29	16.09
1991	490.98	2.53	488.45	26.21	131.38	51.78	120.80	84.94	107.78	15.94
1992	536.46	3.80	532.66	27.61	138.64	51.60	134.25	91.79	122.66	17.71
1993	589.44	8.78	580.66	27.87	145.61	51.50	152.37	102.42	134.02	18.39
1994	668.59	5.33	663.26	27.87	145.61	51.28	152.37	102.42	134.02	18.39
1995	749.57	6.03	743.54	33.18	181.85	56.16	221.43	123.80	159.91	23.39
1996	803.33	8.04	795.29	35.71	204.48	72.75	228.07	128.94	171.98	26.10
1997	876.37	6.66	869.70	39.69	213.77	71.77	253.28	139.81	193.81	29.34
1998	917.18	5.28	911.90	41.24	200.14	50.90	269.56	149.05	216.52	35.39
1995:										
January	60.75	0.25	60.49	2.85	14.44	4.14	17.07	10.93	13.28	1.92
February	60.08	0.24	59.84	2.85	14.48	4.37	17.01	10.65	13.04	1.81
March	62.27	0.88	61.39	2.86	15.12	4.57	17.53	10.71	13.38	1.78
April	63.45	0.89	62.56	2.72	15.61	4.74	18.06	10.99	13.45	1.73
May	63.47	1.16	62.31	2.66	15.63	5.01	18.18	10.40	13.49	1.97
June	63.62	0.92	62.70	2.77	15.63	5.09	18.62	10.25	13.47	1.96
July	62.70	0.22	62.48	2.73	15.40	4.86	18.79	9.94	13.61	2.00
August	62.29	0.25	62.04	2.71	15.05	4.72	18.79	9.97	13.48	2.04
September	63.09	0.24	62.85	2.79	15.39	4.86	19.10	10.21	13.36	1.99
October	62.46	0.43	62.03	2.75	14.77	4.32	19.52	9.67	13.23	2.11
November	62.46	0.32	62.14	2.74	15.11	4.67	19.46	9.80	13.03	2.00
December	62.94	0.22	62.73	2.74	15.23	4.80	19.30	10.28	13.08	2.09
1996:										
January	64.10	0.28	63.83	2.72	15.74	5.21	19.27	10.46	13.59	2.05
February	63.91	0.39	63.52	2.86	15.10	4.57	19.21	10.42	13.81	2.13
March	65.03	1.22	63.81	2.88	15.71	4.88	19.17	10.07	13.83	2.15
April	66.08	1.62	64.46	2.96	16.66	6.00	18.67	10.38	13.58	2.21
May	67.72	1.25	66.46	3.01	17.14	6.29	18.87	11.16	14.10	2.18
June	66.97	0.88	66.09	2.95	17.07	6.27	18.78	10.91	14.18	2.21
July	66.69	0.43	66.25	2.94	17.14	6.24	18.68	11.13	14.17	2.20
August	68.11	0.78	67.33	3.07	17.32	5.91	18.92	11.29	14.62	2.12
September	68.40	0.32	68.08	3.08	17.87	6.74	18.94	11.04	14.92	2.23
October	67.75	0.32	67.42	3.05	18.18	6.98	18.80	10.23	14.98	2.17
November	68.66	0.30	68.36	3.03	17.66	6.33	19.27	11.23	14.90	2.28
December	69.92	0.24	69.68	3.16	18.90	7.34	19.50	10.63	15.32	2.18
1997:										
January	70.07	0.26	69.81	3.05	18.20	6.63	19.45	11.81	15.15	2.16
February	70.73	0.43	70.30	3.13	17.93	6.47	19.69	11.81	15.25	2.47
March	71.39	1.46	69.93	3.19	17.80	6.28	20.12	11.35	15.19	2.28
April	72.39	1.03	71.37	3.27	17.59	5.86	20.70	11.35	16.04	2.43
May	72.73	0.90	71.82	3.35	17.81	6.12	20.91	11.54	15.88	2.36
June	72.66	0.90	71.76	3.26	17.38	5.70	21.04	11.72	15.92	2.44
July	73.64	0.23	73.40	3.44	17.38	5.55	21.74	12.10	16.26	2.47
August	74.31	0.25	74.06	3.41	18.18	6.13	21.83	11.74	16.36	2.53
September	74.42	0.27	74.15	3.45	18.05	5.90	21.93	11.53	16.70	2.50
October	74.53	0.26	74.27	3.39	18.08	6.08	22.06	11.44	16.63	2.69
November	74.11	0.25	73.87	3.34	18.08	5.96	21.44	11.46	17.07	2.49
December	75.40	0.43	74.97	3.42	17.29	5.09	22.38	11.97	17.37	2.54
1998:										
January	74.89	0.58	74.31	3.30	17.13	4.91	21.89	11.84	17.42	2.73
February	74.02	0.23	73.79	3.49	16.84	4.49	22.07	11.92	16.85	2.62
March	76.63	0.51	76.12	3.42	16.69	4.20	22.71	12.57	18.04	2.69
April	76.19	0.33	75.87	3.39	17.27	4.57	22.11	12.14	18.14	2.82
May	77.09	0.29	76.80	3.41	17.48	4.68	22.92	12.41	17.98	2.60
June	75.42	0.36	75.06	3.53	16.69	4.14	22.27	11.79	18.13	2.65
July	75.23	0.36	74.87	3.48	16.59	4.17	22.29	11.03	18.32	3.16
August	76.91	0.70	76.22	3.42	16.88	4.26	22.32	12.29	18.10	3.21
September	77.08	0.55	76.54	3.42	16.51	4.03	22.43	12.75	18.30	3.13
October	78.18	0.59	77.59	3.43	16.55	4.21	22.95	13.05	18.40	3.22
November	78.46	0.52	77.94	3.45	16.24	3.98	23.13	13.38	18.47	3.28
December	77.06	0.27	76.80	3.52	15.29	3.26	22.47	13.89	18.36	3.28

U.S. Exports and Imports of Goods by Principal End-Use Category in Constant Dollars

(Census basis, billions of 1992 dollars, seasonally adjusted)

Year and month	Exports							Imports						
	Total	Foods, feeds, and beverages	Industrial supplies and materials	Capital goods, except auto-motive	Auto-motive vehicles, engines, and parts	Consumer goods (nonfood) except auto-motive	Other goods	Total	Foods, feeds, and beverages	Industrial supplies and materials	Capital goods, except auto-motive	Auto-motive vehicles, engines, and parts	Consumer goods (nonfood) except auto-motive	Other goods
1970	.....	.....	.....	.....	.....	.....	.....	.....	.....	.....	.....	.....	.....	.....
1971	.....	.....	.....	.....	.....	.....	.....	.....	.....	.....	.....	.....	.....	.....
1972	.....	.....	.....	.....	.....	.....	.....	.....	.....	.....	.....	.....	.....	.....
1973	.....	.....	.....	.....	.....	.....	.....	.....	.....	.....	.....	.....	.....	.....
1974	.....	.....	.....	.....	.....	.....	.....	.....	.....	.....	.....	.....	.....	.....
1975	.....	.....	.....	.....	.....	.....	.....	.....	.....	.....	.....	.....	.....	.....
1976	.....	.....	.....	.....	.....	.....	.....	.....	.....	.....	.....	.....	.....	.....
1977	.....	.....	.....	.....	.....	.....	.....	.....	.....	.....	.....	.....	.....	.....
1978	.....	.....	.....	.....	.....	.....	.....	.....	.....	.....	.....	.....	.....	.....
1979	.....	.....	.....	.....	.....	.....	.....	.....	.....	.....	.....	.....	.....	.....
1980	.....	.....	.....	.....	.....	.....	.....	.....	.....	.....	.....	.....	.....	.....
1981	.....	.....	.....	.....	.....	.....	.....	.....	.....	.....	.....	.....	.....	.....
1982	.....	.....	.....	.....	.....	.....	.....	.....	.....	.....	.....	.....	.....	.....
1983	.....	.....	.....	.....	.....	.....	.....	.....	.....	.....	.....	.....	.....	.....
1984	.....	.....	.....	.....	.....	.....	.....	.....	.....	.....	.....	.....	.....	.....
1985	.....	.....	.....	.....	.....	.....	.....	365.40	24.40	101.30	71.80	78.20	79.40	.....
1986	227.20	22.30	57.30	75.80	21.70	.....	.....	406.20	24.80	111.00	84.50	85.00	88.70	.....
1987	254.10	24.30	66.70	86.20	24.60	.....	.....	441.00	24.80	118.30	101.40	87.70	95.90	.....
1988	322.40	32.30	85.10	109.20	29.30	.....	.....	473.20	25.10	132.30	113.30	86.10	102.90	.....
1989	363.80	37.20	99.30	138.80	34.80	.....	.....							
1990	393.60	35.10	104.40	152.70	37.40	39.22	18.70	495.30	26.60	146.20	116.40	87.30	105.70	14.46
1991	421.70	35.70	109.70	166.70	40.00	40.42	21.11	488.50	26.50	131.60	120.70	85.70	108.00	14.15
1992	448.20	40.30	109.10	175.90	47.00	43.60	21.71	532.70	27.60	138.60	134.30	91.80	122.70	15.46
1993	471.17	40.19	111.08	190.02	51.93	54.03	23.91	591.45	28.03	151.26	160.16	100.73	132.92	18.35
1994	522.29	40.43	114.17	225.76	56.54	58.97	26.41	675.05	29.52	168.80	199.56	112.13	144.22	20.82
1995	596.73	44.90	120.50	282.95	59.84	62.35	26.20	754.03	30.04	173.51	259.62	114.00	155.12	21.75
1996	688.10	43.84	128.79	355.58	62.27	66.92	30.70	855.47	32.96	184.32	329.91	117.92	166.08	24.28
1997	834.56	44.18	139.87	476.09	70.31	73.53	30.58	1 038.89	35.90	198.38	460.65	127.45	189.01	27.51
1998	859.15	44.35	139.72	496.99	69.41	75.53	33.14	1 144.84	38.37	218.18	504.52	135.78	214.08	33.93
1995:														
January	46.35	3.78	9.65	20.24	5.37	5.04	2.29	60.74	2.49	14.16	19.03	10.21	13.04	1.82
February	46.68	3.88	9.65	21.05	5.05	5.10	1.96	59.95	2.59	13.99	19.00	9.92	12.74	1.71
March	48.41	3.92	10.25	21.68	5.11	5.19	2.27	61.47	2.51	14.60	19.68	9.95	13.06	1.67
April	47.61	3.88	9.97	21.77	4.84	5.13	2.01	62.26	2.53	14.63	20.25	10.15	13.09	1.62
May	48.57	3.73	9.90	22.52	5.03	5.18	2.22	61.79	2.42	14.43	20.52	9.56	13.05	1.82
June	48.80	3.60	10.10	23.08	4.70	5.21	2.11	62.69	2.53	14.61	21.27	9.43	13.04	1.82
July	48.97	3.60	9.72	23.93	4.67	5.06	1.99	62.88	2.43	14.67	21.68	9.11	13.15	1.84
August	50.75	3.81	9.93	24.64	4.97	5.33	2.07	63.21	2.47	14.50	22.19	9.15	13.02	1.88
September	52.13	3.96	10.48	25.04	5.24	5.28	2.13	64.54	2.53	14.82	23.07	9.36	12.92	1.84
October	51.98	3.55	10.46	25.48	4.98	5.26	2.26	64.30	2.54	14.13	24.03	8.83	12.82	1.95
November	52.86	3.56	10.05	26.58	4.80	5.22	2.65	64.81	2.52	14.53	24.38	8.94	12.60	1.85
December	53.63	3.65	10.34	26.95	5.10	5.33	2.25	65.38	2.49	14.46	24.53	9.39	12.59	1.93
1996:														
January	53.22	3.70	10.17	26.82	5.20	5.37	1.95	66.56	2.62	14.67	24.73	9.57	13.07	1.90
February	54.89	3.64	10.44	27.86	5.16	5.55	2.24	66.75	2.59	14.22	25.14	9.52	13.30	1.97
March	54.71	3.78	10.80	27.78	4.59	5.44	2.33	67.29	2.67	14.53	25.56	9.21	13.33	1.99
April	55.48	3.57	11.03	28.40	4.83	5.46	2.20	67.83	2.63	14.93	25.62	9.50	13.09	2.05
May	56.32	3.56	10.78	28.67	5.18	5.47	2.66	70.51	2.70	15.61	26.38	10.21	13.59	2.03
June	56.73	3.60	10.72	28.84	5.23	5.56	2.78	70.78	2.76	15.81	26.46	10.01	13.69	2.06
July	56.38	3.58	10.26	28.93	5.33	5.42	2.87	71.58	2.77	15.84	27.03	10.19	13.70	2.06
August	57.88	3.47	10.87	29.80	5.36	5.60	2.79	73.13	2.90	15.81	27.98	10.33	14.14	1.98
September	58.54	3.55	10.82	30.02	5.65	5.69	2.81	73.73	2.80	15.93	28.46	10.06	14.40	2.07
October	60.24	3.72	11.04	32.07	5.14	5.77	2.50	73.84	2.77	15.79	29.40	9.36	14.49	2.03
November	62.05	3.93	10.85	33.30	5.42	5.78	2.78	75.80	2.79	15.26	30.94	10.26	14.43	2.12
December	61.66	3.74	11.02	33.09	5.20	5.82	2.79	77.67	2.96	15.94	32.21	9.70	14.83	2.03
1997:														
January	62.69	3.72	10.76	34.53	5.58	5.84	2.26	79.10	2.86	15.51	33.25	10.77	14.70	2.01
February	64.77	3.67	11.28	35.89	5.62	6.03	2.29	80.48	2.87	15.77	33.95	10.78	14.82	2.31
March	66.92	3.51	11.92	37.25	5.56	6.07	2.60	81.44	2.82	16.17	35.16	10.35	14.80	2.13
April	67.90	3.59	11.89	38.29	5.76	6.05	2.34	84.29	2.97	16.54	36.51	10.38	15.62	2.28
May	68.51	3.53	11.69	38.93	5.61	6.14	2.60	85.30	2.99	16.72	37.35	10.55	15.48	2.21
June	70.33	3.61	12.16	39.75	6.05	6.26	2.50	85.92	2.90	16.37	38.16	10.70	15.52	2.28
July	71.75	3.44	11.54	41.57	6.25	6.17	2.79	88.43	3.06	16.54	39.64	11.03	15.85	2.31
August	72.18	3.63	11.75	41.89	5.99	6.19	2.71	89.74	3.06	17.14	40.50	10.70	15.97	2.37
September	72.30	3.70	11.62	42.20	5.89	6.11	2.79	90.48	3.10	17.04	41.17	10.50	16.32	2.35
October	73.33	4.00	11.71	42.54	6.12	6.32	2.65	90.78	3.09	16.92	41.60	10.40	16.24	2.53
November	71.54	3.96	11.66	41.20	6.15	6.22	2.36	90.25	3.06	16.99	40.73	10.42	16.71	2.34
December	72.34	3.82	11.90	42.06	5.74	6.13	2.70	92.68	3.12	16.68	42.62	10.88	16.98	2.39
1998:														
January	71.51	3.76	12.17	40.81	6.10	6.30	2.37	90.94	3.02	17.31	40.20	10.76	17.07	2.59
February	71.01	3.91	11.62	40.74	6.03	6.20	2.50	91.63	3.25	17.45	41.05	10.84	16.55	2.50
March	70.76	3.74	11.73	40.18	6.15	6.14	2.83	94.42	3.23	17.80	41.65	11.42	17.75	2.57
April	69.79	3.61	11.48	39.88	6.01	6.24	2.57	94.14	3.12	18.53	40.86	11.04	17.89	2.69
May	69.32	3.56	11.61	39.61	5.69	6.20	2.65	95.75	3.17	18.79	42.20	11.32	17.78	2.49
June	70.26	3.66	11.26	40.75	5.51	6.42	2.64	94.24	3.27	18.19	41.55	10.75	17.95	2.54
July	69.45	3.47	11.18	40.95	4.82	6.40	2.64	94.64	3.19	18.44	41.76	10.06	18.16	3.03
August	71.43	3.58	11.59	41.25	5.58	6.38	3.06	96.85	3.27	19.04	42.23	11.24	17.98	3.10
September	72.33	3.32	11.57	42.61	5.81	6.37	2.64	96.73	3.18	18.40	42.29	11.66	18.18	3.02
October	74.69	4.07	12.01	43.51	5.84	6.31	2.95	97.93	3.15	18.28	43.23	11.91	18.25	3.10
November	74.63	3.79	12.09	43.10	6.01	6.34	3.30	99.56	3.24	18.28	44.45	12.17	18.28	3.15
December	74.00	3.88	11.43	43.60	5.87	6.23	2.99	98.03	3.28	17.69	43.05	12.61	18.25	3.15

U.S. Exports of Services

(Balance of payments basis, millions of dollars, seasonally adjusted)

Year and month	Total	Travel	Passenger fares	Other transportation	Royalties and license fees	Other private services	Transfers under U.S. military sales contracts [1]	U.S. government miscellaneous services
1970	14 171	2 331	544	3 125	2 331	1 294	4 214	332
1971	16 358	2 534	615	3 299	2 545	1 546	5 472	347
1972	17 841	2 817	699	3 579	2 770	1 764	5 856	357
1973	19 832	3 412	975	4 465	3 225	1 985	5 369	401
1974	22 591	4 032	1 104	5 697	3 821	2 321	5 197	419
1975	25 497	4 697	1 039	5 840	4 300	2 920	6 256	446
1976	27 971	5 742	1 229	6 747	4 353	3 584	5 826	489
1977	31 485	6 150	1 366	7 090	4 920	3 848	7 554	557
1978	36 353	7 183	1 603	8 136	5 885	4 717	8 209	620
1979	39 692	8 441	2 156	9 971	6 184	5 439	6 981	520
1980	47 584	10 588	2 591	11 618	7 085	6 276	9 029	398
1981	57 354	12 913	3 111	12 560	7 284	10 250	10 720	517
1982	64 079	12 393	3 174	12 317	5 603	17 444	12 572	576
1983	64 307	10 947	3 610	12 590	5 778	18 192	12 524	666
1984	71 168	17 177	4 067	13 809	6 177	19 255	9 969	714
1985	73 155	17 762	4 411	14 674	6 678	20 035	8 718	878
1986	86 350	20 385	5 582	15 438	8 113	27 687	8 549	595
1987	98 593	23 563	7 003	17 027	10 183	29 186	11 106	526
1988	111 068	29 434	8 976	19 311	12 146	31 253	9 284	664
1989	127 233	36 205	10 657	20 526	13 818	36 875	8 564	587
1990	147 922	43 007	15 298	22 042	16 634	40 341	9 932	668
1991	164 333	48 385	15 854	22 631	17 819	47 821	11 135	690
1992	175 557	54 742	16 618	21 531	20 841	48 597	12 387	841
1993	184 951	57 875	16 528	21 958	21 695	52 541	13 471	883
1994	199 675	58 417	16 997	23 754	26 712	60 121	12 787	887
1995	217 637	63 395	18 909	26 081	30 289	63 502	14 643	818
1996	237 749	69 751	20 413	26 074	32 470	72 412	15 736	893
1997	258 828	73 301	20 789	27 006	33 781	85 566	17 561	824
1998	263 661	71 250	19 996	25 518	36 808	92 116	17 155	818
1995:								
January	17 515	5 337	1 600	2 052	2 381	5 039	1 033	73
February	16 929	4 789	1 473	2 022	2 408	5 098	1 072	67
March	17 361	4 737	1 465	2 221	2 430	5 144	1 302	62
April	17 780	5 324	1 577	2 190	2 451	5 116	1 072	50
May	17 880	5 223	1 550	2 221	2 474	5 188	1 173	51
June	17 107	4 494	1 373	2 150	2 504	5 272	1 257	57
July	18 440	5 367	1 601	2 134	2 590	5 354	1 309	85
August	18 566	5 304	1 583	2 200	2 612	5 376	1 402	89
September	19 029	5 686	1 685	2 194	2 620	5 426	1 330	88
October	18 701	5 536	1 616	2 191	2 603	5 451	1 239	65
November	19 030	5 696	1 672	2 257	2 604	5 479	1 259	63
December	19 296	5 901	1 713	2 249	2 612	5 558	1 195	68
1996:								
January	18 702	5 507	1 629	2 110	2 633	5 598	1 130	95
February	18 650	5 465	1 643	2 035	2 639	5 727	1 042	99
March	19 576	5 875	1 717	2 118	2 639	5 915	1 217	95
April	19 165	5 551	1 573	2 203	2 622	5 929	1 220	67
May	19 983	6 185	1 783	2 166	2 629	5 940	1 219	61
June	19 694	5 915	1 702	2 121	2 647	5 963	1 287	59
July	19 086	5 262	1 582	2 106	2 704	6 021	1 342	69
August	19 513	5 478	1 651	2 203	2 734	6 039	1 338	70
September	19 505	5 423	1 636	2 129	2 760	6 092	1 394	71
October	21 328	6 435	1 857	2 311	2 820	6 310	1 525	70
November	21 543	6 502	1 870	2 304	2 828	6 430	1 540	69
December	21 000	6 153	1 770	2 267	2 815	6 445	1 482	68
1997:								
January	20 911	6 219	1 719	2 203	2 757	6 575	1 374	64
February	20 760	6 015	1 709	2 219	2 740	6 675	1 338	64
March	21 110	6 097	1 728	2 279	2 735	6 771	1 434	66
April	21 374	6 162	1 730	2 284	2 775	6 889	1 461	73
May	21 709	6 098	1 708	2 273	2 788	7 060	1 708	74
June	21 705	6 073	1 711	2 204	2 809	7 192	1 641	75
July	21 731	6 006	1 703	2 220	2 896	7 270	1 562	74
August	22 075	6 150	1 721	2 249	2 903	7 373	1 606	73
September	22 032	6 374	1 801	2 222	2 891	7 327	1 346	71
October	22 188	6 161	1 777	2 354	2 830	7 534	1 469	63
November	21 682	6 048	1 764	2 242	2 823	7 458	1 284	63
December	21 555	5 898	1 718	2 259	2 835	7 443	1 338	64
1998:								
January	21 649	6 118	1 709	2 189	2 930	7 327	1 304	72
February	21 487	5 967	1 643	2 078	2 964	7 390	1 371	74
March	22 030	5 818	1 564	2 071	2 988	7 585	1 931	73
April	22 710	6 370	1 812	2 136	2 992	7 771	1 564	65
May	22 273	6 050	1 731	2 112	3 002	7 682	1 633	63
June	21 708	5 840	1 642	2 020	3 008	7 843	1 292	63
July	21 660	5 662	1 653	2 094	2 966	7 778	1 441	66
August	21 603	5 718	1 682	2 137	2 999	7 719	1 282	66
September	21 762	5 769	1 717	2 108	3 064	7 781	1 256	67
October	22 424	5 953	1 627	2 253	3 266	7 821	1 435	69
November	22 200	5 904	1 626	2 197	3 314	7 672	1 417	70
December	22 156	6 081	1 590	2 125	3 314	7 747	1 229	70

1. Contains goods that cannot be separately identified.

U.S. Imports of Services

(Balance of payments basis, millions of dollars, seasonally adjusted)

Year and month	Total	Travel	Passenger fares	Other transportation	Royalties and license fees	Other private services	Direct defense expenditures [1]	U.S. government miscellaneous services
1970	14 520	3 980	1 215	2 843	224	827	4 855	576
1971	15 400	4 373	1 290	3 130	241	956	4 819	592
1972	16 868	5 042	1 596	3 520	294	1 043	4 784	589
1973	18 843	5 526	1 790	4 694	385	1 180	4 629	640
1974	21 379	5 980	2 095	5 942	346	1 262	5 032	722
1975	21 996	6 417	2 263	5 708	472	1 551	4 795	789
1976	24 570	6 856	2 568	6 852	482	2 006	4 895	911
1977	27 640	7 451	2 748	7 972	504	2 190	5 823	951
1978	32 189	8 475	2 896	9 124	671	2 573	7 352	1 099
1979	36 689	9 413	3 184	10 906	831	2 822	8 294	1 239
1980	41 491	10 397	3 607	11 790	724	2 909	10 851	1 214
1981	45 503	11 479	4 487	12 474	650	3 562	11 564	1 287
1982	51 749	12 394	4 772	11 710	795	8 159	12 460	1 460
1983	54 973	13 149	6 003	12 222	943	8 001	13 087	1 568
1984	67 748	22 913	5 735	14 843	1 168	9 040	12 516	1 534
1985	72 862	24 558	6 444	15 643	1 170	10 203	13 108	1 735
1986	81 835	25 913	6 505	17 766	1 401	14 834	13 730	1 686
1987	92 349	29 310	7 283	19 010	1 857	18 047	14 950	1 893
1988	99 965	32 114	7 729	20 891	2 601	19 106	15 604	1 921
1989	104 185	33 416	8 249	22 172	2 528	20 636	15 313	1 871
1990	120 021	37 349	10 531	24 966	3 135	24 590	17 531	1 919
1991	121 196	35 322	10 012	24 975	4 035	28 328	16 409	2 116
1992	116 476	38 552	10 603	23 767	5 161	22 296	13 835	2 263
1993	122 281	40 713	11 410	24 524	5 032	26 261	12 086	2 255
1994	131 878	43 782	13 062	26 019	5 852	30 386	10 217	2 560
1995	141 447	44 916	14 663	27 034	6 919	35 249	10 043	2 623
1996	150 797	48 048	15 818	27 403	7 837	37 975	11 029	2 687
1997	166 907	52 051	18 138	28 959	9 390	43 909	11 698	2 762
1998	181 011	56 105	19 797	30 457	11 292	47 670	12 841	2 849
1995:								
January	11 440	3 697	1 136	2 214	512	2 801	851	229
February	11 415	3 638	1 129	2 175	524	2 856	861	232
March	11 678	3 647	1 139	2 365	533	2 903	860	231
April	11 666	3 779	1 209	2 222	541	2 877	824	214
May	11 731	3 725	1 208	2 300	552	2 921	814	211
June	11 839	3 798	1 238	2 259	561	2 963	809	211
July	11 849	3 682	1 243	2 290	589	3 015	809	221
August	11 911	3 669	1 254	2 330	585	3 038	814	221
September	11 905	3 733	1 248	2 241	599	3 041	823	220
October	11 920	3 820	1 275	2 294	638	2 838	843	212
November	12 039	3 828	1 289	2 219	645	2 989	859	210
December	12 056	3 902	1 297	2 126	640	3 004	876	211
1996:								
January	12 062	3 840	1 251	2 236	607	3 005	906	217
February	12 353	4 111	1 343	2 101	596	3 065	917	220
March	12 258	3 991	1 268	2 189	591	3 079	919	221
April	12 351	3 908	1 278	2 354	607	3 091	896	217
May	12 552	3 999	1 331	2 371	604	3 132	896	219
June	12 268	3 861	1 284	2 265	601	3 133	903	221
July	12 964	4 018	1 321	2 375	978	3 113	930	229
August	12 787	4 113	1 348	2 326	708	3 123	938	231
September	12 616	4 008	1 326	2 290	605	3 215	940	232
October	12 891	4 054	1 357	2 387	635	3 304	927	227
November	12 833	4 095	1 364	2 225	646	3 349	927	227
December	12 863	4 050	1 347	2 283	660	3 367	930	226
1997:								
January	13 329	4 306	1 437	2 336	693	3 388	947	222
February	13 422	4 306	1 435	2 328	703	3 483	946	221
March	13 434	4 289	1 423	2 372	708	3 480	939	223
April	13 506	4 214	1 524	2 432	690	3 520	897	229
May	13 718	4 293	1 535	2 472	708	3 578	900	232
June	13 875	4 337	1 556	2 415	740	3 675	917	235
July	14 082	4 360	1 562	2 367	867	3 708	977	241
August	14 149	4 380	1 556	2 355	867	3 745	1 004	242
September	14 415	4 411	1 587	2 481	879	3 794	1 024	239
October	14 250	4 303	1 470	2 499	843	3 851	1 056	228
November	14 323	4 442	1 530	2 370	843	3 868	1 044	226
December	14 403	4 410	1 523	2 531	849	3 819	1 047	224
1998:								
January	14 358	4 561	1 538	2 450	851	3 697	1 036	225
February	14 687	4 600	1 556	2 340	1 236	3 698	1 033	224
March	14 583	4 575	1 535	2 531	868	3 822	1 029	223
April	15 067	4 779	1 680	2 531	893	3 954	1 012	218
May	14 938	4 643	1 631	2 522	894	4 010	1 017	221
June	15 147	4 746	1 647	2 537	907	4 050	1 032	228
July	15 283	4 696	1 730	2 564	926	4 046	1 072	249
August	15 172	4 640	1 669	2 598	889	4 026	1 093	257
September	15 325	4 734	1 686	2 538	906	4 091	1 111	259
October	15 792	4 832	1 771	2 760	950	4 108	1 120	251
November	15 325	4 602	1 695	2 588	974	4 082	1 135	249
December	15 338	4 697	1 659	2 501	999	4 086	1 151	245

1. Contains goods that cannot be separately identified.

U.S. Export and Import Price Indexes

(1995=100, not seasonally adjusted)

Year and month	Exports			Imports		
	All commodities	Agricultural	Nonagricultural	All commodities	Petroleum [1]	Nonpetroleum
1970	.....	.....	.....	.....	.....	.....
1971	.....	.....	.....	.....	.....	.....
1972	.....	.....	.....	.....	.....	.....
1973	.....	.....	.....	.....	.....	.....
1974	.....	.....	.....	.....	.....	.....
1975	.....	.....	.....	.....	.....	.....
1976	.....	.....	.....	.....	.....	.....
1977	.....	.....	.....	.....	.....	.....
1978	.....	.....	.....	.....	.....	.....
1979	.....	.....	.....	.....	.....	.....
1980	.....	.....	.....	.....	.....	.....
1981	.....	.....	.....	.....	.....	.....
1982	.....	.....	.....	.....	.....	.....
1983	.....	.....	.....	.....	.....	.....
1984	.....	.....	.....	.....	.....	.....
1985	.....	.....	.....	.....	.....	.....
1986	.....	.....	.....	.....	.....	.....
1987	.....	.....	.....	.....	.....	.....
1988	.....	.....	.....	.....	.....	.....
1989	91.1	92.8	90.5	90.6	102.3	89.5
1990	91.9	88.3	92.1	93.5	126.3	90.5
1991	92.6	86.9	93.1	93.7	112.6	92.0
1992	92.7	86.1	93.4	94.3	105.3	93.3
1993	93.2	87.7	93.9	94.0	96.5	93.8
1994	95.2	91.9	95.6	95.7	90.8	96.2
1995	100.0	100.0	100.0	100.0	100.0	100.0
1996	100.5	111.4	99.2	101.0	118.9	99.2
1997	99.2	101.3	98.9	98.5	110.4	97.1
1998	95.9	91.4	96.4	92.6	74.9	93.7
1995:						
January	98.0	92.7	98.7	98.2	96.2	98.4
February	98.6	93.1	99.3	98.8	98.7	98.8
March	99.1	94.4	99.7	99.4	100.7	99.2
April	100.0	96.2	100.5	100.3	105.4	99.8
May	100.3	96.9	100.8	101.3	108.8	100.4
June	100.5	98.3	100.8	100.8	105.2	100.4
July	100.8	102.0	100.7	100.5	98.6	100.7
August	100.3	100.6	100.3	100.3	96.0	100.7
September	100.5	103.6	100.1	100.3	97.8	100.5
October	100.6	105.6	99.9	99.8	95.7	100.3
November	100.6	107.9	99.6	100.0	96.3	100.4
December	100.5	108.8	99.4	100.4	100.7	100.4
1996:						
January	101.0	110.6	99.7	100.6	105.5	100.2
February	100.8	110.4	99.5	100.4	104.0	100.1
March	100.6	111.9	99.2	101.0	112.9	99.9
April	101.2	117.3	99.2	101.9	122.5	99.8
May	101.6	120.9	99.1	101.2	118.0	99.5
June	101.4	118.3	99.2	100.1	111.1	99.1
July	100.9	116.0	99.0	100.0	113.2	98.7
August	100.7	115.8	98.8	100.1	115.7	98.6
September	99.9	107.4	99.0	101.3	124.4	99.0
October	99.7	104.6	99.0	101.8	133.2	98.7
November	99.3	102.2	99.0	101.6	132.1	98.6
December	99.3	101.3	99.1	101.9	134.7	98.7
1997:						
January	99.4	101.4	99.1	101.6	135.5	98.3
February	99.6	103.5	99.1	100.7	124.5	98.2
March	99.7	105.1	99.0	99.4	113.7	97.8
April	99.7	104.7	99.0	98.3	105.4	97.3
May	99.4	103.4	99.0	98.3	106.6	97.2
June	99.3	101.3	99.1	98.2	104.5	97.3
July	99.3	100.2	99.1	98.0	103.1	97.1
August	99.3	100.3	99.1	97.9	105.5	96.8
September	99.0	100.2	98.8	97.8	105.7	96.8
October	98.6	98.4	98.6	98.0	111.6	96.5
November	98.6	99.1	98.5	97.6	107.7	96.3
December	98.2	98.3	98.1	96.6	100.4	95.9
1998:						
January	97.5	95.6	97.7	95.3	90.4	95.3
February	97.2	94.2	97.5	94.4	84.5	94.9
March	96.9	93.7	97.2	93.6	76.9	94.6
April	96.5	92.2	97.0	93.3	77.2	94.3
May	96.6	93.1	96.9	93.2	77.6	94.1
June	96.1	93.1	96.4	92.6	74.2	93.7
July	95.8	93.4	96.0	91.8	70.2	93.3
August	95.3	89.6	95.9	91.4	69.8	92.9
September	94.8	87.0	95.7	91.6	74.3	92.7
October	94.7	87.1	95.6	91.8	76.0	92.8
November	94.9	88.6	95.6	91.3	68.6	92.9
December	94.8	89.2	95.4	90.4	59.5	92.7

1. Petroleum and petroleum products.

International Comparisons

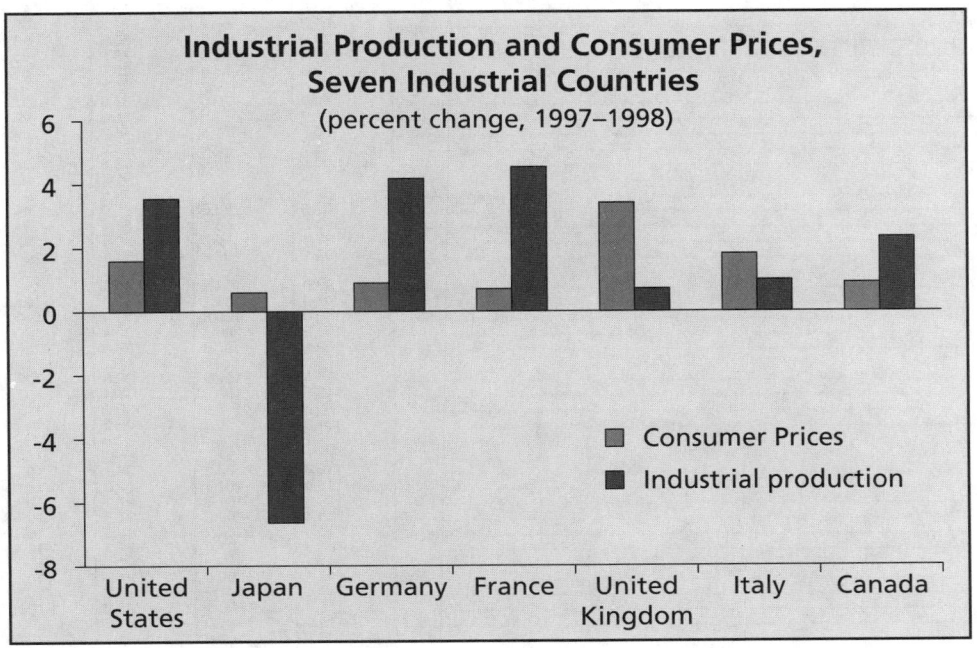

Industrial Production and Consumer Prices, Seven Industrial Countries
(percent change, 1997–1998)

- Consumer prices were relatively stable in all the major industrial countries in 1998. The United Kingdom had the largest price increase, 3.4 percent. The United States and Italy had increases of less than 2 percent; all others were less than one percent.

- Industrial production grew in 1998 in six of the seven countries, the exception being a 6.6 percent decline in Japan, reversing an upward trend since 1993. Strongest growth was in France, with a 4.5 percent increase, and Germany, with a 4.2 percent increase.

- Unemployment rates in five of the seven countries declined in 1998. The exceptions were Japan, with an increase from 3.4 percent in 1997 to 4.1 percent, and Italy, which stayed steady at 12.3 percent.

Industrial Production Indexes

(1992=100, seasonally adjusted)

Year and month	United States	Japan	Germany [1]	France	United Kingdom	Italy	Canada
1970	58.7	47.2	71.5	66.4	75.7	59.7	59.5
1971	59.5	48.4	72.1	70.7	75.4	59.5	62.8
1972	65.3	52.0	74.8	74.6	76.7	62.1	68.4
1973	70.6	59.7	79.7	79.7	83.6	68.1	76.2
1974	69.6	57.3	78.2	81.6	81.9	71.2	77.3
1975	63.5	51.1	73.4	75.7	77.4	64.6	71.6
1976	69.3	56.7	78.3	82.4	80.0	72.7	76.2
1977	74.9	59.0	80.3	83.7	84.1	73.5	78.9
1978	79.3	62.8	78.9	85.6	86.5	74.9	82.2
1979	82.0	67.4	82.9	89.4	89.8	79.9	86.2
1980	79.7	70.5	82.9	91.3	84.0	84.3	83.5
1981	81.0	71.2	81.3	90.5	81.3	82.4	84.0
1982	76.7	71.4	78.7	89.8	82.9	79.9	77.4
1983	79.5	73.8	79.2	89.2	85.9	78.1	81.4
1984	86.6	80.6	81.6	89.5	86.0	80.6	91.7
1985	88.0	83.6	85.5	91.3	90.7	80.7	96.6
1986	89.0	83.5	87.0	91.9	92.9	84.0	96.0
1987	93.2	86.4	87.4	93.1	96.6	86.2	100.2
1988	97.4	94.5	90.5	97.3	101.3	92.1	106.3
1989	99.1	99.9	95.1	100.9	103.4	95.7	105.8
1990	98.9	104.1	99.9	102.4	103.1	101.7	102.9
1991	97.0	106.1	102.3	101.2	99.7	101.3	98.9
1992	100.0	100.0	100.0	100.0	100.0	100.0	100.0
1993	103.5	96.5	92.4	96.1	102.2	97.9	104.5
1994	109.1	97.7	95.6	100.0	107.7	103.9	111.3
1995	114.4	100.9	96.8	102.0	109.5	109.2	116.3
1996	119.5	103.2	97.4	102.2	110.7	107.1	118.3
1997	126.8	107.0	100.8	106.2	111.8	111.2	124.8
1998	131.3	99.9	105.0	111.0	112.6	112.3	127.7
1995:							
January	113.4	99.2	96.3	103.2	108.7	108.4	117.5
February	113.4	101.1	97.3	101.8	109.0	107.0	117.3
March	113.6	101.8	97.1	103.7	109.6	108.8	116.6
April	113.4	102.0	97.3	100.8	109.5	107.1	116.4
May	113.8	100.7	98.3	103.0	110.0	109.4	116.5
June	114.3	101.0	97.3	103.3	109.1	108.7	116.1
July	113.9	98.0	97.2	102.7	109.2	107.9	115.9
August	115.1	101.7	96.2	102.7	109.9	111.0	115.9
September	115.4	100.1	97.2	102.1	110.1	109.7	115.9
October	115.5	101.0	94.8	100.3	109.3	110.3	115.9
November	115.7	101.8	95.8	101.4	109.9	109.9	116.1
December	115.8	102.4	96.1	100.0	110.2	112.0	115.6
1996:							
January	115.5	103.1	97.0	101.8	110.5	110.6	116.9
February	117.0	104.7	95.3	102.3	110.2	110.0	116.8
March	116.8	99.2	96.7	101.6	111.2	108.8	116.2
April	118.2	102.0	96.5	101.3	109.6	106.2	117.0
May	119.2	102.8	97.3	102.7	111.1	107.3	117.4
June	120.0	100.2	97.5	101.9	110.5	106.9	117.9
July	120.3	103.8	97.4	102.7	110.7	107.3	119.1
August	120.9	102.8	98.8	102.7	110.6	108.0	119.3
September	121.1	103.7	98.5	102.7	111.2	105.6	119.5
October	121.2	106.0	97.3	102.8	110.5	107.0	119.0
November	121.9	105.4	98.5	102.6	111.3	106.4	121.1
December	122.3	105.8	98.4	102.6	111.5	105.7	119.3
1997:							
January	123.0	109.7	98.2	102.2	112.6	106.3	121.6
February	123.9	107.4	98.9	103.0	111.8	109.0	122.2
March	124.4	106.1	99.8	102.4	110.6	108.3	121.7
April	125.1	106.2	100.3	106.2	111.6	111.6	123.5
May	125.5	109.3	99.1	105.1	111.4	110.6	124.3
June	126.1	107.2	102.0	105.3	111.7	111.2	123.8
July	127.0	107.9	104.1	108.1	113.5	112.9	126.9
August	127.8	106.4	100.8	108.1	112.0	112.8	125.9
September	128.5	108.4	100.8	107.6	111.5	112.7	126.0
October	129.3	107.5	102.3	109.8	111.9	114.8	126.8
November	129.9	102.8	102.5	107.4	111.6	113.5	126.7
December	130.3	104.8	103.6	109.8	111.6	114.8	127.7
1998:							
January	130.3	106.0	104.7	109.2	111.7	113.2	125.1
February	130.2	102.2	104.7	109.6	111.7	113.6	127.9
March	130.7	101.4	106.1	111.2	112.4	113.3	128.9
April	131.3	99.9	105.2	110.7	113.5	114.4	127.6
May	131.9	97.3	105.6	111.3	112.3	113.9	127.7
June	130.6	99.9	104.8	111.8	113.7	113.6	126.9
July	130.5	98.8	108.0	111.5	113.6	115.0	124.6
August	132.4	98.4	106.9	111.5	113.3	111.4	128.5
September	131.9	100.1	104.3	111.2	112.7	113.9	128.1
October	132.4	98.9	105.2	111.4	112.5	112.7	127.8
November	132.2	98.1	103.4	111.4	112.3	113.2	129.1
December	132.4	98.1	104.3	110.7	111.9	109.7	130.0

1. Data prior to 1991 are for West Germany only.

Consumer Price Indexes

(1982-1984=100, not seasonally adjusted; percent changes are from previous year's average for annual data, from the same month of the previous year for monthly data.)

Year and month	United States Index	Percent change	Japan Index	Percent change	Germany [1] Index	Percent change	France Index	Percent change	United Kingdom Index	Percent change	Italy Index	Percent change	Canada Index	Percent change
1970	38.8	5.7	38.5	6.6	52.8	3.4	28.7	5.7	21.8	6.3	16.8	5.0	35.2	3.4
1971	40.5	4.4	41.0	6.5	55.6	5.2	30.3	5.6	23.8	9.5	17.7	5.0	36.2	2.9
1972	41.8	3.2	42.9	4.7	58.7	5.5	32.2	6.0	25.5	7.1	18.7	5.7	37.9	4.8
1973	44.4	6.2	47.9	11.7	62.8	7.0	34.5	7.4	27.9	9.2	20.6	10.4	40.8	7.7
1974	49.3	11.0	59.1	23.4	67.1	7.0	39.3	13.7	32.3	16.0	24.6	19.4	45.2	10.7
1975	53.8	9.1	65.9	11.5	71.1	5.9	43.9	11.7	40.2	24.2	28.8	17.2	50.1	10.9
1976	56.9	5.8	72.2	9.6	74.2	4.3	48.1	9.6	46.8	16.5	33.6	16.5	53.9	7.5
1977	60.6	6.5	78.0	8.1	76.9	3.7	52.6	9.5	54.2	15.9	40.1	19.4	58.1	7.8
1978	65.2	7.6	81.4	4.3	79.0	2.7	57.5	9.2	58.7	8.2	45.1	12.5	63.3	9.0
1979	72.6	11.3	84.4	3.7	82.2	4.1	63.6	10.6	66.6	13.5	52.1	15.7	69.2	9.2
1980	82.4	13.5	90.9	7.8	86.7	5.5	72.2	13.5	78.5	18.0	63.2	21.2	76.1	10.1
1981	90.9	10.3	95.3	4.8	92.2	6.3	81.8	13.3	87.9	11.9	75.4	19.3	85.6	12.4
1982	96.5	6.2	98.1	2.9	97.1	5.3	91.7	12.0	95.4	8.6	87.7	16.4	94.9	10.9
1983	99.6	3.2	99.8	1.8	100.3	3.3	100.3	9.5	99.8	4.6	100.8	14.9	100.4	5.8
1984	103.9	4.3	102.1	2.3	102.7	2.4	108.0	7.7	104.8	5.0	111.5	10.6	104.7	4.3
1985	107.6	3.6	104.1	2.0	104.8	2.1	114.3	5.8	111.1	6.1	121.1	8.6	109.0	4.0
1986	109.6	1.9	104.8	0.7	104.7	-0.1	117.2	2.5	114.9	3.4	128.5	6.1	113.5	4.1
1987	113.6	3.6	104.8	0.0	104.9	0.2	121.1	3.3	119.7	4.1	134.4	4.6	118.4	4.4
1988	118.3	4.1	105.6	0.7	106.3	1.3	124.3	2.7	125.6	4.9	141.1	5.0	123.2	4.0
1989	124.0	4.8	108.1	2.4	109.2	2.8	128.7	3.5	135.3	7.7	150.4	6.6	129.3	5.0
1990	130.7	5.4	111.4	3.1	112.2	2.7	132.9	3.3	148.2	9.6	159.6	6.1	135.5	4.8
1991	136.2	4.2	115.0	3.2	116.2	3.7	137.2	3.2	156.9	5.9	169.8	6.4	143.1	5.6
1992	140.3	3.0	116.9	1.7	122.1	5.1	140.4	2.4	162.7	3.7	178.8	5.3	145.3	1.5
1993	144.5	3.0	118.4	1.3	127.6	4.4	143.4	2.1	165.3	1.6	186.4	4.2	147.9	1.8
1994	148.2	2.6	119.3	0.7	131.1	2.8	145.8	1.7	169.4	2.5	193.7	3.9	148.2	0.2
1995	152.4	2.8	119.1	-0.1	133.3	1.7	148.4	1.8	175.1	3.4	204.1	5.4	151.4	2.2
1996	156.9	3.0	119.3	0.1	135.2	1.4	151.4	2.0	179.4	2.4	212.0	3.9	153.8	1.6
1997	160.5	2.3	121.4	1.8	137.8	1.9	153.2	1.2	185.0	3.1	215.9	1.8	156.3	1.6
1998	163.0	1.6	122.1	0.6	139.1	0.9	154.2	0.7	191.4	3.4	219.8	1.8	157.8	0.9
1995:														
January	150.3	2.8	119.4	0.6	132.3	2.2	146.9	1.7	171.5	3.3	198.0	3.9	149.9	0.6
February	150.9	2.9	119.0	0.3	132.9	2.0	147.4	1.7	172.6	3.4	199.6	4.3	150.6	1.9
March	151.4	2.9	118.9	-0.3	132.9	1.9	147.8	1.8	173.3	3.5	201.2	5.0	150.9	2.2
April	151.9	3.1	119.3	-0.2	133.1	1.9	147.9	1.6	175.1	3.3	202.2	5.2	151.3	2.4
May	152.2	3.2	119.5	-0.1	133.2	1.7	148.2	1.6	175.8	3.4	203.5	5.5	151.7	2.9
June	152.5	3.0	119.4	0.2	133.5	1.7	148.2	1.6	176.0	3.5	204.5	5.8	151.7	2.7
July	152.5	2.8	118.8	0.2	133.7	1.6	147.9	1.5	175.2	3.5	204.7	5.7	152.0	2.5
August	152.9	2.6	118.9	-0.2	133.7	1.4	148.6	1.9	176.1	3.6	205.5	5.8	151.8	2.3
September	153.2	2.5	119.6	0.1	133.7	1.6	149.1	2.0	176.9	3.9	205.9	5.8	151.9	2.3
October	153.7	2.8	119.3	-0.6	133.5	1.5	149.3	1.8	176.0	3.2	207.1	5.8	151.8	2.4
November	153.6	2.6	118.9	-0.7	133.5	1.4	149.4	1.9	176.0	3.1	208.4	6.0	152.1	2.0
December	153.5	2.5	118.9	-0.4	133.9	1.5	149.5	2.1	177.1	3.2	208.6	5.8	151.9	1.8
1996:														
January	154.4	2.7	118.8	-0.5	134.1	1.4	149.8	2.0	176.5	2.9	209.0	5.6	152.3	1.6
February	154.9	2.7	118.5	-0.4	134.8	1.4	150.3	2.0	177.3	2.7	209.6	5.0	152.4	1.2
March	155.7	2.8	118.8	-0.1	134.9	1.5	151.3	2.3	178.0	2.7	210.2	4.5	153.0	1.4
April	156.3	2.9	119.5	0.2	134.9	1.4	151.5	2.4	179.3	2.4	211.4	4.5	153.4	1.4
May	156.6	2.9	119.7	0.2	135.2	1.5	151.8	2.4	179.6	2.2	212.2	4.3	153.8	1.4
June	156.7	2.8	119.4	0.0	135.3	1.4	151.7	2.3	179.8	2.1	212.7	4.0	153.8	1.4
July	157.0	3.0	119.3	0.4	135.6	1.4	151.4	2.3	179.1	2.2	212.2	3.7	153.8	1.2
August	157.3	2.9	119.1	0.2	135.5	1.3	151.0	1.6	179.9	2.1	212.4	3.4	153.8	1.3
September	157.8	3.0	119.6	0.0	135.5	1.3	151.5	1.6	180.7	2.1	213.1	3.5	154.1	1.5
October	158.3	3.0	119.9	0.5	135.5	1.5	151.9	1.8	180.7	2.7	213.3	3.0	154.4	1.7
November	158.6	3.3	119.5	0.5	135.3	1.4	151.8	1.6	180.8	2.7	213.9	2.6	155.2	2.0
December	158.6	3.3	119.6	0.6	135.9	1.5	152.1	1.7	181.4	2.5	214.1	2.6	155.2	2.1
1997:														
January	159.1	3.0	119.5	0.6	136.8	2.0	152.5	1.8	181.4	2.8	214.5	2.6	155.4	2.1
February	159.6	3.0	119.3	0.6	137.2	1.8	152.7	1.6	182.1	2.7	214.7	2.4	155.7	2.2
March	160.0	2.8	119.4	0.5	137.1	1.6	152.9	1.1	182.6	2.6	215.1	2.3	156.0	2.0
April	160.2	2.5	121.8	1.9	136.8	1.4	152.9	0.9	183.6	2.4	215.3	1.8	156.0	1.7
May	160.1	2.2	122.0	1.9	137.3	1.6	153.1	0.9	184.3	2.6	215.9	1.7	156.2	1.5
June	160.3	2.3	122.0	2.2	137.5	1.6	153.1	1.0	185.1	2.9	215.9	1.5	156.5	1.7
July	160.5	2.2	121.5	1.9	138.5	2.2	152.9	1.0	185.1	3.3	215.9	1.7	156.5	1.7
August	160.8	2.2	121.6	2.1	138.7	2.4	153.3	1.5	186.2	3.5	215.9	1.6	156.8	1.9
September	161.2	2.2	122.5	2.4	138.4	2.2	153.5	1.3	187.2	3.6	216.3	1.5	156.6	1.6
October	161.6	2.1	122.8	2.5	138.3	2.1	153.5	1.0	187.4	3.7	216.9	1.7	156.8	1.5
November	161.5	1.8	122.0	2.1	138.3	2.2	153.8	1.3	187.5	3.7	217.6	1.7	156.5	0.8
December	161.3	1.7	121.8	1.8	138.5	2.0	153.8	1.1	188.0	3.6	217.6	1.6	156.3	0.7
1998:														
January	161.6	1.6	121.6	1.8	138.5	1.3	153.4	0.6	187.4	3.3	218.2	1.7	157.2	1.1
February	161.9	1.4	121.5	1.9	138.8	1.2	153.9	0.8	188.3	3.4	218.6	1.8	157.3	1.0
March	162.2	1.4	122.0	2.2	138.7	1.2	154.2	0.9	188.9	3.5	219.2	1.9	157.5	0.9
April	162.5	1.4	122.2	0.4	138.8	1.5	154.5	1.1	191.0	4.0	219.4	1.9	157.3	0.8
May	162.8	1.7	122.6	0.5	139.2	1.4	154.5	0.9	192.1	4.2	219.8	1.8	157.9	1.1
June	163.0	1.7	122.1	0.1	139.3	1.4	154.7	1.0	192.0	3.7	220.0	1.9	158.1	1.0
July	163.2	1.7	121.4	-0.1	139.7	0.9	154.2	0.9	191.5	3.5	219.6	1.7	158.1	1.0
August	163.4	1.6	121.3	-0.3	139.5	0.6	154.2	0.6	192.3	3.3	219.8	1.8	158.1	0.8
September	163.6	1.5	122.2	-0.2	139.2	0.6	154.2	0.4	193.2	3.2	220.0	1.7	157.8	0.7
October	164.0	1.5	123.1	0.2	138.9	0.5	154.2	0.4	193.3	3.1	220.8	1.8	158.4	1.0
November	164.0	1.5	123.0	0.8	138.9	0.5	154.0	0.2	193.2	3.0	221.0	1.6	158.4	1.2
December	163.9	1.6	122.5	0.6	139.1	0.4	154.2	0.3	193.2	2.7	221.0	1.6	157.9	1.0

1. Data prior to 1991 are for West Germany only.

Unemployment Rates and Civilian Labor Forces [1]

(Quarterly data; seasonally adjusted)

Year and quarter	United States Unemployment rate	United States Labor force (thousands)	Japan Unemployment rate	Japan Labor force (thousands)	Germany [2] Unemployment rate	Germany [2] Labor force (thousands)	France Unemployment rate	France Labor force (thousands)	United Kingdom Unemployment rate	United Kingdom Labor force (thousands)	Italy Unemployment rate	Italy Labor force (thousands)	Canada Unemployment rate	Canada Labor force (thousands)
1970	4.9	78 678	1.2	50 140	0.5	26 100	2.5	20 270	3.1	24 330	3.2	19 080	5.7	7 919
1971	5.9	79 367	1.3	50 480	0.6	26 220	2.8	20 420	3.9	23 970	3.3	19 020	6.2	8 104
1972	5.6	82 153	1.4	50 590	0.7	26 280	2.9	20 540	4.2	24 120	3.8	18 710	6.2	8 344
1973	4.9	85 064	1.3	51 910	0.7	26 590	2.8	20 840	3.2	24 610	3.7	18 870	5.5	8 761
1974	5.6	86 794	1.4	51 710	1.6	26 240	2.9	21 030	3.1	24 680	3.1	19 280	5.3	9 125
1975	8.5	85 846	1.9	51 530	3.4	25 540	4.2	20 860	4.6	24 560	3.4	19 400	6.9	9 284
1976	7.7	88 752	2.0	52 020	3.4	25 400	4.6	21 030	5.9	24 360	3.9	19 500	7.2	9 776
1977	7.1	92 017	2.0	52 720	3.4	25 430	5.2	21 220	6.4	24 400	4.1	19 670	8.1	9 978
1978	6.1	96 048	2.3	53 370	3.3	25 650	5.4	21 320	6.3	24 610	4.1	19 720	8.4	10 320
1979	5.8	98 824	2.1	54 040	2.9	26 080	6.1	21 390	5.4	24 940	4.4	19 930	7.5	10 761
1980	7.1	99 303	2.0	54 600	2.8	26 490	6.5	21 440	7.0	24 670	4.4	20 200	7.5	11 082
1981	7.6	100 397	2.2	55 060	4.0	26 450	7.6	21 330	10.5	23 800	4.9	20 280	7.6	11 398
1982	9.7	99 526	2.4	55 620	5.6	26 150	8.3	21 390	11.3	23 560	5.4	20 250	11.0	11 035
1983	9.6	100 834	2.7	56 550	6.9	25 770	8.6	21 380	11.8	23 470	5.9	20 320	11.9	11 106
1984	7.5	105 005	2.8	56 870	7.1	25 830	10.0	21 200	11.7	23 930	5.9	20 390	11.3	11 402
1985	7.2	107 150	2.6	57 260	7.2	26 010	10.5	21 150	11.2	24 290	6.0	20 490	10.5	11 742
1986	7.0	109 597	2.8	57 740	6.6	26 380	10.6	21 240	11.2	24 470	7.5	20 610	9.6	12 095
1987	6.2	112 440	2.9	58 320	6.3	26 590	10.8	21 320	10.3	25 010	7.9	20 590	8.9	12 422
1988	5.5	114 968	2.5	59 310	6.3	26 800	10.3	21 520	8.6	25 850	7.9	20 870	7.8	12 819
1989	5.3	117 342	2.3	60 500	5.7	27 200	9.6	21 850	7.2	26 510	7.8	20 770	7.5	13 086
1990	5.6	118 793	2.1	61 710	5.0	27 950	9.1	22 100	6.9	26 740	7.0	21 080	8.1	13 165
1991	6.8	117 718	2.1	62 920	4.3	28 480	9.6	22 140	8.8	26 090	6.9	21 360	10.4	12 916
1992	7.5	118 492	2.2	63 620	4.6	28 660	10.4	22 010	10.1	25 530	7.3	21 230	11.3	12 842
1993	6.9	120 259	2.5	63 810	5.7	28 240	11.8	21 750	10.5	25 340	10.2	20 430	11.2	13 015
1994	6.1	123 060	2.9	63 860	6.5	27 910	12.3	21 710	9.7	25 550	11.3	20 080	10.4	13 292
1995	5.6	124 900	3.2	63 890	6.5	27 700	11.8	21 890	8.7	26 000	12.0	19 980	9.5	13 506
1996	5.4	126 708	3.4	64 200	7.2	27 380	12.5	21 950	8.2	26 280	12.1	20 060	9.7	13 676
1997	4.9	129 558	3.4	64 900	7.8	27 120	12.4	22 020	7.0	26 740	12.3	20 050	9.2	13 941
1998	4.5	131 463	4.1	64 440	7.5	27 150	11.8	22 290	6.3	26 930	12.3	20 170	8.3	14 326
1990:														
1st quarter	5.3	.....	2.2	.....	5.2	.....	9.1	.....	6.8	.....	7.3	.....	7.6	.....
2nd quarter	5.3	.....	2.1	.....	5.1	.....	9.0	.....	6.8	.....	6.8	.....	7.5	.....
3rd quarter	5.7	.....	2.1	.....	4.9	.....	9.0	.....	6.8	.....	6.9	.....	8.2	.....
4th quarter	6.1	.....	2.1	.....	4.6	.....	9.1	.....	7.2	.....	6.9	.....	9.3	.....
1991:														
1st quarter	6.6	.....	2.1	.....	4.4	.....	9.1	.....	7.8	.....	6.9	.....	10.2	.....
2nd quarter	6.8	.....	2.1	.....	4.3	.....	9.5	.....	8.6	.....	7.0	.....	10.4	.....
3rd quarter	6.9	.....	2.2	.....	4.3	.....	9.8	.....	9.2	.....	6.8	.....	10.4	.....
4th quarter	7.1	.....	2.1	.....	4.3	.....	9.9	.....	9.5	.....	6.9	.....	10.5	.....
1992:														
1st quarter	7.4	.....	2.1	.....	4.3	.....	10.1	.....	9.7	.....	7.1	.....	10.8	.....
2nd quarter	7.6	.....	2.1	.....	4.4	.....	10.3	.....	9.9	.....	7.0	.....	11.3	.....
3rd quarter	7.6	.....	2.2	.....	4.6	.....	10.5	.....	10.1	.....	7.0	.....	11.6	.....
4th quarter	7.4	.....	2.3	.....	4.9	.....	10.8	.....	10.5	.....	8.3	.....	11.6	.....
1993:														
1st quarter	7.2	.....	2.4	.....	5.3	.....	11.2	.....	10.6	.....	9.2	.....	11.0	.....
2nd quarter	7.1	.....	2.5	.....	5.6	.....	11.6	.....	10.5	.....	10.3	.....	11.4	.....
3rd quarter	6.8	.....	2.6	.....	5.9	.....	12.0	.....	10.4	.....	10.6	.....	11.4	.....
4th quarter	6.6	.....	2.8	.....	6.2	.....	12.4	.....	10.2	.....	10.9	.....	11.2	.....
1994:														
1st quarter	6.6	.....	2.9	.....	6.4	.....	12.5	.....	10.0	.....	11.0	.....	10.9	.....
2nd quarter	6.2	.....	2.9	.....	6.5	.....	12.5	.....	9.8	.....	11.2	.....	10.6	.....
3rd quarter	6.0	.....	3.0	.....	6.5	.....	12.2	.....	9.5	.....	11.3	.....	10.1	.....
4th quarter	5.6	.....	2.9	.....	6.5	.....	12.0	.....	9.1	.....	11.8	.....	9.7	.....
1995:														
1st quarter	5.5	.....	3.0	.....	6.4	.....	12.0	.....	8.9	.....	12.1	.....	9.7	.....
2nd quarter	5.7	.....	3.2	.....	6.5	.....	11.7	.....	8.8	.....	11.8	.....	9.5	.....
3rd quarter	5.7	.....	3.2	.....	6.6	.....	11.6	.....	8.7	.....	12.2	.....	9.5	.....
4th quarter	5.6	.....	3.4	.....	6.7	.....	11.8	.....	8.5	.....	12.0	.....	9.4	.....
1996:														
1st quarter	5.5	.....	3.4	.....	6.9	.....	12.2	.....	8.4	.....	12.1	.....	9.5	.....
2nd quarter	5.5	.....	3.5	.....	7.1	.....	12.5	.....	8.3	.....	12.1	.....	9.6	.....
3rd quarter	5.3	.....	3.4	.....	7.2	.....	12.6	.....	8.1	.....	12.2	.....	9.8	.....
4th quarter	5.3	.....	3.4	.....	7.5	.....	12.6	.....	7.9	.....	12.1	.....	9.9	.....
1997:														
1st quarter	5.2	.....	3.3	.....	7.7	.....	12.4	.....	7.4	.....	12.3	.....	9.6	.....
2nd quarter	5.0	.....	3.4	.....	7.8	.....	12.5	.....	7.2	.....	12.3	.....	9.4	.....
3rd quarter	4.9	.....	3.4	.....	7.8	.....	12.5	.....	6.9	.....	12.2	.....	9.0	.....
4th quarter	4.7	.....	3.5	.....	7.8	.....	12.3	.....	6.6	.....	12.3	.....	8.9	.....
1998:														
1st quarter	4.6	.....	3.7	.....	7.7	.....	12.0	.....	6.4	.....	12.2	.....	8.6	.....
2nd quarter	4.4	.....	4.2	.....	7.6	.....	11.8	.....	6.2	.....	12.3	.....	8.4	.....
3rd quarter	4.5	.....	4.3	.....	7.4	.....	11.7	.....	6.3	.....	12.4	.....	8.3	.....
4th quarter	4.4	.....	4.4	.....	7.3	.....	11.5	.....	6.2	.....	12.4	.....	8.0	.....

1. Data for other countries adjusted to approximate U.S. concepts.
2. Data are for West Germany only.

Stock Price Indexes

(Averages of daily closing values)

Year and month	United States (S&P 500)	Canada (TSE 300)	Brazil (Bovespa)	France (CAC 40)	Germany (DAX)	United Kingdom (FTSE 100)	Hong Kong (Hang Seng)	Japan (Nikkei 225)	Singapore (Straits Times)
1970	83.22	.....	.....	.....	.....	.....	.....	.....	.....
1971	98.29	.....	.....	.....	.....	.....	.....	.....	.....
1972	109.20	.....	.....	.....	.....	.....	.....	.....	.....
1973	107.43	.....	.....	.....	.....	.....	.....	.....	.....
1974	82.85	.....	.....	.....	.....	.....	.....	.....	.....
1975	86.16	.....	.....	.....	.....	.....	.....	.....	.....
1976	102.01	.....	.....	.....	.....	.....	.....	.....	.....
1977	98.20	.....	.....	.....	.....	.....	.....	.....	.....
1978	96.02	.....	.....	.....	.....	.....	.....	.....	.....
1979	103.01	.....	.....	.....	.....	.....	.....	.....	.....
1980	118.78	.....	.....	.....	.....	.....	.....	.....	.....
1981	128.04	.....	.....	.....	.....	.....	.....	.....	.....
1982	119.71	.....	.....	.....	.....	.....	.....	.....	.....
1983	160.41	.....	.....	.....	.....	.....	.....	.....	.....
1984	160.46	.....	.....	.....	.....	.....	.....	10 556.59	.....
1985	186.84	2 683.55	.....	.....	.....	1 307.15	.....	12 552.14	.....
1986	236.34	2 999.33	.....	.....	.....	1 588.21	.....	16 482.73	.....
1987	286.83	3 590.67	.....	.....	.....	2 035.85	2 908.02	23 249.64	.....
1988	265.79	3 288.66	.....	.....	.....	1 803.11	2 555.63	27 046.97	1 000.38
1989	322.84	3 775.62	.....	.....	.....	2 175.55	2 792.82	34 058.49	1 290.32
1990	334.59	3 464.71	.....	.....	.....	2 225.18	3 032.66	29 436.93	1 396.03
1991	376.17	3 457.64	.....	1 766.31	1 579.37	2 466.46	3 798.10	24 295.57	1 428.99
1992	415.74	3 405.84	.....	1 850.49	1 635.87	2 559.42	5 479.33	18 108.70	1 439.72
1993	451.41	3 856.50	.....	2 021.17	1 808.59	2 962.10	7 459.14	19 100.00	1 876.13
1994	460.33	4 274.27	3 164.83	2 058.20	2 120.32	3 140.55	9 532.10	19 936.03	2 270.05
1995	541.64	4 423.47	3 901.76	1 869.74	2 137.91	3 351.10	9 010.28	17 329.66	2 118.97
1996	670.83	5 217.73	5 868.95	2 078.83	2 566.39	3 828.35	11 474.44	21 088.34	2 263.06
1997	873.72	6 473.35	10 386.05	2 759.94	3 721.07	4 696.36	13 375.56	18 397.16	1 961.82
1998	1 085.50	6 792.23	9 261.00	3 693.37	5 016.31	5 628.29	9 418.33	15 362.35	1 254.02
1995:									
January	465.25	4 122.72	3 874.05	1 841.13	2 055.68	3 028.30	7 454.47	18 948.26	2 096.21
February	481.92	4 104.28	3 339.67	1 833.66	2 100.62	3 051.68	8 002.67	18 065.00	2 103.26
March	493.15	4 213.04	2 941.23	1 795.59	1 997.59	3 078.24	8 370.70	16 447.59	2 089.51
April	507.91	4 277.73	3 325.06	1 895.04	1 981.74	3 198.38	8 501.81	16 322.05	2 067.51
May	523.81	4 349.58	3 951.95	1 968.42	2 070.01	3 288.31	8 932.72	16 265.90	2 139.47
June	539.35	4 503.74	3 720.52	1 913.09	2 126.81	3 351.55	9 280.05	15 039.32	2 139.42
July	557.37	4 625.90	3 883.38	1 928.78	2 184.73	3 426.50	9 476.98	16 188.62	2 155.76
August	559.11	4 593.87	4 254.61	1 943.60	2 241.76	3 486.96	9 131.52	17 410.74	2 106.05
September	578.77	4 551.47	4 653.20	1 853.68	2 257.55	3 534.27	9 503.62	18 097.15	2 119.73
October	582.92	4 443.95	4 438.71	1 778.55	2 164.81	3 531.80	9 833.22	17 951.57	2 114.83
November	595.53	4 599.85	4 057.71	1 860.97	2 197.41	3 580.31	9 539.33	18 109.35	2 094.05
December	614.57	4 698.47	4 271.68	1 843.99	2 268.54	3 649.20	9 902.50	19 417.90	2 201.55
1996:									
January	614.42	4 833.76	4 825.05	1 944.18	2 376.43	3 716.69	10 717.38	20 497.21	2 393.10
February	649.54	5 006.85	5 270.72	1 971.76	2 431.31	3 738.08	11 341.84	20 628.55	2 453.87
March	647.07	4 962.09	4 929.24	1 986.76	2 477.10	3 697.50	10 927.46	20 424.35	2 386.85
April	647.17	5 066.41	5 016.65	2 095.12	2 521.55	3 792.32	10 936.64	21 828.67	2 387.17
May	661.23	5 195.73	5 482.18	2 113.97	2 518.07	3 758.41	10 906.83	21 770.76	2 357.37
June	668.50	5 094.69	5 788.47	2 113.26	2 554.47	3 734.02	11 012.58	22 185.45	2 302.31
July	644.07	4 995.16	6 271.87	2 030.68	2 519.99	3 707.21	10 837.12	21 558.52	2 193.62
August	662.68	5 096.06	6 249.36	1 999.89	2 540.95	3 841.75	11 203.53	20 870.27	2 135.63
September	674.89	5 233.30	6 434.24	2 056.10	2 596.70	3 927.10	11 406.33	20 823.68	2 143.58
October	701.46	5 486.12	6 626.82	2 151.19	2 694.68	4 020.99	12 274.82	21 118.95	2 090.17
November	735.67	5 845.10	6 611.45	2 236.06	2 759.32	3 969.54	12 986.34	21 040.70	2 157.08
December	743.25	5 845.25	6 841.42	2 268.10	2 849.49	4 038.89	13 201.13	20 147.25	2 195.69
1997:									
January	766.22	6 027.55	7 595.45	2 395.16	2 963.56	4 164.11	13 456.78	18 050.37	2 235.62
February	798.38	6 177.99	8 604.95	2 587.07	3 192.48	4 316.57	13 398.15	18 562.55	2 222.39
March	792.16	6 147.12	9 253.79	2 634.17	3 358.09	4 349.78	12 974.13	18 244.10	2 139.64
April	763.93	5 824.88	9 596.71	2 568.47	3 340.01	4 312.51	12 460.71	18 177.90	2 051.08
May	833.09	6 266.27	10 598.60	2 690.96	3 579.74	4 622.62	14 021.83	20 046.00	2 064.43
June	876.29	6 477.56	11 934.29	2 750.06	3 727.82	4 649.40	14 673.64	20 505.62	2 014.74
July	925.29	6 678.76	12 712.77	2 963.03	4 161.70	4 842.85	15 416.92	20 148.09	1 965.23
August	927.74	6 772.29	11 637.57	2 941.45	4 191.36	4 945.56	15 945.12	19 090.57	1 919.76
September	937.02	6 868.27	11 396.55	2 939.77	4 044.67	5 010.36	14 454.28	18 248.45	1 897.53
October	951.16	7 032.88	11 898.52	2 936.96	4 078.99	5 145.13	12 609.09	17 274.77	1 783.15
November	938.92	6 748.83	9 168.65	2 782.29	3 824.86	4 846.24	10 327.41	16 103.22	1 678.88
December	962.37	6 647.23	9 707.05	2 899.71	4 133.70	5 087.53	10 806.98	15 917.10	1 620.56
1998:									
January	963.36	6 521.09	9 658.71	3 000.93	4 284.11	5 242.10	9 248.06	15 929.63	1 288.97
February	1 023.74	6 918.26	10 275.00	3 250.75	4 575.55	5 656.07	10 646.23	16 797.79	1 537.52
March	1 076.83	7 382.42	11 521.41	3 616.91	4 915.28	5 861.80	11 314.71	16 840.45	1 616.75
April	1 112.20	7 675.83	11 824.16	3 857.15	5 244.45	5 974.51	11 014.92	15 941.41	1 528.71
May	1 108.42	7 678.67	10 568.65	4 006.74	5 397.79	5 936.72	9 680.72	15 514.28	1 342.95
June	1 108.39	7 336.74	9 793.86	4 124.77	5 719.69	5 846.84	8 318.89	15 231.29	1 115.37
July	1 156.58	7 300.99	10 529.77	4 266.48	6 001.07	5 989.37	8 323.92	16 370.17	1 081.03
August	1 074.62	6 332.50	8 428.71	3 960.53	5 390.41	5 555.77	7 398.00	15 243.98	964.99
September	1 020.64	5 806.89	6 389.05	3 543.34	4 746.55	5 169.88	7 652.51	14 140.69	887.25
October	1 032.47	5 735.72	6 696.57	3 301.96	4 343.36	5 063.84	9 195.26	13 486.91	1 043.87
November	1 144.43	6 401.03	8 256.25	3 693.25	4 828.34	5 595.58	10 298.70	14 525.88	1 297.11
December	1 190.05	6 364.69	7 282.75	3 761.75	4 752.13	5 686.26	10 146.01	14 320.69	1 386.94

Exchange Rates [1]

(Not seasonally adjusted)

Year and month	Trade-weighted exchange indexes				Foreign currency per U.S. dollar						
	G-10 Countries (March 1973=100)	Broad (January 1997=100)	Major Currency (March 1973=100)	Other Important Trading Partners (January 1997=100)	European currency unit	Japanese yen	German mark	French franc	British pound	Italian lira	Canadian dollar
1970	121.06	.....	.....	.....	.....	.....	.....	.....	.....	.....	.....
1971	117.81	.....	.....	.....	.....	348.05	3.4818	5.5108	0.4092	618.37	1.0099
1972	109.07	.....	.....	.....	.....	303.11	3.1889	5.0448	0.4005	583.73	0.9908
1973	99.14	28.71	100.26	1.64	.....	271.40	2.6719	4.4549	0.4084	582.39	1.0002
1974	101.41	29.56	101.85	1.75	.....	291.94	2.5873	4.8104	0.4277	651.18	0.9781
1975	98.50	30.77	102.19	2.01	.....	296.77	2.4614	4.2885	0.4521	653.24	1.0173
1976	105.63	32.81	105.47	2.34	.....	296.48	2.5184	4.7805	0.5567	832.76	0.9861
1977	103.35	34.04	105.31	2.68	.....	268.38	2.3225	4.9149	0.5733	882.69	1.0635
1978	92.39	32.59	96.67	2.88	.....	210.46	2.0090	4.5101	0.5214	849.10	1.1408
1979	88.07	33.07	95.46	3.14	0.7296	219.21	1.8331	4.2545	0.4720	830.92	1.1716
1980	87.38	34.13	95.35	3.48	0.7196	226.58	1.8183	4.2269	0.4304	856.52	1.1694
1981	103.26	37.75	104.04	3.96	0.8946	220.45	2.2606	5.4349	0.4978	1 137.42	1.1989
1982	116.50	43.93	114.67	5.14	1.0195	249.05	2.4281	6.5761	0.5727	1 353.47	1.2339
1983	125.32	49.53	118.56	6.93	1.1218	237.45	2.5545	7.6221	0.6601	1 519.71	1.2326
1984	138.34	56.57	126.27	9.18	1.2673	237.59	2.8483	8.7439	0.7521	1 757.82	1.2952
1985	143.24	63.65	131.08	12.44	1.3118	238.47	2.9443	8.9870	0.7792	1 909.45	1.3659
1986	112.27	59.56	107.89	15.63	1.0166	168.50	2.1711	6.9258	0.6821	1 491.49	1.3898
1987	96.95	58.25	95.47	19.15	0.8663	144.62	1.7976	6.0110	0.6117	1 296.59	1.3262
1988	92.75	59.12	88.74	23.39	0.8447	128.14	1.7561	5.9565	0.5621	1 301.67	1.2309
1989	98.52	65.25	92.36	29.11	0.9071	138.00	1.8792	6.3753	0.6111	1 371.31	1.1841
1990	89.05	70.05	88.39	39.21	0.7841	144.82	1.6159	5.4449	0.5630	1 198.05	1.1670
1991	89.73	73.14	86.91	45.79	0.8052	134.51	1.6585	5.6388	0.5667	1 239.62	1.1460
1992	86.64	76.38	85.45	53.05	0.7726	126.75	1.5624	5.2956	0.5699	1 233.21	1.2088
1993	93.16	84.42	87.73	65.96	0.8546	111.23	1.6537	5.6644	0.6662	1 571.92	1.2902
1994	91.32	90.42	86.25	80.51	0.8431	102.19	1.6219	5.5467	0.6531	1 611.75	1.3659
1995	84.30	92.52	81.40	92.51	0.7731	94.11	1.4331	4.9889	0.6337	1 628.92	1.3727
1996	87.34	97.43	85.22	98.25	0.7987	108.81	1.5048	5.1158	0.6410	1 542.65	1.3637
1997	96.35	104.47	91.85	104.67	0.8845	121.09	1.7339	5.8361	0.6107	1 702.98	1.3849
1998	98.82	116.25	96.49	125.70	0.8908	130.82	1.7593	5.8979	0.6035	1 736.42	1.4836
1995:											
January	88.30	93.88	84.99	90.13	0.8078	99.77	1.5302	5.2912	0.6351	1 611.53	1.4132
February	87.30	93.47	84.08	90.51	0.7990	98.24	1.5022	5.2252	0.6361	1 620.58	1.4005
March	83.69	92.63	81.03	93.37	0.7679	90.52	1.4061	4.9756	0.6249	1 688.99	1.4077
April	81.81	90.04	78.28	91.56	0.7532	83.69	1.3812	4.8503	0.6222	1 710.89	1.3762
May	82.73	89.97	78.75	90.61	0.7649	85.11	1.4096	4.9869	0.6300	1 652.78	1.3609
June	82.27	90.17	78.73	91.13	0.7585	84.64	1.4012	4.9172	0.6270	1 639.75	1.3775
July	81.90	90.21	78.84	91.03	0.7497	87.40	1.3886	4.8307	0.6269	1 609.71	1.3612
August	84.59	92.34	81.43	92.00	0.7724	94.74	1.4456	4.9727	0.6382	1 607.18	1.3552
September	85.69	93.68	82.90	92.89	0.7823	100.55	1.4601	5.0352	0.6414	1 613.41	1.3509
October	84.10	93.56	82.13	93.85	0.7701	100.84	1.4143	4.9374	0.6338	1 605.69	1.3458
November	84.14	94.79	82.49	96.25	0.7718	101.94	1.4173	4.8882	0.6400	1 592.67	1.3534
December	85.07	95.52	83.22	96.84	0.7840	101.85	1.4406	4.9565	0.6491	1 593.88	1.3693
1996:											
January	86.23	96.33	84.32	97.03	0.7935	105.75	1.4635	5.0117	0.6541	1 584.87	1.3669
February	86.42	96.54	84.59	97.11	0.7981	105.79	1.4669	5.0440	0.6510	1 570.00	1.3752
March	86.58	96.52	84.51	97.19	0.7976	105.94	1.4776	5.0583	0.6548	1 562.43	1.3656
April	87.46	96.80	85.02	97.08	0.8044	107.20	1.5044	5.1049	0.6596	1 565.60	1.3592
May	88.28	97.30	85.44	97.58	0.8141	106.34	1.5324	5.1855	0.6600	1 556.71	1.3693
June	88.16	97.77	85.70	98.31	0.8078	108.96	1.5282	5.1787	0.6487	1 542.30	1.3658
July	87.25	97.68	85.36	98.62	0.7955	109.19	1.5025	5.0881	0.6439	1 526.82	1.3697
August	86.54	97.25	84.82	98.45	0.7883	107.87	1.4826	5.0636	0.6452	1 516.62	1.3722
September	87.46	97.77	85.48	98.65	0.7952	109.93	1.5080	5.1307	0.6413	1 520.48	1.3694
October	87.98	98.26	85.83	99.26	0.7976	112.41	1.5277	5.1652	0.6304	1 523.82	1.3508
November	86.97	97.95	85.05	99.77	0.7874	112.30	1.5118	5.1156	0.6016	1 513.66	1.3381
December	88.71	99.01	86.55	99.94	0.8048	113.98	1.5525	5.2427	0.6010	1 528.44	1.3622
1997:											
January	91.01	100.00	88.03	100.00	0.8267	117.91	1.6047	5.4145	0.6030	1 567.91	1.3494
February	94.52	101.87	90.71	100.34	0.8627	122.96	1.6747	5.6536	0.6152	1 655.00	1.3556
March	95.60	102.64	91.43	101.02	0.8728	122.77	1.6946	5.7154	0.6213	1 691.21	1.3725
April	96.39	103.45	92.58	101.22	0.8775	125.64	1.7119	5.7672	0.6138	1 694.52	1.3942
May	95.29	102.39	90.88	101.28	0.8748	119.19	1.7048	5.7482	0.6127	1 684.33	1.3804
June	95.42	102.06	90.38	101.26	0.8846	114.29	1.7277	5.8293	0.6079	1 694.54	1.3843
July	97.48	103.23	91.34	102.54	0.9093	115.38	1.7939	6.0511	0.5990	1 745.91	1.3775
August	99.96	105.12	93.27	104.04	0.9352	117.93	1.8400	6.2010	0.6236	1 797.12	1.3905
September	98.29	105.68	92.93	105.83	0.9107	120.89	1.7862	6.0031	0.6245	1 743.22	1.3872
October	97.07	106.33	92.34	108.26	0.8941	121.06	1.7575	5.8954	0.6124	1 721.09	1.3869
November	96.37	108.23	93.07	111.62	0.8757	125.38	1.7323	5.8001	0.5921	1 697.08	1.4128
December	98.82	112.61	95.27	118.69	0.8994	129.73	1.7788	5.9542	0.6025	1 743.86	1.4271
1998:											
January	100.52	116.29	96.37	125.99	0.9200	129.55	1.8165	6.0832	0.6116	1 787.87	1.4409
February	99.93	114.69	95.39	123.62	0.9180	125.85	1.8123	6.0744	0.6095	1 788.28	1.4334
March	100.48	114.36	95.83	122.07	0.9214	129.08	1.8272	6.1257	0.6017	1 799.07	1.4166
April	100.30	114.13	96.41	120.53	0.9152	131.75	1.8132	6.0782	0.5980	1 791.24	1.4298
May	99.61	115.16	96.88	122.28	0.9012	134.90	1.7753	5.9528	0.6104	1 750.79	1.4452
June	100.90	117.87	98.68	125.97	0.9078	140.33	1.7928	6.0118	0.6059	1 766.32	1.4655
July	101.38	118.17	99.31	125.64	0.9099	140.79	1.7976	6.0280	0.6084	1 772.42	1.4869
August	101.80	120.15	100.96	127.77	0.9062	144.68	1.7869	5.9912	0.6119	1 763.01	1.5346
September	97.17	118.85	96.99	131.38	0.8639	134.48	1.6990	5.6969	0.5944	1 678.92	1.5218
October	93.68	115.46	93.46	129.02	0.8320	121.05	1.6381	5.4925	0.5902	1 620.96	1.5452
November	95.46	115.34	94.23	127.31	0.8561	120.29	1.6827	5.6422	0.6020	1 664.91	1.5404
December	94.60	114.57	93.41	126.80	0.8506	117.07	1.6698	5.5981	0.5985	1 653.23	1.5433

1. Annual data are averages of monthly values.

Part II: Industry Profiles

Mining, Oil, and Gas

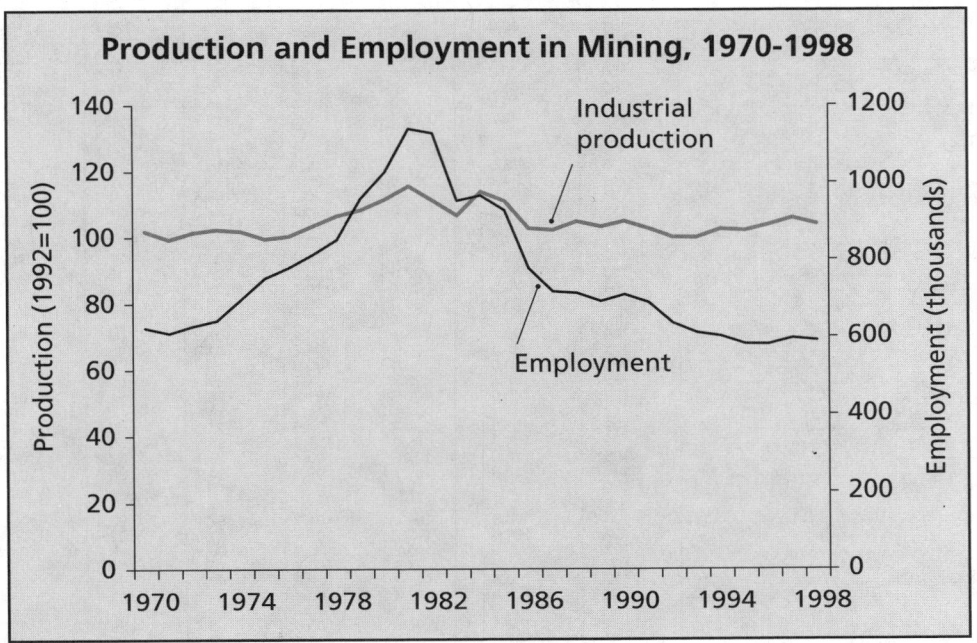

Production and Employment in Mining, 1970-1998

- The mining industries boomed in the late 1970s and peaked in 1981, stimulated by rising prices and shortages of petroleum and other natural resources. Subsequently, both production and employment subsided to near their 1970 levels.

- In oil and gas extraction, the largest of the mining industries, production in 1998 was below 1970, despite an employment increase of 26 percent, illustrating the increasing difficulty of finding and extracting crude oil within the United States.

- The trends in coal mining have been just the opposite. The fastest-growing of the mining industries from 1970 to 1998, coal production rose 76 percent. Increasing mechanization made this increase possible with a 37 percent decline in employment.

- A similar rate of productivity growth occurred in metal mining, with output up 43 percent while employment declined 46 percent.

- Nonmetallic minerals except fuels (stone and earth minerals) had an output increase of 39 percent from 1970 to 1998 while employment fell 5 percent.

Mining Industries—Industrial Production

(Seasonally adjusted, 1992=100)

Year and month	Total mining	Metal mining	Coal mining	Oil and gas extraction						Stone and earth minerals
				Total	Crude oil and natural gas			Natural gas liquids	Oil and gas well drilling	
					Total	Crude oil	Natural gas			
1970	101.8	77.1	62.3	116.5	130.0	137.7	117.6	93.6	85.2	89.5
1971	99.3	68.6	57.3	115.2	128.7	135.2	120.6	94.8	81.8	89.9
1972	101.4	66.3	61.3	117.2	128.9	135.1	121.4	97.5	93.9	93.9
1973	102.3	70.0	60.7	116.6	126.6	131.6	122.0	98.0	101.9	102.5
1974	101.8	68.0	61.6	115.8	120.9	125.7	116.6	95.3	126.4	102.1
1975	99.5	63.5	66.2	113.1	114.3	119.9	107.5	92.0	143.4	91.9
1976	100.3	69.2	68.9	111.2	111.5	116.5	106.2	91.7	144.1	97.2
1977	103.4	61.1	70.6	116.8	112.3	116.8	107.5	93.2	175.0	99.4
1978	106.5	69.5	67.6	121.1	115.4	122.8	106.3	90.7	196.4	104.7
1979	108.3	72.2	78.6	119.5	113.7	120.3	105.8	94.1	190.7	107.1
1980	111.5	65.2	83.4	124.4	115.1	120.5	109.0	93.8	236.8	97.9
1981	115.6	73.5	82.9	129.7	114.5	120.0	108.4	92.9	315.6	94.1
1982	111.2	54.8	84.5	125.6	111.7	120.9	99.5	90.3	296.0	78.7
1983	106.6	52.8	79.0	120.2	108.4	121.4	90.3	90.5	257.6	84.0
1984	113.9	57.2	90.2	126.9	112.9	124.1	97.6	92.6	296.1	94.7
1985	111.0	56.6	89.1	123.0	111.4	125.1	92.3	90.5	259.9	97.9
1986	102.6	59.3	89.7	111.0	108.2	121.1	90.1	87.6	143.3	96.6
1987	102.1	61.9	92.5	108.9	106.6	116.5	93.0	91.4	130.7	100.9
1988	104.7	74.3	95.4	110.4	106.1	113.9	95.3	93.5	150.0	103.2
1989	103.2	85.6	98.9	106.1	102.5	106.5	97.0	90.0	139.9	101.8
1990	104.8	93.1	103.7	106.4	101.6	102.9	99.7	90.8	151.1	103.3
1991	102.6	93.3	100.1	104.7	101.9	103.8	99.3	97.8	128.6	96.7
1992	100.0	100.0	100.0	100.0	100.0	100.0	100.0	100.0	100.0	100.0
1993	99.9	98.8	93.7	101.1	98.0	95.2	101.7	102.1	122.6	102.3
1994	102.4	100.5	102.5	101.7	98.1	92.6	105.6	101.5	127.0	108.6
1995	102.0	101.5	101.9	100.5	96.5	90.6	104.5	103.8	126.4	112.9
1996	103.7	104.0	105.0	101.8	95.9	89.0	105.6	108.7	138.0	114.9
1997	105.8	110.0	107.8	103.1	95.7	87.8	106.6	109.4	149.3	120.3
1998	104.0	110.0	109.7	99.6	94.7	85.5	107.4	103.8	134.7	124.7
1995:										
January	103.0	100.9	104.0	101.1	97.1	92.0	104.1	107.3	125.3	117.2
February	102.5	101.6	102.7	101.1	97.0	92.8	102.9	105.4	126.4	113.0
March	102.1	99.8	105.3	100.1	96.3	90.7	104.0	103.8	124.1	113.6
April	100.6	100.7	94.9	100.4	97.2	91.5	105.1	104.8	120.6	111.5
May	102.4	100.5	101.7	101.6	97.3	91.8	105.0	105.8	128.9	110.9
June	102.3	101.0	103.4	100.8	97.1	91.5	104.9	102.7	125.5	111.5
July	101.9	102.4	98.9	100.6	96.7	90.6	105.1	103.3	126.2	115.3
August	102.1	102.0	103.8	100.4	96.3	90.4	104.6	102.3	127.0	111.8
September	102.1	101.1	104.1	100.0	95.5	88.7	105.0	102.8	128.8	114.8
October	101.1	102.9	102.6	99.2	94.8	88.5	103.5	102.1	127.7	110.9
November	102.3	104.0	103.5	100.6	96.5	90.2	105.2	104.6	126.8	110.8
December	101.3	101.5	98.0	100.1	95.7	89.1	105.0	100.2	129.6	113.9
1996:										
January	100.9	98.9	97.0	100.7	95.5	89.1	104.5	103.1	134.0	109.1
February	102.3	97.7	103.0	101.2	96.1	89.6	105.0	98.9	136.5	111.9
March	103.2	103.4	103.8	101.5	96.3	90.1	105.0	106.6	134.1	113.3
April	104.2	101.5	105.6	102.7	96.8	88.7	108.1	108.6	139.5	113.9
May	104.3	103.2	107.6	102.2	95.9	88.2	106.6	107.3	141.8	114.7
June	104.7	103.6	103.5	103.2	97.3	89.8	107.6	109.3	139.9	117.7
July	105.0	105.4	109.7	102.4	96.3	88.7	106.8	108.9	139.8	116.9
August	105.0	105.2	110.4	102.4	96.4	88.7	107.1	111.0	138.6	116.0
September	104.0	106.5	102.7	102.5	96.5	89.3	106.6	110.6	138.2	114.0
October	104.4	106.8	107.4	101.9	95.7	88.5	105.6	113.1	138.2	117.1
November	103.3	106.6	104.2	100.7	94.4	88.4	102.8	113.0	137.3	118.9
December	103.1	109.0	105.6	100.4	93.9	88.3	101.6	113.8	137.8	115.9
1997:										
January	104.3	109.7	108.2	101.5	95.4	87.3	106.7	109.7	138.4	115.0
February	105.5	108.1	108.9	102.6	95.9	88.0	106.9	112.5	142.7	121.0
March	106.3	109.1	105.6	104.0	96.2	88.0	107.5	112.7	152.4	122.4
April	105.4	108.0	105.9	103.3	96.0	88.6	106.4	108.7	149.2	117.8
May	106.6	108.6	113.4	103.4	96.1	88.0	107.4	108.5	149.8	119.3
June	105.9	110.1	106.5	103.1	95.5	87.7	106.5	110.0	150.3	123.0
July	106.1	109.0	108.1	103.7	95.9	88.2	106.7	110.7	151.9	118.9
August	105.5	109.2	104.3	103.3	95.3	87.3	106.4	110.8	152.9	121.3
September	106.6	111.7	108.9	103.8	96.0	87.7	107.6	110.3	152.4	121.0
October	106.2	113.2	107.7	103.5	96.1	87.7	107.8	108.1	150.6	119.8
November	104.9	115.9	100.3	102.6	95.1	87.7	105.4	101.9	151.6	122.0
December	106.4	107.5	116.1	102.2	94.7	87.6	104.6	108.3	149.6	121.9
1998:										
January	107.6	110.9	112.4	103.6	95.6	87.3	107.1	110.0	153.9	127.5
February	107.5	123.2	104.3	104.6	96.2	87.7	107.9	110.4	157.4	123.1
March	105.8	109.3	103.4	104.0	95.8	87.5	107.4	108.2	155.7	120.0
April	105.7	106.9	107.2	102.9	95.8	87.7	107.1	108.9	147.6	123.3
May	105.4	108.5	106.0	102.4	95.4	87.0	107.0	107.6	147.1	124.4
June	104.7	108.0	110.4	100.4	95.1	86.1	107.6	103.3	136.7	125.6
July	104.6	105.7	112.8	100.0	96.2	87.9	107.8	94.2	131.9	125.4
August	103.7	109.0	109.7	99.2	95.7	86.4	108.5	102.1	127.7	124.3
September	102.4	106.4	115.8	96.8	93.5	82.3	109.1	100.5	123.4	120.3
October	102.0	113.6	110.8	96.8	94.4	84.1	108.7	101.6	119.4	118.8
November	101.1	110.7	108.6	94.2	91.9	82.0	105.6	102.3	115.2	132.1
December	99.0	108.3	114.5	91.0	90.7	80.0	105.7	95.9	103.2	125.6

Mining Industries—Capacity Utilization and Producer Prices

Year and month	Capacity utilization (Output as a percent of capacity, seasonally adjusted)						Producer Prices (December 1984=100, except as noted; not seasonally adjusted)						
				Oil and gas extraction							Crude materials [2]		Nonmetallic minerals, except fuels
	Total mining	Metal mining	Coal mining	Total	Oil and gas well drilling	Stone and earth minerals	Total mining	Metal mining	Coal mining [1]	Oil and gas extraction [1]	Natural gas	Crude petroleum	
1970	88.8	93.6	95.8	87.7	69.7	87.2	.....	.....	.....	.....	7.9	14.5	.....
1971	87.3	83.2	86.0	88.5	68.6	85.9	.....	.....	.....	.....	8.4	15.6	.....
1972	90.3	80.7	89.2	92.3	79.1	87.8	.....	.....	.....	.....	9.0	15.5	.....
1973	92.3	84.6	85.7	94.8	85.2	92.8	.....	.....	.....	.....	9.8	17.2	.....
1974	92.3	82.1	84.2	96.1	98.9	89.6	.....	.....	.....	.....	11.6	28.9	.....
1975	89.7	76.4	87.5	93.8	99.2	79.1	.....	.....	.....	.....	16.1	33.5	.....
1976	89.8	81.0	88.9	92.1	91.5	83.0	.....	.....	.....	.....	21.8	34.6	.....
1977	90.9	69.4	88.2	94.2	101.7	85.4	.....	.....	.....	.....	30.8	37.4	.....
1978	90.9	78.5	80.3	94.7	100.0	89.2	.....	.....	.....	.....	36.5	40.9	.....
1979	91.4	81.4	88.8	92.8	88.2	90.6	.....	.....	.....	.....	47.6	51.3	.....
1980	93.4	72.8	90.3	95.8	95.7	82.7	.....	.....	.....	.....	63.3	75.9	.....
1981	93.9	79.1	86.7	96.1	98.0	79.8	.....	.....	.....	.....	82.1	109.6	.....
1982	86.3	57.5	86.1	88.2	70.3	67.4	.....	.....	.....	.....	100.0	100.0	.....
1983	80.4	57.9	79.1	81.7	52.6	72.6	.....	.....	.....	.....	106.6	92.9	.....
1984	86.0	63.3	88.6	86.7	63.4	81.8	.....	.....	.....	.....	106.1	91.3	.....
1985	84.3	62.7	85.7	84.9	58.5	84.4	.....	.....	.....	.....	102.9	84.5	102.8
1986	77.6	65.9	84.7	76.4	34.3	82.7	77.0	91.2	99.5	76.9	89.6	46.9	104.2
1987	80.3	70.9	85.7	79.3	38.4	85.7	75.0	100.1	96.0	74.3	79.5	55.5	105.1
1988	85.2	80.5	86.8	85.0	56.0	86.9	70.6	100.7	94.6	68.5	77.4	46.2	108.0
1989	86.9	85.4	88.3	87.0	63.7	85.2	76.4	100.3	94.3	75.7	82.0	56.3	111.2
1990	89.8	85.7	90.7	90.3	75.6	86.3	81.8	93.4	96.5	82.7	80.4	71.0	113.7
1991	88.4	82.9	85.7	90.4	69.4	81.1	78.4	82.2	96.3	77.9	79.1	61.9	116.3
1992	86.4	87.1	84.7	87.0	55.2	83.9	76.9	76.6	94.0	76.5	80.6	58.0	117.5
1993	86.0	84.4	79.1	88.1	67.7	82.8	76.4	69.7	93.3	76.2	84.7	51.4	118.8
1994	87.5	86.2	84.5	88.6	70.7	85.4	73.3	81.4	93.2	71.1	78.8	47.1	120.5
1995	86.8	87.6	82.6	87.8	71.2	86.7	71.0	101.4	91.6	66.6	66.6	51.1	123.8
1996	88.5	88.3	84.2	89.8	78.8	85.8	84.4	92.1	91.4	84.8	91.2	62.6	127.1
1997	89.1	91.5	84.9	90.1	85.3	86.1	86.1	85.8	92.2	87.5	101.7	57.5	128.8
1998	86.7	89.8	84.9	86.7	76.0	85.5	70.8	73.2	89.5	68.3	83.9	35.7	132.2
1995:													
January	87.5	87.4	84.4	87.9	70.1	91.0	72.1	101.9	88.4	68.7	72.8	48.4	122.4
February	87.0	88.0	83.3	87.9	70.7	87.6	71.2	102.3	91.3	66.9	67.0	51.0	123.3
March	86.8	86.4	85.4	87.0	69.6	87.8	70.7	103.7	93.7	65.7	65.3	50.6	123.6
April	85.5	87.2	76.9	87.3	67.7	86.0	72.6	105.1	92.6	68.3	66.3	55.3	123.5
May	87.0	86.9	82.4	88.5	72.5	85.3	72.8	100.9	90.4	69.2	67.3	56.0	123.3
June	86.9	87.4	83.8	87.9	70.6	85.6	72.8	101.8	90.7	69.1	68.9	53.3	123.8
July	86.7	88.4	80.2	87.8	71.1	88.4	70.6	103.6	92.5	65.7	67.2	48.3	124.2
August	86.9	88.0	84.1	87.7	71.7	85.6	67.6	101.2	91.8	61.8	59.6	49.1	124.2
September	87.0	87.1	84.3	87.5	72.8	87.8	68.7	99.3	91.7	63.5	60.8	51.4	124.5
October	86.3	88.5	83.1	87.0	72.3	84.6	69.0	97.0	93.0	63.7	63.5	48.3	124.3
November	87.3	89.4	83.8	88.4	71.9	84.4	70.5	100.0	91.4	66.0	67.0	49.0	124.4
December	86.6	87.0	79.4	88.1	73.6	86.7	74.1	100.0	91.3	71.0	73.3	52.2	124.4
1996:													
January	86.3	84.6	78.5	88.7	76.2	82.8	79.1	98.2	89.9	78.0	83.5	56.0	125.9
February	87.5	83.5	83.2	89.3	77.7	84.7	83.4	97.5	91.9	82.6	96.5	52.8	126.4
March	88.3	88.3	83.6	89.6	76.4	85.5	80.9	96.7	92.2	79.2	85.8	57.7	126.7
April	89.1	86.5	84.9	90.7	79.5	85.7	86.0	96.4	91.1	86.2	92.8	66.0	127.1
May	89.2	87.7	86.4	90.2	80.9	86.1	82.9	97.1	93.1	81.8	88.0	61.0	127.6
June	89.5	88.0	83.0	91.1	79.9	88.1	78.1	93.3	91.7	75.9	78.9	57.7	128.1
July	89.7	89.4	87.9	90.4	79.9	87.2	81.0	89.2	90.5	80.7	87.3	59.9	127.2
August	89.6	89.2	88.3	90.4	79.3	86.2	82.6	87.5	92.6	82.7	88.2	62.0	127.2
September	88.6	90.2	82.0	89.8	79.2	84.5	81.3	86.8	90.9	81.3	76.6	67.2	127.5
October	88.9	90.4	85.6	89.8	79.2	86.5	83.0	86.6	90.5	83.7	75.2	72.0	127.3
November	87.8	90.1	82.9	88.6	78.8	87.5	90.4	88.4	91.3	93.4	100.6	68.5	127.3
December	87.6	92.0	84.0	88.2	79.1	84.9	104.2	87.3	90.7	112.1	140.7	70.9	127.1
1997:													
January	88.4	92.5	85.9	89.2	79.5	84.0	111.3	89.9	92.9	121.1	159.5	73.4	127.6
February	89.4	90.9	86.3	90.0	81.9	88.0	95.1	88.5	91.3	99.6	119.9	64.5	127.7
March	89.9	91.5	83.6	91.1	87.4	88.8	78.8	90.9	92.8	77.3	78.5	56.3	127.7
April	88.9	90.4	83.7	90.4	85.5	85.1	77.6	87.7	95.0	75.5	75.5	56.1	128.1
May	89.9	90.7	89.5	90.5	85.8	85.8	80.8	89.7	91.7	80.2	83.7	60.2	128.3
June	89.1	91.7	83.9	90.1	85.9	88.2	79.9	89.4	92.6	78.9	88.7	51.8	128.9
July	89.2	90.5	85.1	90.5	86.8	85.0	79.5	85.7	91.5	78.8	85.8	54.9	129.2
August	88.6	90.5	82.0	90.1	87.3	86.4	80.2	86.4	91.6	79.7	87.1	54.9	129.2
September	89.4	92.3	85.4	90.5	86.9	85.9	82.9	84.0	91.9	83.5	96.9	53.3	129.3
October	89.0	93.3	84.4	90.2	85.8	84.8	90.2	83.2	91.3	93.4	115.7	57.3	129.6
November	87.9	95.2	78.5	89.4	86.3	86.0	93.2	78.9	91.0	98.0	127.3	56.4	129.7
December	89.0	88.1	90.7	89.1	85.0	85.7	83.2	74.8	93.2	84.5	101.4	50.8	129.9
1998:													
January	90.0	90.7	87.7	90.3	87.4	89.3	76.4	73.5	88.2	76.2	90.9	43.4	130.6
February	89.9	100.7	81.2	91.2	89.2	86.0	73.6	74.2	90.2	72.0	81.9	43.2	131.0
March	88.4	89.3	80.5	90.6	88.1	83.6	72.2	74.6	89.7	70.2	86.4	35.8	131.4
April	88.2	87.3	83.3	89.6	83.4	85.6	74.1	76.6	90.7	72.3	90.1	38.1	132.2
May	87.9	88.6	82.2	89.2	82.9	86.0	74.2	75.5	90.2	72.6	90.5	38.3	132.2
June	87.3	88.1	85.5	87.5	77.0	86.6	69.6	73.9	90.2	66.6	81.9	33.6	132.5
July	87.2	88.3	87.1	87.1	74.2	86.2	72.3	74.7	89.9	70.1	89.0	35.9	132.6
August	86.3	88.9	84.7	86.4	71.7	85.1	67.7	71.6	87.6	64.6	82.1	30.4	132.8
September	85.2	86.8	89.3	84.2	69.1	82.1	65.7	72.4	87.3	61.8	69.8	36.0	132.9
October	84.7	92.6	85.3	84.1	66.8	80.8	67.9	71.0	88.8	64.6	77.6	35.2	132.9
November	83.8	90.2	83.6	81.8	64.3	89.5	68.9	71.0	89.6	65.9	83.1	32.7	132.8
December	82.0	88.3	87.9	78.9	57.5	84.8	66.8	69.5	91.4	62.9	83.4	26.1	132.7

1. December 1985=100.
2. 1982=100.

Mining Industries—Employment, Hours, and Earnings

Year and month	Total mining (seasonally adjusted)						Total mining (not seasonally adjusted)					
	Total payroll employees (thousands)	Production workers					Total payroll employees (thousands)	Production workers				
		Employees (thousands)	Average weekly hours	Aggregate weekly hours index (1982=100)	Average earnings (dollars)			Employees (thousands)	Average weekly hours	Aggregate weekly hours index (1982=100)	Average earnings (dollars)	
					Hourly	Weekly					Hourly	Weekly
1970	623	473	42.7	57.6	3.85	164.40	623	473	42.7	57.6	3.85	164.40
1971	609	455	42.4	54.9	4.06	172.14	609	455	42.4	54.9	4.06	172.14
1972	628	475	42.6	57.8	4.44	189.14	628	475	42.6	57.8	4.44	189.14
1973	642	486	42.4	58.8	4.75	201.40	642	486	42.4	58.8	4.75	201.40
1974	697	530	41.9	63.4	5.23	219.14	697	530	41.9	63.4	5.23	219.14
1975	752	571	41.9	68.3	5.95	249.31	752	571	41.9	68.3	5.95	249.31
1976	779	592	42.4	71.5	6.46	273.90	779	592	42.4	71.5	6.46	273.90
1977	813	618	43.4	76.5	6.94	301.20	813	618	43.4	76.5	6.94	301.20
1978	851	638	43.4	79.0	7.67	332.88	851	638	43.4	79.0	7.67	332.88
1979	958	719	43.0	88.2	8.49	365.07	958	719	43.0	88.2	8.49	365.07
1980	1 027	762	43.3	94.1	9.17	397.06	1 027	762	43.3	94.1	9.17	397.06
1981	1 139	841	43.7	104.8	10.04	438.75	1 139	841	43.7	104.8	10.04	438.75
1982	1 128	821	42.7	100.0	10.77	459.88	1 128	821	42.7	100.0	10.77	459.88
1983	952	673	42.5	81.5	11.28	479.40	952	673	42.5	81.5	11.28	479.40
1984	966	686	43.3	84.9	11.63	503.58	966	686	43.3	84.9	11.63	503.58
1985	927	658	43.4	81.4	11.98	519.93	927	658	43.4	81.4	11.98	519.93
1986	777	545	42.2	65.7	12.46	525.81	777	545	42.2	65.7	12.46	525.81
1987	717	511	42.4	61.8	12.54	531.70	717	511	42.4	61.8	12.54	531.70
1988	713	512	42.3	61.7	12.81	540.85	713	512	42.3	61.7	12.80	541.44
1989	692	493	43.0	60.5	13.26	570.18	692	493	43.0	60.5	13.26	570.18
1990	709	509	44.1	63.9	13.68	603.29	709	509	44.1	63.9	13.68	603.29
1991	689	489	44.4	62.0	14.19	630.04	689	489	44.4	62.0	14.19	630.04
1992	635	448	43.9	56.2	14.54	638.31	635	448	43.9	56.2	14.54	638.31
1993	610	431	44.3	54.3	14.60	646.78	610	431	44.3	54.3	14.60	646.78
1994	601	427	44.8	54.6	14.88	666.62	601	427	44.8	54.6	14.88	666.62
1995	581	424	44.7	54.1	15.30	683.91	581	424	44.7	54.1	15.30	683.91
1996	580	430	45.3	55.6	15.62	707.59	580	430	45.3	55.6	15.62	707.59
1997	596	450	45.4	58.3	16.15	733.21	596	450	45.4	58.3	16.15	733.21
1998	590	448	43.9	56.1	16.90	741.91	590	448	43.9	56.1	16.90	741.91
1995:												
January	592	430	45.1	55.3	15.05	678.76	581	419	44.9	53.6	15.23	683.83
February	588	427	44.6	54.3	15.09	673.01	573	414	44.5	52.5	15.24	678.18
March	587	427	44.5	54.2	15.16	674.62	576	417	43.9	52.3	15.22	668.16
April	586	426	44.8	54.4	15.22	681.86	578	420	44.3	53.1	15.30	677.79
May	582	425	44.4	53.8	15.21	675.32	582	424	44.3	53.5	15.19	672.92
June	581	424	44.7	54.1	15.29	683.46	588	430	45.0	55.2	15.23	685.35
July	580	424	44.7	54.1	15.44	690.17	590	432	44.5	54.9	15.34	682.63
August	577	423	44.4	53.6	15.41	684.20	588	433	44.7	55.2	15.29	683.46
September	576	422	44.6	53.7	15.41	687.29	585	430	45.4	55.7	15.35	696.89
October	575	422	44.9	54.1	15.44	693.26	582	428	45.5	55.5	15.33	697.52
November	573	419	44.7	53.4	15.44	690.17	577	424	44.8	54.2	15.35	687.68
December	573	420	44.6	53.4	15.47	689.96	573	420	44.9	53.8	15.54	697.75
1996:												
January	573	420	44.1	52.8	15.45	681.35	562	410	43.9	51.3	15.63	686.16
February	577	426	45.2	54.9	15.46	698.79	563	413	45.1	53.2	15.61	704.01
March	578	427	45.7	55.7	15.46	706.52	566	418	45.0	53.7	15.50	697.50
April	579	429	45.0	55.1	15.48	696.60	572	423	44.9	54.1	15.55	698.20
May	581	430	45.1	55.3	15.55	701.31	579	429	45.1	55.3	15.45	696.80
June	581	432	45.7	56.3	15.61	713.38	587	437	46.0	57.3	15.59	717.14
July	580	431	44.9	55.2	15.66	703.13	591	439	44.8	56.1	15.55	696.64
August	581	433	45.2	55.8	15.70	709.64	592	442	45.2	57.0	15.52	701.50
September	579	432	45.6	56.2	15.70	715.92	587	438	46.0	57.5	15.74	724.04
October	581	433	45.2	55.8	15.66	707.83	587	439	45.9	57.4	15.56	714.20
November	583	435	45.3	56.2	15.77	714.38	588	440	45.4	57.0	15.69	712.33
December	584	436	45.6	56.7	15.89	724.58	584	436	46.0	57.2	15.97	734.62
1997:												
January	587	440	44.7	56.1	16.05	717.44	576	429	44.2	54.0	16.20	716.04
February	592	445	46.0	58.4	15.98	735.08	577	431	45.6	56.1	16.09	733.70
March	592	445	46.5	59.0	15.99	743.54	580	436	45.7	56.9	16.01	731.66
April	593	447	45.2	57.6	16.02	724.10	587	441	45.1	56.7	16.08	725.21
May	596	450	45.7	58.7	16.12	736.68	595	449	45.9	58.8	16.00	734.40
June	596	450	45.6	58.5	16.16	736.90	603	456	45.8	59.6	16.13	738.75
July	598	453	45.3	58.5	16.16	732.05	608	461	45.1	59.4	16.05	723.86
August	599	453	45.5	58.8	16.13	733.92	609	462	45.6	60.1	15.96	727.78
September	601	455	45.2	58.7	16.19	731.79	608	461	45.5	59.9	16.24	738.92
October	601	455	45.0	58.4	16.27	732.15	608	461	45.3	59.6	16.19	733.41
November	601	454	45.1	58.4	16.38	738.74	604	458	45.6	59.6	16.38	746.93
December	602	456	44.9	58.4	16.38	735.46	602	456	45.3	58.9	16.49	747.00
1998:												
January	606	460	45.7	60.0	16.45	751.77	593	448	45.1	57.6	16.60	748.66
February	606	463	44.2	58.4	16.75	740.35	592	448	43.9	56.1	16.85	739.72
March	605	459	44.1	57.7	16.84	742.64	592	449	43.4	55.6	16.85	731.29
April	600	455	44.3	57.5	16.72	740.70	593	450	43.3	55.6	16.79	727.01
May	595	453	44.3	57.2	16.72	740.70	595	453	44.3	57.3	16.67	738.48
June	593	451	43.7	56.2	16.71	730.23	600	457	44.0	57.3	16.68	733.92
July	588	447	44.3	56.5	16.87	747.34	598	456	43.9	57.1	16.76	735.76
August	585	444	43.7	55.3	17.00	742.90	597	454	44.0	57.0	16.88	742.72
September	583	442	43.3	54.6	17.06	738.70	590	448	42.9	54.8	17.11	734.02
October	578	438	43.7	54.6	17.15	749.46	584	444	44.0	55.7	17.07	751.08
November	574	435	43.3	53.7	17.27	747.79	577	439	43.8	54.9	17.29	757.30
December	570	432	43.3	53.4	17.18	743.89	570	432	43.7	53.8	17.29	755.57

Mining Industries—Employment, Hours, and Earnings—Continued

(Not seasonally adjusted)

Year and month	Metal mining					Coal mining				
	Total payroll employees (thousands)	Production workers				Total payroll employees (thousands)	Production workers			
		Employees (thousands)	Average weekly hours	Average earnings (dollars)			Employees (thousands)	Average weekly hours	Average earnings (dollars)	
				Hourly	Weekly				Hourly	Weekly
1970	93	75	43.1	3.88	167.23	145	127	40.5	4.54	183.87
1971	87	69	42.8	4.12	176.34	146	123	40.3	4.78	192.63
1972	83	66	41.4	4.56	188.78	161	140	40.7	5.27	214.49
1973	87	69	41.7	4.84	201.83	162	140	39.8	5.70	226.86
1974	95	76	41.4	5.44	225.22	180	154	37.7	6.22	234.49
1975	94	73	40.7	6.13	249.49	213	182	39.5	7.21	284.80
1976	94	73	41.0	6.76	277.16	225	192	39.8	7.74	308.05
1977	90	68	40.8	7.28	297.02	225	192	41.9	8.25	345.68
1978	94	72	41.3	8.23	339.90	210	173	40.5	9.51	385.16
1979	101	77	41.2	9.27	381.92	259	216	40.7	10.28	418.40
1980	98	74	40.5	10.26	415.53	246	204	40.1	10.86	435.49
1981	104	78	40.5	11.55	467.78	225	186	40.5	11.91	482.36
1982	73	53	39.3	12.31	483.78	237	194	39.9	12.69	506.33
1983	56	41	39.3	12.58	494.39	194	156	39.9	13.73	547.83
1984	55	40	40.5	13.05	528.53	196	158	40.7	14.82	603.17
1985	46	34	40.9	13.38	547.24	187	153	41.1	15.24	626.36
1986	41	31	41.1	13.19	542.11	176	144	40.6	15.40	625.24
1987	44	33	41.9	12.94	542.19	162	132	42.0	15.76	661.92
1988	50	39	42.3	13.24	560.05	151	123	42.2	16.06	677.73
1989	56	44	42.8	13.58	581.22	144	116	43.4	16.26	705.68
1990	58	46	42.8	14.05	601.34	147	119	44.0	16.71	735.24
1991	56	44	43.0	14.87	639.41	136	110	44.6	17.06	760.88
1992	53	42	42.9	15.26	654.65	127	103	44.0	17.15	754.60
1993	50	40	43.1	15.29	659.00	109	86	44.4	17.27	766.79
1994	49	39	43.5	16.08	699.48	112	90	45.2	17.76	802.75
1995	51	41	43.8	16.77	734.53	104	84	44.9	18.45	828.41
1996	54	42	44.0	17.35	763.40	98	80	45.8	18.74	858.29
1997	54	41	44.4	17.82	791.21	96	79	45.4	19.01	863.05
1998	50	38	44.5	18.24	811.68	92	75	44.7	19.15	856.01
1995:										
January	49	40	43.7	16.64	727.17	109	88	46.7	18.51	864.42
February	49	40	43.0	16.57	712.51	107	86	46.1	18.37	846.86
March	50	40	43.5	16.62	722.97	107	86	44.9	18.37	824.81
April	50	41	44.1	16.98	748.82	106	86	44.1	18.34	808.79
May	51	41	42.7	16.61	709.25	105	84	44.5	18.31	814.80
June	52	42	43.5	16.44	715.14	105	84	44.8	18.36	822.53
July	53	43	44.2	16.71	738.58	104	84	41.8	18.38	768.28
August	53	43	43.4	16.84	730.86	104	84	44.8	18.48	827.90
September	52	42	44.7	16.89	754.98	103	84	45.7	18.52	846.36
October	52	41	44.1	16.92	746.17	102	83	45.4	18.46	838.08
November	52	41	44.4	17.06	757.46	102	83	44.8	18.58	832.38
December	52	41	44.5	16.94	753.83	100	82	45.1	18.78	846.98
1996:										
January	52	41	44.4	16.97	753.47	99	81	44.7	18.92	845.72
February	52	41	44.6	16.92	754.63	99	80	47.0	18.79	883.13
March	53	42	44.0	17.14	754.16	98	80	46.7	18.77	876.56
April	53	42	44.7	17.31	773.76	97	80	45.5	18.70	850.85
May	54	43	43.2	17.30	747.36	97	80	45.6	18.61	848.62
June	55	44	43.9	17.25	757.28	98	80	46.7	18.65	870.96
July	55	44	43.6	17.29	753.84	99	80	43.6	18.64	812.70
August	55	44	43.0	17.41	748.63	98	80	45.3	18.59	842.13
September	54	43	44.8	17.58	787.58	97	80	46.1	18.73	863.45
October	54	42	43.6	17.46	761.26	97	79	45.8	18.56	850.05
November	54	42	43.5	17.76	772.56	97	80	46.0	18.80	864.80
December	54	42	44.4	17.80	790.32	97	79	46.2	19.11	882.88
1997:										
January	54	41	45.0	17.53	788.85	97	79	46.6	19.20	894.72
February	53	41	45.1	17.71	798.72	96	80	46.7	19.21	897.11
March	53	41	45.1	17.66	796.47	96	79	46.4	19.02	882.53
April	53	41	44.1	17.87	788.07	97	80	45.1	18.83	849.23
May	54	42	44.0	17.89	787.16	97	80	45.4	18.74	850.80
June	55	43	44.2	17.77	785.43	97	80	45.6	18.91	862.30
July	55	42	44.3	17.70	784.11	96	79	44.1	18.97	836.58
August	55	42	43.8	17.70	775.26	96	78	45.0	18.85	848.25
September	54	41	44.7	17.84	797.45	96	78	45.5	18.94	861.77
October	53	40	43.6	17.94	782.18	95	78	45.0	18.93	851.85
November	53	40	44.4	18.29	812.08	95	78	45.2	19.11	863.77
December	52	39	44.5	18.02	801.89	95	78	44.8	19.47	872.26
1998:										
January	51	39	43.8	17.94	785.77	94	77	45.1	19.30	870.43
February	50	38	44.5	17.97	799.67	94	77	45.3	19.12	866.14
March	50	38	44.9	18.17	815.83	94	77	45.0	19.11	859.95
April	50	38	45.7	18.26	834.48	93	76	44.2	19.10	844.22
May	50	38	44.3	18.24	808.03	93	76	44.5	19.06	848.17
June	51	39	44.2	18.21	804.88	92	75	44.9	19.13	858.94
July	51	39	45.0	18.21	819.45	90	74	42.8	18.95	811.06
August	51	39	44.9	18.31	822.12	91	75	44.5	19.01	845.95
September	50	38	45.4	18.51	840.35	90	74	44.1	19.20	846.72
October	50	38	43.4	18.44	800.30	90	74	45.0	19.13	860.85
November	50	38	44.3	18.45	817.34	90	75	45.8	19.24	881.19
December	50	38	43.8	18.22	798.04	90	74	45.7	19.41	887.04

Mining Industries—Employment, Hours, and Earnings—*Continued*

(Not seasonally adjusted)

Year and month	Oil and gas extraction					Nonmetallic minerals, except fuels				
	Total payroll employees (thousands)	Production workers				Total payroll employees (thousands)	Production workers			
		Employees (thousands)	Average weekly hours	Average earnings (dollars)			Employees (thousands)	Average weekly hours	Average earnings (dollars)	
				Hourly	Weekly				Hourly	Weekly
1970	270	178	43.2	3.57	154.22	115	94	44.7	3.47	155.11
1971	264	173	43.2	3.78	163.30	115	93	44.9	3.70	166.13
1972	268	177	43.4	4.04	175.34	116	93	44.7	3.95	176.57
1973	274	182	43.0	4.33	186.19	119	95	45.5	4.22	192.01
1974	300	203	43.8	4.87	213.31	122	98	45.0	4.50	202.50
1975	329	223	43.7	5.38	235.11	117	92	43.5	4.95	215.33
1976	346	237	44.1	5.85	257.99	115	90	44.2	5.36	236.91
1977	381	267	44.7	6.37	284.74	116	92	44.6	5.81	259.13
1978	429	299	45.0	7.01	315.45	119	94	44.8	6.33	283.58
1979	474	327	44.4	7.72	342.77	124	98	45.0	6.90	310.50
1980	560	389	45.4	8.59	389.99	123	96	43.6	7.52	327.87
1981	692	486	45.6	9.50	433.20	119	91	43.0	8.28	356.04
1982	708	491	44.2	10.25	453.05	110	83	42.7	8.90	380.03
1983	598	398	43.6	10.67	465.21	104	79	43.6	9.31	405.92
1984	606	405	44.4	10.72	475.97	109	83	44.7	9.87	441.19
1985	583	387	44.2	11.06	488.85	110	84	44.5	10.18	453.01
1986	450	287	42.6	11.61	494.59	110	83	44.5	10.38	461.91
1987	402	261	41.7	11.53	480.80	110	85	45.4	10.60	481.24
1988	400	265	41.3	11.85	489.41	112	85	45.5	10.94	497.77
1989	381	248	42.0	12.50	525.00	111	85	45.6	11.25	513.00
1990	395	261	43.9	12.94	568.07	110	83	45.3	11.58	524.57
1991	393	258	44.5	13.53	602.09	105	78	44.5	11.93	530.89
1992	353	228	43.8	14.01	613.64	102	76	44.9	12.26	550.47
1993	350	228	43.8	14.14	619.33	102	76	46.1	12.70	585.47
1994	337	220	44.2	14.13	624.55	104	78	46.5	13.11	609.62
1995	320	218	44.2	14.52	641.78	105	80	46.6	13.39	623.97
1996	322	227	44.7	14.87	664.69	106	81	47.1	13.75	647.63
1997	339	248	45.0	15.64	703.80	108	82	47.3	14.19	671.19
1998	339	252	42.7	16.77	716.08	109	83	46.4	14.70	682.08
1995:										
January	326	219	44.4	14.30	634.92	97	72	44.8	13.09	586.43
February	319	215	44.4	14.38	638.47	98	73	43.7	13.17	575.53
March	318	213	43.1	14.39	620.21	102	77	45.7	13.19	602.78
April	316	213	43.9	14.55	638.75	106	80	45.7	13.25	605.53
May	319	216	43.6	14.46	630.46	108	82	46.6	13.30	619.78
June	323	220	44.3	14.54	644.12	109	83	47.8	13.39	640.04
July	323	222	44.3	14.77	654.31	110	84	48.0	13.43	644.64
August	322	223	43.8	14.50	635.10	109	84	47.9	13.51	647.13
September	321	222	44.3	14.51	642.79	109	83	48.6	13.66	663.88
October	320	221	44.9	14.55	653.30	108	83	47.7	13.61	649.20
November	317	218	44.4	14.50	643.80	107	82	46.2	13.50	623.70
December	319	219	44.9	14.81	664.97	103	78	45.3	13.41	607.47
1996:										
January	314	216	43.8	14.79	647.80	97	72	42.5	13.53	575.03
February	314	218	44.6	14.89	664.09	98	74	45.0	13.40	603.00
March	315	220	44.2	14.67	648.41	102	77	46.3	13.50	625.05
April	317	221	44.0	14.81	651.64	105	81	46.9	13.58	636.90
May	320	224	44.7	14.65	654.86	108	83	47.1	13.68	644.33
June	324	228	45.3	14.87	673.61	110	85	48.2	13.80	665.16
July	326	231	44.0	14.83	652.52	111	85	48.5	13.87	672.70
August	328	234	44.5	14.76	656.82	111	85	48.5	13.91	674.64
September	325	232	45.1	15.04	678.30	110	85	48.9	14.02	685.58
October	326	234	45.4	14.83	673.28	110	84	48.6	13.92	676.51
November	328	236	45.2	14.93	674.84	109	83	46.8	13.85	648.18
December	329	236	45.9	15.34	704.11	105	79	46.7	13.81	644.93
1997:										
January	327	234	43.9	15.62	685.72	99	73	42.2	13.76	580.67
February	328	236	45.5	15.43	702.07	100	74	45.1	13.84	624.18
March	327	238	45.4	15.37	697.80	103	78	46.5	14.02	651.93
April	330	240	44.6	15.59	695.31	107	81	47.1	14.00	659.40
May	334	244	45.3	15.48	701.24	110	84	48.8	14.17	691.50
June	339	248	45.3	15.68	710.30	112	86	48.2	14.19	683.96
July	345	254	44.4	15.52	689.09	113	86	48.8	14.30	697.84
August	346	255	45.1	15.40	694.54	113	86	48.5	14.29	693.07
September	346	256	44.5	15.78	702.21	112	85	48.9	14.49	708.56
October	349	258	44.6	15.76	702.90	111	84	48.6	14.34	696.92
November	348	257	45.6	15.96	727.78	109	83	46.8	14.31	669.71
December	350	259	45.1	16.05	723.86	106	80	46.6	14.36	669.18
1998:										
January	348	258	45.3	16.27	737.03	100	74	44.7	14.24	636.53
February	347	258	43.1	16.76	722.36	100	75	45.2	14.27	645.00
March	345	256	42.3	16.69	705.99	104	78	44.8	14.50	649.60
April	341	253	41.8	16.64	695.55	109	83	46.4	14.55	675.12
May	340	254	43.4	16.44	713.50	111	85	47.0	14.64	688.08
June	345	257	42.5	16.41	697.43	113	86	47.5	14.72	699.20
July	344	256	42.9	16.61	712.57	113	86	47.8	14.85	709.83
August	342	255	42.3	16.76	708.95	113	86	47.9	14.88	712.75
September	337	250	41.2	17.10	704.52	113	86	46.1	14.82	683.20
October	333	247	42.6	17.03	725.48	112	86	47.1	14.93	703.20
November	327	243	42.6	17.33	738.26	111	84	45.8	14.94	684.25
December	322	239	42.2	17.30	730.06	108	81	45.9	14.94	685.75

Petroleum and Petroleum Products—Imports and Stocks

(Not seasonally adjusted)

Year and month	Imports						Stocks (end of period - millions of barrels)		
	Total energy-related petroleum products		Crude petroleum				All oils	Crude petroleum	
	Quantity (thousands of barrels)	Value (millions of dollars)	Quantity (thousands of barrels)		Value (millions of dollars)	Unit price (dollars per barrel)		Total	Strategic petroleum reserve
			Total	Average per day					
1970	.....	.....	.....	.....	.....	.....	1 018	276	.....
1971	.....	.....	.....	.....	.....	.....	1 044	260	.....
1972	.....	.....	.....	.....	.....	.....	959	246	.....
1973	.....	.....	.....	.....	.....	.....	1 008	242	.....
1974	.....	.....	.....	.....	.....	.....	1 074	265	.....
1975	.....	.....	.....	.....	.....	.....	1 133	271	.....
1976	.....	.....	.....	.....	.....	.....	1 112	285	.....
1977	.....	.....	.....	.....	.....	.....	1 312	348	7
1978	.....	.....	.....	.....	.....	.....	1 278	376	67
1979	.....	.....	.....	.....	.....	.....	1 341	430	91
1980	.....	.....	.....	.....	.....	.....	1 392	466	108
1981	.....	.....	.....	.....	.....	.....	1 484	594	230
1982	.....	.....	.....	.....	.....	.....	1 430	644	294
1983	.....	.....	.....	.....	.....	.....	1 454	723	379
1984	.....	.....	.....	.....	.....	.....	1 556	796	451
1985	.....	.....	.....	.....	.....	.....	1 519	814	493
1986	.....	.....	.....	.....	.....	.....	1 593	843	512
1987	.....	.....	.....	.....	.....	.....	1 607	890	541
1988	.....	.....	.....	.....	.....	.....	1 597	890	560
1989	.....	.....	.....	.....	.....	.....	1 581	921	580
1990	.....	.....	.....	.....	.....	.....	1 621	908	586
1991	2 828 953	50 646	2 146 064	5 880	37 463	17.46	1 617	893	569
1992	2 947 582	50 537	2 294 570	6 269	38 553	16.80	1 592	893	575
1993	3 257 008	50 210	2 543 374	6 968	38 469	15.13	1 647	922	587
1994	3 416 045	49 533	2 704 196	7 409	38 479	14.23	1 653	929	592
1995	3 361 882	53 835	2 767 312	7 582	43 750	15.81	1 563	895	592
1996	3 622 385	70 199	2 893 647	7 906	54 931	18.98	1 507	850	566
1997	3 802 574	69 288	3 069 430	8 409	54 226	17.67	1 560	868	571
1998	4 088 027	49 132	3 242 711	8 884	37 252	11.49	1 647	895	575
1995:									
January	260 988	3 994	212 270	6 847	3 196	15.06	1 643	922	592
February	244 696	3 864	195 944	6 998	3 043	15.53	1 608	921	592
March	288 005	4 584	239 741	7 734	3 782	15.78	1 601	931	592
April	251 431	4 247	212 013	7 067	3 553	16.76	1 601	928	592
May	287 411	5 066	240 514	7 759	4 184	17.40	1 612	924	592
June	291 331	4 980	241 982	8 066	4 061	16.78	1 609	920	592
July	299 639	4 717	245 447	7 918	3 807	15.51	1 624	907	592
August	294 480	4 542	240 839	7 769	3 665	15.22	1 614	899	592
September	300 142	4 644	244 875	8 163	3 780	15.44	1 620	898	592
October	274 218	4 232	226 375	7 302	3 451	15.25	1 607	903	592
November	285 510	4 383	231 567	7 719	3 498	15.10	1 604	911	592
December	284 030	4 582	235 746	7 605	3 730	15.82	1 563	895	592
1996:									
January	306 887	5 196	238 990	7 709	3 927	16.43	1 544	895	592
February	252 634	4 181	198 120	6 832	3 189	16.10	1 500	893	592
March	255 345	4 544	201 663	6 505	3 492	17.31	1 482	889	589
April	297 886	5 861	238 198	7 940	4 589	19.27	1 502	890	586
May	323 841	6 274	261 641	8 440	4 945	18.90	1 520	890	586
June	309 546	5 637	253 014	8 434	4 544	17.96	1 546	899	584
July	339 099	6 221	275 225	8 878	4 998	18.16	1 550	891	583
August	307 806	5 844	250 957	8 095	4 681	18.65	1 545	891	578
September	316 593	6 402	260 375	8 679	5 200	19.97	1 551	876	574
October	314 661	6 842	250 694	8 087	5 367	21.41	1 538	882	574
November	275 355	5 998	216 953	7 232	4 638	21.38	1 522	869	570
December	322 733	7 199	247 816	7 994	5 361	21.63	1 507	850	566
1997:									
January	295 029	6 624	224 135	7 230	4 900	21.86	1 501	864	301
February	270 487	5 683	211 073	7 538	4 324	20.48	1 482	860	297
March	315 042	6 048	245 623	7 923	4 608	18.76	1 512	876	313
April	309 804	5 473	250 947	8 365	4 298	17.13	1 518	882	319
May	343 544	6 079	278 223	8 975	4 745	17.06	1 561	889	326
June	313 136	5 431	254 232	8 474	4 285	16.85	1 575	883	320
July	325 451	5 494	266 293	8 590	4 369	16.41	1 559	873	310
August	333 875	5 857	280 897	9 061	4 762	16.95	1 570	864	301
September	335 430	5 823	274 565	9 152	4 593	16.73	1 592	867	304
October	341 352	6 163	280 555	9 050	4 968	17.71	1 598	879	316
November	308 491	5 472	252 757	8 425	4 361	17.25	1 600	887	324
December	310 934	5 141	250 131	8 069	4 014	16.05	1 560	868	305
1998:									
January	332 557	4 877	271 208	8 749	3 881	14.31	1 570	880	317
February	292 678	3 983	230 593	8 235	3 002	13.02	1 569	881	318
March	330 542	4 099	263 407	8 497	3 129	11.88	1 587	897	334
April	357 373	4 415	289 968	9 666	3 412	11.77	1 614	914	351
May	356 929	4 467	282 846	9 124	3 337	11.80	1 652	914	351
June	341 622	4 026	271 314	9 044	3 018	11.12	1 651	895	332
July	366 139	4 165	289 718	9 346	3 122	10.78	1 661	901	338
August	374 808	4 136	300 227	9 685	3 166	10.55	1 669	892	329
September	330 636	3 787	259 951	8 665	2 857	10.99	1 652	873	310
October	342 903	4 183	263 149	8 489	3 069	11.66	1 649	894	330
November	337 814	3 811	267 953	8 932	2 890	10.79	1 672	904	335
December	324 027	3 181	252 378	8 141	2 368	9.38	1 647	895	324

Construction and Housing

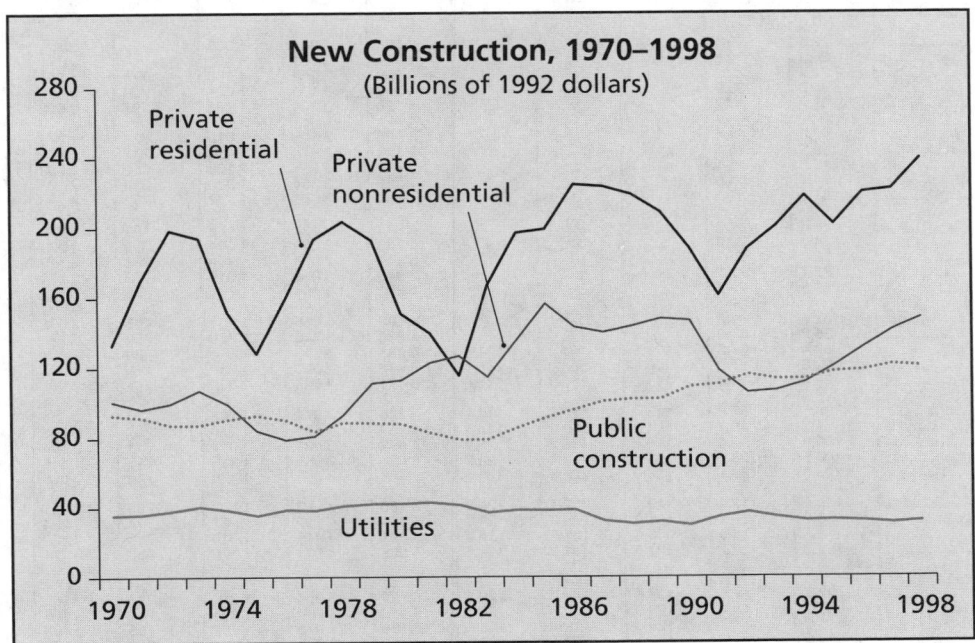

- The construction industry serves several different markets, with different reactions to the general business cycle. In 1998, private residential and nonresidential spending both continued on upward trends, while construction spending by governments and public utilities changed little.

- Residential spending is the most volatile, falling steeply just before and during recessions but responding swiftly to interest-rate reductions.

- Construction workers are relatively well-paid, averaging $16.59 per hour in 1998. Hourly pay was up 3.4 percent in 1998, exceeding the rate of consumer price increase.

- Other indicators confirmed the strength of the residential housing market in 1998. Housing starts, building permits, mobile home shipments, sales of new and existing homes, and median sales prices all increased.

Construction Costs, Prices, Employment, Hours, and Earnings

Year and month	Construction cost indexes (1992=100)		Producer price indexes (June 1986=100, not seasonally adjusted)			Employment, hours, and earnings (seasonally adjusted)								
						Employment (thousands)					Construction workers			
						All construction		General building contractors	Heavy construction, except building	Special trade contractors			Average earnings (dollars)	
	Fixed weight index	Implicit deflator	Inputs to construction industries	Maintenance and repair construction	New construction	Total	Construction workers				Average weekly hours	Aggregate weekly hours index (1982=100)	Hourly	Weekly
1970	28.4	28.4	.....	.....	.....	3 588	2 990	1 066	.....	.....	37.3	101.3	5.24	195.45
1971	30.4	30.3	.....	.....	.....	3 704	3 071	1 102	.....	.....	37.2	103.6	5.69	211.67
1972	32.4	32.2	.....	.....	.....	3 889	3 257	1 165	774	1 951	36.5	107.9	6.06	221.19
1973	35.3	35.0	.....	.....	.....	4 097	3 405	1 221	790	2 087	36.8	113.7	6.41	235.89
1974	39.7	39.7	.....	.....	.....	4 020	3 294	1 192	799	2 029	36.6	109.5	6.81	249.25
1975	43.2	43.4	.....	.....	.....	3 525	2 808	1 012	734	1 779	36.4	92.7	7.31	266.08
1976	45.5	45.5	.....	.....	.....	3 576	2 814	1 022	747	1 806	36.8	94.0	7.71	283.73
1977	49.2	49.1	.....	.....	.....	3 851	3 021	1 108	760	1 983	36.5	100.2	8.10	295.65
1978	54.4	54.6	.....	.....	.....	4 229	3 354	1 229	828	2 173	36.8	112.2	8.66	318.69
1979	61.3	61.1	.....	.....	.....	4 463	3 565	1 272	898	2 293	37.0	119.9	9.27	342.99
1980	68.6	67.8	.....	.....	.....	4 346	3 421	1 173	895	2 278	37.0	115.1	9.94	367.78
1981	74.0	72.9	.....	.....	.....	4 188	3 261	1 094	865	2 229	36.9	109.3	10.82	399.26
1982	76.0	75.7	.....	.....	.....	3 904	2 998	990	795	2 119	36.7	100.0	11.63	426.82
1983	77.7	77.1	.....	.....	.....	3 946	3 031	1 019	753	2 174	37.1	102.2	11.94	442.97
1984	80.6	79.7	.....	.....	.....	4 380	3 404	1 161	758	2 462	37.8	116.8	12.13	458.51
1985	82.9	81.8	.....	.....	.....	4 668	3 655	1 251	765	2 652	37.7	125.3	12.32	464.46
1986	86.2	84.8	.....	.....	.....	4 810	3 770	1 289	750	2 771	37.4	128.2	12.48	466.75
1987	89.4	87.9	101.5	101.3	101.6	4 958	3 870	1 318	739	2 901	37.8	132.7	12.71	480.44
1988	92.6	91.2	106.1	106.0	106.1	5 098	3 980	1 350	743	3 005	37.9	136.9	13.08	495.73
1989	95.8	94.8	111.0	110.9	111.0	5 171	4 035	1 332	767	3 072	37.9	138.9	13.54	513.17
1990	98.5	97.8	113.4	113.6	113.3	5 120	3 974	1 298	770	3 051	38.2	138.0	13.77	526.01
1991	99.3	98.7	114.8	115.1	114.6	4 650	3 549	1 140	727	2 783	38.1	122.8	14.00	533.40
1992	100.0	100.0	116.7	116.2	116.9	4 492	3 431	1 077	711	2 704	38.0	118.4	14.15	537.70
1993	103.7	103.8	121.4	119.4	122.2	4 668	3 589	1 120	713	2 836	38.5	125.4	14.38	553.63
1994	108.0	108.1	125.0	122.3	125.9	4 986	3 858	1 188	740	3 058	38.9	136.4	14.73	573.00
1995	112.5	112.6	129.1	127.1	129.8	5 160	3 993	1 207	752	3 201	38.9	140.9	15.09	587.00
1996	115.0	115.2	131.2	129.3	131.8	5 418	4 199	1 257	777	3 384	39.0	148.7	15.47	603.33
1997	118.7	118.9	133.8	131.5	134.6	5 691	4 415	1 310	799	3 582	39.0	156.2	16.04	625.56
1998	122.0	122.2	133.5	131.3	134.3	5 985	4 641	1 372	838	3 774	38.8	163.7	16.59	643.69
1995:														
January	111.7	111.6	127.6	125.2	128.5	5 129	3 984	1 214	748	3 167	39.1	141.5	14.78	577.90
February	111.7	111.7	127.9	125.7	128.7	5 133	4 004	1 204	744	3 185	37.8	137.5	14.96	565.49
March	111.7	111.7	128.6	126.4	129.3	5 130	3 978	1 206	755	3 169	38.9	140.5	14.98	582.72
April	111.8	111.9	129.1	127.1	129.8	5 136	3 974	1 204	750	3 182	38.8	140.0	15.01	582.39
May	112.1	112.0	129.3	127.4	130.0	5 113	3 956	1 196	744	3 173	38.0	136.5	15.05	571.90
June	112.6	112.5	129.2	127.5	129.8	5 141	3 978	1 199	749	3 193	38.9	140.5	15.11	587.78
July	112.6	112.6	129.5	127.6	130.2	5 153	3 987	1 202	751	3 200	38.9	140.8	15.12	588.17
August	112.6	112.7	129.7	127.8	130.4	5 178	4 006	1 205	754	3 219	38.8	141.2	15.13	587.04
September	113.0	113.1	130.0	127.9	130.6	5 215	4 035	1 212	761	3 242	38.7	141.8	15.16	586.69
October	113.3	113.4	129.6	127.6	130.2	5 236	4 054	1 217	765	3 254	39.1	144.0	15.18	593.54
November	113.3	113.4	129.2	127.4	129.9	5 241	4 049	1 221	760	3 260	38.8	142.7	15.24	591.31
December	113.3	113.5	129.2	127.5	129.8	5 228	4 033	1 222	753	3 253	38.6	141.4	15.10	582.86
1996:														
January	113.6	113.8	129.4	127.8	129.9	5 212	4 057	1 221	741	3 250	37.9	139.6	15.35	581.77
February	113.8	113.9	129.4	127.8	130.0	5 299	4 119	1 234	764	3 301	39.0	145.9	15.25	594.75
March	113.8	114.1	129.8	128.2	130.4	5 337	4 140	1 241	777	3 319	38.8	145.9	15.27	592.48
April	113.7	114.0	130.3	128.7	130.9	5 353	4 145	1 246	770	3 337	38.9	146.4	15.31	595.56
May	114.1	114.2	131.3	129.5	132.0	5 381	4 168	1 254	769	3 358	38.5	145.7	15.37	591.75
June	114.5	114.8	131.5	129.5	132.2	5 417	4 197	1 260	779	3 378	39.0	148.7	15.43	601.77
July	115.2	115.5	131.2	129.4	131.9	5 437	4 214	1 259	781	3 397	38.7	148.1	15.48	599.08
August	115.5	115.7	131.6	129.7	132.3	5 468	4 237	1 268	784	3 416	39.0	150.1	15.53	605.67
September	116.0	116.0	132.3	130.2	133.1	5 488	4 250	1 271	784	3 433	39.0	150.5	15.58	607.62
October	116.3	116.2	132.0	130.1	132.7	5 517	4 280	1 275	789	3 453	38.9	151.2	15.59	606.45
November	116.4	116.3	132.6	130.4	133.3	5 545	4 300	1 283	791	3 471	39.0	152.3	15.62	609.18
December	116.7	116.6	132.5	130.4	133.3	5 558	4 312	1 288	789	3 481	39.0	152.7	15.62	609.18
1997:														
January	117.1	117.2	132.9	130.7	133.7	5 558	4 320	1 287	794	3 477	38.1	149.5	15.82	602.74
February	117.0	117.1	133.4	131.1	134.2	5 601	4 343	1 296	800	3 505	38.8	153.0	15.87	615.76
March	117.6	117.7	133.6	131.2	134.5	5 658	-4 407	1 306	805	3 547	39.1	156.5	15.83	618.95
April	117.8	117.9	134.0	131.6	134.8	5 647	4 371	1 303	793	3 551	39.0	154.8	15.89	619.71
May	118.1	118.3	134.3	131.8	135.2	5 669	4 396	1 305	797	3 567	39.4	157.3	15.94	628.04
June	118.3	118.5	134.2	131.7	135.0	5 670	4 392	1 303	793	3 574	39.1	156.0	15.99	625.21
July	118.6	118.9	134.2	131.7	135.0	5 687	4 406	1 310	791	3 586	39.0	156.1	16.00	624.00
August	118.9	119.3	134.2	131.9	135.1	5 712	4 427	1 311	796	3 605	38.9	156.4	16.07	625.12
September	119.5	119.6	134.1	131.8	134.9	5 734	4 442	1 313	800	3 621	39.3	158.5	16.12	633.52
October	119.9	119.9	133.7	131.5	134.5	5 745	4 449	1 316	800	3 629	39.0	157.6	16.19	631.41
November	120.6	120.4	133.8	131.5	134.6	5 767	4 474	1 325	798	3 644	38.4	156.0	16.23	623.23
December	120.7	120.4	133.5	131.3	134.3	5 813	4 505	1 335	813	3 665	38.9	159.2	16.32	634.85
1998:														
January	120.9	120.7	133.2	131.0	134.0	5 879	4 581	1 341	824	3 714	39.1	162.7	16.34	638.89
February	120.5	120.7	133.3	131.0	134.1	5 885	4 563	1 346	817	3 722	39.3	162.9	16.39	644.13
March	120.5	120.7	133.3	131.0	134.1	5 879	4 570	1 347	823	3 709	38.7	160.6	16.43	635.84
April	120.9	120.9	133.6	131.3	134.4	5 943	4 592	1 357	833	3 753	38.9	162.2	16.48	641.07
May	121.1	121.2	133.6	131.5	134.4	5 932	4 594	1 361	833	3 738	38.9	162.3	16.50	641.85
June	121.8	121.8	133.5	131.3	134.2	5 962	4 617	1 369	835	3 758	38.8	162.7	16.54	641.75
July	122.2	122.1	133.8	131.6	134.6	5 990	4 637	1 377	842	3 771	39.2	165.1	16.63	651.90
August	122.6	122.5	133.9	131.5	134.8	6 005	4 647	1 381	842	3 782	39.2	165.4	16.67	653.46
September	122.8	122.8	133.8	131.5	134.6	6 009	4 641	1 382	837	3 790	38.6	162.7	16.60	640.76
October	123.1	123.3	133.5	131.3	134.2	6 042	4 675	1 389	843	3 810	39.2	164.4	16.72	655.42
November	123.4	123.8	133.3	131.1	134.0	6 085	4 716	1 394	850	3 841	39.1	167.5	16.76	655.32
December	124.1	124.3	133.1	130.9	133.8	6 173	4 787	1 404	876	3 893	39.4	171.3	16.80	661.92

Employment, Hours, and Earnings of Construction Workers

(Not seasonally adjusted)

Year and month	General building contractors				Heavy construction, except building				Special trade contractors			
	Employment (thousands)	Average weekly hours	Average earnings (dollars)		Employment (thousands)	Average weekly hours	Average earnings (dollars)		Employment (thousands)	Average weekly hours	Average earnings (dollars)	
			Hourly	Weekly			Hourly	Weekly			Hourly	Weekly
1970	910	36.3	5.02	182.23	.....	.....	.....	.....	.....	.....	.....	.....
1971	936	36.1	5.33	192.41	.....	.....	.....	.....	1 615	35.8	6.58	235.56
1972	976	35.7	5.58	199.21	666	39.3	5.57	218.90	1 731	36.1	6.97	251.62
1973	1 009	35.8	5.87	210.15	665	39.9	5.85	233.42	1 663	35.8	7.36	263.49
1974	967	35.9	6.24	224.02	663	39.7	6.31	250.51				
1975	799	35.9	6.78	243.40	593	39.2	6.81	266.95	1 416	35.5	7.85	278.68
1976	800	36.4	7.15	260.26	597	39.3	7.31	287.28	1 417	36.0	8.20	295.20
1977	865	36.3	7.52	272.98	594	38.8	7.56	293.33	1 562	35.8	8.65	309.67
1978	955	35.8	8.00	286.40	669	40.1	8.10	324.81	1 730	36.2	9.26	335.21
1979	989	35.9	8.61	309.10	743	40.2	8.65	347.73	1 833	36.4	9.90	360.36
1980	900	36.1	9.22	332.84	720	40.3	9.20	370.76	1 802	36.2	10.63	384.81
1981	825	36.0	9.85	354.60	693	40.1	10.31	413.43	1 743	36.1	11.50	415.15
1982	734	36.2	10.53	381.19	631	40.0	11.45	458.00	1 632	35.7	12.20	435.54
1983	751	36.6	10.73	392.72	604	40.4	11.86	479.14	1 676	36.2	12.53	453.59
1984	862	37.1	10.89	404.02	618	41.5	11.90	493.85	1 925	36.8	12.78	470.30
1985	935	37.1	11.23	416.63	629	41.4	12.08	500.11	2 092	36.9	12.89	475.64
1986	953	37.0	11.43	422.91	623	40.8	12.00	489.60	2 194	36.7	13.09	480.40
1987	963	37.3	11.72	437.16	618	41.5	12.07	500.91	2 290	37.0	13.31	492.47
1988	989	37.5	12.18	456.75	621	41.5	12.46	517.09	2 370	37.1	13.64	506.04
1989	969	37.5	12.71	476.63	639	41.5	13.19	547.39	2 427	37.1	13.98	518.66
1990	938	37.7	13.01	490.48	643	42.0	13.34	560.28	2 393	37.4	14.20	531.08
1991	811	37.6	13.27	498.95	600	41.6	13.77	572.83	2 137	37.4	14.35	536.69
1992	761	37.5	13.45	504.38	588	41.6	13.96	580.74	2 083	37.2	14.47	538.28
1993	790	37.7	13.64	514.23	593	42.1	14.10	593.61	2 206	37.8	14.73	556.79
1994	843	38.1	13.97	532.26	618	42.6	14.44	615.14	2 397	38.3	15.08	577.56
1995	856	38.3	14.33	548.84	626	42.5	14.65	622.63	2 511	38.1	15.47	589.41
1996	888	38.2	14.68	560.78	649	42.8	15.10	646.28	2 662	38.3	15.83	606.29
1997	924	38.2	15.23	581.79	667	42.5	15.58	662.15	2 824	38.4	16.42	630.53
1998	963	38.0	15.91	604.58	703	42.3	16.10	681.03	2 976	38.3	16.94	648.80
1995:												
January	803	37.7	14.17	534.21	503	40.6	13.82	561.09	2 239	37.1	15.12	560.95
February	780	37.1	14.23	527.93	499	39.3	14.15	556.10	2 191	36.4	15.28	556.19
March	791	37.9	14.15	536.29	539	41.2	14.26	587.51	2 275	37.5	15.31	574.13
April	820	37.5	14.21	532.88	603	40.7	14.38	585.27	2 406	37.0	15.33	567.21
May	845	38.0	14.24	541.12	648	41.8	14.56	608.61	2 513	37.8	15.39	581.74
June	886	38.5	14.14	544.39	676	43.8	14.76	646.49	2 618	38.9	15.42	599.84
July	906	38.7	14.26	551.86	688	44.6	14.90	664.54	2 675	39.3	15.51	609.54
August	912	38.8	14.31	555.23	697	44.1	14.95	659.30	2 704	39.0	15.58	607.62
September	898	38.9	14.51	564.44	710	44.4	15.14	672.22	2 684	39.1	15.69	613.48
October	894	39.1	14.57	569.69	709	44.8	15.09	676.03	2 684	39.2	15.69	615.05
November	880	38.3	14.57	558.03	659	41.7	14.76	615.49	2 630	38.0	15.63	593.94
December	857	38.0	14.58	554.04	583	41.2	14.27	587.92	2 511	37.4	15.58	582.69
1996:												
January	803	36.7	14.67	538.39	498	39.8	14.52	577.90	2 320	36.1	15.65	564.97
February	798	38.1	14.57	555.12	517	41.2	14.35	591.22	2 339	37.6	15.57	585.43
March	811	37.9	14.58	552.58	558	41.4	14.35	594.09	2 393	37.5	15.57	583.88
April	846	38.4	14.56	559.10	623	42.4	14.70	623.28	2 534	37.8	15.58	588.92
May	884	38.2	14.61	558.10	674	42.2	14.91	629.20	2 665	38.3	15.64	599.01
June	926	38.6	14.50	559.70	704	43.7	15.20	664.24	2 767	38.9	15.68	609.95
July	944	38.6	14.58	562.79	717	44.2	15.45	682.89	2 846	39.1	15.84	619.34
August	951	38.6	14.61	563.95	727	44.2	15.50	685.10	2 870	39.2	15.92	624.06
September	934	38.5	14.87	572.50	734	44.5	15.68	697.76	2 849	39.0	16.08	627.12
October	930	38.6	14.79	570.89	731	44.5	15.69	698.21	2 850	39.2	16.10	631.12
November	924	38.1	14.84	565.40	689	42.4	15.23	645.75	2 807	38.2	16.01	611.58
December	906	38.1	15.00	571.50	616	41.5	14.76	612.54	2 704	38.1	16.14	614.93
1997:												
January	854	36.2	15.04	544.45	535	38.3	15.01	574.88	2 496	36.1	16.18	584.10
February	849	37.5	15.09	565.88	553	39.6	15.09	597.56	2 511	37.1	16.08	596.57
March	859	38.0	15.05	571.90	581	41.3	15.01	619.91	2 574	37.9	16.10	610.19
April	888	38.4	15.05	577.92	642	42.2	15.24	643.13	2 702	38.1	16.17	616.08
May	919	38.7	15.06	582.82	702	44.1	15.44	680.90	2 837	38.9	16.24	631.74
June	955	38.6	14.95	577.07	715	43.5	15.59	678.17	2 930	39.0	16.31	636.09
July	979	38.8	15.04	583.55	725	44.6	15.76	702.90	3 009	39.5	16.43	648.99
August	981	38.6	15.17	585.56	736	44.1	15.79	696.34	3 032	39.1	16.53	646.32
September	959	38.9	15.39	598.67	744	44.8	16.08	720.38	3 006	39.3	16.66	654.74
October	958	38.7	15.55	601.79	742	44.2	16.09	711.18	2 996	39.1	16.66	651.41
November	950	37.6	15.58	585.81	695	39.4	15.70	618.58	2 947	37.6	16.68	627.17
December	935	38.3	15.69	600.93	632	40.9	15.55	636.00	2 850	38.1	16.82	640.84
1998:												
January	889	37.1	15.64	580.24	556	39.6	15.23	603.11	2 680	37.1	16.72	620.31
February	882	37.7	15.67	590.76	563	41.5	15.31	635.37	2 678	37.3	16.64	620.67
March	884	37.5	15.76	591.00	595	41.3	15.40	636.02	2 692	37.4	16.71	624.95
April	922	37.6	15.84	595.58	672	41.3	15.64	645.93	2 867	37.5	16.72	627.00
May	953	38.1	15.76	600.46	730	43.4	15.92	690.93	2 979	38.7	16.80	650.16
June	999	38.1	15.67	597.03	756	42.8	16.04	686.51	3 081	38.6	16.84	650.02
July	1 026	38.8	15.84	614.59	772	44.6	16.46	734.12	3 160	39.5	16.98	670.71
August	1 028	38.8	15.99	620.41	783	44.7	16.55	739.79	3 178	39.5	17.08	674.66
September	1 000	36.7	16.08	590.14	780	40.5	16.50	668.25	3 132	37.1	17.10	634.41
October	1 004	38.8	16.20	628.56	785	44.6	16.71	745.27	3 136	39.3	17.15	674.00
November	990	37.9	16.18	613.22	747	41.2	16.42	676.50	3 098	38.1	17.13	652.65
December	975	38.5	16.24	625.24	690	41.2	16.25	669.50	3 029	38.8	17.23	668.52

New Construction Put in Place

(Billions of dollars, not seasonally adjusted)

Year and month	Total	Private											Public				
		Total	Residential		Nonresidential buildings [1]					Public utilities			Total	Housing and redevel- opment	Industrial	Military facilities	High- ways and streets
			Total	New housing units	Total	Industrial	Office	Hotels, motels	Other commer- cial buildings	Total	Tele- commun- ications						
1970	105.9	78.0	35.9	27.1	28.2	9.3	9.9	1.5	11.6	11.1	3.0		27.9	1.1	0.3	0.7	10.0
1971	122.4	92.7	48.5	38.7	29.3	7.8	11.8	1.5	13.8	12.0	3.0		29.7	1.1	0.4	0.9	10.7
1972	139.1	109.1	60.7	50.1	32.4	6.7	6.8	2.2	9.8	13.3	3.3		30.0	0.9	0.4	1.1	10.4
1973	153.8	121.4	65.1	54.6	37.6	9.0	7.8	2.5	11.4	15.3	4.0		32.4	0.9	0.5	1.2	10.5
1974	155.2	117.0	56.0	43.4	39.9	11.5	8.0	1.8	11.9	16.9	4.3		38.1	1.0	0.6	1.2	12.1
1975	152.6	109.3	51.6	36.3	35.4	11.7	6.5	1.2	9.5	17.6	3.8		43.3	1.4	0.7	1.4	13.2
1976	172.1	128.2	68.3	50.8	34.6	10.5	6.3	1.0	9.7	20.2	3.9		44.0	1.3	0.7	1.6	12.4
1977	200.5	157.4	92.0	72.2	38.3	11.3	7.0	1.1	11.6	21.4	4.5		43.1	1.5	0.8	1.4	12.5
1978	239.9	189.7	109.8	85.6	48.8	16.2	8.7	1.4	14.7	24.6	5.6		50.2	1.4	0.9	1.5	14.2
1979	272.9	216.2	116.4	89.3	64.8	22.0	12.6	2.5	19.0	28.0	6.9		56.7	1.7	1.1	1.7	17.1
1980	273.9	210.3	100.4	69.6	72.5	20.5	17.8	3.4	20.5	30.9	7.8		63.7	2.0	1.4	1.9	18.2
1981	289.1	224.4	99.2	69.4	85.6	25.4	20.8	4.3	20.8	33.7	8.2		64.7	2.4	1.7	2.0	18.4
1982	279.3	216.3	84.7	57.0	92.7	26.1	31.3	4.8	17.8	33.9	8.5		63.1	2.3	1.6	2.2	17.3
1983	311.6	248.1	125.5	94.7	87.1	19.5	28.3	6.1	18.9	30.8	7.6		63.5	2.6	1.8	2.5	17.9
1984	369.0	298.8	153.9	113.8	107.7	20.9	35.6	8.0	28.0	32.2	8.1		70.2	2.7	1.8	2.8	21.6
1985	401.4	323.6	158.5	114.7	127.5	24.1	43.6	8.8	35.7	32.7	8.4		77.8	2.9	2.0	3.2	23.7
1986	429.9	345.3	187.2	133.2	120.9	21.0	39.4	8.9	35.8	32.9	9.1		84.6	3.0	1.7	3.9	25.3
1987	441.7	351.0	194.7	139.9	123.3	21.2	36.9	8.9	37.3	27.9	9.2		90.7	3.3	1.5	4.3	27.1
1988	455.6	360.9	198.1	139.0	130.9	23.2	39.3	8.3	38.9	27.4	9.6		94.7	3.3	1.4	3.6	29.1
1989	469.8	371.6	196.6	139.2	140.0	28.8	40.1	9.3	39.8	30.1	9.6		98.2	3.4	1.3	3.5	28.8
1990	468.5	361.1	182.9	128.0	143.5	33.6	35.1	10.7	40.1	28.9	9.8		107.5	3.8	1.4	2.7	32.1
1991	424.2	314.1	157.8	110.6	116.6	31.4	26.0	6.9	29.4	34.0	9.0		110.1	3.6	1.8	1.8	32.0
1992	452.1	336.2	187.8	129.6	105.7	29.0	20.3	3.7	29.2	36.8	9.0		115.9	4.1	1.9	2.5	33.1
1993	478.7	362.7	210.5	144.1	110.6	26.5	20.9	4.6	32.5	34.9	9.6		116.0	4.0	1.7	2.5	34.0
1994	519.5	399.3	238.9	167.9	120.3	28.9	22.2	4.6	37.6	34.1	10.1		120.2	3.8	1.5	2.3	37.4
1995	537.4	407.5	230.7	162.9	135.0	32.5	25.6	7.1	42.7	35.9	11.1		129.9	4.7	1.5	3.0	37.6
1996	583.4	449.0	256.5	179.4	150.4	32.7	27.9	10.9	48.2	36.1	11.8		134.5	4.1	1.4	2.6	39.9
1997	618.2	475.1	265.9	187.3	167.6	31.4	34.3	12.9	51.8	35.5	11.7		143.1	3.8	1.0	2.6	44.3
1998	665.4	520.1	294.3	213.9	181.9	32.3	41.5	14.9	53.8	37.3	12.4		145.4	4.0	1.0	2.6	44.8
1995:																	
January	36.1	28.1	15.8	11.7	9.3	2.2	1.9	0.5	2.8	.....	0.8		7.9	0.4	0.1	0.2	1.5
February	35.0	27.3	14.7	10.8	9.7	2.4	1.9	0.5	2.9	.....	0.7		7.7	0.3	0.1	0.2	1.4
March	39.6	30.9	17.0	12.3	10.5	2.6	2.1	0.6	3.3	.....	0.9		8.7	0.4	0.1	0.3	1.8
April	42.2	32.5	18.1	12.6	10.9	2.8	2.2	0.5	3.3	.....	0.9		9.7	0.4	0.1	0.2	2.3
May	45.8	34.6	19.6	13.3	11.4	2.9	2.4	0.6	3.4	.....	0.9		11.1	0.4	0.1	0.2	3.3
June	48.7	36.3	20.7	13.9	11.8	2.8	2.2	0.6	3.9	.....	1.1		12.4	0.4	0.1	0.3	3.8
July	49.2	36.9	21.3	14.6	11.9	2.8	2.3	0.6	3.8	.....	1.0		12.3	0.4	0.1	0.3	4.1
August	51.5	37.9	22.1	15.3	12.0	2.7	2.3	0.6	3.9	.....	1.0		13.7	0.4	0.1	0.3	4.8
September	51.1	37.5	21.6	15.5	*12.2	2.8	2.2	0.6	4.1	.....	0.9		13.5	0.4	0.2	0.4	4.4
October	50.0	37.5	21.6	15.4	12.2	2.8	2.1	0.6	4.1	.....	1.0		12.5	0.4	0.1	0.2	4.5
November	46.9	35.7	20.5	14.8	11.8	2.8	2.0	0.8	3.8	.....	1.0		11.1	0.4	0.1	0.3	3.3
December	41.4	32.1	17.6	12.7	11.4	2.8	2.0	0.8	3.5	.....	0.9		9.3	0.4	0.1	0.3	2.3
1996:																	
January	37.7	29.3	15.9	11.7	10.4	2.5	1.8	0.7	3.2	.....	0.8		8.5	0.4	0.1	0.3	1.7
February	36.2	28.4	15.2	11.2	10.6	2.5	1.9	0.8	3.3	.....	0.8		7.9	0.3	0.1	0.2	1.7
March	40.5	31.9	18.1	13.2	10.9	2.5	1.9	0.8	3.4	.....	0.9		8.6	0.3	0.1	0.2	1.8
April	45.6	35.5	20.3	14.3	11.8	2.6	2.1	0.9	3.7	.....	1.0		10.1	0.3	0.1	0.2	2.6
May	49.8	38.1	22.4	15.3	12.1	2.6	2.4	0.8	4.0	.....	1.0		11.7	0.4	0.1	0.2	3.5
June	53.0	40.9	24.2	16.4	12.9	2.8	2.5	0.9	4.1	.....	0.9		12.2	0.3	0.1	0.2	3.9
July	54.2	41.1	24.7	16.9	12.7	2.6	2.4	0.9	4.1	.....	0.9		13.1	0.4	0.1	0.2	4.5
August	56.4	43.0	25.3	17.3	13.5	2.6	2.5	1.0	4.6	.....	1.1		13.5	0.3	0.1	0.2	4.6
September	56.5	42.3	24.4	17.1	13.9	2.9	2.6	1.0	4.6	.....	0.9		14.3	0.4	0.2	0.3	4.8
October	55.8	42.5	24.1	16.7	14.4	3.2	2.6	1.0	4.7	.....	1.1		13.2	0.4	0.1	0.2	4.8
November	52.2	40.4	22.7	16.0	13.9	3.0	2.6	1.0	4.4	.....	1.1		11.8	0.4	0.1	0.2	3.5
December	45.4	35.7	19.1	13.4	13.1	2.8	2.5	1.1	4.0	.....	1.3		9.7	0.3	0.1	0.2	2.5
1997:																	
January	40.6	32.1	17.0	12.3	12.2	2.4	2.5	0.9	3.8	.....	0.8		8.5	0.3	0.1	0.2	1.8
February	39.8	31.2	16.4	12.0	12.5	2.4	2.6	1.0	3.8	.....	0.8		8.6	0.3	0.1	0.2	1.9
March	44.2	34.6	19.3	14.0	12.7	2.3	2.5	1.0	3.9	.....	0.9		9.6	0.3	0.1	0.2	2.2
April	48.4	37.7	21.2	14.8	13.2	2.4	2.5	1.1	4.1	.....	1.0		10.7	0.3	0.1	0.2	3.1
May	52.4	40.5	23.3	15.9	13.7	2.5	2.6	1.2	4.3	.....	1.0		11.9	0.3	0.1	0.2	3.8
June	55.8	42.5	24.5	16.6	14.2	2.6	2.8	1.2	4.5	.....	1.0		13.3	0.3	0.1	0.2	4.6
July	58.2	44.1	25.1	17.2	14.9	2.7	3.0	1.2	4.7	.....	1.1		14.1	0.3	0.1	0.2	5.0
August	60.1	45.3	25.5	17.7	15.3	2.8	3.1	1.1	4.9	.....	1.0		14.9	0.3	0.1	0.2	5.4
September	59.6	44.7	24.9	17.8	15.4	2.9	3.1	1.1	4.9	.....	1.1		14.9	0.4	0.1	0.3	5.1
October	58.2	44.2	24.9	17.7	15.2	2.8	3.3	1.1	4.7	.....	1.1		14.0	0.4	0.1	0.2	4.9
November	53.3	41.2	23.5	16.9	14.5	2.7	3.2	1.1	4.3	.....	1.0		12.1	0.3	0.1	0.2	3.9
December	47.5	37.0	20.1	14.5	14.0	2.8	3.1	1.1	4.0	.....	1.1		10.5	0.3	0.1	0.2	2.8
1998:																	
January	42.7	33.9	18.3	13.5	12.9	2.4	3.1	1.0	3.6	.....	0.8		8.9	0.3	0.1	0.2	1.9
February	41.7	33.0	17.5	13.0	13.0	2.4	3.1	1.0	3.6	.....	0.9		8.7	0.3	0.1	0.2	1.9
March	47.3	37.8	20.9	15.5	14.0	2.8	3.1	1.1	4.0	.....	1.1		9.5	0.3	0.1	0.2	2.3
April	52.1	41.2	23.1	16.6	14.8	2.7	3.4	1.2	4.2	.....	1.0		10.9	0.3	0.1	0.2	3.1
May	55.2	43.6	25.1	17.6	14.9	2.7	3.5	1.1	4.4	.....	1.0		11.6	0.3	0.1	0.2	3.5
June	61.9	48.1	27.1	19.0	16.1	2.8	3.7	1.3	4.8	.....	1.1		13.8	0.4	0.1	0.2	4.6
July	63.2	48.7	28.2	20.1	15.7	2.6	3.5	1.3	4.9	.....	1.1		14.5	0.4	0.1	0.3	4.9
August	64.4	49.4	28.7	20.4	16.2	2.9	3.5	1.4	5.0	.....	1.1		15.0	0.3	0.1	0.2	5.3
September	64.0	48.5	28.1	20.6	16.3	2.9	3.6	1.4	5.0	.....	1.1		15.5	0.4	0.1	0.2	5.4
October	62.1	48.1	27.9	20.4	16.4	2.8	3.8	1.5	5.0	.....	1.2		14.0	0.3	0.1	0.2	5.2
November	58.5	46.2	26.6	19.9	16.1	2.7	3.7	1.4	4.9	.....	1.0		12.2	0.3	0.1	0.2	3.7
December	52.4	41.6	22.8	17.2	15.5	2.7	3.7	1.3	4.5	.....	1.1		10.8	0.3	0.1	0.2	2.7

1. Includes categories not shown separately.

New Construction Put in Place—*Continued*

(Billions of dollars, seasonally adjusted annual rate)

Year and month	Total	Private									Public				
		Total	Residential		Nonresidential buildings [1]					Tele-commun-ications	Total	Housing and redevel-opment	Industrial	Military facilities	Highways and streets
			Total	New housing units	Total	Industrial	Office	Hotels, motels	Other commer-cial buildings						
1970	105.9	78.0	35.9	27.1	28.2	9.3	9.9	1.5	11.6	3.0	27.9	1.1	0.3	0.7	10.0
1971	122.4	92.7	48.5	38.7	29.3	7.8	11.8	1.5	13.8	3.0	29.7	1.1	0.4	0.9	10.7
1972	139.1	109.1	60.7	50.1	32.4	6.7	6.8	2.2	9.8	3.3	30.0	0.9	0.4	1.1	10.4
1973	153.8	121.4	65.1	54.6	37.6	9.0	7.8	2.5	11.4	4.0	32.4	0.9	0.5	1.2	10.5
1974	155.2	117.0	56.0	43.4	39.9	11.5	8.0	1.8	11.9	4.3	38.1	1.0	0.6	1.2	12.1
1975	152.6	109.3	51.6	36.3	35.4	11.7	6.5	1.2	9.5	3.8	43.3	1.4	0.7	1.4	13.2
1976	172.1	128.2	68.3	50.8	34.6	10.5	6.3	1.0	9.7	3.9	44.0	1.3	0.7	1.6	12.4
1977	200.5	157.4	92.0	72.2	38.3	11.3	7.0	1.1	11.6	4.5	43.1	1.5	0.8	1.4	12.5
1978	239.9	189.7	109.8	85.6	48.8	16.2	8.7	1.4	14.7	5.6	50.2	1.4	0.9	1.5	14.2
1979	272.9	216.2	116.4	89.3	64.8	22.0	12.6	2.5	19.0	6.9	56.7	1.7	1.1	1.7	17.1
1980	273.9	210.3	100.4	69.6	72.5	20.5	17.8	3.4	20.5	7.8	63.7	2.0	1.4	1.9	18.2
1981	289.1	224.4	99.2	69.4	85.6	25.4	23.5	4.3	20.8	8.2	64.7	2.4	1.7	2.0	18.4
1982	279.3	216.3	84.7	57.0	92.7	26.1	31.3	4.8	17.8	8.5	63.1	2.3	1.6	2.2	17.3
1983	311.6	248.1	125.5	94.7	87.1	19.5	28.3	6.1	18.9	7.6	63.5	2.6	1.8	2.5	17.9
1984	369.0	298.8	153.9	113.8	107.7	20.9	35.6	8.0	28.0	8.1	70.2	2.7	1.8	2.8	21.6
1985	401.4	323.6	158.5	114.7	127.5	24.1	43.6	8.8	35.7	8.4	77.8	2.9	2.0	3.2	23.7
1986	429.9	345.3	187.2	133.2	120.9	21.0	39.4	8.9	35.8	9.1	84.6	3.0	1.7	3.9	25.3
1987	441.7	351.0	194.7	139.9	123.3	21.2	36.9	8.9	37.3	9.2	90.7	3.3	1.5	4.3	27.1
1988	455.6	360.9	198.1	139.0	130.9	23.2	39.3	8.3	38.9	9.6	94.7	3.3	1.4	3.6	29.1
1989	469.8	371.6	196.6	139.2	140.0	28.8	40.1	9.3	39.8	9.6	98.2	3.4	1.3	3.5	28.8
1990	468.5	361.1	182.9	128.0	143.5	33.6	35.1	10.7	40.1	9.8	107.5	3.8	1.4	2.7	32.1
1991	424.2	314.1	157.8	110.6	116.6	31.4	26.0	6.9	29.4	9.0	110.1	3.6	1.8	1.8	32.0
1992	452.1	336.2	187.8	129.6	105.7	29.0	20.3	3.7	29.2	9.0	115.9	4.1	1.9	2.5	37.9
1993	478.7	362.7	210.5	144.1	110.6	26.5	20.9	4.6	32.5	9.6	116.0	4.0	1.7	2.5	34.3
1994	519.5	399.3	238.9	167.9	120.3	28.9	22.2	4.6	37.6	10.1	120.2	3.8	1.5	2.3	37.4
1995	537.4	407.5	230.7	162.9	135.0	32.5	25.6	7.1	42.7	11.1	129.9	4.7	1.5	3.0	37.6
1996	583.4	449.0	256.5	179.4	150.4	32.7	27.9	10.9	48.2	11.8	134.5	4.1	1.4	2.6	39.9
1997	618.2	475.1	265.9	187.3	167.6	31.4	34.3	12.9	51.8	11.7	143.1	3.8	1.0	2.6	44.3
1998	665.4	520.1	294.3	213.9	181.9	32.3	41.5	14.9	53.8	12.4	145.4	4.0	1.0	2.6	44.8
1995:															
January	535.6	408.0	238.7	169.5	127.0	29.9	24.4	6.1	40.3	11.1	127.6	4.4	1.7	2.8	36.8
February	538.5	413.0	235.9	166.2	131.8	32.4	24.5	6.2	42.0	10.5	125.5	4.5	1.7	2.6	34.3
March	541.2	411.7	233.9	163.9	134.4	32.5	25.5	7.4	43.4	11.1	129.5	4.6	1.6	3.2	37.6
April	537.3	407.3	228.1	159.7	136.2	35.1	26.2	5.6	42.3	11.9	130.0	4.6	1.6	3.0	36.3
May	531.6	401.9	225.0	157.2	134.7	34.1	27.6	6.2	40.2	10.5	129.7	4.4	1.4	2.9	37.3
June	533.0	400.2	222.8	155.5	135.5	32.8	26.2	6.4	43.4	11.7	132.8	5.0	1.4	2.9	37.7
July	535.6	407.6	225.1	158.2	139.3	34.0	28.0	6.9	43.1	12.4	128.0	4.8	1.5	3.2	37.2
August	532.1	401.3	228.0	161.5	132.7	31.2	26.0	6.8	41.6	10.9	130.8	5.1	1.6	3.1	38.7
September	536.8	406.2	230.5	163.8	135.0	31.8	25.3	7.3	43.0	11.1	130.6	4.6	1.6	3.3	37.6
October	538.8	408.8	232.4	165.8	136.1	31.4	24.4	7.7	44.0	10.9	130.0	4.8	1.4	2.2	39.1
November	541.3	410.5	235.1	167.1	136.8	32.6	23.8	9.1	43.9	10.8	130.8	4.8	1.4	3.2	37.4
December	549.4	419.6	238.7	169.9	140.3	32.7	25.2	10.0	44.7	10.5	129.8	4.7	1.3	3.3	38.7
1996:															
January	560.2	424.6	240.4	170.3	142.3	33.8	23.4	9.6	46.4	11.6	135.6	4.8	1.3	3.3	39.0
February	557.0	427.6	243.8	172.4	141.9	32.7	23.8	9.7	46.9	11.6	129.4	4.2	1.3	3.0	40.4
March	559.3	429.9	247.6	174.8	140.0	32.3	24.0	9.9	45.5	10.9	129.4	4.0	1.5	2.5	38.1
April	575.2	440.5	254.2	179.5	143.8	32.5	25.0	10.4	47.5	11.6	134.7	3.8	1.5	2.8	39.8
May	580.4	442.3	257.7	181.4	143.6	30.8	26.4	9.8	47.5	11.4	138.1	4.5	1.5	2.7	39.5
June	583.9	452.3	260.7	183.6	150.7	32.5	30.4	10.6	46.5	10.7	131.6	3.7	1.6	2.5	38.6
July	580.1	447.1	260.3	182.0	147.4	31.2	28.6	10.4	46.7	10.7	133.1	4.2	1.6	2.3	39.6
August	585.9	454.2	260.9	182.0	151.3	30.3	29.0	11.7	49.2	11.7	131.7	4.0	1.7	2.3	38.3
September	594.3	456.7	261.1	181.5	154.2	32.6	30.0	11.7	48.6	11.4	137.6	4.3	1.7	2.6	41.0
October	600.6	463.8	259.8	180.4	161.1	36.0	30.1	11.7	50.9	11.8	136.8	4.0	0.8	2.6	41.3
November	606.3	466.6	260.7	180.8	162.5	34.8	30.8	12.2	50.9	12.7	139.7	4.1	1.1	2.4	41.0
December	599.8	465.6	259.8	179.5	161.0	32.1	31.1	12.6	50.6	14.5	134.2	3.6	1.0	2.3	42.0
1997:															
January	603.7	466.8	259.4	179.7	166.1	32.3	31.8	12.4	54.3	11.3	136.9	3.4	1.1	2.6	41.8
February	614.4	472.6	264.0	184.7	168.7	32.4	34.0	12.5	54.0	11.2	141.8	3.6	1.0	2.5	44.0
March	612.0	466.4	264.3	184.6	162.1	29.6	31.7	12.0	52.3	11.2	145.6	3.5	1.1	2.3	44.8
April	610.9	468.7	264.8	185.5	162.3	30.2	30.0	12.3	51.8	11.8	142.3	3.5	1.4	2.3	45.1
May	612.5	471.0	266.6	187.9	163.2	29.8	30.7	13.5	51.9	11.3	141.5	3.8	0.9	2.5	44.4
June	611.4	468.8	264.1	185.7	163.6	30.5	32.9	13.4	51.0	11.7	142.6	3.6	1.1	2.6	45.0
July	621.6	478.0	263.7	185.3	171.9	32.9	35.3	13.8	53.3	12.3	143.6	3.8	1.1	2.7	44.6
August	624.5	479.9	264.0	186.5	172.1	32.1	35.9	13.8	52.8	11.5	144.6	3.9	1.0	2.8	45.1
September	624.8	481.3	266.2	188.7	170.6	32.1	36.0	12.4	51.1	12.4	143.5	3.9	0.9	2.6	43.5
October	628.6	483.2	270.2	192.1	170.7	31.8	37.4	13.4	50.1	12.0	145.4	4.7	0.7	2.9	42.1
November	623.3	479.1	270.8	191.9	169.0	30.9	37.7	12.8	49.7	11.7	144.2	4.1	0.8	2.7	46.0
December	626.9	482.3	272.9	194.3	171.6	31.7	38.1	12.7	50.6	11.8	144.6	3.7	0.8	2.2	45.1
1998:															
January	640.0	495.0	277.6	197.7	175.7	32.3	40.9	13.0	51.0	11.7	145.0	3.8	1.0	2.4	46.1
February	644.6	499.9	280.8	200.6	175.4	32.3	39.4	12.7	51.5	12.8	144.7	3.9	1.0	2.8	46.2
March	650.5	506.7	284.0	203.8	178.7	36.0	38.7	12.4	53.0	13.7	143.8	4.0	1.2	2.8	46.5
April	656.3	511.8	287.6	207.4	181.2	33.2	40.4	13.3	53.6	12.2	144.4	4.1	1.0	2.7	46.5
May	648.7	510.9	288.0	207.5	178.3	32.0	41.0	13.7	52.9	12.8	137.8	3.9	1.0	2.5	41.6
June	672.8	525.3	291.9	211.2	185.2	32.8	43.4	15.0	55.0	12.2	147.5	4.2	0.9	2.6	45.3
July	673.7	525.2	297.3	216.8	182.2	31.5	40.8	15.8	55.3	12.0	148.5	4.8	1.1	3.2	44.0
August	670.0	523.7	297.3	216.2	182.5	33.2	40.5	16.2	53.3	12.3	146.4	4.2	1.1	2.8	44.7
September	672.1	524.3	299.8	219.0	181.6	32.4	41.1	16.8	52.1	12.3	147.8	3.8	0.9	2.1	45.1
October	674.3	528.7	302.1	221.6	184.8	30.9	43.8	17.4	53.9	12.9	145.6	3.8	0.8	2.4	46.3
November	680.1	534.7	306.3	226.1	186.6	30.8	43.7	16.2	56.1	12.3	145.4	4.0	1.1	2.3	43.9
December	690.5	541.6	310.3	230.5	190.0	30.3	44.7	15.8	56.9	12.1	148.9	4.1	0.9	2.3	44.6

1. Includes categories not shown separately.

New Construction Put in Place—*Continued*

(Billions of 1992 dollars, seasonally adjusted annual rate)

Year and month	Total	Private											Public				
		Total	Residential		Nonresidential buildings[1]					Public utilities			Total	Housing and redevelopment	Industrial	Military facilities	High-ways and streets
			Total	New housing units	Total	Industrial	Office	Hotels, motels	Other commercial buildings	Total	Tele-commun-ications						
1970	372.3	279.2	133.1	100.5	100.8	33.3	.....	5.2	41.4	35.6	6.6		93.1	4.1	1.1	2.4	30.7
1971	403.8	312.0	170.0	135.5	96.6	25.6	.....	5.0	45.5	36.1	6.6		91.8	4.0	1.3	2.8	30.6
1972	432.2	344.6	198.6	163.9	99.8	20.8	21.1	6.7	30.3	38.0	7.1		87.6	2.9	1.2	3.2	28.7
1973	439.2	351.6	194.2	163.0	107.3	25.7	22.2	7.2	32.4	40.6	7.8		87.6	2.8	1.3	3.2	26.7
1974	391.1	300.3	151.9	117.9	99.4	28.5	19.9	4.6	29.5	38.6	7.3		90.8	2.7	1.4	2.8	27.5
1975	352.0	259.1	128.3	90.3	84.3	27.8	15.5	2.9	22.6	35.5	6.3		92.9	3.4	1.6	3.0	25.7
1976	378.7	288.5	159.6	118.6	79.1	23.9	14.3	2.4	22.1	38.7	6.2		90.3	3.0	1.5	3.4	23.2
1977	408.5	324.8	193.5	151.8	81.2	24.0	14.8	2.3	24.6	38.3	6.7		83.8	3.1	1.8	2.8	23.0
1978	439.1	350.2	203.6	158.6	93.4	30.9	16.7	2.6	28.1	41.0	7.8		88.9	2.6	1.8	2.7	24.0
1979	446.5	358.0	192.9	147.9	111.2	37.9	21.6	4.3	32.5	42.1	8.6		88.6	2.7	1.9	2.6	24.7
1980	403.9	315.8	150.9	104.7	112.9	32.0	27.7	5.3	32.0	42.2	8.6		88.1	3.0	2.2	2.6	22.2
1981	396.3	313.4	139.7	97.7	122.8	36.4	33.7	6.2	29.9	42.8	8.9		82.9	3.3	2.4	2.5	21.0
1982	369.1	290.1	115.5	77.8	126.7	35.7	42.7	6.6	24.4	41.3	9.1		79.1	3.1	2.2	2.8	20.0
1983	403.9	324.8	167.0	125.9	114.7	25.7	37.3	8.1	24.9	37.0	8.5		79.1	3.5	2.4	3.2	21.4
1984	463.1	377.5	197.1	145.9	135.7	26.3	44.8	10.1	35.3	38.4	9.3		85.6	3.4	2.3	3.5	25.6
1985	490.9	399.5	199.1	144.1	156.4	29.6	53.5	10.7	43.8	38.2	9.4		91.4	3.6	2.4	3.8	26.5
1986	507.3	411.2	224.6	159.8	143.1	24.8	46.6	10.5	42.3	38.6	10.4		96.1	3.6	2.0	4.4	27.1
1987	502.5	401.6	223.5	160.7	140.1	24.1	41.9	10.2	42.4	32.1	10.4		100.8	3.8	1.7	4.8	28.7
1988	499.6	397.7	219.0	153.6	143.5	25.4	43.1	9.1	42.6	30.4	10.8		101.9	3.6	1.6	3.8	30.1
1989	495.4	393.3	208.8	147.9	147.8	30.4	42.4	9.8	42.1	31.5	9.8		102.1	3.7	1.4	3.6	28.9
1990	479.0	370.1	188.1	131.6	146.7	34.4	35.8	10.9	40.9	29.5	9.9		108.9	3.9	1.5	2.7	31.8
1991	429.6	319.3	161.0	112.8	118.3	31.9	26.3	7.0	29.8	34.3	9.0		110.4	3.7	1.9	1.8	31.3
1992	452.0	336.1	187.7	129.5	105.6	29.0	20.3	3.7	29.2	36.9	9.0		115.9	4.1	1.9	2.5	33.1
1993	461.1	347.9	200.5	137.2	106.7	25.6	20.2	4.4	31.3	34.1	9.5		113.2	3.8	1.7	2.4	34.2
1994	480.6	367.3	218.0	153.3	111.4	26.8	20.6	4.3	34.8	32.1	9.8		113.4	3.5	1.4	2.2	36.2
1995	477.4	360.0	201.7	142.4	120.6	29.0	22.9	6.4	38.1	32.4	10.1		117.4	4.1	1.4	2.7	34.5
1996	506.5	388.3	220.0	154.0	131.2	28.5	24.3	9.5	42.0	31.8	10.3		118.2	3.5	1.2	2.3	35.3
1997	520.1	398.7	221.8	156.3	141.1	26.4	28.9	10.9	43.6	30.6	10.0		121.4	3.2	0.8	2.2	37.8
1998	544.7	424.4	239.2	173.8	148.0	26.3	33.8	12.1	43.8	31.7	10.6		120.4	3.3	0.8	2.1	37.5
1995:																	
January	480.6	363.6	210.5	149.5	114.4	26.9	22.0	5.5	36.3	.....	10.4		117.0	3.9	1.5	2.6	34.6
February	482.5	367.7	207.6	146.3	118.7	29.2	22.1	5.6	37.9	.....	9.9		114.8	4.0	1.5	2.4	32.2
March	484.9	366.5	205.9	144.3	121.1	29.3	23.0	6.7	39.1	.....	10.4		118.4	4.1	1.4	2.9	35.1
April	480.5	362.1	200.5	140.3	122.5	31.6	23.5	5.0	38.0	.....	11.0		118.4	4.1	1.5	2.7	33.8
May	474.5	356.5	197.2	137.8	120.9	30.6	24.8	5.5	36.1	.....	9.7		118.0	3.8	1.3	2.7	34.6
June	473.6	353.8	194.9	136.0	121.1	29.3	23.4	5.7	38.8	.....	10.6		119.8	4.4	1.2	2.7	34.6
July	475.6	360.3	197.1	138.5	124.4	30.4	25.0	6.1	38.5	.....	11.1		115.3	4.2	1.3	2.9	34.0
August	471.7	353.8	198.8	140.8	118.4	27.8	23.2	6.0	37.1	.....	9.8		117.9	4.4	1.4	2.8	35.4
September	474.2	356.9	200.3	142.3	120.0	28.3	22.5	6.5	38.2	.....	9.9		117.4	4.0	1.4	3.4	34.3
October	475.0	358.6	201.9	144.0	120.6	27.8	21.7	6.8	39.0	.....	9.7		116.4	4.2	1.3	2.0	35.4
November	477.1	360.3	204.5	145.3	121.3	28.9	21.1	8.1	38.9	.....	9.6		116.9	4.1	1.3	2.9	33.7
December	483.8	367.9	207.4	147.6	124.3	28.9	22.3	8.8	39.6	.....	9.3		115.9	4.1	1.2	3.0	34.8
1996:																	
January	492.5	371.9	208.7	147.8	125.8	29.9	20.7	8.5	41.0	.....	10.3		120.7	4.2	1.2	2.9	34.9
February	488.9	374.0	211.5	149.6	125.2	28.9	21.0	8.6	41.4	.....	10.2		114.9	3.7	1.2	2.6	36.0
March	490.5	375.9	215.0	151.7	123.3	28.4	21.2	8.7	40.1	.....	9.6		114.6	3.5	1.4	2.2	33.8
April	504.8	385.4	220.8	155.9	126.8	28.7	22.0	9.2	41.9	.....	10.2		119.4	3.3	1.3	2.5	35.4
May	508.1	385.9	223.3	157.2	126.3	27.1	23.2	8.6	41.8	.....	10.0		122.2	3.9	1.3	2.4	35.2
June	508.6	392.5	224.3	158.0	132.0	28.5	26.6	9.3	40.7	.....	9.3		116.1	3.2	1.4	2.2	34.2
July	502.2	385.4	222.3	155.4	128.4	27.1	24.9	9.0	40.7	.....	9.3		116.9	3.6	1.4	2.0	35.1
August	506.1	390.8	222.4	155.2	131.6	26.4	25.2	10.2	42.8	.....	10.2		115.3	3.4	1.5	2.0	33.8
September	511.9	392.0	222.4	154.6	133.5	28.3	26.0	10.1	42.1	.....	9.8		119.9	3.7	1.5	2.3	36.1
October	516.7	397.5	220.9	153.4	139.2	31.1	26.1	10.1	44.0	.....	10.1		119.2	3.4	0.7	2.3	36.3
November	521.3	399.5	221.3	153.5	140.3	30.1	26.6	10.5	44.0	.....	11.0		121.8	3.5	0.9	2.1	36.1
December	514.4	397.8	220.2	152.1	138.6	27.6	26.8	10.8	43.5	.....	12.5		116.7	3.0	0.9	2.0	37.0
1997:																	
January	515.4	397.2	218.9	151.6	142.3	27.7	27.3	10.6	46.5	.....	9.7		118.2	2.9	1.0	2.2	36.5
February	524.8	402.5	223.0	156.0	144.7	27.8	29.2	10.7	46.3	.....	9.7		122.3	3.0	0.9	2.1	38.3
March	520.3	395.7	223.0	155.8	138.1	25.2	27.0	10.2	44.5	.....	9.6		124.6	2.9	1.0	1.9	38.6
April	518.1	396.8	223.1	156.3	137.9	25.6	25.5	10.5	44.0	.....	10.1		121.4	3.0	1.2	2.0	38.7
May	517.8	397.5	224.0	157.9	138.1	25.2	26.0	11.4	43.9	.....	9.6		120.3	3.2	0.8	2.2	38.0
June	515.8	394.6	221.0	155.4	138.3	25.8	27.8	11.4	43.1	.....	10.0		121.2	3.0	1.0	2.2	38.4
July	522.5	400.7	219.7	154.4	144.5	27.6	29.7	11.6	44.8	.....	10.5		121.8	3.2	0.9	2.3	38.2
August	523.4	401.0	219.3	154.9	144.0	26.9	30.0	11.5	44.2	.....	9.8		122.4	3.3	0.9	2.4	38.6
September	522.2	400.9	220.2	156.1	142.4	26.8	30.1	10.4	42.7	.....	10.6		121.4	3.2	0.7	2.2	37.2
October	524.1	401.6	222.9	158.5	142.4	26.6	31.2	11.2	41.8	.....	10.2		122.5	3.9	0.6	2.5	35.8
November	517.4	396.8	223.3	158.2	140.1	25.6	31.2	10.6	41.2	.....	9.9		120.6	3.4	0.7	2.3	38.7
December	520.5	399.6	225.1	160.3	142.3	26.3	31.6	10.5	42.0	.....	10.0		120.9	3.1	0.7	1.8	37.7
1998:																	
January	530.4	409.2	228.6	162.9	145.2	26.7	33.8	10.8	42.2	.....	9.8		121.2	3.1	0.8	2.0	38.8
February	534.7	413.5	231.5	165.4	145.0	26.7	32.6	10.5	42.6	.....	10.8		121.2	3.2	0.9	2.4	39.0
March	539.3	419.0	234.3	168.2	147.4	29.7	31.9	10.3	43.7	.....	11.5		120.4	3.3	1.0	2.4	39.3
April	542.9	422.1	236.7	170.7	148.9	27.3	33.2	10.9	44.1	.....	10.3		120.8	3.4	0.9	2.3	39.4
May	535.3	420.4	236.4	170.4	146.0	26.2	33.5	11.2	43.3	.....	10.9		114.9	3.2	0.8	2.1	35.2
June	552.1	429.7	237.9	172.2	150.8	26.7	35.3	12.2	44.8	.....	10.5		122.5	3.4	0.7	2.2	38.3
July	551.3	428.3	241.3	176.0	148.0	25.6	33.2	12.8	44.9	.....	10.4		123.0	3.9	0.9	2.7	37.0
August	546.6	425.9	240.9	175.2	147.8	26.9	32.8	13.1	43.2	.....	10.6		120.7	3.4	0.9	2.3	37.3
September	546.8	425.3	242.3	177.0	146.7	26.2	33.2	13.6	42.1	.....	10.5		121.5	3.1	0.8	1.7	37.5
October	546.6	427.1	243.0	178.3	148.8	24.9	35.3	14.0	43.4	.....	11.1		119.5	3.1	0.6	2.0	38.4
November	549.5	430.3	245.0	180.8	149.9	24.8	35.1	13.0	45.1	.....	10.6		119.3	3.2	0.9	1.9	36.5
December	555.5	433.7	246.8	183.4	152.0	24.3	35.8	12.6	45.5	.....	10.3		121.8	3.3	0.7	1.9	37.0

1. Includes categories not shown separately.

Housing Starts and Building Permits; Home Sales and Prices

Year and month	Housing starts and building permits								Home sales and prices				
	New private housing units (thousands)						Manufacturers' shipments of mobile homes (thousands)		New homes			Existing homes	
	Started (not seasonally adjusted)		Seasonally adjusted annual rate						Seasonally adjusted		Median sales price (dollars)	Sold (thousands, seasonally adjusted annual rate)	Median sales price (dollars)
			Started		Authorized by building permits [1]		Not seasonally adjusted	Seasonally adjusted annual rate	Sold (thousands, annual rate)	For sale, end-of-period (thousands)			
	Total	One-family structures	Total	One-family structures	Total	One-family structures							
1970	1 433.6	812.9	1 434	813	1 352	647	401	401	485	220	23 400	1 612	23 000
1971	2 052.2	1 151.0	2 052	1 151	1 925	906	497	497	656	287	25 200	2 018	24 800
1972	2 356.6	1 309.2	2 357	1 309	2 219	1 033	576	576	718	409	27 600	2 252	26 700
1973	2 045.3	1 132.0	2 045	1 132	1 820	882	567	567	634	418	32 500	2 334	28 900
1974	1 337.7	888.1	1 338	888	1 074	644	329	329	519	346	35 900	2 272	32 000
1975	1 160.4	892.2	1 160	892	939	676	213	213	549	313	39 300	2 476	35 300
1976	1 537.5	1 162.4	1 538	1 162	1 296	894	246	246	646	353	44 200	3 064	38 100
1977	1 987.1	1 450.9	1 987	1 451	1 690	1 126	277	277	819	402	48 800	3 650	42 900
1978	2 020.3	1 433.3	2 020	1 433	1 800	1 183	276	276	817	414	55 700	3 986	48 700
1979	1 745.1	1 194.1	1 745	1 194	1 552	982	277	277	709	397	62 900	3 827	55 700
1980	1 292.2	852.2	1 292	852	1 191	710	222	222	545	337	64 600	2 973	62 200
1981	1 084.2	705.4	1 084	705	986	564	241	241	436	275	68 900	2 419	66 400
1982	1 062.2	662.6	1 062	663	1 000	546	240	240	412	253	69 300	1 990	67 800
1983	1 703.0	1 067.6	1 703	1 068	1 605	902	296	296	623	301	75 300	2 697	70 300
1984	1 749.5	1 084.2	1 750	1 084	1 682	922	296	296	639	353	79 900	2 829	72 400
1985	1 741.8	1 072.4	1 742	1 072	1 733	957	284	284	688	346	84 300	3 134	75 500
1986	1 805.4	1 179.4	1 805	1 179	1 769	1 078	244	244	750	357	92 000	3 474	80 300
1987	1 620.5	1 146.4	1 621	1 146	1 535	1 024	233	233	671	366	104 500	3 436	85 600
1988	1 488.1	1 081.3	1 488	1 081	1 456	994	218	218	676	368	112 500	3 513	89 300
1989	1 376.1	1 003.3	1 376	1 003	1 338	932	198	198	650	365	120 000	3 346	93 100
1990	1 192.7	894.8	1 193	895	1 111	794	188	188	534	321	122 900	3 211	95 500
1991	1 013.9	840.4	1 014	840	949	754	171	171	509	284	120 000	3 220	100 300
1992	1 199.7	1 029.9	1 200	1 030	1 095	911	210	210	610	265	121 500	3 520	103 700
1993	1 287.6	1 125.7	1 288	1 126	1 199	987	254	254	666	293	126 500	3 802	106 800
1994	1 457.0	1 198.4	1 457	1 198	1 372	1 069	304	304	670	336	130 000	3 916	107 200
1995	1 354.1	1 076.2	1 354	1 076	1 333	997	340	340	667	370	133 900	3 888	110 500
1996	1 476.8	1 160.9	1 477	1 161	1 426	1 070	363	363	757	322	140 000	4 196	115 800
1997	1 474.0	1 133.7	1 474	1 133	1 441	1 062	354	354	804	283	146 000	4 381	121 800
1998	1 616.9	1 271.4	1 617	1 271	1 612	1 188	373	373	886	295	152 500	4 970	128 400
1995:													
January	84.5	63.6	1 407	1 083	1 282	967	26	348	626	341	127 900	3 710	105 500
February	81.6	65.3	1 316	1 053	1 254	916	24	329	559	346	135 000	3 650	104 300
March	103.8	85.3	1 249	996	1 226	914	29	325	616	346	130 000	3 770	105 400
April	116.9	93.9	1 267	1 013	1 259	925	26	322	621	348	134 000	3 300	105 600
May	130.5	102.3	1 314	1 024	1 271	958	30	330	674	349	133 900	3 730	107 200
June	123.4	100.5	1 281	1 022	1 305	982	31	329	725	348	133 700	3 950	113 400
July	129.1	102.0	1 461	1 133	1 354	1 019	25	336	765	344	131 000	3 820	113 800
August	135.8	108.5	1 416	1 138	1 386	1 045	33	340	701	350	134 900	4 200	115 100
September	122.4	97.7	1 369	1 095	1 421	1 079	30	348	678	353	130 000	4 120	112 600
October	126.2	101.5	1 369	1 128	1 400	1 052	33	354	696	359	135 200	4 100	111 200
November	107.2	82.0	1 452	1 131	1 430	1 060	29	358	664	366	137 000	4 160	111 900
December	92.8	73.7	1 431	1 168	1 442	1 091	24	369	709	370	138 600	4 010	111 700
1996:													
January	90.7	68.9	1 467	1 143	1 387	1 051	27	355	714	369	131 900	4 100	113 000
February	95.9	74.2	1 491	1 158	1 420	1 085	27	344	769	355	139 400	4 210	111 100
March	116.0	96.9	1 424	1 147	1 437	1 108	30	365	721	368	137 000	4 160	113 200
April	146.6	117.9	1 516	1 211	1 463	1 108	32	369	736	368	140 000	4 340	114 100
May	143.9	111.6	1 504	1 156	1 457	1 096	34	363	746	361	136 400	4 400	115 100
June	138.0	115.0	1 467	1 192	1 429	1 089	31	371	721	355	140 000	4 030	119 700
July	137.5	109.1	1 472	1 151	1 450	1 074	29	364	770	350	144 200	4 300	118 600
August	144.2	115.6	1 557	1 252	1 413	1 061	34	369	826	342	137 000	4 240	118 700
September	128.7	99.3	1 475	1 148	1 392	1 037	32	372	770	330	139 000	4 030	115 900
October	130.8	101.0	1 392	1 113	1 358	1 010	36	367	720	328	143 800	4 180	114 600
November	111.5	82.6	1 489	1 121	1 412	1 031	28	358	771	330	143 500	4 180	115 600
December	93.1	68.8	1 370	1 060	1 411	1 015	23	341	805	322	144 900	4 130	116 900
1997:													
January	82.2	66.6	1 373	1 122	1 382	1 046	27	347	821	308	145 000	4 310	117 600
February	94.7	75.1	1 532	1 214	1 445	1 070	26	350	816	301	143 000	4 270	115 400
March	120.4	96.1	1 471	1 137	1 436	1 031	29	351	823	288	148 000	4 100	117 600
April	142.3	109.5	1 487	1 124	1 421	1 054	32	365	757	291	150 000	4 200	118 600
May	136.3	106.2	1 429	1 111	1 414	1 046	31	353	754	288	141 000	4 350	120 900
June	140.4	108.8	1 502	1 124	1 402	1 057	31	355	790	287	145 000	4 230	124 500
July	134.6	107.4	1 437	1 129	1 440	1 050	29	356	806	288	145 900	4 430	124 200
August	126.5	98.8	1 399	1 085	1 449	1 061	31	356	822	285	144 000	4 400	125 600
September	139.2	108.3	1 534	1 204	1 494	1 091	31	354	823	283	146 300	4 540	123 800
October	139.0	99.2	1 519	1 136	1 499	1 098	34	351	816	284	141 500	4 680	122 100
November	112.4	83.7	1 502	1 137	1 469	1 093	26	352	860	282	145 000	4 400	122 400
December	106.0	73.9	1 525	1 126	1 456	1 080	25	354	791	283	145 900	4 670	123 900
1998:													
January	91.2	72.3	1 527	1 227	1 578	1 165	27	361	848	282	148 000	4 590	124 300
February	101.1	78.9	1 644	1 283	1 661	1 200	28	370	887	282	156 000	4 840	122 400
March	132.6	107.2	1 583	1 234	1 606	1 162	32	370	836	285	152 700	5 060	124 600
April	144.9	117.3	1 542	1 235	1 529	1 155	33	369	880	287	148 000	4 930	125 800
May	143.3	114.4	1 541	1 221	1 549	1 174	31	372	893	287	153 200	4 820	128 900
June	159.6	128.7	1 626	1 274	1 531	1 143	33	366	909	286	148 000	5 080	131 300
July	156.0	120.5	1 719	1 306	1 626	1 191	31	380	883	283	149 900	5 170	131 900
August	147.5	115.1	1 615	1 264	1 670	1 202	32	371	836	285	154 900	4 810	130 800
September	141.5	112.4	1 576	1 251	1 569	1 171	33	373	861	289	155 000	4 960	129 400
October	155.5	113.5	1 698	1 298	1 726	1 210	35	379	903	293	154 500	4 940	128 100
November	124.2	101.3	1 654	1 375	1 688	1 254	30	389	985	292	151 000	5 020	129 400
December	119.6	89.8	1 750	1 383	1 708	1 296	27	382	958	295	152 500	5 340	128 500

1. Data beginning with 1994 cover 19,000 permit issuing places; 1984-1993: 17,000 places; 1978-1983: 16,000 places; 1972-1977: 14,000 places; 1970-1971: 13,000 places.

Manufacturing

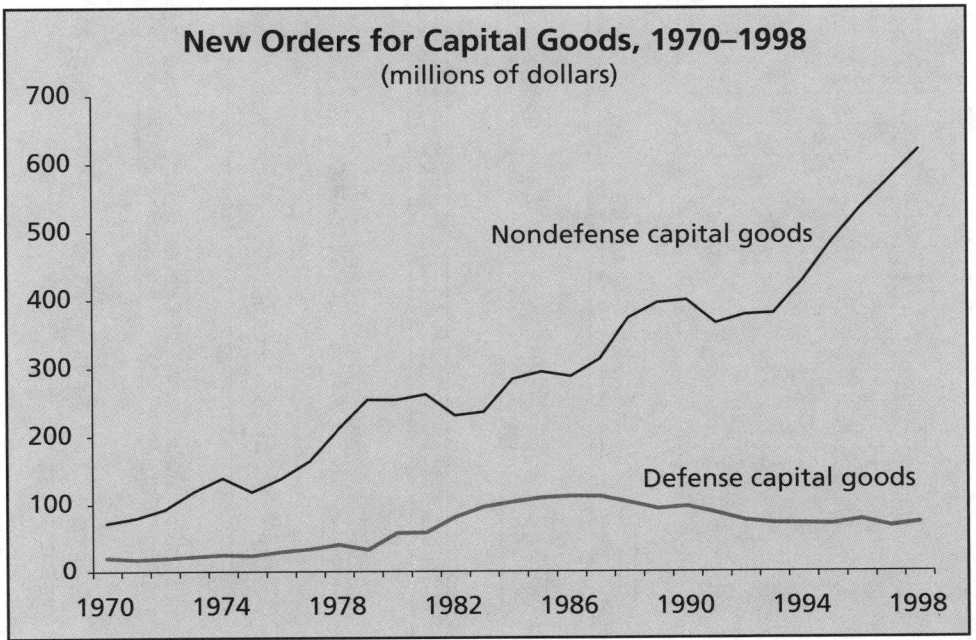

New Orders for Capital Goods, 1970–1998
(millions of dollars)

Nondefense capital goods

Defense capital goods

- U.S. manufacturers received $620 billion worth of new orders for nondefense capital goods (roughly equivalent to business equipment) in 1998, up 7.3 percent from 1997 and continuing the steep upward trend that began in 1994. Orders for defense capital goods, on the other hand, showed little change from 1993 to 1998, and declined from 1987 through 1993. Defense accounted for 23 percent of U.S. capital goods orders in 1970 but only 10 1/2 percent in 1998.

- Production at primary processing industries (such as primary metals) rose 80 percent from 1970 to 1998, and capacity utilization rose from 79.9 to 83.6 percent—still well below earlier highs. Production at advanced processing industries (such as machinery) rose 190 percent, but capacity rose so rapidly that utilization was little higher than in the recession year 1970.

- While total manufacturing production was up 147 percent from 1970 to 1998, payroll employment was lower in 1998 than in 1970. However, the average factory workweek was 41.7 hours in 1998 compared with 39.8 in 1970.

Total Manufacturing—Production, Capacity Utilization, and Prices

(Seasonally adjusted, except as noted)

Year and month	Industrial production (1992=100)					Capacity utilization (output as a percent of capacity)					Producer price index, total manufacturing industries [1]
	Total manufacturing	Primary processing	Advanced processing	Durable goods	Nondurable goods	Total manufacturing	Primary processing	Advanced processing	Durable goods	Nondurable goods	
1970	54.8	67.2	48.9	52.7	58.0	79.4	79.9	78.9	77.2	82.8	.....
1971	55.6	68.7	49.4	52.4	60.3	77.9	78.7	77.1	74.7	82.6	.....
1972	61.5	77.3	54.3	58.5	65.7	83.4	85.5	82.2	81.4	86.4	.....
1973	66.9	84.6	59.0	65.3	69.0	87.7	90.5	86.2	88.0	87.3	.....
1974	65.9	82.0	58.6	64.0	68.5	83.4	85.1	82.5	83.1	83.9	.....
1975	59.4	71.4	53.8	56.1	64.2	72.9	72.1	73.3	70.6	76.3	.....
1976	65.4	80.3	58.6	61.8	70.7	78.2	79.2	77.6	75.7	81.8	.....
1977	71.2	86.7	64.0	68.1	75.7	82.6	83.8	81.9	80.8	85.3	.....
1978	75.8	90.7	68.9	73.6	78.9	85.2	85.9	84.8	84.4	86.4	.....
1979	78.5	92.5	72.0	77.4	79.9	85.3	86.0	84.9	85.6	84.9	.....
1980	75.5	84.4	71.4	73.4	78.3	79.5	77.2	80.8	78.4	81.0	.....
1981	76.7	85.2	72.8	74.6	79.5	78.3	77.2	78.8	76.8	80.4	.....
1982	72.1	75.7	70.5	68.2	77.7	71.8	68.6	73.5	68.0	77.5	.....
1983	76.3	82.1	73.6	72.2	81.9	74.4	74.5	74.4	70.1	80.8	.....
1984	83.8	88.4	81.7	82.7	85.3	79.8	80.0	79.7	77.6	82.9	.....
1985	85.7	88.4	84.5	85.6	86.0	78.8	79.1	78.6	76.8	81.5	.....
1986	88.1	90.0	87.2	87.4	89.1	78.7	79.9	78.1	75.7	82.8	98.4
1987	92.8	95.3	91.6	92.0	93.8	81.3	84.5	79.9	77.9	85.9	100.9
1988	97.1	99.0	96.2	98.1	96.0	83.8	86.8	82.3	81.7	86.4	104.4
1989	99.0	99.9	98.6	100.5	97.3	83.6	86.1	82.5	82.0	85.7	109.6
1990	98.5	99.3	98.2	99.0	97.9	81.4	83.9	80.3	79.0	84.4	114.5
1991	96.2	95.7	96.4	95.5	97.0	77.9	79.6	77.2	74.7	81.9	115.9
1992	100.0	100.0	100.0	100.0	100.0	79.5	82.3	78.3	76.7	82.8	117.4
1993	103.7	103.6	103.8	105.4	101.8	80.5	84.0	79.0	78.8	82.4	119.1
1994	109.9	109.7	110.0	114.2	105.2	82.5	87.1	80.6	81.7	83.6	120.7
1995	115.9	112.1	117.7	124.0	107.1	82.7	86.5	81.0	82.0	83.5	124.2
1996	121.4	114.5	124.8	134.1	107.9	81.4	85.1	79.8	80.7	82.2	127.1
1997	129.7	119.1	134.7	147.1	111.3	82.0	85.3	80.7	81.2	83.1	127.5
1998	135.1	120.7	142.1	157.5	111.9	80.8	83.6	79.9	80.4	81.7	126.2
1995:											
January	115.0	113.6	115.6	121.7	107.7	84.4	89.0	82.3	84.1	84.8	122.6
February	114.8	113.2	115.6	121.8	107.3	83.8	88.4	81.8	83.5	84.3	123.1
March	115.1	112.9	116.1	122.2	107.3	83.6	88.0	81.7	83.1	84.2	123.4
April	115.0	112.2	116.3	122.2	107.2	83.1	87.2	81.3	82.4	84.0	124.1
May	115.1	111.9	116.7	122.4	107.2	82.8	86.7	81.0	81.9	83.9	124.5
June	115.7	111.7	117.6	123.2	107.5	82.7	86.3	81.1	81.8	83.9	124.4
July	115.1	110.7	117.2	122.7	106.9	81.9	85.3	80.4	80.8	83.3	124.4
August	116.2	111.4	118.5	124.7	107.0	82.3	85.6	80.8	81.5	83.2	124.4
September	117.0	112.1	119.3	126.3	106.9	82.4	85.9	80.9	81.9	83.0	124.3
October	117.1	111.9	119.6	126.4	107.2	82.1	85.5	80.6	81.3	83.0	125.1
November	117.2	111.8	119.8	126.9	106.8	81.7	85.1	80.2	81.1	82.5	125.1
December	117.3	111.9	119.9	127.5	106.3	81.3	84.9	79.7	80.8	82.0	125.3
1996:											
January	116.9	111.4	119.6	127.5	105.6	80.7	84.3	79.1	80.1	81.3	125.8
February	118.4	111.7	121.7	129.8	106.3	81.3	84.3	80.0	81.0	81.7	125.7
March	118.1	112.8	120.6	128.6	106.9	80.6	84.8	78.8	79.5	82.0	126.0
April	119.7	112.8	123.1	132.0	106.7	81.3	84.6	79.9	81.0	81.7	126.8
May	120.9	113.9	124.3	133.8	107.3	81.7	85.1	80.2	81.4	81.9	127.4
June	121.8	115.0	125.1	135.2	107.7	81.9	85.6	80.2	81.6	82.1	127.1
July	122.4	114.9	126.1	135.8	108.2	81.9	85.3	80.4	81.4	82.4	127.1
August	123.0	115.7	126.5	136.7	108.5	81.8	85.6	80.2	81.4	82.4	127.4
September	123.3	116.0	126.8	136.6	109.2	81.6	85.6	79.9	80.7	82.8	127.5
October	123.3	116.3	126.7	136.7	109.1	81.2	85.5	79.4	80.2	82.6	128.2
November	124.2	116.5	127.9	138.1	109.5	81.4	85.4	79.7	80.4	82.8	128.0
December	124.7	116.6	128.7	138.7	110.0	81.3	85.2	79.7	80.1	82.9	128.0
1997:											
January	125.3	116.6	129.5	139.8	110.0	81.3	84.9	79.8	80.2	82.8	128.1
February	126.4	117.7	130.7	141.7	110.4	81.7	85.5	80.1	80.7	83.0	127.9
March	127.0	117.9	131.5	142.3	111.0	81.7	85.4	80.2	80.5	83.3	127.8
April	127.7	118.7	132.1	143.6	111.1	81.7	85.7	80.2	80.7	83.3	127.7
May	128.1	118.7	132.8	144.5	111.0	81.6	85.4	80.1	80.6	83.1	127.6
June	129.0	118.8	133.9	146.3	110.9	81.7	85.2	80.4	81.0	82.8	127.2
July	129.8	119.4	134.9	147.7	111.2	81.9	85.3	80.6	81.3	82.9	126.9
August	130.8	119.4	136.5	149.6	111.3	82.2	85.1	81.1	81.8	82.9	127.4
September	131.4	120.0	137.0	150.3	111.8	82.2	85.2	81.1	81.7	83.1	127.3
October	132.2	120.3	138.1	151.8	112.0	82.4	85.2	81.3	82.0	83.1	127.6
November	133.3	121.1	139.3	153.3	112.6	82.6	85.4	81.6	82.2	83.4	127.5
December	133.7	121.5	139.7	154.0	112.7	82.5	85.4	81.4	82.0	83.4	127.0
1998:											
January	133.8	121.6	139.8	153.9	113.1	82.2	85.2	81.0	81.4	83.5	126.4
February	133.7	121.1	140.0	154.0	112.8	81.8	84.7	80.7	81.0	83.1	126.1
March	134.1	121.0	140.6	155.2	112.4	81.6	84.4	80.6	81.1	82.6	125.9
April	134.9	121.5	141.6	156.2	113.0	81.7	84.6	80.7	81.1	82.9	126.2
May	135.4	121.4	142.3	157.2	113.0	81.6	84.3	80.7	81.1	82.7	126.4
June	133.7	120.2	140.4	154.8	112.0	80.2	83.3	79.2	79.3	81.8	126.2
July	133.6	120.7	139.9	154.4	112.1	79.8	83.4	78.5	78.6	81.7	126.2
August	135.7	120.6	143.3	159.8	111.3	80.7	83.1	79.9	80.9	80.9	126.0
September	135.2	119.3	143.2	159.6	110.6	80.1	82.1	79.5	80.3	80.2	125.9
October	136.1	120.1	144.2	161.2	110.9	80.3	82.4	79.6	80.6	80.3	126.4
November	136.4	120.3	144.6	161.0	111.6	80.1	82.4	79.4	80.0	80.7	126.2
December	136.7	121.3	144.4	161.5	111.7	80.0	82.9	79.0	79.8	80.6	125.9

1. December 1984=100, not seasonally adjusted.

Total Manufacturing—Employment and Hours

| Year and month | Employment (thousands, seasonally adjusted) | | | | | | Hours (production workers—seasonally adjusted) | | | | | |
| | Total payroll employees | | | Production workers | | | Average weekly hours | | | Average overtime hours | | |
	Total manufacturing	Durable goods	Nondurable goods	Total manufacturing	Durable goods	Nondurable goods	Total manufacturing	Durable goods	Nondurable goods	Total manufacturing	Durable goods	Nondurable goods
1970	19 367	11 176	8 190	14 044	8 088	5 956	39.8	40.3	39.1	3.0	3.0	3.0
1971	18 623	10 604	8 019	13 544	7 697	5 847	39.9	40.3	39.3	2.9	2.9	3.0
1972	19 151	11 022	8 129	14 045	8 025	6 022	40.5	41.2	39.7	3.5	3.6	3.3
1973	20 154	11 863	8 291	14 834	8 699	6 138	40.7	41.4	39.6	3.8	4.1	3.4
1974	20 077	11 897	8 181	14 638	8 634	6 004	40.0	40.6	39.1	3.3	3.4	3.0
1975	18 323	10 662	7 661	13 043	7 532	5 510	39.5	39.9	38.8	2.6	2.6	2.7
1976	18 997	11 051	7 946	13 638	7 888	5 750	40.1	40.6	39.4	3.1	3.2	3.0
1977	19 682	11 570	8 112	14 135	8 280	5 855	40.3	41.0	39.4	3.5	3.7	3.2
1978	20 505	12 245	8 259	14 734	8 777	5 956	40.4	41.1	39.4	3.6	3.8	3.2
1979	21 040	12 730	8 310	15 068	9 082	5 986	40.2	40.8	39.3	3.3	3.5	3.1
1980	20 285	12 159	8 127	14 214	8 416	5 798	39.7	40.1	39.0	2.8	2.8	2.8
1981	20 170	12 082	8 089	14 020	8 270	5 751	39.8	40.2	39.2	2.8	2.8	2.8
1982	18 780	11 014	7 766	12 742	7 290	5 451	38.9	39.3	38.4	2.3	2.2	2.5
1983	18 432	10 707	7 725	12 528	7 095	5 433	40.1	40.7	39.4	3.0	3.0	3.0
1984	19 372	11 476	7 896	13 280	7 715	5 565	40.7	41.4	39.7	3.4	3.6	3.1
1985	19 248	11 458	7 790	13 084	7 618	5 466	40.5	41.2	39.6	3.3	3.5	3.1
1986	18 947	11 195	7 752	12 864	7 399	5 465	40.7	41.3	39.9	3.4	3.5	3.3
1987	18 999	11 154	7 845	12 952	7 409	5 543	41.0	41.5	40.2	3.7	3.8	3.6
1988	19 314	11 363	7 951	13 193	7 582	5 611	41.1	41.8	40.2	3.9	4.1	3.6
1989	19 391	11 394	7 997	13 230	7 594	5 636	41.0	41.6	40.2	3.8	3.9	3.6
1990	19 076	11 109	7 968	12 947	7 363	5 584	40.8	41.3	40.0	3.6	3.7	3.6
1991	18 406	10 569	7 837	12 434	6 967	5 467	40.7	41.1	40.2	3.6	3.5	3.7
1992	18 104	10 277	7 827	12 287	6 822	5 466	41.0	41.5	40.4	3.8	3.7	3.8
1993	18 075	10 221	7 854	12 341	6 849	5 492	41.4	42.1	40.6	4.1	4.3	4.0
1994	18 321	10 448	7 873	12 632	7 104	5 528	42.0	42.9	40.9	4.7	5.0	4.3
1995	18 524	10 683	7 841	12 826	7 317	5 508	41.6	42.4	40.5	4.4	4.7	4.0
1996	18 495	10 789	7 706	12 776	7 386	5 390	41.6	42.4	40.5	4.5	4.8	4.1
1997	18 675	11 010	7 665	12 907	7 553	5 354	42.0	42.8	40.9	4.8	5.1	4.4
1998	18 772	11 170	7 602	12 930	7 643	5 287	41.7	42.3	40.9	4.6	4.8	4.3
1995:												
January	18 553	10 636	7 917	12 856	7 284	5 572	42.1	43.0	41.0	4.8	5.2	4.3
February	18 554	10 658	7 896	12 861	7 308	5 553	41.9	42.7	40.9	4.7	5.1	4.2
March	18 555	10 673	7 882	12 862	7 321	5 541	41.8	42.7	40.7	4.6	5.0	4.1
April	18 570	10 690	7 880	12 872	7 332	5 540	41.6	42.4	40.6	4.4	4.7	4.0
May	18 544	10 683	7 861	12 851	7 323	5 528	41.5	42.2	40.5	4.3	4.6	3.9
June	18 525	10 672	7 853	12 836	7 313	5 523	41.5	42.3	40.5	4.3	4.6	3.9
July	18 507	10 676	7 831	12 802	7 304	5 498	41.4	42.2	40.4	4.3	4.6	3.9
August	18 515	10 689	7 826	12 817	7 321	5 496	41.5	42.3	40.5	4.4	4.7	4.0
September	18 515	10 699	7 816	12 815	7 328	5 487	41.5	42.3	40.5	4.4	4.7	4.0
October	18 490	10 692	7 798	12 789	7 316	5 473	41.5	42.4	40.4	4.4	4.7	4.0
November	18 474	10 693	7 781	12 769	7 309	5 460	41.5	42.4	40.4	4.4	4.7	3.9
December	18 499	10 737	7 762	12 798	7 358	5 440	41.2	41.9	40.2	4.3	4.6	3.8
1996:												
January	18 465	10 724	7 741	12 765	7 343	5 422	39.9	40.9	38.6	4.1	4.4	3.8
February	18 489	10 743	7 746	12 777	7 353	5 424	41.5	42.2	40.4	4.3	4.6	4.0
March	18 454	10 714	7 740	12 737	7 322	5 415	41.4	42.0	40.5	4.3	4.5	4.0
April	18 467	10 755	7 712	12 752	7 357	5 395	41.5	42.3	40.4	4.4	4.7	4.1
May	18 483	10 775	7 708	12 761	7 374	5 387	41.7	42.5	40.6	4.5	4.8	4.1
June	18 488	10 791	7 697	12 770	7 388	5 382	41.8	42.6	40.7	4.6	4.9	4.1
July	18 491	10 793	7 698	12 770	7 390	5 380	41.7	42.5	40.6	4.5	4.8	4.1
August	18 509	10 816	7 693	12 787	7 408	5 379	41.8	42.6	40.7	4.6	4.9	4.1
September	18 511	10 822	7 689	12 786	7 411	5 375	41.9	42.7	40.7	4.6	4.9	4.2
October	18 519	10 828	7 691	12 792	7 416	5 376	41.7	42.5	40.7	4.5	4.8	4.1
November	18 524	10 841	7 683	12 795	7 423	5 372	41.7	42.5	40.7	4.5	4.8	4.2
December	18 536	10 858	7 678	12 805	7 436	5 369	41.9	42.7	40.9	4.6	4.9	4.3
1997:												
January	18 552	10 875	7 677	12 817	7 452	5 365	41.8	42.5	40.7	4.7	5.0	4.2
February	18 571	10 895	7 676	12 828	7 465	5 363	41.9	42.7	40.8	4.7	5.0	4.3
March	18 601	10 917	7 684	12 847	7 483	5 364	42.1	42.9	40.9	4.9	5.2	4.4
April	18 609	10 933	7 676	12 855	7 492	5 363	42.2	43.1	40.9	4.9	5.3	4.3
May	18 621	10 949	7 672	12 873	7 510	5 363	42.0	42.8	40.8	4.9	5.2	4.4
June	18 649	10 978	7 671	12 887	7 529	5 358	41.9	42.7	40.7	4.7	5.0	4.2
July	18 671	11 013	7 658	12 905	7 553	5 352	41.9	42.8	40.7	4.8	5.1	4.3
August	18 707	11 060	7 647	12 931	7 596	5 335	42.0	42.8	40.8	4.8	5.1	4.3
September	18 716	11 065	7 651	12 939	7 600	5 339	42.0	42.7	40.8	4.8	5.1	4.3
October	18 763	11 106	7 657	12 972	7 627	5 345	42.0	42.8	40.9	4.9	5.2	4.4
November	18 813	11 154	7 659	13 006	7 659	5 347	42.1	42.8	41.0	4.9	5.2	4.5
December	18 838	11 179	7 659	13 023	7 677	5 346	42.1	42.9	41.0	4.9	5.2	4.5
1998:												
January	18 870	11 219	7 651	13 047	7 705	5 342	42.2	42.9	41.1	4.9	5.2	4.4
February	18 875	11 229	7 646	13 051	7 714	5 337	42.0	42.7	41.0	4.8	5.1	4.4
March	18 883	11 237	7 646	13 040	7 709	5 331	41.8	42.5	40.8	4.8	5.0	4.4
April	18 875	11 238	7 637	13 031	7 708	5 323	41.6	42.2	40.8	4.6	4.8	4.2
May	18 852	11 225	7 627	12 999	7 686	5 313	41.8	42.4	40.9	4.6	4.8	4.4
June	18 826	11 210	7 616	12 970	7 668	5 302	41.8	42.3	40.9	4.6	4.8	4.3
July	18 662	11 066	7 596	12 801	7 521	5 280	41.7	42.3	41.0	4.6	4.8	4.4
August	18 754	11 177	7 577	12 891	7 634	5 257	41.7	42.3	40.9	4.5	4.7	4.3
September	18 741	11 159	7 582	12 893	7 628	5 265	41.6	42.2	40.8	4.5	4.7	4.3
October	18 686	11 128	7 558	12 849	7 605	5 244	41.7	42.3	40.9	4.5	4.7	4.3
November	18 639	11 092	7 547	12 808	7 577	5 231	41.7	42.3	40.8	4.5	4.6	4.3
December	18 611	11 074	7 537	12 795	7 568	5 227	41.7	42.2	40.9	4.5	4.6	4.3

Total Manufacturing—Hours and Earnings

(Production workers)

Year and month	Aggregate weekly hours index (seasonally adjusted, 1982=100)			Average hourly earnings (dollars)					Average weekly earnings (dollars, not seasonally adjusted)		
				Seasonally adjusted		Not seasonally adjusted					
	Total manufacturing	Durable goods	Nondurable goods	Total	Excluding overtime	Total manufacturing	Durable goods	Nondurable goods	Total manufacturing	Durable goods	Nondurable goods
1970	112.8	113.0	112.4	3.35	3.23	3.35	3.55	3.08	133.33	143.07	120.43
1971	108.8	107.4	110.8	3.57	3.45	3.57	3.79	3.27	142.44	152.74	128.51
1972	114.8	115.4	114.1	3.82	3.66	3.82	4.07	3.48	154.71	167.68	138.16
1973	121.7	125.8	116.0	4.09	3.91	4.09	4.35	3.70	166.46	180.09	146.52
1974	118.1	122.4	112.1	4.42	4.25	4.42	4.70	4.01	176.80	190.82	156.79
1975	103.8	104.9	102.1	4.83	4.67	4.83	5.15	4.37	190.79	205.49	169.56
1976	110.3	111.9	108.1	5.22	5.02	5.22	5.57	4.71	209.32	226.14	185.57
1977	115.0	118.4	110.2	5.68	5.44	5.68	6.06	5.11	228.90	248.46	201.33
1978	120.1	125.9	112.0	6.17	5.91	6.17	6.58	5.54	249.27	270.44	218.28
1979	122.1	129.1	112.3	6.70	6.43	6.70	7.12	6.01	269.34	290.50	236.19
1980	113.8	117.8	108.1	7.27	7.02	7.27	7.75	6.56	288.62	310.78	255.84
1981	112.5	116.1	107.6	7.99	7.72	7.99	8.53	7.19	318.00	342.91	281.85
1982	100.0	100.0	100.0	8.49	8.25	8.49	9.03	7.75	330.26	354.88	297.60
1983	101.4	100.7	102.4	8.83	8.52	8.83	9.38	8.09	354.08	381.77	318.75
1984	109.0	111.5	105.5	9.19	8.82	9.19	9.73	8.39	374.03	402.82	333.08
1985	106.9	109.5	103.4	9.54	9.16	9.54	10.09	8.72	386.37	415.71	345.31
1986	105.7	106.8	104.2	9.73	9.34	9.73	10.28	8.95	396.01	424.56	357.11
1987	107.0	107.4	106.6	9.91	9.48	9.91	10.43	9.19	406.31	432.85	369.44
1988	109.3	110.5	107.7	10.19	9.73	10.19	10.71	9.45	418.81	447.68	379.89
1989	109.3	110.1	108.2	10.48	10.02	10.48	11.01	9.75	429.68	458.02	391.95
1990	106.4	106.1	106.8	10.83	10.37	10.83	11.35	10.12	441.86	468.76	404.80
1991	102.1	99.3	105.9	11.18	10.71	11.18	11.75	10.44	455.03	482.93	419.69
1992	101.7	98.2	106.6	11.46	10.95	11.46	12.02	10.73	469.86	498.83	433.49
1993	103.1	100.0	107.4	11.74	11.18	11.74	12.33	10.98	486.04	519.09	445.79
1994	107.0	105.5	109.2	12.07	11.43	12.07	12.68	11.24	506.94	543.97	459.72
1995	107.5	107.5	107.6	12.37	11.74	12.37	12.94	11.58	514.59	548.66	468.99
1996	107.2	109.2	104.3	12.77	12.12	12.77	13.33	11.97	531.23	565.19	484.79
1997	109.4	112.9	104.6	13.17	12.45	13.17	13.73	12.34	553.14	587.64	504.71
1998	108.8	112.8	103.3	13.49	12.79	13.49	13.98	12.76	562.53	591.35	521.88
1995:											
January	109.1	109.2	109.1	12.21	11.56	12.25	12.84	11.43	514.50	550.84	465.20
February	108.7	108.9	108.4	12.26	11.61	12.26	12.86	11.41	511.24	547.84	462.11
March	108.5	109.0	107.8	12.26	11.63	12.27	12.86	11.44	511.66	547.83	463.32
April	108.0	108.4	107.5	12.29	11.68	12.30	12.84	11.56	496.92	526.44	457.78
May	107.4	107.8	106.9	12.30	11.69	12.30	12.87	11.50	509.22	543.11	463.45
June	107.4	107.9	106.8	12.34	11.73	12.32	12.89	11.53	512.51	546.54	466.97
July	106.9	107.5	106.2	12.41	11.80	12.40	12.94	11.65	505.92	535.72	467.17
August	107.4	108.1	106.3	12.42	11.79	12.35	12.93	11.56	512.53	546.94	468.18
September	107.3	108.3	106.1	12.43	11.82	12.47	13.06	11.65	523.74	558.97	477.65
October	107.1	108.2	105.6	12.47	11.84	12.43	12.98	11.67	518.33	552.95	473.80
November	106.9	108.1	105.3	12.49	11.87	12.49	13.03	11.73	523.33	557.68	478.58
December	106.3	107.7	104.5	12.52	11.90	12.60	13.13	11.84	529.20	561.96	483.07
1996:											
January	102.7	104.7	100.1	12.62	12.01	12.66	13.17	11.91	503.87	538.65	457.34
February	106.8	108.3	104.8	12.58	11.95	12.57	13.12	11.79	519.14	552.35	472.78
March	106.3	107.4	104.7	12.53	11.91	12.54	13.05	11.83	517.90	548.10	476.75
April	106.8	108.6	104.3	12.72	12.07	12.73	13.28	11.93	524.48	557.76	477.20
May	107.3	109.3	104.5	12.73	12.07	12.70	13.27	11.88	528.32	562.65	479.95
June	107.7	109.9	104.8	12.78	12.11	12.75	13.32	11.92	534.23	568.76	486.34
July	107.4	109.7	104.4	12.81	12.16	12.79	13.35	12.00	525.67	556.70	482.40
August	107.8	110.1	104.6	12.84	12.18	12.79	13.38	11.95	534.62	568.65	488.76
September	107.9	110.3	104.6	12.87	12.20	12.89	13.51	12.01	545.25	582.28	496.01
October	107.6	109.9	104.5	12.87	12.21	12.83	13.41	12.00	537.58	572.61	490.80
November	107.7	110.0	104.6	12.92	12.25	12.92	13.48	12.11	543.93	578.29	498.93
December	108.3	110.8	104.8	12.98	12.29	13.07	13.64	12.23	559.40	594.70	508.77
1997:											
January	107.9	110.6	104.3	13.01	12.32	13.03	13.61	12.20	540.75	574.34	494.10
February	108.4	111.3	104.5	13.02	12.32	13.01	13.57	12.19	541.22	576.73	492.48
March	109.0	112.1	104.8	13.06	12.35	13.07	13.63	12.25	548.94	584.73	498.58
April	109.3	112.6	104.9	13.07	12.35	13.08	13.63	12.26	546.74	582.00	496.53
May	109.0	112.3	104.6	13.10	12.38	13.08	13.63	12.26	548.05	583.36	497.76
June	108.8	112.3	104.1	13.12	12.42	13.09	13.64	12.27	549.78	583.79	499.39
July	109.1	112.7	104.1	13.14	12.43	13.10	13.61	12.37	539.72	570.26	499.75
August	109.4	113.4	104.0	13.20	12.49	13.14	13.69	12.34	551.88	584.56	504.71
September	109.5	113.3	104.2	13.21	12.50	13.23	13.79	12.41	560.95	594.35	513.77
October	110.0	113.9	104.6	13.31	12.57	13.28	13.88	12.40	560.42	596.84	509.64
November	110.4	114.4	104.8	13.34	12.62	13.36	13.95	12.49	569.14	604.04	518.34
December	110.7	115.0	104.8	13.38	12.64	13.47	14.06	12.58	579.21	617.23	525.84
1998:											
January	110.9	115.3	105.0	13.38	12.65	13.40	13.95	12.57	561.46	594.27	514.11
February	110.5	114.9	104.5	13.41	12.69	13.41	13.95	12.58	559.20	592.88	510.75
March	110.0	114.3	104.0	13.45	12.72	13.47	14.01	12.64	561.70	595.43	514.45
April	109.4	113.5	103.8	13.45	12.75	13.46	13.95	12.72	549.17	576.14	508.80
May	109.6	113.7	103.9	13.48	12.77	13.48	13.97	12.72	563.46	593.73	518.98
June	109.2	113.3	103.7	13.48	12.77	13.44	13.93	12.70	561.79	590.63	519.43
July	107.8	110.9	103.4	13.46	12.75	13.38	13.77	12.81	549.92	571.46	520.09
August	108.5	112.6	102.8	13.53	12.82	13.45	13.92	12.75	560.87	587.42	522.75
September	108.3	112.4	102.7	13.58	12.86	13.60	14.07	12.93	564.40	588.13	530.13
October	108.1	112.3	102.4	13.57	12.87	13.55	14.02	12.84	567.75	595.85	527.72
November	107.7	111.8	102.0	13.58	12.88	13.60	14.07	12.90	573.92	602.20	532.77
December	107.5	111.5	102.1	13.60	12.90	13.69	14.16	12.99	583.19	613.13	540.38

Manufacturers' Shipments

(Millions of dollars, adjusted for trading-day and calendar-month variation, but without seasonal adjustment)

Year and month	Total	Durable goods industries									
		Total [1]	Stone, clay, and glass products	Primary metals		Fabricated metal products	Industrial machinery and equipment	Electronic and electric equipment	Transportation equipment		Instruments and products
				Total	Blast furnaces, steel mills				Total	Motor vehicles and parts	
1970	633 663	337 876	16 454	51 995	25 189	44 210	56 893	41 408	74 539	42 538	18 367
1971	670 877	359 089	18 220	51 585	25 791	45 478	56 445	42 377	88 857	58 247	18 613
1972	756 321	407 844	20 875	58 490	28 712	51 487	66 156	47 502	94 706	63 923	21 043
1973	875 173	475 621	23 141	72 791	36 301	58 804	78 207	54 569	110 587	74 799	23 627
1974	1 017 477	530 074	25 503	95 686	49 718	67 212	93 041	58 684	108 244	68 631	27 454
1975	1 039 065	523 178	26 233	80 890	42 281	68 411	96 354	56 068	113 503	70 033	29 547
1976	1 185 563	607 475	29 618	93 082	46 764	77 560	105 847	65 151	141 028	95 380	33 238
1977	1 358 416	710 017	34 209	103 267	50 670	89 938	122 749	77 845	166 954	117 747	38 803
1978	1 522 858	812 776	40 238	118 175	59 228	101 245	143 919	88 679	188 773	131 999	44 655
1979	1 727 234	911 124	44 287	137 488	67 414	113 494	167 014	102 361	201 623	131 378	50 702
1980	1 852 689	929 027	44 473	134 057	61 612	116 071	180 564	112 864	186 516	104 560	59 825
1981	2 017 544	1 004 725	46 220	142 072	70 254	123 535	201 102	122 084	205 223	116 981	66 613
1982	1 960 214	950 541	43 515	104 874	46 928	119 236	186 773	125 728	201 347	112 270	74 918
1983	2 070 564	1 025 770	47 697	109 240	46 398	123 083	178 446	136 138	245 392	148 296	79 637
1984	2 288 184	1 175 276	53 101	120 315	51 978	138 107	211 075	162 362	284 593	181 993	89 398
1985	2 334 456	1 215 352	55 821	112 265	48 904	143 268	218 408	163 951	307 380	193 445	96 207
1986	2 335 881	1 238 859	59 254	107 865	45 718	143 063	213 574	164 811	322 688	198 811	100 798
1987	2 475 906	1 297 532	61 477	120 248	51 815	147 367	217 671	171 287	332 936	205 923	107 325
1988	2 695 432	1 421 501	63 145	149 837	64 294	159 505	244 365	187 301	354 849	222 353	116 009
1989	2 840 375	1 477 900	63 729	155 718	64 783	164 073	256 212	194 598	369 675	233 232	121 523
1990	2 912 228	1 485 313	63 728	148 787	62 826	165 064	259 367	195 898	370 328	217 295	127 978
1991	2 878 167	1 451 998	59 957	136 378	57 267	159 760	247 508	199 278	367 235	209 210	132 836
1992	3 004 727	1 541 866	62 521	138 287	58 449	166 532	258 662	216 764	399 270	238 384	134 941
1993	3 127 625	1 630 635	65 610	142 685	62 466	175 118	278 063	233 622	414 694	267 365	137 387
1994	3 348 019	1 789 510	71 230	161 188	69 887	190 544	313 047	266 405	450 809	314 637	138 400
1995	3 594 663	1 927 029	75 932	180 314	74 927	204 384	353 338	301 447	461 806	327 908	144 719
1996	3 715 460	2 004 159	82 442	178 297	74 552	214 007	381 795	320 616	465 173	329 155	151 017
1997	3 929 419	2 158 699	90 221	188 916	77 023	226 078	408 860	351 554	502 301	346 606	162 981
1998	4 052 248	2 275 987	96 193	180 973	72 767	239 667	442 316	375 970	536 896	359 560	168 952
1995:											
January	268 243	141 891	5 378	14 654	6 072	15 683	23 598	20 795	35 543	26 296	10 683
February	295 196	159 741	5 856	15 589	6 528	16 966	28 079	23 007	41 790	30 761	11 662
March	313 244	172 583	6 119	16 209	6 872	17 725	33 393	25 458	43 299	30 847	12 880
April	292 149	155 826	6 031	15 366	6 328	16 737	27 843	22 609	39 374	28 224	11 193
May	299 386	160 292	6 334	15 580	6 489	17 237	28 844	23 895	39 507	28 680	12 075
June	321 118	174 800	6 847	15 848	6 470	17 933	33 697	27 373	41 872	28 887	13 110
July	264 268	131 592	6 190	13 224	5 401	15 024	24 357	21 757	25 158	15 680	10 318
August	304 662	160 505	6 968	15 021	6 259	17 683	27 878	25 594	37 265	27 028	11 995
September	322 672	175 088	6 978	15 312	6 386	18 075	33 031	28 990	40 861	29 039	13 120
October	310 909	166 873	6 989	15 265	6 477	18 262	29 414	26 206	40 400	30 269	11 790
November	303 583	163 468	6 539	14 577	6 073	16 977	29 459	27 129	39 151	27 944	12 462
December	299 233	164 370	5 703	13 669	5 572	16 082	33 745	28 634	37 586	24 253	13 431
1996:											
January	271 260	142 767	5 769	13 886	5 935	15 922	25 858	22 427	33 464	25 531	10 878
February	300 080	163 354	5 976	14 921	6 331	17 264	31 337	25 286	40 460	30 165	12 204
March	315 500	173 307	6 454	15 258	6 261	17 761	36 959	27 932	38 317	26 135	13 229
April	305 310	163 709	6 910	15 291	6 351	17 889	29 840	24 788	40 220	29 747	11 699
May	314 171	170 574	7 187	15 546	6 407	18 522	30 983	25 733	42 409	30 850	12 626
June	330 105	183 002	7 554	15 308	6 476	19 026	36 898	29 070	42 175	29 620	13 803
July	279 199	141 344	6 964	13 558	5 743	15 888	26 516	22 953	27 451	18 236	11 330
August	314 384	167 129	7 463	14 915	6 271	18 720	30 052	25 752	39 136	27 997	12 473
September	334 219	183 757	7 469	15 256	6 444	19 160	35 929	29 839	42 890	29 806	13 608
October	323 005	173 001	7 801	15 382	6 479	19 122	30 940	27 400	40 498	29 728	12 369
November	317 989	171 489	6 991	14 948	6 057	18 154	30 701	29 102	40 261	28 442	13 079
December	310 238	170 721	5 904	14 028	5 797	16 579	35 782	30 334	37 892	22 898	13 719
1997:											
January	287 787	151 887	6 200	14 808	6 301	18 297	27 167	23 048	36 552	27 495	11 351
February	318 634	175 038	6 882	16 105	6 689	18 491	31 924	27 331	43 165	31 279	13 159
March	335 871	188 904	7 174	16 217	6 614	18 255	38 750	31 270	43 317	29 386	14 197
April	323 369	177 387	7 710	16 430	6 682	18 953	32 421	26 477	43 600	30 579	12 809
May	323 417	176 488	7 718	16 066	6 450	18 401	32 621	27 598	42 090	29 397	12 916
June	349 240	197 434	8 090	16 656	6 784	18 755	40 108	32 148	44 901	30 065	14 985
July	298 607	156 192	7 762	14 462	5 915	18 932	29 766	25 162	31 610	19 687	12 342
August	329 999	178 322	8 044	15 695	6 334	18 995	31 849	29 146	41 490	29 419	13 134
September	356 369	200 122	8 261	16 379	6 538	19 283	39 131	34 583	44 609	30 386	15 477
October	342 277	187 885	8 305	16 264	6 590	19 274	33 894	30 031	44 797	32 999	13 858
November	331 406	181 893	7 381	15 420	6 139	19 143	32 592	30 891	43 769	29 904	13 735
December	332 383	187 147	6 694	14 414	5 987	19 299	38 637	33 869	42 401	26 010	15 018
1998:											
January	298 705	159 937	6 674	15 000	6 339	17 312	30 254	24 951	36 878	26 100	12 181
February	333 973	188 429	7 262	16 331	6 764	19 980	35 503	30 112	46 542	33 024	13 908
March	357 033	205 948	7 690	16 362	6 710	20 575	43 739	33 177	48 839	32 955	15 181
April	332 551	184 959	8 113	16 098	6 583	19 748	35 439	27 883	45 528	31 657	13 226
May	333 343	185 809	8 258	15 551	6 355	20 167	35 449	28 523	45 533	31 928	13 510
June	358 824	204 742	8 712	15 842	6 425	20 951	44 856	33 909	43 265	27 659	15 641
July	302 131	158 992	8 249	13 580	5 460	18 129	32 255	27 019	28 518	16 637	12 608
August	337 377	186 058	8 424	14 961	6 058	20 575	34 028	30 345	44 265	30 383	13 346
September	364 324	209 036	8 608	15 402	6 003	21 460	40 690	36 667	49 441	32 753	15 714
October	350 525	199 125	8 757	14 935	5 851	21 391	35 476	32 427	51 680	35 596	13 698
November	341 167	194 672	8 044	13 914	5 319	20 227	34 464	33 995	49 747	32 539	14 516
December	342 295	198 280	7 402	12 997	4 900	19 152	40 163	36 962	46 660	28 329	15 423

1. Includes categories not shown seperately.

Manufacturers' Shipments—*Continued*

(Millions of dollars, adjusted for trading-day and calendar-month variation, but without seasonal adjustment)

Year and month	Nondurable goods industries							
	Total [1]	Food and products	Tobacco products	Textile mill products	Paper and products	Chemicals and products	Petroleum and coal products	Rubber and plastics products
1970	295 787	98 535	5 350	22 614	24 573	49 195	24 200	16 754
1971	311 788	103 637	5 528	24 034	25 182	51 681	26 198	18 409
1972	348 477	115 054	5 919	28 065	28 004	58 130	27 918	21 662
1973	399 552	135 585	6 341	31 073	32 495	66 003	33 903	25 191
1974	487 403	161 884	7 139	32 790	41 514	85 387	57 229	28 828
1975	515 887	172 054	8 058	31 065	41 497	91 710	67 496	28 128
1976	578 088	180 830	8 786	36 387	47 939	106 467	80 022	32 880
1977	648 399	192 913	9 051	40 550	51 881	120 905	94 702	40 944
1978	710 082	215 989	9 951	42 281	56 777	132 262	100 967	44 823
1979	816 110	235 976	10 602	45 137	64 957	151 887	144 156	48 694
1980	923 662	256 191	12 194	47 256	72 553	168 220	192 969	49 157
1981	1 012 819	272 140	13 130	50 260	79 970	186 909	217 681	55 178
1982	1 009 673	280 529	16 061	47 516	79 698	176 254	203 404	57 307
1983	1 044 794	289 314	16 268	53 733	84 817	189 552	187 788	62 870
1984	1 112 908	304 584	17 473	56 336	95 525	205 963	184 488	72 938
1985	1 119 104	308 606	18 559	54 605	94 679	204 790	176 574	75 590
1986	1 097 022	318 203	19 146	57 188	99 865	205 711	122 605	78 379
1987	1 178 374	329 725	20 757	62 787	108 989	229 546	130 414	86 634
1988	1 273 931	354 084	23 809	64 627	122 882	261 238	131 682	95 485
1989	1 362 475	380 160	25 875	67 265	131 896	283 196	146 487	101 236
1990	1 426 915	391 728	29 856	65 533	132 424	292 802	173 389	105 250
1991	1 426 169	397 893	31 943	65 440	130 131	298 545	159 144	105 804
1992	1 462 861	406 964	35 198	70 753	133 201	305 420	150 227	113 593
1993	1 496 990	422 220	28 383	73 955	133 263	314 907	144 834	122 777
1994	1 558 443	430 963	30 021	78 027	143 649	333 905	143 328	135 145
1995	1 667 634	446 961	32 984	79 874	173 716	361 391	151 439	145 739
1996	1 711 301	461 297	34 482	80 243	160 661	367 674	174 284	150 467
1997	1 770 720	470 447	38 693	83 871	161 992	389 189	177 314	156 599
1998	1 776 261	490 365	41 625	80 624	165 429	391 700	145 673	158 156
1995:								
January	126 352	33 675	2 386	5 828	13 262	28 239	11 299	11 340
February	135 455	35 892	2 612	6 555	14 228	29 807	11 976	12 170
March	140 661	37 280	2 799	7 151	14 523	31 883	11 683	12 804
April	136 323	35 585	2 657	6 418	14 036	30 273	13 100	12 374
May	139 094	36 467	2 979	6 720	14 782	30 434	13 666	12 541
June	146 318	37 884	2 812	7 388	15 742	32 444	13 774	12 965
July	132 676	35 189	2 688	5 824	14 233	28 832	12 859	10 769
August	144 157	38 230	2 796	7 122	15 145	30 486	13 130	12 591
September	147 584	40 376	2 697	7 412	15 126	31 243	12 735	12 818
October	144 036	39 497	2 749	6 845	14 728	29 739	12 412	12 668
November	140 115	38 730	2 988	6 684	14 244	28 955	12 407	11 831
December	134 863	38 156	2 821	5 927	13 667	29 056	12 398	10 868
1996:								
January	128 493	35 484	2 526	5 425	13 283	28 548	11 842	11 041
February	136 726	36 914	2 719	6 341	13 892	29 432	12 372	12 324
March	142 193	38 205	2 954	7 007	13 748	31 234	13 029	12 978
April	141 601	37 217	2 728	6 269	13 279	31 354	15 081	12 949
May	143 597	38 555	2 850	6 719	13 424	31 411	15 286	13 254
June	147 103	38 619	2 869	7 754	13 897	32 026	14 870	13 579
July	137 850	37 150	2 937	6 002	13 065	29 479	14 560	11 769
August	147 255	39 425	3 119	7 095	13 471	30 737	15 049	12 982
September	150 462	40 607	2 814	7 520	13 553	31 813	15 359	13 126
October	150 004	40 862	3 012	6 982	13 375	31 193	15 995	13 053
November	146 500	40 110	2 957	6 840	12 993	30 182	15 627	12 244
December	139 517	38 149	2 997	6 289	12 681	30 265	15 214	11 168
1997:								
January	135 900	36 107	3 048	5 913	12 638	30 628	14 436	11 977
February	143 596	37 802	2 847	6 841	13 249	31 730	14 295	13 049
March	146 967	39 473	3 282	7 409	13 087	33 324	13 742	13 368
April	145 982	38 097	2 912	6 723	13 193	33 822	14 477	13 745
May	146 989	39 547	3 345	7 010	13 077	33 058	15 297	13 281
June	151 806	39 884	3 218	7 624	13 832	34 126	15 172	13 704
July	142 415	37 782	3 179	6 357	13 108	30 988	14 871	12 138
August	151 677	40 045	3 323	7 346	13 635	31 909	16 116	13 121
September	156 247	40 822	3 335	7 828	14 229	33 821	15 437	13 713
October	154 392	40 655	3 430	7 312	14 311	32 330	15 454	13 814
November	149 513	40 600	3 627	7 138	13 706	31 173	14 419	12 615
December	145 236	39 633	3 147	6 370	13 927	32 280	13 598	12 074
1998:								
January	138 768	38 163	2 923	6 283	13 576	31 326	11 944	12 171
February	145 544	39 466	3 480	6 791	13 906	32 013	11 807	13 334
March	151 085	41 268	3 492	7 381	14 092	34 428	11 809	13 753
April	147 592	39 670	3 215	6 486	13 717	33 541	12 725	13 636
May	147 534	40 236	3 431	6 773	13 801	32 920	13 175	13 478
June	154 082	41 619	3 677	7 255	14 452	34 935	12 965	13 817
July	143 139	39 068	3 357	6 292	13 580	30 935	12 428	12 150
August	151 319	41 924	3 611	7 040	14 037	31 647	12 364	13 451
September	155 288	43 044	3 522	7 129	13 981	34 084	12 436	13 875
October	151 400	42 783	3 659	6 836	13 735	31 536	12 267	13 796
November	146 495	42 172	3 346	6 533	13 265	31 044	11 080	12 688
December	144 015	40 952	3 912	5 825	13 287	33 291	10 673	12 007

1. Includes categories not shown seperately.

Manufacturers' Shipments—*Continued*

(Millions of dollars, seasonally adjusted)

Year and month	Total	Durable goods industries									
		Total [1]	Stone, clay, and glass products	Primary metals		Fabricated metal products	Industrial machinery and equipment	Electronic and electric equipment	Transportation equipment		Instruments and products
				Total	Blast furnaces, steel mills				Total	Motor vehicles and parts	
1970	633 663	337 876	16 454	51 995	25 189	44 210	56 893	41 408	74 539	42 538	18 367
1971	670 877	359 089	18 220	51 585	25 791	45 478	56 445	42 377	88 857	58 247	18 613
1972	756 321	407 844	20 875	58 490	28 712	51 487	66 156	47 502	94 706	63 923	21 043
1973	875 173	475 621	23 141	72 791	36 301	58 804	78 207	54 569	110 587	74 799	23 627
1974	1 017 477	530 074	25 503	95 686	49 718	67 212	93 041	58 684	108 244	68 631	27 454
1975	1 039 065	523 178	26 233	80 890	42 281	68 411	96 354	56 068	113 503	70 033	29 547
1976	1 185 563	607 475	29 618	93 082	46 764	77 560	105 847	65 151	141 028	95 380	33 238
1977	1 358 416	710 017	34 209	103 267	50 670	89 938	122 749	77 845	166 954	117 747	38 803
1978	1 522 858	812 776	40 238	118 175	59 228	101 245	143 919	88 679	188 773	131 999	44 655
1979	1 727 234	911 124	44 287	137 488	67 414	113 494	167 014	102 361	201 623	131 378	50 702
1980	1 852 689	929 027	44 473	134 057	61 612	116 071	180 564	112 864	186 516	104 560	59 825
1981	2 017 544	1 004 725	46 220	142 072	70 254	123 535	201 102	122 084	205 223	116 981	66 613
1982	1 960 214	950 541	43 515	104 874	46 928	119 236	186 773	125 728	201 347	112 270	74 918
1983	2 070 564	1 025 770	47 697	109 240	46 398	123 083	178 446	136 138	245 392	148 296	79 637
1984	2 288 184	1 175 276	53 101	120 315	51 978	138 107	211 075	162 362	284 593	181 993	89 398
1985	2 334 456	1 215 352	55 821	112 265	48 904	143 268	218 408	163 951	307 380	193 445	96 207
1986	2 335 881	1 238 859	59 254	107 865	45 718	143 063	213 574	164 811	322 688	198 811	100 798
1987	2 475 906	1 297 532	61 477	120 248	51 815	147 367	217 671	171 287	332 936	205 923	107 325
1988	2 695 432	1 421 501	63 145	149 837	64 294	159 505	244 365	187 301	354 849	222 353	116 009
1989	2 840 375	1 477 900	63 729	155 718	64 783	164 073	256 212	194 598	369 675	233 232	121 523
1990	2 912 228	1 485 313	63 728	148 787	62 826	165 064	259 367	195 898	370 328	217 295	127 978
1991	2 878 167	1 451 998	59 957	136 378	57 267	159 760	247 508	199 278	367 235	209 210	132 836
1992	3 004 727	1 541 866	62 521	138 287	58 449	166 532	258 662	216 764	399 270	238 384	134 941
1993	3 127 625	1 630 635	65 610	142 685	62 466	175 118	278 063	233 622	414 694	267 365	137 387
1994	3 348 019	1 789 576	71 230	161 188	69 887	190 544	313 047	266 405	450 809	314 637	138 400
1995	3 594 663	1 927 029	75 932	180 314	74 927	204 384	353 338	301 447	461 806	327 908	144 719
1996	3 715 460	2 004 159	82 442	178 297	74 552	214 007	381 795	320 616	465 173	329 155	151 017
1997	3 929 419	2 158 699	90 221	188 916	77 023	226 078	408 860	351 554	502 301	346 606	162 981
1998	4 052 248	2 275 987	96 193	180 973	72 767	239 667	442 316	375 970	536 896	359 560	168 952
1995:											
January	296 963	159 920	6 308	15 437	6 261	17 115	27 967	23 992	39 330	27 890	12 116
February	297 287	159 099	6 321	15 192	6 285	16 986	28 590	23 613	39 251	27 787	11 933
March	298 648	160 614	6 263	15 504	6 557	17 023	28 511	24 114	40 078	28 688	12 047
April	294 788	157 020	5 847	14 991	6 202	16 719	29 084	24 029	37 685	26 325	11 777
May	297 738	158 975	6 200	15 155	6 306	16 885	29 513	24 561	37 593	26 404	12 173
June	299 770	159 772	6 277	15 069	6 192	16 830	29 120	25 190	38 461	26 804	11 903
July	294 172	155 735	6 245	14 591	5 929	16 910	28 911	24 864	35 934	25 337	11 576
August	302 528	162 070	6 473	14 975	6 227	17 229	29 850	25 964	37 862	27 123	12 306
September	302 571	162 669	6 421	14 843	6 249	17 120	29 949	26 035	39 007	28 038	12 025
October	301 954	162 533	6 471	14 876	6 300	17 222	30 414	25 842	38 426	27 854	12 032
November	303 049	163 364	6 599	14 823	6 265	17 088	30 637	26 183	38 647	27 269	12 339
December	303 823	164 018	6 558	14 828	6 097	17 328	31 020	26 249	38 793	27 667	12 524
1996:											
January	300 389	161 326	6 735	14 600	6 106	17 391	30 678	26 038	36 997	27 170	12 297
February	302 541	163 002	6 440	14 518	6 083	17 248	32 109	25 996	37 850	27 190	12 396
March	301 083	160 941	6 625	14 661	6 031	17 084	31 379	26 375	35 525	24 361	12 360
April	307 672	164 906	6 697	14 853	6 187	17 794	31 189	26 424	38 430	27 702	12 270
May	312 489	169 351	6 983	15 104	6 216	18 159	31 656	26 456	40 578	28 646	12 759
June	308 248	167 004	6 954	14 538	6 194	17 861	31 696	26 583	39 002	27 690	12 543
July	310 576	167 129	6 966	14 955	6 295	17 864	31 431	26 474	39 028	28 728	12 688
August	312 153	168 808	6 968	14 914	6 274	18 215	32 116	26 228	39 600	27 894	12 797
September	313 159	170 292	6 912	14 790	6 309	18 122	32 371	26 715	40 866	28 670	12 482
October	313 737	168 855	7 205	14 998	6 297	18 051	32 024	27 209	38 581	27 284	12 616
November	317 744	171 970	7 112	15 224	6 266	18 302	32 172	28 185	39 759	27 771	13 006
December	313 779	169 204	6 770	15 240	6 330	17 846	32 690	27 370	38 704	26 350	12 852
1997:											
January	319 150	172 304	7 193	15 552	6 470	18 297	32 400	27 031	40 687	29 411	12 827
February	321 274	174 534	7 402	15 670	6 429	18 491	32 565	28 076	40 442	28 202	13 323
March	320 700	175 504	7 365	15 596	6 388	18 255	32 862	29 456	40 211	27 447	13 242
April	325 639	178 523	7 476	15 906	6 481	18 953	33 688	28 345	41 809	28 491	13 414
May	322 260	175 749	7 476	15 606	6 260	18 401	33 401	28 464	40 515	27 390	13 081
June	326 118	180 038	7 483	15 786	6 461	18 755	34 360	29 329	41 641	28 281	13 642
July	331 331	183 484	7 683	15 904	6 475	18 932	35 124	29 104	43 673	30 472	13 777
August	328 250	180 554	7 555	15 749	6 376	18 995	34 116	29 736	42 022	29 318	13 473
September	333 422	184 966	7 687	15 904	6 416	19 283	35 234	30 809	42 379	29 126	14 172
October	332 321	183 225	7 670	15 858	6 413	19 274	35 090	29 855	42 289	29 936	14 101
November	331 404	182 791	7 574	15 741	6 366	19 143	34 343	29 842	43 285	29 240	13 712
December	336 424	186 007	7 651	15 713	6 513	19 299	35 698	30 495	43 558	30 002	14 100
1998:											
January	331 937	182 303	7 696	15 715	6 484	19 109	35 936	29 532	41 542	28 133	13 760
February	335 883	187 298	7 789	15 838	6 491	19 766	36 209	30 714	43 577	29 678	14 025
March	338 991	189 998	7 872	15 660	6 439	19 742	36 864	30 838	45 208	30 607	14 137
April	335 553	186 843	7 899	15 523	6 358	19 570	36 898	30 056	43 863	29 730	13 836
May	333 622	185 789	7 982	15 716	6 200	19 745	36 561	29 767	43 562	29 461	13 787
June	335 110	186 536	8 033	15 049	6 124	19 755	37 915	30 882	40 857	26 760	14 209
July	335 380	186 907	8 104	14 968	6 006	20 309	37 810	31 216	40 556	27 092	14 042
August	336 445	188 789	8 014	15 056	6 104	20 114	36 711	31 228	44 403	30 017	13 749
September	340 481	192 842	8 077	14 951	5 909	20 235	36 775	32 422	46 588	31 061	14 298
October	340 133	193 818	8 149	14 590	5 729	20 176	37 011	32 219	48 017	31 586	14 040
November	341 423	194 823	8 236	14 286	5 551	20 415	36 623	32 634	48 324	31 581	14 517
December	344 247	195 531	8 317	14 222	5 359	20 523	36 880	33 006	47 908	32 169	14 371

1. Includes categories not shown seperately.

Manufacturers' Shipments—*Continued*

(Millions of dollars, seasonally adjusted)

Year and month	Nondurable goods industries							
	Total [1]	Food and products	Tobacco products	Textile mill products	Paper and products	Chemicals and products	Petroleum and coal products	Rubber and plastics products
1970	295 787	98 535	5 350	22 614	24 573	49 195	24 200	16 754
1971	311 788	103 637	5 528	24 034	25 182	51 681	26 198	18 409
1972	348 477	115 054	5 919	28 065	28 004	58 130	27 918	21 662
1973	399 552	135 585	6 341	31 073	32 495	66 003	33 903	25 191
1974	487 403	161 884	7 139	32 790	41 514	85 387	57 229	28 828
1975	515 887	172 054	8 058	31 065	41 497	91 710	67 496	28 128
1976	578 088	180 830	8 786	36 387	47 939	106 467	80 022	32 880
1977	648 399	192 913	9 051	40 550	51 881	120 905	94 702	40 944
1978	710 082	215 989	9 951	42 281	56 777	132 262	100 967	44 823
1979	816 110	235 976	10 602	45 137	64 957	151 887	144 156	48 694
1980	923 662	256 191	12 194	47 256	72 553	168 220	192 969	49 157
1981	1 012 819	272 140	13 130	50 260	79 970	186 909	217 681	55 178
1982	1 009 673	280 529	16 061	47 516	79 698	176 254	203 404	57 307
1983	1 044 794	289 314	16 268	53 733	84 817	189 552	187 788	62 870
1984	1 112 908	304 584	17 473	56 336	95 525	205 963	184 488	72 938
1985	1 119 104	308 606	18 559	54 605	94 679	204 790	176 574	75 590
1986	1 097 022	318 203	19 146	57 188	99 865	205 711	122 605	78 379
1987	1 178 374	329 725	20 757	62 787	108 989	229 546	130 414	86 634
1988	1 273 931	354 084	23 809	64 627	122 882	261 238	131 682	95 485
1989	1 362 475	380 160	25 875	67 265	131 896	283 196	146 487	101 236
1990	1 426 915	391 728	29 856	65 533	132 424	292 802	173 389	105 250
1991	1 426 169	397 893	31 943	65 440	130 131	298 545	159 144	105 804
1992	1 462 861	406 964	35 198	70 753	133 201	305 420	150 227	113 593
1993	1 496 990	422 220	28 383	73 955	133 263	314 907	144 834	122 777
1994	1 558 443	430 963	30 021	78 027	143 649	333 905	143 328	135 145
1995	1 667 634	446 961	32 984	79 874	173 716	361 391	151 439	145 739
1996	1 711 301	461 297	34 482	80 243	160 661	367 674	174 284	150 467
1997	1 770 720	470 447	38 693	83 871	161 992	389 189	177 314	156 599
1998	1 776 261	490 365	41 625	80 624	165 429	391 700	145 673	158 156
1995:								
January	137 043	36 508	2 690	6 805	13 805	29 745	12 643	12 184
February	138 188	36 722	2 765	6 756	14 165	30 104	13 016	12 128
March	138 034	36 671	2 604	6 760	14 309	30 124	12 684	12 168
April	137 768	36 618	2 884	6 676	14 404	29 260	13 136	12 034
May	138 763	36 288	2 878	6 700	14 827	29 977	13 141	12 086
June	139 998	36 882	2 700	6 651	15 065	30 455	12 933	12 039
July	138 437	36 872	2 744	6 545	14 613	30 446	12 510	11 719
August	140 458	37 563	2 690	6 677	14 861	30 703	12 501	12 285
September	139 902	38 172	2 673	6 658	14 630	30 238	12 172	12 299
October	139 421	38 047	2 792	6 546	14 469	30 388	11 860	12 234
November	139 685	38 072	2 897	6 606	14 353	30 162	12 276	12 335
December	139 805	38 340	2 767	6 512	14 102	30 091	12 699	12 158
1996:								
January	139 063	38 360	2 799	6 330	13 829	29 969	13 151	11 875
February	139 539	37 868	2 788	6 538	13 841	29 802	13 366	12 276
March	140 142	37 723	2 807	6 604	13 582	29 633	14 097	12 394
April	142 766	38 237	2 887	6 538	13 589	30 190	15 103	12 576
May	143 138	38 332	2 741	6 680	13 489	30 861	14 697	12 761
June	141 244	37 639	2 846	6 965	13 310	30 256	14 136	12 659
July	143 447	38 669	2 971	6 737	13 436	31 038	14 264	12 743
August	143 345	38 721	2 982	6 695	13 227	30 972	14 319	12 693
September	142 867	38 601	2 854	6 753	13 090	30 747	14 729	12 586
October	144 882	39 372	2 966	6 683	13 096	31 636	15 247	12 585
November	145 774	39 312	2 823	6 764	13 101	31 451	15 388	12 741
December	144 575	38 524	3 027	6 909	13 089	31 191	15 484	12 518
1997:								
January	146 846	38 858	3 397	6 883	13 148	32 025	15 879	12 904
February	146 740	38 854	2 870	7 054	13 216	32 167	15 504	12 946
March	145 196	39 006	3 146	6 971	12 968	31 695	14 946	12 823
April	147 116	39 084	3 116	7 020	13 455	32 547	14 532	13 321
May	146 511	39 276	3 167	6 969	13 168	32 460	14 701	12 811
June	146 080	38 960	3 215	6 842	13 248	32 365	14 518	12 791
July	147 847	39 164	3 225	7 117	13 464	32 513	14 614	13 078
August	147 696	39 310	3 194	6 959	13 408	32 220	15 311	12 880
September	148 456	38 970	3 358	7 031	13 733	32 662	14 791	13 155
October	149 096	39 315	3 346	6 998	13 987	32 695	14 638	13 301
November	148 613	39 763	3 399	7 050	13 847	32 469	14 139	13 118
December	150 417	40 116	3 252	7 012	14 364	33 092	13 836	13 536
1998:								
January	149 634	40 821	3 260	7 254	14 105	32 697	13 198	13 119
February	148 585	40 556	3 474	6 962	13 880	32 514	12 883	13 185
March	148 993	40 669	3 336	6 891	13 957	32 717	12 913	13 190
April	148 710	40 604	3 393	6 806	13 937	32 380	12 782	13 203
May	147 833	40 143	3 421	6 745	13 938	32 501	12 599	13 045
June	148 574	40 645	3 561	6 640	13 879	32 981	12 416	13 001
July	148 473	40 562	3 444	6 940	13 929	32 468	12 153	13 104
August	147 656	41 117	3 479	6 694	13 761	32 204	11 759	13 196
September	147 639	41 272	3 523	6 491	13 518	32 616	11 885	13 282
October	146 315	41 351	3 466	6 551	13 421	31 960	11 500	13 249
November	146 600	41 387	3 398	6 498	13 489	32 533	11 043	13 209
December	148 716	41 585	3 817	6 472	13 669	33 581	11 060	13 400

1. Includes categories not shown seperately.

Manufacturers' Shipments—*Continued*

(Millions of dollars, seasonally adjusted)

Year and month	By market category[1]						Supplementary series			
	Home goods and apparel	Consumer staples	Machinery and equipment	Automotive equipment	Construction materials and supplies	Other materials, supplies, and intermediate products	Household durables	Capital goods industries		
								Total	Nondefense	Defense
1970	59 987	136 616	96 531	23 038	41 945	210 904	24 259	102 285	78 907	23 378
1971	63 664	143 858	103 931	31 257	45 559	219 088	25 682	98 643	79 148	19 495
1972	72 839	158 995	117 214	34 568	54 119	249 670	29 968	107 198	87 762	19 436
1973	79 588	183 532	137 154	39 808	62 228	295 929	33 285	124 912	103 997	20 915
1974	81 310	225 831	152 937	36 687	69 146	360 524	34 445	143 828	122 674	21 154
1975	81 417	246 958	158 401	37 803	66 984	349 019	34 003	149 687	126 363	23 324
1976	91 278	269 428	176 828	50 088	77 948	408 132	39 178	162 172	135 540	26 632
1977	104 862	294 653	206 927	60 310	91 883	471 894	45 450	185 541	155 956	29 585
1978	113 615	326 611	239 871	67 007	106 017	530 773	50 495	217 165	186 427	30 738
1979	119 089	378 177	278 174	67 095	118 024	605 503	54 211	254 754	222 069	32 685
1980	125 155	437 351	294 260	54 491	118 429	635 014	56 392	287 132	246 797	40 335
1981	132 756	477 864	319 877	60 680	122 875	692 053	59 258	317 191	269 411	47 780
1982	132 734	486 398	304 358	59 108	115 697	640 173	56 080	311 837	251 851	59 986
1983	142 154	491 032	309 492	77 246	127 742	685 041	60 096	315 482	241 867	73 615
1984	152 300	510 760	354 074	93 242	141 355	774 504	65 765	360 211	278 124	82 087
1985	153 426	517 924	372 271	97 330	146 889	765 771	67 107	388 164	293 102	95 062
1986	159 323	503 246	373 070	101 336	153 957	759 499	70 257	395 325	289 599	105 726
1987	162 421	531 263	383 867	104 551	165 109	824 036	69 418	404 229	294 961	109 268
1988	168 393	568 275	426 981	112 474	175 607	926 722	73 535	437 623	333 233	104 390
1989	173 634	615 522	453 994	118 364	180 222	971 154	78 018	449 943	350 357	99 586
1990	174 762	658 106	471 148	109 913	180 459	973 637	78 288	472 738	370 416	102 322
1991	175 076	667 412	470 659	106 157	171 707	953 725	77 951	468 536	370 718	97 818
1992	185 626	677 695	500 089	120 860	184 344	1 000 318	82 226	481 005	388 969	92 036
1993	195 354	691 146	523 514	134 125	199 062	1 048 126	88 415	484 512	399 983	84 529
1994	205 719	705 797	568 643	155 522	217 523	1 154 637	95 026	505 845	428 424	77 421
1995	210 586	741 899	613 109	160 413	228 276	1 284 161	98 626	548 724	475 113	73 611
1996	210 165	780 048	651 871	162 272	237 900	1 306 404	98 395	582 683	510 748	71 935
1997	220 872	809 637	711 111	169 499	252 517	1 382 832	105 872	638 093	562 795	75 298
1998	227 683	831 179	774 197	173 972	260 109	1 392 982	112 671	702 593	623 052	79 541
1995:										
January	18 020	60 460	50 082	13 736	19 368	105 668	8 508	44 420	37 936	6 484
February	17 561	61 186	50 678	13 677	19 383	105 539	8 190	44 783	38 611	6 172
March	17 558	60 675	50 493	13 988	19 158	107 351	8 143	44 832	38 581	6 251
April	17 350	61 290	50 521	12 987	18 557	104 876	8 057	45 337	39 210	6 127
May	17 476	61 299	50 751	13 079	18 686	106 852	8 129	45 794	39 527	6 267
June	17 634	61 896	51 530	13 175	18 777	107 110	8 123	46 160	40 096	6 064
July	17 497	61 599	49 234	12 533	18 630	105 197	8 197	44 363	38 280	6 083
August	17 794	62 591	51 059	13 390	19 222	108 482	8 478	45 948	39 667	6 281
September	17 492	62 525	51 554	13 611	19 255	108 515	8 212	46 252	40 187	6 065
October	17 575	62 411	51 749	13 519	19 235	107 876	8 317	46 227	40 202	6 025
November	17 508	62 643	52 803	13 249	19 103	108 198	8 334	47 193	41 376	5 817
December	17 121	63 324	52 655	13 469	18 902	108 497	7 938	47 415	41 440	5 975
1996:										
January	16 684	63 533	51 018	13 248	19 095	106 949	8 040	45 495	39 410	6 085
February	17 063	63 094	53 489	13 412	18 643	106 950	7 906	47 868	42 010	5 858
March	17 529	63 747	52 414	12 316	18 956	106 109	8 278	47 768	41 684	6 084
April	17 511	65 079	53 255	13 649	19 417	108 207	8 241	47 271	41 416	5 855
May	17 707	64 923	55 070	14 124	19 946	110 122	8 335	48 843	42 821	6 022
June	17 528	63 742	54 440	13 594	19 944	108 560	8 226	48 752	42 665	6 087
July	17 500	65 271	53 750	13 974	20 278	109 399	8 183	47 263	41 568	5 695
August	17 576	65 364	54 972	13 651	20 420	109 598	8 219	49 182	43 156	6 026
September	17 437	65 320	56 228	14 183	20 230	109 286	8 120	49 906	43 849	6 057
October	17 702	66 963	54 971	13 493	20 498	110 078	8 273	48 752	43 079	5 673
November	18 142	66 846	56 259	13 642	20 489	111 180	8 321	50 628	44 312	6 316
December	17 786	66 166	56 005	12 986	19 984	109 966	8 253	50 955	44 778	6 177
1997:										
January	17 812	67 660	55 266	14 316	20 563	112 439	8 300	49 088	43 100	5 988
February	18 215	66 548	56 480	13 767	20 795	113 702	8 530	50 681	44 305	6 376
March	17 830	66 239	57 917	13 423	20 542	113 682	8 621	51 774	45 713	6 061
April	18 520	66 654	58 641	13 834	21 248	115 335	8 620	52 905	46 555	6 350
May	18 102	67 355	58 157	13 283	20 806	113 141	8 588	52 594	46 351	6 243
June	18 266	67 207	59 493	13 856	20 973	114 321	8 947	53 901	47 363	6 538
July	18 515	67 636	61 466	14 908	21 393	115 485	8 828	54 588	48 339	6 249
August	18 221	68 019	59 632	14 272	21 215	115 156	8 633	53 405	47 274	6 131
September	18 793	67 732	61 447	14 237	21 553	117 726	9 156	55 056	49 036	6 020
October	18 569	68 051	60 241	14 524	21 283	117 339	8 984	54 088	47 737	6 351
November	18 795	68 088	59 915	14 272	20 994	116 704	9 147	54 690	47 784	6 906
December	19 234	68 448	62 456	14 807	21 152	117 802	9 518	55 323	49 238	6 085
1998:										
January	19 127	68 815	61 409	13 669	21 050	115 681	9 246	55 821	49 403	6 418
February	19 122	68 668	62 924	14 326	21 401	117 343	9 427	56 941	50 408	6 533
March	18 996	69 077	64 548	14 834	21 608	117 342	9 378	58 223	51 593	6 630
April	19 157	69 101	63 225	14 343	21 403	115 859	9 302	57 305	50 560	6 745
May	18 899	68 662	63 150	14 259	21 428	114 748	9 258	57 144	50 586	6 558
June	18 978	69 586	64 527	13 216	21 852	114 775	9 482	58 709	52 405	6 304
July	19 329	69 212	63 235	13 344	22 063	115 782	9 629	57 811	51 316	6 495
August	18 928	69 369	63 815	14 777	21 656	115 493	9 247	57 910	51 222	6 688
September	18 656	69 893	66 513	15 157	21 705	116 267	9 231	60 025	53 419	6 606
October	18 496	68 901	66 717	15 238	21 719	116 349	9 244	60 938	53 870	7 068
November	18 692	69 370	66 847	15 221	21 914	116 623	9 416	61 154	54 200	6 954
December	19 303	70 525	67 287	15 588	22 310	116 720	9 811	60 612	54 070	6 542

1. Defense products and business supplies not shown.

Manufacturers' Inventories [1]

(Book value, end of period—Millions of dollars)

Year and month	Not seasonally adjusted			Seasonally adjusted											
					Durable goods industries										
							Primary metals					Transportation equipment		
	Total [1]	Durable goods industries	Nondurable goods	Total	Total [2]	Stone, clay, and glass products	Total	Blast furnaces, steel mills	Fabricated metal products	Industrial machinery and equipment	Electronic and electric equipment	Total	Motor vehicles and parts	Instruments and products
1970	101 246	66 187	35 059	101 599	66 651	2 239	8 995	4 990	7 907	14 500	8 410	14 648	4 178	4 196
1971	102 267	65 664	36 603	102 567	66 136	2 302	9 084	4 926	8 098	14 344	8 058	13 799	4 173	4 201
1972	107 900	69 583	38 317	108 121	70 067	2 430	9 617	5 387	8 408	15 142	8 528	14 775	4 670	4 435
1973	124 327	80 608	43 719	124 499	81 192	2 712	10 034	5 302	9 864	18 411	10 532	16 458	5 708	5 233
1974	157 595	100 763	56 832	157 625	101 493	3 403	13 447	6 820	13 387	24 189	12 231	19 197	6 688	6 486
1975	159 844	101 958	57 886	159 708	102 590	3 594	15 742	8 597	13 091	24 156	11 110	19 620	6 101	6 547
1976	174 867	111 366	63 501	174 636	111 988	3 841	17 699	10 035	14 304	25 245	12 594	20 886	7 814	7 214
1977	188 435	120 131	68 304	188 378	120 877	4 095	18 261	10 004	15 527	27 282	13 922	22 423	9 078	8 185
1978	209 113	136 015	73 098	211 691	138 181	4 710	19 420	10 719	17 296	32 086	16 163	26 170	10 357	9 682
1979	239 101	158 146	80 955	242 157	160 734	5 183	22 446	12 012	19 145	37 464	19 566	31 638	10 978	11 415
1980	261 700	171 864	89 836	265 215	174 788	5 674	23 055	12 153	19 532	40 958	21 838	35 900	9 864	13 376
1981	279 453	183 268	96 185	283 413	186 443	6 106	25 794	13 359	20 209	43 652	23 608	37 527	9 047	14 760
1982	307 212	196 663	110 549	311 852	200 444	6 506	24 174	12 556	21 440	47 908	25 100	43 005	8 534	17 038
1983	307 675	196 002	111 673	312 379	199 854	6 628	22 308	11 065	21 752	44 586	26 922	43 791	10 433	17 769
1984	334 236	217 049	117 187	339 516	221 330	7 042	22 444	11 087	23 330	48 760	31 636	50 770	11 680	20 206
1985	329 555	213 978	115 577	334 749	218 193	7 040	19 974	9 709	22 880	46 526	30 549	52 634	11 809	21 569
1986	317 567	207 865	109 702	322 654	211 997	7 093	18 436	8 567	22 094	42 409	28 632	53 363	11 445	22 461
1987	332 619	216 343	116 276	338 109	220 799	7 154	19 076	8 620	22 920	43 141	29 859	56 461	11 937	23 692
1988	363 300	237 510	125 790	369 374	242 468	7 496	22 422	10 495	24 950	47 707	31 645	63 202	12 310	25 346
1989	384 539	252 058	132 481	391 212	257 513	7 792	22 838	10 942	25 427	50 342	33 623	70 968	12 503	26 541
1990	397 850	257 363	140 487	405 073	263 209	8 205	22 560	11 045	25 044	49 673	32 913	77 640	13 504	26 552
1991	383 509	244 121	139 388	390 950	250 019	7 928	20 703	10 236	23 922	47 880	30 981	73 019	13 163	25 778
1992	374 906	232 318	142 588	382 510	238 105	8 006	19 981	9 809	23 815	47 075	30 722	63 290	13 081	24 685
1993	375 982	233 306	142 676	384 039	239 334	7 607	20 132	9 836	23 838	48 602	31 863	60 950	14 099	23 211
1994	395 974	247 001	148 973	404 877	253 624	7 874	22 588	10 697	25 597	52 905	35 847	61 354	15 692	22 965
1995	421 285	261 138	160 147	430 985	268 353	8 567	24 021	11 560	27 003	59 158	39 413	59 735	16 293	24 990
1996	427 130	266 547	167 365	436 729	273 815	8 898	24 289	11 912	27 894	57 944	39 335	64 596	16 369	25 266
1997	446 131	278 766	167 365	456 133	286 372	9 050	24 680	11 727	29 579	60 304	40 488	69 323	16 145	25 903
1998	456 330	287 415	168 915	466 798	295 344	9 331	24 679	12 057	30 855	60 532	39 786	75 701	17 419	26 515
1995:														
January	407 520	254 551	152 969	409 071	255 847	7 934	23 009	10 836	25 917	54 465	36 367	60 767	15 763	22 851
February	414 494	258 998	155 496	412 092	257 193	7 984	23 308	11 068	26 269	54 735	36 963	60 213	15 838	23 068
March	414 835	258 317	156 518	415 625	259 004	8 118	23 475	11 113	26 774	55 193	37 252	60 534	15 950	23 147
April	420 311	261 694	158 617	418 586	260 531	8 329	23 816	11 378	27 031	55 376	37 387	60 455	16 019	23 286
May	425 164	264 982	160 182	421 634	262 135	8 512	23 814	11 395	27 286	55 569	37 514	60 898	16 215	23 264
June	421 625	261 611	160 014	423 425	262 709	8 610	23 999	11 530	27 464	56 376	37 798	59 986	16 153	23 690
July	427 548	266 036	161 512	425 920	264 569	8 738	24 253	11 602	27 590	56 663	38 353	60 174	16 210	23 806
August	429 687	267 589	162 098	426 131	264 748	8 783	24 162	11 622	27 579	56 950	38 616	59 843	16 005	23 967
September	428 165	265 444	162 721	428 522	266 034	8 807	24 095	11 583	27 366	57 567	39 027	59 873	15 909	24 216
October	430 908	267 959	162 949	429 878	267 719	8 748	24 076	11 541	27 356	57 843	39 577	60 215	16 093	24 502
November	429 786	268 180	161 606	429 716	267 826	8 694	24 104	11 465	27 246	58 577	39 008	59 902	16 215	24 812
December	421 285	261 138	160 147	430 985	268 353	8 567	24 021	11 560	27 003	59 158	39 413	59 735	16 293	24 990
1996:														
January	431 902	269 366	162 536	433 597	270 707	8 572	24 084	11 671	27 092	60 045	39 776	60 633	16 537	25 083
February	436 768	273 116	163 652	434 023	271 111	8 609	24 022	11 620	27 386	60 046	39 377	61 056	16 366	25 203
March	433 182	270 291	162 891	434 157	271 251	8 638	24 192	11 827	27 236	59 851	39 099	61 740	16 740	25 331
April	435 707	272 416	163 291	433 815	271 153	8 604	24 043	11 637	27 188	60 061	39 322	61 574	16 489	25 422
May	436 240	274 049	162 191	432 518	270 995	8 537	23 975	11 498	27 132	59 749	39 135	61 778	16 327	25 449
June	430 010	269 373	160 637	432 102	270 682	8 570	24 071	11 529	26 958	58 917	39 331	62 407	16 175	25 212
July	434 354	273 306	161 048	432 854	271 759	8 545	23 898	11 524	27 378	59 172	39 098	63 016	16 483	25 538
August	437 214	275 648	161 566	433 794	272 684	8 627	23 807	11 579	27 592	59 309	39 206	63 093	16 311	25 632
September	434 505	272 469	162 036	434 864	273 092	8 654	24 076	11 758	27 528	58 849	39 367	63 384	16 334	25 624
October	437 488	274 314	163 174	436 428	274 146	8 740	23 969	11 760	27 643	58 708	39 428	64 217	16 513	25 845
November	437 936	275 308	162 628	437 606	274 896	8 778	24 085	11 867	27 746	58 884	39 636	64 721	16 219	25 373
December	427 130	266 547	167 365	436 729	273 815	8 898	24 289	11 912	27 894	57 944	39 335	64 596	16 369	25 266
1997:														
January	437 097	274 261	162 836	438 641	275 517	8 987	24 089	11 755	28 124	58 425	39 024	65 808	16 317	25 483
February	443 876	279 216	164 660	440 915	277 080	9 019	24 228	11 773	28 340	58 512	39 064	66 796	16 547	25 493
March	440 894	276 613	164 281	441 676	277 399	9 003	24 472	11 905	28 595	58 503	38 942	66 827	16 477	25 386
April	446 775	281 269	165 506	444 714	279 880	8 989	24 277	11 824	28 747	59 268	39 422	67 771	16 657	25 566
May	450 616	284 200	166 416	446 888	281 143	9 049	24 278	11 876	28 771	59 462	39 610	68 298	16 943	25 578
June	445 734	280 596	165 138	447 947	282 013	9 093	24 384	11 801	29 012	59 426	39 532	68 637	16 553	25 811
July	451 052	285 204	165 848	449 657	283 723	9 006	24 423	11 715	29 089	59 808	40 120	69 174	16 610	25 959
August	455 123	287 937	167 186	451 737	284 982	9 009	24 544	11 753	29 132	59 842	40 088	69 677	16 246	26 026
September	451 811	283 984	167 827	452 224	284 660	9 065	24 398	11 725	29 360	59 658	39 950	69 534	16 671	25 929
October	456 570	286 770	169 800	455 553	286 654	8 933	24 439	11 718	29 480	60 075	40 052	70 761	16 341	25 909
November	458 113	288 424	169 689	457 766	287 949	9 042	24 474	11 732	29 590	60 093	40 278	71 183	16 163	26 180
December	446 131	278 766	167 365	456 133	286 372	9 050	24 680	11 727	29 579	60 304	40 488	69 323	16 145	25 903
1998:														
January	456 534	286 702	169 832	458 197	288 086	9 097	24 720	11 770	29 775	60 135	40 801	70 371	16 259	26 047
February	464 331	292 368	171 963	461 178	290 153	9 101	24 388	11 767	30 069	61 122	41 250	70 844	16 281	26 113
March	461 334	290 205	171 129	461 948	290 887	9 131	24 241	11 806	30 405	61 011	41 364	70 958	16 721	26 363
April	467 122	295 053	172 069	464 668	293 393	9 067	24 340	11 852	30 580	61 247	41 378	72 542	16 450	26 530
May	469 773	297 637	172 136	465 729	294 375	9 092	24 465	11 986	30 460	61 081	41 236	73 398	16 686	26 797
June	464 495	293 750	170 745	466 701	295 143	9 110	24 612	12 168	30 749	60 900	40 818	74 597	17 046	26 676
July	469 220	297 154	172 066	467 636	295 669	9 112	24 763	12 335	30 939	60 903	40 345	75 032	16 790	26 659
August	471 596	299 838	171 758	468 445	296 913	9 164	24 859	12 437	30 944	60 958	40 526	75 812	16 511	26 651
September	467 407	295 733	171 674	468 552	296 757	9 237	24 898	12 398	31 050	60 938	40 172	75 702	16 701	26 577
October	471 645	298 510	173 135	471 031	298 561	9 235	24 825	12 312	31 093	60 811	40 589	76 999	16 755	26 667
November	471 705	298 755	172 950	471 000	297 981	9 320	24 817	12 215	31 134	60 974	40 315	76 452	17 240	26 679
December	456 330	287 415	168 915	466 798	295 344	9 331	24 679	12 057	30 855	60 532	39 786	75 701	17 419	26 515

1. Data prior to 1982 are not comparable to subsequent periods due to change in inventory valuation methods; see Notes.
2. Includes categories not shown separately.

Manufacturers' Inventories [1]—Continued

(Book value, end of period—Millions of dollars, seasonally adjusted)

Year and month	Durable goods industries by stage of fabrication			Nondurable goods industries								By stage of fabrication		
	Materials and supplies	Work in process	Finished goods	Total [2]	Food and products	Tobacco products	Textile mill products	Paper and products	Chemicals and products	Petroleum and coal products	Rubber and plastics products	Materials and supplies	Work in process	Finished goods
1970	19 149	29 745	17 757	34 948	8 738	2 052	3 676	2 735	6 749	2 161	2 386	13 168	5 271	16 509
1971	19 679	28 550	17 907	36 431	9 258	2 099	3 866	2 828	6 923	2 260	2 453	13 686	5 678	17 067
1972	20 807	30 713	18 547	38 054	9 673	2 355	4 056	2 896	7 079	2 142	2 695	14 677	5 998	17 379
1973	25 944	35 490	19 758	43 307	11 627	2 426	4 592	3 317	7 553	2 476	3 103	18 147	6 729	18 431
1974	35 070	42 530	23 893	56 132	14 625	3 024	5 044	4 816	11 579	3 945	4 023	23 744	8 189	24 199
1975	33 903	43 227	25 460	57 118	14 467	3 290	4 794	4 849	12 073	4 426	4 085	23 565	8 834	24 719
1976	37 457	46 074	28 457	62 648	15 695	3 416	5 232	5 299	13 319	4 711	4 581	25 847	9 929	26 872
1977	40 186	50 226	30 465	67 501	16 329	3 511	5 649	5 667	14 633	5 439	5 116	27 387	10 961	29 153
1978	45 198	58 848	34 135	73 510	18 073	3 669	5 935	6 114	16 018	5 330	5 801	29 619	12 085	31 806
1979	52 670	69 325	38 739	81 423	19 879	3 517	6 148	6 926	17 690	7 458	6 399	32 814	13 910	34 699
1980	55 173	76 945	42 670	90 427	21 710	3 721	6 648	7 802	20 066	9 693	6 435	36 606	15 884	37 937
1981	57 998	80 998	47 447	96 970	21 483	4 436	6 896	8 593	22 438	10 420	6 968	38 165	16 194	42 611
1982	59 136	86 707	54 601	111 408	23 016	6 873	6 723	9 022	24 448	17 009	7 748	44 039	18 612	48 757
1983	60 325	86 899	52 630	112 525	23 609	6 746	7 514	9 192	24 698	14 843	8 070	44 816	18 691	49 018
1984	66 031	98 251	57 048	118 186	24 182	6 533	7 827	10 299	26 420	14 260	8 904	45 692	19 328	53 166
1985	63 904	98 162	56 127	116 556	24 015	5 943	7 439	10 140	26 119	13 975	9 213	44 106	19 442	53 008
1986	61 331	97 000	53 666	110 657	23 884	5 449	7 191	10 254	25 743	8 791	9 285	42 335	18 124	50 198
1987	63 562	102 393	54 844	117 310	24 860	5 331	7 939	11 163	26 585	9 973	10 065	45 319	19 270	52 721
1988	69 611	112 958	59 899	126 906	27 122	5 286	8 384	12 495	29 792	9 196	11 367	49 396	20 559	56 951
1989	72 435	122 251	62 827	133 699	28 459	5 570	8 721	13 404	31 725	10 743	11 533	50 674	21 653	61 372
1990	73 559	124 130	65 520	141 864	29 714	5 974	8 732	13 640	34 001	13 432	12 292	52 645	22 817	66 402
1991	70 834	114 960	64 225	140 931	30 099	6 342	8 484	13 796	34 529	11 671	12 121	53 011	22 815	65 105
1992	69 459	104 424	64 222	144 405	30 996	6 668	8 710	14 010	35 720	11 350	12 541	54 007	23 532	66 866
1993	72 590	102 468	64 276	144 705	31 201	6 322	9 264	13 972	35 771	10 265	12 821	55 072	23 371	66 262
1994	78 468	107 037	68 119	151 253	32 332	5 782	9 804	14 463	37 024	11 121	14 232	58 157	24 638	68 458
1995	85 577	107 209	75 567	162 632	34 527	5 775	10 308	17 352	39 913	11 304	15 220	62 324	26 007	74 301
1996	86 438	111 289	76 088	162 914	35 697	5 904	9 915	16 032	41 110	12 520	15 728	60 416	26 621	75 877
1997	89 844	117 236	79 292	169 761	37 026	5 797	10 184	16 240	44 249	12 218	16 455	61 233	29 498	79 030
1998	91 740	121 246	82 358	171 454	37 299	5 867	10 180	16 362	46 217	10 254	16 766	62 306	29 344	79 804
1995:														
January	78 609	109 016	68 222	153 224	32 869	5 691	9 843	14 749	37 245	11 470	14 481	58 680	24 814	69 730
February	79 591	108 669	68 933	154 899	32 945	5 749	9 897	14 999	37 524	11 611	14 901	59 288	25 013	70 598
March	79 958	108 533	70 513	156 621	33 153	5 617	10 026	15 358	37 654	11 504	15 060	60 558	25 136	70 927
April	80 874	108 628	71 029	158 055	33 077	5 580	10 094	15 706	38 289	11 609	15 312	60 986	25 221	71 848
May	81 603	108 897	71 635	159 499	33 164	5 530	10 180	15 968	38 873	11 712	15 362	61 521	25 415	72 563
June	82 173	107 780	72 756	160 716	33 263	5 559	10 237	16 521	39 272	11 595	15 427	62 217	25 685	72 814
July	82 958	108 290	73 321	161 351	33 416	5 621	10 251	16 772	39 632	11 234	15 460	62 356	25 849	73 146
August	83 889	107 676	73 183	161 383	33 352	5 742	10 250	16 852	39 739	11 079	15 383	62 507	25 690	73 186
September	83 988	107 857	74 189	162 488	33 897	5 944	10 298	17 107	40 029	11 093	15 316	62 666	25 962	73 860
October	85 595	107 534	74 590	162 159	34 231	5 800	10 324	17 308	39 823	10 805	15 265	62 266	25 860	74 033
November	85 605	107 307	74 914	161 890	34 331	5 686	10 347	17 274	39 609	10 886	15 189	62 634	25 778	73 478
December	85 577	107 209	75 567	162 632	34 527	5 775	10 308	17 352	39 913	11 304	15 220	62 324	26 007	74 301
1996:														
January	86 514	108 133	76 060	162 890	34 524	5 776	10 226	17 307	39 985	11 490	15 198	62 320	26 276	74 294
February	86 936	108 179	75 996	162 912	34 707	5 725	10 202	17 316	39 945	11 594	15 217	62 127	26 181	74 604
March	86 872	108 720	75 659	162 662	34 842	5 716	10 102	17 241	40 202	11 959	15 294	61 513	26 325	75 068
April	87 038	108 966	75 149	162 662	35 154	5 612	10 042	16 943	40 377	12 044	15 206	61 436	26 388	74 838
May	86 835	109 053	75 107	161 523	35 028	5 604	9 992	16 633	40 228	11 991	15 138	60 948	26 269	74 306
June	85 718	109 702	75 262	161 420	35 084	5 616	9 916	16 485	40 319	11 942	15 240	60 480	26 477	74 463
July	86 818	109 636	75 305	161 095	35 198	5 502	9 899	16 429	40 157	12 077	15 286	60 403	26 393	74 299
August	86 751	109 850	76 083	161 110	35 175	5 608	9 948	16 457	40 293	12 015	15 335	60 306	26 616	74 188
September	86 946	109 862	76 284	161 772	35 496	5 713	9 908	16 369	40 569	12 252	15 493	60 305	26 562	74 905
October	86 475	111 060	76 611	162 282	35 573	5 783	9 907	16 257	40 670	12 289	15 580	60 712	26 654	74 916
November	86 736	111 659	76 501	162 710	35 756	5 871	9 941	16 144	40 654	12 344	15 619	60 658	26 669	75 383
December	86 438	111 289	76 088	162 914	35 697	5 904	9 915	16 032	41 110	12 520	15 728	60 416	26 621	75 877
1997:														
January	86 626	111 940	76 951	163 124	35 422	5 829	9 956	15 926	41 105	13 039	15 855	60 350	26 924	75 850
February	86 655	112 681	77 744	163 835	35 737	5 796	9 911	15 812	41 328	12 858	15 917	60 822	27 137	75 876
March	87 530	113 067	76 802	164 277	35 866	5 770	9 967	15 918	41 389	12 923	16 031	60 721	27 344	76 212
April	87 649	113 947	78 284	164 834	36 038	5 835	10 060	15 797	41 778	12 656	16 085	60 660	27 586	76 588
May	88 017	114 443	78 683	165 745	36 097	5 836	10 048	15 829	41 883	12 919	16 269	60 843	28 042	76 860
June	88 514	114 629	78 870	165 934	36 248	5 790	10 105	15 682	42 151	12 623	16 281	60 675	27 846	77 413
July	89 322	115 402	78 999	165 934	36 136	5 814	10 121	15 728	42 365	12 338	16 305	60 545	27 994	77 395
August	89 036	116 214	79 732	166 755	36 179	5 779	10 178	15 794	42 471	12 657	16 395	60 577	28 363	77 815
September	89 841	115 538	79 281	167 564	36 331	5 680	10 197	16 016	43 101	12 621	16 348	61 115	28 562	77 887
October	90 147	116 574	79 933	168 899	36 742	5 798	10 213	15 982	43 673	12 559	16 386	61 388	29 053	78 458
November	90 004	117 998	79 947	169 817	36 940	5 890	10 138	16 054	44 324	12 489	16 463	60 770	29 464	79 583
December	89 844	117 236	79 292	169 761	37 026	5 797	10 184	16 240	44 249	12 218	16 455	61 233	29 498	79 030
1998:														
January	90 779	117 542	79 765	170 111	37 359	5 962	10 172	16 351	44 797	11 449	16 562	61 732	29 348	79 031
February	91 428	118 362	80 363	171 025	37 647	5 864	10 217	16 317	45 310	11 478	16 587	62 130	29 622	79 273
March	91 922	118 438	80 527	171 061	37 512	5 882	10 219	16 320	45 368	11 405	16 509	62 364	29 390	79 307
April	92 470	120 494	80 429	171 275	37 488	5 772	10 224	16 363	45 611	11 400	16 484	62 086	29 746	79 443
May	92 778	121 101	80 496	171 354	37 503	5 779	10 254	16 388	45 821	11 169	16 571	61 926	29 800	79 628
June	93 198	121 420	80 525	171 558	37 427	5 716	10 253	16 498	46 061	10 936	16 697	62 374	29 828	79 356
July	93 445	121 367	80 857	171 967	37 424	5 665	10 285	16 584	46 382	10 906	16 650	62 673	29 678	79 616
August	93 042	122 862	81 009	171 532	37 115	5 563	10 245	16 643	46 535	10 759	16 699	62 627	29 275	79 630
September	93 291	122 063	81 403	171 795	37 112	5 783	10 307	16 527	46 313	10 770	16 677	62 838	29 164	79 793
October	93 345	123 446	81 770	172 470	37 459	6 020	10 286	16 511	46 356	10 832	16 678	62 691	29 402	80 377
November	93 115	122 509	82 357	173 019	37 264	5 939	10 194	16 483	46 875	10 965	16 857	62 747	29 795	80 477
December	91 740	121 246	82 358	171 454	37 299	5 867	10 180	16 362	46 217	10 254	16 766	62 306	29 344	79 804

1. Data prior to 1982 are not comparable to subsequent periods due to change in inventory valuation methods; see Notes.
2. Includes categories not shown separately.

Manufacturers' Inventories [1]—Continued

(Book value, end of period—Millions of dollars, seasonally adjusted)

Year and month	By market category [2]						Supplementary series			
	Home goods and apparel	Consumer staples	Machinery and equipment	Automotive equipment	Construction materials and supplies	Other materials, supplies, and intermediate products	Household durables	Capital goods industries		
								Total	Nondefense	Defense
1970	10 162	14 176	24 032	2 355	6 867	34 271	4 711	27 859	22 810	5 049
1971	10 642	14 865	23 978	2 387	7 145	34 562	4 829	26 587	22 455	4 132
1972	11 498	15 596	25 239	2 703	7 603	36 142	5 311	27 667	23 337	4 330
1973	13 398	17 990	29 787	3 174	8 696	41 134	6 319	32 032	27 460	4 572
1974	14 470	23 571	37 403	3 695	11 076	54 267	7 393	39 605	34 583	5 022
1975	13 586	24 083	37 041	3 455	11 267	55 960	6 649	40 181	34 289	5 892
1976	15 324	25 758	37 766	4 163	12 540	63 175	7 453	41 046	34 449	6 597
1977	16 556	27 541	41 529	4 795	13 509	68 042	8 070	44 014	37 781	6 233
1978	18 715	30 063	49 266	5 353	15 100	75 494	9 161	52 237	45 660	6 577
1979	19 157	33 648	58 623	5 630	16 908	87 232	9 533	63 816	55 393	8 423
1980	20 106	37 689	66 157	5 145	17 513	94 117	9 967	74 531	63 692	10 839
1981	21 591	39 589	69 413	4 814	18 328	101 503	10 565	81 112	67 616	13 496
1982	21 738	48 183	76 522	4 865	18 580	106 625	10 926	92 601	73 748	18 853
1983	22 682	47 337	72 066	5 494	19 309	107 999	10 845	89 562	68 420	21 142
1984	24 999	48 555	79 058	6 192	20 552	115 702	12 270	102 615	75 466	27 149
1985	24 229	48 134	75 592	6 214	20 555	111 881	11 704	102 843	71 763	31 080
1986	23 647	44 983	70 923	5 930	20 348	108 766	11 325	99 104	67 631	31 473
1987	25 379	47 186	72 400	6 322	21 158	113 976	12 190	103 167	68 734	34 433
1988	26 723	50 289	81 687	6 448	22 925	125 688	12 948	114 207	77 448	36 759
1989	27 255	54 029	90 697	6 479	23 326	131 807	13 541	124 850	86 897	37 953
1990	27 153	58 161	95 055	6 934	23 714	134 811	13 446	128 997	90 894	38 103
1991	26 303	58 657	93 404	6 559	22 509	130 000	12 678	121 629	88 958	32 671
1992	26 819	60 706	89 589	6 708	22 779	128 441	12 515	110 261	84 351	25 910
1993	28 671	60 225	89 537	6 934	23 979	129 268	13 038	107 012	83 446	23 566
1994	30 826	62 085	95 906	7 508	25 455	139 030	14 452	110 770	90 184	20 586
1995	31 892	66 038	103 724	7 828	26 898	150 711	15 368	116 387	98 241	18 146
1996	29 468	68 270	108 129	8 035	27 222	152 604	14 813	118 829	101 852	16 977
1997	30 671	71 825	115 519	8 134	28 188	157 059	15 193	126 376	108 820	17 556
1998	32 246	72 825	117 856	8 669	28 706	158 957	16 390	130 002	110 184	19 818
1995:										
January	31 065	62 693	96 718	7 557	25 450	141 272	14 592	111 774	91 437	20 337
February	31 370	63 100	97 275	7 607	25 657	142 751	14 761	111 999	91 964	20 035
March	31 761	63 345	98 065	7 662	25 970	144 001	14 745	112 672	92 802	19 870
April	32 033	63 498	98 296	7 691	26 323	145 961	15 016	112 653	93 046	19 607
May	32 134	63 845	99 072	7 718	26 592	147 136	15 044	113 467	93 863	19 604
June	32 102	64 272	99 108	7 671	26 570	148 359	15 115	113 216	93 773	19 443
July	31 979	64 296	99 906	7 706	26 837	150 048	15 068	113 732	94 539	19 193
August	31 823	64 367	100 377	7 677	26 817	150 158	14 929	113 930	94 914	19 016
September	31 856	65 233	101 424	7 594	26 853	150 754	15 053	115 144	96 108	19 036
October	31 933	65 211	102 585	7 731	26 998	150 993	15 176	116 026	97 233	18 793
November	31 933	65 093	102 935	7 804	26 992	150 970	15 198	115 812	97 452	18 360
December	31 892	66 038	103 724	7 828	26 898	150 711	15 368	116 387	98 241	18 146
1996:										
January	31 840	66 439	105 512	7 926	26 906	151 400	15 351	117 625	99 785	17 840
February	31 820	66 499	105 734	7 957	26 839	151 477	15 469	117 867	99 929	17 938
March	31 106	66 978	105 700	8 124	26 747	151 747	15 184	117 653	99 497	18 156
April	30 844	67 045	106 465	8 159	26 522	151 236	15 129	118 172	100 300	17 872
May	30 475	66 891	106 639	8 146	26 560	150 468	15 007	118 055	100 317	17 738
June	30 145	66 943	106 395	8 065	26 571	150 504	14 859	117 842	99 911	17 931
July	29 703	66 871	107 162	8 281	26 646	150 768	14 481	118 354	100 494	17 860
August	29 795	66 976	107 953	8 235	26 731	150 795	14 760	118 997	101 259	17 738
September	29 898	67 611	107 916	8 205	26 837	151 273	14 918	118 846	101 329	17 517
October	29 845	67 705	108 584	8 240	26 923	151 676	14 889	119 517	102 035	17 482
November	29 634	68 077	109 135	8 070	27 121	151 918	14 858	120 509	103 084	17 425
December	29 468	68 270	108 129	8 035	27 222	152 604	14 813	118 829	101 852	16 977
1997:										
January	29 512	68 055	109 645	8 043	27 310	152 604	14 806	120 540	103 224	17 316
February	29 488	68 691	111 002	8 115	27 407	152 900	14 761	121 443	104 468	16 975
March	29 481	68 837	111 208	8 102	27 459	153 348	14 715	121 551	104 785	16 766
April	29 716	69 530	112 767	8 220	27 571	153 540	14 835	122 999	106 154	16 845
May	29 896	69 843	113 413	8 387	27 729	154 114	14 933	123 486	106 762	16 724
June	30 179	69 877	114 392	8 303	27 844	154 072	15 011	124 161	107 658	16 503
July	30 556	69 897	115 481	8 287	27 937	154 315	15 252	125 384	108 751	16 633
August	30 738	69 952	116 125	8 090	28 133	155 137	15 315	126 257	109 616	16 641
September	30 672	70 461	115 181	8 376	28 230	155 216	15 234	125 396	108 456	16 940
October	30 887	71 410	117 298	8 202	28 235	155 594	15 343	127 109	110 425	16 684
November	30 811	71 884	118 194	8 086	28 337	156 350	15 407	127 983	111 299	16 684
December	30 671	71 825	115 519	8 134	28 188	157 059	15 193	126 376	108 820	17 556
1998:										
January	30 747	72 310	116 292	8 180	28 268	157 568	15 322	127 156	109 301	17 855
February	30 933	72 851	117 039	8 166	28 240	158 818	15 432	128 269	110 270	17 999
March	31 163	72 833	116 856	8 331	28 269	159 124	15 566	127 587	109 574	18 013
April	31 136	72 886	118 836	8 277	28 383	159 407	15 623	129 474	111 365	18 109
May	31 205	72 887	119 143	8 410	28 395	159 707	15 767	129 766	111 412	18 354
June	31 308	72 821	119 419	8 532	28 377	160 034	15 819	130 294	111 859	18 435
July	31 564	73 016	119 846	8 535	28 542	159 350	16 041	130 798	111 963	18 835
August	31 724	72 611	120 861	8 330	28 752	159 287	16 164	131 975	112 969	19 006
September	32 107	72 651	120 647	8 287	28 820	159 067	16 393	131 612	112 839	18 773
October	32 345	73 416	121 725	8 364	28 973	159 129	16 556	132 785	113 708	19 077
November	32 512	73 913	120 435	8 577	28 946	159 468	16 633	131 623	112 381	19 242
December	32 246	72 825	117 856	8 669	28 706	158 957	16 390	130 002	110 184	19 818

1. Data prior to 1982 are not comparable to subsequent periods due to change in inventory valuation methods; see Notes.
2. Defense products and business supplies not shown.

Manufacturers' New Orders

(Net, millions of dollars)

Year and month	Not seasonally adjusted			Seasonally adjusted									
					Durable goods industries								
						Primary metals						Transportation equipment	
	Total	Durable goods industries	Nondurable goods industries	Total	Total¹	Total	Blast furnaces, steel mills	Nonferrous and other primary metal	Fabricated metal products	Industrial machinery and equipment	Electronic and electrical equipment	Total	Aircraft, missiles, and parts
1970	624 263	328 079	296 184	624 263	328 079	51 793	25 521	21 883	43 990	55 322	41 117	67 380	17 417
1971	671 051	358 856	312 195	671 051	358 856	51 284	25 571	20 704	44 305	55 886	42 639	89 900	22 459
1972	770 181	420 455	349 726	770 181	420 455	61 447	30 996	24 607	52 879	70 941	48 702	96 501	20 963
1973	912 039	511 525	400 514	912 039	511 525	78 395	39 413	31 417	64 733	89 162	58 275	118 194	26 669
1974	1 047 924	562 339	485 585	1 047 924	562 339	98 831	51 047	38 394	74 281	106 101	58 884	114 081	29 934
1975	1 021 662	503 485	518 177	1 021 662	503 485	75 034	38 611	27 864	64 349	92 863	54 610	109 050	26 869
1976	1 194 151	615 680	578 471	1 194 151	615 680	94 491	47 212	37 378	76 372	107 595	66 864	143 502	31 851
1977	1 381 302	732 422	648 880	1 381 302	732 422	105 689	52 103	42 400	92 028	126 235	80 010	175 446	40 625
1978	1 579 542	867 335	712 207	1 579 542	867 335	124 741	62 648	48 319	105 182	154 051	92 781	213 539	54 600
1979	1 771 243	953 796	817 447	1 771 243	953 796	139 783	66 968	58 420	117 428	174 660	107 314	223 226	67 818
1980	1 876 304	952 701	923 603	1 876 304	952 701	134 416	62 473	60 399	116 195	179 750	115 335	202 584	72 514
1981	2 016 298	1 003 845	1 012 453	2 016 298	1 003 845	137 286	67 457	57 545	123 245	201 576	123 053	203 482	63 530
1982	1 945 684	936 764	1 008 920	1 945 684	936 764	98 445	43 013	46 942	113 399	169 274	127 630	209 325	73 365
1983	2 105 410	1 057 677	1 047 733	2 105 410	1 057 677	113 884	49 123	55 566	122 760	178 879	142 131	261 359	86 952
1984	2 314 549	1 201 964	1 112 585	2 314 549	1 201 964	118 354	50 719	56 030	141 650	212 109	165 541	295 202	91 620
1985	2 348 477	1 228 268	1 120 209	2 348 477	1 228 268	112 276	49 079	52 275	142 300	218 395	163 352	311 482	100 889
1986	2 342 444	1 243 761	1 098 683	2 342 444	1 243 761	108 218	46 408	51 294	143 541	208 567	164 282	327 541	107 993
1987	2 512 663	1 329 712	1 182 951	2 512 663	1 329 712	125 989	54 763	60 302	150 716	221 171	173 210	348 224	114 835
1988	2 739 240	1 464 916	1 274 324	2 739 240	1 464 916	152 578	64 002	75 997	158 170	250 055	189 211	389 635	137 443
1989	2 874 861	1 512 664	1 362 197	2 874 861	1 512 664	152 814	62 752	77 249	160 037	257 051	192 482	411 434	153 430
1990	2 934 086	1 507 001	1 427 085	2 934 086	1 507 001	149 338	63 369	72 944	163 285	258 894	195 748	395 737	150 329
1991	2 865 665	1 438 187	1 427 478	2 865 665	1 438 187	134 657	56 366	66 778	158 401	243 450	197 659	363 366	132 645
1992	2 978 548	1 515 694	1 462 854	2 978 548	1 515 694	136 849	58 002	67 337	165 793	258 608	217 966	377 147	110 830
1993	3 092 381	1 596 974	1 495 407	3 092 381	1 596 974	144 018	63 604	67 112	172 121	277 416	233 991	386 643	88 070
1994	3 356 797	1 794 508	1 562 289	3 356 797	1 794 508	167 685	70 960	81 963	191 099	325 788	266 386	440 817	90 217
1995	3 607 586	1 941 378	1 666 208	3 607 586	1 941 378	178 702	75 811	87 857	205 388	358 910	307 634	465 839	106 062
1996	3 749 299	2 036 536	1 712 763	3 749 299	2 036 536	180 362	74 885	88 773	215 791	383 749	319 157	495 239	129 688
1997	3 952 025	2 180 708	1 771 317	3 952 025	2 180 708	193 987	79 481	96 513	228 567	409 215	356 557	507 667	124 151
1998	4 033 676	2 259 693	1 773 983	4 033 676	2 259 693	175 482	69 444	88 067	238 751	443 332	380 470	524 963	124 111
1995:													
January	277 276	150 075	127 201	299 668	162 131	15 806	6 461	8 052	17 367	29 616	24 632	38 099	6 456
February	299 754	163 609	136 145	300 531	161 869	15 073	6 291	7 386	17 272	29 637	24 370	40 031	9 606
March	315 880	174 471	141 409	301 075	163 038	15 288	6 839	7 217	17 155	30 184	25 834	39 890	8 534
April	291 876	154 811	137 065	293 178	154 998	14 672	6 201	7 151	16 875	29 208	25 099	35 059	6 373
May	298 792	159 407	139 385	298 463	159 671	14 367	6 182	7 036	17 186	29 876	25 745	37 768	8 986
June	314 639	168 428	146 211	296 984	157 187	14 290	6 049	7 097	16 908	30 237	25 125	35 462	5 692
July	265 628	132 535	133 093	293 536	154 831	14 013	5 763	7 113	16 863	28 290	26 511	34 510	7 116
August	302 585	159 496	143 089	302 121	162 432	15 208	6 455	7 461	17 161	29 988	25 637	38 015	8 564
September	320 407	174 555	145 852	305 113	166 313	14 816	6 104	7 413	17 148	29 900	26 416	42 940	11 748
October	313 021	170 322	142 699	302 124	163 267	15 038	6 507	7 189	17 082	30 058	26 494	38 782	8 962
November	303 183	163 216	139 967	304 415	164 674	15 025	6 550	7 207	17 312	31 613	25 272	39 512	9 732
December	304 545	170 453	134 092	309 058	169 839	15 020	6 348	7 529	17 165	30 530	26 030	44 929	14 117
1996:													
January	286 149	156 914	129 235	308 317	168 878	14 703	6 206	7 087	17 327	31 612	25 968	43 577	12 550
February	302 670	165 945	136 725	303 937	164 611	14 886	6 073	7 338	17 365	32 943	25 401	38 151	8 597
March	321 424	179 273	142 151	307 487	167 984	14 245	5 842	7 143	17 223	30 709	26 594	43 753	16 791
April	305 634	163 470	142 164	306 699	163 658	15 059	6 154	7 535	17 843	31 310	26 221	36 960	6 919
May	314 773	170 925	143 848	314 604	171 396	15 539	6 607	7 587	18 507	32 034	25 506	42 770	11 705
June	329 384	181 990	147 394	311 107	169 721	15 347	6 392	7 410	18 045	31 508	26 315	41 891	9 549
July	285 490	147 098	138 392	314 708	171 122	15 492	6 509	7 564	17 959	32 293	27 701	40 788	9 514
August	310 699	163 782	146 917	310 229	166 859	15 470	6 387	7 623	18 299	32 549	26 122	37 359	6 909
September	332 620	182 676	149 944	316 296	173 282	14 820	6 335	7 086	18 442	32 075	26 104	44 565	12 659
October	330 625	181 262	149 363	319 016	173 994	14 761	6 188	7 369	18 264	31 936	30 268	41 009	11 792
November	319 054	171 947	147 107	320 367	173 773	14 814	5 938	7 493	18 444	32 007	28 414	42 246	11 322
December	310 777	171 254	139 523	314 191	169 492	15 262	6 206	7 614	18 049	32 398	23 912	41 869	10 904
1997:													
January	298 991	162 982	136 009	323 321	176 705	15 786	6 497	7 833	18 435	32 911	28 241	42 548	10 530
February	324 279	180 882	143 397	325 819	179 495	15 879	6 362	8 086	18 863	33 468	30 792	40 362	9 845
March	334 621	186 591	148 030	320 729	174 950	15 878	6 195	8 274	18 419	32 862	29 140	39 289	8 812
April	323 346	176 921	146 425	324 449	177 171	16 582	6 898	8 221	19 360	34 184	27 419	39 251	8 494
May	322 077	174 987	147 090	322 213	175 823	16 133	6 516	8 182	18 433	33 279	30 276	38 590	8 494
June	346 439	194 270	152 169	326 998	180 714	15 866	6 709	7 700	19 225	32 985	30 269	41 800	10 703
July	298 815	155 332	143 483	328 799	180 460	16 780	6 781	8 468	19 205	35 411	25 247	41 606	8 457
August	333 072	182 130	150 942	333 083	185 624	16 139	6 442	8 239	19 038	34 420	34 068	42 280	10 746
September	352 126	196 429	155 697	334 091	185 557	17 192	6 683	8 930	19 559	35 499	31 118	41 445	8 479
October	347 068	193 365	153 703	334 576	185 410	15 926	6 754	7 701	19 521	34 991	29 718	44 351	10 429
November	340 579	191 215	149 364	342 310	193 621	16 272	6 881	7 710	19 320	34 395	29 227	53 485	20 719
December	330 612	185 604	145 008	334 974	184 635	15 716	6 803	7 236	19 190	34 853	30 258	42 964	8 043
1998:													
January	310 926	172 138	138 788	336 432	187 048	15 272	6 112	7 707	19 328	35 766	31 417	44 520	13 720
February	333 699	188 167	145 532	334 446	186 033	15 996	6 584	7 722	19 774	36 552	30 714	42 431	9 986
March	351 066	199 682	151 384	334 712	185 963	14 696	6 285	6 688	19 704	37 448	30 850	42 204	8 527
April	336 909	189 159	147 750	337 502	188 921	15 451	6 095	7 891	20 001	36 889	31 707	44 431	12 827
May	327 550	180 165	147 385	330 233	182 777	14 940	6 286	7 168	19 630	36 244	29 114	42 422	10 760
June	349 890	196 102	153 788	331 188	182 986	14 453	5 850	7 325	19 722	36 922	30 072	39 349	8 480
July	306 253	162 637	143 616	334 821	186 617	14 273	5 382	7 521	20 132	37 636	32 840	39 768	10 172
August	335 916	185 341	150 575	337 815	190 304	14 413	5 523	7 298	19 693	37 450	31 116	46 745	13 106
September	359 884	205 297	154 587	340 388	192 783	13 917	5 347	7 186	19 930	38 983	32 870	45 101	9 109
October	347 900	197 533	150 367	334 663	188 523	13 343	4 912	6 927	20 095	35 503	33 348	44 870	9 637
November	333 218	186 550	146 668	335 930	189 193	14 587	5 572	7 447	20 235	35 593	31 933	45 024	9 962
December	340 465	196 922	143 543	343 982	195 574	14 087	5 331	7 323	20 460	38 246	33 859	46 166	7 848

1. Includes categories not shown seperately.

Manufacturers' New Orders—*Continued*

(Net, millions of dollars, seasonally adjusted)

Year and month	Nondurable goods industries		By market category [1]						Supplementary sales		
	Total	Industries with unfilled orders	Home goods and apparel	Consumer staples	Machinery and equipment	Automotive equipment	Construction materials and supplies	Other materials, supplies, and intermediate products	Household durables	Capital goods industries	
										Nondefense	Defense
1970	296 184	72 794	60 053	136 650	90 920	22 920	41 976	208 527	24 360	72 866	21 311
1971	312 195	75 322	63 910	143 889	104 615	31 325	44 769	219 246	25 887	80 185	18 787
1972	349 726	85 481	73 471	159 032	121 439	34 668	54 858	256 608	30 564	92 943	20 467
1973	400 514	95 225	80 190	183 637	151 221	40 271	65 713	310 891	33 804	119 108	23 409
1974	485 585	106 139	80 399	225 842	168 767	36 721	71 972	367 873	33 582	139 131	26 033
1975	518 177	110 975	81 682	247 066	151 278	37 452	64 582	339 984	34 140	118 635	24 765
1976	578 471	126 068	91 453	269 537	179 180	50 230	76 851	411 296	39 289	137 875	30 616
1977	648 880	140 721	105 613	294 776	214 944	60 614	92 881	480 457	46 181	164 168	34 624
1978	712 207	155 601	114 334	326 735	261 585	67 579	107 563	552 092	51 123	211 056	41 511
1979	817 447	172 861	119 157	378 236	305 432	66 949	118 946	619 405	54 117	253 844	33 795
1980	923 603	188 221	124 929	437 370	299 968	54 244	118 449	636 198	56 099	253 619	58 256
1981	1 012 453	206 535	132 987	477 650	312 509	60 834	122 619	688 321	59 342	261 666	58 881
1982	1 008 920	210 918	132 729	486 180	285 408	58 757	112 605	629 399	56 055	230 555	81 415
1983	1 047 733	233 594	143 390	491 092	303 922	77 638	128 440	702 743	60 924	235 489	96 105
1984	1 112 585	255 393	151 993	510 701	359 604	92 714	141 669	776 636	65 706	284 022	103 504
1985	1 120 209	263 955	153 711	518 109	374 954	97 164	147 149	763 711	66 904	294 544	109 505
1986	1 098 683	279 953	159 615	503 299	371 101	101 263	154 725	761 205	70 749	287 786	111 879
1987	1 182 951	308 101	163 728	531 778	400 962	105 265	165 396	838 571	69 526	313 127	111 639
1988	1 274 324	329 100	168 005	569 099	462 470	112 298	176 043	936 836	73 599	373 294	102 728
1989	1 362 197	345 474	174 574	616 054	496 955	118 385	179 546	970 570	78 242	395 855	93 398
1990	1 427 085	353 047	175 162	658 631	500 441	110 181	180 616	972 911	77 946	399 966	96 638
1991	1 427 478	350 693	175 921	667 789	462 856	106 058	172 621	956 041	78 314	365 655	87 213
1992	1 462 854	362 809	185 713	678 613	491 195	120 525	184 385	997 720	82 175	378 293	76 155
1993	1 495 407	370 132	194 976	691 346	505 542	134 526	198 463	1 045 795	88 914	380 329	71 904
1994	1 562 289	392 875	205 505	706 182	567 922	155 702	219 305	1 166 985	95 500	428 364	71 683
1995	1 666 208	430 281	211 040	742 360	624 687	160 887	228 242	1 287 097	98 500	486 134	70 903
1996	1 712 763	427 414	209 912	780 545	672 605	162 310	239 060	1 314 471	97 963	535 575	77 283
1997	1 771 317	439 339	222 405	809 563	729 607	169 310	253 766	1 392 871	107 403	577 978	67 706
1998	1 773 983	1 868 929	226 721	830 983	774 254	174 795	259 859	3 773 817	111 784	620 400	73 169
1995:											
January	137 537	35 483	18 466	60 492	50 900	13 735	19 699	107 179	8 492	39 164	5 701
February	138 662	35 807	17 685	61 240	51 321	13 698	19 444	107 397	8 069	39 408	6 564
March	138 037	35 588	17 695	60 694	51 429	14 019	19 052	107 670	8 296	39 567	7 066
April	138 180	36 128	17 475	61 303	49 071	13 019	18 443	105 624	7 793	37 545	4 978
May	138 792	36 255	18 049	61 326	51 469	13 082	18 767	106 922	8 284	40 962	5 513
June	139 797	36 504	17 604	61 940	50 744	13 203	18 554	106 617	8 284	39 266	4 839
July	138 705	36 302	17 360	61 683	47 456	12 529	18 797	106 619	8 323	36 742	5 333
August	139 689	35 827	17 624	62 625	50 272	13 422	19 444	108 057	8 417	38 778	6 840
September	138 800	35 187	17 121	62 407	55 259	13 647	19 031	106 984	8 199	43 385	7 106
October	138 857	35 470	17 183	62 467	53 244	13 510	19 192	107 306	8 047	40 630	5 777
November	139 741	36 081	17 494	62 678	54 881	13 195	19 039	108 315	8 327	43 730	4 914
December	139 219	35 216	17 245	63 257	58 276	13 449	18 790	107 791	7 887	46 727	6 312
1996:											
January	139 439	35 790	16 810	63 591	57 150	13 297	19 098	107 276	8 113	45 933	7 374
February	139 326	35 252	17 165	63 087	56 122	13 407	18 895	106 231	7 945	44 532	5 081
March	139 503	34 792	17 810	63 675	56 653	12 286	18 946	104 552	8 462	46 136	9 695
April	143 041	35 998	17 574	65 118	52 317	13 639	19 389	108 252	8 275	40 417	5 516
May	143 208	35 690	17 546	64 986	57 149	14 120	19 945	110 402	8 234	45 054	5 846
June	141 386	35 798	17 358	63 716	54 822	13 576	19 976	109 546	8 097	42 638	7 836
July	143 586	35 790	17 190	65 453	56 506	14 021	20 404	111 825	7 938	45 160	4 621
August	143 370	35 570	17 562	65 344	53 280	13 673	20 511	110 492	8 204	41 240	4 845
September	143 014	35 477	17 457	65 254	59 110	14 208	20 431	110 358	8 032	47 118	5 194
October	145 022	35 039	17 847	66 858	57 751	13 445	20 406	113 425	8 419	47 413	4 915
November	146 594	36 291	17 525	66 999	55 433	13 684	20 341	112 890	7 702	44 370	8 315
December	144 699	35 667	17 636	66 203	55 272	12 979	20 478	108 900	8 310	44 169	8 003
1997:											
January	146 616	35 331	17 490	67 733	58 211	14 397	20 722	114 307	8 219	45 919	5 472
February	146 324	35 557	18 183	66 262	59 242	13 795	20 798	116 468	8 698	47 009	5 974
March	145 779	36 181	17 799	66 419	57 428	13 475	20 516	113 852	8 666	45 288	6 032
April	147 278	36 046	18 563	66 741	57 425	13 837	21 582	114 966	8 709	44 763	6 103
May	146 390	35 738	18 357	67 354	57 295	13 267	20 792	114 570	8 849	45 110	5 198
June	146 284	36 395	18 434	67 285	59 773	13 861	21 131	115 062	9 137	47 617	5 904
July	148 339	37 392	19 020	67 727	61 149	14 915	21 681	112 948	9 291	47 731	5 536
August	147 459	36 241	18 086	67 964	60 747	14 302	21 270	119 761	8 460	47 903	5 327
September	148 534	37 134	19 099	67 686	61 767	14 229	21 548	118 772	9 345	49 303	5 247
October	149 166	37 621	18 654	68 004	64 017	14 545	21 521	117 011	8 940	50 450	4 705
November	148 689	37 399	19 287	67 984	71 330	14 216	20 975	116 947	9 486	58 759	5 915
December	150 339	38 066	19 284	68 463	60 418	14 835	21 187	118 234	9 445	47 027	6 496
1998:											
January	149 384	37 807	18 768	68 819	64 672	13 649	21 143	116 171	8 995	52 302	7 455
February	148 413	37 366	18 908	68 675	62 503	14 307	21 585	116 803	9 299	50 436	5 978
March	148 749	37 506	18 556	69 182	63 334	14 819	21 559	116 032	9 028	50 502	5 385
April	148 581	37 600	18 826	69 103	64 295	14 277	21 601	116 922	9 050	51 240	6 865
May	147 456	37 396	18 891	68 622	63 803	14 256	21 424	112 079	9 271	50 834	5 397
June	148 202	37 385	19 020	69 623	63 470	13 212	21 781	112 336	9 509	51 053	5 655
July	148 204	38 043	19 105	69 283	62 709	13 276	21 986	116 895	9 373	50 763	5 522
August	147 511	37 357	19 141	69 360	67 303	14 733	21 523	115 035	9 388	55 371	4 933
September	147 605	36 856	18 792	69 884	67 815	15 223	21 391	114 382	9 285	53 540	7 042
October	146 140	36 598	18 786	68 776	63 403	15 241	21 655	114 849	9 387	50 138	6 353
November	146 737	37 128	18 988	69 552	63 839	15 257	21 783	115 050	9 465	50 675	5 657
December	148 408	36 810	19 341	70 561	64 980	15 644	22 331	117 922	9 854	52 005	7 449

1. Defense products and business supplies not shown.

Manufacturers' Unfilled Orders

(End of period—Millions of dollars)

Year and month	Not seasonally adjusted			Seasonally adjusted										
					Durable goods industries									
						Primary metals						Transportation equipment	
	Total	Durable goods industries	Nondurable goods industries	Total	Total	Total	Blast furnaces, steel mills	Nonferrous and other primary metals	Fabricated metal products	Industrial machinery and equipment	Electronic and electric equipment	Total	Aircraft, missiles, and parts
1970	104 683	100 139	4 544	105 008	100 412	7 796	4 617	2 663	14 877	21 737	11 881	34 720	26 198
1971	104 857	99 906	4 951	105 247	100 225	7 478	4 380	2 552	13 688	21 170	12 148	35 793	26 259
1972	118 717	112 517	6 200	119 349	113 034	10 470	6 681	3 116	15 077	25 968	13 376	37 627	26 151
1973	155 583	148 421	7 162	156 561	149 204	16 129	9 794	4 962	21 019	36 959	17 111	45 248	27 842
1974	186 030	180 686	5 344	187 043	181 519	19 225	11 054	5 952	28 100	50 084	17 319	51 118	30 506
1975	168 627	160 993	7 634	169 546	161 664	13 266	7 345	4 015	24 008	46 580	15 857	46 633	28 244
1976	177 215	169 198	8 017	178 128	169 857	14 684	7 776	4 891	22 810	48 321	17 584	49 078	29 421
1977	200 101	191 603	8 498	202 024	193 323	17 298	9 435	5 483	25 152	52 026	19 999	57 101	37 325
1978	256 785	246 162	10 623	259 169	248 281	23 969	12 932	7 393	29 137	62 233	24 219	81 782	54 417
1979	300 794	288 834	11 960	303 593	291 321	26 320	12 485	9 457	33 131	69 844	29 261	103 555	74 034
1980	324 409	312 508	11 901	327 416	315 202	26 815	13 418	10 096	33 296	68 979	31 751	119 700	88 051
1981	323 163	311 628	11 535	326 547	314 707	22 024	10 589	8 784	33 036	69 405	32 718	118 008	86 794
1982	308 633	297 851	10 782	311 887	300 798	15 500	6 674	7 418	27 117	51 864	34 639	125 879	93 703
1983	343 479	329 758	13 721	347 273	333 114	20 400	9 431	9 594	26 752	52 351	40 794	141 637	105 504
1984	369 844	356 446	13 398	373 529	359 651	18 362	8 103	8 694	30 254	53 466	43 967	152 189	117 923
1985	383 865	369 362	14 503	387 196	372 097	18 331	8 248	8 361	29 197	53 516	43 366	156 155	127 282
1986	390 428	374 264	16 164	393 515	376 699	18 590	8 897	7 783	29 633	48 416	42 793	161 145	133 565
1987	427 185	406 444	20 741	430 426	408 688	24 340	11 828	10 300	32 973	48 416	44 741	176 588	144 987
1988	470 993	449 859	21 134	474 154	452 150	27 079	11 508	12 974	31 661	57 583	46 702	211 575	174 721
1989	505 479	484 623	20 856	508 849	487 098	24 120	9 479	11 824	27 629	58 369	44 616	253 517	217 557
1990	527 337	506 311	21 026	531 131	509 124	24 768	10 120	11 258	25 859	57 872	44 501	279 082	242 208
1991	514 835	492 500	22 335	519 199	495 802	23 075	9 290	10 609	24 516	53 812	42 988	275 260	242 798
1992	488 656	466 328	22 328	492 893	469 381	21 636	8 897	9 925	23 725	53 651	44 348	253 076	222 194
1993	453 412	432 667	20 745	457 810	436 017	23 068	10 163	9 623	20 731	52 952	44 784	225 256	194 154
1994	462 190	437 599	24 591	466 699	440 998	29 661	11 303	14 535	21 290	65 608	44 941	215 171	180 969
1995	475 113	451 948	23 165	479 674	455 459	27 993	12 183	12 195	22 329	71 179	51 470	219 101	186 848
1996	508 952	484 325	24 627	513 062	487 441	29 996	12 432	13 167	24 159	73 042	49 943	249 119	215 171
1997	531 558	506 334	25 224	536 131	509 927	35 160	14 905	14 656	26 649	73 419	55 174	254 579	217 998
1998	512 986	490 040	22 946	519 038	495 172	29 554	11 430	12 666	25 894	74 458	60 530	243 205	204 434
1995:													
January	471 223	445 783	25 440	469 404	443 209	30 030	11 503	14 705	21 542	67 257	45 581	213 940	178 929
February	475 781	449 651	26 130	472 648	445 979	29 911	11 509	14 474	21 828	68 304	46 338	214 720	179 786
March	478 417	451 539	26 878	475 075	448 403	29 665	11 791	14 052	21 960	69 977	48 058	214 532	179 928
April	478 144	450 524	27 620	473 465	446 381	29 376	11 790	13 655	22 116	70 101	49 128	211 906	177 674
May	477 550	449 639	27 911	474 190	447 077	28 588	11 666	13 106	22 417	70 464	50 312	212 081	178 398
June	471 071	443 267	27 804	471 404	444 492	27 809	11 523	12 565	22 495	71 581	50 247	209 082	175 495
July	472 431	444 210	28 221	470 768	443 588	27 231	11 357	12 217	22 448	70 960	51 894	207 658	174 678
August	470 354	443 201	27 153	470 361	443 950	27 464	11 585	12 213	22 380	71 098	51 567	207 811	175 182
September	468 089	442 668	25 421	472 903	447 594	27 437	11 440	12 307	22 408	71 049	51 948	211 744	178 690
October	470 201	446 117	24 084	473 073	448 328	27 599	11 647	12 183	22 268	70 693	52 600	212 100	179 615
November	469 801	445 865	23 936	474 439	449 638	27 801	11 932	12 105	22 492	71 669	51 689	212 965	180 816
December	475 113	451 948	23 165	479 674	455 459	27 993	12 183	12 195	22 329	71 179	51 470	219 101	186 848
1996:													
January	490 002	466 095	23 907	487 602	463 011	28 096	12 283	12 051	22 265	72 113	51 400	225 681	192 279
February	492 592	468 686	23 906	488 998	464 620	28 464	12 273	12 216	22 382	72 947	50 805	225 982	193 115
March	498 516	474 652	23 864	495 402	471 663	28 048	12 084	12 001	22 521	72 277	51 024	234 210	201 821
April	498 840	474 413	24 427	494 429	470 415	28 254	12 051	12 199	22 570	72 398	50 821	232 740	200 862
May	499 442	474 764	24 678	496 544	472 460	28 689	12 442	12 264	22 918	72 776	49 871	234 932	203 497
June	498 721	473 752	24 969	499 403	475 177	29 498	12 640	12 670	23 102	72 588	49 603	237 821	204 867
July	505 012	479 501	25 511	503 535	479 170	30 035	12 854	12 967	23 197	73 450	50 830	239 581	206 685
August	501 327	476 154	25 173	501 611	477 221	30 591	12 967	13 321	23 281	73 883	50 724	237 340	204 607
September	499 728	475 073	24 655	504 748	480 211	30 621	12 993	13 305	23 601	73 587	50 113	241 039	208 275
October	507 348	483 334	24 014	510 027	485 350	30 384	12 884	13 308	23 814	73 499	53 172	243 467	211 491
November	508 413	483 792	24 621	512 650	487 153	29 974	12 556	13 177	23 956	73 334	53 401	245 954	213 658
December	508 952	484 325	24 627	513 062	487 441	29 996	12 432	13 167	24 159	73 042	49 943	249 119	215 171
1997:													
January	520 156	495 420	24 736	517 233	491 842	30 230	12 459	13 290	24 297	73 553	51 153	250 980	216 913
February	525 801	501 264	24 537	521 778	496 803	30 439	12 392	13 493	24 669	74 456	53 869	250 900	217 447
March	524 551	498 951	25 600	521 807	496 249	30 721	12 199	13 879	24 833	74 456	53 553	249 978	216 300
April	524 528	498 485	26 043	520 617	494 897	31 397	12 616	14 082	25 240	74 952	52 627	247 420	214 262
May	523 128	496 984	26 144	520 570	494 971	31 924	12 872	14 265	25 272	74 830	54 439	245 495	212 481
June	520 327	493 820	26 507	521 450	495 647	32 004	13 120	13 998	25 742	73 455	55 379	245 654	212 954
July	520 535	492 960	27 575	518 918	492 623	32 880	13 426	14 463	26 015	73 742	51 522	243 587	210 968
August	523 608	496 768	26 840	523 751	497 693	33 270	13 492	14 730	26 058	74 046	55 854	243 845	211 773
September	519 365	493 075	26 290	524 420	498 284	34 558	13 759	15 601	26 334	74 311	56 163	242 911	210 030
October	524 156	498 555	25 601	526 675	500 469	34 626	14 100	15 338	26 581	74 212	56 026	244 973	210 861
November	533 329	507 877	25 452	537 581	511 299	35 157	14 615	15 092	26 758	74 264	55 411	255 173	220 532
December	531 558	506 334	25 224	536 131	509 927	35 160	14 905	14 656	26 649	73 419	55 174	254 579	217 998
1998:													
January	543 779	518 535	25 244	540 626	514 672	34 717	14 533	14 590	26 868	73 249	57 059	257 557	220 894
February	543 505	518 273	25 232	539 189	513 407	34 875	14 626	14 546	26 876	73 592	57 059	256 411	219 861
March	537 538	512 007	25 531	534 910	509 372	33 911	14 472	13 594	26 838	74 176	57 071	253 407	217 113
April	541 896	516 207	25 689	536 859	511 450	33 839	14 209	13 833	27 269	74 167	58 722	253 975	218 831
May	536 103	510 563	25 540	533 470	508 438	33 603	14 295	13 504	27 154	73 850	58 099	252 835	218 389
June	527 169	501 923	25 246	529 548	504 888	33 007	14 021	13 356	27 121	72 857	57 289	251 327	216 211
July	531 291	505 568	25 723	528 989	504 598	32 312	13 397	13 384	26 944	72 683	58 913	250 539	215 817
August	529 830	504 851	24 979	530 359	506 113	31 669	12 816	13 203	26 523	73 422	58 801	252 881	217 854
September	525 390	501 112	24 278	530 266	506 054	30 635	12 254	12 854	26 218	75 630	59 249	251 394	215 042
October	522 765	499 520	23 245	524 796	500 759	29 388	11 437	12 410	26 137	74 122	60 378	248 247	211 882
November	514 816	491 398	23 418	519 303	495 129	29 689	11 458	12 637	25 957	73 092	59 677	244 947	208 629
December	512 986	490 040	22 946	519 038	495 172	29 554	11 430	12 666	25 894	74 458	60 530	243 205	204 434

Manufacturers' Unfilled Orders—*Continued*

(End of period, millions of dollars, seasonally adjusted)

Year and month	Nondurable goods industries	By market category [1] Home goods and apparel	Consumer staples	Machinery and equipment	Automotive equipment	Construction materials and supplies	Other materials, supplies, and intermediate products	Supplementary sales Household durables	Capital goods industries Nondefense	Defense
1970	4 596	2 245	284	42 704	714	8 880	30 991	2 078	46 544	18 804
1971	5 022	2 509	314	43 386	785	8 073	31 149	2 292	47 576	18 158
1972	6 315	3 168	355	47 635	886	8 810	38 198	2 914	52 781	19 261
1973	7 357	3 831	466	61 767	1 354	12 311	53 339	3 471	67 947	21 756
1974	5 524	2 891	480	77 672	1 400	15 125	60 751	2 582	84 495	26 558
1975	7 882	3 179	596	70 549	1 058	12 694	51 673	2 740	76 773	27 936
1976	8 271	3 376	708	72 941	1 209	11 592	54 856	2 862	79 121	31 826
1977	8 701	4 670	846	81 172	1 481	12 821	63 498	4 135	87 552	36 692
1978	10 888	5 493	978	103 005	2 046	14 408	85 040	4 864	112 277	47 425
1979	12 272	5 547	1 036	130 361	1 899	15 360	99 144	4 754	144 114	48 656
1980	12 214	5 226	1 054	136 142	1 656	15 410	100 488	4 388	150 973	66 636
1981	11 840	5 668	1 113	128 411	1 742	15 213	96 356	4 729	142 802	77 793
1982	11 089	5 784	1 140	109 196	1 563	11 981	84 771	4 860	121 082	99 052
1983	14 159	7 131	1 047	103 626	2 406	12 673	103 680	5 810	114 280	121 177
1984	13 878	6 890	1 083	108 659	2 172	13 102	105 750	5 603	119 424	142 324
1985	15 099	6 996	1 177	111 055	2 036	13 124	103 383	5 253	120 687	156 188
1986	16 816	7 357	1 171	108 830	2 159	13 677	104 644	5 815	118 429	161 705
1987	21 738	8 735	1 148	125 209	2 397	14 140	119 288	5 842	136 171	163 786
1988	22 004	7 999	1 431	160 441	2 220	14 557	129 322	5 703	176 069	161 878
1989	21 751	8 893	1 438	202 960	1 887	13 992	127 879	5 854	221 152	155 314
1990	22 007	9 067	1 276	231 612	1 531	14 021	126 374	5 215	250 314	149 844
1991	23 397	9 810	1 324	224 767	1 705	14 828	128 935	5 498	246 093	139 666
1992	23 512	9 763	1 437	215 353	1 609	14 706	126 420	5 047	234 817	124 047
1993	21 793	9 043	1 507	196 380	1 916	13 980	123 987	5 438	214 248	112 062
1994	25 701	8 430	1 664	195 078	2 218	15 754	136 735	5 788	213 268	106 548
1995	24 215	8 843	1 878	206 290	2 314	15 730	139 058	5 580	224 059	103 880
1996	25 621	8 158	2 113	225 985	2 377	16 649	146 806	4 916	247 491	109 186
1997	26 204	9 542	2 100	243 676	2 552	17 855	156 870	6 289	261 575	101 797
1998	23 866	8 979	2 364	241 602	2 474	17 506	148 367	5 522	257 382	95 947
1995:										
January	26 195	8 876	1 697	195 896	2 217	16 084	138 248	5 772	214 496	105 765
February	26 669	9 000	1 751	196 539	2 238	16 145	140 104	5 651	215 293	106 157
March	26 672	9 137	1 769	197 476	2 269	16 039	140 424	5 804	216 279	106 972
April	27 084	9 261	1 783	196 025	2 302	15 925	141 173	5 540	214 614	105 823
May	27 113	9 834	1 810	196 743	2 304	16 006	141 243	5 695	216 049	105 069
June	26 912	9 804	1 854	195 956	2 333	15 784	140 749	5 856	215 219	103 844
July	27 180	9 666	1 939	194 178	2 329	15 951	142 170	5 982	213 681	103 094
August	26 411	9 496	1 972	193 391	2 361	16 173	141 747	5 921	212 792	103 653
September	25 309	9 125	1 855	197 096	2 397	15 949	140 215	5 908	215 990	104 694
October	24 745	8 733	1 910	198 590	2 388	15 906	139 648	5 638	216 418	104 446
November	24 801	8 719	1 946	200 668	2 334	15 842	139 764	5 631	218 772	103 543
December	24 215	8 843	1 878	206 290	2 314	15 730	139 058	5 580	224 059	103 880
1996:										
January	24 591	8 969	1 937	212 421	2 363	15 733	139 385	5 653	230 582	105 169
February	24 378	9 071	1 929	215 055	2 358	15 985	138 667	5 692	233 104	104 392
March	23 739	9 352	1 857	219 294	2 328	15 974	137 111	5 876	237 556	108 003
April	24 014	9 415	1 896	218 356	2 317	15 946	137 158	5 910	236 557	107 664
May	24 084	9 254	1 960	220 435	2 313	15 945	137 438	5 809	238 790	107 488
June	24 226	9 085	1 933	220 817	2 296	15 977	138 423	5 680	238 763	109 237
July	24 365	8 775	2 115	223 573	2 342	16 103	140 849	5 435	242 355	108 163
August	24 390	8 760	2 095	221 881	2 364	16 195	141 743	5 420	240 439	106 982
September	24 537	8 780	2 028	224 764	2 389	16 395	142 816	5 332	243 708	106 119
October	24 677	8 926	1 923	227 544	2 342	16 303	146 161	5 478	248 042	105 361
November	25 497	8 309	2 076	226 718	2 384	16 155	147 871	4 859	248 100	107 360
December	25 621	8 158	2 113	225 985	2 377	16 649	146 806	4 916	247 491	109 186
1997:										
January	25 391	7 837	2 186	228 930	2 457	16 808	148 674	4 835	250 310	108 670
February	24 975	7 805	1 900	231 692	2 486	16 811	151 440	5 003	253 014	108 268
March	25 558	7 774	2 080	231 204	2 538	16 785	151 609	5 048	252 589	108 239
April	25 720	7 817	2 167	229 988	2 540	17 119	151 242	5 137	250 797	107 992
May	25 599	8 071	2 166	229 125	2 525	17 105	152 672	5 398	249 556	106 947
June	25 803	8 240	2 245	229 405	2 530	17 263	153 411	5 588	249 810	106 313
July	26 295	8 744	2 336	229 088	2 537	17 551	150 875	6 051	249 202	105 600
August	26 058	8 609	2 280	230 203	2 568	17 606	155 480	5 878	249 831	104 796
September	26 136	8 915	2 234	230 523	2 560	17 601	156 525	6 067	250 098	104 023
October	26 206	9 000	2 187	234 298	2 581	17 839	156 198	6 023	252 811	102 377
November	26 282	9 492	2 084	245 713	2 525	17 820	156 440	6 362	263 786	101 386
December	26 204	9 542	2 100	243 676	2 552	17 855	156 870	6 289	261 575	101 797
1998:										
January	25 954	9 183	2 104	246 939	2 532	17 948	157 359	6 038	264 474	102 834
February	25 782	8 968	2 111	246 519	2 514	18 132	156 818	5 910	264 502	102 279
March	25 538	8 528	2 217	245 305	2 499	18 083	155 507	5 560	263 411	101 034
April	25 409	8 198	2 219	246 375	2 433	18 281	156 569	5 308	264 091	101 154
May	25 032	8 189	2 179	247 027	2 431	18 276	153 902	5 321	264 339	99 993
June	24 660	8 232	2 216	245 970	2 426	18 205	151 463	5 348	262 987	99 344
July	24 391	8 007	2 288	245 443	2 358	18 129	152 575	5 092	262 434	98 371
August	24 246	8 219	2 279	248 931	2 314	17 996	152 118	5 233	266 583	96 616
September	24 212	8 356	2 271	250 233	2 380	17 682	150 231	5 287	266 704	97 052
October	24 037	8 646	2 146	246 919	2 382	17 618	148 732	5 430	262 972	96 337
November	24 174	8 941	2 328	243 910	2 418	17 486	147 162	5 479	259 447	95 040
December	23 866	8 979	2 364	241 602	2 474	17 506	148 367	5 522	257 382	95 947

1. Defense products and business supplies not shown.

Manufacturing by Industry—Durable Goods

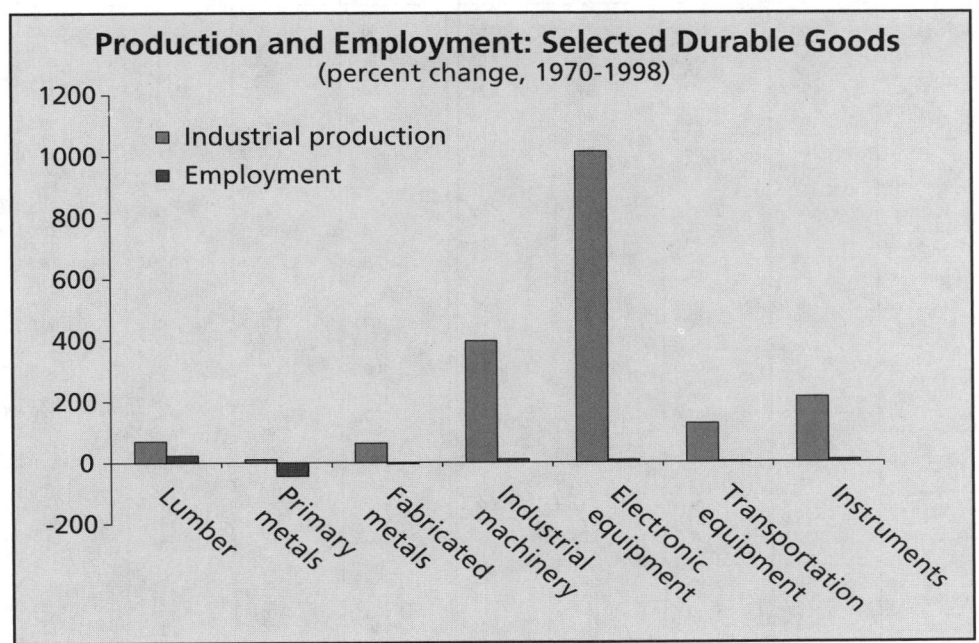

Production and Employment: Selected Durable Goods
(percent change, 1970-1998)

- Industrial production
- Employment

- Over the past 28 years, by far the greatest growth in production has been in industries directly affected by the "high-tech" revolution: electronic and electric machinery and equipment, industrial machinery (which includes computers), and instruments. Production of electronic equipment was up over 1,000 percent; industrial machinery nearly 400 percent; and instruments over 200 percent.

- No durable goods industry has shown much growth in employment, and some have shown declines. The largest employment growth was in lumber, with a 24 percent gain from 1970 to 1998. The largest decline was in primary metals, with a 44 percent drop in employment.

- Measured from the 1989 business cycle peak, the employment picture has been mixed for durable goods. Lumber and wood products; furniture and fixtures; fabricated metals; and industrial machinery all have seen growth in employment. Stone, clay, and glass products; primary metals; electronic equipment; transportation equipment; and instruments have seen declines. Overall, employment in durable goods industries in 1998 was 2 percent below 1989.

Lumber and Wood Products—Production, Capacity Utilization, and Prices

Year and month	Industrial production (1992=100, seasonally adjusted)							Capacity utilization (output as a percent of capacity, seasonally adjusted)	Producer prices (1982=100, except as noted; not seasonally adjusted)		
	Total	Logging and lumber		Lumber products					Lumber and wood products industry (December 1984 =100)	Lumber and wood products commodities	Intermediate materials
		Total	Logging	Total	Millwork and plywood		Manufactured homes				Softwood lumber
					Total	Plywood					
1970	68.6	75.0	70.6	65.8	56.0	70.5	.....	80.5	.....	39.9	35.2
1971	70.4	71.4	62.2	71.9	62.9	80.1	.....	80.0	.....	44.7	44.0
1972	80.6	83.2	74.4	81.3	72.9	88.7	146.6	88.2	.....	50.7	52.1
1973	80.9	80.8	75.6	83.5	76.0	88.9	144.0	85.5	.....	62.2	66.6
1974	73.4	79.3	81.7	71.2	64.1	77.6	101.7	75.8	.....	64.5	65.7
1975	68.3	75.5	76.6	65.1	62.1	75.7	81.5	69.5	.....	62.1	62.4
1976	77.8	83.6	82.5	75.6	70.5	86.5	107.1	78.2	.....	72.2	77.1
1977	86.1	88.6	95.4	84.3	81.3	92.3	118.7	85.7	.....	83.0	92.5
1978	87.5	87.8	91.0	87.5	84.4	95.1	126.0	86.1	.....	96.9	107.6
1979	86.3	86.9	93.1	86.0	82.0	90.4	121.2	83.8	.....	105.5	118.1
1980	80.4	83.6	112.2	77.9	74.8	84.4	99.6	77.7	.....	101.5	107.3
1981	78.1	78.2	104.3	77.9	74.4	85.7	101.8	74.9	.....	102.8	106.6
1982	70.3	70.0	89.9	70.4	65.7	80.0	89.3	66.6	.....	100.0	100.0
1983	83.3	82.0	104.8	84.1	80.3	92.5	110.5	78.8	.....	107.9	115.0
1984	89.9	88.3	112.0	90.8	89.8	95.2	104.7	84.0	.....	108.0	110.0
1985	92.0	91.9	109.1	92.0	93.9	97.8	102.5	84.0	100.3	106.6	107.4
1986	99.6	102.4	118.6	97.7	102.9	109.3	102.5	89.0	101.5	107.2	108.4
1987	104.9	105.8	117.7	104.2	111.8	116.0	106.4	92.1	105.3	112.8	116.1
1988	105.1	106.7	115.0	103.9	111.5	115.6	103.1	91.1	109.2	118.9	120.0
1989	104.3	105.0	113.9	103.7	109.3	111.8	96.3	88.7	115.3	126.7	127.1
1990	101.6	100.5	103.7	102.2	105.4	107.3	94.0	85.1	117.0	129.7	123.8
1991	94.5	95.6	98.2	93.8	95.2	98.1	84.5	78.5	119.4	132.1	125.7
1992	100.0	100.0	100.0	100.0	100.0	100.0	100.0	82.7	129.7	146.6	148.6
1993	100.8	96.2	96.4	104.3	101.8	99.3	115.3	82.6	148.3	174.0	193.0
1994	105.9	99.8	96.5	110.6	108.4	101.0	127.0	84.9	154.4	180.0	198.1
1995	107.9	101.6	96.1	112.8	108.2	102.0	135.8	83.9	154.1	178.1	178.5
1996	110.4	102.4	94.8	116.4	111.2	98.6	144.7	82.9	153.5	176.1	189.5
1997	114.2	107.5	97.4	119.3	114.8	100.4	141.4	82.3	158.9	183.8	206.5
1998	117.0	107.5	92.3	124.2	120.6	101.3	149.2	81.7	157.0	179.1	182.7
1995:											
January	110.3	105.3	98.5	114.2	109.5	105.0	141.3	86.9	155.7	179.6	189.1
February	108.4	101.2	96.2	113.9	111.3	102.7	131.5	85.2	155.0	179.5	183.4
March	106.8	99.7	99.0	112.2	108.2	102.1	130.5	83.7	155.5	180.6	185.4
April	106.9	102.1	93.2	110.6	106.9	99.5	130.2	83.6	155.0	180.4	180.9
May	105.0	98.4	92.4	110.0	107.2	99.2	131.7	81.9	154.5	179.7	178.1
June	105.9	100.5	94.4	110.1	106.1	99.3	132.4	82.4	153.0	178.0	173.7
July	107.2	102.6	94.6	110.8	106.0	100.4	133.2	83.2	154.2	178.2	178.1
August	107.7	100.0	96.8	113.7	108.9	105.6	136.0	83.4	154.2	177.8	177.2
September	109.5	103.4	96.6	114.3	108.6	103.0	138.0	84.6	155.1	178.9	179.9
October	109.2	102.8	97.4	114.1	108.5	102.0	139.1	84.2	153.8	177.2	175.9
November	107.1	98.4	97.2	113.6	108.6	101.0	142.3	82.3	152.1	174.2	170.8
December	110.8	104.5	96.6	115.6	109.2	104.9	147.9	84.9	151.4	173.5	169.3
1996:											
January	106.9	100.0	95.6	112.1	105.9	101.1	141.8	81.7	150.6	172.9	169.2
February	107.3	100.9	96.2	112.2	107.7	99.5	139.6	81.8	150.7	173.0	170.6
March	110.3	104.4	96.9	114.9	108.4	99.4	146.0	83.8	150.9	172.8	174.6
April	110.7	103.0	97.9	116.5	110.5	100.4	146.2	83.8	151.0	171.9	178.5
May	110.7	102.7	95.2	116.7	111.7	102.4	146.7	83.5	153.8	175.8	192.1
June	112.5	103.2	97.0	119.5	113.5	100.6	149.1	84.6	154.5	176.8	196.8
July	109.9	100.5	94.0	117.0	112.8	100.7	144.3	82.4	153.3	175.0	191.6
August	111.8	103.5	92.4	118.0	113.2	99.4	147.7	83.5	154.4	177.0	196.6
September	111.7	102.6	91.3	118.6	113.3	95.0	147.1	83.2	156.6	180.2	203.9
October	110.6	101.0	92.0	117.9	113.7	96.7	146.6	82.1	154.6	177.8	193.7
November	112.3	104.7	94.8	118.0	112.8	97.2	143.2	83.1	156.2	180.2	204.4
December	110.0	103.0	94.5	115.4	111.2	90.3	136.7	81.2	155.9	179.7	202.4
1997:											
January	111.3	105.2	96.8	115.9	111.6	96.0	140.5	81.8	156.4	180.6	202.6
February	113.6	106.4	96.7	119.2	114.7	106.4	142.0	83.2	158.2	183.4	209.5
March	114.4	107.9	96.6	119.3	115.2	103.4	141.8	83.5	159.3	184.8	210.5
April	114.5	106.8	96.3	120.3	114.8	100.3	144.1	83.3	159.9	185.4	215.0
May	115.2	108.7	97.8	120.2	114.6	99.9	142.7	83.5	160.7	186.8	219.6
June	115.6	109.2	97.2	120.5	114.9	101.1	141.7	83.5	159.8	185.4	211.5
July	115.1	108.3	97.0	120.4	115.1	99.6	142.3	82.9	160.1	185.9	212.6
August	114.0	108.1	95.6	118.5	113.3	96.3	140.8	81.8	159.6	185.0	209.1
September	113.2	106.6	97.2	118.3	114.4	100.0	139.7	80.9	158.9	183.7	201.9
October	113.5	106.5	97.4	119.0	115.8	101.1	139.8	80.9	157.3	181.1	194.4
November	114.8	107.9	97.6	120.1	116.5	101.1	141.5	81.5	158.2	181.8	196.2
December	115.0	108.9	101.3	119.7	116.1	98.9	142.3	81.4	157.9	181.5	194.8
1998:											
January	115.2	106.7	93.3	121.7	118.3	101.2	147.1	81.3	157.4	181.1	190.9
February	116.2	108.1	93.6	122.5	119.8	99.7	149.6	81.9	158.2	182.2	192.9
March	115.3	106.5	93.1	121.9	118.0	98.7	148.0	81.0	158.2	182.4	193.7
April	116.1	107.6	92.1	122.6	118.7	102.0	148.0	81.4	158.5	182.5	193.4
May	116.4	106.7	93.3	123.7	119.2	100.3	149.0	81.4	157.4	180.4	187.0
June	116.7	107.3	93.4	123.9	120.3	100.7	146.1	81.5	155.6	177.5	177.1
July	117.5	107.5	93.5	125.0	121.3	103.0	151.1	81.8	157.0	178.5	181.6
August	118.5	110.9	93.4	124.3	120.5	100.3	145.7	82.3	158.2	179.7	183.4
September	117.0	107.0	91.6	124.6	120.7	101.4	147.8	81.1	157.3	178.0	175.2
October	118.0	108.8	92.2	125.0	121.1	100.5	150.9	81.6	155.3	175.5	171.9
November	118.3	106.1	91.5	127.4	123.4	103.4	154.6	81.6	155.2	175.2	170.3
December	121.4	110.9	92.7	129.4	127.7	104.6	156.6	83.6	155.7	175.9	175.1

Lumber and Wood Products—Employment, Hours, and Earnings

Year and month	Producer prices (1982=100, not seasonally adjusted) Intermediate materials—continued Millwork	Plywood	Crude materials: Logs and timber	Employment (thousands, seasonally adjusted) Total payroll employees	Production workers	Production workers Average weekly hours, seasonally adjusted	Aggregate weekly hours index (1982=100), seasonally adjusted	Average earnings (dollars, not seasonally adjusted) Hourly	Weekly
1970	41.5	46.7	.....	658	564	39.6	117.9	2.97	117.61
1971	43.2	49.4	.....	681	588	39.8	123.8	3.18	126.56
1972	46.0	56.3	.....	740	637	40.4	136.1	3.34	134.94
1973	51.6	66.9	.....	774	665	40.0	140.6	3.62	144.80
1974	56.2	69.4	.....	727	618	39.2	128.2	3.90	152.88
1975	57.4	69.4	.....	627	526	38.8	107.8	4.28	166.06
1976	63.3	80.6	.....	693	585	39.9	123.5	4.74	189.13
1977	69.3	91.4	.....	736	626	39.9	132.0	5.11	203.89
1978	84.3	101.5	.....	770	657	39.8	138.3	5.62	223.68
1979	91.0	107.9	.....	782	664	39.5	138.6	6.08	240.16
1980	93.2	106.2	.....	704	587	38.6	119.9	6.57	253.60
1981	97.8	105.9	.....	680	563	38.7	115.1	7.02	271.67
1982	100.0	100.0	100.0	610	497	38.1	100.0	7.46	284.23
1983	108.2	105.2	96.6	671	555	40.1	117.7	7.82	313.58
1984	110.2	104.1	97.0	718	598	39.9	126.3	8.05	321.20
1985	111.7	99.6	96.0	711	592	39.9	124.9	8.25	329.18
1986	113.7	101.4	92.3	724	605	40.4	129.2	8.37	338.15
1987	117.7	102.6	101.8	754	628	40.6	134.9	8.43	342.26
1988	121.9	103.4	117.7	767	639	40.1	135.6	8.59	344.46
1989	127.3	115.9	131.9	756	626	40.1	132.6	8.84	354.48
1990	130.4	114.2	142.8	733	603	40.2	128.2	9.08	365.02
1991	135.5	114.3	144.1	675	553	40.0	116.9	9.24	369.60
1992	143.3	133.3	164.8	680	558	40.6	119.9	9.44	383.26
1993	156.6	152.8	212.3	709	584	40.8	126.1	9.61	392.09
1994	162.4	158.6	219.1	754	623	41.2	135.9	9.84	405.41
1995	163.8	165.3	220.4	769	632	40.6	135.8	10.12	410.87
1996	166.6	156.4	206.8	778	640	40.8	138.0	10.44	425.95
1997	170.9	159.3	214.4	796	655	41.0	142.1	10.76	441.16
1998	171.1	157.3	208.1	813	668	41.1	145.2	11.10	456.21
1995:									
January	163.9	166.0	218.1	771	635	41.0	137.7	9.95	404.97
February	163.4	162.8	224.5	773	637	40.9	137.8	9.94	397.60
March	163.8	164.5	225.9	771	636	40.8	137.2	9.94	401.58
April	163.8	164.0	229.3	768	632	40.6	135.7	9.97	400.79
May	163.7	165.2	228.4	766	630	40.4	134.6	10.01	406.41
June	163.7	159.3	228.8	765	628	40.5	134.5	10.11	412.49
July	163.9	167.6	219.9	765	629	40.4	134.4	10.21	408.40
August	164.0	171.1	216.0	767	629	40.6	135.0	10.20	419.22
September	164.2	173.4	216.0	769	632	40.6	135.7	10.28	422.51
October	164.0	169.9	214.6	771	633	40.8	136.6	10.27	423.12
November	163.4	161.7	211.5	773	634	40.8	136.8	10.22	415.95
December	163.6	157.4	212.3	774	635	40.2	135.0	10.29	415.72
1996:									
January	163.6	154.0	214.5	765	627	38.9	129.0	10.28	396.81
February	163.8	154.2	214.0	772	633	40.7	136.2	10.23	407.15
March	164.1	152.1	209.3	771	632	40.7	136.0	10.29	415.72
April	164.6	151.6	200.2	775	636	40.7	136.9	10.33	420.43
May	165.8	158.3	202.8	776	638	41.0	138.3	10.35	426.42
June	166.7	155.8	201.5	780	641	41.2	139.6	10.45	434.72
July	167.0	154.0	201.7	781	642	41.1	139.5	10.47	426.13
August	167.9	157.4	203.6	783	644	41.1	139.9	10.54	436.36
September	168.7	166.7	206.0	783	643	41.2	140.1	10.57	439.71
October	168.7	160.1	208.8	784	646	41.0	140.0	10.56	437.18
November	169.3	157.9	209.8	787	648	41.0	140.5	10.57	433.37
December	169.3	155.3	209.5	784	646	41.1	140.4	10.62	437.54
1997:									
January	170.1	154.5	213.0	785	646	40.6	138.7	10.58	418.97
February	170.3	158.8	215.9	788	648	40.9	140.1	10.61	426.52
March	170.4	163.6	216.2	791	651	41.1	141.5	10.61	431.83
April	170.8	159.1	215.7	793	653	41.2	142.3	10.65	438.78
May	171.2	158.2	216.6	796	655	41.1	142.3	10.71	442.32
June	171.4	162.7	215.2	796	655	41.1	142.3	10.77	446.96
July	171.5	162.6	215.4	797	655	41.2	142.7	10.82	441.46
August	171.4	161.6	214.8	799	657	41.0	142.4	10.80	446.04
September	171.3	162.6	214.7	799	658	41.1	143.0	10.86	450.69
October	171.0	156.0	211.3	800	659	41.1	143.2	10.87	451.11
November	170.8	157.9	212.1	803	661	41.1	143.6	10.90	451.26
December	171.0	153.6	212.3	805	663	41.0	143.7	10.92	449.90
1998:									
January	170.9	152.9	214.3	806	664	41.1	144.3	10.89	437.78
February	170.8	153.3	216.4	808	665	41.3	145.2	10.90	441.45
March	170.9	151.3	217.0	809	665	41.1	144.5	10.94	445.26
April	171.0	152.4	217.3	811	666	41.2	145.1	10.98	447.98
May	171.2	151.4	213.3	811	666	41.1	144.7	11.05	456.37
June	171.1	151.1	209.0	811	666	41.1	144.7	11.09	461.34
July	170.9	159.1	204.2	812	668	41.2	145.5	11.17	460.20
August	170.8	167.6	204.7	813	668	41.2	145.5	11.18	465.09
September	171.5	170.0	202.9	815	669	40.7	144.0	11.17	452.39
October	171.7	156.7	201.0	817	670	41.1	145.6	11.22	465.63
November	171.5	160.9	199.4	820	673	41.2	146.6	11.24	466.46
December	171.4	161.1	197.9	823	675	41.5	148.1	11.33	472.46

Furniture and Fixtures—Production, Capacity Utilization, Prices, Employment, Hours, and Earnings

Year and month	Industrial production (1992=100, seasonally adjusted)		Capacity utilization (output as a percent of capacity, seasonally adjusted)	Producer prices (1982=100, except as noted; not seasonally adjusted)				Employment (thousands, seasonally adjusted)		Production workers			
				Furniture and fixtures industry (December 1984 = 100)	Finished goods					Average weekly hours, seasonally adjusted	Aggregate weekly hours index (1982= 100), seasonally adjusted	Average earnings (dollars, not seasonally adjusted)	
	Total	Household furniture			Household furniture	Commercial furniture	Public building furniture (December 1984 = 100)	Total payroll employees	Production workers			Hourly	Weekly
1970	56.2	69.2	81.0	.....	48.6	41.6	.....	440	362	39.2	111.6	2.77	108.58
1971	58.6	73.9	80.7	.....	50.0	42.9	.....	444	365	39.8	114.0	2.90	115.42
1972	70.7	90.1	93.0	.....	51.0	43.6	.....	483	400	40.2	126.6	3.08	123.82
1973	75.4	95.0	93.9	.....	53.5	47.0	.....	507	420	40.0	132.0	3.29	131.60
1974	70.1	87.5	82.9	.....	59.4	55.3	.....	489	402	39.1	123.4	3.53	138.02
1975	60.0	75.3	68.9	.....	63.6	60.5	.....	417	337	38.0	100.7	3.78	143.64
1976	67.0	84.4	75.7	.....	66.8	63.0	.....	444	364	38.8	111.0	3.99	154.81
1977	74.8	91.8	82.1	.....	70.6	67.5	.....	464	382	39.0	117.2	4.34	169.26
1978	80.4	98.5	84.5	.....	75.5	73.1	.....	494	406	39.3	125.6	4.68	183.92
1979	80.5	96.4	81.0	.....	81.0	80.5	.....	498	406	38.7	123.5	5.06	195.82
1980	79.1	90.0	77.2	.....	89.1	85.7	.....	466	376	38.1	112.4	5.49	209.17
1981	78.4	90.3	74.7	.....	95.4	93.5	.....	464	374	38.4	112.7	5.91	226.94
1982	74.6	79.6	70.2	.....	100.0	100.0	.....	432	342	37.2	100.0	6.31	234.73
1983	80.2	86.8	74.9	.....	102.1	103.9	.....	448	356	39.4	110.3	6.62	260.83
1984	88.6	92.7	81.4	.....	105.3	107.8	.....	486	390	39.7	121.6	6.84	271.55
1985	88.9	91.1	79.5	101.9	108.5	111.9	102.0	493	394	39.4	121.9	7.17	282.50
1986	93.3	96.6	81.5	103.9	110.3	115.3	105.2	498	397	39.8	124.2	7.46	296.91
1987	100.9	103.0	86.0	106.4	113.0	118.6	106.7	515	412	40.0	129.5	7.67	306.80
1988	101.1	102.5	84.0	111.4	117.6	124.2	109.6	527	420	39.4	130.1	7.95	313.23
1989	102.4	103.0	83.1	115.6	121.8	129.0	113.7	524	418	39.5	129.6	8.25	325.88
1990	100.9	100.9	80.1	119.1	125.1	133.4	116.5	506	400	39.1	122.8	8.52	333.13
1991	94.8	96.7	74.7	121.6	128.0	136.2	117.7	475	373	38.9	113.9	8.76	340.76
1992	100.0	100.0	78.2	122.9	130.0	138.1	119.2	478	377	39.7	117.6	9.01	357.70
1993	104.9	104.5	80.3	125.4	133.4	140.5	122.4	487	385	40.1	121.3	9.27	371.73
1994	108.1	109.3	80.9	129.7	138.0	144.7	131.0	505	400	40.4	127.0	9.55	385.82
1995	111.4	109.9	81.6	133.3	141.8	148.2	134.6	510	403	39.6	125.6	9.82	388.87
1996	113.2	111.9	79.3	136.2	144.5	151.7	138.9	504	398	39.4	123.4	10.15	399.91
1997	117.7	114.1	78.1	138.2	146.2	154.3	141.4	512	407	40.2	128.6	10.55	424.11
1998	121.4	118.5	78.1	139.7	148.4	155.2	141.6	530	423	40.6	134.7	10.90	442.54
1995:													
January	112.2	112.1	83.1	131.5	140.0	146.2	134.0	514	407	40.7	130.2	9.68	393.01
February	114.1	113.7	84.3	132.0	140.4	146.6	134.3	515	408	40.3	129.2	9.67	383.90
March	112.4	111.0	82.9	132.1	140.7	146.6	134.0	516	408	39.7	127.3	9.68	381.39
April	111.1	111.4	81.8	132.6	141.0	147.8	134.0	514	407	39.2	125.4	9.76	367.95
May	109.9	109.4	80.7	132.8	141.6	147.4	133.8	511	404	39.3	124.8	9.71	375.78
June	111.2	109.2	81.5	133.4	141.8	148.1	134.9	508	402	39.5	124.8	9.78	386.31
July	111.0	108.0	81.2	133.4	142.0	148.0	134.6	505	398	39.3	122.9	9.83	381.40
August	111.1	108.5	81.1	133.9	142.2	148.9	135.1	507	401	39.7	125.1	9.89	396.59
September	112.1	109.2	81.6	133.8	142.5	148.5	134.9	507	401	39.4	124.2	9.95	399.99
October	110.7	110.0	80.5	134.4	142.7	149.6	134.9	507	401	39.6	124.8	9.92	397.79
November	110.8	108.4	80.4	134.9	143.2	150.2	135.2	507	400	39.7	124.8	9.92	397.79
December	110.0	108.5	79.6	134.9	143.2	150.4	135.8	508	401	39.4	124.2	10.00	407.00
1996:													
January	111.1	111.1	80.1	135.2	143.6	150.6	136.8	506	399	35.9	112.6	10.01	359.36
February	110.9	109.0	79.5	135.7	143.8	151.4	137.4	504	398	39.2	122.6	9.95	384.07
March	109.6	107.9	78.2	135.6	144.1	150.9	138.0	503	397	39.4	122.9	10.00	390.00
April	110.9	110.5	78.7	135.8	144.2	151.3	137.1	501	395	39.4	122.3	10.06	389.32
May	114.1	115.0	80.6	135.7	144.4	150.7	137.1	503	397	39.6	123.6	10.08	394.13
June	112.6	112.6	79.1	135.9	144.5	151.1	138.1	503	397	39.6	123.6	10.11	399.35
July	112.2	110.2	78.4	136.2	144.6	151.8	139.6	504	398	39.8	124.5	10.13	398.11
August	115.5	114.9	80.3	136.1	144.5	151.5	140.1	505	399	39.7	124.5	10.19	408.62
September	114.6	113.4	79.3	136.4	144.7	151.8	139.5	506	400	39.8	125.1	10.27	414.91
October	116.0	113.7	79.8	137.1	144.9	153.0	140.4	505	400	39.8	125.1	10.28	413.26
November	115.8	113.1	79.3	137.3	145.2	153.2	141.0	506	400	39.9	125.4	10.28	416.34
December	115.3	111.0	78.5	137.4	145.2	153.4	141.0	507	401	40.3	127.0	10.42	433.47
1997:													
January	115.2	110.5	78.1	137.5	145.4	153.6	140.5	507	402	39.6	125.1	10.38	407.93
February	116.4	113.9	78.6	137.6	145.7	153.4	140.3	508	403	39.5	125.1	10.34	402.23
March	116.4	112.4	78.3	137.7	145.9	153.2	141.0	508	403	40.3	127.6	10.43	416.16
April	118.2	114.9	79.2	138.0	146.0	153.9	140.5	509	403	40.2	127.3	10.42	411.59
May	117.1	113.3	78.1	138.2	146.0	154.3	141.7	510	405	40.2	128.0	10.47	416.71
June	117.7	114.0	78.3	138.2	146.1	154.2	141.6	512	406	40.0	127.6	10.51	419.35
July	118.7	116.1	78.6	138.5	146.4	154.7	141.3	514	408	40.1	128.6	10.53	415.94
August	116.6	113.0	76.9	138.3	146.3	154.3	141.5	512	407	40.2	128.6	10.60	429.30
September	117.5	114.3	77.2	138.6	146.6	154.7	142.1	513	409	40.5	130.2	10.70	440.84
October	118.6	114.4	77.6	138.6	146.6	154.6	141.9	516	411	40.3	130.2	10.70	435.34
November	119.7	116.1	78.0	138.9	146.9	155.0	141.8	518	413	40.6	131.8	10.67	435.34
December	120.4	117.0	78.2	138.9	146.8	155.2	142.1	520	414	40.8	132.7	10.79	454.26
1998:													
January	119.4	115.5	77.3	139.1	147.4	154.7	140.6	523	417	40.9	134.0	10.75	437.53
February	118.6	116.0	76.7	139.3	147.6	155.2	141.0	525	419	41.0	135.0	10.78	436.59
March	121.5	117.7	78.5	139.4	147.8	155.2	141.1	527	420	40.7	134.3	10.81	436.72
April	121.0	117.9	78.1	139.4	147.9	155.0	141.6	530	423	40.7	135.3	10.86	431.14
May	120.6	118.9	77.7	139.7	148.2	155.6	141.8	531	423	40.8	135.6	10.80	433.08
June	122.0	120.4	78.5	139.6	148.2	155.3	141.9	531	422	40.9	135.6	10.82	441.46
July	120.8	116.9	77.6	139.6	148.4	155.2	142.0	532	423	40.7	135.3	10.91	439.67
August	120.1	117.8	77.1	139.7	148.5	155.2	141.9	532	424	40.6	135.3	10.96	449.36
September	121.6	119.4	78.0	139.7	148.6	155.2	142.1	532	424	40.2	134.0	10.99	437.40
October	124.5	121.7	79.7	140.1	149.2	155.5	142.1	532	423	40.5	134.6	10.99	449.49
November	123.6	119.6	79.1	140.0	149.2	155.4	141.6	532	424	40.3	134.3	10.99	449.49
December	122.9	119.6	78.5	140.2	149.6	155.4	141.8	534	426	40.2	134.6	11.10	460.65

Stone, Clay, and Glass Products—Production, Capacity Utilization, Shipments and Inventories

(Seasonally adjusted)

Year and month	Industrial production (1992=100)						Capacity utilization (output as a percent of capacity)	Manufacturers' shipments and inventories (millions of dollars)	
	Total	Pressed and blown glass		Cement	Structural clay products	Concrete and miscellaneous		Shipments	Inventories (book value, end of period)
		Total	Glass containers						
1970	74.8	81.5	121.3	102.1	110.4	76.2	73.9	16,454	2,239
1971	78.5	83.4	118.6	110.5	113.8	78.6	75.6	18,220	2,302
1972	86.9	88.8	120.3	117.1	120.9	88.4	81.7	20,875	2,430
1973	93.9	95.0	125.3	125.5	128.4	95.4	86.0	23,141	2,712
1974	92.4	95.8	128.0	115.5	123.2	95.6	81.9	25,503	3,403
1975	81.8	90.2	128.2	97.5	104.8	83.7	70.3	26,233	3,594
1976	91.5	97.9	136.6	102.4	113.7	93.3	77.2	29,618	3,841
1977	98.3	102.2	137.5	110.4	123.3	100.9	81.8	34,209	4,095
1978	106.0	108.0	139.1	117.0	131.2	108.9	86.5	40,238	4,710
1979	106.8	110.0	135.7	118.0	130.4	111.2	85.5	44,287	5,183
1980	96.5	109.2	131.4	100.9	111.1	99.2	76.3	44,473	5,674
1981	94.3	111.3	129.0	102.6	102.5	95.0	75.0	46,220	6,106
1982	84.2	101.4	128.6	89.6	81.5	84.0	67.5	43,515	6,506
1983	91.2	101.8	122.1	99.2	96.8	92.1	73.1	47,697	6,628
1984	98.6	102.8	118.3	110.1	111.2	100.6	78.3	53,101	7,042
1985	98.0	97.0	108.8	109.7	105.3	100.8	76.3	55,821	7,040
1986	101.7	100.4	111.4	111.5	111.8	104.4	78.3	59,254	7,093
1987	104.8	99.1	106.9	113.3	113.4	107.9	79.8	61,477	7,154
1988	107.5	101.8	106.9	113.3	115.2	111.3	81.6	63,145	7,496
1989	107.4	103.3	108.2	111.8	118.7	110.2	81.1	63,729	7,792
1990	105.0	102.4	106.8	110.5	114.2	107.0	78.6	63,728	8,205
1991	97.2	96.7	99.2	96.0	100.3	98.3	72.2	59,957	7,928
1992	100.0	100.0	100.0	100.0	100.0	100.0	74.0	62,521	8,006
1993	102.1	98.5	93.1	96.9	101.6	102.5	75.5	65,610	7,607
1994	107.8	102.4	92.6	106.4	112.1	107.7	80.0	71,230	7,874
1995	110.9	102.0	85.5	112.5	114.4	112.3	79.8	75,932	8,567
1996	118.3	104.2	83.9	114.2	118.9	120.6	80.5	82,442	8,898
1997	122.3	106.1	80.7	120.5	127.5	124.4	80.4	90,221	9,050
1998	126.2	109.1	82.5	127.4	126.9	129.2	81.7	96,193	9,331
1995:									
January	110.4	102.4	87.8	112.6	119.9	110.4	81.7	6,308	7,934
February	110.4	102.7	87.9	111.8	120.9	111.4	81.3	6,321	7,984
March	111.0	105.0	89.6	116.7	120.8	110.7	81.3	6,263	8,118
April	108.9	101.7	85.0	109.3	119.6	109.3	79.3	5,847	8,329
May	110.2	103.8	88.1	107.3	117.2	110.7	79.8	6,200	8,512
June	110.1	102.8	87.1	113.5	114.0	110.8	79.4	6,277	8,610
July	109.2	101.2	83.7	111.8	110.9	110.9	78.3	6,245	8,738
August	110.1	103.3	85.7	112.5	109.3	111.3	78.6	6,473	8,783
September	110.4	98.6	80.2	113.1	109.8	113.1	78.4	6,421	8,807
October	112.3	100.7	85.2	115.4	110.9	114.4	79.3	6,471	8,748
November	114.1	99.6	80.8	115.0	110.8	117.5	80.1	6,599	8,694
December	114.1	101.9	83.7	113.7	108.4	117.1	79.7	6,558	8,567
1996:									
January	114.7	103.6	85.6	113.4	105.2	117.3	79.7	6,735	8,572
February	114.2	102.9	84.3	112.9	103.7	116.3	79.1	6,440	8,609
March	115.2	103.2	84.4	113.5	105.5	118.1	79.5	6,625	8,638
April	114.5	104.5	85.4	117.6	109.7	115.9	78.7	6,697	8,604
May	117.3	107.9	92.5	115.7	114.8	118.6	80.3	6,983	8,537
June	119.3	103.1	82.2	114.3	119.3	122.8	81.4	6,954	8,570
July	121.4	105.5	83.6	115.6	123.0	124.6	82.6	6,966	8,545
August	119.5	104.1	83.9	116.2	125.8	120.9	80.9	6,968	8,627
September	121.0	104.7	82.8	112.5	127.8	123.9	81.6	6,912	8,654
October	121.2	103.5	80.2	115.0	129.3	123.3	81.5	7,205	8,740
November	121.2	104.5	82.3	112.6	130.7	123.1	81.2	7,112	8,778
December	119.8	103.1	79.1	110.7	132.3	121.9	79.9	6,770	8,898
1997:									
January	122.3	105.2	82.0	116.3	133.6	124.3	81.4	7,193	8,987
February	121.8	105.9	81.3	120.7	133.9	123.7	80.8	7,402	9,019
March	121.1	103.5	77.1	125.8	133.0	122.4	80.2	7,365	9,003
April	121.9	106.3	78.5	118.5	131.2	122.9	80.6	7,476	8,989
May	121.1	104.0	77.8	119.1	129.1	123.1	79.9	7,476	9,049
June	121.6	104.9	79.4	118.3	127.2	124.4	80.0	7,483	9,093
July	122.4	105.8	79.4	121.3	125.7	125.1	80.4	7,683	9,006
August	121.7	104.3	79.7	119.0	124.5	124.2	79.7	7,555	9,009
September	122.4	108.3	83.7	123.1	123.5	124.1	80.0	7,687	9,065
October	123.0	104.2	79.3	121.3	122.9	125.2	80.2	7,670	8,933
November	123.7	108.0	83.9	120.8	122.7	126.2	80.5	7,574	9,042
December	125.0	112.7	90.0	124.0	123.1	127.2	81.2	7,651	9,050
1998:									
January	124.6	107.4	81.0	132.9	123.8	127.3	80.9	7,696	9,097
February	124.0	105.8	80.9	126.9	124.5	127.6	80.4	7,789	9,101
March	124.5	107.0	81.8	126.5	125.1	127.3	80.7	7,872	9,131
April	124.0	107.9	81.4	126.4	125.7	125.8	80.4	7,899	9,067
May	124.5	106.8	80.6	124.3	126.5	126.6	80.7	7,982	9,092
June	123.5	108.4	80.3	124.4	127.6	125.0	80.0	8,033	9,110
July	125.4	107.8	81.8	127.5	128.5	128.8	81.2	8,104	9,112
August	127.0	107.7	82.1	124.0	128.7	131.3	82.2	8,014	9,164
September	126.6	111.2	84.9	125.3	128.5	129.4	81.9	8,077	9,237
October	128.3	110.9	83.1	125.0	128.7	132.1	83.1	8,149	9,235
November	130.5	112.9	87.6	134.9	128.5	133.5	84.4	8,236	9,320
December	131.7	114.5	86.0	141.4	128.2	134.6	85.1	8,317	9,331

Stone, Clay, and Glass Products—Prices, Employment, Hours, and Earnings

Year and month	Producer prices (1982=100, except as noted; not seasonally adjusted)						Employment (thousands, seasonally adjusted)		Production workers			
	Stone, clay, and glass products industry (Dec. 1984 =100)	Intermediate materials				Crude materials: Construction sand, gravel, and crushed stone	Total payroll employees	Production workers	Average weekly hours, seasonally adjusted	Aggregate weekly hours index (1982=100), seasonally adjusted	Average earnings (dollars, not seasonally adjusted)	
		Flat glass	Cement	Concrete products	Glass containers						Hourly	Weekly
1970	.....	52.2	.....	37.7	33.9	40.9	610	485	41.2	120.9	3.40	140.08
1971	.....	55.6	36.8	40.5	37.0	42.8	611	486	41.6	122.2	3.67	152.67
1972	.....	55.3	.....	42.2	38.0	43.7	645	516	42.0	131.1	3.94	165.48
1973	.....	54.8	.....	44.2	39.1	44.9	680	546	41.9	138.4	4.22	176.82
1974	.....	58.2	.....	50.9	43.7	48.6	673	539	41.3	134.5	4.54	187.50
1975	.....	62.8	57.1	57.3	50.5	54.3	598	473	40.4	115.6	4.92	198.77
1976	.....	67.7	62.9	60.5	55.0	57.9	613	486	41.1	120.8	5.33	219.06
1977	.....	72.6	67.6	64.4	60.2	61.3	636	505	41.3	125.9	5.81	239.95
1978	.....	78.0	74.3	71.9	68.7	66.7	664	525	41.6	132.1	6.32	262.91
1979	.....	83.0	83.7	82.0	73.4	74.4	674	529	41.5	132.8	6.85	284.28
1980	.....	88.7	91.9	92.0	82.3	85.3	629	486	40.8	119.8	7.50	306.00
1981	.....	96.0	97.4	97.8	92.5	94.0	606	465	40.6	114.1	8.27	335.76
1982	.....	100.0	100.0	100.0	100.0	100.0	548	413	40.1	100.0	8.87	355.69
1983	.....	103.7	100.4	101.4	99.1	101.7	541	412	41.5	103.2	9.27	384.71
1984	.....	101.4	104.0	103.9	101.4	106.0	562	431	42.0	109.5	9.57	401.94
1985	102.1	101.7	106.1	107.5	106.8	110.7	557	427	41.9	108.1	9.84	412.30
1986	103.8	104.5	104.2	109.2	111.9	114.2	554	426	42.2	108.7	10.04	423.69
1987	104.5	107.2	101.9	109.4	113.0	118.1	554	429	42.3	109.7	10.25	433.58
1988	105.8	109.7	102.2	110.0	112.3	120.6	567	443	42.3	113.3	10.56	446.69
1989	107.9	109.7	102.1	111.2	115.2	122.8	568	444	42.3	113.5	10.82	457.69
1990	110.0	107.5	103.7	113.5	120.4	125.4	556	432	42.0	109.7	11.12	467.04
1991	112.3	105.9	106.8	116.6	125.4	128.6	522	403	41.7	101.4	11.36	473.71
1992	112.8	106.5	106.3	117.2	125.1	130.6	513	396	42.2	101.2	11.60	489.52
1993	115.4	107.3	111.7	120.2	125.8	134.0	517	399	42.7	102.9	11.85	506.00
1994	119.6	110.5	119.5	124.6	127.5	137.9	532	411	43.4	107.9	12.13	526.44
1995	124.3	113.2	128.1	129.4	130.5	142.3	540	418	43.0	108.8	12.41	533.63
1996	125.8	110.0	134.0	133.2	129.1	145.6	544	423	43.3	110.8	12.82	555.11
1997	127.4	108.4	139.4	136.0	125.7	148.2	552	431	43.2	112.4	13.18	569.38
1998	129.3	107.1	145.7	140.0	125.9	152.8	563	440	43.5	115.7	13.60	591.60
1995:												
January	122.4	112.9	123.3	127.8	128.7	140.3	539	417	43.6	109.9	12.20	516.06
February	123.1	113.9	124.0	128.1	128.6	140.7	540	418	42.7	107.9	12.24	512.86
March	123.8	114.4	124.0	128.5	130.1	141.2	542	419	43.2	109.4	12.26	522.28
April	124.5	115.5	128.9	129.1	129.9	141.5	543	420	43.0	109.2	12.44	526.21
May	124.6	115.5	129.4	129.3	130.7	141.8	540	418	42.6	107.6	12.32	530.99
June	124.4	112.5	129.3	129.3	130.7	142.5	540	419	43.0	108.9	12.37	539.33
July	124.5	112.8	129.6	129.6	131.0	143.1	539	417	43.0	108.4	12.46	538.27
August	124.6	112.4	129.7	129.7	131.0	143.0	539	418	43.1	108.9	12.47	544.94
September	124.8	112.3	129.9	130.0	131.2	143.3	539	418	43.2	109.2	12.55	552.20
October	124.8	112.3	129.7	130.2	131.2	143.2	538	418	43.1	108.9	12.54	549.25
November	124.9	112.1	129.7	130.8	131.2	143.6	538	418	43.0	108.7	12.57	543.02
December	124.9	111.6	129.4	131.0	131.2	143.6	537	417	42.8	107.9	12.54	534.20
1996:												
January	125.1	112.0	129.3	131.5	130.2	144.5	535	415	42.0	105.4	12.60	515.34
February	125.3	111.9	130.1	132.0	130.2	144.4	539	418	43.3	109.4	12.56	532.54
March	125.3	110.8	130.1	132.4	129.2	144.9	540	420	43.3	109.9	12.60	538.02
April	125.4	110.0	133.3	132.8	129.7	145.5	540	420	43.4	110.2	12.77	551.66
May	125.5	109.4	134.8	133.0	129.6	145.6	542	422	43.2	110.2	12.74	555.46
June	125.5	109.3	135.0	133.2	129.6	145.5	543	422	43.6	111.2	12.82	565.36
July	125.8	109.5	135.0	133.6	129.6	145.9	543	423	43.3	110.7	12.94	562.89
August	125.9	109.4	135.3	133.5	129.6	145.6	545	425	43.4	111.5	12.92	568.48
September	126.3	109.2	136.3	133.8	129.3	146.1	546	426	43.4	111.8	12.99	575.46
October	126.2	109.2	136.4	133.8	127.4	146.1	548	427	43.3	111.8	12.91	568.04
November	126.6	109.6	136.4	134.5	127.4	146.3	549	427	43.2	111.5	12.96	563.76
December	126.5	109.9	135.9	134.7	127.4	146.3	550	429	43.2	112.0	12.93	558.58
1997:												
January	126.8	108.8	136.4	135.0	126.0	147.2	551	429	42.3	109.7	12.99	531.29
February	126.9	108.7	136.7	135.2	126.0	147.0	551	429	43.1	111.8	13.04	547.68
March	127.1	108.2	136.4	135.4	125.9	147.4	552	430	43.2	112.3	13.02	553.35
April	127.5	108.3	139.2	135.9	125.9	148.0	551	429	43.1	111.8	13.06	560.27
May	127.6	108.2	139.6	136.1	125.5	148.4	551	430	43.3	112.6	13.12	573.34
June	127.4	108.1	140.3	135.8	125.5	148.6	550	428	43.1	111.5	13.13	572.47
July	127.4	108.1	140.4	136.2	125.5	148.7	553	432	43.2	112.8	13.20	571.56
August	127.5	108.5	140.9	136.1	125.5	148.6	553	431	43.1	112.3	13.21	578.60
September	127.5	108.2	140.6	136.1	125.7	148.6	553	431	43.3	112.8	13.27	586.53
October	127.8	108.4	140.9	136.5	125.7	148.7	555	433	43.3	113.3	13.32	584.75
November	127.8	108.5	140.6	136.7	125.9	148.7	554	433	43.0	112.6	13.36	575.82
December	127.7	108.5	140.7	136.5	125.9	149.0	555	434	43.7	114.7	13.39	585.14
1998:												
January	127.6	108.0	140.6	136.9	125.9	150.2	563	440	43.7	116.2	13.38	565.97
February	127.8	107.3	141.0	137.4	125.9	150.8	561	439	43.7	116.0	13.45	572.97
March	127.9	107.0	141.2	137.6	125.9	151.2	559	436	43.3	114.1	13.46	573.40
April	128.7	106.8	145.4	139.5	125.9	152.4	561	438	43.4	114.9	13.63	584.73
May	129.0	107.4	145.7	139.9	125.9	152.8	561	437	43.6	115.2	13.58	597.52
June	129.4	107.2	146.9	140.7	125.5	153.3	562	438	43.4	114.9	13.58	596.16
July	129.9	107.9	147.6	141.3	125.5	153.6	563	439	43.6	115.7	13.59	595.24
August	130.1	106.7	147.8	141.3	126.2	153.6	564	440	43.6	116.0	13.63	602.45
September	130.2	106.7	147.9	141.4	126.0	153.6	565	441	43.4	115.7	13.82	606.70
October	130.4	106.9	147.8	141.3	126.0	153.7	566	442	43.6	116.5	13.68	603.29
November	130.3	106.9	148.0	141.4	126.0	153.7	568	443	43.6	116.8	13.65	597.87
December	130.2	106.8	148.0	141.4	126.0	154.2	570	446	43.8	118.1	13.70	600.06

Primary Metals—Production

(Seasonally adjusted)

Year and month	Total	Industrial production (1992=100)												Iron and steel foundries
		Iron and steel												
		Total	Basic steel and mill products											
			Total	Basic iron and steel			Steel mill products							
				Total	Pig iron	Raw steel	Total	Consumer durable steel	Equipment steel	Construction steel	Can and closure steel	Miscellaneous steel		
1970	111.2	139.0	132.6	170.3	178.2	139.2	112.6	130.7	189.3	167.2	186.3	67.5	167.5
1971	104.9	126.3	118.0	152.5	156.9	127.1	99.8	141.5	182.9	137.8	166.2	54.9	164.0
1972	118.3	141.5	133.0	169.5	172.8	143.9	113.4	164.1	206.0	148.4	164.9	64.8	180.7
1973	134.1	161.0	152.2	191.3	196.0	164.3	131.0	196.0	229.2	174.8	182.8	74.7	201.6
1974	129.7	155.7	148.7	185.8	185.4	163.1	128.6	160.8	234.3	181.0	194.3	77.1	187.8
1975	103.4	125.1	119.4	153.0	154.8	128.6	101.4	134.6	205.1	135.2	160.1	55.8	151.9
1976	115.7	137.9	131.2	164.9	166.9	140.9	112.9	186.5	231.0	123.5	171.1	57.7	168.5
1977	119.0	138.0	126.3	158.8	157.1	139.3	108.7	178.6	233.9	117.0	159.1	54.9	180.3
1978	128.0	147.5	137.5	168.6	170.0	154.9	120.6	184.3	265.0	134.3	159.3	64.9	182.4
1979	130.0	148.4	138.4	170.7	168.3	154.4	120.8	159.5	268.9	140.5	156.9	70.3	182.4
1980	108.0	119.0	112.8	139.2	133.5	126.9	98.5	105.9	236.7	119.4	128.3	60.8	138.5
1981	113.9	126.6	121.4	145.7	142.0	138.5	108.6	120.4	252.6	125.8	124.3	70.0	142.0
1982	80.5	80.5	75.9	88.2	83.6	82.6	69.8	81.8	132.9	84.6	108.8	47.0	94.8
1983	88.2	90.0	85.5	95.1	94.3	94.1	81.5	109.7	118.4	91.4	113.9	61.9	104.7
1984	98.7	98.9	92.8	104.0	99.6	102.6	88.1	113.2	132.3	90.1	106.6	70.3	118.9
1985	98.4	98.8	95.0	99.7	96.8	97.7	93.3	124.5	121.1	99.9	104.9	77.1	110.7
1986	91.2	86.8	87.5	88.8	85.0	89.7	87.2	108.6	102.6	93.5	102.9	76.3	85.8
1987	97.8	95.4	93.5	97.7	93.6	98.8	92.3	102.1	106.9	91.9	107.0	86.0	102.5
1988	106.2	107.6	106.4	111.0	107.9	111.2	105.0	115.5	126.0	96.3	113.8	99.3	111.9
1989	104.9	106.2	104.9	109.5	108.0	107.2	103.5	107.3	117.2	102.3	112.6	99.5	110.9
1990	104.0	106.4	106.5	108.5	106.3	108.3	106.0	100.0	123.9	108.0	114.3	103.2	106.0
1991	96.7	96.0	95.7	95.7	93.8	96.2	95.7	87.9	97.9	93.7	109.9	96.6	96.9
1992	100.0	100.0	100.0	100.0	100.0	100.0	100.0	100.0	100.0	100.0	100.0	100.0	100.0
1993	105.7	107.1	107.4	102.8	102.9	104.4	108.8	114.6	112.5	113.0	108.1	106.6	106.2
1994	113.4	113.7	113.2	103.7	103.8	106.6	116.0	131.2	112.5	125.2	109.3	111.6	115.2
1995	116.8	117.7	117.3	109.1	108.7	113.3	119.7	124.5	119.4	128.6	100.3	118.4	118.9
1996	119.8	119.2	118.8	106.2	105.0	112.2	122.5	131.3	125.6	136.7	105.6	118.4	120.6
1997	125.3	124.2	124.2	107.3	106.0	115.9	129.2	132.5	129.0	149.3	108.5	126.3	124.3
1998	123.8	121.1	120.2	104.4	103.0	115.7	124.9	128.9	116.4	152.3	98.4	122.4	124.0
1995:													
January	119.7	120.9	121.3	109.2	109.2	113.3	124.9	131.8	119.9	144.6	88.6	123.2	119.3
February	118.2	119.6	120.0	110.2	109.9	114.9	122.9	133.8	122.8	132.4	99.0	120.1	118.2
March	117.6	119.3	119.3	110.3	110.0	114.7	122.0	135.3	119.5	127.7	106.1	119.1	119.0
April	116.6	116.7	116.1	108.8	108.1	113.4	118.3	125.3	112.6	127.6	102.9	117.4	118.7
May	116.2	117.0	115.7	107.6	106.7	112.0	118.2	125.4	116.8	125.1	102.9	116.4	121.0
June	115.9	116.5	115.7	106.8	105.6	111.7	118.4	121.9	133.5	124.2	98.6	115.1	119.0
July	113.9	112.1	110.6	107.5	106.9	112.0	111.4	113.9	114.6	125.6	93.3	109.0	117.1
August	114.7	116.2	115.8	109.3	109.4	113.2	117.8	122.5	116.2	125.6	100.8	116.7	117.5
September	118.1	121.0	121.5	111.8	111.8	116.9	124.3	123.8	124.5	131.7	107.1	124.4	119.4
October	115.7	114.3	113.0	108.4	108.5	111.2	114.4	118.8	110.0	121.5	96.7	114.2	118.6
November	118.8	121.5	122.4	110.5	110.5	114.4	126.0	124.2	121.0	127.5	98.9	129.2	118.2
December	116.6	117.2	116.2	108.4	107.4	113.9	118.5	116.6	120.2	132.1	110.7	116.9	120.6
1996:													
January	116.1	117.7	117.2	108.4	108.7	112.3	119.8	123.4	124.3	142.2	95.0	116.0	119.2
February	116.8	115.6	114.2	106.6	106.4	111.0	116.5	118.4	118.1	128.3	100.8	114.9	120.0
March	118.7	118.1	118.4	107.6	107.4	112.7	121.6	120.1	125.8	135.3	107.4	120.0	117.0
April	118.2	117.0	117.0	106.0	105.0	111.5	120.3	129.7	124.2	131.1	101.8	116.6	116.8
May	119.2	118.0	118.2	105.7	104.0	112.4	121.9	131.3	124.8	130.9	102.6	118.9	117.1
June	119.9	119.7	121.8	108.6	107.6	114.8	125.7	135.8	127.1	142.0	103.6	121.8	112.4
July	118.5	118.5	120.3	107.6	106.4	114.0	124.1	141.1	129.6	136.0	118.0	117.1	112.2
August	121.5	121.4	121.3	106.7	105.2	113.5	125.6	140.0	135.6	139.4	115.6	118.5	121.6
September	121.8	119.1	118.9	105.4	103.6	112.5	122.9	136.2	128.6	134.6	107.9	117.6	119.7
October	123.1	123.7	121.8	104.9	103.2	112.1	126.8	140.3	132.6	139.5	114.7	121.0	129.8
November	121.9	121.5	118.0	102.3	100.5	109.1	122.6	132.7	123.1	142.5	109.4	117.5	132.7
December	122.2	120.5	118.4	104.2	101.9	112.7	122.5	134.3	113.6	138.9	93.3	120.6	127.2
1997:													
January	120.7	120.8	119.1	103.5	101.1	111.6	123.6	132.5	121.6	140.4	114.2	119.6	126.6
February	122.3	120.6	120.2	105.5	104.5	112.1	124.5	133.1	126.9	140.4	111.7	120.2	122.0
March	121.1	117.8	117.4	106.0	104.4	114.3	120.7	129.1	121.7	141.3	102.4	116.2	119.1
April	124.2	124.8	124.2	106.8	105.6	114.8	129.3	130.3	131.0	150.0	115.2	126.2	126.7
May	124.8	123.9	123.6	107.6	107.1	115.1	128.3	129.0	132.5	150.8	110.6	124.7	124.9
June	126.2	124.5	123.9	106.1	104.6	115.0	129.2	128.9	133.4	151.8	112.8	125.8	126.2
July	126.2	124.5	124.7	106.4	104.4	116.5	130.1	128.6	130.1	150.2	103.1	129.1	123.5
August	126.2	123.4	124.1	106.1	104.0	116.1	129.4	126.7	127.5	149.1	107.2	128.8	121.1
September	127.0	126.6	127.1	109.2	108.0	118.7	132.4	134.1	129.6	151.0	111.4	130.9	125.1
October	128.2	128.2	129.2	109.3	108.4	118.5	135.0	146.9	131.4	157.9	115.7	130.1	125.1
November	129.3	128.0	128.8	110.6	110.0	120.2	134.1	134.5	130.8	155.6	104.4	133.2	125.6
December	127.8	127.6	128.1	110.2	109.7	119.6	133.4	140.1	132.2	152.1	97.1	131.4	125.9
1998:													
January	129.2	128.9	128.1	111.9	111.5	122.5	132.9	126.9	131.7	155.9	112.1	132.2	131.5
February	128.1	128.2	130.1	110.6	109.1	123.3	135.8	136.2	130.4	158.6	106.8	134.9	122.2
March	127.1	127.7	128.5	109.1	108.5	120.0	134.3	139.2	131.6	156.1	106.9	131.8	125.1
April	127.5	126.7	126.0	109.8	109.0	122.4	130.7	132.3	128.2	155.7	103.8	128.5	129.0
May	126.5	125.5	125.6	108.9	108.0	121.9	130.5	130.5	125.3	157.7	99.5	129.0	125.4
June	122.1	119.8	118.0	103.1	101.1	116.0	122.4	113.9	114.0	151.4	102.9	122.6	125.5
July	122.6	120.2	119.6	105.9	104.6	118.3	123.6	107.0	116.7	164.0	100.7	123.8	122.4
August	124.4	122.5	122.5	107.2	105.5	120.3	127.0	131.0	116.4	154.6	97.7	125.3	122.4
September	120.1	113.4	110.7	100.2	97.7	112.6	113.8	122.2	104.6	142.2	93.9	109.8	122.3
October	120.6	114.4	112.7	99.5	98.0	109.7	116.5	137.3	104.8	146.4	96.7	109.5	120.2
November	118.7	109.7	106.9	92.0	89.4	100.2	111.3	127.7	91.2	139.8	97.7	106.7	118.9
December	118.6	114.6	111.9	94.6	93.0	102.0	117.0	142.4	99.5	146.8	70.6	111.9	123.4

Primary Metals—Production and Capacity Utilization

(Seasonally adjusted)

Year and month	Industrial production (1992=100)—continued								Capacity utilization (output as a percent of capacity)					
	Nonferrous metals									Iron and steel		Nonferrous metals		
	Total	Primary nonferrous metals			Nonferrous products			Nonfer-rous foundries	Total	Total	Raw steel	Total	Primary copper	Primary aluminum
		Total	Copper	Aluminum	Total	Nonferrous mill products								
						Total	Aluminum							
1970	75.9	107.2	108.7	89.5	77.5	79.3	67.0	76.3	80.8	84.9	83.4	74.3	88.4	97.4
1971	76.6	101.4	93.2	88.3	78.9	82.4	74.5	72.5	74.8	76.6	76.0	71.7	74.9	88.1
1972	87.0	107.8	107.4	92.5	90.7	93.9	84.9	86.0	83.7	86.2	85.6	79.2	85.1	87.4
1973	98.1	113.6	107.4	101.9	105.2	108.8	106.4	100.1	94.5	98.0	97.1	88.1	85.0	94.0
1974	94.8	112.9	92.9	110.3	101.1	105.5	111.8	93.8	90.7	94.7	96.0	83.7	73.0	100.2
1975	74.3	93.9	82.2	87.3	76.2	79.4	78.9	70.8	71.7	75.9	75.2	64.1	61.9	78.4
1976	85.7	103.1	93.2	95.4	89.9	94.3	92.6	81.6	79.0	82.4	80.7	72.9	67.9	83.1
1977	93.0	101.9	85.5	102.2	98.7	104.8	102.1	86.0	80.1	80.7	78.6	79.4	63.2	87.4
1978	101.1	108.2	91.2	108.2	108.4	115.4	116.3	93.9	86.6	86.5	87.6	86.9	67.9	92.3
1979	104.6	116.1	98.0	113.1	110.0	116.2	118.5	97.3	88.4	88.6	88.3	88.0	71.8	95.7
1980	92.4	106.4	75.9	115.2	95.5	104.8	107.3	74.4	73.5	71.6	73.4	76.9	56.7	95.0
1981	96.1	107.5	91.1	111.4	100.0	110.0	110.3	77.5	77.6	76.4	80.5	79.1	72.0	90.3
1982	80.7	84.4	66.1	81.2	85.3	93.6	86.2	66.8	54.5	48.9	48.3	65.6	54.0	65.9
1983	85.9	86.9	68.6	83.2	92.9	100.7	98.8	75.6	61.7	56.9	57.4	69.6	56.8	67.4
1984	98.6	95.5	77.6	101.5	107.5	109.4	101.1	103.1	71.9	66.5	66.4	81.0	66.9	83.6
1985	98.2	92.2	79.7	86.9	107.4	106.6	97.0	110.0	73.2	68.9	65.8	80.3	71.9	74.9
1986	97.6	80.4	79.4	75.4	108.2	107.1	103.0	111.9	70.1	64.1	63.9	80.3	74.4	71.9
1987	101.2	83.8	80.1	83.0	111.3	112.1	110.6	109.2	79.2	76.2	77.7	84.1	77.2	84.1
1988	104.6	97.3	80.0	97.6	109.2	107.5	107.7	115.0	87.4	87.4	88.9	87.5	78.4	97.4
1989	103.2	98.7	79.0	100.0	106.0	104.1	106.2	112.5	85.2	84.7	84.1	85.9	76.3	98.6
1990	100.9	96.4	81.6	100.4	102.7	102.1	104.0	104.7	83.4	83.6	84.5	83.1	77.8	98.3
1991	97.7	103.2	88.3	102.2	97.4	97.2	102.0	98.0	77.6	75.7	75.8	80.1	81.3	99.6
1992	100.0	100.0	100.0	100.0	100.0	100.0	100.0	100.0	80.7	80.5	80.8	81.2	85.7	97.0
1993	104.0	101.8	116.7	91.7	104.9	104.2	98.7	107.2	85.7	87.6	87.7	83.4	93.6	88.8
1994	113.0	97.6	111.7	81.8	115.4	113.1	106.7	122.9	90.6	91.8	90.8	89.1	87.7	79.1
1995	115.8	101.8	122.0	83.7	116.4	111.6	102.9	132.5	90.5	92.7	94.1	87.9	95.4	80.7
1996	120.6	100.5	103.6	88.5	123.5	118.7	103.3	139.3	90.0	90.7	90.5	89.4	82.4	85.1
1997	126.7	104.8	110.5	89.4	129.9	124.5	111.5	147.6	90.8	90.3	89.5	91.6	90.5	85.8
1998	127.0	105.8	106.4	92.1	128.3	122.4	107.5	147.8	86.8	84.3	83.9	90.2	86.8	88.4
1995:														
January	118.2	99.2	118.5	81.7	120.2	116.3	111.5	133.3	93.8	96.0	95.4	91.2	93.8	78.8
February	116.4	99.1	119.2	81.6	118.1	113.6	108.6	133.1	92.4	94.8	96.5	89.6	94.1	78.6
March	115.6	100.8	123.6	81.6	116.5	114.4	105.3	133.3	91.7	94.4	96.1	88.6	97.4	78.6
April	116.3	101.6	123.2	82.3	117.1	113.1	110.3	130.8	90.7	92.3	94.7	88.9	96.8	79.3
May	115.2	104.0	130.6	83.2	115.6	110.7	102.9	132.2	90.2	92.4	93.3	87.8	102.4	80.1
June	115.2	101.0	120.5	83.6	115.7	111.1	102.3	131.2	89.8	91.9	92.8	87.5	94.3	80.6
July	116.2	102.5	123.4	84.2	115.9	112.1	105.0	128.8	88.1	88.2	92.8	88.0	96.4	81.1
August	112.7	103.2	124.5	84.2	112.3	106.4	93.0	132.3	88.5	91.4	93.5	85.2	97.0	81.2
September	114.5	101.7	119.0	85.1	114.4	108.8	96.5	133.4	91.0	95.0	96.3	86.4	92.6	82.0
October	117.3	103.0	122.6	84.7	118.6	114.2	105.8	133.6	88.9	89.7	91.4	88.2	95.2	81.6
November	115.5	102.8	122.3	85.8	116.2	110.2	94.5	136.3	91.2	95.1	93.8	86.7	94.8	82.7
December	115.9	103.1	116.2	86.9	116.5	110.8	98.8	135.7	89.3	91.6	93.1	86.8	89.9	83.7
1996:														
January	114.2	104.2	114.5	87.6	114.4	107.9	89.2	136.0	88.7	91.8	91.5	85.3	88.8	84.4
February	118.2	102.4	111.1	88.1	120.7	115.6	99.2	137.9	89.0	89.7	90.3	88.3	86.5	84.9
March	119.4	100.7	107.1	88.2	122.4	118.5	106.2	135.3	90.2	91.3	91.5	89.0	83.8	84.9
April	119.7	101.0	106.8	88.7	122.4	118.0	103.4	136.7	89.5	90.0	90.3	89.1	84.0	85.3
May	120.6	99.7	104.0	88.5	124.3	120.1	103.9	138.2	90.0	90.3	90.8	89.7	82.2	85.1
June	120.2	98.7	101.5	88.4	123.4	118.5	102.2	139.7	90.3	91.2	92.6	89.3	80.7	85.0
July	118.5	100.9	102.2	88.2	121.1	116.3	97.0	136.9	88.9	89.9	91.7	87.8	81.6	84.8
August	121.6	97.8	96.4	89.0	125.2	120.5	106.0	140.9	90.9	91.7	91.1	90.0	77.3	85.5
September	125.2	99.8	98.5	88.9	129.3	125.6	110.3	141.5	90.9	89.6	90.1	92.4	79.4	85.4
October	122.3	100.0	102.2	89.0	125.1	119.9	105.3	142.3	91.5	92.6	89.6	90.1	82.8	85.4
November	122.5	100.7	97.2	89.0	125.3	119.9	105.9	142.9	90.3	90.6	87.0	90.1	79.1	85.5
December	124.3	100.3	101.3	88.8	128.7	123.8	111.3	144.6	90.2	89.4	89.7	91.3	82.8	85.2
1997:														
January	120.6	102.5	105.3	88.9	123.3	117.4	99.3	142.9	88.8	89.4	88.5	88.3	86.3	85.3
February	124.4	103.3	104.6	89.3	128.0	123.0	110.1	144.5	89.8	89.0	88.4	90.9	85.7	85.7
March	125.2	104.8	108.8	89.4	128.6	123.7	113.5	144.6	88.7	86.6	89.7	91.3	89.2	85.8
April	123.4	104.0	106.7	89.1	125.9	119.5	103.8	147.0	90.6	91.4	89.7	89.7	87.4	85.5
May	126.0	102.9	99.5	88.9	128.8	123.2	112.1	147.4	90.8	90.5	89.4	91.3	81.5	85.3
June	128.2	105.7	107.5	89.4	130.8	126.0	116.3	146.7	91.6	90.7	88.9	92.7	88.1	85.8
July	128.3	105.1	113.8	89.4	131.2	127.0	114.7	145.1	91.3	90.4	89.6	92.6	93.2	85.8
August	129.6	106.6	113.0	89.4	132.8	127.6	114.9	149.8	91.1	89.4	88.8	93.3	92.5	85.8
September	127.5	102.4	117.0	89.2	131.7	126.3	113.8	149.6	91.4	91.4	90.4	91.6	95.8	85.6
October	128.2	107.1	117.9	89.9	131.4	125.6	111.6	150.3	92.0	92.3	89.7	91.9	96.6	86.3
November	130.9	106.9	115.7	89.9	134.8	130.0	120.0	150.7	92.6	91.9	90.6	93.6	94.8	86.3
December	128.1	106.0	116.4	90.0	131.0	124.7	108.3	151.8	91.3	91.3	89.7	91.5	95.3	86.4
1998:														
January	129.7	105.0	109.6	90.0	131.9	125.9	108.8	151.4	92.1	91.9	91.4	92.4	89.7	86.4
February	128.0	104.7	111.2	90.2	130.1	123.9	108.9	150.6	91.0	91.0	91.5	91.2	91.0	86.5
March	126.4	105.3	107.5	90.9	127.8	121.4	101.3	148.9	90.0	90.2	88.5	89.9	87.9	87.3
April	128.4	106.8	108.9	91.9	130.5	125.2	109.7	148.1	90.0	89.1	89.8	91.2	88.9	88.2
May	127.6	105.0	101.8	92.2	129.4	123.9	109.1	147.5	89.1	87.9	88.9	90.6	83.1	88.5
June	124.9	102.5	103.2	92.6	126.4	121.6	106.3	142.1	85.8	83.5	84.1	88.6	84.2	88.9
July	125.4	108.1	105.1	93.4	125.1	120.3	107.9	140.9	85.9	83.5	85.3	88.9	85.7	89.6
August	126.7	107.8	109.7	93.5	126.7	120.0	103.6	148.8	86.9	84.7	86.3	89.7	89.3	89.7
September	128.1	106.5	103.1	93.8	129.9	124.0	108.7	149.2	83.7	78.1	80.4	90.6	83.9	90.1
October	128.0	106.4	107.7	92.0	130.0	123.4	113.5	151.9	83.7	78.4	77.8	90.4	87.6	88.3
November	129.3	107.4	109.4	92.6	131.4	125.3	115.2	151.2	82.2	74.9	70.7	91.3	88.9	88.9
December	123.4	105.8	100.5	92.1	123.5	115.1	95.7	151.7	81.9	77.9	71.6	87.0	81.6	88.4

Primary Metals—Shipments, Inventories, and Orders

(Seasonally adjusted)

Year and month	Manufacturers' shipments, inventories, and orders (millions of dollars)									
	Shipments		Inventories (book value, end of period)		New orders, net			Unfilled orders, end of period		
	Total	Blast furnaces, steel mills	Total	Blast furnaces, steel mills	Total [1]	Blast furnaces, steel mills	Nonferrous and other primary metals	Total [1]	Blast furnaces, steel mills	Nonferrous and other primary metals
1970	51,995	25,189	8,995	4,990	51,793	25,521	21,883	7,796	4,617	2,663
1971	51,585	25,791	9,084	4,926	51,284	25,571	20,704	7,478	4,380	2,552
1972	58,490	28,712	9,617	5,387	61,447	30,996	24,607	10,470	6,681	3,116
1973	72,791	36,301	10,034	5,302	78,395	39,413	31,417	16,129	9,794	4,962
1974	95,686	49,718	13,447	6,820	98,831	51,047	38,394	19,225	11,054	5,952
1975	80,890	42,281	15,742	8,597	75,034	38,611	27,864	13,266	7,345	4,015
1976	93,082	46,764	17,699	10,035	94,491	47,212	37,378	14,684	7,776	4,891
1977	103,267	50,670	18,261	10,004	105,689	52,103	42,400	17,298	9,435	5,483
1978	118,175	59,228	19,420	10,719	124,741	62,648	48,319	23,969	12,932	7,393
1979	137,488	67,414	22,446	12,012	139,783	66,968	58,420	26,320	12,485	9,457
1980	134,057	61,612	23,055	12,153	134,416	62,473	60,399	26,815	13,418	10,096
1981	142,072	70,254	25,794	13,359	137,286	67,457	57,545	22,024	10,589	8,784
1982	104,874	46,928	24,174	12,556	98,445	43,013	46,942	15,500	6,574	7,418
1983	109,240	46,398	22,308	11,065	113,884	49,123	55,566	20,400	9,431	9,594
1984	120,315	51,978	22,444	11,087	118,354	50,719	56,030	18,362	8,103	8,694
1985	112,265	48,904	19,974	9,709	112,276	49,079	52,275	18,331	8,248	8,361
1986	107,865	45,718	18,436	8,567	108,218	46,408	51,294	18,590	8,897	7,783
1987	120,248	51,815	19,076	8,620	125,989	54,763	60,302	24,340	11,828	10,300
1988	149,837	64,294	22,422	10,495	152,578	64,002	75,997	27,079	11,508	12,974
1989	155,718	64,783	22,838	10,942	152,814	62,752	77,249	24,120	9,479	11,824
1990	148,787	62,826	22,560	11,045	149,338	63,369	72,944	24,768	10,120	11,258
1991	136,378	57,267	20,703	10,236	134,657	56,366	66,778	23,075	9,290	10,609
1992	138,287	58,449	19,981	9,809	136,849	58,002	67,337	21,636	8,897	9,925
1993	142,685	62,466	20,132	9,836	144,018	63,604	67,112	23,068	10,163	9,623
1994	161,188	69,887	22,588	10,697	167,685	70,960	81,963	29,661	11,303	14,535
1995	180,314	74,927	24,021	11,560	178,702	75,811	87,857	27,993	12,183	12,195
1996	178,297	74,552	24,289	11,912	180,362	74,885	88,773	29,996	12,432	13,167
1997	188,916	77,023	24,680	11,727	193,987	79,481	96,513	35,160	14,905	14,656
1998	180,973	72,767	24,679	12,057	175,482	69,444	88,067	29,554	11,430	12,666
1995:										
January	15,437	6,261	23,009	10,836	15,806	6,461	8,052	30,030	11,503	14,705
February	15,192	6,285	23,308	11,068	15,073	6,291	7,386	29,911	11,509	14,474
March	15,504	6,557	23,475	11,113	15,288	6,839	7,217	29,695	11,791	14,052
April	14,991	6,202	23,816	11,378	14,672	6,201	7,151	29,376	11,790	13,655
May	15,155	6,306	23,814	11,395	14,367	6,182	7,036	28,588	11,666	13,106
June	15,069	6,192	23,999	11,530	14,290	6,049	7,097	27,809	11,523	12,565
July	14,591	5,929	24,253	11,602	14,013	5,763	7,113	27,231	11,357	12,217
August	14,975	6,227	24,162	11,622	15,208	6,455	7,461	27,464	11,585	12,213
September	14,843	6,249	24,095	11,583	14,816	6,104	7,413	27,599	11,440	12,307
October	14,876	6,300	24,076	11,541	15,038	6,507	7,189	27,599	11,647	12,183
November	14,823	6,265	24,104	11,465	15,025	6,550	7,207	27,801	11,932	12,105
December	14,828	6,097	24,021	11,560	15,020	6,348	7,529	27,993	12,183	12,195
1996:										
January	14,600	6,106	24,084	11,671	14,703	6,206	7,087	28,096	12,283	12,051
February	14,518	6,083	24,022	11,620	14,886	6,073	7,338	28,464	12,273	12,216
March	14,661	6,031	24,192	11,827	14,245	5,842	7,143	28,048	12,084	12,001
April	14,853	6,187	24,043	11,637	15,059	6,154	7,535	28,254	12,051	12,199
May	15,104	6,216	23,975	11,498	15,539	6,607	7,587	28,689	12,442	12,264
June	14,538	6,194	24,071	11,529	15,347	6,392	7,410	29,498	12,640	12,670
July	14,955	6,295	23,898	11,524	15,492	6,509	7,564	30,035	12,854	12,967
August	14,914	6,274	23,807	11,579	15,470	6,387	7,623	30,591	12,967	13,321
September	14,790	6,309	24,076	11,758	14,820	6,335	7,086	30,621	12,993	13,305
October	14,998	6,297	23,969	11,760	14,761	6,188	7,369	30,384	12,884	13,308
November	15,224	6,266	24,085	11,867	14,814	5,938	7,493	29,974	12,556	13,177
December	15,240	6,330	24,289	11,912	15,262	6,206	7,614	29,996	12,432	13,167
1997:										
January	15,552	6,470	24,089	11,755	15,786	6,497	7,833	30,230	12,459	13,290
February	15,670	6,429	24,228	11,773	15,879	6,362	8,086	30,439	12,392	13,493
March	15,596	6,388	24,472	11,905	15,878	6,195	8,274	30,721	12,199	13,879
April	15,906	6,481	24,277	11,824	16,582	6,898	8,221	31,397	12,616	14,082
May	15,606	6,260	24,278	11,876	16,133	6,516	8,182	31,924	12,872	14,265
June	15,786	6,461	24,384	11,801	15,866	6,709	7,700	32,004	13,120	13,998
July	15,904	6,475	24,423	11,715	16,780	6,781	8,468	32,880	13,426	14,463
August	15,749	6,376	24,544	11,753	16,139	6,442	8,239	33,270	13,492	14,730
September	15,904	6,416	24,398	11,725	17,192	6,683	8,930	34,558	13,759	15,601
October	15,858	6,413	24,439	11,718	15,926	6,754	7,701	34,626	14,100	15,338
November	15,741	6,366	24,474	11,732	16,272	6,881	7,710	35,157	14,615	15,092
December	15,713	6,513	24,680	11,727	15,716	6,803	7,236	35,160	14,905	14,656
1998:										
January	15,715	6,484	24,720	11,770	15,272	6,112	7,707	34,717	14,533	14,590
February	15,838	6,491	24,388	11,767	15,996	6,584	7,722	34,875	14,626	14,546
March	15,660	6,439	24,241	11,806	14,696	6,285	6,688	33,911	14,472	13,594
April	15,523	6,358	24,340	11,852	15,451	6,095	7,891	33,839	14,209	13,833
May	15,176	6,200	24,465	11,986	14,940	6,286	7,168	33,603	14,295	13,504
June	15,049	6,124	24,612	12,168	14,453	5,850	7,325	33,007	14,021	13,356
July	14,968	6,006	24,763	12,335	14,273	5,382	7,521	32,312	13,397	13,384
August	15,056	6,104	24,859	12,437	14,413	5,523	7,298	31,669	12,816	13,203
September	14,951	5,909	24,898	12,398	13,917	5,347	7,186	30,635	12,254	12,854
October	14,590	5,729	24,825	12,312	13,343	4,912	6,927	29,388	11,437	12,410
November	14,286	5,551	24,817	12,175	14,587	5,572	7,447	29,689	11,458	12,637
December	14,222	5,359	24,679	12,057	14,087	5,331	7,323	29,554	11,430	12,666

1. Also includes iron and steel foundries not shown separately.

Primary Metals—Producer Prices

(1982=100, except as noted; not seasonally adjusted)

Year and month	Primary metal industries (December 1984=100)	Intermediate materials						Crude materials				
		Foundry and forge shop products	Steel mill products	Primary nonferrous metals	Aluminum mill shapes	Copper and brass mill shapes	Nonferrous wire and cable	Iron ore	Iron and steel scrap	Nonferrous metal ores (December 1983=100)	Copper base scrap	Aluminum base scrap
1970	.....	32.4	32.7	44.9	36.7	63.4	62.6	35.9	59.6	.....	100.9	34.4
1971	.....	34.6	35.2	40.2	36.4	57.5	57.2	37.0	49.1	.....	80.7	32.7
1972	.....	36.0	37.3	40.7	36.9	60.3	57.4	37.0	52.3	.....	79.3	31.1
1973	.....	38.1	38.4	48.9	37.9	68.8	61.5	38.3	80.7	.....	120.1	46.8
1974	.....	46.7	48.6	69.5	50.1	88.7	84.0	44.2	151.6	.....	138.0	70.9
1975	.....	56.2	56.4	65.0	54.9	72.8	75.2	55.4	105.4	.....	87.3	44.4
1976	.....	63.3	60.0	67.4	59.4	79.6	74.7	61.3	111.2	.....	96.1	74.0
1977	.....	66.7	65.8	72.4	67.7	80.8	77.1	66.8	99.2	.....	90.1	90.2
1978	.....	72.2	72.8	76.8	75.9	83.3	76.6	69.9	113.6	.....	100.3	117.1
1979	.....	80.2	80.2	103.9	82.8	105.0	92.1	77.8	146.8	.....	129.3	169.6
1980	.....	89.7	86.6	132.7	89.3	112.6	107.5	87.8	140.9	.....	138.9	183.9
1981	.....	95.4	96.6	114.7	98.3	107.8	102.5	96.3	140.6	.....	126.3	141.7
1982	.....	100.0	100.0	100.0	100.0	100.0	100.0	100.0	100.0	.....	100.0	100.0
1983	.....	101.6	100.9	106.8	102.2	105.7	100.7	101.2	107.4	.....	110.2	142.3
1984	.....	104.4	104.7	101.3	112.0	106.9	99.9	101.2	123.7	103.5	101.5	167.6
1985	99.4	105.2	104.7	93.6	107.8	106.9	100.9	97.5	112.6	73.2	95.4	123.4
1986	97.0	105.2	99.8	93.8	102.6	106.9	101.8	91.5	109.6	75.7	93.6	124.5
1987	101.0	105.7	102.3	109.3	105.6	121.8	107.0	84.2	128.4	106.0	113.0	156.4
1988	113.0	109.6	110.7	144.3	130.9	162.7	129.6	82.8	177.1	108.1	157.9	219.5
1989	118.8	114.6	114.5	149.2	135.4	182.0	146.1	82.8	173.7	109.6	179.8	204.4
1990	116.5	117.2	112.1	133.4	127.9	174.6	142.6	83.3	166.0	98.3	181.3	172.6
1991	113.1	119.0	109.5	114.0	123.2	160.5	139.2	83.6	147.6	82.6	170.0	143.1
1992	111.7	120.1	106.4	108.1	121.9	166.0	136.7	83.7	139.2	75.4	162.9	137.6
1993	111.4	121.3	108.2	98.1	120.4	150.7	133.1	82.7	172.5	67.2	136.1	129.2
1994	117.0	123.9	113.4	115.7	127.7	167.3	139.8	82.7	192.9	81.4	155.5	172.9
1995	128.2	129.3	120.1	146.8	160.4	195.2	151.5	91.8	202.7	101.6	193.5	209.4
1996	123.7	132.6	115.6	126.2	144.8	179.0	147.5	96.7	191.1	90.2	166.3	173.4
1997	124.7	134.1	116.4	126.2	147.5	177.3	148.1	96.3	188.9	82.2	157.7	195.1
1998	120.9	135.0	113.8	106.7	142.0	153.0	141.1	95.4	165.0	66.6	116.2	162.5
1995:												
January	126.6	126.6	117.9	150.8	158.4	196.3	151.6	82.9	210.6	99.8	188.7	237.9
February	128.2	127.6	119.7	152.5	164.9	194.0	151.3	82.9	208.1	100.2	185.0	237.7
March	129.1	128.4	121.0	151.9	165.1	198.2	150.8	93.5	201.3	100.1	182.0	220.1
April	129.7	128.9	121.7	149.7	165.1	197.7	152.0	93.5	202.9	106.2	191.4	216.7
May	128.9	128.9	121.9	146.0	163.7	188.7	150.0	93.5	202.8	102.8	185.1	208.8
June	128.9	128.9	121.9	145.0	160.9	195.2	151.2	93.5	200.7	103.1	195.1	207.3
July	128.8	129.4	121.9	147.0	159.5	197.6	152.7	93.5	201.0	104.9	200.8	208.5
August	128.8	129.9	121.2	147.9	159.4	197.1	153.2	93.5	210.2	102.1	202.7	212.3
September	128.2	130.1	120.2	146.9	160.3	194.9	150.4	93.5	206.3	100.2	200.4	205.0
October	127.4	130.6	119.1	142.4	158.5	189.1	149.7	93.5	201.4	97.5	199.9	194.1
November	127.1	130.8	117.9	140.6	156.0	194.8	152.6	93.5	193.1	100.9	199.0	183.9
December	126.8	131.0	117.3	141.1	152.4	198.2	152.1	94.0	193.7	100.9	192.5	181.0
1996:												
January	125.7	131.6	116.6	137.5	150.8	188.8	150.0	97.6	199.7	97.9	181.1	179.3
February	124.4	132.1	115.2	131.8	148.0	183.8	148.6	97.6	201.4	96.7	176.7	178.6
March	124.2	132.5	114.7	132.4	148.3	186.3	148.3	97.6	197.8	95.9	179.9	179.3
April	124.1	132.4	114.9	132.4	147.3	182.4	148.6	97.7	197.8	95.5	180.0	183.8
May	124.6	132.6	115.2	135.2	145.3	191.4	150.8	94.8	199.5	97.2	182.9	179.9
June	124.6	132.7	115.6	136.9	147.1	180.9	149.3	94.6	194.8	92.4	167.8	174.6
July	123.2	132.7	115.5	122.4	145.7	172.3	145.9	96.7	190.5	86.6	157.9	167.2
August	122.8	132.8	115.9	117.2	143.2	170.0	145.0	96.7	191.6	84.3	153.2	168.1
September	122.7	132.7	116.3	116.5	142.0	169.6	145.0	96.7	191.7	83.5	151.9	168.4
October	122.7	133.0	116.0	114.4	140.3	169.6	145.6	96.7	183.4	83.2	151.8	160.0
November	122.6	133.0	115.7	115.9	139.0	175.2	145.6	96.7	172.4	85.3	154.5	166.7
December	123.0	133.0	115.6	121.5	140.3	177.1	147.4	96.7	172.2	83.9	157.9	174.8
1997:												
January	123.6	133.6	115.9	125.4	141.8	179.0	147.7	99.7	182.2	86.4	163.6	188.3
February	124.0	134.0	116.1	127.6	144.1	178.5	147.9	99.7	191.1	84.8	164.6	195.5
March	124.8	134.3	116.1	130.3	147.6	183.5	149.4	99.7	186.0	87.8	167.7	202.2
April	125.0	134.2	116.4	129.0	147.2	181.0	149.6	95.2	181.6	84.8	165.4	195.9
May	125.0	134.2	116.2	129.7	146.3	180.6	150.3	95.2	185.4	87.4	170.3	198.9
June	125.4	134.3	116.3	131.6	148.0	184.8	150.2	95.2	185.1	87.0	174.0	196.8
July	125.2	134.4	116.6	126.8	147.3	181.1	149.4	95.2	189.4	82.5	161.9	193.3
August	125.2	134.1	116.6	127.6	148.1	179.0	148.4	95.2	191.7	83.1	156.3	198.1
September	125.2	134.2	116.8	126.6	150.1	173.8	148.3	95.2	189.7	80.2	150.2	193.6
October	124.8	134.1	116.6	122.6	149.7	172.4	146.6	95.2	191.2	79.0	146.6	194.2
November	124.5	134.0	116.6	120.4	149.7	168.3	145.3	95.2	196.0	73.9	140.6	193.0
December	123.9	134.1	116.2	117.2	149.8	165.5	144.1	95.2	197.1	68.8	130.7	191.5
1998:												
January	123.3	134.7	115.9	113.7	147.5	159.7	143.2	95.2	197.3	67.2	122.7	185.8
February	123.0	134.9	115.9	113.8	146.4	159.5	142.0	95.2	193.5	67.9	123.3	184.6
March	122.7	135.0	115.5	111.3	145.3	157.4	142.5	95.2	186.4	68.3	123.6	181.6
April	122.6	135.2	115.4	113.1	144.2	158.4	142.5	95.2	184.1	70.8	124.9	176.8
May	122.1	135.2	115.1	109.4	144.1	156.0	141.3	95.6	184.5	69.4	123.8	171.7
June	121.6	135.2	115.1	106.7	141.2	151.2	141.7	95.5	182.0	67.4	119.0	164.0
July	120.9	134.9	114.8	104.6	139.2	149.0	141.8	95.5	175.7	68.6	114.0	150.5
August	120.6	135.0	114.3	103.0	140.8	149.5	141.3	95.5	162.5	64.5	111.8	149.9
September	120.1	135.0	113.3	103.5	140.7	151.6	140.8	95.6	147.5	65.7	113.1	149.7
October	119.1	134.9	111.8	102.6	139.0	148.8	140.2	95.6	129.1	63.8	111.2	145.8
November	118.0	134.9	110.2	100.6	138.0	149.0	138.3	95.6	119.2	63.8	106.6	145.5
December	116.9	135.0	108.7	97.6	137.1	146.4	137.4	95.2	118.5	61.9	100.5	144.6

Primary Metals—Employment, Hours, and Earnings

Year and month	Primary metals						Blast furnaces and basic steel					
	Employment (thousands, seasonally adjusted)		Production workers				Seasonally adjusted		Not seasonally adjusted			
							Production workers				Average earnings (dollars)	
	Total payroll employees	Production workers	Average weekly hours (seasonally adjusted)	Aggregate weekly hours index (1982=100, seasonally adjusted)	Average earnings (dollars, not seasonally adjusted)		Average weekly hours	Aggregate weekly hours index (1982=100)	Total payroll employees (thousands)	Production workers (thousands)		
					Hourly	Weekly					Hourly	Weekly
1970	1,260	1,000	40.4	152.9	3.93	158.77	40.0	179.5	627	500	4.16	166.40
1971	1,171	923	40.1	140.5	4.23	169.62	39.6	161.5	574	455	4.49	177.80
1972	1,173	933	41.4	146.3	4.66	192.92	40.6	165.1	568	453	5.08	206.25
1973	1,259	1,011	42.3	161.8	5.04	213.19	41.7	181.5	605	485	5.51	229.77
1974	1,289	1,030	41.6	162.4	5.60	232.96	41.3	180.7	610	487	6.27	258.95
1975	1,139	887	40.0	134.3	6.18	247.20	39.5	151.8	548	428	6.94	274.13
1976	1,155	904	40.8	140.0	6.77	276.22	40.3	155.6	549	431	7.59	305.88
1977	1,182	922	41.3	144.2	7.40	305.62	40.5	157.2	554	433	8.36	338.58
1978	1,215	954	41.8	151.3	8.20	342.76	41.5	164.6	561	442	9.39	389.69
1979	1,254	986	41.4	154.8	8.98	371.77	41.2	167.0	571	451	10.41	428.89
1980	1,142	878	40.1	133.4	9.77	391.78	39.4	139.8	512	396	11.39	448.77
1981	1,122	862	40.5	132.5	10.81	437.81	40.4	141.9	506	392	12.60	509.04
1982	922	683	38.6	100.0	11.33	437.34	37.9	100.0	396	294	13.35	505.97
1983	832	620	40.5	95.2	11.35	459.68	39.5	90.8	341	256	12.89	509.16
1984	857	651	41.7	102.9	11.47	478.30	40.7	93.7	334	257	12.98	528.29
1985	808	611	41.5	96.1	11.67	484.31	41.1	85.3	303	232	13.33	547.86
1986	751	565	41.9	89.8	11.86	496.93	41.7	78.2	273	209	13.73	572.54
1987	746	562	43.1	91.8	11.94	514.61	43.4	79.0	268	203	13.77	597.62
1988	770	589	43.5	97.2	12.16	528.96	44.0	85.1	278	215	13.98	615.12
1989	772	589	43.0	96.0	12.43	534.49	43.4	83.9	279	215	14.25	618.45
1990	756	574	42.7	93.0	12.92	551.68	43.4	82.6	276	212	14.82	643.19
1991	723	545	42.2	87.2	13.33	562.53	42.7	76.4	263	200	15.36	655.87
1992	695	525	43.0	85.6	13.66	587.38	43.5	73.7	250	189	15.87	690.35
1993	683	520	43.7	86.2	13.99	611.36	44.1	72.6	240	183	16.36	721.48
1994	698	537	44.7	90.9	14.34	641.00	44.9	73.4	239	182	16.85	756.57
1995	712	553	44.0	92.1	14.62	643.28	44.4	73.6	242	185	17.33	769.45
1996	711	553	44.2	92.6	14.97	661.67	44.5	73.6	240	185	17.80	792.10
1997	711	555	44.9	94.5	15.22	683.38	44.9	72.9	235	181	18.03	809.55
1998	712	557	44.2	93.4	15.49	684.66	44.6	71.7	232	179	18.43	821.98
1995:												
January	712	551	44.9	93.8	14.57	655.65	45.5	75.1	241	183	17.29	784.97
February	712	553	44.6	93.5	14.46	646.36	45.2	74.7	240	184	17.08	768.60
March	712	553	44.5	93.3	14.45	643.03	44.8	74.0	240	184	17.02	760.79
April	714	554	44.3	93.0	14.76	639.11	45.2	75.1	241	184	17.48	793.59
May	714	554	43.8	92.0	14.53	637.87	44.0	73.1	242	185	17.22	757.68
June	712	554	43.9	92.2	14.61	642.84	44.1	73.2	243	187	17.33	762.52
July	709	550	43.3	90.3	14.69	628.73	43.7	72.2	242	185	17.39	758.20
August	711	552	43.7	91.4	14.63	634.94	44.0	73.1	242	185	17.41	762.56
September	711	552	43.7	91.4	14.70	643.86	44.0	72.7	241	184	17.54	775.27
October	711	552	43.8	91.6	14.64	639.77	44.1	72.8	241	184	17.41	766.04
November	712	553	43.9	92.0	14.73	652.54	44.2	73.4	243	185	17.52	781.39
December	712	553	43.7	91.6	14.69	652.24	44.3	74.0	244	186	17.31	772.03
1996:												
January	714	556	43.3	91.3	14.84	644.06	44.2	73.4	242	185	17.62	780.57
February	713	555	43.9	92.4	14.70	648.27	44.8	74.4	241	185	17.46	778.72
March	711	554	43.8	92.0	14.73	645.17	44.3	73.6	241	185	17.57	778.35
April	710	551	43.8	91.5	14.99	653.56	43.9	72.9	240	184	17.88	786.72
May	711	554	44.2	92.8	14.82	653.56	44.3	74.0	241	186	17.52	776.14
June	712	555	44.3	93.2	14.91	660.51	44.5	74.3	242	187	17.65	785.43
July	706	549	44.3	92.2	15.08	657.49	44.6	74.1	241	186	17.97	797.87
August	713	556	44.4	93.6	15.02	662.38	44.3	74.0	242	186	17.85	785.40
September	713	556	44.5	93.8	15.18	680.06	44.4	73.7	241	186	18.11	807.71
October	708	552	44.4	92.9	15.09	670.00	44.6	72.9	236	182	17.96	797.42
November	707	552	44.0	92.1	15.18	675.51	44.6	72.9	237	183	18.07	814.96
December	707	552	44.5	93.1	15.15	686.30	44.7	73.0	237	182	17.94	809.09
1997:												
January	707	552	44.4	92.9	15.12	672.84	44.5	73.1	237	182	17.73	792.53
February	708	552	44.7	93.5	15.09	673.01	44.6	72.9	236	181	17.76	788.54
March	708	552	44.8	93.7	15.16	679.17	44.7	72.6	235	181	17.89	799.68
April	709	553	45.0	94.3	15.15	677.21	44.7	72.6	234	180	17.92	804.61
May	707	553	44.8	93.9	15.09	674.52	44.7	72.2	234	180	17.87	798.79
June	707	553	44.7	93.7	15.16	679.17	44.6	72.1	236	182	18.03	804.14
July	707	554	44.8	94.1	15.28	670.79	44.6	72.1	234	181	18.13	803.16
August	712	558	45.0	95.2	15.16	677.65	45.2	73.0	234	181	18.00	806.40
September	713	557	45.0	95.0	15.27	691.73	45.1	73.3	235	181	18.30	827.16
October	714	559	45.3	96.0	15.33	691.38	45.6	74.1	235	181	18.26	821.70
November	716	561	45.1	95.9	15.38	699.79	45.5	73.9	235	182	18.28	831.74
December	717	562	45.2	96.3	15.43	711.32	45.6	74.1	235	182	18.15	834.90
1998:												
January	720	564	45.3	96.8	15.48	702.79	46.0	75.1	235	182	18.33	846.85
February	719	564	44.8	95.8	15.46	691.06	45.4	74.2	234	181	18.34	828.97
March	719	565	44.5	95.3	15.53	691.09	45.2	73.8	234	181	18.32	828.06
April	718	564	44.1	94.3	15.66	679.64	44.7	72.6	233	180	18.67	836.42
May	716	561	44.3	94.2	15.55	691.98	45.3	73.6	233	181	18.56	842.62
June	716	561	44.4	94.4	15.54	689.98	45.0	72.7	235	182	18.54	834.30
July	705	550	44.0	91.7	15.56	670.64	44.4	71.7	232	180	18.50	812.15
August	713	558	44.1	93.3	15.45	676.71	44.4	71.3	231	179	18.46	815.93
September	712	557	43.9	92.7	15.61	683.72	44.2	70.6	231	178	18.76	832.94
October	705	552	43.7	91.4	15.32	667.95	43.7	69.0	228	176	18.22	787.10
November	700	547	43.8	90.8	15.35	678.47	43.7	68.3	226	174	18.32	800.58
December	699	546	43.7	90.4	15.36	685.06	43.3	68.0	227	175	18.18	794.47

Fabricated Metal Products—Production, Capacity Utilization, Shipments, Inventories, and Orders

(Seasonally adjusted)

Year and month	Industrial production (1992 = 100)							Capacity utilization (output as a percent of capacity)	Manufacturers' shipments, inventories, and orders (millions of dollars)			
	Total	Metal containers	Hardware, tools, and cutlery		Structural metal products	Other fabricated metal products			Shipments	Inventories (book value, end of period)	New orders (net)	Unfilled orders (end of period)
			Total	Hardware and tools		Total	Fasteners, stampings, etc.					
1970	77.7	84.4	83.7	84.4	85.8	70.9	75.3	75.0	44,210	7,907	43,990	14,877
1971	77.3	81.7	88.0	89.5	84.6	69.8	72.1	73.7	45,478	8,098	44,305	13,688
1972	84.8	84.4	98.4	99.7	93.0	76.8	79.3	79.9	51,487	8,408	52,879	15,077
1973	94.3	93.4	105.6	107.3	103.7	86.3	89.5	86.8	58,804	9,864	64,733	21,019
1974	90.5	94.0	101.1	100.4	99.2	83.3	84.4	80.9	67,212	13,387	74,281	28,100
1975	78.4	90.1	87.5	87.4	85.3	71.0	69.8	68.6	68,411	13,091	64,349	24,008
1976	86.9	93.1	102.5	102.4	91.6	79.9	81.2	74.6	77,560	14,304	76,372	22,810
1977	94.7	98.1	110.7	111.0	98.9	88.8	91.2	79.9	89,938	15,527	92,028	25,152
1978	98.2	97.8	109.7	109.8	101.8	93.8	96.4	81.0	101,245	17,296	105,182	29,137
1979	101.6	100.8	115.8	117.9	107.0	96.0	96.8	82.0	113,494	19,145	117,428	33,131
1980	94.4	94.3	99.0	100.2	104.2	88.6	86.1	74.9	116,071	19,532	116,195	33,296
1981	93.0	93.2	100.0	101.6	101.8	87.5	84.5	73.2	123,535	20,209	123,245	33,036
1982	84.9	94.5	85.4	85.3	94.1	79.0	72.8	66.9	119,236	21,440	113,399	27,117
1983	87.2	95.1	91.5	92.0	91.4	82.7	80.3	68.4	123,083	21,752	122,760	26,752
1984	95.2	94.3	99.5	100.8	94.6	93.8	93.9	74.3	138,107	23,330	141,650	30,254
1985	96.5	91.8	100.1	101.1	99.0	94.3	93.1	74.9	143,268	22,880	142,300	29,197
1986	95.6	88.0	100.3	101.7	97.5	93.7	91.4	73.6	143,063	22,094	143,541	29,633
1987	101.9	92.1	105.4	107.8	105.5	99.9	97.9	78.1	147,367	22,920	150,716	32,973
1988	106.1	95.4	107.2	108.9	106.8	106.0	104.3	81.1	159,505	24,950	158,170	31,661
1989	104.8	97.5	107.6	109.2	106.2	103.7	102.4	80.0	164,073	25,427	160,037	27,629
1990	101.2	100.2	102.2	102.6	103.5	99.8	98.0	77.3	165,064	25,044	163,285	25,859
1991	96.2	100.0	96.6	96.8	99.1	94.2	91.4	73.4	159,760	23,922	158,401	24,516
1992	100.0	100.0	100.0	100.0	100.0	100.0	100.0	76.9	166,532	23,815	165,793	23,725
1993	104.4	98.4	105.1	105.1	102.9	105.3	108.9	79.7	175,118	23,838	172,121	20,731
1994	112.2	104.4	116.4	117.2	110.9	112.2	118.4	83.1	190,544	25,597	191,099	21,290
1995	116.4	100.8	117.1	117.7	114.0	118.8	125.9	82.8	204,384	27,003	205,388	22,329
1996	120.2	103.6	122.6	122.8	118.3	121.7	129.8	81.0	214,007	27,894	215,791	24,159
1997	124.7	104.5	125.8	124.3	123.0	126.8	134.3	79.2	226,078	29,579	228,567	26,649
1998	127.3	105.8	127.6	125.8	126.9	129.3	137.6	76.9	239,667	30,855	238,751	25,894
1995:												
January	116.0	97.6	118.3	119.1	114.9	117.1	123.2	84.5	17,115	25,917	17,367	21,542
February	117.0	95.0	118.0	119.3	114.7	119.6	127.1	84.9	16,986	26,269	17,272	21,828
March	116.8	99.3	115.5	116.7	114.8	119.5	126.8	84.3	17,023	26,774	17,155	21,960
April	115.0	99.1	117.0	118.6	113.1	116.8	124.0	82.7	16,719	27,031	16,875	22,116
May	116.2	101.4	116.1	117.1	113.6	118.9	125.9	83.2	16,885	27,286	17,186	22,417
June	116.5	104.5	118.2	119.3	113.1	119.0	126.2	83.0	16,830	27,464	16,908	22,495
July	115.2	97.0	115.1	115.4	113.0	117.6	123.9	81.7	16,910	27,590	16,863	22,448
August	116.7	108.1	115.5	115.7	113.6	119.2	126.1	82.4	17,229	27,579	17,161	22,380
September	117.0	100.0	116.4	116.5	114.3	120.1	127.1	82.2	17,120	27,366	17,148	22,408
October	116.4	103.1	118.2	118.4	113.5	119.0	125.6	81.4	17,222	27,356	17,082	22,268
November	117.0	104.0	117.3	116.9	114.3	119.9	127.6	81.5	17,088	27,246	17,312	22,492
December	117.2	100.8	119.8	120.1	114.9	119.4	126.9	81.3	17,328	27,003	17,165	22,329
1996:												
January	117.7	104.1	119.7	120.0	114.3	120.4	130.2	81.3	17,391	27,092	17,327	22,265
February	118.9	105.4	122.2	122.7	115.3	121.2	129.9	81.8	17,248	27,386	17,365	22,382
March	118.9	102.0	118.4	118.0	116.9	120.8	129.1	81.3	17,084	27,236	17,223	22,521
April	118.7	103.0	119.8	119.6	117.4	120.0	127.7	80.9	17,794	27,188	17,843	22,570
May	119.6	104.4	120.9	120.6	117.4	121.2	129.4	81.1	18,159	27,132	18,507	22,918
June	120.3	101.6	122.3	122.6	118.7	121.7	129.6	81.3	17,861	26,958	18,045	23,102
July	120.8	103.4	122.5	122.8	118.8	122.5	130.3	81.2	17,864	27,378	17,959	23,197
August	121.4	102.1	126.2	126.9	119.2	122.6	130.6	81.2	18,215	27,592	18,299	23,281
September	121.4	103.8	124.6	125.1	119.8	122.5	129.8	80.9	18,122	27,528	18,442	23,601
October	121.6	106.0	125.1	125.3	119.8	122.6	130.6	80.7	18,051	27,643	18,264	23,814
November	121.7	103.4	124.0	124.4	120.7	122.6	130.4	80.4	18,302	27,746	18,444	23,956
December	121.4	104.1	125.4	124.9	120.7	121.9	129.7	79.9	17,846	27,894	18,049	24,159
1997:												
January	121.7	104.1	126.2	125.9	119.5	122.9	131.4	79.6	18,297	28,124	18,435	24,297
February	123.1	103.1	126.7	126.7	122.1	124.2	132.6	80.1	18,491	28,340	18,863	24,669
March	123.6	106.1	124.0	123.3	123.0	124.4	131.4	80.0	18,255	28,595	18,419	24,833
April	124.8	105.4	125.8	124.8	123.4	126.1	134.3	80.4	18,953	28,747	19,360	25,240
May	124.1	103.4	125.7	124.8	122.8	126.0	133.6	79.5	18,401	28,771	18,433	25,272
June	123.7	102.9	123.5	121.3	122.3	126.1	133.3	78.8	18,755	29,012	19,225	25,742
July	125.2	107.7	126.4	124.4	122.3	128.0	136.8	79.3	18,932	29,089	19,205	26,015
August	124.5	102.5	125.2	123.2	123.0	127.1	134.1	78.4	18,995	29,132	19,038	26,058
September	124.7	105.4	125.4	123.0	123.7	126.5	132.0	78.1	19,283	29,360	19,559	26,334
October	126.1	104.7	127.5	125.7	123.6	128.9	136.4	78.6	19,274	29,480	19,521	26,581
November	126.8	101.7	126.2	124.0	124.6	130.2	137.7	78.6	19,143	29,590	19,320	26,758
December	128.2	107.5	127.1	125.3	125.9	131.0	138.6	79.0	19,299	29,579	19,190	26,649
1998:												
January	127.6	104.8	127.8	126.0	126.6	130.2	137.0	78.3	19,109	29,775	19,328	26,868
February	126.6	103.7	125.9	123.7	127.1	128.9	135.0	77.5	19,766	30,069	19,774	26,876
March	127.2	104.5	126.3	124.8	126.9	129.7	136.7	77.6	19,742	30,405	19,704	26,838
April	127.8	106.6	127.0	125.6	126.3	130.6	138.6	77.7	19,570	30,580	20,001	27,269
May	128.7	104.2	129.2	128.2	127.4	131.2	139.8	78.0	19,745	30,460	19,630	27,154
June	128.0	106.0	126.4	125.0	127.4	130.4	138.6	77.3	19,755	30,749	19,722	27,121
July	127.8	103.7	127.2	126.3	128.1	129.7	136.6	77.0	20,309	30,939	20,132	26,944
August	126.3	105.0	125.4	123.5	126.4	128.5	136.0	75.8	20,114	30,944	19,693	26,523
September	126.2	106.6	126.2	123.5	126.0	128.2	136.1	75.6	20,235	31,050	19,930	26,218
October	126.9	107.4	128.1	125.5	127.3	128.5	137.9	75.7	20,176	31,093	20,095	26,137
November	127.7	106.8	131.6	130.0	128.1	128.8	139.2	75.9	20,415	31,134	20,235	25,957
December	128.7	109.7	129.9	128.6	129.8	129.3	139.7	76.4	20,523	30,855	20,460	25,894

Fabricated Metal Products—Prices, Employment, Hours, and Earnings

| Year and month | Producer prices (1982=100, except as noted; not seasonally adjusted) | | | | | | Employment (thousands, seasonally adjusted) | | Production workers | | | |
| | Fabricated metal products industry (December 1984 =100) | Intermediate materials | | | | | Total payroll employees | Production workers | Average weekly hours, seasonally adjusted | Aggregate weekly hours index (1982=100), seasonally adjusted | Average earnings (dollars, not seasonally adjusted) | |
		Metal containers	Hardware	Plumbing fixtures and brass fittings	Heating equipment	Fabricated structural metal products					Hourly	Weekly
1970	.....	34.3	39.8	39.9	46.6	36.7	1,559	1,188	40.7	120.3	3.53	143.67
1971	.....	37.1	41.7	41.8	48.6	38.8	1,479	1,128	40.4	113.2	3.77	152.31
1972	.....	39.2	42.9	43.0	49.8	40.2	1,541	1,189	41.2	121.9	4.05	166.86
1973	.....	41.0	44.5	45.1	50.8	41.8	1,645	1,277	41.6	131.8	4.29	178.46
1974	.....	50.1	50.2	53.5	56.9	52.9	1,632	1,256	40.8	127.4	4.61	188.09
1975	.....	58.5	58.2	58.2	63.5	62.0	1,453	1,090	40.1	108.4	5.05	202.51
1976	.....	61.5	61.8	62.5	66.6	63.6	1,505	1,138	40.8	115.3	5.50	224.40
1977	.....	66.4	66.2	67.0	69.8	67.8	1,577	1,198	41.0	121.9	5.91	242.31
1978	.....	74.1	71.5	71.4	73.5	74.3	1,667	1,269	41.0	129.3	6.35	260.35
1979	.....	81.9	78.0	77.9	78.9	81.6	1,713	1,298	40.7	131.4	6.85	278.80
1980	.....	90.9	85.8	88.5	87.0	88.8	1,609	1,194	40.4	119.8	7.45	300.98
1981	.....	96.1	93.9	96.0	94.5	96.9	1,586	1,171	40.3	117.1	8.20	330.46
1982	.....	100.0	100.0	100.0	100.0	100.0	1,424	1,028	39.2	100.0	8.77	343.78
1983	.....	102.1	103.7	103.8	102.7	99.6	1,368	994	40.6	100.3	9.12	370.27
1984	.....	106.5	105.9	108.6	106.6	101.9	1,462	1,078	41.4	111.0	9.40	389.16
1985	100.6	109.0	109.1	111.9	109.5	103.2	1,464	1,083	41.3	111.2	9.71	401.02
1986	101.0	110.2	109.5	115.5	113.0	103.6	1,422	1,051	41.3	107.8	9.89	408.46
1987	102.1	109.5	109.6	119.7	115.5	105.4	1,399	1,038	41.6	107.1	10.01	416.42
1988	107.4	110.2	113.7	128.7	119.2	114.3	1,428	1,062	41.9	110.5	10.29	431.15
1989	112.6	111.5	120.4	137.7	125.1	120.3	1,445	1,070	41.6	110.6	10.57	439.71
1990	115.1	114.0	125.9	144.3	131.6	121.8	1,419	1,045	41.3	107.1	10.83	447.28
1991	116.6	115.5	130.2	149.7	134.1	122.4	1,355	991	41.2	101.4	11.19	461.03
1992	117.2	113.9	132.7	153.1	137.3	122.1	1,329	975	41.6	100.7	11.42	475.07
1993	118.2	109.7	135.2	155.9	140.4	123.2	1,339	988	42.1	103.3	11.69	492.15
1994	120.3	108.1	137.5	159.6	142.5	127.3	1,388	1,037	42.9	110.5	11.93	511.80
1995	124.8	117.2	141.1	166.0	147.5	135.1	1,437	1,080	42.4	113.6	12.13	514.31
1996	126.2	110.0	143.8	171.1	151.2	137.8	1,449	1,088	42.4	114.5	12.50	530.00
1997	127.6	108.1	145.6	174.5	152.4	140.3	1,479	1,115	42.6	118.1	12.78	544.43
1998	128.7	108.3	147.0	175.1	153.3	142.5	1,501	1,131	42.3	118.8	13.06	552.44
1995:												
January	122.6	109.6	139.4	161.7	145.3	131.9	1,427	1,074	43.2	115.2	12.04	518.92
February	123.6	117.8	139.7	164.8	146.5	132.5	1,434	1,080	42.9	115.1	12.03	513.68
March	124.1	117.8	140.4	165.7	147.0	133.6	1,438	1,083	42.8	115.1	12.05	512.13
April	124.4	118.1	140.8	165.9	147.2	134.4	1,442	1,085	42.1	113.5	12.03	484.81
May	124.6	118.1	140.9	166.5	147.4	134.6	1,441	1,084	42.1	113.3	12.08	508.57
June	125.0	118.3	141.4	166.5	147.6	135.2	1,436	1,079	42.2	113.1	12.05	509.72
July	125.2	118.0	141.5	166.5	147.7	135.8	1,437	1,078	42.1	112.7	12.11	498.93
August	125.5	118.0	141.6	166.7	148.1	136.0	1,437	1,078	42.3	113.3	12.11	511.04
September	125.6	117.8	141.7	166.8	148.2	136.5	1,436	1,077	42.4	113.4	12.22	524.24
October	125.8	117.9	141.7	167.2	148.4	136.6	1,438	1,079	42.4	113.6	12.19	519.29
November	125.8	117.7	141.9	166.7	148.4	136.7	1,439	1,080	42.3	113.5	12.26	525.95
December	125.9	117.8	142.2	166.6	148.5	136.7	1,439	1,081	42.1	113.0	12.42	536.54
1996:												
January	125.9	115.1	142.8	167.6	150.1	136.8	1,439	1,080	41.0	110.0	12.38	506.34
February	125.7	110.5	143.1	170.2	150.5	136.9	1,439	1,080	42.1	112.9	12.32	517.44
March	125.9	110.5	143.5	170.9	150.5	137.1	1,439	1,080	42.1	112.9	12.32	516.21
April	126.0	110.5	143.5	171.0	150.6	137.2	1,438	1,078	42.2	113.0	12.46	520.83
May	126.0	109.7	143.6	171.5	150.8	137.5	1,442	1,082	42.5	114.2	12.45	526.64
June	126.2	109.5	143.7	171.8	151.1	138.0	1,446	1,087	42.6	115.0	12.51	535.43
July	126.2	109.6	143.7	171.6	151.5	138.0	1,452	1,093	42.6	115.6	12.50	520.00
August	126.4	109.6	144.2	171.5	151.8	138.2	1,454	1,093	42.6	115.6	12.52	533.35
September	126.4	109.5	144.2	171.6	151.8	138.4	1,456	1,095	42.5	115.6	12.65	543.95
October	126.5	108.5	144.6	171.6	151.8	138.6	1,458	1,096	42.4	115.4	12.53	535.03
November	126.5	108.4	144.1	171.8	151.8	138.6	1,460	1,098	42.4	115.6	12.59	541.37
December	126.6	109.1	144.2	171.4	151.9	138.6	1,461	1,098	42.5	115.9	12.76	556.34
1997:												
January	126.8	108.0	144.9	171.9	152.0	139.0	1,461	1,099	42.4	115.7	12.72	535.51
February	127.0	108.0	144.7	174.3	152.0	139.1	1,463	1,101	42.6	116.5	12.71	537.63
March	127.1	108.2	145.2	174.5	152.0	139.2	1,466	1,104	42.7	117.1	12.74	541.45
April	127.2	107.9	145.4	174.7	152.2	139.8	1,470	1,107	42.8	117.7	12.75	540.60
May	127.4	107.9	145.5	175.0	151.7	140.2	1,473	1,110	42.6	117.4	12.74	541.45
June	127.5	107.8	145.7	175.1	152.1	140.4	1,476	1,113	42.5	117.5	12.72	541.87
July	127.7	107.6	145.2	174.8	152.7	140.6	1,476	1,114	42.5	117.6	12.65	526.24
August	127.9	107.8	145.9	174.9	152.8	140.8	1,484	1,121	42.5	118.3	12.75	541.88
September	128.0	107.7	145.9	174.6	152.9	141.0	1,487	1,122	42.5	118.4	12.80	550.40
October	128.1	108.9	146.0	174.9	152.9	141.2	1,492	1,126	42.6	119.1	12.85	551.27
November	128.2	108.9	146.0	174.7	153.0	141.3	1,497	1,130	42.7	119.8	12.92	559.44
December	128.1	108.9	146.3	174.3	152.9	141.2	1,501	1,133	42.8	120.4	13.02	572.88
1998:												
January	128.3	109.1	146.5	174.2	152.8	141.4	1,505	1,137	42.9	121.1	12.98	552.95
February	128.4	109.2	147.2	175.6	153.2	141.4	1,507	1,140	42.6	120.6	12.97	548.63
March	128.5	109.3	146.8	175.7	153.1	141.6	1,508	1,139	42.4	119.9	12.99	548.18
April	128.6	108.6	146.9	175.8	153.4	141.9	1,509	1,139	42.1	119.1	12.88	526.79
May	128.8	108.6	146.9	176.1	153.4	142.6	1,507	1,137	42.5	120.0	13.03	553.78
June	128.9	108.5	147.1	175.7	153.0	143.1	1,503	1,131	42.4	119.1	13.01	554.23
July	128.8	108.5	147.3	175.4	153.2	143.0	1,491	1,124	42.4	118.4	12.88	535.81
August	128.8	108.5	147.1	175.2	153.2	142.9	1,502	1,129	42.3	118.6	13.04	550.29
September	128.9	108.5	147.1	174.6	153.2	143.2	1,500	1,130	42.2	118.4	13.16	547.46
October	128.7	107.1	147.2	174.4	153.5	143.2	1,498	1,127	42.3	118.4	13.17	561.04
November	128.8	107.2	147.2	174.5	153.5	143.1	1,494	1,125	42.2	117.9	13.21	565.39
December	128.7	107.1	147.2	174.0	154.0	142.8	1,493	1,123	42.2	117.7	13.34	578.96

Industrial Machinery and Equipment—Production and Capacity Utilization

(Seasonally adjusted)

Year and month	Industrial production (1992=100)								Capacity utilization (output as a percent of capacity)	
	Total	Engines and turbines	Construction and allied	Metal-working	Special industry	General industrial	Computer and office equipment	Service industry machines	Total	Computer and office equipment
1970	41.1	95.9	114.6	99.7	100.1	83.8	2.3	57.7	81.3	90.9
1971	38.2	102.7	114.5	82.9	88.5	76.9	2.0	60.4	73.0	70.9
1972	44.3	109.9	131.6	96.9	98.8	86.9	2.4	74.2	82.5	79.2
1973	51.8	120.9	151.0	116.0	112.2	101.8	2.9	89.1	93.0	86.3
1974	55.2	132.8	168.3	118.7	115.4	106.7	3.5	81.9	94.6	91.7
1975	47.8	110.3	150.9	96.5	98.2	95.7	3.2	60.0	78.4	74.0
1976	50.2	120.6	140.9	95.6	97.0	97.4	3.9	74.1	78.8	75.6
1977	56.6	129.1	163.6	106.0	96.2	105.4	5.1	81.8	83.9	78.1
1978	63.3	138.5	181.8	111.1	102.0	109.1	7.5	89.3	88.2	87.3
1979	70.2	139.7	184.8	120.5	103.4	117.2	10.3	90.9	91.6	89.3
1980	70.5	127.0	176.5	119.0	100.8	111.1	13.9	78.6	85.9	88.2
1981	74.7	127.5	189.0	116.3	94.8	109.9	18.4	82.5	84.8	85.7
1982	65.8	101.5	145.2	87.3	88.0	93.5	21.3	73.7	70.5	74.3
1983	65.2	90.1	101.2	74.2	81.7	89.6	29.5	79.7	66.2	78.7
1984	78.9	115.8	115.8	90.4	90.5	101.3	42.0	89.2	75.7	86.1
1985	81.2	108.2	113.4	92.3	90.4	96.3	50.3	86.3	72.8	80.0
1986	81.8	104.7	105.4	98.2	88.9	92.8	53.7	91.4	70.3	72.5
1987	86.0	97.9	101.4	97.0	96.5	92.9	62.2	96.7	72.1	74.6
1988	97.1	107.6	114.8	106.3	105.5	102.2	74.6	103.3	79.6	79.5
1989	103.0	107.2	121.8	114.0	110.7	103.3	83.0	108.0	83.4	81.2
1990	100.1	100.5	117.6	109.4	107.5	104.0	81.4	97.6	79.4	73.7
1991	95.4	98.4	104.4	98.8	102.1	100.1	82.3	91.9	74.2	68.8
1992	100.0	100.0	100.0	100.0	100.0	100.0	100.0	100.0	75.4	75.1
1993	109.9	109.7	110.4	106.3	107.7	104.8	120.5	107.1	78.7	76.7
1994	124.9	125.0	121.8	115.9	122.2	110.6	149.3	119.8	83.1	77.7
1995	143.9	120.6	133.1	127.5	146.2	117.0	211.3	126.9	86.5	85.3
1996	159.8	125.9	141.2	128.8	152.0	119.3	298.6	133.0	85.4	84.8
1997	179.4	133.6	151.1	134.0	157.0	122.6	423.7	130.6	85.2	82.9
1998	203.7	136.6	170.5	135.0	155.1	124.6	649.1	142.6	85.5	83.6
1995:										
January	138.3	125.3	133.2	124.9	137.5	116.2	181.3	130.6	87.5	84.7
February	138.5	126.2	130.0	125.5	140.0	115.5	190.6	122.8	86.8	86.8
March	139.1	124.3	129.1	125.4	140.7	115.9	194.0	120.8	86.4	86.1
April	140.3	121.8	128.7	126.4	141.9	115.4	200.0	126.0	86.3	86.4
May	141.3	118.8	128.0	126.6	144.6	116.4	204.0	123.4	86.1	85.9
June	142.0	114.3	129.0	126.7	146.2	117.9	205.5	123.3	85.7	84.3
July	142.7	118.7	126.6	125.7	148.2	117.2	213.3	122.9	85.4	85.3
August	145.8	122.5	134.6	129.1	150.6	117.7	216.4	123.3	86.5	84.3
September	147.0	116.9	137.4	128.1	151.6	116.8	220.9	129.6	86.4	83.8
October	149.5	117.7	139.8	128.3	151.1	119.1	230.8	132.9	87.1	85.3
November	150.4	119.5	139.8	131.0	153.6	118.7	235.7	130.1	86.8	84.9
December	152.1	121.0	141.4	131.7	152.1	117.7	243.2	137.6	87.0	85.4
1996:										
January	151.2	119.6	136.9	128.1	150.1	117.9	247.0	129.8	85.6	84.2
February	154.3	117.7	139.7	129.3	152.9	121.4	261.0	132.6	86.5	86.1
March	155.5	120.1	139.4	131.4	152.8	119.6	268.4	132.6	86.2	85.8
April	155.8	121.7	141.5	129.2	153.0	118.3	272.2	130.0	85.5	84.2
May	158.1	124.1	141.8	127.2	153.9	119.0	283.9	131.9	85.8	85.0
June	160.0	126.2	141.9	125.4	153.0	118.8	296.7	140.8	85.9	86.0
July	161.6	124.7	143.8	127.2	153.3	119.4	309.9	132.2	85.9	87.0
August	162.7	129.8	139.6	127.6	150.9	119.6	313.8	135.1	85.6	85.3
September	162.5	129.8	142.8	129.6	151.6	118.3	319.4	134.8	84.7	84.0
October	163.4	132.3	142.4	128.4	151.9	119.6	329.5	128.5	84.3	83.9
November	165.2	132.4	143.8	130.8	151.0	119.5	337.7	132.7	84.3	83.3
December	167.6	132.5	141.2	131.1	151.8	120.5	346.7	135.2	84.7	82.8
1997:										
January	169.0	134.6	146.2	131.7	152.5	120.2	352.3	129.1	84.5	81.6
February	171.5	134.4	145.1	131.3	154.0	121.5	367.2	133.2	85.0	82.5
March	172.8	131.6	147.7	130.3	156.0	121.2	376.2	135.3	84.8	82.1
April	175.5	132.8	149.1	131.5	156.8	123.4	386.1	133.1	85.3	81.8
May	176.3	136.0	149.4	131.7	156.7	122.6	395.1	129.8	84.9	81.3
June	177.9	133.8	148.9	131.7	156.7	120.6	414.3	129.5	84.8	82.7
July	181.1	132.2	148.2	135.9	157.5	123.6	435.1	129.1	85.6	84.3
August	183.7	133.0	157.1	138.5	158.2	122.1	444.5	130.7	86.0	83.7
September	182.7	134.5	152.9	133.2	158.5	123.2	458.1	125.3	84.8	83.7
October	186.4	134.6	155.4	137.5	159.6	124.5	472.0	127.0	85.7	83.7
November	187.3	133.0	155.4	136.4	160.0	122.5	481.3	134.2	85.3	82.9
December	189.0	133.1	158.0	137.2	159.4	125.8	502.2	131.0	85.3	84.0
1998:										
January	191.8	134.9	156.4	134.8	159.8	125.7	526.3	132.1	85.7	85.0
February	192.3	133.3	156.2	131.6	158.8	123.0	552.6	135.4	84.9	85.7
March	198.4	137.1	159.6	137.9	158.5	124.8	589.6	135.6	86.6	87.9
April	200.6	136.5	161.8	135.7	157.8	126.0	605.4	140.8	86.6	86.7
May	202.5	136.0	161.6	133.9	154.1	125.5	623.9	151.2	86.3	85.8
June	205.8	131.8	181.1	135.4	156.7	127.1	641.4	142.3	86.6	84.7
July	209.0	131.0	187.9	136.9	155.6	125.9	657.0	148.8	87.0	83.4
August	207.0	140.4	190.4	132.5	154.5	123.6	673.6	151.7	85.2	82.1
September	207.7	139.6	176.4	131.3	152.6	123.7	695.5	148.0	84.5	81.4
October	211.2	138.4	179.9	134.6	154.0	125.5	718.5	148.0	84.9	80.7
November	211.1	140.0	171.4	137.9	152.7	123.1	746.9	146.9	83.9	80.7
December	212.7	140.2	176.7	138.5	151.2	124.8	761.6	150.4	83.6	79.2

Industrial Machinery and Equipment—Shipments, Inventories, Orders, and Prices

Year and month	Manufacturers' shipments, inventories, and orders (millions of dollars, seasonally adjusted)				Producer prices (1982=100, except as noted, not seasonally adjusted)				
					Industry groups			Commodity groups	
					(December 1984=100)		Electronic computers (December 1998 = 100)	Metalworking machinery and equipment	General purpose machinery and equipment
	Shipments	Inventories (book value, end of period)	New orders (net)	Unfilled orders (end of period)	Machinery, except electrical, total	Office, computing, and accounting machines			
1970	56,893	14,500	55,322	21,737	.....	.....	.....	35.6	37.4
1971	56,445	14,344	55,886	21,170	.....	.....	.....	36.7	39.2
1972	66,156	15,142	70,941	25,968	.....	.....	.....	37.5	40.3
1973	78,207	18,411	89,162	36,959	.....	.....	.....	39.1	41.8
1974	93,041	24,189	106,101	50,084	.....	.....	.....	45.8	49.7
1975	96,354	24,156	92,863	46,580	.....	.....	.....	53.5	58.7
1976	105,847	25,245	107,595	48,321	.....	.....	.....	56.9	62.4
1977	122,749	27,282	126,235	52,026	.....	.....	.....	61.9	66.4
1978	143,919	32,086	154,051	62,233	.....	.....	.....	67.6	71.2
1979	167,014	37,464	174,660	69,844	.....	.....	.....	75.2	77.8
1980	180,564	40,958	179,750	68,979	.....	.....	.....	85.5	87.0
1981	201,102	43,652	201,576	69,405	.....	.....	.....	93.9	95.0
1982	186,773	47,908	169,274	51,864	.....	.....	.....	100.0	100.0
1983	178,446	44,586	178,879	52,351	.....	.....	.....	101.7	101.4
1984	211,075	48,760	212,109	53,466	.....	.....	.....	104.1	103.3
1985	218,408	46,526	218,395	53,516	101.0	.....	.....	106.6	105.7
1986	213,574	42,409	208,567	48,416	102.0	.....	.....	108.4	107.2
1987	217,671	43,141	221,171	48,416	103.2	.....	.....	110.1	108.3
1988	244,365	47,707	250,055	57,583	106.4	.....	.....	113.5	112.8
1989	256,212	50,342	257,051	58,369	110.7	.....	.....	118.2	119.0
1990	259,367	49,673	258,894	57,872	113.9	.....	.....	123.0	123.7
1991	247,508	47,880	243,450	53,812	116.4	.....	334.3	127.6	127.8
1992	258,662	47,075	258,608	53,651	116.7	.....	280.0	130.9	129.9
1993	278,063	48,602	277,416	52,952	116.8	.....	245.8	133.5	132.2
1994	313,047	52,905	325,788	65,608	117.5	.....	225.9	136.5	134.8
1995	353,338	59,158	358,910	71,179	119.0	70.5	202.1	139.8	139.1
1996	381,795	57,944	383,749	73,042	119.2	63.4	169.9	143.1	142.5
1997	408,860	60,304	409,215	73,419	118.5	55.9	137.1	145.3	145.0
1998	442,316	60,532	443,332	74,458	117.7	48.8	109.1	147.2	147.2
1995:									
January	27,967	54,465	29,616	67,257	118.3	72.9	216.7	137.9	136.9
February	28,590	54,735	29,637	68,304	118.6	72.4	213.7	138.6	137.7
March	28,511	55,193	30,184	69,977	118.7	72.0	211.8	138.9	138.1
April	29,084	55,376	29,208	70,101	119.0	71.9	209.8	139.2	138.5
May	29,513	55,969	29,876	70,464	119.1	71.3	206.6	139.7	138.7
June	29,120	56,376	30,237	71,581	119.1	70.7	202.6	139.8	138.9
July	28,911	56,663	28,290	70,960	119.2	70.5	202.0	140.4	139.3
August	29,850	56,950	29,988	71,098	119.1	69.6	197.1	140.5	139.5
September	29,949	57,567	29,900	71,049	119.1	69.2	194.2	140.5	139.7
October	30,414	57,843	30,058	70,693	119.2	68.9	191.9	140.6	140.0
November	30,637	58,577	31,613	71,669	119.3	68.5	190.1	140.8	140.5
December	31,020	59,158	30,530	71,179	119.4	68.3	189.2	140.9	140.8
1996:									
January	30,678	60,045	31,612	72,113	119.7	67.6	186.8	142.0	141.6
February	32,109	60,046	32,943	72,947	119.7	66.4	182.0	142.2	141.9
March	31,379	59,851	30,709	72,277	119.7	65.8	178.9	142.5	142.2
April	31,189	60,061	31,310	72,398	119.3	64.5	175.1	142.7	142.3
May	31,656	59,749	32,034	72,776	119.3	64.2	173.1	143.1	142.3
June	31,696	58,917	31,508	72,588	119.1	63.6	171.3	143.3	142.4
July	31,431	59,172	32,293	73,450	119.1	62.6	167.2	143.3	142.6
August	32,116	59,309	32,549	73,883	119.1	62.4	165.6	143.4	142.7
September	32,371	58,849	32,075	73,587	119.1	62.1	164.7	143.5	142.7
October	32,024	58,708	31,936	73,499	118.9	61.2	161.1	143.6	143.0
November	32,172	58,884	32,007	73,334	118.9	60.6	158.4	144.0	143.3
December	32,690	57,944	32,398	73,042	118.7	60.0	155.0	144.1	143.4
1997:									
January	32,400	58,425	32,911	73,553	119.1	59.7	153.1	144.3	143.8
February	32,565	58,512	33,468	74,456	119.0	59.1	150.6	144.6	144.0
March	32,862	58,503	32,862	74,456	119.1	58.7	148.8	144.7	144.5
April	33,688	59,268	34,184	74,952	119.1	58.3	147.8	145.0	144.9
May	33,401	59,462	33,279	74,830	118.5	56.3	138.3	145.3	144.9
June	34,360	59,426	32,985	73,455	118.3	55.5	135.0	145.4	145.0
July	35,124	59,808	35,411	73,742	118.4	55.0	133.4	145.5	145.2
August	34,116	59,842	34,420	74,046	118.3	54.4	130.5	145.7	145.3
September	35,234	59,658	35,499	74,311	118.2	54.1	129.5	145.8	145.4
October	35,090	60,075	34,991	74,212	118.1	53.6	127.5	145.8	145.4
November	34,343	60,093	34,395	74,264	118.0	53.2	125.6	145.8	145.5
December	35,698	60,304	34,853	73,419	118.0	53.0	124.8	145.9	145.5
1998:									
January	35,936	60,135	35,766	73,249	118.1	52.0	121.0	146.5	146.1
February	36,209	61,122	36,552	73,592	118.0	51.2	117.4	146.9	146.3
March	36,864	61,011	37,448	74,176	117.9	50.7	116.5	147.2	146.5
April	36,898	61,247	36,889	74,167	117.8	49.7	113.0	147.2	146.7
May	36,561	61,081	36,244	73,850	117.7	49.3	111.0	147.3	146.8
June	37,915	60,900	36,922	72,857	117.7	49.0	110.1	147.1	147.1
July	37,810	60,903	37,636	72,683	117.7	48.6	108.7	147.2	147.5
August	36,711	60,958	37,450	73,422	117.5	47.8	104.6	147.3	147.5
September	36,775	60,938	38,983	75,630	117.6	47.6	103.8	147.3	147.9
October	37,011	60,811	35,503	74,122	117.4	47.0	102.5	147.5	147.9
November	36,623	60,974	35,593	73,092	117.4	46.7	101.2	147.5	148.1
December	36,880	60,532	38,246	74,458	117.3	46.1	100.0	147.5	148.3

Industrial Machinery and Equipment—Employment, Hours, and Earnings

Year and month	Industrial machinery and equipment						Computer and office equipment (not seasonally adjusted)				
	Employment (thousands, seasonally adjusted)		Production workers				Employment (thousands)		Production workers		
					Average earnings (dollars, not seasonally adjusted)					Average earnings (dollars)	
	Total payroll employees	Production workers	Average weekly hours, seasonally adjusted	Aggregate weekly hours index (1982=100), seasonally adjusted	Hourly	Weekly	Total payroll employees	Production workers	Average weekly hours	Hourly	Weekly
1970	2,003	1,336	41.1	.....	3.77	154.95	281	138	41.0	3.69	151.30
1971	1,834	1,195	40.6	.....	4.02	163.21	257	116	41.4	3.85	159.40
1972	1,909	1,258	42.1	.....	4.32	181.87	252	112	42.1	3.94	165.90
1973	2,111	1,416	42.8	.....	4.60	196.88	276	127	41.3	4.12	170.20
1974	2,230	1,494	42.1	.....	4.94	207.97	296	137	40.9	4.37	178.70
1975	2,076	1,350	40.8	.....	5.37	219.10	278	119	40.3	4.82	194.30
1976	2,085	1,352	41.2	.....	5.79	238.55	278	119	41.6	5.15	214.20
1977	2,195	1,435	41.5	.....	6.26	259.79	303	136	40.9	5.36	219.20
1978	2,347	1,540	42.0	.....	6.78	284.76	340	154	41.4	5.62	232.70
1979	2,508	1,648	41.7	.....	7.32	305.24	386	173	41.6	6.10	253.80
1980	2,517	1,614	41.0	.....	8.00	328.00	420	181	41.4	6.75	279.50
1981	2,521	1,592	40.9	.....	8.81	360.33	447	182	41.2	7.46	307.40
1982	2,264	1,367	39.7	.....	9.26	367.62	460	184	41.1	7.93	325.90
1983	2,053	1,207	40.5	.....	9.56	387.18	474	190	41.5	8.52	353.60
1984	2,218	1,342	41.9	.....	9.97	417.74	515	205	42.2	8.94	377.30
1985	2,195	1,320	41.5	.....	10.30	427.45	500	184	41.6	9.34	388.50
1986	2,074	1,234	41.6	.....	10.58	440.13	469	163	42.1	9.97	419.70
1987	2,028	1,203	42.2	93.8	10.73	452.81	461	155	42.6	10.28	437.90
1988	2,089	1,256	42.7	98.8	11.08	473.12	459	148	41.7	10.65	444.11
1989	2,125	1,282	42.4	100.3	11.40	483.36	459	145	42.3	10.99	464.88
1990	2,095	1,260	41.9	97.5	11.77	493.16	438	137	42.0	11.51	483.42
1991	2,000	1,193	41.7	91.8	12.15	506.66	415	135	41.5	12.13	503.40
1992	1,929	1,152	42.2	89.6	12.41	523.70	391	128	42.0	12.33	517.86
1993	1,931	1,170	43.0	92.7	12.73	547.39	363	121	41.9	12.54	525.43
1994	1,990	1,233	43.7	99.3	13.00	568.10	354	123	42.7	13.08	558.52
1995	2,067	1,295	43.4	103.5	13.24	574.62	352	123	43.0	13.59	584.37
1996	2,115	1,321	43.1	105.0	13.59	585.73	362	127	42.2	13.87	585.31
1997	2,168	1,364	43.6	109.6	14.07	613.45	376	140	42.2	14.31	603.88
1998	2,203	1,391	42.8	109.8	14.47	619.32	379	146	41.8	15.34	641.21
1995:											
January	2,028	1,266	43.9	102.5	13.16	581.67	350	121	42.8	13.39	573.09
February	2,038	1,273	43.8	102.8	13.17	579.48	349	120	43.3	13.48	583.68
March	2,044	1,279	43.7	103.1	13.17	578.16	347	119	43.2	13.59	587.09
April	2,055	1,288	43.4	103.1	13.07	546.33	347	120	42.7	13.64	582.43
May	2,056	1,290	43.4	103.2	13.17	571.58	348	120	42.8	13.74	588.07
June	2,063	1,293	43.2	103.0	13.17	570.26	352	122	43.0	13.67	587.81
July	2,071	1,297	43.1	103.1	13.23	560.95	353	122	43.1	13.57	584.87
August	2,077	1,299	43.4	104.0	13.25	569.75	353	123	42.5	13.78	585.65
September	2,080	1,303	43.3	104.0	13.34	578.96	354	123	43.0	13.63	586.09
October	2,091	1,310	43.2	104.4	13.33	575.86	357	125	43.0	13.48	579.64
November	2,098	1,315	43.4	105.2	13.39	585.14	359	127	43.1	13.46	580.13
December	2,103	1,320	43.0	104.7	13.47	594.03	360	128	43.4	13.62	591.11
1996:											
January	2,105	1,319	41.9	101.9	13.44	568.51	360	129	41.7	13.42	559.61
February	2,106	1,318	43.1	104.8	13.40	580.22	359	128	42.9	13.65	585.59
March	2,112	1,318	43.1	104.8	13.36	578.49	361	127	43.4	13.61	590.67
April	2,111	1,318	43.1	104.8	13.44	573.89	361	127	42.1	13.70	576.77
May	2,113	1,318	43.2	105.0	13.45	578.35	362	128	42.0	13.76	577.92
June	2,115	1,319	43.2	105.1	13.52	585.42	365	128	42.7	13.99	597.37
July	2,115	1,321	43.1	105.0	13.55	574.52	363	128	41.4	13.93	576.70
August	2,116	1,321	43.1	105.0	13.64	582.43	363	128	41.0	13.96	572.36
September	2,116	1,321	43.2	105.2	13.77	596.24	361	127	42.4	14.06	596.14
October	2,119	1,322	43.1	105.1	13.71	588.16	362	127	41.5	13.95	578.93
November	2,120	1,325	43.1	105.3	13.81	597.97	362	128	42.0	14.08	591.36
December	2,125	1,329	43.4	106.4	13.98	620.71	363	130	43.2	14.33	619.06
1997:											
January	2,133	1,336	43.3	106.7	13.92	602.74	364	129	41.8	14.10	589.38
February	2,139	1,341	43.5	107.6	13.90	606.04	365	130	42.7	14.10	602.07
March	2,145	1,348	43.6	108.4	13.95	611.01	368	135	42.6	14.15	602.79
April	2,151	1,355	44.0	109.9	13.96	608.66	370	137	42.4	14.13	599.11
May	2,156	1,357	43.7	109.4	13.94	606.39	374	140	42.3	13.97	590.93
June	2,162	1,362	43.3	108.8	13.97	606.30	378	142	42.3	14.18	599.81
July	2,169	1,364	43.5	109.4	14.03	600.48	381	143	41.8	14.18	592.72
August	2,178	1,371	43.5	110.0	14.04	605.12	382	144	41.3	14.26	588.94
September	2,182	1,375	43.6	110.6	14.20	620.54	380	143	41.8	14.49	605.68
October	2,193	1,381	43.5	110.8	14.24	616.59	383	145	41.7	14.64	610.49
November	2,201	1,387	43.7	111.8	14.31	629.64	382	144	42.8	14.74	630.87
December	2,207	1,391	43.7	112.1	14.42	646.02	384	145	42.8	14.73	630.44
1998:											
January	2,214	1,397	43.6	112.3	14.35	627.10	384	145	41.9	14.78	619.28
February	2,217	1,399	43.4	112.0	14.38	625.53	383	146	42.5	15.08	640.90
March	2,219	1,400	43.3	111.8	14.38	625.53	383	147	42.5	14.87	631.98
April	2,215	1,399	42.9	110.7	14.34	600.85	381	146	41.4	15.10	625.14
May	2,215	1,398	43.0	110.9	14.38	619.78	381	147	41.1	15.14	622.25
June	2,215	1,400	43.1	111.3	14.42	622.94	381	147	40.7	15.11	614.98
July	2,208	1,392	42.9	110.1	14.43	610.39	381	147	40.8	15.44	629.95
August	2,203	1,391	42.9	110.0	14.46	616.00	379	145	41.7	15.48	645.52
September	2,197	1,389	42.6	109.1	14.55	608.19	377	145	42.8	15.45	661.26
October	2,188	1,383	42.6	108.6	14.57	617.77	375	145	42.3	15.76	666.65
November	2,177	1,376	42.4	107.6	14.64	625.13	373	146	42.4	16.02	679.25
December	2,167	1,369	42.1	106.3	14.73	636.34	371	147	41.7	15.89	662.61

Electronic and Electric Equipment—Production

(1992=100; seasonally adjusted)

Year and month	Electrical machinery	Major electrical equipment and parts		Household appliances							Audio and video equipment
								Miscellaneous			
		Total	Electric distribution equipment	Total	Cooking equipment	Refrigerators and freezers	Laundry	Total	Electrical housewares	Appliances, not elsewhere classified	
1970	26.2	82.5	98.8	57.2	45.0	70.6	67.0	53.1	73.7	48.1	39.0
1971	26.3	83.3	98.2	60.2	50.2	73.8	72.0	55.0	75.1	49.5	43.9
1972	30.1	91.4	106.7	70.6	60.0	86.2	82.4	65.2	91.9	54.6	49.3
1973	34.3	106.2	121.2	79.3	68.1	91.3	88.8	76.1	102.0	65.7	54.1
1974	33.9	107.2	116.3	75.6	60.0	89.2	75.7	76.1	105.3	61.8	47.6
1975	29.2	84.6	91.5	63.1	56.8	69.8	63.6	63.2	92.0	50.1	41.0
1976	32.8	91.0	95.2	70.3	73.9	63.6	68.4	73.3	105.7	59.0	44.6
1977	38.1	99.3	108.0	78.9	80.0	75.9	75.7	80.8	117.2	68.2	51.6
1978	42.2	108.4	115.5	79.1	87.8	77.1	73.7	79.0	112.4	67.4	58.2
1979	46.9	112.6	120.3	81.4	83.9	76.9	74.1	85.4	118.5	74.4	56.7
1980	48.6	105.0	115.6	77.6	88.7	66.6	67.1	82.9	125.7	66.3	57.8
1981	51.0	105.5	110.7	76.9	98.9	69.2	65.3	77.9	111.0	67.7	58.4
1982	51.7	91.8	99.4	68.2	83.2	57.5	58.0	72.2	105.4	59.2	51.8
1983	55.9	87.8	97.3	82.4	121.3	69.2	71.0	81.0	106.0	75.5	69.6
1984	66.7	100.6	106.1	90.3	119.9	83.8	75.1	90.7	107.1	87.1	83.0
1985	68.4	96.9	102.6	83.5	94.1	72.2	79.1	87.9	102.7	88.6	74.8
1986	71.0	96.6	100.8	89.9	104.7	84.6	88.3	88.4	97.9	93.9	77.9
1987	75.6	97.0	101.5	93.6	104.8	88.4	92.6	93.1	100.7	97.9	80.0
1988	82.5	105.8	114.1	96.9	110.6	96.1	94.1	94.2	100.3	94.8	86.8
1989	85.8	105.3	108.8	97.2	101.2	98.5	94.6	96.6	105.3	94.1	93.7
1990	87.7	103.6	107.1	95.3	97.0	87.1	96.1	98.0	104.6	91.7	92.8
1991	89.6	98.4	99.5	92.1	94.2	88.5	92.1	92.9	100.4	87.6	95.9
1992	100.0	100.0	100.0	100.0	100.0	100.0	100.0	100.0	100.0	100.0	100.0
1993	109.6	106.6	99.2	110.5	101.9	105.4	120.8	111.3	106.1	121.4	107.6
1994	131.4	113.0	108.2	122.6	127.4	122.3	142.8	112.1	106.3	128.6	122.7
1995	166.3	123.8	116.4	114.7	128.3	121.5	127.5	101.2	114.8	94.7	138.3
1996	206.0	125.3	116.5	116.0	113.2	128.9	130.2	104.9	106.9	95.6	114.4
1997	253.4	124.7	117.7	115.4	113.1	127.0	128.5	105.1	109.3	94.6	88.4
1998	291.9	125.6	118.2	122.7	117.5	141.4	144.4	107.3	103.2	97.2	65.8
1995:											
January	150.5	116.5	108.3	120.9	137.6	120.4	141.8	105.9	118.4	108.4	143.2
February	153.0	117.4	114.1	119.5	139.4	120.7	135.8	104.3	116.7	103.7	140.3
March	156.9	121.6	115.1	114.8	132.1	114.6	127.5	102.7	118.3	98.0	147.3
April	158.8	121.3	113.4	114.8	139.8	111.9	125.9	101.4	116.1	96.8	132.3
May	161.2	125.0	116.6	114.5	131.5	117.3	131.0	99.6	117.4	91.5	135.5
June	164.0	126.2	116.7	104.2	107.1	113.5	111.2	96.0	113.6	84.5	146.0
July	165.5	125.6	117.2	112.5	144.7	119.5	110.9	98.8	111.0	90.9	127.9
August	170.5	129.4	119.0	113.6	126.6	127.0	121.9	99.8	112.2	91.1	139.9
September	174.5	126.4	117.9	113.3	121.9	125.2	127.0	99.6	114.1	89.1	143.3
October	178.8	125.9	120.4	115.3	119.5	131.9	128.6	101.1	115.5	91.3	139.9
November	180.7	126.1	118.6	115.7	121.0	129.0	132.6	101.1	112.3	92.9	140.5
December	181.5	124.6	118.3	117.1	119.9	127.4	136.1	103.7	112.3	97.9	123.9
1996:											
January	182.3	126.0	118.4	108.8	90.9	129.5	126.3	98.4	107.4	87.6	112.2
February	188.7	127.1	120.5	111.6	105.3	126.0	125.5	101.3	109.4	90.2	124.4
March	192.4	126.2	116.1	114.8	121.9	128.2	116.4	104.9	107.4	96.2	111.1
April	197.7	128.0	117.9	114.3	109.5	125.4	126.0	105.4	104.3	96.0	125.1
May	203.4	126.4	116.6	115.8	109.4	125.9	126.0	108.3	106.7	100.2	125.4
June	208.8	124.6	114.6	122.3	124.7	135.9	136.3	109.1	109.9	101.9	129.3
July	209.8	124.7	117.7	116.6	113.5	125.0	138.5	104.6	114.1	92.4	115.8
August	212.8	124.5	114.9	120.3	121.8	137.8	139.8	104.0	113.0	93.3	110.0
September	215.3	124.7	114.4	118.5	121.7	125.4	135.9	106.8	107.8	100.6	107.8
October	217.6	122.9	116.0	115.1	107.2	123.7	132.7	105.8	104.5	97.6	108.3
November	220.3	124.6	115.4	116.3	114.9	130.4	128.3	104.9	103.6	94.4	108.2
December	223.3	123.8	115.9	117.8	117.1	134.1	131.0	104.8	99.2	97.2	95.6
1997:											
January	226.0	125.5	116.1	112.4	109.3	126.8	122.8	102.1	101.2	92.6	82.3
February	231.6	125.0	116.3	112.7	115.1	124.1	117.1	104.1	106.8	95.7	96.8
March	235.2	122.1	113.8	117.6	123.0	128.0	133.1	104.7	109.6	96.0	87.4
April	240.5	124.5	117.5	115.1	102.1	130.4	132.5	104.7	110.5	95.5	91.6
May	245.6	124.2	116.9	114.8	115.9	125.6	129.2	103.4	110.7	93.6	92.8
June	251.6	123.9	118.4	117.3	115.7	128.5	136.9	104.7	114.2	97.5	83.9
July	259.5	124.0	117.1	116.5	120.9	126.3	142.7	100.6	109.3	93.9	91.8
August	262.6	123.1	116.3	111.5	117.7	125.2	114.6	101.2	112.2	92.4	89.7
September	266.4	123.1	119.7	112.2	110.4	122.8	115.4	105.4	109.2	95.8	86.6
October	269.8	125.5	118.1	116.7	113.8	128.9	129.0	106.5	111.5	88.8	87.6
November	274.9	127.2	120.4	120.5	113.7	131.3	131.3	112.3	109.4	96.9	85.2
December	276.5	127.9	122.4	117.8	97.4	126.5	137.5	111.3	110.4	96.2	85.5
1998:											
January	277.7	126.2	116.5	124.7	122.0	137.1	152.3	109.2	110.5	97.8	84.2
February	278.5	125.3	116.6	124.5	121.1	146.3	147.9	106.7	110.5	98.1	78.1
March	278.2	127.3	118.0	123.0	115.0	141.5	151.7	106.0	108.6	99.5	88.8
April	280.8	126.7	119.8	122.3	119.9	142.9	146.7	104.3	109.1	94.9	78.0
May	282.0	126.8	120.6	123.6	124.3	141.4	147.0	106.4	105.8	98.7	57.4
June	285.5	126.8	118.8	118.9	116.1	135.0	136.2	105.4	104.2	95.6	55.3
July	289.4	125.1	120.1	121.8	124.0	139.2	139.1	106.4	101.6	97.7	59.0
August	290.8	122.8	116.5	119.8	116.2	133.1	132.6	109.0	103.2	102.1	55.6
September	297.7	125.8	118.8	118.2	112.8	135.1	136.1	104.9	101.0	95.2	63.9
October	302.4	124.2	117.4	124.8	123.2	144.8	143.0	109.1	97.9	94.0	55.7
November	304.8	125.0	116.1	127.0	115.8	150.8	148.4	111.3	97.5	96.6	59.4
December	307.3	124.6	119.6	125.6	99.2	156.0	147.5	111.3	98.3	96.2	60.9

Electronic and Electric Equipment—Production, Capacity Utilization, Shipments, Inventories, and Orders

(Seasonally adjusted)

Year and month	Industrial production—Continued (1992=100)				Capacity utilization—Electrical machinery (output as a percent of capacity)	Manufacturers' shipments, inventories, and orders (millions of dollars)			
	Communication equipment	Electronic components	Miscellaneous electrical supplies			Shipments	Inventories (book value, end of period)	New orders (net)	Unfilled orders (end of period)
			Total	Storage batteries					
1970	31.8	4.4	47.0	51.4	76.6	41,408	8,410	41,117	11,881
1971	29.0	4.7	48.9	52.2	73.5	42,377	8,058	42,639	12,148
1972	31.8	5.9	53.8	60.5	81.1	47,502	8,528	48,702	13,376
1973	34.6	7.4	60.6	65.7	88.0	54,569	10,532	58,275	17,111
1974	35.7	7.3	60.5	66.9	81.9	58,684	12,231	58,884	17,319
1975	34.8	6.0	54.7	64.4	67.0	56,068	11,110	54,610	15,857
1976	34.8	7.8	64.6	75.8	72.8	65,151	12,594	66,864	17,584
1977	38.9	9.9	78.6	86.2	80.1	77,845	13,922	80,010	19,999
1978	43.8	12.0	82.2	91.0	83.9	88,679	16,163	92,781	24,219
1979	51.2	15.3	80.9	89.4	87.7	102,361	19,566	107,314	29,261
1980	56.8	18.1	71.3	78.5	84.0	112,864	21,838	115,335	31,751
1981	57.9	21.5	74.4	80.1	81.2	122,084	23,608	123,053	32,718
1982	60.7	25.6	74.1	76.0	76.7	125,728	25,100	127,630	34,639
1983	62.1	29.8	80.9	86.0	77.8	136,138	26,922	142,131	40,794
1984	70.4	40.6	99.3	101.1	85.8	162,362	31,636	165,541	43,967
1985	78.1	41.2	95.8	97.9	80.5	163,951	30,549	163,352	43,366
1986	80.5	44.2	96.9	104.1	77.8	164,811	28,632	164,282	42,793
1987	82.9	51.9	101.4	107.2	78.7	171,287	29,859	173,210	44,741
1988	90.0	58.5	109.3	104.9	82.3	187,301	31,645	189,211	46,702
1989	91.4	65.2	108.1	104.2	81.3	194,598	33,623	192,482	44,616
1990	94.7	72.1	97.3	104.6	78.9	195,898	32,913	195,748	44,501
1991	90.6	80.9	102.5	98.7	76.3	199,278	30,981	197,659	42,988
1992	100.0	100.0	100.0	100.0	80.0	216,764	30,722	217,966	44,348
1993	107.1	115.0	107.7	109.7	81.4	233,622	31,863	233,991	44,784
1994	126.3	154.2	115.8	123.2	86.2	266,405	35,847	266,386	44,941
1995	145.5	243.6	117.4	121.4	88.1	301,447	39,413	307,634	51,470
1996	171.3	356.9	125.2	119.4	83.6	320,616	39,335	319,157	49,943
1997	196.2	523.9	128.7	113.1	81.4	351,554	40,488	356,557	55,174
1998	214.9	675.1	132.4	124.7	77.5	375,970	39,786	380,470	60,530
1995:									
January	137.7	199.8	119.3	126.3	90.2	23,992	36,367	24,632	45,581
February	135.6	208.7	118.4	116.4	89.8	23,613	36,963	24,370	46,338
March	139.1	217.4	115.7	107.8	90.1	24,114	37,252	25,834	48,058
April	139.7	224.3	118.1	119.9	89.2	24,029	37,387	25,099	49,128
May	140.7	230.1	114.2	114.1	88.4	24,561	37,514	25,745	50,312
June	142.8	237.1	115.4	122.3	87.9	25,190	37,798	25,125	50,247
July	144.5	242.6	115.1	119.7	86.9	24,864	38,353	26,511	51,894
August	148.2	252.5	115.4	118.4	87.6	25,964	38,616	25,637	51,567
September	151.6	264.7	118.6	131.7	87.7	26,035	39,027	26,416	51,948
October	156.6	275.4	118.2	119.3	87.9	25,842	39,577	26,494	52,600
November	153.9	283.1	119.0	119.9	86.9	26,183	39,008	25,272	51,689
December	155.2	287.0	121.9	138.2	85.2	26,249	39,413	26,030	51,470
1996:									
January	158.0	289.9	117.8	117.6	83.6	26,038	39,776	25,968	51,400
February	164.1	299.9	124.9	133.6	84.7	25,996	39,377	25,401	50,805
March	167.0	312.7	123.7	129.6	84.4	26,375	39,099	26,594	51,024
April	168.3	328.7	121.9	106.2	84.8	26,424	39,322	26,221	50,821
May	168.5	347.1	124.3	119.4	85.2	26,456	39,135	25,506	49,871
June	172.0	360.1	128.7	133.9	85.4	26,583	39,331	26,315	49,603
July	173.2	366.4	127.0	116.4	84.1	26,474	39,098	27,701	50,830
August	173.3	377.2	127.0	115.9	83.6	26,228	39,206	26,122	50,724
September	175.8	384.9	127.6	115.9	82.9	26,715	39,367	26,104	50,113
October	177.2	396.5	127.7	113.7	82.0	27,209	39,428	30,268	53,172
November	177.5	404.5	125.6	119.8	81.3	28,185	39,636	28,414	53,401
December	180.9	414.9	126.5	115.2	80.6	27,370	39,335	23,912	49,943
1997:									
January	183.0	427.6	125.1	118.9	80.0	27,031	39,024	28,241	51,153
February	185.5	443.4	126.8	115.3	80.6	28,076	39,064	30,792	53,869
March	188.3	459.5	128.5	116.1	80.4	29,456	38,942	29,140	53,553
April	191.3	473.1	127.8	115.5	80.8	28,345	39,422	27,419	52,627
May	192.2	492.5	128.7	117.3	81.0	28,464	39,610	30,276	54,439
June	196.1	517.3	126.5	111.5	81.5	29,329	39,532	30,269	55,379
July	199.4	541.8	129.5	111.5	82.7	29,104	40,120	25,247	51,522
August	197.4	563.4	130.7	117.0	82.4	29,736	40,088	34,068	55,854
September	203.9	576.6	129.3	105.8	82.2	30,809	39,950	31,118	56,163
October	201.3	589.8	127.7	105.5	81.9	29,855	40,052	29,718	56,026
November	208.0	598.0	133.1	126.1	82.0	29,842	40,278	29,227	55,411
December	207.8	604.3	130.3	104.1	81.1	30,495	40,488	30,258	55,174
1998:									
January	209.0	608.8	130.5	108.8	80.2	29,532	40,801	31,417	57,059
February	210.8	612.5	132.4	108.9	79.3	30,714	41,250	30,714	57,059
March	208.1	608.6	134.6	124.0	78.1	30,838	41,364	30,850	57,071
April	214.8	614.4	136.0	126.0	77.7	30,056	41,378	31,707	58,722
May	216.3	621.7	135.8	132.5	76.9	29,767	41,236	29,144	58,099
June	220.1	638.0	133.3	130.0	76.8	30,882	40,818	30,072	57,289
July	220.0	653.9	132.6	125.7	76.8	31,216	40,345	32,840	58,913
August	220.2	672.0	132.5	130.0	76.2	31,228	40,526	31,116	58,801
September	222.7	698.6	132.1	126.8	77.0	32,422	40,172	32,870	59,249
October	220.5	726.3	134.3	136.4	77.2	32,219	40,589	33,348	60,378
November	215.5	747.3	129.6	123.9	76.8	32,634	40,315	31,933	59,677
December	215.4	759.5	129.9	120.3	76.5	33,006	39,786	33,859	60,530

Electronic and Electric Equipment—Prices, Employment, Hours, and Earnings

Year and month	Producer prices (1982=100, except as noted; not seasonally adjusted)					Employment (thousands, seasonally adjusted)		Production workers			
	Industry groups (December 1984 = 100)		Finished goods: Communications and related equipment (December 1985=100)	Intermediate materials		Total payroll employees	Production workers	Average weekly hours, seasonally adjusted	Aggregate weekly hours index (1982=100), seasonally adjusted	Average earnings (dollars, not seasonally adjusted)	
	Electrical and electronic machinery, equipment and supplies	Electronic components and accessories		Switchgear, switchboard, etc.	Electronic components and accessories					Hourly	Weekly
1970	.....	.....	.....	40.5	57.4	1,584	.....	.....	.....	.....	.....
1971	.....	.....	.....	42.3	58.2	1,477	.....	.....	.....	.....	.....
1972	.....	.....	.....	42.2	58.7	1,535	.....	.....	.....	.....	.....
1973	.....	.....	.....	42.9	59.3	1,667	.....	.....	.....	.....	.....
1974	.....	.....	.....	50.3	63.3	1,666	.....	.....	.....	.....	.....
1975	.....	.....	.....	58.6	65.6	1,442	.....	.....	.....	.....	.....
1976	.....	.....	.....	61.9	65.8	1,503	.....	.....	.....	.....	.....
1977	.....	.....	.....	65.9	67.9	1,591	.....	.....	.....	.....	.....
1978	.....	.....	.....	69.8	72.1	1,699	.....	.....	.....	.....	.....
1979	.....	.....	.....	75.8	77.1	1,793	.....	.....	.....	.....	.....
1980	.....	.....	.....	88.4	88.8	1,771	.....	.....	.....	.....	.....
1981	.....	.....	.....	95.1	95.5	1,774	.....	.....	.....	.....	.....
1982	.....	.....	.....	100.0	100.0	1,701	.....	.....	.....	.....	.....
1983	.....	.....	.....	103.3	104.3	1,704	.....	.....	.....	.....	.....
1984	.....	.....	.....	105.0	109.8	1,869	.....	.....	.....	.....	.....
1985	.....	100.5	.....	106.7	112.4	1,859	.....	.....	.....	.....	.....
1986	102.1	102.5	101.2	108.1	114.5	1,790	.....	.....	.....	.....	.....
1987	103.3	102.6	102.5	110.1	115.0	1,750	.....	.....	.....	.....	.....
1988	104.6	104.0	102.8	113.2	117.5	1,764	1,112	41.0	113.1	9.79	401.39
1989	107.1	105.1	104.7	119.0	119.4	1,744	1,102	40.8	111.5	10.05	410.04
1990	108.9	104.9	106.1	124.4	118.4	1,673	1,055	40.8	106.5	10.30	420.24
1991	110.1	104.9	107.4	128.5	118.6	1,591	999	40.7	100.7	10.70	435.49
1992	110.8	104.6	107.9	131.5	117.5	1,528	971	41.2	99.1	11.00	453.20
1993	112.0	105.3	109.1	134.6	117.7	1,526	975	41.8	100.9	11.24	469.83
1994	112.7	104.8	110.8	136.8	116.6	1,571	1,010	42.2	105.7	11.50	485.30
1995	113.3	102.5	112.1	140.3	113.6	1,625	1,045	41.6	107.8	11.69	486.30
1996	113.2	99.3	113.0	142.6	108.9	1,661	1,056	41.5	108.5	12.18	505.47
1997	111.6	95.1	114.0	145.6	104.0	1,689	1,069	42.0	111.1	12.70	533.40
1998	110.4	91.9	114.1	148.4	100.0	1,704	1,068	41.4	109.5	13.09	541.93
1995:											
January	113.1	103.1	111.9	139.4	114.6	1,608	1,041	41.9	108.1	11.58	488.68
February	113.3	103.6	112.1	139.5	115.0	1,609	1,042	41.6	107.4	11.53	478.50
March	113.1	102.8	112.1	140.3	114.3	1,613	1,043	41.7	107.8	11.54	480.06
April	113.3	102.9	112.2	140.3	114.4	1,617	1,043	41.6	107.5	11.52	463.10
May	113.3	102.7	112.1	139.6	114.0	1,621	1,044	41.5	107.3	11.56	477.43
June	113.2	102.5	111.9	139.7	113.7	1,622	1,042	41.5	107.1	11.63	482.65
July	113.2	102.1	111.8	140.4	113.1	1,624	1,042	41.5	107.1	11.74	476.64
August	113.1	102.0	111.9	139.9	112.9	1,626	1,045	41.6	107.7	11.76	488.04
September	113.2	102.1	112.3	140.7	112.9	1,633	1,046	41.8	108.3	11.81	498.38
October	113.3	102.3	112.3	140.5	112.9	1,638	1,049	42.1	109.4	11.79	497.54
November	113.5	102.3	112.3	141.7	113.1	1,641	1,050	41.7	108.5	11.83	500.41
December	113.5	102.2	112.2	141.2	112.9	1,646	1,052	41.1	107.1	11.93	504.64
1996:											
January	113.8	102.0	112.9	142.0	112.5	1,648	1,052	40.1	104.5	11.95	482.78
February	113.9	101.8	113.1	142.0	112.2	1,651	1,053	41.7	108.8	11.88	494.21
March	113.5	100.6	113.0	142.3	110.8	1,651	1,053	41.6	108.5	11.91	494.27
April	113.3	99.7	113.0	141.7	109.4	1,655	1,055	41.2	107.7	12.01	490.01
May	113.1	99.1	112.7	142.1	108.5	1,658	1,056	41.5	108.6	12.09	496.90
June	113.0	98.7	112.6	142.6	107.9	1,661	1,057	41.6	108.9	12.19	507.10
July	113.0	98.7	112.9	142.1	108.0	1,664	1,059	41.4	108.6	12.25	497.35
August	113.1	98.7	113.1	142.7	108.0	1,665	1,057	41.7	109.2	12.28	510.85
September	113.0	98.8	113.1	142.6	108.1	1,667	1,058	41.7	109.3	12.35	518.70
October	112.7	98.0	113.2	142.7	107.3	1,668	1,057	41.5	108.7	12.33	514.16
November	112.8	97.8	113.0	144.8	107.3	1,669	1,057	41.6	108.9	12.35	519.94
December	112.7	97.8	113.9	144.0	107.2	1,670	1,055	41.8	109.3	12.54	537.97
1997:											
January	112.5	97.2	113.9	144.0	106.7	1,670	1,056	41.4	108.3	12.46	513.35
February	112.2	96.6	114.0	144.6	106.0	1,672	1,058	42.0	110.1	12.41	518.74
March	112.2	96.6	113.4	144.8	105.8	1,674	1,059	42.3	111.0	12.49	527.08
April	112.0	96.2	113.5	145.0	105.4	1,675	1,059	42.4	111.2	12.55	525.85
May	111.8	95.4	113.7	145.6	104.5	1,676	1,059	42.1	110.5	12.55	524.59
June	111.8	95.5	113.6	145.7	104.5	1,683	1,063	42.1	110.9	12.59	528.78
July	111.7	95.5	114.4	145.7	104.4	1,691	1,068	42.1	111.4	12.68	522.42
August	111.1	94.2	114.2	145.7	103.0	1,696	1,073	41.9	111.4	12.74	531.26
September	111.1	94.2	114.1	145.5	102.9	1,700	1,076	41.8	111.4	12.84	540.56
October	110.8	93.6	114.1	146.0	101.9	1,707	1,080	41.9	112.1	12.90	540.51
November	110.8	93.3	114.8	147.1	101.6	1,713	1,084	41.9	112.5	12.98	554.25
December	110.8	93.3	114.8	146.9	101.4	1,718	1,089	42.0	113.3	13.11	566.35
1998:											
January	110.8	92.9	114.8	147.8	101.1	1,725	1,091	42.0	113.5	12.98	542.56
February	110.6	92.6	114.8	147.3	100.7	1,725	1,090	41.8	112.9	12.95	538.72
March	110.7	92.5	114.6	147.9	100.7	1,725	1,086	41.5	111.7	13.04	538.55
April	110.5	92.4	114.4	148.1	100.4	1,722	1,082	41.3	110.7	13.06	527.62
May	110.4	92.1	114.1	147.9	100.1	1,718	1,079	41.4	110.7	13.02	536.42
June	110.4	92.0	114.1	148.3	100.0	1,715	1,075	41.4	110.3	13.06	540.68
July	110.4	91.7	113.7	148.3	99.7	1,705	1,067	41.4	109.4	13.13	533.08
August	110.3	91.5	113.6	148.3	99.6	1,698	1,061	41.5	109.1	13.10	543.65
September	110.2	91.3	113.6	148.3	99.5	1,692	1,059	41.4	108.6	13.23	542.43
October	110.0	91.2	113.7	149.0	99.4	1,683	1,051	41.5	108.1	13.13	544.90
November	110.1	91.0	113.7	150.0	99.2	1,673	1,042	41.4	106.9	13.17	554.46
December	110.0	91.0	113.5	149.8	99.1	1,669	1,040	41.1	105.9	13.26	560.90

Transportation Equipment—Production

(1992 = 100, seasonally adjusted)

Year and month	Total	Motor vehicles and parts								Aerospace and miscellaneous transportation equipment			
		Total	Autos	Trucks and truck trailers				Motor vehicle parts	Motor homes	Total	Aircraft and parts	Ships and boats	Railroad and miscellaneous
				Total	Trucks and buses								
					Total	Consumer trucks	Business trucks						
1970	54.1	52.0	63.4	25.0	24.1	14.2	48.0	61.8	.....	62.3	57.1	90.5	53.2
1971	58.5	65.2	86.9	30.5	30.3	20.0	57.1	71.8	.....	55.9	47.9	88.3	59.8
1972	62.4	71.1	90.5	36.2	34.9	25.8	61.2	79.6	.....	57.7	47.6	102.3	65.2
1973	71.1	82.8	100.5	45.2	44.0	33.6	72.1	92.9	.....	63.8	52.7	115.0	71.4
1974	64.6	71.4	78.4	42.8	40.8	31.5	65.5	82.9	.....	62.0	51.2	116.2	68.0
1975	58.2	61.0	74.6	35.3	35.8	28.5	52.8	65.8	.....	59.3	48.1	120.9	65.0
1976	66.3	80.0	96.4	47.9	48.6	40.1	65.0	86.1	.....	56.6	43.9	124.6	63.6
1977	71.9	92.4	107.3	59.5	59.2	50.1	73.2	98.3	.....	55.6	45.0	127.4	58.3
1978	77.5	96.8	108.0	65.2	64.2	55.7	76.4	103.7	.....	62.2	52.8	131.4	62.6
1979	78.7	89.0	102.8	57.0	54.8	45.8	66.6	95.1	.....	71.1	64.2	129.8	68.6
1980	70.3	65.8	82.5	33.6	31.5	24.6	42.3	72.3	.....	74.3	69.7	135.8	65.9
1981	66.9	62.8	82.7	34.5	32.8	26.8	41.6	65.1	.....	70.5	65.1	142.8	61.4
1982	63.0	56.9	68.8	37.9	37.3	34.0	42.3	58.7	.....	68.3	61.9	131.0	63.6
1983	70.5	72.1	95.2	48.9	48.3	45.9	52.4	69.3	.....	69.3	63.7	109.6	68.9
1984	80.5	87.3	111.7	67.0	64.5	60.8	70.6	81.3	.....	75.1	66.7	113.6	81.0
1985	88.8	95.0	120.8	75.1	73.6	68.2	82.2	87.9	.....	83.7	73.8	109.1	96.9
1986	94.1	94.2	118.9	77.3	76.5	70.8	85.2	85.9	.....	94.2	86.4	103.9	107.7
1987	96.1	94.9	111.0	86.2	85.2	80.1	92.9	87.1	114.2	97.5	92.9	107.3	104.2
1988	101.1	100.2	113.7	93.3	92.5	87.0	100.9	92.9	122.7	102.1	95.7	111.2	113.0
1989	105.1	101.2	115.6	96.4	95.7	92.5	100.4	91.9	108.8	109.4	103.9	112.9	120.1
1990	102.3	95.3	106.1	90.9	90.9	88.4	94.6	88.9	89.4	109.8	105.1	113.0	119.0
1991	96.5	88.5	95.7	83.5	83.6	83.4	83.9	85.8	80.3	105.0	105.4	101.3	105.7
1992	100.0	100.0	100.0	100.0	100.0	100.0	100.0	100.0	100.0	100.0	100.0	100.0	100.0
1993	103.6	113.2	106.1	119.9	120.2	120.3	120.0	114.6	106.9	93.9	91.0	95.5	99.7
1994	107.4	130.4	117.1	141.1	141.1	138.2	145.1	134.5	111.2	85.0	80.9	94.4	90.5
1995	106.4	132.7	112.1	144.2	143.2	137.2	152.2	142.6	98.6	80.7	76.2	90.1	87.7
1996	107.9	132.6	109.0	142.3	143.1	143.5	141.8	146.0	107.4	83.8	81.2	91.9	86.1
1997	117.1	139.9	108.3	158.0	158.0	157.1	158.6	153.7	111.0	94.7	97.5	91.1	86.6
1998	123.0	141.1	102.9	169.1	167.4	166.2	168.3	152.4	129.1	104.9	112.4	93.9	86.6
1995:													
January	110.4	138.1	125.2	146.3	145.7	135.4	157.9	143.7	108.6	83.4	79.3	92.5	89.2
February	109.2	135.6	122.7	146.9	146.2	136.5	157.8	139.4	102.4	83.4	79.5	90.4	89.4
March	108.5	134.2	120.3	146.2	144.7	134.5	157.2	138.2	99.8	83.4	79.1	90.3	90.7
April	107.5	133.2	116.1	147.1	146.0	137.2	156.8	136.1	94.9	83.4	79.6	89.5	89.8
May	106.3	130.9	108.4	144.0	143.4	135.7	152.7	141.3	93.1	82.2	78.6	88.6	88.1
June	106.4	131.2	107.0	146.5	145.6	138.8	154.0	141.6	91.8	82.1	78.6	89.0	87.1
July	104.1	127.3	106.0	132.2	130.6	122.5	141.7	142.5	98.5	81.5	77.4	89.5	87.6
August	105.4	130.5	105.6	146.8	146.5	141.8	152.4	140.4	100.9	80.9	77.0	90.9	85.8
September	107.0	133.9	108.9	146.8	145.9	140.3	153.9	146.7	93.6	80.9	76.7	92.1	86.1
October	104.2	132.9	108.4	141.1	140.4	136.0	146.8	148.7	93.5	76.3	70.0	90.5	86.1
November	102.9	131.4	107.4	140.4	139.5	137.1	143.3	145.9	103.0	75.1	68.3	89.0	86.3
December	104.5	133.6	108.8	145.7	144.5	140.6	151.3	146.3	110.6	76.3	70.1	89.5	86.2
1996:													
January	104.8	130.6	102.3	136.2	136.4	135.3	139.2	151.2	102.2	79.7	76.2	86.7	85.1
February	106.7	132.8	107.4	143.5	144.2	143.9	146.2	147.3	105.5	81.3	78.2	87.6	85.4
March	96.3	111.1	81.5	128.6	129.1	128.2	132.1	122.9	116.6	81.6	78.1	90.8	85.8
April	109.1	137.2	113.6	145.7	147.0	148.3	147.2	151.9	107.6	81.7	78.0	91.8	86.0
May	109.7	138.1	114.7	142.6	143.9	144.9	144.6	155.3	114.4	82.0	78.3	92.2	86.1
June	109.6	137.7	119.1	143.9	144.3	144.9	145.6	149.4	115.4	82.3	78.4	94.8	86.0
July	111.8	140.4	122.4	150.6	152.0	156.9	146.6	149.4	95.5	83.9	80.4	91.9	88.8
August	111.1	138.2	118.2	143.0	143.8	148.2	139.0	152.8	100.7	84.8	81.6	94.8	87.8
September	108.9	132.1	114.9	139.0	139.8	143.0	136.4	142.2	113.5	86.2	84.0	94.3	87.1
October	106.8	127.1	100.1	138.5	139.5	144.2	133.4	141.7	110.4	86.8	85.7	93.0	85.6
November	110.1	133.1	109.0	142.7	143.6	145.8	141.5	147.0	108.4	87.5	87.3	92.4	84.5
December	110.0	132.2	104.7	152.7	154.1	157.3	149.8	141.1	96.8	88.3	88.2	92.9	84.8
1997:													
January	112.5	137.0	106.9	154.7	156.0	158.1	153.0	150.0	104.1	88.6	88.5	93.0	85.1
February	113.2	136.7	108.9	154.8	155.9	156.7	154.7	147.5	106.3	90.2	90.1	93.9	86.9
March	113.5	136.1	109.2	154.7	155.4	156.1	153.9	146.1	98.0	91.3	92.0	92.9	86.8
April	112.3	132.4	104.2	143.1	143.0	141.3	145.0	149.0	106.2	92.4	93.9	93.6	86.0
May	112.6	132.4	105.3	148.1	147.7	145.5	150.0	144.2	108.4	93.1	94.9	93.8	86.3
June	115.4	137.3	106.2	153.9	153.7	152.3	154.4	152.1	109.8	93.9	96.5	89.8	86.7
July	114.4	135.0	106.1	138.6	137.9	130.1	149.0	157.7	106.7	94.0	96.4	90.6	87.0
August	120.0	143.6	113.5	162.1	161.2	159.2	162.1	156.3	111.2	96.9	101.0	88.7	87.1
September	121.7	145.5	112.4	165.7	165.9	164.8	165.3	159.0	122.2	98.3	103.2	88.6	86.7
October	121.7	144.9	108.0	168.4	168.5	166.6	169.2	159.2	113.9	98.9	103.8	90.3	87.1
November	123.8	149.0	112.7	178.1	178.1	177.3	176.8	158.5	129.2	99.0	104.5	88.9	86.1
December	124.1	148.6	106.7	173.8	173.2	173.5	170.1	165.5	127.2	100.0	105.3	89.7	87.6
1998:													
January	121.3	141.9	108.5	167.1	166.3	166.1	164.3	151.8	120.6	100.9	106.0	93.2	87.9
February	121.5	140.4	98.8	170.3	169.3	170.5	165.1	154.0	104.6	102.6	108.4	93.9	88.3
March	122.3	140.0	100.4	169.4	168.6	169.8	164.6	151.5	123.2	104.5	111.3	92.7	88.2
April	123.3	140.8	101.1	173.1	172.4	173.8	168.3	150.3	125.8	105.7	113.6	92.0	87.3
May	125.2	144.1	102.0	176.5	175.5	177.1	171.2	155.5	122.5	106.3	114.2	93.9	87.5
June	114.2	121.1	88.2	147.6	145.3	142.2	149.1	128.6	124.8	106.3	113.9	94.0	88.0
July	108.2	107.6	71.3	122.8	118.3	110.0	131.0	125.3	125.7	107.1	115.0	97.7	87.1
August	130.3	154.2	117.1	181.9	179.4	178.9	178.8	165.0	145.9	106.9	114.8	97.1	86.8
September	127.6	149.9	120.8	167.0	164.8	161.1	169.5	162.1	140.6	105.8	113.9	94.0	86.2
October	128.4	150.2	112.8	184.3	182.5	181.0	183.4	156.2	142.6	106.9	115.2	98.1	85.4
November	127.1	148.8	107.0	189.0	187.6	183.2	193.3	154.3	131.1	105.7	113.6	96.3	85.4
December	125.6	146.6	108.7	184.7	183.7	179.1	189.6	149.5	153.8	104.8	112.6	94.9	85.2

Transportation Equipment—Capacity Utilization, Shipments, Inventories, and Orders

(Seasonally adjusted)

Year and month	Capacity utilization (output as a percent of capacity)				Manufacturers' shipments, inventories, and orders (millions of dollars)							
	Total	Motor vehicles and parts		Aerospace and miscellaneous	Shipments		Inventories (book value, end of period)		New orders (net)		Unfilled orders (end of period)	
		Total	Autos and light trucks		Total	Motor vehicles and parts	Total	Motor vehicles and parts	Total	Aircraft, missiles, and parts	Total	Aircraft, missiles, and parts
1970	70.5	66.6	.....	76.7	74,539	42,538	14,648	4,178	67,380	17,417	34,720	26,198
1971	74.2	79.5	.....	68.7	88,857	58,247	13,799	4,173	89,900	22,459	35,793	26,259
1972	76.8	82.5	.....	70.6	94,706	63,923	14,775	4,670	96,501	20,963	37,627	26,151
1973	84.7	91.6	.....	77.3	110,587	74,799	16,458	5,708	118,194	26,669	45,248	27,842
1974	75.0	76.4	.....	73.9	108,244	68,631	19,197	6,688	114,081	29,934	51,118	30,506
1975	65.8	63.1	.....	69.6	113,503	70,033	19,620	6,101	109,050	26,869	46,633	28,244
1976	72.7	80.2	.....	65.3	141,028	95,380	20,886	7,814	143,502	31,851	49,078	29,421
1977	76.4	90.3	89.8	63.2	166,954	117,747	22,423	9,078	175,446	40,625	57,101	37,325
1978	80.7	91.0	88.3	70.2	188,773	131,999	26,170	10,357	213,539	54,600	81,782	54,417
1979	80.2	82.0	78.3	78.4	201,623	131,378	31,638	10,978	223,226	67,818	103,555	74,034
1980	70.9	61.3	57.8	79.1	186,516	104,560	35,900	9,864	202,584	72,514	119,700	88,051
1981	66.1	59.3	60.3	72.2	205,223	116,981	37,527	9,047	203,482	63,530	118,008	86,794
1982	60.9	52.8	53.5	67.8	201,347	112,270	43,005	8,534	209,325	73,365	125,879	93,703
1983	66.7	66.2	71.9	67.2	245,392	148,296	43,791	10,433	261,359	86,952	141,637	105,504
1984	74.1	79.0	81.6	70.0	284,593	181,993	50,770	11,680	295,202	91,620	152,189	117,923
1985	77.9	83.1	81.5	73.8	307,380	193,445	52,634	11,809	311,482	100,889	156,155	127,282
1986	78.6	78.7	76.7	78.5	322,688	198,811	53,363	11,445	327,541	107,993	161,145	133,565
1987	77.5	76.8	74.7	78.1	332,936	205,923	56,461	11,937	348,224	114,835	176,588	144,987
1988	80.6	81.2	79.2	80.0	354,849	222,353	63,202	12,310	389,635	137,443	211,575	174,721
1989	81.8	79.5	79.8	84.4	369,675	233,232	70,968	12,503	411,434	153,430	253,517	217,557
1990	77.7	71.6	71.0	84.0	370,328	217,295	77,640	13,504	395,737	150,329	279,082	242,208
1991	71.8	64.1	64.6	80.8	367,235	209,210	73,019	13,163	363,366	132,645	275,260	242,798
1992	73.8	70.7	71.2	77.2	399,270	238,384	63,290	13,081	377,147	110,830	253,076	222,194
1993	75.7	77.6	78.6	73.5	414,694	267,365	60,950	14,099	386,643	88,070	225,256	194,154
1994	76.9	85.5	86.7	67.2	450,809	314,637	61,354	15,692	440,817	90,217	215,171	180,969
1995	73.4	80.9	80.4	64.1	461,806	327,908	59,735	16,293	465,839	106,062	219,101	186,848
1996	72.1	76.3	79.7	66.5	465,173	329,155	64,596	16,369	495,239	129,688	249,119	215,171
1997	76.6	78.0	83.3	74.8	502,301	346,606	69,323	16,145	507,667	124,151	254,579	217,998
1998	78.8	76.2	82.0	82.4	536,896	359,560	75,701	17,419	524,963	124,111	243,205	204,434
1995:												
January	77.7	87.4	87.4	66.2	39,330	27,890	60,767	15,763	38,099	6,456	213,940	178,929
February	76.5	85.2	86.3	66.1	39,251	27,787	60,213	15,838	40,031	9,606	214,720	179,786
March	75.8	83.7	84.5	66.2	40,078	28,688	60,534	15,950	39,890	8,534	214,532	179,928
April	74.9	81.9	83.1	66.2	37,685	26,325	60,455	16,019	35,059	6,373	211,906	177,674
May	73.7	80.5	79.3	65.3	37,593	26,404	60,898	16,215	37,768	8,986	212,081	178,398
June	73.5	80.2	79.2	65.2	38,461	26,804	59,986	16,153	35,462	5,692	209,082	175,495
July	71.7	77.2	74.0	64.7	35,934	25,337	60,174	16,210	34,510	7,116	207,658	174,678
August	72.3	78.7	78.7	64.3	37,862	27,123	59,843	16,005	38,015	8,564	207,811	175,182
September	73.2	80.2	79.2	64.3	39,007	28,038	59,873	15,909	42,940	11,748	211,744	178,690
October	71.0	79.0	77.6	60.7	38,426	27,854	60,215	16,093	38,782	8,962	212,100	179,615
November	69.8	77.7	77.2	59.7	38,647	27,269	59,902	16,215	39,512	9,732	212,965	180,816
December	70.7	78.5	78.3	60.7	38,793	27,667	59,735	16,293	44,929	14,117	219,101	186,848
1996:												
January	70.7	76.3	74.3	63.4	36,997	27,170	60,633	16,537	43,577	12,550	225,681	192,279
February	71.9	77.4	78.4	64.6	37,850	27,190	61,056	16,366	38,151	8,597	225,982	193,115
March	64.7	64.6	64.5	64.9	35,525	24,361	61,740	16,740	43,753	16,791	234,210	201,821
April	73.2	79.5	81.9	64.9	38,430	27,702	61,574	16,489	36,960	6,919	232,740	200,862
May	73.4	79.8	81.5	65.1	40,578	28,646	61,778	16,327	42,770	11,705	234,932	203,497
June	73.2	79.4	83.2	65.3	39,002	27,690	62,407	16,175	41,891	9,549	237,821	204,867
July	74.6	80.7	87.7	66.6	39,028	28,728	63,016	16,483	40,788	9,514	239,581	206,685
August	74.0	79.3	84.0	67.2	39,600	27,894	63,093	16,311	37,359	6,909	237,340	204,607
September	72.4	75.6	81.5	68.3	40,866	28,670	63,384	16,334	44,565	12,659	241,039	208,275
October	70.8	72.5	76.4	68.7	38,581	27,284	64,217	16,513	41,009	11,792	243,467	211,491
November	72.9	75.7	80.3	69.3	39,759	27,771	64,721	16,219	42,246	11,322	245,954	213,658
December	72.7	75.0	82.0	69.8	38,704	26,350	64,596	16,369	41,869	10,904	249,119	215,171
1997:												
January	74.3	77.5	83.2	70.0	40,687	29,411	65,808	16,317	42,548	10,530	250,980	216,913
February	74.6	77.2	83.6	71.2	40,442	28,202	66,796	16,547	40,362	9,845	250,900	217,447
March	74.7	76.7	83.6	72.1	40,211	27,447	66,827	16,477	39,289	8,812	249,978	216,300
April	73.8	74.4	77.7	73.0	41,809	28,491	67,771	16,657	39,251	8,494	247,420	214,262
May	73.9	74.2	79.3	73.6	40,515	27,390	68,298	16,943	38,590	8,494	245,495	212,481
June	75.6	76.8	81.5	74.2	41,641	28,281	68,637	16,553	41,800	10,703	245,654	212,954
July	74.8	75.3	75.3	74.2	43,673	30,472	69,174	16,610	41,606	8,457	243,587	210,968
August	78.4	79.9	86.0	76.5	42,022	29,318	69,677	16,246	42,280	10,746	243,845	211,773
September	79.3	80.7	87.0	77.6	42,379	29,126	69,534	16,671	41,445	8,479	242,911	210,030
October	79.2	80.1	85.7	78.1	42,289	29,936	70,761	16,341	44,351	10,429	244,973	210,861
November	80.4	82.2	90.3	78.1	43,285	29,240	71,183	16,163	53,485	20,719	255,173	220,532
December	80.5	81.7	86.8	78.9	43,558	30,002	69,323	16,145	42,964	8,043	254,579	217,998
1998:												
January	78.5	77.8	85.3	79.6	41,542	28,133	70,371	16,259	44,520	13,720	257,557	220,894
February	78.5	76.8	82.7	80.8	43,577	29,678	70,844	16,281	42,431	9,986	256,411	219,861
March	78.9	76.4	82.8	82.2	45,208	30,607	70,958	16,721	42,204	8,527	253,407	217,113
April	79.4	76.7	83.9	83.0	43,863	29,730	72,542	16,450	44,431	12,827	253,975	218,831
May	80.5	78.3	84.9	83.4	43,562	29,461	73,398	16,686	42,422	10,760	252,835	218,389
June	73.3	65.7	70.3	83.2	40,857	26,760	74,597	17,046	39,349	8,480	251,327	216,211
July	69.3	58.3	55.3	83.8	40,556	27,092	75,032	16,790	39,768	10,172	250,539	215,817
August	83.3	83.4	90.2	83.5	44,403	30,017	75,812	16,511	46,745	13,106	252,881	217,854
September	81.5	80.9	86.5	82.6	46,588	31,061	75,702	16,701	45,101	9,109	251,394	215,042
October	81.8	80.9	88.8	83.3	48,017	31,586	76,999	16,755	44,870	9,637	248,247	211,882
November	80.8	80.0	87.1	82.3	48,324	31,581	76,452	17,240	45,024	9,962	244,947	208,629
December	79.8	78.7	86.5	81.5	47,908	32,169	75,701	17,419	46,166	7,848	243,205	204,434

Transportation Equipment—Motor Vehicle Sales and Inventories

Year and month	Retail sales of new passenger cars						Retail inventories of new domestic passenger cars (thousands of units, end of period)		
	Thousands of units, not seasonally adjusted			Millions of units, seasonally adjusted annual rate			Not seasonally adjusted	Seasonally adjusted	Inventory to sales ratio
	Total	Domestics	Imports	Total	Domestics	Imports			
1970	8,403	7,119	1,283	8.4	7.1	1.3	1,220	1,294	2.4
1971	10,228	8,662	1,566	10.2	8.7	1.6	1,447	1,512	2.1
1972	10,873	9,253	1,621	10.9	9.3	1.6	1,311	1,379	1.7
1973	11,350	9,589	1,762	11.4	9.6	1.8	1,600	1,654	2.5
1974	8,774	7,362	1,412	8.8	7.4	1.4	1,672	1,730	3.4
1975	8,538	6,951	1,587	8.5	7.0	1.6	1,419	1,468	2.2
1976	9,994	8,492	1,502	10.0	8.5	1.5	1,465	1,494	1.9
1977	11,046	8,971	2,075	11.1	9.0	2.1	1,731	1,743	2.3
1978	11,164	9,164	2,000	11.2	9.2	2.0	1,729	1,731	2.3
1979	10,559	8,230	2,329	10.6	8.2	2.3	1,691	1,667	2.4
1980	8,982	6,581	2,400	9.0	6.6	2.4	1,448	1,440	2.6
1981	8,534	6,209	2,326	8.5	6.2	2.3	1,471	1,495	3.6
1982	7,979	5,758	2,221	8.0	5.8	2.2	1,126	1,127	2.2
1983	9,179	6,793	2,386	9.2	6.8	2.4	1,352	1,350	2.0
1984	10,390	7,952	2,439	10.4	8.0	2.4	1,415	1,411	2.1
1985	10,978	8,205	2,774	11.0	8.2	2.8	1,630	1,619	2.5
1986	11,406	8,215	3,191	11.4	8.2	3.2	1,499	1,515	2.0
1987	10,171	7,081	3,090	10.2	7.1	3.1	1,680	1,716	2.8
1988	10,546	7,539	3,006	10.6	7.5	3.0	1,601	1,601	2.3
1989	9,777	7,078	2,699	9.8	7.1	2.7	1,669	1,687	3.1
1990	9,300	6,897	2,403	9.3	6.9	2.4	1,408	1,418	2.6
1991	8,175	6,137	2,038	8.2	6.1	2.0	1,283	1,296	2.6
1992	8,214	6,277	1,938	8.2	6.3	1.9	1,276	1,288	2.3
1993	8,518	6,734	1,784	8.5	6.7	1.8	1,365	1,378	2.4
1994	8,990	7,255	1,735	9.0	7.3	1.7	1,437	1,449	2.3
1995	8,636	7,129	1,507	8.6	7.1	1.5	1,619	1,582	2.5
1996	8,527	7,254	1,273	8.5	7.3	1.3	1,363	1,354	2.3
1997	8,232	6,876	1,356	8.2	6.9	1.4	1,330	1,331	2.5
1998	8,182	6,794	1,388	8.2	6.8	1.4	1,324	1,179	1.9
1995:									
January	582	472	110	8.9	7.3	1.6	1,530	1,499	2.5
February	649	532	117	8.5	6.8	1.6	1,686	1,569	2.8
March	799	655	144	8.6	7.0	1.6	1,785	1,669	2.8
April	686	562	124	8.1	6.6	1.5	1,808	1,700	3.1
May	825	674	151	8.7	7.0	1.7	1,794	1,677	2.9
June	853	702	151	8.8	7.2	1.6	1,763	1,670	2.8
July	721	594	128	8.5	7.0	1.4	1,505	1,655	2.8
August	806	659	148	9.4	7.9	1.5	1,475	1,572	2.4
September	715	593	122	8.6	7.2	1.4	1,504	1,590	2.7
October	702	593	108	8.6	7.3	1.4	1,580	1,607	2.7
November	645	544	101	8.7	7.3	1.4	1,621	1,600	2.6
December	654	550	105	8.9	7.5	1.4	1,619	1,582	2.5
1996:									
January	567	479	88	8.1	6.8	1.2	1,661	1,566	2.7
February	691	596	95	8.8	7.5	1.3	1,683	1,529	2.4
March	793	674	119	8.8	7.5	1.3	1,514	1,380	2.2
April	761	657	104	8.8	7.5	1.2	1,493	1,364	2.2
May	871	753	118	9.0	7.7	1.3	1,461	1,350	2.1
June	792	677	115	8.5	7.2	1.3	1,473	1,398	2.3
July	732	624	109	8.4	7.1	1.2	1,277	1,451	2.4
August	750	621	129	8.7	7.5	1.3	1,299	1,468	2.4
September	697	593	104	8.7	7.4	1.3	1,326	1,454	2.4
October	678	576	102	8.1	6.8	1.3	1,329	1,398	2.5
November	590	496	95	8.0	6.7	1.3	1,417	1,422	2.5
December	605	508	97	8.3	7.0	1.3	1,363	1,354	2.3
1997:									
January	612	513	99	8.7	7.3	1.4	1,404	1,337	2.2
February	648	550	98	8.5	7.1	1.3	1,443	1,322	2.2
March	766	641	125	8.5	7.2	1.4	1,380	1,285	2.2
April	699	593	106	8.0	6.7	1.3	1,413	1,305	2.3
May	771	653	118	8.0	6.8	1.3	1,384	1,309	2.3
June	740	625	115	8.0	6.7	1.3	1,351	1,276	2.3
July	740	616	124	8.4	7.1	1.4	1,134	1,331	2.3
August	740	601	140	8.8	7.3	1.4	1,167	1,294	2.1
September	669	553	116	8.1	6.7	1.4	1,172	1,284	2.3
October	665	556	109	7.9	6.6	1.3	1,262	1,296	2.4
November	564	469	95	7.9	6.6	1.4	1,363	1,309	2.4
December	618	507	111	7.8	6.5	1.3	1,330	1,331	2.5
1998:									
January	566	462	104	8.5	7.0	1.5	1,390	1,298	2.2
February	615	511	104	8.0	6.6	1.4	1,442	1,274	2.3
March	724	604	120	8.0	6.7	1.4	1,454	1,318	2.4
April	711	598	113	8.2	6.8	1.4	1,412	1,281	2.3
May	793	670	124	8.4	7.0	1.4	1,421	1,245	2.1
June	819	694	125	8.6	7.2	1.4	1,165	1,070	1.8
July	636	510	126	7.2	5.8	1.4	961	930	1.9
August	675	539	136	8.1	6.7	1.4	1,037	1,111	2.0
September	685	584	101	8.2	6.9	1.2	1,114	1,145	2.0
October	712	599	114	8.5	7.2	1.4	1,208	1,181	2.0
November	562	465	98	7.9	6.5	1.4	1,319	1,201	2.2
December	684	559	125	9.1	7.5	1.6	1,324	1,179	1.9

Transportation Equipment—Motor Vehicle Sales

Year and month	Retail sales of new trucks and buses								Unit sales of cars and light trucks (millions of units, seasonally adjusted annual rate)		
	Thousands of units, not seasonally adjusted				Millions of units, seasonally adjusted annual rate						
	Total	0–10,000 pounds		10,001 pounds and over	Total	0–10,000 pounds		10,001 pounds and over	Total	Domestic	Imports
		Domestic	Imports			Domestic	Imports				
1970	.....	1,408.5	.....	337.3	.....	1.4	.....	0.3	.....	8.5	.....
1971	.....	1,592.5	.....	338.9	.....	1.7	.....	0.3	.....	10.4	.....
1972	.....	2,122.5	.....	437.4	.....	2.1	.....	0.4	.....	11.4	.....
1973	.....	2,509.4	.....	495.7	.....	2.5	.....	0.5	.....	12.1	.....
1974	.....	2,180.1	.....	423.9	.....	2.2	.....	0.4	.....	9.6	.....
1975	.....	2,052.6	.....	298.3	.....	2.1	.....	0.3	.....	9.1	.....
1976	3,300.5	2,738.3	237.5	324.7	3.3	2.7	0.2	0.3	12.9	11.2	1.7
1977	3,813.0	3,112.8	323.1	377.1	3.8	3.1	0.3	0.4	14.5	12.1	2.4
1978	4,256.8	3,481.1	335.9	439.8	4.3	3.5	0.3	0.4	15.0	12.7	2.3
1979	3,589.7	2,730.2	469.4	390.1	3.6	2.7	0.5	0.4	13.7	10.9	2.8
1980	2,487.4	1,731.1	484.6	271.7	2.5	1.7	0.5	0.3	11.2	8.3	2.9
1981	2,255.6	1,581.7	447.6	226.3	2.3	1.6	0.4	0.2	10.6	7.8	2.8
1982	2,562.8	1,967.5	410.4	184.9	2.6	2.0	0.4	0.2	10.4	7.8	2.6
1983	3,117.3	2,465.2	463.3	188.8	3.1	2.5	0.5	0.2	12.1	9.3	2.8
1984	4,093.1	3,207.2	607.7	278.2	4.1	3.2	0.6	0.3	14.2	11.2	3.0
1985	4,741.7	3,618.4	828.3	295.0	4.8	3.6	0.8	0.3	15.4	11.8	3.6
1986	4,811.8	3,671.4	866.9	273.5	4.9	3.7	1.0	0.3	16.1	11.9	4.2
1987	5,000.6	3,786.1	912.2	302.3	5.0	3.8	0.9	0.3	14.9	10.9	4.0
1988	5,242.4	4,195.8	697.9	348.7	5.2	4.2	0.7	0.4	15.4	11.7	3.7
1989	5,067.8	4,107.0	630.3	330.5	5.1	4.1	0.6	0.3	14.5	11.2	3.3
1990	4,848.4	3,947.4	602.7	298.3	4.9	4.0	0.6	0.3	13.9	10.9	3.0
1991	4,365.8	3,594.8	528.8	242.2	4.4	3.6	0.5	0.2	12.3	9.7	2.6
1992	4,903.3	4,232.7	395.9	274.7	4.9	4.2	0.4	0.3	12.8	10.5	2.3
1993	5,681.1	4,980.9	364.5	335.7	5.7	5.0	0.4	0.3	13.8	11.7	2.1
1994	6,422.4	5,638.0	396.3	388.1	6.4	5.6	0.4	0.4	15.0	12.9	2.1
1995	6,481.4	5,662.7	390.5	428.2	6.5	5.7	0.4	0.4	14.7	12.8	1.9
1996	6,929.1	6,087.6	430.9	410.6	6.9	6.1	0.4	0.4	15.1	13.4	1.7
1997	7,204.2	6,208.2	567.1	428.9	7.2	6.2	0.6	0.4	15.0	13.1	1.9
1998	7,842.8	6,668.4	650.0	524.4	7.8	6.7	0.7	0.5	15.5	13.5	2.0
1995:											
January	450.0	384.1	32.6	33.3	6.8	5.8	0.5	0.5	15.1	13.1	2.0
February	480.6	418.1	29.8	32.7	6.5	5.6	0.4	0.4	14.4	12.4	2.0
March	604.7	530.2	34.0	40.5	6.5	5.7	0.4	0.4	14.7	12.7	2.0
April	530.0	463.0	28.7	38.3	6.1	5.4	0.4	0.4	13.9	12.0	1.9
May	602.3	528.8	34.3	39.2	6.4	5.6	0.4	0.4	14.7	12.6	2.1
June	624.4	551.0	32.5	40.9	6.6	5.8	0.4	0.4	15.0	13.0	2.0
July	534.0	472.0	28.7	33.3	6.3	5.6	0.3	0.4	14.4	12.6	1.8
August	558.9	487.3	36.8	34.8	6.6	5.8	0.4	0.4	15.6	13.7	1.9
September	499.5	430.6	36.2	32.7	6.3	5.5	0.4	0.4	14.5	12.7	1.8
October	524.3	457.2	30.9	36.2	6.4	5.6	0.4	0.4	14.7	12.9	1.8
November	524.4	461.8	31.7	30.9	6.6	5.8	0.4	0.4	14.9	13.1	1.8
December	548.3	478.6	34.3	35.4	7.0	6.1	0.4	0.4	15.4	13.6	1.8
1996:											
January	483.6	428.9	25.1	29.6	6.8	6.0	0.4	0.4	14.4	12.8	1.6
February	547.4	487.0	28.2	32.2	7.2	6.4	0.4	0.4	15.6	13.9	1.7
March	611.3	537.8	37.6	35.9	6.8	6.0	0.4	0.4	15.2	13.5	1.7
April	598.4	526.6	34.1	37.7	6.8	6.0	0.4	0.4	15.2	13.5	1.7
May	651.8	572.9	40.6	38.3	6.8	5.9	0.5	0.4	15.3	13.6	1.7
June	611.9	535.4	37.1	39.4	6.7	5.9	0.4	0.4	14.8	13.1	1.7
July	584.7	513.9	35.1	35.7	6.7	5.9	0.4	0.4	14.6	13.0	1.6
August	583.6	505.1	44.6	33.9	6.9	6.1	0.4	0.4	15.3	13.6	1.7
September	534.8	470.9	31.9	32.0	7.0	6.2	0.4	0.4	15.3	13.6	1.7
October	618.7	546.1	37.1	35.5	7.3	6.5	0.4	0.4	14.7	13.3	1.7
November	555.8	487.0	40.7	28.1	7.1	6.2	0.5	0.4	14.7	12.9	1.8
December	547.1	476.0	38.8	32.3	7.0	6.1	0.5	0.4	14.9	13.1	1.8
1997:											
January	502.6	435.7	37.5	29.4	7.0	6.0	0.5	0.4	15.2	13.3	1.9
February	529.2	461.5	37.0	30.7	7.1	6.1	0.5	0.4	15.1	13.2	1.9
March	659.8	567.8	53.2	38.8	7.5	6.4	0.6	0.4	15.6	13.6	2.0
April	611.6	528.4	43.9	39.3	6.9	5.9	0.6	0.4	14.5	12.6	1.9
May	664.4	571.6	55.1	37.7	7.2	6.1	0.6	0.4	14.8	12.9	1.9
June	614.9	532.6	45.9	36.4	6.7	5.8	0.5	0.4	14.3	12.5	1.8
July	637.0	547.6	52.4	37.0	7.3	6.3	0.6	0.4	15.4	13.4	2.0
August	607.7	513.6	59.5	34.6	7.3	6.2	0.6	0.4	15.5	13.5	2.0
September	569.5	486.9	48.3	34.3	7.3	6.3	0.6	0.4	15.0	13.0	2.0
October	616.7	529.3	48.3	39.1	7.2	6.2	0.6	0.4	14.7	12.8	1.9
November	582.4	508.4	41.8	32.2	7.6	6.6	0.5	0.5	15.1	13.2	1.9
December	608.4	524.8	44.2	39.4	7.4	6.4	0.5	0.5	14.8	12.9	1.9
1998:											
January	539.2	464.7	42.7	31.8	7.8	6.8	0.6	0.5	15.9	13.8	2.1
February	557.5	480.1	42.8	34.6	7.4	6.4	0.6	0.5	15.0	13.0	2.0
March	680.9	588.3	48.6	44.0	7.6	6.6	0.6	0.5	15.2	13.3	1.9
April	679.9	584.2	48.8	46.9	7.7	6.6	0.6	0.5	15.4	13.4	2.0
May	748.6	649.2	55.3	44.1	8.1	7.0	0.6	0.5	16.0	14.0	2.0
June	787.7	688.2	53.7	45.8	8.6	7.5	0.6	0.5	16.7	14.7	2.0
July	628.9	526.3	58.2	44.4	7.1	5.9	0.7	0.5	13.8	11.7	2.1
August	589.7	480.9	63.8	45.0	7.2	6.0	0.6	0.5	14.7	12.7	2.0
September	629.3	525.9	58.4	45.0	7.8	6.6	0.7	0.6	15.4	13.5	1.9
October	693.8	582.3	62.3	49.2	8.3	7.0	0.7	0.6	16.3	14.2	2.1
November	613.9	518.1	51.7	44.1	8.0	6.7	0.7	0.6	15.3	13.2	2.1
December	693.4	580.2	63.7	49.5	8.7	7.3	0.8	0.6	17.2	14.8	2.4

Transportation Equipment—Producer and Consumer Prices

Year and month	Transportation equipment industry (December 1984 = 100)	Passenger cars	Light motor trucks	Heavy motor trucks	Truck trailers	Civilian aircraft (December 1985 = 100)	Ships (December 1985 = 100)	Railroad equipment	Aircraft engines (December 1985 = 100)	Aircraft parts (June 1985 = 100)	Commodity group: Motor vehicles and equipment	Total	New cars	Used cars and trucks
		Finished goods							Intermediate materials			New vehicles		
1970	.....	50.0	42.0	36.3	.....	.....	.....	33.2	.....	.....	43.3	53.1	53.0	31.2
1971	.....	52.6	45.3	38.4	.....	.....	.....	34.9	.....	.....	45.7	55.3	55.2	33.0
1972	.....	54.0	46.2	39.3	.....	.....	.....	37.1	.....	.....	47.0	54.8	54.7	33.1
1973	.....	54.2	47.0	39.8	.....	.....	.....	38.9	.....	.....	47.4	54.8	54.8	35.2
1974	.....	57.8	52.3	44.5	.....	.....	.....	47.3	.....	.....	51.4	58.0	57.9	36.7
1975	.....	63.0	56.9	50.7	.....	.....	.....	58.1	.....	.....	57.6	63.0	62.9	43.8
1976	.....	66.8	60.4	56.1	.....	.....	.....	62.5	.....	.....	61.2	67.0	66.9	50.3
1977	.....	70.7	64.8	61.2	.....	.....	.....	67.4	.....	.....	65.2	70.5	70.4	54.7
1978	.....	75.9	70.5	66.8	.....	.....	.....	73.0	.....	.....	70.0	75.9	75.8	55.8
1979	.....	81.9	76.4	73.4	.....	.....	.....	80.0	.....	.....	75.8	81.9	81.8	60.2
1980	.....	88.9	83.3	82.3	.....	.....	.....	90.4	.....	.....	83.1	88.5	88.4	62.3
1981	.....	96.2	95.0	92.9	96.9	.....	.....	97.0	.....	.....	94.6	93.9	93.7	76.9
1982	.....	100.0	100.0	100.0	100.0	.....	.....	100.0	.....	.....	100.0	97.5	97.4	88.8
1983	.....	102.2	102.6	103.6	100.6	.....	.....	101.1	.....	.....	102.2	99.9	99.9	98.7
1984	.....	104.0	106.7	108.0	104.0	.....	.....	102.6	.....	.....	104.1	102.6	102.8	112.5
1985	.....	106.9	112.2	108.8	106.2	.....	.....	104.9	.....	.....	106.4	106.1	106.1	113.7
1986	104.4	110.2	117.7	113.4	104.3	100.9	100.5	105.4	99.7	103.4	109.1	110.6	110.6	108.8
1987	105.9	112.9	121.1	111.8	103.4	102.9	100.7	104.7	99.7	105.8	111.7	114.4	114.6	113.1
1988	107.8	113.0	125.0	112.4	106.6	104.5	101.0	107.5	103.2	110.3	113.1	116.5	116.9	118.0
1989	112.1	115.5	129.5	117.2	110.4	108.8	105.4	114.0	106.7	114.5	116.2	119.2	119.2	120.4
1990	115.6	118.3	130.0	120.3	110.8	115.3	110.1	118.6	113.5	117.7	118.2	121.4	121.0	117.6
1991	119.8	124.1	135.5	123.6	112.1	123.0	114.6	122.2	119.2	121.8	122.1	126.0	125.3	118.1
1992	123.0	126.9	142.4	128.6	115.1	128.8	122.1	123.7	125.0	128.0	124.9	129.2	128.4	123.2
1993	126.3	129.8	150.3	133.9	118.2	131.5	129.1	125.2	127.7	131.2	128.0	132.7	131.5	133.9
1994	130.1	133.9	157.1	138.7	122.2	135.4	131.1	129.2	130.7	134.0	131.4	137.6	136.0	141.7
1995	132.2	134.1	159.0	144.1	131.7	141.8	132.8	134.8	132.8	135.7	133.0	141.0	139.0	156.5
1996	134.2	135.4	160.3	144.5	130.7	147.3	138.7	137.2	134.7	139.3	134.1	143.7	141.4	157.0
1997	134.1	133.6	158.9	140.4	130.3	150.0	143.7	134.7	135.7	141.3	132.7	144.3	141.7	151.1
1998	133.6	131.9	155.2	142.4	135.0	150.2	145.7	135.0	137.1	142.9	131.4	143.4	140.7	150.6
1995:														
January	132.2	135.8	160.0	140.4	130.5	139.1	131.9	130.9	131.7	137.5	133.4	139.7	138.0	152.4
February	132.2	135.4	159.5	141.4	130.7	139.7	133.1	132.7	131.6	137.0	133.3	139.8	138.2	153.3
March	132.0	134.5	159.1	142.9	131.3	139.8	133.1	133.2	131.7	136.2	133.1	139.9	138.2	154.8
April	131.9	134.0	159.5	143.3	131.5	140.1	133.1	134.2	131.4	136.1	132.9	140.6	138.8	156.7
May	131.8	133.3	159.5	143.8	131.6	140.7	133.1	134.7	132.4	135.2	132.7	140.9	139.0	157.7
June	131.5	132.3	158.2	144.6	132.1	141.1	133.1	135.2	133.1	135.3	132.2	141.1	139.2	158.3
July	131.4	132.3	158.0	144.6	132.1	142.4	132.3	135.5	133.0	134.4	132.2	141.0	139.0	157.5
August	131.3	131.3	158.1	144.9	132.1	142.6	132.9	135.7	133.6	134.4	131.9	141.2	139.2	157.0
September	129.3	127.2	151.5	144.9	132.0	142.8	132.9	135.6	133.6	134.6	129.1	141.5	139.4	156.5
October	133.9	137.4	160.9	146.3	132.1	144.1	132.9	136.1	133.6	135.3	134.8	141.6	139.4	157.2
November	134.4	138.2	161.7	146.2	132.2	144.5	132.9	136.6	133.8	136.0	135.5	141.9	139.9	157.8
December	134.4	138.0	162.0	145.4	132.1	144.7	132.9	136.9	133.8	136.0	135.4	142.1	139.9	158.2
1996:														
January	134.2	136.2	161.2	145.7	132.1	145.2	135.3	136.7	135.0	139.3	134.5	142.3	140.1	157.9
February	134.2	136.1	160.8	146.6	132.1	145.4	135.3	137.7	134.8	139.6	134.5	142.6	140.4	157.5
March	134.3	136.1	160.6	147.3	132.0	145.6	135.3	137.6	135.5	139.5	134.5	142.8	140.7	157.3
April	134.1	135.2	160.4	147.2	130.5	146.1	138.8	137.8	133.9	139.4	134.1	143.0	140.8	157.4
May	134.1	135.4	159.8	147.9	130.4	146.3	138.3	137.7	134.0	139.4	134.1	143.2	140.9	157.6
June	134.3	135.9	160.1	145.4	130.6	146.9	138.3	137.3	134.1	139.4	134.2	143.6	141.4	157.2
July	133.8	134.1	159.3	145.4	130.6	147.4	138.6	137.3	134.4	139.0	133.5	143.9	141.7	156.9
August	133.8	133.9	158.9	145.7	130.0	148.2	139.6	137.2	134.6	139.1	133.3	144.1	142.0	156.6
September	132.1	130.4	154.1	142.6	130.0	148.5	139.2	137.0	134.7	139.3	131.0	144.7	142.6	157.0
October	135.4	137.3	163.2	142.3	130.0	148.8	144.7	137.0	134.8	139.3	135.2	144.5	142.3	157.0
November	135.2	137.3	162.7	139.5	130.2	149.4	140.7	136.5	135.0	139.3	134.9	144.5	142.1	156.5
December	135.1	136.9	162.4	138.9	130.2	149.3	141.0	136.3	135.6	139.5	134.8	144.7	142.2	155.6
1997:														
January	135.4	136.5	163.0	140.3	130.2	149.4	142.7	142.4	137.7	141.4	134.6	144.6	142.1	154.7
February	135.4	136.7	162.0	140.0	130.2	149.7	142.6	136.6	136.9	141.4	134.5	144.6	142.1	154.4
March	135.3	136.3	161.6	140.5	130.3	149.7	142.6	132.2	137.6	141.7	134.3	144.6	142.1	154.4
April	134.8	135.2	161.0	140.6	130.4	149.7	145.5	131.6	135.7	141.6	133.7	144.6	142.1	154.3
May	133.9	133.0	158.8	140.5	130.4	150.0	141.4	134.2	135.8	141.8	132.5	144.4	141.8	153.9
June	133.8	132.7	158.7	140.6	130.7	150.4	141.3	134.3	135.9	141.5	132.3	144.3	141.7	151.8
July	132.8	130.2	155.7	143.0	129.8	150.5	143.1	133.8	135.2	140.9	131.0	144.4	141.8	149.9
August	132.8	130.0	156.5	141.6	129.7	150.2	144.8	133.5	135.3	141.0	131.0	144.2	141.6	148.5
September	131.8	127.7	154.0	139.9	129.8	150.0	144.9	134.2	134.2	141.0	129.6	144.1	141.5	148.2
October	135.0	136.4	160.4	139.2	129.8	150.1	144.7	134.7	134.1	141.1	133.9	144.1	141.5	147.9
November	134.4	134.8	159.2	139.2	129.9	150.1	145.3	134.2	134.8	141.2	133.1	143.8	141.1	147.6
December	133.7	133.4	156.6	139.8	132.8	150.0	145.3	134.3	134.9	141.2	132.2	143.4	140.8	147.9
1998:														
January	133.8	133.3	156.3	139.8	133.7	150.1	145.4	134.6	136.2	141.7	132.0	143.6	140.9	148.1
February	134.0	133.6	156.4	139.6	133.8	150.1	145.5	134.5	136.3	142.0	132.1	143.6	140.9	148.4
March	133.9	133.2	156.0	141.0	135.0	150.1	145.6	134.5	137.2	141.9	132.0	143.6	140.9	147.3
April	133.8	133.2	156.0	141.5	135.0	150.4	145.8	135.5	137.2	142.2	131.7	143.7	141.0	148.2
May	133.0	130.4	153.7	141.6	135.3	150.2	145.8	135.3	137.6	142.3	130.6	143.1	140.3	150.0
June	132.5	129.3	151.8	141.9	135.6	150.5	145.8	135.6	137.4	142.4	129.9	142.7	140.0	150.9
July	132.7	130.1	152.0	142.0	135.6	150.2	145.8	135.2	136.6	142.6	130.2	143.4	140.7	151.3
August	132.2	128.4	152.4	141.6	135.3	149.8	145.8	135.3	136.6	142.8	129.6	144.0	141.2	151.1
September	131.8	127.0	150.3	144.7	135.1	150.0	145.8	135.3	136.5	144.2	128.8	143.6	140.8	151.9
October	135.4	135.4	160.1	145.0	134.6	150.2	145.8	134.5	138.0	144.6	133.7	143.3	140.5	153.0
November	135.4	135.6	159.3	145.0	135.3	150.5	145.8	134.3	138.1	144.4	133.6	143.3	140.5	154.0
December	134.9	134.1	158.1	145.3	135.3	150.8	145.8	135.2	137.4	143.7	132.9	143.4	140.6	153.1

Note: Producer prices (1982=100, except as noted, not seasonally adjusted). Consumer prices (1982-84=100, seasonally adjusted).

Transportation Equipment—Employment, Hours, and Earnings

Year and month	Employment (thousands, seasonally adjusted)					Production workers							
	Total payroll employees			Production workers		Average weekly hours (seasonally adjusted)		Aggregate weekly hours index (1982=100), seasonally adjusted		Average earnings (dollars, not seasonally adjusted)			
										Hourly		Weekly	
	Total transportation equipment	Motor vehicles and equipment	Aircraft and parts	Total transportation equipment	Motor vehicles and equipment	Total transportation equipment	Motor vehicles and equipment	Total transportation equipment	Motor vehicles and equipment	Total transportation equipment	Motor vehicles and equipment	Total transportation equipment	Motor vehicles and equipment
1970	1,833	799	644	1,223	605	40.3	40.3	114.1	117.7	4.06	4.22	163.62	170.07
1971	1,743	849	509	1,196	655	40.7	41.2	112.6	130.3	4.45	4.72	181.12	194.46
1972	1,777	875	481	1,226	676	41.7	43.0	118.4	140.5	4.81	5.13	200.58	220.59
1973	1,915	977	510	1,324	755	42.1	43.5	129.1	158.5	5.15	5.46	216.82	237.51
1974	1,853	908	524	1,256	688	40.5	40.6	117.9	134.9	5.54	5.87	224.37	238.32
1975	1,700	792	499	1,142	602	40.4	40.3	106.8	117.3	6.07	6.44	245.23	259.53
1976	1,785	881	473	1,223	682	41.7	42.9	117.9	141.2	6.62	7.09	276.05	304.16
1977	1,857	947	467	1,277	735	42.5	44.0	125.6	156.0	7.29	7.85	309.83	345.40
1978	1,987	1,005	511	1,370	782	42.2	43.3	133.6	163.3	7.91	8.50	333.80	368.05
1979	2,059	990	593	1,409	764	41.1	41.1	134.1	151.8	8.53	9.06	350.58	372.37
1980	1,881	789	633	1,220	575	40.6	40.0	114.6	111.0	9.35	9.85	379.61	394.00
1981	1,879	789	626	1,207	586	40.9	40.9	114.2	115.7	10.39	11.02	424.95	450.72
1982	1,718	699	584	1,068	512	40.5	40.5	100.0	100.0	11.11	11.62	449.96	470.61
1983	1,730	754	562	1,085	568	42.1	43.3	105.7	118.9	11.67	12.14	491.31	525.66
1984	1,883	862	575	1,203	664	42.7	43.8	118.9	140.2	12.20	12.73	520.94	557.57
1985	1,960	883	616	1,244	685	42.6	43.5	122.7	143.6	12.71	13.39	541.45	582.47
1986	2,003	872	656	1,258	670	42.3	42.6	123.3	137.7	12.81	13.45	541.86	572.97
1987	2,028	866	678	1,278	673	42.0	42.2	124.3	137.2	12.94	13.53	543.48	570.97
1988	2,036	856	684	1,273	667	42.7	43.5	125.8	140.0	13.29	13.99	567.48	608.57
1989	2,052	859	711	1,278	664	42.4	43.1	125.3	138.0	13.67	14.25	579.61	614.18
1990	1,989	812	712	1,224	617	42.0	42.4	119.1	126.2	14.08	14.56	591.36	617.34
1991	1,890	789	669	1,169	602	41.9	42.3	113.3	122.9	14.75	15.23	618.03	644.23
1992	1,830	813	612	1,147	622	41.8	42.4	110.9	127.3	15.20	15.45	635.36	655.08
1993	1,756	837	542	1,120	642	43.0	44.3	111.4	137.4	15.80	16.10	679.40	713.23
1994	1,761	909	482	1,154	704	44.3	46.0	118.5	156.2	16.51	17.02	731.39	782.92
1995	1,790	971	451	1,200	761	43.8	44.9	121.6	164.9	16.74	17.34	733.21	778.57
1996	1,785	967	458	1,210	764	44.0	44.9	123.1	165.5	17.19	17.74	756.36	796.53
1997	1,845	986	501	1,256	779	44.5	45.0	129.2	169.2	17.55	18.04	780.98	811.80
1998	1,884	990	524	1,258	760	43.4	43.5	126.4	159.7	17.53	17.86	760.80	776.91
1995:													
January	1,800	961	464	1,200	750	44.5	46.1	123.6	166.9	16.68	17.22	738.92	786.95
February	1,802	964	463	1,205	756	44.4	45.8	123.8	167.1	16.78	17.36	746.71	796.82
March	1,805	970	462	1,209	760	44.4	45.6	124.2	167.3	16.75	17.35	747.05	798.10
April	1,806	974	461	1,211	763	43.9	45.0	123.0	165.7	16.56	17.13	698.83	736.59
May	1,803	974	459	1,209	763	43.4	44.2	121.4	162.8	16.65	17.23	729.27	773.63
June	1,795	970	456	1,204	760	43.7	44.6	121.8	163.6	16.71	17.27	733.57	775.42
July	1,794	977	450	1,204	764	43.7	44.5	121.8	164.1	16.72	17.27	705.58	733.98
August	1,792	976	450	1,207	766	43.6	44.5	121.8	164.5	16.66	17.17	724.71	760.63
September	1,790	974	449	1,206	764	43.6	44.7	121.7	164.8	16.95	17.55	752.58	798.53
October	1,765	975	424	1,181	767	43.6	44.7	119.2	165.5	16.74	17.47	731.54	782.66
November	1,750	966	420	1,164	756	43.9	45.1	118.3	164.6	16.79	17.51	743.80	794.95
December	1,782	972	449	1,204	768	42.8	44.1	119.3	163.5	16.88	17.55	741.03	798.53
1996:													
January	1,774	965	450	1,201	764	42.4	43.7	117.9	161.1	16.88	17.42	714.02	756.03
February	1,779	967	451	1,203	766	43.2	44.0	120.3	162.7	16.95	17.47	733.94	770.43
March	1,745	933	451	1,173	734	42.1	41.9	114.3	148.4	16.64	17.04	703.87	720.79
April	1,784	969	453	1,209	766	44.1	45.3	123.4	167.5	17.22	17.89	757.68	812.21
May	1,786	971	455	1,210	767	44.2	45.4	123.8	168.1	17.19	17.84	764.96	818.86
June	1,787	976	451	1,214	771	44.4	45.5	124.8	169.3	17.22	17.83	766.29	814.83
July	1,786	970	455	1,212	766	44.4	45.7	124.5	169.0	17.28	17.88	737.86	775.99
August	1,791	974	456	1,217	769	44.5	45.7	125.3	169.6	17.27	17.78	765.06	808.99
September	1,791	973	459	1,216	769	44.6	45.6	125.5	169.2	17.43	18.03	786.09	832.99
October	1,792	967	467	1,218	763	44.0	44.8	124.0	165.0	17.23	17.71	761.57	795.18
November	1,797	967	472	1,217	762	44.1	44.7	124.2	164.4	17.32	17.83	770.74	804.13
December	1,804	971	475	1,225	766	44.3	44.8	125.6	165.6	17.55	18.09	800.28	841.19
1997:													
January	1,812	976	479	1,232	771	44.8	45.9	127.7	170.8	17.43	17.99	777.38	818.55
February	1,816	976	483	1,233	769	44.5	45.1	127.0	167.4	17.36	17.85	769.05	801.47
March	1,824	981	486	1,237	772	44.7	45.4	128.0	169.2	17.48	17.98	786.60	823.48
April	1,822	973	491	1,234	763	44.8	45.3	128.0	166.8	17.44	17.97	779.57	815.84
May	1,826	974	495	1,241	768	44.4	44.9	127.5	166.4	17.43	17.93	779.12	815.82
June	1,836	979	500	1,247	774	44.5	45.2	128.4	168.9	17.41	17.87	774.75	807.72
July	1,846	984	504	1,256	781	44.3	44.6	128.8	168.1	17.19	17.49	728.86	736.33
August	1,866	999	508	1,276	796	44.5	45.0	131.4	172.9	17.42	17.80	771.71	795.66
September	1,857	989	510	1,270	786	43.9	44.0	129.0	166.9	17.55	17.98	777.47	801.91
October	1,864	990	513	1,274	785	44.2	44.7	130.3	169.4	17.86	18.42	794.77	828.90
November	1,886	1,005	517	1,285	795	44.0	44.3	130.9	170.0	17.91	18.47	797.00	827.46
December	1,886	1,002	520	1,284	790	44.2	44.4	131.4	169.3	18.05	18.59	823.08	860.72
1998:													
January	1,891	1,002	522	1,284	787	44.0	44.1	130.8	167.5	17.72	18.17	776.14	794.03
February	1,898	1,006	525	1,288	789	43.6	43.5	130.0	165.7	17.74	18.23	771.69	793.01
March	1,898	1,003	525	1,285	783	43.5	43.5	129.4	164.4	17.88	18.42	781.36	808.64
April	1,901	1,005	526	1,283	781	42.9	42.9	127.4	161.7	17.67	18.26	731.54	752.31
May	1,897	1,001	525	1,274	774	43.3	43.3	127.7	161.8	17.61	18.07	769.56	796.89
June	1,891	994	526	1,266	767	42.9	42.7	125.7	158.1	17.41	17.75	746.89	757.93
July	1,788	887	526	1,150	648	43.0	42.5	114.5	132.9	16.86	16.79	691.26	664.88
August	1,894	997	526	1,257	758	43.0	43.0	125.1	157.3	17.29	17.52	740.01	744.60
September	1,891	996	525	1,255	759	43.8	44.3	127.2	162.3	17.49	17.77	757.32	778.33
October	1,892	998	523	1,258	760	43.9	44.1	127.8	161.8	17.46	17.63	771.73	784.54
November	1,887	996	520	1,250	757	44.1	44.6	127.6	163.0	17.52	17.68	781.39	799.14
December	1,882	994	518	1,247	755	44.1	44.9	127.3	163.6	17.56	17.73	802.49	829.76

Instruments and Related Products—Production, Capacity Utilization, Shipments, Inventories, Prices, Employment, Hours, and Earnings

Year and month	Industrial production (1992=100, seasonally adjusted)			Capacity utilization (output as a percent of capacity, seasonally adjusted)	Manufacturers' shipments, inventories, and orders (millions of dollars, seasonally adjusted)		Producer prices (1984=100, not seasonally adjusted)	Employment (thousands)		Production workers			
	Total	Scientific and medical			Shipments	Inventories (book value, end of period)		Total payroll employees (seasonally adjusted)	Production workers (not seasonally adjusted)	Average weekly hours, seasonally adjusted	Aggregate weekly hours index (1982=100, seasonally adjusted)	Average earnings (dollars, not seasonally adjusted)	
		Total	Medical									Hourly	Weekly
1970	36.2	32.2	23.6	77.4	18,367	4,196	.....	804	.....	.....	.....	.....	.....
1971	37.9	33.3	26.0	76.3	18,613	4,201	.....	753	.....	.....	.....	.....	.....
1972	42.5	36.6	27.9	81.4	21,043	4,435	.....	786	.....	.....	.....	.....	.....
1973	48.5	41.6	30.0	87.6	23,627	5,233	.....	851	.....	.....	.....	.....	.....
1974	51.4	43.5	30.6	86.5	27,454	6,486	.....	885	.....	.....	.....	.....	.....
1975	48.9	43.0	32.9	77.1	29,547	6,547	.....	804	.....	.....	.....	.....	.....
1976	53.7	46.1	34.5	80.5	33,238	7,214	.....	840	.....	.....	.....	.....	.....
1977	60.1	52.6	36.3	86.1	38,803	8,185	.....	895	.....	.....	.....	.....	.....
1978	66.2	57.2	38.5	89.5	44,655	9,682	.....	952	.....	.....	.....	.....	.....
1979	71.7	62.5	41.3	90.6	50,702	11,415	.....	1,006	.....	.....	.....	.....	.....
1980	73.6	67.9	42.4	87.2	59,825	13,376	.....	1,022	.....	.....	.....	.....	.....
1981	75.4	69.8	46.0	84.8	66,613	14,760	.....	1,041	.....	.....	.....	.....	.....
1982	76.3	72.2	52.3	81.7	74,918	17,038	.....	1,013	.....	.....	.....	.....	.....
1983	77.7	72.6	53.2	79.7	79,637	17,769	.....	990	.....	.....	.....	.....	.....
1984	86.0	80.8	57.8	84.6	89,398	20,206	.....	1,040	.....	.....	.....	.....	.....
1985	89.3	84.3	62.0	83.6	96,207	21,569	101.0	1,045	.....	.....	.....	.....	.....
1986	88.8	85.7	64.2	79.1	100,798	22,461	102.0	1,018	.....	.....	.....	.....	.....
1987	93.8	92.9	72.3	80.2	107,325	23,692	105.0	1,011	.....	.....	.....	.....	.....
1988	97.2	95.4	76.3	80.8	116,009	25,346	107.0	1,031	508	41.4	89.9	10.60	438.84
1989	98.2	96.2	79.0	79.8	121,523	26,541	110.8	1,026	509	41.1	89.6	10.83	445.11
1990	98.4	99.2	87.8	78.5	127,978	26,552	114.6	1,006	499	41.1	87.6	11.29	464.02
1991	99.8	99.8	94.7	78.7	132,836	25,778	116.8	974	479	41.0	84.0	11.64	477.24
1992	100.0	100.0	100.0	77.4	134,941	24,685	118.7	929	457	41.1	80.2	11.89	488.68
1993	100.8	99.8	104.7	77.0	137,387	23,211	120.8	896	438	41.1	77.0	12.23	502.65
1994	99.8	98.5	102.5	75.4	138,400	22,965	122.1	861	422	41.7	75.2	12.47	520.00
1995	103.6	104.0	105.7	76.6	144,719	24,990	124.0	843	417	41.4	73.7	12.71	526.19
1996	107.7	108.4	115.3	78.6	151,017	25,266	125.1	855	423	41.7	75.4	13.13	547.52
1997	110.3	110.6	119.2	80.0	162,981	25,903	125.6	866	427	42.0	76.7	13.52	567.84
1998	113.0	114.0	123.6	80.5	168,952	26,515	126.0	868	432	41.3	76.4	13.81	570.35
1995:													
January	101.8	101.7	104.0	76.2	12,116	22,851	122.9	843	415	41.6	73.8	12.53	525.01
February	101.3	101.3	104.2	75.6	11,993	23,068	123.4	843	415	41.4	73.5	12.62	523.73
March	102.1	102.3	105.3	76.1	12,047	23,147	123.4	840	414	41.5	73.5	12.62	526.25
April	102.9	103.2	105.8	76.5	11,777	23,286	123.6	840	415	41.4	73.5	12.67	513.14
May	102.3	102.7	102.3	75.9	12,173	23,264	123.7	840	414	41.3	73.3	12.65	521.18
June	103.8	104.4	106.0	76.8	11,903	23,690	123.9	845	417	41.4	73.8	12.68	523.68
July	103.4	103.7	102.9	76.4	11,576	23,806	124.2	845	415	41.4	73.8	12.76	520.61
August	105.0	105.9	108.0	77.4	12,306	23,967	124.2	845	418	41.5	74.2	12.70	523.24
September	105.2	105.8	106.6	77.3	12,025	24,216	124.3	845	418	41.4	74.0	12.81	530.33
October	105.0	105.6	105.6	77.0	12,032	24,502	125.3	845	419	41.5	74.3	12.76	528.26
November	105.9	106.7	110.4	77.5	12,339	24,812	125.2	845	419	41.4	74.2	12.83	536.29
December	104.5	105.1	107.4	76.3	12,524	24,990	124.4	846	419	41.3	74.0	12.89	543.96
1996:													
January	105.6	106.3	112.5	77.0	12,297	25,083	125.1	848	419	40.2	72.0	13.00	525.20
February	107.8	108.9	116.3	78.6	12,396	25,203	125.3	850	420	41.7	74.9	12.94	540.89
March	108.0	109.3	115.3	78.8	12,360	25,331	125.2	853	422	41.7	75.1	12.96	543.02
April	107.5	108.3	114.8	78.4	12,270	25,422	125.1	853	422	41.6	75.1	13.03	538.14
May	107.5	108.3	114.9	78.5	12,759	25,449	125.1	856	424	41.7	75.6	13.03	540.75
June	108.2	109.2	116.9	79.0	12,543	25,212	124.9	859	425	42.0	76.0	13.08	549.36
July	107.2	107.9	114.1	78.3	12,688	25,538	125.2	855	419	41.6	74.9	13.17	539.97
August	107.5	108.3	114.2	78.5	12,797	25,632	125.0	858	424	41.7	75.6	13.15	547.04
September	107.8	108.4	115.8	78.7	12,482	25,624	125.0	857	424	41.9	76.0	13.29	558.18
October	108.0	108.6	116.3	78.9	12,616	25,845	125.1	858	426	41.8	76.1	13.24	552.11
November	108.2	108.7	117.0	79.1	13,006	25,373	124.7	858	425	41.9	76.3	13.30	561.26
December	108.6	109.0	115.5	79.4	12,852	25,266	125.2	860	427	42.1	76.9	13.36	574.48
1997:													
January	107.7	108.2	115.7	78.7	12,827	25,483	125.5	858	425	41.7	75.8	13.35	556.70
February	109.1	109.7	118.9	79.6	13,323	25,493	125.4	859	426	41.9	76.1	13.35	560.70
March	108.6	108.8	115.6	79.1	13,242	25,386	125.5	859	426	42.0	76.3	13.42	566.32
April	108.7	109.2	117.1	79.1	13,414	25,566	125.7	861	425	42.0	76.3	13.43	560.03
May	109.8	110.2	118.1	79.8	13,081	25,578	125.7	862	426	42.0	76.3	13.48	562.12
June	110.3	110.5	118.4	80.0	13,642	25,811	125.3	868	429	41.9	76.5	13.52	566.49
July	110.4	110.6	119.2	80.1	13,777	25,959	125.7	868	425	41.8	76.3	13.51	556.61
August	111.4	111.5	120.6	80.6	13,473	26,026	125.8	870	427	42.1	76.9	13.50	568.35
September	111.2	111.2	120.2	80.4	14,172	25,299	125.8	869	428	42.0	76.9	13.65	574.67
October	112.5	112.9	124.1	81.2	14,101	25,909	125.7	871	428	42.0	76.9	13.62	570.68
November	111.8	112.2	120.1	80.6	13,712	26,180	125.8	873	429	42.2	77.6	13.69	583.19
December	112.0	112.1	121.6	80.7	14,100	25,903	125.8	875	431	42.0	77.4	13.71	588.16
1998:													
January	111.5	111.7	117.8	80.2	13,760	26,047	125.6	876	433	41.9	77.8	13.67	572.77
February	112.5	112.7	119.9	80.7	14,025	26,113	125.9	873	434	41.9	77.6	13.71	577.19
March	112.8	113.1	121.3	80.8	14,137	26,363	126.1	876	436	41.5	77.2	13.76	573.79
April	113.0	113.5	121.3	80.8	13,836	26,530	126.3	875	436	41.5	77.2	13.78	560.85
May	113.8	114.8	124.8	81.1	13,787	26,797	126.2	873	435	41.4	77.0	13.78	569.11
June	112.4	113.3	121.1	80.0	14,209	26,676	126.2	875	436	41.4	76.8	13.75	569.25
July	112.6	113.8	122.2	80.0	14,042	26,659	125.8	870	432	41.4	76.6	13.78	560.85
August	113.0	114.1	121.6	80.1	13,749	26,651	125.9	867	431	41.3	76.3	13.79	568.15
September	114.2	115.9	126.1	80.8	14,298	26,577	125.9	864	431	41.1	75.7	13.88	563.53
October	114.6	116.5	128.3	80.9	14,040	26,667	125.8	858	429	41.2	75.7	13.86	569.65
November	114.1	115.9	129.5	80.4	14,517	26,679	126.1	854	427	41.1	75.2	13.91	577.27
December	113.9	115.7	129.7	80.1	14,371	26,515	125.9	850	426	41.1	75.0	14.00	588.00

Manufacturing by Industry— Nondurable Goods

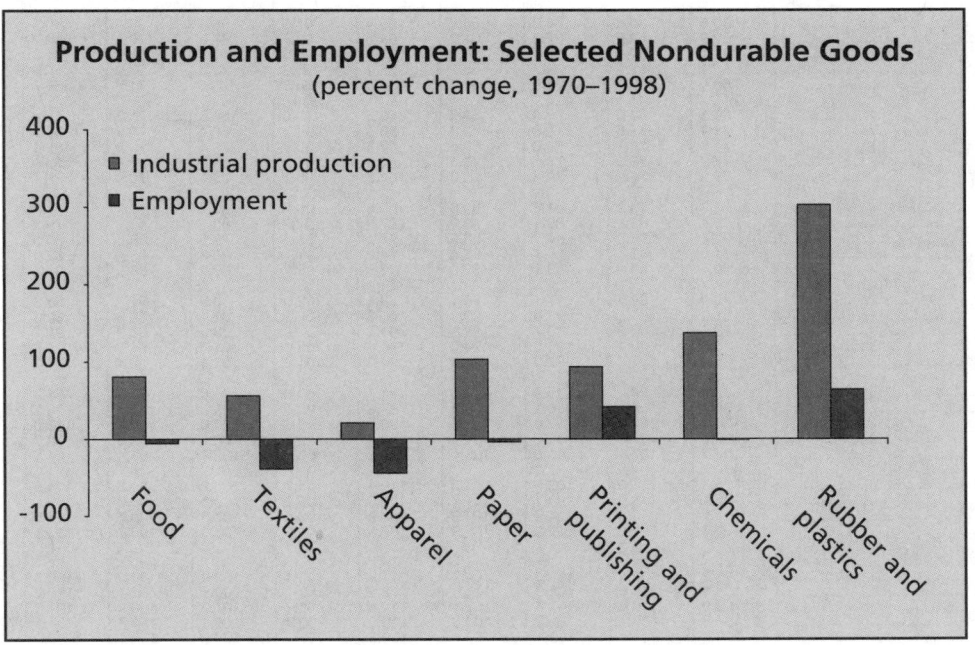

Production and Employment: Selected Nondurable Goods
(percent change, 1970–1998)

- Rubber and plastics products had the most rapid increase in production, rising fourfold from 1970 to 1998. Chemicals was second, growing 136.7 percent. Paper and paper products and printing and publishing followed, doubling and nearly doubling, respectively.

- Leather and leather products (not shown in the above graph) was the only nondurable goods industry to show a drop in production (68 percent) from 1970 to 1998.

- Employment increased in rubber and plastics (63.5 percent) and in printing and publishing (41.8 percent) from 1970 to 1998, but fell in every other nondurable industry. Leather goods (not shown) had the largest drop of all industries in nondurables (74.1 percent), followed by tobacco (50.6 percent, also not shown).

- Food and food products remained the largest industry in nondurables measured by employment, with just under 1,700,000 workers in 1998. Printing and publishing, with over 1,500,000 workers, was the second largest industry.

Food and Food Products—Production, Capacity Utilization, Shipments, and Inventories

(Seasonally adjusted)

Year and month	Industrial production (1992=100)										Capacity utiliza- tion—total foods (output as a percent of capacity)	Manufacturers' shipments and inventories (millions of dollars)	
	Total foods	Meat products	Dairy products	Canned and frozen foods	Grain mill products	Bakery products	Sugar and confec- tionery	Fats and oils	Bev- erages	Coffee and miscella- neous		Ship- ments	Invento- ries (book value, end of period)
1970	60.6	60.5	66.2	58.2	50.4	94.6	66.4	65.8	49.5	56.6	83.6	98 535	8 738
1971	62.5	62.8	67.5	61.2	51.0	93.7	67.8	70.5	52.7	56.2	83.6	103 637	9 258
1972	65.8	67.8	72.3	66.1	53.3	98.0	69.8	66.5	55.2	58.8	85.5	115 054	9 673
1973	67.1	63.9	72.7	68.8	55.1	98.0	72.3	67.0	57.9	63.3	85.0	135 585	11 627
1974	68.0	67.3	74.5	69.3	55.0	96.8	73.7	71.7	59.7	59.4	83.6	161 884	14 625
1975	67.5	64.0	75.0	69.3	56.2	97.5	64.5	70.3	61.4	60.0	80.4	172 054	14 467
1976	71.4	71.8	76.3	72.9	58.9	97.7	68.4	75.3	65.1	65.1	82.4	180 830	15 695
1977	74.6	75.1	78.0	80.5	62.5	98.8	78.4	72.5	69.1	64.6	83.5	192 913	16 329
1978	77.2	75.5	78.1	85.1	62.9	98.2	79.5	78.6	73.0	72.2	83.6	215 989	18 073
1979	77.9	76.2	78.8	83.0	62.8	99.1	79.1	79.6	75.4	75.2	82.0	235 976	19 879
1980	79.7	79.2	81.8	83.6	65.5	96.2	80.7	81.7	77.2	78.3	81.6	256 191	21 710
1981	81.4	81.0	86.8	80.9	67.6	97.7	83.6	83.2	79.3	81.0	81.2	272 140	21 483
1982	82.4	78.8	90.1	83.5	71.6	99.4	79.6	85.6	80.0	80.4	80.2	280 529	23 016
1983	84.6	82.4	94.1	85.4	74.2	97.7	82.9	85.4	82.0	83.1	80.9	289 314	23 609
1984	86.4	83.1	90.1	87.6	77.8	99.7	85.4	85.9	84.4	86.5	81.5	304 584	24 182
1985	88.9	84.4	97.4	88.1	83.5	102.9	83.9	91.7	86.6	86.8	82.2	308 606	24 015
1986	91.2	85.6	98.6	90.9	85.2	106.1	87.1	89.6	89.3	90.2	82.9	318 203	23 884
1987	93.5	87.2	96.7	92.8	91.6	107.3	89.9	90.9	91.7	94.0	84.1	329 725	24 860
1988	94.9	90.1	100.3	94.0	90.8	103.0	91.6	94.7	94.6	96.6	84.4	354 084	27 122
1989	95.9	92.4	97.0	97.8	94.2	101.3	93.1	98.4	94.3	97.0	84.3	380 160	28 459
1990	97.0	93.2	95.9	100.9	97.4	100.6	94.0	99.2	94.9	98.3	83.9	391 728	29 714
1991	98.4	96.1	96.1	104.6	97.6	98.7	95.2	104.4	96.2	100.0	83.4	397 893	30 099
1992	100.0	100.0	100.0	100.0	100.0	100.0	100.0	100.0	100.0	100.0	83.0	406 964	30 996
1993	102.0	101.6	101.0	101.6	103.5	102.3	102.5	98.5	102.0	105.0	83.2	422 220	31 201
1994	103.7	107.4	99.8	103.4	105.2	105.5	102.1	95.4	104.1	101.6	83.3	430 963	32 332
1995	105.8	111.0	103.5	103.3	110.4	105.7	103.2	99.3	105.5	103.0	83.3	446 961	34 527
1996	105.4	112.0	100.1	101.7	101.0	103.5	107.3	98.0	109.7	107.6	81.3	461 297	35 697
1997	108.0	113.8	104.2	102.9	103.9	103.5	107.6	100.7	114.5	111.2	82.0	470 447	37 026
1998	109.6	117.6	104.2	103.9	102.3	104.3	108.9	105.7	117.5	114.0	81.6	490 365	37 299
1995:													
January	105.7	108.6	102.9	104.7	111.0	107.1	103.8	98.6	104.7	103.0	84.2	36 508	32 869
February	104.8	108.6	102.3	105.0	112.4	107.1	100.4	99.1	100.9	100.8	83.2	36 722	32 945
March	105.0	110.4	103.4	102.1	112.1	106.8	101.3	100.3	101.7	102.4	83.3	36 671	33 153
April	105.3	109.4	103.2	103.1	110.2	105.4	106.2	100.6	104.9	100.5	83.4	36 618	33 077
May	106.3	111.1	103.1	106.4	109.5	106.4	104.8	102.1	105.5	102.8	84.0	36 288	33 164
June	107.0	113.0	104.7	101.2	112.5	107.6	105.1	99.5	106.4	106.1	84.4	36 882	33 263
July	106.3	110.5	104.7	104.1	111.1	105.1	105.3	98.6	106.6	103.1	83.7	36 872	33 416
August	106.6	109.1	103.9	106.2	111.4	105.8	102.4	100.4	107.7	103.8	83.7	37 563	33 352
September	106.1	111.6	104.1	102.2	112.5	105.3	100.6	98.4	107.6	102.3	83.2	38 172	33 897
October	106.1	111.4	104.3	101.9	110.6	106.2	102.0	99.3	107.0	104.1	83.1	38 047	34 231
November	105.5	113.8	103.0	100.7	108.2	103.8	101.1	98.1	106.9	104.7	82.4	38 072	34 331
December	104.6	114.1	102.1	101.8	103.2	102.5	105.0	96.8	105.9	102.4	81.5	38 340	34 527
1996:													
January	104.6	112.9	102.1	103.2	100.6	104.3	101.7	96.1	105.7	106.0	81.4	38 360	34 524
February	105.1	115.1	101.4	99.4	102.7	104.2	105.9	95.1	108.5	104.0	81.7	37 868	34 707
March	105.7	112.9	100.7	97.3	101.6	104.7	107.5	95.2	111.3	104.7	82.0	37 723	34 842
April	105.1	114.5	100.5	99.1	103.3	102.3	106.7	98.4	108.5	105.9	81.4	38 237	35 154
May	104.7	112.9	99.3	100.0	100.8	101.2	110.0	98.6	107.5	107.4	81.0	38 332	35 028
June	104.9	111.7	98.2	99.7	100.7	103.0	107.5	98.0	109.8	107.7	81.0	37 639	35 084
July	105.3	111.7	97.8	101.9	101.8	103.9	105.1	100.2	109.2	108.7	81.1	38 669	35 198
August	104.5	111.7	97.6	100.4	98.7	103.9	106.3	98.6	108.4	108.5	80.4	38 721	35 175
September	105.6	109.3	99.5	102.2	99.3	104.7	108.1	96.9	110.4	111.0	81.1	38 601	35 496
October	106.1	111.0	100.1	103.1	99.9	104.6	108.8	99.2	112.2	107.9	81.4	39 372	35 573
November	106.5	110.4	102.1	104.6	100.5	102.4	109.5	98.3	112.1	110.4	81.6	39 312	35 756
December	106.9	110.1	102.2	104.9	101.4	103.1	111.2	101.3	112.9	109.1	81.8	38 524	35 697
1997:													
January	107.1	113.0	100.5	103.0	102.6	103.8	107.9	101.8	112.3	111.6	81.7	38 858	35 422
February	107.4	112.8	103.0	105.6	102.7	104.0	109.7	101.5	111.7	109.6	81.9	38 854	35 737
March	108.7	114.0	104.0	105.0	103.9	103.0	110.1	100.0	116.1	111.7	82.8	39 006	35 866
April	107.6	112.7	103.2	103.8	103.2	103.0	109.3	97.8	113.0	112.6	81.9	39 084	36 038
May	107.7	113.0	104.2	104.0	104.1	102.5	108.0	97.0	113.3	111.8	81.9	39 276	36 097
June	107.6	113.2	105.5	103.4	104.2	102.0	106.4	99.5	113.7	110.8	81.7	38 960	36 248
July	108.7	114.2	106.4	107.0	105.4	105.2	104.5	97.4	113.2	112.0	82.5	39 164	36 136
August	107.9	114.4	105.8	101.9	103.8	102.8	106.7	100.3	114.9	110.9	81.8	39 310	36 179
September	107.6	112.7	106.4	100.9	104.1	102.2	106.4	99.9	115.7	110.1	81.5	38 970	36 331
October	107.5	115.2	104.2	97.4	103.6	103.3	108.1	104.1	115.2	111.1	81.4	39 315	36 742
November	109.1	115.6	104.6	101.5	104.9	105.1	108.4	104.1	118.4	110.3	82.5	39 763	36 940
December	109.0	115.2	103.0	103.8	104.8	105.9	106.2	105.3	116.4	111.9	82.3	40 116	37 026
1998:													
January	110.5	118.0	104.1	107.1	103.5	105.6	111.5	104.8	117.1	114.5	83.3	40 821	37 359
February	110.9	118.2	104.3	104.8	102.9	104.8	112.3	109.5	116.6	112.9	82.7	40 556	37 647
March	109.7	116.5	103.0	106.3	103.3	103.9	109.4	108.0	117.1	114.0	82.4	40 669	37 512
April	110.3	118.0	104.0	107.7	104.2	104.9	111.4	107.1	115.5	113.9	82.5	40 604	37 488
May	110.7	116.0	104.3	105.9	104.3	105.9	111.8	106.6	118.7	115.3	82.7	40 143	37 503
June	109.2	114.2	103.6	105.2	102.9	103.3	110.8	105.1	116.7	113.7	81.3	40 645	37 427
July	109.0	117.1	103.3	104.6	104.2	104.5	109.7	107.0	114.4	111.9	81.0	40 562	37 424
August	107.9	116.9	103.4	99.2	101.6	101.8	110.3	104.3	116.5	111.4	80.0	41 117	37 115
September	107.7	115.8	103.6	99.3	99.0	102.8	108.0	107.2	116.5	112.5	79.6	41 272	37 112
October	109.1	118.8	104.7	99.0	101.1	103.9	107.4	106.2	118.3	115.6	80.5	41 351	37 459
November	111.3	120.6	104.7	103.7	102.2	105.1	107.4	105.4	122.9	116.5	81.8	41 387	37 264
December	111.1	120.7	106.9	107.4	100.6	106.1	105.6	100.8	121.0	115.1	81.6	41 585	37 299

Food and Food Products—Prices, Employment, Hours, and Earnings

Year and month	Producer prices (1982=100, except as noted, not seasonally adjusted)				Consumer prices—Food and beverages (1982-1984 = 100, seasonally adjusted)				Employment (thousands, seasonally adjusted)		Production workers			
	Food and food products industry (December 1984 = 100)	Finished consumer foods	Intermediate materials for food manufacturing	Crude foodstuffs and feedstuffs	Total	Food			Total payroll employees	Production workers	Average weekly hours, seasonally adjusted	Aggregate weekly hours index (1982=100), seasonally adjusted	Average earnings (dollars, not seasonally adjusted)	
						Total	Food at home	Food away from home					Hourly	Weekly
1970	.....	43.8	44.3	45.2	40.1	39.2	39.9	37.5	1 786	1 207	40.5	110.2	3.16	127.98
1971	.....	44.5	45.7	46.1	41.4	40.4	40.9	39.4	1 766	1 203	40.3	109.3	3.38	136.21
1972	.....	46.9	47.0	51.5	43.1	42.1	42.7	41.0	1 745	1 192	40.5	108.7	3.60	145.80
1973	.....	56.5	57.2	72.6	48.8	48.2	49.7	44.2	1 715	1 167	40.4	106.3	3.85	155.54
1974	.....	64.4	82.0	76.4	55.5	55.1	57.1	49.8	1 707	1 164	40.4	106.0	4.19	169.28
1975	.....	69.8	82.1	77.4	60.2	59.8	61.8	54.5	1 658	1 120	40.3	101.8	4.61	185.78
1976	.....	69.6	70.6	76.8	62.1	61.6	63.1	58.2	1 689	1 145	40.5	104.4	4.98	201.69
1977	.....	73.3	71.9	77.5	65.8	65.5	66.8	62.6	1 711	1 161	40.0	104.6	5.37	214.80
1978	.....	79.9	81.0	87.3	72.2	72.0	73.8	68.3	1 724	1 174	39.7	105.1	5.80	230.26
1979	.....	87.3	89.9	100.0	79.9	79.9	81.8	75.9	1 733	1 191	39.9	107.0	6.27	250.17
1980	.....	92.4	103.7	104.6	86.7	86.8	88.4	83.4	1 708	1 175	39.7	105.1	6.85	271.95
1981	.....	97.8	102.1	103.9	93.5	93.6	94.8	90.9	1 671	1 150	39.7	102.8	7.44	295.37
1982	.....	100.0	100.0	100.0	97.3	97.4	98.1	95.8	1 636	1 126	39.4	100.0	7.92	312.05
1983	.....	101.0	101.3	101.8	99.5	99.4	99.1	100.0	1 614	1 114	39.5	99.1	8.19	323.51
1984	.....	105.4	106.3	104.7	103.2	103.2	102.8	104.2	1 611	1 119	39.8	100.3	8.39	333.92
1985	99.0	104.6	101.5	94.8	105.6	105.6	104.3	108.3	1 601	1 117	40.0	100.6	8.57	342.80
1986	100.3	107.3	98.4	93.2	109.1	109.0	107.3	112.5	1 607	1 129	40.0	101.7	8.75	350.00
1987	102.6	109.5	100.8	96.2	113.5	113.5	111.9	117.0	1 617	1 145	40.2	103.7	8.93	358.99
1988	107.1	112.6	106.0	106.1	118.2	118.2	116.6	121.8	1 626	1 155	40.3	105.0	9.12	367.54
1989	112.2	118.7	112.7	111.2	124.9	125.1	124.2	127.4	1 644	1 176	40.7	107.8	9.38	381.77
1990	116.2	124.4	117.9	113.1	132.1	132.4	132.3	133.4	1 661	1 194	40.8	109.7	9.62	392.50
1991	116.5	124.1	115.3	105.5	136.8	136.3	135.8	137.9	1 667	1 205	40.6	110.2	9.90	401.94
1992	116.9	123.3	113.9	105.1	138.7	137.9	136.8	140.7	1 663	1 212	40.6	110.9	10.20	414.12
1993	118.7	125.7	115.6	108.4	141.6	140.9	140.1	143.2	1 680	1 228	40.7	112.6	10.45	425.32
1994	120.1	126.8	118.5	106.5	144.9	144.3	144.1	145.7	1 678	1 231	41.3	114.6	10.66	440.26
1995	121.7	129.0	119.5	105.8	148.9	148.4	148.8	149.0	1 692	1 248	41.1	115.5	10.93	449.22
1996	127.1	133.6	125.3	121.5	153.7	153.3	154.3	152.7	1 692	1 254	41.0	115.9	11.20	459.20
1997	127.9	134.5	123.2	112.2	157.7	157.3	158.1	157.0	1 685	1 252	41.3	116.6	11.48	474.12
1998	126.3	134.3	123.2	103.9	161.1	160.7	161.1	161.1	1 686	1 253	41.7	117.6	11.80	492.06
1995:														
January	120.2	127.9	117.8	102.2	147.2	147.0	147.1	147.4	1 690	1 245	41.5	116.4	10.85	445.94
February	120.8	128.4	118.4	104.1	147.7	147.4	147.6	147.6	1 681	1 237	41.3	115.1	10.82	439.29
March	121.1	128.7	119.0	103.2	147.5	147.1	146.8	148.1	1 680	1 235	41.2	114.7	10.87	441.32
April	120.5	128.7	117.2	101.8	148.5	148.1	148.3	148.3	1 683	1 238	41.0	114.4	10.92	434.62
May	120.3	128.0	116.5	99.6	148.7	148.4	148.7	148.6	1 684	1 240	41.1	114.8	10.90	444.72
June	120.4	127.4	117.3	102.1	148.8	148.5	148.7	148.8	1 695	1 256	41.2	116.6	10.92	449.90
July	121.4	128.5	119.5	104.6	149.0	148.7	148.8	149.1	1 694	1 248	41.3	116.1	10.92	449.90
August	122.0	128.8	120.0	104.8	149.2	148.9	149.0	149.4	1 696	1 250	41.3	116.3	10.89	454.11
September	122.4	130.1	120.5	108.8	149.6	149.4	149.6	149.6	1 701	1 256	41.2	116.6	10.97	461.84
October	123.2	129.9	122.2	109.6	150.1	149.8	150.1	150.0	1 702	1 257	40.9	115.9	10.92	452.09
November	123.8	131.1	122.8	114.2	150.1	149.8	150.0	150.2	1 702	1 258	40.8	115.7	11.05	457.47
December	124.2	131.0	122.9	114.7	150.4	150.2	150.4	150.4	1 701	1 257	40.5	114.7	11.17	460.20
1996:														
January	124.2	130.7	120.7	114.7	150.8	150.5	150.8	150.6	1 701	1 259	39.6	112.3	11.08	435.44
February	124.4	130.7	121.0	115.0	151.3	150.8	151.1	150.9	1 703	1 260	41.1	116.7	11.03	445.61
March	124.3	132.0	120.6	116.2	151.7	151.3	151.7	151.2	1 707	1 261	41.1	116.8	11.10	449.55
April	124.6	131.2	121.6	119.6	152.4	151.9	152.5	151.6	1 697	1 256	41.1	116.3	11.19	449.84
May	126.3	131.5	126.6	127.7	152.5	152.2	152.6	152.0	1 696	1 256	41.0	116.0	11.18	455.03
June	127.6	133.6	128.2	129.0	153.4	153.2	154.1	152.3	1 687	1 250	41.1	115.8	11.22	458.90
July	128.3	133.9	128.5	130.9	154.0	153.8	154.8	152.8	1 687	1 250	40.9	115.2	11.25	459.00
August	129.7	135.3	129.4	129.5	154.4	154.2	155.3	153.1	1 686	1 249	40.9	115.1	11.16	463.14
September	129.7	135.6	129.2	124.9	155.1	154.9	156.1	153.5	1 686	1 249	41.1	115.7	11.19	472.22
October	129.8	136.6	129.2	119.6	155.9	155.8	157.1	154.2	1 687	1 252	41.2	116.2	11.16	464.26
November	128.5	136.1	124.8	117.7	156.5	156.3	157.7	154.7	1 686	1 252	41.2	116.2	11.38	475.68
December	128.2	135.5	123.8	113.6	156.7	156.5	157.7	155.0	1 686	1 254	41.2	116.4	11.45	480.90
1997:														
January	127.4	134.1	122.9	112.2	156.3	156.1	156.9	155.3	1 689	1 255	41.0	116.0	11.41	464.39
February	127.1	133.8	122.9	111.0	156.9	156.7	157.7	155.6	1 687	1 252	41.3	116.5	11.32	460.72
March	128.1	135.2	124.1	114.1	156.8	156.5	157.2	156.0	1 693	1 254	41.3	116.7	11.40	463.98
April	128.3	134.3	123.8	116.7	156.9	156.6	157.1	156.2	1 688	1 255	41.3	116.8	11.45	462.58
May	128.9	135.2	123.9	117.4	157.2	156.8	157.6	156.3	1 685	1 250	41.3	116.3	11.47	470.27
June	128.3	134.0	122.7	111.3	157.4	157.1	157.8	156.6	1 685	1 251	41.0	115.6	11.44	466.75
July	128.0	134.0	122.3	112.0	157.8	157.5	158.1	157.1	1 683	1 250	41.2	116.1	11.52	473.47
August	128.6	134.9	122.9	111.6	158.3	158.0	158.8	157.4	1 675	1 243	41.3	115.7	11.51	481.12
September	127.9	134.7	123.1	110.6	158.6	158.3	158.9	157.8	1 682	1 250	41.2	116.1	11.51	486.87
October	127.5	135.1	122.4	110.1	158.8	158.5	159.1	158.2	1 684	1 250	41.4	116.6	11.45	478.61
November	127.5	134.6	124.2	110.4	159.1	158.9	159.4	158.6	1 686	1 252	41.5	117.1	11.59	487.94
December	127.1	134.4	123.2	109.0	159.3	159.0	159.3	159.0	1 686	1 252	41.6	117.4	11.71	496.50
1998:														
January	125.8	133.1	119.9	105.5	159.9	159.6	160.1	159.2	1 685	1 252	41.7	117.6	11.66	482.72
February	126.0	133.6	121.6	105.1	159.8	159.5	159.9	159.6	1 684	1 253	41.5	117.2	11.63	475.67
March	125.5	133.4	121.0	106.3	159.8	159.5	159.7	159.9	1 685	1 252	41.5	117.1	11.69	478.12
April	125.5	133.8	121.7	105.8	159.9	159.6	159.7	160.2	1 686	1 253	41.5	117.2	11.74	474.30
May	125.9	133.6	123.7	106.2	160.7	160.4	160.7	160.6	1 687	1 255	41.7	117.9	11.78	488.87
June	126.4	133.8	123.0	106.2	160.7	160.4	160.6	160.7	1 686	1 254	41.7	117.8	11.76	488.04
July	126.6	134.7	122.9	103.7	161.1	160.9	161.1	161.1	1 684	1 252	41.8	117.9	11.80	490.88
August	127.4	135.2	124.6	103.3	161.6	161.3	161.6	161.5	1 675	1 240	41.7	116.5	11.76	493.92
September	127.1	135.4	125.1	101.3	161.6	161.4	161.3	162.1	1 687	1 253	41.7	117.7	11.95	507.88
October	126.6	135.5	125.4	103.7	162.4	162.2	162.5	162.3	1 685	1 252	41.6	117.4	11.82	496.44
November	126.6	134.9	125.5	102.4	162.7	162.4	162.7	162.6	1 690	1 257	41.7	118.1	11.95	506.68
December	126.1	134.5	124.0	97.0	162.8	162.5	162.7	163.0	1 693	1 261	42.0	119.3	12.02	514.46

Tobacco Products—Production, Shipments, Inventories, Prices, Employment, Hours, and Earnings

Year and month	Industrial production (1992=100), seasonally adjusted	Manufacturers' shipments and inventories (millions of dollars, seasonally adjusted)		Producer prices (not seasonally adjusted)			Employment (thousands, seasonally adjusted)		Production workers			
		Shipments	Inventories (book value, end of period)	Tobacco manufactures (December 1984 = 100)	Cigarette manufacture (December 1982= 100)	Leaf tobacco (1982 =100)	Total payroll employees	Production workers	Average weekly hours, not seasonally adjusted	Aggregate weekly hours index (1982 =100) seasonally adjusted	Average earnings (dollars, not seasonally adjusted)	
											Hourly	Weekly
1970	94.3	5 350	2 052	.....	28.1	40.3	83	69	37.8	129.2	2.91	110.00
1971	93.1	5 528	2 099	.....	28.8	41.9	77	63	37.8	118.7	3.16	119.45
1972	96.6	5 919	2 355	.....	29.0	45.7	75	62	37.6	115.9	3.47	130.47
1973	101.7	6 341	2 426	.....	30.2	47.7	78	65	38.6	124.0	3.76	145.14
1974	99.4	7 139	3 024	.....	33.1	54.7	77	64	38.3	120.9	4.12	157.80
1975	101.7	8 058	3 290	.....	37.4	.....	76	62	38.2	118.1	4.55	173.81
1976	106.8	8 786	3 416	.....	41.0	60.6	77	64	37.5	118.2	4.98	186.75
1977	102.8	9 051	3 511	.....	45.5	65.1	71	57	37.8	106.8	5.54	209.41
1978	107.4	9 951	3 669	.....	50.2	70.8	71	56	38.1	106.1	6.13	233.55
1979	106.9	10 602	3 517	.....	55.2	76.7	70	56	38.0	104.4	6.67	253.46
1980	108.5	12 194	3 721	.....	62.5	82.1	69	54	38.1	101.2	7.74	294.89
1981	109.9	13 130	4 436	.....	68.2	91.2	70	55	38.8	105.1	8.88	344.54
1982	106.2	16 061	6 873	.....	83.1	100.0	69	53	37.8	100.0	9.79	370.06
1983	101.6	16 268	6 746	.....	93.5	101.3	68	52	37.4	96.3	10.38	388.21
1984	101.7	17 473	6 533	.....	102.3	101.5	64	49	38.9	93.5	11.22	436.46
1985	101.8	18 559	5 943	106.6	110.7	101.2	64	48	37.2	88.4	11.96	444.91
1986	100.3	19 146	5 449	115.5	120.9	89.8	59	44	37.4	81.6	12.88	481.71
1987	104.7	20 757	5 331	126.5	133.5	85.8	55	42	39.0	80.1	14.07	548.73
1988	106.5	23 809	5 286	141.8	150.8	87.2	54	41	39.8	80.1	14.67	583.87
1989	105.4	25 875	5 570	161.4	173.1	93.8	50	37	38.6	70.6	15.31	590.97
1990	105.4	29 856	5 974	183.2	197.6	95.8	49	36	39.2	70.6	16.23	636.22
1991	98.9	31 943	6 342	207.5	225.0	101.1	49	36	39.1	70.2	16.77	655.71
1992	100.0	35 198	6 668	230.2	250.5	101.0	48	36	38.6	68.2	16.92	653.11
1993	84.1	28 383	6 322	218.0	235.2	100.3	44	33	37.4	60.7	16.89	631.69
1994	104.4	30 021	5 782	187.8	198.9	100.2	43	33	39.3	64.1	19.07	749.45
1995	111.8	32 984	5 775	193.2	204.3	102.5	42	32	39.6	62.8	19.41	768.64
1996	113.5	34 482	5 904	199.1	210.5	105.1	41	32	40.0	63.3	19.35	774.00
1997	110.9	38 693	5 797	210.8	223.3	.....	41	32	38.9	61.4	19.24	748.44
1998	106.0	41 625	5 867	243.1	260.4	105.1	41	32	38.3	59.8	18.55	710.47
1995:												
January	108.7	2 690	5 691	188.1	198.5	110.5	43	33	39.1	65.0	18.60	727.26
February	107.8	2 765	5 749	188.7	199.2	112.5	42	32	38.5	62.1	19.53	751.91
March	111.1	2 604	5 617	190.6	201.4	100.2	41	32	38.1	61.3	20.30	773.43
April	113.0	2 884	5 580	190.7	201.5	90.0	42	32	38.4	63.5	19.98	767.23
May	111.4	2 878	5 530	195.3	206.7	.....	42	32	40.0	63.7	20.97	838.80
June	118.7	2 700	5 559	195.3	206.7	.....	42	32	41.6	64.5	21.85	908.96
July	120.6	2 744	5 621	195.2	206.6	103.5	42	32	39.3	64.3	21.71	853.20
August	110.7	2 690	5 742	195.0	206.2	102.0	43	33	40.4	65.7	18.49	747.00
September	106.7	2 673	5 944	195.0	206.1	107.6	43	32	40.0	60.9	17.57	702.80
October	108.8	2 792	5 800	195.0	206.1	106.7	42	32	40.4	62.0	18.09	730.84
November	111.1	2 897	5 686	195.0	206.1	108.5	41	31	40.6	61.0	19.48	790.89
December	113.3	2 767	5 775	195.0	206.0	108.5	42	32	39.1	60.7	17.71	692.46
1996:												
January	108.9	2 799	5 776	195.1	205.9	111.4	41	32	35.8	57.9	18.38	658.00
February	113.0	2 788	5 725	195.0	205.9	118.8	42	32	38.7	62.5	18.13	701.63
March	117.3	2 807	5 716	195.1	205.9	102.6	41	32	39.4	63.5	19.34	762.00
April	113.8	2 887	5 612	195.1	205.9	94.4	42	32	39.3	63.4	20.40	801.72
May	112.3	2 741	5 604	201.1	213.0	.....	41	32	39.9	63.2	21.06	840.29
June	115.3	2 846	5 616	201.0	212.8	.....	42	32	41.0	63.4	21.40	877.40
July	115.0	2 971	5 502	201.1	212.7	94.1	41	32	38.6	63.2	20.98	809.83
August	114.2	2 982	5 608	201.4	212.9	102.6	40	31	40.0	61.3	20.24	809.60
September	118.7	2 854	5 713	201.0	212.8	110.5	42	32	42.0	64.3	18.39	772.38
October	110.3	2 966	5 783	201.1	212.6	112.6	42	32	41.2	63.1	17.75	731.30
November	112.7	2 823	5 871	201.1	212.7	112.9	42	33	41.2	65.7	18.65	768.38
December	110.0	3 027	5 904	201.2	212.6	113.2	42	33	41.9	66.9	18.68	782.69
1997:												
January	117.7	3 397	5 829	201.4	212.4	118.2	42	32	39.2	63.1	18.58	728.34
February	112.8	2 870	5 796	201.2	212.1	120.8	42	32	39.1	64.5	18.59	726.87
March	120.5	3 146	5 770	203.3	214.5	111.7	42	32	39.1	63.1	19.46	760.89
April	109.2	3 116	5 835	208.4	220.6	.....	41	31	38.4	59.9	20.34	781.06
May	107.0	3 167	5 836	209.2	221.4	.....	41	32	38.7	61.2	20.75	803.03
June	105.3	3 215	5 790	209.6	221.8	.....	41	32	39.2	60.5	21.12	827.90
July	108.1	3 225	5 814	209.4	221.6	93.2	42	32	35.3	57.9	20.93	738.83
August	108.2	3 194	5 779	209.4	221.5	94.1	41	31	37.8	58.0	19.79	748.06
September	112.1	3 358	5 680	219.4	233.7	103.2	41	32	39.4	60.4	18.26	719.44
October	112.0	3 346	5 798	219.4	233.6	105.5	41	32	39.6	61.8	18.00	712.80
November	112.1	3 399	5 890	219.3	233.4	108.5	42	32	39.5	62.1	17.80	703.10
December	106.4	3 252	5 797	219.3	233.2	112.9	41	32	40.1	62.1	18.63	747.06
1998:												
January	110.1	3 260	5 962	219.6	233.1	112.9	40	32	37.8	61.0	18.36	694.01
February	112.7	3 474	5 864	223.7	237.9	112.9	41	32	37.4	61.7	18.12	677.69
March	105.3	3 336	5 882	223.7	237.7	106.7	42	33	37.1	61.6	18.42	683.38
April	109.8	3 393	5 772	231.0	246.2	99.6	42	33	37.0	62.5	18.84	697.08
May	111.5	3 421	5 779	237.7	254.0	.....	41	32	39.0	62.0	20.24	789.36
June	104.7	3 561	5 716	237.9	254.3	.....	40	31	39.9	59.6	20.78	829.12
July	106.0	3 444	5 665	237.9	254.3	95.8	40	31	39.3	61.6	20.59	809.19
August	107.0	3 479	5 563	246.4	264.7	95.2	40	31	39.3	60.2	18.96	745.13
September	104.2	3 523	5 783	247.0	265.2	105.2	40	31	37.4	57.9	17.92	670.21
October	101.9	3 466	6 020	247.7	266.0	109.6	40	31	39.1	59.1	16.95	662.75
November	99.8	3 398	5 939	248.4	266.0	112.0	40	31	38.9	59.1	17.31	673.36
December	100.0	3 817	5 867	316.0	345.9	112.3	40	31	37.5	56.2	17.05	639.38

Textile Mill Products—Production, Capacity Utilization, Shipments, and Inventories

(Seasonally adjusted)

Year and month	Industrial production (1992=100)					Capacity utilization (output as a percent of capacity)	Manufacturers' shipments and inventories (millions of dollars)	
	Total	Fabrics	Knit goods	Carpeting	Yarns and miscellaneous		Shipments	Inventories (book value, end of period)
1970	71.8	105.9	60.4	52.4	60.3	83.5	22 614	3 676
1971	75.8	103.7	63.9	57.6	67.2	84.7	24 034	3 866
1972	83.1	101.6	75.7	66.9	74.8	88.6	28 065	4 056
1973	86.5	108.4	79.4	73.2	73.7	89.7	31 073	4 592
1974	78.7	101.3	69.7	63.2	67.4	80.5	32 790	5 044
1975	75.0	92.5	68.7	58.1	66.5	76.1	31 065	4 794
1976	83.3	106.5	71.8	67.3	75.2	83.6	36 387	5 232
1977	88.3	107.5	76.0	82.8	78.8	87.2	40 550	5 649
1978	88.6	100.3	78.5	87.0	82.7	86.0	42 281	5 935
1979	91.5	107.2	78.5	96.5	83.8	87.7	45 137	6 148
1980	89.0	107.7	79.5	84.8	77.4	84.8	47 256	6 648
1981	86.3	105.3	76.3	79.2	76.1	81.6	50 260	6 896
1982	80.1	92.2	76.7	75.8	69.7	75.5	47 516	6 723
1983	89.9	102.5	82.6	91.0	80.4	85.3	53 733	7 514
1984	90.4	100.1	81.9	99.6	82.0	85.8	56 336	7 827
1985	86.5	91.9	80.9	99.5	79.4	81.5	54 605	7 439
1986	90.5	95.0	82.2	104.7	86.6	85.4	57 188	7 191
1987	96.3	100.6	85.6	105.2	96.6	90.5	62 787	7 939
1988	95.0	102.4	82.0	106.7	95.7	88.0	64 627	8 384
1989	96.5	100.1	88.8	105.2	97.9	87.9	67 265	8 721
1990	93.2	94.4	87.7	100.9	96.4	83.5	65 533	8 732
1991	92.7	96.3	92.6	88.0	92.7	81.7	65 440	8 484
1992	100.0	100.0	100.0	100.0	100.0	87.3	70 753	8 710
1993	105.3	104.6	107.0	105.9	103.9	89.6	73 955	9 264
1994	110.6	111.1	111.0	107.4	111.4	91.2	78 027	9 804
1995	110.2	113.3	110.5	107.4	111.7	88.5	79 874	10 308
1996	108.9	108.9	110.6	108.8	111.4	85.8	80 243	9 915
1997	112.2	110.5	115.8	109.0	118.6	85.3	83 871	10 184
1998	112.2	105.7	119.8	112.9	117.7	83.2	80 624	10 180
1995:								
January	114.9	119.6	110.0	111.7	117.0	93.0	6 805	9 843
February	113.3	117.2	107.9	113.8	116.5	91.6	6 756	9 897
March	113.6	117.9	113.2	104.7	116.8	91.7	6 760	10 026
April	113.6	114.7	112.2	113.7	117.2	91.6	6 676	10 094
May	110.8	118.0	109.0	100.8	113.4	89.2	6 700	10 180
June	109.5	113.3	113.0	98.8	112.0	88.0	6 651	10 237
July	105.0	106.4	107.5	109.9	104.6	84.3	6 545	10 251
August	110.1	113.3	112.4	105.7	111.3	88.2	6 677	10 250
September	108.5	109.8	109.1	110.7	111.2	86.8	6 658	10 298
October	108.7	111.1	112.7	103.8	107.4	86.9	6 546	10 324
November	106.9	109.1	111.0	102.5	106.6	85.3	6 606	10 347
December	107.0	109.2	107.7	112.8	106.2	85.3	6 512	10 308
1996:								
January	103.6	106.1	105.6	102.5	102.7	82.4	6 330	10 226
February	106.1	106.6	109.1	104.1	108.6	84.2	6 538	10 202
March	109.3	108.6	110.4	118.1	109.9	86.7	6 604	10 102
April	107.8	110.4	109.7	103.8	108.8	85.3	6 538	10 042
May	109.1	111.5	111.4	104.2	109.9	86.2	6 680	9 992
June	111.8	109.8	111.7	127.0	111.2	88.1	6 965	9 916
July	110.0	110.9	113.7	103.3	111.1	86.6	6 737	9 899
August	110.8	109.7	112.8	108.2	114.0	87.0	6 695	9 948
September	109.8	109.6	110.4	110.2	112.8	86.0	6 753	9 908
October	109.8	109.2	110.4	106.7	114.8	85.9	6 683	9 907
November	110.1	109.1	110.0	110.0	115.6	85.9	6 764	9 941
December	108.9	105.2	111.6	107.9	117.4	84.8	6 909	9 915
1997:								
January	109.9	108.8	112.8	107.3	115.8	85.4	6 883	9 956
February	110.0	109.8	114.0	99.0	116.2	85.1	7 054	9 911
March	111.2	107.5	114.1	115.3	116.1	85.7	6 971	9 967
April	112.4	113.7	115.8	107.0	116.9	86.3	7 020	10 060
May	110.5	107.9	114.6	109.3	116.8	84.5	6 969	10 048
June	112.3	108.6	115.3	115.8	118.0	85.5	6 842	10 105
July	114.0	114.1	118.1	105.7	119.2	86.5	7 117	10 121
August	112.8	108.7	117.9	113.6	119.6	85.2	6 959	10 178
September	112.8	111.2	116.6	106.7	121.7	84.9	7 031	10 197
October	113.1	112.8	115.7	109.2	119.8	84.8	6 998	10 213
November	114.1	111.1	115.7	118.8	120.2	85.2	7 050	10 138
December	113.1	111.5	118.7	99.7	123.3	84.1	7 012	10 184
1998:								
January	115.0	105.8	118.8	130.2	120.1	85.3	7 254	10 172
February	113.2	109.9	116.8	115.4	117.3	84.0	6 962	10 217
March	112.6	108.8	120.9	104.3	117.8	83.5	6 891	10 219
April	113.3	109.3	121.0	109.9	116.7	84.0	6 806	10 224
May	114.5	108.4	119.5	119.8	118.4	84.8	6 745	10 254
June	112.0	108.8	118.1	107.1	117.1	83.0	6 640	10 253
July	113.2	108.3	117.6	118.5	117.8	83.9	6 940	10 285
August	111.8	102.9	120.0	113.6	118.4	82.8	6 694	10 245
September	111.2	104.7	121.0	107.1	116.1	82.3	6 551	10 307
October	112.4	105.2	118.3	116.3	118.4	83.2	6 498	10 286
November	108.8	97.8	120.5	111.4	115.1	80.5	6 498	10 194
December	109.4	97.3	124.8	108.7	116.9	80.9	6 472	10 180

Textile Mill Products—Prices, Employment, Hours, and Earnings

Year and month	Producer prices (1982=100, except as noted; not seasonally adjusted)							Employment (thousands, seasonally adjusted)		Production workers			
	Textile mill products (December 1984 = 100)	Intermediate materials					Crude materials: Raw cotton	Total payroll employees	Production workers	Average weekly hours, seasonally adjusted	Aggregate weekly hours index (1982=100), seasonally adjusted	Average earnings (dollars, not seasonally adjusted)	
		Synthetic fibers	Processed yarns and thread	Gray fabrics	Finished fabrics	Industrial textile products						Hourly	Weekly
1970	.....	.....	.....	.....	.....	.....	43.6	975	855	39.9	141.8	2.45	97.76
1971	.....	.....	.....	.....	.....	.....	47.2	955	837	40.6	141.3	2.57	104.34
1972	.....	.....	.....	.....	.....	.....	57.0	986	867	41.3	148.9	2.75	113.58
1973	.....	.....	.....	.....	.....	.....	93.4	1 010	886	40.9	150.7	2.95	120.66
1974	.....	.....	.....	.....	.....	.....	96.4	965	843	39.5	138.5	3.20	126.40
1975	.....	63.2	71.9	73.0	81.2	.....	75.1	868	752	39.3	122.9	3.42	134.41
1976	.....	63.2	71.9	73.0	81.2	.....	113.3	919	800	40.1	133.3	3.69	147.97
1977	.....	66.2	73.0	72.1	83.3	.....	101.1	910	792	40.4	132.9	3.99	161.20
1978	.....	67.6	74.0	81.6	83.3	77.7	96.0	899	783	40.4	131.6	4.30	173.72
1979	.....	73.4	78.9	87.5	86.2	82.4	104.2	885	771	40.4	129.3	4.66	188.26
1980	.....	83.1	88.6	95.0	92.9	91.7	135.7	848	737	40.1	122.7	5.07	203.31
1981	.....	96.5	99.8	101.0	100.5	98.5	120.0	823	713	39.6	117.3	5.52	218.59
1982	.....	100.0	100.0	100.0	100.0	100.0	100.0	749	642	37.5	100.0	5.83	218.63
1983	.....	96.7	100.1	101.2	98.9	99.9	114.0	741	639	40.4	107.4	6.18	249.67
1984	.....	98.5	103.2	105.8	101.7	100.2	113.5	746	646	39.9	107.0	6.46	257.75
1985	99.7	95.5	102.1	104.4	101.4	102.5	97.7	702	606	39.7	100.1	6.70	265.99
1986	100.3	92.5	101.7	103.7	101.4	106.5	88.0	703	608	41.1	103.8	6.93	284.82
1987	102.6	91.8	103.8	107.2	104.2	106.1	105.8	725	630	41.8	109.4	7.17	299.71
1988	106.8	97.3	108.0	114.0	109.4	107.7	95.5	728	632	41.0	107.7	7.38	302.58
1989	109.3	104.8	110.4	115.2	113.6	109.2	105.6	720	622	40.9	105.6	7.67	313.70
1990	111.6	106.7	112.6	117.2	116.0	112.0	118.2	691	593	39.9	98.4	8.02	320.00
1991	112.5	105.3	112.6	117.4	117.5	113.8	116.2	670	574	40.6	97.0	8.30	336.98
1992	113.6	103.4	110.8	120.6	118.8	114.7	89.8	674	577	41.1	98.6	8.60	353.46
1993	113.6	103.6	107.8	118.6	119.5	115.5	91.9	675	575	41.4	98.9	8.88	367.63
1994	113.6	104.1	108.4	116.8	119.2	116.6	121.3	676	575	41.6	99.4	9.13	379.81
1995	116.5	109.4	112.8	121.2	121.7	119.0	156.2	663	560	40.8	94.9	9.41	383.93
1996	118.2	111.3	114.7	121.4	123.6	125.6	130.0	627	529	40.6	89.2	9.69	393.41
1997	118.8	111.1	114.0	121.9	123.8	127.9	116.5	616	522	41.4	89.8	10.03	415.24
1998	118.6	109.9	112.7	121.6	123.9	130.2	111.0	598	507	41.0	86.4	10.39	425.99
1995:													
January	114.7	106.8	110.6	118.6	120.0	118.0	144.4	681	576	41.7	99.8	9.34	387.61
February	115.5	107.0	111.1	120.5	120.6	117.7	150.2	681	576	41.5	99.3	9.31	382.64
March	115.7	106.4	112.0	120.7	121.0	118.1	181.4	679	574	41.2	98.3	9.29	382.75
April	116.1	108.4	112.2	121.0	121.3	118.2	176.2	680	575	41.0	98.0	9.35	373.07
May	116.6	108.6	113.1	121.7	121.7	118.5	166.4	672	568	40.6	95.8	9.34	378.27
June	116.6	108.4	113.2	122.0	121.8	119.0	179.9	667	563	40.4	94.5	9.37	382.30
July	116.8	109.6	112.9	121.4	122.0	118.8	164.4	659	556	40.5	93.6	9.39	373.72
August	116.9	111.0	113.5	121.4	122.3	119.1	139.7	658	555	40.8	94.1	9.45	387.45
September	117.2	111.6	113.4	122.5	122.3	119.2	148.3	653	551	40.6	92.9	9.50	390.45
October	117.4	112.4	113.5	121.8	122.4	119.6	143.4	648	547	40.5	92.0	9.49	385.29
November	117.2	111.8	113.9	120.9	122.3	120.8	140.8	645	545	40.5	91.7	9.53	389.78
December	117.3	110.9	113.8	121.6	122.3	121.0	138.9	640	540	40.3	90.4	9.57	389.50
1996:													
January	117.4	111.0	114.4	120.8	123.1	121.7	137.0	632	531	36.1	79.6	9.56	344.16
February	117.5	111.2	114.5	120.8	123.2	121.5	136.0	635	536	40.4	90.0	9.55	383.91
March	117.7	111.2	114.1	121.9	123.1	121.5	133.0	632	534	40.7	90.3	9.55	388.69
April	118.1	111.2	114.7	122.4	123.6	121.6	143.5	627	530	40.3	88.7	9.65	386.97
May	118.3	111.0	114.5	121.6	123.5	127.4	138.2	627	529	40.8	89.7	9.62	390.57
June	118.0	109.5	114.6	120.9	123.7	127.3	136.5	626	529	41.0	90.1	9.68	400.75
July	118.3	111.7	114.5	121.1	123.7	127.4	128.8	626	528	41.0	89.9	9.69	389.54
August	118.4	111.8	114.3	121.4	123.9	127.8	128.9	624	529	41.1	90.3	9.72	401.44
September	118.5	112.1	116.4	121.3	123.8	128.1	123.2	621	526	41.0	89.6	9.78	404.89
October	118.6	112.0	114.9	121.6	123.7	128.1	120.3	623	528	41.0	89.9	9.73	399.90
November	118.6	111.7	114.8	121.2	123.9	127.1	113.3	620	525	41.2	89.9	9.78	407.83
December	118.6	111.6	114.6	121.5	123.6	127.5	120.8	620	525	41.5	90.5	9.93	417.06
1997:													
January	118.6	112.7	114.2	121.4	123.7	126.2	116.6	621	526	41.1	89.8	9.94	407.54
February	118.8	111.4	114.4	121.7	123.8	126.1	116.7	619	525	40.8	89.0	9.90	399.96
March	118.8	111.4	114.4	121.6	123.6	127.7	122.5	621	526	41.3	90.3	9.93	410.11
April	118.2	111.5	114.0	121.4	123.9	127.7	114.7	618	524	41.6	90.6	9.95	411.93
May	118.5	111.3	113.9	121.8	124.0	127.8	115.5	616	522	41.4	89.8	9.95	409.94
June	118.6	111.0	113.7	121.9	123.9	127.9	116.8	616	522	41.3	89.6	9.98	416.17
July	118.8	110.9	113.5	121.9	123.9	127.7	119.4	617	524	41.4	90.1	10.02	406.81
August	118.8	111.0	113.6	121.7	123.8	127.5	120.5	614	520	41.4	89.4	10.02	416.83
September	118.9	110.5	113.7	122.4	123.9	127.8	117.6	613	519	41.5	89.5	10.10	424.20
October	119.1	110.5	114.0	122.1	124.1	127.7	116.0	613	520	41.4	89.4	10.11	418.55
November	119.0	110.4	114.2	121.7	123.7	130.6	114.6	612	519	41.5	89.5	10.16	425.70
December	119.2	110.4	114.6	122.7	123.6	130.6	107.3	612	520	41.6	89.9	10.25	431.53
1998:													
January	119.0	111.2	113.3	123.4	123.6	130.3	103.3	609	517	41.7	89.6	10.26	426.82
February	119.3	111.2	113.4	123.4	123.9	130.2	108.0	608	517	41.5	89.1	10.26	421.69
March	119.2	110.9	113.3	123.0	124.5	130.2	110.1	606	514	41.3	88.2	10.29	423.95
April	119.1	111.0	113.3	123.2	124.6	130.5	101.2	606	514	41.2	88.0	10.39	417.68
May	119.1	110.9	113.2	123.0	124.7	130.4	108.0	604	513	41.2	87.8	10.37	426.21
June	119.0	110.7	113.3	122.8	124.2	130.3	118.7	601	510	41.2	87.3	10.36	429.94
July	118.7	110.8	113.0	121.6	124.0	130.4	121.8	597	505	41.0	86.0	10.36	418.54
August	118.7	110.8	112.8	121.4	124.2	130.2	116.6	594	503	41.0	85.7	10.37	427.24
September	118.3	109.5	112.7	120.6	123.7	130.3	119.4	593	502	40.4	84.3	10.48	424.44
October	117.8	107.9	111.9	118.7	123.5	130.4	114.0	590	499	41.1	85.2	10.45	429.50
November	117.8	107.2	111.3	118.9	122.7	130.4	112.3	586	495	40.8	83.9	10.51	431.96
December	117.6	106.9	111.3	118.8	122.5	128.7	98.7	582	492	40.8	83.4	10.56	437.18

Apparel—Production, Capacity Utilization, Prices, Employment, Hours, and Earnings

| Year and month | Apparel products (seasonally adjusted) | | Producer prices (1982=100, except as noted; not seasonally adjusted) | | | | Consumer prices: Apparel (1982-1984 =100, seasonally adjusted) | Employment (thousands, seasonally adjusted) | | Production workers | | | |
| | Industrial production (1992 =100) | Capacity utilization (output as a percent of capacity) | Apparel industry (December 1984 = 100) | Finished apparel | | | | Total payroll employees | Production workers | Average weekly hours, seasonally adjusted | Aggregate weekly hours index (1982 =100), seasonally adjusted | Average earnings (dollars, not seasonally adjusted) | |
				Women's	Men's and boys'	Girls', children's and infants'						Hourly	Weekly
1970	81.8	78.9	.....	62.8	51.2	58.8	59.2	1 364	1 196	35.3	123.9	2.39	84.37
1971	82.9	78.6	.....	64.1	52.7	60.3	61.1	1 343	1 178	35.6	122.9	2.49	88.64
1972	87.9	82.0	.....	64.6	53.6	60.7	62.3	1 383	1 208	36.0	127.8	2.60	93.60
1973	88.5	81.4	.....	66.7	56.1	61.9	64.6	1 438	1 250	35.9	131.7	2.76	99.08
1974	84.5	76.5	.....	70.0	63.4	68.9	69.4	1 363	1 175	35.2	121.3	2.97	104.54
1975	77.4	69.3	.....	71.3	66.3	70.0	72.5	1 243	1 067	35.2	110.2	3.17	111.58
1976	91.1	80.3	.....	73.5	71.1	72.1	75.2	1 318	1 134	35.8	119.3	3.40	121.72
1977	98.0	84.8	.....	75.6	77.1	73.2	78.6	1 316	1 129	35.6	117.9	3.62	128.87
1978	100.4	85.9	.....	77.4	80.2	76.6	81.4	1 332	1 145	35.6	119.5	3.94	140.26
1979	95.3	80.5	.....	81.1	84.7	81.0	84.9	1 304	1 117	35.3	115.6	4.23	149.32
1980	95.4	79.4	.....	86.9	91.3	87.1	90.9	1 264	1 079	35.4	112.2	4.56	161.42
1981	97.3	80.6	.....	95.0	96.0	97.1	95.3	1 244	1 060	35.7	111.0	4.97	177.43
1982	96.3	79.7	.....	100.0	100.0	100.0	97.8	1 161	981	34.7	100.0	5.20	180.44
1983	100.3	82.6	.....	102.1	101.3	100.5	100.2	1 163	984	36.2	104.5	5.38	194.76
1984	102.2	84.1	.....	103.7	103.5	103.2	101.1	1 185	1 002	36.4	107.2	5.55	202.02
1985	98.6	80.4	101.1	105.4	105.0	103.1	105.0	1 120	944	36.4	100.7	5.73	208.57
1986	101.8	82.3	102.3	106.8	106.4	103.8	105.9	1 100	926	36.7	99.7	5.84	214.33
1987	105.5	85.2	103.9	108.4	108.6	106.7	110.6	1 097	922	37.0	100.1	5.94	219.78
1988	103.6	83.6	107.2	111.3	113.0	107.5	115.4	1 085	912	37.0	99.0	6.12	226.44
1989	100.3	80.9	110.2	113.5	116.8	110.5	118.6	1 076	907	36.9	98.3	6.35	234.32
1990	97.2	78.3	113.3	116.1	120.2	115.3	124.1	1 036	869	36.4	92.9	6.57	239.15
1991	97.8	78.7	116.0	117.9	122.7	117.8	128.7	1 006	841	37.0	91.3	6.77	250.49
1992	100.0	80.1	118.0	119.9	126.0	119.0	131.9	1 007	844	37.2	92.2	6.95	258.54
1993	102.4	81.3	119.2	120.2	127.7	120.1	133.7	989	829	37.2	90.4	7.09	263.75
1994	106.3	83.4	119.7	119.7	128.5	119.9	133.4	974	815	37.5	89.7	7.34	275.25
1995	107.1	82.5	120.6	119.6	130.3	121.6	132.0	936	776	37.0	84.2	7.64	282.68
1996	104.7	79.5	122.3	119.9	132.1	122.4	131.7	868	711	37.0	77.2	7.96	294.52
1997	102.8	77.1	123.4	120.5	132.7	122.9	132.9	824	673	37.3	73.7	8.25	307.73
1998	99.2	74.2	124.8	122.3	133.2	121.8	133.0	763	614	37.3	67.2	8.52	317.80
1995:													
January	109.1	85.0	120.0	119.9	129.2	119.1	132.2	972	813	37.6	89.7	7.55	280.86
February	108.8	84.5	120.3	120.1	129.8	121.2	131.9	963	804	37.5	88.5	7.49	280.13
March	109.5	85.0	120.6	120.2	129.9	120.9	132.2	960	800	37.3	87.6	7.53	280.87
April	107.3	83.1	120.4	119.4	130.1	121.1	132.0	955	795	37.0	86.3	7.62	271.27
May	108.3	83.7	120.5	119.8	130.1	121.6	131.6	948	789	37.0	85.7	7.57	280.09
June	106.6	82.2	120.4	119.4	130.0	122.1	131.3	940	779	36.9	84.4	7.62	283.46
July	106.0	81.6	120.7	120.1	130.3	121.4	131.4	934	771	36.9	83.5	7.64	278.86
August	106.5	81.8	120.6	119.4	130.4	121.4	132.4	929	768	36.8	83.0	7.68	284.16
September	106.5	81.7	120.9	120.2	130.4	122.7	132.3	921	761	36.9	82.4	7.72	287.18
October	106.1	81.1	121.0	120.2	130.8	122.8	132.4	910	752	36.7	81.0	7.73	285.24
November	105.6	80.6	120.7	118.2	130.9	122.8	132.0	901	743	36.8	80.3	7.77	288.27
December	104.3	79.4	120.7	118.7	130.8	122.7	132.2	895	736	36.8	79.5	7.83	292.06
1996:													
January	101.7	77.4	121.4	119.7	131.7	122.4	132.7	885	727	33.7	71.9	7.87	262.07
February	105.0	79.9	121.6	119.9	132.1	121.7	132.0	889	729	36.9	79.0	7.82	287.78
March	104.1	79.1	121.6	119.9	132.2	121.8	132.6	880	723	36.9	78.3	7.86	290.82
April	105.1	79.9	121.5	118.9	132.2	121.8	132.0	877	720	36.8	77.8	7.95	289.38
May	105.4	80.1	122.2	119.5	132.2	121.8	131.9	873	716	37.3	78.4	7.94	296.16
June	105.3	80.0	122.5	120.2	132.3	121.8	131.5	868	712	37.5	78.4	7.99	302.82
July	105.1	79.8	122.6	120.2	132.4	121.8	131.3	868	711	37.3	77.8	7.95	292.56
August	106.2	80.6	122.5	119.4	132.0	121.8	130.4	861	705	37.5	77.6	7.94	299.34
September	105.7	80.2	123.0	120.4	131.9	123.1	131.2	859	703	37.4	77.2	7.99	300.42
October	104.8	79.5	123.1	120.6	132.2	122.5	131.5	856	700	37.4	76.8	8.02	301.55
November	104.4	79.2	122.9	120.0	132.4	123.5	131.6	852	696	37.4	76.4	8.01	301.18
December	103.7	78.6	123.1	120.1	132.3	123.9	131.9	847	693	37.4	76.1	8.14	308.51
1997:													
January	103.1	78.0	122.9	120.0	132.4	124.0	132.2	844	691	37.2	75.4	8.12	299.63
February	102.7	77.6	122.9	120.2	132.3	124.0	132.8	844	690	37.1	75.1	8.18	301.02
March	103.7	78.2	123.2	120.2	132.7	124.0	132.3	837	685	37.4	75.2	8.23	308.63
April	103.4	77.9	122.9	119.8	132.4	124.0	133.2	834	682	37.4	74.9	8.21	304.59
May	103.2	77.6	123.3	120.4	132.5	122.6	133.3	830	680	37.2	74.2	8.22	305.78
June	103.2	77.5	123.4	120.4	132.7	122.6	133.1	827	677	37.3	74.1	8.25	311.03
July	103.0	77.2	123.4	120.4	132.8	122.6	133.2	821	671	37.1	73.1	8.19	299.75
August	102.5	76.7	123.5	120.7	133.0	122.6	132.4	818	667	37.1	72.6	8.23	307.80
September	102.5	76.6	123.7	120.8	133.0	122.2	132.9	812	662	37.3	72.5	8.33	312.38
October	102.7	76.6	123.4	120.6	133.1	122.2	133.0	811	661	37.3	72.4	8.33	313.21
November	101.8	75.8	124.2	121.3	132.6	122.2	132.9	807	657	37.3	71.9	8.33	313.21
December	102.3	76.1	124.2	121.2	132.5	122.3	133.2	803	652	37.5	71.8	8.42	320.80
1998:													
January	102.5	76.2	124.4	122.2	133.1	122.6	132.7	798	647	37.6	71.4	8.42	314.07
February	101.1	75.2	124.3	122.2	132.9	122.6	132.8	792	641	37.3	70.2	8.38	310.90
March	101.6	75.6	124.5	121.9	132.9	122.5	132.7	788	637	37.1	69.4	8.43	313.60
April	101.0	75.2	124.7	121.9	133.0	122.2	132.7	781	629	37.5	69.2	8.48	309.52
May	100.4	74.9	124.9	121.9	133.1	122.1	132.9	773	622	37.4	68.3	8.47	316.78
June	100.5	75.0	124.9	121.8	133.3	122.2	133.1	768	618	37.3	67.7	8.50	321.30
July	100.1	74.8	124.9	121.7	133.6	122.2	132.7	764	614	37.4	67.4	8.48	312.91
August	99.2	74.2	124.9	121.7	133.5	121.2	134.0	755	606	37.4	66.5	8.54	321.10
September	98.3	73.5	125.1	122.7	133.5	120.5	133.2	751	603	37.2	65.8	8.63	316.72
October	97.3	72.9	125.3	123.2	133.5	121.2	133.2	738	591	37.3	64.7	8.65	325.24
November	95.5	71.6	125.0	123.0	133.2	121.0	133.1	729	581	37.3	63.6	8.64	325.73
December	95.4	71.6	124.9	123.1	133.3	121.0	132.3	724	579	37.3	63.4	8.71	330.11

Paper and Paper Products—Production, Capacity Utilization, Shipments, and Inventories

(Seasonally adjusted)

| Year and month | Industrial production (1992=100) | | | | | | | | Capacity utilization (output as a percent of capacity) | | Manufacturers' shipments and inventories (millions of dollars) | |
| | Total | Pulp and paper | | | | Paper products | | | Total | Pulp and paper | Shipments | Inventories (book value, end of period) |
		Total	Wood pulp	Paper	Paper-board	Total	Paper-board containers	Converted paper productss				
1970	56.7	60.3	63.9	57.3	61.9	54.3	55.7	51.8	86.5	92.2	24 573	2 735
1971	59.1	62.8	67.2	59.1	64.8	56.7	57.9	54.2	87.4	93.3	25 182	2 828
1972	64.3	67.2	71.1	63.0	70.8	62.6	64.1	60.0	91.9	95.8	28 004	2 896
1973	68.8	69.7	73.8	65.7	73.0	68.3	68.4	67.0	95.4	96.1	32 495	3 317
1974	68.2	69.1	73.0	66.4	71.0	67.7	64.6	69.1	91.9	93.5	41 514	4 816
1975	59.4	59.4	62.4	58.1	60.1	59.5	57.9	60.0	78.1	79.4	41 497	4 849
1976	67.4	67.8	71.6	65.6	69.0	67.2	65.0	68.3	87.0	89.8	47 939	5 299
1977	70.1	68.6	71.6	67.9	69.0	71.5	68.1	72.3	90.1	90.8	51 881	5 667
1978	73.4	70.7	71.9	69.7	72.2	75.6	73.1	75.8	92.5	92.4	56 777	6 114
1979	76.0	74.4	76.0	74.2	74.4	77.4	74.9	77.5	92.6	94.6	64 957	6 926
1980	75.2	74.7	77.6	74.2	74.6	75.8	72.0	77.0	88.4	92.2	72 553	7 802
1981	76.6	76.4	79.1	76.2	75.8	76.9	73.6	77.8	87.2	91.3	79 970	8 593
1982	74.3	73.6	75.4	75.1	69.4	75.0	70.4	77.0	83.1	86.2	79 698	9 022
1983	81.0	79.8	80.3	81.1	76.9	82.1	75.7	85.4	89.5	91.7	84 817	9 192
1984	85.0	83.7	84.6	85.0	80.5	86.2	80.0	89.3	92.1	93.4	95 525	10 299
1985	83.8	82.4	82.7	84.0	78.6	85.1	80.0	87.7	88.2	90.4	94 679	10 140
1986	88.3	86.8	87.1	87.8	84.5	89.6	84.9	92.2	90.3	94.0	99 865	10 254
1987	90.9	90.6	91.0	91.1	89.5	91.3	89.1	92.5	90.8	95.7	108 989	11 163
1988	93.8	93.4	93.3	94.5	91.3	94.1	92.1	95.3	92.2	95.6	122 882	12 495
1989	95.4	94.3	94.9	95.3	92.1	96.6	94.0	97.9	91.1	93.9	131 896	13 404
1990	96.0	96.7	96.9	97.8	94.2	95.5	95.1	95.7	88.9	93.9	132 424	13 640
1991	96.8	97.3	97.6	97.6	96.6	96.4	95.7	96.8	86.7	91.7	130 131	13 796
1992	100.0	100.0	100.0	100.0	100.0	100.0	100.0	100.0	87.5	92.1	133 201	14 010
1993	104.0	103.3	98.6	104.0	103.3	104.6	105.8	103.9	88.9	93.2	133 263	13 972
1994	108.4	107.1	101.1	106.8	109.3	109.3	112.2	107.7	90.8	94.9	143 649	14 463
1995	109.6	108.8	103.0	108.3	111.5	110.0	111.8	109.1	90.1	94.2	173 716	17 352
1996	108.8	107.5	100.3	105.1	114.1	109.7	112.6	108.0	86.7	90.9	160 661	16 032
1997	114.4	113.1	102.7	110.8	120.2	115.4	116.7	114.7	89.2	94.3	161 992	16 240
1998	115.0	113.0	100.5	111.5	119.0	116.4	118.0	115.5	87.1	92.6	165 429	16 362
1995:												
January	111.9	110.6	104.3	109.3	114.9	112.8	119.8	108.9	93.0	96.9	13 805	14 749
February	111.1	110.2	104.8	109.3	113.4	111.6	115.4	109.6	92.2	96.3	14 165	14 999
March	110.9	110.7	104.7	109.6	114.7	110.8	112.6	109.9	91.9	96.6	14 309	15 358
April	110.8	110.3	103.8	108.8	115.2	110.9	113.5	109.6	91.7	96.0	14 404	15 706
May	110.8	111.6	104.8	110.6	115.5	110.1	110.4	110.0	91.6	96.9	14 827	15 968
June	109.4	110.2	105.8	108.1	115.7	108.5	109.7	108.0	90.2	95.5	15 065	16 521
July	109.6	109.7	104.8	109.1	112.3	109.4	108.1	110.3	90.2	94.8	14 613	16 772
August	108.6	108.5	102.8	108.2	110.6	108.5	108.4	108.7	89.1	93.5	14 861	16 852
September	108.2	106.9	102.3	106.9	108.1	109.2	111.5	108.0	88.5	91.9	14 630	17 107
October	109.8	108.7	102.1	109.8	108.4	110.6	109.3	111.5	89.6	93.2	14 469	17 308
November	106.4	104.6	97.1	104.8	106.3	107.7	109.6	106.7	86.5	89.4	14 353	17 274
December	107.6	104.2	99.1	105.1	104.0	110.3	115.0	107.8	87.2	88.9	14 102	17 352
1996:												
January	106.3	104.6	99.4	104.1	106.9	107.6	110.2	106.2	85.9	89.0	13 829	17 307
February	104.7	103.7	97.6	101.5	109.6	105.4	109.5	103.2	84.4	88.1	13 841	17 316
March	106.3	104.5	99.1	103.0	109.2	107.6	112.2	105.0	85.5	88.8	13 582	17 241
April	108.2	107.1	99.0	105.6	112.4	109.0	111.3	107.7	86.8	90.8	13 589	16 943
May	108.3	106.7	101.4	104.1	113.3	109.3	112.6	107.6	86.6	90.4	13 489	16 633
June	109.3	106.9	100.8	105.6	111.1	111.1	115.0	109.0	87.2	90.4	13 310	16 485
July	109.9	108.6	101.6	105.8	116.3	110.9	114.2	109.1	87.5	91.7	13 436	16 429
August	109.1	108.7	102.6	104.4	119.4	109.5	112.9	107.6	86.7	91.7	13 227	16 457
September	109.5	108.0	101.6	104.5	117.2	110.6	116.7	107.3	86.8	91.1	13 090	16 369
October	109.3	109.3	100.8	106.2	118.2	109.3	109.5	109.2	86.5	92.1	13 096	16 257
November	111.4	110.2	102.2	107.6	117.8	112.3	114.6	111.1	88.1	92.7	13 101	16 144
December	112.6	111.6	98.7	109.0	120.3	113.4	114.1	113.1	88.9	93.8	13 089	16 032
1997:												
January	111.7	110.4	98.7	108.3	117.9	112.5	113.8	111.9	87.9	92.7	13 148	15 926
February	113.6	112.7	105.9	110.2	119.8	114.2	115.7	113.5	89.3	94.5	13 216	15 812
March	114.0	113.1	105.8	110.9	119.3	114.6	115.3	114.4	89.5	94.7	12 968	15 918
April	113.4	111.5	102.5	109.9	117.2	114.7	116.4	113.8	88.8	93.3	13 455	15 797
May	113.9	112.1	100.9	110.7	117.9	115.1	115.7	115.0	89.0	93.7	13 168	15 829
June	113.4	111.5	101.3	110.0	117.2	114.7	118.3	112.8	88.5	93.1	13 248	15 682
July	114.4	112.6	101.4	110.7	119.4	115.7	117.0	115.1	89.1	93.8	13 464	15 728
August	115.5	114.3	103.3	111.4	123.5	116.3	118.6	115.1	89.7	95.2	13 408	15 794
September	116.0	115.0	103.3	112.8	122.8	116.8	117.7	116.3	90.0	95.6	13 733	16 016
October	115.0	114.9	102.7	112.3	123.6	115.1	112.8	116.4	89.0	95.4	13 987	15 982
November	116.1	114.2	103.9	110.7	124.4	117.5	122.5	114.9	89.6	94.7	13 847	16 054
December	116.2	114.5	103.6	112.5	121.5	117.4	118.8	116.7	89.4	94.7	14 364	16 240
1998:												
January	115.7	114.6	102.1	111.8	123.9	116.4	116.6	116.3	88.8	94.7	14 105	16 351
February	115.9	114.0	103.3	111.6	121.7	117.2	118.0	116.9	88.8	94.0	13 880	16 317
March	115.0	113.1	102.0	110.8	120.7	116.4	118.3	115.4	87.9	93.1	13 957	16 320
April	115.2	113.6	102.6	111.5	121.0	116.3	116.8	116.0	87.8	93.5	13 937	16 363
May	115.0	112.7	104.9	111.2	118.0	116.6	119.0	115.3	87.4	92.6	13 938	16 388
June	114.9	113.5	100.6	111.4	121.3	115.8	117.6	114.9	87.1	93.1	13 879	16 498
July	115.9	114.1	101.7	112.0	121.8	117.2	118.7	116.4	87.7	93.5	13 929	16 584
August	115.3	113.2	100.0	112.3	118.7	116.8	118.3	116.0	87.0	92.6	13 761	16 643
September	113.9	111.9	98.1	111.6	116.2	115.2	117.1	114.3	85.7	91.4	13 518	16 527
October	115.4	113.3	97.4	113.5	117.2	116.9	114.3	118.4	86.7	92.4	13 421	16 511
November	112.3	109.7	97.9	108.8	114.6	114.2	120.1	111.0	84.2	89.3	13 489	16 483
December	115.3	111.6	96.0	112.4	113.9	117.9	123.8	114.8	86.2	90.8	13 669	16 362

Paper and Paper Products—Prices, Employment, Hours, and Earnings

Year and month	Paper and paper products (December 1984 =100)	Intermediate materials					Crude materials: waste paper	Total payroll employees	Production workers	Average weekly hours, seasonally adjusted	Aggregate weekly hours index (1982 =100), seasonally adjusted	Average earnings (dollars, not seasonally adjusted)	
		Woodpulp	Paper	Paperboard	Paper boxes and containers	Building paper and board						Hourly	Weekly
1970	.....	28.9	38.8	39.7	43.3	42.2	103.2	701	540	41.9	110.2	3.44	144.14
1971	.....	29.6	39.9	40.2	44.7	42.9	92.5	677	518	42.1	106.4	3.67	154.51
1972	.....	29.4	40.6	41.4	46.4	44.4	110.3	679	528	42.8	110.3	3.95	169.06
1973	.....	33.8	42.4	45.2	49.9	47.1	162.9	694	540	42.9	112.7	4.20	180.18
1974	.....	57.5	51.9	59.7	58.5	51.6	219.2	696	541	42.2	111.2	4.53	191.17
1975	.....	74.8	60.4	66.8	63.3	53.1	90.9	633	477	41.6	96.8	5.01	208.42
1976	.....	75.5	63.7	69.1	66.0	57.9	152.6	666	505	42.5	104.7	5.47	232.48
1977	.....	74.2	67.8	69.1	67.1	65.6	154.6	682	515	42.9	107.6	5.96	255.68
1978	.....	70.3	72.0	70.5	69.9	78.2	157.8	689	521	42.9	109.0	6.52	279.71
1979	.....	82.9	80.2	79.3	79.1	76.2	170.5	697	532	42.6	110.5	7.13	303.74
1980	.....	100.3	89.7	92.0	89.4	86.1	172.2	685	519	42.2	106.9	7.84	330.85
1981	.....	104.8	97.7	101.2	97.7	96.7	145.0	681	515	42.5	106.8	8.60	365.50
1982	.....	100.0	100.0	100.0	100.0	100.0	100.0	655	491	41.8	100.0	9.32	389.58
1983	.....	91.5	98.5	98.4	99.5	104.4	.....	654	491	42.6	102.1	9.93	423.02
1984	.....	104.8	105.8	110.4	105.7	108.2	198.2	674	508	43.1	106.8	10.41	448.67
1985	98.8	91.4	106.0	107.7	108.8	107.4	122.9	671	508	43.1	106.8	10.83	466.77
1986	99.5	94.7	107.0	106.6	107.8	108.8	142.6	667	507	43.2	106.9	11.18	482.98
1987	104.9	111.5	111.5	118.1	115.4	111.2	181.4	674	512	43.4	108.5	11.43	496.06
1988	113.7	136.7	123.2	133.2	123.5	113.3	183.6	689	516	43.3	108.9	11.69	506.18
1989	120.8	157.4	129.6	140.1	129.8	115.6	157.1	696	521	43.3	109.9	11.96	517.87
1990	121.9	151.3	128.8	135.7	129.9	112.2	138.9	697	522	43.3	110.4	12.31	533.02
1991	121.1	119.2	126.9	130.2	128.6	111.8	124.4	688	517	43.3	109.3	12.72	550.78
1992	121.2	118.9	123.2	134.3	130.6	119.6	117.5	690	520	43.6	110.5	13.07	569.85
1993	120.2	104.2	123.8	130.0	129.9	132.7	117.4	692	522	43.6	110.9	13.42	585.11
1994	123.7	115.9	126.0	140.5	136.1	144.1	209.5	692	524	43.9	112.3	13.77	604.50
1995	146.7	183.2	159.0	183.1	163.8	144.9	371.1	693	525	43.1	110.5	14.23	613.31
1996	138.6	133.1	149.4	155.1	153.9	137.2	141.6	684	519	43.3	109.5	14.67	635.21
1997	133.5	128.6	143.9	144.4	144.7	129.6	163.3	683	521	43.7	111.0	15.05	657.69
1998	136.2	122.6	145.4	151.6	154.7	132.9	145.4	675	514	43.4	108.9	15.51	673.13
1995:													
January	136.0	144.6	141.9	165.3	151.0	147.3	343.5	695	528	43.9	113.0	14.00	616.00
February	139.1	158.8	146.9	170.5	155.6	148.0	387.5	695	527	43.6	112.0	14.01	606.63
March	141.4	168.4	150.6	172.3	157.3	147.3	465.0	694	527	43.4	111.5	14.02	604.26
April	143.9	173.7	155.2	183.8	159.0	146.6	508.9	695	528	43.3	111.5	14.26	603.20
May	146.2	181.1	157.5	188.2	162.9	145.4	544.9	695	528	43.0	110.7	14.15	605.62
June	148.8	191.7	161.0	189.6	167.6	141.3	511.3	694	527	43.0	110.5	14.13	606.18
July	150.3	196.3	164.2	189.9	169.0	141.4	452.4	694	527	43.0	110.5	14.41	616.75
August	150.9	200.5	164.8	190.6	169.4	142.3	394.2	695	526	43.0	110.3	14.20	606.34
September	151.2	198.2	166.4	190.3	168.8	145.8	310.6	693	525	43.0	110.1	14.33	621.92
October	151.2	198.7	167.3	188.8	168.6	146.3	215.8	691	523	42.9	109.4	14.31	616.76
November	150.8	195.4	166.6	185.7	168.8	145.5	170.5	688	521	43.0	109.2	14.38	624.09
December	150.2	191.3	165.6	182.2	167.8	141.9	148.5	688	521	42.9	109.0	14.51	634.09
1996:													
January	147.8	176.6	163.1	175.7	165.3	138.5	163.4	687	521	41.5	105.4	14.58	607.99
February	146.1	160.4	160.9	172.6	163.9	138.2	163.0	685	519	43.1	109.1	14.43	617.60
March	143.0	141.4	157.5	166.6	161.1	136.3	142.0	684	518	43.1	108.8	14.44	618.03
April	140.5	120.3	152.6	161.8	157.6	136.2	123.1	681	516	43.2	108.7	14.61	626.77
May	138.2	114.1	149.4	154.0	155.3	137.9	124.1	682	516	43.3	108.9	14.58	626.94
June	137.2	120.0	148.4	150.6	152.3	135.9	128.6	682	516	43.4	109.2	14.63	634.94
July	136.3	125.5	146.4	148.0	151.1	137.4	134.9	681	516	43.3	108.9	14.78	638.50
August	135.3	127.3	144.5	145.5	148.5	137.3	136.9	682	518	43.5	109.9	14.69	637.55
September	135.1	127.8	143.5	145.6	148.6	140.5	142.2	683	520	43.5	110.3	14.73	648.12
October	134.9	128.2	142.3	146.6	148.0	138.7	146.2	683	521	43.4	110.2	14.73	642.23
November	134.6	127.6	141.7	146.9	147.3	136.2	147.8	684	521	43.6	110.8	14.85	654.89
December	134.7	128.2	142.1	147.6	147.4	133.7	146.6	685	522	43.7	111.2	14.93	664.39
1997:													
January	134.5	127.4	141.7	147.1	148.1	132.4	150.3	684	521	43.7	111.0	14.82	649.12
February	133.5	125.2	140.9	144.2	146.3	130.9	157.5	684	522	43.8	111.5	14.76	637.63
March	132.5	124.5	140.8	139.7	144.6	130.9	155.9	685	522	43.8	111.5	14.92	649.02
April	131.5	121.9	141.8	137.2	142.8	129.1	151.0	684	522	43.7	111.2	14.98	650.13
May	131.5	123.5	142.8	136.8	142.0	128.1	154.0	684	522	43.7	111.2	14.97	649.70
June	131.7	125.5	143.3	137.5	141.4	128.7	154.6	683	521	43.4	110.2	14.97	649.70
July	132.0	130.0	144.4	137.8	141.5	127.4	165.4	682	520	43.5	110.3	15.16	656.43
August	132.8	132.7	145.2	143.8	140.2	127.0	192.3	682	519	43.5	110.1	15.11	655.77
September	134.1	133.3	145.5	148.4	144.1	128.4	182.1	681	519	43.6	110.3	15.17	669.00
October	134.6	133.2	146.1	150.1	145.2	127.9	168.4	682	520	43.7	110.8	15.18	664.88
November	135.9	132.8	146.5	154.4	148.2	133.8	164.8	682	520	43.9	111.3	15.22	675.77
December	137.3	133.4	147.5	156.1	151.9	131.0	163.6	681	520	43.8	111.0	15.28	683.02
1998:													
January	137.7	130.7	147.9	155.9	154.9	127.3	163.5	682	522	43.7	111.2	15.19	663.80
February	137.8	127.8	147.8	156.1	156.0	128.6	164.4	681	520	43.6	110.5	15.21	654.03
March	137.5	126.4	147.6	156.0	155.5	128.2	162.4	681	520	43.4	110.0	15.28	658.57
April	137.0	121.5	146.9	155.2	154.7	131.0	153.7	679	519	43.1	109.1	15.45	656.63
May	137.0	120.8	146.4	154.2	156.3	132.0	151.8	678	517	43.5	109.6	15.51	671.58
June	136.7	123.9	145.6	153.7	155.9	131.6	149.6	676	515	43.5	109.2	15.46	672.51
July	136.7	126.1	145.5	152.2	155.8	136.2	146.7	674	513	43.6	109.0	15.64	674.08
August	136.3	123.3	145.3	150.9	154.6	141.9	145.5	673	512	43.3	108.1	15.54	669.77
September	135.5	121.1	144.2	149.0	154.7	142.8	140.5	672	511	43.6	108.6	15.84	698.54
October	134.6	116.9	143.5	146.9	153.1	134.6	132.8	669	509	43.5	108.0	15.60	680.16
November	134.0	116.1	142.6	144.7	153.0	131.3	117.3	666	507	43.5	107.5	15.64	686.60
December	133.5	116.7	141.4	143.6	151.9	129.3	116.3	666	506	43.4	107.1	15.78	699.05

Printing and Publishing—Production, Capacity Utilization, Prices, Employment, Hours, and Earnings

Year and month	Industrial production (1992=100, seasonally adjusted)			Capacity utilization (output as a percent of capacity, seasonally adjusted)	Producer prices (December 1984=100, not seasonally adjusted)	Employment (thousands, seasonally adjusted)		Production workers			
	Total	Newspapers	Job printing			Total payroll employees	Production workers	Average weekly hours, seasonally adjusted	Aggregate weekly hours index (1982=100), seasonally adjusted	Average earnings (dollars, not seasonally adjusted)	
										Hourly	Weekly
1970	54.4	89.8	38.9	86.9	.....	1 104	679	37.7	98.9	3.92	147.78
1971	54.8	90.2	38.7	85.3	.....	1 081	658	37.5	95.3	4.20	157.50
1972	58.5	95.9	43.7	88.3	.....	1 094	664	37.7	96.5	4.51	170.03
1973	60.1	98.4	46.0	87.7	.....	1 111	670	37.7	97.4	4.75	179.08
1974	59.1	98.6	44.2	83.9	.....	1 111	660	37.5	95.5	5.03	188.63
1975	55.4	92.8	41.2	77.0	.....	1 083	624	36.9	88.9	5.38	198.52
1976	60.5	95.0	46.8	82.6	.....	1 099	625	37.5	90.3	5.71	214.13
1977	66.3	97.6	52.2	89.4	.....	1 141	647	37.7	94.1	6.12	230.72
1978	70.1	103.6	54.3	91.7	.....	1 192	672	37.6	97.5	6.51	244.78
1979	72.0	107.3	56.3	89.5	.....	1 235	697	37.5	101.0	6.94	260.25
1980	72.4	105.8	56.8	85.8	.....	1 252	699	37.1	100.1	7.53	279.36
1981	74.3	106.9	58.0	83.9	.....	1 266	699	37.3	100.6	8.19	305.49
1982	77.5	106.4	63.0	83.8	.....	1 272	699	37.1	100.0	8.74	324.25
1983	81.4	111.3	66.9	85.2	.....	1 298	712	37.6	103.3	9.11	342.54
1984	87.0	119.8	71.7	87.7	.....	1 375	758	37.9	110.9	9.41	356.64
1985	90.2	121.7	75.6	86.4	103.6	1 426	788	37.8	114.9	9.71	367.04
1986	93.4	125.3	78.5	85.6	107.8	1 456	816	38.0	119.6	9.99	379.62
1987	102.5	129.3	93.3	91.0	112.2	1 503	839	38.0	123.2	10.28	390.64
1988	103.4	124.9	95.5	89.5	118.2	1 543	864	38.0	126.7	10.53	400.14
1989	103.5	121.9	96.8	87.7	124.7	1 556	863	37.9	126.2	10.88	412.35
1990	103.1	116.0	97.8	85.2	130.5	1 569	871	37.9	127.5	11.24	426.00
1991	99.1	105.9	95.2	80.8	136.4	1 536	847	37.7	123.3	11.48	432.80
1992	100.0	100.0	100.0	81.4	140.8	1 507	833	38.1	122.3	11.74	447.29
1993	100.7	98.4	100.6	81.7	145.6	1 517	839	38.3	123.9	11.93	456.92
1994	100.7	98.7	101.5	81.2	149.7	1 537	846	38.6	125.9	12.14	468.60
1995	101.4	97.2	102.1	81.2	159.0	1 546	848	38.2	125.0	12.33	471.01
1996	101.6	94.2	103.0	81.0	165.6	1 540	841	38.2	124.0	12.65	483.23
1997	105.2	97.1	106.0	83.8	169.1	1 552	847	38.5	126.0	13.06	502.81
1998	105.1	97.8	108.0	82.5	174.0	1 565	845	38.3	124.9	13.45	515.14
1995:											
January	101.0	100.1	101.4	81.2	154.7	1 547	849	38.4	125.8	12.25	466.73
February	101.7	99.0	102.3	81.7	155.6	1 549	850	38.4	126.0	12.25	467.95
March	101.2	98.2	101.8	81.3	156.4	1 548	849	38.4	125.8	12.27	471.17
April	101.4	97.7	101.8	81.4	157.2	1 547	849	38.4	125.8	12.22	461.92
May	101.4	97.5	101.8	81.4	157.9	1 545	848	38.3	125.4	12.23	464.74
June	101.3	97.4	101.3	81.2	158.9	1 547	848	38.2	125.0	12.25	464.28
July	101.4	97.5	101.2	81.2	159.7	1 546	848	38.2	125.0	12.33	467.31
August	101.7	97.5	102.0	81.4	160.1	1 544	847	38.1	124.6	12.36	472.15
September	101.8	96.8	102.5	81.5	160.5	1 544	846	38.1	124.4	12.50	482.50
October	101.0	95.3	102.2	80.8	161.6	1 543	844	38.1	124.1	12.44	476.45
November	101.7	95.2	103.2	81.3	162.6	1 544	845	38.3	124.9	12.41	480.27
December	100.6	93.9	103.0	80.4	163.0	1 544	844	37.9	123.5	12.50	481.25
1996:											
January	99.0	92.5	100.6	79.0	164.5	1 542	843	37.0	120.4	12.49	458.38
February	100.4	91.4	102.6	80.1	164.8	1 540	843	38.1	124.0	12.49	473.37
March	100.4	92.0	102.5	80.2	164.8	1 543	844	38.2	124.5	12.53	478.65
April	100.5	93.6	101.6	80.2	165.1	1 538	841	38.2	124.0	12.53	474.89
May	101.6	93.9	103.5	81.1	165.3	1 538	840	38.3	124.2	12.54	476.52
June	101.2	94.8	102.7	80.7	165.4	1 538	840	38.3	124.2	12.54	475.27
July	101.6	95.4	102.5	81.1	165.2	1 539	840	38.3	124.2	12.63	479.94
August	102.2	95.5	102.9	81.5	165.5	1 540	841	38.3	124.3	12.70	490.22
September	102.6	95.4	103.7	81.8	166.1	1 541	840	38.3	124.2	12.82	497.42
October	102.8	95.5	103.8	81.9	166.4	1 543	841	38.2	124.0	12.81	493.19
November	103.1	94.7	104.5	82.2	166.7	1 541	841	38.3	124.3	12.82	496.13
December	103.4	95.4	104.6	82.4	166.9	1 541	840	38.4	124.5	12.90	503.10
1997:											
January	102.7	95.6	105.6	81.8	168.0	1 541	840	38.3	124.2	12.86	486.11
February	103.9	97.5	104.7	82.8	168.1	1 543	841	38.5	125.0	12.89	491.11
March	104.1	97.9	104.2	82.9	168.0	1 545	842	38.7	125.8	13.01	503.49
April	105.0	98.2	105.7	83.7	168.5	1 550	846	38.5	125.7	12.98	497.13
May	105.3	97.8	105.8	83.8	168.2	1 553	852	38.5	126.6	12.93	492.63
June	104.8	96.8	104.5	83.5	168.4	1 556	852	38.4	126.3	12.90	490.20
July	105.1	96.1	105.5	83.7	168.7	1 555	851	38.4	126.1	13.01	495.68
August	105.2	96.7	105.3	83.8	168.9	1 555	849	38.4	125.8	13.07	504.50
September	105.8	97.9	105.7	84.3	169.2	1 556	847	38.7	126.5	13.22	518.22
October	106.4	98.0	108.0	84.7	170.7	1 557	849	38.7	126.8	13.20	513.48
November	107.1	96.7	108.0	85.3	171.1	1 559	850	38.7	127.0	13.25	520.73
December	107.0	96.3	109.1	85.2	171.3	1 561	850	38.6	126.7	13.31	521.75
1998:											
January	106.4	97.2	108.0	84.6	173.2	1 563	850	38.5	126.3	13.28	504.64
February	106.4	98.4	108.7	84.4	173.0	1 564	849	38.6	126.5	13.34	509.59
March	105.4	99.2	107.1	83.3	173.1	1 564	848	38.4	125.7	13.38	515.13
April	105.5	99.3	108.0	83.1	174.0	1 565	847	38.3	125.2	13.34	504.25
May	105.6	99.5	108.3	83.0	173.9	1 566	847	38.4	125.6	13.33	507.87
June	105.5	98.4	109.1	82.7	173.6	1 568	847	38.3	125.2	13.34	506.92
July	105.4	97.3	108.9	82.4	173.7	1 567	846	38.4	125.4	13.44	512.06
August	104.9	97.3	106.8	81.7	173.7	1 566	844	38.5	125.4	13.47	519.94
September	104.6	97.5	107.0	81.3	174.3	1 565	844	38.2	124.5	13.65	526.89
October	104.2	97.2	107.3	80.8	174.9	1 565	843	38.2	124.3	13.61	522.62
November	105.4	96.6	110.6	81.4	175.2	1 564	840	38.1	123.5	13.57	525.16
December	105.1	96.6	110.7	81.0	175.2	1 560	836	38.1	123.0	13.68	530.78

Chemicals and Chemical Products—Production and Capacity Utilization

(Seasonally adjusted)

Year and month	Industrial production (1992=100)								Capacity utilization (output as a percent of capacity)		
	Total	Basic chemicals	Inorganic chemicals, not elsewhere classified	Industrial organic chemicals	Synthetic materials	Drugs and medicines	Soap and toiletries	Agricultural chemicals	Total	Plastic materials	Synthetic fibers
1970	48.8	69.4	81.1	.....	35.9	36.0	62.2	43.5	77.7	82.3	81.9
1971	51.9	71.9	74.8	.....	40.0	40.0	62.1	45.2	77.5	81.3	87.6
1972	58.4	81.4	81.5	63.0	49.1	42.0	71.0	50.6	82.3	98.5	87.6
1973	63.9	85.0	83.5	73.5	55.6	45.7	75.4	58.0	85.5	98.5	91.5
1974	66.2	89.1	88.8	74.0	59.0	48.3	78.5	63.4	84.4	93.8	89.9
1975	60.3	74.4	72.3	61.4	50.0	49.0	72.4	66.5	73.3	64.8	76.3
1976	67.5	79.6	77.3	75.2	57.7	53.4	79.1	67.8	78.4	74.5	77.7
1977	72.4	83.9	84.2	85.1	64.3	55.7	82.1	73.2	80.8	80.6	81.1
1978	76.4	85.6	84.9	86.5	71.2	59.0	87.7	74.4	82.7	85.3	86.5
1979	79.2	88.1	86.4	89.5	77.5	60.4	89.4	77.7	83.7	86.7	91.4
1980	75.9	83.1	81.0	81.5	64.0	62.8	94.5	80.4	78.4	75.2	65.3
1981	77.3	83.6	82.2	85.2	71.9	63.4	89.2	85.8	78.1	76.9	81.2
1982	71.0	75.0	74.6	71.2	64.5	64.8	81.5	74.6	70.7	71.2	68.6
1983	76.0	79.8	78.8	79.0	75.7	67.4	83.4	73.6	75.2	82.3	84.9
1984	79.3	84.0	81.9	82.1	80.1	68.1	82.7	85.7	77.4	86.3	85.4
1985	79.4	83.3	81.1	82.7	78.7	69.4	83.4	80.7	75.6	85.7	78.4
1986	82.4	81.8	78.0	83.5	82.9	75.8	88.3	74.8	77.6	89.4	86.3
1987	87.0	85.4	81.7	87.9	90.7	78.4	91.3	84.6	81.3	98.7	92.1
1988	92.2	89.4	84.6	98.1	94.5	82.2	97.2	90.0	84.0	95.5	91.7
1989	95.1	92.6	88.0	103.5	97.5	85.1	98.0	97.2	83.7	90.3	94.8
1990	97.3	101.2	101.1	104.9	95.9	88.3	99.9	100.4	83.0	87.1	86.7
1991	96.4	97.7	97.4	99.9	92.9	93.2	98.7	97.6	80.1	81.4	85.6
1992	100.0	100.0	100.0	100.0	100.0	100.0	100.0	100.0	80.2	89.0	86.0
1993	101.5	96.0	92.5	99.7	100.9	100.5	107.1	100.8	78.7	86.7	87.7
1994	104.7	91.3	86.1	107.2	108.7	104.5	106.4	100.5	78.9	95.9	85.8
1995	107.3	93.3	90.0	109.8	109.4	108.6	112.2	100.3	79.0	91.7	86.1
1996	110.0	94.7	92.3	110.5	110.8	113.3	116.2	102.4	78.2	89.1	85.3
1997	114.9	97.1	93.1	118.2	118.0	119.1	120.0	103.6	79.5	91.7	87.3
1998	115.5	91.4	84.4	116.5	120.7	119.5	122.2	108.3	77.8	91.1	85.3
1995:											
January	107.9	94.4	90.3	109.0	116.6	108.8	107.8	100.2	80.4	102.4	86.9
February	107.3	94.6	91.7	109.8	113.9	108.0	107.9	99.2	79.8	97.2	89.3
March	107.4	95.5	92.6	110.4	111.6	108.4	108.2	99.0	79.7	94.8	90.3
April	106.6	94.6	91.3	110.7	110.7	107.1	108.5	99.6	78.9	94.3	85.4
May	107.0	93.8	89.3	111.0	110.7	107.8	108.7	99.9	79.1	92.1	88.5
June	107.5	92.7	88.9	111.3	109.4	109.0	111.1	100.2	79.3	90.8	87.0
July	106.7	93.6	90.2	111.3	106.0	108.2	110.3	100.6	78.5	88.9	82.7
August	106.8	91.9	87.8	110.9	105.2	108.3	114.4	100.5	78.3	85.7	84.6
September	107.3	91.7	88.5	109.8	107.7	108.6	115.3	99.8	78.5	89.0	85.0
October	108.2	92.8	89.5	108.5	107.0	109.5	118.0	101.9	78.9	88.6	84.3
November	108.0	92.7	89.9	107.5	108.1	109.2	118.8	101.1	78.5	88.9	85.8
December	107.3	91.6	89.6	107.3	105.8	109.6	116.7	101.7	77.8	87.3	83.5
1996:											
January	107.5	92.3	89.8	107.5	106.5	108.8	119.0	102.2	77.7	88.1	81.3
February	107.7	91.8	89.7	108.0	106.6	110.0	116.9	102.8	77.6	88.5	81.2
March	107.6	90.9	89.0	108.4	107.3	110.7	115.4	103.1	77.3	88.5	81.1
April	107.4	92.5	89.7	108.8	107.6	110.2	112.9	100.4	76.9	88.3	80.8
May	108.4	94.5	90.9	109.1	109.5	110.2	115.7	98.9	77.4	89.6	83.5
June	108.5	94.5	92.4	109.4	111.0	109.6	114.5	102.2	77.2	89.9	84.7
July	110.4	95.1	93.8	109.9	111.3	114.2	115.3	102.5	78.4	88.8	86.9
August	111.0	96.0	94.3	110.6	111.7	113.2	118.0	104.5	78.6	89.6	86.6
September	111.9	96.6	94.9	111.7	112.7	117.4	114.7	103.2	79.0	89.9	86.5
October	112.9	98.0	94.2	113.0	115.7	117.2	118.0	104.0	79.5	89.6	91.9
November	112.8	96.7	94.2	114.3	113.4	118.7	116.0	102.4	79.2	88.5	88.8
December	113.8	97.6	94.1	115.3	115.7	118.6	117.5	102.0	79.7	89.7	90.1
1997:											
January	114.0	97.5	95.1	116.1	116.4	117.5	118.8	102.4	79.7	89.7	92.5
February	113.8	98.3	95.6	116.7	115.6	117.6	117.3	102.4	79.4	90.5	87.0
March	113.0	98.3	95.4	117.1	116.0	116.3	115.0	102.8	78.7	91.3	86.8
April	115.4	98.6	96.0	117.2	118.7	119.6	119.6	104.1	80.3	90.9	93.4
May	114.8	98.1	95.8	116.8	115.2	121.6	116.5	105.3	79.6	90.9	83.8
June	114.8	97.8	95.2	116.0	115.2	119.7	121.3	104.2	79.5	91.3	83.4
July	114.1	95.0	88.7	115.5	119.7	117.7	119.4	104.1	78.8	92.9	88.5
August	114.6	94.9	89.9	116.3	118.0	119.4	121.4	103.6	79.0	91.8	86.0
September	115.5	98.1	92.3	118.8	120.9	118.1	121.5	104.5	79.5	92.9	87.9
October	116.3	96.1	90.7	121.7	118.9	120.5	122.6	104.5	79.8	91.7	86.1
November	116.2	94.6	89.3	123.4	119.1	119.9	122.6	103.2	79.5	93.1	83.6
December	117.3	96.1	90.1	122.9	122.1	120.8	123.5	102.3	80.1	93.6	88.1
1998:											
January	117.0	96.8	90.0	121.0	121.9	121.2	121.1	106.3	79.7	93.4	87.9
February	116.7	95.8	87.9	119.4	121.0	121.2	120.8	105.4	79.3	91.0	90.2
March	116.6	95.9	89.2	118.9	119.8	121.2	121.2	105.7	79.1	89.5	89.5
April	117.7	94.8	87.8	119.1	122.0	122.5	124.3	104.3	79.7	91.7	90.0
May	116.9	93.7	87.4	118.8	120.4	122.5	122.1	107.3	79.0	90.5	86.4
June	116.2	90.4	83.0	117.5	119.4	121.0	126.0	108.8	78.3	89.7	86.3
July	115.7	87.2	78.6	115.6	121.2	120.6	124.9	112.2	77.9	91.6	85.5
August	114.3	84.3	74.5	114.1	121.8	116.9	122.8	113.0	76.7	92.9	85.0
September	113.3	84.6	74.7	113.7	118.9	116.8	120.1	111.0	75.9	87.1	85.5
October	113.1	88.4	81.5	111.8	118.8	115.7	119.9	111.3	75.7	89.1	81.7
November	114.7	92.9	88.6	112.9	122.7	117.7	122.1	108.0	76.6	94.1	79.6
December	114.0	92.4	89.4	114.7	120.0	117.8	120.4	106.6	76.1	93.1	76.2

Chemicals and Chemical Products—Shipments, Inventories, Prices, Employment, Hours, and Earnings

Year and month	Manufacturers' shipments and inventories (millions of dollars, seasonally adjusted)		Producer prices (1982=100, except as noted; not seasonally adjusted)			Employment (thousands, seasonally adjusted)		Production workers			
			Chemical industry (December 1984 = 100)	Commodity groups		Total payroll employees	Production workers	Average weekly hours, seasonally adjusted	Aggregate weekly hours index (1982=100), seasonally adjusted	Average earnings (dollars, not seasonally adjusted)	
	Shipments	Inventories (book value, end of period)		Drugs and pharmaceuticals	Agricultural chemicals					Hourly	Weekly
1970	49 195	6 749	.....	48.2	30.3	1 049	604	41.6	102.5	3.69	153.50
1971	51 681	6 923	.....	48.8	31.5	1 011	588	41.6	99.8	3.97	165.15
1972	58 130	7 079	.....	49.0	31.4	1 009	593	41.7	100.9	4.26	177.64
1973	66 003	7 553	.....	49.6	33.0	1 038	611	41.8	104.2	4.51	188.52
1974	85 387	11 579	.....	53.6	47.1	1 061	623	41.5	105.7	4.88	202.52
1975	91 710	12 073	.....	60.3	69.6	1 015	580	41.0	97.1	5.39	220.99
1976	106 467	13 319	.....	63.8	64.4	1 043	600	41.6	102.0	5.91	245.86
1977	120 905	14 633	.....	66.9	64.2	1 074	616	41.7	105.0	6.43	268.13
1978	132 262	16 018	.....	70.5	67.8	1 096	628	41.9	107.4	7.02	294.14
1979	151 887	17 690	.....	75.9	73.3	1 109	633	41.9	108.3	7.60	318.44
1980	168 220	20 066	.....	83.0	87.9	1 107	626	41.5	106.0	8.30	344.45
1981	186 909	22 438	.....	92.1	97.4	1 109	628	41.6	106.8	9.12	379.39
1982	176 254	24 448	.....	100.0	100.0	1 075	599	40.9	100.0	9.96	407.36
1983	189 552	24 698	.....	107.6	95.9	1 043	579	41.6	98.3	10.58	440.13
1984	205 963	26 420	.....	114.2	97.4	1 049	583	41.9	99.8	11.07	463.83
1985	204 790	26 119	100.7	122.0	96.2	1 044	577	41.9	98.9	11.56	484.36
1986	205 711	25 743	100.5	130.1	94.2	1 021	568	41.9	97.3	11.98	501.96
1987	229 546	26 585	103.6	139.1	96.4	1 025	575	42.3	99.3	12.37	523.25
1988	261 238	29 792	113.0	148.4	104.5	1 057	596	42.2	102.9	12.71	536.36
1989	283 196	31 725	119.6	160.0	108.7	1 074	603	42.4	104.5	13.09	555.02
1990	292 802	34 001	121.0	170.8	107.4	1 086	600	42.6	104.3	13.54	576.80
1991	298 545	34 529	124.4	182.6	111.7	1 076	580	42.9	101.6	14.04	602.32
1992	305 420	35 720	125.8	192.2	110.3	1 084	567	43.1	100.0	14.51	625.38
1993	314 907	35 771	127.2	200.9	109.9	1 081	573	43.1	100.9	14.82	638.74
1994	333 905	37 024	130.0	206.0	119.9	1 057	578	43.2	102.0	15.13	653.62
1995	361 391	39 913	143.4	210.9	130.1	1 038	580	43.2	102.5	15.62	674.78
1996	367 674	41 110	145.8	214.7	133.7	1 034	575	43.2	101.5	16.17	698.54
1997	389 189	44 249	147.1	219.1	132.7	1 036	573	43.2	101.2	16.57	715.82
1998	391 700	46 217	148.7	242.6	128.5	1 043	586	43.2	103.4	17.12	739.58
1995:											
January	29 745	37 245	138.4	207.8	126.9	1 045	577	43.4	102.3	15.37	665.52
February	30 104	37 524	140.6	208.9	129.6	1 043	577	43.3	102.1	15.39	664.85
March	30 124	37 654	141.4	208.9	131.5	1 040	576	43.3	101.9	15.39	666.39
April	29 260	38 289	144.8	210.4	132.5	1 039	577	43.4	102.3	15.69	679.38
May	29 977	38 873	145.0	210.4	132.1	1 038	578	43.2	102.0	15.49	667.62
June	30 455	39 272	143.9	210.2	131.1	1 037	579	43.3	102.4	15.49	670.72
July	30 446	39 632	144.5	210.8	129.4	1 037	582	43.2	102.7	15.68	671.10
August	30 703	39 739	144.3	210.9	127.9	1 036	583	43.1	102.7	15.56	665.97
September	30 238	40 029	144.7	211.9	128.2	1 036	583	43.2	102.9	15.71	678.67
October	30 388	39 823	144.7	213.1	128.7	1 037	584	43.2	103.1	15.79	682.13
November	30 162	39 609	144.6	213.4	130.7	1 037	583	43.0	102.4	15.88	689.19
December	30 091	39 913	144.3	213.8	132.7	1 033	582	43.1	102.5	16.03	703.72
1996:											
January	29 969	39 985	144.6	213.5	135.2	1 035	582	42.5	101.1	16.08	681.79
February	29 802	39 945	144.5	213.4	136.3	1 035	581	43.2	102.6	15.96	687.88
March	29 633	40 202	145.0	214.4	138.2	1 037	580	43.1	102.1	16.00	689.60
April	30 190	40 377	145.3	214.1	136.9	1 035	578	43.0	101.6	16.15	691.22
May	30 861	40 228	146.0	214.8	134.9	1 034	576	43.2	101.7	16.04	689.72
June	30 256	40 319	146.0	215.0	132.9	1 033	576	43.4	102.1	16.11	699.17
July	31 038	40 157	145.9	215.4	129.9	1 033	574	43.3	101.6	16.16	691.65
August	30 972	40 293	146.1	215.1	129.9	1 035	574	43.2	101.3	16.22	695.84
September	30 747	40 569	146.8	215.1	131.1	1 033	573	43.1	100.9	16.26	704.06
October	31 636	40 670	146.8	215.4	132.2	1 033	571	43.1	100.6	16.29	702.10
November	31 451	40 654	146.3	214.8	132.7	1 033	571	43.3	101.0	16.38	715.81
December	31 191	41 110	146.4	215.4	133.7	1 033	570	43.5	101.3	16.45	730.38
1997:											
January	32 025	41 105	146.8	217.4	134.1	1 034	569	43.1	100.2	16.37	705.55
February	32 167	41 328	146.8	218.2	133.8	1 033	569	43.3	100.7	16.49	710.72
March	31 695	41 389	146.9	218.6	134.1	1 035	570	43.2	100.6	16.42	709.34
April	32 547	41 778	147.0	217.7	134.6	1 035	570	43.2	100.6	16.42	706.06
May	32 460	41 883	147.0	218.3	134.3	1 036	571	43.3	101.0	16.48	710.29
June	32 365	42 151	147.0	218.6	132.7	1 036	570	43.1	100.4	16.53	712.44
July	32 513	42 365	147.1	219.1	132.0	1 033	571	43.1	100.6	16.58	707.97
August	32 220	42 471	147.2	219.3	132.0	1 034	572	43.2	101.0	16.57	712.51
September	32 662	43 101	147.1	219.3	131.7	1 037	575	43.2	101.5	16.62	722.97
October	32 695	43 673	147.3	220.4	131.3	1 038	577	43.3	102.1	16.64	720.51
November	32 469	44 324	147.3	221.2	131.2	1 040	579	43.4	102.7	16.84	735.91
December	33 092	44 249	147.3	221.4	130.4	1 041	581	43.2	102.6	16.91	744.04
1998:											
January	32 697	44 797	147.3	221.6	130.7	1 040	583	43.5	103.6	16.88	732.59
February	32 514	45 310	147.1	224.5	129.9	1 041	585	43.4	103.7	16.92	732.64
March	32 717	45 368	149.2	243.3	130.0	1 043	586	43.4	103.9	16.96	736.06
April	32 380	45 611	149.8	243.4	129.0	1 042	587	43.2	103.6	17.15	735.74
May	32 501	45 821	149.7	244.1	129.7	1 044	588	43.1	103.6	17.11	734.02
June	32 981	46 061	149.5	245.9	129.8	1 044	588	43.2	103.8	17.04	734.42
July	32 468	46 382	149.5	247.7	129.1	1 044	587	43.1	103.4	17.19	734.01
August	32 204	46 535	149.1	247.2	128.9	1 044	586	43.2	103.4	17.14	737.02
September	32 616	46 313	148.5	247.2	126.2	1 043	586	43.2	103.4	17.30	750.82
October	31 960	46 356	148.3	248.6	127.2	1 042	585	43.2	103.3	17.21	743.47
November	32 533	46 875	148.1	248.5	126.3	1 043	585	42.9	102.5	17.27	746.06
December	33 581	46 217	147.9	249.1	125.5	1 042	586	42.7	102.2	17.31	752.99

Petroleum and Coal Products—Production, Capacity Utilization, Shipments and Inventories

(Seasonally adjusted)

| Year and month | Industrial production–Petroleum products (1992=100) | | | | | | | | Capacity utilization: Petroleum products (output as a percent of capacity) | Manufacturers' shipments and inventories (millions of dollars) | |
| | Total | Petroleum refining and miscellaneous | | | | | | Paving and roofing materials | | Shipments | Inventories (book value, end of period) |
		Total	Miscellaneous petroleum products	Distillate fuel oil	Residual fuel oil	Aviation fuel and kerosene	Automotive gasoline				
1970	80.8	80.8	79.9	82.5	79.2	78.6	80.7	74.8	93.9	24 200	2 161
1971	83.5	83.5	82.0	83.9	84.1	77.2	84.6	78.2	91.8	26 198	2 260
1972	87.4	87.3	86.2	88.3	89.3	76.2	88.9	82.0	92.8	27 918	2 142
1973	92.2	92.3	92.0	94.9	109.3	77.0	92.4	85.7	94.2	33 903	2 476
1974	89.0	89.9	90.4	89.5	120.7	71.1	90.0	79.2	87.1	57 229	3 945
1975	88.0	89.9	83.4	89.0	138.8	72.7	92.0	71.8	83.7	67 496	4 426
1976	93.6	95.6	87.6	98.2	154.6	75.8	96.8	76.0	85.2	80 022	4 711
1977	101.5	103.3	97.3	110.5	196.9	81.1	99.6	83.4	87.6	94 702	5 439
1978	104.9	105.9	109.9	106.5	186.9	79.6	101.5	94.0	87.6	100 967	5 330
1979	103.9	104.9	112.7	106.1	188.8	84.1	96.9	93.2	84.1	144 156	7 458
1980	95.9	97.2	105.6	89.6	177.1	80.0	92.1	81.8	74.7	192 969	9 693
1981	91.2	92.3	95.0	88.0	148.0	76.4	90.7	78.0	70.7	217 681	10 420
1982	86.6	87.5	80.7	87.6	120.2	76.3	89.7	76.5	70.1	203 404	17 009
1983	86.9	86.0	81.7	82.5	95.6	78.9	89.8	95.0	73.4	187 788	14 843
1984	89.9	89.5	83.4	90.2	99.8	86.9	91.5	95.0	77.8	184 488	14 260
1985	89.5	89.7	84.7	90.1	98.7	88.7	90.9	90.2	78.4	176 574	13 975
1986	95.7	94.9	92.0	94.0	99.6	96.9	95.6	103.3	83.7	122 605	8 791
1987	97.0	95.8	94.6	91.7	99.2	99.0	96.9	107.0	83.5	130 414	9 973
1988	98.8	97.9	95.5	96.1	103.8	100.9	98.5	106.9	85.3	131 682	9 196
1989	99.3	98.5	95.6	97.5	106.9	102.8	98.6	106.0	87.0	146 487	10 743
1990	100.3	99.6	98.7	98.3	106.5	106.5	98.6	106.5	87.6	173 389	13 432
1991	99.1	99.2	97.2	99.6	104.8	102.6	98.8	98.4	86.6	159 144	11 671
1992	100.0	100.0	100.0	100.0	100.0	100.0	100.0	100.0	92.1	150 227	11 350
1993	102.9	102.0	101.7	105.3	93.6	102.1	101.4	109.1	92.1	144 834	10 265
1994	102.7	101.9	102.5	107.8	92.6	104.5	99.7	107.5	91.1	143 328	11 121
1995	104.5	103.6	104.6	106.1	88.3	102.0	103.6	111.2	91.9	151 439	11 304
1996	106.8	105.4	103.3	111.5	81.3	109.4	105.0	117.8	93.8	174 284	12 520
1997	109.8	108.6	110.2	114.1	78.9	111.7	107.6	118.6	95.3	177 314	12 218
1998	112.0	110.0	112.3	115.1	85.3	110.8	109.0	127.5	96.1	145 673	10 254
1995:											
January	104.4	103.9	105.8	106.8	94.7	100.6	103.2	107.3	91.6	12 643	11 470
February	104.2	103.9	106.4	106.2	83.8	101.1	103.9	106.2	91.5	13 016	11 611
March	105.2	104.5	108.1	111.1	88.5	95.0	103.4	110.4	92.4	12 684	11 504
April	103.7	102.7	102.4	105.4	91.8	98.8	103.4	110.5	91.1	13 136	11 609
May	103.4	102.5	104.8	104.4	84.9	100.9	102.5	109.6	90.9	13 141	11 712
June	104.6	103.3	106.0	103.9	87.4	100.7	103.5	113.9	92.0	12 933	11 595
July	105.4	104.4	108.0	103.5	94.3	102.7	104.2	112.4	92.8	12 510	11 234
August	104.7	103.6	106.3	106.3	91.4	101.3	102.7	112.3	92.2	12 501	11 079
September	105.7	105.2	104.7	108.1	91.8	104.8	105.4	107.5	93.1	12 172	11 093
October	103.4	102.0	99.3	103.1	85.0	104.5	103.4	114.3	91.2	11 860	10 805
November	104.0	102.7	101.8	106.2	75.8	106.5	103.1	112.9	91.7	12 276	10 886
December	105.3	103.9	101.6	107.9	89.4	106.1	103.9	115.4	92.9	12 699	11 304
1996:											
January	105.6	104.3	101.1	108.6	82.9	112.8	103.9	114.9	93.1	13 151	11 490
February	106.5	105.4	100.2	112.3	85.2	109.9	105.6	114.5	93.9	13 366	11 594
March	106.2	105.1	101.1	109.1	80.7	109.1	106.2	114.0	93.5	14 097	11 959
April	105.8	104.7	101.6	111.5	79.0	109.4	104.4	113.8	93.1	15 103	12 044
May	106.3	104.9	102.9	108.9	84.7	105.0	105.7	116.8	93.5	14 697	11 991
June	106.6	105.3	103.5	109.7	86.0	108.1	105.3	116.0	93.6	14 136	11 942
July	105.6	104.2	102.1	106.4	76.3	105.6	106.1	116.0	92.7	14 264	12 077
August	107.7	105.8	104.6	110.7	83.1	108.0	105.8	122.2	94.4	14 319	12 015
September	107.3	105.7	105.2	111.4	80.2	117.3	103.4	119.0	94.0	14 729	12 252
October	108.7	107.0	106.1	118.1	81.6	110.4	104.3	121.6	95.1	15 247	12 289
November	108.0	106.3	105.2	116.1	76.7	107.0	105.1	121.6	94.5	15 388	12 344
December	107.6	106.0	106.2	114.0	79.0	109.1	104.3	120.2	94.1	15 484	12 520
1997:											
January	107.6	106.0	109.3	109.2	82.9	107.6	104.8	120.2	93.9	15 879	13 039
February	108.6	106.8	109.1	110.4	83.4	110.2	105.6	122.3	94.7	15 504	12 858
March	108.3	106.7	105.4	113.0	73.7	110.5	106.6	120.7	94.3	14 946	12 923
April	110.0	108.6	111.8	112.5	73.6	111.0	107.9	120.9	95.7	14 532	12 656
May	111.8	110.5	114.0	117.8	72.2	112.8	108.8	121.0	97.2	14 701	12 919
June	111.4	110.3	110.5	117.5	85.5	113.7	108.6	120.1	96.7	14 518	12 623
July	109.0	107.9	108.8	114.5	76.4	114.5	106.0	117.4	94.5	14 614	12 338
August	110.1	109.1	109.0	115.6	73.0	113.0	108.7	117.2	95.4	15 311	12 657
September	110.1	109.3	109.2	113.3	77.0	113.2	109.4	115.7	95.3	14 791	12 621
October	111.1	110.4	111.5	114.9	80.9	111.1	110.3	116.0	96.0	14 638	12 559
November	109.1	108.2	112.2	113.0	84.6	114.0	105.3	115.5	94.2	14 139	12 489
December	110.6	109.5	112.1	115.3	81.7	109.6	108.2	118.3	95.4	13 836	12 218
1998:											
January	111.2	110.6	116.0	116.3	79.4	107.5	108.9	115.7	95.8	13 198	11 449
February	110.5	109.0	112.0	117.8	70.6	107.4	107.6	122.6	95.2	12 883	11 478
March	113.0	110.9	112.0	118.6	91.7	113.7	108.4	129.4	97.2	12 913	11 405
April	112.8	111.3	110.6	116.7	102.2	113.3	109.8	124.0	96.9	12 782	11 400
May	111.5	109.9	108.7	117.7	90.7	112.5	108.3	123.9	95.7	12 599	11 169
June	111.6	109.9	107.8	117.8	87.9	112.3	109.1	124.2	95.7	12 416	10 936
July	113.4	111.6	112.1	121.9	93.0	106.5	109.7	127.3	97.2	12 153	10 906
August	114.1	111.9	113.1	117.1	88.4	116.3	110.3	131.7	97.7	11 759	10 759
September	110.7	108.1	112.2	111.6	83.8	105.2	107.2	131.8	94.7	11 885	10 770
October	110.4	108.2	112.9	105.1	78.6	107.0	109.7	128.2	94.4	11 500	10 832
November	112.8	110.5	117.5	109.7	79.7	115.9	109.0	131.3	96.3	11 043	10 965
December	112.5	109.6	113.1	110.6	81.4	111.7	109.5	135.8	96.0	11 060	10 254

Petroleum and Coal Products—Prices, Employment, Hours, and Earnings

Year and month	Producer prices (1982=100, except as noted, not seasonally adjusted)								Consumer prices: Motor fuel (1982-1984=100, seasonally adjusted)		Employment (thousands, seasonally adjusted)		Production workers			
	Petroleum refining and related industries, (December 1984=100)	Intermediate materials				Finished goods		Petroleum refining industry					Average weekly hours, not seasonally adjusted	Aggregate weekly hours index (1982=100), seasonally adjusted	Average earnings (dollars, not seasonally adjusted)	
		Liquefied petroleum gas	Jet fuels	Number 2 diesel fuel	Residual fuel	Gasoline	Number 2 fuel oil		Total	Gasoline	Total payroll employees	Production workers			Hourly	Weekly
1970	.....	.....	.....	.....	10.6	14.4	.....	.....	27.9	27.9	191	118	42.8	96.2	4.28	183.18
1971	.....	15.2	.....	.....	14.0	15.1	.....	.....	28.1	28.1	194	124	42.8	100.9	4.57	195.60
1972	.....	14.9	.....	.....	13.4	15.5	.....	.....	28.4	28.4	195	125	42.7	101.5	4.96	211.79
1973	.....	18.0	.....	14.3	16.1	18.2	13.9	.....	31.2	31.2	193	124	42.4	99.9	5.28	223.87
1974	.....	29.2	.....	27.7	41.1	29.2	26.3	.....	42.2	42.2	197	126	42.1	100.9	5.68	239.13
1975	.....	35.2	28.4	31.2	41.9	34.5	30.1	.....	45.1	45.1	194	123	41.2	96.3	6.48	266.98
1976	.....	45.8	31.1	34.1	38.3	38.0	32.7	.....	47.0	47.0	199	128	42.1	102.3	7.21	303.54
1977	.....	57.3	35.7	38.5	44.2	41.3	37.6	47.9	49.7	49.7	202	131	42.7	106.6	7.83	334.34
1978	.....	54.7	39.6	39.7	42.1	43.4	39.0	50.3	51.8	51.8	208	136	43.6	112.2	8.63	376.27
1979	.....	64.7	53.7	57.1	57.9	60.0	56.4	68.8	70.1	70.2	210	137	43.8	114.0	9.36	409.97
1980	.....	102.3	87.5	85.8	81.3	93.3	82.8	104.6	97.4	97.5	198	125	41.8	99.1	10.10	422.18
1981	.....	112.0	104.5	105.0	104.8	108.0	104.1	123.9	108.5	108.5	214	134	43.2	110.0	11.38	491.62
1982	.....	100.0	100.0	100.0	100.0	100.0	100.0	117.1	102.8	102.8	201	120	43.9	100.0	12.46	546.99
1983	.....	113.5	91.5	87.9	89.6	90.2	87.8	106.8	99.4	99.4	196	118	43.9	98.4	13.28	582.99
1984	.....	99.1	87.0	86.3	94.7	84.6	87.3	103.7	97.9	97.8	189	111	43.7	92.5	13.44	587.33
1985	.....	86.3	81.0	81.2	83.2	83.3	81.6	98.3	98.7	98.6	179	109	43.0	88.7	14.06	604.58
1986	66.6	61.0	53.8	48.6	44.5	54.7	50.5	64.3	77.1	77.0	169	106	43.8	88.1	14.19	621.52
1987	70.5	57.4	54.2	55.4	53.1	58.8	55.9	68.6	80.2	80.1	164	107	44.0	89.4	14.58	641.52
1988	67.7	51.6	52.1	49.7	41.1	57.3	49.5	65.4	80.9	80.8	160	104	44.4	88.1	14.97	664.67
1989	75.7	52.7	58.1	58.9	47.6	65.1	58.0	73.6	88.5	88.5	156	102	44.3	85.7	15.41	682.66
1990	91.4	77.4	76.0	74.1	57.7	78.7	73.3	90.1	101.2	101.0	157	103	44.6	87.2	16.24	724.30
1991	83.1	75.4	66.4	65.6	49.1	69.9	65.2	80.9	99.4	99.2	160	103	44.1	86.7	17.04	751.46
1992	80.3	65.8	61.9	61.9	45.9	68.1	61.7	78.3	99.0	99.0	158	103	43.8	86.0	17.90	784.02
1993	77.6	63.6	59.0	60.5	49.6	63.9	59.1	75.2	98.0	97.7	152	99	44.2	83.1	18.53	819.03
1994	74.8	58.2	53.9	56.0	48.2	61.7	56.0	72.2	98.5	98.2	149	97	44.4	81.4	19.07	846.71
1995	77.2	65.1	55.0	57.0	52.6	63.7	56.6	74.5	100.0	99.8	145	94	43.7	77.9	19.36	846.03
1996	87.4	84.7	66.7	70.0	59.8	72.8	69.5	85.3	106.3	105.9	142	92	43.6	76.3	19.32	842.35
1997	85.6	84.5	62.9	64.5	59.5	71.9	64.8	83.1	106.2	105.8	141	93	43.1	76.1	20.20	870.62
1998	66.3	60.1	46.1	47.4	43.8	53.4	48.1	62.3	92.2	91.6	140	93	43.6	76.7	20.92	912.11
1995:																
January	74.3	63.8	53.3	54.0	50.4	60.2	56.4	71.5	100.9	100.9	148	96	43.8	80.3	19.18	840.08
February	74.6	67.0	53.0	53.1	54.0	60.4	54.2	71.8	101.1	100.9	148	96	44.4	81.6	19.55	868.02
March	75.3	65.5	52.2	55.0	54.8	61.6	54.0	72.5	100.5	100.3	148	96	43.3	79.9	19.37	838.72
April	80.2	65.7	53.6	58.2	54.7	67.7	56.3	77.7	100.8	100.6	147	95	43.9	80.4	19.55	858.25
May	83.4	65.9	55.4	59.4	56.9	71.8	59.3	81.1	102.5	102.3	147	95	43.2	78.7	19.17	828.14
June	81.9	68.5	53.9	56.8	61.2	70.6	54.5	79.5	103.0	103.1	146	94	43.7	78.1	19.16	837.29
July	78.1	64.5	53.7	53.7	57.1	65.9	53.2	75.3	101.3	101.2	145	94	44.1	78.6	19.25	848.93
August	77.5	61.7	53.9	56.0	54.0	64.5	55.3	74.7	99.8	99.6	144	93	43.2	76.7	19.14	826.85
September	77.6	62.4	55.8	58.5	45.9	64.2	58.1	74.8	98.4	98.3	143	93	43.8	76.0	19.41	850.16
October	75.4	64.4	56.5	58.8	46.8	60.8	56.8	72.4	97.9	97.6	143	93	44.3	77.3	19.68	871.82
November	73.4	65.2	58.5	59.7	47.0	57.2	59.6	70.2	95.9	95.6	142	91	43.8	74.7	19.46	852.35
December	75.4	66.9	59.5	60.2	48.5	59.8	62.0	72.4	97.6	97.3	142	91	43.2	74.2	19.44	839.81
1996:																
January	79.4	73.0	62.8	62.2	55.8	64.1	64.3	76.7	100.6	100.4	143	92	43.1	75.6	19.41	836.57
February	77.3	76.0	57.0	59.4	57.1	62.2	61.1	74.5	101.1	100.9	143	92	42.8	75.6	19.54	836.31
March	81.8	77.4	58.9	62.6	56.8	68.0	65.9	79.2	104.6	104.4	143	92	42.9	75.7	19.21	824.11
April	90.5	81.0	66.7	75.4	56.2	76.4	75.6	88.6	110.0	109.7	142	91	43.3	75.4	19.32	836.56
May	92.8	76.3	68.8	74.5	61.9	80.1	69.4	91.0	111.7	111.2	142	91	42.6	74.6	18.98	808.55
June	87.3	74.7	62.1	64.9	61.0	75.8	60.1	85.2	108.1	107.8	142	92	44.7	78.4	18.88	843.94
July	86.3	76.0	62.0	66.1	61.5	73.6	62.6	84.1	106.8	106.5	142	92	44.3	77.1	19.01	842.14
August	86.9	80.8	66.0	66.6	61.6	72.6	67.2	84.7	105.1	104.7	142	92	43.9	76.8	18.98	833.22
September	89.9	88.4	73.0	74.7	58.4	73.6	72.8	87.9	104.9	104.4	142	92	44.2	76.6	19.34	854.83
October	92.0	95.4	75.5	80.2	61.7	74.1	80.6	90.2	105.3	104.5	141	92	43.6	75.4	19.34	843.22
November	92.5	102.5	72.6	77.0	61.7	76.6	77.1	90.7	107.0	106.5	142	92	43.9	75.9	19.61	860.88
December	92.5	114.7	75.0	76.0	64.4	76.0	77.5	90.7	109.6	109.0	141	92	43.9	76.1	20.25	888.98
1997:																
January	92.9	114.8	75.1	73.2	64.6	76.6	75.8	91.1	110.5	110.0	141	93	44.9	78.2	20.11	902.94
February	91.2	103.1	74.8	73.1	61.4	75.0	72.4	89.3	111.3	110.7	141	93	43.4	77.4	20.39	884.93
March	87.3	86.0	66.7	66.5	57.6	73.5	64.0	85.0	109.9	109.3	141	93	43.0	76.4	20.48	880.64
April	85.8	79.9	60.9	66.1	56.8	72.7	64.9	83.4	107.5	107.0	141	93	42.4	75.7	19.94	845.46
May	85.5	73.8	58.7	63.6	56.2	72.8	66.2	83.1	104.0	103.4	141	93	42.4	75.9	19.96	846.30
June	83.6	76.9	59.5	61.0	57.0	71.2	60.9	80.9	103.1	102.5	141	92	42.9	75.2	19.92	854.57
July	81.3	73.0	57.6	57.7	53.1	69.3	58.8	78.5	102.1	101.5	141	93	42.8	75.2	20.02	856.86
August	85.3	75.8	59.7	62.1	55.4	73.7	61.6	82.8	106.4	106.1	141	93	43.0	75.9	19.99	859.57
September	86.1	80.4	58.4	61.3	59.8	75.3	60.2	83.7	108.2	108.0	141	93	43.3	75.9	20.27	877.69
October	84.8	83.6	62.1	64.7	69.2	70.5	66.0	82.3	105.8	105.6	141	93	43.3	75.9	20.32	879.86
November	83.6	85.2	63.7	65.8	62.9	67.9	66.5	81.0	103.6	103.2	141	93	43.3	76.4	20.42	884.19
December	79.1	81.1	58.3	58.9	59.5	64.6	60.7	76.2	102.4	101.9	142	94	42.2	74.9	20.58	868.48
1998:																
January	73.8	74.6	54.8	53.9	51.5	59.4	55.1	70.4	99.4	99.0	140	92	44.5	76.4	20.66	919.37
February	70.1	70.5	52.1	51.3	47.3	55.8	54.1	66.4	96.9	96.4	140	92	42.2	74.5	20.95	884.09
March	65.6	66.0	47.2	47.6	42.6	51.7	49.7	61.5	94.0	93.5	141	92	43.1	75.7	21.20	913.72
April	67.9	62.4	47.3	50.0	49.3	54.0	51.2	64.0	93.2	92.7	141	92	42.8	75.2	21.02	899.66
May	70.2	63.4	47.9	50.0	47.1	58.3	50.6	66.6	93.3	92.8	141	92	42.9	76.1	20.81	892.75
June	68.0	59.2	43.5	45.8	46.3	57.4	46.5	64.1	92.5	91.9	141	93	43.2	76.6	20.74	895.97
July	67.0	55.7	42.9	44.7	47.7	56.0	45.5	63.1	92.2	91.6	140	92	44.8	77.7	20.83	933.18
August	63.6	54.5	43.5	44.4	38.2	51.6	43.1	59.4	90.6	89.9	140	92	44.0	76.6	20.80	915.20
September	64.2	52.5	43.1	48.1	39.0	51.0	48.0	60.0	89.1	88.5	140	92	43.2	76.3	20.83	899.86
October	65.5	52.8	47.6	47.3	41.7	52.5	47.9	61.5	89.8	89.3	140	92	44.0	76.3	21.06	926.64
November	63.3	55.2	46.2	46.1	39.0	49.8	46.3	59.1	88.6	88.2	140	93	43.9	77.3	20.96	920.14
December	56.3	54.7	37.4	39.0	35.8	43.2	38.8	51.6	86.4	85.9	140	94	44.7	79.4	21.22	948.53

Rubber and Plastics Products—Production, Capacity Utilization, Shipments, and Inventories

(Seasonally adjusted)

Year and month	Industrial production (1992=100)				Capacity utilization (output as a percent of capacity)	Manufacturers' shipments and inventories	
	Total	Tires	Other rubber products	Plastic products, not elsewhere classified		Shipments	Inventories (book value, end of period)
1970	33.0	41.7	69.5	23.8	81.2	16 754	2 386
1971	35.9	48.1	70.1	26.1	82.6	18 409	2 453
1972	43.7	54.5	79.4	33.6	91.6	21 662	2 695
1973	49.0	55.9	87.4	39.6	93.3	25 191	3 103
1974	47.9	59.1	86.2	37.3	84.9	28 828	4 023
1975	41.6	54.5	74.0	31.7	70.1	28 128	4 085
1976	48.1	54.0	80.4	40.0	78.5	32 880	4 581
1977	56.0	70.2	85.1	47.1	88.3	40 944	5 116
1978	59.3	69.9	88.0	51.4	89.2	44 823	5 801
1979	58.7	68.9	88.6	50.7	84.2	48 694	6 399
1980	53.3	55.3	78.0	48.1	73.9	49 157	6 435
1981	57.5	64.2	82.0	51.1	77.9	55 178	6 968
1982	56.8	63.4	73.1	52.0	74.4	57 307	7 748
1983	64.0	68.2	77.1	60.3	79.2	62 870	8 070
1984	72.1	78.8	85.7	67.9	84.3	72 938	8 904
1985	73.8	76.8	85.3	70.6	82.1	75 590	9 213
1986	78.2	75.0	86.6	76.8	82.9	78 379	9 285
1987	86.0	83.3	93.5	84.7	89.0	86 634	10 065
1988	88.2	88.2	98.3	85.8	87.8	95 485	11 367
1989	91.2	91.8	97.2	89.6	87.4	101 236	11 533
1990	92.2	91.0	97.6	91.1	84.6	105 250	12 292
1991	90.7	87.3	92.9	90.8	80.3	105 804	12 121
1992	100.0	100.0	100.0	100.0	84.7	113 593	12 541
1993	106.9	105.3	106.2	107.4	86.2	122 777	12 821
1994	116.5	110.0	112.7	118.5	89.6	135 145	14 232
1995	119.7	117.1	118.5	120.4	88.0	145 739	15 220
1996	123.3	116.8	120.0	125.0	86.6	150 467	15 728
1997	128.2	122.3	122.9	130.3	85.6	156 599	16 455
1998	132.6	127.6	125.4	135.1	84.6	158 156	16 766
1995:							
January	120.6	113.9	115.3	122.9	90.5	12 184	14 481
February	120.8	115.0	117.9	122.4	90.3	12 128	14 901
March	119.9	112.8	118.9	121.2	89.3	12 168	15 060
April	120.6	121.7	118.7	121.0	89.5	12 034	15 312
May	118.7	114.6	118.3	119.4	87.7	12 086	15 362
June	118.5	116.3	119.3	118.7	87.3	12 039	15 427
July	117.4	121.6	115.5	117.3	86.1	11 719	15 460
August	119.1	117.5	120.8	119.0	87.1	12 285	15 383
September	120.0	118.0	120.4	120.2	87.4	12 299	15 316
October	120.4	118.4	119.8	120.9	87.4	12 234	15 265
November	120.4	118.8	119.9	120.8	87.1	12 335	15 189
December	119.7	116.3	117.1	120.8	86.3	12 158	15 220
1996:							
January	120.0	118.7	118.2	120.7	86.3	11 875	15 198
February	120.5	114.2	119.3	121.7	86.2	12 276	15 217
March	121.3	118.1	118.3	122.5	86.5	12 394	15 294
April	120.7	113.7	118.5	122.3	85.7	12 576	15 206
May	122.8	113.5	120.3	124.8	86.9	12 761	15 138
June	124.1	117.1	120.1	126.1	87.4	12 659	15 240
July	124.0	114.5	118.7	126.7	87.0	12 743	15 286
August	125.2	116.1	120.5	127.6	87.4	12 693	15 335
September	125.8	122.0	119.5	127.9	87.5	12 586	15 493
October	124.4	119.3	122.4	125.7	86.2	12 585	15 580
November	124.6	117.9	121.0	126.5	85.9	12 741	15 619
December	126.0	116.4	123.6	128.0	86.6	12 518	15 728
1997:							
January	124.8	117.8	121.3	126.7	85.3	12 904	15 855
February	126.6	121.5	122.0	128.5	86.2	12 946	15 917
March	127.2	125.3	119.0	129.5	86.3	12 823	16 031
April	126.4	114.3	122.6	129.0	85.3	13 321	16 085
May	127.2	116.9	120.9	130.1	85.5	12 811	16 269
June	127.5	124.3	121.9	129.4	85.4	12 791	16 281
July	127.9	124.6	122.8	129.6	85.3	13 078	16 305
August	129.7	129.2	123.3	131.4	86.1	12 880	16 395
September	129.6	123.6	124.2	131.7	85.7	13 155	16 348
October	129.2	119.7	125.5	131.4	85.1	13 301	16 386
November	130.9	126.4	125.7	132.9	85.9	13 118	16 466
December	130.9	123.5	125.4	133.3	85.5	13 536	16 455
1998:							
January	131.0	122.1	125.3	133.6	85.3	13 119	16 562
February	131.1	124.9	122.5	134.1	85.0	13 185	16 587
March	131.4	125.3	123.3	134.2	84.9	13 190	16 509
April	133.2	128.0	126.6	135.5	85.7	13 203	16 484
May	133.1	134.8	125.4	134.8	85.3	13 045	16 571
June	132.4	121.1	126.1	135.5	84.6	13 001	16 697
July	132.7	125.9	123.6	135.8	84.4	13 104	16 650
August	132.2	133.6	121.0	134.8	83.7	13 196	16 699
September	132.6	126.0	124.5	135.5	83.7	13 282	16 607
October	133.4	125.3	125.5	136.4	83.8	13 249	16 678
November	135.0	131.4	129.2	137.0	84.5	13 209	16 857
December	136.0	132.2	132.3	137.6	84.8	13 400	16 766

Rubber and Plastics Products—Prices, Employment, Hours, and Earnings

Year and month	Producer prices (1982=100, except as noted, not seasonally adjusted)						Employment (thousands, seasonally adjusted)		Production workers			
	Rubber and plastics products (December 1984=100)	Finished tires and tubes	Intermediate materials				Total payroll employees	Production workers	Average hours, seasonally adjusted	Aggregate hours index (1982=100), seasonally adjusted	Average earnings (dollars, not seasonally adjusted)	
			Synthetic rubber	Plastic construction products	Plastic film and sheet	Plastic parts for manufacturing					Hourly	Weekly
1970	.....	42.7	34.0	65.5	.....	.....	617	473	40.3	86.3	3.21	129.36
1971	.....	42.8	34.0	63.7	47.3	.....	617	479	40.4	87.5	3.41	137.76
1972	.....	42.8	34.1	62.9	46.2	.....	667	525	41.2	97.8	3.63	149.56
1973	.....	43.7	34.3	63.4	46.9	.....	731	579	41.2	107.9	3.84	158.21
1974	.....	52.3	44.1	80.1	61.6	.....	733	577	40.6	105.8	4.09	166.05
1975	.....	58.2	49.3	83.5	69.6	.....	643	493	39.9	89.0	4.42	176.36
1976	.....	63.3	52.6	85.7	72.5	.....	675	522	40.7	96.1	4.71	191.70
1977	.....	66.6	56.1	89.7	75.0	.....	750	588	41.1	109.2	5.21	214.13
1978	.....	70.2	60.4	91.8	76.2	.....	793	622	40.9	115.3	5.57	227.81
1979	.....	80.7	70.3	99.4	81.4	82.5	821	643	40.6	118.2	6.02	244.41
1980	.....	92.8	85.3	103.9	89.3	90.8	764	588	40.0	106.7	6.58	263.20
1981	.....	98.2	98.0	104.3	95.7	96.6	772	597	40.3	109.0	7.22	290.97
1982	.....	100.0	100.0	100.0	100.0	100.0	729	558	39.6	100.0	7.70	304.92
1983	.....	96.1	97.0	110.1	102.4	101.8	743	574	41.2	107.2	8.06	332.07
1984	.....	94.9	96.8	115.5	106.6	103.5	813	632	41.7	119.6	8.35	348.20
1985	100.0	93.0	96.8	108.6	106.1	103.5	818	632	41.1	117.6	8.60	353.46
1986	100.3	91.7	91.5	106.4	105.1	107.9	823	639	41.4	119.6	8.79	363.91
1987	100.9	91.0	98.0	108.4	106.8	108.1	842	653	41.6	123.1	8.98	373.57
1988	106.7	94.0	108.9	121.1	113.9	110.0	866	674	41.7	127.3	9.19	383.22
1989	110.2	97.2	108.5	120.1	119.9	111.3	888	692	41.4	129.6	9.46	391.64
1990	111.3	96.8	111.9	117.2	119.0	112.9	888	687	41.1	127.9	9.76	401.14
1991	113.7	98.2	106.1	115.1	120.6	113.5	862	662	41.1	123.2	10.07	413.88
1992	114.2	98.9	103.8	112.7	120.3	113.3	878	677	41.7	127.8	10.36	432.01
1993	115.4	98.9	105.7	116.6	121.4	113.9	909	703	41.8	133.2	10.57	441.83
1994	117.1	98.6	108.9	122.9	122.8	113.5	953	742	42.2	141.9	10.70	451.54
1995	123.3	100.2	126.3	133.8	135.6	115.9	980	763	41.5	143.4	10.91	452.77
1996	123.1	97.0	122.2	130.9	132.7	117.5	983	762	41.5	143.2	11.24	466.46
1997	122.8	95.2	119.3	128.2	131.7	117.2	996	773	41.8	146.4	11.57	483.63
1998	122.1	94.0	117.2	126.2	128.0	117.1	1 009	783	41.7	147.9	11.87	494.98
1995:												
January	121.3	98.7	118.9	129.9	132.7	114.3	985	768	42.1	146.4	10.81	456.18
February	121.8	98.8	121.9	131.8	134.4	114.5	985	768	42.1	146.4	10.75	451.50
March	122.5	99.8	124.7	132.9	135.2	114.6	983	767	41.9	145.6	10.79	451.02
April	123.2	99.9	126.2	134.8	135.4	115.6	984	767	41.7	144.9	10.76	434.70
May	123.6	99.8	127.4	136.1	135.9	115.8	983	766	41.5	144.0	10.85	451.36
June	124.1	101.0	127.3	135.3	136.9	115.8	980	762	41.4	142.9	10.90	454.53
July	124.1	101.3	127.9	135.2	136.4	115.8	975	758	41.0	140.8	11.01	443.70
August	124.2	101.0	129.0	136.3	136.0	116.4	976	759	41.3	142.0	10.93	449.22
September	124.2	101.0	129.1	134.8	137.0	116.8	977	758	41.5	142.5	10.99	459.38
October	124.0	101.0	128.3	134.0	137.0	116.8	978	760	41.5	142.9	11.01	456.92
November	123.6	101.0	127.8	132.6	136.0	116.8	979	763	41.5	143.4	11.01	460.22
December	123.2	99.7	126.6	131.8	134.7	117.0	977	759	41.3	142.0	11.15	470.53
1996:												
January	123.0	98.4	124.5	130.5	133.8	117.0	976	758	40.2	138.0	11.13	448.54
February	122.9	97.7	123.0	130.9	133.6	117.6	975	755	41.4	141.6	11.14	460.08
March	122.8	97.2	123.2	129.8	133.5	117.7	975	755	41.4	141.6	11.15	460.50
April	122.6	96.9	122.3	130.7	131.3	117.7	976	756	41.5	142.1	11.20	460.32
May	123.0	97.4	122.0	130.6	131.6	117.7	978	757	41.6	142.6	11.20	465.92
June	123.0	96.2	122.0	131.7	132.0	117.7	982	761	41.6	143.4	11.16	465.37
July	123.2	96.3	122.1	131.8	133.3	117.6	985	764	41.5	143.6	11.25	459.00
August	123.4	97.2	122.0	131.9	132.4	117.4	988	767	41.7	144.9	11.23	467.17
September	123.5	97.3	121.4	131.2	132.8	117.4	988	767	41.8	145.2	11.30	475.73
October	123.1	96.2	121.5	130.5	132.5	117.4	989	767	41.5	144.2	11.28	469.25
November	123.3	95.9	120.8	131.4	133.1	117.4	991	770	41.4	144.4	11.33	471.33
December	123.3	97.2	121.2	130.3	133.0	117.4	989	767	41.7	144.9	11.51	490.33
1997:												
January	122.9	96.7	121.2	127.7	132.3	117.5	988	766	41.6	144.3	11.48	475.27
February	122.8	95.7	121.1	128.1	132.3	117.5	990	768	41.7	145.1	11.45	475.18
March	122.4	95.6	120.7	127.4	131.2	117.4	992	769	41.8	145.6	11.50	480.70
April	122.8	96.4	119.3	128.6	131.2	117.3	993	770	42.1	146.8	11.53	480.80
May	122.9	95.8	120.2	128.4	131.8	117.3	994	771	41.7	145.6	11.50	479.55
June	122.9	95.1	119.4	128.0	131.8	117.1	995	772	41.5	145.1	11.52	480.38
July	123.0	94.8	117.6	128.7	132.0	117.1	994	772	41.7	145.8	11.57	474.37
August	123.1	94.8	118.1	129.2	132.2	117.2	997	773	41.8	146.3	11.57	482.47
September	122.9	95.5	118.3	127.9	131.7	117.1	999	775	41.7	146.4	11.64	488.88
October	122.7	94.1	118.5	128.1	131.3	117.1	1 001	776	41.9	147.3	11.64	487.72
November	122.8	94.3	118.4	128.1	131.3	117.1	1 002	778	42.0	148.0	11.64	494.70
December	122.8	94.1	118.9	127.7	131.5	117.1	1 004	779	42.1	148.5	11.76	505.68
1998:												
January	122.7	94.0	118.7	127.6	130.1	117.3	1 007	781	42.1	148.9	11.74	491.91
February	122.6	94.5	118.6	127.1	129.8	117.3	1 008	782	41.9	148.4	11.77	489.63
March	122.5	94.5	117.7	127.3	128.5	117.3	1 010	784	41.6	147.7	11.78	488.87
April	122.5	94.2	117.4	127.4	128.6	117.2	1 010	785	41.7	148.3	11.83	485.03
May	122.3	93.8	117.4	127.5	128.8	117.2	1 009	783	41.8	148.2	11.85	496.52
June	122.1	94.0	117.2	126.0	128.4	117.0	1 009	783	41.9	148.6	11.81	496.02
July	121.9	93.7	117.4	125.6	127.6	117.0	1 004	778	41.9	147.6	11.91	489.50
August	121.9	93.7	117.3	125.7	127.9	117.0	1 009	782	41.7	147.7	11.84	491.36
September	121.9	94.0	116.8	125.6	126.6	117.1	1 010	783	41.7	147.9	11.98	495.97
October	121.6	94.0	116.4	125.0	126.7	117.1	1 009	782	41.8	148.1	11.88	496.58
November	121.7	94.0	115.8	125.1	126.3	117.1	1 010	783	41.6	147.5	11.97	503.94
December	121.8	93.9	115.8	124.9	126.9	117.2	1 012	784	41.7	148.1	12.08	515.82

Leather and Leather Products—Production, Capacity Utilization, Prices, Employment, Hours, and Earnings

Year and month	Industrial production (1992=100, seasonally adjusted)		Capacity utilization (output as a percent of capacity, seasonally adjusted)	Producer prices (1982=100, except as noted, not seasonally adjusted)				Employment (thousands, seasonally adjusted)		Production workers			
	Total	Shoes		Leather and leather products (December 1984=100)	Finished footwear	Leather	Cattle hides	Total payroll employees	Production workers	Average weekly hours, seasonally adjusted	Aggregate weekly hours index (1982=100), seasonally adjusted	Average earnings (dollars, not seasonally adjusted)	
												Hourly	Weekly
1970	235.0	296.8	81.8	.....	46.2	34.6	30.4	320	273	37.2	156.4	2.49	92.63
1971	225.7	283.1	79.9	.....	47.7	36.2	32.3	299	257	37.7	148.7	2.59	97.64
1972	234.2	280.2	84.2	.....	50.8	45.1	69.4	296	256	38.3	150.7	2.68	102.64
1973	217.9	258.9	79.6	.....	53.3	51.4	76.9	284	245	37.8	142.3	2.79	105.46
1974	207.2	235.1	77.4	.....	57.1	49.6	55.1	271	232	36.9	131.8	2.99	110.33
1975	206.6	230.9	79.7	.....	60.3	48.7	51.8	248	213	37.1	121.3	3.21	119.09
1976	205.1	223.2	81.7	.....	64.8	60.4	78.1	263	227	37.4	130.6	3.40	127.16
1977	200.6	223.1	83.3	.....	68.8	64.6	85.8	255	218	36.9	123.9	3.61	133.21
1978	201.6	223.4	86.8	.....	74.7	76.6	111.2	257	220	37.1	125.5	3.89	144.32
1979	184.4	211.2	82.2	.....	89.0	114.6	169.3	246	209	36.5	117.1	4.22	154.03
1980	181.6	204.0	84.1	.....	95.2	99.8	104.6	233	197	36.7	110.7	4.58	168.00
1981	176.0	197.3	83.9	.....	98.3	102.7	104.5	238	201	36.7	113.6	4.99	183.13
1982	163.1	190.5	80.7	.....	100.0	100.0	100.0	219	183	35.6	100.0	5.33	189.75
1983	158.3	180.4	82.8	.....	102.1	106.2	109.8	205	171	36.8	96.8	5.54	203.87
1984	141.9	160.4	78.6	.....	102.7	119.6	143.8	189	158	36.8	89.3	5.71	210.13
1985	126.1	140.5	74.1	101.3	104.8	113.4	126.1	165	137	37.2	78.1	5.83	216.88
1986	115.0	128.0	71.9	103.0	106.9	122.9	147.7	149	123	36.9	69.5	5.92	218.45
1987	112.4	120.0	74.7	106.6	109.4	140.9	179.9	143	120	38.2	70.3	6.08	232.26
1988	112.0	121.6	78.7	113.4	115.1	167.5	205.8	143	118	37.5	67.9	6.28	235.50
1989	111.9	117.0	82.5	118.0	120.8	170.4	213.1	138	114	37.9	66.4	6.59	249.76
1990	107.8	112.2	82.7	122.6	125.6	177.5	217.8	133	109	37.4	62.8	6.91	258.43
1991	98.4	96.4	78.8	124.8	128.6	168.4	173.4	124	100	37.5	57.7	7.18	269.25
1992	100.0	100.0	83.0	127.0	132.0	163.7	171.4	120	97	38.0	56.6	7.42	281.96
1993	101.0	100.1	86.1	129.0	134.4	168.6	180.2	117	94	38.6	55.6	7.63	294.52
1994	93.6	97.8	81.4	130.6	135.5	179.6	200.9	113	90	38.5	53.0	7.97	306.85
1995	86.9	92.2	74.6	134.1	139.2	191.4	209.9	106	83	38.0	48.3	8.17	310.46
1996	87.3	82.8	72.3	134.7	141.6	177.9	186.5	96	74	38.1	43.3	8.57	326.52
1997	81.9	77.3	68.1	137.1	143.7	182.7	196.1	91	69	38.4	40.6	8.97	344.45
1998	75.3	67.3	63.9	137.1	144.7	178.4	153.6	83	62	37.6	36.0	9.32	350.43
1995:													
January	89.7	96.0	78.4	133.3	137.5	192.2	221.2	111	87	38.1	50.9	8.10	306.18
February	88.9	94.8	77.5	133.7	138.6	194.7	223.7	109	86	38.5	50.9	8.11	307.37
March	88.5	95.6	76.8	133.8	138.7	195.2	232.0	109	85	38.3	50.0	8.10	308.61
April	86.8	94.6	75.2	134.2	138.8	198.4	223.7	108	84	38.3	49.4	8.28	307.19
May	86.9	93.9	75.0	134.4	138.9	199.5	236.8	107	84	38.4	49.6	8.15	313.78
June	86.4	92.3	74.3	134.3	139.0	195.3	216.7	105	83	38.1	48.6	8.10	313.47
July	84.5	91.6	72.5	134.3	139.2	193.9	217.7	105	82	37.3	47.0	8.01	293.17
August	86.4	92.5	73.9	134.2	139.3	190.0	207.1	105	82	38.2	48.1	8.14	314.20
September	87.3	93.0	74.3	134.1	139.3	186.5	200.1	105	82	37.9	47.7	8.24	318.06
October	85.7	89.0	72.7	134.4	140.1	184.6	185.8	104	81	37.8	47.0	8.23	314.39
November	85.9	89.1	72.6	134.4	140.4	183.5	176.7	102	80	37.6	46.2	8.23	312.74
December	85.4	86.2	72.0	134.5	140.5	182.4	177.4	100	78	37.6	45.1	8.33	317.37
1996:													
January	85.2	84.4	71.6	134.6	140.6	182.3	172.7	99	77	35.0	41.4	8.51	294.45
February	87.1	84.7	73.0	134.6	141.1	181.0	175.7	99	77	37.6	44.5	8.41	312.01
March	87.3	84.0	73.0	134.8	141.3	181.2	177.1	98	76	37.9	44.2	8.46	319.79
April	87.8	83.4	73.2	134.1	141.2	176.1	175.6	97	75	37.9	43.7	8.40	315.00
May	87.3	82.9	72.6	134.5	141.2	178.1	178.1	97	74	38.4	43.7	8.43	322.03
June	88.7	83.7	73.5	134.4	141.6	175.2	181.2	97	74	38.6	43.9	8.48	331.57
July	88.2	82.1	72.9	134.1	141.7	172.7	186.0	96	73	38.5	43.2	8.44	318.19
August	88.1	82.0	72.6	134.2	142.0	173.4	190.7	95	73	38.8	43.5	8.63	335.71
September	87.9	82.1	72.2	135.3	142.0	176.0	186.3	94	73	38.7	43.4	8.71	341.43
October	86.9	82.4	71.2	135.1	142.2	177.4	204.8	94	72	38.6	42.7	8.73	341.34
November	86.4	81.8	70.6	135.2	142.2	179.4	204.4	92	71	38.9	42.4	8.74	343.48
December	87.0	82.7	70.9	136.0	142.3	182.5	205.4	94	73	38.7	43.4	8.85	347.81
1997:													
January	86.3	82.8	70.3	136.8	143.1	183.2	207.5	93	72	38.3	42.4	8.86	334.02
February	84.2	81.7	68.9	137.3	143.3	185.3	209.4	93	71	38.5	42.0	8.94	337.93
March	85.1	81.9	69.8	137.2	143.5	185.5	211.7	93	71	38.7	42.2	8.89	342.27
April	84.4	80.4	69.5	137.4	143.5	188.1	211.9	92	70	38.6	41.5	8.89	338.71
May	83.3	79.7	68.8	136.9	143.7	183.6	208.9	92	70	38.4	41.3	8.92	340.74
June	82.3	77.4	68.3	136.2	142.2	180.2	198.8	91	69	38.3	40.6	8.94	346.87
July	82.3	77.3	68.5	136.9	144.1	179.7	180.1	90	68	38.6	40.3	8.77	331.51
August	78.9	76.0	66.0	136.9	144.3	178.0	186.2	90	68	38.2	39.9	8.89	341.38
September	78.9	75.0	66.2	137.0	144.4	178.4	180.3	89	67	38.5	39.6	9.11	356.20
October	80.0	75.0	67.4	137.5	144.2	182.1	183.0	89	67	38.4	39.5	9.15	353.19
November	78.7	72.4	66.5	137.9	144.1	185.2	190.3	88	67	37.9	39.0	9.13	351.51
December	78.8	71.8	66.9	137.4	144.2	182.4	185.5	88	66	38.2	38.7	9.21	357.35
1998:													
January	77.3	70.6	65.7	137.4	144.5	180.5	156.0	87	66	38.3	38.8	9.31	350.99
February	78.3	72.1	66.5	137.4	144.7	179.3	154.6	87	66	38.5	39.0	9.28	351.71
March	77.9	70.1	66.2	137.4	144.7	178.9	145.8	86	65	37.8	37.7	9.30	350.61
April	76.3	68.3	64.8	137.1	144.7	176.6	152.2	85	64	37.5	36.9	9.27	338.36
May	75.8	67.6	64.4	137.2	144.6	177.4	153.1	84	64	37.5	36.9	9.31	348.19
June	74.5	67.3	63.3	137.2	144.7	177.2	175.3	83	63	37.6	36.4	9.33	355.47
July	75.3	67.3	63.9	137.3	144.5	179.7	160.6	82	62	37.3	35.5	9.14	337.27
August	74.0	65.9	62.8	137.1	144.6	179.5	164.4	81	61	37.9	35.5	9.28	356.35
September	73.5	65.5	62.4	137.2	144.7	179.0	162.0	81	60	37.4	34.5	9.35	348.76
October	72.8	63.9	61.8	137.1	144.7	178.0	142.6	80	60	37.4	34.5	9.45	355.32
November	74.3	65.8	63.0	136.5	144.7	177.1	133.1	79	59	37.4	33.9	9.44	358.72
December	73.0	64.6	62.0	136.7	144.9	177.9	143.7	78	58	37.5	33.4	9.43	359.28

Transportation, Communications, and Utilities

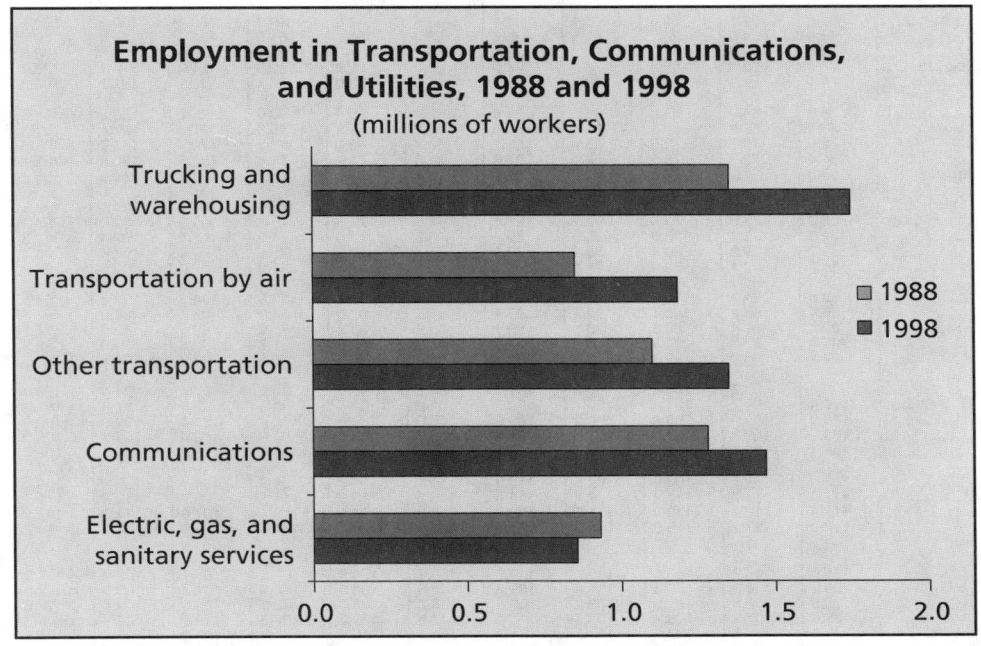

Employment in Transportation, Communications, and Utilities, 1988 and 1998
(millions of workers)

- From 1988 to 1998, employment in air transportation and in trucking and warehousing grew 39 and 29 percent, respectively, with both higher than the average for all private nonfarm employment.

- Employment rose at a fairly steady rate from 1970 to 1998 in the communications and transportation industries. In electric, gas, and sanitary services, however, employment increased from 1970 to 1991, but fell thereafter to a 16 year low.

- Electricity generation doubled between 1970 and 1992, with greater growth in nuclear and hydro production. However, after 1992, growth of generation by fossil fuels slightly outpaced that of nuclear and hydro.

- Output of gas utilities, on the other hand, has declined since 1970.

Electric and Gas Utilities—Industrial Production

(1992=100)

| Year and month | Total | Seasonally adjusted — Electric | | | | | | | | Seasonally adjusted — Gas | | | | Not seasonally adjusted | |
| | | Total | Generation | | | Sales | | | | Total | Residential | Commercial and other | Gas transmission | Electric | Gas |
			Total	Fossil fuel	Hydro and nuclear	Total	Residential	Nonresidential Total	Industrial						
1970	66.5	51.1	53.4	65.1	31.4	49.4	49.8	49.0	130.4	130.5	104.1	90.0	169.6	51.1	130.4
1971	69.6	54.0	56.3	67.5	35.5	52.3	53.2	51.5	134.4	134.4	106.6	94.2	175.2	54.0	134.4
1972	74.1	58.4	61.0	73.3	38.1	56.7	57.6	55.8	136.4	136.5	108.8	94.6	177.8	58.4	136.4
1973	77.0	62.4	63.6	76.1	41.3	61.2	62.0	60.3	134.2	134.4	106.0	97.8	176.7	62.4	134.2
1974	76.1	61.9	62.6	73.3	47.1	61.0	62.0	60.1	131.1	131.2	106.3	97.6	169.5	61.9	131.1
1975	76.8	64.0	65.0	74.5	54.6	62.9	65.5	60.9	125.2	125.2	108.8	95.0	158.6	64.0	125.2
1976	79.9	67.1	69.8	80.8	55.3	65.2	64.5	65.5	127.0	127.1	111.9	100.9	157.6	67.1	127.0
1977	82.0	70.7	73.9	85.6	55.1	68.7	68.6	68.7	120.7	120.7	102.3	92.4	156.9	70.7	120.7
1978	84.4	73.3	76.0	84.9	65.4	71.5	71.7	71.4	122.6	122.6	105.1	93.8	158.8	73.3	122.6
1979	86.8	75.2	77.8	88.5	62.6	73.6	73.0	73.9	126.6	126.6	105.6	99.1	166.5	75.2	126.6
1980	87.3	76.4	78.9	90.6	61.5	74.8	76.5	73.6	124.8	124.8	103.2	94.2	166.5	76.4	124.8
1981	85.0	78.0	79.5	91.1	62.4	77.0	77.3	76.7	109.3	109.3	97.9	91.5	127.1	78.0	109.3
1982	82.3	76.7	78.3	85.8	69.2	75.6	78.0	74.0	102.4	102.4	98.8	92.7	115.7	76.7	102.4
1983	83.7	79.2	80.4	86.9	73.1	78.3	80.7	76.5	100.4	100.4	94.4	87.2	124.2	79.2	100.4
1984	86.7	82.4	83.8	91.1	75.5	81.5	82.6	81.0	102.6	102.6	97.2	90.6	118.9	82.4	102.6
1985	88.8	84.6	85.9	93.3	77.6	83.7	84.7	83.0	104.3	104.3	93.6	86.1	130.0	84.6	104.3
1986	86.4	86.2	87.1	92.2	82.4	85.5	87.5	84.2	83.8	87.0	92.2	83.4	86.7	86.2	87.0
1987	89.4	89.4	89.5	96.5	82.4	89.3	90.9	88.2	87.5	89.0	92.1	86.7	87.4	89.4	89.0
1988	93.9	93.6	94.1	100.8	87.4	93.2	95.5	91.7	92.8	94.5	98.9	95.4	91.8	93.6	94.5
1989	97.1	96.8	97.9	102.9	92.7	96.0	96.7	95.5	95.9	98.1	102.1	97.1	96.2	96.8	98.1
1990	98.3	99.2	100.5	100.9	100.1	98.2	98.6	98.0	97.0	94.4	93.8	93.6	94.6	99.2	94.4
1991	100.4	101.2	101.9	100.1	103.7	100.6	102.5	99.3	97.8	97.3	97.3	97.5	97.3	101.2	97.3
1992	100.0	100.0	100.0	100.0	100.0	100.0	100.0	100.0	100.0	100.0	100.0	100.0	100.0	100.0	100.0
1993	103.9	103.8	103.0	103.8	102.3	104.3	106.5	102.9	102.0	104.3	105.9	102.4	103.5	103.8	104.3
1994	105.3	105.5	104.1	104.8	103.3	106.5	107.7	105.6	102.8	104.6	103.4	103.3	106.2	105.5	104.6
1995	109.0	109.5	108.9	104.8	113.0	110.0	111.6	108.9	104.9	107.2	103.4	108.2	110.5	109.5	107.2
1996	112.6	112.7	111.9	107.1	116.8	113.3	115.9	111.5	106.7	112.3	111.7	112.7	112.5	112.7	112.3
1997	112.8	113.2	112.3	111.6	112.9	113.8	114.5	113.4	107.0	111.2	107.3	117.5	112.5	113.2	111.2
1998	113.9	117.2	115.0	115.5	114.4	118.8	121.1	117.1	109.3	101.9	94.2	109.7	108.3	117.2	101.9
1995:															
January	104.9	105.7	105.5	100.7	110.7	105.8	104.0	107.0	105.1	102.0	97.8	100.6	105.4	111.8	180.1
February	106.2	106.6	106.8	104.6	109.2	106.5	106.5	106.4	104.2	105.0	102.5	105.5	106.9	106.3	167.0
March	106.5	107.3	105.9	102.2	109.8	108.2	108.0	108.2	105.3	103.4	98.6	102.4	108.5	102.3	142.4
April	106.6	107.2	106.8	103.6	110.0	107.6	107.2	107.8	104.8	104.3	99.2	103.0	110.3	96.1	108.3
May	108.6	108.6	107.6	103.3	111.9	109.4	110.7	108.3	105.3	108.3	104.6	110.3	111.8	100.3	80.6
June	108.5	109.0	107.8	103.3	112.4	109.8	110.5	109.1	105.3	106.6	104.6	106.3	109.1	112.3	61.7
July	109.9	109.8	110.2	106.8	113.6	109.7	110.7	108.8	104.5	110.1	107.2	109.9	113.8	124.3	61.3
August	114.7	116.2	114.5	116.4	112.5	117.3	124.6	112.0	106.2	109.0	101.2	111.6	116.9	130.3	60.5
September	109.9	110.3	108.4	104.2	112.5	111.6	115.1	108.9	104.2	108.4	104.8	111.5	110.9	113.2	58.6
October	109.3	111.0	111.2	101.1	121.4	111.0	112.3	110.0	104.6	102.9	95.6	108.1	107.7	102.7	72.8
November	111.2	111.0	110.3	104.0	116.8	111.4	113.5	109.9	104.4	112.0	109.2	114.3	112.9	102.9	121.9
December	112.1	111.4	111.4	106.0	116.8	111.5	113.7	109.9	105.3	114.6	112.0	117.5	114.5	111.6	171.1
1996:															
January	113.1	112.9	112.2	106.9	117.6	113.3	117.2	110.5	106.1	114.1	112.3	113.8	113.9	119.7	201.1
February	114.2	114.0	112.6	106.5	118.9	114.9	118.2	112.4	107.9	115.3	113.7	114.7	114.2	113.7	181.1
March	114.5	114.1	113.3	106.5	120.3	114.7	118.5	111.8	107.4	116.1	115.0	114.9	114.5	108.8	160.0
April	113.5	112.9	113.2	105.2	121.5	112.8	117.1	109.7	104.7	115.6	113.1	116.2	113.9	100.9	117.6
May	114.0	114.5	114.5	109.0	120.3	114.5	117.5	112.3	106.7	112.0	108.7	109.3	111.7	105.8	81.8
June	113.3	113.7	112.6	108.7	116.6	114.6	118.4	111.8	106.1	111.5	107.7	105.8	112.9	117.5	63.2
July	109.7	110.5	109.4	104.8	114.2	111.2	113.0	109.9	106.7	106.8	102.2	104.0	108.0	125.0	58.0
August	111.8	112.3	111.3	108.1	114.7	113.0	114.7	111.8	106.5	109.5	106.6	105.1	109.7	125.8	57.9
September	111.1	111.1	110.1	106.3	114.1	111.9	112.5	111.4	106.8	111.1	109.0	106.3	110.6	114.2	58.6
October	111.7	111.8	111.1	107.2	115.1	112.4	113.2	111.7	107.5	111.2	108.2	108.5	111.5	103.8	76.8
November	112.6	112.6	111.6	110.2	113.1	113.3	114.6	112.3	107.3	113.0	110.3	112.2	112.7	104.7	123.8
December	112.1	112.3	110.8	106.4	115.5	113.3	114.6	112.4	107.5	111.3	108.0	113.8	111.0	112.8	167.3
1997:															
January	113.4	113.7	113.5	111.3	115.7	114.0	114.8	113.4	107.2	112.1	109.6	114.2	112.2	120.2	197.3
February	111.0	111.4	111.2	107.3	115.2	111.6	111.3	111.9	106.4	109.7	105.9	112.1	111.2	110.8	171.7
March	109.6	111.0	111.3	108.8	113.8	110.9	110.2	111.3	105.4	104.0	97.4	105.8	109.6	105.7	148.5
April	112.7	113.0	112.1	110.7	113.5	113.6	114.2	113.1	106.9	111.8	109.0	117.1	112.4	101.1	112.1
May	111.4	110.3	108.9	107.9	109.8	111.3	110.9	111.4	106.2	116.2	115.3	126.5	112.8	102.2	86.2
June	111.4	110.8	110.9	108.6	113.2	110.8	108.7	112.3	106.9	114.1	110.4	127.5	113.2	114.5	65.4
July	113.7	114.0	113.4	113.5	113.3	114.5	115.6	113.6	106.6	112.6	106.6	123.5	115.7	129.1	62.7
August	113.1	113.4	112.7	110.5	114.9	114.0	115.8	112.6	107.1	111.9	107.5	122.3	113.7	126.8	60.4
September	114.4	114.5	114.8	116.3	113.4	115.5	115.9	115.2	108.7	110.5	103.3	125.3	114.1	118.4	59.9
October	116.1	117.4	114.3	116.0	112.6	119.4	122.2	117.4	107.8	110.2	105.0	123.6	112.0	109.1	77.2
November	113.6	114.1	112.7	113.3	112.1	115.1	116.2	114.2	107.4	111.0	108.5	120.2	111.5	106.2	124.5
December	113.1	113.8	111.5	116.0	107.1	115.2	116.1	114.5	107.1	109.9	106.3	114.8	113.1	114.2	168.2
1998:															
January	109.8	111.4	109.4	108.8	109.9	112.8	112.1	113.1	106.8	102.2	96.4	107.2	107.1	117.4	179.2
February	109.0	111.2	111.5	108.9	114.0	111.1	107.8	113.3	109.3	99.3	94.4	102.6	103.5	110.3	154.8
March	114.0	115.7	114.5	114.7	114.4	116.5	118.0	115.3	108.3	106.3	102.7	108.4	110.1	110.2	148.9
April	112.8	115.2	113.5	114.8	112.3	116.3	116.5	116.1	108.8	102.0	97.0	104.4	107.2	102.8	104.2
May	115.2	118.9	116.8	120.2	113.5	120.2	122.1	118.8	111.4	98.3	89.5	104.2	105.8	110.1	73.6
June	118.7	121.0	118.5	122.4	114.8	122.6	128.9	118.0	109.5	108.4	101.8	114.5	113.5	124.9	62.4
July	118.3	119.8	117.3	120.0	114.6	121.4	128.0	117.6	108.3	111.7	102.0	126.8	117.0	135.9	61.9
August	120.2	121.2	116.3	121.9	111.0	124.3	130.9	119.6	110.8	115.7	105.4	140.0	118.6	135.6	62.0
September	120.3	122.6	119.7	122.5	116.8	124.4	130.7	119.9	109.3	109.7	95.1	137.3	116.7	125.9	59.5
October	116.5	120.3	116.2	111.7	120.2	122.9	130.1	117.7	107.7	98.7	86.8	114.3	106.6	111.4	69.1
November	110.6	114.6	112.2	107.6	116.2	116.2	113.4	118.0	109.7	92.0	82.1	100.0	99.5	106.6	102.1
December	111.8	115.2	114.0	111.1	116.5	115.9	112.5	118.3	112.2	96.0	86.6	102.9	103.3	115.6	145.2

Transportation, Communications, and Utilities—Capacity Utilization and Prices

Year and month	Capacity utilization—Electric and gas utilities (percent of capacity, seasonally adjusted)			Producer prices (not seasonally adjusted)							
				Industries				Commodities			
				Motor freight transportation and warehousing (June 1993 = 100)	Water transportation (December 1992= 100)	Transportation by air (December 1992= 100)	Pipelines, except natural gas (December 1986= 100)	Electric (1982=100)		Natural gas (December 1990=100)	
	Total	Electric	Gas					Commercial	Industrial	Commercial	Industrial
1970	96.2	98.9	91.9	.....	.....	.....	.....	30.8	22.5	.....	.....
1971	94.6	96.5	92.3	.....	.....	.....	.....	33.7	24.8	.....	.....
1972	95.2	97.0	92.5	.....	.....	.....	.....	34.8	26.2	.....	.....
1973	93.5	95.4	90.7	.....	.....	.....	.....	36.8	28.0	.....	.....
1974	87.3	87.3	88.6	.....	.....	.....	.....	44.8	36.4	.....	.....
1975	84.4	84.8	84.8	.....	.....	.....	.....	51.4	44.3	.....	.....
1976	85.2	85.1	86.6	.....	.....	.....	.....	54.7	47.9	.....	.....
1977	85.0	86.0	83.2	.....	.....	.....	.....	60.7	54.3	.....	.....
1978	85.4	85.3	85.5	.....	.....	.....	.....	64.6	59.1	.....	.....
1979	86.6	85.3	89.5	.....	.....	.....	.....	68.7	64.5	.....	.....
1980	85.9	84.7	89.3	.....	.....	.....	.....	80.6	77.8	.....	.....
1981	82.5	84.3	79.1	.....	.....	.....	.....	91.6	89.2	.....	.....
1982	79.3	81.3	74.9	.....	.....	.....	.....	100.0	100.0	.....	.....
1983	79.7	82.3	74.4	.....	.....	.....	.....	102.5	103.1	.....	.....
1984	81.9	84.0	77.1	.....	.....	.....	.....	108.0	108.4	.....	.....
1985	83.5	84.7	79.8	.....	.....	.....	.....	110.3	112.8	.....	.....
1986	80.6	84.9	67.6	.....	.....	.....	.....	110.5	114.5	.....	.....
1987	82.5	86.1	69.9	.....	.....	.....	97.9	108.9	111.9	.....	.....
1988	84.9	87.8	73.7	.....	.....	.....	94.8	109.5	112.6	.....	.....
1989	86.3	89.4	75.7	.....	.....	.....	94.4	113.0	116.2	.....	.....
1990	85.7	89.6	72.9	.....	.....	.....	95.8	115.3	119.6	.....	.....
1991	86.3	89.1	75.1	.....	.....	.....	96.1	122.3	128.1	95.9	93.6
1992	84.5	86.8	77.2	.....	.....	.....	96.4	124.4	129.6	96.7	94.2
1993	87.2	88.8	80.4	.....	99.7	105.6	96.6	127.2	130.6	102.7	101.6
1994	87.4	89.2	80.4	101.9	100.0	108.5	102.6	128.8	129.2	103.7	99.5
1995	89.2	91.1	82.0	104.5	103.0	113.7	110.8	131.7	130.8	96.5	90.9
1996	90.5	91.8	84.8	106.3	103.7	121.1	104.6	131.6	131.6	103.2	98.9
1997	89.7	91.5	82.2	108.9	104.2	125.3	98.8	131.7	130.8	109.8	109.3
1998	90.9	94.6	75.2	111.6	105.6	124.5	99.2	130.4	130.0	106.4	103.6
1995:											
January	86.5	88.9	78.2	103.1	102.6	108.1	110.9	127.2	127.6	102.6	97.6
February	87.5	89.4	80.5	104.2	102.8	109.6	110.9	127.6	128.0	101.3	95.4
March	87.5	89.8	79.2	104.4	102.6	110.1	110.9	127.7	128.3	99.9	93.6
April	87.5	89.6	79.9	104.3	102.0	110.0	110.9	126.5	126.4	98.0	92.3
May	89.0	90.6	82.9	104.4	102.3	113.2	110.9	129.8	130.2	94.2	89.5
June	88.8	90.7	81.6	104.7	102.2	114.1	110.7	138.5	135.3	94.3	90.2
July	89.8	91.3	84.2	104.4	102.4	115.2	110.7	139.7	136.6	93.8	88.4
August	93.6	96.3	83.3	104.8	103.3	115.8	110.7	139.7	136.5	92.7	87.2
September	89.6	91.3	82.9	104.7	104.5	117.1	110.7	137.8	133.7	93.0	86.4
October	89.0	91.7	78.6	104.9	104.2	117.2	110.6	131.3	131.4	92.5	86.8
November	90.3	91.5	85.5	104.9	103.7	118.0	110.6	127.1	127.6	97.4	91.0
December	90.9	91.7	87.5	104.7	104.0	115.9	110.6	127.6	127.7	98.5	92.3
1996:											
January	91.6	92.7	87.0	105.1	103.9	117.2	110.6	127.6	127.9	101.8	95.4
February	92.4	93.4	87.8	105.9	103.8	119.1	110.6	126.0	127.1	103.0	96.8
March	92.5	93.4	88.2	105.8	104.2	119.9	110.6	126.8	127.8	104.2	98.0
April	91.5	92.3	87.7	105.9	103.8	120.2	103.7	126.6	129.1	102.6	96.6
May	91.8	93.4	84.8	106.0	103.0	120.8	103.7	129.6	135.0	100.3	97.0
June	91.1	92.7	84.2	106.9	102.9	121.4	103.7	138.4	137.5	100.5	97.2
July	88.1	89.9	80.5	106.2	103.0	122.5	104.0	139.1	136.0	101.2	98.0
August	89.6	91.3	82.4	106.4	103.0	121.8	104.0	139.6	136.2	102.3	99.0
September	88.9	90.2	83.4	106.6	103.8	121.9	101.0	139.5	136.2	99.7	96.9
October	89.2	90.6	83.4	106.9	104.6	122.4	100.9	131.3	131.2	99.4	96.1
November	89.8	91.1	84.6	107.1	104.5	123.5	100.9	126.8	127.1	108.3	103.5
December	89.2	90.7	83.1	107.2	104.2	122.7	100.9	127.5	127.7	115.0	112.9
1997:											
January	90.2	91.8	83.6	108.0	104.1	128.8	98.8	127.7	128.3	121.2	130.2
February	88.3	89.9	81.7	108.5	104.2	128.9	98.8	127.7	128.1	119.1	121.9
March	87.1	89.6	77.3	108.6	104.1	124.6	98.8	127.6	128.2	110.3	107.3
April	89.6	91.3	83.0	108.8	104.2	125.1	98.8	127.1	127.3	103.0	100.4
May	88.5	89.1	86.1	108.8	104.3	125.1	98.9	129.2	129.7	102.3	99.9
June	88.5	89.6	84.5	109.0	104.8	126.2	98.9	138.6	135.1	103.3	100.5
July	90.4	92.2	83.2	109.1	104.4	126.5	98.7	139.2	135.9	104.5	100.4
August	89.9	91.8	82.6	109.3	104.7	125.4	98.7	138.1	134.7	103.7	100.6
September	90.9	93.2	81.4	109.4	103.8	122.5	98.7	139.4	136.0	105.7	102.7
October	92.3	95.0	81.0	109.3	104.6	123.7	98.7	131.2	130.1	110.0	111.0
November	90.3	92.4	81.5	109.0	104.1	123.4	98.7	127.0	127.9	118.5	120.3
December	89.9	92.2	80.6	109.4	103.3	123.3	98.7	127.5	128.3	116.0	116.4
1998:											
January	87.2	90.2	74.8	110.5	103.0	122.6	99.3	126.8	127.4	112.0	111.4
February	86.6	90.0	72.6	110.6	102.7	123.7	99.3	126.4	127.2	108.4	108.2
March	90.5	93.6	77.6	110.7	102.3	123.7	99.3	125.7	126.7	108.1	106.6
April	89.5	93.1	74.4	110.9	102.2	124.3	99.3	125.7	126.4	106.2	103.3
May	91.3	96.0	71.6	111.3	105.3	124.3	99.3	128.0	129.2	105.8	103.3
June	94.0	97.7	78.9	111.5	106.1	124.2	99.3	136.3	133.8	102.9	100.3
July	93.7	96.7	81.2	111.9	107.9	124.2	99.2	137.6	134.8	103.8	100.7
August	95.1	97.8	84.0	112.1	108.1	124.3	99.2	137.8	135.2	103.7	99.6
September	95.0	98.8	79.6	112.4	108.9	125.2	99.2	137.7	135.2	102.9	98.7
October	92.0	96.9	71.5	112.6	108.4	125.4	99.2	130.7	130.4	104.5	100.4
November	87.3	92.2	66.5	112.5	107.3	126.1	99.2	127.1	127.6	108.1	105.1
December	88.2	92.6	69.4	112.7	105.7	126.5	99.2	125.2	126.6	110.6	105.1

Transportation, Communications, and Utilities—Employment, Hours, and Earnings

Year and month	Total payroll employment (thousands, seasonally adjusted)						Nonsupervisory workers				
	Total	Transportation			Communications	Electric, gas, and sanitary services	Seasonally adjusted			Average earnings (dollars, not seasonally adjusted)	
		Total	Trucking and warehousing	Transportation by air			Employment	Average weekly hours	Aggregate weekly hours index (1982=100)	Hourly	Weekly
1970	4 515	2 694	.....	.....	1 129	692	3 914	40.5	96.9	3.85	155.93
1971	4 476	2 639	.....	.....	1 143	698	3 872	40.1	95.1	4.21	168.82
1972	4 541	2 676	.....	.....	1 152	713	3 943	40.4	97.3	4.65	187.86
1973	4 656	2 746	.....	.....	1 180	731	4 034	40.5	99.9	5.02	203.31
1974	4 725	2 779	.....	.....	1 203	744	4 079	40.2	100.4	5.41	217.48
1975	4 542	2 634	.....	.....	1 176	733	3 894	39.7	94.6	5.88	233.44
1976	4 582	2 678	.....	.....	1 169	735	3 918	39.8	95.5	6.45	256.71
1977	4 713	2 781	.....	.....	1 185	747	4 008	39.9	97.9	6.99	278.90
1978	4 923	2 905	.....	.....	1 240	778	4 142	40.0	101.3	7.57	302.80
1979	5 136	3 019	.....	.....	1 309	807	4 299	39.9	104.9	8.16	325.58
1980	5 146	2 960	.....	.....	1 357	829	4 293	39.6	104.1	8.87	351.25
1981	5 165	2 920	.....	.....	1 391	854	4 283	39.4	103.3	9.70	382.18
1982	5 081	2 787	.....	.....	1 417	877	4 190	39.0	100.0	10.32	402.48
1983	4 952	2 742	.....	.....	1 324	886	4 072	39.0	97.3	10.79	420.81
1984	5 156	2 914	.....	.....	1 340	902	4 258	39.4	102.8	11.12	438.13
1985	5 233	2 997	.....	.....	1 319	916	4 335	39.5	104.6	11.40	450.30
1986	5 247	3 051	.....	.....	1 275	921	4 339	39.2	104.0	11.70	458.64
1987	5 362	3 156	.....	.....	1 282	925	4 446	39.2	106.5	12.03	471.58
1988	5 512	3 301	1 351	850	1 280	931	4 555	38.2	108.2	12.24	467.57
1989	5 614	3 404	1 379	897	1 272	938	4 655	38.3	111.1	12.57	481.43
1990	5 777	3 511	1 395	968	1 309	957	4 781	38.4	114.5	12.92	496.13
1991	5 755	3 495	1 378	962	1 299	961	4 774	38.1	113.4	13.20	502.92
1992	5 718	3 495	1 385	964	1 269	954	4 768	38.3	113.6	13.43	514.37
1993	5 811	3 598	1 444	988	1 269	944	4 862	39.3	118.2	13.55	532.52
1994	5 984	3 761	1 526	1 023	1 295	928	5 012	39.7	122.4	13.78	547.07
1995	6 132	3 904	1 587	1 068	1 318	911	5 140	39.4	123.9	14.13	556.72
1996	6 253	4 019	1 637	1 107	1 351	884	5 260	39.6	127.5	14.45	572.22
1997	6 408	4 123	1 677	1 134	1 419	866	5 366	39.7	130.5	14.92	592.32
1998	6 600	4 276	1 745	1 183	1 469	855	5 471	39.5	132.1	15.31	604.75
1995:											
January	6 092	3 873	1 576	1 056	1 299	920	5 110	39.5	123.5	14.01	549.19
February	6 108	3 876	1 581	1 053	1 314	918	5 117	39.5	123.7	13.97	547.62
March	6 114	3 881	1 585	1 053	1 317	916	5 121	39.4	123.4	13.98	546.62
April	6 123	3 893	1 593	1 053	1 315	915	5 121	39.4	123.4	14.04	554.58
May	6 110	3 883	1 581	1 058	1 314	913	5 117	39.3	123.0	13.96	545.84
June	6 112	3 884	1 580	1 063	1 316	912	5 118	39.4	123.4	14.02	553.79
July	6 109	3 881	1 572	1 065	1 318	910	5 119	39.4	123.4	14.16	566.40
August	6 137	3 910	1 586	1 071	1 318	909	5 146	39.3	123.7	14.14	561.36
September	6 139	3 908	1 575	1 076	1 323	908	5 152	39.2	123.6	14.25	562.88
October	6 182	3 948	1 606	1 085	1 327	907	5 188	39.2	124.4	14.35	566.83
November	6 201	3 971	1 611	1 102	1 326	904	5 205	39.3	125.1	14.34	563.56
December	6 185	3 957	1 596	1 102	1 326	902	5 202	39.4	125.4	14.32	562.78
1996:											
January	6 199	3 976	1 620	1 100	1 325	898	5 208	39.1	124.6	14.32	551.32
February	6 202	3 982	1 622	1 099	1 326	894	5 223	39.6	126.5	14.34	563.56
March	6 207	3 989	1 625	1 104	1 327	891	5 225	39.8	127.2	14.33	564.60
April	6 229	4 009	1 631	1 113	1 331	889	5 238	39.4	126.3	14.40	563.04
May	6 242	4 017	1 637	1 110	1 338	887	5 249	39.5	126.8	14.35	563.96
June	6 264	4 033	1 647	1 111	1 347	884	5 271	39.6	127.7	14.41	577.84
July	6 285	4 050	1 653	1 117	1 355	880	5 285	39.5	127.7	14.45	573.67
August	6 285	4 043	1 648	1 114	1 363	879	5 283	39.7	128.3	14.50	581.45
September	6 280	4 034	1 641	1 110	1 368	878	5 284	39.7	128.3	14.59	587.98
October	6 281	4 035	1 638	1 112	1 370	876	5 284	39.8	128.7	14.51	576.05
November	6 298	4 045	1 642	1 114	1 377	876	5 294	39.8	128.9	14.59	580.68
December	6 282	4 027	1 632	1 103	1 380	875	5 292	39.8	128.9	14.63	583.74
1997:											
January	6 333	4 073	1 645	1 132	1 387	873	5 323	39.5	128.6	14.75	573.78
February	6 356	4 088	1 652	1 138	1 396	872	5 343	39.5	129.1	14.69	580.26
March	6 377	4 101	1 659	1 141	1 405	871	5 367	39.9	131.0	14.74	583.70
April	6 398	4 119	1 665	1 143	1 410	869	5 383	39.6	130.4	14.80	581.64
May	6 407	4 123	1 671	1 142	1 416	868	5 388	39.6	130.5	14.76	580.07
June	6 419	4 134	1 674	1 144	1 418	867	5 394	39.4	130.0	14.81	590.92
July	6 425	4 137	1 679	1 143	1 422	866	5 391	39.3	129.6	14.98	591.71
August	6 283	3 994	1 687	987	1 427	862	5 211	40.1	127.8	15.03	608.72
September	6 454	4 164	1 695	1 154	1 427	863	5 389	40.0	131.9	15.04	606.11
October	6 480	4 179	1 698	1 163	1 439	862	5 396	39.8	131.4	15.07	599.79
November	6 483	4 182	1 699	1 163	1 442	859	5 395	39.9	131.7	15.17	612.87
December	6 474	4 168	1 694	1 152	1 447	859	5 389	39.9	131.5	15.15	602.97
1998:											
January	6 505	4 192	1 708	1 160	1 453	860	5 400	39.9	131.8	15.24	598.93
February	6 528	4 214	1 718	1 164	1 455	859	5 401	39.9	131.8	15.25	608.48
March	6 545	4 228	1 724	1 167	1 459	858	5 413	39.7	131.5	15.21	599.27
April	6 559	4 238	1 732	1 170	1 465	856	5 421	39.6	131.3	15.24	595.88
May	6 577	4 254	1 738	1 175	1 467	856	5 442	39.7	132.2	15.18	599.61
June	6 589	4 265	1 744	1 179	1 470	854	5 450	39.5	131.7	15.19	601.52
July	6 606	4 281	1 749	1 183	1 472	853	5 474	39.5	132.3	15.27	606.22
August	6 625	4 305	1 755	1 190	1 467	853	5 502	39.4	132.6	15.30	610.47
September	6 637	4 313	1 759	1 196	1 472	852	5 509	39.3	132.5	15.41	605.61
October	6 657	4 327	1 766	1 199	1 480	850	5 527	39.3	132.9	15.39	604.83
November	6 671	4 335	1 770	1 201	1 484	852	5 540	39.2	132.9	15.48	614.56
December	6 684	4 340	1 769	1 205	1 492	852	5 561	39.1	133.0	15.50	606.05

Transportation, Communications, and Utilities—Employment, Hours, and Earnings—*Continued*

Year and month	Trucking and warehousing				Communications				Electric, gas, and sanitary services			
	Employment (thousands)	Average weekly hours	Average earnings Hourly	Average earnings Weekly	Employment (thousands)	Average weekly hours	Average earnings Hourly	Average earnings Weekly	Employment (thousands)	Average weekly hours	Average earnings Hourly	Average earnings Weekly
1970	.....	.....	.....	.....	886	39.3	3.41	134.01	.....	.....	.....	.....
1971	.....	.....	.....	.....	896	38.1	3.69	140.59	.....	.....	.....	.....
1972	.....	.....	.....	.....	909	39.3	4.15	163.10	609	41.5	4.82	200.03
1973	.....	.....	.....	.....	934	39.6	4.48	177.41	620	41.8	5.13	214.43
1974	.....	.....	.....	.....	943	39.6	4.91	194.44	628	41.5	5.52	229.08
1975	.....	.....	.....	.....	911	38.9	5.54	215.51	614	41.1	6.03	247.83
1976	.....	.....	.....	.....	902	38.9	6.19	240.79	611	41.2	6.58	271.10
1977	.....	.....	.....	.....	907	39.6	6.74	266.90	618	41.3	7.11	293.64
1978	.....	.....	.....	.....	939	39.9	7.33	292.47	637	41.8	7.65	319.77
1979	.....	.....	.....	.....	987	39.8	7.85	312.43	660	41.7	8.25	344.03
1980	.....	.....	.....	.....	1 014	39.9	8.50	339.15	678	41.7	8.90	371.13
1981	.....	.....	.....	.....	1 040	39.8	9.48	377.30	699	41.4	9.89	409.45
1982	.....	.....	.....	.....	1 072	39.5	10.19	402.51	711	41.4	10.78	446.29
1983	.....	.....	.....	.....	996	39.4	10.77	424.34	712	41.4	11.50	476.10
1984	.....	.....	.....	.....	1 018	39.9	11.26	449.27	719	41.5	12.20	506.30
1985	.....	.....	.....	.....	1 005	40.2	11.75	472.35	730	41.7	12.83	535.01
1986	.....	.....	.....	.....	972	40.1	12.15	487.22	733	41.8	13.39	559.70
1987	.....	.....	.....	.....	972	40.0	12.45	498.00	733	41.5	13.79	572.29
1988	1 176	38.3	10.95	419.39	951	39.8	12.85	511.43	736	41.5	14.27	592.21
1989	1 203	38.4	11.35	435.84	950	39.4	13.18	519.29	742	41.9	14.72	616.77
1990	1 215	38.5	11.68	449.68	978	39.4	13.51	532.29	759	41.6	15.23	633.57
1991	1 197	38.4	11.83	454.27	986	39.2	13.96	547.23	762	41.6	15.69	652.70
1992	1 205	38.7	12.07	467.11	981	39.4	14.42	568.15	753	41.9	16.08	673.75
1993	1 254	39.5	12.26	484.27	985	39.6	14.91	590.44	744	42.3	16.71	706.83
1994	1 328	39.9	12.50	498.75	993	39.6	15.24	603.50	734	42.4	17.24	730.98
1995	1 382	39.6	12.73	504.11	1 017	39.8	15.56	619.29	719	42.4	17.68	749.63
1996	1 426	39.8	12.95	515.41	1 058	40.4	16.03	647.61	699	42.2	18.26	770.57
1997	1 467	40.2	13.23	531.85	1 090	40.2	16.92	680.18	689	42.1	19.10	804.11
1998	1 529	40.0	13.62	544.80	1 069	40.8	17.31	706.25	684	42.2	19.99	843.58
1995:												
January	1 341	38.6	12.57	485.20	997	40.2	15.53	624.31	723	42.1	17.42	733.38
February	1 342	38.6	12.63	487.52	1 007	39.1	15.39	601.75	719	42.1	17.42	733.38
March	1 350	38.9	12.67	492.86	1 010	39.1	15.47	604.88	719	41.7	17.44	727.25
April	1 360	39.1	12.60	492.66	1 009	39.4	15.38	605.97	716	42.6	17.61	750.19
May	1 368	39.3	12.66	497.54	1 010	39.4	15.34	604.40	718	42.0	17.51	735.42
June	1 389	40.2	12.64	508.13	1 017	39.6	15.40	609.84	726	42.2	17.48	737.66
July	1 384	39.9	12.64	504.34	1 019	40.4	15.51	626.60	727	42.6	17.75	756.15
August	1 401	40.3	12.77	514.63	1 021	40.4	15.56	628.62	725	42.3	17.56	742.79
September	1 394	40.4	12.88	520.35	1 021	40.1	15.63	626.76	717	42.4	17.73	751.75
October	1 427	40.4	12.87	519.95	1 027	40.2	15.88	638.38	718	42.8	17.96	768.69
November	1 421	39.9	12.91	515.11	1 031	39.9	15.79	630.02	714	43.2	18.13	783.22
December	1 410	39.9	12.84	512.32	1 029	40.0	15.79	631.60	712	42.6	18.11	771.49
1996:												
January	1 377	37.7	12.75	480.68	1 021	39.9	15.80	630.42	705	42.0	17.98	755.16
February	1 382	39.1	12.82	501.26	1 031	39.9	15.77	629.22	701	42.4	18.09	767.02
March	1 385	39.5	12.88	508.76	1 035	39.8	15.82	629.64	698	42.2	18.06	762.13
April	1 396	39.4	12.89	507.87	1 038	39.9	15.90	634.41	697	42.1	18.11	762.43
May	1 420	39.7	12.94	513.72	1 046	40.1	15.88	636.79	699	41.9	18.11	758.81
June	1 447	40.4	12.87	519.95	1 059	41.2	16.00	659.20	704	42.2	18.02	760.44
July	1 456	39.9	12.86	513.11	1 067	40.9	15.99	653.99	704	41.9	18.01	754.62
August	1 460	40.4	12.97	523.99	1 074	41.0	16.11	660.51	702	41.9	18.13	759.65
September	1 453	40.4	13.09	528.84	1 077	41.5	16.25	674.38	695	42.5	18.53	787.53
October	1 452	40.3	13.12	528.74	1 078	40.3	16.17	651.65	695	42.2	18.52	781.54
November	1 446	40.2	13.11	527.02	1 082	40.1	16.23	650.82	694	42.5	18.81	799.43
December	1 436	40.1	13.07	524.11	1 081	40.5	16.44	665.82	693	42.1	18.73	788.53
1997:												
January	1 401	38.8	12.99	504.01	1 075	40.1	16.67	668.47	690	41.8	18.76	784.17
February	1 408	39.4	13.04	513.78	1 083	40.0	16.54	661.60	688	41.8	18.76	784.17
March	1 416	39.8	13.07	520.19	1 092	40.1	16.69	669.27	689	41.9	18.92	792.75
April	1 428	39.9	13.14	524.29	1 095	40.0	16.66	666.40	688	42.4	19.00	805.60
May	1 455	40.1	13.18	528.52	1 098	39.8	16.60	660.68	692	42.0	18.95	795.90
June	1 469	40.7	13.15	535.21	1 105	40.5	16.90	684.45	696	42.2	19.00	801.80
July	1 486	40.3	13.16	530.35	1 100	40.5	17.04	690.12	696	42.0	19.04	799.68
August	1 505	41.2	13.30	547.96	1 099	40.5	17.15	694.58	693	42.1	19.07	802.85
September	1 513	40.7	13.36	543.75	1 090	40.5	17.18	695.79	687	42.0	19.25	808.50
October	1 516	40.5	13.37	541.49	1 085	39.9	17.17	685.08	684	42.2	19.31	814.88
November	1 504	40.4	13.41	541.76	1 082	40.6	17.21	698.73	681	42.7	19.60	836.92
December	1 497	40.3	13.47	542.84	1 075	40.4	17.22	695.69	681	41.8	19.51	815.52
1998:												
January	1 461	39.0	13.47	525.33	1 067	40.6	17.42	707.25	681	42.1	19.81	834.00
February	1 467	39.3	13.53	531.73	1 057	41.2	17.31	713.17	680	42.0	19.83	832.86
March	1 477	39.3	13.55	532.52	1 051	40.7	17.17	698.82	681	41.9	19.76	827.94
April	1 494	39.2	13.59	532.73	1 048	40.3	17.00	685.10	681	41.6	19.87	826.59
May	1 516	40.0	13.61	544.40	1 060	40.5	17.03	689.72	685	42.0	19.90	835.80
June	1 542	40.4	13.59	549.04	1 068	41.0	17.15	703.15	690	42.2	19.79	835.14
July	1 554	40.4	13.58	548.63	1 075	41.3	17.19	709.95	692	42.0	19.82	832.44
August	1 570	40.7	13.58	552.71	1 076	40.4	17.36	701.34	690	42.3	19.96	844.31
September	1 570	40.1	13.66	547.77	1 073	41.0	17.46	715.86	683	42.8	20.26	867.13
October	1 574	40.7	13.68	556.78	1 080	40.6	17.46	708.88	681	42.6	20.16	858.82
November	1 563	40.3	13.74	553.72	1 087	40.9	17.53	716.98	684	43.2	20.47	884.30
December	1 560	40.4	13.78	556.71	1 091	40.6	17.65	716.59	683	42.1	20.23	851.68

Retail and Wholesale Trade

Employment in Wholesale and Retail Trade, 1970 and 1998
(millions of workers)

- The 1970 to 1998 time period saw employment in retail trade more than double and employment in wholesale grow by 71 percent, but 1998 saw employment in wholesale trade increase more rapidly, growing by 2.8 percent to 6.8 million. Employment in retail trade grew by 1.5 percent to 22.3 million from 22 million. Fully a third of the increase in retail came from eating and drinking establishments, reflecting a long-standing trend of much more rapid growth in this sector.

- Average weekly earnings of nonsupervisory workers in retail trade averaged $253.17, up over 5 percent from 1997, reflecting both a 4.8 percent increase in hourly wages and a small growth in average weekly hours. Low weekly earnings in this industry reflect both low hourly wages and a short average workweek.

- Average weekly earnings of nonsupervisory workers in wholesale trade grew to $539.90, reflecting a 4.5 percent increase in average hourly earnings.

- The value of retail sales increased by 5 percent in 1998. Durable goods sales increased by nearly 7 percent, with particularly strong growth for building materials and furniture and home furnishings sales. Sales of nondurable goods increased by 3.8 percent. Though most nondurable goods stores recorded larger increases, food stores, with over 25 percent of the nondurable total, only grew by 3.1 percent in 1998. Gasoline service stations actually saw their sales value fall by 5.5 percent to $162 billion, the lowest level since 1995; gasoline prices were down 13 percent in 1998, so this still represented a rise in sales volume.

Retail and Wholesale Trade—Employment

(Total payroll employment—Thousands, seasonally adjusted)

Year and month	Wholesale trade			Retail trade						Nonsupervisory workers	
	Total	Durable goods	Nondura-ble goods	Total	General merchan-dise stores	Food stores	Auto dealers and service stations	Apparel and accessory stores	Eating and drinking places	Wholesale trade	Retail trade
1970	4 006	.....	.....	11 034	.....	1 731	1 617	761	2 575	3 340	10 034
1971	4 014	.....	.....	11 338	.....	1 752	1 642	779	2 700	3 327	10 288
1972	4 127	2 336	1 791	11 822	2 149	1 805	1 723	784	2 860	3 418	10 717
1973	4 291	2 457	1 835	12 315	2 229	1 856	1 778	795	3 054	3 560	11 155
1974	4 447	2 578	1 869	12 539	2 210	1 948	1 666	811	3 231	3 683	11 316
1975	4 430	2 539	1 891	12 630	2 113	2 007	1 677	806	3 380	3 650	11 373
1976	4 562	2 615	1 946	13 193	2 155	2 039	1 744	842	3 656	3 759	11 890
1977	4 723	2 732	1 991	13 792	2 204	2 106	1 801	870	3 949	3 892	12 424
1978	4 985	2 917	2 068	14 556	2 308	2 199	1 861	909	4 277	4 109	13 110
1979	5 221	3 098	2 123	14 972	2 287	2 297	1 812	949	4 513	4 290	13 458
1980	5 292	3 139	2 153	15 018	2 245	2 384	1 689	957	4 626	4 328	13 484
1981	5 375	3 182	2 193	15 171	2 230	2 448	1 653	968	4 749	4 375	13 582
1982	5 295	3 107	2 188	15 158	2 184	2 477	1 632	942	4 829	4 261	13 594
1983	5 283	3 087	2 197	15 587	2 165	2 556	1 674	963	5 038	4 239	13 989
1984	5 568	3 291	2 277	16 512	2 267	2 636	1 798	1 008	5 381	4 466	14 736
1985	5 727	3 402	2 325	17 315	2 323	2 774	1 889	1 039	5 699	4 607	15 421
1986	5 761	3 395	2 365	17 880	2 365	2 896	1 941	1 075	5 902	4 623	15 925
1987	5 848	3 437	2 411	18 422	2 411	2 958	2 001	1 123	6 086	4 685	16 378
1988	6 030	3 564	2 466	19 023	2 472	3 074	2 071	1 165	6 258	4 858	16 869
1989	6 187	3 653	2 534	19 475	2 544	3 164	2 092	1 197	6 402	4 981	17 262
1990	6 173	3 614	2 559	19 601	2 540	3 215	2 063	1 183	6 509	4 959	17 358
1991	6 081	3 531	2 550	19 284	2 453	3 204	1 984	1 151	6 476	4 872	17 006
1992	5 997	3 446	2 552	19 356	2 451	3 180	1 966	1 131	6 609	4 817	17 048
1993	5 981	3 433	2 549	19 773	2 488	3 224	2 014	1 144	6 821	4 823	17 428
1994	6 162	3 559	2 604	20 507	2 583	3 291	2 116	1 144	7 078	4 972	18 056
1995	6 378	3 715	2 663	21 187	2 681	3 366	2 190	1 125	7 354	5 163	18 639
1996	6 482	3 805	2 677	21 597	2 702	3 436	2 267	1 098	7 517	5 238	19 002
1997	6 648	3 927	2 721	21 966	2 701	3 478	2 311	1 109	7 646	5 355	19 337
1998	6 831	4 042	2 789	22 296	2 730	3 482	2 341	1 143	7 760	5 476	19 591
1995:											
January	6 311	3 661	2 650	21 008	2 680	3 330	2 166	1 147	7 259	5 105	18 487
February	6 339	3 681	2 658	21 065	2 678	3 338	2 173	1 148	7 278	5 133	18 541
March	6 356	3 696	2 660	21 047	2 643	3 342	2 179	1 142	7 291	5 144	18 526
April	6 363	3 701	2 662	21 126	2 678	3 355	2 181	1 139	7 310	5 153	18 584
May	6 368	3 707	2 661	21 123	2 677	3 357	2 182	1 129	7 312	5 154	18 577
June	6 381	3 716	2 665	21 192	2 688	3 367	2 184	1 130	7 354	5 170	18 639
July	6 391	3 721	2 670	21 213	2 688	3 368	2 186	1 125	7 374	5 179	18 667
August	6 395	3 726	2 669	21 254	2 686	3 380	2 193	1 124	7 392	5 181	18 701
September	6 401	3 733	2 668	21 293	2 691	3 382	2 199	1 109	7 413	5 185	18 730
October	6 403	3 740	2 663	21 276	2 699	3 379	2 205	1 104	7 401	5 184	18 718
November	6 410	3 747	2 663	21 310	2 682	3 392	2 211	1 107	7 421	5 187	18 741
December	6 418	3 754	2 664	21 335	2 674	3 403	2 219	1 102	7 435	5 192	18 753
1996:											
January	6 421	3 759	2 662	21 339	2 677	3 404	2 226	1 098	7 438	5 191	18 748
February	6 426	3 765	2 661	21 394	2 686	3 407	2 234	1 098	7 453	5 196	18 828
March	6 434	3 772	2 662	21 447	2 691	3 411	2 242	1 099	7 476	5 204	18 884
April	6 442	3 780	2 662	21 460	2 681	3 413	2 250	1 095	7 485	5 206	18 891
May	6 457	3 790	2 667	21 540	2 711	3 425	2 259	1 098	7 498	5 217	18 954
June	6 472	3 799	2 673	21 574	2 710	3 430	2 269	1 098	7 505	5 229	18 985
July	6 479	3 808	2 671	21 621	2 709	3 439	2 277	1 099	7 522	5 233	19 030
August	6 499	3 817	2 682	21 655	2 704	3 445	2 282	1 097	7 534	5 249	19 049
September	6 517	3 830	2 687	21 681	2 704	3 451	2 286	1 098	7 532	5 263	19 073
October	6 539	3 841	2 698	21 770	2 716	3 458	2 289	1 102	7 573	5 284	19 163
November	6 550	3 851	2 699	21 801	2 711	3 465	2 294	1 102	7 581	5 295	19 180
December	6 559	3 860	2 699	21 852	2 715	3 467	2 296	1 101	7 593	5 295	19 216
1997:											
January	6 563	3 867	2 696	21 839	2 687	3 472	2 299	1 100	7 608	5 299	19 223
February	6 585	3 880	2 705	21 842	2 677	3 474	2 303	1 095	7 619	5 315	19 223
March	6 605	3 894	2 711	21 895	2 701	3 479	2 306	1 098	7 626	5 336	19 290
April	6 614	3 902	2 712	21 920	2 702	3 479	2 307	1 101	7 633	5 335	19 305
May	6 626	3 912	2 714	21 917	2 694	3 477	2 307	1 100	7 636	5 341	19 303
June	6 633	3 917	2 716	21 945	2 698	3 476	2 306	1 102	7 650	5 345	19 324
July	6 656	3 934	2 722	21 933	2 697	3 481	2 308	1 104	7 624	5 361	19 315
August	6 669	3 947	2 722	21 986	2 704	3 481	2 314	1 111	7 647	5 368	19 351
September	6 678	3 952	2 726	22 012	2 698	3 477	2 317	1 116	7 664	5 369	19 375
October	6 699	3 963	2 736	22 047	2 704	3 482	2 318	1 128	7 666	5 384	19 413
November	6 712	3 973	2 739	22 109	2 715	3 481	2 321	1 127	7 690	5 393	19 458
December	6 732	3 984	2 748	22 139	2 732	3 475	2 321	1 130	7 691	5 408	19 468
1998:											
January	6 755	3 995	2 760	22 142	2 712	3 482	2 322	1 137	7 703	5 419	19 470
February	6 767	4 006	2 761	22 149	2 711	3 479	2 321	1 134	7 720	5 427	19 473
March	6 780	4 014	2 766	22 155	2 709	3 477	2 323	1 134	7 719	5 434	19 494
April	6 798	4 023	2 775	22 177	2 716	3 474	2 327	1 139	7 718	5 447	19 490
May	6 814	4 032	2 782	22 237	2 725	3 478	2 333	1 142	7 736	5 460	19 558
June	6 826	4 039	2 787	22 257	2 725	3 474	2 338	1 145	7 740	5 470	19 568
July	6 836	4 046	2 790	22 321	2 728	3 484	2 343	1 148	7 767	5 482	19 623
August	6 846	4 055	2 791	22 353	2 733	3 483	2 345	1 149	7 779	5 488	19 633
September	6 871	4 066	2 805	22 382	2 745	3 486	2 349	1 150	7 782	5 507	19 651
October	6 876	4 068	2 808	22 392	2 744	3 485	2 356	1 144	7 787	5 510	19 657
November	6 891	4 074	2 817	22 443	2 750	3 488	2 361	1 148	7 808	5 523	19 699
December	6 901	4 077	2 824	22 525	2 758	3 487	2 370	1 147	7 857	5 534	19 750

Retail and Wholesale Trade—Hours and Earnings

(Nonsupervisory workers)

Year and month	Average weekly hours (seasonally adjusted)		Aggregate weekly hours index (1982=100, seasonally adjusted)		Average earnings (dollars, not seasonally adjusted)								
					Hourly							Weekly	
	Whole-sale trade	Retail trade	Whole-sale trade	Retail trade	Whole-sale trade	Retail trade	General mer-chan-dise stores	Food stores	Auto dealer and service stations	Apparel and acces-sory stores	Eating and drinking places	Whole-sale trade	Retail trade
1970	39.9	33.8	81.7	83.4	3.43	2.44	.....	2.71	.....	2.26	1.86	136.86	82.47
1971	39.4	33.7	80.4	85.3	3.64	2.60	.....	2.94	.....	2.36	1.96	143.42	87.62
1972	39.4	33.4	82.5	88.2	3.85	2.75	2.62	3.18	3.18	2.52	2.07	151.69	91.85
1973	39.2	33.1	85.6	90.9	4.07	2.91	2.76	3.38	3.38	2.63	2.18	159.54	96.32
1974	38.8	32.7	87.6	91.0	4.38	3.14	2.98	3.74	3.64	2.83	2.37	169.94	102.68
1975	38.6	32.4	86.4	90.6	4.72	3.36	3.21	4.08	3.84	3.03	2.55	182.19	108.86
1976	38.7	32.1	89.1	93.9	5.02	3.57	3.41	4.41	4.14	3.26	2.69	194.27	114.60
1977	38.8	31.6	92.5	96.5	5.39	3.85	3.71	4.77	4.49	3.45	2.93	209.13	121.66
1978	38.8	31.0	97.7	100.0	5.88	4.20	4.05	5.23	4.93	3.72	3.22	228.14	130.20
1979	38.8	30.6	102.0	101.5	6.39	4.53	4.38	5.67	5.31	4.01	3.45	247.93	138.62
1980	38.4	30.2	101.9	100.1	6.95	4.88	4.77	6.24	5.66	4.30	3.69	266.88	147.38
1981	38.5	30.1	103.3	100.6	7.55	5.25	5.15	6.85	6.07	4.65	3.95	290.68	158.03
1982	38.3	29.9	100.0	100.0	8.08	5.48	5.39	7.22	6.31	4.85	4.09	309.46	163.85
1983	38.5	29.8	99.9	102.7	8.54	5.74	5.61	7.51	6.76	5.02	4.27	328.79	171.05
1984	38.5	29.8	105.3	108.2	8.88	5.85	5.64	7.64	7.13	5.11	4.26	341.88	174.33
1985	38.4	29.4	108.4	111.7	9.15	5.94	5.92	7.35	7.41	5.25	4.33	351.36	174.64
1986	38.3	29.2	108.5	114.3	9.34	6.03	6.30	7.06	7.68	5.37	4.35	357.72	176.08
1987	38.1	29.2	109.4	117.9	9.59	6.12	6.47	6.95	7.81	5.56	4.42	365.38	178.70
1988	38.1	29.1	113.3	121.0	9.98	6.31	6.45	7.01	8.24	5.79	4.57	380.24	183.62
1989	38.0	28.9	116.1	122.9	10.39	6.53	6.64	7.15	8.57	6.01	4.75	394.82	188.72
1990	38.1	28.8	115.7	123.0	10.79	6.75	6.83	7.31	8.92	6.25	4.97	411.10	194.40
1991	38.1	28.6	113.7	119.5	11.15	6.94	7.04	7.33	9.07	6.60	5.18	424.82	198.48
1992	38.2	28.8	112.8	120.6	11.39	7.12	7.18	7.56	9.34	6.88	5.29	435.10	205.06
1993	38.2	28.8	112.8	123.4	11.74	7.29	7.29	7.80	9.66	7.01	5.35	448.47	209.95
1994	38.4	28.9	116.9	128.6	12.06	7.49	7.44	7.94	10.09	7.17	5.47	463.10	216.46
1995	38.3	28.8	121.1	132.2	12.43	7.69	7.53	8.15	10.41	7.47	5.59	476.07	221.47
1996	38.3	28.8	122.9	134.6	12.87	7.99	7.86	8.40	10.90	7.74	5.79	492.92	230.11
1997	38.4	28.9	126.1	137.7	13.45	8.33	8.16	8.68	11.41	8.07	6.06	516.48	240.74
1998	38.4	29.0	128.8	140.0	14.06	8.73	8.59	9.05	12.06	8.47	6.35	539.90	253.17
1995:													
January	38.4	28.8	120.1	131.0	12.33	7.63	7.44	8.08	10.15	7.42	5.52	471.01	215.17
February	38.3	28.7	120.5	130.9	12.31	7.63	7.50	8.11	10.15	7.43	5.52	469.01	214.40
March	38.3	28.7	120.8	130.8	12.27	7.63	7.53	8.10	10.18	7.47	5.53	467.49	215.93
April	38.3	28.8	121.0	131.7	12.47	7.65	7.51	8.06	10.43	7.49	5.53	477.60	221.09
May	38.2	28.8	121.0	131.7	12.35	7.64	7.51	8.13	10.31	7.48	5.57	470.54	219.27
June	38.2	28.8	121.0	132.1	12.34	7.65	7.51	8.08	10.47	7.49	5.56	472.62	222.62
July	38.2	28.7	121.3	131.8	12.46	7.66	7.53	8.11	10.54	7.44	5.57	479.71	227.50
August	38.3	28.8	121.6	132.5	12.41	7.65	7.51	8.11	10.45	7.39	5.60	475.30	225.68
September	38.3	28.8	121.7	132.7	12.52	7.77	7.59	8.23	10.62	7.52	5.64	479.52	224.55
October	38.2	28.7	121.4	132.2	12.56	7.77	7.59	8.27	10.50	7.55	5.65	483.56	223.78
November	38.2	28.8	121.4	132.8	12.55	7.78	7.54	8.27	10.51	7.50	5.66	479.41	222.51
December	38.2	28.7	121.6	132.4	12.63	7.80	7.55	8.25	10.57	7.47	5.70	483.73	226.20
1996:													
January	38.0	28.5	120.9	131.5	12.66	7.89	7.73	8.38	10.38	7.73	5.69	476.02	216.98
February	38.2	28.8	121.7	133.4	12.68	7.87	7.74	8.38	10.53	7.73	5.69	481.84	221.93
March	38.3	28.9	122.2	134.3	12.69	7.90	7.81	8.38	10.77	7.71	5.69	483.49	225.15
April	38.2	28.7	121.9	133.4	12.78	7.92	7.91	8.40	10.80	7.74	5.70	486.92	224.93
May	38.3	28.8	122.5	134.3	12.75	7.92	7.88	8.37	10.88	7.73	5.72	487.05	227.30
June	38.4	28.8	123.1	134.6	12.98	7.98	7.89	8.30	11.20	7.77	5.76	499.74	234.61
July	38.1	28.7	122.2	134.4	12.83	7.93	7.86	8.28	10.89	7.66	5.76	488.82	233.14
August	38.3	28.8	123.2	135.0	12.85	7.95	7.87	8.31	10.97	7.62	5.78	493.44	234.53
September	38.4	28.9	123.9	135.6	13.04	8.06	7.93	8.44	11.08	7.77	5.82	503.34	234.55
October	38.3	28.8	124.0	135.8	12.95	8.11	7.93	8.51	11.03	7.80	5.92	495.99	232.76
November	38.3	28.8	124.3	135.9	13.07	8.13	7.86	8.53	11.13	7.78	5.92	500.58	232.52
December	38.4	28.9	124.6	136.7	13.21	8.15	7.92	8.52	11.11	7.77	5.97	511.23	238.80
1997:													
January	38.3	28.9	124.4	136.7	13.19	8.24	7.97	8.61	11.00	7.96	5.95	499.90	229.90
February	38.4	28.9	125.1	136.7	13.27	8.24	8.07	8.61	11.22	7.95	5.93	510.90	236.49
March	38.4	29.0	125.6	137.7	13.29	8.26	8.15	8.65	11.33	7.97	5.95	511.67	237.06
April	38.4	28.9	125.6	137.3	13.35	8.27	8.12	8.71	11.35	8.01	5.96	511.31	236.52
May	38.5	28.9	126.0	137.3	13.34	8.27	8.08	8.66	11.39	8.09	5.99	513.59	238.18
June	38.4	28.8	125.8	137.0	13.38	8.27	8.12	8.61	11.44	8.09	5.98	517.81	243.14
July	38.4	28.9	126.2	137.4	13.39	8.26	8.10	8.61	11.44	7.98	5.98	512.84	244.50
August	38.4	29.0	126.3	138.1	13.50	8.29	8.10	8.59	11.55	7.95	6.04	519.75	246.21
September	38.4	28.9	126.4	137.8	13.55	8.44	8.25	8.75	11.59	8.17	6.18	520.32	244.76
October	38.4	28.9	126.7	138.1	13.59	8.46	8.30	8.78	11.47	8.20	6.22	521.86	243.65
November	38.5	29.0	127.3	138.9	13.79	8.50	8.27	8.79	11.65	8.21	6.21	533.67	244.80
December	38.4	28.9	127.3	138.5	13.76	8.50	8.29	8.81	11.52	8.18	6.28	528.38	248.20
1998:													
January	38.5	29.0	127.9	138.9	13.81	8.61	8.43	8.93	11.56	8.30	6.24	526.16	241.94
February	38.4	29.0	127.7	139.0	13.89	8.60	8.44	8.93	11.71	8.39	6.23	534.77	246.82
March	38.3	29.0	127.6	139.1	13.90	8.64	8.58	8.97	11.82	8.41	6.26	533.76	247.97
April	38.3	29.0	127.9	139.1	13.95	8.69	8.72	8.98	12.01	8.42	6.29	531.50	249.40
May	38.4	29.1	128.5	140.1	14.00	8.69	8.66	9.01	12.12	8.48	6.31	537.60	252.01
June	38.3	29.0	128.4	139.6	13.94	8.68	8.59	8.95	12.17	8.50	6.33	535.30	254.32
July	38.4	29.1	129.0	140.5	14.04	8.69	8.53	8.97	12.21	8.40	6.33	537.73	258.96
August	38.4	29.0	129.2	140.1	14.18	8.72	8.61	9.00	12.27	8.37	6.37	548.77	260.73
September	38.3	29.0	129.3	140.2	14.16	8.88	8.73	9.40	12.18	8.57	6.43	539.50	258.41
October	38.3	29.1	129.3	140.8	14.19	8.84	8.62	9.16	12.14	8.59	6.45	543.48	255.48
November	38.4	29.0	130.0	140.6	14.34	8.86	8.56	9.18	12.24	8.60	6.45	554.96	256.05
December	38.4	29.0	130.2	140.9	14.32	8.88	8.62	9.14	12.20	8.59	6.53	549.89	259.30

Retail Sales

(All retail stores—Millions of dollars, not seasonally adjusted)

Year and month	Total	Durable goods stores				Nondurable goods stores							
		Total	Building materials group [1]	Automotive dealers	Furniture and home furnishings and equipment	Total	General merchandise group stores	Food stores	Gasoline service stations	Apparel and accessory stores	Eating and drinking places	Drug and proprietary stores	Liquor stores
1970	374 989	114 586	18 080	65 241	17 043	260 403	49 163	89 990	28 903	22 095	30 476	14 567	8 412
1971	413 969	135 113	20 924	80 718	18 183	278 856	54 365	94 002	30 620	24 178	32 321	15 143	9 294
1972	458 267	155 937	24 123	92 335	21 199	302 330	59 656	100 589	33 072	26 367	35 738	16 139	9 814
1973	511 570	176 817	27 466	104 893	24 244	334 753	65 825	111 817	36 942	29 109	40 290	17 190	10 288
1974	541 686	172 497	27 347	97 551	25 982	369 189	69 540	126 312	43 054	30 077	44 606	18 595	11 087
1975	587 704	185 479	27 299	107 348	27 046	402 225	73 759	138 665	47 603	32 398	51 067	19 995	11 896
1976	655 859	219 908	33 259	130 169	30 300	435 951	79 500	148 218	52 037	34 706	57 331	21 710	12 442
1977	722 109	249 078	38 913	150 129	33 308	473 031	87 824	158 444	56 638	37 165	63 370	23 381	13 031
1978	804 019	280 899	45 170	168 065	36 832	523 120	97 215	175 425	59 889	42 649	71 828	25 607	13 630
1979	896 561	306 561	51 016	178 641	42 417	590 000	103 817	197 985	73 521	46 070	82 110	28 455	15 194
1980	956 921	298 618	50 794	164 149	44 238	658 303	108 955	220 224	94 093	49 296	90 058	30 951	16 882
1981	1 038 163	324 211	52 230	181 903	46 900	713 952	120 534	236 188	103 072	53 998	98 118	33 999	17 702
1982	1 068 747	335 587	50 994	192 440	46 761	733 160	124 624	246 122	97 440	55 570	104 593	36 440	18 146
1983	1 170 163	390 849	58 739	229 979	54 691	779 314	135 959	256 018	102 927	60 192	113 281	40 591	19 121
1984	1 286 914	454 481	67 077	273 320	61 432	832 433	150 283	271 909	107 565	64 341	121 321	44 011	18 273
1985	1 375 027	498 125	71 196	303 199	68 287	876 902	158 636	285 062	113 341	70 195	127 949	46 994	19 532
1986	1 449 636	540 688	77 104	326 138	75 714	908 948	169 397	297 019	102 093	75 626	139 415	50 546	19 929
1987	1 541 299	575 863	83 454	342 896	78 072	965 436	181 970	309 461	104 769	79 322	153 461	54 142	19 826
1988	1 656 202	629 154	91 056	372 570	85 390	1 027 048	192 521	325 493	110 341	85 307	167 993	57 842	19 638
1989	1 758 971	657 154	92 379	386 011	91 301	1 101 817	206 306	347 045	122 882	92 341	177 829	63 343	20 099
1990	1 844 611	668 835	94 640	387 605	91 545	1 175 776	215 514	368 333	138 504	95 819	190 149	70 558	21 722
1991	1 855 937	649 974	91 496	372 647	91 676	1 205 963	226 730	374 523	137 295	97 441	194 424	75 540	22 454
1992	1 951 589	703 604	100 838	406 935	96 947	1 247 985	246 420	377 099	136 950	104 212	200 164	77 788	21 698
1993	2 083 029	782 264	111 014	459 317	105 545	1 300 765	264 147	382 930	141 603	107 588	212 690	79 784	21 561
1994	2 250 033	887 443	125 868	525 379	119 171	1 362 590	282 332	394 671	148 673	110 735	221 882	82 156	22 136
1995	2 361 793	948 652	131 711	562 867	128 437	1 413 141	297 996	403 205	156 939	111 970	229 526	86 093	22 053
1996	2 506 141	1 020 861	141 935	608 781	135 149	1 485 280	313 342	415 390	168 320	116 101	238 474	92 169	23 216
1997	2 615 669	1 066 087	150 482	632 885	140 776	1 549 582	330 216	425 170	171 527	120 575	253 551	99 301	24 147
1998	2 746 011	1 138 286	165 331	668 658	152 044	1 607 725	351 436	438 212	162 095	126 939	266 544	106 713	25 114
1995:													
January	168 433	65 441	8 366	39 305	9 629	102 992	18 279	32 165	11 961	6 562	17 109	6 848	1 558
February	165 285	65 402	8 144	40 221	8 945	99 883	18 411	30 186	11 423	6 716	16 739	6 634	1 504
March	193 560	79 513	10 499	50 139	10 040	114 047	22 282	33 470	12 767	8 663	19 092	7 156	1 729
April	188 910	76 026	11 178	46 519	9 303	112 884	22 765	32 898	12 678	8 949	19 127	6 975	1 702
May	202 984	84 596	13 006	51 324	10 022	118 388	23 918	34 296	13 911	9 016	19 916	7 296	1 811
June	204 197	86 615	12 558	53 432	10 230	117 582	23 992	34 120	14 183	8 898	19 935	7 055	1 866
July	196 444	80 249	11 600	48 611	10 108	116 195	23 207	34 595	13 985	8 526	20 242	6 813	1 890
August	206 003	85 574	12 048	51 832	10 882	120 429	24 654	34 403	14 157	9 845	20 590	7 056	1 864
September	194 651	79 388	11 519	47 472	10 621	115 263	23 204	33 230	13 185	9 372	19 303	6 879	1 849
October	195 985	78 895	11 738	47 003	10 718	117 090	24 138	32 980	13 162	9 070	19 429	7 104	1 793
November	204 647	78 896	10 853	44 539	12 275	125 751	30 072	33 602	12 623	10 858	18 458	7 230	1 884
December	240 694	88 057	10 202	42 470	15 664	152 637	43 074	37 260	12 904	15 495	19 586	9 047	2 603
1996:													
January	177 259	70 610	8 477	43 438	10 077	106 649	18 705	32 963	12 429	6 637	17 386	7 153	1 682
February	184 487	75 510	8 665	48 072	9 806	108 977	20 617	31 971	12 177	7 541	18 156	7 209	1 654
March	204 139	84 868	10 311	54 184	10 798	119 271	23 388	34 320	13 488	9 024	19 940	7 530	1 840
April	203 496	85 451	12 618	52 536	10 332	118 045	23 528	33 377	13 967	9 210	19 513	7 447	1 802
May	218 902	92 878	14 105	56 539	10 794	126 024	25 965	35 651	15 224	9 621	20 787	7 779	1 961
June	209 761	88 566	13 665	53 393	10 671	121 195	24 937	34 629	14 804	9 124	20 343	7 288	1 961
July	209 910	88 509	13 448	53 427	10 808	121 401	23 776	35 586	14 802	8 815	20 673	7 511	2 038
August	217 519	89 745	13 024	53 826	11 466	127 774	26 471	36 019	14 995	10 623	21 495	7 659	2 068
September	200 917	82 812	12 321	49 664	10 862	118 105	23 853	33 462	13 846	9 263	19 524	7 240	1 786
October	213 341	87 233	12 992	52 489	11 329	126 108	26 034	34 850	14 446	9 785	20 392	7 850	1 866
November	215 784	82 748	11 452	46 556	12 513	133 036	31 114	35 242	13 964	11 014	20 008	7 742	1 999
December	250 626	91 931	10 857	44 657	15 693	158 695	44 954	37 320	14 178	15 444	20 257	9 761	2 559
1997:													
January	191 430	76 010	9 247	46 761	10 440	115 420	20 820	34 536	13 691	7 155	19 068	7 944	1 717
February	188 803	77 382	9 278	48 510	9 954	111 421	21 360	31 798	12 827	7 423	18 868	7 671	1 631
March	215 770	88 809	11 598	55 950	10 969	126 961	25 468	35 822	14 201	9 650	21 114	8 392	1 865
April	210 561	88 762	13 544	54 446	10 619	121 799	24 250	33 960	14 124	8 877	20 834	7 944	1 828
May	224 921	93 311	14 862	56 162	11 165	131 610	27 253	36 865	14 871	9 925	22 376	8 359	2 073
June	217 884	92 136	14 239	55 703	10 920	125 748	26 126	34 793	14 745	9 327	21 564	8 019	2 012
July	222 040	93 497	14 151	56 656	11 368	128 543	25 594	36 676	15 033	9 416	22 386	8 109	2 107
August	226 032	93 118	13 118	56 286	11 909	132 914	27 880	36 555	15 298	11 114	23 012	8 042	2 086
September	212 931	88 798	13 435	53 053	11 370	124 133	24 643	34 436	14 497	9 599	21 045	7 964	1 894
October	222 035	90 178	13 589	53 712	11 732	131 857	27 644	35 857	14 773	10 233	21 719	8 328	2 049
November	220 005	84 390	11 693	46 868	13 087	135 615	32 751	35 550	13 629	11 428	20 344	8 150	2 076
December	263 257	99 696	11 728	48 778	17 243	163 561	46 427	38 322	13 838	16 428	21 221	10 379	2 809
1998:													
January	198 479	80 133	10 012	48 073	11 658	118 346	21 966	35 142	12 880	7 650	20 042	8 485	1 826
February	195 093	80 508	9 996	49 198	10 964	114 585	22 850	32 263	11 916	7 936	19 719	8 126	1 745
March	220 426	93 356	12 674	58 124	11 832	127 070	25 886	35 235	13 011	9 553	21 906	8 630	1 865
April	225 008	95 525	14 813	58 366	11 247	129 483	27 412	35 762	13 310	10 383	21 780	8 752	1 931
May	236 370	100 397	16 098	60 602	11 743	135 973	29 214	37 577	14 271	10 413	23 389	8 848	2 105
June	234 836	103 681	16 028	63 304	11 986	131 155	27 639	36 198	14 313	9 844	22 734	8 652	2 028
July	232 611	98 245	15 448	58 160	12 413	134 366	27 217	38 293	14 716	10 119	23 314	8 743	2 177
August	231 685	95 851	14 329	56 072	12 813	135 834	28 903	37 336	14 288	11 423	23 460	8 718	2 092
September	222 104	93 393	14 548	54 944	12 251	128 711	26 500	35 967	13 404	9 778	21 978	8 556	2 011
October	234 928	97 193	14 867	57 702	12 639	137 735	29 271	37 388	13 841	10 816	23 385	9 033	2 148
November	232 852	91 559	13 171	50 953	13 978	141 293	34 787	36 396	12 844	11 870	21 742	8 936	2 149
December	281 619	108 445	13 347	53 160	18 520	173 174	49 791	40 655	13 301	17 154	23 095	11 234	3 037

1. Includes building materials; hardware; plants and garden supplies; and manufactured (mobile) homes.

Retail Sales—Continued

(All retail stores—Millions of dollars, seasonally adjusted)

Year and month	Total	Durable goods stores										Nondurable goods stores, total
		Total	Building materials group [1]			Automotive dealers			Furniture and home furnishings and equipment			
			Total	Building materials and supply stores	Hardware stores	Total	Motor vehicle and miscellaneous automotive dealers	Auto and home supply stores	Total	Furniture and home furnishings	Household appliances and electronics	
1970	374 989	114 586	18 080	11 343	2 979	65 241	59 243	5 998	17 043	10 442	5 571	260 403
1971	413 969	135 113	20 924	13 070	3 230	80 718	73 747	6 971	18 183	11 439	5 634	278 856
1972	458 267	155 937	24 123	15 112	3 620	92 335	84 477	7 858	21 199	13 480	6 274	302 330
1973	511 570	176 817	27 466	17 314	4 187	104 893	96 121	8 772	24 244	15 430	7 210	334 753
1974	541 686	172 497	27 347	17 874	4 604	97 551	88 310	9 241	25 982	18 544	7 427	369 189
1975	587 704	185 479	27 299	17 947	5 165	107 348	97 275	10 073	27 046	16 460	8 218	402 225
1976	655 859	219 908	33 259	22 484	5 591	130 169	119 063	11 116	30 300	18 383	9 129	435 951
1977	722 109	249 078	38 913	27 123	6 139	150 129	150 129	13 095	33 308	20 384	10 046	473 031
1978	804 019	280 899	45 170	31 910	6 652	168 065	168 065	14 165	36 832	22 538	10 780	523 120
1979	896 561	306 561	51 016	36 245	7 937	178 641	152 458	16 183	42 417	25 642	12 936	590 000
1980	956 921	298 618	50 794	34 997	8 349	164 149	146 190	17 959	44 238	26 332	14 010	658 303
1981	1 038 163	324 211	52 230	35 738	8 475	181 903	162 271	19 632	46 900	27 499	15 402	713 952
1982	1 068 747	335 587	50 994	35 144	8 727	192 440	172 359	20 081	46 761	27 093	15 774	733 160
1983	1 170 163	390 849	58 739	41 256	9 140	229 979	207 871	22 108	54 691	31 296	19 280	779 314
1984	1 286 914	454 481	67 077	47 127	10 354	273 320	250 193	23 127	61 432	35 587	21 474	832 433
1985	1 375 027	498 125	71 196	50 766	10 471	303 199	277 995	25 204	68 287	38 270	25 147	876 902
1986	1 449 636	540 688	77 104	56 510	10 734	326 138	301 083	25 055	75 714	43 030	27 037	908 948
1987	1 541 299	575 863	83 454	61 302	11 036	342 896	316 274	26 622	78 072	44 477	27 121	965 436
1988	1 656 202	629 154	91 056	66 796	11 894	372 570	343 217	29 353	85 390	47 617	30 608	1 027 048
1989	1 758 971	657 154	92 379	67 457	12 637	386 011	356 485	29 526	91 301	51 202	32 666	1 101 817
1990	1 844 611	668 835	94 640	70 341	12 524	387 605	356 764	30 841	91 545	50 524	33 035	1 175 776
1991	1 855 937	649 974	91 496	68 196	12 148	372 647	343 018	29 629	91 676	49 469	33 569	1 205 963
1992	1 951 589	703 604	100 838	75 358	12 729	406 935	377 118	29 817	96 947	52 348	35 802	1 247 985
1993	2 083 029	782 264	111 014	83 435	13 066	459 317	428 636	30 681	105 545	54 741	41 397	1 300 765
1994	2 250 033	887 443	125 868	95 209	13 852	525 379	492 662	32 717	119 171	59 013	49 745	1 362 590
1995	2 361 793	948 652	131 711	99 181	13 793	562 867	529 138	33 729	128 437	60 790	56 572	1 413 141
1996	2 506 141	1 020 861	141 935	106 859	13 989	608 781	573 557	35 224	135 149	63 887	59 792	1 485 280
1997	2 615 669	1 066 087	150 482	114 187	14 039	632 885	597 069	35 816	140 776	67 537	61 735	1 549 582
1998	2 746 011	1 138 286	165 331	124 365	14 630	668 658	631 689	36 969	152 044	71 377	68 532	1 607 725
1995:												
January	194 807	77 593	11 176	8 637	1 071	45 657	42 846	2 811	10 571	5 039	4 585	117 214
February	191 635	76 049	10 952	8 338	1 126	44 693	41 938	2 755	10 389	4 946	4 561	115 586
March	193 235	77 115	11 050	8 298	1 155	45 566	42 772	2 794	10 355	4 905	4 579	116 120
April	193 768	77 095	10 740	8 094	1 126	45 720	42 925	2 795	10 320	4 954	4 489	116 673
May	195 870	78 347	10 764	8 034	1 154	46 417	43 629	2 788	10 517	4 961	4 674	117 523
June	197 529	79 393	10 761	8 124	1 185	47 509	44 740	2 769	10 612	5 021	4 684	118 136
July	197 195	79 395	10 821	8 149	1 160	47 388	44 600	2 788	10 611	5 062	4 624	117 800
August	199 045	80 847	10 968	8 157	1 154	48 373	45 560	2 813	10 864	5 096	4 778	118 198
September	198 960	80 118	11 001	8 227	1 160	47 653	44 799	2 854	10 930	5 186	4 798	118 842
October	198 786	80 494	11 201	8 482	1 138	47 872	45 028	2 844	10 971	5 180	4 848	118 292
November	200 973	81 718	11 360	8 486	1 193	48 513	45 614	2 899	11 130	5 271	4 895	119 255
December	202 317	82 066	11 431	8 649	1 172	48 748	45 858	2 890	11 105	5 210	4 967	120 251
1996:												
January	201 610	81 782	11 114	8 390	1 163	49 158	46 259	2 899	10 884	5 028	4 907	119 828
February	204 520	83 626	11 147	8 435	1 184	50 926	48 020	2 906	10 929	5 158	4 810	120 944
March	205 955	84 530	11 175	8 507	1 141	51 051	48 139	2 912	11 273	5 302	4 995	121 425
April	207 142	84 088	11 615	8 693	1 197	49 894	46 975	2 919	11 306	5 298	5 027	123 054
May	208 566	85 279	11 716	8 896	1 179	50 469	47 531	2 938	11 312	5 301	5 034	123 287
June	207 568	84 511	12 106	9 040	1 167	49 873	46 948	2 925	11 314	5 337	4 996	123 057
July	208 074	84 952	12 056	9 069	1 152	50 410	47 494	2 916	11 185	5 352	4 867	123 122
August	208 414	84 771	11 986	9 045	1 139	50 298	47 382	2 916	11 293	5 340	4 997	123 643
September	210 571	85 977	12 032	9 062	1 124	51 475	48 546	2 929	11 447	5 394	5 117	124 594
October	212 329	86 609	12 088	9 038	1 163	51 684	48 697	2 987	11 458	5 443	5 091	125 720
November	212 216	85 945	12 096	9 096	1 167	51 024	48 085	2 939	11 290	5 380	4 972	126 271
December	213 061	85 969	12 089	9 063	1 189	51 091	48 130	2 961	11 256	5 377	4 934	127 092
1997:												
January	215 250	87 435	12 224	9 195	1 199	52 335	49 342	2 993	11 229	5 447	4 863	127 815
February	217 338	89 191	12 378	9 371	1 174	53 650	50 692	2 958	11 421	5 477	5 005	128 147
March	217 731	88 772	12 572	9 547	1 149	53 000	50 009	2 991	11 478	5 497	5 035	128 959
April	215 044	87 594	12 485	9 527	1 149	51 844	48 897	2 947	11 648	5 547	5 173	127 450
May	213 890	85 935	12 423	9 570	1 158	50 399	47 444	2 955	11 635	5 602	5 091	127 955
June	216 311	87 557	12 518	9 465	1 172	51 748	48 763	2 985	11 632	5 587	5 115	128 754
July	218 992	89 260	12 566	9 518	1 195	53 184	50 154	3 030	11 729	5 609	5 177	129 732
August	220 627	90 423	12 503	9 446	1 195	54 305	51 221	3 084	11 869	5 718	5 195	130 204
September	220 430	89 863	12 689	9 596	1 188	53 399	50 413	2 986	11 806	5 675	5 164	130 567
October	219 841	89 367	12 742	9 642	1 207	52 650	49 679	2 971	11 900	5 698	5 214	130 474
November	220 740	90 312	12 746	9 604	1 159	53 216	50 237	2 979	12 098	5 801	5 315	130 428
December	221 660	91 578	12 862	9 740	1 106	54 355	51 398	2 957	12 215	5 846	5 354	130 082
1998:												
January	223 038	92 538	13 320	9 982	1 134	54 159	51 208	2 951	12 419	5 874	5 523	130 500
February	224 158	92 576	13 300	9 970	1 170	54 297	51 258	3 039	12 479	5 930	5 552	131 582
March	224 508	92 689	13 519	10 039	1 219	54 395	51 365	3 030	12 404	5 875	5 532	131 819
April	226 659	93 990	13 611	10 195	1 220	55 568	52 529	3 039	12 368	5 894	5 459	132 669
May	228 631	94 915	13 757	10 189	1 214	56 157	53 068	3 089	12 457	5 881	5 556	133 716
June	229 520	95 671	13 552	10 213	1 213	56 929	53 827	3 102	12 568	5 885	5 660	133 849
July	228 189	93 620	13 775	10 392	1 214	54 503	51 404	3 099	12 727	5 942	5 772	134 569
August	228 410	93 774	13 678	10 359	1 241	54 557	51 449	3 108	12 761	5 886	5 850	134 636
September	229 283	94 545	13 790	10 497	1 271	55 300	52 205	3 095	12 778	5 937	5 801	134 738
October	232 379	96 724	13 991	10 565	1 224	56 895	53 773	3 122	12 839	6 001	5 780	135 655
November	234 504	97 782	14 296	10 864	1 235	57 615	54 506	3 109	12 969	6 077	5 900	136 722
December	236 786	99 500	14 583	11 085	1 266	58 778	55 614	3 164	13 151	6 196	5 970	137 286

1. Includes building materials; hardware; plants and garden supplies; and manufactured (mobile) homes.

Retail Sales—*Continued*

(All retail stores—Millions of dollars, seasonally adjusted)

	Nondurable goods stores —Continued												
	General merchandise group stores			Food stores		Gasoline service stations	Apparel and accessory stores				Eating and drinking places	Drug and proprietary stores	Liquor stores
Year and month	Total	Depart-ment stores[1]	Variety stores	Total	Grocery stores		Total	Men's and boys' clothing and furnish-ings	Women's clothing and acces-sories	Shoe stores			
1970	49 163	36 187	6 082	89 990	82 558	28 903	22 095	4 544	8 239	4 458	30 476	14 567	8 412
1971	54 365	40 472	6 111	94 002	86 419	30 620	24 178	4 903	9 222	4 524	32 321	15 143	9 294
1972	59 656	44 451	6 598	100 589	92 856	33 072	26 367	5 684	9 739	4 884	35 738	16 139	9 814
1973	65 825	49 342	7 207	111 817	103 555	36 942	29 109	6 193	10 732	5 600	40 290	17 190	10 288
1974	69 540	52 059	7 594	126 312	117 182	43 054	30 077	6 190	11 338	5 405	44 606	18 595	11 087
1975	73 759	55 702	7 893	138 665	129 087	47 603	32 398	6 619	12 438	5 751	51 067	19 995	11 896
1976	79 500	61 500	7 101	148 218	137 992	52 037	34 706	6 815	13 426	8 249	57 331	21 710	12 442
1977	87 824	68 856	6 987	158 444	148 116	56 638	37 165	7 042	12 537	7 058	63 370	23 381	13 031
1978	97 215	76 137	7 176	175 425	164 234	59 889	42 649	7 537	15 995	8 305	71 828	25 607	13 630
1979	103 817	81 161	7 770	197 985	185 318	73 521	46 070	7 763	17 030	9 693	82 110	28 455	15 194
1980	108 955	85 464	7 791	220 224	205 630	94 093	49 296	7 664	17 592	10 530	90 058	30 951	16 882
1981	120 534	95 638	8 202	236 188	220 580	103 072	53 998	7 910	19 060	11 821	98 118	33 999	17 702
1982	124 624	99 841	8 211	246 122	230 696	97 440	55 570	7 803	20 017	11 419	104 593	36 440	18 146
1983	135 959	108 637	8 367	256 018	240 402	102 927	60 192	7 958	21 847	11 949	113 281	40 591	19 121
1984	150 283	120 487	8 700	271 909	258 465	107 565	64 341	8 206	23 764	12 306	121 321	44 011	18 273
1985	158 636	126 412	8 459	285 062	269 546	113 341	70 195	8 458	26 149	13 054	127 949	46 994	19 532
1986	169 397	134 486	7 447	297 019	280 833	102 093	75 626	8 646	28 600	13 947	139 415	50 546	19 929
1987	181 970	144 017	7 134	309 461	290 979	104 769	79 322	9 017	29 208	14 594	153 461	54 142	19 826
1988	192 521	151 523	7 458	325 493	307 173	110 341	85 307	9 826	30 567	15 444	167 993	57 842	19 638
1989	206 306	160 524	7 936	347 045	328 072	122 882	92 341	10 507	32 231	17 290	177 829	63 343	20 099
1990	215 514	165 808	8 306	368 333	348 243	138 504	95 819	10 450	32 812	18 043	190 149	70 558	21 722
1991	226 730	172 922	8 341	374 523	354 331	137 295	97 441	10 435	32 865	17 504	194 424	75 540	22 454
1992	246 420	186 423	9 516	377 099	358 148	136 950	104 212	10 197	35 750	18 122	200 164	77 788	21 698
1993	264 147	199 845	9 729	382 930	363 625	141 603	107 588	9 986	36 426	18 509	212 690	79 784	21 561
1994	282 332	217 499	9 464	394 671	374 730	148 673	110 735	10 064	35 117	19 349	221 882	82 156	22 136
1995	297 903	231 303	9 750	403 205	382 378	156 939	111 970	9 353	33 831	19 755	229 526	86 093	22 053
1996	313 342	244 783	10 481	415 390	393 568	168 320	116 101	9 592	34 055	20 609	238 474	92 169	23 216
1997	330 216	259 985	11 120	425 170	402 540	171 527	120 575	10 123	34 222	20 802	253 551	99 301	24 147
1998	351 436	276 697	11 480	438 212	414 667	162 095	126 939	10 922	34 330	21 227	266 544	106 713	25 114
1995:													
January	24 841	19 108	892	33 719	32 009	12 973	9 404	818	2 917	1 615	18 801	7 089	1 826
February	23 949	18 604	746	33 457	31 751	12 995	9 055	799	2 822	1 493	18 682	7 103	1 803
March	24 273	18 760	768	33 305	31 614	13 028	9 268	775	2 884	1 653	18 903	7 064	1 824
April	24 541	18 909	783	33 493	31 782	13 070	9 189	770	2 815	1 657	19 089	7 088	1 813
May	24 602	19 000	811	33 596	31 911	13 249	9 315	773	2 857	1 664	19 150	7 160	1 813
June	25 019	19 392	816	33 636	31 942	13 330	9 321	764	2 823	1 685	19 113	7 177	1 826
July	25 115	19 565	792	33 570	31 837	13 269	9 237	755	2 820	1 652	19 241	7 067	1 807
August	24 898	19 340	792	33 608	31 867	13 194	9 227	759	2 800	1 641	19 315	7 185	1 836
September	25 246	19 676	820	33 623	31 861	13 067	9 576	777	2 852	1 663	19 342	7 264	1 875
October	24 984	19 450	823	33 733	31 956	12 942	9 292	777	2 810	1 658	19 294	7 286	1 872
November	25 239	19 711	831	33 750	31 954	12 947	9 500	783	2 763	1 702	19 368	7 370	1 878
December	25 284	19 593	857	34 113	32 302	13 114	9 542	796	2 795	1 662	19 373	7 410	1 886
1996:													
January	25 096	19 604	833	34 212	32 412	13 350	9 347	791	2 709	1 685	19 169	7 269	1 945
February	25 479	19 861	828	34 048	32 268	13 381	9 684	816	2 843	1 679	19 439	7 394	1 912
March	25 309	19 650	852	34 252	32 453	13 820	9 520	798	2 746	1 687	19 549	7 493	1 939
April	25 941	20 224	885	34 413	32 602	14 165	9 781	801	2 841	1 797	19 651	7 499	1 929
May	26 040	20 307	883	34 332	32 505	14 403	9 702	806	2 867	1 741	19 722	7 619	1 924
June	25 903	20 210	872	34 490	32 651	14 180	9 710	790	2 919	1 714	19 655	7 568	1 944
July	25 962	20 242	889	34 650	32 843	13 899	9 587	795	2 788	1 729	19 802	7 680	1 960
August	26 331	20 541	888	34 565	32 753	13 884	9 628	793	2 810	1 724	19 848	7 760	1 968
September	26 476	20 734	859	34 791	32 989	13 958	9 812	816	2 887	1 698	19 963	7 760	1 918
October	26 635	20 831	892	34 953	33 135	14 135	9 846	803	2 904	1 722	20 170	7 945	1 910
November	26 553	20 777	866	35 008	33 166	14 264	9 658	800	2 856	1 700	20 669	7 908	1 918
December	27 071	21 262	909	35 028	33 183	14 438	9 733	799	2 854	1 710	20 420	8 021	1 927
1997:													
January	27 102	21 257	917	35 232	33 365	14 596	9 818	825	2 888	1 704	20 771	8 049	1 949
February	27 101	21 242	936	35 271	33 392	14 626	9 863	827	2 898	1 752	20 895	8 152	1 951
March	27 330	21 523	938	35 685	33 782	14 701	9 906	821	2 881	1 752	20 946	8 179	1 976
April	26 581	20 810	887	35 167	33 317	14 281	9 774	811	2 800	1 706	20 960	8 181	1 976
May	27 190	21 373	889	35 216	33 356	14 029	9 899	827	2 800	1 711	20 971	8 171	1 993
June	27 392	21 556	911	35 189	33 314	14 110	10 023	836	2 846	1 749	21 100	8 293	2 039
July	27 726	21 786	945	35 380	33 506	14 155	10 175	872	2 850	1 744	21 279	8 308	2 018
August	27 896	21 934	1 004	35 473	33 554	14 324	10 266	878	2 870	1 741	21 407	8 291	2 017
September	27 781	21 880	984	35 718	33 808	14 425	10 158	853	2 850	1 717	21 474	8 419	2 013
October	28 051	22 134	936	35 678	33 773	14 357	10 111	863	2 820	1 729	21 377	8 387	2 068
November	28 067	22 189	937	35 753	33 851	14 212	10 233	866	2 852	1 742	21 236	8 463	2 053
December	28 054	22 201	896	35 579	33 670	13 964	10 263	853	2 894	1 776	21 435	8 459	2 079
1998:													
January	28 300	22 348	918	35 613	33 701	13 702	10 359	867	2 913	1 756	21 574	8 579	2 036
February	28 654	22 642	918	35 819	33 867	13 603	10 503	875	2 849	1 815	21 765	8 608	2 082
March	28 619	22 530	921	35 964	33 995	13 441	10 565	906	2 852	1 792	21 862	8 630	2 045
April	28 996	22 865	919	36 264	34 260	13 458	10 664	932	2 899	1 761	21 824	8 743	2 048
May	29 221	23 084	929	36 363	34 397	13 578	10 613	909	2 882	1 770	22 044	8 813	2 062
June	29 219	22 997	943	36 523	34 553	13 567	10 565	935	2 813	1 755	22 158	8 811	2 022
July	29 185	22 986	937	36 657	34 670	13 753	10 717	930	2 909	1 788	22 078	8 912	2 058
August	29 283	23 061	936	36 867	34 907	13 454	10 633	940	2 834	1 787	22 111	9 006	2 080
September	29 535	23 193	952	36 755	34 772	13 431	10 333	911	2 770	1 683	22 404	9 044	2 115
October	29 739	23 354	993	36 928	34 962	13 412	10 575	917	2 799	1 783	22 726	9 088	2 127
November	30 169	23 639	1 037	37 111	35 169	13 365	10 699	918	2 881	1 768	22 959	9 231	2 171
December	30 129	23 730	1 009	37 390	35 436	13 449	10 703	895	2 931	1 792	23 141	9 223	2 231

1. Excluding leased departments.

Retail Inventories [1]

(All retail stores—Book value, end of period, millions of dollars, not seasonally adjusted)

Year and month	Total	Durable goods stores				Nondurable goods stores				
		Total	Building materials group [2]	Automotive dealers	Furniture and home furnishings and equipment	Total	General merchandise group stores		Food stores	Apparel and accessory stores
							Total	Department stores [3]		
1970	42 808	17 482	2 877	8 410	3 330	25 326	8 834	6 283	5 166	4 245
1971	48 895	21 273	3 547	11 136	3 546	27 622	10 013	6 997	5 685	4 618
1972	53 791	23 820	4 097	11 665	4 379	29 971	10 928	7 639	6 071	4 976
1973	61 835	28 065	4 641	14 270	4 776	33 770	12 173	8 349	7 050	5 530
1974	69 644	32 590	4 910	16 770	5 428	37 054	12 595	8 890	8 164	5 798
1975	70 273	33 130	5 239	16 478	5 711	37 143	12 426	9 070	8 190	5 758
1976	77 617	37 607	6 215	18 623	6 115	40 010	13 643	10 143	8 840	6 229
1977	87 411	42 742	7 179	22 142	6 511	44 669	15 821	12 067	9 474	7 340
1978	100 242	49 717	8 036	25 490	7 750	50 525	18 110	13 598	10 305	8 566
1979	108 408	53 630	8 604	27 256	8 533	54 778	19 139	14 353	11 456	9 143
1980	117 857	55 084	9 307	25 667	9 097	62 773	20 984	15 301	13 589	10 383
1981	129 073	60 261	9 793	28 137	9 687	68 812	23 509	17 544	14 866	11 598
1982	130 797	60 492	9 805	28 437	9 607	70 305	24 068	17 897	15 473	11 698
1983	143 513	67 921	11 224	33 030	11 105	75 592	25 996	19 331	16 488	12 658
1984	162 773	78 125	12 310	39 280	12 334	84 648	31 236	23 510	17 826	13 675
1985	176 941	87 630	13 054	46 399	13 693	89 311	31 517	23 330	19 480	14 575
1986	181 651	89 586	13 373	46 190	14 297	92 065	32 528	24 167	19 772	14 830
1987	203 210	105 654	14 184	57 800	15 005	97 556	34 874	26 032	20 019	15 880
1988	214 824	112 970	15 462	60 915	16 295	101 854	35 768	27 468	21 812	16 524
1989	233 143	122 220	16 437	66 436	17 297	110 923	39 487	30 916	23 821	17 713
1990	236 152	122 141	16 368	65 517	17 477	114 011	38 969	30 716	25 402	17 957
1991	239 478	119 977	16 099	63 134	17 737	119 501	42 168	33 257	26 045	18 500
1992	248 198	124 046	16 596	66 501	18 077	124 152	44 938	35 104	26 275	20 336
1993	265 058	135 843	18 215	72 177	20 374	129 215	48 449	38 009	26 654	20 522
1994	289 601	153 821	20 538	82 695	23 032	135 780	51 211	40 441	27 453	21 353
1995	305 476	165 784	21 923	90 331	24 304	139 692	54 012	43 015	28 242	20 826
1996	315 582	171 468	22 963	93 885	24 503	144 114	54 890	44 308	29 255	20 966
1997	325 120	177 130	24 177	97 622	23 948	147 990	54 998	45 296	29 577	22 411
1998	335 457	181 797	26 058	99 491	25 021	153 660	55 921	45 495	30 231	23 320
1995:										
January	289 462	154 639	20 829	83 846	22 246	134 823	51 400	40 564	26 998	20 932
February	294 615	157 749	21 180	86 561	21 963	136 866	53 285	42 226	26 592	22 126
March	301 955	162 215	22 181	89 607	22 385	139 740	54 664	42 992	26 750	23 222
April	305 275	165 043	22 691	90 574	22 605	140 232	54 950	43 292	26 629	23 476
May	304 568	164 714	22 711	89 997	22 575	139 854	54 894	43 385	26 512	23 062
June	301 327	162 235	22 172	87 915	22 827	139 092	54 438	42 969	26 612	22 432
July	296 118	155 007	21 928	80 700	22 560	141 111	55 266	43 738	26 668	23 367
August	300 413	155 446	22 007	78 570	23 745	144 967	57 026	45 210	26 658	24 321
September	309 494	158 677	22 201	79 266	25 085	150 817	60 913	48 397	27 124	24 987
October	329 570	168 191	22 596	84 505	26 895	161 379	66 938	53 254	28 125	26 594
November	337 595	174 625	22 315	89 085	28 147	162 970	68 570	54 659	28 631	26 437
December	305 476	165 784	21 923	90 331	24 304	139 692	54 012	43 015	28 242	20 826
1996:										
January	302 867	164 531	21 990	90 367	23 369	138 336	53 659	42 720	27 654	20 389
February	307 261	167 081	22 633	91 866	23 524	140 180	54 806	44 008	27 284	21 477
March	309 110	166 959	23 699	89 930	23 757	142 151	56 285	45 219	27 452	22 357
April	310 939	168 157	23 976	89 288	24 389	142 782	56 738	45 621	27 534	21 909
May	310 139	168 271	24 015	89 531	24 381	141 868	56 365	45 285	27 374	21 411
June	306 685	166 340	23 849	88 597	23 941	140 345	55 552	44 571	27 232	21 222
July	306 274	161 879	23 463	83 531	24 172	144 395	57 032	45 716	27 415	22 498
August	309 084	161 890	22 892	82 783	24 830	147 194	58 978	47 476	27 297	23 275
September	319 488	165 987	22 847	84 767	26 031	153 501	62 969	50 582	27 833	23 960
October	340 397	176 194	23 160	89 115	28 356	164 203	68 685	55 256	29 157	25 756
November	344 498	178 325	23 068	91 086	28 334	166 173	70 003	56 631	29 851	26 191
December	315 582	171 468	22 963	93 885	24 503	144 114	54 890	44 308	29 255	20 966
1997:										
January	311 782	169 221	22 881	92 861	24 085	142 561	53 847	43 588	28 678	20 614
February	317 939	173 361	23 518	95 639	23 790	144 578	55 452	45 119	28 145	21 834
March	320 963	174 836	24 720	96 044	23 770	146 127	56 422	46 136	28 454	22 332
April	324 712	177 089	25 276	96 600	23 739	147 623	57 571	47 068	28 127	22 974
May	321 774	175 295	25 383	94 218	23 911	146 479	57 044	46 612	28 049	22 686
June	318 703	173 433	24 976	93 125	23 626	145 270	56 079	45 775	28 110	22 513
July	316 370	167 912	24 493	87 061	24 006	148 458	56 919	46 368	28 006	23 777
August	316 085	165 687	24 129	85 286	23 848	150 398	57 915	47 284	28 215	24 385
September	329 051	170 691	24 574	87 172	24 870	158 360	62 430	50 961	28 789	25 754
October	348 171	180 275	24 754	91 914	27 231	167 896	67 682	55 615	29 760	27 362
November	353 308	183 721	24 332	94 698	27 790	169 587	69 035	56 956	30 483	27 141
December	325 120	177 130	24 177	97 622	23 948	147 990	54 998	45 296	29 577	22 411
1998:										
January	322 248	174 051	24 512	96 013	23 196	148 197	54 913	45 167	29 276	22 246
February	327 124	177 178	25 787	97 692	23 172	149 946	56 347	46 463	28 665	23 281
March	334 614	180 866	26 703	99 006	23 785	153 748	57 852	47 756	29 125	24 566
April	337 793	183 034	27 051	99 757	24 319	154 759	58 433	48 156	29 152	24 644
May	330 027	177 470	26 488	95 430	23 859	152 557	57 044	46 936	28 882	24 196
June	325 913	173 201	26 298	91 239	23 767	152 712	56 705	46 514	29 123	24 367
July	322 405	166 781	25 897	84 289	24 294	155 624	57 918	47 715	29 138	25 634
August	324 047	165 726	26 046	82 566	24 472	158 321	59 402	48 892	28 892	26 364
September	337 131	171 303	25 990	86 470	25 403	165 828	64 172	52 568	29 241	27 730
October	356 274	181 590	26 246	91 414	27 779	174 684	70 034	57 310	30 385	28 906
November	364 018	187 832	26 127	96 020	28 843	176 186	71 165	58 336	31 190	28 529
December	335 457	181 797	26 058	99 491	25 021	153 660	55 921	45 495	30 231	23 320

1. Data prior to 1980 are not comparable to subsequent periods due to change inventory valuation methods; see Notes.
2. Includes building materials; hardware; plants and garden supplies; and manufactured (moblie) homes.
3. Excluding leased departments.

Retail Inventories [1]—*Continued*

(All retail stores—Book value, end of period, millions of dollars, seasonally adjusted)

Year and month	Total	Durable goods stores				Nondurable goods stores				
		Total	Building materials [2]	Automotive dealers	Furniture and home furnishings and equipment	Total	General merchandise group stores		Food stores	Apparel and accessory stores
							Total	Department stores [3]		
1970	43 867	17 908	2 981	8 679	3 374	25 959	9 438	6 713	5 095	4 422
1971	50 063	21 687	3 683	11 363	3 585	28 376	10 728	7 499	5 601	4 820
1972	55 079	24 238	4 268	11 855	4 414	30 841	11 743	8 214	5 981	5 200
1973	63 237	28 418	4 844	14 356	4 800	34 819	13 137	9 016	6 946	5 791
1974	71 067	32 861	5 131	16 737	5 439	38 206	13 647	9 632	8 043	6 071
1975	71 744	33 356	5 474	16 347	5 717	38 388	13 521	9 848	8 069	6 029
1976	79 273	37 841	6 481	18 420	6 115	41 432	14 886	11 037	8 709	6 516
1977	89 444	43 071	7 502	21 879	6 610	46 373	17 307	13 145	9 362	7 646
1978	102 694	50 136	8 397	25 188	7 876	52 558	19 853	14 829	10 193	8 914
1979	111 098	54 108	8 981	26 933	8 681	56 990	21 033	15 686	11 343	9 514
1980	121 078	55 799	9 685	25 553	9 207	65 279	23 171	16 814	13 390	10 929
1981	132 719	61 050	10 180	28 026	9 795	71 669	25 951	19 279	14 649	12 234
1982	134 628	61 316	10 203	28 352	9 714	73 312	26 548	19 645	15 248	12 392
1983	147 833	68 856	11 716	32 919	11 217	78 977	28 651	21 196	16 282	13 466
1984	167 812	79 074	12 890	39 004	12 433	88 738	34 392	25 750	17 624	14 641
1985	181 881	88 315	13 683	45 798	13 762	93 566	34 683	25 525	19 283	15 689
1986	186 510	89 983	14 033	45 246	14 340	96 527	35 743	26 412	19 612	16 067
1987	207 836	105 481	14 868	56 161	15 050	102 355	38 285	28 450	19 898	17 280
1988	219 047	112 453	16 157	58 907	16 311	106 594	39 179	29 987	21 601	18 079
1989	237 234	121 347	17 122	64 072	17 280	115 887	43 107	33 678	23 543	19 422
1990	239 815	121 194	17 015	63 107	17 442	118 621	42 377	33 387	25 038	19 690
1991	243 389	119 189	16 718	60 881	17 649	124 200	45 764	36 110	25 580	20 263
1992	252 185	123 152	17 234	64 134	17 934	129 033	48 630	38 033	25 738	22 249
1993	269 303	135 088	18 895	69 730	20 232	134 215	52 305	41 091	26 043	22 453
1994	294 052	153 019	21 305	79 897	22 963	141 033	55 216	43 673	26 779	23 362
1995	310 276	165 108	22 742	87 354.	24 377	145 168	58 189	46 402	27 551	22 811
1996	320 601	170 849	23 821	90 733	24 726	149 752	59 127	47 797	28 539	22 989
1997	330 308	176 483	25 080	94 244	24 263	153 825	59 239	48 863	28 853	24 600
1998	340 760	181 070	27 031	95 965	25 376	159 690	60 217	49 078	29 494	25 598
1995:										
January	297 969	156 120	21 495	82 180	22 958	141 849	55 834	44 043	26 845	23 414
February	299 510	157 041	21 244	83 206	23 070	142 469	56 648	44 731	26 892	23 439
March	302 054	159 361	21 452	85 373	23 173	142 693	56 371	44 276	26 866	23 672
April	304 161	161 286	21 756	86 336	23 304	142 875	56 195	44 176	26 881	23 858
May	306 316	162 454	21 754	87 262	23 345	143 862	56 724	44 773	26 921	23 923
June	306 980	162 480	21 737	86 910	23 729	144 500	57 310	45 326	26 983	23 588
July	305 494	161 414	21 928	85 951	23 476	144 080	57 196	45 324	27 143	23 320
August	308 770	163 319	22 319	85 943	24 180	145 451	57 544	45 621	27 327	23 521
September	308 619	163 401	22 654	85 420	24 378	145 218	57 420	45 701	27 383	23 374
October	311 056	164 906	22 847	87 067	24 186	146 150	57 943	46 187	27 343	23 472
November	313 453	167 026	22 840	88 349	24 712	146 427	58 348	46 479	27 322	23 354
December	310 276	165 108	22 742	87 354	24 377	145 168	58 189	46 402	27 551	22 811
1996:										
January	311 493	166 040	22 717	88 397	24 217	145 453	58 325	46 435	27 476	22 781
February	311 995	166 154	22 747	88 071	24 684	145 841	58 217	46 619	27 622	22 775
March	309 364	164 151	22 920	85 562	24 670	145 213	58 157	46 666	27 560	22 767
April	309 629	164 078	22 944	84 827	25 117	145 551	58 096	46 600	27 815	22 311
May	312 253	166 266	23 047	86 985	25 239	145 987	58 300	46 782	27 847	22 234
June	312 786	166 941	23 381	87 894	24 913	145 845	58 490	47 016	27 665	22 292
July	316 480	168 952	23 486	89 373	25 101	147 528	59 077	47 423	27 905	22 476
August	318 148	170 368	23 241	90 701	25 259	147 780	59 551	47 956	27 964	22 553
September	318 718	170 945	23 266	91 254	25 297	147 773	59 341	47 764	28 103	22 372
October	321 153	172 408	23 394	91 573	25 431	148 745	59 439	47 882	28 328	22 693
November	319 714	170 384	23 611	90 248	24 811	149 330	59 462	48 033	28 437	23 137
December	320 601	170 849	23 821	90 733	24 726	149 752	59 127	47 797	28 539	22 989
1997:										
January	320 527	170 836	23 662	90 681	25 089	149 691	58 557	47 430	28 495	23 007
February	322 714	172 415	23 660	91 548	24 989	150 299	58 871	47 796	28 499	23 154
March	320 987	171 684	23 907	91 312	24 735	149 303	58 387	47 661	28 580	22 718
April	322 666	172 184	24 141	91 521	24 373	150 482	58 988	48 127	28 437	23 419
May	324 143	173 365	24 407	91 799	24 727	150 778	59 070	48 203	28 532	23 582
June	325 290	174 349	24 462	92 725	24 610	150 941	59 042	48 286	28 585	23 623
July	326 937	175 410	24 518	93 421	24 825	151 527	58 905	48 050	28 511	23 730
August	325 596	174 640	24 521	93 628	24 260	150 956	58 479	47 762	28 880	23 652
September	328 245	175 725	24 974	93 730	24 193	152 520	58 811	48 122	29 071	24 047
October	328 645	176 383	25 004	94 288	24 379	152 262	58 537	48 152	28 917	24 107
November	328 371	175 665	24 905	93 827	24 335	152 706	58 601	48 268	29 006	23 997
December	330 308	176 483	25 080	94 244	24 263	153 825	59 239	48 863	28 853	24 600
1998:										
January	331 323	175 817	25 401	93 730	24 213	155 506	59 730	49 148	29 071	24 773
February	331 938	176 200	25 943	93 510	24 340	155 738	59 790	49 219	29 034	24 636
March	334 282	177 346	25 800	93 946	24 750	156 936	59 845	49 284	29 240	24 991
April	335 270	177 584	25 812	94 322	24 892	157 686	59 867	49 233	29 496	25 147
May	332 728	175 598	25 518	93 158	24 648	157 130	59 139	48 588	29 379	25 178
June	333 042	174 303	25 757	91 015	24 783	158 739	59 766	49 117	29 616	25 569
July	332 881	174 098	25 897	90 536	25 071	158 783	59 932	49 446	29 670	25 583
August	333 432	174 523	26 496	90 677	24 870	158 909	59 970	49 386	29 572	25 596
September	335 965	176 303	26 386	92 966	24 735	159 662	60 433	49 639	29 524	25 868
October	335 911	177 448	26 511	93 609	24 847	158 463	60 569	49 619	29 521	25 490
November	338 348	179 586	26 769	95 043	25 257	158 762	60 430	49 437	29 648	25 225
December	340 760	181 070	27 031	95 965	25 376	159 690	60 217	49 078	29 494	25 598

1. Data prior to 1980 are not comparable to subsequent periods due to change inventory valuation methods; see Notes.
2. Includes building materials; hardware; plants and garden supplies; and manufactured (moblie) homes.
3. Excluding leased departments.

Merchant Wholesalers—Sales and Inventories

(Millions of dollars)

Year and month	Not seasonally adjusted						Seasonally adjusted					
	Sales			Inventories (book value, end of period)			Sales			Inventories (book value, end of period)		
	Total	Durable goods establishments	Nondurable goods establishments	Total	Durable goods establishments	Nondurable goods establishments	Total	Durable goods establishments	Nondurable goods establishments	Total	Durable goods establishments	Nondurable goods establishments
1970	289 999	133 778	156 221	.....	.....	.....	289 999	133 778	156 221	.....	.....	.....
1971	317 899	147 761	170 138	.....	.....	.....	317 899	147 761	170 138	.....	.....	.....
1972	358 388	168 879	189 509	.....	.....	.....	358 388	168 879	189 509	.....	.....	.....
1973	457 378	208 554	248 824	.....	.....	.....	457 378	208 554	248 824	.....	.....	.....
1974	575 786	255 863	319 923	.....	.....	.....	575 786	255 863	319 923	.....	.....	.....
1975	559 606	235 723	323 883	.....	.....	.....	559 606	235 723	323 883	.....	.....	.....
1976	608 381	263 605	344 776	.....	.....	.....	608 381	263 605	344 776	.....	.....	.....
1977	673 633	304 721	368 912	.....	.....	.....	673 633	304 721	368 912	.....	.....	.....
1978	796 961	372 176	424 785	.....	.....	.....	796 961	372 176	424 785	.....	.....	.....
1979	948 614	436 254	512 360	.....	.....	.....	948 614	436 254	512 360	.....	.....	.....
1980	1 117 187	486 509	630 678	124 015	78 849	45 166	1 117 187	486 509	630 678	122 631	79 372	43 259
1981	1 214 156	525 607	688 549	130 709	85 371	45 338	1 214 156	525 607	688 549	129 654	85 856	43 798
1982	1 142 535	480 318	662 217	128 514	84 806	43 708	1 142 535	480 318	662 217	127 428	85 222	42 206
1983	1 190 705	523 080	667 625	131 306	84 709	46 597	1 190 705	523 080	667 625	130 075	85 180	44 895
1984	1 346 392	622 361	724 031	143 458	94 895	48 563	1 346 392	622 361	724 031	142 452	95 474	46 978
1985	1 361 507	651 864	709 643	148 403	96 659	51 744	1 361 507	651 864	709 643	147 409	97 371	50 038
1986	1 379 514	681 691	697 823	154 081	101 369	52 712	1 379 514	681 691	697 823	153 574	102 349	51 225
1987	1 475 613	730 592	745 021	164 310	106 820	57 490	1 475 613	730 592	745 021	163 903	108 112	55 791
1988	1 614 249	801 751	812 498	179 828	115 613	64 215	1 614 249	801 751	812 498	178 801	117 045	61 756
1989	1 725 123	851 550	873 573	187 897	120 701	67 196	1 725 123	851 550	873 573	187 009	122 237	64 772
1990	1 794 072	880 767	913 305	196 881	124 839	72 042	1 794 072	126 413	913 305	195 775	880 767	69 362
1991	1 779 673	860 138	919 535	201 777	125 921	75 856	1 779 673	860 138	919 535	200 376	127 342	73 034
1992	1 849 798	908 917	940 881	209 675	130 044	79 631	1 849 798	908 917	940 881	208 244	131 458	76 786
1993	1 934 675	990 282	944 393	218 419	135 473	82 946	1 934 675	990 282	944 393	216 974	137 042	79 932
1994	2 066 847	1 091 483	975 364	236 710	149 016	87 694	2 066 847	1 091 483	975 364	235 413	150 928	84 485
1995	2 254 673	1 196 306	1 058 367	254 921	161 110	93 811	2 254 673	1 196 306	1 058 367	253 565	163 474	90 091
1996	2 384 019	1 246 078	1 137 941	256 490	163 621	92 869	2 384 019	1 246 078	1 137 941	255 871	166 185	89 686
1997	2 480 049	1 312 427	1 167 622	274 517	174 967	99 550	2 480 049	1 312 427	1 167 622	273 885	177 746	96 139
1998	2 535 008	1 359 989	1 175 019	287 997	184 769	103 228	2 535 008	1 359 989	1 175 019	287 484	187 734	99 750
1995:												
January	172 627	89 977	82 650	242 657	152 085	90 572	183 833	97 858	85 975	237 694	152 238	85 456
February	168 331	88 641	79 690	243 155	154 470	88 685	185 230	98 562	86 668	239 721	154 136	85 585
March	195 118	104 747	90 371	243 524	155 494	88 030	183 820	97 934	85 886	242 390	155 829	86 561
April	177 813	93 121	84 692	247 024	158 279	88 745	185 688	97 961	87 727	245 128	157 028	88 100
May	194 362	102 422	91 940	244 591	159 333	85 258	186 906	99 694	87 212	246 090	158 159	87 931
June	195 069	104 278	90 791	244 093	159 066	85 027	188 772	99 797	88 975	247 884	159 202	88 682
July	180 311	94 509	85 802	248 543	162 069	86 474	186 860	98 180	88 680	250 361	160 083	90 278
August	199 662	106 643	93 019	245 125	160 647	84 478	190 101	100 869	89 232	250 762	160 203	90 559
September	189 587	102 899	86 688	246 230	159 948	86 282	190 050	100 752	89 298	251 878	160 913	90 965
October	201 469	108 151	93 318	255 059	161 937	93 122	190 760	100 759	90 001	253 145	162 259	90 886
November	192 401	101 617	90 784	255 999	162 076	93 923	192 886	102 406	90 480	253 286	163 172	90 114
December	187 923	99 301	88 622	254 921	161 110	93 811	195 152	103 951	91 201	253 565	163 474	90 091
1996:												
January	186 047	95 494	90 553	260 515	164 077	96 438	193 316	101 900	91 416	254 994	164 493	90 501
February	183 825	95 646	88 179	258 374	164 427	93 947	192 945	101 577	91 368	254 442	164 108	90 334
March	197 394	105 102	92 292	255 583	163 409	92 174	195 015	102 661	92 354	254 119	163 720	90 399
April	198 468	103 147	95 321	260 154	166 263	93 891	195 754	102 215	93 539	258 113	164 970	93 143
May	204 299	105 853	98 446	256 007	165 751	90 256	197 145	103 610	93 535	258 029	164 437	93 592
June	193 740	102 400	91 340	252 736	164 287	88 449	197 040	103 062	93 978	257 041	164 170	92 871
July	201 849	104 214	97 635	255 533	167 173	88 360	199 510	102 810	96 700	257 407	165 050	92 357
August	204 862	106 618	98 244	251 499	166 010	85 489	200 368	103 508	96 860	256 716	165 433	91 283
September	199 109	106 251	92 858	250 008	164 974	85 034	199 641	104 135	95 506	255 036	165 939	89 097
October	218 284	115 068	103 216	257 664	165 228	92 436	202 293	105 277	97 016	255 818	165 657	90 161
November	196 992	103 074	93 918	258 273	165 098	93 175	202 744	106 278	96 466	256 152	166 442	89 710
December	199 150	103 211	95 939	256 490	163 621	92 869	200 426	104 701	95 725	255 871	166 185	89 686
1997:												
January	195 131	98 665	96 466	262 962	166 761	96 201	204 254	106 325	97 929	258 316	167 292	91 024
February	189 546	98 207	91 339	261 559	167 657	93 902	207 557	108 738	98 819	258 249	167 400	90 849
March	209 043	109 672	99 371	261 074	168 757	92 317	204 996	106 755	98 241	259 631	168 848	90 783
April	207 746	109 310	98 436	262 057	171 108	90 949	205 892	108 890	97 002	260 020	169 656	90 364
May	209 447	109 029	100 418	259 661	172 303	87 358	205 864	108 659	97 205	261 155	170 836	90 319
June	208 772	112 191	96 581	262 348	175 196	87 152	206 602	109 755	96 847	265 759	174 939	90 820
July	209 357	112 281	97 076	263 339	175 369	87 970	206 627	110 726	95 901	264 610	173 180	91 430
August	203 910	108 833	95 077	261 136	173 889	87 247	205 694	108 986	96 708	265 874	173 326	92 548
September	214 933	117 451	97 482	263 799	174 636	89 163	208 966	111 483	97 483	269 025	175 648	93 377
October	224 322	120 852	103 470	271 617	174 576	97 041	208 956	111 410	97 546	269 667	175 116	94 551
November	195 878	104 074	91 804	274 186	174 409	99 777	207 263	110 560	96 703	271 728	175 953	95 775
December	211 964	111 862	100 102	274 517	174 967	99 550	208 111	110 907	97 204	273 885	177 746	96 139
1998:												
January	195 743	102 395	93 348	278 169	178 008	100 161	209 635	112 602	97 033	273 523	178 685	94 838
February	191 126	101 585	89 541	279 657	181 013	98 644	209 112	112 224	96 888	276 503	180 803	95 700
March	220 251	120 001	100 250	279 740	182 419	97 321	210 555	113 400	97 155	278 013	182 230	95 783
April	213 811	114 593	99 218	279 198	183 936	95 262	211 441	114 414	97 027	277 163	182 385	94 778
May	208 002	110 314	97 688	277 406	184 391	93 015	210 436	112 993	97 443	278 837	182 755	96 082
June	220 052	120 596	99 456	275 757	182 801	92 956	211 135	114 077	97 058	279 060	182 433	96 627
July	214 065*	115 715	98 350	277 765	184 468	93 297	211 930	114 485	97 445	278 768	182 189	96 579
August	208 102	113 002	95 100	277 278	184 761	92 517	209 144	113 303	95 841	281 915	184 028	97 887
September	216 827	118 172	98 655	279 244	184 305	94 939	211 964	112 979	98 985	284 832	185 366	99 466
October	222 269	119 632	102 637	286 558	185 559	100 999	211 366	112 441	98 925	284 496	186 129	98 367
November	205 584	108 648	96 936	288 222	184 640	103 582	212 367	112 597	99 770	286 145	186 525	99 620
December	219 176	115 336	103 840	287 997	184 769	103 228	215 550	114 522	101 028	287 484	187 734	99 750

Finance, Insurance, Real Estate, and Private Services

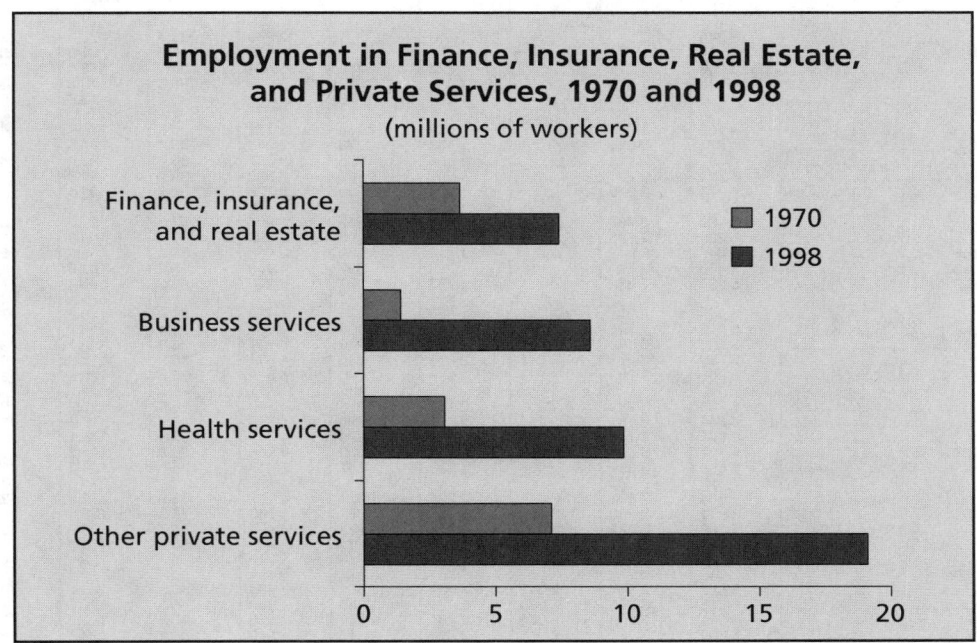

Employment in Finance, Insurance, Real Estate, and Private Services, 1970 and 1998
(millions of workers)

- Finance, insurance, and real estate, business services, health services, and other private services all grew strongly from 1970 to 1998. The strongest employment growth was in business services, a large and heterogeneous category that ranges from janitors and temporary help ("help supply") to computer and data processing services.

- Since the last business cycle employment peak in 1989, total finance, insurance and real estate payroll employment rose, but employment in the subindustry of depository institutions fell by 10.2 percent.

- From 1989 to 1998 the fastest growing service industry continued to be business services. In total, employment in the industry grew 73.7 percent in the period, buoyed by growth in help supply of 136 percent and computer and data processing services of 117 percent.

- Hourly earnings for those employed in help supply averaged $10.18 per hour in 1998, 20 percent below the average for all private nonfarm industries. Hourly earnings for nonsupervisory workers in computer services, on the other hand, averaged $21.31 in 1998.

Finance, Insurance, and Real Estate—Employment, Hours, and Earnings

Year and month	Payroll employment (thousands, seasonally adjusted)					Nonsupervisory workers						
	Total	Finance		Insurance	Real estate	Employment (thousands, seasonally adjusted)	Weekly hours worked		Average earnings (dollars, not seasonally adjusted)			
		Total	Depository institutions				Average hours, not seasonally adjusted	Aggregate hours index (1982=100, seasonally adjusted)	Hourly		Weekly	
									Total	Depository institutions	Total	Depository institutions
1970	3 645	.....	.....	.....	.....	2 879	36.7	73.0	3.07	.....	112.67	.....
1971	3 772	.....	.....	.....	.....	2 936	36.6	74.3	3.22	.....	117.85	.....
1972	3 908	1 778	.....	1 373	756	3 024	36.6	76.5	3.36	.....	122.98	.....
1973	4 046	1 866	.....	1 401	778	3 121	36.6	78.9	3.53	.....	129.20	.....
1974	4 148	1 936	.....	1 434	778	3 169	36.5	79.8	3.77	.....	137.61	.....
1975	4 165	1 964	.....	1 442	760	3 173	36.5	79.9	4.06	.....	148.19	.....
1976	4 271	2 026	.....	1 468	776	3 243	36.4	81.5	4.27	.....	155.43	.....
1977	4 467	2 113	.....	1 528	826	3 397	36.4	85.4	4.54	.....	165.26	.....
1978	4 724	2 233	.....	1 591	900	3 593	36.4	90.3	4.89	.....	178.00	.....
1979	4 975	2 369	.....	1 643	963	3 776	36.2	94.4	5.27	.....	190.77	.....
1980	5 160	2 483	.....	1 688	989	3 907	36.2	97.8	5.79	.....	209.60	.....
1981	5 298	2 593	.....	1 713	992	3 999	36.3	105.5	6.31	.....	229.05	.....
1982	5 340	2 647	.....	1 723	970	3 996	36.2	100.0	6.78	.....	245.44	.....
1983	5 466	2 741	.....	1 728	997	4 066	36.2	101.6	7.29	.....	263.90	.....
1984	5 684	2 852	.....	1 765	1 067	4 226	36.5	106.4	7.63	.....	278.50	.....
1985	5 948	2 974	.....	1 840	1 135	4 410	36.4	110.9	7.94	.....	289.02	.....
1986	6 273	3 145	.....	1 944	1 184	4 637	36.4	116.7	8.36	.....	304.30	.....
1987	6 533	3 264	.....	2 027	1 242	4 797	36.3	120.1	8.73	.....	316.90	.....
1988	6 630	3 274	2 255	2 075	1 280	4 811	35.9	119.2	9.06	7.77	325.25	277.39
1989	6 668	3 283	2 273	2 090	1 296	4 829	35.8	119.5	9.53	8.13	341.17	289.43
1990	6 709	3 268	2 251	2 126	1 315	4 860	35.8	120.2	9.97	8.43	356.93	300.11
1991	6 646	3 187	2 164	2 161	1 299	4 795	35.7	118.3	10.39	8.70	370.92	307.98
1992	6 602	3 160	2 096	2 152	1 290	4 772	35.8	118.1	10.82	8.90	387.36	315.06
1993	6 757	3 238	2 089	2 197	1 322	4 908	35.8	121.2	11.35	9.10	406.33	320.32
1994	6 896	3 299	2 066	2 236	1 361	5 018	35.8	124.0	11.83	9.37	423.51	329.82
1995	6 806	3 231	2 025	2 225	1 351	4 961	35.9	122.9	12.32	9.62	442.29	341.51
1996	6 911	3 303	2 019	2 226	1 382	5 043	35.9	125.0	12.80	9.92	459.52	349.18
1997	7 109	3 424	2 027	2 264	1 421	5 193	36.1	129.6	13.34	10.29	481.57	363.24
1998	7 407	3 593	2 042	2 344	1 471	5 442	36.4	136.6	14.06	10.82	511.78	384.11
1995:												
January	6 822	3 244	2 040	2 227	1 351	4 964	36.3	123.1	12.17	9.58	441.77	347.75
February	6 815	3 236	2 035	2 230	1 349	4 957	35.8	122.6	12.20	9.59	436.76	338.53
March	6 811	3 233	2 034	2 234	1 344	4 956	35.5	122.2	12.21	9.61	433.46	336.35
April	6 800	3 224	2 031	2 233	1 343	4 949	36.3	122.4	12.32	9.62	447.22	348.24
May	6 793	3 222	2 026	2 227	1 344	4 948	35.4	122.0	12.24	9.60	433.30	335.04
June	6 790	3 218	2 022	2 225	1 347	4 954	35.6	122.5	12.19	9.54	433.96	336.76
July	6 793	3 222	2 022	2 221	1 350	4 955	36.3	122.7	12.32	9.61	447.22	347.88
August	6 801	3 225	2 020	2 222	1 354	4 962	35.6	122.7	12.27	9.56	436.81	337.47
September	6 805	3 228	2 019	2 222	1 355	4 967	35.7	123.5	12.39	9.63	442.32	338.98
October	6 812	3 233	2 018	2 221	1 358	4 972	36.4	123.3	12.52	9.70	455.73	350.17
November	6 818	3 239	2 018	2 218	1 361	4 978	35.7	123.1	12.48	9.68	445.54	338.80
December	6 827	3 247	2 019	2 215	1 365	4 983	35.7	123.2	12.56	9.73	448.39	340.55
1996:												
January	6 831	3 257	2 020	2 216	1 358	4 981	35.5	122.8	12.61	9.77	447.66	340.00
February	6 851	3 267	2 021	2 215	1 369	4 995	35.7	123.5	12.69	9.84	453.03	344.40
March	6 859	3 271	2 018	2 216	1 372	5 003	35.7	124.0	12.73	9.86	454.46	344.11
April	6 870	3 280	2 017	2 217	1 373	5 014	35.6	124.0	12.75	9.84	453.90	343.42
May	6 890	3 291	2 017	2 222	1 377	5 028	35.6	124.3	12.74	9.86	453.54	343.13
June	6 905	3 300	2 018	2 225	1 380	5 040	36.5	125.3	12.76	9.89	465.74	358.02
July	6 919	3 307	2 017	2 228	1 384	5 052	35.6	124.9	12.69	9.85	451.76	345.74
August	6 935	3 319	2 017	2 228	1 388	5 063	35.8	125.5	12.72	9.89	455.38	348.13
September	6 949	3 324	2 018	2 234	1 391	5 073	36.5	126.8	12.91	10.02	471.22	361.72
October	6 962	3 335	2 020	2 233	1 394	5 085	35.7	126.1	12.88	9.99	459.82	347.65
November	6 973	3 339	2 018	2 236	1 398	5 091	35.8	126.6	12.99	10.08	465.04	352.80
December	6 989	3 349	2 018	2 238	1 402	5 101	36.7	127.2	13.04	10.13	478.57	365.69
1997:												
January	7 004	3 359	2 019	2 241	1 404	5 110	35.7	126.7	13.02	10.12	464.81	353.19
February	7 015	3 364	2 019	2 244	1 407	5 124	36.7	127.4	13.17	10.27	483.34	367.67
March	7 033	3 376	2 021	2 246	1 411	5 133	36.5	127.6	13.22	10.23	482.53	362.14
April	7 058	3 391	2 023	2 250	1 417	5 152	35.9	128.4	13.12	10.10	471.01	354.51
May	7 074	3 402	2 024	2 253	1 419	5 167	36.7	128.8	13.21	10.27	474.24	358.42
June	7 086	3 411	2 025	2 258	1 417	5 175	36.7	129.0	13.26	10.19	486.64	367.86
July	7 113	3 424	2 028	2 264	1 425	5 196	35.9	129.5	13.21	10.18	474.24	358.34
August	7 134	3 439	2 029	2 269	1 426	5 212	36.1	130.3	13.38	10.32	483.02	364.30
September	7 155	3 453	2 028	2 273	1 429	5 227	35.8	130.3	13.48	10.32	482.58	361.20
October	7 181	3 468	2 032	2 281	1 432	5 250	35.9	130.9	13.56	10.36	486.80	360.53
November	7 207	3 485	2 036	2 288	1 434	5 272	36.7	131.8	13.73	10.53	503.89	380.13
December	7 233	3 502	2 041	2 299	1 432	5 297	35.9	131.7	13.64	10.55	489.68	368.20
1998:												
January	7 258	3 513	2 037	2 304	1 441	5 321	36.1	133.4	13.71	10.56	494.93	370.66
February	7 282	3 527	2 039	2 309	1 446	5 344	37.1	134.3	13.95	10.74	517.55	388.79
March	7 317	3 547	2 041	2 317	1 453	5 374	36.8	134.7	13.98	10.76	514.46	385.21
April	7 348	3 559	2 042	2 326	1 463	5 398	36.1	135.3	13.98	10.70	504.68	375.57
May	7 374	3 574	2 043	2 336	1 464	5 416	36.1	135.8	13.99	10.73	505.04	375.55
June	7 400	3 589	2 043	2 343	1 468	5 440	36.0	136.0	13.94	10.73	501.84	378.77
July	7 430	3 606	2 043	2 349	1 475	5 462	36.1	136.9	13.94	10.73	503.23	379.84
August	7 445	3 616	2 043	2 355	1 474	5 473	36.9	137.2	14.12	10.89	521.03	395.31
September	7 467	3 623	2 040	2 362	1 482	5 484	35.9	137.5	14.10	10.87	506.19	383.71
October	7 494	3 642	2 044	2 367	1 485	5 508	36.1	138.1	14.20	10.94	512.62	385.09
November	7 520	3 651	2 044	2 375	1 494	5 528	36.9	138.6	14.43	11.08	532.47	403.31
December	7 542	3 663	2 047	2 379	1 500	5 542	36.2	138.9	14.40	11.11	521.28	391.07

Private Services—Prices and Employment

Year and month	Producer prices (not seasonally adjusted) Hotels and motels (June 1993 = 100)	Health services (Dec. 1994 = 100)	Legal services (Dec. 1996 = 100)	Total All workers	Nonsupervisory workers	Agricultural services	Hotels and other lodging places	Personal services	Business services Total	Personnel supply services Total	Help supply	Computer and data processing	Auto repair services and parking	Miscellaneous repair services	Motion pictures
1970	.....	.....	.....	11 548	10 481	.....	.....	898	1 397	.....	.....	.....	.....	189	.....
1971	.....	.....	.....	11 797	10 655	.....	.....	848	1 402	.....	.....	.....	.....	193	.....
1972	.....	.....	.....	12 276	11 059	.....	813	828	1 491	214	.....	107	399	199	.....
1973	.....	.....	.....	12 857	11 606	.....	854	823	1 610	247	.....	120	422	205	.....
1974	.....	.....	.....	13 441	12 100	.....	878	807	1 686	257	.....	135	430	217	.....
1975	.....	.....	.....	13 892	12 479	.....	898	782	1 697	242	.....	143	439	218	.....
1976	.....	.....	.....	14 551	13 043	184	929	790	1 806	293	.....	159	466	227	.....
1977	.....	.....	.....	15 302	13 683	197	956	806	1 958	357	.....	187	498	241	.....
1978	.....	.....	.....	16 252	14 476	217	988	827	2 181	438	.....	224	549	261	.....
1979	.....	.....	.....	17 112	15 193	234	1 060	821	2 410	508	.....	271	575	282	.....
1980	.....	.....	.....	17 890	15 921	246	1 076	818	2 564	543	.....	304	571	289	.....
1981	.....	.....	.....	18 615	16 562	258	1 119	828	2 700	585	.....	337	574	293	.....
1982	.....	.....	.....	19 021	16 867	267	1 133	844	2 722	541	417	365	589	287	.....
1983	.....	.....	.....	19 664	17 429	287	1 172	869	2 948	619	488	416	619	287	.....
1984	.....	.....	.....	20 746	18 284	328	1 263	918	3 353	797	643	474	682	310	.....
1985	.....	.....	.....	21 927	19 305	361	1 331	957	3 679	891	732	542	730	319	.....
1986	.....	.....	.....	22 957	20 163	389	1 378	991	3 957	990	837	588	762	322	.....
1987	.....	.....	.....	24 110	21 132	411	1 464	1 027	4 278	1 177	989	629	794	321	.....
1988	.....	.....	.....	25 504	22 323	447	1 540	1 056	4 638	1 350	1 126	673	834	350	341
1989	.....	.....	.....	26 907	23 532	465	1 596	1 086	4 941	1 455	1 216	736	884	374	375
1990	.....	.....	.....	27 934	24 387	490	1 631	1 104	5 139	1 535	1 288	772	914	374	408
1991	.....	.....	.....	28 336	24 712	487	1 589	1 112	5 086	1 485	1 268	797	882	341	411
1992	.....	.....	.....	29 052	25 347	490	1 576	1 116	5 315	1 629	1 411	836	881	347	401
1993	.....	.....	.....	30 197	26 380	519	1 596	1 137	5 735	1 906	1 669	893	925	349	412
1994	102.6	.....	.....	31 579	27 632	564	1 631	1 140	6 281	2 272	2 017	959	968	338	441
1995	106.1	102.4	.....	33 117	28 979	582	1 668	1 163	6 812	2 476	2 189	1 090	1 020	359	488
1996	110.1	104.6	.....	34 454	30 144	627	1 715	1 180	7 293	2 654	2 352	1 228	1 080	372	525
1997	115.6	106.1	102.5	36 040	31 518	678	1 746	1 186	7 988	2 985	2 656	1 409	1 120	374	550
1998	119.9	107.7	106.1	37 526	32 763	706	1 776	1 195	8 584	3 230	2 872	1 599	1 144	382	573
1995:															
January	104.3	101.5	.....	32 500	28 417	574	1 652	1 154	6 629	2 440	2 167	1 020	1 000	352	465
February	105.3	101.6	.....	32 652	28 572	575	1 657	1 157	6 654	2 453	2 175	1 034	1 002	356	477
March	106.7	101.8	.....	32 809	28 708	582	1 661	1 162	6 691	2 451	2 173	1 046	1 006	356	477
April	107.3	101.9	.....	32 870	28 767	581	1 657	1 161	6 703	2 447	2 164	1 058	1 008	358	484
May	106.2	101.9	.....	32 933	28 812	575	1 662	1 163	6 733	2 437	2 155	1 074	1 011	357	486
June	105.6	102.0	.....	33 032	28 899	577	1 668	1 164	6 761	2 431	2 149	1 085	1 017	358	485
July	105.9	102.4	.....	33 102	28 950	581	1 673	1 167	6 780	2 435	2 150	1 097	1 021	360	491
August	106.0	102.6	.....	33 297	29 118	583	1 677	1 165	6 863	2 474	2 185	1 110	1 026	361	490
September	106.6	102.6	.....	33 409	29 255	585	1 679	1 164	6 930	2 530	2 228	1 123	1 026	363	497
October	106.9	103.3	.....	33 487	29 330	589	1 679	1 163	6 956	2 520	2 228	1 134	1 035	362	500
November	106.2	103.4	.....	33 587	29 390	588	1 675	1 164	7 004	2 544	2 246	1 145	1 040	364	504
December	105.8	103.5	.....	33 688	29 492	600	1 678	1 168	7 028	2 543	2 243	1 160	1 047	366	502
1996:															
January	107.4	104.0	.....	33 720	29 479	607	1 679	1 170	7 011	2 491	2 203	1 165	1 052	367	510
February	108.3	104.2	.....	33 937	29 703	616	1 690	1 174	7 100	2 555	2 258	1 176	1 059	369	508
March	109.8	104.2	.....	34 082	29 832	617	1 700	1 176	7 141	2 572	2 272	1 186	1 067	372	518
April	110.1	104.3	.....	34 170	29 907	615	1 705	1 178	7 182	2 596	2 297	1 196	1 069	373	520
May	110.0	104.3	.....	34 296	30 018	620	1 711	1 180	7 217	2 623	2 321	1 205	1 073	373	526
June	110.6	104.5	.....	34 430	30 126	628	1 732	1 182	7 261	2 653	2 353	1 213	1 077	373	527
July	110.7	104.6	.....	34 526	30 210	631	1 719	1 181	7 310	2 672	2 372	1 229	1 084	372	531
August	110.9	104.7	.....	34 668	30 337	634	1 719	1 182	7 393	2 707	2 407	1 243	1 090	372	526
September	110.7	104.8	.....	34 734	30 390	635	1 722	1 182	7 419	2 727	2 425	1 257	1 092	372	532
October	111.1	105.2	.....	34 815	30 474	639	1 724	1 185	7 413	2 697	2 394	1 273	1 098	371	533
November	110.4	105.2	.....	34 994	30 597	643	1 730	1 186	7 516	2 765	2 454	1 289	1 099	374	533
December	110.9	105.3	100.0	35 089	30 687	645	1 736	1 185	7 561	2 775	2 467	1 304	1 103	373	533
1997:															
January	112.5	105.7	101.6	35 234	30 805	651	1 737	1 184	7 626	2 811	2 505	1 322	1 105	371	536
February	113.7	105.8	101.9	35 406	30 946	656	1 742	1 186	7 719	2 852	2 538	1 339	1 111	370	535
March	116.3	105.9	102.0	35 552	31 081	661	1 743	1 184	7 797	2 892	2 574	1 358	1 115	372	537
April	117.3	105.9	102.0	35 736	31 255	670	1 747	1 182	7 873	2 931	2 607	1 374	1 118	373	539
May	115.1	105.9	102.1	35 888	31 386	679	1 743	1 185	7 933	2 958	2 630	1 390	1 121	373	543
June	115.8	106.0	102.2	35 989	31 480	679	1 739	1 184	7 985	2 985	2 652	1 407	1 116	374	549
July	116.7	106.2	102.3	36 155	31 648	683	1 738	1 184	8 041	3 020	2 686	1 418	1 120	375	551
August	116.0	106.2	102.5	36 219	31 690	686	1 737	1 185	8 055	3 004	2 673	1 431	1 120	376	556
September	115.9	106.3	102.6	36 370	31 824	690	1 746	1 188	8 127	3 045	2 711	1 447	1 124	375	559
October	116.2	106.3	102.8	36 492	31 918	693	1 758	1 190	8 158	3 067	2 727	1 460	1 126	375	561
November	115.8	106.2	103.7	36 619	32 018	690	1 758	1 194	8 230	3 107	2 767	1 470	1 128	375	563
December	115.5	106.4	104.1	36 782	32 153	689	1 759	1 187	8 302	3 153	2 804	1 491	1 132	376	570
1998:															
January	116.8	107.0	105.1	36 905	32 251	688	1 766	1 184	8 362	3 185	2 829	1 505	1 134	376	570
February	117.7	107.1	105.6	37 003	32 332	687	1 764	1 190	8 398	3 198	2 844	1 520	1 130	377	573
March	119.7	107.3	105.9	37 103	32 411	692	1 766	1 193	8 428	3 200	2 846	1 537	1 131	376	572
April	120.6	107.4	106.0	37 194	32 486	696	1 771	1 195	8 457	3 195	2 843	1 555	1 130	378	570
May	119.9	107.5	106.1	37 334	32 604	694	1 774	1 197	8 513	3 212	2 858	1 573	1 137	380	573
June	119.5	107.5	106.1	37 460	32 713	698	1 777	1 196	8 573	3 248	2 886	1 593	1 142	381	564
July	120.3	107.8	106.2	37 576	32 818	704	1 782	1 197	8 601	3 234	2 873	1 613	1 146	381	573
August	120.6	107.9	106.4	37 688	32 895	709	1 784	1 197	8 649	3 249	2 887	1 626	1 150	382	575
September	120.1	108.0	106.5	37 780	32 979	712	1 785	1 195	8 654	3 230	2 874	1 639	1 153	384	577
October	121.8	108.3	106.5	37 929	33 089	716	1 784	1 194	8 729	3 254	2 891	1 658	1 155	386	577
November	120.8	108.3	106.5	38 070	33 199	726	1 782	1 198	8 779	3 267	2 903	1 675	1 160	388	575
December	120.4	108.4	106.7	38 207	33 301	739	1 783	1 202	8 829	3 292	2 922	1 691	1 163	390	577

Private Services—Employment—*Continued*

(Thousands, seasonally adjusted)

Year and month	Amusement and recreation	Legal services	Educational services	Social services	Museums, botanical gardens, and zoos	Membership organizations	Engineering and management	Health services				
								Total	Hospitals	Offices and clinics of medical doctors	Nursing and personal care facilities	Home health care services
1970	.....	.....	940	.....	.....	.....	.....	3 053	1 863	.....	.....	.....
1971	.....	.....	948	.....	.....	.....	.....	3 239	1 935	.....	.....	.....
1972	.....	271	958	553	.....	1 403	.....	3 412	1 980	467	591	.....
1973	.....	296	975	552	.....	1 410	.....	3 641	2 051	519	659	.....
1974	.....	326	990	625	.....	1 438	.....	3 887	2 160	567	708	.....
1975	.....	341	1 001	690	.....	1 452	.....	4 134	2 274	608	759	.....
1976	.....	364	1 013	763	.....	1 487	.....	4 350	2 363	644	809	.....
1977	.....	394	1 031	855	.....	1 495	.....	4 584	2 465	681	860	.....
1978	.....	427	1 062	991	.....	1 502	.....	4 792	2 538	720	911	.....
1979	.....	460	1 090	1 081	.....	1 516	.....	4 993	2 608	761	951	.....
1980	.....	498	1 138	1 134	.....	1 539	.....	5 278	2 750	802	997	.....
1981	.....	532	1 179	1 149	.....	1 527	.....	5 562	2 904	845	1 029	.....
1982	.....	565	1 199	1 149	.....	1 526	.....	5 811	3 014	887	1 067	.....
1983	.....	602	1 225	1 188	.....	1 510	.....	5 986	3 037	934	1 106	.....
1984	.....	645	1 270	1 222	.....	1 504	.....	6 118	3 004	977	1 147	.....
1985	.....	692	1 359	1 325	.....	1 517	.....	6 293	2 997	1 028	1 198	.....
1986	.....	747	1 421	1 406	.....	1 536	.....	6 528	3 037	1 081	1 245	.....
1987		801	1 449	1 454	.....	1 614	.....	6 794	3 142	1 139	1 283	.....
1988	977	845	1 567	1 552	58	1 740	2 230	7 105	3 294	1 200	1 311	216
1989	1 033	880	1 647	1 644	62	1 836	2 389	7 463	3 439	1 268	1 356	244
1990	1 076	908	1 661	1 734	66	1 946	2 478	7 814	3 549	1 338	1 415	291
1991	1 122	912	1 710	1 845	69	1 982	2 433	8 183	3 655	1 405	1 493	345
1992	1 188	914	1 678	1 959	73	1 973	2 471	8 490	3 750	1 463	1 533	398
1993	1 258	924	1 711	2 070	76	2 035	2 521	8 756	3 779	1 506	1 585	469
1994	1 334	924	1 850	2 200	79	2 082	2 579	8 992	3 763	1 545	1 649	559
1995	1 417	921	1 965	2 336	80	2 146	2 731	9 230	3 772	1 609	1 691	629
1996	1 476	928	2 030	2 413	85	2 201	2 844	9 478	3 812	1 678	1 730	675
1997	1 552	944	2 104	2 518	90	2 277	2 988	9 703	3 860	1 739	1 756	710
1998	1 601	973	2 177	2 644	93	2 361	3 185	9 846	3 926	1 803	1 762	672
1995:												
January	1 360	923	1 923	2 296	79	2 123	2 666	9 117	3 762	1 575	1 671	602
February	1 380	923	1 943	2 308	79	2 127	2 685	9 139	3 760	1 583	1 676	607
March	1 418	923	1 949	2 320	80	2 133	2 697	9 163	3 764	1 589	1 678	611
April	1 425	922	1 952	2 327	80	2 134	2 707	9 178	3 770	1 594	1 681	614
May	1 412	921	1 963	2 332	80	2 139	2 715	9 190	3 767	1 599	1 682	617
June	1 417	919	1 966	2 336	80	2 144	2 731	9 213	3 769	1 605	1 687	625
July	1 418	920	1 967	2 321	81	2 148	2 741	9 235	3 770	1 610	1 691	632
August	1 427	921	1 984	2 347	81	2 158	2 751	9 262	3 773	1 616	1 697	641
September	1 434	921	1 977	2 357	81	2 155	2 757	9 281	3 775	1 624	1 702	643
October	1 435	921	1 983	2 358	81	2 153	2 766	9 301	3 779	1 630	1 704	646
November	1 427	920	1 984	2 361	82	2 165	2 775	9 327	3 784	1 638	1 710	650
December	1 422	920	1 993	2 371	82	2 171	2 781	9 351	3 788	1 646	1 712	656
1996:												
January	1 436	922	1 986	2 372	83	2 172	2 786	9 357	3 792	1 646	1 713	654
February	1 449	924	2 002	2 384	83	2 179	2 801	9 387	3 798	1 655	1 717	660
March	1 459	924	2 009	2 391	83	2 181	2 816	9 413	3 803	1 661	1 722	662
April	1 471	923	2 014	2 399	84	2 185	2 809	9 430	3 804	1 668	1 724	667
May	1 469	926	2 017	2 406	85	2 195	2 833	9 454	3 808	1 672	1 728	671
June	1 474	927	2 030	2 411	85	2 199	2 844	9 471	3 808	1 678	1 732	673
July	1 479	928	2 045	2 417	86	2 199	2 846	9 490	3 810	1 683	1 734	675
August	1 488	930	2 047	2 422	86	2 212	2 856	9 505	3 810	1 689	1 734	679
September	1 482	928	2 038	2 428	86	2 216	2 871	9 527	3 819	1 692	1 737	683
October	1 498	931	2 051	2 438	87	2 221	2 878	9 547	3 823	1 695	1 739	687
November	1 502	933	2 060	2 446	87	2 227	2 890	9 569	3 829	1 700	1 741	693
December	1 505	933	2 063	2 449	89	2 231	2 901	9 585	3 833	1 704	1 744	695
1997:												
January	1 520	936	2 069	2 460	89	2 235	2 906	9 613	3 836	1 711	1 745	704
February	1 529	937	2 074	2 471	89	2 239	2 926	9 628	3 842	1 719	1 746	703
March	1 537	939	2 078	2 482	89	2 245	2 935	9 645	3 848	1 720	1 747	708
April	1 541	942	2 089	2 495	89	2 256	2 953	9 669	3 849	1 726	1 753	714
May	1 556	942	2 092	2 502	90	2 265	2 964	9 692	3 853	1 736	1 757	712
June	1 563	943	2 100	2 512	90	2 272	2 976	9 691	3 856	1 736	1 756	712
July	1 565	945	2 111	2 535	90	2 283	2 994	9 715	3 861	1 742	1 758	715
August	1 556	946	2 117	2 536	90	2 290	3 009	9 727	3 865	1 742	1 760	714
September	1 557	948	2 123	2 545	91	2 296	3 022	9 738	3 870	1 747	1 760	713
October	1 558	950	2 127	2 554	91	2 305	3 042	9 756	3 876	1 755	1 762	713
November	1 557	952	2 132	2 560	91	2 309	3 053	9 771	3 882	1 761	1 764	709
December	1 567	955	2 134	2 569	91	2 325	3 071	9 790	3 888	1 772	1 767	707
1998:												
January	1 565	957	2 142	2 579	91	2 336	3 087	9 796	3 896	1 773	1 763	702
February	1 571	959	2 147	2 589	92	2 345	3 099	9 801	3 898	1 777	1 766	695
March	1 573	962	2 154	2 600	93	2 354	3 114	9 807	3 902	1 782	1 766	689
April	1 580	964	2 158	2 611	92	2 356	3 130	9 817	3 912	1 787	1 765	680
May	1 584	968	2 164	2 624	92	2 357	3 158	9 830	3 918	1 793	1 766	675
June	1 587	971	2 171	2 638	92	2 360	3 178	9 842	3 925	1 798	1 765	674
July	1 599	974	2 177	2 650	92	2 362	3 201	9 847	3 931	1 803	1 762	665
August	1 608	977	2 176	2 660	93	2 365	3 214	9 859	3 937	1 811	1 760	661
September	1 622	980	2 189	2 672	93	2 369	3 231	9 873	3 943	1 818	1 761	658
October	1 626	985	2 206	2 682	93	2 374	3 248	9 883	3 948	1 825	1 759	654
November	1 641	986	2 214	2 695	94	2 375	3 273	9 892	3 950	1 831	1 757	651
December	1 647	988	2 223	2 708	94	2 380	3 292	9 899	3 952	1 833	1 756	651

Private Services—Hours and Earnings

(Nonsupervisory workers)

Year and month	Average weekly hours (Seasonally adjusted)	Aggregate weekly hours index (1982= 100, seasonally adjusted)	Average earnings (dollars, not seasonally adjusted)											
			Hourly						Weekly					
			All private services	Business services			Auto repair services and parking	Amusement and recreation	All private services	Business services			Auto repair services and parking	Amusement and recreation
				Total	Help supply	Computer and data processing				Total	Help supply	Computer and data processing		
1970	34.4	65.3	2.81	.....	.....	.....	.....	.....	96.66	.....	.....	.....	.....	.....
1971	33.9	65.6	3.04	.....	.....	.....	.....	.....	103.06	.....	.....	.....	.....	.....
1972	33.9	68.0	3.27	.....	.....	4.53	3.26	.....	110.85	.....	.....	163.53	122.25	.....
1973	33.8	71.3	3.47	.....	.....	4.79	3.47	.....	117.29	.....	.....	173.88	130.13	.....
1974	33.6	73.9	3.75	.....	.....	5.02	3.75	.....	126.00	.....	.....	184.74	140.25	.....
1975	33.5	76.0	4.02	.....	.....	5.26	3.99	.....	134.67	.....	.....	196.20	150.02	.....
1976	33.3	78.8	4.31	.....	.....	5.18	4.31	.....	143.52	.....	.....	190.62	163.35	.....
1977	33.0	82.0	4.65	.....	.....	5.32	4.61	.....	153.45	.....	.....	197.90	172.41	.....
1978	32.8	86.3	4.99	.....	.....	5.76	5.03	.....	163.67	.....	.....	211.39	188.12	.....
1979	32.7	90.2	5.36	.....	.....	6.35	5.59	.....	175.27	.....	.....	231.78	209.63	.....
1980	32.6	94.3	5.85	.....	.....	7.16	6.10	.....	190.71	.....	.....	260.62	229.36	.....
1981	32.6	98.2	6.41	.....	.....	7.92	6.44	.....	208.97	.....	.....	294.62	244.08	.....
1982	32.6	100.0	6.92	.....	.....	9.00	6.76	.....	225.59	.....	161.79	338.40	254.85	.....
1983	32.7	103.6	7.31	.....	.....	10.10	6.94	.....	239.04	.....	171.57	387.84	260.94	.....
1984	32.6	108.2	7.59	.....	.....	10.50	7.21	.....	247.43	.....	185.63	400.05	270.38	.....
1985	32.5	114.0	7.90	.....	.....	10.98	7.40	.....	256.75	.....	198.25	422.73	276.76	.....
1986	32.5	119.2	8.18	.....	.....	11.63	7.55	.....	265.85	.....	206.82	444.27	282.37	.....
1987	32.5	124.9	8.49	.....	.....	12.29	7.78	.....	275.93	.....	218.15	460.88	285.53	.....
1988	32.6	132.2	8.88	8.61	7.41	13.21	8.16	7.39	289.49	286.71	231.93	499.34	299.47	201.01
1989	32.6	139.3	9.38	9.08	7.73	14.19	8.47	7.82	305.79	301.46	237.31	539.22	310.85	214.27
1990	32.5	144.2	9.83	9.48	8.09	15.11	8.77	8.11	319.48	313.79	249.17	575.69	320.98	220.59
1991	32.4	145.3	10.23	9.76	8.31	15.57	8.96	8.04	331.45	322.08	256.78	591.66	326.14	215.47
1992	32.5	149.3	10.54	9.97	8.29	15.81	9.16	8.08	342.55	329.01	257.82	602.36	333.42	218.16
1993	32.5	155.4	10.78	10.12	8.24	16.46	9.33	8.32	350.35	333.96	257.91	627.13	338.68	227.97
1994	32.5	162.9	11.04	10.31	8.38	17.17	9.58	8.49	358.80	341.26	266.48	649.03	347.75	228.38
1995	32.4	170.5	11.39	10.71	8.80	17.79	9.92	8.74	369.04	354.50	279.84	672.46	356.13	235.98
1996	32.4	177.4	11.79	11.23	9.20	18.78	10.20	8.83	382.00	372.84	295.32	708.01	368.22	238.41
1997	32.6	186.6	12.28	11.83	9.65	20.13	10.60	9.18	400.33	396.31	312.66	770.98	383.72	246.94
1998	32.6	194.3	12.85	12.58	10.18	21.31	11.09	9.59	418.91	421.43	329.83	820.44	398.13	256.05
1995:														
January	32.4	167.3	11.36	10.60	8.67	17.55	9.84	9.07	368.06	351.92	276.57	675.68	350.30	238.54
February	32.4	168.2	11.35	10.62	8.75	17.65	9.79	9.09	366.61	350.46	277.38	667.17	347.55	240.89
March	32.4	169.0	11.32	10.58	8.76	17.51	9.82	9.01	364.50	350.20	281.20	654.87	350.57	236.06
April	32.4	169.3	11.38	10.72	8.77	17.80	9.85	8.90	369.85	351.62	269.24	678.18	353.62	242.08
May	32.3	169.1	11.31	10.62	8.76	17.69	9.90	8.82	363.05	348.34	275.06	656.30	352.44	231.97
June	32.5	170.6	11.22	10.63	8.78	17.76	9.88	8.33	364.65	351.85	280.08	662.45	358.64	233.24
July	32.4	170.4	11.26	10.80	8.86	17.97	9.90	8.15	369.33	356.40	279.09	682.86	359.37	236.35
August	32.4	171.4	11.22	10.64	8.79	17.68	9.94	8.18	366.89	352.18	282.16	663.00	360.82	233.13
September	32.4	172.2	11.45	10.74	8.80	17.83	9.97	8.80	369.84	354.42	278.08	673.97	357.92	232.32
October	32.3	172.1	11.54	10.79	8.78	17.99	10.02	8.90	376.20	358.23	278.33	694.41	360.72	234.07
November	32.4	173.0	11.57	10.77	8.85	17.87	10.01	9.11	373.71	358.64	286.74	675.49	358.36	239.59
December	32.4	173.6	11.66	10.91	8.94	18.13	10.04	9.18	376.62	362.21	286.97	679.88	356.42	241.43
1996:														
January	32.2	172.4	11.73	11.08	9.07	18.15	10.05	9.09	373.01	356.78	279.36	675.18	354.77	236.34
February	32.3	174.3	11.72	11.09	9.15	18.25	10.07	9.13	377.38	363.75	286.40	686.20	361.51	241.03
March	32.4	175.6	11.72	11.08	9.13	18.32	10.12	9.05	377.38	367.86	293.99	688.83	365.33	236.21
April	32.3	175.5	11.71	11.13	9.13	18.35	10.12	8.90	377.06	366.18	289.42	691.80	363.31	237.63
May	32.4	176.7	11.67	11.10	9.12	18.45	10.18	8.80	375.77	367.41	292.75	691.88	366.48	229.68
June	32.5	177.9	11.66	11.20	9.14	18.80	10.14	8.38	382.45	376.32	297.05	720.04	371.12	232.96
July	32.3	177.3	11.61	11.16	9.16	18.68	10.17	8.26	377.33	369.40	294.95	694.90	369.17	234.58
August	32.4	178.6	11.63	11.17	9.09	18.87	10.18	8.25	380.30	373.08	295.43	711.40	373.61	235.13
September	32.5	179.4	11.90	11.33	9.18	19.16	10.27	8.88	387.94	378.42	294.68	733.83	372.80	233.54
October	32.4	179.4	11.94	11.30	9.24	19.15	10.30	9.07	386.86	376.29	298.45	721.96	373.89	240.36
November	32.4	180.1	12.04	11.43	9.39	19.32	10.37	9.31	390.10	380.62	304.24	730.30	375.39	247.65
December	32.5	181.2	12.16	11.59	9.53	19.65	10.45	9.44	397.63	388.27	307.82	750.63	376.20	254.88
1997:														
January	32.4	181.3	12.19	11.68	9.62	19.54	10.51	9.35	390.08	383.10	303.03	734.70	375.21	242.17
February	32.6	183.3	12.24	11.76	9.60	19.87	10.44	9.43	400.25	393.96	311.04	765.00	376.88	251.78
March	32.6	184.1	12.24	11.75	9.59	19.86	10.48	9.41	399.02	394.80	312.63	762.62	378.33	249.37
April	32.5	184.5	12.19	11.72	9.58	19.76	10.48	9.30	394.96	391.45	309.43	754.83	376.23	243.66
May	32.6	185.9	12.16	11.76	9.69	19.86	10.48	9.11	393.98	392.78	313.96	756.67	378.33	239.59
June	32.5	185.9	12.14	11.80	9.62	20.13	10.49	8.73	398.19	395.30	307.84	777.02	383.93	240.08
July	32.5	186.9	12.06	11.72	9.55	19.97	10.50	8.49	395.57	390.28	309.42	756.86	384.30	241.12
August	32.7	188.3	12.12	11.78	9.56	20.16	10.61	8.61	398.75	396.99	314.52	772.13	389.39	243.66
September	32.6	188.5	12.36	11.87	9.58	20.34	10.69	9.31	401.70	396.46	310.39	776.99	386.98	242.06
October	32.6	189.0	12.41	11.91	9.67	20.47	10.76	9.46	404.57	398.99	314.28	784.00	389.51	249.74
November	32.7	190.2	12.57	12.10	9.77	20.73	10.87	9.81	412.30	407.77	317.53	808.47	390.23	262.91
December	32.6	190.4	12.61	12.11	9.87	20.67	10.88	9.82	411.09	406.90	321.76	793.73	389.50	261.21
1998:														
January	32.7	191.6	12.66	12.26	10.02	20.61	10.94	9.75	410.18	409.48	326.65	787.30	387.28	256.43
February	32.6	191.5	12.75	12.41	10.08	21.02	10.91	9.81	418.20	416.98	327.60	815.58	389.49	259.97
March	32.6	192.0	12.77	12.44	10.11	21.08	10.91	9.82	416.30	416.74	327.56	811.58	389.49	256.30
April	32.6	192.4	12.77	12.48	10.14	21.05	11.00	9.65	413.75	413.09	320.42	804.11	390.50	252.83
May	32.7	193.7	12.76	12.49	10.19	21.13	11.04	9.56	414.70	419.66	333.21	809.28	396.34	248.56
June	32.6	193.7	12.71	12.50	10.16	21.22	11.06	9.18	415.62	421.25	333.25	816.97	397.05	246.94
July	32.7	195.0	12.68	12.57	10.23	21.24	11.09	9.05	417.17	422.35	334.52	813.49	404.79	256.12
August	32.7	195.4	12.75	12.60	10.13	21.50	11.12	9.12	423.30	428.40	334.29	840.65	406.99	259.01
September	32.5	194.7	12.97	12.78	10.23	21.51	11.16	9.65	418.93	412.79	304.85	825.98	399.53	248.97
October	32.7	196.6	13.01	12.68	10.20	21.61	11.21	9.81	424.11	427.32	333.54	831.99	403.56	256.04
November	32.7	197.2	13.15	12.84	10.28	21.89	11.26	10.06	431.32	433.99	334.10	855.90	400.86	265.58
December	32.6	197.8	13.18	12.82	10.36	21.73	11.32	10.14	429.67	434.60	341.88	832.26	402.99	266.68

Selected Service Industries—Receipts of Taxable Firms

(By kind of business and SIC code, millions of dollars)

Year	Arrangement of passenger transportation (472)	Real estate agents and managers (653)	Hotels, rooming houses, camps and other lodging places, except on membership bases (70, ex.704)	Personal services (72)	Business services (73)	Automotive repair, services, and parking (75)	Miscellaneous repair services (76)	Motion pictures (78)
1986	7 465	48 360	47 634	39 587	170 250	53 867	22 478	23 740
1987	8 196	52 919	53 630	43 247	188 856	58 278	24 599	27 754
1988	9 521	58 980	58 637	48 329	223 369	66 053	27 659	31 746
1989	11 041	62 325	61 229	51 832	251 648	70 961	30 064	36 173
1990	12 276	63 023	64 225	54 736	280 699	73 722	32 848	39 982
1991	11 438	63 180	65 284	54 620	287 214	71 542	32 401	42 838
1992	11 926	73 115	71 038	59 597	309 439	78 511	35 238	45 662
1993	12 396	79 206	74 149	62 597	337 403	84 324	36 772	49 799
1994	13 125	80 947	79 555	66 105	375 067	91 865	40 683	53 504
1995	14 192	82 667	84 093	70 607	425 075	99 227	44 870	57 184
1996	15 354	90 186	88 961	73 905	484 242	106 638	46 101	60 279
1997	16 584	99 202	94 024	76 938	552 488	111 837	48 054	63 010

Year	Amusement and recreation services (79)	Health services (80)	Legal services (81)	Vocational schools (824)	Social services (83)	Museums, art galleries, and botanical and zoological gardens (84)	Engineering, accounting, research, management and related services (87)
1986	33 984	173 885	63 390	3 327	.....	.....	127 885
1987	36 646	196 212	72 115	3 400	.....	.....	139 897
1988	41 272	221 741	81 636	4 263	.....	.....	160 446
1989	44 539	241 558	89 144	4 577	.....	.....	183 528
1990	50 126	271 212	97 640	4 519	15 509	144	198 395
1991	51 654	293 907	100 027	4 183	16 365	154	202 696
1992	57 699	321 653	108 443	4 429	18 201	192	215 624
1993	63 651	335 108	112 145	4 507	20 146	222	222 853
1994	68 453	351 419	114 603	4 710	22 498	231	235 447
1995	77 452	376 279	116 000	5 285	24 858	247	263 835
1996	85 733	398 353	124 659	6 190	27 694	273	292 260
1997	93 794	421 317	132 784	7 104	30 506	322	322 205

Selected Service Industries—Revenue of Tax-exempt Firms

(By kind of business and SIC code, millions of dollars)

Year	Camps and membership lodging (703, 704)	Selected amusement and recreation services (792, 7991, 7997, 7999)	Health services (80)	Legal aid societies and similar legal services (81)	Libraries (823)	Vocational schools (824)	Social services (83)	Museums, art galleries, and botanical and zoological gardens (84)	Selected membership organizations (86 [pt])	Research, development, and testing services (873)	Commercial, physical, and biological research (8731)	Non-commercial research organizations (8733)	Management and public relations services (874, ex.8744)
1986	.....	5 070	.....	563	.....	.....	.....	.....	.....	7 125	.....	.....	791
1987	.....	5 858	.....	665	.....	.....	.....	.....	.....	8 304	.....	.....	902
1988	.....	6 506	.....	775	.....	.....	.....	.....	.....	9 014	.....	.....	1 201
1989	.....	7 163	.....	944	.....	.....	.....	.....	.....	9 975	.....	.....	1 494
1990	798	7 922	267 858	1 088	476	507	45 255	2 871	31 458	11 035	.....	.....	1 933
1991	782	8 160	298 168	1 162	481	486	49 055	3 048	33 288	11 463	.....	.....	2 150
1992	808	8 993	324 416	1 161	527	549	53 673	3 199	36 256	12 534	.....	.....	2 246
1993	817	10 279	345 081	1 190	606	569	59 052	3 615	39 426	13 180	.....	.....	2 588
1994	836	11 560	363 112	1 241	655	612	63 493	3 972	41 907	13 919	.....	.....	3 119
1995	846	12 778	385 210	1 278	730	696	70 303	4 295	45 873	14 493	5 951	7 688	3 732
1996	877	13 299	401 047	1 259	754	772	75 240	4 729	48 897	14 906	5 703	8 293	4 821
1997	929	14 600	414 990	1 446	850	871	83 235	6 231	51 098	16 839	5 950	9 953	6 583

Government

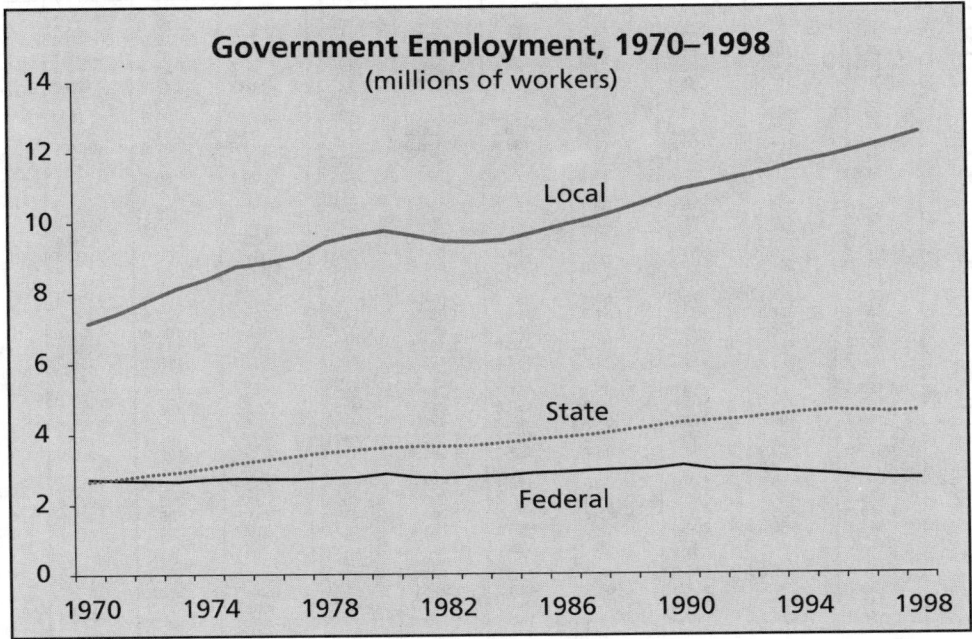

Government Employment, 1970–1998
(millions of workers)

- Federal government employment declined slightly in 1998 and was no higher than it had been in 1970. Job growth continued at the state and local levels. Local governments added over 5 million jobs over the 1970–1998 period, 57 percent of which were accounted for by education. State governments added nearly 2 million, 42 percent due to education.

- The federal government achieved a budget surplus of $69 billion in fiscal year 1998, the first since 1969. The surplus was used mainly to repay debt held by the public—also a first since 1969—and the ratio of debt to GDP dropped to 44.2 percent. On the national income and product accounts (NIPA) basis, the federal government displayed a similar swing to surplus in calendar 1998.

- State and local governments have had substantial and growing surpluses of receipts over current expenditures for the entire 1970–1998 period. Their investment spending, which is outside their NIPA current budget, also has grown; it exceeds their current surplus and is substantially greater than federal investment.

Federal Government Receipts and Current Expenditures

(Calendar years—Billions of dollars, quarterly data are seasonally adjusted annual rates)

Year and quarter	Receipts					Current expenditures						Surplus or deficit (—), national income and product accounts		
	Total	Personal tax and nontax receipts	Corporate profits tax accruals	Indirect business tax and nontax accruals	Contributions to social insurance	Total	Consumption expenditures	Transfer payments (net)	Grants in-aid to state and local governments	Net interest paid	Subsidies less surplus government enterprises	Total	Social insurance funds	Other
1970	195.1	92.2	30.6	19.5	52.8	209.1	100.5	63.6	24.4	14.1	6.5	-14.1	3.6	-17.7
1971	203.3	89.9	33.5	20.5	59.4	228.6	103.8	75.4	29.0	13.8	6.6	-25.3	0.7	-26.1
1972	232.6	107.8	36.6	20.1	68.1	253.1	110.1	83.5	37.5	14.4	8.0	-20.5	3.0	-23.6
1973	264.0	114.3	43.3	21.5	84.9	275.1	112.9	96.2	40.6	18.0	7.4	-11.1	9.3	-20.4
1974	295.1	130.9	45.1	22.1	97.1	312.0	123.3	118.2	43.9	20.7	5.5	-16.9	7.0	-23.9
1975	297.4	125.4	43.6	24.2	104.2	371.3	135.0	150.3	54.6	23.0	8.6	-73.9	-11.2	-62.7
1976	343.1	146.6	54.6	23.8	118.2	400.3	141.7	163.0	61.1	26.8	7.8	-57.2	-9.7	-47.5
1977	389.6	169.1	61.6	25.6	133.3	435.9	155.4	173.6	67.5	29.1	10.4	-46.3	-5.6	-40.7
1978	446.5	193.8	71.4	28.9	152.4	478.1	168.8	186.2	77.3	34.6	11.4	-31.7	3.7	-35.4
1979	511.1	229.7	74.4	30.1	176.8	529.5	185.9	209.7	80.5	42.1	11.3	-18.4	9.8	-28.2
1980	561.5	256.2	70.3	39.7	195.3	622.5	215.2	252.0	88.7	52.7	13.9	-61.0	-4.4	-56.6
1981	649.3	297.2	65.7	57.3	229.1	707.1	246.0	287.1	87.9	71.7	14.4	-57.8	-1.3	-56.5
1982	646.4	302.9	49.0	49.7	244.8	781.0	270.0	323.4	83.9	84.4	19.4	-134.7	-19.8	-114.8
1983	671.9	293.0	61.3	53.3	264.2	846.3	293.0	347.7	87.0	92.8	25.4	-174.4	-20.7	-153.6
1984	746.9	308.3	75.2	57.9	305.3	902.9	314.1	354.3	94.4	113.3	27.1	-156.0	21.9	-177.9
1985	811.3	343.7	76.3	58.2	333.1	974.2	342.5	379.0	100.3	126.9	25.2	-162.9	33.1	-196.0
1986	850.1	358.3	83.8	53.2	354.7	1 027.6	362.3	399.1	107.6	130.5	28.0	-177.5	40.0	-217.5
1987	937.4	402.4	103.2	57.8	374.1	1 066.3	378.2	413.0	102.9	137.8	34.4	-128.9	49.7	-178.6
1988	997.2	414.4	111.0	60.9	410.9	1 118.5	387.8	437.2	111.2	148.4	33.8	-121.3	73.8	-195.1
1989	1 079.3	463.4	117.1	61.7	437.1	1 192.7	405.2	471.7	118.2	166.7	30.8	-113.4	80.9	-194.2
1990	1 129.8	485.7	118.0	65.1	461.1	1 284.5	426.6	513.3	132.4	179.9	32.4	-154.7	80.1	-234.8
1991	1 149.0	476.9	109.8	79.7	482.6	1 345.0	445.9	522.2	153.4	192.7	30.8	-196.0	65.0	-261.0
1992	1 198.5	490.8	118.6	81.9	507.1	1 479.4	451.0	625.1	172.2	195.8	35.1	-280.9	48.4	-329.3
1993	1 275.1	522.6	138.3	86.9	527.3	1 525.7	447.3	659.9	185.8	192.7	40.1	-250.7	44.6	-295.2
1994	1 374.8	562.3	156.7	98.7	557.1	1 561.4	443.2	683.0	199.2	200.0	35.9	-186.7	59.2	-245.8
1995	1 460.3	606.1	179.3	92.5	582.4	1 634.7	442.8	720.3	212.0	224.8	34.8	-174.4	54.7	-229.1
1996	1 584.7	687.0	193.0	94.5	610.2	1 695.0	450.9	764.2	218.9	228.4	32.7	-110.3	54.6	-164.9
1997	1 719.9	769.1	210.0	93.8	647.0	1 741.0	460.4	791.9	225.0	231.2	32.5	-21.1	70.3	-91.4
1998	1 844.2	858.0	204.9	95.9	685.4	1 771.4	461.0	816.6	231.1	226.1	36.6	72.8	94.2	-21.5
1990:														
1st quarter	1 107.3	477.4	111.6	63.2	455.1	1 261.5	421.7	504.2	128.4	176.2	30.9	-154.1	76.7	-230.8
2nd quarter	1 132.7	490.7	118.5	64.2	459.3	1 276.9	423.7	509.6	132.2	179.7	31.7	-144.1	82.2	-226.3
3rd quarter	1 144.1	489.7	124.3	65.5	464.5	1 286.7	423.2	513.2	131.8	185.8	32.7	-142.6	84.1	-226.7
4th quarter	1 135.2	484.9	117.4	67.4	465.6	1 313.0	437.7	526.1	137.1	177.8	34.4	-177.7	77.5	-255.2
1991:														
1st quarter	1 140.1	478.4	107.3	77.2	477.2	1 274.7	450.5	461.7	144.8	186.3	31.6	-134.6	66.0	-200.6
2nd quarter	1 142.6	474.3	108.9	79.1	480.3	1 339.3	449.1	515.5	151.8	192.6	30.0	-196.7	63.6	-260.3
3rd quarter	1 152.3	476.0	111.8	79.9	484.7	1 366.3	443.7	545.6	154.4	191.9	30.7	-214.0	66.8	-280.8
4th quarter	1 160.9	479.0	111.1	82.8	488.1	1 399.8	440.5	565.8	162.7	200.0	30.9	-238.8	63.7	-302.5
1992:														
1st quarter	1 183.4	481.0	119.6	80.8	502.0	1 450.7	445.8	611.1	165.4	196.8	31.8	-267.4	48.2	-315.6
2nd quarter	1 193.1	481.6	125.3	80.2	506.1	1 472.8	446.3	621.9	173.0	198.4	33.1	-279.6	47.6	-327.2
3rd quarter	1 187.0	490.7	106.0	80.2	510.1	1 484.5	454.4	624.2	174.2	196.4	35.3	-297.5	50.2	-347.7
4th quarter	1 230.5	510.0	123.7	86.5	510.3	1 509.5	457.7	643.3	176.3	191.8	40.3	-279.0	47.6	-326.6
1993:														
1st quarter	1 227.1	500.8	125.2	82.6	518.5	1 505.3	447.1	647.1	177.2	192.2	41.7	-278.2	41.0	-319.2
2nd quarter	1 268.8	519.1	138.5	85.5	525.8	1 518.0	445.8	655.7	181.9	193.1	41.6	-249.2	44.6	-293.8
3rd quarter	1 277.2	527.1	135.0	85.9	529.3	1 527.8	447.0	661.3	187.3	192.9	39.2	-250.6	44.3	-294.9
4th quarter	1 327.2	543.4	154.5	93.8	535.5	1 551.9	449.2	675.5	196.9	192.5	37.8	-224.6	48.3	-273.0
1994:														
1st quarter	1 324.5	542.0	136.9	98.2	547.4	1 533.5	442.4	670.6	194.5	189.9	36.0	-209.0	54.6	-263.6
2nd quarter	1 381.1	574.3	153.4	98.1	555.3	1 544.3	439.2	676.9	196.2	196.6	35.4	-163.2	58.7	-221.9
3rd quarter	1 383.8	561.6	163.4	99.3	559.5	1 571.4	450.5	683.8	199.6	202.8	34.8	-187.6	60.7	-248.3
4th quarter	1 409.5	571.1	173.2	99.0	566.2	1 596.4	440.8	700.7	206.6	210.8	37.5	-186.8	62.7	-249.6
1995:														
1st quarter	1 426.2	582.9	172.5	96.0	574.7	1 615.8	443.0	707.8	212.4	218.3	34.4	-189.6	57.1	-246.7
2nd quarter	1 459.3	609.4	176.6	94.6	578.7	1 637.1	444.7	717.1	216.4	224.3	34.6	-177.9	52.8	-230.6
3rd quarter	1 469.1	608.2	186.2	89.2	585.5	1 646.0	447.2	724.8	211.0	227.8	35.2	-176.9	54.2	-231.2
4th quarter	1 486.8	623.9	182.1	90.3	590.5	1 639.8	436.5	731.5	208.1	228.7	35.1	-153.0	54.8	-207.8
1996:														
1st quarter	1 529.9	652.6	191.2	89.9	596.2	1 680.0	445.7	757.8	214.3	227.7	34.4	-150.1	47.4	-197.5
2nd quarter	1 581.7	691.4	195.2	88.5	606.7	1 694.4	453.1	757.9	223.8	226.1	33.5	-112.6	51.7	-164.3
3rd quarter	1 593.7	693.8	194.3	90.5	615.0	1 693.8	452.9	762.5	219.0	228.6	30.8	-100.1	57.9	-158.0
4th quarter	1 633.5	710.0	191.4	109.2	622.9	1 711.9	451.8	778.6	218.4	231.1	32.0	-78.3	61.5	-139.8
1997:														
1st quarter	1 671.1	741.7	203.9	90.7	634.8	1 722.3	456.8	783.4	220.7	229.4	32.0	-51.2	60.8	-112.0
2nd quarter	1 703.6	759.1	206.5	95.5	642.4	1 738.4	464.8	787.1	223.2	231.6	31.6	-34.8	66.7	-101.5
3rd quarter	1 739.6	776.9	217.0	95.1	650.6	1 739.9	460.0	791.2	224.4	231.9	32.5	-0.3	72.9	-73.3
4th quarter	1 765.5	798.6	212.8	93.8	660.3	1 763.4	460.1	805.9	231.8	231.8	33.7	2.2	80.9	-78.7
1998:														
1st quarter	1 809.1	836.5	204.8	93.9	673.9	1 750.3	450.9	808.5	228.7	228.8	33.4	58.8	84.5	-25.7
2nd quarter	1 838.3	855.7	206.2	95.2	681.2	1 763.9	464.0	811.1	226.9	228.3	33.5	74.4	90.6	-16.2
3rd quarter	1 858.8	863.8	207.5	98.3	689.2	1 766.7	458.7	817.0	231.4	225.7	34.0	92.0	96.4	-4.4
4th quarter	1 870.4	875.9	201.0	96.0	697.5	1 804.6	470.6	829.8	237.4	221.4	45.4	65.8	105.4	-39.6

State and Local Government Receipts and Current Expenditures

(Calendar years—Billions of dollars, quarterly data are at seasonally adjusted annual rates)

Year and quarter	Receipts						Current expenditures						Surplus or deficit (—), national income and product accounts		
	Total	Personal tax and nontax receipts	Corporate profits tax accruals	Indirect business tax and nontax accruals	Contributions to social insurance	Federal grants-in-aid	Total	Consumption expenditures	Transfer payments to persons	Net interest paid	Less: dividends received by government	Subsidies less surplus government enterprises	Total	Social insurance funds	Other
1970	129.0	16.7	3.7	74.8	9.2	24.4	108.2	91.6	20.1	-1.8	0.2	-1.6	20.8	6.9	13.9
1971	145.3	18.7	4.3	83.1	10.2	29.0	123.7	102.9	24.0	-1.4	0.3	-1.4	21.7	7.6	14.1
1972	169.7	24.2	5.3	91.2	11.5	37.5	137.5	113.4	27.5	-1.5	0.3	-1.6	32.2	8.7	23.5
1973	185.3	26.3	6.0	99.5	13.0	40.6	152.0	126.4	30.4	-2.9	0.5	-1.5	33.4	9.6	23.8
1974	200.6	28.2	6.7	107.2	14.6	43.9	170.2	144.0	32.3	-4.4	0.9	-0.9	30.5	10.9	19.5
1975	225.6	31.0	7.3	115.8	16.8	54.6	198.0	164.9	38.9	-4.5	0.9	-0.4	27.6	13.1	14.5
1976	253.9	35.8	9.6	127.8	19.5	61.1	217.9	179.7	43.6	-4.1	0.9	-0.4	35.9	15.6	20.4
1977	281.9	41.0	11.4	139.9	22.1	67.5	237.1	196.1	47.4	-4.7	1.3	-0.3	44.7	17.9	26.8
1978	309.3	46.3	12.1	148.9	24.7	77.3	256.7	214.5	52.4	-8.1	1.7	-0.3	52.6	20.2	32.4
1979	330.6	50.5	13.6	158.6	27.4	80.5	278.3	235.9	57.2	-13.3	2.0	0.4	52.3	23.7	28.6
1980	361.4	56.2	14.5	172.3	29.7	88.7	307.0	261.3	65.7	-19.3	1.9	1.2	54.4	26.9	27.5
1981	390.8	63.0	15.4	192.0	32.5	87.9	335.4	285.3	73.6	-23.6	2.3	2.4	55.4	29.8	25.6
1982	409.0	68.5	14.0	206.8	35.8	83.9	357.7	307.9	79.9	-28.9	2.9	1.7	51.3	36.6	14.7
1983	443.6	76.2	15.9	226.8	37.7	87.0	378.8	326.2	86.6	-31.0	3.4	0.2	64.9	41.6	23.3
1984	492.0	87.1	18.8	251.5	40.2	94.4	405.1	350.8	93.9	-34.1	3.9	-1.6	86.9	42.9	44.0
1985	528.7	94.0	20.2	271.4	42.8	100.3	437.8	382.6	101.9	-38.9	4.5	-3.3	91.0	47.0	44.0
1986	570.6	101.6	22.7	291.5	47.3	107.6	475.7	412.7	111.8	-40.7	5.1	-3.0	94.9	52.8	42.1
1987	594.9	111.8	23.9	307.1	49.2	102.9	511.1	441.1	120.7	-41.5	5.9	-3.4	83.8	54.8	29.0
1988	631.4	117.6	26.0	324.6	51.9	111.2	545.5	471.3	131.0	-44.6	6.9	-5.3	85.9	56.7	29.2
1989	681.0	131.4	24.2	353.0	54.1	118.2	585.9	507.2	144.5	-51.2	8.1	-6.6	95.1	60.2	34.9
1990	728.9	139.1	22.5	377.6	57.4	132.4	648.8	550.1	166.5	-51.7	9.0	-7.1	80.1	59.9	20.2
1991	784.2	147.8	23.6	398.4	60.9	153.4	708.4	579.4	199.0	-53.3	9.5	-7.2	75.8	64.3	11.5
1992	844.3	159.7	24.4	423.7	64.3	172.2	758.0	603.6	227.2	-54.7	10.1	-8.0	86.3	68.0	18.3
1993	894.4	167.4	26.9	445.6	68.7	185.8	807.0	631.6	247.2	-52.4	10.5	-9.0	87.4	67.8	19.7
1994	949.2	176.8	29.9	469.8	73.4	199.2	852.3	663.8	264.3	-55.1	11.4	-9.3	96.8	68.9	27.9
1995	997.7	188.9	31.7	488.7	76.5	212.0	886.0	695.2	281.2	-68.2	12.5	-9.7	111.7	74.6	37.0
1996	1 045.2	203.5	33.1	511.9	77.8	218.9	922.6	724.7	293.5	-71.3	13.7	-10.7	122.6	70.4	52.2
1997	1 094.3	219.9	36.0	533.4	79.9	225.0	960.1	758.8	304.1	-77.4	14.8	-10.6	134.1	68.1	66.0
1998	1 148.1	240.3	35.2	559.4	82.1	231.1	997.9	789.1	317.4	-83.0	16.1	-9.5	150.2	67.6	82.5
1990:															
1st quarter	710.3	135.6	21.4	368.9	56.0	128.4	624.8	535.3	156.5	-51.2	8.7	-7.1	85.5	59.3	26.2
2nd quarter	721.3	137.5	22.7	371.9	56.9	132.2	638.5	543.9	162.4	-51.7	9.0	-7.1	82.8	59.5	23.3
3rd quarter	736.2	141.2	23.7	381.8	57.9	131.8	655.5	554.0	169.3	-51.8	9.0	-7.0	80.7	60.0	20.7
4th quarter	748.0	142.3	22.2	387.7	58.7	137.1	676.5	567.3	177.7	-52.0	9.3	-7.1	71.5	60.9	10.6
1991:															
1st quarter	758.5	143.9	22.8	387.5	59.6	144.8	689.8	572.1	186.9	-52.6	9.4	-7.2	68.8	62.5	6.3
2nd quarter	775.8	146.3	23.4	393.8	60.5	151.8	702.1	576.9	195.0	-53.0	9.5	-7.2	73.7	63.9	9.8
3rd quarter	791.4	147.7	24.3	403.8	61.3	154.4	714.3	581.5	203.1	-53.6	9.5	-7.2	77.1	64.9	12.2
4th quarter	811.0	153.5	24.2	408.4	62.2	162.7	727.2	587.3	210.8	-54.0	9.6	-7.2	83.8	66.0	17.7
1992:															
1st quarter	823.4	155.7	24.3	414.9	63.1	165.4	738.6	592.6	217.7	-54.7	9.8	-7.2	84.8	67.1	17.6
2nd quarter	838.8	158.4	25.7	417.7	64.0	173.0	752.2	600.8	224.1	-54.9	10.1	-7.7	86.6	68.1	18.5
3rd quarter	847.3	159.9	21.6	427.0	64.7	174.2	765.4	607.4	231.2	-54.8	10.1	-8.3	82.0	68.4	13.6
4th quarter	867.7	164.9	25.9	435.2	65.4	176.3	775.9	613.6	235.8	-54.2	10.3	-8.9	91.7	68.4	23.3
1993:															
1st quarter	867.6	161.6	24.1	438.0	66.8	177.2	789.8	621.4	240.4	-53.1	10.2	-8.7	77.8	67.8	10.0
2nd quarter	883.9	166.5	26.9	440.4	68.2	181.9	802.6	628.9	245.2	-52.3	10.4	-8.8	81.3	67.7	13.6
3rd quarter	899.9	168.4	26.3	448.5	69.4	187.3	812.9	635.0	249.5	-51.9	10.5	-9.1	86.9	67.7	19.3
4th quarter	926.3	172.9	30.4	455.5	70.6	196.9	822.6	641.1	253.8	-52.3	10.8	-9.2	103.7	67.9	35.9
1994:															
1st quarter	922.0	170.8	26.1	458.7	71.8	194.5	837.2	651.6	257.9	-53.2	11.1	-7.9	84.7	68.4	16.3
2nd quarter	941.0	176.1	29.4	466.3	72.9	196.2	846.2	659.2	262.3	-54.5	11.3	-9.5	94.8	68.9	25.9
3rd quarter	956.9	178.3	31.3	473.8	73.9	199.6	858.4	668.6	266.6	-55.6	11.4	-9.7	98.4	69.0	29.4
4th quarter	976.8	182.0	32.9	480.4	74.9	206.6	867.5	676.0	270.5	-57.2	11.7	-10.1	109.3	69.4	40.0
1995:															
1st quarter	985.9	184.2	30.4	483.1	75.8	212.4	875.5	684.8	275.2	-62.7	12.1	-9.8	110.4	72.9	37.6
2nd quarter	996.0	186.3	31.0	486.0	76.4	216.4	883.4	693.5	279.2	-67.4	12.3	-9.7	112.6	74.8	37.7
3rd quarter	1 001.9	190.8	32.9	490.4	76.8	211.0	888.9	698.4	283.4	-70.5	12.6	-9.7	113.0	75.7	37.3
4th quarter	1 007.1	194.4	32.2	495.3	77.1	208.1	896.4	704.2	286.9	-72.1	12.9	-9.9	110.7	75.2	35.5
1996:															
1st quarter	1 025.3	197.1	32.7	504.0	77.2	214.3	908.0	712.6	289.6	-70.5	13.2	-10.4	117.3	72.0	45.3
2nd quarter	1 047.9	201.9	33.4	511.3	77.6	223.8	918.8	721.6	292.3	-70.7	13.7	-10.7	129.1	70.9	58.2
3rd quarter	1 049.1	205.6	33.3	513.3	78.0	219.0	926.9	727.8	294.9	-71.4	13.7	-10.8	122.3	69.8	52.5
4th quarter	1 058.3	209.7	32.8	519.1	78.4	218.4	936.6	736.7	297.3	-72.5	14.0	-10.9	121.7	68.8	52.9
1997:															
1st quarter	1 075.2	213.9	34.9	526.5	79.2	220.7	946.8	747.2	299.7	-75.0	14.4	-10.7	128.4	68.6	59.8
2nd quarter	1 084.5	216.7	35.4	529.5	79.7	223.2	954.4	754.0	302.5	-76.7	14.7	-10.6	130.1	68.5	61.6
3rd quarter	1 100.8	222.1	37.3	536.9	80.2	224.4	964.3	762.2	305.5	-78.2	14.8	-10.5	136.6	67.9	68.7
4th quarter	1 116.5	226.9	36.5	540.7	80.6	231.8	975.1	771.5	308.6	-79.5	15.2	-10.3	141.4	67.6	73.8
1998:															
1st quarter	1 123.3	230.4	35.1	548.0	81.1	228.7	983.0	776.7	312.6	-80.7	15.7	-9.9	140.2	67.5	72.7
2nd quarter	1 133.8	237.2	35.4	552.5	81.7	226.9	992.5	784.7	315.6	-82.2	16.0	-9.6	141.3	67.7	73.6
3rd quarter	1 152.3	244.6	35.7	558.2	82.4	231.4	1 003.6	793.9	318.8	-83.7	16.0	-9.4	148.7	67.4	81.3
4th quarter	1 183.1	248.9	34.5	579.1	83.2	237.4	1 012.6	801.2	322.5	-85.3	16.6	-9.1	170.5	67.9	102.6

Government Consumption Expenditures and Gross Investment[1]

(Calendar years—Billions of dollars, quarterly data are at seasonally adjusted annual rates)

Year and quarter	Total	Federal		Nondefense							
					Consumption expenditures				Services		
		Total	Defense	Total	Total	Durable [2]	Nondurable	Consumption expenditures	Compensation of general government employees	Capital consumption [3]	Other services
1970	236.1	115.9	90.6	25.3	21.9	-0.2	1.9	20.1	11.6	2.0	6.6
1971	249.9	117.1	88.7	28.3	24.6	-0.2	2.0	22.8	13.3	2.1	7.4
1972	268.9	125.1	93.2	31.9	27.8	-0.3	2.3	25.9	14.7	2.2	9.0
1973	287.6	128.2	94.7	33.5	29.2	-0.5	1.8	27.9	15.9	2.3	9.7
1974	323.2	139.9	101.9	38.0	33.2	-0.5	2.5	31.3	17.8	2.5	10.9
1975	362.6	154.5	110.9	43.6	38.0	-0.4	2.7	35.8	20.3	2.8	12.6
1976	385.9	162.7	116.1	46.6	40.4	-0.6	3.3	37.7	23.0	2.9	11.8
1977	416.9	178.4	125.8	52.6	45.7	-0.7	3.8	42.6	26.2	3.1	13.3
1978	457.9	194.4	135.6	58.9	50.4	-0.8	3.9	47.4	28.2	3.3	15.9
1979	507.1	215.0	151.2	63.8	55.2	-1.0	3.9	52.3	30.0	3.6	18.6
1980	572.8	248.4	174.2	74.2	64.3	-0.4	5.6	59.0	33.9	4.1	21.0
1981	633.4	284.1	202.0	82.2	71.7	-0.2	9.4	62.6	36.2	4.6	21.7
1982	684.8	313.2	230.9	82.3	72.3	0.1	7.3	65.0	37.8	5.0	22.2
1983	735.7	344.5	255.0	89.4	78.2	0.1	8.8	69.2	39.8	5.3	24.2
1984	796.6	372.6	282.7	89.9	77.9	0.1	5.0	72.8	41.7	5.6	25.4
1985	875.0	410.1	312.4	97.7	84.9	0.0	8.2	76.8	43.5	6.0	27.2
1986	938.5	435.2	332.4	102.9	89.7	-0.2	11.7	78.2	44.3	6.4	27.5
1987	992.8	455.7	350.4	105.3	90.7	-0.2	6.0	84.9	46.7	6.8	31.4
1988	1 032.0	457.3	354.0	103.3	89.9	-0.4	-0.7	91.1	51.0	7.2	32.8
1989	1 095.1	477.2	360.6	116.7	101.9	-0.3	5.2	97.1	54.0	7.8	35.4
1990	1 176.1	503.6	373.1	130.4	113.9	0.0	5.1	108.8	59.2	8.4	41.3
1991	1 225.9	522.6	383.5	139.1	120.6	0.0	5.6	115.0	64.1	8.9	42.0
1992	1 263.8	528.0	375.8	152.2	131.4	0.3	6.5	124.6	67.7	9.3	47.6
1993	1 283.4	518.3	360.7	157.7	136.2	0.5	6.9	128.8	72.5	9.7	46.6
1994	1 313.0	510.2	349.2	161.0	141.6	1.0	6.8	133.8	74.4	10.2	49.3
1995	1 356.4	509.1	344.4	164.7	144.7	0.8	6.5	137.3	76.1	10.7	50.5
1996	1 405.2	518.4	351.0	167.4	146.8	1.0	5.8	140.0	77.5	11.1	51.5
1997	1 454.6	520.2	346.0	174.3	154.2	1.0	6.8	146.3	80.2	11.5	54.7
1998	1 487.1	520.6	340.4	180.2	159.6	-0.3	7.9	152.0	82.7	12.1	57.2
1990:											
1st quarter	1 153.0	496.4	369.7	126.7	110.0	0.0	4.4	105.7	57.7	8.1	39.9
2nd quarter	1 164.3	500.1	370.6	129.5	112.9	-0.2	4.5	108.6	58.6	8.3	41.7
3rd quarter	1 176.9	501.2	368.9	132.3	115.9	-0.1	5.9	110.2	59.7	8.4	42.0
4th quarter	1 210.4	516.7	383.3	133.3	116.7	0.2	5.5	110.9	60.9	8.6	41.5
1991:											
1st quarter	1 220.6	525.6	389.7	136.0	119.3	0.5	6.7	112.1	63.6	8.7	39.8
2nd quarter	1 227.4	528.2	389.3	138.9	120.5	0.2	6.5	113.8	63.5	8.8	41.5
3rd quarter	1 226.5	520.9	382.1	138.8	120.6	-0.9	5.3	116.2	64.2	8.9	43.1
4th quarter	1 229.2	515.5	373.0	142.6	122.0	0.3	4.0	117.7	65.2	9.0	43.5
1992:											
1st quarter	1 247.9	521.8	372.8	149.0	128.5	0.5	5.1	122.9	66.8	9.1	46.9
2nd quarter	1 256.4	523.2	374.1	149.1	129.1	0.2	6.6	122.3	66.9	9.2	46.2
3rd quarter	1 270.7	532.0	380.9	151.1	130.9	-0.2	6.8	124.3	67.5	9.4	47.5
4th quarter	1 280.0	535.0	375.3	159.7	137.0	0.6	7.6	128.9	69.5	9.4	50.0
1993:											
1st quarter	1 271.5	521.3	363.6	157.7	134.7	0.3	6.9	127.5	71.8	9.6	46.1
2nd quarter	1 281.2	517.8	361.7	156.1	134.3	0.6	6.6	127.1	71.7	9.7	45.7
3rd quarter	1 285.3	515.7	358.0	157.7	136.4	0.5	6.4	129.5	73.1	9.8	46.6
4th quarter	1 295.5	518.5	359.4	159.1	139.4	0.7	7.5	131.3	73.5	9.9	47.9
1994:											
1st quarter	1 291.0	506.9	344.9	162.0	142.6	1.0	7.2	134.4	75.3	10.0	49.1
2nd quarter	1 300.8	505.3	348.5	156.8	138.5	0.8	7.0	130.7	75.4	10.2	45.2
3rd quarter	1 332.3	520.4	359.7	160.7	141.8	1.0	5.8	135.0	73.6	10.3	51.1
4th quarter	1 328.0	508.3	343.6	164.7	143.5	1.0	7.1	135.3	73.3	10.4	51.7
1995:											
1st quarter	1 344.1	512.3	346.1	166.2	144.3	1.1	7.0	136.2	76.0	10.5	49.7
2nd quarter	1 357.8	511.7	348.1	163.6	144.5	1.0	6.0	137.6	76.0	10.6	51.0
3rd quarter	1 362.3	511.2	345.5	165.7	146.1	0.8	6.6	138.7	76.5	10.8	51.5
4th quarter	1 361.4	501.2	337.9	163.3	143.8	0.5	6.5	136.8	76.1	10.9	49.8
1996:											
1st quarter	1 387.5	517.1	350.3	166.8	145.6	1.2	6.3	138.0	77.4	11.0	49.7
2nd quarter	1 406.0	523.1	355.6	167.4	147.2	1.1	5.8	140.3	77.7	11.0	51.6
3rd quarter	1 408.6	519.0	351.3	167.7	147.4	1.0	5.5	140.9	77.5	11.1	52.2
4th quarter	1 418.8	514.6	346.7	167.9	147.0	0.6	5.6	140.8	77.3	11.2	52.3
1997:											
1st quarter	1 439.4	517.0	341.1	175.9	153.0	1.1	6.5	145.4	80.2	11.3	53.9
2nd quarter	1 451.5	522.9	349.1	173.8	154.4	1.3	6.7	146.5	80.7	11.5	54.4
3rd quarter	1 459.5	521.0	347.1	173.9	154.0	0.9	6.7	146.4	80.3	11.5	54.6
4th quarter	1 468.1	520.1	346.5	173.6	155.3	0.9	7.4	147.0	79.5	11.7	55.8
1998:											
1st quarter	1 464.9	511.6	331.6	180.0	157.6	1.2	7.3	149.1	81.5	11.8	55.8
2nd quarter	1 481.2	520.7	339.8	180.9	160.9	1.3	7.6	152.0	82.3	11.9	57.9
3rd quarter	1 492.3	519.4	343.7	175.7	155.8	-4.8	8.1	152.5	82.7	12.2	57.5
4th quarter	1 510.2	530.7	346.4	184.3	164.0	1.1	8.4	154.5	84.4	12.4	57.8

1. Gross government investment consists of general government enterprise expenditures for fixed assets; inventory is included in government consumption expenditures.
2. Consumption expenditures for durable goods excludes expenditures classified as investment, except for goods transferred to foreign countries by the federal government. Total includes items not shown separately.
3. Consumption of general government fixed capital, or depreciation, is a partial measure of the value of the services of general government fixed assets; a zero net rate of return on these assets is assumed.

Government Consumption Expenditures and Gross Investment [1]—Continued

(Calendar years—Billions of dollars, quarterly data are at seasonally adjusted annual rates)

Year and quarter	Federal—Continued Nondefense—Continued Gross investment			State and local	Consumption expenditures			Gross investment		
	Total	Structures	Equipment	Total	Total [2]	Compensation of general government employees	Capital consumption [3]	Total	Structures	Equipment
1970	3.4	2.1	1.3	120.2	91.6	70.4	7.6	28.6	25.8	2.8
1971	3.8	2.5	1.3	132.8	102.9	78.5	8.5	29.9	27.0	2.9
1972	4.0	2.7	1.3	143.8	113.4	87.0	9.2	30.4	27.1	3.3
1973	4.3	3.1	1.2	159.4	126.4	97.1	10.2	33.0	29.1	3.8
1974	4.8	3.4	1.4	183.3	144.0	106.7	12.6	39.3	34.7	4.6
1975	5.5	4.1	1.4	208.1	164.9	120.2	14.3	43.2	38.1	5.1
1976	6.2	4.6	1.6	223.1	179.7	132.1	15.0	43.4	38.1	5.3
1977	6.9	5.0	1.9	238.5	196.1	144.1	15.9	42.4	36.9	5.4
1978	8.5	6.1	2.3	263.4	214.5	157.7	17.2	48.9	42.8	6.1
1979	8.6	6.3	2.4	292.0	235.9	173.2	19.3	56.1	49.0	7.1
1980	9.9	7.1	2.9	324.4	261.3	191.7	22.2	63.1	55.1	8.1
1981	10.5	7.7	2.8	349.2	285.3	208.7	25.3	64.0	55.4	8.5
1982	9.9	6.8	3.2	371.6	307.9	226.3	27.4	63.6	54.2	9.4
1983	11.3	6.7	4.5	391.2	326.2	242.0	28.3	65.0	54.2	10.8
1984	12.0	7.0	5.0	424.0	350.8	259.9	29.2	73.2	60.5	12.7
1985	12.8	7.3	5.4	464.9	382.6	283.4	30.7	82.3	67.6	14.8
1986	13.2	8.0	5.2	503.3	412.7	305.8	32.8	90.6	74.2	16.4
1987	14.6	9.0	5.6	537.2	441.1	327.2	35.2	96.0	78.8	17.2
1988	13.4	6.8	6.6	574.7	471.3	351.2	37.3	103.4	84.8	18.6
1989	14.7	6.9	7.9	617.9	507.2	377.5	39.7	110.6	88.7	21.9
1990	16.6	8.0	8.6	672.6	550.1	411.0	42.3	122.5	98.5	23.9
1991	18.5	9.2	9.3	703.4	579.4	434.8	44.7	123.9	100.5	23.4
1992	20.8	10.3	10.5	735.8	603.6	456.7	46.6	132.2	108.1	24.0
1993	21.5	11.2	10.2	765.0	631.6	479.5	48.8	133.4	108.7	24.7
1994	19.5	10.4	9.0	802.8	663.8	502.6	51.3	138.9	113.4	25.6
1995	20.0	10.9	9.1	847.3	695.2	524.0	54.4	152.1	123.1	29.0
1996	20.6	10.9	9.8	886.8	724.7	542.9	57.4	162.1	130.9	31.2
1997	20.1	10.0	10.0	934.4	758.8	566.7	60.5	175.6	142.4	33.2
1998	20.7	10.8	9.8	966.5	789.1	590.9	63.5	177.4	141.9	35.5
1990:										
1st quarter	16.7	8.2	8.5	656.6	535.3	399.5	41.3	121.3	97.7	23.6
2nd quarter	16.5	8.1	8.4	664.2	543.9	407.6	41.9	120.4	96.5	23.9
3rd quarter	16.4	8.1	8.3	675.7	554.0	415.0	42.8	121.7	97.6	24.1
4th quarter	16.6	7.6	9.1	693.7	567.3	421.8	43.4	126.5	102.4	24.1
1991:										
1st quarter	16.7	7.7	9.0	695.0	572.1	427.4	43.9	123.0	99.3	23.7
2nd quarter	18.4	9.1	9.3	699.2	576.9	433.1	44.5	122.4	99.0	23.3
3rd quarter	18.2	9.1	9.1	705.5	581.5	436.7	45.0	124.1	100.8	23.2
4th quarter	20.6	10.8	9.8	713.6	587.3	442.1	45.5	126.3	102.9	23.4
1992:										
1st quarter	20.4	10.3	10.1	726.1	592.6	448.0	45.8	133.5	109.9	23.6
2nd quarter	20.0	10.2	9.9	733.2	600.8	454.4	46.4	132.4	108.6	23.8
3rd quarter	20.2	9.6	10.5	738.7	607.4	459.4	46.9	131.3	107.1	24.2
4th quarter	22.6	11.0	11.6	745.1	613.6	464.9	47.4	131.5	106.9	24.6
1993:										
1st quarter	23.0	11.5	11.5	750.1	621.4	471.3	48.0	128.7	104.1	24.6
2nd quarter	21.7	10.9	10.8	763.4	628.9	476.9	48.6	134.5	109.9	24.6
3rd quarter	21.4	11.3	10.1	769.6	635.0	482.3	49.1	134.6	109.8	24.8
4th quarter	19.7	11.1	8.6	777.0	641.1	487.4	49.6	135.9	111.1	24.8
1994:										
1st quarter	19.4	10.3	9.1	784.1	651.6	494.2	50.3	132.5	107.2	25.3
2nd quarter	18.3	9.7	8.6	795.5	659.2	499.8	50.9	136.3	110.8	25.5
3rd quarter	18.9	9.9	8.9	811.9	668.6	505.7	51.7	143.3	117.6	25.8
4th quarter	21.2	11.8	9.4	819.6	676.0	510.9	52.3	143.6	117.9	25.8
1995:										
1st quarter	21.9	11.5	10.4	831.8	684.8	517.4	53.3	147.0	119.6	27.4
2nd quarter	19.1	10.8	8.3	846.2	693.5	522.3	54.0	152.6	124.0	28.6
3rd quarter	19.6	11.1	8.5	851.1	698.4	525.6	54.8	152.8	123.3	29.5
4th quarter	19.5	10.2	9.3	860.2	704.2	530.5	55.6	156.0	125.6	30.4
1996:										
1st quarter	21.2	10.5	10.7	870.4	712.6	534.9	56.4	157.9	127.4	30.5
2nd quarter	20.2	11.1	9.1	882.9	721.6	540.5	57.0	161.3	130.4	30.9
3rd quarter	20.3	10.9	9.4	889.6	727.8	545.5	57.8	161.7	130.3	31.4
4th quarter	20.9	11.0	9.9	904.2	736.7	550.7	58.5	167.5	135.6	31.9
1997:										
1st quarter	22.9	10.7	12.2	922.4	747.2	557.6	59.3	175.2	142.7	32.4
2nd quarter	19.3	10.0	9.4	928.6	754.0	563.7	60.1	174.6	141.6	32.9
3rd quarter	19.8	10.8	9.1	938.5	762.2	570.1	60.8	176.3	142.8	33.4
4th quarter	18.3	8.7	9.6	947.9	771.5	575.4	61.8	176.4	142.6	33.9
1998:										
1st quarter	22.4	10.6	11.8	953.3	776.7	581.1	62.4	176.6	142.0	34.6
2nd quarter	20.0	10.4	9.6	960.4	784.7	587.8	62.9	175.7	140.6	35.2
3rd quarter	19.9	11.3	8.6	972.9	793.9	594.2	63.9	179.0	143.2	35.8
4th quarter	20.4	11.0	9.4	979.5	801.2	600.3	64.8	178.3	141.8	36.5

1. Gross government investment consists of general government enterprise expenditures for fixed assests; inventory is included in government consumption expenditures.
2. Consumption expenditures for durable goods excludes expenditures classified as investment, except for goods transferred to foreign countries by the federal government. Total includes items not shown separately.
3. Consumption of general government fixed capital, or depreciation, is a partial measure of the value of the services of general government fixed assets; a zero net rate of return on these assets is assumed.

Real Government Consumption Expenditures and Gross Investment [1]

(Calendar years—Billions of chained [1992] dollars, quarterly data are at seasonally adjusted annual rates)

		Federal									
				Nondefense							
					Consumption expenditures						
								Services			
Year and quarter	Total	Total	Defense	Total	Total	Durable [2]	Nondurable	Consumption expenditures	Compensation of general government employees	Capital consumption [3]	Other services
1970	866.8	427.2	349.0	83.1	74.6	-1.2	2.8	75.1	48.8	5.4	21.6
1971	851.0	397.0	313.7	86.3	77.5	-1.1	3.0	78.2	50.3	5.3	23.2
1972	854.1	390.2	300.3	91.9	83.0	-1.3	3.8	83.4	51.8	5.3	26.8
1973	848.4	371.1	281.2	91.5	82.3	-1.2	3.0	84.3	52.1	5.3	27.4
1974	862.9	368.8	273.6	96.4	87.3	-1.3	4.2	87.7	54.8	5.3	28.3
1975	876.3	367.9	269.7	99.1	89.9	-1.2	4.0	90.2	55.9	5.2	29.8
1976	876.8	364.3	264.7	100.4	90.2	-1.4	4.8	89.4	58.8	5.2	26.5
1977	884.7	370.1	266.4	104.3	93.6	-1.3	5.2	92.2	60.1	5.3	27.9
1978	910.6	377.7	266.8	111.4	98.1	-1.3	5.2	97.1	61.7	5.4	31.1
1979	924.9	383.3	271.0	112.7	100.4	-1.6	5.2	100.0	61.6	5.5	33.7
1980	941.4	399.3	280.7	119.0	106.0	-0.6	6.2	102.4	63.3	5.7	34.2
1981	947.7	415.9	296.0	120.4	107.9	-0.5	10.5	98.6	61.5	5.8	32.1
1982	960.1	429.4	316.5	113.3	102.3	-0.1	7.6	95.7	60.3	5.9	30.3
1983	987.3	452.7	334.6	118.5	105.9	0.0	7.4	98.3	61.2	6.2	31.7
1984	1 018.4	463.7	348.1	115.9	102.3	0.0	5.2	99.2	61.2	6.5	32.1
1985	1 080.1	495.6	374.1	121.8	107.4	-0.2	7.5	101.0	61.4	6.9	33.2
1986	1 135.0	518.4	393.4	125.2	110.6	-0.4	9.7	99.9	60.5	7.2	32.7
1987	1 165.9	534.4	409.2	125.3	109.2	-0.4	4.3	105.3	61.5	7.5	36.4
1988	1 180.9	524.6	405.5	119.1	104.8	-0.7	-1.2	107.8	63.1	7.8	37.0
1989	1 213.9	531.5	401.6	130.1	114.8	-0.5	5.2	110.0	63.5	8.1	38.5
1990	1 250.4	541.9	401.5	140.5	123.8	-0.2	5.2	118.9	66.6	8.6	43.8
1991	1 258.0	539.4	397.5	142.0	123.6	-0.2	5.3	118.4	66.5	8.9	43.0
1992	1 263.8	528.0	375.8	152.2	131.4	0.3	6.5	124.6	67.7	9.3	47.6
1993	1 252.1	505.7	354.4	151.2	129.9	0.6	6.4	122.9	67.4	9.6	45.9
1994	1 252.3	486.6	336.9	149.5	130.4	1.1	6.1	123.2	65.5	9.9	47.9
1995	1 254.5	470.6	323.5	146.9	127.5	1.0	5.8	120.8	62.9	10.2	47.9
1996	1 268.2	465.6	319.1	146.2	126.1	1.2	5.2	119.6	61.2	10.6	48.3
1997	1 285.0	458.0	308.9	148.6	128.7	1.4	6.1	121.4	60.8	11.0	50.3
1998	1 296.9	453.3	300.4	152.1	131.5	0.3	7.2	124.2	61.5	11.6	52.1
1990:											
1st quarter	1 246.5	542.9	404.1	138.9	122.0	-0.2	4.5	117.8	66.5	8.4	42.9
2nd quarter	1 248.2	543.0	402.8	140.4	123.7	-0.4	4.5	119.8	66.8	8.5	44.4
3rd quarter	1 246.8	538.2	396.1	142.2	125.7	-0.3	5.9	120.2	67.4	8.6	44.2
4th quarter	1 259.9	543.5	403.1	140.5	124.0	0.0	5.9	118.0	65.8	8.7	43.5
1991:											
1st quarter	1 262.6	547.3	408.4	139.0	122.4	0.3	6.0	116.1	66.1	8.8	41.2
2nd quarter	1 263.8	547.1	405.0	142.2	123.8	0.0	6.3	117.5	65.9	8.9	42.7
3rd quarter	1 255.1	536.3	395.0	141.4	123.2	-1.1	5.2	119.2	66.2	9.0	44.0
4th quarter	1 250.7	526.9	381.7	145.3	124.7	0.1	3.8	120.8	67.7	9.1	44.0
1992:											
1st quarter	1 258.5	525.1	374.2	150.8	130.4	0.4	5.2	124.7	68.2	9.2	47.3
2nd quarter	1 257.5	523.3	373.3	150.0	129.9	0.1	6.6	123.2	67.6	9.3	46.4
3rd quarter	1 266.5	529.6	378.7	150.9	130.7	-0.2	6.8	124.1	67.5	9.3	47.3
4th quarter	1 272.5	534.0	376.8	157.1	134.5	0.6	7.5	126.3	67.3	9.4	49.6
1993:											
1st quarter	1 250.1	512.1	359.2	152.9	130.0	0.4	6.4	123.1	68.0	9.5	45.6
2nd quarter	1 253.1	507.8	356.7	151.1	129.5	0.7	6.2	122.6	67.9	9.6	45.1
3rd quarter	1 250.5	501.5	351.1	150.3	129.1	0.6	5.8	122.7	67.2	9.6	45.8
4th quarter	1 254.7	501.3	350.8	150.4	130.8	0.8	7.0	123.1	66.5	9.7	46.9
1994:											
1st quarter	1 241.9	487.2	335.1	151.9	132.7	1.1	6.7	124.9	67.0	9.8	48.1
2nd quarter	1 243.3	481.2	335.9	145.1	127.1	0.9	6.5	119.7	65.7	9.9	44.0
3rd quarter	1 268.1	496.4	347.0	149.4	130.8	1.1	5.1	124.4	65.2	9.9	49.6
4th quarter	1 255.8	481.7	329.6	151.7	131.1	1.2	6.3	123.6	64.0	10.0	49.9
1995:											
1st quarter	1 256.2	478.6	328.3	150.0	128.8	1.2	6.3	121.4	63.9	10.1	47.6
2nd quarter	1 259.9	476.2	328.4	147.6	129.0	1.1	5.2	122.8	64.4	10.2	48.4
3rd quarter	1 257.6	473.1	323.9	148.8	129.9	0.9	5.9	123.0	64.3	10.3	48.7
4th quarter	1 244.5	454.6	313.3	141.1	122.3	0.7	5.8	115.9	58.9	10.4	47.1
1996:											
1st quarter	1 254.5	463.5	318.7	144.5	124.0	1.4	5.6	117.0	60.0	10.5	47.0
2nd quarter	1 276.2	472.6	325.0	147.3	127.5	1.3	5.2	121.0	62.3	10.6	48.5
3rd quarter	1 271.1	467.0	319.8	146.8	127.0	1.3	4.9	120.7	61.7	10.7	48.9
4th quarter	1 271.2	459.5	313.0	146.1	125.7	1.0	5.2	119.7	60.8	10.8	48.7
1997:											
1st quarter	1 277.7	456.3	305.0	150.7	128.5	1.4	5.8	121.3	61.1	10.9	50.0
2nd quarter	1 284.4	460.4	311.7	148.2	129.0	1.6	5.9	121.6	61.3	11.0	50.0
3rd quarter	1 288.9	458.9	310.2	148.2	128.5	1.3	6.0	121.3	61.0	11.1	50.0
4th quarter	1 289.2	456.5	308.7	147.3	129.0	1.3	6.6	121.2	59.9	11.2	51.1
1998:											
1st quarter	1 283.0	446.1	293.3	151.9	130.0	1.5	6.6	122.0	60.7	11.3	51.0
2nd quarter	1 294.8	454.1	300.3	152.9	132.9	1.7	6.9	124.5	61.4	11.4	52.8
3rd quarter	1 299.6	452.5	303.5	148.4	128.4	-3.3	7.6	124.5	61.5	11.7	52.2
4th quarter	1 310.3	460.6	304.6	155.2	134.6	1.4	7.8	125.8	62.6	11.8	52.3

1. Gross government investment consists of general government enterprise expenditures for fixed assests; inventory is included in government consumption expenditures.
2. Consumption expenditures for durable goods excludes expenditures classified as investment, except for goods transferred to foreign countries by the federal government. Total includes items not shown separately.
3. Consumption of general government fixed capital, or depreciation, is a partial measure of the value of the services of general government fixed assets; a zero net rate of return on these assets is assumed.

Real Government Consumption Expenditures and Gross Investment [1]—Continued

(Calendar years—Billions of chained [1992] dollars, quarterly data are at seasonally adjusted annual rates)

Year and quarter	Federal—Continued / Nondefense—Continued / Gross investment			State and local	Consumption expenditures			Gross investment		
	Total	Structures	Equipment	Total	Total [2]	Compensation of general government employees	Capital consumption [3]	Total	Structures	Equipment
1970	8.8	7.1	1.9	440.0	344.1	297.1	23.0	91.3	86.0	6.7
1971	9.1	7.9	1.8	454.4	362.1	309.6	23.9	88.6	83.1	6.8
1972	9.4	8.1	1.8	464.5	376.0	321.4	24.8	85.6	78.9	7.6
1973	9.5	8.7	1.6	478.5	389.9	333.6	25.7	86.0	78.3	8.5
1974	9.6	8.5	1.8	495.6	406.8	344.8	26.6	86.7	78.1	9.3
1975	9.8	8.9	1.7	510.0	423.2	353.1	27.5	85.8	77.4	9.0
1976	10.6	9.5	1.9	514.3	429.5	357.3	28.3	84.3	76.1	8.8
1977	11.1	9.8	2.1	516.4	437.7	362.9	29.0	79.3	71.3	8.6
1978	13.2	11.3	2.7	534.7	448.1	371.2	29.8	86.4	78.1	9.0
1979	12.5	10.6	2.6	543.5	452.3	377.4	30.7	90.5	81.4	9.8
1980	13.2	10.7	3.1	543.6	451.7	381.4	31.5	91.1	81.3	10.3
1981	12.8	10.5	2.9	532.8	450.3	380.4	32.2	83.0	73.3	10.1
1982	11.5	8.6	3.2	531.4	455.6	382.0	32.7	77.4	67.0	10.7
1983	12.9	8.4	4.7	534.9	458.2	379.2	33.4	78.3	66.3	12.1
1984	13.8	8.7	5.2	555.0	467.9	380.9	34.5	87.8	73.8	14.2
1985	14.5	8.9	5.7	584.7	487.8	391.0	35.7	97.2	80.9	16.4
1986	14.7	9.4	5.4	616.9	513.3	403.3	37.1	103.9	85.9	18.0
1987	16.1	10.3	5.9	631.8	525.5	410.7	38.5	106.5	87.8	18.8
1988	14.4	7.6	6.8	656.6	545.3	424.5	39.9	111.5	91.6	20.0
1989	15.3	7.4	7.9	682.6	566.3	437.4	41.6	116.5	93.5	23.0
1990	16.8	8.3	8.5	708.6	583.2	448.1	43.2	125.4	100.7	24.7
1991	18.4	9.3	9.2	718.7	593.8	452.0	44.9	124.9	101.3	23.6
1992	20.8	10.3	10.5	735.8	603.6	456.7	46.6	132.2	108.1	24.0
1993	21.3	11.0	10.3	746.4	615.8	463.2	48.1	130.6	106.1	24.5
1994	19.0	9.9	9.1	765.7	633.4	471.6	49.4	132.2	107.1	25.2
1995	19.3	9.9	9.4	783.9	644.0	477.8	50.9	139.9	111.5	28.6
1996	20.2	9.6	10.7	802.7	656.8	484.5	52.7	145.8	114.9	31.1
1997	19.8	8.6	11.6	827.1	672.3	492.8	54.8	154.8	121.0	34.3
1998	20.7	8.9	12.1	843.8	689.3	501.9	57.0	154.4	117.5	38.3
1990:										
1st quarter	17.0	8.5	8.5	703.8	578.1	444.9	42.6	125.6	101.0	24.6
2nd quarter	16.8	8.4	8.3	705.4	581.6	447.3	43.0	123.8	99.0	24.8
3rd quarter	16.5	8.4	8.2	708.7	585.0	449.3	43.4	123.8	99.0	24.8
4th quarter	16.7	7.7	8.9	716.5	588.2	450.8	43.8	128.3	103.7	24.6
1991:										
1st quarter	16.7	7.9	8.8	715.5	590.9	451.4	44.3	124.6	100.6	23.9
2nd quarter	18.4	9.2	9.2	716.8	593.5	452.4	44.7	123.3	99.7	23.7
3rd quarter	18.2	9.1	9.0	718.8	594.2	451.7	45.1	124.7	101.2	23.5
4th quarter	20.6	10.9	9.7	723.8	596.7	452.8	45.6	127.1	103.7	23.4
1992:										
1st quarter	20.5	10.4	10.1	733.5	599.0	454.1	46.0	134.4	110.8	23.6
2nd quarter	20.1	10.2	9.8	734.2	601.7	455.5	46.4	132.6	108.8	23.8
3rd quarter	20.1	9.6	10.5	736.9	605.9	458.2	46.9	131.0	106.8	24.2
4th quarter	22.6	10.9	11.7	738.5	607.9	459.0	47.3	130.6	106.1	24.6
1993:										
1st quarter	23.0	11.4	11.5	738.0	610.8	460.7	47.6	127.1	102.7	24.5
2nd quarter	21.6	10.7	10.9	745.3	613.5	462.3	47.9	131.8	107.4	24.4
3rd quarter	21.2	11.0	10.2	749.1	617.5	464.0	48.3	131.5	107.0	24.5
4th quarter	19.5	10.8	8.7	753.4	621.5	466.0	48.6	131.9	107.2	24.7
1994:										
1st quarter	19.1	9.9	9.2	754.7	627.2	467.9	48.9	127.6	102.7	24.9
2nd quarter	18.0	9.3	8.7	762.2	631.6	470.8	49.2	130.6	105.5	25.0
3rd quarter	18.4	9.4	9.0	771.7	635.9	473.1	49.5	135.8	110.6	25.2
4th quarter	20.7	11.1	9.6	774.1	639.0	474.6	49.9	135.0	109.6	25.4
1995:										
1st quarter	21.2	10.7	10.6	777.6	641.0	476.4	50.3	136.6	109.6	27.0
2nd quarter	18.4	9.8	8.5	783.7	642.8	477.3	50.7	140.9	112.7	28.2
3rd quarter	18.9	10.0	8.8	784.5	644.3	477.8	51.1	140.1	111.2	29.1
4th quarter	18.8	9.2	9.7	790.0	647.8	479.9	51.5	142.1	112.3	30.0
1996:										
1st quarter	20.5	9.4	11.3	791.0	648.1	478.1	52.0	142.9	112.9	30.2
2nd quarter	19.8	9.9	9.9	803.6	657.9	486.4	52.5	145.7	115.1	30.8
3rd quarter	19.9	9.6	10.3	804.2	659.1	486.2	53.0	145.1	114.0	31.4
4th quarter	20.4	9.6	11.0	811.8	662.2	487.4	53.5	149.6	117.8	32.1
1997:										
1st quarter	22.5	9.3	13.8	821.5	665.9	489.0	54.0	155.5	122.7	33.0
2nd quarter	19.1	8.5	10.8	824.2	670.1	491.7	54.5	154.0	120.6	33.9
3rd quarter	19.6	9.2	10.6	830.1	674.7	494.4	55.0	155.3	121.0	34.8
4th quarter	18.1	7.3	11.3	832.9	678.5	496.2	55.6	154.3	119.5	35.5
1998:										
1st quarter	22.2	8.8	14.1	837.1	682.8	498.1	56.1	154.2	118.5	36.7
2nd quarter	19.9	8.6	11.7	840.9	687.3	500.9	56.7	153.5	117.0	37.7
3rd quarter	19.9	9.3	10.7	847.3	691.6	503.4	57.2	155.6	118.2	38.8
4th quarter	20.5	9.0	11.8	850.0	695.6	505.3	57.8	154.3	116.1	39.8

1. Gross government investment consists of general government enterprise expenditures for fixed assests; inventory is included in government consumption expenditures.
2. Consumption expenditures for durable goods excludes expenditures classified as investment, except for goods transferred to foreign countries by the federal government. Total includes items not shown separately.
3. Consumption of general government fixed capital, or depreciation, is a partial measure of the value of the services of general government fixed assets; a zero net rate of return on these assets is assumed.

National Defense Consumption Expenditures and Gross Investment [1]

(Calendar years—Billions of dollars, quarterly data are at seasonally adjusted annual rates)

Year and quarter	Total	Consumption expenditures Total	Durable goods [2] Aircraft	Missiles	Ships	Vehicles	Electronics	Other durable goods	Nondurable goods Petroleum products	Ammunition	Other nondurable goods	Services Employee compensation	Capital consumption [3]	Research and development
1970	90.6	78.6	.....	.....	.....	.....	.....	.....	.....	.....	.....	.....	.....	.....
1971	88.7	79.2	.....	.....	.....	.....	.....	.....	.....	.....	.....	.....	.....	.....
1972	93.2	82.3	3.0	1.2	0.2	0.4	0.8	0.2	1.8	2.0	0.9	40.5	15.6	5.2
1973	94.7	83.7	2.8	1.2	0.2	0.4	0.8	-0.1	1.7	1.7	0.9	41.4	17.1	5.4
1974	101.9	90.1	2.2	1.4	0.2	0.5	0.8	-0.5	2.8	1.4	1.1	44.1	18.9	5.9
1975	110.9	97.0	2.3	1.6	0.3	0.8	0.9	0.6	2.9	1.1	1.1	47.9	20.5	6.1
1976	116.1	101.3	2.2	1.3	0.3	0.6	0.7	0.9	2.5	0.6	1.4	50.2	21.7	6.6
1977	125.8	109.6	3.3	1.5	0.5	0.8	0.8	0.9	2.4	0.8	1.3	53.6	23.1	7.1
1978	135.6	118.4	3.6	2.3	0.7	1.1	1.0	1.0	2.5	1.0	1.3	57.5	24.8	7.4
1979	151.2	130.7	4.9	2.2	0.9	1.2	1.1	1.3	3.6	1.2	1.5	61.7	26.9	8.1
1980	174.2	150.9	5.6	2.3	0.7	1.5	1.4	1.3	6.8	1.4	1.9	68.5	28.9	10.4
1981	202.0	174.3	7.8	2.7	0.6	1.7	1.7	1.5	7.7	1.6	2.6	78.8	31.3	12.6
1982	230.9	197.6	10.3	3.0	0.4	1.7	2.0	1.7	6.8	2.1	2.7	87.4	33.6	14.4
1983	255.0	214.9	13.6	3.7	1.2	2.3	2.4	1.9	6.4	2.5	2.5	92.4	35.9	16.4
1984	282.7	236.3	14.0	4.0	1.0	2.8	2.7	2.4	5.9	2.2	2.3	107.5	35.8	18.7
1985	312.4	257.6	15.4	3.9	0.8	2.9	3.2	3.0	5.8	1.3	2.9	115.3	38.6	23.0
1986	332.4	272.7	17.2	4.6	0.8	3.2	3.3	2.7	3.6	3.6	3.1	118.7	41.6	25.4
1987	350.4	287.6	18.2	4.7	1.0	3.1	3.7	3.0	3.9	2.8	3.6	124.4	43.3	26.9
1988	354.0	297.9	18.3	5.1	1.1	2.6	3.6	3.1	3.5	3.5	3.6	126.4	45.3	32.4
1989	360.6	303.3	16.0	5.1	1.0	1.6	3.8	3.7	4.2	3.1	3.6	131.4	47.3	32.6
1990	373.1	312.7	16.3	5.3	1.7	1.5	3.8	3.5	5.3	2.8	2.9	134.8	50.2	30.8
1991	383.5	325.4	16.5	5.5	1.9	1.7	3.4	4.8	4.7	2.7	3.4	142.3	52.8	25.0
1992	375.8	319.7	14.0	4.8	2.1	1.3	3.3	4.6	3.5	2.6	3.4	143.1	54.2	26.1
1993	360.7	311.1	11.4	4.1	2.3	1.3	3.5	4.4	3.2	2.4	2.8	138.8	55.7	26.0
1994	349.2	301.6	9.4	3.5	1.6	0.8	3.1	4.6	3.0	1.7	2.8	133.8	56.7	25.0
1995	344.4	298.2	8.9	3.0	1.2	0.9	2.5	4.6	2.8	1.2	2.4	131.2	57.3	22.8
1996	351.0	304.1	9.0	3.0	0.9	0.8	2.5	4.9	3.4	1.3	2.9	133.8	56.8	25.9
1997	346.0	306.3	9.6	2.6	0.7	0.9	2.6	4.3	2.9	1.5	3.0	133.3	56.3	28.9
1998	340.4	301.5	10.1	2.4	0.6	1.0	2.5	4.6	1.9	1.7	3.1	132.2	54.8	27.0
1990:														
1st quarter	369.7	311.7	15.8	5.7	1.4	1.3	4.1	4.0	4.4	2.9	2.8	133.7	49.2	34.0
2nd quarter	370.6	310.8	15.9	4.9	1.8	1.5	3.4	4.7	4.1	2.9	3.1	134.0	49.4	32.3
3rd quarter	368.9	307.3	15.4	5.6	1.7	1.5	4.2	3.0	4.1	2.4	2.9	134.6	50.3	28.4
4th quarter	383.3	321.0	18.1	4.9	1.9	1.6	3.4	2.3	8.7	3.0	2.9	137.0	52.1	28.5
1991:														
1st quarter	389.7	331.3	16.4	5.7	1.7	1.6	3.7	5.3	6.6	2.8	3.8	143.9	51.7	24.8
2nd quarter	389.3	328.6	16.5	5.7	2.0	2.2	4.0	4.2	3.9	2.7	3.2	143.3	52.8	24.6
3rd quarter	382.1	323.1	16.4	5.9	2.2	1.6	3.3	4.7	4.5	2.4	3.0	141.7	53.1	24.4
4th quarter	373.0	318.5	16.6	4.8	1.9	1.4	2.8	4.8	3.6	2.7	3.5	140.1	53.5	26.3
1992:														
1st quarter	372.8	317.2	15.0	4.8	2.0	1.2	3.2	4.8	3.3	1.8	3.6	144.6	53.7	26.2
2nd quarter	374.1	317.3	13.8	4.6	1.9	1.3	3.1	4.2	3.6	3.4	3.3	145.4	54.2	23.2
3rd quarter	380.9	323.5	13.8	5.1	2.1	1.3	3.5	4.7	4.0	2.5	3.5	144.0	54.3	26.2
4th quarter	375.3	320.7	13.2	4.6	2.4	1.4	3.3	4.8	3.1	2.4	3.3	138.4	54.7	28.8
1993:														
1st quarter	363.6	312.4	11.4	4.3	1.9	1.3	3.6	4.4	3.0	2.4	2.7	142.4	55.1	26.0
2nd quarter	361.7	311.5	12.3	4.2	3.6	1.5	3.9	4.6	3.5	2.6	2.7	139.4	55.3	25.1
3rd quarter	358.0	310.6	11.6	4.1	1.7	1.2	3.4	4.3	3.4	2.6	3.1	138.1	56.1	25.2
4th quarter	359.4	309.8	10.3	4.0	1.8	1.0	3.0	4.3	2.9	2.1	2.6	135.4	56.4	27.7
1994:														
1st quarter	344.9	299.8	9.1	3.9	1.7	0.8	3.3	4.4	2.5	1.8	2.5	135.6	56.6	24.4
2nd quarter	348.5	300.7	8.5	3.3	1.6	0.8	3.2	4.7	3.4	1.5	2.2	135.2	56.9	26.0
3rd quarter	359.7	308.7	10.7	3.8	1.6	0.8	3.1	4.9	3.5	1.4	3.2	133.2	56.5	26.1
4th quarter	343.6	297.3	9.1	2.9	1.5	0.9	2.9	4.6	2.8	2.3	3.1	131.5	56.8	23.6
1995:														
1st quarter	346.1	298.7	9.9	2.6	1.1	0.9	2.6	4.5	2.6	1.1	2.3	132.6	57.1	22.7
2nd quarter	348.1	300.2	7.0	3.3	1.3	1.0	2.4	4.8	2.8	1.3	2.5	131.0	57.4	24.2
3rd quarter	345.5	301.1	10.5	3.6	1.6	1.1	2.7	4.4	3.3	1.1	2.3	131.2	57.3	22.5
4th quarter	337.9	292.7	8.0	2.7	0.9	0.7	2.2	4.6	2.4	1.1	2.4	130.0	57.5	21.9
1996:														
1st quarter	350.3	300.1	8.8	2.7	0.7	0.8	2.2	4.6	3.1	1.4	2.4	133.8	57.0	23.9
2nd quarter	355.6	305.9	9.0	3.2	0.9	0.7	2.8	5.4	3.4	1.6	3.1	134.1	57.0	25.1
3rd quarter	351.3	305.5	9.3	3.4	1.3	0.9	2.8	5.1	4.1	1.3	3.2	134.2	56.6	25.5
4th quarter	346.7	304.7	9.0	2.7	0.6	0.8	2.2	4.7	3.0	0.9	3.0	133.0	56.7	29.0
1997:														
1st quarter	341.1	303.8	9.7	2.5	0.7	0.9	2.6	4.2	3.1	1.7	3.0	134.6	56.7	26.5
2nd quarter	349.1	310.4	10.3	2.6	0.7	0.9	2.7	4.5	3.1	1.5	2.7	133.5	56.7	31.3
3rd quarter	347.1	306.0	8.7	2.5	0.7	0.9	2.7	4.1	3.1	1.2	3.2	133.1	56.0	29.3
4th quarter	346.5	304.8	9.7	2.7	0.7	1.0	2.4	4.4	2.5	1.7	3.1	131.9	55.7	28.6
1998:														
1st quarter	331.6	293.3	9.3	2.4	0.7	1.0	2.6	4.4	2.0	1.4	3.1	133.4	55.3	22.0
2nd quarter	339.8	303.0	10.1	2.2	0.6	0.9	2.5	4.6	2.0	1.2	3.1	132.2	54.8	27.5
3rd quarter	343.7	302.9	9.9	2.7	0.6	1.0	2.5	5.1	2.0	2.3	3.0	132.3	54.5	28.4
4th quarter	346.4	306.7	10.9	2.3	0.7	1.0	2.4	4.4	1.7	1.8	3.2	130.9	54.7	29.9

1. Gross government investment consits of general government and government enterprise expenditures for fixed assets; inventory investment is included is included in government consumption expenditures.
2. Consumption expenditures for durable goods excludes expenditures classified as investment, except for goods transferred to foreign countries by the federal government.
3. Consumption of general government fixed capital, or depreciation, is a partial measure of the value of the services of general government fixed assets; a zero net rate of return on these assets is assumed.

National Defense Consumption Expenditures and Gross Investment [1]—*Continued*

(Calendar years—Billions of dollars, quarterly data are at seasonally adjusted annual rates)

Year and quarter	Consumption expenditures—*Continued* Services—*Continued*						Gross investment							
							Total	Structures	Equipment					
	Installation support	Weapons support	Personnel support	Transportation of material	Travel of persons	Other services			Aircraft	Missiles	Ships	Vehicles	Electronics	Other equipment
1970	.....	.....	.....	.....	.....	.....	12.1	1.3	.....	.....	.....	.....	.....	.....
1971	.....	.....	.....	.....	.....	.....	9.5	1.8	.....	.....	.....	.....	.....	.....
1972	4.4	1.6	1.9	1.8	0.9	-0.2	10.9	1.8	2.6	1.5	1.8	0.4	0.6	2.2
1973	4.3	1.6	1.8	1.6	1.0	-0.1	11.0	2.1	2.3	1.5	1.6	0.3	0.6	2.5
1974	4.7	1.8	2.0	1.7	1.1	-0.2	11.9	2.2	2.3	1.7	2.2	0.3	0.6	2.6
1975	4.9	1.7	2.2	1.8	1.0	-0.8	14.0	2.3	3.6	1.3	2.2	0.3	0.7	3.6
1976	5.4	1.9	2.4	1.8	1.0	-0.2	14.8	2.1	3.4	1.4	2.4	0.5	0.8	4.2
1977	6.2	2.1	2.4	1.9	1.2	-0.4	16.2	2.4	3.7	1.2	3.1	0.6	0.9	4.2
1978	6.3	2.4	2.8	1.9	1.4	-0.5	17.1	2.5	3.7	1.1	3.9	0.8	1.1	4.0
1979	7.3	2.9	3.0	2.2	1.3	-0.5	20.6	2.5	4.8	1.8	4.3	0.9	1.2	5.0
1980	8.8	4.4	3.4	2.6	1.6	-0.7	23.3	3.2	6.1	2.3	4.1	1.2	1.6	4.8
1981	9.9	5.2	4.5	2.8	2.1	-0.8	27.7	3.2	7.5	2.8	5.1	1.1	2.0	6.1
1982	14.0	6.0	6.3	3.1	2.6	-0.7	33.3	4.0	8.4	3.4	6.2	2.1	2.4	6.8
1983	14.3	7.3	6.8	3.4	2.4	-0.5	40.2	4.8	10.1	4.6	7.1	3.4	2.9	7.3
1984	15.5	8.6	7.2	3.3	2.9	-0.7	46.4	4.9	10.9	5.7	8.0	4.2	3.4	9.3
1985	17.2	9.8	8.9	3.1	3.1	-0.7	54.8	6.2	13.4	6.6	9.0	3.7	4.3	11.5
1986	18.6	10.4	9.9	3.4	3.3	-0.8	59.7	6.8	17.9	7.9	8.9	3.8	4.6	9.9
1987	20.1	11.0	11.6	3.5	3.7	-0.8	62.8	7.7	17.6	8.7	8.8	4.3	5.1	10.6
1988	20.3	10.7	12.1	3.6	3.7	-1.1	56.1	7.4	13.6	7.8	8.6	3.7	4.9	10.1
1989	20.0	9.9	12.7	4.0	4.0	-1.0	57.3	6.4	12.2	8.9	10.0	3.1	4.7	12.0
1990	21.9	10.7	13.4	4.8	4.1	-1.1	60.4	6.1	12.2	10.9	10.8	3.2	4.7	12.5
1991	23.5	9.7	13.4	8.8	7.0	-1.6	58.1	4.6	9.6	10.7	10.2	3.4	4.2	15.4
1992	23.3	8.8	15.7	5.9	5.4	-2.3	56.1	5.2	8.7	10.5	10.1	2.8	4.2	14.7
1993	25.3	7.4	15.5	4.6	4.9	-2.6	49.6	5.1	9.3	7.9	8.7	1.9	4.4	12.3
1994	26.1	8.4	16.9	3.8	4.4	-4.0	47.6	5.8	10.4	5.7	8.1	1.0	4.0	12.6
1995	26.7	7.6	18.2	4.3	4.2	-1.6	46.2	6.3	9.0	4.7	8.0	1.1	3.5	13.6
1996	27.2	5.7	18.8	4.9	4.0	-1.9	46.9	6.7	9.2	4.3	6.8	1.1	3.5	15.3
1997	26.3	6.4	20.1	4.6	3.6	-1.3	39.7	5.7	6.0	3.0	6.1	1.5	3.6	13.9
1998	25.5	6.1	20.8	4.7	3.5	-1.0	38.9	5.2	5.6	2.9	6.4	1.5	3.4	13.8
1990:														
1st quarter	22.6	10.4	13.5	3.7	3.4	-1.1	58.0	6.3	10.8	10.4	10.0	3.1	5.0	12.3
2nd quarter	20.7	10.8	13.8	4.4	4.2	-1.1	59.8	6.3	12.9	9.6	10.6	3.3	4.4	12.7
3rd quarter	21.9	10.6	12.5	5.2	4.2	-1.1	61.6	6.4	13.0	11.3	10.3	3.5	5.0	12.1
4th quarter	22.4	11.1	13.8	5.9	4.5	-1.0	62.3	5.3	12.2	12.4	12.2	2.9	4.2	13.0
1991:														
1st quarter	24.4	11.3	13.6	9.5	6.1	-1.6	58.4	4.8	9.0	11.6	9.8	2.9	4.5	15.7
2nd quarter	23.2	9.7	12.6	11.0	8.4	-1.5	60.7	4.8	10.6	11.1	10.6	4.3	4.8	14.5
3rd quarter	21.9	8.6	12.7	9.6	9.4	-2.2	59.0	4.5	10.1	10.6	10.2	4.3	4.0	15.3
4th quarter	24.6	8.9	14.7	5.1	4.1	-1.0	54.5	4.5	8.4	9.4	10.2	2.3	3.6	16.0
1992:														
1st quarter	22.2	8.9	15.2	4.7	4.1	-2.1	55.6	5.2	7.9	9.8	10.7	2.4	4.4	15.2
2nd quarter	22.0	8.1	14.2	8.0	6.1	-3.1	56.9	5.5	10.1	10.9	10.4	2.2	3.7	14.0
3rd quarter	22.3	8.8	15.3	7.6	7.1	-2.8	57.4	4.8	9.0	11.0	9.9	3.4	4.5	14.9
4th quarter	26.6	9.4	18.0	3.5	4.2	-1.4	54.6	5.5	7.7	10.2	9.3	3.1	4.1	14.6
1993:														
1st quarter	24.6	8.2	16.2	3.3	4.2	-2.5	51.2	4.8	8.2	8.7	9.2	3.0	4.7	12.7
2nd quarter	24.9	6.4	14.8	4.3	5.0	-2.6	50.3	4.9	7.9	8.4	9.0	1.8	5.0	13.4
3rd quarter	25.2	6.6	15.5	6.2	5.8	-3.6	47.4	5.4	9.6	6.5	8.2	1.4	4.3	12.0
4th quarter	26.3	8.4	15.6	4.8	4.8	-1.7	49.6	5.3	11.8	8.0	8.2	1.3	3.8	11.3
1994:														
1st quarter	26.5	7.9	15.5	3.9	3.6	-4.1	45.1	5.4	7.9	6.6	7.6	1.1	4.3	12.3
2nd quarter	26.0	8.2	16.1	4.0	4.4	-5.2	47.7	5.5	9.9	5.6	8.7	1.2	4.0	12.8
3rd quarter	25.7	9.5	18.1	3.7	5.8	-2.8	51.1	6.1	12.5	5.7	8.8	0.8	4.1	13.0
4th quarter	26.2	7.9	17.8	3.6	3.8	-4.0	46.3	6.1	11.5	4.8	7.1	1.0	3.7	12.2
1995:														
1st quarter	26.6	7.7	17.9	3.8	4.1	-1.5	47.4	6.9	9.3	4.1	8.7	1.2	3.9	13.3
2nd quarter	27.2	8.0	18.2	4.2	4.3	-0.6	47.9	6.1	9.1	5.8	8.5	1.0	3.2	14.1
3rd quarter	26.7	7.6	18.4	4.3	4.3	-1.8	44.5	6.0	8.1	5.1	7.6	1.2	3.7	13.0
4th quarter	26.1	7.1	18.4	4.9	4.2	-2.3	45.2	6.5	9.5	3.7	7.2	1.0	3.2	14.2
1996:														
1st quarter	26.2	6.1	18.8	5.0	4.2	-1.5	50.2	6.7	13.7	4.4	7.0	1.3	3.2	13.9
2nd quarter	27.8	5.4	18.7	5.1	4.0	-1.5	49.8	7.2	9.9	4.7	7.2	1.2	3.7	15.9
3rd quarter	27.5	5.0	18.5	4.9	3.9	-2.1	45.8	6.5	7.6	4.5	6.6	1.1	3.9	15.6
4th quarter	27.5	6.3	19.2	4.7	3.8	-2.3	42.0	6.4	5.4	3.7	6.3	1.0	3.2	15.8
1997:														
1st quarter	25.8	5.3	19.4	4.6	3.7	-1.3	37.3	5.8	4.7	2.9	5.6	1.4	3.7	13.2
2nd quarter	26.8	6.3	19.7	4.5	3.6	-1.0	38.7	5.6	3.7	2.9	6.7	1.5	3.8	14.7
3rd quarter	26.9	6.9	20.4	4.5	3.6	-1.5	41.1	5.7	7.1	3.1	6.4	1.5	3.6	13.6
4th quarter	25.7	7.0	21.0	4.7	3.6	-1.4	41.7	5.7	8.3	3.1	5.8	1.4	3.2	14.3
1998:														
1st quarter	25.1	5.6	18.6	4.6	3.5	-1.8	38.3	5.4	5.1	3.2	6.3	1.3	3.4	13.6
2nd quarter	25.8	6.4	21.5	4.7	3.5	-0.6	36.8	4.9	4.3	2.7	6.0	1.8	3.6	13.5
3rd quarter	25.2	5.8	20.3	4.7	3.5	-0.8	40.9	5.5	6.1	2.9	6.5	1.5	3.3	15.1
4th quarter	25.7	6.7	22.7	5.0	3.5	-0.7	39.7	5.0	7.1	3.0	6.8	1.4	3.2	13.1

1. Gross government investment consits of general government and government enterprise expenditures for fixed assets; inventory investment is included is included in government consumption expenditures.

Federal Government Receipts and Outlays by Fiscal Year [1]

(Millions of dollars)

| Year and month | Receipts, outlays, deficit, and financing | | | | | Receipts by source | | | | | |
| | | | | Sources of financing | | | | Social insurance taxes and contributions | | | |
	Receipts (net)	Outlays (net)	Budget surplus or deficit (-)	Borrowing from the public	Other financing	Individual income taxes	Corporate income taxes	Employment taxes and contributions	Unemployment insurance	Other retirement contributions	Excise taxes
1970	192 807	195 649	-2 842	5 090	-2 248	90 412	32 829	39 133	3 464	1 765	15 705
1971	187 139	210 172	-23 033	19 839	3 194	86 230	26 785	41 699	3 674	1 952	16 614
1972	207 309	230 681	-23 373	19 340	4 032	94 737	32 166	46 120	4 357	2 097	15 477
1973	230 799	245 707	-14 908	18 533	-3 625	103 246	36 153	54 876	6 051	2 187	16 260
1974	263 224	269 359	-6 135	2 789	3 346	118 952	38 620	65 888	6 837	2 347	16 844
1975	279 090	332 332	-53 242	51 001	2 241	122 386	40 621	75 199	6 771	2 565	16 551
1976	298 060	371 792	-73 732	82 704	-8 972	131 603	41 409	79 901	8 054	2 814	16 963
1977	355 559	409 218	-53 659	71 699	-18 040	157 626	54 892	92 199	11 312	2 974	17 548
1978	399 561	458 746	-59 186	58 022	1 163	180 988	59 952	103 881	13 850	3 237	18 376
1979	463 302	504 032	-40 729	33 183	7 547	217 841	65 677	120 058	15 387	3 494	18 745
1980	517 112	590 947	-73 835	69 530	4 305	244 069	64 600	138 748	15 336	3 719	24 329
1981	599 272	678 249	-78 976	75 500	3 477	285 917	61 137	162 973	15 763	3 984	40 839
1982	617 766	745 755	-127 989	134 447	-6 458	297 744	49 207	180 686	16 600	4 212	36 311
1983	600 562	808 380	-207 818	211 811	-3 993	288 938	37 022	185 766	18 799	4 429	35 300
1984	666 499	851 888	-185 388	168 902	16 487	298 415	56 893	209 658	25 138	4 580	37 361
1985	734 165	946 499	-212 334	199 410	12 924	334 531	61 331	234 646	25 758	4 759	35 992
1986	769 260	990 505	-221 245	236 801	-15 556	348 959	63 143	255 062	24 098	4 742	32 919
1987	854 396	1 004 164	-149 769	151 971	-2 203	392 557	83 926	273 028	25 575	4 715	32 457
1988	909 303	1 064 489	-155 187	162 119	-6 933	401 181	94 508	305 093	24 584	4 638	35 227
1989	991 190	1 143 671	-152 481	139 083	13 398	445 690	103 291	332 859	22 011	4 546	34 386
1990	1 031 969	1 253 163	-221 194	220 840	544	466 884	93 507	353 891	21 635	4 522	35 345
1991	1 055 041	1 324 400	-269 359	277 415	-8 246	467 827	98 086	370 526	20 922	4 568	42 402
1992	1 090 453	1 380 793	-290 339	310 696	-20 294	475 964	100 270	385 491	23 410	4 788	45 569
1993	1 153 226	1 408 532	-255 306	248 594	6 503	509 680	117 520	396 939	26 556	4 805	48 057
1994	1 258 411	1 461 359	-202 948	184 583	18 427	543 055	140 385	428 810	28 004	4 661	55 225
1995	1 351 495	1 515 410	-163 916	171 363	-4 247	590 244	157 004	451 045	28 878	4 550	57 484
1996	1 452 765	1 560 210	-107 445	129 657	-22 380	656 417	171 824	476 361	28 584	4 469	54 014
1997	1 578 955	1 600 910	-21 956	38 171	-15 553	737 466	182 294	506 750	28 202	4 418	56 926
1998	1 721 465	1 652 224	69 241	-51 049	-18 192	828 597	188 677	540 016	27 484	4 335	57 669
1995:											
January	131 801	115 171	16 630	13 337	-29 967	79 162	3 258	38 990	1 069	383	4 555
February	82 544	120 527	-37 983	38 964	-981	33 863	2 060	35 667	2 630	357	3 485
March	92 532	143 074	-50 542	13 645	36 897	26 846	14 863	38 646	320	413	5 143
April	165 392	115 673	49 719	-27 638	-22 081	76 441	23 482	50 423	3 061	354	4 602
May	90 405	129 958	-39 553	44 740	-5 187	29 729	2 193	37 226	10 601	355	4 770
June	147 868	135 054	12 814	8 491	-21 305	61 457	35 876	40 605	320	416	4 897
July	92 749	106 328	-13 579	10 627	2 952	42 819	3 397	34 514	1 636	349	5 074
August	96 560	130 411	-33 851	16 071	17 780	44 122	2 501	34 914	4 454	436	4 757
September	143 219	135 933	7 286	-9 845	2 559	60 909	32 989	39 304	235	364	5 706
October	95 674	118 252	-22 578	13 353	9 406	51 840	2 180	30 549	1 214	342	4 453
November	90 086	128 538	-38 452	38 339	113	39 524	1 694	34 919	2 940	340	5 154
December	138 347	133 064	5 283	-18 358	13 071	53 179	38 021	37 123	223	416	4 870
1996:											
January	142 999	123 543	19 456	-4 802	-14 654	86 192	5 158	40 742	1 081	374	4 241
February	89 428	133 775	-44 347	47 022	-2 727	40 327	1 692	36 011	2 546	403	4 308
March	89 087	136 158	-47 071	38 189	9 086	.....	.....	.....	.....	.....	.....
April	203 468	131 064	72 404	-35 466	-36 938	107 513	24 937	56 615	3 628	346	4 577
May	90 122	143 173	-53 051	20 633	32 418	29 914	2 570	29 938	10 155	417	4 113
June	151 995	117 655	34 340	-8 619	-25 721	60 816	36 957	44 888	400	295	4 310
July	103 893	130 749	-26 856	29 098	-3 263	49 814	4 975	36 946	1 939	372	4 508
August	99 996	141 828	-41 832	16 160	25 672	46 105	3 074	36 562	3 994	397	4 033
September	157 670	122 412	35 258	-5 892	-29 366	68 672	35 105	42 817	206	348	5 315
October	99 656	139 461	-39 805	15 588	24 671	53 600	863	34 428	1 330	346	3 923
November	97 850	135 728	-37 878	45 459	-7 581	46 271	2 339	36 967	2 574	411	4 678
December	148 488	129 999	18 489	-12 321	-7 041	59 423	38 956	40 057	259	371	4 559
1997:											
January	150 718	137 354	13 364	-16 776	3 413	87 239	4 808	47 302	1 137	355	1 212
February	90 293	134 303	-44 010	35 968	8 042	37 400	2 237	38 969	2 423	391	5 106
March	108 074	129 397	-21 323	28 833	-7 510	36 434	18 724	43 547	311	339	3 998
April	228 588	134 649	93 939	-39 001	-54 937	134 291	27 422	50 771	3 532	341	4 768
May	94 493	142 988	-48 494	-19 054	67 548	30 690	4 253	39 835	9 963	422	4 808
June	173 361	118 726	54 635	-11 147	-43 377	74 381	39 373	47 933	343	336	5 185
July	109 178	134 802	-25 624	-1 408	27 032	53 868	3 703	38 066	2 081	425	5 369
August	103 483	138 672	-35 189	30 348	4 841	45 669	2 279	41 861	4 002	338	4 593
September	174 772	124 832	49 941	-18 318	-30 968	78 199	37 338	47 013	247	342	5 719
October	114 898	150 866	-35 968	6 315	29 273	60 680	3 254	36 928	1 443	414	5 082
November	103 481	120 830	-17 349	29 108	-11 758	46 596	3 913	39 629	2 526	334	5 171
December	167 998	154 359	13 639	-1 771	-11 867	69 060	44 037	44 297	425	427	5 167
1998:											
January	162 610	137 231	25 379	-24 807	-572	95 798	4 407	50 395	1 036	333	4 679
February	97 952	139 701	-41 749	30 565	11 185	42 209	829	41 825	2 589	335	4 791
March	117 930	131 743	-13 813	20 137	-6 324	39 662	19 491	47 389	301	337	4 499
April	261 002	136 400	124 602	-60 587	-64 016	158 284	27 361	56 544	4 589	332	5 742
May	95 278	134 057	-38 779	-8 597	47 376	29 974	3 259	42 560	8 273	406	4 841
June	187 858	136 752	51 106	-12 618	-38 488	81 587	39 785	54 807	292	369	5 370
July	119 723	143 807	-24 084	-16 370	40 454	58 969	4 072	41 130	2 301	385	6 127
August	111 741	122 907	-11 166	33 989	-22 823	55 300	1 468	41 973	3 502	331	3 181
September	180 995	143 569	37 426	-46 413	8 191	90 479	36 800	42 540	206	333	2 961
October	119 974	152 413	-32 439	15 330	17 131	60 255	1 758	39 690	1 142	405	9 630
November	113 978	130 915	-16 937	22 364	-5 248	51 341	3 440	42 940	2 655	331	6 021
December	178 646	183 803	-5 157	-5 390	10 800	75 988	42 374	47 869	315	417	5 446

1. Fiscal years through 1976 are from July 1 through June 30. Beginning with October 1976 (fiscal year 1977), fiscal years are from October 1 through September 30. The period from July 1 through September 30, 1976 (not shown here) is a separate fiscal period known as the transition quarter and not included in any fiscal year.

Federal Government Receipts and Outlays by Fiscal Year [1]—*Continued*

(Millions of dollars)

Year and month	Receipts by source—*Continued*			Outlays by function							
	Estate and gift taxes	Customs deposits	Miscellaneous receipts	National defense	International affairs	General science, space, and technology	Energy	Natural resources and environment	Agriculture	Commerce and housing credit	Transportation
1970	3 644	2 430	3 424	81 692	4 330	4 511	997	3 065	5 166	2 112	7 008
1971	3 735	2 591	3 858	78 872	4 159	4 182	1 035	3 915	4 290	2 366	8 052
1972	5 436	3 287	3 632	79 174	4 781	4 175	1 296	4 241	5 259	2 222	8 392
1973	4 917	3 188	3 920	76 681	4 149	4 032	1 237	4 775	4 854	931	9 066
1974	5 035	3 334	5 368	79 347	5 710	3 980	1 303	5 697	2 230	4 705	9 172
1975	4 611	3 676	6 712	86 509	7 097	3 991	2 916	7 346	3 036	9 947	10 918
1976	5 216	4 074	8 027	89 619	6 433	4 373	4 204	8 184	3 170	7 619	13 739
1977	7 327	5 150	6 531	97 241	6 353	4 736	5 770	10 032	6 787	3 093	14 829
1978	5 285	6 573	7 419	104 495	7 482	4 926	7 992	10 983	11 357	6 254	15 521
1979	5 411	7 439	9 252	116 342	7 459	5 235	9 180	12 135	11 236	4 686	18 079
1980	6 389	7 174	12 748	133 995	12 714	5 832	10 156	13 858	8 839	9 390	21 329
1981	6 787	8 083	13 790	157 513	13 104	6 469	15 166	13 568	11 323	8 206	23 379
1982	7 991	8 854	16 161	185 309	12 300	7 200	13 527	12 998	15 944	6 256	20 625
1983	6 053	8 655	15 600	209 903	11 848	7 935	9 353	12 672	22 901	6 681	21 334
1984	6 010	11 370	17 073	227 413	15 876	8 317	7 086	12 593	13 613	6 959	23 669
1985	6 422	12 079	18 647	252 748	16 176	8 627	5 685	13 357	25 565	4 337	25 838
1986	6 958	13 327	20 053	273 375	14 152	8 976	4 735	13 639	31 449	5 059	28 117
1987	7 493	15 085	19 560	281 999	11 649	9 216	4 115	13 363	26 606	6 435	26 222
1988	7 594	16 198	20 259	290 361	10 471	10 841	2 297	14 606	17 210	19 164	27 272
1989	8 745	16 334	23 328	303 559	9 573	12 838	2 706	16 182	16 919	29 710	27 608
1990	11 500	16 707	27 978	299 331	13 764	14 444	3 341	17 080	11 958	67 600	29 485
1991	11 138	15 949	23 623	273 292	15 851	16 111	2 436	18 559	15 183	76 271	31 099
1992	11 143	17 359	27 284	298 350	16 107	16 409	4 500	20 025	15 205	10 919	33 333
1993	12 577	18 802	19 465	291 086	17 248	17 030	4 319	20 239	20 363	-21 853	35 004
1994	15 225	20 099	23 164	281 642	17 083	16 227	5 219	21 064	15 046	-4 228	38 066
1995	14 763	19 301	28 226	272 066	16 434	16 724	4 936	22 078	9 778	-17 808	39 350
1996	17 189	18 670	25 232	265 748	13 496	16 709	2 836	21 614	9 159	-10 646	39 565
1997	19 845	17 927	25 149	270 084	15 423	18 510	1 583	20 977	10 663	-13 963	39 725
1998	24 076	18 297	32 270	270 407	13 144	19 632	1 359	21 897	14 306	907	36 610
1995:											
January	1 005	1 539	1 839	18 499	999	1 194	488	1 571	1 049	-1 469	3 080
February	916	1 435	2 131	21 461	1 108	1 374	260	1 374	1 264	-2 978	2 799
March	1 218	1 470	3 612	26 533	425	1 628	569	1 951	1 195	-1 853	3 167
April	1 906	1 349	3 774	17 753	95	1 298	196	1 587	623	-1 092	2 560
May	1 339	1 471	2 719	22 194	1 282	1 596	244	1 820	236	-1 988	3 154
June	1 040	1 583	1 674	26 148	818	1 521	601	1 698	328	-3 041	3 432
July	1 037	1 603	2 320	18 069	517	1 355	547	1 811	-482	-733	3 324
August	1 500	1 794	2 081	23 882	1 877	1 668	13	2 116	-462	-2 592	3 359
September	1 289	1 634	789	26 040	1 479	1 612	969	1 915	-102	2 490	3 719
October	1 160	1 786	2 070	18 353	1 074	1 427	348	2 835	1 109	-1 661	3 128
November	1 349	1 593	2 496	21 234	1 616	1 474	489	2 245	2 291	-1 465	3 284
December	1 383	1 439	1 618	25 376	431	1 274	-163	1 711	708	-451	3 117
1996:											
January	1 288	1 482	2 364	.....	.....	1 326	54	.....	345	-1 024	2 960
February	1 090	1 456	1 517	21 691	2 604	1 381	131	1 817	-62	-1 443	2 864
March	.....	.....	.....	22 479	1 391	1 534	17	1 592	-249	-1 741	2 864
April	2 704	1 388	1 680	22 725	988	1 584	216	1 660	-175	256	3 324
May	1 415	1 427	1 929	26 609	1 165	1 536	822	1 757	-124	-1 368	3 185
June	1 141	1 450	1 663	19 769	837	1 660	187	1 543	843	-304	3 648
July	1 259	1 712	2 287	22 541	497	1 526	153	2 062	627	-1 678	3 583
August	1 566	1 807	2 459	26 000	969	1 689	563	1 821	3 309	1 559	3 540
September	1 698	1 604	1 902	19 738	1 007	1 447	-207	1 914	2 347	-167	3 870
October	1 547	1 432	2 187	22 284	4 112	1 586	-96	1 758	1 405	-4 535	3 386
November	1 394	1 219	1 997	24 911	814	1 590	201	1 888	2 240	-1 335	3 209
December	1 371	1 520	1 973	23 085	1 371	1 429	-62	2 150	2 159	-1 531	2 895
1997:											
January	1 615	1 468	2 574	22 127	1 405	1 417	211	2 018	-96	-1 460	2 842
February	1 180	1 379	1 208	20 897	898	1 478	490	1 508	26	-2 986	2 810
March	1 468	1 315	1 962	19 854	1 094	1 395	28	1 410	-206	-2 314	2 955
April	3 308	1 492	2 662	21 789	1 654	1 655	129	1 545	-205	-62	3 320
May	1 412	1 443	1 667	26 152	256	1 565	-5	1 719	-255	891	3 224
June	1 494	1 522	2 793	20 613	472	1 763	238	1 622	-35	-415	3 667
July	1 552	1 799	2 315	22 944	1 541	1 643	48	1 909	121	-1 917	3 730
August	1 655	1 749	1 338	24 259	494	1 543	598	1 555	3 152	1 601	3 818
September	1 849	1 590	2 474	21 076	1 312	1 586	-163	2 071	2 983	-629	3 913
October	2 198	1 802	3 097	26 374	724	1 606	-68	1 710	1 425	-714	3 014
November	1 510	1 354	2 450	17 883	955	1 899	-267	1 566	2 846	-1 144	3 681
December	1 498	1 416	1 671	26 944	4 534	1 498	291	2 388	1 958	-403	2 762
1998:											
January	1 808	1 387	2 768	20 738	750	1 404	-43	1 638	330	-1 065	2 504
February	1 500	1 454	2 420	20 492	364	1 617	40	1 746	283	-972	2 734
March	1 845	1 412	2 994	20 326	979	1 702	-34	1 556	119	-814	2 511
April	4 198	1 428	2 525	22 065	1 460	1 548	42	1 575	-451	791	2 746
May	1 845	1 297	2 823	23 212	720	1 657	661	1 574	140	-20	3 127
June	1 775	1 568	2 307	22 329	347	1 711	122	1 964	176	-1 223	3 327
July	1 825	1 777	3 135	25 865	815	1 581	-113	2 217	1 656	-1 423	3 218
August	1 718	1 732	2 535	18 502	443	1 824	892	1 855	2 780	8 147	3 997
September	2 356	1 701	3 572	24 748	1 123	1 550	-135	2 115	3 287	1 078	3 455
October	2 089	1 776	3 228	25 730	169	1 558	-218	1 859	5 620	-701	3 447
November	2 132	1 380	3 738	18 173	4 924	1 918	151	2 080	3 238	-1 821	3 400
December	2 239	1 472	2 527	27 178	822			2 545			

1. Fiscal years through 1976 are from July 1 through June 30. Beginning with October 1976 (fiscal year 1977), fiscal years are from October 1 through September 30. The period from July 1 through September 30, 1976 (not shown here) is a separate fiscal period known as the transition quarter and not included in any fiscal year.

Federal Government Receipts and Outlays by Fiscal Year [1]—Continued

(Millions of dollars)

Year and month	Community and regional development	Education, employment, and social services	Health	Medicare	Income security	Social security	Veterans benefits and services	Administration of justice	General government	Net interest	Undistributed offsetting receipts
1970	2 392	8 634	5 907	6 213	15 655	30 270	8 669	959	2 320	14 380	-8 632
1971	2 917	9 849	6 843	6 622	22 946	35 872	9 768	1 306	2 442	14 841	-10 107
1972	3 423	12 529	8 674	7 479	27 650	40 157	10 720	1 653	2 960	15 478	-9 583
1973	4 605	12 745	9 356	8 052	28 276	49 090	12 003	2 141	9 774	17 349	-13 409
1974	4 229	12 457	10 733	9 639	33 713	55 867	13 374	2 470	10 032	21 449	-16 749
1975	4 322	16 022	12 930	12 875	50 176	64 658	16 584	2 955	10 408	23 244	-13 602
1976	5 442	18 910	15 734	15 834	60 799	73 899	18 419	3 328	9 747	26 727	-14 386
1977	7 021	21 104	17 302	19 345	61 060	85 061	18 022	3 605	12 833	29 901	-14 879
1978	11 841	26 710	18 524	22 768	61 505	93 861	18 961	3 813	12 015	35 458	-15 720
1979	10 480	30 223	20 494	26 495	66 376	104 073	19 914	4 173	12 293	42 636	-17 476
1980	11 252	31 843	23 169	32 090	86 557	118 547	21 169	4 584	13 028	52 538	-19 942
1981	10 568	33 709	26 866	39 149	99 742	139 584	22 973	4 769	11 429	68 774	-28 041
1982	8 347	27 029	27 445	46 567	107 737	155 964	23 938	4 712	10 914	85 044	-26 099
1983	7 560	26 606	28 641	52 588	122 621	170 724	24 824	5 105	11 235	89 828	-33 976
1984	7 673	27 579	30 417	57 540	112 694	178 223	25 588	5 663	11 817	111 123	-31 957
1985	7 680	29 342	33 542	65 822	128 230	188 623	26 262	6 270	11 588	129 504	-32 698
1986	7 233	30 585	35 936	70 164	119 824	198 757	26 327	6 572	12 564	136 047	-33 007
1987	5 051	29 724	39 967	75 120	123 282	207 353	26 750	7 553	7 565	138 652	-36 455
1988	5 294	31 938	44 487	78 878	129 374	219 341	29 386	9 236	9 464	151 838	-36 967
1989	5 362	36 674	48 390	84 964	136 066	232 542	30 031	9 474	9 017	169 266	-37 212
1990	8 498	38 755	57 716	98 102	147 076	248 623	29 058	9 993	10 734	184 221	-36 615
1991	6 811	43 354	71 183	104 489	170 320	269 015	31 305	12 276	11 661	194 541	-39 356
1992	6 838	45 248	89 497	119 024	197 022	287 585	34 064	14 426	12 990	199 421	-39 280
1993	9 052	50 012	99 415	130 552	207 299	304 585	35 671	14 955	13 009	198 811	-37 386
1994	10 454	46 307	107 122	144 747	214 089	319 565	37 585	15 256	11 303	202 957	-37 772
1995	10 641	54 263	115 418	159 855	220 493	335 846	37 890	16 216	13 835	232 169	-44 455
1996	10 685	52 001	119 378	174 225	225 989	349 676	36 985	17 548	11 892	241 090	-37 620
1997	11 695	51 509	123 430	189 970	230 359	365 257	39 313	20 224	12 750	244 058	-49 973
1998	10 437	52 214	131 015	192 820	232 949	379 226	41 782	22 612	13 903	243 353	-47 194
1995:											
January	1 140	4 650	9 440	11 923	16 326	27 811	1 996	1 568	-233	19 568	-2 911
February	228	4 078	8 918	11 829	20 583	27 632	3 023	1 099	1 170	18 002	-2 688
March	971	4 678	10 625	15 409	24 708	27 800	4 642	1 488	1 680	19 671	-2 829
April	896	3 647	9 281	11 510	18 963	27 953	1 850	1 359	299	20 017	-3 121
May	860	4 205	9 952	14 390	20 633	27 997	3 204	1 129	1 109	20 295	-2 956
June	1 035	4 480	10 543	15 663	16 426	32 058	4 552	1 419	1 781	18 617	-3 127
July	1 191	2 869	8 777	12 016	15 310	27 998	1 591	1 664	421	20 245	-10 163
August	909	5 785	10 422	14 840	16 919	27 950	3 267	1 400	1 464	20 619	-3 022
September	1 043	4 802	9 401	14 430	19 591	28 175	4 517	1 335	1 385	18 929	-5 796
October	943	3 556	9 657	12 671	14 522	28 061	1 594	1 223	1 712	20 565	-2 765
November	1 087	4 185	10 189	14 058	18 134	27 889	3 280	1 258	717	19 058	-2 565
December	912	3 623	8 567	14 794	19 738	28 505	4 435	1 233	1 924	19 934	-2 683
1996:											
January	.....	.....	.....	.....	.....	.....	.....	.....	.....	.....	.....
February	396	4 498	9 542	14 117	23 812	28 833	2 901	1 281	1 575	19 771	-2 855
March	1 007	4 270	10 306	14 123	25 968	29 116	3 300	1 342	766	20 244	-2 490
April	1 026	4 014	10 458	15 124	21 417	29 092	2 974	1 585	-25	20 463	-2 932
May	826	3 961	11 201	17 571	21 407	29 156	5 254	1 683	180	20 359	-2 991
June	896	3 903	9 762	12 049	11 332	32 682	1 570	1 327	1 755	18 977	-2 636
July	959	3 108	10 077	16 111	18 189	29 265	3 255	1 989	53	20 311	-3 543
August	1 021	5 037	10 352	16 983	20 125	29 222	4 657	1 460	1 390	21 460	-2 880
September	1 191	5 082	10 004	12 546	13 664	29 147	1 641	1 382	1 548	19 243	-6 466
October	1 247	4 176	10 378	16 067	18 544	29 353	3 336	1 311	1 657	21 472	140 209
November	990	4 973	10 060	16 479	19 714	29 457	5 156	1 897	200	20 144	-2 635
December	706	3 799	10 558	15 220	17 278	29 559	3 088	1 563	1 687	19 997	-6 839
1997:											
January	1 005	4 676	10 762	16 205	19 587	30 376	3 281	1 745	982	21 092	-2 555
February	608	5 100	9 169	15 027	26 346	29 946	3 384	2 074	119	19 362	-3 049
March	920	3 843	10 478	13 703	23 639	30 232	1 772	1 612	1 447	20 410	-2 810
April	1 067	4 123	10 439	16 533	20 706	30 290	3 342	1 454	1 519	21 132	-2 803
May	883	3 799	10 374	18 466	22 357	30 421	4 333	1 875	484	21 162	-4 128
June	1 207	3 702	10 595	13 498	11 298	34 060	1 583	1 883	1 897	19 543	-8 556
July	958	3 542	9 821	17 323	17 921	30 537	3 409	1 863	366	21 046	-3 594
August	865	4 055	10 024	18 107	19 702	30 576	4 806	1 484	747	21 049	-3 262
September	1 115	5 804	10 771	13 283	13 718	30 448	1 833	1 470	1 440	17 061	-6 630
October	1 014	4 289	11 905	18 900	20 292	30 571	5 234	1 584	1 460	21 805	-3 067
November	916	4 517	9 870	12 329	14 694	30 535	1 864	1 747	713	20 592	-2 613
December	843	4 688	11 159	19 511	19 951	30 989	4 931	2 051	2 504	20 480	-3 629
1998:											
January	783	5 081	11 162	15 686	20 093	31 243	3 331	1 718	836	20 570	-2 504
February	669	6 535	9 735	15 539	28 194	31 271	3 386	2 026	108	19 901	-3 394
March	503	2 888	10 876	14 394	22 853	31 421	1 883	1 764	1 012	20 651	-3 064
April	1 121	4 428	11 259	17 016	20 757	31 335	4 056	1 757	1 178	20 961	-6 054
May	873	2 798	10 419	15 341	18 705	31 490	3 604	1 781	925	20 855	-2 916
June	914	4 237	11 602	16 139	14 554	35 430	3 355	2 241	2 080	19 407	-3 408
July	917	3 645	11 033	19 388	21 198	31 721	4 958	2 256	308	20 791	-5 416
August	770	4 708	10 704	12 817	14 281	31 423	1 749	2 012	579	21 366	-3 221
September	1 115	4 455	11 293	15 758	17 309	31 797	3 432	1 675	2 199	15 976	-7 909
October	1 260	4 861	12 572	18 824	20 104	31 720	5 465	1 899	2 377	19 442	-3 078
November	1 405	4 111	10 477	12 088	14 644	31 640	1 841	2 067	1 418	19 350	-2 828
December	1 505	5 465	11 757	17 982	21 945	61 651	5 305	2 132	2 198	20 029	-3 343

1. Fiscal years through 1976 are from July 1 through June 30. Beginning with October 1976 (fiscal year 1977), fiscal years are from October 1 through September 30. The period from July 1 through September 30, 1976 (not shown here) is a separate fiscal period known as the transition quarter and not included in any fiscal year.

Federal Government Debt by Fiscal Year [1]; Government Employment

| Year and month | Federal government debt at end of fiscal year | | Government employment (payroll employment, thousands, seasonally adjusted, except as noted) | | | | | | |
| | Federal debt held by the public (billions of dollars) | Federal debt/GDP ratio (percent) | Total | Federal | | State | | Local | |
				Total	Department of Defense (not seasonally adjusted)	Total	Education	Total	Education
1970	283	28.1	12 554	2 731	1 044	2 664	1 104	7 158	4 004
1971	303	28.1	12 881	2 696	1 009	2 747	1 149	7 437	4 188
1972	322	27.4	13 334	2 684	995	2 859	1 188	7 790	4 363
1973	341	26.1	13 732	2 663	961	2 923	1 205	8 146	4 537
1974	344	23.9	14 170	2 724	964	3 039	1 267	8 407	4 692
1975	395	25.4	14 686	2 748	955	3 179	1 323	8 758	4 834
1976	477	27.6	14 871	2 733	929	3 273	1 371	8 865	4 899
1977	549	27.9	15 127	2 727	918	3 377	1 385	9 023	4 974
1978	607	27.4	15 672	2 753	910	3 474	1 367	9 446	5 075
1979	640	25.7	15 947	2 773	895	3 541	1 378	9 633	5 107
1980	710	26.1	16 241	2 866	893	3 610	1 398	9 765	5 210
1981	785	25.8	16 031	2 772	913	3 640	1 420	9 619	5 216
1982	920	28.6	15 837	2 739	939	3 640	1 433	9 458	5 169
1983	1 132	33.1	15 869	2 774	947	3 662	1 450	9 434	5 139
1984	1 301	34.1	16 024	2 807	963	3 734	1 488	9 482	5 196
1985	1 500	36.6	16 394	2 875	988	3 832	1 540	9 687	5 344
1986	1 737	39.7	16 693	2 899	983	3 893	1 561	9 901	5 484
1987	1 889	41.0	17 010	2 943	985	3 967	1 586	10 100	5 598
1988	2 051	41.4	17 386	2 971	964	4 076	1 621	10 339	5 722
1989	2 190	40.9	17 779	2 988	973	4 182	1 668	10 609	5 875
1990	2 411	42.4	18 304	3 085	951	4 305	1 730	10 914	6 042
1991	2 688	45.9	18 402	2 966	921	4 355	1 768	11 081	6 136
1992	2 999	48.8	18 645	2 969	917	4 408	1 799	11 267	6 220
1993	3 248	50.2	18 841	2 915	870	4 488	1 834	11 438	6 353
1994	3 432	50.1	19 128	2 870	825	4 576	1 882	11 682	6 479
1995	3 603	50.1	19 305	2 822	779	4 635	1 919	11 849	6 606
1996	3 733	49.4	19 419	2 757	740	4 606	1 911	12 056	6 748
1997	3 771	47.2	19 557	2 699	698	4 582	1 904	12 276	6 918
1998	3 719	44.2	19 819	2 686	665	4 612	1 916	12 521	7 082
1995:									
January	.....	.....	19 252	2 840	797	4 645	1 919	11 767	6 543
February	.....	.....	19 267	2 836	791	4 649	1 924	11 782	6 555
March	.....	.....	19 278	2 832	788	4 653	1 926	11 793	6 564
April	.....	.....	19 290	2 828	783	4 647	1 922	11 815	6 582
May	.....	.....	19 275	2 831	787	4 640	1 922	11 804	6 579
June	.....	.....	19 296	2 833	789	4 638	1 921	11 825	6 585
July	.....	.....	19 289	2 828	787	4 626	1 922	11 835	6 592
August	.....	.....	19 295	2 827	781	4 628	1 916	11 840	6 596
September	.....	.....	19 295	2 816	770	4 621	1 912	11 858	6 613
October	.....	.....	19 323	2 804	760	4 626	1 917	11 893	6 623
November	.....	.....	19 328	2 794	757	4 623	1 916	11 911	6 636
December	.....	.....	19 334	2 789	756	4 621	1 913	11 924	6 651
1996:									
January	.....	.....	19 320	2 780	751	4 613	1 907	11 927	6 645
February	.....	.....	19 359	2 782	750	4 626	1 918	11 951	6 660
March	.....	.....	19 397	2 780	748	4 626	1 921	11 991	6 687
April	.....	.....	19 388	2 774	745	4 620	1 918	11 994	6 701
May	.....	.....	19 418	2 770	749	4 621	1 919	12 027	6 712
June	.....	.....	19 404	2 762	753	4 615	1 916	12 027	6 728
July	.....	.....	19 404	2 756	752	4 603	1 915	12 045	6 743
August	.....	.....	19 420	2 739	745	4 600	1 912	12 081	6 764
September	.....	.....	19 433	2 740	734	4 598	1 910	12 095	6 778
October	.....	.....	19 429	2 732	719	4 586	1 901	12 111	6 792
November	.....	.....	19 430	2 727	717	4 584	1 899	12 119	6 803
December	.....	.....	19 444	2 725	716	4 580	1 897	12 139	6 815
1997:									
January	.....	.....	19 461	2 730	708	4 575	1 894	12 156	6 829
February	.....	.....	19 459	2 714	708	4 576	1 895	12 169	6 843
March	.....	.....	19 469	2 711	706	4 572	1 892	12 186	6 856
April	.....	.....	19 490	2 707	703	4 576	1 896	12 207	6 867
May	.....	.....	19 494	2 704	705	4 577	1 900	12 213	6 871
June	.....	.....	19 537	2 699	707	4 577	1 904	12 261	6 903
July	.....	.....	19 584	2 694	706	4 600	1 922	12 290	6 919
August	.....	.....	19 585	2 689	699	4 581	1 904	12 315	6 937
September	.....	.....	19 582	2 682	691	4 583	1 908	12 317	6 953
October	.....	.....	19 618	2 684	684	4 585	1 906	12 349	6 963
November	.....	.....	19 638	2 686	682	4 588	1 908	12 364	6 972
December	.....	.....	19 650	2 685	679	4 581	1 905	12 384	6 982
1998:									
January	.....	.....	19 660	2 680	674	4 577	1 900	12 403	6 996
February	.....	.....	19 678	2 677	672	4 574	1 898	12 427	7 014
March	.....	.....	19 694	2 674	669	4 583	1 904	12 437	7 021
April	.....	.....	19 726	2 675	666	4 591	1 908	12 460	7 034
May	.....	.....	19 763	2 675	669	4 597	1 908	12 491	7 052
June	.....	.....	19 776	2 677	673	4 598	1 911	12 501	7 060
July	.....	.....	19 799	2 675	672	4 612	1 915	12 512	7 078
August	.....	.....	19 869	2 688	667	4 633	1 931	12 548	7 109
September	.....	.....	19 891	2 689	661	4 647	1 939	12 555	7 103
October	.....	.....	19 913	2 711	655	4 633	1 923	12 569	7 108
November	.....	.....	19 948	2 723	654	4 637	1 923	12 588	7 132
December	.....	.....	19 973	2 701	653	4 652	1 932	12 620	7 148

1. Fiscal years through 1976 are from July 1 through June 30. Beginning with October 1976 (fiscal year 1977), fiscal years are from October 1 through September 30. The period from July 1 through September 30, 1976 (not shown here) is a separate fiscal period known as the transition quarter and not included in any fiscal year.

Part III: Historical Data

Gross Domestic Product

(Billions of dollars, quarterly data are at seasonally adjusted annual rates)

Year and quarter	Gross domestic product	Personal consumption expenditures	Gross private domestic investment					Exports and imports of goods and services			Government consumption expenditures and gross investment			Addendum: Final sales of domestic product
			Total	Fixed investment		Change in business inventories		Net exports	Exports	Imports	Total	Federal	State and local	
				Nonres-idential	Residen-tial	Nonfarm	Farm							
1962	585.2	363.4	87.9	52.8	29.0	5.5	0.6	2.4	27.4	25.0	131.4	76.5	55.0	579.1
1963	617.4	383.0	93.4	55.6	32.1	5.2	0.5	3.3	29.4	26.1	137.7	78.1	59.6	611.7
1964	663.0	411.4	101.7	62.4	34.3	6.2	-1.2	5.5	33.6	28.1	144.4	79.4	65.0	658.0
1965	719.1	444.3	118.0	74.1	34.2	8.9	0.8	3.9	35.4	31.5	153.0	81.8	71.2	709.4
1966	787.8	481.9	130.4	84.4	32.3	14.3	-0.5	1.9	38.9	37.1	173.6	94.1	79.5	774.0
1967	833.6	509.5	128.0	85.2	32.4	9.6	0.9	1.4	41.4	39.9	194.6	106.6	88.1	823.1
1968	910.6	559.8	139.9	92.1	38.7	7.8	1.4	-1.3	45.3	46.6	212.1	113.8	98.3	901.4
1969	982.2	604.7	155.0	102.9	42.6	9.5	0.0	-1.2	49.3	50.5	223.8	115.8	108.0	972.7
1970	1 035.6	648.1	150.2	106.7	41.4	3.0	-0.8	1.2	57.0	55.8	236.1	115.9	120.2	1 033.4
1971	1 125.4	702.5	176.0	111.7	55.8	6.8	1.7	-3.0	59.3	62.3	249.9	117.1	132.8	1 116.9
1972	1 237.3	770.7	205.6	126.1	69.7	9.6	0.3	-8.0	66.2	74.2	268.9	125.1	143.8	1 227.4
1973	1 382.6	851.6	242.9	150.0	75.3	15.9	1.5	0.6	91.8	91.2	287.6	128.2	159.4	1 365.2
1974	1 496.9	931.2	245.6	165.6	66.0	16.9	-2.8	-3.1	124.3	127.5	323.2	139.9	183.3	1 482.8
1975	1 630.6	1 029.1	225.4	169.0	62.7	-9.7	3.4	13.6	136.3	122.7	362.6	154.5	208.1	1 636.9
1976	1 819.0	1 148.8	286.6	187.2	82.5	17.8	-0.8	-2.3	148.9	151.1	385.9	162.7	223.1	1 802.0
1977	2 026.9	1 277.1	356.6	223.2	110.3	18.5	4.5	-23.7	158.8	182.4	416.9	178.4	238.5	2 003.8
1978	2 291.4	1 428.8	430.8	272.0	131.6	25.8	1.4	-26.1	186.1	212.3	457.9	194.4	263.4	2 264.2
1979	2 557.5	1 593.5	480.9	323.0	141.0	13.3	3.6	-24.0	228.7	252.7	507.1	215.0	292.0	2 540.6
1980	2 784.2	1 760.4	465.9	350.3	123.2	-1.5	-6.1	-14.9	278.9	293.8	572.8	248.4	324.4	2 791.9
1981	3 115.9	1 941.3	556.2	405.4	122.6	19.4	8.8	-15.0	302.8	317.8	633.4	284.1	349.2	3 087.8
1982	3 242.1	2 076.8	501.1	409.9	105.7	-20.2	5.8	-20.5	282.6	303.2	684.8	313.2	371.6	3 256.6
1983	3 514.5	2 283.4	547.1	399.4	152.5	10.4	-15.4	-51.7	277.0	328.6	735.7	344.5	391.2	3 519.4
1984	3 902.4	2 492.3	715.6	468.3	179.8	61.8	5.7	-102.0	303.1	405.1	796.6	372.6	424.0	3 835.0
1985	4 180.7	2 704.8	715.1	502.0	186.9	20.4	5.8	-114.2	303.0	417.2	875.0	410.1	464.9	4 154.5
1986	4 422.2	2 892.7	722.5	494.8	218.1	11.1	-1.5	-131.5	320.7	452.2	938.5	435.2	503.3	4 412.6
1987	4 692.3	3 094.5	747.2	495.4	227.6	30.7	-6.4	-142.1	365.7	507.9	992.8	455.7	537.2	4 668.1
1988	5 049.6	3 349.7	773.9	530.6	232.5	22.8	-11.9	-106.1	447.2	553.2	1 032.0	457.3	574.7	5 038.7
1989	5 438.7	3 594.8	829.2	566.2	231.3	31.7	0.0	-80.4	509.3	589.7	1 095.1	477.2	617.9	5 407.0
1962:														
1st quarter	575.3	355.3	89.3	51.4	28.4	8.0	1.5	2.3	26.6	24.3	128.4	74.5	53.9	565.8
2nd quarter	582.8	361.3	87.9	53.0	29.2	5.4	0.2	3.2	28.1	24.9	130.4	75.9	54.5	577.1
3rd quarter	589.9	365.4	89.1	53.7	29.2	5.9	0.2	2.9	28.0	25.1	132.6	77.3	55.3	583.7
4th quarter	592.9	371.7	85.4	53.2	29.1	2.7	0.4	1.5	27.0	25.6	134.3	78.1	56.2	589.8
1963:														
1st quarter	602.2	375.1	90.3	53.1	30.2	5.1	1.9	2.0	27.2	25.2	134.7	76.9	57.8	595.1
2nd quarter	610.9	379.4	91.8	54.7	32.2	4.8	0.1	3.7	29.6	25.9	135.9	77.3	58.7	606.0
3rd quarter	623.7	386.4	94.7	56.3	32.5	6.6	-0.6	3.1	29.8	26.7	139.5	79.1	60.4	617.8
4th quarter	632.8	391.1	96.6	58.1	33.7	4.2	0.6	4.4	31.1	26.8	140.7	79.0	61.7	627.9
1964:														
1st quarter	649.4	400.5	100.6	59.6	35.4	6.2	-0.6	5.9	32.9	27.0	142.4	79.4	62.9	643.8
2nd quarter	658.4	408.3	100.4	61.4	34.2	6.1	-1.2	4.9	32.6	27.7	144.8	80.1	64.6	653.6
3rd quarter	669.2	417.1	101.5	63.5	33.7	6.1	-1.8	5.4	33.9	28.4	145.1	79.4	65.7	664.9
4th quarter	675.1	419.8	104.4	65.2	33.8	6.5	-1.1	5.7	35.0	29.3	145.3	78.6	66.7	669.7
1965:														
1st quarter	695.6	430.6	115.8	69.7	33.9	11.9	0.3	3.0	31.5	28.5	146.2	78.3	67.9	683.4
2nd quarter	708.2	437.8	115.8	72.4	34.2	8.0	1.1	4.7	36.3	31.7	149.9	79.9	70.1	699.0
3rd quarter	725.0	447.2	119.1	75.3	34.3	8.7	0.8	3.7	35.7	32.0	155.0	82.4	72.7	715.5
4th quarter	747.7	461.5	121.3	78.9	34.5	6.8	1.0	4.1	38.0	33.9	160.9	86.5	74.3	739.9
1966:														
1st quarter	770.5	472.0	130.5	82.2	34.8	12.8	0.6	3.2	38.2	35.0	164.8	88.5	76.3	757.0
2nd quarter	780.0	477.1	129.9	84.2	33.2	14.1	-1.7	2.0	38.2	36.2	171.1	92.9	78.2	767.5
3rd quarter	793.6	486.4	129.4	85.3	31.9	12.7	-0.6	0.8	39.0	38.2	176.9	96.7	80.2	781.4
4th quarter	807.1	492.0	132.0	85.7	29.2	17.4	-0.4	1.5	40.4	38.8	181.6	98.4	83.3	790.1
1967:														
1st quarter	817.5	496.8	127.7	84.3	28.3	13.3	1.7	2.3	41.7	39.4	190.8	105.1	85.6	802.5
2nd quarter	823.3	506.2	123.0	84.5	31.6	4.6	2.1	2.1	41.1	39.0	191.9	105.0	87.0	816.5
3rd quarter	838.9	513.7	128.5	84.7	33.4	9.9	0.5	1.1	40.7	39.5	195.6	107.0	88.6	828.5
4th quarter	854.7	521.2	133.0	87.2	36.0	10.6	-0.9	0.2	41.9	41.7	200.3	109.1	91.2	845.0
1968:														
1st quarter	880.5	539.5	135.7	90.6	36.9	5.1	3.0	-1.2	43.2	44.4	206.6	112.4	94.2	872.4
2nd quarter	904.9	553.2	141.9	89.9	38.2	9.6	4.3	-0.6	44.8	45.4	210.4	113.1	97.3	891.0
3rd quarter	920.1	569.1	138.7	91.8	38.9	7.8	0.2	-1.3	47.0	48.2	213.6	114.2	99.5	912.1
4th quarter	936.8	577.5	143.5	96.0	40.9	8.6	-2.0	-1.9	46.2	48.2	217.7	115.5	102.3	930.2
1969:														
1st quarter	960.0	588.8	154.7	99.5	43.2	10.2	1.8	-1.9	41.9	43.8	218.4	114.1	104.3	948.1
2nd quarter	974.1	599.4	154.4	101.4	43.4	8.3	1.4	-1.8	50.9	52.7	222.0	114.8	107.2	964.5
3rd quarter	993.6	609.2	159.0	105.1	43.2	11.9	-1.2	-1.3	51.0	52.4	226.7	117.6	109.2	982.9
4th quarter	1 001.0	621.1	152.0	105.6	40.7	7.7	-1.9	0.1	53.2	53.1	227.8	116.7	111.1	995.2
1970														
1st quarter	1 013.9	632.4	148.5	105.8	40.7	0.4	1.6	1.1	54.7	53.5	231.8	117.1	114.7	1 011.9
2nd quarter	1 029.5	642.7	151.1	107.1	39.4	4.2	0.4	2.4	57.6	55.2	233.4	115.5	117.9	1 025.0
3rd quarter	1 047.8	655.2	153.8	108.2	40.4	7.1	-1.8	0.9	57.3	56.4	237.9	115.3	122.5	1 042.6
4th quarter	1 051.3	662.1	147.6	105.7	45.0	0.4	-3.5	0.4	58.3	57.9	241.2	115.7	125.5	1 054.4
1971														
1st quarter	1 096.8	681.6	169.3	108.2	48.6	9.9	2.5	0.8	59.5	58.7	245.1	116.2	128.8	1 084.3
2nd quarter	1 117.7	695.8	177.1	111.1	54.6	7.3	4.2	-3.8	59.5	63.3	248.7	116.8	131.9	1 106.3
3rd quarter	1 137.3	708.2	181.1	112.4	58.3	8.1	2.3	-3.1	62.4	65.5	251.1	117.3	133.8	1 126.9
4th quarter	1 149.8	724.5	176.6	115.3	61.5	2.1	-2.3	-6.0	56.0	61.9	254.6	117.8	136.8	1 150.0
1972:														
1st quarter	1 190.2	741.9	191.8	120.6	66.6	5.0	-0.5	-8.6	63.5	72.2	265.2	125.2	140.0	1 185.6
2nd quarter	1 224.4	759.9	204.2	123.5	68.2	10.4	2.0	-8.3	63.1	71.4	268.6	127.3	141.3	1 211.9
3rd quarter	1 247.8	778.1	209.8	126.3	69.6	13.0	1.0	-7.9	66.2	74.1	267.9	123.1	144.7	1 233.8
4th quarter	1 286.8	802.9	216.8	133.8	74.3	10.1	-1.4	-7.1	72.1	79.2	274.1	124.7	149.4	1 278.1

Gross Domestic Product—*Continued*

(Billions of dollars, quarterly data are at seasonally adjusted annual rates)

Year and quarter	Gross domestic product	Personal con- sumption expendi- tures	Gross private domestic investment						Exports and imports of goods and services			Government consumption expenditures and gross investment			Adden- dum: Final sales of domestic product
			Total	Fixed investment		Change in business inventories			Net exports	Exports	Imports	Total	Federal	State and local	
				Nonres- idential	Residen- tial	Nonfarm	Farm								
1973:															
1st quarter	1 337.5	827.2	232.9	141.2	77.9	18.1	-4.2	-4.4	81.0	85.4	281.8	128.3	153.5	1 323.6
2nd quarter	1 369.4	842.1	242.4	149.0	75.8	12.7	5.0	-1.1	88.3	89.5	286.0	129.1	157.0	1 351.7
3rd quarter	1 391.4	860.8	240.3	153.7	75.0	9.0	2.6	3.2	94.3	91.1	287.1	126.0	161.1	1 379.8
4th quarter	1 432.3	876.1	255.8	156.4	72.7	24.0	2.8	4.7	103.4	98.7	295.6	129.6	166.1	1 405.6
1974:															
1st quarter	1 446.5	894.4	241.2	159.0	69.0	16.6	-3.3	4.3	114.6	110.3	306.6	133.7	172.9	1 433.3
2nd quarter	1 482.5	922.4	247.5	163.7	67.5	15.3	1.0	-5.6	123.8	129.4	318.2	137.2	181.0	1 466.2
3rd quarter	1 511.7	950.1	242.8	168.5	67.4	6.9	-0.1	-9.1	124.5	133.6	328.0	140.9	187.1	1 504.9
4th quarter	1 546.8	957.8	251.0	171.0	60.0	28.7	-8.7	-2.2	134.4	136.6	340.1	147.8	192.3	1 526.8
1975:															
1st quarter	1 560.3	982.7	212.2	166.3	57.7	-18.8	7.1	13.1	138.0	124.9	352.3	150.5	201.8	1 572.1
2nd quarter	1 597.8	1 012.4	211.2	166.0	59.9	-17.8	3.1	16.6	131.8	115.2	357.7	153.0	204.6	1 612.5
3rd quarter	1 657.1	1 046.3	234.3	169.7	64.6	-0.8	0.8	11.6	133.7	122.1	364.9	154.7	210.2	1 657.1
4th quarter	1 707.3	1 075.1	243.7	173.9	68.7	-1.3	2.5	12.9	141.7	128.7	375.5	159.7	215.9	1 706.1
1976:															
1st quarter	1 767.3	1 110.2	271.3	179.1	76.2	16.5	-0.5	4.2	143.1	138.9	381.7	159.3	222.3	1 751.3
2nd quarter	1 797.9	1 130.2	285.8	183.4	80.7	23.6	-1.8	-1.1	146.0	147.1	383.0	160.8	222.2	1 776.1
3rd quarter	1 830.4	1 159.8	289.5	189.8	80.6	17.1	2.0	-5.0	150.9	155.8	386.0	163.1	222.9	1 811.3
4th quarter	1 880.3	1 195.0	299.8	196.4	92.5	13.9	-3.0	-7.2	155.4	162.7	392.8	167.7	225.0	1 869.4
1977:															
1st quarter	1 934.4	1 230.7	321.3	208.8	97.6	16.2	-1.3	-21.6	154.8	176.4	403.9	172.7	231.2	1 919.4
2nd quarter	2 005.1	1 259.1	353.2	218.5	111.7	17.7	5.3	-21.7	161.3	183.0	414.6	177.8	236.8	1 982.1
3rd quarter	2 063.2	1 290.3	373.8	226.8	115.0	27.6	4.4	-21.1	161.8	182.9	420.2	179.5	240.7	2 031.3
4th quarter	2 104.7	1 328.1	378.0	238.8	116.9	12.5	9.8	-30.3	157.1	187.4	428.9	183.7	245.2	2 082.5
1978:															
1st quarter	2 147.7	1 358.3	392.9	243.8	121.1	28.7	-0.6	-39.3	164.0	203.3	435.8	186.3	249.5	2 119.6
2nd quarter	2 273.7	1 417.4	425.6	268.2	130.5	26.5	0.4	-23.3	185.6	208.8	453.9	192.5	261.4	2 246.8
3rd quarter	2 333.9	1 450.6	443.5	281.3	135.8	19.2	7.2	-24.6	190.5	215.1	464.4	196.1	268.3	2 307.5
4th quarter	2 410.2	1 488.7	461.2	294.8	139.1	28.9	-1.5	-17.3	204.5	221.8	477.5	202.9	274.6	2 382.8
1979:															
1st quarter	2 464.5	1 529.3	471.1	308.2	138.6	20.1	4.2	-19.2	210.7	229.8	483.3	206.5	276.8	2 440.2
2nd quarter	2 522.3	1 563.9	482.4	314.2	140.9	24.2	3.1	-23.4	219.7	243.1	499.3	212.0	287.3	2 495.0
3rd quarter	2 592.8	1 617.4	486.4	331.4	143.5	4.9	6.6	-24.4	232.9	257.3	513.4	216.0	297.4	2 581.2
4th quarter	2 650.4	1 663.5	483.5	338.0	141.2	4.0	0.3	-29.0	251.5	280.5	532.3	225.6	306.6	2 646.1
1980															
1st quarter	2 722.3	1 713.1	493.0	350.0	134.5	9.0	-0.6	-37.2	267.1	304.3	553.4	236.3	317.1	2 713.9
2nd quarter	2 719.4	1 716.9	449.8	338.9	111.2	4.9	-5.2	-16.7	275.9	292.6	569.5	247.8	321.7	2 719.8
3rd quarter	2 783.4	1 774.9	430.8	348.7	115.9	-21.3	-12.5	3.3	282.5	279.2	574.5	248.5	325.9	2 817.2
4th quarter	2 911.8	1 836.8	490.1	363.5	131.3	1.4	-6.1	-8.9	290.3	299.2	593.8	261.1	332.8	2 916.5
1981															
1st quarter	3 040.2	1 890.3	549.9	379.7	132.0	31.5	6.8	-17.0	302.8	319.7	616.9	271.3	345.6	3 001.9
2nd quarter	3 070.3	1 923.5	534.7	396.4	128.9	-0.4	9.9	-16.4	305.5	322.0	628.5	282.8	345.7	3 060.8
3rd quarter	3 167.7	1 967.4	576.1	413.4	120.2	30.7	11.8	-10.2	299.7	309.9	634.4	285.4	348.9	3 125.2
4th quarter	3 185.5	1 983.9	564.1	432.2	109.6	15.8	6.5	-16.3	303.2	319.4	653.7	296.9	356.8	3 163.1
1982:															
1st quarter	3 178.6	2 021.4	511.1	426.7	104.8	-25.5	5.1	-17.2	292.3	309.5	663.6	301.6	361.9	3 199.1
2nd quarter	3 231.6	2 046.1	514.1	415.0	102.8	-8.1	4.3	-5.0	294.2	299.1	676.3	307.6	368.7	3 235.3
3rd quarter	3 259.1	2 091.1	509.3	402.6	102.3	-4.7	9.0	-30.3	279.0	309.3	689.1	314.8	374.3	3 254.8
4th quarter	3 299.1	2 148.7	469.8	395.1	112.8	-42.7	4.6	-29.7	265.1	294.9	710.3	328.9	381.4	3 337.2
1983:															
1st quarter	3 361.0	2 185.0	481.3	383.7	130.9	-26.0	-7.3	-24.6	270.6	295.3	719.4	334.5	384.8	3 394.3
2nd quarter	3 469.2	2 257.2	526.0	385.8	148.2	4.9	-13.0	-45.5	272.5	318.0	731.5	343.8	387.7	3 477.2
3rd quarter	3 563.3	2 316.8	561.7	400.9	162.6	30.6	-32.4	-65.2	278.2	343.4	750.0	355.5	394.5	3 565.0
4th quarter	3 664.6	2 374.7	619.4	427.4	168.5	32.2	-8.8	-71.3	286.7	358.0	741.9	344.0	397.9	3 641.2
1984:															
1st quarter	3 791.1	2 422.5	695.6	440.4	175.6	74.0	5.5	-94.3	293.7	388.0	767.4	358.1	409.3	3 711.6
2nd quarter	3 879.7	2 475.6	716.2	464.0	181.4	65.2	5.6	-103.5	303.0	406.5	791.4	372.6	418.8	3 808.9
3rd quarter	3 942.2	2 510.5	731.7	478.4	180.8	65.6	6.8	-103.1	306.5	409.6	803.1	373.3	429.8	3 869.8
4th quarter	3 996.7	2 560.6	718.8	490.3	181.3	42.2	5.0	-107.1	309.2	416.4	824.5	386.3	438.2	3 949.5
1985:															
1st quarter	4 081.2	2 623.8	705.6	496.6	183.4	17.7	7.9	-91.4	305.9	397.3	843.1	395.2	448.0	4 055.6
2nd quarter	4 134.8	2 673.4	711.2	504.1	182.8	20.1	4.2	-114.7	303.9	418.6	864.8	404.4	460.4	4 110.5
3rd quarter	4 221.4	2 742.3	706.3	498.2	187.7	13.9	6.6	-117.2	297.0	414.2	890.0	418.6	471.4	4 201.0
4th quarter	4 285.3	2 779.6	737.2	508.9	193.9	30.0	4.3	-133.6	305.3	438.9	902.1	422.2	479.9	4 250.9
1986:															
1st quarter	4 358.2	2 823.3	752.1	502.4	204.5	42.5	2.5	-126.9	312.2	439.1	909.7	418.6	491.1	4 313.2
2nd quarter	4 385.6	2 855.6	729.7	492.6	218.3	22.3	-3.5	-128.8	314.5	443.4	929.1	431.1	498.0	4 366.8
3rd quarter	4 443.3	2 926.2	699.4	488.6	224.1	-10.1	-3.1	-138.0	320.5	458.5	955.7	448.4	507.3	4 456.5
4th quarter	4 501.7	2 965.6	708.9	495.6	225.6	-10.5	-1.8	-132.3	335.4	467.7	959.5	442.8	516.7	4 513.9
1987:															
1st quarter	4 565.7	3 002.4	729.6	480.0	225.3	31.9	-7.7	-139.4	337.4	476.9	973.2	447.9	525.3	4 541.5
2nd quarter	4 645.1	3 070.0	732.3	490.1	229.2	23.7	-10.7	-144.7	356.9	501.6	987.4	454.9	532.6	4 632.1
3rd quarter	4 722.6	3 134.2	734.0	504.6	227.4	6.0	-4.0	-142.4	373.9	516.4	996.8	456.5	540.4	4 720.6
4th quarter	4 835.9	3 171.3	792.8	506.8	228.4	61.0	-3.3	-142.0	394.7	536.7	1 013.8	463.4	550.4	4 778.2
1988:															
1st quarter	4 898.2	3 247.1	756.5	515.9	228.4	14.4	-2.2	-120.9	421.1	542.0	1 015.5	456.3	559.1	4 886.0
2nd quarter	5 000.4	3 310.2	767.3	529.4	231.4	16.4	-9.9	-103.3	442.1	545.4	1 026.2	454.6	571.6	4 993.9
3rd quarter	5 094.5	3 382.3	776.5	533.2	233.6	23.1	-13.4	-95.8	456.2	552.0	1 031.5	453.5	578.1	5 084.8
4th quarter	5 205.3	3 459.2	795.5	543.7	236.6	37.2	-22.0	-104.2	469.3	573.5	1 054.8	465.0	589.9	5 190.1
1989:															
1st quarter	5 316.8	3 506.1	829.0	553.0	237.2	33.6	5.2	-83.7	492.6	576.3	1 065.3	465.5	599.9	5 277.9
2nd quarter	5 413.2	3 569.7	836.0	562.0	232.2	35.9	5.8	-81.2	512.8	594.0	1 088.7	476.5	612.1	5 371.4
3rd quarter	5 486.9	3 627.3	832.0	579.0	229.1	28.5	-4.7	-79.3	509.7	589.0	1 107.0	484.9	622.1	5 463.0
4th quarter	5 537.8	3 676.1	819.9	570.9	226.6	28.8	-6.5	-77.5	522.1	599.7	1 119.4	482.0	637.4	5 515.4

Real Gross Domestic Product

(Billions of chained [1992] dollars, quarterly data are at seasonally adjusted annual rates)

Year and quarter	Gross domestic product	Personal consumption expenditures	Gross private domestic investment						Exports and imports of goods and services			Government consumption expenditures and gross investment			Addendum: Final sales of domestic product
			Total	Fixed investment		Change in business inventories		Net exports	Exports	Imports	Total	Federal	State and local	
				Nonres-idential	Residen-tial	Nonfarm	Farm							
1962	2 454.8	1 533.8	302.1	168.0	133.9	18.1	1.5	-26.5	93.0	119.5	686.0	393.2	292.1	2 445.4
1963	2 559.4	1 596.6	321.6	176.4	149.6	16.4	1.3	-22.7	100.0	122.7	701.9	391.8	309.7	2 552.4
1964	2 708.4	1 692.3	348.3	197.2	158.3	19.5	-3.7	-15.9	113.3	129.2	715.9	385.2	330.9	2 705.1
1965	2 881.1	1 799.1	397.2	231.3	153.7	27.7	2.4	-27.4	115.6	143.0	737.6	385.2	353.2	2 860.4
1966	3 069.2	1 902.0	430.6	259.4	140.0	44.7	-1.3	-40.9	123.4	164.2	804.6	429.1	375.9	3 033.5
1967	3 147.2	1 958.6	411.8	255.3	135.6	29.6	2.5	-50.1	126.1	176.2	865.6	471.7	394.2	3 125.1
1968	3 293.9	2 070.2	433.3	266.4	154.0	23.0	3.7	-67.2	135.3	202.5	892.4	476.3	416.5	3 278.0
1969	3 393.6	2 147.5	458.3	285.6	158.6	27.3	0.0	-71.3	142.7	214.0	887.5	459.9	428.0	3 377.2
1970	3 397.6	2 197.8	426.1	282.8	149.1	8.3	-2.4	-65.0	158.1	223.1	866.8	427.2	440.0	3 406.5
1971	3 510.0	2 279.5	474.9	282.4	190.0	18.0	4.0	-75.8	159.2	235.0	851.0	397.0	454.4	3 499.8
1972	3 702.3	2 415.9	531.8	307.7	223.8	25.4	0.3	-89.0	172.0	261.0	854.1	390.2	464.5	3 689.5
1973	3 916.3	2 532.6	595.5	352.5	222.3	38.5	1.4	-63.0	209.6	272.6	848.4	371.1	478.5	3 883.9
1974	3 891.2	2 514.7	546.5	354.4	176.4	31.9	-4.7	-35.6	229.8	265.3	862.9	368.8	495.6	3 873.4
1975	3 873.9	2 570.0	446.6	317.3	153.5	-18.5	6.1	-7.2	228.2	235.4	876.3	367.9	510.0	3 906.4
1976	4 082.9	2 714.3	537.4	332.6	189.7	32.1	-1.3	-39.9	241.6	281.5	876.8	364.3	514.3	4 061.7
1977	4 273.6	2 829.8	622.1	371.8	229.8	31.7	6.8	-64.2	247.4	311.7	884.7	370.1	516.4	4 240.8
1978	4 503.0	2 951.6	693.4	422.6	245.0	41.4	2.6	-65.6	273.1	338.6	910.6	377.7	534.7	4 464.4
1979	4 630.6	3 020.2	709.8	463.3	236.0	19.3	3.8	-45.3	299.0	344.3	924.9	383.3	543.5	4 614.4
1980	4 615.0	3 009.7	628.3	461.1	186.1	-1.5	-7.1	10.1	331.4	321.3	941.4	399.3	543.6	4 641.9
1981	4 720.7	3 046.4	686.0	485.7	171.2	22.8	9.6	5.6	335.3	329.7	947.7	415.9	532.8	4 691.6
1982	4 620.3	3 081.5	587.2	464.3	140.1	-22.9	7.3	-14.1	311.4	325.5	960.1	429.4	531.4	4 651.2
1983	4 803.7	3 240.6	642.1	456.4	197.6	12.1	-16.9	-63.3	303.3	366.6	987.3	452.7	534.9	4 821.2
1984	5 140.1	3 407.6	833.4	535.4	226.4	69.1	6.4	-127.3	328.4	455.7	1 018.4	463.7	555.0	5 061.6
1985	5 323.5	3 566.5	823.8	568.4	229.5	23.3	6.9	-147.9	337.3	485.2	1 080.1	495.6	584.7	5 296.9
1986	5 487.7	3 708.7	811.8	548.5	257.0	12.4	-1.6	-163.9	362.2	526.1	1 135.0	518.4	616.9	5 480.9
1987	5 649.5	3 822.3	821.5	542.4	257.6	34.2	-8.8	-156.2	402.0	558.2	1 165.9	534.4	631.8	5 626.0
1988	5 865.2	3 972.7	828.2	566.0	252.5	24.7	-12.6	-114.4	465.8	580.2	1 180.9	524.6	656.6	5 855.1
1989	6 062.0	4 064.6	863.5	588.8	243.2	33.5	0.0	-82.7	520.2	603.0	1 213.9	531.5	682.6	6 028.7
1962:														
1st quarter	2 422.6	1 508.4	305.2	163.3	130.9	26.3	2.2	-27.0	89.5	116.5	674.9	386.2	288.0	2 400.3
2nd quarter	2 448.0	1 526.7	301.9	168.6	135.0	17.0	0.6	-23.6	95.4	119.0	682.4	391.7	290.0	2 440.7
3rd quarter	2 471.9	1 539.6	306.5	170.8	134.9	19.7	1.1	-25.4	95.2	120.5	691.4	397.0	293.6	2 462.0
4th quarter	2 476.7	1 560.6	295.0	169.3	134.7	9.3	1.9	-30.2	91.9	122.0	695.4	398.0	296.7	2 478.7
1963:														
1st quarter	2 508.7	1 571.2	313.1	168.7	139.6	17.0	6.9	-27.0	92.1	119.2	691.1	388.3	302.3	2 492.4
2nd quarter	2 538.1	1 586.3	316.2	173.7	149.6	14.9	0.9	-21.4	100.6	122.0	694.5	388.8	305.3	2 533.8
3rd quarter	2 586.3	1 607.6	327.4	178.8	152.4	21.2	-1.4	-23.7	101.3	125.0	713.3	399.5	313.4	2 578.0
4th quarter	2 604.6	1 621.1	329.7	184.5	157.0	12.7	-1.0	-18.7	106.0	124.7	708.6	390.5	317.9	2 605.3
1964:														
1st quarter	2 666.7	1 653.6	346.1	189.4	166.7	19.6	-3.8	-12.8	111.7	124.6	712.5	389.5	322.9	2 663.1
2nd quarter	2 697.5	1 683.1	344.2	194.1	158.2	19.3	-4.3	-16.6	110.8	127.4	721.4	391.6	329.9	2 695.0
3rd quarter	2 729.6	1 713.9	349.1	200.6	155.7	18.7	-4.1	-16.6	114.2	130.8	714.9	381.7	333.6	2 727.6
4th quarter	2 739.8	1 718.6	353.9	204.5	152.8	20.3	-2.7	-17.6	116.6	134.2	714.7	377.9	337.3	2 734.5
1965:														
1st quarter	2 808.9	1 756.2	392.0	218.7	153.4	38.2	0.6	-26.9	102.5	129.4	713.9	374.2	340.4	2 777.2
2nd quarter	2 846.3	1 776.1	391.6	226.6	154.6	26.0	2.8	-26.0	118.7	144.7	728.4	380.2	349.0	2 826.8
3rd quarter	2 898.8	1 806.1	400.9	235.0	155.2	25.6	3.2	-28.8	116.6	145.3	746.3	388.2	359.1	2 879.8
4th quarter	2 970.5	1 858.0	404.3	244.9	151.8	21.1	3.0	-27.8	124.7	152.5	761.7	398.3	364.2	2 957.8
1966:														
1st quarter	3 042.4	1 885.6	436.1	255.6	155.2	41.4	0.6	-33.3	123.1	156.3	776.3	407.7	369.4	3 008.8
2nd quarter	3 055.5	1 890.9	429.8	259.3	142.8	43.6	-2.9	-38.0	122.2	160.2	800.0	428.1	372.3	3 023.1
3rd quarter	3 076.5	1 912.4	426.7	262.0	138.2	39.7	-1.7	-46.3	123.0	169.3	812.5	436.6	376.3	3 047.2
4th quarter	3 102.4	1 919.1	429.8	260.8	123.7	53.9	-1.3	-46.0	125.2	171.1	829.6	444.2	385.8	3 054.9
1967:														
1st quarter	3 127.2	1 931.2	415.8	255.0	120.0	39.9	5.5	-46.6	127.0	173.6	864.4	474.4	390.2	3 085.6
2nd quarter	3 129.5	1 957.5	399.3	254.4	133.6	15.0	7.0	-46.8	125.6	172.4	860.2	468.3	392.2	3 119.0
3rd quarter	3 154.2	1 967.1	411.5	253.4	140.3	30.8	0.5	-50.4	124.4	174.8	865.4	471.8	393.9	3 134.2
4th quarter	3 178.0	1 978.5	420.6	258.6	148.4	32.5	-3.0	-56.6	127.4	184.0	872.5	472.3	400.6	3 161.5
1968:														
1st quarter	3 236.2	2 025.1	425.2	266.4	149.3	15.4	6.5	-64.5	130.3	194.7	887.3	480.5	407.1	3 225.3
2nd quarter	3 292.1	2 056.4	442.9	261.6	153.1	27.7	11.5	-65.2	132.5	197.7	892.2	477.7	414.9	3 258.0
3rd quarter	3 316.1	2 095.1	430.1	264.9	155.9	23.1	0.9	-68.9	140.7	209.6	893.6	473.6	420.4	3 303.9
4th quarter	3 331.2	2 104.4	434.9	272.7	157.8	25.6	-4.4	-70.2	137.6	207.8	896.6	473.5	423.6	3 325.1
1969:														
1st quarter	3 381.9	2 128.0	463.3	280.4	163.5	29.7	3.8	-65.1	123.2	188.3	891.6	466.4	425.7	3 357.5
2nd quarter	3 390.2	2 141.4	458.9	283.2	161.7	24.3	3.8	-75.9	149.5	225.3	890.8	462.5	428.8	3 373.0
3rd quarter	3 409.7	2 152.0	468.2	290.6	160.5	33.9	-2.9	-74.8	147.7	222.4	888.7	459.8	429.3	3 389.6
4th quarter	3 392.6	2 168.8	442.6	288.4	148.7	21.4	-4.6	-69.6	150.4	220.0	878.8	451.0	428.2	3 388.9
1970														
1st quarter	3 386.5	2 182.3	427.6	285.9	149.0	0.4	2.3	-65.6	153.8	219.4	871.8	439.7	432.5	3 397.6
2nd quarter	3 391.6	2 192.9	427.3	284.3	139.1	11.6	0.9	-64.6	159.0	223.6	863.2	428.5	435.0	3 391.9
3rd quarter	3 423.0	2 211.6	435.9	285.8	146.4	19.8	-4.6	-64.3	158.7	223.0	866.7	422.0	445.0	3 421.9
4th quarter	3 389.4	2 204.6	413.8	275.3	161.9	1.2	-8.1	-65.6	160.9	226.5	865.5	418.3	447.5	3 414.8
1971														
1st quarter	3 481.4	2 246.5	465.0	277.9	170.6	25.5	5.7	-64.3	159.6	223.9	856.4	406.7	450.0	3 458.9
2nd quarter	3 501.0	2 266.5	480.6	281.8	187.8	18.7	9.8	-81.5	159.4	240.9	852.6	399.7	453.1	3 481.2
3rd quarter	3 523.8	2 283.9	484.1	282.3	197.0	18.8	5.4	-78.1	168.1	246.1	848.8	394.8	454.3	3 509.4
4th quarter	3 533.8	2 321.1	470.0	287.7	204.6	9.1	-5.1	-79.5	149.7	229.2	846.4	386.8	460.0	3 549.5
1972:														
1st quarter	3 604.7	2 352.0	502.4	297.6	218.3	14.4	-1.6	-95.6	167.4	263.0	858.8	397.0	462.2	3 608.1
2nd quarter	3 687.9	2 394.9	533.3	302.5	222.6	27.4	4.6	-88.3	164.8	253.1	859.9	399.7	460.5	3 665.7
3rd quarter	3 726.2	2 430.6	542.4	307.3	223.1	35.8	1.3	-85.7	172.4	258.2	848.4	384.8	464.3	3 700.0
4th quarter	3 790.4	2 486.1	549.1	323.6	231.1	24.0	-2.9	-86.1	183.5	269.6	849.2	379.3	470.8	3 784.3

Real Gross Domestic Product—*Continued*

(Billions of chained [1992] dollars, quarterly data are at seasonally adjusted annual rates)

Year and quarter	Gross domestic product	Personal consumption expenditures	Gross private domestic investment					Exports and imports of goods and services			Government consumption expenditures and gross investment			Addendum: Final sales of domestic product
			Total	Fixed investment		Change in business inventories		Net exports	Exports	Imports	Total	Federal	State and local	
				Nonres-idential	Residen-tial	Nonfarm	Farm							
1973:														
1st quarter	3 892.2	2 530.4	588.6	339.0	238.8	47.0	-7.3	-81.2	200.3	281.5	854.6	381.8	473.8	3 867.0
2nd quarter	3 919.0	2 527.5	601.0	352.5	226.7	29.2	9.3	-64.7	209.0	273.8	852.3	378.6	474.7	3 884.5
3rd quarter	3 907.1	2 539.9	583.0	358.2	217.0	22.2	2.1	-55.9	210.3	266.2	839.1	360.6	479.9	3 890.9
4th quarter	3 947.1	2 532.6	609.2	360.5	206.8	55.6	1.4	-50.3	218.8	269.1	847.7	363.6	485.5	3 893.1
1974:														
1st quarter	3 908.2	2 512.7	565.5	360.2	191.6	35.0	-6.4	-34.1	226.4	260.6	857.5	367.6	491.3	3 889.1
2nd quarter	3 922.6	2 522.7	561.1	359.2	183.2	27.7	-0.7	-34.7	236.4	271.2	866.9	370.7	497.6	3 899.7
3rd quarter	3 880.0	2 532.4	530.3	354.5	177.1	11.0	-1.0	-41.1	225.0	266.1	861.8	366.6	496.7	3 882.5
4th quarter	3 854.1	2 490.9	529.2	343.7	153.9	53.7	-10.8	-32.3	231.1	263.4	865.6	370.4	496.6	3 822.2
1975:														
1st quarter	3 800.9	2 513.2	431.2	321.5	144.3	-39.5	10.5	-6.8	230.5	237.3	875.7	368.5	508.8	3 848.3
2nd quarter	3 835.2	2 556.3	419.9	312.8	147.4	-32.8	6.4	2.5	220.9	218.4	871.6	368.2	504.9	3 887.9
3rd quarter	3 907.0	2 591.8	462.5	315.9	157.7	-0.7	3.6	-11.9	224.7	236.6	875.7	366.9	510.5	3 922.7
4th quarter	3 952.5	2 618.7	472.8	319.1	164.6	-1.1	3.9	-12.7	236.7	249.3	882.2	368.1	515.9	3 966.7
1976:														
1st quarter	4 044.6	2 674.2	519.7	324.9	181.4	31.1	-1.3	-29.2	236.0	265.2	886.2	365.3	522.8	4 027.0
2nd quarter	4 072.2	2 697.9	540.5	328.4	186.7	42.6	-2.1	-38.4	238.1	276.5	876.8	364.4	514.1	4 039.1
3rd quarter	4 088.5	2 724.9	539.9	335.4	183.6	29.9	2.7	-42.8	244.7	287.5	872.8	363.6	511.0	4 061.7
4th quarter	4 126.4	2 760.8	549.6	341.6	207.0	25.0	-4.7	-49.2	247.7	296.8	871.5	363.8	509.4	4 119.0
1977:														
1st quarter	4 176.3	2 794.3	577.7	357.6	212.8	28.4	-2.2	-67.0	243.8	310.8	878.1	366.0	513.9	4 161.4
2nd quarter	4 260.1	2 810.3	622.7	367.8	236.6	30.3	7.9	-63.2	250.1	313.3	887.6	372.3	517.0	4 228.4
3rd quarter	4 329.5	2 836.9	652.8	374.6	236.4	47.5	11.1	-56.9	252.2	309.1	887.4	372.2	516.9	4 270.0
4th quarter	4 328.3	2 877.7	635.3	387.1	233.5	20.7	10.3	-69.9	243.6	313.5	885.8	369.8	517.7	4 303.3
1978:														
1st quarter	4 345.5	2 893.1	650.5	389.1	235.1	48.4	-0.9	-84.9	249.5	334.4	887.5	370.8	518.5	4 306.0
2nd quarter	4 510.7	2 954.6	691.0	421.0	246.2	42.8	1.2	-59.7	275.5	335.1	910.9	378.6	534.2	4 474.6
3rd quarter	4 552.1	2 968.3	710.7	433.8	249.7	30.3	10.8	-62.0	278.3	340.3	917.8	379.3	540.5	4 511.6
4th quarter	4 603.7	2 990.6	721.5	446.5	249.0	44.2	-0.9	-55.7	289.1	344.7	925.9	382.2	545.7	4 565.4
1979:														
1st quarter	4 605.7	3 008.1	717.8	456.8	243.2	28.8	5.9	-55.7	288.9	344.6	916.2	381.3	536.8	4 579.0
2nd quarter	4 615.6	3 003.5	722.9	455.9	238.9	34.4	5.0	-56.1	289.7	345.7	924.8	384.8	541.9	4 577.0
3rd quarter	4 644.9	3 028.7	708.2	470.3	235.7	7.2	6.7	-40.2	299.8	340.0	925.6	383.1	544.5	4 639.2
4th quarter	4 656.2	3 040.2	690.1	470.2	226.4	6.6	-2.2	-29.1	317.8	346.9	932.9	384.0	550.9	4 662.5
1980														
1st quarter	4 679.0	3 037.2	689.6	475.9	210.3	13.2	-2.7	-20.0	327.7	347.8	946.5	395.1	553.2	4 675.3
2nd quarter	4 566.6	2 968.8	614.5	450.4	169.9	6.8	-6.2	11.3	333.9	322.7	948.3	403.7	546.1	4 579.0
3rd quarter	4 562.3	2 998.6	570.7	454.1	173.0	-28.0	-14.0	33.4	332.8	299.4	936.4	399.3	538.6	4 637.1
4th quarter	4 651.9	3 034.2	638.3	464.3	191.3	1.9	-5.3	15.7	331.1	315.4	934.4	399.2	536.6	4 676.2
1981														
1st quarter	4 739.2	3 045.6	699.8	471.3	188.0	37.4	6.8	8.3	336.8	328.5	946.1	406.7	540.7	4 692.9
2nd quarter	4 696.8	3 045.9	662.4	479.5	180.8	-0.2	10.3	9.5	338.9	329.4	947.7	418.4	530.3	4 699.0
3rd quarter	4 753.0	3 058.8	704.6	490.7	166.5	35.9	13.4	5.5	331.4	325.9	945.5	418.1	528.2	4 702.5
4th quarter	4 693.8	3 035.3	677.1	501.4	149.6	18.3	7.8	-0.9	334.1	335.0	951.7	420.5	532.0	4 672.0
1982:														
1st quarter	4 615.9	3 054.0	605.8	488.0	141.1	-29.0	7.0	-5.3	320.4	325.7	949.0	420.2	529.6	4 655.4
2nd quarter	4 634.9	3 062.1	601.6	469.6	136.5	-9.6	5.7	2.6	322.8	320.2	954.7	424.3	531.2	4 651.2
3rd quarter	4 612.1	3 080.1	593.7	454.2	134.8	-4.9	11.5	-26.5	308.2	334.7	961.2	431.0	530.8	4 616.9
4th quarter	4 618.3	3 129.7	547.6	445.5	147.8	-47.9	5.0	-27.3	294.3	321.7	975.5	442.1	533.8	4 681.3
1983:														
1st quarter	4 663.0	3 156.5	563.9	435.9	170.8	-29.7	-8.5	-29.8	298.9	328.8	978.4	444.6	534.1	4 719.4
2nd quarter	4 763.6	3 220.0	617.7	440.6	192.9	5.3	-14.6	-54.6	299.8	354.5	985.0	452.5	532.7	4 785.3
3rd quarter	4 849.0	3 267.1	661.4	459.2	210.5	35.9	-34.8	-78.0	304.3	382.2	1 001.8	465.1	536.6	4 860.7
4th quarter	4 939.2	3 318.6	725.3	490.0	216.3	36.9	-9.8	-90.8	310.2	401.0	984.1	448.4	536.0	4 919.5
1984:														
1st quarter	5 053.6	3 354.0	812.2	505.5	224.0	83.5	4.5	-115.5	317.5	433.0	994.1	450.8	543.8	4 961.0
2nd quarter	5 132.9	3 397.5	835.6	530.8	229.6	72.5	7.2	-125.5	325.7	451.2	1 016.6	465.9	550.9	5 050.0
3rd quarter	5 170.3	3 418.4	850.8	546.3	226.6	72.6	7.8	-130.5	332.0	462.5	1 022.5	463.1	559.9	5 085.6
4th quarter	5 203.7	3 460.6	834.9	558.8	225.5	47.8	6.2	-137.7	338.3	476.1	1 040.4	475.1	565.6	5 149.9
1985:														
1st quarter	5 257.3	3 511.2	816.6	564.6	226.9	20.7	8.7	-127.3	338.7	466.0	1 053.2	482.3	571.1	5 231.7
2nd quarter	5 283.7	3 540.8	821.1	572.7	225.7	23.5	3.6	-151.6	337.3	489.0	1 072.8	491.5	581.5	5 261.0
3rd quarter	5 359.6	3 602.1	816.0	563.5	230.2	16.1	9.6	-152.6	332.0	484.6	1 095.7	505.2	590.5	5 336.9
4th quarter	5 393.6	3 612.1	841.8	572.9	235.1	32.9	5.6	-160.0	341.4	501.3	1 098.9	503.4	595.6	5 358.0
1986:														
1st quarter	5 460.8	3 644.0	855.3	563.8	245.1	50.5	2.2	-149.7	351.3	501.0	1 108.3	500.1	608.7	5 410.5
2nd quarter	5 466.9	3 683.0	824.0	548.0	259.2	27.6	-5.2	-167.1	355.9	523.0	1 129.6	514.8	615.1	5 448.4
3rd quarter	5 496.3	3 742.8	781.3	538.7	262.5	-12.7	-3.7	-173.9	364.1	538.1	1 154.5	533.9	620.8	5 518.2
4th quarter	5 526.8	3 764.8	786.7	543.4	261.2	-15.6	0.1	-164.9	377.5	542.3	1 147.7	524.8	623.2	5 546.6
1987:														
1st quarter	5 561.8	3 765.7	808.6	526.2	258.8	36.3	-7.7	-161.2	377.7	538.8	1 153.4	526.9	626.8	5 535.8
2nd quarter	5 618.0	3 814.0	807.1	537.5	260.8	27.4	-14.1	-160.2	393.5	553.7	1 162.8	534.3	628.8	5 608.4
3rd quarter	5 667.4	3 852.9	806.3	553.8	256.2	7.7	-6.8	-152.2	411.1	563.2	1 165.9	534.2	632.0	5 671.5
4th quarter	5 750.6	3 856.5	864.0	552.0	254.7	65.6	-6.3	-151.3	425.7	577.0	1 181.5	542.2	639.6	5 688.3
1988:														
1st quarter	5 785.3	3 924.2	817.8	556.1	251.3	16.8	-3.3	-125.9	448.8	574.8	1 172.5	527.6	645.1	5 774.2
2nd quarter	5 844.0	3 952.2	823.2	567.1	252.2	17.7	-11.7	-106.9	461.4	568.3	1 177.0	522.2	655.0	5 840.1
3rd quarter	5 878.7	3 985.1	830.0	568.0	252.9	25.5	-13.6	-110.6	469.4	580.0	1 176.1	517.9	658.4	5 869.2
4th quarter	5 952.8	4 029.1	841.7	572.9	253.7	38.8	-21.8	-114.3	483.5	597.8	1 198.1	530.6	667.8	5 937.0
1989:														
1st quarter	6 011.0	4 032.8	870.5	579.5	252.6	36.2	5.0	-88.7	502.0	590.7	1 193.5	521.4	672.3	5 970.0
2nd quarter	6 055.6	4 047.4	873.1	586.6	244.3	37.8	6.1	-79.8	522.0	601.9	1 211.1	532.0	679.4	6 010.9
3rd quarter	6 088.0	4 083.2	864.0	600.5	240.1	30.4	-4.6	-84.5	521.3	605.8	1 222.6	537.7	685.1	6 063.1
4th quarter	6 093.5	4 095.0	846.3	588.8	236.0	29.6	-6.3	-77.9	535.5	613.5	1 228.4	535.0	693.7	6 070.8

Price Indexes for Gross Domestic Product and Domestic Purchases

(Index numbers, 1992=100; quarterly data are seasonally adjusted)

Year and quarter	Gross domestic product	Personal con- sumption expendi- tures	Private fixed investment			Exports and imports of goods and services		Government consumption expenditures and gross investment			Adden- dum: Final sales of domestic purchases
			Total	Nonres- idential	Residen- tial	Exports	Imports	Total	Federal	State and local	
1962	23.8	23.7	28.0	31.5	21.7	29.5	20.9	19.2	19.4	18.8	23.3
1963	24.1	24.0	28.0	31.5	21.5	29.4	21.3	19.6	19.9	19.3	23.6
1964	24.5	24.3	28.2	31.7	21.7	29.6	21.8	20.2	20.6	19.6	23.9
1965	25.0	24.7	28.6	32.1	22.3	30.6	22.1	20.7	21.2	20.2	24.4
1966	25.7	25.3	29.3	32.6	23.1	31.6	22.6	21.6	21.9	21.1	25.1
1967	26.5	26.0	30.1	33.4	23.9	32.8	22.7	22.5	22.6	22.4	25.8
1968	27.6	27.0	31.3	34.6	25.1	33.5	23.0	23.7	23.8	23.6	27.0
1969	28.9	28.2	32.9	36.0	26.9	34.5	23.6	25.2	25.1	25.2	28.2
1970	30.5	29.5	34.3	37.8	27.7	36.0	25.0	27.2	27.1	27.3	29.7
1971	32.1	30.8	36.1	39.6	29.4	37.3	26.5	29.3	29.4	29.2	31.3
1972	33.4	31.9	37.6	41.0	31.1	38.5	28.4	31.5	32.0	31.0	32.7
1973	35.3	33.6	39.7	42.6	33.9	43.8	33.4	33.9	34.5	33.3	34.6
1974	38.5	37.0	43.7	46.8	37.4	54.1	48.0	37.5	37.9	37.0	38.2
1975	42.1	40.0	49.2	53.3	40.9	59.7	52.1	41.4	42.0	40.8	41.7
1976	44.6	42.3	52.1	56.3	43.5	61.6	53.7	44.0	44.6	43.4	44.2
1977	47.4	45.1	56.2	60.1	48.0	64.2	58.5	47.1	48.2	46.2	47.2
1978	50.9	48.4	61.1	64.4	53.7	68.2	62.7	50.3	51.5	49.3	50.7
1979	55.2	52.8	66.7	69.7	59.8	76.5	73.4	54.8	56.1	53.7	55.2
1980	60.3	58.5	73.0	76.0	66.2	84.2	91.5	60.9	62.2	59.7	61.1
1981	66.0	63.7	79.9	83.5	71.6	90.3	96.4	66.8	68.3	65.6	66.7
1982	70.2	67.4	84.5	88.3	75.5	90.8	93.1	71.3	72.9	69.9	70.6
1983	73.2	70.5	84.4	87.5	77.2	91.3	89.6	74.5	76.1	73.2	73.3
1984	75.9	73.1	85.0	87.5	79.4	92.3	88.9	78.2	80.4	76.4	75.9
1985	78.5	75.8	86.2	88.3	81.5	89.8	86.0	81.0	82.7	79.5	78.3
1986	80.6	78.0	88.6	90.2	84.9	88.5	86.0	82.7	84.0	81.6	80.4
1987	83.1	81.0	90.4	91.3	88.3	91.0	91.0	85.2	85.3	85.0	83.1
1988	86.1	84.3	93.3	93.7	92.1	96.0	95.4	87.4	87.2	87.5	86.1
1989	89.7	88.4	95.9	96.2	95.1	97.9	97.8	90.2	89.8	90.5	89.8
1962:											
1st quarter	23.7	23.6	28.1	31.5	21.7	29.7	20.9	19.0	19.3	18.7	23.2
2nd quarter	23.8	23.7	28.1	31.5	21.7	29.4	20.9	19.1	19.3	18.8	23.2
3rd quarter	23.9	23.7	28.0	31.5	21.7	29.4	20.8	19.2	19.4	18.8	23.3
4th quarter	24.0	23.8	28.0	31.4	21.6	29.4	20.9	19.3	19.6	19.0	23.4
1963:											
1st quarter	24.0	23.9	28.0	31.5	21.6	29.5	21.1	19.5	19.8	19.1	23.5
2nd quarter	24.1	23.9	28.0	31.5	21.5	29.5	21.2	19.6	19.8	19.2	23.5
3rd quarter	24.1	24.0	27.9	31.6	21.3	29.4	21.4	19.5	19.8	19.3	23.6
4th quarter	24.3	24.1	28.0	31.5	21.4	29.4	21.5	19.9	20.2	19.4	23.7
1964:											
1st quarter	24.3	24.2	27.9	31.5	21.2	29.5	21.7	20.0	20.4	19.5	23.8
2nd quarter	24.4	24.3	28.1	31.7	21.6	29.4	21.8	20.1	20.5	19.6	23.9
3rd quarter	24.5	24.3	28.2	31.7	21.6	29.7	21.8	20.3	20.8	19.7	24.0
4th quarter	24.6	24.4	28.5	31.9	22.1	30.0	21.8	20.3	20.7	19.8	24.1
1965:											
1st quarter	24.8	24.5	28.5	31.9	22.1	30.7	22.0	20.5	20.9	20.0	24.2
2nd quarter	24.9	24.7	28.6	32.0	22.1	30.6	21.9	20.6	21.0	20.1	24.3
3rd quarter	25.0	24.8	28.6	32.1	22.1	30.6	22.1	20.8	21.2	20.2	24.4
4th quarter	25.2	24.8	28.9	32.2	22.7	30.5	22.3	21.1	21.7	20.4	24.6
1966:											
1st quarter	25.3	25.0	28.8	32.2	22.4	31.0	22.4	21.2	21.7	20.7	24.7
2nd quarter	25.5	25.2	29.3	32.5	23.2	31.3	22.6	21.3	21.6	21.0	24.9
3rd quarter	25.8	25.4	29.3	32.6	23.1	31.7	22.6	21.8	22.2	21.3	25.2
4th quarter	26.0	25.6	29.7	32.9	23.6	32.3	22.7	21.9	22.1	21.6	25.4
1967:											
1st quarter	26.2	25.7	29.8	33.1	23.6	32.8	22.7	22.1	22.1	22.0	25.5
2nd quarter	26.3	25.9	29.9	33.3	23.7	32.8	22.6	22.3	22.4	22.2	25.7
3rd quarter	26.6	26.1	30.1	33.5	23.8	32.7	22.6	22.6	22.6	22.5	25.9
4th quarter	26.9	26.4	30.5	33.8	24.3	32.9	22.7	22.9	23.1	22.8	26.2
1968:											
1st quarter	27.2	26.7	30.8	34.1	24.7	33.1	22.8	23.3	23.3	23.2	26.5
2nd quarter	27.5	26.9	31.1	34.4	25.0	33.8	23.0	23.6	23.6	23.5	26.8
3rd quarter	27.8	27.2	31.3	34.7	25.0	33.4	23.0	23.9	24.1	23.7	27.1
4th quarter	28.1	27.4	32.0	35.3	25.9	33.6	23.2	24.3	24.4	24.2	27.4
1969:											
1st quarter	28.4	27.7	32.4	35.5	26.4	34.1	23.3	24.5	24.4	24.5	27.7
2nd quarter	28.7	28.0	32.7	35.8	26.8	34.1	23.4	24.9	24.8	25.0	28.0
3rd quarter	29.1	28.3	33.0	36.2	26.9	34.6	23.6	25.5	25.5	25.4	28.4
4th quarter	29.5	28.6	33.4	36.6	27.3	35.4	24.2	25.9	25.8	26.0	28.8
1970											
1st quarter	29.9	29.0	33.7	37.0	27.3	35.5	24.4	26.6	26.6	26.5	29.2
2nd quarter	30.4	29.3	34.5	37.7	28.3	36.3	24.7	27.0	26.9	27.1	29.6
3rd quarter	30.6	29.6	34.3	37.9	27.6	36.1	25.3	27.4	27.3	27.5	29.9
4th quarter	31.0	30.0	34.7	38.4	27.8	36.2	25.6	27.8	27.6	28.1	30.3
1971											
1st quarter	31.5	30.3	35.3	39.0	28.5	37.3	26.2	28.6	28.6	28.6	30.8
2nd quarter	31.9	30.7	35.9	39.5	29.1	37.3	26.3	29.1	29.2	29.1	31.2
3rd quarter	32.3	31.0	36.3	39.8	29.7	37.1	26.6	29.5	29.6	29.5	31.5
4th quarter	32.5	31.2	36.7	40.1	30.1	37.3	27.0	30.0	30.4	29.7	31.8
1972:											
1st quarter	33.0	31.6	37.1	40.6	30.5	37.9	27.5	30.8	31.5	30.3	32.3
2nd quarter	33.2	31.7	37.4	40.9	30.7	38.3	28.2	31.2	31.8	30.7	32.5
3rd quarter	33.5	32.0	37.7	41.1	31.2	38.4	28.7	31.5	31.9	31.2	32.8
4th quarter	33.9	32.3	38.3	41.4	32.1	39.4	29.4	32.2	32.8	31.7	33.2

Price Indexes for Gross Domestic Product and Domestic Purchases —*Continued*

(Index numbers, 1992=100; quarterly data are seasonally adjusted)

Year and quarter	Gross domestic product	Personal consumption expenditures	Private fixed investment			Exports and imports of goods and services		Government consumption expenditures and gross investment			Addendum: Final sales of domestic purchases
			Total	Nonres-idential	Residen-tial	Exports	Imports	Total	Federal	State and local	
1973:											
1st quarter	34.4	32.7	38.7	41.7	32.6	40.6	30.2	32.9	33.5	32.4	33.7
2nd quarter	35.0	33.3	39.4	42.3	33.4	42.4	32.6	33.6	34.1	33.1	34.3
3rd quarter	35.6	33.9	40.2	43.0	34.5	44.9	34.2	34.2	34.9	33.6	35.0
4th quarter	36.2	34.6	40.7	43.4	35.1	47.2	36.7	34.8	35.5	34.2	35.6
1974:											
1st quarter	37.0	35.6	41.5	44.1	35.9	50.6	42.6	35.7	36.2	35.2	36.6
2nd quarter	37.8	36.6	42.7	45.6	36.8	52.3	47.7	36.7	37.1	36.4	37.6
3rd quarter	38.9	37.5	44.4	47.5	37.9	55.3	50.1	38.1	38.4	37.7	38.7
4th quarter	40.1	38.4	46.2	49.8	39.0	58.2	51.7	39.3	39.9	38.8	39.8
1975:											
1st quarter	41.0	39.1	47.9	51.7	40.0	60.0	52.6	40.2	40.8	39.7	40.7
2nd quarter	41.7	39.6	49.0	53.1	40.7	59.7	52.7	41.0	41.5	40.5	41.3
3rd quarter	42.4	40.4	49.6	53.8	41.1	59.4	51.6	41.6	42.1	41.2	42.1
4th quarter	43.2	41.1	50.4	54.6	41.8	59.8	51.6	42.6	43.4	41.8	42.8
1976:											
1st quarter	43.7	41.5	50.9	55.2	42.0	60.6	52.4	43.1	43.6	42.5	43.3
2nd quarter	44.2	41.9	51.8	55.9	43.3	61.3	53.3	43.7	44.1	43.2	43.8
3rd quarter	44.8	42.6	52.5	56.7	44.0	61.7	54.2	44.2	44.8	43.6	44.4
4th quarter	45.6	43.3	53.4	57.5	44.7	62.8	54.8	45.0	46.1	44.2	45.2
1977:											
1st quarter	46.3	44.0	54.4	58.5	45.9	63.6	56.8	46.0	47.1	45.0	46.0
2nd quarter	47.1	44.8	55.6	59.5	47.3	64.6	58.4	46.7	47.7	45.8	46.8
3rd quarter	47.7	45.5	56.8	60.6	48.7	64.1	59.2	47.3	48.2	46.6	47.6
4th quarter	48.6	46.2	58.0	61.7	50.1	64.5	59.8	48.4	49.6	47.4	48.4
1978:											
1st quarter	49.4	47.0	59.2	62.6	51.6	65.8	60.8	49.1	50.2	48.1	49.2
2nd quarter	50.4	48.0	60.5	63.9	53.1	67.5	62.3	49.9	50.9	49.0	50.2
3rd quarter	51.3	48.9	61.7	64.9	54.4	68.6	63.3	50.6	51.7	49.6	51.1
4th quarter	52.4	49.8	63.0	66.1	55.9	70.9	64.4	51.6	53.1	50.3	52.1
1979:											
1st quarter	53.5	50.9	64.3	67.5	57.0	73.0	66.9	52.8	54.2	51.6	53.2
2nd quarter	54.7	52.1	66.0	69.0	58.9	76.0	70.5	54.0	55.1	53.0	54.5
3rd quarter	55.8	53.4	67.6	70.5	60.8	77.8	75.6	55.5	56.4	54.6	55.9
4th quarter	56.9	54.7	69.0	71.8	62.3	79.2	80.7	57.0	58.6	55.7	57.3
1980											
1st quarter	58.3	56.4	70.6	73.4	63.9	81.5	87.2	58.5	59.8	57.3	58.9
2nd quarter	59.6	57.8	72.3	75.2	65.4	82.6	90.7	60.1	61.4	58.9	60.4
3rd quarter	60.9	59.2	73.8	76.8	66.9	84.9	93.2	61.3	62.2	60.5	61.8
4th quarter	62.6	60.5	75.4	78.4	68.6	87.7	94.7	63.6	65.4	62.0	63.3
1981											
1st quarter	64.2	62.1	77.4	80.6	70.1	90.0	97.2	65.2	66.8	63.9	65.0
2nd quarter	65.4	63.2	79.3	82.8	71.2	90.3	97.8	66.3	67.5	65.2	66.2
3rd quarter	66.7	64.3	80.7	84.3	72.1	90.4	95.2	67.2	68.4	66.1	67.3
4th quarter	67.9	65.4	82.3	86.2	73.2	90.6	95.5	68.7	70.5	67.1	68.5
1982:											
1st quarter	68.9	66.2	83.5	87.4	74.2	91.2	95.2	69.9	71.7	68.3	69.4
2nd quarter	69.7	66.8	84.5	88.3	75.3	91.2	93.5	70.9	72.5	69.4	70.2
3rd quarter	70.7	67.9	84.9	88.7	76.0	90.5	92.3	71.7	73.1	70.5	71.1
4th quarter	71.5	68.7	85.0	88.7	76.3	90.1	91.6	72.8	74.4	71.5	71.9
1983:											
1st quarter	72.1	69.2	84.6	88.1	76.7	90.6	89.7	73.5	75.3	72.1	72.3
2nd quarter	72.8	70.1	84.3	87.6	76.9	91.0	89.8	74.3	76.0	72.8	73.0
3rd quarter	73.5	70.9	84.2	87.3	77.3	91.4	89.8	74.8	76.3	73.5	73.7
4th quarter	74.2	71.6	84.4	87.2	77.9	92.3	89.3	75.4	76.8	74.2	74.2
1984:											
1st quarter	75.0	72.3	84.5	87.1	78.4	92.5	89.6	77.2	79.4	75.3	75.0
2nd quarter	75.6	72.9	84.9	87.5	79.0	93.2	90.1	77.9	80.0	76.1	75.7
3rd quarter	76.3	73.4	85.2	87.6	79.8	92.2	88.5	78.6	80.7	76.8	76.2
4th quarter	76.8	74.0	85.5	87.7	80.4	91.3	87.4	79.2	81.3	77.5	76.7
1985:											
1st quarter	77.6	74.7	85.8	87.9	80.8	90.3	85.4	80.1	81.9	78.5	77.4
2nd quarter	78.3	75.5	85.9	88.0	81.0	90.2	85.7	80.7	82.4	79.2	78.0
3rd quarter	78.8	76.1	86.3	88.4	81.5	89.4	85.5	81.2	82.8	79.8	78.6
4th quarter	79.4	77.0	86.9	88.8	82.5	89.3	87.3	82.1	83.9	80.6	79.4
1986:											
1st quarter	79.8	77.5	87.4	89.2	83.5	88.9	87.5	82.1	83.7	80.7	79.8
2nd quarter	80.3	77.6	88.2	89.9	84.3	88.5	84.7	82.3	83.8	81.0	80.0
3rd quarter	80.8	78.2	89.0	90.7	85.4	88.0	85.4	82.8	83.9	81.7	80.6
4th quarter	81.4	78.8	89.7	91.1	86.4	88.8	86.3	83.6	84.4	82.9	81.3
1987:											
1st quarter	82.1	79.7	89.9	91.1	87.1	89.3	88.5	84.4	85.0	83.8	82.1
2nd quarter	82.7	80.5	90.2	91.2	87.9	90.7	90.8	85.0	85.2	84.7	82.7
3rd quarter	83.4	81.4	90.5	91.2	88.8	91.2	91.6	85.5	85.4	85.5	83.4
4th quarter	84.1	82.3	91.2	91.9	89.6	92.8	93.1	85.8	85.5	86.1	84.2
1988:											
1st quarter	84.7	82.8	92.2	92.8	90.9	93.9	94.3	86.6	86.5	86.7	84.8
2nd quarter	85.6	83.8	92.9	93.4	91.8	95.9	96.1	87.2	87.0	87.3	85.7
3rd quarter	86.7	84.9	93.4	93.9	92.4	97.2	95.1	87.7	87.5	87.8	86.6
4th quarter	87.5	85.9	94.4	94.9	93.2	97.1	95.9	88.1	87.7	88.3	87.4
1989:											
1st quarter	88.4	86.9	95.0	95.4	93.9	98.2	97.6	89.3	89.3	89.2	88.5
2nd quarter	89.4	88.2	95.6	95.8	95.0	98.3	98.8	89.9	89.6	90.1	89.5
3rd quarter	90.1	88.8	96.1	96.4	95.4	97.7	97.2	90.5	90.1	90.8	90.1
4th quarter	90.9	89.8	96.7	97.0	96.0	97.4	97.6	91.2	90.2	91.9	91.0

Per Capita Product and Income and U.S. Population

(Dollars, except as noted; quarterly data are at seasonally adjusted annual rates)

Year and quarter	Current dollars							Chained (1992) dollars						Population (Mid-period, thousands)
	Gross domestic product	Personal income	Disposable personal income	Personal consumption expenditures				Gross domestic product	Disposable personal income	Personal consumption expenditures				
				Total	Durable goods	Non-durable goods	Services			Total	Durable goods	Non-durable goods	Services	
1962	3 136	2 449	2 156	1 948	251	873	824	13 156	9 098	8 220	606	3 465	4 199	186 590
1963	3 261	2 536	2 229	2 023	273	888	862	13 520	9 294	8 434	655	3 487	4 325	189 300
1964	3 455	2 681	2 389	2 144	295	931	918	14 112	9 825	8 817	706	3 608	4 525	191 927
1965	3 700	2 864	2 546	2 286	325	986	975	14 825	10 311	9 257	785	3 753	4 706	194 347
1966	4 007	3 081	2 720	2 451	347	1 062	1 042	15 612	10 735	9 674	842	3 913	4 888	196 599
1967	4 194	3 274	2 882	2 563	354	1 092	1 117	15 835	11 081	9 854	846	3 932	5 069	198 752
1968	4 536	3 559	3 101	2 789	402	1 174	1 212	16 408	11 468	10 313	930	4 069	5 278	200 745
1969	4 845	3 844	3 302	2 982	424	1 249	1 310	16 739	11 726	10 593	953	4 136	5 479	202 736
1970	5 050	4 082	3 550	3 160	414	1 326	1 419	16 566	12 039	10 717	912	4 189	5 634	205 089
1971	5 419	4 334	3 811	3 383	467	1 375	1 541	16 900	12 366	10 975	990	4 211	5 768	207 692
1972	5 894	4 710	4 082	3 671	526	1 467	1 678	17 637	12 794	11 508	1 105	4 349	6 014	209 924
1973	6 524	5 226	4 562	4 018	583	1 619	1 816	18 479	13 566	11 950	1 207	4 449	6 225	211 939
1974	6 998	5 685	4 941	4 353	572	1 797	1 984	18 192	13 344	11 756	1 114	4 322	6 317	213 898
1975	7 550	6 107	5 383	4 765	618	1 948	2 199	17 936	13 444	11 899	1 103	4 344	6 474	215 981
1976	8 341	6 692	5 856	5 268	728	2 101	2 438	18 721	13 837	12 446	1 231	4 516	6 681	218 086
1977	9 201	7 336	6 383	5 797	822	2 256	2 719	19 400	14 142	12 846	1 332	4 587	6 892	220 289
1978	10 292	8 201	7 123	6 418	905	2 470	3 043	20 226	14 715	13 258	1 387	4 697	7 139	222 629
1979	11 361	9 133	7 888	7 079	950	2 772	3 357	20 571	14 951	13 417	1 365	4 752	7 285	225 106
1980	12 226	10 069	8 697	7 730	938	3 054	3 739	20 265	14 867	13 216	1 241	4 677	7 336	227 726
1981	13 547	11 167	9 601	8 440	1 002	3 296	4 142	20 524	15 064	13 245	1 243	4 671	7 374	230 008
1982	13 961	11 731	10 132	8 943	1 030	3 388	4 525	19 896	15 034	13 270	1 229	4 654	7 442	232 218
1983	14 998	12 352	10 776	9 744	1 194	3 543	5 007	20 499	15 293	13 829	1 397	4 747	7 720	234 332
1984	16 508	13 585	11 912	10 543	1 375	3 738	5 430	21 744	16 286	14 415	1 586	4 872	7 966	236 394
1985	17 529	14 427	12 592	11 341	1 514	3 889	5 938	22 320	16 604	14 954	1 725	4 941	8 290	238 506
1986	18 374	15 122	13 211	12 019	1 656	3 977	6 385	22 801	16 939	15 409	1 863	5 052	8 482	240 682
1987	19 323	15 968	13 851	12 743	1 716	4 175	6 851	23 264	17 109	15 740	1 873	5 103	8 758	242 842
1988	20 605	17 052	14 881	13 669	1 840	4 411	7 417	23 934	17 650	16 211	1 973	5 200	9 028	245 061
1989	21 984	18 176	15 771	14 531	1 911	4 704	7 915	24 504	17 833	16 430	2 006	5 269	9 145	247 387
1962:													
1st quarter	3 101	2 410	2 128	1 915	243	866	806	13 056	9 033	8 129	588	3 453	4 142	185 553
2nd quarter	3 130	2 443	2 152	1 940	249	870	821	13 147	9 093	8 199	601	3 458	4 192	186 203
3rd quarter	3 156	2 461	2 164	1 955	251	874	829	13 224	9 117	8 236	605	3 470	4 213	186 926
4th quarter	3 159	2 481	2 178	1 980	261	881	839	13 196	9 147	8 315	630	3 478	4 247	187 680
1963:													
1st quarter	3 198	2 498	2 193	1 992	266	883	843	13 323	9 187	8 344	641	3 480	4 255	188 299
2nd quarter	3 234	2 516	2 211	2 008	271	884	853	13 436	9 243	8 397	653	3 483	4 289	188 906
3rd quarter	3 289	2 545	2 238	2 038	274	893	870	13 638	9 309	8 477	659	3 497	4 356	189 631
4th quarter	3 324	2 583	2 276	2 054	279	893	883	13 682	9 434	8 516	667	3 486	4 398	190 362
1964:													
1st quarter	3 401	2 622	2 322	2 097	289	912	897	13 965	9 587	8 660	690	3 542	4 453	190 954
2nd quarter	3 437	2 660	2 379	2 132	295	926	910	14 082	9 807	8 786	706	3 596	4 503	191 560
3rd quarter	3 481	2 701	2 412	2 170	304	941	924	14 198	9 909	8 915	727	3 648	4 548	192 256
4th quarter	3 499	2 739	2 442	2 176	292	945	939	14 200	9 996	8 908	701	3 647	4 593	192 938
1965:													
1st quarter	3 596	2 784	2 468	2 226	320	956	950	14 519	10 067	9 077	765	3 680	4 624	193 467
2nd quarter	3 650	2 828	2 506	2 257	318	973	966	14 672	10 167	9 155	765	3 711	4 678	193 994
3rd quarter	3 725	2 892	2 578	2 297	327	989	981	14 893	10 412	9 279	790	3 751	4 725	194 647
4th quarter	3 829	2 953	2 632	2 363	337	1 024	1 002	15 211	10 595	9 515	821	3 869	4 795	195 279
1966:													
1st quarter	3 936	3 005	2 667	2 411	352	1 044	1 015	15 541	10 656	9 632	858	3 894	4 828	195 763
2nd quarter	3 974	3 047	2 689	2 431	338	1 060	1 033	15 567	10 657	9 634	820	3 918	4 875	196 277
3rd quarter	4 031	3 106	2 738	2 471	350	1 072	1 049	15 627	10 764	9 714	846	3 932	4 902	196 877
4th quarter	4 087	3 166	2 785	2 492	350	1 072	1 069	15 710	10 864	9 718	843	3 905	4 946	197 481
1967:													
1st quarter	4 129	3 212	2 828	2 509	342	1 080	1 088	15 796	10 995	9 755	825	3 926	4 999	197 967
2nd quarter	4 148	3 240	2 859	2 551	358	1 087	1 107	15 769	11 054	9 864	860	3 935	5 049	198 455
3rd quarter	4 215	3 299	2 903	2 581	357	1 095	1 128	15 849	11 116	9 884	850	3 927	5 103	199 012
4th quarter	4 283	3 344	2 939	2 612	361	1 107	1 144	15 924	11 157	9 914	849	3 937	5 126	199 572
1968:													
1st quarter	4 403	3 434	3 018	2 697	386	1 140	1 171	16 181	11 329	10 126	900	4 015	5 181	199 995
2nd quarter	4 514	3 526	3 093	2 760	394	1 164	1 202	16 423	11 499	10 259	916	4 056	5 256	200 452
3rd quarter	4 578	3 606	3 123	2 831	415	1 191	1 226	16 498	11 497	10 423	955	4 109	5 311	200 997
4th quarter	4 648	3 670	3 168	2 865	415	1 201	1 250	16 529	11 544	10 442	947	4 097	5 363	201 538
1969:													
1st quarter	4 754	3 728	3 194	2 916	424	1 220	1 272	16 746	11 543	10 537	961	4 127	5 410	201 955
2nd quarter	4 812	3 808	3 259	2 961	424	1 241	1 296	16 749	11 641	10 579	957	4 138	5 455	202 419
3rd quarter	4 895	3 891	3 352	3 001	424	1 257	1 320	16 797	11 838	10 602	952	4 134	5 495	202 986
4th quarter	4 917	3 947	3 402	3 051	423	1 277	1 351	16 664	11 878	10 653	944	4 147	5 555	203 584
1970													
1st quarter	4 968	3 988	3 447	3 099	416	1 304	1 379	16 593	11 895	10 693	925	4 180	5 595	204 086
2nd quarter	5 029	4 076	3 532	3 139	420	1 318	1 401	16 567	12 051	10 711	931	4 176	5 609	204 721
3rd quarter	5 101	4 116	3 598	3 190	423	1 332	1 434	16 663	12 144	10 766	931	4 190	5 656	205 419
4th quarter	5 100	4 145	3 623	3 212	398	1 351	1 463	16 443	12 063	10 695	861	4 209	5 675	206 130
1971													
1st quarter	5 304	4 221	3 716	3 296	448	1 355	1 492	16 838	12 249	10 865	954	4 209	5 706	206 763
2nd quarter	5 390	4 318	3 802	3 355	461	1 370	1 525	16 883	12 387	10 930	973	4 212	5 743	207 362
3rd quarter	5 468	4 366	3 842	3 405	470	1 378	1 556	16 941	12 391	10 980	997	4 200	5 776	208 000
4th quarter	5 511	4 431	3 882	3 473	487	1 395	1 592	16 937	12 436	11 125	1 037	4 221	5 845	208 642
1972:													
1st quarter	5 691	4 554	3 938	3 547	502	1 415	1 631	17 236	12 484	11 246	1 060	4 237	5 925	209 142
2nd quarter	5 840	4 621	3 996	3 625	516	1 452	1 658	17 592	12 594	11 424	1 084	4 332	5 973	209 637
3rd quarter	5 937	4 740	4 110	3 702	530	1 482	1 690	17 728	12 839	11 564	1 110	4 381	6 030	210 181
4th quarter	6 106	4 926	4 281	3 810	555	1 521	1 734	17 987	13 256	11 797	1 164	4 445	6 127	210 737

Per Capita Product and Income and U.S. Population—*Continued*

(Dollars, except as noted; quarterly data are at seasonally adjusted annual rates)

Year and quarter	Current dollars							Chained (1992) dollars						Popu-lation (Mid-period, thou-sands)
	Gross domestic product	Personal income	Dispos-able personal income	Personal consumption expenditures				Gross domestic product	Dispos-able personal income	Personal consumption expenditures				
				Total	Durable goods	Non-durable goods	Services			Total	Durable goods	Non-durable goods	Services	
1973:														
1st quarter	6 333	5 025	4 384	3 917	593	1 564	1 760	18 430	13 411	11 981	1 239	4 482	6 168	211 192
2nd quarter	6 470	5 151	4 504	3 979	586	1 592	1 800	18 515	13 520	11 941	1 216	4 434	6 220	211 663
3rd quarter	6 557	5 269	4 600	4 057	583	1 638	1 835	18 413	13 572	11 970	1 204	4 455	6 246	212 191
4th quarter	6 734	5 457	4 760	4 119	569	1 680	1 869	18 556	13 760	11 906	1 170	4 425	6 267	212 708
1974:														
1st quarter	6 786	5 518	4 809	4 196	558	1 732	1 906	18 336	13 509	11 789	1 136	4 361	6 268	213 144
2nd quarter	6 940	5 610	4 875	4 318	576	1 781	1 962	18 364	13 332	11 810	1 144	4 336	6 312	213 602
3rd quarter	7 059	5 768	5 007	4 437	601	1 829	2 006	18 118	13 346	11 825	1 151	4 331	6 325	214 147
4th quarter	7 204	5 842	5 071	4 461	553	1 848	2 061	17 951	13 189	11 602	1 025	4 260	6 363	214 700
1975:														
1st quarter	7 253	5 891	5 119	4 568	573	1 880	2 116	17 668	13 091	11 682	1 048	4 272	6 403	215 135
2nd quarter	7 409	6 019	5 417	4 694	595	1 927	2 173	17 784	13 679	11 854	1 067	4 351	6 470	215 652
3rd quarter	7 662	6 177	5 428	4 837	638	1 977	2 222	18 064	13 447	11 983	1 132	4 375	6 484	216 289
4th quarter	7 873	6 339	5 565	4 958	666	2 006	2 286	18 227	13 556	12 076	1 162	4 379	6 539	216 848
1976:														
1st quarter	8 132	6 493	5 704	5 109	709	2 049	2 350	18 612	13 739	12 306	1 222	4 456	6 608	217 314
2nd quarter	8 256	6 606	5 785	5 190	718	2 078	2 394	18 699	13 809	12 388	1 222	4 507	6 638	217 776
3rd quarter	8 383	6 758	5 907	5 312	731	2 118	2 463	18 725	13 875	12 478	1 231	4 535	6 695	218 338
4th quarter	8 589	6 909	6 026	5 459	755	2 158	2 546	18 849	13 923	12 611	1 249	4 564	6 782	218 917
1977:														
1st quarter	8 815	7 064	6 127	5 609	791	2 204	2 613	19 033	13 910	12 735	1 298	4 583	6 823	219 427
2nd quarter	9 116	7 226	6 288	5 724	813	2 237	2 675	19 386	14 035	12 777	1 327	4 569	6 841	219 956
3rd quarter	9 354	7 413	6 464	5 850	830	2 260	2 760	19 628	14 213	12 862	1 342	4 563	6 923	220 573
4th quarter	9 515	7 640	6 651	6 004	855	2 322	2 828	19 567	14 410	13 009	1 361	4 631	6 978	221 201
1978:														
1st quarter	9 687	7 821	6 819	6 126	842	2 364	2 920	19 599	14 523	13 048	1 325	4 645	7 060	221 719
2nd quarter	10 229	8 098	7 048	6 376	920	2 441	3 016	20 293	14 691	13 292	1 423	4 681	7 142	222 281
3rd quarter	10 469	8 317	7 210	6 507	918	2 504	3 085	20 419	14 753	13 315	1 397	4 711	7 170	222 933
4th quarter	10 780	8 567	7 413	6 659	939	2 571	3 149	20 590	14 891	13 376	1 403	4 750	7 182	223 583
1979:														
1st quarter	10 995	8 800	7 620	6 823	942	2 648	3 233	20 547	14 988	13 420	1 385	4 759	7 249	224 152
2nd quarter	11 223	8 978	7 764	6 959	934	2 715	3 310	20 538	14 911	13 365	1 350	4 724	7 283	224 737
3rd quarter	11 502	9 246	7 977	7 175	969	2 818	3 388	20 606	14 938	13 436	1 384	4 750	7 282	225 418
4th quarter	11 721	9 503	8 189	7 357	957	2 906	3 494	20 592	14 966	13 445	1 341	4 775	7 324	226 117
1980														
1st quarter	12 006	9 773	8 465	7 555	968	2 995	3 592	20 635	15 007	13 394	1 320	4 746	7 334	226 754
2nd quarter	11 959	9 831	8 490	7 551	876	3 017	3 658	20 083	14 681	13 056	1 169	4 669	7 269	227 389
3rd quarter	12 204	10 128	8 744	7 782	931	3 064	3 787	20 004	14 772	13 147	1 220	4 642	7 334	228 070
4th quarter	12 733	10 539	9 086	8 032	975	3 139	3 918	20 341	15 009	13 268	1 255	4 652	7 407	228 689
1981														
1st quarter	13 267	10 838	9 335	8 249	1 015	3 251	3 982	20 681	15 041	13 290	1 291	4 684	7 340	229 155
2nd quarter	13 368	10 981	9 427	8 375	990	3 290	4 095	20 450	14 928	13 262	1 235	4 681	7 391	229 674
3rd quarter	13 754	11 380	9 766	8 543	1 035	3 311	4 197	20 638	15 183	13 282	1 271	4 664	7 385	230 301
4th quarter	13 796	11 466	9 873	8 592	968	3 333	4 291	20 328	15 105	13 145	1 175	4 654	7 379	230 903
1982:														
1st quarter	13 737	11 497	9 897	8 736	1 008	3 351	4 377	19 948	14 953	13 198	1 212	4 648	7 393	231 395
2nd quarter	13 935	11 717	10 094	8 823	1 016	3 354	4 453	19 986	15 106	13 204	1 213	4 639	7 408	231 906
3rd quarter	14 018	11 781	10 203	8 994	1 024	3 407	4 562	19 837	15 029	13 248	1 219	4 649	7 438	232 498
4th quarter	14 155	11 926	10 330	9 219	1 073	3 440	4 705	19 815	15 046	13 428	1 273	4 678	7 528	233 074
1983:														
1st quarter	14 391	11 991	10 420	9 356	1 090	3 448	4 818	19 966	15 053	13 515	1 284	4 690	7 594	233 546
2nd quarter	14 824	12 231	10 625	9 645	1 174	3 517	4 954	20 355	15 157	13 759	1 379	4 721	7 698	234 028
3rd quarter	15 188	12 425	10 879	9 875	1 223	3 587	5 066	20 669	15 342	13 926	1 428	4 774	7 754	234 603
4th quarter	15 584	12 757	11 176	10 098	1 290	3 620	5 189	21 004	15 619	14 113	1 497	4 803	7 832	235 153
1984:														
1st quarter	16 091	13 142	11 535	10 282	1 337	3 673	5 272	21 449	15 970	14 236	1 553	4 820	7 874	235 605
2nd quarter	16 434	13 478	11 835	10 486	1 374	3 739	5 373	21 742	16 243	14 391	1 586	4 887	7 923	236 082
3rd quarter	16 658	13 787	12 090	10 608	1 373	3 755	5 481	21 847	16 462	14 445	1 579	4 886	7 990	236 657
4th quarter	16 847	13 930	12 185	10 793	1 416	3 783	5 594	21 935	16 469	14 587	1 626	4 895	8 074	237 232
1985:														
1st quarter	17 171	14 191	12 292	11 040	1 472	3 826	5 742	22 120	16 449	14 773	1 680	4 913	8 185	237 673
2nd quarter	17 360	14 327	12 615	11 224	1 488	3 875	5 861	22 184	16 708	14 866	1 696	4 933	8 241	238 176
3rd quarter	17 679	14 473	12 621	11 484	1 578	3 902	6 004	22 445	16 578	15 085	1 799	4 948	8 331	238 789
4th quarter	17 901	14 714	12 837	11 611	1 517	3 953	6 141	22 531	16 682	15 089	1 724	4 968	8 404	239 387
1986:														
1st quarter	18 170	14 931	13 066	11 771	1 544	3 986	6 241	22 767	16 864	15 192	1 752	5 020	8 422	239 861
2nd quarter	18 245	15 028	13 151	11 880	1 601	3 950	6 330	22 744	16 961	15 322	1 811	5 057	8 447	240 368
3rd quarter	18 440	15 208	13 290	12 144	1 751	3 966	6 427	22 810	16 999	15 533	1 961	5 051	8 495	240 962
4th quarter	18 637	15 319	13 336	12 278	1 729	4 007	6 542	22 881	16 930	15 587	1 927	5 080	8 561	241 539
1987:														
1st quarter	18 866	15 582	13 621	12 406	1 629	4 103	6 674	22 982	17 084	15 560	1 801	5 096	8 665	242 009
2nd quarter	19 153	15 814	13 601	12 659	1 706	4 166	6 786	23 165	16 897	15 726	1 870	5 115	8 735	242 520
3rd quarter	19 425	16 035	13 921	12 892	1 788	4 198	6 906	23 311	17 113	15 848	1 942	5 100	8 794	243 120
4th quarter	19 842	16 438	14 258	13 012	1 740	4 234	7 038	23 595	17 339	15 823	1 881	5 101	8 838	243 721
1988:														
1st quarter	20 057	16 667	14 559	13 296	1 819	4 281	7 197	23 690	17 595	16 069	1 969	5 139	8 951	244 208
2nd quarter	20 433	16 923	14 736	13 527	1 832	4 363	7 332	23 881	17 594	16 150	1 972	5 176	8 992	244 716
3rd quarter	20 764	17 172	15 002	13 785	1 822	4 459	7 504	23 960	17 676	16 242	1 948	5 221	9 067	245 354
4th quarter	21 163	17 444	15 226	14 064	1 888	4 542	7 634	24 202	17 734	16 381	2 003	5 264	9 102	245 966
1989:														
1st quarter	21 573	17 904	15 560	14 226	1 876	4 594	7 755	24 389	17 897	16 363	1 982	5 256	9 117	246 460
2nd quarter	21 914	18 118	15 686	14 451	1 913	4 694	7 844	24 515	17 785	16 385	2 011	5 245	9 117	247 017
3rd quarter	22 152	18 225	15 825	14 644	1 956	4 738	7 950	24 578	17 814	16 485	2 048	5 281	9 142	247 698
4th quarter	22 296	18 453	16 011	14 800	1 899	4 790	8 111	24 534	17 836	16 487	1 982	5 294	9 203	248 374

Private Fixed Investment by Type

(Billions of dollars, quarterly data are at seasonally adjusted annual rates)

Year and quarter	Total	Nonresidential									Residential			
		Structures				Producers' durable equipment					Structures			Producers' durable equipment
		Total	Nonresidential buildings, including farm	Utilities	Mining exploration, shafts, and wells	Total	Information processing and related equipment		Industrial equipment	Transportation and related equipment	Total	Single family	Multi-family	
							Computers [1]	Other						
1962	81.8	20.8	13.7	4.6	2.5	32.1	0.3	5.1	9.2	9.8	28.4	15.1	4.8	0.5
1963	87.7	21.2	13.9	5.0	2.3	34.4	0.7	5.3	10.0	9.4	31.5	16.0	6.4	0.6
1964	96.7	23.7	15.8	5.4	2.4	38.7	0.9	5.8	11.4	10.6	33.6	17.6	6.4	0.6
1965	108.3	28.3	19.5	6.1	2.4	45.8	1.2	6.6	13.6	13.2	33.5	17.8	6.0	0.7
1966	116.7	31.3	21.3	7.1	2.5	53.0	1.7	7.9	16.1	14.5	31.6	16.6	5.2	0.7
1967	117.6	31.5	20.6	7.8	2.4	53.7	1.9	8.1	16.8	14.3	31.6	16.8	4.7	0.7
1968	130.8	33.6	21.1	9.2	2.6	58.5	1.9	8.6	17.2	17.6	37.9	19.5	7.2	0.9
1969	145.5	37.7	24.4	9.6	2.8	65.2	2.4	10.4	18.9	18.9	41.6	19.7	9.5	1.0
1970	148.1	40.3	25.4	11.1	2.8	66.4	2.7	11.6	20.2	16.2	40.2	17.5	9.5	1.1
1971	167.5	42.7	27.1	11.9	2.7	69.1	2.8	12.1	19.4	18.4	54.5	25.8	12.9	1.3
1972	195.7	47.2	30.1	13.1	3.1	78.9	3.5	13.1	21.3	21.8	68.1	32.8	17.2	1.5
1973	225.4	55.0	35.5	15.0	3.5	95.1	3.5	16.3	25.9	26.6	73.6	35.2	19.4	1.7
1974	231.5	61.2	38.3	16.5	5.2	104.3	3.9	19.0	30.5	26.3	64.1	29.7	13.7	1.9
1975	231.7	61.4	35.6	17.1	7.4	107.6	3.6	19.9	31.1	25.2	60.8	29.6	6.7	1.9
1976	269.6	65.9	35.9	20.0	8.6	121.2	4.4	22.8	33.9	30.0	80.4	43.9	6.9	2.1
1977	333.5	74.6	39.9	21.5	11.5	148.7	5.7	27.5	39.2	39.3	107.9	62.2	10.0	2.4
1978	403.6	91.4	49.7	24.1	15.4	180.6	7.6	34.2	47.4	47.3	128.9	72.8	12.8	2.7
1979	464.0	114.9	65.7	27.5	19.0	208.1	10.2	39.8	55.8	53.6	137.9	72.3	17.0	3.2
1980	473.5	133.9	73.7	30.2	27.4	216.4	12.5	46.4	60.4	48.4	119.9	53.0	16.7	3.4
1981	528.1	164.6	86.3	33.0	42.5	240.9	17.1	52.3	65.2	50.6	119.0	52.0	17.5	3.6
1982	515.6	175.0	94.5	32.5	44.8	234.9	18.9	53.9	62.2	46.8	102.0	41.5	15.5	3.7
1983	552.0	152.7	90.5	28.7	30.0	246.7	23.9	58.1	58.2	53.7	148.3	72.2	22.4	4.2
1984	648.1	176.0	110.0	30.0	31.3	292.3	31.6	67.0	67.4	64.8	175.1	85.6	28.2	4.7
1985	688.9	193.3	128.0	30.6	27.9	308.7	33.7	70.5	71.7	69.7	181.9	86.1	28.5	5.1
1986	712.9	175.8	123.3	31.2	15.7	319.0	33.4	75.4	74.6	71.8	212.6	102.2	31.0	5.5
1987	722.9	172.1	126.0	26.5	13.1	323.3	35.8	74.0	75.9	70.4	221.8	114.5	25.5	5.8
1988	763.1	181.3	133.3	27.1	15.7	349.3	38.1	80.1	82.9	76.0	226.4	116.6	22.3	6.1
1989	797.5	192.3	142.7	29.4	14.4	373.9	43.3	83.8	91.5	71.2	225.1	116.9	22.3	6.2
1962:														
1st quarter	79.8	20.0	12.8	4.6	2.5	31.4	0.3	5.3	9.4	9.3	27.8	15.0	4.3	0.5
2nd quarter	82.2	20.8	13.6	4.6	2.6	32.2	0.3	5.2	9.5	9.6	28.7	15.3	4.7	0.5
3rd quarter	82.9	21.4	14.2	4.6	2.5	32.3	0.4	4.9	9.1	10.1	28.6	15.2	5.1	0.6
4th quarter	82.4	20.9	13.9	4.6	2.3	32.3	0.4	4.9	8.9	10.1	28.6	15.0	5.3	0.6
1963:														
1st quarter	83.3	20.2	13.2	4.7	2.3	32.9	0.6	5.1	9.3	9.5	29.6	15.2	5.8	0.6
2nd quarter	86.9	21.2	13.9	5.0	2.3	33.5	0.7	5.3	9.8	9.0	31.6	15.9	6.4	0.6
3rd quarter	88.8	21.4	14.1	5.0	2.3	34.9	0.8	5.4	10.2	9.3	31.9	16.0	6.6	0.6
4th quarter	91.8	21.9	14.5	5.2	2.2	36.2	0.8	5.4	10.5	9.9	33.1	16.8	6.9	0.6
1964:														
1st quarter	95.0	22.4	14.8	5.3	2.3	37.2	1.0	5.6	10.8	10.2	34.8	18.4	6.8	0.6
2nd quarter	95.6	23.4	15.5	5.4	2.4	38.0	0.9	5.7	10.8	10.6	33.5	17.5	6.5	0.6
3rd quarter	97.2	24.3	16.2	5.4	2.4	39.3	0.9	5.7	11.4	11.3	33.1	17.2	6.3	0.6
4th quarter	99.0	24.8	16.6	5.5	2.5	40.3	0.9	6.2	12.4	10.3	33.2	17.5	6.1	0.6
1965:														
1st quarter	103.5	26.1	17.7	5.8	2.4	43.5	1.0	6.2	12.6	12.9	33.2	17.2	6.2	0.7
2nd quarter	106.6	28.2	19.3	6.0	2.6	44.3	1.1	6.5	13.3	12.8	33.5	17.5	6.1	0.7
3rd quarter	109.6	28.5	19.7	6.1	2.4	46.8	1.2	6.8	14.1	13.3	33.6	18.1	5.9	0.7
4th quarter	113.4	30.4	21.2	6.4	2.3	48.5	1.3	7.0	14.4	13.8	33.8	18.5	5.8	0.7
1966:														
1st quarter	117.0	31.1	21.2	6.7	2.5	51.1	1.4	7.5	15.0	14.7	34.1	18.7	5.9	0.7
2nd quarter	117.4	31.2	21.1	7.1	2.4	53.0	1.6	7.8	16.0	14.7	32.5	17.7	5.6	0.7
3rd quarter	117.3	31.9	21.6	7.3	2.5	53.4	1.8	8.0	16.4	14.2	31.2	15.8	5.1	0.7
4th quarter	114.9	31.2	21.1	7.2	2.4	54.5	2.0	8.2	16.7	14.4	28.5	14.0	4.4	0.7
1967:														
1st quarter	112.7	31.7	21.4	7.3	2.4	52.7	1.9	8.0	17.1	13.3	27.7	14.3	4.1	0.7
2nd quarter	116.2	30.9	20.2	7.7	2.5	53.6	1.9	8.1	17.0	14.0	31.0	15.8	4.2	0.7
3rd quarter	118.1	31.5	20.4	7.9	2.4	53.2	1.8	8.0	16.3	14.7	32.7	17.9	4.9	0.7
4th quarter	123.3	32.0	20.5	8.4	2.4	55.3	1.9	8.5	16.9	15.1	35.2	19.2	5.7	0.8
1968:														
1st quarter	127.5	33.1	20.9	8.8	2.5	57.6	1.9	8.7	17.2	17.2	36.1	19.0	6.3	0.8
2nd quarter	128.0	33.2	21.0	9.0	2.5	56.7	1.9	8.5	17.0	16.6	37.3	19.6	6.9	0.8
3rd quarter	130.7	33.2	20.6	9.4	2.6	58.6	2.0	8.7	17.0	17.7	38.0	19.3	7.5	0.9
4th quarter	137.0	34.8	21.8	9.5	2.7	61.3	1.9	8.7	17.6	19.0	40.0	20.2	8.0	0.9
1969:														
1st quarter	142.7	35.8	23.1	9.5	2.6	63.7	2.1	9.4	18.2	19.4	42.3	21.0	9.0	0.9
2nd quarter	144.8	36.7	23.6	9.4	2.8	64.7	2.4	10.1	18.7	19.1	42.4	20.2	9.7	1.0
3rd quarter	148.3	38.9	25.2	9.6	2.9	66.1	2.6	10.8	19.4	19.0	42.2	19.2	9.7	1.0
4th quarter	146.2	39.4	25.4	10.1	2.9	66.2	2.7	11.3	19.4	18.1	39.6	18.3	9.7	1.1
1970														
1st quarter	146.5	39.5	25.5	10.2	2.8	66.4	3.1	11.4	20.1	16.8	39.6	17.0	9.4	1.1
2nd quarter	146.5	40.3	25.7	10.9	2.8	66.8	3.0	11.7	20.2	16.5	38.3	16.5	9.2	1.1
3rd quarter	148.6	40.6	25.2	11.6	2.7	67.6	2.4	11.6	20.4	17.1	39.3	17.4	9.4	1.1
4th quarter	150.6	40.8	25.1	11.6	2.8	64.9	2.4	11.8	20.0	14.6	43.8	19.3	10.1	1.2
1971														
1st quarter	156.8	41.5	25.8	11.8	2.7	66.7	2.3	11.6	19.2	17.7	47.4	22.0	11.0	1.2
2nd quarter	165.7	42.3	26.7	12.1	2.5	68.8	2.8	12.2	19.6	18.3	53.3	25.3	12.2	1.3
3rd quarter	170.7	43.1	27.5	12.0	2.7	69.3	2.9	12.2	19.3	18.2	57.1	27.1	13.7	1.3
4th quarter	176.8	43.8	28.2	11.9	2.8	71.5	3.1	12.5	19.9	19.5	60.2	28.7	14.6	1.4
1972:														
1st quarter	187.2	45.8	29.0	12.8	2.9	74.9	3.7	12.6	19.9	21.0	65.1	31.4	16.2	1.5
2nd quarter	191.7	46.6	29.5	13.0	3.0	76.9	3.4	12.7	20.9	21.2	66.7	32.2	17.1	1.5
3rd quarter	195.8	47.3	30.3	13.1	3.1	78.9	3.5	13.0	21.8	21.0	68.0	33.0	17.2	1.6
4th quarter	208.1	49.0	31.4	13.5	3.2	84.9	3.2	13.9	22.6	24.2	72.7	34.9	18.5	1.6

1. New computers and peripheral equipment.

Private Fixed Investment by Type—*Continued*

(Billions of dollars, quarterly data are at seasonally adjusted annual rates)

Year and quarter	Total	Nonresidential									Residential			
		Structures				Producers' durable equipment					Structures			Producers' durable equipment
		Total	Nonresidential buildings, including farm	Utilities	Mining exploration, shafts, and wells	Total	Information processing and related equipment		Industrial equipment	Transportation and related equipment	Total	Single family	Multi-family	
							Computers [1]	Other						
1973:														
1st quarter	219.0	51.3	33.3	13.9	3.2	89.9	3.4	15.1	23.6	25.2	76.1	36.9	19.3	1.7
2nd quarter	224.7	54.1	35.2	14.6	3.3	94.9	3.7	15.9	25.3	26.9	74.0	36.9	19.6	1.7
3rd quarter	228.7	56.8	36.6	15.5	3.6	96.8	3.4	16.6	26.5	27.1	73.3	35.1	20.1	1.7
4th quarter	229.1	57.7	36.9	15.9	3.8	98.6	3.7	17.5	28.1	27.0	71.0	31.8	18.7	1.8
1974:														
1st quarter	228.0	59.0	37.6	16.2	4.1	100.0	3.5	18.0	29.1	26.8	67.1	29.7	16.8	1.9
2nd quarter	231.2	61.3	38.7	16.3	5.1	102.3	3.2	18.6	30.3	26.8	65.6	30.5	14.8	1.9
3rd quarter	235.9	61.4	37.8	16.8	5.5	107.1	4.4	19.3	31.1	27.4	65.4	30.3	13.0	1.9
4th quarter	231.0	63.2	39.1	16.8	5.9	107.8	4.4	20.3	31.5	24.2	58.2	28.3	10.3	1.8
1975:														
1st quarter	223.9	61.7	37.2	16.6	6.6	104.6	4.1	20.0	30.3	24.0	55.8	26.4	8.5	1.8
2nd quarter	225.9	60.4	35.1	16.9	7.1	105.6	3.5	19.8	30.7	23.9	58.0	27.3	6.4	1.9
3rd quarter	234.4	61.3	35.0	17.1	7.6	108.4	3.3	19.8	31.5	25.8	62.7	30.8	5.8	1.9
4th quarter	242.6	62.0	34.9	17.7	8.1	111.8	3.5	19.8	31.9	27.0	66.7	34.0	6.0	2.0
1976:														
1st quarter	255.2	64.1	36.5	17.8	8.4	115.0	3.7	20.6	33.1	28.3	74.1	38.2	6.0	2.0
2nd quarter	264.0	65.1	35.7	19.8	8.2	118.3	4.4	21.9	33.6	29.0	78.6	42.8	6.3	2.1
3rd quarter	270.4	66.7	35.6	21.2	8.7	123.1	4.5	23.5	34.0	30.2	78.5	45.6	7.1	2.2
4th quarter	288.9	67.8	35.9	21.3	9.2	128.6	5.0	25.2	35.0	32.4	90.3	48.8	8.3	2.2
1977:														
1st quarter	306.4	69.7	37.3	20.7	10.2	139.1	5.2	25.9	36.5	36.9	95.5	53.7	8.9	2.1
2nd quarter	330.2	73.6	39.2	21.8	11.2	144.8	5.6	27.0	37.6	38.4	109.4	62.8	10.1	2.3
3rd quarter	341.8	76.4	40.9	21.6	12.0	150.4	5.8	27.7	40.1	39.3	112.5	65.0	10.6	2.5
4th quarter	355.7	78.5	42.1	21.7	12.5	160.3	6.1	29.2	42.5	42.6	114.3	67.3	10.5	2.7
1978:														
1st quarter	364.8	79.2	43.3	22.2	11.8	164.5	6.3	31.0	44.0	43.1	118.5	68.3	10.8	2.6
2nd quarter	398.8	88.6	47.9	23.7	14.7	179.6	7.3	33.7	46.4	48.4	127.8	71.5	12.6	2.7
3rd quarter	417.1	95.8	52.4	24.7	16.4	185.6	8.0	35.4	49.0	48.3	133.0	75.1	13.8	2.8
4th quarter	433.9	102.0	55.2	25.9	18.8	192.8	8.7	36.7	50.2	49.6	136.2	76.3	14.1	2.9
1979:														
1st quarter	446.8	104.8	57.5	26.2	18.9	203.4	9.3	38.3	53.7	54.1	135.6	73.8	14.6	2.9
2nd quarter	455.1	110.0	63.6	27.2	16.7	204.3	9.8	38.5	54.6	52.5	137.7	72.8	16.5	3.1
3rd quarter	474.9	119.1	68.7	28.3	19.3	212.2	10.4	40.2	55.9	55.4	140.2	73.3	17.9	3.3
4th quarter	479.2	125.7	73.2	28.4	21.2	212.3	11.1	42.1	59.1	52.6	137.9	69.3	19.0	3.3
1980														
1st quarter	484.6	130.3	75.3	29.7	22.4	219.7	10.9	45.1	60.0	51.7	131.2	60.7	18.9	3.4
2nd quarter	450.1	129.8	73.5	30.1	23.4	209.1	11.9	45.4	59.4	45.6	107.9	46.5	16.2	3.3
3rd quarter	464.6	133.6	71.6	30.2	29.3	215.1	13.5	47.3	59.7	48.1	112.5	47.2	15.2	3.4
4th quarter	494.8	141.9	74.3	30.9	34.4	221.6	13.8	47.9	62.5	48.1	127.9	57.5	16.6	3.5
1981														
1st quarter	511.6	147.5	81.2	32.4	31.5	232.1	15.4	50.2	63.8	50.5	128.4	59.6	18.7	3.6
2nd quarter	525.3	158.3	84.4	32.7	38.5	238.1	15.9	52.2	64.6	50.0	125.3	56.6	18.5	3.6
3rd quarter	533.6	166.8	89.1	33.4	41.2	246.6	17.2	53.4	66.0	52.0	116.5	49.7	17.0	3.7
4th quarter	541.8	185.7	90.3	33.6	58.6	246.5	20.0	53.5	66.4	49.8	105.9	42.3	15.7	3.7
1982:														
1st quarter	531.5	183.8	92.6	34.0	54.1	242.9	20.8	54.6	64.2	49.5	101.2	39.0	15.6	3.6
2nd quarter	517.8	179.6	95.1	33.2	48.1	235.4	18.1	53.8	63.6	46.8	99.1	38.9	14.9	3.7
3rd quarter	505.0	170.4	94.9	32.1	40.1	232.2	18.3	54.2	61.9	43.9	98.6	39.6	15.5	3.7
4th quarter	507.9	166.2	95.3	30.8	36.7	228.9	18.2	52.9	59.0	47.1	109.0	48.3	16.2	3.8
1983:														
1st quarter	514.6	156.7	90.2	28.8	34.2	227.0	21.3	54.5	56.2	47.2	126.9	59.1	18.8	4.0
2nd quarter	534.0	147.8	86.7	29.2	28.2	238.0	23.3	56.7	56.7	49.6	144.1	70.3	21.2	4.1
3rd quarter	563.4	151.0	92.2	26.9	28.4	249.9	25.2	57.3	59.1	55.1	158.2	78.7	23.7	4.3
4th quarter	596.0	155.5	92.9	30.1	29.2	272.0	25.8	64.0	60.9	63.1	164.1	80.7	26.1	4.5
1984:														
1st quarter	616.0	164.5	101.5	29.0	30.5	275.9	27.7	63.1	64.6	60.8	171.0	85.1	26.8	4.6
2nd quarter	645.4	174.4	109.5	30.1	30.6	289.6	30.1	67.0	66.8	64.8	176.7	87.9	27.2	4.7
3rd quarter	659.3	181.0	112.6	30.9	32.3	297.5	32.9	67.5	68.2	66.5	176.1	85.5	29.4	4.7
4th quarter	671.6	184.2	116.4	30.1	31.7	306.1	35.7	70.2	70.2	67.2	176.5	83.9	29.4	4.8
1985:														
1st quarter	680.0	193.5	123.7	30.9	32.3	303.1	33.3	70.1	69.5	67.1	178.5	86.1	29.1	4.9
2nd quarter	686.9	194.1	128.2	30.7	28.1	310.0	35.0	70.2	71.9	69.6	177.8	83.8	28.5	5.0
3rd quarter	685.8	191.0	128.5	30.2	25.9	307.2	32.4	70.1	71.3	71.4	182.6	85.7	28.4	5.1
4th quarter	702.8	194.6	131.5	30.4	25.4	314.3	34.2	71.4	74.3	70.7	188.6	88.9	28.2	5.3
1986:														
1st quarter	707.0	190.9	128.3	31.7	23.4	311.5	33.7	72.1	74.0	68.1	199.2	94.0	29.9	5.4
2nd quarter	710.9	173.9	121.9	32.1	14.6	318.7	34.3	74.0	73.8	72.0	212.9	100.1	32.2	5.4
3rd quarter	712.6	168.3	120.1	31.2	12.2	320.3	32.3	76.1	75.4	74.0	218.5	106.7	31.2	5.6
4th quarter	721.1	170.1	122.8	29.7	12.6	325.5	33.3	79.5	75.3	73.0	219.9	107.8	30.9	5.6
1987:														
1st quarter	705.3	165.4	120.5	27.6	11.8	314.6	35.0	72.9	75.1	67.5	219.7	110.9	27.7	5.6
2nd quarter	719.3	167.3	123.1	26.3	11.1	322.8	35.1	73.2	74.9	73.8	223.5	114.0	25.5	5.7
3rd quarter	732.0	175.3	128.7	26.0	13.8	329.3	36.3	75.2	76.2	72.3	221.5	115.6	24.1	5.9
4th quarter	735.1	180.3	131.8	26.0	15.5	326.5	36.7	74.7	77.2	68.2	222.4	117.3	24.6	6.0
1988:														
1st quarter	744.3	177.4	130.6	26.1	15.3	338.5	36.7	77.6	78.4	74.5	222.5	114.5	23.1	5.9
2nd quarter	760.9	182.5	134.5	26.3	16.5	346.9	37.8	79.9	81.9	75.5	225.3	116.1	21.7	6.1
3rd quarter	766.8	181.9	133.6	27.7	15.7	351.3	38.7	80.6	84.5	74.9	227.4	116.2	21.9	6.1
4th quarter	780.3	183.3	134.6	28.2	15.2	360.4	39.0	82.3	86.7	79.0	230.3	119.8	22.4	6.2
1989:														
1st quarter	790.1	188.3	140.0	29.6	13.1	364.7	41.2	81.4	90.0	71.7	230.9	121.3	22.6	6.2
2nd quarter	794.2	188.0	138.3	29.6	14.4	374.0	44.0	83.7	91.2	72.3	226.0	117.7	23.1	6.2
3rd quarter	808.1	196.4	146.6	29.0	15.0	382.5	44.5	85.1	93.3	72.5	223.0	114.5	22.8	6.1
4th quarter	797.5	196.6	145.7	29.2	14.9	374.3	43.4	85.0	91.5	68.1	220.4	114.2	20.7	6.2

1. New computers and peripheral equipment.

Real Private Fixed Investment by Type

(Billions of chained [1992] dollars, quarterly data are at seasonally adjusted annual rates)

Year and quarter	Total	Nonresidential Structures Total	Nonresidential buildings, including farm	Utilities	Mining exploration, shafts, and wells	Producers durable equipment Total	Computers[1]	Other	Industrial equipment	Transportation and related equipment	Residential Structures Total	Single family	Multi-family	Producers' durable equipment
1962	292.0	98.1	67.4	19.0	11.1	81.0	0.0	12.5	41.8	33.4	134.2	69.1	23.9	1.0
1963	313.7	99.2	67.5	20.4	10.4	87.1	0.0	13.0	45.1	32.1	150.0	73.8	32.1	1.2
1964	343.7	109.5	75.0	22.2	11.1	98.1	0.0	14.1	51.0	36.3	158.7	81.0	31.9	1.2
1965	378.5	126.9	89.4	24.4	11.0	115.9	0.0	16.0	60.2	45.5	153.6	79.1	28.6	1.4
1966	399.1	135.6	94.2	27.8	10.4	133.8	0.0	18.9	69.2	50.1	139.5	70.5	24.0	1.4
1967	391.0	132.2	88.7	29.8	9.9	132.5	0.0	18.9	69.5	48.4	135.0	69.1	20.9	1.4
1968	418.1	134.1	86.2	33.3	10.0	140.5	0.0	19.5	68.1	58.2	153.2	75.9	30.1	1.7
1969	442.9	141.3	92.7	33.4	10.4	152.2	0.1	22.8	72.6	60.5	157.4	72.1	37.5	2.0
1970	432.1	141.7	91.1	35.7	9.8	149.5	0.1	24.5	73.7	49.7	147.4	62.6	36.7	2.1
1971	464.9	139.4	89.4	36.1	9.1	150.7	0.1	24.7	67.7	53.6	188.4	86.9	46.7	2.4
1972	520.3	143.7	91.8	37.6	9.7	169.8	0.2	26.0	73.0	62.3	221.8	103.3	58.5	2.9
1973	567.5	155.4	100.3	40.0	10.4	201.2	0.2	31.7	86.2	75.0	219.8	101.1	60.1	3.2
1974	530.2	152.2	97.6	37.6	12.4	205.4	0.2	34.8	92.8	67.9	173.2	77.6	38.7	3.3
1975	471.0	136.2	82.5	34.4	14.4	183.9	0.2	33.3	78.6	58.5	150.4	70.8	17.3	3.1
1976	517.6	139.6	80.6	38.0	15.6	195.2	0.3	36.6	79.0	65.0	186.7	98.6	16.7	3.2
1977	593.7	146.4	83.6	38.2	18.1	225.6	0.5	43.8	83.6	79.1	226.8	126.2	21.9	3.5
1978	660.8	162.3	95.3	40.0	20.0	259.6	1.0	52.4	93.0	87.3	241.7	130.9	25.0	3.8
1979	695.6	182.7	113.5	41.3	21.3	280.7	1.5	59.5	99.8	91.0	232.2	116.0	30.5	4.2
1980	648.4	195.0	114.4	41.3	30.0	268.2	2.4	64.9	95.5	74.2	182.0	76.3	27.3	4.2
1981	660.6	210.4	122.8	42.0	34.9	278.2	3.8	68.5	94.1	72.0	167.0	69.5	26.3	4.2
1982	610.4	207.2	126.6	39.5	32.2	260.3	4.7	67.0	85.5	63.7	135.9	53.2	21.4	4.0
1983	654.2	185.7	117.6	34.2	26.7	272.4	7.1	70.4	78.5	71.7	193.2	92.0	29.3	4.5
1984	762.4	212.2	137.6	35.4	30.3	324.6	11.6	79.0	89.9	85.1	221.5	106.2	35.8	5.0
1985	799.3	227.8	155.2	35.6	27.0	342.4	14.5	81.9	94.1	88.4	224.2	104.8	34.9	5.4
1986	805.0	203.3	144.5	36.5	15.8	345.9	16.7	84.6	93.5	85.6	251.3	119.3	35.9	5.8
1987	799.4	195.9	142.4	30.7	15.5	346.9	21.0	80.2	91.1	82.1	251.6	128.3	28.3	6.1
1988	818.3	196.8	145.3	30.0	15.8	369.2	24.0	85.7	95.3	87.1	246.3	126.1	23.4	6.3
1989	832.0	201.2	150.2	30.9	13.9	387.6	29.4	88.1	101.5	78.9	237.0	121.9	23.3	6.3
1962:														
1st quarter	284.5	94.8	63.7	19.1	11.3	79.0	0.0	13.1	42.7	31.5	131.3	68.4	21.1	1.0
2nd quarter	293.6	98.3	67.3	19.1	11.3	81.4	0.0	12.7	43.1	33.1	135.4	69.9	23.4	1.0
3rd quarter	296.0	100.9	70.4	19.0	11.0	81.7	0.0	12.2	41.4	34.6	135.1	69.6	25.1	1.1
4th quarter	294.1	98.4	68.2	19.0	10.6	81.8	0.0	12.1	40.1	34.3	134.9	68.5	26.0	1.1
1963:														
1st quarter	297.2	95.0	64.5	19.3	10.4	83.2	0.0	12.5	42.2	32.1	139.8	69.4	28.6	1.1
2nd quarter	310.5	99.4	67.6	20.6	10.5	84.7	0.0	12.9	44.2	30.6	150.0	73.0	31.8	1.1
3rd quarter	318.4	100.1	68.2	20.4	10.5	88.4	0.0	13.3	46.4	31.8	152.8	75.0	33.4	1.2
4th quarter	328.5	102.1	69.6	21.4	10.1	92.0	0.0	13.2	47.6	34.1	157.5	77.8	34.5	1.2
1964:														
1st quarter	341.4	104.8	71.7	21.7	10.5	94.4	0.0	13.7	48.7	34.9	167.2	86.5	34.5	1.2
2nd quarter	340.2	108.4	73.8	22.1	11.2	96.2	0.0	14.0	48.7	36.3	158.6	80.2	32.2	1.2
3rd quarter	345.5	112.0	77.1	22.3	11.2	99.5	0.0	13.9	51.3	38.8	155.9	79.0	31.2	1.3
4th quarter	347.7	112.8	77.5	22.5	11.6	102.2	0.0	14.9	55.4	35.3	153.0	78.1	29.5	1.2
1965:														
1st quarter	364.0	118.6	82.6	23.4	11.0	110.4	0.0	15.0	56.2	44.3	153.4	77.2	29.6	1.3
2nd quarter	373.8	126.9	88.9	24.1	11.8	112.1	0.0	15.7	58.8	44.1	154.6	78.4	29.3	1.3
3rd quarter	383.8	128.2	90.8	24.6	10.7	118.2	0.0	16.5	62.2	45.9	155.1	81.3	28.6	1.4
4th quarter	392.2	134.1	95.4	25.5	10.4	122.9	0.0	17.0	63.5	47.8	151.5	79.6	27.1	1.5
1966:														
1st quarter	406.8	137.3	96.4	26.6	10.7	129.7	0.0	18.1	65.8	51.0	155.0	82.3	28.1	1.4
2nd quarter	401.2	134.6	93.3	27.9	10.2	134.3	0.0	18.8	69.6	50.9	142.4	74.5	25.3	1.4
3rd quarter	400.5	137.6	95.6	28.6	10.7	134.7	0.0	19.2	70.4	49.1	137.7	67.3	23.1	1.4
4th quarter	387.7	133.0	91.7	28.2	10.0	136.5	0.0	19.4	70.8	49.2	123.1	57.9	19.6	1.4
1967:														
1st quarter	378.3	134.3	92.7	28.5	9.9	130.9	0.0	18.7	71.7	45.7	119.3	59.3	18.3	1.4
2nd quarter	388.4	130.5	87.2	29.5	10.2	132.7	0.0	18.8	70.5	47.7	133.1	65.5	18.8	1.4
3rd quarter	392.6	131.9	88.0	30.0	9.9	131.0	0.0	18.5	67.1	49.7	139.8	73.8	21.6	1.4
4th quarter	404.9	132.1	86.8	31.4	9.8	135.2	0.0	19.6	68.6	50.6	147.8	77.6	24.7	1.6
1968:														
1st quarter	414.3	134.7	87.2	32.5	10.1	140.1	0.0	19.9	69.6	57.5	148.6	75.2	27.1	1.6
2nd quarter	412.0	133.5	86.6	32.8	9.7	136.8	0.0	19.3	67.7	55.1	152.4	76.7	29.3	1.7
3rd quarter	417.9	132.6	84.4	33.8	10.0	140.2	0.1	19.6	66.8	58.4	155.0	75.8	31.7	1.8
4th quarter	428.1	135.4	86.7	34.1	10.2	145.0	0.0	19.4	68.4	61.8	156.9	75.9	32.4	1.8
1969:														
1st quarter	441.2	137.4	90.1	33.5	9.9	150.2	0.1	20.8	70.6	63.1	162.6	77.8	35.9	1.9
2nd quarter	442.8	138.5	90.7	32.7	10.4	151.8	0.1	22.2	72.0	61.9	160.5	74.1	38.4	2.0
3rd quarter	449.9	145.1	95.5	33.2	10.8	153.9	0.1	23.6	74.2	60.3	159.2	70.4	38.0	2.0
4th quarter	437.9	144.1	94.4	34.0	10.6	152.7	0.1	24.4	73.5	56.8	147.1	66.0	37.6	2.0
1970														
1st quarter	435.5	143.0	94.2	34.0	10.1	151.4	0.1	24.4	75.0	52.1	147.4	61.6	36.8	2.1
2nd quarter	425.6	141.5	91.4	35.4	9.9	150.9	0.1	24.8	74.1	51.0	137.3	57.1	34.3	2.1
3rd quarter	433.2	142.1	90.4	37.1	9.3	151.8	0.1	24.3	73.9	52.1	144.7	62.9	36.7	2.1
4th quarter	434.1	140.4	88.2	36.3	9.9	143.9	0.1	24.6	71.6	43.6	160.2	69.0	39.0	2.2
1971														
1st quarter	444.0	140.0	88.3	36.5	9.6	146.3	0.1	24.0	68.2	51.6	168.9	76.8	41.5	2.3
2nd quarter	462.3	139.7	89.2	36.9	8.6	149.9	0.1	24.9	67.0	52.9	186.2	86.3	44.7	2.4
3rd quarter	470.5	139.2	89.8	35.8	9.0	150.7	0.1	24.7	67.0	52.9	195.5	90.6	49.1	2.4
4th quarter	482.7	138.8	90.3	35.1	9.1	155.7	0.1	25.2	68.5	57.2	203.0	94.1	51.5	2.5
1972														
1st quarter	504.7	142.4	90.7	37.3	9.6	161.8	0.2	25.1	68.4	60.3	216.5	101.1	56.0	2.7
2nd quarter	513.6	143.2	91.4	37.3	9.7	165.5	0.2	25.4	71.6	60.7	220.8	103.0	59.0	2.8
3rd quarter	519.2	143.5	92.3	37.4	9.6	169.6	0.2	25.8	74.6	59.5	221.0	103.5	58.3	2.9
4th quarter	543.6	145.7	93.0	38.4	10.1	182.5	0.2	27.5	77.2	68.9	228.9	105.7	60.5	3.0

1. New computers and peripheral equipment.

Real Private Fixed Investment by Type—*Continued*

(Billions of chained [1992] dollars, quarterly data are at seasonally adjusted annual rates)

Year and quarter	Total	Nonresidential									Residential			
		Structures				Producers durable equipment					Structures			Producers' durable equipment
		Total	Nonresidential buildings, including farm	Utilities	Mining exploration, shafts, and wells	Total	Information processing and related equipment		Industrial equipment	Transportation and related equipment	Total	Single family	Multi-family	
							Computers [1]	Other						
1973:														
1st quarter	566.8	150.5	97.4	38.9	9.9	192.7	0.2	29.6	80.1	72.6	236.5	110.3	62.2	3.2
2nd quarter	571.2	155.2	100.7	39.8	10.1	201.4	0.2	31.0	84.9	76.5	224.1	107.7	61.7	3.2
3rd quarter	569.1	158.7	102.1	40.9	10.7	203.8	0.2	32.3	87.8	75.9	214.4	98.7	61.0	3.2
4th quarter	562.7	157.3	101.0	40.3	11.0	207.0	0.2	33.9	92.1	74.9	204.0	87.7	55.4	3.3
1974:														
1st quarter	549.4	156.4	101.2	39.3	11.3	207.4	0.2	34.5	93.9	72.3	188.4	80.2	48.8	3.4
2nd quarter	541.0	155.8	100.7	38.0	12.7	206.9	0.2	34.4	95.0	70.3	179.8	80.8	42.1	3.4
3rd quarter	530.9	149.2	94.4	37.4	12.7	207.9	0.3	34.7	93.3	69.6	173.9	78.1	36.0	3.3
4th quarter	499.6	147.3	94.0	35.8	12.8	199.4	0.3	35.5	89.1	59.2	150.9	71.2	27.9	3.0
1975:														
1st quarter	467.8	139.8	87.2	34.4	13.6	185.0	0.2	34.2	80.9	57.4	141.3	64.8	22.5	3.0
2nd quarter	461.1	134.4	81.5	34.2	14.0	181.2	0.2	33.2	78.3	55.6	144.4	65.6	16.6	3.0
3rd quarter	473.0	135.3	81.0	34.2	14.9	183.3	0.2	33.1	77.9	59.7	154.6	73.4	14.8	3.1
4th quarter	482.2	135.4	80.4	34.8	15.2	186.2	0.2	32.7	77.4	61.1	161.5	79.5	15.2	3.1
1976:														
1st quarter	502.4	139.1	83.7	34.5	15.8	188.6	0.3	33.6	79.0	62.7	178.5	89.5	15.2	3.1
2nd quarter	510.6	138.6	80.4	37.8	15.0	192.2	0.3	35.2	79.0	63.7	183.7	96.7	15.3	3.2
3rd quarter	515.5	140.1	79.2	39.9	15.5	197.4	0.3	37.5	78.7	65.1	180.6	101.4	16.9	3.2
4th quarter	541.9	140.5	79.0	39.7	16.0	202.7	0.4	40.2	79.2	68.3	204.1	106.9	19.6	3.3
1977:														
1st quarter	564.2	141.8	80.7	37.8	17.2	216.3	0.4	41.1	81.0	77.0	210.3	114.5	20.5	3.1
2nd quarter	595.2	146.3	83.2	39.0	18.0	222.1	0.5	43.0	81.2	79.0	233.8	130.0	22.6	3.4
3rd quarter	602.3	148.3	84.9	38.1	18.4	226.8	0.5	44.2	84.4	78.6	233.2	129.4	22.7	3.7
4th quarter	613.1	149.2	85.6	37.7	18.6	237.5	0.6	46.8	87.8	81.8	230.1	130.7	21.8	3.9
1978:														
1st quarter	616.6	147.1	86.0	38.0	16.8	241.0	0.7	48.3	88.9	81.3	231.8	128.5	21.9	3.7
2nd quarter	660.2	159.8	93.0	39.8	19.7	260.3	0.9	51.9	92.2	90.0	242.9	130.1	24.7	3.9
3rd quarter	676.8	168.3	99.7	40.6	20.9	265.2	1.0	53.9	95.3	88.3	246.4	133.3	26.7	3.8
4th quarter	689.5	174.3	102.3	41.6	22.9	272.1	1.2	55.6	95.5	89.5	245.6	131.7	26.6	3.9
1979:														
1st quarter	695.1	174.3	104.3	41.0	22.0	281.6	1.3	57.8	99.8	94.8	239.7	124.9	27.3	4.0
2nd quarter	690.4	177.6	111.5	41.4	19.0	278.1	1.4	57.9	98.9	89.7	235.1	118.3	30.1	4.2
3rd quarter	702.6	186.5	116.8	41.8	21.2	284.1	1.6	60.2	98.7	93.2	231.7	114.9	31.7	4.3
4th quarter	694.1	192.5	121.3	40.9	23.2	279.0	1.8	62.2	101.8	86.1	222.4	106.1	32.9	4.3
1980														
1st quarter	685.5	195.8	121.4	41.8	25.1	281.5	1.9	65.4	99.5	82.1	206.2	90.5	31.8	4.3
2nd quarter	622.5	191.1	115.6	41.4	26.1	261.5	2.2	64.1	95.3	70.7	165.7	68.1	26.9	4.1
3rd quarter	629.3	193.5	109.9	40.9	32.4	262.9	2.7	65.2	92.7	72.5	168.9	67.3	24.5	4.2
4th quarter	656.3	199.8	110.9	40.9	36.4	267.1	2.9	64.8	94.6	71.4	187.1	79.5	26.0	4.2
1981														
1st quarter	660.7	198.6	118.7	42.3	29.6	274.9	3.3	67.1	94.7	74.2	183.8	80.8	28.8	4.3
2nd quarter	662.6	205.9	121.2	41.9	33.2	276.4	3.4	68.7	93.8	71.4	176.7	75.8	28.0	4.2
3rd quarter	661.6	210.8	125.9	42.1	33.2	282.7	3.8	69.6	94.3	73.3	162.3	65.9	25.3	4.2
4th quarter	657.6	226.4	125.4	41.9	43.4	278.7	4.6	68.7	93.5	69.1	145.4	55.5	22.9	4.2
1982:														
1st quarter	636.0	219.2	126.4	41.7	38.6	272.3	5.1	68.6	89.6	68.0	136.9	50.6	22.2	4.0
2nd quarter	612.8	211.9	128.0	40.5	34.0	261.2	4.5	67.0	87.4	63.9	132.3	50.0	20.7	4.0
3rd quarter	595.0	200.9	126.2	38.8	28.9	256.3	4.5	67.2	84.6	59.3	130.6	50.6	21.0	4.0
4th quarter	597.7	197.0	125.8	37.0	27.5	251.5	4.5	65.3	80.4	63.5	143.7	61.7	21.7	4.0
1983:														
1st quarter	608.4	189.0	118.3	34.3	28.3	249.5	5.7	66.6	76.1	63.4	166.4	75.5	24.8	4.3
2nd quarter	633.4	179.9	113.1	34.8	24.9	262.5	6.7	69.1	76.3	66.3	188.5	89.8	27.8	4.4
3rd quarter	668.9	184.2	119.5	32.0	25.8	276.5	7.7	69.2	79.6	73.4	206.0	100.4	30.9	4.6
4th quarter	706.1	189.9	119.4	35.8	27.7	301.1	8.2	76.8	81.9	83.7	211.7	102.2	33.7	4.7
1984:														
1st quarter	729.3	200.8	128.9	34.5	29.8	306.2	9.4	75.3	86.6	80.1	219.3	106.7	34.4	4.8
2nd quarter	760.7	210.8	137.9	35.5	29.5	321.5	10.8	79.2	89.0	85.2	224.7	109.6	34.8	5.0
3rd quarter	773.9	217.4	140.1	36.4	31.3	330.5	12.3	79.4	90.6	87.2	221.7	105.5	37.1	5.0
4th quarter	785.7	219.9	143.6	35.3	30.7	340.3	13.8	82.2	93.3	87.7	220.5	103.1	36.9	5.1
1985:														
1st quarter	792.9	229.3	151.5	36.1	31.0	337.3	13.5	81.9	92.3	86.7	221.8	105.5	36.0	5.2
2nd quarter	800.1	229.5	156.2	35.8	27.3	345.0	14.8	81.8	94.9	89.0	220.4	102.5	35.0	5.3
3rd quarter	794.9	224.6	155.3	35.2	25.1	340.6	14.2	81.5	93.1	90.2	224.9	104.1	34.6	5.4
4th quarter	809.1	227.6	157.6	35.4	24.7	346.9	15.6	82.4	96.1	87.9	229.5	106.9	33.9	5.6
1986:														
1st quarter	809.3	222.3	152.6	37.1	22.9	343.0	16.6	82.3	94.0	83.7	239.4	112.1	35.4	5.7
2nd quarter	806.6	201.4	143.5	37.6	14.5	347.2	17.4	83.6	92.8	86.2	253.5	117.8	37.5	5.8
3rd quarter	800.4	194.2	140.1	36.5	12.5	344.8	16.1	84.5	93.9	87.4	256.8	124.0	35.8	5.9
4th quarter	803.9	195.2	141.6	34.7	13.4	348.5	16.7	88.1	93.3	84.9	255.4	123.5	35.0	5.9
1987:														
1st quarter	784.2	190.0	137.9	32.2	13.8	336.7	19.2	79.4	91.5	78.6	252.9	125.8	31.3	5.9
2nd quarter	797.7	191.3	139.7	30.6	13.4	346.5	20.5	79.4	90.3	86.1	254.9	128.2	28.5	6.0
3rd quarter	809.5	199.4	145.0	30.1	16.7	354.7	22.1	81.6	91.6	84.1	250.1	129.3	26.7	6.2
4th quarter	806.3	202.8	147.2	29.7	18.1	349.6	22.2	80.3	91.2	79.8	248.5	130.0	26.9	6.2
1988:														
1st quarter	807.1	195.9	144.0	29.7	16.3	360.3	22.5	83.0	91.5	86.9	245.2	124.9	24.5	6.2
2nd quarter	819.0	199.1	147.2	29.4	16.7	368.0	23.8	85.8	94.3	87.3	246.0	126.1	22.8	6.3
3rd quarter	820.6	196.4	145.1	30.5	15.5	371.6	24.7	86.6	97.2	85.3	246.6	125.4	22.9	6.3
4th quarter	826.4	195.9	144.9	30.6	14.7	377.0	25.1	87.5	98.1	88.9	247.4	128.0	23.3	6.4
1989:														
1st quarter	831.9	199.8	149.5	31.7	12.9	379.7	26.8	85.8	101.0	80.5	246.2	128.3	23.7	6.4
2nd quarter	830.9	197.2	145.9	31.3	14.0	389.4	29.7	88.1	102.0	80.5	238.0	122.6	24.0	6.4
3rd quarter	840.5	204.6	153.7	30.3	14.5	395.5	30.5	89.3	103.2	80.3	233.9	118.8	23.8	6.2
4th quarter	824.7	203.2	151.7	30.2	14.4	385.6	30.7	89.1	100.0	74.3	229.7	117.9	21.5	6.3

1. New computers and peripheral equipment.

Federal Government Receipts and Current Expenditures

(Calendar years—Billions of dollars, quarterly data are at seasonally adjusted annual rates)

Year and quarter	Receipts					Current expenditures						Surplus or deficit (—), national income and product accounts		
	Total	Personal tax and nontax receipts	Corporate profits tax accruals	Indirect business tax and nontax accruals	Contributions to social insurance	Total	Consumption expenditures	Transfer payments (net)	Grants-in-aid to state and local governments	Net interest paid	Subsidies less surplus of government enterprises	Total	Social insurance funds	Other
1962	107.2	48.5	22.5	14.7	21.5	104.4	59.1	27.7	8.0	6.8	2.9	2.8	0.7	2.1
1963	115.5	51.3	24.6	15.4	24.3	110.2	62.0	29.1	9.1	7.3	2.6	5.4	2.2	3.2
1964	116.2	48.4	26.1	16.3	25.4	115.4	63.9	30.0	10.4	8.0	3.1	0.9	2.8	-1.9
1965	125.8	53.7	28.9	16.6	26.6	122.4	67.2	32.4	11.1	8.4	3.4	3.4	2.0	1.4
1966	143.5	61.5	31.4	15.7	34.9	140.9	77.0	35.7	14.4	9.2	4.6	2.6	7.5	-4.8
1967	152.6	67.2	30.0	16.5	38.9	160.9	88.3	42.3	15.9	9.8	4.5	-8.3	6.1	-14.5
1968	176.8	79.3	36.1	18.2	43.2	179.7	97.0	48.1	18.6	11.3	4.6	-2.8	5.2	-8.1
1969	199.5	94.7	36.1	19.2	49.5	190.8	100.1	52.6	20.3	12.7	5.1	8.7	7.7	1.0
1970	195.1	92.2	30.6	19.5	52.8	209.1	100.5	63.6	24.4	14.1	6.5	-14.1	3.6	-17.7
1971	203.3	89.9	33.5	20.5	59.4	228.6	103.8	75.4	29.0	13.8	6.6	-25.3	0.7	-26.1
1972	232.6	107.8	36.6	20.1	68.1	253.1	110.1	83.5	37.5	14.4	8.0	-20.5	3.0	-23.6
1973	264.0	114.3	43.3	21.5	84.9	275.1	112.9	96.2	40.6	18.0	7.4	-11.1	9.3	-20.4
1974	295.1	130.9	45.1	22.1	97.1	312.0	123.3	118.2	43.9	20.7	5.5	-16.9	7.0	-23.9
1975	297.4	125.4	43.6	24.2	104.2	371.3	135.0	150.3	54.6	23.0	8.6	-73.9	-11.2	-62.7
1976	343.1	146.6	54.6	23.8	118.2	400.3	141.7	163.0	61.1	26.8	7.8	-57.2	-9.7	-47.5
1977	389.6	169.1	61.6	25.6	133.3	435.9	155.4	173.6	67.5	29.1	10.4	-46.3	-5.6	-40.7
1978	446.5	193.8	71.4	28.9	152.4	478.1	168.8	186.2	77.3	34.6	11.4	-31.7	3.7	-35.4
1979	511.1	229.7	74.4	30.1	176.8	529.5	185.9	209.7	80.5	42.1	11.3	-18.4	9.8	-28.2
1980	561.5	256.2	70.3	39.7	195.3	622.5	215.2	252.0	88.7	52.7	13.9	-61.0	-4.4	-56.6
1981	649.3	297.2	65.7	57.3	229.1	707.1	246.0	287.1	87.9	71.7	14.4	-57.8	-1.3	-56.5
1982	646.4	302.9	49.0	49.7	244.8	781.0	270.0	323.4	83.9	84.4	19.4	-134.7	-19.8	-114.8
1983	671.9	293.0	61.3	53.3	264.2	846.3	293.0	347.7	87.0	92.8	25.4	-174.4	-20.7	-153.6
1984	746.9	308.3	75.2	57.9	305.3	902.9	314.1	354.3	94.4	113.3	27.1	-156.0	21.9	-177.9
1985	811.3	343.7	76.3	58.2	333.1	974.2	342.5	379.0	100.3	126.9	25.2	-162.9	33.1	-196.0
1986	850.1	358.3	83.8	53.2	354.7	1 027.6	362.3	399.1	107.6	130.5	28.0	-177.5	40.0	-217.5
1987	937.4	402.4	102.2	57.8	374.1	1 066.3	378.2	413.0	102.9	137.8	34.4	-128.9	49.7	-178.6
1988	997.2	414.4	111.0	60.9	410.9	1 118.5	387.8	437.2	111.2	148.4	33.8	-121.3	73.8	-195.1
1989	1 079.3	463.4	117.1	61.7	437.1	1 192.7	405.2	471.7	118.2	166.7	30.8	-113.4	80.9	-194.2
1962:														
1st quarter	104.4	46.3	22.3	14.5	21.2	101.8	57.2	27.6	7.8	6.4	2.8	2.5	0.7	1.9
2nd quarter	106.1	48.0	22.1	14.5	21.5	103.7	59.0	27.2	7.9	6.6	3.0	2.5	0.7	1.8
3rd quarter	108.4	49.2	22.7	15.0	21.6	104.9	59.6	27.6	7.9	6.9	2.8	3.5	1.0	2.6
4th quarter	109.9	50.4	22.8	14.9	21.8	107.3	60.6	28.4	8.3	7.1	2.9	2.6	0.5	2.1
1963:														
1st quarter	112.7	50.9	22.9	15.0	23.9	108.3	61.0	29.4	8.5	7.1	2.4	4.4	1.1	3.4
2nd quarter	115.2	51.2	24.5	15.4	24.2	108.7	61.5	28.6	8.8	7.2	2.6	6.5	2.5	4.0
3rd quarter	116.4	51.4	25.2	15.4	24.4	110.6	62.3	28.9	9.4	7.4	2.7	5.8	2.7	3.1
4th quarter	117.8	51.7	25.8	15.6	24.8	113.1	63.3	29.5	9.9	7.6	2.7	4.7	2.6	2.1
1964:														
1st quarter	116.7	50.2	25.9	15.7	24.9	114.7	63.6	30.1	10.1	7.8	3.0	2.0	1.8	0.2
2nd quarter	113.4	46.2	26.0	16.0	25.2	116.0	64.7	29.8	10.4	7.9	3.2	-2.6	2.8	-5.3
3rd quarter	116.5	47.9	26.6	16.5	25.6	115.6	64.0	29.9	10.5	8.0	3.3	1.0	3.0	-2.1
4th quarter	118.3	49.5	26.1	17.0	25.8	115.2	63.1	30.1	10.7	8.4	2.9	3.1	3.5	-0.4
1965:														
1st quarter	124.1	53.2	27.5	17.5	26.0	116.5	63.5	31.0	10.5	8.1	3.3	7.7	2.3	5.3
2nd quarter	125.9	54.4	28.4	16.8	26.3	119.2	65.6	31.0	11.0	8.3	3.3	6.7	3.3	3.4
3rd quarter	124.6	53.1	28.9	15.9	26.7	124.9	67.6	34.3	11.3	8.4	3.4	-0.3	0.4	-0.8
4th quarter	128.7	54.4	30.8	16.2	27.4	129.2	72.0	33.1	11.6	8.8	3.7	-0.5	2.0	-2.5
1966:														
1st quarter	138.0	57.4	31.7	15.1	33.8	132.7	71.9	34.7	13.3	8.7	4.1	5.3	7.6	-2.3
2nd quarter	142.9	61.0	31.7	15.9	34.3	138.5	76.6	34.0	14.4	9.0	4.6	4.4	7.9	-3.5
3rd quarter	145.4	62.6	31.4	15.8	35.5	144.0	79.4	35.5	14.9	9.3	4.9	1.4	8.0	-6.6
4th quarter	147.8	64.9	30.8	16.2	35.9	148.4	80.3	38.5	15.0	9.7	5.0	-0.6	6.4	-7.0
1967:														
1st quarter	149.0	65.7	29.7	16.1	37.5	157.9	86.7	41.3	15.3	9.9	4.7	-8.9	5.4	-14.3
2nd quarter	149.7	65.4	29.4	16.4	38.5	158.3	87.5	41.9	14.9	9.6	4.5	-8.6	5.9	-14.6
3rd quarter	153.6	68.2	29.6	16.5	39.3	161.2	88.1	43.1	16.0	9.7	4.3	-7.5	6.4	-13.9
4th quarter	158.0	69.6	31.4	16.8	40.2	166.2	90.9	43.1	17.5	10.2	4.6	-8.2	6.8	-15.1
1968:														
1st quarter	166.1	71.4	35.3	17.5	41.9	172.6	95.1	44.8	17.6	10.6	4.5	-6.5	6.6	-13.1
2nd quarter	171.2	74.3	35.9	18.1	42.9	178.7	96.3	47.9	18.7	11.3	4.6	-7.6	4.8	-12.3
3rd quarter	182.4	84.0	36.1	18.6	43.7	181.7	97.6	49.3	18.8	11.4	4.7	0.7	5.0	-4.2
4th quarter	187.7	87.7	36.9	18.7	44.4	185.6	99.2	50.4	19.3	11.9	4.7	2.1	4.7	-2.5
1969:														
1st quarter	197.8	93.6	37.5	18.6	48.1	183.9	96.8	51.0	19.0	12.2	5.0	13.9	7.1	6.8
2nd quarter	201.1	96.5	36.5	19.2	48.9	189.6	99.6	52.7	19.8	12.5	5.1	11.5	6.9	4.6
3rd quarter	198.8	93.8	35.3	19.6	50.1	192.8	101.5	52.8	20.6	12.7	5.2	6.0	8.4	-2.3
4th quarter	200.2	95.0	35.0	19.3	51.0	196.9	102.3	53.9	22.0	13.5	5.1	3.4	8.5	-5.1
1970														
1st quarter	195.6	94.0	30.4	19.2	51.9	197.7	101.7	55.7	23.1	13.8	5.9	-2.1	9.1	-11.2
2nd quarter	197.5	94.8	30.5	19.5	52.6	211.8	100.0	65.1	24.1	13.9	6.7	-14.4	1.3	-15.7
3rd quarter	193.8	89.6	31.4	19.5	53.2	211.7	100.2	65.2	25.0	14.5	6.5	-17.9	3.3	-21.2
4th quarter	193.4	90.6	30.1	19.5	53.2	215.3	100.0	68.5	25.7	14.3	6.9	-22.0	0.8	-22.8
1971														
1st quarter	199.1	87.0	33.3	20.8	58.1	220.4	102.6	69.6	27.0	14.3	6.9	-21.2	4.5	-25.8
2nd quarter	201.7	88.5	34.0	20.2	59.1	229.9	103.7	76.9	29.5	13.5	6.3	-28.1	-1.8	-26.4
3rd quarter	203.4	90.0	33.2	20.4	59.9	230.5	104.1	77.0	29.2	13.8	6.4	-27.1	0.4	-27.5
4th quarter	208.8	94.3	33.4	20.5	60.5	233.6	104.9	78.2	30.3	13.7	6.6	-24.8	-0.2	-24.6
1972:														
1st quarter	228.0	106.3	35.0	19.8	66.9	243.7	110.3	80.4	31.4	14.2	7.3	-15.7	3.7	-19.4
2nd quarter	229.3	106.7	35.2	19.9	67.6	253.5	111.8	80.5	39.1	14.2	7.8	-24.2	4.9	-29.0
3rd quarter	232.7	107.8	36.3	20.2	68.5	246.3	108.3	81.4	33.5	14.4	8.8	-13.7	5.5	-19.1
4th quarter	240.3	110.5	39.9	20.6	69.3	268.9	110.2	91.6	46.1	14.9	8.2	-28.6	-2.0	-26.6

Federal Government Receipts and Current Expenditures—*Continued*

(Calendar years—Billions of dollars, quarterly data are at seasonally adjusted annual rates)

Year and quarter	Receipts					Current expenditures						Surplus or deficit (—), national income and product accounts		
	Total	Personal tax and nontax receipts	Corporate profits tax accruals	Indirect business tax and nontax accruals	Contributions to social insurance	Total	Consumption expenditures	Transfer payments (net)	Grants-in-aid to state and local governments	Net interest paid	Subsidies less surplus of government enterprises	Total	Social insurance funds	Other
1973:														
1st quarter	256.9	109.8	43.1	21.3	82.6	270.1	112.3	92.7	41.3	16.3	7.6	-13.2	11.7	-24.9
2nd quarter	260.3	111.2	43.6	21.8	83.8	274.6	113.3	95.3	40.9	17.4	7.6	-14.3	9.5	-23.8
3rd quarter	264.4	115.4	42.1	21.2	85.6	274.1	111.9	97.1	39.2	18.8	7.0	-9.7	8.2	-17.9
4th quarter	274.4	120.8	44.3	21.7	87.6	281.7	114.2	99.8	40.8	19.6	7.4	-7.4	7.8	-15.2
1974:														
1st quarter	282.5	124.3	42.5	21.6	94.0	294.1	119.0	107.6	42.4	19.7	5.4	-11.6	12.0	-23.6
2nd quarter	292.3	129.3	44.8	22.1	96.1	305.2	120.1	115.6	44.0	20.2	4.8	-12.9	8.0	-20.9
3rd quarter	304.4	134.0	49.5	22.3	98.7	317.4	124.2	121.7	43.3	21.2	5.5	-13.0	6.0	-18.9
4th quarter	301.4	136.0	43.7	22.3	99.5	331.5	129.7	128.1	46.0	21.5	6.2	-30.1	2.2	-32.3
1975:														
1st quarter	296.7	136.5	36.6	21.9	101.8	348.5	131.7	138.0	49.4	21.8	7.7	-51.8	-4.4	-47.4
2nd quarter	264.6	99.3	39.3	23.4	102.6	370.1	134.1	152.1	53.6	22.2	8.1	-105.5	-10.1	-95.4
3rd quarter	309.6	130.6	48.7	25.4	104.9	378.5	135.1	154.2	57.3	23.1	8.9	-68.9	-16.1	-52.8
4th quarter	318.5	135.1	49.7	26.1	107.6	388.0	139.2	156.7	57.9	24.8	9.5	-69.4	-14.3	-55.1
1976:														
1st quarter	331.2	137.6	55.7	23.1	114.8	389.6	138.7	159.0	58.7	25.7	7.6	-58.4	-9.4	-49.0
2nd quarter	339.1	143.6	54.9	23.7	117.0	392.5	141.0	158.6	59.2	26.3	7.5	-53.4	-7.0	-46.4
3rd quarter	347.2	149.4	54.4	24.1	119.3	404.5	141.4	167.6	61.0	26.9	7.8	-57.3	-11.3	-46.0
4th quarter	354.8	155.6	53.3	24.2	121.7	414.5	145.9	166.6	65.5	28.4	8.2	-59.7	-11.0	-48.7
1977:														
1st quarter	376.7	166.7	56.9	24.5	128.6	419.3	149.8	169.6	63.2	28.0	8.7	-42.5	-6.4	-36.1
2nd quarter	384.9	165.9	61.7	25.2	132.1	427.9	154.0	170.3	66.2	28.5	9.0	-43.0	-3.9	-39.1
3rd quarter	392.7	167.7	63.9	26.3	134.8	442.0	156.2	176.1	70.9	28.8	10.0	-49.3	-6.2	-43.1
4th quarter	404.0	176.0	63.9	26.4	137.7	454.2	161.4	178.1	69.9	30.9	14.0	-50.2	-5.7	-44.5
1978:														
1st quarter	412.7	178.1	60.4	27.3	147.0	463.8	163.4	181.2	74.4	32.7	12.2	-51.1	2.7	-53.8
2nd quarter	440.2	187.5	73.0	28.9	150.8	470.8	167.3	181.4	77.6	33.5	11.2	-30.6	6.6	-37.2
3rd quarter	456.9	199.9	74.0	29.2	153.7	481.5	169.7	189.3	77.4	35.2	10.1	-24.7	2.1	-26.8
4th quarter	476.1	209.8	78.2	30.2	157.9	496.4	174.9	192.8	79.6	37.1	12.0	-20.3	3.6	-23.9
1979:														
1st quarter	492.7	216.3	75.4	29.9	171.1	505.7	179.7	197.6	78.0	39.7	10.5	-13.0	13.7	-26.7
2nd quarter	505.0	224.6	75.6	30.2	174.5	517.2	184.4	202.1	78.0	41.4	11.3	-12.2	13.9	-26.1
3rd quarter	517.5	234.1	74.8	29.9	178.7	536.5	184.0	216.9	81.9	42.3	11.3	-19.0	5.8	-24.8
4th quarter	529.1	243.7	71.9	30.5	183.0	558.7	195.3	222.3	84.1	44.9	12.1	-29.6	5.7	-35.3
1980														
1st quarter	546.3	243.4	79.9	32.8	190.2	583.5	203.2	232.3	85.5	49.9	12.6	-37.3	8.5	-45.8
2nd quarter	543.0	249.8	61.8	39.1	192.4	606.1	214.8	236.9	87.4	53.4	13.5	-63.1	3.1	-66.2
3rd quarter	563.1	258.9	66.4	41.9	195.9	638.5	216.1	266.2	89.3	52.3	14.6	-75.5	-16.2	-59.3
4th quarter	593.7	272.9	73.2	44.8	202.7	661.7	226.6	272.4	92.5	55.2	15.1	-68.1	-13.0	-55.0
1981														
1st quarter	639.3	283.9	73.8	57.8	223.8	683.1	236.4	274.7	90.4	66.8	14.7	-43.8	4.5	-48.3
2nd quarter	645.5	294.9	64.4	58.8	227.4	694.5	244.9	277.5	90.2	68.8	13.1	-49.0	5.6	-54.6
3rd quarter	663.2	307.7	67.6	56.6	231.4	717.5	246.2	296.6	86.7	73.1	15.2	-54.2	-7.0	-47.2
4th quarter	649.2	302.4	56.9	55.9	234.0	733.3	256.5	299.8	84.2	78.1	14.7	-84.1	-8.4	-75.7
1982:														
1st quarter	645.8	303.9	48.4	51.9	241.7	745.8	262.1	305.1	82.7	80.5	15.4	-100.1	-5.2	-94.8
2nd quarter	653.0	309.1	50.9	48.7	244.2	761.0	263.1	313.3	84.9	83.4	16.3	-108.0	-12.3	-95.7
3rd quarter	642.8	296.9	50.8	48.9	246.2	795.6	271.8	328.8	83.5	87.0	24.5	-152.7	-24.7	-128.0
4th quarter	643.8	301.6	46.0	49.2	247.0	821.8	282.8	346.4	84.3	86.8	21.5	-178.0	-37.1	-140.8
1983:														
1st quarter	649.6	295.5	46.5	49.6	257.9	826.1	286.8	343.3	86.5	86.9	22.6	-176.4	-25.9	-150.6
2nd quarter	680.7	301.6	63.0	54.0	262.1	848.2	293.8	350.5	86.9	90.0	25.8	-167.5	-28.0	-139.5
3rd quarter	675.0	284.4	70.4	54.4	265.9	858.5	302.7	345.8	87.7	95.2	26.7	-183.5	-16.8	-166.7
4th quarter	682.4	290.7	65.4	55.3	271.1	852.6	288.8	351.4	86.9	99.0	26.5	-170.1	-12.3	-157.9
1984:														
1st quarter	732.6	294.8	82.7	57.3	298.0	876.3	301.5	349.4	91.9	104.6	29.2	-143.7	14.4	-158.0
2nd quarter	743.7	301.0	81.2	58.1	303.5	893.8	314.8	351.5	94.7	107.8	25.1	-150.1	19.7	-169.8
3rd quarter	750.4	313.7	70.0	58.3	308.4	913.1	317.3	355.4	93.2	117.6	29.4	-162.7	25.0	-187.6
4th quarter	760.7	323.9	67.1	58.1	311.6	928.3	322.9	360.8	97.6	123.0	24.5	-167.6	28.7	-196.3
1985:														
1st quarter	820.4	360.0	75.6	57.6	327.2	951.2	332.9	373.3	96.2	124.6	24.3	-130.8	29.4	-160.2
2nd quarter	781.1	314.5	73.6	62.3	330.7	966.6	338.0	376.2	99.4	127.7	24.2	-185.5	32.4	-218.0
3rd quarter	818.3	347.8	78.7	57.4	334.4	982.0	346.9	382.1	101.2	126.3	25.5	-163.6	32.8	-196.5
4th quarter	825.2	352.5	77.1	55.5	340.1	997.0	352.4	384.5	104.3	128.9	26.9	-171.7	37.7	-209.4
1986:														
1st quarter	834.2	348.9	81.3	54.1	349.8	1 003.3	351.6	389.6	104.5	130.3	27.3	-169.1	39.8	-208.9
2nd quarter	837.3	352.0	80.8	52.4	352.1	1 027.7	360.8	397.9	109.5	131.4	28.1	-190.4	39.5	-229.9
3rd quarter	850.5	360.1	82.0	52.5	356.0	1 044.6	369.7	404.5	113.1	128.9	28.4	-194.1	38.2	-232.3
4th quarter	878.3	372.2	91.3	53.9	360.9	1 034.8	367.3	404.6	103.2	131.5	28.3	-156.5	42.6	-199.0
1987:														
1st quarter	881.4	367.4	90.3	55.6	368.1	1 045.5	373.6	406.4	100.9	132.9	31.7	-164.1	46.1	-210.2
2nd quarter	952.5	420.2	103.2	57.6	371.6	1 062.5	376.4	412.2	105.4	134.3	34.3	-110.0	45.8	-155.8
3rd quarter	948.2	404.5	109.3	58.3	376.1	1 065.2	376.2	413.3	102.8	138.2	35.0	-117.1	50.6	-167.6
4th quarter	967.7	417.3	110.0	59.5	380.9	1 092.0	386.7	420.3	102.5	145.9	36.4	-124.3	56.3	-180.6
1988:														
1st quarter	966.9	401.6	102.9	60.6	401.8	1 110.7	388.7	433.0	108.8	143.1	37.1	-143.8	63.8	-207.5
2nd quarter	995.8	418.0	109.5	60.2	408.1	1 109.2	384.4	433.1	111.6	147.2	33.0	-113.4	70.8	-184.3
3rd quarter	1 002.1	414.0	113.0	61.4	413.7	1 116.8	383.9	437.0	112.2	150.0	33.7	-114.7	77.2	-191.9
4th quarter	1 023.9	423.9	118.6	61.5	419.9	1 137.1	394.3	445.8	112.3	153.1	31.6	-113.2	83.4	-196.6
1989:														
1st quarter	1 072.6	451.8	127.0	62.1	431.6	1 164.6	395.4	459.4	115.9	162.6	31.3	-92.0	81.4	-173.5
2nd quarter	1 084.2	469.1	119.1	60.8	435.2	1 184.4	406.2	463.7	117.1	166.6	30.8	-100.2	82.0	-182.2
3rd quarter	1 073.7	461.6	110.3	62.6	439.1	1 198.4	409.0	475.3	118.4	165.4	30.4	-124.7	80.9	-205.6
4th quarter	1 086.9	471.1	111.8	61.5	442.4	1 223.3	410.1	488.6	121.4	172.4	30.7	-136.5	79.1	-215.6

State and Local Government Receipts and Current Expenditures

(Calendar years—Billions of dollars, quarterly data are at seasonally adjusted annual rates)

Year and quarter	Receipts						Current expenditures						Surplus or deficit (—), national income and product accounts		
	Total	Personal tax and nontax receipts	Corporate profits tax accruals	Indirect business tax and nontax accruals	Contributions for social insurance	Federal grants-in-aid	Total	Consumption expenditures	Transfer payments to persons	Net interest paid	Less: dividends received by government	Subsidies less surplus of government enterprises	Total	Social insurance funds	Other
1962	56.6	6.3	1.5	37.0	3.9	8.0	44.8	39.1	7.0	0.2	.....	-1.4	11.7	2.6	9.1
1963	61.1	6.7	1.7	39.4	4.2	9.1	48.1	42.2	7.5	0.1	.....	-1.7	13.0	2.8	10.2
1964	67.1	7.5	1.8	42.6	4.7	10.4	52.4	46.0	8.2	-0.1	.....	-1.7	14.7	3.2	11.5
1965	72.3	8.1	2.0	46.1	5.0	11.1	57.2	50.5	8.8	-0.3	.....	-1.7	15.1	3.4	11.6
1966	81.5	9.5	2.2	49.7	5.7	14.4	64.3	56.5	10.1	-0.6	.....	-1.7	17.3	4.0	13.3
1967	89.8	10.6	2.6	53.9	6.7	15.9	72.5	62.9	12.1	-0.9	.....	-1.6	17.3	4.8	12.5
1968	102.7	12.7	3.3	60.8	7.2	18.6	82.6	70.8	14.5	-1.0	0.1	-1.6	20.0	5.2	14.8
1969	114.8	15.2	3.6	67.4	8.3	20.3	93.7	79.8	16.7	-1.2	0.2	-1.5	21.1	5.8	15.3
1970	129.0	16.7	3.7	74.8	9.2	24.4	108.2	91.6	20.1	-1.8	0.2	-1.6	20.8	6.9	13.9
1971	145.3	18.7	4.3	83.1	10.2	29.0	123.7	102.9	24.0	-1.4	0.3	-1.4	21.7	7.6	14.1
1972	169.7	24.2	5.3	91.2	11.5	37.5	137.5	113.4	27.5	-1.5	0.3	-1.6	32.2	8.7	23.5
1973	185.3	26.3	6.0	99.5	13.0	40.6	152.0	126.4	30.4	-2.9	0.5	-1.5	33.4	9.6	23.8
1974	200.6	28.2	6.7	107.2	14.6	43.9	170.2	144.0	32.3	-4.4	0.9	-0.9	30.5	10.9	19.5
1975	225.6	31.0	7.3	115.8	16.8	54.6	198.0	164.9	38.9	-4.5	0.9	-0.4	27.6	13.1	14.5
1976	253.9	35.8	9.6	127.8	19.5	61.1	217.9	179.7	43.6	-4.1	0.9	-0.4	35.9	15.6	20.4
1977	281.9	41.0	11.4	139.9	22.1	67.5	237.1	196.1	47.4	-4.7	1.3	-0.3	44.7	17.9	26.8
1978	309.3	46.3	12.1	148.9	24.7	77.3	256.7	214.5	52.4	-8.1	1.7	-0.3	52.6	20.2	32.4
1979	330.6	50.5	13.6	158.6	27.4	80.5	278.3	235.9	57.2	-13.3	2.0	0.4	52.3	23.7	28.6
1980	361.4	56.2	14.5	172.3	29.7	88.7	307.0	261.3	65.7	-19.3	1.9	1.2	54.4	26.9	27.5
1981	390.8	63.0	15.4	192.0	32.5	87.9	335.4	285.3	73.6	-23.6	2.3	2.4	55.4	29.8	25.6
1982	409.0	68.5	14.0	206.8	35.8	83.9	357.7	307.9	79.9	-28.9	2.9	1.7	51.3	36.6	14.7
1983	443.6	76.2	15.9	226.8	37.7	87.0	378.8	326.2	86.6	-31.0	3.4	0.2	64.9	41.6	23.3
1984	492.0	87.1	18.8	251.5	40.2	94.4	405.1	350.8	93.9	-34.1	3.9	-1.6	86.9	42.9	44.0
1985	528.7	94.0	20.2	271.4	42.8	100.3	437.8	382.6	101.9	-38.9	4.5	-3.3	91.0	47.0	44.0
1986	570.6	101.6	22.7	291.5	47.3	107.6	475.7	412.7	111.8	-40.7	5.1	-3.0	94.9	52.8	42.1
1987	594.9	111.8	23.9	307.1	49.2	102.9	511.1	441.1	120.7	-41.5	5.9	-3.4	83.8	54.8	29.0
1988	631.4	117.6	26.0	324.6	51.9	111.2	545.5	471.3	131.0	-44.6	6.9	-5.3	85.9	56.7	29.2
1989	681.0	131.4	24.2	353.0	54.1	118.2	585.9	507.2	144.5	-51.2	8.1	-6.6	95.1	60.2	34.9
1962:															
1st quarter	55.3	6.0	1.5	36.2	3.8	7.8	44.0	38.3	6.8	0.2	.....	-1.4	11.3	2.5	8.8
2nd quarter	56.1	6.2	1.5	36.7	3.8	7.9	44.6	38.9	6.9	0.1	.....	-1.4	11.5	2.5	9.0
3rd quarter	56.9	6.4	1.5	37.2	3.9	7.9	45.0	39.3	7.0	0.1	.....	-1.4	11.9	2.6	9.3
4th quarter	58.0	6.5	1.5	37.7	4.0	8.3	45.8	40.0	7.1	0.2	.....	-1.5	12.2	2.6	9.6
1963:															
1st quarter	58.9	6.5	1.5	38.2	4.1	8.5	46.6	40.8	7.3	0.2	.....	-1.6	12.2	2.7	9.6
2nd quarter	60.1	6.6	1.6	38.9	4.2	8.8	47.5	41.7	7.4	0.1	.....	-1.6	12.6	2.8	9.9
3rd quarter	61.9	6.8	1.7	39.8	4.3	9.4	48.4	42.5	7.5	0.0	.....	-1.7	13.5	2.9	10.7
4th quarter	63.4	6.9	1.7	40.5	4.4	9.9	49.7	43.6	7.7	0.1	.....	-1.7	13.8	2.9	10.8
1964:															
1st quarter	65.0	7.2	1.8	41.4	4.5	10.1	50.9	44.6	7.9	0.0	.....	-1.6	14.1	3.1	11.0
2nd quarter	66.5	7.5	1.8	42.1	4.7	10.4	51.9	45.5	8.1	0.0	.....	-1.6	14.5	3.2	11.3
3rd quarter	68.0	7.7	1.9	43.2	4.7	10.5	52.8	46.4	8.2	-0.1	.....	-1.7	15.2	3.2	12.0
4th quarter	68.9	7.9	1.8	43.7	4.8	10.7	54.0	47.5	8.4	-0.2	.....	-1.8	14.9	3.2	11.7
1965:															
1st quarter	69.9	8.0	1.9	44.6	4.9	10.5	55.2	48.6	8.5	-0.2	.....	-1.7	14.7	3.3	11.4
2nd quarter	71.4	8.0	1.9	45.5	4.9	11.0	56.4	49.7	8.7	-0.3	.....	-1.8	15.0	3.4	11.6
3rd quarter	73.1	8.1	2.0	46.6	5.1	11.3	58.1	51.1	8.9	-0.2	.....	-1.7	15.0	3.4	11.6
4th quarter	74.9	8.3	2.1	47.7	5.2	11.6	59.3	52.4	9.0	-0.4	.....	-1.7	15.5	3.6	12.0
1966:															
1st quarter	78.0	8.8	2.3	48.4	5.4	13.3	61.2	54.0	9.3	-0.5	.....	-1.6	16.8	3.7	13.1
2nd quarter	80.6	9.3	2.3	49.1	5.6	14.4	63.3	55.6	9.9	-0.6	.....	-1.6	17.4	3.8	13.5
3rd quarter	82.9	9.8	2.2	50.2	5.8	14.9	65.2	57.3	10.3	-0.7	.....	-1.6	17.7	4.1	13.6
4th quarter	84.6	10.3	2.2	51.1	6.1	15.0	67.4	59.0	10.9	-0.8	.....	-1.7	17.2	4.3	12.9
1967:															
1st quarter	86.3	10.3	2.6	51.8	6.3	15.3	68.9	60.3	11.2	-0.9	.....	-1.6	17.3	4.3	13.0
2nd quarter	87.2	10.3	2.6	52.8	6.6	14.9	71.2	61.8	11.8	-0.8	.....	-1.7	16.0	4.5	11.5
3rd quarter	90.9	10.8	2.6	54.7	6.8	16.0	73.7	63.8	12.4	-1.0	.....	-1.5	17.1	5.0	12.1
4th quarter	94.7	11.1	2.7	56.4	6.9	17.5	76.1	65.6	13.1	-1.0	.....	-1.6	18.6	5.3	13.4
1968:															
1st quarter	98.1	11.8	3.2	58.4	7.0	17.6	78.7	67.8	13.6	-1.0	0.1	-1.6	19.5	5.2	14.3
2nd quarter	101.5	12.4	3.3	60.0	7.1	18.7	81.3	69.6	14.4	-1.0	0.1	-1.6	20.1	5.2	15.0
3rd quarter	104.1	13.0	3.3	61.7	7.3	18.8	83.8	71.6	14.7	-0.9	0.1	-1.5	20.3	5.2	15.0
4th quarter	106.9	13.6	3.4	63.1	7.5	19.3	86.6	74.0	15.2	-1.0	0.1	-1.5	20.3	5.4	14.9
1969:															
1st quarter	109.4	14.2	3.8	64.6	7.8	19.0	89.1	75.9	15.9	-1.1	0.1	-1.5	20.3	5.4	14.8
2nd quarter	112.7	14.7	3.7	66.4	8.1	19.8	91.9	78.4	16.3	-1.1	0.1	-1.5	20.8	5.7	15.1
3rd quarter	116.7	15.7	3.5	68.4	8.5	20.6	95.2	81.0	17.0	-1.1	0.2	-1.5	21.5	5.9	15.6
4th quarter	120.4	16.1	3.4	70.2	8.7	22.0	98.4	83.9	17.7	-1.5	0.2	-1.6	22.0	6.2	15.8
1970															
1st quarter	124.2	16.4	3.8	72.0	8.9	23.1	102.4	87.3	18.6	-1.7	0.2	-1.6	21.8	6.6	15.3
2nd quarter	127.5	16.7	3.7	73.9	9.1	24.1	106.1	90.1	19.6	-1.9	0.2	-1.6	21.4	6.8	14.6
3rd quarter	130.8	16.9	3.8	75.8	9.4	25.0	110.1	93.0	20.7	-1.7	0.3	-1.6	20.7	7.1	13.7
4th quarter	133.4	17.0	3.6	77.5	9.6	25.7	114.1	95.9	21.8	-1.8	0.3	-1.5	19.2	7.2	12.0
1971															
1st quarter	138.1	17.4	4.1	79.8	9.8	27.0	118.7	99.3	22.7	-1.6	0.3	-1.5	19.4	7.3	12.1
2nd quarter	144.0	18.4	4.2	81.8	10.1	29.5	122.4	101.8	23.6	-1.4	0.3	-1.4	21.6	7.5	14.1
3rd quarter	147.3	19.0	4.4	84.5	10.3	29.2	125.5	104.3	24.4	-1.2	0.3	-1.4	21.9	7.7	14.2
4th quarter	151.9	20.2	4.5	86.4	10.5	30.3	128.1	106.3	25.3	-1.3	0.3	-1.4	23.8	7.9	15.9
1972:															
1st quarter	158.1	22.6	5.0	88.1	11.0	31.4	133.2	109.4	26.4	-1.3	0.3	-1.5	24.9	8.3	16.6
2nd quarter	170.0	24.2	5.0	90.3	11.3	39.1	135.6	111.8	27.0	-1.4	0.3	-1.6	34.4	8.6	25.9
3rd quarter	167.1	24.6	5.2	92.2	11.6	33.5	139.4	114.8	28.1	-1.5	0.3	-1.7	27.7	8.8	18.9
4th quarter	183.7	25.4	5.7	94.4	12.0	46.1	142.0	117.6	28.3	-1.9	0.3	-1.7	41.7	9.0	32.6

State and Local Government Receipts and Current Expenditures—*Continued*

(Calendar years—Billions of dollars, quarterly data are at seasonally adjusted annual rates)

Year and quarter	Receipts						Current expenditures						Surplus or deficit (—), national income and product accounts		
	Total	Personal tax and nontax receipts	Corporate profits tax accruals	Indirect business tax and nontax accruals	Contributions for social insurance	Federal grants-in-aid	Total	Consumption expenditures	Transfer payments to persons	Net interest paid	Less: dividends received by government	Subsidies less surplus of government enterprises	Total	Social insurance funds	Other
1973:															
1st quarter	182.2	25.4	6.0	97.0	12.4	41.3	146.0	121.0	29.3	-2.2	0.4	-1.6	36.1	9.3	26.9
2nd quarter	183.8	25.6	6.1	98.4	12.8	40.9	150.2	124.6	30.2	-2.7	0.5	-1.6	33.6	9.5	24.1
3rd quarter	185.6	26.5	5.8	100.8	13.1	39.2	153.7	128.2	30.6	-3.1	0.5	-1.5	31.9	9.7	22.2
4th quarter	189.8	27.5	6.1	101.9	13.6	40.8	157.9	131.8	31.5	-3.4	0.6	-1.4	31.9	10.0	21.9
1974:															
1st quarter	192.8	26.8	6.3	103.3	14.0	42.4	160.6	136.3	30.2	-3.9	0.7	-1.3	32.2	10.4	21.8
2nd quarter	199.1	27.7	6.6	106.3	14.4	44.0	166.7	141.3	31.6	-4.3	0.8	-1.1	32.4	10.7	21.7
3rd quarter	203.5	28.9	7.3	109.2	14.8	43.3	173.2	146.5	33.0	-4.6	0.9	-0.8	30.3	11.1	19.2
4th quarter	207.1	29.4	6.4	110.0	15.3	46.0	180.2	151.8	34.5	-4.6	0.9	-0.6	26.9	11.6	15.4
1975:															
1st quarter	212.4	29.6	6.0	111.5	15.8	49.4	188.5	157.5	36.8	-4.6	0.9	-0.4	23.9	12.1	11.7
2nd quarter	221.5	30.5	6.6	114.2	16.5	53.6	195.8	163.3	38.4	-4.6	0.8	-0.4	25.7	12.7	12.9
3rd quarter	231.6	31.4	8.3	117.5	17.2	57.3	201.1	167.8	39.2	-4.5	0.9	-0.4	30.5	13.4	17.1
4th quarter	236.8	32.6	8.5	119.9	17.8	57.9	206.4	171.0	41.2	-4.3	0.9	-0.6	30.4	14.0	16.4
1976:															
1st quarter	244.4	33.9	9.7	123.6	18.5	58.7	211.5	174.6	42.4	-4.1	0.8	-0.5	32.9	14.6	18.3
2nd quarter	249.6	35.2	9.6	126.3	19.2	59.2	215.4	178.0	42.8	-4.1	0.9	-0.4	34.1	15.3	18.8
3rd quarter	255.8	36.4	9.7	128.9	19.9	61.0	220.3	181.3	44.3	-4.0	0.9	-0.3	35.4	15.9	19.6
4th quarter	265.7	37.6	9.6	132.5	20.5	65.5	224.4	184.9	44.8	-4.0	1.0	-0.3	41.3	16.5	24.8
1977:															
1st quarter	269.5	39.0	10.5	135.7	21.1	63.2	229.3	189.2	45.6	-4.1	1.1	-0.3	40.2	17.0	23.1
2nd quarter	278.2	40.5	11.4	138.4	21.7	66.2	235.2	193.5	47.6	-4.5	1.2	-0.3	43.0	17.6	25.4
3rd quarter	287.9	41.4	11.9	141.3	22.4	70.9	239.6	198.5	47.7	-4.9	1.4	-0.3	48.3	18.2	30.1
4th quarter	291.9	42.9	11.9	144.1	23.1	69.9	244.4	203.2	48.5	-5.4	1.5	-0.4	47.4	18.8	28.7
1978:															
1st quarter	298.8	44.2	10.5	146.0	23.7	74.4	249.9	208.2	50.3	-6.5	1.7	-0.4	48.9	19.4	29.5
2nd quarter	311.1	45.9	12.4	150.9	24.3	77.6	254.9	212.0	52.4	-7.5	1.7	-0.3	56.2	19.8	36.4
3rd quarter	309.4	46.9	12.5	147.6	25.0	77.4	258.8	216.6	53.1	-8.6	1.8	-0.2	50.7	20.5	30.2
4th quarter	317.7	48.2	13.1	151.2	25.7	79.6	263.0	221.2	53.8	-9.7	1.8	-0.1	54.7	21.1	33.6
1979:															
1st quarter	320.7	48.3	13.8	154.3	26.4	78.0	268.9	227.4	54.8	-11.3	1.9	0.1	51.8	22.2	29.6
2nd quarter	323.9	48.4	13.8	156.5	27.1	78.0	275.5	232.5	56.2	-12.5	1.9	0.4	48.4	23.2	25.2
3rd quarter	335.1	51.9	13.6	159.9	27.8	81.9	281.1	239.0	57.5	-13.9	2.0	0.5	54.0	24.2	29.8
4th quarter	342.6	53.4	13.0	163.7	28.4	84.1	287.7	244.7	60.2	-15.5	2.1	0.6	55.0	25.2	29.7
1980															
1st quarter	351.1	53.4	16.3	167.0	28.8	85.5	296.6	252.1	62.8	-17.2	2.0	0.7	54.5	26.0	28.5
2nd quarter	352.8	55.1	12.7	168.9	28.8	87.4	302.0	258.5	63.2	-18.7	1.9	1.0	50.8	26.1	24.8
3rd quarter	364.4	56.9	13.8	174.0	30.3	89.3	311.0	264.5	67.1	-20.1	1.8	1.3	53.3	27.5	25.8
4th quarter	377.3	59.3	15.0	179.4	31.1	92.5	318.4	270.0	69.5	-21.2	1.8	1.8	58.9	28.1	30.8
1981															
1st quarter	386.0	60.5	17.3	186.3	31.5	90.4	327.1	277.4	71.3	-21.9	2.0	2.3	58.9	28.2	30.7
2nd quarter	389.4	62.0	15.2	189.9	32.1	90.2	334.0	282.8	73.6	-22.8	2.2	2.6	55.4	29.0	26.5
3rd quarter	393.9	64.0	15.7	194.7	32.8	86.7	338.4	287.9	74.5	-24.1	2.4	2.6	55.5	30.2	25.3
4th quarter	394.0	65.5	13.5	197.2	33.6	84.2	342.2	293.1	74.9	-25.6	2.6	2.3	51.8	32.0	19.9
1982:															
1st quarter	398.1	66.3	14.1	200.4	34.7	82.7	348.9	299.8	76.9	-27.2	2.8	2.2	49.3	34.2	15.1
2nd quarter	407.1	67.3	14.4	204.9	35.6	84.9	355.6	305.8	79.5	-28.5	2.9	1.8	51.5	36.0	15.5
3rd quarter	412.7	70.0	14.4	208.6	36.3	83.5	360.6	310.5	81.2	-29.5	3.0	1.5	52.1	37.5	14.6
4th quarter	418.1	70.5	13.3	213.1	36.8	84.3	365.8	315.7	82.1	-30.2	3.1	1.3	52.3	38.8	13.5
1983:															
1st quarter	424.4	71.3	12.4	217.1	37.1	86.5	373.0	320.6	85.0	-30.3	3.2	0.8	51.4	40.3	11.1
2nd quarter	438.8	74.4	16.4	223.8	37.4	86.9	376.3	324.2	85.8	-30.7	3.3	0.4	62.4	41.4	21.0
3rd quarter	451.9	78.3	18.1	230.1	37.8	87.7	380.5	328.1	87.0	-31.1	3.4	0.0	71.4	42.1	29.3
4th quarter	459.5	81.0	16.8	236.3	38.4	86.9	385.3	332.0	88.8	-31.8	3.5	-0.2	74.2	42.5	31.8
1984:															
1st quarter	479.1	84.0	20.6	243.4	39.2	91.9	394.8	340.1	91.6	-32.5	3.7	-0.7	84.3	42.2	42.1
2nd quarter	490.8	86.7	20.2	249.3	39.9	94.7	401.7	347.0	93.1	-33.5	3.8	-1.2	89.2	42.5	46.6
3rd quarter	493.1	87.9	17.5	253.9	40.6	93.2	408.6	354.5	94.4	-34.6	3.9	-1.8	84.5	43.1	41.4
4th quarter	505.1	89.9	16.8	259.6	41.1	97.6	415.4	361.6	96.4	-35.9	4.1	-2.6	89.6	43.7	45.9
1985:															
1st quarter	512.6	91.2	19.9	263.8	41.6	96.2	423.7	369.7	98.7	-37.4	4.2	-3.0	89.0	45.0	44.0
2nd quarter	523.7	93.3	19.4	269.3	42.3	99.4	432.0	377.7	100.6	-38.6	4.5	-3.3	91.7	46.1	45.6
3rd quarter	534.2	94.3	21.0	274.5	43.2	101.2	442.5	387.1	102.9	-39.4	4.6	-3.5	91.7	47.7	44.1
4th quarter	544.4	97.0	20.7	278.1	44.3	104.3	452.9	395.9	105.2	-40.1	4.7	-3.4	91.5	49.0	42.5
1986:															
1st quarter	560.9	98.3	21.2	291.3	45.5	104.5	462.0	402.5	107.9	-40.3	4.9	-3.2	98.9	50.5	48.3
2nd quarter	564.0	99.3	21.9	286.8	46.5	109.5	469.5	407.5	110.7	-40.6	5.0	-3.1	94.5	51.9	42.6
3rd quarter	577.0	102.1	22.4	292.1	47.4	113.1	478.9	414.8	113.1	-40.8	5.2	-2.9	98.1	53.1	45.0
4th quarter	580.6	106.7	25.1	295.7	49.9	103.2	492.4	426.1	115.4	-41.0	5.4	-2.7	88.2	55.8	32.4
1987:															
1st quarter	576.8	107.3	20.8	299.4	48.4	100.9	498.9	431.1	117.3	-41.0	5.6	-2.9	77.9	54.2	23.7
2nd quarter	599.4	116.6	23.9	304.7	48.9	105.4	507.6	438.1	119.6	-41.2	5.8	-3.1	91.8	54.6	37.2
3rd quarter	597.7	109.4	25.4	310.7	49.4	102.8	514.7	443.6	121.9	-41.5	5.9	-3.4	83.0	55.0	28.0
4th quarter	605.6	114.0	25.5	313.4	50.1	102.5	523.1	451.7	124.0	-42.3	6.1	-4.1	82.4	55.4	27.0
1988:															
1st quarter	613.6	113.4	24.1	316.4	50.9	108.8	533.0	459.7	126.9	-42.6	6.4	-4.6	80.6	55.5	25.1
2nd quarter	627.6	117.1	25.8	321.5	51.7	111.6	541.6	467.8	129.4	-43.7	6.9	-5.1	86.1	56.3	29.7
3rd quarter	636.0	118.3	26.5	326.7	52.2	112.2	548.9	474.6	132.3	-45.3	7.1	-5.6	87.1	57.0	30.1
4th quarter	648.2	121.7	27.7	333.7	52.8	112.3	558.4	483.1	135.5	-47.0	7.2	-6.0	89.9	57.8	32.1
1989:															
1st quarter	663.6	125.9	26.8	341.7	53.2	115.9	568.0	493.3	138.5	-49.8	7.6	-6.4	95.6	59.5	36.1
2nd quarter	677.5	131.6	24.7	350.5	53.7	117.1	579.2	502.7	142.2	-51.0	8.0	-6.7	98.3	60.3	38.1
3rd quarter	686.5	133.0	22.6	358.1	54.4	118.4	590.6	511.0	146.5	-51.7	8.2	-6.9	95.9	60.5	35.4
4th quarter	696.3	135.3	22.9	361.6	55.1	121.4	605.9	522.0	150.9	-52.2	8.5	-6.3	90.4	60.5	29.9

U.S. International Transactions

(Millions of dollars, seasonally adjusted)

Year and quarter	Exports of goods, services, and income				Imports of goods, services, and income [1]				Unilateral current transfers, net [2]	U.S.-owned assets abroad, net [3]				
													U.S. private assets, net	
	Total	Goods	Services	Income receipts	Total	Goods	Services	Income payments		Total	U.S. official reserve assets, net	U.S. government assets, other than official reserve assets, net	Total	Direct investment
1962	33 340	20 781	6 941	5 618	-25 676	-16 260	-8 092	-1 324	-4 277	-4 174	1 535	-1 085	-4 623	-2 851
1963	35 776	22 272	7 348	6 157	-26 970	-17 048	-8 362	-1 560	-4 392	-7 270	378	-1 662	-5 986	-3 483
1964	40 165	25 501	7 840	6 824	-29 102	-18 700	-8 619	-1 783	-4 240	-9 560	171	-1 680	-8 050	-3 760
1965	42 722	26 461	8 824	7 437	-32 708	-21 510	-9 111	-2 088	-4 583	-5 716	1 225	-1 605	-5 336	-5 011
1966	46 454	29 310	9 616	7 528	-38 468	-25 493	-10 494	-2 481	-4 955	-7 321	570	-1 543	-6 347	-5 418
1967	49 353	30 666	10 667	8 021	-41 476	-26 866	-11 863	-2 747	-5 294	-9 757	53	-2 423	-7 386	-4 805
1968	54 911	33 626	11 917	9 367	-48 671	-32 991	-12 302	-3 378	-5 629	-10 977	-870	-2 274	-7 833	-5 295
1969	60 132	36 414	12 806	10 913	-53 998	-35 807	-13 322	-4 869	-5 735	-11 585	-1 179	-2 200	-8 206	-5 960
1970	68 387	42 469	14 171	11 748	-59 901	-39 866	-14 520	-5 515	-6 156	-8 470	3 348	-1 589	-10 229	-7 590
1971	72 384	43 319	16 358	12 707	-66 414	-45 579	-15 400	-5 435	-7 402	-11 758	3 066	-1 884	-12 940	-7 618
1972	81 986	49 381	17 841	14 765	-79 237	-55 797	-16 868	-6 572	-8 544	-13 787	706	-1 568	-12 925	-7 747
1973	113 050	71 410	19 832	21 808	-98 997	-70 499	-18 843	-9 655	-6 913	-22 874	158	-2 644	-20 388	-11 353
1974	148 484	98 306	22 591	27 587	-137 274	-103 811	-21 379	-12 084	-9 249	-34 745	-1 467	366	-33 643	-9 052
1975	157 936	107 088	25 497	25 351	-132 745	-98 185	-21 996	-12 564	-7 075	-39 703	-849	-3 474	-35 380	-14 244
1976	172 090	114 745	27 971	29 375	-162 109	-124 228	-24 570	-13 311	-5 686	-51 269	-2 558	-4 214	-44 498	-11 949
1977	184 655	120 816	31 485	32 354	-193 764	-151 907	-27 640	-14 217	-5 226	-34 785	-375	-3 693	-30 717	-11 890
1978	220 516	142 075	36 353	42 088	-229 870	-176 002	-32 189	-21 680	-5 788	-61 130	732	-4 660	-57 202	-16 056
1979	287 965	184 439	39 692	63 834	-281 657	-212 007	-36 689	-32 961	-6 593	-64 915	6	-3 746	-61 176	-25 222
1980	344 440	224 250	47 584	72 606	-333 774	-249 750	-41 491	-42 532	-8 349	-85 815	-7 003	-5 162	-73 651	-19 222
1981	380 928	237 044	57 354	86 529	-364 196	-265 067	-45 503	-53 626	-11 702	-113 054	-4 082	-5 097	-103 875	-9 624
1982	366 926	211 157	64 079	91 690	-355 964	-247 642	-51 749	-56 572	-17 139	-127 825	-4 965	-6 131	-116 729	-4 499
1983	356 156	201 799	64 307	90 050	-377 577	-268 901	-54 973	-53 703	-17 778	-66 423	-1 196	-5 006	-60 222	-12 578
1984	400 052	219 926	71 168	108 958	-474 144	-332 418	-67 748	-73 977	-20 661	-40 515	-3 131	-5 489	-31 896	-16 546
1985	387 806	215 915	73 155	98 736	-484 106	-338 088	-72 862	-73 156	-22 762	-44 946	-3 858	-2 821	-38 268	-19 121
1986	406 060	223 344	85 442	97 274	-530 478	-368 425	-80 147	-81 905	-24 818	-111 933	312	-2 022	-110 224	-24 205
1987	456 227	250 208	97 591	108 428	-594 825	-409 765	-90 787	-94 273	-24 047	-79 540	9 149	1 006	-89 694	-35 278
1988	567 260	320 230	110 030	137 000	-664 167	-447 189	-98 526	-118 452	-26 139	-106 860	-3 912	2 967	-105 915	-22 815
1989	649 902	362 120	126 216	161 566	-721 686	-477 365	-102 479	-141 842	-27 116	-175 662	-25 293	1 233	-151 602	-43 726
1963:														
1st quarter	8 428	5 063	1 849	1 516	-6 478	-4 064	-2 057	-357	-1 107	-1 922	32	-482	-1 472	-980
2nd quarter	9 244	5 599	2 150	1 495	-6 674	-4 226	-2 066	-382	-1 371	-2 631	124	-654	-2 101	-874
3rd quarter	8 832	5 671	1 620	1 541	-6 893	-4 372	-2 122	-399	-918	-887	227	-86	-1 028	-721
4th quarter	9 275	5 939	1 731	1 605	-6 926	-4 386	-2 118	-422	-999	-1 831	-5	-440	-1 386	-908
1964:														
1st quarter	9 885	6 242	1 922	1 721	-6 982	-4 416	-2 140	-426	-993	-2 086	-51	-288	-1 747	-822
2nd quarter	9 975	6 199	2 088	1 688	-7 179	-4 598	-2 142	-439	-1 269	-2 018	303	-386	-1 935	-970
3rd quarter	10 009	6 423	1 851	1 735	-7 349	-4 756	-2 153	-440	-935	-2 255	70	-414	-1 911	-1 018
4th quarter	10 299	6 637	1 982	1 680	-7 594	-4 930	-2 186	-478	-1 043	-3 200	-151	-592	-2 457	-949
1965:														
1st quarter	9 689	5 768	2 047	1 874	-7 395	-4 711	-2 187	-497	-1 037	-1 576	843	-374	-2 045	-1 606
2nd quarter	11 263	6 876	2 448	1 939	-8 208	-5 428	-2 269	-511	-1 478	-1 270	69	-536	-803	-1 250
3rd quarter	10 625	6 643	2 120	1 862	-8 307	-5 516	-2 263	-528	-1 013	-1 454	42	-254	-1 242	-1 030
4th quarter	11 149	7 174	2 212	1 763	-8 802	-5 855	-2 393	-554	-1 058	-1 416	271	-441	-1 246	-1 125
1966:														
1st quarter	11 190	7 242	2 124	1 824	-9 068	-6 012	-2 483	-573	-1 140	-1 465	424	-321	-1 568	-1 115
2nd quarter	11 726	7 169	2 705	1 852	-9 390	-6 195	-2 601	-594	-1 547	-1 967	68	-504	-1 531	-1 373
3rd quarter	11 470	7 290	2 301	1 879	-9 912	-6 576	-2 693	-643	-1 073	-1 681	83	-339	-1 425	-1 314
4th quarter	12 068	7 609	2 487	1 972	-10 098	-6 710	-2 717	-671	-1 194	-2 208	-5	-380	-1 823	-1 616
1967:														
1st quarter	12 439	7 751	2 731	1 957	-10 248	-6 708	-2 866	-674	-1 315	-1 203	1 027	-643	-1 587	-1 186
2nd quarter	12 275	7 693	2 666	1 916	-10 136	-6 475	-2 986	-675	-1 472	-2 339	-419	-543	-1 377	-964
3rd quarter	12 134	7 530	2 540	2 064	-10 262	-6 526	-3 059	-677	-1 309	-3 155	-375	-551	-2 229	-1 359
4th quarter	12 506	7 692	2 731	2 083	-10 833	-7 157	-2 955	-721	-1 199	-3 060	-180	-685	-2 195	-1 297
1968:														
1st quarter	13 016	7 998	2 816	2 202	-11 571	-7 796	-2 997	-778	-1 249	-1 299	912	-706	-1 505	-981
2nd quarter	13 577	8 324	2 936	2 317	-11 885	-8 051	-2 990	-844	-1 363	-2 427	-135	-632	-1 660	-1 172
3rd quarter	14 155	8 745	3 039	2 411	-12 611	-8 612	-3 129	-870	-1 445	-3 447	-572	-568	-2 307	-1 573
4th quarter	14 126	8 559	3 129	2 438	-12 604	-8 532	-3 185	-887	-1 573	-3 803	-1 075	-368	-2 360	-1 568
1969:														
1st quarter	12 921	7 468	2 884	2 569	-11 622	-7 444	-3 174	-1 004	-1 177	-2 595	-45	-406	-2 144	-1 556
2nd quarter	15 492	9 536	3 283	2 673	-13 978	-9 527	-3 303	-1 148	-1 645	-3 428	-298	-632	-2 498	-1 663
3rd quarter	15 439	9 400	3 245	2 794	-14 072	-9 380	-3 368	-1 324	-1 319	-3 361	-685	-703	-1 973	-1 548
4th quarter	16 279	10 010	3 394	2 875	-14 329	-9 456	-3 481	-1 392	-1 593	-2 199	-151	-459	-1 589	-1 192
1970:														
1st quarter	16 461	10 258	3 235	2 968	-14 458	-9 587	-3 449	-1 422	-1 383	-2 611	481	-399	-2 693	-1 958
2nd quarter	17 419	10 744	3 645	3 030	-14 861	-9 766	-3 690	-1 405	-1 586	-1 725	1 025	-348	-2 402	-2 144
3rd quarter	17 267	10 665	3 625	2 977	-15 141	-10 049	-3 715	-1 377	-1 611	-2 146	802	-423	-2 525	-1 718
4th quarter	17 241	10 802	3 666	2 773	-15 443	-10 464	-3 668	-1 311	-1 576	-1 989	1 040	-419	-2 610	-1 771
1971:														
1st quarter	17 980	10 920	4 048	3 012	-15 551	-10 600	-3 724	-1 227	-1 746	-2 747	868	-573	-3 042	-2 033
2nd quarter	18 163	10 878	4 087	3 198	-16 764	-11 614	-3 867	-1 283	-1 808	-2 534	839	-567	-2 806	-1 949
3rd quarter	18 676	11 548	3 972	3 156	-17 460	-12 171	-3 861	-1 428	-1 752	-3 390	1 377	-387	-4 380	-2 308
4th quarter	17 564	9 973	4 251	3 340	-16 639	-11 194	-3 948	-1 497	-2 098	-3 084	-18	-355	-2 711	-1 327
1972:														
1st quarter	19 757	11 833	4 473	3 451	-19 153	-13 501	-4 173	-1 479	-2 297	-3 585	620	-212	-3 993	-2 187
2nd quarter	19 427	11 618	4 233	3 576	-19 105	-13 254	-4 228	-1 623	-2 011	-2 125	-60	-271	-1 794	-1 481
3rd quarter	20 788	12 351	4 634	3 803	-19 767	-14 022	-4 095	-1 650	-2 306	-3 952	96	-518	-3 530	-2 435
4th quarter	22 015	13 579	4 503	3 933	-21 212	-15 020	-4 371	-1 821	-1 933	-4 125	50	-566	-3 609	-1 644

1. A minus sign indicates imports of goods, services, or income.
2. A minus sign indicates unilateral transfers to foreigners.
3. A minus sign indicates capital outflow or a increase in official reserve assets.

U.S. International Transactions—*Continued*

(Millions of dollars, seasonally adjusted)

Year and quarter	Exports of goods, services, and income				Imports of goods, services, and income [1]				Unilateral current transfers, net [2]	U.S.-owned assets abroad, net [3]				
	Total	Goods	Services	Income receipts	Total	Goods	Services	Income payments		Total	U.S. official reserve assets, net	U.S. government assets, other than official reserve assets, net	U.S. private assets, net	
													Total	Direct investment
1973:														
1st quarter	24 681	15 474	4 579	4 628	-23 000	-16 285	-4 613	-2 102	-1 536	-7 886	213	-572	-7 527	-3 785
2nd quarter	27 127	17 112	4 828	5 187	-24 301	-17 168	-4 741	-2 392	-1 953	-4 154	11	-423	-3 742	-2 691
3rd quarter	29 329	18 271	5 145	5 913	-24 841	-17 683	-4 640	-2 518	-1 751	-3 189	-23	-608	-2 558	-2 159
4th quarter	31 912	20 553	5 279	6 080	-26 855	-19 363	-4 849	-2 643	-1 674	-7 646	-43	-1 042	-6 561	-2 718
1974:														
1st quarter	34 698	22 614	5 189	6 895	-29 643	-21 952	-4 985	-2 706	-3 443	-5 914	-246	1 389	-7 057	900
2nd quarter	37 295	24 500	5 691	7 104	-34 710	-26 346	-5 359	-3 005	-2 475	-10 318	-358	267	-10 227	-1 790
3rd quarter	37 385	24 629	5 633	7 123	-36 004	-27 368	-5 360	-3 276	-1 676	-7 694	-1 002	-354	-6 338	-4 385
4th quarter	39 105	26 563	6 078	6 464	-36 918	-28 145	-5 675	-3 098	-1 656	-10 818	139	-938	-10 019	-3 776
1975:														
1st quarter	40 047	27 480	6 454	6 113	-33 797	-24 980	-5 580	-3 237	-2 043	-10 576	-327	-877	-9 372	-4 022
2nd quarter	38 675	25 866	6 807	6 002	-31 284	-22 832	-5 309	-3 143	-2 377	-9 591	-28	-875	-8 688	-3 990
3rd quarter	38 347	26 109	5 886	6 352	-33 078	-24 487	-5 379	-3 212	-1 189	-5 099	-333	-745	-4 021	-1 495
4th quarter	40 868	27 633	6 351	6 884	-34 588	-25 886	-5 729	-2 973	-1 467	-14 436	-161	-977	-13 298	-4 736
1976:														
1st quarter	41 183	27 575	6 556	7 052	-37 464	-28 176	-5 883	-3 405	-1 153	-12 364	-777	-749	-10 838	-3 923
2nd quarter	42 309	28 256	6 660	7 393	-39 494	-30 182	-5 980	-3 332	-1 167	-11 701	-1 580	-914	-9 207	-2 017
3rd quarter	43 818	29 056	7 311	7 451	-41 737	-32 213	-6 231	-3 293	-2 165	-10 618	-408	-1 428	-8 782	-3 327
4th quarter	44 780	29 858	7 444	7 478	-43 416	-33 657	-6 478	-3 281	-1 201	-16 588	207	-1 124	-15 671	-2 682
1977:														
1st quarter	44 916	29 668	7 494	7 754	-46 360	-36 585	-6 676	-3 099	-1 243	-1 198	-420	-1 062	284	-1 880
2nd quarter	46 796	30 852	7 901	8 043	-48 401	-38 063	-6 940	-3 398	-1 426	-12 182	-24	-885	-11 273	-3 783
3rd quarter	47 125	30 752	7 991	8 382	-48 511	-38 005	-6 894	-3 612	-1 371	-6 297	112	-1 001	-5 408	-2 762
4th quarter	45 818	29 544	8 098	8 176	-50 495	-39 254	-7 133	-4 108	-1 185	-15 109	-43	-746	-14 320	-3 466
1978:														
1st quarter	48 847	30 470	8 704	9 673	-54 471	-42 487	-7 612	-4 372	-1 396	-15 219	187	-1 009	-14 397	-4 771
2nd quarter	54 213	35 674	8 772	9 767	-56 513	-43 419	-7 768	-5 326	-1 477	-5 606	248	-1 257	-4 597	-3 720
3rd quarter	56 058	36 523	9 203	10 332	-58 300	-44 422	-8 248	-5 630	-1 425	-9 703	115	-1 394	-8 424	-2 753
4th quarter	61 399	39 408	9 673	12 318	-60 587	-45 674	-8 561	-6 352	-1 491	-30 601	182	-999	-29 784	-4 812
1979:														
1st quarter	64 530	41 475	9 664	13 391	-63 492	-47 582	-8 649	-7 261	-1 462	-7 841	-2 446	-1 094	-4 301	-5 465
2nd quarter	68 445	43 885	9 713	14 847	-67 584	-50 778	-8 960	-7 846	-1 552	-15 565	322	-970	-14 917	-7 220
3rd quarter	74 411	47 104	9 936	17 371	-71 856	-54 002	-9 329	-8 525	-1 632	-27 156	2 779	-779	-29 156	-7 166
4th quarter	80 577	51 975	10 378	18 224	-78 726	-59 645	-9 751	-9 330	-1 949	-14 353	-649	-904	-12 800	-5 370
1980:														
1st quarter	85 274	54 237	10 997	20 040	-86 559	-65 815	-10 335	-10 409	-2 174	-12 662	-2 116	-1 441	-9 105	-5 188
2nd quarter	83 441	55 967	11 491	15 983	-82 734	-62 274	-10 106	-10 354	-1 648	-24 724	502	-1 159	-24 067	-2 659
3rd quarter	86 148	55 830	12 543	17 775	-79 906	-59 010	-10 292	-10 604	-1 909	-19 666	-109	-1 382	-17 175	-4 156
4th quarter	89 578	58 216	12 554	18 808	-84 577	-62 651	-10 760	-11 166	-2 618	-28 761	-4 279	-1 178	-23 304	-7 219
1981:														
1st quarter	94 665	60 317	13 684	20 664	-91 024	-67 004	-11 360	-12 660	-2 678	-21 922	-3 436	-1 361	-17 125	-2 044
2nd quarter	96 294	60 141	14 392	21 761	-92 303	-67 181	-11 447	-13 675	-2 763	-24 158	-905	-1 491	-21 762	-5 709
3rd quarter	95 013	58 031	14 835	22 147	-89 787	-64 407	-11 236	-14 144	-3 145	-17 945	-4	-1 268	-16 673	-1 124
4th quarter	94 958	58 555	14 446	21 957	-91 082	-66 475	-11 460	-13 147	-3 117	-49 028	262	-976	-48 314	-745
1982:														
1st quarter	93 981	55 163	16 032	22 786	-90 327	-63 502	-12 749	-14 076	-4 103	-36 310	-1 089	-800	-34 421	-2 670
2nd quarter	96 042	55 344	16 187	24 511	-88 312	-60 580	-13 096	-14 636	-4 097	-42 736	-1 132	-1 727	-39 877	1 092
3rd quarter	90 915	52 089	16 003	22 823	-90 937	-63 696	-12 794	-14 447	-4 169	-23 537	-794	-2 524	-20 219	913
4th quarter	85 989	48 561	15 857	21 571	-86 384	-59 864	-13 109	-13 411	-4 771	-25 242	-1 950	-1 080	-22 213	-3 834
1983:														
1st quarter	86 149	49 198	16 239	20 712	-85 108	-59 757	-12 951	-12 400	-3 685	-28 893	-787	-1 136	-26 970	-865
2nd quarter	87 223	49 340	16 093	21 790	-91 114	-64 783	-13 557	-12 774	-4 076	-2 983	16	-1 263	-1 736	-1 851
3rd quarter	89 935	50 324	16 308	23 303	-98 507	-70 370	-14 133	-14 004	-4 455	-12 207	529	-1 171	-11 565	-4 877
4th quarter	92 853	52 937	15 671	24 245	-102 856	-73 991	-14 337	-14 528	-5 562	-22 340	-953	-1 436	-19 951	-4 984
1984:														
1st quarter	96 028	52 991	17 353	25 684	-112 618	-79 740	-16 131	-16 747	-4 448	-8 366	-657	-2 033	-5 676	-1 865
2nd quarter	100 290	54 626	18 045	27 619	-119 271	-83 798	-16 885	-18 588	-4 557	-25 751	-566	-1 342	-23 844	-2 000
3rd quarter	102 333	55 893	17 936	28 504	-120 593	-83 918	-17 168	-19 507	-5 217	15 261	-799	-1 392	17 452	-3 246
4th quarter	101 402	56 416	17 834	27 152	-121 659	-84 962	-17 564	-19 133	-6 441	-21 659	-1 110	-720	-19 830	-9 437
1985:														
1st quarter	97 840	54 866	18 227	24 747	-116 328	-80 319	-17 707	-18 302	-5 184	-5 537	-233	-760	-4 544	-2 829
2nd quarter	97 485	54 154	18 214	25 117	-120 975	-84 565	-18 276	-18 134	-5 410	-2 388	-356	-1 053	-979	-4 422
3rd quarter	94 820	52 836	17 961	24 023	-120 372	-83 909	-18 151	-18 312	-6 012	-5 825	-121	-453	-5 251	-4 747
4th quarter	97 663	54 059	18 756	24 848	-126 436	-89 295	-18 732	-18 409	-6 157	-31 197	-3 148	-555	-27 495	-7 124
1986:														
1st quarter	100 072	53 536	20 741	25 795	-129 425	-89 220	-19 855	-20 350	-5 348	-17 457	-115	-266	-17 076	-9 832
2nd quarter	101 946	56 828	20 600	24 518	-131 773	-91 743	-19 066	-20 964	-6 368	-24 997	16	-230	-24 783	-7 350
3rd quarter	101 029	55 645	21 657	23 727	-132 963	-92 801	-20 448	-19 714	-6 633	-32 668	280	-1 554	-31 394	-5 028
4th quarter	103 017	57 335	22 449	23 233	-136 318	-94 661	-20 778	-20 879	-6 471	-36 807	132	29	-36 968	-1 992
1987:														
1st quarter	104 539	56 696	23 334	24 509	-138 977	-96 023	-21 273	-21 681	-5 310	8 120	1 956	-5	6 169	-6 604
2nd quarter	111 434	60 202	24 472	26 760	-146 219	-100 648	-22 537	-23 034	-5 696	-26 798	3 419	-168	-30 049	-7 601
3rd quarter	116 483	64 217	24 719	27 547	-151 208	-104 412	-22 833	-23 963	-5 890	-27 853	32	310	-28 195	-8 857
4th quarter	123 766	69 093	25 062	29 611	-158 425	-108 682	-24 146	-25 597	-7 149	-33 008	3 742	868	-37 618	-12 215
1988:														
1st quarter	134 789	75 655	26 385	32 749	-161 916	-109 963	-24 503	-27 450	-6 272	2 822	1 502	-1 597	2 917	-5 107
2nd quarter	139 842	79 542	27 353	32 947	-163 373	-110 836	-24 282	-28 255	-5 867	-23 500	39	-854	-22 685	-2 666
3rd quarter	143 702	80 941	28 204	34 557	-166 008	-110 901	-24 588	-30 519	-6 118	-50 037	-7 380	1 960	-44 617	-7 863
4th quarter	148 928	84 092	28 089	36 747	-172 875	-115 489	-25 157	-32 229	-7 884	-36 147	1 925	3 457	-41 529	-7 178
1989:														
1st quarter	156 807	87 426	30 358	39 023	-176 160	-116 477	-25 140	-34 543	-6 306	-53 771	-4 000	961	-50 732	-12 204
2nd quarter	164 011	92 208	30 892	40 911	-182 839	-120 907	-25 241	-36 691	-5 963	-8 270	-12 095	-306	4 131	-7 754
3rd quarter	162 832	90 163	32 098	40 571	-180 488	-118 873	-25 792	-35 823	-6 866	-51 748	-5 996	489	-46 241	-8 774
4th quarter	166 254	92 323	32 870	41 061	-182 199	-121 108	-26 306	-34 785	-7 983	-61 876	-3 202	87	-58 761	-14 995

1. A minus sign indicates imports of goods, services, or income.
2. A minus sign indicates unilateral transfers to foreigners.
3. A minus sign indicates capital outflow or a increase in official reserve assets.

U.S. International Transactions—*Continued*

(Millions of dollars, seasonally adjusted)

Year and quarter	U.S. private assets, net—Continued — Foreign securities	U.S. claims — on unaffiliated foreigners reported by U.S. nonbanking concerns	U.S. claims — reported by U.S. banks, not included elsewhere	Foreign-owned assets in the U.S., net[1] — Total	Foreign official assets in the United States, net	Other foreign assets in the U.S., net — Total	Direct investment	U.S. Treasury securities and U.S. currency flows	U.S. securities other than U.S. Treasury securities	U.S. liabilities to unaffiliated foreigners reported by U.S. nonbanking concerns	reported by U.S. banks, not included elsewhere	Statistical discrepancy[2]	Balance on Goods and services	Current account
1962	-969	-354	-450	1 911	1 270	641	346	-66	134	-110	336	-1 124	3 370	3 387
1963	-1 105	157	-1 556	3 217	1 986	1 231	231	-149	287	-37	898	-360	4 210	4 414
1964	-677	-1 108	-2 505	3 643	1 660	1 983	322	-146	-85	75	1 818	-907	6 022	6 823
1965	-759	341	93	742	134	607	415	-131	-358	178	503	-457	4 664	5 431
1966	-720	-442	233	3 661	-672	4 333	425	-356	906	476	2 882	629	2 940	3 031
1967	-1 308	-779	-495	7 379	3 451	3 928	698	-135	1 016	584	1 765	-205	2 604	2 583
1968	-1 569	-1 203	233	9 928	-774	10 703	807	136	4 414	1 475	3 871	438	250	611
1969	-1 549	-126	-570	12 702	-1 301	14 002	1 263	-68	3 130	792	8 886	-1 516	91	399
1970	-1 076	-596	-967	6 359	6 908	-550	1 464	81	2 189	2 014	-6 298	-219	2 254	2 331
1971	-1 113	-1 229	-2 980	22 970	26 879	-3 909	367	-24	2 289	369	-6 911	-9 779	-1 303	-1 433
1972	-618	-1 054	-3 506	21 461	10 475	10 986	949	-39	4 507	815	4 754	-1 879	-5 443	-5 795
1973	-671	-2 383	-5 980	18 388	6 026	12 362	2 800	-216	4 041	1 035	4 702	-2 654	1 900	7 140
1974	-1 854	-3 221	-19 516	35 341	10 546	24 796	4 760	1 797	378	1 844	16 017	-2 558	-4 292	1 962
1975	-6 247	-1 357	-13 532	17 170	7 027	10 143	2 603	4 090	2 503	319	628	4 417	12 404	18 116
1976	-8 885	-2 296	-21 368	38 018	17 693	20 326	4 347	4 283	1 284	-578	10 990	8 955	-6 082	4 295
1977	-5 460	-1 940	-11 427	53 219	36 816	16 403	3 728	2 434	2 437	1 086	6 719	-4 099	-27 246	-14 335
1978	-3 626	-3 853	-33 667	67 036	33 678	33 358	7 897	5 178	2 254	1 889	16 141	9 236	-29 763	-15 143
1979	-4 726	-5 014	-26 213	40 852	-13 665	54 516	11 877	7 060	1 351	1 621	32 607	24 349	-24 565	-285
1980	-3 568	-4 023	-46 838	62 612	15 497	47 115	16 918	7 145	5 457	6 852	10 743	20 886	-19 407	2 317
1981	-5 699	-4 377	-84 175	86 232	4 960	81 272	25 195	6 127	6 905	917	42 128	21 792	-16 172	5 030
1982	-7 983	6 823	-111 070	96 578	3 593	92 986	1 262	11 027	6 085	-2 383	65 633	37 224	-24 156	-6 177
1983	-6 762	-10 954	-29 928	88 783	5 845	82 938	10 461	14 089	8 164	-118	50 342	16 630	-57 767	-39 198
1984	-4 756	533	-11 127	117 973	3 140	114 833	24 689	27 101	12 568	16 626	33 849	17 059	-109 073	-94 753
1985	-7 481	-10 342	-1 323	146 452	-1 119	147 570	20 079	25 633	50 962	9 851	41 045	17 242	-121 880	-119 062
1986	-4 271	-21 773	-59 975	230 345	35 648	194 696	35 756	7 909	70 969	3 325	76 737	30 524	-139 786	-149 236
1987	-5 251	-7 046	-42 119	249 016	45 387	203 629	58 852	-2 243	42 120	18 363	86 537	-7 196	-152 753	-162 645
1988	-7 980	-21 193	-53 927	246 948	39 758	207 190	58 161	26 039	26 353	32 893	63 744	-17 535	-115 455	-123 046
1989	-22 070	-27 646	-58 160	225 307	8 503	216 804	68 653	35 518	38 767	22 086	51 780	48 920	-91 509	-98 900
1963:														
1st quarter	-522	-27	57	1 191	946	245	40	25	14	-36	202	-112	791	843
2nd quarter	-536	-108	-583	1 527	910	617	108	-109	119	69	430	-95	1 457	1 199
3rd quarter	-100	47	-254	205	56	149	105	1	52	11	-20	-339	797	1 021
4th quarter	53	245	-776	295	75	220	-22	-66	102	-80	286	186	1 166	1 350
1964:														
1st quarter	20	-206	-739	462	393	69	87	32	-42	0	-8	-286	1 608	1 910
2nd quarter	-206	-166	-593	630	227	403	109	-108	14	19	369	-139	1 547	1 527
3rd quarter	2	-532	-363	769	275	494	56	-65	-30	37	496	-239	1 365	1 725
4th quarter	-494	-204	-810	1 781	763	1 018	70	-5	-27	19	961	-243	1 503	1 662
1965:														
1st quarter	-198	286	-527	208	-202	410	184	60	57	3	106	111	917	1 257
2nd quarter	-147	165	429	-330	-194	-136	-21	64	-243	63	1	23	1 627	1 577
3rd quarter	-209	-19	16	587	115	472	147	-149	-227	49	652	-438	984	1 305
4th quarter	-205	-91	175	280	421	-141	104	-106	54	63	-256	-153	1 138	1 289
1966:														
1st quarter	-437	-159	143	458	-164	622	143	-102	173	68	340	25	871	982
2nd quarter	-115	-68	25	961	-57	1 018	133	-316	518	78	605	217	1 078	789
3rd quarter	-115	-105	109	909	-342	1 251	-37	66	107	195	920	287	322	485
4th quarter	-53	-110	-44	1 332	-111	1 443	187	-4	108	135	1 017	100	669	776
1967:														
1st quarter	-265	-107	-29	401	708	-307	169	-6	133	219	-822	-74	908	876
2nd quarter	-261	-69	-83	1 884	1 100	784	174	-61	329	66	276	-212	898	667
3rd quarter	-419	-40	-411	2 513	548	1 965	127	-36	520	164	1 190	79	485	563
4th quarter	-363	-563	28	2 584	1 098	1 486	228	-32	34	135	1 121	2	311	474
1968:														
1st quarter	-449	-231	156	1 374	-533	1 907	367	22	855	207	456	-271	21	196
2nd quarter	-283	-567	362	2 192	-2 007	4 199	133	86	1 122	478	2 380	-94	219	329
3rd quarter	-318	-213	-203	2 809	442	2 367	148	-8	1 124	315	788	499	43	139
4th quarter	-519	-191	-82	3 550	1 321	2 229	160	36	1 312	474	247	304	-29	-51
1969:														
1st quarter	-366	-132	-90	3 664	-1 117	4 781	359	-125	1 388	90	3 069	-1 191	-266	122
2nd quarter	-498	-21	-316	3 896	-766	4 662	267	-35	365	181	3 884	-337	-11	-131
3rd quarter	-546	141	-20	3 833	1 256	2 577	261	79	396	345	1 496	-520	-103	48
4th quarter	-139	-114	-144	1 311	-672	1 983	376	13	981	176	437	531	467	357
1970:														
1st quarter	-306	-366	-63	2 160	2 830	-670	592	16	304	222	-1 804	-169	457	620
2nd quarter	80	-73	-265	848	694	154	212	-35	374	534	-931	-95	933	972
3rd quarter	-517	-157	-133	1 940	1 411	529	357	1	720	510	-1 059	-309	526	515
4th quarter	-333	0	-506	1 413	1 975	-562	303	99	792	748	-2 504	354	336	222
1971:														
1st quarter	-408	-355	-246	3 092	5 178	-2 086	196	179	559	-62	-2 958	-1 028	644	683
2nd quarter	-368	-131	-358	5 154	5 630	-476	140	1 862	196	-34	-2 640	-2 211	-516	-409
3rd quarter	-346	-337	-1 389	8 726	10 367	-1 641	-293	-795	626	79	-1 258	-4 800	-512	-536
4th quarter	9	-406	-987	5 997	5 704	293	324	-1 270	908	386	-55	-1 740	-918	-1 173
1972:														
1st quarter	-476	-248	-1 082	4 367	2 762	1 605	-136	-3	1 059	-14	699	911	-1 368	-1 693
2nd quarter	-318	-185	190	4 277	1 103	3 174	373	-83	961	250	1 673	-463	-1 631	-1 689
3rd quarter	203	-241	-1 057	6 382	4 740	1 642	310	-12	718	216	410	-1 145	-1 132	-1 285
4th quarter	-28	-380	-1 557	6 437	1 871	4 566	403	59	1 769	363	1 972	-1 182	-1 309	-1 130

1. A minus sign indicates capital outflow or decrease in foreign official assets in the United States.
2. Sum of credits and debits with the signs reversed.

U.S. International Transactions—*Continued*

(Millions of dollars, seasonally adjusted)

Year and quarter	U.S.-owned assets abroad, net [1]—Continued / U.S. private assets, net—Continued / U.S. claims: Foreign securities	on unaffiliated foreigners reported by U.S. nonbanking concerns	reported by U.S. banks, not included elsewhere	Foreign-owned assets in the United States, net [1]: Total	Foreign official assets in the United States, net	Other foreign assets in the United States, net: Total	Direct investment	U.S. Treasury securities and U.S. currency flows	U.S. securities other than U.S. Treasury securities	U.S. liabilities: to unaffiliated foreigners reported by U.S. nonbanking concerns	reported by U.S. banks, not included elsewhere	Statistical discrepancy [2]	Balance on: Goods and services	Current account
1973:														
1st quarter	55	-809	-2 988	10 743	9 937	806	631	-119	1 718	246	-1 670	-3 002	-845	145
2nd quarter	-86	-202	-763	3 056	-403	3 458	835	-185	489	54	2 265	225	31	873
3rd quarter	-196	-502	299	2 168	-772	2 940	539	-205	1 173	454	979	-1 716	1 093	2 737
4th quarter	-445	-870	-2 528	2 423	-2 736	5 159	795	293	662	281	3 128	1 840	1 620	3 383
1974:														
1st quarter	-600	-2 113	-5 244	6 514	-1 138	7 652	1 784	336	712	354	4 466	-2 212	866	1 612
2nd quarter	-272	-588	-7 577	9 962	4 434	5 528	539	60	363	390	4 176	246	-1 514	110
3rd quarter	-282	273	-1 944	9 303	3 062	6 241	1 610	400	227	239	3 765	-1 314	-2 466	-295
4th quarter	-699	-793	-4 751	9 563	4 188	5 375	828	1 001	-925	861	3 610	724	-1 179	531
1975:														
1st quarter	-1 931	353	-3 772	2 788	3 419	-631	278	892	344	359	-2 504	3 581	3 374	4 207
2nd quarter	-985	112	-3 825	4 371	2 244	2 127	870	10	385	55	807	206	4 532	5 014
3rd quarter	-938	-939	-649	2 991	-1 731	4 722	86	2 424	737	-163	1 638	-1 972	2 129	4 080
4th quarter	-2 393	-883	-5 286	7 021	3 095	3 926	1 369	764	1 038	68	687	2 602	2 369	4 813
1976:														
1st quarter	-2 467	-747	-3 701	7 769	3 699	4 070	1 471	737	1 036	154	672	2 029	72	2 566
2nd quarter	-1 405	-999	-4 786	8 453	4 039	4 414	1 086	-91	134	-231	3 516	1 600	-1 246	1 648
3rd quarter	-2 751	616	-3 320	9 120	2 958	6 162	999	3 325	64	-184	1 958	1 582	-2 077	-84
4th quarter	-2 262	-1 166	-9 561	12 677	6 997	5 680	790	312	51	-317	4 844	3 748	-2 833	163
1977:														
1st quarter	-749	-771	3 684	3 062	5 554	-2 492	980	1 181	749	-98	-5 304	823	-6 099	-2 687
2nd quarter	-1 784	-1 124	-4 582	14 781	7 888	6 893	965	-799	589	-102	6 240	432	-6 250	-3 031
3rd quarter	-2 177	1 310		14 676	8 257	6 419	1 023	1 651	337	768	2 640	-5 622	-6 156	-2 757
4th quarter	-749	-1 355	-8 750	20 703	15 117	5 586	761	401	763	518	3 143	268	-8 745	-5 862
1978:														
1st quarter	-1 115	-2 241	-6 270	18 684	15 448	3 236	1 356	1 381	396	507	-404	3 555	-10 925	-7 020
2nd quarter	-1 094	315	-98	1 551	-5 113	6 664	2 313	1 493	1 082	304	1 472	7 832	-6 741	-3 777
3rd quarter	-510	-29	-5 132	17 582	4 903	12 679	2 620	-368	296	912	9 219	-4 212	-6 944	-3 667
4th quarter	-907	-1 898	-22 167	29 220	18 440	10 780	1 608	2 672	480	166	5 854	2 060	-5 154	-679
1979:														
1st quarter	-908	-3 854	5 926	2 707	-8 697	11 404	1 554	2 964	409	-296	6 773	5 558	-5 092	-424
2nd quarter	-492	716	-7 921	7 663	-9 775	17 438	3 354	743	524	799	12 018	8 593	-6 140	-691
3rd quarter	-2 331	-1 826	-17 833	25 349	6 036	19 313	3 382	2 402	166	210	13 153	884	-6 291	923
4th quarter	-995	-50	-6 385	5 134	-1 228	6 362	3 588	951	252	908	663	9 317	-7 043	-98
1980:														
1st quarter	-787	-1 927	-1 203	9 582	-7 413	16 995	3 321	4 300	2 435	340	6 599	6 539	-10 916	-3 459
2nd quarter	-1 387	144	-20 165	11 373	7 731	3 643	5 756	229	496	1 671	-4 509	14 292	-4 922	-941
3rd quarter	-944	365	-12 440	14 930	7 564	7 366	4 713	222	263	1 252	916	403	-929	4 333
4th quarter	-450	-2 605	-13 030	26 726	7 614	19 112	3 128	2 394	2 263	3 590	7 737	-348	-2 641	2 383
1981:														
1st quarter	-473	-2 944	-11 664	9 819	5 502	4 317	3 146	2 486	2 357	121	-3 793	11 140	-4 363	963
2nd quarter	-1 564	513	-15 002	15 364	-3 159	18 523	5 294	1 641	3 512	13	8 063	7 566	-4 095	1 228
3rd quarter	-697	458	-15 310	17 531	-5 992	23 523	5 505	-248	704	1 084	16 478	-1 667	-2 777	2 081
4th quarter	-2 966	-2 404	-42 199	43 519	8 609	34 910	11 251	2 248	332	-301	21 380	4 750	-4 934	759
1982:														
1st quarter	-628	2 220	-33 343	27 231	-3 265	30 496	2 145	1 297	1 263	-65	25 856	9 473	-5 056	-449
2nd quarter	-471	-1 095	-39 403	35 254	1 534	33 720	2 939	4 193	2 486	-2 023	26 125	3 797	-2 145	3 633
3rd quarter	-3 397	3 670	-21 405	18 662	2 694	15 968	2 848	2 091	555	-282	10 756	9 018	-8 398	-4 191
4th quarter	-3 488	2 028	-16 919	15 429	2 629	12 800	4 690	3 446	1 781	-13	2 896	14 935	-8 555	-5 166
1983:														
1st quarter	-1 549	-4 253	-20 303	16 277	-38	16 315	1 265	3 713	2 873	-2 763	11 227	15 209	-7 271	-2 644
2nd quarter	-2 813	-590	3 518	16 343	1 612	14 731	3 305	4 616	2 470	-64	4 404	-5 445	-12 907	-7 967
3rd quarter	-1 308	-1 764	-3 616	20 446	-2 689	23 135	4 085	2 308	1 777	1 311	13 654	4 735	-17 871	-13 027
4th quarter	-1 093	-4 347	-9 527	35 716	6 960	28 756	1 805	3 452	1 044	1 398	21 057	2 136	-19 720	-15 565
1984:														
1st quarter	758	-3 012	-1 557	23 344	-2 956	26 300	4 900	2 450	1 333	6 092	11 525	6 004	-25 527	-21 038
2nd quarter	-764	-934	-20 146	42 740	-156	42 896	8 676	8 036	362	4 232	21 590	6 492	-28 012	-23 538
3rd quarter	-1 106	3 987	17 817	7 628	-884	8 512	4 492	1 447	6 103	1 662	-5 192	528	-27 257	-23 477
4th quarter	-3 644	492	-7 241	44 260	7 136	37 124	6 620	10 512	9 426	4 640	5 926	4 035	-28 276	-26 698
1985:														
1st quarter	-2 474	475	284	18 421	-10 962	29 383	4 992	3 390	9 615	-720	12 106	10 717	-24 933	-23 672
2nd quarter	-2 219	2 337	3 325	29 418	8 502	20 916	4 460	6 888	7 194	1 724	650	1 794	-30 473	-28 900
3rd quarter	-1 572	-2 779	3 847	38 350	2 506	35 844	4 926	9 136	11 669	2 801	7 312	-1 042	-31 263	-31 564
4th quarter	-1 217	-10 375	-8 779	60 266	-1 165	61 431	5 705	6 219	22 484	6 046	20 977	5 774	-35 212	-34 930
1986:														
1st quarter	-5 930	-6 230	4 916	41 572	2 712	38 860	3 514	6 420	18 730	696	9 500	10 502	-34 798	-34 701
2nd quarter	-1 051	-2 722	-13 660	53 793	15 918	37 875	5 603	4 620	22 752	1 635	3 265	7 323	-33 381	-36 195
3rd quarter	181	-7 638	-18 909	70 960	15 789	55 171	8 830	-854	17 107	1 947	28 141	205	-35 947	-38 567
4th quarter	2 529	-5 183	-32 322	64 019	1 229	62 790	17 809	-2 277	12 380	-953	35 831	12 489	-35 655	-39 772
1987:														
1st quarter	-1 749	-5 715	20 237	42 337	14 199	28 138	12 973	-2 326	18 372	6 151	-7 032	-10 796	-37 266	-39 748
2nd quarter	-287	712	-22 873	57 425	10 444	46 981	8 687	-731	15 960	5 595	17 470	9 763	-38 511	-40 481
3rd quarter	-1 159	-1 319	-16 860	83 242	764	82 478	20 860	-1 835	12 676	6 656	44 121	-14 868	-38 309	-40 615
4th quarter	-2 056	-724	-22 623	66 011	19 980	46 031	16 331	2 649	-4 888	-39	31 978	8 712	-38 673	-41 808
1988:														
1st quarter	-4 504	-3 454	15 982	32 134	24 925	7 209	8 531	6 511	2 423	12 593	-22 849	-1 666	-32 426	-33 399
2nd quarter	1 318	-9 954	-11 383	74 639	6 006	68 633	13 825	7 673	9 702	6 742	30 691	-21 859	-28 223	-29 398
3rd quarter	-1 500	-5 217	-30 037	52 904	-1 974	54 878	13 885	4 743	7 464	6 399	22 387	25 427	-26 344	-28 424
4th quarter	-3 294	-2 568	-28 489	87 271	10 801	76 470	21 920	7 112	6 764	7 159	33 515	-19 429	-28 465	-31 831
1989:														
1st quarter	-2 225	-9 293	-27 010	66 761	7 700	59 061	18 679	10 961	8 544	6 637	14 240	12 541	-23 833	-25 659
2nd quarter	-6 192	-5 767	23 844	11 074	-5 115	16 188	15 419	4 789	9 365	12 000	-25 385	21 854	-23 048	-24 791
3rd quarter	-9 149	-5 924	-22 394	74 162	13 060	61 102	11 613	12 744	10 270	-1 121	27 596	1 969	-22 404	-24 522
4th quarter	-4 504	-6 662	-32 600	73 311	-7 142	80 453	22 942	7 024	10 588	4 570	35 329	12 557	-22 221	-23 928

1. A minus sign indicates capital outflow or decrease in foreign official assets in the United States.
2. Sum of credits and debits with the signs reversed.

Productivity and Related Data

(Seasonally adjusted, 1992=100)

Year and quarter	Business sector								Nonfarm business sector							
	Output per hour of all persons	Output	Hours of all persons	Compensation per hour	Real compensation per hour	Unit labor costs	Unit nonlabor payments	Implicit price deflator	Output per hour of all persons	Output	Hours of all persons	Compensation per hour	Real compensation per hour	Unit labor costs	Unit nonlabor payments	Implicit price deflator
1962	55.7	37.2	66.8	14.8	68.9	26.6	25.7	26.3	59.2	37.0	62.6	15.4	71.5	26.0	25.3	25.8
1963	57.9	38.9	67.2	15.4	70.6	26.6	26.3	26.5	61.2	38.7	63.3	15.9	73.0	26.0	25.9	26.0
1964	60.6	41.4	68.3	16.2	73.3	26.7	26.8	26.8	63.8	41.3	64.8	16.7	75.4	26.1	26.6	26.3
1965	62.7	44.2	70.6	16.8	74.8	26.8	28.0	27.2	65.8	44.2	67.3	17.2	76.7	26.2	27.6	26.7
1966	65.2	47.2	72.5	17.9	77.6	27.5	28.6	27.9	68.0	47.4	69.7	18.2	78.9	26.8	28.2	27.3
1967	66.6	48.1	72.3	18.9	79.5	28.4	29.2	28.7	69.2	48.2	69.7	19.3	81.0	27.8	28.8	28.2
1968	68.9	50.5	73.3	20.5	82.5	29.7	30.0	29.8	71.6	50.7	70.9	20.8	83.8	29.0	29.7	29.3
1969	69.2	52.0	75.2	21.9	83.8	31.7	30.0	31.1	71.7	52.3	72.9	22.2	84.9	31.0	29.6	30.5
1970	70.6	52.0	73.6	23.6	85.4	33.5	30.6	32.4	72.7	52.1	71.8	23.8	86.1	32.8	30.3	31.9
1971	73.6	54.0	73.3	25.1	87.1	34.2	33.4	33.9	75.7	54.1	71.5	25.4	87.9	33.5	33.0	33.3
1972	76.0	57.6	75.7	26.7	89.6	35.1	34.8	35.0	78.3	57.8	73.9	27.0	90.6	34.5	34.0	34.3
1973	78.4	61.6	78.5	29.0	91.6	37.0	36.6	36.8	80.7	62.0	76.9	29.2	92.3	36.2	34.3	35.5
1974	77.1	60.6	78.6	31.8	90.6	41.3	38.6	40.3	79.4	61.1	76.9	32.1	91.3	40.4	36.7	39.1
1975	79.8	60.0	75.2	35.1	91.5	44.0	44.5	44.2	81.6	60.0	73.6	35.3	92.2	43.3	43.0	43.2
1976	82.5	64.0	77.5	38.2	94.1	46.2	47.1	46.5	84.5	64.3	76.1	38.4	94.7	45.4	46.0	45.6
1977	84.0	67.6	80.6	41.2	95.3	49.0	50.0	49.4	85.8	67.9	79.1	41.5	96.0	48.3	49.0	48.6
1978	84.9	71.7	84.5	44.9	96.5	52.8	53.3	53.0	87.0	72.3	83.1	45.2	97.3	52.0	51.8	51.9
1979	84.5	73.9	87.4	49.2	95.0	58.2	56.5	57.6	86.3	74.3	86.1	49.5	95.7	57.4	54.7	56.4
1980	84.2	73.0	86.6	54.5	92.8	64.7	59.6	62.8	86.0	73.4	85.4	54.8	93.4	63.8	58.6	61.9
1981	85.8	74.8	87.2	59.6	92.1	69.6	67.1	68.7	87.0	74.8	86.0	60.2	92.8	69.2	65.6	67.9
1982	85.3	72.5	85.0	64.1	93.2	75.1	68.3	72.7	86.3	72.4	83.9	64.6	93.9	74.8	67.4	72.2
1983	88.0	76.1	86.4	66.8	94.0	75.8	74.6	75.4	89.9	76.8	85.4	67.3	94.8	74.9	74.3	74.7
1984	90.2	82.5	91.5	69.7	94.1	77.2	78.5	77.7	91.4	82.8	90.6	70.2	94.8	76.8	77.4	77.0
1985	91.7	85.7	93.5	73.1	95.3	79.7	80.5	80.0	92.3	85.8	92.9	73.4	95.7	79.5	79.9	79.6
1986	94.1	88.5	94.1	76.8	98.4	81.7	81.7	81.7	94.7	88.7	93.6	77.2	98.8	81.5	81.3	81.4
1987	94.0	91.1	96.9	79.8	98.6	84.9	81.9	83.8	94.5	91.3	96.6	80.1	98.9	84.7	81.4	83.6
1988	94.7	94.6	99.9	83.6	99.1	88.3	84.1	86.8	95.3	94.6	99.8	83.7	99.3	87.8	83.8	86.4
1989	95.5	97.8	102.4	85.9	97.2	90.0	91.3	90.4	95.8	98.1	102.4	86.0	97.3	89.7	90.7	90.0
1962:																
1st quarter	55.0	36.7	66.8	14.6	68.0	26.5	25.6	26.2	58.9	36.6	62.2	15.2	70.9	25.9	25.3	25.6
2nd quarter	55.3	37.1	67.2	14.8	68.6	26.7	25.5	26.3	58.6	36.9	63.0	15.3	71.1	26.1	25.2	25.8
3rd quarter	56.1	37.5	66.9	14.9	68.9	26.6	25.9	26.3	59.3	37.3	62.9	15.4	71.4	26.0	25.5	25.8
4th quarter	56.5	37.5	66.3	15.1	69.7	26.7	25.7	26.3	59.8	37.3	62.4	15.6	72.0	26.1	25.4	25.8
1963:																
1st quarter	57.0	38.1	66.8	15.2	69.9	26.6	25.9	26.4	60.2	37.8	62.7	15.7	72.5	26.1	25.5	25.9
2nd quarter	57.3	38.5	67.2	15.2	70.0	26.6	26.1	26.4	60.7	38.3	63.2	15.8	72.6	26.0	25.7	25.9
3rd quarter	58.5	39.3	67.2	15.5	70.6	26.4	26.6	26.5	61.8	39.2	63.4	16.0	72.9	25.8	26.3	26.0
4th quarter	58.7	39.6	67.5	15.6	71.2	26.7	26.6	26.6	61.9	39.5	63.8	16.2	73.7	26.1	26.1	26.1
1964:																
1st quarter	60.3	40.7	67.5	16.0	72.4	26.5	26.9	26.6	63.5	40.7	64.2	16.4	74.4	25.8	26.7	26.1
2nd quarter	60.4	41.2	68.2	16.1	72.7	26.6	26.8	26.7	63.9	41.2	64.5	16.5	74.9	25.9	26.8	26.2
3rd quarter	60.9	41.7	68.5	16.3	73.6	26.7	26.8	26.8	64.3	41.7	64.9	16.8	75.9	26.1	26.7	26.3
4th quarter	60.6	41.8	69.0	16.4	73.8	27.1	26.6	26.9	63.6	41.7	65.6	16.9	76.0	26.6	26.2	26.4
1965:																
1st quarter	61.7	43.1	69.8	16.6	74.2	26.9	27.4	27.0	64.6	43.0	66.6	17.0	76.0	26.2	27.1	26.6
2nd quarter	61.8	43.7	70.7	16.7	74.2	27.0	27.5	27.2	65.1	43.7	67.2	17.1	76.2	26.3	27.2	26.6
3rd quarter	63.1	44.5	70.5	16.9	75.0	26.7	28.2	27.3	66.1	44.5	67.3	17.3	76.8	26.1	27.8	26.7
4th quarter	64.1	45.7	71.4	17.0	75.3	26.6	28.8	27.4	67.2	45.8	68.1	17.5	77.3	26.0	28.2	26.8
1966:																
1st quarter	65.2	47.0	72.1	17.4	76.4	26.8	28.9	27.5	68.2	47.1	69.1	17.8	77.9	26.1	28.3	26.9
2nd quarter	65.0	47.1	72.5	17.8	77.2	27.4	28.4	27.7	67.9	47.3	69.7	18.1	78.6	26.7	28.1	27.2
3rd quarter	65.0	47.3	72.7	18.1	77.6	27.8	28.5	28.0	67.8	47.5	70.1	18.3	78.9	27.0	28.1	27.4
4th quarter	65.5	47.6	72.6	18.3	78.2	28.0	28.7	28.3	68.2	47.7	69.9	18.6	79.3	27.2	28.6	27.7
1967:																
1st quarter	66.2	47.9	72.4	18.5	78.9	28.0	29.0	28.4	68.8	48.0	69.7	18.9	80.3	27.4	28.7	27.9
2nd quarter	66.7	47.9	71.8	18.8	79.7	28.3	28.9	28.5	69.1	47.9	69.4	19.1	81.0	27.7	28.6	28.0
3rd quarter	66.7	48.2	72.3	19.0	79.8	28.6	29.3	28.8	69.4	48.3	69.6	19.4	81.2	28.0	28.9	28.3
4th quarter	66.9	48.6	72.6	19.3	79.8	28.8	29.5	29.1	69.6	48.7	70.0	19.7	81.4	28.3	29.2	28.6
1968:																
1st quarter	68.3	49.6	72.6	19.9	81.6	29.1	29.8	29.4	71.1	49.8	70.0	20.2	83.0	28.5	29.6	28.9
2nd quarter	69.1	50.5	73.1	20.3	82.4	29.3	30.3	29.7	71.9	50.8	70.6	20.6	83.7	28.7	30.1	29.2
3rd quarter	69.1	50.9	73.6	20.6	82.7	29.9	29.9	29.9	71.7	51.1	71.2	20.9	83.9	29.2	29.7	29.4
4th quarter	69.0	51.1	74.0	21.1	83.4	30.5	29.9	30.3	71.6	51.3	71.7	21.4	84.6	29.8	29.6	29.7
1969:																
1st quarter	69.2	52.0	75.1	21.2	82.7	30.6	30.6	30.6	72.2	52.2	72.3	21.6	84.7	30.0	30.2	30.0
2nd quarter	69.2	52.0	75.2	21.7	83.6	31.4	30.1	30.9	71.6	52.2	73.0	22.0	84.7	30.7	29.7	30.4
3rd quarter	69.3	52.3	75.5	22.2	84.2	32.0	29.9	31.2	71.5	52.5	73.4	22.4	85.0	31.3	29.6	30.7
4th quarter	69.1	51.9	75.1	22.6	84.7	32.8	29.5	31.6	71.2	52.1	73.1	22.8	85.4	32.1	29.0	31.0
1970:																
1st quarter	69.3	51.8	74.7	23.1	85.0	33.3	29.5	31.9	71.4	52.0	72.9	23.2	85.6	32.6	29.1	31.3
2nd quarter	70.1	51.9	74.0	23.4	84.8	33.3	30.6	32.3	72.4	52.1	71.9	23.6	85.7	32.6	30.3	31.8
3rd quarter	71.6	52.5	73.3	23.9	85.8	33.3	31.1	32.5	73.8	52.7	71.4	24.1	86.6	32.7	30.7	32.0
4th quarter	71.2	51.7	72.7	24.2	85.6	33.9	31.3	33.0	73.1	51.9	70.9	24.3	86.2	33.3	31.0	32.4
1971:																
1st quarter	73.3	53.5	72.9	24.6	86.5	33.6	33.0	33.4	75.3	53.6	71.2	24.8	87.2	33.0	32.5	32.8
2nd quarter	73.4	53.8	73.4	24.9	86.7	34.0	33.4	33.8	75.6	54.0	71.4	25.2	87.8	33.4	33.0	33.2
3rd quarter	74.2	54.2	73.1	25.4	87.6	34.2	33.9	34.1	76.2	54.4	71.3	25.6	88.3	33.6	33.5	33.6
4th quarter	73.4	54.3	74.0	25.5	87.4	34.8	33.5	34.3	75.4	54.5	72.3	25.8	88.1	34.2	32.9	33.7
1972:																
1st quarter	74.4	55.7	74.9	26.2	88.8	35.2	33.8	34.7	76.8	56.1	73.1	26.4	89.6	34.4	33.4	34.0
2nd quarter	76.0	57.3	75.4	26.5	89.3	34.8	34.8	34.8	78.2	57.6	73.7	26.7	90.2	34.2	34.1	34.2
3rd quarter	76.4	58.0	75.9	26.8	89.6	35.1	35.1	35.1	78.7	58.3	74.1	27.1	90.8	34.5	34.1	34.3
4th quarter	77.2	59.2	76.6	27.4	90.6	35.4	35.6	35.5	79.2	59.3	74.9	27.7	91.6	34.9	34.2	34.6

Productivity and Related Data—*Continued*

(Seasonally adjusted, 1992=100)

Year and quarter	Business sector								Nonfarm business sector							
	Output per hour of all persons	Output	Hours of all persons	Compensation per hour	Real compensation per hour	Unit labor costs	Unit nonlabor payments	Implicit price deflator	Output per hour of all persons	Output	Hours of all persons	Compensation per hour	Real compensation per hour	Unit labor costs	Unit nonlabor payments	Implicit price deflator
1973:																
1st quarter	78.9	61.2	77.5	28.2	92.0	35.8	36.0	35.8	81.3	61.8	75.9	28.5	92.8	35.0	34.5	34.8
2nd quarter	78.7	61.7	78.4	28.6	91.5	36.4	36.5	36.4	81.0	62.1	76.8	28.9	92.2	35.7	34.4	35.2
3rd quarter	77.9	61.3	78.8	29.2	91.6	37.6	36.5	37.2	80.5	62.1	77.2	29.4	92.2	36.6	33.9	35.6
4th quarter	78.2	62.0	79.3	29.8	91.1	38.1	37.5	37.9	79.9	62.1	77.7	30.1	91.8	37.6	34.4	36.4
1974:																
1st quarter	77.0	61.1	79.3	30.4	90.1	39.4	37.4	38.7	79.7	61.6	77.3	30.8	91.3	38.6	34.8	37.2
2nd quarter	77.6	61.3	79.0	31.4	90.7	40.5	37.9	39.5	79.7	61.7	77.4	31.7	91.5	39.7	36.3	38.5
3rd quarter	76.7	60.3	78.6	32.4	91.0	42.2	38.6	40.9	78.8	60.8	77.2	32.6	91.5	41.3	36.9	39.7
4th quarter	77.0	59.8	77.6	33.1	90.2	43.0	40.7	42.2	79.3	60.2	76.0	33.4	91.0	42.1	38.7	40.9
1975:																
1st quarter	78.2	58.6	75.0	34.2	91.2	43.7	42.1	43.1	80.0	58.8	73.4	34.4	91.7	42.9	40.8	42.2
2nd quarter	79.6	59.2	74.4	34.8	91.7	43.7	43.8	43.7	81.4	59.3	72.8	35.0	92.4	43.0	42.5	42.8
3rd quarter	80.6	60.6	75.2	35.3	91.2	43.8	45.8	44.5	82.4	60.6	73.5	35.6	92.2	43.2	44.1	43.5
4th quarter	80.6	61.5	76.3	36.0	91.5	44.7	46.2	45.3	82.3	61.6	74.8	36.3	92.1	44.1	44.5	44.2
1976:																
1st quarter	82.0	63.3	77.2	37.0	92.9	45.1	46.8	45.7	83.9	63.6	75.8	37.2	93.3	44.3	45.4	44.7
2nd quarter	82.5	63.8	77.4	37.7	93.9	45.8	46.7	46.1	84.5	64.1	75.9	37.9	94.4	44.9	45.7	45.2
3rd quarter	82.5	64.1	77.7	38.5	94.3	46.7	46.9	46.8	84.6	64.4	76.1	38.8	95.0	45.9	45.9	45.9
4th quarter	83.1	64.8	78.0	39.3	95.0	47.4	47.9	47.5	84.8	65.0	76.7	39.5	95.4	46.6	47.0	46.7
1977:																
1st quarter	83.5	65.8	78.8	40.1	94.9	48.0	48.8	48.3	85.3	66.1	77.5	40.2	95.4	47.2	47.8	47.4
2nd quarter	83.7	67.4	80.5	41.0	94.7	48.6	49.9	49.0	85.9	67.9	78.9	41.0	95.6	47.7	49.0	48.2
3rd quarter	84.7	68.7	81.2	41.5	95.4	49.1	50.6	49.6	86.6	69.1	79.8	41.8	96.1	48.3	49.9	48.9
4th quarter	83.8	68.6	81.9	42.3	95.8	50.5	50.6	50.5	85.4	68.7	80.5	42.7	96.6	50.0	49.4	49.8
1978:																
1st quarter	83.5	68.7	82.3	43.5	96.7	52.1	50.2	51.4	85.5	69.2	80.9	43.9	97.6	51.3	48.8	50.4
2nd quarter	85.1	72.0	84.7	44.2	96.3	52.0	53.4	52.5	87.2	72.6	83.2	44.6	97.1	51.2	51.7	51.4
3rd quarter	85.3	72.7	85.2	45.2	96.2	53.0	54.2	53.4	87.3	73.1	83.8	45.6	96.9	52.2	52.7	52.4
4th quarter	85.4	73.5	86.1	46.3	96.3	54.2	55.2	54.6	87.6	74.3	84.8	46.7	97.0	53.3	53.8	53.4
1979:																
1st quarter	84.6	73.5	86.9	47.5	96.3	56.2	55.1	55.8	86.5	74.0	85.5	47.8	97.0	55.3	53.1	54.6
2nd quarter	84.6	73.6	87.0	48.6	95.4	57.4	56.4	57.0	86.4	74.1	85.8	48.9	96.0	56.5	54.6	55.9
3rd quarter	84.5	74.2	87.8	49.7	94.5	58.8	57.2	58.2	86.2	74.6	86.5	50.0	95.1	58.0	55.4	57.1
4th quarter	84.2	74.2	88.1	50.8	93.8	60.4	57.3	59.3	86.0	74.6	86.7	51.2	94.5	59.6	55.6	58.2
1980																
1st quarter	84.8	74.4	87.7	52.4	92.9	61.7	58.7	60.6	86.5	74.9	86.6	52.6	93.4	60.9	57.6	59.7
2nd quarter	83.6	71.9	86.0	53.8	92.5	64.4	58.0	62.1	85.2	72.3	84.9	54.2	93.0	63.6	57.8	61.5
3rd quarter	83.8	71.8	85.7	55.2	93.0	65.8	59.7	63.6	85.6	72.3	84.5	55.5	93.6	64.9	58.6	62.6
4th quarter	84.6	73.6	87.0	56.4	92.6	66.7	62.2	65.1	86.5	74.2	85.8	56.9	93.3	65.8	60.4	63.9
1981																
1st quarter	85.9	75.3	87.6	57.9	92.3	67.3	65.7	66.7	87.6	75.6	86.3	58.4	93.1	66.6	64.1	65.7
2nd quarter	85.3	74.4	87.2	59.1	92.3	69.3	65.8	68.0	86.5	74.5	86.1	59.6	93.1	68.8	64.2	67.2
3rd quarter	86.4	75.4	87.2	60.4	91.8	69.8	68.7	69.4	87.4	75.2	86.1	60.9	92.6	69.6	66.9	68.7
4th quarter	85.3	74.1	86.9	61.2	91.6	71.8	68.2	70.5	86.2	73.9	85.7	61.8	92.4	71.6	67.1	70.0
1982:																
1st quarter	84.5	72.5	85.8	62.6	92.8	74.1	66.8	71.4	85.4	72.3	84.6	63.1	93.5	73.8	65.8	71.0
2nd quarter	85.2	72.8	85.4	63.7	93.1	74.7	68.0	72.3	86.2	72.7	84.3	64.1	93.8	74.4	67.1	71.8
3rd quarter	85.3	72.3	84.7	64.7	93.0	75.8	68.5	73.2	86.4	72.2	83.6	65.2	93.7	75.5	67.5	72.6
4th quarter	86.1	72.4	84.1	65.4	93.7	75.9	70.1	73.8	87.1	72.3	83.0	65.9	94.4	75.7	69.3	73.4
1983:																
1st quarter	86.8	73.3	84.5	65.9	94.4	76.0	71.5	74.4	88.1	73.5	83.4	66.5	95.3	75.6	70.6	73.8
2nd quarter	88.1	75.3	85.5	66.6	94.2	75.5	74.3	75.1	89.9	76.0	84.4	67.1	95.0	74.6	73.8	74.3
3rd quarter	88.3	77.0	87.2	66.8	93.7	75.7	75.7	75.7	90.6	78.0	86.1	67.5	94.6	74.5	75.9	75.0
4th quarter	88.8	78.7	88.6	67.7	93.9	76.2	76.7	76.4	90.8	79.7	87.8	68.1	94.5	75.0	76.6	75.5
1984:																
1st quarter	89.7	81.0	90.3	68.5	93.8	76.4	77.8	76.9	91.1	81.5	89.4	69.0	94.4	75.7	76.6	76.0
2nd quarter	90.4	82.5	91.3	69.3	93.9	76.7	78.6	77.4	91.6	82.8	90.4	69.8	94.6	76.2	77.5	76.7
3rd quarter	90.4	83.1	91.9	70.1	94.1	77.5	78.7	77.9	91.5	83.3	91.0	70.6	94.9	77.1	77.8	77.4
4th quarter	90.5	83.5	92.3	70.8	94.3	78.2	78.9	78.5	91.5	83.7	91.5	71.3	94.9	77.9	77.9	77.9
1985:																
1st quarter	90.8	84.6	93.1	71.6	94.5	78.8	79.8	79.2	91.7	84.7	92.3	72.0	95.1	78.6	78.8	78.7
2nd quarter	91.0	85.0	93.4	72.4	94.7	79.5	80.2	79.8	91.8	85.1	92.7	72.8	95.2	79.3	79.5	79.4
3rd quarter	92.4	86.4	93.5	73.5	95.6	79.5	81.4	80.2	92.9	86.4	93.0	73.8	95.9	79.5	81.0	80.0
4th quarter	92.6	86.9	93.9	74.7	96.2	80.7	80.9	80.8	93.0	87.0	93.6	75.0	96.5	80.6	80.3	80.5
1986:																
1st quarter	93.9	88.2	93.9	75.6	96.8	80.5	82.1	81.0	94.5	88.3	93.4	75.9	97.2	80.3	81.9	80.9
2nd quarter	94.2	88.2	93.6	76.3	98.2	81.0	82.0	81.4	95.0	88.4	93.1	76.7	98.7	80.8	81.8	81.1
3rd quarter	94.2	88.7	94.1	77.2	98.7	82.0	81.8	81.9	94.8	88.8	93.7	77.5	99.2	81.8	81.2	81.6
4th quarter	94.0	89.1	94.8	78.2	99.3	83.2	80.9	82.4	94.6	89.3	94.4	78.6	99.8	83.1	80.3	82.1
1987:																
1st quarter	93.5	89.7	96.0	78.7	98.7	84.2	80.7	82.9	94.0	89.9	95.6	79.0	99.1	84.1	80.2	82.7
2nd quarter	94.0	90.7	96.5	79.3	98.3	84.4	81.8	83.4	94.6	90.9	96.1	79.6	98.7	84.2	81.3	83.2
3rd quarter	93.9	91.4	97.3	79.8	97.9	85.0	82.4	84.1	94.4	91.6	97.0	80.1	98.3	84.8	82.0	83.8
4th quarter	94.7	92.8	98.1	81.4	98.9	86.0	82.6	84.8	95.1	93.0	97.8	81.6	99.2	85.9	82.1	84.5
1988:																
1st quarter	94.6	93.3	98.7	82.0	98.9	86.7	82.6	85.2	94.8	93.4	98.4	82.2	99.1	86.6	81.9	84.9
2nd quarter	94.5	94.3	99.8	83.3	99.3	88.1	82.7	86.2	95.0	94.7	99.6	83.5	99.5	87.9	82.3	85.9
3rd quarter	94.7	94.8	100.1	84.2	99.2	88.9	84.7	87.4	95.4	95.4	100.0	84.3	99.3	88.5	84.3	86.9
4th quarter	94.9	96.0	101.1	84.8	98.8	89.3	86.3	88.2	96.0	96.2	101.0	84.9	98.9	88.5	86.5	87.8
1989:																
1st quarter	95.1	97.1	102.1	84.9	97.8	89.3	89.0	89.2	95.5	97.4	102.0	85.0	98.0	89.0	88.1	88.7
2nd quarter	95.6	97.8	102.3	85.4	96.9	89.4	91.6	90.2	95.8	98.0	102.3	85.4	96.8	89.1	91.0	89.8
3rd quarter	95.6	98.1	102.7	86.1	96.8	90.0	92.3	90.8	96.0	98.4	102.6	86.1	96.9	89.7	91.9	90.5
4th quarter	95.7	98.2	102.7	87.2	97.2	91.1	92.2	91.5	96.1	98.6	102.6	87.3	97.3	90.8	91.7	91.1

Productivity and Related Data—*Continued*

(Seasonally adjusted, 1992=100)

Year and quarter	Nonfinancial corporations										Manufacturing					
	Output per hour of all persons	Output	Employee hours	Compensation per hour	Real compensation per hour	Unit costs Total	Labor costs	Nonlabor costs	Implicit price deflator	Unit nonlabor payments	Output per hour of all persons	Output	Hours of all persons	Compensation per hour	Real compensation per hour	Unit labor costs
1962	58.6	31.9	54.4	16.7	77.8	27.7	28.6	25.4	29.9	43.4	44.5	41.5	93.4	15.9	74.1	35.9
1963	60.6	33.7	55.7	17.3	79.2	27.7	28.5	25.3	30.1	45.1	46.0	43.4	94.4	16.4	75.3	35.7
1964	63.1	36.1	57.2	18.0	81.6	27.7	28.6	25.2	30.4	47.1	47.7	46.0	96.4	17.1	77.4	35.9
1965	64.6	39.1	60.5	18.5	82.6	27.8	28.7	25.1	30.9	48.0	48.8	49.8	102.0	17.5	77.8	35.8
1966	65.5	41.8	63.9	19.5	84.6	28.6	29.8	25.1	31.6	48.6	49.3	53.6	108.6	18.3	79.1	37.1
1967	66.4	42.9	64.5	20.6	86.6	29.9	31.0	26.6	32.4	50.5	51.1	55.2	108.0	19.3	80.9	37.7
1968	68.7	45.6	66.4	22.2	89.4	31.3	32.3	28.4	33.6	52.3	52.9	57.9	109.6	20.7	83.5	39.2
1969	68.7	47.4	69.0	23.7	90.6	33.5	34.5	30.6	35.1	53.1	53.8	59.6	110.9	22.2	85.1	41.4
1970	69.1	47.0	68.0	25.4	91.7	36.1	36.7	34.3	36.6	54.7	54.4	56.8	104.4	23.8	86.2	43.8
1971	72.0	48.9	67.9	27.0	93.4	37.1	37.5	36.0	38.0	58.3	58.2	58.5	100.5	25.3	87.6	43.5
1972	73.9	52.7	71.4	28.5	95.8	37.9	38.6	35.9	39.2	60.5	60.7	63.7	105.1	26.6	89.3	43.9
1973	74.5	55.8	74.9	30.8	97.2	40.3	41.3	37.5	41.5	62.2	61.9	68.3	110.4	28.7	90.6	46.3
1974	72.7	54.8	75.3	33.7	95.9	45.5	46.3	43.3	45.6	62.9	61.6	66.5	107.9	31.8	90.6	51.7
1975	75.6	53.9	71.3	37.1	96.6	49.0	49.0	48.9	50.1	64.8	64.7	62.9	97.2	35.7	93.1	55.2
1976	78.2	58.3	74.6	40.2	99.0	50.7	51.4	48.8	52.4	67.4	67.4	68.6	101.9	38.7	95.3	57.4
1977	80.1	62.6	78.1	43.3	100.3	53.1	54.0	50.4	55.1	69.7	70.1	74.3	106.1	42.0	97.3	60.0
1978	80.8	66.7	82.6	47.0	101.2	57.1	58.2	53.8	59.0	70.6	70.7	78.2	110.6	45.4	97.7	64.2
1979	79.4	68.2	85.8	51.4	99.3	63.4	64.7	59.8	64.3	70.1	70.2	79.1	112.7	49.9	96.4	71.0
1980	80.4	68.3	85.1	56.7	96.5	70.2	70.5	69.2	69.7	70.5	70.4	75.7	107.5	55.8	95.0	79.3
1981	82.9	71.5	86.2	61.9	95.5	75.8	74.7	79.0	75.8	71.5	71.1	76.0	107.0	61.3	94.7	86.3
1982	84.2	70.5	83.7	66.3	96.3	80.4	78.7	85.4	79.3	75.2	74.7	73.1	97.9	67.3	97.8	90.1
1983	86.9	73.7	84.9	68.7	96.8	80.9	79.1	85.8	81.1	77.9	77.1	76.3	98.9	69.1	97.4	89.6
1984	89.6	81.0	90.3	71.7	96.8	81.1	80.0	84.3	82.8	80.3	79.8	84.0	105.3	71.5	96.5	89.6
1985	91.1	84.2	92.5	75.0	97.8	83.1	82.3	85.2	84.4	83.3	82.8	86.6	104.6	75.3	98.2	91.0
1986	93.7	86.9	92.7	78.8	100.8	84.9	84.0	87.5	85.2	87.0	86.5	89.1	103.0	78.7	100.7	91.0
1987	95.2	91.1	95.8	81.6	100.8	86.2	85.7	87.5	87.1	89.3	88.8	92.1	103.8	80.9	99.9	91.2
1988	96.9	95.9	99.1	84.9	100.7	88.2	87.7	89.7	89.6	90.9	90.5	96.5	106.6	84.2	99.9	93.0
1989	95.5	97.5	102.0	87.1	98.5	92.5	91.1	96.3	92.8	96.2	90.7	97.1	107.1	86.9	98.3	95.8
1962:																
1st quarter	58.3	31.4	53.8	16.6	77.1	27.6	28.4	25.3	29.9	43.7	44.5	41.1	92.5	15.8	73.5	35.5
2nd quarter	58.1	31.7	54.6	16.7	77.3	27.8	28.7	25.3	29.9	43.3	44.1	41.4	93.9	15.9	73.7	36.0
3rd quarter	58.6	32.1	54.8	16.8	77.7	27.8	28.6	25.5	29.9	43.6	44.5	41.7	93.8	16.0	74.0	36.0
4th quarter	59.3	32.5	54.7	16.9	78.2	27.7	28.6	25.4	30.0	44.1	44.8	41.9	93.5	16.1	74.5	36.0
1963:																
1st quarter	59.7	32.8	55.0	17.1	78.6	27.8	28.6	25.4	30.0	44.6	45.3	42.4	93.7	16.2	74.7	35.9
2nd quarter	60.3	33.6	55.7	17.1	78.7	27.6	28.4	25.2	30.1	45.5	46.0	43.4	94.3	16.3	75.0	35.4
3rd quarter	60.9	34.1	55.9	17.3	79.1	27.6	28.4	25.3	30.1	45.6	46.0	43.6	94.6	16.5	75.1	35.7
4th quarter	61.5	34.5	56.1	17.5	79.9	27.7	28.5	25.3	30.3	46.2	46.6	44.2	94.9	16.7	76.0	35.8
1964:																
1st quarter	62.8	35.3	56.2	17.8	80.7	27.5	28.4	25.1	30.3	46.9	47.2	44.8	95.0	16.9	76.6	35.8
2nd quarter	62.9	35.9	57.0	17.9	81.2	27.6	28.5	25.1	30.3	47.4	47.7	45.8	96.1	17.0	77.2	35.7
3rd quarter	63.5	36.6	57.5	18.2	82.0	27.7	28.6	25.2	30.4	47.5	47.8	46.4	97.0	17.2	77.9	36.0
4th quarter	63.0	36.8	58.3	18.2	81.9	28.0	28.9	25.5	30.6	47.8	48.1	46.9	97.5	17.3	77.8	35.9
1965:																
1st quarter	64.2	38.1	59.4	18.3	82.1	27.6	28.5	25.2	30.7	48.1	48.4	48.6	100.3	17.3	77.7	35.8
2nd quarter	64.3	38.7	60.1	18.4	82.1	27.7	28.7	25.1	30.8	48.5	48.9	49.4	101.0	17.4	77.6	35.6
3rd quarter	64.5	39.2	60.8	18.6	82.6	27.9	28.8	25.1	30.9	48.6	49.1	50.3	102.4	17.5	77.8	35.7
4th quarter	65.1	40.3	61.9	18.8	83.1	27.9	28.9	25.0	31.0	48.4	48.8	50.9	104.2	17.6	78.0	36.1
1966:																
1st quarter	65.5	41.2	63.0	19.1	83.6	28.0	29.2	24.6	31.2	48.5	48.9	52.2	106.7	17.9	78.3	36.6
2nd quarter	65.4	41.7	63.7	19.4	84.2	28.4	29.6	24.9	31.5	48.7	49.1	53.3	108.6	18.1	78.7	37.0
3rd quarter	65.3	42.0	64.3	19.7	84.7	28.9	30.1	25.3	31.7	49.1	49.4	54.0	109.4	18.4	79.1	37.2
4th quarter	65.6	42.4	64.6	19.9	85.1	29.2	30.4	25.6	32.0	49.6	49.8	54.7	109.8	18.6	79.5	37.4
1967:																
1st quarter	65.8	42.4	64.4	20.2	86.0	29.5	30.7	26.0	32.1	50.0	50.2	54.7	108.8	18.9	80.3	37.5
2nd quarter	66.3	42.5	64.1	20.5	86.7	29.7	30.9	26.4	32.2	50.6	50.8	54.6	107.5	19.1	80.8	37.6
3rd quarter	66.5	42.9	64.6	20.7	86.9	30.1	31.2	26.9	32.5	51.0	51.1	54.9	107.4	19.4	81.3	38.0
4th quarter	67.0	43.7	65.2	21.0	87.0	30.3	31.3	27.3	32.8	51.2	52.3	56.6	108.2	19.7	81.4	37.6
1968:																
1st quarter	67.9	44.4	65.3	21.6	88.7	30.8	31.9	27.7	33.2	52.5	52.6	57.2	108.7	20.2	82.9	38.4
2nd quarter	68.7	45.3	66.0	22.0	89.4	31.0	32.0	28.0	33.5	52.8	52.9	57.8	109.2	20.6	83.7	38.9
3rd quarter	68.9	46.1	66.8	22.3	89.4	31.4	32.4	28.6	33.7	52.5	52.7	57.9	109.9	20.8	83.4	39.5
4th quarter	69.2	46.6	67.4	22.7	90.1	31.9	32.9	29.1	34.2	52.9	53.2	58.8	110.4	21.3	84.1	39.9
1969:																
1st quarter	68.9	47.0	68.3	23.0	90.1	32.4	33.4	29.5	34.5	53.3	53.8	59.6	110.8	21.6	84.7	40.2
2nd quarter	68.8	47.4	68.9	23.4	90.3	33.1	34.1	30.2	34.9	53.1	53.6	59.6	111.2	22.0	84.7	41.0
3rd quarter	68.6	47.7	69.5	23.9	90.7	33.8	34.8	30.9	35.3	53.5	53.9	60.0	111.4	22.5	85.3	41.7
4th quarter	68.4	47.5	69.5	24.4	91.1	34.6	35.6	31.7	35.7	53.8	53.9	59.4	110.2	22.9	85.7	42.5
1970																
1st quarter	67.9	46.9	69.1	24.7	91.1	35.5	36.4	33.0	36.1	53.5	53.1	57.5	108.4	23.2	85.5	43.8
2nd quarter	68.8	47.0	68.3	25.1	91.2	35.9	36.5	34.0	36.6	54.8	54.0	57.1	105.6	23.7	86.1	43.9
3rd quarter	69.9	47.4	67.8	25.6	92.1	36.1	36.7	34.4	36.7	55.8	54.9	56.8	103.6	24.1	86.6	43.9
4th quarter	69.7	46.6	66.9	25.9	91.9	36.9	37.2	35.8	37.1	56.6	55.7	55.6	99.9	24.4	86.4	43.8
1971																
1st quarter	71.5	48.1	67.3	26.5	92.9	36.6	37.0	35.6	37.6	57.8	57.0	57.4	100.6	24.9	87.5	43.7
2nd quarter	71.5	48.5	67.8	26.8	93.3	37.0	37.5	35.8	38.0	58.4	57.8	58.1	100.5	25.2	87.7	43.6
3rd quarter	72.2	49.0	67.8	27.2	93.7	37.3	37.7	36.2	38.2	58.9	58.4	58.4	100.0	25.4	87.7	43.6
4th quarter	72.5	49.9	68.8	27.4	93.7	37.4	37.8	36.3	38.4	59.8	59.4	60.0	100.9	25.6	87.8	43.1
1972:																
1st quarter	73.0	51.1	70.0	28.0	95.0	37.7	38.4	35.7	38.8	60.5	60.2	62.0	102.9	26.1	88.7	43.4
2nd quarter	73.5	52.3	71.1	28.3	95.4	37.9	38.5	36.1	38.9	60.6	60.3	63.2	104.7	26.4	89.1	43.8
3rd quarter	74.0	53.0	71.7	28.6	95.8	37.9	38.7	35.8	39.2	60.8	60.6	63.8	105.2	26.7	89.4	44.1
4th quarter	74.7	54.4	72.8	29.2	96.5	38.2	39.0	35.9	39.7	61.8	61.5	66.1	107.4	27.2	90.0	44.2

Productivity and Related Data—*Continued*

(Seasonally adjusted, 1992=100)

Year and quarter	Nonfinancial corporations										Manufacturing					
	Output per hour of all persons	Output	Employee hours	Compensation per hour	Real compensation per hour	Unit costs Total	Labor costs	Nonlabor costs	Implicit price deflator	Unit nonlabor payments	Output per hour of all persons	Output	Hours of all persons	Compensation per hour	Real compensation per hour	Unit labor costs
1973:																
1st quarter	75.6	55.9	73.9	30.0	97.7	38.7	39.6	36.0	40.2	62.1	61.7	67.5	109.4	27.9	91.0	45.2
2nd quarter	74.5	55.7	74.8	30.4	97.1	39.9	40.8	37.2	41.0	62.4	61.8	68.2	110.4	28.4	90.5	45.9
3rd quarter	74.0	55.6	75.1	31.0	97.1	40.9	41.9	38.1	41.9	63.2	62.3	68.8	110.4	28.9	90.5	46.4
4th quarter	73.7	55.9	75.9	31.6	96.5	41.8	42.9	38.8	42.8	62.9	61.7	68.7	111.4	29.5	90.0	47.8
1974:																
1st quarter	72.9	55.3	75.9	32.3	95.8	43.3	44.3	40.4	43.7	62.0	60.4	66.5	110.0	30.3	89.8	50.1
2nd quarter	73.4	55.6	75.7	33.2	96.0	44.4	45.3	41.9	44.6	63.3	61.5	66.9	108.8	31.4	90.6	51.0
3rd quarter	72.4	54.8	75.6	34.1	95.9	46.4	47.1	44.2	46.3	63.9	62.1	67.4	108.4	32.3	90.7	52.0
4th quarter	72.0	53.4	74.2	35.0	95.5	48.1	48.6	46.7	47.9	64.1	62.6	65.5	104.5	33.5	91.3	53.4
1975:																
1st quarter	73.2	52.1	71.2	36.0	96.2	49.0	49.2	48.5	49.0	63.5	62.6	60.9	97.3	34.6	92.4	55.3
2nd quarter	75.3	53.0	70.4	36.7	96.7	48.8	48.7	49.2	49.6	64.7	64.1	61.3	95.6	35.4	93.4	55.2
3rd quarter	76.8	54.8	71.4	37.3	96.5	48.7	48.6	48.9	50.4	66.2	65.8	63.8	96.9	36.1	93.2	54.8
4th quarter	76.8	55.7	72.5	38.1	96.7	49.5	49.6	49.1	51.2	66.5	66.2	65.6	99.2	36.6	93.0	55.3
1976:																
1st quarter	77.9	57.5	73.9	38.9	97.6	49.4	50.0	47.9	51.6	66.9	66.5	67.4	101.3	37.5	94.0	56.4
2nd quarter	77.9	58.0	74.4	39.6	98.6	50.3	50.9	48.5	51.9	67.4	66.9	68.0	101.7	38.3	95.2	57.2
3rd quarter	78.4	58.6	74.8	40.6	99.3	51.0	51.8	48.9	52.5	68.1	67.6	68.9	102.0	39.1	95.6	57.8
4th quarter	78.3	58.9	75.3	41.4	100.0	52.1	52.9	49.9	53.3	69.0	68.5	70.2	102.4	39.9	96.2	58.2
1977:																
1st quarter	78.6	59.9	76.3	42.0	99.5	52.6	53.4	50.4	54.1	69.7	69.4	72.0	103.8	40.8	96.6	58.7
2nd quarter	80.0	62.2	77.9	42.8	99.8	52.7	53.6	50.0	54.8	70.3	70.1	74.4	106.1	41.5	96.8	59.2
3rd quarter	81.4	64.1	78.8	43.7	100.4	52.7	53.7	49.9	55.2	70.7	70.5	75.4	106.9	42.5	97.7	60.3
4th quarter	80.3	64.1	79.7	44.5	100.8	54.4	55.4	51.4	56.4	70.3	70.2	75.6	107.8	43.3	98.0	61.7
1978:																
1st quarter	80.1	64.2	80.2	45.6	101.4	56.0	56.9	53.4	57.2	70.1	69.9	75.6	108.2	44.1	98.2	63.2
2nd quarter	81.1	66.9	82.6	46.4	101.0	56.2	57.3	53.2	58.4	71.0	70.7	78.2	110.6	44.8	97.4	63.3
3rd quarter	80.9	67.4	83.4	47.4	100.8	57.4	58.6	53.8	59.4	71.4	71.0	79.1	111.4	45.7	97.2	64.4
4th quarter	80.9	68.4	84.5	48.5	100.9	58.7	60.0	54.9	60.8	71.4	71.0	79.9	112.5	46.9	97.4	66.0
1979:																
1st quarter	79.7	68.1	85.4	49.6	100.6	60.9	62.2	56.9	62.3	70.7	70.3	79.9	113.6	47.9	97.1	68.1
2nd quarter	79.4	67.9	85.6	50.8	99.8	62.6	63.9	59.0	63.7	71.0	70.6	79.5	112.6	49.3	96.9	69.9
3rd quarter	79.0	68.1	86.1	51.9	98.8	64.4	65.7	60.7	65.0	70.2	69.8	78.7	112.9	50.4	95.9	72.2
4th quarter	79.4	68.6	86.4	53.1	98.0	65.7	66.9	62.5	66.0	70.4	70.0	78.4	112.0	51.7	95.4	73.9
1980:																
1st quarter	79.9	69.0	86.3	54.5	96.7	67.3	68.2	64.6	67.4	70.9	70.4	78.4	111.4	53.2	94.4	75.5
2nd quarter	79.6	67.4	84.6	56.0	96.1	69.9	70.3	68.8	68.8	70.5	70.0	74.7	106.7	55.1	94.5	78.7
3rd quarter	80.4	67.5	84.0	57.4	96.7	71.4	71.4	71.3	70.5	70.7	70.1	73.6	105.0	56.7	95.6	80.9
4th quarter	81.3	69.5	85.5	58.8	96.4	72.3	72.3	72.3	72.1	71.6	70.9	76.1	107.3	58.3	95.6	82.2
1981																
1st quarter	82.1	70.8	86.2	60.0	95.7	73.7	73.0	75.4	73.8	70.9	70.6	76.0	107.7	59.2	94.5	83.9
2nd quarter	82.4	71.1	86.3	61.3	95.8	75.3	74.4	78.0	75.2	71.4	71.0	76.6	107.9	60.7	94.9	85.5
3rd quarter	83.8	72.5	86.5	62.6	95.2	75.9	74.7	79.4	76.5	71.9	71.4	76.7	107.4	62.0	94.3	86.8
4th quarter	83.1	71.5	86.0	63.6	95.1	78.2	76.5	83.0	77.6	71.5	71.1	74.6	105.0	63.4	94.8	89.2
1982:																
1st quarter	83.2	70.7	85.0	64.8	96.2	79.4	77.9	83.7	78.4	73.2	72.7	74.0	101.8	65.3	96.8	89.8
2nd quarter	84.3	70.8	84.0	65.9	96.4	80.0	78.2	85.0	79.1	75.4	74.8	74.0	98.9	67.1	98.1	89.6
3rd quarter	84.6	70.4	83.2	66.9	96.1	80.7	79.0	85.5	79.8	76.4	75.8	73.1	96.5	68.2	97.9	90.0
4th quarter	84.7	69.9	82.5	67.4	96.6	81.6	79.6	87.4	80.0	76.1	75.4	71.4	94.7	68.6	98.3	91.0
1983:																
1st quarter	85.4	70.6	82.7	67.9	97.1	81.1	79.5	85.8	80.3	77.1	76.2	72.8	95.4	68.8	98.6	90.3
2nd quarter	86.8	72.9	83.9	68.4	96.8	80.5	78.8	85.3	80.9	77.6	76.7	74.9	97.7	68.9	97.5	89.8
3rd quarter	87.3	74.6	85.5	68.8	96.5	80.4	78.8	84.8	81.3	78.5	77.6	77.7	100.1	69.1	96.8	89.0
4th quarter	87.9	76.8	87.3	69.8	96.9	81.5	79.4	87.5	81.8	78.5	77.7	79.7	102.6	69.6	96.6	89.5
1984:																
1st quarter	88.6	78.8	88.9	70.4	96.3	80.5	79.4	83.8	82.3	79.5	78.9	82.4	104.5	70.2	96.0	89.0
2nd quarter	89.6	80.7	90.1	71.3	96.6	80.6	79.5	83.5	82.6	80.0	79.5	83.9	105.6	70.9	96.1	89.2
3rd quarter	89.9	81.6	90.8	72.2	97.0	81.3	80.3	84.2	83.0	80.7	80.3	84.8	105.6	71.9	96.7	89.6
4th quarter	90.3	82.6	91.5	72.9	97.1	82.0	80.7	85.7	83.3	80.8	80.4	84.9	105.6	72.9	97.1	90.6
1985:																
1st quarter	90.2	83.1	92.1	73.6	97.1	82.3	81.5	84.5	83.9	81.5	81.1	85.5	105.4	74.1	97.8	91.4
2nd quarter	90.4	83.5	92.4	74.4	97.3	83.2	82.3	85.8	84.3	83.3	82.7	86.5	104.5	74.7	97.8	90.3
3rd quarter	92.0	85.1	92.5	75.3	98.0	82.6	81.9	84.8	84.5	83.9	83.4	86.9	104.2	75.7	98.4	90.8
4th quarter	91.7	85.1	92.8	76.6	98.6	84.2	83.6	85.9	84.9	84.4	83.9	87.4	104.1	76.9	98.9	91.6
1986:																
1st quarter	93.8	87.0	92.8	77.6	99.3	83.8	82.7	87.0	84.9	85.8	85.3	88.5	103.8	77.7	99.4	91.0
2nd quarter	93.5	86.4	92.4	78.3	100.8	84.6	83.7	87.1	84.9	86.7	86.3	88.9	103.0	78.2	100.6	90.6
3rd quarter	93.3	86.4	92.6	79.1	101.1	85.7	84.7	88.3	85.4	87.1	86.7	89.0	102.7	79.0	101.0	91.1
4th quarter	94.3	87.8	93.1	80.1	101.8	85.7	85.0	87.8	85.7	88.1	87.6	90.0	102.7	79.9	101.5	91.2
1987:																
1st quarter	94.1	88.9	94.4	80.6	101.0	86.1	85.6	87.4	86.2	88.3	87.8	90.4	103.0	80.4	100.8	91.6
2nd quarter	94.9	90.4	95.2	81.1	100.5	86.0	85.4	87.5	86.8	89.3	88.8	91.4	103.0	80.6	99.9	90.7
3rd quarter	95.5	92.0	96.3	81.6	100.2	85.9	85.4	87.2	87.3	89.4	88.9	92.5	104.0	81.1	99.5	91.2
4th quarter	96.1	93.3	97.1	83.1	101.1	86.9	86.5	88.0	87.9	90.0	89.5	94.2	105.3	81.5	99.1	91.1
1988:																
1st quarter	96.4	94.3	97.8	83.3	100.5	87.0	86.4	88.6	88.3	90.2	89.8	95.1	105.9	82.9	100.0	92.3
2nd quarter	96.7	95.4	98.7	84.7	101.0	87.9	87.5	89.0	89.1	90.8	90.4	96.1	106.4	83.7	99.8	92.6
3rd quarter	96.7	96.2	99.4	85.5	100.7	88.8	88.4	90.1	90.2	91.2	90.8	96.9	106.7	84.5	99.6	93.1
4th quarter	97.3	97.9	100.6	86.0	100.2	89.1	88.4	91.2	90.8	91.4	91.1	97.7	107.3	85.7	99.9	94.1
1989:																
1st quarter	95.6	97.3	101.7	86.2	99.3	91.1	90.1	93.9	91.6	94.7	91.0	98.2	107.8	86.2	99.4	94.7
2nd quarter	95.3	97.2	102.0	86.5	98.1	92.1	90.8	95.9	92.6	96.5	90.9	97.6	107.4	86.1	97.6	94.7
3rd quarter	95.7	97.7	102.1	87.1	98.0	92.7	91.1	97.4	93.3	97.7	90.1	96.4	107.0	87.0	97.9	96.5
4th quarter	95.4	97.7	102.4	88.4	98.4	94.0	92.6	97.9	93.7	95.9	90.8	96.3	106.0	88.3	98.4	97.2

New Plant and Equipment Spending [1]

(Billions of dollars, seasonally adjusted annual rates)

Year and quarter	Mining	Manufacturing								
		Total	Durables							
			Total	Stone, clay, and glass products	Primary metals	Blast furnaces and steel mills	Non-ferrous metals	Fabricated metals	Machinery except electrical	Electrical machinery
1961	1.26	15.53	7.43	0.70	1.28	0.86	0.29	0.52	1.11	1.05
1962	1.41	16.03	7.81	0.72	1.25	0.76	0.34	0.59	1.26	0.99
1963	1.26	17.27	8.64	0.70	1.51	0.88	0.46	0.69	1.24	1.02
1964	1.33	21.23	10.98	0.81	2.22	1.44	0.56	0.85	1.61	1.17
1965	1.36	25.41	13.49	0.86	2.57	1.59	0.71	0.86	2.24	1.69
1966	1.42	31.37	17.23	1.13	3.06	1.72	1.01	1.14	2.91	2.51
1967	1.38	32.25	17.83	0.92	3.31	1.90	1.11	1.29	3.02	3.13
1968	1.44	32.34	17.93	0.89	3.45	2.01	1.11	1.36	2.90	3.16
1969	1.77	36.27	19.97	1.12	3.29	1.83	1.06	1.34	3.63	3.27
1970	2.02	36.99	19.80	1.06	3.24	1.63	1.18	1.22	3.78	3.49
1971	2.67	33.60	16.78	0.94	2.69	1.27	1.02	1.20	3.15	3.03
1972	2.88	35.42	18.22	1.34	2.44	1.07	0.97	1.43	3.23	2.83
1973	3.30	42.35	22.63	1.58	2.94	1.25	1.22	1.81	3.95	3.48
1974	4.58	52.48	26.77	1.65	4.27	1.97	1.77	1.93	5.13	3.80
1975	6.12	53.66	25.37	1.67	5.43	3.08	1.72	1.96	4.86	3.08
1976	7.63	58.53	27.50	1.91	5.32	3.13	1.42	2.20	5.43	3.61
1977	9.81	67.48	32.77	2.30	4.97	2.88	1.30	2.45	6.35	4.61
1978	10.55	78.13	39.02	3.05	5.07	2.65	1.45	2.93	7.19	5.92
1979	11.05	95.13	47.72	3.69	5.96	3.36	1.60	3.17	9.80	7.69
1980	12.71	112.60	54.82	3.69	6.65	3.70	2.02	3.26	10.68	10.20
1981	15.81	128.68	58.93	3.03	7.19	3.87	2.34	3.42	12.39	11.41
1982	14.11	123.97	54.58	2.70	6.78	4.27	1.72	2.81	12.28	12.21
1983	10.64	117.35	51.61	2.62	5.89	3.66	1.57	2.56	11.98	12.68
1984	11.86	139.61	64.57	3.13	6.83	3.99	1.96	3.14	13.62	16.22
1985	12.00	152.88	70.87	3.58	7.45	4.66	1.75	3.25	13.83	17.09
1986	8.15	137.95	65.68	3.13	6.74	3.76	1.75	3.61	11.36	15.64
1987	8.28	141.06	68.03	3.32	8.59	5.30	1.98	3.62	11.87	16.84
1988	9.29	163.45	77.04	3.63	10.99	7.01	2.51	3.91	13.70	20.84
1989	9.21	183.80	82.56	4.00	12.03	7.87	2.64	4.17	14.58	20.46
1990	9.88	192.61	82.58	3.29	12.16	7.78	2.88	4.39	13.66	22.04
1991	10.02	182.81	77.64	2.89	10.74	6.53	2.81	4.03	12.68	20.97
1992	8.88	174.02	73.32	3.36	9.76	5.64	2.67	3.67	10.64	20.42
1993	10.08	179.47	81.45	4.31	9.87	5.64	2.59	3.92	9.71	24.41
1985:										
1st quarter	12.13	147.69	68.84	3.36	7.22	4.34	1.87	3.13	13.87	17.66
2nd quarter	12.56	155.97	72.87	3.77	7.33	4.61	1.71	3.03	14.69	18.73
3rd quarter	12.14	154.76	70.77	3.69	7.46	4.68	1.73	3.38	13.65	16.78
4th quarter	11.19	151.98	70.61	3.47	7.69	4.88	1.72	3.44	13.20	15.72
1986:										
1st quarter	9.71	142.28	65.33	3.18	7.19	4.29	1.71	3.65	12.02	14.42
2nd quarter	8.16	138.09	65.38	2.81	6.57	3.42	1.82	3.62	11.07	16.26
3rd quarter	7.35	133.95	65.53	2.95	6.29	3.61	1.55	3.52	11.25	14.97
4th quarter	7.52	138.07	66.31	3.51	6.95	3.75	1.89	3.64	11.18	16.55
1987:										
1st quarter	7.49	135.22	67.34	3.07	7.47	4.57	1.59	3.57	11.12	16.51
2nd quarter	7.86	137.20	66.48	3.18	8.17	4.95	1.94	3.51	11.00	16.35
3rd quarter	8.60	142.75	68.57	3.57	8.81	5.44	2.09	3.61	12.29	17.07
4th quarter	9.03	146.91	69.43	3.42	9.53	5.94	2.24	3.79	12.72	17.29
1988:										
1st quarter	9.29	155.63	73.68	3.44	10.29	6.35	2.49	3.86	13.68	19.40
2nd quarter	9.59	159.99	76.04	3.71	10.66	6.80	2.41	4.05	13.45	21.05
3rd quarter	9.25	165.72	77.43	3.53	11.61	7.48	2.59	3.88	13.01	21.04
4th quarter	9.01	169.85	80.02	3.78	11.22	7.21	2.57	3.87	14.48	21.60
1989:										
1st quarter	8.99	173.07	79.84	4.03	11.10	7.15	2.48	4.00	14.26	20.46
2nd quarter	9.18	180.51	82.14	4.13	11.88	7.72	2.61	4.10	14.77	19.95
3rd quarter	9.22	185.92	83.80	4.12	12.17	7.97	2.67	4.38	14.49	21.14
4th quarter	9.39	191.98	83.86	3.78	12.66	8.40	2.78	4.19	14.77	20.36
1990:										
1st quarter	9.70	191.73	85.75	3.61	12.60	8.23	2.90	4.52	14.64	23.07
2nd quarter	9.76	194.70	83.74	3.32	12.32	7.92	2.87	4.43	14.50	22.09
3rd quarter	9.89	195.06	83.16	3.26	11.91	7.46	2.91	4.44	13.85	22.15
4th quarter	10.13	189.25	79.01	3.02	11.94	7.63	2.84	4.20	12.16	21.25
1991:										
1st quarter	10.05	190.50	80.31	2.92	11.91	7.54	2.92	4.18	13.12	21.18
2nd quarter	10.09	187.18	78.89	2.78	11.03	6.79	2.88	4.05	12.67	20.81
3rd quarter	9.97	178.24	75.54	2.82	10.75	6.70	2.69	4.01	12.59	21.08
4th quarter	9.98	178.33	76.85	3.02	9.72	5.53	2.75	3.89	12.49	20.95
1992:										
1st quarter	8.99	173.14	73.26	3.00	9.82	5.76	2.67	3.65	10.31	20.27
2nd quarter	9.20	172.52	73.74	3.13	10.01	5.92	2.54	3.62	11.46	20.93
3rd quarter	8.96	173.05	72.63	3.32	9.58	5.58	2.64	3.49	10.54	20.55
4th quarter	8.43	176.74	73.64	3.83	9.67	5.41	2.80	3.88	10.29	20.08
1993:										
1st quarter	8.98	173.99	78.19	4.16	8.94	5.22	2.26	3.54	10.39	24.04
2nd quarter	9.10	177.55	80.33	4.32	9.62	5.52	2.58	3.95	8.48	24.30
3rd quarter	11.09	182.48	82.74	4.27	10.16	5.80	2.64	4.02	9.93	23.91
4th quarter	10.92	182.15	83.64	4.44	10.53	5.88	2.81	4.12	10.05	25.20
1994:										
1st quarter	11.43	185.04	86.03	5.03	11.28	6.93	2.31	3.99	9.10	25.33
2nd quarter	10.70	193.99	91.71	5.42	12.08	7.26	2.55	3.92	9.17	28.36

1. These series were discontinued in mid-1994; see Notes.

New Plant and Equipment Spending [1]—Continued

(Billions of dollars, seasonally adjusted annual rates)

| Year and quarter | Manufacturing—Continued | | | | | | | | | |
| | Durables—Continued | | | Nondurables | | | | | | |
	Transportation equipment	Motor vehicles	Aircraft	Total	Food and beverages	Textiles	Paper	Chemicals	Petroleum	Rubber
1961	1.78	1.38	0.30	8.10	1.50	0.35	0.62	1.60	2.97	0.36
1962	1.98	1.45	0.40	8.22	1.45	0.39	0.62	1.58	3.08	0.38
1963	2.37	1.82	0.44	8.63	1.50	0.43	0.70	1.72	3.10	0.39
1964	3.08	2.48	0.41	10.25	1.75	0.59	0.91	2.10	3.51	0.47
1965	3.74	3.00	0.53	11.92	1.87	0.79	1.07	2.82	3.88	0.59
1966	4.61	3.13	1.17	14.15	2.11	0.96	1.32	3.35	4.48	0.65
1967	4.44	2.85	1.25	14.42	2.05	0.77	1.49	3.08	4.84	0.67
1968	4.25	2.67	1.23	14.40	2.20	0.65	1.27	2.80	4.96	0.96
1969	4.80	2.99	1.29	16.31	2.76	0.86	1.62	3.01	5.26	1.07
1970	4.65	3.05	0.88	17.19	3.32	0.80	1.74	3.38	5.16	0.92
1971	3.54	2.42	0.63	16.82	3.35	0.90	1.29	3.27	5.21	0.79
1972	4.41	3.00	0.68	17.20	3.28	1.06	1.46	3.38	4.79	1.03
1973	5.60	3.83	0.79	19.72	3.74	1.02	1.99	4.17	4.61	1.56
1974	6.60	4.29	1.21	25.71	4.25	1.06	2.88	6.18	7.04	1.61
1975	5.46	3.33	1.19	28.28	4.38	0.86	2.93	7.12	9.07	1.20
1976	5.79	3.60	1.02	31.03	5.39	0.98	2.99	7.37	10.02	1.37
1977	8.32	5.82	1.14	34.71	5.72	1.18	3.48	7.35	11.82	1.77
1978	10.97	7.10	1.77	39.10	6.59	1.32	3.78	7.58	13.68	2.22
1979	13.47	8.06	2.71	47.41	7.42	1.45	5.18	9.24	16.77	2.18
1980	16.10	8.54	3.60	57.77	8.51	1.60	6.39	10.62	22.75	1.68
1981	16.91	9.10	3.40	69.75	10.13	1.76	5.95	11.99	31.94	1.77
1982	13.55	7.13	3.45	69.39	9.43	1.55	5.47	11.44	33.50	1.72
1983	11.86	6.56	2.95	65.74	8.46	1.63	5.73	11.59	29.47	2.05
1984	16.63	10.17	3.63	75.04	9.71	2.00	6.90	13.46	32.56	2.62
1985	19.61	13.39	3.51	82.01	11.35	1.82	8.14	14.35	34.06	3.34
1986	18.86	12.79	3.86	72.28	11.62	1.71	8.26	14.54	23.05	3.30
1987	16.73	10.88	3.60	73.03	12.10	2.00	8.54	13.92	22.06	2.94
1988	15.76	9.75	3.49	86.41	14.16	2.18	10.92	16.62	26.03	3.26
1989	18.71	11.49	4.17	101.24	15.89	2.25	15.58	18.47	30.08	3.79
1990	17.89	11.28	4.02	110.04	16.36	2.18	16.53	20.63	34.79	3.48
1991	17.19	10.20	4.05	105.17	17.43	1.96	11.50	21.52	35.59	3.43
1992	16.06	8.67	4.36	100.69	18.95	2.05	10.53	23.15	29.59	3.85
1993	19.16	12.28	3.23	98.02	18.78	2.27	10.31	21.83	28.71	3.32
1985:										
1st quarter	17.87	11.32	3.59	78.85	10.70	2.06	7.58	14.28	32.98	2.99
2nd quarter	19.32	13.16	3.46	83.10	11.45	1.87	7.74	14.70	35.72	3.03
3rd quarter	19.59	12.97	3.79	83.99	11.46	1.78	8.23	14.45	35.10	3.34
4th quarter	20.89	15.26	3.22	81.37	11.62	1.55	8.75	14.00	32.34	3.89
1986:										
1st quarter	18.73	12.67	3.87	76.95	10.62	1.54	8.52	13.85	29.34	3.92
2nd quarter	18.59	12.60	3.89	72.71	11.47	1.77	8.50	14.26	23.59	3.46
3rd quarter	20.46	14.62	3.69	68.41	11.96	1.58	8.35	14.07	19.50	3.16
4th quarter	17.85	11.43	3.98	71.76	12.26	1.92	7.77	15.67	20.79	2.81
1987:										
1st quarter	18.93	13.27	3.57	67.88	12.13	1.94	7.79	12.78	19.43	2.71
2nd quarter	17.49	11.47	3.71	70.72	11.85	2.10	8.14	13.76	20.47	3.03
3rd quarter	15.88	9.92	3.69	74.17	12.09	1.91	8.56	14.33	23.05	3.03
4th quarter	15.32	9.54	3.45	77.48	12.36	2.03	9.35	14.54	24.14	2.94
1988:										
1st quarter	15.25	9.47	3.32	81.95	13.80	2.11	9.60	15.53	25.19	3.25
2nd quarter	15.26	9.35	3.44	83.95	13.84	2.14	10.48	16.54	25.42	2.82
3rd quarter	16.02	10.01	3.57	88.28	14.04	2.26	11.10	18.02	25.89	3.53
4th quarter	16.36	10.04	3.60	89.83	14.83	2.19	12.01	16.29	26.95	3.43
1989:										
1st quarter	17.39	9.93	4.49	93.23	14.91	2.16	13.81	17.46	26.58	3.40
2nd quarter	18.54	11.62	3.95	98.37	16.26	2.20	14.39	17.90	28.31	3.82
3rd quarter	18.65	11.75	3.74	102.12	15.73	2.29	15.67	18.35	30.52	3.96
4th quarter	19.83	12.27	4.50	108.12	16.45	2.33	17.75	19.75	33.26	3.90
1990:										
1st quarter	18.80	12.03	4.30	105.98	15.98	2.23	17.30	20.08	31.50	3.52
2nd quarter	18.19	11.33	4.12	110.95	16.89	2.17	18.53	20.24	33.80	3.59
3rd quarter	18.28	11.63	4.03	111.90	16.36	2.21	16.72	20.40	36.01	3.50
4th quarter	16.63	10.43	3.69	110.24	16.21	2.10	14.20	21.44	36.61	3.33
1991:										
1st quarter	17.50	10.99	3.63	110.19	17.21	2.09	12.85	20.97	39.34	3.52
2nd quarter	17.86	11.23	3.84	108.29	16.82	1.95	11.64	21.51	38.74	3.34
3rd quarter	16.09	8.97	4.07	102.70	17.69	1.85	11.39	21.75	33.80	3.26
4th quarter	17.56	9.89	4.66	101.48	18.02	1.95	10.57	21.61	32.17	3.58
1992:										
1st quarter	17.02	9.26	4.93	99.87	18.65	1.94	11.01	22.02	30.15	3.73
2nd quarter	15.42	7.96	4.52	98.78	18.59	2.17	9.84	22.75	29.01	3.64
3rd quarter	15.69	8.23	4.46	100.42	18.72	2.12	10.25	23.31	29.56	3.81
4th quarter	16.16	9.28	3.56	103.09	19.81	1.98	10.94	24.05	29.67	4.15
1993:										
1st quarter	17.23	10.22	3.51	95.80	19.79	2.05	10.60	21.42	26.07	3.00
2nd quarter	19.95	13.02	3.40	97.22	19.24	2.16	10.37	21.57	28.38	3.24
3rd quarter	20.27	13.68	3.00	99.74	18.99	2.37	9.79	22.10	30.44	3.41
4th quarter	18.86	11.89	3.02	98.51	17.29	2.50	10.45	22.09	29.30	3.54
1994:										
1st quarter	21.49	15.16	2.52	99.02	17.01	2.20	10.01	21.93	29.60	3.44
2nd quarter	21.07	14.10	2.81	102.28	18.77	2.41	10.35	22.91	28.83	4.30

1. These series were discontinued in mid-1994; see Notes.

New Plant and Equipment Spending [1]—Continued

(Billions of dollars, seasonally adjusted annual rates)

Year and quarter	Transportation				Public utilities			Communi-cations	Wholesale and retail trade	Finance and insurance	Personal and business services
	Total	Railroads	Air	Other	Total	Electric	Gas and other				
1961	3.14	1.19	0.73	1.22	5.20	3.78	1.42	3.59	4.14	1.39	4.08
1962	3.59	1.43	0.53	1.63	5.12	3.76	1.36	4.02	4.53	1.46	4.69
1963	3.64	1.72	0.35	1.57	5.33	4.01	1.32	4.19	4.91	1.68	5.39
1964	4.71	2.20	0.92	1.60	5.80	4.27	1.53	4.75	5.72	1.90	5.84
1965	5.66	2.60	1.08	1.98	6.49	4.76	1.73	5.47	6.51	2.21	6.41
1966	6.68	3.09	1.66	1.93	7.82	5.73	2.09	6.23	7.09	2.23	7.57
1967	6.57	2.50	2.28	1.79	9.33	7.30	2.03	6.61	6.88	2.46	7.27
1968	6.91	2.15	2.54	2.23	10.52	7.97	2.54	7.07	7.04	3.03	8.09
1969	7.23	2.61	2.28	2.34	11.70	9.05	2.65	8.57	7.62	3.62	8.96
1970	7.17	2.48	2.50	2.18	13.03	10.56	2.46	10.40	8.78	3.91	9.62
1971	6.42	2.39	1.33	2.71	14.70	12.28	2.42	10.96	9.32	4.66	10.58
1972	7.14	2.35	1.93	2.86	16.26	13.60	2.66	12.27	10.95	6.37	12.11
1973	8.00	2.91	1.89	3.21	17.99	15.07	2.92	13.30	13.18	7.75	14.16
1974	9.16	3.63	1.80	3.73	19.96	16.85	3.11	14.46	15.02	8.45	15.56
1975	9.95	3.88	1.54	4.53	20.23	16.94	3.29	12.90	14.77	9.96	14.83
1976	11.10	4.25	1.13	5.72	22.90	19.29	3.61	13.66	17.61	9.19	17.83
1977	12.20	4.67	2.15	5.38	27.83	23.24	4.58	16.27	20.84	10.13	20.28
1978	12.07	4.93	3.00	4.14	32.10	26.70	5.40	19.79	26.14	13.52	24.52
1979	13.91	5.86	3.73	4.32	37.53	30.78	6.75	23.55	30.81	18.23	25.06
1980	13.56	5.91	3.66	3.98	41.32	33.30	8.01	26.80	31.95	22.57	24.89
1981	12.67	5.03	3.48	4.15	47.17	37.37	9.80	30.09	35.68	28.38	26.26
1982	11.75	4.28	3.61	3.86	53.58	43.65	9.93	30.06	36.78	30.35	25.58
1983	10.81	3.85	3.38	3.57	52.95	44.87	8.08	27.85	44.45	32.04	25.08
1984	13.44	5.32	3.31	4.81	57.53	45.18	12.35	31.60	53.39	37.89	28.52
1985	14.57	5.65	4.11	4.81	59.58	44.01	15.58	37.08	60.10	45.15	28.76
1986	15.05	5.33	5.17	4.55	56.61	41.03	15.58	38.22	65.37	49.57	28.44
1987	15.07	4.72	5.34	5.01	56.26	39.10	17.17	37.17	68.53	54.06	30.07
1988	16.63	5.52	5.63	5.48	60.37	40.90	19.47	37.24	76.37	59.22	32.93
1989	18.84	6.26	6.73	5.85	66.28	44.81	21.47	39.83	84.52	70.30	34.62
1990	21.47	6.40	8.87	6.20	67.21	44.10	23.11	43.13	95.63	68.96	33.72
1991	22.66	5.95	10.17	6.54	66.57	43.76	22.82	42.68	104.99	63.98	34.67
1992	22.64	6.67	8.93	7.04	72.21	48.22	23.99	41.53	116.23	72.76	38.32
1993	21.77	6.14	6.42	9.22	75.98	52.55	23.43	45.02	131.37	80.47	42.57
1985:											
1st quarter	13.50	5.35	3.40	4.75	59.17	44.80	14.37	36.07	58.32	41.74	28.61
2nd quarter	14.29	5.79	3.33	5.17	59.52	44.13	15.39	37.56	60.57	43.31	28.54
3rd quarter	14.86	5.86	4.60	4.39	59.50	43.48	16.02	38.50	60.24	46.41	27.96
4th quarter	15.35	5.47	5.00	4.88	59.66	43.51	16.15	36.08	61.01	48.07	29.89
1986:											
1st quarter	14.82	5.25	5.31	4.26	57.86	42.31	15.55	39.33	62.15	49.84	28.17
2nd quarter	15.28	5.38	5.50	4.39	56.98	41.26	15.72	40.24	64.68	46.18	28.04
3rd quarter	14.77	5.50	4.69	4.58	56.30	40.85	15.46	36.33	66.13	50.92	28.54
4th quarter	15.11	5.16	5.10	4.84	55.44	39.78	15.66	37.17	67.97	50.86	29.00
1987:											
1st quarter	14.70	4.49	5.58	4.64	54.52	38.59	15.93	36.26	66.16	52.40	28.88
2nd quarter	14.53	4.66	4.94	4.93	54.49	39.03	15.46	36.15	67.72	51.78	29.72
3rd quarter	15.27	4.84	5.14	5.29	57.47	38.97	18.50	37.87	67.72	54.23	30.39
4th quarter	15.58	4.84	5.64	5.11	57.76	39.47	18.29	38.08	71.96	56.84	31.25
1988:											
1st quarter	15.97	5.32	5.32	5.33	57.43	38.86	18.56	36.25	73.68	56.20	32.06
2nd quarter	16.50	5.54	5.44	5.52	58.67	39.62	19.05	37.81	74.84	61.36	33.27
3rd quarter	16.65	5.43	5.74	5.48	61.08	41.54	19.54	37.44	77.50	59.51	32.83
4th quarter	17.26	5.73	5.94	5.58	63.21	42.77	20.44	37.22	79.05	59.28	33.55
1989:											
1st quarter	17.60	6.10	5.56	5.94	65.92	43.86	22.06	39.46	81.63	65.46	35.07
2nd quarter	18.42	5.81	6.79	5.83	68.74	46.70	22.05	38.16	83.71	68.10	35.05
3rd quarter	20.68	6.29	8.44	5.96	65.30	44.62	20.67	39.77	86.33	71.07	35.43
4th quarter	18.69	6.81	6.22	5.66	65.23	43.91	21.33	41.49	85.97	75.21	33.10
1990:											
1st quarter	21.74	6.51	9.07	6.16	65.45	43.68	21.77	42.41	94.11	71.68	34.33
2nd quarter	21.72	6.64	9.23	5.85	65.05	42.96	22.09	43.44	94.63	72.39	33.93
3rd quarter	20.47	5.55	9.08	5.85	67.96	44.12	23.84	42.78	94.42	68.82	33.98
4th quarter	22.06	6.95	8.25	6.85	69.39	45.18	24.21	43.55	99.10	64.32	32.68
1991:											
1st quarter	23.00	5.74	10.88	6.39	67.15	43.56	23.59	43.14	100.80	65.82	33.19
2nd quarter	22.79	6.29	9.93	6.57	65.02	43.09	21.93	41.84	104.36	60.86	33.25
3rd quarter	21.93	6.49	8.99	6.45	67.10	43.67	23.43	42.54	107.29	64.88	35.13
4th quarter	23.13	5.18	11.23	6.73	66.76	44.37	22.39	43.13	106.65	64.88	37.01
1992:											
1st quarter	21.82	6.79	8.73	6.30	69.09	46.06	23.03	39.26	110.90	73.49	37.54
2nd quarter	23.32	6.40	9.77	7.15	72.56	48.45	24.12	41.35	113.18	71.61	37.55
3rd quarter	23.66	6.87	9.36	7.43	72.48	48.37	24.11	42.18	117.79	72.02	37.68
4th quarter	21.66	6.64	7.80	7.22	73.79	49.37	24.42	42.72	121.83	73.87	40.35
1993:											
1st quarter	22.38	6.16	7.26	8.96	73.78	49.98	23.79	43.79	124.11	77.60	38.84
2nd quarter	21.50	5.94	6.63	8.92	74.45	50.61	23.83	45.68	127.91	79.13	43.63
3rd quarter	21.32	5.89	6.70	8.74	75.94	52.96	22.98	45.06	133.21	82.46	43.01
4th quarter	21.84	6.55	5.06	10.23	78.87	55.60	23.27	45.28	138.74	82.29	44.42
1994:											
1st quarter	22.47	7.46	4.23	10.77	73.20	48.68	24.51	43.56	145.46	88.51	49.67
2nd quarter	19.59	5.36	4.53	9.70	76.51	53.55	22.96	42.97	152.63	91.53	49.16

1. These series were discontinued in mid-1994; see Notes.

Personal Income and its Disposition

(Billions of dollars, seasonally adjusted annual rate)

Year and month	Personal income	Wage and salary disburse-ments	Other labor income	Proprietors' income [1]		Rental income of persons [2]	Personal dividend income	Personal interest income	Transfer payments to persons	Less: Personal contribu-tions for social insurance	Personal tax and nontax payments	Disposable personal income
				Farm	Nonfarm							
1971:												
January	868.4	567.4	34.5	14.8	68.0	24.4	23.8	73.7	92.0	30.1	103.5	764.9
February	871.8	570.0	34.8	15.1	67.4	23.5	23.6	74.4	93.3	30.2	104.5	767.3
March	878.1	572.7	35.1	15.2	68.7	24.3	23.3	74.9	94.2	30.3	105.1	773.0
April	884.1	576.3	35.6	15.3	69.6	24.6	23.3	74.9	94.9	30.4	106.2	777.9
May	890.7	581.1	36.0	15.3	70.2	24.9	23.4	75.0	95.5	30.6	107.0	783.7
June	911.4	582.6	36.4	15.3	70.8	24.9	23.5	75.3	113.1	30.6	107.5	803.9
July	902.1	584.2	36.8	14.8	71.6	24.9	23.5	76.0	101.0	30.7	107.9	794.2
August	909.2	589.8	37.3	14.8	72.0	24.7	23.6	76.6	101.3	31.0	108.8	800.4
September	913.2	590.0	37.7	15.1	72.5	24.7	23.6	77.0	103.5	30.9	110.1	803.0
October	916.2	591.6	38.2	16.3	73.1	24.6	23.7	76.9	102.9	30.9	111.6	804.6
November	923.5	595.2	38.7	16.4	74.3	24.6	23.9	77.0	104.5	31.0	115.2	808.2
December	933.6	605.5	39.2	16.4	74.7	24.9	22.5	77.4	104.6	31.5	116.6	817.0
1972:												
January	942.6	613.4	39.6	14.8	75.7	25.4	24.6	77.7	104.9	33.5	126.1	816.5
February	954.2	620.5	40.2	14.9	75.3	25.8	24.8	78.2	108.3	33.9	129.1	825.1
March	960.6	624.0	40.9	15.4	75.9	25.7	24.8	78.9	109.0	33.9	131.6	829.0
April	967.1	627.9	41.8	17.0	77.1	25.2	24.9	79.5	107.6	34.0	132.4	834.7
May	972.6	630.5	42.4	17.8	77.6	24.7	25.2	80.1	108.4	34.1	130.2	842.4
June	966.3	633.9	43.0	18.6	75.4	14.6	25.3	81.0	108.8	34.2	130.3	836.1
July	984.6	636.1	43.5	19.5	79.0	24.4	25.7	81.9	109.5	35.1	130.8	853.7
August	998.0	642.8	44.1	20.7	81.1	24.4	25.8	82.9	110.8	34.6	132.5	865.5
September	1 005.9	648.6	44.5	21.9	80.2	24.7	25.8	84.0	110.7	34.7	133.6	872.3
October	1 026.0	656.2	44.9	23.8	81.4	25.2	26.0	84.6	118.9	35.0	135.1	891.0
November	1 040.0	661.9	45.4	24.6	83.0	25.6	26.1	85.7	122.9	35.2	136.0	904.0
December	1 048.0	668.2	45.9	24.9	83.8	25.4	26.4	87.2	121.5	35.3	136.3	911.7
1973:												
January	1 051.2	676.1	46.6	23.4	84.5	24.6	26.3	88.5	122.6	41.3	137.5	913.8
February	1 061.6	684.2	47.1	23.9	84.3	24.1	26.6	89.6	123.4	41.7	134.9	926.7
March	1 070.6	689.2	47.6	25.4	83.6	24.4	26.9	90.3	124.9	41.8	133.3	937.3
April	1 078.9	695.3	47.9	29.0	82.5	23.6	27.3	90.2	125.1	42.0	134.3	944.6
May	1 091.5	699.9	48.3	30.7	83.4	26.7	27.2	90.6	126.8	42.2	137.7	953.8
June	1 100.4	705.5	48.8	32.0	83.8	26.8	27.4	91.9	126.6	42.4	138.6	961.8
July	1 106.5	711.4	49.2	31.2	84.4	25.1	27.5	93.6	126.8	42.8	140.2	966.3
August	1 117.3	715.1	49.8	33.2	84.3	24.8	27.9	95.6	129.6	43.0	141.7	975.6
September	1 130.0	721.7	50.3	35.3	84.5	25.3	28.1	97.5	130.6	43.3	144.0	986.1
October	1 149.1	728.5	50.9	42.2	84.6	27.3	28.3	98.6	131.9	43.3	145.9	1 003.2
November	1 163.0	736.7	51.5	43.2	85.1	28.4	28.6	100.1	133.0	43.7	148.5	1 014.5
December	1 170.3	740.7	52.1	41.9	85.2	29.0	29.5	102.2	133.4	43.7	150.4	1 019.9
1974:												
January	1 171.1	744.1	52.6	35.9	85.9	28.6	29.2	103.7	137.7	46.5	149.1	1 022.0
February	1 176.3	748.3	53.2	32.5	87.4	28.0	28.9	105.6	139.3	46.8	151.5	1 024.8
March	1 180.8	751.8	53.8	28.9	88.6	27.4	29.2	107.5	140.4	46.9	152.8	1 027.9
April	1 185.5	756.6	54.4	23.8	88.2	25.2	29.3	109.1	146.0	47.1	153.8	1 031.7
May	1 199.3	766.0	55.2	21.7	89.5	26.6	29.6	110.5	147.8	47.6	157.4	1 041.9
June	1 209.9	774.6	55.9	20.9	89.5	26.4	29.9	112.2	148.6	48.0	159.9	1 050.0
July	1 227.5	780.9	56.8	22.8	91.3	26.6	29.9	113.4	154.2	48.4	161.8	1 065.7
August	1 234.6	783.3	57.6	23.4	92.1	26.4	29.8	114.9	155.4	48.5	162.7	1 071.8
September	1 243.5	789.1	58.5	24.0	92.0	25.4	30.0	116.2	157.2	48.8	164.1	1 079.3
October	1 253.5	795.1	59.4	25.6	91.0	23.6	29.8	117.9	160.0	49.0	165.6	1 087.9
November	1 251.5	790.6	60.2	25.6	90.9	22.3	29.7	118.5	162.4	48.7	165.1	1 086.3
December	1 257.6	791.2	60.9	24.9	91.7	22.1	29.3	119.1	167.1	48.7	165.5	1 092.1
1975:												
January	1 262.1	792.3	61.3	22.0	94.0	23.1	29.2	119.2	170.6	49.6	166.1	1 096.0
February	1 267.7	790.0	61.9	21.2	94.2	24.1	29.1	119.8	176.8	49.4	165.8	1 101.9
March	1 272.3	792.7	62.6	20.9	93.1	24.8	29.1	120.3	178.4	49.5	166.4	1 105.8
April	1 279.0	793.5	63.2	21.3	94.3	24.9	28.9	120.3	182.0	49.5	147.5	1 131.5
May	1 291.7	800.6	64.1	21.8	95.6	25.0	28.8	120.9	184.6	49.8	87.4	1 204.3
June	1 323.2	806.3	65.0	22.8	96.6	25.0	28.8	122.0	207.0	50.0	154.5	1 168.8
July	1 321.0	810.9	66.1	25.3	98.1	24.9	28.9	123.0	193.8	50.2	159.7	1 161.4
August	1 337.8	823.1	67.2	26.3	98.7	24.8	29.1	124.2	195.2	50.7	162.6	1 175.2
September	1 349.3	829.1	68.3	26.9	100.0	24.8	29.6	125.3	196.5	51.0	163.6	1 185.7
October	1 364.6	837.8	69.4	27.4	101.4	24.8	29.9	126.4	199.1	51.4	165.9	1 198.7
November	1 374.4	846.1	70.6	26.9	102.7	25.0	30.3	127.0	197.6	51.8	167.8	1 206.7
December	1 384.7	852.6	71.8	25.8	104.2	25.2	29.0	127.8	200.4	52.1	169.6	1 215.2
1976:												
January	1 401.2	864.9	73.1	22.8	106.0	25.5	31.2	128.3	203.5	53.9	171.0	1 230.2
February	1 412.3	871.7	74.3	21.4	108.3	25.6	32.3	128.7	204.1	54.2	171.7	1 240.6
March	1 419.6	876.2	75.5	20.1	110.4	25.4	32.5	130.1	203.7	54.4	172.0	1 247.6
April	1 429.9	883.3	76.8	19.2	111.3	25.1	33.4	131.5	203.7	54.7	176.5	1 253.4
May	1 439.3	890.7	78.0	18.5	112.4	24.8	34.5	132.9	202.5	55.0	179.0	1 260.3
June	1 446.7	893.3	79.2	17.9	114.1	23.4	35.0	134.4	204.9	55.1	180.8	1 265.9
July	1 464.2	900.6	80.4	17.6	116.3	23.9	35.6	134.7	210.9	55.6	183.3	1 280.9
August	1 476.1	909.4	81.6	17.3	117.3	23.4	36.0	135.5	211.3	56.0	185.9	1 290.2
September	1 486.0	914.6	82.8	17.1	119.1	23.4	36.4	137.1	211.9	56.2	188.2	1 297.8
October	1 493.7	920.1	83.8	16.9	118.7	23.5	37.1	138.7	211.5	56.5	190.5	1 303.1
November	1 515.2	930.9	85.0	17.0	122.4	23.7	37.7	140.6	215.0	57.0	193.5	1 321.6
December	1 528.6	938.0	86.3	17.4	123.4	23.9	38.1	142.3	216.6	57.3	195.6	1 333.0

1. Includes inventory valuation and capital consumption adjustments.
2. Includes capital consumption adjustment.

Personal Income and its Disposition—*Continued*

(Billions of dollars, seasonally adjusted annual rate)

Year and month	Personal income	Wage and salary disburse- ments	Other labor income	Proprietors' income [1] Farm	Proprietors' income [1] Nonfarm	Rental income of persons [2]	Personal dividend income	Personal interest income	Transfer payments to persons	Less: Personal contribu- tions for social insurance	Personal tax and nontax payments	Disposable personal income
1977:												
January	1 533.8	939.3	87.9	19.0	124.0	23.9	37.8	144.9	215.9	58.7	196.6	1 337.2
February	1 550.8	950.5	89.2	18.9	124.7	23.8	38.3	146.9	217.8	59.3	216.3	1 334.5
March	1 565.4	959.5	90.4	18.4	125.7	23.7	38.7	148.8	219.9	59.7	204.1	1 361.3
April	1 577.3	969.8	91.3	16.3	127.3	22.1	38.8	150.3	221.5	60.2	205.2	1 372.2
May	1 590.1	981.5	92.6	15.5	128.4	23.0	38.4	152.2	219.3	60.7	208.5	1 381.5
June	1 600.8	990.6	93.8	15.0	127.7	22.7	39.3	154.1	218.6	61.1	205.5	1 395.3
July	1 620.5	999.5	95.3	14.5	131.1	22.4	39.9	155.9	223.5	61.6	207.1	1 413.3
August	1 634.2	1 005.4	96.6	14.7	131.9	22.2	40.1	158.1	227.1	61.8	208.6	1 425.6
September	1 650.3	1 016.8	98.0	16.1	131.8	22.2	40.3	160.4	227.0	62.3	211.7	1 438.6
October	1 669.6	1 030.5	99.2	19.0	131.9	22.2	40.5	163.2	226.0	62.9	216.4	1 453.2
November	1 692.7	1 038.5	100.5	21.0	135.6	22.4	40.9	165.7	231.4	63.2	219.0	1 473.6
December	1 707.9	1 044.7	101.9	21.7	138.9	22.8	41.3	168.2	231.9	63.4	221.3	1 486.6
1978:												
January	1 714.5	1 051.5	103.2	21.3	136.2	23.7	41.7	170.6	232.9	66.7	223.0	1 491.4
February	1 731.8	1 062.2	104.5	21.0	138.4	24.0	41.8	173.1	233.8	67.1	222.7	1 509.1
March	1 756.0	1 078.1	105.9	21.2	141.1	24.0	42.1	175.6	235.7	67.8	221.1	1 534.9
April	1 782.2	1 096.4	107.3	22.8	145.5	23.1	42.5	178.2	234.9	68.6	227.6	1 554.6
May	1 799.3	1 104.0	108.6	23.6	147.2	23.3	42.8	180.7	238.0	68.9	232.3	1 567.1
June	1 818.3	1 118.2	109.8	23.9	148.8	23.7	43.5	183.1	236.8	69.6	240.4	1 577.9
July	1 837.1	1 128.2	111.0	23.7	145.7	25.0	44.1	185.3	244.4	70.2	243.8	1 593.3
August	1 854.9	1 136.3	112.1	23.1	148.8	25.6	45.2	187.8	246.5	70.5	246.7	1 608.2
September	1 870.3	1 147.5	113.2	22.6	149.3	26.0	46.0	190.5	246.2	71.0	250.0	1 620.3
October	1 897.5	1 164.8	114.2	19.9	156.8	25.9	46.6	192.9	248.2	71.8	254.5	1 642.9
November	1 914.0	1 174.9	115.3	20.8	155.1	26.3	47.3	196.1	250.6	72.3	257.8	1 656.2
December	1 934.7	1 187.5	116.5	22.1	155.4	26.8	48.0	199.7	251.7	72.9	261.6	1 673.1
1979:												
January	1 953.0	1 198.1	117.8	26.6	151.7	28.5	48.2	204.5	255.7	78.1	261.9	1 691.0
February	1 970.6	1 208.7	118.9	27.6	153.7	28.6	48.7	208.2	254.7	78.6	264.2	1 706.4
March	1 994.1	1 223.3	120.1	27.8	155.8	28.3	49.0	211.6	257.6	79.4	267.6	1 726.5
April	2 000.0	1 225.1	121.1	24.7	158.3	24.6	49.4	214.3	262.0	79.6	268.4	1 731.6
May	2 018.0	1 236.0	122.3	24.7	159.5	25.6	50.0	217.4	262.5	80.0	272.3	1 745.7
June	2 035.4	1 250.2	123.5	24.8	160.5	25.2	50.3	220.5	261.0	80.7	278.1	1 757.3
July	2 066.6	1 261.3	124.8	26.0	161.3	25.0	50.5	222.7	276.4	81.3	282.8	1 783.8
August	2 085.3	1 269.5	126.0	25.7	164.6	25.3	50.6	226.5	278.7	81.7	285.7	1 799.6
September	2 100.8	1 282.0	127.3	25.3	163.1	23.3	51.2	230.9	280.1	82.3	289.7	1 811.1
October	2 125.1	1 292.7	128.5	25.3	161.9	28.0	51.8	236.0	283.6	82.8	293.3	1 831.8
November	2 147.7	1 305.3	129.9	23.9	162.0	29.3	52.5	241.7	286.3	83.3	297.0	1 850.7
December	2 173.5	1 318.8	131.3	21.6	164.2	30.7	53.3	248.1	289.5	84.0	301.0	1 872.5
1980:												
January	2 203.4	1 326.6	133.0	17.9	168.6	33.5	55.2	257.7	297.6	86.7	293.3	1 910.1
February	2 216.7	1 338.2	134.3	14.3	165.7	33.9	55.4	263.5	298.3	86.9	296.5	1 920.2
March	2 228.4	1 350.7	135.6	10.5	161.3	35.3	56.3	267.9	297.5	86.9	300.6	1 927.8
April	2 225.1	1 349.7	136.7	2.4	158.7	35.4	56.7	270.7	301.1	86.4	301.9	1 923.2
May	2 232.1	1 353.4	137.9	0.8	157.4	33.9	57.0	272.9	305.4	86.7	304.7	1 927.4
June	2 249.4	1 361.3	139.1	1.8	159.3	34.4	57.6	274.0	309.2	87.3	308.1	1 941.3
July	2 284.9	1 364.4	140.2	9.1	162.5	33.1	57.7	270.2	335.8	88.0	310.6	1 974.4
August	2 307.0	1 381.9	141.4	12.4	163.3	30.9	58.0	272.2	336.0	89.2	316.1	1 990.9
September	2 338.0	1 395.2	142.8	15.4	166.8	30.0	58.2	276.1	343.3	89.8	320.5	2 017.5
October	2 380.3	1 420.3	144.4	19.1	169.7	31.5	58.5	284.2	343.6	91.1	327.2	2 053.0
November	2 409.9	1 439.0	145.7	21.0	168.7	36.0	59.0	290.2	342.2	91.9	332.7	2 077.2
December	2 440.4	1 451.2	146.9	21.7	170.4	39.0	59.9	296.5	347.3	92.5	336.9	2 103.5
1981:												
January	2 464.2	1 465.8	148.1	20.4	174.0	43.9	61.0	304.2	348.2	101.4	340.6	2 123.6
February	2 481.7	1 473.5	149.0	20.4	173.5	43.8	62.4	309.9	350.9	101.8	344.0	2 137.7
March	2 504.9	1 485.1	149.9	20.4	174.4	43.6	63.6	314.9	355.4	102.4	348.5	2 156.4
April	2 503.4	1 494.0	150.3	19.7	164.1	42.8	65.2	315.4	354.9	102.9	352.1	2 151.3
May	2 519.7	1 501.1	151.1	20.6	162.2	42.7	66.6	321.8	356.9	103.3	357.4	2 162.3
June	2 543.0	1 512.4	152.1	22.1	160.8	42.8	67.9	330.4	358.4	103.9	361.1	2 181.9
July	2 599.2	1 522.8	153.3	27.5	164.7	43.2	69.5	348.0	375.2	104.9	367.0	2 232.2
August	2 625.3	1 538.0	154.4	27.9	165.4	43.8	69.8	355.9	375.9	105.7	372.8	2 252.5
September	2 637.8	1 544.3	155.5	26.8	164.9	44.7	70.3	361.0	376.5	106.1	375.4	2 262.4
October	2 639.7	1 554.3	156.5	20.9	162.2	46.8	70.3	358.6	376.8	106.8	364.1	2 275.6
November	2 652.0	1 560.5	157.6	18.6	162.5	47.6	70.2	361.3	380.8	107.2	368.3	2 283.7
December	2 651.1	1 559.1	158.7	16.9	160.0	48.1	69.7	364.5	381.3	107.1	371.4	2 279.7
1982:												
January	2 646.4	1 567.6	159.9	16.6	150.5	47.1	64.9	368.1	382.4	110.6	366.1	2 280.3
February	2 662.9	1 576.2	161.0	15.6	151.9	46.7	63.9	372.4	386.4	111.1	372.5	2 290.5
March	2 671.5	1 577.1	162.1	14.9	152.8	46.1	63.5	377.3	389.0	111.2	371.9	2 299.6
April	2 702.9	1 577.8	163.2	14.3	166.6	45.7	62.9	387.5	396.1	111.2	366.6	2 336.3
May	2 721.6	1 590.5	164.2	14.0	169.2	45.3	62.6	390.1	397.7	112.1	378.3	2 343.3
June	2 727.6	1 593.5	165.2	13.6	168.4	45.5	62.4	389.8	401.4	112.3	384.6	2 343.1
July	2 733.7	1 601.0	166.2	14.0	162.3	45.5	62.6	382.0	413.0	113.0	365.1	2 368.6
August	2 739.4	1 604.2	167.1	13.2	164.6	46.2	62.9	379.4	414.8	113.1	367.6	2 371.8
September	2 744.1	1 602.2	167.9	12.5	166.9	46.8	63.4	377.4	419.9	112.9	367.8	2 376.3
October	2 764.7	1 606.8	168.5	13.9	174.4	49.4	64.3	375.7	424.9	113.1	369.9	2 394.8
November	2 781.5	1 609.9	169.2	15.6	175.9	48.5	65.4	375.1	435.3	113.2	371.7	2 409.8
December	2 793.0	1 620.3	169.8	15.2	177.9	45.2	66.4	375.3	436.4	113.7	374.7	2 418.3

1. Includes inventory valuation and capital consumption adjustments.
2. Includes capital consumption adjustment.

Personal Income and its Disposition—*Continued*

(Billions of dollars, seasonally adjusted annual rate)

Year and month	Personal income	Sources of personal income									Disposition of personal income	
		Wage and salary disburse-ments	Other labor income	Proprietors' income [1]		Rental income of persons [2]	Personal dividend income	Personal interest income	Transfer payments to persons	Less: Personal contribu-tions for social insurance	Personal tax and nontax payments	Disposable personal income
				Farm	Nonfarm							
1983:												
January	2 791.1	1 629.3	169.8	9.9	177.0	46.7	67.1	376.1	432.1	116.9	365.0	2 426.2
February	2 795.5	1 624.7	170.8	15.0	174.0	46.2	68.1	378.3	434.8	116.5	366.6	2 428.9
March	2 814.5	1 635.6	172.3	15.2	172.9	45.9	68.8	381.7	439.2	117.0	368.8	2 445.8
April	2 838.7	1 647.9	175.3	9.4	182.5	45.9	69.3	386.5	439.6	117.6	367.4	2 471.3
May	2 868.2	1 666.6	176.9	7.0	183.9	45.9	70.2	391.8	444.7	118.7	378.5	2 489.8
June	2 880.2	1 675.4	178.2	2.9	185.6	46.0	70.6	397.9	442.9	119.1	382.0	2 498.2
July	2 902.7	1 690.9	178.9	-2.4	192.6	46.3	71.5	406.4	438.4	119.9	360.3	2 542.4
August	2 904.5	1 697.3	179.7	-5.7	190.5	39.6	72.2	412.8	438.3	120.3	362.6	2 541.9
September	2 937.8	1 710.6	180.4	-4.5	196.5	47.0	72.8	418.8	437.1	121.0	365.0	2 572.8
October	2 970.3	1 738.7	180.6	-4.7	196.4	47.8	73.4	424.7	436.1	122.6	369.7	2 600.6
November	2 998.8	1 745.7	181.3	0.4	199.1	48.1	73.8	429.6	443.9	123.0	371.2	2 627.7
December	3 030.4	1 760.6	182.2	6.9	202.4	48.2	74.0	433.8	446.1	123.8	374.4	2 656.0
1984:												
January	3 060.3	1 781.5	183.5	16.0	204.2	48.4	74.1	434.4	446.8	128.6	375.3	2 685.0
February	3 099.5	1 793.8	184.5	22.7	218.1	48.2	75.1	439.4	447.1	129.3	379.4	2 720.1
March	3 129.3	1 806.4	185.4	26.4	221.9	47.7	75.8	446.0	449.7	130.1	381.4	2 747.9
April	3 163.9	1 828.8	186.4	24.1	226.4	45.8	76.1	455.8	451.9	131.4	383.6	2 780.4
May	3 174.9	1 833.2	187.3	23.4	225.2	45.8	75.8	464.1	451.6	131.6	386.9	2 788.0
June	3 206.7	1 851.7	188.2	23.9	228.0	46.5	75.6	472.6	452.9	132.7	392.8	2 814.0
July	3 231.0	1 866.8	188.6	22.6	224.6	48.6	75.2	484.7	453.3	133.5	398.0	2 833.1
August	3 263.3	1 874.2	189.7	22.5	238.0	50.2	74.7	491.0	456.7	133.9	400.9	2 862.4
September	3 293.8	1 891.9	190.9	22.8	244.8	51.9	75.4	495.0	455.9	134.8	406.0	2 887.7
October	3 282.4	1 894.1	192.7	23.9	222.8	54.4	75.6	493.9	459.9	134.9	408.2	2 874.2
November	3 307.8	1 910.3	194.2	24.5	224.9	56.8	75.7	495.1	461.9	135.6	413.7	2 894.1
December	3 323.6	1 928.0	195.6	25.0	227.6	56.6	75.9	496.0	455.4	136.5	419.6	2 903.9
1985:												
January	3 353.0	1 933.3	197.1	26.1	240.0	53.5	77.4	494.8	476.0	145.1	419.3	2 933.7
February	3 370.3	1 942.6	198.3	26.1	243.7	52.3	77.7	496.2	479.1	145.6	452.1	2 918.2
March	3 394.9	1 963.5	199.4	25.5	244.0	51.1	78.2	498.4	481.6	146.8	482.2	2 912.7
April	3 397.7	1 964.9	200.0	23.6	242.4	49.4	78.5	503.4	482.4	146.9	425.8	2 971.9
May	3 409.4	1 974.7	201.1	22.8	242.1	48.6	79.0	505.8	482.8	147.5	359.0	3 050.4
June	3 430.0	1 993.0	202.3	22.2	242.1	48.3	79.5	507.6	483.7	148.6	438.6	2 991.4
July	3 442.5	1 994.4	203.7	21.4	244.7	49.3	79.8	506.6	491.4	148.8	438.8	3 003.7
August	3 455.6	2 008.7	204.9	21.3	244.9	49.3	79.9	508.8	487.6	149.8	442.2	3 013.4
September	3 469.7	2 025.1	206.0	21.8	245.3	39.7	80.1	512.2	490.5	150.9	445.5	3 024.1
October	3 503.5	2 036.1	207.2	24.2	250.1	47.9	80.4	516.9	492.4	151.7	447.0	3 056.6
November	3 512.7	2 045.1	208.1	24.3	250.3	39.7	81.0	522.1	494.5	152.4	448.6	3 064.1
December	3 551.1	2 069.3	208.9	23.6	250.3	47.7	80.9	527.9	496.5	154.1	452.8	3 098.3
1986:												
January	3 565.1	2 067.4	209.0	20.8	251.9	47.1	82.8	538.4	505.9	158.1	446.1	3 119.0
February	3 578.3	2 075.5	209.8	20.0	251.3	46.4	84.3	542.9	507.1	158.9	447.4	3 130.9
March	3 600.6	2 091.5	210.7	19.6	252.1	45.6	85.2	545.3	510.8	160.2	448.3	3 152.3
April	3 599.0	2 087.1	211.9	19.3	255.3	44.9	86.0	542.4	512.1	160.1	447.7	3 151.3
May	3 610.8	2 094.5	213.2	20.2	255.0	43.8	86.5	543.0	515.4	160.7	450.0	3 160.8
June	3 627.2	2 105.4	214.6	21.9	255.4	42.6	87.1	543.8	517.9	161.5	456.0	3 171.2
July	3 649.5	2 113.9	216.3	26.7	255.1	40.6	87.1	546.4	525.5	162.2	458.0	3 191.5
August	3 664.2	2 128.1	217.9	28.4	258.1	39.3	87.2	546.6	521.7	163.1	462.7	3 201.6
September	3 679.9	2 135.0	219.5	29.3	264.0	38.2	87.4	545.9	524.2	163.6	465.9	3 214.0
October	3 682.7	2 153.8	221.2	27.8	252.6	36.1	87.4	542.4	526.2	164.8	471.1	3 211.6
November	3 697.1	2 169.5	222.9	27.9	251.3	35.1	87.5	541.3	527.1	165.7	477.6	3 219.5
December	3 720.7	2 176.9	224.7	28.2	261.2	38.1	87.2	540.8	529.7	166.1	488.1	3 232.5
1987:												
January	3 743.4	2 192.2	226.5	27.8	264.2	40.7	88.5	539.8	533.0	169.3	474.3	3 269.1
February	3 774.2	2 210.6	228.3	29.8	268.4	42.7	87.9	540.9	535.8	170.2	471.3	3 302.9
March	3 795.7	2 226.0	230.1	30.5	268.7	43.8	87.7	543.1	536.9	171.0	478.4	3 317.3
April	3 808.8	2 231.4	232.4	32.2	268.6	41.1	87.5	548.0	539.0	171.4	608.3	3 200.6
May	3 842.1	2 250.1	233.8	31.6	271.6	41.2	88.5	551.6	546.2	172.5	499.5	3 342.6
June	3 855.1	2 259.2	234.8	30.9	273.1	42.3	89.0	555.2	543.4	172.9	502.5	3 352.6
July	3 867.9	2 267.2	234.1	31.2	275.3	41.0	89.8	557.5	545.3	173.5	507.3	3 360.7
August	3 903.8	2 294.0	235.5	31.5	276.6	43.0	90.6	562.4	545.3	175.0	515.1	3 388.7
September	3 923.4	2 299.9	237.5	31.9	277.7	44.9	91.6	568.5	546.7	175.2	519.5	3 403.9
October	3 972.8	2 323.3	242.0	32.5	278.1	50.8	92.7	580.8	548.9	176.3	523.4	3 449.3
November	3 998.8	2 340.4	244.1	32.6	278.9	52.3	93.9	585.4	548.6	177.3	528.6	3 470.2
December	4 047.6	2 377.9	245.4	35.9	281.4	53.6	94.6	587.3	550.8	179.4	541.9	3 505.7
1988:												
January	4 045.6	2 364.7	244.9	37.9	287.7	52.1	97.6	583.1	566.2	188.7	518.0	3 527.6
February	4 070.1	2 382.4	245.8	39.1	291.1	52.6	98.3	582.3	568.3	189.7	509.1	3 561.0
March	4 095.2	2 395.6	246.9	39.6	294.8	52.5	99.0	581.5	575.8	190.4	517.8	3 577.4
April	4 123.8	2 421.4	248.4	34.5	305.5	54.5	100.1	577.3	574.0	191.9	551.5	3 572.4
May	4 136.5	2 433.4	249.7	29.7	307.8	54.1	101.2	579.0	574.2	192.6	529.8	3 606.7
June	4 163.6	2 452.3	250.9	27.5	311.9	54.0	102.5	583.3	575.0	193.8	524.0	3 639.6
July	4 194.7	2 471.1	251.9	30.5	309.7	51.4	104.1	593.6	577.6	195.2	529.6	3 665.1
August	4 210.5	2 471.6	253.2	29.3	313.0	51.9	106.2	600.3	580.2	195.2	531.4	3 679.1
September	4 234.4	2 486.2	254.7	24.0	315.2	54.9	107.8	606.9	581.0	196.2	536.0	3 698.4
October	4 269.2	2 517.8	256.4	12.2	317.3	58.9	109.8	611.1	584.0	198.3	542.9	3 726.3
November	4 281.7	2 515.2	258.0	9.0	318.8	62.1	111.4	619.1	586.4	198.3	544.3	3 737.3
December	4 321.1	2 531.3	259.7	16.4	321.1	62.5	112.1	628.9	588.8	199.6	549.7	3 771.3

1. Includes inventory valuation and capital consumption adjustments.
2. Includes capital consumption adjustment.

Personal Income and its Disposition—*Continued*

(Billions of dollars, seasonally adjusted annual rate)

Year and month	Personal income	Wage and salary disbursements	Other labor income	Proprietors' income [1] Farm	Nonfarm	Rental income of persons [2]	Personal dividend income	Personal interest income	Transfer payments to persons	Less: Personal contributions for social insurance	Personal tax and nontax payments	Disposable personal income
1989:												
January	4 382.1	2 552.2	261.3	29.9	323.5	58.1	116.9	643.4	604.1	207.3	580.8	3 801.3
February	4 407.6	2 550.3	263.1	41.9	322.3	57.1	119.0	653.9	607.2	207.3	571.0	3 836.6
March	4 448.3	2 565.4	265.2	45.3	322.9	56.0	121.2	663.7	617.2	208.5	581.4	3 866.9
April	4 469.4	2 581.3	267.5	39.3	319.3	58.2	123.2	675.3	615.0	209.6	618.5	3 850.9
May	4 468.6	2 570.5	269.7	38.6	317.8	56.8	124.7	681.4	618.0	209.0	596.0	3 872.6
June	4 488.3	2 582.6	271.9	37.3	317.1	55.5	126.3	684.8	622.5	209.9	587.6	3 900.7
July	4 505.8	2 604.9	274.2	33.9	316.2	51.6	128.1	682.1	626.3	211.4	592.2	3 913.6
August	4 513.8	2 601.2	276.5	32.9	321.3	50.7	129.2	682.4	630.9	211.2	593.7	3 920.1
September	4 523.4	2 615.1	278.7	32.6	320.0	40.9	130.2	682.4	635.5	212.1	598.0	3 925.4
October	4 554.1	2 646.9	280.6	34.1	320.4	33.4	131.7	680.4	640.7	214.2	604.2	3 949.9
November	4 587.7	2 647.3	283.0	34.6	325.5	50.5	132.8	681.2	647.0	214.2	605.5	3 982.2
December	4 607.7	2 659.7	285.6	34.9	327.3	51.8	132.4	683.1	647.7	214.8	609.3	3 998.4
1990:												
January	4 661.6	2 678.4	288.9	36.9	333.6	54.1	135.0	687.4	668.8	221.5	607.7	4 053.9
February	4 698.0	2 707.8	291.5	33.4	332.3	55.2	136.2	690.6	670.4	219.4	613.6	4 084.4
March	4 723.9	2 725.7	293.8	36.2	330.6	56.2	137.2	693.9	672.4	222.1	617.5	4 106.3
April	4 764.6	2 748.8	295.7	38.3	335.9	56.3	138.2	697.5	674.1	220.3	624.4	4 140.2
May	4 767.3	2 744.4	297.8	38.5	337.5	57.5	135.3	701.0	676.8	221.6	627.9	4 139.4
June	4 799.4	2 765.7	299.9	38.1	338.0	59.0	135.9	704.6	683.3	225.0	632.4	4 167.0
July	4 829.2	2 782.4	302.1	35.8	341.4	62.6	135.4	709.3	686.0	225.9	631.4	4 197.8
August	4 833.4	2 775.7	304.0	34.8	344.5	64.4	134.7	711.9	688.6	225.4	629.5	4 203.9
September	4 864.5	2 795.2	305.9	34.1	345.1	66.0	134.1	713.7	697.1	226.5	631.6	4 232.9
October	4 858.2	2 780.0	307.8	34.4	341.2	66.1	133.2	715.0	706.2	225.7	627.1	4 231.1
November	4 865.2	2 782.8	309.3	33.3	341.9	66.9	132.3	714.6	710.0	226.0	625.6	4 239.6
December	4 889.2	2 803.0	310.6	31.6	340.8	67.1	130.9	712.9	719.9	227.6	628.7	4 260.5
1991:												
January	4 878.2	2 788.9	310.7	27.7	333.6	66.7	134.8	707.5	741.2	232.9	625.3	4 252.9
February	4 882.5	2 787.6	312.2	25.0	336.3	66.3	137.4	705.2	745.5	232.9	621.6	4 260.9
March	4 896.5	2 791.6	314.2	26.8	338.0	66.1	137.0	703.5	752.5	233.1	620.1	4 276.5
April	4 922.8	2 799.0	317.4	32.0	342.4	65.9	137.3	703.6	758.8	233.5	619.9	4 302.9
May	4 945.1	2 809.1	319.7	34.8	345.5	66.0	138.3	702.3	763.6	234.1	619.1	4 326.0
June	4 977.7	2 837.3	322.0	33.3	348.2	66.2	138.8	700.8	767.3	236.1	622.6	4 355.0
July	4 965.8	2 825.2	324.1	28.0	350.9	65.8	139.3	698.7	769.8	236.0	620.7	4 345.1
August	4 982.4	2 835.9	326.3	27.0	351.2	66.8	139.2	697.0	775.7	236.7	622.8	4 359.6
September	5 007.9	2 855.3	328.4	26.9	352.8	68.6	139.1	695.4	779.3	237.9	627.5	4 380.4
October	5 011.7	2 848.5	330.1	27.6	352.1	66.8	138.2	695.9	790.5	237.8	629.7	4 382.0
November	5 034.6	2 862.2	332.4	30.9	354.8	74.1	137.1	692.8	788.8	238.4	631.0	4 403.6
December	5 082.5	2 890.7	334.9	31.5	360.4	75.9	135.4	688.3	805.9	240.5	636.9	4 445.6
1992:												
January	5 109.9	2 889.3	338.2	34.6	372.8	76.4	133.5	677.7	830.9	243.4	634.7	4 475.2
February	5 155.6	2 925.3	340.8	37.5	374.3	77.2	132.7	673.5	840.1	245.8	642.1	4 513.5
March	5 168.7	2 934.9	343.3	35.4	375.9	78.0	132.3	671.2	844.0	246.4	633.3	4 535.4
April	5 194.1	2 942.2	345.1	34.6	382.4	78.3	132.9	674.9	850.3	246.5	637.5	4 556.6
May	5 218.6	2 959.0	347.5	36.0	383.6	79.4	133.7	673.4	853.6	247.6	640.2	4 578.4
June	5 238.3	2 967.5	350.1	40.6	385.4	80.7	135.0	670.6	856.5	248.1	642.3	4 596.0
July	5 249.5	2 974.3	353.6	40.0	387.3	82.3	136.6	663.5	860.8	248.8	646.5	4 603.1
August	5 236.6	2 996.5	356.0	39.1	387.0	45.2	138.7	660.8	863.6	250.2	652.2	4 584.4
September	5 280.4	2 993.7	358.0	37.8	388.5	81.1	140.4	659.3	871.6	250.0	653.3	4 627.1
October	5 325.0	3 010.5	358.4	37.8	399.9	88.6	143.0	660.7	877.5	251.4	658.9	4 666.1
November	5 349.1	3 032.7	360.8	36.6	403.5	91.0	145.8	660.4	870.8	252.5	663.7	4 685.4
December	5 542.0	3 210.9	363.9	35.0	399.6	94.1	149.7	660.0	879.2	250.4	701.9	4 840.1
1993:												
January	5 329.0	2 975.2	371.3	30.0	409.5	99.5	139.4	661.3	897.6	254.9	661.0	4 668.0
February	5 337.7	2 979.4	374.4	29.2	412.3	102.3	140.5	660.4	894.7	255.6	663.1	4 674.5
March	5 329.6	2 971.7	375.7	29.9	410.0	97.4	141.5	659.3	899.4	255.2	663.2	4 666.4
April	5 445.5	3 064.6	379.2	36.1	413.9	104.6	142.7	656.3	906.3	258.1	682.2	4 763.3
May	5 480.3	3 091.9	383.9	37.5	417.9	105.6	144.1	653.3	906.2	260.1	687.8	4 792.5
June	5 472.5	3 081.5	383.8	35.2	416.1	106.6	145.7	651.3	911.7	259.5	686.7	4 785.7
July	5 479.3	3 097.5	386.9	26.8	417.7	100.6	147.4	649.8	913.2	260.6	691.2	4 788.1
August	5 518.4	3 119.4	390.6	23.4	422.9	108.3	149.2	647.7	918.9	262.1	697.0	4 821.4
September	5 519.5	3 116.3	390.9	26.6	421.3	109.5	151.1	645.9	919.8	262.0	698.3	4 821.2
October	5 541.4	3 130.0	393.3	32.2	423.3	107.6	153.1	644.2	921.9	263.1	702.8	4 838.7
November	5 564.8	3 137.7	394.6	39.0	426.8	111.8	154.8	641.0	922.9	263.8	705.9	4 858.9
December	5 754.5	3 310.1	396.7	42.7	430.3	115.0	155.9	641.1	931.2	268.7	740.5	5 014.0
1994:												
January	5 529.1	3 138.4	399.8	46.5	389.8	93.6	157.2	639.5	936.3	272.0	711.8	4 817.4
February	5 595.1	3 128.5	398.3	47.9	430.5	120.7	158.9	640.8	941.0	271.4	711.0	4 884.1
March	5 625.8	3 148.0	400.4	44.8	432.4	124.0	161.2	643.9	943.9	272.7	715.8	4 910.0
April	5 707.1	3 214.5	402.2	41.1	434.9	124.5	164.3	651.0	949.6	275.0	780.6	4 926.4
May	5 743.1	3 241.8	405.0	38.8	436.5	126.0	166.8	656.3	948.8	276.8	735.7	5 007.5
June	5 749.2	3 239.7	403.9	36.7	436.3	127.5	169.2	661.9	951.0	276.9	735.2	5 014.0
July	5 777.7	3 256.6	406.8	34.9	435.6	127.9	171.8	666.9	955.3	278.1	737.5	5 040.2
August	5 800.2	3 262.2	406.4	33.2	438.8	130.2	174.4	673.8	959.9	278.5	738.8	5 061.4
September	5 834.3	3 281.9	407.5	31.6	440.8	132.1	177.5	681.6	961.1	279.8	743.2	5 091.1
October	5 894.2	3 319.6	411.0	31.2	444.3	129.8	180.7	693.5	966.6	282.4	751.6	5 142.6
November	5 902.7	3 318.6	409.1	29.3	446.5	128.9	184.0	700.9	967.9	282.4	751.8	5 150.9
December	5 936.8	3 338.5	409.3	27.0	450.2	128.0	186.2	706.8	974.7	283.8	755.7	5 181.1

1. Includes inventory valuation and capital consumption adjustments.
2. Includes capital consumption adjustment.

Personal Income and its Disposition—*Continued*

(Billions of dollars, except as noted; seasonally adjusted annual rate)

Year and month	Personal outlays					Personal saving		Disposable personal income	Constant (1992) dollars			
	Total	Personal consumption expenditures				Billions of dollars	Percent of disposable personal income		Personal consumption expenditures			
		Total	Durable goods	Nondurable goods	Services				Total	Durable goods	Nondurable goods	Services
1971:												
January	696.9	678.5	92.1	280.6	305.8	68.1	8.9	2 529.2	2 243.4	196.5	872.9	1 174.4
February	700.3	681.8	91.9	281.0	308.9	67.0	8.7	2 529.4	2 247.6	195.3	873.0	1 181.4
March	703.0	684.4	94.2	279.2	311.0	70.0	9.1	2 539.3	2 248.4	200.1	865.2	1 183.3
April	710.0	691.2	94.9	282.7	313.7	67.9	8.7	2 544.7	2 261.3	200.9	872.6	1 187.6
May	712.5	693.7	94.2	283.2	316.3	71.2	9.1	2 553.5	2 260.2	199.2	870.9	1 191.7
June	721.3	702.4	97.5	286.4	318.5	82.6	10.3	2 607.4	2 278.0	205.5	876.9	1 193.6
July	720.6	701.4	95.5	284.9	321.0	73.6	9.3	2 567.8	2 267.8	201.0	871.3	1 196.6
August	726.8	707.5	96.6	287.2	323.7	73.6	9.2	2 579.3	2 280.0	204.6	874.4	1 200.5
September	735.2	715.7	101.3	288.0	326.5	67.9	8.4	2 584.8	2 303.7	216.3	874.9	1 206.9
October	738.3	718.6	101.5	288.0	329.1	66.4	8.2	2 584.6	2 308.4	216.7	873.6	1 213.1
November	743.6	723.8	101.5	291.3	331.0	64.6	8.0	2 591.2	2 320.4	216.6	882.5	1 216.2
December	751.2	731.2	101.6	293.6	336.0	65.8	8.0	2 608.4	2 334.6	216.0	886.1	1 229.1
1972:												
January	754.5	734.6	104.7	291.5	338.4	61.9	7.6	2 596.9	2 336.5	221.6	876.2	1 233.6
February	759.1	739.0	103.5	295.0	340.5	66.0	8.0	2 613.6	2 341.0	218.8	882.3	1 236.2
March	772.3	752.0	106.4	301.1	344.5	56.8	6.8	2 622.3	2 378.6	224.6	900.2	1 247.5
April	775.7	755.2	106.9	301.8	346.5	59.0	7.1	2 635.6	2 384.6	225.0	901.7	1 251.8
May	781.2	760.5	108.5	305.4	346.6	61.3	7.3	2 654.8	2 396.6	228.1	910.6	1 249.3
June	784.9	764.0	108.8	305.9	349.4	51.2	6.1	2 629.9	2 403.3	228.5	911.8	1 255.1
July	793.2	772.2	110.5	309.2	352.6	60.5	7.1	2 676.2	2 420.6	231.6	917.7	1 262.4
August	799.8	778.6	112.1	310.9	355.6	65.7	7.6	2 704.6	2 433.2	234.7	920.4	1 268.3
September	804.8	783.4	111.7	314.3	357.4	67.5	7.7	2 714.5	2 438.0	233.4	924.0	1 271.6
October	818.9	797.3	115.7	319.8	361.8	72.1	8.1	2 767.0	2 476.3	242.6	937.7	1 283.2
November	824.6	802.8	117.0	320.2	365.6	79.4	8.8	2 799.1	2 485.9	245.4	935.8	1 292.1
December	830.5	808.5	118.4	321.5	368.6	81.2	8.9	2 814.4	2 495.9	248.0	936.5	1 298.3
1973:												
January	840.9	818.8	122.9	326.9	369.0	72.8	8.0	2 812.2	2 519.9	257.3	946.1	1 298.4
February	850.4	828.0	125.2	331.3	371.5	76.3	8.2	2 836.7	2 534.5	261.5	950.4	1 302.8
March	857.5	834.8	127.6	332.8	374.4	79.8	8.5	2 848.1	2 536.7	266.2	942.9	1 306.9
April	860.4	837.4	125.4	334.6	377.4	84.3	8.9	2 849.5	2 525.9	260.6	938.6	1 309.2
May	866.4	843.1	126.1	336.3	380.7	87.4	9.2	2 864.3	2 531.8	261.4	936.8	1 316.8
June	869.4	845.8	120.9	340.1	384.8	92.4	9.6	2 871.0	2 524.8	250.3	940.1	1 323.4
July	879.6	855.8	123.0	346.7	386.1	86.8	9.0	2 875.2	2 546.3	254.1	956.1	1 321.3
August	879.1	855.1	121.7	345.0	388.5	96.5	9.9	2 872.9	2 518.2	251.0	933.7	1 322.4
September	895.5	871.4	126.7	351.2	393.6	90.5	9.2	2 891.4	2 555.2	261.3	946.3	1 332.3
October	896.0	870.3	122.3	352.9	395.1	107.2	10.7	2 923.5	2 536.3	251.9	941.3	1 332.2
November	904.9	879.1	121.9	359.1	398.1	109.6	10.8	2 933.0	2 541.4	250.4	945.1	1 335.8
December	904.9	879.0	119.0	360.3	399.7	115.0	11.3	2 924.0	2 520.1	244.1	937.5	1 331.1
1974:												
January	912.0	887.1	119.0	365.1	403.0	110.0	10.8	2 904.5	2 521.2	243.5	935.7	1 335.5
February	917.3	892.2	117.0	369.3	405.8	107.5	10.5	2 878.4	2 506.0	238.4	929.3	1 334.5
March	928.9	903.8	120.6	373.0	410.2	99.0	9.6	2 855.7	2 510.9	244.5	923.4	1 337.8
April	938.2	913.0	121.4	377.3	414.3	93.5	9.1	2 847.2	2 519.6	244.0	927.3	1 343.7
May	949.8	924.4	124.3	380.7	419.4	92.1	8.8	2 848.2	2 527.0	247.5	925.9	1 348.5
June	955.3	929.8	123.3	383.0	423.5	94.7	9.0	2 847.6	2 521.6	241.5	925.6	1 352.4
July	964.9	939.4	126.1	387.5	425.7	100.8	9.5	2 870.0	2 529.8	243.9	929.7	1 352.7
August	981.5	955.8	133.4	393.0	429.4	90.3	8.4	2 856.0	2 546.9	255.4	930.0	1 353.6
September	980.9	955.2	126.8	394.4	433.9	98.4	9.1	2 848.0	2 520.4	240.0	922.8	1 357.2
October	984.2	958.5	122.6	396.7	439.2	103.7	9.5	2 849.5	2 510.4	228.5	921.6	1 365.8
November	980.5	954.8	116.8	397.6	440.5	105.8	9.7	2 825.3	2 483.3	216.6	916.3	1 360.4
December	985.6	960.0	116.5	396.0	447.5	106.5	9.7	2 820.2	2 479.1	215.0	905.8	1 372.1
1975:												
January	998.6	973.0	121.0	402.1	450.0	97.4	8.9	2 815.2	2 499.3	223.0	915.6	1 369.7
February	1 012.5	986.8	126.2	404.7	456.0	89.4	8.1	2 816.5	2 522.3	231.0	919.0	1 379.3
March	1 013.9	988.3	122.5	406.3	459.5	91.9	8.3	2 817.4	2 518.1	222.2	922.8	1 383.7
April	1 018.7	993.4	123.8	405.4	464.2	112.8	10.0	2 871.5	2 521.0	222.4	919.3	1 391.5
May	1 043.0	1 017.7	129.6	419.5	468.7	161.3	13.4	3 043.6	2 572.1	232.8	948.5	1 396.0
June	1 051.2	1 025.9	131.4	421.6	472.9	117.6	10.1	2 934.5	2 575.8	235.4	947.1	1 398.0
July	1 064.5	1 038.9	136.2	424.8	477.8	96.8	8.3	2 890.9	2 585.9	243.1	943.9	1 401.6
August	1 071.6	1 046.1	136.5	429.3	480.3	103.4	8.8	2 911.4	2 591.5	242.3	948.6	1 403.1
September	1 079.8	1 053.9	141.1	429.0	483.8	105.9	8.9	2 922.9	2 598.0	249.2	946.2	1 402.8
October	1 085.6	1 059.6	139.2	429.7	490.8	113.1	9.4	2 938.1	2 597.2	244.4	941.7	1 415.4
November	1 100.8	1 074.6	144.1	436.2	494.2	105.9	8.8	2 938.7	2 617.1	252.0	951.9	1 413.0
December	1 117.4	1 091.0	149.9	439.2	502.0	97.8	8.0	2 942.4	2 641.8	259.7	954.9	1 425.5
1976:												
January	1 133.7	1 107.0	152.1	446.9	507.9	96.6	7.9	2 968.1	2 670.7	262.7	969.9	1 434.8
February	1 134.9	1 108.0	155.0	443.5	509.6	105.7	8.5	2 988.4	2 668.9	266.9	964.6	1 432.8
March	1 142.7	1 115.6	155.3	445.5	514.8	104.9	8.4	3 000.4	2 682.9	267.4	970.6	1 440.6
April	1 153.2	1 126.0	158.1	450.1	517.8	100.2	8.0	3 006.6	2 701.0	270.5	980.9	1 443.4
May	1 150.8	1 123.4	152.7	449.8	520.9	109.5	8.7	3 007.8	2 681.1	259.9	975.2	1 444.7
June	1 169.0	1 141.3	158.1	457.8	525.5	96.9	7.7	3 007.6	2 711.6	268.3	988.8	1 449.0
July	1 178.3	1 150.3	159.6	459.2	531.5	102.6	8.0	3 026.3	2 717.8	269.6	987.5	1 455.9
August	1 187.1	1 158.9	158.4	462.9	537.6	103.1	8.0	3 030.7	2 722.4	267.2	991.0	1 460.6
September	1 198.6	1 170.1	160.8	465.3	544.0	99.3	7.6	3 031.4	2 733.1	269.3	991.6	1 468.7
October	1 207.7	1 179.0	160.7	469.9	548.4	95.4	7.3	3 026.4	2 738.0	266.2	997.5	1 472.0
November	1 220.5	1 191.6	163.1	470.5	557.9	101.1	7.6	3 054.5	2 753.9	270.0	995.2	1 487.0
December	1 243.7	1 214.4	172.1	476.7	565.6	89.3	6.7	3 063.0	2 790.5	284.0	1 004.6	1 495.2

Personal Income and its Disposition—*Continued*

(Billions of dollars, except as noted; seasonally adjusted annual rate)

Year and month	Personal outlays					Personal saving		Constant (1992) dollars				
	Total	Personal consumption expenditures				Billions of dollars	Percent of disposable personal income	Disposable personal income	Personal consumption expenditures			
		Total	Durable goods	Nondurable goods	Services				Total	Durable goods	Nondurable goods	Services
1977:												
January	1 247.4	1 217.6	167.9	479.5	570.2	89.8	6.7	3 056.1	2 782.8	275.2	1 005.5	1 499.1
February	1 263.8	1 233.8	173.6	486.4	573.8	70.7	5.3	3 027.3	2 798.9	285.0	1 008.5	1 498.2
March	1 271.2	1 240.8	179.4	485.2	576.3	90.1	6.6	3 073.3	2 801.3	293.9	1 002.6	1 494.3
April	1 280.8	1 250.0	178.3	489.9	581.7	91.4	6.7	3 079.9	2 805.6	292.3	1 006.4	1 497.1
May	1 291.5	1 260.3	178.1	493.6	588.6	90.1	6.5	3 083.8	2 813.1	290.9	1 008.0	1 505.9
June	1 298.5	1 266.9	179.7	492.6	594.6	96.8	6.9	3 097.3	2 812.2	292.6	1 000.7	1 511.3
July	1 315.5	1 283.6	181.0	498.8	603.9	97.8	6.9	3 120.4	2 834.0	293.2	1 009.8	1 524.0
August	1 321.5	1 289.1	183.2	497.5	608.4	104.2	7.3	3 133.6	2 833.6	296.1	1 003.9	1 526.2
September	1 331.0	1 298.2	184.9	499.2	614.0	107.7	7.5	3 150.8	2 843.3	298.5	1 005.9	1 531.2
October	1 348.0	1 314.8	185.7	507.3	621.7	105.2	7.2	3 166.0	2 864.4	297.3	1 017.8	1 542.3
November	1 364.0	1 330.3	189.2	517.1	624.0	109.7	7.4	3 192.3	2 881.7	301.8	1 030.9	1 538.9
December	1 373.6	1 339.3	192.3	516.1	630.9	112.9	7.6	3 204.1	2 886.7	303.8	1 024.4	1 549.5
1978:												
January	1 368.5	1 333.3	180.1	514.9	638.3	122.9	8.2	3 194.5	2 855.8	284.3	1 017.0	1 553.7
February	1 395.2	1 359.4	187.0	523.9	648.5	114.0	7.6	3 215.5	2 896.5	294.5	1 030.4	1 567.6
March	1 418.7	1 382.3	193.2	533.5	655.6	116.2	7.6	3 250.0	2 926.9	302.8	1 042.2	1 574.9
April	1 438.1	1 401.0	201.9	535.6	663.6	116.5	7.5	3 265.2	2 942.7	314.4	1 036.5	1 582.0
May	1 455.7	1 417.9	205.2	543.0	669.7	111.4	7.1	3 265.9	2 955.0	317.5	1 041.0	1 585.7
June	1 471.8	1 433.2	206.2	549.2	677.8	106.2	6.7	3 265.6	2 966.1	317.0	1 044.2	1 595.1
July	1 473.9	1 434.7	203.3	552.0	679.3	119.4	7.5	3 278.2	2 952.0	310.8	1 043.7	1 589.0
August	1 495.3	1 455.4	209.9	556.8	688.7	112.9	7.0	3 291.2	2 978.5	319.1	1 048.0	1 601.4
September	1 502.0	1 461.6	201.0	565.6	695.0	118.2	7.3	3 297.0	2 974.2	304.2	1 059.2	1 605.1
October	1 515.7	1 474.6	208.2	565.9	700.5	127.2	7.7	3 318.6	2 978.6	313.1	1 052.2	1 605.4
November	1 529.1	1 487.3	209.7	575.1	702.6	127.1	7.7	3 327.3	2 988.1	313.4	1 062.5	1 602.8
December	1 546.7	1 504.2	211.6	583.6	709.0	126.4	7.6	3 342.5	3 005.2	314.7	1 071.7	1 609.0
1979:												
January	1 555.6	1 512.9	208.4	585.1	719.4	135.4	8.0	3 349.8	2 996.9	308.7	1 062.7	1 619.9
February	1 574.3	1 531.1	212.0	592.4	726.6	132.1	7.7	3 357.1	3 012.2	311.7	1 065.6	1 629.3
March	1 587.7	1 543.9	213.0	602.8	728.2	138.8	8.0	3 371.8	3 015.2	311.2	1 071.7	1 625.8
April	1 591.5	1 547.2	210.6	599.0	737.6	140.0	8.1	3 354.4	2 997.3	305.4	1 054.1	1 636.2
May	1 609.2	1 564.3	212.2	608.9	743.2	136.5	7.8	3 351.4	3 003.1	306.8	1 059.3	1 634.3
June	1 625.7	1 580.3	206.9	622.4	751.0	131.6	7.5	3 347.2	3 010.1	298.3	1 071.4	1 639.9
July	1 637.5	1 591.4	213.5	622.5	755.3	146.3	8.2	3 367.4	3 004.2	306.1	1 058.8	1 637.2
August	1 667.6	1 620.8	218.8	637.3	764.7	132.1	7.3	3 372.2	3 037.1	312.6	1 075.0	1 644.6
September	1 687.3	1 639.9	222.9	646.0	771.0	123.8	6.8	3 362.8	3 044.9	316.9	1 078.5	1 642.6
October	1 697.1	1 648.8	215.8	648.8	784.1	134.7	7.4	3 373.9	3 036.9	304.8	1 075.1	1 655.9
November	1 714.7	1 665.7	216.1	659.8	789.8	136.1	7.4	3 384.7	3 046.3	303.0	1 085.1	1 656.6
December	1 725.4	1 676.0	217.0	662.7	796.3	147.1	7.9	3 393.6	3 037.5	302.0	1 078.9	1 655.9
1980:												
January	1 758.7	1 708.6	226.9	675.2	806.5	151.4	7.9	3 423.6	3 062.4	312.6	1 082.7	1 663.7
February	1 762.9	1 712.5	220.3	677.9	814.3	157.2	8.2	3 405.4	3 037.0	300.2	1 076.1	1 661.5
March	1 768.9	1 718.3	211.1	684.4	822.8	158.9	8.2	3 379.5	3 012.3	285.2	1 069.7	1 663.8
April	1 757.6	1 707.1	199.6	684.8	822.7	165.6	8.6	3 349.9	2 973.6	267.9	1 065.1	1 651.2
May	1 762.8	1 712.4	195.7	686.5	830.3	164.6	8.5	3 330.8	2 959.4	261.2	1 062.3	1 648.4
June	1 781.6	1 731.2	202.2	686.8	842.1	159.7	8.2	3 334.1	2 973.2	268.3	1 057.8	1 659.4
July	1 809.8	1 759.1	213.7	691.6	853.8	164.6	8.3	3 364.1	2 997.3	282.6	1 056.8	1 667.3
August	1 826.6	1 775.5	211.0	701.7	862.8	164.3	8.3	3 363.8	2 999.9	276.5	1 062.7	1 671.8
September	1 841.4	1 790.0	212.5	703.4	874.1	176.1	8.7	3 379.5	2 998.5	275.6	1 056.4	1 679.3
October	1 875.8	1 823.9	223.1	713.1	887.8	177.2	8.6	3 414.9	3 033.9	288.7	1 064.2	1 690.7
November	1 883.8	1 831.6	223.7	714.7	893.2	193.4	9.3	3 429.3	3 023.8	287.5	1 059.1	1 687.3
December	1 907.5	1 854.7	222.3	725.5	906.9	195.9	9.3	3 453.2	3 044.8	284.8	1 068.1	1 703.9
1981:												
January	1 929.9	1 873.5	226.6	740.3	906.6	193.8	9.1	3 453.1	3 046.4	289.2	1 079.6	1 684.7
February	1 945.8	1 888.9	233.9	744.8	910.1	191.9	9.0	3 440.8	3 040.3	297.0	1 071.0	1 677.2
March	1 966.2	1 908.5	237.3	750.1	921.1	190.3	8.8	3 446.1	3 050.0	301.0	1 069.4	1 684.4
April	1 968.2	1 909.8	228.1	754.0	927.7	183.1	8.5	3 422.6	3 038.3	286.6	1 074.0	1 686.3
May	1 978.5	1 919.5	226.3	753.2	939.9	183.8	8.5	3 423.5	3 039.1	282.0	1 072.3	1 696.1
June	2 000.6	1 941.2	227.8	759.3	954.1	181.2	8.3	3 439.4	3 060.0	282.3	1 079.3	1 710.5
July	2 009.9	1 949.8	231.6	759.1	959.1	222.3	10.0	3 494.9	3 052.6	285.8	1 073.8	1 704.0
August	2 036.1	1 975.5	246.9	763.0	965.6	216.4	9.6	3 502.5	3 071.5	303.1	1 074.9	1 699.4
September	2 038.6	1 976.9	236.6	765.4	974.9	223.8	9.9	3 492.9	3 052.1	289.3	1 074.7	1 698.9
October	2 036.5	1 974.2	223.9	767.7	982.7	239.1	10.5	3 498.7	3 035.4	272.8	1 074.7	1 701.8
November	2 042.5	1 980.0	223.7	766.9	989.3	241.2	10.6	3 491.6	3 027.2	271.2	1 070.9	1 699.4
December	2 060.2	1 997.6	223.2	773.9	1 000.5	219.5	9.6	3 473.1	3 043.4	269.7	1 078.3	1 710.6
1982:												
January	2 068.2	2 004.7	227.9	770.2	1 006.6	212.2	9.3	3 454.2	3 036.7	274.3	1 069.9	1 706.9
February	2 092.1	2 028.8	235.7	780.9	1 012.1	198.4	8.7	3 459.2	3 064.0	283.5	1 081.9	1 709.8
March	2 094.0	2 030.6	235.8	775.2	1 019.6	205.7	8.9	3 466.7	3 061.2	283.5	1 074.8	1 715.4
April	2 096.8	2 033.0	231.4	775.3	1 026.3	239.5	10.3	3 519.6	3 062.7	277.5	1 080.4	1 718.8
May	2 115.3	2 051.0	243.1	777.9	1 030.0	228.0	9.7	3 507.8	3 070.3	290.1	1 077.4	1 713.1
June	2 119.1	2 054.4	232.4	780.3	1 041.7	224.0	9.6	3 482.1	3 053.2	276.6	1 069.8	1 722.3
July	2 143.3	2 078.4	233.7	794.8	1 049.9	225.3	9.5	3 498.7	3 069.9	277.6	1 084.5	1 721.7
August	2 150.9	2 085.6	234.7	789.7	1 061.2	220.9	9.3	3 494.4	3 072.7	279.4	1 077.8	1 730.1
September	2 175.0	2 109.3	246.0	792.1	1 071.2	201.3	8.5	3 489.8	3 097.8	293.0	1 080.3	1 736.1
October	2 196.5	2 130.2	240.0	801.4	1 088.9	198.3	8.3	3 496.6	3 110.2	284.5	1 090.1	1 750.0
November	2 219.7	2 152.5	254.0	799.9	1 098.5	190.2	7.9	3 508.1	3 133.5	301.7	1 086.7	1 756.3
December	2 230.9	2 163.3	256.4	804.3	1 102.6	187.3	7.7	3 516.1	3 145.4	304.0	1 094.0	1 757.6

Personal Income and its Disposition—*Continued*

(Billions of dollars, except as noted; seasonally adjusted annual rate)

Year and month	Personal outlays					Personal saving		Constant (1992) dollars				
	Total	Personal consumption expenditures				Billions of dollars	Percent of disposable personal income	Disposable personal income	Personal consumption expenditures			
		Total	Durable goods	Nondurable goods	Services				Total	Durable goods	Nondurable goods	Services
1983:												
January	2 242.4	2 174.6	254.0	802.8	1 117.8	183.8	7.6	3 510.6	3 146.6	299.7	1 091.6	1 767.4
February	2 244.7	2 176.2	252.6	800.8	1 122.9	184.2	7.6	3 509.1	3 144.2	297.6	1 090.6	1 768.7
March	2 273.3	2 204.3	257.1	812.5	1 134.7	172.5	7.1	3 526.8	3 178.6	302.3	1 104.2	1 784.2
April	2 302.4	2 232.8	267.0	814.3	1 151.5	169.0	6.8	3 539.4	3 197.8	313.7	1 097.7	1 797.3
May	2 325.3	2 255.3	274.0	822.9	1 158.5	164.5	6.6	3 550.8	3 216.4	322.2	1 102.9	1 800.3
June	2 354.5	2 283.5	283.0	832.2	1 168.3	143.7	5.8	3 551.3	3 246.1	332.1	1 113.6	1 807.1
July	2 377.6	2 305.3	288.0	839.1	1 178.2	164.8	6.5	3 599.1	3 263.4	337.1	1 119.4	1 812.9
August	2 389.2	2 316.0	285.5	840.5	1 189.9	152.7	6.0	3 584.5	3 266.0	333.3	1 118.1	1 822.1
September	2 402.8	2 329.0	287.0	844.7	1 197.3	170.0	6.6	3 614.5	3 271.9	334.4	1 122.5	1 822.2
October	2 430.8	2 355.6	297.9	848.8	1 208.9	169.8	6.5	3 642.6	3 299.5	346.6	1 126.3	1 831.7
November	2 445.7	2 369.0	299.8	853.0	1 216.2	182.0	6.9	3 670.4	3 309.0	347.6	1 132.6	1 833.6
December	2 476.9	2 399.4	312.3	851.6	1 235.5	179.1	6.7	3 705.4	3 347.4	361.9	1 129.5	1 860.0
1984:												
January	2 506.2	2 428.8	320.3	869.6	1 238.9	178.7	6.7	3 731.1	3 375.2	371.8	1 146.0	1 858.6
February	2 485.4	2 406.6	312.3	860.8	1 233.5	234.7	8.6	3 764.6	3 330.8	362.9	1 128.5	1 842.1
March	2 511.3	2 431.9	312.6	865.7	1 253.7	236.6	8.6	3 791.9	3 356.0	362.9	1 132.5	1 864.8
April	2 536.9	2 456.9	319.4	876.2	1 261.3	243.4	8.8	3 823.2	3 378.4	368.8	1 145.1	1 867.0
May	2 555.5	2 474.2	324.8	879.6	1 269.8	232.5	8.3	3 827.0	3 396.2	374.9	1 150.0	1 872.8
June	2 578.3	2 495.8	329.0	892.5	1 274.3	235.7	8.4	3 853.7	3 417.9	379.4	1 166.4	1 871.8
July	2 574.1	2 491.4	324.6	882.7	1 284.1	259.0	9.1	3 869.9	3 403.2	374.3	1 151.8	1 879.0
August	2 591.8	2 508.6	322.8	886.2	1 299.6	270.6	9.5	3 896.5	3 414.8	371.4	1 153.1	1 893.7
September	2 615.3	2 531.6	327.3	896.9	1 307.5	272.4	9.4	3 920.8	3 437.3	375.5	1 164.4	1 899.9
October	2 616.1	2 531.5	325.7	890.4	1 315.5	258.1	9.0	3 891.7	3 427.6	374.3	1 152.3	1 904.5
November	2 656.8	2 571.7	340.5	902.2	1 328.9	237.3	8.2	3 911.2	3 475.4	390.4	1 167.5	1 918.5
December	2 664.5	2 578.5	341.9	899.9	1 336.7	239.4	8.2	3 917.8	3 478.8	392.6	1 163.7	1 923.5
1985:												
January	2 693.9	2 607.0	347.6	901.7	1 357.6	239.8	8.2	3 943.3	3 504.1	398.5	1 163.3	1 943.6
February	2 716.5	2 628.7	346.8	913.0	1 368.9	201.7	6.9	3 904.9	3 517.5	395.5	1 172.6	1 951.3
March	2 724.8	2 635.8	355.0	913.2	1 367.7	187.9	6.5	3 880.9	3 512.0	404.1	1 167.1	1 940.8
April	2 739.0	2 649.4	347.1	923.4	1 379.0	233.0	7.8	3 949.2	3 520.7	395.2	1 177.0	1 950.2
May	2 778.1	2 687.9	365.4	924.4	1 398.1	272.3	8.9	4 040.6	3 560.4	416.8	1 177.8	1 964.7
June	2 773.5	2 682.8	350.8	921.4	1 410.6	217.9	7.3	3 948.8	3 541.4	400.1	1 170.2	1 973.6
July	2 796.3	2 704.9	357.2	925.7	1 422.1	207.4	6.9	3 956.8	3 563.2	407.6	1 174.6	1 982.6
August	2 828.8	2 737.1	370.5	931.9	1 434.8	184.6	6.1	3 958.7	3 595.8	421.9	1 182.4	1 991.0
September	2 877.9	2 784.9	402.9	937.5	1 444.5	146.3	4.8	3 960.5	3 647.1	459.3	1 187.4	1 994.3
October	2 846.1	2 752.8	359.0	939.3	1 454.5	210.4	6.9	3 987.7	3 591.5	407.9	1 185.7	1 999.7
November	2 866.7	2 772.8	360.2	948.7	1 463.8	197.4	6.4	3 981.6	3 603.0	409.2	1 192.8	2 002.7
December	2 907.8	2 813.2	370.3	950.9	1 492.0	190.5	6.1	4 010.7	3 641.6	420.7	1 189.3	2 033.0
1986:												
January	2 922.7	2 826.8	380.3	959.9	1 486.6	196.3	6.3	4 022.4	3 645.6	431.0	1 198.3	2 015.1
February	2 916.1	2 819.6	368.2	953.1	1 498.2	214.8	6.9	4 038.0	3 636.5	418.0	1 197.5	2 022.0
March	2 920.4	2 823.6	362.5	955.3	1 505.8	231.9	7.4	4 075.0	3 650.1	412.0	1 216.3	2 023.4
April	2 934.6	2 837.3	381.9	942.4	1 513.0	216.7	6.9	4 077.7	3 671.5	434.2	1 210.3	2 025.3
May	2 959.7	2 861.8	391.4	951.3	1 519.1	201.2	6.4	4 078.1	3 692.4	442.8	1 218.2	2 028.4
June	2 965.8	2 867.8	380.9	954.5	1 532.4	205.4	6.5	4 075.1	3 685.2	429.0	1 217.9	2 037.8
July	2 987.6	2 888.9	392.7	955.1	1 541.1	203.9	6.4	4 094.5	3 706.3	441.0	1 219.0	2 044.3
August	3 006.7	2 907.8	410.7	953.3	1 543.8	194.9	6.1	4 097.5	3 721.6	459.7	1 215.2	2 042.1
September	3 081.5	2 981.8	462.6	958.2	1 561.0	132.6	4.1	4 096.4	3 800.4	517.0	1 216.7	2 054.7
October	3 044.9	2 944.3	411.2	966.0	1 567.1	166.7	5.2	4 086.1	3 746.0	459.5	1 227.8	2 054.4
November	3 041.8	2 941.3	396.7	962.5	1 582.1	177.7	5.5	4 087.1	3 733.9	442.5	1 221.3	2 068.7
December	3 111.4	3 011.2	445.0	974.9	1 591.3	121.1	3.7	4 094.9	3 814.6	494.2	1 231.8	2 080.4
1987:												
January	3 055.5	2 956.3	376.0	976.6	1 603.6	213.6	6.5	4 115.2	3 721.4	416.6	1 221.3	2 086.3
February	3 120.2	3 021.0	402.4	1 003.6	1 615.0	182.6	5.5	4 140.7	3 787.3	445.1	1 244.6	2 096.6
March	3 129.2	3 029.9	404.3	998.5	1 627.1	188.1	5.7	4 148.0	3 788.6	445.8	1 234.2	2 108.0
April	3 155.4	3 055.4	412.4	1 006.0	1 637.0	45.1	1.4	3 988.6	3 807.7	453.0	1 239.2	2 114.1
May	3 164.9	3 065.0	409.1	1 010.4	1 645.5	177.7	5.3	4 153.7	3 808.7	448.8	1 241.6	2 117.6
June	3 190.0	3 089.8	419.8	1 015.0	1 655.0	162.6	4.8	4 151.0	3 825.5	458.8	1 241.0	2 123.9
July	3 212.0	3 110.9	426.4	1 016.3	1 668.2	148.7	4.4	4 150.2	3 841.7	464.5	1 239.6	2 135.5
August	3 249.4	3 148.3	442.9	1 022.6	1 682.8	139.4	4.1	4 165.2	3 869.7	481.2	1 241.4	2 143.1
September	3 244.6	3 143.5	434.7	1 023.1	1 685.7	159.3	4.7	4 166.1	3 847.4	470.7	1 238.5	2 135.4
October	3 255.0	3 154.5	417.6	1 026.2	1 710.7	194.3	5.6	4 204.7	3 845.3	451.5	1 238.9	2 155.0
November	3 264.4	3 164.2	421.2	1 030.7	1 712.3	205.8	5.9	4 217.5	3 845.5	454.7	1 241.1	2 149.2
December	3 295.7	3 195.3	433.3	1 038.9	1 723.0	210.0	6.0	4 255.4	3 878.6	468.9	1 249.7	2 158.1
1988:												
January	3 333.3	3 232.5	444.8	1 039.1	1 748.6	194.4	5.5	4 271.6	3 914.2	481.8	1 247.5	2 182.1
February	3 336.4	3 235.4	442.1	1 038.2	1 755.1	224.6	6.3	4 307.2	3 913.4	479.2	1 248.3	2 183.4
March	3 374.7	3 273.5	445.6	1 058.9	1 768.9	202.7	5.7	4 311.4	3 945.1	481.6	1 268.8	2 192.0
April	3 382.4	3 281.1	442.2	1 061.0	1 777.9	190.0	5.3	4 282.6	3 933.4	477.1	1 261.8	2 192.5
May	3 414.3	3 312.8	450.3	1 068.9	1 793.7	192.5	5.3	4 307.3	3 956.4	484.9	1 268.9	2 199.8
June	3 438.5	3 336.7	452.2	1 073.5	1 811.0	201.1	5.5	4 326.8	3 966.7	485.7	1 269.6	2 208.9
July	3 464.3	3 362.8	448.2	1 084.8	1 829.7	200.8	5.5	4 335.8	3 978.2	480.6	1 274.3	2 221.5
August	3 489.1	3 387.1	446.9	1 094.6	1 845.6	190.0	5.2	4 337.5	3 993.2	478.0	1 283.7	2 230.1
September	3 499.1	3 397.0	446.2	1 102.6	1 848.2	199.3	5.4	4 337.4	3 984.0	475.3	1 285.0	2 222.2
October	3 541.5	3 438.7	456.2	1 112.0	1 870.5	184.8	5.0	4 353.1	4 017.2	484.5	1 292.5	2 238.3
November	3 558.3	3 454.8	459.6	1 119.9	1 875.3	179.0	4.8	4 354.3	4 025.1	487.5	1 298.5	2 236.7
December	3 588.6	3 484.1	477.6	1 119.4	1 887.1	182.7	4.8	4 378.5	4 045.1	506.0	1 293.5	2 241.7

Personal Income and its Disposition—*Continued*

(Billions of dollars, except as noted; seasonally adjusted annual rate)

Year and month	Personal outlays					Personal saving		Constant (1992) dollars				
	Total	Personal consumption expenditures				Billions of dollars	Percent of disposable personal income	Disposable personal income	Personal consumption expenditures			
		Total	Durable goods	Nondurable goods	Services				Total	Durable goods	Nondurable goods	Services
1989:												
January	3 611.0	3 503.4	472.8	1 135.5	1 895.1	190.3	5.0	4 388.6	4 044.7	499.4	1 304.9	2 236.9
February	3 612.2	3 503.6	456.9	1 128.5	1 918.2	224.3	5.8	4 414.6	4 031.5	481.8	1 292.6	2 255.6
March	3 620.7	3 511.4	457.7	1 132.8	1 920.9	246.2	6.4	4 429.5	4 022.2	483.8	1 288.4	2 248.4
April	3 669.1	3 558.8	478.4	1 151.2	1 929.2	181.9	4.7	4 381.0	4 048.6	503.8	1 291.5	2 249.9
May	3 679.9	3 568.7	468.1	1 161.8	1 938.7	192.7	5.0	4 387.7	4 043.4	492.3	1 296.0	2 252.8
June	3 693.3	3 581.6	471.0	1 165.8	1 944.8	207.3	5.3	4 410.9	4 050.1	494.4	1 299.3	2 253.8
July	3 713.4	3 601.3	476.8	1 167.1	1 957.4	200.2	5.1	4 413.3	4 061.0	499.4	1 299.1	2 259.8
August	3 752.2	3 639.3	498.0	1 172.2	1 969.1	167.9	4.3	4 416.5	4 100.2	521.7	1 309.3	2 265.1
September	3 754.4	3 641.2	479.0	1 181.4	1 980.8	171.0	4.4	4 407.6	4 088.5	501.0	1 316.2	2 268.3
October	3 772.4	3 657.6	473.8	1 182.7	2 001.0	177.5	4.5	4 412.8	4 086.2	494.6	1 309.4	2 279.9
November	3 780.0	3 664.7	469.7	1 186.6	2 008.3	202.2	5.1	4 436.3	4 082.6	489.5	1 311.7	2 279.5
December	3 821.7	3 705.9	471.7	1 200.1	2 034.1	176.7	4.4	4 440.9	4 116.1	492.5	1 323.8	2 297.9
1990:												
January	3 867.4	3 751.4	514.8	1 208.2	2 028.4	186.5	4.6	4 472.8	4 139.1	534.6	1 312.7	2 287.4
February	3 866.9	3 750.1	483.4	1 224.4	2 042.3	217.4	5.3	4 487.3	4 120.1	500.2	1 322.2	2 295.4
March	3 893.0	3 776.1	481.6	1 229.5	2 065.0	213.4	5.2	4 488.6	4 122.5	498.7	1 322.5	2 304.4
April	3 914.7	3 797.8	484.8	1 226.8	2 086.1	225.5	5.4	4 507.9	4 135.1	502.5	1 317.2	2 313.4
May	3 918.0	3 800.4	474.0	1 223.3	2 104.2	221.3	5.3	4 492.2	4 124.4	491.2	1 310.3	2 322.0
June	3 955.5	3 837.3	473.8	1 241.4	2 122.1	211.5	5.1	4 500.8	4 144.7	492.4	1 323.2	2 328.0
July	3 974.3	3 854.7	475.4	1 245.5	2 133.8	223.4	5.3	4 519.3	4 150.0	493.3	1 322.7	2 332.8
August	4 001.1	3 881.0	469.3	1 257.1	2 154.6	202.8	4.8	4 495.4	4 150.1	486.5	1 321.4	2 341.3
September	4 022.5	3 901.9	474.9	1 266.1	2 160.9	210.5	5.0	4 497.1	4 145.5	491.4	1 315.4	2 337.8
October	4 029.0	3 908.2	466.2	1 273.3	2 168.7	202.2	4.8	4 466.9	4 125.9	480.0	1 310.0	2 335.4
November	4 030.8	3 909.7	463.6	1 278.5	2 167.6	208.8	4.9	4 466.2	4 118.6	477.8	1 313.4	2 326.8
December	4 024.0	3 903.1	455.8	1 270.5	2 176.7	236.5	5.6	4 480.5	4 104.6	471.1	1 301.8	2 331.5
1991:												
January	4 001.3	3 879.8	432.3	1 264.6	2 183.0	251.6	5.9	4 450.4	4 060.0	443.5	1 293.2	2 323.9
February	4 026.2	3 904.4	444.3	1 266.9	2 193.3	234.7	5.5	4 447.1	4 075.1	452.8	1 298.9	2 323.7
March	4 069.9	3 947.9	470.4	1 273.3	2 204.1	206.6	4.8	4 461.0	4 118.3	479.4	1 309.9	2 328.3
April	4 064.0	3 941.8	450.7	1 273.2	2 217.8	239.0	5.6	4 476.5	4 100.8	458.1	1 304.4	2 338.4
May	4 089.2	3 966.8	450.8	1 284.2	2 231.8	236.8	5.5	4 486.5	4 114.0	458.0	1 312.0	2 344.0
June	4 096.7	3 974.4	456.5	1 281.8	2 236.2	258.3	5.9	4 509.4	4 115.3	465.3	1 307.8	2 342.1
July	4 119.0	3 996.7	462.8	1 286.1	2 247.8	226.2	5.2	4 487.4	4 127.6	468.6	1 313.0	2 345.9
August	4 116.9	3 994.4	457.8	1 282.5	2 254.1	242.7	5.6	4 488.6	4 112.6	463.6	1 305.8	2 343.2
September	4 135.8	4 013.7	465.3	1 281.5	2 266.9	244.6	5.6	4 494.5	4 118.3	469.9	1 302.5	2 345.9
October	4 122.5	3 999.8	454.0	1 273.5	2 272.3	259.5	5.9	4 487.0	4 095.6	457.3	1 295.0	2 343.4
November	4 153.2	4 030.6	457.1	1 280.4	2 293.1	250.4	5.7	4 491.4	4 111.0	460.2	1 296.3	2 354.6
December	4 173.6	4 050.8	460.7	1 283.3	2 306.8	272.0	6.1	4 522.4	4 120.7	466.9	1 295.8	2 358.1
1992:												
January	4 234.2	4 112.1	473.3	1 303.7	2 335.0	241.0	5.4	4 538.6	4 170.3	477.3	1 317.5	2 375.5
February	4 247.8	4 125.2	478.7	1 303.7	2 342.9	265.7	5.9	4 564.5	4 171.9	480.3	1 315.5	2 375.8
March	4 267.8	4 145.6	470.2	1 302.0	2 373.3	267.6	5.9	4 572.1	4 179.1	470.6	1 310.1	2 398.5
April	4 279.3	4 157.3	469.3	1 304.2	2 383.8	277.3	6.1	4 581.1	4 179.6	469.6	1 310.8	2 399.3
May	4 308.0	4 186.3	483.3	1 311.6	2 391.4	270.5	5.9	4 593.4	4 199.9	482.5	1 316.0	2 401.3
June	4 327.1	4 205.6	491.4	1 309.4	2 404.7	269.0	5.9	4 600.6	4 209.7	491.3	1 309.2	2 409.1
July	4 352.8	4 232.1	487.8	1 318.4	2 425.9	250.3	5.4	4 590.3	4 220.4	487.4	1 314.7	2 418.2
August	4 329.2	4 208.6	492.8	1 329.5	2 386.3	255.2	5.6	4 583.0	4 207.3	492.1	1 324.4	2 390.9
September	4 396.4	4 276.0	496.9	1 331.0	2 448.1	230.7	5.0	4 601.5	4 252.3	496.3	1 324.3	2 431.7
October	4 428.4	4 307.5	505.4	1 344.8	2 457.3	237.7	5.1	4 622.0	4 266.8	503.5	1 336.1	2 427.2
November	4 444.6	4 324.3	496.8	1 349.3	2 478.3	240.8	5.1	4 634.0	4 276.8	494.7	1 340.2	2 441.9
December	4 476.9	4 357.0	516.4	1 354.3	2 486.2	363.2	7.5	4 780.5	4 303.4	516.7	1 343.1	2 443.7
1993:												
January	4 488.5	4 365.2	519.8	1 359.1	2 486.3	179.5	3.8	4 596.3	4 298.1	517.2	1 346.1	2 435.0
February	4 500.6	4 377.3	501.9	1 361.3	2 514.0	173.9	3.7	4 588.2	4 296.4	499.5	1 342.6	2 454.3
March	4 476.2	4 353.7	497.4	1 342.9	2 513.4	190.2	4.1	4 572.5	4 266.0	495.4	1 323.8	2 446.7
April	4 535.7	4 413.4	520.0	1 365.6	2 527.8	227.7	4.8	4 654.2	4 312.3	515.1	1 345.5	2 451.8
May	4 543.6	4 422.7	525.0	1 366.6	2 531.1	248.9	5.2	4 677.3	4 316.4	520.4	1 347.0	2 449.2
June	4 569.2	4 448.2	527.6	1 366.7	2 554.0	216.5	4.5	4 669.0	4 339.7	522.3	1 350.9	2 466.6
July	4 594.3	4 473.2	539.0	1 372.1	2 562.2	193.8	4.0	4 666.3	4 359.4	533.0	1 355.6	2 471.1
August	4 607.9	4 486.6	535.8	1 372.4	2 578.3	213.5	4.4	4 689.7	4 364.0	528.4	1 354.0	2 481.7
September	4 627.1	4 505.9	536.8	1 377.3	2 591.8	194.0	4.0	4 682.4	4 376.2	528.2	1 360.8	2 487.3
October	4 657.5	4 536.8	548.1	1 385.6	2 603.0	181.2	3.7	4 678.3	4 386.4	537.3	1 360.7	2 488.6
November	4 674.2	4 554.2	553.6	1 387.9	2 612.8	184.8	3.8	4 690.2	4 396.0	542.2	1 361.0	2 493.0
December	4 693.9	4 573.8	557.6	1 390.6	2 625.6	320.1	6.4	4 836.3	4 411.7	546.8	1 363.6	2 501.5
1994:												
January	4 681.6	4 559.6	550.4	1 385.1	2 624.0	135.8	2.8	4 645.4	4 396.8	539.4	1 360.4	2 497.2
February	4 757.2	4 635.8	567.2	1 407.7	2 660.9	126.9	2.6	4 696.6	4 457.8	554.9	1 381.8	2 521.5
March	4 775.8	4 654.4	572.0	1 420.2	2 662.1	134.1	2.7	4 708.7	4 463.6	557.7	1 392.8	2 513.9
April	4 784.7	4 662.8	578.1	1 408.4	2 676.4	141.7	2.9	4 716.4	4 464.1	563.9	1 379.9	2 520.8
May	4 797.8	4 675.3	567.5	1 414.3	2 693.5	209.6	4.2	4 786.9	4 469.4	550.5	1 385.6	2 533.5
June	4 827.3	4 703.5	571.6	1 425.2	2 706.6	186.7	3.7	4 779.2	4 483.2	552.9	1 390.9	2 539.7
July	4 841.7	4 718.0	576.8	1 431.3	2 709.9	198.5	3.9	4 786.9	4 480.8	556.0	1 389.5	2 535.7
August	4 886.3	4 760.9	587.0	1 442.5	2 731.4	175.1	3.5	4 790.7	4 506.2	565.3	1 395.1	2 546.4
September	4 900.4	4 772.9	586.1	1 444.6	2 742.2	190.7	3.7	4 808.0	4 507.6	563.9	1 394.9	2 549.3
October	4 935.0	4 806.4	595.3	1 451.3	2 759.8	207.6	4.0	4 845.0	4 528.2	573.4	1 401.3	2 554.2
November	4 953.7	4 823.2	603.1	1 454.1	2 766.1	197.2	3.8	4 844.3	4 536.1	580.0	1 403.5	2 553.6
December	4 963.4	4 830.9	599.4	1 455.7	2 775.9	217.8	4.2	4 867.0	4 538.0	576.3	1 402.6	2 559.9

Industrial Production and Capacity Utilization

(Seasonally adjusted)

Year and month	Total industrial production	Industrial production indexes (1992=100)										Capacity utilization (output as a percent of capacity)					
		Major market groups					Major industry groups					Total industry	Manufacturing			Mining	Utilities
		Products				Materials	Manufacturing			Mining	Utilities		Total	Primary processing	Advanced processing		
		Total	Consumer goods	Business equipment	Construction supplies		Total	Durables	Nondurables								
1971:																	
January	58.8	57.0	62.8	42.7	70.6	61.1	54.7	52.0	58.7	102.4	68.7	79.6	77.7	78.7	76.9	89.7	95.9
February	58.7	57.1	62.7	42.9	71.0	60.7	54.8	52.1	58.6	101.0	68.3	79.2	77.6	78.6	76.8	88.5	94.8
March	58.6	56.9	62.9	42.5	70.7	60.8	54.7	51.9	58.6	101.5	68.9	78.9	77.2	78.5	76.2	89.0	95.2
April	59.0	57.2	63.4	42.3	71.4	61.2	54.9	51.9	59.3	102.0	69.1	79.2	77.4	79.0	76.2	89.6	95.0
May	59.3	57.3	63.5	42.0	71.7	61.9	55.3	52.6	59.3	101.9	69.7	79.4	77.8	79.5	76.4	89.6	95.4
June	59.5	57.5	64.0	42.2	72.5	62.2	55.5	52.4	59.9	101.5	70.3	79.5	77.8	79.5	76.4	89.3	95.7
July	59.3	58.1	65.0	42.2	73.2	60.7	55.5	52.1	60.5	98.2	70.0	79.1	77.7	78.1	77.0	86.4	94.9
August	59.0	57.8	64.2	42.9	71.9	60.4	54.9	51.0	60.5	99.4	69.5	78.4	76.6	75.9	76.5	87.5	93.7
September	60.0	58.6	64.8	43.9	74.6	61.5	56.0	52.4	61.2	99.1	70.0	79.5	77.9	78.1	77.4	87.3	93.9
October	60.4	59.2	65.7	44.3	75.6	61.7	56.8	53.3	61.9	90.3	71.1	79.9	78.9	79.2	78.3	79.7	94.9
November	60.7	59.6	66.2	44.5	75.9	61.8	57.0	53.4	62.3	94.0	70.2	80.0	79.0	79.0	78.5	83.0	93.3
December	61.4	59.9	66.7	44.8	77.2	63.1	57.6	53.9	62.9	100.0	69.9	80.7	79.5	79.8	79.0	88.4	92.5
1972:																	
January	62.7	61.0	67.6	45.9	79.1	64.9	58.9	55.5	63.9	100.3	71.7	82.3	81.2	82.8	80.7	88.8	94.3
February	63.2	61.5	67.8	46.5	79.5	65.1	59.4	56.1	64.0	100.1	73.0	82.6	81.5	82.7	81.1	88.7	95.7
March	63.7	61.9	68.1	47.3	80.2	65.7	59.9	56.6	64.6	100.7	73.0	83.1	82.0	83.5	81.2	89.3	95.2
April	64.7	62.9	69.4	48.3	81.4	66.8	60.9	57.7	65.4	102.0	74.4	84.2	83.1	84.5	82.3	90.6	96.6
May	64.5	62.6	68.7	48.4	81.8	66.9	60.7	57.7	65.1	100.5	73.1	83.8	82.7	84.9	81.4	89.4	94.5
June	64.7	62.9	69.0	48.6	82.3	66.9	60.9	57.7	65.6	101.1	73.0	83.8	82.7	84.7	81.5	90.0	94.0
July	64.6	62.8	68.7	48.4	82.8	67.0	60.9	57.9	65.4	101.7	73.1	83.5	82.5	84.9	81.0	90.6	93.7
August	65.5	63.6	69.9	49.1	83.7	68.0	61.8	58.6	66.3	101.4	74.0	84.4	83.4	85.8	81.8	90.5	94.4
September	66.2	64.2	70.2	50.2	84.8	68.9	62.3	59.4	66.4	102.7	74.5	85.1	83.9	86.4	82.3	91.8	94.7
October	67.2	65.0	71.1	51.2	85.8	70.0	63.3	60.8	66.9	102.4	76.1	86.1	85.0	87.8	83.4	91.6	96.2
November	68.0	65.7	71.4	52.5	87.0	70.9	64.1	61.9	67.2	101.9	76.7	86.9	85.9	88.8	84.2	91.2	96.6
December	68.6	66.3	72.2	53.0	86.4	71.8	64.9	62.6	68.0	101.4	76.8	87.5	86.7	89.3	85.3	90.9	96.3
1973:																	
January	68.7	66.2	71.5	54.1	86.8	71.9	65.0	63.2	67.5	101.3	76.1	87.3	86.6	89.1	85.2	90.9	95.0
February	69.7	67.2	72.5	55.0	88.3	72.8	65.9	64.2	68.2	101.9	77.4	88.3	87.6	90.6	85.9	91.6	96.2
March	69.6	67.2	72.6	55.3	88.7	72.7	66.1	64.2	68.6	100.3	75.5	88.0	87.5	90.4	86.0	90.2	93.3
April	69.9	67.4	72.4	56.1	88.1	73.2	66.3	64.4	68.7	100.1	76.4	88.1	87.5	90.3	86.0	90.2	93.9
May	70.2	67.6	72.5	56.8	88.6	73.6	66.5	64.8	68.8	100.8	76.6	88.3	87.6	90.5	86.1	90.9	93.7
June	70.7	68.1	72.7	57.6	88.8	74.2	67.0	65.5	68.9	101.8	77.7	88.7	87.9	90.4	86.6	91.9	94.6
July	71.2	68.3	72.6	58.0	88.8	75.0	67.3	65.8	69.3	103.4	77.9	89.0	88.1	91.1	86.6	93.4	94.3
August	71.1	68.2	72.5	58.2	88.9	75.1	67.4	65.7	69.6	103.6	77.6	88.7	88.0	91.0	86.5	93.7	93.5
September	71.7	69.1	73.8	59.5	89.1	75.0	67.8	66.5	69.4	103.3	79.6	89.2	88.2	90.5	87.1	93.5	95.3
October	71.9	69.2	73.4	60.0	89.1	75.6	68.2	66.8	70.0	103.5	78.1	89.2	88.5	90.9	87.2	93.8	93.2
November	72.0	69.2	73.3	60.1	89.5	75.7	68.3	67.1	69.9	103.4	76.7	89.0	88.5	91.2	87.0	93.8	91.0
December	70.8	67.8	71.2	58.7	88.9	75.1	67.1	65.7	68.8	103.8	74.5	87.4	86.6	90.2	84.7	94.3	88.0
1974:																	
January	69.8	66.9	70.2	58.4	86.7	74.0	66.3	64.3	68.9	103.0	74.5	85.9	85.3	88.4	83.6	93.6	87.5
February	69.6	66.7	69.7	58.6	86.2	73.5	66.0	63.9	68.9	103.4	74.0	85.4	84.7	87.7	83.1	94.0	86.5
March	69.9	67.3	70.6	59.1	86.4	73.4	66.3	63.9	69.7	102.7	75.4	85.5	84.8	87.4	83.4	93.3	87.8
April	69.8	67.5	70.4	59.7	86.8	72.7	66.0	63.8	69.0	102.6	75.9	85.1	84.2	87.0	82.7	93.1	88.0
May	70.6	68.1	71.0	60.8	86.6	73.9	66.8	64.9	69.5	103.5	77.5	85.8	85.0	87.2	83.8	93.9	89.5
June	70.8	68.4	71.5	61.0	85.9	73.9	67.1	65.2	69.6	102.4	77.8	85.8	85.1	87.1	84.0	92.9	89.5
July	70.5	68.0	71.0	61.1	83.6	73.8	66.7	64.7	69.5	103.6	75.4	85.2	84.3	86.4	83.2	94.0	86.4
August	70.2	67.8	71.4	60.1	82.7	73.4	66.7	64.7	69.4	100.7	76.7	84.7	84.1	85.9	83.1	91.3	87.4
September	70.5	68.1	71.2	61.6	81.9	73.7	66.8	65.0	69.1	102.0	77.3	84.8	83.9	85.3	83.2	92.5	87.7
October	70.0	67.6	70.9	61.4	79.5	73.1	66.2	64.6	68.3	103.2	77.0	83.9	83.0	83.5	82.6	93.6	87.1
November	68.0	66.4	69.0	60.9	77.3	69.8	64.4	62.8	66.5	96.8	75.8	81.3	80.4	80.1	80.6	87.8	85.3
December	65.2	64.1	67.1	57.4	73.6	66.1	61.3	59.5	63.8	97.1	75.9	77.7	76.3	74.9	77.2	88.0	85.0
1975:																	
January	63.5	62.2	64.3	56.4	71.7	64.7	59.5	57.5	62.2	101.3	74.5	75.5	73.9	72.7	74.5	91.7	83.2
February	62.5	61.7	64.4	55.2	71.3	62.8	58.3	56.0	61.5	101.1	75.6	74.1	72.3	71.0	73.0	91.5	84.2
March	61.3	60.9	64.0	53.7	69.7	61.2	57.0	54.9	59.9	99.9	77.6	72.6	70.5	68.2	71.8	90.3	86.2
April	61.9	61.5	65.7	53.5	69.7	61.6	57.6	55.1	61.2	99.2	78.7	73.1	71.1	68.9	72.3	89.6	87.1
May	61.7	61.5	66.1	52.9	69.3	61.1	57.5	54.6	61.7	98.7	76.3	72.7	70.8	69.0	71.8	89.0	84.2
June	62.5	62.3	67.4	52.6	69.7	62.0	58.4	54.6	63.8	100.0	76.7	73.5	71.7	70.2	72.4	90.2	84.3
July	62.9	62.8	68.8	52.4	70.3	62.1	58.9	54.9	64.8	97.9	76.6	73.8	72.3	71.2	72.7	88.2	84.0
August	64.0	63.4	69.3	52.9	72.1	64.1	59.6	56.0	65.7	98.3	77.9	75.0	73.3	73.1	73.4	88.5	85.2
September	64.7	63.7	70.0	52.9	72.9	65.3	60.7	56.7	66.6	98.2	77.4	75.6	74.1	74.9	73.6	88.3	84.4
October	65.0	63.8	69.9	53.1	73.4	66.0	61.1	57.0	67.2	99.2	76.3	75.8	74.5	75.0	74.1	89.1	83.0
November	65.6	64.4	70.7	53.5	73.5	66.7	61.6	57.4	67.9	100.2	77.5	76.4	74.9	75.5	74.5	89.9	84.0
December	66.1	64.8	71.3	53.6	73.3	67.5	62.2	58.1	68.4	99.9	76.7	76.8	75.5	76.1	75.2	89.6	82.9
1976:																	
January	66.8	65.4	72.0	53.5	75.9	68.4	62.9	58.9	68.8	100.3	78.4	77.5	76.2	77.2	75.6	89.9	84.6
February	68.0	66.6	73.5	54.7	77.9	69.4	64.3	60.5	70.0	99.8	77.1	78.7	77.7	78.8	77.2	89.4	83.0
March	67.9	66.3	72.9	54.5	77.5	69.7	64.1	60.3	69.6	99.0	78.0	78.3	77.2	78.5	76.6	88.7	83.8
April	68.1	66.3	73.1	54.5	77.9	70.2	64.3	60.6	69.7	98.8	78.9	78.4	77.2	78.5	76.7	88.5	84.6
May	68.9	67.1	74.0	55.0	79.0	71.0	65.1	61.8	69.9	100.1	79.3	79.1	78.1	78.9	77.7	89.6	84.8
June	69.0	67.0	74.0	54.8	79.3	71.3	65.0	61.6	70.0	100.0	79.3	79.0	77.8	79.1	77.2	89.5	84.6
July	69.4	67.6	74.3	55.4	80.5	71.5	65.6	62.3	70.6	99.3	79.7	79.3	78.3	79.3	77.8	89.9	84.8
August	69.8	67.8	74.7	55.5	81.2	72.1	65.9	63.0	70.2	99.8	79.8	79.6	78.5	79.5	78.0	89.3	84.8
September	70.0	68.0	74.4	55.6	81.4	72.4	66.2	62.3	71.8	101.6	79.5	79.7	78.6	80.2	77.6	90.9	84.3
October	70.2	68.4	74.7	56.0	82.0	72.4	66.4	62.4	72.4	101.5	80.8	79.8	78.7	80.2	77.7	90.8	85.6
November	71.4	69.8	76.7	57.9	82.8	73.1	67.3	63.8	72.5	101.6	84.0	80.9	79.6	80.0	79.2	90.9	88.8
December	72.0	70.4	77.4	58.9	81.9	73.7	68.0	64.5	73.1	101.6	83.9	81.4	80.2	80.5	79.8	90.8	88.4

Industrial Production and Capacity Utilization—*Continued*

(Seasonally adjusted)

Year and month	Total indus-trial produc-tion	Industrial production indexes (1992=100)										Capacity utilization (output as a percent of capacity)					
		Major market groups					Major industry groups					Manufacturing					
		Products				Mater-ials	Manufacturing			Mining	Utilities	Total industry	Total	Primary process-ing	Ad-vanced process-ing	Mining	Utilities
		Total	Con-sumer goods	Busi-ness equip-ment	Con-struc-tion supplies		Total	Dura-bles	Non-dura-bles								
1977:																	
January	72.4	70.9	78.1	59.1	81.6	73.8	68.5	64.9	73.8	100.3	83.0	81.6	80.6	80.5	80.5	89.6	87.3
February	72.4	70.6	77.3	59.1	81.9	74.5	68.7	65.2	73.7	102.1	79.9	81.5	80.6	81.5	79.9	91.0	83.7
March	73.3	71.2	78.0	59.2	84.0	75.8	69.6	65.9	74.8	103.6	78.8	82.3	81.4	82.8	80.5	92.0	82.4
April	74.3	72.3	78.7	60.9	86.2	76.5	70.6	67.3	75.3	104.4	79.9	83.3	82.3	83.8	81.5	92.4	83.4
May	75.0	72.9	79.2	61.1	87.5	77.5	71.2	67.9	76.0	104.7	81.9	83.9	82.9	84.7	81.8	92.4	85.2
June	75.6	73.5	79.7	61.8	88.5	78.0	71.8	68.6	76.3	105.4	82.7	84.3	83.3	85.2	82.2	92.7	85.8
July	75.6	73.8	80.0	62.4	89.3	77.7	71.8	68.9	75.9	104.5	83.7	84.2	83.2	84.7	82.2	91.7	86.7
August	75.9	74.3	80.7	62.8	89.4	77.8	72.4	69.4	76.7	101.9	83.1	84.3	83.6	85.0	82.8	89.1	85.8
September	76.3	74.5	80.4	64.4	88.8	78.4	72.5	69.8	76.2	106.8	82.8	84.6	83.5	84.2	83.1	93.2	85.4
October	76.2	74.4	80.7	64.0	89.0	78.2	72.4	69.7	76.2	105.5	83.0	84.2	83.2	84.4	82.5	91.7	85.4
November	76.2	74.5	80.8	64.4	88.7	78.2	72.5	69.5	76.8	105.0	81.9	84.1	83.2	84.2	82.6	91.0	84.1
December	75.9	75.0	81.0	65.1	89.0	76.7	72.8	70.2	76.5	96.8	82.8	83.5	83.4	84.0	83.0	83.6	84.8
1978:																	
January	75.7	74.4	79.6	64.6	89.2	76.9	72.6	69.5	77.0	96.0	83.0	83.0	82.9	84.2	82.1	82.7	84.9
February	75.7	74.8	80.6	65.0	89.4	76.3	72.6	69.5	76.9	95.9	83.5	82.8	82.6	83.4	82.2	82.5	85.2
March	76.4	75.7	81.4	65.8	89.3	76.9	73.1	70.2	77.1	100.3	83.7	83.4	83.0	82.9	83.0	86.1	85.3
April	79.0	77.5	83.1	67.9	92.0	80.7	75.2	72.6	78.9	109.9	83.6	86.0	85.2	85.7	84.9	94.1	85.0
May	79.1	77.2	82.4	67.9	91.8	81.1	75.3	72.7	78.8	109.4	84.5	85.8	85.0	86.3	84.2	93.6	85.7
June	79.9	78.5	83.8	69.1	93.1	81.5	76.2	73.6	79.8	110.0	84.7	86.6	85.8	86.4	85.4	93.9	85.8
July	80.2	78.5	83.5	69.6	92.7	82.0	76.4	74.3	79.4	110.4	84.5	86.6	85.8	86.2	85.6	94.1	85.3
August	80.4	78.7	83.3	70.9	92.2	82.2	76.6	74.9	79.3	109.3	84.5	86.6	85.9	86.5	85.6	93.0	85.3
September	80.8	79.1	83.7	71.1	93.0	82.7	77.2	75.4	79.7	109.0	85.3	86.7	86.2	86.8	85.8	92.6	85.9
October	81.2	79.2	83.4	72.1	93.3	83.4	77.6	76.0	79.6	109.4	85.4	86.9	86.3	87.3	85.8	93.2	85.8
November	81.7	79.8	83.2	73.6	94.1	83.7	78.2	76.8	80.1	109.4	84.9	87.2	86.8	87.6	86.3	92.6	85.1
December	82.0	80.1	83.4	73.8	95.0	84.1	78.6	77.4	80.2	108.7	85.3	87.3	86.9	88.1	86.3	91.9	85.3
1979:																	
January	81.6	80.1	82.8	75.7	93.5	83.1	78.3	77.4	79.4	106.7	85.5	86.7	86.4	86.2	86.5	90.1	85.4
February	82.2	80.5	82.7	76.6	94.3	84.0	78.9	78.2	79.6	106.4	88.5	87.1	86.7	87.0	86.6	89.8	88.4
March	82.4	80.7	82.8	77.3	94.1	84.3	79.2	78.5	80.0	106.2	87.8	87.1	86.9	87.1	86.7	89.6	87.6
April	81.6	79.6	81.1	76.4	93.3	83.9	78.0	76.5	80.0	108.2	89.3	86.1	85.3	86.6	84.6	91.3	89.1
May	82.6	80.8	82.4	78.1	93.7	84.5	79.2	78.3	80.3	107.7	88.6	86.9	86.4	86.8	86.1	90.9	88.4
June	82.6	80.6	82.2	78.2	93.4	84.8	79.3	78.7	80.0	108.0	86.7	86.7	86.3	87.0	85.8	91.1	86.5
July	82.0	80.1	80.9	77.9	93.9	84.2	78.9	78.0	80.0	106.4	85.2	85.9	85.6	87.0	84.6	89.8	85.0
August	81.7	79.7	80.3	77.3	92.3	83.9	78.1	76.8	79.8	109.2	85.9	85.4	84.5	85.8	83.7	92.2	85.6
September	81.7	79.9	80.5	77.8	92.4	83.7	78.1	77.1	79.4	110.1	85.8	85.3	84.3	85.1	83.8	92.9	85.5
October	82.1	80.4	80.9	78.3	92.7	83.9	78.5	77.2	80.2	110.0	86.2	85.5	84.5	85.0	84.2	92.8	85.8
November	81.7	79.9	80.5	77.2	92.2	83.5	77.9	76.4	79.9	110.6	86.8	84.9	83.6	84.2	83.3	93.3	86.4
December	81.5	79.9	81.0	76.5	91.6	83.2	77.8	76.3	79.9	109.9	86.0	84.5	83.3	83.7	83.1	92.7	85.5
1980:																	
January	81.9	79.7	80.3	76.9	90.9	84.4	78.0	76.1	80.5	113.9	84.2	84.7	83.3	83.9	82.9	96.0	83.6
February	81.9	80.4	80.7	78.3	91.2	83.6	78.2	76.7	80.0	112.0	85.2	84.6	83.3	82.9	83.5	94.3	84.5
March	81.9	80.4	81.0	77.8	90.4	83.5	77.9	76.5	79.6	113.0	87.8	84.4	82.7	82.1	83.1	95.0	86.9
April	80.3	78.9	79.6	77.3	84.2	81.8	76.2	74.5	78.6	111.7	86.1	82.6	80.8	79.2	81.8	93.8	85.0
May	78.3	77.4	77.8	75.9	80.9	79.2	73.9	71.7	76.8	112.4	85.6	80.4	78.1	74.8	80.0	94.3	84.4
June	77.3	77.0	77.7	75.2	79.8	77.4	72.8	70.3	76.2	111.5	86.0	79.2	76.7	72.8	79.0	93.4	84.6
July	76.8	77.2	78.1	75.2	79.1	76.0	72.2	69.6	75.9	109.8	88.1	78.5	75.9	71.0	78.9	91.9	86.5
August	77.7	78.2	79.0	75.5	82.7	76.8	73.4	70.9	76.9	108.5	88.8	79.3	77.0	72.7	79.6	90.7	87.1
September	78.9	78.9	80.1	75.7	83.9	78.5	74.5	71.9	78.2	110.5	89.3	80.3	77.9	74.5	79.9	92.2	87.4
October	79.5	79.3	80.3	76.7	84.4	79.3	75.4	73.2	78.4	109.7	88.8	80.7	78.6	75.7	80.3	91.4	86.8
November	80.7	79.9	80.4	77.5	85.8	81.4	76.7	75.0	78.8	111.4	89.3	81.8	79.7	78.3	80.5	92.8	87.2
December	81.1	80.1	80.5	78.2	85.7	82.0	76.9	74.9	79.5	113.6	88.9	82.1	79.7	78.4	80.4	94.4	86.7
1981:																	
January	80.4	79.6	80.2	76.5	85.6	81.1	76.4	74.2	79.4	113.0	84.6	81.2	79.0	78.6	79.2	93.8	82.5
February	80.8	80.2	80.6	78.0	84.6	81.3	76.9	74.7	79.8	114.1	83.0	81.4	79.2	78.9	79.4	94.3	80.8
March	81.2	80.4	80.4	78.2	85.6	81.9	77.1	75.1	79.8	115.2	84.1	81.6	79.3	78.8	79.6	94.9	81.9
April	80.6	80.5	80.3	78.1	85.4	80.5	77.2	75.2	79.9	109.6	82.9	80.9	79.3	78.8	79.5	90.0	80.7
May	81.3	81.2	81.0	79.2	85.1	81.1	77.8	76.0	80.2	110.3	85.2	81.4	79.6	78.8	80.1	90.3	82.8
June	81.8	81.2	80.3	80.0	83.3	82.3	77.7	75.9	80.0	115.0	86.6	81.8	79.3	78.3	79.9	93.7	84.1
July	82.6	81.6	81.1	79.8	83.0	83.4	78.2	76.3	80.7	117.8	86.9	82.3	79.6	78.8	80.1	95.6	84.4
August	82.2	81.0	80.4	78.4	83.0	83.4	77.5	75.8	79.9	119.4	85.6	81.8	78.8	78.9	78.8	96.6	83.1
September	81.5	80.5	79.8	78.0	80.4	82.5	76.9	74.9	79.7	118.6	84.5	80.9	78.0	77.4	78.4	95.5	82.0
October	80.9	80.2	79.4	77.9	79.0	81.5	76.1	74.1	78.7	118.7	85.6	80.1	77.0	75.4	77.8	95.2	82.9
November	79.8	79.5	78.9	76.0	77.2	79.8	74.9	72.4	78.3	117.3	85.2	78.8	75.6	73.5	76.8	93.7	82.5
December	78.9	79.1	78.2	75.6	74.9	78.3	73.7	71.1	77.3	117.7	85.5	77.7	74.2	70.7	76.1	93.7	82.8
1982:																	
January	77.6	78.1	77.8	72.9	74.0	76.7	72.2	68.8	76.9	116.8	86.3	76.3	72.6	69.3	74.3	92.6	83.5
February	79.3	80.0	79.4	75.0	77.3	78.1	74.3	71.1	78.7	117.7	84.2	77.8	74.6	71.5	76.2	92.9	81.4
March	78.7	79.5	78.9	74.8	75.8	77.5	73.8	70.6	78.3	116.8	83.8	77.1	73.9	70.4	75.7	91.9	81.0
April	78.0	78.9	78.7	73.5	75.4	76.5	73.1	69.9	77.6	115.1	83.8	76.2	73.1	69.3	75.1	90.2	80.9
May	77.4	78.4	78.8	72.3	76.5	75.9	72.8	69.6	77.4	113.1	82.0	75.4	72.7	68.7	74.7	88.3	79.1
June	77.1	78.2	79.4	71.7	76.4	75.5	72.8	69.5	77.5	111.1	81.6	75.0	72.6	68.9	74.4	86.3	78.7
July	76.5	77.7	79.1	70.9	76.3	74.7	72.2	68.8	77.0	109.7	81.6	74.2	71.8	68.0	73.8	85.0	78.6
August	76.1	77.2	79.5	68.9	76.6	74.4	71.9	67.7	77.8	108.4	81.8	73.7	71.4	68.4	72.9	83.6	78.7
September	75.5	76.7	78.9	68.3	76.0	73.8	71.5	67.0	77.9	106.9	80.7	73.0	70.9	68.2	72.2	82.1	77.6
October	74.9	76.0	78.7	66.6	75.2	73.3	70.7	65.6	78.0	107.0	81.1	72.2	69.9	67.4	71.2	81.8	77.9
November	74.7	75.9	78.7	65.8	75.9	72.9	70.5	65.2	77.9	106.4	81.7	71.9	69.6	67.2	70.8	81.0	78.4
December	74.1	75.7	77.8	66.4	73.7	71.9	70.0	65.1	77.0	105.9	79.2	71.1	69.0	66.2	70.4	80.3	75.9

Industrial Production and Capacity Utilization—*Continued*

(Seasonally adjusted)

Year and month	Total indus-trial produc-tion	Industrial production indexes (1992=100)										Capacity utilization (output as a percent of capacity)					
		Major market groups					Major industry groups					Total industry	Manufacturing			Mining	Utilities
		Products				Materials	Manufacturing			Mining	Utilities		Total	Primary process-ing	Ad-vanced process-ing		
		Total	Con-sumer goods	Busi-ness equip-ment	Con-struc-tion supplies		Total	Dura-bles	Non-dura-bles								
1983:																	
January	75.7	76.7	79.6	65.6	77.8	74.1	71.8	66.8	78.9	107.1	79.4	72.5	70.6	69.0	71.4	81.0	76.1
February	75.5	76.5	79.8	65.1	79.0	74.0	72.1	67.4	78.8	104.4	77.6	72.3	70.8	69.9	71.3	79.0	74.2
March	76.2	77.1	80.1	65.7	79.6	75.0	73.1	68.6	79.6	103.1	78.7	72.9	71.8	71.2	72.0	77.9	75.2
April	77.2	78.0	81.4	65.8	82.1	75.9	74.0	69.5	80.3	104.2	81.1	73.7	72.5	72.3	72.5	78.7	77.4
May	78.1	78.8	82.3	66.1	83.0	77.0	75.0	70.5	81.4	104.0	82.7	74.5	73.4	73.9	73.1	78.6	78.9
June	78.6	79.6	83.1	66.6	84.2	77.0	75.6	71.2	81.9	104.1	81.8	74.8	73.9	74.1	73.7	78.6	77.9
July	80.0	80.5	83.9	67.3	86.6	79.0	76.7	72.7	82.4	106.2	85.5	76.1	74.8	75.5	74.5	80.1	81.3
August	81.0	81.6	85.1	68.3	86.5	80.1	77.6	73.6	83.2	107.9	88.0	77.0	75.6	76.1	75.4	81.3	83.6
September	82.4	83.2	86.3	71.1	87.1	81.2	79.3	75.7	84.4	109.1	86.2	78.2	77.2	77.4	77.0	82.2	81.8
October	83.1	83.3	85.5	71.7	88.5	82.6	79.8	76.6	84.3	110.4	87.4	78.7	77.6	78.4	77.2	83.2	82.9
November	83.0	83.4	85.2	72.7	88.0	82.2	80.1	77.0	84.3	109.8	84.5	78.6	77.7	78.2	77.5	82.7	80.1
December	83.4	84.2	85.7	73.6	87.3	82.1	80.0	77.5	83.5	109.0	91.9	78.9	77.5	77.8	77.4	82.0	87.0
1984:																	
January	85.1	85.4	86.9	76.0	89.0	84.6	82.0	80.1	84.6	112.9	88.0	80.4	79.3	79.5	79.2	84.9	83.3
February	85.0	85.3	86.5	75.6	90.3	84.4	82.4	80.5	85.1	111.6	83.3	80.1	79.5	80.2	79.2	84.0	78.8
March	85.9	85.9	86.6	77.1	90.9	85.7	83.0	81.3	85.4	112.3	88.5	80.8	79.8	80.7	79.4	84.5	83.7
April	86.4	86.5	87.5	77.4	91.0	86.0	83.4	81.9	85.5	113.7	88.3	81.0	80.0	80.5	79.8	85.6	83.4
May	86.9	86.8	86.8	78.2	90.4	86.7	83.7	82.4	85.6	115.6	88.8	81.3	80.1	80.9	79.6	87.1	83.9
June	87.3	87.5	87.2	79.5	90.6	86.7	84.3	83.0	86.0	116.0	87.5	81.5	80.3	81.0	80.1	87.5	82.6
July	87.5	87.8	87.1	80.6	90.6	86.8	84.5	83.6	85.8	117.0	85.8	81.5	80.4	80.3	80.4	88.4	81.1
August	87.5	87.5	86.0	81.2	90.2	87.1	84.6	84.2	85.2	115.6	86.8	81.3	80.2	80.2	80.2	87.4	82.0
September	87.3	87.4	86.2	80.8	90.0	87.0	84.4	83.9	85.2	116.1	86.3	81.0	79.8	80.1	79.7	87.9	81.4
October	86.9	87.6	86.6	81.1	90.1	85.8	84.5	83.8	85.4	112.3	86.0	80.5	79.6	79.4	79.8	85.1	81.1
November	87.0	87.9	86.8	81.2	90.9	85.5	84.5	83.9	85.4	112.0	86.4	80.4	79.5	79.2	79.6	85.0	81.5
December	86.6	87.5	86.4	81.4	90.4	85.2	84.3	83.8	85.0	111.2	85.0	79.8	79.0	78.2	79.4	84.6	80.2
1985:																	
January	86.9	87.6	86.4	81.4	89.4	85.7	84.4	84.1	84.7	110.0	89.8	79.9	78.9	78.5	79.1	83.7	84.6
February	87.7	88.3	87.0	81.9	90.8	86.6	84.9	84.6	85.2	112.1	91.5	80.4	79.1	79.2	79.0	85.4	86.3
March	87.9	88.7	87.2	82.3	92.0	86.6	85.4	85.2	85.7	112.1	88.7	80.4	79.3	79.3	79.4	85.4	83.6
April	88.0	88.9	86.8	83.2	93.3	86.6	85.6	85.5	85.7	112.1	89.1	80.3	79.2	79.6	79.1	85.4	83.9
May	88.2	89.6	87.5	83.4	94.1	86.2	86.0	85.7	86.3	112.1	87.2	80.3	79.4	79.2	79.5	85.4	82.1
June	88.0	89.3	87.6	82.1	94.0	86.1	85.7	85.6	86.0	112.2	86.9	79.9	78.9	79.2	78.7	85.5	81.8
July	87.6	88.8	87.0	82.5	93.8	85.9	85.4	85.4	85.5	110.7	87.4	79.4	78.3	79.0	78.0	84.2	82.2
August	88.2	89.6	87.9	82.9	95.0	86.0	86.1	86.2	86.1	110.0	87.2	79.6	78.8	79.4	78.5	83.6	82.0
September	88.7	90.1	88.6	83.0	95.1	86.6	86.4	86.0	87.0	110.8	89.7	79.9	78.8	79.4	78.5	84.1	84.2
October	87.9	89.2	88.1	81.3	94.4	86.0	85.7	85.3	86.4	109.8	88.5	79.0	77.9	77.4	77.4	83.2	83.0
November	88.4	90.1	88.3	83.4	95.4	86.0	86.7	86.7	86.7	108.1	87.3	79.2	78.5	79.0	78.3	81.8	81.8
December	89.0	90.3	88.6	82.8	94.3	87.1	86.6	86.5	86.8	111.2	92.0	79.5	78.2	78.9	77.9	83.9	86.2
1986:																	
January	89.6	91.4	90.0	83.5	97.8	87.0	87.9	87.4	88.4	111.0	86.9	79.8	79.1	79.9	78.8	83.6	81.3
February	89.0	90.4	89.7	82.5	96.8	86.8	87.4	87.0	88.0	108.8	86.3	79.2	78.6	79.6	78.2	81.9	80.7
March	88.1	89.6	88.7	82.0	96.1	85.9	86.6	86.3	87.0	106.5	85.7	78.2	77.8	78.6	77.4	80.2	80.1
April	88.7	90.7	90.8	82.2	97.3	86.0	87.8	87.3	88.4	103.3	85.3	78.7	78.7	79.5	78.4	77.8	79.7
May	88.6	90.3	90.4	81.9	97.0	86.0	87.7	87.1	88.6	102.2	85.4	78.4	78.5	79.6	78.0	77.0	79.7
June	88.2	90.0	90.6	80.3	96.9	85.7	87.5	86.4	88.9	100.7	85.9	78.1	78.1	79.4	77.6	75.9	80.1
July	88.5	90.4	90.8	81.6	97.2	85.8	87.7	86.9	88.8	100.6	87.0	78.2	78.2	79.0	77.9	75.4	81.2
August	88.8	90.7	90.9	81.9	98.1	86.0	88.2	87.3	89.5	99.7	85.5	78.3	78.6	80.2	77.9	75.4	79.7
September	88.7	90.7	90.5	82.3	99.1	85.8	88.2	87.8	88.9	98.2	85.8	78.2	78.4	80.1	77.7	74.5	80.0
October	89.5	91.6	91.3	82.2	100.4	86.5	88.9	87.9	90.3	99.4	87.3	78.8	78.9	80.4	78.2	75.5	81.3
November	89.9	91.9	91.6	81.4	101.8	87.2	89.3	88.2	90.6	100.6	88.0	79.1	79.1	81.3	78.1	76.7	82.0
December	90.8	93.1	93.0	82.3	102.5	87.5	90.3	89.1	91.8	100.0	87.9	79.7	79.9	81.8	79.0	76.5	81.9
1987:																	
January	90.2	92.1	91.5	81.4	101.5	87.4	89.6	88.5	91.0	100.6	87.6	79.1	79.1	81.1	78.3	77.3	81.5
February	91.2	93.3	92.8	83.2	102.3	88.2	91.0	90.2	92.0	100.5	86.2	80.0	80.2	82.1	79.4	77.6	80.1
March	91.6	93.7	93.3	83.0	102.4	88.5	91.2	90.2	92.4	100.4	88.4	80.2	80.3	82.5	79.3	78.0	82.0
April	92.0	93.9	92.8	83.4	103.4	89.1	91.6	90.8	92.8	100.5	88.2	80.5	80.6	83.5	79.3	78.4	81.7
May	92.4	94.3	93.2	83.3	103.6	89.5	91.9	90.8	93.3	100.9	89.8	80.7	80.7	83.8	79.3	79.1	83.1
June	93.2	95.3	93.9	85.3	106.0	90.1	92.8	91.9	94.1	101.0	89.9	81.4	81.4	84.4	80.0	79.5	83.0
July	93.7	95.7	94.1	85.4	105.9	90.9	93.4	92.1	95.2	100.4	90.9	81.8	81.8	85.6	80.1	79.4	83.8
August	93.8	95.8	94.4	85.0	106.5	91.0	93.3	92.2	94.7	103.1	91.7	81.8	81.5	85.0	80.0	81.7	84.5
September	93.7	95.6	93.6	86.0	105.3	91.1	93.4	92.4	94.6	103.1	89.3	81.6	81.5	85.5	79.8	81.9	82.2
October	95.0	96.8	94.7	87.8	106.9	92.4	94.6	94.6	94.8	104.3	91.1	82.6	82.5	86.1	80.8	83.1	83.7
November	95.3	96.9	94.8	88.1	106.8	92.9	95.1	94.9	95.3	105.0	89.4	82.8	82.8	86.7	80.9	83.8	82.0
December	95.9	97.2	95.0	89.1	106.3	93.8	95.6	95.6	95.8	105.3	90.1	83.2	83.1	87.5	81.2	84.2	82.5
1988:																	
January	95.9	97.7	95.9	89.4	105.2	93.4	95.4	95.6	95.3	104.1	94.0	83.2	82.9	86.4	81.3	83.4	85.9
February	96.2	98.1	96.0	90.2	106.1	93.6	95.8	95.9	95.8	104.4	93.9	83.4	83.1	86.8	81.4	83.8	85.7
March	96.3	97.8	95.6	90.0	106.2	93.9	95.7	95.8	95.7	105.6	93.9	83.3	82.9	86.9	81.1	85.0	85.6
April	96.8	98.6	96.6	91.9	106.7	94.2	96.7	97.2	96.2	104.7	91.4	83.7	83.7	87.0	82.1	84.5	83.2
May	96.9	98.5	96.2	92.9	106.9	94.5	96.6	97.7	95.3	105.6	92.7	83.7	83.5	86.7	82.0	85.4	84.1
June	97.0	98.3	96.0	93.1	106.2	94.9	96.6	97.8	95.1	105.6	93.5	83.6	83.4	86.5	81.9	85.7	84.7
July	97.6	98.9	96.3	94.1	106.9	95.6	97.3	98.4	96.0	105.2	94.7	84.1	83.8	86.9	82.4	85.6	85.6
August	98.1	99.6	97.3	95.1	105.9	95.9	97.5	98.5	96.4	105.7	98.0	84.5	84.0	86.5	82.8	86.3	88.4
September	97.8	99.3	96.8	95.3	106.1	95.5	97.7	99.3	96.0	104.0	93.0	84.1	84.0	86.6	82.8	85.2	83.7
October	98.0	99.6	97.5	95.2	106.3	95.7	97.9	99.3	96.4	104.0	93.9	84.2	84.1	86.6	82.9	85.6	84.4
November	98.8	100.2	97.9	97.1	106.2	96.6	98.9	100.7	96.7	103.7	93.6	84.8	84.8	87.2	83.6	85.6	83.9
December	99.3	100.8	98.5	97.9	107.2	97.0	99.4	101.2	97.4	103.9	93.7	85.1	85.1	87.9	83.8	86.1	83.8

Industrial Production and Capacity Utilization—*Continued*

(Seasonally adjusted)

Year and month	Total indus-trial produc-tion	Industrial production indexes (1992=100)										Capacity utilization (output as a percent of capacity)					
		Major market groups					Major industry groups					Manufacturing					
		Products				Mater-ials	Manufacturing			Mining	Utilities	Total industry	Manufacturing			Mining	Utilities
		Total	Con-sumer goods	Busi-ness equip-ment	Con-struc-tion supplies		Total	Dura-bles	Non-dura-bles				Total	Primary process-ing	Ad-vanced process-ing		
1989:																	
January	99.8	101.4	98.8	98.5	109.3	97.5	100.3	102.4	97.9	103.4	91.7	85.4	85.7	88.9	84.2	86.0	81.9
February	99.0	100.5	98.0	97.6	106.7	96.9	99.1	101.0	97.0	101.9	95.6	84.6	84.5	87.0	83.4	85.0	85.3
March	100.0	101.5	99.1	98.5	106.4	97.7	99.9	101.3	98.4	102.3	98.4	85.3	85.0	87.9	83.7	85.4	87.7
April	100.2	101.8	98.8	100.5	106.2	97.9	100.0	101.9	97.9	104.9	98.0	85.3	85.0	87.1	83.9	87.9	87.2
May	99.6	100.9	98.0	99.2	105.1	97.6	99.4	101.0	97.6	104.8	97.2	84.7	84.2	86.6	83.1	88.0	86.5
June	99.4	101.1	97.6	100.9	104.8	97.0	99.4	101.1	97.5	103.4	96.0	84.4	84.1	86.3	83.0	87.0	85.3
July	98.4	99.7	96.0	99.4	104.9	96.5	98.3	100.0	96.5	102.8	95.6	83.4	83.0	85.6	81.8	86.7	84.8
August	98.8	100.2	96.6	99.6	104.5	96.8	98.7	100.4	96.8	103.8	96.1	83.6	83.1	85.4	82.0	87.7	85.2
September	98.6	100.2	96.6	99.2	104.3	96.3	98.4	100.1	96.5	103.7	96.6	83.3	82.7	84.6	81.8	87.8	85.6
October	98.2	99.3	97.1	96.1	104.2	96.5	97.8	98.4	97.3	102.8	97.6	82.8	82.1	85.0	80.7	87.2	86.4
November	98.6	99.9	97.2	97.1	104.7	96.6	98.2	98.7	97.7	103.5	98.1	83.0	82.2	84.9	81.0	88.0	86.7
December	99.0	100.9	98.4	99.5	105.1	96.3	98.3	99.6	96.9	101.2	104.8	83.2	82.1	83.7	81.4	86.2	92.6
1990:																	
January	98.6	100.2	96.8	97.7	105.6	96.2	98.1	98.0	98.2	105.2	97.3	82.7	81.8	84.8	80.5	89.7	85.8
February	99.1	100.6	97.7	98.1	105.7	96.9	99.0	99.4	98.6	104.6	94.8	83.0	82.5	85.2	81.2	89.2	83.4
March	99.6	101.1	98.2	98.5	105.5	97.3	99.3	100.2	98.4	104.4	97.6	83.3	82.6	84.8	81.6	89.2	85.7
April	99.0	100.0	97.4	96.8	104.6	97.4	98.6	99.2	97.8	104.9	97.9	82.7	81.8	84.7	80.5	89.6	85.8
May	99.4	100.5	97.5	98.4	103.6	97.6	99.0	99.9	97.9	104.7	98.6	82.9	82.0	84.6	80.8	89.5	86.2
June	99.3	100.3	98.2	97.8	103.2	97.8	98.9	100.0	97.6	104.5	99.8	82.7	81.8	84.3	80.6	89.5	87.0
July	99.3	100.4	97.6	98.9	102.5	97.7	98.8	99.8	97.8	104.9	99.0	82.6	81.6	84.0	80.6	89.9	86.2
August	99.5	100.4	97.8	99.7	101.5	98.0	99.1	100.1	98.0	104.4	99.3	82.6	81.7	84.3	80.5	89.5	86.3
September	99.6	100.6	98.4	99.4	101.7	98.0	99.0	100.1	97.9	105.4	100.6	82.6	81.5	83.8	80.5	90.4	87.3
October	99.1	100.0	97.2	99.2	101.0	97.6	98.4	99.1	97.8	105.9	99.5	82.0	80.9	83.1	79.9	91.0	86.2
November	97.7	98.6	95.9	97.3	100.0	96.4	97.2	96.8	97.5	105.1	97.3	80.8	79.7	82.1	78.6	90.4	84.1
December	97.2	98.2	95.3	96.2	99.2	95.6	96.6	95.7	97.5	103.7	97.8	80.2	79.0	80.9	78.2	89.2	84.5
1991:																	
January	96.7	97.6	95.9	95.9	95.5	95.3	95.8	94.7	96.9	104.0	100.4	79.6	78.2	79.8	77.5	89.5	86.6
February	95.9	96.8	94.8	95.8	94.6	94.6	95.0	93.9	96.4	105.3	97.0	78.9	77.5	79.1	76.8	90.6	83.6
March	95.0	96.0	94.8	94.8	93.9	93.5	94.1	93.1	95.1	104.1	97.6	78.1	76.6	77.7	76.1	89.6	84.1
April	95.4	96.4	95.0	95.3	95.0	93.8	94.4	93.7	95.2	103.5	98.9	78.2	76.8	77.9	76.2	89.1	85.2
May	96.1	97.1	96.7	94.9	94.8	94.6	95.0	94.0	96.2	103.0	102.2	78.7	77.1	78.1	76.7	88.7	87.9
June	97.2	98.5	98.1	96.1	98.2	95.3	96.3	95.7	97.0	103.0	102.1	79.6	78.1	79.2	77.6	88.7	87.8
July	97.3	97.9	97.9	95.1	96.8	96.4	96.6	95.9	97.3	101.8	101.7	79.5	78.2	79.9	77.4	87.7	87.4
August	97.4	97.7	97.4	95.2	97.1	97.1	96.8	96.1	97.5	101.4	101.5	79.5	78.2	80.4	77.3	87.4	87.1
September	98.4	98.9	98.9	97.1	97.7	97.5	97.8	97.5	98.2	101.6	101.4	80.2	79.0	80.8	78.2	87.6	86.9
October	98.3	98.5	98.6	96.7	96.3	97.9	97.8	97.3	98.3	101.5	100.9	80.0	78.9	80.8	78.0	87.6	86.3
November	98.1	98.5	98.6	96.6	97.6	97.5	97.6	97.4	97.7	100.8	102.3	79.8	78.6	80.5	77.7	87.0	87.4
December	97.5	97.7	97.9	95.5	96.4	97.2	97.1	96.5	97.7	100.9	99.3	79.2	78.1	80.3	77.1	87.2	84.7
1992:																	
January	97.7	97.5	97.4	95.1	97.5	98.0	97.4	96.5	98.4	100.4	98.5	79.2	78.2	80.8	77.1	86.8	83.9
February	98.2	98.3	98.2	97.4	99.3	98.2	98.1	98.0	98.2	99.3	99.0	79.5	78.6	81.0	77.6	85.9	84.1
March	98.9	98.9	99.0	97.3	99.2	99.0	98.9	98.5	99.3	99.5	99.1	79.9	79.1	81.9	77.9	86.0	84.1
April	99.6	99.7	99.8	99.2	99.7	99.6	99.5	99.3	99.7	100.5	100.6	80.3	79.4	82.2	78.3	86.9	85.3
May	99.9	99.9	99.9	99.4	100.9	99.9	99.9	100.2	99.4	100.5	99.5	80.4	79.6	82.3	78.4	86.9	84.2
June	99.7	99.4	99.3	99.7	99.7	100.2	99.9	99.9	99.9	99.5	98.2	80.1	79.5	82.5	78.1	86.1	83.0
July	100.5	100.4	100.3	101.1	101.2	100.7	100.6	100.5	100.7	101.0	98.8	80.6	79.9	83.1	78.5	87.3	83.4
August	100.2	100.5	100.5	100.8	101.3	99.7	100.4	100.2	100.5	99.1	98.7	80.2	79.6	82.2	78.4	85.6	83.2
September	100.6	100.6	100.5	101.2	100.1	100.6	100.7	100.5	100.9	99.8	100.0	80.4	79.7	82.5	78.5	86.3	84.3
October	101.2	101.2	101.4	102.0	100.4	101.1	101.2	101.6	100.8	100.5	101.3	80.8	79.9	82.8	78.7	86.8	85.4
November	101.7	101.8	101.8	103.1	100.5	101.5	101.8	102.2	101.3	99.8	102.1	81.0	80.2	83.1	79.0	86.1	86.0
December	101.8	102.0	102.0	103.9	100.3	101.4	101.7	102.6	100.7	100.1	104.2	81.0	80.0	82.6	78.9	86.4	87.7
1993:																	
January	102.2	102.4	102.3	104.7	101.4	102.0	102.6	103.6	101.5	99.5	101.0	81.2	80.5	83.6	79.2	85.9	85.0
February	102.7	102.7	102.7	104.4	102.3	102.7	102.8	103.9	101.6	99.2	104.7	81.4	80.6	83.8	79.2	85.5	88.0
March	102.9	102.8	102.7	105.5	101.1	103.0	103.0	104.4	101.4	99.2	105.1	81.4	80.5	83.3	79.3	85.5	88.4
April	103.3	103.1	102.8	106.0	101.5	103.5	103.6	105.2	101.9	98.9	103.5	81.5	80.8	83.8	79.6	85.2	87.0
May	102.7	102.8	102.3	106.1	102.7	102.7	103.2	104.9	101.3	98.6	101.2	81.0	80.4	83.3	79.1	84.9	85.0
June	103.0	102.5	102.4	105.2	101.8	103.8	103.2	104.7	101.5	100.3	103.2	81.0	80.1	83.7	78.7	86.4	86.7
July	103.2	103.0	103.1	105.6	102.8	103.4	103.4	104.8	101.8	99.1	104.5	81.0	80.1	83.8	78.6	85.3	87.7
August	102.8	102.6	102.8	103.6	103.5	103.2	102.9	104.0	101.6	99.4	105.3	80.6	79.6	83.7	77.8	85.5	88.3
September	103.9	103.6	103.5	105.7	104.6	104.3	104.1	106.0	102.0	100.1	104.5	81.3	80.4	84.2	78.8	86.0	87.6
October	104.3	103.9	103.8	106.2	105.6	104.9	104.5	107.0	101.8	101.1	104.4	81.4	80.5	84.3	78.9	86.9	87.4
November	104.8	104.1	103.9	106.6	105.7	105.9	105.1	107.7	102.2	101.8	104.5	81.7	80.8	84.9	79.0	87.4	87.4
December	105.7	104.8	104.4	108.0	108.0	107.1	106.0	109.3	102.5	101.9	105.0	82.2	81.4	85.6	79.6	87.5	87.7
1994:																	
January	105.9	105.4	105.0	109.7	107.1	106.7	106.1	109.5	102.4	100.7	108.0	82.2	81.2	85.3	79.4	86.4	90.1
February	106.4	105.6	105.5	110.0	106.0	107.6	106.7	110.1	102.9	101.4	107.1	82.3	81.4	85.4	79.7	87.0	89.3
March	107.2	106.0	105.9	110.0	106.7	109.0	107.6	110.7	104.2	103.7	105.0	82.6	81.8	86.2	80.0	88.9	87.4
April	107.6	106.4	106.4	110.5	109.1	109.6	108.4	112.0	104.5	102.0	103.5	82.7	82.2	86.8	80.2	87.3	86.1
May	108.4	106.8	107.1	111.1	109.6	110.9	109.3	113.0	105.3	102.6	103.2	83.1	82.5	87.3	80.5	87.8	85.7
June	108.9	107.2	107.6	111.6	110.4	111.7	109.5	113.2	105.4	103.2	107.6	83.2	82.4	87.0	80.4	88.2	89.3
July	109.3	107.1	106.8	113.2	112.2	112.7	110.1	114.9	104.8	102.3	105.9	83.2	82.6	87.3	80.5	87.4	87.8
August	109.8	107.5	108.0	113.3	111.6	113.6	110.7	115.2	105.8	103.5	105.5	83.4	82.8	87.3	80.8	88.3	87.4
September	110.0	107.5	107.3	113.9	112.3	114.0	111.1	116.1	105.7	102.0	104.9	83.3	82.7	87.4	80.7	86.9	86.8
October	110.8	108.7	108.2	115.9	113.8	114.0	112.0	117.1	106.4	101.1	105.0	83.5	83.1	87.6	81.2	86.1	86.8
November	111.6	109.0	108.3	116.7	113.0	115.8	113.0	118.3	107.2	102.5	103.6	83.9	83.6	88.1	81.6	87.2	85.6
December	112.9	109.8	108.9	118.2	115.7	117.6	114.3	120.6	107.4	103.9	104.1	84.6	84.2	89.2	82.1	88.3	86.0

Civilian Population, Labor Force, Employment, and Unemployment

(Thousands of persons, 16 years of age and over, seasonally adjusted, except as noted)

Year and month	Noninsti-tutional population (Not seasonally adjusted)	Labor force		Employed		Unemployed		By age and sex					
		Thousands of persons	Participa-tion rate [1]	Thousands of persons	Ratio: Employ-ment to popula-tion [2]	Total	Long-term [3]	Men 20 years and over		Women 20 years and over		Both sexes, 16 to 19 years	
								Employed	Unem-ployed	Employed	Unem-ployed	Employed	Unem-ployed
1971:													
January	138 795	83 850	60.4	78 864	56.8	4 986	1 113	45 527	2 100	27 173	1 637	6 164	1 249
February	139 021	83 603	60.1	78 700	56.6	4 903	1 068	45 455	2 069	27 040	1 629	6 205	1 205
March	139 285	83 575	60.0	78 588	56.4	4 987	1 098	45 520	2 055	26 967	1 687	6 101	1 245
April	139 566	83 946	60.1	78 987	56.6	4 959	1 149	45 789	2 049	26 984	1 700	6 214	1 210
May	139 826	84 135	60.2	79 139	56.6	4 996	1 173	45 917	2 093	27 056	1 662	6 166	1 241
June	140 090	83 706	59.8	78 757	56.2	4 949	1 167	45 879	2 061	27 013	1 623	5 865	1 265
July	140 343	84 340	60.1	79 305	56.5	5 035	1 251	46 000	2 079	27 054	1 610	6 251	1 346
August	140 596	84 673	60.2	79 539	56.6	5 134	1 261	46 041	2 160	27 171	1 694	6 327	1 280
September	140 869	84 731	60.1	79 689	56.6	5 042	1 239	46 090	2 142	27 390	1 657	6 209	1 243
October	141 146	84 872	60.1	79 918	56.6	4 954	1 268	46 132	2 029	27 538	1 650	6 248	1 275
November	141 393	85 458	60.4	80 297	56.8	5 161	1 277	46 209	2 166	27 721	1 701	6 367	1 294
December	141 666	85 625	60.4	80 471	56.8	5 154	1 283	46 280	2 178	27 791	1 674	6 400	1 302
1972:													
January	142 736	85 978	60.2	80 959	56.7	5 019	1 257	46 471	2 071	27 956	1 624	6 532	1 324
February	143 017	86 036	60.2	81 108	56.7	4 928	1 292	46 600	1 993	28 016	1 506	6 492	1 429
March	143 263	86 611	60.5	81 573	56.9	5 038	1 232	46 821	2 034	28 126	1 625	6 626	1 379
April	143 483	86 614	60.4	81 655	56.9	4 959	1 203	46 863	2 019	28 114	1 619	6 678	1 321
May	143 760	86 809	60.4	81 887	57.0	4 922	1 168	46 950	2 006	28 184	1 698	6 753	1 218
June	144 033	87 006	60.4	82 083	57.0	4 923	1 141	47 147	1 981	28 175	1 666	6 761	1 276
July	144 285	87 143	60.4	82 230	57.0	4 913	1 154	47 244	1 960	28 225	1 702	6 761	1 251
August	144 522	87 517	60.6	82 578	57.1	4 939	1 156	47 321	1 898	28 382	1 684	6 875	1 357
September	144 761	87 392	60.4	82 543	57.0	4 849	1 131	47 394	1 878	28 417	1 657	6 732	1 314
October	144 988	87 491	60.3	82 616	57.0	4 875	1 123	47 354	1 910	28 438	1 689	6 824	1 276
November	145 211	87 592	60.3	82 990	57.2	4 602	1 040	47 529	1 791	28 567	1 523	6 894	1 288
December	145 446	87 943	60.5	83 400	57.3	4 543	1 006	47 747	1 742	28 698	1 512	6 955	1 289
1973:													
January	145 720	87 487	60.0	83 161	57.1	4 326	947	47 701	1 688	28 596	1 552	6 864	1 086
February	145 943	88 364	60.5	83 912	57.5	4 452	894	47 884	1 693	28 995	1 492	7 033	1 267
March	146 230	88 846	60.8	84 452	57.8	4 394	889	48 117	1 695	29 110	1 498	7 225	1 201
April	146 459	89 018	60.8	84 559	57.7	4 459	809	48 098	1 670	29 304	1 480	7 157	1 309
May	146 719	88 977	60.6	84 648	57.7	4 329	816	48 068	1 671	29 432	1 403	7 148	1 255
June	146 981	89 548	60.9	85 185	58.0	4 363	779	48 244	1 628	29 505	1 541	7 436	1 194
July	147 233	89 604	60.9	85 299	57.9	4 305	756	48 452	1 566	29 592	1 532	7 255	1 207
August	147 471	89 509	60.7	85 204	57.8	4 305	788	48 353	1 575	29 578	1 546	7 273	1 184
September	147 731	89 838	60.8	85 488	57.9	4 350	785	48 408	1 543	29 710	1 539	7 370	1 268
October	147 980	90 131	60.9	85 987	58.1	4 144	793	48 631	1 467	29 885	1 416	7 471	1 261
November	148 219	90 716	61.2	86 320	58.2	4 396	832	48 764	1 560	30 071	1 518	7 485	1 318
December	148 479	90 890	61.2	86 401	58.2	4 489	767	48 902	1 628	29 991	1 573	7 508	1 288
1974:													
January	148 753	91 199	61.3	86 555	58.2	4 644	799	49 107	1 755	29 893	1 598	7 555	1 291
February	148 982	91 485	61.4	86 754	58.2	4 731	829	49 057	1 809	30 146	1 600	7 551	1 322
March	149 225	91 453	61.3	86 819	58.2	4 634	849	48 986	1 735	30 293	1 581	7 540	1 318
April	149 478	91 287	61.1	86 669	58.0	4 618	889	48 853	1 796	30 376	1 579	7 440	1 243
May	149 750	91 596	61.2	86 891	58.0	4 705	880	49 039	1 736	30 424	1 618	7 428	1 351
June	150 012	91 868	61.2	86 941	58.0	4 927	926	48 946	1 800	30 512	1 670	7 483	1 457
July	150 248	92 212	61.4	87 149	58.0	5 063	924	48 883	1 833	30 869	1 733	7 397	1 497
August	150 493	92 059	61.2	87 037	57.8	5 022	960	48 950	1 957	30 662	1 764	7 425	1 301
September	150 753	92 488	61.4	87 051	57.7	5 437	1 021	48 978	1 978	30 569	1 918	7 504	1 541
October	151 009	92 518	61.3	86 995	57.6	5 523	1 072	48 959	2 129	30 570	1 846	7 466	1 548
November	151 256	92 766	61.3	86 626	57.3	6 140	1 128	48 833	2 380	30 424	2 166	7 369	1 594
December	151 494	92 780	61.2	86 144	56.9	6 636	1 326	48 458	2 727	30 431	2 295	7 255	1 614
1975:													
January	151 755	93 128	61.4	85 627	56.4	7 501	1 555	48 086	3 127	30 343	2 629	7 198	1 745
February	151 990	92 776	61.0	85 256	56.1	7 520	1 841	47 927	3 214	30 215	2 595	7 114	1 711
March	152 217	93 165	61.2	85 187	56.0	7 978	2 074	47 776	3 476	30 334	2 742	7 077	1 760
April	152 443	93 399	61.3	85 189	55.9	8 210	2 442	47 759	3 632	30 410	2 831	7 020	1 747
May	152 704	93 884	61.5	85 451	56.0	8 433	2 643	47 835	3 772	30 483	2 838	7 133	1 823
June	152 976	93 575	61.2	85 355	55.8	8 220	2 843	47 754	3 627	30 618	2 753	6 983	1 840
July	153 309	94 021	61.3	85 894	56.0	8 127	2 943	48 050	3 611	30 794	2 679	7 050	1 837
August	153 580	94 162	61.3	86 234	56.1	7 928	2 862	48 239	3 453	30 966	2 643	7 029	1 832
September	153 848	94 202	61.2	86 279	56.1	7 923	2 906	48 126	3 585	30 979	2 600	7 174	1 738
October	154 082	94 267	61.2	86 370	56.1	7 897	2 689	48 165	3 489	31 121	2 657	7 084	1 751
November	154 338	94 250	61.1	86 456	56.0	7 794	2 789	48 203	3 497	31 135	2 624	7 118	1 673
December	154 589	94 409	61.1	86 665	56.1	7 744	2 868	48 266	3 346	31 268	2 638	7 131	1 760
1976:													
January	154 853	94 934	61.3	87 400	56.4	7 534	2 713	48 592	3 161	31 595	2 619	7 213	1 754
February	155 066	94 998	61.3	87 672	56.5	7 326	2 519	48 721	3 041	31 680	2 575	7 271	1 710
March	155 306	95 215	61.3	87 985	56.7	7 230	2 441	48 836	3 012	31 842	2 518	7 307	1 700
April	155 529	95 746	61.6	88 416	56.8	7 330	2 210	49 097	3 002	31 951	2 545	7 368	1 783
May	155 765	95 847	61.5	88 794	57.0	7 053	2 115	49 193	2 968	32 147	2 384	7 454	1 701
June	156 027	95 885	61.5	88 563	56.8	7 322	2 332	49 010	3 167	32 267	2 498	7 286	1 657
July	156 276	96 583	61.8	89 093	57.0	7 490	2 316	49 236	3 136	32 334	2 673	7 523	1 681
August	156 525	96 741	61.8	89 223	57.0	7 518	2 378	49 417	3 046	32 437	2 673	7 369	1 799
September	156 779	96 553	61.6	89 173	56.9	7 380	2 296	49 485	3 075	32 390	2 635	7 298	1 670
October	156 993	96 704	61.6	89 274	56.9	7 430	2 292	49 524	3 076	32 412	2 638	7 338	1 716
November	157 235	97 254	61.9	89 634	57.0	7 620	2 354	49 561	3 241	32 753	2 644	7 320	1 735
December	157 438	97 348	61.8	89 803	57.0	7 545	2 375	49 599	3 227	32 914	2 597	7 290	1 721

1. Civilian labor force as a percent of the civilian noninstitutional population.
2. Civilian employment as a percent of the civilian population.
3. Fifteen weeks and over.

Civilian Population, Labor Force, Employment, and Unemployment—*Continued*

(Thousands of persons, 16 years of age and over, seasonally adjusted, except as noted)

Year and month	Noninstitutional population (Not seasonally adjusted)	Labor force		Employed		Unemployed		By age and sex					
		Thousands of persons	Participation rate [1]	Thousands of persons	Ratio: Employment to population [2]	Total	Long-term [3]	Men 20 years and over		Women 20 years and over		Both sexes, 16 to 19 years	
								Employed	Unemployed	Employed	Unemployed	Employed	Unemployed
1977:													
January	157 688	97 208	61.6	89 928	57.0	7 280	2 200	49 738	3 046	32 872	2 527	7 318	1 707
February	157 913	97 785	61.9	90 342	57.2	7 443	2 174	49 838	3 136	32 997	2 616	7 507	1 691
March	158 131	98 115	62.0	90 808	57.4	7 307	2 057	50 031	2 939	33 246	2 642	7 531	1 726
April	158 371	98 330	62.1	91 271	57.6	7 059	1 936	50 185	2 824	33 470	2 562	7 616	1 673
May	158 657	98 665	62.2	91 754	57.8	6 911	1 928	50 280	2 847	33 851	2 408	7 623	1 656
June	158 929	99 093	62.4	91 959	57.9	7 134	1 918	50 544	2 769	33 678	2 577	7 737	1 788
July	159 185	98 913	62.1	92 084	57.8	6 829	1 907	50 597	2 698	33 749	2 492	7 738	1 639
August	159 430	99 366	62.3	92 441	58.0	6 925	1 836	50 745	2 720	33 809	2 542	7 887	1 663
September	159 674	99 453	62.3	92 702	58.1	6 751	1 853	50 825	2 532	34 218	2 538	7 659	1 681
October	159 915	99 815	62.4	93 052	58.2	6 763	1 789	51 046	2 679	34 187	2 462	7 819	1 622
November	160 129	100 576	62.8	93 761	58.6	6 815	1 804	51 316	2 584	34 536	2 589	7 909	1 642
December	160 377	100 491	62.7	94 105	58.7	6 386	1 717	51 492	2 509	34 668	2 416	7 945	1 461
1978													
January	160 617	100 873	62.8	94 384	58.8	6 489	1 643	51 542	2 535	34 948	2 375	7 894	1 579
February	160 831	100 837	62.7	94 519	58.8	6 318	1 584	51 578	2 483	35 118	2 210	7 823	1 625
March	161 038	101 092	62.8	94 755	58.8	6 337	1 531	51 635	2 468	35 310	2 238	7 810	1 631
April	161 263	101 574	63.0	95 394	59.2	6 180	1 502	51 912	2 335	35 546	2 263	7 936	1 582
May	161 518	101 896	63.1	95 769	59.3	6 127	1 420	52 050	2 298	35 597	2 283	8 122	1 546
June	161 795	102 371	63.3	96 343	59.5	6 028	1 352	52 240	2 200	35 828	2 322	8 275	1 506
July	162 034	102 399	63.2	96 090	59.3	6 309	1 373	52 190	2 232	35 764	2 464	8 136	1 613
August	162 259	102 511	63.2	96 431	59.4	6 080	1 242	52 228	2 229	35 856	2 295	8 347	1 556
September	162 502	102 795	63.3	96 670	59.5	6 125	1 308	52 284	2 229	36 274	2 308	8 112	1 588
October	162 783	103 080	63.3	97 133	59.7	5 947	1 319	52 448	2 222	36 525	2 158	8 160	1 567
November	163 017	103 562	63.5	97 485	59.8	6 077	1 242	52 802	2 216	36 559	2 281	8 124	1 580
December	163 272	103 809	63.6	97 581	59.8	6 228	1 269	52 807	2 330	36 686	2 278	8 088	1 620
1979:													
January	163 516	104 057	63.6	97 948	59.9	6 109	1 250	53 072	2 277	36 697	2 262	8 179	1 570
February	163 726	104 502	63.8	98 329	60.1	6 173	1 297	53 233	2 291	36 904	2 312	8 192	1 570
March	164 027	104 589	63.8	98 480	60.0	6 109	1 365	53 120	2 270	37 159	2 289	8 201	1 550
April	164 162	104 172	63.5	98 103	59.8	6 069	1 272	53 085	2 253	36 944	2 238	8 074	1 578
May	164 459	104 171	63.3	98 331	59.8	5 840	1 239	53 178	2 117	37 134	2 189	8 019	1 534
June	164 721	104 638	63.5	98 679	59.9	5 959	1 171	53 309	2 193	37 221	2 251	8 149	1 515
July	164 970	105 002	63.6	99 006	60.0	5 996	1 123	53 384	2 302	37 514	2 196	8 108	1 498
August	165 198	105 096	63.6	98 776	59.8	6 320	1 203	53 336	2 350	37 548	2 406	7 892	1 564
September	165 431	105 530	63.8	99 340	60.0	6 190	1 172	53 510	2 345	37 798	2 254	8 032	1 591
October	165 813	105 700	63.7	99 404	59.9	6 296	1 219	53 478	2 417	37 931	2 300	7 995	1 579
November	166 051	105 812	63.7	99 574	60.0	6 238	1 239	53 435	2 449	38 065	2 264	8 074	1 525
December	166 300	106 258	63.9	99 933	60.1	6 325	1 277	53 555	2 435	38 259	2 319	8 119	1 571
1980:													
January	166 544	106 562	64.0	99 879	60.0	6 683	1 353	53 501	2 724	38 367	2 380	8 011	1 579
February	166 759	106 697	64.0	99 995	60.0	6 702	1 358	53 686	2 726	38 389	2 395	7 920	1 581
March	166 984	106 442	63.7	99 713	59.7	6 729	1 457	53 353	2 842	38 406	2 341	7 954	1 546
April	167 197	106 591	63.8	99 233	59.4	7 358	1 694	53 035	3 292	38 427	2 565	7 771	1 501
May	167 407	106 929	63.9	98 945	59.1	7 984	1 740	52 915	3 598	38 335	2 624	7 695	1 762
June	167 643	106 780	63.7	98 682	58.9	8 098	1 760	52 712	3 662	38 312	2 656	7 658	1 780
July	167 932	107 159	63.8	98 796	58.8	8 363	1 995	52 733	3 820	38 374	2 733	7 689	1 810
August	168 103	107 105	63.7	98 824	58.8	8 281	2 162	52 815	3 770	38 511	2 762	7 498	1 749
September	168 297	107 098	63.6	99 077	58.9	8 021	2 309	52 866	3 747	38 595	2 601	7 616	1 673
October	168 503	107 405	63.7	99 317	58.9	8 088	2 306	53 094	3 584	38 620	2 788	7 603	1 716
November	168 695	107 568	63.8	99 545	59.0	8 023	2 329	53 210	3 550	38 795	2 767	7 540	1 706
December	168 883	107 352	63.6	99 634	59.0	7 718	2 406	53 333	3 332	38 737	2 775	7 564	1 611
1981:													
January	169 104	108 026	63.9	99 955	59.1	8 071	2 389	53 392	3 468	39 042	2 824	7 521	1 779
February	169 280	108 242	63.9	100 191	59.2	8 051	2 344	53 445	3 483	39 280	2 777	7 466	1 791
March	169 453	108 553	64.1	100 571	59.4	7 982	2 276	53 662	3 445	39 464	2 770	7 445	1 767
April	169 641	108 925	64.2	101 056	59.6	7 869	2 231	53 886	3 350	39 628	2 772	7 542	1 747
May	169 829	109 222	64.3	101 048	59.5	8 174	2 221	53 879	3 580	39 759	2 844	7 410	1 750
June	170 042	108 396	63.7	100 298	59.0	8 098	2 250	53 576	3 526	39 682	2 832	7 040	1 740
July	170 246	108 556	63.8	100 693	59.1	7 863	2 166	53 814	3 365	39 683	2 855	7 196	1 643
August	170 399	108 725	63.8	100 689	59.1	8 036	2 241	53 718	3 519	39 723	2 834	7 248	1 683
September	170 593	108 294	63.5	100 064	58.7	8 230	2 261	53 625	3 550	39 342	2 942	7 097	1 738
October	170 809	109 024	63.8	100 378	58.8	8 646	2 303	53 482	3 819	39 843	3 029	7 053	1 798
November	170 996	109 236	63.9	100 207	58.6	9 029	2 345	53 335	4 026	39 908	3 115	6 964	1 888
December	171 166	108 912	63.6	99 645	58.2	9 267	2 374	53 149	4 280	39 708	3 173	6 788	1 814
1982:													
January	171 335	109 089	63.7	99 692	58.2	9 397	2 409	53 103	4 358	39 821	3 131	6 768	1 908
February	171 489	109 467	63.8	99 762	58.2	9 705	2 758	53 172	4 435	39 859	3 304	6 731	1 966
March	171 667	109 567	63.8	99 672	58.1	9 895	2 965	53 054	4 624	39 936	3 403	6 682	1 868
April	171 844	109 820	63.9	99 576	57.9	10 244	3 086	53 081	4 742	39 848	3 544	6 647	1 958
May	172 026	110 451	64.2	100 116	58.2	10 335	3 276	53 234	4 788	40 121	3 555	6 761	1 992
June	172 190	110 081	63.9	99 543	57.8	10 538	3 451	52 933	5 072	40 219	3 564	6 391	1 902
July	172 364	110 342	64.0	99 493	57.7	10 849	3 555	52 896	5 183	40 228	3 655	6 369	2 011
August	172 511	110 514	64.1	99 633	57.8	10 881	3 696	52 797	5 240	40 336	3 627	6 500	2 014
September	172 690	110 721	64.1	99 504	57.6	11 217	3 889	52 760	5 536	40 275	3 681	6 469	2 000
October	172 881	110 744	64.1	99 215	57.4	11 529	4 185	52 624	5 711	40 105	3 805	6 486	2 013
November	173 058	111 050	64.2	99 112	57.3	11 938	4 485	52 537	5 853	40 111	4 029	6 464	2 056
December	173 199	111 083	64.1	99 032	57.2	12 051	4 662	52 497	5 903	40 164	4 122	6 371	2 026

1. Civilian labor force as a percent of the civilian noninstitutional population.
2. Civilian employment as a percent of the civilian population.
3. Fifteen weeks and over.

Civilian Population, Labor Force, Employment, and Unemployment—*Continued*

(Thousands of persons, 16 years of age and over, seasonally adjusted, except as noted)

Year and month	Noninsti-tutional population (Not seasonally adjusted)	Labor force Thousands of persons	Labor force Participa-tion rate [1]	Employed Thousands of persons	Employed Ratio: Employ-ment to popula-tion [2]	Unemployed Total	Unemployed Long-term [3]	Men 20 years and over Employed	Men 20 years and over Unem-ployed	Women 20 years and over Employed	Women 20 years and over Unem-ployed	Both sexes, 16 to 19 years Employed	Both sexes, 16 to 19 years Unem-ployed
1983:													
January	173 354	110 695	63.9	99 161	57.2	11 534	4 668	52 487	5 618	40 268	3 987	6 406	1 929
February	173 505	110 634	63.8	99 089	57.1	11 545	4 641	52 453	5 738	40 336	3 948	6 300	1 859
March	173 656	110 587	63.7	99 179	57.1	11 408	4 612	52 615	5 630	40 368	3 876	6 196	1 902
April	173 794	110 828	63.8	99 560	57.3	11 268	4 370	52 814	5 643	40 542	3 735	6 204	1 890
May	173 953	110 796	63.7	99 642	57.3	11 154	4 538	52 922	5 609	40 538	3 721	6 182	1 824
June	174 125	111 879	64.3	100 633	57.8	11 246	4 470	53 515	5 347	40 695	3 874	6 423	2 025
July	174 306	111 756	64.1	101 208	58.1	10 548	4 329	53 835	5 170	41 041	3 503	6 332	1 875
August	174 440	112 231	64.3	101 608	58.2	10 623	4 070	53 837	5 162	41 314	3 539	6 457	1 922
September	174 602	112 298	64.3	102 016	58.4	10 282	3 854	53 983	5 036	41 650	3 482	6 383	1 764
October	174 779	111 926	64.0	102 039	58.4	9 887	3 648	54 146	4 817	41 597	3 356	6 296	1 714
November	174 951	112 228	64.1	102 729	58.7	9 499	3 535	54 499	4 605	41 788	3 261	6 442	1 633
December	175 121	112 327	64.1	102 996	58.8	9 331	3 379	54 662	4 422	41 852	3 302	6 482	1 607
1984:													
January	175 533	112 209	63.9	103 201	58.8	9 008	3 254	54 975	4 275	41 812	3 182	6 414	1 551
February	175 679	112 615	64.1	103 824	59.1	8 791	2 991	55 213	4 128	42 196	3 120	6 415	1 543
March	175 824	112 713	64.1	103 967	59.1	8 746	2 881	55 281	4 052	42 328	3 126	6 358	1 568
April	175 969	113 098	64.3	104 336	59.3	8 762	2 858	55 373	4 077	42 512	3 148	6 451	1 537
May	176 123	113 649	64.5	105 193	59.7	8 456	2 884	55 661	3 879	43 071	3 094	6 461	1 483
June	176 284	113 817	64.6	105 591	59.9	8 226	2 612	55 996	3 754	42 944	2 992	6 651	1 480
July	176 440	113 972	64.6	105 435	59.8	8 537	2 638	55 921	3 869	42 979	3 158	6 535	1 510
August	176 583	113 682	64.4	105 163	59.6	8 519	2 604	55 930	3 876	42 885	3 182	6 348	1 461
September	176 763	113 857	64.4	105 490	59.7	8 367	2 538	56 095	3 851	42 967	2 993	6 428	1 523
October	176 956	114 019	64.4	105 638	59.7	8 381	2 526	56 183	3 745	43 052	3 177	6 403	1 459
November	177 135	114 170	64.5	105 972	59.8	8 198	2 438	56 274	3 734	43 244	3 074	6 454	1 390
December	177 306	114 581	64.6	106 223	59.9	8 358	2 401	56 313	3 812	43 472	3 051	6 438	1 495
1985:													
January	177 384	114 725	64.7	106 302	59.9	8 423	2 284	56 184	3 765	43 589	3 151	6 529	1 507
February	177 516	114 876	64.7	106 555	60.0	8 321	2 389	56 216	3 739	43 787	3 114	6 552	1 468
March	177 667	115 328	64.9	106 989	60.2	8 339	2 394	56 356	3 715	44 035	3 160	6 598	1 464
April	177 799	115 331	64.9	106 936	60.1	8 395	2 393	56 374	3 812	44 000	3 187	6 562	1 396
May	177 944	115 234	64.8	106 932	60.1	8 302	2 292	56 531	3 640	43 905	3 192	6 496	1 470
June	178 096	114 965	64.6	106 505	59.8	8 460	2 310	56 288	3 861	43 958	3 178	6 259	1 421
July	178 263	115 320	64.7	106 807	59.9	8 513	2 329	56 435	3 757	43 975	3 140	6 397	1 616
August	178 405	115 291	64.6	107 095	60.0	8 196	2 258	56 655	3 675	44 103	3 144	6 337	1 377
September	178 572	115 905	64.9	107 657	60.3	8 248	2 242	56 845	3 694	44 395	3 153	6 417	1 401
October	178 770	116 145	65.0	107 847	60.3	8 298	2 295	56 969	3 678	44 565	3 044	6 313	1 576
November	178 940	116 135	64.9	108 007	60.4	8 128	2 207	56 972	3 642	44 617	3 052	6 418	1 434
December	179 112	116 354	65.0	108 216	60.4	8 138	2 208	56 995	3 606	44 889	3 038	6 332	1 494
1986:													
January	179 670	116 682	64.9	108 887	60.6	7 795	2 089	57 637	3 489	44 944	2 908	6 306	1 398
February	179 821	116 882	65.0	108 480	60.3	8 402	2 308	57 269	3 758	44 804	3 156	6 407	1 488
March	179 985	117 220	65.1	108 837	60.5	8 383	2 261	57 353	3 766	44 960	3 164	6 524	1 453
April	180 148	117 316	65.1	108 952	60.5	8 364	2 162	57 358	3 700	45 081	3 119	6 513	1 545
May	180 311	117 528	65.2	109 089	60.5	8 439	2 232	57 287	3 836	45 289	3 119	6 513	1 484
June	180 503	118 084	65.4	109 576	60.7	8 508	2 320	57 471	3 832	45 621	3 136	6 484	1 540
July	180 682	118 129	65.4	109 810	60.8	8 319	2 269	57 514	3 859	45 837	3 005	6 459	1 455
August	180 828	118 150	65.3	110 015	60.8	8 135	2 276	57 597	3 701	45 926	3 006	6 492	1 428
September	180 997	118 395	65.4	110 085	60.8	8 310	2 318	57 630	3 862	45 972	2 986	6 483	1 462
October	181 186	118 516	65.4	110 273	60.9	8 243	2 188	57 660	3 823	46 046	3 010	6 567	1 410
November	181 363	118 634	65.4	110 475	60.9	8 159	2 202	57 941	3 775	46 070	2 957	6 464	1 427
December	181 547	118 611	65.3	110 728	61.0	7 883	2 161	58 185	3 713	46 132	2 812	6 411	1 358
1987:													
January	181 827	118 845	65.4	110 953	61.0	7 892	2 168	58 264	3 635	46 219	2 866	6 470	1 391
February	181 998	119 122	65.5	111 257	61.1	7 865	2 117	58 279	3 596	46 444	2 834	6 534	1 435
March	182 179	119 270	65.5	111 408	61.2	7 862	2 070	58 362	3 539	46 549	2 907	6 497	1 416
April	182 344	119 336	65.4	111 794	61.3	7 542	2 091	58 503	3 415	46 746	2 756	6 545	1 371
May	182 533	120 000	65.7	112 434	61.6	7 574	2 104	58 713	3 462	47 052	2 706	6 669	1 406
June	182 703	119 644	65.5	112 246	61.4	7 398	2 087	58 581	3 477	47 102	2 627	6 563	1 294
July	182 885	119 902	65.6	112 634	61.6	7 268	1 921	58 740	3 380	47 229	2 642	6 665	1 246
August	183 002	120 318	65.7	113 057	61.8	7 261	1 878	58 810	3 294	47 322	2 660	6 925	1 307
September	183 161	120 011	65.5	112 909	61.6	7 102	1 866	58 964	3 147	47 285	2 670	6 660	1 285
October	183 311	120 509	65.7	113 282	61.8	7 227	1 794	59 073	3 200	47 533	2 629	6 676	1 398
November	183 470	120 540	65.7	113 505	61.9	7 035	1 797	59 210	3 102	47 622	2 604	6 673	1 329
December	183 620	120 729	65.7	113 793	62.0	6 936	1 767	59 217	3 051	47 781	2 588	6 795	1 297
1988:													
January	183 822	120 969	65.8	114 016	62.0	6 953	1 714	59 346	3 077	47 862	2 574	6 808	1 302
February	183 969	121 156	65.9	114 227	62.1	6 929	1 738	59 535	3 049	47 919	2 628	6 773	1 252
March	184 111	120 913	65.7	114 037	61.9	6 876	1 744	59 393	3 086	48 090	2 490	6 554	1 300
April	184 232	121 251	65.8	114 650	62.2	6 601	1 563	59 832	2 869	48 147	2 466	6 671	1 266
May	184 374	121 071	65.7	114 292	62.0	6 779	1 647	59 644	3 080	47 946	2 489	6 702	1 210
June	184 562	121 473	65.8	114 927	62.3	6 546	1 531	59 751	2 930	48 146	2 453	7 030	1 163
July	184 729	121 665	65.9	115 060	62.3	6 605	1 601	59 888	2 876	48 186	2 517	6 986	1 212
August	184 830	122 125	66.1	115 282	62.4	6 843	1 639	59 877	3 117	48 467	2 463	6 938	1 263
September	184 962	121 960	65.9	115 356	62.4	6 604	1 569	59 980	2 877	48 511	2 468	6 865	1 259
October	185 114	122 206	66.0	115 638	62.5	6 568	1 562	60 023	2 932	48 859	2 431	6 756	1 205
November	185 244	122 637	66.2	116 100	62.7	6 537	1 468	60 042	2 989	49 254	2 448	6 804	1 100
December	185 402	122 622	66.1	116 104	62.6	6 518	1 490	60 059	2 945	49 257	2 395	6 788	1 178

1. Civilian labor force as a percent of the civilian noninstitutional population.
2. Civilian employment as a percent of the civilian population.
3. Fifteen weeks and over.

Civilian Population, Labor Force, Employment, and Unemployment—*Continued*

(Thousands of persons, 16 years of age and over, seasonally adjusted, except as noted)

Year and month	Noninstitutional population (Not seasonally adjusted)	Labor force Thousands of persons	Labor force Participation rate [1]	Employed Thousands of persons	Employed Ratio: Employment to population [2]	Unemployed Total	Unemployed Long-term [3]	Men 20 years and over Employed	Men 20 years and over Unemployed	Women 20 years and over Employed	Women 20 years and over Unemployed	Both sexes, 16 to 19 years Employed	Both sexes, 16 to 19 years Unemployed
1989:													
January	185 644	123 390	66.5	116 708	62.9	6 682	1 480	60 477	2 898	49 529	2 467	6 702	1 317
February	185 777	123 135	66.3	116 776	62.9	6 359	1 304	60 588	2 838	49 497	2 341	6 691	1 180
March	185 897	123 227	66.3	117 022	62.9	6 205	1 353	60 795	2 710	49 503	2 410	6 724	1 085
April	186 024	123 565	66.4	117 097	62.9	6 468	1 397	60 764	2 864	49 565	2 443	6 768	1 161
May	186 181	123 474	66.3	117 099	62.9	6 375	1 348	60 795	2 720	49 583	2 486	6 721	1 169
June	186 329	123 995	66.5	117 418	63.0	6 577	1 300	61 054	2 787	49 542	2 518	6 822	1 272
July	186 483	123 967	66.5	117 472	63.0	6 495	1 435	60 947	2 804	49 693	2 562	6 832	1 129
August	186 598	124 166	66.5	117 655	63.1	6 511	1 302	60 915	2 849	49 804	2 472	6 936	1 190
September	186 726	123 944	66.4	117 354	62.8	6 590	1 360	60 668	3 002	50 015	2 389	6 671	1 199
October	186 871	124 211	66.5	117 581	62.9	6 630	1 392	60 958	2 935	49 871	2 507	6 752	1 188
November	187 017	124 637	66.6	117 912	63.0	6 725	1 418	60 958	2 992	50 221	2 502	6 733	1 231
December	187 165	124 497	66.5	117 830	63.0	6 667	1 375	61 068	2 962	50 116	2 500	6 646	1 205
1990:													
January	188 413	125 833	66.8	119 081	63.2	6 752	1 412	61 742	3 063	50 436	2 489	6 903	1 200
February	188 516	125 710	66.7	119 059	63.2	6 651	1 350	61 805	2 946	50 438	2 506	6 816	1 199
March	188 630	125 801	66.7	119 203	63.2	6 598	1 331	61 832	2 974	50 463	2 471	6 908	1 153
April	188 778	125 649	66.6	118 852	63.0	6 797	1 376	61 579	3 107	50 457	2 519	6 816	1 171
May	188 913	125 893	66.6	119 151	63.1	6 742	1 415	61 778	3 043	50 646	2 515	6 727	1 184
June	189 058	125 573	66.4	118 983	62.9	6 590	1 436	61 762	3 066	50 550	2 412	6 671	1 112
July	189 188	125 732	66.5	118 810	62.8	6 922	1 534	61 683	3 183	50 514	2 575	6 613	1 164
August	189 342	125 990	66.5	118 802	62.7	7 188	1 607	61 715	3 291	50 635	2 641	6 452	1 256
September	189 528	125 892	66.4	118 524	62.5	7 368	1 695	61 608	3 387	50 587	2 735	6 329	1 246
October	189 710	125 995	66.4	118 536	62.5	7 459	1 689	61 606	3 487	50 616	2 721	6 314	1 251
November	189 872	126 070	66.4	118 306	62.3	7 764	1 831	61 545	3 700	50 541	2 778	6 220	1 286
December	190 017	126 142	66.4	118 241	62.2	7 901	1 804	61 506	3 794	50 530	2 796	6 205	1 311
1991:													
January	190 163	125 955	66.2	117 940	62.0	8 015	1 866	61 383	3 766	50 472	2 856	6 085	1 393
February	190 271	126 020	66.2	117 755	61.9	8 265	1 955	61 117	4 051	50 523	2 924	6 115	1 290
March	190 381	126 238	66.3	117 652	61.8	8 586	2 137	61 144	4 206	50 422	3 019	6 086	1 361
April	190 517	126 548	66.4	118 109	62.0	8 439	2 206	61 280	4 183	50 760	2 944	6 069	1 312
May	190 650	126 176	66.2	117 440	61.6	8 736	2 252	61 052	4 168	50 457	3 196	5 931	1 372
June	190 800	126 331	66.2	117 639	61.7	8 692	2 533	61 147	4 229	50 585	3 122	5 907	1 341
July	190 946	126 154	66.1	117 568	61.6	8 586	2 388	61 179	4 245	50 636	2 956	5 753	1 385
August	191 116	126 150	66.0	117 484	61.5	8 666	2 460	61 122	4 235	50 601	3 087	5 761	1 344
September	191 302	126 650	66.2	117 928	61.6	8 722	2 497	61 279	4 307	50 864	3 077	5 785	1 338
October	191 497	126 642	66.1	117 800	61.5	8 842	2 638	61 174	4 276	50 811	3 196	5 815	1 370
November	191 657	126 701	66.1	117 770	61.4	8 931	2 718	61 201	4 332	50 759	3 240	5 810	1 359
December	191 798	126 664	66.0	117 466	61.2	9 198	2 892	61 074	4 453	50 728	3 305	5 664	1 440
1992:													
January	191 953	127 261	66.3	117 978	61.5	9 283	3 060	61 116	4 651	51 095	3 261	5 767	1 371
February	192 067	127 207	66.2	117 753	61.3	9 454	3 182	61 062	4 657	51 033	3 372	5 658	1 425
March	192 204	127 604	66.4	118 144	61.5	9 460	3 196	61 363	4 650	51 204	3 389	5 577	1 421
April	192 354	127 841	66.5	118 426	61.6	9 415	3 130	61 468	4 699	51 323	3 441	5 635	1 275
May	192 503	128 119	66.6	118 375	61.5	9 744	3 444	61 513	4 859	51 245	3 474	5 617	1 411
June	192 663	128 459	66.7	118 419	61.5	10 040	3 758	61 537	4 890	51 383	3 512	5 499	1 638
July	192 826	128 563	66.7	118 713	61.6	9 850	3 614	61 641	4 779	51 458	3 598	5 614	1 473
August	193 018	128 613	66.6	118 826	61.6	9 787	3 579	61 681	4 768	51 386	3 584	5 759	1 435
September	193 229	128 501	66.5	118 720	61.4	9 781	3 504	61 663	4 723	51 359	3 540	5 698	1 518
October	193 442	128 026	66.2	118 628	61.3	9 398	3 505	61 550	4 709	51 373	3 409	5 705	1 280
November	193 621	128 441	66.3	118 876	61.4	9 565	3 397	61 644	4 666	51 535	3 432	5 697	1 467
December	193 784	128 554	66.3	118 997	61.4	9 557	3 651	61 721	4 529	51 524	3 606	5 752	1 422
1993:													
January	193 962	128 400	66.2	119 075	61.4	9 325	3 346	61 895	4 434	51 505	3 477	5 675	1 414
February	194 108	128 458	66.2	119 275	61.4	9 183	3 190	61 963	4 400	51 573	3 378	5 739	1 405
March	194 248	128 598	66.2	119 542	61.5	9 056	3 115	62 007	4 489	51 808	3 162	5 727	1 405
April	194 398	128 584	66.1	119 474	61.5	9 110	3 014	62 032	4 397	51 732	3 332	5 710	1 381
May	194 549	129 264	66.4	120 115	61.7	9 149	3 101	62 309	4 367	51 996	3 348	5 810	1 434
June	194 719	129 411	66.5	120 290	61.8	9 121	3 141	62 409	4 392	52 183	3 313	5 698	1 416
July	194 882	129 397	66.4	120 467	61.8	8 930	3 046	62 497	4 349	52 088	3 258	5 882	1 323
August	195 063	129 619	66.4	120 856	62.0	8 763	3 026	62 634	4 230	52 294	3 197	5 928	1 336
September	195 259	129 268	66.2	120 554	61.7	8 714	3 042	62 437	4 188	52 241	3 222	5 876	1 304
October	195 444	129 573	66.3	120 823	61.8	8 750	3 029	62 614	4 140	52 379	3 269	5 830	1 341
November	195 625	129 711	66.3	121 169	61.9	8 542	2 986	62 732	3 949	52 531	3 251	5 906	1 342
December	195 794	129 941	66.4	121 464	62.0	8 477	2 968	62 760	3 941	52 813	3 249	5 891	1 287
1994:													
January	195 953	130 596	66.6	121 966	62.2	8 630	3 060	62 798	3 990	53 052	3 270	6 116	1 370
February	196 090	130 669	66.6	122 086	62.3	8 583	3 118	62 708	4 001	53 266	3 237	6 112	1 345
March	196 213	130 400	66.5	121 930	62.1	8 470	3 055	62 780	3 844	53 099	3 296	6 051	1 330
April	196 363	130 621	66.5	122 290	62.3	8 331	2 921	62 906	3 726	53 274	3 164	6 110	1 441
May	196 510	130 779	66.6	122 864	62.5	7 915	2 836	63 116	3 511	53 624	3 062	6 124	1 342
June	196 693	130 561	66.4	122 634	62.3	7 927	2 735	63 041	3 553	53 393	3 047	6 200	1 327
July	196 859	130 652	66.4	122 706	62.3	7 946	2 822	63 034	3 679	53 531	2 955	6 141	1 312
August	197 043	131 275	66.6	123 342	62.6	7 933	2 750	63 294	3 591	53 744	3 027	6 304	1 315
September	197 248	131 421	66.6	123 687	62.7	7 734	2 746	63 631	3 402	53 991	3 045	6 065	1 287
October	197 430	131 744	66.7	124 112	62.9	7 632	2 955	63 818	3 450	54 071	2 862	6 223	1 320
November	197 607	131 891	66.7	124 516	63.0	7 375	2 666	64 080	3 336	54 168	2 884	6 268	1 155
December	197 765	131 951	66.7	124 721	63.1	7 230	2 488	64 359	3 202	54 054	2 737	6 308	1 291

1. Civilian labor force as a percent of the civilian noninstitutional population.
2. Civilian employment as a percent of the civilian population.
3. Fifteen weeks and over.

Civilian Employment and Selected Unemployment Rates

(Seasonally adjusted)

Year and month	Employment by industry (Thousands of persons)		All civilian workers	Unemployment rates (percent of civilian labor force in group)					Persons of Hispanic origin	By marital or family status			Wage and salary workers, by industry of last job			
				20 years and over		Both sexes, 16 to 19 years	By race			By marital or family status			Private nonagricultural			
	Agricultural	Nonagricultural		Men	Women		White	Black		Married men, spouse present	Married women, spouse present	Women who maintain families	Total	Construction	Manufacturing	Agricultural
1971:																
January	3 393	75 471	5.9	4.4	5.7	16.8	5.5	.....	.....	3.3	5.7	6.4	6.4	11.5	6.9	8.7
February	3 288	75 412	5.9	4.4	5.7	16.3	5.3	.....	.....	3.2	5.7	7.3	6.3	11.1	6.9	9.3
March	3 356	75 232	6.0	4.3	5.9	16.9	5.5	.....	.....	3.2	6.0	6.9	6.3	11.1	6.8	7.4
April	3 574	75 413	5.9	4.3	5.9	16.3	5.4	.....	.....	3.1	6.0	7.1	6.3	10.1	7.0	6.8
May	3 449	75 690	5.9	4.4	5.8	16.8	5.4	.....	.....	3.2	5.7	7.8	6.4	9.9	6.8	7.2
June	3 334	75 423	5.9	4.3	5.7	17.7	5.5	.....	.....	3.1	5.7	7.3	6.3	10.5	6.7	6.3
July	3 386	75 919	6.0	4.3	5.6	17.7	5.5	.....	.....	3.1	5.6	7.2	6.2	9.5	6.7	8.4
August	3 395	76 144	6.1	4.5	5.9	16.8	5.6	.....	.....	3.2	5.6	7.3	6.3	9.6	7.1	8.9
September	3 367	76 322	6.0	4.4	5.7	16.7	5.4	.....	.....	3.3	5.6	7.6	6.3	9.4	7.1	8.3
October	3 405	76 513	5.8	4.2	5.7	16.9	5.4	.....	.....	3.0	5.7	7.3	6.1	9.8	6.5	7.3
November	3 410	76 887	6.0	4.5	5.8	16.9	5.6	.....	.....	3.4	5.7	7.3	6.3	10.3	6.7	8.2
December	3 371	77 100	6.0	4.5	5.7	16.9	5.4	.....	.....	3.2	5.5	8.5	6.3	10.9	6.7	7.8
1972:																
January	3 366	77 593	5.8	4.3	5.5	16.9	5.2	11.2	.....	3.0	5.3	7.2	6.0	10.3	6.1	8.6
February	3 358	77 750	5.7	4.1	5.1	18.0	5.1	11.2	.....	2.9	5.3	7.0	6.0	10.8	6.0	8.1
March	3 438	78 135	5.8	4.2	5.5	17.2	5.2	10.7	.....	2.8	5.4	7.0	6.0	10.3	6.0	6.9
April	3 382	78 273	5.7	4.1	5.4	16.5	5.3	9.8	.....	·2.8	5.5	7.2	5.9	10.5	5.8	6.3
May	3 412	78 475	5.7	4.1	5.7	15.3	5.1	10.2	.....	2.8	5.6	7.0	5.9	10.9	5.9	8.0
June	3 402	78 681	5.7	4.0	5.6	15.9	5.1	10.2	.....	2.8	5.6	7.7	5.7	9.7	5.7	7.6
July	3 461	78 769	5.6	4.0	5.7	15.6	5.1	10.5	.....	2.8	5.7	7.3	5.9	10.4	5.9	6.7
August	3 603	78 975	5.6	3.9	5.6	16.5	5.1	10.6	.....	2.7	5.6	7.3	5.9	11.3	5.6	6.7
September	3 568	78 975	5.5	3.8	5.5	16.3	5.0	10.4	.....	2.8	5.3	7.2	5.6	8.9	5.3	8.9
October	3 634	78 982	5.6	3.9	5.6	15.8	5.1	10.6	.....	2.8	5.2	8.3	5.8	10.1	5.4	9.9
November	3 517	79 473	5.3	3.6	5.1	15.7	4.7	10.0	.....	2.5	5.0	6.5	5.3	10.1	4.8	8.2
December	3 596	79 804	5.2	3.5	5.0	15.6	4.6	9.4	.....	2.4	5.0	6.3	5.1	9.7	4.6	7.1
1973:																
January	3 456	79 705	4.9	3.4	5.1	13.7	4.5	9.1	.....	2.4	4.9	7.1	5.0	9.4	4.8	6.8
February	3 415	80 497	5.0	3.4	4.9	15.3	4.5	9.5	.....	2.4	4.8	6.6	5.1	9.3	4.4	7.3
March	3 469	80 983	4.9	3.4	4.9	14.3	4.4	9.4	7.3	2.4	4.6	7.0	4.9	8.9	4.4	6.6
April	3 407	81 152	5.0	3.4	4.8	15.5	4.5	9.9	7.9	2.4	4.6	6.9	4.9	9.1	4.3	7.4
May	3 376	81 272	4.9	3.4	4.6	14.9	4.3	9.6	8.1	2.3	4.6	6.7	4.8	8.8	4.5	8.9
June	3 509	81 676	4.9	3.3	5.0	13.8	4.3	9.8	7.9	2.2	4.7	8.0	4.8	8.0	4.4	7.0
July	3 540	81 759	4.8	3.1	4.9	14.3	4.2	9.8	7.2	2.1	4.7	7.0	4.8	9.1	4.0	5.7
August	3 425	81 779	4.8	3.2	5.0	14.0	4.3	9.2	7.4	2.2	5.0	6.5	4.9	8.4	4.2	7.5
September	3 342	82 146	4.8	3.1	4.9	14.7	4.3	9.7	7.7	2.1	4.7	6.8	4.8	9.0	4.4	6.4
October	3 424	82 563	4.6	2.9	4.5	14.4	4.1	8.8	8.0	2.2	4.3	7.0	4.6	8.9	4.1	6.8
November	3 593	82 727	4.8	3.1	4.8	15.0	4.3	9.3	8.1	2.2	4.6	8.0	4.9	9.0	4.4	7.4
December	3 658	82 743	4.9	3.2	5.0	14.6	4.4	9.0	7.6	2.3	4.7	7.1	5.0	8.4	4.4	6.7
1974:																
January	3 756	82 799	5.1	3.5	5.1	14.6	4.6	9.5	7.6	2.4	4.8	6.7	5.1	9.5	4.8	6.7
February	3 824	82 930	5.2	3.6	5.0	14.9	4.6	9.8	7.8	2.4	5.0	6.4	5.3	8.5	5.1	6.9
March	3 726	83 093	5.1	3.4	5.0	14.9	4.5	9.8	7.6	2.3	4.7	6.5	5.1	8.6	5.0	7.0
April	3 582	83 087	5.1	3.5	4.9	14.3	4.5	9.5	7.0	2.4	4.5	6.6	5.2	9.9	4.9	7.3
May	3 529	83 362	5.1	3.4	5.0	15.4	4.6	9.7	7.3	2.2	4.7	7.0	5.2	9.5	4.8	7.0
June	3 386	83 555	5.4	3.5	5.2	16.3	4.8	10.1	8.6	2.5	4.8	6.7	5.5	9.9	5.2	7.4
July	3 436	83 713	5.5	3.6	5.3	16.8	4.9	10.4	8.8	2.7	5.1	6.2	5.6	10.2	5.4	8.3
August	3 429	83 608	5.5	3.8	5.4	14.9	5.0	9.9	8.1	2.8	5.3	6.6	5.7	10.9	5.7	7.4
September	3 460	83 591	5.9	3.9	5.9	17.0	5.4	10.8	8.1	2.8	5.8	7.4	6.1	11.6	6.0	7.3
October	3 431	83 564	6.0	4.2	5.7	17.2	5.4	11.5	8.2	3.0	5.3	7.3	6.2	12.1	6.5	8.3
November	3 405	83 221	6.6	4.6	6.6	17.8	6.0	12.4	8.6	3.4	6.5	8.5	6.9	13.6	7.5	7.6
December	3 361	82 783	7.2	5.3	7.0	18.2	6.4	13.1	9.1	3.8	7.0	8.3	7.7	15.3	8.7	7.7
1975:																
January	3 401	82 226	8.1	6.1	8.0	19.5	7.4	14.1	10.7	4.6	8.1	9.0	8.7	15.7	10.4	10.7
February	3 361	81 895	8.1	6.3	7.9	19.4	7.4	14.4	11.2	4.7	8.0	9.7	8.7	16.3	10.7	9.1
March	3 358	81 829	8.6	6.8	8.3	19.9	7.8	15.1	12.1	5.1	8.4	9.9	9.3	17.8	11.3	10.6
April	3 315	81 874	8.8	7.1	8.5	19.9	8.0	15.3	12.4	5.5	8.7	9.6	9.8	19.2	12.0	11.3
May	3 560	81 891	9.0	7.3	8.5	20.4	8.4	15.1	14.3	5.7	8.7	10.5	10.1	21.5	12.3	9.4
June	3 368	81 987	8.8	7.1	8.2	20.9	8.1	15.0	11.7	5.5	8.2	10.2	9.8	19.8	12.1	10.4
July	3 457	82 437	8.6	7.0	8.0	20.7	8.0	14.1	11.6	5.4	7.6	10.4	9.5	19.5	11.4	9.0
August	3 429	82 805	8.4	6.7	7.9	20.7	7.7	15.2	12.1	5.2	7.6	9.8	9.2	19.1	10.7	11.3
September	3 508	82 771	8.4	6.9	7.7	19.5	7.7	15.4	12.7	5.3	7.6	9.8	9.1	18.5	10.5	11.1
October	3 397	82 973	8.4	6.8	7.9	19.8	7.7	14.9	13.0	5.2	7.5	10.4	9.0	17.8	10.1	10.8
November	3 331	83 125	8.3	6.8	7.8	19.0	7.6	14.6	12.4	4.9	7.3	10.1	8.9	17.4	9.9	10.3
December	3 259	83 406	8.2	6.5	7.8	19.8	7.4	14.5	12.1	4.7	7.2	10.4	8.7	16.8	9.2	11.7
1976:																
January	3 387	84 013	7.9	6.1	7.7	19.6	7.2	14.3	11.4	4.4	7.2	10.6	8.3	15.5	8.5	11.4
February	3 304	84 368	7.7	5.9	7.5	19.0	6.9	14.4	10.7	4.2	7.2	10.2	8.0	15.4	8.2	10.6
March	3 296	84 689	7.6	5.8	7.3	18.9	6.9	13.5	11.0	4.2	6.9	9.5	7.8	15.7	7.7	10.9
April	3 438	84 978	7.7	5.8	7.4	19.5	6.9	13.8	11.7	4.1	7.0	9.6	7.7	15.6	7.8	11.5
May	3 367	85 427	7.4	5.7	6.9	18.6	6.7	13.2	10.5	4.1	6.8	9.2	7.7	14.7	7.7	12.9
June	3 310	85 253	7.6	6.1	7.2	18.5	6.9	14.3	11.1	4.4	7.0	9.6	7.9	16.3	7.8	11.5
July	3 358	85 735	7.8	6.0	7.6	18.3	7.1	13.9	11.7	4.4	7.3	10.1	8.1	16.8	7.7	11.7
August	3 380	85 843	7.8	5.8	7.6	19.6	7.1	14.3	12.4	4.1	7.4	10.5	8.1	16.6	7.8	11.0
September	3 278	85 895	7.6	5.9	7.5	18.6	7.0	13.7	11.8	4.4	7.2	10.6	8.0	15.7	7.7	11.3
October	3 316	85 958	7.7	5.8	7.5	19.0	7.0	13.9	11.6	4.2	7.2	10.5	7.9	14.7	7.8	11.2
November	3 263	86 371	7.8	6.1	7.5	19.2	7.1	14.0	11.7	4.3	7.0	9.8	8.0	15.4	7.7	13.5
December	3 251	86 552	7.8	6.1	7.3	19.1	7.0	14.1	11.7	4.2	6.9	10.3	7.9	14.3	8.1	13.6

Civilian Employment and Selected Unemployment Rates—*Continued*

(Seasonally adjusted)

Year and month	Employment by industry (Thousands of persons) Agricultural	Nonagricultural	All civilian workers	20 years and over Men	Women	Both sexes, 16 to 19 years	By race White	Black	Persons of Hispanic origin	By marital or family status Married men, spouse present	Married women, spouse present	Women who maintain families	Wage and salary workers, by industry of last job Private nonagricultural Total	Construction	Manufacturing	Agricultural
1977:																
January	3 185	86 743	7.5	5.8	7.1	18.9	6.8	13.8	11.2	4.1	6.6	9.5	7.6	14.8	7.3	13.0
February	3 222	87 120	7.6	5.9	7.3	18.4	6.9	14.2	11.4	4.1	6.9	9.5	7.7	14.7	7.5	12.8
March	3 212	87 596	7.4	5.5	7.4	18.6	6.7	13.9	11.2	3.8	7.0	9.7	7.6	13.9	7.0	12.7
April	3 313	87 958	7.2	5.3	7.1	18.0	6.4	12.8	9.6	3.7	6.7	9.3	7.1	12.5	6.9	12.5
May	3 432	88 322	7.0	5.4	6.6	17.8	6.3	13.5	9.9	3.6	6.5	8.9	7.2	13.4	6.5	11.6
June	3 340	88 619	7.2	5.2	7.1	18.8	6.4	13.9	10.1	3.5	6.7	9.4	7.0	12.6	6.5	11.8
July	3 247	88 837	6.9	5.1	6.9	17.5	6.0	13.9	9.5	3.4	6.5	9.2	6.9	12.0	6.5	9.4
August	3 260	89 181	7.0	5.1	7.0	17.4	6.0	15.1	9.4	3.4	6.4	9.9	6.9	11.5	6.6	10.1
September	3 201	89 501	6.8	4.7	6.9	18.0	6.0	14.5	9.7	3.3	6.4	10.4	6.7	10.5	6.7	10.5
October	3 272	89 780	6.8	5.0	6.7	17.2	5.9	14.5	9.4	3.6	6.2	9.3	6.8	11.8	6.6	10.0
November	3 375	90 386	6.8	4.8	7.0	17.2	5.8	14.7	9.3	3.3	6.4	9.4	6.7	11.4	6.4	9.6
December	3 320	90 785	6.4	4.6	6.5	15.5	5.5	13.6	8.8	3.2	6.0	8.1	6.3	10.8	5.8	10.0
1978																
January	3 434	90 950	6.4	4.7	6.4	16.7	5.5	13.9	9.3	3.1	5.8	8.3	6.4	11.6	5.9	9.4
February	3 320	91 199	6.3	4.6	5.9	17.2	5.5	13.1	9.9	3.0	5.5	7.8	6.3	11.1	6.0	9.8
March	3 351	91 404	6.3	4.6	6.0	17.3	5.4	13.1	9.5	3.1	5.4	8.7	6.2	11.0	5.7	10.1
April	3 349	92 045	6.1	4.3	6.0	16.6	5.3	12.9	8.5	2.8	5.1	9.9	6.0	9.8	5.4	8.2
May	3 325	92 444	6.0	4.2	6.0	16.0	5.2	13.0	9.6	2.8	5.8	9.1	5.9	9.7	5.6	8.0
June	3 483	92 860	5.9	4.0	6.1	15.4	5.0	12.8	9.1	2.8	5.5	8.7	5.7	9.6	5.6	8.9
July	3 441	92 649	6.2	4.1	6.4	16.5	5.3	13.0	9.5	2.6	5.6	9.9	5.9	9.8	5.4	9.2
August	3 401	93 030	5.9	4.1	6.0	15.7	5.1	12.3	9.1	2.7	5.6	8.2	5.7	9.2	5.4	8.5
September	3 400	93 270	6.0	4.1	6.0	16.4	5.2	11.9	8.9	2.7	5.7	8.4	5.9	10.9	5.3	8.7
October	3 409	93 724	5.8	4.1	5.6	16.1	5.0	11.8	8.5	2.6	5.2	7.6	5.6	11.2	5.1	9.4
November	3 284	94 201	5.9	4.0	5.9	16.3	5.0	12.7	8.4	2.5	5.5	7.8	5.7	10.8	5.2	8.2
December	3 396	94 185	6.0	4.2	5.8	16.7	5.2	12.4	8.7	2.7	5.6	8.0	5.9	12.2	5.3	8.3
1979:																
January	3 305	94 643	5.9	4.1	5.8	16.1	5.1	12.4	8.2	2.7	5.4	7.9	5.8	10.8	5.2	7.5
February	3 373	94 956	5.9	4.1	5.9	16.1	5.1	13.1	7.7	2.8	5.3	8.5	5.8	11.5	5.1	9.0
March	3 368	95 112	5.8	4.1	5.8	15.9	5.1	12.5	7.9	2.7	5.3	8.3	5.8	10.3	5.4	8.1
April	3 291	94 812	5.8	4.1	5.7	16.3	5.0	12.9	8.2	2.7	5.2	8.1	5.7	10.3	5.5	8.9
May	3 272	95 059	5.6	3.8	5.6	16.1	4.8	12.4	7.9	2.4	5.0	8.6	5.6	9.5	5.3	9.3
June	3 331	95 348	5.7	4.0	5.7	15.7	4.9	12.2	8.4	2.6	5.1	9.0	5.6	9.7	5.3	8.3
July	3 335	95 671	5.7	4.1	5.5	15.6	4.9	12.1	8.1	2.8	4.9	8.1	5.7	9.7	5.6	9.9
August	3 374	95 402	6.0	4.2	6.0	16.5	5.3	12.4	8.7	2.9	5.4	8.2	6.0	9.1	6.0	9.6
September	3 371	95 969	5.9	4.2	5.6	16.5	5.2	11.7	7.6	2.8	5.0	8.1	5.9	9.1	6.1	10.4
October	3 325	96 079	6.0	4.3	5.7	16.5	5.2	12.3	8.7	2.9	5.2	8.4	5.9	10.0	6.0	9.5
November	3 436	96 138	5.9	4.4	5.6	15.9	5.2	11.9	9.2	3.0	4.8	8.4	5.9	10.5	6.0	10.6
December	3 400	96 533	6.0	4.3	5.7	16.2	5.2	12.2	9.1	2.9	5.1	8.4	5.9	11.1	6.0	9.7
1980:																
January	3 316	96 563	6.3	4.8	5.8	16.5	5.5	13.0	8.7	3.5	5.3	8.9	6.3	11.7	6.8	10.1
February	3 397	96 598	6.3	4.8	5.9	16.6	5.5	12.9	8.9	3.3	5.4	8.8	6.3	11.4	6.8	9.6
March	3 418	96 295	6.3	5.1	5.7	16.3	5.6	12.9	9.2	3.5	5.3	8.8	6.4	13.2	6.7	10.3
April	3 326	95 907	6.9	5.8	6.3	16.2	6.1	13.8	10.4	4.1	5.7	9.0	7.1	14.6	8.2	12.0
May	3 382	95 563	7.5	6.4	6.4	18.6	6.6	14.4	10.1	4.5	5.9	8.3	7.9	16.1	9.6	11.4
June	3 296	95 386	7.6	6.5	6.5	18.9	6.7	14.6	10.1	4.7	6.1	8.4	8.0	15.4	9.5	10.1
July	3 319	95 477	7.8	6.8	6.6	19.1	6.9	15.3	10.8	4.9	6.2	8.9	8.2	15.8	9.9	11.6
August	3 234	95 590	7.7	6.7	6.7	18.9	6.9	14.6	10.8	4.9	6.2	9.4	8.1	16.5	9.5	13.2
September	3 443	95 634	7.5	6.6	6.3	18.0	6.6	14.8	11.4	4.7	5.9	9.1	7.9	15.5	9.2	11.7
October	3 372	95 945	7.5	6.3	6.7	18.4	6.6	15.1	10.6	4.5	6.0	10.1	7.8	14.1	9.1	11.3
November	3 396	96 149	7.5	6.3	6.7	18.5	6.5	15.1	9.9	4.3	5.8	9.8	7.8	14.5	8.8	10.1
December	3 492	96 142	7.2	5.9	6.7	17.6	6.3	15.0	10.3	4.1	5.8	10.2	7.5	13.6	8.5	10.5
1981:																
January	3 429	96 526	7.5	6.1	6.7	19.1	6.7	14.6	10.6	4.2	6.1	10.3	7.6	13.7	8.4	10.8
February	3 345	96 846	7.4	6.1	6.6	19.3	6.6	14.7	11.3	4.2	5.8	10.0	7.6	13.8	8.5	12.4
March	3 365	97 206	7.4	6.0	6.6	19.2	6.5	15.1	10.2	4.2	5.9	9.7	7.4	14.9	8.2	12.1
April	3 529	97 527	7.2	5.9	6.5	18.8	6.4	14.7	9.5	3.8	5.8	9.8	7.3	14.5	7.7	9.5
May	3 369	97 679	7.5	6.2	6.7	19.1	6.6	14.8	10.0	4.0	5.7	10.4	7.6	15.9	7.8	10.9
June	3 334	96 964	7.5	6.2	6.7	19.8	6.5	15.7	10.3	4.3	5.7	10.5	7.4	16.3	7.5	12.6
July	3 296	97 397	7.2	5.9	6.7	18.6	6.3	15.0	10.0	4.0	5.7	11.3	7.3	15.3	7.5	11.4
August	3 379	97 310	7.4	6.1	6.7	18.8	6.3	16.3	10.0	4.1	5.5	10.3	7.4	16.1	7.3	12.4
September	3 361	96 703	7.6	6.2	7.0	19.7	6.6	15.9	9.6	4.3	6.0	10.6	7.7	15.8	7.9	11.7
October	3 412	96 966	7.9	6.7	7.1	20.3	6.9	16.7	10.7	4.6	6.1	10.6	8.0	17.4	8.5	13.3
November	3 415	96 792	8.3	7.0	7.2	21.3	7.3	16.8	11.2	4.9	6.5	10.9	8.3	17.6	9.3	13.8
December	3 227	96 418	8.5	7.5	7.4	21.1	7.5	17.2	11.7	5.4	6.5	10.4	8.9	17.6	10.5	14.0
1982:																
January	3 393	96 299	8.6	7.6	7.3	22.0	7.6	17.3	11.7	5.4	6.3	10.4	8.8	18.8	10.4	15.0
February	3 375	96 387	8.9	7.7	7.7	22.6	7.8	17.7	12.1	5.4	6.9	10.4	9.1	18.3	10.6	13.4
March	3 372	96 300	9.0	8.0	7.9	21.8	8.0	18.1	12.2	5.7	7.0	10.6	9.4	18.3	10.8	13.9
April	3 351	96 225	9.3	8.2	8.2	22.8	8.3	18.2	12.9	6.0	7.7	11.3	9.8	19.3	11.3	14.8
May	3 434	96 682	9.4	8.3	8.1	22.8	8.2	18.5	13.9	6.1	7.2	11.9	9.9	18.8	11.6	18.0
June	3 331	96 212	9.6	8.7	8.1	22.9	8.5	18.5	13.8	6.5	7.0	12.1	10.0	19.5	12.4	15.2
July	3 402	96 091	9.8	8.9	8.3	24.0	8.7	18.8	14.2	6.7	7.3	12.3	10.3	20.4	12.4	14.6
August	3 408	96 225	9.8	9.0	8.3	23.7	8.7	18.9	14.8	6.8	7.2	11.8	10.2	20.4	12.4	14.7
September	3 385	96 119	10.1	9.5	8.4	23.6	9.0	19.7	14.4	7.1	7.5	12.2	10.6	21.7	13.6	13.4
October	3 489	95 726	10.4	9.8	8.7	23.7	9.2	20.1	15.0	7.4	7.9	11.3	11.0	22.6	13.7	12.5
November	3 510	95 602	10.8	10.0	9.1	24.1	9.6	20.2	15.2	7.5	8.5	12.6	11.4	21.7	14.5	15.7
December	3 414	95 618	10.8	10.1	9.3	24.1	9.7	20.9	15.7	7.5	8.2	13.5	11.5	21.5	14.3	16.2

Civilian Employment and Selected Unemployment Rates—*Continued*

(Seasonally adjusted)

Year and month	Employment by industry (Thousands of persons)		Unemployment rates (percent of civilian labor force in group)												
			All civilian workers	20 years and over		Both sexes, 16 to 19 years	By race		Persons of Hispanic origin	By marital or family status			Wage and salary workers, by industry of last job			
	Agricultural	Nonagricultural		Men	Women		White	Black		Married men, spouse present	Married women, spouse present	Women who maintain families	Private nonagricultural			Agricultural
													Total	Construction	Manufacturing	
1983:																
January	3 439	95 722	10.4	9.7	9.0	23.1	9.1	21.2	15.3	7.2	7.8	13.3	10.9	20.4	13.0	15.6
February	3 382	95 707	10.4	9.9	8.9	22.8	9.3	19.9	15.5	7.2	7.6	13.0	10.9	19.8	13.3	16.3
March	3 360	95 819	10.3	9.7	8.8	23.5	9.1	20.1	15.6	7.2	7.5	13.2	10.8	20.5	12.9	16.1
April	3 341	96 219	10.2	9.7	8.4	23.4	8.9	20.4	14.8	7.1	7.3	13.0	10.5	20.4	12.4	17.6
May	3 328	96 314	10.1	9.6	8.4	22.8	8.8	20.3	14.0	7.0	7.4	12.8	10.5	20.2	12.4	17.2
June	3 462	97 171	10.1	9.1	8.7	24.0	8.7	20.7	14.3	6.6	7.8	12.6	10.1	18.2	11.6	17.3
July	3 481	97 727	9.4	8.8	7.9	22.8	8.2	19.4	12.4	6.1	6.9	12.1	9.6	17.8	10.8	14.5
August	3 502	98 106	9.5	8.7	7.9	22.9	8.2	19.7	13.0	6.4	6.8	11.6	9.7	18.0	11.1	15.0
September	3 347	98 669	9.2	8.5	7.7	21.7	8.0	18.8	12.9	6.0	6.7	11.8	9.2	17.9	10.0	15.8
October	3 303	98 736	8.8	8.2	7.5	21.4	7.7	18.2	12.1	5.7	6.3	11.3	9.0	15.6	9.5	16.0
November	3 291	99 438	8.5	7.8	7.2	20.2	7.4	17.5	12.3	5.5	6.2	10.4	8.6	15.2	8.9	15.6
December	3 332	99 664	8.3	7.5	7.3	19.9	7.1	17.8	11.6	5.2	6.3	11.2	8.4	16.3	8.5	15.7
1984:																
January	3 293	99 908	8.0	7.2	7.1	19.5	6.9	17.3	11.4	5.0	5.9	10.9	8.0	15.3	8.2	15.4
February	3 353	100 471	7.8	7.0	6.9	19.4	6.8	16.2	10.4	4.8	5.9	10.7	7.8	14.9	7.7	13.8
March	3 233	100 734	7.8	6.8	6.9	19.8	6.7	16.6	11.5	4.7	5.8	10.8	7.7	13.5	7.6	15.1
April	3 291	101 045	7.7	6.9	6.9	19.2	6.7	16.5	11.6	4.7	5.8	10.5	7.8	14.6	7.6	13.0
May	3 343	101 850	7.4	6.5	6.7	18.7	6.4	15.7	10.6	4.6	5.7	9.9	7.2	14.9	7.1	13.9
June	3 383	102 208	7.2	6.3	6.5	18.2	6.2	15.6	10.3	4.5	5.7	9.7	7.0	14.7	7.3	12.8
July	3 344	102 091	7.5	6.5	6.8	18.8	6.3	16.7	10.4	4.5	5.8	10.0	7.4	14.6	7.5	13.9
August	3 286	101 877	7.5	6.5	6.9	18.7	6.4	16.0	10.7	4.6	5.9	10.1	7.5	14.2	7.4	12.5
September	3 393	102 097	7.3	6.4	6.5	19.2	6.4	15.0	10.5	4.6	5.7	9.7	7.2	13.8	7.3	13.9
October	3 194	102 444	7.4	6.2	6.9	18.6	6.3	15.3	10.8	4.5	5.8	10.4	7.3	13.4	7.3	13.6
November	3 394	102 578	7.2	6.2	6.6	17.7	6.2	15.0	10.2	4.4	5.5	10.9	7.2	13.9	7.2	11.3
December	3 385	102 838	7.3	6.3	6.6	18.8	6.3	15.2	10.4	4.5	5.5	10.1	7.3	13.7	7.4	12.9
1985:																
January	3 317	102 985	7.3	6.3	6.7	18.8	6.3	15.2	10.5	4.5	5.7	10.2	7.3	13.5	7.5	15.9
February	3 317	103 238	7.2	6.2	6.6	18.3	6.2	15.8	9.8	4.4	5.3	10.9	7.2	13.3	7.6	13.2
March	3 250	103 739	7.2	6.2	6.7	18.2	6.2	15.1	10.5	4.2	5.8	10.2	7.2	13.3	7.6	12.8
April	3 306	103 630	7.3	6.3	6.8	17.5	6.3	15.1	10.4	4.3	5.8	10.9	7.3	13.7	8.0	13.5
May	3 280	103 652	7.2	6.0	6.8	18.5	6.2	15.2	10.6	4.0	5.7	10.6	7.1	10.5	7.7	11.3
June	3 161	103 344	7.4	6.4	6.7	18.5	6.5	14.4	10.7	4.6	5.9	9.7	7.3	13.9	7.7	12.9
July	3 143	103 664	7.4	6.2	6.7	20.2	6.4	15.2	11.2	4.4	5.6	10.4	7.2	13.5	8.0	13.9
August	3 121	103 994	7.1	6.1	6.7	17.9	6.2	14.3	10.4	4.3	5.4	10.7	7.2	13.3	7.9	13.3
September	3 064	104 593	7.1	6.1	6.6	17.9	6.1	15.2	10.4	4.4	5.7	11.1	7.2	13.7	7.7	12.8
October	3 051	104 796	7.1	6.1	6.4	20.0	6.1	15.0	11.1	4.1	5.4	10.5	7.1	13.2	7.6	13.0
November	3 062	104 945	7.0	6.0	6.4	18.3	5.9	15.6	10.6	4.2	5.4	10.1	7.1	13.2	7.7	13.1
December	3 141	105 075	7.0	6.0	6.3	19.1	6.0	15.0	10.5	4.3	5.3	9.7	7.0	12.5	7.3	11.0
1986:																
January	3 287	105 600	6.7	5.7	6.1	18.1	5.7	14.5	10.2	4.3	5.0	9.9	6.7	12.8	6.9	11.2
February	3 083	105 397	7.2	6.2	6.6	18.8	6.3	14.4	11.9	4.4	5.4	9.9	7.2	13.2	7.2	13.8
March	3 200	105 637	7.2	6.2	6.6	18.2	6.2	14.6	10.7	4.5	5.5	10.1	7.1	13.0	7.1	12.2
April	3 153	105 799	7.1	6.1	6.5	19.2	6.1	14.8	10.3	4.2	5.3	9.6	7.2	12.4	6.9	13.9
May	3 150	105 939	7.2	6.3	6.4	18.6	6.2	14.6	10.8	4.5	5.5	9.9	7.2	12.9	7.3	15.1
June	3 193	106 383	7.2	6.3	6.4	19.2	6.2	15.1	10.6	4.5	5.4	9.9	7.2	12.5	7.5	13.7
July	3 141	106 669	7.0	6.3	6.2	18.4	6.1	14.4	10.7	4.5	5.2	9.3	7.2	13.3	7.0	11.5
August	3 082	106 933	6.9	6.0	6.1	18.0	5.9	14.8	10.9	4.3	5.1	10.1	7.0	12.2	7.0	12.9
September	3 171	106 914	7.0	6.3	6.1	18.4	6.0	14.9	11.1	4.3	5.1	9.8	7.0	12.9	7.0	12.7
October	3 128	107 145	7.0	6.2	6.1	17.7	6.0	14.6	10.4	4.5	5.0	8.9	7.1	13.5	7.4	11.7
November	3 220	107 255	6.9	6.1	6.0	18.1	6.0	14.3	9.3	4.4	4.9	9.9	7.0	14.9	7.2	9.9
December	3 148	107 580	6.6	6.0	5.7	17.5	5.8	13.7	10.5	4.3	4.7	9.9	6.7	13.5	6.9	11.3
1987:																
January	3 143	107 810	6.6	5.9	5.8	17.7	5.7	14.0	10.6	4.2	4.7	9.7	6.6	12.2	6.6	11.3
February	3 208	108 049	6.6	5.8	5.8	18.0	5.7	13.8	9.8	4.1	4.7	9.6	6.6	11.6	6.7	11.3
March	3 214	108 194	6.6	5.7	5.9	17.9	5.7	13.8	9.3	4.1	4.5	9.7	6.6	12.5	6.8	10.9
April	3 246	108 548	6.3	5.5	5.6	17.3	5.4	12.9	8.9	4.0	4.5	9.4	6.3	12.1	6.3	9.4
May	3 345	109 089	6.3	5.6	5.4	17.4	5.4	13.6	8.6	4.0	4.2	9.4	6.3	12.2	6.3	8.3
June	3 216	109 030	6.2	5.6	5.3	16.5	5.4	12.9	8.5	4.1	4.1	9.6	6.2	11.8	5.8	9.2
July	3 235	109 399	6.1	5.4	5.3	15.8	5.2	12.9	8.1	3.9	4.2	9.1	6.1	10.9	6.0	11.5
August	3 112	109 945	6.0	5.3	5.3	15.9	5.1	12.6	7.9	3.7	4.2	9.1	5.9	11.1	5.5	10.4
September	3 189	109 720	5.9	5.1	5.3	16.2	5.1	12.6	8.3	3.7	4.2	8.8	5.9	12.3	5.7	8.2
October	3 219	110 063	6.0	5.1	5.2	17.3	5.2	12.3	8.4	3.7	4.2	8.9	5.9	11.3	5.8	10.8
November	3 145	110 360	5.8	5.0	5.2	16.6	5.0	12.1	8.8	3.5	4.2	8.6	5.8	10.5	5.5	11.6
December	3 213	110 580	5.7	4.9	5.1	16.0	4.9	12.1	8.1	3.4	4.3	8.2	5.6	10.6	5.1	11.6
1988:																
January	3 247	110 769	5.7	4.9	5.1	16.1	5.0	12.0	7.6	3.5	4.1	8.9	5.7	11.8	5.4	11.4
February	3 201	111 026	5.7	4.9	5.2	15.6	4.9	12.4	8.5	3.4	4.0	8.4	5.7	10.9	5.6	10.7
March	3 169	110 868	5.7	4.9	4.9	16.6	4.8	12.7	8.4	3.4	4.0	7.6	5.6	10.8	5.3	11.0
April	3 224	111 426	5.4	4.6	4.9	16.0	4.6	12.2	8.8	3.0	3.8	8.6	5.3	10.6	5.2	10.4
May	3 121	111 171	5.6	4.9	4.9	15.3	4.7	12.3	8.8	3.3	3.9	8.3	5.6	10.7	5.4	12.0
June	3 111	111 816	5.4	4.7	4.8	14.2	4.6	11.5	8.8	3.2	3.8	7.9	5.4	10.3	4.9	9.6
July	3 060	112 000	5.4	4.6	5.0	14.8	4.7	11.6	7.9	3.1	4.0	8.1	5.4	10.4	5.2	11.1
August	3 119	112 163	5.6	4.9	4.8	15.4	4.8	11.4	8.1	3.4	4.0	7.5	5.6	10.7	5.5	11.1
September	3 165	112 191	5.4	4.6	4.8	15.5	4.8	11.0	7.4	3.1	3.8	8.1	5.5	9.6	5.6	11.1
October	3 231	112 407	5.4	4.7	4.7	15.1	4.7	11.1	7.8	3.1	3.7	7.9	5.5	10.1	5.3	10.2
November	3 241	112 859	5.3	4.7	4.7	13.9	4.6	11.0	7.9	3.3	3.8	7.7	5.5	10.6	5.2	9.5
December	3 194	112 910	5.3	4.7	4.6	14.8	4.6	11.3	7.6	3.1	3.6	8.2	5.3	10.2	5.1	8.8

Civilian Employment and Selected Unemployment Rates—*Continued*

(Seasonally adjusted)

Year and month	Employment by industry (Thousands of persons)		Unemployment rates (percent of civilian labor force in group)													
				20 years and over			By race			By marital or family status			Wage and salary workers, by industry of last job			
						Both sexes, 16 to 19 years			Persons of Hispanic origin				Private nonagricultural			
	Agricultural	Nonagricultural	All civilian workers	Men	Women		White	Black		Married men, spouse present	Married women, spouse present	Women who maintain families	Total	Construction	Manufacturing	Agricultural
1989:																
January	3 287	113 421	5.4	4.6	4.7	16.4	4.6	11.8	8.6	3.1	3.7	8.1	5.5	10.3	5.2	9.5
February	3 234	113 542	5.2	4.5	4.5	15.0	4.3	11.9	7.0	3.1	3.4	8.1	5.2	10.1	4.8	9.2
March	3 198	113 824	5.0	4.3	4.6	13.9	4.2	11.1	6.6	2.9	3.5	7.9	5.1	9.7	4.8	8.8
April	3 162	113 935	5.2	4.5	4.7	14.6	4.5	11.1	8.1	3.1	4.1	7.7	5.2	9.7	4.8	10.1
May	3 125	113 974	5.2	4.3	4.8	14.8	4.4	11.2	7.9	2.9	3.8	8.4	5.2	9.5	5.0	10.1
June	3 068	114 350	5.3	4.4	4.8	15.7	4.5	11.7	8.2	2.8	3.8	8.0	5.3	10.0	5.1	10.2
July	3 227	114 245	5.2	4.4	4.9	14.2	4.5	11.0	8.8	3.0	3.9	8.2	5.4	10.2	5.1	8.5
August	3 284	114 371	5.2	4.5	4.7	14.6	4.5	11.1	8.8	3.1	3.8	7.9	5.3	10.3	5.2	8.8
September	3 219	114 135	5.3	4.7	4.6	15.2	4.5	11.7	8.1	3.3	3.8	7.7	5.5	10.4	5.3	8.0
October	3 215	114 366	5.3	4.6	4.8	15.0	4.5	11.7	8.0	3.1	4.0	7.7	5.4	9.1	5.4	10.1
November	3 132	114 780	5.4	4.7	4.7	15.5	4.6	11.7	7.9	3.1	3.7	8.2	5.5	9.8	5.4	12.0
December	3 188	114 642	5.4	4.6	4.8	15.3	4.6	11.6	8.3	3.1	3.8	8.0	5.4	9.7	5.6	9.5
1990:																
January	3 210	115 871	5.4	4.7	4.7	14.8	4.6	11.1	7.3	3.4	3.7	7.9	5.5	9.2	6.0	8.9
February	3 188	115 871	5.3	4.5	4.7	15.0	4.6	11.0	7.5	3.1	3.7	7.8	5.4	9.2	5.6	9.1
March	3 260	115 943	5.2	4.6	4.7	14.3	4.5	10.9	7.4	3.1	3.6	8.2	5.3	10.0	5.5	9.3
April	3 231	115 621	5.4	4.8	4.8	14.7	4.7	10.7	8.5	3.3	3.6	7.6	5.6	10.3	5.6	12.3
May	3 266	115 885	5.4	4.7	4.7	15.0	4.6	10.6	7.9	3.2	3.6	7.9	5.5	11.4	5.6	8.8
June	3 245	115 738	5.2	4.7	4.6	14.3	4.5	10.5	7.7	3.1	3.6	8.2	5.3	9.8	5.0	9.4
July	3 192	115 618	5.5	4.9	4.9	15.0	4.7	11.4	8.0	3.4	3.8	8.4	5.6	10.5	5.8	9.8
August	3 197	115 605	5.7	5.1	5.0	16.3	4.9	11.7	8.3	3.5	4.0	8.3	5.8	11.6	5.9	9.9
September	3 206	115 318	5.9	5.2	5.1	16.4	5.0	12.1	8.3	3.5	4.0	9.0	6.0	12.1	6.1	10.0
October	3 270	115 266	5.9	5.4	5.1	16.5	5.1	12.1	8.5	3.7	4.1	8.7	6.1	13.0	5.9	9.3
November	3 189	115 117	6.2	5.7	5.2	17.1	5.3	12.4	8.9	3.9	4.2	9.0	6.4	13.8	6.3	9.6
December	3 245	114 996	6.3	5.8	5.2	17.4	5.4	12.4	9.9	3.9	4.1	9.0	6.5	14.2	6.8	11.9
1991:																
January	3 208	114 732	6.4	5.8	5.4	18.6	5.6	11.9	9.1	4.1	4.1	9.3	6.5	14.4	6.9	12.0
February	3 270	114 485	6.6	6.2	5.5	17.4	5.8	12.2	9.2	4.3	4.4	9.2	6.9	15.4	7.2	11.2
March	3 177	114 475	6.8	6.4	5.6	18.3	6.0	12.5	9.8	4.4	4.7	9.0	7.0	14.1	7.6	13.0
April	3 241	114 868	6.7	6.4	5.5	17.8	5.9	12.7	9.8	4.5	4.6	9.5	7.0	14.8	7.5	11.7
May	3 275	114 165	6.9	6.4	6.0	18.8	6.1	12.8	10.0	4.4	4.7	9.5	7.1	14.9	7.5	12.2
June	3 300	114 339	6.9	6.5	5.8	18.5	6.2	12.5	10.1	4.5	4.6	9.2	7.2	15.2	7.7	11.7
July	3 319	114 249	6.8	6.5	5.5	19.4	6.2	11.9	9.6	4.3	4.5	8.3	7.2	16.4	7.0	10.8
August	3 313	114 171	6.9	6.5	5.7	18.9	6.2	12.4	10.5	4.4	4.5	9.5	7.1	15.4	7.3	11.8
September	3 319	114 609	6.9	6.6	5.7	18.8	6.2	12.3	10.9	4.5	4.6	9.4	7.1	15.9	7.0	11.9
October	3 289	114 511	7.0	6.5	5.9	19.1	6.2	13.3	10.7	4.3	4.5	9.7	7.1	16.2	6.9	12.4
November	3 296	114 474	7.0	6.6	6.0	19.0	6.3	12.5	10.4	4.7	4.6	9.5	7.4	16.9	7.2	12.0
December	3 146	114 320	7.3	6.8	6.1	20.3	6.5	12.9	10.2	4.9	4.9	9.2	7.6	16.8	7.5	11.2
1992:																
January	3 155	114 823	7.3	7.1	6.0	19.2	6.4	13.5	11.0	4.9	4.8	9.2	7.5	17.1	7.5	11.2
February	3 239	114 514	7.4	7.1	6.2	20.1	6.5	14.2	11.3	5.1	5.0	9.6	7.7	17.9	7.7	11.2
March	3 236	114 908	7.4	7.0	6.2	20.3	6.5	14.1	11.2	4.8	5.0	10.0	7.7	17.2	7.5	10.1
April	3 245	115 181	7.4	7.1	6.3	18.5	6.5	14.1	11.0	4.9	5.1	10.0	7.7	16.5	7.7	11.9
May	3 213	115 162	7.6	7.3	6.3	20.1	6.6	14.7	11.7	5.1	5.1	10.1	7.9	16.8	7.9	14.6
June	3 297	115 122	7.8	7.4	6.4	23.0	6.9	14.6	12.1	5.2	5.2	10.2	7.9	17.1	8.2	13.0
July	3 285	115 428	7.7	7.2	6.5	20.8	6.7	14.4	11.7	5.2	5.2	10.4	7.9	16.5	8.1	13.9
August	3 279	115 547	7.6	7.2	6.5	19.9	6.7	14.2	11.7	5.3	5.0	10.7	8.0	16.8	7.9	11.1
September	3 274	115 446	7.6	7.1	6.4	21.0	6.7	13.9	11.8	5.3	5.0	9.6	7.9	17.4	8.0	16.0
October	3 254	115 374	7.3	7.1	6.2	18.3	6.5	14.3	11.8	5.2	5.0	9.4	7.8	16.0	8.1	13.1
November	3 207	115 669	7.4	7.0	6.2	20.5	6.5	14.1	12.0	5.0	5.0	11.0	7.6	15.4	7.9	14.2
December	3 259	115 738	7.4	6.8	6.5	19.8	6.5	14.3	11.5	4.9	5.0	10.1	7.7	16.3	7.5	12.3
1993:																
January	3 222	115 853	7.3	6.7	6.3	19.9	6.3	14.1	11.3	4.6	5.0	10.4	7.4	14.5	7.5	11.4
February	3 125	116 150	7.1	6.6	6.1	19.7	6.2	13.5	11.5	4.6	4.6	10.2	7.3	14.3	7.4	12.2
March	3 119	116 423	7.0	6.8	5.8	19.7	6.1	13.7	11.3	4.6	4.4	9.2	7.2	14.9	7.4	11.6
April	3 074	116 400	7.1	6.6	6.1	19.5	6.1	14.0	11.0	4.6	5.0	9.6	7.3	14.6	7.4	12.3
May	3 100	117 015	7.1	6.5	6.0	19.8	6.2	13.1	10.2	4.6	4.7	10.0	7.3	15.2	7.2	11.3
June	3 108	117 182	7.0	6.6	6.0	19.9	6.2	13.4	10.4	4.5	4.7	9.9	7.2	15.0	7.5	11.9
July	3 126	117 341	6.9	6.5	5.9	18.4	6.1	12.7	10.7	4.5	4.7	9.7	7.1	16.2	7.2	12.0
August	3 026	117 830	6.8	6.3	5.8	18.4	6.0	12.3	9.8	4.4	4.4	9.2	7.0	14.8	7.4	12.4
September	3 174	117 380	6.7	6.3	5.8	18.2	5.9	12.5	10.0	4.3	4.6	9.2	7.0	14.2	7.2	10.8
October	3 084	117 739	6.8	6.2	5.9	18.7	6.2	11.8	11.4	4.4	4.7	9.4	7.0	13.9	6.8	12.3
November	3 157	118 012	6.6	5.9	5.8	18.5	5.7	12.6	10.5	4.1	4.5	9.6	6.8	12.8	6.6	11.0
December	3 116	118 348	6.5	5.9	5.8	17.9	5.8	11.7	10.6	4.0	4.5	10.0	6.7	13.1	6.7	11.5
1994:																
January	3 302	118 664	6.6	6.0	5.8	18.3	5.7	13.1	10.5	4.1	4.4	9.1	6.9	13.3	6.2	13.0
February	3 339	118 747	6.6	6.0	5.7	18.0	5.7	12.8	10.1	4.4	4.4	9.6	6.9	13.2	6.3	13.8
March	3 354	118 576	6.5	5.8	5.8	18.0	5.7	12.4	9.9	4.1	4.4	9.4	6.7	13.3	6.1	13.0
April	3 428	118 862	6.4	5.6	5.6	19.1	5.6	11.9	10.8	3.9	4.1	9.4	6.5	12.3	5.8	10.6
May	3 409	119 455	6.1	5.3	5.4	18.0	5.2	11.7	9.6	3.7	4.1	9.0	6.2	11.5	5.4	8.8
June	3 299	119 335	6.1	5.3	5.4	17.6	5.3	11.3	10.3	3.6	4.2	8.8	6.2	12.2	5.3	8.5
July	3 333	119 373	6.1	5.5	5.2	17.6	5.3	10.9	10.1	3.6	4.0	7.7	6.2	11.4	5.5	13.4
August	3 451	119 891	6.0	5.4	5.3	17.3	5.2	11.2	9.8	3.5	4.2	8.9	6.1	10.7	5.4	12.7
September	3 430	120 257	5.9	5.1	5.3	17.5	5.1	10.6	10.1	3.3	4.1	8.9	6.0	10.6	5.4	10.8
October	3 490	120 622	5.8	5.1	5.0	17.5	5.0	11.3	9.5	3.3	3.9	8.8	5.9	10.6	5.2	9.9
November	3 574	120 942	5.6	4.9	5.1	15.6	4.8	10.8	8.9	3.3	3.9	8.5	5.8	10.5	4.8	9.7
December	3 577	121 144	5.5	4.7	4.8	17.0	4.8	9.9	9.3	3.2	3.7	9.0	5.6	11.1	4.9	9.8

Nonagricultural Employment

(Wage and salary workers on nonagricultural payrolls—Thousands, seasonally adjusted)

Year and month	Total	Goods-producing industries [1]		Manufacturing			Service-producing industries						Government	
		Total	Construction	Total	Durable goods	Nondurable goods	Total	Transportation and public utilities	Wholesale trade	Retail trade	Finance, insurance, and real estate	Services (private)	Total	Federal
1971:														
January	70 718	22 944	3 582	18 737	10 694	8 043	47 774	4 465	3 996	11 176	3 709	11 692	12 736	2 684
February	70 657	22 840	3 542	18 679	10 650	8 029	47 817	4 481	3 999	11 194	3 716	11 683	12 744	2 682
March	70 746	22 827	3 604	18 602	10 586	8 016	47 919	4 480	3 995	11 225	3 725	11 714	12 780	2 680
April	70 936	22 915	3 676	18 616	10 591	8 025	48 021	4 470	3 997	11 265	3 739	11 729	12 821	2 685
May	71 129	22 980	3 681	18 673	10 633	8 040	48 149	4 491	4 010	11 293	3 751	11 758	12 846	2 685
June	71 163	22 919	3 695	18 599	10 594	8 005	48 244	4 515	3 990	11 315	3 773	11 787	12 864	2 685
July	71 219	22 886	3 717	18 564	10 568	7 996	48 333	4 511	4 003	11 353	3 779	11 801	12 886	2 693
August	71 220	22 851	3 718	18 513	10 518	7 995	48 369	4 469	4 011	11 395	3 787	11 786	12 921	2 707
September	71 527	22 989	3 746	18 617	10 593	8 024	48 538	4 501	4 029	11 423	3 801	11 857	12 927	2 708
October	71 532	22 940	3 793	18 589	10 589	8 000	48 592	4 461	4 037	11 436	3 813	11 877	12 968	2 706
November	71 734	23 046	3 846	18 637	10 607	8 030	48 688	4 454	4 048	11 437	3 829	11 915	13 005	2 702
December	71 996	23 073	3 791	18 654	10 624	8 030	48 923	4 486	4 058	11 530	3 840	11 956	13 053	2 698
1972:														
January	72 303	23 210	3 852	18 730	10 691	8 039	49 093	4 485	4 059	11 585	3 848	11 990	13 126	2 703
February	72 525	23 260	3 810	18 824	10 762	8 062	49 265	4 497	4 067	11 653	3 854	12 024	13 170	2 698
March	72 808	23 384	3 847	18 909	10 822	8 087	49 424	4 527	4 090	11 677	3 865	12 065	13 200	2 691
April	73 061	23 487	3 877	18 999	10 883	8 106	49 574	4 519	4 102	11 703	3 878	12 133	13 239	2 695
May	73 341	23 590	3 897	19 069	10 942	8 127	49 751	4 522	4 108	11 745	3 886	12 201	13 289	2 691
June	73 643	23 677	3 911	19 139	10 985	8 154	49 966	4 543	4 132	11 791	3 914	12 330	13 256	2 676
July	73 636	23 586	3 878	19 086	10 972	8 114	50 050	4 535	4 129	11 805	3 917	12 320	13 344	2 645
August	73 929	23 700	3 911	19 161	11 039	8 122	50 229	4 533	4 142	11 852	3 926	12 367	13 409	2 666
September	74 115	23 797	3 918	19 244	11 101	8 143	50 318	4 564	4 151	11 871	3 933	12 362	13 437	2 671
October	74 527	24 003	3 951	19 418	11 247	8 171	50 524	4 578	4 161	11 943	3 945	12 440	13 457	2 674
November	74 881	24 121	3 930	19 558	11 353	8 205	50 760	4 584	4 181	12 035	3 959	12 499	13 502	2 678
December	75 235	24 179	3 848	19 703	11 470	8 233	51 056	4 611	4 200	12 174	3 967	12 562	13 542	2 684
1973:														
January	75 474	24 368	3 932	19 808	11 555	8 253	51 106	4 598	4 216	12 139	3 976	12 630	13 547	2 673
February	75 908	24 610	4 020	19 957	11 677	8 280	51 298	4 605	4 241	12 176	4 000	12 689	13 587	2 665
March	76 137	24 690	4 027	20 031	11 734	8 297	51 447	4 623	4 249	12 211	4 015	12 730	13 619	2 664
April	76 312	24 754	4 045	20 077	11 769	8 308	51 558	4 630	4 258	12 226	4 021	12 759	13 664	2 667
May	76 516	24 814	4 078	20 104	11 811	8 293	51 702	4 644	4 261	12 295	4 033	12 773	13 696	2 670
June	76 738	24 928	4 125	20 167	11 863	8 304	51 810	4 643	4 290	12 314	4 045	12 793	13 725	2 655
July	76 758	24 940	4 154	20 145	11 887	8 258	51 818	4 645	4 300	12 314	4 059	12 779	13 721	2 624
August	77 018	24 992	4 143	20 202	11 925	8 277	52 026	4 663	4 319	12 324	4 064	12 885	13 771	2 645
September	77 164	24 978	4 145	20 185	11 921	8 264	52 186	4 693	4 318	12 372	4 072	12 981	13 750	2 654
October	77 502	25 113	4 138	20 323	12 024	8 299	52 389	4 711	4 335	12 413	4 075	13 021	13 834	2 659
November	77 833	25 214	4 147	20 408	12 081	8 327	52 619	4 703	4 350	12 483	4 089	13 099	13 895	2 668
December	77 992	25 264	4 168	20 431	12 102	8 329	52 728	4 716	4 360	12 500	4 100	13 133	13 919	2 680
1974:														
January	77 953	25 175	4 144	20 359	12 043	8 316	52 778	4 737	4 399	12 420	4 113	13 172	13 937	2 683
February	78 177	25 211	4 251	20 284	11 986	8 298	52 966	4 738	4 419	12 431	4 131	13 239	14 008	2 699
March	78 177	25 134	4 216	20 242	11 958	8 284	53 043	4 737	4 422	12 437	4 133	13 280	14 034	2 705
April	78 261	25 102	4 156	20 260	12 004	8 256	53 159	4 731	4 430	12 479	4 137	13 303	14 079	2 711
May	78 407	25 067	4 131	20 244	11 987	8 257	53 340	4 733	4 441	12 529	4 145	13 390	14 102	2 719
June	78 434	25 017	4 064	20 258	12 017	8 241	53 417	4 734	4 455	12 541	4 157	13 444	14 086	2 723
July	78 517	24 925	3 975	20 250	12 035	8 215	53 592	4 740	4 461	12 563	4 158	13 515	14 155	2 729
August	78 478	24 833	3 966	20 157	11 951	8 206	53 645	4 734	4 468	12 542	4 158	13 533	14 210	2 732
September	78 498	24 721	3 921	20 089	11 915	8 174	53 777	4 713	4 463	12 608	4 161	13 552	14 280	2 739
October	78 569	24 582	3 882	19 978	11 874	8 104	53 987	4 716	4 476	12 685	4 164	13 616	14 330	2 737
November	78 238	24 216	3 827	19 663	11 666	7 997	54 022	4 704	4 481	12 647	4 164	13 646	14 380	2 738
December	77 565	23 653	3 774	19 185	11 345	7 840	53 912	4 688	4 459	12 574	4 158	13 636	14 397	2 738
1975:														
January	77 145	23 266	3 757	18 769	11 076	7 693	53 879	4 645	4 438	12 478	4 151	13 649	14 518	2 735
February	76 742	22 781	3 641	18 397	10 831	7 566	53 961	4 596	4 418	12 500	4 144	13 696	14 607	2 736
March	76 419	22 481	3 522	18 216	10 716	7 500	53 938	4 565	4 402	12 491	4 141	13 722	14 617	2 737
April	76 298	22 335	3 461	18 134	10 617	7 517	53 963	4 548	4 405	12 443	4 149	13 769	14 649	2 737
May	76 459	22 359	3 471	18 139	10 581	7 558	54 100	4 543	4 402	12 524	4 150	13 813	14 668	2 739
June	76 388	22 291	3 454	18 091	10 524	7 567	54 097	4 519	4 400	12 595	4 151	13 792	14 640	2 738
July	76 626	22 254	3 447	18 060	10 455	7 605	54 372	4 521	4 416	12 636	4 157	13 947	14 695	2 750
August	76 980	22 448	3 484	18 205	10 529	7 676	54 532	4 519	4 427	12 696	4 169	14 018	14 703	2 750
September	77 188	22 607	3 508	18 350	10 613	7 737	54 581	4 522	4 449	12 717	4 178	14 001	14 714	2 756
October	77 499	22 723	3 516	18 447	10 638	7 809	54 776	4 520	4 456	12 772	4 192	14 058	14 778	2 757
November	77 619	22 765	3 527	18 473	10 640	7 833	54 854	4 519	4 469	12 805	4 194	14 103	14 764	2 754
December	77 915	22 891	3 547	18 567	10 700	7 867	55 024	4 496	4 482	12 883	4 207	14 159	14 797	2 753
1976:														
January	78 326	23 070	3 588	18 703	10 793	7 910	55 256	4 539	4 497	12 934	4 211	14 242	14 833	2 750
February	78 606	23 165	3 589	18 798	10 856	7 942	55 441	4 550	4 516	13 029	4 218	14 293	14 835	2 744
March	78 819	23 237	3 572	18 887	10 929	7 958	55 582	4 559	4 528	13 051	4 228	14 367	14 849	2 739
April	79 134	23 360	3 587	18 999	11 005	7 994	55 774	4 568	4 549	13 137	4 240	14 435	14 845	2 736
May	79 192	23 320	3 564	18 985	11 050	7 935	55 872	4 568	4 560	13 177	4 250	14 481	14 836	2 733
June	79 258	23 315	3 555	18 992	11 069	7 923	55 943	4 575	4 562	13 168	4 262	14 541	14 835	2 723
July	79 485	23 359	3 564	19 015	11 078	7 937	56 126	4 595	4 569	13 207	4 266	14 622	14 867	2 723
August	79 581	23 356	3 567	19 031	11 117	7 914	56 225	4 595	4 570	13 261	4 275	14 639	14 885	2 724
September	79 842	23 498	3 565	19 152	11 177	7 975	56 344	4 615	4 587	13 307	4 300	14 665	14 870	2 727
October	79 842	23 406	3 571	19 049	11 094	7 955	56 436	4 597	4 592	13 315	4 319	14 708	14 905	2 726
November	80 141	23 555	3 601	19 161	11 196	7 965	56 586	4 605	4 600	13 341	4 330	14 775	14 935	2 732
December	80 338	23 580	3 590	19 186	11 218	7 968	56 758	4 631	4 611	13 386	4 347	14 836	14 947	2 728

1. Includes mining, not shown seperately.

Nonagricultural Employment—*Continued*

(Wage and salary workers on nonagricultural payrolls—Thousands, seasonally adjusted)

| Year and month | Total | Goods-producing industries [1] | | | | | Service-producing industries | | | | | | | |
| | | Total | Construc-tion | Manufacturing | | | Total | Transpor-tation and public utilities | Wholesale trade | Retail trade | Finance, insurance, and real estate | Services (private) | Government | |
				Total	Durable goods	Nondur-able goods							Total	Federal
1977:														
January	80 517	23 628	3 542	19 276	11 276	8 000	56 889	4 647	4 624	13 441	4 363	14 893	14 921	2 723
February	80 794	23 803	3 665	19 321	11 288	8 033	56 991	4 656	4 633	13 475	4 375	14 939	14 913	2 724
March	81 221	24 000	3 739	19 436	11 381	8 055	57 221	4 657	4 653	13 580	4 401	15 014	14 916	2 729
April	81 610	24 186	3 813	19 546	11 446	8 100	57 424	4 678	4 675	13 634	4 422	15 086	14 929	2 723
May	81 977	24 308	3 843	19 639	11 520	8 119	57 669	4 701	4 692	13 704	4 437	15 147	14 988	2 724
June	82 381	24 431	3 879	19 723	11 582	8 141	57 950	4 707	4 713	13 762	4 454	15 232	15 082	2 724
July	82 760	24 515	3 908	19 799	11 658	8 141	58 245	4 725	4 735	13 806	4 469	15 336	15 174	2 720
August	82 974	24 508	3 911	19 796	11 656	8 140	58 466	4 727	4 754	13 872	4 484	15 411	15 218	2 726
September	83 431	24 612	3 935	19 851	11 704	8 147	58 819	4 766	4 776	13 942	4 513	15 529	15 293	2 731
October	83 661	24 656	3 944	19 878	11 731	8 147	59 005	4 747	4 787	13 998	4 538	15 600	15 335	2 729
November	84 031	24 739	3 967	19 926	11 762	8 164	59 292	4 764	4 809	14 091	4 565	15 693	15 370	2 731
December	84 271	24 746	3 991	20 057	11 868	8 189	59 525	4 784	4 831	14 169	4 581	15 750	15 410	2 746
1978														
January	84 464	24 780	3 941	20 145	11 942	8 203	59 684	4 804	4 848	14 222	4 600	15 745	15 465	2 739
February	84 808	24 870	3 968	20 203	11 987	8 216	59 938	4 825	4 872	14 249	4 631	15 837	15 524	2 740
March	85 338	25 055	4 065	20 277	12 034	8 243	60 283	4 858	4 898	14 338	4 650	15 947	15 592	2 740
April	86 083	25 458	4 220	20 358	12 100	8 258	60 625	4 896	4 930	14 402	4 666	16 066	15 665	2 748
May	86 404	25 507	4 211	20 413	12 153	8 260	60 897	4 908	4 956	14 485	4 688	16 153	15 707	2 752
June	86 811	25 656	4 283	20 491	12 212	8 279	61 155	4 938	4 983	14 560	4 718	16 237	15 719	2 757
July	87 037	25 717	4 304	20 523	12 258	8 265	61 320	4 906	4 991	14 613	4 740	16 330	15 740	2 760
August	87 324	25 778	4 310	20 570	12 308	8 262	61 546	4 929	5 020	14 651	4 755	16 435	15 756	2 761
September	87 434	25 820	4 311	20 616	12 363	8 253	61 614	4 953	5 039	14 688	4 772	16 475	15 687	2 764
October	87 797	25 972	4 336	20 729	12 462	8 267	61 825	4 993	5 069	14 752	4 794	16 496	15 721	2 764
November	88 249	26 116	4 347	20 851	12 548	8 303	62 133	5 021	5 095	14 835	4 827	16 612	15 743	2 764
December	88 559	26 235	4 352	20 956	12 624	8 332	62 324	5 044	5 122	14 860	4 845	16 691	15 762	2 746
1979:														
January	88 728	26 264	4 309	21 019	12 677	8 342	62 464	5 062	5 148	14 914	4 871	16 692	15 777	2 757
February	88 985	26 319	4 326	21 043	12 717	8 326	62 666	5 082	5 160	14 938	4 891	16 799	15 796	2 757
March	89 426	26 511	4 456	21 102	12 768	8 334	62 915	5 101	5 182	15 004	4 907	16 908	15 813	2 754
April	89 363	26 462	4 423	21 092	12 766	8 326	62 901	5 005	5 188	14 968	4 924	16 955	15 861	2 758
May	89 681	26 527	4 467	21 110	12 781	8 329	63 154	5 109	5 206	14 958	4 952	17 042	15 887	2 769
June	89 955	26 599	4 493	21 162	12 828	8 334	63 356	5 166	5 230	14 931	4 971	17 120	15 938	2 776
July	90 019	26 606	4 505	21 148	12 819	8 329	63 413	5 163	5 235	14 881	4 986	17 148	16 000	2 782
August	90 159	26 474	4 506	21 003	12 698	8 305	63 685	5 188	5 242	14 901	5 015	17 221	16 118	2 811
September	90 149	26 471	4 495	21 012	12 745	8 267	63 678	5 178	5 247	14 945	5 014	17 261	16 033	2 776
October	90 360	26 467	4 496	20 998	12 705	8 293	63 893	5 183	5 264	15 033	5 039	17 337	16 037	2 775
November	90 466	26 383	4 497	20 908	12 631	8 277	64 083	5 198	5 280	15 098	5 055	17 390	16 062	2 778
December	90 617	26 451	4 533	20 929	12 655	8 274	64 166	5 196	5 266	15 083	5 068	17 471	16 082	2 785
1980:														
January	90 729	26 448	4 570	20 892	12 614	8 278	64 281	5 195	5 290	15 095	5 092	17 506	16 103	2 790
February	90 876	26 386	4 550	20 834	12 611	8 223	64 490	5 186	5 310	15 125	5 108	17 617	16 144	2 820
March	90 995	26 307	4 461	20 833	12 617	8 216	64 688	5 182	5 315	15 142	5 122	17 703	16 224	2 881
April	90 780	25 979	4 380	20 573	12 384	8 189	64 801	5 165	5 296	15 025	5 125	17 746	16 444	3 111
May	90 316	25 630	4 333	20 258	12 117	8 141	64 686	5 151	5 280	14 986	5 139	17 804	16 326	2 958
June	89 974	25 331	4 287	20 003	11 925	8 078	64 643	5 126	5 266	14 942	5 152	17 847	16 310	2 946
July	89 676	25 042	4 246	19 777	11 761	8 016	64 634	5 120	5 263	14 921	5 161	17 919	16 250	2 891
August	89 964	25 197	4 259	19 929	11 852	8 077	64 767	5 118	5 270	14 955	5 173	17 990	16 261	2 829
September	90 046	25 254	4 271	19 959	11 894	8 065	64 792	5 120	5 288	14 967	5 184	18 051	16 182	2 783
October	90 334	25 371	4 286	20 048	11 974	8 074	64 963	5 136	5 297	14 992	5 211	18 095	16 232	2 794
November	90 550	25 485	4 282	20 146	12 066	8 080	65 065	5 130	5 310	15 019	5 223	18 156	16 227	2 797
December	90 774	25 585	4 306	20 199	12 112	8 087	65 189	5 139	5 325	15 045	5 230	18 240	16 210	2 799
1981:														
January	91 003	25 594	4 265	20 236	12 151	8 085	65 409	5 150	5 347	15 096	5 261	18 357	16 198	2 797
February	91 095	25 575	4 272	20 197	12 105	8 092	65 520	5 159	5 358	15 146	5 271	18 400	16 186	2 789
March	91 206	25 654	4 306	20 227	12 132	8 095	65 552	5 163	5 365	15 163	5 277	18 439	16 145	2 781
April	91 219	25 567	4 313	20 274	12 173	8 101	65 652	5 161	5 381	15 208	5 290	18 487	16 125	2 780
May	91 142	25 511	4 240	20 277	12 167	8 110	65 631	5 157	5 376	15 204	5 297	18 533	16 064	2 774
June	91 285	25 634	4 194	20 286	12 174	8 112	65 651	5 163	5 380	15 185	5 298	18 581	16 044	2 780
July	91 410	25 630	4 168	20 278	12 151	8 127	65 780	5 180	5 381	15 170	5 305	18 624	16 120	2 787
August	91 320	25 559	4 144	20 219	12 104	8 115	65 761	5 184	5 381	15 199	5 310	18 682	16 005	2 772
September	91 191	25 564	4 119	20 240	12 120	8 120	65 627	5 176	5 380	15 217	5 311	18 725	15 818	2 752
October	91 216	25 443	4 117	20 119	12 048	8 071	65 773	5 169	5 385	15 203	5 315	18 805	15 896	2 756
November	91 014	25 264	4 092	19 960	11 916	8 044	65 750	5 170	5 388	15 135	5 316	18 848	15 893	2 751
December	90 831	25 044	4 075	19 756	11 751	8 005	65 787	5 151	5 382	15 145	5 318	18 896	15 895	2 743
1982:														
January	90 448	24 695	3 930	19 555	11 621	7 934	65 753	5 147	5 368	15 090	5 325	18 945	15 878	2 740
February	90 474	24 709	4 014	19 479	11 553	7 926	65 765	5 139	5 358	15 128	5 327	18 964	15 849	2 738
March	90 337	24 544	3 981	19 344	11 467	7 877	65 793	5 128	5 353	15 134	5 333	18 977	15 868	2 736
April	90 031	24 292	3 953	19 136	11 308	7 828	65 739	5 108	5 333	15 140	5 331	18 954	15 873	2 737
May	89 965	24 165	3 977	19 013	11 211	7 802	65 800	5 113	5 324	15 177	5 332	18 984	15 870	2 724
June	89 703	23 898	3 919	18 828	11 075	7 753	65 805	5 095	5 303	15 175	5 342	18 996	15 894	2 742
July	89 380	23 670	3 888	18 663	10 967	7 696	65 710	5 079	5 288	15 172	5 341	19 025	15 805	2 749
August	89 177	23 479	3 867	18 519	10 807	7 712	65 698	5 065	5 272	15 182	5 341	19 035	15 803	2 743
September	88 995	23 396	3 853	18 471	10 761	7 710	65 599	5 043	5 254	15 191	5 345	19 040	15 726	2 718
October	88 787	23 126	3 837	18 242	10 558	7 684	65 661	5 033	5 241	15 175	5 348	19 059	15 805	2 740
November	88 649	22 964	3 844	18 095	10 446	7 649	65 685	5 023	5 231	15 139	5 356	19 118	15 818	2 748
December	88 675	22 894	3 840	18 047	10 412	7 635	65 781	5 016	5 220	15 209	5 360	19 152	15 824	2 746

1. Includes mining, not shown seperately.

Nonagricultural Employment—*Continued*

(Wage and salary workers on nonagricultural payrolls—Thousands, seasonally adjusted)

Year and month	Total	Goods-producing industries [1]					Service-producing industries						Government	
		Total	Construction	Manufacturing			Total	Transportation and public utilities	Wholesale trade	Retail trade	Finance, insurance, and real estate	Services (private)	Total	Federal
				Total	Durable goods	Nondurable goods								
1983:														
January	88 826	22 930	3 877	18 062	10 424	7 638	65 896	4 977	5 214	15 254	5 375	19 202	15 874	2 772
February	88 758	22 846	3 820	18 060	10 427	7 633	65 912	4 969	5 213	15 264	5 389	19 217	15 860	2 766
March	88 946	22 826	3 793	18 077	10 435	7 642	66 120	4 977	5 209	15 333	5 398	19 337	15 866	2 765
April	89 211	22 911	3 808	18 159	10 495	7 664	66 300	4 989	5 225	15 383	5 421	19 430	15 852	2 763
May	89 497	23 041	3 841	18 260	10 575	7 685	66 456	4 995	5 239	15 427	5 432	19 496	15 867	2 768
June	89 886	23 172	3 902	18 330	10 620	7 710	66 714	4 994	5 263	15 505	5 444	19 622	15 886	2 769
July	90 313	23 334	3 946	18 443	10 712	7 731	66 979	4 999	5 278	15 608	5 470	19 729	15 895	2 775
August	89 973	23 430	3 993	18 495	10 750	7 745	66 543	4 366	5 299	15 687	5 494	19 819	15 878	2 775
September	91 088	23 628	4 031	18 654	10 868	7 786	67 460	5 045	5 325	15 781	5 517	19 922	15 870	2 784
October	91 408	23 809	4 069	18 788	10 978	7 810	67 599	5 047	5 349	15 846	5 529	19 976	15 852	2 786
November	91 727	23 961	4 108	18 901	11 069	7 832	67 766	5 034	5 377	15 910	5 548	20 048	15 849	2 778
December	92 110	24 058	4 132	18 972	11 130	7 842	68 052	5 037	5 406	16 024	5 571	20 150	15 864	2 781
1984:														
January	92 524	24 199	4 174	19 066	11 202	7 864	68 325	5 087	5 443	16 121	5 585	20 221	15 868	2 778
February	93 043	24 430	4 296	19 172	11 287	7 885	68 613	5 103	5 480	16 201	5 603	20 337	15 889	2 784
March	93 312	24 496	4 269	19 263	11 360	7 903	68 816	5 117	5 500	16 258	5 624	20 422	15 895	2 788
April	93 650	24 586	4 294	19 329	11 403	7 926	69 064	5 127	5 521	16 325	5 634	20 520	15 937	2 794
May	93 952	24 675	4 334	19 372	11 446	7 926	69 277	5 144	5 536	16 353	5 651	20 627	15 966	2 802
June	94 325	24 783	4 387	19 420	11 498	7 922	69 542	5 164	5 555	16 447	5 670	20 718	15 988	2 806
July	94 647	24 865	4 405	19 484	11 554	7 930	69 782	5 166	5 587	16 522	5 685	20 768	16 054	2 813
August	94 885	24 897	4 421	19 498	11 584	7 914	69 988	5 186	5 602	16 568	5 705	20 825	16 102	2 817
September	95 186	24 893	4 455	19 462	11 580	7 882	70 293	5 184	5 626	16 663	5 725	20 986	16 109	2 817
October	95 499	24 909	4 467	19 480	11 598	7 882	70 590	5 196	5 642	16 768	5 752	21 082	16 150	2 824
November	95 829	24 917	4 495	19 467	11 596	7 871	70 912	5 196	5 656	16 929	5 773	21 181	16 177	2 831
December	95 997	24 963	4 535	19 483	11 614	7 869	71 034	5 200	5 671	16 958	5 798	21 257	16 150	2 834
1985:														
January	96 249	24 968	4 550	19 472	11 616	7 856	71 281	5 213	5 687	16 972	5 817	21 391	16 201	2 834
February	96 397	24 914	4 549	19 420	11 580	7 840	71 483	5 223	5 689	17 034	5 836	21 477	16 224	2 835
March	96 734	24 953	4 615	19 393	11 568	7 825	71 781	5 204	5 707	17 150	5 859	21 598	16 263	2 846
April	96 896	24 918	4 640	19 328	11 520	7 808	71 978	5 220	5 710	17 209	5 884	21 670	16 285	2 856
May	97 163	24 893	4 664	19 285	11 497	7 788	72 270	5 231	5 717	17 291	5 907	21 795	16 329	2 868
June	97 280	24 843	4 659	19 246	11 469	7 777	72 437	5 232	5 725	17 343	5 928	21 858	16 351	2 878
July	97 465	24 786	4 659	19 200	11 428	7 772	72 679	5 241	5 728	17 353	5 950	21 915	16 492	2 888
August	97 696	24 795	4 688	19 186	11 407	7 779	72 901	5 227	5 737	17 413	5 978	22 055	16 491	2 896
September	97 878	24 761	4 724	19 124	11 358	7 766	73 117	5 243	5 745	17 443	6 008	22 186	16 492	2 894
October	98 098	24 768	4 740	19 124	11 365	7 759	73 330	5 253	5 756	17 475	6 038	22 287	16 521	2 895
November	98 286	24 754	4 750	19 108	11 351	7 757	73 532	5 254	5 761	17 511	6 071	22 405	16 530	2 903
December	98 500	24 765	4 765	19 110	11 342	7 768	73 735	5 257	5 762	17 579	6 103	22 482	16 552	2 910
1986:														
January	98 599	24 787	4 793	19 105	11 341	7 764	73 812	5 260	5 756	17 584	6 116	22 527	16 569	2 914
February	98 718	24 738	4 789	19 077	11 313	7 764	73 980	5 255	5 755	17 618	6 150	22 588	16 614	2 914
March	98 796	24 679	4 795	19 039	11 283	7 756	74 117	5 246	5 744	17 684	6 174	22 663	16 606	2 914
April	98 974	24 651	4 823	19 016	11 266	7 750	74 323	5 242	5 755	17 734	6 208	22 762	16 622	2 911
May	99 096	24 567	4 800	18 986	11 238	7 748	74 529	5 251	5 763	17 801	6 235	22 833	16 646	2 901
June	98 973	24 472	4 784	18 924	11 177	7 747	74 501	5 148	5 730	17 836	6 262	22 895	16 630	2 885
July	99 276	24 431	4 792	18 883	11 152	7 731	74 845	5 250	5 779	17 903	6 294	22 978	16 641	2 879
August	99 435	24 429	4 811	18 881	11 148	7 733	75 006	5 222	5 767	17 985	6 320	23 061	16 651	2 888
September	99 747	24 415	4 812	18 879	11 130	7 749	75 332	5 261	5 767	18 051	6 343	23 153	16 757	2 896
October	99 980	24 407	4 827	18 860	11 105	7 755	75 573	5 259	5 768	18 092	6 365	23 255	16 834	2 895
November	100 145	24 407	4 831	18 860	11 097	7 763	75 738	5 285	5 770	18 111	6 383	23 334	16 855	2 895
December	100 394	24 446	4 868	18 867	11 093	7 774	75 948	5 290	5 776	18 159	6 419	23 431	16 873	2 901
1987:														
January	100 543	24 444	4 884	18 852	11 080	7 772	76 099	5 297	5 786	18 139	6 434	23 554	16 889	2 909
February	100 772	24 512	4 916	18 890	11 109	7 781	76 260	5 310	5 802	18 197	6 453	23 620	16 878	2 913
March	101 005	24 517	4 911	18 899	11 108	7 791	76 488	5 314	5 809	18 247	6 474	23 737	16 907	2 922
April	101 367	24 542	4 925	18 909	11 101	7 808	76 825	5 342	5 822	18 325	6 507	23 861	16 968	2 932
May	101 564	24 586	4 951	18 924	11 109	7 815	76 978	5 343	5 827	18 342	6 524	23 973	16 969	2 938
June	101 713	24 584	4 951	18 920	11 103	7 817	77 129	5 343	5 834	18 394	6 534	24 047	16 977	2 945
July	102 047	24 643	4 951	18 976	11 107	7 869	77 404	5 351	5 844	18 438	6 555	24 186	17 030	2 945
August	102 266	24 706	4 965	19 021	11 159	7 862	77 560	5 367	5 858	18 455	6 566	24 296	17 018	2 948
September	102 430	24 761	4 962	19 072	11 194	7 878	77 669	5 394	5 874	18 500	6 573	24 350	16 978	2 953
October	102 980	24 856	5 007	19 117	11 225	7 892	78 124	5 410	5 891	18 627	6 590	24 472	17 134	2 962
November	103 200	24 933	5 020	19 183	11 261	7 922	78 267	5 429	5 902	18 666	6 584	24 539	17 147	2 971
December	103 544	24 992	5 047	19 216	11 287	7 929	78 552	5 439	5 923	18 722	6 599	24 669	17 200	2 976
1988:														
January	103 623	24 910	4 979	19 204	11 266	7 938	78 713	5 450	5 918	18 747	6 608	24 779	17 211	2 972
February	104 046	24 990	5 022	19 240	11 294	7 946	79 056	5 458	5 944	18 875	6 608	24 920	17 251	2 973
March	104 311	25 057	5 073	19 261	11 308	7 953	79 254	5 476	5 964	18 867	6 619	25 026	17 302	2 973
April	104 537	25 098	5 092	19 285	11 334	7 951	79 439	5 482	5 983	18 906	6 620	25 145	17 303	2 967
May	104 811	25 111	5 091	19 302	11 340	7 962	79 700	5 496	6 003	18 962	6 623	25 275	17 341	2 963
June	105 132	25 156	5 118	19 325	11 363	7 962	79 976	5 506	6 027	19 010	6 630	25 440	17 363	2 962
July	105 400	25 170	5 125	19 333	11 385	7 948	80 230	5 519	6 048	19 062	6 634	25 591	17 376	2 961
August	105 599	25 136	5 125	19 300	11 362	7 938	80 463	5 535	6 058	19 102	6 633	25 715	17 420	2 964
September	105 814	25 157	5 132	19 321	11 384	7 937	80 657	5 537	6 076	19 121	6 632	25 846	17 445	2 976
October	106 091	25 193	5 128	19 363	11 410	7 953	80 898	5 544	6 094	19 165	6 639	25 962	17 494	2 983
November	106 368	25 236	5 131	19 410	11 445	7 965	81 132	5 562	6 108	19 202	6 648	26 085	17 527	2 986
December	106 691	25 265	5 135	19 437	11 469	7 968	81 426	5 573	6 135	19 283	6 651	26 218	17 566	2 985

1. Includes mining, not shown seperately.

Nonagricultural Employment—*Continued*

(Wage and salary workers on nonagricultural payrolls—Thousands, seasonally adjusted)

Year and month	Total	Goods-producing industries [1]		Manufacturing			Service-producing industries						Government	
		Total	Construc-tion	Total	Durable goods	Nondur-able goods	Total	Transpor-tation and public utilities	Wholesale trade	Retail trade	Finance, insurance, and real estate	Services (private)	Total	Federal
1989:														
January	106 993	25 340	5 182	19 466	11 485	7 981	81 653	5 578	6 160	19 336	6 649	26 334	17 596	2 982
February	107 244	25 303	5 143	19 471	11 486	7 985	81 941	5 607	6 185	19 414	6 656	26 448	17 631	2 985
March	107 438	25 308	5 134	19 483	11 482	8 001	82 130	5 581	6 205	19 448	6 658	26 586	17 652	2 986
April	107 637	25 323	5 159	19 472	11 477	7 995	82 314	5 600	6 199	19 467	6 659	26 708	17 681	2 986
May	107 738	25 303	5 160	19 453	11 453	8 000	82 435	5 610	6 194	19 469	6 662	26 767	17 733	3 000
June	107 838	25 254	5 153	19 421	11 420	8 001	82 584	5 618	6 186	19 470	6 668	26 878	17 764	3 000
July	107 933	25 222	5 170	19 382	11 380	8 002	82 711	5 627	6 190	19 480	6 672	26 951	17 791	3 001
August	108 048	25 251	5 181	19 374	11 370	8 004	82 797	5 526	6 190	19 491	6 679	27 039	17 872	2 994
September	108 178	25 200	5 177	19 327	11 330	7 997	82 978	5 614	6 183	19 489	6 680	27 144	17 868	2 984
October	108 290	25 183	5 201	19 284	11 290	7 994	83 107	5 629	6 183	19 522	6 676	27 213	17 884	2 984
November	108 571	25 216	5 226	19 290	11 287	8 003	83 355	5 649	6 185	19 564	6 683	27 347	17 927	2 983
December	108 692	25 137	5 170	19 268	11 269	7 999	83 555	5 734	6 182	19 571	6 685	27 433	17 950	2 978
1990:														
January	108 946	25 114	5 270	19 140	11 139	8 001	83 832	5 741	6 191	19 626	6 687	27 549	18 038	3 002
February	109 263	25 267	5 307	19 254	11 259	7 995	83 996	5 760	6 177	19 617	6 699	27 670	18 073	3 007
March	109 461	25 212	5 269	19 238	11 244	7 994	84 249	5 762	6 168	19 622	6 694	27 801	18 202	3 093
April	109 499	25 123	5 194	19 220	11 219	8 001	84 376	5 770	6 173	19 631	6 701	27 811	18 290	3 155
May	109 790	25 074	5 183	19 181	11 181	7 985	84 716	5 785	6 173	19 635	6 708	27 898	18 529	3 349
June	109 869	25 031	5 159	19 159	11 181	7 978	84 838	5 788	6 184	19 635	6 716	27 958	18 557	3 340
July	109 707	24 950	5 120	19 118	11 148	7 970	84 757	5 781	6 185	19 638	6 719	28 008	18 426	3 168
August	109 543	24 861	5 085	19 067	11 096	7 971	84 682	5 773	6 183	19 621	6 726	28 048	18 331	3 042
September	109 457	24 783	5 056	19 016	11 051	7 965	84 674	5 783	6 176	19 605	6 723	28 075	18 312	2 992
October	109 274	24 657	4 993	18 955	11 012	7 943	84 617	5 787	6 163	19 559	6 718	28 084	18 306	2 981
November	109 074	24 460	4 953	18 797	10 884	7 913	84 614	5 780	6 154	19 538	6 709	28 125	18 308	2 964
December	108 965	24 375	4 909	18 754	10 860	7 894	84 590	5 799	6 148	19 499	6 702	28 138	18 304	2 943
1991:														
January	108 759	24 175	4 805	18 660	10 783	7 877	84 584	5 812	6 121	19 423	6 707	28 203	18 318	2 952
February	108 500	24 058	4 799	18 549	10 688	7 861	84 442	5 774	6 106	19 362	6 699	28 169	18 332	2 951
March	108 330	23 926	4 744	18 473	10 633	7 840	84 404	5 758	6 093	19 336	6 699	28 172	18 346	2 950
April	108 145	23 822	4 685	18 432	10 613	7 819	84 323	5 757	6 084	19 271	6 680	28 165	18 366	2 954
May	108 107	23 791	4 677	18 413	10 597	7 816	84 316	5 753	6 077	19 249	6 665	28 200	18 372	2 957
June	108 200	23 741	4 661	18 383	10 562	7 821	84 459	5 742	6 078	19 275	6 651	28 278	18 435	2 973
July	108 131	23 688	4 634	18 365	10 552	7 813	84 443	5 754	6 081	19 254	6 631	28 297	18 426	2 970
August	108 215	23 687	4 619	18 384	10 543	7 841	84 528	5 756	6 070	19 265	6 619	28 384	18 434	2 973
September	108 223	23 648	4 612	18 360	10 519	7 841	84 575	5 746	6 076	19 256	6 610	28 469	18 418	2 979
October	108 209	23 574	4 578	18 326	10 487	7 839	84 635	5 744	6 069	19 237	6 605	28 535	18 445	2 984
November	108 115	23 467	4 520	18 285	10 447	7 838	84 648	5 738	6 060	19 223	6 598	28 549	18 480	2 983
December	108 121	23 409	4 522	18 229	10 395	7 834	84 712	5 725	6 055	19 233	6 594	28 604	18 501	2 981
1992:														
January	108 084	23 317	4 513	18 151	10 324	7 827	84 767	5 706	6 045	19 245	6 578	28 670	18 523	2 978
February	108 077	23 263	4 489	18 125	10 315	7 810	84 814	5 709	6 038	19 253	6 583	28 681	18 550	2 982
March	108 119	23 239	4 488	18 103	10 295	7 808	84 880	5 708	6 036	19 253	6 575	28 726	18 582	2 984
April	108 301	23 258	4 482	18 133	10 306	7 827	85 043	5 711	6 024	19 319	6 583	28 807	18 599	2 983
May	108 495	23 274	4 493	18 140	10 310	7 830	85 221	5 709	6 016	19 362	6 593	28 917	18 624	2 984
June	108 541	23 247	4 481	18 132	10 298	7 834	85 294	5 715	6 005	19 353	6 599	28 996	18 626	2 976
July	108 595	23 227	4 473	18 123	10 290	7 833	85 368	5 712	5 985	19 362	6 593	29 072	18 644	2 965
August	108 741	23 209	4 487	18 097	10 268	7 829	85 532	5 718	5 975	19 373	6 601	29 149	18 716	2 962
September	108 807	23 178	4 483	18 074	10 247	7 827	85 629	5 726	5 964	19 380	6 613	29 236	18 710	2 969
October	108 941	23 179	4 493	18 064	10 234	7 830	85 762	5 732	5 965	19 423	6 622	29 333	18 687	2 949
November	109 119	23 182	4 500	18 060	10 233	7 827	85 937	5 732	5 965	19 471	6 631	29 433	18 705	2 944
December	109 266	23 209	4 518	18 069	10 230	7 839	86 057	5 738	5 948	19 463	6 648	29 541	18 719	2 945
1993:														
January	109 502	23 240	4 520	18 098	10 246	7 852	86 262	5 763	5 957	19 509	6 658	29 648	18 727	2 944
February	109 816	23 323	4 605	18 104	10 248	7 856	86 493	5 773	5 951	19 576	6 670	29 767	18 756	2 942
March	109 749	23 259	4 550	18 093	10 236	7 857	86 490	5 773	5 944	19 534	6 675	29 809	18 755	2 935
April	110 055	23 261	4 576	18 072	10 215	7 857	86 794	5 780	5 954	19 640	6 695	29 954	18 771	2 923
May	110 398	23 324	4 643	18 067	10 202	7 865	87 074	5 795	5 974	19 711	6 719	30 069	18 806	2 915
June	110 539	23 306	4 650	18 049	10 186	7 863	87 233	5 812	5 968	19 744	6 741	30 152	18 816	2 906
July	110 744	23 312	4 678	18 030	10 187	7 843	87 432	5 823	5 984	19 790	6 766	30 250	18 819	2 904
August	110 957	23 344	4 700	18 044	10 190	7 854	87 613	5 820	5 982	19 853	6 781	30 337	18 840	2 907
September	111 204	23 383	4 715	18 066	10 211	7 855	87 821	5 834	5 998	19 893	6 807	30 420	18 869	2 903
October	111 525	23 441	4 757	18 081	10 230	7 851	88 084	5 848	6 010	19 967	6 833	30 529	18 897	2 901
November	111 780	23 480	4 781	18 097	10 246	7 851	88 300	5 864	6 022	19 988	6 857	30 650	18 919	2 897
December	112 034	23 536	4 808	18 112	10 265	7 847	88 498	5 847	6 036	20 056	6 877	30 731	18 951	2 895
1994:														
January	112 302	23 583	4 815	18 155	10 305	7 850	88 719	5 894	6 054	20 088	6 892	30 817	18 974	2 897
February	112 532	23 606	4 832	18 167	10 316	7 851	88 926	5 914	6 067	20 165	6 909	30 883	18 988	2 896
March	112 982	23 700	4 898	18 198	10 341	7 857	89 282	5 938	6 088	20 266	6 927	31 042	19 021	2 888
April	113 350	23 785	4 949	18 234	10 372	7 862	89 565	5 906	6 109	20 347	6 927	31 218	19 058	2 884
May	113 697	23 834	4 971	18 264	10 397	7 867	89 863	5 972	6 130	20 393	6 918	31 350	19 100	2 872
June	113 980	23 890	4 986	18 305	10 437	7 868	90 090	5 982	6 145	20 454	6 917	31 498	19 094	2 862
July	114 333	23 935	5 005	18 333	10 449	7 884	90 398	5 998	6 161	20 535	6 908	31 687	19 109	2 857
August	114 673	23 995	5 015	18 383	10 493	7 890	90 678	6 013	6 195	20 604	6 901	31 818	19 147	2 861
September	114 980	24 056	5 050	18 406	10 520	7 886	90 924	6 021	6 220	20 680	6 885	31 935	19 183	2 866
October	115 235	24 090	5 057	18 437	10 548	7 889	91 145	6 034	6 240	20 743	6 865	32 063	19 200	2 861
November	115 641	24 179	5 097	18 485	10 592	7 893	91 462	6 055	6 258	20 845	6 853	32 230	19 221	2 852
December	115 918	24 220	5 112	18 513	10 609	7 904	91 698	6 087	6 285	20 894	6 836	32 361	19 235	2 848

1. Includes mining, not shown seperately.

Average Hours and Earnings

(Production or nonsupervisory workers on private nonagricultural payrolls—Seasonally adjusted, except as noted)

Year and month	Average weekly hours					Indexes of aggregate weekly hours (1982=100)		Average hourly earnings (Dollars)					Average weekly earnings (Dollars)			
	All indus-tries[1]	Con-struction	Manufacturing		Retail trade	All indus-tries[1]	Manufac-turing	All industries[1]		Con-struction	Manufac-turing	Retail trade	All indus-tries[1]	Not seasonally adjusted		
			Average weekly hours	Overtime hours				Current dollars	1982 dollars					Con-struction	Manufac-turing	Retail trade
1971:																
January	36.9	37.5	39.9	2.8	33.6	85.3	109.2	3.34	8.07	5.48	3.47	2.51	123.25	198.36	137.86	83.74
February	36.9	36.7	39.7	2.8	33.6	85.2	108.4	3.36	8.10	5.52	3.51	2.53	123.98	196.32	137.94	84.07
March	36.9	37.4	39.8	2.8	33.6	85.3	108.3	3.39	8.17	5.54	3.52	2.54	125.09	203.87	139.74	84.41
April	36.9	37.1	39.7	2.8	33.7	85.6	108.2	3.40	8.15	5.58	3.53	2.56	125.46	204.06	139.48	85.58
May	36.9	36.8	39.9	2.9	33.6	85.8	109.3	3.43	8.21	5.64	3.55	2.58	126.57	207.38	141.65	86.25
June	36.9	37.2	40.0	2.9	33.6	85.8	109.2	3.44	8.19	5.68	3.57	2.59	126.94	212.24	143.51	88.06
July	36.7	37.1	39.9	2.9	33.7	85.3	108.7	3.45	8.18	5.70	3.58	2.61	126.62	214.70	142.09	90.83
August	36.9	37.1	39.8	2.9	33.7	85.7	108.0	3.48	8.23	5.74	3.59	2.62	128.41	218.50	142.09	90.48
September	36.6	35.8	39.4	2.9	33.7	85.5	107.8	3.48	8.23	5.77	3.59	2.63	127.37	214.54	143.32	88.89
October	36.9	37.3	39.9	2.9	33.8	86.1	109.0	3.50	8.25	5.80	3.60	2.64	129.15	223.65	144.00	88.70
November	37.0	38.5	40.0	2.9	33.7	86.6	109.6	3.51	8.26	5.82	3.60	2.65	129.87	221.51	145.12	88.18
December	37.0	36.7	40.2	3.0	33.9	86.9	110.3	3.54	8.29	5.84	3.66	2.67	130.98	213.81	150.22	90.63
1972:																
January	36.9	37.0	40.2	3.1	33.7	87.4	111.0	3.61	8.43	5.91	3.71	2.69	133.21	211.23	148.06	89.70
February	37.0	36.9	40.4	3.2	33.5	87.7	112.2	3.61	8.41	5.93	3.73	2.70	133.57	211.46	149.20	89.43
March	37.0	36.8	40.4	3.3	33.6	88.3	112.9	3.64	8.47	5.96	3.75	2.71	134.68	215.49	151.13	90.03
April	37.1	36.5	40.7	3.6	33.6	88.8	114.3	3.66	8.51	6.00	3.78	2.72	135.79	215.39	153.09	90.64
May	36.9	36.2	40.5	3.4	33.4	88.6	114.2	3.67	8.52	6.03	3.79	2.72	135.42	217.80	153.50	90.36
June	37.0	36.4	40.6	3.5	33.5	89.2	114.9	3.67	8.50	6.02	3.80	2.74	135.79	219.78	155.04	92.89
July	36.9	36.4	40.5	3.4	33.4	88.9	114.2	3.69	8.50	6.03	3.81	2.75	136.16	223.05	153.52	94.88
August	36.9	36.6	40.6	3.5	33.3	89.3	114.9	3.72	8.55	6.07	3.85	2.77	137.27	228.09	155.09	94.33
September	37.0	36.7	40.6	3.5	33.3	89.6	115.5	3.74	8.56	6.10	3.87	2.78	138.38	231.99	158.69	92.85
October	37.1	36.7	40.7	3.6	33.4	90.5	117.0	3.77	8.59	6.17	3.89	2.79	139.87	234.00	158.30	92.63
November	37.0	36.0	40.8	3.7	33.3	90.9	118.3	3.78	8.59	6.21	3.91	2.81	139.86	221.25	159.92	92.40
December	36.8	35.3	40.5	3.7	33.3	90.8	118.6	3.81	8.62	6.27	3.95	2.83	140.21	220.92	163.58	94.42
1973:																
January	36.8	36.0	40.4	3.9	33.3	91.4	118.8	3.83	8.63	6.37	3.98	2.82	140.94	221.15	159.60	92.87
February	37.0	35.8	40.9	4.0	33.3	92.3	121.5	3.84	8.61	6.29	3.99	2.85	142.08	218.61	161.60	93.81
March	37.1	36.6	40.8	3.8	33.3	92.8	121.7	3.86	8.58	6.31	4.00	2.86	143.21	226.97	162.80	94.14
April	37.1	36.8	40.9	4.1	33.1	93.0	122.1	3.89	8.59	6.33	4.03	2.88	144.32	228.86	164.02	94.79
May	37.0	36.9	40.7	3.9	33.2	93.0	121.7	3.90	8.55	6.34	4.05	2.89	144.30	233.10	164.84	95.08
June	37.0	36.9	40.6	3.8	33.2	93.3	121.8	3.92	8.56	6.35	4.06	2.91	145.04	236.88	166.05	97.78
July	37.0	36.8	40.7	3.8	33.2	93.2	121.7	3.96	8.63	6.39	4.10	2.92	146.52	239.02	166.05	99.86
August	36.9	36.8	40.5	3.7	33.0	93.3	121.4	3.96	8.46	6.40	4.12	2.93	146.12	241.16	165.65	98.94
September	36.9	36.7	40.7	3.8	33.0	93.4	121.8	3.99	8.51	6.46	4.14	2.95	147.23	244.60	170.15	97.65
October	36.8	36.5	40.6	3.8	32.9	93.6	122.4	4.01	8.48	6.50	4.17	2.96	147.57	246.09	169.31	96.79
November	37.0	37.8	40.7	3.9	33.0	94.5	123.2	4.04	8.47	6.54	4.19	2.98	149.48	245.15	171.37	97.12
December	36.8	36.7	40.6	3.7	32.9	94.1	123.1	4.06	8.46	6.56	4.21	3.01	149.41	239.94	174.69	98.94
1974:																
January	36.7	36.1	40.5	3.6	32.9	93.8	122.0	4.07	8.39	6.55	4.22	3.01	149.37	227.01	169.60	97.57
February	36.8	37.2	40.4	3.5	32.8	94.1	121.2	4.10	8.35	6.60	4.24	3.02	150.88	237.60	170.02	97.87
March	36.7	36.5	40.4	3.5	32.8	93.8	120.7	4.12	8.31	6.62	4.26	3.04	151.20	237.83	171.25	98.82
April	36.4	35.9	39.3	2.8	33.0	93.1	117.4	4.13	8.29	6.65	4.27	3.05	150.33	234.60	166.96	100.06
May	36.7	36.4	40.3	3.5	32.7	93.9	120.4	4.19	8.31	6.69	4.36	3.11	153.77	242.36	175.71	101.08
June	36.6	36.7	40.2	3.4	32.7	93.9	120.0	4.24	8.35	6.75	4.42	3.14	155.18	249.83	178.16	103.93
July	36.6	36.7	40.2	3.4	32.6	93.7	119.8	4.25	8.30	6.76	4.45	3.16	155.55	252.30	177.60	106.18
August	36.5	36.4	40.2	3.3	32.7	93.5	119.0	4.29	8.28	6.92	4.50	3.19	156.59	257.74	179.25	106.51
September	36.6	36.8	40.0	3.2	32.7	93.4	118.1	4.33	8.25	7.00	4.54	3.21	158.48	264.79	183.37	104.97
October	36.4	36.8	40.0	3.2	32.5	93.1	117.0	4.36	8.24	7.00	4.60	3.22	158.70	266.92	184.06	104.01
November	36.2	36.8	39.5	2.8	32.5	91.7	113.4	4.36	8.15	7.04	4.61	3.23	157.83	258.08	183.02	103.68
December	36.1	37.0	39.3	2.7	32.5	90.4	109.2	4.40	8.16	7.09	4.64	3.25	158.84	262.41	186.73	105.62
1975:																
January	36.1	37.1	39.2	2.5	32.4	89.7	105.9	4.41	8.12	7.13	4.66	3.26	159.20	253.46	181.12	104.29
February	35.9	35.9	38.9	2.4	32.4	88.3	102.3	4.43	8.11	7.11	4.70	3.29	159.04	248.86	180.95	105.27
March	35.8	35.2	38.8	2.4	32.4	87.4	101.0	4.45	8.12	7.29	4.74	3.30	159.31	250.16	183.44	105.92
April	35.9	36.1	39.2	2.4	32.2	87.4	101.6	4.46	8.11	7.26	4.76	3.32	160.11	259.56	184.78	106.23
May	35.9	36.5	39.0	2.3	32.4	87.7	101.2	4.48	8.13	7.28	4.78	3.34	160.83	264.97	186.03	107.55
June	36.0	35.8	39.2	2.5	32.4	87.8	101.4	4.51	8.13	7.35	4.81	3.35	162.36	263.90	189.60	109.88
July	36.0	36.2	39.4	2.6	32.3	88.2	101.8	4.53	8.09	7.36	4.83	3.36	163.08	271.57	188.94	111.89
August	36.2	36.8	39.7	2.8	32.5	89.2	103.8	4.57	8.13	7.34	4.87	3.38	165.43	275.98	192.15	112.22
September	36.2	36.9	39.9	2.8	32.3	89.5	105.3	4.60	8.11	7.36	4.90	3.39	166.52	278.26	197.38	109.50
October	36.2	36.3	39.8	2.8	32.3	89.8	105.9	4.61	8.09	7.33	4.92	3.41	166.88	276.02	196.80	109.46
November	36.2	36.4	39.9	2.9	32.4	90.1	106.2	4.66	8.12	7.41	4.96	3.43	168.69	269.31	198.90	109.78
December	36.3	36.6	40.2	3.0	32.3	90.7	107.9	4.67	8.09	7.44	4.99	3.45	169.52	273.39	205.73	111.83
1976:																
January	36.3	37.7	40.5	3.1	32.5	91.5	109.5	4.70	8.10	7.44	5.02	3.47	170.61	268.17	201.60	111.30
February	36.3	37.1	40.3	3.1	32.4	91.8	109.8	4.73	8.16	7.48	5.06	3.47	171.70	269.69	202.40	111.33
March	36.1	36.1	40.2	3.2	32.2	91.6	110.1	4.75	8.18	7.53	5.10	3.49	171.48	265.19	204.11	111.30
April	36.1	36.6	39.6	2.6	32.4	92.0	109.2	4.77	8.18	7.59	5.11	3.50	172.20	275.23	199.92	112.67
May	36.2	36.6	40.3	3.3	32.2	92.4	110.9	4.81	8.22	7.68	5.16	3.53	174.12	280.42	207.55	112.96
June	36.2	36.9	40.2	3.2	32.1	92.3	110.6	4.84	8.23	7.65	5.19	3.54	175.21	284.25	209.79	115.05
July	36.2	36.6	40.3	3.2	32.0	92.7	111.0	4.87	8.24	7.73	5.23	3.55	176.29	288.75	209.32	117.15
August	36.1	36.6	40.1	3.1	31.9	92.5	110.3	4.91	8.27	7.77	5.28	3.60	177.25	290.60	210.53	117.10
September	36.0	36.2	39.8	3.2	31.9	92.6	110.5	4.94	8.26	7.80	5.32	3.64	177.84	289.14	214.13	116.12
October	36.0	37.1	40.0	3.1	31.8	92.6	109.9	4.97	8.27	7.86	5.32	3.67	178.92	302.48	213.33	115.66
November	36.0	37.0	40.1	3.2	31.8	92.8	110.9	5.01	8.31	7.88	5.38	3.69	180.36	290.24	216.81	115.61
December	36.0	36.8	40.0	3.2	31.8	93.0	110.8	5.04	8.32	7.91	5.42	3.72	181.44	291.77	222.22	118.50

1. Includes industries not shown seperately.

Average Hours and Earnings—*Continued*

(Production or nonsupervisory workers on private nonagricultural payrolls—Seasonally adjusted, except as noted)

| Year and month | Average weekly hours | | | | | Indexes of aggregate weekly hours (1982=100) | | Average hourly earnings (Dollars) | | | | | Average weekly earnings (Dollars) | | | |
	All industries [1]	Construction	Manufacturing Average weekly hours	Manufacturing Overtime hours	Retail trade	All industries [1]	Manufacturing	All industries [1] Current dollars	All industries [1] 1982 dollars	Construction	Manufacturing	Retail trade	All industries [1]	Not seasonally adjusted Construction	Not seasonally adjusted Manufacturing	Not seasonally adjusted Retail trade
1977:																
January	35.8	35.6	39.7	3.3	31.7	92.8	110.5	5.06	8.30	7.99	5.48	3.71	181.15	271.88	215.05	116.25
February	36.1	37.5	40.3	3.3	31.7	94.0	112.4	5.10	8.29	7.99	5.48	3.75	184.11	289.38	218.65	117.94
March	36.0	36.9	40.2	3.3	31.7	94.5	113.3	5.13	8.30	8.01	5.52	3.77	184.68	289.38	221.90	118.63
April	36.0	36.7	40.4	3.6	31.6	95.2	114.5	5.17	8.31	8.03	5.58	3.79	186.12	291.77	222.96	118.94
May	36.1	36.7	40.4	3.5	31.7	95.7	115.1	5.20	8.32	8.03	5.61	3.82	187.72	294.09	226.24	120.33
June	36.0	36.3	40.5	3.5	31.5	96.1	116.0	5.23	8.31	8.08	5.66	3.84	188.28	296.37	230.52	122.50
July	36.0	36.4	40.3	3.5	31.6	96.4	115.8	5.27	8.34	8.07	5.70	3.87	189.72	300.27	228.17	125.45
August	36.0	36.1	40.4	3.5	31.5	96.5	115.7	5.28	8.33	8.10	5.73	3.88	190.08	299.26	229.31	124.74
September	36.0	36.2	40.4	3.5	31.5	97.0	116.2	5.32	8.35	8.15	5.77	3.91	191.52	303.14	235.65	122.85
October	36.0	36.3	40.5	3.5	31.6	97.4	116.4	5.36	8.39	8.20	5.82	3.93	192.96	308.39	236.29	123.09
November	35.9	36.5	40.4	3.6	31.3	97.7	116.7	5.39	8.38	8.22	5.85	3.96	193.50	298.19	238.10	122.53
December	35.9	36.2	40.4	3.5	31.3	97.8	117.3	5.41	8.37	8.26	5.88	3.99	194.22	299.27	243.72	124.90
1978																
January	35.5	34.7	39.6	3.4	31.0	97.0	115.8	5.47	8.42	8.32	5.95	4.05	194.19	275.55	234.02	124.23
February	35.6	35.7	39.9	3.7	30.9	97.7	117.0	5.50	8.42	8.37	5.98	4.06	195.80	288.22	236.81	124.64
March	35.9	36.6	40.5	3.5	31.2	99.1	118.9	5.54	8.42	8.45	6.01	4.09	198.89	304.08	242.80	126.59
April	36.0	36.9	40.8	3.9	31.1	100.4	120.3	5.60	8.45	8.48	6.05	4.13	201.60	309.96	244.02	127.82
May	35.9	36.6	40.4	3.5	31.1	100.3	119.6	5.63	8.42	8.57	6.09	4.16	202.12	312.68	245.23	128.54
June	35.9	37.2	40.5	3.6	31.1	101.1	120.2	5.67	8.41	8.63	6.12	4.18	203.55	324.80	249.29	130.94
July	35.9	37.3	40.6	3.6	31.1	101.3	120.6	5.71	8.41	8.67	6.18	4.21	204.99	330.05	249.05	134.40
August	35.8	37.2	40.5	3.5	31.0	101.4	120.4	5.74	8.40	8.73	6.21	4.23	205.49	331.25	249.27	133.56
September	35.8	37.0	40.6	3.6	30.9	101.6	121.1	5.79	8.42	8.78	6.27	4.27	207.28	333.38	256.00	131.63
October	35.9	37.1	40.5	3.6	30.9	102.1	121.6	5.84	8.39	8.81	6.33	4.30	209.66	337.31	257.00	132.13
November	35.8	36.9	40.6	3.7	30.8	102.6	122.7	5.87	8.39	8.87	6.39	4.33	210.15	324.85	261.35	131.89
December	35.8	37.1	40.6	3.6	30.9	103.0	123.4	5.91	8.38	8.91	6.43	4.36	211.58	331.67	268.27	134.90
1979:																
January	35.7	36.5	40.5	3.6	30.6	102.9	123.5	5.95	8.38	8.95	6.47	4.42	212.42	311.95	260.65	133.95
February	35.7	36.7	40.5	3.6	30.7	103.3	123.6	6.00	8.36	9.06	6.53	4.43	214.20	320.57	262.51	134.55
March	35.8	37.4	40.6	3.7	30.7	104.2	124.0	6.03	8.32	9.03	6.56	4.45	215.87	333.53	266.34	135.74
April	35.4	35.7	39.2	2.9	30.9	102.6	119.9	6.03	8.22	9.12	6.56	4.48	213.46	321.82	254.80	137.70
May	35.7	37.2	40.2	3.4	30.6	103.9	122.9	6.09	8.21	9.20	6.65	4.49	217.41	341.30	265.86	136.50
June	35.7	37.2	40.2	3.4	30.7	104.4	123.1	6.13	8.17	9.21	6.68	4.51	218.84	347.32	269.47	139.50
July	35.7	36.9	40.2	3.4	30.7	104.3	123.0	6.18	8.14	9.29	6.72	4.53	220.63	350.03	268.13	142.38
August	35.7	37.4	40.1	3.2	30.6	104.2	121.4	6.21	8.11	9.33	6.75	4.56	221.70	355.85	268.00	142.24
September	35.7	37.4	40.2	3.2	30.6	104.3	121.6	6.27	8.10	9.42	6.79	4.59	223.84	361.76	274.04	140.61
October	35.6	36.9	40.2	3.2	30.5	104.3	121.4	6.28	8.04	9.40	6.82	4.61	223.57	357.77	274.85	139.54
November	35.6	37.0	40.1	3.2	30.6	104.5	120.4	6.32	8.01	9.48	6.87	4.64	224.99	348.07	277.55	140.45
December	35.6	37.2	40.2	3.2	30.6	104.8	120.7	6.38	7.99	9.54	6.93	4.67	227.13	356.00	285.48	142.91
1980:																
January	35.5	36.4	40.0	3.1	30.5	104.7	120.0	6.40	7.90	9.42	6.94	4.73	227.84	334.29	277.41	142.44
February	35.5	36.9	40.1	3.0	30.4	104.7	119.4	6.45	7.88	9.61	7.00	4.74	228.98	342.72	278.60	142.44
March	35.3	36.4	39.8	3.1	30.3	104.1	118.4	6.51	7.82	9.70	7.07	4.79	229.80	349.69	281.39	143.82
April	35.2	36.9	39.5	2.9	29.9	103.1	116.1	6.54	7.79	9.77	7.11	4.79	230.86	355.62	279.74	142.56
May	35.1	36.8	39.3	2.6	30.1	102.1	112.5	6.57	7.75	9.83	7.16	4.82	231.26	361.86	280.60	144.12
June	35.2	37.4	39.2	2.4	30.2	101.5	110.1	6.63	7.74	9.89	7.22	4.85	232.71	372.78	284.07	147.14
July	35.0	36.9	39.1	2.5	30.0	100.9	108.4	6.66	7.76	9.95	7.29	4.91	233.10	374.98	282.85	150.61
August	35.2	36.9	39.4	2.6	30.1	101.6	110.3	6.71	7.77	10.05	7.36	4.93	235.52	376.24	288.01	151.41
September	35.2	37.2	39.6	2.7	30.1	102.2	111.1	6.76	7.76	10.10	7.42	4.96	237.95	387.60	295.71	149.49
October	35.3	37.5	39.8	2.8	30.2	102.7	111.9	6.83	7.76	10.18	7.51	4.99	241.10	390.26	298.50	149.90
November	35.4	37.6	40.0	3.0	30.2	103.1	113.2	6.90	7.75	10.26	7.60	5.02	243.57	378.96	305.52	150.60
December	35.4	37.3	40.3	3.1	30.0	103.5	114.1	6.94	7.73	10.33	7.64	5.03	244.98	385.39	314.16	152.20
1981:																
January	35.5	37.5	40.1	3.1	30.3	104.2	114.3	6.99	7.72	10.37	7.69	5.13	248.15	381.79	308.43	152.52
February	35.4	36.5	40.0	3.0	30.3	104.1	113.6	7.05	7.71	10.41	7.75	5.16	249.57	366.80	306.13	153.62
March	35.4	37.5	40.0	3.0	30.3	104.3	113.8	7.11	7.74	10.48	7.81	5.18	251.69	390.90	311.62	154.96
April	35.4	37.2	40.1	2.9	30.2	104.3	114.4	7.14	7.72	10.54	7.87	5.21	252.76	387.76	312.84	156.60
May	35.3	36.6	40.1	3.0	30.0	103.7	114.3	7.18	7.71	10.64	7.93	5.21	253.45	391.46	317.59	156.08
June	35.2	36.6	39.9	2.9	30.0	103.8	113.8	7.22	7.70	10.77	7.97	5.23	254.14	396.55	320.39	158.17
July	35.3	36.8	39.9	2.9	30.1	104.1	113.4	7.26	7.65	10.88	8.01	5.26	256.28	408.62	317.59	161.92
August	35.3	36.7	39.9	2.9	30.2	104.0	113.1	7.34	7.67	10.97	8.09	5.29	259.10	409.16	320.40	162.23
September	35.1	36.8	39.7	2.7	30.1	103.7	112.6	7.39	7.66	11.02	8.16	5.36	259.39	397.38	322.32	161.87
October	35.1	37.2	39.7	2.6	29.9	103.7	111.5	7.41	7.65	11.10	8.19	5.30	260.09	419.63	323.95	157.64
November	35.2	37.8	39.5	2.6	30.1	103.4	109.8	7.46	7.67	11.26	8.22	5.30	262.59	414.77	325.94	158.24
December	35.0	37.3	39.4	2.5	29.6	102.4	107.7	7.46	7.65	11.21	8.23	5.35	261.10	418.86	329.97	160.89
1982:																
January	34.4	34.2	38.0	2.3	29.8	100.2	102.5	7.52	7.69	11.57	8.38	5.38	258.69	388.61	312.38	157.18
February	35.2	37.2	39.6	2.5	30.1	102.6	106.5	7.54	7.69	11.36	8.33	5.38	265.41	408.12	326.93	159.35
March	34.9	37.2	39.1	2.4	29.8	101.6	104.2	7.57	7.72	11.42	8.37	5.40	264.19	422.17	327.27	159.35
April	34.8	36.9	38.9	2.2	29.9	100.8	102.3	7.59	7.72	11.43	8.41	5.43	264.13	417.28	325.85	161.02
May	34.9	37.1	39.0	2.4	29.9	100.8	101.7	7.65	7.71	11.57	8.46	5.45	266.99	431.63	329.55	162.71
June	34.9	36.9	39.1	2.3	29.8	100.3	100.7	7.67	7.64	11.60	8.51	5.48	267.68	430.50	334.05	164.65
July	34.8	37.0	39.2	2.3	29.8	99.9	99.8	7.71	7.64	11.68	8.54	5.49	268.31	441.18	332.60	167.38
August	34.8	36.9	39.0	2.3	29.9	99.6	98.6	7.75	7.66	11.72	8.56	5.51	269.70	439.17	331.50	167.38
September	34.8	37.0	39.0	2.3	30.0	99.3	98.2	7.75	7.66	11.67	8.58	5.51	269.70	433.94	333.76	165.85
October	34.7	36.8	38.9	2.3	29.9	98.7	96.5	7.78	7.65	11.80	8.58	5.55	269.97	441.49	333.45	165.09
November	34.8	36.9	39.1	2.3	29.9	98.6	96.0	7.80	7.68	11.78	8.61	5.57	271.44	423.45	337.98	165.17
December	34.8	37.0	39.1	2.4	29.8	98.6	95.8	7.83	7.74	11.88	8.63	5.59	272.48	440.13	344.60	169.28

1. Includes industries not shown seperately.

Average Hours and Earnings—*Continued*

(Production or nonsupervisory workers on private nonagricultural payrolls—Seasonally adjusted, except as noted)

Year and month	Average weekly hours					Indexes of aggregate weekly hours (1982=100)		Average hourly earnings (Dollars)					Average weekly earnings (Dollars)			
	All indus-tries[1]	Con-struction	Manufacturing		Retail trade	All indus-tries[1]	Manufac-turing	All industries[1]		Con-struction	Manufac-turing	Retail trade	All indus-tries[1]	Not seasonally adjusted		
			Average weekly hours	Overtime hours				Current dollars	1982 dollars					Con-struction	Manufac-turing	Retail trade
1983:																
January	35.0	37.9	39.4	2.4	30.1	99.5	96.7	7.88	7.78	11.85	8.66	5.63	275.80	439.39	341.04	166.13
February	34.6	36.8	39.3	2.4	29.4	98.4	96.5	7.91	7.81	11.95	8.72	5.67	273.69	424.80	338.72	163.88
March	34.8	36.7	39.6	2.5	29.7	99.1	97.6	7.92	7.80	11.95	8.72	5.67	275.62	434.62	345.71	166.72
April	34.9	36.7	39.8	2.7	29.8	99.8	98.6	7.95	7.77	11.95	8.74	5.69	277.46	435.17	348.25	168.15
May	35.0	37.0	40.0	2.8	29.8	100.4	99.7	7.99	7.78	11.89	8.78	5.72	279.65	442.44	349.92	169.88
June	35.0	37.2	40.1	2.9	29.8	101.1	100.7	8.01	7.78	11.91	8.80	5.74	280.35	446.84	354.24	172.47
July	35.0	37.2	40.3	3.0	29.9	101.9	101.9	8.04	7.79	11.91	8.83	5.76	281.40	451.91	353.60	175.34
August	35.0	37.2	40.3	3.1	29.8	101.0	102.4	8.01	7.72	11.93	8.84	5.77	280.35	451.82	352.96	174.46
September	35.1	37.1	40.6	3.3	29.8	103.3	104.3	8.09	7.79	11.97	8.90	5.78	283.96	457.45	362.71	172.82
October	35.2	37.0	40.7	3.3	30.0	104.1	105.4	8.14	7.81	11.99	8.94	5.80	286.53	450.96	362.23	173.12
November	35.1	37.1	40.7	3.3	29.9	104.4	106.2	8.14	7.80	12.00	8.98	5.80	285.71	433.79	366.38	172.56
December	35.2	37.1	40.6	3.4	30.1	104.9	106.5	8.16	7.81	11.99	9.00	5.81	287.23	444.18	372.86	177.45
1984:																
January	35.2	37.4	40.7	3.5	30.0	105.4	107.4	8.21	7.81	12.08	9.05	5.82	288.99	441.41	369.05	171.70
February	35.3	38.4	41.1	3.5	30.0	106.5	109.0	8.21	7.80	12.03	9.06	5.82	289.81	446.59	369.15	171.70
March	35.1	37.1	40.7	3.5	29.9	106.2	108.6	8.23	7.82	12.07	9.09	5.83	288.87	442.60	370.37	172.58
April	35.3	37.6	40.9	3.5	30.0	107.1	109.6	8.28	7.85	12.10	9.11	5.85	292.28	451.88	373.01	174.04
May	35.2	37.6	40.7	3.4	29.9	107.2	109.2	8.27	7.82	12.14	9.13	5.84	291.10	460.63	371.18	174.03
June	35.2	38.0	40.7	3.4	29.9	107.6	109.3	8.31	7.84	12.15	9.16	5.85	292.51	464.74	373.32	176.95
July	35.1	37.5	40.6	3.4	29.8	107.9	109.4	8.34	7.83	12.17	9.19	5.85	292.73	465.08	370.36	177.51
August	35.1	37.6	40.5	3.3	29.8	107.9	109.3	8.34	7.77	12.15	9.23	5.84	292.73	465.02	370.06	176.60
September	35.1	37.6	40.5	3.3	29.7	108.5	109.0	8.38	7.77	12.16	9.26	5.84	294.14	472.01	377.40	174.33
October	35.0	37.6	40.5	3.3	29.6	108.5	108.8	8.38	7.75	12.15	9.29	5.86	293.30	465.50	374.63	172.58
November	35.1	38.1	40.5	3.4	29.6	109.1	108.6	8.41	7.78	12.15	9.32	5.89	295.19	452.08	379.32	173.46
December	35.1	38.0	40.6	3.4	29.7	109.4	108.8	8.44	7.79	12.21	9.36	5.87	296.24	461.73	387.69	177.26
1985:																
January	35.0	37.6	40.4	3.3	29.6	109.4	108.4	8.44	7.77	12.26	9.39	5.88	295.40	448.81	380.43	171.09
February	34.9	37.9	40.1	3.3	29.6	109.3	107.0	8.47	7.76	12.33	9.43	5.90	295.60	452.74	375.17	171.67
March	35.0	38.2	40.5	3.2	29.6	110.1	107.8	8.50	7.76	12.27	9.45	5.91	297.50	461.83	382.18	173.16
April	34.9	37.9	40.3	3.3	29.3	109.8	106.8	8.52	7.76	12.30	9.49	5.91	297.35	464.28	380.95	172.27
May	34.9	37.6	40.4	3.1	29.6	110.4	106.8	8.52	7.75	12.29	9.50	5.93	297.35	465.73	382.45	174.94
June	34.9	37.5	40.5	3.2	29.5	110.5	106.7	8.57	7.77	12.28	9.53	5.93	299.09	464.06	387.46	176.71
July	34.9	37.7	40.4	3.2	29.4	110.2	106.3	8.57	7.76	12.31	9.55	5.94	299.09	471.69	382.96	177.59
August	34.9	37.6	40.6	3.3	29.4	110.8	106.7	8.59	7.77	12.33	9.57	5.95	299.79	471.94	384.75	177.29
September	34.9	37.7	40.6	3.3	29.4	111.0	106.3	8.63	7.80	12.38	9.58	5.97	301.19	481.73	390.46	175.81
October	34.9	37.8	40.7	3.3	29.3	111.3	106.5	8.63	7.76	12.34	9.60	5.96	301.19	476.45	390.05	174.03
November	34.9	37.4	40.7	3.4	29.3	111.4	106.3	8.65	7.74	12.32	9.63	5.97	301.89	451.41	394.28	174.02
December	34.9	37.4	41.0	3.6	29.2	111.9	107.2	8.71	7.76	12.44	9.70	6.02	303.98	462.50	406.58	178.80
1986:																
January	35.1	38.5	40.8	3.5	29.4	112.5	106.9	8.68	7.71	12.32	9.66	6.00	304.67	461.77	394.79	173.35
February	34.8	36.5	40.6	3.4	29.2	111.7	106.2	8.71	7.76	12.37	9.69	6.01	303.11	436.13	391.31	173.03
March	34.9	36.9	40.8	3.5	29.3	112.1	106.2	8.73	7.82	12.29	9.72	6.01	304.68	447.49	396.01	174.27
April	34.8	37.5	40.6	3.4	29.1	111.9	105.7	8.72	7.85	12.37	9.70	6.01	303.46	462.38	393.26	173.98
May	34.8	37.4	40.7	3.5	29.2	112.1	105.8	8.74	7.85	12.42	9.73	6.01	304.15	469.20	394.63	174.89
June	34.7	37.2	40.6	3.4	29.1	111.6	105.2	8.75	7.83	12.45	9.73	6.02	303.63	467.21	396.17	177.00
July	34.7	37.4	40.6	3.5	29.1	112.0	104.8	8.75	7.83	12.45	9.74	6.02	303.63	472.15	391.55	178.20
August	34.8	37.6	40.8	3.5	29.2	112.5	105.4	8.77	7.84	12.50	9.75	6.03	305.20	478.46	393.98	178.50
September	34.7	37.7	40.7	3.5	29.1	112.6	105.3	8.77	7.81	12.52	9.74	6.04	304.32	485.87	399.34	176.35
October	34.6	37.2	40.6	3.5	29.1	112.6	104.9	8.80	7.83	12.60	9.76	6.06	304.48	481.33	396.58	175.74
November	34.7	37.1	40.8	3.5	29.2	113.1	105.4	8.85	7.85	12.68	9.78	6.07	307.10	462.82	401.39	176.32
December	34.7	37.3	40.9	3.6	28.9	113.2	105.7	8.85	7.83	12.74	9.80	6.08	307.10	471.04	409.76	178.46
1987:																
January	34.7	38.5	40.9	3.6	29.0	113.7	105.8	8.87	7.80	12.58	9.81	6.05	307.79	469.84	401.84	172.35
February	34.9	38.2	41.2	3.7	29.3	114.5	106.7	8.89	7.78	12.55	9.83	6.05	310.26	463.10	401.88	174.50
March	34.8	37.8	41.0	3.7	29.3	114.5	106.3	8.91	7.77	12.67	9.85	6.06	310.07	472.74	403.27	175.42
April	34.7	37.3	40.9	3.7	29.3	114.6	106.2	8.92	7.74	12.66	9.86	6.08	309.52	471.99	398.75	177.83
May	34.8	38.2	41.0	3.7	29.3	115.4	106.7	8.95	7.75	12.71	9.88	6.09	311.46	489.06	403.68	177.83
June	34.8	37.7	41.0	3.7	29.3	115.4	106.6	8.95	7.72	12.76	9.88	6.10	311.46	483.99	405.66	179.97
July	34.7	37.8	41.0	3.8	29.2	115.6	107.0	8.96	7.70	12.69	9.87	6.12	310.91	486.75	400.72	182.40
August	34.9	37.8	41.0	3.8	29.4	116.4	107.3	9.02	7.72	12.73	9.93	6.13	314.80	489.83	403.27	183.31
September	34.8	37.7	40.9	3.8	29.5	116.3	107.5	9.03	7.70	12.71	9.99	6.18	314.24	467.57	407.59	182.90
October	34.8	37.9	41.1	3.8	29.2	116.8	108.3	9.06	7.70	12.74	9.98	6.15	315.29	498.19	410.94	179.26
November	34.8	37.6	41.1	3.9	29.2	117.2	108.7	9.10	7.72	12.85	10.00	6.16	316.68	477.11	414.41	179.22
December	34.7	38.1	41.1	3.9	28.8	117.1	108.8	9.12	7.72	12.79	10.02	6.19	316.46	482.78	420.93	181.37
1988:																
January	34.7	37.7	41.1	3.9	29.1	117.2	108.7	9.14	7.72	13.02	10.05	6.21	317.16	468.50	413.28	177.22
February	34.7	37.4	41.0	3.8	29.1	118.0	108.6	9.13	7.70	12.92	10.05	6.22	316.81	464.61	409.44	178.46
March	34.6	37.8	41.0	3.8	29.1	117.8	108.6	9.15	7.69	12.86	10.07	6.24	316.59	481.50	412.27	178.46
April	34.6	37.6	40.8	3.7	29.1	118.2	108.3	9.20	7.70	12.99	10.12	6.26	318.32	491.18	415.33	181.83
May	34.6	37.7	41.0	3.8	29.1	118.5	108.9	9.24	7.71	12.99	10.15	6.28	319.70	495.84	416.15	182.12
June	34.6	37.9	41.0	3.8	29.1	118.9	109.2	9.26	7.69	13.04	10.17	6.30	320.40	501.94	419.00	184.97
July	34.7	37.6	41.0	3.8	29.2	119.4	109.2	9.28	7.67	13.09	10.18	6.32	322.02	502.43	414.33	189.03
August	34.5	37.6	40.9	3.8	29.0	119.0	108.7	9.30	7.65	13.11	10.21	6.32	320.85	503.58	414.73	186.55
September	34.6	37.5	40.9	3.8	29.1	119.5	108.9	9.35	7.66	13.15	10.24	6.36	323.51	508.24	423.74	185.66
October	34.7	37.8	41.0	3.9	29.2	120.3	109.5	9.40	7.67	13.17	10.28	6.38	326.18	517.92	424.15	186.59
November	34.6	37.9	41.1	3.9	29.1	120.3	110.1	9.40	7.65	13.15	10.31	6.41	325.24	496.32	428.70	185.18
December	34.6	37.6	41.0	3.9	29.2	120.8	109.9	9.44	7.67	13.27	10.33	6.41	326.62	495.13	432.22	190.67

1. Includes industries not shown seperately.

Average Hours and Earnings—*Continued*

(Production or nonsupervisory workers on private nonagricultural payrolls—Seasonally adjusted, except as noted)

Year and month	Average weekly hours					Indexes of aggregate weekly hours (1982=100)		Average hourly earnings (Dollars)					Average weekly earnings (Dollars)			
	All indus-tries [1]	Con-struction	Manufacturing		Retail trade	All indus-tries [1]	Manufac-turing	All industries [1]		Con-struction	Manufac-turing	Retail trade	All indus-tries [1]	Not seasonally adjusted		
			Average weekly hours	Overtime hours				Current dollars	1982 dollars					Con-struction	Manufac-turing	Retail trade
1989:																
January	34.6	37.5	41.1	3.9	29.1	121.1	110.5	9.49	7.67	13.37	10.37	6.43	328.35	487.64	425.99	184.40
February	34.6	37.3	41.2	4.0	29.0	121.4	110.7	9.53	7.68	13.37	10.41	6.46	329.74	481.21	424.32	183.10
March	34.6	37.8	41.1	3.9	29.0	121.7	110.6	9.55	7.65	13.41	10.43	6.46	330.43	500.41	427.22	184.40
April	34.6	37.9	41.3	4.0	28.9	122.0	110.9	9.58	7.62	13.47	10.42	6.48	331.47	509.38	427.22	188.14
May	34.5	37.4	40.9	3.7	28.9	121.7	109.7	9.59	7.59	13.46	10.42	6.48	330.86	506.31	426.59	186.62
June	34.5	37.1	40.9	3.7	28.9	121.5	109.2	9.62	7.59	13.49	10.45	6.50	331.89	507.86	429.50	188.92
July	34.5	38.2	40.9	3.7	28.9	121.7	108.8	9.66	7.60	13.53	10.48	6.52	333.27	525.15	424.85	193.10
August	34.5	38.0	40.9	3.7	28.9	121.7	108.7	9.68	7.62	13.53	10.52	6.55	333.96	526.32	427.41	191.81
September	34.5	37.7	40.8	3.6	28.8	121.9	108.3	9.72	7.63	13.55	10.53	6.57	335.34	528.05	435.07	190.45
October	34.5	38.1	40.7	3.7	28.9	122.1	107.8	9.75	7.62	13.62	10.56	6.59	336.38	538.61	430.68	190.74
November	34.5	38.1	40.8	3.6	28.8	122.4	108.0	9.79	7.62	13.72	10.58	6.60	337.76	522.73	433.78	189.33
December	34.4	37.6	40.6	3.6	28.8	122.2	107.5	9.83	7.63	13.79	10.62	6.65	338.15	514.95	440.67	193.89
1990:																
January	34.5	38.7	40.7	3.7	28.9	122.9	106.7	9.83	7.56	13.65	10.57	6.67	339.14	512.86	429.95	188.55
February	34.5	38.4	40.8	3.6	28.9	123.2	107.8	9.88	7.57	13.69	10.68	6.69	340.86	508.77	431.07	188.94
March	34.6	38.4	40.9	3.7	28.9	123.5	107.9	9.92	7.56	13.72	10.75	6.71	343.23	518.85	437.12	190.85
April	34.5	38.1	40.8	3.5	28.9	123.1	107.6	9.93	7.56	13.66	10.74	6.71	342.59	508.40	427.45	194.79
May	34.5	38.0	40.9	3.7	28.8	123.2	107.5	9.97	7.58	13.75	10.79	6.73	343.97	525.86	441.72	193.15
June	34.5	38.3	40.9	3.7	28.9	123.4	107.4	10.01	7.57	13.77	10.83	6.76	345.35	534.89	445.52	196.52
July	34.4	37.6	40.8	3.7	28.7	122.8	106.9	10.03	7.55	13.77	10.86	6.76	345.03	528.00	440.24	199.58
August	34.4	38.1	40.8	3.6	28.7	122.8	106.3	10.05	7.49	13.78	10.87	6.77	345.72	537.42	441.05	197.57
September	34.4	38.4	40.8	3.7	28.7	122.7	106.2	10.08	7.46	13.84	10.91	6.78	346.75	545.84	451.41	196.13
October	34.3	37.0	40.7	3.6	28.6	121.9	105.5	10.11	7.43	13.83	10.97	6.80	346.77	531.50	447.45	193.40
November	34.3	38.3	40.5	3.5	28.6	121.8	103.9	10.13	7.43	13.85	10.96	6.81	347.46	529.45	447.17	193.29
December	34.4	39.0	40.6	3.5	28.6	121.8	103.9	10.15	7.43	13.82	10.99	6.81	349.16	534.14	456.37	198.85
1991:																
January	34.2	37.3	40.4	3.4	28.5	120.8	102.7	10.18	7.43	14.03	11.02	6.83	348.16	506.80	443.81	189.61
February	34.3	38.2	40.3	3.3	28.6	120.6	101.6	10.19	7.43	13.96	11.03	6.84	349.52	515.69	439.30	191.12
March	34.2	37.9	40.3	3.3	28.6	120.2	101.1	10.22	7.44	13.93	11.07	6.85	349.52	518.47	443.51	193.05
April	34.1	37.8	40.4	3.4	28.5	119.7	101.2	10.26	7.46	14.01	11.11	6.90	349.87	528.07	445.51	195.14
May	34.2	38.0	40.4	3.4	28.6	120.0	101.2	10.30	7.46	13.98	11.15	6.92	352.26	533.90	449.35	196.94
June	34.3	38.0	40.8	3.6	28.6	120.2	102.0	10.32	7.46	13.97	11.18	6.94	353.98	537.77	457.26	202.06
July	34.2	37.9	40.7	3.6	28.6	120.0	102.0	10.35	7.47	13.97	11.22	6.96	353.97	538.86	453.29	202.76
August	34.3	37.9	40.9	3.6	28.6	120.3	102.5	10.37	7.47	14.01	11.23	6.97	355.69	544.36	457.26	202.46
September	34.3	38.3	40.9	3.7	28.6	120.4	102.5	10.39	7.46	14.01	11.26	6.98	356.38	552.87	466.99	201.19
October	34.3	38.2	40.9	3.7	28.6	120.3	102.4	10.39	7.45	14.01	11.29	6.99	356.38	553.90	462.79	198.80
November	34.3	37.9	41.0	3.7	28.7	120.1	102.3	10.42	7.44	13.99	11.32	7.01	357.41	529.20	467.10	199.65
December	34.3	38.5	41.0	3.7	28.6	120.1	102.0	10.45	7.44	14.05	11.32	7.03	358.44	535.15	474.55	204.28
1992:																
January	34.3	38.5	40.9	3.5	28.6	120.0	101.2	10.45	7.43	14.07	11.29	7.03	358.44	516.37	458.78	195.84
February	34.3	38.1	41.1	3.7	28.6	120.0	101.6	10.47	7.43	14.02	11.34	7.04	359.12	510.50	460.00	199.80
March	34.3	38.0	41.0	3.7	28.6	120.1	101.5	10.50	7.43	14.12	11.38	7.07	360.15	524.81	465.03	200.36
April	34.4	38.8	41.1	3.8	28.9	120.9	101.9	10.52	7.43	14.11	11.41	7.08	361.89	537.09	461.37	202.35
May	34.5	38.4	41.2	3.9	28.8	121.3	102.2	10.54	7.42	14.12	11.44	7.09	363.63	548.49	470.60	203.48
June	34.3	38.1	41.1	3.8	28.6	120.8	102.0	10.57	7.42	14.23	11.46	7.11	362.55	551.07	473.30	204.90
July	34.4	38.2	41.1	3.8	28.6	121.1	102.0	10.59	7.42	14.14	11.48	7.13	364.30	548.49	466.42	207.74
August	34.4	38.2	41.1	3.8	28.8	121.3	101.9	10.62	7.42	14.20	11.52	7.15	365.33	556.78	470.60	209.57
September	34.4	37.8	41.0	3.7	29.0	121.5	101.6	10.62	7.40	14.09	11.51	7.19	365.33	527.93	472.73	209.09
October	34.4	38.2	41.1	3.8	28.8	121.8	101.7	10.65	7.40	14.20	11.51	7.18	366.36	559.52	474.54	205.35
November	34.4	37.9	41.2	3.8	28.8	122.0	102.0	10.67	7.39	14.22	11.54	7.19	367.05	534.38	480.48	205.92
December	34.4	37.8	41.2	3.9	28.8	122.1	102.1	10.69	7.39	14.23	11.57	7.20	367.74	531.59	487.30	209.95
1993:																
January	34.5	38.1	41.4	4.0	28.8	122.8	102.9	10.72	7.39	14.22	11.60	7.22	369.84	514.40	477.17	202.55
February	34.5	38.1	41.4	4.2	28.9	123.4	103.1	10.73	7.38	14.25	11.62	7.24	370.19	518.57	477.17	204.73
March	34.3	38.2	41.1	3.9	28.3	122.5	102.2	10.78	7.41	14.34	11.64	7.26	369.75	535.88	475.67	202.11
April	34.5	38.5	41.6	4.4	28.7	123.8	103.5	10.78	7.39	14.33	11.68	7.25	371.91	539.41	479.70	206.18
May	34.5	38.6	41.3	4.1	28.8	124.2	103.2	10.80	7.38	14.36	11.70	7.28	372.60	561.74	483.62	210.10
June	34.4	38.5	41.3	4.1	28.7	124.2	102.5	10.82	7.39	14.35	11.72	7.28	372.21	560.03	484.79	210.54
July	34.5	38.8	41.4	4.1	28.8	124.9	102.9	10.84	7.39	14.41	11.74	7.29	373.98	569.45	480.52	214.60
August	34.5	38.7	41.5	4.1	28.8	125.1	103.0	10.86	7.39	14.41	11.77	7.31	374.67	574.06	485.55	215.33
September	34.6	38.8	41.8	4.3	28.8	125.6	103.8	10.89	7.40	14.38	11.82	7.31	376.79	556.88	491.78	211.55
October	34.6	38.4	41.6	4.3	29.0	126.1	103.7	10.91	7.38	14.43	11.84	7.34	377.49	559.31	493.24	211.68
November	34.6	39.0	41.6	4.3	28.8	126.3	104.0	10.93	7.39	14.45	11.87	7.35	378.18	559.31	498.54	210.50
December	34.6	38.8	41.7	4.4	28.9	126.7	104.3	10.96	7.39	14.48	11.92	7.37	379.22	556.03	508.80	215.65
1994:																
January	34.6	38.4	41.7	4.4	28.8	127.0	104.6	10.99	7.41	14.49	11.93	7.40	380.25	535.35	496.34	210.09
February	34.4	37.6	41.2	4.5	28.7	126.7	103.7	11.02	7.42	14.62	12.01	7.42	379.09	524.18	490.80	209.35
March	34.7	38.9	42.1	4.7	28.9	128.5	106.1	11.03	7.40	14.55	11.99	7.43	382.74	553.14	502.38	212.33
April	34.7	38.4	41.9	4.4	29.0	128.9	106.0	11.05	7.41	14.60	12.00	7.46	383.44	557.57	504.42	214.39
May	34.7	39.2	42.0	4.6	28.9	129.4	106.7	11.07	7.41	14.66	12.01	7.47	384.13	580.81	504.84	215.88
June	34.7	38.9	42.0	4.7	29.0	129.9	107.0	11.09	7.39	14.68	12.04	7.49	384.82	579.62	507.67	218.58
July	34.7	38.8	42.1	4.7	29.0	130.4	107.4	11.12	7.38	14.75	12.05	7.50	385.86	587.45	501.28	222.31
August	34.6	38.8	42.0	4.7	29.0	130.5	107.5	11.14	7.37	14.74	12.08	7.51	385.44	589.44	504.42	220.97
September	34.6	38.7	41.9	4.6	28.9	130.8	107.6	11.17	7.37	14.82	12.11	7.53	386.48	599.60	515.16	218.66
October	34.7	38.6	42.1	4.8	29.0	131.5	108.3	11.21	7.39	14.92	12.15	7.55	388.99	597.17	512.25	220.29
November	34.6	38.9	42.1	4.8	28.9	131.8	108.6	11.22	7.38	14.85	12.17	7.56	388.21	573.65	517.65	217.26
December	34.6	39.1	42.1	4.8	28.9	132.4	108.8	11.25	7.39	14.85	12.18	7.59	389.25	576.96	526.38	222.39

1. Includes industries not shown seperately.

Consumer Price Indexes

(All urban consumers; 1982–1984=100, seasonally adjusted)

Year and month	All items	Food	Housing					Apparel	Transportation			Medical care	Energy	All items less food and energy
			Total	Shelter		Fuels and utilities	House-hold furnish-ings and oper-ations		Total	New vehicles	Motor fuel			
				Total	Rent of primary residence									
1971:														
January	39.9	39.4	37.5	36.8	.....	30.3	47.7	60.4	39.2	56.2	28.5	35.2	26.3	42.1
February	39.9	39.5	37.5	36.6	.....	30.5	47.8	60.6	39.4	56.3	28.1	35.4	26.2	42.2
March	40.0	39.8	37.4	36.4	.....	30.7	47.9	60.6	39.4	56.1	27.9	35.6	26.2	42.2
April	40.1	40.1	37.4	36.4	.....	30.7	48.1	60.7	39.4	56.1	27.5	35.8	26.1	42.4
May	40.3	40.3	37.6	36.5	.....	30.9	48.5	61.1	39.4	56.2	27.5	36.0	26.2	42.6
June	40.5	40.5	37.9	36.9	.....	31.0	48.7	61.2	39.6	56.3	27.6	36.2	26.3	42.8
July	40.6	40.6	38.1	37.0	.....	31.3	48.8	61.3	39.6	56.6	27.3	36.4	26.3	42.9
August	40.7	40.6	38.2	37.2	.....	31.5	49.0	61.1	39.7	54.7	28.4	36.5	26.8	43.0
September	40.8	40.6	38.4	37.4	.....	31.6	49.0	61.3	39.5	53.6	28.5	36.7	26.9	43.0
October	40.9	40.7	38.5	37.5	.....	31.7	49.1	61.4	39.5	53.6	28.6	36.5	27.0	43.1
November	41.0	40.9	38.6	37.7	.....	31.7	49.1	61.5	39.4	53.6	28.4	36.6	26.9	43.2
December	41.1	41.3	38.7	37.8	.....	31.9	49.2	61.6	39.4	54.0	28.5	36.7	27.0	43.3
1972:														
January	41.2	41.1	38.9	38.0	.....	32.0	49.2	61.7	39.7	54.7	28.2	36.8	27.0	43.5
February	41.4	41.7	39.0	38.1	.....	32.1	49.2	61.9	39.6	54.7	28.1	36.9	26.8	43.6
March	41.4	41.6	39.0	38.2	.....	32.2	49.4	61.9	39.6	54.9	28.1	37.0	26.9	43.6
April	41.5	41.6	39.1	38.3	.....	32.3	49.4	62.1	39.6	55.0	27.8	37.1	26.9	43.8
May	41.6	41.7	39.2	38.4	.....	32.4	49.6	62.2	39.7	55.0	28.0	37.2	27.0	43.9
June	41.7	41.9	39.4	38.6	.....	32.5	49.6	62.2	39.7	55.0	27.7	37.3	27.0	44.0
July	41.8	42.1	39.6	38.8	.....	32.6	49.7	62.2	39.8	55.1	28.0	37.3	27.1	44.1
August	41.9	42.2	39.7	39.0	.....	32.7	49.8	62.0	40.0	55.3	28.4	37.4	27.3	44.3
September	42.1	42.5	39.8	39.0	.....	32.8	49.9	62.5	40.2	55.6	29.0	37.4	27.6	44.3
October	42.2	42.8	39.8	39.1	.....	32.9	49.9	62.8	40.1	54.1	29.1	37.8	27.7	44.4
November	42.4	43.0	39.9	39.2	.....	33.0	50.0	63.0	40.3	54.0	29.3	37.8	27.9	44.4
December	42.5	43.2	40.1	39.3	.....	33.0	50.2	63.2	40.4	54.2	29.3	37.9	27.8	44.6
1973:														
January	42.7	44.0	40.1	39.4	.....	33.1	50.2	63.2	40.4	54.1	29.4	38.0	27.9	44.6
February	43.0	44.6	40.2	39.5	.....	33.4	50.3	63.4	40.6	54.3	29.6	38.1	28.2	44.8
March	43.4	45.8	40.4	39.6	.....	33.5	50.4	63.8	40.7	54.5	29.7	38.2	28.3	45.0
April	43.7	46.5	40.5	39.7	.....	33.7	50.6	64.2	41.0	54.7	30.2	38.3	28.6	45.1
May	43.9	47.1	40.6	39.9	.....	33.8	50.7	64.4	41.0	54.8	30.4	38.5	28.8	45.3
June	44.2	47.6	40.9	40.0	.....	34.0	51.0	64.6	41.2	54.8	31.0	38.6	29.2	45.4
July	44.2	47.7	41.0	40.1	.....	34.1	51.1	64.6	41.2	55.1	31.0	38.6	29.2	45.5
August	45.0	50.5	41.3	40.5	.....	34.4	51.3	64.9	41.2	55.2	31.0	38.7	29.4	45.7
September	45.2	50.4	41.7	41.0	.....	34.5	51.5	65.2	41.1	55.2	30.8	38.9	29.4	46.0
October	45.6	50.7	42.1	41.6	.....	35.1	51.7	65.4	41.4	55.0	32.2	39.6	30.3	46.3
November	45.9	51.4	42.5	41.8	.....	35.8	52.0	65.7	41.8	55.0	33.7	39.7	31.5	46.5
December	46.3	51.9	42.8	42.1	.....	36.7	52.2	66.0	42.2	54.8	35.2	39.9	32.5	46.7
1974:														
January	46.8	52.5	43.3	42.4	.....	37.9	52.7	66.3	42.8	55.1	37.2	40.1	34.1	46.9
February	47.3	53.6	43.6	42.7	.....	38.6	53.1	67.0	43.4	55.2	39.3	40.3	35.4	47.2
March	47.8	54.2	44.1	43.0	.....	38.9	53.9	67.5	44.2	55.5	42.1	40.7	36.9	47.6
April	48.1	54.1	44.4	43.2	.....	39.6	54.4	68.2	44.7	55.8	42.7	41.0	37.6	47.9
May	48.6	54.5	44.9	43.5	.....	40.1	55.5	68.7	45.3	56.6	43.6	41.4	38.3	48.5
June	49.0	54.5	45.4	43.9	.....	40.5	56.3	69.2	45.9	57.5	43.6	42.1	38.6	49.0
July	49.3	54.3	45.9	44.4	.....	41.0	57.1	69.5	46.4	58.6	43.7	42.6	38.9	49.5
August	49.9	55.1	46.5	44.9	.....	41.6	58.1	70.8	46.6	59.0	43.4	43.2	39.2	50.2
September	50.6	56.2	47.1	45.5	.....	42.0	59.0	71.0	47.0	59.8	43.2	43.7	39.3	50.7
October	51.0	56.8	47.7	46.0	.....	42.3	59.8	71.2	47.3	60.9	42.6	44.1	39.2	51.2
November	51.5	57.5	48.1	46.3	.....	42.6	60.6	71.7	47.6	61.0	42.4	44.4	39.4	51.6
December	51.9	58.2	48.6	46.9	.....	42.8	61.2	71.7	47.9	61.0	42.5	44.8	39.6	52.0
1975:														
January	52.3	58.4	49.0	47.3	.....	43.4	61.6	71.8	48.0	60.3	42.8	45.3	40.0	52.3
February	52.6	58.5	49.4	47.7	.....	43.8	62.1	72.0	48.3	61.1	42.8	45.8	40.3	52.8
March	52.8	58.4	49.7	47.9	.....	44.0	62.4	72.1	48.7	62.7	43.0	46.3	40.6	53.0
April	53.0	58.3	50.0	48.2	.....	44.5	62.8	72.1	48.8	63.0	43.0	46.7	41.0	53.3
May	53.1	58.6	50.2	48.3	.....	44.8	63.1	72.2	48.9	62.7	43.5	47.0	41.3	53.5
June	53.5	59.2	50.5	48.7	.....	45.2	63.4	72.2	49.4	62.9	44.5	47.4	41.7	53.8
July	54.0	60.3	50.7	48.9	.....	45.4	63.6	72.6	50.2	62.9	46.1	47.8	42.5	54.0
August	54.2	60.3	51.0	49.0	.....	45.8	63.8	72.6	50.6	63.3	46.5	48.1	42.8	54.2
September	54.6	60.7	51.3	49.3	.....	46.4	64.1	72.7	51.4	63.7	46.9	48.5	43.2	54.5
October	54.9	61.3	51.5	49.6	.....	46.7	64.4	73.0	51.7	64.0	47.3	48.9	43.5	54.8
November	55.3	61.7	52.0	50.0	.....	47.4	64.6	73.2	52.4	64.2	47.3	48.8	43.9	55.2
December	55.6	62.1	52.3	50.3	.....	47.7	64.8	73.4	52.6	65.3	47.2	49.3	44.1	55.5
1976:														
January	55.8	61.9	52.6	50.5	.....	48.0	65.7	73.7	53.0	65.5	47.1	49.7	44.5	55.9
February	55.9	61.3	52.8	50.6	.....	48.3	66.1	74.0	53.3	65.8	46.7	50.2	44.4	56.2
March	56.0	60.9	52.9	50.7	.....	48.4	66.5	74.2	53.8	66.1	46.3	50.7	44.1	56.5
April	56.1	60.9	53.1	50.7	.....	48.6	66.7	74.3	54.0	66.3	45.7	51.0	43.9	56.7
May	56.4	61.1	53.2	50.9	.....	48.7	66.8	74.6	54.3	66.4	46.1	51.4	44.1	57.0
June	56.7	61.3	53.5	51.2	.....	48.8	67.1	74.9	54.8	66.5	46.7	51.8	44.4	57.2
July	57.0	61.6	53.8	51.6	.....	49.1	67.4	75.3	55.1	66.7	46.8	52.3	44.8	57.6
August	57.3	61.8	54.1	51.9	.....	49.6	67.6	75.8	55.4	67.1	46.9	52.6	45.2	57.9
September	57.6	62.1	54.4	52.2	.....	50.0	67.8	76.1	56.0	67.6	47.2	53.0	45.7	58.2
October	57.9	62.4	54.6	52.3	.....	50.5	68.1	76.2	56.6	68.7	47.8	53.2	46.1	58.5
November	58.1	62.3	54.8	52.4	.....	51.4	68.4	76.5	57.0	68.4	48.2	53.9	46.8	58.7
December	58.4	62.5	55.1	52.4	.....	52.3	68.6	76.8	57.3	68.6	48.3	54.2	47.5	58.9

Consumer Price Indexes—*Continued*

(All urban consumers; 1982–1984=100, seasonally adjusted)

Year and month	All items	Food	Housing Total	Shelter Total	Rent of primary residence	Fuels and utilities	House-hold furnish-ings and oper-ations	Apparel	Transportation Total	New vehicles	Motor fuel	Medical care	Energy	All items less food and energy
1977:														
January	58.7	62.7	55.6	52.9	.....	53.3	68.9	77.2	57.8	68.8	48.5	54.6	48.1	59.3
February	59.3	63.9	55.9	53.2	.....	53.5	69.2	77.6	58.2	68.9	49.2	54.9	48.1	59.7
March	59.6	64.2	56.2	53.5	.....	53.9	69.4	77.5	58.7	69.3	49.7	55.5	48.4	60.0
April	60.0	65.0	56.5	54.0	.....	54.1	69.5	77.6	59.0	69.4	49.7	56.0	48.6	60.3
May	60.2	65.3	56.8	54.3	.....	54.0	69.8	78.1	59.1	69.7	50.0	56.5	48.9	60.6
June	60.5	65.7	57.1	54.7	.....	54.1	70.2	78.5	59.1	70.0	49.7	57.0	48.9	61.0
July	60.8	65.9	57.6	55.2	.....	54.5	70.5	79.1	59.0	70.3	49.4	57.3	49.1	61.2
August	61.1	66.2	57.9	55.5	.....	55.0	70.8	79.2	58.9	70.6	49.4	57.7	49.5	61.5
September	61.3	66.4	58.3	55.9	.....	55.4	71.0	79.1	59.1	70.9	49.6	58.2	49.8	61.8
October	61.6	66.6	58.6	56.2	.....	55.7	71.3	79.3	59.3	72.1	50.1	58.4	50.5	62.0
November	62.0	67.1	59.0	56.6	.....	56.8	71.5	79.8	59.5	72.6	50.5	58.6	51.3	62.3
December	62.3	67.4	59.4	57.0	.....	56.8	71.9	80.1	59.8	73.6	50.9	59.0	51.6	62.7
1978:														
January	62.7	67.9	59.7	57.5	.....	56.7	72.2	80.1	60.1	74.2	50.9	59.3	51.1	63.1
February	63.0	68.6	60.1	57.8	.....	57.1	72.3	79.5	60.2	74.5	50.6	59.9	50.6	63.4
March	63.4	69.5	60.5	58.3	.....	57.5	72.8	79.9	60.3	74.8	50.7	60.2	51.0	63.8
April	63.9	70.6	61.0	58.8	.....	58.0	73.3	80.7	60.4	74.7	50.4	60.7	51.4	64.3
May	64.5	71.6	61.6	59.4	.....	58.3	73.8	81.3	60.7	74.9	50.5	61.1	51.7	64.7
June	65.0	72.7	62.1	60.0	.....	58.4	74.4	81.6	61.1	75.4	50.7	61.5	51.9	65.2
July	65.5	73.0	62.7	60.7	.....	58.4	74.8	81.5	61.6	75.7	51.1	61.9	52.1	65.6
August	65.9	73.3	63.1	61.3	.....	58.6	75.3	81.7	62.0	76.0	51.8	62.4	52.6	66.1
September	66.5	73.6	63.8	62.1	.....	58.8	75.8	81.9	62.6	76.6	52.5	62.8	53.2	66.7
October	67.1	74.2	64.5	62.8	.....	59.4	76.4	82.4	63.3	77.3	53.5	63.3	54.1	67.2
November	67.5	74.7	64.9	63.3	.....	59.6	76.9	82.6	63.9	77.9	54.4	63.8	54.9	67.6
December	67.9	75.1	65.2	63.5	.....	60.0	77.4	82.6	64.5	78.6	55.4	64.1	55.9	68.0
1979:														
January	68.5	76.4	65.7	64.0	.....	60.4	77.9	83.0	64.6	79.0	56.0	64.8	55.8	68.5
February	69.2	77.7	66.5	64.9	.....	60.8	78.2	83.3	65.2	79.8	56.4	65.2	55.9	69.2
March	69.9	78.4	67.0	65.5	.....	61.3	78.6	83.6	66.4	80.3	59.0	65.7	57.4	69.8
April	70.6	79.0	67.7	66.3	.....	61.9	79.0	84.0	67.8	81.2	62.1	66.1	59.5	70.3
May	71.4	79.7	68.4	67.1	.....	62.7	79.3	84.5	69.1	81.6	65.2	66.6	62.0	70.8
June	72.2	80.0	69.3	68.0	.....	64.0	79.7	84.7	70.5	81.9	69.1	67.1	64.7	71.3
July	73.0	80.5	70.2	69.0	.....	65.1	80.0	84.8	71.7	82.4	72.7	67.7	67.3	71.9
August	73.7	80.4	71.2	70.1	.....	66.4	80.4	85.0	72.7	82.7	75.9	68.2	69.7	72.7
September	74.4	80.9	72.1	71.1	.....	67.4	80.7	85.6	73.5	82.9	78.8	68.7	71.9	73.3
October	75.2	81.5	73.1	72.3	.....	68.2	81.2	86.1	74.0	83.2	80.4	69.2	73.5	74.0
November	76.0	82.0	74.2	73.5	.....	68.8	82.0	86.6	74.7	83.8	81.7	69.8	74.8	74.8
December	76.9	82.8	75.2	74.6	.....	69.6	82.5	87.3	75.8	84.2	83.8	70.6	76.8	75.7
1980:														
January	78.0	83.3	76.2	75.9	.....	70.4	83.0	88.1	78.0	85.2	89.8	71.4	79.1	76.7
February	79.0	83.4	77.2	76.8	.....	71.5	83.6	88.7	79.8	86.3	94.1	72.3	81.9	77.5
March	80.1	84.1	78.3	78.1	.....	72.6	84.4	89.7	81.8	86.5	99.6	73.0	84.5	78.6
April	80.9	84.7	79.4	79.3	.....	73.7	84.9	90.1	82.2	87.4	98.7	73.6	85.4	79.5
May	81.7	85.2	80.5	80.5	.....	74.5	85.5	90.3	82.8	88.0	98.7	74.2	86.4	80.1
June	82.5	85.7	82.0	82.3	.....	75.5	86.1	90.6	82.7	87.9	98.1	74.7	86.5	81.0
July	82.6	86.6	81.5	81.3	.....	76.3	86.6	90.9	83.1	88.5	97.9	75.2	86.7	80.8
August	83.2	88.0	81.8	81.4	.....	76.9	87.2	91.4	83.7	89.8	97.8	75.6	87.2	81.3
September	83.9	89.1	82.3	82.0	.....	77.3	87.9	92.0	84.6	90.5	97.7	76.3	87.5	82.1
October	84.7	89.8	83.4	83.4	.....	77.5	88.3	92.7	85.3	90.3	98.5	76.9	88.0	83.0
November	85.6	90.8	84.4	84.7	.....	78.1	88.6	93.1	86.1	90.6	98.7	77.3	88.8	83.9
December	86.4	91.3	85.5	85.8	.....	79.2	89.1	93.3	86.8	90.6	99.4	77.8	90.7	84.9
1981:														
January	87.2	91.6	86.1	86.3	84.7	80.7	89.6	93.4	88.5	90.9	103.5	78.6	92.1	85.4
February	88.0	92.1	86.6	86.3	85.2	82.7	90.3	93.9	90.7	90.9	109.9	79.2	95.2	85.9
March	88.6	92.6	87.1	86.7	85.9	83.8	90.9	94.3	91.8	90.4	113.0	79.9	97.4	86.4
April	89.1	92.8	87.8	87.3	86.5	84.8	91.7	94.7	91.7	91.9	110.6	80.7	97.6	87.0
May	89.7	92.8	88.8	88.6	87.1	85.2	92.1	94.8	92.2	93.9	109.0	81.4	97.9	87.8
June	90.5	93.2	89.8	89.9	87.6	85.7	92.7	95.0	92.7	94.7	107.8	82.3	97.3	88.6
July	91.5	93.9	91.3	91.5	87.9	87.0	93.3	95.4	93.5	95.1	107.2	83.4	97.3	89.8
August	92.2	94.4	92.2	92.5	88.8	87.9	93.9	95.9	93.9	94.8	107.2	84.3	97.8	90.7
September	93.1	94.8	93.4	93.9	89.5	88.8	94.4	96.1	94.6	95.1	107.7	85.1	98.6	91.8
October	93.4	95.0	93.4	93.8	90.0	88.9	94.8	96.4	95.5	95.6	108.3	85.9	99.2	92.1
November	93.8	95.1	93.8	94.0	90.6	89.9	95.5	96.4	96.2	96.1	108.9	86.8	100.5	92.5
December	94.1	95.3	94.1	94.3	91.3	90.4	95.8	96.7	96.4	96.8	108.6	87.5	101.5	93.0
1982:														
January	94.4	95.6	94.4	94.4	91.9	91.3	96.2	96.7	96.7	96.9	108.1	88.2	100.6	93.3
February	94.7	96.3	94.7	94.7	92.3	91.7	96.7	97.0	96.2	96.3	106.0	88.8	98.0	93.8
March	94.7	96.2	94.6	94.2	92.9	92.6	97.1	97.3	95.8	96.0	103.6	89.6	96.6	93.9
April	95.0	96.4	95.4	95.3	93.2	93.1	97.3	97.5	94.5	96.8	97.3	90.5	94.2	94.7
May	95.9	97.2	96.7	96.8	93.8	93.8	97.8	97.6	95.1	97.2	97.8	91.3	95.7	95.4
June	97.0	98.1	97.7	98.0	94.3	94.5	98.0	97.7	97.2	97.7	102.8	92.2	98.4	96.1
July	97.5	98.2	98.1	98.5	95.0	94.9	98.3	98.1	98.1	98.1	104.3	93.0	99.3	96.7
August	97.7	98.0	98.4	98.9	95.5	95.4	98.3	98.1	98.2	98.3	104.1	93.9	99.8	97.1
September	97.7	98.2	98.2	98.4	95.7	96.1	98.5	98.1	98.0	98.0	103.2	94.7	100.3	97.2
October	98.1	98.2	98.6	98.4	96.5	97.7	98.9	98.3	98.2	98.0	103.2	95.5	101.7	97.5
November	98.0	98.2	98.3	97.9	97.0	98.4	98.8	98.3	98.2	97.9	102.8	96.5	102.5	97.3
December	97.7	98.2	97.5	96.5	97.4	98.9	99.1	98.2	97.7	98.3	100.4	97.2	102.8	97.2

Consumer Price Indexes—*Continued*

(All urban consumers; 1982–1984=100, seasonally adjusted)

Year and month	All items	Food	Housing Total	Shelter Total	Shelter Rent of primary residence	Fuels and utilities	House-hold furnish-ings and oper-ations	Apparel	Transportation Total	Transportation New vehicles	Transportation Motor fuel	Medical care	Energy	All items less food and energy
1983:														
January	97.9	98.1	98.0	97.2	98.0	99.4	99.3	98.6	97.6	98.6	99.0	97.9	99.6	97.6
February	98.0	98.2	98.2	97.5	98.5	99.2	99.4	99.1	96.9	98.9	95.9	98.8	97.7	98.0
March	98.1	98.8	98.3	97.6	98.8	99.0	99.6	99.1	96.5	99.0	94.2	99.0	96.8	98.2
April	98.8	99.2	98.9	98.4	99.3	99.5	100.0	99.3	97.8	99.2	98.0	99.4	98.9	98.6
May	99.2	99.5	99.1	98.7	99.5	99.9	99.9	99.9	98.6	99.5	100.5	99.9	100.4	98.9
June	99.4	99.6	99.3	99.0	99.9	99.9	100.1	100.3	99.0	99.7	101.0	100.4	100.6	99.2
July	99.8	99.6	99.7	99.4	100.2	100.3	100.3	100.9	99.6	99.8	101.3	100.8	100.9	99.8
August	100.1	99.7	99.8	99.6	100.6	100.2	100.3	101.0	100.4	100.3	102.1	101.4	101.2	100.1
September	100.4	100.0	100.1	100.1	101.1	100.6	100.3	100.8	100.7	100.6	101.2	101.8	101.0	100.5
October	100.8	100.3	100.4	100.3	101.3	100.8	100.6	100.6	101.1	100.8	100.7	102.3	100.8	101.0
November	101.1	100.3	100.8	100.7	101.7	101.3	100.9	100.9	101.5	101.0	99.5	102.8	100.5	101.5
December	101.4	100.6	101.0	101.1	102.1	101.2	101.2	101.1	101.5	101.3	98.6	103.4	100.0	101.8
1984:														
January	102.1	102.0	101.5	101.4	102.5	102.4	101.2	101.5	102.0	101.4	98.9	104.0	100.2	102.5
February	102.6	102.7	102.1	101.8	102.9	104.2	101.0	101.2	102.2	101.6	99.4	105.0	101.4	102.8
March	102.9	102.9	102.3	102.3	103.5	103.6	101.2	101.3	102.9	101.9	100.1	105.2	101.4	103.2
April	103.3	102.9	102.9	103.0	104.3	104.3	101.4	101.2	103.3	102.1	99.9	105.8	101.7	103.7
May	103.5	102.7	103.1	103.2	104.6	104.4	101.6	101.4	103.7	102.3	99.5	106.2	101.6	104.1
June	103.7	103.1	103.3	103.6	105.1	104.3	101.7	101.3	103.9	102.5	98.3	106.7	100.8	104.5
July	104.1	103.3	103.9	104.3	105.6	105.3	101.5	101.9	103.7	102.8	96.4	107.2	100.5	105.0
August	104.4	103.9	104.2	104.7	106.1	105.6	102.0	102.5	103.8	103.0	95.4	107.7	100.1	105.4
September	104.7	103.8	104.7	105.1	106.5	106.0	102.5	102.7	104.1	103.3	96.1	108.1	100.6	105.8
October	105.1	104.0	104.9	105.5	107.0	105.8	102.6	103.0	104.8	103.5	97.4	108.7	101.1	106.2
November	105.3	104.1	105.1	105.8	107.4	105.9	102.6	103.0	104.9	103.6	97.0	109.3	100.8	106.4
December	105.5	104.5	105.3	106.4	108.1	105.4	102.7	103.1	104.7	103.7	96.0	109.8	100.1	106.8
1985:														
January	105.7	104.7	105.5	106.7	108.5	105.6	102.5	103.2	105.1	104.4	96.4	110.2	100.3	107.1
February	106.3	105.2	106.0	107.4	109.2	105.3	103.3	104.1	105.6	104.9	96.5	110.8	100.3	107.7
March	106.8	105.5	106.4	107.8	109.7	106.0	103.6	104.5	106.3	105.3	98.1	111.4	101.3	108.1
April	107.0	105.4	106.7	108.1	110.2	106.3	104.0	104.5	106.8	105.5	99.8	112.0	102.3	108.4
May	107.2	105.2	107.4	109.2	111.0	106.4	103.9	104.4	106.5	105.7	99.4	112.6	102.2	108.8
June	107.5	105.5	107.6	109.6	111.6	106.6	103.7	105.1	106.5	106.0	99.8	113.3	102.2	109.1
July	107.7	105.5	107.9	110.1	112.0	106.7	103.5	105.2	106.6	106.2	100.0	113.9	102.2	109.4
August	107.9	105.6	108.3	110.8	112.6	106.4	103.7	105.3	106.2	106.4	98.7	114.6	101.2	109.8
September	108.1	105.8	108.5	111.0	113.0	106.8	103.8	105.5	106.2	106.8	98.2	115.2	101.2	110.0
October	108.5	105.8	108.9	111.5	113.8	106.8	104.4	105.7	106.5	106.8	98.2	115.8	101.2	110.5
November	109.0	106.5	109.5	112.3	114.6	107.3	104.6	106.0	107.0	107.3	98.9	116.5	101.8	111.1
December	109.5	107.3	109.8	112.7	115.0	107.7	104.5	106.1	107.5	107.4	99.7	117.1	102.4	111.4
1986:														
January	109.9	107.5	110.1	113.2	115.4	107.8	104.5	106.1	108.0	107.8	100.1	118.0	102.6	111.9
February	109.7	107.3	110.0	113.5	115.6	106.4	104.6	105.4	107.0	108.1	95.9	118.8	99.5	112.2
March	109.1	107.5	110.3	114.3	116.4	105.3	104.9	105.0	103.6	108.4	83.5	119.7	92.6	112.5
April	108.7	107.7	110.4	115.0	116.7	104.4	104.9	105.0	101.0	109.0	74.3	120.4	87.2	112.9
May	109.0	108.2	110.4	115.2	117.8	103.7	105.0	104.9	101.4	109.9	75.5	121.2	87.2	113.1
June	109.4	108.3	110.9	115.6	118.2	104.7	105.1	104.9	102.3	110.7	77.9	121.8	88.8	113.4
July	109.5	109.1	110.9	115.9	118.9	103.6	105.2	105.2	101.1	111.3	72.9	122.5	85.6	113.8
August	109.6	110.1	111.1	116.3	119.0	103.6	105.2	106.4	100.1	111.6	69.0	123.2	83.6	114.2
September	110.0	110.2	111.5	116.9	119.4	103.4	105.7	106.9	100.6	111.8	70.8	124.0	84.4	114.6
October	110.2	110.5	111.6	117.5	120.0	102.4	105.7	106.6	100.5	112.3	69.2	124.7	82.8	115.0
November	110.4	111.1	111.6	117.8	120.4	101.7	105.5	106.9	100.8	113.1	68.6	125.5	82.1	115.3
December	110.8	111.4	111.9	118.1	120.7	101.8	106.1	107.2	101.1	113.4	69.1	126.2	82.5	115.6
1987:														
January	111.5	111.9	112.2	118.4	121.2	102.2	106.3	108.0	102.7	113.9	74.1	126.8	85.1	116.1
February	111.9	112.3	112.6	118.9	121.6	102.2	106.5	108.6	103.6	112.9	78.4	127.3	87.1	116.4
March	112.3	112.5	112.9	119.3	122.0	102.4	106.8	109.2	103.9	112.9	78.7	127.9	87.3	116.8
April	112.8	112.7	113.4	120.1	122.2	102.3	107.2	109.8	104.4	113.3	79.3	128.7	87.3	117.5
May	113.1	113.3	113.7	120.5	122.5	102.5	107.1	110.3	104.5	113.8	77.8	129.3	86.8	117.9
June	113.6	114.0	114.0	120.8	122.5	103.1	107.1	110.3	105.2	114.3	79.5	130.1	88.2	118.1
July	113.9	113.8	114.2	120.9	123.0	103.3	107.2	110.3	106.0	114.9	81.2	130.7	88.9	118.5
August	114.4	114.0	114.8	121.7	123.8	104.0	107.3	111.0	106.7	115.0	83.1	131.3	90.2	118.9
September	114.8	114.5	115.1	122.2	124.2	104.0	107.5	111.6	107.0	115.3	82.7	132.0	90.0	119.4
October	115.1	114.7	115.4	122.9	124.6	103.3	107.4	112.3	107.1	115.4	82.6	132.5	89.3	120.0
November	115.5	114.7	115.7	123.2	124.6	103.7	107.4	113.0	107.4	115.8	82.7	133.1	89.7	120.3
December	115.7	115.3	116.0	123.9	125.5	103.4	107.3	112.7	107.3	115.4	82.1	133.6	89.2	120.6
1988:														
January	116.1	115.8	116.3	124.4	125.9	103.2	107.5	113.2	107.1	115.1	81.2	134.6	88.5	121.1
February	116.2	115.8	116.7	124.9	126.2	103.5	107.7	112.1	107.1	115.1	80.8	135.4	88.4	121.3
March	116.6	116.0	117.1	125.3	126.6	103.5	108.3	113.4	107.1	115.1	80.0	136.0	88.1	121.9
April	117.2	116.6	117.6	125.8	126.9	103.9	109.1	115.1	107.5	115.4	80.6	136.8	88.5	122.5
May	117.6	117.0	117.8	126.1	127.2	103.7	109.3	115.1	108.0	115.8	80.3	137.7	88.2	122.9
June	118.1	117.7	118.2	126.6	127.6	104.2	109.6	115.5	108.4	116.3	80.2	138.4	88.6	123.4
July	118.6	118.9	118.5	127.0	127.9	104.3	109.8	115.9	108.9	116.6	81.2	139.3	89.1	123.8
August	119.0	119.6	118.9	127.6	128.4	104.4	109.7	114.5	109.7	117.1	82.5	139.9	89.8	124.1
September	119.6	120.2	119.4	128.1	128.9	105.0	110.1	116.3	110.0	117.9	81.4	140.7	89.5	124.8
October	120.0	120.5	119.8	128.4	129.1	105.7	110.3	117.5	110.0	117.9	80.8	141.6	89.5	125.3
November	120.4	120.7	120.1	129.0	129.5	105.6	110.6	117.7	110.3	118.0	80.8	142.1	89.5	125.8
December	120.8	121.2	120.5	129.4	129.9	106.2	110.6	118.2	110.4	118.0	80.3	142.9	89.3	126.2

Consumer Price Indexes—*Continued*

(All urban consumers; 1982–1984=100, seasonally adjusted)

Year and month	All items	Food	Housing Total	Shelter Total	Shelter Rent of primary residence	Fuels and utilities	Household furnishings and operations	Apparel	Transportation Total	New vehicles	Motor fuel	Medical care	Energy	All items less food and energy
1989:														
January	121.3	121.8	120.8	129.6	130.4	106.6	111.0	118.4	111.0	118.3	81.1	144.0	89.9	126.7
February	121.7	122.6	121.1	130.1	130.9	106.4	110.7	117.1	111.7	118.5	82.6	145.1	90.5	127.0
March	122.3	123.4	121.4	130.8	131.2	106.7	110.3	118.1	112.5	118.7	84.4	145.9	91.5	127.5
April	123.2	124.1	121.8	131.1	131.6	107.1	110.5	118.6	115.1	118.9	93.8	146.8	96.2	128.0
May	123.8	124.9	122.2	131.8	132.0	107.4	110.6	118.9	115.9	119.1	95.7	147.6	97.0	128.5
June	124.1	125.3	122.6	132.2	132.6	107.5	111.0	118.7	115.8	119.1	94.4	148.8	96.5	128.9
July	124.6	125.8	123.3	133.0	133.0	108.1	111.1	118.3	115.4	119.1	93.2	149.7	96.3	129.4
August	124.6	126.1	123.6	133.4	133.5	108.3	111.4	117.1	114.5	119.0	89.1	150.8	94.6	129.7
September	124.9	126.5	123.8	133.7	133.7	108.3	111.5	118.7	114.0	118.8	86.9	151.9	93.4	130.1
October	125.5	127.0	124.4	134.6	134.4	108.4	111.9	119.6	114.6	119.3	87.8	152.9	94.1	130.8
November	125.9	127.5	124.8	135.2	135.0	108.8	111.9	120.0	114.5	120.3	86.2	154.2	93.6	131.3
December	126.4	128.0	125.3	135.7	135.3	109.3	112.0	119.8	114.8	120.9	86.1	155.1	93.9	131.8
1990:														
January	127.6	129.8	126.0	136.1	135.8	111.1	112.4	119.9	117.1	121.3	93.5	156.2	98.6	132.3
February	128.1	131.0	126.1	136.4	136.1	110.7	112.6	122.0	117.3	121.2	93.3	157.2	97.8	132.9
March	128.6	131.2	126.7	137.4	136.7	110.7	112.6	123.8	117.3	120.9	92.5	158.5	97.2	133.7
April	129.0	131.0	127.0	138.0	137.2	110.5	112.6	124.1	117.8	120.8	92.9	159.8	97.2	134.2
May	129.2	131.3	127.3	138.4	137.6	110.2	112.8	124.0	117.6	120.9	91.8	161.0	96.4	134.6
June	130.0	132.3	128.0	139.4	138.2	110.7	113.0	124.2	118.1	120.8	92.7	162.2	97.0	135.3
July	130.6	133.0	128.6	140.5	138.7	109.9	113.2	124.2	118.5	120.8	93.1	163.6	96.8	136.0
August	131.7	133.4	129.6	141.6	139.3	111.4	113.3	124.5	120.8	121.1	101.2	165.0	101.3	136.8
September	132.6	133.7	130.1	141.9	139.7	112.6	113.8	125.4	123.3	121.2	109.6	166.1	106.2	137.3
October	133.5	134.3	130.5	142.2	140.2	113.7	114.3	125.4	125.7	121.8	117.2	167.4	110.5	137.8
November	133.8	134.7	130.7	142.4	140.5	114.1	114.0	125.4	126.2	122.5	117.4	168.9	110.8	138.2
December	134.3	134.8	130.9	143.0	141.0	113.4	114.0	126.2	126.9	123.4	117.8	170.0	110.6	138.8
1991:														
January	134.8	135.2	131.9	143.9	141.2	115.0	114.4	126.9	125.6	124.2	110.9	171.2	108.1	139.7
February	134.9	135.3	132.3	144.2	141.6	115.1	115.4	127.3	123.9	124.8	102.6	172.3	104.2	140.4
March	134.9	135.5	132.5	144.6	142.1	114.9	115.5	127.0	122.8	125.3	97.7	173.4	101.5	140.7
April	135.2	136.3	132.6	145.0	142.6	114.2	115.6	127.5	122.6	125.5	97.6	174.5	100.8	141.1
May	135.7	136.8	133.0	145.3	143.0	114.7	116.0	128.0	123.3	125.7	99.4	175.4	101.8	141.5
June	136.1	137.6	133.1	145.7	143.2	114.4	115.8	127.9	123.5	126.0	98.2	176.6	100.8	142.0
July	136.3	136.8	133.5	146.1	143.7	115.0	116.0	128.7	123.4	126.3	96.4	177.6	100.3	142.5
August	136.7	136.3	133.7	146.4	143.7	115.0	116.2	129.9	124.1	126.4	97.7	179.0	100.8	143.1
September	137.1	136.5	134.2	146.9	144.4	115.5	116.4	130.0	124.1	126.4	97.8	180.1	101.1	143.6
October	137.3	136.4	134.6	147.4	144.4	116.0	116.4	130.1	124.0	126.7	97.3	181.0	101.2	143.9
November	137.9	136.9	135.1	148.0	144.8	116.5	116.6	131.0	124.5	127.0	98.4	182.1	102.0	144.4
December	138.3	137.2	135.5	148.6	145.1	116.8	116.6	130.7	125.2	127.5	99.5	183.3	102.7	144.9
1992:														
January	138.4	136.7	135.8	149.1	145.4	116.4	117.0	130.9	124.6	127.6	97.1	184.5	101.2	145.3
February	138.7	137.3	136.0	149.3	145.7	116.4	117.1	131.0	124.6	127.9	96.7	185.8	100.8	145.6
March	139.2	137.7	136.3	149.8	146.5	116.4	117.4	131.3	125.1	128.3	97.0	187.0	100.8	146.1
April	139.5	137.6	136.6	150.0	146.2	117.0	117.7	130.7	125.6	128.6	96.8	188.1	101.1	146.5
May	139.8	137.4	136.8	150.3	146.5	117.2	117.6	131.6	126.0	129.0	97.6	188.9	101.6	147.0
June	140.2	137.7	137.3	150.9	146.7	117.5	118.1	132.1	126.5	129.3	99.8	189.8	102.9	147.3
July	140.6	137.6	137.6	151.1	147.0	117.9	118.2	132.7	126.9	129.3	100.4	190.8	103.3	147.8
August	140.9	138.5	137.8	151.5	147.0	118.1	118.2	132.3	127.0	129.8	99.8	191.7	103.1	148.1
September	141.2	139.1	138.0	151.6	147.1	118.4	118.2	132.2	127.1	130.0	99.5	192.6	103.2	148.3
October	141.8	139.1	138.5	152.3	147.9	118.7	118.4	132.5	128.2	130.0	100.8	193.7	103.9	149.0
November	142.2	138.9	138.9	152.7	148.4	119.5	118.6	132.7	128.7	130.4	101.2	194.7	104.7	149.4
December	142.4	139.0	139.1	152.9	148.5	119.5	118.5	132.8	128.9	130.5	101.7	195.5	104.9	149.8
1993:														
January	142.8	139.3	139.5	153.6	148.9	119.6	118.4	132.8	129.3	130.9	101.5	196.6	104.7	150.3
February	143.2	139.8	139.5	153.8	149.1	118.9	118.5	134.0	129.7	131.1	101.6	197.6	104.0	150.8
March	143.4	139.7	139.9	154.0	149.1	120.3	118.4	134.0	129.4	131.3	100.8	198.3	104.5	151.0
April	143.9	140.2	140.5	154.7	149.7	120.7	118.9	134.0	129.7	131.7	100.1	199.3	104.5	151.6
May	144.3	141.2	140.7	155.0	150.0	121.0	118.9	133.5	129.9	132.2	98.1	200.7	103.9	152.0
June	144.4	140.8	141.1	155.5	150.4	121.4	119.0	133.0	129.9	132.3	96.8	201.6	103.5	152.3
July	144.6	140.8	141.2	155.6	150.4	121.7	118.6	132.8	130.1	132.9	95.6	202.4	103.1	152.5
August	144.9	141.3	141.6	156.0	150.8	122.0	119.1	134.0	130.5	133.4	95.3	203.0	103.0	153.0
September	145.1	141.6	141.9	156.3	151.0	122.4	119.5	133.7	130.4	133.6	94.2	203.8	102.6	153.1
October	145.7	142.2	142.2	156.6	151.3	122.6	120.0	133.8	132.0	134.2	99.2	204.7	105.0	153.6
November	146.0	142.5	142.5	157.0	151.5	122.3	120.4	134.4	132.3	134.6	97.8	205.3	104.0	154.1
December	146.4	143.0	142.9	157.6	151.9	122.5	120.6	134.1	132.2	134.9	96.3	206.0	103.3	154.5
1994:														
January	146.4	143.1	143.1	157.9	152.2	122.2	120.7	133.3	131.8	135.3	94.8	206.6	102.4	154.7
February	146.8	142.9	143.6	158.6	152.7	123.0	120.3	133.2	132.3	135.7	96.7	207.4	103.8	155.0
March	147.2	142.9	143.9	159.1	153.2	123.4	120.3	133.8	132.7	136.1	96.3	208.1	103.9	155.5
April	147.3	143.2	143.9	159.2	153.3	122.8	120.3	133.5	132.9	136.4	96.1	209.2	103.4	155.8
May	147.6	143.5	144.3	159.7	153.4	122.8	121.0	134.0	132.5	137.0	94.5	209.9	102.4	156.2
June	148.0	144.0	144.5	159.9	153.5	122.7	121.4	134.8	133.3	137.5	95.3	210.7	102.7	156.7
July	148.5	144.8	144.7	160.1	154.0	122.8	121.4	134.2	134.5	138.1	98.1	211.5	104.1	156.9
August	149.1	145.3	145.2	161.0	154.5	123.0	121.3	133.2	136.1	138.4	102.6	212.4	106.3	157.4
September	149.4	145.5	145.4	161.4	155.0	122.7	121.3	133.6	136.2	138.9	102.0	213.3	105.7	157.7
October	149.5	145.5	145.6	161.8	155.1	122.5	121.3	133.0	136.3	139.2	101.4	214.3	105.3	158.0
November	149.9	145.8	145.9	162.3	155.5	122.7	121.2	132.5	136.8	139.2	102.1	215.2	105.7	158.4
December	150.2	147.0	145.9	162.3	155.7	122.6	121.0	132.1	137.2	139.4	102.0	216.1	105.5	158.6

Producer Price Indexes

(By stage of processing—1982=100, seasonally adjusted)

Year and month	Finished goods								Intermediate materials, supplies, and components					Crude materials for further processing		
			Consumer goods													
					Consumer goods, except foods											
	Total	Total less food and energy	Total	Foods	Total	Nondurable goods, except food	Durable goods	Capital equipment	Total	Materials and components for manufacturing	Materials and components for construction	Processed fuels and lubricants	Supplies	Total	Foodstuffs and feedstuffs	Nonfood materials
1971:																
January	39.9	.....	39.5	43.2	38.5	33.4	48.4	41.3	36.0	.....	.....	.....	.....	34.8	44.2	24.2
February	40.1	.....	39.7	43.6	38.5	33.3	48.6	41.4	36.1	.....	.....	.....	.....	35.9	46.1	24.3
March	40.2	.....	39.8	43.9	38.5	33.3	48.6	41.5	36.3	.....	.....	.....	.....	35.4	45.3	24.2
April	40.3	.....	40.0	44.4	38.4	33.2	48.7	41.6	36.3	.....	.....	.....	.....	36.0	46.4	24.5
May	40.5	.....	40.1	44.7	38.5	33.3	48.8	41.7	36.5	.....	.....	.....	.....	36.0	46.3	24.4
June	40.6	.....	40.3	45.0	38.6	33.4	48.9	41.7	36.7	.....	.....	.....	.....	36.2	46.4	24.6
July	40.4	.....	40.1	44.1	38.8	33.5	49.0	41.9	36.9	.....	.....	.....	.....	35.9	45.8	24.7
August	40.7	.....	40.4	44.7	38.8	33.6	49.1	42.0	37.2	.....	.....	.....	.....	35.8	45.9	24.6
September	40.7	.....	40.3	44.5	38.9	33.7	49.1	41.9	37.2	.....	.....	.....	.....	35.7	45.0	24.9
October	40.7	.....	40.4	44.9	38.9	33.7	48.9	41.8	37.1	.....	.....	.....	.....	36.4	46.4	25.1
November	40.8	.....	40.6	45.2	38.9	33.7	49.0	41.8	37.2	.....	.....	.....	.....	37.0	47.4	25.2
December	41.1	.....	40.9	45.7	39.1	33.8	49.5	42.1	37.4	.....	.....	.....	.....	37.2	47.6	25.6
1972:																
January	41.0	.....	40.7	45.5	39.0	33.6	49.6	42.3	37.5	.....	.....	.....	.....	37.8	48.4	25.8
February	41.3	.....	40.9	45.9	39.1	33.6	49.8	42.5	37.7	.....	.....	.....	.....	38.1	48.9	26.0
March	41.3	.....	40.9	45.7	39.2	33.7	49.9	42.6	37.8	.....	.....	.....	.....	38.1	48.4	26.4
April	41.3	.....	40.9	45.7	39.2	33.8	49.9	42.7	37.9	.....	.....	.....	.....	38.7	49.4	26.6
May	41.5	.....	41.1	46.3	39.3	33.9	49.9	42.8	38.0	.....	.....	.....	.....	39.3	50.1	26.9
June	41.7	.....	41.4	46.8	39.4	33.9	50.0	42.8	38.0	.....	.....	.....	.....	39.4	50.4	27.0
July	41.8	.....	41.6	47.1	39.5	34.0	50.1	42.9	38.1	.....	.....	.....	.....	40.0	51.5	27.1
August	42.0	.....	41.7	47.3	39.6	34.1	50.4	42.9	38.2	.....	.....	.....	.....	40.3	52.2	27.2
September	42.2	.....	42.0	47.8	39.8	34.3	50.6	43.0	38.5	.....	.....	.....	.....	40.5	52.4	27.1
October	42.0	.....	41.9	47.6	39.6	34.4	49.7	42.8	38.7	.....	.....	.....	.....	40.9	53.0	27.3
November	42.3	.....	42.1	48.3	39.7	34.6	49.7	42.9	39.0	.....	.....	.....	.....	42.0	54.6	28.1
December	42.7	.....	42.6	49.3	39.8	34.6	50.0	43.0	39.6	.....	.....	.....	.....	43.8	57.7	28.6
1973:																
January	43.0	.....	43.0	50.5	39.9	34.7	49.8	43.0	39.8	41.5	44.1	20.8	.....	45.0	59.3	29.1
February	43.5	.....	43.5	51.2	40.3	35.2	50.0	43.3	40.4	41.9	44.7	21.0	.....	47.1	62.5	30.0
March	44.4	.....	44.7	53.9	40.5	35.4	50.2	43.6	41.1	42.6	45.6	21.2	.....	49.3	66.1	30.6
April	44.7	.....	45.0	54.5	40.8	35.6	50.6	43.8	41.3	43.1	46.3	21.3	.....	50.1	67.3	31.0
May	45.0	.....	45.3	55.0	40.9	35.8	50.9	44.1	42.2	43.5	46.8	21.6	.....	52.5	70.5	32.6
June	45.5	.....	45.9	56.2	41.1	36.0	51.0	44.2	43.0	44.0	46.7	22.0	.....	55.0	74.0	34.0
July	45.4	.....	45.7	55.7	41.2	36.0	51.2	44.3	42.3	44.1	46.3	22.1	.....	52.5	69.7	33.4
August	47.0	.....	47.7	61.0	41.4	36.1	51.4	44.4	43.5	44.8	46.5	22.2	.....	64.1	89.9	35.9
September	46.9	.....	47.5	60.3	41.5	36.3	51.4	44.6	43.0	45.0	47.0	22.5	.....	60.9	81.3	38.2
October	46.8	.....	47.4	59.6	41.7	36.8	51.0	44.7	43.4	45.4	47.4	23.1	.....	58.5	76.9	38.0
November	47.2	.....	47.9	59.8	42.2	37.4	51.4	44.9	43.8	45.9	48.3	23.8	.....	59.0	77.4	38.6
December	47.6	.....	48.3	60.1	42.8	38.1	51.7	45.3	44.8	46.9	48.9	25.1	.....	59.1	75.7	40.4
1974:																
January	48.8	49.7	49.6	62.2	43.7	39.2	52.4	45.8	45.9	48.2	49.7	26.4	.....	63.3	82.3	42.0
February	49.7	50.0	50.7	63.8	44.6	40.2	52.7	46.2	46.8	49.1	50.3	28.6	.....	64.3	83.5	42.8
March	50.2	50.5	51.1	63.5	45.5	41.3	53.1	46.8	48.1	50.7	51.4	30.5	.....	62.3	78.9	43.4
April	50.7	51.1	51.5	63.0	46.4	42.3	53.6	47.4	49.0	52.1	52.7	31.6	.....	60.6	74.7	44.2
May	51.3	52.2	52.0	62.9	47.2	43.2	54.4	48.7	50.6	53.9	54.2	33.1	.....	58.3	71.8	42.6
June	51.3	53.1	51.8	60.8	48.0	44.2	55.0	49.7	51.5	55.4	55.2	33.8	.....	55.4	65.8	43.0
July	52.7	54.0	53.2	63.1	49.0	45.0	55.9	50.7	53.4	57.3	56.4	35.7	.....	59.8	72.4	45.0
August	53.7	55.0	54.1	64.6	49.6	45.7	56.4	52.1	55.8	59.2	57.4	36.7	.....	62.9	78.1	45.3
September	54.3	55.7	54.6	65.1	50.1	46.2	56.9	53.1	55.9	59.9	58.0	35.9	.....	60.9	74.3	45.3
October	55.3	56.7	55.6	66.3	50.9	46.7	58.3	54.2	57.2	60.9	58.0	36.9	.....	63.2	78.6	45.6
November	56.4	57.4	56.7	69.1	51.2	47.0	58.8	55.0	57.8	62.6	58.3	37.0	.....	64.2	80.4	45.7
December	56.4	57.9	56.6	68.0	51.6	47.3	59.3	55.5	57.8	62.3	58.6	37.3	.....	61.5	76.8	44.1
1975:																
January	56.7	58.3	56.8	68.0	51.9	47.6	59.6	56.2	58.0	62.5	58.9	38.1	.....	59.6	74.0	43.0
February	56.6	58.7	56.6	67.3	52.0	47.6	60.0	56.7	57.8	62.2	59.2	37.5	.....	57.9	70.9	42.9
March	56.6	59.0	56.4	66.7	52.1	47.6	60.3	57.2	57.4	61.6	59.2	37.9	.....	57.1	70.0	42.2
April	57.1	59.2	56.9	67.8	52.3	47.8	60.4	57.5	57.5	61.4	59.3	38.3	.....	59.5	74.4	42.5
May	57.4	59.3	57.3	68.5	52.5	48.1	60.5	57.8	57.3	60.9	59.6	38.2	.....	61.2	76.8	43.4
June	57.9	59.5	57.8	69.5	52.7	48.4	60.7	58.0	57.3	60.9	60.0	38.5	.....	61.5	77.4	43.3
July	58.4	59.8	58.4	70.5	53.1	48.8	60.7	58.4	57.5	61.0	60.0	38.9	.....	62.4	79.3	43.3
August	58.9	59.9	59.0	71.3	53.5	49.3	61.1	58.5	58.0	61.3	60.1	39.9	.....	63.0	80.2	43.6
September	59.3	60.2	59.4	71.8	53.9	49.7	61.3	58.9	58.2	61.5	60.3	40.5	.....	64.5	81.9	44.7
October	59.8	60.6	59.9	72.4	54.3	50.1	61.8	59.3	58.8	62.0	61.0	41.0	.....	65.1	83.0	44.8
November	60.0	61.0	60.1	72.3	54.8	50.5	62.4	59.7	59.0	62.2	61.2	41.8	.....	64.4	81.6	44.8
December	60.1	61.4	60.1	71.9	55.1	50.8	62.5	60.0	59.2	62.3	61.9	41.8	.....	64.0	80.1	45.7
1976:																
January	60.0	61.7	59.9	70.9	55.2	51.0	62.7	60.4	59.4	62.7	62.1	41.6	63.3	63.0	78.4	45.5
February	59.9	61.9	59.6	69.7	55.4	51.1	63.0	60.7	59.6	62.6	62.3	41.5	63.6	62.1	77.2	44.8
March	60.0	62.2	59.6	69.5	55.5	51.2	63.1	61.1	59.8	62.8	62.9	41.4	63.5	61.5	75.8	45.3
April	60.3	62.3	60.0	70.7	55.5	51.3	62.9	61.3	60.0	63.0	63.1	41.5	63.5	63.9	79.0	46.5
May	60.4	62.4	60.0	70.6	55.5	51.3	62.9	61.5	60.3	63.2	63.5	41.3	64.3	63.6	77.8	47.4
June	60.5	62.8	60.1	69.8	56.0	51.9	63.3	61.8	60.8	63.7	63.7	41.5	66.0	65.2	79.9	48.3
July	60.7	63.1	60.3	69.5	56.4	52.4	63.4	62.1	61.1	64.2	64.1	41.9	66.8	64.8	77.7	50.0
August	60.9	63.5	60.4	68.9	56.8	52.9	63.8	62.5	61.3	64.5	64.5	42.3	67.0	63.6	76.1	49.4
September	61.1	63.9	60.5	68.5	57.2	53.1	64.4	62.9	61.6	64.9	65.1	42.9	68.3	63.0	75.6	49.5
October	61.4	64.1	60.9	68.7	57.7	53.7	64.7	63.1	62.0	65.0	65.6	43.2	67.7	63.0	74.0	50.5
November	61.9	64.6	61.4	68.6	58.4	54.6	65.2	63.4	62.4	65.4	66.1	43.9	67.4	63.4	73.9	51.3
December	62.4	64.9	61.9	70.1	58.4	54.5	65.3	64.0	62.8	65.7	66.7	44.2	68.3	64.5	76.8	50.3

Producer Price Indexes—Continued

(By stage of processing—1982=100, seasonally adjusted)

Year and month	Finished goods								Intermediate materials, supplies, and components					Crude materials for further processing		
	Total	Total less food and energy	Consumer goods					Capital equipment	Total	Materials and components for manufacturing	Materials and components for construction	Processed fuels and lubricants	Supplies	Total	Foodstuffs and feedstuffs	Nonfood materials
			Total	Foods	Consumer goods, except foods											
					Total	Nondurable goods, except food	Durable goods									
1977:																
January	62.5	65.1	62.1	70.2	58.6	54.7	65.6	64.0	63.0	65.7	66.8	44.8	68.6	64.3	77.6	49.1
February	63.2	65.4	62.8	71.5	59.2	55.4	65.9	64.3	63.3	65.8	66.7	46.0	68.8	65.7	78.6	50.9
March	63.7	65.7	63.4	72.6	59.5	55.8	66.2	64.7	63.9	66.3	67.3	46.6	69.0	66.6	79.9	51.4
April	64.0	65.9	63.7	72.8	59.9	56.2	66.3	65.0	64.4	66.6	67.7	47.2	70.3	68.3	82.6	51.9
May	64.4	66.1	64.2	73.7	60.1	56.5	66.6	65.3	64.9	67.1	68.2	47.5	70.8	67.6	81.0	52.4
June	64.6	66.5	64.2	73.2	60.4	56.7	67.0	65.7	64.9	67.3	68.7	47.8	70.0	65.5	77.6	51.5
July	64.8	66.8	64.5	73.7	60.6	56.9	67.2	66.0	65.1	67.7	69.5	48.2	68.5	64.7	76.4	51.3
August	65.2	67.3	64.8	74.1	60.9	57.1	67.8	66.6	65.4	68.0	70.1	48.5	68.8	63.9	74.3	51.8
September	65.5	67.8	65.0	73.7	61.4	57.5	68.4	67.0	65.7	68.3	71.1	48.7	68.9	63.7	73.8	52.1
October	65.9	68.2	65.3	73.9	61.7	57.7	68.9	67.6	65.8	68.4	71.3	49.1	68.7	64.0	74.4	52.1
November	66.4	68.8	65.8	74.6	62.2	58.1	69.4	68.1	66.3	68.8	71.5	49.2	69.9	65.4	76.6	52.5
December	66.7	69.0	66.1	74.9	62.4	58.3	69.6	68.6	66.6	69.1	72.1	49.3	69.9	66.4	77.7	53.5
1978:																
January	67.0	69.2	66.4	75.6	62.6	58.4	70.0	68.8	66.9	69.3	72.8	49.5	70.3	67.3	79.3	53.6
February	67.5	69.5	66.9	77.1	62.6	58.4	70.3	69.1	67.4	69.7	73.7	49.4	70.3	68.4	81.2	53.7
March	67.8	69.9	67.3	77.6	63.0	58.6	70.8	69.6	67.8	70.2	74.2	49.3	71.2	69.8	83.5	54.1
April	68.6	70.6	68.2	79.1	63.6	58.8	72.3	69.9	68.1	70.7	74.9	49.1	71.5	72.1	86.9	55.3
May	69.1	71.1	68.6	79.4	64.1	59.0	73.0	70.5	68.7	71.2	75.6	49.6	72.3	72.8	87.4	56.2
June	69.7	71.7	69.3	80.5	64.6	59.5	73.5	71.0	69.2	71.7	76.4	50.2	72.5	74.6	89.8	57.4
July	70.3	72.3	69.9	80.7	65.2	60.0	74.5	71.5	69.4	72.0	76.8	49.6	72.9	74.2	88.1	58.3
August	70.4	72.8	69.9	80.0	65.6	60.2	75.2	72.0	69.9	72.6	77.5	49.5	73.7	73.7	86.8	58.6
September	71.1	73.5	70.6	80.8	66.3	60.7	76.1	72.6	70.5	73.2	77.9	49.8	74.1	75.1	88.7	59.5
October	71.4	73.4	71.0	82.2	66.3	61.3	75.3	72.8	71.3	74.0	78.6	50.4	75.0	77.0	91.4	60.4
November	72.0	74.1	71.5	82.4	66.9	62.0	75.6	73.5	71.9	74.6	79.6	51.0	75.3	77.4	91.6	61.1
December	72.8	74.7	72.5	83.6	67.7	62.7	76.6	74.0	72.4	75.0	79.8	51.5	76.1	78.0	92.4	61.7
1979:																
January	73.7	75.3	73.3	85.0	68.4	63.3	77.4	74.5	73.1	76.0	80.9	51.8	76.5	80.1	95.8	62.0
February	74.4	75.9	74.2	86.5	69.0	63.8	78.2	75.2	73.7	76.6	81.4	52.0	77.4	82.1	98.4	63.5
March	75.0	76.4	74.8	87.2	69.6	64.4	78.8	75.7	74.6	77.6	82.1	52.9	77.6	83.8	100.0	65.2
April	75.8	77.0	75.6	87.6	70.5	65.5	79.2	76.4	75.7	78.8	82.9	54.7	78.0	84.4	100.7	65.7
May	76.2	77.4	75.9	86.8	71.4	66.6	79.7	76.8	76.6	79.5	83.4	57.1	78.6	84.7	99.8	67.4
June	76.6	78.0	76.4	85.9	72.4	67.9	80.4	77.3	77.5	80.2	83.7	59.5	79.4	85.6	99.1	70.0
July	77.4	78.5	77.3	86.2	73.6	69.5	80.9	77.8	78.7	81.4	84.2	61.9	80.9	86.5	100.5	70.3
August	78.2	78.8	78.3	86.7	74.7	71.4	80.7	77.8	79.8	82.1	84.8	65.2	81.3	85.5	98.6	70.6
September	79.5	79.7	79.8	87.8	76.4	73.1	82.4	78.7	81.1	83.1	86.0	68.3	82.0	87.9	100.9	73.0
October	80.4	80.4	80.6	87.8	77.7	74.6	83.2	79.2	82.4	84.2	87.1	70.8	83.1	88.8	101.1	74.6
November	81.4	81.0	81.8	89.5	78.6	75.6	84.1	79.8	83.2	85.1	87.1	72.4	83.3	90.0	102.0	76.1
December	82.2	81.7	82.6	90.0	79.5	76.6	84.8	80.6	84.0	86.0	87.1	73.4	84.3	91.2	102.9	77.7
1980:																
January	83.4	83.3	83.9	89.5	81.6	78.3	87.6	81.7	86.0	88.2	88.1	76.8	84.7	90.9	100.0	80.2
February	84.6	84.2	85.2	89.3	83.6	80.6	89.0	82.3	87.6	89.5	89.2	80.0	87.1	92.6	101.8	81.9
March	85.5	84.7	86.1	90.0	84.7	82.4	88.7	83.1	88.2	89.5	90.3	82.5	87.8	90.8	99.1	81.2
April	86.2	85.5	86.7	88.6	86.1	84.6	89.1	84.4	88.5	89.6	90.4	84.0	87.8	88.3	94.0	81.7
May	86.6	85.7	87.1	89.1	86.4	85.0	89.0	84.6	89.0	90.4	90.4	84.2	88.2	89.5	96.3	81.5
June	87.3	86.6	87.9	89.8	87.2	85.6	90.3	85.1	89.8	91.3	90.7	84.7	88.6	90.1	97.1	81.8
July	88.7	87.7	89.4	92.8	88.1	86.2	91.7	86.2	90.5	91.6	91.6	86.2	90.1	94.6	104.2	83.4
August	89.7	88.4	90.5	95.2	88.6	86.7	92.2	87.0	91.5	92.8	92.2	86.4	91.3	99.0	110.9	85.3
September	90.1	88.8	90.8	95.3	89.0	87.0	92.8	87.5	91.9	92.9	92.6	87.3	92.3	100.4	111.9	87.1
October	90.8	89.6	91.3	96.1	89.5	87.4	93.5	88.8	92.8	94.2	93.1	87.4	92.8	102.2	113.9	88.6
November	91.4	90.1	92.0	96.5	90.2	88.3	93.7	89.3	93.5	94.9	93.9	88.9	93.8	103.5	114.6	90.6
December	91.8	90.4	92.4	96.6	90.7	89.3	93.7	89.7	94.4	95.5	94.8	91.5	93.8	102.7	111.7	92.3
1981:																
January	92.8	91.4	93.3	96.8	92.0	91.0	93.9	90.8	95.6	96.3	95.4	94.0	94.6	103.4	111.1	94.4
February	93.6	92.0	94.1	96.5	93.1	92.5	94.4	91.7	96.1	96.5	95.2	96.7	94.6	104.2	107.6	100.1
March	94.7	92.6	95.3	97.2	94.6	94.6	92.4	92.4	97.1	97.1	96.0	100.6	95.1	103.8	106.0	101.1
April	95.7	93.5	96.4	97.2	96.1	96.4	95.5	93.1	98.3	97.8	97.6	103.1	96.2	104.2	105.6	102.4
May	96.0	94.0	96.6	97.4	96.2	96.2	96.2	93.8	98.7	98.2	97.9	103.3	97.0	103.8	103.8	103.7
June	96.5	94.6	97.0	98.0	96.6	96.5	96.6	94.4	99.0	98.7	98.4	102.4	97.4	104.9	105.8	103.8
July	96.7	94.8	97.1	99.0	96.4	96.3	96.4	95.0	99.2	99.4	98.7	100.9	97.8	105.0	105.6	104.0
August	96.8	95.3	97.1	98.9	96.4	96.3	96.7	95.4	99.7	100.0	98.8	101.6	97.9	104.0	102.2	103.1
September	97.2	95.9	97.5	98.7	97.1	97.0	97.2	96.1	99.7	100.1	98.8	101.2	97.9	102.7	102.2	103.1
October	97.6	96.5	97.8	98.5	97.5	97.1	98.1	96.9	99.8	100.0	99.2	101.1	98.1	101.2	100.5	101.8
November	97.9	97.0	98.0	98.1	98.0	97.6	98.7	97.5	99.9	100.2	99.4	101.1	98.2	99.7	98.2	101.3
December	98.3	97.6	98.4	98.1	98.5	98.3	98.9	98.1	100.0	100.2	99.6	101.3	98.7	98.8	96.1	101.7
1982:																
January	98.9	98.1	99.0	98.9	99.0	98.9	99.1	98.6	100.4	100.0	99.7	102.7	99.0	99.7	99.2	100.4
February	98.8	98.1	99.0	99.2	98.8	99.0	98.4	98.2	100.3	100.3	99.6	101.2	99.4	100.0	100.1	99.8
March	98.8	98.7	98.8	99.0	98.7	98.5	98.9	98.7	99.9	100.2	99.7	99.7	99.6	99.7	100.4	98.9
April	99.0	99.0	98.9	100.2	98.4	98.1	98.9	99.0	99.7	100.2	99.6	98.6	99.8	100.2	101.9	98.4
May	99.0	99.4	98.8	100.9	98.0	97.3	99.3	99.5	99.7	100.4	99.7	97.3	100.4	101.9	104.4	99.2
June	99.8	99.9	99.8	101.6	99.0	98.5	99.9	100.0	99.8	100.1	100.1	98.4	100.6	101.8	104.0	99.5
July	100.2	100.1	100.1	100.1	100.1	100.1	100.2	100.3	100.0	99.8	100.0	100.6	100.4	100.7	101.1	100.3
August	100.6	100.6	100.5	100.1	100.7	100.8	100.7	100.7	99.9	99.6	99.7	100.9	100.2	99.8	99.6	100.0
September	100.7	100.8	100.7	100.7	100.9	101.1	100.6	101.0	100.0	99.9	100.4	99.7	100.1	99.2	98.1	100.3
October	101.0	101.3	101.0	100.0	101.3	101.6	100.9	101.1	99.9	99.9	100.4	99.7	100.1	98.7	97.1	100.5
November	101.4	101.6	101.4	100.0	102.0	102.4	101.4	101.3	100.1	99.9	100.6	100.2	100.3	99.2	97.2	101.3
December	101.8	102.2	101.7	100.1	102.4	102.8	101.7	101.9	100.1	99.8	100.7	100.5	100.4	98.8	97.3	100.4

Producer Price Indexes—*Continued*

(By stage of processing—1982=100, seasonally adjusted)

Year and month	Finished goods								Intermediate materials, supplies, and components					Crude materials for further processing		
			Consumer goods													
					Consumer goods, except foods											
	Total	Total less food and energy	Total	Foods	Total	Nondurable goods, except food	Durable goods	Capital equipment	Total	Materials and components for manufacturing	Materials and components for construction	Processed fuels and lubricants	Supplies	Total	Foodstuffs and feedstuffs	Nonfood materials
1983:																
January	101.0	101.8	100.8	99.6	101.2	101.1	101.7	101.8	99.8	99.8	101.2	98.3	100.4	98.8	97.7	100.1
February	101.1	102.2	100.8	100.3	100.9	100.2	102.4	102.1	100.0	100.5	101.6	96.1	100.6	100.0	100.2	99.8
March	101.0	102.5	100.7	100.5	100.5	99.6	102.5	102.2	99.7	100.1	101.9	95.1	100.7	100.5	100.4	100.7
April	101.1	102.4	100.7	101.1	100.3	99.3	102.5	102.3	99.5	100.3	102.0	92.7	101.0	101.2	102.2	99.9
May	101.4	102.6	101.0	101.1	100.8	99.8	102.8	102.5	99.8	100.5	102.3	93.7	101.1	100.9	101.6	100.1
June	101.6	102.8	101.3	100.7	101.4	100.8	102.9	102.6	100.2	100.8	102.6	95.2	101.3	100.5	100.3	100.6
July	101.6	103.1	101.3	100.2	101.5	100.8	103.1	102.8	100.5	101.4	102.9	95.0	101.4	99.5	98.5	100.6
August	101.9	103.5	101.6	100.6	101.8	101.2	103.3	103.1	100.9	101.6	103.2	95.5	102.2	102.2	103.1	101.2
September	102.2	103.5	101.8	101.5	101.8	101.1	103.3	103.3	101.6	102.3	103.4	96.3	103.1	103.3	104.9	101.6
October	102.2	103.6	101.9	102.4	101.5	101.0	102.8	103.4	101.7	102.3	103.7	97.0	103.2	103.2	105.2	101.0
November	102.0	103.8	101.5	101.6	101.3	100.5	103.2	103.5	101.8	102.5	104.0	95.6	103.5	102.3	103.2	101.3
December	102.3	104.1	101.9	102.3	101.5	100.6	103.5	103.8	101.9	102.9	104.2	94.8	103.6	103.5	104.9	101.9
1984:																
January	103.0	104.5	102.7	104.8	101.6	100.6	103.7	104.1	102.1	103.2	104.2	94.6	103.8	104.6	106.8	102.2
February	103.4	104.7	103.1	105.3	101.9	101.0	103.9	104.5	102.5	103.5	104.8	95.5	103.8	103.8	104.5	103.0
March	103.8	105.2	103.6	106.2	102.2	101.1	104.5	104.6	103.0	104.2	105.3	95.8	104.1	105.7	108.4	102.8
April	103.9	105.3	103.5	105.2	102.5	101.6	104.4	105.3	103.2	104.4	105.4	96.2	104.2	105.2	107.0	103.1
May	103.8	105.3	103.5	104.7	102.7	102.0	104.4	105.1	103.4	104.5	105.3	97.2	104.3	104.5	105.3	103.6
June	103.8	105.5	103.4	104.5	102.6	101.9	104.4	105.2	103.6	104.6	105.4	97.5	104.3	103.3	103.3	103.2
July	104.0	105.7	103.6	105.9	102.3	101.3	104.6	105.5	103.4	104.5	105.7	96.4	104.1	104.0	105.2	102.8
August	103.8	105.9	103.3	105.8	102.0	100.7	104.7	105.6	103.2	104.4	106.0	95.0	104.5	103.3	104.0	102.4
September	103.8	106.2	103.2	105.5	101.9	100.4	105.0	105.9	103.1	104.1	106.2	94.9	104.2	102.8	103.5	102.1
October	103.6	105.9	103.1	105.2	101.9	100.9	104.2	105.6	103.2	104.0	106.4	95.2	104.2	101.5	101.5	101.4
November	104.0	106.2	103.4	105.6	102.2	101.1	104.7	105.8	103.3	104.2	106.5	95.2	104.0	101.9	103.3	100.4
December	104.0	106.3	103.5	105.6	102.3	101.0	105.0	105.6	103.2	104.1	106.7	94.7	104.1	101.4	102.9	99.8
1985:																
January	104.0	106.9	103.4	105.4	102.3	100.6	105.7	106.3	103.1	103.9	106.8	94.5	104.3	99.9	101.2	98.5
February	104.1	107.3	103.4	106.0	102.0	100.0	105.9	106.9	102.8	103.7	106.7	92.9	104.4	99.4	100.5	98.1
March	104.1	107.6	103.3	105.4	102.1	100.2	106.0	107.1	102.7	103.5	106.6	92.5	104.4	97.6	97.8	97.4
April	104.6	107.6	103.9	104.8	103.3	101.9	106.1	107.1	102.9	103.6	106.6	94.4	104.2	96.7	95.8	97.8
May	104.9	107.8	104.2	103.8	104.1	103.0	106.5	107.4	103.2	103.5	107.4	95.6	104.1	95.8	93.6	98.1
June	104.6	108.2	103.8	103.7	103.6	102.0	106.8	107.6	102.6	103.5	107.9	91.7	104.1	95.2	93.5	97.1
July	104.7	108.4	103.8	104.3	103.4	101.6	106.9	107.7	102.3	103.3	107.7	90.6	104.3	94.9	92.9	97.1
August	104.5	108.5	103.6	103.8	103.3	101.4	107.1	107.9	102.3	103.2	107.7	90.4	104.5	92.9	89.9	96.1
September	103.8	107.9	102.9	102.5	102.9	101.6	105.6	107.2	102.2	103.1	107.5	90.5	104.6	91.8	87.9	96.0
October	104.9	108.9	103.9	103.9	103.7	102.1	107.0	108.3	102.3	102.9	107.6	91.3	104.8	94.1	92.2	96.1
November	105.5	109.1	104.6	105.3	104.1	102.5	107.3	108.5	102.5	102.9	107.6	92.5	104.9	95.7	96.0	95.4
December	106.0	109.1	105.3	106.1	104.6	103.4	107.4	108.6	102.9	103.0	107.8	94.3	105.0	95.5	95.9	95.1
1986:																
January	105.5	109.3	104.6	105.8	103.8	102.2	107.1	108.6	102.4	102.6	107.8	92.0	105.2	94.2	93.3	95.2
February	104.1	109.5	102.8	104.8	101.6	98.8	107.4	108.7	101.2	102.3	107.9	85.5	105.3	90.5	91.8	89.2
March	102.8	109.6	101.0	104.8	99.1	94.9	107.6	108.9	99.9	102.3	107.8	77.6	105.5	88.2	91.0	85.1
April	102.3	110.1	100.3	105.0	97.9	92.7	108.4	109.2	98.9	101.9	108.2	73.0	105.5	85.6	89.0	82.0
May	102.8	110.2	101.0	106.1	98.4	93.4	108.4	109.3	98.7	101.7	108.2	71.7	105.4	86.5	91.2	81.5
June	103.1	110.5	101.2	106.2	98.7	93.8	108.6	109.6	98.6	101.7	108.1	71.2	105.6	86.2	90.9	81.1
July	102.3	110.7	100.2	107.6	96.5	90.3	108.9	109.7	98.0	101.9	108.0	66.7	105.6	86.4	93.5	78.3
August	102.7	110.8	100.7	109.5	96.4	90.2	108.9	109.8	98.0	102.1	108.0	65.7	105.6	86.7	96.3	75.8
September	102.9	110.7	100.9	109.0	97.0	91.3	108.4	109.7	98.5	102.3	108.2	68.1	105.8	86.6	94.9	77.1
October	103.5	111.8	101.5	109.8	97.4	90.7	110.7	110.6	98.3	102.4	108.2	66.8	105.6	87.4	95.9	77.7
November	103.4	112.0	101.4	109.5	97.4	90.6	110.9	110.8	98.3	102.5	108.3	66.7	105.8	87.6	96.0	78.2
December	103.6	112.1	101.5	109.3	97.7	91.0	111.1	110.9	98.5	102.5	108.1	67.5	105.9	86.9	94.4	78.3
1987:																
January	104.1	112.5	102.1	108.0	99.2	92.7	111.5	111.3	99.0	102.8	108.1	69.5	106.1	89.3	92.6	83.2
February	104.4	112.3	102.5	108.6	99.5	93.5	110.5	111.1	99.8	103.1	108.3	71.7	106.5	90.2	93.6	84.1
March	104.5	112.4	102.6	108.3	99.8	94.0	110.7	111.1	99.9	103.4	108.4	71.5	106.5	90.5	93.1	84.8
April	105.1	112.9	103.3	109.6	100.2	94.3	111.4	111.6	100.3	103.9	108.5	72.0	106.8	92.5	97.4	85.4
May	105.2	113.0	103.4	110.5	100.0	94.0	111.3	111.6	100.8	104.5	108.7	72.8	107.3	93.8	99.1	86.3
June	105.5	113.1	103.8	110.4	100.5	94.7	111.3	111.5	101.4	105.1	109.2	73.7	107.5	94.5	98.2	87.9
July	105.7	113.3	104.0	110.2	100.9	95.3	111.5	111.7	101.9	105.5	109.7	75.1	107.7	95.6	97.1	90.3
August	105.9	113.6	104.2	109.4	101.4	96.2	111.6	112.0	102.4	105.9	110.2	76.2	107.8	96.5	96.8	91.9
September	106.2	113.9	104.5	110.3	101.0	96.0	112.0	112.0	102.6	106.4	110.8	74.7	108.2	96.0	97.4	90.8
October	106.0	114.0	104.4	109.9	102.1	96.0	112.0	112.0	103.1	107.2	111.3	74.5	108.8	95.8	97.3	90.6
November	106.0	114.2	104.3	109.9	101.8	95.9	112.0	112.1	103.5	107.6	112.0	74.3	109.5	95.1	96.2	90.1
December	105.8	114.3	104.1	109.1	101.8	96.1	111.6	112.2	103.8	108.3	112.6	73.3	110.0	94.9	96.9	89.3
1988:																
January	106.4	115.0	104.6	110.7	101.6	95.8	112.4	112.8	104.1	109.4	113.7	70.6	110.5	94.2	98.5	87.3
February	106.3	115.3	104.4	109.9	101.8	95.9	112.6	113.0	104.4	109.9	113.9	70.7	110.7	95.2	100.7	87.5
March	106.6	115.6	104.7	110.3	102.0	96.1	112.7	113.2	104.8	110.5	114.3	70.4	111.1	94.1	99.8	86.3
April	107.0	115.9	105.2	110.4	102.7	97.1	112.8	113.5	105.5	111.5	114.8	70.8	111.8	95.4	100.9	87.8
May	107.2	116.2	105.4	110.7	102.8	97.1	113.2	113.8	106.2	112.2	115.2	71.4	112.2	95.8	101.3	88.1
June	107.5	116.6	105.7	111.7	102.8	97.0	113.3	114.0	107.4	112.9	115.7	74.1	113.7	97.0	106.3	87.0
July	108.4	117.2	106.6	113.0	103.5	97.9	113.9	114.4	108.3	114.1	116.4	74.1	115.1	96.7	109.1	85.2
August	108.8	117.7	107.1	113.7	103.8	97.9	114.6	114.9	108.5	114.5	116.7	73.6	115.1	97.0	110.5	84.5
September	109.0	118.1	107.3	115.3	103.4	97.3	114.8	115.2	108.7	115.0	117.1	72.4	115.6	97.0	113.6	83.0
October	109.2	118.4	107.5	114.9	103.8	97.8	115.0	115.5	108.6	115.4	117.7	69.3	116.0	96.6	113.6	82.0
November	109.6	118.7	107.9	115.1	104.3	98.5	115.1	115.7	108.8	116.2	118.3	68.1	116.2	95.2	109.7	82.1
December	110.0	119.2	108.3	115.7	104.7	98.8	115.5	116.1	109.4	117.0	118.9	69.2	116.3	98.1	111.3	85.6

Producer Price Indexes—*Continued*

(By stage of processing—1982=100, seasonally adjusted)

Year and month	Finished goods — Total	Total less food and energy	Consumer goods — Total	Foods	Consumer goods, except foods — Total	Nondurable goods, except food	Durable goods	Capital equipment	Intermediate materials, supplies, and components — Total	Materials and components for manufacturing	Materials and components for construction	Processed fuels and lubricants	Supplies	Crude materials for further processing — Total	Foodstuffs and feedstuffs	Nonfood materials
1989:																
January	111.1	119.9	109.5	116.9	105.9	100.2	116.3	116.9	110.8	117.8	119.5	72.6	117.2	102.0	114.1	90.1
February	111.9	120.5	110.5	117.6	106.9	101.4	116.7	117.3	111.3	118.3	120.0	73.6	117.5	101.7	112.2	90.7
March	112.3	120.7	110.9	118.2	107.4	102.1	116.6	117.5	111.9	118.6	120.4	75.2	118.1	102.9	113.2	92.0
April	113.1	120.8	111.9	117.8	109.0	104.5	116.5	117.6	112.5	118.7	120.7	78.4	118.1	104.1	111.2	95.1
May	114.0	121.6	112.9	118.3	110.3	105.9	117.2	118.3	112.6	118.8	121.1	78.5	118.1	104.5	110.9	95.9
June	114.0	122.2	112.7	118.0	110.1	105.5	117.7	118.9	112.5	118.5	121.4	78.2	118.0	103.2	109.4	94.7
July	113.8	122.1	112.4	118.4	109.5	104.8	117.2	118.9	112.2	118.2	121.5	77.2	118.3	103.5	108.9	95.5
August	113.4	122.7	111.7	118.7	108.3	102.9	117.9	119.3	111.8	117.9	121.7	75.5	118.3	101.2	110.1	91.2
September	114.0	123.1	112.5	118.7	109.4	104.1	118.7	119.7	112.1	117.8	122.0	76.4	118.5	102.5	109.6	93.5
October	114.6	123.5	113.1	119.9	109.8	104.6	118.6	120.0	112.2	117.9	122.5	76.8	118.4	102.7	109.3	94.0
November	114.8	123.9	113.2	120.5	109.6	104.4	118.7	120.4	112.0	117.8	122.3	76.1	118.4	103.5	112.2	93.6
December	115.5	124.2	114.1	121.8	110.3	105.2	119.1	120.6	112.2	117.5	122.1	78.0	118.4	105.1	114.6	94.5
1990:																
January	117.7	124.5	116.9	124.2	113.3	109.5	118.7	121.0	113.7	117.7	121.9	85.9	118.7	106.7	114.6	97.0
February	117.6	124.9	116.7	124.9	112.7	108.5	119.0	121.4	112.8	117.5	121.9	81.5	118.4	106.8	114.6	97.2
March	117.5	125.3	116.3	124.5	112.4	108.0	119.1	121.8	112.9	117.8	122.4	80.4	118.6	105.1	114.1	94.8
April	117.4	125.5	116.1	123.3	112.6	108.2	119.4	122.1	113.1	118.1	122.9	80.3	118.8	102.7	114.3	91.1
May	117.5	126.0	116.3	123.8	112.5	108.1	119.5	122.1	113.1	118.3	123.0	79.0	119.4	103.1	113.4	92.3
June	117.6	126.4	116.3	123.6	112.8	108.0	120.5	122.5	112.9	118.3	122.7	78.4	119.2	100.6	113.5	88.2
July	117.9	126.6	116.6	124.5	112.7	107.9	120.7	122.9	112.8	118.4	122.9	76.9	119.6	101.0	114.4	88.3
August	119.2	127.1	118.2	124.7	115.0	111.0	120.8	123.3	114.0	118.6	123.0	83.5	119.4	110.5	113.1	103.9
September	120.7	127.7	120.0	124.3	117.9	114.5	121.9	123.8	115.8	119.3	123.4	90.9	119.8	115.8	111.7	113.1
October	121.9	128.0	121.5	124.7	120.0	117.6	121.5	124.1	117.4	120.0	123.5	97.7	120.1	125.8	112.3	128.3
November	122.6	128.4	122.3	125.4	120.7	118.4	122.0	124.5	117.7	120.2	123.6	98.2	120.3	117.8	111.3	116.4
December	122.0	128.6	121.4	124.7	119.8	117.0	122.4	124.8	116.9	119.9	123.7	94.3	120.5	110.8	109.5	106.6
1991:																
January	122.6	129.5	122.0	125.0	120.5	117.8	123.0	125.6	116.9	119.9	124.0	93.7	120.9	113.3	108.3	110.9
February	121.8	129.8	120.8	124.7	118.9	115.5	123.4	125.8	115.9	119.5	123.8	89.8	121.1	104.1	107.3	98.0
March	121.3	130.1	120.2	125.0	117.9	114.0	123.7	126.0	114.7	118.8	123.9	85.1	121.2	100.5	108.0	92.3
April	121.3	130.4	120.2	125.2	117.8	114.0	123.7	126.1	114.2	118.5	124.2	83.7	121.3	100.2	107.7	92.0
May	121.6	130.6	120.4	125.3	118.1	114.5	123.4	126.5	114.1	118.0	124.4	84.0	121.3	100.9	105.8	94.0
June	121.4	130.7	120.1	124.9	117.8	114.1	123.4	126.6	113.9	117.8	125.1	83.4	121.4	99.2	105.9	91.3
July	121.1	131.0	119.6	124.3	117.4	113.5	123.4	126.7	113.6	117.4	125.3	82.5	121.2	99.4	104.7	92.3
August	121.3	131.3	119.9	123.0	118.3	114.7	123.6	126.8	113.8	117.3	124.7	83.7	121.6	99.1	102.7	93.0
September	121.5	131.8	120.1	122.8	118.7	115.0	124.2	127.2	114.0	117.3	124.8	84.7	121.7	98.4	104.1	91.2
October	121.9	132.3	120.5	123.1	119.2	115.4	124.9	127.6	114.0	117.5	124.6	84.1	121.6	100.8	104.9	94.3
November	122.4	132.5	121.0	123.4	119.8	116.2	124.9	127.8	114.1	117.4	124.5	84.7	121.8	100.7	103.9	94.7
December	122.3	132.6	120.8	122.8	119.8	116.1	125.0	128.0	114.0	117.4	124.6	84.7	121.8	98.2	102.6	91.6
1992:																
January	122.0	133.0	120.4	122.8	119.1	115.2	125.2	128.2	113.4	117.2	124.9	81.5	122.0	97.2	104.5	88.9
February	122.3	133.1	120.8	123.5	119.4	115.7	124.9	128.3	113.8	117.4	125.8	82.6	122.0	98.6	106.1	90.1
March	122.4	133.4	120.8	123.1	119.6	115.7	125.4	128.6	113.9	117.4	126.5	82.0	122.3	97.1	105.4	88.1
April	122.5	133.8	120.9	122.6	119.9	116.2	125.6	129.0	114.1	117.6	126.6	82.5	122.4	98.1	104.1	90.5
May	122.9	134.3	121.4	122.5	120.7	117.2	125.7	129.0	115.1	118.2	126.6	86.4	122.7	101.6	106.4	94.7
June	123.4	134.1	121.9	122.9	121.3	118.1	125.9	129.0	115.1	118.2	126.3	86.4	122.7	101.6	105.0	95.6
July	123.3	134.3	121.9	122.7	121.3	118.0	125.8	129.1	115.2	118.2	126.3	86.6	122.7	101.6	105.0	95.6
August	123.4	134.3	121.9	123.3	121.1	117.6	126.0	129.4	115.1	118.3	126.4	86.0	122.8	100.7	103.9	94.7
September	123.7	134.6	122.3	123.5	121.5	118.3	125.8	129.4	115.3	118.4	126.9	86.2	123.1	102.8	103.9	98.0
October	124.2	134.9	122.8	123.9	122.0	119.0	126.0	129.7	115.3	118.2	126.9	86.6	123.3	102.8	105.8	96.9
November	124.1	135.1	122.6	123.8	121.9	118.6	126.3	129.9	115.1	118.1	127.1	85.3	123.4	102.5	104.3	97.4
December	124.2	135.2	122.7	124.7	121.7	118.3	126.4	130.1	115.1	118.1	127.9	84.8	123.6	101.3	105.4	94.8
1993:																
January	124.4	135.6	122.9	124.8	121.9	118.5	126.6	130.4	115.4	118.4	129.1	84.6	124.1	101.7	106.2	95.0
February	124.7	135.9	123.2	124.7	122.3	118.9	127.2	130.7	115.9	118.7	130.8	85.2	124.2	101.2	105.8	94.5
March	125.0	136.1	123.4	124.5	122.7	119.4	127.3	130.9	116.3	118.8	132.4	86.0	124.2	101.7	106.5	94.7
April	125.7	136.5	124.3	126.5	123.1	119.8	127.9	131.1	116.6	119.0	132.6	86.3	124.7	103.4	109.4	95.3
May	125.7	136.6	124.4	126.8	123.1	119.8	127.9	131.2	116.3	118.8	131.9	85.7	124.6	105.6	110.6	98.4
June	125.2	136.4	123.7	125.3	122.7	119.1	128.0	131.1	116.3	118.8	131.3	86.4	124.7	103.8	106.5	98.0
July	125.1	136.6	123.4	125.0	122.5	118.7	128.3	131.5	116.3	118.9	131.1	85.3	125.2	101.6	107.8	93.7
August	123.9	134.9	121.9	125.0	120.4	115.6	128.6	131.6	116.2	119.0	131.6	84.0	125.6	100.8	108.1	92.2
September	124.1	134.9	122.1	125.5	120.4	115.6	128.5	131.7	116.3	119.0	132.4	84.3	125.5	101.2	108.0	93.0
October	124.2	135.0	122.3	125.4	120.7	116.1	128.2	131.8	116.4	119.0	132.6	84.8	125.6	103.7	107.2	97.4
November	124.4	135.3	122.3	126.8	120.3	115.2	128.9	132.2	116.5	119.2	133.4	83.7	125.8	103.0	111.3	93.7
December	124.4	135.7	122.3	127.5	119.9	114.5	129.2	132.4	116.2	119.3	134.3	81.0	126.2	101.7	113.3	90.5
1994:																
January	124.8	136.3	122.6	127.4	120.4	115.0	129.9	132.9	116.5	119.5	135.1	81.1	126.4	103.8	113.6	93.6
February	125.0	136.3	122.9	126.9	121.0	115.9	129.9	133.1	116.9	119.7	135.1	83.1	126.5	102.1	114.3	90.5
March	125.1	136.4	122.9	127.3	120.9	115.6	130.1	133.3	117.1	120.0	135.5	83.0	126.5	103.8	114.0	93.3
April	125.1	136.6	122.9	127.2	120.9	115.4	130.3	133.7	117.1	120.3	135.0	82.3	126.5	103.8	113.4	93.8
May	125.1	137.0	122.7	126.5	120.8	115.1	130.9	134.1	117.2	120.7	135.2	81.5	126.6	102.2	108.4	94.3
June	125.2	137.2	122.8	126.0	121.2	115.6	131.1	134.3	117.8	121.2	136.2	82.4	126.9	102.7	106.8	96.1
July	125.7	137.3	123.4	126.3	121.9	116.5	131.4	134.4	118.3	121.7	136.2	84.0	126.9	101.7	102.6	97.2
August	126.2	137.6	124.0	126.1	122.9	117.7	131.8	134.6	119.1	122.5	136.7	85.3	126.9	101.6	100.7	98.2
September	125.9	137.7	123.5	126.0	122.2	116.7	131.7	134.9	119.6	123.7	137.5	84.0	127.2	99.7	100.7	95.1
October	125.5	137.4	123.1	126.0	121.7	116.2	131.2	134.4	120.1	124.5	138.1	82.9	127.6	98.6	99.1	94.5
November	126.1	137.6	123.9	126.8	122.4	117.2	131.4	134.5	121.0	125.6	139.2	83.9	128.0	99.8	101.1	95.0
December	126.6	137.9	124.4	128.7	122.4	117.1	131.7	134.9	121.5	126.3	139.5	83.7	128.4	101.1	102.6	96.3

Money Stock and Selected Components

(Averages of daily figures; billions of dollars, seasonally adjusted)

Year and month	Money stock measures [1]			Selected components					
	M1	M2	M3	Currency	Demand deposits	Other checkable deposits	Savings deposits	Small time deposits	Large time deposits
1971:									
January	215.5	633.0	685.5	48.9	165.6	0.1	263.6	153.8	47.1
February	217.4	641.0	695.8	49.2	167.1	0.2	266.1	157.5	49.4
March	218.8	649.9	706.5	49.4	168.2	0.2	269.4	161.7	51.0
April	220.0	658.4	713.7	49.7	169.1	0.2	272.6	165.8	48.9
May	222.0	666.7	723.3	50.0	170.9	0.2	275.7	169.0	49.8
June	223.5	673.0	730.1	50.4	171.9	0.2	278.2	171.3	51.0
July	224.9	679.6	738.3	50.9	172.8	0.2	280.8	174.0	52.3
August	225.6	685.5	744.0	51.2	173.2	0.2	283.4	176.6	52.0
September	226.5	692.5	751.7	51.4	173.8	0.2	286.0	180.0	52.4
October	227.2	698.4	760.2	51.6	174.3	0.2	288.2	183.0	54.6
November	227.8	704.6	768.3	51.8	174.7	0.2	290.3	186.6	55.9
December	228.3	710.3	776.0	52.0	175.1	0.2	292.2	189.8	57.6
1972:									
January	230.1	717.7	783.8	52.3	176.6	0.2	294.7	192.9	58.3
February	232.3	725.7	792.9	52.6	178.4	0.2	297.2	196.2	59.2
March	234.3	733.5	800.6	53.0	180.1	0.2	299.5	199.8	58.8
April	235.6	738.4	807.9	53.1	181.2	0.2	301.1	201.7	60.5
May	235.9	743.3	816.1	53.4	181.2	0.2	302.7	204.8	63.9
June	236.6	749.7	824.5	53.7	181.6	0.2	304.9	208.1	65.4
July	238.8	759.5	835.5	54.0	183.5	0.2	307.7	213.0	66.0
August	240.9	768.7	846.6	54.4	185.2	0.2	311.1	216.6	67.5
September	243.2	778.4	856.4	54.8	187.0	0.2	314.3	221.0	68.4
October	245.0	786.9	865.8	55.3	188.4	0.2	316.6	225.3	69.2
November	246.4	793.9	875.8	55.7	189.3	0.2	319.2	228.4	71.7
December	249.2	802.3	885.9	56.2	191.6	0.2	321.4	231.7	73.3
1973:									
January	251.5	810.3	896.3	56.6	193.4	0.2	322.7	236.2	74.3
February	252.2	814.1	906.1	56.9	193.8	0.3	323.0	238.9	79.3
March	251.7	815.3	915.0	57.2	193.0	0.3	323.6	240.1	86.9
April	252.7	819.7	922.4	57.8	193.4	0.3	323.8	243.1	90.2
May	254.9	826.8	932.2	58.1	195.2	0.3	325.1	246.8	92.7
June	256.7	833.2	940.7	58.5	196.6	0.3	326.6	250.0	93.4
July	257.5	836.5	950.2	58.8	197.1	0.3	327.4	251.6	98.0
August	257.8	838.8	959.0	59.1	197.0	0.3	325.8	255.1	104.0
September	257.9	839.3	965.8	59.6	196.7	0.3	325.1	256.4	109.0
October	259.0	842.6	972.0	59.9	197.5	0.3	325.5	258.1	110.4
November	261.0	848.9	977.4	60.3	199.0	0.3	325.9	262.0	110.2
December	262.9	855.5	985.0	60.8	200.3	0.3	326.7	265.8	111.0
1974:									
January	263.8	859.7	993.9	61.3	200.7	0.3	327.5	268.3	115.1
February	265.3	864.2	1 002.4	61.8	201.7	0.3	327.8	271.0	118.4
March	266.7	870.1	1 010.7	62.3	202.5	0.4	328.8	274.6	119.5
April	267.2	872.9	1 020.8	63.0	202.3	0.4	329.6	276.1	126.8
May	267.6	874.6	1 029.2	63.4	202.3	0.4	329.7	277.1	132.7
June	268.4	877.8	1 037.7	63.7	202.9	0.4	330.4	278.7	136.8
July	269.3	881.4	1 043.9	64.1	203.3	0.4	331.7	280.0	139.5
August	270.1	884.2	1 048.7	64.7	203.5	0.4	332.0	281.4	140.9
September	271.1	888.2	1 053.1	65.2	203.8	0.4	332.7	283.5	141.4
October	272.4	893.6	1 058.8	65.8	204.4	0.4	334.3	285.8	142.2
November	273.7	898.9	1 064.0	66.5	205.1	0.4	336.2	287.4	141.7
December	274.2	902.4	1 070.2	67.0	205.1	0.4	338.6	287.9	144.7
1975:									
January	273.9	906.6	1 076.3	67.4	204.3	0.5	341.0	289.5	147.0
February	275.0	914.4	1 082.9	67.8	204.9	0.5	343.9	293.0	145.7
March	276.4	925.4	1 090.2	68.4	205.6	0.6	348.4	297.9	142.4
April	276.2	935.5	1 096.2	68.5	205.2	0.6	353.5	302.9	137.9
May	279.2	948.3	1 106.8	69.1	207.6	0.6	358.8	307.2	135.8
June	282.4	963.4	1 118.8	70.0	209.8	0.7	365.6	312.3	133.1
July	283.7	975.5	1 128.6	70.5	210.5	0.7	370.6	318.2	130.2
August	284.2	983.5	1 135.1	71.0	210.5	0.7	374.2	322.3	128.6
September	285.7	991.9	1 146.0	71.2	211.7	0.7	377.7	325.6	129.0
October	285.4	998.3	1 153.9	71.7	210.8	0.8	380.6	329.4	130.3
November	286.8	1 007.4	1 164.0	72.3	211.5	0.8	384.6	333.1	131.2
December	287.1	1 016.6	1 171.9	72.8	211.3	0.9	388.8	337.8	129.7
1976:									
January	288.4	1 027.1	1 182.5	73.2	212.0	1.0	394.3	341.6	127.2
February	290.8	1 040.9	1 193.9	73.9	213.5	1.1	402.7	344.8	124.6
March	292.7	1 050.5	1 204.9	74.7	214.5	1.2	408.5	346.6	125.2
April	294.7	1 061.3	1 217.2	75.5	215.5	1.4	413.8	350.3	125.0
May	295.9	1 072.6	1 228.5	76.1	215.9	1.5	418.4	355.8	122.2
June	296.2	1 078.1	1 236.3	76.6	215.6	1.7	420.0	359.4	124.9
July	297.2	1 086.9	1 246.1	77.1	215.9	1.8	423.4	363.7	125.5
August	299.0	1 099.2	1 259.4	77.6	216.9	2.0	428.5	369.3	122.5
September	299.7	1 111.4	1 268.4	78.1	216.8	2.2	433.5	375.8	120.7
October	302.0	1 125.6	1 281.1	78.6	218.6	2.3	439.8	381.4	118.8
November	303.6	1 138.9	1 294.9	79.1	219.4	2.5	447.2	385.7	117.8
December	306.2	1 152.6	1 312.3	79.5	221.5	2.7	453.2	390.7	118.1

1. See Notes for definitions of M1, M2, and M3.

Money Stock and Selected Components—*Continued*

(Averages of daily figures; billions of dollars, seasonally adjusted)

Year and month	Money stock measures [1]			Selected components					
	M1	M2	M3	Currency	Demand deposits	Other checkable deposits	Savings deposits	Small time deposits	Large time deposits
1977:									
January	308.3	1 165.8	1 323.4	80.2	222.6	2.8	459.1	396.1	117.6
February	311.5	1 178.2	1 336.2	80.8	225.1	3.0	463.3	401.0	118.3
March	313.9	1 189.2	1 349.0	81.3	226.8	3.1	466.3	406.6	118.5
April	316.0	1 200.3	1 361.2	82.1	228.1	3.1	470.0	411.9	118.8
May	317.2	1 209.7	1 374.9	82.5	228.7	3.2	472.7	417.6	120.3
June	318.7	1 218.4	1 388.0	83.1	229.6	3.3	474.5	423.0	123.4
July	320.2	1 227.5	1 400.8	83.9	230.0	3.5	477.6	427.5	126.1
August	322.3	1 237.8	1 415.6	84.5	231.4	3.6	481.8	431.4	129.5
September	324.5	1 247.0	1 428.4	85.2	232.7	3.7	484.9	435.3	132.2
October	326.4	1 254.7	1 442.3	85.9	233.8	3.9	487.2	438.7	136.5
November	328.6	1 263.2	1 457.8	86.6	235.1	4.0	490.5	441.5	140.9
December	330.9	1 271.1	1 472.7	87.4	236.4	4.2	492.2	445.5	145.2
1978:									
January	334.4	1 280.5	1 487.2	88.0	239.1	4.3	494.6	448.8	149.1
February	335.3	1 286.3	1 498.9	88.7	239.1	4.4	496.4	451.8	153.2
March	337.0	1 293.0	1 513.8	89.4	240.0	4.6	497.5	455.5	158.6
April	339.9	1 301.2	1 529.3	90.0	242.2	4.7	498.6	459.4	164.8
May	344.9	1 311.4	1 545.2	90.8	246.1	4.9	499.7	463.3	170.8
June	346.8	1 319.3	1 556.1	91.5	247.3	4.9	498.4	470.3	173.7
July	347.6	1 325.0	1 567.8	92.0	247.5	5.0	494.2	479.2	177.1
August	349.7	1 334.4	1 583.9	92.7	248.6	5.1	494.4	486.0	180.8
September	352.3	1 346.0	1 597.8	93.6	250.3	5.2	495.1	493.7	182.6
October	353.4	1 353.3	1 612.0	94.4	250.4	5.3	493.4	501.2	184.5
November	355.4	1 360.1	1 631.2	95.2	250.2	6.7	488.8	510.0	191.8
December	357.3	1 366.9	1 646.5	96.0	249.5	8.5	481.9	520.9	195.6
1979:									
January	358.6	1 372.5	1 657.8	96.8	248.5	10.0	472.6	533.3	198.6
February	359.9	1 378.8	1 670.2	97.4	248.1	11.1	466.6	542.9	201.0
March	362.5	1 388.9	1 684.2	98.0	248.8	12.3	463.2	552.3	201.7
April	368.0	1 403.3	1 701.9	98.8	252.4	13.4	459.2	563.3	201.3
May	369.6	1 411.3	1 712.1	99.5	252.7	14.0	455.8	571.2	201.0
June	373.3	1 424.0	1 729.0	100.3	254.7	14.9	456.2	577.7	199.4
July	377.2	1 435.7	1 744.2	101.2	257.0	15.7	456.3	582.9	201.0
August	378.8	1 447.6	1 762.5	102.1	257.1	16.1	457.1	589.8	204.0
September	379.3	1 455.2	1 783.8	103.1	256.2	16.4	452.6	598.8	210.6
October	380.9	1 461.5	1 797.7	103.9	256.9	16.5	441.6	611.1	217.4
November	380.8	1 467.0	1 800.1	104.3	256.5	16.5	429.2	625.7	220.3
December	381.8	1 474.7	1 810.1	104.8	256.6	16.8	423.8	634.2	223.1
1980:									
January	385.8	1 483.8	1 824.2	106.0	258.9	17.4	417.2	641.5	225.7
February	389.7	1 495.5	1 842.7	106.7	261.7	18.0	410.5	650.6	229.5
March	388.1	1 500.8	1 851.1	107.5	258.9	18.5	400.1	665.5	233.5
April	383.4	1 503.5	1 855.5	107.7	253.4	19.0	386.4	686.3	238.6
May	384.6	1 513.4	1 868.1	108.7	253.4	19.2	382.2	696.0	239.5
June	389.5	1 530.8	1 886.0	109.6	255.3	20.6	390.8	694.9	233.6
July	394.9	1 547.6	1 905.3	110.5	257.8	22.0	402.7	691.1	228.8
August	400.1	1 563.5	1 923.1	111.6	260.6	23.2	414.6	688.4	229.0
September	405.4	1 575.7	1 936.9	112.5	264.2	24.5	419.0	690.5	232.9
October	409.1	1 586.0	1 954.9	113.4	266.1	25.7	419.8	695.7	238.3
November	410.4	1 596.5	1 976.2	114.8	264.2	27.9	414.7	709.1	247.1
December	408.1	1 600.4	1 996.3	115.3	261.2	28.1	400.2	728.5	260.2
1981:									
January	410.8	1 607.7	2 021.3	115.3	248.2	43.8	382.2	748.7	271.7
February	414.4	1 619.7	2 040.3	116.2	241.3	53.3	375.0	758.0	276.4
March	418.7	1 637.7	2 059.2	117.0	238.8	59.3	372.0	765.6	275.2
April	427.1	1 661.0	2 088.1	117.9	239.5	66.0	372.5	767.5	274.3
May	424.4	1 665.5	2 103.5	118.3	236.3	66.0	367.0	775.5	281.2
June	425.5	1 672.0	2 120.2	118.7	234.6	67.9	360.9	784.3	286.0
July	427.9	1 684.2	2 140.3	119.5	233.7	69.8	360.0	786.2	290.5
August	427.8	1 696.6	2 159.6	119.9	232.2	70.7	354.0	796.3	295.5
September	427.5	1 707.8	2 181.0	120.1	230.5	72.3	348.2	804.4	298.7
October	428.5	1 723.2	2 203.7	120.5	230.4	73.4	343.6	815.9	299.0
November	430.9	1 736.9	2 225.4	121.4	229.8	76.0	343.1	820.6	300.3
December	436.2	1 756.1	2 254.9	122.5	231.4	78.7	343.9	823.1	303.9
1982:									
January	442.1	1 771.2	2 278.6	123.2	233.6	81.8	346.5	824.7	307.1
February	441.5	1 775.6	2 287.0	123.9	231.3	82.6	345.3	833.1	312.6
March	442.4	1 787.7	2 305.6	124.5	229.8	84.4	344.2	844.0	316.1
April	446.8	1 806.2	2 333.4	125.5	229.9	87.6	344.3	853.2	320.3
May	446.5	1 816.8	2 344.8	126.7	228.8	87.1	344.0	860.5	319.4
June	447.9	1 827.9	2 362.1	127.4	227.6	88.3	343.5	865.4	320.8
July	449.1	1 836.9	2 374.7	128.1	226.8	88.9	342.0	873.9	323.9
August	452.5	1 851.9	2 399.7	129.0	227.3	91.0	344.2	876.3	325.7
September	457.5	1 865.4	2 415.5	129.9	229.0	93.9	346.7	877.6	325.4
October	464.6	1 876.2	2 436.1	130.8	230.8	98.6	355.3	870.4	329.0
November	471.1	1 889.4	2 449.5	131.6	233.2	102.5	362.6	866.8	330.6
December	474.3	1 911.2	2 460.9	132.5	234.1	104.1	400.1	850.9	324.9

1. See Notes for definitions of M1, M2, and M3.

Money Stock and Selected Components—*Continued*
(Averages of daily figures; billions of dollars, seasonally adjusted)

Year and month	Money stock measures [1]			Selected components					
	M1	M2	M3	Currency	Demand deposits	Other checkable deposits	Savings deposits	Small time deposits	Large time deposits
1983:									
January	476.7	1 964.3	2 490.9	133.6	233.6	106.0	521.5	794.9	302.4
February	483.8	2 001.8	2 519.2	135.0	234.1	111.0	601.8	755.0	289.9
March	490.2	2 020.1	2 536.0	136.4	235.5	114.4	639.2	736.6	285.3
April	492.8	2 034.0	2 555.8	137.4	234.5	116.9	660.7	731.9	287.0
May	499.8	2 048.1	2 570.7	138.7	236.9	120.0	678.1	726.6	284.4
June	504.3	2 059.0	2 588.1	139.6	237.7	122.3	687.1	726.0	288.2
July	509.0	2 070.9	2 598.7	140.5	238.3	124.6	688.9	733.5	289.0
August	511.6	2 079.9	2 612.8	141.4	238.9	125.8	687.6	742.0	294.5
September	513.4	2 088.6	2 629.1	142.7	238.7	126.9	687.3	750.3	300.0
October	517.2	2 104.1	2 648.2	144.1	238.8	129.7	686.3	763.2	302.4
November	518.5	2 116.8	2 675.9	145.3	238.2	130.8	684.9	776.0	309.4
December	520.8	2 127.8	2 699.2	146.2	238.5	132.1	684.9	784.0	316.5
1984:									
January	524.4	2 142.5	2 716.8	147.4	240.2	132.7	685.5	793.2	322.1
February	527.0	2 162.8	2 744.9	148.0	240.5	134.2	690.8	802.2	327.0
March	530.8	2 179.7	2 773.1	149.1	241.0	136.3	696.7	807.7	333.7
April	534.0	2 196.1	2 802.7	150.1	242.3	137.2	702.1	813.8	341.4
May	536.6	2 209.3	2 830.5	150.7	241.8	139.4	701.9	822.0	353.5
June	540.5	2 220.7	2 852.4	151.9	242.6	140.8	698.1	832.1	364.9
July	542.1	2 230.0	2 874.7	152.8	242.0	141.2	693.1	843.1	375.7
August	542.4	2 236.9	2 888.9	153.5	241.4	141.3	686.3	857.6	381.4
September	543.9	2 250.2	2 907.7	154.3	241.3	142.7	685.5	868.8	385.5
October	543.9	2 264.4	2 933.6	154.7	240.9	143.4	687.1	878.1	395.4
November	547.3	2 286.7	2 961.4	155.5	242.3	145.1	694.4	884.4	398.7
December	551.2	2 311.7	2 992.8	156.1	243.4	147.4	704.7	888.8	403.2
1985:									
January	555.7	2 336.7	3 018.7	156.9	244.9	149.5	720.2	887.9	402.4
February	562.5	2 358.4	3 042.5	157.9	247.4	152.7	736.1	884.7	403.4
March	565.7	2 370.7	3 058.1	158.5	247.6	155.1	744.3	883.9	407.1
April	569.5	2 380.1	3 063.6	159.4	248.6	156.9	748.4	886.1	410.9
May	575.1	2 395.2	3 080.7	160.5	251.0	158.6	755.8	890.0	410.9
June	583.2	2 419.3	3 106.6	161.7	253.2	162.4	767.9	891.6	408.3
July	590.8	2 436.9	3 116.7	162.8	255.5	165.5	780.1	888.7	404.5
August	598.1	2 451.4	3 134.8	164.3	257.6	169.1	791.6	884.1	405.8
September	604.5	2 463.2	3 152.9	165.2	261.2	171.8	798.7	882.3	410.7
October	607.9	2 473.9	3 169.6	166.2	261.5	174.6	806.6	881.8	414.4
November	611.8	2 483.0	3 184.5	167.1	262.0	177.7	812.7	881.9	418.3
December	619.4	2 497.4	3 209.8	167.9	266.9	179.8	815.2	885.7	422.4
1986:									
January	620.4	2 506.8	3 233.2	168.5	265.3	181.8	817.2	889.6	431.5
February	624.1	2 517.3	3 252.1	169.5	265.7	183.9	819.7	891.7	435.1
March	632.8	2 537.8	3 278.4	170.8	269.8	186.9	824.1	895.0	434.5
April	640.3	2 562.6	3 308.6	171.5	272.8	190.8	835.1	895.6	433.9
May	652.0	2 590.7	3 333.3	172.8	277.3	196.5	850.5	891.8	430.0
June	661.5	2 611.7	3 355.7	173.7	279.9	201.4	863.2	887.0	428.2
July	672.2	2 634.6	3 387.0	174.8	283.4	206.3	875.2	884.8	429.6
August	680.8	2 654.8	3 412.1	176.0	285.0	212.0	889.4	881.2	430.1
September	688.5	2 675.3	3 439.4	177.0	287.6	216.9	903.9	877.5	429.1
October	695.3	2 694.4	3 458.1	178.4	288.0	222.7	919.6	869.9	424.1
November	705.2	2 707.6	3 469.7	179.5	291.4	228.8	931.1	861.8	421.2
December	724.3	2 734.0	3 501.2	180.7	302.8	235.6	940.9	858.4	420.2
1987:									
January	729.3	2 749.2	3 526.2	182.1	299.3	242.6	952.1	856.0	423.0
February	729.8	2 752.9	3 535.4	183.5	295.8	245.0	959.1	852.2	424.4
March	733.0	2 759.0	3 543.6	184.2	295.0	248.0	964.5	850.1	426.6
April	743.4	2 773.2	3 564.4	185.6	299.2	252.9	970.2	847.9	428.9
May	746.0	2 779.2	3 581.3	186.6	298.8	254.6	972.8	847.4	435.0
June	743.7	2 781.2	3 596.2	187.8	294.2	254.8	969.8	854.0	440.1
July	745.0	2 787.3	3 603.8	188.9	292.3	255.6	966.0	862.1	441.7
August	747.0	2 796.4	3 626.0	190.2	290.9	257.5	962.9	870.0	444.6
September	748.7	2 806.8	3 649.5	191.5	290.3	259.3	960.4	877.7	448.2
October	756.5	2 821.1	3 672.1	193.3	295.3	261.3	953.0	889.6	454.7
November	752.8	2 825.0	3 684.3	195.5	291.1	260.3	941.4	908.1	462.4
December	749.7	2 832.8	3 692.0	196.9	287.6	259.5	937.4	921.0	467.0
1988:									
January	755.6	2 853.8	3 715.2	198.0	289.0	262.6	936.5	933.1	465.9
February	757.1	2 876.8	3 742.6	199.1	287.3	264.5	938.0	949.5	470.1
March	761.2	2 897.3	3 767.3	200.4	287.8	266.7	941.2	960.9	474.1
April	767.6	2 917.2	3 795.3	202.0	289.3	270.1	945.0	968.6	476.0
May	771.7	2 932.9	3 821.5	203.4	288.5	273.3	949.7	974.7	478.7
June	779.1	2 946.0	3 842.5	204.8	291.0	275.9	952.6	979.5	484.3
July	783.4	2 956.8	3 860.4	206.2	289.7	278.9	952.0	985.4	491.7
August	785.1	2 961.5	3 872.5	207.4	290.1	279.0	946.2	993.6	498.3
September	784.8	2 966.0	3 883.7	208.8	289.1	279.0	938.4	1 005.9	506.4
October	783.6	2 974.0	3 899.4	209.9	287.3	279.4	933.4	1 019.1	511.9
November	784.5	2 988.0	3 918.7	211.0	287.0	280.1	931.9	1 028.2	513.5
December	786.3	2 995.8	3 935.2	212.2	287.0	280.9	926.3	1 037.1	518.3

1. See Notes for definitions of M1, M2, and M3.

Money Stock and Selected Components—*Continued*

(Averages of daily figures; billions of dollars, seasonally adjusted)

Year and month	Money stock measures [1]			Selected components					
	M1	M2	M3	Currency	Demand deposits	Other checkable deposits	Savings deposits	Small time deposits	Large time deposits
1989:									
January	784.9	2 999.0	3 942.0	213.1	284.9	280.7	916.3	1 050.1	524.3
February	783.4	2 999.8	3 949.3	213.6	283.2	280.2	904.3	1 061.7	531.2
March	782.7	3 007.3	3 970.0	214.9	282.8	278.6	894.1	1 073.6	537.7
April	778.8	3 013.3	3 981.7	215.4	279.7	277.4	881.1	1 091.1	545.8
May	774.8	3 019.4	3 987.7	216.4	279.3	272.5	866.1	1 110.3	548.9
June	774.2	3 036.3	4 009.3	217.4	277.1	272.4	861.9	1 124.3	549.4
July	779.7	3 061.7	4 033.0	218.2	279.1	274.1	863.6	1 133.1	549.6
August	781.1	3 083.9	4 043.0	218.8	278.3	275.6	867.8	1 140.1	547.7
September	782.2	3 101.8	4 050.8	219.4	277.2	278.0	872.9	1 142.7	545.4
October	787.0	3 123.0	4 062.7	220.1	279.2	280.8	879.0	1 145.7	543.3
November	788.0	3 141.4	4 078.3	221.0	278.0	282.5	887.2	1 147.7	542.6
December	792.6	3 159.9	4 091.0	222.6	278.7	285.1	893.7	1 151.4	541.5
1990:									
January	794.9	3 173.4	4 099.1	224.3	278.3	286.0	900.7	1 150.6	539.5
February	797.7	3 185.6	4 102.2	225.9	278.1	287.1	904.9	1 151.6	532.2
March	801.3	3 197.1	4 105.9	227.9	277.5	289.2	908.7	1 154.5	527.2
April	806.2	3 209.9	4 111.1	229.9	277.1	292.6	912.1	1 157.1	520.7
May	804.4	3 207.4	4 110.9	231.6	274.8	291.1	911.9	1 158.4	516.8
June	810.3	3 222.3	4 121.2	233.8	275.4	293.3	914.8	1 161.6	512.9
July	811.8	3 232.5	4 131.6	235.9	275.6	291.4	917.4	1 164.7	511.2
August	817.8	3 251.2	4 146.7	238.8	278.0	291.8	920.7	1 166.1	505.0
September	821.8	3 263.4	4 153.7	241.7	278.6	292.8	922.8	1 166.9	496.9
October	820.3	3 266.5	4 155.7	243.9	276.9	291.4	922.6	1 169.1	492.8
November	822.1	3 270.5	4 150.8	245.5	276.8	292.4	923.0	1 170.6	490.5
December	824.6	3 279.1	4 155.6	247.0	276.9	293.7	923.2	1 173.4	482.1
1991:									
January	826.7	3 294.3	4 178.8	251.1	274.0	294.5	927.3	1 174.5	484.4
February	832.4	3 311.9	4 196.7	254.1	274.6	296.6	934.6	1 174.2	484.3
March	838.6	3 329.3	4 204.8	256.0	274.8	300.7	946.0	1 169.2	478.9
April	842.7	3 339.1	4 210.7	256.3	275.8	303.6	957.5	1 161.4	472.5
May	849.0	3 348.9	4 210.6	257.0	277.6	307.1	970.8	1 150.8	466.9
June	858.3	3 360.3	4 212.7	258.2	280.4	311.9	983.2	1 139.6	462.6
July	863.0	3 363.8	4 207.4	259.6	280.3	314.4	993.2	1 128.8	454.7
August	868.6	3 363.2	4 200.9	261.4	280.2	318.3	1 000.0	1 119.9	446.9
September	871.6	3 362.3	4 192.9	262.6	279.5	321.2	1 007.1	1 109.8	439.9
October	878.4	3 366.2	4 195.7	264.3	282.5	324.0	1 019.1	1 096.1	431.1
November	888.0	3 373.1	4 202.0	265.9	285.8	329.2	1 031.4	1 081.5	423.9
December	896.7	3 379.8	4 208.6	267.5	289.7	332.5	1 044.4	1 065.7	417.6
1992:									
January	910.5	3 388.8	4 216.7	269.1	296.3	337.9	1 065.1	1 043.6	413.6
February	925.1	3 407.3	4 234.5	270.8	302.7	344.4	1 087.4	1 020.4	406.5
March	936.0	3 410.6	4 234.8	271.8	308.5	348.5	1 102.7	1 001.2	402.1
April	943.9	3 407.4	4 224.3	273.6	311.9	351.3	1 115.4	982.7	395.6
May	950.8	3 407.4	4 219.0	275.1	313.3	355.2	1 125.9	964.0	388.9
June	954.7	3 403.1	4 216.9	276.7	313.3	356.7	1 132.6	950.7	383.4
July	964.6	3 404.6	4 218.9	279.5	317.2	359.1	1 141.3	937.3	378.8
August	975.7	3 410.3	4 228.9	282.4	320.5	363.7	1 151.4	922.8	374.1
September	988.8	3 420.0	4 234.5	285.4	327.4	367.1	1 163.7	909.8	369.2
October	1 004.3	3 433.7	4 232.4	287.8	334.1	373.9	1 175.0	894.8	362.0
November	1 016.0	3 436.0	4 228.7	289.9	337.3	381.1	1 183.2	879.9	357.6
December	1 024.4	3 434.0	4 220.0	292.5	340.0	384.4	1 186.7	868.2	354.5
1993:									
January	1 030.9	3 431.3	4 205.3	294.6	340.2	388.6	1 188.7	857.8	348.5
February	1 033.2	3 425.0	4 203.0	296.7	341.6	387.5	1 189.1	850.8	344.4
March	1 038.0	3 421.3	4 203.2	298.8	343.1	388.5	1 187.0	843.1	340.2
April	1 047.5	3 423.8	4 210.5	301.4	349.0	389.6	1 189.4	835.4	343.6
May	1 066.2	3 448.9	4 238.5	304.2	357.9	396.3	1 200.1	827.1	344.2
June	1 075.6	3 454.8	4 238.9	306.8	361.6	398.9	1 205.5	819.4	342.1
July	1 085.9	3 455.6	4 237.6	309.7	364.8	402.4	1 206.6	811.1	338.1
August	1 095.6	3 459.7	4 239.3	312.4	369.6	404.5	1 209.3	803.9	338.0
September	1 105.4	3 466.8	4 249.1	315.6	374.6	406.7	1 211.4	797.9	335.7
October	1 113.8	3 471.5	4 255.7	317.7	377.7	410.3	1 213.2	792.4	335.5
November	1 123.9	3 483.0	4 271.0	319.8	384.1	412.5	1 216.7	787.0	334.4
December	1 129.3	3 487.4	4 279.7	322.0	385.4	414.6	1 219.1	782.1	334.5
1994:									
January	1 132.2	3 491.9	4 284.1	325.4	386.5	412.9	1 224.8	775.9	339.7
February	1 136.1	3 493.5	4 266.7	328.7	388.4	411.7	1 226.9	770.4	334.1
March	1 139.9	3 495.7	4 273.2	331.7	387.9	412.8	1 225.7	766.4	331.7
April	1 141.4	3 501.6	4 283.4	334.1	387.9	411.9	1 223.4	764.2	332.1
May	1 142.9	3 507.0	4 289.2	337.3	385.3	412.5	1 221.3	764.8	334.8
June	1 145.6	3 496.7	4 288.7	340.1	384.8	412.2	1 211.9	767.7	337.8
July	1 151.5	3 504.9	4 309.4	343.1	385.7	413.3	1 206.4	772.2	340.5
August	1 151.4	3 501.6	4 309.8	345.4	385.5	411.0	1 197.9	778.6	344.9
September	1 152.4	3 502.1	4 318.2	347.7	386.7	408.9	1 190.3	785.1	350.6
October	1 150.4	3 501.2	4 327.4	350.2	385.6	406.0	1 179.1	795.2	354.0
November	1 150.4	3 502.9	4 341.3	352.9	384.7	404.8	1 165.7	806.2	359.9
December	1 149.7	3 502.0	4 353.9	354.2	383.6	404.1	1 150.0	816.5	364.5

1. See Notes for definitions of M1, M2, and M3.

Interest Rates, Bond Yields, and Stock Price Indexes

(Not seasonally adjusted)

Year and month	Short-term rates					U.S. Treasury securites			Bond yields				Stock price indexes	
	Federal funds	Federal Reserve discount rate [1]	U.S. Treasury bills, 3-month	U.S. Treasury bills, 6-month	Bank prime rate	One-year	Ten-year	Long-term composite [2]	Domestic corporate (Moody's)		State and local bonds (Bond Buyer)	Fixed-rate first mortgages	Dow Jones industrials (30 stocks)	Standard and Poor's composite (500 stocks) [3]
									Aaa	Baa				
1971:														
January	4.14	5.23	4.49	4.51	6.29	4.57	6.24	5.91	7.36	8.74	5.35	.....	849.04	93.49
February	3.72	4.91	3.78	3.81	5.88	3.89	6.11	5.84	7.08	8.39	5.23	.....	879.69	97.11
March	3.71	4.75	3.33	3.43	5.44	3.69	5.70	5.71	7.21	8.46	5.17	.....	901.29	99.60
April	4.15	4.75	3.78	3.93	5.28	4.30	5.83	5.75	7.25	8.45	5.37	7.31	932.54	103.04
May	4.63	4.75	4.14	4.37	5.46	5.04	6.39	5.96	7.53	8.62	5.90	7.43	925.49	101.64
June	4.91	4.75	4.70	4.89	5.50	5.64	6.52	5.94	7.64	8.75	5.95	7.53	900.43	99.72
July	5.31	4.88	5.41	5.58	5.91	6.04	6.73	5.91	7.64	8.76	6.06	7.60	887.81	99.00
August	5.56	5.00	5.08	5.36	6.00	5.80	6.58	5.78	7.59	8.76	5.82	7.70	875.40	97.24
September	5.55	5.00	4.67	4.93	6.00	5.41	6.14	5.56	7.44	8.59	5.37	7.69	901.22	99.40
October	5.20	5.00	4.49	4.63	5.90	4.91	5.93	5.46	7.39	8.48	5.06	7.63	872.15	97.29
November	4.91	4.90	4.19	4.34	5.53	4.67	5.81	5.44	7.26	8.38	5.20	7.55	822.11	92.78
December	4.14	4.63	4.02	4.20	5.49	4.60	5.93	5.62	7.25	8.38	5.21	7.48	869.90	99.17
1972:														
January	3.50	4.50	3.41	3.66	5.18	4.28	5.95	5.62	7.19	8.23	5.12	7.44	904.65	103.30
February	3.29	4.50	3.18	3.59	4.75	4.27	6.08	5.67	7.27	8.23	5.28	7.33	914.37	105.24
March	3.83	4.50	3.72	4.09	4.75	4.67	6.07	5.66	7.24	8.24	5.31	7.30	939.23	107.69
April	4.17	4.50	3.72	4.22	4.97	4.96	6.19	5.74	7.30	8.24	5.43	7.29	958.16	108.81
May	4.27	4.50	3.65	4.07	5.00	4.64	6.13	5.64	7.30	8.23	5.30	7.37	948.22	107.65
June	4.46	4.50	3.87	4.27	5.04	4.93	6.11	5.59	7.23	8.20	5.33	7.37	943.43	108.01
July	4.55	4.50	4.06	4.59	5.25	4.96	6.11	5.57	7.21	8.23	5.41	7.40	925.92	107.21
August	4.80	4.50	4.01	4.53	5.27	4.98	6.21	5.54	7.19	8.19	5.30	7.40	958.34	111.01
September	4.87	4.50	4.65	5.09	5.50	5.52	6.55	5.70	7.22	8.09	5.36	7.42	950.58	109.39
October	5.04	4.50	4.72	5.12	5.73	5.52	6.48	5.69	7.21	8.06	5.18	7.42	944.10	109.56
November	5.06	4.50	4.78	5.08	5.75	5.27	6.28	5.50	7.12	7.99	5.02	7.43	1 001.19	115.05
December	5.33	4.50	5.06	5.29	5.79	5.52	6.36	5.63	7.08	7.93	5.05	7.44	1 020.32	117.50
1973:														
January	5.94	4.77	5.31	5.53	6.00	5.89	6.46	5.94	7.15	7.90	5.05	7.44	1 026.82	118.42
February	6.58	5.05	5.56	5.75	6.02	6.19	6.64	6.14	7.22	7.97	5.13	7.44	974.04	114.16
March	7.09	5.50	6.05	6.43	6.30	6.85	6.71	6.20	7.29	8.03	5.29	7.46	957.35	112.42
April	7.12	5.50	6.29	6.53	6.61	6.85	6.67	6.11	7.26	8.09	5.15	7.54	944.10	110.27
May	7.84	5.90	6.35	6.62	7.01	6.89	6.85	6.22	7.29	8.06	5.15	7.65	922.41	107.22
June	8.49	6.33	7.19	7.24	7.49	7.31	6.90	6.32	7.37	8.13	5.17	7.73	893.90	104.75
July	10.40	6.98	8.02	8.08	8.30	8.39	7.13	6.53	7.45	8.24	5.40	8.05	903.61	105.83
August	10.50	7.29	8.67	8.70	9.23	8.82	7.40	6.81	7.68	8.53	5.48	8.50	883.73	103.80
September	10.78	7.50	8.48	8.54	9.86	8.31	7.09	6.42	7.63	8.63	5.10	8.82	909.98	105.61
October	10.01	7.50	7.16	7.26	9.94	7.40	6.79	6.26	7.60	8.41	5.05	8.77	967.62	109.84
November	10.03	7.50	7.87	7.82	9.75	7.57	6.73	6.31	7.67	8.42	5.18	8.58	878.98	102.03
December	9.95	7.50	7.37	7.45	9.75	7.27	6.74	6.35	7.68	8.48	5.12	8.54	824.08	94.78
1974:														
January	9.65	7.50	7.76	7.63	9.73	7.42	6.99	6.56	7.83	8.48	5.22	8.54	857.24	96.11
February	8.97	7.50	7.06	6.88	9.21	6.88	6.96	6.54	7.85	8.53	5.20	8.46	831.34	93.45
March	9.35	7.50	7.99	7.83	8.85	7.76	7.21	6.81	8.01	8.62	5.40	8.41	874.00	97.44
April	10.51	7.60	8.23	8.17	10.02	8.62	7.51	7.04	8.25	8.87	5.73	8.58	847.79	92.46
May	11.31	8.00	8.43	8.50	11.25	8.78	7.58	7.07	8.37	9.05	6.02	8.97	829.84	89.67
June	11.93	8.00	8.15	8.23	11.54	8.67	7.54	7.03	8.47	9.27	6.13	9.09	831.43	89.79
July	12.92	8.00	7.75	8.03	11.97	8.80	7.81	7.18	8.72	9.48	6.68	9.28	783.00	82.82
August	12.01	8.00	8.75	8.85	12.00	9.36	8.04	7.33	9.00	9.77	6.71	9.59	729.30	76.03
September	11.34	8.00	8.37	8.60	12.00	8.87	8.04	7.30	9.24	10.18	6.76	9.96	651.28	68.12
October	10.06	8.00	7.24	7.56	11.68	8.05	7.90	7.22	9.27	10.48	6.57	9.98	638.62	69.44
November	9.45	8.00	7.59	7.55	10.83	7.66	7.68	6.93	8.89	10.60	6.61	9.79	642.10	71.74
December	8.53	7.81	7.18	7.09	10.50	7.31	7.43	6.78	8.89	10.63	7.05	9.62	596.50	67.07
1975:														
January	7.13	7.40	6.49	6.53	10.05	6.83	7.50	6.68	8.83	10.81	6.82	9.43	659.09	72.56
February	6.24	6.82	5.59	5.68	8.96	5.98	7.39	6.61	8.62	10.65	6.39	9.11	724.89	80.10
March	5.54	6.40	5.55	5.64	7.93	6.11	7.73	6.73	8.67	10.48	6.73	8.90	765.06	83.78
April	5.49	6.25	5.69	6.01	7.50	6.90	8.23	7.03	8.95	10.58	6.95	8.82	790.93	84.72
May	5.22	6.12	5.32	5.65	7.40	6.39	8.06	6.99	8.90	10.69	6.97	8.91	836.56	90.10
June	5.55	6.00	5.20	5.47	7.07	6.29	7.86	6.86	8.77	10.62	6.94	8.89	845.70	92.40
July	6.10	6.00	6.17	6.49	7.15	7.11	8.06	6.89	8.84	10.55	7.07	8.89	856.28	92.49
August	6.14	6.00	6.46	6.94	7.66	7.70	8.40	7.06	8.95	10.59	7.17	8.94	815.51	85.71
September	6.24	6.00	6.38	6.87	7.88	7.75	8.43	7.29	8.95	10.61	7.44	9.13	818.28	84.67
October	5.82	6.00	6.08	6.38	7.96	6.95	8.14	7.29	8.86	10.62	7.39	9.22	831.26	88.57
November	5.22	6.00	5.47	5.75	7.53	6.49	8.05	7.21	8.78	10.56	7.43	9.15	845.51	90.07
December	5.20	6.00	5.50	5.93	7.26	6.60	8.00	7.17	8.79	10.56	7.31	9.10	840.80	88.70
1976:														
January	4.87	5.79	4.96	5.24	7.00	5.81	7.74	6.94	8.60	10.41	7.07	9.02	929.34	96.86
February	4.77	5.50	4.85	5.14	6.75	5.91	7.79	6.92	8.55	10.24	6.94	8.81	971.70	100.64
March	4.84	5.50	5.05	5.49	6.75	6.21	7.73	6.87	8.52	10.12	6.91	8.76	988.55	101.08
April	4.82	5.50	4.88	5.20	6.75	5.92	7.56	6.73	8.40	9.94	6.60	8.73	992.51	101.93
May	5.29	5.50	5.19	5.60	6.75	6.40	7.90	6.99	8.58	9.86	6.87	8.77	988.82	101.16
June	5.48	5.50	5.45	5.79	7.20	6.52	7.86	6.92	8.62	9.89	6.87	8.85	985.59	101.77
July	5.31	5.50	5.28	5.60	7.25	6.20	7.83	6.85	8.56	9.82	6.79	8.93	993.20	104.20
August	5.29	5.50	5.15	5.42	7.01	6.00	7.77	6.79	8.45	9.64	6.61	9.00	981.63	103.29
September	5.25	5.50	5.08	5.31	7.00	5.84	7.59	6.70	8.38	9.40	6.51	8.98	994.37	105.45
October	5.02	5.50	4.93	5.07	6.77	5.50	7.41	6.65	8.32	9.29	6.30	8.93	951.95	101.89
November	4.95	5.43	4.81	4.94	6.50	5.29	7.29	6.62	8.25	9.23	6.29	8.81	944.58	101.19
December	4.65	5.25	4.36	4.51	6.35	4.89	6.87	6.39	7.98	9.12	5.94	8.79	976.86	104.66

1. Discount window borrowing, Federal Reserve Bank of New York.
2. Maturities of more than ten years.
3. 1941–1943=10.

Interest Rates, Bond Yields, and Stock Price Indexes—*Continued*

(Not seasonally adjusted)

Year and month	Federal funds	Federal Reserve discount rate [1]	U.S. Treasury bills, 3-month	U.S. Treasury bills, 6-month	Bank prime rate	One-year	Ten-year	Long-term composite [2]	Domestic corporate (Moody's) Aaa	Baa	State and local bonds (Bond Buyer)	Fixed-rate first mortgages	Dow Jones industrials (30 stocks)	Standard and Poor's composite (500 stocks) [3]
1977:														
January	4.61	5.25	4.60	4.79	6.25	5.29	7.21	6.68	7.96	9.08	5.87	8.72	970.62	103.81
February	4.68	5.25	4.66	4.90	6.25	5.47	7.39	7.15	8.04	9.12	5.88	8.67	941.77	100.96
March	4.69	5.25	4.61	4.88	6.25	5.50	7.46	7.20	8.10	9.12	5.89	8.69	946.11	100.57
April	4.73	5.25	4.54	4.79	6.25	5.44	7.37	7.13	8.04	9.07	5.72	8.75	929.10	99.05
May	5.35	5.25	4.94	5.19	6.41	5.84	7.46	7.17	8.05	9.01	5.75	8.82	926.31	98.76
June	5.39	5.25	5.00	5.20	6.75	5.80	7.28	6.99	7.95	8.91	5.62	8.86	916.56	99.29
July	5.42	5.25	5.14	5.35	6.75	5.94	7.33	6.97	7.94	8.87	5.63	8.94	908.20	100.18
August	5.90	5.27	5.50	5.81	6.83	6.37	7.40	7.00	7.98	8.82	5.62	8.94	872.26	97.75
September	6.14	5.75	5.77	5.99	7.13	6.53	7.34	6.94	7.92	8.80	5.51	8.90	853.30	96.23
October	6.47	5.80	6.19	6.41	7.52	6.97	7.52	7.08	8.04	8.89	5.64	8.92	823.96	93.74
November	6.51	6.00	6.16	6.43	7.75	6.95	7.58	7.14	8.08	8.95	5.49	8.92	828.51	94.28
December	6.56	6.00	6.06	6.38	7.75	6.96	7.69	7.23	8.19	8.99	5.57	8.96	818.80	93.82
1978:														
January	6.70	6.37	6.45	6.69	7.93	7.28	7.96	7.50	8.41	9.17	5.71	9.02	781.09	90.25
February	6.78	6.50	6.46	6.74	8.00	7.34	8.03	7.60	8.47	9.20	5.62	9.16	763.57	88.98
March	6.79	6.50	6.32	6.65	8.00	7.31	8.04	7.63	8.47	9.22	5.61	9.20	756.37	88.82
April	6.89	6.50	6.31	6.70	8.00	7.45	8.15	7.74	8.56	9.32	5.79	9.36	794.66	92.71
May	7.36	6.84	6.43	7.02	8.27	7.82	8.35	7.87	8.69	9.49	6.03	9.58	838.56	97.41
June	7.60	7.00	6.71	7.20	8.63	8.09	8.46	7.94	8.76	9.60	6.22	9.71	840.26	97.66
July	7.81	7.23	7.08	7.48	9.00	8.39	8.64	8.09	8.88	9.60	6.28	9.74	831.71	97.19
August	8.04	7.43	7.04	7.36	9.01	8.31	8.41	7.87	8.69	9.48	6.12	9.79	887.93	103.92
September	8.45	7.83	7.84	7.95	9.41	8.64	8.42	7.82	8.69	9.42	6.09	9.76	878.64	103.86
October	8.96	8.26	8.13	8.49	9.94	9.14	8.64	8.07	8.89	9.59	6.13	9.86	857.69	100.58
November	9.76	9.50	8.79	9.20	10.94	10.01	8.81	8.16	9.03	9.83	6.19	10.11	804.29	94.71
December	10.03	9.50	9.12	9.40	11.55	10.30	9.01	8.35	9.16	9.94	6.50	10.35	807.94	96.11
1979:														
January	10.07	9.50	9.35	9.50	11.75	10.41	9.10	8.43	9.25	10.13	6.46	10.39	837.39	99.71
February	10.06	9.50	9.27	9.35	11.75	10.24	9.10	8.43	9.26	10.08	6.31	10.41	825.18	98.23
March	10.09	9.50	9.46	9.46	11.75	10.25	9.12	8.45	9.37	10.26	6.33	10.43	847.84	100.11
April	10.01	9.50	9.49	9.50	11.75	10.12	9.18	8.44	9.38	10.33	6.28	10.50	864.96	102.07
May	10.24	9.50	9.58	9.53	11.75	10.12	9.25	8.55	9.50	10.47	6.25	10.69	837.41	99.73
June	10.29	9.50	9.05	9.06	11.65	9.57	8.91	8.32	9.29	10.38	6.12	11.04	838.65	101.73
July	10.47	9.69	9.27	9.19	11.54	9.64	8.95	8.35	9.20	10.29	6.13	11.09	836.95	102.71
August	10.94	10.24	9.45	9.45	11.91	9.98	9.03	8.42	9.23	10.35	6.20	11.09	873.55	107.36
September	11.43	10.70	10.18	10.13	12.90	10.84	9.33	8.68	9.44	10.54	6.52	11.30	878.50	108.60
October	13.77	11.77	11.47	11.34	14.39	12.44	10.30	9.44	10.13	11.40	7.08	11.64	840.39	104.47
November	13.18	12.00	11.87	11.86	15.55	12.39	10.65	9.80	10.76	11.99	7.30	12.83	815.78	103.66
December	13.78	12.00	12.07	11.85	15.30	11.98	10.39	9.59	10.74	12.06	7.22	12.90	836.14	107.78
1980:														
January	13.82	12.00	12.04	11.85	15.25	12.06	10.80	10.03	11.09	12.42	7.35	12.88	860.74	110.87
February	14.13	12.52	12.82	12.72	15.63	13.92	12.41	11.55	12.38	13.57	8.16	13.04	878.22	115.34
March	17.19	13.00	15.53	15.10	18.31	15.82	12.75	11.87	12.96	14.45	9.16	15.28	803.56	104.69
April	17.61	13.00	14.00	13.62	19.77	13.30	11.47	10.83	12.04	14.19	8.63	16.33	786.33	102.97
May	10.98	12.94	9.15	9.15	16.57	9.39	10.18	9.82	10.99	13.17	7.59	14.26	828.19	107.69
June	9.47	11.40	7.00	7.22	12.63	8.16	9.78	9.40	10.58	12.71	7.63	12.71	869.86	114.55
July	9.03	10.87	8.13	8.10	11.48	8.65	10.25	9.83	11.07	12.65	8.13	12.19	909.79	119.83
August	9.61	10.00	9.26	9.45	11.12	10.24	11.10	10.53	11.64	13.15	8.67	12.56	947.33	123.50
September	10.87	10.17	10.32	10.55	12.23	11.52	11.51	10.94	12.02	13.70	8.94	13.20	946.67	126.51
October	12.81	11.00	11.58	11.57	13.79	12.49	11.75	11.20	12.31	14.23	9.11	13.79	949.17	130.22
November	15.85	11.47	13.89	13.61	16.06	14.15	12.68	11.83	12.97	14.64	9.56	14.21	971.08	135.65
December	18.90	12.87	15.66	14.77	20.35	14.88	12.84	11.89	13.21	15.14	10.20	14.79	945.96	133.48
1981:														
January	19.08	13.00	14.73	13.88	20.16	14.08	12.57	11.65	12.81	15.03	9.66	14.90	962.13	132.97
February	15.93	13.00	14.91	14.14	19.43	14.57	13.19	12.23	13.35	15.37	10.09	15.13	945.50	128.40
March	14.70	13.00	13.48	12.98	18.05	13.71	13.12	12.15	13.33	15.34	10.16	15.40	987.18	133.19
April	15.72	13.00	13.63	13.43	17.15	14.32	13.68	12.62	13.88	15.56	10.62	15.58	1 004.86	134.43
May	18.52	13.87	16.29	15.34	19.61	16.20	14.10	12.96	14.32	15.95	10.77	16.40	979.52	131.73
June	19.10	14.00	14.56	13.95	20.03	14.86	13.47	12.39	13.75	15.80	10.67	16.70	996.27	132.28
July	19.04	14.00	14.70	14.40	20.39	15.72	14.28	13.05	14.38	16.17	11.14	16.83	947.94	129.13
August	17.82	14.00	15.61	15.55	20.50	16.72	14.94	13.78	14.89	16.34	12.26	17.29	926.25	129.63
September	15.87	14.00	14.95	15.06	20.08	16.52	15.32	14.14	15.49	16.92	12.92	18.16	853.38	118.27
October	15.08	14.00	13.87	14.01	18.45	15.38	15.15	14.13	15.40	17.11	12.83	18.45	853.24	119.80
November	13.31	13.03	11.27	11.53	16.84	12.41	13.39	12.68	14.22	16.39	11.89	17.83	860.44	122.92
December	12.37	12.10	10.93	11.47	15.75	12.85	13.72	12.88	14.23	16.55	12.91	16.92	878.28	123.79
1982:														
January	13.22	12.00	12.41	12.93	15.75	14.32	14.59	13.73	15.18	17.10	13.28	17.40	853.41	117.28
February	14.78	12.00	13.78	13.71	16.56	14.73	14.43	13.63	15.27	17.18	12.97	17.60	833.15	114.50
March	14.68	12.00	12.49	12.62	16.50	13.95	13.86	12.98	14.58	16.82	12.82	17.16	844.96	110.84
April	14.94	12.00	12.82	12.86	16.50	13.98	13.87	12.84	14.46	16.78	12.58	16.89	848.36	116.31
May	14.45	12.00	12.15	12.22	16.50	13.34	13.62	12.67	14.26	16.64	11.95	16.68	846.72	116.35
June	14.15	12.00	12.11	12.31	16.50	14.07	14.30	13.32	14.81	16.92	12.44	16.70	804.37	109.70
July	12.59	11.81	11.92	12.24	16.26	13.24	13.95	12.97	14.61	16.80	12.28	16.82	818.41	109.38
August	10.12	10.68	9.01	10.11	14.39	11.43	13.06	12.15	13.71	16.32	11.23	16.27	832.11	109.65
September	10.31	10.00	8.20	9.54	13.50	10.85	12.34	11.48	12.94	15.63	10.66	15.43	917.27	122.43
October	9.71	9.68	7.75	8.30	12.52	9.32	10.91	10.51	12.12	14.73	9.68	14.61	988.71	132.66
November	9.20	9.35	8.04	8.32	11.85	9.16	10.55	10.18	11.68	14.30	10.06	13.83	1 027.76	138.10
December	8.95	8.73	8.02	8.22	11.50	8.91	10.54	10.33	11.83	14.14	9.96	13.62	1 033.08	139.37

1. Discount window borrowing, Federal Reserve Bank of New York.
2. Maturities of more than ten years.
3. 1941–1943=10.

Interest Rates, Bond Yields, and Stock Price Indexes—*Continued*

(Not seasonally adjusted)

Year and month	Federal funds	Federal Reserve discount rate[1]	U.S. Treasury bills, 3-month	U.S. Treasury bills, 6-month	Bank prime rate	One-year	Ten-year	Long-term composite[2]	Domestic corporate (Moody's) Aaa	Baa	State and local bonds (Bond Buyer)	Fixed-rate first mortgages	Dow Jones industrials (30 stocks)	Standard and Poor's composite (500 stocks)[3]
1983:														
January	8.68	8.50	7.81	7.90	11.16	8.62	10.46	10.37	11.79	13.94	9.50	13.25	1 064.29	144.27
February	8.51	8.50	8.13	8.24	10.98	8.92	10.72	10.60	12.01	13.95	9.58	13.04	1 087.43	146.80
March	8.77	8.50	8.30	8.33	10.50	9.04	10.51	10.34	11.73	13.61	9.20	12.80	1 129.58	151.88
April	8.80	8.50	8.25	8.35	10.50	8.98	10.40	10.19	11.51	13.29	9.04	12.78	1 168.43	157.71
May	8.63	8.50	8.19	8.20	10.50	8.90	10.38	10.21	11.46	13.09	9.11	12.63	1 212.86	164.10
June	8.98	8.50	8.82	8.89	10.50	9.66	10.85	10.64	11.74	13.37	9.52	12.87	1 221.47	166.39
July	9.37	8.50	9.12	9.29	10.50	10.20	11.38	11.10	12.15	13.39	9.53	13.42	1 213.93	166.96
August	9.56	8.50	9.39	9.53	10.89	10.53	11.85	11.42	12.51	13.64	9.72	13.81	1 189.21	162.42
September	9.45	8.50	9.05	9.19	11.00	10.16	11.65	11.26	12.37	13.55	9.58	13.73	1 237.04	167.16
October	9.48	8.50	8.71	8.90	11.00	9.81	11.54	11.21	12.25	13.46	9.66	13.54	1 252.20	167.65
November	9.34	8.50	8.71	8.89	11.00	9.94	11.69	11.32	12.41	13.61	9.74	13.44	1 250.00	165.23
December	9.47	8.50	8.96	9.14	11.00	10.11	11.83	11.44	12.57	13.75	9.89	13.42	1 257.64	164.36
1984:														
January	9.56	8.50	7.14	9.06	11.00	9.90	11.67	11.29	12.20	13.65	9.63	13.37	1 258.89	166.39
February	9.59	8.50	9.03	9.13	11.00	10.04	11.84	11.44	12.08	13.59	9.64	13.23	1 164.46	157.25
March	9.91	8.50	9.08	9.32	11.21	10.59	12.32	11.90	12.57	13.99	9.94	13.39	1 161.97	157.44
April	10.29	8.87	9.69	9.83	11.93	10.90	12.63	12.17	12.81	14.31	9.96	13.65	1 152.71	157.60
May	10.32	9.00	9.90	10.31	12.39	11.66	13.41	12.89	13.28	14.74	10.49	13.94	1 143.42	156.55
June	11.06	9.00	9.94	10.55	12.60	12.08	13.56	13.04	13.55	15.05	10.67	14.42	1 121.14	153.12
July	11.23	9.00	10.13	10.58	13.00	12.03	13.36	12.82	13.44	15.15	10.42	14.67	1 113.27	151.08
August	11.64	9.00	10.49	10.65	13.00	11.82	12.72	12.23	12.87	14.63	9.99	14.47	1 212.82	164.42
September	11.30	9.00	10.41	10.51	12.97	11.58	12.52	11.97	12.66	14.35	10.10	14.35	1 213.51	166.11
October	9.99	9.00	9.97	10.05	12.58	10.90	12.16	11.66	12.63	13.94	10.25	14.13	1 199.30	164.82
November	9.43	8.83	8.79	8.99	11.77	9.82	11.57	11.25	12.29	13.48	10.17	13.64	1 211.30	166.27
December	8.38	8.37	8.16	8.36	11.06	9.33	11.50	11.21	12.13	13.40	9.95	13.18	1 188.96	164.48
1985:														
January	8.35	8.00	7.76	8.03	10.61	9.02	11.38	11.15	12.08	13.26	9.51	13.08	1 238.16	171.61
February	8.50	8.00	8.17	8.28	10.50	9.29	11.51	11.35	12.13	13.23	9.65	12.92	1 283.23	180.88
March	8.58	8.00	8.57	8.92	10.50	9.86	11.86	11.78	12.56	13.69	9.77	13.17	1 268.83	179.42
April	8.27	8.00	8.00	8.31	10.50	9.14	11.43	11.42	12.23	13.51	9.42	13.20	1 266.36	180.62
May	7.97	7.81	7.56	7.75	10.31	8.46	10.85	10.96	11.72	13.15	9.01	12.91	1 279.40	184.90
June	7.53	7.50	7.01	7.16	9.78	7.80	10.16	10.36	10.94	12.40	8.69	12.22	1 314.00	188.89
July	7.88	7.50	7.05	7.16	9.50	7.86	10.31	10.51	10.97	12.43	8.81	12.03	1 343.17	192.54
August	7.90	7.50	7.18	7.35	9.50	8.05	10.33	10.59	11.05	12.50	9.08	12.19	1 326.18	188.31
September	7.92	7.50	7.08	7.27	9.50	8.07	10.37	10.67	11.07	12.48	9.27	12.19	1 317.95	184.06
October	7.99	7.50	7.17	7.32	9.50	8.01	10.24	10.56	11.02	12.36	9.08	12.14	1 351.58	186.18
November	8.05	7.50	7.20	7.26	9.50	7.88	9.78	10.08	10.55	11.99	8.54	11.78	1 432.88	197.45
December	8.27	7.50	7.07	7.09	9.50	7.67	9.26	9.59	10.16	11.58	8.42	11.26	1 517.02	207.26
1986:														
January	8.14	7.50	7.04	7.13	9.50	7.73	9.19	9.51	10.05	11.44	8.08	10.88	1 534.86	208.19
February	7.86	7.50	7.03	7.08	9.50	7.61	8.70	9.07	9.67	11.11	7.44	10.71	1 652.73	219.37
March	7.48	7.10	6.59	6.60	9.10	7.03	7.78	8.13	9.00	10.50	7.08	10.08	1 757.35	232.33
April	6.99	6.83	6.06	6.07	8.83	6.44	7.30	7.59	8.79	10.19	7.19	9.94	1 807.05	237.98
May	6.85	6.50	6.12	6.16	8.50	6.65	7.71	8.02	9.09	10.29	7.54	10.14	1 801.80	238.46
June	6.92	6.50	6.21	6.28	8.50	6.73	7.80	8.23	9.13	10.34	7.87	10.68	1 867.70	245.30
July	6.56	6.16	5.84	5.85	8.16	6.27	7.30	7.86	8.88	10.16	7.51	10.51	1 809.92	240.18
August	6.17	5.82	5.57	5.58	7.90	5.93	7.17	7.72	8.72	10.18	7.21	10.20	1 843.45	245.00
September	5.89	5.50	5.19	5.31	7.50	5.77	7.45	8.08	8.89	10.20	7.11	10.01	1 813.47	238.27
October	5.85	5.50	5.18	5.26	7.50	5.72	7.43	8.04	8.86	10.24	7.08	9.97	1 817.04	237.36
November	6.04	5.50	5.35	5.42	7.50	5.80	7.25	7.81	8.68	10.07	6.84	9.70	1 883.65	245.09
December	6.91	5.50	5.49	5.53	7.50	5.87	7.11	7.67	8.49	9.97	6.87	9.31	1 924.07	248.61
1987:														
January	6.43	5.50	5.45	5.47	7.50	5.78	7.08	7.60	8.36	9.72	6.66	9.20	2 065.13	264.51
February	6.10	5.50	5.59	5.60	7.50	5.96	7.25	7.69	8.38	9.65	6.61	9.08	2 202.34	280.93
March	6.13	5.50	5.56	5.56	7.50	6.03	7.25	7.62	8.36	9.61	6.65	9.04	2 292.61	292.47
April	6.37	5.50	5.76	5.93	7.75	6.50	8.02	8.31	8.85	10.04	7.55	9.83	2 302.64	289.32
May	6.85	5.50	5.75	6.11	8.14	7.00	8.61	8.79	9.33	10.51	8.00	10.60	2 291.11	289.12
June	6.73	5.50	5.69	5.99	8.25	6.80	8.40	8.63	9.32	10.52	7.79	10.54	2 384.02	301.38
July	6.58	5.50	5.78	5.86	8.25	6.68	8.45	8.70	9.42	10.61	7.72	10.28	2 481.72	310.09
August	6.73	5.50	6.00	6.14	8.25	7.03	8.76	8.97	9.67	10.80	7.82	10.33	2 655.01	329.36
September	7.22	5.95	6.32	6.57	8.70	7.67	9.42	9.58	10.18	11.31	8.26	10.89	2 570.80	318.66
October	7.29	6.00	6.40	6.86	9.07	7.59	9.52	9.61	10.52	11.62	8.70	11.26	2 224.59	280.16
November	6.69	6.00	5.81	6.23	8.78	6.96	8.86	8.99	10.01	11.23	7.95	10.65	1 931.86	245.01
December	6.77	6.00	5.80	6.36	8.75	7.17	8.99	9.12	10.11	11.29	7.96	10.65	1 910.07	240.96
1988:														
January	6.83	6.00	5.90	6.31	8.75	6.99	8.67	8.82	9.88	11.07	7.69	10.43	1 947.35	250.48
February	6.58	6.00	5.69	5.96	8.51	6.64	8.21	8.41	9.40	10.62	7.49	9.89	1 980.65	258.13
March	6.58	6.00	5.69	5.91	8.50	6.71	8.37	8.61	9.39	10.57	7.74	9.93	2 044.31	265.74
April	6.87	6.00	5.92	6.21	8.50	7.01	8.72	8.91	9.67	10.90	7.81	10.20	2 036.13	262.61
May	7.09	6.00	6.27	6.53	8.84	7.40	9.09	9.24	9.90	11.04	7.91	10.46	1 988.91	256.12
June	7.51	6.00	6.50	6.76	9.00	7.49	8.92	9.04	9.86	11.00	7.78	10.46	2 104.94	270.68
July	7.75	6.00	6.73	6.97	9.29	7.75	9.06	9.20	9.96	11.11	7.76	10.43	2 104.22	269.05
August	8.01	6.37	7.02	7.36	9.84	8.17	9.26	9.33	10.11	11.21	7.79	10.60	2 051.29	263.73
September	8.19	6.50	7.23	7.43	10.00	8.09	8.98	9.06	9.82	10.90	7.66	10.48	2 080.06	267.97
October	8.30	6.50	7.34	7.50	10.00	8.11	8.80	8.89	9.51	10.41	7.46	10.30	2 144.31	277.40
November	8.35	6.50	7.68	7.76	10.05	8.48	8.96	9.07	9.45	10.48	7.46	10.27	2 099.04	271.02
December	8.76	6.50	8.09	8.24	10.50	8.99	9.11	9.13	9.57	10.65	7.61	10.61	2 148.58	276.51

1. Discount window borrowing, Federal Reserve Bank of New York.
2. Maturities of more than ten years.
3. 1941–1943=10.

Interest Rates, Bond Yields, and Stock Price Indexes—*Continued*

(Not seasonally adjusted)

Year and month	Short-term rates					U.S. Treasury securites			Bond yields				Stock price indexes	
	Federal funds	Federal Reserve discount rate [1]	U.S. Treasury bills, 3-month	U.S. Treasury bills, 6-month	Bank prime rate	One-year	Ten-year	Long-term composite [2]	Domestic corporate (Moody's) Aaa	Domestic corporate (Moody's) Baa	State and local bonds (Bond Buyer)	Fixed-rate first mortgages	Dow Jones industrials (30 stocks)	Standard and Poor's composite (500 stocks) [3]
1989:														
January	9.12	6.50	8.29	8.38	10.50	9.05	9.09	9.07	9.62	10.65	7.35	10.73	2 234.68	285.41
February	9.36	6.59	8.48	8.49	10.93	9.25	9.17	9.16	9.64	10.61	7.44	10.65	2 304.30	294.01
March	9.85	7.00	8.83	8.87	11.50	9.57	9.36	9.33	9.80	10.67	7.59	11.03	2 283.11	292.71
April	9.84	7.00	8.70	8.73	11.50	9.36	9.18	9.18	9.79	10.61	7.49	11.05	2 348.91	302.25
May	9.81	7.00	8.40	8.39	11.50	8.98	8.86	8.95	9.57	10.46	7.25	10.77	2 439.55	313.93
June	9.53	7.00	8.22	8.00	11.07	8.44	8.28	8.40	9.10	10.03	7.02	10.20	2 494.90	323.73
July	9.24	7.00	7.92	7.63	10.98	7.89	8.02	8.19	8.93	9.87	6.96	9.88	2 554.03	331.93
August	8.99	7.00	7.91	7.72	10.50	8.18	8.11	8.26	8.96	9.88	7.06	9.99	2 691.11	346.61
September	9.02	7.00	7.72	7.74	10.50	8.22	8.19	8.31	9.01	9.91	7.26	10.13	2 693.41	347.33
October	8.84	7.00	7.63	7.61	10.50	7.99	8.01	8.15	8.92	9.81	7.22	9.95	2 692.01	347.40
November	8.55	7.00	7.65	7.46	10.50	7.77	7.87	8.03	8.89	9.81	7.14	9.77	2 642.49	340.22
December	8.45	7.00	7.64	7.45	10.50	7.72	7.84	8.02	8.86	9.82	6.98	9.74	2 728.47	348.57
1990:														
January	8.23	7.00	7.64	7.52	10.11	7.92	8.21	8.39	8.99	9.94	7.10	9.90	2 679.24	339.97
February	8.24	7.00	7.76	7.72	10.00	8.11	8.47	8.66	9.22	10.14	7.22	10.20	2 614.18	330.45
March	8.28	7.00	7.87	7.83	10.00	8.35	8.59	8.74	9.37	10.21	7.29	10.27	2 700.13	338.47
April	8.26	7.00	7.78	7.82	10.00	8.40	8.79	8.92	9.46	10.30	7.39	10.37	2 708.26	338.18
May	8.18	7.00	7.78	7.82	10.00	8.32	8.76	8.90	9.47	10.41	7.35	10.48	2 793.81	350.25
June	8.29	7.00	7.74	7.64	10.00	8.10	8.48	8.62	9.26	10.22	7.24	10.16	2 894.82	360.39
July	8.15	7.00	7.66	7.57	10.00	7.94	8.47	8.64	9.24	10.20	7.19	10.04	2 934.23	360.03
August	8.13	7.00	7.44	7.36	10.00	7.78	8.75	8.97	9.41	10.41	7.32	10.10	2 681.89	330.75
September	8.20	7.00	7.38	7.33	10.00	7.76	8.89	9.11	9.56	10.64	7.43	10.18	2 550.69	315.41
October	8.11	7.00	7.19	7.20	10.00	7.55	8.72	8.93	9.53	10.74	7.49	10.18	2 460.54	307.12
November	7.81	7.00	7.07	7.04	10.00	7.31	8.39	8.60	9.30	10.62	7.18	10.01	2 518.56	315.29
December	7.31	6.79	6.81	6.76	10.00	7.05	8.08	8.31	9.05	10.43	7.09	9.67	2 610.92	328.75
1991:														
January	6.91	6.50	6.30	6.34	9.52	6.64	8.09	8.33	9.04	10.45	7.08	9.64	2 587.60	325.49
February	6.25	6.00	5.95	5.93	9.05	6.27	7.85	8.12	8.83	10.07	6.91	9.37	2 863.04	362.26
March	6.12	6.00	5.91	5.91	9.00	6.40	8.11	8.38	8.93	10.09	7.10	9.50	2 920.11	372.28
April	5.91	5.98	5.67	5.73	9.00	6.24	8.04	8.29	8.86	9.94	7.02	9.49	2 925.53	379.68
May	5.78	5.50	5.51	5.65	8.50	6.13	8.07	8.33	8.86	9.86	6.95	9.47	2 928.42	377.99
June	5.90	5.50	5.60	5.76	8.50	6.36	8.28	8.54	9.01	9.96	7.13	9.62	2 968.13	378.29
July	5.82	5.50	5.58	5.71	8.50	6.31	8.27	8.50	9.00	9.89	7.05	9.58	2 978.18	380.23
August	5.66	5.50	5.39	5.47	8.50	5.78	7.90	8.17	8.75	9.65	6.90	9.24	3 006.08	389.40
September	5.45	5.20	5.25	5.29	8.20	5.57	7.65	7.96	8.61	9.51	6.80	9.01	3 010.35	387.20
October	5.21	5.00	5.03	5.08	8.00	5.33	7.53	7.88	8.55	9.49	6.68	8.86	3 019.73	386.88
November	4.81	4.58	4.60	4.66	7.58	4.89	7.42	7.83	8.48	9.45	6.73	8.71	2 986.12	385.92
December	4.43	4.11	4.12	4.16	7.21	4.38	7.09	7.58	8.31	9.26	6.69	8.50	2 958.64	388.51
1992:														
January	4.03	3.50	3.84	3.88	6.50	4.15	7.03	7.48	8.20	9.13	6.54	8.43	3 227.06	416.08
February	4.06	3.50	3.84	3.94	6.50	4.29	7.34	7.78	8.29	9.23	6.74	8.76	3 257.27	412.56
March	3.98	3.50	4.05	4.19	6.50	4.63	7.54	7.93	8.35	9.25	6.76	8.94	3 247.41	407.36
April	3.73	3.50	3.81	3.93	6.50	4.30	7.48	7.88	8.33	9.21	6.67	8.85	3 294.08	407.41
May	3.82	3.50	3.66	3.78	6.50	4.19	7.39	7.80	8.28	9.13	6.57	8.67	3 376.78	414.81
June	3.76	3.50	3.70	3.81	6.50	4.17	7.26	7.72	8.22	9.05	6.49	8.51	3 337.79	408.27
July	3.25	3.02	3.28	3.36	6.02	3.60	6.84	7.40	8.07	8.84	6.13	8.13	3 329.40	415.05
August	3.30	3.00	3.14	3.23	6.00	3.47	6.59	7.19	7.95	8.65	6.16	7.98	3 307.45	417.93
September	3.22	3.00	2.97	3.01	6.00	3.18	6.42	7.08	7.92	8.62	6.25	7.92	3 293.92	418.48
October	3.10	3.00	2.84	2.98	6.00	3.30	6.59	7.26	7.99	8.84	6.41	8.09	3 198.69	412.50
November	3.09	3.00	3.14	3.35	6.00	3.68	6.87	7.43	8.10	8.96	6.36	8.31	3 238.49	422.84
December	2.92	3.00	3.25	3.39	6.00	3.71	6.77	7.30	7.98	8.81	6.22	8.22	3 303.15	435.64
1993:														
January	3.02	3.00	3.06	3.17	6.00	3.50	6.60	7.17	7.91	8.67	6.16	8.02	3 277.71	435.23
February	3.03	3.00	2.95	3.08	6.00	3.39	6.26	6.89	7.71	8.39	5.87	7.68	3 367.26	441.70
March	3.07	3.00	2.97	3.08	6.00	3.33	5.98	6.65	7.58	8.15	5.64	7.50	3 440.73	450.16
April	2.96	3.00	2.89	3.00	6.00	3.24	5.97	6.64	7.46	8.14	5.76	7.47	3 423.62	443.08
May	3.00	3.00	2.96	3.07	6.00	3.36	6.04	6.68	7.43	8.21	5.73	7.47	3 478.17	445.25
June	3.04	3.00	3.10	3.23	6.00	3.54	5.96	6.55	7.33	8.07	5.63	7.42	3 513.81	448.06
July	3.06	3.00	3.05	3.15	6.00	3.47	5.81	6.34	7.17	7.93	5.57	7.21	3 529.43	447.29
August	3.03	3.00	3.05	3.17	6.00	3.44	5.68	6.18	6.85	7.60	5.45	7.11	3 597.01	454.13
September	3.09	3.00	2.96	3.06	6.00	3.36	5.36	5.94	6.66	7.34	5.29	6.92	3 592.28	459.24
October	2.99	3.00	3.04	3.13	6.00	3.39	5.33	5.90	6.67	7.31	5.25	6.83	3 625.80	463.90
November	3.02	3.00	3.12	3.27	6.00	3.58	5.72	6.25	6.93	7.66	5.47	7.16	3 674.69	462.89
December	2.96	3.00	3.08	3.25	6.00	3.61	5.77	6.27	6.93	7.69	5.35	7.17	3 743.62	465.95
1994:														
January	3.05	3.00	3.02	3.19	6.00	3.54	5.75	6.24	6.92	7.65	5.31	7.06	3 868.36	472.99
February	3.25	3.00	3.21	3.38	6.00	3.87	5.97	6.44	7.08	7.76	5.40	7.15	3 905.62	471.58
March	3.34	3.00	3.52	3.79	6.06	4.32	6.48	6.90	7.48	8.13	5.91	7.68	3 816.98	463.81
April	3.56	3.00	3.74	4.13	6.45	4.82	6.97	7.32	7.88	8.52	6.23	8.32	3 661.48	447.23
May	4.01	3.24	4.19	4.64	6.99	5.31	7.18	7.47	7.99	8.62	6.19	8.60	3 707.99	450.90
June	4.25	3.50	4.18	4.58	7.25	5.27	7.10	7.43	7.97	8.65	6.11	8.40	3 737.58	454.83
July	4.26	3.50	4.39	4.81	7.25	5.48	7.30	7.61	8.11	8.80	6.23	8.61	3 718.30	451.40
August	4.47	3.76	4.50	4.91	7.51	5.56	7.24	7.55	8.07	8.74	6.21	8.51	3 797.48	464.24
September	4.73	4.00	4.64	5.02	7.75	5.76	7.46	7.81	8.34	8.98	6.28	8.64	3 880.60	466.96
October	4.76	4.00	4.96	5.39	7.75	6.11	7.74	8.02	8.57	9.20	6.52	8.93	3 868.10	463.81
November	5.29	4.40	5.25	5.69	8.15	6.54	7.96	8.16	8.68	9.32	6.97	9.17	3 792.43	461.01
December	5.45	4.75	5.64	6.21	8.50	7.14	7.81	7.97	8.46	9.10	6.80	9.20	3 770.31	455.19

1. Discount window borrowing, Federal Reserve Bank of New York.
2. Maturities of more than ten years.
3. 1941–1943=10.

Part IV: State and Regional Data

Personal Income and Employment

(Millions of dollars, except as noted)

Year	Total	Nonfarm	Farm	Earnings by place of work	Less: Personal contributions for social insurance	Plus: Adjustment for residence	Equals: Net earnings by place of residence	Dividends, interest, and rent	Transfer payments	Per capita (dollars) Total	Per capita (dollars) Disposable	Population (thousands)	Total employment (thousands)
UNITED STATES													
1969	772 952	754 726	18 226	619 495	26 013	-176	593 306	109 299	70 347	3 840	3 297	201 298	91 057
1970	830 848	812 276	18 572	657 814	27 624	-186	630 004	116 198	84 646	4 077	3 545	203 799	91 282
1971	894 815	875 703	19 112	701 512	30 457	-210	670 845	123 763	100 207	4 327	3 804	206 818	91 586
1972	983 311	960 097	23 214	774 294	34 247	-244	739 803	131 529	111 979	4 699	4 071	209 275	94 317
1973	1 101 241	1 065 317	35 924	868 143	42 376	-263	825 504	147 560	128 177	5 211	4 548	211 349	98 433
1974	1 210 981	1 179 837	31 144	939 618	47 695	-282	891 641	167 661	151 679	5 676	4 933	213 334	100 118
1975	1 314 384	1 284 442	29 942	997 365	50 184	-336	946 845	176 931	190 608	6 100	5 377	215 457	98 907
1976	1 455 441	1 429 541	25 900	1 108 418	55 250	-358	1 052 810	193 828	208 803	6 690	5 854	217 554	101 597
1977	1 611 733	1 586 583	25 150	1 231 242	60 966	-402	1 169 874	217 993	223 866	7 334	6 381	219 761	105 049
1978	1 820 240	1 791 065	29 175	1 394 282	69 478	-441	1 324 363	253 571	242 306	8 196	7 117	222 098	109 688
1979	2 047 659	2 016 745	30 914	1 556 345	80 661	-427	1 475 257	300 895	271 507	9 118	7 874	224 569	113 288
1980	2 286 358	2 265 084	21 274	1 686 882	88 283	-488	1 598 111	366 045	322 202	10 062	8 690	227 225	114 231
1981	2 557 139	2 529 185	27 954	1 846 125	104 069	-487	1 741 569	448 858	366 712	11 144	9 578	229 466	115 304
1982	2 714 034	2 689 505	24 529	1 928 363	111 843	-559	1 815 961	489 421	408 652	11 715	10 116	231 664	114 521
1983	2 888 851	2 871 762	17 089	2 048 345	119 234	-553	1 928 558	520 321	439 972	12 356	10 781	233 792	116 020
1984	3 200 479	3 169 105	31 374	2 281 282	132 207	-617	2 148 458	597 834	454 187	13 571	11 898	235 825	121 051
1985	3 428 478	3 397 199	31 279	2 454 846	148 470	-647	2 305 729	635 818	486 931	14 410	12 575	237 924	124 473
1986	3 627 522	3 595 293	32 229	2 599 801	161 501	-622	2 437 678	671 054	518 790	15 106	13 196	240 133	126 941
1987	3 863 177	3 825 231	37 946	2 798 603	173 054	-656	2 624 893	695 009	543 275	15 945	13 827	242 289	130 371
1988	4 165 890	4 129 090	36 800	3 027 680	193 506	-689	2 833 485	754 822	577 583	17 038	14 867	244 499	134 676
1989	4 480 624	4 437 068	43 556	3 212 991	210 125	-740	3 002 126	852 535	625 963	18 153	15 748	246 819	137 318
1990	4 778 306	4 734 233	44 073	3 414 296	223 152	-790	3 190 354	900 214	687 738	19 156	16 657	249 439	139 185
1991	4 947 591	4 908 585	39 006	3 508 762	235 010	-785	3 272 967	904 818	769 806	19 623	17 148	252 127	138 786
1992	5 239 364	5 194 429	44 935	3 745 439	247 816	-778	3 496 845	884 375	858 144	20 547	18 000	254 995	139 411
1993	5 469 485	5 424 921	44 564	3 916 346	259 745	-2 840	3 653 761	903 830	911 894	21 220	18 547	257 746	142 006
1994	5 741 050	5 698 217	42 833	4 103 160	276 992	-3 219	3 822 949	963 501	954 600	22 056	19 221	260 289	145 650
1995	6 059 091	6 025 806	33 285	4 308 382	293 083	-3 501	4 011 798	1 031 489	1 015 804	23 059	20 037	262 765	149 361
1996	6 408 103	6 361 601	46 502	4 531 745	305 832	-3 530	4 222 383	1 117 844	1 067 876	24 164	20 810	265 190	152 657
1997	6 770 650	6 725 875	44 775	4 824 055	325 765	-3 812	4 494 478	1 165 828	1 110 344	25 288	21 598	267 744	156 410
1998	7 158 176	7 114 828	43 348	5 169 822	346 910	-4 162	4 818 751	1 190 497	1 148 929	26 482	22 424	270 299	.....
ALABAMA													
1969	9 431	9 128	303	7 699	339	142	7 502	935	994	2 742	2 411	3 440	1 411
1970	10 225	9 948	278	8 182	366	144	7 959	1 036	1 230	2 964	2 648	3 450	1 413
1971	11 174	10 864	311	8 867	400	155	8 622	1 104	1 449	3 195	2 862	3 497	1 423
1972	12 405	12 022	383	9 899	455	178	9 622	1 158	1 624	3 504	3 113	3 540	1 471
1973	14 026	13 461	566	11 177	567	194	10 804	1 317	1 906	3 917	3 484	3 581	1 526
1974	15 599	15 229	370	12 221	652	205	11 773	1 542	2 285	4 300	3 817	3 628	1 552
1975	17 320	16 885	436	13 199	714	216	12 701	1 702	2 918	4 706	4 221	3 681	1 543
1976	19 566	19 070	496	15 051	827	234	14 458	1 872	3 236	5 235	4 669	3 737	1 594
1977	21 627	21 230	397	16 683	916	262	16 030	2 123	3 474	5 717	5 089	3 783	1 651
1978	24 520	23 996	523	19 035	1 040	284	18 279	2 458	3 783	6 395	5 681	3 834	1 714
1979	27 382	26 841	541	20 952	1 186	310	20 077	2 927	4 379	7 076	6 255	3 869	1 739
1980	30 178	29 947	231	22 321	1 299	343	21 364	3 663	5 151	7 737	6 822	3 900	1 736
1981	33 418	32 912	506	24 170	1 492	379	23 057	4 568	5 794	8 528	7 495	3 919	1 724
1982	35 102	34 686	416	24 821	1 588	404	23 636	5 035	6 430	8 942	7 931	3 925	1 692
1983	37 395	37 102	293	26 548	1 733	400	25 214	5 246	6 934	9 505	8 464	3 934	1 721
1984	41 165	40 683	482	29 484	1 914	430	28 001	5 960	7 204	10 417	9 315	3 952	1 786
1985	44 227	43 758	469	31 844	2 132	441	30 153	6 393	7 682	11 133	9 889	3 973	1 830
1986	46 846	46 394	452	33 748	2 216	461	31 993	6 790	8 063	11 736	10 432	3 992	1 867
1987	49 765	49 249	517	36 152	2 355	480	34 276	7 105	8 384	12 394	10 970	4 015	1 922
1988	53 471	52 680	791	38 916	2 622	484	36 777	7 786	8 908	13 288	11 885	4 024	1 983
1989	57 497	56 568	929	41 295	2 851	502	38 947	8 781	9 770	14 266	12 695	4 030	2 020
1990	61 589	60 757	832	43 908	3 029	513	41 392	9 241	10 957	15 213	13 554	4 048	2 058
1991	65 008	63 883	1 125	46 235	3 234	516	43 518	9 442	12 049	15 895	14 202	4 090	2 075
1992	69 582	68 606	976	49 518	3 434	546	46 630	9 474	13 479	16 817	15 076	4 138	2 113
1993	72 930	71 892	1 039	51 976	3 638	548	48 885	9 591	14 454	17 398	15 553	4 192	2 174
1994	76 999	75 981	1 018	54 761	3 908	595	51 447	10 345	15 206	18 163	16 170	4 239	2 189
1995	81 315	80 521	794	57 243	4 185	631	53 689	11 152	16 475	19 041	16 930	4 270	2 249
1996	85 129	84 230	898	59 308	4 322	638	55 624	12 053	17 452	19 838	17 588	4 291	2 279
1997	89 348	88 304	1 044	62 383	4 563	669	58 488	12 503	18 357	20 672	18 234	4 322	2 325
1998	93 567	92 368	1 199	65 679	4 763	757	61 673	12 780	19 114	21 500	18 876	4 352	.....

Personal Income and Employment—*Continued*

(Millions of dollars, except as noted)

Year	Total	Nonfarm	Farm	Earnings by place of work	Less: Personal contributions for social insurance	Plus: Adjustment for residence	Equals: Net earnings by place of residence	Dividends, interest, and rent	Transfer payments	Total	Disposable	Population (thousands)	Total employment (thousands)
ALASKA													
1969	1 375	1 373	2	1 279	55	-27	1 198	110	67	4 643	3 930	296	144
1970	1 543	1 541	2	1 446	64	-47	1 336	119	88	5 070	4 362	304	149
1971	1 686	1 684	2	1 580	71	-62	1 448	127	111	5 325	4 607	316	153
1972	1 844	1 842	2	1 735	79	-77	1 579	138	128	5 648	4 811	326	158
1973	2 164	2 162	2	1 916	96	-95	1 725	161	277	6 493	5 623	333	167
1974	2 671	2 669	2	2 573	132	-212	2 229	192	250	7 748	6 533	345	189
1975	3 759	3 755	4	4 067	204	-619	3 244	222	293	10 133	8 466	371	227
1976	4 521	4 517	4	5 102	251	-893	3 958	257	306	11 500	9 602	393	243
1977	4 650	4 645	5	4 685	233	-460	3 992	298	360	11 703	9 789	397	237
1978	4 737	4 731	6	4 554	229	-333	3 993	353	391	11 777	10 004	402	237
1979	5 006	5 002	4	4 727	248	-292	4 187	423	397	12 405	10 358	404	241
1980	5 624	5 620	4	5 282	280	-332	4 669	482	473	13 875	11 803	405	244
1981	6 505	6 503	2	6 158	346	-445	5 367	579	559	15 543	12 911	418	253
1982	7 779	7 777	2	7 123	395	-536	6 192	685	903	17 302	14 617	450	278
1983	8 778	8 776	3	7 976	444	-596	6 936	855	987	17 973	15 268	488	298
1984	9 295	9 293	2	8 506	478	-608	7 420	991	884	18 093	15 815	514	310
1985	10 078	10 076	2	8 901	517	-602	7 783	1 111	1 184	18 925	16 695	532	318
1986	10 051	10 043	8	8 680	510	-547	7 624	1 146	1 281	18 466	16 496	544	311
1987	9 719	9 710	10	8 239	499	-514	7 226	1 158	1 336	18 021	15 870	539	312
1988	9 998	9 987	11	8 426	540	-540	7 347	1 203	1 449	18 447	16 304	542	319
1989	10 927	10 921	6	9 250	605	-616	8 030	1 311	1 586	19 970	17 265	547	331
1990	11 656	11 648	8	9 823	644	-653	8 527	1 387	1 742	21 073	18 124	553	341
1991	12 233	12 224	9	10 302	683	-694	8 926	1 407	1 901	21 496	18 676	569	350
1992	12 951	12 942	8	10 844	706	-724	9 415	1 445	2 092	22 073	19 275	587	354
1993	13 557	13 546	10	11 221	742	-737	9 743	1 511	2 302	22 711	19 897	597	361
1994	14 065	14 057	8	11 471	766	-752	9 953	1 720	2 392	23 417	20 290	601	367
1995	14 421	14 411	10	11 613	795	-758	10 061	1 830	2 531	23 971	20 525	602	369
1996	14 713	14 705	9	11 697	822	-771	10 104	1 909	2 701	24 310	20 765	605	373
1997	15 222	15 212	11	11 976	857	-768	10 352	1 941	2 930	24 969	21 203	610	380
1998	15 824	15 812	12	12 455	885	-801	10 769	1 972	3 082	25 771	21 741	614	.....
ARIZONA													
1969	6 024	5 811	214	4 705	203	-26	4 477	972	576	3 468	3 019	1 737	711
1970	6 848	6 659	189	5 248	227	-30	4 992	1 155	701	3 815	3 334	1 795	747
1971	7 786	7 573	213	5 955	266	-29	5 660	1 283	843	4 106	3 626	1 896	786
1972	8 946	8 725	220	6 892	314	-32	6 546	1 426	975	4 453	3 896	2 009	850
1973	10 383	10 130	253	8 006	405	-31	7 569	1 644	1 170	4 885	4 335	2 125	925
1974	11 716	11 312	404	8 922	465	-41	8 418	1 886	1 413	5 267	4 646	2 224	955
1975	12 461	12 232	229	9 080	484	-47	8 550	1 992	1 919	5 450	4 914	2 286	935
1976	14 009	13 661	348	10 277	550	-47	9 681	2 191	2 137	5 966	5 342	2 348	976
1977	15 797	15 515	282	11 679	646	-55	10 978	2 490	2 329	6 508	5 779	2 427	1 047
1978	18 701	18 366	336	13 880	767	-68	13 046	3 019	2 636	7 427	6 549	2 518	1 149
1979	22 205	21 794	412	16 486	937	-69	15 480	3 720	3 005	8 416	7 374	2 639	1 241
1980	25 624	25 129	495	18 560	1 059	-79	17 423	4 574	3 628	9 359	8 233	2 738	1 285
1981	29 141	28 707	434	20 555	1 265	-12	19 278	5 633	4 230	10 370	9 039	2 810	1 317
1982	30 584	30 172	412	21 227	1 344	-5	19 878	5 986	4 721	10 583	9 246	2 890	1 319
1983	33 482	33 151	331	23 138	1 472	5	21 671	6 652	5 159	11 277	10 000	2 969	1 383
1984	37 957	37 402	555	26 603	1 676	9	24 937	7 594	5 427	12 375	10 952	3 067	1 511
1985	42 278	41 758	521	29 718	1 922	22	27 817	8 415	6 046	13 280	11 710	3 184	1 631
1986	46 251	45 752	499	32 423	2 123	41	30 342	9 318	6 591	13 980	12 335	3 308	1 711
1987	50 287	49 653	634	35 214	2 246	68	33 035	10 046	7 206	14 631	12 870	3 437	1 777
1988	53 898	53 128	770	37 880	2 507	111	35 484	10 611	7 803	15 246	13 515	3 535	1 851
1989	57 663	56 978	685	39 548	2 674	169	37 043	11 803	8 817	15 919	14 015	3 622	1 883
1990	61 104	60 464	640	41 681	2 799	234	39 115	12 129	9 860	16 608	14 632	3 679	1 907
1991	63 848	63 123	725	43 512	3 013	224	40 723	12 119	11 007	16 971	14 960	3 762	1 921
1992	68 001	67 354	647	46 523	3 208	242	43 558	11 908	12 535	17 583	15 579	3 867	1 945
1993	72 962	72 138	824	50 150	3 452	218	46 916	12 508	13 537	18 270	16 126	3 994	2 030
1994	79 335	78 825	510	54 857	3 838	215	51 234	13 583	14 519	19 127	16 806	4 148	2 167
1995	86 479	85 706	773	60 088	4 236	223	56 075	14 842	15 562	20 078	17 595	4 307	2 291
1996	93 391	92 716	676	65 012	4 571	251	60 692	16 334	16 366	21 071	18 284	4 432	2 407
1997	100 160	99 530	631	70 388	4 978	273	65 684	17 353	17 124	21 998	18 914	4 553	2 502
1998	108 086	107 421	666	77 524	5 452	284	72 356	17 898	17 832	23 152	19 777	4 669	.....

Personal Income and Employment—*Continued*

(Millions of dollars, except as noted)

Year	Total	Nonfarm	Farm	Derivation of personal income						Per capita (dollars)		Population (thou-sands)	Total employ-ment (thou-sands)
				Earnings by place of work	Less: Personal contribu-tions for social insurance	Plus: Adjustment for residence	Equals: Net earnings by place of residence	Dividends, interest, and rent	Transfer payments	Total	Disposable		
ARKANSAS													
1969	5 021	4 662	359	3 936	162	27	3 801	584	636	2 624	2 326	1 913	800
1970	5 494	5 063	432	4 250	175	17	4 093	651	750	2 847	2 538	1 930	805
1971	6 081	5 660	421	4 672	199	15	4 488	710	883	3 083	2 781	1 972	831
1972	6 862	6 356	506	5 339	230	13	5 123	752	987	3 400	3 050	2 018	867
1973	8 141	7 207	934	6 368	289	9	6 089	859	1 194	3 955	3 542	2 058	902
1974	9 098	8 246	852	6 945	333	2	6 614	1 033	1 451	4 331	3 850	2 100	927
1975	9 931	9 124	807	7 315	356	-1	6 959	1 150	1 822	4 601	4 162	2 158	905
1976	11 036	10 388	648	8 166	401	-12	7 753	1 270	2 014	5 089	4 542	2 169	941
1977	12 352	11 624	728	9 174	450	-20	8 705	1 475	2 172	5 596	5 009	2 207	981
1978	14 396	13 202	1 195	10 812	516	-26	10 271	1 741	2 384	6 424	5 758	2 241	1 022
1979	15 869	14 859	1 010	11 685	589	-29	11 067	2 081	2 721	6 993	6 220	2 269	1 033
1980	17 111	16 727	384	11 962	638	-19	11 305	2 581	3 225	7 476	6 609	2 289	1 035
1981	19 304	18 433	870	13 267	741	-41	12 485	3 176	3 643	8 418	7 449	2 293	1 030
1982	20 114	19 471	644	13 451	786	-42	12 624	3 516	3 974	8 767	7 698	2 294	1 014
1983	21 369	20 971	397	14 319	846	-70	13 404	3 679	4 286	9 267	8 268	2 306	1 043
1984	23 809	22 947	862	16 349	934	-90	15 325	4 067	4 418	10 263	9 195	2 320	1 083
1985	25 408	24 565	843	17 340	1 044	-94	16 203	4 444	4 762	10 919	9 781	2 327	1 104
1986	26 605	25 830	775	18 151	1 126	-117	16 908	4 672	5 025	11 409	10 260	2 332	1 116
1987	27 738	26 802	937	19 253	1 179	-136	17 938	4 600	5 200	11 842	10 609	2 342	1 143
1988	29 605	28 329	1 276	20 704	1 306	-164	19 234	4 888	5 483	12 637	11 337	2 343	1 178
1989	31 331	30 160	1 171	21 723	1 430	-167	20 126	5 256	5 949	13 353	11 950	2 346	1 197
1990	33 020	32 128	892	22 823	1 516	-213	21 095	5 488	6 438	14 025	12 542	2 354	1 210
1991	35 003	34 011	992	24 284	1 622	-232	22 430	5 500	7 074	14 766	13 245	2 370	1 239
1992	37 845	36 596	1 249	26 625	1 761	-270	24 595	5 395	7 856	15 807	14 202	2 394	1 265
1993	39 704	38 457	1 248	27 974	1 866	-322	25 786	5 487	8 431	16 380	14 705	2 424	1 305
1994	41 881	40 527	1 353	29 751	2 022	-356	27 373	5 734	8 774	17 090	15 261	2 451	1 335
1995	44 478	43 082	1 396	31 340	2 162	-326	28 853	6 198	9 428	17 934	15 947	2 480	1 378
1996	47 116	45 301	1 816	32 964	2 239	-322	30 403	6 769	9 944	18 808	16 682	2 505	1 405
1997	49 442	47 799	1 643	34 537	2 370	-299	31 868	7 154	10 420	19 595	17 314	2 523	1 431
1998	51 763	50 225	1 538	36 417	2 498	-312	33 608	7 345	10 810	20 393	17 884	2 538	.....
CALIFORNIA													
1969	89 193	87 458	1 736	70 063	3 176	-66	66 822	13 458	8 913	4 525	3 917	19 711	9 033
1970	95 743	94 008	1 735	73 880	3 338	-57	70 485	14 412	10 846	4 782	4 207	20 023	9 057
1971	101 679	99 945	1 734	77 505	3 596	-46	73 863	15 329	12 487	4 998	4 442	20 346	9 036
1972	111 196	108 980	2 216	85 662	4 217	-35	81 411	16 227	13 559	5 402	4 707	20 585	9 369
1973	122 804	119 841	2 963	94 714	5 095	-32	89 588	18 227	14 990	5 885	5 185	20 868	9 844
1974	137 198	133 526	3 672	104 529	5 561	-24	98 944	20 530	17 724	6 480	5 698	21 173	10 163
1975	150 729	147 432	3 297	112 967	5 919	123	107 172	21 583	21 975	6 999	6 225	21 537	10 286
1976	169 161	165 674	3 488	127 102	6 507	228	120 822	23 789	24 550	7 712	6 793	21 935	10 653
1977	188 443	184 880	3 563	142 483	7 312	76	135 247	26 734	26 462	8 431	7 372	22 350	11 119
1978	216 040	212 531	3 509	163 369	8 358	47	155 057	32 241	28 742	9 459	8 242	22 839	11 802
1979	247 641	242 993	4 648	186 411	9 856	32	176 587	39 385	31 669	10 649	9 229	23 255	12 462
1980	281 589	275 847	5 742	207 494	10 411	14	197 097	47 654	36 838	11 831	10 233	23 801	12 777
1981	315 375	310 921	4 454	226 308	12 745	137	213 701	58 550	43 126	12 986	11 254	24 286	12 969
1982	336 098	331 411	4 687	239 569	13 951	155	225 772	62 961	47 365	13 541	11 809	24 820	12 896
1983	361 590	357 300	4 289	259 288	15 096	170	244 361	66 832	50 396	14 258	12 522	25 360	13 215
1984	402 979	397 977	5 002	290 819	17 060	135	273 895	77 322	51 763	15 593	13 680	25 844	13 848
1985	436 898	431 867	5 030	317 108	19 233	99	297 974	81 779	57 145	16 523	14 397	26 441	14 356
1986	467 657	462 164	5 493	341 654	21 478	68	320 243	86 008	61 406	17 255	15 029	27 102	14 785
1987	504 862	498 232	6 630	374 269	23 852	11	350 427	89 806	64 630	18 175	15 636	27 777	15 392
1988	548 302	541 316	6 985	407 649	26 814	-11	380 824	98 632	68 846	19 263	16 672	28 464	16 164
1989	590 962	584 154	6 808	435 992	28 997	-6	406 989	109 523	74 450	20 226	17 338	29 218	16 578
1990	639 297	632 292	7 006	469 356	31 082	-44	438 229	118 406	82 663	21 363	18 391	29 926	16 955
1991	653 172	647 282	5 891	476 910	32 610	-6	444 294	117 574	91 305	21 491	18 693	30 393	16 907
1992	684 674	677 969	6 706	498 151	33 823	34	464 362	115 589	104 723	22 191	19 467	30 854	16 554
1993	698 130	690 350	7 780	506 522	34 561	-391	471 570	116 424	110 137	22 430	19 702	31 124	16 532
1994	718 322	711 508	6 813	517 994	36 012	-452	481 531	122 721	114 070	22 953	20 084	31 295	16 736
1995	754 788	748 094	6 694	539 606	37 241	-479	501 888	133 351	119 549	23 983	20 828	31 472	17 099
1996	798 580	791 161	7 420	567 889	38 553	-494	528 843	145 128	124 610	25 142	21 503	31 762	17 585
1997	846 839	839 332	7 507	607 976	40 818	-562	566 596	152 202	128 041	26 314	22 310	32 182	18 017
1998	900 900	893 096	7 804	657 898	43 812	-641	613 445	155 672	131 783	27 579	23 119	32 667	.....

Personal Income and Employment—*Continued*

(Millions of dollars, except as noted)

Year	Total	Nonfarm	Farm	Earnings by place of work	Less: Personal contributions for social insurance	Plus: Adjustment for residence	Equals: Net earnings by place of residence	Dividends, interest, and rent	Transfer payments	Per capita (dollars) Total	Per capita (dollars) Disposable	Population (thousands)	Total employment (thousands)
COLORADO													
1969	8 035	7 772	263	6 315	256	2	6 060	1 250	725	3 709	3 194	2 166	1 001
1970	9 031	8 729	302	7 042	285	2	6 759	1 394	878	4 061	3 543	2 224	1 032
1971	10 145	9 827	318	7 932	329	3	7 605	1 515	1 024	4 404	3 866	2 304	1 072
1972	11 481	11 128	353	9 092	381	4	8 714	1 622	1 145	4 774	4 128	2 405	1 149
1973	13 201	12 743	459	10 461	485	3	9 979	1 880	1 343	5 289	4 596	2 496	1 243
1974	14 807	14 250	558	11 643	558	4	11 089	2 151	1 567	5 827	5 041	2 541	1 276
1975	16 251	15 765	486	12 579	589	8	11 998	2 315	1 938	6 284	5 510	2 586	1 285
1976	18 049	17 695	354	13 996	653	9	13 351	2 549	2 150	6 857	5 986	2 632	1 339
1977	20 234	19 953	281	15 730	752	11	14 990	2 888	2 356	7 505	6 499	2 696	1 411
1978	23 439	23 221	218	18 315	875	20	17 460	3 405	2 574	8 472	7 330	2 767	1 505
1979	27 163	26 946	217	21 170	1 056	21	20 135	4 143	2 886	9 534	8 205	2 849	1 594
1980	31 264	30 976	288	23 975	1 209	27	22 793	5 094	3 378	10 748	9 261	2 909	1 654
1981	35 969	35 698	271	27 188	1 460	6	25 734	5 945	3 945	12 079	10 348	2 978	1 722
1982	39 309	39 143	167	29 518	1 629	2	27 891	6 951	4 468	12 840	10 964	3 062	1 765
1983	42 179	41 833	346	31 473	1 731	-1	29 742	7 526	4 911	13 460	11 797	3 134	1 794
1984	46 273	45 844	430	34 557	1 907	7	32 657	8 522	5 095	14 597	12 860	3 170	1 891
1985	48 850	48 455	395	36 524	2 124	16	34 417	9 020	5 413	15 224	13 366	3 209	1 926
1986	50 412	50 016	396	37 442	2 255	20	35 207	9 355	5 850	15 571	13 715	3 237	1 924
1987	52 647	52 160	487	39 080	2 317	32	36 794	9 572	6 281	16 147	14 192	3 260	1 914
1988	55 410	54 835	576	41 161	2 518	46	38 689	10 080	6 641	16 985	14 938	3 262	1 986
1989	59 325	58 709	616	43 387	2 725	62	40 723	11 345	7 256	18 110	15 801	3 276	2 019
1990	63 733	62 823	910	46 757	2 920	81	43 918	11 938	7 877	19 290	16 758	3 304	2 052
1991	67 698	67 055	643	49 560	3 186	80	46 454	12 458	8 787	20 099	17 432	3 368	2 105
1992	72 690	72 067	624	53 844	3 431	81	50 495	12 447	9 749	21 005	18 150	3 461	2 154
1993	78 783	77 819	964	58 784	3 723	47	55 109	13 157	10 517	22 117	19 060	3 562	2 252
1994	84 115	83 634	481	62 238	4 019	38	58 257	14 786	11 071	23 019	19 732	3 654	2 368
1995	90 853	90 323	530	67 082	4 360	40	62 762	15 844	12 248	24 304	20 887	3 738	2 464
1996	97 735	97 097	638	72 051	4 672	46	67 425	17 426	12 884	25 627	21 829	3 814	2 551
1997	105 143	104 482	661	78 156	5 084	43	73 115	18 434	13 595	27 015	22 787	3 892	2 652
1998	114 449	113 546	904	86 858	5 602	30	81 285	18 976	14 188	28 821	24 128	3 971	.....
CONNECTICUT													
1969	14 564	14 491	73	10 733	421	680	10 991	2 538	1 035	4 855	4 052	3 000	1 417
1970	15 448	15 369	79	11 325	444	670	11 551	2 645	1 252	5 084	4 357	3 039	1 414
1971	16 175	16 098	77	11 670	481	696	11 885	2 729	1 562	5 283	4 594	3 061	1 388
1972	17 444	17 368	76	12 679	534	735	12 879	2 891	1 674	5 683	4 848	3 070	1 416
1973	19 060	18 972	87	14 026	663	748	14 111	3 144	1 805	6 210	5 350	3 069	1 480
1974	20 772	20 682	90	15 178	751	775	15 202	3 456	2 115	6 753	5 838	3 076	1 511
1975	22 123	22 042	81	15 767	774	837	15 830	3 539	2 754	7 172	6 293	3 085	1 468
1976	24 121	24 033	88	17 216	832	911	17 294	3 865	2 961	7 816	6 775	3 086	1 493
1977	26 643	26 555	88	19 118	915	1 003	19 206	4 308	3 129	8 626	7 470	3 089	1 546
1978	29 760	29 675	85	21 485	1 040	1 149	21 594	4 928	3 238	9 616	8 272	3 095	1 616
1979	33 652	33 571	81	24 178	1 224	1 311	24 265	5 790	3 597	10 856	9 282	3 100	1 675
1980	38 362	38 277	85	26 989	1 375	1 534	27 148	7 070	4 144	12 322	10 471	3 113	1 709
1981	42 960	42 876	84	29 461	1 621	1 670	29 511	8 668	4 781	13 730	11 616	3 129	1 732
1982	46 190	46 080	110	31 400	1 769	1 797	31 428	9 416	5 346	14 715	12 421	3 139	1 731
1983	49 397	49 286	111	33 882	1 899	1 930	33 913	9 738	5 746	15 620	13 456	3 162	1 748
1984	55 207	55 074	132	37 870	2 124	2 078	37 824	11 401	5 982	17 360	15 014	3 180	1 831
1985	59 319	59 187	132	41 371	2 415	2 221	41 177	11 792	6 350	18 531	15 887	3 201	1 889
1986	63 880	63 735	145	44 789	2 671	2 369	44 488	12 639	6 754	19 815	16 857	3 224	1 948
1987	70 101	69 957	144	49 904	2 977	2 516	49 443	13 560	7 099	21 588	18 176	3 247	1 997
1988	77 541	77 383	158	55 281	3 347	2 706	54 641	15 290	7 611	23 699	20 245	3 272	2 057
1989	83 421	83 275	145	58 292	3 589	2 647	57 350	17 651	8 419	25 407	21 765	3 283	2 050
1990	87 002	86 817	185	60 375	3 726	2 913	59 562	17 919	9 521	26 453	22 792	3 289	2 017
1991	87 837	87 674	164	60 670	3 897	2 958	59 732	17 445	10 661	26 721	22 965	3 287	1 940
1992	92 749	92 559	191	63 760	4 023	3 751	63 489	16 836	12 425	28 345	23 980	3 272	1 921
1993	95 588	95 363	225	66 158	4 128	3 635	65 665	16 997	12 926	29 232	24 617	3 270	1 942
1994	98 966	98 790	176	68 308	4 333	3 611	67 586	17 967	13 413	30 310	25 558	3 265	1 927
1995	104 616	104 448	169	71 266	4 569	4 186	70 882	19 350	14 385	32 073	26 841	3 262	1 952
1996	110 904	110 739	165	74 423	4 756	5 030	74 697	21 407	14 801	33 979	28 035	3 264	1 987
1997	117 173	117 009	164	80 012	5 120	4 533	79 425	22 300	15 449	35 863	29 215	3 267	2 029
1998	123 431	123 261	170	85 206	5 403	4 888	84 691	22 703	16 037	37 700	30 317	3 274	.....

Personal Income and Employment—*Continued*

(Millions of dollars, except as noted)

Year	Total	Nonfarm	Farm	Earnings by place of work	Less: Personal contributions for social insurance	Plus: Adjustment for residence	Equals: Net earnings by place of residence	Dividends, interest, and rent	Transfer payments	Per capita (dollars) Total	Disposable	Population (thousands)	Total employment (thousands)
DELAWARE													
1969	2 400	2 343	58	1 968	73	-61	1 835	414	151	4 445	3 612	540	271
1970	2 541	2 505	37	2 087	77	-69	1 942	418	181	4 618	3 786	550	275
1971	2 759	2 719	40	2 285	86	-87	2 112	431	215	4 881	4 046	565	280
1972	3 032	2 980	51	2 540	98	-98	2 344	448	239	5 283	4 361	574	293
1973	3 373	3 275	98	2 865	128	-119	2 619	475	280	5 825	4 805	579	305
1974	3 655	3 570	85	3 062	146	-124	2 793	517	345	6 267	5 190	583	302
1975	3 908	3 813	95	3 221	152	-129	2 941	513	454	6 637	5 562	589	292
1976	4 290	4 203	87	3 542	165	-145	3 233	563	494	7 236	5 986	593	296
1977	4 648	4 590	58	3 818	179	-163	3 477	629	543	7 814	6 478	595	296
1978	5 101	5 038	63	4 230	201	-190	3 840	690	571	8 527	7 103	598	304
1979	5 619	5 564	56	4 630	232	-212	4 187	782	651	9 383	7 758	599	312
1980	6 315	6 301	14	5 102	259	-259	4 584	945	786	10 614	8 757	595	312
1981	6 943	6 900	43	5 491	300	-290	4 901	1 157	884	11 649	9 533	596	314
1982	7 445	7 378	67	5 898	328	-322	5 249	1 251	946	12 425	10 315	599	317
1983	7 967	7 887	80	6 343	356	-367	5 620	1 333	1 014	13 159	11 074	605	326
1984	8 740	8 643	97	6 952	389	-412	6 151	1 516	1 074	14 291	12 123	612	341
1985	9 553	9 448	105	7 606	440	-451	6 715	1 687	1 150	15 451	13 115	618	359
1986	10 202	10 055	147	8 080	477	-458	7 146	1 809	1 247	16 257	13 747	628	372
1987	11 097	10 983	115	8 876	516	-521	7 840	1 937	1 321	17 423	14 852	637	389
1988	12 226	12 041	185	9 803	585	-576	8 642	2 143	1 441	18 878	16 202	648	406
1989	13 536	13 342	194	10 779	654	-672	9 454	2 516	1 566	20 563	17 615	658	418
1990	14 445	14 306	138	11 478	693	-735	10 050	2 702	1 693	21 590	18 485	669	422
1991	15 135	15 005	130	11 914	729	-773	10 412	2 822	1 901	22 241	19 151	680	418
1992	15 875	15 762	113	12 429	748	-800	10 882	2 836	2 157	23 004	19 823	690	417
1993	16 482	16 369	114	12 953	781	-881	11 291	2 926	2 265	23 542	20 248	700	424
1994	17 344	17 235	109	13 596	837	-962	11 798	3 101	2 445	24 465	20 937	709	428
1995	18 401	18 323	78	14 387	897	-1 063	12 428	3 350	2 623	25 603	21 976	719	441
1996	19 723	19 624	99	15 317	953	-1 217	13 147	3 732	2 844	27 125	23 100	727	452
1997	20 947	20 861	85	16 319	1 022	-1 149	14 148	3 896	2 903	28 493	24 076	735	465
1998	22 258	22 117	141	17 659	1 100	-1 271	15 288	3 970	3 001	29 932	25 077	744	.....
DISTRICT OF COLUMBIA													
1969	3 473	3 473	0	5 851	269	-3 002	2 580	475	418	4 558	3 861	762	678
1970	3 793	3 793	0	6 345	302	-3 260	2 784	493	516	5 023	4 273	755	674
1971	4 149	4 149	0	6 802	324	-3 494	2 984	531	635	5 528	4 762	751	668
1972	4 522	4 522	0	7 352	357	-3 791	3 203	570	748	6 079	5 202	744	671
1973	4 802	4 802	0	7 823	402	-4 052	3 368	600	833	6 545	5 591	734	664
1974	5 263	5 263	0	8 496	445	-4 411	3 641	654	969	7 302	6 267	721	676
1975	5 746	5 746	0	9 252	478	-4 870	3 904	655	1 187	8 089	6 976	710	680
1976	6 139	6 139	0	10 003	517	-5 325	4 162	713	1 265	8 816	7 487	696	677
1977	6 608	6 608	0	10 841	550	-5 788	4 503	777	1 328	9 692	8 294	682	683
1978	7 016	7 016	0	11 870	600	-6 504	4 767	855	1 395	10 472	8 904	670	696
1979	7 455	7 455	0	12 892	670	-7 284	4 938	957	1 559	11 370	9 546	656	709
1980	7 922	7 922	0	14 028	736	-8 262	5 031	1 107	1 785	12 412	10 450	638	706
1981	8 626	8 626	0	14 892	822	-8 773	5 297	1 355	1 974	13 544	11 239	637	696
1982	9 231	9 231	0	15 761	883	-9 244	5 634	1 491	2 107	14 556	12 103	634	680
1983	9 655	9 655	0	16 767	999	-9 767	6 001	1 498	2 156	15 267	12 853	632	676
1984	10 527	10 527	0	18 287	1 092	-10 604	6 592	1 696	2 239	16 620	13 995	633	699
1985	11 124	11 124	0	19 548	1 223	-11 296	7 030	1 837	2 258	17 531	14 711	635	713
1986	11 703	11 703	0	20 681	1 309	-11 901	7 470	1 890	2 343	18 335	15 377	638	733
1987	12 462	12 462	0	22 434	1 391	-12 942	8 101	1 927	2 434	19 566	16 241	637	746
1988	13 732	13 732	0	24 865	1 542	-14 374	8 949	2 204	2 579	21 782	18 461	630	770
1989	14 630	14 630	0	26 487	1 678	-15 416	9 393	2 614	2 623	23 438	19 779	624	778
1990	15 484	15 484	0	28 410	1 802	-16 578	10 031	2 645	2 809	25 646	21 752	604	787
1991	16 050	16 050	0	29 648	1 907	-17 461	10 281	3 126	2 643	27 028	23 138	594	775
1992	16 726	16 726	0	31 252	1 995	-18 536	10 721	2 613	3 393	28 597	24 640	585	768
1993	17 265	17 265	0	32 556	2 081	-19 360	11 115	2 596	3 553	29 912	25 572	577	768
1994	17 660	17 660	0	33 395	2 141	-20 008	11 247	2 804	3 608	31 212	26 568	566	748
1995	17 899	17 899	0	33 733	2 167	-20 131	11 435	2 869	3 594	32 398	27 857	552	733
1996	18 463	18 463	0	34 040	2 185	-20 269	11 586	3 115	3 763	34 213	28 950	540	716
1997	18 920	18 920	0	35 024	2 259	-20 940	11 825	3 135	3 959	35 704	29 914	530	712
1998	19 526	19 526	0	37 129	2 379	-22 457	12 293	3 159	4 074	37 325	30 776	523	.....

Personal Income and Employment—*Continued*

(Millions of dollars, except as noted)

Year	Total	Nonfarm	Farm	Derivation of personal income						Per capita (dollars)		Population (thousands)	Total employment (thousands)
				Earnings by place of work	Less: Personal contributions for social insurance	Plus: Adjustment for residence	Equals: Net earnings by place of residence	Dividends, interest, and rent	Transfer payments	Total	Disposable		
FLORIDA													
1969	24 309	23 652	657	17 477	735	-21	16 721	4 983	2 606	3 660	3 191	6 641	2 857
1970	27 298	26 728	570	19 334	822	-19	18 493	5 635	3 170	3 988	3 516	6 845	2 966
1971	30 568	29 895	673	21 400	943	-13	20 445	6 307	3 816	4 267	3 781	7 163	3 082
1972	35 206	34 432	774	24 851	1 104	-11	23 736	6 973	4 498	4 681	4 073	7 520	3 338
1973	41 275	40 409	867	29 149	1 435	-10	27 704	8 136	5 436	5 207	4 562	7 927	3 666
1974	46 399	45 460	939	32 036	1 588	-2	30 447	9 394	6 559	5 579	4 911	8 317	3 766
1975	50 125	49 087	1 038	33 272	1 578	-11	31 683	10 038	8 404	5 868	5 267	8 542	3 676
1976	55 120	54 046	1 074	36 293	1 719	8	34 583	11 155	9 382	6 339	5 651	8 695	3 730
1977	61 779	60 703	1 075	40 565	1 930	19	38 654	12 722	10 403	6 950	6 170	8 889	3 929
1978	71 733	70 447	1 286	47 064	2 267	21	44 818	15 340	11 576	7 856	6 948	9 132	4 235
1979	83 239	81 873	1 367	53 859	2 715	16	51 160	18 719	13 361	8 789	7 729	9 471	4 457
1980	97 980	96 223	1 756	61 883	3 152	11	58 741	23 306	15 933	9 957	8 714	9 840	4 695
1981	112 971	111 501	1 470	69 114	3 838	34	65 311	29 103	18 558	11 083	9 676	10 193	4 881
1982	121 683	119 781	1 902	73 782	4 237	63	69 608	31 136	20 939	11 620	10 054	10 471	4 969
1983	134 039	131 379	2 661	81 992	4 666	86	77 413	33 853	22 774	12 469	11 019	10 750	5 183
1984	148 770	146 834	1 936	91 625	5 297	131	86 460	38 500	23 811	13 476	12 028	11 040	5 527
1985	163 083	161 137	1 946	100 613	6 104	174	94 682	42 391	26 011	14 367	12 643	11 351	5 807
1986	176 203	174 111	2 092	108 747	6 772	233	102 207	45 977	28 020	15 102	13 227	11 668	6 054
1987	191 969	189 723	2 246	120 415	7 356	300	113 359	48 688	29 923	16 001	14 028	11 997	6 139
1988	210 337	207 473	2 865	132 495	8 363	372	124 504	53 333	32 501	17 092	15 062	12 306	6 452
1989	232 601	229 982	2 619	140 871	9 263	458	132 066	64 500	36 035	18 405	16 196	12 638	6 661
1990	249 004	246 774	2 230	150 415	9 822	558	141 151	67 907	39 946	19 127	16 901	13 019	6 787
1991	258 495	255 771	2 725	154 754	10 347	612	145 019	68 628	44 848	19 451	17 325	13 290	6 785
1992	268 828	266 269	2 559	164 944	11 021	653	154 576	63 710	50 542	19 910	17 691	13 502	6 833
1993	289 052	286 229	2 823	176 426	11 746	524	165 204	69 465	54 383	21 080	18 701	13 712	7 071
1994	303 647	301 707	1 941	184 805	12 614	532	172 723	73 055	57 870	21 761	19 235	13 954	7 315
1995	321 549	319 499	2 050	195 888	13 447	547	182 987	76 374	62 188	22 676	19 959	14 180	7 534
1996	343 806	341 976	1 830	207 367	14 044	575	193 899	84 081	65 827	23 834	20 723	14 425	7 770
1997	363 980	362 086	1 893	220 986	14 971	607	206 623	88 023	69 335	24 799	21 379	14 677	8 033
1998	386 654	384 392	2 263	240 215	16 163	635	224 687	89 734	72 234	25 922	22 134	14 916	.....
GEORGIA													
1969	14 429	13 986	443	12 191	496	-53	11 642	1 566	1 220	3 170	2 751	4 551	2 119
1970	15 658	15 234	424	12 996	535	-48	12 414	1 744	1 499	3 400	2 994	4 605	2 121
1971	17 269	16 785	484	14 220	600	-43	13 577	1 907	1 785	3 666	3 261	4 710	2 167
1972	19 430	18 924	506	16 056	692	-36	15 328	2 081	2 021	4 042	3 543	4 807	2 253
1973	22 050	21 230	819	18 232	873	-31	17 328	2 377	2 345	4 494	3 973	4 907	2 356
1974	24 288	23 584	704	19 612	983	-25	18 604	2 768	2 916	4 863	4 298	4 995	2 374
1975	26 045	25 387	658	20 373	1 010	-11	19 352	2 912	3 781	5 149	4 640	5 059	2 313
1976	29 135	28 492	644	23 052	1 134	-24	21 894	3 139	4 102	5 684	5 071	5 126	2 399
1977	32 247	31 878	370	25 700	1 265	-28	24 407	3 486	4 356	6 187	5 486	5 212	2 503
1978	36 746	36 168	577	29 387	1 459	-3	27 925	4 072	4 749	6 951	6 136	5 286	2 622
1979	41 404	40 789	616	32 875	1 698	4	31 182	4 844	5 379	7 680	6 701	5 391	2 704
1980	46 229	46 170	58	35 665	1 932	8	33 741	6 048	6 440	8 426	7 382	5 486	2 747
1981	52 116	51 598	518	39 603	2 275	13	37 340	7 437	7 339	9 359	8 156	5 568	2 785
1982	56 170	55 488	682	42 352	2 490	-30	39 833	8 274	8 063	9 942	8 711	5 650	2 801
1983	61 533	61 066	466	46 411	2 719	-68	43 624	9 185	8 725	10 742	9 402	5 728	2 885
1984	70 184	69 229	954	53 368	3 104	-104	50 160	10 862	9 161	12 028	10 586	5 835	3 080
1985	77 087	76 310	777	58 908	3 577	-118	55 214	11 919	9 955	12 928	11 304	5 963	3 224
1986	83 773	82 957	815	64 373	3 994	-163	60 216	12 882	10 674	13 768	12 059	6 085	3 353
1987	90 406	89 535	871	69 852	4 286	-168	65 398	13 670	11 338	14 562	12 698	6 208	3 454
1988	98 473	97 334	1 139	75 882	4 773	-157	70 953	15 243	12 278	15 591	13 689	6 316	3 572
1989	105 563	104 227	1 337	80 144	5 137	-108	74 899	17 206	13 460	16 466	14 390	6 411	3 635
1990	113 112	111 920	1 193	85 363	5 483	-93	79 788	18 356	14 969	17 385	15 214	6 506	3 681
1991	118 746	117 235	1 511	88 443	5 764	-81	82 598	19 073	17 075	17 930	15 784	6 623	3 650
1992	127 686	126 129	1 557	96 052	6 151	-96	89 805	18 908	18 973	18 888	16 664	6 760	3 729
1993	135 613	134 082	1 532	102 333	6 597	-115	95 621	19 502	20 490	19 668	17 212	6 895	3 898
1994	145 373	143 543	1 831	109 446	7 140	-142	102 166	21 303	21 905	20 632	18 013	7 046	4 057
1995	155 959	154 200	1 759	117 310	7 704	-204	109 403	23 079	23 478	21 696	18 897	7 189	4 224
1996	167 956	165 962	1 993	125 807	8 228	-265	117 314	25 458	25 184	22 900	19 798	7 334	4 363
1997	178 875	176 696	2 179	134 876	8 843	-272	125 761	26 914	26 200	23 882	20 495	7 490	4 470
1998	191 865	189 695	2 170	146 982	9 588	-349	137 045	27 678	27 143	25 106	21 359	7 642	.....

Personal Income and Employment—*Continued*

(Millions of dollars, except as noted)

| Year | Total | Nonfarm | Farm | Derivation of personal income | | | | | | Per capita (dollars) | | Population (thousands) | Total employment (thousands) |
				Earnings by place of work	Less: Personal contributions for social insurance	Plus: Adjustment for residence	Equals: Net earnings by place of residence	Dividends, interest, and rent	Transfer payments	Total	Disposable		
HAWAII													
1969	3 332	3 211	121	2 760	122	0	2 638	477	216	4 484	3 803	743	416
1970	3 811	3 676	135	3 147	141	0	3 006	530	276	4 996	4 266	763	434
1971	4 112	3 978	133	3 339	159	0	3 180	580	353	5 194	4 508	792	437
1972	4 524	4 390	134	3 667	174	0	3 493	610	420	5 530	4 732	818	453
1973	5 028	4 889	139	4 050	207	0	3 843	702	484	5 973	5 128	842	473
1974	5 762	5 405	357	4 631	238	0	4 394	786	582	6 714	5 796	858	485
1975	6 195	5 985	210	4 904	264	0	4 640	811	745	7 079	6 252	875	499
1976	6 726	6 551	175	5 283	286	0	4 997	855	873	7 537	6 602	892	505
1977	7 288	7 101	187	5 737	313	0	5 425	927	936	7 958	6 924	916	509
1978	8 091	7 921	170	6 333	353	0	5 980	1 093	1 018	8 711	7 532	929	527
1979	9 196	8 998	198	7 154	405	0	6 750	1 319	1 127	9 679	8 347	950	556
1980	10 563	10 173	391	8 169	452	0	7 716	1 543	1 304	10 916	9 427	968	575
1981	11 376	11 170	206	8 528	514	0	8 014	1 844	1 519	11 630	10 032	978	569
1982	12 046	11 804	242	9 074	565	0	8 509	1 867	1 670	12 121	10 670	1 013	568
1983	13 193	12 850	344	9 855	604	0	9 251	2 095	1 847	13 028	11 433	1 028	579
1984	14 123	13 890	234	10 457	647	0	9 810	2 394	1 920	13 740	12 165	1 028	585
1985	15 070	14 855	215	11 181	700	0	10 481	2 539	2 050	14 494	12 703	1 040	601
1986	16 118	15 858	260	11 983	739	0	11 245	2 685	2 189	15 325	13 427	1 052	616
1987	17 367	17 136	231	13 112	800	0	12 312	2 791	2 264	16 262	14 040	1 068	647
1988	19 237	18 983	254	14 644	914	0	13 731	3 087	2 420	17 815	15 335	1 080	675
1989	21 230	20 993	238	16 130	1 031	0	15 099	3 498	2 633	19 395	16 439	1 095	703
1990	23 957	23 706	250	18 084	1 143	0	16 941	3 882	3 134	21 529	18 340	1 113	730
1991	25 098	24 891	207	19 083	1 228	0	17 856	4 012	3 231	22 171	18 987	1 132	753
1992	26 372	26 173	200	20 328	1 297	0	19 031	3 700	3 642	22 906	19 736	1 151	755
1993	27 511	27 326	186	20 844	1 320	0	19 524	4 028	3 959	23 638	20 391	1 164	751
1994	28 332	28 152	180	21 072	1 354	0	19 718	4 363	4 251	24 090	20 834	1 176	747
1995	29 396	29 232	165	21 187	1 372	0	19 814	4 806	4 777	24 848	21 736	1 183	740
1996	29 784	29 620	164	21 213	1 375	0	19 838	5 010	4 937	25 086	21 824	1 187	741
1997	30 514	30 356	159	21 702	1 413	0	20 290	5 079	5 147	25 598	22 145	1 192	745
1998	31 268	31 097	171	22 180	1 427	0	20 753	5 158	5 358	26 210	22 500	1 193	.....
IDAHO													
1969	2 286	2 024	263	1 853	71	12	1 794	281	212	3 234	2 870	707	315
1970	2 518	2 239	280	2 016	77	13	1 951	313	254	3 511	3 141	717	324
1971	2 747	2 484	263	2 155	87	14	2 081	366	301	3 719	3 325	739	332
1972	3 135	2 796	339	2 488	101	15	2 402	391	343	4 107	3 689	763	347
1973	3 642	3 174	468	2 891	129	17	2 779	472	392	4 656	4 152	782	365
1974	4 290	3 643	647	3 412	152	20	3 280	536	474	5 310	4 698	808	381
1975	4 572	4 170	402	3 545	171	25	3 398	588	585	5 495	4 898	832	393
1976	5 170	4 813	357	4 000	194	31	3 839	664	669	6 033	5 373	857	419
1977	5 655	5 405	251	4 347	215	31	4 164	767	725	6 401	5 683	883	435
1978	6 545	6 221	324	5 074	245	38	4 867	898	779	7 184	6 372	911	460
1979	7 203	6 969	234	5 463	287	43	5 219	1 081	904	7 723	6 835	933	470
1980	8 129	7 722	407	5 985	310	56	5 731	1 314	1 084	8 575	7 593	948	466
1981	8 894	8 499	395	6 348	358	51	6 040	1 615	1 239	9 244	8 099	962	463
1982	9 197	8 810	387	6 316	374	59	6 001	1 777	1 419	9 445	8 356	974	453
1983	9 939	9 350	589	6 984	398	58	6 645	1 788	1 506	10 122	9 037	982	464
1984	10 681	10 178	504	7 522	434	70	7 157	1 990	1 534	10 780	9 665	991	474
1985	11 264	10 803	461	7 890	480	76	7 487	2 096	1 681	11 331	10 117	994	476
1986	11 549	11 073	477	8 017	499	92	7 610	2 161	1 778	11 663	10 464	990	476
1987	12 081	11 495	586	8 501	519	101	8 083	2 179	1 820	12 265	10 949	985	490
1988	12 920	12 285	635	9 205	593	116	8 730	2 252	1 940	13 108	11 657	986	513
1989	14 203	13 344	859	10 144	661	130	9 612	2 505	2 086	14 283	12 548	994	529
1990	15 528	14 551	977	11 140	719	150	10 570	2 680	2 278	15 346	13 470	1 012	552
1991	16 267	15 465	802	11 576	787	165	10 955	2 773	2 539	15 664	13 700	1 039	571
1992	17 700	16 892	808	12 778	850	167	12 096	2 814	2 790	16 607	14 535	1 066	591
1993	19 475	18 339	1 136	14 197	919	151	13 429	3 007	3 038	17 699	15 507	1 100	614
1994	20 628	19 979	650	14 959	1 017	161	14 103	3 303	3 222	18 186	15 898	1 134	651
1995	22 062	21 371	691	15 894	1 109	185	14 970	3 583	3 510	18 961	16 562	1 164	675
1996	23 418	22 644	774	16 641	1 169	212	15 684	3 920	3 814	19 741	17 214	1 186	696
1997	24 651	23 958	693	17 503	1 257	248	16 495	4 166	3 991	20 392	17 658	1 209	715
1998	25 901	25 254	647	18 504	1 329	277	17 452	4 295	4 154	21 080	18 129	1 229	.....

Personal Income and Employment—*Continued*

(Millions of dollars, except as noted)

Year	Total	Nonfarm	Farm	Derivation of personal income Earnings by place of work	Less: Personal contributions for social insurance	Plus: Adjustment for residence	Equals: Net earnings by place of residence	Dividends, interest, and rent	Transfer payments	Per capita (dollars) Total	Disposable	Population (thousands)	Total employment (thousands)
ILLINOIS													
1969	48 262	47 312	951	39 216	1 620	125	37 722	6 943	3 598	4 372	3 715	11 039	5 179
1970	51 044	50 271	773	41 150	1 702	62	39 509	7 261	4 275	4 588	3 913	11 125	5 144
1971	54 689	53 759	929	43 833	1 872	23	41 983	7 589	5 117	4 880	4 229	11 206	5 105
1972	59 325	58 283	1 042	47 569	2 071	7	45 505	8 057	5 764	5 270	4 505	11 258	5 156
1973	66 435	64 578	1 858	53 091	2 542	-3	50 545	9 115	6 776	5 900	5 087	11 260	5 351
1974	72 783	71 083	1 700	57 585	2 878	-3	54 705	10 349	7 729	6 456	5 545	11 274	5 442
1975	78 720	76 264	2 456	61 210	2 991	-18	58 201	10 774	9 745	6 962	6 058	11 306	5 342
1976	86 290	84 571	1 720	67 023	3 273	13	63 763	11 697	10 831	7 596	6 549	11 360	5 458
1977	95 213	93 461	1 752	74 116	3 567	88	70 637	13 098	11 478	8 347	7 169	11 406	5 587
1978	105 573	104 020	1 553	82 193	4 008	187	78 373	14 979	12 221	9 233	7 921	11 434	5 748
1979	116 428	114 620	1 808	89 924	4 561	284	85 647	17 512	13 270	10 193	8 695	11 423	5 811
1980	126 028	125 703	325	93 515	4 873	386	89 027	20 974	16 026	11 021	9 421	11 435	5 688
1981	139 612	137 931	1 680	101 066	5 599	319	95 785	25 451	18 376	12 200	10 416	11 443	5 684
1982	144 863	144 034	829	102 846	5 881	255	97 221	27 377	20 266	12 681	10 976	11 423	5 581
1983	150 369	150 890	-521	105 808	6 108	230	99 930	28 830	21 609	13 180	11 462	11 409	5 540
1984	166 014	164 956	1 059	118 159	6 697	154	111 616	32 511	21 887	14 547	12 750	11 412	5 744
1985	174 664	173 149	1 515	125 209	7 431	93	117 871	33 514	23 279	15 322	13 387	11 400	5 812
1986	183 406	182 186	1 219	132 025	8 043	40	124 022	35 049	24 335	16 106	14 077	11 387	5 925
1987	194 399	193 166	1 233	141 743	8 591	-43	133 109	36 083	25 207	17 066	14 735	11 391	6 070
1988	207 437	206 902	535	152 154	9 607	-135	142 412	38 727	26 299	18 212	15 836	11 390	6 240
1989	221 653	219 820	1 832	160 121	10 393	-166	149 561	44 074	28 018	19 427	16 769	11 410	6 347
1990	234 593	233 210	1 383	169 224	11 010	-265	157 950	46 456	30 187	20 494	17 688	11 447	6 427
1991	241 788	241 233	556	174 022	11 606	-283	162 133	46 887	32 768	20 966	18 200	11 533	6 422
1992	258 288	256 915	1 373	187 671	12 170	-329	175 171	45 974	37 142	22 209	19 355	11 630	6 406
1993	268 281	267 145	1 137	196 180	12 847	-437	182 896	46 704	38 682	22 895	19 847	11 718	6 497
1994	282 546	280 927	1 619	206 635	13 719	-493	192 423	49 916	40 207	23 956	20 665	11 794	6 677
1995	298 246	298 113	133	216 484	14 372	-597	201 515	53 609	43 123	25 135	21 620	11 866	6 850
1996	314 960	313 272	1 688	227 469	14 734	-625	212 109	57 781	45 071	26 393	22 494	11 934	6 969
1997	331 966	330 294	1 672	241 851	15 633	-835	225 384	59 989	46 593	27 688	23 377	11 989	7 098
1998	349 030	348 029	1 000	257 283	16 572	-927	239 784	61 210	48 036	28 976	24 277	12 045	.....
INDIANA													
1969	19 034	18 420	614	16 042	625	5	15 423	2 225	1 386	3 701	3 186	5 143	2 327
1970	19 740	19 291	449	16 326	636	34	15 724	2 381	1 635	3 793	3 304	5 204	2 291
1971	21 448	20 774	674	17 526	701	91	16 917	2 571	1 960	4 085	3 594	5 250	2 290
1972	23 451	22 867	584	19 259	798	123	18 584	2 705	2 163	4 428	3 849	5 296	2 367
1973	26 995	25 703	1 292	22 198	1 008	161	21 351	3 108	2 536	5 065	4 446	5 329	2 483
1974	28 893	28 097	796	23 256	1 135	209	22 330	3 580	2 984	5 401	4 666	5 350	2 492
1975	30 965	29 809	1 157	24 221	1 158	246	23 309	3 911	3 745	5 787	5 096	5 351	2 405
1976	34 742	33 605	1 138	27 472	1 293	287	26 466	4 314	3 962	6 468	5 638	5 372	2 489
1977	38 562	37 759	803	30 550	1 436	335	29 448	4 894	4 220	7 134	6 192	5 405	2 578
1978	43 175	42 369	806	34 241	1 645	385	32 981	5 556	4 639	7 927	6 864	5 446	2 671
1979	47 732	47 043	689	37 406	1 884	452	35 974	6 466	5 293	8 718	7 519	5 475	2 713
1980	51 210	50 826	384	38 233	1 964	574	36 843	7 795	6 572	9 327	8 098	5 491	2 632
1981	55 917	55 589	328	40 793	2 280	619	39 132	9 447	7 339	10 203	8 810	5 480	2 611
1982	57 423	57 140	283	40 694	2 342	685	39 038	10 203	8 183	10 502	9 141	5 468	2 529
1983	59 961	60 218	-258	42 279	2 456	742	40 566	10 624	8 771	11 001	9 666	5 450	2 549
1984	66 588	65 905	683	47 437	2 705	905	45 639	11 858	9 092	12 199	10 770	5 458	2 653
1985	70 118	69 532	586	50 175	3 005	988	48 158	12 405	9 555	12 844	11 291	5 459	2 708
1986	73 701	73 233	469	52 659	3 235	1 083	50 507	13 024	10 170	13 513	11 911	5 454	2 769
1987	78 395	77 747	648	56 842	3 451	1 151	54 542	13 312	10 540	14 324	12 575	5 473	2 865
1988	83 645	83 485	159	60 932	3 861	1 255	58 326	14 101	11 218	15 231	13 397	5 492	2 955
1989	90 013	89 173	841	65 411	4 215	1 343	62 539	15 413	12 061	16 296	14 182	5 524	3 030
1990	95 364	94 637	727	68 728	4 451	1 488	65 765	16 406	13 193	17 167	14 962	5 555	3 083
1991	98 710	98 586	124	70 848	4 722	1 517	67 643	16 435	14 632	17 624	15 415	5 601	3 094
1992	105 968	105 403	565	76 562	5 020	1 669	73 211	16 237	16 520	18 763	16 488	5 648	3 144
1993	112 016	111 341	675	81 398	5 363	1 752	77 787	16 656	17 574	19 649	17 110	5 701	3 217
1994	119 029	118 474	555	86 712	5 805	1 899	82 807	17 976	18 246	20 734	17 951	5 741	3 313
1995	123 987	123 832	156	90 439	6 143	2 035	86 331	19 061	18 595	21 427	18 556	5 787	3 402
1996	129 570	128 738	831	93 825	6 360	2 198	89 663	20 323	19 584	22 234	19 160	5 827	3 447
1997	136 074	135 116	958	98 835	6 713	2 672	94 794	21 046	20 234	23 202	19 849	5 865	3 508
1998	143 362	142 612	751	105 377	7 132	2 840	101 086	21 476	20 800	24 302	20 660	5 899	.....

Personal Income and Employment—*Continued*

(Millions of dollars, except as noted)

| Year | Total | Nonfarm | Farm | Derivation of personal income | | | | | | Per capita (dollars) | | Population (thousands) | Total employment (thousands) |
				Earnings by place of work	Less: Personal contributions for social insurance	Plus: Adjustment for residence	Equals: Net earnings by place of residence	Dividends, interest, and rent	Transfer payments	Total	Disposable		
IOWA													
1969	10 187	8 945	1 242	8 012	327	72	7 757	1 529	902	3 632	3 171	2 805	1 289
1970	10 846	9 628	1 218	8 410	340	77	8 147	1 648	1 052	3 835	3 372	2 829	1 295
1971	11 345	10 336	1 010	8 670	375	73	8 369	1 778	1 198	3 978	3 534	2 852	1 297
1972	12 708	11 233	1 476	9 828	417	74	9 485	1 927	1 297	4 443	3 880	2 861	1 316
1973	15 341	12 626	2 715	12 065	523	68	11 609	2 241	1 491	5 356	4 728	2 864	1 374
1974	15 893	14 191	1 702	12 180	613	63	11 630	2 533	1 730	5 542	4 756	2 868	1 407
1975	17 637	15 689	1 948	13 372	659	72	12 785	2 731	2 122	6 121	5 332	2 881	1 407
1976	18 851	17 652	1 199	14 140	721	61	13 481	3 016	2 353	6 492	5 598	2 904	1 455
1977	20 908	19 686	1 222	15 645	779	33	14 899	3 482	2 527	7 174	6 190	2 914	1 488
1978	24 258	21 830	2 428	18 351	879	27	17 499	3 986	2 773	8 310	7 221	2 919	1 514
1979	26 155	24 610	1 545	19 371	1 034	38	18 375	4 667	3 113	8 967	7 714	2 917	1 557
1980	27 669	27 051	618	19 547	1 101	53	18 499	5 496	3 674	9 495	8 136	2 914	1 541
1981	31 373	29 656	1 718	21 656	1 218	76	20 515	6 703	4 156	10 789	9 252	2 908	1 513
1982	31 745	31 004	741	20 639	1 263	136	19 512	7 500	4 734	10 991	9 489	2 888	1 476
1983	32 203	32 264	-61	20 645	1 288	147	19 503	7 641	5 059	11 218	9 735	2 871	1 479
1984	35 618	34 336	1 282	23 602	1 396	169	22 374	8 126	5 118	12 460	11 030	2 859	1 506
1985	36 905	35 371	1 534	24 557	1 515	204	23 246	8 162	5 497	13 042	11 553	2 830	1 502
1986	38 216	36 294	1 923	25 534	1 602	197	24 129	8 352	5 735	13 688	12 188	2 792	1 501
1987	40 152	37 823	2 329	27 611	1 736	193	26 068	8 231	5 854	14 511	12 809	2 767	1 523
1988	41 200	39 852	1 348	28 461	1 936	231	26 756	8 317	6 127	14 882	13 073	2 768	1 568
1989	44 490	42 382	2 109	30 940	2 123	240	29 058	8 917	6 516	16 058	14 006	2 771	1 610
1990	46 933	44 928	2 005	32 467	2 258	261	30 470	9 460	7 003	16 885	14 682	2 780	1 642
1991	48 294	46 843	1 451	33 275	2 378	288	31 185	9 487	7 623	17 304	15 061	2 791	1 664
1992	51 557	49 422	2 135	36 073	2 496	309	33 885	9 470	8 201	18 368	16 082	2 807	1 680
1993	52 073	51 593	480	36 077	2 630	247	33 694	9 618	8 762	18 461	16 163	2 821	1 705
1994	56 485	54 190	2 295	40 178	2 836	236	37 578	9 848	9 059	19 964	17 528	2 829	1 741
1995	57 983	56 794	1 190	40 940	3 017	278	38 201	10 261	9 521	20 412	17 875	2 841	1 790
1996	62 759	59 718	3 041	44 535	3 142	293	41 686	11 133	9 942	22 032	19 246	2 849	1 824
1997	65 993	63 062	2 931	46 897	3 340	374	43 931	11 813	10 250	23 120	20 058	2 854	1 856
1998	68 720	66 598	2 121	49 307	3 561	375	46 121	12 077	10 522	24 007	20 689	2 862	.....
KANSAS													
1969	7 913	7 452	462	5 906	254	432	6 083	1 086	744	3 539	3 079	2 236	1 029
1970	8 532	7 929	604	6 333	267	429	6 496	1 164	872	3 796	3 325	2 248	1 018
1971	9 254	8 554	701	6 870	297	419	6 992	1 265	998	4 120	3 660	2 246	1 023
1972	10 343	9 365	978	7 792	341	441	7 892	1 374	1 077	4 586	4 035	2 256	1 049
1973	11 858	10 467	1 390	8 998	423	457	9 033	1 566	1 259	5 237	4 603	2 264	1 091
1974	12 885	11 817	1 068	9 575	485	470	9 559	1 866	1 460	5 682	4 936	2 268	1 123
1975	14 000	13 184	815	10 241	532	483	10 192	2 045	1 763	6 144	5 397	2 279	1 134
1976	15 342	14 747	595	11 233	589	500	11 144	2 233	1 965	6 674	5 849	2 299	1 170
1977	16 768	16 259	509	12 211	628	538	12 121	2 496	2 151	7 234	6 291	2 318	1 209
1978	18 672	18 376	296	13 582	728	587	13 441	2 887	2 344	8 004	6 953	2 333	1 254
1979	21 491	20 762	729	15 724	851	631	15 504	3 402	2 586	9 155	7 880	2 347	1 300
1980	23 571	23 468	104	16 545	940	704	16 309	4 188	3 074	9 950	8 540	2 369	1 314
1981	26 653	26 377	277	18 206	1 099	742	17 849	5 266	3 539	11 176	9 489	2 385	1 328
1982	28 581	28 020	561	19 109	1 169	756	18 696	5 907	3 979	11 903	10 133	2 401	1 312
1983	29 645	29 328	317	19 862	1 214	727	19 374	6 037	4 234	12 273	10 660	2 416	1 329
1984	32 534	31 822	712	22 193	1 331	780	21 642	6 586	4 305	13 421	11 806	2 424	1 372
1985	34 277	33 507	770	23 325	1 458	825	22 692	6 991	4 595	14 121	12 368	2 427	1 377
1986	35 767	34 876	891	24 451	1 559	806	23 698	7 198	4 870	14 703	12 979	2 433	1 377
1987	37 481	36 332	1 148	25 907	1 640	872	25 139	7 298	5 044	15 327	13 394	2 445	1 431
1988	39 491	38 411	1 079	27 331	1 809	879	26 400	7 763	5 328	16 040	14 086	2 462	1 445
1989	41 549	40 801	748	28 399	1 953	924	27 370	8 373	5 806	16 802	14 607	2 473	1 466
1990	44 503	43 154	1 349	30 419	2 067	965	29 317	8 898	6 288	17 940	15 652	2 481	1 484
1991	46 113	45 144	968	31 405	2 194	932	30 143	9 067	6 903	18 492	16 187	2 494	1 502
1992	48 967	47 626	1 341	34 049	2 309	972	32 712	8 703	7 552	19 447	17 125	2 518	1 516
1993	50 883	49 523	1 361	35 611	2 437	1 003	34 177	8 787	7 920	20 048	17 595	2 538	1 538
1994	52 794	51 648	1 146	37 019	2 610	979	35 388	8 989	8 418	20 638	18 048	2 558	1 567
1995	55 304	54 723	581	38 217	2 764	1 052	36 505	10 051	8 748	21 481	18 702	2 575	1 601
1996	58 689	57 479	1 210	40 789	2 904	1 059	38 943	10 745	9 002	22 707	19 617	2 585	1 638
1997	62 363	61 158	1 205	43 575	3 123	1 275	41 727	11 341	9 295	23 972	20 561	2 601	1 685
1998	65 855	64 591	1 263	46 650	3 325	1 280	44 605	11 679	9 571	25 049	21 322	2 629	.....

Personal Income and Employment—*Continued*

(Millions of dollars, except as noted)

Year	Total	Nonfarm	Farm	Earnings by place of work	Less: Personal contributions for social insurance	Plus: Adjustment for residence	Equals: Net earnings by place of residence	Dividends, interest, and rent	Transfer payments	Per capita Total	Per capita Disposable	Population (thousands)	Total employment (thousands)
KENTUCKY													
1969	9 419	8 958	461	7 540	308	179	7 412	997	1 010	2 945	2 559	3 198	1 332
1970	10 193	9 761	432	8 057	333	170	7 895	1 106	1 191	3 155	2 769	3 231	1 336
1971	11 064	10 617	446	8 719	369	115	8 464	1 197	1 403	3 354	2 973	3 298	1 360
1972	12 268	11 710	558	9 724	416	110	9 418	1 287	1 563	3 677	3 211	3 336	1 392
1973	13 834	13 208	626	10 962	516	78	10 525	1 450	1 860	4 103	3 628	3 372	1 461
1974	15 595	14 890	704	12 220	595	53	11 679	1 696	2 220	4 564	3 960	3 417	1 495
1975	16 939	16 427	513	12 901	639	48	12 310	1 864	2 765	4 883	4 331	3 469	1 465
1976	19 075	18 493	583	14 641	714	26	13 953	2 070	3 051	5 403	4 772	3 530	1 523
1977	21 502	20 791	711	16 645	796	43	15 892	2 358	3 253	6 015	5 264	3 575	1 579
1978	24 067	23 431	637	18 703	910	57	17 850	2 728	3 489	6 664	5 820	3 611	1 645
1979	27 116	26 413	703	20 862	1 050	55	19 867	3 214	4 036	7 442	6 500	3 644	1 668
1980	29 709	29 139	570	21 911	1 126	80	20 865	3 987	4 858	8 108	7 124	3 664	1 646
1981	33 063	32 086	977	23 854	1 301	78	22 631	4 949	5 483	9 008	7 870	3 670	1 639
1982	34 824	33 932	893	24 559	1 378	77	23 258	5 563	6 003	9 454	8 270	3 683	1 620
1983	35 823	35 595	228	24 851	1 433	110	23 528	5 827	6 468	9 696	8 545	3 694	1 629
1984	40 051	38 960	1 091	28 285	1 590	86	26 781	6 573	6 697	10 838	9 643	3 695	1 682
1985	41 671	40 837	834	29 369	1 765	93	27 696	6 943	7 032	11 278	9 976	3 695	1 706
1986	43 203	42 611	592	30 303	1 893	119	28 529	7 297	7 378	11 715	10 378	3 688	1 741
1987	45 825	45 127	698	32 731	2 036	88	30 782	7 390	7 653	12 441	10 976	3 683	1 774
1988	48 527	47 859	668	34 641	2 275	82	32 449	7 927	8 151	13 187	11 670	3 680	1 828
1989	52 231	51 190	1 042	36 951	2 482	45	34 515	8 831	8 886	14 204	12 474	3 677	1 877
1990	55 702	54 742	960	39 091	2 637	60	36 514	9 403	9 785	15 085	13 226	3 693	1 915
1991	58 417	57 435	983	40 500	2 810	43	37 733	9 520	11 164	15 719	13 842	3 716	1 916
1992	62 678	61 509	1 169	44 161	3 017	-130	41 014	9 382	12 282	16 677	14 721	3 758	1 964
1993	65 279	64 268	1 012	46 322	3 181	-199	42 942	9 344	12 994	17 207	15 162	3 794	2 005
1994	68 343	67 335	1 009	48 734	3 417	-292	45 026	9 835	13 483	17 872	15 722	3 824	2 049
1995	71 727	71 149	578	50 509	3 653	-331	46 525	10 627	14 575	18 601	16 280	3 856	2 103
1996	75 612	74 769	844	52 874	3 832	-377	48 666	11 490	15 457	19 475	16 983	3 883	2 136
1997	80 435	79 234	1 202	56 509	4 078	-486	51 945	12 004	16 486	20 570	17 837	3 910	2 189
1998	84 834	83 383	1 451	60 160	4 293	-509	55 359	12 277	17 199	21 551	18 587	3 936	.....
LOUISIANA													
1969	10 470	10 220	250	8 544	351	3	8 196	1 213	1 061	2 893	2 557	3 619	1 440
1970	11 281	10 986	295	9 076	368	3	8 711	1 289	1 282	3 091	2 770	3 650	1 429
1971	12 281	11 950	332	9 829	409	-9	9 411	1 396	1 474	3 310	2 968	3 711	1 445
1972	13 451	13 085	366	10 806	460	-22	10 324	1 495	1 633	3 576	3 179	3 762	1 488
1973	15 049	14 455	594	12 095	570	-38	11 488	1 667	1 894	3 972	3 549	3 789	1 550
1974	17 157	16 535	622	13 622	661	-54	12 906	2 028	2 223	4 491	3 979	3 821	1 598
1975	19 161	18 736	425	15 091	738	-82	14 271	2 171	2 719	4 930	4 412	3 887	1 641
1976	21 834	21 378	456	17 359	848	-111	16 400	2 386	3 048	5 525	4 898	3 952	1 702
1977	24 463	24 011	452	19 495	934	-136	18 425	2 699	3 339	6 092	5 380	4 016	1 756
1978	28 125	27 752	373	22 532	1 082	-184	21 267	3 223	3 635	6 905	6 063	4 073	1 848
1979	32 101	31 590	511	25 622	1 268	-228	24 127	3 865	4 109	7 755	6 763	4 139	1 899
1980	37 083	36 901	182	28 999	1 459	-332	27 207	4 943	4 932	8 781	7 632	4 223	1 968
1981	42 694	42 446	248	33 083	1 796	-354	30 935	6 211	5 548	9 968	8 587	4 283	2 036
1982	45 471	45 217	255	34 500	1 920	-332	32 248	6 851	6 373	10 447	9 123	4 353	2 028
1983	47 135	46 915	220	34 802	1 908	-312	32 583	7 393	7 160	10 724	9 498	4 395	1 990
1984	50 256	49 943	312	36 947	2 028	-305	34 615	8 273	7 369	11 421	10 179	4 400	2 031
1985	52 349	52 124	225	37 754	2 171	-275	35 308	8 871	8 170	11 876	10 601	4 408	2 019
1986	52 009	51 793	216	36 492	2 142	-221	34 128	8 966	8 915	11 802	10 695	4 407	1 938
1987	52 175	51 804	371	36 690	2 119	-188	34 383	8 745	9 048	12 010	10 877	4 344	1 914
1988	55 022	54 458	564	38 887	2 321	-171	36 395	9 074	9 553	12 829	11 662	4 289	1 949
1989	57 925	57 527	399	40 352	2 518	-137	37 697	9 898	10 332	13 620	12 303	4 253	1 967
1990	62 332	61 984	349	43 563	2 714	-125	40 725	10 299	11 309	14 773	13 272	4 219	2 018
1991	66 135	65 715	421	46 039	2 914	-132	42 994	10 259	12 882	15 593	14 043	4 241	2 047
1992	69 971	69 519	452	48 528	3 012	-117	45 398	9 962	14 611	16 381	14 830	4 272	2 058
1993	73 424	72 976	449	50 373	3 148	-136	47 089	10 216	16 119	17 133	15 466	4 286	2 105
1994	77 893	77 378	515	53 022	3 406	-138	49 479	10 812	17 602	18 086	16 305	4 307	2 148
1995	81 484	80 951	533	55 864	3 647	-152	52 065	11 506	17 914	18 826	16 925	4 328	2 204
1996	85 100	84 419	680	58 162	3 811	-170	54 181	12 467	18 453	19 609	17 526	4 340	2 248
1997	89 067	88 569	498	61 527	4 067	-179	57 281	12 952	18 833	20 458	18 123	4 354	2 296
1998	93 430	93 058	373	65 273	4 293	-179	60 800	13 214	19 416	21 385	18 810	4 369	.....

Personal Income and Employment—*Continued*

(Millions of dollars, except as noted)

Year	Total	Nonfarm	Farm	Earnings by place of work	Less: Personal contributions for social insurance	Plus: Adjustment for residence	Equals: Net earnings by place of residence	Dividends, interest, and rent	Transfer payments	Per capita (dollars) Total	Per capita (dollars) Disposable	Population (thousands)	Total employment (thousands)
MAINE													
1969	3 122	3 045	77	2 447	102	-21	2 324	444	354	3 147	2 775	992	443
1970	3 408	3 327	81	2 640	110	-16	2 514	470	424	3 419	3 048	997	446
1971	3 659	3 589	70	2 769	120	-15	2 635	521	504	3 603	3 254	1 016	443
1972	4 006	3 937	69	3 039	132	-18	2 889	550	566	3 871	3 478	1 035	453
1973	4 517	4 365	152	3 417	161	-8	3 248	602	667	4 316	3 849	1 046	470
1974	5 026	4 826	200	3 738	184	-4	3 551	672	803	4 741	4 232	1 060	478
1975	5 365	5 282	83	3 860	196	-14	3 650	705	1 011	4 999	4 506	1 073	475
1976	6 182	6 016	166	4 535	222	-16	4 298	777	1 108	5 672	5 095	1 090	498
1977	6 723	6 592	130	4 901	242	-16	4 643	881	1 198	6 082	5 465	1 105	513
1978	7 445	7 354	91	5 451	276	-13	5 162	991	1 291	6 674	5 971	1 115	532
1979	8 329	8 253	76	6 031	313	-5	5 713	1 163	1 453	7 404	6 592	1 125	546
1980	9 356	9 310	46	6 598	348	-2	6 248	1 413	1 695	8 302	7 368	1 127	555
1981	10 365	10 247	118	7 103	401	1	6 703	1 736	1 927	9 149	8 045	1 133	554
1982	11 079	10 975	105	7 491	435	5	7 062	1 899	2 119	9 747	8 495	1 137	556
1983	11 942	11 870	72	8 086	466	11	7 632	2 027	2 283	10 431	9 213	1 145	568
1984	13 290	13 173	117	9 022	515	19	8 526	2 381	2 383	11 500	10 229	1 156	591
1985	14 306	14 203	103	9 777	581	38	9 234	2 540	2 532	12 301	10 857	1 163	610
1986	15 529	15 437	93	10 655	646	71	10 080	2 799	2 650	13 272	11 636	1 170	634
1987	17 049	16 915	134	11 884	709	87	11 263	3 073	2 714	14 392	12 503	1 185	657
1988	18 704	18 590	114	13 127	807	108	12 428	3 394	2 882	15 537	13 560	1 204	693
1989	20 274	20 145	128	14 124	886	93	13 331	3 847	3 096	16 618	14 509	1 220	708
1990	21 127	20 970	157	14 620	912	94	13 801	3 893	3 433	17 159	15 059	1 231	706
1991	21 362	21 257	104	14 446	937	89	13 598	3 822	3 941	17 300	15 277	1 235	684
1992	22 231	22 061	170	15 038	983	105	14 161	3 738	4 332	18 463	16 389	1 236	687
1993	22 823	22 672	151	15 435	1 032	128	14 531	3 720	4 573	19 190	16 944	1 235	699
1994	23 699	23 576	122	15 871	1 099	162	14 935	4 001	4 763	19 190	16 944	1 235	711
1995	24 658	24 574	84	16 393	1 168	201	15 426	4 197	5 035	19 995	17 661	1 233	720
1996	25 934	25 823	111	17 019	1 209	225	16 035	4 563	5 336	20 948	18 394	1 238	731
1997	27 243	27 182	62	17 940	1 281	254	16 913	4 718	5 613	21 937	19 061	1 242	747
1998	28 620	28 528	91	19 084	1 349	280	18 015	4 790	5 815	23 002	19 811	1 244	.....
MARYLAND													
1969	16 187	16 037	150	11 468	515	2 002	12 955	2 019	1 213	4 185	3 450	3 868	1 679
1970	17 799	17 656	143	12 471	567	2 315	14 220	2 125	1 455	4 520	3 795	3 938	1 702
1971	19 315	19 197	118	13 443	631	2 488	15 299	2 271	1 745	4 802	4 085	4 023	1 729
1972	21 174	21 020	155	14 793	699	2 684	16 777	2 392	2 004	5 188	4 336	4 081	1 781
1973	23 538	23 304	234	16 479	857	2 873	18 495	2 706	2 338	5 728	4 821	4 109	1 846
1974	25 862	25 674	189	17 908	967	3 067	20 008	3 118	2 736	6 257	5 226	4 133	1 868
1975	27 887	27 659	228	18 917	1 025	3 330	21 223	3 297	3 367	6 708	5 697	4 157	1 846
1976	30 582	30 385	197	20 816	1 117	3 574	23 273	3 621	3 688	7 330	6 228	4 172	1 866
1977	33 218	33 071	147	22 553	1 201	3 845	25 197	4 027	3 993	7 919	6 659	4 195	1 919
1978	37 066	36 862	204	25 146	1 349	4 182	27 979	4 687	4 400	8 801	7 406	4 212	2 003
1979	41 195	41 023	172	27 671	1 547	4 523	30 647	5 544	5 004	9 754	8 163	4 223	2 061
1980	46 191	46 128	64	30 126	1 706	4 949	33 369	6 828	5 996	10 926	9 199	4 228	2 074
1981	51 569	51 428	140	32 955	1 955	5 307	36 308	8 385	6 875	12 100	10 074	4 262	2 102
1982	55 176	55 030	147	34 591	2 081	5 740	38 250	9 206	7 721	12 883	10 772	4 283	2 090
1983	59 747	59 658	89	37 658	2 296	6 186	41 549	9 816	8 383	13 852	11 792	4 313	2 158
1984	66 698	66 426	271	42 064	2 562	6 798	46 299	11 603	8 796	15 279	12 968	4 365	2 252
1985	72 614	72 330	284	46 243	2 988	7 374	50 630	12 621	9 364	16 454	14 072	4 413	2 356
1986	78 346	78 052	293	50 179	3 259	7 867	54 786	13 547	10 013	17 461	14 945	4 487	2 443
1987	85 215	84 916	299	55 242	3 473	8 643	60 413	14 311	10 491	18 665	15 774	4 566	2 571
1988	93 528	93 171	357	60 793	3 954	9 642	66 482	15 800	11 246	20 079	17 169	4 658	2 672
1989	101 490	101 136	354	65 171	4 323	10 404	71 251	18 139	12 100	21 469	18 237	4 727	2 729
1990	107 858	107 520	338	69 162	4 601	10 924	75 485	19 139	13 234	22 482	19 149	4 797	2 757
1991	111 089	110 800	289	70 104	4 771	11 420	76 752	19 407	14 929	22 877	19 580	4 856	2 687
1992	115 446	115 125	321	72 895	4 917	12 127	80 105	19 072	16 271	23 548	20 270	4 903	2 661
1993	120 033	119 735	299	75 748	5 105	12 482	83 125	19 710	17 198	24 283	20 864	4 943	2 686
1994	126 277	126 024	253	79 042	5 410	12 831	86 463	21 102	18 712	25 329	21 698	4 985	2 737
1995	131 318	131 146	172	82 412	5 654	12 971	89 730	22 597	18 992	26 141	22 357	5 023	2 789
1996	138 068	137 764	304	86 003	5 859	13 330	93 473	24 417	20 178	27 298	23 151	5 058	2 833
1997	146 090	145 855	235	91 509	6 250	14 065	99 324	25 325	21 441	28 674	24 031	5 095	2 907
1998	154 164	153 790	375	97 538	6 602	15 142	106 078	25 798	22 287	30 023	24 983	5 135	.....

Personal Income and Employment—*Continued*

(Millions of dollars, except as noted)

Year	Total	Nonfarm	Farm	Earnings by place of work	Less: Personal contributions for social insurance	Plus: Adjustment for residence	Equals: Net earnings by place of residence	Dividends, interest, and rent	Transfer payments	Per capita Total	Per capita Disposable	Population (thousands)	Total employment (thousands)
MASSACHUSETTS													
1969	24 179	24 107	71	18 519	735	-115	17 669	4 086	2 423	4 279	3 618	5 650	2 679
1970	25 938	25 862	75	19 784	774	-98	18 912	4 149	2 876	4 547	3 897	5 704	2 679
1971	27 570	27 499	70	20 835	847	-103	19 885	4 272	3 413	4 804	4 169	5 739	2 644
1972	29 743	29 673	70	22 596	932	-108	21 555	4 431	3 757	5 162	4 399	5 762	2 697
1973	32 389	32 312	77	24 676	1 136	-132	23 409	4 789	4 191	5 600	4 813	5 784	2 787
1974	35 089	35 013	76	26 217	1 253	-151	24 814	5 316	4 960	6 074	5 218	5 777	2 811
1975	37 427	37 352	75	27 156	1 285	-163	25 709	5 355	6 363	6 495	5 671	5 762	2 728
1976	40 482	40 399	83	29 639	1 373	-188	28 078	5 751	6 653	7 042	6 119	5 749	2 756
1977	44 140	44 055	85	32 559	1 501	-238	30 821	6 386	6 933	7 684	6 635	5 744	2 833
1978	49 021	48 911	110	36 446	1 710	-290	34 446	7 174	7 402	8 536	7 368	5 743	2 959
1979	54 889	54 795	94	40 710	1 992	-365	38 354	8 323	8 213	9 552	8 181	5 746	3 079
1980	61 945	61 835	110	45 169	2 264	-482	42 423	10 109	9 413	10 780	9 192	5 746	3 142
1981	69 096	68 978	118	49 310	2 648	-609	46 053	12 371	10 672	11 978	10 118	5 769	3 155
1982	74 706	74 573	134	52 912	2 892	-733	49 287	13 795	11 625	12 945	11 030	5 771	3 155
1983	81 243	81 073	170	58 384	3 190	-896	54 299	14 581	12 363	14 009	11 936	5 799	3 229
1984	91 717	91 527	190	66 349	3 617	-1 156	61 575	17 303	12 839	15 703	13 446	5 841	3 420
1985	99 042	98 873	169	72 931	4 161	-1 333	67 437	18 328	13 277	16 842	14 321	5 881	3 531
1986	106 839	106 655	185	79 133	4 683	-1 443	73 008	19 647	14 185	18 100	15 315	5 903	3 628
1987	116 329	116 172	156	87 259	5 074	-1 628	80 558	20 994	14 776	19 600	16 511	5 935	3 660
1988	128 075	127 896	179	96 217	5 721	-1 856	88 640	23 469	15 966	21 417	18 332	5 980	3 778
1989	136 152	135 986	166	100 012	6 117	-1 991	91 904	26 442	17 806	22 634	19 317	6 015	3 751
1990	139 687	139 536	152	101 547	6 253	-2 103	93 191	26 747	19 750	23 210	19 813	6 018	3 646
1991	141 466	141 293	173	101 024	6 390	-2 180	92 455	26 415	22 597	23 590	20 210	5 997	3 486
1992	147 039	146 863	177	107 119	6 628	-2 299	98 191	25 213	23 635	24 538	20 992	5 992	3 517
1993	152 204	152 023	181	111 609	6 933	-2 502	102 174	25 664	24 367	25 333	21 584	6 008	3 587
1994	159 317	159 170	147	116 493	7 391	-2 711	106 392	27 333	25 593	26 433	22 387	6 027	3 660
1995	170 211	170 068	144	123 381	7 804	-2 794	112 783	30 265	27 164	28 097	23 702	6 058	3 747
1996	179 998	179 834	164	130 378	8 102	-3 058	119 219	32 943	27 836	29 591	24 623	6 083	3 825
1997	191 008	190 826	182	139 516	8 690	-3 305	127 522	34 297	29 190	31 239	25 740	6 114	3 923
1998	202 252	202 087	165	149 796	9 286	-3 573	136 937	35 061	30 254	32 902	26 824	6 147	.....
MICHIGAN													
1969	35 847	35 456	391	29 646	1 182	104	28 569	4 510	2 770	4 082	3 472	8 781	3 640
1970	36 917	36 534	384	29 892	1 194	109	28 808	4 641	3 469	4 150	3 583	8 897	3 558
1971	40 150	39 795	356	32 379	1 337	102	31 144	4 865	4 141	4 475	3 900	8 972	3 571
1972	44 595	44 114	481	36 155	1 514	110	34 750	5 149	4 696	4 941	4 228	9 025	3 687
1973	50 049	49 439	610	40 879	1 940	136	39 075	5 651	5 323	5 517	4 763	9 072	3 858
1974	53 586	52 890	697	42 562	2 086	137	40 613	6 408	6 565	5 883	5 106	9 109	3 854
1975	56 602	55 988	615	43 275	2 082	151	41 344	6 759	8 500	6 215	5 472	9 108	3 695
1976	64 060	63 552	508	49 874	2 341	192	47 726	7 456	8 879	7 026	6 097	9 117	3 844
1977	72 276	71 684	593	57 005	2 597	216	54 625	8 422	9 230	7 893	6 781	9 157	4 016
1978	80 921	80 374	547	64 091	2 929	261	61 423	9 708	9 790	8 794	7 503	9 202	4 188
1979	89 172	88 597	575	69 672	3 313	301	66 659	11 304	11 209	9 641	8 231	9 249	4 234
1980	95 312	94 760	552	70 373	3 365	343	67 352	13 301	14 660	10 298	8 919	9 256	4 039
1981	101 864	101 350	514	73 859	3 856	366	70 370	15 873	15 621	11 061	9 536	9 209	3 992
1982	103 544	103 122	422	72 832	3 894	378	69 316	16 787	17 441	11 359	9 905	9 115	3 836
1983	109 866	109 659	206	77 276	4 173	408	73 511	17 898	18 457	12 143	10 601	9 048	3 879
1984	121 804	121 280	524	86 269	4 681	472	82 060	21 065	18 680	13 460	11 796	9 049	4 058
1985	131 970	131 339	630	95 004	5 408	489	90 085	22 504	19 380	14 540	12 617	9 076	4 256
1986	140 002	139 552	450	101 076	5 898	468	95 645	23 918	20 438	15 338	13 321	9 128	4 372
1987	146 072	145 490	583	105 292	6 248	487	99 532	24 921	21 620	15 899	13 785	9 187	4 510
1988	156 250	155 737	513	113 515	6 981	498	107 032	26 641	22 577	16 950	14 769	9 218	4 617
1989	166 441	165 539	903	119 814	7 579	477	112 712	29 766	23 963	17 987	15 550	9 253	4 745
1990	174 103	173 430	672	124 183	7 869	457	116 771	31 341	25 991	18 699	16 266	9 311	4 810
1991	178 612	178 058	554	125 226	8 166	476	117 536	31 777	29 300	19 022	16 586	9 390	4 757
1992	187 979	187 424	555	133 918	8 624	535	125 829	31 239	30 911	19 861	17 374	9 465	4 789
1993	199 411	198 815	597	143 426	9 168	519	134 777	31 644	32 991	20 939	18 254	9 523	4 849
1994	214 135	213 664	471	154 750	10 095	593	145 248	35 448	33 439	22 338	19 376	9 586	5 030
1995	226 179	225 576	604	163 367	10 778	628	153 217	37 783	35 179	23 407	20 177	9 663	5 182
1996	233 571	233 112	459	167 090	11 169	675	156 596	40 405	36 570	23 996	20 507	9 734	5 295
1997	244 073	243 570	503	175 715	11 821	792	164 686	41 103	38 285	24 956	21 126	9 780	5 387
1998	255 039	254 673	366	185 223	12 378	857	173 703	41 682	39 655	25 979	21 832	9 817	.....

Personal Income and Employment—*Continued*

(Millions of dollars, except as noted)

Year	Total	Nonfarm	Farm	Earnings by place of work	Less: Personal contributions for social insurance	Plus: Adjustment for residence	Equals: Net earnings by place of residence	Dividends, interest, and rent	Transfer payments	Per capita Total	Per capita Disposable	Population (thousands)	Total employment (thousands)
MINNESOTA													
1969	14 112	13 359	753	11 408	473	-33	10 902	1 957	1 253	3 755	3 233	3 758	1 691
1970	15 318	14 402	915	12 314	502	-29	11 784	2 052	1 483	4 015	3 503	3 815	1 699
1971	16 316	15 479	837	12 973	551	-29	12 393	2 201	1 722	4 236	3 731	3 852	1 706
1972	17 721	16 709	1 012	14 152	613	-32	13 508	2 305	1 908	4 583	3 968	3 867	1 780
1973	20 866	18 646	2 219	16 834	771	-39	16 025	2 620	2 221	5 371	4 713	3 885	1 878
1974	22 508	20 823	1 685	17 781	889	-35	16 857	3 041	2 611	5 774	4 963	3 898	1 921
1975	24 108	22 807	1 301	18 669	946	-36	17 687	3 297	3 125	6 141	5 321	3 926	1 920
1976	26 275	25 461	814	20 287	1 053	-44	19 190	3 622	3 463	6 641	5 727	3 957	1 977
1977	29 656	28 124	1 532	23 061	1 149	-57	21 855	4 107	3 694	7 451	6 408	3 980	2 034
1978	33 447	31 796	1 652	26 186	1 327	-72	24 788	4 681	3 979	8 352	7 164	4 005	2 123
1979	37 436	36 162	1 273	29 168	1 557	-91	27 520	5 483	4 433	9 270	7 882	4 038	2 222
1980	41 489	40 570	919	31 373	1 711	-100	29 562	6 629	5 299	10 156	8 678	4 085	2 254
1981	45 805	44 830	976	33 759	1 982	-135	31 642	8 088	6 076	11 140	9 483	4 112	2 241
1982	48 617	47 815	802	34 993	2 122	-158	32 713	9 065	6 839	11 768	10 054	4 131	2 200
1983	50 981	50 904	77	36 592	2 295	-186	34 112	9 514	7 355	12 310	10 568	4 141	2 227
1984	58 105	56 729	1 376	42 434	2 540	-246	39 648	10 766	7 690	13 975	12 142	4 158	2 335
1985	61 744	60 501	1 244	45 340	2 844	-295	42 201	11 275	8 268	14 756	12 826	4 184	2 399
1986	65 291	63 756	1 534	48 065	3 078	-336	44 651	11 933	8 706	15 526	13 488	4 205	2 431
1987	69 790	67 795	1 995	52 076	3 307	-388	48 382	12 250	9 158	16 479	14 145	4 235	2 525
1988	73 530	72 376	1 154	55 245	3 703	-472	51 071	12 754	9 705	17 115	14 731	4 296	2 601
1989	79 838	77 856	1 983	59 697	4 042	-457	55 199	14 254	10 384	18 404	15 782	4 338	2 654
1990	84 886	82 999	1 887	63 383	4 306	-485	58 593	15 003	11 290	19 348	16 542	4 387	2 707
1991	87 866	86 776	1 089	65 157	4 559	-497	60 101	15 520	12 244	19 845	17 000	4 428	2 739
1992	94 472	93 310	1 163	70 827	4 874	-535	65 418	15 730	13 324	21 126	18 104	4 472	2 785
1993	97 202	97 178	24	72 687	5 133	-595	66 959	16 063	14 180	21 488	18 306	4 524	2 842
1994	104 110	102 949	1 160	78 001	5 541	-649	71 811	17 343	14 956	22 802	19 397	4 566	2 933
1995	109 304	108 822	482	81 801	5 927	-688	75 187	18 292	15 825	23 736	20 095	4 605	3 029
1996	117 293	115 494	1 798	88 385	6 287	-782	81 316	19 496	16 482	25 235	21 035	4 648	3 096
1997	123 010	122 021	989	93 276	6 717	-880	85 680	20 362	16 969	26 243	21 647	4 687	3 166
1998	130 737	129 915	822	100 683	7 225	-985	92 473	20 813	17 451	27 667	22 719	4 725	.....
MISSISSIPPI													
1969	5 292	4 923	369	4 341	177	34	4 198	497	597	2 384	2 157	2 220	909
1970	5 804	5 387	417	4 655	190	35	4 500	555	750	2 613	2 352	2 221	917
1971	6 422	5 968	454	5 082	211	55	4 926	607	889	2 834	2 588	2 266	939
1972	7 326	6 809	517	5 838	246	69	5 661	658	1 006	3 175	2 854	2 307	979
1973	8 395	7 684	711	6 680	308	90	6 461	762	1 172	3 573	3 237	2 350	1 019
1974	9 255	8 723	532	7 138	356	118	6 899	911	1 445	3 891	3 489	2 379	1 031
1975	9 965	9 578	387	7 441	380	143	7 204	986	1 775	4 152	3 780	2 400	1 001
1976	11 392	10 811	582	8 620	428	173	8 365	1 068	1 959	4 688	4 233	2 430	1 039
1977	12 733	12 119	614	9 667	478	213	9 403	1 197	2 133	5 176	4 689	2 460	1 071
1978	14 191	13 732	459	10 726	558	269	10 437	1 410	2 344	5 704	5 114	2 488	1 102
1979	16 116	15 398	718	12 110	648	326	11 789	1 666	2 662	6 426	5 741	2 508	1 117
1980	17 507	17 299	208	12 470	688	411	12 192	2 125	3 190	6 932	6 190	2 525	1 114
1981	19 613	19 256	357	13 697	802	446	13 341	2 658	3 615	7 725	6 843	2 539	1 110
1982	20 663	20 242	422	14 091	861	457	13 686	2 995	3 982	8 082	7 291	2 557	1 082
1983	21 497	21 405	91	14 437	902	509	14 044	3 084	4 369	8 372	7 532	2 568	1 091
1984	23 516	23 042	473	16 039	982	569	15 626	3 438	4 451	9 122	8 266	2 578	1 121
1985	24 704	24 268	435	16 908	1 085	598	16 420	3 518	4 766	9 545	8 650	2 588	1 129
1986	25 672	25 487	185	17 372	1 175	583	16 781	3 814	5 078	9 898	9 015	2 594	1 136
1987	27 139	26 605	535	18 541	1 217	623	17 948	3 885	5 306	10 484	9 523	2 589	1 147
1988	28 994	28 331	663	19 876	1 360	666	19 182	4 147	5 665	11 236	10 291	2 580	1 176
1989	30 882	30 378	505	20 946	1 505	707	20 148	4 590	6 144	11 996	10 941	2 574	1 196
1990	32 748	32 414	334	22 033	1 588	752	21 197	4 814	6 737	12 706	11 575	2 577	1 208
1991	34 658	34 198	460	23 155	1 680	786	22 261	4 953	7 444	13 376	12 252	2 591	1 217
1992	36 967	36 442	525	24 937	1 793	806	23 950	4 783	8 235	14 163	13 011	2 610	1 242
1993	39 272	38 854	418	26 726	1 940	816	25 602	4 809	8 861	14 900	13 604	2 636	1 297
1994	42 308	41 665	643	29 128	2 140	828	27 816	5 123	9 369	15 886	14 457	2 663	1 347
1995	44 591	44 104	487	30 301	2 306	911	28 906	5 487	10 198	16 574	15 085	2 690	1 378
1996	47 150	46 333	817	31 787	2 419	952	30 320	5 910	10 921	17 398	15 803	2 710	1 401
1997	49 437	48 761	677	33 345	2 581	1 109	31 872	6 173	11 392	18 098	16 363	2 732	1 426
1998	52 283	51 438	846	35 706	2 740	1 179	34 146	6 319	11 818	18 998	17 107	2 752	.....

Personal Income and Employment—*Continued*

(Millions of dollars, except as noted)

Year	Total	Nonfarm	Farm	Earnings by place of work	Less: Personal contributions for social insurance	Plus: Adjustment for residence	Equals: Net earnings by place of residence	Dividends, interest, and rent	Transfer payments	Total	Disposable	Population (thousands)	Total employment (thousands)
MISSOURI													
1969	16 493	16 023	471	13 977	579	-753	12 647	2 302	1 545	3 555	3 053	4 640	2 216
1970	17 931	17 386	545	14 940	613	-700	13 627	2 463	1 840	3 827	3 331	4 685	2 203
1971	19 337	18 750	587	15 914	675	-681	14 558	2 646	2 133	4 094	3 592	4 723	2 200
1972	21 070	20 324	746	17 356	746	-707	15 904	2 845	2 322	4 433	3 837	4 753	2 242
1973	23 543	22 300	1 243	19 324	911	-746	17 669	3 198	2 676	4 931	4 325	4 775	2 325
1974	25 195	24 526	668	20 184	1 017	-777	18 391	3 641	3 163	5 265	4 586	4 785	2 341
1975	27 358	26 642	716	21 384	1 064	-790	19 530	3 877	3 951	5 705	5 037	4 795	2 291
1976	30 274	29 792	482	23 769	1 175	-869	21 725	4 287	4 263	6 276	5 497	4 824	2 365
1977	33 676	32 957	719	26 596	1 288	-1 008	24 299	4 849	4 528	6 950	6 086	4 845	2 424
1978	37 769	36 834	935	29 867	1 467	-1 174	27 227	5 617	4 926	7 754	6 760	4 871	2 513
1979	42 440	41 234	1 206	33 270	1 676	-1 335	30 259	6 612	5 570	8 680	7 539	4 889	2 579
1980	46 093	45 856	237	34 550	1 809	-1 555	31 186	8 154	6 753	9 365	8 138	4 922	2 554
1981	51 506	50 682	824	37 624	2 090	-1 636	33 899	10 042	7 566	10 443	9 037	4 932	2 549
1982	54 179	53 857	322	38 768	2 239	-1 699	34 830	11 072	8 277	10 991	9 431	4 929	2 524
1983	57 581	57 714	-133	41 195	2 390	-1 739	37 065	11 647	8 869	11 647	10 216	4 944	2 570
1984	63 982	63 619	363	46 157	2 650	-1 898	41 609	13 239	9 135	12 860	11 342	4 975	2 678
1985	68 690	67 978	712	49 843	2 974	-2 024	44 845	13 935	9 911	13 737	12 076	5 000	2 752
1986	72 245	71 776	469	52 358	3 222	-2 088	47 048	14 703	10 494	14 383	12 642	5 023	2 816
1987	76 275	75 622	653	55 874	3 437	-2 212	50 226	15 102	10 948	15 084	13 219	5 057	2 853
1988	80 846	80 264	582	59 374	3 789	-2 305	53 279	15 922	11 644	15 909	14 019	5 082	2 907
1989	86 429	85 585	844	62 651	4 094	-2 451	56 106	17 798	12 524	16 961	14 872	5 096	2 959
1990	90 424	89 823	600	65 049	4 280	-2 563	58 205	18 816	13 403	17 639	15 444	5 126	2 987
1991	94 410	93 930	480	66 717	4 483	-2 556	59 677	19 058	15 675	18 305	16 126	5 158	2 964
1992	99 302	98 646	656	71 113	4 696	-2 667	63 751	18 956	16 595	19 120	16 872	5 194	2 981
1993	102 826	102 514	312	73 982	4 930	-2 791	66 260	18 618	17 948	19 632	17 290	5 238	3 062
1994	108 872	108 309	564	78 707	5 328	-2 862	70 518	19 760	18 595	20 576	18 049	5 291	3 138
1995	114 966	114 901	66	82 636	5 703	-3 051	73 882	21 173	19 911	21 540	18 870	5 337	3 210
1996	121 265	120 466	799	86 916	5 940	-3 135	77 841	22 505	20 919	22 586	19 656	5 369	3 277
1997	127 795	126 800	994	92 444	6 333	-3 651	82 460	23 373	21 962	23 629	20 395	5 408	3 352
1998	132 956	132 653	303	96 691	6 633	-3 766	86 292	23 854	22 809	24 447	20 952	5 439	.....
MONTANA													
1969	2 245	1 999	247	1 766	80	-1	1 685	328	233	3 235	2 804	694	298
1970	2 481	2 182	299	1 935	87	-1	1 846	364	270	3 558	3 139	697	301
1971	2 636	2 377	259	2 039	95	-1	1 943	377	316	3 707	3 310	711	307
1972	3 072	2 656	416	2 417	109	-1	2 307	414	351	4 271	3 768	719	319
1973	3 583	2 996	588	2 814	134	0	2 681	497	405	4 926	4 334	727	333
1974	3 887	3 411	476	2 985	152	1	2 834	576	477	5 272	4 623	737	344
1975	4 245	3 838	408	3 203	164	2	3 041	630	574	5 667	5 013	749	344
1976	4 581	4 351	230	3 422	187	3	3 238	699	644	6 039	5 293	759	359
1977	4 971	4 902	70	3 658	213	4	3 449	813	710	6 445	5 609	771	372
1978	5 889	5 578	311	4 399	243	3	4 160	949	780	7 511	6 598	784	390
1979	6 351	6 237	115	4 613	275	6	4 344	1 130	877	8 047	6 963	789	397
1980	6 975	6 859	116	4 896	297	13	4 612	1 331	1 032	8 842	7 678	789	394
1981	7 876	7 672	204	5 371	342	25	5 055	1 631	1 191	9 903	8 626	795	396
1982	8 275	8 112	164	5 464	361	17	5 120	1 820	1 336	10 293	9 056	804	392
1983	8 673	8 557	116	5 705	377	9	5 338	1 880	1 455	10 654	9 351	814	400
1984	9 237	9 192	45	6 004	406	5	5 604	2 098	1 536	11 252	10 001	821	410
1985	9 445	9 516	-71	6 047	435	3	5 615	2 196	1 634	11 486	10 216	822	409
1986	9 863	9 620	243	6 303	448	-2	5 852	2 255	1 756	12 120	10 836	814	404
1987	10 159	9 882	278	6 524	458	-4	6 062	2 282	1 816	12 619	11 098	805	408
1988	10 366	10 280	85	6 625	507	-3	6 116	2 334	1 916	12 954	11 365	800	419
1989	11 349	10 946	403	7 266	548	-4	6 715	2 545	2 090	14 193	12 329	800	427
1990	12 028	11 664	363	7 654	584	-6	7 065	2 653	2 310	15 038	13 136	800	436
1991	12 883	12 351	531	8 394	634	-16	7 744	2 684	2 456	15 947	14 019	808	447
1992	13 605	13 193	412	8 911	690	-8	8 213	2 725	2 667	16 541	14 500	822	460
1993	14 761	13 985	776	9 863	741	-18	9 105	2 776	2 879	17 571	15 480	840	473
1994	15 038	14 734	304	9 906	787	-19	9 099	2 937	3 002	17 590	15 413	855	497
1995	15 881	15 582	299	10 355	838	-19	9 499	3 137	3 245	18 286	16 151	868	513
1996	16 546	16 303	243	10 802	882	-16	9 905	3 268	3 373	18 872	16 591	877	527
1997	17 276	16 959	317	11 333	926	-28	10 380	3 384	3 513	19 660	17 143	879	534
1998	17 827	17 731	95	11 730	972	-29	10 730	3 458	3 639	20 247	17 530	880	.....

Personal Income and Employment—*Continued*

(Millions of dollars, except as noted)

Year	Total	Nonfarm	Farm	Derivation of personal income — Earnings by place of work	Less: Personal contributions for social insurance	Plus: Adjustment for residence	Equals: Net earnings by place of residence	Dividends, interest, and rent	Transfer payments	Per capita (dollars) — Total	Per capita — Disposable	Population (thousands)	Total employment (thousands)
NEBRASKA													
1969	5 265	4 670	596	4 255	172	-98	3 986	820	460	3 572	3 118	1 474	704
1970	5 638	5 100	538	4 501	184	-104	4 214	888	537	3 789	3 337	1 488	715
1971	6 178	5 493	685	4 938	203	-106	4 630	941	608	4 107	3 679	1 504	728
1972	6 855	6 040	815	5 481	224	-115	5 144	1 041	672	4 515	3 967	1 518	748
1973	8 007	6 777	1 230	6 425	282	-117	6 027	1 182	799	5 239	4 620	1 529	775
1974	8 359	7 588	771	6 533	321	-126	6 087	1 353	919	5 436	4 732	1 538	793
1975	9 433	8 321	1 112	7 346	343	-131	6 873	1 445	1 115	6 119	5 428	1 541	790
1976	9 910	9 319	591	7 659	376	-138	7 145	1 567	1 199	6 398	5 646	1 549	811
1977	10 749	10 217	531	8 216	403	-136	7 679	1 775	1 295	6 915	6 018	1 554	831
1978	12 535	11 428	1 107	9 709	463	-157	9 089	2 013	1 433	8 031	7 055	1 561	855
1979	13 566	12 811	755	10 360	539	-184	9 637	2 335	1 594	8 672	7 515	1 564	877
1980	14 369	14 273	95	10 494	588	-204	9 703	2 800	1 866	9 139	7 918	1 572	879
1981	16 634	15 785	849	11 976	674	-226	11 076	3 415	2 142	10 538	9 225	1 579	874
1982	17 445	16 715	730	12 264	721	-233	11 310	3 771	2 365	11 029	9 477	1 582	863
1983	18 063	17 585	478	12 569	753	-246	11 571	3 946	2 547	11 401	10 025	1 584	870
1984	20 108	19 007	1 102	14 379	834	-286	13 259	4 224	2 626	12 658	11 307	1 589	889
1985	21 222	19 823	1 400	15 375	927	-312	14 136	4 265	2 821	13 392	11 972	1 585	902
1986	21 843	20 487	1 356	15 781	986	-312	14 483	4 394	2 966	13 875	12 398	1 574	902
1987	22 925	21 277	1 648	16 862	1 062	-311	15 489	4 383	3 052	14 634	13 021	1 567	929
1988	24 376	22 413	1 964	18 095	1 179	-344	16 572	4 590	3 214	15 511	13 808	1 571	954
1989	25 782	24 001	1 781	18 874	1 282	-355	17 237	5 116	3 429	16 371	14 437	1 575	970
1990	27 717	25 570	2 148	20 401	1 367	-371	18 663	5 335	3 720	17 536	15 401	1 581	992
1991	28 652	26 681	1 970	21 100	1 446	-389	19 264	5 365	4 023	18 012	15 814	1 591	999
1992	30 697	28 673	2 025	22 450	1 517	-424	20 510	5 804	4 383	19 157	16 932	1 602	1 006
1993	31 785	30 068	1 718	23 242	1 609	-453	21 180	5 887	4 719	19 714	17 421	1 612	1 028
1994	33 029	31 434	1 594	24 569	1 739	-465	22 365	5 762	4 902	20 365	17 954	1 622	1 070
1995	34 391	33 238	1 155	25 470	1 857	-500	23 113	6 069	5 210	21 029	18 367	1 635	1 098
1996	37 653	35 280	2 372	28 003	1 936	-521	25 547	6 559	5 547	22 847	19 965	1 648	1 126
1997	39 135	37 588	1 547	28 912	2 070	-578	26 265	7 061	5 809	23 618	20 415	1 657	1 146
1998	41 212	39 514	1 698	30 733	2 177	-609	27 947	7 250	6 014	24 786	21 318	1 663	.....
NEVADA													
1969	2 157	2 122	35	1 825	72	-35	1 717	287	153	4 493	3 778	480	244
1970	2 419	2 382	37	2 025	79	-41	1 906	330	183	4 904	4 284	493	256
1971	2 683	2 646	38	2 227	91	-43	2 093	365	225	5 160	4 558	520	267
1972	3 001	2 955	46	2 480	103	-47	2 330	404	267	5 488	4 811	547	280
1973	3 431	3 372	59	2 845	133	-57	2 656	464	311	6 030	5 303	569	304
1974	3 803	3 766	37	3 097	153	-60	2 884	535	384	6 373	5 588	597	317
1975	4 255	4 220	35	3 407	163	-62	3 183	557	516	6 865	6 176	620	326
1976	4 882	4 845	38	3 911	181	-72	3 659	638	586	7 548	6 675	647	349
1977	5 695	5 667	29	4 582	207	-89	4 286	743	667	8 399	7 387	678	384
1978	6 942	6 919	24	5 615	248	-124	5 244	941	757	9 651	8 424	719	432
1979	8 122	8 112	11	6 492	302	-139	6 050	1 188	885	10 616	9 199	765	468
1980	9 420	9 360	60	7 417	345	-168	6 905	1 440	1 075	11 626	10 123	810	490
1981	10 691	10 666	26	8 232	417	-181	7 635	1 762	1 295	12 613	10 991	848	502
1982	11 222	11 182	40	8 487	440	-181	7 867	1 909	1 446	12 730	11 156	882	497
1983	11 863	11 830	32	8 941	531	-186	8 225	2 061	1 577	13 151	11 671	902	502
1984	13 041	13 000	42	9 767	513	-204	9 050	2 327	1 665	14 100	12 419	925	528
1985	14 190	14 154	36	10 583	584	-212	9 787	2 557	1 845	14 920	13 082	951	550
1986	15 332	15 300	32	11 379	640	-229	10 510	2 770	2 053	15 635	13 663	981	577
1987	16 806	16 761	45	12 598	707	-253	11 639	2 937	2 231	16 422	14 285	1 023	623
1988	19 016	18 953	62	14 405	825	-291	13 289	3 282	2 445	17 688	15 301	1 075	671
1989	21 706	21 628	78	16 161	951	-336	14 874	4 041	2 791	19 084	16 583	1 137	720
1990	24 628	24 548	80	18 307	1 062	-370	16 875	4 573	3 180	20 209	17 527	1 219	763
1991	26 468	26 394	74	19 273	1 136	-373	17 765	4 821	3 882	20 596	17 994	1 285	781
1992	28 956	28 895	61	21 198	1 223	-386	19 589	4 974	4 393	21 730	18 904	1 333	789
1993	30 945	30 847	98	22 959	1 326	-447	21 187	5 104	4 655	22 388	19 293	1 382	831
1994	34 105	34 039	65	25 450	1 494	-496	23 460	5 737	4 908	23 391	20 241	1 458	914
1995	37 508	37 448	60	27 865	1 652	-543	25 669	6 463	5 376	24 541	21 177	1 528	970
1996	41 413	41 354	58	30 763	1 824	-610	28 330	7 353	5 730	25 877	22 084	1 600	1 036
1997	44 510	44 454	56	33 243	1 990	-653	30 600	7 780	6 130	26 514	22 431	1 679	1 090
1998	47 795	47 704	91	36 216	2 154	-712	33 350	8 025	6 420	27 360	22 959	1 747	.....

Personal Income and Employment—*Continued*

(Millions of dollars, except as noted)

Year	Total	Nonfarm	Farm	Derivation of personal income						Per capita (dollars)		Population (thousands)	Total employment (thousands)
				Earnings by place of work	Less: Personal contributions for social insurance	Plus: Adjustment for residence	Equals: Net earnings by place of residence	Dividends, interest, and rent	Transfer payments	Total	Disposable		
NEW HAMPSHIRE													
1969	2 733	2 710	23	1 940	79	225	2 086	414	233	3 774	3 320	724	334
1970	2 908	2 889	19	2 055	84	214	2 185	445	278	3 919	3 425	742	334
1971	3 144	3 126	18	2 194	92	222	2 324	484	336	4 124	3 667	762	336
1972	3 482	3 462	20	2 443	105	243	2 581	529	373	4 454	3 894	782	350
1973	3 934	3 910	24	2 772	132	272	2 912	587	435	4 906	4 346	802	374
1974	4 344	4 328	16	2 986	150	316	3 151	671	522	5 317	4 693	817	381
1975	4 687	4 667	19	3 125	158	347	3 315	711	661	5 646	5 050	830	370
1976	5 338	5 318	21	3 614	178	392	3 829	795	715	6 302	5 594	847	394
1977	6 029	6 008	20	4 100	204	458	4 355	902	771	6 914	6 103	872	418
1978	6 966	6 945	21	4 790	236	539	5 093	1 029	844	7 792	6 835	894	446
1979	8 007	7 984	24	5 473	281	644	5 836	1 210	961	8 781	7 703	912	469
1980	9 166	9 151	14	6 059	316	800	6 543	1 494	1 129	9 917	8 730	924	483
1981	10 371	10 347	24	6 670	371	904	7 202	1 857	1 313	11 073	9 716	937	494
1982	11 234	11 217	18	7 180	414	986	7 753	2 039	1 443	11 854	10 505	948	500
1983	12 466	12 450	16	8 059	460	1 101	8 700	2 223	1 543	13 011	11 483	958	520
1984	14 182	14 161	21	9 104	521	1 313	9 895	2 686	1 602	14 518	12 855	977	556
1985	15 790	15 765	26	10 288	616	1 436	11 108	2 984	1 699	15 842	13 903	997	589
1986	17 460	17 433	27	11 525	702	1 497	12 320	3 339	1 801	17 033	14 793	1 025	621
1987	19 359	19 315	44	13 043	789	1 623	13 876	3 623	1 860	18 362	15 983	1 054	639
1988	21 363	21 315	48	14 408	896	1 770	15 282	4 081	2 000	19 733	17 355	1 083	666
1989	22 708	22 660	49	15 032	962	1 869	15 939	4 555	2 214	20 559	18 112	1 105	666
1990	23 047	23 005	42	14 921	978	1 968	15 910	4 649	2 488	20 728	18 455	1 112	648
1991	23 678	23 636	42	14 770	998	2 034	15 806	4 641	3 231	21 390	19 148	1 107	622
1992	24 758	24 702	56	15 793	1 062	2 108	16 839	4 479	3 440	22 234	19 843	1 114	635
1993	25 484	25 430	54	16 484	1 115	2 200	17 568	4 563	3 353	22 710	20 191	1 122	648
1994	27 337	27 291	46	17 483	1 209	2 296	18 571	4 951	3 815	24 119	21 463	1 133	673
1995	29 014	28 965	49	18 673	1 308	2 297	19 662	5 243	4 109	25 313	22 459	1 146	696
1996	30 633	30 583	50	19 734	1 381	2 474	20 827	5 740	4 067	26 418	23 140	1 160	716
1997	32 546	32 501	45	21 242	1 493	2 663	22 411	5 970	4 164	27 766	24 104	1 172	736
1998	34 626	34 573	53	23 007	1 605	2 842	24 244	6 085	4 298	29 219	25 188	1 185	.....
NEW JERSEY													
1969	32 201	32 086	116	22 963	976	2 991	24 979	4 781	2 442	4 539	3 909	7 095	3 061
1970	34 800	34 686	114	24 859	1 058	2 927	26 729	5 102	2 970	4 840	4 212	7 190	3 125
1971	37 421	37 315	107	26 499	1 177	2 980	28 302	5 505	3 615	5 139	4 530	7 282	3 119
1972	40 593	40 490	103	28 850	1 303	3 158	30 703	5 844	4 046	5 533	4 806	7 337	3 184
1973	44 366	44 227	139	31 712	1 595	3 267	33 383	6 447	4 535	6 048	5 304	7 335	3 288
1974	48 202	48 050	152	34 069	1 782	3 429	35 716	7 170	5 316	6 571	5 743	7 335	3 301
1975	51 574	51 462	112	35 447	1 858	3 669	37 258	7 474	6 842	7 025	6 229	7 341	3 191
1976	56 399	56 281	118	38 906	1 995	3 947	40 858	8 079	7 462	7 679	6 743	7 344	3 248
1977	61 788	61 661	126	42 715	2 175	4 313	44 853	8 969	7 967	8 416	7 298	7 342	3 325
1978	68 923	68 780	143	47 795	2 478	4 884	50 200	10 241	8 482	9 369	8 126	7 356	3 464
1979	77 002	76 867	134	52 869	2 850	5 602	55 621	11 976	9 404	10 444	8 975	7 373	3 555
1980	86 872	86 748	124	58 047	3 156	6 606	61 497	14 581	10 794	11 777	10 102	7 376	3 608
1981	96 827	96 669	158	63 227	3 695	7 189	66 720	17 958	12 150	13 072	11 175	7 407	3 643
1982	104 026	103 855	171	67 395	4 042	7 731	71 084	19 543	13 400	13 999	11 963	7 431	3 650
1983	112 615	112 412	203	73 365	4 404	8 045	77 007	21 201	14 408	15 080	12 954	7 468	3 751
1984	125 357	125 155	202	81 394	4 961	8 455	84 888	25 530	14 939	16 680	14 433	7 515	3 932
1985	134 719	134 486	233	88 527	5 602	8 840	91 764	27 330	15 625	17 807	15 244	7 566	4 047
1986	144 056	143 821	235	95 617	6 280	9 387	98 724	28 865	16 467	18 900	16 115	7 622	4 145
1987	156 412	156 149	263	105 428	6 972	9 976	108 432	30 630	17 350	20 391	17 296	7 671	4 247
1988	171 997	171 739	258	116 947	7 875	10 373	119 444	34 017	18 536	22 302	19 127	7 712	4 355
1989	183 505	183 254	251	122 816	8 383	10 114	124 547	38 959	19 999	23 751	20 441	7 726	4 391
1990	193 035	192 809	227	128 786	8 805	10 511	130 493	40 519	22 024	24 883	21 500	7 758	4 338
1991	197 153	196 936	217	130 235	9 179	10 394	131 450	40 739	24 965	25 328	21 910	7 784	4 209
1992	209 344	209 129	215	138 824	9 669	11 746	140 901	39 882	28 561	26 749	23 113	7 826	4 208
1993	216 183	215 933	251	144 366	9 867	11 698	146 197	40 228	29 757	27 457	23 631	7 873	4 238
1994	224 290	224 043	246	149 966	10 455	11 586	151 097	42 559	30 634	28 333	24 266	7 916	4 279
1995	235 425	235 175	250	156 304	10 961	12 408	157 751	45 070	32 604	29 568	25 328	7 962	4 345
1996	247 381	247 120	261	162 797	11 407	14 042	165 431	48 110	33 840	30 892	26 248	8 008	4 400
1997	260 736	260 536	200	171 907	11 977	16 133	176 063	49 708	34 965	32 356	27 286	8 058	4 494
1998	275 532	275 331	200	184 531	12 751	17 067	188 848	50 528	36 156	33 953	28 329	8 115	.....

Personal Income and Employment—Continued

(Millions of dollars, except as noted)

Year	Total	Nonfarm	Farm	Derivation of personal income						Per capita (dollars)		Population (thousands)	Total employment (thousands)
				Earnings by place of work	Less: Personal contributions for social insurance	Plus: Adjustment for residence	Equals: Net earnings by place of residence	Dividends, interest, and rent	Transfer payments	Total	Disposable		
NEW MEXICO													
1969	2 940	2 822	119	2 393	102	-21	2 270	361	309	2 908	2 567	1 011	395
1970	3 242	3 100	142	2 591	110	-21	2 460	396	386	3 168	2 810	1 023	399
1971	3 586	3 444	142	2 830	125	-21	2 684	448	454	3 405	3 072	1 053	416
1972	4 022	3 872	150	3 182	142	-18	3 021	489	512	3 732	3 340	1 078	440
1973	4 530	4 337	193	3 567	176	-16	3 375	554	602	4 102	3 674	1 104	461
1974	5 101	4 939	161	3 958	206	-15	3 738	638	725	4 515	4 025	1 130	478
1975	5 783	5 591	191	4 452	230	-11	4 210	689	883	4 973	4 510	1 163	491
1976	6 500	6 365	135	5 004	258	-11	4 735	766	1 000	5 438	4 878	1 195	512
1977	7 333	7 186	148	5 674	293	-10	5 372	882	1 078	5 985	5 367	1 225	539
1978	8 425	8 243	182	6 536	338	-10	6 189	1 050	1 187	6 730	5 989	1 252	568
1979	9 588	9 370	218	7 361	394	-9	6 959	1 268	1 361	7 487	6 657	1 281	593
1980	10 802	10 612	190	8 068	445	-2	7 621	1 558	1 623	8 250	7 350	1 309	598
1981	12 215	12 090	125	8 938	533	-1	8 405	1 956	1 855	9 165	8 058	1 333	613
1982	13 212	13 090	122	9 498	582	-1	8 916	2 248	2 049	9 687	8 478	1 364	621
1983	14 044	13 914	131	10 090	674	5	9 420	2 396	2 228	10 072	9 063	1 394	633
1984	15 386	15 236	150	11 061	688	13	10 386	2 673	2 328	10 861	9 774	1 417	658
1985	16 673	16 458	215	11 932	763	18	11 187	2 955	2 532	11 592	10 430	1 438	678
1986	17 290	17 092	198	12 208	806	24	11 426	3 139	2 725	11 820	10 710	1 463	684
1987	18 122	17 890	232	12 769	840	36	11 965	3 232	2 925	12 257	10 996	1 479	703
1988	19 173	18 858	315	13 528	926	44	12 646	3 372	3 155	12 865	11 537	1 490	740
1989	20 482	20 103	379	14 298	1 004	51	13 345	3 698	3 438	13 619	12 189	1 504	755
1990	22 009	21 595	414	15 329	1 073	56	14 311	3 939	3 758	14 480	12 938	1 520	766
1991	23 314	22 901	413	16 370	1 167	59	15 262	3 842	4 210	15 069	13 486	1 547	791
1992	24 917	24 445	473	17 553	1 233	63	16 384	3 871	4 663	15 762	14 116	1 581	804
1993	26 749	26 211	538	18 981	1 329	52	17 704	3 984	5 061	16 559	14 748	1 615	832
1994	28 362	27 968	394	19 981	1 449	57	18 590	4 333	5 439	17 150	15 257	1 654	866
1995	30 357	30 006	351	21 266	1 577	60	19 749	4 585	6 023	18 029	16 091	1 684	899
1996	31 826	31 472	354	21 912	1 653	69	20 328	5 025	6 473	18 634	16 540	1 708	908
1997	33 269	32 890	379	23 008	1 758	73	21 323	5 243	6 704	19 298	17 000	1 724	923
1998	34 753	34 380	373	24 183	1 839	94	22 438	5 355	6 961	20 008	17 574	1 737	.....
NEW YORK													
1969	83 490	83 014	475	66 858	2 854	-3 227	60 777	14 082	8 631	4 611	3 848	18 105	8 496
1970	89 116	88 659	457	71 054	3 019	-3 144	64 891	14 200	10 024	4 877	4 142	18 272	8 468
1971	95 023	94 575	448	74 869	3 283	-3 212	68 375	14 512	12 136	5 174	4 450	18 365	8 347
1972	101 639	101 239	400	79 966	3 550	-3 417	72 999	15 021	13 619	5 538	4 709	18 352	8 350
1973	108 610	108 100	509	85 238	4 281	-3 565	77 391	16 220	14 999	5 969	5 112	18 195	8 467
1974	116 935	116 451	484	90 113	4 685	-3 732	81 696	17 945	17 295	6 470	5 525	18 073	8 395
1975	124 787	124 377	410	93 905	4 827	-4 013	85 065	18 261	21 462	6 920	5 994	18 032	8 175
1976	133 522	133 097	425	100 283	5 085	-4 347	90 850	19 659	23 014	7 428	6 406	17 975	8 128
1977	144 207	143 859	348	108 408	5 432	-4 819	98 157	21 776	24 274	8 078	6 938	17 852	8 202
1978	157 873	157 423	451	119 192	5 974	-5 466	107 752	24 619	25 502	8 909	7 645	17 720	8 381
1979	173 911	173 362	550	131 018	6 791	-6 264	117 963	28 669	27 280	9 862	8 416	17 634	8 590
1980	193 986	193 453	534	143 996	7 461	-7 376	129 160	33 549	31 278	11 043	9 385	17 567	8 622
1981	216 042	215 499	543	157 768	8 827	-8 319	140 622	40 167	35 253	12 298	10 344	17 568	8 700
1982	232 028	231 509	518	169 360	9 675	-9 123	150 561	42 932	38 534	13 191	11 041	17 590	8 706
1983	248 289	247 926	363	181 057	10 357	-9 671	161 029	45 726	41 535	14 038	11 946	17 687	8 768
1984	277 105	276 645	459	200 941	11 505	-10 362	179 074	54 333	43 699	15 615	13 333	17 746	9 054
1985	295 573	295 053	520	216 858	12 965	-11 022	192 871	56 692	46 010	16 613	14 079	17 792	9 289
1986	315 807	315 182	626	233 656	14 248	-11 860	207 549	59 254	49 005	17 709	14 975	17 833	9 491
1987	337 195	336 501	694	252 992	15 367	-12 696	224 928	61 246	51 020	18 871	15 798	17 869	9 549
1988	366 602	366 014	588	275 142	17 248	-13 502	244 392	68 205	54 006	20 433	17 277	17 941	9 779
1989	392 398	391 683	716	286 976	18 486	-13 343	255 146	79 189	58 063	21 820	18 319	17 983	9 852
1990	415 971	415 260	711	303 541	19 632	-14 145	269 764	82 588	63 620	23 106	19 568	18 002	9 802
1991	425 460	424 865	594	305 905	20 219	-14 025	271 661	81 711	72 089	23 600	20 124	18 028	9 579
1992	448 371	447 740	631	326 925	21 274	-16 250	289 402	77 739	81 230	24 801	21 185	18 079	9 511
1993	460 250	459 597	652	335 073	21 744	-16 203	297 126	77 514	85 610	25 373	21 588	18 139	9 538
1994	476 331	475 810	522	342 640	22 523	-16 138	303 979	82 291	90 061	26 242	22 312	18 152	9 585
1995	500 563	500 176	387	358 782	23 306	-17 740	317 736	86 604	96 223	27 587	23 442	18 145	9 653
1996	526 390	525 856	533	376 627	24 281	-20 215	332 131	92 480	101 778	29 015	24 378	18 142	9 756
1997	548 927	548 594	333	396 903	25 578	-21 719	349 606	95 425	103 896	30 250	25 160	18 146	9 908
1998	575 768	575 201	567	422 391	27 011	-23 162	372 218	96 894	106 656	31 679	26 005	18 175	.....

Personal Income and Employment—*Continued*

(Millions of dollars, except as noted)

Year	Total	Nonfarm	Farm	Earnings by place of work	Less: Personal contributions for social insurance	Plus: Adjustment for residence	Equals: Net earnings by place of residence	Dividends, interest, and rent	Transfer payments	Per capita (dollars) Total	Disposable	Population (thousands)	Total employment (thousands)
NORTH CAROLINA													
1969	15 238	14 519	719	12 990	527	13	12 477	1 544	1 218	3 029	2 627	5 031	2 458
1970	16 619	15 893	727	13 946	571	10	13 386	1 749	1 484	3 259	2 853	5 099	2 469
1971	18 059	17 371	688	15 073	645	7	14 435	1 878	1 746	3 472	3 063	5 201	2 490
1972	20 428	19 606	822	17 173	743	0	16 430	2 036	1 963	3 857	3 353	5 296	2 602
1973	23 250	22 021	1 229	19 572	936	-4	18 632	2 331	2 287	4 320	3 789	5 382	2 720
1974	25 631	24 459	1 173	21 152	1 068	1	20 085	2 707	2 840	4 693	4 093	5 461	2 743
1975	27 497	26 387	1 110	21 868	1 120	3	20 751	2 885	3 862	4 968	4 435	5 535	2 647
1976	30 775	29 590	1 185	24 602	1 255	4	23 351	3 214	4 211	5 502	4 858	5 593	2 754
1977	33 913	33 027	886	27 099	1 384	8	25 723	3 650	4 540	5 983	5 257	5 668	2 851
1978	38 449	37 278	1 171	30 956	1 598	5	29 362	4 175	4 912	6 698	5 872	5 740	2 948
1979	42 618	41 842	776	33 964	1 848	-1	32 115	4 904	5 599	7 346	6 385	5 802	3 051
1980	47 723	47 064	658	36 947	2 046	-3	34 899	6 120	6 704	8 090	7 030	5 899	3 060
1981	53 616	52 556	1 060	40 741	2 412	-36	38 292	7 621	7 703	9 001	7 802	5 957	3 082
1982	56 817	55 760	1 057	42 602	2 595	-48	39 960	8 283	8 574	9 439	8 290	6 019	3 050
1983	61 815	61 188	627	46 482	2 846	-67	43 569	9 017	9 229	10 172	8 895	6 077	3 137
1984	70 042	68 748	1 294	53 072	3 191	-104	49 778	10 667	9 598	11 363	9 965	6 164	3 305
1985	75 900	74 739	1 162	57 731	3 620	-170	53 941	11 649	10 311	12 136	10 589	6 254	3 409
1986	81 548	80 409	1 138	62 141	4 013	-233	57 895	12 576	11 077	12 900	11 252	6 322	3 511
1987	87 841	86 753	1 088	67 672	4 335	-316	63 021	13 152	11 669	13 717	11 877	6 404	3 630
1988	95 977	94 567	1 410	73 887	4 871	-377	68 640	14 721	12 616	14 810	12 948	6 481	3 777
1989	103 911	102 257	1 654	79 100	5 337	-432	73 332	16 666	13 913	15 827	13 727	6 565	3 865
1990	110 830	108 714	2 116	83 717	5 668	-480	77 569	17 729	15 533	16 649	14 553	6 657	3 918
1991	115 494	113 097	2 397	86 264	5 968	-485	79 811	17 947	17 735	17 115	15 010	6 748	3 893
1992	124 565	122 272	2 294	94 127	6 436	-534	87 158	17 810	19 598	18 230	16 021	6 833	3 995
1993	132 981	130 283	2 698	100 299	6 891	-617	92 791	18 438	21 753	19 137	16 784	6 949	4 121
1994	140 667	137 972	2 695	106 370	7 443	-688	98 239	19 870	22 558	19 920	17 358	7 061	4 241
1995	150 877	148 328	2 549	112 627	8 008	-777	103 843	21 820	25 215	20 996	18 258	7 186	4 382
1996	161 180	158 242	2 937	119 054	8 457	-848	109 749	24 267	27 164	22 053	19 134	7 309	4 485
1997	172 154	169 064	3 090	127 747	9 090	-907	117 750	25 794	28 611	23 168	19 953	7 431	4 612
1998	182 036	179 495	2 541	136 221	9 665	-971	125 585	26 561	29 890	24 122	20 578	7 546	.....
NORTH DAKOTA													
1969	1 869	1 501	368	1 527	63	-51	1 412	268	189	3 009	2 672	621	274
1970	1 947	1 656	291	1 578	71	-53	1 453	272	221	3 146	2 815	619	281
1971	2 245	1 831	414	1 819	80	-55	1 685	300	261	3 583	3 257	627	284
1972	2 703	2 041	662	2 230	88	-58	2 083	330	290	4 284	3 890	631	288
1973	3 838	2 326	1 512	3 280	112	-62	3 106	405	327	6 068	5 541	632	300
1974	3 803	2 655	1 148	3 154	133	-73	2 948	479	377	5 997	5 299	634	308
1975	3 957	3 032	926	3 196	149	-78	2 968	548	442	6 198	5 486	638	314
1976	3 890	3 428	463	3 050	165	-93	2 793	607	491	6 028	5 323	645	326
1977	4 049	3 792	257	3 063	162	-99	2 802	701	545	6 236	5 537	649	331
1978	5 144	4 297	846	4 051	187	-111	3 754	798	592	7 905	7 019	651	346
1979	5 308	4 815	494	4 080	216	-127	3 737	919	653	8 140	7 203	652	354
1980	5 106	5 454	-348	3 552	242	-141	3 169	1 164	773	7 803	6 762	654	356
1981	6 617	6 311	306	4 645	282	-162	4 201	1 532	884	10 034	8 708	660	360
1982	7 154	6 879	275	4 849	306	-163	4 380	1 781	992	10 693	9 485	669	361
1983	7 511	7 185	326	5 112	319	-167	4 626	1 785	1 099	11 100	9 841	677	367
1984	8 079	7 528	551	5 571	337	-167	5 068	1 850	1 161	11 871	10 663	680	368
1985	8 336	7 699	638	5 766	364	-165	5 237	1 851	1 249	12 314	11 058	677	366
1986	8 453	7 811	642	5 780	382	-162	5 237	1 845	1 371	12 625	11 394	670	359
1987	8 620	7 975	645	5 973	398	-165	5 411	1 771	1 438	13 037	11 690	661	365
1988	7 957	8 106	-149	5 359	431	-169	4 760	1 738	1 459	12 142	10 764	655	369
1989	8 835	8 510	325	6 032	463	-173	5 395	1 851	1 590	13 669	12 107	646	373
1990	9 729	9 137	592	6 627	498	-181	5 949	2 060	1 720	15 264	13 580	637	376
1991	9 817	9 415	402	6 767	532	-189	6 047	1 973	1 797	15 479	13 693	634	385
1992	10 718	9 959	759	7 566	552	-208	6 806	1 957	1 956	16 866	15 039	635	390
1993	10 860	10 516	344	7 591	585	-237	6 769	1 986	2 106	17 040	15 178	637	399
1994	11 612	10 955	657	8 333	621	-251	7 461	1 993	2 159	18 156	16 241	640	414
1995	11 640	11 532	108	8 199	663	-273	7 263	2 140	2 238	18 149	16 162	641	425
1996	12 983	12 158	825	9 338	692	-289	8 356	2 267	2 360	20 197	18 077	643	434
1997	12 886	12 716	170	9 102	727	-298	8 078	2 325	2 482	20 103	17 768	641	441
1998	13 855	13 253	603	9 996	757	-308	8 931	2 361	2 562	21 708	19 162	638	.....

Personal Income and Employment—*Continued*

(Millions of dollars, except as noted)

Year	Total	Nonfarm	Farm	Derivation of personal income						Per capita (dollars)		Population (thousands)	Total employment (thousands)
				Earnings by place of work	Less: Personal contributions for social insurance	Plus: Adjustment for residence	Equals: Net earnings by place of residence	Dividends, interest, and rent	Transfer payments	Total	Disposable		
OHIO													
1969	41 296	40 820	476	34 270	1 411	-228	32 632	5 419	3 245	3 909	3 361	10 563	4 695
1970	43 290	42 790	500	35 607	1 464	-219	33 924	5 554	3 812	4 058	3 534	10 669	4 683
1971	45 940	45 454	485	37 309	1 591	-180	35 538	5 889	4 513	4 279	3 784	10 735	4 627
1972	49 885	49 303	581	40 599	1 746	-185	38 668	6 212	5 006	4 642	4 035	10 747	4 710
1973	55 574	54 840	734	45 306	2 174	-217	42 917	6 898	5 760	5 161	4 498	10 767	4 902
1974	60 878	60 020	858	48 913	2 430	-204	46 279	7 727	6 872	5 655	4 917	10 766	4 964
1975	64 649	63 785	864	50 504	2 443	-186	47 875	8 103	8 671	6 002	5 264	10 770	4 809
1976	71 639	70 807	831	56 342	2 707	-212	53 423	8 781	9 435	6 662	5 814	10 753	4 889
1977	79 516	78 791	726	62 915	3 052	-231	59 632	9 813	10 071	7 382	6 397	10 771	5 034
1978	88 258	87 582	676	69 925	3 467	-252	66 206	11 183	10 869	8 175	7 079	10 795	5 207
1979	97 968	97 167	800	76 815	3 976	-274	72 566	13 057	12 345	9 072	7 806	10 799	5 298
1980	106 861	106 271	590	80 235	4 198	-311	75 727	15 747	15 388	9 894	8 561	10 801	5 215
1981	116 103	115 961	142	85 028	4 806	-369	79 853	19 077	17 174	10 762	9 254	10 788	5 151
1982	120 577	120 317	260	85 717	4 941	-494	80 283	20 394	19 900	11 209	9 740	10 757	4 982
1983	127 243	127 332	-89	89 798	5 193	-611	83 994	21 965	21 285	11 850	10 339	10 738	4 976
1984	140 414	139 597	817	100 329	5 763	-751	93 814	24 600	22 000	13 077	11 500	10 738	5 182
1985	148 599	147 801	798	106 889	6 438	-836	99 615	25 615	23 368	13 843	12 123	10 735	5 314
1986	155 139	154 537	602	111 293	6 896	-871	103 526	26 779	24 835	14 458	12 691	10 730	5 429
1987	163 078	162 419	659	117 884	7 276	-916	109 692	27 361	26 026	15 156	13 190	10 760	5 581
1988	174 795	174 121	674	127 102	8 026	-963	118 112	29 315	27 367	16 187	14 170	10 799	5 726
1989	186 297	185 246	1 052	133 723	8 705	-1 010	124 007	32 610	29 680	17 203	14 968	10 829	5 848
1990	196 777	195 714	1 062	140 658	9 171	-1 078	130 409	34 328	32 040	18 116	15 786	10 862	5 898
1991	203 194	202 651	543	143 651	9 620	-1 114	132 917	34 882	35 396	18 589	16 245	10 931	5 892
1992	214 356	213 421	935	153 164	10 049	-1 180	141 935	33 583	38 838	19 482	17 093	11 003	5 907
1993	223 793	223 058	735	160 551	10 628	-1 257	148 666	34 535	40 592	20 228	17 600	11 063	6 010
1994	235 724	234 790	935	169 876	11 490	-1 334	157 051	36 342	42 331	21 237	18 448	11 100	6 197
1995	247 449	246 741	708	177 653	12 281	-1 362	164 010	38 959	44 480	22 217	19 234	11 138	6 370
1996	257 507	256 552	955	183 715	12 832	-1 391	169 493	41 827	46 188	23 054	19 821	11 170	6 475
1997	270 450	268 972	1 479	194 487	13 618	-1 576	179 293	43 271	47 887	24 163	20 618	11 193	6 597
1998	282 920	281 802	1 118	205 520	14 314	-1 689	189 518	44 056	49 347	25 239	21 329	11 209	.....
OKLAHOMA													
1969	8 089	7 806	283	6 295	262	62	6 095	1 052	943	3 191	2 786	2 535	1 107
1970	8 875	8 506	369	6 857	285	63	6 635	1 147	1 094	3 458	3 057	2 566	1 120
1971	9 653	9 305	347	7 368	317	63	7 113	1 271	1 268	3 687	3 299	2 618	1 132
1972	10 608	10 168	440	8 183	351	72	7 904	1 302	1 401	3 992	3 517	2 657	1 183
1973	12 117	11 363	754	9 334	437	83	8 979	1 546	1 592	4 497	4 005	2 694	1 221
1974	13 526	13 057	469	10 239	508	106	9 837	1 794	1 894	4 950	4 337	2 732	1 256
1975	15 097	14 680	417	11 236	553	140	10 823	1 950	2 324	5 446	4 834	2 772	1 269
1976	16 759	16 412	347	12 459	608	176	12 026	2 150	2 583	5 936	5 253	2 823	1 305
1977	18 655	18 471	184	13 955	689	152	13 418	2 441	2 796	6 509	5 713	2 866	1 359
1978	21 252	21 070	182	16 014	803	150	15 361	2 869	3 022	7 295	6 352	2 913	1 428
1979	24 867	24 202	666	18 763	949	164	17 978	3 438	3 452	8 373	7 278	2 970	1 483
1980	28 776	28 465	311	21 342	1 108	171	20 405	4 357	4 015	9 463	8 170	3 041	1 551
1981	33 597	33 238	359	24 681	1 370	194	23 505	5 518	4 574	10 851	9 220	3 096	1 630
1982	37 254	36 771	483	27 080	1 532	200	25 748	6 346	5 160	11 620	9 785	3 206	1 678
1983	37 896	37 710	187	26 919	1 555	239	25 603	6 653	5 641	11 517	10 078	3 290	1 642
1984	40 668	40 289	379	28 939	1 648	288	27 579	7 319	5 770	12 378	10 913	3 286	1 671
1985	42 182	41 792	390	29 751	1 780	328	28 298	7 714	6 169	12 894	11 398	3 271	1 655
1986	42 019	41 371	648	29 298	1 823	376	27 851	7 571	6 598	12 918	11 712	3 253	1 595
1987	41 949	41 375	575	29 170	1 820	424	27 773	7 279	6 897	13 068	11 659	3 210	1 606
1988	43 811	43 033	778	30 411	1 986	469	28 894	7 548	7 368	13 833	12 342	3 167	1 619
1989	46 280	45 450	830	31 883	2 154	493	30 222	8 201	7 858	14 691	13 010	3 150	1 632
1990	49 135	48 314	822	33 818	2 289	546	32 075	8 595	8 466	15 613	13 601	3 147	1 663
1991	50 981	50 339	643	35 141	2 444	576	33 273	8 438	9 270	16 100	14 160	3 166	1 679
1992	53 937	53 154	783	37 175	2 574	610	35 210	8 471	10 256	16 832	14 918	3 204	1 692
1993	56 252	55 232	1 021	39 090	2 673	615	37 032	8 380	10 841	17 419	15 462	3 229	1 719
1994	58 417	57 605	812	40 170	2 808	664	38 026	8 975	11 416	17 984	15 927	3 248	1 753
1995	60 661	60 306	355	41 179	2 957	698	38 920	9 340	12 402	18 544	16 405	3 271	1 795
1996	63 750	63 393	357	43 210	3 089	719	40 840	9 947	12 964	19 342	17 008	3 296	1 842
1997	67 444	66 632	813	46 091	3 235	739	43 595	10 352	13 498	20 305	17 755	3 322	1 889
1998	70 469	70 146	324	48 514	3 405	795	45 904	10 563	14 003	21 056	18 292	3 347	.....

Personal Income and Employment—*Continued*

(Millions of dollars, except as noted)

Year	Total	Nonfarm	Farm	Earnings by place of work	Less: Personal contributions for social insurance	Plus: Adjustment for residence	Equals: Net earnings by place of residence	Dividends, interest, and rent	Transfer payments	Per capita (dollars) Total	Disposable	Population (thousands)	Total employment (thousands)
OREGON													
1969	7 574	7 331	242	6 069	263	-85	5 721	1 118	734	3 673	3 123	2 062	920
1970	8 222	7 984	238	6 428	280	-61	6 087	1 240	895	3 914	3 388	2 100	926
1971	9 002	8 772	230	6 974	313	-53	6 608	1 353	1 042	4 187	3 657	2 150	951
1972	10 101	9 810	292	7 906	360	-53	7 494	1 459	1 149	4 601	3 976	2 195	1 001
1973	11 416	11 018	398	8 936	451	-60	8 424	1 638	1 354	5 099	4 423	2 239	1 058
1974	12 938	12 433	504	9 972	519	-72	9 382	1 889	1 667	5 672	4 888	2 281	1 089
1975	14 190	13 777	413	10 661	556	-45	10 061	2 035	2 095	6 104	5 341	2 325	1 105
1976	16 184	15 795	388	12 256	626	-33	11 596	2 284	2 303	6 822	5 914	2 372	1 156
1977	18 149	17 815	335	13 810	715	-96	12 999	2 623	2 527	7 440	6 358	2 439	1 223
1978	20 910	20 574	336	16 008	837	-155	15 016	3 121	2 773	8 332	7 112	2 510	1 297
1979	23 796	23 397	399	18 101	976	-229	16 897	3 786	3 114	9 229	7 853	2 578	1 352
1980	26 327	25 847	480	19 403	1 060	-278	18 064	4 565	3 698	9 968	8 529	2 641	1 353
1981	28 273	27 885	389	19 947	1 190	-269	18 489	5 518	4 267	10 597	9 094	2 668	1 324
1982	28 702	28 424	279	19 652	1 228	-256	18 168	5 732	4 802	10 770	9 251	2 665	1 274
1983	30 380	30 096	284	20 669	1 284	-242	19 143	6 074	5 163	11 451	9 933	2 653	1 300
1984	33 091	32 682	409	22 746	1 406	-284	21 057	6 752	5 283	12 409	10 841	2 667	1 348
1985	34 918	34 486	432	24 211	1 546	-323	22 342	6 961	5 614	13 065	11 354	2 673	1 378
1986	36 649	36 092	558	25 521	1 657	-365	23 499	7 347	5 802	13 657	11 761	2 684	1 414
1987	38 575	38 081	495	27 231	1 777	-422	25 031	7 517	6 027	14 282	12 325	2 701	1 464
1988	41 978	41 308	670	30 054	2 030	-484	27 540	8 011	6 427	15 313	13 389	2 741	1 534
1989	45 729	45 114	616	32 458	2 258	-535	29 665	9 130	6 934	16 387	14 021	2 791	1 587
1990	49 805	49 148	657	35 488	2 433	-629	32 426	9 688	7 691	17 423	15 099	2 859	1 638
1991	52 230	51 572	658	37 082	2 636	-674	33 772	9 901	8 557	17 895	15 400	2 919	1 649
1992	55 550	54 887	663	39 664	2 816	-745	36 103	9 977	9 470	18 678	16 022	2 974	1 668
1993	59 234	58 410	824	42 433	3 011	-883	38 540	10 490	10 205	19 518	16 705	3 035	1 713
1994	63 309	62 679	631	45 468	3 258	-983	41 227	11 419	10 664	20 508	17 455	3 087	1 798
1995	67 908	67 373	535	48 593	3 531	-1 115	43 948	12 336	11 624	21 618	18 474	3 141	1 870
1996	73 156	72 493	663	52 357	3 783	-1 338	47 236	13 466	12 454	22 894	19 467	3 195	1 942
1997	77 579	76 982	597	56 353	4 079	-1 763	50 511	14 258	12 811	23 920	20 096	3 243	2 001
1998	81 310	80 692	618	59 453	4 267	-1 818	53 368	14 671	13 271	24 775	20 678	3 282	.....
PENNSYLVANIA													
1969	44 816	44 413	403	36 398	1 532	-422	34 444	5 980	4 392	3 817	3 292	11 741	5 250
1970	48 037	47 609	428	38 435	1 615	-390	36 431	6 201	5 405	4 067	3 533	11 812	5 226
1971	50 862	50 484	378	40 097	1 767	-360	37 970	6 488	6 404	4 280	3 758	11 884	5 159
1972	55 497	55 099	398	43 763	1 956	-362	41 445	6 807	7 245	4 662	4 004	11 905	5 247
1973	61 071	60 542	529	48 201	2 391	-333	45 477	7 546	8 048	5 138	4 448	11 885	5 402
1974	67 125	66 612	513	52 323	2 693	-342	49 288	8 440	9 397	5 658	4 877	11 864	5 419
1975	72 799	72 329	472	55 325	2 815	-372	52 137	8 860	11 803	6 119	5 358	11 898	5 302
1976	80 099	79 542	557	60 585	3 046	-367	57 173	9 725	13 201	6 738	5 881	11 887	5 353
1977	87 893	87 386	507	66 487	3 310	-358	62 820	10 931	14 143	7 397	6 413	11 882	5 429
1978	97 314	96 763	550	73 764	3 690	-362	69 712	12 391	15 211	8 202	7 098	11 865	5 564
1979	108 195	107 506	690	81 293	4 209	-393	76 692	14 400	17 103	9 112	7 851	11 874	5 672
1980	119 039	118 576	464	86 665	4 557	-413	81 695	17 692	19 653	10 030	8 656	11 868	5 638
1981	130 870	130 199	671	92 689	5 238	-387	87 065	21 714	22 091	11 036	9 454	11 859	5 605
1982	138 167	137 593	574	94 592	5 498	-231	88 863	24 068	25 237	11 664	10 056	11 845	5 493
1983	144 410	144 031	379	97 927	5 731	-75	92 122	25 278	27 009	12 199	10 645	11 838	5 452
1984	155 960	155 120	840	106 546	6 375	114	100 285	28 601	27 074	13 200	11 523	11 815	5 603
1985	166 011	165 174	838	112 870	7 038	262	106 095	31 053	28 864	14 104	12 304	11 771	5 712
1986	174 917	174 034	882	118 891	7 703	378	111 567	32 946	30 405	14 845	12 965	11 783	5 806
1987	186 194	185 335	860	128 658	8 181	477	120 954	33 962	31 279	15 765	13 677	11 811	5 996
1988	200 511	199 811	701	139 223	9 144	685	130 765	36 863	32 884	16 927	14 738	11 846	6 171
1989	216 716	215 774	942	148 650	9 868	841	139 623	41 787	35 307	18 264	15 891	11 866	6 270
1990	230 427	229 521	907	157 505	10 434	981	148 052	44 258	38 118	19 371	16 886	11 896	6 343
1991	238 558	237 951	606	161 172	10 935	973	151 210	44 393	42 954	19 975	17 466	11 943	6 275
1992	251 004	249 977	1 027	171 425	11 570	1 086	160 941	42 891	47 172	20 950	18 310	11 981	6 280
1993	260 110	259 173	936	177 936	12 212	1 127	166 850	43 333	49 926	21 635	18 952	12 022	6 315
1994	269 002	268 258	745	184 002	12 890	1 286	172 399	45 521	51 082	22 343	19 539	12 040	6 392
1995	280 147	279 645	503	190 565	13 447	1 577	178 696	48 422	53 030	23 268	20 269	12 040	6 469
1996	295 230	294 340	890	198 406	13 749	1 709	186 364	52 641	56 225	24 533	21 255	12 034	6 555
1997	308 325	307 760	565	208 694	14 448	1 486	195 733	54 162	58 430	25 670	22 022	12 011	6 694
1998	322 706	321 918	788	221 165	15 210	1 701	207 657	54 894	60 155	26 889	22 883	12 001	.....

Personal Income and Employment—*Continued*

(Millions of dollars, except as noted)

| Year | Total | Nonfarm | Farm | Derivation of personal income | | | | | | Per capita (dollars) | | Population (thousands) | Total employment (thousands) |
				Earnings by place of work	Less: Personal contributions for social insurance	Plus: Adjustment for residence	Equals: Net earnings by place of residence	Dividends, interest, and rent	Transfer payments	Total	Disposable		
RHODE ISLAND													
1969	3 590	3 581	9	2 744	130	65	2 678	525	387	3 852	3 363	932	440
1970	3 888	3 877	10	2 941	139	67	2 870	546	472	4 090	3 602	951	440
1971	4 111	4 101	9	3 074	151	63	2 986	567	558	4 264	3 758	964	436
1972	4 485	4 476	9	3 381	167	59	3 272	597	617	4 594	4 004	976	447
1973	4 831	4 824	7	3 600	204	72	3 468	661	702	4 940	4 316	978	452
1974	5 144	5 135	10	3 702	219	87	3 570	748	828	5 395	4 709	954	439
1975	5 519	5 509	10	3 833	224	80	3 689	752	1 078	5 831	5 194	946	424
1976	6 084	6 073	10	4 299	245	87	4 141	826	1 116	6 402	5 650	950	442
1977	6 670	6 661	9	4 722	268	102	4 557	932	1 182	6 983	6 168	955	459
1978	7 349	7 339	10	5 239	301	99	5 037	1 049	1 263	7 677	6 696	957	475
1979	8 185	8 177	8	5 823	345	107	5 585	1 201	1 399	8 555	7 384	957	484
1980	9 189	9 181	8	6 344	380	119	6 083	1 497	1 609	9 685	8 413	949	486
1981	10 231	10 222	9	6 804	429	160	6 535	1 852	1 844	10 735	9 352	953	486
1982	10 952	10 924	29	7 143	462	213	6 895	2 030	2 027	11 478	10 048	954	476
1983	11 757	11 718	39	7 701	504	268	7 465	2 136	2 156	12 293	10 859	956	482
1984	13 024	12 990	35	8 532	560	336	8 307	2 518	2 199	13 540	11 952	962	507
1985	13 956	13 911	45	9 203	616	394	8 981	2 603	2 372	14 403	12 683	969	522
1986	14 984	14 937	47	9 977	689	417	9 706	2 797	2 482	15 331	13 388	977	540
1987	16 242	16 198	44	10 933	755	486	10 664	2 991	2 588	16 412	14 195	990	550
1988	17 836	17 788	49	12 042	847	560	11 755	3 334	2 747	17 900	15 634	996	565
1989	19 197	19 162	35	12 705	900	621	12 427	3 806	2 964	19 184	16 747	1 001	566
1990	19 789	19 756	33	12 985	942	662	12 706	3 811	3 273	19 698	17 285	1 005	555
1991	20 057	20 022	35	12 656	976	693	12 374	3 702	3 982	19 982	17 577	1 004	529
1992	20 828	20 790	38	13 415	1 034	721	13 102	3 581	4 145	20 819	18 348	1 000	534
1993	21 688	21 642	46	13 898	1 083	766	13 581	3 643	4 465	21 735	19 123	998	539
1994	22 170	22 138	33	14 189	1 140	852	13 901	3 762	4 507	22 315	19 564	993	539
1995	23 269	23 233	36	14 864	1 189	876	14 552	3 955	4 762	23 520	20 692	989	548
1996	24 067	24 033	34	15 266	1 216	936	14 985	4 219	4 863	24 356	21 274	988	552
1997	25 340	25 306	34	16 113	1 269	993	15 837	4 329	5 174	25 667	22 225	987	561
1998	26 614	26 576	38	17 102	1 331	1 081	16 852	4 384	5 378	26 924	23 145	988	.....
SOUTH CAROLINA													
1969	7 206	7 004	202	6 047	246	106	5 907	677	622	2 804	2 475	2 570	1 170
1970	7 877	7 675	202	6 505	265	107	6 347	753	777	3 032	2 704	2 598	1 196
1971	8 619	8 402	218	7 054	298	117	6 872	839	908	3 238	2 891	2 662	1 215
1972	9 674	9 441	232	7 953	342	134	7 744	901	1 028	3 559	3 116	2 718	1 262
1973	11 069	10 752	318	9 067	434	147	8 780	1 060	1 229	3 988	3 516	2 775	1 328
1974	12 502	12 146	356	10 117	506	158	9 768	1 190	1 544	4 397	3 868	2 843	1 365
1975	13 501	13 215	285	10 463	527	166	10 102	1 327	2 071	4 655	4 197	2 900	1 326
1976	15 215	14 977	239	11 909	599	196	11 506	1 471	2 238	5 173	4 601	2 941	1 376
1977	16 713	16 523	190	13 086	657	216	12 645	1 668	2 401	5 591	4 956	2 989	1 411
1978	18 952	18 703	249	14 912	756	233	14 389	1 917	2 647	6 232	5 518	3 041	1 467
1979	21 360	21 093	267	16 696	874	253	16 076	2 255	3 030	6 920	6 060	3 087	1 510
1980	23 974	23 931	43	18 165	971	284	17 479	2 823	3 673	7 648	6 718	3 135	1 527
1981	26 914	26 732	182	20 058	1 149	301	19 211	3 477	4 226	8 466	7 394	3 179	1 541
1982	28 362	28 171	191	20 733	1 224	332	19 840	3 869	4 652	8 842	7 793	3 208	1 518
1983	30 779	30 732	46	22 519	1 348	345	21 516	4 294	4 969	9 517	8 388	3 234	1 551
1984	34 413	34 147	265	25 447	1 521	377	24 303	4 960	5 150	10 518	9 319	3 272	1 631
1985	37 014	36 825	190	27 142	1 709	431	25 865	5 454	5 695	11 206	9 909	3 303	1 663
1986	39 359	39 281	78	28 841	1 889	498	27 450	5 850	6 059	11 774	10 424	3 343	1 706
1987	42 332	42 090	242	31 361	2 018	549	29 892	6 128	6 312	12 522	11 053	3 381	1 748
1988	45 953	45 621	332	34 231	2 282	566	32 515	6 678	6 760	13 468	11 983	3 412	1 821
1989	49 016	48 672	345	36 596	2 532	520	34 584	6 841	7 591	14 180	12 485	3 457	1 871
1990	53 979	53 711	268	39 420	2 717	501	37 205	8 240	8 535	15 427	13 650	3 499	1 921
1991	55 907	55 541	366	40 357	2 843	490	38 003	8 291	9 613	15 710	14 003	3 559	1 900
1992	59 065	58 725	340	42 674	2 986	514	40 202	8 188	10 675	16 410	14 685	3 599	1 913
1993	62 123	61 797	326	44 878	3 168	513	42 222	8 443	11 458	17 091	15 231	3 635	1 948
1994	65 688	65 241	447	47 089	3 384	592	44 296	9 106	12 286	17 914	15 908	3 667	1 997
1995	69 506	69 157	350	49 413	3 625	699	46 487	9 836	13 183	18 789	16 596	3 699	2 045
1996	73 435	73 008	427	51 482	3 797	806	48 492	10 851	14 092	19 651	17 272	3 737	2 084
1997	77 686	77 192	494	54 732	4 056	881	51 558	11 314	14 814	20 508	17 913	3 788	2 147
1998	82 040	81 671	369	58 398	4 307	959	55 050	11 564	15 426	21 387	18 598	3 836	.....

Personal Income and Employment—*Continued*

(Millions of dollars, except as noted)

Year	Total	Nonfarm	Farm	Derivation of personal income						Per capita (dollars)		Population (thousands)	Total employment (thousands)
				Earnings by place of work	Less: Personal contributions for social insurance	Plus: Adjustment for residence	Equals: Net earnings by place of residence	Dividends, interest, and rent	Transfer payments	Total	Disposable		
SOUTH DAKOTA													
1969	1 976	1 626	350	1 564	61	6	1 508	266	203	2 958	2 668	668	303
1970	2 144	1 776	367	1 674	66	6	1 615	296	233	3 216	2 929	667	305
1971	2 346	1 949	398	1 822	71	6	1 757	319	270	3 494	3 214	671	306
1972	2 718	2 152	567	2 145	80	6	2 072	348	299	4 013	3 697	677	309
1973	3 453	2 425	1 027	2 806	104	7	2 709	398	346	5 085	4 670	679	323
1974	3 445	2 758	687	2 673	122	8	2 559	479	407	5 066	4 580	680	326
1975	3 760	3 054	706	2 866	137	10	2 740	537	483	5 517	5 058	681	326
1976	3 729	3 451	278	2 737	149	12	2 600	592	537	5 429	4 899	687	336
1977	4 228	3 789	439	3 120	155	13	2 979	673	576	6 137	5 612	689	342
1978	4 906	4 289	618	3 670	176	15	3 509	771	626	7 117	6 488	689	355
1979	5 433	4 778	656	4 021	206	16	3 831	895	708	7 885	7 176	689	360
1980	5 424	5 310	115	3 697	220	18	3 494	1 101	829	7 852	7 040	691	354
1981	6 277	5 877	400	4 183	246	14	3 950	1 377	950	9 102	8 193	690	349
1982	6 573	6 263	310	4 198	260	12	3 950	1 565	1 058	9 517	8 512	691	345
1983	6 779	6 598	181	4 348	277	5	4 076	1 565	1 138	9 782	8 871	693	354
1984	7 751	7 129	623	5 204	304	-1	4 899	1 666	1 186	11 117	10 167	697	364
1985	7 990	7 442	548	5 343	335	-3	5 004	1 707	1 279	11 440	10 480	698	366
1986	8 361	7 772	589	5 576	361	-10	5 205	1 812	1 344	12 012	11 005	696	368
1987	8 828	8 066	762	6 046	393	-17	5 636	1 804	1 389	12 683	11 523	696	383
1988	9 204	8 523	682	6 346	434	-24	5 888	1 852	1 464	13 183	12 003	698	390
1989	9 780	9 104	676	6 704	479	-34	6 191	2 002	1 587	14 038	12 678	697	398
1990	10 790	9 821	968	7 524	513	-50	6 961	2 114	1 715	15 488	13 930	697	411
1991	11 335	10 480	855	7 911	552	-61	7 299	2 187	1 849	16 014	14 404	708	423
1992	12 195	11 262	934	8 591	589	-76	7 925	2 240	2 030	17 055	15 359	715	434
1993	12 717	11 874	843	9 027	624	-100	8 303	2 244	2 170	17 600	15 843	723	445
1994	13 541	12 531	1 010	9 782	677	-127	8 978	2 284	2 279	18 568	16 848	729	468
1995	13 753	13 295	459	9 731	727	-153	8 851	2 452	2 451	18 724	16 898	735	481
1996	15 076	13 901	1 175	10 865	756	-183	9 926	2 555	2 596	20 450	18 513	737	490
1997	15 549	14 705	844	11 118	804	-200	10 114	2 761	2 675	21 076	18 952	738	499
1998	16 388	15 509	879	11 842	852	-214	10 775	2 859	2 754	22 201	19 866	738	.....
TENNESSEE													
1969	11 530	11 244	285	9 792	389	-161	9 243	1 216	1 071	2 959	2 600	3 897	1 789
1970	12 502	12 202	301	10 416	413	-162	9 842	1 344	1 317	3 176	2 814	3 937	1 785
1971	13 746	13 449	297	11 380	471	-173	10 736	1 470	1 541	3 428	3 060	4 010	1 817
1972	15 461	15 094	367	12 901	545	-199	12 157	1 595	1 708	3 782	3 365	4 088	1 924
1973	17 653	17 122	531	14 679	692	-197	13 791	1 847	2 016	4 266	3 798	4 138	2 025
1974	19 530	19 174	356	15 945	797	-214	14 935	2 136	2 460	4 648	4 144	4 202	2 055
1975	21 105	20 825	279	16 630	826	-218	15 587	2 318	3 200	4 953	4 459	4 261	1 983
1976	23 791	23 394	397	18 876	920	-224	17 733	2 535	3 523	5 495	4 928	4 329	2 052
1977	26 449	26 126	324	21 164	1 041	-281	19 843	2 838	3 770	6 009	5 376	4 402	2 135
1978	30 200	29 854	346	24 315	1 200	-347	22 769	3 304	4 127	6 769	6 035	4 462	2 228
1979	33 849	33 468	382	26 933	1 383	-400	25 150	3 931	4 768	7 467	6 657	4 533	2 282
1980	37 467	37 229	239	28 824	1 504	-469	26 851	4 883	5 733	8 145	7 250	4 600	2 264
1981	41 600	41 194	405	31 388	1 757	-497	29 135	5 975	6 490	8 989	7 997	4 628	2 263
1982	43 788	43 494	294	32 443	1 880	-471	30 093	6 550	7 145	9 425	8 415	4 646	2 224
1983	46 622	46 655	-32	34 569	1 983	-492	32 094	6 878	7 651	10 005	8 957	4 660	2 246
1984	52 129	51 739	391	38 987	2 188	-526	36 273	7 943	7 914	11 123	10 046	4 687	2 353
1985	55 982	55 667	315	42 015	2 471	-555	38 989	8 477	8 517	11 872	10 662	4 715	2 410
1986	59 823	59 625	198	44 904	2 706	-591	41 607	9 035	9 181	12 624	11 364	4 739	2 489
1987	64 487	64 234	253	48 935	2 939	-630	45 366	9 393	9 728	13 483	12 094	4 783	2 591
1988	69 840	69 536	304	52 798	3 269	-663	48 866	10 462	10 511	14 482	13 072	4 822	2 682
1989	74 944	74 584	360	56 055	3 559	-697	51 799	11 746	11 400	15 438	13 888	4 854	2 754
1990	79 761	79 416	345	59 238	3 771	-731	54 737	12 289	12 736	16 309	14 693	4 891	2 790
1991	83 961	83 557	403	61 895	4 011	-723	57 162	12 357	14 442	16 976	15 331	4 946	2 797
1992	91 505	90 999	506	67 959	4 289	-643	63 027	12 255	16 223	18 256	16 483	5 012	2 862
1993	97 273	96 824	450	72 770	4 607	-775	67 388	12 405	17 480	19 139	17 262	5 082	2 957
1994	103 614	103 103	511	77 870	5 019	-858	71 993	13 384	18 238	20 088	18 060	5 158	3 080
1995	110 511	110 233	278	82 244	5 363	-929	75 953	14 675	19 883	21 109	18 927	5 235	3 176
1996	115 698	115 490	207	85 142	5 542	-919	78 681	16 035	20 981	21 800	19 406	5 307	3 221
1997	121 934	121 670	264	90 325	5 897	-1 068	83 360	16 663	21 911	22 699	20 066	5 372	3 286
1998	128 244	128 097	148	95 803	6 220	-1 139	88 444	17 032	22 768	23 615	20 745	5 431	.....

Personal Income and Employment—*Continued*

(Millions of dollars, except as noted)

Year	Total	Nonfarm	Farm	Derivation of personal income						Per capita (dollars)		Population (thousands)	Total employment (thousands)
				Earnings by place of work	Less: Personal contributions for social insurance	Plus: Adjustment for residence	Equals: Net earnings by place of residence	Dividends, interest, and rent	Transfer payments	Total	Disposable		
TEXAS													
1969	37 408	36 457	952	30 757	1 229	-86	29 442	4 917	3 049	3 387	2 943	11 045	5 005
1970	41 040	39 845	1 195	33 334	1 324	-96	31 914	5 479	3 647	3 652	3 215	11 237	5 045
1971	44 412	43 359	1 054	35 790	1 471	-102	34 218	5 938	4 256	3 859	3 430	11 510	5 123
1972	49 274	47 952	1 323	39 801	1 650	-128	38 023	6 457	4 795	4 190	3 680	11 759	5 334
1973	56 187	53 980	2 208	45 340	2 087	-155	43 099	7 354	5 735	4 675	4 122	12 019	5 608
1974	63 570	62 363	1 208	50 681	2 444	-131	48 107	8 599	6 864	5 182	4 534	12 268	5 822
1975	71 923	70 576	1 347	57 051	2 706	-130	54 215	9 224	8 484	5 723	5 067	12 568	5 938
1976	81 720	80 412	1 308	65 384	3 082	-94	62 208	10 102	9 411	6 333	5 569	12 903	6 207
1977	91 775	90 486	1 289	73 943	3 496	-309	70 139	11 391	10 245	6 957	6 059	13 192	6 521
1978	106 428	105 392	1 036	85 800	4 097	-431	81 271	13 726	11 431	7 885	6 902	13 498	6 898
1979	123 735	121 953	1 782	99 378	4 925	-437	94 015	16 729	12 990	8 910	7 711	13 887	7 222
1980	142 504	141 824	681	112 556	5 720	-548	106 289	20 889	15 326	9 939	8 558	14 338	7 511
1981	167 489	165 427	2 062	131 481	7 145	-384	123 953	26 068	17 468	11 358	9 673	14 746	7 925
1982	182 418	181 117	1 301	141 351	7 908	-452	132 991	29 576	19 851	11 898	10 235	15 331	8 096
1983	192 258	190 586	1 672	147 911	8 183	-432	139 295	30 837	22 125	12 206	10 674	15 752	8 086
1984	211 731	210 111	1 621	162 488	8 921	-489	153 078	35 619	23 034	13 227	11 637	16 007	8 466
1985	227 488	225 966	1 521	174 007	10 001	-516	163 491	39 089	24 908	13 980	12 301	16 273	8 718
1986	231 390	230 157	1 233	174 512	10 331	-456	163 725	40 357	27 308	13 972	12 464	16 561	8 558
1987	237 150	235 196	1 954	178 992	10 448	-452	168 091	40 154	28 905	14 267	12 704	16 622	8 771
1988	251 975	250 102	1 873	190 208	11 413	-456	178 339	42 933	30 703	15 118	13 538	16 667	8 943
1989	270 749	268 846	1 903	202 672	12 476	-464	189 733	47 486	33 530	16 110	14 366	16 807	9 065
1990	294 697	291 957	2 740	221 450	13 504	-500	207 446	49 754	37 498	17 290	15 379	17 045	9 287
1991	312 020	309 329	2 691	236 061	14 542	-574	220 946	49 173	41 901	17 985	16 091	17 349	9 467
1992	333 570	330 513	3 056	252 466	15 470	-583	236 414	48 541	48 614	18 886	16 945	17 662	9 550
1993	353 092	349 180	3 912	268 344	16 330	-721	251 293	49 446	52 352	19 606	17 583	18 009	9 854
1994	372 673	369 723	2 950	282 248	17 546	-783	263 919	53 171	55 584	20 312	18 218	18 348	10 192
1995	398 555	396 204	2 351	301 997	19 009	-892	282 096	56 170	60 290	21 320	19 097	18 694	10 531
1996	425 299	423 274	2 024	321 029	20 170	-926	299 933	61 140	64 226	22 345	19 861	19 033	10 815
1997	459 586	456 833	2 753	350 411	22 037	-1 058	327 318	64 775	67 493	23 707	20 980	19 386	11 239
1998	494 544	491 874	2 670	382 848	23 973	-1 211	357 664	66 542	70 338	25 028	21 999	19 760	.....
UTAH													
1969	3 196	3 119	77	2 652	121	2	2 533	380	284	3 053	2 680	1 047	444
1970	3 546	3 463	83	2 902	134	2	2 771	431	344	3 327	2 953	1 066	455
1971	3 943	3 861	83	3 191	151	3	3 042	491	411	3 583	3 205	1 101	467
1972	4 432	4 335	97	3 585	170	5	3 420	542	471	3 906	3 477	1 135	494
1973	4 965	4 827	138	4 033	210	7	3 831	582	552	4 248	3 778	1 169	523
1974	5 575	5 472	104	4 500	244	11	4 267	671	637	4 651	4 126	1 199	545
1975	6 195	6 122	73	4 942	268	14	4 688	717	790	5 021	4 506	1 234	553
1976	7 070	6 990	80	5 689	307	17	5 399	795	876	5 556	4 922	1 272	580
1977	8 024	7 955	69	6 487	351	22	6 157	901	966	6 095	5 375	1 316	613
1978	9 241	9 163	78	7 476	406	27	7 097	1 063	1 081	6 773	5 978	1 364	651
1979	10 522	10 430	92	8 469	489	36	8 015	1 278	1 229	7 430	6 528	1 416	679
1980	11 812	11 749	64	9 311	546	50	8 815	1 536	1 463	8 021	7 065	1 473	689
1981	13 301	13 261	40	10 345	649	57	9 753	1 845	1 704	8 777	7 683	1 515	699
1982	14 309	14 264	45	10 975	701	57	10 330	2 031	1 948	9 182	8 005	1 558	709
1983	15 284	15 247	36	11 660	747	45	10 959	2 207	2 118	9 582	8 564	1 595	721
1984	16 919	16 857	62	13 012	822	41	12 231	2 534	2 154	10 429	9 311	1 622	764
1985	18 100	18 037	63	13 903	899	42	13 046	2 740	2 315	11 017	9 815	1 643	792
1986	18 924	18 831	93	14 460	957	36	13 539	2 876	2 510	11 380	10 124	1 663	805
1987	19 906	19 781	125	15 112	966	26	14 172	3 018	2 716	11 862	10 518	1 678	835
1988	21 032	20 823	209	16 046	1 046	24	15 024	3 156	2 852	12 450	11 017	1 689	871
1989	22 581	22 379	203	17 124	1 140	22	16 006	3 438	3 138	13 238	11 701	1 706	903
1990	24 586	24 340	246	18 750	1 228	16	17 538	3 570	3 479	14 214	12 405	1 730	943
1991	26 302	26 080	222	20 106	1 333	9	18 782	3 651	3 870	14 855	13 010	1 771	968
1992	28 303	28 033	271	21 819	1 433	5	20 392	3 683	4 228	15 561	13 629	1 819	986
1993	30 624	30 322	302	23 609	1 544	-3	22 061	3 954	4 609	16 359	14 273	1 872	1 033
1994	33 021	32 820	201	25 666	1 695	-7	23 964	4 300	4 757	17 004	14 733	1 942	1 112
1995	35 954	35 788	166	27 957	1 848	-10	26 100	4 708	5 146	18 054	15 568	1 991	1 175
1996	38 856	38 687	169	30 169	1 989	1	28 182	5 228	5 446	19 214	16 533	2 022	1 235
1997	41 682	41 500	182	32 610	2 160	1	30 452	5 525	5 705	20 185	17 267	2 065	1 283
1998	44 297	44 065	232	34 976	2 297	4	32 683	5 686	5 929	21 096	17 920	2 100	.....

Personal Income and Employment—*Continued*

(Millions of dollars, except as noted)

Year	Total	Nonfarm	Farm	Earnings by place of work	Less: Personal contributions for social insurance	Plus: Adjustment for residence	Equals: Net earnings by place of residence	Dividends, interest, and rent	Transfer payments	Per capita (dollars) Total	Disposable	Population (thousands)	Total employment (thousands)
VERMONT													
1969	1 481	1 419	62	1 180	48	-27	1 105	222	155	3 389	2 904	437	203
1970	1 618	1 551	67	1 271	53	-27	1 191	241	186	3 625	3 128	446	205
1971	1 749	1 683	67	1 346	58	-24	1 263	266	221	3 850	3 416	454	206
1972	1 936	1 861	75	1 479	64	-22	1 394	293	249	4 178	3 619	463	211
1973	2 130	2 052	78	1 623	79	-20	1 525	324	283	4 547	3 994	469	220
1974	2 296	2 232	64	1 707	87	-17	1 603	356	337	4 852	4 280	473	222
1975	2 482	2 416	66	1 791	91	-11	1 689	371	422	5 171	4 582	480	220
1976	2 779	2 697	81	2 021	100	-6	1 915	407	456	5 728	5 108	485	228
1977	3 023	2 954	69	2 195	109	-2	2 083	464	476	6 143	5 428	492	236
1978	3 486	3 387	98	2 580	129	-2	2 449	531	506	6 995	6 188	498	252
1979	3 946	3 838	108	2 892	149	5	2 748	625	574	7 803	6 864	506	261
1980	4 423	4 312	111	3 136	165	13	2 985	755	684	8 629	7 568	513	266
1981	4 951	4 827	125	3 427	200	19	3 245	923	783	9 603	8 385	516	271
1982	5 260	5 138	122	3 583	207	24	3 400	990	870	10 132	8 915	519	272
1983	5 659	5 574	84	3 873	216	23	3 680	1 058	921	10 813	9 491	523	278
1984	6 244	6 164	81	4 272	239	29	4 062	1 238	945	11 857	10 459	527	290
1985	6 785	6 686	99	4 725	276	31	4 480	1 316	989	12 800	11 224	530	302
1986	7 303	7 206	97	5 135	307	35	4 863	1 412	1 029	13 675	11 930	534	313
1987	7 969	7 850	119	5 707	338	43	5 412	1 501	1 056	14 750	12 777	540	323
1988	8 768	8 646	122	6 285	386	51	5 950	1 696	1 123	15 948	13 909	550	337
1989	9 601	9 473	128	6 770	427	53	6 395	1 984	1 222	17 215	14 950	558	345
1990	9 979	9 875	104	6 978	446	53	6 585	2 030	1 364	17 677	15 434	564	344
1991	10 147	10 055	92	6 998	465	54	6 587	2 041	1 520	17 899	15 700	567	338
1992	10 762	10 601	161	7 504	492	55	7 068	2 014	1 681	18 883	16 611	570	345
1993	11 128	11 007	122	7 815	516	53	7 352	2 014	1 762	19 392	17 029	574	353
1994	11 688	11 573	116	8 130	547	59	7 643	2 184	1 862	20 196	17 767	579	363
1995	12 375	12 281	94	8 464	580	66	7 951	2 412	2 013	21 246	18 757	582	370
1996	13 005	12 874	131	8 867	604	71	8 334	2 606	2 065	22 179	19 328	586	377
1997	13 549	13 439	110	9 268	637	81	8 713	2 693	2 144	23 017	19 905	589	383
1998	14 310	14 137	172	9 923	673	94	9 344	2 747	2 219	24 217	20 815	591	.....
VIRGINIA													
1969	16 359	16 120	239	12 757	547	910	13 120	1 921	1 318	3 545	3 019	4 614	2 148
1970	17 584	17 339	244	13 693	592	797	13 899	2 088	1 596	3 773	3 229	4 660	2 158
1971	19 253	19 027	227	14 905	667	805	15 044	2 298	1 911	4 051	3 498	4 753	2 196
1972	21 452	21 157	295	16 670	758	850	16 762	2 475	2 215	4 443	3 778	4 828	2 263
1973	24 200	23 810	390	18 762	937	917	18 742	2 819	2 640	4 932	4 233	4 907	2 384
1974	27 011	26 657	354	20 633	1 072	1 012	20 573	3 274	3 165	5 426	4 624	4 978	2 451
1975	29 609	29 309	299	21 989	1 142	1 234	22 080	3 555	3 973	5 856	5 110	5 056	2 425
1976	33 015	32 749	266	24 496	1 266	1 414	24 644	3 947	4 425	6 432	5 580	5 133	2 501
1977	36 687	36 495	192	27 173	1 399	1 600	27 374	4 454	4 859	7 047	6 069	5 206	2 584
1978	41 732	41 416	316	30 771	1 579	1 917	31 110	5 264	5 359	7 898	6 776	5 284	2 697
1979	46 902	46 724	178	34 123	1 827	2 259	34 554	6 240	6 108	8 809	7 554	5 325	2 769
1980	53 439	53 351	88	37 646	2 036	2 742	38 353	7 796	7 291	9 954	8 539	5 368	2 802
1981	60 096	59 792	303	41 569	2 369	2 883	42 083	9 630	8 383	11 039	9 401	5 444	2 820
1982	64 522	64 405	117	44 369	2 599	2 910	44 679	10 644	9 200	11 747	10 055	5 493	2 831
1983	70 053	70 007	46	48 402	2 882	2 950	48 470	11 672	9 911	12 589	10 887	5 565	2 904
1984	78 597	78 281	317	54 484	3 183	3 092	54 394	13 944	10 260	13 926	12 152	5 644	3 053
1985	85 190	84 972	218	59 641	3 616	3 166	59 191	15 078	10 922	14 906	12 915	5 715	3 197
1986	92 037	91 774	263	64 958	4 010	3 193	64 141	16 297	11 600	15 837	13 723	5 812	3 333
1987	100 162	99 796	365	71 738	4 387	3 361	70 712	17 237	12 213	16 884	14 504	5 932	3 500
1988	109 052	108 550	501	78 031	4 926	3 726	76 831	19 126	13 095	18 064	15 646	6 037	3 588
1989	117 776	117 155	621	83 523	5 405	3 954	82 072	21 580	14 124	19 244	16 558	6 120	3 685
1990	124 401	123 762	639	87 322	5 689	4 528	86 161	22 824	15 417	20 021	17 330	6 214	3 720
1991	128 807	128 226	581	89 306	5 951	4 918	88 274	23 545	16 989	20 498	17 805	6 284	3 669
1992	135 857	135 252	605	94 742	6 247	5 240	93 735	23 205	18 917	21 280	18 532	6 384	3 688
1993	143 137	142 641	496	99 619	6 568	5 620	98 671	24 317	20 150	22 133	19 201	6 467	3 761
1994	150 591	150 037	555	104 309	6 988	5 823	103 144	26 115	21 333	23 031	19 858	6 539	3 851
1995	158 066	157 605	461	109 224	7 364	5 737	107 597	27 654	22 816	23 943	20 611	6 602	3 940
1996	166 351	165 897	455	114 794	7 683	5 456	112 566	29 481	24 304	24 950	21 344	6 667	4 021
1997	175 911	175 565	346	122 579	8 220	5 310	119 669	30 716	25 526	26 109	22 130	6 737	4 123
1998	186 686	186 327	359	131 951	8 789	5 624	128 786	31 390	26 511	27 489	23 105	6 791	.....

Personal Income and Employment—*Continued*

(Millions of dollars, except as noted)

Year	Total	Nonfarm	Farm	Derivation of personal income						Per capita (dollars)		Population (thousands)	Total employment (thousands)
				Earnings by place of work	Less: Personal contributions for social insurance	Plus: Adjustment for residence	Equals: Net earnings by place of residence	Dividends, interest, and rent	Transfer payments	Total	Disposable		
WASHINGTON													
1969	13 681	13 263	418	10 888	471	85	10 502	1 904	1 275	4 092	3 562	3 343	1 539
1970	14 323	13 960	363	11 019	484	68	10 602	2 047	1 675	4 191	3 719	3 417	1 491
1971	15 079	14 670	410	11 364	521	66	10 910	2 205	1 965	4 375	3 917	3 447	1 457
1972	16 309	15 777	532	12 360	576	76	11 860	2 322	2 127	4 732	4 186	3 447	1 481
1973	18 447	17 667	780	14 033	725	93	13 402	2 649	2 396	5 305	4 688	3 477	1 558
1974	20 918	20 005	913	15 802	870	138	15 070	3 011	2 837	5 896	5 217	3 548	1 621
1975	23 446	22 519	927	17 562	983	208	16 786	3 188	3 472	6 479	5 753	3 619	1 659
1976	26 260	25 491	769	19 728	1 074	258	18 912	3 547	3 801	7 115	6 302	3 691	1 739
1977	29 222	28 606	616	22 084	1 174	238	21 147	4 013	4 063	7 746	6 838	3 772	1 815
1978	34 206	33 432	774	26 064	1 385	281	24 961	4 807	4 438	8 802	7 710	3 886	1 939
1979	39 535	38 781	755	30 029	1 645	336	28 719	5 820	4 995	9 852	8 560	4 013	2 061
1980	44 818	43 928	890	33 130	1 834	396	31 691	7 054	6 074	10 787	9 387	4 155	2 109
1981	49 954	49 110	845	35 947	2 147	450	34 249	8 667	7 038	11 794	10 239	4 236	2 126
1982	52 429	51 662	768	37 006	2 276	482	35 211	9 303	7 915	12 260	10 835	4 277	2 101
1983	55 579	54 488	1 091	38 956	2 389	505	37 072	10 014	8 493	12 925	11 561	4 300	2 147
1984	59 702	58 662	1 040	41 532	2 573	560	39 518	11 212	8 972	13 745	12 363	4 344	2 223
1985	63 503	62 753	750	44 111	2 867	605	41 849	11 866	9 789	14 432	12 918	4 400	2 290
1986	67 871	66 804	1 068	47 475	3 142	622	44 956	12 553	10 363	15 243	13 661	4 453	2 364
1987	72 236	71 177	1 058	50 994	3 359	670	48 305	13 107	10 824	15 939	14 168	4 532	2 486
1988	78 342	77 397	946	55 701	3 787	747	52 661	14 097	11 583	16 884	15 023	4 640	2 622
1989	86 435	85 378	1 057	61 047	4 246	830	57 632	16 172	12 632	18 211	16 029	4 746	2 741
1990	96 079	94 995	1 085	68 111	4 680	944	64 376	17 738	13 967	19 605	17 201	4 901	2 862
1991	102 310	101 158	1 152	72 844	5 138	993	68 699	17 889	15 723	20 401	17 971	5 015	2 903
1992	110 238	108 821	1 418	79 301	5 577	1 078	74 803	18 205	17 231	21 436	18 919	5 143	2 932
1993	115 598	113 915	1 683	82 799	5 787	1 094	78 106	18 977	18 514	22 024	19 519	5 249	2 973
1994	121 059	119 897	1 162	86 061	6 155	1 159	81 063	20 472	19 523	22 687	20 037	5 336	3 086
1995	128 637	127 465	1 172	90 809	6 560	1 248	85 497	22 210	20 930	23 677	20 884	5 433	3 158
1996	137 741	136 122	1 619	97 198	6 974	1 444	91 668	24 198	21 875	24 958	21 774	5 519	3 247
1997	148 500	147 368	1 132	105 959	7 622	1 811	100 149	25 752	22 600	26 451	22 914	5 614	3 363
1998	159 674	158 348	1 326	116 101	8 293	1 855	109 664	26 534	23 476	28 066	24 119	5 689	.....
WEST VIRGINIA													
1969	4 868	4 831	38	3 971	172	-84	3 715	518	635	2 788	2 428	1 746	652
1970	5 420	5 386	34	4 353	188	-87	4 079	567	775	3 103	2 734	1 747	660
1971	5 947	5 913	34	4 711	213	-105	4 393	607	947	3 360	2 974	1 770	670
1972	6 591	6 550	42	5 205	240	-119	4 846	656	1 089	3 668	3 230	1 797	684
1973	7 235	7 181	54	5 621	288	-122	5 211	742	1 282	4 008	3 556	1 805	700
1974	8 045	8 006	40	6 192	326	-138	5 729	863	1 453	4 435	3 894	1 814	711
1975	9 096	9 073	23	6 948	360	-163	6 426	953	1 717	4 942	4 352	1 841	717
1976	10 207	10 196	11	7 859	406	-198	7 256	1 056	1 896	5 437	4 764	1 877	739
1977	11 421	11 416	5	8 873	448	-235	8 190	1 188	2 043	5 993	5 258	1 906	758
1978	12 747	12 728	19	9 914	504	-275	9 136	1 353	2 258	6 638	5 847	1 920	781
1979	14 258	14 231	27	10 925	579	-289	10 058	1 574	2 626	7 353	6 438	1 939	791
1980	15 757	15 742	15	11 713	633	-315	10 765	1 937	3 055	8 075	7 047	1 951	784
1981	17 056	17 073	-17	12 275	718	-300	11 256	2 357	3 443	8 728	7 621	1 954	764
1982	18 024	18 051	-27	12 607	763	-256	11 588	2 657	3 778	9 245	8 117	1 950	743
1983	18 317	18 335	-18	12 329	756	-215	11 357	2 803	4 157	9 417	8 320	1 945	735
1984	19 582	19 563	20	13 211	815	-169	12 226	3 147	4 210	10 158	9 008	1 928	735
1985	20 294	20 277	17	13 638	886	-154	12 598	3 220	4 476	10 643	9 473	1 907	735
1986	21 024	20 986	38	13 905	926	-137	12 842	3 437	4 745	11 169	9 997	1 882	735
1987	21 608	21 605	4	14 302	961	-75	13 266	3 468	4 874	11 632	10 406	1 858	742
1988	22 693	22 664	29	14 951	1 046	-50	13 855	3 683	5 155	12 399	11 202	1 830	755
1989	23 756	23 699	56	15 435	1 118	28	14 344	3 965	5 447	13 149	11 779	1 807	762
1990	25 409	25 371	38	16 501	1 180	72	15 394	4 174	5 841	14 176	12 652	1 792	782
1991	26 641	26 618	23	16 975	1 249	71	15 797	4 273	6 571	14 815	13 253	1 798	784
1992	28 310	28 263	47	17 974	1 312	90	16 752	4 223	7 334	15 679	14 125	1 806	795
1993	29 620	29 562	58	18 664	1 381	91	17 374	4 201	8 045	16 306	14 654	1 817	807
1994	30 822	30 770	52	19 712	1 477	126	18 361	4 384	8 077	16 948	15 197	1 819	829
1995	31 771	31 763	8	20 239	1 541	155	18 853	4 563	8 355	17 441	15 605	1 822	843
1996	32 976	32 989	-14	20 795	1 562	177	19 409	4 909	8 658	18 116	16 193	1 820	854
1997	33 988	34 004	-16	21 402	1 596	228	20 035	5 005	8 949	18 724	16 649	1 815	864
1998	35 087	35 078	9	22 152	1 634	302	20 820	5 057	9 211	19 373	17 131	1 811	.....

Personal Income and Employment—*Continued*

(Millions of dollars, except as noted)

Year	Total	Nonfarm	Farm	Earnings by place of work	Less: Personal contributions for social insurance	Plus: Adjustment for residence	Equals: Net earnings by place of residence	Dividends, interest, and rent	Transfer payments	Per capita Total	Per capita Disposable	Population (thousands)	Total employment (thousands)
WISCONSIN													
1969	16 189	15 519	670	12 769	546	245	12 468	2 273	1 448	3 698	3 139	4 378	1 944
1970	17 333	16 655	678	13 473	573	249	13 149	2 474	1 709	3 916	3 370	4 426	1 954
1971	18 578	17 840	737	14 299	626	259	13 932	2 640	2 006	4 165	3 634	4 460	1 957
1972	20 291	19 505	786	15 708	701	281	15 288	2 771	2 232	4 511	3 887	4 498	2 014
1973	22 716	21 749	968	17 694	876	306	17 124	3 073	2 520	5 027	4 346	4 518	2 116
1974	24 967	24 109	857	19 164	1 003	330	18 491	3 485	2 991	5 501	4 731	4 538	2 159
1975	27 020	26 109	909	20 324	1 058	336	19 602	3 706	3 711	5 913	5 143	4 570	2 148
1976	29 903	29 102	800	22 585	1 136	378	21 827	4 021	4 055	6 522	5 654	4 585	2 211
1977	33 520	32 332	1 187	25 477	1 226	419	24 670	4 490	4 360	7 266	6 253	4 613	2 293
1978	37 634	36 450	1 184	28 619	1 404	473	27 688	5 143	4 803	8 125	6 951	4 632	2 382
1979	42 367	40 914	1 453	31 991	1 637	509	30 863	6 016	5 489	9 080	7 802	4 666	2 465
1980	46 644	45 166	1 478	33 970	1 762	534	32 742	7 230	6 672	9 899	8 523	4 712	2 449
1981	50 638	49 470	1 169	35 714	2 022	583	34 275	8 794	7 570	10 714	9 163	4 726	2 424
1982	53 089	52 059	1 030	36 480	2 111	601	34 970	9 662	8 457	11 226	9 677	4 729	2 381
1983	55 694	55 251	444	37 761	2 122	653	36 291	10 337	9 066	11 796	10 287	4 721	2 384
1984	61 284	60 334	950	41 952	2 307	767	40 412	11 650	9 222	12 941	11 314	4 736	2 478
1985	64 502	63 560	942	44 143	2 519	856	42 480	12 165	9 857	13 586	11 944	4 748	2 509
1986	67 932	66 710	1 222	46 680	2 701	939	44 918	12 733	10 281	14 285	12 520	4 756	2 551
1987	71 751	70 501	1 250	50 006	2 892	1 046	48 160	12 960	10 632	15 017	13 064	4 778	2 620
1988	76 224	75 481	744	53 601	3 268	1 206	51 539	13 644	11 041	15 806	13 716	4 822	2 704
1989	81 719	80 159	1 560	57 439	3 587	1 245	55 097	14 840	11 782	16 827	14 518	4 857	2 760
1990	86 726	85 577	1 150	60 743	3 807	1 325	58 261	15 750	12 715	17 692	15 275	4 902	2 829
1991	90 320	89 610	710	62 881	4 040	1 362	60 204	16 102	14 014	18 237	15 759	4 953	2 862
1992	96 746	95 957	789	68 212	4 335	1 458	65 335	16 223	15 188	19 331	16 717	5 005	2 917
1993	101 159	100 725	434	71 916	4 582	1 462	68 797	16 476	15 887	20 009	17 244	5 056	2 974
1994	107 063	106 563	500	76 378	4 954	1 590	73 015	17 520	16 528	21 012	18 037	5 095	3 070
1995	112 807	112 596	211	79 742	5 246	1 694	76 190	19 099	17 517	21 960	18 818	5 137	3 148
1996	118 941	118 451	490	83 531	5 437	1 846	79 940	20 926	18 075	22 987	19 521	5 174	3 203
1997	125 082	124 917	165	88 417	5 794	2 067	84 691	21 657	18 734	24 048	20 235	5 201	3 268
1998	131 547	131 048	499	94 035	6 102	2 247	90 179	22 058	19 311	25 184	21 029	5 224	.....
WYOMING													
1969	1 171	1 096	75	934	41	0	893	180	98	3 558	3 119	329	158
1970	1 285	1 201	83	1 019	46	0	974	197	114	3 849	3 389	334	159
1971	1 429	1 335	93	1 121	51	-1	1 069	226	134	4 201	3 724	340	165
1972	1 603	1 469	134	1 286	59	-3	1 225	231	147	4 620	4 140	347	172
1973	1 877	1 718	160	1 512	74	-7	1 431	275	171	5 312	4 694	353	182
1974	2 206	2 089	117	1 787	90	-13	1 684	326	196	6 051	5 247	365	194
1975	2 485	2 414	71	2 019	103	-16	1 901	350	235	6 530	5 746	380	203
1976	2 772	2 723	50	2 257	119	-22	2 117	391	266	7 011	6 079	395	214
1977	3 256	3 210	46	2 677	137	-29	2 511	448	297	7 910	6 876	412	231
1978	3 933	3 864	69	3 252	170	-38	3 044	553	335	9 127	7 928	431	250
1979	4 640	4 541	99	3 845	206	-54	3 586	669	386	10 269	8 781	452	267
1980	5 439	5 353	86	4 453	233	-74	4 146	833	460	11 469	9 831	474	280
1981	6 175	6 124	51	4 977	281	-86	4 610	1 019	546	12 558	10 691	492	290
1982	6 381	6 348	33	5 026	310	-82	4 634	1 120	627	12 600	10 853	506	288
1983	6 304	6 262	42	4 776	267	-59	4 450	1 122	732	12 352	10 897	510	275
1984	6 555	6 537	18	4 960	281	-53	4 626	1 215	715	12 983	11 529	505	277
1985	6 830	6 809	22	5 166	305	-52	4 810	1 255	766	13 669	12 200	500	278
1986	6 668	6 627	42	4 919	299	-40	4 579	1 244	845	13 455	12 115	496	265
1987	6 478	6 420	59	4 688	291	-25	4 372	1 248	859	13 582	12 172	477	260
1988	6 659	6 610	49	4 795	315	-20	4 461	1 302	897	14 317	12 776	465	265
1989	7 121	7 039	82	5 026	334	-13	4 680	1 484	957	15 535	13 671	458	267
1990	7 787	7 643	144	5 445	359	-9	5 078	1 662	1 048	17 174	15 168	453	273
1991	8 399	8 187	213	5 846	387	0	5 459	1 772	1 169	18 348	16 290	458	280
1992	8 670	8 466	204	6 072	410	-9	5 654	1 725	1 291	18 704	16 574	464	282
1993	9 164	8 887	276	6 477	429	-18	6 031	1 745	1 388	19 535	17 243	469	287
1994	9 434	9 345	89	6 575	454	-24	6 097	1 865	1 472	19 865	17 509	475	301
1995	9 895	9 817	78	6 792	473	-24	6 296	2 040	1 560	20 685	18 271	478	307
1996	10 333	10 271	63	6 939	484	-21	6 433	2 239	1 661	21 524	18 570	480	311
1997	10 847	10 741	105	7 326	509	-20	6 797	2 318	1 732	22 596	19 333	480	315
1998	11 169	11 199	-29	7 560	529	-18	7 013	2 361	1 795	23 225	19 678	481	.....

Personal Income and Employment—*Continued*

(Millions of dollars, except as noted)

Year	Total	Nonfarm	Farm	Derivation of personal income						Per capita (dollars)		Population (thousands)	Total employment (thousands)
				Earnings by place of work	Less: Personal contributions for social insurance	Plus: Adjustment for residence	Equals: Net earnings by place of residence	Dividends, interest, and rent	Transfer payments	Total	Disposable		
NEW ENGLAND													
1969	49 668	49 353	315	37 561	1 516	808	36 853	8 228	4 586	4 232	3 592	11 735	5 516
1970	53 207	52 875	332	40 016	1 604	811	39 223	8 497	5 488	4 479	3 861	11 878	5 518
1971	56 407	56 096	311	41 888	1 748	838	40 977	8 837	6 593	4 702	4 107	11 996	5 454
1972	61 095	60 776	319	45 614	1 933	889	44 570	9 290	7 234	5 054	4 340	12 088	5 573
1973	66 860	66 436	424	50 115	2 374	932	48 673	10 106	8 081	5 504	4 763	12 148	5 783
1974	72 670	72 215	456	53 527	2 643	1 006	51 889	11 217	9 564	5 978	5 177	12 157	5 843
1975	77 601	77 268	333	55 530	2 726	1 076	53 880	11 432	12 289	6 373	5 603	12 176	5 685
1976	84 985	84 536	449	61 323	2 950	1 180	59 554	12 421	13 010	6 962	6 080	12 207	5 811
1977	93 226	92 824	402	67 595	3 238	1 307	65 663	13 873	13 690	7 606	6 617	12 257	6 007
1978	104 025	103 611	415	75 990	3 692	1 483	73 781	15 701	14 544	8 455	7 330	12 303	6 280
1979	117 007	116 617	390	85 107	4 303	1 697	82 500	18 311	16 196	9 478	8 162	12 345	6 515
1980	132 439	132 066	373	94 294	4 847	1 983	91 430	22 337	18 673	10 705	9 186	12 372	6 641
1981	147 974	147 498	477	102 775	5 670	2 144	99 249	27 407	21 319	11 899	10 145	12 436	6 692
1982	159 421	158 905	516	109 709	6 177	2 292	105 824	30 168	23 429	12 787	10 946	12 468	6 691
1983	172 462	171 970	492	119 985	6 734	2 438	115 688	31 763	25 011	13 748	11 852	12 544	6 825
1984	193 664	193 089	575	135 148	7 576	2 617	130 190	37 525	25 949	15 319	13 263	12 642	7 195
1985	209 197	208 624	574	148 295	8 666	2 787	142 416	39 563	27 219	16 420	14 112	12 741	7 444
1986	225 995	225 402	593	161 214	9 696	2 946	154 464	42 631	28 900	17 610	15 038	12 833	7 686
1987	247 049	246 407	641	178 729	10 640	3 126	171 215	45 742	30 092	19 075	16 186	12 951	7 826
1988	272 286	271 617	669	197 359	12 003	3 338	188 694	51 263	32 329	20 810	17 899	13 085	8 095
1989	291 352	290 701	651	206 934	12 880	3 291	197 345	58 285	35 722	22 103	19 001	13 182	8 086
1990	300 630	299 958	673	211 427	13 258	3 587	201 755	59 046	39 829	22 741	19 618	13 220	7 917
1991	304 546	303 936	610	210 563	13 661	3 648	200 550	58 066	45 931	23 078	19 952	13 197	7 598
1992	318 366	317 574	792	222 629	14 222	4 441	212 849	55 861	49 657	24 150	20 774	13 183	7 640
1993	328 914	328 136	779	231 398	14 807	4 280	220 870	56 600	51 444	24 903	21 346	13 208	7 767
1994	343 175	342 537	639	240 474	15 717	4 269	229 026	60 196	53 953	25 934	22 168	13 233	7 873
1995	364 142	363 567	574	253 040	16 617	4 832	241 255	65 421	57 466	27 439	23 363	13 271	8 033
1996	384 540	383 885	655	265 686	17 268	5 678	254 096	71 477	58 967	28 872	24 269	13 319	8 189
1997	406 858	406 263	595	284 091	18 490	5 218	270 820	74 305	61 733	30 427	25 309	13 372	8 379
1998	429 852	429 163	689	304 119	19 646	5 611	290 083	75 769	64 000	32 007	26 346	13 430	.....
MIDEAST													
1969	182 567	181 366	1 202	145 505	6 218	-1 718	137 569	27 750	17 248	4 335	3 664	42 111	19 435
1970	196 086	194 908	1 178	155 251	6 636	-1 620	146 995	28 540	20 552	4 612	3 950	42 517	19 469
1971	209 528	208 438	1 089	163 995	7 267	-1 685	155 043	29 736	24 749	4 888	4 238	42 870	19 303
1972	226 456	225 349	1 106	177 262	7 964	-1 825	167 473	31 082	27 901	5 267	4 498	42 992	19 526
1973	245 760	244 251	1 509	192 316	9 653	-1 930	180 733	33 994	31 033	5 737	4 937	42 837	19 973
1974	267 041	265 619	1 422	205 971	10 717	-2 113	193 141	37 843	36 057	6 253	5 362	42 709	19 960
1975	286 700	285 384	1 316	216 067	11 155	-2 386	202 527	39 059	45 115	6 710	5 839	42 728	19 485
1976	311 029	309 645	1 384	234 134	11 924	-2 663	219 547	42 359	49 124	7 290	6 312	42 667	19 568
1977	338 361	337 176	1 185	254 822	12 846	-2 970	239 006	47 108	52 248	7 953	6 841	42 547	19 854
1978	373 294	371 883	1 411	281 997	14 292	-3 455	264 251	53 482	55 561	8 800	7 564	42 421	20 411
1979	413 376	411 775	1 601	310 374	16 298	-4 027	290 049	62 327	61 001	9 759	8 338	42 358	20 899
1980	460 325	459 127	1 199	337 964	17 875	-4 755	315 335	74 700	70 290	10 890	9 294	42 272	20 961
1981	510 875	509 320	1 554	367 022	20 836	-5 273	340 913	90 736	79 227	12 069	10 215	42 329	21 061
1982	546 073	544 597	1 476	387 595	22 506	-5 449	359 640	98 489	87 944	12 885	10 906	42 382	20 936
1983	582 683	581 568	1 115	413 118	24 143	-5 647	383 328	104 850	94 505	13 696	11 746	42 544	21 131
1984	644 386	642 516	1 870	456 183	26 884	-6 012	423 287	123 280	97 820	15 096	12 981	42 687	21 881
1985	689 594	687 615	1 979	491 651	30 255	-6 293	455 104	131 220	103 271	16 114	13 792	42 794	22 476
1986	735 030	732 846	2 184	527 104	33 275	-6 588	487 241	138 310	109 479	17 097	14 618	42 991	22 989
1987	788 574	786 345	2 230	573 630	35 900	-7 063	530 667	144 012	113 896	18 258	15 474	43 190	23 498
1988	858 596	856 508	2 088	626 773	40 348	-7 753	578 673	159 232	120 692	19 767	16 902	43 435	24 153
1989	922 275	919 818	2 457	660 878	43 392	-8 072	609 415	183 203	129 657	21 160	18 036	43 585	24 438
1990	977 220	974 900	2 320	698 882	45 966	-9 042	643 875	191 849	141 497	22 349	19 149	43 726	24 447
1991	1 003 443	1 001 607	1 836	708 977	47 740	-9 473	651 765	191 714	159 965	22 865	19 683	43 885	23 943
1992	1 056 766	1 054 459	2 307	753 749	50 171	-10 627	692 952	185 032	178 783	23 982	20 668	44 064	23 845
1993	1 090 322	1 088 070	2 251	778 632	51 790	-11 138	715 705	186 308	188 309	24 637	21 185	44 255	23 968
1994	1 130 903	1 129 028	1 875	802 640	54 255	-11 403	736 982	197 379	196 542	25 489	21 872	44 368	24 169
1995	1 183 752	1 182 363	1 390	836 183	56 431	-11 977	767 776	208 911	207 065	26 636	22 829	44 442	24 430
1996	1 245 254	1 243 167	2 087	873 188	58 434	-12 621	802 132	224 495	218 627	27 978	23 765	44 509	24 711
1997	1 303 943	1 302 525	1 418	920 354	61 533	-12 123	846 698	231 651	225 594	29 252	24 609	44 576	25 180
1998	1 369 952	1 367 882	2 071	980 414	65 052	-12 980	902 383	235 242	232 328	30 652	25 512	44 693	.....

Personal Income and Employment—*Continued*

(Millions of dollars, except as noted)

| Year | Total | Nonfarm | Farm | Derivation of personal income | | | | | | Per capita (dollars) | | Population (thousands) | Total employment (thousands) |
				Earnings by place of work	Less: Personal contributions for social insurance	Plus: Adjustment for residence	Equals: Net earnings by place of residence	Dividends, interest, and rent	Transfer payments	Total	Disposable		
GREAT LAKES													
1969	160 627	157 526	3 101	131 944	5 382	251	126 812	21 370	12 446	4 025	3 436	39 904	17 785
1970	168 323	165 541	2 783	136 448	5 569	234	131 114	22 312	14 899	4 175	3 602	40 320	17 630
1971	180 803	177 623	3 181	145 346	6 126	294	139 513	23 554	17 737	4 451	3 891	40 622	17 549
1972	197 546	194 071	3 475	159 289	6 831	336	152 794	24 893	19 859	4 839	4 167	40 824	17 933
1973	221 768	216 308	5 460	179 167	8 539	383	171 011	27 843	22 915	5 416	4 695	40 947	18 710
1974	241 107	236 199	4 908	191 479	9 531	468	182 417	31 548	27 142	5 875	5 078	41 037	18 911
1975	257 955	251 955	6 000	199 533	9 731	529	190 331	33 253	34 371	6 275	5 493	41 105	18 399
1976	286 634	281 637	4 997	223 295	10 750	659	213 204	36 268	37 162	6 959	6 039	41 187	18 891
1977	319 086	314 027	5 060	250 063	11 878	827	239 011	40 715	39 359	7 716	6 652	41 353	19 508
1978	355 561	350 795	4 766	279 069	13 452	1 053	266 670	46 569	42 322	8 566	7 363	41 510	20 195
1979	393 666	388 340	5 326	305 806	15 370	1 272	291 707	54 354	47 605	9 461	8 106	41 611	20 520
1980	426 054	422 726	3 328	316 325	16 161	1 526	301 690	65 047	59 317	10 219	8 811	41 694	20 024
1981	464 135	460 301	3 834	336 460	18 563	1 517	319 415	78 641	66 079	11 144	9 567	41 648	19 862
1982	479 495	476 671	2 823	338 570	19 169	1 425	320 827	84 422	74 246	11 556	10 030	41 492	19 309
1983	503 133	503 350	-217	352 922	20 052	1 421	334 291	89 654	79 188	12 163	10 611	41 366	19 329
1984	556 103	552 071	4 032	394 146	22 153	1 547	373 540	101 683	80 880	13 435	11 792	41 393	20 113
1985	589 851	585 381	4 470	421 419	24 801	1 590	398 208	106 203	85 439	14 241	12 449	41 418	20 599
1986	620 180	616 218	3 961	443 733	26 773	1 658	418 619	111 501	90 059	14 960	13 088	41 455	21 045
1987	653 694	649 323	4 372	471 767	28 458	1 725	445 033	114 637	94 025	15 718	13 649	41 590	21 646
1988	698 350	695 726	2 625	507 303	31 743	1 860	477 421	122 428	98 502	16 739	14 603	41 721	22 241
1989	746 123	739 936	6 187	536 506	34 479	1 889	503 917	136 702	105 504	17 819	15 432	41 873	22 731
1990	787 562	782 568	4 995	563 535	36 308	1 928	529 155	144 282	114 126	18 717	16 221	42 076	23 048
1991	812 624	810 138	2 487	576 627	38 153	1 959	540 432	146 082	126 110	19 163	16 686	42 406	23 028
1992	863 337	859 121	4 216	619 526	40 197	2 152	581 481	143 255	138 600	20 195	17 647	42 749	23 163
1993	904 660	901 084	3 576	653 470	42 588	2 039	612 921	146 014	145 725	21 009	18 250	43 061	23 547
1994	958 497	954 418	4 079	694 350	46 062	2 256	650 544	157 202	150 751	22 128	19 143	43 316	24 287
1995	1 008 668	1 006 857	1 811	727 685	48 819	2 399	681 264	168 510	158 895	23 140	19 954	43 590	24 951
1996	1 054 547	1 050 126	4 422	755 629	50 532	2 703	707 800	181 259	165 488	24 055	20 578	43 839	25 388
1997	1 107 644	1 102 868	4 777	799 305	53 578	3 120	748 847	187 066	171 732	25 158	21 335	44 028	25 857
1998	1 161 898	1 158 164	3 734	847 438	56 497	3 328	794 269	190 481	177 148	26 290	22 119	44 195	.....
PLAINS													
1969	57 816	53 576	4 241	46 648	1 929	-425	44 295	8 227	5 295	3 568	3 094	16 202	7 506
1970	62 355	57 877	4 478	49 750	2 042	-373	47 335	8 782	6 238	3 814	3 342	16 350	7 516
1971	67 021	62 390	4 631	53 006	2 251	-374	50 382	9 449	7 190	4 068	3 604	16 475	7 545
1972	74 119	67 864	6 255	58 983	2 507	-390	56 086	10 169	7 864	4 475	3 910	16 563	7 731
1973	86 904	75 567	11 337	69 731	3 124	-431	66 177	11 609	9 118	5 226	4 611	16 628	8 065
1974	92 087	84 358	7 730	72 079	3 579	-469	68 031	13 392	10 665	5 524	4 791	16 672	8 220
1975	100 253	92 729	7 524	77 074	3 830	-470	72 774	14 479	13 000	5 988	5 258	16 743	8 182
1976	108 270	103 848	4 422	82 874	4 227	-571	78 076	15 924	14 269	6 420	5 599	16 864	8 440
1977	120 031	114 823	5 209	91 911	4 563	-715	86 634	18 083	15 315	7 082	6 161	16 950	8 658
1978	136 729	128 849	7 881	105 415	5 225	-885	99 306	20 751	16 673	8 029	6 986	17 028	8 959
1979	151 828	145 171	6 657	115 991	6 078	-1 052	108 861	24 311	18 655	8 880	7 667	17 097	9 249
1980	163 721	161 982	1 739	119 757	6 610	-1 225	111 922	29 531	22 268	9 514	8 205	17 208	9 252
1981	184 866	179 516	5 349	132 047	7 590	-1 326	123 132	36 422	25 312	10 708	9 213	17 264	9 214
1982	194 293	190 553	3 741	134 819	8 079	-1 350	125 390	40 660	28 243	11 236	9 657	17 292	9 081
1983	202 762	201 578	1 184	140 321	8 535	-1 460	130 327	42 134	30 301	11 703	10 196	17 325	9 195
1984	226 177	220 168	6 008	159 539	9 391	-1 649	148 499	46 457	31 221	13 012	11 470	17 382	9 512
1985	239 165	232 320	6 845	169 549	10 417	-1 770	157 362	48 185	33 618	13 744	12 099	17 402	9 664
1986	250 175	242 770	7 405	177 546	11 191	-1 904	164 452	50 237	35 486	14 384	12 685	17 393	9 754
1987	264 070	254 889	9 180	190 348	11 971	-2 027	176 351	50 838	36 882	15 152	13 260	17 428	10 010
1988	276 602	269 944	6 659	200 210	13 282	-2 203	184 726	52 936	38 941	15 776	13 833	17 533	10 233
1989	296 703	288 237	8 466	213 297	14 436	-2 305	196 556	58 312	41 836	16 863	14 695	17 595	10 430
1990	314 981	305 432	9 549	225 869	15 289	-2 422	208 157	61 686	45 137	17 807	15 495	17 688	10 598
1991	326 485	319 270	7 216	232 332	16 145	-2 472	213 716	62 656	50 113	18 339	16 002	17 803	10 675
1992	347 907	338 896	9 011	250 668	17 032	-2 628	231 008	62 860	54 039	19 390	16 971	17 943	10 791
1993	358 347	353 265	5 082	258 215	17 947	-2 928	237 341	63 201	57 804	19 807	17 291	18 092	11 018
1994	380 442	372 015	8 427	276 588	19 351	-3 139	254 098	65 978	60 367	20 863	18 186	18 235	11 330
1995	397 342	393 303	4 040	286 993	20 657	-3 334	263 002	70 436	63 904	21 631	18 781	18 369	11 634
1996	425 718	414 497	11 221	308 829	21 657	-3 558	283 614	75 258	66 846	23 039	19 861	18 478	11 885
1997	446 730	438 050	8 680	325 324	23 113	-3 957	298 254	79 035	69 442	24 034	20 536	18 587	12 146
1998	469 721	462 032	7 689	345 901	24 529	-4 226	317 145	80 892	71 684	25 126	21 339	18 695	.....

Personal Income and Employment—*Continued*

(Millions of dollars, except as noted)

| Year | Total | Nonfarm | Farm | Derivation of personal income | | | | | | Per capita (dollars) | | Population (thousands) | Total employment (thousands) |
				Earnings by place of work	Less: Personal contributions for social insurance	Plus: Adjustment for residence	Equals: Net earnings by place of residence	Dividends, interest, and rent	Transfer payments	Total	Disposable		
SOUTHEAST													
1969	133 570	129 246	4 324	107 285	4 446	1 094	103 932	16 650	12 988	3 075	2 683	43 440	19 085
1970	145 954	141 601	4 354	115 463	4 815	968	111 616	18 516	15 822	3 319	2 925	43 974	19 254
1971	160 481	155 898	4 582	125 913	5 424	925	121 414	20 317	18 751	3 565	3 164	45 013	19 635
1972	180 551	175 185	5 366	142 414	6 230	968	137 152	22 065	21 333	3 923	3 436	46 019	20 523
1973	206 177	198 540	7 637	162 363	7 843	1 033	155 553	25 365	25 258	4 388	3 868	46 992	21 636
1974	230 110	223 109	7 002	177 831	8 937	1 115	170 009	29 540	30 561	4 799	4 215	47 955	22 069
1975	250 292	244 032	6 260	187 488	9 387	1 324	179 426	31 860	39 006	5 130	4 587	48 788	21 642
1976	280 160	273 582	6 578	210 924	10 516	1 486	201 894	35 181	43 085	5 658	5 020	49 514	22 350
1977	311 886	305 943	5 944	235 322	11 695	1 662	225 289	39 857	46 740	6 199	5 478	50 312	23 208
1978	355 856	348 706	7 151	269 124	13 467	1 953	257 611	46 984	51 262	6 962	6 133	51 113	24 308
1979	402 214	395 119	7 095	300 607	15 662	2 276	287 220	56 217	58 776	7 738	6 779	51 977	25 019
1980	454 155	449 723	4 432	328 504	17 483	2 739	313 760	70 211	70 184	8 588	7 515	52 881	25 378
1981	512 459	505 580	6 879	362 817	20 649	2 908	345 076	87 160	80 224	9 556	8 328	53 627	25 676
1982	545 538	538 695	6 843	380 309	22 320	3 064	361 053	95 372	89 112	10 056	8 796	54 249	25 570
1983	586 374	581 349	5 025	407 659	24 021	3 176	386 815	102 930	96 629	10 689	9 425	54 856	26 104
1984	652 511	644 114	8 398	457 296	26 746	3 390	433 941	118 331	100 241	11 754	10 436	55 515	27 387
1985	702 908	695 478	7 430	492 901	30 178	3 535	466 258	128 354	108 296	12 508	11 033	56 199	28 234
1986	748 100	741 258	6 843	523 931	32 861	3 625	494 696	137 592	115 813	13 157	11 615	56 861	28 977
1987	801 447	793 321	8 127	567 640	35 188	3 887	536 340	143 461	121 647	13 929	12 253	57 536	29 705
1988	867 942	857 401	10 542	615 298	39 413	4 315	580 199	157 066	130 677	14 933	13 223	58 120	30 761
1989	937 432	926 396	11 036	652 990	43 136	4 673	614 527	179 857	143 049	15 961	14 060	58 733	31 490
1990	1 001 887	991 691	10 196	693 393	45 812	5 345	652 926	190 762	158 200	16 847	14 880	59 469	32 006
1991	1 047 271	1 035 287	11 985	718 206	48 391	5 784	675 599	193 788	177 884	17 380	15 429	60 257	31 971
1992	1 112 858	1 100 580	12 278	772 239	51 457	6 059	726 842	187 294	198 723	18 223	16 200	61 068	32 458
1993	1 180 409	1 167 861	12 547	818 359	54 731	5 946	769 575	196 216	214 618	19 073	16 904	61 887	33 448
1994	1 247 824	1 235 256	12 567	864 995	58 956	6 022	812 061	209 063	226 699	19 893	17 563	62 727	34 438
1995	1 321 835	1 310 593	11 242	912 202	63 004	5 963	855 161	222 969	243 705	20 804	18 312	63 538	35 456
1996	1 401 507	1 388 616	12 891	959 534	65 936	5 703	899 301	243 771	258 435	21 787	19 049	64 328	36 267
1997	1 482 256	1 468 943	13 313	1 020 946	70 330	5 594	956 210	255 215	270 832	22 751	19 744	65 151	37 201
1998	1 568 488	1 555 226	13 262	1 094 956	74 952	5 997	1 026 000	260 949	281 538	23 793	20 488	65 922	.....
SOUTHWEST													
1969	54 461	52 894	1 567	44 150	1 796	-71	42 283	7 303	4 876	3 335	2 904	16 328	7 219
1970	60 004	58 110	1 894	48 030	1 946	-83	46 001	8 176	5 827	3 610	3 178	16 621	7 311
1971	65 436	63 681	1 756	51 943	2 179	-88	49 676	8 940	6 822	3 832	3 410	17 077	7 457
1972	72 850	70 717	2 133	58 056	2 456	-106	55 494	9 674	7 683	4 162	3 659	17 503	7 807
1973	83 217	79 809	3 407	66 246	3 105	-120	63 022	11 097	9 098	4 638	4 102	17 943	8 215
1974	93 913	91 671	2 242	73 801	3 622	-80	70 099	12 917	10 897	5 117	4 487	18 354	8 511
1975	105 262	103 078	2 184	81 818	3 973	-47	77 797	13 854	13 610	5 602	4 980	18 789	8 633
1976	118 988	116 850	2 139	93 123	4 499	25	88 649	15 209	15 131	6 175	5 452	19 270	9 001
1977	133 558	131 657	1 902	105 252	5 124	-222	99 906	17 205	16 448	6 776	5 931	19 710	9 466
1978	154 806	153 071	1 735	122 231	6 006	-359	115 866	20 663	18 277	7 671	6 722	20 180	10 043
1979	180 395	177 318	3 077	141 987	7 204	-351	134 432	25 155	20 808	8 683	7 541	20 777	10 539
1980	207 706	206 030	1 676	160 526	8 331	-459	151 737	31 377	24 591	9 694	8 387	21 426	10 944
1981	242 441	239 461	2 980	185 656	10 313	-202	175 141	39 174	28 126	11 027	9 430	21 985	11 485
1982	263 468	261 150	2 318	199 155	11 365	-258	187 532	44 155	31 781	11 560	9 941	22 791	11 714
1983	277 680	275 360	2 321	208 058	11 884	-184	195 990	46 538	35 153	11 864	10 409	23 405	11 744
1984	305 742	303 037	2 705	229 091	12 932	-179	215 980	53 205	36 558	12 859	11 338	23 776	12 305
1985	328 621	325 974	2 647	245 407	14 467	-147	230 794	58 173	39 655	13 599	11 990	24 166	12 682
1986	336 950	334 372	2 577	248 441	15 082	-15	233 344	60 384	43 221	13 706	12 243	24 585	12 548
1987	347 508	344 114	3 395	256 144	15 354	75	240 865	60 711	45 933	14 042	12 490	24 748	12 857
1988	368 856	365 119	3 736	272 026	16 831	167	255 362	64 464	49 030	14 838	13 262	24 860	13 152
1989	395 173	391 377	3 796	288 402	18 308	249	270 343	71 187	53 643	15 755	14 015	25 083	13 336
1990	426 944	422 330	4 614	312 277	19 665	335	292 947	74 417	59 581	16 815	14 904	25 391	13 623
1991	450 163	445 691	4 472	331 083	21 165	285	310 203	73 572	66 387	17 432	15 534	25 824	13 857
1992	480 423	475 465	4 959	353 718	22 485	332	331 565	72 792	76 067	18 257	16 327	26 315	13 990
1993	509 054	502 761	6 294	376 564	23 784	164	352 945	74 319	81 791	18 961	16 941	26 847	14 436
1994	538 786	534 121	4 665	397 255	25 641	153	371 768	80 061	86 957	19 666	17 554	27 397	14 978
1995	576 052	572 222	3 830	424 529	27 779	89	396 839	84 937	94 276	20 605	18 369	27 956	15 516
1996	614 265	610 855	3 410	451 162	29 481	111	421 793	92 444	100 029	21 577	19 086	28 469	15 972
1997	660 459	655 883	4 575	489 899	32 007	27	457 918	97 722	104 818	22 787	20 049	28 985	16 553
1998	707 853	703 820	4 033	533 068	34 669	-38	498 362	100 358	109 134	23 985	20 967	29 512	.....

Personal Income and Employment—*Continued*

(Millions of dollars, except as noted)

Year	Total	Nonfarm	Farm	Earnings by place of work	Less: Personal contributions for social insurance	Plus: Adjustment for residence	Equals: Net earnings by place of residence	Dividends, interest, and rent	Transfer payments	Per capita (dollars) Total	Per capita (dollars) Disposable	Population (thousands)	Total employment (thousands)
ROCKY MOUNTAIN													
1969	16 933	16 009	924	13 519	569	13	12 964	2 418	1 551	3 426	2 979	4 943	2 216
1970	18 860	17 814	1 045	14 914	628	15	14 301	2 700	1 859	3 744	3 295	5 038	2 271
1971	20 899	19 884	1 016	16 436	713	18	15 741	2 974	2 185	4 024	3 564	5 194	2 343
1972	23 722	22 383	1 339	18 866	819	21	18 068	3 198	2 456	4 419	3 880	5 368	2 482
1973	27 268	25 457	1 811	21 711	1 032	20	20 700	3 706	2 862	4 933	4 332	5 527	2 646
1974	30 766	28 864	1 901	24 327	1 195	22	23 154	4 261	3 351	5 445	4 756	5 650	2 740
1975	33 749	32 308	1 440	26 288	1 294	32	25 026	4 599	4 123	5 837	5 159	5 782	2 778
1976	37 643	36 572	1 071	29 365	1 460	38	27 942	5 097	4 604	6 363	5 586	5 916	2 912
1977	42 139	41 422	717	32 898	1 668	40	31 270	5 816	5 053	6 932	6 050	6 079	3 060
1978	49 045	48 045	1 000	38 515	1 937	51	36 629	6 867	5 550	7 839	6 845	6 257	3 257
1979	55 879	55 123	756	43 560	2 313	51	41 298	8 300	6 281	8 678	7 526	6 439	3 406
1980	63 618	62 658	961	48 620	2 595	71	46 096	10 105	7 417	9 650	8 382	6 592	3 482
1981	72 215	71 255	960	54 228	3 091	54	51 191	12 400	8 624	10 710	9 250	6 743	3 571
1982	77 471	76 676	795	57 297	3 374	53	53 976	13 699	9 797	11 221	9 698	6 904	3 607
1983	82 377	81 248	1 129	60 600	3 520	53	57 133	14 522	10 723	11 710	10 330	7 035	3 653
1984	89 665	88 606	1 059	66 054	3 850	70	62 275	16 358	11 033	12 613	11 180	7 109	3 816
1985	94 489	93 619	870	69 530	4 243	85	65 373	17 308	11 809	13 183	11 659	7 168	3 881
1986	97 416	96 166	1 250	71 140	4 459	106	66 787	17 891	12 738	13 530	12 003	7 200	3 875
1987	101 271	99 737	1 535	73 905	4 550	129	69 484	18 297	13 490	14 054	12 414	7 206	3 907
1988	106 387	104 833	1 554	77 833	4 978	164	73 018	19 124	14 245	14 771	13 033	7 203	4 054
1989	114 580	112 417	2 163	82 946	5 408	198	77 736	21 316	15 527	15 839	13 868	7 234	4 146
1990	123 662	121 021	2 641	89 746	5 810	232	84 168	22 502	16 992	16 943	14 775	7 299	4 258
1991	131 549	129 137	2 412	95 481	6 326	238	89 393	23 337	18 820	17 674	15 419	7 443	4 371
1992	140 968	138 650	2 318	103 424	6 812	236	96 848	23 394	20 726	18 472	16 079	7 631	4 473
1993	152 805	149 351	3 454	112 930	7 355	159	105 735	24 639	22 432	19 482	16 927	7 844	4 660
1994	162 235	160 511	1 724	119 343	7 973	149	111 520	27 191	23 524	20 128	17 399	8 060	4 928
1995	174 645	172 881	1 764	128 080	8 627	173	119 626	29 311	25 708	21 194	18 340	8 240	5 134
1996	186 887	185 001	1 886	136 601	9 195	222	127 629	32 080	27 179	22 304	19 163	8 379	5 319
1997	199 598	197 640	1 958	146 927	9 935	245	137 237	33 826	28 536	23 414	19 946	8 525	5 499
1998	213 643	211 795	1 849	159 628	10 729	263	149 163	34 775	29 706	24 668	20 854	8 661	.....
FAR WEST													
1969	117 310	114 757	2 553	92 884	4 158	-127	88 599	17 354	11 358	4 404	3 805	26 635	12 295
1970	126 060	123 552	2 509	97 944	4 386	-138	93 420	18 677	13 963	4 651	4 087	27 101	12 313
1971	134 240	131 694	2 546	102 988	4 750	-137	98 101	19 957	16 182	4 869	4 321	27 570	12 300
1972	146 974	143 753	3 221	113 810	5 509	-135	108 167	21 159	17 649	5 264	4 589	27 918	12 742
1973	163 288	158 949	4 340	126 494	6 707	-151	119 636	23 841	19 812	5 764	5 070	28 328	13 405
1974	183 288	177 804	5 484	140 605	7 473	-230	132 902	26 943	23 444	6 364	5 585	28 801	13 865
1975	202 574	197 688	4 886	153 567	8 088	-395	145 085	28 395	29 095	6 903	6 125	29 346	14 103
1976	227 733	222 872	4 861	173 380	8 926	-511	163 944	31 370	32 419	7 609	6 691	29 929	14 625
1977	253 446	248 713	4 733	193 381	9 954	-331	183 096	35 337	35 014	8 295	7 243	30 553	15 287
1978	290 924	286 107	4 818	221 943	11 409	-283	210 251	42 554	38 119	9 299	8 091	31 285	16 234
1979	333 296	327 283	6 013	252 914	13 432	-292	239 190	51 920	42 186	10 427	9 022	31 965	17 140
1980	378 341	370 775	7 567	280 893	14 382	-369	266 142	62 738	49 461	11 542	9 981	32 780	17 549
1981	422 175	416 254	5 921	305 120	17 358	-308	287 454	76 919	57 802	12 627	10 931	33 434	17 744
1982	448 277	442 259	6 018	320 910	18 854	-337	301 720	82 457	64 100	13 151	11 474	34 086	17 613
1983	481 382	475 340	6 042	345 684	20 347	-349	324 988	87 931	68 463	13 866	12 190	34 716	18 040
1984	532 231	525 503	6 728	383 826	22 676	-401	360 749	100 996	70 486	15 068	13 257	35 321	18 842
1985	574 655	568 191	6 465	416 095	25 446	-433	390 216	106 813	77 626	15 946	13 941	36 037	19 494
1986	613 678	606 260	7 417	446 692	28 166	-451	418 076	112 508	83 094	16 669	14 565	36 815	20 067
1987	659 564	651 096	8 468	486 442	30 994	-508	454 940	117 313	87 311	17 523	15 143	37 641	20 923
1988	716 872	707 943	8 928	530 879	34 910	-578	495 392	128 311	93 169	18 600	16 159	38 542	21 985
1989	776 988	768 187	8 802	571 038	38 088	-662	532 289	143 674	101 026	19 654	16 899	39 534	22 660
1990	845 422	836 335	9 086	619 168	41 044	-752	577 373	155 672	112 377	20 839	17 984	40 569	23 288
1991	871 511	863 520	7 990	635 494	43 430	-754	591 311	155 604	124 597	21 095	18 359	41 313	23 342
1992	918 740	909 686	9 055	669 486	45 442	-743	623 301	153 890	141 549	21 853	19 143	42 041	23 051
1993	944 975	934 394	10 582	686 777	46 745	-1 363	638 670	156 533	149 772	22 208	19 474	42 551	23 162
1994	979 190	970 331	8 858	707 514	49 039	-1 525	656 951	166 432	155 807	22 797	19 918	42 953	23 648
1995	1 032 656	1 024 021	8 635	739 672	51 150	-1 646	686 876	180 995	164 785	23 816	20 697	43 360	24 206
1996	1 095 386	1 085 454	9 933	781 116	53 330	-1 768	726 018	197 062	172 307	24 969	21 408	43 869	24 925
1997	1 163 164	1 153 703	9 460	837 210	56 778	-1 935	778 497	207 009	177 658	26 127	22 210	44 520	25 595
1998	1 236 770	1 226 748	10 022	904 302	60 836	-2 117	841 348	212 031	183 390	27 367	23 027	45 192	.....

Notes

These notes pertain to the data on pages 23 through 404. The notes are arranged by page number, with the pages to which they pertain and the general subject heading shown at the top of each group of notes. The notes provide information about data sources, definitions, methodology, revisions, and sources of additional information.

The tables on pages 23 through 404 are divided into four main parts.

Part I (pages 23–184) pertains to the U.S. economy as a whole.

Part II (pages 185–297) presents data by industry or industry group, arranged in accordance with the 1987 U.S. Standard Industrial Classification (SIC). The SIC classifies economic activity into divisions such as mining, manufacturing, retail trade, etc. and into a hierarchy of more detailed industry groups within each division. The tables in Part II present data for each SIC division and within manufacturing, for each major ("2-digit") industry group. Some of these data are repeated from the tables in Part I, giving the user the convenience of a profile of the industry in a single location. Where data are repeated in this way, these notes will normally cross reference earlier discussions of the data, rather than repeat the discussion.

The 1987 SIC is published in *Standard Industrial Classification Manual, 1987*, Executive Office of the President, Office of Management and Budget (Washington, DC: U.S. Government Printing Office, 1988). Brief descriptions adapted from the SIC manual are provided in these notes for the industry groups in Part II. These descriptions list only the main activities for each industry group; the SIC Manual should be consulted for complete detail.

For industry data to be collected and published in the future, the SIC is being replaced by the North American Industry Classification System (NAICS) as the official U.S. system for the classification of data. However, as few data using the new system have as yet been published, this edition of *Business Statistics* continues to present data on an SIC basis. A description of the NAICS and agency plans for implementation is given in a lead article in the 1998 edition of *Business Statistics*. Additional information is available on the Census Bureau internet site (www.census.gov).

Part III (pages 299–371) contains additional historical data for selected quarterly and monthly series. In most cases, quarterly data are shown beginning with 1962 and monthly data beginning with 1971.

Part IV (pages 373–404) contains data on personal income, population, and employment by state and region. The data are annual and cover 1969 through 1998.

The column headings for the data tables normally indicate that the data are "seasonally adjusted" or "not seasonally adjusted" or "at a seasonally adjusted annual rate." These headings refer to the monthly or quarterly, rather than the annual, data. Seasonal adjustment removes from the time series the average impact of variations that normally occur at about the same time each year due to, for example, weather, holidays, and tax payment dates. Data that are presented at annual rates show values at their annual equivalents—the values that would be registered if the rate of activity measured during a particular month or quarter were maintained for a full year.

The statistical method used to achieve the seasonal adjustment may vary from one data set to another. Many of the data are adjusted by a method known as X-12 ARIMA, developed by the Bureau of the Census. A description of the method is found in "New Capabilities and Methods of the X-12-ARIMA Seasonal Adjustment Program," David F. Findley, Brian C. Monsell, William R. Bell, Mark C. Otto and Bor-Chung Chen, *Journal of Business and Economic Statistics*, April 1998. A preprint version of this article can be downloaded from the Bureau of the Census web site.

Most of the data in this volume are from federal government sources and may be reproduced freely. A few are from private sources and are used with permission; further use may be subject to copyright restrictions. A list of data sources, including addresses, phone numbers, E-mail addresses, internet addresses, and complete citations for the government periodicals cited may be found at the end of these Notes.

The tables in this volume incorporate data revisions and corrections released by the source agencies through August 1999.

PAGES 26–34 AND 301–308
NATIONAL PRODUCT AND INCOME

Source: U.S. Department of Commerce, Bureau of Economic Analysis (BEA).

All data on these pages are from the national income and product accounts (NIPAs). The data are as published in the 1996 comprehensive NIPA revisions and as subsequently updated and revised through September 1999.

REVISIONS

NIPA data normally undergo revision at the end of July each year. Typically these annual revisions cover annual and quarterly data for the previous three years, but may also include more limited revisions to data for earlier years. Approximately once every five years the NIPA data undergo "benchmark" revision, on which occasions some definitional changes may affect data back to 1929—the earliest year for which official national account data are available.

COMPREHENSIVE REVISIONS RELEASED IN 1999. Comprehensive NIPA revisions were released in October 1999, too late to be included in this volume. These revised estimates that are being released in 1999 begin with 1959; comparable estimates back to 1929 will be released early in 2000. These revisions will incorporate a number of major definitional, conceptual, and methodological changes which are outlined in the "Current Issues in Economic Measurement" article found in the front of this book.

REVISIONS RELEASED IN 1998. The 1998 annual revisions to the NIPA data cover 1995 through the first quarter of 1998 and appear in the August, September, and October 1998 issues of the BEA publication *Survey of Current Business*.

REVISIONS TO PERSONAL INCOME. Released at the same time as these annual revisions were revisions to personal income and related series beginning with data for 1982. These revisions were due to a change in the NIPA definition of dividend payments. Dividends were redefined to exclude distributions that reflect capital gains income. In practice this means that capital gains distributions by mutual funds now have been excluded from personal income. (Other capital gains income included in dividends is not separately identifiable but is believed to be small.) The rationale for the definitional change is to achieve closer conformity with the conceptual definition of income used in the NIPAs, a definition that excludes all identifiable forms of capital gains. The revisions reduce dividends and raise estimates of undistributed corporate profits. Since dividends are a component of personal income, estimates of personal income (total, disposable, and per capita, in current and constant dollars), personal saving, and the personal saving rate also are affected. GDP and national saving, already measured to exclude capital gains, were not affected. (See the August 1998 *Survey of Current Business*.)

DEFINITIONS AND NOTES ON THE DATA

The NIPAs show the composition of production and the distribution to labor and capital of the income resulting from production.

GROSS DOMESTIC PRODUCT (GDP), the featured measure of U.S. output, is the market value of the goods and services produced by labor and property located in the United States. GDP is the sum of personal consumption expenditures, gross private domestic investment (including change in business inventories and before deduction of charges for consumption of fixed capital), net exports of goods and services, and government consumption expenditures and gross investment. GDP excludes intermediate purchases of goods and services by business, since their value is included in the final product.

GDP, rather than gross national product (GNP), has been the featured measure of U.S. production since the comprehensive NIPA revisions in 1991. GDP refers to production taking place within the geographic boundaries of the United States, including production from capital and labor supplied by nonresidents; GNP refers to production by labor and property supplied by U.S. residents, whether located in the United States or abroad. GDP is consistent in coverage with other national economic indicators such as employment and productivity. It also is the measure used by almost all other countries and thus facilitates comparison of economic activity in the United States with that of other countries.

PERSONAL CONSUMPTION EXPENDITURES (PCE) is goods and services purchased by persons residing in the United States. PCE consists mainly of purchases of new goods and services by individuals from business. In addition, PCE includes purchases of new goods and services by nonprofit institutions, net purchases of used goods by individuals and nonprofit institutions, and purchases abroad of goods and services by U.S. residents traveling or working in foreign countries. (See the notes for pages 50–57 for additional information.)

GROSS PRIVATE DOMESTIC INVESTMENT consists of private fixed investment and changes in business inventories.

PRIVATE FIXED INVESTMENT consists of both nonresidential and residential fixed investment. It consists of purchases of fixed assets, which are commodities that will be used in a production process for more than one year, including replacements and additions to the capital stock, and it is measured before a deduction for consumption of fixed capital. It covers all investment by private businesses and nonprofit institutions in the United States, regardless of whether the investment is owned by U.S. residents. It does not include purchases of the same types of equipment and structures by government agencies, which are included in government gross investment, or investment by U.S. residents in other countries.

NONRESIDENTIAL FIXED INVESTMENT consists of both structures and producers' durable equipment (PDE).

NONRESIDENTIAL STRUCTURES consists of new construction, brokers' commissions on sales of structures, and net purchases of used structures by private business and by nonprofit institutions from government agencies. New construction also includes hotels and motels and mining exploration, shafts, and wells.

NONRESIDENTIAL PRODUCERS' DURABLE EQUIPMENT (PDE) consists of private business purchases, on capital account, of new machinery, equipment, and vehicles; dealers' margins on sales of used equipment; and net purchases of used equipment from government agencies, persons, and the rest of the world. (It does not, however, include the personal-use portion of equipment purchased for both business and personal use, which is included in PCE.)

RESIDENTIAL PRIVATE FIXED INVESTMENT consists of both structures and residential producers' durable equipment—equipment owned by landlords and rented to tenants. Investment in structures consists of new units, improvements to existing units, mobile homes, brokers' commissions on the sale of residential property, and net purchases of used structures from government agencies. CHANGE IN BUSINESS INVENTORIES is the change in the physical volume of inventories held by business, valued at the average price of the period. It differs from the change in the book value of inventories reported by most businesses; an inventory valuation adjustment converts historical cost valuations of inventories to replacement cost.

NET EXPORTS OF GOODS AND SERVICES is exports of goods and services less imports of goods and services. It does not include factor income or transfer payments to and from the rest of the world .

GOVERNMENT CONSUMPTION EXPENDITURES is purchases by governments (federal, state, and local) of goods and services for current consumption. It includes compensation of general government employees and an allowance for consumption of general government fixed capital (i.e., depreciation). Receipts for certain services provided by government—primarily tuition payments for higher education and charges for medical care—are defined as government sales, which are treated as deductions from government purchases.

GROSS GOVERNMENT INVESTMENT consists of general government and government enterprise expenditures for fixed assets (structures and durable equipment). Government inventory investment is included in government consumption expenditures.

REAL, OR CHAINED (1992) DOLLAR, ESTIMATES are estimates from which the effect of price change has been removed. Prior to the 1996 comprehensive revisions, constant-dollar measures were obtained by combining real output measures for different goods and services using the relative prices of a single year as weights. The current measure changes the weights as relative prices shift over time. Therefore, the chained-dollar estimates are usually not additive; that is, the components in any given table usually do not add to the total. In time periods close to the base year, the residual usually is quite small.

GDP PRICE INDEXES are chain-type measures that use a series of annual weights, chained together, to form a time series that allows for the effect of changes in the composition of output over time.

IMPLICIT PRICE DEFLATORS are GDP price measures consisting of the ratios of current-dollar to real GDP components (multiplied by 100).

FINAL SALES OF DOMESTIC PRODUCT is GDP minus change in business inventories. Thus, it is the sum of personal consumption expenditures, gross private domestic fixed investment, government consumption expenditures and gross investment, and net exports of goods and services.

GROSS DOMESTIC PURCHASES is the market value of goods and services purchased by U.S. residents, regardless of where those goods and services were produced. It is GDP minus net exports of goods and services; equivalently, it is the sum of personal consumption expenditures, gross private domestic investment, and government consumption expenditures and gross investment.

FINAL SALES TO DOMESTIC PURCHASERS is gross domestic purchases minus change in business inventories.

GROSS NATIONAL PRODUCT (GNP) refers to production by labor and property supplied by U.S. residents, whether located in the United States or abroad. It is equal to gross domestic product (GDP) plus receipts of factor income from the rest of the world less payments of factor income to the rest of the world. More information is given above under gross domestic product.

NET NATIONAL PRODUCT is the net market value of goods and services attributable to the labor and property supplied by U.S. residents and is equal to GNP less the consumption of fixed capital. The measure of fixed capital consumption used relates only to fixed capital located in the United States. Investment in that capital is measured by private fixed investment and government gross investment.

NATIONAL INCOME is the income received by labor and capital as a result of their participation in the production process. It consists of compensation of employees; proprietors' income with inventory valuation and capital consumption adjustments; rental income of persons with capital consumption adjustment; corporate profits with inventory valuation and capital consumption adjustments; and net interest. Conceptually, national income can be derived from net national product by deducting indirect business tax and nontax liability and business transfer payments and adding subsidies less current surplus of government enterprises. In practice, the product and income sides of the national accounts are estimated separately from different source data and there is always some statistical discrepancy between the two sides of the accounts.

COMPENSATION OF EMPLOYEES is the income accruing to employees as remuneration for their work. It is the sum of wage and salary accruals and of supplements to wages and salaries.

WAGE AND SALARY ACCRUALS consists of the monetary remuneration of employees, including the compensation of corporate officers; commissions, tips, and bonuses; voluntary employee contributions to certain deferred compensation plans, such as 401(k) plans; and receipts in kind that represent income. WAGE AND SALARY DISBURSEMENTS is wages and salaries as just defined except that retroactive wage payments are recorded when paid, rather than when earned. In the NIPAs, wages accrued is the appropriate measure for national income, and wages disbursed is the appropriate measure for personal income.

SUPPLEMENTS TO WAGES AND SALARIES consists of employer contributions for social insurance and other labor income. Employer contributions for social insurance consists of employer payments under the following federal, state, and local government programs: Old-age, survivors, and disability insurance (social security); hospital insurance; unemployment insurance; railroad retirement; government employee retirement; pension benefit guaranty; veterans life insurance; publicly administered workers' compensation; military medical insurance; and temporary disability insurance. Other labor income consists of employer payments (including payments in kind) to private pension and profit-sharing plans, private group health and life insurance plans, privately administered workers' compensation plans, and supplemental unemployment benefit plans; corporate directors' fees; and several minor categories of employee compensation, including judicial fees to jurors and witnesses, compensation of prison inmates, and marriage fees to justices of the peace.

PROPRIETORS' INCOME WITH INVENTORY VALUATION AND CAPITAL CONSUMPTION ADJUSTMENTS is the current-production income (including income in kind) of sole proprietorships and partnerships and of tax-exempt cooperatives. The imputed net rental income of owner-occupants of farm dwellings is included, but the imputed net rental income of owner-occupants of nonfarm dwellings is included in rental income of persons. Proprietors' income excludes dividends and monetary interest received by nonfinancial business and rental incomes received by persons not primarily engaged in the real estate business; these incomes are included in dividends, net interest, and rental income of persons.

RENTAL INCOME OF PERSONS WITH CAPITAL CONSUMPTION ADJUSTMENT is the net current-production income of persons from the rental of real property except for the income of persons primarily engaged in the real estate business; the imputed net rental income of owner-occupants of nonfarm dwellings; and the royalties received by persons from patents, copyrights, and rights to natural resources.

CORPORATE PROFITS WITH INVENTORY VALUATION AND CAPITAL CONSUMPTION ADJUSTMENTS is the net current-production income of organizations treated as corporations in the NIPAs. These organizations consist of all entities required to file federal corporate tax returns, including mutual financial institutions and cooperatives subject to federal income tax; private noninsured pension funds; nonprofit institutions that primarily serve business; Federal Reserve banks; and federally sponsored credit agencies. With several differences, this income is measured as receipts less expenses as defined in federal tax law. Among these differences: Receipts exclude capital gains and dividends received; expenses exclude depletion and capital losses and losses resulting from bad debts; inventory withdrawals are valued at replacement cost; and depreciation is on a consistent accounting basis and is valued at replacement cost. Because national income is defined as the income of U.S. residents, its profits component includes income earned abroad by U.S. corporations and excludes income earned in the United States by the rest of the world.

PROFITS BEFORE TAX is the income of organizations treated as corporations in the NIPAs, except that it reflects the inventory- and depreciation-accounting practices used for federal income tax returns. It consists of profits tax liability, dividends, and undistributed corporate profits.

PROFITS TAX LIABILITY is the sum of federal, state, and local income taxes on all income subject to taxes; this income includes capital gains and other income excluded from profits before tax. The taxes are measured on an accrual basis, net of applicable tax credits.

PROFITS AFTER TAX is profits before tax less profits tax liability. It consists of dividends and undistributed corporate profits.

DIVIDENDS is payments in cash or other assets, excluding the corporations' own stock, that are made by corporations located in the United States and abroad to stockholders who are U.S. residents. The payments are measured net of dividends received by U.S. corporations. Dividends paid to state and local government social insurance funds and general government are included.

UNDISTRIBUTED PROFITS is corporate profits after tax less dividends.

INVENTORY VALUATION ADJUSTMENT (IVA) for corporations is the difference between the cost of inventory withdrawals as valued in the source data used to determine profits before tax and the cost of withdrawals valued at replacement cost. The adjustment is needed because inventories as reported in the source data are often valued at their acquisition (historical) cost rather than at their replacement cost. As prices change, companies that value inventory at acquisition cost may realize profits or losses. In the NIPAs, inventory profits or losses are shown as adjustments to business income (corporate profits and nonfarm proprietors' income); they are shown as the IVA with the sign reversed. No adjustment is needed to farm proprietors' income because farm inventories are measured on a current-market-cost basis.

CONSUMPTION OF FIXED CAPITAL is a charge for the using up of private and government fixed capital located in the United States. It is based on studies of prices of used equipment and structures in resale markets. For general government and for nonprofit institutions that primarily serve individuals, it is recorded in government consumption expenditures and in personal consumption expenditures, respectively, as the value of the current services of the fixed capital assets owned and used by these entities. PRIVATE CAPITAL CONSUMPTION ALLOWANCES consists of tax-return-based depreciation charges for corporations and nonfarm proprietorships and of historical-cost depreciation (calculated by BEA using a geometric pattern of price declines) for farm proprietorships, rental income of persons, and nonprofit institutions. The PRIVATE CAPITAL CON-SUMPTION ADJUSTMENT is the difference between private capital consumption allowances and private consumption of fixed capital.

NET INTEREST is the interest paid by private business less the interest received by private business, plus the interest received from the rest of the world less the interest paid to the rest of the world. Interest payments on mortgage and home improvement loans and on home equity loans are counted as interest paid by business because home owner-ship is treated as a business in the NIPAs. In addition to monetary interest, net interest includes imputed interest, which is paid by corporate financial business and is meas-ured as the difference between the property income received on depositors' or policyholders' funds and the amount of property income paid out explicitly. The imput-ed interest paid by life insurance carriers and noninsured pension plans attributes their investment income to per-sons in the period it is earned.

PRODUCT AND INCOME OF NONFINANCIAL CORPORATE BUSI-NESS provide consistent information for the nonfinancial corporate sector of the economy on gross product, income, and the distribution of the total value of output among capital consumption, employee compensation, profits, and interest. Excluded from nonfinancial corporate business are households, institutions, general government, all non-corporate business, and financial business.

DATA AVAILABILITY; REVISION POLICY
Annual data are available beginning with 1929; quarterly data begin with 1946. Not all data are available for all time periods.

New data normally are released toward the end of each month. The first estimates for each calendar quarter are released in the month after the quarter's end. Revisions for the most recent quarter are released in the second and third months after the quarter's end. In addition, "annual" revisions to the data for the last several years typically occur each July. "Comprehensive" revisions to the data for all time periods typically occur about once every five years.

The most recent data are published each month in the *Survey of Current Business*, may be purchased on diskette from BEA, or may be obtained from the BEA internet site (http://www.bea.doc.gov). Full historical data also may be purchased on diskette from BEA or may be obtained from the STAT-USA subscription internet site (http://www.stat-usa.gov).

REFERENCES

For information about the 1999 comprehensive revisions, see press releases issued in October by the Commerce Department; the STAT-USA subscription internet site (http://www.stat-usa.gov); the *Survey of Current Business*: "A Preview of the 1999 Comprehensive Revision of the National Income and Product Accounts: Definitional and

Classificational Changes", August 1999; and "A Preview of the 1999 Comprehensive Revision of the National Income and Product Accounts: New and Redesigned Tables", September 1999.

For the data prior to the 1999 revision, complete historical data through 1994, plus definitions and a discussion of methodology and source data, are found in *National Income and Product Accounts of the United States, 1929-94* (Bureau of Economic Analysis, 1998), available from the Government Printing Office (stock number 003-010-00272-7). Historical data are also available on CD-ROM, *NIPA Historical Data, 1929-97*, (BEA product number NCN-0198) includes the complete NIPA tables, as well as summary tables of the most frequently used series and a selection of related articles from the *Survey of Current Business*.

For recent summaries of BEA's definitions, methodology, and principal source data, see *Survey of Current Business*: "Updated Summary NIPA Methodologies," September 1998, and "A Guide to the NIPA's," March 1998.

More detailed, but less recent, information on BEA methodology is found in the following methodology papers available on the BEA internet site or by purchase from the National Technical Information Service: *MP-1: Introduction to National Economic Accounting* (March 1985); *MP-2: Corporate Profits: Profits Before Tax, Profits Tax Liability, and Dividends* (May 1985); *MP-3: Foreign Transactions* (May 1987); *MP-5: Government Transactions* (Nov 1988); *MP-6: Personal Consumption Expenditures* (June 1990).

For information about 1998 revisions, see *Survey of Current Business*: "Annual Revision of the National Income and Product Accounts: Annual Estimates, 1995-97, and Quarterly Estimates, 1995:I-1998:I" and "Annual NIPA Revision: Revised Estimates for 1982- 94," August 1998 and "Annual NIPA Revision: Newly Available Table," September 1998.

For discussion of alternative measures of change in output and prices, see *Survey of Current Business*: "BEA's Chain Indexes, Time Series, and Measures of Long-Term Economic Growth," May 1997; "Alternative Measures of Change in Real Output and Prices, Quarterly Estimates for 1959-92," March 1993; "Alternative Measures of Change in Real Output and Prices," April 1992.

PAGE 35
COMPOSITE INDEXES OF ECONOMIC ACTIVITY

Sources: U.S. Department of Commerce, Bureau of Economic Analysis and The Conference Board.

The composite indexes of leading, coincident, and lagging indicators are intended to help predict peaks and troughs in the business cycle. They are calculated from sets of com-ponent series selected for their utility as indicators of stages of the business cycle. The component series originate with a variety of sources, as indicated below. Several of the component series appear on the page with the composite indexes; other components can be found on the pages indicated below.

Late in 1995, responsibility for compilation and publication of the composite indexes was transferred from the Bureau of Economic Analysis to The Conference Board.

INDEX COMPONENTS

The *index of leading economic indicators* consists of the following ten components, with monthly data seasonally adjusted except as noted:

AVERAGE WEEKLY HOURS are average hours worked per week by production workers in manufacturing. Source: Bureau of Labor Statistics. (See page 123)

INITIAL CLAIMS, UNEMPLOYMENT INSURANCE are average weekly claims for unemployment insurance under state programs. Source: U.S. Department of Labor, Employment and Training Administration. (See page 116)

MANUFACTURERS' NEW ORDERS, CONSUMER GOODS AND MATERIALS are net new orders in billions of 1992 dollars. Source: Bureau of the Census, with inflation adjustment by The Conference Board.

VENDOR PERFORMANCE, SLOWER DELIVERIES DIFFUSION INDEX tracks the relative speed with which goods-producing companies receive deliveries from their suppliers. An increase in this series indicates a slowdown in deliveries and is generally caused by increased demand for manufacturing supplies. The survey asks purchasing managers if their suppliers' deliveries were obtained faster, slower, or the same as the previous month's deliveries. The index records the percentage reporting slower deliveries plus one-half of the percentage reporting no change in delivery speed. Source: National Association of Purchasing Managers.

MANUFACTURERS' NEW ORDERS, NONDEFENSE CAPITAL GOODS are in billions of 1992 dollars. Source: Bureau of the Census, with inflation adjustment by The Conference Board. (See page 216 for new orders of nondefense capital goods in current dollars.)

BUILDING PERMITS, NEW PRIVATE HOUSING UNITS is the number of new private housing units authorized by local building permits. Source: Bureau of the Census. (See page 201)

STOCK PRICES: 500 COMMON STOCKS is an index based on 1941-1943=10. Source: Standard and Poor's Corporation. (See page 153)

MONEY SUPPLY (M2) is in billions of 1992 dollars. Source: Federal Reserve Board of Governors, with inflation adjustment by The Conference Board. (See page 142 for the M2 money supply in current dollars.)

INTEREST RATE SPREAD is equal to the rate on 10-year treasury bonds less the rate on federal funds. The interest rate series are not seasonally adjusted. Source: Federal Reserve Board of Governors.

INDEX OF CONSUMER EXPECTATIONS is based on the first quarter of 1966=100. The monthly data are not seasonally adjusted. Source: University of Michigan, Survey Research Center. This is a copyrighted series used by permission; it may not be reproduced without written permission from the source.

The *index of coincident economic indicators* consists of the following four components, with monthly data seasonally adjusted:

EMPLOYEES ON NONAGRICULTURAL PAYROLLS are total wage and salary employees, in thousands. Source: Bureau of Labor Statistics. (See page 117)

PERSONAL INCOME LESS TRANSFER PAYMENTS is in billions of chained 1992 dollars (seasonally adjusted annual rate). Source: Bureau of Economic Analysis, with inflation adjustment by The Conference Board. (See pages 50–51 for total personal income and transfer payments in current dollars.)

INDEX OF INDUSTRIAL PRODUCTION is an index of the output of the mining, manufacturing, and utility sectors of the U.S. economy. The index is based on 1992=100. Source: Federal Reserve, Board of Governors. (See page 60)

MANUFACTURING AND TRADE SALES are in millions of 1992 dollars. Sources: Bureau of the Census, with inflation adjustment by The Conference Board. (See page 83 for manufacturing and trade sales in current dollars.)

The *index of lagging economic indicators* consists of the following seven components, with monthly data seasonally adjusted except as noted.

AVERAGE DURATION OF UNEMPLOYMENT is in weeks. Source: Bureau of Labor Statistics (See page 113).

RATIO: MANUFACTURING AND TRADE INVENTORIES TO SALES is calculated from sales and inventories in chained 1992 dollars. Source: Bureau of Economic Analysis. (See page 86)

MANUFACTURING LABOR COST PER UNIT OF OUTPUT is the smoothed percent change in this index.

AVERAGE PRIME INTEREST RATE is the average percentage rate per annum charged by banks for prime business loans; not seasonally adjusted. Source: Federal Reserve Board of Governors. (See page 151)

COMMERCIAL AND INDUSTRIAL LOANS OUTSTANDING is in billions of 1992 dollars. Sources: Federal Reserve Board of Governors, with inflation adjustment by The Conference Board. (See page 145)

CONSUMER INSTALLMENT CREDIT OUTSTANDING is expressed as a percent of personal income. Sources: Bureau of Economic Analysis and Federal Reserve, Board of Governors.

CONSUMER PRICE INDEX FOR SERVICES is the smoothed percent change in this index from the previous month. Monthly changes are expressed at a seasonally adjusted annual rate. Source: Bureau of Labor Statistics. (See page 95)

NOTES ON THE DATA

Each composite index is scaled so that its average monthly value equals 100 in a base year, currently 1992.

Each of the composite indexes measures the average behavior of a group of economic time series that show similar timing at business cycle turns but represent widely differing activities or sectors of the economy. The procedures used to construct the indexes are designed to neutralize the tendency of the more volatile series to dominate the average and to enhance the usefulness of the three indexes as a consistent system.

Comprehensive revisions of the composite indexes were introduced in 1996, 1993, and 1989. Changes made to the components of the leading index in the 1996 revision included:

- Adding the interest rate spread as a component;

- Removing manufacturers' unfilled orders and sensitive material prices as components;

- Replacing contracts and orders for plant and equipment with manufacturers' new orders for nondefense capital goods;

- Showing building permits in units rather than as an index number.

In addition, all the indexes were moved to 1992 as the base year, and deflators that follow BEA's chain-weighting procedures were introduced for all the constant-dollar components.

Details about these changes and others introduced at the same time can be found in the November and December 1996 and January 1997 issues of The Conference Board monthly publication Business Cycle Indicators, as well as on The Conference Board Business Cycle Indicators website (www.tcb-indicators.org).

DATA AVAILABILITY

Data are published each month by The Conference Board. Their monthly report Business Cycle Indicators is available by subscription from The Conference Board, 845 Third Avenue, New York, NY 10022. A monthly press release from The Conference Board at http://www.tcb-indicators.org. The full historical database is available by subscription from the same internet site.

REFERENCES

In addition of The Conference Board's Business Cycle Indicators (referenced above), see the following articles in the Survey of Current Business: "Business Cycle Indicators: Upcoming Revision of the Composite Indexes" (October 1993); "Composite Index of Coincident Indicators and Alternative Composite Indexes" (June 1992); "Leading Indicators and the 'Prime Mover' View" (August 1989); "Business Cycle Indicators: Revised Composite Indexes" (January 1989); "Composite Indexes of Leading, Coincident, and Lagging Indicators" (November 1987). See also Handbook of Cyclical Indicators (Bureau of Economic Analysis, 1984).

PAGES 38–47
INCOME DISTRIBUTION AND POVERTY

Source: U.S. Department of Commerce, Bureau of the Census

All data in this chapter are derived from the Current Population Survey (CPS), which is also the source of data on labor force, employment, and unemployment (see the notes for pages 112–115). In March of each year, the 50,000 households in this monthly survey are asked questions about earnings and other income in the previous year. In most of the tables, the latest data available are data for 1998 collected in March 1999. State-by-state data are only shown through 1997, however. Averages for states for the years 1997-98 have been published but the data for the year 1998 were not available as Business Statistics went to press.

The population covered by the survey is the civilian non-institutional population of the United States and members of the Armed Forces in the United States living off post or with their families on post, but excluding all other members of the Armed Forces. Because it is a survey of households, homeless persons are not included.

DEFINITIONS

HOUSEHOLDS consist of all persons who occupy a housing unit. A household includes the related family members and all the unrelated persons, if any, such as lodgers, foster children, wards, or employees who share the housing unit. A person living alone in a housing unit or a group of unrelated persons sharing a housing unit as partners is also counted as a household. The count of households excludes group quarters.

A FAMILY is a group of two or more persons related by birth, marriage, or adoption who reside together.

MEDIAN INCOME is the amount that divides the income distribution into two equal groups, half having incomes above the median, half having incomes below the median. The medians for persons are based on persons 15 years old and over with income.

All historical income figures are shown in constant *1998 dollars*. They are converted from current-dollar values using the *CPI-U-X1*. This index uses a historically consistent method of measuring changes in the cost of home ownership, and is similar in concept and behavior to the deflators used in the NIPAs for consumer income and spending. See the notes for pages 90–95 for further explanation of this price index.

MEAN INCOME is the amount obtained by dividing the total aggregate income of a group by the number of units in that group.

EARNINGS include wages, salaries, armed forces pay, commissions, tips, piece-rate payments, and cash bonuses before deductions such as taxes, bonds, pensions, and union dues; net income from nonfarm self-employment; and net income from farm self-employment.

INCOME, in the official definition used in the survey, is money income including earnings as defined above; unemployment compensation; workers' compensation; Social Security; Supplemental Security Income; cash public assistance (welfare payments); veterans' payments; survivor benefits; disability benefits; pension or retirement income; interest income; dividends (but not capital gains); rents, royalties, and payments from estates or trusts; educational assistance, such as scholarships or grants; child support; alimony; financial assistance from outside of the household; and other cash income regularly received, such as foster child payments, military family allotments, and foreign government pensions. Receipts not counted as income include capital gains or losses, withdrawals of bank deposits, money borrowed, tax refunds, gifts, and lump-sum inheritances or insurance payments.

The GINI COEFFICIENT (also known as Gini ratio or index of income concentration) is a statistical measure of income inequality ranging from 0 to 1. A measure of 1 indicates "perfect" inequality; i.e., one household having all the income and the rest having none. A measure of 0 indicates "perfect" equality; i.e., all households having equal shares of income. For more detailed discussion, see *Current Population Reports*, Series P-60, No. 123. There are small differences between the Gini coefficients presented in the report's main tables and those presented in the tables comparing alternative definitions of income. In the latter, the coefficients were recalculated, for comparability with the other income definitions, using a slightly different method.

THE POVERTY POPULATION is the number of persons with family or individual incomes below a specified level intended to measure the cost of a minimum standard of living. These minimum levels vary by size and composition of family and are known as *poverty thresholds*. The poverty thresholds are based on a definition developed by Mollie Orshansky of the Social Security Administration in 1964 and are adjusted each year for price increase, using the percent change in the Consumer Price Index for all urban consumers (CPI-U). For more detail and further references, see Bureau of the Census, *Current Population Reports: Consumer Income, P60-207*, "Poverty in the United States: 1998," pp. A2-A4. The *poverty rate* for a demographic group is the number of poor persons or families in that group expressed as a percentage of the total number of persons or families in the group.

UNRELATED INDIVIDUALS are persons 15 years and over who are not living with any relatives. The poverty status of unrelated individuals is determined independently of income of other persons with whom they may share a household.

A person with WORK EXPERIENCE is one who, during the preceding calendar year, did any work for pay or profit or worked without pay on a family-operated farm or business at any time during the year, on a part-time or full-time basis. A year-round worker is one who worked for 50 weeks or more during the preceding calendar year. A person is classified as having worked full time if he or she worked 35 hours or more per week during a majority of the weeks worked. A year-round, full-time worker is a person who worked 35 or more hours per week and 50 or more weeks during the previous calendar year.

NOTES ON THE DATA

The following changes may affect year-to-year comparability of income and poverty data from the CPS.

With 1972 data, 1970 census sample design and population controls were introduced; previous data used 1960.

With 1984 data, 1980 census sample design was introduced; 1980 population controls were introduced, and were extended back to 1979 data.

With 1993 data, there was a major redesign of the CPS, including computer-assisted interviewing. The limits used to code income amounts were changed, resulting in reporting of higher income values for the highest income families and, consequently, an exaggerated year-to-year increase in income inequality. In addition, 1990 Census population controls were introduced, and were extended back to the 1992 data.

ALTERNATIVE DEFINITIONS OF INCOME

ALTERNATIVE DEFINITIONS OF INCOME

In June 1999, the Census Bureau published a report on "Experimental Poverty Measures, 1990 to 1997." This report is discussed in the article "Current Issues in Economic Measurement" at the beginning of this year's *Business Statistics*. The experimental measures are still under development and encompass significant revisions of both the concept of the poverty threshold and the resources with which that threshold is compared. They are not included in this chapter.

The Census Bureau also calculates "alternative" income and poverty measures based on a number of different definitions of income, but the same concept of the poverty threshold, as the official measure. These measures in many cases require simulation—use of data from sources other than the CPS to estimate elements of family and individual income as reported in the CPS. *Business Statistics* shows income and poverty rates according to three of these alternative definitions, with the official definition also shown for comparison in the same table. As of this year the Census Bureau no longer publishes the alternative poverty rates, but they are still available on the Census website.

DEFINITION 1 is the official Census definition of money income described above.

DEFINITION 4 is Definition 1 income *minus* government cash transfers (Social Security, unemployment compensation, workers' compensation, veteran's payments, railroad retirement, Black Lung payments, government education assistance, Supplemental Security Income, and welfare payments), *plus* realized capital gains and employers' payments for health insurance coverage. Capital gains and health insurance are not collected in the CPS but are simulated using statistical data from the Internal Revenue Service and the National Medical Care Expenditure Survey. Definition 4 is, in effect, the income generated by the workings of the economy before government interventions in the form of taxes and transfer payments.

DEFINITION 14 is income after all government tax and transfer interventions. It consists of Definition 4 income *minus* payroll taxes and federal and state income taxes, *plus* the Earned Income Credit; all of the cash transfers listed above as being subtracted in Definition 4; the "fungible" value of Medicare and Medicaid; the value of regular-price school lunches provided by government; and the value of noncash transfers, including food stamps, rent subsidies, and free and reduced-price school lunches. The tax information is not collected in the CPS but is simulated using statistical data from the Internal Revenue Service, Social Security payroll tax formulas, and a model of each state's income tax regulations. The "fungible" value approach to medical benefits counts such benefits as income only to the extent that they free up resources that could have been spent on medical care; if family income is not sufficient to cover the family's basic food and housing requirements, Medicare and Medicaid are treated as having no income value. Data on average Medicare and Medicaid outlays per enrollee were used in the valuation process. Food stamp values are reported in the March CPS. Estimates of other government subsidy payments used data from the Department of Agriculture (for school lunches) and the 1985 American Housing Survey.

DEFINITION 15 is Definition 14 income plus the net imputed return on equity in owner-occupied housing—the calculated annual benefit of converting one's home equity into an annuity, net of property taxes. (It also can be thought of as measuring the extent to which home ownership relieves the owner of the need for rental or mortgage payments.) Information from the 1987 American Housing Survey was used to assign values of home equity and amounts of property taxes. Because disposable personal income in the NIPAs includes the imputed rent on owner-occupied housing plus most of the cash and in-kind transfers included in Definitions 14 and 15, Definition 15 is the Census income definition closest to the NIPA concept.

Alternative poverty rates are also calculated and shown in this table using poverty thresholds that have been adjusted for price increase using the CPI-U-X1, instead of the CPI-U, which is used in the official thresholds.

The STANDARD ERROR is a measure of the variability that arises from the use of a sample to estimate data for an entire population. The sample estimate and its standard error can be used to construct a "confidence interval." For example, if all possible samples were surveyed, the average result from about 90 percent of samples would fall within the interval from 1.645 standard errors below the estimate to 1.645 standard errors above the estimate. Standard errors are shown for the estimates of median income and poverty by state to indicate the necessary degree of caution in making comparisons among states or over time.

DATA AVAILABILITY

Data are published annually, in September or October, by the Bureau of the Census, in a series with the general title *Current Population Reports: Consumer Income, P60*. Data in this report were derived from P60-206, "Money Income in the United States: 1998," and P60-207, "Poverty in the United States: 1998," issued in September 1999. These reports also contain extensive explanations and references to other relevant sources.

Data are available on the Census internet site (http://www.census.gov).

PAGES 50–57 AND 328–335
SOURCES AND DISPOSITION OF PERSONAL INCOME; PERSONAL CONSUMPTION EXPENDITURE BY MAJOR TYPE OF PRODUCT

Source: U.S. Department of Commerce, Bureau of Economic Analysis.

All personal income and personal consumption expenditure series are from the national income and product accounts (NIPAs). All series are shown at a seasonally adjusted annual rate and, except for the per capita series and the saving rate, are in billions of dollars.

REVISIONS

Data in this book reflect revisions to the NIPAs available through August 1999. (See the notes for pages 26–34 for additional information, and see "Current Issues in Economic Measurement" at the front of this book for information on changes introduced in October 1999.)

In addition to the regular periodic revisions, other revisions to some series related to personal income were released in 1998. These revisions begin with data for 1982 and were due to a change in the NIPA definition of dividend payments. Dividends were redefined to exclude distributions that reflect capital gains income. In practice, this means that capital gains distributions by mutual funds now have been excluded from personal income. (Other capital gains income included in dividends is not separately identifiable, but is believed to be small.) The rationale for the definitional change is to achieve closer conformity with the conceptual definition of income used in the NIPAs, a definition that excludes all identifiable forms of capital gains. Since dividends are a component of personal income, estimates of personal income (total, disposable, and per capita, in current and constant dollars), personal saving, and the personal saving rate also are affected. (See the August 1998 *Survey of Current Business*.)

In 1997, historical revisions stemming from BEA's revised estimates of reproducible tangible wealth were introduced. The series affected included proprietors' income, rental income of persons, and total personal income. (See the May 1997 *Survey of Current Business*.)

DEFINITIONS

PERSONAL INCOME is the income received by persons from participation in production, government and business transfer payments, and government interest, which is treated like a transfer payment. *Persons* refers to individuals, nonprofit institutions that primarily serve individuals, private noninsured welfare funds, and private trust funds. Proprietors' income is treated in its entirety as received by individuals. Life insurance carriers and private noninsured pension funds are not counted as persons, but their saving is credited to persons.

Personal income is the sum of wage and salary disbursements, other labor income, proprietors' income with inventory valuation and capital consumption adjustments, rental income of persons with capital consumption adjustment, personal dividend income, personal interest income, and transfer payments to persons, less personal contributions for social insurance.

Personal income differs from national income in that it includes transfer payments and interest received by persons, regardless of source, while it excludes both employee and employer contributions for social insurance, business interest paid (other than to persons), and undistributed corporate profits.

WAGE AND SALARY DISBURSEMENTS consists of the monetary remuneration of employees, including the compensation of corporate officers; commissions, tips, and bonuses; voluntary employee contributions to certain deferred compensation plans such as 401(k) plans; and receipts in kind that represent income. As explained in the notes to pages 26–35, wage and salary *disbursements* are the appropriate concept for personal income whereas wage and salary *accruals* are used in computing national income.

COMMODITY-PRODUCING INDUSTRIES consists of the following Standard Industrial Classification (SIC) divisions: Agriculture, forestry, and fishing; mining; construction; and manufacturing. DISTRIBUTIVE INDUSTRIES consists of the following SIC divisions: Transportation (excluding the U.S. Postal Service); communications; electric, gas, and sanitary services; wholesale trade; and retail trade. SERVICE INDUSTRIES consists of the rest-of-the-world sector and the following SIC divisions: Finance, insurance, and real estate; and services. GOVERNMENT consists of federal, state, and local general government and government enterprises.

OTHER LABOR INCOME consists of employer payments to private pension and profit-sharing plans, private group health and life insurance plans, privately administered workers' compensation plans, and supplemental unemployment benefit plans; corporate directors' fees; and several minor categories of employee compensation, including judicial fees to jurors and witnesses, compensation of prison inmates, and marriage fees to justices of the peace.

PROPRIETORS' INCOME WITH INVENTORY VALUATION AND CAPITAL CONSUMPTION ADJUSTMENTS is the current-production income (including income-in-kind) of sole proprietors and partnerships and of tax-exempt cooperatives. The imputed net rental income of owner-occupants of farm dwellings is included. Dividends and monetary interest received by proprietors of nonfinancial business and rental incomes received by persons not primarily engaged in the real estate business are excluded; these incomes are included in dividends, net interest, and rental income of persons. The two valuation adjustments are designed to obtain income measures in which inventory withdrawals are valued at replacement, rather than historical, cost and charges for depreciation are on a consistent accounting basis and are valued at replacement cost.

RENTAL INCOME OF PERSONS with capital consumption adjustment is the net current-production income of persons from the rental of real property, except income of persons primarily engaged in the real estate business; the imputed net rental income of owner-occupants of nonfarm dwellings; and the royalties received by persons from patents, copyrights, and rights to natural resources. The capital consumption adjustment is described in the preceding paragraph.

PERSONAL DIVIDEND INCOME is the dividend income of persons from all sources, excluding capital gains distributions (See "Revisions" above). It equals net dividends paid by corporations less dividends received by government. Dividends received by government consists of dividends received by state and local general government, primarily by their retirement systems.

PERSONAL INTEREST INCOME is the interest income (monetary and imputed) of persons from all sources.

TRANSFER PAYMENTS TO PERSONS is income payments to persons for which no current services are performed. It consists of business transfer payments to persons and government transfer payments. Government transfer payments consists of benefits from the following social insurance funds: Old-age, survivors, and disability insurance (social security); hospital insurance; supplementary medical insurance; unemployment insurance; government employee retirement; railroad retirement; pension benefit guaranty; veterans' life insurance; workers' compensation; military medical insurance; and temporary disability insurance. Government transfer payments also includes benefits from certain other programs, including the value of benefits received in-kind as well as cash transfers. Among the programs included are veterans' benefits, in addition to veterans' life insurance; food stamps; black lung; supplemental security income; public assistance (including Medicaid); and educational assistance. Government payments to nonprofit institutions, other than for work under research and development contracts, also are included.

PERSONAL CONTRIBUTIONS FOR SOCIAL INSURANCE, which is subtracted to arrive at personal income, includes payments by employees, self-employed, and other individuals who participate in the following programs: Old-age, survivors, and disability insurance (social security); hospital insurance; supplementary medical insurance; unemployment insurance; government employee retirement; railroad retirement; veterans' life insurance; and temporary disability insurance.

PERSONAL TAX AND NONTAX PAYMENTS is tax payments (net of refunds) by persons residing in the United States that are not chargeable to business expense and certain other personal payments to government agencies (except government enterprises) that are treated like taxes. Personal taxes includes taxes on income, including realized net capital gains; on transfers of estates and gifts; and on personal property. Nontaxes includes donations and fees, fines, and forfeitures. Personal contributions for social insurance is not included.

DISPOSABLE PERSONAL INCOME is personal income less personal tax and nontax payments. It is the income available to persons for spending or saving. Disposable personal income in chained (1992) dollars represents the inflation-adjusted value of disposable personal income.

PERSONAL OUTLAYS is the sum of personal consumption expenditures, interest paid by persons, and personal transfer payments to the rest of the world (net). The last item is personal remittances in cash and in kind to the rest of the world less such remittances from the rest of the world.

PERSONAL SAVING is derived by subtracting personal outlays and personal tax and nontax payments from personal income. It is the current saving of individuals (including proprietors), nonprofit institutions that primarily serve individuals, life insurance carriers, private noninsured welfare funds, and private trust funds. Conceptually, personal saving may also be viewed as the sum of the net acquisition of financial assets and the change in physical assets less the sum of net borrowing and consumption of fixed capital. In either case, it is defined to exclude capital gains.

PERSONAL CONSUMPTION EXPENDITURES is goods and services purchased by persons residing in the United States. Persons are defined as individuals and nonprofit institutions that primarily serve individuals. Most of personal consumption expenditures (PCE) consists of purchases of new goods and services by individuals from business. In addition, PCE includes purchases of new goods and services by nonprofit institutions, net purchases of used goods by individuals and nonprofit institutions, and purchases abroad of goods and services by U.S. residents traveling or working in foreign countries. PCE also includes purchases for certain services provided by the government—such as water and sewer services and tuition payments for higher education. Finally, PCE includes imputed purchases that keep PCE invariant to changes in the way that certain activities are carried out. For example, to take account of the value of the services provided by owner-occupied housing, PCE includes an imputation equal to the estimated rent homeowners would pay if they rented their houses from themselves. (Actual purchases of residential structures by individuals are classified as gross private domestic investment.)

In general, DURABLE GOODS are commodities that can be stored or inventoried and that have an average life of at least 3 years. NONDURABLE GOODS are all other commodities that can be stored or inventoried.

DATA AVAILABILITY

Data are released monthly in a BEA press release, normally the first business day following the monthly release of the latest national income and product account (NIPA) estimates. Data are subsequently published each month in the *Survey of Current Business*. Annual and quarterly historical data incorporating revisions through September 7, 1999 are published in the August 1999 *Survey of Current Business*. Current data are available on the BEA internet site (http://www.bea.doc.gov), and full historical data may be purchased on diskette from BEA or obtained from the STAT-USA subscription internet site (http://www.stat-usa.gov).

REFERENCES

A discussion of monthly estimates of personal income and its disposition appears in the November 1979 *Survey of Current Business*. A more detailed description of concepts, sources, and methods used in estimating personal consumption expenditures appears in *Personal Consumption Expenditures* (NIPA Methodology Paper No. 6, 1990), available on the BEA internet site from the National Technical Information Service (NTIS Accession No. PB 90-254244). Additional and more recent information can be found in the articles listed in the notes for pages 26–34.

PAGES 60–73 AND 336–339
INDUSTRIAL PRODUCTION AND CAPACITY UTILIZATION

Source: Board of Governors of the Federal Reserve System.

THE INDUSTRIAL PRODUCTION INDEX measures changes in the physical volume or quantity of output of manufacturing, mining, and electric and gas utilities. *Capacity utilization* is calculated by dividing a seasonally adjusted industrial production index for an industry or group of industries by a related index of productive capacity.

Around the 15th day of each month, the Federal Reserve issues estimates of industrial production and capacity utilization for the previous month. The production estimates are in the form of index numbers (currently 1992=100) reflecting the monthly levels of total output of the nation's factories, mines, and gas and electric utilities. Capacity estimates are expressed as index numbers, 1992 output=100, and capacity utilization represents the production index as a percent of the capacity index. Monthly estimates are subject to revision in each of the three subsequent months.

DEFINITIONS AND NOTES ON THE DATA

The index of industrial production measures a large portion of the goods output of the national economy on a monthly basis. That portion, together with construction, accounts for the bulk of the variation in output over the course of the business cycle. The index, with its substantial industrial detail, also is helpful in illuminating structural developments in the economy.

The total industrial production index and indexes for its major components are constructed from individual industry series (267 series for data from 1992 forward) based on the 1987 Standard Industrial Classification (SIC). The individual series are grouped in two ways: market groups and industry groups.

MARKET GROUPS. For analyzing market trends and product flows, the individual series are grouped into final products, intermediate products, and materials. Final products are assumed to be purchased by consumers, businesses, or government for final use. Intermediate products are expected to become inputs in nonindustrial sectors, such as construction, agriculture, and services. Materials are industrial output requiring further processing within the industrial sector. Total products comprise final and intermediate products, and final products are divided into consumer goods and equipment.

INDUSTRY GROUPS typically are groupings by 2-digit SIC and major aggregates of these industries—for example, durable and nondurable manufacturing, mining, and utilities. Indexes are also calculated for primary processing and advanced processing. PRIMARY PROCESSING manufacturing includes textile mill products, paper and products, industrial chemicals, synthetic materials and fertilizers, petroleum products, rubber and plastic products, lumber and products, primary metals, fabricated metals, and stone, clay, and glass products. ADVANCED PROCESSING manufacturing includes foods, tobacco products, apparel products, printing and publishing, chemical products and other agricultural chemicals, leather and products, furniture and fixtures, industrial machinery and equipment, electrical machinery, transportation equipment, instruments, and miscellaneous manufactures.

The index of industrial production is constructed with data from a variety of sources. Current monthly estimates of production in some industries are based on measures of physical output. For industries in which direct measurement is not possible, output is inferred from production-worker hours or the use of electric power, adjusted for trends in output relative to input derived from annual and benchmark revisions. In annual and benchmark revisions, the individual indexes are revised using data from the quinquennial Censuses of Manufactures and Mineral Industries and the Annual Survey of Manufactures, prepared by the Bureau of the Census; the Minerals Yearbook, prepared by the Department of the Interior; publications of the Department of Energy, and other sources.

The weights used in computing the indexes are based on value added—the difference between the value of production and the cost of materials and supplies consumed. Important changes in weighting methods were introduced during 1997 (See *Revisions* below).

To separate seasonal movements from cyclical patterns and underlying trends, components of the index are adjusted for two kinds of short-time recurring fluctuations, differences in the number of working days from month to month and seasonal variation. Individual series are seasonally adjusted by the X-11 ARIMA method.

The index does not cover production on farms, in the construction industry, in transportation, or in various trade and service industries. A number of groups and subgroups include data for individual series not published separately.

CAPACITY UTILIZATION is calculated for the manufacturing, mining, and electric and gas utilities industries. Output is measured by seasonally-adjusted indexes of industrial production. The capacity indexes attempt to capture the concept of sustainable practical capacity, which is defined as the greatest level of output that a plant can maintain within the framework of a realistic work schedule, taking account of normal downtime, and assuming sufficient availability of inputs to operate the machinery and equipment in place. The 76 individual capacity indexes are based on a variety of data, including capacity data measured in physical units compiled by trade associations, Census Bureau surveys of utilization rates and investment, and estimates of growth of the capital stock.

REVISIONS

Revisions to data for recent years normally occur annually, taking into account additional source data that have become available. Annual revisions introduced in December 1998 affected data from 1992 forward.

Comprehensive revisions introduced in 1997 moved the reference year from 1987 to 1992=100 and introduced new aggregation methods beginning with the data for 1977. Under the new aggregation methods, the value-added weights for each industry are updated annually, rather than quinquennially. The more frequent updating takes more accurate account of changes in the relative valuations of the individual industry series and thus provides a more accurate overall index, eliminating an upward bias.

DATA AVAILABILITY

Data are available monthly in Federal Reserve release G.17. Selected data are subsequently published monthly in the *Federal Reserve Bulletin*. Historical data may be purchased on diskette from Publications Services, Board of Governors of the Federal Reserve System. Current and historical data are available on the Federal Reserve internet site (http://www.bog.frb.fed.us/releases/)

REFERENCES

Descriptions of recent revisions are found in *Federal Reserve Bulletin*: "Industrial Production and Capacity Utilization: 1998 Annual Revision," vol. 85 no. 1 (January 1999) and "Industrial Production and Capacity Utilization: Historical Revision and Recent Developments," vol. 83, no. 2 (February 1997). For information on seasonal adjustment methods, see "A Revision to Industrial Production and Capacity Utilization, 1991-1995," vol. 82 (January 1996). A detailed description of the industrial production index, together with a history of the index, a glossary of terms, and a bibliography is presented in *Industrial Production—1986 Edition*, available from the Publication Services, Board of Governors of the Federal Reserve System.

PAGES 76–82 AND 309–312
GROSS SAVING AND INVESTMENT ACCOUNT

Sources: U.S. Department of Commerce, Bureau of Economic Analysis

REVISIONS

Data in this book reflect revisions to the NIPAs available through September 1999. (See the notes for pages 26–34 for additional information)

For information concerning the October 1999 redefinition of certain types of equipment as investment and reclassification of certain forms of saving, see the article in the front of this book "Current Issues in Economic Measurement".

DEFINITIONS

PERSONAL SAVING is derived by subtracting personal outlays and personal tax and nontax payments from personal income. It is the current saving of individuals (including proprietors), nonprofit institutions that primarily serve individuals, life insurance carriers, private noninsured welfare funds, and private trust funds. Conceptually, personal saving may also be viewed as the sum of the net acquisition of financial assets and the change in physical assets less the sum of net borrowing and consumption of fixed capital. In either case, it is defined to exclude capital gains. UNDISTRIBUTED PROFITS is corporate profits after tax less dividends.

CONSUMPTION OF FIXED CAPITAL is a charge for the using up of private and government fixed capital located in the United States. It is based on studies of prices of used equipment and structures in resale markets. For general government and for nonprofit institutions that primarily serve individuals, it is recorded in government consumption expenditures and in personal consumption expenditures, respectively, as the value of the current services of the fixed capital assets owned and used by these entities. PRIVATE CAPITAL CONSUMPTION ALLOWANCES consists of tax-return-based depreciation charges for corporations and nonfarm proprietorships and of historical-cost depreciation (calculated by BEA using a geometric pattern of price declines) for farm proprietorships, rental income of persons, and nonprofit institutions. The PRIVATE CAPITAL CONSUMPTION ADJUSTMENT is the difference between private capital consumption allowances and private consumption of fixed capital.

GROSS PRIVATE DOMESTIC INVESTMENT consists of private fixed investment and changes in business inventories.

PRIVATE FIXED INVESTMENT consists of both nonresidential and residential fixed investment. It consists of purchases of fixed assets, which are commodities that will be used in a production process for more than one year, including replacements and additions to the capital stock, and it is measured before a deduction for consumption of fixed capital. It covers all investment by private businesses and nonprofit institutions in the United States, regardless of whether the investment is owned by U.S. residents. It does not include purchases of the same types of equipment and structures by government agencies, which are included in government gross investment, or investment by U.S. residents in other countries.

NONRESIDENTIAL FIXED INVESTMENT consists of both structures and producers' durable equipment (PDE).

NONRESIDENTIAL STRUCTURES consists of new construction, brokers' commissions on sales of structures, and net purchases of used structures by private business and by nonprofit institutions from government agencies. New construction also includes hotels and motels and mining exploration, shafts, and wells.

NONRESIDENTIAL PRODUCERS' DURABLE EQUIPMENT (PDE) consists of private business purchases, on capital account, of new machinery, equipment, and vehicles; dealers' margins on sales of used equipment; and net purchases of used equipment from government agencies, persons, and the rest of the world. (It does not, however, include the personal-use portion of equipment purchased for both business and personal use, which is included in PCE.)

RESIDENTIAL PRIVATE FIXED INVESTMENT consists of both structures and residential producers' durable equipment—equipment owned by landlords and rented to tenants. Investment in structures consists of new units, improvements to existing units, mobile homes, brokers' commissions on the sale of residential property, and net purchases of used structures from government agencies.

DATA AVAILABILITY

Current data are included in the monthly release of the latest national income and product account (NIPA) estimates and are subsequently published each month in the *Survey of Current Business*. Full historical data may be purchased from BEA or may be obtained from the STAT-USA subscription internet site (http://www.stat-usa.gov).

REFERENCES

Sources of information about the NIPAs are listed in the notes for pages 26–34.

PAGES 83–86
MANUFACTURING AND TRADE SALES AND INVENTORIES

Sources: U.S. Department of Commerce, Bureau of the Census (current dollar series) and U.S. Department of Commerce, Bureau of Economic Analysis (constant dollar series)

The current dollar data on these pages draw together summary data from the separate series on manufacturers' shipments, inventories, and orders; merchant wholesalers' sales and inventories; and retail sales and inventories included in Part II of this book. See the notes to pages 207–218 and 272–276 for information about these data.

Estimates of real sales, inventories, and inventory-sales ratios are published by the Bureau of Economic Analysis.

Annual values of inventory-sales ratios in this volume are averages of monthly data.

DATA AVAILABILITY

Sales, inventories and inventory-sales ratios for manufacturers, merchant wholesalers, and retailers are published monthly by the Bureau of the Census in a press release entitled "Manufacturing and Trade Inventories and Sales"; recent data are available on the web (www.census.gov/mtis/www/mtis.html). Sales and inventories in constant dollars are published regularly by the Bureau of Economic Analysis in the *Survey of Current Business*; recent data are available on the BEA internet site (http://www.bea.doc.gov) or from the STAT-USA subscription internet site (http://www.stat-usa.gov).

REFERENCES

For information about the 1996 historical revisions to sales and inventories in constant dollars, see "Real Inventories, Sales, and Inventory-Sales Ratios for Manufacturing and Trade, 1977-95," *Survey of Current Business*, May 1996.

PAGE 87
ANNUAL CAPITAL EXPENDITURE

Source: U.S. Department of Commerce, Bureau of the Census

These data are from the Census Bureau's Annual Capital Expenditures Survey (ACES). The survey provides detailed information on capital investment in new and used structures and equipment by nonfarm businesses. The program was initiated with a small test survey in 1992 and currently provides data for the latest two years (1996 and 1997).

In the 1997 survey, data were collected from a sample of approximately 32,000 companies with employees and 14,000 non-employer businesses. For companies with employees, the data are reported for 97 separate industry categories based on 2-digit and selected 3-digit Standard Industrial Classification (SIC) codes. Total capital expenditures, with no industry detail, are shown for the nonemployer businesses.

CAPITAL EXPENDITURES include all capitalized costs during the year for both new and used structures and equipment chargeable to fixed asset accounts for which depreciation or amortization accounts are ordinarily maintained. For projects lasting longer than one year, this definition includes gross additions to construction-in-progress accounts, even if the asset was not in use and not yet depreciated. For capital leases, the company using the asset (lessee) is asked to include the cost or present value of the leased assets in the year in which the lease was entered. Also included in capital expenditures are capitalized leasehold improvements and capitalized interest charges on loans used to finance capital projects.

DATA AVAILABILITY

The "Annual Capital Expenditure Survey: 1997" was published by the Census Bureau in May 1999 and contains data for 1996 and 1997.

PAGES 90-95 AND 356–359
CONSUMER PRICE INDEXES

Source: U.S. Department of Labor, Bureau of Labor Statistics (BLS)

The Consumer Price Index (CPI) is a statistical measure of the average change in the cost to consumers of a fixed market basket of goods and services purchased by urban consumers. The reference base for most indexes currently is 1982-84=100. Except as noted, the indexes in this volume are for all urban consumers (CPI-U); recent data represent the 1993-95 buying habits of about 87 percent of the noninstitutional population of the United States at that time. An alternative index, the CPI-W, represents the buying habits only of urban wage earners and clerical workers. Major revisions to the CPI were incorporated into data beginning with January 1998, and are reflected in the tables on pages 90–95, which contain data through 1998. Further CPI revisions adopted in 1999 or planned for the future are discussed in an article in the front of this book.

NOTES ON THE DATA

The CPI is based on prices of food, clothing, shelter, fuel, utilities, transportation, medical care, and other goods and services that people buy for day-to-day living. The quantity and quality of these items are kept essentially constant between major revisions so that only price changes will be measured. All taxes directly associated with the purchase and use of items are included in the index.

As of 1999, data collected from more than 23,000 retail establishments and about 5,800 housing units in 87 urban areas across the country are used to develop the U.S. city average.

Periodic major revisions of the indexes update the content and weights of the market basket of goods and services priced for the CPI; update the statistical sample of urban areas, outlets, and unique items used in calculating the CPI; and improve the statistical methods used. In addition, retail outlets and items are resampled on a rotating 5-year basis; adjustments for changing quality are made at times of major product changes, such as the annual auto model changeover; and other methodological changes are introduced from time to time. Data in this book incorporate the major revision that became effective with the data for January 1998.

The most basic aspect of the 1998 revision is the incorporation of a new set of expenditure weights. Consumer Expenditure Survey data from 1993–95 are used to calculate a new expenditure weight for each item strata category in every CPI index area. These new market baskets took effect with the index for January 1998. At the same time, many of the samples underlying the CPI were replaced. These samples include geographic areas, items selected for pricing, and outlets in which items are priced.

CPI weights for 1964–77 were derived from reported expenditures of a sample of wage-earner and clerical-worker families and individuals in 1960–61 and adjusted for price changes between the survey dates and 1963. Weights for 1978–86 were derived from a consumer expenditure survey (CES) undertaken over the 1972–74 period and adjusted for price change between the survey dates and December 1977. For 1987–1997, the spending patterns reflected in the CPI were derived from a CES undertaken over the 1982–84 period. The reported expenditures were adjusted for price change between the survey dates and December 1986.

The CES is composed of two separate surveys: an interview survey and a diary survey, both conducted by the Bureau of the Census for BLS. Each expenditure reported in the two surveys is coded to detailed categories, which are then combined in expenditure classes and ultimately into major expenditure groups. Data as of 1998 are grouped into eight such groups: (1) food and beverages, (2) housing, (3) apparel, (4) transportation, (5) medical care, (6) recreation, (7) education and communication, and (8) other goods and services. Education and communication and recreation are new groups, and several subcategories have been rearranged as well.

Seasonally adjusted national CPI indexes are published for selected series for which there is a significant seasonal pattern of price change. The factors currently in use were derived by the X-12-ARIMA seasonal adjustment method. Seasonally adjusted indexes and seasonal factors for the preceding 5 years are updated annually based on data through the previous December. Detailed descriptions of BLS seasonal adjustment procedures are available upon request from the Bureau of Labor Statistics.

DEFINITIONS

As noted, definitions were modified beginning with the data for January 1998. The definitions below are the current definitions.

The FOOD AND BEVERAGE INDEX includes both food at home and food away from home (restaurant meals and other food bought and eaten away from home).

The HOUSING INDEX measures changes in rental costs and

in expenses connected with the acquisition and operation of a home. The CPI-U, beginning with data for January 1983, and the CPI-W, beginning with data for January 1985, reflect a change in the methodology used to compute the homeownership component. A rental equivalence measure replaced the asset-price approach. The central purpose of the change was to separate shelter costs from the investment component of home-ownership so that the index would reflect only the cost of shelter services provided by owner-occupied homes. In addition to these measures of the cost of shelter, the housing category includes insurance, fuel, utilities, and household furnishings and operations.

The APPAREL INDEX includes the purchase of apparel and footwear.

The PRIVATE TRANSPORTATION INDEX includes prices paid by urban consumers on such items as new and used automobiles and other vehicles, gasoline, motor oil, tires, repairs and maintenance, insurance, registration fees, driver's licenses, parking fees, etc. Auto finance charges are no longer included in the CPI. City bus, streetcar, subway, taxicab, intercity bus, airplane, and railroad coach fares are some of the components of the PUBLIC TRANSPORTATION INDEX.

The MEDICAL CARE INDEX includes prices for professional medical services; hospital and related services; prescription and nonprescription drugs; and other medical care commodities. The portion of health insurance premiums used to cover the costs of these medical goods and services is distributed among the items; the portion of health insurance costs attributable to administrative expenses and profits of insurance providers constitutes a separate health insurance item. Effective with the January 1997 data, the method of calculating the hospital cost component was changed from the pricing of individual commodities and services to a more comprehensive cost-of-treatment approach.

RECREATION includes components formerly in housing, apparel, entertainment, and "other".

EDUCATION AND COMMUNICATION is a new group including components formerly in housing and "other", such as telephone services and computers.

OTHER GOODS AND SERVICES now includes tobacco, personal care, and miscellaneous.

The CPI-U-X1 is a special version of the CPI that is used by many researchers to provide a historically consistent series. As explained in the previous paragraph, the official CPI-U treated homeownership on an asset price basis until January 1983 and then changed to a rental equivalence method. The CPI-U-X1 incorporates a rental equivalence approach to homeowners' costs for the years 1967–82 as well. It is rebased to the December 1982 value of the CPI-U (1982–84=100); thus it is identi-

cal with CPI-U data for December 1982 and all subsequent periods.

The CPI-U-RS is a research series CPI that retroactively incorporates all changes implemented as of 1998, including rental equivalence method, quality adjustments for used cars and housing, the new Consumer Expenditure Survey-based market basket, and others mentioned in the prices article in the front of the book. These data go back to 1977, incorporating changes made subsequently up to 1998.

DATA AVAILABILITY

The indexes are initially issued in a press release about two weeks following the month to which the data pertain. The *CPI Detailed Report* is issued about a month after the press release. Selected CPI data are published monthly in the *Monthly Labor Review*, which also contains periodic articles analyzing price developments. Complete historical data are available on the BLS internet site (http://stats.bls.gov).

REFERENCES

Two special issues of the *Monthly Labor Review* cover the CPI in detail. The December 1996 issue describes the subsequently-implemented 1997 and 1998 revisions in a series of articles, and the December 1993 issue on "The Anatomy on Price Change" includes: "The Consumer Price Index: Underlying Concepts and Caveats"; "Basic Components of the CPI: Estimation of Price Changes"; "The Commodity Substitution Effect in CPI Data, 1982–91"; and "Quality Adjustment of Price Indexes." A new formula for calculating basic components is described in "Incorporating a geometric mean formula into the CPI", *Monthly Labor Review*, October 1998.

For a detailed discussion of the treatment of homeownership, see "Changing the Homeownership Component of the Consumer Price Index to Rental Equivalence," *CPI Detailed Report* (January 1983).

BLS Handbook of Methods Bulletin 2490 (April 1997), Chapter 17 "Consumer Price Indexes" describes the methodology used in computing the CPI.

General discussions of the nature and quality of the CPI include: "Using Survey Data to Assess Bias in the Consumer Price Index," *Monthly Labor Review* (April 1998); Joel Popkin "Improving the CPI: The Record and Suggested Next Steps," *Business Economics*, Vol. XXXII, No. 3 (July 1997), pages 42–47; *Measurement Issues in the Consumer Price Index*, Bureau of Labor Statistics, U.S. Department of Labor, June 1997; *Toward a More Accurate Measure of the Cost of Living*, Final Report to the Senate Finance Committee from the Advisory Commission to Study the Consumer Price Index, December 4, 1996 (the "Boskin Commission" report); and *Government Price Statistics*, U.S. Congress Joint Economic Committee, 87th

Congress, 1st Session, January 24, 1961 (the "Stigler Committee" report).

PAGES 96–100 AND 360–363
PRODUCER PRICE INDEXES

Source: U.S. Department of Labor, Bureau of Labor Statistics

Producer Price Indexes (PPI) measure average changes in prices received by domestic producers of commodities by stage of processing, by industry, and by product. Most of the indexes currently are published on a base of 1982=100, but there are a number of exceptions, identified in this book in the column headings for the individual series. Pages 96–100 present data by stage of processing. The industry tables in Part II of this book present a number of additional PPI series by commodity, industry, or product.

DEFINITIONS

The STAGE-OF-PROCESSING PPI indexes organize products by class of buyer and degree of fabrication. These have been the featured measures since 1978. The three major indexes are (1) *finished goods*, commodities that will not undergo further processing and are ready for sale to the ultimate user (e.g., automobiles, meats, apparel, machine tools); (2) *intermediate materials, supplies, and components*, commodities that have been processed but require further processing before they become finished goods (e.g., steel mill products, cotton yarns, lumber, flour), as well as physically complete goods that are purchased by business firms as inputs for their operations (e.g., diesel fuel and paper boxes); and (3) *crude materials* for further processing, products entering the market for the first time which have not been manufactured or fabricated but which will be processed before becoming finished goods (e.g., scrap metals, crude petroleum, raw cotton, livestock).

The traditional COMMODITY indexes organize products by similarity of end use or material composition. Each individual product is grouped under one of 15 major commodity groups, two of which comprise the Farm Products and Processed Foods and Feeds Index and the other 13 of which compose the Industrial Commodities Index; the All Commodities Index is composed of all 15 major commodity groups.

The INDUSTRY AND PRODUCT indexes organize data in accordance with the Standard Industrial Classification (SIC) and the product code extension of the SIC developed by the Bureau of the Census.

NOTES ON THE DATA

The sample used for calculating the PPI contained (as of mid-1999) about 25,000 establishments providing close to 100,000 price quotations per month, selected to represent the movement of prices of all commodities produced in the manufacturing; agriculture, forestry, and fishing; mining; and gas and electricity and public utility sectors.

To the extent possible, prices used in calculating the PPI represent prices received by domestic producers in the first important commercial transaction for each commodity. These indexes attempt to measure only price changes; i.e., price changes not influenced by changes in quality, quantity, terms of sale, or level of distribution. Most quotations are the selling prices of selected manufacturers or other producers, although a few prices are those quoted on organized exchanges or markets. Transaction prices are sought instead of list or book prices.

Price data are generally collected monthly, primarily by mail questionnaire. Most prices are obtained directly from producing companies on a voluntary and confidential basis. Prices generally are reported for the Tuesday of the week containing the 13th day of the month.

The name "Producer Price Index" became effective with the release of March 1978 data, replacing the term "Wholesale Price Index." The change was made to reflect the coverage of the data more accurately. At the same time, there was a shift in analytical emphasis from the All Commodities Index and other traditional commodity grouping indexes to the Finished Goods Index and other stage-of-processing indexes.

For analysis of general price trends, stage-of-processing indexes are more useful than commodity grouping indexes. Commodity grouping indexes sometimes produce exaggerated or misleading signals of price changes by reflecting the same price movement through various stages of processing.

The BLS revises the Producer Price Index weighting structure periodically when data from economic censuses become available. Beginning with data for January 1996, the weights used to construct the PPI reflect 1992 shipment values as measured by the 1992 Economic Censuses and other sources. Data for 1992 through 1995 reflect 1987 shipment values; 1987 through 1991 reflect 1982 values; 1976 through 1986 reflect 1972 values; and 1967 through 1975 reflect 1963 values.

BLS has been working for a number of years on a comprehensive overhaul of the theory, methods, and procedures use to construct the PPI. One aspect of this overhaul was the already mentioned shift in emphasis beginning in 1978 to the stage-of-processing measures. Other changes that have been phased in since 1978 include the replacement of judgment sampling with probability sampling techniques; expansion to systematic coverage of the net output of virtually all industries in the mining and manufacturing sectors; introduction of measures for selected service industries; a shift from a commodity to an industry orientation; the exclusion of imports from, and the inclusion of exports in, the survey universe. These changes have resulted in a system of indexes that is easier to use in conjunction with data on wages, productivity, employment, and other series that are organized in terms of the SIC and the Bureau of the Census product class designations.

Seasonal factors for the PPI are revised annually to take into account the most recent 12 months of data. Seasonally adjusted data for the previous 5 years are subject to these annual revisions.

DATA AVAILABILITY

The indexes are initially issued in a press release about two weeks following the month to which the data pertain and subsequently are published in greater detail in the monthly BLS publication, *PPI Detailed Report*. Selected PPI data also are published monthly in the *Monthly Labor Review,* which also contains periodic articles analyzing price developments. Historical data tables providing annual and monthly data for all available periods for all published series are available on request from BLS. Complete historical data are available on the BLS internet site (http://stats.bls.gov).

REFERENCES

The following *Monthly Labor Review* articles and technical notes contain background information: "Comparing PPI Energy Indexes to Alternative Data Sources" (December 1998); "Are Producer Prices Good Proxies for Export Prices" (October 1997); "Effect of 1992 Weights on Producer Price Indexes" (July 1996); "Hospital Price Inflation: What Does the PPI Tell Us?" (July 1996); "Seasonal Adjustment of Producer Price Index for Passenger Cars" (June 1996); "Effect of Updated Weights on Producer Price Indexes" (March 1993); "Milestones in the Producer Price Index Methodology and Presentation" (August 1989); "New Stage of Process Price System Developed for the Producer Price Index" (April 1988); "Improving the Measurement of Producer Price Changes" (April 1977).
BLS Handbook of Methods Bulletin 2490 (April 1997), Chapter 14, "Producer Prices" describes the methodology used in computing the PPI.

PAGE 100
PURCHASING POWER OF THE DOLLAR

Source: U.S. Department of Labor, Bureau of Labor Statistics

The purchasing power of the dollar measures changes in the quantity of goods and services a dollar will buy at a particular date compared with a selected base date. It must be defined in terms of: (1) The specific commodities and services that are to be purchased with the dollar; (2) the market level (producer, retail, etc.) at which they are purchased; and (3) the dates for which the comparison is to be made. Thus, the purchasing power of the dollar for a selected period, compared with another period, may be measured in terms of a single commodity or a large group of commodities; for example, all goods and services purchased by consumers at retail, or all finished commodities sold in primary markets.

The BLS publishes two basic price indexes that may be used to calculate the purchasing power of the dollar in the United States: (1) The Producer Price Index (PPI) for Finished Goods, which relates to prices received by the producers of finished commodities at the primary market level, and (2) the Consumer Price Index (CPI-W, through 1977; CPI-U, beginning 1978), which measures average changes in retail prices of goods and services. These indexes are described in the sections of the notes pertaining to the Producer Price Index and the Consumer Price Index, respectively.

The purchasing power of the dollar is computed by dividing the price index number for the base period by the price index number for the date to be compared, and expressing the result in dollars and cents. The base period is the period in which the price index equals 100 (and the purchasing power is $1.00). In this book, 1982 through 1984 is used as the base period for the two indexes shown so that they can be readily compared.

PAGE 101
PRICES RECEIVED AND PAID BY FARMERS

Source: U.S. Department of Agriculture, National Agricultural Statistics Service (NASS)

The data on prices received and paid by farmers represent prices farmers received for commodities sold, as well as prices paid for production input goods and services. Prices are weighted and aggregated into price indexes. These indexes provide measures of relative price changes for agricultural outputs and inputs. These price measures are based on voluntary reports from agribusiness firms, merchants, dealers, and farmers. Data are collected at regular intervals using mailed inquiries, telephone, and personal enumeration. In January 1995, these data were converted to a reference base of 1990–1992=100. Prices-paid indexes were available only quarterly for several years but have been published monthly beginning with January 1996, with monthly indexes for 1995 constructed for historical comparison.

DEFINITIONS

PRICES RECEIVED by farmers represent sales from producers to first buyers. They include all grades and qualities. The average commodity price from the survey multiplied by the total quantity marketed theoretically should give the total cash receipts for the commodity.

PRICES PAID by farmers represent the average costs of inputs purchased by farmers and ranchers to produce agricultural commodities. Conceptually, the average price when multiplied by quantity purchased should equal total producer expenditures for the item.

RATIO OF PRICES RECEIVED TO PRICES PAID is the ratio of the index of prices received for all farm products to the index of prices paid for all commodities and services. (For some years, prices paid are available only for the first month of each quarter. Each month's ratio of prices received to prices paid is based on the latest data available.)

NOTES ON THE DATA

In 1995, NASS reweighted and reconstructed the prices paid and received indexes. The indexes are now based on five-year moving average weights compared with fixed weights previously. The changes in the construction of the indexes simplified updating component items and reference periods while maintaining appropriate weights. The overall changes to the weighting and construction of the indexes did not have a significant effect on the index levels and therefore had little effect on the level of parity prices. Indexes are now published on a 1990–92=100 base. As required by law, the parity ratio (ratio of prices received to prices paid) also continues to be published on a base of 1910–1914=100.

PRICES PAID. Since 1995, the Prices Paid Survey of items purchased by farm establishments has been conducted annually in April. Surveys are conducted for feed, seed, fertilizer, agricultural chemicals, fuel, and farm machinery. About 135 selected items are priced to represent groups of similar items purchased which make up the major production expenditure categories. The number of input items consumed on farms is so extensive that it is not feasible to collect price data for all of the inputs. Items on the questionnaire are described in the simplest way consistent with definite identification. Firms are requested to report the prices for the most commonly sold item that meets the general specification on the questionnaire.

Reported data are summarized to regional estimates and then weighted to U.S. prices. Weights are based on available consumption or expenditure information. Average prices, including state and local taxes, are used in computing the indexes and are published in *Agricultural Prices* for the same month as the survey. Regional prices are published for feed, fuel, and fertilizer. U.S. prices are published for the remaining items surveyed.

Bureau of Labor Statistics (BLS) indexes are used to measure price change for the months when no survey data are collected. The BLS indexes measure price changes for farm supplies and repairs, autos and trucks, building materials, and marketing containers. Before 1995, quarterly prices-paid surveys were conducted by NASS. Quarterly feeder livestock surveys still are conducted.

REVISIONS: PRICES PAID. Any revisions are published in the monthly and in annual issues of "Agricultural Prices". The basis for revision must be supported by additional data that directly affect the level of the estimate. More revisions are likely in April when separate prices paid surveys are conducted.

SURVEY PROCEDURES: PRICES RECEIVED: Primary sales data used to determine grain prices are obtained from probability samples of mills and elevators. These procedures ensure that virtually all grain moving into commercial channels has a chance of being included in the survey. Livestock prices are obtained from packers, stockyards, auctions, dealers, and market check data. Inter-farm sales of grain and livestock are not included since they represent very small percentages of the total marketings. Grain marketed for seed is also excluded. Fruit and vegetable prices are obtained from sample surveys and market check data.

SUMMARY AND ESTIMATION PROCEDURES: PRICES RECEIVED: Survey quantities sold are expanded by strata to state levels and used to weight average strata prices to a state average. State prices are then weighted to a U.S. price.

REVISIONS: PRICES RECEIVED: For most items, the current month's price represents a 3–5 day period around the mid-month. Previous month's prices represent actual dollars received for quantities sold during the entire month. Revisions are published in monthly issues of *Agricultural Prices* and in the annual summary published in July. A schedule of monthly revisions is published in the December issue of *Agricultural Prices* and in the July annual summary.

RELIABILITY: PRICES RECEIVED: U.S. price estimates generally have a sampling error of less than one-half percent for the major commodities such as corn, wheat, soybeans, cotton, and rice.

DATA AVAILABILITY

Prices paid and received by farmers are available each month in a press release issued around the end of the month. Data are subsequently published monthly in *Agricultural Prices*. Data also are available on the NASS internet site (http://www.usda.gov/nass/).

REFERENCE

"Revised Prices Received and Paid Indexes, United States, 1975–93 for Base Periods 1910–14=100 and 1990–92=100," Statistical Bulletin number 917 (National Agricultural Statistics Service, February 1995).

PAGES 104–105
EMPLOYMENT COST INDEXES

Source: U.S. Department of Labor, Bureau of Labor Statistics (BLS)

The Employment Cost Index (ECI) is a quarterly measure of the change in the cost of labor, free from the influence of employment shifts among occupations and industries. It uses a fixed market basket of labor, similar in concept to the Consumer Price Index's fixed market basket of goods and services, to measure changes over time in employer costs of employing labor. Data are quarterly in all cases; in most cases, index levels have a base period of June 1989=100.

DEFINITIONS

TOTAL COMPENSATION includes wages, salaries, and the employer's costs for employee benefits. Excluded from wages and salaries and employee benefits are such items as payment-in-kind, free room and board, and tips.

WAGES AND SALARIES consist of earnings before payroll deductions, including production bonuses, incentive earnings, commissions, and cost-of-living adjustments.

BENEFITS include the cost to employers for paid leave, supplemental pay (including nonproduction bonuses), insurance, retirement and savings plans, and legally required benefits (such as Social Security, workers' compensation, and unemployment insurance).

PRIVATE INDUSTRY WORKERS are workers in private nonfarm industry excluding proprietors, the self-employed, and household workers.

CIVILIAN WORKERS includes private nonfarm industry workers and workers in state and local government. Federal workers are not included.

NOTES ON THE DATA

Employee benefit costs are calculated as cents per hour worked for benefits ranging from employer payments for Social Security to paid time off for holidays.

The data are collected from a probability sample of occupational observations in sample establishments in private industry and state and local governments. The sample establishments are classified in industry categories based on the 1987 Standard Industrial Classification (SIC). Within an establishment, specific job categories are selected to represent broader occupational definitions. On average, each reporting unit provides wage and compensation information on five well-specified occupations. Data are collected each quarter for the pay period including the 12th day of March, June, September, and December.

Beginning with March 1995, ECI measures are based on 1990 fixed employment counts. From June 1986 through December 1994, ECI measures were based on 1980 fixed employment counts, while prior to June 1986, they were base on 1970 employment counts. Use of fixed weights ensures that changes in the indexes reflect only changes in compensation, not employment shifts among industries or occupations with different levels of wages and compensation.

DATA AVAILABILITY

Data for wages and salaries for the private nonfarm economy are available beginning with data for 1975; data for compensation begin with 1980. The series for state and local government and the civilian nonfarm economy begin with 1981. Historical data are published in the March issue of the BLS periodical *Compensation and Working Conditions.* Complete historical data are available on the BLS internet site (http://stats.bls.gov).

Wage and salary change and compensation cost change data also are available from BLS by major occupational and industry groups, as well as by region and bargaining status. Wage and salary change information is available from 1975 to the present for most of these series. Compensation cost change data are available from 1980 to the present for most series. For 10 occupational and industry series, benefit cost change data are available from the early 1980s to the present. For state and local governments and the civilian economy (state and local governments plus private industry), wage and salary change and compensation cost change data are available for major occupational and industry series. The data for all these series are provided from June 1981 to present.

Updates are available about four weeks following the end of the reference quarter. Reference quarters end in March, June, September, and December.

REFERENCES

Chapter 8 "National Compensation Measures" *BLS Handbook of Methods* Bulletin 2490 (April 1997); *Employment Cost Indexes and Levels, 1975–1997*, BLS Bulletin 2504 (1998); and the following *Monthly Labor Review* articles: "Is the ECI Sensitive to the Method of Aggregation" (June 1997); "Employment Cost Index Rebased to June 1989" (April 1990); "Measuring the Precision of the Employment Cost Index" (March 1989); "Employment Cost Index to Replace Hourly Earnings Index" (July 1988).

PAGES 106–107 AND 321–324 PRODUCTIVITY

Source: U.S. Department of Labor, Bureau of Labor Statistics (BLS)

Productivity measures relate real physical output to real input. As such, they encompass a family of measures that includes single-factor input measures, such as output per unit of labor input or output per unit of capital input, as well as measures of multifactor productivity (output per unit of combined labor and capital inputs). The indexes published in this book are indexes of labor productivity expressed in terms of output per hour. Data are provided for four sectors of the economy: Business, nonfarm business, the nonfinancial corporate sector, and manufacturing. All data are presented as indexes, 1992=100.

DEFINITIONS

OUTPUT PER HOUR OF ALL PERSONS (labor productivity) is

the value of goods and services in constant prices produced per hour of labor input.

COMPENSATION PER HOUR is the wages and salaries of employees plus employers' contributions for social insurance and private benefit plans, and the wages, salaries, and supplementary payments for the self-employed—the sum of these divided by hours at work.

REAL COMPENSATION PER HOUR is compensation per hour deflated by the change in the Consumer Price Index for All Urban Consumers.

UNIT LABOR COSTS are the labor costs expended in the production of a unit of output and are derived by dividing compensation by output.

UNIT NONLABOR PAYMENTS include profits, depreciation, interest, and indirect taxes per unit of output. They are computed by subtracting compensation of all persons from current-dollar value of output and dividing by output.

UNIT NONLABOR COSTS contain all the components of unit nonlabor payments except unit profits.

HOURS OF ALL PERSONS are the total hours at work of payroll workers, self-employed persons, and unpaid family workers.

NOTES ON THE DATA

The output for the business sector is equal to constant-dollar gross domestic product less the following: the rental value of owner-occupied dwellings; the output of nonprofit institutions; the output of paid employees of private households; and general government output. The measures are derived from data supplied by the U.S. Department of Commerce, Bureau of Economic Analysis (BEA). For manufacturing, annual estimates of sectoral output are produced by the BLS. Quarterly manufacturing output indexes from the Federal Reserve Board of Governors are adjusted to these annual measures by the BLS.

Compensation and hours data are developed from BLS and BEA data. Data on hours at work are obtained from the annual BLS Hours at Work Survey. Hours at work replaced a former measure based primarily on hours paid in 1989. For paid employees, hours at work differs from hours paid in that it excludes paid vacation and holidays, paid sick leave, and other paid personal or administrative leave. When the hours at work concept was introduced in 1989, the historical data were revised to reflect the change in concept.

Although the labor productivity measures relate output to labor input, they do not measure the contribution of labor or any other specific factor of production. Rather, they reflect the joint effect of many influences, including changes in technology; capital investment; level of output;

utilization of capacity, energy, and materials; the organization of production; managerial skill; and the characteristics and efforts of the work force.

REVISIONS

Data for recent years are revised frequently to take account of revisions in the output and labor input measures that underlie the estimates. Traditionally, all revisions to source data are reflected in the release following the source data revision.

DATA AVAILABILITY

Most of the series begin in 1959. Series are available quarterly and annually. Quarterly measures are based entirely on seasonally adjusted data. For some manufacturing series, only annual averages are available. Updates are performed near the end of the first two months of each quarter, reflecting new data from the preceding quarter. Complete historical data are available on the BLS internet site (http://stats.bls.gov).

BLS also publishes productivity estimates for a number of individual industries. A listing is given in *Productivity Measures for Selected Industries and Government Services*, BLS Bulletin 2440.

REFERENCES

Chapter 10 "Productivity Measures: Business Sector and Major Subsectors" *BLS Handbook of Methods* Bulletin 2490 (April 1997), and the following *Monthly Labor Review* articles: "Possible measurement bias in aggregate productivity growth" (February 1999); "Improvements to the Quarterly Productivity Measures" (October 1995); "Hours of Work: A New Base for BLS Productivity Statistics" (February 1990); and "New Sector Definitions for Productivity Series" (October 1976).

PAGES 108–110
CORPORATE PROFITS AND DIVIDENDS

Source: U.S. Department of Commerce, Bureau of the Census (since 1983); Federal Trade Commission (prior to 1983); and Securities and Exchange Commission (prior to 1972).
The corporate profits and dividend data are taken from the Quarterly Financial Report (QFR) data set. The QFR, which is based on an extensive sample survey, provides estimates of income and retained earnings, balance sheets, and related financial and operating ratios for industry groups, classified according to the SIC.

NOTES ON THE DATA

PURPOSE OF THE QFR: The QFR provides data on business financial conditions for use by government and private sector organizations and individuals. Among its users, the Commerce Department regularly employs QFR data as an important component in determining corporate profits for the national income and product accounts (NIPAs), and the Treasury Department estimates aggregate corporate tax liability through use of QFR data.

The QFR program designs and maintains probability samples of corporate enterprises; collects, analyzes, and summarizes periodic confidential reports from those corporations; estimates national aggregates based upon the individual company reports; and publishes the resulting aggregates.

CLASSIFICATION BY INDUSTRY: The industry combinations used in the QFR are based on the 1987 SIC. A reporting corporation is initially classified into the SIC division accounting for more gross receipts than any other SIC division. To be in scope for the QFR, more gross receipts of the reporting corporation must be accounted for by either (not a combination of) SIC Division B (Mining), Division D (Manufacturing), Division F (Wholesale Trade), or Division G (Retail Trade) than by any other SIC division.

For the most part, after a corporation is assigned to a division, it is further classified by the 2-digit SIC major group accounting for more gross receipts than any other 2-digit group within the division. In certain cases, corporations are further classified into 3-digit SIC groups. QFR data are published for these major groups when precision criteria are satisfied.

Note that these procedures may lead to a conglomerate corporation being assigned to a major group from which only a small proportion of its receipts are obtained. For example, if a corporation obtains 25 percent of its gross receipts from mining activities, 30 percent from manufacturing, 20 percent from wholesale, and 25 percent from retail, it would be classified in the Manufacturing Division. Furthermore, if the 30 percent of manufacturing activity was conducted in two major groups, 20 percent in one and 10 percent in the other, the activities of the corporation as a whole would be classified in the major group accounting for 20 percent of total receipts.

SAMPLE. Nearly all corporations whose operations are within the scope of the QFR and which have total assets greater than $250 million are included in the sample. They are permanent sample members. For smaller corporations (as measured by asset size), a replacement scheme is used which provides that one-eighth of the sample be replaced each quarter. Corporations removed are those that have been in the reporting group the longest (usually eight quarters). Therefore, samples of small corporations for adjacent quarters are seven-eighths identical. The composition of the sample changes each quarter to reflect the effects of corporate births, deaths, acquisitions, divestitures, mergers, consolidations, and the like.

COMPARISONS WITH OTHER STATISTICS: QFR estimates will not necessarily agree with other financial and industrial statistics compilations whether based upon a sample or complete canvass. For example:

• The QFR eliminates multiple counting of interplant and other intra-company transfers included in census establishment statistics.

• The conventional accounting concept of profits is used in the QFR estimates. This differs from the concept of profits employed in the national income and product accounts.

• Corporations' QFR submissions generally embody the accounting conventions adopted for financial reporting purposes. As such, they may differ from those used by corporations for reporting income to the IRS.

• QFR estimates by corporation size are based upon the total assets of consolidated corporate enterprises. They differ from estimates based upon other criteria such as value of shipments or number of employees. They differ also from estimates based upon other reporting units such as establishments, nonconsolidated corporations, or enterprises consolidated differently than in the QFR.

• QFR estimates are based upon a changing sample of audited, unaudited, and estimated reports required to be submitted within 25 days after the end of each quarterly reporting period by corporations. Aggregated for any four consecutive quarters, the QFR estimates will differ from similar aggregations of finalized and audited annual reports.

CHANGES IN THE SERIES. A number of changes in accounting, industry classification, and sample design affect the comparability of the QFR data over time. When the QFR series began in 1947, corporations were instructed to consolidate all of their subsidiaries that were taxable under the U.S. Internal Revenue Code and that were fully consolidated in their latest report to stockholders. The income tax liability rule was expected to eliminate most foreign operations. However, as the number of multinational corporations increased between 1947 and 1973, foreign operations gradually became more significant in the QFR data. New consolidation rules were put into effect in the fourth quarter of 1973 to maximize coverage and minimize the impact of foreign operations on QFR statistics. As a result of these changes, foreign operations are included on an investment basis. The change in consolidation rules and the creation of a line item to reflect equity in earnings from nonconsolidated subsidiaries significantly lessened the comparability of pre- and post-fourth quarter 1973 reports. There was a net decrease in sales and in net income before taxes. The net effect of the rule changes on net income after taxes was small, as, under both rules, foreign activity should be included above the net income after tax line.

Industry classification from 1959 through the third quarter of 1972 was based on the 1957 SIC (the 1967 SIC revision did not affect the level of aggregation used in the QFR); from the fourth quarter of 1972 through 1987, on the 1972 SIC; and from 1988 forward, on the 1987 SIC. Prior to the first quarter of 1974, a corporation was classified as a manufacturer only if 50 percent or more of its gross receipts were derived from manufacturing operations. The new classification rules are more inclusive.

DATA AVAILABILITY

QFR data are scheduled for release approximately 75 days after the end of the first, second, and third calendar quarters and approximately 95 days after the end of the fourth calendar quarter. The QFR publishes information on the most recently closed quarter for manufacturing, mining, and wholesaling and the preceding quarter's data for retailing except in the fourth quarter, when the 95-day publication lag permits synchronized presentation. Current data are available in press releases and on the Bureau of the Census internet site (http://www.census.gov). Historical data may be purchased on diskette from the Bureau of the Census.

The QFR is prepared by the Bureau of the Census. The Federal Trade Commission had been responsible for the program from inception in 1947 until December 1982. That responsibility was shared with the Securities and Exchange Commission until 1971.

PAGES 112–115 AND 340–347
LABOR FORCE, EMPLOYMENT, AND UNEMPLOYMENT

Source: U.S. Department of Labor, Bureau of Labor Statistics (BLS)

The labor force, employment and unemployment data are derived from the Current Population Survey (CPS), a sample survey of households conducted each month by the Bureau of the Census for the Bureau of Labor Statistics. The data pertain to the U.S. civilian noninstitutional population 16 years of age and over.

Due to changes in questionnaire design and survey methodology, data for 1994 and subsequent years are not fully comparable with data for 1993 and earlier years. In addition, data beginning with 1990 incorporate 1990 census-based population controls adjusted for the estimated undercount. See "Notes on the Data" below for additional information.

DEFINITIONS

The CIVILIAN NONINSTITUTIONAL POPULATION comprises all civilians 16 years of age and older who are not inmates of penal or mental institutions, sanitariums, or homes for the aged, infirm, or needy.

CIVILIAN EMPLOYMENT includes those civilians who (1) worked for pay or profit at any time during the week that includes the 12th day of the month (the survey week) or who worked unpaid for 15 hours or more in a family-operated enterprise or (2) were temporarily absent from their regular jobs because of vacation, illness, industrial dispute, bad weather, or similar reasons. Each employed person is counted only once; those who hold more than one job are counted in the job at which they worked the greatest number of hours during the survey week.

UNEMPLOYED PERSONS are all civilians who did not work during the survey week, but were available for work, except for temporary illness, and had made specific efforts to find employment sometime during the prior 4 weeks. Persons who did not look for work because they were on layoff are also counted as unemployed.

The CIVILIAN LABOR FORCE comprises all civilians classified as employed or unemployed.

The civilian LABOR FORCE PARTICIPATION RATE represents the proportion of the civilian noninstitutional population (age 16 and over) that is in the civilian labor force.

The EMPLOYMENT TO POPULATION RATIO represents the proportion of the civilian noninstitutional population (age 16 and over) that is employed.

The LONG-TERM UNEMPLOYED are persons unemployed 15 consecutive weeks or longer. If a person ceases to look for work for 2 weeks or more (or is employed), the continuity of long-term unemployment is broken.

MEDIAN AND AVERAGE WEEKS UNEMPLOYED are summary measures of the length of time that persons classified as unemployed have been looking for work. For persons on layoff, the duration represents the number of full weeks they have been on layoff. Mean number of weeks is the arithmetic average computed by aggregating all the weeks of unemployment experienced by all unemployed persons (during their current spell of unemployment) and dividing by the number of unemployed. Median number of weeks unemployed is the number of weeks of unemployment experienced by the person at the midpoint of the distribution of all unemployed persons, ranked by duration of unemployment.

The CIVILIAN UNEMPLOYMENT RATE is the number of unemployed as a percent of the civilian labor force. The unemployment rates for groups within the civilian population (such as, for example, males 20 years and over) are the number of unemployed in a group as a percent of the labor force in that group. The unemployment rates by industry and occupation refer to experienced wage and salary workers and are based on industry or occupation of the last job held.

Civilians in the noninstitutional population, 16 years of age and over, who are not classified as employed or unemployed are defined as *"not in the labor force."* This group includes those engaged in own-home housework, in school, unable to work because of long-term illness, retired, too old, seasonal workers for whom the survey week fell in an "off" season (not reported as unemployed), persons who became discouraged and gave up the search for work, and the voluntarily idle. Also included are those doing only incidental work (less than 15 hours) in a family business during the survey week.

NOTES ON THE DATA

The CPS data are collected monthly by trained interviewers from sample households selected to represent the U.S. population 16 years of age and older. Sample size was about 60,000 households from mid-1989 to mid-1995 but has since been reduced in two stages to about 50,000 household beginning in January 1996. The data collected are based on the activity or status reported for the calendar week, Sunday through Saturday, that includes the 12th day of the month. Households are interviewed on a rotating basis so that three-fourths of the sample is the same for any two consecutive months.

Data relating to 1994 and subsequent years are not fully comparable with data for 1993 and earlier years because of the introduction of a major redesign of the survey questionnaire and collection methodology. The redesign included new and revised questions for the classification of individuals as employed or unemployed, the collection of new data on multiple job holding, a change in the definition of discouraged workers, and the implementation of more completely automated data collection.

The 1994 redesign of the CPS was the most extensive in many years. However, there are also several earlier periods of noncomparability in the labor force data, which resulted from the introduction of new decennial census data into the CPS estimation procedures, expansions of the sample, and other improvements made to increase the reliability of the estimates. For strict comparability, the following allowances should be made when making certain data comparisons. In general, more detailed explanations of the changes listed below can be found in the February issue of the BLS publication *Employment and Earnings* for the year in which the change was introduced.

1. Beginning in 1953, the introduction of 1950 census data added about 600,000 to the population and about 350,000 to the labor force, total employment, and agricultural employment.

2. Beginning in 1960, the inclusion of Alaska and Hawaii added about 500,000 to the population, about 300,000 to the labor force, and about 240,000 to nonagricultural employment.

3. Beginning in 1962, the introduction of 1960 census data reduced the population by about 50,000, and the labor force and total employment by about 200,000.

4. Beginning in 1972, the introduction of 1970 census data added about 800,000 to the population, and a little over 300,000 to the labor force and total employment. A subsequent adjustment in March 1973 (based on 1970 census data), which substantially affected major categories for white and black and other workers, resulted in a net increase of 60,000 in the labor force and total employment.

5. Beginning in 1978, an expansion in the sample and changes in the estimation procedures added about 250,000 to the labor force and total employment.

6. Beginning in 1982, changes in the estimation procedures and the introduction of 1980 census data caused substantial increases in the population and estimates of persons in all labor force categories. Rates on labor force characteristics, however, were essentially unchanged. In order to avoid major breaks in series, some 30,000 labor force series were adjusted back to 1970. The revisions did not, however, smooth out the breaks in series occurring between 1972 and 1979 that are described above.

7. Beginning in 1986, the population controls used in the estimation procedures were revised to reflect an explicit estimate of the number of undocumented immigrants (largely Hispanic) since 1980 and an improved estimate of the number of legal foreign-born immigrants for the same time period. As a result, the civilian population and labor force estimates were raised by nearly 400,000; civilian employment was increased by about 350,000. The Hispanic-origin civilian population and labor force estimates were raised by about 425,000 and 305,000 respectively, and civilian employment by 270,000. Total and subgroup unemployment levels and rates were not significantly affected. Because of the magnitude of the adjustments for Hispanics, data were revised back to January 1980 to the extent possible.

8. Effective February 1996, 1990 census-based population controls, adjusted for the estimated undercount, were introduced into estimates for 1990 through 1993. (They already had been introduced in January 1994 for the data beginning with that month.) The new controls raised the estimate of the civilian noninstitutional population for 1990 by about 1.1 million; employment by about 880,000; and unemployment by about 175,000. The overall unemployment rate was increased by about 0.1 percentage point.

9. Beginning in January 1997, the population controls were revised to reflect updated information on immigrants to, and emigrants from, the United States. These revisions raised the estimate of the civilian noninstitutional population by about 470,000; the civilian labor force by about 320,000; and employment by about 290,000.

10. Effective with the data for January 1998, new composite estimation procedures and minor revisions in the population controls were introduced, resulting in relatively minor changes in the civilian labor force, employment, and unemployment estimates.

Nonagricultural employment estimates from the CPS differ in level and trend from estimates compiled from establishment payrolls (pages 117–122). The differences are attributable in part to differences in definitions and coverage and in part to differences in sample design, collection methodology, and the sampling variability inherent in the surveys. The CPS data include domestics and other private household workers, self-employed persons, and unpaid family workers who worked 15 hours or more in the survey week in family-operated enterprises, whereas the payroll or establishment survey covers only employees on payrolls of nonfarm establishments; persons holding more than one job during the survey week are counted once in the household survey, but multiple jobholders are counted each time (i.e., on each payroll) in the establishment survey; and persons with a job but not at work (i.e., absent because of bad weather, work stoppages, personal reasons, etc.) are included in the household survey but are excluded from the payroll survey if on leave without pay for the entire payroll period. See "Current Issues in Economic Measurement" at the front of this book.

The monthly labor force, employment and unemployment data are seasonally adjusted by the X-11 ARIMA method. All seasonally adjusted civilian labor force and unemployment rate statistics, as well as the major employment and unemployment estimates, are computed by aggregating independently adjusted series. For example, the seasonally adjusted level of total unemployment is the sum of the seasonally adjusted levels of unemployment for the four sex-age groups (men and women 16 to 19, and men and women 20 years and over). Seasonally adjusted employment is the sum of the seasonally adjusted level of employment for eight sex-age-industry groups (men and women 16 to 19, and men and women 20 years and over, employed in nonagricultural and agricultural industries). The seasonally adjusted civilian labor force is the sum of all 12 components. Finally, the seasonally adjusted civilian worker unemployment rate is calculated by taking total seasonally adjusted unemployment as a percent of the total seasonally adjusted civilian labor force. Seasonal adjustment factors are revised at the end of each year to reflect recent experience, and the revisions affect the preceding three years as well.

DATA AVAILABILITY

Data for each month usually are released on the first Friday of the following month in a press release that also contains data from the establishment survey (pages 117–135). Data are subsequently published in the BLS monthly periodical *Employment and Earnings*, which also contains detailed explanatory notes. Selected data are published each month in the *Monthly Labor Review*, which also contains frequent articles analyzing labor force, employment, and unemployment developments.

Monthly and annual data beginning with 1948 are available. Historical unadjusted data are published in *Labor Force Statistics Derived from the Current Population Survey*, BLS Bulletin 2307. Historical seasonally-adjusted data are available from BLS upon request. Complete historical data are available on the BLS internet site (http://stats.bls.gov).

REFERENCES

Historical background on the CPS, as well as a description of the 1994 redesign, are found in three articles in the September 1993 *Monthly Labor Review*: "Why Is It Necessary to Change"; "Redesigning the Questionnaire"; and "Evaluating Changes in the Estimates." The redesign also is described in the February 1994 issue of *Employment and Earnings*. Information on the introduction of the 1990 census-based population controls is found in the March 1996 issue of *Employment and Earnings*. See also Chapter 1, "Labor Force Data Derived from the Current Population Survey," *BLS Handbook of Methods*, Bulletin 2490 (April 1997).

PAGE 116
INSURED UNEMPLOYMENT

Source: U.S. Department of Labor, Employment and Training Administration

State programs of unemployment insurance cover operations of regular programs under state unemployment insurance laws. In 1976, the law was amended to extend coverage (effective January 1, 1978) to include virtually all state and local government employees plus many agricultural and domestic workers.

The federal civilian employees unemployment insurance program (UCFE) provides unemployment insurance protection to civilian employees of the federal government or of wholly or partially owned instrumentalities, with the following exceptions: Elective officers in the executive and legislative branches of government, certain foreign service personnel, temporary emergency workers, and other small groups.

Unemployment compensation for ex-service members (UCX) provides unemployment insurance protection to veterans under the law of the state in which the claim for compensation is filed.

An INITIAL CLAIM is the first claim in a benefit year filed by a worker after losing his job, or the first claim filed at the beginning of a subsequent period of unemployment in the same benefit year. The initial claim establishes the starting date for any insured unemployment that may result if the claimant is unemployed for one week or longer. Transitional claims (filed by persons as they start a new benefit year in a continuing spell of unemployment) are excluded; therefore, the data more closely represent instances of new unemployment.

Monthly averages in this book are averages of the weekly data published by the Employment and Training Administration. Annual data are averages of the monthly data.

DATA AVAILABILITY

Data are published in weekly press releases from the Employment and Training Administration. These releases are available on their internet site (www.doleta.gov). Also, historical data on weekly claims is available at the Department of Labor's Information Technology Support Center (www.itsc.state.md.us).

PAGES 117–122 AND 348–351
NONAGRICULTURAL EMPLOYMENT

Source: U.S. Department of Labor, Bureau of Labor Statistics (BLS)

The nonagricultural employment data, as well as the hours and earnings data on pages 123–135, are compiled from payroll records. Information is reported monthly on a voluntary basis to the BLS and its cooperating state agencies by a large sample of establishments representing all industries except agriculture. In most industries, the sampling probabilities are based on the size of the establishment; most large establishments are therefore in the sample. These data often are referred to as the "establishment data" or the "payroll data." The data by industry conform to the definitions in the 1987 Standard Industrial Classification (SIC).

DEFINITIONS

An ESTABLISHMENT is an economic unit which produces goods or services (such as a factory or store) at a single location and is engaged in one type of economic activity.

EMPLOYED PERSONS are all persons who received pay (including holiday and sick pay) for any part of the payroll period including the 12th day of the month (except in government—see below). Included are all full-time and part-time workers in nonfarm establishments. Persons holding more than one job are counted in each establishment that reports them. Not covered are proprietors, the self-employed, unpaid volunteer or family workers, farm workers, domestic workers in households, and military personnel; salaried officers of corporations are included.

Persons on an establishment payroll who are on paid sick leave (when pay is received directly from the employer), on paid holiday or vacation, or who work during a portion of the pay period even though they are unemployed or on strike during the rest of the period are counted as employed. Not counted as employed are persons who are laid off, on leave without pay, or on strike for the entire period, or who are hired but have not been paid during the period.

Intermittent workers are counted if they performed any service during the month. BLS considers regular full-time teachers (private and governmental) to be employed during the summer vacation period whether or not they are specifically paid in those months.

The government division of the SIC includes federal, state, and local activities such as legislative, executive, and judicial functions, as well as all government-owned and government-operated business enterprises, establishments, and institutions (arsenals, navy yards, hospitals, etc.), and government force account construction. Federal government employment is civilian employment only and pertains to the last day of the month. Employees of the Central Intelligence Agency and the National Security Agency are not included.

Nonagricultural employment in these series differs from the measures in the household survey (pages 112–115) in that, among other factors, it excludes domestics and other private household workers, self-employed persons, and unpaid family workers. Persons holding more than one job during the survey week are counted once in the household survey, but multiple jobholders are counted each time (i.e., on each payroll) in the establishment survey. Persons with a job but not at work (i.e., absent because of bad weather, work stoppages, personal reasons, etc.) are included in the household survey but are excluded from the payroll survey if on leave without pay for the entire payroll period. See "Current Issues in Economic Measurement" at the front of this book.

THE DIFFUSION INDEX OF EMPLOYMENT CHANGE, for 356 nonagricultural industries, represents the percent of industries in which employment was rising over a six-month span, plus one-half of the industries with unchanged employment. It is based on seasonally adjusted data and centered within the span; i.e., the diffusion index reported for June represents the change from March to September. *Business Statistics* uses the June value to represent the year. Diffusion indexes measure the dispersion of economic gains and losses, with values below 50 percent associated with recessions.

PRODUCTION OR NONSUPERVISORY WORKERS. The data refer to the private, nonfarm sector and cover all production and related workers in mining and manufacturing; construction workers in construction; and nonsupervisory workers in transportation, communication, electric, gas, and sanitary services; wholesale and retail trade; finance, insurance, and real estate; and services. These groups account for about four-fifths of the total employment on private nonagricultural payrolls.

Included are full-time and part-time workers who are on payrolls of private nonfarm establishments and who received pay for all or any part of the pay period that includes the 12th day of the month. Not counted are persons who are laid off, on leave without pay, or on strike for the entire period. Persons who worked in more than one establishment during a single reporting period are counted each time reported, whether the duplication is due to turnover or dual jobholding. The manufacturing series exclude manufacturing operations in government establishments such as arsenals and navy yards; these are included in government employment.

Production and related workers include working supervisors and all nonsupervisory workers (including group leaders and trainees) engaged in fabricating, processing, assembling, inspecting, receiving, storing, handling, packing, warehousing, shipping, trucking, hauling, maintenance, repair, janitorial, guard services, product development, auxiliary production for plant's own use (e.g., power plant), record keeping, and other services closely associated with these production operations.

Construction workers include the following employees in the construction division of the SIC: Working supervisors, qualified craft workers, mechanics, apprentices, laborers, etc., engaged in new work, alterations, demolition, repair, maintenance, etc., whether working at the site of construction or working in shops or yards at jobs (such as precutting and preassembling) ordinarily performed by members of the construction trades.

Nonsupervisory employees include employees (not above the working supervisory level) such as office and clerical workers, repairers, salespersons, operators, drivers, physicians, lawyers, accountants, nurses, social workers, research aides, teachers, drafters, photographers, beauticians, musicians, restaurant workers, custodial workers, attendants, line installers and repairers, laborers, janitors, guards, and other employees at similar occupational levels whose services are closely associated with those of the employees listed.

NOTES ON THE DATA

BENCHMARK ADJUSTMENTS. The establishment survey data are adjusted annually to comprehensive counts of employment (called "benchmarks"). Benchmark information on employment, by industry, is compiled by state agencies from reports of establishments covered under state unemployment insurance laws. These tabulations cover about 98 percent of all employees on nonfarm payrolls. Benchmark data for the residual are obtained from the records of the Social Security Administration and a number of other agencies in private industry or government.

The estimates for the benchmark month are compared with new benchmark levels, industry by industry. If revisions are necessary, the monthly series of estimates between benchmark periods are adjusted by graduated amounts between the new benchmark and the preceding

one, and the new benchmark for each industry is then carried forward progressively to the current month by use of the sample trends. Thus, under this procedure, the benchmark is used to establish the level of employment; the sample is used to measure the month-to-month changes in the level. Data for all months since the last benchmark to which the series has been adjusted are subject to revision.

SEASONAL ADJUSTMENT. The seasonal movements that recur periodically (such as warm and cold weather, holidays, vacations, etc.) are generally the largest single component of month-to-month changes in employment. After adjusting the data to remove such seasonal variation, the basic trends are more evident. Since the early 1980s the BLS has used the X-11-ARIMA procedure to seasonally adjust the establishment-based series. Seasonal adjustment factors are directly applied to the component levels. Seasonally adjusted totals for employment series are then obtained by aggregating seasonally adjusted components directly, while hours and earnings series represent weighted averages of the seasonally adjusted component series. Seasonally adjusted data are not published for a small number of series characterized by small seasonal components relative to their trend and/or irregular components. Theses series, however, are used in aggregating to broader seasonally adjusted levels.

Seasonal adjustment factors for federal government employment are derived from unadjusted data that include Christmas temporary workers employed by the Postal Service. The number of temporary census workers for the decennial census is removed, however, prior to the calculation of seasonal adjustment factors.

Revisions of the seasonally adjusted data, usually for the most recent five year period, are made once a year coincident with the benchmark revisions.

DATA AVAILABILITY

Employment data by industry division are available beginning with 1919. Data for each month usually are released on the first Friday of the following month in a press release that also contains data from the household survey (pages 112–115). Data are subsequently published in the BLS monthly periodical *Employment and Earnings*, which also contains detailed explanatory notes. Selected data are published each month in the *Monthly Labor Review*, which also contains frequent articles analyzing labor force, employment, and unemployment developments. Complete historical data are available on the BLS internet site (http://stats.bls.gov).

REFERENCES

Chapter 2 "Employment, Hours, and Earnings from the Establishment Survey," *BLS Handbook of Methods*, Bulletin 2490 (April 1997).

PAGES 123–128 AND 352–355
AVERAGE HOURS PER WEEK; AGGREGATE EMPLOYEE HOURS

Source: U.S. Department of Labor, Bureau of Labor Statistics (BLS)

The nonagricultural employment, hours, and earnings data are compiled from payroll records. Information is reported monthly on a voluntary basis to the BLS and its cooperating state agencies by a large sample of establishments representing all industries except agriculture. These data often are referred to as the "establishment data" or the "payroll data." The data by industry conform to the definitions in the 1987 Standard Industrial Classification (SIC). See the notes for pages 117–122 for a general description of the establishment survey.

DEFINITIONS

HOURS represent the average weekly hours for which production or nonsupervisory workers received pay; average weekly hours are different from standard or scheduled hours. Such factors as unpaid absenteeism, labor turnover, part-time work, and work stoppages cause average weekly hours to be lower than scheduled hours of work for an establishment.

OVERTIME HOURS represent the portion of average weekly hours which was in excess of regular hours and for which overtime premiums were paid. Weekend and holiday hours are included only if overtime premiums were paid. Hours for which only shift differential, hazard, incentive, or other similar types of premiums were paid are excluded.

PRODUCTION OR NONSUPERVISORY WORKERS. See the notes to pages 117–122 for definition.

NOTES ON THE DATA

BENCHMARK ADJUSTMENTS. Independent benchmarks are not available for the hours and earnings series. At the time of the annual adjustment of the employment series to new benchmarks, the levels of hours and earnings may be affected slightly by the revised employment weights (which are used in computing the industry averages for hours and earnings), as well as by the changes in seasonal adjustment factors also introduced with the benchmark revision.

METHOD OF COMPUTING INDUSTRY SERIES. "Average weekly hours" for individual industries are computed by dividing production or nonsupervisory worker hours (reported by establishments classified in each industry) by the number of production or nonsupervisory workers reported for the same establishments. Estimates for SIC divisions and major industry groups are averages (weighted by employment) of the figures for component industries.

SEASONAL ADJUSTMENT. Hours and earnings series are sea-

sonally adjusted by applying factors directly to the corresponding unadjusted series. Data for some industries are not seasonally adjusted because the seasonal component is small relative to the trend-cycle and/or irregular components and consequently cannot be separated with sufficient precision.

AGGREGATE HOURS. Data pertain to production and nonsupervisory workers in nonfarm establishments. The indexes are obtained by multiplying seasonally adjusted production or nonsupervisory worker employment by seasonally adjusted average weekly hours and dividing by the monthly average for the 1982 period. For total private, goods-producing, service-producing, and major industry divisions, the indexes are obtained by summing the seasonally adjusted aggregate weekly employee hours for the component industries and dividing by the monthly average for the 1982 period.

DATA AVAILABILITY

Data for each month usually are released on the first Friday of the following month in a press release that also contains employment data from the household and establishment surveys (pages 112–115 and 117–122). Data subsequently are published in the BLS monthly periodical *Employment and Earnings*, which also contains detailed explanatory notes. Selected data are published each month in the *Monthly Labor Review*. Complete historical data are available on the BLS internet site (http://stats.bls.gov).

REFERENCES

Chapter 2 "Employment, Hours, and Earnings from the Establishment Survey," *BLS Handbook of Methods*, Bulletin 2490 (April 1997).

PAGES 129–135 AND 352–355
HOURLY AND WEEKLY EARNINGS

Source: U.S. Department of Labor, Bureau of Labor Statistics (BLS)

The nonagricultural employment, hours, and earnings data are compiled from payroll records. Information is reported monthly on a voluntary basis to the BLS and its cooperating state agencies by a large sample of establishments representing all industries except agriculture. These data often are referred to as the "establishment data" or the "payroll data." The data by industry conform to the definitions in the 1987 Standard Industrial Classification (SIC). See the notes for pages 117–122 for a general description of the establishment survey.

DEFINITIONS

EARNINGS are the payments production or nonsupervisory workers receive during the survey period (before deductions for taxes and other items), including premium pay for overtime or late-shift work but excluding irregular bonuses and other special payments.

REAL EARNINGS are earnings adjusted to reflect the effects of changes in consumer prices as measured by the Consumer Price Index for Urban Wage Earners and Clerical Workers (CPI-W).

PRODUCTION OR NONSUPERVISORY WORKERS. See the notes to pages 117–122 for definition.

NOTES ON THE DATA

The hours and earnings series are based on reports of gross payroll and corresponding paid hours for full- and part-time production and related workers, construction workers, or nonsupervisory workers who received pay for any part of the pay period that included the 12th of the month.

Total payrolls are before deductions; e.g., for the employee share of old-age and unemployment insurance, group insurance, withholding taxes, bonds, and union dues. The payroll figures also include pay for overtime, holidays, vacations, and sick leave (paid directly by the employer for the period reported). Excluded from the payroll figures are fringe benefits (health and other types of insurance, contributions to retirement, etc., paid by the employer, and the employer share of payroll taxes); bonuses (unless earned and paid regularly each pay period); other pay not earned in the pay period reported (e.g., retroactive pay); tips; and the value of free rent, fuel, meals, or other payment in kind.

Average hourly earnings data are on a "gross" basis; that is, they reflect not only changes in basic hourly and incentive wage rates but also such variable factors as premium pay for overtime and late-shift work, and changes in output of workers paid on an incentive basis. Also, shifts in the volume of employment between relatively high-paid and low-paid work affect the general average of hourly earnings.

Averages of hourly earnings should not be confused with *wage rates*, which represent the rates stipulated for a given unit of work or time, while earnings refer to the actual return to the worker for a stated period of time. The earnings series do not represent total labor cost to the employer because of the exclusion of irregular bonuses, retroactive items, the cost of employer-provided benefits, payroll taxes paid by employers, and earnings for those employees not covered under the production-worker or nonsupervisory-worker definition. Similarly, average weekly earnings are not the amounts available to workers for spending, since they do not reflect such deductions as those for income and social security taxes, etc.

METHOD OF COMPUTING INDUSTRY SERIES. Average hourly earnings are obtained by dividing the reported total production or nonsupervisory worker payroll by the total production or nonsupervisory worker hours. Estimates for both hours and hourly earnings for nonfarm divisions and major industry groups are employment-weighted averages of the figures for component industries.

Average weekly earnings are computed by multiplying average hourly earnings by average weekly hours. In addition to the factors mentioned above, which exert varying influences upon average hourly earnings, average weekly earnings are affected by changes in the length of the workweek, part-time work, work stoppages, labor turnover, and absenteeism. Persistent long-term increases in the proportion of part-time workers in retail trade and many of the service industries have reduced average workweeks and have affected the average weekly earnings series.

INDEPENDENT BENCHMARKS are not available for the hours and earnings series. At the time of the annual adjustment of the employment series to new benchmarks, the levels of hours and earnings may be affected slightly by the revised employment weights (which are used in computing the industry averages for hours and earnings), as well as by the changes in seasonal adjustment factors also introduced with the benchmark revision.

SEASONAL ADJUSTMENT. Hours and earnings series are seasonally adjusted by applying factors directly to the corresponding unadjusted series; seasonally adjusted average weekly earnings are the product of seasonally adjusted hourly earnings and weekly hours. Weekly earnings in constant dollars, seasonally adjusted, are obtained by dividing seasonally adjusted average weekly earnings by the seasonally adjusted Consumer Price Index for Urban Wage Earners and Clerical Workers (CPI-W).

DATA AVAILABILITY

Data for each month usually are released on the first Friday of the following month in a press release that also contains employment data from the household and establishment surveys (pages 112–115 and 117–122). Data subsequently are published in the BLS monthly periodical *Employment and Earnings*, which also contains detailed explanatory notes. Selected data are published each month in the *Monthly Labor Review*. Complete historical data are available on the BLS internet site (http://stats.bls.gov).

REFERENCES

Chapter 2 "Employment, Hours, and Earnings from the Establishment Survey," *BLS Handbook of Methods*, Bulletin 2490 (April 1997).

PAGES 138–139
ENERGY SUPPLY AND CONSUMPTION

Sources: U.S. Department of Energy, Energy Information Administration; U.S. Department of Commerce, Bureau of Economic Analysis

NOTES ON THE DATA

These data are published in the *Monthly Energy Review*, Tables 1.3, 2.2, and 1.9. Consumption by end-use sector is based on total, not net, consumption. The gross domestic product (GDP) data used to calculate energy consumption per dollar of GDP are from the Bureau of Economic Analysis and include revisions through August 1999.

ENERGY PRODUCTION: Crude oil includes lease condensates. Hydroelectric power includes electrical utility and industrial generation. Other energy production includes energy generated for distribution from wood, waste, photovoltaic, and solar thermal energy.

Because of a lack of consistent monthly historical data, some renewable energy sources are not included in total consumption. In 1998, for example, 3.5 quadrillion Btu of renewable energy used by electric utilities to generate electricity for distribution and 0.1 quadrillion Btu of ethanol blended into motor gasoline is included, but an estimated 3.4 quadrillion Btu used by residential, commercial, and industrial consumers is not. In 1997, 3.9 quadrillion Btu used by electric utilities to generate electricity for distribution is included, but an estimated 3.2 quadrillion Btu used by residential, commercial, and industrial consumers is not. In 1996, 3.9 quadrillion Btu used by electric utilities to generate electricity for distribution is included, but an estimated 3.4 quadrillion Btu used by residential, commercial, and industrial consumers is not. In 1995, 3.4 quadrillion Btu used by electric utilities to generate electricity for distribution is included, but an estimated 3.3 quadrillion Btu used by residential, commercial, and industrial consumers is not.

REFERENCES

Energy Information Administration, *Monthly Energy Review*. Current and historical data are available on the EIA internet site (http://www.eia.doe.gov).

PAGES 142–143 AND 364–367
MONEY STOCK, LIQUID ASSETS, AND DEBT; COMPONENTS OF THE MONEY STOCK

Source: Board of Governors of the Federal Reserve System

Estimates of three monetary aggregates (M1, M2, and M3), a debt aggregate, and the components of these measures are published weekly. The monthly data are averages of daily figures.

DEFINITIONS

M1 consists of (1) currency outside the U.S. Treasury, Federal Reserve Banks, and the vaults of depository institutions; (2) travelers checks of nonbank issuers; (3) demand deposits at all commercial banks other than those due to depository institutions, the U.S. government, and foreign banks and official institutions, less cash items in the process of collection and Federal Reserve float; and (4) other checkable deposits, consisting of negotiable order of withdrawal (NOW) and automatic transfer service (ATS) accounts at depository institutions, credit union share draft accounts, and demand deposits at thrift institutions.

M2 consists of M1 plus savings deposits (including money market deposit accounts), small-denomination time deposits (time deposits—including retail repurchase agreements [RPs]—in amounts of less than $100,000), and balances in retail money market mutual funds. It excludes individual retirement account (IRA) and Keogh balances at depository institutions and money market funds.

M3 consists of M2 plus large-denomination time deposits (in amounts of $100,000 or more), balances in institutional money funds, RP liabilities (overnight and term) issued by all depository institutions, and Eurodollars (overnight and term) held by U.S. residents at foreign branches of U.S. banks worldwide and at all banking offices in the United Kingdom and Canada. It excludes amounts held by depository institutions, the U.S. government, money funds, and foreign banks and official institutions.

DEBT is the outstanding credit market debt of the domestic nonfinancial sectors—the federal sector (U.S. government, not including government-sponsored enterprises or federally related mortgage pools) and the nonfederal sectors (state and local governments, households and nonprofit organizations, nonfinancial corporate and nonfarm noncorporate businesses, and farms). Domestic nonfinancial debt is monitored by the Federal Reserve as an indicator of the effect of monetary policy. Nonfederal debt consists of mortgages, tax-exempt and corporate bonds, consumer credit, bank loans, commercial paper, and other loans. The data, which are derived from the Federal Reserve Board's flow of funds accounts, are break-adjusted (that is, discontinuities in the data have been smoothed into the series) and month-averaged (that is, the data have been derived by averaging adjacent month-end levels).

CURRENCY consists of currency outside the U.S. Treasury, the Federal Reserve Banks and the vaults of depository institutions.

DEMAND DEPOSITS consists of demand deposits at commercial banks and foreign-related institutions other than those due to depository institutions, the U.S. government, and foreign banks and official institutions, less cash items in the process of collection and Federal Reserve float.

OTHER CHECKABLE DEPOSITS consists of NOW and ATS balances at all depository institutions; credit union share draft balances; and demand deposits at thrift institutions.

SAVINGS DEPOSITS include money market deposit accounts.

SMALL TIME DEPOSITS are those issued at commercial banks and thrift institutions in amounts of less than $100,000. Retail RPs are included. All IRA and Keogh account balances at commercial banks and thrift institutions are subtracted from small time deposits.

LARGE TIME DEPOSITS are those issued in amounts of $100,000 or more at commercial banks and thrift institutions, excluding those booked at international banking facilities. Deposits held at commercial banks by money market mutual funds, depository institutions, the U.S. government, and foreign banks and official institutions also are excluded.

NOTES ON THE DATA

SEASONAL ADJUSTMENT. Seasonally-adjusted M1 is calculated by summing currency, travelers checks, demand deposits, and other checkable deposits, each seasonally adjusted separately. Seasonally-adjusted M2 is computed by adjusting each of its non-M1 components and then adding this result to seasonally-adjusted M1. Similarly, seasonally-adjusted M3 is obtained by adjusting each of its non-M2 components and then adding this result to seasonally-adjusted M2.

REVISIONS. Money stock measures are revised annually, usually in February, based on a benchmark and seasonal factor review. These revisions typically extend back a number of years. The monetary aggregates were redefined in major revisions in 1980.

The 1998 revisions incorporate historical data for a number of money market mutual funds that began reporting for the first time during 1997. The level of M3 was raised by amounts that reached $18 billion by mid-1997.

There was a minor definitional change in M2 at the time of the 1996 revisions: Overnight wholesale repurchase agreements (RPs) and overnight Eurodollars were removed from M2 and are now included in the non-M2 component of M3. Although the revision lowered M2 for all years since 1969, it had no effect on quarterly and annual percent changes in M2.

DATA AVAILABILITY

Estimates are released weekly in Federal Reserve Statistical Release H.6, "Money Stock, Liquid Assets, and Debt Measures" and are subsequently published each month in the *Federal Reserve Bulletin*. Historical data beginning with 1959 are available from Publications Services, Board of Governors of the Federal Reserve System. Current and historical data are available on the Federal Reserve internet site (http://www.federalreserve.gov/releases/).

REFERENCES

An explanation of the 1980 redefinition of the monetary aggregates is found in the *Federal Reserve Bulletin* for February 1980.

PAGE 144
AGGREGATE RESERVES OF DEPOSITORY INSTITUTIONS AND MONETARY BASE

Source: Board of Governors of the Federal Reserve System

The data presented here are in millions of dollars, seasonally adjusted and adjusted for changes in reserve requirements ("break-adjusted"). Monthly data are averages of daily figures. Annual data are for December.

DEFINITIONS

TOTAL RESERVES consists of reserve balances with Federal Reserve Banks plus vault cash used to satisfy reserve requirements. Seasonally-adjusted, break-adjusted total reserves equal seasonally-adjusted, break-adjusted required reserves plus unadjusted excess reserves.

Seasonally-adjusted, break-adjusted NONBORROWED RESERVES equal seasonally adjusted, break-adjusted total reserves less unadjusted total borrowings of depository institutions from the Federal Reserve.

EXTENDED CREDIT consists of borrowing at the discount window under the terms and conditions established for the extended credit program to help depository institutions deal with sustained liquidity pressures. Because there is not the same need to repay such borrowing promptly as there is with traditional short-term adjustment credit, the money market impact of extended credit is similar to that of nonborrowed reserves.

To adjust *required reserves* for discontinuities due to regulatory changes in reserve requirements, a multiplicative procedure is used to estimate what required reserves would have been in past periods had current reserve requirements been in effect. Break-adjusted required reserves include required reserves against transactions deposits and personal time and savings deposits (but not reservable nondeposit liabilities).

The seasonally-adjusted, break-adjusted MONETARY BASE consists of (1) seasonally adjusted, break-adjusted total reserves plus (2) the seasonally-adjusted currency component of the money stock plus (3) for all quarterly reporters on the "Report of Transaction Accounts, Other Deposits and Vault Cash" and for all those weekly reporters whose vault cash exceeds their required reserves, the seasonally adjusted, break-adjusted difference between current vault cash and the amount applied to satisfy current reserve requirements.

DATA AVAILABILITY

Data are released weekly in Federal Reserve release H.3 and subsequently published in the *Federal Reserve Bulletin*. Historical data are available from the Money and Reserves Projections Section, Division of Monetary Affairs, Board of Governors of The Federal Reserve System, Washington, D.C. 20551. Current and historical data also are available on the Federal Reserve internet site (http://www.federalreserve.gov/releases/).

PAGES 145–147
ASSETS AND LIABILITIES OF COMMERCIAL BANKS

Source: Board of Governors of the Federal Reserve System

These data on the assets and liabilities of commercial banks were introduced by the Federal Reserve in 1994, replacing several discontinued data sets as noted below. Weekly data are Wednesday figures; monthly data are pro rata averages of the weekly figures; annual data are for December.

DEFINITIONS AND NOTES ON THE DATA

The current Federal Reserve data set H.8, Assets and Liabilities of Commercial Banks in the United States, was introduced in March 1994. It incorporates key items from three statistical releases that were discontinued: the previous version of the H.8, Assets and Liabilities of Insured Domestically Chartered and Foreign-Related Institutions; the G.7, Loans and Securities at Commercial Banks; and the G.10, Major Nondeposit Funds of Commercial Banks. The new data series are available beginning with 1988.

The new H.8 contains monthly and weekly balance sheets for all commercial banks, domestically chartered banks, small domestic banks, large domestic banks, and foreign-related institutions. The data are adjusted for known reclassifications between balance sheet items and are available both seasonally adjusted and not seasonally adjusted.

The data for *all commercial banks in the United States* cover the following types of institutions in the 50 states and the District of Columbia: domestically chartered commercial banks that submit a weekly report of condition (large domestic); other domestically chartered commercial banks (small domestic); branches and agencies of foreign banks, and Edge Act and agreement corporations (foreign-related institutions). International banking facilities are excluded. Small domestic banks and foreign-related institutions are estimated based on weekly samples and on quarter-end condition reports. Data are adjusted for breaks caused by reclassifications of assets and liabilities.

LOANS AND LEASES IN BANK CREDIT excludes federal funds sold to, reverse repurchase agreements with, and loans to commercial banks in the United States; all of these are in interbank loans.

SECURITY LOANS consists of reverse repurchase agreements with broker-dealers and loans to purchase and carry securities.

INTERBANK LOANS consists of federal funds sold to, reverse repurchase agreements with, and loans to commercial banks in the United States.

CASH ASSETS includes vault cash, cash items in process of collection, demand balances due from depository institutions, and balances due from Federal Reserve Banks.

OTHER ASSETS AND OTHER LIABILITIES exclude the due-from position with related foreign offices, which is included in net due to related foreign offices.

TOTAL ASSETS excludes unearned income, reserves for losses on loans and leases, and reserves for transfer risk.

RESIDUAL: ASSETS LESS LIABILITIES. This balancing item is not intended as a measure of equity capital for use in capital adequacy analysis. On a seasonally adjusted basis this item reflects any differences in the seasonal patterns estimated for total assets and total liabilities.

REVISIONS

Data are revised annually to reflect new benchmark information and revised seasonal factors.

DATA AVAILABILITY

Assets and Liabilities of Commercial Banks, Federal Reserve release H.8, is released each Friday around 4:30 p.m. eastern time. Selected data are subsequently published in the *Federal Reserve Bulletin*. Historical data may be purchased on diskette from Publications Services, Board of Governors of the Federal Reserve System. Current and historical data are available on the Federal Reserve internet site (http://www.federalreserve.gov/releases/).

PAGES 148–149
CREDIT MARKET DEBT OUTSTANDING AND DEBT SERVICE BURDENS

Source: Board of Governors of the Federal Reserve System

The flow of funds accounts compiled quarterly by the Federal Reserve Board supplement the national income and product and international transactions accounts by providing a comprehensive and detailed accounting of financial transactions. Included in the accounts and reproduced here are aggregate data on U.S. credit market debt outstanding owed by domestic financial and nonfinancial sectors and by foreigners.

DEFINITIONS AND NOTES ON THE DATA

Quarterly data on debt outstanding are shown on an end-of-period basis, not adjusted for seasonal variation or for "breaks" or discontinuities in the series. For these and other reasons they differ from the monthly debt aggregates shown on page 142.

Data for the current and preceding years are revised each year to reflect revisions in source data.

In DOMESTIC FINANCIAL SECTORS, FEDERAL GOVERNMENT-RELATED sectors include federally sponsored credit agencies, federally related mortgage pools, and the monetary authority (Federal Reserve). The PRIVATE sector includes commercial banks, thrift institutions, insurance and pension funds (except federal government), mutual funds, investment trusts, and other financial institutions.

In DOMESTIC NONFINANCIAL SECTORS, THE FEDERAL GOVERNMENT consists of all federal government agencies and funds that are in the unified budget, except for the District of Columbia government, which is included in the state and local sector. Federal government debt is shown on a consolidated basis so that the securities liability reported is smaller than the official public debt, which also includes securities held by agencies within the U.S. government (e.g., in the Social Security trust funds). Therefore, *treasury securities* in the flow of funds accounts corresponds with the "debt held by the public" shown on page 297. *Budget agency securities and mortgages* are those issued by government-owned corporations and agencies, such as the Export-Import Bank, that issue securities individually.

HOUSEHOLDS also include personal trusts and nonprofit organizations.

In the nonfinancial sector, STATE AND LOCAL GOVERNMENTS reflects general funds only; retirement funds are included in the financial sector.

FOREIGN CREDIT MARKET DEBT HELD IN THE UNITED STATES is included along with the debt of domestic financial and nonfinancial sectors in TOTAL CREDIT MARKET DEBT OUTSTANDING.

DELINQUENCY RATES OF CREDIT CARD ACCOUNTS HELD AT BANKS are compiled from the quarterly FFIEC (Federal Financial Institutions Examination Council) Consolidated Reports of Condition and Income (FFIEC 031 through 034). Data for each calendar quarter become available approximately sixty days after the end of the quarter.

MORTGAGE DELINQUENCY RATES of over 90 days are compiled by the Mortgage Bankers Association of America in their National Delinquency Survey.

DATA AVAILABILITY

Estimates are released quarterly, about nine weeks following the end of a quarter, in Federal Reserve Statistical Release Z.1, "Flow of Funds Accounts of the United States," and are subsequently published in the *Federal Reserve Bulletin*. Releases and data on diskettes are available from Publications Services, Board of Governors of the Federal Reserve System. Current and historical data also are available on the Federal Reserve internet site (http://www.federalreserve.gov/releases). Delinquency rates of credit card accounts held at banks are also available on the Federal Reserve internet site, listed under Charge-Off and Delinquency Rates on Loans at Commercial Banks.

Mortgage delinquency rates can be obtained from the Mortgage Bankers Association of America for length of delinquency (30, 60, 90 days or more) and type of loan, as well as for various levels of geography. MBAA statistical information can be found on their internet site (http://www.mbaa.org/marketdata/).

REFERENCES

A *Guide to the Flow of Funds Accounts* is available from Publications Services, Board of Governors of the Federal Reserve System.

PAGE 150
CONSUMER INSTALLMENT CREDIT

Source: Board of Governors of the Federal Reserve System

The consumer installment credit series cover most short- and intermediate-term credit extended to individuals through regular business channels, usually to finance the purchase of consumer goods and services or to refinance debts originally incurred for such purposes, and scheduled to be repaid (or with the option of repayment) in two or more installments. Consumer installment credit is categorized by major holders and by major types of credit.

DEFINITIONS AND NOTES ON THE DATA

Categories of holders include commercial banks, finance companies, credit unions, savings institutions, nonfinancial businesses, and pools of securitized assets. Retailers and gasoline companies are included in the nonfinancial businesses category. *Pools of securitized assets* comprises the outstanding balances of pools upon which securities have been issued; these balances are no longer carried on the balance sheets of the loan originators.

Types of credit include revolving, automobile, and "other." *Revolving credit* includes credit arising from purchases on credit card plans of retail stores and banks, cash advances and check credit plans of banks, and some overdraft credit arrangements. *Non-revolving credit* includes automobile loans (new and passenger automobiles), mobile home loans, and all other installment loans not included in revolving credit, such as loans for education, boats, trailers, or vacations. These loans may be secured or unsecured. *Automobile credit* and *"other"* credit were combined in *non-revolving credit* in July 1999. This change owes to an assessment that the split between the two categories has become unreliable because of shifts in the composition of the monthly commercial bank panel and the lack of suitable benchmarks for the commercial bank automobile and "other" credit series. Seasonal adjustment factors have been estimated or the entire history of the consolidated series.

Debt secured by real estate (including first liens, junior liens, and home equity loans) is excluded. Credit extended to governmental agencies and nonprofit or charitable organizations, as well as credit extended to business or to individuals exclusively for business purposes, is excluded.

The consumer credit series are based on comprehensive benchmark data that become available periodically. Current monthly estimates are brought forward from the latest benchmarks in accordance with weighted changes indicated by sample data. Classifications are made on a "holder" basis. Thus, installment paper sold by retail outlets is included in figures for the banks and finance companies that purchased the paper.

The amount of outstanding credit represents the sum of the balances in the installment receivable accounts of financial institutions and retail outlets at the end of each month. Net change measures the change during the month in the amount of consumer installment credit outstanding. It is defined as the amount of consumer installment credit extended less the amount liquidated (including repayments, chargeoffs, and other credits) during the month. Each monthly change is computed by subtracting the seasonally-adjusted amount outstanding at the end of the previous month from the amount outstanding at the end of the current month. Information is not available to make separate estimates of the amount of extensions, liquidations, and chargeoffs of bad debts.

The estimates of the amount of credit outstanding and net change include any finance and insurance charges included as part of the installment contract. Unearned income on loans is included in some cases where lenders cannot separate the components.

The seasonally-adjusted data are adjusted for differences in the number of trading days and for seasonal influences. The seasonal factors used are derived by the X-11-ARIMA process.

REVISIONS

Consumer credit data were revised in December 1997 to incorporate updated seasonal factors and a change in the estimation procedures for commercial banks that brings data for such institutions into alignment with Call Reports. In addition, some loans for light trucks that had been included in the "other" consumer credit category were reclassified as automobile loans. A previous revision in August 1997 benchmarked company components to the June 1996 Survey of Finance Companies. As part of the August 1997 revisions, the revolving credit category was expanded to include the revolving credit held by finance companies and the "other credit" category was reduced by the same amount.

DATA AVAILABILITY

Current data are available monthly in the Federal Reserve statistical release G.19, Consumer Credit, and in the *Federal Reserve Bulletin*. The data for earlier years may be purchased on diskette from Publication Services, Board of Governors of the Federal Reserve System. Current and historical data are available on the Federal Reserve internet site (http://www.federalreserve.gov/releases/).

PAGES 151–153 AND 368–371 INTEREST RATES, BOND YIELDS, STOCK PRICES AND YIELDS

Sources: Board of Governors of the Federal Reserve System; Moody's Investors Service; The Bond Buyer; Dow Jones, Inc.; Standard and Poor's Corporation; New York Stock Exchange

DEFINITIONS AND NOTES ON THE DATA

INTEREST RATES AND BOND YIELDS are percents per year and are averages of business day figures, except as noted.

The daily effective FEDERAL FUNDS RATE is a weighted average of rates on trades through New York brokers. Monthly figures include each calendar day in the month. Annualized figures use a 360-day year.

The FEDERAL RESERVE DISCOUNT RATE is the rate for discount window borrowing at the Federal Reserve Bank of New York. Annualized figures use a 360-day year.

The EURODOLLAR RATE shown is the bid rate for Eurodollar deposits at 11 a.m. London time for one-month deposits.

The U.S. TREASURY BILLS, 3-MONTH RATE and the U.S. TREASURY BILLS, 6-MONTH RATE shown are the auction averages; the monthly averages are computed on an issue-date basis. The rates are quoted on a discount basis, and annualized figures use a 360-day year.

BANKERS' ACCEPTANCES, 3-MONTH RATES are representative closing yields for acceptances of the highest rated money center banks. The rates are quoted on a discount basis, and annualized figures use a 360-day year.

CDs (SECONDARY MARKET), 3-MONTH RATES are averages of dealer offering rates on nationally traded certificates of deposit. Annualized figures use a 360-day year.

DISCONTINUED SERIES. The Federal Reserve interest rate series on 6-month *commercial paper* and *finance company paper* were discontinued as of September 1997 due to a change in the way the Federal Reserve obtains its information on commercial paper rates and amounts outstanding. This information is now obtained from the Depository Trust Company (DTC), the national clearinghouse for the settlements of securities trades. DTC generates the data through the normal course of business, and use of their data eliminates the need for the Federal Reserve to impose a separate reporting burden on market participants. The interest rate series obtained from the DTC data are thought to be more accurate than the previous series, but they are sufficiently different to represent a break in series. Series with a 6-month maturity are no longer published.

The BANK PRIME RATE is one of several base rates used by banks to price short-term business loans. Monthly and annual figures include each calendar day in the month or year. U.S. TREASURY SECURITIES. The rates shown for 1-year, 10-year, and 30-year securities are yields on actively traded issues adjusted to constant maturities. Yields on Treasury securities at "constant maturity" are interpolated by the U.S. Treasury from the daily yield curve. This curve, which relates the yield on a security to its time to maturity, is based on the closing market bid yields on actively traded Treasury securities in the over-the-counter market. These market yields are calculated from composites of quotations reported by five leading U.S. Government securities dealers to the Federal Reserve Bank of New York. The constant maturity yield values are read from the yield curve at fixed maturities, currently 1, 2, 3, 5, 7, 10, 20, and 30 years. This method provides a yield for a 10-year maturity, for example, even if no outstanding security has exactly 10 years remaining to maturity. The *long-term composite* is the unweighted average of rates on all outstanding bonds neither due nor callable in less than 10 years.

DOMESTIC CORPORATE BOND YIELDS. The rates shown are for general obligation bonds based on Thursday figures and are provided by Moody's Investors Service and republished by the Federal Reserve.

The A-RATED UTILITY BOND rate shown is an estimate compiled by the Federal Reserve of the yield on a recently offered A-rated utility bond with a maturity of 30 years and call protection of 5 years; Friday quotations.

The STATE AND LOCAL BOND YIELDS are the Bond Buyer index as republished by the Federal Reserve. The index is based on 20 state and local government general obligation bonds maturing in 20 years or less.

The FIXED RATE MORTGAGE rates are contract interest rates on commitments for fixed-rate first mortgages. The rates are obtained by the Federal Reserve from the Federal Home Loan Mortgage Corporation (FHLMC).

STOCK PRICE INDEXES. The Dow Jones industrial average is an average of 30 stocks compiled by Dow Jones, Inc. The Standard and Poor's composite is an index of 500 stocks based on 1941–1943=10 compiled by Standard and Poor's Corporation. The New York Stock Exchange indexes are compiled by the New York Stock Exchange and are based on December 31, 1965=50, except for the utility index, which is based on December 31, 1965=100. The monthly and annual data are averages of daily figures.

DATA AVAILABILITY

Interest rates and bond yields are published weekly in the Federal Reserve's H.15 release. Most are subsequently published in the *Federal Reserve Bulletin*, as are the stock indexes. The starting dates for individual interest rate series vary; some date back to 1911, and many begin in the 1950s and 1960s. Historical data may be purchased on diskette from Publications Services, Board of Governors of the Federal Reserve System. Current and historical data are available on the Federal Reserve internet site (http://www.federalreserve.gov/releases/).

PAGES 156–161 AND 317–320
INTERNATIONAL TRANSACTIONS

Source: U.S. Department of Commerce, Bureau of Economic Analysis.

The U.S. international transactions accounts, or "balance of payments," provide a comprehensive view of economic transactions between the United States and foreign countries. The accounts include estimates of exports and imports of goods and of travel, transportation, and other services; receipts and payments of income between U.S. and foreign residents; foreign aid and other transfers; and private and official capital flows, including direct investment. Data in the accounts have undergone extensive revision in the last few years to incorporate improved data sources and methodology. The detailed categories of service exports and imports are shown in the table on pages 176–177 and discussed in the notes for pages 162–177.

DEFINITIONS

CREDITS (+): The following items are treated as credits in the international transactions accounts: Exports of goods and services and income receipts; unilateral current transfers to the United States; capital account transactions receipts; financial inflows—increase in foreign-owned assets (U.S. liabilities) or decrease in U.S.-owned assets (U.S. claims).

DEBITS (-): The following items are treated as debits in the international transactions accounts, indicated by minus signs in the data cells: Imports of goods and services and income payments; unilateral current transfers to foreigners; capital accounts transactions payments; financial outflows—decrease in foreign-owned assets (U.S. liabilities) or increase in U.S.-owned assets (U.S. claims).

The BALANCE ON GOODS is the excess of exports of goods over imports of goods. (A minus sign indicates an excess of imports over exports.)

The BALANCE ON SERVICES is the excess of service exports over service imports. (A minus sign indicates an excess of imports over exports.)

The BALANCE ON GOODS AND SERVICES is the sum of the balance on goods and the balance on services.

The BALANCE ON INCOME is the excess of income receipts from abroad over income payments to foreigners. (A minus sign indicates an excess of payments over receipts.) The BALANCE ON GOODS, SERVICES, AND INCOME is the excess of exports of goods, services, and income over imports of goods, services, and income. It is equal to the sum of the balance on goods and services and the balance on income. (A minus sign indicates an excess of imports over exports.)

The BALANCE ON UNILATERAL TRANSFERS is equal to unilateral transfers, net.

The BALANCE ON CURRENT ACCOUNT is equal to the sum of the balance on goods, services, and income and the balance on unilateral transfers.

The CAPITAL ACCOUNT covers net capital transfers and the acquisition and disposal of nonproduced nonfinancial assets. The major types of *capital transfers* are debt forgiveness and assets that accompany immigrants. *Nonproduced nonfinancial assets* include rights to natural resources, patents, copyrights, trademarks, franchises, and leases.

The FINANCIAL ACCOUNT includes all other inflows and outflows of capital, i.e. changes in U.S.-owned assets abroad and foreign-owned assets in the United States, including official reserve assets, direct investment, securities, currency, and bank deposits.

In concept, the balance on current account is necessarily offset exactly by the net financial and capital inflow or outflow; for example, a U.S. current account deficit results in more dollars held by foreigners, which must be reflected in additional claims on the United States held by foreigners, whether in the form of U.S. currency, securities, loans, or other forms of obligation. But because of different and incomplete data sources, the financial and capital accounts do not exactly offset the current account. The *statistical discrepancy* in the U.S. international accounts—the sum of all credits and debits, with the sign reversed—measures the amount by which the net financial and capital flow would have to be augmented to offset the current account balance exactly. (In the quarterly accounts, a part of this discrepancy, the *seasonal adjustment discrepancy*, results from separate seasonal adjustment.) The statistical discrepancy in the international accounts is not the same as the statistical discrepancy in the national income and product accounts, which arises from measurement differences between domestic output and domestic income.

NOTES ON THE DATA

EXPORTS AND IMPORTS OF GOODS in the international transactions account exclude exports of goods under U.S. military agency sales contracts identified in Census Bureau export documents and imports of goods under direct defense expenditures identified in import documents. They also reflect various other adjustments (for valuation, coverage, and timing) of Census Bureau statistics to a balance-of-payments basis.

SERVICES include some goods, mainly military equipment (included in transfers under military agency sales contracts); major equipment, other materials, supplies, and petroleum products purchased abroad by U.S. military agencies (included in direct defense expenditures abroad); and fuels purchased by airline and steamship operators (included in other transportation).

U.S. GOVERNMENT GRANTS include transfers of goods and services under U.S. military grant programs. The data for 1974 include extraordinary U.S. government transactions with India.

Beginning in 1982, PRIVATE REMITTANCES AND OTHER TRANSFERS includes taxes paid by U.S. private residents to foreign governments and taxes paid by private nonresidents to the U.S. government.

At the present time, all U.S. Treasury-owned *gold* is held in the United States.

Beginning with the data for 1982, DIRECT INVESTMENT INCOME and the reinvested earnings component of DIRECT INVESTMENT financial flows are measured on a current-cost (replacement-cost) basis after adjustment to reported depreciation, depletion, and expensed exploration and development costs. For prior years, depreciation is valued in terms of the historical cost of assets and reflects a mix of prices for the various years in which capital investments were made. See *Survey of Current Business,* July 1999, pp 65–67, and *Survey of Current Business*, June 1992, pages 72ff.

REPAYMENTS ON U.S. CREDITS AND OTHER LONG-TERM ASSETS includes sales of foreign obligations to foreigners. The data for 1974 include extraordinary U.S. government transactions with India, described in "Special U.S. Government Transactions," *Survey of Current Business,* June 1974, page 27.

FOREIGN OFFICIAL ASSETS IN THE UNITED STATES. U.S. TREASURY SECURITIES consists of bills, certificates, marketable bonds and notes, and nonmarketable convertible and nonconvertible bonds and notes; OTHER U.S. GOVERNMENT SECURITIES consists of U.S. Treasury and Export-Import Bank obligations, not included elsewhere, and of debt securities of U.S. government corporations and agencies; OTHER U.S. GOVERNMENT LIABILITIES includes, primarily, U.S. government liabilities associated with military agency sales contracts and other transactions arranged with or through foreign official agencies; OTHER FOREIGN OFFICIAL ASSETS consists of investments in U.S. corporate stocks and in debt securities of private corporations and state and local governments.

Estimates of U.S. CURRENCY FLOWS ABROAD were introduced for the first time as part of the July 1997 revisions. Data for 1974 and subsequent years were affected (see *Survey of Current Business*, July 1997). Beginning with the 1998 revisions, currency flows are published separately from U.S. treasury securities.

For 1978–83, U.S. TREASURY SECURITIES includes foreign currency-denominated notes sold to private residents abroad.

RELATION OF BALANCE ON CURRENT ACCOUNT TO NET FOREIGN INVESTMENT. Conceptually, "net foreign investment" in the national income and product accounts (NIPAs) is equal to the balance on current account plus allocation of special drawing rights. However, the foreign transactions account in the NIPAs includes (a) adjustments to the international transactions accounts for the treatment of gold, (b) adjustments for the different geographical treatment of transactions with U.S. territories and Puerto Rico, and (c) services furnished without payment by financial pension plans except life insurance carriers and private noninsured pension plans. A reconciliation of the balance on goods and services from the international accounts and the NIPA net exports appears periodically in the "Reconciliation and Other Special Tables" section of the *Survey of Current Business*. A reconciliation of the other foreign transactions in the two sets of accounts appears in Table 4.5 of the NIPAs.

REVISIONS

The international transactions accounts are revised annually in July. Changes in definitions and methodology, as well as the incorporation of newly available source data, are introduced in these revisions.

Revisions incorporated in July 1999 include:

- The accounts are now divided into three groups— current account, capital account, and financial account. This change is made to provide a more focused picture of different types of transactions and to remove certain capital transactions from the current account that may distort the analysis of underlying trends in the balance of goods, services, income, and current transfers. Previously, the accounts were divided into a current account and a capital account. The latter measured the concept now renamed the financial account.

- Compensation of employees, previously included in the services account, is now reclassified to the income account, and its coverage has been expanded for 1986–1998. This change places all income transactions together; consequently, both the services account and income account are redefined.

- In the direct investment account and financial accounts, new measures of the current-cost adjustment are introduced for 1982–1998. This change more closely aligns the accounts with economic, rather than business, accounting requirements.

- In the investment income account, greatly improved estimates of income receipts are introduced based on preliminary results of a benchmark survey of the stock of U.S. portfolio investment in long-term foreign securities as of December 31, 1997. The updated position estimates enable BEA to develop improved estimates of bond interest and dividend receipts for 1994–1998.

- In the services account, results from a one-time survey are incorporated into estimates of travel payments for 1997–1998, and revised methodology and updated source data for medical services receipts are introduced for 1995–1998.

- In the new capital account, new estimates of immigrants transfers are introduced for 1982–1998; these estimates are a key component of this account.

- In the income account, new estimates of the compensation of temporary nonagricultural workers in the United States are introduced for 1986–1998.

- In the goods account, improvements to the seasonal adjustment of exports for 1996–1998 have reduced the amount of "residual" seasonality.

DATA AVAILABILITY

Quarterly and annual data are available. Data first are reported in a press release and subsequently published in the *Survey of Current Business*. Revisions to historical data are published annually. The most recent historical revisions appear in the July 1999 issue of the *Survey*. Complete historical data may be purchased on diskette from BEA. Historical data also are available on the BEA internet site (http://www.bea.doc.gov)

REFERENCES

Discussions of the impact of changes in methodology and incorporation of new data sources are found in the July (June for 1995 and earlier) issues of the *Survey of Current Business*, the most recent being "U.S. International Transactions, Revised Estimates for 1982–98" (July 1999).

The Balance of Payments of the United States: Concepts, Data Sources, and Estimating Procedures (May 1990), available on the BEA internet site or from NTIS (Accession No. PB 90-268715) describes the methodology in detail and provides a list of data sources.

PAGES 162–177
EXPORTS AND IMPORTS OF GOODS AND SERVICES

Sources: U.S. Department of Commerce, Bureau of the Census and Bureau of Economic Analysis (BEA)

Monthly and annual data on exports and imports of goods are compiled by the Bureau of the Census from documents collected by the U.S. Customs Service. BEA makes certain adjustments to these data (described below) to place the estimates on a "balance of payments" basis—a basis consistent with the national and international accounts. Data on exports and imports of services are prepared by BEA from a variety of sources. Monthly data on services are available from the beginning of 1992. Annual and quarterly data for earlier years are available as part of the international transactions accounts. Current data on goods and services are available each month in a joint Census-BEA press release.

DEFINITIONS: GOODS

GOODS: CENSUS BASIS. The Census basis goods data are compiled from the documents collected by the U.S. Customs Service and reflect the movement of goods between foreign countries and the 50 states, the District of Columbia, Puerto Rico, the U.S. Virgin Islands, and U.S. Foreign Trade Zones. They include government and non-government shipments of goods. They exclude shipments between the United States and its territories and possessions, transactions with U.S. military, diplomatic and consular installations abroad, U.S. goods returned to the United States by its Armed Forces, personal and household effects of travelers, and in-transit shipments. The general import values reflect the total arrival of merchandise from foreign countries that immediately enters consumption channels, warehouses, or Foreign Trade Zones.

For IMPORTS, the value reported is the U. S. Customs Service appraised value of merchandise (generally, the price paid for merchandise for export to the United States). Import duties, freight, insurance, and other charges incurred in bringing merchandise to the United States are excluded.

EXPORTS are valued at the f.a.s. (free alongside ship) value of merchandise at the U.S. port of export, based on the transaction price including inland freight, insurance, and other charges incurred in placing the merchandise alongside the carrier at the U.S. port of exportation.

GOODS: BALANCE OF PAYMENTS (BOP) BASIS. Goods on a Census basis are adjusted by the BEA to goods on a BOP basis to bring the data in line with the concepts and definitions used to prepare the international and national accounts. Broadly, the adjustments include changes in ownership that occur without goods passing into or out of the customs territory of the United States. These adjustments are necessary to supplement coverage of the Census basis data, to eliminate duplication of transactions recorded elsewhere in the international accounts, and to value transactions according to a standard definition.

The EXPORT adjustments include: (1) Deduction of *U.S. military sales contracts*, because the Census Bureau has included these contracts in the goods data, but BEA includes them in the service category "Transfers Under U.S. Military Sales Contracts." BEA's source material for these contracts is more comprehensive, but does not dis-

tinguish between goods and services. (2) Addition of *private gift parcels* mailed to foreigners by individuals through the U.S. Postal Service. (Only commercial shipments are covered in Census goods exports.) (3) Addition to *nonmonetary gold exports* of gold purchased by foreign official agencies from private dealers in the United States and held at the Federal Reserve Bank of New York. The Census data include only gold that leaves the customs territory. (4) *Smaller adjustments* include deductions for repairs of goods, and for exposed motion picture film, and military grant aid; and additions for sales of fish in U.S. territorial waters, exports of electricity to Mexico, and vessels and oil rigs that change ownership without export documents being filed.

The IMPORT adjustments include: (1) On *inland freight in Canada*, the customs value for imports for certain Canadian goods is the point of origin in Canada. The BEA makes an addition for the inland freight charges of transporting these Canadian goods to the U.S. border. (2) An addition is made to *nonmonetary gold imports* for gold sold by foreign official agencies to private purchasers out of stock held at the Federal Reserve Bank of New York. The Census Bureau data include only gold that enters the customs territory. (3) A deduction is made for *imports by U.S. military agencies* because the Census Bureau has included these contracts in the goods data, but BEA includes them in the service category "Direct Defense Expenditures." BEA's source material is more comprehensive, but does note distinguish between goods and services. (4) *Smaller adjustments* include deductions for repairs of goods and for exposed motion picture film; and additions for imported electricity from Mexico, conversion of vessels for commercial use, and repairs to U.S. vessels abroad.

DEFINITIONS: SERVICES

The statistics are estimates of service transactions between foreign countries and the 50 states, the District of Columbia, Puerto Rico, the U.S. Virgin Islands, and other U.S. territories and possessions. Transactions with U.S. military, diplomatic, and consular installations abroad are excluded because they are considered to be part of the U.S. economy. Services are shown in the broad categories described below. For six of these, the categories are the same for imports and exports. For the seventh, exports is "Transfers under U.S. Military Sales Contracts" while for imports the category is "Direct Defense Expenditures."

TRAVEL—Purchases of services and goods by U.S. travelers abroad and by foreign visitors to the United States. A traveler is defined as a person who stays for a period of less than one year in a country of which the person is not a resident. Included are expenditures for food, lodging, recreation, gifts, and other items incidental to a foreign visit.

PASSENGER FARES—Fares paid by residents of one country to residents in other countries. Receipts consist of fares received by U.S. carriers from foreign residents for travel between the United States and foreign countries and between two foreign points. Payments consist of fares paid by U.S. residents to foreign carriers for travel between the United States and foreign countries.

BREAK IN SERIES: TRAVEL AND PASSENGER FARES — Beginning with data for 1984, these items incorporate results from a survey administered by the U.S. Travel and Tourism Administration. See *Survey of Current Business,* June 1989, pages 57ff.

OTHER TRANSPORTATION — Charges for the transportation of goods by ocean, air, waterway, pipeline, and rail carriers to and from the United States. Includes freight charges, operating expenses that transportation companies incur in foreign ports, and payments for vessel charter and aircraft and freight car rentals. (*Break in series.* Estimates of freight charges for the transportation of goods by truck between the United States and Canada are included in the data beginning with 1986. Reliable estimates for earlier years are not available. See *Survey of Current Business,* June 1994, pages 70ff.)

ROYALTIES AND LICENSE FEES — Transactions with foreign residents involving intangible assets and proprietary rights, such as the use of patents, techniques, processes, formulas, designs, know-how, trademarks, copyrights, franchises, and manufacturing rights. The term "royalties" generally refers to payments for the utilization of copyrights or trademarks, and "license fees" generally refers to payments for the use of patents or industrial processes.

OTHER PRIVATE SERVICES — Transactions with affiliated foreigners for which no identification by type is available and transactions with unaffiliated foreigners. (The term "affiliated" refers to a direct investment relationship, which exists when a U.S. person has ownership or control, directly or indirectly, of 10 percent or more of a foreign business enterprise, or when a foreign person has a similar interest in a U.S. enterprise.) Transactions with unaffiliated foreigners consist of education services; financial services; insurance premiums and losses; telecommunications services; and business, professional, and technical services. Included in the last group are advertising services; computer and data processing services; database and other information services; research, development, and testing services; management, consulting, and public relations services; legal services; construction, engineering, architectural, and mining services; industrial engineering services; installation, maintenance and repair of equipment; and other services, including medical services and film and tape rental.

BEA conducts surveys of international transactions in financial services and "selected services" (largely business, professional, and technical services). Beginning with data for 1986, *other private services* includes estimates of business, professional, and technical services from the BEA surveys of selected services. (See *Survey of Current Business,* June 1989, pages 57ff.)

BREAKS IN SERIES: ROYALTIES AND LICENSE FEES AND OTHER PRIVATE SERVICES — These items are presented on a gross basis beginning in 1982. The definition of exports is revised to exclude U.S. parents' payments to foreign affiliates and to include U.S. affiliates' receipts from foreign parents. The definition of imports is revised to include U.S. parents' payments to foreign affiliates and to exclude U.S. affiliates' receipts from foreign parents.

TRANSFERS UNDER U.S. MILITARY SALES CONTRACTS (exports only) — Exports of goods and services in which U.S. government military agencies participate. Includes both goods, such as equipment, and services, such as repair services and training, that cannot be separately identified. Transfers of goods and services under U.S. military grant programs are included.

DIRECT DEFENSE EXPENDITURES (imports only) — Expenditures incurred by U.S. military agencies abroad, including expenditures by U.S. personnel, payments of wages to foreign residents, construction expenditures, payments for foreign contractual services, and procurement of foreign goods. Included are both goods and services that cannot be separately identified.

U.S. GOVERNMENT MISCELLANEOUS SERVICES — Transactions of U.S. Government nonmilitary agencies with foreign residents. Most of these transactions involve the provision of services to, or purchases of services from, foreigners; transfers of some goods are also included.

Services estimates are based on quarterly, annual, and benchmark surveys and partial information generated from monthly reports. Service transactions are estimated at market prices. Estimates are seasonally adjusted when statistically significant seasonal patterns are present.

DEFINITIONS: AREA GROUPINGS

NORTH AMERICA — Canada, Mexico

SOUTH/CENTRAL AMERICA — Anguilla, Antigua and Barbuda, Argentina, Aruba, Bahamas, Barbados, Belize, Bermuda, Bolivia, Brazil, British Virgin Islands, Cayman Islands, Chile, Colombia, Costa Rica, Cuba, Dominica, Dominican Republic, Ecuador, El Salvador, Falkland Islands, French Guiana, Grenada, Guadeloupe, Guatemala, Guyana, Haiti, Honduras, Jamaica, Martinique, Montserrat, Netherlands Antilles, Nicaragua, Panama, Paraguay, Peru, St. Kitts and Nevis, St. Lucia, St. Vincent and the Grenadines, Suriname, Trinidad and Tobago, Turks and Caicos Islands, Uruguay, Venezuela.

WESTERN EUROPE — Andorra, Austria, Belgium, Bosnia-Herzegovina, Croatia, Cyprus, Denmark, Faroe Islands, Finland, France, Germany, Gibraltar, Greece, Iceland, Ireland, Italy, Liechtenstein, Luxembourg, Malta and Gozo, Macedonia, Monaco, Netherlands, Norway, Portugal, San Marino, Slovenia, Spain, Svalbard, Sweden, Switzerland, Turkey, United Kingdom, Vatican City, Yugoslavia.

EUROPEAN UNION—Austria, Belgium, Denmark, Finland, France, Germany, Greece, Ireland, Italy, Luxembourg, Netherlands, Portugal, Spain, Sweden, United Kingdom.

EUROPEAN FREE TRADE ASSOCIATION—Iceland, Liechtenstein, Norway, Sweden, Switzerland.

EASTERN EUROPE AND FORMER SOVIET REPUBLICS—Albania, Armenia, Azerbaijan, Belarus, Bulgaria, Czech Republic, Estonia, Georgia, Hungary, Kazakhstan, Kyrgyzstan, Latvia, Lithuania, Moldova, Poland, Romania, Russia, Slovakia, Tajikistan, Turkmenistan, Ukraine, Uzbekistan.

ASEAN—Association of Southeast Asian Nations: Brunei, Indonesia, Malaysia, Philippines, Singapore, Thailand.

MERCOSUR (SOUTHERN COMMON MARKET)—Argentina, Brazil, Paraguay, Uruguay.

CENTRAL AMERICAN COMMON MARKET—Costa Rica, El Salvador, Guatemala, Honduras, Nicaragua.

NEWLY INDUSTRIALIZED COUNTRIES—Hong Kong, South Korea, Singapore, Taiwan.

ORGANIZATION OF PETROLEUM EXPORTING COUNTRIES (OPEC)—Algeria, Gabon, Indonesia, Iran, Iraq, Kuwait, Libya, Nigeria, Qatar, Saudi Arabia, United Arab Emirates, Venezuela.

PACIFIC RIM COUNTRIES—Australia, Brunei, China, Hong Kong, Indonesia, Japan, Korea, Macao, Malaysia, New Zealand, Papua New Guinea, Philippines, Singapore, Taiwan.

NOTES ON THE DATA

U.S./CANADA DATA EXCHANGE AND SUBSTITUTION. The data for U.S. exports to Canada are derived from import data compiled by Canada. The use of Canada's import data to produce U.S. export data requires several alignments in order to compare the two series: *Coverage*: Canadian imports are based on country of origin. U.S. goods shipped from a third country are included. U.S. exports exclude these foreign shipments. U.S. export coverage also excludes certain Canadian postal shipments. *Valuation*: Canadian imports are valued at point of origin in the United States. However, U.S. exports are valued at the port of exit in the United States and include inland freight charges, making the U.S. export value slightly larger. Canada requires inland freight to be reported. *Reexports*: U.S. exports include reexports of foreign goods. Again, the aggregate U.S. export figure is slightly larger. *Exchange Rate*: Average monthly exchange rates are applied to convert the published data to U.S. currency.

END-USE CATEGORIES AND SEASONAL ADJUSTMENT OF TRADE IN GOODS. Goods are initially classified under the Harmonized System, which describes and measures the characteristics of goods traded. Combining trade into approximately 140 export and 140 import end-use categories makes it possible to examine goods according to their principal uses. These categories are used as the basis for computing the seasonal and working-day adjusted data. These adjusted data are then summed to the six end-use aggregates for publication.

The seasonal adjustment procedure is based on a model that estimates the monthly movements as percentages above or below the general level of each end-use commodity series (unlike other methods that redistribute the actual series values over the calendar year). Imports of petroleum and petroleum products are adjusted for the length of the month.

DATA AVAILABILITY

Data are released in a monthly joint Census-BEA press release (FT-900) about six weeks after the end of the month to which the data pertain. The data on trade in goods by end-use category (BOP basis) and trade in services are subsequently published each month in the *Survey of Current Business*. Additional data and information on goods is obtainable from the Foreign Trade Division, Bureau of the Census, Washington, DC 20233. Additional data and information on services is obtainable from the Balance of Payments Division, Bureau of Economic Analysis, Washington, DC 20230. Current releases and some historical data are available on the Bureau of the Census internet site (http://www.census.gov/foreign-trade/www/).

REVISIONS

Data for recent years normally are revised annually. Data on trade in services may be subject to extensive revision as part of BEA's annual revision of the international transactions accounts, usually released each June or July.

The services account has been redefined in order to bring it into alignment with the concepts used in the U.S. national income and product accounts and into closer conformance with international guidelines established by the International Monetary Fund. Compensation of foreign workers temporarily employed in the United States and of U.S. workers temporarily employed abroad, which until now has been included indistinguishably as a component of "Other private services", is removed from both services receipts and payments. (The amounts removed are reclassified to the income account of the international transactions accounts, which are released separately by the Bureau of Economic Analysis). As a result of this redefinition, service payments are reduced more than service receipts, thereby increasing the services surplus. Other revisions to the services account result from the use of newly developed data for travel payments for 1997-98, the incorporation of results from annual surveys, and newly available and updated source data.

REFERENCES

Discussion of the impact of changes in methodology and incorporation of new data sources are found in discussions of annual revisions of the international transactions accounts in the June or July issue of the BEA publication, *Survey of Current Business*, the most recent being "U.S. International Transactions, Revised Estimates for 1982–98" (July 1999).

PAGE 178
EXPORT AND IMPORT PRICE INDEXES

Source: U.S. Department of Labor, Bureau of Labor Statistics (BLS)

The BLS International Price Program produces monthly and quarterly export and import price indexes for nonmilitary goods traded between the United States and the rest of the world.

DEFINITIONS

The EXPORT price index provides a measure of price change for all products sold by U.S. residents (i.e., businesses and individuals located within the geographic boundaries of the United States, whether or not owned by U.S. citizens) to foreign buyers.

The IMPORT price index provides a measure of price change for goods purchased from other countries by U.S. residents.

NOTES ON THE DATA

The product universe for both the import and export indexes includes raw materials, agricultural products, and manufactures. Price data are collected primarily by mail questionnaire, in all but a few cases directly from the exporter or importer.

To the extent possible, the data refer to prices at the U.S. border for exports and at either the foreign border or the U.S. border for imports. For nearly all products, the prices refer to transactions completed during the first week of the month and represent the actual price for which the product was bought or sold, including discounts, allowances, and rebates.

The indexes are weighted indexes of the Laspeyres type. The values assigned to each weight category are based on trade value figures compiled by the Bureau of the Census. The weights currently used refer to 1990. Adjustments are made to account for changes in product characteristics in order to obtain a "pure" measure of price change.

For the export price indexes, the preferred pricing basis is f.a.s. (free alongside ship) U.S. port of exportation. Where necessary, adjustments are made to reported prices to place them on this basis. An attempt is made to collect two prices for imports: f.o.b. (free on board) at the port of exportation and c.i.f. (cost, insurance, and freight) at the U.S. port of importation.

DATA AVAILABILITY

Indexes are published monthly in a press release and a more detailed report. Selected data subsequently are published in the *Monthly Labor Review*. Indexes are published for detailed product categories, as well as for all commodities. Aggregate import indexes by country or region of origin also are available, as are indexes for selected categories of internationally traded services. Additional information is available from the Division of International Prices, Bureau of Labor Statistics. Complete historical data are available on the BLS internet site (http://stats.bls.gov).

REFERENCES

"BLS to Produce Monthly Indexes of Export and Import Prices," *Monthly Labor Review* (December 1988) and Chapter 15 "International Price Indexes," *BLS Handbook of Methods* Bulletin 2490 (April 1997).

PAGES 180–184
INTERNATIONAL COMPARISONS: PRODUCTION, PRICES, LABOR FORCE, UNEMPLOYMENT RATES, STOCK INDEXES, AND EXCHANGE RATES

Sources: Industrial Production—Board of Governors of the Federal Reserve System and Department of Commerce, International Trade Administration, Office of Trade and Economic Analysis. Consumer Price Indexes—Department of Labor, Bureau of Labor Statistics and Department of Commerce, International Trade Administration, Office of Trade and Economic Analysis. Unemployment rate and labor force—Department of Labor, Bureau of Labor Statistics. Stock Price Indexes—Commodity Systems, Inc. Exchange Rates—Board of Governors of the Federal Reserve System.

INDUSTRIAL PRODUCTION. The index base is 1992=100. The German data before 1991 apply to West Germany only. The indexes for countries other than the United States are from the Office of Trade and Economic Analysis. Data for the United States are from the Federal Reserve (See the notes for pages 60–73).

CONSUMER PRICE INDEXES. The index base is 1982–1984=100. The data for Germany prior to 1991 are for West Germany only. Data for countries other than the United States are provided by the Office of Trade and Economic Analysis. Data for the United States are from the Bureau of Labor Statistics.

UNEMPLOYMENT RATES AND LABOR FORCES. These data are from the U.S. Bureau of Labor Statistics (BLS), and have been adjusted by BLS to approximate U.S. concepts and definitions. The quarterly unemployment rates for France, Germany, and the United Kingdom before 1992 should be taken as less precise approximations of the U.S. concept of unemployment than the annual data. The German data are for West Germany only and do not cover former East Germany.

No adjustment is made to unemployment rates from Canada. Slight adjustments are made to those from Japan. Substantial adjustments were made to the Italian data prior to a 1992 definitional change. For France, Germany, and the United Kingdom before 1992, unemployment adjustment factors were based on annual household labor force surveys.

The concept of "layoffs" differ from country to country. In the United States and Canada, persons who are laid off are classified as unemployed. The employees do not remain on the payroll, receive no payments from their firms, and are frequently not rehired. However, in Europe and Japan, these people are classified as employed. In general, employers reduce hours or days worked, rather than letting people go for weeks without work. The workers continue to receive pay, which is supplemented by a subsidy for time not worked. Because of these differences, the strict U.S. definition of unemployment is not applied on this point.

The adjusted statistics use the age at which compulsory schooling ends in each country instead of the U.S. standard of 16 years and older. This is 16 years in France and in the United Kingdom since 1973; 15 years in Canada, Japan, Germany, Italy since 1993, and the United Kingdom before 1973; and 14 years in Italy before 1993. Data pertain to the noninstitutional population except in Japan and Germany, where the institutionalized population of working age is included.

There are several breaks in the series due to changes in methods or definitions. Among the more important of these are ones for the United States (1994), France (1992), Germany (1983), and Italy (1986, 1991, and 1993).

These data and more in-depth information on measurement procedures and standards are available from the Bureau of Labor Statistics internet site (http://stats.bls.gov).

STOCK PRICE INDEXES. Daily closing averages (except for the S&P 500) are provided by Commodity Systems, Inc. (CSI) and averaged by months and years by the editors. The daily data are available for a fee from CSI in a variety of forms, including electronically. CSI can be contacted at www.csidata.com, or by telephone at (800) 274-4727. These data cannot be reproduced without permission from the source. The Standard and Poor's composite is an index of 500 stocks based on 1941–1943=10 compiled by Standard and Poor's Corporation.

EXCHANGE RATES. The monthly data shown are averages of the daily exchange rates. The annual data are averages of the monthly figures. The established G-10 index and three newer trade-weighted indexes of the value of the dollar against groups of foreign currency appear first in this table. These newer indexes have been developed by the Federal Reserve as a response to two major developments. One is the growing trade between the United States and countries other than the G-10 members. The other is the establishment of the European Economic and Monetary Union (EMU), of which five G-10 countries are members. As members, their national currencies are being replaced by the euro. Thus, the G-10 index was discontinued as of the end of 1998, and these new indexes take its place.

These indexes are weighted based on trade flows. The weighting scheme can be summarized as the country's share of U.S. imports, the country's share of U.S. exports, and the country's share of exports that go to another country that is a large importer of U.S. goods.

THE BROAD INDEX (January 1997=100): Share of U.S. exports determines the selection of a country's currency for the index. Basically, currencies were selected from countries that had a share of U.S. nonoil or nonagricultural exports of at least 0.5 percent. These countries are then divided up into the Major Currency and Other Important Trading Partners below. The selection of countries is updated annually when currency weights are adjusted.

MAJOR CURRENCY INDEX (March 1973=100): This index serves purposes similar to the G-10 index, namely a measure of the competitiveness of U.S. goods and a gauge of financial pressure on the dollar. The index includes countries whose currencies are traded in deep and relatively liquid financial markets and for which information on short and long-term interests rates are readily available. A benefit of this country group is that it excludes economies that have been subject to high inflation. The large depreciation of those currencies would mask movement of the dollar's value against other currencies. As of October 1998, this index includes the currencies of the following countries: Canada, Euro area (Germany, France, Italy, Netherlands, Belgium and Luxembourg, Spain, Ireland, Austria, Finland, and Portugal), Japan, United Kingdom, Switzerland, Australia, and Sweden.

OTHER IMPORTANT TRADING PARTNERS (OITP) INDEX (January 1997=100): This index captures the competitiveness of U.S. goods in key emerging markets in Latin America, Asia, the Middle East, and Eastern Europe. Because of the episodes of hyperinflation that some of the countries have experienced, this index is more useful for analysis of short-term exchange rate movements. The countries that make up this index include, as of October 1998, Mexico, China, Taiwan, South Korea, Singapore, Hong Kong, Malaysia, Brazil, Thailand, Indonesia, Philippines, Russia, India, Saudi Arabia, Israel, Argentina, Venezuela, Chile, and Columbia.

G-10 INDEX (March 1973=100): This measure is an index of the weighted average exchange value of the U.S. dollar against the currencies of other G-10 (industrialized) countries, which are Belgium, Canada, France, Germany, Italy, Japan, the Netherlands, Sweden, Switzerland, and the United Kingdom. This index was revised in August 1978. Unlike the previous three indexes, the weights on this index were fixed, and annual revisions were not necessary. These data are from the Federal Reserve and were published weekly in the H.10 release. The Federal Reserve ceased to calculate this index as of December 1998.

More information on the dollar value indexes can be found in the article "New Summary Measures of the Foreign Exchange Value of the Dollar," *Federal Reserve Bulletin*, vol. 84 (October 1998). This is available on the Federal Reserve web site, www.federalreserve.gov.

Foreign exchange rates shown are averages of the daily noon buying rates in New York City for cable transfers payable in foreign currencies. These data are published in the Federal Reserve H.10 statistical release, available on the Federal Reserve web site, www.federalreserve.gov. Additional information can be found on the Federal Reserve Bank of St. Louis web site, http://www.stls.frb.org/fred/data/exchange.html.

PAGES 188–192
MINING INDUSTRIES

Sources: Industrial production and capacity utilization: Board of Governors of the Federal Reserve System (see notes to pages 60–73); producer prices and employment, hours, and earnings: U.S. Department of Labor, Bureau of Labor Statistics (see notes to pages 96–100 and 117–122)

Mining (SIC Division B) includes all establishments primarily engaged in mining. The term mining is used in the broad sense to include the extraction of naturally occurring solids (such as coals and ores), liquids (such as crude petroleum), and gases (such as natural gas). Quarrying, well operations, and other preparation customarily done at the mine site are included, as are exploration and development of mineral properties.

Oil and gas extraction (SIC Major Group 13) is classified in mining and includes producing crude petroleum and natural gas; extracting oil from oil sands and shale; producing natural gas and cycle condensate; and producing gas and hydrocarbon liquids from coal at the mine site. Petroleum refining is classified in Manufacturing, Major Group 39. Pipeline transportation of oil and gas is classified in Division E, Transportation.

NOTES ON THE DATA

INDUSTRIAL PRODUCTION AND CAPACITY UTILIZATION. These indexes are for industry groups as defined by the SIC code. The indexes for *total mining* cover SIC Division B as described above; *metal mining* covers Major Group 10, which includes mining for iron, copper, lead, zinc, gold, silver, and ferroalloy ores; *coal mining* covers SIC Major

Group 12, which includes mining for bituminous coal and lignite and anthracite coal; *oil and gas extraction* covers Major Group 13, which includes extraction of crude oil and natural gas, production of natural gas liquids, and oil field services; *crude oil and natural gas* covers SIC 131, oil and gas extraction; *natural gas liquids* is SIC 132; and *oil and gas well drilling* is SIC 138, which also includes other oil and gas field services. *Stone and earth minerals* is Major Group 14, which includes mining and quarrying of stone, sand and gravel, clay, and chemical and fertilizer minerals.

The PRODUCER PRICE indexes and EMPLOYMENT, HOURS, AND EARNINGS data for metal mining and coal mining cover SICs 10 and 12, respectively; *oil and gas extraction* covers SIC 13; the indexes for crude materials use the stage-of-processing classification. The data for *nonmetallic minerals except fuel* cover SIC 14.

PAGE 193
PETROLEUM AND PETROLEUM PRODUCTS—IMPORTS AND STOCKS

Sources: Imports: U.S. Department of Commerce, Bureau of the Census (see notes to pages 162–177); stocks U.S. Department of Energy, Energy Information Administration.

NOTES ON THE DATA

The import data are published as Exhibit 17: "Imports of Energy-related Petroleum Products, including Crude Petroleum" of the monthly Census-BEA foreign trade press release. *Total energy-related petroleum products* include the following standard international trade classification (SITC) commodity groupings: crude oil, petroleum preparations, and liquefied propane and butane gas.

The data on petroleum stocks are derived from the Department of Energy's weekly petroleum supply reporting system and are published in the Energy Information Administration publication "Petroleum Supply Monthly." Stock totals are as of the end of the period. Geographic coverage includes the 50 states and the District of Columbia.

DATA AVAILABILITY

Data on stocks are available from the Energy Information Administration internet site (http://www.eia.doe.gov). See the notes to pages 162–177 for availability of import data.

PAGES 196–197
CONSTRUCTION COSTS, PRICES, EMPLOYMENT, HOURS, AND EARNINGS

Sources: Construction cost indexes: U.S. Department of Commerce, Bureau of the Census; producer prices; employment, hours, and earnings: U.S. Department of Labor, Bureau of Labor Statistics (see notes to pages 96–100 and 117–122)

Construction (SIC Division C) includes establishments primarily engaged in construction, including new work, additions, alterations, reconstruction, installations, and repairs. Construction of buildings and heavy construction other than buildings are included. Specialized construction activities, such as plumbing, painting, and electrical work, also are included.

General building contractors is SIC Major Group 15 and includes both residential and nonresidential building; heavy construction except building is Major Group 16 and includes highways, pipelines, power lines, water mains, and other heavy construction; special trade contractors is Major Group 17 and includes plumbing, painting, carpentry, and other specialized building trades.

The *Construction Cost Indexes* are included in the Bureau of the Census "Construction Put in Place" release (C-30 release). See the notes to pages 198–200 for additional information on availability.

PAGES 198–200
CONSTRUCTION PUT IN PLACE

Source: U.S. Department of Commerce, Bureau of the Census

The Census Bureau's estimates of the value of new construction put in place are intended to provide monthly estimates of the total dollar value of construction work done in the United States.

DEFINITIONS AND NOTES ON THE DATA

The estimates cover all construction work done each month on new residential and nonresidential buildings and structures, public construction, and improvements to existing buildings and structures. Included are the cost of labor and materials; cost of architectural and engineering work; overhead costs assigned to the project; interest and taxes paid during construction; and contractor's profits.

The total value put-in-place for a given period is the sum of the value of work done on all projects underway during this period, regardless of when work on each individual project was started or when payment was made to the contractors. For some categories, estimates are derived by distributing the total construction cost of the project by means of historic construction progress patterns.

The statistics on the value of construction put in place result from direct measurement and indirect estimation. A series results from direct measurement when it is based on reports of the actual value of construction progress or construction expenditures obtained from a complete census or sample survey. All other series are developed by indirect estimation using related construction statistics. On an annual basis, the estimates for series directly measured monthly, quarterly, or annually accounted for about 71 percent of total construction in 1998 (private multifamily

residential, private residential improvements, private nonresidential buildings, farm nonresidential construction, public utility construction, all other private construction, and virtually all of public construction). On a monthly basis, directly measured data are available for about 55 percent of the value-in-place estimates.

The data shown are divided into three categories: not seasonally adjusted, seasonally adjusted at annual rate, and constant 1992 dollars, seasonally adjusted at annual rate. The seasonally adjusted at annual rate data are obtained by removing normal seasonal movement from the unadjusted data to bring out underlying trends and business cycles. Seasonal adjustment accounts for month-to-month variations resulting from normal or average changes in any phenomena affecting the data such as weather conditions, the differing lengths of months, and the varying number of weekdays and weekends within each month. It neither adjusts for abnormal conditions within each month nor for year-to-year variations in weather. The seasonally adjusted annual rate is the seasonally adjusted monthly rate multiplied by 12.

The constant 1992 dollar series are converted from monthly estimates in current dollars using cost indexes derived for each category of construction. The deflators for the various categories are related indexes or combinations of related indexes from private companies and federal agencies. The selection of the indexes and procedures used for developing the deflators for each category resulted primarily from recommendations made jointly by the Bureau of Economic Analysis and the Census Bureau.

NEW HOUSING UNITS includes new houses, apartments, condominiums, and town houses. The classification excludes residential units in buildings that are primarily nonresidential. It also excludes mobile homes and houseboats. *Improvements* (included in total residential but not shown separately) includes remodeling, additions, and major replacements to properties subsequent to completion of original building. It includes construction of additional housing units in existing residential structures; finishing of basements and attics; and modernization of kitchens, bathrooms, etc. Also included are improvements outside of residential structures, such as the addition of swimming pools and garages, and replacement of major equipment items such as water heaters, furnaces, and central air-conditioners. Maintenance and repair work is not included.

NONRESIDENTIAL BUILDINGS includes industrial, office, hotels and motels, and other commercial buildings. It also includes categories not shown separately in this book, including religious, educational, cultural, and health care facilities.

INDUSTRIAL includes all buildings and structures at manufacturing sites. OFFICE includes office and professional buildings used primarily for office space. HOTELS, MOTELS includes hotels, motels, resort lodging, tourist courts and cabins, and similar facilities. OTHER COMMERCIAL includes buildings and structures which are intended for use by wholesale, retail, or service trade establishments. For example, shopping centers or malls, department stores, low-rise banks and financial institutions, drug stores, parking garages, auto service stations and repair garages, beauty schools, grocery stores, restaurants, and dry cleaning stores are included in this category. Also included are warehouses and storage buildings, cold storage plants, grain elevators and silos, except such facilities at industrial sites.

PUBLIC UTILITIES construction expenditures are classified in terms of the industry rather than the function of the building or structure. Construction expenditures made by the following types of privately owned public utility companies or cooperatives are included in this category: Railroad, telephone, telegraph, television cable, petroleum pipelines, electric light and power, and gas manufacturing, transmission, and distribution.

Also included in total private construction are farm construction and privately-built streets and bridges, dams and reservoirs, sewer and water facilities, golf courses, parks and playgrounds, and airfields.

PUBLIC CONSTRUCTION includes both state and local construction and federal construction. State and local construction includes housing and redevelopment, educational facilities, hospitals, general administrative buildings, police and fire buildings, industrial buildings, parking and transportation facilities, highways, streets, and buildings, sewer systems, water systems, erosion control and other resource protective construction, and miscellaneous nonbuilding construction.

HOUSING AND REDEVELOPMENT includes houses, apartment buildings, and all other residential structures. HIGHWAYS AND STREETS includes highways, streets, bridges, overpasses, tunnels, toll facilities, street lighting, and miscellaneous road erosion control.

FEDERAL CONSTRUCTION in general is classified based on the agency responsible for the work; for example, Veterans Administration expenditures are classified as "hospital," and Bureau of Reclamation expenditures are classified as "conservation and development." However, the expenditures reported by a few agencies are subdivided into two or more types of construction.

HOUSING includes new family housing units and the rehabilitation of existing units constructed for the armed services. Military barracks, bachelor officers' quarters, and family housing for Coast Guard personnel are classified under "military facilities." Housing for forest rangers and national park employees is classified under "conservation and development."

INDUSTRIAL includes construction done at Department of Energy research and development facilities. It also includes manufacturing, assembling, and processing buildings and their related facilities, such as arsenals, ordnance works, and shipyards.

MILITARY FACILITIES, with the specific exceptions noted below, covers construction owned by the Department of Defense and the Coast Guard. This category includes troop housing, administration and training buildings, warehouses, mess halls, recreation centers, educational facilities, airfields and airport buildings, missile sites, etc. The following specific types of construction owned by the Department of Defense are classified in other categories: Family housing for the armed services, civil works, industrial facilities, military hospitals, and soldiers' homes.

HIGHWAYS AND STREETS includes streets, bridges, vehicular tunnels, viaducts, and forest and park roads owned by federal agencies other than the Department of Defense. Also included are the following built in connection with a federal road: culverts, drainage, erosion control, lighting, guard rails, and earthwork protective structures.

The monthly and annual estimates of construction put in place are derived by combining data from sample surveys, direct reporting by federal agencies, and indirect estimates for categories not available directly. Among the sample surveys from which data are derived are the Census Bureau's Construction Progress Reporting Survey, Housing Starts Survey, and Housing Sales Survey, and the Bureau of Labor Statistics' Consumer Expenditure Survey.

REVISIONS

Revised data for recent years normally are published each May. The revisions incorporate data not previously available. Seasonally-adjusted statistics are also revised using newly computed seasonal factors. Data for 1995 and subsequent years were revised in May 1999. Information on the revisions is found in the May 1999 issue of the Bureau of the Census monthly publication "Current Construction Reports—Value of Construction Put in Place" (the C-30 Report). The full report is available on the Bureau of the Census internet site.

DATA AVAILABILITY

The construction put in place data are first issued in a monthly press release. A full report (the C-30 report) follows. Data are shown by type of construction, seasonally-adjusted and unadjusted, and in current and constant dollars. Statistics are available monthly at the U.S. level, and, for selected categories, are available annually by the nine geographic divisions. The Census Bureau has derived monthly estimates of new construction put in place since 1960.

Press releases on expenditures for residential improvements and repairs are issued quarterly. An annual supplement shows data by specific kind of job (e.g., painting) and by region.

Current data and some historical data are available on the Bureau of the Census internet site (http://www.census.gov)

Additional data related to the value of construction put in place can be found in the following issues of the Bureau of the Census publication *Current Construction Reports, Value of Construction Put in Place* (the C30 Report):

- May 1999, C30/99-5, containing annual data for 1994 to 1998 and monthly data for 1996 to 1998. This report also describes the relationship of the Construction Put in Place Estimates to estimates of the construction components of the GDP and provides detailed definitions and descriptions of sources and methodology.

- June 1999, C30/99-6, containing annual value of construction put in place for private nonresidential buildings by geographic area and detailed types of construction for 1994 to 1998.

- July 1997, C30/97-7, containing annual value of construction put in place for private nonresidential buildings by geographic area and detailed types of construction for 1973 to 1996.

- October 1992, C30/92-10, containing total time and monthly progress from start to completion for private nonresidential buildings and for state and local construction.

and in these additional Bureau of the Census publications:

- Current Construction Reports, Value of New Construction Put in Place in the United States, 1964 to 1980, C30-80 supplement, 1981 containing annual data for 1915 to 1963.
- Current Construction Reports Special Study, "Expenditures for Nonresidential Improvements and Repairs: 1992," 1994.

PAGE 201
HOUSING STARTS AND PERMITS; HOME SALES AND PRICES

Sources: U.S. Department of Commerce, Bureau of the Census and National Association of Realtors

These data are mainly from two Bureau of the Census Surveys. The *Building Permits Survey* provides current data on new residential construction authorized by building permits. The *Survey of Construction* covers housing starts and completions. A *Housing Sales Survey* is a subset of the Survey of Construction and covers new homes sold and for sale. Data on sales of existing homes are from the Existing Homes Survey of the National Association of Realtors.

NOTES ON THE DATA

The BUILDING PERMITS SURVEY covers all places that issue permits to authorize new private residential buildings or changes in or demolition of existing structures. Data are collected through a mail-out/mail-back monthly survey of selected permit-issuing places and an annual mail-out/mail-back census of the permit-issuing places that do not report monthly.

Data on housing units authorized by local building permits relate to the time of issuance rather than to the actual start of construction. They do, however, provide some indication of residential building activity in advance of the start of actual construction. Although construction is started on most residential buildings in the same month in which the permit is issued, several months sometimes may pass before start of construction.

The 19,000 areas with local building permit systems for which figures are currently published account for a major portion of residential building in the United States. For the country as a whole, approximately 96 percent of private housing units are now constructed in permit-issuing places. Beginning with 1994, data are based upon 19,000 places. Data for 1984 through 1993 are for 17,000 places; data for 1978 through 1983 are for 16,000 places; data for 1972 through 1977 are for 14,000 places; data for 1967 through 1971 are for 13,000 places.

The SURVEY OF CONSTRUCTION provides current data on starts and completions of new single- and multi-family housing units and sales of new one-family houses. It covers new residential buildings currently authorized by a building permit or started in areas not requiring a building permit. The data collected include start date, completion date, sale date, sales price (for single-family houses only), and physical characteristics of each housing unit, such as square footage and number of bedrooms. Data are collected through telephone or personal interviews.

The start of construction of a privately owned housing unit is when excavation begins for the footings or foundation of a building intended primarily as a housekeeping residential structure and designed for nontransient occupancy. All housing units in a multifamily building are defined as being started when excavation for the building has begun.

The HOUSING SALES SURVEY (a subset of the Survey of Construction) is conducted by the Bureau of the Census under contract with the U.S. Department of Housing and Urban Development. Statistics are estimates derived from a survey of new one-family houses sold or for sale for which building permits have been issued in permit-issuing places, or which have been started in nonpermit areas. The information is obtained by monthly interviews with the builders or owners of the new houses in the sample. These monthly interviews continue until the house is sold or withdrawn from the sales market.

The SALES PRICE used in this survey is the price agreed upon between the purchaser and the seller at the time the first sales contract is signed or deposit made. It includes the price of the improved lot. The *median sales price* is the sales price of the house which falls on the middle point of the total number of houses sold. Half of the houses sold have a sales price less than the median; half have a greater price. Changes in the median sales price reflect the changing proportion of houses of different size, locations, etc., as well as any changes in the sales price of houses of identical characteristics.

Beginning with the data for 1977, data on MOBILE HOME SHIPMENTS are compiled from manufacturers' reports to the National Conference of States on Building Codes and Standards (NCSBCS). Data for earlier years are those provided by the Manufactured Housing Institute (MHI).

A mobile home (also referred to as a manufactured home) is defined as a movable dwelling, 8 feet or more wide and 40 feet or more long, designed to be towed on its own chassis, with transportation gear integral to the unit when it leaves the factory and without need of a permanent foundation. These mobile homes include multiwides and expandable mobile homes. Excluded are travel trailers, motor homes, and modular housing. The shipments figures are based on reports submitted by manufacturers on the number of mobile homes actually shipped during the survey month. Shipments to dealers may not necessarily be placed for residential use in the same month as they are shipped. The number of mobile "homes" used for nonresidential purposes is not known.

Data on SALES OF EXISTING SINGLE-FAMILY homes pertain to homes occupied prior to sale and represent closed or pending sales contracts. These data are from the National Association of Realtors.

DATA AVAILABILITY

Housing start and building permit data have been collected by the Bureau of the Census monthly since 1959. Prior to 1959, building permit data were collected by the Bureau of Labor Statistics.

Housing Starts and Building Permits press releases contain the first available start and permit data and are released three weeks after the reference month. New One Family Homes Sold (C25) reports are released six weeks after the reference month and provide data on houses sold and for sale, average and median sale prices, and sale prices by type of financing. Both releases contain national and regional data.

Housing Starts (C20) reports are available four weeks after the reference period and Housing Units Authorized by Building Permits reports six weeks after. These contain more detailed data than the earlier press releases.

These reports are available on the Bureau of the Census internet site (http://www.census.gov)

Historical statistics on new one-family houses sold and for sale from 1963 to date are available from Residential Construction Branch, Manufacturing and Construction

Division, Bureau of the Census, Washington, DC 20233-6900. Telephone: 301-457-1321.

Existing-homes sales data are published monthly in *Real Estate Outlook: Market Trends and Insights*, available by subscription from the National Association of Realtors and also are available on the National Association of Realtors internet site (http://nar.realtor.com).

REFERENCES

Definitions and methodological descriptions for the Census Bureau surveys are provided in the January 1999 issues of the Bureau's Housing Starts (C20) and New One Family Homes Sold (C25) monthly publications.

For further information on NCSBCS mobile home data collection procedures, write to NCSBCS, 505 Huntmar Park Drive, Suite 210, Herndon, VA 20170.

PAGES 204–206
TOTAL MANUFACTURING: PRODUCTION, CAPACITY, PRICES, EMPLOYMENT, HOURS, AND EARNINGS

Sources: Industrial production and capacity utilization: Board of Governors of the Federal Reserve System (see notes to pages 60–75); producer prices and employment, hours, and earnings: U.S. Department of Labor, Bureau of Labor Statistics (see notes to pages 96–100 and 117–135)

Manufacturing (SIC Division D) includes establishments engaged in the mechanical or chemical transformation of materials or substances into new products. These establishments typically are described as plants, factories, or mills. The Division is subdivided into 20 Major Groups, each of which is described briefly at the beginning of the notes for the pages on which data for the group are presented.

There are numerous borderline cases between manufacturing and other divisions of the SIC. Logging, for example, is included in manufacturing, while threshing and cotton ginning fall under Agriculture, Forestry, and Fishing. Dressing of ores and crushing and grinding of sand and gravel are classified under Mining. Production of computer software is classified under Services.

NOTES ON THE DATA

Many data series divide manufacturing into durable and nondurable goods. *Durable goods* include SIC Major Groups 24, 25, and 32 through 39 (lumber and wood products; furniture and fixtures; stone, clay, and glass; primary metals industries; fabricated metal products; industrial and commercial machinery and computer equipment; electronic and other electrical equipment; transportation equipment; instruments; and miscellaneous manufactures). *Nondurable goods* include Major Groups 20 through 23 and 26 through 31 (food and kindred products; tobacco products; textile mill products; apparel and related products; paper and allied products; printing and publishing; chemicals; petroleum refining; rubber and miscellaneous plastic products; and leather and leather products).

PAGES 207–218
MANUFACTURERS' SHIPMENTS, INVENTORIES, AND ORDERS

Source: U.S. Department of Commerce, Bureau of the Census.

These data are from the Bureau of the Census monthly M3 survey, a survey covering all manufacturing and intended to provide measures of changes in domestic manufacturing activity and indications of future production commitments.

DEFINITIONS AND NOTES ON THE DATA

SHIPMENTS. The value of shipments data represent net selling values, f.o.b. (free on board) plant, after discounts and allowances and excluding freight charges and excise taxes. For multi-establishment companies, the M3 reports typically are company- or division-level reports that encompass groups of plants or products. The data reported are usually net sales and receipts from customers and do not include the value of interplant transfers. The reported sales are used to calculate month-to-month changes which bring forward the universe estimates developed from the Annual Survey of Manufactures (ASM). The value of products made elsewhere under contract from materials owned by the plant is also included in shipments, as well as receipts for contract work performed for others, resales, miscellaneous activities such as the sale of scrap and refuse, installation and repair work performed by employees of the plant, and the receipts for research and development performed at the plant.

INVENTORIES. Inventories in the M3 survey are collected on a current cost or pre-LIFO basis. Because different inventory valuation methods are reflected in the reported data, the estimates differ slightly from replacement cost estimates. Companies using the LIFO (last in, first out) method for valuing inventories report their pre-LIFO value; that is, the adjustment to their base-period prices is excluded. In the ASM, inventories are collected according to this same definition. However, there are discontinuities in the historical data in both surveys. Inventory data prior to 1982 are not comparable to later years because of changes in valuation methods. Until 1982, respondents were asked in the ASM to report their inventories at book values; that is, according to whatever method they used for tax purposes (LIFO, FIFO [first in, first out], and so forth.) Because of this, the value of aggregate inventories for an industry was not precise. The change in instructions for reporting current cost inventories was carried to the monthly survey beginning in January 1987. The data for 1982 to 1987 were redefined (but not recollected) on a pre-LIFO or current cost basis.

Inventory data are requested from respondents by stage of fabrication; that is, finished goods, work in process, and raw materials and supplies. There are several limitations to the quality of these data for two reasons. First, response to the stage of fabrication inquiries is lower than for total inventories because all companies do not keep their data monthly at this level of detail. Second, a product considered to be a finished good in one industry, such as steel mills shapes, may be reported as a raw material in another industry, such as stamping plants. Therefore, within the two-digit SIC major groups the same type of inventory may be included under different stage of fabrication categories. Like total inventories, stage of fabrication inventories are also benchmarked to the ASM data, but the stage of fabrication data are benchmarked at the two-digit major group level.

NEW ORDERS RECEIVED AND UNFILLED ORDERS. New orders, as reported in the monthly survey, are net of order cancellations and include orders received and filled during the month as well as orders received for future delivery. They also include the value of contract changes that increase or decrease the value of the unfilled orders to which they relate. Orders are defined to include those supported by binding legal documents such as signed contracts, letters of award, or letters of intent, although in some industries this definition may not be strictly applicable. Unfilled orders include orders (as defined above) that have not been reflected as shipments. Generally, unfilled orders at the end of the reporting period are equal to unfilled orders at the beginning of the period plus net new orders received less net shipments.

COVERAGE. The M3 survey covers companies that have employees and are classified in SIC Division D, Manufacturing. The monthly estimates are based on information obtained from most manufacturing companies with $500 million or more in annual shipments, as well as from selected smaller companies.

BENCHMARKING AND REVISIONS

Data beginning with 1982 were revised in mid-1996. The revisions were the result of: (1) benchmarking the shipments and inventory data to the revised, drift adjusted, 1988-1991 ASM; 1992 Census of Manufactures; and 1993-1994 ASM; (2) benchmarking the defense shipments series to the 1992 MC9675, "Shipments to Federal Government Agencies"; (3) adjusting new and unfilled orders to be consistent with the benchmarked shipments and inventory data; (4) correcting monthly data for late receipts, reclassification of reported data, and revisions to previously reported data; (5) updating the trading day adjustment factors for the shipments series; and (6) updating the seasonal adjustment factors for all series, including re-evaluating options used.

Data beginning with 1987 were further revised in July 1999. The revisions reflect benchmarking to the 1995-1996 ASM, revision of seasonal factors, and other adjustments.

Data have been collected monthly since 1958.

An Advance Report on Durable Goods Manufacturers' Shipments and Orders is available as a press release about 17 working days after the end of each month. Content includes seasonally and not seasonally adjusted estimates of shipments, new orders, and unfilled orders for durable goods industries.

The Manufacturers' Shipments, Inventories, and Orders reports are released about 22 working days after the end of each month. Content includes revisions to the advance report plus estimates for inventories and nondurable goods industries, tabulations by market category, and ratios of shipments to inventories and to unfilled orders. Revisions include selected data for the two previous months.

Computer diskettes, including data back to 1958, can be purchased from Manufacturing & Construction Division, Manufacturers' Shipments, Inventories, and Orders Branch, Bureau of the Census, Washington, D.C. 20233, (301) 457-4804. The data also are available on the Census Bureau internet site (http://www.census.gov).

REFERENCES

Bureau of the Census publication M3-1(97), "Manufacturers' Shipments, Inventories, and Orders 1987-1997" contains the 1998 revisions. Report M3-1(95), (July 1996) contains revised data beginning with 1982. These reports can be purchased from Census Bureau's customer services on (301) 457-4100.

PAGES 220–221
LUMBER AND WOOD PRODUCTS

Sources: Industrial production and capacity utilization: Board of Governors of the Federal Reserve System (see notes to pages 60–73); producer prices and employment, hours, and earnings: U.S. Department of Labor, Bureau of Labor Statistics (see notes to pages 96–100 and 117–135)

Lumber and wood products (SIC Major Group 24) includes timber and pulpwood cutting; sawmills and other mills engaged in producing basic wooden materials; and manufacture of finished articles made entirely or mostly of wood. However, furniture, office fixtures, musical instruments, toys, and some other wooden articles are classified elsewhere.

INDUSTRIAL PRODUCTION: *Logging* (SIC 241) covers timber cutting and production of rough products in the field, including wood chips; *lumber* (SIC 242) covers sawmills and planing mills; *lumber products* includes millwork, veneer, plywood, and structural wood members (SIC 243), wood containers (SIC 244), wood buildings and mobile homes (SIC 245), and miscellaneous wood products (SIC 249); *plywood* includes hardwood and softwood veneer and plywood (SIC 2435, 2436); *manufactured homes* (SIC

245) includes mobile homes (as distinct from motor homes, which are in SIC 371) and prefabricated wood buildings and components.

PAGE 222
FURNITURE AND FIXTURES

Sources: Industrial production and capacity utilization: Board of Governors of the Federal Reserve System (see notes to pages 60–73); producer prices and employment, hours, and earnings: U.S. Department of Labor, Bureau of Labor Statistics (see notes to pages 96–100 and 117–135)

FURNITURE AND FIXTURES (SIC Major Group 25) includes manufacture of household, office, public building, and restaurant furniture and of office and store fixtures.

INDUSTRIAL PRODUCTION: *Household furniture* (SIC 251) includes household furniture, including upholstered, made of wood, metal, or other materials.

PAGES 223–224
STONE, CLAY, AND GLASS

Sources: Industrial production and capacity utilization: Board of Governors of the Federal Reserve System (see notes to pages 60–73); manufacturers' shipments, and inventories: U.S. Department of Commerce, Bureau of the Census (see notes to pages 207–218); producer prices and employment, hours, and earnings: U.S. Department of Labor, Bureau of Labor Statistics (see notes to pages 96–100 and 117–135)

Stone, clay, glass, and concrete products (SIC Major Group 32) includes manufacture of flat glass and other glass products, cement, structural clay products, pottery, concrete and gypsum products, cut stone, abrasive and asbestos products, and other products from materials taken from the earth principally in the form of stone, clay, and sand. When separate reports are available, mining and quarrying are classified in Division B, Mining.

INDUSTRIAL PRODUCTION: *Pressed and blown glass* (SIC 322) includes manufacture of pressed, blown, or shaped glass and glassware from glass produced in the same establishment; *glass containers* (SIC 3221) covers manufacture of glass containers for commercial packing and bottling and for home canning; *cement* (SIC 324) covers hydraulic cement, including portland, natural, masonry, and pozzolana cements; *structural clay products* (SIC 325) covers brick and structural clay tile; *concrete and miscellaneous* covers pottery and related products (SIC 326), concrete, gypsum, and plaster products (SIC 327), cut stone and stone products (SIC 328), and abrasive, asbestos, and miscellaneous nonmetallic mineral products (SIC 329).

PAGES 225–229
PRIMARY METALS

Sources: Industrial production and capacity utilization: Board of Governors of the Federal Reserve System (see notes to pages 60–73); manufacturers' shipments, inventories, and orders: U.S. Department of Commerce, Bureau of the Census (see notes to pages 207–218); producer prices and employment, hours, and earnings: U.S. Department of Labor, Bureau of Labor Statistics (see notes to pages 96–100 and 117–135)

Primary metal industries (SIC Major Group 33) includes smelting and refining of ferrous and nonferrous metals from ore, pig, or scrap; rolling, drawing, and alloying metals; manufacture of castings and other basic metal products; and manufacture of nails, spikes, and insulated wire and cable. The production of coke is included. Manufacture of metal forgings or stampings are classified in Major Group 34, Fabricated Metal Products.

INDUSTRIAL PRODUCTION: *iron and steel* includes steel works, blast furnaces, and rolling and finishing mills (SIC 331) and iron and steel foundries (SIC 332); *basic steel and mill products* is SIC 331.

PAGES 230–231
FABRICATED METAL PRODUCTS

Sources: Industrial production and capacity utilization: Board of Governors of the Federal Reserve System (see notes to pages 60–73); manufacturers' shipments, inventories, and orders: U.S. Department of Commerce, Bureau of the Census (see notes to pages 207–218); producer prices and employment, hours, and earnings: U.S. Department of Labor, Bureau of Labor Statistics (see notes to pages 96–100 and 117–135)

Fabricated metal products, except machinery and transportation equipment (SIC Major Group 34) includes fabricating ferrous and nonferrous metal products, such as metal cans, tinware, hand tools, cutlery, nonelectrical heating apparatus, structural metal products, metal forgings and stampings, ordnance (except vehicles and guided missiles), and a variety of metal and wire products not elsewhere classified. Some important segments of metal fabricating industries, such as machinery, transportation equipment, scientific and controlling instruments, jewelry, and silverware, are not included.

INDUSTRIAL PRODUCTION: *metal containers* (SIC 341) covers metal cans and shipping containers; *hardware, tools, and cutlery* (SIC 342) covers cutlery, handtools, and general hardware; *hardware and tools* covers hand and edge tools (SIC 3423), saw blades and handsaws (SIC 3425), and hardware, not elsewhere classified (SIC 3429); *structural metal products* (SIC 344) covers fabricated structural metal products including structural metal, doors, plate work, sheet metal work, and ornamental metal work; *other fabricated metal products* includes screw machine products and bolts, nuts, screws, rivets, and washers (SIC 345), metal forgings and stampings (SIC 346), coatings, engraving, and allied services (SIC 347), ordnance and accessories, except vehicles and guided missiles (SIC 348), and miscellaneous fabricated metal products (SIC 349); *fasteners, stampings, etc.* is SIC 345, 346, and 347.

PAGES 232–234
INDUSTRIAL MACHINERY AND EQUIPMENT

Sources: Industrial production and capacity utilization: Board of Governors of the Federal Reserve System (see notes to pages 60–73); manufacturers' shipments, inventories, and orders: U.S. Department of Commerce, Bureau of the Census (see notes to pages 207–218); producer prices and employment, hours, and earnings: U.S. Department of Labor, Bureau of Labor Statistics (see notes to pages 96–100 and 117–135)

Industrial and commercial machinery and computer equipment (SIC Major Group 35) includes manufacture of industrial and commercial machinery and equipment and computers. Included are manufacture of engines and turbines; farm and garden machinery; construction, mining, and oil field machinery; elevators and conveying equipment; hoists and cranes; metalworking machinery; computer and peripheral equipment; office machinery; and refrigeration machinery. Motor-powered machines ordinarily are included, except for electrical household appliances. Equipment for the generation and transmission of electricity is not included. Hand tools are not included unless powered.

INDUSTRIAL PRODUCTION: *engines and turbines* (SIC 351) includes steam, gas, and hydraulic turbines and turbine generator set units and internal combustion engines, not elsewhere classified (aircraft engines and automotive engines, except diesel are classified elsewhere); *construction and allied machinery* (SIC 353) includes construction, mining, and materials handling machinery and equipment; *metalworking machinery* (SIC 354) includes machine tools and accessories, power-driven handtools, rolling mill machinery, and welding and soldering equipment; *special industry machinery* (SIC 355) includes textile machinery, woodworking machinery, paper industries machinery, printing machinery, food products machinery, and others; *general industrial machinery* (SIC 356) includes pumps, bearings, compressors, fans, industrial process furnaces, and others; *computer and office equipment* (SIC 357) includes electronic computers (mainframe, micro, mini, and personal), computer storage devices and peripheral equipment, and calculating machines; *service industry machines* (SIC 358) includes automatic vending machines, commercial laundry machines, air-conditioning and warm air heating equipment, commercial refrigeration equipment, and others.

PAGES 235–237
ELECTRONIC AND ELECTRIC EQUIPMENT

Sources: Industrial production and capacity utilization: Board of Governors of the Federal Reserve System (see notes to pages 60–73); manufacturers' shipments, invento-

ries, and orders: U.S. Department of Commerce, Bureau of the Census (see notes to pages 207–218); producer prices and employment, hours, and earnings: U.S. Department of Labor, Bureau of Labor Statistics (see notes to pages 96–100 and 117–135)

Electronic and other electrical equipment and components, except computer equipment (SIC Major Group 36) includes manufacture of machinery, apparatus, and supplies for the generation, storage, transmission, transformation, and utilization of electrical energy. Included are electricity distribution equipment; electrical industrial apparatus; household appliances; electrical lighting and wiring equipment; radio and television receiving equipment; communications equipment; and other electrical equipment and supplies. Industrial machinery and equipment powered by electric motors are not included, nor are measuring and controlling instruments.

INDUSTRIAL PRODUCTION: *electrical machinery* is SIC Major Group 36; *major electrical equipment and parts* includes electric transmission and distribution equipment (SIC 361) and electrical industrial apparatus (SIC 362); *electric distribution equipment* is SIC 361; *household appliances* (SIC 363) includes *cooking equipment* (SIC 3631); *refrigerators and freezers* (SIC 3632); *household laundry equipment* (SIC 3633) and *miscellaneous household appliances* (SIC 3634, 3635, and 3639); *audio and video equipment* (SIC 365) includes household radios, TV, tape players, and phonograph records, tapes, and disks; *communications equipment* (SIC 366) includes telephone and telegraph apparatus and broadcasting and communications equipment; *electronic components* (SIC 367) includes tubes, circuit boards, semiconductors, capacitors, resistors, coils, and connectors; *miscellaneous electrical supplies* (SIC 369) includes *storage batteries* (SIC 3691), magnetic and optical recording media (such as blank computer diskettes), and electrical machinery, not elsewhere classified.

PAGES 238–243
TRANSPORTATION EQUIPMENT, INCLUDING MOTOR VEHICLES

Sources: Industrial production and capacity utilization: Board of Governors of the Federal Reserve System (see notes to pages 60–73); manufacturers' shipments, inventories, and orders: U.S. Department of Commerce, Bureau of the Census (see notes to pages 207–218); retail sales of cars and trucks: U.S. Department of Commerce, Bureau of Economic Analysis; producer prices, consumer prices, and employment, hours, and earnings: U.S. Department of Labor, Bureau of Labor Statistics (see notes to pages 96–100, 90–95, and 117–135)

Transportation equipment (SIC Major Group 37) includes manufacture of equipment for transportation of passengers and cargo by land, air, and water, including motor vehicles, aircraft, guided missiles and space vehicles, ships, boats, and railroad equipment. Manufacture of equipment for moving materials on farms and work sites

is included in Major Group 35, industrial machinery and equipment.

INDUSTRIAL PRODUCTION AND CAPACITY UTILIZATION: *Motor vehicles and parts* (SIC 371) includes motor vehicles, *motor vehicle parts and accessories* (SIC 3714), truck trailers, and *motor homes* (SIC 3716); *aerospace and miscellaneous transportation equipment* includes *aircraft and parts* (SIC 372), *ships and boats* (SIC 373), and *railroad and miscellaneous* (SIC 374—railroad equipment, 375—motorcycles, bicycles, and parts, 376—guided missiles, space vehicles, and parts, and 379—miscellaneous transportation equipment).

RETAIL SALES AND INVENTORIES OF CARS, TRUCKS, AND BUSES. These estimates are prepared by the Bureau of Economic Analysis based on data from the American Automobile Manufacturers Association, Ward's Automotive Reports, and other sources. Data are available in BEA press releases and on the STAT-USA subscription internet site (http://www.stat-usa.gov).

PAGE 244
INSTRUMENTS AND RELATED PRODUCTS

Sources: Industrial production and capacity utilization: Board of Governors of the Federal Reserve System (see notes to pages 60–73); manufacturers' shipments and inventories: U.S. Department of Commerce, Bureau of the Census (see notes to pages 207–218); producer prices and employment, hours, and earnings: U.S. Department of Labor, Bureau of Labor Statistics (see notes to pages 96–100 and 117–135)

Measuring, analyzing, and controlling instruments; photographic, medical and optical goods; watches and clocks (SIC Major Group 38) includes manufacture of instruments (including professional and scientific) for measuring, testing, analyzing, and controlling, and their associated sensors and accessories; hydrological, hydrographic, meteorological, and geophysical equipment; navigation and guidance systems; surgical and medical instruments, equipment, and supplies; photographic equipment and supplies; and watches and clocks.

INDUSTRIAL PRODUCTION: *Scientific and medical instruments* includes search, detection, navigation, guidance, aeronautical, and nautical systems, instruments, and equipment (SIC 381); laboratory apparatus and analytical, optical, measuring, and controlling instruments (SIC 382); and surgical, medical, and dental instruments and supplies (SIC 384); *medical instruments* is SIC 384.

PAGES 246–247
FOOD AND KINDRED PRODUCTS

Sources: Industrial production and capacity utilization: Board of Governors of the Federal Reserve System (see notes to pages 60–73); manufacturers' shipments and inventories: U.S. Department of Commerce, Bureau of the

Census (see notes to pages 207–218); producer prices, consumer prices, and employment, hours, and earnings: U.S. Department of Labor, Bureau of Labor Statistics (see notes to pages 96–100, 90–95, and 117–135)

Food and kindred products (SIC Major Group 20) includes manufacture or processing of foods for human consumption and prepared feeds for animals.

INDUSTRIAL PRODUCTION: *meat products* (SIC 201) includes meat packing plants, production of sausages and other prepared meat products, and poultry slaughtering and processing; *dairy products* (SIC 202) includes manufacture of creamery butter, cheese, dry and condensed dairy products, and ice cream and frozen desserts and processing of fluid milk; *canned and frozen foods* (SIC 203) includes canning, freezing, drying, dehydrating, and pickling of fruits, vegetables, and specialty foods; *grain mill products* (SIC 204) includes flour milling, breakfast cereal manufacture, rice milling, prepared mixes and doughs, wet corn milling, and dog and cat food; *bakery products* (SIC 205) includes bread, cookies, crackers, and frozen bakery products; *sugar and confectionery* (SIC 206) includes manufacture and refining of sugar and syrup from cane and sugar beets, candy and confectionery, chocolate and cocoa products, chewing gum, and salted and roasted nuts; *fats and oils* (SIC 207) includes cottonseed, soybean, and vegetable oil mills and manufacture of animal and marine fats and oils; *beverages* (SIC 208) includes alcoholic and nonalcoholic beverages and flavoring extracts and syrups; *coffee and miscellaneous* includes roasted coffee, seafoods, snack foods, macaroni and spaghetti, and miscellaneous food preparations.

PAGE 248
TOBACCO PRODUCTS

Sources: Industrial production: Board of Governors of the Federal Reserve (see notes to pages 60–73); manufacturers' shipments and inventories: U.S. Department of Commerce, Bureau of the Census (see notes to pages 207–218); producer prices and employment, hours, and earnings: U.S. Department of Labor, Bureau of Labor Statistics (see notes to pages 96–100 and 117–135)

TOBACCO PRODUCTS (SIC Major Group 21) includes manufacture of cigarettes, cigars, smoking and chewing tobacco, and snuff and stemming and redrying of tobacco. It also includes manufacture of nontobacco cigarettes.

PAGES 249–250
TEXTILE MILL PRODUCTS

Sources: Industrial production and capacity utilization: Board of Governors of the Federal Reserve System (see notes to pages 60–73); manufacturers' shipments and inventories: U.S. Department of Commerce, Bureau of the Census (see notes to pages 207–218); producer prices and employment, hours, and earnings: U.S. Department of Labor, Bureau of Labor Statistics (see notes to pages 96–100 and 117–135)

TEXTILE MILL PRODUCTS (SIC Major Group 22) includes (1) preparation of fiber and manufacture of yarn, thread, twine, and cordage; (2) manufacture of broad woven, narrow woven, and knit fabrics and carpet and rugs from yarn; (3) dyeing and finishing fiber, yarn, fabrics, and knit apparel; (4) coating, waterproofing, or otherwise treating fabrics; (5) integrated manufacture of finished articles from yarn; and (6) manufacture of felt goods, lace, nonwoven fabrics, and miscellaneous textiles.

INDUSTRIAL PRODUCTION: *Fabrics* (SIC 221, 222, 223, and 224) includes broadwoven and narrow woven fabrics of cotton, wool, silk, and manmade fiber; *knit goods* (SIC 225) includes knitting of hosiery, underwear, and outerwear; *carpeting* (SIC 227) includes manufacture of carpets and rugs from textile materials and from materials such as reeds, sisal, or jute; *yarns and miscellaneous* (SIC 228 and 229) includes yarn and thread mills, coated fabrics (not rubberized), tire cord, nonwoven fabrics, cordage and twine, linen goods, and textiles not elsewhere classified.

PAGE 251
APPAREL

Sources: Industrial production and capacity utilization: Board of Governors of the Federal Reserve System (see notes to pages 60–73); producer prices, consumer prices, and employment, hours, and earnings: U.S. Department of Labor, Bureau of Labor Statistics (see notes to pages 96–100, 90–95, and 117–135)

Apparel and other finished products made from fabrics and similar materials (SIC Major Group 23) includes production of clothing and other products by cutting and sewing purchased woven or knit fabrics, leather, rubberized fabrics, plastics, and furs. Also includes manufacture of clothing by cutting and joining (for example, by adhesives) materials such as paper and nonwoven fabrics.

PAGES 252–253
PAPER AND ALLIED PRODUCTS

Sources: Industrial production and capacity utilization: Board of Governors of the Federal Reserve System (see notes to pages 60–73); manufacturers' shipments and inventories: U.S. Department of Commerce, Bureau of the Census (see notes to pages 207–218); producer prices and employment, hours, and earnings: U.S. Department of Labor, Bureau of Labor Statistics (see notes to pages 96–100 and 117–135)

Paper and allied products (SIC Major Group 26) includes manufacture of pulps from wood and other cellulose fibers and rags; manufacture of paper and paperboard and paper products such as bags, boxes, and envelopes. Also included is manufacture of plastic bags.

INDUSTRIAL PRODUCTION AND CAPACITY UTILIZATION: *Pulp and paper* includes pulp mills (SIC 261), paper mills (SIC

262), and paperboard mills (SIC 263); *paper products* includes paperboard containers and boxes (SIC 265) and converted paper and paperboard products, except containers and boxes (SIC 267).

PAGE 254
PRINTING AND PUBLISHING

Sources: Industrial production and capacity utilization: Board of Governors of the Federal Reserve System (see notes to pages 60–73); producer prices and employment, hours, and earnings: U.S. Department of Labor, Bureau of Labor Statistics (see notes to pages 96–100 and 117–135)

Printing, publishing, and allied industries (SIC Major Group 27) includes printing, lithography, and services performed for the printing trade, such as bookbinding and plate making. Also included are publishers of newspapers, books, and periodicals.

INDUSTRIAL PRODUCTION: *Newspapers* (SIC 271) includes publishing and printing of newspapers; *commercial printing* (SIC 275) includes lithographic, offset, and gravure printing.

PAGES 255–256
CHEMICALS AND CHEMICAL PRODUCTS

Sources: Industrial production and capacity utilization: Board of Governors of the Federal Reserve System (see notes to pages 60–73); manufacturers' shipments and inventories: U.S. Department of Commerce, Bureau of the Census (see notes to pages 207–218); producer prices and employment, hours, and earnings: U.S. Department of Labor, Bureau of Labor Statistics (see notes to pages 96–100 and 117–135)

Chemicals and allied products (SIC Major Group 28) includes production of basic chemicals and manufacture of products by predominantly chemical processes. Three general classes of products are included: (1) basic chemicals; (2) chemical products to be used in further manufacture, including synthetic fibers and plastic materials; (3) finished chemical products, including drugs, cosmetics, paints, fertilizers, and explosives. The mining of natural chemicals and fertilizers is classified in Division B, Mining.

INDUSTRIAL PRODUCTION AND CAPACITY UTILIZATION: *Basic chemicals* (SIC 281—Industrial Inorganic Chemicals) includes alkalies, chlorine, industrial gases, inorganic pigments, and industrial organic chemicals not elsewhere classified (SIC 2819); *synthetic materials* (SIC 282) includes plastic materials, synthetic resins, and nonvulcanizable elastomers (SIC 2821), synthetic fibers (SIC 2823 and 2824), and synthetic rubber (vulcanizable elastomers); *drugs and medicines* (SIC 283) includes medicinal chemicals and pharmaceutical products; *soaps and toiletries* (SIC 284) includes soap, detergents, cleaning preparations, perfumes, cosmetics, and other toiletries; *industrial organic chemicals* (SIC 286) includes noncyclic organic chemicals,

solvents, polyhydric alcohols, synthetic perfumes and flavorings, rubber processing chemicals, plasticizers, synthetic tanning agents, and others; *agricultural chemicals* (SIC 287) includes nitrogenous and phosphatic fertilizers, pesticides, and agricultural chemicals not elsewhere classified.

PAGES 257–258
PETROLEUM AND COAL PRODUCTS

Sources: Industrial production and capacity utilization: Board of Governors of the Federal Reserve System (see notes to pages 60–73); manufacturers' shipments and inventories: U.S. Department of Commerce, Bureau of the Census (see notes to pages 207–218); producer prices, consumer prices, and employment, hours, and earnings: U.S. Department of Labor, Bureau of Labor Statistics (see notes to pages 96–100, 90–95, and 117–135)

Petroleum refining and related industries (SIC Major Group 29) includes refining petroleum, manufacturing paving and roofing materials, and compounding lubricating oils and greases from purchased materials. Producing coke and byproducts is classified in Major Group 33, Primary Metals. Gas distribution is classified in public utilities.

INDUSTRIAL PRODUCTION: *Petroleum refining and miscellaneous* (SIC 291, 299) includes petroleum refining, blending and compounding lubricating oils and greases, and production of petroleum and coal products not elsewhere classified; *paving and roofing materials* (SIC 295) includes manufacture of asphalt and tar paving materials and asphalt roofing materials.

PAGES 259–260
RUBBER AND PLASTICS PRODUCTS

Sources: Industrial production and capacity utilization: Board of Governors of the Federal Reserve System (see notes to pages 60–73); manufacturers' shipments and inventories: U.S. Department of Commerce, Bureau of the Census (see notes to pages 207–218); producer prices and employment, hours, and earnings: U.S. Department of Labor, Bureau of Labor Statistics (see notes to pages 96–100 and 117–135)

Rubber and miscellaneous plastics products (SIC Major Group 30) includes manufacturing products, not elsewhere classified, from plastic resins and from natural, synthetic, or reclaimed rubber. Many products made from these materials, including boats, toys, buckles, and buttons, are classified elsewhere. Tire manufacture is included, but recapping and retreading are classified in Services. Manufacture of synthetic rubber and synthetic plastic resins is classified in Chemicals, Major Group 28.

INDUSTRIAL PRODUCTION: *Tires* (SIC 301) includes manufacture of pneumatic casings, inner tubes, and solid and cushion tires for all types of vehicles, airplanes, and farm equipment and of tire repair and retreading materials; *other rub-*

ber products includes manufacture of rubber and plastics footwear (SIC 302), gaskets, packing, and sealing devices and rubber and plastic hosing and belting (SIC 305), and fabricated rubber products not elsewhere classified (SIC 306); *plastics products, not elsewhere classified* (SIC 308) includes manufacture of unsupported and laminated plastic film, sheet, and profile shapes, plastics pipe, plastics bottles, plastics foam products, and plastics plumbing fixtures.

PAGE 261
LEATHER AND LEATHER PRODUCTS

Sources: Industrial production and capacity utilization: Board of Governors of the Federal Reserve System (see notes to pages 60–73); producer prices and employment, hours, and earnings: U.S. Department of Labor, Bureau of Labor Statistics (see notes to pages 96–100 and 117–135)

Leather and leather products (SIC Major Group 31) includes tanning, currying, and finishing hides and skins and manufacturing finished leather and artificial leather products and some similar products made of other materials.

INDUSTRIAL PRODUCTION: *Shoes* (SIC 314) includes manufacture of footwear, except rubber or plastic footwear.

PAGES 264–267
TRANSPORTATION, COMMUNICATIONS, AND UTILITIES

Sources: Industrial production and capacity utilization: Board of Governors of the Federal Reserve System (see notes to pages 60–73); producer prices and employment, hours, and earnings: U.S. Department of Labor, Bureau of Labor Statistics (see notes to pages 96–100 and 117–135

Transportation, communications, and electric, gas, and sanitary services (SIC Division E) includes establishments providing to the general public or to other business enterprises passenger and freight transportation, communications services, or electricity, gas, steam, water or sanitary services. Private courier and delivery services are included. The U.S. Postal Service is classified in this group in the SIC, but postal service employment is counted by BLS in the government sector and is not included in the employment data in this chapter.

INDUSTRIAL PRODUCTION: *Electric utilities* includes the generation, transmission, and/or distribution of electric energy for sale (SIC 491) and part of SIC 493—combination electric, gas, and other utility services; *gas utilities* includes natural gas transmission and distribution and manufacture and distribution of liquefied petroleum gas (SIC 493) and part of SIC 493.

EMPLOYMENT, HOURS, AND EARNINGS: *Trucking and warehousing* (SIC Major Group 42) includes local and long-distance trucking, warehousing and storage, and courier services (except by air); *communications* (SIC Major Group 48) includes telephone, telegraph, radio and television, and other communications services; *electric, gas, and sanitary services* (SIC Major Group 49) includes electricity and gas production and distribution, water supply, sewerage systems, and refuse systems.

PAGES 270–271
RETAIL AND WHOLESALE TRADE: EMPLOYMENT, HOURS, AND EARNINGS

Sources: Employment, hours, and earnings: U.S. Department of Labor, Bureau of Labor Statistics (see notes to pages 117–135)

WHOLESALE TRADE (SIC Division F) includes establishments primarily engaged in selling merchandise to retailers; to commercial, professional, or institutional purchasers; or to other wholesalers. Certain establishments that sell merchandise both for commercial and professional use, such as paint stores and gasoline service stations, are classified in Retail Trade. Wholesale trade includes merchant wholesalers—wholesalers who take title to the goods they sell—as well as sales branches of manufacturing or mining enterprises (apart from their plants or mines) and commodity brokers and commission merchants. The data in this book pertain to merchant wholesalers only.

RETAIL TRADE (SIC Division G) includes establishments primarily engaged in selling merchandise for personal or household consumption and rendering services incidental to the sales of the goods. However, establishments engaged in selling such merchandise as plumbing equipment, electrical supplies, and office furniture are classified in Wholesale Trade, even if a higher proportion of their sales is made to individuals for personal or household use.

GENERAL MERCHANDISE STORES (SIC Major Group 53) includes department stores, variety stores, and general stores; *food stores* (SIC Major Group 54) includes grocery stores, meat markets, bakeries, and other food specialty stores; *auto dealers and service stations* (SIC Major Group 55) includes new and used motor vehicle dealers, auto supply stores, and gasoline service stations; *apparel and accessory stores* (SIC Major Group 56) includes men's, women's, and children's clothing stores, shoe stores, and accessory stores; *eating and drinking places* (SIC Major Group 58) includes restaurant, carry-outs, institutional food service, bars, and taverns.

PAGES 272–276
RETAIL SALES AND INVENTORIES

Source: U.S. Department of Commerce, Bureau of the Census
Each month the Bureau of the Census prepares estimates of retail sales and inventories by kind of business based on a mail-out/mail-back survey of a sample of companies with one or more establishments that sell merchandise and related services to final consumers.

INVENTORY DATA prior to 1980 are not comparable to later years due to changes in valuation methods. Prior to 1980, inventories are book values of merchandise on hand at the end of the period and are valued according to the valuation method used by each respondent. Thus the aggregates are a mixture of LIFO (last-in-first-out) and non-LIFO values. Beginning with 1980, inventories are valued using methods other than LIFO in order to better reflect the current costs of goods held as inventory.

The SURVEY SAMPLE is stratified by kind of business and estimated sales. All firms with sales above an applicable size cutoff are included. Firms are selected randomly from the remaining strata. To reduce reporting burden, only specially selected panels report each month, with the remainder reporting quarterly in three rotating panels.

DATA AVAILABILITY

An *Advance Monthly Retail Sales* report is released about nine working days after the close of the reference month, based on responses from a sub-sample of the complete retail sample.

Revised and more complete monthly *Retail Trade, Sales, and Inventories* reports are released 6 weeks after the close of the reference month. They contain preliminary figures for the current month and final figures for the prior 12 months. Statistics include retail sales, inventories, and ratios of inventories to sales. Data are both seasonally adjusted and unadjusted.

The *Annual Benchmark Report for Retail Trade* is released annually each spring. It includes updated seasonal adjustment factors; revised and benchmarked monthly estimates of sales and inventories; monthly data for the most recent 10 years; detailed annual estimates and ratios for the United States by kind of business; and comparable prior-year statistics and year-to-year changes.

Data are available on the Bureau of the Census internet site (http://www.census.gov)

PAGE 277
MERCHANT WHOLESALERS: SALES AND INVENTORIES

Source: U.S. Department of Commerce, Bureau of the Census

These data pertain to merchant wholesalers and are based on a monthly survey conducted by the Bureau of the Census.

NOTES ON THE DATA

INVENTORY DATA prior to 1980 are not comparable to later years because of changes in valuation methods and are not included in this book. Prior to 1980, inventories are book values of stocks on hand at the end of the period and are valued according to the valuation method used by each respondent. Thus the aggregates are a mixture of LIFO (last-in-first-out) and non-LIFO values. Beginning with 1980 inventories are valued using methods other than LIFO in order to better reflect the current costs of goods held as inventory.

THE SURVEY covers wholesale companies with employment that are primarily engaged in merchant wholesale trade in the United States (SIC Division F). These include merchant wholesalers that take title of the goods they sell, and jobbers, industrial distributors, exporters, and importers. Excluded are non-merchant wholesalers such as manufacturers' sales branches and offices; agents, merchandise or commodity brokers, and commission merchants; and other businesses whose primary activities are other than wholesale trade.

Companies provide data on dollar values of merchant wholesale sales, end-of-month inventories, and methods of inventory valuation.

A survey has been conducted monthly since 1946. A mail-out/mail-back survey of selected wholesale firms is used. Firms are first stratified by merchant wholesale sales, inventories and major kind of business (determined from the latest census of wholesale trade). All firms with wholesale sales or inventories above applicable size cutoffs for each major kind of business are included in the survey. Remaining firms are stratified by major kind of business and estimated sales, and a simple random sample is selected from each stratum. Companies selected with certainty report each month. To minimize reporting burden, randomly selected firms are put in one of three rotating panels and report once each quarter for the two preceding months.

New samples are drawn every five years, and the samples are updated every quarter to add new businesses and drop companies that are no longer active.

DATA AVAILABILITY

Monthly Wholesale Trade, Sales and Inventories reports are released 6 weeks after the close of the reference month. They contain preliminary current-month figures and final figures for the previous month. Statistics include sales, inventories, and stock/sale ratios by 3-digit SIC code, along with standard errors. Data are both seasonally adjusted and unadjusted.

The *Annual Benchmark Report for Wholesale Trade* is released annually each spring. It contains estimated annual sales, monthly and year-end inventories, inventory/sales ratios, purchases, gross margins, and gross margin/sales ratios by kind of business. Annual estimates are benchmarked to the most recent census of wholesale trade. These reports also present the results of a benchmarking operation that revises monthly sales and inventories estimates. Estimates are both seasonally adjusted and unadjusted.

Data are available on the Bureau of the Census internet site (http://www.census.gov)

PAGE 280
FINANCE, INSURANCE, AND REAL ESTATE

Sources: Employment, hours, and earnings: U.S. Department of Labor, Bureau of Labor Statistics (see notes to pages 117–135)

Finance, insurance, and real estate (SIC Division H) includes establishments operating primarily in these fields. FINANCE includes *depository institutions* (SIC Major Group 60), *nondepository credit institutions* (Major Group 61), and *securities brokers and dealers and exchanges* (Major Groups 62 and 67). INSURANCE (SIC Major Groups 63 and 64) covers carriers, agents, and brokers of all types of insurance. REAL ESTATE (SIC Major Group 65) includes buyers, sellers, agents, developers, and owners of real estate.

PAGES 281–283
PRIVATE SERVICES

Sources: Producer prices, employment, hours, and earnings: U.S. Department of Labor, Bureau of Labor Statistics (see notes to pages 117–135)

Services (SIC Division I) includes establishments engaged in providing a wide variety of services to individuals, businesses, government, and other organizations. Personal, business, repair, health, amusement, legal, and engineering services and hotels and other lodging places are among the categories included.

The SIC Division definition includes both governmental and private activities, classified according to the type of service provided. However, the employment, hours, and earnings data shown on these pages pertain only to the private, nonfarm economy. On the other hand, the BLS data include one industry—agricultural services—which the SIC places in Division A (agriculture, forestry, and fishing).

AGRICULTURAL SERVICES (SIC Major Group 7) includes soil preparation and crop services, veterinary services, and landscape services.

HOTELS AND OTHER LODGING PLACES (SIC Major Group 70) includes hotels, motels, rooming houses, and RV camps; PERSONAL SERVICES (SIC Major Group 72) includes laundry, photography, hair care, shoe repair, and funeral services; BUSINESS SERVICES (SIC Major Group 73) includes *personnel supply services* (SIC 736), *computer and data processing services* (SIC 737), and also advertising, equipment rental, and other business services. Personnel supply

services includes employment agencies and *help supply services* (SIC 7363), which supply temporary or continuing help on a contract or fee basis.

AUTO REPAIR, SERVICES, AND PARKING (SIC Major Group 75) includes auto rental, parking, and repair; MISCELLANEOUS REPAIR SERVICES (SIC Major Group 76) includes electrical and watch and clock repair, reupholstery and furniture repair, and other repair services.

MOTION PICTURES (SIC Major Group 78) includes motion picture production and distribution, motion picture theaters, and video tape rental; AMUSEMENT AND RECREATION (SIC Major Group 79) includes theaters, sports events, and sports facilities, such as golf courses and health clubs; LEGAL SERVICES (SIC Major Group 81) includes establishments headed by attorneys; EDUCATIONAL SERVICES (SIC Major Group 82) includes private schools and colleges, libraries, and vocational schools; SOCIAL SERVICES (SIC Major Group 83) includes private family services, day care, and job training.

MUSEUMS, BOTANICAL GARDENS, AND ZOOS (SIC Major Group 84) includes museums, galleries, botanical gardens, and zoos; MEMBERSHIP ORGANIZATIONS (SIC Major Group 86) includes business and professional associations, labor unions, and civic, religious, and political organizations; ENGINEERING AND MANAGEMENT (SIC Major Group 87) includes engineering, accounting, research, and management services.

HEALTH SERVICES (SIC Major Group 80) includes *hospitals* (SIC 806), *offices and clinics of medical doctors* (SIC 801), *nursing and personal care facilities* (SIC 805), *home health care services* (SIC 808), and also dental offices, medical and dental laboratories, and other health care practitioners.

PAGE 284
SELECTED SERVICE INDUSTRIES—RECEIPTS AND REVENUE

Source: U.S. Department of Commerce, Bureau of the Census

The Census Service Annual Survey, based on a sample of establishments, provides, for selected service industries, annual estimates of operating receipts of taxable firms, and revenues of firms exempt from federal income taxation.

DEFINITIONS AND NOTES ON THE DATA

Many of the service industries covered are described in the preceding section of the Notes. In addition to those, the survey includes *arrangement of passenger transportation* (SIC 472) and *real estate agents and managers* (SIC 653). It excludes elementary and secondary schools (SIC 821); colleges, universities, professional schools, and junior colleges (SIC 822); miscellaneous educational services (SIC 829); labor unions and similar labor organizations

(SIC 863); political organizations (SIC 865); religious organizations (SIC 866); private households (SIC 881); and services not elsewhere classified (SIC 899).

Separate estimates were developed for taxable and non-taxable firms in camps and membership lodging; selected amusement and recreation services; selected health services; legal services; libraries; vocational schools; social services; museums, art galleries, botanical gardens, and zoos; research, development, and testing services; and selected management and public relations services. Firms considered tax-exempt include membership lodging, membership organizations, and noncommercial research organizations. Firms in all remaining SICs were defined to be taxable. For tax-exempt firms, employer firms only were sampled; for all other kinds of business, data represent combined estimates for employer and nonemployer firms. Government-operated hospitals were included, while all other government establishments were excluded.

DATA AVAILABILITY

Data are published annually as *Current Business Reports, Service Annual Survey.* They are available on the Bureau of the Census internet site (http://www.census.gov).

PAGES 286–293 AND 313–316
GOVERNMENT RECEIPTS AND EXPENDITURES

Source: U.S. Department of Commerce, Bureau of Economic Analysis

These data are from the national income and product accounts (NIPAs), as published in the 1996 comprehensive NIPA revisions and as subsequently revised and updated through August 1999. The 1996 comprehensive revisions for the first time separated government expenditures into those for current consumption and those for gross investment.

Because of the October 1999 comprehensive NIPA revision (which was released too late to be included in this volume), there was no 1999 annual revision. For more information on the 1999 comprehensive revision, see the notes for pages 26–34 and the article "Current Issues in Economic Measurement" in the front of this volume.

NOTES ON THE DATA

The data on government receipts and expenditures record transactions of governments (federal, state, and local) with other U.S. residents and foreigners. Each entry in the government receipts and expenditures account has a corresponding entry elsewhere in the NIPAs. Thus, for example, the sum of personal tax and nontax receipts by federal and state and local governments is equal to personal tax and nontax payments as shown in the personal income table.

The government receipts and expenditures estimates are derived primarily from financial statements on federal, state, and local governments. However, a number of adjustments are made to place the data on the basis required for the NIPAs. Annual data are placed on a calendar year basis. Data are converted from the cash basis usually found in financial statements to the timing bases required for the NIPAs. In the NIPAs receipts from businesses generally are on an accrual basis, purchases of goods and services are recorded when delivered, and receipts from and transfer payments to persons are on a cash basis.

The federal receipts and expenditure data from the NIPAs on pages 286–293 thus differ from the federal receipts and outlay data on pages 294–296 in that, among other differences, the latter are by fiscal year and are on a modified cash basis.

DEFINITIONS

PERSONAL TAX AND NONTAX RECEIPTS is personal tax payments that are not chargeable to business expense and certain other personal payments to government agencies (except government enterprises) that are treated like taxes. Personal taxes includes taxes on income, including realized net capital gains; on transfers of estates and gifts; and on personal property. Nontaxes includes donations and fees, fines, and forfeitures. Personal contributions for social insurance are not included.

CORPORATE PROFITS TAX ACCRUALS is the sum of federal, state, and local income taxes on all corporate earnings, including realized net capital gains. These taxes are net of refunds and applicable tax credits.

INDIRECT BUSINESS TAX AND NONTAX ACCRUALS is tax liabilities that are chargeable to business expense in the calculation of profit-type incomes and certain other business liabilities to government agencies (except government enterprises) that are treated like taxes. Examples are sales and property taxes and regulatory and inspection fees. Employer contributions for social insurance are not included.

CONTRIBUTIONS FOR SOCIAL INSURANCE includes employer and personal contributions for social security, unemployment insurance, government employee retirement, and other government social insurance programs.

GOVERNMENT CONSUMPTION EXPENDITURES is purchases by governments (federal, state, and local) of goods and services for current consumption. It includes compensation of general government employees and an allowance for consumption of general government fixed capital (i.e., depreciation). Receipts for certain services provided by government—primarily tuition payments for higher education and charges for medical care—are defined as government sales, which are treated as deductions from government purchases.

TRANSFER PAYMENTS includes payments to persons for which they do not render current services. Examples are social security benefits, Medicare, Medicaid, unemployment benefits, and public assistance. U.S. government non-military grants to other countries also are included.

FEDERAL GRANTS-IN-AID are net payments from federal to state and local governments to help finance programs such as highway construction, public assistance, and education.

NET INTEREST PAID is interest paid to U.S. and foreign persons and businesses and to foreign governments less interest received from business and from foreigners. Interest paid consists of monetary interest paid on public debt and other financial obligations. Interest received consists of monetary and imputed interest received on loans and investments, including the balance of state and local social insurance funds.

SUBSIDIES LESS CURRENT SURPLUS OF GOVERNMENT ENTERPRISES. Subsidies are the monetary grants paid by government to business, including government enterprises at another level of government. The current surplus of government enterprises is their current operating revenue and subsidies received from other levels of government less their current expenses. No deduction is made for depreciation charges and net interest paid.

SURPLUS OR DEFICIT (-), NATIONAL INCOME AND PRODUCT ACCOUNTS is the sum of government receipts less the sum of current government expenditures.

GROSS GOVERNMENT INVESTMENT consists of general government and government enterprise expenditures for fixed assets (structures and durable equipment). Government inventory investment is included in government consumption expenditures.

CAPITAL CONSUMPTION. Consumption of fixed capital, or depreciation, is included in government consumption expenditures as a partial measure of the value of the services of general government fixed assets; use of depreciation assumes a zero net return on these assets.

DATA AVAILABILITY

The most recent data are published each month in the Survey of Current Business; may be purchased on diskette from BEA; or may be obtained from the BEA internet site (http://www.bea.doc.gov). Full historical data also may be purchased on diskette from BEA or may be obtained from the STAT-USA subscription internet site (http://www.stat-usa.gov).

REFERENCES

For information on the 1996 comprehensive revisions, see these articles in the Survey of Current Business: "The Measurement of Depreciation in the U.S. National Income and Product Accounts," July 1997; "Improved Estimates of the National Income and Product Accounts for 1959-95: Results of the Comprehensive Revision,"

January/February 1996; and "Preview of the Comprehensive Revision of the National Income and Product Accounts: Recognition of Government Investment and Incorporation of a New Methodology for Calculating Depreciation," September 1995. Other sources of general information about the NIPAs are listed in the Notes for pages 26–34.

PAGES 294–297
FEDERAL GOVERNMENT RECEIPTS AND OUTLAYS; FEDERAL DEBT

Source: U.S. Department of the Treasury

The data on government receipts and outlays are from the *Monthly Treasury Statement* and are on a modified cash basis. Annual data are by federal fiscal years: July 1 to June 30 through 1976 and October 1 to September 30 for subsequent years. There are numerous differences in timing and definition between these estimates and the NIPA estimates on pages 286–293. *Outlays* occur when the federal government liquidates an obligation through a cash payment, when interest accrues on public debt issues, or when a government-owned asset is sold on credit terms. *Outlays by function* present outlays according to the major purpose of the spending. Functional classifications cut across departmental and agency lines.

DATA AVAILABILITY

Data are published monthly in the *Monthly Treasury Statement* prepared by the Financial Management Service, U.S. Department of the Treasury. The publication is available on the Financial Management Service internet site (http://www.fms.treas.gov)

PAGE 297
GOVERNMENT EMPLOYMENT

Source: U.S. Department of Labor, Bureau of Labor Statistics (see notes to pages 117–122).

The government division of the SIC includes federal, state, and local activities such as legislative, executive, and judicial functions, as well as all government-owned and government-operated business enterprises, establishments, and institutions (arsenals, navy yards, hospitals, etc.), and government force account construction. The figures relate to civilian employment only. BLS considers regular full-time teachers (private and governmental) to be employed during the summer vacation period whether or not they are specifically paid in those months.

Employment in federal government establishments represents those who occupied positions the last day of the month. Intermittent workers are counted if they performed any service during the month. Federal government employment excludes employees of the Central Intelligence Agency and the National Security Agency.

PAGES 301–308
SELECTED NATIONAL INCOME AND PRODUCT ACCOUNT DATA

See the notes for pages 26–34.

PAGES 309–312
PRIVATE FIXED INVESTMENT

See the notes for pages 76–81.

PAGES 313–316
GOVERNMENT RECEIPTS AND EXPENDITURES

See the notes for pages 286–293.

PAGES 317–320
U.S. INTERNATIONAL TRANSACTIONS

See the notes for pages 156–161.

PAGES 321–324
PRODUCTIVITY AND RELATED DATA

See the notes for pages 106–107.

PAGES 325–327
NEW PLANT AND EQUIPMENT SPENDING

Source: U.S. Bureau of Economic Analysis and Bureau of the Census

The data on new plant and equipment spending are from the *Plant and Equipment Survey*. This survey program, which began in 1947, was concluded with the data released in September 1994 and was replaced by a new semi-annual Investment Plans Survey (IPS). The IPS was, in turn, discontinued as of March 1996, due to budgetary limitations at the Bureau of the Census. Although an annual capital expenditure survey (ACES) now provides annual data (see notes for page 87), there is no longer any official survey of capital spending by industry on a less-than-annual basis or of future investment plans. The ACES differs significantly in survey design, scope, and publication detail from the former Plant and Equipment Survey.

To provide a historical time series on new investment by U.S. businesses, the back data from the Plant and Equipment Survey are included in the historical statistics section of this book.

COVERAGE. The survey covered businesses classified in SIC Divisions A (excluding agricultural producers), B through H, and I (except private households).

CONTENT. Basic data on spending for plant and equipment were collected for each quarter, with additional data obtained for the 3rd and 4th quarters. Quarterly data included actual expenditures for the prior quarter and planned spending for each of the next three quarters.

METHODS. The Census Bureau conducted this survey from the third quarter of 1988 through 1994; the Bureau of Economic Analysis conducted it for prior periods. A mail-out/mail-back quarterly survey of selected large companies, and a mail-out/mail-back annual survey of additional companies in selected industries was used. The survey panels were benchmarked in 1982. Beginning in 1989, a survey panel maintenance program was used to assess and improve industry coverage based on information from other censuses and surveys. Beginning with 1991, companies not responding to voluntary quarterly survey requests received mandatory annual requests for comparable information.

DATA AVAILABILITY

Quarterly and annual data from the Plant and Equipment Survey covering 1947 through mid-1994 are available from the Bureau of the Census.

PAGES 328–335
PERSONAL INCOME

See the notes for pages 50–57.

PAGES 336–339
INDUSTRIAL PRODUCTION AND CAPACITY UTILIZATION

See the notes for pages 60–73.

PAGES 340–347
CIVILIAN POPULATION, LABOR FORCE, EMPLOYMENT, AND UNEMPLOYMENT

See the notes for pages 112–115.

PAGES 348–355
NONAGRICULTURAL EMPLOYMENT, HOURS, AND EARNINGS

See the notes for pages 117–135.

PAGES 356–359
CONSUMER PRICE INDEXES

See the notes for pages 90-95.

PAGES 360–363
PRODUCER PRICE INDEXES

See the notes for pages 96–100.

PAGES 364–367
MONEY STOCK AND SELECTED COMPONENTS

See the notes for pages 142–143.

PAGES 368–371
INTEREST RATE, BOND YIELDS, AND STOCK PRICES

See the notes for pages 151–153.

PAGES 375–404
STATE AND REGIONAL DATA, ANNUAL, 1969-1998

This appendix contains annual time-series data on personal income and employment for the United States, each state, the District of Columbia and eight geographic regions. All data are from the Bureau of Economic Analysis, U.S. Department of Commerce. All revisions available through September 1999 are included. These data utilize the same concepts and definitions as the personal income estimates contained in the national income and product accounts (NIPAs). Summaries of these definitions can be found in the Notes for pages 50-57 of this volume.

ADDITIONAL NOTES ON THE STATE AND REGIONAL DATA

The U.S. data that accompany the state differ from those in the NIPAs in that the NIPA totals include the labor income of U.S. residents temporarily living and working abroad. The population estimates shown are the ones used in the calculation of per capita amounts. These are midyear estimates from the Bureau of the Census.

The dividends, interest, and rent total includes the capital consumption adjustment for rental income of persons.

Total employment is the average annual number of jobs, full-time plus part-time; each job that a person holds is counted at full weight. The estimates are on a place-of-work basis. Both wage and salary employment and self-employment are included. The main source for the wage and salary employment estimates are Bureau of Labor Statistics estimates from the unemployment insurance data (the ES-202 data). Self-employment is estimated mainly from individual and partnership federal income tax returns.

The employment estimates correspond closely in coverage to the earnings estimates. However, the earnings estimates include the income of limited partnerships and of tax-exempt cooperatives, for which there are no corresponding employment estimates. The state-level earnings estimates included in *Business Statistics* have been adjusted to a place-of-residence basis to adjust for interstate commuting; the difference between earnings by place of residence and earnings by place of work is shown in the "Adjustment for residence" column.

The states are divided into regions as follows:

- New England: Connecticut, Maine, Massachusetts, New Hampshire, Rhode Island, Vermont

- Mideast: Delaware, District of Columbia, Maryland, New Jersey, New York, Pennsylvania,

- Great Lakes: Illinois, Indiana, Michigan, Ohio, Wisconsin

- Plains: Iowa, Kansas, Minnesota, Missouri, Nebraska, North Dakota, South Dakota

- Southeast: Alabama, Arkansas, Florida, Georgia, Kentucky, Louisiana, Mississippi, North Carolina, South Carolina, Tennessee, Virginia, West Virginia

- Southwest: Arizona, New Mexico, Oklahoma, Texas

- Rocky Mountain: Colorado, Idaho, Montana, Utah, Wyoming

- Far West: Alaska, California, Hawaii. Nevada, Oregon, Washington

These regional groupings are the ones used by the Bureau of Economic Analysis. They differ from the region and division definitions used by the U.S. Bureau of the Census.

The data provided here are from a larger data set maintained by the Bureau of Economic Analysis. Comprehensive revisions are described in "State Personal Income, Revised Estimates for 1982–1997," Survey of Current Business (September 1997). Data for 1998 and revised data for 1982–1997, consistent with the July 1999 revisions to national income and product accounts, were released by BEA in July 1999.

DATA SOURCES

Most of the data in this volume are from the government agencies and private sources listed below. The specific source(s) for the individual data sets are identified at the beginning of the notes for the relevant data pages.

Board of Governors of the Federal Reserve System
20th Street and Constitution Ave., NW Washington, DC 20551

Data Inquiries and Publication Sales:
Publications Services
Mail Stop 127
Board of Governors of the
Federal Reserve System
Washington, DC 20551
Telephone: (202) 452-3244

Monthly Publication:
Federal Reserve Bulletin

Internet Address:
http://www.federalreserve.gov/

**Bureau of the Census,
U.S. Department of Commerce**
Washington, DC 20233

Data Inquiries:
General Information: (301) 457-4100
Foreign Trade Information: (301) 457-3041

Internet Address:
http://www.census.gov

**Bureau of Economic Analysis,
U.S. Department of Commerce**
Washington, DC 20230

Data Inquiries:
Public Information Office:
(202) 606-9900

Monthly Publication:
Survey of Current Business
Available by subscription from the Superintendent of Documents

Internet Address:
http://www.bea.doc.gov

Bureau of Labor Statistics,
U.S. Department of Labor
2 Massachusetts Ave., NE
Washington, DC 20212

Data Inquiries:
General: (202) 606-5886
24-Hour Hotline: (202) 606-7828

Monthly Publications:
Monthly Labor Review
Employment and Earnings
Compensation and Working Conditions
Producer Price Indexes
CPI Detailed Report
Available by subscription from the Superintendent of Documents

Internet Address:
http://stats.bls.gov

Commodity Systems, Inc. (CSI)
200 West Palmetto Park Road, Suite 200
Boca Raton, FL 33432

Data Orders:
(800) 274-4727
(561) 392-8663

Internet Address:
http://www.csidata.com

Conference Board, The
845 Third Avenue, New York, NY 10022

Data Inquiries:
Michael Boldin
E-mail: lei@conference-board.org

Publication Sales:
Customer Service: (212) 339-0345

Monthly Publication:
Business Cycle Indicators

Internet Address:
http://www.tcb-indicators.org

**Financial Management Service,
U.S. Department of the Treasury**
401 14th Street, SW,
Washington, DC 20227

Data Inquiries:
Budget Reports Branch:
(202) 874-9880

Monthly Publication:
Monthly Treasury Statement
Available by subscription from the Superintendent of Documents

Internet Address:
http://www.fms.treas.gov

Employment and Training Administration
U.S. Department of Labor
200 Constitution Avenue, NW
Washington, DC 20210

Data Inquiries:
    (202) 219-6871

Internet Address:
    http://www.doleta.gov

Energy Information Administration
U.S. Department of Energy
1000 Independence Ave., SW
Washington, DC 20585

Data Inquiries and Publications:
    National Energy Information Center
    Phone: (202) 586-8800
    E-mail: infoctr@eia.doe.gov

Monthly Publication:
Monthly Energy Review

Internet Address:
    http://www.eia.doe.gov

Mortgage Bankers Association of America
1125 15th Street NW
Washington, DC 20005
Data Inquiries:
    (202) 861-6500

Internet Address:
    http://www.mbaa.org

National Agricultural Statistics Service
U.S. Department of Agriculture
14th & Independence Ave., SW
Washington, DC 20250

Data Inquiries:
    Information Hotline: (800) 727-9540

Publication Sales:
    Telephone: (800) 999-6779
    Fax: (703) 834-0110

Internet Address:
    http://www.usda.gov/nass/

To order government publications:
    Superintendent of Documents
    P.O. Box 371954
    Pittsburgh, PA 15250-7954
    (202) 512-1800

Index